For Reference

Not to be taken from this room

Asheville-Buncombe
Technical Community College
Learning Resources Center
340 Victoria Rd.
Asheville, NC 28801

Discarded
Date SEP 1 3 2024

Academic American Encyclopedia

Grolier Incorporated

Danbury, Connecticut

Library of Congress Cataloging-in-Publication Data

Academic American encyclopedia.
    p.   cm.
  Includes bibliographical references and index.
  ISBN 0-7172-2059-1
  1. Encyclopedias and dictionaries. I. Grolier Incorporated.
AE5.A23   1995
031—dc20   94–42537
                                                     CIP

Copyright © 1995 by Grolier Incorporated

Copyright © by Grolier Incorporated.
1994, 1993, 1992, 1991, 1990, 1989, 1988, 1987, 1986,
1985, 1984, 1983, 1982, 1981, 1980.

Copyright © Philippines by Grolier International, Inc.
1995, 1994, 1993, 1992, 1991, 1990, 1989, 1988, 1987,
1986, 1985, 1984, 1983.

Copyright © Republic of China by Grolier International,
Inc.
1995, 1994, 1993, 1992, 1991, 1990, 1989, 1988, 1987,
1986, 1985, 1984, 1983.

All rights reserved. No part of this book may be reproduced
or transmitted in any form by any means electronic, mechanical,
or otherwise, whether now or hereafter devised, including
photocopying, recording, or by any information storage and
retrieval system without express written prior permission from
the publisher.

Printed and manufactured in the United States of America.

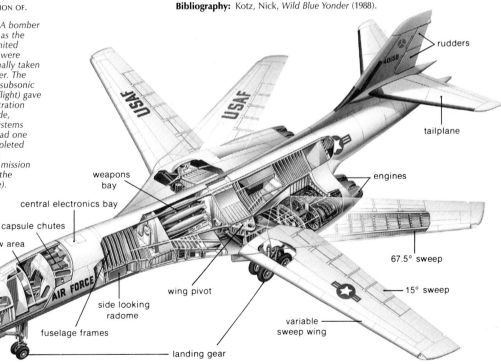

PHOENICIAN

EARLY HEBREW

EARLY ARAMAIC

EARLY GREEK

CLASSICAL GREEK

Bb
MODERN LATIN

ETRUSCAN

EARLY LATIN

CLASSICAL LATIN

RUSSIAN-CYRILLIC

GERMAN-GOTHIC

B

B/b is the second letter of the English alphabet; its form and position were inherited from the Latin alphabet by way of the Etruscan and Greek. The Greek letter *beta* was in turn derived from a Semitic (probably Phoenician) writing system, in which the name of the sign is *beth*.

In modern Greek, the letter *beta* is pronounced similarly to v. Thus, in the Cyrillic (Eastern Slavic) alphabet, which developed from the late Greek, the symbol *B* represents the sound v, and a new symbol for the sound b, Б, was devised.

In English, the letter *b* represents a consonant that is a voiced labial stop made by interrupting the flow of air with the lips and vibrating the vocal cords, as in *bat, label,* and *slab.* In some instances, *b* is not pronounced when preceded by *m* or followed by *t,* as in *dumb* or *doubt.*

Because the sound *b* is very closely related to other labial consonants, such *p, v, f (ph), m,* and *w (wh),* these sounds are frequently interchanged in words of different languages that have a common origin: thus, Latin *frater,* Greek *phrater,* Sanskrit *bhratr,* German *Bruder,* and English *brother.* At times, this interchange is found in words in a single language: English *burse, bourse, bursar, purse,* and *purser* are derived from Latin *bursa.*   I. J. GELB AND R. M. WHITING

See also: WRITING SYSTEMS, EVOLUTION OF.

The supersonic, variable-wing B-1A bomber was designed to replace the B-52 as the primary nuclear bomber of the United States—although only prototypes were produced, and its role was eventually taken over by the B-2, or Stealth, bomber. The B-1A's variable wing (forward for subsonic flight; swept back for supersonic flight) gave it a near-sonic, low-altitude penetration capability, as well as a high-altitude, supersonic capability. All its subsystems were duplicated. If a subsystem had one failure, the mission could be completed (fail-operative); if a second failure occurred in the same system, the mission could still be safely aborted, and the bomber returned to base (fail-safe).

B-1 bomber

The Rockwell International B-1 bomber was developed to replace the B-52 STRATOFORTRESS. In 1965 the U.S. Air Force began planning for an Advanced Manned Strategic Aircraft. In June 1970, North American Rockwell received the contract for the airframe, with General Electric to supply the engines. Designated B-1 (later, B-1A), the original supersonic, variable-geometry, strategic bomber prototype emerged as a monoplane with swing wings of 41.67 m (136 ft 8½ in) extended span and 15 degrees sweepback, and a spread of 23.84 m (78 ft 2½ in) in the fully swept position (67.5 degrees). The craft was powered by four 17,000-lb static thrust (75.62 × 103 newtons) F101-GE100 turbofans mounted in two pairs on the underside. The first B-1 was flown on Dec. 23, 1974.

In 1977, President Jimmy Carter canceled the entire B-1 program. In 1981, however, President Ronald Reagan revived the program, with funding now going to the development of a new model, the B-1B, with a maximum speed of approximately Mach 1.25 and a substantially reduced radar cross-section. Reagan's goal of a fleet of 100 B-1Bs was reached in 1988, although three craft were destroyed in crashes. The entire fleet was grounded five times over the next two years because of engine and other problems.

Bibliography: Kotz, Nick, *Wild Blue Yonder* (1988).

rudders

tailplane

engines

67.5° sweep

15° sweep

weapons bay

central electronics bay

capsule chutes

crew area

pilots' cabin

forward electronics bay

forward radar

side looking radome

fuselage frames

wing pivot

variable sweep wing

landing gear

canard surface

B-17 Flying Fortress

The Boeing B-17 Flying Fortress, a long-range, high-altitude bomber, was one of the most famous aircraft of World War II. About 13,000 Flying Fortresses were built before the craft was superseded by the B-29 Superfortress.

The Boeing B-17 Flying Fortress was a World War II bomber that was used for daylight bombing raids over Europe and the Pacific. The powerful four-engine, low-wing, 31.62-m-span (103.75-ft) monoplane, with its five defensive machine-gun positions, represented a significant advance in bomber evolution. The prototype made its first flight on July 28, 1935. It was an all-metal design with a circular-section fuselage, wings embodying a deep root section equal to half the fuselage diameter, and large wing-mounted flaps. The fuselage bomb bay accommodated a 2,177-kg (4,800-lb) offensive load.

The B-17E was able to attain a top speed of 510 km/h (317 mph) at an altitude of 7,620 m (25,000 ft). It incorporated various improvements, including an enlarged tail to improve stability, power operation for three gun turrets, a tail turret, a ventral "ball" turret, and use of 0.50-in machine guns throughout, except for a 0.30-in caliber pair in the nose. The greatly improved B-17G represented the ultimate form of the B-17 and was produced in greater number than any other variant.
PETER M. H. LEWIS

B-2 bomber: see STEALTH BOMBER.

B-24 Liberator

The Consolidated B-24 Liberator was developed in response to a U.S. Army Air Corps specification of September 1938 for a heavy bomber capable of exceeding the performance of the B-17. It evolved as a four-engine aircraft with an advanced low-drag, high-aspect-ratio, 33.5-m-span (110-ft) wing, designed by David R. Davis specifically to achieve the mandatory long range. The impressive high-wing monoplane had a large fuselage and a tricycle landing gear. The initial flight of the prototype XB-24 was on Dec. 29, 1939. Ultimately, the Liberator became the celebrated partner of the B-17 during World War II in the daylight raids over Europe. The B-24's long range also made it invaluable for operations in the Pacific. Throughout its production life (1939–45), the various models of the B-24 were equipped with progressively improved versions of the Pratt & Whitney R-1830 radial engine and increasingly powerful defensive armament. The versatile Liberator was also used extensively for maritime patrol, transport, and photographic reconnaissance.
PETER M. H. LEWIS

B-29 Superfortress

The Boeing B-29 Superfortress, the successor to the B-17, was a U.S. bomber of World War II. Design of the B-29 was initiated in 1940 by the need for a "Hemisphere Defense Weapon"—an airplane with a speed of 644 km/h (400 mph) and the ability to carry a 907-kg (2,000 lb) bomb load for 8,583 km (5,333 mi). The B-29 is best known as the aircraft that dropped the only atomic bombs of World War II—on Aug. 6, 1945, at Hiroshima, and on Aug. 9, 1945, at Nagasaki. Earlier, the 43.05-m-span (141.25-ft) medium strategic bomber monoplane carried out high-altitude raids against Japanese-defended targets and numerous low-altitude night bombings. The B-29 was also used as a flight-refueling tanker. It usually carried a crew of ten. High performance was ensured by the incorporation of high–aspect-ratio wings mid-mounted on a circular-section fuselage. Careful design decreased the drag of the nacelles (housing) on the four 2,200-hp Wright radial engines. The bomb load of the B-29 eventually reached 9,000 kg (20,000 lb). Development of the basic design continued after VJ-Day, resulting in the B-50 Superfortress.
PETER M. H. LEWIS

B-52 Stratofortress

The Boeing B-52 Stratofortress was a long-distance U.S. bomber, first built in the 1950s. Intended initially to be equipped with turboprop engines to attain the necessary range, the massive 56-m-span (185-ft), 35-degree-sweptwing B-52 eventually entered the Strategic Air Command in 1955 with eight powerful Pratt & Whitney turbojet engines. The B-52G version, developed in 1958, was the most significant bomber in the world's most powerful air force and was able to carry nuclear weapons to any global target at short notice. Major changes gave the B-52G integral fuel tanks in the wings, a remote-controlled tail-gun turret, and underwing attachment points for transporting North American GAM-77 Hound Dog missiles. In 1962 the B-52H, with TF-33 turbofan engines, flew nonstop without refueling from Okinawa to Madrid (20,147 km/12,519 mi) in 22 hours and 10 minutes. In 1977 the Stratofortress was designated to carry the air-launched CRUISE MISSILE (ALCM). During the Gulf War (1991), B-52s, modified and equipped with advanced electronics, were used against entrenched Iraqi forces.
PETER M. H. LEWIS

Bibliography: Boyne, Walter, *Boeing B-52* (1982); Davis, L., *B-52 Stratofortress in Action* (1993).

Ba Jin (Pa Chin) [bah-jin]

Ba Jin is the pseudonym of Li Feigan (Li Fei-kan), b. Nov. 25, 1904, a Chinese novelist. He is best known for the trilogy *Jiliu* (*Chi-liu*, or Torrent, 1933–40, Eng. trans. of first part, *Family*, 1958), which attacked the traditional family system. Exalted by the Communist regime after 1949, Ba Jin was denounced as a counterrevolutionary during the 1966–69 Cultural Revolution but reappeared during the late 1970s.

Bibliography: Lang, Olga, *Pa Chin and His Writings* (1967); Munoz, V., *Li Fei-kan and Chinese Anarchism* (1988).

Ba Xian (Pa Hsien) [bay shee-en]

In Chinese mythology, the Ba Xian (Eight Immortals) were Daoist (Taoist) holy men (similar to saints). Unconnected as historical persons, each was believed to have earned the right to immortality and to be endowed with miraculous powers. The classic group of eight was formed during the Yuan period (1260–1368); they are often shown together in Chinese art.

Bibliography: Ho, Kwok Man, and O'Brian, J., eds. and trans., *The Eight Immortals of Taoism* (1991); Lai, T. C., *The Eight Immortals* (1972).

Baade, Walter [bahd'-e]

Wilhelm Heinrich Walter Baade, b. Mar. 24, 1893, d. June 25, 1960, was a German-born American astronomer who established through extragalactic studies that the universe is twice as large as had been previously thought. After graduating from the University of Göttingen, Baade worked for 11 years at the observatory of the University of Hamburg at Bergedorf, where he discovered the asteroids Hidalgo and Icarus. In 1931 he arrived at Mount Wilson Observatory in California and began a fruitful collaboration on extragalactic astronomy with Edwin P. HUBBLE. The wartime blackout in Los Angeles enhanced observational opportunities, and Baade's study of the Andromeda galaxy during this period led to his distinction between the star types now known as population I and II stars (see POPULATION, STELLAR). From these studies Baade concluded that the Andromeda galaxy was more than twice as far away as had been estimated up until then.

Bibliography: Richardson, R. S., *The Star Lovers* (1967).

Baal   [bay'-uhl]

Baal, the name of the fertility god or gods of the ancient Canaanite religions, was one of the chief characters mentioned in the 14th-century BC UGARIT tablets. Called the lord of the universe, he was killed by monsters but restored to life. His death and resurrection were celebrated annually as a part of Canaanite fertility rituals. The cult of Baal—and particularly the human sacrifice and temple prostitution associated with it—was frequently denounced by Old Testament prophets.

Baal Shem Tov   [bah'-ahl shaym tohv]

Israel ben Eliezer, b. Ukraine, c.1700, d. 1760, known as Baal Shem Tov ("Master of the Good Name") or by the acronym Besht, was the founder of the 18th-century Eastern European Jewish sect of HASIDISM. Little is known of his life, and that little is encrusted with legend.

Baal Shem Tov was reputed to be a wonder-worker and healer by virtue of his knowledge of the secret name of God (hence, "Master of the Good Name"). His reputation for deep knowledge of the rabbinic tradition, as well as for clairvoyance and mystical penetration, is, in all probability, a later legendary accretion. In reaction to the intellectualism and casuistry of the rabbinical legalists, he stressed the joyous and enthusiastic experience of religious participation. Song and dance, fervent prayer, and ecstatic communion with God were the keys to unlock spiritual powers. Humility completes the list of cardinal virtues. Whatever in his teaching was drawn from the earlier Zoharic form of the KABBALAH or its later Lurianic form was developed in a way that emphasized the elements of adherence (*devekut*) to God through a recognition of the divine immanence in nature. Attainment of this adherence demanded the total concentrated devotion (*kavvanah*) of the person in fervent communion with God.

JOSEPH L. BLAU

Bibliography: Buber, Martin, *The Legend of the Ba'al Shem*, trans. by Maurice Friedman (1955; repr. 1969); Heschel, Abraham, ed., *The Circle of the Baal Shem Tov* (1985).

Baalbek   [bay'-uhl-bek]

Baalbek is a village in eastern Lebanon, about 55 km (34 mi) northwest of Damascus, Syria, and about 64 km (40 mi) northeast of Beirut. A desert oasis on the western slopes of the Anti-Lebanon Mountains, it has a population of 14,000 (1982 est.) and has become a base for the Iranian-backed HEZBOLLAH.

Baalbek was probably an ancient center for the worship of the Phoenician god BAAL, although its early history is obscure. The Greeks, who identified Baal with Helios and called the city Heliopolis, occupied the site as part of their conquest of Syria in 332 BC. It became a Roman colony under Augustus in 16 BC. In 1759 an earthquake destroyed much of the city. Just west of the village are some well-preserved Roman ruins, including remains of the Temple of Jupiter, the Temple of Bacchus, the Temple of Venus, and parts of the city wall.

Baath party   [bah'-ahth]

The Baath party is a secular Arab political party that advocates a single socialist Arab nation; since 1953 it has been formally known as the Arab Socialist Resurrection Party. The first Baath party congress was held in Damascus in 1947, and the party soon developed organizations in most Arab countries and among Arabs in non-Arab countries. The more conservative and nationalistic military wing of the party eventually seized control of the governments of Iraq (in 1968) and Syria (in 1970), where the Baath party is strongest.

Bibliography: Baram, A., *Culture, History, and Ideology in the Formation of Ba'thist Iraq, 1968–1989* (1991); Devlin, John F., *The Ba'th Party* (1976); Hinnebusch, R., *Authoritarian Power and State Formation in Ba'thist Syria* (1990).

Bab el-Mandeb   [bahb el-mahn'-deb]

The Bab el-Mandeb is a strait that connects the Gulf of Aden and the Red Sea. An important shipping lane for Suez Canal traffic, it is about 26 km (16 mi) long and 32 km (20 mi) wide. It has a maximum depth of 311 m (1,020 ft). Eritrea and Djibouti are on its western shore; Yemen is to the east.

Babangida, Ibrahim

Maj.-Gen. Ibrahim Babangida was head of state in Nigeria from August 1985 to August 1993. Babangida participated in the 1983 coup led by Maj.-Gen. Mohammed BUHARI. He then served on the ruling Supreme Military Council and as army chief of staff. As popular discontent with Buhari mounted, Babangida seized power to restore the prestige of the army. He initiated a plan for a gradual return to civilian rule by 1993 but annulled its final step, the June 1993 presidential election, when the pro-army candidate lost. In August he turned power over to an interim civilian president, who was overthrown by Gen. Sani Abacha in November.

Babbage, Charles

The British mathematician Charles Babbage, b. Dec. 26, 1792, d. Oct. 18, 1871, designed an "analytical engine," a mechanical progenitor of the digital computer. Elected (1816) a fellow of the Royal Society, he was Lucasian Professor of Mathematics at Cambridge (1828–39). In 1830 he published *Reflections on the Decline of Science in England*, a controversial work that resulted in the formation, in 1831, of the British Association for the Advancement of Science. Two years later, Babbage published his most influential work, *On the Economy of Machinery and Manufactures*, in which he proposed an early form of OPERATIONS RESEARCH. The computation of logarithms had made him aware of the drudgery and inaccuracy of human calculation, and he became so obsessed with the mechanization of computation that he spent his family fortune in pursuit of it. Although Babbage never built an operational, mechanical computer, his design concepts have been proved correct.

DAVID HOUNSHELL

Bibliography: Blaug, Mark, *Whewell, Lardner, Babbage: Pioneers in Economics* (1991); Campbell-Kelley, Martin, ed., *The Works of Charles Babbage*, 11 vols. (1988); Collier, Bruce, *The Little Engines That Could've* (1990); Hyman, A., *Charles Babbage* (1982; repr. 1984).

Babbitt

Babbitt (1922), a novel by Sinclair LEWIS, is a devastating attack on American small-town life. It is set in a fictional Zenith, nicknamed Zip City by its residents, who are inordinately proud and chauvinistic. The central character is George F. Babbitt, a middle-aged real-estate broker who devoutly believes in progress and esteems "good fellowship, optimism, and good business." Although financially successful, Babbitt is dissatisfied with his life. The novel traces his semiridiculous attempts to vary the monotony of his existence. The term *Babbittry* now describes unthinking conformity to prevailing middle-class standards.

CHARLOTTE D. SOLOMON

Babbitt, Irving

Irving Babbitt, b. Dayton, Ohio, Aug. 2, 1865, d. July 15, 1933, a literary critic and teacher, strongly advocated the New Humanism, an early 20th-century intellectual movement that sought inspiration in the classical tradition. In *The New Laokoön* (1910) and *Rousseau and Romanticism* (1919), he vigorously criticized romanticism and opposed his contemporaries who applauded spontaneity and unconscious impulse. On the positive side, Babbitt upheld reason, self-discipline, and tradition. He taught French literature at Harvard from 1912 until his death.

CHARLES CANTALUPO

Bibliography: Brennan, S. C., and Yarbrough, S. R., *Irving Babbitt* (1987); Nevin, T. R., *Irving Babbitt: An Intellectual Study* (1984); Panichas, G. A., and Ryn, C. G., *Irving Babbitt in Our Time* (1986).

Babbitt, Milton

Composer Milton Babbitt, b. Philadelphia, May 10, 1916, received traditional training in music and later in mathematics.

His encounter with the music of Arnold Schoenberg at the age of 16 confirmed his decision to become a composer. He studied with Roger Sessions and began writing twelve-tone music (see TWELVE-TONE SYSTEM), but came to the realization that he wanted total organization and total control of all musical elements in his compositions.

Babbitt has been a member of the faculty of Princeton University since 1938. His work with the Columbia-Princeton Electronic Music Center and with the journal *Perspectives of New Music* has been admired by music critics. Babbitt's music does not appeal to the general public, nor does he desire this, wishing instead to enjoy the intellectual status of the mathematician, the scientist, or the philosopher.

The following are representative works: *Composition for Four Instruments* (1947–48); *Philomel*, for voice and synthesizer (1963–64); *Relata II*, for orchestra (1968); and *A Solo Requiem*, for soprano and two pianos (1976–77).   DIKA NEWLIN

Bibliography: Babbitt, Milton, "Who Cares If You Listen?" in *Contemporary Composers on Contemporary Music*, ed. by E. Schwartz and B. Childs (1967; repr. 1978); Burbank, R., *20th Century Music* (1984); Griffiths, P., *Modern Music: The Avant Garde since 1945* (1981); Morgan, R. P., *20th Century Music* (1988); Peyser, J., *The New Music: The Sense behind the Sound* (1971); Sablosky, I. L., *American Music* (1985); Slonimsky, N., *Music since 1900,* 4th ed. (1971), and *Supplement* (1986).

See also: ELECTRONIC MUSIC; SERIAL MUSIC.

babbitt metals

Babbitt metals, also called white metals, are soft alloys of tin (or lead), copper, and antimony in various proportions, used to reduce friction in BEARINGS. These alloys were developed by the American manufacturer Isaac Babbitt (1799–1862) in 1839. Babbitt metals are used as linings between bearings and shafts. Linings of 0.025 to 0.5 mm (0.001 to 0.02 in) are used. Thick linings are used in bearings subjected to steady loads, for example, in railroad journal bearings.   MERLE C. NUTT

babbler

The babblers are nearly 300 species of songbirds that make up the babbler family, Timaliidae, order Passeriformes. They are an extremely diversified group that ranges through Africa, Australia, and the Orient. The family is poorly defined, with some members superficially resembling types of wren, thrush, titmouse, or pitta. They are 9–40 cm (3.5–16 in) long; most have in common soft lax plumage, dull coloration (a few are boldly marked), short rounded wings, and strong legs. The babblers are named for the chattering songs of many species. The birds feed on insects, other small animals, and fruit; the cuplike, or domed, nest has a side entrance.

WM. EARL GODFREY

Babcock, Horace Welcome

The American astronomer Horace Welcome Babcock, b. Pasadena, Calif., Sept. 13, 1912, served as director of Mount Wilson and Palomar observatories from 1964 to 1978. A graduate (1938) of the University of California, Babcock investigated the magnetic fields of the Sun and stars and, with his father, Harold D. Babcock, invented the solar magnetograph for this purpose. A specialist in telescope design and instrumentation, he played an important role in the founding of Las Campanas Observatory in Chile.   STEVEN J. DICK

Babcock, Stephen Moulton

An American agricultural chemist, Stephen Moulton Babcock, b. Bridgewater, N.Y., Oct. 22, 1843, d. July 1, 1931, developed (1890) the Babcock test, a simple method for determining the butterfat content of milk. The test was an important factor in modernizing the dairy industry, since it permitted accurate grading of milk, discouraged adulteration and, by furnishing a practical means for testing the milk of individual cows, encouraged the development of more productive dairy strains. For most of his career, Babcock was a professor at the University of Wisconsin.

See also: DAIRYING.

Babel, Isaak Emmanuilovich   [bah'-buhl, ee'-sahk em-ahn-weel'-oh-vich]

Isaak Emmanuilovich Babel, b. Odessa, July 13, 1894, ranks as one of the finest Russian short-story writers of the Soviet period. He received a traditional Hebrew religious training as well as a secular education. As a result, his tales bear the imprint of four literary traditions, the Russian, the Hebrew, the Yiddish, and the French. Babel's most important works are about 50 short stories, contained in two collections, *The Red Cavalry* (1926; Eng. trans., 1929) and *Odessa Tales* (1927; *Collected Stories*, 1955). The first is a series of vignettes based on his experiences as a soldier in the Polish-Soviet war. The second describes an exotic Jewish Odessa, which Babel populates with gangsters, beggars, and other picturesque characters. He also wrote a novel, *Benia Krik* (1927; Eng. trans., 1935), and such plays as *Sunset* (1928) and *Maria* (1935). In 1939 Babel was arrested on unknown charges; he died or was killed in prison in 1941. His works were again published, in censored form, in the 1950s after Stalin's death.

MAURICE FRIEDBERG

Bibliography: Bloom, H., intro., *Isaac Babel* (1987); Carden, P., *The Art of Isaac Babel* (1972); Ehre, M., *Isaac Babel* (1986); Falen, J., *Isaac Babel* (1974); Hallett, R. W., *Isaac Babel* (1973).

Babel, Tower of   [bay'-buhl]

According to the Bible, the tower of Babel was erected by the descendants of Noah, who were attempting to unite all peoples in building a city and tower that would reach to heaven. God thwarted their efforts by turning their language into babblings (Gen. 11). The story may be an early attempt to explain the origin of languages.

Babesia   [buh-bee'-zhee-uh]

Babesia, *Babesia*, are any of several intracellular Protozoa parasites found in vertebrate animals and transmitted by ticks. One species, *B. bigemina*, causes one of the most serious diseases of domestic animals: Texas, or red water, fever. The transmission of the disease by ticks was first demonstrated (1893) by Theobald Smith.   J. F. McCLELLAN

Babeuf, François Noël   [bah-buf', frahn-swah' noh-el']

François Noël ("Gracchus") Babeuf, a minor figure in the French Revolution, has received considerable attention as a precursor of modern communism. Born of humble parents on Nov. 23, 1760, he became an ardent revolutionary while employed as an agent for the assessment of local manorial dues in Picardy. Repeatedly imprisoned after 1789, he gained notoriety in 1795 through his paper *The Tribune of the People*, and on May 10, 1796, he and others were arrested for conspiring to overthrow the Directory. A fiasco, this "Conspiracy for Equality" was also a landmark in the theory and practice of revolution, because Babeuf had evolved both an advanced technique for the seizure of power and a belief that an era of universal equality could be inaugurated by a final revolution in which all private property would be destroyed by a ruthless popular dictatorship. After a prolonged public trial, he was condemned and guillotined on May 27, 1797.

M. J. SYDENHAM

Bibliography: Rose, R. B., *Gracchus Babeuf, the First Revolutionary Communist* (1978); Thomson, David, *The Babeuf Plot* (1947).

babirusa   [bab-uh-roos'-uh]

The babirusa, *Babyrousa babyrussa*, is a mammal belonging to the swine family, Suidae, order Artiodactyla. It is 1 m (40 in) long and weighs about 90 kg (200 lb). The almost hairless skin is rough and loose. The upper canine teeth, or tusks, grow through the snout upward to a length of 20–25 cm (8–9 in). Useless for rooting out food or for combat, the tusks may have sexual significance. Babirusas live in jungles of the Moluccas and Sulawesi, where they forage at night for roots and grubs.   EVERETT SENTMAN

A babirusa, B. babyrussa, *has tusklike upper canine teeth that pierce its snout and curve backward over its forehead.*

Babism [bah'-bizm]

Babism is a religious movement founded by Mirza Ali Muhammad of Shiraz (Iran), who announced his divine election as the Bab in 1844. This title, meaning "doorway to knowledge," was understood by many to imply that Muhammad of Shiraz claimed to have received a divine manifestation surpassing in significance the revelation granted to the prophet Muhammad, and that his book of revelation, the *Bayan,* overshadowed the Koran.

Understandably, serious tensions arose, and the Bab was executed (1850). When an attempt to assassinate the Shah failed in 1852, the persecution of the Babis intensified. The Bab's successor fled to Baghdad with his half brother Mirza Husayn Ali, who was later on recognized by most followers as the BAHAULLAH ("Splendor of God"). The religious movement led by the Bahaullah became known as BAHA'I.

WILLEM A. BIJLEFELD

Bibliography: Balyuzi, H. M., *The Bab* (1973); Smith, Peter, *The Babi and Baha'i Religions* (1987).

baboon

Baboons are bulky, ground-dwelling monkeys in the order Primate, family Cercopithecidae. They are classified into two genera. Members of the genus *Chaeropithecus* are the blackish gray chacma (*C. ursinus*) of eastern and southern Africa, largest of the baboons; the yellow baboon (*C. cynocephalus*) of central and southern Africa; the brown doguera baboon (*C. doguera*) of east central Africa; and the reddish brown western baboon (*C. papio*) of west central Africa, smallest of the baboons.

The sole member of the genus *Comopithecus* is the hamadryas, or sacred Anubis, baboon, which lives in Egypt, Arabia, Sudan, Ethiopia, and Somalia.

Baboons range in length from 50 to 110 cm (20 to 43 in), plus a tail that is 35 to 68 cm (14 to 27 in) long. They weigh from 13.5 to 39.6 kg (30 to 87 lb). The hamadryas grows up to 75 cm (30 in) long, has a 50-cm (20-in) tail, and weighs about 18 kg (40 lb). The body hair is coarse and rough, and the buttocks have naked pads. The adult male hamadryas baboon has an impressive wide mane and side whiskers. In the wild, baboons keep themselves clean by frequently grooming each other's coat. The canine teeth are long, the jaws powerful, and the limbs extremely strong, making the baboon a formidable fighter.

Baboons walk or gallop on all fours, sniffing the air with their long, doglike muzzles, and carry their tails in an arch. They are social and travel in large troops of as many as 50. The strongest and most dominant males travel near the center of the troop, along with the infants and their mothers. The older juveniles are nearby in play groups. The young adults on the troop's periphery warn of danger. The dominant males are usually those with the largest canine teeth. They support each other in maintaining order within the troop; thus fighting among wild baboons is rare. Baboons do, however, fight in captivity. The dominant males also defend the troop against such predators as cheetahs.

Baboons prefer to live on rocky plains or in hilly regions, although sometimes they are found in sparse forests. They usually feed during the day and sleep in trees at night. Occasionally they raid farms at night, killing lambs and other young animals. Baboons may even attack humans if they see no gun being carried. Their usual diet includes scorpions, small animals, and most plants.

Baboons breed year round. Gestation lasts six months. The infant is born black and changes to adult coloration 4 to 6 months later. Usually, one a year is born.

Bibliography: Abegglen, J., *On Socialization in Hamadryas Baboons* (1984); Altman, Stuart A., *Baboon Ecology* (1970); Smuts, B. B., *Sex and Friendship in Baboons* (1985); Strum, S. C., *Almost Human: A Journey into the World of Baboons* (1987).

A male hamadryas baboon, C. hamadryas, *has a thick, silver mane and coat, as well as long canine teeth, all of which the female lacks. A female carries her young on her back. Common to regions near the Red Sea, these baboons were considered sacred in ancient Egypt.*

Babur, Mogul emperor of India [bah'-bur]

Babur, b. Feb. 15, 1483, d. Dec. 26, 1530, was the founder and first emperor of the MOGUL dynasty in India. A direct descendant of GENGHIS KHAN and TIMUR, he became king of the petty principality of Fergana in 1495 and captured Samarkand in 1497. After losing both kingdoms, he occupied Kabul in 1504 and established a kingdom in Afghanistan. In 1525, Babur invaded India. He defeated (1526) the Lodi sultan at Panipat and took Delhi, where he was declared king. During his brief reign Babur conquered northern India as far as Bengal, but he did not have time to establish a secure administration before his death and the succession of his son HUMAYUN. Also called Zahir ud-Din Muhammad, Babur was a poet and the author of memoirs (Eng. trans., 1921–22). The name Babur (meaning "tiger") is also transliterated as Baber or Babar.

Bibliography: Lal, Muni, *Babar: Life and Times* (1977); Lamb, Harold, *Babur, the Tiger: First of the Great Moguls* (1961); Williams, L. F., *Empire Builder of the 16th Century* (1962).

Babylon

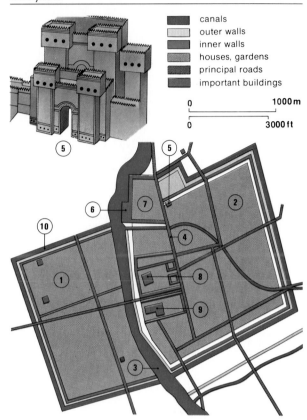

canals
outer walls
inner walls
houses, gardens
principal roads
important buildings

| 0 | 1000 m |
| 0 | 3000 ft |

As this layout of ancient Babylon (c.6th century BC) depicts, the older (1) and newer (2) sections of the city were separated by the Euphrates River (3). The Processional Way (4) entered the city through the Ishtar Gate (5), passing a fortress (6) and the main citadel complex (7) of administrative structures. This main avenue then passed the ziggurat (8) of the Etemenanki enclosure and the temple of Marduk (9). Navigable canals (10) formed a protective moat around the city.

The ruins of Babylon (from Bab-ili, meaning "Gate of God"), the 2d–1st millennium BC capital of southern Mesopotamia (BABYLONIA), stand beside the Euphrates about 90 km (55 mi) south of modern Baghdad, Iraq. Occupied in prehistoric times but first mentioned in the late 3d millennium BC, the city became important when its AMORITE king HAMMURABI (r. 1792–1750 BC) gained control of all southern Mesopotamia. Raided by the HITTITES about 1595 BC, Babylon then came under KASSITE rule about 1570 BC, only to be sacked again about 1158 BC by the Elamites, who removed many Babylonian monuments to SUSA, including the famous Law Code stela of Hammurabi (now in the Louvre). Dominated by Assyria from the 9th century until that country's fall to the Medes in 612 BC, Babylon once more became a major political power under the 6th-century CHALDEAN kings, in particular NEBUCHADNEZZAR II (r. 605–562), builder of much of the existing city. Surrendered to CYRUS THE GREAT in 539 BC and possibly the intended capital of Alexander the Great, who died there in 323 BC, Babylon declined after the founding of SELEUCIA, the new Greek capital.

Nebuchadnezzar's triple-walled city measured at least 18 km (11 mi) in circumference. In the old city, on the east bank of the Euphrates, stood Esagila, the temple of Marduk, the city god, and the associated seven-staged ziggurat Etemenanki, popularly associated with the Tower of BABEL. Northward from Esagila, the Processional Way, decorated with animals in glazed and relief brickwork, led through the Ishtar Gate (now in the Berlin Museum) to the New Year (Akitu) temple. Northwest of the Processional Way stood Nebuchadnezzar's

palace. Vaulted structures at its northwest corner may be remains of the legendary Hanging Gardens, numbered among the SEVEN WONDERS OF THE WORLD.

The site was first excavated in 1811, but the principal German investigations begun by Robert Koldewey took place in 1899 to 1917. The Iraq Department of Antiquities has carried out recent restoration work.   KATE FIELDEN

Bibliography: Koldewey, Robert, *The Excavations at Babylon* (1914); Oates, Joan, *Babylon* (1986); Saggs, H. W. F., *The Greatness That Was Babylon* (1962).

Babylonia

Babylonia was an ancient name for the lower Tigris-Euphrates valley in MESOPOTAMIA (now in Iraq). It was applied to an area beginning a little north of modern Baghdad and running in a southeasterly direction to the Persian Gulf. Babylonia took its name from its capital city, BABYLON, which first rose to prominence under the Amorite, or Old Babylonian, dynasty shortly after 1900 BC.

The AMORITES were a Semitic-speaking people who came down the Euphrates River from Syria and conquered the northern part of Babylonia (formerly called AKKAD). Under the sixth king of the dynasty, HAMMURABI (r. 1792–50 BC), famous for his code of laws, all of Babylonia, including SUMER (the south), was united into a single state. The Amorites held sway until the coming (c.1550 BC) of the KASSITES, who established a regime that lasted to the 12th century. Then the Middle Babylonian kings restored native rule, which continued to about 1000 BC. Thereafter the country came under the domination of a succession of foreign masters, of whom the most important were from ASSYRIA. After exacting tribute from the Babylonians for many years, the Assyrian kings finally took (729) the title of king in Babylonia in addition to reigning separately as kings of Assyria. Eventually, a successful revolt against Assyria reestablished (626) Babylonian independence under the so-called CHALDEAN dynasty, the most notable of whose kings was NEBUCHADNEZZAR II (r. 605–562). Chaldean rule ended when the Persians under CYRUS THE GREAT captured Babylon in 539 BC. Henceforth, Babylonia was merely a province in a succession of large empires: Persian, Seleucid, Parthian, and Sassanian (539 BC–AD 650). Its capital was moved from Babylon to nearby SELEUCIA by the Seleucids; later CTESIPHON, near Seleucia, was the administrative center of the Parthians and Sassanians.

Babylonia owed its long prosperity to its location astride important trade routes. Babylon itself commanded the north-

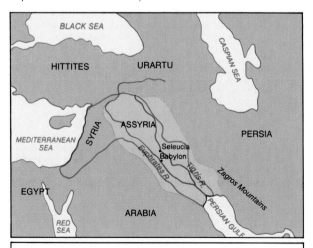

BABYLONIAN EMPIRE

Babylonian Empire c.1750 BC

Boundary of Neo-Babylonian (Chaldean) Empire c.600 BC

south route of the Tigris River running down from Assyria to the Persian Gulf; the Euphrates River gave access to the west; and a caravan route led eastward through the Zagros Mountains to Iran. Babylon was not only the capital of the country but also a religious center. It became the most populous city of the Near East, and under Nebuchadnezzar II it was a legendary showplace with its great walls and ziggurat, gates and temples, and the fabled Hanging Gardens.   TOM B. JONES

Bibliography: Dandamaev, Muhammad, *Slavery in Babylonia*, trans. by V. Powell (1984); King, Leonard W., *A History of Babylon from the Foundation of the Monarchy to the Persian Conquest* (1915; repr. 1980); Saggs, H. W. F., *Everyday Life in Babylonia and Assyria* (1965; repr. 1987).

See also: HAMMURABI, CODE OF; MESOPOTAMIA.

Babylonian Captivity

The Babylonian Captivity is the name given to the period between 586 and 538 BC when the JEWS of the Kingdom of JUDAH lived in exile in Babylonia. After NEBUCHADNEZZAR II captured Jerusalem and destroyed the first temple in 586, he deported the Judeans to various Babylonian cities (Jer. 52:28–32). When CYRUS THE GREAT conquered Babylonia in 538, he permitted the Jews to return to their homeland.   NAHUM N. GLATZER

baby's breath

Baby's breath is the common name for two species of flowering plants, *Gypsophila paniculata* (a perennial) and *G. elegans* (an annual), belonging to the PINK family, Caryophyllaceae. The plants reach heights of 60–90 cm (24–36 in), have lance-shaped leaves, and produce clouds of small, white—sometimes reddish or purplish—flowers. Native to Eurasia but now widespread, they are cultivated as border plants in gardens and for use in bouquets. Some species of BEDSTRAW, *Galium*, are known as false baby's breath.

Bacall, Lauren   [buh-kawl']

Lauren Bacall is the stage name of Betty Joan Perske, b. New York City, Sept. 16, 1924, an actress who, after an unsuccessful period on Broadway, achieved overnight stardom with her first film, *To Have and Have Not* (1944). She married the film's star, Humphrey BOGART, in 1945 and appeared with him in *The Big Sleep* (1946) and *Key Largo* (1948). Among her other films are *The Shootist* (1976) and *Mr. North* (1988). She returned to the stage in *Cactus Flower* (1965) and won Tony Awards for *Applause* (1970) and *Woman of the Year* (1981).

Bibliography: Bacall, Lauren, *Lauren Bacall by Myself* (1978); Hyams, Joe, *Bogart and Bacall* (1975); Quirk, L. J., *Lauren Bacall* (1986).

Baccaloni, Salvatore   [bahk-kah-loh'-nee]

Salvatore Baccaloni, b. Rome, Apr. 14, 1900, d. Dec. 31, 1969, was considered the best Italian basso-buffo of his generation. In 1922 he made his debut at Rome's Teatro Adriano as Bartolo in Rossini's *Barber of Seville*. It was to remain one of his most acclaimed roles, along with that of Dr. Bartolo in Mozart's *Marriage of Figaro*, the title role in Donizetti's *Don Pasquale*, and Leporello in Mozart's *Don Giovanni*. Baccaloni appeared at the major opera houses and festivals in England, Europe, and South America and in 1940 made his debut at the Metropolitan Opera, where he appeared for 22 seasons. He was highly regarded for his vocal characterizations and for his acting ability. Baccaloni later appeared in films.   ELLA MALIN

baccarat   [bah-kah-rah']

Baccarat is a card game played by a banker, or dealer, and as many as ten other participants. The role of banker is awarded in an auction to the highest bidder, who then finances the bank with the amount of the winning bid. The banker plays against the *table* in an order usually determined by the amount each player has bid.

Baccarat is played with at least three and as many as eight, but usually six, 52-card decks. They are shuffled together and are not reshuffled until the bank changes hands or until seven cards or fewer remain undealt.

The banker deals three hands of two cards each, face down, and one at a time—one to the left, one to the right, and one to himself or herself. The players, called *punters*, may then bet that either the left hand or the right hand, or both, will beat the banker.

Face cards and tens count 0, aces 1 each, and other cards their numerical value. When the total of one hand exceeds 10, the tens unit is dropped. For example, a seven and a six, totaling 13 count as 3. The aim of each player, including the dealer, is to be as close to 9 as possible. Each player is entitled to request one more card, dealt face up. The rules require that a player draw another card if his or her count is 4 or less and stand if the count is 6 or more; if the count is 5, the player may stand or draw. The banker is always free to stand or draw.

The banker is committed to pay off only to the amount of money in the bank at the moment of play and may not remove any of the bank's money except to pay losses. The banker may withdraw from play, however, after a deal has been completed and the bets settled. If the banker loses the entire bank or withdraws from the game, the bank is auctioned again and a new game started.

Once a highly popular game most often played for high stakes in the casinos of France, baccarat has never enjoyed favor in the United States and has been replaced worldwide by CHEMIN DE FER.

Bibliography: Korfman, Tony, *Baccarat* (1986); Stuart, Lyle, *Lyle Stuart on Baccarat* (1984); Tamburin, H. J., and Rahm, D., *Winning Baccarat Strategies* (1983).

Bacchae, The   [bak'-ee]

The Bacchae, a tragic play by EURIPIDES first produced in Athens in 405 BC, is the most demonic extant work of the ancient Attic theater. It takes as its overt theme the punishment that the wine god Dionysus visits upon Thebes and its youthful king, the puritanical Pentheus, for rejecting his divinity. Euripides here advances an almost bewildering array of dramatic techniques and hypotheses as to the nature of the play's action. Divine, human, animal, and sexual identities are confused; miracles and distortions of physical and behavioral phenomena abound. *The Bacchae* constitutes the most explicit dramatization of Euripides' preoccupations with the ambiguities, paradoxes, and deceptions innate in the human condition.   GERALD FITZGERALD

Bibliography: Barlow, Shirley A., *The Imagery of Euripides* (1986); Burnett, Anne P., *Catastrophe Survived: Euripides' Plays of Mixed Reversal* (1985); Foley, Helene P., *Ritual Irony: Poetry and Sacrifice in Euripides* (1985); Soyinka, Wole, *The Bacchae of Euripides: A Communion Rite* (1975); Winnington-Ingram, R. P., *Euripides and Dionysus* (1969).

Bacchanalia   [bak-uh-nayl'-ee-uh]

The Bacchanalia was a Roman festival celebrated for three days each year in honor of BACCHUS, the god of wine. Drunken orgies and other excesses characterizing its observance eventually caused its prohibition in 186 BC.

Bacchus   [bak'-uhs]

In Roman mythology, Bacchus was the god of wine and revelry. The son of SEMELE and JUPITER, Bacchus was known to the Greeks as DIONYSUS. His wife was ARIADNE.

Bacchylides   [buh-kil'-i-deez]

A Greek lyric poet, Bacchylides, fl. 5th century BC, was the nephew of SIMONIDES. He wrote choral poetry and epigrams. He was best at mythical narration full of color and exuberant detail. A rival of PINDAR, he nevertheless won several coveted commissions from Hieron of Syracuse, whose court he visited (c.476–70). Substantial portions of his poetry survive because of a papyrus found in Egypt in 1896 containing 15 victory odes and 6 dithyrambs.   CHARLES SEGAL

Bibliography: Burnett, A. P., *The Art of Bacchylides* (1985).

Bach, Carl Philipp Emanuel   [bahk]

Known as the "Hamburg" or "Berlin" Bach, Carl Philipp Emanuel Bach, b. Mar. 8, 1714, d. Dec. 14, 1788, was one of the leading composers and keyboard players of the mid-18th century. The second surviving son of Johann Sebastian Bach, he studied law at the universities of Leipzig and Frankfurt an der Oder but received all his training in composition and keyboard from his father. In 1738 he visited the court of FREDER-ICK II of Prussia, and in 1740 he became his official harpsichordist in Berlin. Bach grew dissatisfied in Berlin and went to Hamburg in 1768 as the musical director for the principal churches of the city. He remained in Hamburg until his death.

Bach wrote much church and chamber music, but his most important compositions are the keyboard sonatas and fantasies written for his favorite instrument, the clavichord. These works were widely known and helped form the transition from the baroque style of his father to the classical style of Wolfgang Amadeus Mozart and Franz Josef Haydn. Like his symphonies, they are notable for their surprise effects and their exceptionally expressive character. His treatise on playing keyboard instruments is the most informative of its kind from the period.   ROBERT L. MARSHALL

Bibliography: Barford, Philip, *The Keyboard Music of C. P. E. Bach* (1965); Clark, S., ed., *C. P. E. Bach Studies* (1988); Geiringer, Karl, *The Bach Family* (1954; repr. 1981); Ottenberg, Hans-Gunter, *Carl Philipp Emanuel Bach* (1987).

Bach, Johann Christian

Called the "English" Bach, Johann Christian Bach, b. Sept. 5, 1735, d. Jan. 1, 1782, was a German preclassical composer who had a profound influence on English musical life. The youngest son of Johann Sebastian Bach, he studied in Berlin with his brother Carl Philipp Emanuel and in Bologna with Padre Giovanni Battista Martini. In 1762, Bach moved to England and became the master of music to King GEORGE III. In 1764, Bach and Carl Friedrich Abel started the Bach-Abel concerts that lasted two decades and helped end England's musical isolation. Bach's sonatas, concertos, and symphonies (his best works) were important in the evolution of these forms and influenced Haydn and Mozart. Bach's pleasant and melodious music was greatly admired by Mozart.

Bibliography: Terry, C. S., *Johann Christian Bach* (1929; repr. 1980); Wolff, C., et al., *The New Grove Bach Family*, rev. ed. (1983); Wesley, Samuel J., ed., *The Bach Letters* (1878; repr. 1981); Young, Percy, *The Bachs* (1970; repr. 1978–79).

Bach, Johann Sebastian

Johann Sebastian Bach, one of the greatest composers in Western musical history, created masterpieces of choral and instrumental music, both sacred and secular. More than 1,000 of his compositions survive, including works in virtually every musical form and genre in use in 18th-century Germany. During his lifetime he enjoyed greater renown as an organist than as a composer, and although such later composers as Mozart and Beethoven held his work in great esteem, it was not until nearly a century after his death that the broader musical public came to appreciate the level of craftsmanship his works embody. Bach's music is now regarded as the high point of the baroque era, which lasted from 1600 to 1750, the year of his death (see BAROQUE MUSIC).

Life. Bach was born in Eisenach, Germany, on Mar. 21, 1685, into a family of musicians. His parents died when he was nine years old, and in 1695 he went to live with his brother Johann Christoph, who was an organist at Ohrdruf. He remained there until 1700, learning the fundamentals of the keyboard from his brother and studying composition on his own, using works of older composers as models.

Johann Sebastian Bach, the great German composer and organ virtuoso, brought baroque music to its peak. Much of Bach's finest music was written for the church, including the St. Matthew Passion (1792) and the Mass in B-minor. His orchestral music includes the six Brandenburg Concertos.

In 1703 he took an orchestral post in Weimar and after six months was appointed organist at the Neukirche in Arnstadt, where he composed his earliest surviving organ works. In 1705 he went to Lübeck (he traveled the 320 km/200 mi, reportedly, on foot) to hear Dietrich Buxtehude, one of the great northern German organist-composers. His Arnstadt tenure lasted two more years and was marked by clashes with the authorities about the scope of his duties. Such difficulties with his employers were constantly to mar his career.

In 1707, Bach married his first cousin Maria Barbara and was appointed organist in Mühlhausen. Almost immediately, the congregation objected to the innovative harmonized music he was introducing, and by the end of the year he moved back to Weimar, where he served as court organist for nine years. There he began composing a cycle of weekly cantatas, and his duties expanded, but he was not granted the position of music director *(Kapellmeister)* he had hoped for, and he sought a post elsewhere. When he found one, at Cöthen, in 1717, he asked for release from his duties at Weimar in a manner so antagonistic that he was imprisoned for a month.

Bach remained at Cöthen until 1723. After the death of his first wife, he married (1721) Anna Magdalena Wilcken. In all he fathered 20 children, of whom several—including Wilhelm Friedemann, Carl Philipp Emanuel, and Johann Christian—became well-known composers. Because his patron at Cöthen, Prince Leopold, enjoyed music, Bach composed both secular and sacred works. After the prince married, however, music played a less important role in court life, and again Bach sought employment elsewhere.

He found it in Leipzig, where in 1723 he was appointed choir leader and *Kapellmeister* of Saint Thomas Church—a prestigious post that made Bach, in effect, the director of music for the entire city. He remained in Leipzig for the rest of his life and wrote many of his greatest works there. Bach died in Leipzig on July 28, 1750.

Music. Bach's duties required that he write compositions of many kinds—organ and choral music for the church, chamber music for court use, and fairly straightforward harpsichord works for teaching the instrument. These compositions make up the bulk of his output. In addition, there are difficult solo works composed either for his own use or for that of friends, and there are also works that are clearly theoretical exercises, such as the Mass in B-minor and the *Art of Fugue*. These were, in a sense, Bach's private explorations. They were not performed during his lifetime. Today, however, they stand as some of the most glorious of baroque works.

One considerable body of Bach's music is his cantata series, of which more than 200 survive. (It is believed that over half of his secular cantatas and more than a third of his sacred ones have been lost.) The secular cantatas, by far the smaller of the two groups, were composed for public and private festivities and use allegorical or mythological texts. Most of the sacred cantatas were composed as parts of cycles, with a specific work intended for each Sunday in the year. Their texts tend to be either biblical or based on church hymns, although some also include poetry. In the greatest of these, which were composed in Leipzig, the chorale melody often serves as an underlying theme that unifies the complete cantata. Besides the cantatas, Bach is believed to have composed five Passion settings, although only the *St. John* and *St. Matthew* Passions survive. Also prominent among his sacred works are the Easter and Christmas oratorios, the motets, and the Mass in B-minor.

The sacred works show one side of Bach—that of a composer working in, and responding to, the Lutheran tradition. Another side, that of the keyboard virtuoso, is seen in his organ and harpsichord works. The organ works run the gamut from fairly simple chorale settings to ornate fantasias, toccatas, fugues, and sonatas. Among the harpsichord works, the *Goldberg Variations* and the two books of *The Well-Tempered Clavier* remain at the peak of music for the keyboard.

Bach's command of other instruments and their resources is evident in the six cello suites, the six violin sonatas and partitas, the four lute suites, and the accompanied sonatas for flute, violin, viola, and viola da gamba (now usually played on the cello). For chamber orchestra, he composed four extended suites, as well as the six *Brandenburg Concertos,* and concertos for harpsichord, violin, and oboe.

Bach performance style has varied greatly over the years. As scholars have unearthed new evidence and offered new theories about how the music was performed in Bach's time, approaches have changed radically. Thus the massive chorale presentations of the *St. John* and *St. Matthew* Passions and the Mass in B-minor that were common through the 1960s have given way to performances by much smaller ensembles. One theory that gained prominence in the early 1980s suggested that the choral and many of the instrumental works were performed with one singer and one player to a part. Since the 1950s the practice of using instruments constructed as they were during Bach's time has become an increasingly important aspect of Bach performance.

Significance. At the start of his career, Bach built on the foundations laid by Buxtehude and others of the north German school, but he quickly developed not only a distinctive compositional voice, but an unparalleled sense of structure. These qualities did not always serve him well politically. As an employee of a German church establishment, he was required to provide music of the kind to which the congregation had become accustomed. There were, therefore, those who in the early years found Bach's counterpoint too florid and his harmonization too bold. Later in his life, as musical styles moved toward the elegant simplicity of the *stil galant* (the basis of the classical style, of which his son, Johann Christian, was a pioneer), Bach came to be regarded as a musical arch-conservative, an adherent to an antiquated style.

He was keenly aware of these changes, however, and in the last decade of his life he composed works of great complexity using the musical techniques that most interested him. An example is his final work, the *Art of Fugue.* Begun during the 1740s but left incomplete at his death, this compilation is a thorough examination of a sublime musical form by a master who knew that the form was falling out of fashion.

Counterpoint, or the interplay of independent musical strands, is certainly one of the salient features of Bach's work, and his brilliant use of this technique is something on which both professional musicians and general listeners can focus easily. Yet Bach's appeal lies in the more human qualities the music embodies. Combined with its cerebral aspects are exquisite melodies and complex figuration, and a sense of passion that comes through both in his text settings and in his instrumental works.   ALLAN KOZINN

Bibliography: Arnold, D., *Bach* (1984); Boyd, M., *Bach* (1983); David, H., and Mendel, A., eds., *The Bach Reader* (1966); Dowley, T., *Bach: His Life and Times* (1983); Felix, W., *J. S. Bach* (1985); Robertson, A., *Bach* (1977); Schweitzer, A., *J. S. Bach,* 2 vols. (Eng. trans., 1911; repr. 1962); Spitta, P., *Johann Sebastian Bach,* 2 vols. (1873–80; Eng. trans., 1884–99); Terry, C. S., *The Music of Bach: An Introduction* (1933); Wolff, C., et al., *The New Grove Bach Family,* rev. ed. (1983).

Bach, Wilhelm Friedemann

Wilhelm Friedemann Bach, b. Nov. 22, 1710, d. July 1, 1784, was a German virtuoso organist and composer whose compositions, although showing bursts of genius, never fulfilled his early promise. Called the "Halle" Bach, he was the eldest son of Johann Sebastian BACH, who considered Friedemann his most talented son and wrote the instructional *Clavier-Büchlein* for him. After holding organist posts in Dresden (1733–47) and Halle (from 1746 until his dismissal in 1764 for "irregular" behavior), Bach moved in 1770 to Berlin, where he subsisted on recitals, lessons, and charity.

Bibliography: Geiringer, Karl, *The Bach Family* (1954; repr. 1981); Young, Percy, *The Bachs* (1970; repr. 1978–79).

Bacharach, Burt   [bak'-rak]

Burt Bacharach, b. Kansas City, Mo., May 12, 1929, is a popular American songwriter. Teamed with lyricist Hal David from 1957, he has written many songs with uncommonly sophisticated harmony and structure, including such hits as "Walk on By" (1964) and "I'll Never Fall in Love Again" (1969) for the pop-soul singer Dionne Warwick. His Academy Award-winning "Raindrops Keep Falling on My Head" (1969) sold 3 million records. Bacharach's stage and film scores include *Promises, Promises* (1969) and *Butch Cassidy and the Sundance Kid* (1969).   JONATHAN KAMIN

bachelor's button

Bachelor's button is another common name for the cornflower, *Centaurea cyanus.* The name "yellow bachelor's button" is sometimes applied to a MILKWORT, *Polygala lutea,* also known as candyweed; a biennial of the eastern United States, it grows to about 30 cm (12 in) high. The leaves form a rosette, and the orange yellow flowers develop in racemes.

Bacher, Robert Fox   [bak'-ur]

The American physicist Robert Fox Bacher, b. Loudonville, Ohio, Aug. 31, 1905, played a major role in the development of nuclear technology. After graduating (1930) from the University of Michigan, he joined the faculty of Cornell University in 1935. Bacher undertook secret research on radar from 1940 to 1943 and collaborated (1943–45) on the development of the atomic bomb. At Los Alamos, N.Mex., on July 12, 1945, he assembled the first atomic bomb, with his own hands, in an old ranch house. President Harry Truman awarded him the Medal of Merit and named him a commissioner of the Atomic Energy Commission in 1946, but Bacher resigned in 1949 to return to teaching. He chaired the physical science division at the California Institute of Technology until 1962 and then served as provost until 1970.   KENNETH THIBODEAU

Bachmann, Ingeborg   [bahk'-mahn]

Ingeborg Bachmann, b. Klagenfurt, Austria, June 25, 1926, d. Rome, Oct. 16, 1973, was one of the most significant writers of postwar Austria. She wrote in many genres but is best known for her lyric poetry. Her first volume of poems, *Die gestundete Zeit* (Borrowed Time, 1953), earned her international recognition. Bachmann's themes center on the threat of existence and on social protest, strongly stated in her collection of short stories, *The Thirtieth Year* (1961, Eng. trans., 1964). Her existential pessimism is balanced by the hope of finding a better human order through new language; thus her work deals fundamentally with the problem of language.

                                     MARILYN SIBLEY FRIES

Bachofen, Johann Jakob [bahk'-ohf-en]

Johann Jakob Bachofen, b. Dec. 22, 1815, d. Nov. 25, 1887, was a Swiss jurist who made important contributions to the study of primitive law and religion. His many works include the well-known *Das Mutterrecht* (The Mother Right, 1861), an evolutionary history of the family. In this work he introduced the notion that the matriarchal family (see MATRIARCHY) antedated the patriarchal family and was the foundation upon which human society was first built. His works influenced early anthropological theorists, notably Lewis Henry MORGAN and Sir Edward B. TYLOR.   JAMES W. HERRICK

Baciccio, Il: see GAULLI, GIOVANNI BATTISTA.

Bacillus: see BACTERIA.

bacitracin: see ANTIBIOTICS.

backgammon

Backgammon is a two-person game played on a square or rectangular board that is divided into two equal halves by the *bar*. For purposes of play, one side is called the *inner table*; the other side is the *outer table*.

Projecting toward the center from the edge of each side of the board are 12 elongated triangles called *points*. Each player has a set of 15 pieces, called *men, stones,* or *counters*. The sets are made of contrasting colors, most frequently black and white or red and white. All 30 pieces are placed on the points at the start of the game, in the manner shown here.

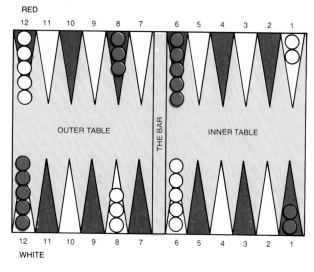

RED
12 11 10 9 8 7 6 5 4 3 2 1

OUTER TABLE | THE BAR | INNER TABLE

12 11 10 9 8 7 6 5 4 3 2 1
WHITE

The equipment also includes two dice cups, four dice, and a *doubling cube*, whose six faces bear the numbers 2, 4, 8, 16, 32, and 64. This is used to double bets when gambling.

Rules. The object of the game is to be the first to move all 15 men into the inner table and then *bear them off*, that is, remove them from the board. Play commences with each player throwing a single die. Whoever rolls the higher number moves first by playing the numbers on both dice. After that, each player in turn rolls two dice, each of which is counted separately and used to move one or two men, as strategy dictates. Whenever two or more men belong to the same player on a single point, they are safe from attack, and the opposing men may not even stop on such a point, regardless of what numbers a roll of the dice produces.

When a point is occupied by a single man (a *blot*), and an opponent's man can land on that point, the blot is removed from the point, placed on the bar, and made to start over. At this juncture, the player with the man on the bar cannot make another move until that man is able to enter the table, and if the count corresponding to the roll of the dice should block this entrance, the player loses that turn.

History. Backgammon is thought to be about 5,000 years old, and a reference to the game appears in Plato's writings. Popular in France and England from the 1600s, the game was described by Edmond Hoyle in 1743. With the formulation (1931) of the current set of rules by Wheaton Vaughan of New York City and others, the game's U.S. popularity blossomed in the 1930s. Another revival occurred in the 1970s. With or without wagering, backgammon remains a favorite board pastime. The game has no worldwide governing body, but the annual tournaments in Monte Carlo, the Bahamas, Boston, and Reno, Nev., are large, international events.

Bibliography: Barr, Ted, *Barr on Backgammon* (1981); Goren, Charles H., *Goren's Modern Backgammon Complete* (1974); Heyken, Enno, and Fischer, M. B., *The Backgammon Handbook* (1991).

background radiation

Background radiation is low-temperature electromagnetic radiation that pervades the universe at microwave wavelengths. Its source is thought to have been the extremely hot fireball with which the universe began, according to the BIG BANG THEORY. Its existence was first predicted in 1948 by Hans BETHE, George GAMOW, and R. A. Alpher. According to their proposal—based on Einstein's theory of general relativity—the first chemical elements were formed under the conditions of extremely high temperature that existed in the earliest moments of the universe. As the universe expanded and cooled, the radiation field corresponding to the high-temperature state decayed in a similar manner. Using data available at the time, Bethe, Gamow, and Alpher calculated that the radiation's temperature would by now be about 25 K (25 degrees Kelvin, or 25 degrees above absolute zero). When they made this proposal, however, no experimental technique was sensitive enough to detect such a weak field.

It was not until 1964, during the course of measurements made for another purpose, that Robert W. WILSON and Arno A. Penzias of Bell Telephone Laboratories discovered the existence of a uniform background radiation at a temperature around 3.5 K. This was identified as the predicted radiation field. Its temperature has since been more accurately determined as 2.73 K. The discovery of background radiation demonstrated the correctness of the application of Einstein's theory of general relativity to cosmology. In addition, its support of the big-bang concept of the singular origin of the universe further entrenched the big bang as the prevailing cosmological concept.

In the 1980s a sophisticated expansion of the big bang theory was developed, called inflationary theory (see COSMOLOGY). It tried to account for the fact that the universe is not featureless but has structure—particles, atoms, stars, galaxies. An initial universe that left behind an absolutely uniform background radiation could not have produced such structure. If the big-bang concept was to survive, therefore, it became essential to find spatially widespread variations—however minute—in the temperature of the background radiation. Such variations were at last detected by NASA's COBE (Cosmic Background Explorer) satellite in the early 1990s. This finding lends further support to but does not constitute final proof of the big bang theory.   HONG YEE CHIU

Bibliography: Gribbin, John, *In Search of the Big Bang* (1985); Hawking, Stephen, *A Brief History of Time* (1988); Henbest, Nigel, "Big Bang Echoes through the Universe," *New Scientist,* May 2, 1992; Stroh, Michael, "COBE Causes Big Bang in Cosmology," *Science News,* May 2, 1992; Weinberg, Steven, *The First Three Minutes* (1988).

Backhaus, Wilhelm [bahk'-hows]

The German pianist Wilhelm Backhaus, b. Mar. 26, 1884, d. July 5, 1969, was renowned for his interpretations of Beethoven and Brahms. After studies in Leipzig and in Frankfurt am Main, the latter under Eugen d'Albert, he began (1900) his career as a concert artist. He taught in London (1905), where he won the Rubinstein piano prize, Sondershausen, Germany

(1907), and at the Curtis Institute in Philadelphia (1925–26). His performances were noted for their clarity, force, lack of obtrusive mannerisms, and faithfulness to the scores. He made many recordings, including a notable set of the complete Beethoven piano sonatas.

F. E. KIRBY

backswimmer

The backswimmer is any of several aquatic insects that constitute the family Notonectidae, order HEMIPTERA. The name is derived from the insects' ability to swim rapidly upside down, using the hind legs as oars. Their usually light-colored, boat-shaped bodies are 2–17 mm (0.08–0.66 in) long, with a convex dorsal surface.

Backswimmers are predators of other insects, crustaceans, snails, tadpoles, and small fish, sucking out their body juices, and can inflict a painful wound when handled by humans. Two genera, *Notonecta* and *Buenoa*, are found in the United States.

STEPHEN CHARLES REINGOLD

bacon

Bacon is the meat product resulting from the curing and smoking of pork. In the United States, about 900 million kg (2 billion lb) of bacon annually is produced from pork bellies; Canadian bacon is made from pork loin, and in Europe the ham and shoulder are used.

Fresh pork bellies range in weight from 3.5 to 11 kg (8 to 25 lb). The ingredients most often used to cure bacon are salt, sugar, sodium nitrite, sodium erythorbate, and the sodium phosphates. These ingredients may be rubbed into the meat or dissolved in water to make a pickling brine. Most commercially produced bacon is pickle-cured; the brine is injected uniformly into the bellies with a multiple-needle machine. The bellies are then placed in a smokehouse, at temperatures of 54.5° to 60° C (130° to 140° F) and humidities of 25 to 45 percent. The time required for cooking and smoking is from two to ten days, depending on the size of the bellies, the internal temperature desired, and air velocity. The bacon is then chilled, pressed, and formed into slabs of uniform width and thickness to facilitate slicing in high-speed slicers. Slabs are sliced to three thicknesses: thin, 0.08 cm (0.031 in); regular, 0.16 cm (0.062 in); and thick, 0.32 cm (0.111 in).

Home-cured bacon, which was a staple food in Europe for hundreds of years, is made by rubbing a salt and spice mixture into the meat, or by soaking it in brine and then hanging it in wood smoke. The curing process takes up to four months.

REX L. GILBREATH

Bibliography: Business Trend Analysts, eds., *Processed Meat Industry* (1985).

Bacon, Francis (painter)

Francis Bacon, b. Oct. 28, 1909, d. Apr. 28, 1992, is considered by many critics to be the outstanding British painter of the second half of the 20th century. Bacon's subjects—nightmarishly distorted faces, bodies, and animals, frequently set in ominously confined spaces—seem to embody the calamities of modern civilization, although the artist avoided stating their meaning.

Bacon's paintings were often comments on the old masters. Two famous paintings, *Pope Innocent X* by Diego Velázquez and *Butchered Ox* by Rembrandt, were sources for Bacon's startling "pope" series, in which an enthroned pontiff, mouth often agape in a shriek (derived from the Odessa Steps sequence in Eisenstein's 1925 film *Battleship Potemkin*), is trapped within the icy perspectives of a glass cage. In *Head Surrounded by Sides of Beef* (1954; The Art Institute of Chicago), a screaming figure is flanked by the split carcass of an ox.

Bacon's later works, many of them triptychs of grotesque male forms writhing in sequence across the panels, reveal such disparate influences as Vincent van Gogh and Eadweard Muybridge's photographic motion studies.

Bibliography: Alley, R., and Rothenstein, J., *Francis Bacon* (1964); Davies, H. M., and Yard, S., *Francis Bacon* (1986); Demetrion, J. T., et al., *Francis Bacon* (1989); Leiris, M., *Francis Bacon* (1988); Sylvester, D., *Interviews with Francis Bacon,* rev. ed. (1981; repr. 1988).

Francis Bacon's Study of Velázquez's Portrait of Innocent X *(1953) transforms the stately image of the 17th-century pope into a symbol of isolation, separation, and entrapment. (Marlborough Gallery, London.)*

Bacon, Francis (philosopher)

Francis Bacon, b. Jan. 22, 1561, d. Apr. 9, 1626, was an English essayist, lawyer, statesman, and philosopher who had a major influence on the philosophy of science. When he was 12 years old, he began studies at Trinity College, Cambridge. In 1576 he entered Gray's Inn to pursue a career in law. He was first elected to Parliament in 1584.

Bacon's opposition to royal tax measures would probably have brought an end to his political advancement, but he had the support of the earl of ESSEX, whose prosecution for treason he later managed. Knighted (1603) after the succession of JAMES I, Bacon became solicitor-general (1609), attorney-general (1613), lord keeper of the great seal (1617), and lord chancellor (1618); he was also created Baron Verulam (1618), and Viscount St. Albans (1621). Bacon retained James's favor by steadfast defense of royal prerogative, but in 1621 he was found guilty of accepting bribes and was removed from his offices. Retiring to Gorhambury, he devoted himself to writing and scientific work.

Philosophically, Bacon sought to purge the mind of what he called "idols," or tendencies to error. These came from human nature ("idols of the tribe"), from individual temperament and experience ("idols of the cave"), from language ("idols of the marketplace"), and from false philosophies ("idols of the theater"). Of earlier philosophers, he particularly criticized Aristotle.

Bacon planned a large work, the *Instauratio Magna* (Great Restoration), setting forth his concepts for the restoration of humankind to mastery over nature. It was intended to contain six parts: (1) a classification of sciences; (2) a new inductive logic; (3) a gathering of empirical and experimental facts; (4) examples to show the efficacy of his new approach; (5) generalizations derivable from natural history; and (6) a new philosophy that would be a complete science of nature.

Francis Bacon held high political offices under James I of England but is best known for his philosophical writings. He influenced scientists to rely on knowledge gained through methodical observation rather than on theory.

Bacon completed only two parts, however: *The Advancement of Learning* (1605), later expanded as *De Dignitate et Augmentis Scientiarum* (On the Dignity and Growth of Sciences, 1623); and the *Novum Organum* (The New *Organon*, 1620), which was to replace Aristotle's *Organon*. Sciences were classified under the general headings of history, poetry, and philosophy. Their culmination was an inductive philosophy of nature, in which Bacon proposed to find the "forms," or natural laws, of bodily action. To this end, he devised so-called tables of induction (of presence, absence, and degrees) designed to discover such forms with the goal of mastery over nature.

Although Bacon was not a great scientist, he gave impetus to the development of modern inductive science. His works were held in esteem by Robert BOYLE, Robert HOOKE, Sir Isaac NEWTON, and Thomas HOBBES. In the 18th century, VOLTAIRE and DIDEROT considered him the father of modern science. Other works of Bacon's include his *Essays* (1597–1625) and *The New Atlantis* (1627). Some 19th-century writers suggested that Bacon was the real author of William SHAKESPEARE's plays, but this theory is discounted by most scholars.

JOHN P. DOYLE

Bibliography: Anderson, F. H., *Francis Bacon* (1962; repr. 1978); Davies, D. W., and Wrigley, E. S., eds., *A Concordance to the Essays of Francis Bacon* (1973); Farrington, Benjamin, *Francis Bacon: Philosopher of Planned Science* (1963); Wallace, Karl, *Francis Bacon on the Nature of Man* (1967); Whitney, Charles, *Francis Bacon and Modernity* (1986).

Bacon, Peggy

Peggy Bacon, b. Ridgefield, Conn., May 2, 1895, d. Jan. 4, 1987, was a printmaker, author, book illustrator, and painter. She studied at the Art Students League of New York primarily with John SLOAN and Kenneth Hayes Miller, with whom she shared a commitment to the depiction of the life of New York City. Best known in the 1920s and '30s as a printmaker and pastelist, she did caricatures of the people in her artistic circle, many reproduced in her witty book *Off with Their Heads!* (1934). During her marriage (1920–40) to the painter Alexander BROOK, she gave up painting in oil, but she returned to that medium in the 1950s.

MARIAN BURLEIGH-MOTLEY

Bibliography: Bacon, Peggy, *The True Philosopher and Other Cat Tales* (1919); Tarbell, Roberta K., *Peggy Bacon* (1975).

Bacon, Roger

Because of his emphasis on the importance of mathematics and experimentation, the English scholastic philosopher

Roger Bacon, c.1220–92, is often considered an early advocate of the methods of modern science.

Most of what is known today about Bacon comes from autobiographical references in his own writings. He received much of his university training in Paris, where he taught philosophy from about 1240 to 1247; after that he went to Oxford, where he was influenced by the ideas of Robert GROSSETESTE. About 1257, Bacon became a Franciscan friar, and for the rest of his life his outspokenness and unorthodox opinions involved him in frequent difficulties with the superiors of his order.

In 1267–68, at the request of Pope Clement IV, Bacon prepared three works, the *Opus maius, Opus minus,* and *Opus tertium,* in which he outlined proposals for a reform of education, arguing that a study of the natural world using observation and exact measurement was the surest foundation for a knowledge of the world's creator. In place of the curriculum followed in medieval universities, he recommended the study of languages, mathematics, alchemy, and experimental sciences—especially optics. In later works, the *Compendium of the Study of Philosophy* (1272) and *Compendium of the Study of Theology* (1292), he harshly criticized the philosophical and theological methods of his day.

Suspected of promoting "dangerous novelties," Bacon was imprisoned for a time (probably between 1277 and 1279) by order of the minister-general of the Franciscans. After his death Bacon acquired the reputation of having been a sorcerer and wonder-worker. Later, because he had speculated about such things as gunpowder, flying machines, telescopes, and mechanically driven carriages, he became celebrated for his foresight. Modern research has shown that although Bacon borrowed many of his ideas from others, he did have a real influence on subsequent scientific thought.

Bibliography: Crowley, Theodore, *Roger Bacon: The Problem of the Soul in His Philosophical Commentaries* (1950); Easton, S. C., *Roger Bacon and His Search for a Universal Science* (1952); Westacott, Evelyn, *Roger Bacon in Life and Legend* (1953; repr. 1974).

Bacon's Rebellion

Bacon's Rebellion was a short-lived revolt in colonial Virginia. It began in May 1676 when Nathaniel Bacon (1647–76), a young, well-placed Virginian, led a small army of his fellow colonists in combat against both the royal governor, Sir William BERKELEY, and the Indians on the frontier. The participants in the rebellion were motivated by a variety of concerns. Some resented Berkeley's growing personal power, others were anxious to strengthen the popular voice in the political process, and nearly all were opposed to the governor's Indian policy, which threatened to restrict their expansion into western lands occupied by Indians.

Bacon and his men enjoyed some initial success. In June 1676 an assembly dominated by Bacon's supporters passed laws extending the rights of freemen and restricting still further the rights of Indians. Bacon died of swamp fever, however, in October 1676, and by January 1677, Berkeley was once again in control of the colony.

RICHARD R. BEEMAN

Bibliography: Washburn, Wilcomb E., *The Governor and the Rebel* (1957; repr. 1972); Wertenbaker, Thomas J., *Torchbearer of the Revolution: The Story of Bacon's Rebellion and Its Leader* (1940) and *Bacon's Rebellion, 1676* (1980).

bacteria

Bacteria is the common name for a vast group of one-celled microscopic organisms that encompasses the smallest, simplest, and perhaps first form of CELL life that evolved. They constitute one of two divisions in the kingdom MONERA. They are unicellular and furnish both the raw material and the chemical machinery for their own reproduction, whereas viruses, for example, do not. The oldest sign of life is a fossilized bacterial cell discovered in a rock in Africa and estimated at about 3.5 billion years old. The study of bacteria is called bacteriology, which belongs to the broader science of MICROBIOLOGY, or the study of all types of microorganisms, in-

Bacteria are arranged into three basic cell shapes: coccus, or spherical (top); bacillus, or cylindrical (center); and spirillum, or spiral (bottom). Bacteria of the genus Staphylococcus (1) *are arranged in clusters.* Diplococcus *species (2) generally consist of two spheres encased in a membrane, and* Streptococcus *species (3) form chains. Most cocci are unable to move independently because they lack flagella, which are whiplike appendages.*

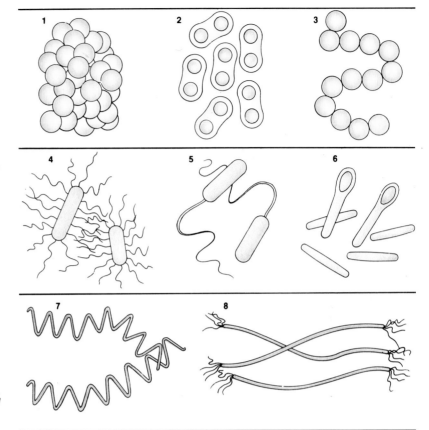

Most bacilli are freely mobile because they have flagella to propel them through water by a beating motion. Some species have flagella distributed around the body (4) and others have a single flagellum (5). Bacilli form spores (6) that are resistant to heat, lack of water, and toxic chemicals. Each spore germinates and forms new bacilli.

Spirilla may be tightly coiled into an accordion shape, such as Leptospira (7), *which is a genus of pathogenic spirochetes.* Spirillum *species (8) curve in a fairly loose to moderately tight helix. Unlike spirochetes, which are flexible,* Spirillum *species are rigid and need flagella in order to move. Other spirilla are regularly or irregularly coiled.*

cluding one-celled protozoa, yeasts, and algae. Medical microbiology is concerned with the behavior and control of pathogens, which are microorganisms that cause INFECTIOUS DISEASES in humans and other animals.

SIZE AND HABITAT
Thirty trillion bacteria of average size weigh about 28 g (1 oz). Bacteria are measured in microns (0.001 μm, about 0.00004 in) and most types range from 0.1 to 4.0 microns in width and 0.2 to 50 microns in length. Bacteria are found everywhere. Approximately 2,000 species have been identified, many of them living in conditions that would destroy other organisms. They have been found in the almost airless reaches of the upper atmosphere, 10 km (6 mi) below the surface of the ocean, in frozen soil, and on rocks in hot springs. Some bacteria produce a resting stage, the endospore, which is the most resistant living thing known and can be killed only by boiling in steam under pressure for many hours.

CLASSIFICATION
Advances in biology during the 19th century indicated that bacteria and certain other organisms were neither plant nor animal. Both bacteria and plants have rigid cell walls, but unlike plants, most kinds of bacteria move about and use organic foods for energy and growth; only a few use photosynthesis. Although bacteria are classified as plants in the traditional two-kingdom classification system, in one of the five-kingdom classification systems used today the one-celled PROKARYOTES (bacteria and cyanobacteria, or BLUE-GREEN ALGAE) are classified in the kingdom Monera and the one-celled EUKARYOTES (protozoa) are placed in the kingdom Protista.

On the basis of their shapes, bacteria may be grouped into three main types: the rod-shaped bacilli, which often have small whiplike structures known as FLAGELLA that propel the organism, usually in a rolling or tumbling motion; the spherical cocci (singular coccus), which may grow in chains (STREP-TOCOCCI, or ''strep germs,'' as in STREP THROAT) or which may clump together like a bunch of grapes (STAPHYLOCOCCI); and the comma- or spiral-shaped spirilla and SPIROCHETES. Another

kind of bacteria, called the MYCOPLASMAS, have no rigid cell walls and consequently are formless. These are the smallest bacteria and are often called pleuropneumonialike organisms (PPLO), because they cause a contagious pneumonia in cows and human beings. Recently, a new classification system has been proposed that arranges species according to genetic makeup. In this new system, ARCHAEBACTERIA, a group of highly specialized bacteria, are differentiated from the eubacteria, a group that includes the vast majority of bacteria, on the basis of the sequence of ribosomal RNA.

An important, widely used technique for identifying bacteria is gram staining, perfected by the Danish bacteriologist Hans Christian Gram in 1884. In this process the bacteria are treated with a special dye, or stain, and other chemicals. The treated bacteria fall into two groups: gram-positive bacteria, which appear deep violet in color, and gram-negative bacteria, which appear red in color. Physicians often use gram staining in choosing the proper ANTIBIOTIC for treating a bacterial infection. Gram-positive bacteria are more susceptible

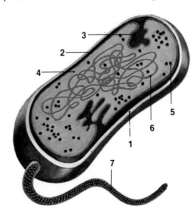

A simplified bacterium has a tough cell wall (1) and a semipermeable membrane (2). A mesosome (3) is an invagination of the membrane into the cytoplasm (4). The cytoplasm contains small bodies such as ribosomes (5), which have the RNA that synthesizes proteins. Bacterial DNA (6) is circular and 1,000 times longer than the cell. Many bacteria have flagella (7).

to penicillin, whereas gram-negative bacteria are usually more susceptible to other antibiotics such as streptomycin. The basis of this difference in staining properties is still a mystery, but evidence indicates that the difference lies in the composition of the bacterial cell wall.

Although bacterial and plant cells are enclosed by rigid walls, they differ in composition. Plant cell walls derive their strength largely from cellulose, whereas bacterial cell walls are stiffened primarily by murein (a compound made of amino acids and sugar). This important difference is the basis for the selective activity of certain drugs such as penicillin. Nontoxic to plants and animals, penicillin is toxic to growing bacteria because it inhibits formation of murein and thus interferes with bacterial reproduction.

PHYSIOLOGY

The only organisms comparable to bacteria in size and simplicity are the cyanobacteria, still often known as the blue-green algae, Cyanophyta (see ALGAE). The kingdom MONERA is composed of only two groups and classified separately from all other forms of cellular life. Other life forms, including human beings, are eukaryotic, that is, their cells contain organelles such as the nucleus, chloroplast, chromoplast, lysosome, mitochondrion, endoplasmic reticulum, and golgi apparatus. Cells of monerans are prokaryotic (prenuclear) and lack organelles but not the functions controlled by them.

In terms of metabolism, the diversity of life is much more evident in bacteria (and blue-green algae) than in other organisms. Bacteria display a staggering variety of mechanisms for obtaining energy that have no parallel in higher organisms.

Bacteria may be classified on the basis of their requirements for free atmospheric oxygen. Those requiring oxygen are aerobes; those which cannot live in the presence of oxygen are obligate ANAEROBES; and those which do well with oxygen but can survive without it are facultative anaerobes. Many photosynthetic bacteria are anaerobic. The sulfur bacteria that live in oxygen-poor environments produce sulfur instead of the oxygen gas given off by green plants. Anaerobes obtain sufficient energy for their needs through FERMENTATION (breaking down organic molecules with enzymes). Other bacteria are chemosynthetic; unlike photosynthetic bacteria, which use light as an energy source, they use nitrogen- and sulfur-containing compounds to obtain the necessary energy for food manufacture.

REPRODUCTION

Most bacteria reproduce asexually by binary fission (see REPRODUCTION), in which a single cell divides in two. Many species divide as often as every 20 minutes under favorable conditions. If all the descendants survived, the initial cell would result in about 500,000 new cells after 6 hours. Such rapid increases help to explain the rapid development of disease, food spoilage, decay, and the speed at which certain chemical processes used in industry take place.

Certain bacteria such as E. coli reproduce by conjugation, which resembles sexual reproduction, in that the two bacteria join (mate) and exchange genes. As in true sexual reproduction, the genetic material, or "nuclear" chromosomes, recombine with one another (see GENETICS). In the process of recombination, a fragment of a chromosome transmitted from one bacterium is incorporated in the chromosome of the recipient. Conjugation and recombination increase the total number of different hereditary characteristics in a population of bacteria, increasing the bacteria's chances of survival.

ECONOMIC IMPORTANCE

The beneficial role of bacteria is worth emphasizing, as the popular idea that all bacteria are hostile stems from the prominent historical connection between bacteria and disease. Most important bacteria are harmless to humans, and many are essential to the existence of plant and animal life. Only a small fraction of bacteria cause disease; most bacteria attack organic matter only after it is dead. Were it not for bacteria that decompose animal waste matter and the bodies of dead animals and plants, these materials would accumulate almost indefinitely. Bacteria also enrich the soil in various ways. The so-called nitrogen-fixing bacteria take nitrogen gas from the atmosphere and convert it to a form (nitrate) that

green plants use for growth. Small nodules in the roots of leguminous plants contain bacteria, genus Rhizobium, that help fix nitrogen in usable form, and a number of cyanobacteria fix atmospheric nitrogen (see NITROGEN CYCLE). Bacteria also create FERTILIZER by breaking down compost heaps made of soil and dead plant matter.

Bacteria are important industrially in the production of cheese, yogurt, buttermilk, vinegar, and sauerkraut; in the preparation of antibiotics such as Streptomycin, which is extracted from soil bacteria; in the tanning of leather and hides and the curing of tobacco; and in sewage disposal plants to render organic wastes harmless. Cattle, sheep, and goats live on grass; yet without bacteria they would not be able to digest the tough fibers of plant cellulose.

Stored foods that have been improperly processed are subject to spoilage by bacteria. Poisonous toxins are sometimes produced by such food-spoiling bacteria as Staphylococci, Streptococci, and SALMONELLA. They cause severe illness in humans eating affected food. Clostridium botulinum, growing in canned or smoked foods that have been improperly processed, produces a toxin that causes a frequently fatal disease called BOTULISM.

DESTRUCTION OF BACTERIA

High temperature usually kills most bacteria. Most disease-producing bacteria in milk, for example, can be killed by maintaining the temperature at 62° C (143° F) for 30 minutes, a process called PASTEURIZATION. "Flash pasteurization," done at 71° C (160° F) for 15 seconds, is now commonly used. Most nonspore-forming bacteria are destroyed by boiling water and can be killed by various disinfectants. ANTISEPTICS may kill bacteria or prevent infection by inhibiting their growth. Among the most potent disinfectants are phenol (carbolic acid), chlorine gas (drinking water is treated with chlorine to render it safe), and alcohol in a 50- to 70-percent solution, as in rubbing alcohol. Bichloride of mercury and other mercury-containing compounds (mercurochrome and merthiolate) are often used as disinfectants and antiseptics.

The above chemicals are poisonous in the human body and should not be taken internally. Antibiotics, however, are substances produced by living organisms (usually bacteria and MOLDS) that are used internally for inhibiting the growth of bacteria or destroying them; antimicrobial agents are natural or artificial chemicals having the same use.

BACTERIA AND DISEASE

A century ago in the United States, and even today in the less developed countries, at least 25 percent of the children died of bacterial infections before reaching puberty. In the United States and other Western nations, this figure is now below 5 percent as a result of improved sanitation, hygiene, nutrition, and medical care.

The control of TYPHOID FEVER alone is perhaps the greatest triumph of organized PREVENTIVE MEDICINE. As late as 1900, the annual death rate from typhoid fever in the United States was more than 30 per 100,000; by 1944, the rate had decreased to 0.4 per 100,000. For the world as a whole, however, typhoid fever remains a major disease.

History. To account for the spread of certain diseases from person to person, thoughtful men since ancient times postulated the existence of transmissible agents of infection invisible to the naked eye. In his book on contagious diseases, published in 1546, the Italian physician Girolamo FRACASTORO described the transmission of disease by "seminaria," or living germs. Although Fracastoro proposed the true germ theory of disease, visualization of the germs could not take place until the microscope had been invented. Bacteria and other microscopic organisms were first seen in 1676 by a Dutch linen-draper, Antoni van LEEUWENHOEK, who made single-lens microscopes with sufficient magnification to observe the major types of bacteria as well as protozoa, yeasts, and one-celled algae. Leeuwenhoek is regarded as the father of bacteriology. By keeping secret the methods of making and using his instruments, he remained the sole occupant of the field he had created for the rest of his life.

The first important classification of bacteria was made in the early 1800s. In 1829, Christian Gottfried established the ge-

(Above) *Robert Koch, a German bacteriologist, received the 1905 Nobel Prize for physiology or medicine for his discovery of and research into the bacilli that cause tuberculosis. He also isolated the bacteria responsible for anthrax and cholera.*

(Right) *The life cycle of anthrax bacilli, B. anthracis, was sketched by Robert Koch in 1876. New bacilli (1a) are found among red blood cells. These immature bacteria (2a) grow and develop elongated cell bodies (3a). Mature, rod-shaped bacilli (3b) develop spores that form long chains (4) when released from the parent bacilli. Eventually the chains break apart so that individual spores can develop new bacilli.*

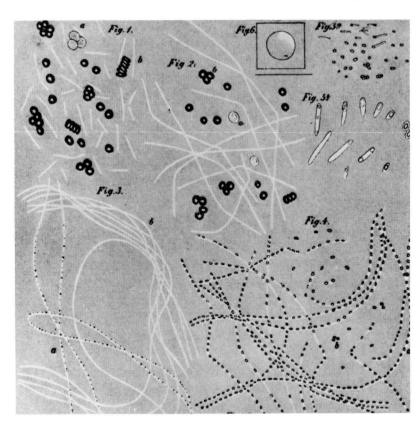

nus *Bacterium,* using a term formed from the Greek word *bacterion,* signifying a rod. The entire subject of bacteriology has taken its common name from the prominence of rodlike forms of bacteria, now called bacilli. Eventually, bacteria were classified in the plant kingdom, and this remained the dominant view until the 1960s. Historically, living organisms have been classified as either plant or animal. In this traditional classification, bacteria are regarded as the simplest forms of FUNGI and are named Schizomycetes, or "fission fungi," because they multiply by fission (splitting in two). Bacteria are now classified as Monerans, and the name Schizophyta is the scientific designation of these organisms.

An experimental science of bacteriology emerged slowly and required the development of special methodology. The key was the use of sterile (germ-free) materials and antiseptic techniques. Although the chemist defines purity in terms of the percentage of contaminating material, a single contaminating cell can ruin an experiment in bacteriology. Only after learning to avoid such contamination could investigators recognize the existing variety of bacteria, their distribution, and their major roles.

Bacteria in Disease. In Vienna in the mid-1840s, Ignaz Philip SEMMELWEISS, a Hungarian obstetrician, tried to convince his disbelieving colleagues that the disease that swept through maternity wards and killed hundreds of women each year could be prevented. Childbed fever (puerperal sepsis) was caused by a strain of Streptococcus spread by medical students going from the dissecting room to the patients without first washing. Semmelweiss had the students on his wards wash their hands in disinfectant before each delivery, and this precaution greatly reduced the amount of infection. In spite of the remarkable drop in the number of deaths, he was discredited by his colleagues. Ironically, he died of an infection from a cut received during an AUTOPSY.

The role of bacteria in a disease was first proved (1876) by the German bacteriologist Robert KOCH for ANTHRAX, and was confirmed by Louis PASTEUR. Koch meticulously developed the techniques that are used today in culturing bacteria for study and set down rules still used for proving that a given infec-

(Below) *Anthrax bacilli, B. anthracis, infect the blood and skin of domestic animals such as sheep, pigs, and cattle. Humans who sort wool or handle skins may contract anthrax, but sanitation and vaccination have prevented epidemics during the 20th century.*

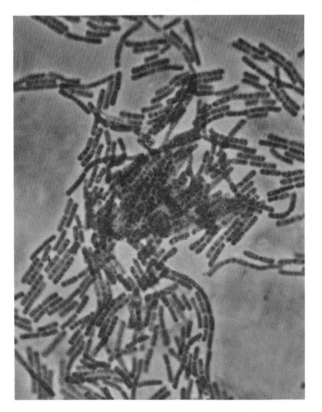

tion is caused by particular bacteria, the pathogenic bacteria. These rules are called Koch's postulates and may be summarized as follows: the bacteria must be present in the infected tissue in every case of the infection; they must be isolated in pure culture on an artificial medium; innoculation of this culture into experimental animals must cause a similar disease; and the organisms must be recovered from the infected tissue. About ten years before Koch isolated anthrax, Joseph LISTER virtually eliminated wound infections by soaking bandages in carbolic acid. This was the start of modern aseptic surgical techniques.

Following Koch's initial discovery, medical scientists raced to identify other pathogens. Pasteur, however, devoted himself to developing vaccines, which are materials made from specially treated organisms and inoculated into humans and other animals to develop immunity to a specific infectious disease. Studies of the response of the body's defense mechanisms to bacteria later gave rise to the field of IMMUNOLOGY. Immunology is thus inseparable from bacteriology, although, strictly speaking, it is a branch of medicine.

It is now known that bacteria are transmitted by air, insects, water, food, and direct contact with human beings, animals, and objects. Not all of the bacteria associated with human beings cause disease, however; a natural flora exists in the body, and the *E. coli* of the large intestine help to control the body's water balance and to provide certain vitamins. Their presence in drinking water may be taken as a measure of contamination, however, suggesting that pathogens may be present.

Plasmids. Many bacteria contain PLASMIDS, which are tiny pieces of DNA (see NUCLEIC ACID) that are much smaller than and independent of chromosomal DNA and generally carry nonessential bacterial genes. First observed in *E. coli,* some plasmids carry traits such as resistance to antibiotics. How they acquire their extra DNA controlling resistance and virulence is not known, although many authorities believe that overuse of antibiotics is the main cause.

In GENETIC ENGINEERING, plasmids are isolated, opened up for insertion of pieces of DNA from other sources, and then resealed; this hybrid DNA is called recombinant DNA. The new plasmid is placed into a receptor cell, "infecting" it as if it were a virus. The inserted genes then express themselves along with the normal genetic complement of the cell. A bacterium may be programmed in this way to produce a useful substance; human insulin, for example, is produced when human genes controlling insulin production are placed into a plasmid and then inserted into a bacterium.

Transduction. Bacteria also exchange chromosomal material through transduction, which occurs when bacteria are infected by viruses called bacteriophages. Transduction involves the accidental transfer of bacterial genes between bacterial cells by a bacteriophage and the incorporation of these genes into the recipient bacterium. This transfer requires that the bacteriophage infect a bacterial strain that is destroyed by the virus and that the recipient strain of bacteria be the one that harbors the virus but that is not usually destroyed by it. This alternation between destruction of bacterial cells by bacteriophage and harboring the virus with no sign of infection is called lysogeny. A process analogous to lysogeny is believed to be the reason viruses cause certain cancers in animals and perhaps humans.

BACTERIA IN MODERN BIOLOGY

Until the 1950s, bacteriology was a branch of medicine concerned almost solely with pathogenic bacteria. Eventually, however, bacteria were found particularly suitable for studying many basic problems common to all cells, such as metabolism, the molecular aspects of genetics that involve the structure and function of DNA and the way in which cellular action is regulated, and the synthesis of proteins in the cell. These studies revealed many instances of a resemblance between microbial cells and cells of higher organisms, in their building blocks, enzymes, and metabolic pathways. The advantages of bacteria for such studies include their relatively simple structure; homogenous cell populations (each cell is exactly like the others); extremely rapid growth; and the ease

with which billions of individual cells can be cultivated and selected to yield mutants and mutant HYBRIDS. Mutants obtained in this way have permitted scientists to identify the role of various genes and protein molecules in cell actions as well as reasons for bacterial resistance to antibiotics. These developments have led to an interdisciplinary activity known as molecular biology or biochemical genetics.

Reviewed by LAWRENCE J. CROCKETT

Bibliography: Bainbridge, B. W., *Genetics of Microbes* (1986); Fletcher, M. M., and Floodgate, G. D., eds., *Bacteria in Their Natural Environments* (1985); Gunsalus, I. C., et al., eds., *The Bacteria,* 8 vols. (1960–85); Singleton, P., and Sainsbury, D., *Introduction to Bacteria* (1981); Sinha, U., and Srivastava, S., *An Introduction to Bacteria* (1983); VanDemark, P. J., and Batzing, B. L., *The Microbes: An Introduction to Their Nature and Importance* (1987).

bacteriology: see MICROBIOLOGY.

Bactria   [bak'-tree-uh]

Bactria was an ancient land on both sides of the upper Oxus River, today called the Amu Darya, in present-day northern Afghanistan and southern Tadzhik SSR. The heart of Bactria was the plain south of the river and its principal city, Bactra (the present-day Balkh). The northern and southern tributaries of the Oxus made the valleys of Bactria leading to the alluvial plain rich centers of agriculture, but Bactria was more important for its strategic location between China, India, and the West. The prophet ZOROASTER is said to have made his first converts in Bactria and to have died there. Bactria became an important province of the ACHAEMENID Empire, and after the conquests of ALEXANDER THE GREAT it became the center of an independent Greek kingdom whose rulers struck fine Greek coins. The kingdom lasted until 128 BC, when northern nomads overran it. Bactria then became part of the Kushan empire and remained so until the 4th century AD, when Sassanian governors became its rulers. The nomadic Hephthalites (White Huns) took control in the following century, ruling until the Arab conquest at the end of the 7th century.

RICHARD N. FRYE

Bibliography: Rawlinson, Hugh G., *Bactria* (1912); Tarn, William W., *The Greeks in Bactria and India* (1951).

Badaga   [buh-dah'-guh]

The Badaga are the largest of the four main groups of people in the Nilgiri Hills of western Tamil Nadu (Madras) state in southern India. The Badaga, estimated to number more than 100,000, speak a DRAVIDIAN dialect that closely resembles the Kannada language of neighboring Karnataka state. The name *Badaga* means "northerner," suggesting an origin outside the Nilgiris. The Badaga were probably driven into the hills by stronger political groups several centuries ago.

The Badaga are divided into six ritually ranked sections, which resemble the wider CASTE system of Indian society. The two highest sections are traditionally cultivators and vegetarians, and the other four are artisans. Although traditionally dependent for essential goods and services upon the Kotas, Todas, and Kurumbas with whom they share the Nilgiris, the Badaga have increasingly dissociated themselves from these other, more tribal groups in their attempts to raise their status by becoming accepted as high-caste Hindus. Such self-improvement has been made possible by their success in agriculture. The traditional interdependence between the Badaga and their neighbors has gradually broken down, and the Badaga have begun to treat these same neighbors as UNTOUCHABLES.

HILARY STANDING AND R. L. STIRRAT

Bibliography: Mandelbaum, D. G., *Society in India,* 2 vols. (1970).

Badajoz   [bah-thah-hohs']

Badajoz is the capital of Badajoz province in southwestern Spain, at the Portuguese border on the southern bank of the Guadiana River. Its population is 114,361 (1981). The city is Spain's most important center of trade with Portugal and serves as the market center for the surrounding agricultural region. Industrialized since the 1940s, it processes wheat, pepper, coffee, tuna, cooking oil, building materials, and textiles. Industrialization has caused a rapid rise in population, principally by emigration from the countryside.

Badajoz was settled by the Romans, who built (late 1st century BC) a fortress later occupied (1010–1229) by Moors. The city is still surrounded by walls, with bastions and a moat; also remaining are a Roman bridge, ruins of a Moorish castle, and a cathedral begun during the 13th century that houses paintings by Luís de MORALES, a native of Badajoz. The city was the scene of a massacre after its surrender to General Franco's forces in 1936.

Badalona   [bahd-uh-loh'-nuh]

Badalona (1987 est. pop., 224,233) is an industrial suburb and port in northeastern Spain, on the Mediterranean coast about 8 km (5 mi) north of Barcelona. Badalona is one of the country's most important and diversified industrial centers, producing metals, textiles, glassware, and petroleum products. As Baetulo, it was important during Roman times.

Baden   [bah'-den]

Baden is a former state in the extreme southwest of Germany. It is now part of Baden-Württemberg, one of the 15 *länder* (states) of Germany (see WÜRTTEMBERG). The region's physical relief is dominated by the Rhine River valley in the west and the BLACK FOREST to the south. Baden's historic capital is KARLSRUHE; other important cities include FREIBURG IM BREISGAU, HEIDELBERG, MANNHEIM, and Konstanz.

Baden became a political entity in 1112 when a member of the Zähringen family, Hermann, grandson of Bertold, duke of Carinthia, took the title of margrave of Baden. For the next 600 years, however, the region was divided into numerous petty states, and it suffered particularly from religious rivalries following the Reformation. In 1771, Baden was reunited under the house of Zähringen (combining the margraviates of Baden-Baden and Baden-Durlach). Charles Frederick of Baden allied (1796) himself with Napoleon I. In 1806, Baden, with expanded territory, became a duchy in Napoleon's Confederation of the Rhine. In 1815, Baden became a member of the German Confederation, and in 1836 it joined the ZOLLVEREIN. Revolutionary activity in 1848 was suppressed by Prussian troops. In 1871, Baden became part of the German Empire as a grand duchy. The last grand duke was deposed in 1918, and Baden joined the Weimar Republic. Baden was made an administrative district of Germany in 1933. In 1952 it was incorporated into the West German State of Baden-Württemberg.

BRUCE L. LaROSE

Bibliography: Lee, Lloyd, *The Politics of Harmony: Civil Service and Social Reform in Baden, 1800–1850* (1980).

Baden-Baden

Baden-Baden is a city in the state of Baden-Württemberg in southwestern Germany. Located in the BLACK FOREST, it is a health resort known for hot mineral baths and has a population of 50,761 (1989 est.). Average annual rainfall is 1,102 mm (43 in). The ruins there, dating from the early 3d century, attest to the importance of Baden-Baden as a spa since Roman times. From 1112 to 1705 it was the residence of the margraves of Baden. In the 19th century it became one of Europe's most fashionable resorts. It served as the seat of the French zone of occupation after World War II. Important buildings include the casino, a 7th-century church with tombs of the margraves, and two castles.

Baden-Powell, Robert Stephenson Smyth, 1st Baron Baden-Powell of Gilwell
[bay-den-poh'-ul]

Robert Baden-Powell, b. Feb. 22, 1857, d. Jan. 8, 1941, was a British soldier who founded the Boy Scout and Girl Guide (Girl Scout) movement. During the SOUTH AFRICAN WAR (1899–1902) he won renown for holding Mafeking against a Boer

siege for 217 days. He later organized the South African constabulary. Having formed the Boy Scouts (1908) and, with his sister Agnes Baden-Powell, the Girl Guides (1909), Baden-Powell devoted the rest of his life to the SCOUTING movement. He wrote many books on scouting.

Bibliography: Jeal, Tim, *The Boy-Man: The Life of Lord Baden-Powell* (1990); Kiernan, R. H., *Baden-Powell* (1939; repr. 1970).

badger

The American badger, Taxidea taxus, *is a solitary, fierce animal that hibernates in winter. It is the only New World species of badger.*

Badger is the common name of several nocturnal carnivores belonging to the family Mustelidae, order Carnivora, which also includes weasels and skunks. Six genera and eight species exist. Seven species live in Eurasia and one in North America, in habitats ranging from prairies to mountain areas.

The badger has a broad, flat body, a small head, and short, heavy-clawed legs. It is a rapid burrower and a fierce fighter. The body may be up to 76 cm (30 in) long, excluding a short tail, and the weight up to 11 kg (25 lb). All badgers have scent glands, which may be used defensively. The stiff fur of the badger has been used for making brushes and as trim for coats and jackets. Most badgers are ground dwellers, but certain badgers of China, Burma, and Java can climb trees. Badgers eat gophers, mice, ground squirrels, other small animals, and some plant material. Gestation lasts more than 180 days because of delayed implantation of the fertilized egg on the wall of the uterus. The female gives birth to a litter of one to seven young.

EVERETT SENTMAN

Bibliography: Kruuk, Hans, *The Social Badger* (1989); Neal, E., *The Natural History of Badgers* (1986).

Badings, Henk   [bah'-dingz]

Hendrik Herman Henk Badings, b. Bandoeng, Java, Jan. 17, 1907, of Dutch parents, d. June 26, 1987, was a prolific Dutch composer whose compositions show strong contrapuntal skills and striking orchestral effects. Early works such as the Third Symphony (1934) are thickly polyphonic, but later ones such as the Concerto for Two Violins (1954) are lighter in texture. Badings also explored different scale systems. In the 1950s he began to write electronic music, a medium he used throughout his remaining career, along with traditional instruments.

badlands

Badlands are elevated areas that have been severely eroded and are deeply incised with gullies. They are usually formed in dry regions and lack a protective vegetation cover. Occasional heavy rainfall will form runoff gullies in the softer strata. Uneven resistance of different rocks can create a tortured landscape of pinnacles and buttes.

The term *badlands* was first used for a region of the northern Great Plains of the United States, specifically in southwest South Dakota and the Little Missouri River region of North Dakota. Two protected badlands areas in the United States remain in their natural state. The Badlands National Monument southeast of Rapid City, S.Dak., covers 985 km² (380 mi²); fossil remains of the saber-toothed cat, the three-toed horse, and other early mammals, reptiles, and birds have been found there. The Theodore Roosevelt National Memorial Park in North Dakota includes 285 km² (110 mi²) of badlands. Little vegetation or animal life exists in these regions, but the multi-colored formations of shales and limestones make the parks tourist attractions.

badminton   [bad'-min-tuhn]

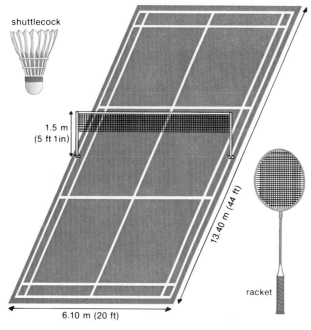

shuttlecock

1.5 m
(5 ft 1in)

13.40 m (44 ft)

6.10 m (20 ft)

racket

Badminton, introduced by British troops returning from India, grew popular in England, where the first set of rules was codified in 1895.

Badminton is an Olympic sport for two or four players in which long-handled rackets are used to hit a shuttlecock (also called a shuttle or bird) over a net stretched across a marked court. Badminton's growth both as a backyard recreation and as a highly developed competitive indoor sport has been greatest since the end of World War II, although the game dates back to the 1800s. The International Badminton Federation (IBF) has members in more than 90 nations and an annual world Grand Prix circuit for both men and women.

History. The game is believed to have been invented in India in a version called *poona*. British army officers learned the game about 1870. In 1873 the duke of Beaufort introduced the sport at his country estate, Badminton, from which the game derives its name. In 1887 the Bath Badminton Club was formed; it was replaced in 1893 by the Badminton Association of England, which codified the rules that still govern competitive play. In the United States, meanwhile, the first badminton club was formed in 1878 in New York City.

The IBF was founded in 1934 with nine nations represented. The introduction of Thomas Cup play for men in 1949 and Uber Cup competition for women in 1957 brought to public attention outstanding stars such as Judy Devlin Hashman, of Baltimore, Md., winner of ten all-England titles.

Equipment. Rackets are lightweight, much smaller than those used in tennis. The 5-g (0.18-oz) shuttlecock is usually made of cork and feathers, which can cause the shuttle suddenly to stop, drop, or turn in midair. The court is about 5.2 by 13.4 m (17 by 44 ft) for singles and 1 m (3 ft) wider for doubles.

Scoring. In order to score, a player has to serve, or put the shuttle into play. A server can score when the opponent lets the shuttle fall to the ground or by a fault. A fault occurs

when the opponent, in an attempt to return the shuttle safely, allows it to go into or under the net, hits it out of the playing area, touches the net, or is touched by the shuttle.

In doubles or men's singles, 15 points wins a game; in women's singles, 11 points. A match is the best two out of three games.   JIM BENAGH

Bibliography: Bloss, M. V., and Hales, R. S., *Badminton*, 6th ed. (1990); Davis, Pat, *Badminton: A Complete Practical Guide* (1989).

Badoglio, Pietro   [bah-dohl'-ee-oh, pee-et'-troh]

Pietro Badoglio, b. Sept. 28, 1871, d. Nov. 1, 1956, was an Italian general who was supreme commander in the Italian conquest of Ethiopia (1935–36) and in the disastrous Italian invasion of Greece (1940). After Benito Mussolini's fall, Badoglio became (July 25, 1943) prime minister and negotiated an armistice with the Allies. He resigned in June 1944.

Baeck, Leo   [bek]

Leo Baeck, b. May 23, 1873, d. Nov. 2, 1956, was the chief rabbi of German Reform Judaism and an outstanding leader of progressive Judaism during the Nazi period. His theoretical position developed gradually. In the beginning he espoused an extreme form of rationalism, which is seen in his *Essence of Judaism* (1905; Eng. trans., 1936). Toward the end of his life, he promoted a Jewish existentialism, which grew out of his experiences in the concentration camp of Theresienstadt and took expression in *This People Israel* (1955–57; Eng. trans., 1965). After 1945, Baeck chaired the World Union for Progressive Judaism and taught at the Hebrew Union College in Cincinnati. Both the Leo Baeck College—a liberal Jewish training school in England—and the Leo Baeck Institute in New York City—a center for historical study of German-Jewish life—were named in his honor to preserve the memory of his efforts on behalf of his coreligionists.   JOSEPH L. BLAU

Bibliography: Bach, H. I., *The German Jew* (1984); Baker, Leonard, *Days of Pain and Sorrow: Leo Baeck and the Berlin Jews* (1980); Friedlander, A. H., *Leo Baeck, Teacher of Theresienstadt* (1968).

Baedeker, Karl   [bay'-duh-kur]

Karl Baedeker, b. Nov. 3, 1801, d. Oct. 4, 1859, was the founder of a publishing firm specializing in travel books that were extremely popular not only in their original German editions but also in English and French translations. The first of the "Baedekers," a guide to Germany and the Low Countries, appeared in 1839; it was followed by guides to most of Europe, North America, and the Far East. Still published, the guides now present information alphabetically, not geographically.

Baer, Karl Ernst von   [bair]

Karl Ernst von Baer, b. Feb. 29, 1792, d. Nov. 28, 1876, was a German-Russian biologist and a founder of modern embryology. He was the first to observe and identify the mammalian ovum, or egg cell, differentiating it from the fluid-filled sac, or Graafian follicle, that surrounds it and establishing that mammalian eggs are similar to those of lower animals. Baer also discovered that a developing egg forms several distinct layers of cells, which he called germ layers, and that these layers become the specialized tissues of the body organs. He compared the development of embryos among various vertebrates and thus helped to establish comparative embryology.

Bibliography: Willier, Benjamin H., and Oppenheimer, Jane M., eds., *Foundations of Experimental Embryology*, 2d ed. (1974).

Baeyer, Adolf von   [bah'-yur]

The German chemist Adolf von Baeyer, b. Oct. 31, 1835, d. Aug. 20, 1917, carried out important research on DYES. He discovered a new group of dyes—the phthaleins—demonstrated their chemical nature, and, with Heinrich Caro, developed these compounds into dyestuffs. For this research on dyes and his synthesis of indigo, he was awarded the Nobel Prize for chemistry in 1905.

He also carried out notable synthetic and theoretical work on compounds resulting from the reduction of benzene derivatives. Baeyer synthesized (1864) barbituric acid, obtained (1892) the first synthesis of a terpene, and investigated the organic peroxides.   VIRGINIA F. McCONNELL

Baez, Joan   [by-ez']

Joan Baez, b. Staten Island, N.Y., Jan. 9, 1941, is a folksinger and guitarist noted for her strong, pure soprano voice. A singer in Cambridge, Mass., coffeehouses in the mid-1950s, Baez first reached a national audience at the 1959 Newport Folk Festival. Several of her early recordings, primarily of Anglo-American folk ballads, each sold more than 1 million copies. An early Bob DYLAN enthusiast, Baez recorded many of his songs, as well as those she herself had composed. Prominent during the 1960s in the civil rights and antiwar movements, in the 1970s Baez more or less retired from singing while continuing to work for other political causes. In 1985 she returned to the stage, opening the immensely successful Live Aid concert. Her autobiography, *And a Voice to Sing With*, was published in 1987.

Baffin, William   [baf'-in]

William Baffin, b. *c*.1584, d. Jan. 23, 1622, was a British navigator who piloted two expeditions searching for the NORTHWEST PASSAGE. On the second voyage (1616), Baffin's ship *Discovery* passed north through Davis Strait and went about 485 km (300 mi) beyond previous exploration. Finding it an unlikely route for passage to the Orient, he recommended a search for other routes. Baffin is said to have been the first person to attempt determination of longitude by observing the Moon. Baffin Bay and Baffin Island were named for him.

Baffin Bay

Baffin Bay is between Greenland on the east and the Arctic Archipelago of Canada on the west. On the south it connects with the Atlantic Ocean through Davis Strait and on the north with the Arctic Ocean by a chain of sounds. It is 1,127 km (700 mi) long and has a maximum width of 644 km (400 mi). Ice covers the bay much of the year.

Baffin Island

Baffin Island is in the Arctic Archipelago of Canada and is part of the Franklin district of the Northwest Territories. The fifth-largest island in the world, it is about 1,530 km (950 mi) long and up to 725 km (450 mi) wide. Its area is about 476,100 km^2 (183,800 mi^2). Peaks rise to 2,042 m (6,700 ft).

Bagehot, Walter   [baj'-uht]

Walter Bagehot, b. Feb. 3, 1826, d. Mar. 24, 1877, was an English social scientist and the editor of The ECONOMIST from 1860 until his death. He joined the family banking business in 1852 and went to *The Economist* six years later. His knowledge of the money market as it functioned between 1850 and 1870 formed the basis of his influential book *Lombard Street* (1873). Bagehot also wrote *The English Constitution* (1867), which depicted the daily workings of British government; *Physics and Politics* (1869), an application of Darwinism to political theory; and *Economic Studies* and *Literary Studies*, which appeared after his death.

Bibliography: Irvine, William, *Walter Bagehot* (1939; repr. 1987).

Baggara   [buh-gah'-ruh]

Baggara, also Baqqarah or Bakkara, which means "cattle-men" in Arabic, is the name applied to nomadic tribes of Arabic-speaking pastoralists in Sudan and Chad who migrate seasonally in the zone of cattle-supporting savanna between the Nile River and Lake Chad. Most of these culturally related, Muslim tribes claim distant kinship with one another. Their population numbers more than 5 million.

The Baggara graze their cattle in the riverine country of the south in the dry season, and they move north each year to exploit seasonal grasslands during the wet season. On their way north they sow grain, especially millet and sorghum, and cotton, which they then harvest on their return south at the beginning of each dry season. Drought and civil strife, however, have disrupted their way of life.

Most of the Baggara are descendants of Arab tribes that migrated west out of Egypt in the Middle Ages and later moved south, arriving in their present habitat in the 18th and 19th centuries. They turned from camels to cattle as an adaptation to local conditions. They played an important part in the uprising of the MAHDI at the end of the 19th century. Due to intermarriage with dark-skinned indigenous people (as slave-wives) they are now indistinguishable in appearance from neighboring populations such as the FULANI.   BRIAN SPOONER

Bibliography: Cunnison, Ian, *Baggara Arabs* (1966).

Baghdad

Baghdad is the largest city and the capital of Iraq. It is also the capital of Baghdad province. Situated on both banks of the Tigris River in the center of the country, it lies about 40 km (25 mi) north of the parallel river, the Euphrates. The

During the Gulf War of 1991, Baghdad was the target of massive allied air attacks. The precision bombing destroyed much of the city's infrastructure, including several bridges over the Tigris, as well as military and government sites. Most city landmarks were spared, however, and reconstruction after the war was rapid.

name, which in Persian means the "God-given," has been applied to the city since the 8th century. Baghdad is situated in a rich river valley with an extensive irrigation network and stands at the junction of many of the great trade routes that have shaped the politics and economics of the Middle East. Baghdad has grown greatly in recent decades, and the population of the city is 3,844,608 (1987).

Contemporary City. Ancient Baghdad was extensively rebuilt and expanded in the 20th century until it became a largely modern city. Among the few remaining historical buildings are the 13th-century al-Mustansiriya Madrasah Mosque and the 10th-century minaret of Suq al-Ghazi. The University of Baghdad was founded in 1958.

The population, although mostly Arab, also has considerable Persian, Armenian, and Kurdish elements. The major trade of the city is in carpets, hides, wool, gum, and dates. Industries include distilling, oil refining, food processing, tanning, and metalworking. Baghdad continues to fill its traditional roles as an important center of communication and trade. The city is the terminus of the Baghdad Railway (from Istanbul), a project sponsored by the Germans in the early 1900s and a sensitive topic in pre–World War I diplomacy, although traffic on the line was not possible until 1940.

History. The present city was founded in 762 on the west bank by the Abbasid caliph al-Mansur. From that time its commercial supremacy in the region was unchallenged. The period of the city's greatest glory was under Caliph Harun al-Rashid during the 8th and 9th centuries, when it was one of the greatest cities of Islam. A period of decline set in, however, and in 1258 the Mongols sacked the city. It was again sacked by Timur (1401) and the Persian shah Esmail I (1508). Thereafter Baghdad was repeatedly conquered by Persians and Turks until 1638, when it became part of the Ottoman Empire. The city was captured by the British in 1917. In 1921 it became the capital of the new Kingdom of Iraq, which was made a republic in 1958. Baghdad was extensively damaged by allied bombing during the 1991 GULF WAR, and its economy was hurt by the trade embargo before and after the war. A massive reconstruction effort is under way.

ARTHUR CAMPBELL TURNER

Baghdad Pact: see CENTRAL TREATY ORGANIZATION.

Bagley, Sarah G.

The New Hampshire–born labor organizer Sarah G. Bagley, fl. 1835–47, worked (1836–45) in a cotton mill in Lowell, Mass., where she founded (1844) the Lowell Female Labor Reform Association to agitate for improved conditions in the mills and a 10-hour workday. After leaving the mill she organized factory workers elsewhere in New England, wrote tracts denouncing the mill owners, and served (1846) as a delegate to the National Industrial Congress.   BARBARA CUNNINGHAM

Bagnold, Enid   [bag'-nohld]

Enid Bagnold, later Lady Roderick Jones, b. Oct. 27, 1889, d. Mar. 31, 1981, was an English novelist and playwright. Her most popular novel, *National Velvet* (1935; film, 1944), is the story of a girl who rides her horse to victory in the Grand National steeplechase. Her other works include the novel *The Loved and Envied* (1951) and the plays *The Chalk Garden* (1956) and *The Chinese Prime Minister* (1964). She published her autobiography in 1969.

bagpipe

The bagpipe is a musical instrument having reed pipes that are actuated by air pressure from a windbag to which the pipes are attached. The melody is played on one pipe (the chanter) or two (the double chanter) having finger holes. Most chanters have a melodic range limited to one octave, or, at most, a ninth, although in some instruments keys are used to extend the range. The other pipes—up to six—are called drones; usually rested on the shoulder, they play one sustained tone each and furnish the accompaniment. In modern

instruments pipes are inserted in stocks that are permanently sewn into the bag. In some bagpipes—the Scottish, for example—air is supplied by the player blowing into a tube connected to the bag. In others, such as the French *musette,* the air is supplied by bellows, usually placed under the arm of the player, who regulates the pressure.

In the earlier, Eastern instruments, both the chanter and the drone pipes have single reeds; in some modern types, all the pipes have double reeds, as in those used in Italy and parts of France, or the drones have single reeds and the chanter has a double reed, as in those of Ireland, Scotland, and Brittany. Bags have been made from the whole skin of a sheep, goat, or other animal. Modern bags are sometimes cut from leather, rubber, or some other, synthetic material. Originally of bone or ivory, pipes are now normally made of hardwood.

The bagpipe is believed to have originated in the Orient, and it was known in ancient Rome. Its penetrating melody with drone accompaniment, characteristic of much medieval music, made the bagpipe a useful instrument during that period. Since the Renaissance it has been used mostly for folk and military music, notably in the British Isles.

Bibliography: Baines, Anthony, *Bagpipes* (1960); Collinson, Francis M., *The Bagpipe* (1975); Flood, W. G., *The Story of the Bagpipe* (1911; repr. 1976).

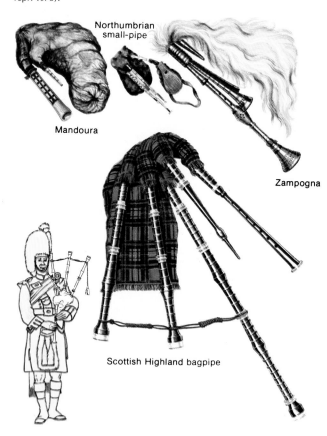

Northumbrian small-pipe

Mandoura

Zampogna

Scottish Highland bagpipe

The bagpipe is a musical wind instrument that consists of an air reservoir in the form of a bag, which is inflated by either a mouth pipe or a bellows. The Scottish Highland bagpipe is the most familiar type. A mouth-blown bagpipe, it comprises a tartan-covered bag, a mouthpiece, a conical double-reed chanter with seven finger holes in front and a thumb hole in the rear, two tenor drones, and a bass drone. The Mandoura is a mouth-blown bagpipe from Crete with a kidskin bag and a chanter made of a double pipe; each pipe has five finger holes and a single reed. The Zampogna, of Italy and Sicily, is a mouth-blown bagpipe consisting of a sheepskin bag, blowpipe, two conical double-reed chanters, and two double-reed drones. The Northumbrian small-pipe, dating to the late 17th century, is a bellows-blown bagpipe with a cylindrical double-reed chanter and four single-reed drones of which no more than three are used at once.

Baguio [bah-gee'-oh]

Baguio (1989 est. pop., 152,193), a city on the island of Luzon in the Philippines, is the traditional summer capital of the country and a popular mountain resort. Copper and gold are mined in the rugged surrounding mountains.

bagworm

The bagworm is the larva of the bagworm moth of the worldwide family Psychidae, order Lepidoptera. Bagworm larvae feed on the leaves of a wide variety of trees, especially evergreens. The evergreen bagworm, *Thyridopteryx ephemeraeformis*, attacks juniper and arborvitae.

Baha'i [bah-hah'-ee]

Baha'i is a religious movement founded in the 19th century by the Persian BAHAULLAH. It claims members in practically every country of the world. Objecting to polygamy, slavery of any kind, religious prejudices, and politicized religion, Baha'is call for world peace and harmony. The ideals of a world federalist government and a new world language are also a part of their teachings. Recognition of the common ground of all religions is seen as fostering this move toward global unity; Krishna, Buddha, Moses, Zarathustra, Jesus, and Muhammad are all recognized as divine manifestations, a series of prophets culminating in Bahaullah. Nonresistance, respect for persons, and legal recognition of the equal rights of both sexes constitute additional aspects of Baha'i teaching.

By the time of Bahaullah's death in 1892, the Baha'i faith had won adherents throughout the Middle East. Under his son Abbas Effendi (or Abdul Baha, 1844–1921), who succeeded him as the movement's leader, it spread to Europe and the United States. Abbas Effendi was succeeded by his grandson, Shoghi Effendi (1897–1957). Since Shoghi Effendi's death, the Baha'is have been governed by elected leaders. Divided into more than 130 national assemblies and more than 26,000 local assemblies, they are estimated to number about 2 million worldwide. Since the establishment of the Islamic Republic of Iran in 1979, the discrimination to which Baha'is have always been subjected in Iran has escalated into persecution.

Bibliography: Hatcher, W., and Martin, J. D., *The Baha'i Faith* (1985); Savi, Julio, *The Eternal Quest for God* (1990); Smith, P., *The Babi and Baha'i Religions* (1987).

Bahama Islands

COMMONWEALTH OF THE BAHAMAS

LAND. Area: 13,939 km² (5,382 mi²). Capital and largest city: Nassau (1990 est. pop., 172,196).
PEOPLE. Population (1993 est.): 268,726; density: 19.3 persons per km² (49.9 per mi²). Distribution (1993 est.): 64% urban, 36% rural. Annual growth (1990): 1.5%. Official language: English. Major religions: Roman Catholicism, Greek Orthodoxy, Judaism.
EDUCATION AND HEALTH. Literacy (1992): 89% of adult population. Universities: (1993): none. Hospital beds (1988): 1,009. Physicians (1988): 303. Life expectancy (1993 est.): women—76; men—68. Infant mortality (1993 est.): 31.6 per 1,000 live births.
ECONOMY. GDP (1991 est.): $2.6 billion; $10,200 per capita. Labor distribution (1990): govt.—28%; tourism—28%; constr.—7.8%; transp. and commun.—7%; finance—7%; agric.—4%; manuf.—3.6%. Foreign trade (1991 est.): imports—$1.14 billion; exports—$306 million; principal trade partners—United States, European Union, Canada, Nigeria. Currency: 1 Bahamian dollar=100 cents.
GOVERNMENT. Type: independent state within Commonwealth of Nations. Legislature: Parliament.
COMMUNICATIONS. Railroads (1993): none. Roads (1990): 3,370 km (2,094 mi) total. Major ports: 2. Major airfields: 2.

BAHAMA ISLANDS

+ Spot Elevation or Depth

Scale 1:10,839,000

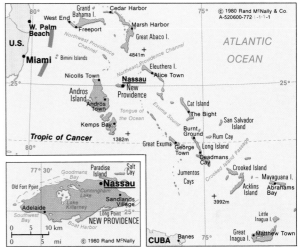

The Commonwealth of the Bahamas, an independent member of the Commonwealth of Nations, is composed of about 700 islands and more than 2,000 cays, islets, and rocks in the Atlantic Ocean. Located about 97 km (60 mi) off the southern Florida coast, they extend some 1,224 km (760 mi) southeastward to within 80 km (50 mi) of Cuba and spread over more than 233,000 km² (90,000 mi²) of the Atlantic. Scenic beaches and mild climate make the Bahamas a major tourist resort.
Land and People. The main islands include Andros (the largest), New Providence, Grand Bahama, Eleuthera, Great Abaco, and Great Inagua. The archipelago generally comprises an undulating limestone platform that is derived from coral. The climate is semitropical, with an average summer temperature of 28° C (83° F) and an average winter temperature of 21° C (70° F). Annual rainfall averages 1,168 mm (46 in) and is concentrated in May–June and September–October. Large Caribbean pine forests thrive on several of the islands.

More than 80% of the population are black. Only 22 of the islands have permanent residents. Almost two-thirds of the total population live on the small island of New Providence, the site of the capital, NASSAU. Other important settlements are FREEPORT and West End on Grand Bahama.
Economy. Tourism is the Bahamas' major source of revenue. Climate, gambling casinos, and sport fishing on the out islands contribute to the continued attraction of tourist revenues. Also, liberal tax laws have encouraged expatriates to settle in the Bahamas from countries such as the United States, Britain, and Canada. The tax structure has also attracted many foreign banks, which have major offices on New Providence. Agriculture has played only a minor role in the economy, although the government is promoting agriculture and fishing to lessen the dependence on imported foodstuffs.

The Bahamas has long served as an oil transshipment point to the United States, but the health of oil-related industries (including a government-owned refinery on Grand Bahama) fluctuates with the world demand for oil.
History. Many scholars believe that Christopher COLUMBUS made his first landing (Oct. 12, 1492) in the Western Hemisphere on SAN SALVADOR Island of the Bahamas. The first British settlement on the islands was established on Eleuthera·in 1648. When the islands became (1670) a British colony, New Providence was made the seat of government. After attempts at farming and fishing proved unsuccessful, the

Tourists are drawn to Nassau's Paradise Beach by the temperate climate and clean, uncrowded recreational areas. Tourism remains the Bahamas' most important source of revenue, despite government efforts to broaden the country's economic base.

economy eventually settled on tourism after World War II. In 1964 the Bahamas were granted internal self-government, and the first elections under universal suffrage were held in 1967. The islands became fully independent on July 10, 1973. The British monarch appoints the governor-general, but actual governmental control is in the hands of the prime minister and the bicameral parliament. From 1967 to 1992, Sir Lynden Pindling's Progressive Liberal party held power. In elections in 1992, after a decade of illicit drug trading in the islands, repeated charges of government corruption, and strained U.S. relations, Hubert Ingraham's Free National Movement ousted Pindling's regime. THOMAS D. BOSWELL

Bibliography: Ajlouny, J., *The Bahamas* (1989); Evans, F. C., and Young, N., *The Bahamas* (1977).

Bahaullah [bah-hah-ul-lah']

Bahaullah, or Baha'u'llah ("Splendor of God"), was the title assumed by the Iranian religious leader Mirza Husayn Ali, b. Nov. 12, 1817, d. May 29, 1892, the founder of the BAHA'I faith. Bahaullah proclaimed (1863) himself to be the person announced by the Bab (see BABISM) as the one who would bring the Bab's work to completion. His teachings concerning the oneness of God, the oneness of religion, and the oneness of humankind became the central principles of the Baha'i religion. Bahaullah died a prisoner of the Ottoman authorities in Acre, Palestine.

Bibliography: Balyuzi, H. M., *Baha'u'llah* (1980); Effendi, Shoghi, *The World Order of Baha'u'llah,* 2d rev. ed. (1974); Taherzadeh, Adib, *The Revelation of Baha'u'llah,* 4 vols. (1989).

Bahia: see SALVADOR.

Bahía Blanca [bah-hee'-ah blahng'-kah]

Bahía Blanca, a city in Argentina, is a major seaport, naval base, and industrial and transportation center. It is located about 570 km (350 mi) southwest of Buenos Aires on Bahía Blanca ("white bay"), an inlet of the Atlantic Ocean.The city has a population of 242,000 (1985 est.). It is the processing

center for cereals, meat products, cowhide, wool, sheepskin, and other items produced in the Pampas.

Located on one of Argentina's best natural harbors, the city was founded in 1828 as a fort; Puerto Belgrano, a large naval base, is now located there. Because of its strategic location, Bahía Blanca prospered as a regional city and has grown particularly fast since World War II. The National University of the South (1956) is located in Bahía Blanca, as is the Bernardino Rivadavia Library (1882). RICHARD W. WILKIE

Bahrain [bah-rayn']

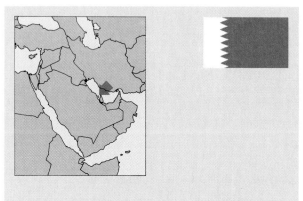

BAHRAIN

LAND. Area: 678 km² (262 mi²). Capital and largest city: Manama (1988 est. pop., 151,500).
PEOPLE. Population (1992 est.): 500,000; density: 737 persons per km² (1,908 per mi²). Distribution (1992): 81% urban, 19% rural. Annual growth (1992): 2.4%. Official language: Arabic. Major religion: Islam.
EDUCATION AND HEALTH. Literacy (1990 est.): 77% of adult population. Universities (1990): 1. Hospital beds (1987): 1,612. Physicians (1989): 664. Life expectancy (1992): women—74; men—70. Infant mortality (1992): 20 per 1,000 live births.
ECONOMY. GDP (1989 est.): $3.4 billion; $7,000 per capita. Labor distribution (1986): agriculture—2%; mining—3%; manufacturing—8%; construction—21%; services—37%; utilities, transportation, and communications—11%; trade and finance—18%. Foreign trade (1989 est.): imports—$3.0 billion; exports—$2.7 billion; principal trade partners—Saudi Arabia, United States, Japan, United Arab Emirates. Currency: 1 Bahrain dinar = 1,000 fils.
GOVERNMENT. Type: monarchy. Legislature: National Assembly (dissolved 1975). Political subdivisions: 12 municipalities.
COMMUNICATIONS. Railroads (1992): none. Roads (1988): 2,614 km (1,624 mi) total. Major ports: 1. Major airfields: 1.

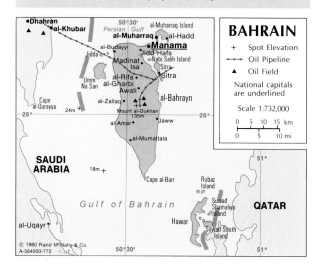

BAHRAIN
+ Spot Elevation
Oil Pipeline
▲ Oil Field

National capitals are underlined

Scale 1:732,000

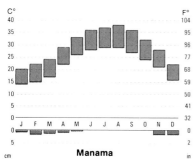

C° / F° chart

Bars indicate the monthly ranges of temperatures (red) and precipitation (blue) of Manama, capital of Bahrain, with a desert climate.

Manama

Bahrain is an independent emirate comprising a group of low-lying islands located in the Persian Gulf between the Saudi Arabian mainland and the Qatar peninsula. The archipelago's major island, Bahrain, is about 48 km (30 mi) long and 16 km (10 mi) wide. About 40% of the country's population lives in MANAMA, the capital city. The name *Bahrain* is derived from the Arabic for "two seas." Bahrain's importance as an oil-producer is waning, but it continues to be a commercial center because of its strategic location.

LAND AND PEOPLE
The two most important islands are Bahrain and al-Muharraq, which are connected by causeway; other islands include Sitra, Umm Nassan, An Nabi Salih, Jidda, and the Hawar group. All the islands are small and low-lying. The central region of the main island, however, is a barren limestone plateau that rises to a maximum elevation of 135 m (445 ft).

The climate is hot, and rainfall is sparse. Summer temperatures average 34° C (93° F), with daytime temperatures in excess of 41° C (106° F); winter temperatures average about 17° C (63° F). Relative humidity is 70% to 80% for most of the year, but annual rainfall averages only about 76 mm (3 in).

The population of Bahrain is mostly Arab, more than 65% of Bahrainis being native-born. Many Indians, Persians, Pakistanis, Europeans, and Americans also reside in the country. Arabic is the official language, although Persian and English are understood widely. Islam, practiced by 95% of the population, is the official religion. The SUNNITE sect predominates in the urban centers and accounts for about one-third of the population, including the ruling family. The SHIITE sect is important in rural areas. Urban services—including hospitals, utilities, highways, and education—have reached a high standard as a result of the influx of oil revenues, although oil income declined in the 1980s. Housing and transportation are state subsidized, and health services and education are free.

ECONOMIC ACTIVITY
Oil, first discovered in 1931, was Bahrain's principal product for many years, but since reserves are small and will probably be depleted by the end of the 20th century, major efforts have been made to diversify the economy and develop other sources of income. These include a large oil refinery, which processes local oil and oil piped from Saudi Arabia; a huge aluminum smelter, for which electric power is obtained from natural gas; a plant producing steel pellets; and ancillary industries based on oil refining and aluminum smelting.

Bahrain receives a variety of subsidies from the richer Gulf states. It has become a major regional banking and communications center. Also important are the engineering workshops, warehousing facilities, and ship-repair facilities (including a dry dock for the repair of supertankers) related to Bahrain's position as a transportation and trade center for the Persian Gulf. The airport at al-Muharraq is a major international airport, and the port of Mina Sulman offers a free trade zone. A causeway linking Bahrain Island to Saudi Arabia was officially opened in 1986.

Dates and alfalfa can be grown extensively, especially on the northern shore of Bahrain Island, because of the spring waters there. Rice, citrus fruits, and vegetables are also grown, although yields are low, and food must be imported.

HISTORY AND GOVERNMENT
As early as the 3d millennium BC, Bahrain was the site of the thriving commercial center DILMUN. In ancient times Bahrain

was known for its pearling industry. After nearly eight centuries of independence as an Arab Muslim state, Bahrain came under the rule of Portugal (1521–1602) and Persia (1602–1783). Since 1783 the al-Khalifa family has ruled the country. British-Bahrain treaties were signed in 1820 and 1861, and Bahrain was under British protection from 1861. Upon independence in 1971, Bahrain elected not to join the UNITED ARAB EMIRATES. A constitution was adopted in 1973, but the National Assembly, which met for the first time in 1973, was dissolved in 1975, and the emir has since ruled by decree. Bahrain, which first granted U.S. forces the right to use naval installations there in 1949, was a member of the allied coalition against Iraq during the 1991 GULF WAR.   IRA M. SHESKIN

Bibliography: Abu Hakima, A. M., *History of Eastern Arabia, 1750–1800* (1965); Adamiyat, F., *Bahrein Islands* (1955); Khuri, F. I., *Tribe and State in Bahrain* (1981); Lawson, F. H., *Bahrain* (1989); Nugent, J., and Thomas, T., *Bahrain and the Gulf* (1985); Sadik, M. T., and Snavely, W. P., *Bahrain, Qatar, and the United Arab Emirates* (1972).

Baikal, Lake   [by-kahl']

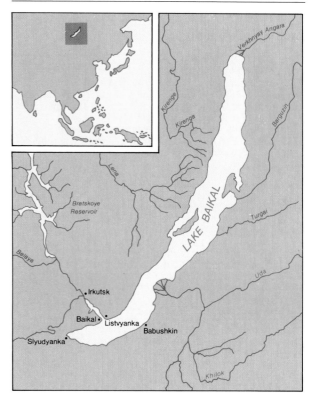

The most remarkable freshwater lake in the world, Russia's Lake Baikal, or Baykal, is located in southeastern Siberia, west of the Yablonovy Mountains. It covers 31,494 km² (12,160 mi²), making it the largest freshwater lake by area in Eurasia. Baikal measures 636 km (395 mi) long and 29–81 km (18–50 mi) wide and is fed by more than 300 rivers and streams. Its only outlet, however, is the Angara River, which flows past Irkutsk. Near the center of the lake is Olkhon Island, Baikal's largest, with a maximum length of about 73.6 km (46 mi).

Baikal is most notable because it lies in a deep rocky fault produced by a massive shift in the Earth's crust. It contains about 23,000 km³ (5,500 mi³) of water. This is equivalent to the total volume of North America's Great Lakes and represents 20 percent of the world's liquid freshwater resources. Thus Baikal is the world's largest freshwater lake by volume. It is also the deepest, reaching a maximum of 1,620 m (5,315 ft). Because it formed some 20 to 30 million years ago—making Baikal the world's oldest freshwater lake as well—the nearly 6.5 km (4 mi) of bottom sediment that has accumulated could be added to this depth. The region continues to be geologically active and shaken by earthquakes. Some geologists conjecture that the Asian continent is splitting apart at this site and that Baikal is an ocean in the making, a view supported in 1990 by the discovery of lake-bottom HYDROTHERMAL VENTS, which are usually found on mid-oceanic ridges.

Baikal's huge volume has a moderating effect on local weather, but the lake is buffeted by wind-generated storms. The water stays cold, with temperatures rising to no more than 14° C (57° F) in summer. From December to May the lake is frozen. Baikal's exceptionally mineral-free waters support an unusual population of organisms, including many species endemic to the lake and its vents. The lake is a popular summer resort. Forest and mineral resources have been processed along its shores. In the 1960s, however, iron-ore production and forest exploitation began to present a serious threat to the ecology of the region, and by the 1980s the government of the former USSR had placed severe restrictions on activities that were polluting Baikal.

Bibliography: Tilzer, M. M., and Serruya, Colette, eds., *Large Lakes* (1990).

Baikonur Cosmodrome: see SPACE PROGRAMS, NATIONAL.

bail

Bail is the procedure by which a judge releases from custody a person charged with a CRIME, upon receiving security in the form of cash or a promise that the released prisoner will appear in court at a specified time to answer the charge. The usual form of security is a bail bond provided by a bonding company. Depending on the amount of bail fixed by the judge, the defendant may have to pay a fee of 10 percent and also put up collateral in the form of securities or property.

In fixing bail the court may consider the nature of the offense, the weight of evidence, the accused's reputation in the community, and the accused's ability to obtain bail. Critics contend that deserving poor people stay in jail because they cannot afford bail, whereas the professional criminals easily find someone to pay. In some cases, poor defendants are released on their "personal recognizance"—their promise to appear for trial. The U.S. Comprehensive Crime Control Act of 1984 allowed judges to deny bail to defendants charged with serious federal crimes (see CRIMINAL JUSTICE).

Bailey, F. Lee

Francis Lee Bailey, b. Waltham, Mass., June 10, 1933, has become one of the best-known criminal lawyers of his day because of his aggressive courtroom tactics. "Criminal law," he once said, "has made me a rebel by profession." Among his early successful cases was that of Samuel Sheppard, a Cleveland, Ohio, physician who had been sentenced to life imprisonment for the 1954 murder of his wife. Bailey became Sheppard's lawyer in 1961, a year after he had been admitted to the bar, and took his case to the U.S. Supreme Court in 1965. The Court in 1966 overturned Sheppard's conviction on the ground that prejudicial publicity before and during his prosecution had denied him a fair trial. A second trial resulted in a verdict of not guilty. In 1977, Bailey represented Patricia Hearst at her trial for involvement in a bank robbery conducted by the Symbionese Liberation Army. His books include *The Defense Never Rests* (1971), *How to Protect Yourself* (1984), and a novel, *Secrets* (1979).

Bailey, Liberty Hyde

Liberty Hyde Bailey, b. South Haven, Mich., Mar. 15, 1858, d. Dec. 25, 1954, an American botanist, systematized the study of horticulture and trained a generation of agriculturalists. He graduated from Michigan State Agricultural College and studied under the Harvard botanist Asa GRAY. As a professor of botany and dean of the College of Agriculture at Cornell University (1888–1913), Bailey brought botanists, plant physiolo-

gists, and geneticists together to work in the field of horticulture, and he established a laboratory, the Bailey Hortorium, which is still an important research center. His published works—about 700 papers and 66 books—include *The Standard Cyclopedia of Horticulture* (1914), still used as a reference source, and *Hortus,* revised and republished as *Hortus Third: A Concise Dictionary of Plants Cultivated in the United States and Canada.*

Bailey bridge

The Bailey bridge is a temporary BRIDGE made of standard sections that can be put together quickly. Sir Donald Coleman Bailey (1901–85) designed the bridge for military use in World War II. He foresaw the need for a bridge constructed of lightweight standardized panels that could be put together quickly in a wide range of spans and carry light or heavy loads.

The standard panels, measuring 3 by 1.5 m (10 by 4.75 ft), were prefabricated in all-welded high-tensile steel and could be joined end to end by interlocking pin connections to make spans up to 73 m (240 ft) long that could carry convoys of heavy tanks. To support such weight, up to four panels could be assembled side by side if necessary, and the depth could be increased by placing one panel on top of another to make girders of double or triple thicknesses.

The Bailey bridge proved so useful in wartime that it is now also used in the civilian market as a temporary structure either before or during the construction of a permanent bridge, or as an emergency structure.   HUBERT SHIRLEY-SMITH

Bailey v. Drexel Furniture Company

In *Bailey* v. *Drexel Furniture Company* (1922), known as the Child Labor Tax Case, the Supreme Court declared unconstitutional the federal child labor law of 1919. Under that law a 10 percent tax was levied on the net profits of any firm employing children under 14 years of age. The Drexel Furniture Company of North Carolina had been assessed more than $6,000 for having employed a boy under 14 during 1919. Speaking through Chief Justice William Howard TAFT, the Court invalidated the law on two grounds: first, it was an attempt to regulate a matter reserved to the states; and second, the tax was a penalty rather than a revenue-raising measure. Said Taft, ". . . to give such magic to the word 'tax' would be to break down all constitutional limitation of the powers of Congress and completely wipe out the sovereignties of the states." Although the Supreme Court thus prevented Congress from outlawing CHILD LABOR through its taxing power, Congress was able to resolve the problem in the late 1930s under the commerce power.   ROBERT J. STEAMER

Baily, Francis

The English astronomer Francis Baily, b. Apr. 28, 1774, d. Aug. 30, 1844, is best known for his description of the solar ECLIPSE phenomenon now called Baily's beads. Baily was an explorer and stockbroker before turning to astronomy at about age 50. He helped found what became the Royal Astronomical Society of London, revised star catalogs, and did work in meteorology. It was during the annular eclipse of May 15, 1836, that Baily described the fleeting phenomenon of a string of bright points, like "beads," along the circumference of the otherwise totally eclipsed Sun. The beads are caused by sunlight shining between mountains on the Moon's limb.

Bainbridge, William

The American naval officer William Bainbridge, b. Princeton, N.J., May 7, 1774, d. July 27, 1833, was commissioned (1798) in the newly created U.S. Navy during the undeclared war with France (1798–1800) that followed the XYZ AFFAIR. His first ship, the *Retaliation,* was captured by the French, but he was later so successful in running blockades and convoying American merchantmen in the French West Indies that he was promoted to captain in 1800. Given command of the frigate *Philadelphia* during the TRIPOLITAN WAR (1801–05), Bainbridge was again captured when he ran aground at Tripoli in 1803. During the WAR OF 1812, he successfully advocated a strategy of fleet dispersion and commerce raiding. Commanding the U.S.S. CONSTITUTION, he captured the British frigate *Java* off Brazil on Dec. 29, 1812.   KENNETH J. HAGAN

Bibliography: Barnes, James, *Commodore Bainbridge* (1897); Dearborn, Henry A. S., *The Life of William Bainbridge, Esq.* (1931).

Baird, Bil and Cora

The American puppeteers Bil Baird, b. Grand Island, Nebr., Aug. 15, 1904, d. Mar. 18, 1987, and his wife, actress Cora Burlar, b. New York City, Jan. 26, 1912, d. Dec. 7, 1967, were for nearly 30 years the creative spirits behind such well-loved marionettes as Groovy the disc-jockey rabbit and Heathcliff the talking horse. The couple presented puppet shows in theaters and nightclubs and, in the 1950s, on television. After his wife's death Baird concentrated on television commercials and his Greenwich Village theater, where he presented puppet versions of children's classics.

Baird, John Logie

Television inventor John Logie Baird, b. Scotland, Aug. 13, 1888, d. June 14, 1946, began experimenting with television in 1922. By 1926, using homemade equipment, he succeeded in transmitting the first television picture, a crude, 30-line image of a human face sent electrically to a small screen (see VIDEO). In 1929 the British Broadcasting Corporation adopted Baird's system with its mechanical 30-line scanner, although they eventually abandoned it in favor of the Marconi Company's 405-line system. Baird demonstrated color TV and transmitted the first transatlantic TV signal (both, 1928), and invented the first videodisc, the Phonodisc.

Baird, Spencer F.

Spencer Fullerton Baird, b. Reading, Pa., Feb. 3, 1823, d. Aug. 19, 1887, was an American zoologist and a skilled administrator of scientific institutions. As assistant secretary (1850) and then as secretary (1878) of the Smithsonian Institution, he directed the Smithsonian until his death. The first commissioner (1871) of the U.S. Fish Commission, he established the WOODS HOLE Marine Biological Laboratory. His most significant scientific publications were studies of birds and animals.

Bibliography: Allard, D., *Spencer Fullerton Baird*, rev. ed. (1978).

Baire, René   [bayr]

René Baire, b. Jan. 21, 1874, d. July 5, 1932, was one of the most influential French mathematicians of the early 20th century. His interest in FUNCTIONS and CONTINUITY was reinforced by Vito Volterra. As professor of analysis at the Faculty of Science in Dijon (from 1905), he wrote an important treatise on discontinuous functions. Baire's category theorem bears his name today, as do two other important mathematical concepts, Baire functions and Baire classes.   J. W. DAUBEN

Baj, Enrico   [by]

Enrico Baj, b. Oct. 31, 1924, is a contemporary Italian artist who founded several influential art groups and the journal *Il gesto* (Milan, 1955–59) during the 1950s and '60s. After initially being influenced by the drip paintings of Jackson Pollock, Baj produced work closely related to the tradition of surrealism. The strange humanoid forms that inhabit his paintings recall those of Jean Dubuffet, and his parodies of older works by Pablo Picasso and Georges Seurat are close to American pop art. He is perhaps best known outside Italy for his assemblages and graphic works.   MARIAN BURLEIGH-MOTLEY

Bibliography: Sanesi, R., and van der Marck, J., *Baj: Graphic Works* (1986); Van der Marck, J., *Baj* (1971).

Baja California   [bah'-hah]

Baja California (English: Lower California) is a mountainous, arid peninsula of northwestern Mexico. Extending about 1,220 km (760 mi) south from the U.S. border, it ranges in width from 40 to 240 km (25 to 150 mi) and is connected to the Mexican mainland by a narrow strip across the delta of the Colorado River. The peninsula is divided into the Mexican states of Baja California Norte (1990 pop., 1,660,855), whose capital city is MEXICALI, and Baja California Sur (1990 pop., 317,764; made a state in 1974), whose capital city is LA PAZ.

The peninsula retains much unspoiled desert land. Some indigenous plants, including the boogum and elephant trees, exist only there. Most of the peninsula's population is concentrated in the cities clustered near the U.S. border—TIJUANA, Mexicali, and Ensenada. The economy is based in agriculture, fishing, and tourism.

Bakelite

The first commercially successful synthetic RESIN, developed in 1909 by the Belgian-American chemist Dr. Leo Hendrik Baekeland (1863–1944), Bakelite is a polymer of phenol and formaldehyde, often compounded with reinforcing fillers such as asbestos, wood fibers, or cotton linters. When heat is applied, the mixture becomes a very hard mass, colorless or light yellow, with excellent solvent and heat resistance. Because it is almost noncombustible, it soon replaced CELLULOID and is used today, instead of rubber, as an electrical insulator, in adhesives, and in varnishes and molding powders.

Baker, Sir Benjamin

The English engineer Benjamin Baker, b. Mar. 31, 1840, d. May 19, 1907, helped to design the great railroad bridge across Scotland's Firth of Forth, a 1,630-m-long (5,349-ft) steel structure completed in 1890. Involved in the building of the first ASWAN Dam, Baker also designed a cylindrical ship to transport an obelisk, Cleopatra's Needle, from Egypt to London. In the United States he assisted in the construction of the Eads Bridge across the Mississippi River at St. Louis and designed a pneumatic tunneling shield that made possible the completion of the first Hudson River tunnel at New York City.

Baker, George Pierce

George Pierce Baker, b. Providence, R.I., Apr. 4, 1866, d. Jan. 6, 1935, was an educator who laid the groundwork for theater-arts training programs in U.S. universities. In 1906, Baker established a playwriting class at Harvard University that became known (from its course number) as the "47 Workshop." It was devoted to the production of plays written by students, among them Eugene O'Neill. In 1925, Baker moved to Yale University, where he joined a new drama department that later became the Yale School of Drama.   COLETTE BROOKS

Bibliography: Kinne, W. P., *George Pierce Baker* (1954; repr. 1968).

Baker, Howard

Howard Henry Baker, Jr., b. Huntsville, Tenn., Nov. 15, 1925, Republican senator from Tennessee (1967–85), gained national prominence in 1973 as a member of the Senate committee investigating WATERGATE. Baker became Senate minority leader in 1977 and, after an unsuccessful bid for the Republican presidential nomination in 1980, majority leader in 1981. He declined to run for reelection in 1984 but in 1987 became President Ronald Reagan's chief of staff during the investigation of the IRAN-CONTRA AFFAIR. He retired to Tennessee in 1988.

Baker, James A.

James Addison Baker III, b. Houston, Tex., Apr. 28, 1930, was U.S. secretary of state (1989–92) under George Bush, whose presidential campaigns he managed. A graduate (1952) of Princeton with a law degree (1957) from the University of Texas, Baker practiced law in Houston. He served President Ronald Reagan first as chief of staff (1981–85), earning a reputation as a master of compromise, and then as secretary of the treasury (1985–88).

Baker, Janet

Dame Janet Baker, b. York, England, Aug. 21, 1933, a mezzo-soprano, is world renowned as a recitalist, concert soloist, and opera singer. She studied with Helene Isepp in London, at the Mozarteum in Salzburg, and with Lotte Lehmann. Baker first became known by giving recitals at the Edinburgh Festival and by appearing at the Royal Albert Hall, where she sang Sosostrice's aria from Michael Tippett's *A Midsummer Marriage*. In 1966 she made her debut in San Francisco and in New York in Mahler's *Das Lied von der Erde*. Her repertoire ranges from classical works to modern opera, from Bach cantatas to the heroines of the operas of Benjamin Britten: Nancy in *Albert Herring*, Kate Julian in *Owen Wingrave*, and the title role in *The Rape of Lucretia*. She was awarded a D.B.E. (Dame Commander of the British Empire) in 1976. She retired from the operatic stage in 1982. Her memoirs, *Full Circle*, were published in 1982.

Bibliography: Blyth, Alan, *Janet Baker* (1973); Christiansen, Rupert, *Prima Donna* (1985).

Baker, Josephine

Josephine Baker, b. St. Louis, Mo., June 3, 1906, d. Apr. 12, 1975, an entertainer, personified *le jazz hot* for the French in the 1920s and '30s. At the age of 16 she joined the chorus of the all-black musical *Shuffle Along* on a post–Broadway American tour and soon attracted attention with her brilliant clowning and dancing. In 1924 she was featured on Broadway in *The Chocolate Dandies*. In 1925 she starred in Paris in *La Revue Nègre* and created a sensation as a dancer clad only in a string of bananas. She remained in Paris as a star at the Folies Bergère, a blues singer, and a film actress, and became a French citizen in 1937. Baker was honored by France for her work in the French resistance during World War II. After the war she devoted much of her time and resources to her "rainbow tribe," a group of babies of all races whom she had adopted. Baker remained a glamorous international star for half a century, despite intermittent periods of retirement. She enjoyed notably triumphant appearances on Broadway in 1964 and 1973.   DALE HARRIS

Bibliography: Baker, Josephine, and Bouillon, Jo, *Josephine*, trans. by Mariana Fitzpatrick (1977; repr. 1988); Papich, Stephen, *Remembering Josephine* (1976); Rose, Phyllis, *Jazz Cleopatra* (1989).

Baker, Newton Diehl

Newton Diehl Baker, b. Martinsburg, W.Va., Dec. 3, 1871, d. Dec. 25, 1937, was secretary of war (1916–21) under President Woodrow Wilson and administered the U.S. war effort in World War I. He was early influenced by the reform Democratic mayor of Cleveland, Tom Loftin Johnson, under whom he served as city solicitor (1903–12). He was himself mayor of Cleveland from 1912 to 1916.

Appointed secretary of war in March 1916, Baker, a pacifist, took little action until the United States entered (April 1917) World War I. Then he proved himself a vigorous administrator. He implemented military conscription, reorganized the War Department, and efficiently administered the huge war budget. Increasingly conservative in his later life, he opposed the New Deal policies of President Franklin D. Roosevelt.

Bibliography: Cramer, Clarence H., *Newton D. Baker* (1961); Palmer, Frederick, *Newton D. Baker: America at War*, 2 vols. (1931; repr. 1969).

Baker, Ray Stannard

Ray Stannard Baker, b. Lansing, Mich., Apr. 17, 1870, d. July 12, 1946, was a prolific American journalist and editor who won a 1940 Pulitzer Prize for his *Woodrow Wilson: Life and Letters* (8 vols., 1927–39). A friend and European envoy of the World War I president, Baker also coedited *The Public Papers of Woodrow Wilson* (6 vols., 1925–26). Initially a reporter for the *Chicago Record* (1892–98), he wrote (1899–1905) muckraking articles for *McClure's Magazine* and helped found and edit (1906–15) *American Magazine*. He also wrote several volumes of essays, including *Adventures in Contentment*

(1907), under the pseudonym David Grayson. His *Native American* (1941) and *American Chronicle* (1945) are autobiographical.
F. M. PAULSEN

Baker, Russell

Russell Baker, b. Loudoun County, Va., Aug. 14, 1925, is the author of the "Observer," a *New York Times* column that is one of the most popular U.S. humor commentaries. In 1993 he became the host of public television's *Masterpiece Theatre*. Formerly a reporter on the *Baltimore Sun* (1947–54) and in the Washington bureau of the *Times* (1954–62), Baker began writing the "Observer" in 1962. Seldom permitting his wit to become cruel, Baker penetrates to the heart of topics in the news. His columns have been collected in anthologies: *An American in Washington* (1961), *No Cause for Panic* (1964), *All Things Considered* (1965), *Poor Russell's Almanac* (1972), *So This Is Depravity* (1980), *The Rescue of Miss Yaskell and Other Pipe Dreams* (1983), and *There's a Country in My Cellar* (1990). He received a Pulitzer Prize for commentary in 1979 and another in 1983 for the first volume of his autobiography, *Growing Up* (1982). The second volume, *The Good Times* (1989), covers his days as a reporter.   CALDER M. PICKETT

Baker, Sir Samuel White

Sir Samuel White Baker, b. June 8, 1821, d. Dec. 30, 1893, was an English explorer in Africa whose expeditions—with those of John Hanning SPEKE—finally settled the question of the source of the Nile. In 1861, Baker and his wife explored the Nile's tributaries in Ethiopia. Two years later they followed the river farther south and discovered (Mar. 14, 1864) Lake Albert Nyanza, determining that the Nile flowed through the lake. Baker was later appointed (1869) governor of the region by the Egyptian khedive and suppressed the slave trade there.
ROBIN BUSS

Bibliography: Middleton, Dorothy, *Baker of the Nile* (1949); Moorhead, Alan, *The White Nile*, rev. ed. (1971).

Baker v. Carr

In *Baker* v. *Carr* (1962), the U.S. Supreme Court made a landmark decision that opened the way to ending unequal APPORTIONMENT of state legislatures. The state of Tennessee had not reapportioned its legislative districts in more than 50 years, even though the migration from rural to urban areas in that time had left rural counties with a disproportionately large representation in the legislature. Charles Baker, a voter, sued Joe Carr, a state official in charge of elections, contending that he (Baker) had been deprived of the equal protection of the law in violation of the 14th Amendment to the Constitution. The district court dismissed the complaint, ruling that it lacked jurisdiction over a state political issue. Up to that time the federal judiciary had refused to become involved in state apportionment questions; on Baker's appeal, however, the Supreme Court held that the matter was within the purview of federal courts and ordered the district court in Tennessee to decide the issue. The Supreme Court subsequently received appeals from 15 states; in REYNOLDS V. SIMS (1964), it held that, under the 14th Amendment, seats in a state legislature must be apportioned on a population basis.

Bakersfield

Bakersfield is a city in the San Joaquin Valley in south central California with a population of 174,820 (1990). Founded in 1869, the city developed rapidly after petroleum was discovered nearby in 1899. It now depends on petroleum-based industries, manufacturing, and agriculture.

Bakhtiari   [bahk-tee-ah'-ree]

The Bakhtiari tribe, which numbers more than 800,000, inhabits an area of approximately 67,000 km² (25,000 mi²) that straddles the central Zagros Mountains in Iran. Although only about a third of the tribe is nomadic (the rest are settled agriculturalists), the nomads embody the Bakhtiari cultural ideals. They specialize in producing meat and dairy products and migrate seasonally with their sheep, cattle, or goat herds from high plateau pastures, where they spend the summer, west of the city of Isfahan, to lowland plains in the province of Khuzistan for winter herd grazing. Their migration is among the most spectacular known among nomadic pastoralists anywhere. They are obliged to cross mountain passes at about 3,050 m (10,000 ft) and therefore have to time their movement with extreme care in order to minimize the danger of early snowfall, flooding mountain rivers, and lack of grazing. Traditionally these dangers took a heavy toll, but in recent years the government has helped the migration by building bridges, improving the route, and setting up fodder supplies en route.

The Bakhtiari speak a dialect of Persian called Luri and are Shiite Muslims. Politically, the tribe used to form a confederacy under a chief appointed by the shah, but this position has now been abolished. The confederacy was most effective in the late 19th and early 20th centuries, and the Bakhtiari played an important role on the national level in Iran's constitutional movement. More recently, many tribesmen have left the traditional way of life for employment in the oil industry in the cities.   BRIAN SPOONER

Bibliography: Metz, Helen, *Iran: A Country Study*, 4th ed. (1989); Moss, W., *Peoples of the World: Mid East, North Africa* (1992).

baking industry

The manufacture of bakery products is a significant part of the worldwide food industry. In the United States the industry produces and sells billions of dollars worth of goods annually. Bread and cake products lead in total sales value, followed by cookies, crackers, pretzels, and similar low-moisture products.

The industry consists of large wholesale bakeries, which sell their products to retail outlets or food service operations; retail bakeries owned, and usually run, by independent bakers; franchised retail outlets; and in-store bakeries—as they are known in the trade—which are specialty sections of supermarkets.

Small neighborhood bakeries owned by the baker, and often staffed by members of his family, were the principal suppliers of bread, rolls, and pastries in the United States until after World War II, when the growth of large wholesale bakeries could put small operations at a disadvantage. Large plants could mass-produce bread and rolls on automated lines, and the labor costs per unit of product were lower, as were their expenses for ingredients and for energy, especially for heating ovens. The better control of processing conditions and ingredient characteristics in larger bakeries also enabled them to maintain more uniform product quality, and they had an additional advantage in that they delivered their products to supermarkets, so that grocery shoppers could buy them without having to visit another store. Factory technologies have now penetrated other countries. The French fear the disappearance of their famous *pain* as factory-made breads take over supermarket shelves. Even in such traditionally non–bread-eating countries as Japan, mass-produced bread is becoming a staple.

Some small neighborhood bakeries attempt to adapt to the difficult competitive situation by making ethnic specialties, cakes decorated for special occasions, gourmet-quality goods, and other products that can be sold at prices high enough to justify their large labor input but for which demand is too limited to attract the wholesale baker. In addition, there has been a remarkable increase in the number of small bakeries that sell their products in shopping malls. These stores usually specialize in a product that is in demand at the moment: chocolate chip cookies, for example, or croissants, or oversize muffins. Doughnut franchise shops sell dazzling varieties of doughnuts prepared on the premises from recipes supplied by the franchiser. Finally, in recent years, bakeries have opened in many supermarkets, whose owners have found that a bakery on the premises increases store traffic and improves the sale of baked goods. Supermarket bakeries either mix their own doughs and batters, or—more commonly—obtain frozen or refrigerated doughs from a central facility belonging to the supermarket chain, and bake and decorate the products within each store.   SAMUEL A. MATZ

Bibliography: Business Trend Analysts, *Bakery Products* (1985); Matz, S. A., *Bakery Technology: Nutrition, Packaging, Product Development* (1989).

baking powder

Baking powder is a mixture of baking soda (sodium bicarbonate), an acid salt such as cream of tartar, and small amounts of starch, to simplify measuring and improve the stability of the mixture. It is used as a leavening agent in baking.

Carbon dioxide, the leavening gas produced by baking powder, originates from baking soda. Addition of an acidic compound promotes a rapid release of gas. The rate of gas release controls the size of the bubbles in the dough and influences the grain, volume, and texture of the baked product.

Some bakery products, such as pie crusts, are unleavened: they do not increase in volume while baking. Puff pastry doughs and cakes based on whipped eggs are leavened primarily by the expansion of water vapor and entrapped air during baking. BREADS and sweet-dough pastries are usually YEAST leavened. Most layer cakes, cupcakes, and many kinds of cookies are leavened by chemicals such as baking powder. Although yeast often produces a finer texture and flavor, baked goods made with baking powder are usually easier to prepare.   SAMUEL A. MATZ

baking soda: see SODA.

Bakke case: see UNIVERSITY OF CALIFORNIA V. BAKKE.

Bakst, Léon

The Russian artist Léon Bakst, b. Feb. 8, 1866, d. Dec. 24, 1924, is primarily known for his association with Serge DIAGHILEV and his BALLETS RUSSES. His sumptuous decors for such ballets as *Schéhérezade* (1910) and *L'Après-midi d'une Faune* (AFTERNOON OF A FAUN, 1912) contributed to the success of the dance company and, as well, launched a craze for exotic colors and patterns in fashion and interior decoration. Bakst (originally named Lev Samoylovich Rosenberg) studied painting at the Saint Petersburg Academy of Arts (1883–87) and then at the Académie Julian in Paris with Jean Léon GÉRÔME. In the 1890s he met Diaghilev in Saint Petersburg and became cofounder of the luxurious art magazine *Mir iskusstva* (World of Art) in 1899. His first sets were for a mime staged by Marius PETIPA at the Hermitage court theater in 1902. After his success with the Ballets Russes in Paris in the first decade of the 1900s, Bakst returned to Russia, where he founded a school of painting. His last years were spent in Paris designing sets for plays, ballets, and operas.

Bibliography: Bakst, Léon, *The Decorative Art of Léon Bakst*, trans. by H. Melvill (1913; repr. 1969); Levinson, André, *Bakst: The Story of the Artist's Life* (1923; repr. 1969); Pruzhan, Irina, *Léon Bakst* (1988).

Baku   [buh-koo']

Baku is the capital of the republic of Azerbaijan, formerly part of the USSR. It is situated on the south shore of the beak-shaped Apsheron Peninsula on the Caspian Sea. The population of the city proper is 1,150,000, and that of the metropolitan area, which encompasses the entire peninsula, is 2,020,000 (1989). The name *Baku* is believed to mean "windy place," an allusion to the strong winds that sweep across the area. Baku has a dry climate, with an annual precipitation of about 200 mm (8 in), hot, dry summers, and short, mild winters.

The city's economy revolves around the historic oil fields on the Apsheron Peninsula and offshore, and several oil refineries, oil-equipment manufacturing plants, and other industries associated with oil are located there. Petroleum, in the form of incoming crude oil and outgoing refined products, constitutes most of the cargo of the port, which is the largest on the Caspian Sea. The population is ethnically mixed, including 46% Azerbaijanis, 28% Russians, and 16% Armenians.

First mentioned in the 9th century, Baku passed from Persian to Russian control in 1806. Commercial oil development began in the 1870s. By the start of the 20th century, Baku was the world's largest producer, a position it was unable to maintain with the development of major oil fields elsewhere. In the USSR, oil produced in Baku now represents only 3% of the national total.

THEODORE SHABAD

Bakunin, Mikhail Aleksandrovich   [buh-koon'-yin, mee-kuh-yel' ul-yek-sahn'-droh-vich]

Mikhail Aleksandrovich Bakunin, b. May 30, 1814, d. July 1, 1876, was a Russian aristocrat who became revolutionist and a leading theorist of ANARCHISM. He left Russia in 1840 to study philosophy in Germany but was attracted to revolutionary socialism. After being actively involved in the Revolutions of 1848 in Germany, France, and Austria, he was arrested in Dresden in 1849 and deported to Russia. Escaping from Siberia in 1861, he went to England and Western Europe and resumed his revolutionary work.

Bakunin taught that man is basically good but corrupted by existing institutions. Accordingly, he advocated the violent overthrow of the state, the churches, and the economic system to permit men to start over again in voluntary associations of free individuals. He was a bitter critic of MARXISM, which he saw as authoritarian. Although Bakunin was never precise about how his ends would be achieved in practice, he won a substantial following in Italy and Spain. He died in Bern, Switzerland.

ROBERT BASS

Bibliography: Aldred, Guy, *Bakunin* (1971); Kelley, Aileen, *Mikhail Bakunin* (1982); Mendel, Arthur P., *Michael Bakunin* (1981); Ravindranathan, T. R., *Bakunin and the Italians* (1988); Saltman, Richard B., *The Social and Political Thought of Michael Bakunin* (1983).

Balaguer, Joaquín   [bah-lah-gair', hwah-keen']

Joaquín Balaguer y Ricardo, b. Sept. 1, 1907, was elected president of the Dominican Republic five times. A scholar, poet, and lawyer, he held important posts during the dictatorship of Rafael TRUJILLO Molina, including that of nominal president (1960–62). After Trujillo's assassination in 1961, the country fell into disorder; Balaguer resigned and went into U.S. exile for three years. He was elected president in 1966 and reelected in 1970 and 1974. A moderate conservative, he attempted to restore financial stability to his country. In the 1978 elections, economic troubles and reports of repression and corruption in his government contributed to his defeat by Antonio Guzmán. In 1986, elderly and blind, Balaguer narrowly won a fourth term. He won a fifth term in 1990 in a close election that resulted in a recount. He is the author of *Dominican Reality* (1947; Eng. trans., 1949) and *History of Dominican Literature* (1955; Eng. trans., 1978).

Balakirev, Mily Alekseyevich   [buh-lahk'-yir-yef, mee'-lee ul-yek-syay'-yih-vich]

Mily Alekseyevich Balakirev, b. Jan. 2, 1837, d. May 29, 1910, was a leading Russian nationalist composer. Balakirev received his earliest musical training from his mother. He was precocious, and at the age of 14 he was made conductor of an orchestra of the nobleman Aleksandr Oulibishev, who became his patron. In 1855, Balakirev moved to Saint Petersburg, where he met Mikhail GLINKA, who encouraged him, and for a brief period he was a concert pianist. Within a few years he had become the leader of a famous group of musicians known as The FIVE (which included Aleksandr BORODIN, César CUI, Modest MUSSORGSKY, and Nikolai RIMSKY-KORSAKOV). As a champion of nationalism, he wrote a number of works based on Russian folk themes and collected and arranged many Russian folk songs. Balakirev was one of the founders (1862) of the Free Music School in Saint Petersburg and was director (1883–95) of the Court Chapel. Among his best-known works are the piano fantasy *Islamey*, the overture *Russia*, and the

symphonic poem *Tamara*. He also wrote symphonies, piano concertos, chamber music, choral works, and many songs.

MILOS VELIMIROVIĆ

Bibliography: Garden, Edward, *Balakirev* (1967).

Balaklava, Battle of   [bah-lah-klah'-vah]

The Battle of Balaklava, fought on Oct. 25, 1854, in the CRIMEAN WAR, was brought about by an unsuccessful Russian attempt to raise the siege of Sevastopol by British, French, and Turkish forces. It is famous primarily for the senseless but heroic British cavalry charge against Russian field artillery, commemorated in Tennyson's CHARGE OF THE LIGHT BRIGADE. More than one-third of the 673 British troops, commanded by the earl of Cardigan (1797–1868), were killed or wounded.

Bibliography: Selby, John, *Balaclava: Gentlemen's Battle* (1970); Woodham-Smith, Cecil, *The Reason Why* (1953; repr. 1982).

balalaika   [bal-uh-ly'-kuh]

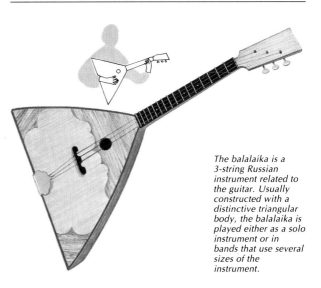

The balalaika is a 3-string Russian instrument related to the guitar. Usually constructed with a distinctive triangular body, the balalaika is played either as a solo instrument or in bands that use several sizes of the instrument.

The balalaika, a popular Russian instrument of the guitar family, originated in the 17th century. It has a triangular body with a flat back and a slightly arched belly, a long fretted neck, and three rib-fastened gut (or now sometimes metal) strings. V. V. Andreyev transformed the balalaika and the dombra, the immediate ancestor of the balalaika, from folk to popular instruments late in the 19th century, creating six sizes of balalaika, from piccolo to contrabass, which he used to form the basis of an all-Russian orchestra. Such orchestras, playing arrangements usually scored in the style of Nikolai RIMSKY-KORSAKOV, have toured Europe and America. Typically, the instruments are played by plucking the strings with the fingers.

ROBERT A. WARNER

Bibliography: Marcuse, Sybil, *A Survey of Musical Instruments* (1975).

balance

A balance is a mechanical device for weighing. The term is properly applied to an instrument that opposes equal weights in two pans suspended from the ends of a lever that has its fulcrum precisely in the middle. The balance is basically a lever in which equal force is applied to its two arms at points equidistant from the fulcrum. Balances were used by the Egyptians as early as 5000 BC and have been used ever since.

DEVELOPMENT

The most primitive balance was a straight stick suspended at midpoint by a string and having pouches attached at either end. By the Middle Ages much more precise devices were in use. These had a stone or metal fulcrum and balanced metal weighing-pans. In modern times balances are widely used in

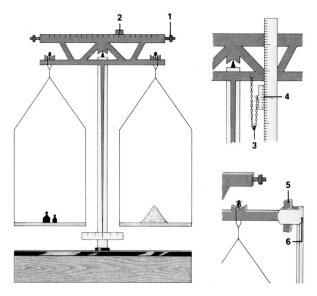

The balance is an ancient weighing instrument that makes use of various high-sensitivity devices. Screw weights (1) ensure that the long, vertical indicator needle is centered. A rider weight (2) slides along the balance arm for fine adjustment, or a fine gold chain (3) suspended between the balance arm and the vertical scale (4) may be used to increase accuracy; as the vertical scale moves, the weight of the gold chain supported by the balance arm varies. An aluminum plate (5) between poles of a magnet (6) may be used to damp the oscillating balance arm and reduce delay in taking a reading.

commerce, science, and industry. The basic concept of balancing forces at the ends of levers is still the most widely used principle in weighing, although not all balances have arms of equal length. Some use a short arm for the load and a long one for the counterbalancing weights. The ratio of arm length (long:short) times the counterbalance weight is used to calculate the true weight of the load. Many such devices are further modified by spring tension, which is used in place of weights; these devices are actually scales rather than balances.

TYPES

Analytical Balance. Instruments that weigh very small amounts with extreme accuracy are analytical balances. An accuracy of 1 part in 100,000,000 is theoretically possible using the best equipment. The simplest modern analytical balance is an equal-arm balance with two pans, enclosed in a glass case to protect against dust and air currents. The material to be weighed is placed on one pan, and weights are added to the other until the two are in exact balance. When small weighings are made, the swings of the balance pointer to the right and left are averaged, and the deviation from absolute center is used to calculate the precise weight.

The fulcrum at the center of the beam is called a knife-edge. It is a triangular piece of hard material, such as synthetic sapphire, that balances on a smooth surface of the same material. This mounting arrangement is delicate and easily disturbed. It includes pan rests and supporting guides, which can be retracted to allow the pans to swing free during the weighing. A balance such as this can accept weights up to 200 g and weigh with a sensitivity of about 0.1 mg.

Many refinements of this basic design have been made. One such refinement is a damping device that shortens the time required for the swinging of the weighing arm to cease. This damping can be supplied by a partially closed cylinder that entraps air under the swinging arm.

Substitution Balance. In substitution balances, built-in weights counterbalance the load and are removed until the centering pointer comes to rest. The weights may be removed by levers actuated by buttons labeled with the corresponding weight values. The sum of the weights left on the beam may be indicated by a digital readout.

Apothecary Balance. Less-accurate laboratory, or apothecary, balances for weighing heavier samples have a platform or swinging pan on the short end of the beam and sliding weights that may be moved along the long end to offset the load by furnishing greater leverage. Double- and triple-beam balances have riders of different weights on separate calibrated bars. Thus the heaviest rider may supply 0 to 100 g; the second, 0 to 10 g; and the third, 0 to 1 g. When all riders are in their highest position, they would exactly offset 111 g.

The standard weights used with balances are made of special noncorrosive metal alloys, such as chrome-nickel steel, and are manufactured to conform to standards set by the U.S. Bureau of Standards. The tolerance within which they conform to these values is indicated by a grade marking. Weights should always be handled with forceps to keep oil, dirt, or moisture from altering their true values.   LESLIE W. LEE

Bibliography: Kisch, Bruno, *Scales and Weights* (1965).

balance of payments

Every country maintains a record of its financial and economic relations with other countries. Just as a household's accounts show various sources of income balanced off against expenditures, so a national government maintains a balance of its international receipts and payments. While each country has its own procedures, the International Monetary Fund (IMF) recommends certain standard practices for all countries to follow. The balance of payments is organized into the current account and the capital account.

The current account covers imports and exports of goods (this part is known as the merchandise account) and of such services as transportation, insurance, and banking. In terms of value the merchandise account is by far the most important component of the current account. Also included in the current account are purchases and sales of military equipment, earnings from investments in other countries, and payments on foreign investments in the home country. Not all of these items will be in balance. The country may have spent more for imported goods than it earned from sales of its own goods abroad; its merchandise account will then be in debit, and it will be said to have a negative balance of trade. Many people feel that their country should export more goods than it imports to have a positive, or favorable, balance of trade, but this is not necessary. A negative balance of trade may be offset by other accounts in the balance of payments—for example, by the export of services or by earnings on investments abroad (see INTERNATIONAL TRADE).

The capital account covers the import and export of capital, both government and private. Capital moves from one country to another in the form of short-term or long-term investments and as debt payments. If a large corporation in one country establishes a plant in some other country, that will cause a long-term outflow of capital from the first country—and a long-term inflow to the second—to cover the investment. Thus if one of the oil-producing Arab countries buys a hotel in London, it will register on the British government's books as a long-term inflow of capital. Short-term capital movements include such transactions as short-term loans or rapid shifts of company funds from one country to another.

When the current and capital account balances are added together, the result shows the total payments and receipts. If a deficit exists, it must be made up in some way. The deficit may be covered by drawing upon the country's previous accumulation of foreign assets, or by borrowing from the central banks of other countries or from the IMF.

When a country runs a sizable balance of payments deficit, it means that its currency supply in the international money market will be greater than the demand. Under the system of floating exchange rates in existence since 1973, the value of the currency will tend to fall until demand and supply are equal. In theory at least, the decline in value will cause foreigners to buy more of the country's goods and services, while its citizens will buy fewer goods from other countries.

Beginning in the 1970s major shifts in the world balance of payments occurred, initially mostly because of inflationary crude-oil price increases by the Organization of Petroleum Exporting Countries (OPEC). International financial instability resulted because many nations, especially less-developed countries dependent on imported oil, incurred serious trade deficits. By the 1980s some of these countries had incurred such debt that banks and the IMF were forced to act to prevent disruption of the international banking system.

In the case of the United States, relatively high domestic interest rates and the fall in inflation in the early 1980s combined to attract a substantial and sustained net inflow of financial capital, which caused the U.S. dollar to appreciate significantly. This created a mounting deficit in the current account as foreign goods and services became cheaper. In the mid-1980s the central banks of the major industrial nations took concerted actions to depreciate the dollar in order to slow this continuing trend.   ROBERT M. STERN

Bibliography: De Vries, Margaret G., *Balance of Payment Adjustment from 1945 to 1986* (1987).

balance of power

A balance of power among nations is a state of equilibrium in which no nation or group of nations is able to dominate others. The notion of a balance of power as the goal of foreign policy was adopted by the Italian city-states of the 15th century and by William of Orange (later WILLIAM III of England), whose wars against France between 1672 and 1701 may be seen as an attempt to restore a power balance. In 1713 the Peace of Utrecht (see UTRECHT, PEACE OF) prevented either France or Austria from dominating Europe.

The 19th century saw the peak of balance-of-power policies. The CONGRESS SYSTEM established in 1815 sought to achieve a balance in Europe and to guard against a revival of French power. Although the formal arrangements made in 1815 broke down quickly, the system whereby the major European powers entered into alliances in order to maintain stable power relations lasted until World War I.

After World War II the COLD WAR rivalry between the United States and the Soviet Union and the development of nuclear weapons produced a bipolar "balance of terror." For the next 45 years this confrontation was a dominant factor in most international relations. The U.S.-USSR relationship was characterized by periods of greater or lesser tension, but alliances and regional security pacts were created throughout the world, distinguishing the "Eastern bloc" from the "Western bloc," and polarizing international organizations.

Beginning in 1989, the formal structures of this balance of power began to disappear. An end to the cold war was pronounced, Germany was reunited, the WARSAW TREATY ORGANIZATION unraveled, and the United Nations began to function more effectively, giving rise to hopes for a "New World Order." Nuclear and conventional arms control agreements between the superpowers, the growth of regional power centers such as the EUROPEAN COMMUNITY, and the increased importance of so-called North/South issues such as development, trade, drugs, and terrorism have meant that the bipolar balance of power has been increasingly superseded by a more complex multipolar system.

Bibliography: Gulick, E. V., *Europe's Classical Balance of Power* (1967); Keal, P., *Unspoken Rules and Superpower Dominance* (1984); Wright, M., ed., *Theory and Practice of the Balance of Power* (1975).

balance sheet: see ACCOUNTING; BOOKKEEPING.

Balanchine, George   [bal'-uhn-cheen or bal-ahn-sheen']

George Balanchine, b. Georgi Melitonovich Balanchivadze in Saint Petersburg (now Leningrad), Jan. 22 (N.S.), 1904, d. Apr. 30, 1983, is considered the most influential and prolific ballet choreographer of the 20th century. After graduating with honors from the Imperial Ballet Academy in 1921, he joined the

George Balanchine, the artistic director and one of the founders of New York City Ballet, rehearses two of his dancers. One of the most influential and demanding choreographers of the 20th century, he emphasized in his work the primacy of pure dance over plot.

corps de ballet of what is now the Kirov Ballet. In 1924, while touring Europe with a Soviet company, he joined the Ballets Russes de Serge Diaghilev and became that company's chief choreographer the following year.

Balanchine created ten dances for Ballets Russes, two of which, *Apollo* (1928) and *Prodigal Son* (1929), are still performed. *Apollo,* originally *Apollon-Musagète* (Apollo, Leader of the Muses), marks the definition of Balanchine's neoclassical style. After Ballets Russes was disbanded following Diaghilev's death in 1929, Balanchine worked for various companies before accepting Lincoln KIRSTEIN's invitation to come to the United States to direct a school and, eventually, a company. The School of American Ballet was founded in New York City in 1934; that same year Balanchine created his first ballet in the United States, *Serenade,* for its students. The work, an homage to ballet's past and set to Peter Ilich Tchaikovsky's Serenade in C Major for String Orchestra, has since become the signature piece of NEW YORK CITY BALLET.

Between 1934 and 1948, Balanchine and Kirstein directed various financially unsuccessful forerunners of New York City Ballet, and Balanchine choreographed for other dance companies and for Broadway and Hollywood. From 1948 until his death, however, Balanchine devoted himself almost exclusively to New York City Ballet—for which he created more than 200 ballets—while at the same time generously permitting his works to be restaged for other companies around the world.

Balanchine's neoclassical style was based on the classical ballet vocabulary of the French-Russian choreographer Marius Petipa. Balanchine extended, distorted, and recombined this vocabulary in unexpected ways, but always within a classical context. He did, however, occasionally use movements derived from the musical theater. Perhaps the most outstanding element in Balanchine's works is their musicality. He began studying piano at the age of five and attended the Saint Petersburg Conservatory of Music. He often used and commissioned scores by composers not yet popularly accepted and closely collaborated with Igor Stravinsky for almost 50 years. Balanchine did not alter tempos to suit his dancers; they earned their reputation for being the world's fastest.

Although Balanchine occasionally created a story ballet, most of his ballets are nonnarrative, and many are nonrepresentational. Because the dancing was always of primary—and often exclusive—importance, costumes and decor were deemphasized, as was the role of the star performer. Although Balanchine was famous for his ability to discern unique qualities in individual dancers, and to reveal these choreographically, New York City Ballet has no star system. The Balanchine legacy continues at New York City Ballet.   ROBERT J. PIERCE

Bibliography: Balanchine, George, and Mason, Francis, *Balanchine's Book of Ballet* (1977); Buckle, Richard, with John Taras, *George Balanchine* (1988); Caras, Steven, *Balanchine* (1985); Kirstein, Lincoln, *Portrait of Mr. B.* (1984); Taper, Bernard, *Balanchine*, 3d rev. ed. (1987); Tracy, Robert, and DeLano, Sharon, *Balanchine's Ballerinas* (1986).

balantidiasis   [bal-uhn-ti-dy'-uh-sis]

Balantidiasis is a protozoal disease—primarily in the Philippines—that affects the digestive tract of humans and other animals. It is caused by *Balantidium coli,* a ciliated, oval-shaped protozoa that is a parasite of pigs. The encysted form is transmitted from the pig's feces to humans through contaminated water. The parasite then develops into a motile form, penetrates the intestinal lining, and feeds on red blood cells. Balantidiasis is characterized by dysentery and ulcers of the large intestine. The disease is usually cured by treatment with a combination of drugs including tetracycline, emetine, and diiodohydroxyquin.

Balard, Antoine Jérôme   [bahl-ahr']

The French experimental chemist and pharmacist, Antoine Jérôme Balard, b. Sept. 30, 1802, d. Mar. 30, 1876, discovered (1825) the element BROMINE. This, his first and greatest achievement, was a by-product of his more general studies of the sea and its creatures. The discovery was especially important in that it made clear the existence of the most obvious family of chemical elements—the HALOGENS, or salt formers.
      GEORGE B. KAUFFMAN

Balaton, Lake   [bal'-uh-tahn]

Lake Balaton (German: Plattensee) is a lake in west central Hungary about 88 km (55 mi) southwest of Budapest. The largest lake in central Europe, it is 77 km (48 mi) long and an average of 13 km (8 mi) wide. It is shallow and fed mainly by the Zala River. Its outlet is the Sió River. Many resorts are on its shores, and prehistoric artifacts have been found.

Balbo, Italo

Italo Balbo, b. June 6, 1896, d. June 28, 1940, was an Italian Fascist leader and aviator. As air minister (1929–33), he developed the Italian air force and organized mass demonstration flights to Brazil and the United States. From 1933 to 1940 he was governor of Libya. He died there when his plane was shot down, possibly by Italian antiaircraft guns, in battle against British forces.

Bibliography: Segre, C. G., *Italo Balbo* (1987).

Balboa, Vasco Núñez de

Vasco Núñez de Balboa, b. 1475, d. January 1519, a Spanish conquistador and explorer, was the first European to sight the eastern shore of the Pacific Ocean; he opened the way for Spanish exploration and settlement of South America's western coast. The son of a poor nobleman, he set sail for the New World in 1500 as part of an expedition to Colombia. He settled on the island of Hispaniola and tried his hand unsuccessfully at farming. In 1510, to escape his creditors, he stowed away on a ship heading for the mainland, where he founded the colony of Darién on the Isthmus of Panama.

In 1513, Balboa led an expedition to the west, and on September 25 or 27 he sighted the Pacific Ocean, which he named the South Sea. King Ferdinand II of Aragon appointed Pedrarias Dávila as governor of Darién and named Balboa to serve under Pedrarias as governor of an area on the Pacific coast, where Balboa founded the settlement of Acla. Pedrarias had Balboa beheaded in Acla on false charges of treason.

Bibliography: Anderson, Charles L., *Life and Letters of Vasco Núñez de Balboa* (1941; repr. 1977); Garrison, Omar, *Balboa* (1971).

Balch, Emily Greene   [bawlch]

Emily Greene Balch, b. Jamaica Plain, Mass., Jan. 8, 1867, d. Jan. 9, 1961, was a pacifist who, with J. R. Mott, was corecipient of the Nobel Peace Prize in 1946. She taught economics and political science at Wellesley College but was dismissed in 1918 for opposing U.S. entry into World War I. She became one of the founders of the Women's International League for Peace and Freedom.

bald cypress

Bald cypress, T. distichum, *grows in swamps and rivers of the southeastern United States and the Mississippi Valley. Its needlelike leaves alternate along stems, and its flowers harden into cones by October. Its root growths, or "knees," project above the water.*

The bald cypress, *Taxodium distichum,* is an attractive coniferous tree of the southeastern United States. It grows mainly in swampy areas, sometimes reaching a height of 45 m (150 ft). Not a true cypress, the tree is deciduous, shedding its needlelike leaves and short branches in winter—hence its name. It is noted for its long life; trees as old as 1,200 years have been reported. When it stands in water, unique structures called "knees" (conical outgrowths of lateral roots) develop and usually project above the water. Bald cypress wood is decay-resistant and is valued for construction and siding. The taller Montezuma, or Mexican, cypress, *T. mucronatum,* of Mexico is not deciduous, although it may be so in cooler regions. These two species are all that remain of a genus that was widely distributed a few million years ago. They are members of the redwood family, Taxodiaceae.

Balder

In Norse mythology, Balder was the god of light and beauty. The most beloved of the gods, he was the son of Odin and Frigg and the husband of Nanna, goddess of the Moon. A famous Norse myth tells how LOKI, the evil giant, had Balder killed with a dart made of mistletoe, the only thing in the world that had not promised his mother it would never harm him. By his refusal to weep for Balder, Loki also thwarted the gods' effort to secure Balder's release from death and return to Asgard, home of the gods.

Baldinucci, Filippo   [bahl-dee-noo'-chee]

Filippo Baldinucci, b. 1624, d. Jan. 1, 1696, was a 17th-century connoisseur and historian of the arts. He was curator of Cardinal Leopoldo de'Medici's drawing collection, and his own fine collection of drawings is now one of the treasures of the Louvre. Among Baldinucci's many writings are a number of perceptive and well-documented biographies of artists. *Notizie de' professori del disegno* (Accounts of the Professors of Design, 1681–1728) was published in six volumes. He also wrote a *Life of Bernini* (1682; Eng. trans., 1966), a history of engraving and etching (1686), and a dictionary of artistic terms (1686).   TANIA BAYARD

baldness

Baldness, or alopecia, is total or partial loss of scalp hair. The condition may be temporary or permanent. The most common type of alopecia is pattern baldness, a hereditary trait that is expressed more often in males than in females because it depends on the influence of the male hormone testosterone. Pattern baldness in males extends until only a sparse growth of hair remains on the back and sides of the head. In women, the baldness usually extends until only a sparse growth remains on the crown. Neither hair tonics nor any other medical measure can prevent or reverse such baldness.

Premature baldness may partly result from an imbalance of sex hormones. Sudden temporary hair loss sometimes occurs as a result of typhoid fever, influenza, pneumonia, or stress. Gradual thinning of the hair may be caused by severe nutritional deficiency, tuberculosis, cancer, and disorders of the thyroid gland or pituitary gland. Temporary baldness also may be caused by exposure to nuclear radiation or X rays or by the internal use of certain anticancer drugs. Plugs of hair-containing skin from the back of a bald person's head are sometimes successfully transplanted on bare areas of the scalp; more painstakingly, individual hair follicles may be transplanted. The hypertension drug minoxidil has been found to restore hair growth. Although originally not approved for such use because of concern over serious side effects, it was approved for sale as a hair restorer (Rogaine) in Canada in 1986 and the United States in 1987. It is expensive, must be used daily, and seems to work mainly on young men who only recently began to lose hair.

Baldovinetti, Alesso   [bahl-doh-vee-net'-tee, ah-les'-soh]

Alesso Baldovinetti, b. Oct. 14, 1425, d. Aug. 29, 1499, was an Italian painter and mosaicist who made important contributions to landscape painting during the early Florentine Renaissance. As a youth he was apprenticed to DOMENICO VENEZIANO and was influenced by Fra ANGELICO. Baldovinetti was one of the most respected artists in Florence during the 1460s, renowned for such elegant paintings as his *Annunciation* (c.1460; Uffizi, Florence) and the *Madonna and Child* (c.1460; Louvre, Paris). His paintings blend sophistication and naïveté, using precisely drawn elongated figures and subtle gradations of tone and light. His refined style, however, became conservative and archaistic toward the end of his career. He painted a solemn *Annunciation* (1466) above Antonio ROSSELLINO's elaborate tomb of the Cardinal of Portugal in the church of San Miniato al Monte above Florence.

Baldovinetti also designed and executed several stained-glass windows and made ambitious wood-inlay (tarsia) panels and numerous mosaics, such as those (1453–55) above Lorenzo Ghiberti's two bronze doors to the Florence Baptistery. In 1483 he was appointed curator and restorer of the Baptistery mosaics.   ALAN P. DARR

Bibliography: Kennedy, R. W., *Alesso Baldovinetti* (1938).

Baldung-Grien, Hans   [bahl'-doong-green]

Hans Baldung, or Baldung-Grien, b. c.1484, was a German painter who spent most of his artistic life in the Rhineland. He became a citizen of Strasbourg in 1509 and died there in 1545. Although his art was strongly influenced by Albrecht

The Three Ages of Women and Death *(1539) by Hans Baldung-Grien is an allegory that displays this German Renaissance artist's typical combination of the macabre and the erotic. The young woman, the old woman, and Death have linked their arms, while the infant clasps Death's flail. (Prado, Madrid.)*

DÜRER, with whom Baldung studied in Nuremberg between 1502 and 1504, Baldung's distinctive fervor was soon evident. His works included altarpieces, isolated panels, designs for stained glass, woodcut prints, BOOK ILLUSTRATIONS, drawings, and portraits of nobility. His most memorable images are fantasy creations of witches and allegories of love and death.

Baldung signed and dated paintings and other works throughout his career. His earliest altarpiece commissions are from 1507, and his earliest dated drawings and prints appeared in 1503 and 1505. Most important and extensive of the Baldung altarpiece commissions is the giant *Mary* altarpiece (1513–16) for the high altar of the cathedral at Freiburg im Breisgau. In this work, Baldung revealed his assimilation of the massive, full-scale figures of Dürer, which were combined with the energetic motion, vibrant colors, and spiritual passion found in the work of another great German painter, Mattias GRÜNEWALD. In his smaller religious works, Baldung favored images of the Holy Family.

Baldung's fascination with both the supernatural and the erotic gave rise to his most bizarre subjects. An early woodcut (1510) with color-toned blacks (CHIAROSCURO) depicts a witches' sabbath in the depths of a nocturnal forest. Witches, shown as old and young nude women, are also featured in a large number of Baldung's drawings and in a painting, *The Meteorologic Witches* (1523; Städelsches Kunstinstitut, Frankfurt am Main), in which they are shown evoking storms. Baldung also used images of nude women to convey allegorically the ages of humankind and the vanity of sensual pleasures in the face of death. Several panels on the theme of ''Death and the Maiden'' contrast a lustrous fleshy female nude with the spectral skeleton of Death. A typical masterwork in this genre is the image *Eve, the Serpent, and Death* (c.1510–12; National Gallery of Canada, Ottawa), where original sin is presented as the cause of man's mortality, a theme related to the pessimistic visions of Baldung's contemporary, Hieronymus BOSCH.   LARRY A. SILVER

Bibliography: Benesch, Otto, *German Painting: From Dürer to Holbein* (1966); Koch, Robert A., *Hans Baldung-Grien: Eve, the Serpent, and Death* (1974); Von der Osten, Gert, and Vey, Horst, *Painting and Sculpture in Germany and the Netherlands, 1500–1600* (1969).

Baldwin, James

James Arthur Baldwin, b. Harlem, New York City, Aug. 2, 1924, d. Nov. 30, 1987, was a vital literary voice during the era of civil rights activism in the 1950s and '60s. The son of a minister, at the age of 14 Baldwin himself became a preacher in a small evangelical Harlem church. Within three years, he had transferred his faith from religion to literature, but the impassioned cadences of black religious ritual ring through his writings. His first novel, *Go Tell It on the Mountain* (1953), is a partially autobiographical account of his youth. The essay collections—*Notes of a Native Son* (1955), *Nobody Knows My Name* (1961), and The FIRE NEXT TIME (1963)—influenced a large white audience.

After 1948, Baldwin made his home primarily in France,

James Baldwin, a highly acclaimed black American author, conveys in his writing attitudes of blacks living in a white-dominated society. Baldwin's plays and short stories, which are to some degree autobiographical, established him as a leading literary figure in the American civil rights movement.

although he returned to the United States often to teach and lecture. His novels include *Giovanni's Room* (1956), about a white American expatriate who must come to terms with his homosexuality, and *Another Country* (1962), about racial and sexual tensions among New York intellectuals. His play, *Blues for Mister Charlie*, was produced in 1964. The short-story collection *Going to Meet the Man* (1965) and the novel *Tell Me How Long the Train's Been Gone* (1968) added to his bitterly incisive descriptions of American racism. *The Evidence of Things Not Seen* (1985) is Baldwin's analysis of the Atlanta child murders of 1979 and 1980.

Bibliography: Bloom, Harold, intro. by, *James Baldwin* (1986); O'Daniel, T. B., *James Baldwin: A Critical Evaluation* (1977); Sylvander, C. W., *James Baldwin* (1981).

Baldwin, Matthias W.

Matthias William Baldwin, b. Elizabethtown, N.J., Dec. 10, 1795, d. Sept. 7, 1866, was an American locomotive designer and philanthropist. Trained as a jeweler, he became a toolmaker, manufactured bookbinders' tools, and devised machinery for fabric printing. In 1832 he built *Old Ironsides*, Pennsylvania's first locomotive, and went on to establish what became the Baldwin Locomotive Works, the largest such company in the world. His engines could carry more steam pressure than any others then available. During his lifetime he sold more than 1,500 of them throughout the United States, except in the South where his products were boycotted because he was an abolitionist.

Baldwin, Robert

Robert Baldwin, a 19th-century political reformer, was a leader in establishing parliamentary rule in Canada. Baldwin promoted responsible government by a system that made Canada's executive and cabinet accountable to an elected parliament.

Robert Baldwin, b. May 12, 1804, d. Dec. 9, 1858, was a respected political leader of pre-Confederation Canada who has become identified with the theory and practice of responsible government. Baldwin was a lawyer who first entered the legislature in 1829 as a moderate reformer. Frequent confrontations between the elected assembly of Upper Canada (Ontario) and the British-appointed governor led Baldwin to advocate responsible government, the principle by which the governor should act on the advice of ministers who possessed the confidence of the majority in the popular legislature. Twice while serving (1836, 1841) as a minister, Baldwin unsuccessfully pressed this view on governors, resigning when his advice was not taken. On the first occasion he set down his ideas in a memorandum, from which they were incorporated by the earl of DURHAM in his famous *Report* (1839) offering remedies for political dissatisfaction in the Canadas.

In 1842, Baldwin joined with his French-speaking colleague Louis Hippolyte LAFONTAINE to form an administration devoted to the achievement of responsible government. When the governor, Sir Charles (later Baron) METCALFE, failed to take their advice on appointments, Baldwin and Lafontaine and most of the cabinet resigned. In 1847 the reformers won victory in the elections, and early in 1848 Baldwin and Lafontaine were invited to collaborate in a second ministry as joint premiers and attorneys general for their sections of the Province of Canada (created by the union of Upper and Lower Canada in 1840). Responsible government became firmly established when the new governor, the 8th earl of ELGIN, accepted the ministry's recommendation of a bill granting compensation for losses in the rebellions of 1837–38 despite his own dislike for it.

The Baldwin-Lafontaine government, sometimes called the Great Ministry, provided amnesty to those taking part in the Rebellions of 1837–38, established municipal institutions for Canada West (Ontario), and gave public aid to railroad building. Baldwin resigned his office in 1851. His party became a major element in the national Conservative party subsequently constructed by Sir John A. MACDONALD.   D. M. L. FARR

Bibliography: Careless, J. M. S., ed., *The Pre-Confederation Premiers* (1980); Wilson, G. E., *The Life of Robert Baldwin* (1933).

Baldwin, Stanley, 1st Earl Baldwin of Bewdley

Stanley Baldwin was prime minister of Great Britain three times between 1923 and 1937. Born on Aug. 3, 1867, he was the son of a prominent industrialist in Worcestershire and a cousin of Rudyard Kipling. He was elected to Parliament as a Conservative in 1908, became parliamentary private secretary to Andrew Bonar LAW (1916) and joint financial secretary of the treasury (1917), and in 1921 entered the cabinet as president of the Board of Trade.

In 1922, Baldwin played a leading part in persuading the Conservatives to withdraw their support of David LLOYD

Stanley Baldwin was prime minister of Great Britain three times between World Wars I and II. Although called by one Conservative rival "a man of the utmost insignificance," he was a skilled political leader who retained confidence through a series of crises, including the General Strike of 1926 and the abdication of Edward VIII ten years later.

GEORGE's coalition government. After a general election, he became chancellor of the exchequer in the new Conservative government and then found himself unexpectedly prime minister when Bonar Law had to resign in 1923. Although the Conservatives lost the general election at the end of that year, Baldwin returned to office in November 1924 and remained in power until 1929. During a period of rising unemployment and unrest culminating in the General Strike of 1926, Baldwin gained a reputation for reasonableness and political skill.

After losing the election of 1929, Baldwin spent an unhappy two years as leader of the opposition. When the Labour government collapsed during the economic crisis of 1931, he joined the coalition government of Ramsay MACDONALD as lord president of the council. Baldwin preferred this post to the premiership; he was much less gifted as an executive than as a parliamentarian and conciliator. By the time he succeeded MacDonald as prime minister in the summer of 1935, Baldwin was tired and aging. He won an election that year on a platform that included substantial rearmament but was severely shaken by the government's failure to settle the crisis provoked by the Italian invasion of Ethiopia in 1935–36. Nonetheless, he managed the abdication (1936) of King EDWARD VIII with dignity and sensitivity. Baldwin retired in May 1937, was created a peer, and died on Dec. 14, 1947.

In retirement, Baldwin was bitterly criticized. It was suggested that he had deceived the people about rearmament, which was not true, and that he had underestimated the threat to peace posed by Nazi Germany, which was true—but he was not alone in this. More recently, Baldwin's reputation has risen as understanding of Britain's predicament in the 1930s has deepened. Baldwin may be admired for his deft handling of the General Strike and of the abdication; his firm support of the Government of India Act (1935), in many respects a blueprint for Indian independence; and his efforts to assuage class strife.   DAVID DILKS

Bibliography: Young, Kenneth, *Stanley Baldwin* (1976).

Bale, John

John Bale, b. Nov. 21, 1495, d. November 1563, was an English bishop, playwright, and author of a catalog of British writers. His miracle plays, written to support the Reformation, are often virulent and crude anti-Catholic propaganda. His *Kynge Johan* (c.1548) is an early historical drama.   ROBIN BUSS

Bibliography: Fairfield, L. P., *John Bale* (1976).

Balearic Islands   [bal-ee-ar'-ik]

The Balearic Islands, an archipelago in the western Mediterranean, form the Spanish province of Baleares. The population of 675,400 (1986 est.) is concentrated on the densely inhabited four main islands—IBIZA, MAJORCA, MINORCA, and Formentera. The numerous smaller islands are mostly uninhabited. Total area is 5,014 km² (1,936 mi²), and the highest

elevation, Torrellas (Puig Mayor), is 1,363 m (4,471 ft). The Balearics are actually partially submerged peaks that are a continuation of the mountains of southeastern Spain. The climate and good soil promote the growing of grapes, olives, citrus fruits, and pines (for lumber). Other economic activities include fishing and livestock raising, and some minerals (lead, lignite, and marble) are found, but the economy is heavily dependent on tourism. PALMA, the capital, on Majorca, has a permanent population of 304,422 (1981).

Successively occupied by the Phoenicians, Carthaginians, Romans, and Byzantines, the Balearics came under Moorish control in the 8th century and were used as pirate bases. James I of Aragon captured them in 1235. After maintaining independence from 1276 to 1343, they returned to Spanish control. During the Spanish Civil War (1936–39), Majorca and Ibiza were held by insurgents; Minorca remained Loyalist.

The locator map shows the position of the Balearic Islands, an archipelago in the Mediterranean that is part of Spain.

Balenciaga, Cristóbal   [bah-len-see-ah'-gah, krees-toh'-bahl]

Cristóbal Balenciaga, b. Jan. 21, 1895, d. Mar. 24, 1972, was a master couturier from the 1930s through the 1960s; he was the only designer, beside Madeleine Vionnet, who could cut, fit, and sew his own designs. He feminized the suit and popularized the chemise dress in 1955. Balenciaga was born in a Basque fishing village in Spain. His abilities as a dressmaker were discovered by the marquesa de Casas Torres, who encouraged him in his career. By the 1930s Balenciaga had fashion houses in Barcelona and Madrid, but he left Spain during its civil war and opened a couture house in Paris in 1937.

In 1947, Christian DIOR introduced the "new look," with lengthened skirts and softened shoulders, but by the 1950s Balenciaga's ideas were dominant. He softened dresses, coats, and suits by loosening the fit, removing lapels, rounding collars, and adding three-quarter-length sleeves. His puffed evening dresses were marvels of engineering and yet devoid of excess; in his clothes the mature woman could be fashionable.

Balenciaga's disciples were André Courrèges and Hubert de Givenchy. Discouraged by the youth revolution in the late 1960s, Balenciaga gave up his business and retired to Spain, where he died.   E. M. PLUNKETT

Bibliography: Brogden, Jean, *Fashion Design* (1971); Garland, Madge, *The Changing World of Fashion* (1970); Lyman, Ruth, *Couture* (1972).

Balewa, Sir Abubakar Tafawa   [bah-leh-wah', ah-boo-bah-kar' tah-fah'-wah]

Sir Abubakar Tafawa Balewa, b. December 1912, d. January 1966, was the first federal prime minister of Nigeria. A teacher, he served in the House of Assembly of the Northern Region from 1947 and the federal House of Representatives from 1952. As leader of the large Northern People's Congress, he became prime minister of the federation in 1957, continuing in that position when Nigeria became independent (1960). Many thought him too closely identified with the interests of the Northern Region. He was killed in an army coup.
          ROBIN BUSS

Balfe, Michael William   [balf]

Michael William Balfe, b. May 15, 1808, d. Oct. 20, 1870, was a celebrated Irish composer and baritone best known for his opera *The Bohemian Girl*, which premiered in London in 1843. In 1827 he won recognition when he was engaged by Gioacchino Rossini, then director of the Italian Opera in Paris, to sing the part of Figaro in Rossini's *Barber of Seville*. In London in 1835, he established his fame as a composer by producing his opera *The Siege of Rochelle*.

Bibliography: Walker, Ernest, *A History of Music in England*, 3d ed., rev. by J. A. Westrup (1952; repr. 1978).

Balfour, Arthur, 1st Earl of Balfour   [bal'-fur]

Arthur James Balfour, b. July 25, 1848, d. Mar. 19, 1930, succeeded his uncle, the 3d marquess of Salisbury, as British prime minister (1902–05) and was leader of the Conservative party until 1911. He held high office again during World War I and at intervals until 1929.

Balfour was born into a family with political connections and academic distinction. Entering Parliament in 1874, he received his first cabinet appointment in 1886. As chief secretary for Ireland (1887–91) he earned the nickname "Bloody Balfour" by firm suppression of unrest, but at the same time he promoted land reforms.

Balfour rendered invaluable assistance to the marquess of Salisbury by acting as government leader in the House of Commons in 1891–92 and again from 1895 to 1902. He established a reputation as one of the best debaters of his day. Although Balfour's time as prime minister was marked by party dissensions, his government introduced (1902) educational reforms, concluded (1904) the Anglo-French Entente (see TRIPLE ENTENTE), and established (1904) the Committee of Imperial Defence.

The government split, however, over Joseph CHAMBERLAIN's tariff proposals, and in 1905 Balfour resigned. After the defeat of the Conservatives in the election of 1906, he led the party in opposition until 1911.

In the wartime coalition governments, Balfour served as first lord of the Admiralty (1915–16) and as foreign secretary (1916–19). In 1917 he issued the celebrated Balfour Declaration in favor of a Jewish national home. At the Paris Peace Conference he mitigated some of the harsher terms of the Treaty of Versailles (1919). Balfour, who held office several more times during the 1920s, was created a peer in 1922.

Balfour enjoyed great social prestige and a considerable reputation as a philosopher; it was said of him that "no finer mind has been given to politics in our generation." His writings include *A Defence of Philosophic Doubt* (1879), *The Foundations of Belief* (1895), and *Chapters of Autobiography* (1930).   DAVID DILKS

Bibliography: Dugdale, Blanche E., *Arthur James Balfour*, 2 vols. (1936; repr. 1970); Mackay, R. F., *Balfour: Intellectual Statesman* (1985); Shannon, C. B., *Arthur J. Balfour and Ireland, 1874–1922* (1987); Young, Kenneth, *Arthur James Balfour* (1963).

Balfour Declaration

The Balfour Declaration was a statement of British policy concerning ZIONISM contained in a letter from Foreign Secretary Arthur Balfour to Lord Rothschild, head of the British Zionist Federation, dated Nov. 2, 1917. Ultimately written into the League of Nations mandate for Palestine (1922), the declaration endorsed the establishment of "a national home" for the Jewish people in Palestine, stipulated that such a national home not prejudice the rights of non-Jewish communities in Palestine, and added that the rights and political status enjoyed by Jews in other countries should not be compromised by the creation of this national home. The declaration reflected a combination of wartime expediencies and fundamentalist Christian yearnings among members of the British government.   SAUL S. FRIEDMAN

Bibliography: Friedman, I., and Sachar, H. M., eds., *Britain Enters into a Compact with Zionism* (1987); Stein, L. J., *The Balfour Declaration* (1961).

Bali

Bali, a province of Indonesia, is part of the Lesser Sunda Islands, 3.2 km (2 mi) east of Java. Its area is about 5,623 km^2 (2,171 mi^2), and its highest peak, Mount Agung, reaches 3,142 m (10,308 ft). The population is 2,709,200 (1986 est.).

Volcanic in origin, Bali has a dry, mountainous north coastal section and a southern plain with a rainy monsoon season. The annual mean temperature is 28° C (82° F). Teak forests have economic importance, but the giant waringin trees are locally sacred. Wild animals include tigers and deer. Most Balinese, of Malayan origin, follow a form of Hinduism. Largely agricultural, they raise rice, maize, cassava, pigs, and cattle for local use; produce copra, coffee, and tobacco for export; and are noted for weaving and wood carving. Cities of Bali include the capital, Denpasar (1980 pop., 88,142), and Singaradja (1980 pop., 42,289).

The Dutch EAST INDIA COMPANY traded with Bali from 1597, but the Dutch gained full control only in 1908. After Japanese occupation during World War II, Dutch rule was reestablished until Indonesia received independence in 1949.

Balinese

The Balinese are the major ethnic group occupying the island of Bali in Indonesia. Their language, affiliated with the Malayo-Polynesian linguistic family, is written in both a Javanese script and the Roman alphabet (see MALAYO-POLYNESIAN LANGUAGES).

Nearly all of the more than 2 million Balinese live in villages in narrow river valleys or along the coastal lowlands. The major crops of their small, irrigated fields are rice, corn, cassava, vegetables, and fruit. Balinese villages vary in population from a few hundred to several thousand. The houses are usually surrounded by a walled courtyard. Genealogical descent is traced through the male line, and the family is the most important social group. Polygamy is permitted, but most men have only one wife. Divorce is common.

Balinese culture was indirectly influenced in the past by Indian civilization as traders passed through the Indonesian islands. During the 16th century the ruling class of the predominantly Hindu Java adopted Islam. As a result, many Javanese took refuge in Bali, carrying with them Hindu beliefs and traditions. Today Balinese practice a blend of Hinduism, Buddhism, and animism that stresses dramatic rituals rather than philosophy and mysticism. The Balinese adopted a modified form of the Hindu caste system. The people are noted for their graceful dances, lively music, and superb handicrafts—silver and gold jewelry, painting, and woodcarving.

DONN V. HART

Bibliography: Belo, Jane, ed., *Traditional Balinese Culture* (1970) and *Trance in Bali* (1970); Geertz, H. and C., *Kinship in Bali* (1978); Lansing, J. S., *Three Worlds of Bali* (1983).

Balinese cat

The Balinese cat, which was bred from Siamese cats in the United States, has a long, silky coat similar to that of Persian cats and an insistent voice like that of its Siamese forebears.

The Balinese cat originated as a sport, or mutation, from the Siamese cat in the early 1950s, when some purebred Siamese produced longhaired kittens. The longhairs bred true, and eventually the new breed was established. The Balinese has the same body conformation and color points as the Siamese but has a medium-long silky coat. The ears are large and the eyes blue.   EVERETT SENTMAN

Baliol, John de   [bay'-lee-ul]

John de Baliol (or Balliol), c.1250–1314, king of Scotland (1292–96), was the youngest son of John de Baliol (d. 1269), the founder of Balliol College, Oxford. In 1290, with the death of King Alexander III's heir, Margaret, "Maid of Norway," John became one of the chief competitors for the Scottish crown along with Robert de Bruce, grandfather of King Robert I. EDWARD I of England was made adjudicator between the claimants and decided in favor of Baliol. John was crowned at Scone on Nov. 30, 1292, and later did homage to Edward at Newcastle.

By 1296, John had fallen out with Edward, who had invaded Scotland and reduced the Scottish king to a *toom tabard* ("empty cloak"). John was later imprisoned in the Tower of London. In 1299 the pope intervened for his release, and John fled to Normandy. John's son **Edward de Baliol**, d. 1364, was crowned king in 1332 and soon acknowledged EDWARD III as overlord of Scotland. He later resigned (1356) his kingdom and title to the English king.   CHARLES H. HAWS

Balkan Wars

The Balkan Wars of 1912–13 were two short wars fought over the disposition of the Ottoman Empire's former Balkan territories. Tsarist Russia supported the efforts of Bulgaria and Serbia in 1911 to establish an alliance that would check Austria-Hungary's advances southeastward into the Balkans. In the aftermath of the 1908 revolt of the YOUNG TURKS, these two smaller states were additionally interested in dividing the remaining Turkish-controlled territory in Europe, specifically MACEDONIA. On Mar. 13, 1912, Serbia and Bulgaria signed a treaty of mutual assistance. Greece joined in a pact with Bulgaria on May 29, 1912, and Montenegro arranged agreements with Bulgaria and Serbia in late September.

With Turkey already involved in a war with Italy over Libya, and despite protests from the great powers, the Balkan League began its war against the Ottoman Empire on Oct. 8, 1912. To the surprise of most observers, the Balkan allies won quick, decisive victories. The Treaty of London (May 30, 1913) forced the Ottoman Empire to cede virtually all of its remaining European territory—except for the region immediately adjacent to Constantinople—to the Balkan states.

Subsequently, the allies disputed the division of the territorial gains. Bulgaria challenged, in particular, Greek and Serbian claims to Macedonia. Overestimating its strength, Bulgaria launched an attack on its former allies on June 30, 1913. This second Balkan War soon found Romania and Turkey joining the fighting with Greece and Serbia. Thus attacked from all sides, Bulgaria had to sign an armistice on July 31. The Treaty of Bucharest (Aug. 10, 1913) stripped Bulgaria of some recently conquered territory. Greece, which in the earlier conflict had taken Crete and some Aegean islands from Turkey, now formally acquired the important port of Salonika (Thessaloníki) and most of coastal Macedonia, while Serbia received north and central Macedonia. Romania obtained a large section of the DOBRUJA from Bulgaria, which also had to yield the greater part of Thrace to Turkey.

Although all the Balkan states significantly increased the size of their territories at the expense of Turkey, Bulgaria remained embittered by its defeat in the second Balkan War, and its neighboring states sought still other lands for expansion. The Balkan disputes were to be continued in the larger context of WORLD WAR I.   S. VICTOR PAPACOSMA

Bibliography: Jelavich, Barbara, *History of the Balkans: Twentieth Century* (1983); Young, George, *Nationalism and War in the Near East* (1915; repr. 1970).

Balkans

The Balkans are the states that occupy the mountainous Balkan Peninsula of southeastern Europe, a region that was long part of the Ottoman Empire. Although the peninsula's boundaries are imprecise, it is usually defined as including ALBANIA, BULGARIA, GREECE, ROMANIA, European TURKEY, the states that were formerly part of Yugoslavia (BOSNIA AND HERCEGOVINA, CROATIA, MACEDONIA, and SLOVENIA), and presentday YUGOSLAVIA (SERBIA and MONTENEGRO). The Balkans are bounded on the west by the Adriatic and Ionian seas, on the south by the Mediterranean, and on the east by the Black and Aegean seas.

LAND

Mountains are the dominant topographic feature of the peninsula; *Balkan* means "forested mountain" in Turkish. The mountains form two distinct systems. Toward the west lie the DINARIC ALPS, which border the Adriatic from Slovenia in the north to Albania in the south. In the east, the CARPATHIAN MOUNTAINS and Transylvanian Alps cover northern and central Romania; in Bulgaria, the Stara Planina, or Balkan Mountains, cover the central portion, and the Rhodope Massif is in the south. The heavily wooded mountains are a source of mineral wealth and, where less wooded, are used for grazing.

The rivers and their valleys are the major arteries of movement between the mountains. The DANUBE RIVER flows east across the northern portion of the peninsula to the Black Sea, creating a deep gorge, the IRON GATE, where it cuts between the Carpathian and Balkan mountains. Flowing from south to north are the Morava River, one of the Danube's main tributaries, and the Vardar River, which empties into the Aegean Sea at Salonika, Greece. Agriculture is practiced in the few river valleys and narrow coastal plains. Cereals, tobacco, cotton, olives, and grapes are the principal products.

PEOPLE

The people of the Balkans possess great cultural, linguistic, and religious diversity, a heritage of the many distinct groups who invaded the region. As the invaders settled, they often became isolated because of the mountainous terrain, which has preserved their differences. By the 2d century AD, three main groups occupied the peninsula: Greeks in the south and Thracians and Illyrians in the north. The modern Albanian language is descended from Illyrian.

During the 2d and 3d centuries, the Romans penetrated the region. They influenced Romania, which was the Roman province of Dacia, most strongly, and the Romanian language is derived from Latin.

During the 5th to the 7th century the Balkans were penetrated from the north by the SLAVS. After settling, they split into distinct tribes that are reflected in the different languages remaining today: Serbo-Croatian, Slovenian, and Macedonian; and Bulgarian. (See SLAVIC LANGUAGES.)

The lack of clear divisions between ethnic communities has made it difficult to delimit political boundaries, which has often led to prolonged conflict among the peoples of the peninsula. One of the worst of these occurred with the disintegration of Yugoslavia in the early 1990s. The existence of a Serbian minority in Croatia and of a patchwork of Serbian, Croatian, and Slavic Muslim communities in Bosnia-Hercegovina led to fighting between the different groups once these states had broken free of the Yugoslav federation. In addition, Greece refused to recognize the former Yugoslav state of Macedonia, challenging its right to use that name.

Three major religions are practiced in the Balkans: Orthodoxy, Islam, and Roman Catholicism. After the Christian church split in 1054, Constantinople (now Istanbul) became the center of the Orthodox church, which spread throughout and still dominates the Balkans today. After the Ottoman conquest, many people converted to Islam; this influence remains in Albania, Bosnia, and Bulgaria. The largest Roman Catholic communities are in Croatia and Slovenia, which were under Hungarian and Austrian control. Catholic minorities, however, live in the other primarily Orthodox countries. Jewish and Protestant minorities also live in the region.

HISTORY

The most important early civilization to arise in the Balkans

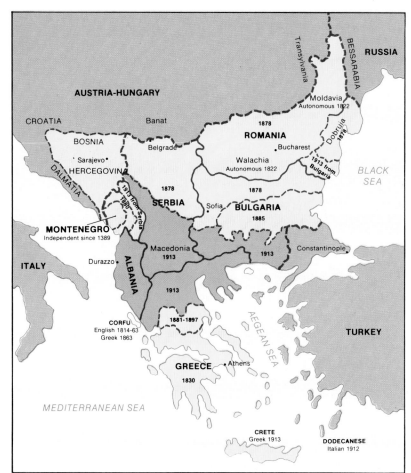

Growth of Balkan Independence 1822-1913

1913	Years in which independence was gained from Ottoman Empire
	Territory lost by Ottoman Empire as a result of the Balkan war of 1913

The map below shows the boundaries in effect after World War II — until the distintegration of Yugoslavia and the USSR in 1991.

was that of the Greeks. With the fall of Greek civilization, Rome became the major power, and by the 3d century it ruled the entire peninsula. In 395 the Roman Empire was divided between east and west, with most of the Balkans falling in the eastern portion, called the BYZANTINE EMPIRE. Byzantine rule continued until the 10th century, when the empire controlled only the southern Balkan Peninsula. In the north, the independent states of SERBIA, CROATIA, and Bulgaria arose.

During the 14th century, the Ottomans began to penetrate the Balkans; some areas of the peninsula remained under their rule for about 500 years (see OTTOMAN EMPIRE). They took Adrianople (now Edirne) in 1365, Serbia in 1389, Constantinople in 1453, and Belgrade in 1521. Ottoman rule was often characterized by harsh and oppressive methods. Because they failed to encourage any form of social or economic development, the Balkans remained backward compared with the rest of Europe. By the 17th century, Ottoman rule in Europe had begun to decline, and in 1699, under provisions of the Treaty of Karlowitz, the Ottomans were forced to surrender Transylvania, Croatia, and Slavonia to the Habsburgs, and DALMATIA and the PELOPONNESUS to Venice.

The 19th century ushered in the age of nationalism throughout the Balkans and the resulting struggle for independence from the Ottomans. Serbia was the first to revolt, in 1804, and gained limited autonomy in 1815. The Greek revolution (1821–29) focused the attention of the European powers (Britain, France, Russia, Austria) on the Balkans for the first time, as each sought to further its own interests in the region. The problems of the Balkans were thereafter a part of the EASTERN QUESTION. Britain, France, and Russia entered the Greek revolution on the side of Greece, defeating the Ottomans and assuring Greek independence. Following the RUSSO-TURKISH WAR of 1828–29, the Ottomans were forced to affirm Serbian self-government and also to grant virtual autonomy to MOLDAVIA

and WALACHIA. In 1861, Moldavia and Walachia united and proclaimed the independent state of Romania. During the Russo-Turkish War of 1877–78 the Ottomans were again defeated. At the ensuing Congress of Berlin (see BERLIN, CONGRESS OF), Bulgaria was divided, the northern portion becoming autonomous and the southern portion remaining under modified Ottoman control; Bosnia and Hercegovina were granted to the Habsburgs.

With independence, the Balkan states' own territorial ambitions increased. In 1912, Bulgaria, Greece, MONTENEGRO, and Serbia united, forming the Balkan League, and declared war on the Ottomans. The two BALKAN WARS followed (1912–13), in which the Ottomans were virtually expelled from Europe. Following the wars, the state of Albania was formed, and the other states expanded their territory. Meanwhile a movement for unification and independence from Austria-Hungary had arisen among Croatians, Serbians, and Slovenes. It reached a peak in 1914 with the assassination by a Serbian nationalist of Archduke Franz Ferdinand, heir to the Austrian throne, precipitating the outbreak of WORLD WAR I. Following the war and the dissolution of Habsburg Austria-Hungary, Yugoslavia was created and Romania expanded. The southern Balkans, however, remained virtually unchanged.

The interwar period was marked by political instability in the Balkans. During World War II, Bulgaria and Romania became German allies, but the other states attempted to remain neutral. Both Greece and Yugoslavia were invaded by Germany in 1941. After Germany's defeat in 1945, Communist regimes were established in Romania, Bulgaria, and Yugoslavia. Only Greece remained within the capitalist orbit. This situation continued until the early 1990s, when Communist rule ended in Romania, Bulgaria, and Albania. At the same time Croatia, Slovenia, Bosnia-Hercegovina, and Macedonia seceded from Yugoslavia, which led to destructive civil wars among the ethnic groups of Croatia and Bosnia, and Serbian intervention in both states. In 1992, Serbia and Montenegro formed a new and smaller Yugoslavia.

The term *balkanization* has been used to refer to the breaking up of a geographic area into small and often hostile units.

NORMAN J. G. POUNDS

Bibliography: Fine, John, *The Early Medieval Balkans* (1991) and *The Late Medieval Balkans* (1987); Jelavich, Barbara, *History of the Balkans*, 2 vols. (1983); Sjoberg, Orjan, and Wyzan, Michael, eds., *Economic Crisis and Reform in the Balkans* (1991).

Balkhash, Lake [bahl-kahsh']

Lake Balkhash is in eastern Kazakhstan, about 160 km (100 mi) west of the Chinese border. It is about 605 km (376 mi) long and 10–74 km (6–46 mi) wide and is subject to climate-induced fluctuations. Its maximum depth is 26 m (85 ft). The lake, which has no outlet, supports a fishing and salt extraction industry. Copper is mined on the northern shore and smelted in the lake's major town, Balkhash.

Ball, Lucille

Lucille Ball, an American actress, comedienne, and producer, rose to stardom as the scatterbrained housewife in "I Love Lucy" (1951–57), one of television's most successful situation comedies. Two later series, "The Lucy Show" (1962–68) and "Here's Lucy" (1968–74), established Lucille Ball as one of America's most durably popular performers. A 1986 series, "Life with Lucy," was less successful.

Lucille Ball, b. Jamestown, N.Y., Aug. 6, 1911, d. Apr. 26, 1989, was a comedienne and TV producer best known for her television series "I Love Lucy," which ran almost continuously from 1951 to 1957 and also featured her husband, bandleader Desi Arnaz. Ball began her career as a model, then appeared—first as bit player, then as featured star—in more than 50 Hollywood films. After the success of the "Lucy" series, and her divorce from Arnaz, she became head of two major TV production companies and the star of three subsequent "Lucy" series. She also starred in the Broadway show *Wildcat* (1960), the film *Mame* (1974), and occasionally in TV specials.

FRANK MANCHEL

Bibliography: Harris, Warren, *Lucy and Desi* (1990); Morella, J., and Epstein, E. Z., *Forever Lucy* (1986).

Ball, Thomas

Thomas Ball, b. Charlestown, Mass., June 3, 1819, d. Dec. 11, 1911, was one of several 19th-century American sculptors who spent a large portion of their careers in Italy. Ball worked in Florence, producing marble portrait busts, in the 1850s and again in the 1860s. He was one of the first American sculptors to work on large-scale public monuments in bronze, for which he received many commissions from the U.S. government in the 1870s. Ball's best-known bronze is an equestrian portrait of George Washington in the Boston Public Gardens (unveiled 1875). Ball was greatly admired in his own time, but in this century his numerous public monuments, such as those in Central Park, New York, and in Washington, D.C., have fallen out of favor. His best-known pupil was Daniel Chester French.

MARIAN BURLEIGH-MOTLEY

Bibliography: Craven, Wayne, *Sculpture in America,* 2d ed. (1983); Reynolds, G. A., *American Bronze Sculpture: 1850 to the Present* (1984).

Balla, Giacomo

Giacomo Balla, b. July 18, 1871, d. Mar. 1, 1958, was the oldest of the Italian painters who signed (1910) the *Technical Manifesto of Futurist Painting* in Milan. He was the teacher of both Umberto BOCCIONI and Gino SEVERINI and became the link to the second generation of futurists after World War I (see FUTURISM).

After early work in the divisionist (pointillist) technique, and under the influence of the cinematograph and of photography, Balla, in 1912, adopted cubist fragmentation as a means of expressing the dynamism of modern life. This fragmentation is evident in such works as *Speeding Automobile* (1912; Museum of Modern Art, New York). His studies, during that same year, of the interpenetration of light were among the earliest abstract paintings.

MARIAN BURLEIGH-MOTLEY

Bibliography: Dell'Arco, M. F., *Balla* (1988); Dortch-Dorazio, Virginia, *Giacomo Balla: An Album of His Life and Work* (n.d.); Martin, Marianne W., *Futurist Art and Theory; 1909–1915* (1968); Robinson, Susan B., *Giacomo Balla: Divisionism and Futurism, 1871–1912* (1981).

ballad

A ballad is a poem that tells a dramatic story in a simple, direct style suitable for setting to music. The form is characterized by informal diction, by a narrative largely dependent on action and dialogue, by thematic intensity, and by a stress on repetition. The typical ballad stanza is a quatrain containing rhymed second and fourth lines accentuated by alternating lines of trimeter and tetrameter verse.

The four types of ballads are folk, literary, broadside, and sentimental. Folk ballads are derived from medieval oral tradition. English folk ballads were first collected by Bishop Thomas Percy in his *Reliques of Ancient English Poetry* (1765). These were supplemented by the more definitive *English and Scottish Popular Ballads* published (1883–98) by Francis Child, an American. Many English ballads, such as "Edward" and "Barbara Allen," have survived in American versions. (See FOLK MUSIC.)

A literary ballad is the result of a deliberate attempt by an author to capture the naive charm of the folk ballad. Literary ballads were part of the romantic impetus toward the natural. Wordsworth's "Preface" to his *Lyrical Ballads* (1798) is a manifesto of this movement.

Broadside ballads were printed on large, double-columned sheets that included a suggested tune in keeping with the rhythm. In the 18th century they were sold for a penny and hence became known as penny ballads. Their human interest and sometimes sensational subject matter served the function of the modern tabloid.

Sentimental ballads, songs with banal tunes and melodramatic lyrics, were popular at the turn of the 20th century. Simple popular songs written since then have also been called ballads.

JANE COLVILLE BETTS

Bibliography: Child, F. J., *English and Scottish Popular Ballads*, ed. by H. C. Sargent and G. L. Kittredge, 5 vols. (1965); Coffin, T. P., and Renwick, R. D., *The British Traditional Ballad in North America*, rev. ed. (1977); Fowler, D. C., *A Literary History of the Popular Ballad* (1968); Grigson, G., ed., *Penguin Book of Ballads* (1976); Kinsley, J., ed., *The Oxford Book of Ballads* (1971; repr. 1982); Richmond, W. E., *Ballads and Ballad Scholarship* (1986).

ballade [bal-ahd']

The ballade is both a musical and an Old French poetic form. Originally, it was a dance form as well. The ballade consists of three stanzas and an envoy, written in iambic or anapestic meter, with an octave stanza in the rhyme scheme *a b a b b c b C* and an envoy in the scheme *b c b C* (see VERSIFICATION). Thus the rhymes are carried throughout the poem; stanzas and envoy both end with a refrain (*C*).

Sung ballades were popular in 14th- and 15th-century France. Guillaume de Machaut, poet and musician to French nobility, excelled at the courtly ballade. His influence is apparent in the work of the English poet Geoffrey Chaucer, who wrote several poems in ballade form. François VILLON, however, was the greatest master of the ballade.

The envoy of the ballade is addressed to an important person, usually a patron. Although many French ballades end with an envoy saluting ''ma dame,'' the tradition seems to have as much to do with being a courtier as it does with amorous courting. Chaucer's ballade ''A Complaint to His Empty Purse'' ends with an envoy that is both a compliment and a request for money.

Thomas MORLEY, in his *Plaine and Easie Introduction to Practical Musicke* (1597), speaks of the ballade as a dance form, but by the time that Charles Burney had published his encompassing *General History of Music* (1776–89), the ballade had long been dissociated from dancing. In the 19th century composers turned to the ballade as a romantic musical form. Brahms, Chopin, Grieg, and Liszt all wrote ballades for the piano; and Schubert used the ballade as a song form.

JANE COLVILLE BETTS

Balladur, Edouard   [bahl-ah-duer']

Edouard Balladur, b. May 2, 1929, became prime minister of France in 1993. Balladur, of the neo-Gaullist Rassemblement pour la république (RPR), served as finance minister in Jacques Chirac's cabinet from 1986 to 1988. As premier, he has implemented stringent economic reforms and pursued a policy of industrial privatization. He is considered likely to be a candidate for the presidency in 1995.

Ballard, J. G.

James Graham Ballard, b. Nov. 15, 1930, is an English novelist whose work in science fiction has extended the boundaries of that genre's content, style, and imagery. Ballard was born to English parents residing in Shanghai. His comfortable childhood was abruptly ended, however, when, after the Japanese attacked Pearl Harbor in 1941, they interned enemy foreigners living in Shanghai, separating Ballard from his family. His recollections of the war years provide the substance of his autobiographical novel, *Empire of the Sun* (1984; film, 1987). The visual motifs in that work—objects in landscapes of desolation that hint at events of cruelty and horror—are also found

in much of his fiction. Ballard thinks of them as ''psychological landscapes,'' externalizations, perhaps, of the collective psyche of industrialized humanity. Among Ballard's most successful science fiction novels are *The Crystal World* (1966), *The Atrocity Exhibition* (1970), *Concrete Island* (1974), and *The Day of Creation* (1988). *The Kindness of Women* (1991) is a sequel to *Empire of the Sun.*

Bibliography: Brigg, Peter, *J. G. Ballard* (1985).

ballet   [bal-lay']

Ballet is a formalized type of dancing in which the performers, through planned movement to accompanying music, present a story or develop an abstract concept. It is an elaborated form of lyric theater, and its history is a 400-year record of invention and performance. Like opera, with whose history it frequently intermingles, ballet is a tradition European in origin and Renaissance in its ideal of harmonious collaboration between artists—dancers, mimes, choreographers, musicians, and designers of costumes and decor. Since World War II, ballet has achieved a renaissance of its own throughout the world with the establishment of national companies, or private companies with national identities, supported variously by government subsidy, philanthropic funding, and burgeoning public enthusiasm.

BALLET HISTORY

The roots of ballet are in the public celebrations—parades, masques, pageants, and equestrian demonstrations—of Italy and France in the 15th, 16th, and 17th centuries. In Italy the impulse toward dramatic representation resulted in the *balletto*—from *ballo* (''dance'') and *ballare* (''to dance'')—an enormous spectacle lasting hours (or even days) and utilizing dance, recited poetry, song, and elaborate scenic effects, all organized around an allegorical plot and with the masked and richly costumed men and boys of the local court taking the principal roles. The spectacles were presented in large halls or on tennis courts. (Modern theaters as such were not built until the late 16th century.) The audience for this matrix of ballet and opera was the courtiers, who themselves employed dancing masters for instruction in social skills and for mounting amateur theatricals. In 1460, Domenico da Piacenza wrote one of the first dance manuals.

Karen Kain and Frank Augustyn dance in the National Ballet of Canada's version of Swan Lake, a four-act ballet with music by Peter Ilich Tchaikovsky. Although considered a failure when first performed in 1877, Swan Lake has since become one of the world's most popular full-length ballets.

French Court Ballets. When Henry II of France married Catherine de Médicis, in 1533, she imported the Italian *balletto* to her new home in France, where it became the *ballet*. In 1573, she staged *Ballet des Polonais* to music of Roland de LASSUS, the poetry of Pierre de RONSARD, and the dances of Balthazar de BEAUJOYEUX. Beaujoyeux's most famous work was *Ballet Comique de la Reine*, presented in 1581.

Louis XIV, patron of the arts and himself a dancer in court ballets (*ballets de cour*), founded L'ACADÉMIE ROYALE DE DANSE in 1661, which brought this form to a culmination. His dancing master, Pierre Beauchamps, codified the positions of the feet in classical ballet technique (the *danse d'école*) and invented many ballets, divertissements, and *comédies-ballets* (a spoken comedy with dance scenes interspersed) in collaboration with MOLIÈRE and the composer Jean Baptiste LULLY. *Le Triomphe de l'Amour* (1681) was the masterpiece of Beauchamps and Lully; in it appeared LaFontaine, the first woman to dance professionally in a ballet. The French love of *la danse* found a home at the Paris Opéra, and the terminology for ballet technique was henceforth in the French language (see the accompanying *Glossary of Ballet Terms*).

Emergence of Professional Ballet. In the early 18th century, ballet became a profession, with schools, theaters, paid performers, and rival aesthetic movements. Two French dancers, Marie Sallé and Marie Camargo, achieved fame through their reforms of stage dress and their refinements in dance technique. The most distinguished composer of ballet music of the time was Jean Philippe RAMEAU. The dominant progressive style of dance theater in the century was the *ballet d'action*, an attempt to unify the spectacle around clear narrative indicated in heroic mime and dance. No present-day equivalent to such a style exists, except perhaps in some of the dance-mimes of Mikhail FOKINE. The choreographers John Weaver of England, Franz Hilverding of Vienna, Gaspardo Angiolini of Italy, and Jean Georges NOVERRE of France spread the form throughout Europe and into Russia. Noverre alone created 150 ballets and worked in England, Austria, Italy, and Germany; his *Letters on the Dance* (1760) are still read today. The new narrative realism of stage action finally banished masks, and costumes began to suggest period style. Testifying to the international dynasties of dancers now possible, the Italian dancer and dancing master Gaetano Vestris (see VESTRIS family) fathered Auguste Vestris in Paris in 1760, and the son danced at the Paris Opéra for almost four decades as the "god of the dance," a title inherited from his father.

Romantic Ballet. At the end of the 18th and the beginning of the 19th century ballet began to produce works still revived in the present time and thus capable of direct experience. The French ballet *La Fille Mal Gardée* (1789) is the oldest regularly performed work in current world repertoire. Choreographed by Jean DAUBERVAL, the ballet used peasant characters and occasional rustic dances, thereby prefiguring the style of the French romantic ballet of the 1830s and '40s. The technical reforms that resulted in the romantic movement were achieved by the Italian ballet masters Salvatore VIGANÒ and Carlo BLASIS, and by the Frenchman Charles Didelot, who encouraged the use of *pointe* technique in "toe shoes" (shoes with blocked toes) for women.

The romantic ballet announced itself in Filippo Taglioni's *La Sylphide* (1832), a ballet for his daughter, Marie Taglioni (see TAGLIONI family). The supernatural subject was expressed through the long, calf-length *tutu* of the sylphs' costume as well as by dancers "flown" by means of wires and pulleys. More importantly, *La Sylphide* marked an advance in dance technique for the simulation of an "unearthly" floating continuity in the dance movement. The work allowed some point-work for Taglioni, and its choreography featured reactive effects for the *corps de ballet* and waltzlike partnering and adagio passages for the leads. In this ballet and in Adolphe ADAM's *Giselle* (1841) the modern idea of the ballerina was born, not only in her sheer authority but in her mastery of dance discourse. Carlotta GRISI was the first Giselle; her dances were choreographed by Jules PERROT, who is known as well for the *Pas de Quatre* (1845), a dance divertissement choreographed for Taglioni, Fanny CERRITO, Grisi, and Lucile GRAHN, the four reigning ballerinas of their age. French ballet music reached a peak of expression in the ballets composed by Léo DELIBES: *Coppélia* (1870), choreographed by Arthur SAINT-LÉON, and *Sylvia* (1876), choreographed by Louis Mérante.

In addition to the French, the other major—although little known at the time—European school of ballet was the Danish

(Left) *Ballet Comique de la Reine, often considered the first true ballet, was performed in 1581 in Paris. The ballet spectacle was staged by Balthazar de Beaujoyeux for Queen Catherine Médicis and her court.*

(Right) *King Louis XIV of France wears an elaborate costume for his performance in* Le Ballet de la Nuit, *danced in 1653 in Paris. Louis XIV's appearance at the age of 14 in the role of the Sun earned him the soubriquet "the Sun King."*

(Above) *The French dancer Marie Camargo, as portrayed by Nicolas Lancret, was the most popular and technically accomplished ballerina of the 18th century. She is also credited with raising the skirts of the ballet costume just above the ankle.*

(Below) *Anna Pavlova and Mikhail Fokine dance in Marius Petipa's* Les Millions d'Arlequin, *or* Harlequinade, *based on* commedia dell'arte *and first performed (1900) at St. Petersburg's Maryinsky Theater. Both Pavlova and Fokine later danced with the Ballets Russes de Serge Diaghilev.*

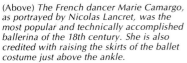

(Above) *Isadora Duncan, as portrayed in a sketch by André Dunoyer de Segonzac, was a pioneer of modern dance. Duncan rejected the formal conventions of ballet for improvisation. She abandoned traditional costumes and danced barefoot in tunics.*

under the direction of August BOURNONVILLE, a pupil of Auguste Vestris. Bournonville's version of *La Sylphide,* which premiered in 1836, is still performed today. The legacy of Bournonville, especially his French-derived technical emphasis on buoyancy and unexpected movement transitions, still awaits full absorption into international ballet language. Bournonville's many works include *The Conservatory, Napoli,* and *The Guards at Amager.*

Russian Ballet. In Russia, the tsars' rapt imitation of European court manners included the importation of dancing masters, choreographers, and dancers throughout the 18th century. The French ballet master Didelot and the Swedish teacher Christian Johansson brought their art to St. Petersburg (now Leningrad). The great achievement of establishing a Russian classical school of dance, however, was the work of a Frenchman, Marius PETIPA, the chief ballet master of the Imperial School and the Maryinsky (now Kirov) Ballet from 1869 to 1903. His many ballets (at least 60 full-length) form the Western idea of Russian theatrical art, especially those ballets set to the music of Peter Ilich TCHAIKOVSKY, *The Sleeping Beauty* (1890) and *Swan Lake* (first perf. 1877; Petipa version 1895). Petipa was assisted by Lev IVANOV, and together their *corps de ballet* experiments, sophistication of *pointe* technique, and clear differentiation between classical and character dance styles remain as definitive of ballet. Ivanov choreographed *The Nutcracker* to Tchaikovsky's score and to Petipa's scenario in 1892. Perhaps the best loved of all ballets, *The Nutcracker* is believed to be the most frequently staged ballet in history.

Fokine and Diaghilev. The beginnings of American theatrical dance proved influential on Russian ballet through the work of Isadora DUNCAN as dancer and choreographer in the first years of the 20th century. Performing to serious concert scores not intended for dance and wearing light "Greek" costumes, Duncan revolted against the declining French ballet and its European and American progeny, declaring the birth of a "free dance" that her barefoot style was to herald. Her immediate influence was less on American choreographers—Ruth ST. DENIS, Martha GRAHAM, or Doris HUMPHREY—than on the Russian choreographer Mikhail Fokine. As chief choreographer for the impresario Serge DIAGHILEV, Fokine conquered Paris and all Europe when the BALLETS RUSSES DE SERGE DIAGHILEV opened in the French capital in 1909. For the next 20 years

Diaghilev's company ruled world ballet. The greatest of his choreographers was Fokine, whose *Petrouchka* (1911) combined the music of Igor STRAVINSKY, the decor of Aleksandr BENOIS, and the dancing of Vaslav NIJINSKY (the new "god of the dance"), Tamara KARSAVINA, and Enrico Cecchetti. Fokine's mastery of plastic values and his effects of dance-mime created a new theatrical style. His ballets include *Les Sylphides* (1909; orig. *Chopiniana,* 1907), *Le Pavillon d' Armide* (1907), *Le Carnaval* (1910), and *L'Oiseau de Feu (Firebird,* 1910). Numerous dancers were associated with the Diaghilev company: Adolf Bolm, Alexandra DANILOVA, Anton DOLIN, Alicia MARKOVA, and Olga SPESSIVTSEVA. The Russian ballerina Anna PAVLOVA danced only briefly with Diaghilev's company; with her own troupe she traveled throughout the world educating audiences in classical dance.

From the Diaghilev period a tradition of great collaboration was born. Such world-famous choreographers as Vaslav Nijinsky, his sister Bronislava NIJINSKA, Leonid MASSINE, and George BALANCHINE were all sponsored by Diaghilev. Splendid scenic contributions were made by Benois, Léon BAKST, Michel LARIONOV, and Natalia GONCHAROVA, as well as by artists of the modern French school, including Fernand LÉGER, Georges BRAQUE, Pablo PICASSO, and Henri MATISSE. The greatest ballet composer of this century, Stravinsky, began his career with the Ballets Russes.

CONTEMPORARY BALLET

Following Diaghilev's death in 1929, various national ballet companies were established, many of them by his former associates. The earliest to emerge (1932) was the BALLETS RUSSES DE MONTE CARLO, in the first of its several forms. The British school combined the teaching of Marie RAMBERT and the directorial skills of Ninette de VALOIS. The resultant national company, the SADLER'S WELLS (later, ROYAL) BALLET, developed a great classical choreographer in Frederick ASHTON, whose many ballets—among them *Les Patineurs* (1937), *Les Rendezvous* (1933), *Façade* (1931), *Sylvia* (1952), *Birthday Offering* (1956), and *La Fille Mal Gardée* (1960)—and favored ballerina, Margot FONTEYN, have achieved world acclaim. Recent British dancers of renown have been Antoinette SIBLEY, Lynn SEYMOUR, Anthony DOWELL, and David Blair. The choreographer Kenneth MACMILLAN has produced such widely admired full-length ballets as *Romeo and Juliet* (1965), *Anastasia* (1971), and *Manon* (1974).

(Left) *The dancer-choreographer Vaslav Nijinsky and the composer Igor Stravinsky collaborated on the ballet* Petrouchka. *The ballet was first performed in Paris in 1911 by the Ballets Russes de Serge Diaghilev.*

(Right) *George Balanchine rehearses the New York City Ballet for the 1962 television premiere of* Noah and the Flood, *with music by Igor Stravinsky. His collaboration with Stravinsky produced over 20 works, which include* Apollo *(1928),* Agon *(1957), and* Orpheus *(1948).*

(Left) *Robert Kovich and Chris Komar dance in* Summerspace, *by the revolutionary choreographer Merce Cunningham. The sets and costumes of the dance, first performed in 1958, were designed by Robert Rauschenberg.* (Right) *A poster from the New York City Ballet, with the drawings by Edward Gorey, illustrates the five basic positions of the feet in classical ballet; all ballet steps begin and end with one of these positions.*

The French ballet has achieved no renaissance in the 20th century, despite the efforts of such longtime Opéra Ballet choreographers as Léo Staats and Serge LIFAR and other influential French choreographers, including Roland PETIT and Maurice BÉJART. The ROYAL DANISH BALLET periodically retrenches itself around its Bournonville riches, and its academy continues to produce great male dancers. The STUTTGART BALLET, with a history dating from the 1600s, gained new prominence under John CRANKO, who was its director (1961–73). The Hamburg Ballet is also influential. The Russian schools associated with the BOLSHOI BALLET of Moscow and the Leningrad KIROV BALLET have produced such great performers as Galina ULANOVA, Maya PLISETSKAYA, Irina Kolpakova, and Vladimir Vasiliev, as well as the sensational Kirov defectors to the West, Rudolf NUREYEV, Natalia MAKAROVA, and Mikhail BARYSHNIKOV.

Ballet in North America. Canada has three major ballet companies, which also tour the United States: Royal Winnipeg Ballet (1939) received its Royal Charter from Queen Elizabeth II in 1953; NATIONAL BALLET OF CANADA (1951) is based in Toronto; Les Grands Ballets Canadiens (1956) makes its home in Montreal.

In the United States, three companies dominate. The JOFFREY BALLET (1960) offers a museum repertoire of modern classics and occasional works by contemporary choreographers. AMERICAN BALLET THEATRE (1939) presents a repertoire of 19th-century classics along with modern works by Jerome ROBBINS, Britain's Antony TUDOR, Eliot FELD, and Twyla THARP, interpreted by a continually changing performance roster that has included such recent stars as Cynthia GREGORY, Gelsey KIRKLAND, Martine van HAMEL, and the imported Russians Makarova, Nureyev, and Baryshnikov.

The largest ballet academy in the Western Hemisphere is the School of American Ballet, established in 1934 by Lincoln KIRSTEIN and choreographer George Balanchine and today the official school of NEW YORK CITY BALLET. In a series of great modern works—*Apollo* (1928), *Serenade* (1934), *The Four Temperaments* (1946; revised 1951), *Orpheus* (1948), *Agon* (1957)—Balanchine re-created the idea of dance classicism and ballet technique. His collaborations with Stravinsky are models of sensitivity to musical values. The core of Balanchine's repertoire, including *Concerto Barocco* (1940), *Ballet Imperial* (1941; retitled *Piano Concerto #2*), *Symphony in C* (1947, as *Palais de Cristal*), *Divertimento No. 15* (1956), *Liebeslieder Walzer* (1960), *Jewels* (1967), and *Violin Concerto* (1972; first version, *Balustrade*, 1941), has made him the most influential ballet choreographer in the second half of this century.

A number of great dancers have associated with New York City Ballet, among them Diana Adams, Mikhail Baryshnikov, Jacques D'Amboise, André Eglevsky, Suzanne Farrell, Melissa Hayden, Allegra Kent, Tanaquil LeClercq, Patricia McBride, Peter Martins, Maria Tallchief, and Edward Villella. Arthur Mitchell, also a principal dancer with the company, withdrew to found the first black classical ballet school and company, Dance Theatre of Harlem, following Martin Luther King's assassination in 1968; the company made its auspicious debut two years later.

Ballet has recently become enormously popular outside New York City, although the oldest American company, the Atlanta Ballet, was founded in 1929. Among the prestigious companies now presenting regular seasons are the Dayton Ballet (1937) in Ohio, the San Francisco Ballet (1938), the Tulsa Ballet (1956), the Boston Ballet (1963), the Minnesota Dance Theater (1962) in Minneapolis, the Houston Ballet (1968), and the Pennsylvania and Milwaukee Ballet (merged 1987) in Philadelphia and Milwaukee. Ballet West, founded (1952) in Salt Lake City by the University of Utah, is the most notable of university-affiliated companies.

These groups, and the many professional ballet and dance schools in the United States, have become the source of fresh talent for ballet companies throughout the Western world.

Don Daniels

Bibliography: Anderson, Jack, *Ballet and Modern Dance: A Concise History* (1986); Balanchine, George, and Mason, Francis, *Balanchine's Book of Ballets* (1977); Beaumont, Cyril, *Complete Book of Ballets* (1949); Benois, Aleksandr, *Memoirs*, 2 vols., trans. by Moura Budberg (1960); Chujoy, Anatole, and Manchester, P. W., *The Dance Encyclopedia* (1967); Denby, Edwin, *Looking at the Dance* (1949; repr. 1968); Guest, Ivor, *The Romantic Ballet in Paris* (1966); Karsavina, Tamara, *Theatre Street* (1961); Kirstein, Lincoln, *Dance* (1969) and *Movement and Metaphor* (1970); Koegler, Horst, *The Concise Oxford Dictionary of Ballet*, 2d ed. (1982); Noverre, Jean Georges, *Letters on Dancing and Ballets*, trans. by Cyril Beaumont (1966); Roslavleva, Natalia, *Era of the Russian Ballet* (1966); Stravinsky, Vera, and Craft, Robert, *Stravinsky in Pictures and Documents* (1979).

See also: CHOREOGRAPHY; DANCE; FOLK DANCE; MUSICAL COMEDY; OPERA; THEATER ARCHITECTURE AND STAGING.

GLOSSARY OF BALLET TERMS

Adagio 1. A sequence of exercises in slow tempo, performed in ballet class to develop strength in sustaining extensions and balances. 2. A passage in a *pas de deux* in which the man supports the woman in turns and balances. 3. The technique of partnering.

Air, en l' "In the air." May be used to describe steps performed with the working leg off the floor, for example, *rond de jambe en l'air;* or jumping steps, for example, *tour en l'air.*

Allegro Sequences of steps in fast tempo, performed in ballet class to develop speed and clarity of execution.

Arabesque A position in which the dancer stands on one leg, straight or bent, with the other extended to the back, usually at right angles to the body, but higher in *arabesque penchée* (leaning), when the dancer leans forward and raises the leg higher to follow the line of the torso.

Assemblé A jumping step in which the dancer thrusts one leg up and out to the front, side, or back, at the same time springing off the other, and brings the legs together in the air before landing.

Attitude A position originally derived from Giovanni da Bologna's statue of Mercury, in which the dancer stands on one leg with the other extended to the front or back and bent at the knee, which should be held at a higher level than the foot.

Ballabile A group dance, usually for the corps de ballet.

Ballerina Literally, "female dancer," but usually used of one who dances leading roles, *prima ballerina*, first dancer.

Ballet master/mistress Before the word *choreographer* was used in its contemporary sense, the ballet master was responsible for arranging ballets. Today, the term more usually denotes the person who rehearses ballets created by someone else and also performs certain administrative duties such as drawing up rehearsal schedules; casting of minor roles is often the province of the ballet master.

Ballon Literally, "bounce." The quality of smooth, springing ascent and descent in jumping steps, achieved primarily by the pliant use of the feet.

Barre The horizontal wooden bar that runs around the wall of the ballet studio at waist height, and that the dancer holds on to during the first part of class; by extension, this part of ballet class is also usually referred to as the *barre*.

Basque, saut de A jumping step in which the working leg is raised to the side and the foot of the other is drawn up to the knee of the working leg as the body turns in the air, landing in that position.

These are the five basic positions:

first   second   third   fourth   fifth

Battement   A generic term to describe the various movements in which the leg makes a beating motion. They are performed at the *barre* in a systematic progression to exercise all the leg muscles: *Battement tendu*, in which the leg is extended to front, side, and back with the toe resting on the floor; *battement tendu jeté*, in which the leg is extended to front, side, and back with the toe leaving the floor very slightly (also called *glissé* or *dégagé*); *battement frappé*, in which the foot is sharply extended to front, side, and back from the ankle of the supporting leg; *petit battement*, in which the working foot beats from front to back, or back to front, against the ankle of the supporting leg; *battement fondu*, in which the working leg is extended to front, side, or back, either to point *tendu* or in the air, from a position in which the working foot is pointed in front or in back of the supporting ankle; both knees are bent at the beginning and straighten simultaneously; *grand battement jeté*, in which the leg is lifted, straight, to front, side, and back, attaining waist level or higher; *grand battement développé*, in which the foot is drawn up to the knee of the standing leg and then extended to front, side, or back, until the leg is straight.

Batterie   A generic term referring to steps in which the

in which the knees bend, bringing the feet together beneath the body before landing again in fifth position.

Coda   The fast final section of a *pas de deux*, in which the dancers may have brief solo passages as well as dancing together in a brilliant conclusion, as in the "Bluebird" *pas de deux* of Tchaikovsky's *Sleeping Beauty*.

Corps de ballet   The ensemble of dancers in a ballet company, who appear in support of the soloists.

Coryphée   A dancer (of either sex) who has moved out of the *corps de ballet* to dance minor solo roles.

Croisé   Literally "crossed." A position of the body in which the dancer turns obliquely to the audience, so that when the working leg is raised, it crosses the supporting leg.

Développé   See *grand battement développé*.

Divertissement   1. A section of a ballet comprising dances that have no connection with the plot, for example, the fairytale dances in *The Sleeping Beauty*, Act III, or the "Peasant" *pas de deux* in *Giselle*, Act I. 2. A short dance or excerpt from a longer ballet given as a separate item in a program.

Effacé   A position of the body in which the dancer turns

attitude devant   attitude derrière   arabesque   battement

feet beat together or cross in the air, either as an embellishment to add brilliance to jumping steps, or as the essential characteristic of the step, as in *entrechats* or *brisés*.

Bourrée, pas de   A linking step in which the weight is transferred from one foot to the other in three small steps. *Pas de bourrée chaîné* or *couru* is a series of small, even steps on *pointe* which give the impression that the dancer is gliding across the surface of the stage.

Brisé, pas   Literally, "broken step." A small traveling *assemblé* embellished with a beat. *Brisé volé*: a series of *brisés* to front and back alternately, landing on one foot, giving the impression that the dancer is skimming over the surface of the stage.

Cabriole   A jumping step in which the dancer beats straight legs together in the air.

Changement de pieds   The dancer jumps straight up in the air with legs together and reverses the position of his feet before landing.

Chassé, pas   A linking step in which the dancer slides one foot out to front, side, or back, bringing the other up to it in fifth position before continuing into the next movement.

Chat, pas de   Literally, "cat's step." A light, jumping step

slightly away from the audience; the working leg is the one farther from the audience.

Elevation   The ability to jump high in the air and give the impression of remaining suspended there for an instant.

Enchaînement   A combination of steps into a dance phrase.

Entrechat   A vertical jump in fifth position, with the feet changing in the air, twice (*entrechat quatre*), three times (*entrechat six*), four times (*entrechat huit*), and, exceptionally, five times (*entrechat dix*). The term *entrechat deux* is not used: when the feet beat once and change this is called *changement battu* or *royale*. In all of these the dancer returns to fifth position. In *entrechat trois, cinq,* and *sept* the dancer lands on one foot with the other touching the supporting leg after one, two, or three beats.

Épaulement   Literally, "shouldering." The slight turning of the shoulders, *croisé* or *effacé*, in relation to the head and legs, distinguishes the classic style, particularly of the Italian, Russian, and British Schools. In the old French and the Danish Schools it is rarely used.

Fouetté   Literally, "whipped." A turning step, usually done in a series, in which the working leg whips out to the side in a *rond de jambe* and then in to the knee as the dancer turns on the supporting leg, rising on to the *pointe* at each revolution. The 32 *fouettés* performed by Odile in *Swan Lake*, Act III, are a supposed touchstone of female virtuosity.

Glissade Literally, "sliding." A linking step in which the dancer moves to the side, front, or back from fifth position to fourth or fifth position, with a moment of transition in which the feet should be fully stretched.

Jeté Literally, "thrown." A jump from one foot on to the other. It may be a small jump, or large (*grand jeté*), landing in a position such as *arabesque* or *attitude*. The jump may be beaten (*battu*) or done with a turn (*en tournant*).

Leotard A one-piece garment covering the whole torso, with or without sleeves, worn with tights for practice or, in many contemporary ballets, as a stage costume. Originally designed by the French acrobat Jules Léotard (1830–70).

Maître or maîtresse de ballet See *ballet master/mistress.*

Pas Literally, "step." The technical terms for ballet steps often include the word *pas*, or sometimes *temps* (literally "time"), as in *pas de chat* or *temps de poisson*. *Pas* is also used in the sense of "dance," as in *pas de deux/trois/*

spread flat on the floor and the rest of the foot raised (*relevé*) from the metatarsal.

Port de bras Literally, "carriage of the arms." Used in this general sense, and also to denote exercises designed to develop the graceful and harmonious use of the arms. For instance, when a dancer, at the *barre*, bends the whole torso forward and back, this exercise is called *port de bras* even though its correct execution involves the entire body. There are positions of the arms corresponding to positions of the feet.

Positions There are five basic positions of the feet in which all steps in classic ballet begin and end, with the legs turned out from the pelvis: First position: heels touching, feet in a straight line; Second position: feet wide apart, in a straight line; Third position: one foot in front of the other, and heel against the instep; Fourth position: feet apart, one in front of the other, opposite fifth; Fifth position: one foot in front of the other, the heel against the joint of the big toe.

Relevé Literally, "lifted." The raising of the body on to half or full *pointe.*

Rond de jambe Literally, "circle of the leg." The working

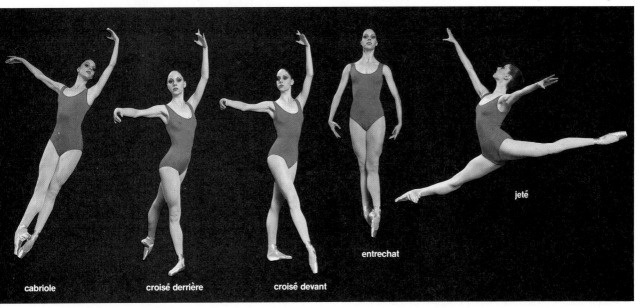

cabriole   croisé derrière   croisé devant   entrechat   jeté

quatre (dance for two, three, four people) or more, or as in *pas de l'ombre* (dance of the shadow) from *Ondine*, or *pas des patineurs* (dance of the skaters). *Pas d'action* signifies a sequence in a ballet in which the narrative is carried forward by means of dancing, as in the so-called Rose Adagio in Act I of *The Sleeping Beauty.*

Pirouette A complete turn of the body performed on one leg; the working leg may be placed against the ankle or drawn up to the knee of the supporting leg, or extended to the side or to the back, in *arabesque* or *attitude.*

Plié Literally, a "bending." The first exercises done in every class to loosen the muscles, the foundation of the dancer's technique. The dancer stands erect at the *barre* and slowly bends the knees, keeping them in line with the turned-out feet. *Pliés* are practiced in all five positions. Nearly every step begins and ends in *demi-plié* (half-), giving impetus to a jump and cushioning a landing.

Pointe The tip of the toe. Women, and infrequently men, dance *sur les pointes* in blocked shoes. The introduction of this technique in the early 19th century made possible the development of female virtuosity, with such feats as multiple *fouettés* and sustained balances on one leg. *Demi-pointe* is when the dancer stands with the toes

leg describes a circle either on the floor (*à terre*) or in the air (*en l'air*).

Sissonne A jump from both feet on to one foot with the working leg opening to the side, front, or back in a scissor-like motion. May be performed with a beat.

Tour A complete turn of the body. See *pirouette. Tour en l'air*, a turn in the air, executed as the dancer jumps up vertically. Male dancers are expected to perform double *tours en l'air*, and some are capable of triples. Rarely performed by women.

Tournant, en Literally, "turning." Many steps may be performed, either singly or in series, while the dancer makes a revolution of the body or describes a circle on the floor.

Turn-out (French: *en dehors.*) The turning out of the legs from the pelvis, essential for speed, flexibility, elegance, and the ability to move in any direction.

Tutu Ballet skirt, either calf-length as in romantic ballets (as in *Les Sylphides*) or projecting straight out at hip level as in classic ballets (as in *Swan Lake*), with many layers of ruffles underneath. The term *tutu* is actually a slang word referring to the latter part of the costume, or rather to the part of the anatomy it conceals.

Variation Solo dance.   DAVID VAUGHAN

Ballets Jooss: see JOOSS, KURT.

Ballets Russes de Monte Carlo   [bah-lay roos duh mahn'-tay kahr'-loh]

Ballets Russes de Monte Carlo, an outgrowth of the great BALLETS RUSSES DE SERGE DIAGHILEV, was created in 1931, two years after the death of DIAGHILEV. The new company included the best dancers and choreographers from the parent company, such as Leonid MASSINE, George BALANCHINE (until 1933), André EGLEVSKY, Alexandra DANILOVA, and Tamara Toumanova, under the joint directorship of René Blum and Colonel W. de Basil. It opened to great acclaim at Monte Carlo in 1932; a three-week London season in 1933 proved so successful that it was extended to four months. The same year Ballets Russes made its New York debut, followed by an extensive American tour. This sequence—opening in Monte Carlo, followed by tours to London and the United States—was followed until 1936, when the company split into two factions, one headed by Blum and the other by de Basil. By 1938 dissension led to litigation between the two; Blum's company emerged as the Ballet Russe de Monte Carlo. Its rival, called by de Basil the Original Ballet Russe, never achieved stability and died of financial starvation after a decade of unsuccessful world tours.

Ballet Russe de Monte Carlo, on the other hand, achieved triumphant success immediately under the leadership of Blum and Massine. For its first American tour in 1938, the dancers Alicia MARKOVA, Igor YOUSKEVITCH, Frederic FRANKLIN, and Serge LIFAR, among many others, joined the company. The outbreak of World War II in 1939 forced the company to remain in the United States where, headquartered in New York, it continued to tour. Blum was seized by the Gestapo in Paris and died at Auschwitz in 1942. By 1948, when Ballet Russe celebrated its tenth anniversary in the United States with a gala performance at New York's Old Metropolitan Opera House, it had made itself a nonprofit foundation, one that long maintained an office to oversee its remaining assets after its dissolution. It gave its final New York season in 1957, with Alicia ALONSO and Youskevitch as guest artists. Although the company toured occasionally until it was dissolved in 1962, its days as a major force in ballet history were over long before then. Ballet Russe is remembered for maintaining the Diaghilev tradition and enhancing it and for preparing Western audiences for the unprecedented growth of their own national companies after 1950.

Bibliography: Anderson, Jack, *The One and Only: The Ballet Russe de Monte Carlo* (1981); Clarke, Mary, and Crisp, Clement, *Ballet: An Illustrated History* (1978); Lawson, Joan, *A History of Ballet and Its Makers* (1972); Lieven, Peter, *The Birth of Ballets-Russes*, trans. by L. Zarine (1973); Walker, Katherine S., *De Basil's Ballets Russes* (1983).

Ballets Russes de Serge Diaghilev   [sir-gay' dee-ah'-gil-yif]

A ballet company that became legendary in its own time for its brilliant synthesis of dance, decor, and music, the Ballets Russes de Serge Diaghilev, founded in 1909 by the impresario DIAGHILEV, revolutionized and revitalized BALLET by departing from the romantic style of such full-length ballets as Adolphe ADAM's *Giselle* to create shorter, more novel ballets, such as *L'Après-midi d'un faune* (AFTERNOON OF A FAUN), in a modern, expressive style. When the company opened in Paris at the Théâtre du Châtelet on May 19, 1909, the era of modern ballet began.

Called the "Diaghilev Miracle" when it burst upon the European scene, the Ballets Russes was a unique combination of such luminaries as Vaslav NIJINSKY, Anna PAVLOVA, and Tamara KARSAVINA, the dancer-choreographer Mikhail FOKINE, the composer Igor STRAVINKSY, and the designers Aleksandr BENOIS, Léon BAKST, and Nikolai Roerich. Under Diaghilev these artists together transformed ballet into a new form, a vivid combination of movement, sound, passion, fantasy, and color.

Despite the company's name, it never performed as a group in Russia, although it did tour the Continent, England, and

The poster of Vaslav Nijinsky in L'Après-midi d'un faune *is by Léon Bakst, who also designed the scenery and costumes for the ballet. First performed by the Ballets Russes in 1912, the ballet was choreographed and danced by Nijinsky to music by Debussy.*

the United States. But the artistic unity of the troupe's first Paris production, *Le Pavillon d'Armide* (Armida's Pavilion), created an immediate sensation and began a string of artistic triumphs that would last 20 years. Pavlova (who was a member of the troupe only for the first season) and Fokine danced the lead roles, and Nijinsky created a furor in the smaller virtuoso role of Armida's princely slave. The first season included the "Polovtsian Dances" from Aleksandr BORODIN's opera *Prince Igor*, and *Le Festin* (*The Banquet*) to Mikhail GLINKA's music.

Shéhérazade (to Nikolai RIMSKY-KORSAKOV's score) and *The Firebird* (with Stravinsky's music and Fokine's choreography) both premiered in 1910 and are typical of the early Ballets Russes style. Based on the first story from *A Thousand and One Nights*, *Shéhérazade* highlighted Diaghilev's preference for exotic themes and colorful fairy-tale settings and costumes. Bakst's designs, and the ballet, were an escape into a febrile world of sensuality and fantasy. The *Firebird*, derived from Russian fairy tales, continued in the same quasi-Oriental vein, but added Stravinsky's brilliantly dissonant score.

Petrushka (1911), another Stravinsky-Fokine collaboration, was a success, particularly in Nijinsky's interpretation of the title role. But one of the greatest uproars in modern theater history occurred two years later at the premiere of *Le Sacre du printemps* (*The Rite of Spring*), which represented a primitive fertility rite ending with a human sacrifice set to Stravinsky's wild and searing music, with Roerich's strange designs and Nijinsky's highly controversial choreography. The audience, violently divided in opinion, rioted and almost halted the performance, which concluded with the arrival of the police, according to some accounts.

After 1913, the Ballets Russes moved in another direction, less Russian and more French, with new dancers and designers; nevertheless, it continued to experiment. Its production of *Parade* (1917), half-danced and half-pantomimed, had a scenario by Jean COCTEAU and was choreographed by Leonid MASSINE. *Parade* became a major influence on postwar French productions, largely because of Pablo PICASSO's cubist settings and costumes and Erik SATIE's score, a collage of sounds incorporating typewriters and street noises with instrumental music.

During the 1920s Nijinsky's sister, Bronislava NIJINSKA, became an important choreographer for the troupe, and in 1925 George BALANCHINE was appointed chief choreographer. For Serge LIFAR, the last of the great male dancers, after Nijinsky and Massine, to be discovered by Diaghilev, Balanchine created both *Apollo* (1928) and *The Prodigal Son* (1929), two of his most important works.

The company was frequently on the verge of bankruptcy, but during the two decades of its existence, until Diaghilev's death in 1929, about 68 ballets were presented. The company did not have a school, but many dancers and choreographers later joined the BALLETS RUSSES DE MONTE CARLO, founded in 1931 to succeed the Ballets Russes de Serge Diaghilev, while others such as Balanchine and Ninette de VALOIS went on to found their own companies.

Bibliography: Buckle, Richard, *Diaghilev* (1984); Kochno, Boris, *Diaghilev and the Ballets Russes* (1970); Macdonald, Nesta, *Diaghilev Observed* (1975; repr. 1986).

Ballinger, Richard A.

Richard Achilles Ballinger, b. Boonesboro, Iowa, July 9, 1858, d. June 6, 1922, U.S. secretary of the interior (1909–11) under President William H. TAFT, became the focus of attacks upon Taft's conservation policies. An expert in mining law, he served (1907–08) as commissioner of the General Land Office. As interior secretary, Ballinger in 1909 fired a subordinate who had accused him of impeding investigation of allegedly fraudulent Alaskan coal-land claims. He was denounced by Forestry Bureau chief Gifford PINCHOT and others who felt Taft was betraying former president Theodore ROOSEVELT's conservationist policies. A joint congressional committee cleared Ballinger of wrongdoing, but he resigned in March 1911. The controversy helped create the split in the Republican party that led to the formation of the BULL MOOSE PARTY in 1912.

Bibliography: Penick, J. L., *Progressive Politics and Conservation: The Ballinger-Pinchot Affair* (1968).

ballistic missile

A ballistic missile is a type of self-propelled weapon. It is termed *unguided* because after its rocket motor burns out in flight, the subsequent trajectory (called a ballistic trajectory) is determined by gravity. A weapon of considerable sophistication, it is able to reach remote targets with a high degree of accuracy.

The initial acceleration imparted to such a missile may be controlled by varying the amount and duration of thrust applied by the rocket motors. The direction of thrust may also be varied by means of deflectors or by nozzle steering to control the missile's orientation and attitude. After the rocket motors have burned out, further corrections to the trajectory can be made by small thruster motors under the control of the missile guidance system. The guidance is usually based upon inertial navigation techniques. (See GUIDANCE AND CONTROL SYSTEMS.)

The booster stages of the propulsion motor separate one by one from the main missile, either at burnout or at a predetermined instant, leaving the payload—the warhead, guidance package, and other subsystems—to continue to the target in the reentry vehicle. This vehicle may be equipped with some form of terminal guidance to increase accuracy in the final phase of the trajectory. Multiple warheads, or MRVs, may be carried.

Categories of ballistic missiles include the ICBM (Intercontinental Ballistic Missile), SLBM (Submarine-Launched Ballistic Missile), IRBM (Intermediate Range Ballistic Missile), and the Tactical Ballistic Missile.   R. T. PRETTY

Bibliography: *Jane's Weapon Systems* (annual); Taylor, Michael H., *Missiles of the World*, 3d ed. (1980).

See also: MIRV MISSILE; ROCKETS AND MISSILES.

Ballistic Missile Early Warning System: see BMEWS.

ballistics

Ballistics is the scientific study of the propulsion and motion of projectiles such as bullets, ARTILLERY shells, rockets, and guided missiles (see ROCKETS AND MISSILES). The field of ballistics also includes the study of the destructive action of such projectiles. The theory and techniques of ballistics have broad applications in technology. Such applications include the formation of metal parts by explosive means, the development of cartridge-actuated devices for industry, and the development of heat shields and aluminum bumpers for spacecraft. Scientific research in fields such as geophysics, geodesy, meteoritics, and planetary exploration may also make use of the science of ballistics.

DEVELOPMENT OF BALLISTIC THEORY

The first systematic treatment of the ballistics of gunnery was given by the Italian Niccolò Fontana, better known to historians of science as TARTAGLIA, in his *Nuova scienzia*, which was published in 1537. A professional military engineer, Tartaglia served as a consultant on scientific problems to the rulers of several principalities. The master of ordnance at the castle of Verona suggested that he consider what angular elevation of a gun barrel would yield the greatest range for a shot. Tartaglia found that an elevation of one-half of a right angle—in traditional measure, 45°—was the inclination required.

The theory of exterior ballistics was rapidly developed early in the 18th century, after the principles of dynamics and the methods of the calculus had been established by Galileo, Newton, and Leibniz. But this important work in theory was largely an exercise in pure mathematics that had no immediate effect on practical gunnery, because no acceptably accurate way existed to measure the muzzle velocity of any firearm. Such a method was first suggested by the astronomer Cassini in 1707; the instrument itself, the ballistic pendulum, was invented by the Englishman Benjamin Robins in 1740. In this device, a large pendulum bob is suspended from a tripod. A bullet of small mass is fired into the bob, causing a swing of large amplitude that can be carefully measured. The velocity of the striking bullet can be determined from the known masses of the bullet and bob and the amplitude of the swing, using the basic laws of physics.

Drawing on his own experience and the writings of others as far back as Leonardo da Vinci, Robins suggested some useful directions for research and development in gun and projectile design. Noting that large quantities of gas escaped past round shot in the smooth-bore weapons of this time, he proposed the use of breech-loading weapons (loaded at the rear of the bore) with rifled barrels (containing spiral grooves), and elongated projectiles of close fit in the bore. He described these design proposals in his *New Principles of Gunnery*; they were gradually incorporated into ordnance-engineering practice during the 19th century. A breech-loading infantry rifle, the needle gun, so called because of its long, sharp firing pin, was invented by Johann Dreyse and issued to some Prussian regiments in 1841. A serviceable breech-loading artillery rifle was developed by Major Cavalli of Sardinia in 1845. Pointed cylindrical projectiles became standard issue for both small arms and artillery. Bullets were made of soft metal so they could be seated at the base of the rifling in small arms, and copper rotating bands were added near the base of artillery shells. By these means, the gases produced by the burning powder were retained behind the projectiles, which were induced to spin as their seating grooves were forced forward along the helical curve of the rifling.

INTERIOR BALLISTICS

Interior ballistics is the study of the propulsion of projectiles by forces derived from the expansion of gases burning within a gun or rocket motor. Although the burning proceeds by similar stages in a gun and in a solid-propellant rocket, the pressures developed within a closed gun breech are much higher than those in a nozzled rocket motor; therefore, the metal parts of a gun system—the chamber, barrel, and recoil mechanism—are more complicated and must be much stronger than those of a nearly recoilless rocket launcher. In addition, motion is imparted in quite different ways to projectiles fired from guns and to missiles carrying both warheads and gas-reaction motors.

Guns. During the early development of the interior ballistics of guns, the muzzle velocity and the maximum pressure of the gas in the chamber were considered the two most important physical variables to predict and measure. These quantities were found to be functions of given firing conditions, usually the known characteristics of projectile, charge, and gun. Four physical principles—governing the transformation of energy, the rate of change of projectile momentum, the linear buring rate, and the granulation geometry—suffice for a solution of the problem of computing projectile travel, speed, and chamber pressure as functions of time. These quantities may then be used for comparison with data obtained from experimental firings.

Rockets. Rocket propellants may be either solid or liquid; if solid, the propellant should contain all the materials needed to maintain steady combustion; if liquid, the fuel and the oxidizer are kept in separate containers and come in contact only in the motor chamber. In either case, the process must be stringently controlled; a good pressure-time curve for a rocket is roughly trapezoidal, rising steadily to a plateau that is maintained during thrust and dropping rapidly at burnout. The mechanical strength of the chamber should not greatly exceed the maximum chamber pressure that can occur in practice, since the extra wall-mass can reduce acceleration.

The shape of the nozzle or nozzles is a critical feature in the design of rockets. The contour chosen for the longitudinal section should steadily increase the speed of the gas into the throat, where it may flow at the speed of sound; beyond this point, the gas pressure declines and its speed increases.

If gravity and air-drag are ignored, the motion of a rocket can be calculated by using an equation derived directly from Newton's second law of motion. If the rocket begins at rest, its velocity v at any time t is given by

$$v = q \log_e \frac{M + m_o}{M + m_t}$$

where M denotes the mass of the solid part of the rocket, m_o the initial mass of propellant, m_t the mass of propellant that is still unburned, and q the exhaust speed of the gas. This equation suggests that high-velocity rockets should permit exhaust gases to escape at high speeds and should carry a mass of propellant that is large in comparison to the mass of the rest of the rocket.

A high initial propellant temperature will increase the chamber pressure in a rocket, which will in turn increase the thrust. However, too high propellant temperature will cause burnout to occur quickly and will have no substantial effect on the final speed of the rocket.

EXTERIOR BALLISTICS
Exterior ballistics, in the classical sense, deals with the flight of projectiles moving under the influence of gravitational and aerodynamic forces. The study of certain types of projectile, however, may require that forces not treated in the classical theory of the subject be considered. Guided missiles, for example, may be acted upon by corrective forces, such as motor thrust or aerodynamic lift due to fin movement, when their trajectories depart from prescribed paths in space.

Trajectory in a Vacuum. Galileo found that the path of a cannonball rolled off the end of a plank was the descending branch of a parabola, similar to the trajectory of a very heavy modern bomb dropped from an aircraft in horizontal flight. The trajectory of a projectile fired in a vacuum from an inclined gun barrel would include both the ascending and the descending branches of a parabola. The equation of the Galilean parabola, or trajectory *in vacuo*, is usually written in the form

$$y = x \tan \phi - \frac{gx^2}{2v_0^2} \sec \phi$$

In this equation, x denotes the horizontal range coordinate of the projectile, y its height, ϕ the quadrant angle of departure, v_o the muzzle velocity, and g the constant value of terrestrial gravity, 9.8 m/sec².

Galileo assumed—incorrectly, because he was unaware of a small angle called the jump—that the elevation of the initial tangent to the trajectory, ϕ, was equal to the quadrant elevation of the bore. From his range-elevation relation he found, as Tartaglia had, that the maximum range was obtained when

the elevation was 45°. He also found "that of other shots, those which exceed or fall short of forty-five degrees by equal amounts, have equal ranges."

Drag. Galileo and Newton were both greatly interested in the force called air resistance, now usually called aerodynamic drag, which reduces the speed of a projectile. Galileo had compared the times of fall of oak and lead balls dropped from heights of "150 or 200 cubits" and found small but definite differences in their times of descent. He concluded that the deceleration due to drag varied with the projectile's shape, increased with its speed, and decreased with its density—more accurately, this should have been the modern sectional density, or mass divided by diameter squared. By dropping pellets from different altitudes, Newton found that the drag was apparently proportional to the square of the velocity of the projectile. He was aware that what is now called the drag coefficient depended upon the projectile's shape, but he regarded it as constant with respect to other variables.

The first determinations of the drag of projectiles in flight were made by Benjamin Robins, using the ballistic pendulum. He found that the average value of drag-induced deceleration was about 80 times the acceleration of gravity. This demonstration amply established the importance of drag as a force affecting the motion of projectiles.

Robins next undertook to determine drag as a function of speed. He obtained data approximately in accord with the Newtonian square law up to speeds of about 275 m/sec (900 ft/sec), but beyond this point he found great differences between his experimental results and those predicted by Newton's law. Robins, who made measurements up to speeds of about 520 m/sec (1,700 ft/sec), did not fully understand the significance of the differences between his measurements and Newton's predictions. It is now known that these differences chiefly result from the augmentation of the drag caused by the bow wave that forms at the head of a projectile moving at a speed near that of sound because of the compressibility of the air. In modern terms, the effects of the compressibility of the air are expressed through dependence of the dimensionless aerodynamic coefficients upon the MACH NUMBER, which is the ratio of the speed of the projectile to the speed of sound.

The drag of a projectile moving head on is now usually divided into three parts: bow resistance, due to air pressure at the head of the projectile; skin friction, caused by the friction of air moving along the middle portion of the body; and base drag, due to the under-pressure and disturbance of the air behind the base. At speeds slightly greater than that of sound, head drag can be diminished by a sharp, extended point; skin friction by a smooth, somewhat streamlined body; and base drag by a boattail. At Mach numbers of about 3, projectiles with slender, sharply pointed heads and boattails have about half the drag of more obtusely coned, square-based projectiles of the same diameter.

The equations of motion of a particle acted upon by aerodynamic drag and terrestrial gravity can be written by using Newton's second law of motion. In the early 18th century, Johann Bernoulli of Switzerland examined the problem of a particle moving under the influence of gravity and drag proportional to the nth power of the velocity. He changed the equations of motion by substituting, for time, the angle of inclination of the tangent to the trajectory as the independent variable. The Bernoulli solution, obtained in 1719, was widely employed to compute trajectories during the 19th century and continues to have some application for the motion of projectiles fired at low velocities.

Leonhard EULER of Switzerland was the first major writer on ballistics whose work was presented in analytical rather than geometrical form. In the mid-18th century he wrote equations of motion for a particle projectile and devised approximate methods of solving them that have been used repeatedly by later writers. A somewhat more convenient method was devised by James GREGORY about the same time and served as the basis for the important method for computing trajectories developed by American astronomer F. R. Moulton during World War I.

At sufficiently great altitudes and ranges, exterior ballistics merges with the field of CELESTIAL MECHANICS. Problems encountered under such conditions fall within the province of a new science, sometimes called geoballistics.

Projectile Stability. Most projectiles, such as bombs, artillery shells, and rockets, are somewhat elongated and have warheads placed toward the forward end of the body. Satisfactory fuse action for such missiles requires that they travel roughly head-on in their trajectories. This type of nearly head-on motion is called stable flight and is roughly synonymous with reasonably close trailing of some longitudinal line in the projectile along the tangent to its space path. Artillerists generally compare stability of motion with two other conditions, called instability and superstability; an unstable projectile may yaw violently or tumble, while a superstable projectile may maintain a fixed attitude in space regardless of how the tangent to its trajectory turns. Both instability and superstability are undesirable conditions for most conventional projectiles: for example, an unstable bomb may tumble and strike far short of its target because of excessive drag due to yaw; a superstable howitzer shell fired at a high angle of elevation may land base down, so that its point fuse may fail to operate.

Stability in flight is ordinarily achieved by placing fins on the rear of the projectile or by giving it a rapid spin about a long axis by rifling in the bore of a gun. Bombs and darts are said to be fin-stabilized; rifle bullets and artillery shells are spin-stabilized. Both methods of stabilization are based on ancient principles: for example, arrows are finned with trimmed feathers, and flywheels resist forces that tend to cant their axes.

TERMINAL BALLISTICS

Terminal ballistics deals with the destructive actions and effects that occur at the end of the projectile's flight as an integral and undeformed body. The flight may end in one of two ways: the projectile may strike a solid obstruction, or its metal case may be broken by the explosion of a bursting charge. The phenomena of impact of a solid missile on a solid target develop as a continuous physical process; they have been extensively studied by flash radiography and are more readily predictable than those of the bursting of a high-explosive charge, whatever the nature of the surrounding medium.

Impact Studies. Impact studies consider the mechanical impulse delivered by a solid projectile striking a target and the resulting internal forces, motions, and deformations affecting the two bodies. Traditional types of solid projectiles designed to achieve high penetration include steel-jacketed rifle bullets and armor-piercing bombs and shot. The projectile may strike into a target to some depth, leaving an indentation, or crater, or it may create an opening all the way through the target; a crater is said to result from a partial penetration, while an opening all the way through is called a perforation.

The mechanical impulse delivered to the target is greatest when the projectile's long axis is aligned on its path and the path is perpendicular to the face of the target. Empirical formulas for spherical projectiles indicate that the depth of penetration is proportional to $\cos^{2/3}\theta$, when θ denotes the angle between the path of the projectile and the perpendicular to the face of the target. Such formulas do not hold for impact angles close to the critical values at which a ricochet may occur. Ricochets occur more frequently as the impact angle increases; for firings at a given speed, the angle at which one-half of the rounds ricochet is called the ricochet angle. Experimental studies also indicate that the depth of penetration increases with the projectile's speed and its sectional density (the ratio of the projectile's mass to the square of its diameter). Heavy, needle-shaped projectiles penetrate better than light, blunt ones.

Detonation and Fragmentation. The physical action of high explosives is called detonation. Unlike propellants—in which the chemical reaction proceeds relatively slowly—the chemical reaction of high explosives can keep pace with the physical disturbance resulting from the reaction. The resulting narrow-reaction zone is called a detonation wave and can move in explosive materials at speeds as great as 6.3 km/sec

(4 mi/sec). The gaseous products behind the front may have pressures of 50,000 atmospheres and temperatures of 3,000 to 5,000° C. If the wave strikes a solid material, it will deliver a mechanical impulse whose principal destructive effect is fragmentation. It is possible to control the masses, sizes, shapes, velocities, and directions of motion of fragments by varying the characteristics of the case, for example, by corrugation or surface shaping.   F. V. RENO

Bibliography: Farrar, C. L., and Leeming, D. W., *Military Ballistics* (1983); Krier, Herman, and Summerfield, Martin, eds., *Interior Ballistics of Guns* (1979); Laible, Roy C., *Ballistic Materials and Penetration Mechanics* (1980); McShane, E. J., et al., *Exterior Ballistics* (1953); Matunas, Edward, *American Ammunition and Ballistics* (1979); Sutton, G. P., and Ross, D. M., *Rocket Propulsion Elements*, 5th ed. (1986).

balloon

A balloon is a type of AIRCRAFT that becomes airborne because of the buoyancy, or lift, supplied by a gas that is less dense than the air surrounding the balloon. (See ARCHIMEDES' PRINCIPLE; ATMOSPHERE.)

The first public balloon flight was made by the MONTGOLFIER BROTHERS, Joseph and Etienne, at Annonay, France, on June 5, 1783. Made of linen and paper, this unmanned balloon had a volume of 660 m³ (23,308 ft³) and was buoyed up by heated air. The balloon rose to an altitude of 1,800 m (5,906 ft) and flew 1.6 km (1 mi) from its starting point. On Nov. 21, 1783, Pilâtre de Rozier and the marquis d'Arlandes used a Montgolfier balloon to make the first manned flight, from the center of Paris to the city's suburbs. On Aug. 27, 1783, French chemist J. A. C. CHARLES inflated a balloon with hydrogen and launched it on an unmanned flight from the Champ de Mars in Paris. In December of that year he and an assistant made the first manned flight in a hydrogen balloon, from Paris to the village of Nesle, 104 km (65 mi) to the north.

Hydrogen was found to be superior to hot air for filling a balloon because hydrogen has inherent buoyancy, whereas

The Double Eagle II *floats above the French countryside toward the end of its historic Atlantic crossing in 1978, the first such flight made by a balloon. The craft was piloted by an American team.*

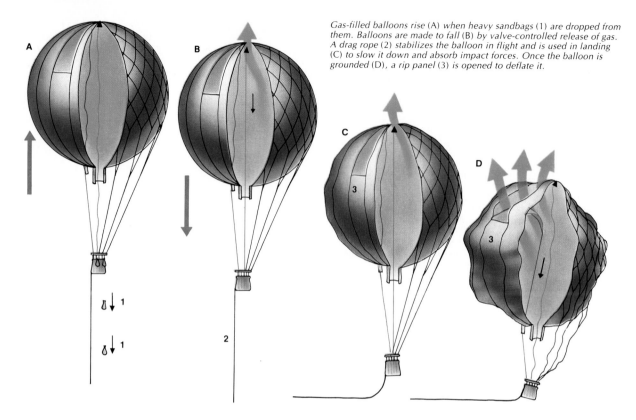

Gas-filled balloons rise (A) when heavy sandbags (1) are dropped from them. Balloons are made to fall (B) by valve-controlled release of gas. A drag rope (2) stabilizes the balloon in flight and is used in landing (C) to slow it down and absorb impact forces. Once the balloon is grounded (D), a rip panel (3) is opened to deflate it.

the ability of hot air to supply lift decreases as the air cools. The preference for hydrogen lasted well into the 20th century, although coal gas was popular for a brief time in the 19th century because it was used for streetlights and was readily available. Helium, discovered in 1895, did not become commercially available until after 1918; it was also expensive and could not supply as much lift as hydrogen. The great advantage of helium, however, is its safety. Hydrogen is highly flammable and potentially explosive, but helium is not.

Once launched, a balloon will rise until its average density exactly equals that of the surrounding atmosphere. In order to go higher, the pilot must discard some ballast (bags of sand are often used). To descend, the pilot releases some of the buoyant gas through a valve. When the balloon lands, a ripping panel is opened; this allows the remaining gas to escape so that the balloon will not be dragged over the ground.

Toward the end of the 18th century a balloon craze swept Europe and the United States. On Jan. 9, 1783, at Philadelphia, Jean Pierre BLANCHARD made the first U.S. balloon flight. As late as the 1930s, balloon flights, races, and ascents in tethered balloons anchored by cables were popular events.

MILITARY USE

The balloon was put into early use by the military. In the Battle of Fleurus between France and Austria (June 26, 1794), the French used a tethered balloon to observe the battlefield and direct artillery fire. A balloon corps, the world's first air force, was organized, and more balloons were built. The corps, however, was soon abolished.

When the Austrians besieged Venice in 1849, they used 200 small hot-air balloons to carry bombs that were released by preset controls. Because of unpredictable winds, however, the results of this first aerial bombing were negligible.

Balloons were also used in the American Civil War (1861–65). Again, however, results were negligible.

In the five-month-long siege of Paris during the Franco-Prussian War (1870–71), balloons were the only means of communication and transportation between Paris and the rest of France. Balloons launched from Paris carried mail, passengers, and homing pigeons for carrying messages back to Paris.

The spherical balloon was excellent for free flight, but tethered spherical balloons were subject to bucking and rotation about their anchor cables. This made them unsuitable for military operations, for which a steady platform was required. By 1900, sausage-shaped balloons had been developed that combined the aerodynamics of the KITE with the aerostatics of the balloon. They foreshadowed the motorized AIRSHIP. Thousands of these kite balloons were used during World War I as observation posts and as aerial barrages (aprons of cables were suspended between the balloons to create hazards for enemy airplanes). Barrage balloons were also used during World War II. During the war the Japanese launched 9,000 balloons carrying bombs that they hoped would be blown across the Pacific Ocean to North America. Only about 300 are known to have reached North America, their bombs falling mostly in uninhabited areas. When the cold war developed between the United States and the USSR after 1948, the Central Intelligence Agency (CIA) launched camera-carrying balloons from Western Europe, which were then carried across the USSR, including Siberia, to the Pacific, where the camera packages were retrieved. Because the flight path of the balloons could not be controlled, the operation had little success. After 1956 the CIA's balloon effort was superseded by the Lockheed U-2 photoreconnaisance plane (see U-2) and later by a series of military spy satellites.

TRANSCONTINENTAL CROSSING

The great dream of 19th-century balloonists was intercontinental air travel. Because the prevailing wind in the Northern Hemisphere blows from west to east, the Atlantic crossing is easier from North America to Europe; thus most attempts have been eastward. John Wise, a 19th-century American balloonist, detected a "constant current of wind" that he was certain, would carry him to Europe; but Wise was killed in a ballooning accident before he could try. Today, Wise's current of wind is known as the JET STREAM.

In 1978, 1980, and 1981, respectively, the first transatlantic, transcontinental (North America), and transpacific flights were made, in helium balloons. In 1984 the first solo transatlantic flight was made.

SPORT BALLOONING

In the 1960s hot-air ballooning was revived as a sport. The Montgolfiers had had to place their heat source on the ground, so their flights were short. The recent development of a small, lightweight, propane burner, however, now allows the heat source to be carried aloft. New, tough, synthetic balloon fabrics have also been produced. The first hot-air-balloon crossing of the Atlantic was achieved in 1987.

SCIENTIFIC USE

Since the 1890s the main scientific use of balloons has been in meteorological research. Small pilot balloons are regularly launched and tracked to determine wind direction and velocity; other balloons containing packages of METEOROLOGICAL INSTRUMENTATION record data from the upper atmosphere. Until the development in the 1930s of the RADIOSONDE, a small and inexpensive radio transmitter, it was necessary to retrieve these packages in order to obtain their data.

Extremely high-altitude balloons are used by astronomers and physicists to detect cosmic rays and gamma rays arriving from outer space. These balloons are sometimes several hundred meters high, and their reusable instrument packages are returned to Earth by parachute. Development of very thin, tough balloon materials such as Astrofilm E accelerated such balloon use in the 1980s. RICHARD K. SMITH

Bibliography: Crouch, T. D., *The Eagle Aloft* (1983); Kirschner, E. J., *Aerospace Balloons* (1985); Lawler, B. P., *With a Light Heart* (1988); Maran, S. P., "Little Missions, Big Returns," *Astronomy*, January 1989.

balloonflower

The balloonflower, or Chinese bellflower, P. grandiflorum, produces buds that swell like balloons and then unfold as flowers.

The balloonflower, *P. grandiflorum*, is the only species of the genus *Platycodon* in the BELLFLOWER family, Campanulaceae. Balloonflowers are perennial herbs native to eastern Asia and Japan. The large flowers are dark to pale blue, lilac, or white and are borne at the ends of the branches. The leaves are oval, and the buds are balloonlike before opening, hence the name. The balloonflower and its varieties are commonly planted as garden borders. HUGH M. RAUP

ballot

A ballot is a means for indicating a choice between alternatives in an ELECTION. The devices used have ranged from balls and shells in ancient times to tickets, printed forms, and VOTING MACHINES in the present day.

The so-called Australian ballot, introduced to eliminate corruption in elections, requires that all candidates' names appear on a single, official ballot, which is printed at public expense and distributed at a polling place. It also allows secrecy while voting.

The length of the ballot and the arrangement of candidates' names on it, are often controversial because they are thought to influence the decisions of voters. RITA J. IMMERMAN

Bibliography: Bain, Henry M., and Hecock, Donald S., *Ballot Position and Voter's Choice* (1957; repr. 1973); Fredman, L. E., *Australian Ballot: The Story of an American Reform* (1968).

Ballou, Hosea [buh-loo']

Hosea Ballou, b. Richmond, N.H., Apr. 30, 1771, d. June 7, 1852, was an American theologian and clergyman instrumental in formulating the tenets of UNIVERSALISM. After rejecting the Calvinist position on salvation of the elect, he began teaching that all people are saved (universal salvation). Ballou was minister of the Second Universalist Society in Boston (1817–52). As editor of the *Universalist Magazine* (1819–21), he was a key figure in moving Universalists toward the position of UNITARIANISM. His numerous writings include *A Treatise on the Atonement* (1805) and *An Examination of the Doctrine of Future Retribution* (1834).

Bibliography: Cassara, Ernest, *Hosea Ballou and the Rise of American Religious Liberalism* (1958), *Hosea Ballou: The Challenge to Orthodoxy* (1961), and *Universalism in America* (1984).

balm

A balm is an aromatic substance. Several species of plants in the MINT family, Labiatae, are known as balm. The common balm, *Melissa officinalis*, is native to Eurasia but is widely cultivated in temperate areas as a garden herb. It is sometimes called bee balm or lemon balm. *M. officinalis* is an upright, leafy perennial bearing white, yellowish, or pinkish flowers that attract bees. The lemon-scented flowers can be used for seasonings.

Other plants in the mint family known as balm are the American bee balm, *Monarda didyma*, the bastard balm, *Melittis melissophyllum*, the Canary balm, *Cedronella canariensis*, the field balm, *Glechoma hederacea*, and the Molucca balm, *Moluccella laevis*. The Mecca BALSAM, *Commiphora opobalsamum*, of the torchwood family, Burseraceae, yields balm of Gilead, a resin used for incense. HUGH M. RAUP

Balmaceda, José [bahl-mah-say'-dah]

José Manuel Balmaceda Fernández, b. July 19, 1840, d. Sept. 19, 1891, was president of Chile from 1886 to 1891. A Liberal party leader, he held several cabinet offices before winning the presidency. His administration, noted for its progressive social policies, inaugurated a massive program of public works. The legislature opposed Balmaceda's strong assertion of presidential power, however, and a bitter civil war broke out in 1891. The congressional forces were victorious. In September, Balmaceda took refuge in the Argentine legation, where he committed suicide.

Bibliography: Hervey, Maurice H., *Dark Days in Chile: An Account of the Revolution of 1891* (1892; repr. 1979); Zeitlin, Maurice, *The Civil Wars in Chile* (1984).

Balmain, Pierre: see FASHION DESIGN.

Balmer, Johann Jakob [bahl'-mur]

Johann Jakob Balmer, b. May 1, 1825, d. Mar. 12, 1898, was a Swiss mathematician and physicist who developed the first mathematical organization of spectroscopic data. Balmer taught mathematics at a girls' secondary school in Basel from 1859 until his death and did not become involved in spectroscopy until late in life. Other workers had tried to establish a mechanical acoustical relationship among spectral lines of an element; Balmer found, by empirical means, a simple formula for accurately generating the known lines of the HYDROGEN SPECTRUM. Using this formula, he also predicted other spectral series that were subsequently discovered.

Balmer series: see HYDROGEN SPECTRUM.

Balmont, Konstantin Dmitriyevich

[bahl'-mawnt, kun-stahn-teen' dim-ee'-tree-ev-ich]

The Russian poet Konstantin Dmitriyevich Balmont, b. June 15, 1867, d. Dec. 24, 1942, was a highly influential representative of early Russian SYMBOLISM, originally known as decadence. His brilliant verses helped to create among Russian readers a taste for extreme subject matter (sex, evil, madness, death), esoteric knowledge, the exaltation of the human spirit and intuitive understanding, and the refined aesthetic qualities characteristic of decadent poetry. A master of the sonnet, Balmont is also remembered for his experiments with poetic form, the musical qualities of his verse, his exoticism, and his moods of romantic solitude and individualism. His works include *Pod severnym nebom* (Under the Northern Sky, 1894), *Tishina* (Silence, 1898), and *Goryashchie zdaniya* (Burning Buildings, 1900). Cosmopolitan and multilingual, he was particularly fond of poetry in English and translated extensively from it (Blake, Coleridge, Poe, Shelley, Whitman, and Wilde). He also translated the poetry of Baudelaire and that of Czech and Japanese writers. In 1918 he emigrated to Paris, where he spent the rest of his life.   KENNETH N. BROSTROM

Bibliography: Mirsky, D., *Contemporary Russian Literature, 1881–1925,* (1926); Markov, Vladimir, and Sparks, Merrill, eds., *Modern Russian Poetry* (1966); Proffer, Carl and Ellendea, eds., *The Silver Age of Russian Culture* (1971).

balsa

Balsa, O. pyramidale, *is a tropical American tree with deltoid leaves and an elongated fruit* (center). *Balsa wood resembles cork in its properties of extreme light weight and buoyancy.*

The balsa, *Ochroma pyramidale,* is a tropical American tree of the Bombax family, Bombacaceae, found in the West Indies and Central and South America. It is best known for its low-density and lightweight wood. The peoples who navigate the coastal and inland waters of Central and South America have used it extensively for canoes and rafts. In 1947 the anthropologist Thor HEYERDAHL went to Peru, built a raft of balsa logs, and with five companions sailed it from the port of Callao across the Pacific Ocean to the Tuamotu Islands in the South Pacific.

Balsa trees may grow to a height of 18 m (about 60 ft), with the trunk growing up to 76 cm (30 in) in diameter in about six years. They are now produced most successfully in plantations. The properties of balsa wood are much like those of CORK; most of its commercial use exploits its insulating qualities against heat or cold, its lightness for flotation equipment, and its capacity for deadening sound or mechanical vibrations. It is widely used for toys and for model building.

HUGH M. RAUP

balsam

Balsam is a fragrant, resinous substance derived from evergreen plants. Balsams used in perfumes include the Central American balsam of Peru. Oleoresins (oil-bearing resins) that are sometimes called balsams are Canada balsam, from the bark of the North American BALSAM FIR, used in optical work; copaiba balsam, from Brazil and Venezuela, used in varnishes and lacquers; and storax, from southwestern Asia, used medicinally and in incense. Balm of Gilead, a resin from the Middle East used for incense, is also sometimes referred to as Mecca balsam.

Balsam also refers to plants in the genus *Impatiens,* family Balsaminaceae.   FRANCES GIES

balsam fir

The balsam fir, A. balsamea, *flourishes in moist soil, reaching a height of 12–18 m (40–60 ft). The cones, 5–10 cm (2–4 in) long, have fanlike scales and a covering of short, fine hairs. The needles are flat.*

The balsam fir, *Abies balsamea,* is a small- to medium-sized evergreen conifer tree of the northern forest regions of North America. It belongs to the pine family, Pinaceae, and grows in Canada from Labrador to Alberta and, in the United States, Minnesota, Wisconsin, Michigan, northern Pennsylvania, New York, and the New England states. Sensitive to warm temperatures, this tree cannot stand hot, dry summers and seldom survives being brought to elevations much below its natural mountain habitat. Balsam fir is short-lived, often decaying after 70 to 80 years.

Balsam fir is a popular Christmas tree. Canada BALSAM, a liquid resin collected from the bark blisters of balsam fir, is used to mount specimens on microscope slides.

Balthus   [bahl-toos']

The Polish-French artist Balthus (Balthasar Klossowski de Rola), b. Feb. 2, 1908, is a major 20th-century figurative painter, mainly self-taught. His large paintings, which he sometimes takes years to finish, have disconcerting, dreamlike undercurrents. Balthus has notably portrayed young girls in unsettling, often erotic, attitudes. His many exhibits include one at New York's Metropolitan Museum in 1984.

Bibliography: Carandente, Giovanni, *Balthus* (1983); Rewald, Sabine, *Balthus,* ed. by Kathleen Howard (1984).

Baltic languages

The Baltic languages are classified among the Northern INDO-EUROPEAN LANGUAGE group, a branch that includes the Slavic and Germanic languages. Two Baltic languages, Lithuanian and Lettish, or Latvian, survive. In addition are found some scant traces of Old Prussian as well as evidence of a fourth distinct dialect, Curonian. These four languages retain archaic elements of ancient Indo-European and of their common ancestor Proto-Baltic. The Baltic, Slavic, and Germanic language groups are the only Indo-European languages to have the sound *m* in the dative plural ending, which indicates their close relationship.

Traditionally, Baltic has been more closely associated with the Slavic languages than with the Germanic. Indeed, the term *Balto-Slavic* has been used, at least since the 19th century, to imply an especially close relationship between these two Indo-European subgroups. Many scholars, however, contend that the term *Balto-Slavic* is not appropriate and that the two subgroups, Baltic and Slavic, should be kept separate. Efforts to form a Balto-Germanic subgroup have received little support. Scholars, particularly in the former USSR, have attempted to demonstrate that the Baltic languages correspond to Dacian and Thracian, the ancient languages of the Balkans.

Each of the extant languages, Lithuanian and Latvian, is divided into dialects; Prussian is known only through surviving manuscripts; and Curonian has been absorbed into the living languages.

Lithuanian. This East Baltic language has existed in written form since the late 16th century and is spoken by more than 3 million persons. Lithuanian has retained more features of the original Indo-European than any other surviving language. For example, its declension of nouns has retained the dual—a grammatical number indicating two, used in addition to the singular and plural. Its accentuation patterns have retained early Indo-European characteristics, as have its vowels and most of its consonants. It has two principal dialects, Samogitian, or Low Lithuanian, and High Lithuanian. These have been further refined, and the western dialect of High Lithuanian has become the basis for the modern literary language.

Lettish, or Latvian. The East Baltic language Lettish is spoken by 2 million persons and has three principal dialects: Tamian, or Livonian; High Latvian; and a central dialect, which is the basis for the modern literary language. As in Lithuanian, texts in this language exist only from the late 16th century. Lettish is less conservative than Lithuanian. For example, it no longer has a movable accent; all words are accented on the initial syllable. No neuter gender exists, and the dual appears only in rare forms.

Prussian. This West Baltic language, sometimes called Old Prussian, became extinct near the end of the 17th century and is known only slightly from written documents, the oldest of which is the *Elbing Vocabulary,* a short German-Prussian glossary written between 1300 and 1400. Prussian texts did not appear until the mid-16th century. These writings indicate that Prussian is the most conservative of all Baltic languages, containing more archaisms than Lithuanian and differing significantly from that language and from Lettish.

Curonian. This East Baltic dialect was absorbed into both Lithuanian and Lettish by the mid-16th century. No texts in Curonian exist, and knowledge of Curonian comes primarily from proper names that survived after the language became extinct.   JOHN A. C. GREPPIN

Bibliography: Dambriunas, Leonadas, et al., *Introduction to Modern Lithuanian,* 4th ed. (1990); Endzelins, J., *Comparative Phonology and Morphology of the Baltic Languages,* trans. by William Schmalsteig and Benjamin Jegers (1971); Fennel, T. G., and Gelsen, H., *A Grammar of Modern Latvian,* 3 vols. (1980); Magner, Thomas F., and Schmalsteig, William, eds., *Baltic Linguistics* (1970); Millers, Antonia, *The Latvian Language for the Use of Students* (1985).

Baltic Sea

The Baltic Sea is an arm of the Atlantic Ocean and is connected to the North Sea by two relatively narrow passages, the KATTEGAT and SKAGERRAK. Touching on Finland, Russia, the Baltic States, Poland, Germany, Denmark, and Sweden, the sea has long been important in trade and commerce. With an area of about 420,000 km² (160,000 mi²), the Baltic is a shrinking remnant of a large water body created by Ice Age glacial melt and is generally shallow. Many rivers feed it, notably the ODER and VISTULA, and it has a shallow outlet to the

Atlantic Ocean; the water is brackish (5 to 15 parts salt per 1,000), and the tide is negligible. Ice becomes a barrier to shipping in winter. Temperatures in Saint Petersburg at the eastern tip of the Gulf of Finland average −9° C (15° F) in January.

In the Middle Ages the Baltic Sea was the center of trade between ports of the HANSEATIC LEAGUE dealing in fish—particularly herring—timber, grains, furs, and amber. In the 17th century Sweden dominated the area, and from the late 17th century, Russia. Its importance declined when modern ships became too large to pass through the Kattegat, its shallow entrance between Denmark and Sweden. The Kiel Canal crosses the base of the Danish peninsula, shortening distances to southern Europe. Connecting the Baltic and North seas, it can accommodate medium-size ships and is one of the most heavily used canals in the world.

Baltic States

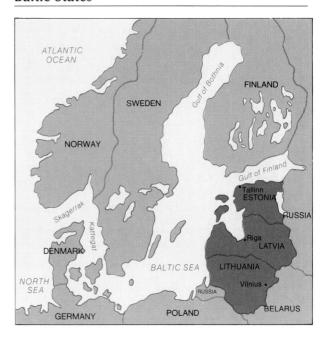

The Baltic States are ESTONIA, LATVIA, and LITHUANIA, three small countries located between Poland and the Gulf of Finland on the forested eastern shore of the Baltic Sea. Before 1918 they were part of the Russian empire. After World War I they became independent, but in 1940 they were forcibly annexed by the USSR. Nationalist movements developed in the Baltic States during the 1980s. In 1990, Lithuania declared its independence; Estonia and Latvia did the same in 1991. The USSR, weakened by internal dissension, was forced to recognize the independence of all three Baltic States shortly before its own demise in late 1991. The Baltic enclave of KALININGRAD (formerly Königsberg), between Poland and Lithuania, remains part of the Russian Federation. (See also LIVONIA.)

Baltimore

Baltimore, the largest city in Maryland and among the largest in the United States, has one of the nation's biggest seaports and is a wholesaling and manufacturing center. Situated about 65 km (40 mi) northeast of Washington, D.C., the city occupies about 204 km² (79 mi²) along the Patapsco River estuary on Chesapeake Bay.

The population of the city is 736,014 (1990); that of the metropolitan area is 2,382,172 (1990). Baltimore's population is nearly 60% black and also includes many people of Italian, German, and central European ancestry.

The climate is moderate, with temperatures averaging 2° C (35° F) in January and 25° C (77° F) in July. Rainfall averages about 1,065 mm (42 in) annually.

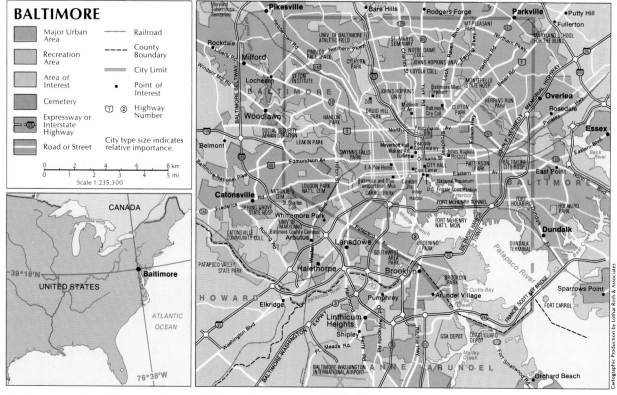

BALTIMORE

▦ Major Urban Area	┼─┼─ Railroad
▦ Recreation Area	┄┄┄ County Boundary
▦ Area of Interest	▨▨ City Limit
▦ Cemetery	■ Point of Interest
▦ Expressway or Interstate Highway	① ② Highway Number
▨ Road or Street	City type size indicates relative importance.

Scale 1:235,300

0   2   4   6   8 km
0   1   2   3   4   5 mi

Cartographic Production by Lothar Roth & Associates

Contemporary City. Industry and port activities are the main employers. The manufacturing and service industries are especially important. The port has extensive shipbuilding and repair facilities and modern freight-handling equipment and ranks 7th in the nation in terms of cargo value (1989). Baltimore has excellent rail, road, and air connections with other major U.S. cities.

Among the colleges and universities in the Baltimore area are the JOHNS HOPKINS UNIVERSITY (1876), the College of Notre Dame of Maryland (1873), the Peabody Institute of Johns Hopkins University (formerly the Peabody Conservatory of Music; f. 1857), and Goucher College (1885) in suburban Towson, Md. The Baltimore Museum of Art, the Peale Museum, and the WALTERS ART GALLERY have notable collections of art, and the B & O Railroad Museum houses an impressive collection of railroad memorabilia. Meyerhoff Symphony Hall, FORT MC-HENRY (the defense of which, in 1814, inspired Francis Scott Key to write "The Star-Spangled Banner"), the first Roman Catholic cathedral built in the United States, and the National Aquarium are other major attractions. Pimlico Race Track, site of the Preakness Stakes, is nearby. Druid Hill Park contains the city zoo and a natural history museum. The U.S.S. CONSTELLATION, launched in Baltimore in 1797 and the oldest U.S. warship afloat, is docked in the harbor.

Plagued for years by urban deterioration, Baltimore underwent a dramatic rejuvenation in the 1980s, sparked by a commercial and residential building boom, particularly alongside the Inner Harbor. In the downtown area, streets are laid out in a grid pattern, but toward the suburbs, to conform with the topography, radial streets become more common. Charles and Baltimore streets divide the city; at their intersection the Charles Center, a renewal area of office and apartment buildings, and the Civic Center dominate the skyline.

History. Baltimore, founded in 1729, was named for the baronial title of the CALVERT family, who were the proprietors of Maryland. The city's strategic location spurred its growth, and by the time of the American Revolution it was a thriving seaport. The city served (1776–77) as the seat of the Continental Congress while Philadelphia was under British siege. The threat to Baltimore's commerce posed by the opening of the

Erie Canal in 1825 prompted construction of the first U.S. railroad here, the Baltimore and Ohio, begun in 1827.

The site of numerous riots between Southern and Northern sympathizers during the Civil War, Baltimore remained within the Union but under martial law throughout the war. During the latter half of the 19th century the city was transformed from a mercantile to an industrial center. In 1904 a fire destroyed most of the downtown business district, but recovery was rapid. Baltimore's continued growth in the 20th century has been due in large part to its port facilities, which have grown from the original all-purpose piers to the present 72 km (45 mi) of developed waterfront.   PAUL A. GROVES

Bibliography: Beirne, F. F., *The Amiable Baltimoreans* (1984); Miles, Priscilla L., *Historic Baltimore* (1987); Nast, L. H., et al., eds., *Baltimore: A Living Renaissance* (1982); Vexler, R. I., *Baltimore: A Chronological and Documentary History, 1632–1970* (1975).

Baltimore, David

The American biochemist David Baltimore, b. New York City, Mar. 7, 1938, shared the 1975 Nobel Prize for medicine with Renato DULBECCO and Howard TEMIN for the discovery of reverse transcriptase, an enzyme that carries out one of the basic molecular processes in a cell. A graduate of Swarthmore College (1960) and Rockefeller University (1964), Baltimore worked at the Salk Institute of Biological Studies, then became a professor of microbiology at the Massachusetts Institute of Technology in 1968 and director of its institute for biomedical research. At the Salk Institute, Baltimore worked with Dulbecco on the mechanism of replication of the poliovirus in a cell. This led to his discovery of reverse transcriptase in 1970, independently of Temin. The discovery that viral RNA can pass information to DNA and replicate was a conceptual breakthrough in molecular biology. It has also been an important tool in the study of viruses and cancer. In 1990, Baltimore was chosen president of Rockefeller University. After a paper he coauthored but was not the primary researcher for was found fraudulent, he resigned in 1991.

Baltimore Canyon: see SUBMARINE CANYON.

Baltimore oriole: see ORIOLE.

Baluch   [buh-looch']

The Baluch (Baloch) are a group of tribes that inhabit the province of Baluchistan in western Pakistan, southeast Iran, and southwest Afghanistan; small groups also live in northeast Iran, northwest Afghanistan, Soviet Turkmenistan, northwest India, the Arab states of the Persian Gulf, and on the coast and islands of East Africa. Of an estimated total Baluch population of more than 2,000,000, about 60 percent reside in Pakistan. Numerous Baluch migrations from the early 19th century, primarily for raiding and for employment as mercenaries, have resulted in their present wide distribution across the Middle East. The groups that stayed among the TURKMEN on the northern edge of the Iranian plateau in what is now Afghanistan and the Turkmen SSR developed the styles of Baluchi rugs for which the Baluch are famous.

The origin of the Baluch is unclear. Although the name *Baluch* is known from earlier records in Iran, the present tribes cannot be traced back beyond the 17th century, when they rose to power under their chief Kambar. The Baluch share a common identity based on Baluchi—an Iranian language—and adherence to Sunni Islam. They have never formed a political unit, although the khan of the former Indian state of Kalat, in present-day Pakistan, briefly exerted suzerainty over a large portion of them in the 19th century. Traditional Baluch society consists of pastoral nomadic groups, small agricultural settlements, and remnants of a Negroid slave population that earlier functioned as agricultural serfs and personal retainers for the chiefs. This organization is now breaking down as the Baluch are integrated into the social organization of the countries in which they reside.   BRIAN SPOONER

Baluchistan   [buh-loo-chi-stahn']

Baluchistan, meaning "land of Baluchs," is a province in western Pakistan, bordered by Afghanistan on the northwest, the Arabian Sea on the south, and Iran on the west. The area, approximately 347,188 km² (134,050 mi²), is mainly mountainous with barren and rugged terrain. The mean annual temperature ranges from 37° C (98° F) in the inland deserts to 24° C (76° F) in the mountainous regions. Rainfall ranges from 100 to 400 mm (4 to 16 in) annually.

Primitive agriculture, nomadism, and karez (tunnel-type) irrigation are the main bases of economic life. Some coking coal is mined near Quetta, the capital. The most important food crops are wheat, rice, and millet. Most of the 4,611,000 (1983 est.) inhabitants are Muslim. Baluchistan was a part of the Indian Maurya Empire (3d century BC) and fell under the control of various Turk and Arab empires until it was annexed by the Mogul Empire in 1595. It came under British rule in 1879. Since 1947 it has been a part of independent Pakistan. In 1972, 55,000 Baluch tribesmen launched a revolt for autonomy, which was harshly suppressed.   ASHOK K. DUTT

Baluchitherium   [buh-loo-chi-thir'-ee-uhm]

Baluchitherium is an extinct rhinoceros of the order Perissodactyla, class Mammalia, that lived during the late Oligocene and early Miocene epochs of the TERTIARY PERIOD (about 20–30 million years ago). It is believed to be the largest land mammal that ever lived. The first baluchitheres were found in central Mongolia. Unlike its modern descendants, *Baluchitherium* was hornless, but other features clearly indicate that this huge beast was a rhinoceros. Its skull was about 1.2 m (4 ft) long, and it stood about 5.5 m (18 feet) high at the shoulder. A long neck and huge, pillarlike legs enabled the animal to browse among the higher branches of trees. Baluchitheres were probably limited to Asia, for their remains have not been found elsewhere.   WILLIAM H. MATTHEWS III

Bibliography: Broadhead, T. W., ed., *Mammals* (1984); Romer, Alfred S., *The Procession of Life* (1968); Savage, R. J. G., and Long, M. R., *Mammal Evolution: An Illustrated Guide* (1986); Schoch, Robert M., ed., *Vertebrate Paleontology* (1984).

The Baluchitherium *was a hornless rhinoceros of late Oligocene and early Miocene times. Considered the largest land mammal ever to have lived, it stood nearly 5.5 m (18 ft) at the shoulder. Its long neck and forelegs probably enabled it to eat leaves from high branches.*

Balzac, Honoré de   [bahl-zahk', oh-nohr-ay' duh]

A traditionalist in morality and a reactionary in politics, the great French novelist Balzac was himself a product of the bourgeois society he so vehemently criticized. In fact, without the middle-class society that developed after the French Revolution, he would have lacked the subject matter of his monumental creation, *La Comédie humaine.* Produced between 1829 and 1847, it consists of nearly 100 completed novels and some 50 others left in drafts. Presenting the human character as fixed but often possessed by its hereditary, geographical, historical, and social environment, Balzac's microcosm of French society consists of 2,000 recurring characters and spans five decades of postrevolutionary France. *La Comédie humaine* is divided into three categories: Analytical Studies, which demonstrate the principles that govern society; Philosophical Studies, which are concerned with the motives behind human behavior; and Studies of Social Mores, which depict the effects of these two causes in six *scènes* of private, provincial, Parisian, military, political, and country life. (See COMÉDIE HUMAINE, LA.)

Early Life. Born in Tours on May 20, 1799, to a new member of the prospering middle class, Balzac (who later added the *de* to his name) was particularly devoted to his unobliging mother, who dominated him all his life and outlived him. At the age of 8, he was sent to a boarding school, where he consoled himself by reading, but to such excess that by the time he was 14 he suffered from nervous exhaustion and returned home to attend the local *lycée* (secondary school). In 1814, he moved to Paris with his family and reluctantly began to study law. After completing his studies he was apprenticed to a law firm, but he finally persuaded his family to subsidize his literary career for two years. In a miserable Paris garret, with a meager stipend, Balzac embarked on the regimen he was to follow the rest of his life: a workday that began before dawn (16 hours were normal for him) and the consumption of innumerable cups of coffee.

Balzac's first and abiding ambition was to write for the theater. His first play, *Cromwell* (1819), was so bad, however, that he was advised to try anything but writing. He then turned his hand to Gothic thrillers, using a variety of pen names and working with several collaborators.

In 1821 he met Laure de Berny, the mother of nine children and 22 years his senior, who braved ridicule to become his

Honoré de Balzac, a French novelist of the 19th century, is renowned for his fictional work concerning French middle-class society. The major portion of his work, a vast collection of novels and shorter fiction, was published as La Comédie humaine *(1829–47).*

mistress. For 10 years Balzac remained devoted to this remarkable woman who was a major influence in his life.

Business Debts. In 1825 a venture that was to publish new editions of French classics turned into a financial disaster. Within three years Balzac amassed up to 100,000 francs in debts for his triple failures: publishing, a printing establishment, and a type foundry. He was rescued by his family, but for the rest of his life he was pursued by debts and driven by a hunger for renown. His capacity for work was titanic: three or four novels a year, scores of articles and reviews, historical dramas, and a voluminous correspondence.

Success. The first novel published under his own name, *The Chouans* (1829; Eng. trans., 1921), attracted considerable notice; *The Physiology of Marriage* (1829; Eng. trans., 1943) was a major success; and *The Wild Ass's Skin* (1831; Eng. trans., 1954) definitively launched his career. His expenses, however, always exceeded his income. He bought properties, *objets d'art*, entertained lavishly, and traveled in style. By 1838 he was 230,000 francs further in debt, but he managed to stay out of prison by ruses and speculations that would have seemed extravagant in his novels. As massive in size as he was in talent (see Auguste RODIN's statue of him), he churned through life like a ship under full steam, leading the life of a celebrity. Women from all over Europe wrote to him; aristocratic ladies became his mistresses. His sensitive portrayals of women won him the devotion of countless feminine readers.

On Mar. 2, 1850, after an 18–year courtship, Balzac married the Polish countess Mme. Hanska, who had signed herself *L'Étrangère* ("the foreign lady") in an anonymous fan letter. Her wealth would have protected him from bill collectors. But on August 18, five months after the wedding, he was dead, worn out by having been what he called "a galley slave of the pen."   BETH ARCHER BROMBERT

Bibliography: Hunt, H. J., *Honoré de Balzac: A Biography* (1957; repr. 1969); Kanes, Martin, *Balzac's Comedy of Words* (1975); McCarthy, M. S., *Balzac and His Reader* (1983); Maurois, André, *Prometheus: The Life of Balzac* (1965; repr. 1983); Pritchett, V. S., *Balzac* (1973); Stowe, W. W., *Balzac, James, and the Realistic Novel* (1986).

Bamako   [bah-mah-koh']

Bamako, the capital of Mali in western Africa, is situated in the southwestern section of the country, on the upper Niger River. Bamako has a population of 801,500 (1985 est.). A bustling river port and trade hub, the city is also a road and air nexus and an administrative and military center. It has commercial fishing fleets, and cattle are traded and local handicrafts displayed in the colorful markets. Bamako has several colleges, a notable national museum, a large zoo, and botanical gardens. Although it was a Muslim center in the ancient Mali empire, it had declined to a village of fewer than 1,000 when the French arrived in 1880. Its growth was spurred by the opening of the railroad in 1904 and by the city's designation as colonial capital in 1908.

Bambara kingdoms   [bahm-bar'-uh]

The Bambara kingdoms of the western Sudan (present-day Mali) were founded in the latter part of the 17th century by former slave-warriors (*ton dyoñ*) of the SONGHAI empire. Some historians regard their establishment as an anti-Muslim response to the Islamic-style government under which Songhai had exercised its authority. The main Bambara capitals were at Segu (Ségou), on the Niger River, and Kaarta, in the grasslands region between the Niger and Senegal rivers.

Segu's founder was Kaladian Kulubali (r. 1652–82). Under Mamari "Biton" Kulubali (r. 1712–55) all the Bambara were unified in a state that extended from Bamako in the southwest to Timbuktu in the north. A period of disorder followed, however, during which one group of Bambara established a new kingdom at Kaarta. In the mid-19th century both kingdoms were attacked and defeated by the Muslim reformer al-Hajj UMAR. Many Bambara continued armed resistance against their new Muslim overlords. Others were recruited into French colonial military service near the end of the century. Both kingdoms were incorporated into the French colonial empire by 1900.   ROBERT R. GRIFFETH

Bamboccianti   [bahm-baw-chee-ahn'-tee]

Bamboccianti are GENRE PAINTINGS depicting everyday Italian life in the 17th century. The term derives from the nickname given to Pieter van LAER (*c.*1592–1642), a Dutch painter who settled in Rome around 1625. Because he was physically deformed, Laer was called *il Bamboccio* ("the simpleton"). The word *bamboccianti* was applied to his paintings, which, because they depicted peasants and street people, aroused the hostility of certain artists and critics, who held classical ideals and moral subject matter to be the chief concerns of art.

Laer, whose style reflects the naturalism of CARAVAGGIO, was at the center of a group of Dutch and Flemish painters (Bamboccianti) who painted, and took part in, the coarser side of life in 17th-century Rome. They were not accepted in official artistic circles, where their work was considered decadent, but they had a large following of private patrons. In rejecting idealized subject matter in favor of lowlife scenes, the Bamboccianti were the precursors of later 17th-century Dutch genre painting.   TANIA BAYARD

Bibliography: Wittkower, Rudolf, *Art and Architecture in Italy: 1600–1750,* 3d ed. (1973).

bamboo

Bamboos are plants of great economic importance in several regions of the world. The name is applied in general to members of the tribe Bambuseae in the GRASS family. Some 76 genera and over 1,000 species have been described. Most are tropical or subtropical, but a few reach the temperate zones or grow at high altitudes. Some common bamboos, such as *Bambusa vulgaris* and *Arundinaria amabilis*, have been in cultivation so long that their origins are uncertain.

Bamboos are perennial plants. Their woody stems are hollow and segmented, with partitions between the segments. The leaves, usually long and narrow, rise from the nodes of the stems. Some species are only shrublike, but others grow to heights of 30 m (100 ft) or more, with stem diameters of 20–30 cm (8–12 in). Bamboo stems are light, strong, durable, flexible, and easily split lengthwise. Depending on size, they are used in making houses, furniture, piping, a wide range of domestic goods, baskets, and musical instruments. They are also pulverized for paper pulp. Bamboo hay is a protein-rich food for livestock, and the fresh sprouts of some species are widely used in cookery. In the United States, bamboo is grown mainly as an ornamental.

One striking characteristic of bamboo is that most species produce seeds only once in their lifetime, which may range to more than 100 years. (They can also reproduce asexually by producing seedless clones, or rhizomes.) Researchers in 1990 announced development of a promising technique for making bamboos flower more rapidly, which would be of major importance to bamboo cultivators.   HUGH M. RAUP

Bamboo, a fast-growing grass of tropical Asia, Africa, and America, has hollow, segmented stems. It provides material for making furniture, wickerwork, poles, and other products.

Bibliography: Farrelly, David, *The Book of Bamboo* (1984); Wang, Dajun, *Bamboos of China* (1987).

Bamian   [bahm-yahn']

Bamian (Bamiyan), a town in the Bamian River valley (elevation 2,590 m/8,480 ft) northwest of Kabul, in Afghanistan, was for centuries an important commercial and religious center on the caravan route between central Asia and India. During the 2d to 9th century, numerous Buddhist monuments were constructed along the conglomerate cliffs that wall the valley. They include caves fashioned into temples and monasteries, many containing well-preserved frescolike wall paintings, and a famous colossal statue of the Buddha, standing 53 m (175 ft) high, the tallest stone sculpture of its kind in the world. This standing Buddha and another measuring about 37 m (120 ft) are set within niches carved into the cliff. The statues, which probably date from the 3d to 5th century, are mentioned by the Chinese monk Hsüan-Tsang, who visited Bamian c.630 on his way to India. Mongol invaders under Genghis Khan destroyed the town in 1221.

Bibliography: Allchim, F. R., and Hammond, N., eds., *The Archaeology of Afghanistan* (1979).

Bamileke   [bam-i-lee'-kee]

The Bamileke (Mileke) are a people who live in the highlands of Cameroon, in Equatorial Africa, known for their distinctive art forms, particularly wood carving, and their pyramidal-roofed houses. Numbering more than 700,000, they speak a Bantu language of the Benue-Niger subfamily of the Niger-Congo stock (see AFRICAN LANGUAGES). They are subsistence farmers and live in chiefdoms, in which each chief is supported by his staff and by various military and religious societies. Residence is in neighborhoods made up of dispersed homesteads. High population density has promoted migration of large numbers of the Bamileke to cities.

Bamileke religion consists chiefly of ancestor worship. Descent is traced through the father's line. Marriage is polygynous, with cowives and their children living in separate houses. Marriage is formalized by the payment of BRIDE-PRICE to the wife's people. The hierarchical structure of Bamileke

society is reflected in their wood carvings of chiefs and their wives, chiefs' thrones, and dignitaries' carved doorjambs and lintels. Other objects carved in wood include dance masks, drums, and stools. Bamileke also make statuettes, goblets, horns, and bracelets of carved ivory.   PHOEBE MILLER

Ban Chiang

The village of Ban Chiang, in northeastern Thailand, is the site of a large and rich Late Neolithic settlement occupied through the Bronze and Iron ages. Its ancient red-on-buff painted pottery resembles the pottery of the Yang-shao Neolithic (5000–2500 BC) of northern China. Similar pottery was found in Bronze Age deposits at NON NOK THA.

Initial faulty dating suggested that Ban Chiang's bronze artifacts preceded the earliest-known bronze artifacts found in the Near East, and some scientists still believe that metallurgy developed there independently. It is now thought that the area was settled about 4000 BC, with pottery dating back to as early as 3500 BC, bronzework between 2500 and 1500 BC, and iron implements about 1000 to 500 BC. Since excavation of the site began in 1967, Ban Chiang pottery has become renowned in the international art market.   ROBERT E. DEWAR

Bibliography: Hingham, C. F., *The Ban Chiang Culture in Wider Perspective* (1985).

Banach, Stefan   [bah-nahk']

Stefan Banach, b. Mar. 30, 1892, d. Aug. 31, 1945, was a Polish mathematician who helped found modern functional analysis and made major contributions to the theory of topological vector spaces. In addition, he contributed to measure theory, integration, and orthogonal series.

Banach lectured in mathematics at the Institute of Technology in Lvov and eventually became a professor at the University of Lvov. His best-known work is the *Théorie des opérations linéaires* (Theory of Linear Operations, 1932). Banach algebra and Banach spaces (an important class of vector spaces) were named for him.   H. HOWARD FRISINGER

banana

The banana family consists of large plants that flourish in moist areas throughout the tropics. The edible fruit is rich in carbohydrates and is a source of vitamins A and C and the minerals potassium and phosphorus. The most familiar banana is the yellow-skinned, sweet, pulpy fruit of international trade. Of the many varieties, only a few are widely grown and only two are exported. Wild banana plants tend to spring up where tropical forest has been felled or burned.

Bananas are a significant food crop in the tropics. From 80 to 85 percent of the world's banana crop is grown locally for domestic consumption. Consumers in the tropics not only eat the raw, ripe fruit but also cook bananas as a starchy vegetable food similar to the potato. Some are fermented to make beer, and others are dried. In upland East Africa, especially in the Buganda province of Uganda, bananas even attain the status of a staple foodstuff.

Origin and Types. Bananas originated primarily in Malaysia and the neighboring archipelago probably about 4,000 years ago. Diversity developed over a much wider area, from India to the Philippines and New Guinea. About 2,000 years ago, travelers carried bananas eastward through the Pacific and westward across the Indian Ocean to tropical Africa. Shortly after the discovery of America, Europeans took banana plants from Africa or the Canary Islands to Hispaniola (modern Haiti and the Dominican Republic).

The banana family, *Musaceae*, contains only two genera, *Ensete* and *Musa*. They range in height from 1 m (3 ft) to more than 9 m (30 ft) and are actually gigantic herbs. What looks like the trunk of a banana plant is neither woody nor a true stem. The true stem is underground, and the above-ground portion is called a pseudostem. Even when as large as 60 cm (2 ft) across, the pseudostem is made solely of overlapping, concentric leaf sheaths wrapped tightly.

The banana plant is among the largest herbaceous plants. Its trunk is formed by the bases of closely overlapping leaves. A banana plant flowers and fruits only once in its life span and then dies. The striking flower is seen at right.

A slender flowering stalk several centimeters across grows up through the center of the pseudostem and bears a terminal cluster of flowers. The flowers emerge from a purple bract and are tubular, with yellow petals. When plants are in the wild state, bees and bats pollinate the female flowers, each of which produces a banana. Wild banana fruit is seedy and inedible; the edible, cultivated types are seedless because they are set without pollination and have evolved sterility.

A Southeast Asian species, *Musa textilis,* supplies the Philippine Islands with a principal export—Manila HEMP, or abaca. In parts of Ethiopia the 6-m (20-ft) leaves of *E. ventricosum* provide building material, fiber, and a starchy food. Several of the smaller species of *Musa* are grown as ornamentals.

World Production and Trade. The world crop of bananas (including plantains, which are never reliably distinguished in statistics) is not accurately recorded; estimates vary from about 35 million to more than 40 million metric tons. Many countries, including those in Africa, consume most of what they grow. Banana exporters, who supply the North American and European markets, are led by Brazil, which is by far the world's largest producer. India follows, growing somewhat less than half of Brazil's crop. The Philippines, Ecuador, Colombia, and Honduras are also important producers. In the United States only Hawaii grows significant amounts. The United States is the world's leading banana importer. Banana shipments are transported in special refrigerator units.

From small beginnings in the early years of the 19th century, the trade became important toward the end of the century, aided by the development of fast refrigerated sea transport, improved local transport in the producing countries (such as Central American railways), and vertical integration of production from plantation to point of retail. The United Fruit Company, formed in 1899, became the first big international name in the export business; in 1970 it was merged into United Brands. Standard Fruit and Steamship Company was established in 1923 as a competitor; since 1968 it has been a subsidiary of Castle and Cook. Del Monte Corporation entered the banana trade in 1968 by purchasing the West Indies Fruit Company. Large landholdings and one-crop economies made the multinational companies important influences in some Latin American countries, particularly in the early days of the banana industry.

The export trades have always been based on only two basic varieties: Gros Michel (or Martinique) and several mutants (called "sports") of the Cavendish banana. Dwarf or semi-dwarf mutants of the latter have been especially important because they can be planted densely and are less susceptible to damage by wind than are tall bananas. In the early days, fruit bunches, especially of Gros Michel, were mostly shipped unwrapped; parceling, or wrapping of bunches, was also practiced by some trades, but today most fruit is cut and boxed for transport. Fruit is always cut and carried green and ripened just before delivery to retail stores by the use of ethylene gas in special chambers.

Diseases. Export production has been bedeviled by epidemic diseases promoted by large-scale monoculture. Panama disease, or banana wilt, caused by a soil-borne fungus; Sigatoka disease, or leaf-spot, caused by an airborne fungus; bacterial wilt; banana nematode; and bunchy-top, caused by a virus, have contributed substantially to the fluctuations in the banana trade's economic fortunes. Efforts are being made to breed new, disease-resistant varieties.   N. W. SIMMONDS

Bibliography: Reynolds, P. K., *The Banana: Its History and Cultivation* (1977); Simmonds, N. W., *Bananas,* 2d ed. (1978; repr. 1982).

bananaquit   [buh-nan'-uh-kwit]

The bananaquit, or banana bird, is a small songbird of the West Indies, except Cuba; it also ranges from Mexico to Argentina. It is found in gardens, scrub vegetation, and open woodlands; its domed nest is constructed of banana-leaf fibers. The sexes are similar in appearance: dark gray above and yellow below, black crowned, and often with a white stripe above the eye and a white patch on the wing. The bill is curved, with a tubular tongue for drawing nectar from flowers. Insects are the main diet, however. The species, *Coereba flaveola,* is usually classified with the wood-warbler family, Parulidae, but some taxonomists place it in a separate honeycreeper family, Coerebidae.   ROBERT J. RAIKOW

Bancroft, Anne

Anne Bancroft is the stage name of Anna Maria Italiano, b. New York City, Sept. 17, 1931, a stage and film actress. She achieved Broadway and Hollywood fame in the role of Annie Sullivan, Helen Keller's teacher, in *The Miracle Worker* (1960; film, 1962), for which she won an Academy Award. Other notable films include *The Graduate* (1967); *The Turning Point* (1977); *Fatso* (1979), which she also wrote and directed; *To Be or Not To Be* (1983), with her husband, Mel BROOKS; and *84 Charing Cross Road* (1987). Bancroft won an Emmy award in 1970 for her television work, and starred in the Broadway production *Golda* (1977), about the life of Israeli leader Golda Meier.   LESLIE HALLIWELL

Bancroft, George

George Bancroft, b. Worcester, Mass., Oct. 3, 1800, d. Jan. 17, 1891, was a historian, diplomat, and statesman whose comprehensive 10-volume work, *A History of the United States, from the Discovery of America to the Inauguration of Washington* (1834–74; rev. in 1876 and 1883–85), is considered a classic. After teaching at Harvard and at the Round Hill School in Northampton, Mass., he began a writing career.

A series of partisan essays, published in the *North American Review* in the 1820s and '30s, in which he defended the positions of the Jacksonian Democrats, drew Bancroft into politics. In 1844 he ran unsuccessfully for the governorship of Massachusetts. As secretary of the navy (1845–46) under James K. Polk, Bancroft actively supported American expansion even at the cost of war with Mexico. He then served (1846–49) as U.S. minister in London. Opposed to slavery, he abandoned his party during the sectional crisis to support Abraham Lincoln, whose eulogy he delivered before Congress following the president's assassination. From 1867 to 1874 he served as the U.S. minister in Berlin. In addition to his history of the United States, Bancroft also wrote *History of the Formation of the Constitution of the United States* (2 vols., 1882) and a biography of Martin Van Buren (1889).   JOEL COLTON

Bibliography: Canary, Robert H., *George Bancroft* (1974); Handlin, Lillian, *George Bancroft* (1984); Howe, M. De Wolfe, *Life and Letters of George Bancroft,* 2 vols. (1908; repr. 1971).

Bancroft, Hubert Howe

Hubert Howe Bancroft, b. Granville, Ohio, May 5, 1832, d. Mar. 2, 1918, was an American historian, bookseller, and publisher. In 1856 he opened a bookstore in San Francisco and began to take an active interest in the region's history. Bancroft compiled and published several volumes on the history of American Indians, Spanish settlements, and the early years of the West. Although they were issued as the *Works of Hubert Howe Bancroft* (1883–90), little of the writing was actually done by him. His collection of maps, manuscripts, and rare books was donated to the University of California and forms the nucleus of the Bancroft Library.　　JOEL COLTON

Bibliography: Caughey, John W., *Hubert Howe Bancroft, Historian of the West* (1946); Clark, Harry, *A Venture in History* (1973) .

Bancroft, Sir Squire

Sir Squire Bancroft, b. May 4, 1841, d. Apr. 19, 1926, was a British actor who, with his actress wife, Marie Effie Wilton (1839–1921), was partly responsible for the popularity of drawing-room comedy on the 19th-century English stage. As managers of the Prince of Wales Theatre from 1865, the couple employed the then-innovative boxset and raised actors' pay scales. Bancroft was knighted (1897) in recognition of these achievements.

Bibliography: Bancroft, Marie and Squire, *The Bancrofts* (1909).

band

Bands originated in the outdoor ensembles of the Renaissance. In modern usage, the term *band* denotes an instrumental ensemble consisting mainly or entirely of wind instruments and percussion instruments. In its broadest sense, the term may designate almost any instrumental group, such as a jazz band, dance band, or balalaika band. The various types of bands include brass, marching, military, and concert or symphonic. The largest of these, the concert band, usually includes a full complement of woodwinds (piccolos, flutes, oboes, clarinets, bassoons, and saxophones), a large brass section (cornets, trumpets, horns, trombones, and tubas), and a large percussion section. Cellos and double basses are sometimes used to reinforce the bass.

Notable concert bands were the Grand Boston Band founded by Patrick S. Gilmore in 1859 and the famous John Philip SOUSA band founded in 1892. Gilmore, who took his 22d Regiment Band of New York on a worldwide tour, is generally regarded as the father of the U. S. concert band.

Marching bands use neither oboes nor bassoons, the number of clarinets and saxophones is much reduced, and flutes are usually replaced by fifes. Brass bands are smaller yet, eliminating all woodwind instruments except, sometimes, the alto saxophone. The modern brass band dates from the decade of the 1830s, when valves began to be used in brass instruments, greatly increasing their versatility. Military bands are usually larger than marching bands but smaller than concert bands; today's larger groups, connected with various branches of the armed services, are highly polished ensembles capable of playing the most difficult music written for wind instruments. The size and instrumentation of each type of band varies, particularly among the amateur groups found in the United States.

Bibliography: Goldman, R. F., *The Concert Band* (1946) and *The Wind Band: Its Literature and Technique* (1961); Hazen, M. H. and R. M., *The Music Then: An Illustrated History of Brass Bands in America, 1800–1920* (1987); Rehrig, W. H., *The Heritage Encyclopedia of Band Music*, 2 vols. (1991); Simon, George, *The Big Bands* (1981).

Banda, H. Kamuzu   [ban'-duh, kah-moo'-zoo]

Hastings Kamuzu Banda, b. 1906?, was president of Malawi (formerly Nyasaland) from 1966 to 1994. Banda, the son of poor peasants, went to the United States in 1923, where he received a medical degree. He continued his studies in Scotland and practiced medicine in England and the Gold Coast (Ghana). Long active in the African independence movement,

Banda returned to Nyasaland in 1958 and was imprisoned (1959–60) for his nationalist activities. In 1961, under a constitution he had helped negotiate, Banda's Malawi Congress party won a majority in the legislature. Banda became prime minister in 1963, when Britain granted Nyasaland internal self-government, and retained the post after independence. When Malawi became a republic, Banda became president; he was sworn in as president-for-life in 1971. Domestic opposition to the increasingly dictatorial Banda emerged in the early 1990s, and he lost a 1993 referendum on one-party rule. After his defeat in Malawi's first multiparty presidential elections, held in 1994, Banda ceded power peacefully and was honored by the new legislature for his contributions as a founder of the nation.

Bibliography: Short, Philip, *Banda* (1974).

Bandaranaike   (family)   [bahn-drah-ny'-kee]

Sri Lanka's Sirimavo Bandaranaike was the world's first woman prime minister. Her husband, Solomon W. R. D. Bandaranaike, whom she married in 1940, had been prime minister of Sri Lanka from 1956 to 1959. She held that post three times (1960–65, 1970–77, and 1994–   ). Their daughter, Chandrika Bandaranaike Kumaratunga, became prime minister in August 1994 and president in November. Their son, Anura Bandaranaike, served (1993–94) in the cabinet of the rival United National party.

Solomon West Ridgeway Dias Bandaranaike, b. Jan. 8, 1899, d. Sept. 26, 1959, became prime minister of Ceylon (now Sri Lanka) in 1956. An Oxford-educated lawyer elected to the legislative assembly in 1931, he served in the cabinet when Ceylon became independent in 1947. He resigned from the ruling United National party (UNP) in 1951 and founded the Sri Lanka Freedom party (SLFP). In 1956 he formed the leftist coalition People's United Front, which won the elections of 1956. Bandaranaike promoted neutrality in international affairs and Sinhalese nationalism at home. He was assassinated by a Buddhist monk in 1959.

His widow, **Sirimavo Bandaranaike**, b. Apr. 17, 1916, became the world's first woman prime minister when she led the SLFP to victory in the 1960 election. She served as prime minister until 1965 and returned to office from 1970 to 1977 as head of a pro-Sinhalese left-wing coalition that promoted state control of the economy. After losing the post to the UNP's J. R. JAYAWARDENE, she remained head of the SLFP.

The Bandaranaikes' daughter, **Chandrika Kumaratunga**, b. June 29, 1945, was elected president of Sri Lanka in November 1994 and immediately named her mother prime minister. After her husband was assassinated by a Sinhalese nationalist in 1988, Kumaratunga went to London. She returned in 1991 and rejoined the SLFP, which she had left in 1984. She became prime minister in August 1994 as head of a 10-party left-center coalition that included the SLFP. She pledged to continue the free-market policies introduced after her mother's 1977 defeat while increasing services to the poor. In the November presidential election, she attracted voters across ethnic lines by promising to negotiate with Sri Lanka's Tamil rebels.

Bibliography: Manor, James, *The Expedient Utopian* (1990).

Bandello, Matteo   [bahn-del'-loh, maht-tay'-oh]

Matteo Bandello, b. *c.*1485, d. Sept. 13, 1561, is considered the most important short-story writer of the Italian Renaissance. Each of his 214 short stories is preceded by a dedicatory letter to a famous personality of the time; written between 1510 and 1560, the stories are collected under the title *Novelle.* His work was a source for the writings of Lord Byron, Alfred de Musset, Shakespeare, and Lope de Vega.   OSCAR BÜDEL

bandicoot

The long-nosed bandicoot, Perameles nasuta, *is common to eastern Australia. It often lives close enough to towns to be a garden pest.*

A bandicoot is any of 8 genera and about 19 species of marsupial mammals that constitute the family Peramelidae. Bandicoots are found in Australia, New Guinea, and several South Pacific islands. The name was first applied by the explorer George Bass in 1799 because of the animals' supposed resemblance to India's bandicoot rat—from Telegu words meaning "pig-rat."

The bandicoot's coarsely haired body is from 28 to 76 cm (11 to 30 in) long, including the usually ratlike tail. The muzzle is long and pointed, and the hind legs are longer than the forelegs. The forefeet look three-toed because the outer toes are vestigial. The second and third toes of the hind feet are fused, and the first toes are sometimes absent. The female usually bears a litter of two to six young, and her marsupial pouch opens backward and downward.

Bandicoots are solitary, lively, mainly nocturnal animals that feed on insects, worms, and plants and build grassy nests in burrows. Their digging can damage crops, and some species have been considered pests. Several species are endangered or perhaps extinct; in Australia, however, bandicoots are now protected.   EVERETT SENTMAN

Bibliography: Sherman, Geraldine, *Animals with Pouches: The Marsupials* (1978); Tyndale-Biscoe, Hugh, *Life of Marsupials* (1973).

Bandinelli, Baccio   [bahn-dee-nel'-lee]

Baccio (or Bartolomeo) Bandinelli, b. Nov. 12, 1493, d. Feb. 7, 1560, was a Florentine Mannerist sculptor, painter, and goldsmith. He was trained by his father, an eminent goldsmith, and later entered the workshop of the sculptor Giovanni Francesco Rustici. Bandinelli worked mostly for the MEDICI family, producing, among numerous other works, a copy of the LAOCOÖN (completed 1525, Uffizi Gallery, Florence), tombs of the popes Leo X and Clement VII (after 1536; both in Santa Maria sopra Minerva, Rome), and a portrait bust of Cosimo I de'Medici (*c.*1544; Bargello, Florence). His life was marked by intense rivalry with Benvenuto CELLINI and MICHELANGELO. Bandinelli boasted that his major sculpture, *Hercules and Cacus* (1525–34; Piazza della Signoria, Florence), would surpass Michelangelo's DAVID, then standing nearby. Instead, it appeared labored and awkward in comparison and was much criticized. The choir screen that Bandinelli began in 1547 for the Duomo (Cathedral) of Florence was not successful either, for it was later altered and partially dismantled. His best work is probably *Dead Christ Supported by Nicodemus*

(1554–59), begun by his son Clemente in his own memorial chapel in the church of Santissimo Annunziata, Florence.
                                                   GIULIA BARTRUM

Bibliography: Pope-Hennessy, John, *Italian High Renaissance and Baroque Sculpture* (1963); Vasari, Giorgio, *The Lives of the Painters, Sculptors, and Architects,* trans. by A. B. Hinds (1963).

Bandung

Bandung (1983 est. pop., 1,602,000) is the capital city of West Java province on the island of Java, Indonesia. About 120 km (75 mi) southeast of Jakarta, the city is a Sundanese cultural and educational center and has a relatively moderate climate because of its altitude of 768 m (2,520 ft). The city is hemmed in by a series of volcanic peaks covered with tangled upland vegetation. Bandung is the center of Indonesia's quinine industry, with cinchona grown on nearby plantations. It is also noted for its ceramics and textiles.

Settled around 1810, the city has grown rapidly in the 20th century. It is the home of the Institute for Technical Research, the Padjadjaran State University, and a nuclear research center. Just outside the city is the Tangkubanprahu (Upside-Down Boat), a volcanic crater that can be entered.

In 1955, Bandung was the site of a conference of 29 African and Asian nations—the first of its kind—which helped prepare the way for the establishment of the NONALIGNED NATIONS MOVEMENT.

baneberry

The baneberry is any plant of the genus *Actaea* in the buttercup family, Ranunculaceae. They are perennial herbs with terminal clusters of small, white flowers. The baneberry is found in rich, shady woods in temperate North America and northern Eurasia. The white berries on the white baneberry, or snakeroot, and the red berries on the red baneberry, or cohosh, are poisonous.   HUGH M. RAUP

Banff   (Alberta)

Banff is an unincorporated Canadian town on the Bow River in southwestern Alberta, near the British Columbian border. It is situated in the Rocky Mountains at an altitude of 1,382 m (4,534 ft) and is mainly a tourist center with a seasonally fluctuating population. The town is the headquarters of Banff National Park (established 1885), renowned for its magnificent mountain and glacier scenery, including Lake Louise, and for its abundant wildlife. The Banff School of Fine Arts, part of the University of Alberta, is located there.

Banff   (Scotland)

Banff (also called Banffshire) was a county in northeastern Scotland until 1975, when it became part of the Grampian administrative region. On the south shore of Moray Firth, it is between the North Sea coast, to the north, and the Cairngorm Mountains, a range of the Grampian Mountains, to the south. Banff, a seaport at the mouth of the Deveron River, was the county town. The rivers Avon, Deveron, and Spey drain the mainly livestock-raising and dairy-farming region. Marble and granite are quarried, and fishing and tourism are important in the coastal river towns. Industries include distilling, boatbuilding, food processing, and textile manufacturing. The remains of an ancient castle, built as a defense against Viking raids, still stand.

Because of the commercial advantages afforded by membership in the HANSEATIC LEAGUE, Banff was an important port during the Middle Ages. The entire county was a center of the JACOBITES after 1689.

Bang, Herman

The Danish writer Herman Joachim Bang, b. Apr. 20, 1857, d. Jan. 29, 1912, was noted for his critical essays, verse, impressionistic short stories, and psychologically insightful provincial novels. While studying at the University of Copenhagen, he began writing stories and essays and published his first novel, *Håbløse Slaegter* (Hopeless Generations), in 1880. Bang began a career as a journalist and from 1884 was chief correspondent for the paper *National-Tidende*. He continued writing, however, and produced novels probing the depression, frustration, and loneliness of life. Among these are *Tine* (1889), which was greatly admired by Ibsen; *Ida Brandt* (1896; Eng. trans., 1928); *Det hvide hus* (The White House, 1898); and *Denied a Country* (1906; Eng. trans., 1927).

Bibliography: Rossei, Sven, *A History of Scandinavian Literature: 1870 to 1980,* trans. by A. Culmer (1982).

Bangalore   [bang'-guh-lohr]

Bangalore, the capital of the Karnataka (formerly Mysore) state of India, is situated on a ridge in the southern Mysore Plateau at an elevation of 949 m (3,113 ft). The city has a population of 4,100,000 (1991 prelim.). Its pleasant climate has made it a noted retirement site.

After World War II the city experienced rapid growth and rose in rank to the sixth largest city in India, mainly because of rapid industrialization. Bangalore is a center of diversified industries, producing cotton textiles, electronics, machinery, and aircraft. The city has several institutes of learning, including the Indian Institute of Science.

Kempe Gowda, founder of the city in 1537, erected a mud fort, which was rebuilt in stone in 1761. Some remains of TIPPU SULTAN's palace are in the center of the oval fort. Lord CORNWALLIS captured the fort in 1791 for the British. It became the administrative capital in 1831 and was the center of British rule until 1881. Surrounding the fort, the old city is congested, but the planned gridiron suburbs in the north and south, along with the cantonment area in the east, are open and garden-like. The notable botanic gardens of Lal Bagh were laid out in the 18th century.   ASHOK K. DUTT

Bangkok   [bang'-kahk]

Bangkok is the capital and chief port of Thailand and one of the most important cities in Southeast Asia. It is located on the east bank of the Chao Phraya River 40 km (24 mi) upstream from the Gulf of Thailand. Bangkok's Thai name is Krung Thep ("City of Angels"). The population of Bangkok Metropolis, which includes the industrial city of Thon Buri on the west bank of the river, is 5,716,779 (1988 est.).

Bangkok was known during the 19th century as the Venice of the East because of its many canals, which served as streets and commercial thoroughfares. The city has undergone extensive development in recent years, however, and many of the canals have been paved over. The surrounding region, the river's delta plain, is flat and swampy, and heavy rains frequently cause flooding during the rainy season (May to October).

Most of the citizens of contemporary Bangkok are Thais, although a significant number of Chinese, many of whom are merchants, also live there. Houses perched on stilts lining the banks of the canals can still be seen. Although the city has many modern skyscrapers and buildings that reflect a European influence, perhaps its most distinctive features are the approximately 400 Buddhist temples, called *wats*. Bangkok is a regional center for many United Nations agencies and the site of Chulalongkorn, Kasetsart, Thammasat, Mahidol, and other universities.

Bangkok is Thailand's economic center. The city's industries are based primarily on the products of the surrounding region. Processed rice and lumber are most important. Others include sugar, paper, textiles, cigarettes, soap, matches, metal, and processed foods. Tourism is also important.

Bangkok is the center of Thailand's transportation system. The modern port of Klongtoi, 7 km (4 mi) downstream from central Bangkok, handles about 90% of Thailand's foreign trade. Much of the local commerce was long distributed by canals—the city's first road was not built until 1860. The busy Don Muang international airport is nearby.

At first a small agricultural community, Bangkok became the capital of Siam in 1782 when Chao Phraya Chakkri (Rama

The ornate spires of a Buddhist wat, *or monastery, rise above the Chao Phraya River, Bangkok's major avenue of commerce. The historic river port has been the capital of Thailand since the city's founding in 1782.*

I), founder of the Chakkri dynasty, moved his government from Thon Buri. Rama I built the walled Grand Palace, which contains the Wat Po and the Wat Emerald Buddha. The first major secular construction projects were undertaken during the reign (1851–68) of Mongkut (Rama IV). During the 20th century, and especially since World War II, the city has grown rapidly.   ASHOK K. DUTT

Bibliography: *Baedeker's Bangkok,* rev. ed. (1987); Hookin, John, *Bangkok* (1991); Hürliman, Martin, *Bangkok* (1963); Seidenfaden, Erik, *Guide to Bangkok with Notes on Siam* (1985).

Bangladesh   [bahng-glah-desh']

Bangladesh (formerly East Pakistan) is an independent country in southern Asia located on the Bay of Bengal, bounded on most of its borders by India and to the southeast by Burma. It occupies a total area of 142,776 km² (55,126 mi²). Bangladesh is one of the world's most densely populated and fastest-growing countries. DHAKA (Dacca) is the capital city. Bangladesh is an overwhelmingly agricultural country, with rich farmland and major crops of rice and jute. Before 1947, most of the territory now in Bangladesh was part of the province of British-ruled India known as East BENGAL, which in 1947 joined with the Sylhet district of Assam and became East Pakistan in the new state of Pakistan. Growing economic and political differences with West Pakistan led East Pakistan to declare independence in 1971 as the new nation of Bangladesh. The name *Bangladesh* means "the Bengal nation." Not all who speak the Bengali language and otherwise identify with the cultural history of Bengal, however, are included within Bangladesh boundaries; many Bengalis live to the west of Bangladesh in the Indian province of West Bengal.

THE LAND AND RESOURCES

The Chittagong Hills in eastern and southeastern Bangladesh include the highest and most rugged parts of the nation, with elevations rising to more than 1,200 m (4,000 ft) above sea level. The remainder of Bangladesh is generally low-lying, with elevations approaching only 300 m (900 ft) in the hills of the northwest and northeast and considerably lower on the vast deltaic plains on the BRAHMAPUTRA, GANGES, and Meghna rivers in the south. The lowlands of the delta region are crisscrossed by numerous distributaries of the main rivers.

About 6% of the total land area of Bangladesh is permanently under water, and two-thirds is flooded for part of the year. The floods often result in great loss of life, crops, and property damage but are, nonetheless, of special value to agricultural Bangladesh for the sediments (alluvium) that the muddy floodwaters deposit on the land. These alluvial soils are rich in minerals and other nutrients needed for plant growth. The fertility of the soil has attracted thousands of landless laborers to shifting silt islands (*chars*) off the coast, despite their vulnerability to natural disasters.

Climate. Bangladesh has a tropical monsoon-type climate, with a hot and rainy summer and a pronounced dry season in the cooler months. January is the coolest month of the year, with temperatures averaging near 26° C (78° F), and April the warmest month, with temperatures ranging between 33° C and 36° C (91° F and 96° F). The climate is one of the wettest in the world; most places receive more than 1,525 mm (60 in) of rain a year, and areas near the hills receive 5,080 mm (200 in). Most rain falls in the monsoon (June–September) season.

Vegetation and Animal Life. About 15% of Bangladesh is still forested; the three principal forest regions are the Madhupur jungle, the tidal forest in the coastal Sundarbans (a swamp region in the Ganges delta), and the tropical rain forest of the Chittagong Hills. Bamboo and rattan are abundant. Tigers and other game are found in the Madhupur jungle and Sundarbans, crocodiles in the Sundarbans, and elephants, rhinoceroses, and leopards in the hill areas.

Natural Resources. The principal resources of Bangladesh are the fertile soils of the delta region, the long growing season, and the heavy rainfall suitably distributed over the year for growing rice and jute. The nation's abundant water supplies are used to produce hydroelectric power and for irrigating farmlands during the dry season. A pact with India, signed in 1977, provides Bangladesh with a share of the waters of the Ganges.

Although minerals have traditionally been economically unimportant, the country has large reserves of natural gas and some petroleum deposits. Natural gas is piped into Dhaka and CHITTAGONG for industrial use. There are also large deposits of low-grade coal, mined at Jamalpur.

THE PEOPLE

About 98% of the people of Bangladesh are Bengalis, a generally short, brown-skinned people; most of the remainder are tribal peoples, who have distinctly Mongoloid features and live mainly in the hills. About 85% of the population are Muslim and, except for the tribal peoples who are mainly animistic in religious outlook, most of the remaining people are Hindu. Bengali, the national language, is spoken by all but the tribal hill people, who speak a variety of languages.

Demography. Bangladesh has one of the highest birthrates and population densities in the world. Nearly half of the total population are under 15 years old, which means that even if birthrates can be made to decline in the near future, the total population is likely, nonetheless, to expand rapidly in the next 20 years. Cholera, tuberculosis, leprosy, and malaria occur widely, aided by the generally unsanitary conditions; and, despite a doubling of facilities in recent years, medical personnel, facilities, and supplies are in chronically short supply.

Most people live in the countryside. The largest cities are Dhaka and the port of Chittagong. Villages are often located on the highest available ground, with houses further raised on earthen plinths. The number of landless laborers is rising steadily as landholdings become increasingly fragmented.

Education. About one-fourth of the population is literate; and

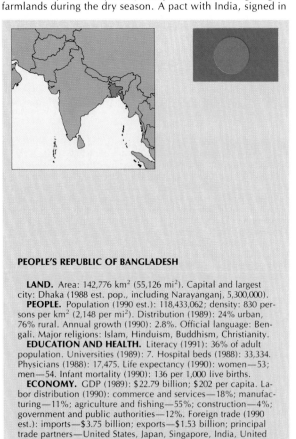

PEOPLE'S REPUBLIC OF BANGLADESH

LAND. Area: 142,776 km² (55,126 mi²). Capital and largest city: Dhaka (1988 est. pop., including Narayanganj, 5,300,000).

PEOPLE. Population (1990 est.): 118,433,062; density: 830 persons per km² (2,148 per mi²). Distribution (1989): 24% urban, 76% rural. Annual growth (1990): 2.8%. Official language: Bengali. Major religions: Islam, Hinduism, Buddhism, Christianity.

EDUCATION AND HEALTH. Literacy (1991): 36% of adult population. Universities (1989): 7. Hospital beds (1988): 33,334. Physicians (1988): 17,475. Life expectancy (1990): women—53; men—54. Infant mortality (1990): 136 per 1,000 live births.

ECONOMY. GDP (1989): $22.79 billion; $202 per capita. Labor distribution (1990): commerce and services—18%; manufacturing—11%; agriculture and fishing—55%; construction—4%; government and public authorities—12%. Foreign trade (1990 est.): imports—$3.75 billion; exports—$1.53 billion; principal trade partners—United States, Japan, Singapore, India, United Kingdom. Currency: 1 taka = 100 paisa.

GOVERNMENT. Type: republic. Legislature: Parliament. Political subdivisions: 4 divisions, 64 districts.

COMMUNICATIONS. Railroads (1987): 2,872 km (1,785 mi) total. Roads (1989): 176,876 km (109,906 mi) total. Major ports: 2. Major airfields: 3.

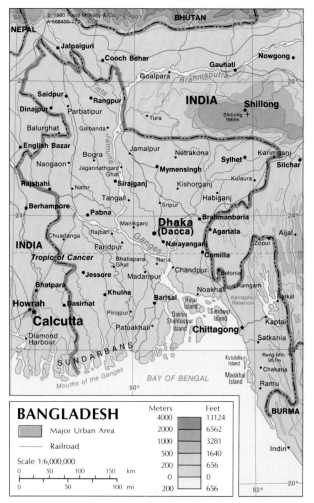

BANGLADESH

▨ Major Urban Area

— Railroad

Scale 1:6,000,000

Meters	Feet
4000	13124
2000	6562
1000	3281
500	1640
200	656
0	0
200	656

(Right) *Sailing and motor vessels move leisurely along the Burhi Ganga River as it flows past Dhaka, the capital and largest city of Bangladesh.*

(Below) *Vegetables are unloaded at a market on the Dhaka waterfront. Although the alluvial soils of Bangladesh are fertile, food production has not fully recovered from the tidal waves and cyclones of 1970 and 1985 or from the war of independence in 1971.*

for each literate woman, three men can read and write. Literacy rates are higher in urban areas. About 60% of all children attend primary schools; far fewer attend a technical school or one of the six universities. The largest university is the University of Dhaka (see SOUTH ASIAN UNIVERSITIES).

The Arts. Bengali literature—rooted in folk legend, ballads, and religious stories—has long flourished. Rabindranath TAGORE, the renowned Bengali poet, remains popular today. Art and architectural traditions conform distinctly to 16th- and 17th-century Islamic styles.

ECONOMIC ACTIVITY

Before the Industrial Revolution, Bangladesh was known for its fine cotton textiles, but this industry was eclipsed in the 18th and 19th centuries by the production of cheaper mill cloth overseas in Europe. Thereafter, the economy of Bangladesh was primarily agricultural, with major exports in the 18th and 19th centuries of opium and indigo and, in the 20th century, of jute and jute products. Industrial development was not encouraged by the British, and many factories established following partition from India in 1947 were destroyed in the struggle for independence from Pakistan.

Agriculture. The economy today remains primarily agricultural, and nearly two-thirds of the land area is under cultivation. Double and triple crops are obtained where water is available for irrigation during the dry season. Farms are generally small,

(Above) *Near Dhaka, a Bengali fisherman hangs his nets to dry above the surrounding rice paddies. Although fishing is both productive and profitable, the industry cannot satisfy the food needs of populous Bangladesh.*

(Right) *Bars indicate monthly ranges of temperatures (red) and precipitation (blue) of Chittagong. Bangladesh has a monsoon climate and has tropical wet-dry influences in the north.*

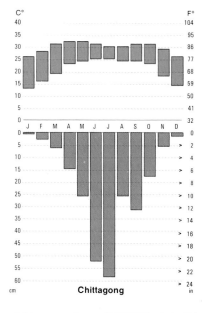

Chittagong

and many are so small that normal agricultural crises, such as floods, other natural disasters, and price fluctuations, have forced many small landowners to sell their land and seek other employment. Rice, planted on 90% of the cultivated land, is the leading crop, but even in good years the output is insufficient to feed the rapidly growing population. The government is encouraging increased planting of wheat as a food crop. The principal cash crops are jute, which is grown in flooded fields on the delta, and tea, which is produced mainly in the Sylhet and the Chittagong Hills regions.

Manufacturing. Jute processing is the principal factory industry. Bangladesh supplies more than half of the world's jute, but the paper and plastic-packaging revolution has reduced world demand for jute products, and the Bangladesh economy has suffered accordingly. Other manufactures include textiles, cigarettes, steel, cement, fertilizers, and chemicals. Many of the industries nationalized by the government in 1972 have since been returned to private ownership.

The chief sources of power are natural gas and thermal electricity produced from oil, natural gas, and coal.

Transportation and Trade. The transportation and communication system was severely damaged during the war of independence and again in 1988, when the worst flooding in 70 years left three-quarters of the country under water. The economy was dealt a further blow by the 1990 Iraqi invasion of Kuwait and the 1991 GULF WAR, which cost the nation an estimated 3 percent of its gross national product in increased oil prices, trade losses, and lost remittances from Bangladeshi workers formerly employed in the Persian Gulf region.

Bangladesh has an unfavorable balance of trade and depends heavily on international aid and large economic development loans from overseas to feed its population and finance economic development. The principal exports are jute and jute products, tea, leather goods, and fish. Imports include food, chemicals, manufactured goods, and machinery.

GOVERNMENT

Bangladesh's constitution of 1972 provided for a parliamentary government headed by a prime minister; it was revised in 1975 to a presidential system with a strong, elected president as chief executive. After the first president, Sheikh MUJIBUR RAHMAN, was assassinated, periods of military rule alternated with elected governments. A constitutional referendum in September 1991 approved a return to a parliamentary system of government.

HISTORY

Bangladesh, independent only since 1971 and thus one of the world's youngest nations, has a long history of domination by larger political entities. In the late 16th century the area that is now Bangladesh was conquered by the Mogul emperor AKBAR, and, under Mogul rule, most of the population, which had hitherto been predominantly Buddhist, was converted to Islam. After 1707, Mogul control weakened, and Bangladesh was caught up in the struggle by European trading and financial interests, including the British EAST INDIA COMPANY, for control of the Indian subcontinent. In 1757, Robert CLIVE led British forces in the famous victory over the French at Plassey, and in 1764 the Mogul emperor acknowledged the dominance of the British, who remained in control until 1947.

In the early 20th century, conflicts between Hindu and Muslim interests became intense. In 1947, when the British withdrew, the two independent nations of Pakistan, which was predominantly Muslim and included modern Bangladesh, and India, which was largely Hindu, were created. In this partition, East Bengal, where most of the jute was produced, became part of East Pakistan, and West Bengal, where the jute-processing factories were located, became part of India.

The two provinces of the new Pakistan nation had almost nothing in common other than the shared Islamic faith; moreover, East Pakistan was separated by more than 1,600 km (1,000 mi) from West Pakistan, and, with more than half the population of the new nation, it felt underrepresented in a government dominated by West Pakistan. In the 1970 national elections, East Pakistan's Awami League, under Sheikh Mujibur Rahman, won a majority of seats in the Pakistan National Assembly but was denied power by delays in the opening of

the assembly. On Mar. 26, 1971, East Pakistan proclaimed its independence as the new state of Bangladesh. The national government of Pakistan responded by invading the eastern province, but, with assistance from India, the Pakistani army was driven back before the end of 1971 (see INDIA-PAKISTAN WARS). Sheikh Mujibur Rahman became the first prime minister and, under the amended constitution of 1975, the first president. Mujibur was overthrown and assassinated on Aug. 15, 1975, in a military coup led by Khondaker Moshtaque Ahmed, who was in turn overthrown in a military counter coup in November 1975. Gen. Ziaur Rahman then assumed power and was president from 1977 until his assassination in an unsuccessful military coup in May 1981. Former vice-president Abdus Sattar, elected president in November 1981, was deposed in March 1982 in a coup led by Lt. Gen. H. M. ERSHAD.

Ershad proclaimed himself president in 1983, and in a 1985 referendum voters approved his policies. In 1986 martial law was lifted and the constitution revived after Ershad's Jatiya party won a majority in parliament and Ershad won the presidency in an election boycotted by the opposition. New parliamentary elections held in 1988 after a wave of antigovernment protests were also boycotted by the opposition, and there was further violence when Islam was declared the state religion later that year. In December 1990, Ershad suddenly resigned under pressure. A caretaker government was formed, and Ershad was later placed under house arrest and charged with corruption and misuse of power. New elections were held in February 1991. Begum Khaleda Zia, head of the center-right Bangladesh Nationalist party and widow of former president Ziaur Rahman, became the nation's first woman prime minister on Mar. 20, 1991. On Apr. 30, 1991, the fragile new democracy was severely tested when a devastating cyclone left more than 125,000 people dead and thousands more threatened by famine and disease. DAVID DICKASON

Bibliography: Baxter, C., *Bangladesh* (1985); Jansen, E. G., *Rural Bangladesh* (1987); Kahn, A. R., and Hossain, M., *The Strategy of Development in Bangladesh* (1990); Kahn, M. T., and Thorp, J. P., *Bangladesh* (1985); O'Donnell, C. P., *Bangladesh* (1984).

See also: INDIA, HISTORY OF.

Bangor

Bangor (1990 pop., 33,181) is a city in east central Maine and the seat of Penobscot County. A port of entry, it is located at the head of navigation on the Penobscot River, 29 km (18 mi) from the Atlantic Ocean. Bangor is a commercial and industrial center that manufactures paper, electronics equipment, and machinery. It is surrounded by Maine's vast timber stands and is a leading lumber port. Settled in 1769, it grew considerably after 1830 with the advent of shipbuilding and expansion of the lumber industry.

Bang's disease: see BRUCELLOSIS.

Bangui   [bahn-gee']

Bangui (1988 est. pop., 596,776) is the capital city of the Central African Republic in central Africa and lies at the head of navigation of the Ubangi River. Bangui has many small industries and handles the country's exports, mainly timber, cotton, sisal, and coffee. A network of road and rail lines connects it with Cameroon, Chad, and Sudan. The University of Bangui was founded in 1969.

banjo

The banjo is a plucked string instrument that has a long fretted neck piercing a circular frame over which a membrane is tightened with thumbscrews, often containing a resonator over the open back. A descendant of the West African long-necked lute, it came to the Americas with the slave trade. In the 19th century a more highly developed banjo, popular especially in blackface minstrel shows, was exported to England. In the early 20th century it became an important rhythmic instrument of the jazz band, and it is now cultivated as a folk instrument. The standard form is the finger-style banjo, originally gut-strung, its five strings plucked with bare fingers.

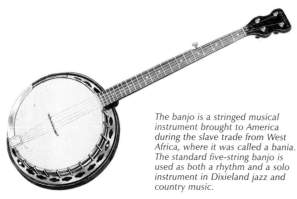

The banjo is a stringed musical instrument brought to America during the slave trade from West Africa, where it was called a bania. The standard five-string banjo is used as both a rhythm and a solo instrument in Dixieland jazz and country music.

Banjul   [bahn'-jool]

Banjul, the capital of Gambia, has a population of 40,000 (1986 est.). Located on Saint Mary's Island at the mouth of the Gambia River, it is linked to the mainland by ferry. Banjul is the economic center and major port of the country. Its major industry is groundnut processing; beaches and abundant birdlife attract tourists. Founded as a British trading post in 1816, Banjul was the capital of the British crown colony of Gambia from 1889 to 1965, when Gambia became independent. Until 1973, it was known as Bathurst.

Bank of Canada

The Bank of Canada is that country's CENTRAL BANK. Founded in 1934 and nationalized in 1938, it was assigned the task of regulating credit and currency in the national interest. Although Canada's highly centralized banking system consists of only nine Canadian-owned commercial banks (1994), these have a total of almost 8,000 branches. The Bank of Canada is both the note-issuing authority and the holder of reserve deposits for the commercial banks. It can therefore influence the national economy by adjusting interest rates on the loans it makes to commercial banks, by changing the banks' reserve requirements, and by buying and selling securities.

Bank of Credit and Commerce International

Founded in 1972 with Middle Eastern capital, the Bank of Credit and Commerce International (BCCI) was at the center of one of the largest international banking scandals. Several hundred thousand BCCI creditors worldwide lost an estimated $10 billion in the bank's collapse.

Based in Luxembourg and the Cayman Islands, BCCI was managed by Pakistani financiers from London and eventually largely owned by the emirate of Abu Dhabi. In 1991 it achieved notoriety when bank regulators on several continents seized its assets, charging that it had concealed losses for years. In 1993, BCCI's former treasurer, Syed Ziaudin Ali Akbar, pleaded guilty in England to false accounting and was sentenced to prison. Britain and the United States meanwhile were still seeking extradition of a dozen other former BCCI officers on fraud and forgery charges. In 1994, U.S. charges against Abu Dhabi were dropped in exchange for the emirate's agreement to pay $180 million in fines and to extradite BCCI's former chairman, Swaleh Naqvi, who pleaded guilty to federal fraud charges and was sentenced to prison that year.

BCCI's illegal acquisition of First American Bankshares, Inc., the largest bank in the District of Columbia, led to the forced resignation of First American's chairman, Clark CLIFFORD, and indictments for fraud, larceny, bribery, and money laundering (later dropped because of Clifford's age and ill health).

Bank of England

The Bank of England was the first CENTRAL BANK. It serves as the banker to the government of the United Kingdom, with sole authority to issue notes in England and Wales, and also as the banker to the country's commercial banks. Until 1946 the bank was privately owned, but it had long governed its operations in the national interest. Chartered as a joint-stock company in 1694, the bank helped fund the national debt arising from William III's wars in Ireland and against France. Today the bank is able to adjust the country's supply of money through the purchase and sale of securities. It also controls interest rates and sets limits on the amount of bank credit.

Bank for International Settlements

The Bank for International Settlements (BIS) was established in 1930 in Basel, Switzerland, to promote cooperation among CENTRAL BANKS and generally to facilitate international financial operations by acting as a "central banks' bank." The bank's authorized capital is 1.5 billion gold francs, divided into 600,000 shares. Subscribing to these shares are the central banks (or surrogate institutions) of 28 European countries and 5 other nations, which exercise the right of representation and voting at annual meetings in proportion to their shares (some shares are in private hands with no participation at annual meetings). The BIS is thus a limited-share company but also an international organization governed by international law.

Bank of the United States

The first Bank of the United States was established in 1791. A private corporation operating under a federal charter, the bank was designed by Secretary of the Treasury Alexander HAMILTON as a way to secure the safety of public funds, stabilize the currency, and provide a source of credit for the federal government and private business.

The federal government subscribed for 20 percent of the bank's stock of $10 million. In return the bank served as the government's fiscal agent. Although it had no direct legal power to regulate state banks, the Bank of the United States was able to prevent abuses by state-chartered banks by collecting their notes and demanding redemption in specie. Doubts about the constitutional power of the federal government to charter a private corporation, however, had been raised by Thomas Jefferson in 1791, and despite the bank's excellent record in the handling of public funds and in stabilizing the currency, these doubts persisted. In 1811, when the bank's charter expired, it was not renewed.

The instability of state banks, however, led to the chartering of the Second Bank of the United States in 1816. The charter of the second bank resembled the first, but the U.S. president was now empowered to name 5 of the bank's 25 directors. Under its first president, William Jones, the bank engaged in inflationary lending policies that undermined the bank's stability. The second president, Langlon Cheves (1819–23), created ill will by foreclosing on bank loans, but he restored the bank's role as a conservative influence in the nation's economy. He was succeeded in 1823 by Nicholas BIDDLE.

President Andrew JACKSON, disturbed by misgivings about the bank's constitutionality and angered by political opposition from some of the bank's officers, opposed renewal of the bank's charter. Biddle's efforts to defeat Jackson through an alliance with Henry CLAY were unavailing. Jackson vetoed a recharter bill, won reelection in 1832, and by executive order withdrew all federal deposits from the bank in 1833. Crippled by loss of government patronage, the bank had ceased to be an effective force for national economic stability by the time its charter expired in 1836.   ALFRED A. CAVE

Bibliography: Holdsworth, J. T., and Dewey, D. R., *First and Second Banks of the United States* (1910); Remini, R. V., *Andrew Jackson and the Bank War* (1967); Taylor, G. R., ed., *Jackson versus Biddle's Bank* (1972); Wilburn, J. A., *Biddle's Bank: The Crucial Years* (1967).

Bankhead, Tallulah

Tallulah Brockman Bankhead, b. Huntsville, Ala., Jan. 31, 1903, d. Dec. 12, 1968, was an American actress who starred in numerous New York and London stage productions and intermittently in films. She won the New York Drama Critics best actress awards for *The Little Foxes* (1939) and *The Skin of Our Teeth* (1942). Her most memorable film role was in Alfred Hitchcock's *Lifeboat* (1943), for which she won the New York Film Critics top award in 1944. Her autobiography *Tallulah* (1952) was a best seller.

Bibliography: Israel, Lee, *Miss Tallulah Bankhead* (1973); Tunney, Kieran, *Tallulah: Darling of the Gods* (1974).

banking systems

Commercial banks, usually called just "banks," in the United States are institutions that provide checking accounts to the public and have a substantial proportion of their assets invested in loans to business firms. Owing to deregulation in the 1980s and 1990s, the difference between commercial banks and savings banks (see SAVINGS INDUSTRY) has been disappearing. Commercial banks now offer individual savings services, and savings institutions increasingly offer checking services, while both kinds of institutions have extended their lending to each other's traditional markets.

Banks today accept checkable deposits, such as DEMAND DEPOSITS and NOW (Negotiable Order of Withdrawal) accounts, as well as time deposits, and use their depositors' funds mainly to make loans and buy securities. (Currently about one-quarter of their total portfolio of loans and securities consists of securities, close to one-quarter of commercial and industrial loans, almost a third of real estate loans, and about one-eighth of consumer loans.)

Banks thus operate as financial intermediaries, standing between the primary lenders (depositors) and the ultimate borrowers. In this way they provide many services. One is the pooling of risks. A bank that makes many loans is spreading its risks. It is highly likely to experience losses on a few loans but most unlikely to experience losses on all or most. (In contrast, someone who makes only a single loan faces an all-or-nothing situation.) Another service of banks is providing liquidity. Someone who opens a checking account in a bank can get her money back whenever she wants. The bank meanwhile can make loans with her deposits and others' deposits, while keeping only a small fraction of such deposits as a liquid reserve. Because it has many depositors, who usually want to withdraw deposits at different times, a bank normally can meet the demands of those depositors who want to withdraw their deposits.

Another service that banks provide is expert judgment in making loans. Most savers cannot evaluate the creditworthiness of those who wish to borrow. Hence, instead of lending directly to the ultimate borrowers, they "lend" their savings to banks, by depositing them, and the banks then use those savings to make loans to the ultimate borrowers. Banks have a particular advantage in making loans to corporate accounts that are constrained in borrowing directly from the public (through issuance of BONDS and other securities) because the public cannot judge whether they are creditworthy. Banks generally are expert in evaluating the credit standing of such borrowers, partly because they specialize in lending to local businesses, about which they have information that distant lenders do not have. Moreover, once they have made loans, banks are in a good position to ensure compliance with terms of the loans.

Banks have an incentive to take risks because risky loans have a higher rate of return. All of these higher earnings accrue to the banks. But most of the funds at risk belong to depositors. Accordingly, much of the risk that banks take is borne by depositors and by the FEDERAL DEPOSIT INSURANCE CORPORATION (FDIC), which insures their deposits. This is one reason why banks are heavily regulated by the government. Another, perhaps even more important reason is that banks are custodians of the checkable deposits that make up most of society's circulating medium of exchange. If banks fail, and there is no deposit insurance, then depositors have to reduce their expenditures. As a result, sales fall, and firms have to throw employees out of work. The widespread bank failures of the DEPRESSION OF THE 1930s may well have accounted for much of the severity of that depression.

Fractional Reserve System. The banking system can create more than one dollar of deposits for every dollar of reserves it has. This is possible because deposits are not physical objects but, rather, abstract property rights documented by entries on computer tape. No physical object is created; it is all a matter of accounting. Suppose someone deposits $1,000 of currency in a bank. The bank credits the $1,000 to the depositor's account and then lends most of it out. It cannot lend all of it, however. The law and prudence require that it keep a reserve against the deposit, say 10%. It therefore lends out only $900. The borrower then buys something with this $900, and the seller deposits her $900 check in the bank. The bank then keeps $90 as a reserve against this $900 deposit, and lends out $810, which then becomes a deposit and so on. Ultimately, all of the original $1,000 is held in reserves in one bank or another. And because reserves are 10% of deposits, total deposits will then be ten times the original deposit, or 10,000. This hypothetical example overstates the actual case—the actual "deposit multiplier" is closer to 2 than to 10—in large part because at each stage the public withdraws some of its deposits in order to hold more currency.

History. Banking existed in ancient Babylon, and imperial Rome had an extensive banking system. In medieval Europe banking declined, largely because the Roman Catholic church condemned the practice of USURY. Banking revived in Renaissance Italy by the early 14th century, and government supervision of banking was established in 1502. During the 14th century the Florentine Bardi and Peruzzi banks had agencies in many countries. The most famous of the Florentine bankers were the Medici. English banking developed from the custom of goldsmiths safekeeping their customers' precious metals. In doing so, the goldsmiths discovered that they could safely lend these metals out. They gave their customers receipts, which the customers used to pay their own bills. The BANK OF ENGLAND was established privately in 1694 and chartered by the government in return for a loan. The bank was allowed, among other things, to issue its own notes. Although started as a private bank, it gradually evolved into a CENTRAL BANK.

In the United States the first bank, in the modern sense, was established in 1782. In 1791, Congress established a national bank, the First BANK OF THE UNITED STATES, but its charter lapsed in 1811. In 1816 the Second Bank of the United States was chartered, but its charter was not renewed in 1836. Subsequently the states allowed the establishment of banks, with little restraint, and many of those banks failed, often because of defaults on the states' bonds that they were holding. In 1863 the federal government started a system of nationally chartered banks that were required to back their notes with federal government securities. In 1913 this system was superseded by the FEDERAL RESERVE SYSTEM.

Banking in the United States. To open a NATIONAL BANK one needs a charter from the federal government and to open a state bank a charter from a state. All national banks must, and state banks may (though few do), become Federal Reserve member banks and be regulated by the Federal Reserve. Nearly all banks are members of the FDIC, which insures their deposits up to $100,000 and also regulates them. About one-third of all U.S. banks are national banks. They hold about 60% of all deposits. Frequently, when a bank fails, the FDIC, instead of paying off depositors, merges the failing bank with another bank. In that case even deposits over $100,000 are protected. Traditionally, branch banking has been tightly regulated. Most states limited or altogether prohibited branching, and banks could not open branches in other states. As a result, the United States, unlike most industrialized countries, has a great number of small banks. Recently the limitations on branch banking have been greatly eased. Within-state branching is now standard, and as of 1991 all states except Hawaii and Montana have entered into compacts with other states, usually in their own regions, that allow bank holding companies located in one of the states to own banks in the other states.

As noted, commercial banks compete with other institutions that offer some of the same services. Savings and loan associations, savings banks (also called mutual savings banks), and CREDIT UNIONS compete with banks for deposits of households and nonprofit institutions. Their accounts are also insured up to $100,000 by government agencies. Savings and loan associations and savings banks invest most of their funds in MORTGAGES and compete with commercial banks in this market. Along with credit unions and FINANCE COMPANIES, they also compete with banks for consumer loans and are now allowed to make business loans within certain limits.

Money market funds also compete with banks. They invest in very short-term, extremely safe securities and generally allow their customers to write large checks against their accounts. Competition among banks is strong in cities with many banks, as it is for the business of firms that are large enough and well enough known to borrow outside their localities. However, small borrowers located in cities with just a few banks may find that banks have considerable market power.

Banking in Other Countries. The banking systems of many countries differ sharply from the U.S. system by being much more concentrated. For example, in Britain four banks hold the great bulk of domestic deposits, and in Canada there are only eight chartered banks. Control over banks also differs. The United States, with about 15,000 banks, relies on formal regulation. In contrast, Britain relies primarily on moral suasion. Another way in which banks differ in various countries is in the types of assets they hold. U.S. commercial banks make business loans in more or less arm's-length transactions, whereas in many other countries ordinary banking activities and INVESTMENT BANKING activities are carried out by the same institutions. Thus, German banks finance firms by making loans and by buying stock in them and place their managers on the boards of those companies. In many less developed countries (LDCs) much of the banking activity is carried out by branches of large multinational banks, although some countries prohibit foreign banks.

International Banking. In recent years banking has become much more internationalized. U.S. banks have many branches and subsidiaries in foreign countries, while foreign banks account for a significant share of all industrial and commercial bank loans in the United States. Some small islands, such as the Cayman Islands, along with Luxembourg, have become "monetary havens," akin to tax havens. Their relaxed business regulations have attracted, for example, the BANK OF CREDIT AND COMMERCE INTERNATIONAL.

Banking in Renaissance Europe was often conducted as a family enterprise. This painting (c.1515) by Quentin Massys portrays a money-changer and his wife. For a fee, they would exchange gold for silver coins or convert coins of one currency into another.

The First Bank of the United States, which had its headquarters in Philadelphia, was chartered by the U.S. government in 1791 to serve as a repository for federal funds and as a loan source for private citizens and businesses. The bank was strongly opposed by President James Madison, and its charter was allowed to lapse in 1811.

Unresolved Issues and Developments. In the 1970s, mainly owing to the OPEC oil shocks, large U.S. banks made very large loans to the LDCs, both to oil importers and to oil exporters. Many of these countries, particularly Latin American ones, which had borrowed massively, in effect defaulted on these loans. The banks avoided formal defaults only by devices such as rescheduling repayment of the loans, reducing the interest rates, or lending the debtors additional funds that they could then use to pay the interest on the previous loans. The banks then built up their reserves for loan losses and their capital sufficiently that they would no longer be ruined by defaults on these debts.

Then, in the 1980s, as oil prices fell, U.S. banks, particularly those in the Southwest, took large losses on loans they had made to the faltering oil industry and to real estate developers. When, owing to massive overbuilding of commercial real estate, the real estate slump spread to other regions, banks in those regions also suffered large losses, and some failed.

Bank failures, which for the four previous decades had been rare and usually involved only small banks, rose substantially in the 1970s. Then in the 1980s and early 1990s they rose very steeply, as some large banks failed along with small ones. In 1984, when Continental Illinois, then the eighth-largest U.S. bank, was about to fail, the FDIC stepped in, protected all of its creditors, and, in effect, temporarily nationalized it. Subsequently the FDIC had to deal with the failures of several large Texas banks. With the FDIC insurance fund falling rapidly, Congress in 1991 provided that the FDIC could borrow up to $75 billion from the Treasury. How much it will actually have to borrow and whether it will be able to repay all it borrows is uncertain.

Extensive failures are not the only problem that the U.S. banking industry faces. As a result of increased sophistication and falling costs of gathering, processing, and communicating information, the bank's advantage as repository of specialized knowledge about borrowers is being eroded, while at the same time cheaper communications and automated teller machines expose it to more competition in the deposit market. One response of banks has been to offer various new services to customers, such as guaranteeing their credit, another to seek permission to enter other industries.   THOMAS MAYER

Bibliography: Benston, George J., et al., *Perspectives on Safe and Sound Banking: Past, Present, and Future* (1986); Klebaner, Benjamin J., *Commercial Banking in the United States: A History* (1974); Mayer, Martin, *The Money Bazaars: Understanding the Banking Revolution around Us* (1984); Mayer, Thomas, et al., *Money, Banking and the Economy,* 4th ed. (1990).

bankruptcy

Bankruptcy, in law, is a system of procedures by which an insolvent debtor may be released from, or can modify, DEBT obligations. Under the U.S. Constitution, bankruptcy is a matter of federal law and is currently governed by the Bankruptcy Reform Acts of 1978 and 1984; the latter chiefly restructured the bankruptcy courts and curtailed some liberal 1978 provisions concerning consumer bankruptcy. Generally, individuals, corporations, and associations whose assets are less than their liabilities can file.

Major Types. The Bankruptcy Code provides for three major types of bankruptcy proceedings. In Chapter 7, or liquidation, cases, the debtor's property is sold off by a trustee to pay the debts owed to creditors. An individual debtor can keep a modest amount of household property or realty under federal or state exemptions. Individuals with a regular income who cannot pay their debts can, instead of liquidation, elect adjustment (Chapter 13) proceedings. In these cases, claims of creditors are frozen until the individual, with the assistance of a trustee, presents a plan to pay off the creditors from income. With court and creditor approval, debts may be stretched out or compromised and repossessions prevented, while the debtor retains all property. In Chapter 11, or business reorganizations, the business is continued by its management or a trustee while creditors' claims are frozen pending their approval of a plan. With court approval, the plan can modify or forgive debts, recapitalize a corporation, provide for mergers or takeovers, or dispose of assets.

Procedure. The 1984 law gave U.S. district courts original jurisdiction over all Title II bankruptcy proceedings. It also authorized the regional federal appeals courts to appoint a total of 232 bankruptcy judges, who are adjuncts of the district courts and have 14-year terms. Trustees are either elected by the creditors in a particular proceeding or appointed by the government. Almost all U.S. bankruptcy cases are voluntarily instituted by debtors, although creditors can force a debtor into involuntary liquidation.

In liquidations the trustee inventories the debtor's assets and lists creditors and their claims. The trustee can void unperformed contracts and leases or recover property that the debtor has transferred fraudulently to others or preferentially to creditors. The trustee also administers the property and distributes the proceeds. In nonliquidation cases the trustee and the debtor split these duties. A debtor in liquidation or one who completes a plan may be discharged from the obligation to repay a prebankruptcy debt.

England and Canada. English law follows a similar approach. Creditors may petition a court to appoint an official receiver as a trustee of the insolvent debtor's estate. The receiver will try to arrange a settlement among the parties. If this fails, a formal adjudication of bankruptcy will follow. Canadian law also allows both voluntary and involuntary bankruptcy.

THOMAS W. DUNFEE

Bibliography: Drake, W. Homer, and Herzog, Richard B., *Bankruptcy: A Concise Guide for Debtors and Creditors* (1983); Jackson, Thomas, *The Logic and Limits of Bankruptcy Law* (1986); Tay, Catherine S. K., *Bankruptcy: The Law and Practice* (1987).

Banks, Sir Joseph

Sir Joseph Banks, b. Feb. 13, 1743, d. June 19, 1820, was an English botanist, a patron of the sciences, and president of the Royal Society of London for 42 years, during which time he influenced European scientific investigation. A member of the wealthy landed gentry, Banks was educated at Harrow, Eton, and Oxford. His interest in botany and the natural sciences prompted him to make voyages of scientific exploration. From his first, to Labrador and Newfoundland in 1766, he brought back botanical specimens that were the beginning of the Banks Herbarium, a collection now in the British Museum. In 1768 he financed and accompanied a botanical expedition to the South Seas with Capt. James COOK and collected more than 800 previously unknown specimens. As honorary director of the Royal Botanical Gardens at Kew,

Banks was instrumental in efforts to grow tropical crops throughout the British Empire. At Banks's suggestion the ship BOUNTY attempted to bring breadfruit to the West Indies.

Bibliography: Beaglehole, J. C., ed., *The Endeavour Journal of Joseph Banks, 1768–1771*, 2 vols. (1962); Cameron, Hector C., *Sir Joseph Banks, K.B., P.R.S.: The Autocrat of the Philosophers* (1952).

Banks, Nathaniel Prentiss

Nathaniel Prentiss Banks, b. Waltham, Mass., Jan. 30, 1816, d. Sept. 1, 1894, was Speaker of the U.S. House of Representatives (1856–57) and an inept Union general during the Civil War. He also served in the Massachusetts legislature (1849–53) and as governor (1858–60). Banks, an abolitionist, was appointed a general in the Union army. Although pugnacious and combative, he was not a capable army commander and suffered military defeats in the Shenandoah Valley, at Cedar Mountain, and in Louisiana; he did, however, capture Port Hudson, Miss., in 1863. After the war Banks again served in Congress.
WARREN W. HASSLER, JR.

Bibliography: Harrington, Fred Harvey, *Fighting Politician* (1948).

banksia [bank'-see-uh]

The giant banksia, Banksia grandis, *flourishes in western Australia and has the largest flower spikes, 30 cm (1 ft), of the* Banksia *genus. The tree grows to 12 m (40 ft), and its leaves are 30 cm (1 ft) long.*

The banksia is any of a number of Australian evergreen trees or shrubs of the genus *Banksia* in the family Proteaceae. The leaves are lance-shaped or linear and are variously toothed or incised. They are leathery, dark green above and whitish or brown beneath. The yellowish and occasionally reddish flowers are borne in densely crowded spikes that are terminal or rise from the axils of the leaves; they mature as conelike structures. The genus is characteristic of the scrub vegetation found in mountains of southeastern and southern Australia, and also in southwest Australia.
HUGH M. RAUP

Banneker, Benjamin

Benjamin Banneker, b. near Ellicott's Lower Mills, Md., Nov. 9, 1731, d. Oct. 9, 1806, achieved fame as a compiler of almanacs. A free black tobacco farmer, he acquired his astronomical knowledge through self-teaching, aided by the loan of books by George Ellicott, a Quaker millowner. He served (1791) as scientific assistant to Maj. Andrew Ellicott in surveying the boundaries for the new District of Columbia. Banneker's series of six almanacs (1791–1802) were widely distributed to counter the prevailing opinion that blacks were inherently intellectually inferior to whites.

Bibliography: Bedini, Silvio A., *The Life of Benjamin Banneker* (1972; repr. 1984).

Bannister, Roger

Roger Gilbert Bannister, b. Mar. 23, 1929, an English runner, made track history on May 6, 1954, when he became the first person to run a mile in less than 4 minutes. Then an Oxford medical student, he broke the so-called 4–minute barrier with a time of 3:59.4. John Landy set a new record (3:58.0) just 46 days later, but Bannister beat Landy on August 7 in a historic Commonwealth Games mile, retired shortly thereafter, and then wrote *First Four Minutes* (1955). Bannister, who became a neurologist, was knighted in 1975.

Bannock

The Bannock are a North American Indian people whose traditional homeland was the Snake River drainage basin in present-day Idaho and neighboring states. They spoke a Shoshonian language related to that of the Northern PAIUTE of eastern Oregon. A hunting and gathering people, the Bannock lived in small, seminomadic bands; their population probably never exceeded 2,000. They exploited bison herds, fished for salmon, and gathered roots and pine nuts. They sometimes gathered in large groups for ceremonial events or to ally with the SHOSHONI against their enemies, the BLACKFOOT.

The Bannock remained only loosely united until threatened by white encroachment. Several outbreaks of hostility toward the whites occurred between 1859 and 1863. In 1866, Fort Hall Reservation was established for the Bannock and the Shoshoni. NEZ PERCÉ resistance in 1877 incited the Bannock to further conflict with the U.S. government. In 1878, Buffalo Horn, a former cavalry scout, led the uprising known as the Bannock War. Today the combined Bannock/Shoshoni population at Fort Hall numbers about 6,900.   ERNEST L. SCHUSKY

Bibliography: Madsen, Brigham D., *The Bannock of Idaho* (1958).

Bannockburn, Battle of

The Battle of Bannockburn, which took place in Stirlingshire, Scotland, on June 24, 1314, was a major victory for the Scottish king ROBERT I over the much larger English forces of EDWARD II. The English army, attempting to relieve the siege of Stirling Castle, suffered heavy losses against the Scottish pikemen and were routed by supporting Scottish troops.

Banpocun   (Pan-p'o-tsun)   [bahn-po-tsoon]

Banpocun, near modern Xi'an (Sian), in Shaanxi (Shensi) province, northern China, was the site of a large settlement occupied (c.4100–3600 BC) during the Painted Pottery, or Yangshao (Yang-shao) phase of the Neolithic in China (see CHINESE ARCHAEOLOGY). Although only a small portion of the site has been excavated, about 50 separate dwellings have been found, along with more than 100 burials nearby. Originally excavated in 1954–57, much of the site has been preserved as a museum and is open to public view.   CHARLES E. DEWAR

banteng

The male banteng, B. banteng, has a darker coat than a female, whose hide is reddish brown. Domesticated bantengs are called Bali cattle.

The banteng, *Bos banteng,* is a wild ox belonging to the family Bovidae, order Artiodactyla; this family includes other wild and domestic CATTLE. The banteng is about 2 m (6.5 ft) long and 1.2 to 1.5 m (4 to 5 ft) tall at the shoulder. It has slender, curved horns and a black to reddish brown coat. These shy cattle roam in herds through Southeast Asian lowlands and forested hills eating grass, bamboo shoots, and other plants. Some have been domesticated.   EVERETT SENTMAN

Banting, Sir Frederick G.

Canadian physician Sir Frederick Grant Banting, b. Alliston, Ontario, Nov. 14, 1891, d. Feb. 21, 1941, extracted, with Charles H. BEST, the hormone INSULIN from the pancreas, making possible the treatment of DIABETES mellitus, a disease in which an abnormal buildup of glucose takes place in the body. Earlier work had shown that the pancreas produced a substance that regulates glucose metabolism. In 1922, Banting and Best successfully isolated this substance, insulin, from the islets of Langerhans in the pancreas. Insulin was given to diabetic dogs and restored their health. Insulin also proved effective in treating human diabetes mellitus. Banting was a corecipient of the 1923 Nobel Prize for physiology or medicine.

Bibliography: Abbott, David, ed., *The Biographical Dictionary of Scientists: Biologists* (1985).

Bantu   [ban'-too]

Bantu, meaning "the people," is the name of a major linguistic group in Africa. In Africa to the south of a line drawn roughly from Douala, Cameroon, on the Atlantic coast to Kenya's Tana River on the Indian Ocean, more than 90 million people speak Bantu languages, which number nearly 700 and include numerous dialects.

Linguists have tried to explain the enormous geographical spread along with the considerable degree of linguistic convergence in Bantu grammar and vocabulary. According to one theory, the ultimate source of the Bantu people was in the central Benue Valley in eastern Nigeria. Migration then took Bantu speakers southward and eastward into the Congo Basin and ultimately across the continent. Another theory is that their origins were in the north, perhaps central Cameroon or the Central African Republic. From there a major center was established in the LUBA country of northern Shaba, Zaire, in an area of light woodland. Gradually, areas of higher rainfall were colonized as the Bantu speakers, who subsisted mainly by fishing and agriculture, spread south and east of the equatorial forest.

Archaeological evidence for the latter part of the last millennium BC points to expansion by Iron Age invaders cultivating sorghum and millet at the expense of indigenous Late Stone Age hunter-gatherers. At least by the 5th century AD the invaders, presumably Bantu speakers, had brought the Iron Age as far south as Swaziland and, by the 9th century, into northern Namibia. Archaeologists generally agree that the ancestors of such Bantu speakers as the Kalanga, Karanga, and Venda achieved a peak of material cultural development in the 10th–15th centuries and built the elegant structures, terraces, pits, and fortresses (including the ZIMBABWE RUINS) that appear across Zimbabwe into Botswana and at MAPUNGUBWE in the Transvaal.   RICHARD P. WERBNER

Bibliography: Hammond-Tooke, W. D., ed., *The Bantu-Speaking Peoples of Southern Africa* (1974; repr. 1980); Vasina, J., *Paths in the Rainforests* (1990).

See also: AFRICAN LANGUAGES; AFRICAN PREHISTORY.

Banville, Théodore de   [bahn-veel']

Théodore Faullain de Banville, b. Mar. 14, 1823, d. Mar. 13, 1891, was a French poet, dramatist, and member of the PARNASSIAN movement. His verse, particularly in the volumes *Les Cariatides* (The Caryatids, 1842) and *Odes funambulesques* (Fantastic Odes, 1857), shows his skill with a new style of French versification. He wrote a valuable treatise on poetics,

Petit traité de poésie française (Small Treatise Concerning French Poetry, 1872). He was also a critic, principally of theater, noted for his witty observations. His *Ballades* (1873) was translated in 1913, and his most famous play, *Gringoire* (1866), was produced in 1888.

banyan

The banyan, F. benghalensis, sacred to Hindus, may shade a huge area beneath its canopy. Secondary, supporting trunks are formed by aerial roots growing from the branches. The paired, edible figs (bottom right) are about 1.25 cm (0.5 in) in diameter.

The banyan, *Ficus benghalensis,* is a large fig tree belonging to the mulberry family, Moraceae. It grows in India and Bangladesh and is held sacred in both places. The tree begins life as an epiphyte on a host tree, gathering its nourishment and water from the air. As it grows, its lateral branches send down aerial supporting roots that become absorbing roots when they reach the ground. Eventually, the host tree is smothered as the banyan continues to send out more branches and roots. The mature banyan's canopy may cover an area more than 300 m (1,000 ft) in diameter. The stems below the canopy form a kind of columned room, sometimes used as a market shelter by merchants called *banians* in India. The leathery, evergreen leaves are up to 20 cm (8 in) long. The reddish figs are eaten by birds and bats.   HUGH M. RAUP

Banzer Suárez, Hugo   [bahn-sair' swah'-res, oo'-goh]

Gen. Hugo Banzer Suárez, b. May 10, 1926, served as president of Bolivia from 1971 to 1978. Director of the Military College from 1969 to 1971, he rose to power in a military coup that ousted Juan José Torres. Banzer himself was overthrown by the military in 1978; he unsuccessfully sought reelection in 1979 and 1980.

Bao Dai, Emperor of Annam   [bow dy]

Bao Dai, b. Oct. 22, 1913, was emperor of France's Indochinese protectorate of ANNAM (now part of Vietnam) from 1925 to 1945. During World War II he was forced to collaborate with the Japanese occupation forces. He abdicated in 1945 under pressure from the nationalist-Communist leader HO CHI MINH. Later made (1949) Vietnam's chief of state by France, he was deposed in 1955, when NGO DINH DIEM became South Vietnam's president.   RICHARD BUTWELL

Bibliography: Fall, Bernard, *The Two Vietnams: A Political and Military Analysis,* 2d ed. (1967; repr. 1985); Marr, David G., *Vietnamese Tradition on Trial, 1920 to 1945* (1981).

baobab   [bow'-bab]

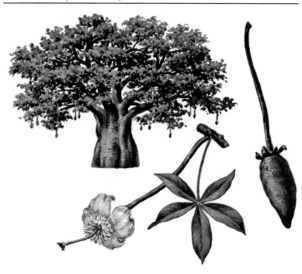

Baobab, A. digitata, one of the largest trees in the world, is one of the few trees found on the African savanna. It has compound leaves, fragrant flowers, and a woody, elongated fruit.

The baobab tree, *Adansonia digitata,* is one of the most unusual deciduous trees of Africa. The interior of its trunk, which may reach 9 m (30 ft) in diameter, and the lower branches are soft and spongy and can store large quantities of water. Baobabs are specially adapted for long dry seasons. They are leafless during this time of year, thus reducing transpiration, or water loss. The baobab is an extremely slow-growing tree, reaching up to 18 m (60 ft) in height, and giant specimens may be several thousand years old. Pollination of the flowers is performed by bats. Many animals use the baobab for food and shelter.

baptism

Baptism is a SACRAMENT of the Christian church in which candidates are immersed in water or water is poured over them in the name of the Father, Son, and Holy Spirit. It is derived from the practice of John the Baptist, who baptized Jesus, and probably from the Jewish *tebilah* (a ritual bath). Matthew 28:19 calls upon Christians to make disciples and to baptize them.

In the early church, baptism was administered after a period of preparation (catechumenate), preferably at Easter. It was performed in conjunction with the rites later called confirmation and Eucharist. The effects of baptism were believed

The baptism of Christ, as portrayed in this early fresco, shows Christ being immersed in the River Jordan by John the Baptist. A dove, symbolizing the Holy Spirit, hovers overhead, and angels watch.

to be union with Jesus in his death and resurrection, forgiveness of sin, the gift of the Holy Spirit, membership in the church, and rebirth to new life in Christ. Some scholars believe infants were included among the candidates from the beginning; others believe that infant baptism began in the 3d century. Today Baptists and Disciples of Christ do not practice infant baptism and do insist on immersion. Most other churches baptize infants and permit the pouring of water. A few Protestant groups, such as the Quakers, reject outward baptism altogether. The Christian rite is in some ways similar to rites of purification used in other religions.

L. L. MITCHELL

Bibliography: Beasley-Murray, G. R., *Baptism in the New Testament* (1973); Eastman, A. Theodore, *The Baptizing Community* (1982); Martin, Francis, *Baptism in the Holy Spirit: A Scriptural Foundation* (1986); Marty, Martin, *Baptism* (1977); Schmemann, Alexander, *Of Water and the Spirit: A Liturgical Study of Baptism* (1974); Wainwright, Geoffrey, *Christian Initiation* (1969).

baptistery

A baptistery is a building adjacent or attached to a church, or sometimes a chamber within a church, in which the ritual of baptism takes place. Baptisteries probably derived their form from ancient Greek and Roman *tholoi*, or round temples, such as the Temple of the Vestal Virgins in the Roman Forum. One of the oldest surviving examples is the domed octagonal baptistery adjoining the basilica of Saint John in the Lateran in Rome. Built during the reign (430–40) of Pope Sixtus III and subsequently altered many times, the building nevertheless was the prototypical baptistery for many centuries. Since total immersion was widely practiced at this time, the central fea-

The Florence Baptistery, an octagonal Romanesque structure dedicated to St. John the Baptist, is most famous for its outstanding gilded bronze doors, the great "Gates of Paradise" (1424–52) by Lorenzo Ghiberti, which depict ten scenes from the Old Testament.

ture was usually a large basin or pool directly beneath the dome. As affusion (pouring water over the head) replaced immersion in some baptismal rites, the basins became much smaller, were usually placed on pedestal bases, and were called baptismal FONTS.

The octagonal form for baptisteries persisted as the preferred one through the Romanesque and Gothic periods, particularly in Italy. The Florence Baptistery (consecrated in 1059) is perhaps the best known: sheathed in white marble with green marble trim, the large slant-roofed octagon is directly opposite the central door of the Duomo (Cathedral), a symbolic reminder that baptism is the first rite of Christian life. Inside the baptistery a huge octagonal dome is revealed, completely covered with mosaics, part of an exceedingly rich decorative scheme.

As baptismal practices became simplified, separate baptisteries became a rarity. They survive most frequently today as a font placed near the church door, although some contemporary churches include separate baptisteries. In churches of religious groups that practice baptismal immersion, the basin or pool is usually placed prominently behind the chancel.

Bibliography: Davies, John G., *The Architectural Setting of Baptism* (1962); Krautheimer, Richard, *Early Christian and Byzantine Architecture* (1965); Smith, Christine, *The Baptistery of Pisa* (1978).

Baptists

The Baptists form one of the largest Protestant denominations, with worldwide membership of nearly 35 million. The following distinguish the Baptists from other Protestant communions: (1) their insistence on baptism of adult believers only; (2) their concern for freedom of speech and conscience and for freedom from interference by any civil or ecclesiastical authority; (3) the primacy they seek to give to Scripture in matters of faith, doctrine, and morals; and (4) the authority they give to the congregation in church affairs.

The forerunners of present-day Baptists were the ANABAPTISTS of the REFORMATION period. Some Anabaptist congregations were settled in Holland in the early 17th century when groups of Puritan Independents, or Congregationalists, fled from England to Holland. Influenced by the Anabaptists, some of these Independents were persuaded that Christian baptism was appropriate only for adults with a personal faith and commitment. Returning to England, this group formed the first Baptist congregation in 1611. Shortly thereafter, Roger WILLIAMS formed (1639) the first Baptist congregation in Providence, R.I. The Baptists grew rapidly in the United States. The democratic, informal, Scripture-centered, relatively untheological mode of Baptist service was ideal for any unsettled, rural, or frontier situation. Thus the South, the Midwest, and the Far West were heavily populated—more than were the Northeast or the Middle Atlantic—by Baptists, a pattern that remains true to this day.

Baptists view the Christian life as one of personal faith and of serious dedication to live according to the highest Christian precepts. Each person is thus to be born again, converted into a new life, and gathered into the church community. For Baptists, the church is essentially the result of conversion and of GRACE, a gathered community of committed believers; it is not the mother of Christian experience or the source (rather than the effect) of grace, as in the Catholic tradition. The church is, therefore, holy only because the faith and life of its people are holy; conceptually, the church has in itself (at least in principle) no authority over its members, over their freedom of conscience, or over their churchly affairs.

More than most church groups, Baptists have manifested startlingly opposite characteristics in their history. Because of their emphasis on the Bible, on a strict puritan, or Victorian, ethic, and on the absolute necessity of personal faith and personal holiness, most Baptists around the world have remained conservative, even fundamentalist, in matters of both faith and morals (see FUNDAMENTALISM). They have been impatient with theological compromises with science, with modern philosophy, and with liberal politics. The pure gospel, that is, the Bible interpreted literally, traditional Baptist principles, and a pure Christian ethic are fundamentals that many Baptist groups will not relinquish. For this reason, many Baptist conventions still refuse to join the ecumenical movement in any official way. They have also largely ignored the social gospel (a concern for establishing social justice in political, social, and economic life) while retaining a deep loyalty to the efficacy of individualistic revivalism. On the other hand, because of their emphasis on freedom of conscience and of personal believing, on the importance of Christian life and works rather than on ritual, on their distaste for creeds, dogmas, and ecclesiastical authority, some Baptists have been leaders in theological and social liberalism. Many Baptist seminaries and churches are known for their liberal theology, style of worship, and social attitudes; Baptists were consistently important leaders in establishing the ecumenical movement of the early 20th century. In those controversies that have dominated 20th-century American religion—the modernist-fundamentalist, the social gospel–individualist, and the ecumenical-exclusivist controversies—Baptists have appeared in leading roles on both sides.

LANGDON GILKEY

Bibliography: Brackney, W., *Baptists* (1988); Richards, W., *The Winds of Doctrine: The Origin and Development of Southern Baptist Theology* (1991); Torbet, R. G., *A History of the Baptists*, rev. ed. (1973); Tull, J. E., *Shapers of Baptist Thought* (1972).

bar code

A bar code is a pattern of bars and lines that appears on many retail items. When an item is purchased, its code is scanned by a laser that ''reads'' the code as a number sequence into a central computer (see SCANNING). The computer identifies the item in its database, determines the current price, and relays the data to the cash register. In North America, bar codes are administered by the Universal Product Code (UPC) Council. Some UPC versions, when preceded by a zero symbol, can be scanned in the European Article Numbering (EAN) bar-code system, in use in more than 65 other nations. Similar codes have been developed for warehouses, hospitals, and elsewhere, and are also employed in some passport systems.

Bar Harbor

The town of Bar Harbor (1990 pop., 4,443), on Mount Desert Island in southeast Maine, was settled in 1763 and became a famous 19th-century resort. In 1947 most of the town was destroyed by fire. Acadia National Park is located nearby.

Bar Kochba [bar kohk'-buh]

Bar Kochba, also known as Simeon ben Koseva, d. AD 135, was the leader of the Jewish rebellion against Rome, in AD 132–35. Although most contemporary scholars considered a revolt futile, Rabbi AKIBA BEN JOSEPH saw in him ''the Son of the Star'' (Bar Kochba) and supported the uprising. The rebels avoided open battles, fighting instead from underground fortifications. Jerusalem was conquered. Emperor HADRIAN recalled Severus from Britain to oppose Bar Kochba. After a lengthy and heroic defense, the rebellion failed. Fifty fortresses and a thousand villages were destroyed; Jerusalem was renamed Aelia Capitolina (Hadrian's name was Aelius); and a temple to Jupiter was built on the ruins of Solomon's Temple. Bar Kochba died in battle.

NAHUM N. GLATZER

Bibliography: Yadin, Yigael, *Bar-Kokhba* (1971).

bar mitzvah

A bar mitzvah (''son of the commandment'') is a male Jew who has reached his 13th birthday and is recognized as fully responsible for his own religious and moral actions. A bat (or bas) mitzvah is the corresponding female Jew. A rite in the synagogue, which is also commonly referred to as bar mitzvah, marks the attainment of the status of bar mitzvah. In Conservative and Reform Judaism, a similar rite is used for the bat mitzvah as well. When reaching puberty, a young man or woman is called upon to read a prophetic passage from Scripture to the synagogue congregation. Thereupon, he or she

is recognized as a full member of the congregation, able to count as a member of the required quorum of ten. On that occasion the parents say a blessing: ''Blessed is God who has now freed me from bearing full responsibility for this person.'' In the 19th century, Reform Judaism created the rite of confirmation instead of, or in addition to, the bar mitzvah. It is held on the festival of Shavuoth, or Pentecost, which marks the revelation of the Torah. This rite is now common in Reform and Conservative synagogues.

JACOB NEUSNER

Bibliography: Schoenfeld, Stuart, et al., *Bar Mitzvah* (1985).

Bar Sauma, Rabban

Rabban Bar Sauma, a Nestorian Christian monk, b. Beijing (Peking), c.1220, d. Baghdad, 1294, traveled (1287–88) to Europe at the direction of the Mongol emperor KUBLAI KHAN. He visited Rome, Genoa, and Florence and met England's Edward I and France's Philip IV, as well as Pope Nicholas IV. In many respects he was the Asian counterpart of Marco POLO.

RICHARD BUTWELL

Bibliography: Budge, E. A. T. W., *The Monks of Kublai Khan, Emperor of China* (1928; repr. 1973).

Bara, Theda

Theda Bara, an American star of the silent screen, achieved widespread popularity for her many roles portraying a coldhearted seductress. During her 5-year screen contract, she appeared in about 40 films, including Carmen *(1915),* Romeo and Juliet *(1916),* Cleopatra *(1917), and* Salome *(1918). After the expiration of her contract in 1919 she returned to the stage and made only a few later films.*

Theda Bara was the stage name of Theodosia Goodman, b. Cincinnati, Ohio, July 20, 1890, d. Apr. 7, 1955, who was molded by Hollywood into the screen's first sex symbol. She was hired by the producer William Fox to play a femme fatale in the silent film *A Fool There Was* (1915) and was immediately dubbed ''the vamp.'' A vast publicity campaign continued to promote this image. Even after leaving Hollywood in 1920, she could not escape typecasting. Bara retired from show business in the late 1920s.

Barabbas [buh-rab'-uhs]

In the Bible, Barabbas was the prisoner who, by popular choice of the Jews, was released instead of Christ (Matt. 27, Mark 15, Luke 23, John 18). The Roman governor customarily granted one such pardon each year at Passover time.

Baraga, Frederick [bahr'-uh-guh]

Frederick Baraga, b. June 29, 1797, d. Jan. 19, 1868, known as the Apostle of the Ottawas and Chippewas, was a Slovenian-born Catholic missionary to the Indians in the Great Lakes region. Educated in Ljubljana and at the University of Vienna, he sought ordination to the priesthood and volunteered for missionary work in the United States. Baraga had great talent with languages, and shortly after reaching Cincinnati in 1831 he began mastering the Ottawa dialect of the Algonquian tongue. In that year he was assigned to an Ottawa town at Harbor Springs, near the tip of Michigan's lower peninsula. He went on to found missions at Grand Rapids and Keweenaw Bay, Mich., and La Pointe, Wisc. Traveling by foot and by canoe, he endured great hardships to reach all the Indians of the area. As whites came into the Keweenaw Bay area to mine copper, he ministered to them as well.

In 1836 and again in 1853 Baraga made trips to Europe, where he travelled widely, raising funds and recruiting priests to work in the Great Lakes missions. In 1853 he was made bishop and vicar-apostolic of Upper Michigan, and in 1865 he became the first bishop of Marquette, Mich. Baraga was the author (1850) of the first grammar of the Ojibwa (Chippewa) language, and of a comprehensive Ojibwa dictionary (1853).   HENRY WARNER BOWDEN

Bibliography: Gregorich, J., *The Apostle of the Chippewas* (1932).

Baraka, Imamu Amiri   [bah-rah'-kah, ee-mah'-moo ah-mee'-ree]

Imamu Amiri Baraka, formerly LeRoi Jones, is an American playwright and poet whose works express hostility toward and mistrust of white society. The politically active Baraka founded the Black Community Development and Defense Organization, a Muslim group, and was a leader of the National Black Political Caucus.

A poet, playwright, and community leader, Imamu Amiri Baraka, originally named Everett LeRoi Jones, b. Newark, N.J., Oct. 7, 1934, is best known for his play *Dutchman* (1964), which depicts blacks and whites in a shocking symbolic confrontation. The play won a 1964 Obie Award. As LeRoi Jones, Baraka produced his first major work, an accomplished volume of poetry, *Preface to a Twenty-Volume Suicide Note* (1961). His increasingly militant stance was reflected in two plays, *The Slave* and *The Toilet*, both produced Off Broadway in 1965. In 1968 he discarded his ''slave name'' for a Muslim one and assumed leadership of his own black Muslim organization, Kawaida, dedicated to coalescing black power in Newark. His *The Autobiography of LeRoi Jones* was published in 1984.

Bibliography: Bigsby, C. W. E., ed., *The Black American Writer*, vol. 2 (1969); Clurman, H., *The Naked Image: Observations on the Modern Theatre* (1966); Cruse, H., *The Crisis of the Negro Intellectual* (1967); Harris, W. J., *The Poetry and Politics of Amiri Baraka* (1987).

Baranov, Aleksandr Andreyevich   [buh-rah'-nawf, ahl-ik-sahn'-dur ahn-dray'-uh-vich]

Aleksandr Andreyevich Baranov, b. 1747, d. Apr. 28, 1819, was head of the RUSSIAN-AMERICAN COMPANY and the first governor (1799–1818) of Russian Alaska. Baranov Island is named after him. A successful fur trader, he reached Alaska in 1790, extended the Russian settlements, and sold furs to the United States, to the Spanish in California and Manila, and to Guangzhou (Canton), China. In 1809, Baranov's new settlement at Sitka replaced Kodiak as the trading capital.

Bibliography: Chevigny, H., *Lord of Alaska* (1942; repr. 1970); Tikhmenov, P. A., et al., eds., *History of the Russian-American Company*, trans. by D. Krenov (1979).

Bárány, Robert   [bah'-rahn-ee]

Robert Bárány, b. Apr. 22, 1876, d. Apr. 8, 1936, was an Austrian physician who pioneered work on the function of the inner ear in maintaining balance. He was awarded the 1914 Nobel Prize for physiology or medicine ''for his work on the physiology and pathology of the vestibular apparatus.'' Bárány's experiments, which demonstrated how fluid movement affects vestibular organs in the inner ear's semicircular canals and causes changes in the sense of equilibrium, resulted in improved methods of diagnosing and treating inner ear disorders. Bárány became associated with the University of Uppsala, Sweden, in 1917 and wrote several textbooks.

Barbados

Barbados is an independent country, formerly a British colony, and the most easterly island of the West Indies. Its capital and only port of entry is BRIDGETOWN.

The island is underlain with folded sedimentary deposits, and a surface layer of coral attains 90 m (300 ft) in thickness. In the northeastern parts, erosion has exposed rugged ridges

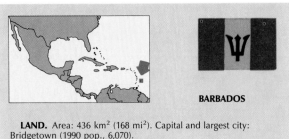

BARBADOS

LAND. Area: 436 km² (168 mi²). Capital and largest city: Bridgetown (1990 pop., 6,070).

PEOPLE. Population (1992): 259,000; density (1992): 594 per km² (1,542 per mi²). Distribution (1992): 42% urban, 58% rural. Annual growth (1991): 0.8%. Official language: English. Major religions: Anglicanism, Pentecostalism, Methodism.

EDUCATION AND HEALTH. Literacy (1985): 98%. Universities: (1994): 1. Hospital beds (1987): 2,111. Physicians (1986): 243. Life expectancy (1990–95): women—77.9; men—72.9. Infant mortality (1991): 11.8 per 1,000 live births.

ECONOMY. GNP (1991): $1.8 billion; $7,000 per capita. Labor distribution (1991): commerce and services—74.5%; manufacturing and construction—19.9%. Foreign trade (1991): imports—$1.4 billion; exports—$412 million; principal trade partners—United States, Caribbean Community, Britain. Currency: 1 Barbadian dollar = 100 cents.

GOVERNMENT. Type: independent state within Commonwealth of Nations. Legislature: Parliament. Political subdivisions: 11 parishes, Bridgetown.

COMMUNICATIONS. Railroads (1995): none. Roads (1990): 1,573 km (977 mi) total. Major ports: 1. Major airfields: 1.

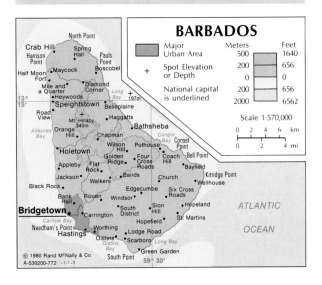

BARBADOS

	Major Urban Area	Meters	Feet
		500	1640
+	Spot Elevation or Depth	200	656
		0	0
	National capital is underlined	200	656
		2000	6562

Scale 1:570,000

0 2 4 6 km
0   2   4 mi

North Point
Crab Hill
Harrison   Spring   Pauls
Point   Hall   Point
Half Moon   Maycock   Boscobel
Fort
Mile and   Diamond
a Quarter   Corner   Long   197m
Heywoods   Bay
13°
15'   Speightstown   Belleplaine
Road
View   Haggatts
Mt. Hillaby   Bathsheba
340m
Alleynes   Orange
Bay   Hill   Chapman   Conset
Congor   Bay   Point
Wilson   Pothouse
Holetown   Hill   Four   Coach   Bell Point
Golden   Cross   Hill
Appleby   Flat   Ridge   Roads
Jackson   Rock   Bairds   Church   Bayfield
Kitridge Point
Walkers   Edgecumbe   Wellhouse
Black Rock   Six Cross
Bank   Rouen   Windsor   Roads
Hall   Sion
Carrington   South   Hill   Hopeland
Bridgetown   District   St. Martins
Needham's Point   Worthing   Hopefield
Hastings   Lodge Road
Oistins   Scarboro   Long Bay
Bay   Green Garden
© 1980 Rand McNally & Co.   South Point
A-530200-772   59° 30'

ATLANTIC

OCEAN

and ravines. The climate is warm and pleasant. The average annual temperature is about 27° C (80° F), and little daily or annual variation occurs. A dry season (from December to May) alternates with a wet season. The average annual rainfall is about 1,500 mm (60 in).

Barbados is one of the world's most densely populated countries. Nearly 90% of the island's population is black.

The production of sugarcane and its by-products, molasses and rum, long a mainstay of the Barbadian economy, has been replaced by tourism as the chief industry. The development of light industry and the diversification of agriculture have been encouraged by the government.

Barbados was settled by English colonists in 1627. To work the sugarcane plantations, slaves were brought from Africa, a practice abolished throughout the British Empire in 1834. Dominance by a small group of British landowners continued, and a political rights movement began, resulting in the founding of the Barbados Labour party (BLP) in 1938 and an offshoot, the Democratic Labour party (DLP), in 1955. Barbados became independent on Nov. 30, 1966. Errol Barrow of the DLP, the first premier, was succeeded by Tom Adams of the BLP, who held office from 1976 until his death in 1985. The DLP returned to power under Barrow (1986–87) and Lloyd Erskine Sandiford (1987–94). Owen Arthur of the BLP became premier after elections in 1994.   THOMAS D. BOSWELL

Bibliography: Davis, K., *Cross and Crown in Barbados* (1983); Levy, C., *Emancipation, Sugar, and Federalism* (1980); Payne, A. J., and Sutton, P. K., eds., *Dependency under Challenge: The Political Economy of the Commonwealth Caribbean* (1984).

Barbados cherry

The Barbados cherry, *Malpighia glabra,* is a shrub or small tree in the family Malpighiaceae. Native to the West Indies, it is found from southern Texas to South America and grows up to 4.6 m (15 ft) tall. The ovate leaves are shiny, leathery, and green, and pale pink to rose-colored flowers bloom throughout the summer. The red fruits are cherrylike, with an acid flavor. Because the fruits have a high vitamin C content, the pulp is used for beverages and in making preserves.

Barbari, Jacopo de'   [bahr'-bahr-ee, yah'-koh-po day]

Jacopo de'Barbari, *c.*1440–*c.*1516, was a well-known painter, engraver, and designer of woodcuts during the Italian Renaissance. He was the first major Italian artist to travel to Germany and the Netherlands. His correspondence with Albrecht Dürer, who knew and admired him, contains the information that Jacopo was born in Venice and that he was active there as a painter and engraver in the late 1490s. Jacopo is believed to have designed the large, topographical woodcut *View of Venice* (1498–1500). Between 1500 and 1508 he is recorded as working in Germany for Holy Roman Emperor Maximilian I, Frederick III (the Wise), elector of Saxony, and others. During this time Dürer and Jacopo influenced one another, as is evident in Jacopo's painting, for example, in *Still Life with Partridge and Iron Gauntlet* (1504; Alte Pinakothek, Munich), and his engravings, such as *St. Catherine* (*c.*1501–03), *Judith with the Head of Holofernes* (*c.*1501–03), and *Satyr's Family* (*c.*1503–04).

After 1509, Jacopo worked in the Netherlands at the humanist court of Margaret of Austria. His Italianate interest in the nude and in mythological subjects influenced the Flemish painters Jan Gossaert (Mabuse) and Bernard van Orley. Jacopo's mark was the caduceus, another sign of his humanist approach.   ALAN P. DARR

Bibliography: Borenius, Tancred, *Four Early Italian Engravers* (1923); Levenson, Jay, and Oberhuber, Konrad, *Early Italian Engravings from the National Gallery of Art* (1973).

Barbary ape

The barbary ape, so called since ancient times, is a monkey, not an ape. More precisely, it is a MACAQUE, *Macaca sylvana.* The Barbary ape is 38–76 cm (15–30 in) long and weighs up

The Barbary ape, M. sylvana, *the only wild monkey existing in Europe, was probably brought from Africa by Arabs during the Middle Ages.*

to 13 kg (28 lb). The thick fur is yellowish brown to black, and the hairless face is whitish pink. Barbary apes are the only wild monkeys now living in Europe; they occupy caves on the Rock of Gibraltar. They also live in rocky areas of Morocco and Algeria. The young are usually born singly. The life span in captivity is more than 30 years.   EVERETT SENTMAN

Barbary States

The Barbary States is a former name for the coastal region of North Africa extending from the Atlantic Ocean to Egypt and comprising the present states of Morocco, Algeria, Tunisia, and Libya. The name is derived from the BERBERS, the oldest known inhabitants of the region.

In ancient times, parts of the region were colonized by the Phoenicians, who founded CARTHAGE, and the Greeks, who established CYRENE. By the middle of the 1st century AD the area was in Roman hands. It remained Roman until the VANDALS invaded in the 5th century, was briefly recovered (533–34) by the Eastern Roman (Byzantine) Empire, and was overrun by the Muslim Arabs in the 7th century.

In the 16th century the Arab principalities of North Africa came under the nominal rule of the Ottoman Empire. They were in fact conquered for Turkey by a corsair, or pirate, known as Barbarossa (d. 1546) to prevent their falling to Christian Spain. Thereafter, the Barbary States became a base for piracy against European shipping in the Mediterranean. The booty—and tribute paid to gain immunity from attacks—were the chief source of revenue for the local rulers.

In 1801 the newly independent United States, whose ships had also been attacked, launched the TRIPOLITAN WAR (1800–05) against Tripoli (now Libya). In 1815 the United States also fought against Algiers, which was then bombarded by an Anglo-Dutch fleet (1816). Nevertheless, it was not until the French conquest (1830) of Algeria that the piracy was effectively ended. Subsequently, the entire region came under colonial rule (by France and Italy) until the mid-20th century.

Bibliography: Hopkins, J. F., *Medieval Muslim Government in Barbary* (1958); Irwin, Ray W., *Diplomatic Relations of the U.S. with the Barbary Powers, 1776–1816* (1931; repr. 1971).

barbed wire

Barbed wire is a form of cattle fencing made of steel wire strands into which sharp wire barbs are twisted or welded. It is also used in warfare as a defense against the advance of infantry units.

Homesteaders settling the western plains of the United States in the 19th century found that wood for fencing was scarce and, in any case, ineffective in protecting fields against grazing cattle herds. Thorned shrubs such as the osage orange were often planted as cattle-breaks, but an immediately effective fence could be created by incorporating jagged bits of metal in a wire strand. In 1874, Joseph F. Glidden, an Illinois farmer, patented the type of barbed wire still used. In

1885 alone, about 400 patents were issued for barbed wire and for machines and other devices associated with the new industry. In the decade 1875–85 the manufacture of barbed wire jumped from 272 to 91,000 metric tons (300 to 100,000 U.S. tons). Its widespread use, often violently opposed by cattle ranchers, ended the era of the open range in the West.

Bibliography: McCallum, Henry and Frances, *The Wire That Fenced the West* (1965; repr. 1985).

barbel [bahr'-bul]

Barbels are freshwater fish in the CARP family, Cyprinidae, and are found in European rivers. *Barbus barbus* is the true barbel, although more than 100 species in the genus *Barbus* can be called barbel. The common name refers to the four fleshy tentacles that protrude from the mouth. These bear taste buds that enable the fish to detect bottom-dwelling animals in rivers. Like most minnows, they spawn in the spring over gravel in shallow water.

Barbels lay an average of 9,000 eggs and usually reach a weight of 3 kg (6.5 lb) and a length of 75 cm (30 in). Although not good to eat, they are often sought after by anglers for their sporting qualities.

barber

A barber earns a living by cutting and grooming hair and shaving beards. Barbering is an ancient occupation, allied at one time with surgery. (The striped red-and-white barber's pole signifies blood and bandages.)

History. The early barbers were those personal servants of ancient rulers and nobility who attended to the appearance, clothing, and armor of their masters. The biblical prophet Ezekiel spoke of the use of a barber's razor, probably one made of bronze. References to barbers in ancient Egyptian writings and wall paintings indicate their role in preparing the shaved scalps favored by the Egyptians. Barbershops were operated in some ancient Greek city-states, notably Athens, where a carefully curled and shaped beard was a mark of gentility and status. The Roman legions enlisted barbers, whose duties in the field included care of the wounded.

By the Middle Ages, European barbers were performing surgery and other bloodletting medical tasks scorned by physicians. In France there were barber-surgeons on the faculty of the University of Paris in the early 1500s. Ambroise PARÉ, the father of modern surgery, began his career as a barber. By the 19th century, however, surgery had become a medical specialty and barbers were confined to cutting hair.

Current American Barbering. The United States has about 150,000 barbers, most of whom have been licensed by state examining boards. To become a barber, it is necessary to attend an accredited school for six months to a year; to serve, in some states, as an apprentice barber for one or two years; and to pass examinations that test practical as well as theoretical skill. Although shops are not as crowded as they were in the days of the twice-monthly haircut, the industry in the U.S. earns more than $1 billion annually.

Bibliography: Thorpe, Sidney C., *The Practice and Science of Standard Barbering*, rev. ed. (1967).

Barber, Samuel

Samuel Barber, b. West Chester, Pa., Mar. 9, 1910, d. Jan. 23, 1981, was a prominent modern American composer. After studying at the Curtis Institute of Music in Philadelphia, he attracted notice in 1933 with his overture to *The School for Scandal*. In 1935 his Symphony no. 1 (in one movement) was performed in Rome and at the Salzburg Festival (the first work by an American to be played there). Arturo Toscanini conducted Barber's Adagio for Strings (based on the slow movement of his String Quartet) and First Essay for Orchestra with the NBC Symphony in 1938. In 1958, Barber won a Pulitzer Prize in music for his opera *Vanessa* (premiere by the Metropolitan Opera, New York City) and again in 1963 for his Piano Concerto. His major works include *Capricorn* Concerto

Although the American composer Samuel Barber assimilated some aspects of modernism, his lyrical style retained traditional elements of melodic structure. Many of his compositions were inspired by literature; his two Essays for Orchestra (1938, 1942) are musical analogues of the literary form.

(1944), *Knoxville: Summer of 1915* (1948) for soprano and orchestra, and *Prayers of Kierkegaard* (1954) for soprano, chorus, and orchestra. He also wrote the opera *Antony and Cleopatra* for the opening of the new Metropolitan Opera at Lincoln Center in 1966. Barber's music is characterized by full-blooded lyricism, rich orchestration, and idiomatic writing for voices and instruments.   DAVID EWEN

Bibliography: Broder, Nathan, *Samuel Barber* (1954; repr. 1985); Ewen, David, ed., *The New Book of Modern Composers* (1967).

Barber of Seville, The

Although the premiere of Gioacchino Rossini's opera buffa *The Barber of Seville*, at the Argentina Theater in Rome on Feb. 20, 1816, was far from successful, the work won popularity within a short time and has retained it to this day. Young Rosina, attractive and desirable as a potential heiress, is jealously kept under lock and key by her guardian, Doctor Bartolo, who plans to marry her himself. In act 1 the dashing Count Almaviva, who has seen the girl in Madrid and pursued her to Seville, tries to gain access to Rosina and turns for advice to the resourceful Figaro, Seville's most popular barber, who is only too willing—on receipt of bonus—to further the count's intrigues.

Not only does Bartolo oppose Almaviva and Figaro, but Bartolo's shifty music master, Don Basilio, advises him to spread slander about Almaviva. The project goes forward. First, Almaviva gains entrance to Bartolo's house by posing as a military man assigned to garrison duty. The ruse does not work. Then he tries to pass himself off as a music master (act 2) come in place of the allegedly indisposed Don Basilio. This plan also fails when Almaviva is discovered caressing his pupil, Rosina. An elopement is planned as the last resort, but matters are finally resolved happily and the lovers are married.

The Barber of Seville is one of the few great comic operas, along with Mozart's *The Marriage of Figaro*, Donizetti's *Don Pasquale*, Verdi's *Falstaff*, and Richard Strauss's *Der Rosenkavalier*. Lacking the warmth and sentiment of other masterpieces, however, it has survived by virtue of such brilliant individual numbers as Figaro's "Largo al factotum" and Rosina's "Una voce poco fa" and by its sparkling ensembles. The libretto, by Cesare Sterbini, is based on the first play of a trilogy by the French playwright Caron de BEAUMARCHAIS, about the adventures of Count Almaviva, his countess, and their valet, Figaro, in his youth, maturity, and late years. Mozart triumphed with his setting of the second of these plays, *The Marriage of Figaro*, and in the 20th century, Darius Milhaud adapted the third, *La Mère coupable*. Rossini's *The Barber of Seville* had its American premiere in New York City at the Park Theater on May 3, 1819.

Bibliography: Beyle, Marie Henri (Stendhal), *The Life of Rossini*, trans. by Richard N. Coe (1956; repr. 1970); Toye, F., *Rossini* (1934; repr. 1987); Weinstock, H., *Rossini: A Biography* (1968; repr. 1987).

Barberini Faun   [bahr-bair-ee'-nee]

The Barberini Faun is a Roman marble statue of a sleeping satyr. Dating from about 200 BC, it is a copy of a Hellenistic Greek original by an unknown sculptor. The 2.1-m (7-ft) statue, found between 1624 and 1641 near the Castel Sant' Angelo in Rome, was first displayed in the Palazzo Barberini, but it has been in the Munich Glyptothek since 1820. It was restored by Giovanni Lorenzo Bernini in the 17th century, and by Camillo Pacetti (following Bernini's scheme) in the 19th century, both somewhat incorrectly. Its highly realistic portrayal of a sprawled, nude satyr stirring restlessly in drunken slumber made it immensely popular. Frequently copied, it exerted considerable influence on sculptors from Bernini to Daniel Chester French.

Bibliography: Bieber, Margarete, *The Sculpture of the Hellenistic Age*, rev. ed. (1980); Natalini, Adolfo, *Figures of Stone* (1985); Vermeule, Cornelius, *European Art and the Classical Past* (1964) and *Greek Sculpture and Roman Taste* (1977).

barberry

The barberry is a thorny shrub represented by nearly 500 species of the genus *Berberis* in the barberry family, Berberidaceae. Barberries have simple, alternate leaves, bright yellow flowers, and red, yellow, or black fruit. They make excellent specimen plants and hedges. Some, like the Japanese barberry, *B. thunbergii*, retain their fruits all winter. Approximately 140 different species, forms, and hybrids of barberry have been found to act as alternate hosts for the fungus that causes black stem rust of wheat. Thus, barberries should not be planted in areas where wheat is grown.

barbershop quartet

The American barbershop quartet probably assumed its present form in the late 19th century, when the informal group singing associated with barbershop bonhomie became more formalized and professional quartets became popular. Present-day quartets specialize in songs from the turn of the century, such as "Sweet Adeline" and "Down by the Old Mill Stream." The Society for the Preservation and Encouragement of Barber Shop Quartet Singing in America was founded in 1938.

The barbershop music tradition is an old one. In Europe, barbers were often amateur musicians, and "barber's music" came to mean any rough, extemporaneous music-making.

barbet   [bahr'-bit]

The toucan barbet, Semnornis ramphastinus, *is one of the New World's tiniest barbets, 21 cm (8.3 in) long. It makes its home in tropical forests of the Andes in Ecuador and Colombia.*

The barbet is any of a number of birds of the family Capitonidae. They are small or medium sized, stocky and big headed, heavy billed, and often gaudily colored; many are bright green with contrasting markings of other brilliant hues. Of 72 species, 12 are found in tropical America; the rest inhabit tropical Africa or southern Asia. Forest birds, barbets tend to be sedentary, but they are extremely noisy. They eat both vegetable and animal food and nest in holes; both sexes incubate and care for the young.   WILLIAM A. LUNK

Barbey d'Aurevilly, Jules Amédée   [bahr-bay' dor-vee-yee', zhool ah-may-day']

Jules Barbey d'Aurevilly, b. Nov. 2, 1808, d. Apr. 23, 1889, was a French poet, novelist, literary critic, and dandy perhaps best known for the decadent and satanic short stories included in *The Diaboliques* (1874; Eng. trans., 1925). An impoverished aristocrat noted for his staunch royalist and Catholic views, he successfully blended the realistic and the mystical, equally favoring Balzac and Baudelaire. His other works include *The Anatomy of Dandyism* (1845; Eng. trans., 1928) and such novels as *Bewitched* (1854; Eng. trans., 1928) and *Le Chevalier des Touches* (1864).

Bibliography: Chartier, Armand B., *Barbey d'Aurevilly* (1977); Rogers, Brian G., *The Novels and Stories of Barbey d'Aurevilly* (1967).

Barbirolli, Sir John   [bar-bi-rah'-lee]

Sir John Barbirolli, b. Dec. 2, 1899, d. July 29, 1970, was one of England's most beloved conductors. Born to Italian parents, and originally named Giovanni Battista, Barbirolli grew up in a musical family; his father and grandfather had played violin in the orchestra at La Scala for the world premiere of Verdi's *Otello* (1887). Barbirolli studied cello and conducting and formed his own chamber orchestra in 1925. In 1926 he made his opera debut. His appointments included the Scottish Orchestra (1933–37), the New York Philharmonic (1937–43), and the Hallé Orchestra (beginning 1943). Barbirolli conducted mostly symphonic music but turned again to opera late in his career, making several highly regarded recordings, among these *Madame Butterfly* with Renata Scotto. He was knighted in 1949. Barbirolli was noted for the warmth of his performances and for his excellence in accompanying soloists.

STEPHANIE VON BUCHAU

Bibliography: Atkins, H., and Cotes, P., *The Barbirollis: A Musical Marriage* (1985); Kennedy, M., *Barbirolli* (1971; repr. 1982).

barbiturate

Barbiturates are habit-forming drugs used as sedatives and hypnotics. They are white, crystalline, odorless derivatives of the chemical compound barbituric acid ($C_4H_4N_2O_3$). Medically, these drugs are used to induce sleep, relieve anxiety and neuroses by inducing drowsiness, and control epileptic seizures. Barbiturates are also among the most widely abused drugs, being taken to cause a state of euphoria. Sometimes they are used in suicide attempts.

Barbiturates act to depress the central nervous system. The duration of action depends on how quickly one of the drugs passes through the blood-brain barrier and affects the brain. Long-acting barbiturates such as amobarbital penetrate this barrier slowly and short-acting drugs, such as secobarbital, penetrate faster and are used to alleviate an inability to sleep. Ultrashort barbiturates, such as thiopental, pass through the blood-brain barrier so rapidly that sleep occurs in seconds; these are used as adjuncts to anesthesia.

Side effects of barbiturates include drowsiness and an effect similar to that of an alcoholic hangover. Judgment and motor control are usually impaired, and mood changes (such as depression) may occur. An overdose depresses the respiratory rate and may result in coma and death. Other depressant drugs—such as alcohol, antihistamines, and tranquilizers—if taken simultaneously, increase the effect of barbiturates. The human body develops a tolerance for barbiturates, and withdrawal symptoms (for example, depression, aggressiveness, and irritability) occur once a person who is physically dependent on these drugs stops taking them.

Bibliography: Henningfield, J. E., and Ator, Nancy, *Barbiturates* (1985); Jones, Kenneth L., et al., *Drugs and Alcohol*, 2d ed. (1973); Smith, David, and Wesson, Donald, *Barbiturates: Their Use, Misuse, and Abuse* (1977) and *Uppers and Downers* (1974).

Barbizon school

Théodore Rousseau's Edge of the Forest at Fontainebleau *(1848) exemplifies the Barbizon school's moody, atmospheric approach to landscape painting. The style owed much to the custom of painting outdoors, directly from nature, in order to catch the play of light, especially at sunset. (Louvre, Paris.)*

The term *Barbizon school* refers to a group of French landscape painters active between 1830 and 1880. They include Théodore ROUSSEAU, Charles François DAUBIGNY, Narcisse Virgile DIAZ DE LA PEÑA, and Constant TROYON. Less well known are Jules Dupré, Achille Etna Michallon, and Georges MICHEL. Not all of them actually painted in Barbizon, a village bordering the Fontainbleau forest, about 50 km (30 mi) south of Paris. Dupré made his home in the Oise Valley, and Daubigny lived in Auvers.

The members of the Barbizon school were primarily landscape painters interested in both the look of their native countryside and the moods it evoked. Because they usually painted in restrained hues and often at twilight, their work differs from the classical, mythological scenes based on Nicolas POUSSIN and the bright, deliberately picturesque landscapes of such romantic painters as Eugène DELACROIX.

The Barbizon artists painted outdoors, *en plein air*. Unlike the later impressionists, however, whom they influenced, they usually finished their original sketches in the atelier. An exception was Daubigny, who liked to complete his canvases at the original site, the better to capture coloristic and atmospheric nuances.

The Barbizon school had its roots in the work of such 17th-century Dutch painters as Meindert HOBBEMA and Jacob van RUISDAEL. The English landscapists Richard Parkes BONINGTON and John CONSTABLE were also influential.

Each of the Barbizon painters had a distinctive style and preferred subjects: Rousseau's somber landscapes are often dominated by clumps of dark oaks; Diaz frequently included gypsies and nymphs in his thickly painted, gleaming forests; Troyon's bucolic scenes featured grazing sheep and cattle; and Daubigny, who often painted in a canopied rowboat, produced light-filled river scenes. Two other painters, Camille COROT and Jean François MILLET, are sometimes included in this group because they also painted at Barbizon.

Although the Barbizon painters had the support of the influential critic Théophile Thoré, they were often criticized for the "sketchy" qualities of their canvases, which looked unfinished to the public. At the Paris World Exhibition of 1855, however, the Barbizon painters finally achieved both success and popularity.

Bibliography: Bouret, Jean, *The Barbizon School* (1973); Herbert, Robert L., *Barbizon Revisited* (1962); Leymarie, Jean, *French Painting in the Nineteenth Century* (1962); Sprague, Charles R., *The Barbizon School and the Paintings of Corot* (1982).

See also: LANDSCAPE PAINTING.

Barbour, John

John Barbour, b. *c.*1316, d. Mar. 13, 1395, is often considered Scotland's first identifiable poet. While archdeacon of Aberdeen (1357–95) he wrote the national epic romance *The Bruce* (1375). This work, based largely on fact, celebrates Scotland's victory under King Robert the Bruce over the English at the Battle of Bannockburn (1314). ROBIN BUSS

Barbusse, Henri   [bar-bues']

Henri Barbusse, b. May 17, 1873, d. Aug. 30, 1935, French novelist and journalist, owes his fame to the war novel *Under Fire* (1916; Eng. trans., 1917), which describes life in the trenches and the agonizing existence of the soldier. All of his works reflect his pacifist and socialist views. His first novel, *The Inferno* (1908; Eng. trans., 1918), is a social novel in the manner of Roger MARTIN DU GARD. JOSEPH A. REITER

Barcelona

Barcelona is the second-largest city in Spain, with a population of 1,707,286 (1990 est.). The capital of Barcelona province and of the autonomous region of CATALONIA, it covers an area of 91 km² (35 mi²) and is Spain's leading seaport. Located on a narrow Mediterranean coastal plain of northeastern Spain, the port developed under the shelter and protection of Montjuic, an isolated hill rising 192 m (630 ft). The valleys of the Besós and Llobregat rivers afford transportation routes through the mountains behind Montjuic and have facilitated communications with the interior.

The Contemporary City. Barcelona's metropolitan area, including many small industrial towns, spreads over 487 km² (188 mi²) and has a population of 4,040,000 (1988 est.). Barcelona, the leading manufacturing center of Spain, is an important banking and financial area.

Barcelona's citizens pride themselves on being Catalans. The Catalan language, suppressed under the Franco regime, is once again widely used, and the city's importance as a regional center is strongly emphasized.

The old city lies close to the harbor. Its chief feature is the Rambla—a broad, tree-lined avenue leading to the Plaça de Catalunya. Wide boulevards occupying the site of the ancient walls surround the precinct. The old city contains remains of a Roman settlement, a medieval cathedral, and many ancient palaces and houses. Residential and industrial suburbs en-

Crowned by four spires, the bold and original entrance facade of Antonio Gaudí's unfinished Templo de la Sagrada Familia (Church of the Holy Family) is one of Barcelona's most striking monuments.

close the area on the north and west and extend over the outlying foothills toward the mountains.

Approximately one-fifth of all industrial production in Spain is from Barcelona. Traditionally, the textile industry, especially woolens and cottons, dominated, and many mills are located in the metropolitan area rather than in the city itself. Recently, engineering industries, including automobile producers and chemical manufacturers, have been added. Approximately 11 km (7 mi) of quays and a number of specialized docks for oil, grain, and other commodities facilitate transport for domestic consumption and export.

Barcelona is the site of the University of Barcelona. Founded (1430) by Alfonso V, king of Aragon, it is one of the largest and most important universities in Spain. In 1968 a second university was established. A number of museums and galleries, including an important collection of Picasso's works, are also there. The city is a cultural center, especially for the Catalans, and is noted for its innovative architecture, much of it built during the 1980s and 1990s. The Sant Jordi sports stadium, designed by the Japanese architect Arata Isozaki, was constructed for the 1992 Summer Olympics, held in Barcelona. The city's most famous building, however, is probably Antonio GAUDÍ's unfinished Sagrada Familia church, begun in the late 19th century.

History. Barcelona was a Carthaginian city, and the name is believed to have been derived from the Punic family of Barca. The Romans developed the city, and it was later ruled briefly by the Moors. It achieved independence in the 11th century under the counts of Barcelona. Absorbed (1137) into the kingdom of Aragon, it grew to be one of the leading Mediterranean centers of commerce, rivaling Venice and Genoa in wealth. It declined in the 16th century. Toward the end of the 19th century, the port was modernized, and Barcelona again became a center of commerce. During the SPANISH CIVIL WAR it was a stronghold of the anti-Franco forces.

NORMAN J. G. POUNDS

Bibliography: Hughes, Robert, *Barcelona* (1992).

Barclay, Alexander

Alexander Barclay, c.1475–1552, was the first English writer to describe his work as satire. The work was his verse translation based on Sebastian BRANT's *Das Narren Schyff* (1494; *The Shyp of Folys of the Worlde*, 1509). Barclay's other works, which were popular in his time, include his *Eclogues* (c.1513), said to be the first English eclogues.

ROBIN BUSS

Barclay de Tolly, Mikhail Bogdanovich
[buhrk-lee' de taw'-lyi]

Mikhail Bogdanovich Barclay de Tolly, b. Dec. 27 (N.S.), 1761, d. May 26 (N.S.), 1818, was a Russian military leader of Scottish descent prominent in the Napoleonic Wars. As war minister (1810–12), Barclay effected major reforms in the Russian army. During the French invasion of 1812 he was removed from command after being defeated by Napoleon at Smolensk, but the strategy of withdrawal he initiated eventually led to the exhaustion of the invading army. After Napoleon's defeat, Barclay commanded (1814–15) Russian occupation forces in France.

Bibliography: Josselson, Michael and Diana, *The Commander* (1980).

Bard College

Founded in 1860 as Saint Stephen's College by the Episcopal church, and affiliated with Columbia University from 1928 to 1944, Bard (enrollment: 700; library: 150,000 volumes) is a private coeducational liberal arts college in Annandale-on-Hudson, N.Y. It has earned a reputation for being academically innovative.

Bardeen, John

The American physicist John Bardeen, b. Madison, Wis., May 23, 1908, d. Jan. 30, 1991, shared the 1956 Nobel Prize for physics with William B. SHOCKLEY and Walter H. BRATTAIN for the invention of the TRANSISTOR, and the 1972 Nobel Prize for physics with Leon N. COOPER and John SCHRIEFFER for the development of the theory of SUPERCONDUCTIVITY. A graduate of the University of Wisconsin (1928) and Princeton University (1936), Bardeen served as an assistant professor of physics at the University of Minnesota (1938–41) and as a physicist at the U.S. Naval Ordnance Laboratory in Washington, D.C. (1941–45), and at Bell Telephone Laboratories (1945–51). From 1951 to 1975 he was a professor of physics at the University of Illinois, Urbana.

Bardot, Brigitte   [bahr-doh']

The French film actress Brigitte Bardot, b. Sept. 28, 1934, achieved international celebrity for the sexy image she projected on and off screen. She was most successful in the films *And God Created Woman* (1956), *The Devil Is a Woman* (1958), *The Truth* (1961), *Contempt* (1964), and *Viva Maria* (1965).

LESLIE HALLIWELL

Bibliography: Beauvoir, Simone de, *Brigitte Bardot and the Lolita Syndrome* (1960; repr. 1972); Crawley, Tony, *Bebe* (1977); Vadim, Roger, *Bardot, Deneuve, Fonda*, trans. by M. Porter (1987).

Barenboim, Daniel   [bar'-en-boym]

Daniel Barenboim, b. Buenos Aires, Nov. 15, 1942, is a celebrated pianist and conductor, who gave his first recital at the age of 7 and embarked on his professional career at 14. After two decades of concertizing, conducting, and recording, he became musical director of the Orchestre de Paris in 1975, a post he held until 1987, when he was appointed artistic director of the new Paris Opéra de la Bastille. In 1989, however, a new government administration took the controversial step of dismissing him, allegedly because of his large salary (over $1 million) and costly plans. He became head of the Chicago Symphony in 1991, replacing the retiring Sir Georg Solti. Barenboim was married to the English cellist Jacqueline du Pré (1945–87).

Barents, Willem

The Dutch navigator Willem Barents, b. c.1550, d. June 20, 1597, is the most famous of the early explorers of the Arctic. Seeking the NORTHEAST PASSAGE, he reached the archipelago of Novaya Zemlya on his first two voyages (1594, 1595). He embarked again in 1596, discovering Spitsbergen and rounding the northern point of Novaya Zemlya. Caught in the ice, Barents and his crew survived the winter in a shelter built on Novaya Zemlya. In June 1597 they set out for the mainland in two open boats, but Barents soon died. One survivor was Gerrit de Veer, who chronicled the voyages in *The Three Voyages of William Barents to the Arctic Regions* (Eng. trans., 1876). In 1871 the shelter in which Barents wintered was found. The Barents Sea is named for him.

Barents Sea

The Barents Sea (formerly called the Murmean Sea) is an extension of the Arctic Ocean lying north of Norway and Russia, named in 1853 for Willem Barents, the 16th-century Dutch explorer. Its area is about 1,400,000 km² (540,000 mi²). In northern sections of the sea, the average winter air temperature is −25° C (−13° F), but the Russian port of MURMANSK remains ice-free in winter, partly due to the North Cape Current.

barge

A barge is a flat-bottomed boat of heavy construction used to transport materials in bulk on rivers and canals and in short-distance coastal traffic. Animal haulage of unpowered (dumb) canal barges was used from the Middle Ages to the early 19th century. Mechanical cable haulage, and later steam and diesel power, largely replaced the unpowered barge, although today, on large rivers and canals, several dumb barges are sometimes lashed together in an assembly known as a push tow, which is propelled by a tugboat. On the Mississippi River, barge assemblies of as many as 40 barges may extend 457 m (1,500 ft) ahead of the tug. New barge technology has created the LASH

(Lighter Aboard Ship), a vessel that carries cargo in small steel barges that can be stowed on deck or lowered into the water by crane. FRANCES GIES

See also: CONTAINERIZATION.

Barges laden with coal are pushed by a modern tug boat on the Rhine River, where cargo hauling has been used effectively since 1960.

Bargello [bahr-jel'-oh]

The Bargello, or *Palazzo del Podestà*, in Florence, Italy, was built between 1254 and 1346 as the armory, city jail, and residence of the chief of police. Remodeled in the 19th century as the Museo Nazionale (National Museum), it now houses a rich collection of Tuscan sculpture, ceramics, and armor produced during the Middle Ages and the Renaissance. Its principal monuments include Lorenzo Ghiberti's and Filippo Brunelleschi's competitive bronze reliefs for the Florence Baptistery doors (1401); Donatello's *St. George* (c.1415–20) and *David* (c.1430); Andrea del Verrocchio's *David* (c.1476); Antonio Pollaiuolo's *Hercules and Antaeus*; glazed terracottas from the della Robbia workshop (active c.1440–1530); four marbles by Michelangelo—*Bacchus* (1796–97), *Brutus* (after 1539), the *Pitti Tondo* (c.1504–05), and *Apollo* (completed 1530); bronzes and marbles by Benvenuto Cellini, and Giovanni da Bologna's *Mercury* (1580). ADELHEID M. GEALT

Bibliography: Berti, Luciano, *Il Bargello, National Museum*, trans. by Peggy Haines (1970); Pope-Hennessy, John, *Italian Renaissance Sculpture*, 2d ed. (1971); Seymour, Charles, Jr., *Sculpture in Italy, 1400–1500* (1966).

Barham, Richard Harris

The Englishman Richard Barham, b. Dec. 6, 1788, d. June 17, 1845, wrote a series of tales in verse under the pseudonym of Thomas Ingoldsby. Called *The Ingoldsby Legends*, they parodied contemporary and superstitious practices. The tales first appeared in *Bentley's Miscellany* from 1837. Charming and erudite, they reflect the character of their clergyman author. ROBIN BUSS

Bari [bah'-ree]

Bari is the capital city of Bari province and of the Apulia region in southeast Italy. Situated on the Adriatic Sea northwest of Brindisi, it is a major seaport for trade with the countries

of the Balkans and the Middle East. Bari has a population of 369,576 (1983 est.). It is the center of a rich agricultural district. Its industries include food processing, flour milling, oil refining, and textiles, chemicals, and tobacco.

Possibly inhabited since 1500 BC, Bari was first under Greek, then Roman, control. During the early Middle Ages it was controlled by Goths, Lombards, Saracens, and Byzantines, until the Normans took it in 1071. An important Crusader embarkation point from 1096, it was revitalized under the German emperor Frederick II (1194–1250) and was later ruled by the Sforzas of Milan before being passed to the kingdom of Naples in 1557. Bari was badly damaged during World War II; its remaining monuments include the 11th-century Romanesque Basilica of San Nicola with relics of St. Nicholas (Bari's patron saint), a 12th-century Romanesque cathedral, and the Hohenstaufen castle (1223). DANIEL R. LESNICK

barite

Barite minerals are found in various forms of transparent to opaque crystals with a glassy luster. Normally white to light gray, they are often tinged blue, green, yellow, brown, or red. Illustrated here is a concentric group of crystals called a "desert rose," found in such desert areas as the Sahara.

The chief ore and most common mineral of barium is barite, barium sulfate, $BaSO_4$. It forms vitreous, white or tinted, tabular or prismatic crystals (ORTHORHOMBIC SYSTEM) and crystal aggregates ("desert roses"), as well as coarsely laminated or granular masses, stalactites, and nodules. Hardness is $3–3\frac{1}{2}$; specific gravity is 4.3–4.6, high for a nonmetallic mineral. Barite mud is used in drilling oil wells to help control oil and gas pressure and prevent drill-hole cave-ins. Barite is the chief component of the white pigment lithopone. Also called heavy spar, it is widespread in metal ore veins, in limestones and in clays formed from weathered limestones, in sandstones, and in extensive beds as a lake or marine deposit.

See also: SULFATE MINERALS.

baritone

Baritone is the term applied to the singing VOICE midway between bass and tenor. The baritone quality may be either lyric or robust; the range is generally from G on the lowest line of the bass stave to G two octaves above. The total number of natural baritones exceeds the total number of tenors or basses, and baritones are more frequently called for in operatic works. Choral music also offers numerous parts for baritones. The term *baritone* is also used to designate an instrument next in range to the bass of a family, such as baritone horn and baritone saxophone.

barium

Barium is a chemical element—a silvery, soft metal—and it is the fifth of the ALKALINE EARTH METALS forming Group IIA in the periodic table. Its symbol is Ba; its atomic number is 56; and its atomic weight is 137.34. The density of barium is 3.75 g/cm^3 at 20° C; its melting point is approximately 725° C, and its boiling point is approximately 1,640° C. The name *barium* is derived from the Greek *barus*, meaning "heavy."

Barium is widely distributed in nature. The principal ore is barite (barium sulfate), also called heavy spar. The presence of barium oxide in barite was discovered (1779) by K. W. SCHEELE, and the metal was first isolated (1808) by Sir Humphry DAVY. Pure barium oxidizes readily, a property that makes it useful as a "getter" for removing oxygen from vacuum tubes. Useful alloys of barium and aluminum or magnesium are made by reacting these metals with barium oxide. Barium is highly electropositive and very reactive. It readily forms the Ba^{2+} ion, which behaves as a typical divalent ion and can be used to precipitate larger anions. Barium hydroxide, $Ba(OH)_2$, is soluble in water and is a strong base. Barium oxide, BaO, is used as a laboratory source of small amounts of peroxide. The oxidation of BaO in air produces BaO_2, barium peroxide, which, reacting with diluted sulfuric acid, H_2SO_4, yields hydrogen peroxide, H_2O_2.

Barium carbonate, $BaCO_3$, is used as a raw material for other barium compounds, as an ingredient in optical glass and fine glassware, and in the preparation of ceramic permanent magnets for loudspeakers. It is also used as a rat poison.

Barium sulfate, $BaSO_4$, is used medically as a contrast agent when taking X-ray images of the gastrointestinal tract to look for tumors, polyps, or other abnormal conditions (see RADIOLOGY). The procedure is known as a barium enema.

RICHARD L. CARLIN

bark

Bark is the external, relatively impervious covering on the stems of TREES and SHRUBS. Two different tissues in the mature stems of PLANTS continuously produce cells as the stem grows: an inner vascular cambium and an outer cork cambium. (Cambium is an embryonic tissue in vascular plants.) The vascular cambium produces inner layers of xylem (water-conducting) cells, which become wood, and an outer layer of phloem (nutrient-conducting) cells, which eventually become part of bark. The cork cambium produces cork cells, which constitute most of the bark.

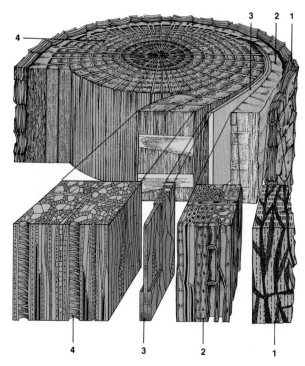

Bark protects trees just as skin protects people. It comprises two basic layers, the cork cambium, or periderm (1), and the secondary phloem (2). Cork cambium is old tissue, which consists of cork cells and dead phloem tissue. Cork cells contain fatty material that makes the entire tissue impermeable to air and water. Old bark cracks, splits, or peels off as the tree trunk grows; a tree can be identified by the outer bark's distinct color and pattern of splitting. Phloem is vascular tissue of a tree and transports or stores food from photosynthetic sites such as leaves. If the phloem is damaged by gouging or chopping, the food supply is cut off and the tree dies. Bark insulates and provides nutrition for the inner cambium (3) and xylem (4).

As the plant stem increases in girth, the layers from the vascular cambium outward rupture and die and produce the characteristic bark patterns of the different types of plants. The layer of dead cork cells is the outer bark of the older stem or root. The inner bark is the phloem tissue. In some species the outer bark is slowly and continuously sloughed off; in others it is held tightly to the stem. The thickness of bark in mature plants varies from less than 3 cm (1.2 in) to the more than 30 cm (1 ft) found in giant redwoods.

New xylem cells produced early in the growing season, when conditions are best, grow larger than cells produced later in the season, thus forming a series of concentric annual rings visible in cross sections of the stem. Each ring consists of an inner area of spring wood (large cells) and an outer area of winter wood (smaller cells). The number of rings furnishes a rough estimate of the age of a tree. Because ring widths vary with climatic conditions, a study of the rings of a large sample of old trees also gives clues to the climate of an area in past ages (see DENDROCHRONOLOGY).

Bibliography: Cutler, E. F., and Alvin, K. L., *The Plant Cuticle* (1982); Esau, Katherine, *Plant Anatomy*, 3d ed. (1988).

bark beetle

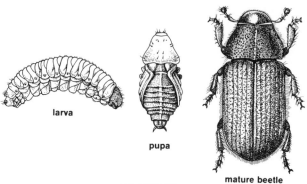

larva

pupa

mature beetle

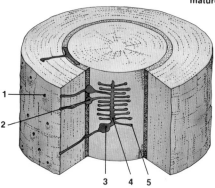

A bark beetle of the genus Dendroctonus *bores through tree bark (1) until it reaches outer sapwood. There, the male excavates a nuptial chamber (2) and mates with a female. The female beetle continues digging, occasionally making a materials chamber (3) where she dumps debris. She burrows vertically into the wood, creating a birth chamber (4), and lays her eggs. Each larva then tunnels perpendicularly (5) away from the birth chamber and stops to develop into a pupa. It finally emerges from the tree as a mature beetle.*

The bark beetle is an insect of the family Scolytidae of the order Coleoptera and is also known as the engraver beetle. It is elongate and cylindrical and usually lives beneath the bark of trees, where it tunnels between the bark and wood. Adult and larval tunneling can greatly weaken or kill a tree.

The ELM bark beetle, *Scolytus multistriatus*, is the chief vector, or transmitter, of Dutch elm disease, which has killed millions of elms in North America and Eurasia.

Bibliography: Martineau, Rene, *Insects Harmful to Forest Trees* (1984).

Women of Fiji decorate bark cloth with bold geometric designs. This cloth, which is made from the inner bark of trees, is used for clothing, bedding, ritual gifts, and sometimes kites.

bark cloth

Bark cloth, made by beating the inner bark of certain trees, was traditionally and widely used in the non-Western world for clothing, bed coverings, decorative objects, and ceremonial gifts. The use of bark cloth is known from such widely scattered areas as South America, Africa, India, Madagascar, Indonesia, Malaysia, Japan, New Guinea, Melanesia, and Polynesia. It was particularly important in areas where the loom was not known. Bark cloth is often referred to as tapa, a word adopted from the Polynesian area, although in most Polynesian languages bark cloth is not known as tapa.

Technique. In making bark cloth, the outer and inner bark are removed from the tree and the outer bark scraped away. The thick inner bark is softened by soaking, then beaten on anvils with special wood or stone implements. The beating thins and greatly widens the bark. Pieces are then pasted, felted, or sewn to form larger pieces. In areas such as Tonga, huge ceremonial pieces might measure about 5.5 m (18 ft) wide and hundreds of feet long. The quality of the product depends on the plant species, the care of the growing plant, and the skill of the craftsperson. Some of the finest bark cloth was made from the paper mulberry, *Broussonetia papyrifera,* cultivated so as to prevent side branches from growing. In many societies the making of bark cloth traditionally was women's work, but in some areas it was carried out by men.

Decoration. The finished product is often elaborately decorated with geometric or other patterns. The bark cloth might be dipped into a dye, or colored substances such as charcoal or ocher might be beaten into it. Freehand or stamped designs are sometimes also used to decorate the surface. Among the finest bark cloth was that made in Hawaii in the early 19th century, in which one layer of design was impressed into the cloth by beating it with a beater incised with designs, and a second layer of design was printed on the upper surface with intricately carved bamboo stamps.   ADRIENNE L. KAEPPLER

Bibliography: Kaeppler, Adrienne L., *The Fabric of Hawaii (Bark Cloth)* (1975); Kooijman, Simon, *Ornamented Bark-Cloth in Indonesia* (1963) and *Tapa in Polynesia* (1972).

Barker, Harley Granville: see GRANVILLE-BARKER, HARLEY.

barking frog

The barking frog, *Hylactophryne augusti,* of the family Leptodactylidae, is a large (6.5–7.5 cm/2.5–3 in) and toadlike frog that ranges from central Texas southward across the Mexican Plateau to the Isthmus of Tehuantepec. It frequently hides in limestone areas, and at a distance its call is often mistaken for a dog's bark. About 50 eggs are laid in a moist place, and the tadpoles develop within the egg; thus, completely metamorphosed froglets emerge. The male remains with the eggs and moistens them periodically with water from his bladder.   JONATHAN CAMPBELL

Barkla, Charles Glover   [bahrk'-luh]

The English physicist Charles Glover Barkla, b. June 27, 1877, d. Oct. 23, 1944, received the 1917 Nobel Prize for physics for his discovery that each element emits a characteristic X-ray spectrum. He had achieved an international reputation in X-ray research by 1911, was elected a fellow of the Royal Society (1912), and taught physics at the University of Edinburgh from 1913 until his death.   E. ROBERT PAUL

Barkley, Alben W.

Alben William Barkley, b. Graves County, Ky., Nov. 24, 1877, d. Apr. 30, 1956, was vice-president of the United States (1949–53) under President Harry S. TRUMAN. Son of a Kentucky tobacco farmer, Barkley graduated (1897) from Marvin College in Clinton, Ky., and attended the University of Virginia Law School. Returning to Kentucky, he began legal practice in the town of Paducah and was a county judge from 1909 to 1913.

Barkley, a Democrat, represented Kentucky in the U.S. House of Representatives (1913–27) and Senate (1927–49). In the Senate he was majority leader (1937–47) and a key spokesman for President Franklin D. Roosevelt's New Deal legislation. After serving as vice-president, Barkley sought the 1952 Democratic presidential nomination, but criticism of his age caused him to bow out of the race. In 1954, Barkley was again elected to the Senate and served until his death. His autobiography, *That Reminds Me,* was published in 1954.

Bibliography: Barzman, Sol, *Madmen and Geniuses* (1974); Libbey, J. K., *Dear Alben* (1979).

Barlach, Ernst   [bahr'-lahk]

Ernst Barlach, b. Jan 2, 1870, d. Oct. 24, 1938, was a German sculptor, graphic artist, and dramatist whose work is a sculptural form of expressionism and of social protest, opposed to the laws of classical beauty. Barlach used distortion and grotesque interpretations of the human form to express spiritual states rather than to achieve individual representations.

Barlach attended the Hamburg School of Applied Arts from 1883 to 1891 with the intention of becoming a drawing teacher; he studied (1891–95) at the Dresden Academy and in 1895 went to Paris, where he attended the Académie Julian briefly. Barlach was indifferent to the then-dominant art of Auguste RODIN, preferring instead the work of Jean François MILLET, the Belgian sculptor Constantin MEUNIER, and Vincent VAN GOGH. A visit to Russia in 1906 was to be decisive for Barlach's art. His expressionist sensibilities were stirred by the Russian peasants, who became prototypes for his heavy, blocky forms, which are closely related to both Russian peasant woodcarving and German medieval art. In 1908, Barlach carved his first works in wood, *Seated Woman* (Herbert Kurz collection, Wolframs-Eschenbach) and *Shepherd in a Storm* (Kunsthalle, Bremen); he had cast his first bronzes, *Beggarwoman with Child* (William Landmann collection, Toronto) and *The Melon Eater* (Beloit College Art Collections, Beloit, Wisc.), in 1908. In 1910 he moved to Güstrow, where he remained for the rest of his life.

The social criticism of such writers as Émile ZOLA had a lasting effect on Barlach as well as on his contemporary Käthe

The Reunion, carved in 1926 in walnut by Ernst Barlach, is one of his many wood sculptures in the medieval German tradition he revived. Barlach, a sculptor, graphic artist, and playwright, was a major German expressionist. (Ernst Barlach House, Hamburg.)

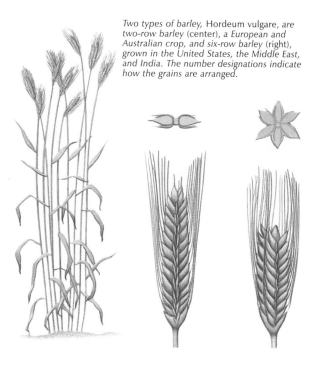

Two types of barley, Hordeum vulgare, are two-row barley (center), a European and Australian crop, and six-row barley (right), grown in the United States, the Middle East, and India. The number designations indicate how the grains are arranged.

KOLLWITZ, whose work is closely related to Barlach's type of social and political statement. By the outbreak of World War I in 1914, Barlach was producing works such as *In Time of War* (lithograph), *Hunger* (wood relief, location unknown), and *The Avenger* (plaster, Barlach Estate, Güstrow; bronze, Wallraf-Richartz Museum, Cologne). His major figures in bronze are massive groupings of figures or single forms usually swathed in heavy, deeply folded drapery.

During the 1930s, Barlach's works were under constant attack by the Nazis. As he was being made an honorary member of the Vereinigung Bildender Künstler (Artists' Alliance) of the Vienna SECESSION MOVEMENT in 1936, his work, along with that of Kollwitz and Wilhelm LEHMBRUCK, was removed from the jubilee exhibition of the Berlin Akademie der Künste (Art Academy) before its opening. In 1937 his *Warrior of the Spirit* (1928) in Kiel was damaged by the Nazis (restored 1954), and his Güstrow Memorial, *The Hovering Angel* (1927), was removed. In America, the 1931 exhibition of Barlach's works at New York's Museum of Modern Art exerted considerable influence on younger artists, especially those committed to social realism. Barlach's powerful conceptions convey agony, compassion, and earthy solidity.   BARBARA CAVALIERE

Bibliography: Carls, C. D., *Ernst Barlach*, rev. ed. (1969); Chick, E. M., *Ernst Barlach* (1967); Hooper, K., *Ernst Barlach's Literary and Visual Art* (1987).

See also: EXPRESSIONISM (art).

barley

Barley is probably the world's oldest domesticated grain crop, having been cultivated in Egypt as early as 6000 BC. It is a grass of the family Gramineae, generally classified in three types, six-row, two-row, and hull-less. The two- and six-row types —referring to the arrangement of the grains in the head— commercially are the most important.

Barley can be grown under a greater variety of climatic conditions than any other grain, and—although it produces less abundantly than in regions where it can grow for at least three months—is planted even where the growing season is ex-

tremely short, as in Lapland or the Himalayas, or where heat and lack of moisture prevent the growth of other cereals. The normal height of the plant is 76 cm (30 in), with grain heads forming at the tops of the stems. Like most cereal grains, it is composed of 8–10% protein, 62–65% starch, 1–3% fat, and 2–3% mineral matter. It can be harvested by a combine, or cut and windrowed in swaths to dry. The kernels require careful threshing to avoid the skinning or breaking that will harm germination, if they are to be used for seed.

Barley is the fourth most important cereal crop, after wheat, rice, and corn. Total annual world production in the early 1990s was 164 million metric tons (181 million U.S. tons), with Russia producing by far the largest crop—almost three times as much as Germany, Canada, or France, the next most important producers. North Dakota, Montana, and Idaho are the main barley-growing areas in the United States.

Approximately 60% of all barley produced is ground or rolled and mixed with other ingredients to produce formulated animal feeds. The ground meal is often pelleted. The major food use of barley is in the production of MALT for the brewing of BEER. The grain is eaten in soups and porridge and is used in making flour for flat breads. Pearled barley is produced by subjecting the kernel to abrasion to remove the hull and outer bran.   J. A. SHELLENBERGER

Bibliography: Rasmussen, D. C., *Barley* (1985).

Barlow, Joel

The development of the early American poet and statesman Joel Barlow, b. Redding, Conn., Mar. 24, 1754, d. Dec. 24, 1812, closely paralleled that of the young nation. His poems, "The Prospect of Peace" (1778), and *The Vision of Columbus* (1787)—the first version of what was to become a lifelong work—reflect the conservative religious, political, and literary ideas that made him one of the CONNECTICUT WITS.

During prolonged travels in Europe, Barlow was exposed to political turmoil and became acquainted with the humanitarian and democratic ideas of Jefferson and Paine. These influences became evident when his *Vision* received its final epic form in *The Columbiad* (1807). This conventional narrative written in heroic couplets traces the history of the New World and looks forward with hope to its future.

Barlow's most popular poetic work is still "The Hasty Pudding" (1796), a mock-heroic praise of the uniquely American

cornmeal mush. Some believe that his best writings are his political letters and proposals, which have a simplicity and forcefulness not found in the more ambitious poetry.
PAULA HART

Bibliography: Ford, Arthur L., *Joel Barlow* (1971); Woodress, James L., *A Yankee's Odyssey: The Life of Joel Barlow* (1958; repr. 1969).

barn

The word *barn* refers to an agricultural building or structure, usually large, that stores or houses animals, feed, machines, and farm products. Single-purpose barns are named for their function: horse barn, hay barn, dairy barn, tobacco barn.

In the United States, many farms have barns that are of a traditional two-story design; one type, called Switzer barns, was first built by the Pennsylvania Dutch in colonial times. The upper story houses hay and other forage feed along with bedding materials such as straw, wood shavings, and sawdust. These can be passed down to the first, or basement, floor where cattle and other livestock are housed.

Barns differ in size, shape, and internal construction, to accommodate the topography of the area and the type of farming practiced. The modern dairy barn, a common type, is either a single-story building or two stories, and cows are kept on the ground floor. It is commonly about 11 to 12 m (36 to 40 ft) wide to accommodate two rows of stanchions with three alleyways, two feed alleys, and one alley for milking and gutter cleaning. The length of the barn is usually determined by the number of mature cows to be housed and tended; roughly, 60 cm (24 in) of length are needed for each cow.

An increasing number of dairy farmers are building or remodeling dairy barns to include milking parlors. These units are two-level structures. The upper level holds cows while they are being milked and fed a mixed feed, and the farm workers perform the machine milking-operation on the lower level. Usually barns are equipped with air-ventilator fans and have a water supply. Dairy farms may have glass pipes for the flow of milk from cow stalls to the milk house, vacuum lines for the milking equipment, electric lines for lighting, and outlets for milkers or clippers. With stanchions or stalls, there will usually be gutters where manure accumulates. Gutter cleaners of chains, paddles, sprockets, and a motor move the manure out to a pit or manure spreader.
E. W. FOSS

Bibliography: Schuler, Stanley, *American Barns* (1984); Sloane, Eric, *An Age of Barns* (1985).

Barnabas, Saint

St. Barnabas was one of the earliest Christian converts at Jerusalem and one of the first missionaries. He introduced St. PAUL to the apostles after Paul's conversion (Acts 9). Barnabas led the missionary effort in Antioch and went to Cyprus with St. Paul, although he and Paul later disagreed over an assistant named John Mark (Acts 15) and separated. Feast day: June 11.

barnacle

Barnacle is the common name for members of the invertebrate subclass Cirripedia in the class Crustacea of the arthropod phylum. This group of about 1,000 exclusively marine species includes the only crustaceans that are sessile (permanently attached to a surface). Most live attached to rocks, shells, ship bottoms, and other submerged objects; some live on whales, turtles, and fish; and two groups are parasitic on other marine invertebrates.

Larval barnacles have six pairs of thoracic limbs, reduced abdomens, and mouthparts. A carapace forms a bivalvelike pair of shells around the body. Upon metamorphosis to the adult stage, the larva settles and attaches to a substrate headdown, using cement secreted by glands at the base of the first pair of antennae. Calcareous plates replace the carapace and surround the animal. In one group, a fleshy stalk supports the plates and body. Within the protective plates, the barnacle body consists of a cephalic region and thoracic region containing six pairs of long, feathery appendages (called cirri) that rhythmically emerge to catch food.

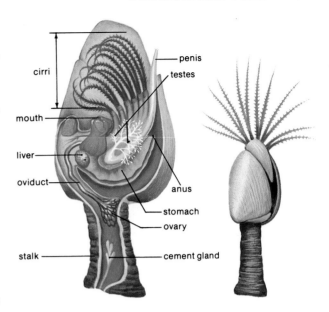

The goose barnacle is a deep-sea animal that attaches itself to driftwood and ship bottoms. A cross section of this barnacle (left) shows a cement gland, which secretes a gluelike substance. A barnacle also has both male and female sex organs and can fertilize itself. Its outer structure (right) includes a fleshy stalk, a thin shell covering its body, and six pairs of cirri, which capture food.

Internally, the barnacle possesses a U-shaped gut with a simple stomach and a blood pump to aid circulation. Gills are absent, and gas exchange occurs across the mantle and cirri surfaces. The barnacle is mostly hermaphroditic.

Barnacles form encrustations on ship bottoms that can reduce ship speed by 30 percent and cause significant increases in fuel costs.
STEPHEN C. REINGOLD

Bibliography: Barnes, R. D., *Invertebrate Zoology*, 4th ed. (1980).

Barnard, Christiaan

Christiaan Barnard, b. Nov. 8, 1922, is the South African surgeon who, on Dec. 3, 1967, performed the first successful human heart transplant. In 1974 he was the first to implant a second heart in a human being and to link the hearts to work together to provide blood circulation. Barnard served as professor of surgical science at the University of Cape Town from 1968 until 1983, at which time he retired from active surgical practice.

Bibliography: Cooper, D. K., and Lanza, R. P., eds., *Heart Transplantation* (1984); Leopold, L. E., *Dr. Christiaan Barnard: The Man with the Golden Hands* (1971).

Barnard, Edward Emerson

The foremost American observational astronomer of his time, Edward Emerson Barnard, b. Nashville, Tenn., Dec. 16, 1857, d. Feb. 6, 1923, studied at Vanderbilt University. He worked first at Lick Observatory, and then, during the last 28 years of his life, at Yerkes Observatory. Barnard was well known for his frequent discovery of comets and nebulae, for the novel application of photography to astronomy on a regular basis, and for his discoveries of BARNARD'S STAR and the fifth moon of Jupiter. Especially remarkable were his photographs of the Milky Way, an achievement that required long exposures and extreme patience. A measure of Barnard's devotion to astronomy is found in the circumstances of his final observation, an occultation of Venus by the Moon. It was made from his bed less than a month before his death.

Bibliography: Ashbrook, Joseph, *The Astronomical Scrapbook* (1985); Cruikshank, D. P., "Barnard's Satellite of Jupiter," *Sky & Telescope*, September 1982; Struve, Otto, and Zebergs, Velta, *Astronomy of the 20th Century* (1962).

Barnard, Frederick Augustus Porter

Frederick Barnard, b. Sheffield, Mass., May 5, 1809, d. Apr. 27, 1889, was president (1864–1889) of Columbia College, now Columbia University, in New York City. During his tenure, enrollment grew tenfold to 1,500, the elective system was introduced, the School of Mines and Teachers College were established, and graduate research and education were introduced. In 1883 he briefly opened the college to women; in 1889, BARNARD COLLEGE, an institution for women that soon affiliated with Columbia, was founded.

Barnard, Henry

Henry Barnard, b. Hartford, Conn., Jan. 24, 1811, d. July 5, 1900, was the first U.S. commissioner of education and a leader of the movement to establish American public school systems. Educated at Yale, Barnard served three terms (1837–39) in the Connecticut legislature, where he introduced the bill creating a state board of "commissioners of common schools." After moving to Rhode Island, Barnard served as the first state commissioner of public schools (1843–49), traveling to more than 1,100 meetings to promote the cause of public education and public libraries. In 1849 he returned to Connecticut to become superintendent of common schools. In helping to establish successful school systems in Connecticut and Rhode Island, Barnard was following after Horace MANN, who struggled for public schools in Massachusetts.

Barnard founded (1855) the *American Journal of Education* and edited it for a quarter century. It was an important national source of information about education, contributing to the professionalization of American education. In 1867, when Congress established the Bureau of Education, he became commissioner, serving until 1870.

Barnard College

Barnard College (1889; enrollment: 2,132; library: 162,991 volumes) is a private, 4-year, women's liberal-arts college in New York City. It is affiliated with COLUMBIA UNIVERSITY, with which it has cross-registration, dual-degree programs, and the sharing of faculty and facilities. After talks of a merger with its coordinate college, Columbia, Barnard remained independent; Columbia opted for coeducation in 1983.

Barnard's Star

Barnard's Star is the star of largest known PROPER MOTION, 10.3 seconds of arc per year. Its velocity is 140 km (87 mi) per second. The fourth nearest star to the Sun (see table in STAR), it lies 5.9 light-years away in the constellation Ophiuchus. It is a faint, cool dwarf star of spectral type M5 and magnitude 9.54. Variations in its motion have suggested that it has planets, but the evidence is inconclusive.   R. H. GARSTANG

Barnburners: see HUNKERS AND BARNBURNERS.

Barnes, Clive

Clive Alexander Barnes, b. London, May 13, 1927, is an Anglo-American dance and drama critic who has used the journalistic forum to popularize dance. After covering the performing arts and dance for several British publications, including *The Times* (1958–65), he emigrated to the United States where he was named (1965) dance critic for the *New York Times* and, in 1967, one of its drama critics. In 1978, Barnes left the *Times* to become dance and drama critic for the *New York Post*. He has written *Ballet in Britain since the War* (1953), *Frederick Ashton and His Ballets* (1961), *Inside American Ballet Theatre* (1977), and *Nureyev* (1982).   TOBI TOBIAS

Barnes, Djuna

Djuna Barnes, b. Cornwall-on-Hudson, N.Y., June 12, 1892, d. June 18, 1982, was an American writer and illustrator whose fame came with the publication of a single book, *Nightwood* (1936). The novel was described by T. S. Eliot in his admir-

ing introduction as a poetic work with "a quality of horror and doom very nearly related to that of Elizabethan tragedy." A contributor to New York City newspapers and magazines in the early 1900s—a collection of her pieces was published in *The Book of Repulsive Women* (1915)—Barnes moved to Paris in 1920. Here she was to write and illustrate the works upon which her literary celebrity rests today: *A Book* (1923), containing one-act plays, stories, and poems; *Ladies Almanack* (1928), a satiric description of the Parisian lesbian literary circle of the 1920s; *Ryder* (1928), a novel; and finally, *Nightwood*. From 1940, Barnes led a reclusive life in New York City's Greenwich Village. Much of her work has now been republished—for example, *Smoke and Other Early Stories* (1988).

Bibliography: Barry, Alyce, ed., *Interviews* (1985); Broe, Mary L., ed., *Silence and Power: A Reevaluation of Djuna Barnes* (1991); Field, Andrew, *Djuna: The Formidable Miss Barnes* (1985).

Barnes, Edward Larrabee

Edward Larrabee Barnes, b. Chicago, Apr. 22, 1915, is an architect and planner. He continued the design orientation of Marcel BREUER, in whose office Barnes worked after completing (1942) his training at Harvard University. In independent practice since 1949, he has designed a variety of buildings in the United States that have won numerous awards; in the words of one citation, his work is remarkable for having "no intrusive artifices of architecture." Among his major commissions are the campus plan for the New York State University College at Potsdam (1972), the Sarah Scaife Gallery (1975) of the Carnegie Institute in Pittsburgh, Kansas City's Crown Center (coordinating architect, 1967 on), and the Asia Society building (1981) in New York City.   J. MEREDITH NEIL

Barnes Foundation

The Barnes Foundation is an art museum in Merion, Pa., founded in 1922 to house the collection of Albert C. Barnes (1872–1951), a wealthy American manufacturer of pharmaceuticals and a prodigious collector of art. A pre–World War I trip to Paris inspired Barnes's first art purchases, and over the years he acquired an immense collection of paintings by Renoir, Matisse, Cézanne, and Picasso, as well as works of the European old masters and a trove of African art.

His interest in Afro-American culture prompted Barnes to leave control of his foundation to Lincoln University, a black institution of higher learning. Although during Barnes's lifetime the museum was essentially closed to the public—one had to receive permission from Barnes himself to tour the galleries—a legal suit in 1960 forced the trustees to allow limited public visits. In 1993, hoping to raise funds to finance needed museum renovations, the trustees assembled a traveling exhibit of "Great Paintings from the Barnes Foundation" —marking the first time any of these works had been seen outside the Foundation walls.

barnstorming

Barnstorming is a form of aerial showmanship that reached its peak in the 1920s. In the years preceding World War I, flying-exhibition teams thrilled spectators at carnivals, county fairs, and flying meets across the United States. After the war, when thousands of surplus military planes were sold at bargain prices, ex-military pilots earned money by taking adventurous passengers up for a ride. Many also entertained at fairs and air shows, demonstrating wartime aerobatics, parachute jumps, wing-walking, and other stunts. Barnstorming accidents in the 1920s and '30s gave aviation a poor reputation, although many fliers established reputable fixed-base operations, offering flight training, charter flights, aerial photography, and other services that helped develop commercial aviation. With stringent safety precautions, the tradition of barnstorming continues in present-day air shows and other events.

ROGER E. BILSTEIN

Bibliography: Caidin, Martin, *Barnstorming* (1991); O'Neil, Paul, *Barnstormers and Speed Kings* (1981).

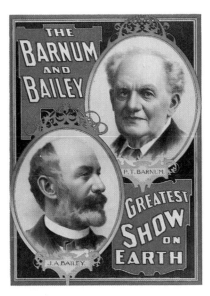

A 19th-century handbill advertises the "Greatest Show on Earth," the famous circus formed in 1881 by P. T. Barnum and his competitor James Bailey. A consummate and cynical showman, Barnum maintained "There's a sucker born every minute." Barnum made a fortune exhibiting such sensational attractions as Siamese twins, midgets, and exotic animals.

Barnum, P. T.

Phineas Taylor Barnum, b. Bethel, Conn., July 5, 1810, d. Apr. 7, 1891, was the most famous U.S. showman and a self-proclaimed "Prince of Humbugs." After starting out as a merchant and lottery-ticket salesman, he fell into the occupation of showman in 1835 with the purchase of a decrepit hymn-singing black woman, Joice Heth, said to be 161 years old, whom he brazenly exhibited as the nurse of George Washington. Graduating to the equally sensational "Feejee Mermaid" (in reality the upper half of a monkey sewn to the body of a fish), he later made fortunes out of the midget TOM THUMB and the Swedish singer Jenny LIND. In these, as in all his enterprises, Barnum was one of the first impresarios to realize the value of massive publicity campaigns.

Between 1841 and 1868, Barnum was the proprietor of the American Museum in New York City, where thousands of curiosities, freaks, and wild animals were displayed, and he produced such edifying melodramas as *The Drunkard* in a large, well-equipped theater known as the "lecture room." Stressing education and innocent amusement, the museum became one of New York's most popular places of entertainment. In 1871, Barnum launched a mammoth traveling CIRCUS, museum, and menagerie. A merger with James A. Bailey's London Circus ten years later led to the concern that eventually became known as the Barnum & Bailey Show, which in turn was acquired by the Ringling Brothers in 1907.

Barnum served four terms in the Connecticut state legislature and one term as mayor of Bridgeport, where the Barnum Museum exists today.   A. H. SAXON

Bibliography: Fleming, A. P., *P. T. Barnum* (1993); Saxon, A. H., *P. T. Barnum: The Legend and the Man* (1989).

Barnum & Bailey: see BARNUM, P. T.; CIRCUS; RINGLING (family).

Barocci, Federico   [bah-rawt'-chee]

Federico Barocci, c.1535–1612, was an Italian painter noted for his innovative style. His work was deeply influenced by CORREGGIO. Both Barocci and Correggio painted soft, melting forms that move through diagonal compositions aglow with bright pastel colors. In 1550, Barocci made the first of two trips to Rome to study the works of RAPHAEL. During his second visit in 1560, Barocci worked on frescoes in the Vatican. He spent the remainder of his career in Urbino, his birthplace. Barocci's reputation spread from Urbino; he sent paintings to Florence, Rome, Genoa, and even to Vienna and Madrid. Barocci was never strongly attracted to the artificial Mannerist style of his period (see MANNERISM). On the contrary, the movement and fervor of many of his canvases anticipate the baroque style of Peter Paul RUBENS and Giovanni Lorenzo BERNINI. Among Barocci's works are *The Martyrdom of Saint Sebastian* (c.1557–58; Urbino Cathedral) and *The Last Supper* (1604–07; Santa Maria Sopra Minerva, Rome).   THOMAS BUSER

Bibliography: Olsen, Harald, *Federico Barocci* (1962).

Baroda   [buh-roh'-duh]

Baroda (Vadodara), a city in west central India, is located about 403 km (250 mi) north of Bombay on the fertile Gujarat plain. One of the largest cities in Gujarat state, it has a population of 1,021,084 (1991). The city is an industrial center for calico prints, dyed fabrics, soap, and cigarettes.

A walled city with four gates, Baroda was the capital of the native state of the Maratha Gaekwars from 1734 to 1947. Mandwi Gate, in the old city, was built in 1736 to commemorate the Maratha victory over the Moguls in Gujarat. Maharaja Sayajirao University (1949) was named after Sayaji Rao III, who ruled (1875–1939) when most of the modern city was built.   ASHOK K. DUTT

Baroja y Nessi, Pio   [bah-roh'-hah ee nes'-ee]

The Spanish novelist Pio Baroja y Nessi, b. Dec. 28, 1872, d. Oct. 30, 1956, was a member of the Generation of '98, a group of writers dedicated to the cultural rebirth of Spain after its defeat (1898) in the Spanish-American War. The best known of his 11 trilogies is *The Struggle for Existence* (1904; Eng. trans., 1922–24), concerning the struggle of the poor in Madrid's underworld. His 22-volume cycle of novels, collectively called *Memorias de un hombre de acción* (Memoirs of a Man of Action, 1913–35) has as its hero a 19th-century political nonconformist.

Bibliography: Patt, B., *Pio Baroja* (1971); Ramsden, H., *Baroja* (1982).

barometer

The barometer, the single most important meteorological instrument, measures atmospheric pressure.

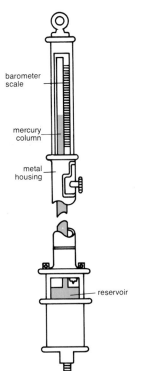

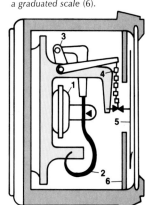

barometer scale

mercury column

metal housing

reservoir

A mercury barometer (left) consists of a mercury-filled glass tube with its lower end submerged in an adjustable mercury reservoir, and a scale marked in inches and centimeters for reading the mercury column height. A cross-section of an aneroid barometer (below) reveals a small metal box, from which air has been withdrawn, with a movable end (1) that expands and contracts with changes in air pressure. Any motion of the movable end is transmitted by means of a spring (2), a system of levers (3), and a chain (4) to a rotating needle (5), which indicates the air pressure on a graduated scale (6).

Mercury Barometer. The invention of the mercury barometer (1643) by Evangelista TORRICELLI depended on his realization that air has weight. He noted that if the open end of a glass tube filled with mercury is inverted in a bowl of mercury, the atmospheric pressure on the bowl of mercury will affect the height of the column of mercury in the glass tube. The greater the air pressure, the longer is the mercury column. The atmospheric pressure may be calculated by multiplying the height of the mercury column by the mercury density and the acceleration due to gravity. At sea level, atmospheric pressure is equal to about 15 lb per in^2, or 29.9 in. of mercury. This is equivalent to 101.3 kilopascals, the pressure unit meteorologists now use, besides millibars.

Mercury is ideal for a liquid barometer, since its high density permits a short column, whereas a water barometer would be 10 m (33 ft) tall at one atmosphere. Another advantage of mercury is its negligible vapor pressure, important because the few mercury vapor molecules in the empty space above the mercury column will add only slightly to the pressure exerted by the column itself. In a water barometer the vapor would cause an error of 2 percent at 15° C (59 ° F).

Aneroid Barometer. Most barometers are of the aneroid type and function without liquid. The aneroid barometer, dating from 1843, consists of a small metal box, almost totally evacuated of air. One side is immovable, and the opposite side is connected to a strong spring to keep the box from collapsing. The movable side will expand if the air pressure decreases and will compress if the air pressure increases. The position of the movable side is indicated by a pointer. The aneroid barometer can be easily converted into a barograph, or recording barometer, by adding a pen to the pointer. The ink in the pen describes a trace (barogram) on the paper wrapped around a cylinder. The cylinder usually rotates once a day or once a week. An aneroid barometer is checked regularly against a mercury barometer for calibration.

The mercury barometer is used in research laboratories and in the most important weather stations. Aneroid barometers, used in the home, on board ships, and in all weather stations, are also a prominent part of RADIOSONDE instruments.

WILLEM VAN DER BIJL

Bibliography: Bolle, Bert, *Barometers* (1984); Middleton, W. E. K., *Invention of the Meteorological Instruments* (1969); Wang, J.-Y., *Instruments for Physical Environmental Measurements*, 2d ed. (1983).

Baron, Salo Wittmayer   [buh-rohn', sah'-loh wit'-my-ur]

Salo Wittmayer Baron, b. Tarnow, Austria (now Poland), May 26, 1895, d. Nov. 25, 1989, was a Jewish historian. He received his doctorate from the University of Vienna in 1917 and lectured at the Juedisches Paedagogium from 1919 to 1925. Baron emigrated to the United States in 1926. His principal tenure (1930–63) was as professor of Jewish history at Columbia University. He also was associated with the Center of Israel and Jewish Studies, the Jewish Theological Seminary of America, and Hebrew (Jerusalem), Rutgers, and Brown universities. Baron edited *Jewish Social Studies* (1939–89) and authored works ranging from the political theory of Ferdinand Lassalle to essays on Maimonides. His major works include *A Social and Religious History of the Jews* (18 vols.; rev. ed., 1952–83), *History and Jewish Historians* (1964), and *Ancient and Medieval Jewish History: Essays* (1972).   SAUL S. FRIEDMAN

Baronius, Caesar   [buh-rohn'-ee-uhs]

Caesar Baronius, b. Oct. 31, 1583, d. June 30, 1607, was an Italian Roman Catholic church historian. An ordained priest, he served as confessor to Pope Clement VIII, who elevated him to the rank of cardinal in 1596 and appointed him librarian of the Vatican. Baronius scrupulously compiled documents for his *Annales ecclesiastici a Christo nato ad annum 1198* (Annals of the Church from the Birth of Christ until the Year 1198; 1588–1607) in an attempt to refute the claims of Protestant authors. Although biased, the work is valued for its source materials.   JOEL COLTON

Bibliography: Pullapilly, Cyriac, *Caesar Baronius* (1975).

Barons' War

The Barons' War is the name given to the armed conflict (1263–67) between HENRY III, king of England, and a group of barons led by Simon de MONTFORT, earl of Leicester.

The conflict stemmed from Henry's renunciation of the Provisions of Oxford of 1258 and the Provisions of Westminster of 1259, which had created a baronial council with substantial governmental powers. In 1261 and again in 1262 the pope absolved Henry from his oath to observe the provisions. The following year the barons took up arms to force the king to renew his oath of adherence to the provisions. They agreed, however, to submit the dispute for arbitration by King LOUIS IX of France. In his judgment, rendered in the Mise of Amiens of January 1264, Louis took Henry's side and condemned the provisions. As a result the English barons renewed the war.

On May 14, 1264, Montfort defeated Henry's army in the Battle of Lewes and temporarily became effective ruler of England. Early in 1265 he summoned a PARLIAMENT, including for the first time both gentry from the shires and burgesses from the towns, to bolster his support. Disputes soon arose among the barons, however, and Henry's eldest son (later King EDWARD I) gathered an army that defeated and killed Montfort at the Battle of Evesham on Aug. 4, 1265. Despite the barons' defeat, some elements of these reforms were incorporated in the constitutional changes of the reign of Edward I.

Bibliography: Powicke, F. M., *King Henry III and the Lord Edward* (1947); Treharne, R. F., and Sanders, I. J., eds., *Documents of the Baronial Movement of Reform and Rebellion* (1973).

baron: see TITLES OF NOBILITY AND HONOR.

baroque art and architecture   [buh-rohk']

Baroque art and architecture, broadly speaking, is the art and architecture of Europe and its Latin American colonies in the 17th and the first half of the 18th centuries. In a more specific sense, the term refers to the most characteristic of the styles created in that period—that is, to the art that arose in Italy and Flanders soon after 1600, dominated ITALIAN ART AND AR-

Peter Paul Rubens's exuberant, opulent style is shown in Rape of the Daughters of Leucippus *(c.1616). Its rich, warm colors, voluptuous female nudes, and dramatic vitality are characteristic of the baroque Flemish painter. (Alte Pinakothek, Munich.)*

(Left) *A detail from Pietro da Cortona's ceiling fresco* Triumph of Divine Providence *(1633–39) shows the use of illusionism, or visual techniques such as perspective and foreshortening, to create a three-dimensional effect incorporating simulated sculpture and architecture. The subject is an allegory glorifying the Barberini family. (Palazzo Barberini, Rome.)*
(Below) *The enormous baldachino (1624–33) in St. Peter's, Rome, designed by Giovanni Lorenzo Bernini, stands over the high altar. The gilded bronze canopy combines architecture and sculpture in its twisting columns and rich ornamental decoration.*

CHITECTURE until the classical revival of the mid-18th century, and produced echoes of varying intensity in all other countries. This style is associated, above all, with Peter Paul RUBENS and Giovanni Lorenzo BERNINI.

ORIGINS

The label *baroque* was first applied to the art of this period in the late 18th century, when the style itself had gone out of fashion; as is not uncommon in art history, it was initially employed as a term of abuse. The word may be derived either from the Portuguese *barocco*, meaning an irregularly shaped pearl (in which sense it is still used by jewelers) or, as is perhaps more likely, from *baroco*, a scholastic term coined as a mnemonic aid for a tortuous argument in logic. As used by late 18th-century art critics, it signified "absurd," "willful," "grotesque"—in other words, a wanton defiance of the classical rules. Eventually, however, as the classical rules lost their hold in the next hundred years and art historians began to look more objectively at the art of the past, *baroque* lost its derogatory significance. By the early 20th century, first specialists and later a wider art-loving public saw that baroque artists and architects had made a positive and original contribution to European art and had not merely gone off on a wrong track.

Baroque art at its greatest and most intense is found in Roman Catholic countries, and a close association, if not an ideological link, existed between the style and the Roman Catholic church in the later stages of the COUNTER-REFORMATION. During that period, the church was reemphasizing its traditional spiritual doctrines in opposition to the rising forces of PROTESTANTISM and scientific progress and was simultaneously engaging in intense missionary activity. For both purposes, it needed vivid and compelling imagery. This the baroque artists and architects, with their capacity for creating spectacular visual effects and representing supernatural beings in a seemingly realistic way, were able to supply. They were also fitted to provide suitably sumptuous palaces for monarchs and other secular patrons anxious to impress their subjects (and each other) with their power and wealth. Because of its associations with authoritarian regimes in both church and state, the baroque succeeded best in traditional societies, such as those of Italy, Spain, and central Europe, whereas it met with some resistance in the more progressive societies of northern Europe (including France).

inward at the sides, outward in the middle—used for facades, doorways, and furniture.

Leaving aside their various origins, the principal characteristics of the baroque may thus be summarized. In architecture, besides those already mentioned, the primary features are twisted columns and fantastical pediments. A baroque PEDIMENT may be varied in many ways, such as by interrupting it in the center, turning the sloping sides into scrolls, and curving it in its vertical plane. In sculpture, the style is characterized by fluttering draperies, realistic surfaces, and the use of bronze, white and colored marbles, and sometimes other materials in the same work. In painting, the main features are illusionistic ceilings, bold foreshortening, and a new, powerful kind of realism, obtained chiefly through the use of light and shade.

The expression of emotion was increasingly emphasized in both painting and sculpture. In larger works, such as tombs and church interiors, two or more arts were often harnessed into one overwhelming effect, producing what has been called the baroque *Gesamtkunstwerk* (''total art work'').

The result was a style of great richness and flexibility that could encompass effects both on the grandest possible scale and on the scale of a small oil sketch or pen drawing. Popular as well as sophisticated, it could be used equally for didactic purposes and for decoration.

HISTORICAL DEVELOPMENT

The development of the baroque style began in Italy around 1600, when a group of painters, of whom the most important were Michelangelo da CARAVAGGIO and Annibale CARRACCI, brought about a revival of art in Rome following the breakdown of Mannerism.

The first to turn this revival decisively toward a baroque aesthetic, however, was the Flemish painter Rubens, who, after studying in Italy from 1600 to 1608, created a baroque style

(Above) *Francesco Borromini used the typical baroque device of alternating concave and convex surfaces in the facade (1665–67) of San Carlo alle Quattro Fontane, Rome. Also called San Carlino, the church was begun in 1638.*

(Right) *The focal point of Johann Balthasar Neumann's pilgrimage church of Vierzehnheiligen near Bamberg, Germany, is the Grace Altar, dedicated to the 14 Saints of Divine Intercession.*

CHARACTERISTICS

For all its dynamism, the baroque style was not absolutely new, in the sense that Gothic art or cubism were new. Formally, it owed much to RENAISSANCE ART AND ARCHITECTURE and the intervening phase, MANNERISM; it was also influenced by the antique—Greek and Roman art and architecture. The classical orders of architecture and the idealized human figure are as much features of baroque art as they are of those earlier styles. A strong connection exists also between baroque and Renaissance (bypassing Mannerist) methods of representing reality. What was new in all these cases was the way in which the forms were used or the methods applied. To cite a slightly different example, some of the features correctly regarded as most typically baroque, such as the inward-curving FACADE and oval groundplan, were anticipated by prototypes occurring as sidelines, often in underdeveloped form, in the art of the past. (By the same token, baroque ILLUSIONISM was not without precedents, either.) Finally, baroque artists and architects did create some, although not many, entirely new forms, of which perhaps the most important was the double curve—

of marvelous color, vitality, and realism. He used the style in paintings for the Roman Catholic church and for the court of the Spanish Netherlands as well as other courts he visited. An example is his series of allegorical paintings (1629–35) glorifying the Stuart monarchy, on the ceiling of Inigo JONES's Banqueting House, WHITEHALL PALACE, London.

The main center of the baroque in the first three-quarters of the 17th century, however, was Rome, where a greater number of important works of art were created, and far more artists were active, than in all the rest of Europe. The dominant personalities were the sculptor and architect Bernini, the architect Francesco BORROMINI, and the architect and painter Pietro da CORTONA, the latter a master of illusionistic ceiling painting (*Triumph of Divine Providence,* 1633–39; Palazzo Barberini, Rome). Bernini's most outstanding contribution is to be seen in his additions to ST. PETER'S BASILICA (1624–78), comprising the colonnade, the tombs of Popes URBAN VIII and Alexander VII, the statue of *St. Longinus,* the baldachino (canopy) over the high altar, and the altar of the *cathedra* (chair) of St. Peter behind it. This is the most astounding group of baroque works in any one place and the most complete expression anywhere of the Roman Catholic spirit in the later stages of the Counter-Reformation. Although Borromini's architecture was confined to a narrower compass, his small churches, such as SAN CARLO ALLE QUATTRO FONTANE (1638–41; 1662–67), with its undulating walls and facade and its highly original ornament, are in some ways even more ingenious than its larger baroque counterparts.

INFLUENCE IN NORTHERN EUROPE, IBERIA, AND COLONIAL AMERICA

Outside Italy and Flanders, the baroque was mainly a late 17th- and 18th-century phenomenon, although signs of it appeared earlier in most places. Each region interpreted the style in a different way. Probably its most radiant flowering was in Germany, in such churches as Vierzehnheiligen (Fourteen Saints; 1743–72), near Bamberg, by Johann Balthasar NEUMANN. In Spain and Portugal and their American colonies, the interpretation was more pious and popular, as can be seen in Bartolomé MURILLO's painting of the *Immaculate Conception* (c.1660; Prado, Madrid) or in the facade of Santiago de Compostela Cathedral (finished 1750), the plain surface of which is encrusted with carved forms partly of traditional Spanish origin. In France, full acceptance of the baroque was prevented by the cult of reason, which favored classical restraint, but the resulting "classical-baroque" style produced the greatest of all royal palaces, VERSAILLES (1669–1703). In the Protestant Netherlands the full baroque was confined to sculpture, but the art of REMBRANDT was affected by the style (*The Night Watch*, 1642; Rijksmuseum, Amsterdam). In Protestant England a temperate form of baroque was applied in the design of large country houses and, most notably, SAINT PAUL'S CATHEDRAL, London (1675–1708), by Sir Christopher WREN.

In the early 18th century the baroque gave way in France and Germany to the ROCOCO STYLE, and in the second half of the century both styles were superseded by NEOCLASSICISM.

MICHAEL KITSON

Bibliography: Bazin, G., *Baroque and Rococo* (1985); Blunt, A., *Art and Architecture in France, 1500–1700*, 3d ed. (1973); Downes, K., *English Baroque Architecture* (1986); Haskell, F., *Patrons and Painters*, rev. ed. (1980); Hempel, E., *Baroque Art and Architecture in Central Europe* (1965); Johnston, C., *Vatican Splendor* (1986); Kitson, M., *The Age of Baroque*, 3d ed. (1976); Kubler, G., and Soria, M., *Art and Architecture in Spain and Portugal and Their American Dominions, 1500–1800* (1959); Varriano, J., *Italian Baroque and Rococo Architecture* (1986).

baroque music

The term *baroque* refers to music written during the period extending roughly from 1600 to 1750, beginning with the first attempts at opera, in Italy, and ending with the death of Johann Sebastian BACH, whose works represent the zenith of the era's contrapuntal style. Baroque music is, however, a broad category that can be divided both chronologically and by distinct national styles.

In the late 18th century—a period during which the dominant style stressed elegance and simplicity—writers began to use the word *baroque* to describe earlier music (as well as painting, sculpture, and architecture) that seemed to them to be distorted by a profusion of unnatural ornamentation. (*Baroque*, a French word, means an irregularly shaped pearl, of the type often used in the extremely fanciful jewelry of the post-Renaissance period.)

By the end of the 16th century, Italian composers had perfected the MADRIGAL, a popular form of polyphonic text setting in which the music reflected the intensity of the emotions suggested in the poetry. The solo song forms of the time reflected this realistic emotionalism too. Gradually, song forms were extended into longer dramatic settings.

Claudio MONTEVERDI was chief among the early experimenters in vocal music; his operas and books of madrigals stand as the high points of this early period of the baroque.

The early Italian CANTATA was a form in which a story—usually secular—was related by a solo singer through recitatives and arias, to a sparse basso continuo (a lute or harpsichord, usually with a bass viol emphasizing the bass line). Over the course of 150 years, this form traveled through Europe and was greatly transformed, particularly in Germany, where it evolved into works that could include several singers and a chorus. By the end of the baroque era, Bach was composing cantatas in which sacred hymn tunes played a central and unifying role, and that frequently ended with grand chorale settings.

The ORATORIO, an extended dramatic work on a religious theme, had its roots in Rome and spread throughout Europe through the work of the German-English composer George Frideric HANDEL. It was in England, and in English, that he composed the most popular of all oratorios, the *Messiah* (1741).

The SONATA, an instrumental work, is another form that had its genesis in the early baroque. In Italy the term *sonata* meant a group of slow and fast dance movements, or an abstract work in contrasting slow and fast sections, the latter known as a "church sonata." Among the Italian composers who wrote in both styles, perhaps the most inventive was Arcangelo CORELLI.

Outside Italy the dance sets were called suites and followed their own evolutionary path. The sonata's evolution was more dramatic, however. Like the MOTET and the cantata, it expanded from a single-movement two- or three-part form, such as that found in the keyboard sonatas of Domenico SCARLATTI, into multimovement forms such as those Bach composed. The early sonatas could be either for solo instruments or for small ensembles. Toward the end of the 17th century, as the middle baroque period gave way to the late, or high, baroque, the ensemble sonata gave way to the concerto grosso, where an opposition is set up between the full ensemble (the ripieno, or "filling") and a smaller group, typically composed of two violins and continuo (the concertino). From the concerto grosso emerged the solo CONCERTO, in which a solo instrument is set against the forces of the full ensemble. Bach's *Brandenburg Concertos* are fine examples of the concerto grosso style; his solo concertos, along with those of Antonio VIVALDI, are models of the genre.

Central in the development of the sonata and the concerto, and the various vocal forms as well, is another of the baroque era's novel elements: tonality. By the middle of the 16th century the old system of church modes was being replaced by a new concept of key relationships. Throughout the early baroque period, composers moved freely from one key to another through modulations, usually involving chords common to more than one key as jumping-off points. They produced, for the time, daringly chromatic music.

Gradually, a system evolved whereby the relationship between keys was established in an orderly way (see MUSIC). Bach's *Well-Tempered Clavier* illustrates these relationships. It also demonstrates two other important baroque forms, the freely invented PRELUDE and the complex, tightly structured FUGUE.

The great baroque forms emerged during the era's early and middle periods. The late baroque saw the expansion and re-

Water Music by George Frideric Handel, the great composer of the late baroque period, is a set of orchestral pieces written for King George I of England. Water Music was first performed about 1717 on a barge during a royal procession down the River Thames.

finement of these forms, as well as the further development of distinct national schools. Thus, while the models were by-and-large Italian, German and French variants were immediately distinguishable through certain hallmarks. One such French trait was the use of dotted rhythms, which gave dance movements, as well as preludes and overtures, an especially lively character that came to be associated with France, even when used by composers elsewhere. In Germany, elements of both Italian basic style and French fashion were prevalent, but these were tempered by a more staid Lutheran musical tradition and by a fascination with contrapuntal complexity.

In all countries, musicians were expected to add ornamentation and embellishment to the music they found on the printed page—much the same way a jazz player today is expected to add improvised filigree to the shape of a standard tune. A series of signs developed representing frequently used ornaments—the trill, turn, grace note or appoggiatura, tremolo, and so forth. The sign indicated how an ornament should sound, but the performer had wide improvisational leeway. Instrumental music was often highly ornamented. The FIGURED BASS, another baroque-era innovation, allowed the players of the bass accompaniment to improvise around a given harmonic outline. Singers of *opera seria* often displayed astonishingly lengthy series of embellishments in their improvised CADENZAS. Some of the era's music—Bach's, for instance—is notated so densely that it probably includes a great deal of what might originally have been ornamentation. Most scores of the time leave ample room for the interpreter's input.

The baroque era in music was a crucial link in the development of the modern musical language. During this century and a half, forms emerged that have remained standard. The codification of tonality and the establishment of the tempered tuning system were of vital importance. Equally important, though, is the fact that the prolific composers of the era left works that continue to speak eloquently over a distance of centuries.   ALLAN KOZINN

Bibliography: Anthony, J. R., *French Baroque Music,* rev. ed. (1978); Arnold, D., et al., *The New Grove Italian Baroque Masters* (1984); Boroff, Edith, *The Music of the Baroque* (1970; repr. 1978); Bukofzer, M., *Music in the Baroque Era* (1947); Hutchings, A., *The Baroque Concerto,* 4th ed. (1978); Palisca, C. V., *Baroque Music* (1968); Robinson, M. F., *Opera before Mozart* (1966); Rosand, Ellen, ed., *Baroque Music I: 17th Century* and *Baroque Music II: 18th Century* (1986).

Barr, Alfred H., Jr.

The American art historian and museum administrator Alfred Hamilton Barr, Jr., b. Detroit, Jan. 28, 1902, d. Aug. 15, 1981, founded the MUSEUM OF MODERN ART, New York City, and became, at the age of 27, its first director. Barr studied art history at Princeton University from 1918 to 1923 and then taught at Harvard University and Wellesley College. During his tenure as director (1929–43), and later as director of museum collections (1947–67), Barr was responsible for building an unprecedented collection comprising outstanding examples of all the contemporary visual arts, including architectural designs, cinema, photography, and the decorative and industrial arts. Through exhibitions and writings, he was instrumental in developing popular interest in modern art in the United States. After his retirement in 1967, Barr was active as a writer and as an advisor to major art institutions throughout the world. Among his many influential books are *Cubism and Abstract Art* (1936; repr. 1974) and *What Is Modern Painting?* (6th ed., 1956; repr. 1966).   MARIAN BURLEIGH-MOTLEY

Bibliography: Hunter, Sam, intro. by, *The Museum of Modern Art, New York: The History and the Collection* (1984); Marquis, Alice Goldfarb, *Alfred H. Barr, Jr., Missionary for the Modern* (1989).

barracuda   [bair-uh-koo′-duh]

Barracuda are predaceous fish of the family Sphyraenidae, order Perciformes, that inhabit temperate and tropical waters throughout the world. They have a long-bodied form with a sharp set of fangs and jutting lower jaw. The most common species along the western Atlantic coast is the great barracuda, *Sphyraena barracuda,* which is most abundant in the

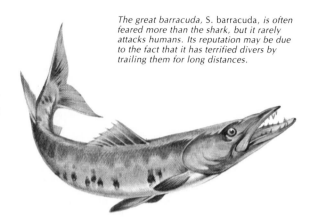

The great barracuda, S. barracuda, is often feared more than the shark, but it rarely attacks humans. Its reputation may be due to the fact that it has terrified divers by trailing them for long distances.

West Indies. The great barracuda may grow to more than 3 m (10 ft) in length; the larger ones tend to live in the deeper waters of the coral reefs, where they feed on fish. Barracuda can be dangerous to humans when provoked, being attracted to erratic movement and bright colors. Overall, however, the low number of alleged attacks does not completely support its dangerous reputation.   ALFRED PERLMUTTER

Bibliography: Caillet, G. M., et al., *Fishes: A Guide to Their Structure, Systematics, and Natural History* (1986).

barracudina   [bair-uh-koo-dee′-nuh]

Barracudinas are among the most common mid-water (to a depth of 3.2 km/2 mi) marine fishes found in all oceans. Barracudinas are slender-bodied and resemble their namesakes, the barracudas, in having an impressive array of teeth. Unlike most mid-water fishes, the majority of barracudinas lack luminescent organs, the genus *Lestidium* being an exception.

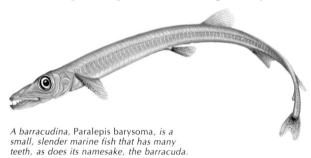

A barracudina, Paralepis barysoma, is a small, slender marine fish that has many teeth, as does its namesake, the barracuda.

The largest measured species, *Paralepis barysoma,* grows to about 61 cm (24 in). Barracudinas are the favorite food of many larger fishes, including the tunas. The barracudinas are members of the family Paralepididae.   EDWARD O. WILEY

Barragán, Luis   [bah-rah-gahn′]

The Mexican architect Luis Barragán, b. 1902, d. Nov. 22, 1988, is known for his abstract minimalist building designs and visually dramatic landscape settings, which often include the evocative use of still or running water. In numerous residential buildings in Mexico City, notably the luxurious Jardines de Pedregal (1945–50), and at the spare and ascetic chapel for the Capuchinas Sacramentarius in Tlalpan (1952–53), he used vast unbroken walls that give the impression of abstract, planar sculpture.

Barragán's frequent use of such vibrant colors as coral, pink, lemon, and magenta on the exteriors of his buildings evokes the richness of traditional Mexican village and ranch architecture, by which he was strongly influenced. He also found inspiration in SURREALISM, in the French architect LE CORBUSIER, and in Moorish gardens, with their fountains and walled enclosures. An effect of great refinement and serenity characterizes Las Arboledas (1958–61) and the Folke Egerstrom house and stable (1967–68) in Mexico City, designs in which expanses of controlled water are used as reflective sheeting. He was awarded the 1980 Pritzker Architecture Prize.

DONALD ROBERTSON AND MARTHA ROBERTSON

Bibliography: Ambasz, Emilio, *The Architecture of Luis Barragán* (1976); Kirby, Rosina G., *Mexican Landscape Architecture* (1972); Portugal, A. S., *The Architecture of Light, Color, and Form* (1992); Smith, Clive B., *Builders in the Sun: Five Mexican Architects* (1967).

Barranquilla   [bah-rahn-kee′-ah]

Barranquilla (1992 est. pop., 1,018,763), a city on the Río Magdalena in northern Colombia, 16 km (10 mi) from the Caribbean Sea and Colombia's principal Caribbean port, is the capital of Atlántico department. The port ships cotton from the surrounding agricultural region and coffee and petroleum from the interior. Diversified industries in the city produce textiles, shoes, beverages, foodstuffs, furniture, cement, and petrochemicals. Several publishing firms are located there. With an international airport and modern railroad and highway connections, Barranquilla draws tourists to its colorful carnivals. Atlántico University (1941) and the University of the North (1966) are located there. Settled in 1629, the city grew in importance when steamboats began to navigate the river. During the 1930s sandbars at the river's mouth were dredged.

Barraqué, Jean   [bah-rah-kay′]

Jean Barraqué, b. Jan. 17, 1928, d. Aug. 17, 1973, was a French composer best known for his SERIAL MUSIC. He studied with Jean Langlais and Olivier Messiaen. Beginning in 1961 he investigated problems of musical aesthetics at the Centre National de la Recherche Scientifique in Paris. Although a serialist composer, Barraqué was a romanticist and a firm opponent of musical collage and aleatory music. Most of his works written after 1956 are related to his huge cycle for voices and instruments, *The Death of Virgil*, after Hermann BROCH. Barraqué's principal supporter was the French jazz expert André Hodeir, who, in *Since Debussy* (1961), ranked Barraqué the highest among contemporary French composers. Most critics do not share this assessment.   DIKA NEWLIN

Bibliography: Myers, R., *Modern French Music* (1971; repr. 1984); Rostand, C., *French Music Today* (1955; repr. 1973).

Barras, Paul François Jean Nicolas, Vicomte de   [bah-rahs′]

The vicomte de Barras, b. June 30, 1775, d. Jan. 29, 1829, a French revolutionary, was a leading member of the five-man DIRECTORY government (1795–99). He joined the Jacobins and was elected to the National Convention in 1792.

Becoming opposed to the Reign of Terror, he helped depose (July 1794) Maximilien ROBESPIERRE and subsequently commanded the Army of the Interior and the police. In 1795 he chose Napoléon Bonaparte (later NAPOLEON I) to put down a revolt in Paris against the Directory. As a director he lived in luxury, sustained by bribes. Bonaparte's coup of Nov. 10, 1799, forced him to retire from government. Napoleon exiled him from France twice: he lived in Belgium from 1801 to 1805 and in Rome from 1813 to 1814.

barratry   [bar′-uh-tree]

Barratry, in criminal law, is the offense of stirring up lawsuits that have no grounds. A closely related offense is champerty, a bargain between a party to a suit and a third person, in which the latter agrees to help pay the costs of the suit in return for a share of the proceeds. In maritime law, barratry is an act, committed by the master or crew of a vessel, that injures the vessel's owners.

Barrault, Jean Louis   [bah-roh′]

A French actor, director, and mime, Jean Louis Barrault, b. 1910, d. Jan. 22, 1994, was a student of Charles Dullin at Théâtre de l'Atelier and of the mime Étienne Decroux. His performances in Ben Jonson's *Volpone* and William Faulkner's *As I Lay Dying* brought him to the attention of Antonin ARTAUD, who taught him not to "intellectualize" his roles but to feel them. Barrault joined the Comédie Française in 1940 and staged plays by Aeschylus, Shakespeare, and Paul Claudel. With his wife, Madeleine Renaud, he founded the Compagnie Renaud-Barrault (1947), where he directed and acted in André Gide's translation of *Hamlet*, Franz Kafka's *The Trial*, and plays by Albert Camus, Jean Anouilh, Eugène Ionesco, Samuel Beckett, and Jean Genet. Later, he began staging collage spectacles: *Rabelais* (1968), *Jarry* (1970), and *Zarathustra* (1974). His most noteworthy film role was in *Children of Paradise* (1944) by Marcel Carné.

Barrault wrote in his autobiographies, *Reflections on the Theatre* (1945; Eng. trans., 1951) and *The Theatre of Jean-Louis Barrault* (1961; Eng. trans., 1961), that actors must learn the art of diction, breath control, and the use of the body and face to exteriorize their emotions. They must use their hearts and imaginations as they listen to the author and the characters they conjure up before audiences.   BETTINA KNAPP

Barre   [bair′-ee]

Barre (1990 pop., 9,482) is a city in Washington County in central Vermont. The area was settled in 1788; the town, organized in 1793 as Wildersburgh, was renamed for Barre, Mass. Since the War of 1812 its chief industries have been granite quarrying and finishing, which have attracted skilled European stonecutters to the area. The Rock of Ages granite quarry, the world's largest, is open to visitors. Goddard College (1863) is also nearby.

Barre, Raymond   [bahr]

Raymond Barre, b. Apr. 12, 1924, was prime minister of France under President Valéry Giscard d'Estaing from 1976 until 1981. He also served as minister of finance and economic affairs from 1976 to 1978. Backed by the conservative Union pour la démocratie française, he was an unsuccessful candidate for the presidency in 1988. Barre has been a professor of economics since 1951 (at Tunis, Caen, and Paris) and was vice-president (1967–72) of the European Commission.

barrel

A barrel is a round container or cask, usually made of wood or metal. Originally, all barrels were made of wooden staves bound together with iron or wooden hoops. The staves were bowed to make the barrels wider in the middle than at the ends, a shape that enabled them to better withstand expansion pressure from within.

Cooperage, the craft of barrel making, is ancient. The Roman scholar Pliny claimed that it originated among the inhabitants of the Alpine valleys, where wood was plentiful. Barrels became especially important for use in shipping, which expanded enormously after the Middle Ages. For centuries most commodities were shipped in barrels.

Two kinds of wood barrels are made today: slack barrels for dry goods and tight barrels for liquids. Slack barrels are usually made of pine but can be fashioned from other softwoods, and they do not require precise workmanship. Tight barrels, on the other hand, are carefully constructed. To prevent undesirable odors from forming in the barrel's contents, only high-grade woods are used—usually white oak but occasionally red oak, gum, ash, or Douglas fir. Barrel interiors are often coated with glue, sodium silicate, paraffin, or other materials. In addition, tight barrels usually have an opening, called a bunghole, for filling and emptying.

Barrel making begins with cutting and planing the staves, which are jointed at the edges so that the barrel will have a uniform bulge and taper. The staves are then stood upright, arranged in a circle, and fitted with temporary hoops. After the ends of the staves are trimmed and fitted with flat headpieces, permanent hoops are put into place, and the finished barrel is tested for leaks.

Barrel making began with tapering the staves, held on a block (1) or hook (2) or clamped on a shaving horse (3). The staves were beveled on a jointer plane (4), then arranged upright in a circle and fitted with temporary hoops (5). Finally, headpiece grooves were cut (6). The craft of barrel making, or cooperage, has become rare, and the manufacture of modern barrels is usually a mechanized process.

Once a skilled handicraft, cooperage is now largely mechanized. Modern coopers make tanks, vats, and other wooden vessels as well as barrels. Barrels are used primarily in the brewing and distilling industries for storing and maturing beer, wine, whiskey, and other alcoholic beverages.

Bibliography: Dyer, Walter, *Early American Craftsmen* (1978); Jupo, Frank, *To Carry and to Keep: The Story of Containers* (1976); Newman, Thelma and Jay H., *The Container Book* (1977).

barrel organ

The barrel organ is a mechanical pipe organ that uses a revolving cylinder with projecting pins to produce a melody. The cylinder is turned by means of a handle that also operates a bellows, forcing air through the organ pipes. Some barrel organs are operated by means of a clockwork system.

The barrel organ, a mechanical instrument operated by a handle or clockwork, was popular in English country churches beginning in the 18th century. This instrument is often confused with the HURDY-GURDY, a medieval instrument, and with the barrel piano, a mechanical instrument used by street musicians. The action of the barrel organ operates the bellows and rotates a barrel from which pins project. These open valves on the pipes, allowing air to enter and the pipes to sound. Barrel organs had as few as eight pitches and as many as the full chromatic range.   ELWYN A. WIENANDT

Bibliography: Chapuis, A., *History of the Musical Box and of Mechanical Music* (1980); Ord-Hume, A. W., *Clockwork Music* (1973) and *The Musical Box* (1980).

Barrès, Maurice   [bah-res']

Maurice Barrès, b. Aug. 19, 1862, d. Dec. 5, 1923, was a French novelist, essayist, and politician best known for the mystic na-

tionalism and the egoism that underlie such works as *Le Culte du moi* (The Cult of Ego, 1888–91). *Sous l'oeil des barbares* (Under the Eye of Barbarians, 1888), *Les Déracinés* (The Uprooted, 1897), and *La Colline inspirée* (The Inspired Hill, 1913) stressed the role of race, nation, and heritage in the creation of the individual. A political reactionary and anti-Dreyfusard, Barrès presented his views in ironic, biting articles in various newspapers, particularly, *L'Echo de Paris.*

JOSEPH A. REITER

Barrie, Sir James

James Matthew Barrie, b. May 9, 1860, d. June 19, 1937, was a Scottish novelist and playwright whose works include the enduring children's play PETER PAN. He also wrote a number of other entertaining plays, highly popular in their day, and interesting fictional and autobiographical works.

Barrie received a strict upbringing in the village of Kirriemuir, which, as the imaginary Thrums, furnished the setting and material for much of his fiction, including *Auld Licht Idylls* (1888) and *A Window in Thrums* (1889). He went to Edinburgh University and then became a journalist in Nottingham. He later moved to London as a free-lance writer, but soon relied solely on literature for his livelihood. With the publication in 1891 of the novel *The Little Minister* and the play *Richard Savage*, he became prominent. His other early work includes *The Professor's Love Story* (1892), a play char-

Sir James M. Barrie, a Scottish novelist and playwright, wrote a succession of popular plays during the early 20th century. His most memorable works include the classic children's play Peter Pan (1904) and the comedy What Every Woman Knows (1908).

acterized by its humor and sentimentality, and *Margaret Ogilvy* (1896), a biography of his mother, to whom he was closely attached. He found the writing of novels difficult and turned more and more to drama. His dramatic reputation was established with the romantic *Quality Street* and *The Admirable Crichton* (both 1902) with its social satire. Despite the influence of IBSEN at that time, Barrie wrote only one problem play, *The Wedding Guest* (1900), in which the former mistress of the bridegroom, with their child, invades his wedding. His later plays include *What Every Woman Knows* (1908) and, perhaps his best, *Dear Brutus* (1917), a mixture of fairy tale and realism. *Peter Pan or the Boy Who Would Not Grow Up* was first performed on Dec. 27, 1904, and was published as the story *Peter and Wendy* in 1911 and as a play in 1928. It has been translated into many languages, and its hero has taken his place in English folklore. The play is a mixture of adventure story and fairy tale about pirates, human flight, and eternal childhood. Its setting is the imaginative world of children, and its universal attraction is the celebration of youth, a theme that has tragic overtones for adults.

RICHARD M. FORD

Bibliography: Birkin, Andrew, *J. M. Barrie and the Lost Boys* (1979); Dunbar, Janet, *J. M. Barrie: The Man Behind the Image* (1970).

Barrios, Eduardo

Eduardo Barrios, b. Oct. 27, 1884, d. Sept. 13, 1963, was a Chilean author celebrated for his probing psychological novels. His *El niño que enloqueció de amor* (The Boy Who Went Mad from Love, 1915) is an analysis of a boy's erotic obsession with an older woman. *Brother Ass* (1922; Eng. trans., 1942), about a religious mania, is often considered his best work. Other noted novels include *Un perdido* (The Failure, 1918), about an alcoholic, *Gran señor y rajadiablos* (Gentleman and Hell-Raiser, 1948), and *Los hombres del hombre* (The Men of the Man, 1950). Barrios also wrote short stories and plays and served Chile as minister of education.

GERARDO LUZURIAGA

Bibliography: Davidson, Ned J., *Eduardo Barrios* (1970).

Barrios, Justo Rufino

As president of Guatemala (1873–85), Justo Rufino Barrios, b. 1835, was noted for his harsh antichurch policies and his aggressive liberal reforms. He severely limited church authority while strengthening the provincial governments. He improved education, built roads, and encouraged the development of coffee growing. Barrios also tried and failed to unite all the Central American countries under his leadership. Having invaded El Salvador, he was killed at the Battle of Chalchuapa on Apr. 2, 1885.

barrister

In England and Wales, under a distinction that has become increasingly blurred, a barrister has traditionally been the lawyer who tries cases in higher courts, as opposed to a solicitor, who briefs the barrister, handles pretrial preparations, and represents clients in lower court cases.

Barron, Clarence Walker

Clarence Barron, b. Boston, July 2, 1855, d. Oct. 2, 1928, was a newspaperman who, as publisher of the *Wall Street Journal* from 1902 to 1928, gave American economic journalism its modern interpretative role. Until then, it had been heavily statistical. He started the Boston News Bureau, a financial bulletin service, in 1887, later expanding his control to the *Philadelphia Financial News*, which he founded in 1895. Barron took over the *Wall Street Journal* seven years later. In 1921 he founded *Barron's National Business and Financial Weekly,* thus consolidating his hegemony over American financial reporting. Barron wrote books about the Boston stock exchange (1893), the Federal Reserve Act (1914), and military finance (1919). In *They Told Barron* (2 vols.; 1930, 1931), he described many of the financial personalities of his day.

Barrow

Barrow is a village in northern Alaska, located 14 km (9 mi) southwest of Point Barrow, the northernmost part of the United States. Its population of 3,469 (1990) is predominantly Eskimo. Whaling and handicrafts are important industries, and the area has vast oil and gas reserves. The U.S. Navy maintains the Barrow Arctic Science Research Station. The city was incorporated in 1959.

barrow

The term *barrow* is applied to a variety of burial monuments in European prehistory, ranging from the stone-built chambered tombs of the NEOLITHIC PERIOD in the Atlantic west to the Iron Age burial mounds of the HALLSTATT and LA TÈNE cultures of Britain and Europe. Specifically, however, it refers to the unchambered earthen tumuli, often originally built over internal structures of timber, that characterize BRONZE AGE cemeteries. The cemeteries of the WESSEX CULTURE of southern England are of this type; some are outstanding for the wealth of their grave goods, including bronze weapons, gold ornaments, and necklaces of amber and faïence.

DENNIS W. HARDING

Barrow, Clyde

Clyde Barrow, b. Tellice, Tex., Mar. 24, 1909, was a murderer and bank robber whose story was dramatized in the film *Bonnie and Clyde* (1967). For four years he and Bonnie Parker (b. Rowena, Tex., Oct. 1, 1910) wandered the southwestern United States, holding up gas stations, luncheonettes, and small-town banks. The pair killed 12 people before they themselves were killed in a police ambush in Louisiana on May 23, 1934.

Bibliography: Grove, Larry, and Hinton, Ted, *Ambush* (1979).

Barrow, Isaac

The English theologian and natural philosopher Isaac Barrow, b. Oct. 1630, d. May 4, 1677, is known for his work in mathematics and for his influence on Sir Isaac NEWTON. A graduate of Trinity College, Cambridge (1648, 1652), Barrow served (1663–69) as the first Lucasian professor of mathematics at Cambridge. He was succeeded in this position by Newton, who attended his lectures and who addressed many of the important problems in physics as a result of Barrow's influence. Barrow was ordained an Anglican minister in 1659 and served as chaplain to Charles II from 1670. With his *Lectiones geometricae* (Geometrical Lectures, 1670), he anticipated the development of the calculus.

Bibliography: Child, J. M., ed., *The Geometrical Lectures of Isaac Barrow* (1916); Osmond, P. H., *Isaac Barrow: His Life and Times* (1944).

Barrow, Sir John

Sir John Barrow, b. June 19, 1764, d. Nov. 23, 1848, was an English administrator and geographer. An official of the Admiralty from 1804 to 1845, he encouraged exploration of the Arctic, particularly the expeditions of William PARRY and John FRANKLIN. Barrow Strait, Point Barrow, and Cape Barrow are named for him. He wrote a history of Arctic exploration (1846) and accounts of his own travels in China and Africa.

Barry, Sir Charles

Sir Charles Barry, b. May 23, 1795, d. May 12, 1860, was one of the leading architects in England in the second quarter of the 19th century. He achieved fame as a designer in the revivals of Greek, Gothic, and Italianate styles. Barry is best known for designing the Houses of Parliament (he won the competition in 1836), which he completed with assistance on the Gothic decoration by Augustus PUGIN. Barry's most characteristic works include the Travellers' Club (1829–31) and Reform Club (1837–41) in London, designed in the Italian *palazzo* mode; the Royal Institution in Manchester (1824–35; now City Art Gallery) in the Greek Revival manner; such Gothic Revival churches as Saint Peter, Brighton (1824–28); and country houses, among them Cliveden, Buckinghamshire (1850–51).

Bibliography: Fleetwood-Hesketh, Peter, "Sir Charles Barry," in *Victorian Architecture*, ed. by Peter Ferriday (1963); Hitchcock, Henry-Russell, *Early Victorian Architecture in Britain*, 2 vols. (1954).

Barry, John

John Barry, b. 1745, d. Sept. 13, 1803, was a U.S. naval commander in the AMERICAN REVOLUTION. Born in Ireland, he immigrated to America in the early 1770s. In 1776 he was commissioned a captain in the Continental Navy. Commanding the brigantine *Lexington*, Barry captured (Apr. 17, 1776) the British tender *Edward*—the first British ship to be taken at sea by the Americans. His subsequent commands were the *Effingham*, the *Raleigh*, and the *Alliance*; in the last, he captured two British ships in 1781 and fought (Mar. 10, 1783) the final naval engagement of the war, against the British *Sybil*.

During the undeclared war with France (1798–1800), Barry was in command of U.S. forces in the Caribbean. Because of his role in training Stephen DECATUR and other prominent second-generation naval officers, Barry is sometimes called the father of the U.S. Navy.

Bibliography: Clark, William B., *Gallant John Barry, 1745–1803* (1938).

Barry, Philip

Philip Barry, b. Rochester, N.Y., June 18, 1896, d. Dec. 3, 1949, was an American dramatist. He first thought of entering politics, but instead studied playwriting in George Pierce Baker's 47 Workshop at Harvard. He is best known for such witty, elegant social comedies as *Holiday* (1928; films, 1930, 1938), *The Animal Kingdom* (1932; films, 1932, 1946), and *The Philadelphia Story* (1939; film, 1940). He also wrote serious plays of a psychological and moral nature, including *Hotel Universe* (1930) and *Here Come the Clowns* (1938).

Barrymore   (family)

The Barrymores were an Anglo-American family of actors who became prominent first on the New York stage and then in Hollywood films. Their close-knit, imperious, and tempestuous lives were the thinly disguised subject of *The Royal Family* (1927), a play by George S. KAUFMAN and Edna FERBER.

The patriarch of the family, **Maurice Barrymore** (1847–1905), gave up the law and a projected career in the civil service to devote himself to the theater. He made his debut in London in 1872 and immigrated to America in 1875. That same year, in New York, he appeared in Augustin DALY's melodrama *Under the Gaslight*. Barrymore acted opposite most of the famous actresses of his day, and in 1876 married one, **Georgianna Drew** (1856–93), who had begun her career at the age of 16 in the acting company of her parents, John and Louisa Lane Drew. Together, the Barrymores appeared in

The Barrymores (left to right), John, Ethel, and Lionel, belonged to the second generation of a prominent family of American actors. In 1932 the three starred in the film Rasputin and the Empress, *the only production in which the family appeared together.*

such plays as *Diplomacy* (1886) and as leading players in Helena Modjeska's company. Georgianna also played opposite Edwin Booth, but ill health led to an early death.

The Barrymores' eldest son, **Lionel**, b. Apr. 28, 1878, d. Nov. 15, 1954, first appeared in his grandmother's company and later achieved fame in such plays as *The Copperhead*. He left the stage for Hollywood, won the Academy Award as best actor in *Free Soul* (1931), and appeared in *Grand Hotel* (1932) and *Dinner at Eight* (1933). He also played the gruff but kindly Dr. Gillespie in 15 Dr. Kildare movies, beginning with *Young Dr. Kildare* (1938). A serious hip injury forced him into a wheel chair in 1938, but he continued to work in films and radio. *We Barrymores*, his biography of the family, was published in 1951.

Lionel's sister, **Ethel Barrymore**, b. Aug. 15, 1879, d. June 18, 1959, became one of America's foremost stage actresses. After her debut in 1894 and a brief appearance in London with the English actor Henry Irving, she achieved immediate success in 1901 as Madame Trentoni in Clyde Fitch's *Captain Jinks of the Horse Marines*. She also played Shakespeare's heroines Juliet and Portia, Dumas *fils'* Camille, and Ibsen's Nora in *A Doll's House*. Her most notable performance was Miss Moffat in *The Corn Is Green* (1940). She also received an Academy Award for her supporting role in the film *None But the Lonely Heart* (1944). Her autobiography, *Memories*, appeared in 1955.

Lionel's brother, **John Barrymore**, b. Feb. 15, 1882, d. May 29, 1942, known for his superb profile and erratic temper, was the most famous member of the family. Following his debut in 1903 he became a matinee idol before turning to films in the 1920s. In 1922–23 he appeared in a record 101 performances as Hamlet, considered his finest stage role. Barrymore also acted in the screen comedies *A Bill of Divorcement* (1932) and *Twentieth Century* (1934). His private life was troubled by four marriages, alcoholism, and a belittling sense of himself. Barrymore's autobiography, *Confessions of an Actor*, was published in 1926.

Although the Barrymores never appeared together on stage, they did act together in the film *Rasputin and the Empress* (1932).   ANDREW J. KELLY

Bibliography: Alpert, Hollis, *The Barrymores* (1964); Barrymore, Elaine, *All My Sins Remembered* (1964); Barrymore, John, *The Life and Times of John Barrymore* (1943; repr. 1978); Fowler, Gene, *Good Night, Sweet Prince* (1943); Garton, Joseph W., *The Film Acting of John Barrymore* (1980); Kotsilibas-Davis, James, *Great Times, Good Times: The Odyssey of Maurice Barrymore* (1977).

Barth, Heinrich

Heinrich Barth, b. Feb. 16, 1821, d. Nov. 25, 1865, was a German explorer who traveled in North and Central Africa. From 1845 to 1847 he journeyed through North Africa and the Middle East, examining antiquities. In 1850 he joined an expedition across the Sahara, taking charge after the death of its leader. He continued to Central Africa and contributed to knowledge of the region.

Barth, John

John Simmons Barth, b. Cambridge, Md., May 27, 1930, is one of the first American writers to win both popular and academic acclaim for his experimental fiction. His early novels *The Floating Opera* (1956) and *The End of the Road* (1958; film, 1970) drew heavily on the philosophy of EXISTENTIALISM and the fiction of Albert CAMUS and Jean Paul SARTRE. With *The Sot-Weed Factor* (1960), however, Barth abandoned conventional storytelling and moralizing in favor of a literature that criticizes itself through the use of burlesque and parody.

Barth's theory of fiction, explained in his essay "The Literature of Exhaustion" (*Atlantic Monthly*, August 1967) is perhaps best illustrated in his novel *Giles Goat-Boy* (1966) and his collection of short fiction entitled *Lost in the Funhouse* (1968). Barth has been strongly influenced by his long experience as an English professor at Pennsylvania State University, the State University of New York at Buffalo, and The Johns Hopkins University, and by the literary theory of the Argentine writer Jorge Luis Borges. He argued in the essay that the —in his view—apparent exhaustion of all literary forms makes it imperative that the contemporary writer "confront an intellectual dead end and employ it against himself to accomplish new human work." His collection of three novellas, *Chimera* (1972), received a 1973 National Book Award for fiction; *Letters* (1979), *Sabbatical* (1982), and *The Tidewater Tales* (1987) are more recent novels.   JEROME KLINKOWITZ

Bibliography: Harris, C. B., *Passionate Virtuosity* (1983); Klinkowitz, J., *Literary Disruptions* (1975); Waldmeir, J. J., *Critical Essays on John Barth* (1980); Walkiewicz, E. P., *John Barth* (1986).

Barth, Karl   (bahrt)

Karl Barth, b. Basel, Switzerland, May 10, 1886, d. Dec. 9, 1968, is considered by some the greatest Protestant theologian of the 20th century and possibly the greatest since the Reformation. More than anyone else, Barth inspired and led the renaissance of theology that took place from about 1920 to 1950. He studied at the universities of Bern, Berlin, Tübingen, and Marburg and held pastorates in Switzerland between 1909 and 1921. During this time, he became known as a radical critic both of the prevailing liberal theology and of the social order. Liberal theology, Barth believed, had accommodated Christianity to modern culture. The crisis of World War I was in part a symptom of this unholy alliance. In his famous commentary on Romans (1919), Barth stressed the discontinuity between the Christian message and the world. God is the wholly other; he is known only in his revelation; he is not the patron saint of culture, but its judge.

Between 1921 and 1935, Barth held professorships at Göttingen, Münster, and Bonn. He engaged in controversy with Adolf von HARNACK, holding that the latter's scientific theology is only a preliminary to the true task of theology, which is identical with that of preaching. With the rise of Adolf Hitler, Barth emerged as a leader of the church opposition to Nazi control, expressed in the Barmen Declaration of 1934.

Deprived of his chair at Bonn, he returned to Switzerland and from 1935 until his retirement in 1962 was professor at Basel, exercising a worldwide influence. During this period he worked on his *Church Dogmatics* (1932–67), a multivolume work of great richness that was unfinished at his death. Although he modified some of his early positions, he continued to maintain that theology is concerned only with unfolding the revealed word attested in the Bible and has no place for natural theology or the insights of non-Christian religions. He held that religion is humankind's attempt to grasp at God and is therefore diametrically opposed to revelation, in which God has come to humans through Christ.

Although Barth's uncompromising position was a great strength during the period of Nazi power, his views were increasingly subjected to criticism in the following decades. Some argue that he was too negative in his estimate of humankind and its reasoning powers and too narrow in limiting revelation to the biblical tradition, thus excluding the non-Christian religions.   JOHN MACQUARRIE

Bibliography: Anderson, W. P., *Aspects of the Theology of Karl Barth* (1981); Jungel, E., *Karl Barth: A Theological Legacy* (1986); Küng, H., *Justification: The Doctrine of Karl Barth and a Catholic Reflection* (1964); Sykes, S. W., *Karl Barth: Studies of His Theological Method* (1979); Villa-Vicencio, C., ed., *On Reading Karl Barth in South Africa* (1988); Willis, R. E., *The Ethics of Karl Barth* (1971).

Barthelme, Donald   [bahr'-tuhl-mee]

Short-story writer and novelist Donald Barthelme, b. Philadelphia, Apr. 7, 1931, d. July 23, 1989, was a major figure among Americans who write outside the realist tradition. A newspaper reporter, art-museum director, and university publicist, Barthelme became a full-time writer after the publication of his first short-fiction collection, *Come Back Dr. Caligari* (1964). Barthelme's novels, *Snow White* (1967), *The Dead Father* (1975), and *Paradise* (1986), deftly satirize American life and reveal a sharp eye for the absurdities concealed beneath familiar customs. *60 Stories* (1981), *Overnight to Many Distant Cities* (1983), and *40 Stories* (1987) are short-story collections.

Donald's brother Frederick, b. Houston, Tex., Oct. 10, 1943, is both artist and writer. His spare style mimics the emotional sparseness of the suburban lives he describes in short-story collections (*Moon Deluxe*, 1983) and such novels as *Two against One* (1988).   JEROME KLINKOWITZ

Bibliography: Couturier, M., and Durand, R., *Donald Barthelme* (1982); Klinkowitz, J., *The Life of Fiction* (1977); Molesworth, C. F., *Donald Barthelme's Fiction* (1982); Stengel, W. B., *The Shape of Art in the Short Stories of Donald Barthelme* (1985).

Barthes, Roland   [bahrt]

The distinguished French literary critic and intellectual Roland Barthes, b. Nov. 12, 1915, d. Mar. 25, 1980, was a leading exponent of the application of STRUCTURALISM and SEMIOTICS to the study of literature. Barthes believed that language is a system of signs reflecting the assumptions of a particular society at a particular time. He expressed this view in *Writing Degree Zero* (1953; Eng. trans., 1977) and *Critical Essays* (1964; Eng. trans., 1972). Signs and symbols are themselves a form of language, and Barthes's work in this area produced *The Empire of Signs* (1970; Eng. trans., 1982), which applies semiotics to Japanese culture. Other influential Barthes works include *S/Z* (1970; Eng. trans., 1974) and *The Pleasure of the Text* (1973; Eng. trans., 1975). *The Barthes Reader* (1983), edited by Susan Sontag, contains selections in English from his writings.

Bibliography: Culler, J. D., *Roland Barthes* (1983); Lavers, A., *Roland Barthes* (1982); Thody, P., *Roland Barthes: A Conservative Estimate* (1984); Wiseman, M., *The Ecstacies of Roland Barthes* (1988).

Bartholdi, Frédéric Auguste   [bahr-tohl-dee']

The French sculptor Frédéric Auguste Bartholdi, b. Aug. 2, 1834, d. Oct. 4, 1904, studied architecture and painting in Paris before exhibiting his first sculpture in 1853. Thereafter he received many commissions for public monumental sculpture, including that for the colossal bronze STATUE OF LIBERTY (*Liberty Enlightening the World*, erected 1886) in New York Harbor. After the Franco-Prussian War of 1870–71, he received several commissions for war memorials, of which the huge red sandstone *Lion of Belfort* (1875–80) in Belfort, France, is the best known. Besides the Statue of Liberty, Bartholdi also made other sculptures reflecting Franco-American friendship, such as his statue (1873–76) of the Marquis de Lafayette for Union Square, New York City, and a group (1896) of George Washington and Lafayette for the Place des États-Unis, Paris.   MARIAN BURLEIGH-MOTLEY

Bartholomew, Saint

Saint Bartholomew was one of the apostles, mentioned only in the lists of the Twelve (Matt. 10:3; Mark 3:18; Luke 6:14; Acts 1:13). His name means "son of Tolmai," and he is frequently identified with Nathanael (John 1). According to tradition, he was martyred in Armenia. Feast day: Aug. 24 (Western); June 11 (Eastern).

Bartlett, Jennifer

The American artist Jennifer Losch Bartlett, b. Long Beach, Calif., Mar. 14, 1941, achieved fame in 1976 with the exhibition of *Rhapsody* (1975) in New York City. Consisting of 988 enameled steel plates, with both figurative and abstract images, *Rhapsody* established Bartlett's characteristic mode of working on a single theme through subthemes, by dissection and variation. Her series *In the Garden* (1979–80) consists of 200 drawings in pencil, pen, watercolor, and other media; this suite gave rise in 1983 to 8 large oil paintings. In 1985, Bartlett published *Rhapsody* as well as *History of the Universe*, the latter with her photomontages.

Bartók, Béla   [bahr'-tohk, bel'-uh]

Béla Bartók, b. Mar. 25, 1881, d. Sept. 26, 1945, was one of the greatest composers of the 20th century. A Hungarian, he stud-

Béla Bartók, the 20th-century Hungarian composer, was a student and collector of folk music. He combined its rhythmic, melodic, and textural elements with traditional classical forms to produce a highly individual style of composition.

ied piano and composition at the Budapest Academy of Music, where he was appointed professor of piano in 1907.

Embittered by the hostile reception of his early works, Bartók began to collect Hungarian and other folk music. Until 1936 he traversed the Balkans, Turkey, and parts of North Africa searching for indigenous material, and with his friend, the composer Zoltán KODÁLY, he produced a series of important studies, anthologies, and arrangements of folk songs.

During the 1920s, Budapest audiences became less hostile to Bartók's music, and performances of his one-act opera *Duke Bluebeard's Castle* (1911) and ballets *The Wooden Prince* (1914–16) and *The Miraculous Mandarin* (1919) were well received. Bartók traveled widely in Europe as a pianist, and in 1927–28 he toured the United States.

The Piano Sonata of 1926 initiated Bartók's most fruitful period, which includes *Mikrokosmos* (1926–37), a large set of piano pieces designed for students; Piano Concertos Nos. 1 (1927) and 2 (1931); String Quartets Nos. 3–6 (1927–39), widely considered the most important contributions to the genre by a 20th-century composer; Music for Strings, Percussions, and Celesta (1936); Sonata for Two Pianos and Percussion (1937); and Violin Concerto No. 2 (1937–38). In 1940, in reaction to the growing Nazification of Hungary, Bartók went to the United States, where he remained until his death. These years were full of disappointment, financial hardship, and illness, yet during this time he completed the Concerto for Orchestra (1943) and all but the final bars of Piano Concerto No. 3, which were concluded by his friend Tibor Serly. Bartók died of leukemia in New York City.

The stark strength of Bartók's music, particularly the rhythmic drive of his fast movements, derives in large part from his affinity for folk music. His harmony is often dissonant, full of irregular chords and tone clusters; many of his melodies are based on the folk patterns of the pentatonic (5-tone) scale. The characteristic percussive quality and novel tone color of his music are achieved with traditional instruments.

Bibliography: Antokoletz, Elliott, *The Music of Bela Bartók* (1984); Demeny, Janos, ed., *Béla Bartók: Letters* (1972); Griffiths, Paul, *Bartók* (1984); Stevens, Halsey, *Life and Music of Béla Bartók*, rev. ed. (1967).

Bartolommeo, Fra   [bahr-toh-loh-may'-oh]

Fra Bartolommeo, also called Baccio della Porta, b. Mar. 28, 1472, d. Oct. 31, 1517, was the foremost painter in the High Renaissance in Florence after Leonardo da Vinci. Baccio's early painting style was influenced by Domenico GHIRLANDAIO, in whose workshop he trained. Baccio joined the Dominican Order in 1500, taking the name Fra Bartolommeo. By 1510, Bartolommeo had become the leading painter in Florence. His monumentalized style combines the geometrical compositions developed in the 15th century with the classical figural style that he helped to develop from Leonardo's work. A typical large altarpiece is *The Mystic Marriage of Saint Catherine* (1511; Louvre, Paris), which combines faultless

technique, complex spatial organization, and subtle use of color.

Bibliography: Freedberg, Sydney J., *Painting in Italy 1500–1600* (1970).

Bartolozzi, Francesco   [bahr-toh-loht'-tsee]

Francesco Bartolozzi, b. 1727, d. Mar. 7, 1815, was an Italian engraver who helped refine stipple engraving, a technique employing dots (stipples) rather than lines. Bartolozzi learned standard engraving techniques from his father, a goldsmith, and was soon famous for engraving facsimiles of paintings. In 1763 he came to England to reproduce the paintings in the Royal Collection. The graphic artist William Ryland taught him stipple technique, and Bartolozzi became its foremost exponent, producing over 1,500 plates.

Barton, Clara

Clarissa Harlowe Barton, b. North Oxford, Mass., Dec. 25, 1821, d. Apr. 12, 1912, founded the American RED CROSS. Known as the "Angel of the Battlefield," she cared for the wounded during the Civil War and helped gather identification records for the missing and the dead. After becoming familiar with the work of the International Red Cross in Europe, she organized a similar group in the United States in 1881.

Bibliography: Barton, Clara, *The Story of My Childhood* (1907; repr. 1980); Barton, William E., *The Life of Clara Barton*, 2 vols. (1922); Pryor, Elizabeth B., *Clara Barton: Professional Angel* (1987).

Barton, Derek

The English chemist Derek Harold Richard Barton, b. Sept. 8, 1918, received, with Odd HASSEL, the 1969 Nobel Prize for chemistry for his work on the three-dimensional structure of complex organic molecules. He later discovered (1960) a method for synthesizing the hormone ALDOSTERONE. Barton was serving (1949–50) as visiting professor at Harvard when his chief conclusions on molecular structure were announced. Thereafter he taught at the University of London, the University of Glasgow, and the Imperial College of Science and Technology. In 1978 he became director of France's Institut de Chimie des Substances Naturelles. He was knighted in 1972.

Barton, Sir Edmund

Edmund Barton, b. Jan. 18, 1849, d. Jan. 7, 1920, was the first prime minister of the Commonwealth of Australia (1901–03). From 1891 he led the federal movement, helping to draft the Commonwealth constitution. He served in the government of New South Wales in several positions, including that of acting prime minister. Knighted in 1902, he served as a senior judge of the Australian High Court from 1903 until his death.

Bibliography: Reynolds, John, *Edmund Barton* (1948).

Bartram, John

John Bartram, b. near Darby, Pa., Mar. 23, 1699, d. Sept. 22, 1777, a self-educated botanist, is considered by many to be the father of American botany. He founded (1728) a botanical garden at Kingsessing, Pa.—the first in the American colonies—where he performed hybridization experiments. In 1765, King George III named him botanist for the colonies. Bartram traveled in the eastern and southern United States and published descriptions of the soil, climate, and life forms of the regions he visited; he also introduced some European plants into the New World, and New World plants into Europe. His *Observations* (1751) described the Lake Ontario area.

Bibliography: Berkeley, Edmund and D. S., *The Life and Travels of John Bartram* (1982); Herbst, Josephine, *New Green World* (1954); Hindle, Brooke, *The Pursuit of Science in Revolutionary America, 1734–1789* (1956).

Bartsch, Adam von   [bahrch]

Adam von Bartsch, b. Aug. 17, 1757, d. Aug. 21, 1821, was an Austrian engraver, scholar, and cataloger. For many years he was director of the print collection of the Imperial Library in

Vienna. He compiled numerous catalogs of master engravings. His major publication was a monumental 21-volume work, *Le Peintre Graveur* (1803–21), which includes the engravings of 500 Flemish, Dutch, German, and Italian artists. His efforts contributed to the eventual recognition of printmaking as an important art form.   TANIA BAYARD

Baruch, Bernard M.   [buh-rook']

Bernard Mannes Baruch, b. Camden, S.C., Aug. 19, 1870, d. June 20, 1965, an American financier and confidant of presidents, began his career in a Wall Street brokerage house and made a fortune in stocks while still a young man. During World War I he was chairman of the War Industries Board, and following the war he was a U.S. delegate and an economic advisor to the Paris Peace Conference. In later years he often served as an economic advisor to government. Every president from Woodrow Wilson to John F. Kennedy consulted Baruch, and other government officials often conferred with him while seated on a park bench in Lafayette Square opposite the White House. He wrote about his life in *Baruch: My Own Story* (1957) and *Baruch: The Public Years* (1960).

Bibliography: Coit, M. L., *Mr. Baruch* (1957; repr. 1975); Grant, J., *Bernard M. Baruch* (1983); Schwarz, J. A., *The Speculator* (1981).

Baruch, Book of   [bair'-uhk]

Baruch, considered a canonical book of the Bible by Roman Catholics, follows the Book of Lamentations. It is not found in the Hebrew Bible and is included in the APOCRYPHA by Protestants. The book, a brief compilation of verses from the books of Job, Daniel, Isaiah, and Jeremiah, is named after Baruch (fl. 600 BC), secretary of the prophet Jeremiah. Its dependence upon later works such as Daniel, however, suggests a composition date in the 2d century BC. Written in three sections, it contains liturgical prayers and a homily on wisdom.

Barye, Antoine Louis   [bah-ree']

Antoine Louis Barye, b. Sept. 24, 1796, d. June 25, 1875, was a French sculptor renowned for his unparalleled bronzes of wild animals. At 13 he was apprenticed to a goldsmith; he entered the studio of sculptor François Bosio in 1816 and studied painting with Antoine Gros in 1817. Barye made direct observations of animals in the Paris zoos and attended lectures on animal physiology. The resultant watercolors are among the finest animal paintings in the world.

Barye's bronze *Tiger Devouring a Crocodile* (Louvre, Paris) won a medal in the Paris Salon of 1831, but five large hunting groups (Walters Art Gallery, Baltimore) were rejected for the Salon of 1837, a rebuff he answered by not submitting any works for years. Barye's studies in Greek art gave a neoclassic monumentality to his later works, as in the dynamic bronze *Theseus and the Minotaur* (1846; Hirschhorn Museum, Washington, D.C.) and in his powerful stone allegories *War, Peace, Force, and Order* (1854; Louvre). Barye became professor of zoological drawing at the Jardin des Plantes in Paris in 1854, and in 1868 he joined the Académie des Beaux-Arts.

Bibliography: Benge, G. F., *Antoine Louis Barye* (1984); Lengyel, Alfonz, *Life and Art of Antoine Louis Barye* (1963).

Barylambda   [bair-i-lam'-duh]

Barylambda, an extinct genus of pantodont mammal, was one of the largest land animals of the late Paleocene Epoch, about 55 million years ago (see TERTIARY PERIOD). It was quite unlike modern mammals, with an unusually heavy skeleton and a relatively small skull and short face. It stood about 1.2 m (4 ft) high at the shoulder and was approximately 2.4 m (8 ft) in length. Like other pantodonts, *Barylambda* appears to have been a plant eater. Its feet bore claws, which were probably used for digging roots.   WILLIAM H. MATTHEWS III

baryon   [bair'-ee-ahn]

A baryon is any member of a class of relatively heavy FUNDAMENTAL PARTICLES (from the Greek *barys*, meaning "heavy")

that comprises the proton (the lightest member), the neutron, and several particles called hyperons, denoted by the Greek letters *lambda*, *sigma*, *xi*, and *omega*. The hyperons have lifetimes of about 10^{-10} seconds and decay into nucleons and some number of MESONS or lighter particles. Each baryon is assumed to have a corresponding antibaryon.

See also: HADRON.

Baryshnikov, Mikhail   [buh-rish'-ni-kawf, meek-hyl']

Mikhail Baryshnikov, the Latvian-born virtuoso dancer, performs (1978) in Jerome Robbins's version of Afternoon of a Faun. *Famous for his brilliant but highly disciplined technique, Baryshnikov left the Kirov Ballet in 1974 for the chance to extend his repertoire in modern ballets.*

Mikhail Nikolaievich Baryshnikov, b. Riga, Latvian SSR, Jan. 27, 1948, is considered by many the greatest male classical dancer of his generation. He began his studies in Riga, then became a pupil of Aleksandr Pushkin at the Leningrad Choreographic School. He joined the Kirov Ballet in 1967, creating the title role in Konstantin Sergeyev's *Hamlet* (1970).

While on tour with Soviet dancers in Canada in 1974, he decided to remain in the West, because he wanted to dance a more extensive repertoire, particularly of contemporary works, than was available to him in the USSR. Soon afterward, he joined American Ballet Theatre (ABT). Although he continued to dance such classic ballets as *Giselle, La Bayadère*, and *La Sylphide*, he also added to his repertoire ballets by Frederick Ashton (*Les Patineurs* or The Skaters), George Balanchine (*Theme and Variations*), and Antony Tudor (*Shadowplay*). Twyla Tharp created *Push Comes to Shove* for him in 1976. Baryshnikov also appeared with Britain's Royal Ballet, dancing Ashton's *La Fille mal gardée* (Vain Precautions) and Kenneth MacMillan's *Romeo and Juliet*, and with other companies. Although he is capable of prodigious feats of virtuosity, his dancing is notable for the concealment of effort and of obvious preparation.

In 1976, Baryshnikov made his debut as a choreographer with *The Nutcracker* for ABT. A *Don Quixote* followed in 1978. That year he left ABT and joined New York City Ballet. He returned to ABT as director in 1980 and continued to choreograph (*Cinderella*, 1984) and to dance (premiering *The Mollino Room*, 1986). Differences with the ABT management led to his resignation in 1989. Soon after, he premiered in a revival of Martha Graham's *American Document*. Baryshnikov also has pursued a film career, appearing in *The Turning Point* (1977), *White Nights* (1985), and *Dancers* (1987).

DAVID VAUGHAN

Bibliography: Smakov, Gennady, *Baryshnikov* (1981).

Barzun, Jacques   [bahr'-zuhn]

Jacques Barzun, b. Créteil, France, Nov. 30, 1907, is an American historian, author, and teacher. He began studying at Columbia University before he was 16 and graduated at the top of his class in 1927. Columbia awarded him a doctorate in

French history in 1932. He taught there from 1929, later serving as dean of the graduate faculties (1955–58) and as dean of faculties (1958–67).

Barzun has written on a wide range of topics, including the mystery story, but is particularly known for his works on music, education, the role of the intellect, and 19th-century romanticism. Among his works are *Berlioz and the Romantic Century* (1950), a 2-volume study, and *Science: The Glorious Entertainment* (1964), in which he attacked the domination of modern thought by science.

In his controversial book *The House of Intellect* (1959), Barzun accused the American educational system of producing "deep hostility to intellect." He wrote, "The notion of helping a child has in the United States displaced that of teaching him." Barzun opposes specialization and vocationalism in education. He was one of the sponsors of a 2-year liberal education course at Columbia focusing on "great books." One of his later books is *Simple and Direct* (rev. ed., 1985).

Bibliography: Weiner, Dora B., and Keylor, William R., *From Parnassus: Essays in Honor of Jacques Barzun* (1976).

bas-relief   [bah-ree-leef']

Bas-relief, or low relief, is a sculptural term used to describe an object with a design slightly projecting from the surface. It is the opposite of high relief, in which the design appears almost wholly detached by undercutting from its background, being attached only where functionally necessary. Bas-relief designs are not raised high enough to appear detached from the surface; unlike high reliefs, bas-reliefs incorporate both surface plane and carving in their design. The degrees of projection from the surface plane in bas-reliefs remain variable and have depended on style, function, placement, or material.

This Assyrian bas-relief is from the palace of Ashurbanipal at Nineveh in present-day Iraq. Dating from about 700–650 BC, the relief represents scenes from a royal lion hunt. The king (lower right), shown drawing his bow, has an elaborately curled beard and wears a flowered tunic. The relief is in the British Museum, London.

This marble relief, a classical Greek work from the west frieze of the Parthenon, represents two horsemen. Dating from about 440 BC, it stands 103 cm (43 in) high. The relief, displayed at the British Museum, London, is part of the Elgin Marbles.

Early Use. The ancient Egyptians used a simple outline cut into the stone, with virtually no modeling and no projection beyond the level of the surface. This style is typical of the flat, two-dimensional nature of their art, which concentrated on illustrating a hierarchic view of life. The reliefs decorating the palaces of the Assyrian kings are in very low relief, with a particular interest in the naturalistic modeling of animal details. They exemplify the narrative use of bas-reliefs: battle scenes and lion hunts are depicted in long friezes; a fragment appears meaningless until seen within its context in the composition. Narrative friezes were also commonly used to decorate Greek temples, where an interest in representing depth was emphasized by an increasing number of superimposed planes. In parts of the Parthenon frieze, five or six planes are sometimes used, yet the actual thickness of the relief is only a little more than 5 cm (2 in).

Bas-Reliefs in Asia and Europe. Other ornamental reliefs are found in Indian temple-sculpture and in such Khmer temples as ANGKOR WAT. In Europe, Romanesque church decoration featured sculpture controlled by the architectural shape—a bas-relief is particularly suitable for decorating a flat pillar. Bas-reliefs were widely used for sculptured CAPITALS, varying from simple geometric ornamentation, as in English Norman cathedrals, to depictions of figures and vegetation, as in Romanesque and Gothic sculpture, or the elegant stylization of Early Christian and Byzantine sculpture. Byzantine art emphasized the purely decorative, as opposed to figurative, potential of bas-reliefs by concentrating on an extreme intricacy of carving to create flowing, lively patterns. The leafy basket capitals in HAGIA SOPHIA (AD 532–37), Istanbul, and the delicate marble pluteus (panel; 6th century) in Sant' Apollinare Nuovo, Ravenna, are prime examples of Byzantine sculpture.

Renaissance Illusionism. Pictorial illusionism is fully exploited in the *rilievo schiacciato* ("flat relief") refined by DONATELLO during the Renaissance. An extremely shallow, almost two-dimensional relief, it is delicately modeled to suggest a much greater depth through a trick of optical perspective. The success of this apparent contradiction shows a display of virtuosity that is typical of Renaissance ideals.

The very nature of these bas-reliefs, which, in a sense, are stone paintings, gives them stronger pictorial qualities than sculpture in the round. They have sometimes been used instead of paintings, as for example in the decoration of altarpieces: Donatello's *Ascension and Delivery of the Keys to St. Peter* (1428–30; Victoria and Albert Museum, London) may have served this function. The durability of bas-reliefs, as opposed to the relative fragility of paintings, was also a consideration in decoration of tombs, fonts, pulpits, and portals. Lorenzo GHIBERTI's east doors, called the *Gates of Paradise* (1425–52), of the Florence Baptistery are a supreme example of bas-relief in gilded bronze.

Bas-Reliefs on Small Objects. Not sharing the monumentality of three-dimensional sculpture, low relief is particularly suitable for the decoration of smaller objects. Private devotional

A superb example of bas-relief is seen in this detail from the Jacob and Esau panel of Lorenzo Ghiberti's masterpiece Gates of Paradise (1425–52). The work, one of ten rectangular panels depicting Old Testament themes, appears on the gilded bronze doors at the east portal of the Florence Baptistery. To achieve an illusion of space and perspective, the artist varies the depth of relief from fine lines to almost fully rounded figures.

Basalt, one of the two most common surface rocks, is a heavy, fine-grained volcanic mineral composed mainly of dark-colored silicates. Uniform cooling and contraction of vertical basaltic lava flows develop fractured columnar blocks, such as this specimen from the Columbia River plateau. Crushed into stones, it is used extensively in highway construction.

images in the form of diptychs (two panels) carved of ivory or cast in metal were common in Byzantine art and in the art of the Middle Ages, when manuscript covers were frequently decorated with ivory bas-reliefs. They have also been used for jewelry. Coincidental with the development of ornamental reliefs in Greek art, the CAMEO flowered as an art form in the classical and the Hellenistic periods. The Romans used cameos for both decoration and personal adornment; the *Gemma Augustea* (1st century AD; Kunsthistorisches Museum, Vienna) is one of the largest (20 by 23 cm/8 by 9 in) and most sumptuous extant examples. Throughout history, periods of classical revival have witnessed a specialized production of the cameo, and it has been highly prized as a collector's item since the Renaissance. Low relief was also used to decorate Chinese BRONZES as well as such jade objects as amuletic jewelry. PRE-COLUMBIAN jade ornaments are an example of the profusion of bas-reliefs in PRIMITIVE ART. Chinese lacquer work exploits varying levels of relief, in which intricate patterns are carved through differently colored layers of lacquer. Two of the earliest types of relief are on coins and seals, which served the practical purpose of imparting necessary information. Being impressed on a soft material, the actual seals have not survived as well as the engraved gems, either cylindrical or flat, from which the seal impressions were made; examples of such seal stones date from about 5000 BC in West Asia and were also widely used in the ancient Near East. GIULIA BARTRUM

Bibliography: Bazin, Germain, *The History of World Sculpture*, trans. by Madeline Jay (1976); Verhelst, Wilbert, *Sculpture*, 2d ed. (1987); Wittkower, Rudolf, *Sculpture: Processes and Principles* (1977).

See also: INTAGLIO; IVORY CARVING; SCULPTURE; SCULPTURE TECHNIQUES.

basal metabolism: see METABOLISM.

basalt [buh-sawlt']

Basalt is the most abundant of the Earth's volcanic rocks (see IGNEOUS ROCK). It is dark, dense, and hard, and usually has a texture so fine-grained that individual crystals can be seen only under a microscope. Most basalts occur in LAVA flows and sheets; coarser-grained basalts occur in DIKES. (GABBRO is a coarse-grained plutonic rock, crystallizing at great depth, that is chemically and mineralogically equivalent to basalt.) Basalts typically contain 42%–54% silicon dioxide (SiO_2), 13%–18% aluminum oxide (Al_2O_3), 8%–15% total iron, 3%–9% magnesium oxide (MgO), 6%–12% calcium oxide (CaO), 3%–6% sodium oxide (Na_2O), 1%–3% titanium oxide (TiO_2), 1%–2% potassium oxide (K_2O), and minor amounts of manganese oxide and other substances.

Mineralogically, basalts are made up of silicates such as plagioclase feldspar and pyroxene. They may also contain amphiboles. Small amounts of other minerals, including magnetite, ilmenite, apatite, and sphene, are always present. Natural glass is common in the matrix. Basalts of suboceanic origin may contain abundant olivine but varieties called tholeiites, often originating at or near the margins of continental plates, are olivine-free. Near rapidly cooled edges of flows or dikes, escaping gas produces a basalt full of holes, or vesicles, which may be filled with gemstones such as opal and chalcedony, or with zeolites.

Basaltic magma is believed to form by partial melting of mantle rocks near the base of the crust (tholeiites) and deeper in the mantle (olivine basalts). It then rises through oceanic or continental rifts to cover vast areas of the ocean floors or continents. Rocks that are basaltic in mineralogy, texture, and composition also cover much of the surface area of the Moon.
WILLIAM D. ROMEY

Bibliography: Hess, H. H., and Poldervaart, A., eds., *Basalts* (1968); MacDonald, G. A., *Volcanoes* (1972); Ragland, P., and Rogers, J., eds., *Basalts* (1984).

See also: PETROGRAPHY; SEAFLOOR SPREADING; VOLCANO.

Basawan [ba-sah'-wahn]

Basawan, a Hindu artist who flourished in the 16th century, was a master of miniature painting at the Mogul court of Emperor Akbar (1556–1605) in India. He was among the first Indian artists to take an interest in Western techniques of painting, particularly in the use of strong contrasts of light and shade.

Little is known of Basawan's life. He seems to have been an accomplished painter before going to Akbar's court, where he came under the influence of the renowned master Khwaja Abd-us-Samad. His contemporaries considered him matchless in his delineation of backgrounds, his sensitive rendering of human expression, and his subtle distribution of colors. Basawan's signed works are found principally in manuscripts, including the illustrations of the *Razmnama* (Jaipur Library, India), the *Akbar-nama* (Victoria and Albert Museum, London), the *Darab-nama* (British Museum, London), the *Baharistan of Jami* (Bodleian Library, Oxford), and the *Akbar-nama* and the *Jami al-Tawarikh* (Gulistan Library, Tehran). S. A. A. RIZVI

Bibliography: Desai, V. N., *Life at Court* (1985); Verma, S. P., *Art and Material Culture in the Paintings of Akbar's Court* (1978).

base (chemistry): see ACIDS AND BASES.

base   (mathematics)

In any NUMERAL system, the base of the system is the number that determines the place values for numerals written in that system. For example, in the numeral 3467, the numerals 3, 4, 6, and 7 separately indicate a multiple of the value of the place each holds in the numeral as a whole.

In the DECIMAL system, which is the one most widely used worldwide, the number 10 is the base. This means that each place in a numeral written in the base-10 system has the value of increasing powers of 10, reading from right to left. Thus, using the example 3467, the 7 indicates $7 \times 1 (10^0) = 7$; the 6 indicates $6 \times 10^1 = 60$; the 4 indicates $4 \times 102 = 400$; and the 3 indicates $3 \times 10^3 = 3000$.

It is not necessary to use base 10. Any positive integer greater than 1 may also be used. For example, BINARY NUMBERS, base 2, are useful in digital computers; octal numbers, base 8, are useful in reading the cumbersome binary numbers; and duodecimal numbers (see DUODECIMAL SYSTEM), base 12, are used because they simplify certain calculations.

In the octal system, the number 3467 would mean

$$(3 \times 8^3) + (4 \times 8^2) + (6 \times 8) + (7 \times 1);$$

this equals 1847 in base 10. A subscript is used to indicate the base of the number. For example, $3467_8 = 1847_{10}$.

In writing numbers in base 10, the digits 0, 1, 2, 3, 4, 5, 6, 7, 8, and 9 are needed. (Invention of the digit 0 as a place holder was crucial for the development of the system.) In the octal system, only the digits 0, 1, 2, 3, 4, 5, 6, and 7 are needed. In base 12, two extra digits corresponding to 10_{10} and 11_{10} are needed, and symbols must be chosen for them. The expression 10 in any base stands for this base—that is, $10_8 = 8_{10}$, $10_2 = 2_{10}$, $10_{12} = 12_{10}$, and so on. Arithmetic operations are performed as usual in any of these systems, except that the number regrouped depends on the base. For example,

$$\begin{array}{r} 3476_8 \\ +2615_8 \\ \hline 6313_8 \end{array} \quad \text{Also,} \quad \begin{array}{r} 23_8 \\ \times 43_8 \\ \hline 71_8 \\ 114_8 \\ \hline 1231_8 \end{array}$$

WILLIAM W. ADAMS

Bibliography: Shapiro, H., *Arithmetic* (1992).

baseball

Baseball is an immensely popular American game, known as the "national pastime," played between two teams of nine players each. The basic implements used in the game are a leather-covered ball, wooden bats for hitting the ball, and gloves for catching it. Baseball is played on a large scale in Latin America, Japan, and other places besides the United States, but it is in the United States that it thrives most both as a participant's and spectator's sport. It is played at its highest level in the United States and two Canadian cities, divided into the American and National Leagues, each with three divisions, East, Central, and West. Combined, these leagues are called major-league (professional) baseball.

Most players who reach the major leagues have worked their way up through Little League, scholastic, college, and minor-league (professional) ball. The vast majority of major-league players are American-reared, although since the 1960s the sport has seen an influx of Latin American players.

Following a regular season of 162 games, a playoff is held with the winners awarded each league's pennant; the American and National League champions then compete in the World Series. All rounds of competition employ best-of-seven series of games.

Baseball's popularity is in part a result of the fact that almost every American boy plays the game at one time or another, and the lore of the game is intertwined with American life. Baseball has supplied the American culture with a wide range of legendary heroes, as well as books, magazines, movies, and songs. The game has contributed hundreds of words and phrases to the American language.

The History of Baseball. The popular myth that Abner DOUBLE-DAY invented baseball in Cooperstown, N.Y., in 1839, is without foundation. Actually, baseball evolved from cricket and rounders, with town ball and the New York game, popular in the eastern United States by the 1820s, as intermediaries.

On June 19, 1846, a New York team defeated the Knickerbocker Baseball Club of New York, which had drafted (1845) rules establishing the nine-player team and the four-base diamond. The score at Elysian Fields in Hoboken, N.J., that day was 23-1 in four innings.

In 1857 a convention of baseball clubs established the length of a game as nine innings instead of 21 runs. One year later the first organized league, the National Association of Base Ball Players, was formed.

Opening-game ceremonies for the 1983 World Series—between the Baltimore Orioles (American League) and the Philadelphia Phillies (National League)—were held at Memorial Stadium in Baltimore, Md. Although the Phillies won the first game, the Orioles were victorious in the next four to take the Series.

The first professional team, the Cincinnati Red Stockings, won 91 and tied 1 of their first 92 games in 1869–70. Their success helped spread professionalism, and the National Association of Professional Base-Ball Players operated a loose league for five years (1871–75) until the owners formed the National League of Professional Base Ball Clubs in 1876.

The independent American Association (1882–91) prospered by allowing Sunday games and the sale of beer in the stadium. Both leagues survived the rival Union Association's challenge in 1884, but in 1890 the athletes formed the Players League, which financially pressed the National League (NL) and mortally wounded the American Association. In 1892 the 8-team NL absorbed 4 American Association teams, but it reverted to 8 teams after 1899.

In 1901 the American League (AL) declared itself a major league, invaded NL cities, and raided the older league for players. The result of the eventual truce was the World Series, which was played yearly from 1903—except 1904, when the New York Giants refused to meet the AL champions (Boston).

The major leagues successfully met the challenge of the Federal League (1914–15). But further problems arose with the revelation that eight members of the Chicago White Sox had conspired to throw the 1919 World Series to Cincinnati. Only the appointment of Judge Kenesaw Mountain LANDIS as commissioner and the introduction of a livelier ball saved the game. Landis enforced strict regulations regarding integrity of players, and the livelier ball significantly increased the number of crowd-pleasing home runs.

Star players, reared in a minor-league system that comprised 59 leagues in 1949, increased baseball's popularity and caused it to be called America's pastime. The annual All-Star Game between teams composed of the best players in each league was begun in 1933. The introduction of night baseball (1935) and the entry to the majors of black players (1947), previously consigned to all-black leagues, changed the style of play and expanded the potential talent pool.

In 1950 a $6-million World Series television contract made baseball the financial giant among sports. In 1953 the Boston Braves moved to Milwaukee, and one year later the St. Louis Browns became the Baltimore Orioles. In 1958 the Brooklyn Dodgers moved to Los Angeles and the New York Giants moved to San Francisco, making baseball a truly national game. Both leagues have since added teams throughout the United States and Canada. In 1969 both leagues set up divisional play,

with the winners playing a championship to determine the World Series contestants. In 1994 each league was divided into 3 divisions, and league playoffs were established.

Baseball's popularity fell in the 1960s and early '70s, particularly with the rise of professional football, but rose strongly through the late '80s. Labor disputes (players' strikes in 1980, 1981, and 1985; an owners' lock-out in 1990) and increasing salary demands by the players cost fan support in the early '90s. Baseball's popularity was on the rebound in 1994, with the possibility of players breaking long-standing records, but the season was ended by a strike in mid-August. For the first time since 1904, the World Series was not played.

Playing the Game. Baseball is played on an infield of standard proportions and an outfield of varied dimensions. The infield is 90 ft (27.4 m) on each side. The corner farthest from the outfield fence is home plate, and the other bases—first, second, and third—run counterclockwise. The pitcher's mound, an 18-ft (5.5-m) circle inclining upward toward a small rectangular rubber slab in the center, lies inside the square 60 ft 6 in. (18 m) from home plate. The outfield ends at an outer fence, the distance of which from home plate varies with the field. It is usually about 76 to 137 m (250 to over 450 ft).

The teams play 9 innings, alternating in the field and at bat, with the home team batting last. The infielders—first baseman, second baseman, shortstop, and third baseman—usually position themselves along the two sides of the square between the bases. The outfielders—left, center, and right fielders—cover those portions of the outfield. The pitcher stands on the rubber, and the catcher crouches behind the batter. The AL decided in 1973 to allow a tenth player, a designated hitter, to bat for the pitcher. U.S. colleges also adopted the rule.

The team at bat sends its nine men to the plate in a specified sequence. Each batter attempts to hit the pitcher's deliveries, which the latter tries to vary in speed and in placement within the strike zone (the area over home plate and between the batter's knees and armpits). Substitutions are allowed throughout the game but preclude a player's return.

The defending players wear a leather glove on one hand. The catcher's glove, the largest, is round and heavily padded. The first baseman's mitt is more flexible and has one compartment for the thumb and another for the other fingers. The remaining players use gloves with separate compartments for each finger and a webbing between the thumb and index finger. The bat, up to 2.75 in (7 cm) thick and 42 in (106.7 cm)

Spectator enthusiasm for baseball, even during the sport's formative years, is evident in this Currier and Ives print from 1866. The game depicted, between the Brooklyn Atlantics and the Philadelphia Athletics, was played only three years before the first professional team—the Cincinnati Red Stockings—was organized.

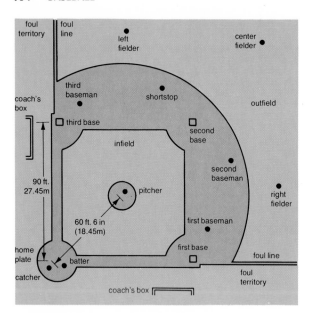

(Left) The diagram illustrates the layout and standard dimensions of a baseball field, known as a diamond. Dots indicate a batter and the typical fielding positions of the nine defensive players.

foul territory
foul line
left fielder
center fielder
third baseman
shortstop
outfield
coach's box
third base
second base
infield
90 ft. 27.45m
pitcher
second baseman
right fielder
60 ft. 6 in (18.45m)
first baseman
home plate
batter
first base
foul line
catcher
foul territory
coach's box

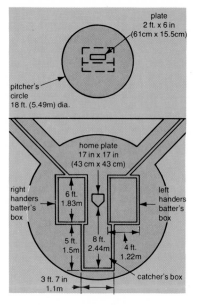

plate
2 ft. x 6 in (61cm x 15.5cm)
pitcher's circle 18 ft. (5.49m) dia.

(Right) The pitching circle (top) is a gently sloping mound topped by a rectangular plate. The batting area (bottom), consisting of the batter's boxes, the catcher's box, and home plate, is the focal point of offensive activity.

home plate 17 in x 17 in (43 cm x 43 cm)
right handers batter's box
6 ft. 1.83m
left handers batter's box
5 ft. 1.5m
8 ft. 2.44m
4 ft. 1.22m
3 ft. 7 in 1.1m
catcher's box

(Below) Baseball, at its most fundamental level, requires only a bat (1), or tapering cylinder of wood, and a ball (2), usually a multilayered sphere covered with hide. Formal competition requires considerably more specialized equipment, either for protection or to enhance an athlete's performance. Outfielders, pitchers, and infielders wear a standard fielding glove (3), except for the first baseman, whose glove (4) is adapted for his position. At the plate, a batting helmet (5) is worn, its single flap covering the ear and temple closest to the pitcher. Shoes (6) are light, strong, and cleated for added traction. The catcher's mitt (7), wider and less flexible than other fielding gloves, has additional padding to protect its wearer's hand. A catcher's mask (8) affords protection for the face, while the body is guarded by a chest protector (9) and shin guards (10). During a game, the plate umpire (11) is positioned behind the catcher (12), where both the batter (13) and the pitcher (14) can be observed. Like the catcher, the umpire wears protective gear. Once the ball is pitched, the batter attempts to drive it along a path that will elude the defense presented by outfielders (15) and infielders (16) or over the outfield fence in fair territory before touching the ground.

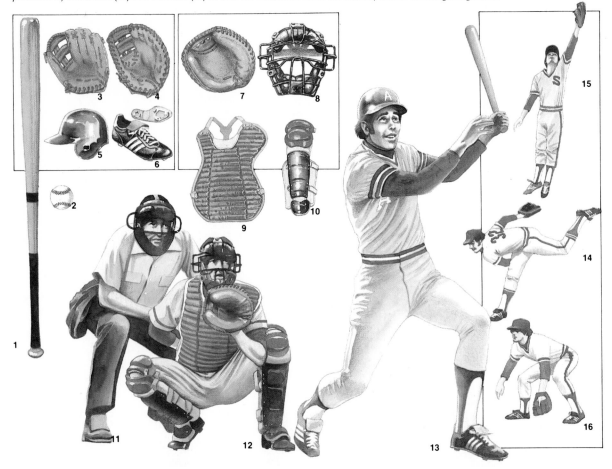

MAJOR LEAGUE WORLD SERIES
(Series Winner in Italics)

Year	National League Team (Wins)	American League Team (Wins)	Year	National League Team (Wins)	American League Team (Wins)	Year	National League Team (Wins)	American League Team (Wins)
1903	Pittsburgh (3)	*Boston* (5)	1935	Chicago (2)	*Detroit* (4)	1966	Los Angeles (0)	*Baltimore* (4)
1905	*New York* (4)	Philadelphia (1)	1936	New York (2)	*New York* (4)	1967	*St. Louis* (4)	Boston (3)
1906	Chicago (2)	*Chicago* (4)	1937	New York (1)	*New York* (4)	1968	St. Louis (3)	*Detroit* (4)
1907	*Chicago* (4)	Detroit (0)	1938	Chicago (0)	*New York* (4)	1969	*New York* (4)	Baltimore (1)
1908	*Chicago* (4)	Detroit (1)	1939	Cincinnati (0)	*New York* (4)	1970	Cincinnati (1)	*Baltimore* (4)
1909	*Pittsburgh* (4)	Detroit (3)	1940	*Cincinnati* (4)	Detroit (3)	1971	*Pittsburgh* (4)	Baltimore (3)
1910	Chicago (1)	*Philadelphia* (4)	1941	Brooklyn (1)	*New York* (4)	1972	Cincinnati (3)	*Oakland* (4)
1911	New York (2)	*Philadelphia* (4)	1942	*St. Louis* (4)	New York (1)	1973	New York (3)	*Oakland* (4)
1912	New York (3)	*Boston* (4)	1943	St. Louis (1)	*New York* (4)	1974	Los Angeles (1)	*Oakland* (4)
1913	New York (1)	*Philadelphia* (4)	1944	*St. Louis* (4)	St. Louis (2)	1975	*Cincinnati* (4)	Boston (3)
1914	*Boston* (4)	Philadelphia (0)	1945	Chicago (3)	*Detroit* (4)	1976	*Cincinnati* (4)	New York (0)
1915	Philadelphia (1)	*Boston* (4)	1946	*St. Louis* (4)	Boston (3)	1977	Los Angeles (2)	*New York* (4)
1916	Brooklyn (1)	*Boston* (4)	1947	Brooklyn (3)	*New York* (4)	1978	Los Angeles (2)	*New York* (4)
1917	New York (2)	*Chicago* (4)	1948	Boston (2)	*Cleveland* (4)	1979	*Pittsburgh* (4)	Baltimore (3)
1918	Chicago (2)	*Boston* (4)	1949	Brooklyn (1)	*New York* (4)	1980	*Philadelphia* (4)	Kansas City (2)
1919	*Cincinnati* (5)	Chicago (3)	1950	Philadelphia (0)	*New York* (4)	1981	*Los Angeles* (4)	New York (2)
1920	Brooklyn (2)	*Cleveland* (5)	1951	New York (2)	*New York* (4)	1982	*St. Louis* (4)	Milwaukee (3)
1921	*New York* (5)	New York (3)	1952	Brooklyn (3)	*New York* (4)	1983	Philadelphia (1)	*Baltimore* (4)
1922	*New York* (4)	New York (0)	1953	Brooklyn (2)	*New York* (4)	1984	San Diego (1)	*Detroit* (4)
1923	New York (2)	*New York* (4)	1954	*New York* (4)	Cleveland (0)	1985	St. Louis (3)	*Kansas City* (4)
1924	New York (3)	*Washington* (4)	1955	*Brooklyn* (4)	New York (3)	1986	*New York* (4)	Boston (3)
1925	*Pittsburgh* (4)	Washington (3)	1956	Brooklyn (3)	*New York* (4)	1987	St. Louis (3)	*Minnesota* (4)
1926	*St. Louis* (4)	New York (3)	1957	*Milwaukee* (4)	New York (3)	1988	*Los Angeles* (4)	Oakland (1)
1927	Pittsburgh (0)	*New York* (4)	1958	Milwaukee (3)	*New York* (4)	1989	San Francisco (0)	*Oakland* (4)
1928	St. Louis (0)	*New York* (4)	1959	*Los Angeles* (4)	Chicago (2)	1990	*Cincinnati* (4)	Oakland (0)
1929	Chicago (1)	*Philadelphia* (4)	1960	*Pittsburgh* (4)	New York (3)	1991	Atlanta (3)	*Minnesota* (4)
1930	St. Louis (2)	*Philadelphia* (4)	1961	Cincinnati (1)	*New York* (4)	1992	Atlanta (2)	*Toronto* (4)
1931	*St. Louis* (4)	Philadelphia (3)	1962	San Francisco (3)	*New York* (4)	1993	Philadephia (2)	*Toronto* (4)
1932	Chicago (0)	*New York* (4)	1963	*Los Angeles* (4)	New York (0)	1994	Series not played	
1933	*New York* (4)	Washington (1)	1964	*St. Louis* (4)	New York (3)			
1934	*St. Louis* (4)	Detroit (3)	1965	*Los Angeles* (4)	Minnesota (3)			

MAJOR LEAGUE TEAMS

American League		National League
	Eastern Division	
Baltimore Orioles		Atlanta Braves
Boston Red Sox		Florida Marlins
Detroit Tigers		Montreal Expos
New York Yankees		New York Mets
Toronto Blue Jays		Philadelphia Phillies
	Central Division	
Chicago White Sox		Chicago Cubs
Cleveland Indians		Cincinnati Reds
Kansas City Royals		Houston Astros
Milwaukee Brewers		Pittsburgh Pirates
Minnesota Twins		St. Lous Cardinals
	Western Division	
California Angels		Colorado Rockies
Oakland Athletics		Los Angeles Dodgers
Seattle Mariners		San Diego Padres
Texas Rangers		San Francisco Giants

CY YOUNG AWARD WINNERS*

Year	Player, Team, League
1956	Don Newcombe, Brooklyn, NL
1957	Warren Spahn, Milwaukee, NL
1958	Bob Turley, New York, AL
1959	Early Wynn, Chicago, AL
1960	Vernon Law, Pittsburgh, NL
1961	Whitey Ford, New York, AL
1962	Don Drysdale, Los Angeles, NL
1963	Sandy Koufax, Los Angeles, NL
1964	Dean Chance, Los Angeles, AL
1965	Sandy Koufax, Los Angeles, NL
1966	Sandy Koufax, Los Angeles, NL
1967	Jim Lonborg, Boston, AL; Mike McCormick, San Francisco, NL
1968	Dennis McLain, Detroit, AL; Bob Gibson, St. Louis, NL
1969	Mike Cuellar, Baltimore, and Dennis McLain, Detroit, tied in AL; Tom Seaver, New York, NL
1970	Jim Perry, Minnesota, AL; Bob Gibson, St. Louis, NL
1971	Vida Blue, Oakland, AL; Ferguson Jenkins, Chicago, NL
1972	Gaylord Perry, Cleveland, AL; Steve Carlton, Philadelphia, NL
1973	Jim Palmer, Baltimore, AL; Tom Seaver, New York, NL
1974	Catfish Hunter, Oakland, AL; Mike Marshall, Los Angeles, NL
1975	Jim Palmer, Baltimore, AL; Tom Seaver, New York, NL
1976	Jim Palmer, Baltimore, AL; Randy Jones, San Diego, NL
1977	Sparky Lyle, New York, AL; Steve Carlton, Philadelphia, NL
1978	Ron Guidry, New York, AL; Gaylord Perry, San Diego, NL
1979	Mike Flanagan, Baltimore, AL; Bruce Sutter, Chicago, NL
1980	Steve Stone, Baltimore, AL; Steve Carlton, Philadelphia, NL
1981	Rollie Fingers, Milwaukee, AL; Fernando Valenzuela, L.A., NL
1982	Pete Vuckovich, Milwaukee, AL; Steve Carlton, Phila., NL
1983	LaMarr Hoyt, Chicago, AL; John Denny, Philadelphia, NL
1984	Willie Hernández, Detroit, AL; Rick Sutcliffe, Chicago, NL
1985	Bret Saberhagen, K.C., AL; Dwight Gooden, New York, NL
1986	Roger Clemens, Boston, AL; Mike Scott, Houston, NL
1987	Roger Clemens, Boston, AL; Steve Bedrosian, Phila., NL
1988	Frank Viola, Minnesota, AL; Orel Hershiser, L.A., NL
1989	Bret Saberhagen, K.C., AL; Mark Davis, San Diego, NL
1990	Bob Welch, Oakland, AL; Doug Drabek, Pittsburgh, NL
1991	Roger Clemens, Boston, AL; Tom Glavine, Atlanta, NL
1992	Dennis Eckersley, Oakland, AL; Greg Maddux, Chicago, NL
1993	Jack McDowell, Chicago, AL; Greg Maddux, Atlanta, NL
1994	David Cone, K.C., AL; Greg Maddux, Atlanta, NL

* Best pitcher as selected by Baseball Writers Association.

long, is round and wooden (in amateur games, aluminum is allowed). The ball consists of three layers: a cork-and-rubber sphere in the central core; wool yarn tightly wound around the core; and a leather casing stitched together around the whole. A regulation baseball is 9–9.25 in (22.9–23.5 cm) in circumference and weighs 5–5.25 oz (141.7–148.8 g).

Each team's half-inning consists of three outs. An out occurs most commonly when a ball is caught before bouncing (a fly ball), when a ground ball is caught and thrown to first base before the batter arrives, when a base runner is not touching a base and is tagged by a fielder holding the ball, when a fielder who has the ball touches a base other than first when there is a runner approaching that base and each previous base, when a player has left a base and is unable to get back before a caught fly ball is thrown to the base, and when the pitcher gets three strikes on a batter.

A strike is any pitch the batter swings at and misses, any pitch that travels through the strike zone, and any batted ball that lands outside the straight lines running from home plate through first base and from home plate through third base

(Far left) Ty Cobb played 24 seasons (1905–28) in the major leagues, winning the American League batting championship a dozen times en route to his .367 lifetime batting average. Cobb, a fierce base runner, stole 892 career bases, a total unsurpassed until Lou Brock broke the record 49 years later.

(Left) Babe Ruth, the great New York Yankee of the 1920s and '30s and the most famous baseball player in history, hits one of his 714 career home runs, a record that stood until 1974. Ruth, who was an outstanding pitcher before becoming an outfielder, was the first baseball player to earn more than $1 million during his career.

(Below) Joe DiMaggio, who is regarded as one of the most graceful outfielders ever to play baseball, led the New York Yankees to 10 American League championships in his 13 seasons. DiMaggio set one of the sport's most durable records in 1941, hitting safely in 56 consecutive games.

MOST VALUABLE PLAYER*

Year	Player, Team (AL)	Player, Team (NL)
1931	Lefty Grove, Philadelphia	Frank Frisch, St. Louis
1932	Jimmy Foxx, Philadelphia	Chuck Klein, Philadelphia
1933	Jimmy Foxx, Philadelphia	Carl Hubbell, New York
1934	Mickey Cochrane, Detroit	Dizzy Dean, St. Louis
1935	Hank Greenberg, Detroit	Gabby Hartnett, Chicago
1936	Lou Gehrig, New York	Carl Hubbell, New York
1937	Charley Gehringer, Detroit	Joe Medwick, St. Louis
1938	Jimmy Foxx, Boston	Ernie Lombardi, Cincinnati
1939	Joe DiMaggio, New York	Bucky Walters, Cincinnati
1940	Hank Greenberg, Detroit	Frank McCormick, Cincinnati
1941	Joe DiMaggio, New York	Dolph Camilli, Brooklyn
1942	Joe Gordon, New York	Mort Cooper, St. Louis
1943	Spurgeon Chandler, New York	Stan Musial, St. Louis
1944	Hal Newhouser, Detroit	Marty Marion, St. Louis
1945	Hal Newhouser, Detroit	Phil Cavarretta, Chicago
1946	Ted Williams, Boston	Stan Musial, St. Louis
1947	Joe DiMaggio, New York	Bob Elliot, Boston
1948	Lou Boudreau, Cleveland	Stan Musial, St. Louis
1949	Ted Williams, Boston	Jackie Robinson, Brooklyn
1950	Phil Rizzuto, New York	Jim Konstanty, Philadelphia
1951	Yogi Berra, New York	Roy Campanella, Brooklyn
1952	Bobby Shantz, Philadelphia	Hank Sauer, Chicago
1953	Al Rosen, Cleveland	Roy Campanella, Brooklyn
1954	Yogi Berra, New York	Willie Mays, New York
1955	Yogi Berra, New York	Roy Campanella, Brooklyn
1956	Mickey Mantle, New York	Don Newcombe, Brooklyn
1957	Mickey Mantle, New York	Henry Aaron, Milwaukee
1958	Jackie Jensen, Boston	Ernie Banks, Chicago
1959	Nellie Fox, Chicago	Ernie Banks, Chicago
1960	Roger Maris, New York	Dick Groat, Pittsburgh
1961	Roger Maris, New York	Frank Robinson, Cincinnati
1962	Mickey Mantle, New York	Maury Wills, Los Angeles
1963	Elston Howard, New York	Sandy Koufax, Los Angeles
1964	Brooks Robinson, Baltimore	Ken Boyer, St. Louis
1965	Zoilo Versalles, Minnesota	Willie Mays, San Francisco
1966	Frank Robinson, Baltimore	Roberto Clemente, Pittsburgh
1967	Carl Yastrzemski, Boston	Orlando Cepeda, St. Louis
1968	Dennis McLain, Detroit	Bob Gibson, St. Louis
1969	Harmon Killebrew, Minnesota	Willie McCovey, San Francisco
1970	John Boog Powell, Baltimore	Johnny Bench, Cincinnati
1971	Vida Blue, Oakland	Joe Torre, St. Louis
1972	Dick Allen, Chicago	Johnny Bench, Cincinnati
1973	Reggie Jackson, Oakland	Pete Rose, Cincinnati
1974	Jeff Burroughs, Texas	Steve Garvey, Los Angeles
1975	Fred Lynn, Boston	Joe Morgan, Cincinnati
1976	Thurman Munson, New York	Joe Morgan, Cincinnati
1977	Rod Carew, Minnesota	George Foster, Cincinnati
1978	Jim Rice, Boston	Dave Parker, Pittsburgh
1979	Don Baylor, California	Willie Stargell, Pittsburgh
		Keith Hernandez, St. Louis
1980	George Brett, Kansas City	Mike Schmidt, Philadelphia
1981	Rollie Fingers, Milwaukee	Mike Schmidt, Philadelphia
1982	Robin Yount, Milwaukee	Dale Murphy, Atlanta
1983	Cal Ripken, Jr., Baltimore	Dale Murphy, Atlanta
1984	Willie Hernández, Detroit	Ryne Sandberg, Chicago
1985	Don Mattingly, New York	Willie McGee, St. Louis
1986	Roger Clemens, Boston	Mike Schmidt, Philadelphia
1987	George Bell, Toronto	Andre Dawson, Chicago
1988	Jose Canseco, Oakland	Kirk Gibson, Los Angeles
1989	Robin Yount, Milwaukee	Kevin Mitchell, San Francisco
1990	Rickey Henderson, Oakland	Barry Bonds, Pittsburgh
1991	Cal Ripken, Jr., Baltimore	Terry Pendleton, Atlanta
1992	Dennis Eckersley, Oakland	Barry Bonds, Pittsburgh
1993	Frank Thomas, Chicago	Barry Bonds, San Francisco
1994	Frank Thomas, Chicago	Jeff Bagwell, Houston

* Selected by Baseball Writers Association.

to the outfield fence (called a foul). If the batter has two strikes, a foul is not considered a strike unless it is a foul bunt or a tipped foul caught by the catcher before it bounces.

The team at bat tries to get players on base and advance them until they round all four bases to score runs. The team with more runs after nine innings wins. If the score is tied at the end of nine innings, the teams play extra innings until one team scores more than the other and both teams have had an equal number of turns at bat.

(Left) Willie Mays hit 660 home runs in the major leagues, a number surpassed only by Henry Aaron and Babe Ruth. Mays's unorthodox ''basket'' catches and a powerful throwing arm made him one of baseball's finest defensive outfielders.

(Below) Jackie Robinson, a daring base runner, slides safely into home plate. Robinson made his debut with the Brooklyn Dodgers in 1947, becoming the first black to play in modern major league baseball.

A batter reaches base if hit by a pitch, if he or she receives a walk by taking four pitches (called balls) outside the strike zone, if a defensive player misplays the ball for an error, if the catcher interferes with a swing, and if the catcher fails to catch the pitcher's throw on a third strike and does not throw the ball to first base before the batter reaches the base. But the most common way of reaching base is with a hit.

Hits come in many forms: deliberately gentle bunts to unreachable parts of the infield, hard-hit ground balls that travel between infielders, bloopers popped in an arc beyond the infield but out of the outfielders' reach, line drives in front of or between the outfielders, and clouts smashed over the fence. Both the batter and runners may advance as far as possible on any hit. A one-base hit is a single, a two-base hit a double, a three-base hit a triple, and a four-base hit a home run. The most common kind of home run is a fair ball over the fence on a fly, but a batter may also run around all the bases before the fielders can retrieve a ball hit inside the park and throw it to the plate.

Runners may also advance by stealing a base, on a balk (improper procedure by a pitcher), on a sacrifice (a bunt intended to move the runner even though the batter probably will be out), or on a sacrifice fly (a fly ball caught by an outfielder but not returned to the proper base before the runner reaches it—provided the runner does not leave his or her original base before the ball is caught).

Four umpires, one near each base, regulate the game, enforce the rules, and call balls and strikes, foul and fair balls, and safe or out. The umpires may also eject players from the game for improper behavior and call a forfeit for serious infractions. Some amateur games have only one or two umpires; the playoff series in both the American and National leagues and the World Series have six.

Baseball has two basic styles of play. Inside baseball, prevalent until the 1920s, emphasizes speed, defense, and good pitching. The second style emphasizes power hitting. The New York Yankees dominated baseball with the latter, winning 29 pennants and 20 World Series between 1921 and 1964. The use of relief pitchers and artificial turf has returned inside baseball to favor, but power hitting remains an appealing factor in the game. Reviewed by JIM BENAGH

Bibliography: Angell, Roger, *The Summer Game* (1973); Blake, Mike, *Baseball Chronicles* (1994); Honig, Donald, *Baseball: When the Grass Was Real* (1975); James, Bill, *The Bill James Historical Baseball Abstract*, rev. ed. (1988); Peterson, Robert, *Only the Ball Was White* (1970; repr. 1985); Reichler, Joseph L., *The Great All-Time Baseball Record Book*, rev. ed. (1993); Ritter, Lawrence S., *The Glory of Their Times* (1984) and *The Negro Leagues* (1995); Seymour, Harold, *Baseball: The Early Years* (1960) and *Baseball: The Golden Age* (1971); Ward, Geoffrey C., and Burns, Ken, *Baseball: An Illustrated History* (1994).

(Left) Sandy Koufax, star lefthander of the Los Angeles Dodgers, pitched four no-hit games. Plagued by arm injuries, he retired in 1966 at the height of his career.

(Right) Reggie Jackson, named the Most Valuable Player of the 1977 World Series, capped a brilliant hitting performance with three home runs in the New York Yankees' final victory over the Los Angeles Dodgers. In 1986, Jackson surpassed Mickey Mantle's career total of 536 home runs, placing him sixth on the all-time list.

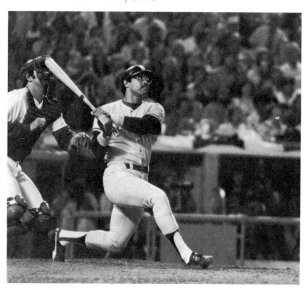

Basel [bah'-zuhl]

Basel (also Basle; French: Bâle) is the capital of the half canton of Basel Stadt, in northern Switzerland. The population of the city proper is 171,036 (1991 est.), and that of the conurbation, 360,350.

Located on the Rhine River, where it joins with the Birs and Weise rivers, Basel is a major industrial center and commercial port. Manufactures include chemicals, pharmaceuticals, machinery, and textiles. Basel is also a center for banking and finance; the Bank for International Settlements has its headquarters there. Basel University, founded by Pope Pius II in 1460, is the oldest in Switzerland. Landmarks include the cathedral (consecrated 1019), a Romanesque and Gothic building containing the tomb of Erasmus; the town hall (1504–14); the Church of Saint Martin; and several museums, including a gallery exhibiting the works of Hans Holbein.

Known as Basilia to the Romans, Basel became the seat of a bishopric in the 5th century. It was an imperial free city of the Holy Roman Empire from 1096 to 1501 and was the site of the ecumenical Council of Basel in 1431–49. Basel joined the Swiss Confederation in 1501 and quickly became an intellectual center of the Swiss Reformation, with Holbein residing in the city and Erasmus teaching at the university. In 1831 the original canton was divided in half when the rural population revolted and proclaimed independence from the city.

Basel, Council of

The Council of Basel convened in 1431 as the 17th ecumenical council of the Roman Catholic church. Its ostensible purpose was to initiate church reform and bring an end to the difficulties with the HUSSITES, but it originated in a decree of the Council of Constance (1417) that required the calling of councils at regular intervals. Almost from the beginning the council fell into conflict with Pope Eugene IV, who was suspicious of it. When in 1437 he ordered the council transferred to Ferrara (see FERRARA-FLORENCE, COUNCIL OF), some of its members refused to comply. They declared the pope deposed and, to replace him, elected a layman, Amadeus VII, duke of Savoy; as antipope he took the name Felix V. Thereafter, the prestige of the Basel assembly declined, and it became increasingly involved in the political quarrels of Germany. It expired ingloriously in 1449. Although the council accomplished a partial reconciliation with the Hussites, its efforts at reform were largely ineffective. Moreover, the failure of its challenge to papal authority marked the triumph of the papacy over CONCILIARISM.   T. TACKETT

Bibliography: Gill, J., *Eugene IV* (1962); Hay, Denys, ed., *De Gestis Concilii Basiliensis Commentariorum*, libri II (1992).

baselevel

The baselevel of a river is the level at which it enters a large standing body of water, such as a lake or an ocean. Because erosion effectively ceases when the flow of a river ends, baselevel is the lowest level to which a river can erode the surrounding land, and changes in baselevel have a strong effect on rates of erosion (see RIVER AND STREAM). For most purposes, SEA LEVEL may be regarded as an ultimate baselevel; overall rates of erosion on the Earth's surface have thus altered dramatically as sea level has risen and fallen in the past.

basement rock

Basement rock is the term for crystalline IGNEOUS ROCKS and METAMORPHIC ROCKS on which rest younger rocks, both layered sedimentary and volcanic. The basement is believed to extend downward to the Mohorovičić discontinuity, the boundary between the Earth's crust and its mantle. Basement rocks are commonly Precambrian in age, at least 570 million years old; in some cases they are the stable remnants of ancient continents (see CONTINENTAL SHIELD). Geologists often use the term *basement* in a relative sense, however, referring to any complex on which a younger complex has been deposited.
                    WILLIAM D. ROMEY

basenji [buh-sen'-jee]

The basenji is a smooth-coated dog that stands about 41–43 cm (16–17 in) at the shoulder and weighs about 10–11 kg (22–24 lb). Its coat may be red, black, tricolor, or brindle, and it may have white markings on the chest, muzzle, legs, and tip of tail. The ears are erect, and the tail is carried erect and tightly curled to one side of the back.

The basenji was raised in ancient times in Central Africa. The first basenjis brought to England in 1895 died before the breed became established, and the dog did not reappear in England —or arrive in the United States—until the mid-1930s. It was recognized by the American Kennel Club in 1943.

Bibliography: Coe, S., *The Basenji* (1990).

The basenji is a short-coated African dog that does not bark but sometimes produces a yelping sound. It is one of the oldest breeds of dogs and was first raised to kill small predators. The name is a Bantu word meaning "natives."

Basho [bah-shoh]

Basho was the pseudonym of Matsuo Munefusa, b. 1644, d. Oct. 12, 1694, the finest writer of Japanese HAIKU during the formative years of the genre. As a young man he served as a samurai. From 1667 he lived in Edo (now Tokyo), where he began to compose haiku. His attention to the natural world transformed this verse form from a frivolous social pastime into a major genre of Japanese poetry. From 1684, Basho traveled widely, keeping diaries, such as *The Narrow Road to the Far North* (1689; Eng. trans., 1974), and collaborating with local poets on the linked-verse forms known as *renga*.

Bibliography: Basho, Matsuo, *Basho's "The Narrow Road to the Far North" and Selected Haiku*, trans. by Nobuyuki Yuasa (1974); Ueda, Makoto, *Basho and His Interpreters* (1992).

BASIC

BASIC is a high-level COMPUTER LANGUAGE developed at Dartmouth College (Hanover, N.H.) in 1964. Its creators, Thomas E. Kurtz and John G. Kemeny, conceived BASIC as a simple language for students first learning about computers. As such, BASIC was one of the first to use English words for many of its functions and to allow programmers to use decimal notation rather than forcing them to use BINARY NUMBERS or HEXADECIMAL numbers. Its ease of use popularized BASIC in the computing community, and versions of BASIC were available for most minicomputers by the early 1970s. With the advent of the personal computer (see COMPUTER, PERSONAL), BASIC found an even larger community of users. In the 1980s and early 1990s, BASIC was standard issue for virtually every personal computer sold in the United States.

Although other general-purpose high-level languages, such as PASCAL and C, have superseded BASIC in academic and programming communities, BASIC is still widely used. The newer versions—notably Microsoft Corporation's *Visual BASIC* —incorporate such features as object-oriented programming and "plug-in elements" that generate hundreds of lines of code for generic, often-repeated tasks.   PHILIP STOREY

Basie, Count

The pianist and bandleader William "Count" Basie, b. Red Bank, N.J., Aug. 21, 1904, d. Apr. 26, 1984, was one of the great exponents of SWING. He studied with Fats Waller, a major influence on his work, and played with New York and Kansas City jazz groups in the 1920s and early '30s before forming his own band in 1935. Basie's band was celebrated for its polished, rhythmic versions of blues melodies. Famous musicians who performed with Basie include the singer Billie Holiday and saxophonist Lester Young.

Bibliography: Basie, Count, and Murray, Albert, *Good Morning Blues: The Autobiography of Count Basie* (1985); Dance, Stanley, *The World of Count Basie* (1980); Horricks, R., *Count Basie and His Orchestra* (1971).

basil

Common, or sweet, basil, O. basilicum, is an annual herb that produces shiny, green leaves that have a spicy fragrance. Its small, white flowers bloom in August and can be pinched off to promote more leaf growth. Leaves of basil are commonly used to flavor tomato dishes and are an ingredient of fines herbes, *an herbal mixture used in French cooking.*

Basil are herbs of the genus *Ocimum*, belonging to the mint family Labiatae. Native to tropical Asia and Africa, common, or sweet, basil, *O. basilicum,* grows about 30 cm (1 ft) high. Crushed basil leaves are used to flavor tomato products, meats, fish and egg dishes, and salads. Basil's essential oil is used in perfumes, and it is one of the herbs used in chartreuse liqueur.
ARTHUR O. TUCKER

Basil I, Byzantine Emperor (Basil the Macedonian)

Basil I, b. *c.*812, d. Aug. 29, 886, ruled the Byzantine Empire from 867 to 886 and founded the Macedonian dynasty, which governed during a prosperous, expansionist period. Born of Armenian parents in Macedonia, he rose as a favorite of Emperor Michael III, whom he then murdered (Sept. 24, 867). As emperor, by conquering the PAULICIANS, he continued Byzantium's expansion eastward toward the Euphrates; he also strengthened the empire's hold on southern Italy. In church affairs he reconciled the moderate and extremist factions led by patriarchs PHOTIUS and St. Ignatius of Constantinople.

Basil ordered a recodification of Byzantine law similar to that of JUSTINIAN I, but in his lifetime only two abridged versions were completed. His construction of the Nea Ecclesia (New Church) set a pattern for later Byzantine architecture. Basil was succeeded by his son LEO VI, and the Macedonian dynasty ruled the empire until 1056.
C. M. BRAND

Basil II, Byzantine Emperor (Basil Bulgaroktonus)

Basil II, c.958–1025, Byzantine emperor (960–1025), was coemperor with his brother Constantine VIII. Crowned when he was 2 years old, he did not exercise power until he was 18 and then had to overcome serious rebellions. Basil main-tained Byzantine interests in Syria, Armenia, and Georgia. In Europe he campaigned (996–1018) ferociously against the Bulgars (hence his sobriquet "Bulgar slayer") and finally incorporated their kingdom into his empire.

Basil III, Grand Duke of Moscow: see Vasily III, Grand Duke of Moscow.

Basil the Great, Saint

Saint Basil the Great, b. *c.*329, d. Jan. 1, 379, was one of the Cappadocian Fathers, the other two being his brother, Gregory of Nyssa, and his friend, Gregory of Nazianzus. The Cappadocians brought to fulfillment the theological work of Athanasius against ARIANISM.

The son of devout parents, Basil was born at Caesarea in Cappadocia. He received his higher education in Constantinople and Athens but renounced a promising career to become a monk. Impressed by the ascetic life, he settled as a hermit near Neo-Caesarea by the Iris River, where he was joined by Gregory of Nazianzus. In 364 the bishop of Caesarea, Eusebius, persuaded Basil to accept ordination. Basil agreed and became an able defender of orthodoxy among the churches of Anatolia, which had suffered from divisions caused by the Arian controversy. In 370 he succeeded Eusebius as bishop. A leader who had brilliant organizational gifts, Basil established hospitals, fostered monasticism, and reformed the liturgy. His Rule, a code for monastic life, became the basis of eastern monasticism, and the liturgy of Saint Basil, probably compiled by him though later revised, is still used on certain Sundays in Orthodox churches.

Basil wrote numerous letters and treatises and is known mainly for the treatise *On the Holy Spirit* (375) and three books entitled *Against Eunomius* (363–65), who was an Arian protagonist. Feast day: Jan. 1 (Eastern); Jan. 2 (Western; formerly June 14).
ROSS MACKENZIE

Bibliography: Clarke, W. K. L., *St. Basil the Great* (1913); Fedwick, Paul, *The Church and the Charisma of Leadership in Basil of Caesarea* (1979).

Basile, Giovanni Battista   [bah-zee'-lay]

The Italian soldier and courtier Giovanni Battista (Giambattista) Basile, b. *c.*1575, d. Feb. 23, 1632, was the author of *Lo cunto de li cunti* (Tale of Tales, 1634; trans. as *The Pentamerone,* 1932), one of the earliest published collections of European fairy tales. The tales, which are written in the Neapolitan dialect, include versions of such classic folk stories as "Beauty and the Beast," "Cinderella," "Puss in Boots," and "Snow White." Ten women entertain a prince for five days with the tales, and the teller of the last tale, who recounts the story of her own real life, wins the prince's hand in marriage.

basilica   [buh-sil'-i-kuh]

In the Roman Catholic church *basilica* is an honorary name given to certain churches. The original and still the most important basilicas are the four principal churches of Rome: SAINT PETER'S BASILICA, San Giovanni in Laterano, Santa Maria Maggiore, and San Paolo Fuori le Mura.

The term *basilica* also refers to a particular architectural form. In Roman architecture a basilica was a large, oblong building used particularly as a court of law and a place of public assembly. In Early Christian and Merovingian times the function of the basilica became exclusively religious, and the plan was often varied by TRANSEPTS, or side wings, frequently with DOMES over the resultant crossing.

Although the name is derived from the Greek *Basilikē* (meaning "royal"), the Basilica Porcia, the earliest known, was built (184 BC) by Cato the Elder in republican Rome. It was so useful that others were built throughout the Roman world, usually adjoining the FORUM or AGORA of a town. The earliest preserved basilica (2d century BC) has been found in POMPEII. Its main entrances were at one end of the rectangle, but it also had a doorway in the center of each long wall. An inner,

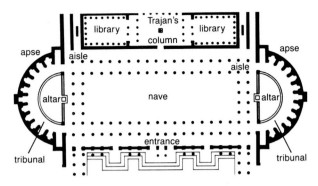

The Basilica Ulpia (98–112) in Trajan's Forum, Rome, was designed by Apollodorus of Damascus. The plan reveals a typical basilican structure with a wide central nave, double side aisles, and raised tribunals in semicircular apses with sacrificial altars at either end.

rectangular COLONNADE supported the roof, but the center may have been open to the sky (in later basilicas these colonnades were reorganized to form aisles). At the end opposite the main doors was a rectangular tribunal, two stories high, with a subsidiary room on either side. Although the ends of basilicas could be rectangular or semicircular (forming an APSE) and could include the side rooms or not, the scheme remained basically constant in Roman practice. VITRUVIUS (active 46–30 BC) gave detailed directions for building such basilicas in his treatise on Roman architecture.

The form of the basilica lent itself to public assembly for religious rites. A rare pagan religious basilica dating from the reign (AD 14–37) of Tiberius was discovered in Rome near Porta Maggiore. The form was widely used, however, for synagogues in Palestine and at Sardis, Turkey, from at least the 2d century AD. When early Christian congregations grew too large to meet in *titulae* (houses), they adopted the basilican form for their own use. Constantine's 4th-century donations of monumental basilicas at all the major holy sites throughout the Roman world strengthened the popularity of the form. Although variations were many, the hall remained long and rectangular. If it was extremely wide, it might be divided by colonnades or arches into three or more aisles, the center aisle, or NAVE, remaining the most important. In many basilicas the ceiling of the nave was raised by placing a wall pierced with windows (the CLERESTORY) above the side colonnades. The hall might be beam-roofed, vaulted, or domed. An ALTAR took the place of the Roman tribunal. The rooms on either side, when they were retained, could be used as the *prothesis* and *diakonikon* (rooms in which the sacraments, books, and vestments were stored) in the Byzantine church. In Western churches they became side altars, CHAPELS, and sacristies as Romanesque and Gothic architecture developed.

The basilica thus served as the basic plan for the majority of churches in the past, and it continues to be the most popular form for houses of worship today.

JOHN STEPHENS CRAWFORD

Bibliography: Boethius, Axel, and Ward-Perkins, J. B., *Etruscan and Roman Architecture* (1969); Krautheimer, Richard, *Early Christian and Byzantine Architecture* (1965; repr. 1975); Robertson, Donald, *A Handbook of Greek and Roman Architecture*, 2d ed. (1969); Vitruvius, *The Ten Books on Architecture* (1960).

See also: CATHEDRALS AND CHURCHES; MONASTIC ART AND ARCHITECTURE.

Basilicata   [bah-zee-lee-kah'-tah]

Basilicata, a region in southern Italy comprising Matera and Potenza provinces, is located on the Gulf of Taranto. It covers 9,992 km² (3,858 mi²) and has a population of 617,265 (1985 est.). The capital is Potenza. Basilicata has a low-lying coastal plains area, but inland, traversed by the Apennines, it is primarily mountainous, reaching 1,327 m (4,354 ft) at Monte Vulture in the north. The Basento, Bradano, and Senni rivers drain the region. Although the soil is poor and stony, agriculture is the primary economic activity, and tobacco, grains,

and fruits are grown. Chemical manufacturing is the most important industry, and natural gas is produced.

Known as Lucania by the 4th century BC, Basilicata was controlled by the Romans (272 BC), Lombards (6th century AD), Byzantines and Normans (11th century), and by the kingdom of Naples from the 13th century until 1860, when it became part of unified Italy.

Basilides   [bas-i-ly'-deez]

Basilides was a 2d-century proponent of GNOSTICISM at Alexandria. His major work was *Exegetica*, a biblical commentary in 24 books. He claimed to follow secret traditions derived from Saint Peter and Saint Matthias. Only fragments of his writings survive. His followers formed a sect, the Basilideans, that flourished until the 4th century.

basilisk   [baz'-uh-lisk]

In Greek and Roman mythology, the basilisk, or cockatrice, was a serpent with the head and wings of a cock and the tail of a dragon. Its glance killed whatever it encountered.

basin and range province

The most familiar basin and range province is found in the western United States. In such an area, fault-block mountains trending north to south rise abruptly above intermontane (between-mountain) DESERT basins. Most of Nevada and parts of Oregon, Idaho, California, Arizona, New Mexico, and northern Mexico are included in the area. Much of the province has interior drainage; rivers terminate either in salt lakes that have no outlets (such as Great Salt Lake, Utah) or in the low parts of desert basins (bolsons), where they feed PLAYA lakes that evaporate during dry seasons. The mountains have been so deeply eroded that in places only remnants (INSELBERGS) remain. Material washed down from the mountains by FLASH FLOODS fills the intermontane basins and piles up as ALLUVIAL FANS that slope away from the canyon mouths. The province has more than 150 separate ranges, and a number are still being uplifted by active FAULTS.

JOHN A. SHIMER

See also: EROSION AND SEDIMENTATION; MOUNTAIN.

Basin Street

Basin Street, which runs one block north of New Orleans's famed French Quarter, was the main artery of Storyville, a district where legalized prostitution flourished from 1897 to 1917. In the brothels of Storyville, pianists like Jelly Roll MORTON played a form of jazz, and the name Basin Street has become synonymous with the early JAZZ of New Orleans.

Baskerville, John

John Baskerville, b. Jan. 28, 1706, d. Jan. 8, 1775, was an English writing master who became a type designer and printer. His beautiful round Roman TYPEFACE, modeled on his earlier penmanship, had an important influence on type design. Baskerville made outstanding contributions to modern typography through other innovations: the use of wove paper, the invention of rich inks that were truly black, generous leading (space between lines), and wide spacing within display lines made up of capitals. He also introduced glossy-surface paper that was vastly different from the rough, antique laid paper of the time. In 1757 he printed his first book, a quarto edition of Vergil, which was the forerunner of more than 50 other Baskerville productions. He was printer to Cambridge University from 1758 to 1768. His printed folio Bible of 1763, under the license of the university, ranks as one of the finest examples of printing in the 18th century. In it, Baskerville achieved a particularly harmonious combination of type, paper, layout, and ink.

M. C. FAIRLEY

Bibliography: Gaskell, Philip, *John Baskerville: A Bibliography*, rev. ed. (1973); McKitterick, David, *Four Hundred Years of Printing and Publishing in Cambridge* (1985).

Basket Makers: see ANASAZI.

basketball

Basketball, extremely popular around the world, is a court game played by two teams of five players each. The object is to put a ball through a hoop, or basket, and thus score more points than the opposing team.

Although basketball can by played outdoors, it was invented to serve as an exciting indoor exercise for the winter months in a northern climate. It quickly became a spectator sport, however, and now attracts large audiences to gymnasiums and arenas, especially in the United States, South America, and Europe.

The sport is played on the amateur level by high schools, colleges, other groups, and, since 1936, by national teams in the Olympic Games. It also is played by professional athletes, notably in the United States and Europe. The foremost championships contended for are those of the National Basketball Association (U.S. professionals), the National Collegiate Athletic Association (U.S. colleges), and the Olympic Games.

HISTORY

James Naismith, an instructor in physical education at the International Young Men's Christian Association (YMCA) Training School in Springfield, Mass., devised basketball in December 1891. Naismith, who later became a doctor of medicine, hung up two peach baskets, one at either end of the gymnasium, as goals. His YMCA athletes played the first game with a soccer ball, passing it back and forth until one team was able to throw it into its assigned basket. That first game was governed by 13 axioms formulated by Naismith. The rules of basketball, based on those axioms, were established later by the YMCA and the Amateur Athletic Union. All 13 axioms are still incorporated in today's rule books.

Word of the new game spread swiftly, and basketball soon was being played in YMCA gymnasiums throughout the eastern United States. Its growth was so rapid that the first men's intercollegiate game was played in 1897, the first professional

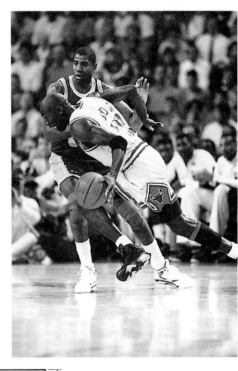

(Above) *Center Patrick Ewing grabs a rebound at Madison Square Garden.* (Right) *Preeminent passer Magic Johnson, in purple, and Michael Jordan, in white, combined quickness and height to revolutionize the guard position in the 1980s.*

(Right) *Three diagrams illustrate layouts and standardized dimensions used in basketball. Basketball courts (A) vary in size depending on the level of competition. Backboards (B) may be either rectangular (professional and collegiate) or fan-shaped (some high schools), but the basket's height (C) is a globally recognized 10 ft (3.05 m).*

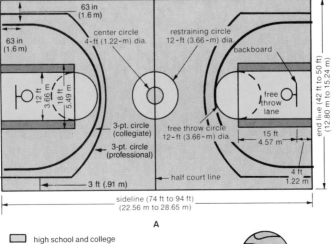

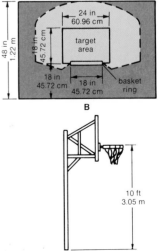

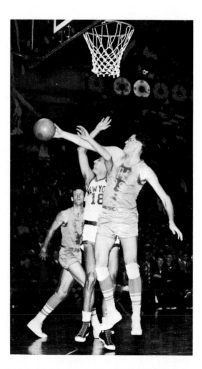

(Left) *The first basketball team poses with the game's inventor, James Naismith (suited, center row). Naismith, a physical education instructor, developed basketball in 1891 to provide young men with a competitive athletic diversion during winter.*

(Right) *George Mikan, professional basketball's first dominating center, lunges for a rebound. Before retiring in 1956, the 6-ft 10-in (2-m 8-cm) Mikan won the scoring title three times while leading the Minneapolis Lakers to five championships.*

league was founded in 1898, and the first collegiate association—the Eastern Intercollegiate League—was formed in 1902. Women also took up the game before 1900.

The growing popularity of basketball resulted in improvements in equipment and skills. The metal hoop was introduced in 1893, and backboards in 1895. The soccer ball was replaced by the first basketball. As playing skills also became more sophisticated, the game attracted more and more spectators.

Until the late 1930s, scores were low, sometimes in single digits. After each score, opposing centers (one of the five positions, the others being two guards and two forwards) lined up in the middle of the court and jumped for the ball. Then the team that got the ball would pass or dribble until a player was about 3 m (10 ft) from the basket before trying a shot. The slow pace did not inhibit the growth of the game, however. By the 1920s, basketball was being played all over the United States, and tournaments were being conducted in high school and college gymnasiums. Most states held high school championships for boys.

Several events in the 1930s spurred the growth of the game as a spectator sport and at the same time made basketball more exciting for the players. The first of these came in the 1932–33 season (basketball seasons tend to be between football in fall and baseball in spring), when rules designed to speed up play were adopted. It became mandatory, under penalty of losing possession, to move the ball past midcourt in less than ten seconds. In addition, no player was permitted to remain within the foul lanes for more than three seconds. Then in 1934 a New York sportswriter, Ned Irish, persuaded the promoters at New York's Madison Square Garden, a large arena, to schedule doubleheaders between college teams. These events proved successful, and similar promotions followed in other cities. Before long, colleges began building their own arenas for basketball.

Another significant advance occurred in 1936, when a Stanford University team traveled from California to a Madison Square Garden promotion to challenge the eastern powers in the "cradle of basketball." Opponents and fans were stunned by the Stanford style of shooting—one-handed while jumping, which contrasted to the prevalent method of taking two-handed shots while standing still. One Stanford player, Hank LUISETTI, was so adept at the "jump shot" that he could outscore an entire opposing team. The new style gained universal acceptance, and basketball scores rose remarkably.

In the 1937–38 season the center jump following each field goal was eliminated. At the end of the next season, Madison Square Garden brought in college teams from around the nation for the National Invitation Tournament (NIT), a post-season play-off that was adopted (1939) on a wider scale by

the National Collegiate Athletic Association (NCAA). Although the NIT is still held annually, the NCAA tournament serves as the official intercollegiate championship.

The University of Kentucky (coached, 1930–72, by Adolph Rupp), St. John's (in New York), the University of North Carolina, Western Kentucky, Kansas University, and Indiana University have been among the leading college basketball teams for years. From 1964 to 1975 the University of California at Los Angeles (UCLA), coached by John WOODEN and led by the centers Lew Alcindor (see ABDUL-JABBAR, KAREEM) and Bill WALTON, dominated the intercollegiate play-offs, winning the title an unprecedented 10 times in 12 years. The 1,250 college teams in the United States now draw about 30 million spectators per season.

Although women have played the game since the 1890s, and even though a few states (Iowa, for instance) have shown great participatory and spectator interest in secondary-school women's basketball for some decades, significant growth and serious recognition of women's basketball in the United States and elsewhere did not occur until the 1970s. Almost all U.S. states now hold girls' high school tournaments, and basketball is the fastest-growing women's intercollegiate sport.

PROFESSIONAL BASKETBALL

From 1898 on, many attempts were made to establish professional basketball as a spectator sport—but success did not come until 1946. The best of the early efforts was made by the HARLEM GLOBETROTTERS, an all-black team that toured first only the United States and then internationally to play local professional or semiprofessional teams. The Globetrotters, founded in 1926, were not affiliated with a league. Their style was and is often showy because, at least into the early 1950s, they could dominate all opponents.

In 1946 serious professional basketball had acquired a following among American sports fans, who wanted to see the former collegians in action. That year the Basketball Association of America, with teams from the United States and one from Toronto, began competing in large arenas in the major cities. Another professional league, the National Basketball League, was already in existence, with many franchises in medium-sized midwestern cities. The two leagues merged in 1949 as the National Basketball Association (NBA) and pared away the weaker franchises.

With the signing of the country's best collegians through

what was called a player draft, the NBA could display both talent and balance. The NBA's greatest spurt of growth occurred in the 1960s and 1970s. Although the Boston Celtics, led by Bill RUSSELL, Bob COUSY, and John HAVLICEK and coached by Red AUERBACH, won 11 of 13 NBA titles beginning in 1957, fans also closely followed such stars as Philadelphia's Wilt CHAMBERLAIN, Cincinnati's Oscar ROBERTSON, and Los Angeles's Jerry WEST and Elgin BAYLOR. The NBA of the 1970s and 1980s exhibited a welcome balance of power: from 1970 until 1988 no team won consecutive NBA titles, though the New York Knicks (with Willis Reed, Walt Frazier, and Bill BRADLEY) won twice; the Boston Celtics, 5 times (3 with Larry BIRD); and the Los Angeles Lakers, 6 times (5 with Kareem Abdul-Jabbar and Magic JOHNSON).

In the 1970s the NBA expanded from 9 teams to 22, including some franchises acquired when the American Basketball Association (1968–76) merged with the NBA. During the late 1970s and early 1980s several women's professional leagues were begun; all of them failed financially.

(Left) *Oscar Robertson, who became the NBA's all-time leader in assists (passes to teammates resulting in field goals) while with the Cincinnati Royals and the Milwaukee Bucks, attempts a jump shot. A superb scorer and rebounder as well as passer, active in the 1960s and early 1970s, Robertson is considered by many experts to have been the game's greatest all-around player.*

(Left) *Bob Cousy, one of the first great ball-handling guards, dribbles the ball downcourt. The flashy floor leader earned Most Valuable Player honors in 1957.*

(Below) *Julius Erving ("Doctor J") three-time scoring champion and MVP of the defunct American Basketball Association, leaps for a lay-up. He excelled for the Philadelphia 76ers in the late 1970s and 1980s.*

(Above) *The leading center of the 1960s, 7 ft-2 in. (2 m-18 cm) tall Wilt Chamberlain works the ball in against Jerry Lucas. Chamberlain was the NBA's all-time leading scorer and rebounder.* (Left) *Jerry West, the outstanding guard of the Los Angeles Lakers in the 1960s and early 1970s, drives past defensive players en route to a field goal. West's single-season record for free throws testified to the aggressiveness of his playing style.*

NBA* PLAYOFF WINNERS
(NBA champion in italics)

Year	Eastern Conference	Western Conference
1947	*Philadelphia Warriors*	Chicago Stags
1948	Philadelphia Warriors	*Baltimore Bullets*
1949	Washington Capitols	*Minneapolis Lakers*
1950	Syracuse Nationals	*Minneapolis Lakers*
1951	New York Knickerbockers	*Rochester Royals*
1952–53	New York Knickerbockers	*Minneapolis Lakers*
1954	Syracuse Nationals	*Minneapolis Lakers*
1955	*Syracuse Nationals*	Ft. Wayne Pistons
1956	*Philadelphia Warriors*	Ft. Wayne Pistons
1957	*Boston Celtics*	St. Louis Hawks
1958	Boston Celtics	*St. Louis Hawks*
1959	*Boston Celtics*	Minneapolis Lakers
1960–61	*Boston Celtics*	St. Louis Hawks
1962–63	*Boston Celtics*	Los Angeles Lakers
1964	*Boston Celtics*	San Francisco Warriors
1965–66	*Boston Celtics*	Los Angeles Lakers
1967	*Philadelphia 76ers*	San Francisco Warriors
1968–69	*Boston Celtics*	Los Angeles Lakers
1970	*New York Knickerbockers*	Los Angeles Lakers
1971	Baltimore Bullets	*Milwaukee Bucks*
1972	New York Knickerbockers	*Los Angeles Lakers*
1973	*New York Knickerbockers*	Los Angeles Lakers
1974	*Boston Celtics*	Milwaukee Bucks
1975	Washington Bullets	*Golden State Warriors*
1976	*Boston Celtics*	Phoenix Suns
1977	Philadelphia 76ers	*Portland Trail Blazers*
1978	*Washington Bullets*	Seattle SuperSonics
1979	Washington Bullets	*Seattle SuperSonics*
1980	Philadelphia 76ers	*Los Angeles Lakers*
1981	*Boston Celtics*	Houston Rockets
1982	Philadelphia 76ers	*Los Angeles Lakers*
1983	*Philadelphia 76ers*	Los Angeles Lakers
1984	*Boston Celtics*	Los Angeles Lakers
1985	Boston Celtics	*Los Angeles Lakers*
1986	*Boston Celtics*	Houston Rockets
1987	Boston Celtics	*Los Angeles Lakers*
1988	Detroit Pistons	*Los Angeles Lakers*
1989	*Detroit Pistons*	Los Angeles Lakers
1990	*Detroit Pistons*	Portland Trail Blazers
1991	*Chicago Bulls*	Los Angeles Lakers
1992	*Chicago Bulls*	Portland Trail Blazers
1993	*Chicago Bulls*	Phoenix Suns
1994	New York Knickerbockers	*Houston Rockets*

*National Basketball Association (in 1947–49, Basketball Association of America).

NBA SCORING LEADERS

Year	Player, Team	Average
1947	Joe Fulks, Philadelphia	23.2
1948	Max Zaslofsky, Chicago	21.0
1949–51	George Mikan, Minneapolis	28.3, 27.4, 28.4
1952	Paul Arizin, Philadelphia	25.4
1953–55	Neil Johnston, Philadelphia	22.3, 24.4, 22.7
1956	Bob Pettit, St. Louis	25.7
1957	Paul Arizin, Philadelphia	25.6
1958	George Yardley, Detroit	27.8
1959	Bob Pettit, St. Louis	29.2
1960–62	Wilt Chamberlain, Philadelphia	37.9, 38.4, 50.4
1963–64	Wilt Chamberlain, San Francisco	44.8, 36.5
1965	Wilt Chamberlain, San Fran., Phila.	34.7
1966	Wilt Chamberlain, Philadelphia	33.5
1967	Rick Barry, San Francisco	35.6
1968	Dave Bing, Detroit	27.1
1969	Elvin Hayes, San Diego	28.4
1970	Jerry West, Los Angeles	31.2
1971	Lew Alcindor, Milwaukee	31.7
1972	Kareem Abdul-Jabbar (Alcindor), Milwaukee	34.8
1973	Nate Archibald, Kansas City–Omaha	34.0
1974–76	Bob McAdoo, Buffalo	30.6, 34.5, 31.1
1977	Pete Maravich, New Orleans	31.1
1978–80	George Gervin, San Antonio	27.2, 29.6, 33.1
1981	Adrian Dantley, Utah	30.7

Year	Player, Team	Average
1982	George Gervin, San Antonio	32.3
1983	Alex English, Denver	28.4
1984	Adrian Dantley, Utah	30.6
1985	Bernard King, New York	32.9
1986	Dominique Wilkins, Atlanta	30.3
1987–93	Michael Jordan, Chicago	37.1, 35.0, 32.5, 33.6, 31.5, 30.1, 32.6
1994	David Robinson, San Antonio	29.8

NBA MOST VALUABLE PLAYER*

Year	Player, Team	Year	Player, Team
1956	Bob Pettit, St. Louis	1975	Bob McAdoo, Buffalo
1957	Bob Cousy, Boston	1976–77	K. Abdul-Jabbar, L.A.
1958	Bill Russell, Boston	1978	Bill Walton, Portland
1959	Bob Pettit, St. Louis	1979	Moses Malone,
1960	Wilt Chamberlain,		Houston
	Philadelphia	1980	K. Abdul-Jabbar, L.A.
1961–63	Bill Russell, Boston	1981	Julius Erving,
1964	Oscar Robertson,		Philadelphia
	Cincinnati	1982–83	Moses Malone,
1965	Bill Russell, Boston		Houston, Phila.
1966–68	Wilt Chamberlain,	1984–86	Larry Bird, Boston
	Philadelphia	1987	Earvin Johnson, L.A.
1969	Wes Unseld, Baltimore	1988	Michael Jordan, Chicago
1970	Willis Reed, New York	1989–90	Earvin Johnson, L.A.
1971–72	Lew Alcindor (Kareem	1991–92	Michael Jordan, Chicago
	Abdul-Jabbar),	1993	Charles Barkley, Phoenix
	Milwaukee	1994	Hakeem Olajuwon,
1973	Dave Cowens, Boston		Houston
1974	K. Abdul-Jabbar,		
	Milwaukee		

*Selected by NBA players.

NCAA* BASKETBALL CHAMPIONS

Year	Team	Year	Team
1939	Oregon	1966	Texas Western
1940	Indiana	1967–73	UCLA
1941	Wisconsin	1974	North Carolina State
1942	Stanford	1975	UCLA
1943	Wyoming	1976	Indiana
1944	Utah	1977	Marquette
1945–46	Oklahoma A & M	1978	Kentucky
1947	Holy Cross	1979	Michigan State
1948–49	Kentucky	1980	Louisville
1950	CCNY	1981	Indiana
1951	Kentucky	1982	North Carolina
1952	Kansas	1983	North Carolina State
1953	Indiana	1984	Georgetown
1954	La Salle	1985	Villanova
1955–56	San Francisco	1986	Louisville
1957	North Carolina	1987	Indiana
1958	Kentucky	1988	Kansas
1959	California	1989	Michigan
1960	Ohio State	1990	UNLV
1961–62	Cincinnati	1991–92	Duke
1963	Loyola (Ill.)	1993	North Carolina
1964–65	UCLA	1994	Arkansas

*National Collegiate Athletic Association.

RULES AND EQUIPMENT

Professional, college, and high school games are similar except in length and in range of basic skills. Professional games are 48 minutes long, divided into quarters; college games, 40 minutes, played in halves; and high school games, 32 minutes, broken into quarters. If a game is tied at the end of regulation time, an overtime (3 to 5 minutes, depending on the level of competition) is played.

Although no set of dimensions for a basketball court is universally accepted, the recommended size is 94 ft (28.65 m) long and 50 ft (15.24 m) wide.

Two points are given for a field goal, which is a shot that goes through the hoop—10 ft (3 m) high—while the ball is in play. The NBA instituted, beginning with the 1979–80 season, the 3-point field goal, awarded to a player who scores from beyond a semicircle (see diagram) at a distance of an even 22 ft

NBA TEAMS

Eastern Conference	Western Conference
Atlantic Division	**Midwest Division**
Boston Celtics	Dallas Mavericks
Miami Heat	Denver Nuggets
New Jersey Nets	Houston Rockets
New York Knickerbockers	Minnesota Timberwolves
Orlando Magic	San Antonio Spurs
Philadelphia 76ers	Utah Jazz
Washington Bullets	
Central Division	**Pacific Division**
Atlanta Hawks	Golden State Warriors
Charlotte Hornets	Los Angeles Clippers
Chicago Bulls	Los Angeles Lakers
Cleveland Cavaliers	Phoenix Suns
Detroit Pistons	Portland Trail Blazers
Indiana Pacers	Sacramento Kings
Milwaukee Bucks	Seattle Supersonics

(6.7 m) all the way around the basket. The NCAA followed suit, beginning in 1986–87, with a 3-point semicircle that averages 19.75 ft (6 m) from the basket. One point is awarded for a free throw, or foul shot, which is attempted by a player who has been fouled, or impeded physically, by an opponent. Free throws are attempted, undefended, from a line drawn 15 ft (4.57 m) from the basket.

On the offensive, a player may advance the ball by passing or even rolling it to a teammate or by dribbling, which is bouncing it along the floor with one-hand taps. The defensive team can get the ball back by intercepting passes, blocking shots, or even by literally stealing it out of an opponent's hand, provided that no illegal body contact occurs. After a basket is made, the ball is awarded to the other team, which puts it back in play. If a field-goal attempt is missed and the ball remains in bounds, it is kept in play by the team that recovers (rebounds) it.

LOUIS SABIN

Bibliography: Ashe, Arthur R., Jr., *A Hard Road to Glory—Basketball* (1994); Axthelm, Pete, *The City Game* (1982); Bradley, Bill, *Life on the Run* (1976); Feinstein, John, *Season on the Brink* (1989); Fox, Robert A., *Basketball: The Complete Handbook of Individual Skills* (1988); Head-Summit, Pat, and Jennings, Deborah K., *Basketball: Fundamentals and Team Play* (1991); National Basketball Association Staff, *The Official NBA Basketball Encyclopedia* (1989); Pluto, Terry, *Loose Balls* (1991); Wooden, John R., *Practical Modern Basketball*, 3d ed. (1988).

basketry

Basketry, the art of twisting together strands of material to form objects, is one of the oldest and most widespread handicrafts. Basketry is most often employed to make containers, but it has also been used in the construction of such other items as houses (of osier, or willow), boats, sails, carts, coffins, clothing, armor, masks, fish weirs, and furniture.

Most of the baskets that survive from ancient times are found in dry caves or burials located in arid or semiarid places, including coastal Peru, the Nile Valley, and the Southwest region of the United States. Basketry has also been found preserved in peat bogs, in permafrost, and under water, or in a carbonized state. In regions with wet climates, ancient basketry is best known from impressions left in mud or pottery or from its representation in paintings and carvings.

Construction Methods. Basketry is generally either woven or sewn. Basket-weaving requires that one element, called the weft, is passed over and under a foundation element called the warp. Techniques include plaiting or checkerwork, when warp and weft elements are of equal width, thickness, and flexibility; twilling, when two or more weft strands are passed over and under two or more warps; wickerwork, when relatively inflexible warp and relatively slender and flexible weft elements are used; and twining, when two or more weft elements are passed around each warp. In sewn baskets a foundation is coiled around itself and stitched in place.

Materials. Most baskets are made of vegetal materials that may be as fine and flexible as grass or as thick and rigid as a tree trunk—although wire, whalebone, leather, and other materials are also used. Its materials are often the key in identifying a basket's origin.

Willow has been the favored basketmaking material of northern Europe for millennia. Relatively rigid, it is usually woven by wicker techniques when the rods are whole or by plaiting when they are split. Other frequently used basketry materials include bamboo in the Far East, rattan in tropical Asia and Indonesia, and cane in parts of tropical Africa and America. The weaving characteristics of these materials are similar to those of willow. In areas where softer and more flexible materials such as palm leaf, tree roots, bark, yucca, or grasses are available, plaiting, twining, and coiling are generally the dominant techniques.

Decorative Methods. Methods of decorating basketry vary greatly from place to place. Self-patterns are those which are woven or sewn into a basket as it is made. Additive designs are those which are applied to completed baskets. The most basic self-patterns are textural and are created by the construction method used. Others are made by varying the color or texture of weft, warp, stitch, or foundation coil. Additive decorations include false embroidery, imbrication (overlapping), and the sewing of beads or feathers to the foundation of a coil basket as it is made.

Because of their flexibility, the twine and coil methods are most conducive to decoration. The greatest variety of decorated baskets come from regions where such techniques are widely employed, including East Africa and the Southwest and Northwest Coast regions of aboriginal North America. The elaborately decorated baskets of the Pomo Indians of California are among the finest in the world. Also known for fine decorative detail are the traditional plaited basketry of the southwestern United States, Mexico, the Caribbean, the Philippines, China, and Japan, and the small wickerwork from Scandinavia, Great Britain, and Appalachia.

In the industrialized West, where machinery was replacing hand-weaving in basket-making, the Art Nouveau movement led to a revival of the use of wicker furniture and objects around the end of the 19th century. At about the same time, native-American basketry began to be appreciated, valued, and

A young man of the Meo tribe of Thailand demonstrates the technique of plaiting as he makes a basket from split bamboo, a relatively rigid material. Plaiting is a basket-weaving technique that uses a warp and weft of identical thickness, width, and flexibility.

collected as an art form and was widely imitated by non-Indian hobbyists.   J. J. BRODY

Bibliography: Bobart, H. H., *Basketwork through the Ages* (1936; repr. 1971); Harvey, V. I., *The Techniques of Basketry* (1986); James, G. W., *Indian Basketry* (1901; repr. 1972); Kollath, R., and Frew, T., *Baskets* (1989); Wetherbee, M., et al., *Shaker Baskets* (1987).

Baskin, Leonard

Leonard Baskin, b. New Brunswick, N.J., Aug. 15, 1922, is an artist who is known as a sculptor in wood and bronze, as a watercolorist, engraver, maker of woodcuts and lithographs, and as an illustrator and occasional author of books. In his work with the human figure, Baskin often uses biblical or mythological themes—as in *A Passover Haggadah* (1974), for which he provided watercolors of events in the biblical Exodus and hand-lettered much of the Hebrew text as well. He may be better known for his animal prints—his illustrations for poet Ted Hughes's *Crow* (1970), for example, or his own *The Raptors and Other Birds* (1985), which makes birds seem messengers of a malign nature.

Bibliography: Baskin, L., *Baskin: Sculpture, Drawings, Prints* (1970); Fern, A., and O'Sullivan, J., *The Complete Prints of Leonard Baskin* (1984); Jaffe, I., *The Sculpture of Leonard Baskin* (1980).

Basov, Nikolai Gennadiyevich   [bah'-sawf, nik'-oh-ly gen-nad-ee-ye'-vich]

The Russian physicist Nikolai Gennadiyevich Basov, b. Dec. 14, 1922, shared the 1964 Nobel Prize for physics with Aleksandr Prokhorov and Charles H. Townes for his work on the theory of the MASER. A maser is a microwave amplifier; it operates on the same principle as a laser but in a different region of the spectrum. Basov, a graduate of the Moscow Engineering and Physics Institute in 1950, has served as director of the Lebedev Institute since 1973 and is editor of the popular science journal *Priroda* (Nature).

Basque language

Basque, or Euskara, is a language spoken by about a million people in northern Spain and southwestern France. Although attempts have been made to link it to ancient Iberian, the Hamito-Semitic group, and Caucasian, its origins remain uncertain.

The sound pattern resembles that of Spanish, with its five pure vowels and such peculiarities as a trilled *r* and palatal *n* and *l*. In spite of this, and the presence of numerous Latinate loanwords, Basque has maintained its distinctiveness throughout two millennia of external contacts. For example, it still places a unique emphasis on suffixes to denote case and number and to form new words.

Basque is the only language remaining of those spoken in southwestern Europe before the Roman conquest. Since the 10th century, it has gradually been supplanted by Castilian Spanish, and under the Franco regime its use in Spain was outlawed altogether. The ethnic insularity of the Basques, however, has fostered revivals. Attempts are now being made to standardize the orthography.

Bibliography: Russell, H., et al., *Basque Essay* (1974); Tovar, A., *The Basque Language* (1957); Vallie, F., *Literature of the Basques* (1974).

Basques

The Basques are a people whose homeland is the westernmost part of the Pyrenees Mountains and the immediately surrounding regions. This area comprises four provinces in Spain (Guipúzcoa, Vizcaya, Álava, and Navarra) and the department of Pyrénées-Atlantiques in France. Known to the Spanish as *vascos* and to the French as *basques*, the Basques call themselves *Euskaldunak* and their homeland *Euskadi*. Basque speakers number about 890,000 in Spain and 80,000 in France (1987 est.), but a larger number identify themselves as Basques in each country.

The origins of the Basques are still a mystery. Their language is unrelated to any Indo-European language. Although they look much like their French and Spanish neighbors, Basques possess the lowest frequency of blood-type B and the highest frequencies of types O and Rh-negative of any population in Europe. They are staunchly Roman Catholic and noted for their distinctive folklore, folk theater, games, music, and a light-footed, acrobatic form of dancing.

Traditionally a fiercely independent peasant and fishing people, they were known as early as the Middle Ages as skilled boat makers and courageous whale hunters and cod fishermen who often ranged far into the Atlantic. Their characteristic settlement is the isolated farm. The growth of villages is a relatively recent response to increased industry and trade in the Basque country.

A large number of Basques have migrated to North and South America. Historically, this migration has been the result partly of adverse political circumstances (most Basques opposed the Franco regime in Spain) and partly of the inheritance rule known as primogeniture, by which the oldest son inherits the family farm. Younger sons generally have either sought employment in coastal settlements as industrial workers or fishermen, or they have migrated to the New World, frequently finding work as sheepherders.

Isolated in their mountainous homeland, the Basques repulsed incursions by Romans, Germanic tribes, Moors, and others until the 1700s. They lost their autonomy in France after the French Revolution (1789) and in Spain by the early 1800s. A movement for Basque separatism rose in the 19th and 20th centuries, which since 1959 has been led by the militant separatist organization ETA (a Basque acronym for "Basqueland and Freedom"). Spain's Basques were granted home rule in 1980, but ETA violence continued. Basque separatists won about 16% of the vote in regional elections in October 1990.
                                      ROBERT T. ANDERSON

Bibliography: Clark, Robert P., *The Basques* (1980); Douglass, W. A., ed., *Basque Politics* (1985); Heiberg, Marianne, *The Making of the Basque Nation* (1989); Payne, S. G., *Basque Nationalism* (1975).

Basra   [bas'-rah]

Basra, Iraq's second-largest city and the capital of Basra province in southeastern Iraq, is situated on the SHATT-AL-ARAB, about 115 km (71 mi) from the Persian Gulf. Two-thirds of the population of 616,700 (1985 est.) is Shiite. Until recently, the economy was based on oil shipping and refining and the making of petrochemicals and fertilizers.

The city was founded in 636 by Caliph Umar I. An important center of letters, science, poetry, finance, and commerce under the early ABBASIDS, it declined in later centuries but revived with the completion of the railroad to Baghdad in the early 20th century. Occupied by the British in World Wars I and II, it was an important staging post on the Allied supply route to the USSR after 1941. Basra's rapid commercial development after World War II was due to its advantageous location as a port and to the major oil fields nearby. The IRAN-IRAQ WAR (1980–88) virtually closed the port. In 1991 the city was virtually destroyed by allied bombing during the GULF WAR and by subsequent fighting between Shiite rebels and government forces.
                                      ARTHUR TURNER CAMPBELL

bass   (fish)   [bas]

The bass is any of several percoid, or perchlike, fish, including some important food fish and some of the most popular game species. Most bass are members of three related families: Serranidae, or sea bass, including GROUPERS; Percichthyidae, or temperate bass; and Centrarchidae, including the CRAPPIE and SUNFISH, including some bream. The first two families are primarily marine shore fish distributed worldwide in tropical and temperate seas, but a few species are found in brackish or fresh water; together they number more than 400 species. The Centrarchidae, about 30 species, are freshwater fish of temperate North America.

Bass are spiny-finned fish with generalized, laterally compressed bodies and usually only slightly forked tail fins. They range in size from the giant sea bass, *Stereolepis gigas*, a temperate bass of the Pacific coast of North America that reaches

Bass are popular North American food and game fish. Shown are the striped bass, Morone saxatilis (top); the yellow bass, M. mississippiensis (middle), and the largemouth bass, Micropterus salmoides (bottom).

lengths of 2.1 m (7 ft) and weights of more than 250 kg (550 lb), to sea bass species that reach lengths of no more than 10 cm (4 in). The majority of bass are carnivorous.

Among common sea bass of North America are the Pacific coast's kelp bass, *Paralabrax clathratus;* the barred sand bass, *P. nebulifer;* and the spotted sand bass, *P. maculatofasciatus.* On the Atlantic coast, the black sea bass, *Centropristis striata,* is a popular game fish.

Several temperate bass, including the giant sea bass, are important game fish as well. The most desirable species, the striped bass, *Morone saxatilis,* can weigh more than 45 kg (100 lb). It is native to the Atlantic coast and was introduced to the California coast in the late 19th century. Two smaller freshwater relatives, the white bass, *M. chrysops,* and the yellow bass, *M. mississippiensis,* are native to eastern North America.

Probably the best-known bass to North American freshwater anglers are the various sunfish species of the genus *Micropterus.* The largemouth bass, *M. salmoides,* occurs naturally in eastern North America but has been introduced throughout the rest of the continent. It is one of the most popular of all freshwater game fish; the angling record is 10 kg (22.25 lb). The smallmouth bass, *M. dolomieui,* is a more northern species that prefers cooler waters and grows to about half the size of the largemouth. Another common species is the spotted bass, *M. punctulatus,* found from Ohio to Florida and westward into Kansas and Texas; it grows to about 1.8 kg (4 lb). The Guadalupe bass, *M. treculi,* is found only in the Guadalupe River drainage basin in Texas; the Suwannee bass, *M. notius,* is restricted to northern Florida; and the redeye bass, *M. coosae,* is restricted to the Alabama River drainage basin. None of these last three species reaches more than 0.9 kg (2 lb).

The white sea bass, *Cynoscion nobilis,* of California is actually a drum, family Sciaenidae.   EDWARD O. WILEY

Bibliography: Lee, D. S., et al., *Atlas of North American Freshwater Fishes* (1980); Migdalski, Edward C., and Fichter, George S., *The Fresh and Salt Water Fishes of the World* (1976).

bass   (music)   [bays]

The bass is the lowest part of a musical composition, the foundation on which the HARMONY, in the traditional sense, is built. The lowest adult male singing voice is also called the bass. When referring to a musical instrument, the term *bass* indicates either the lowest member of a family, or, when a contrabass instrument is used, the next lowest, as in bass CLARINET. The DOUBLE BASS, the lowest instrument of the violin family, is sometimes called simply the bass. The bass clef is the F clef on the fourth line of the musical staff.

Bass, Sam   [bas]

Sam Bass, b. near Mitchell, Ind., July 21, 1851, d. July 21, 1878, was an outlaw in the American West. In 1869 he left Indiana for Texas, where he became a cowboy and a deputy sheriff. About 1875 he began robbing stage coaches in the Dakota Territory to recoup gambling losses. Bass participated in a $65,000 Nebraska train holdup in 1877. Returning to Texas, he organized a gang that robbed four trains. He was shot by Texas Rangers during a bank robbery at Round Rock, Tex., and died two days later.

Bibliography: Gard, Wayne, *Sam Bass* (1936; repr. 1976); Martin, Charles L., *Sketch of Sam Bass, the Bandit* (1956; repr. 1968).

bass drum: see DRUM (musical instrument).

Bass Strait   [bas]

The Bass Strait lies between Australia and its island state, Tasmania. It was named in 1798 for George Bass, a British surgeon and navigator. The strait is 298 km (185 mi) long and varies from 129 to 242 km (80 to 150 mi) wide. Its average depth is 70 m (230 ft).

Bassani, Giorgio   [bah-sah'-nee]

The Italian poet and novelist Giorgio Emilio Bassani, b. Apr. 4, 1916, is regarded as one of his country's most interesting contemporary writers. A rigorous, elegant stylist, he is at his best in depicting his native Ferrara, particularly its Jewish community, during the fascist era and the persecutions of the late 1930s and '40s. His novel *The Garden of the Finzi-Continis* (1962; Eng. trans., 1965; film, 1971) and many of his other works have been translated, including *Five Stories of Ferrara* (1965; Eng. trans., 1971), *The Heron* (1968; Eng. trans., 1986), and a collection of poems published in English (1982) as *Rolls Royce and Other Poems.*   SERGIO PACIFICI

Bibliography: Radcliff-Umstead, Douglas, *The Exile into Eternity* (1987).

Bassano   (family)   [bah-sah'-noh]

Jacopo Bassano's The Adoration of the Shepherds *(1568) demonstrates his realistic portrayal of the lower classes. Bassano was known for his robust style and his use of vivid colors, dramatic chiaroscuro, and elongated human figures. (Galleria Nazionale, Rome.)*

The Bassano family of Venetian painters was active for about 100 years from the early 16th century to the early 17th century. Their name was derived from the town of Bassano, where the family lived at various times. The painters were Francesco da Ponte, the Elder, *c.*1480–1540; Jacopo, *c.*1517–1592; Giovanni Battista, 1553–1613; Leandro, 1557–1622; and Gerolamo, 1556–1621.

Francesco the Elder painted for churches in and near Bassano. His style was somewhat old-fashioned and provincial; a painting such as *Madonna Enthroned between Saints Peter and Paul* (1519; Museo Civico, Bassano) reflects the work of Bartolommeo Montagna, Giovanni Battista CIMA, and Giovanni Caroto.

Francesco's son **Jacopo** was far more important. After early training with his father, Jacopo came under the influence of Bonifazio di Pitati; this is evident in *The Story of Nebuchadnezzar* (1534–36; Museo Civico, Bassano). Less direct influences came from TITIAN, Palma Vecchio, and Paris BORDONE. His *Portrait of a Man* (late 1530s; National Gallery, Washington, D.C.) is related to the art of Lorenzo LOTTO. Beginning in the 1540s, MANNERISM reached Jacopo through prints, especially of the works of PARMIGIANINO. *The Holy Trinity* (Church of the Trinity, Angarano), with elongated figures and decorative effects achieved through bold swirls of drapery, owes much to the Florentine Mannerists; it also resembles certain works by EL GRECO. Later in his career, Jacopo often portrayed groups of rustic figures in compositions such as *Adoration of the Shepherds* (*c.*1568; Galleria Nazionale, Rome). This sensitive rendering of realistic genre figures, combined with an often dramatic contrast of light and shadow (CHIAROSCURO), has led some critics to call Jacopo's later painting style "pre-Caravaggesque," that is, prefiguring the style of CARAVAGGIO. He was also expert at painting animals, as in *Adoration of the Shepherds* (*c.*1545; Hampton Court, England).

Jacopo's increasingly realistic style was continued both in the family's workshop in Bassano and in the Venice studio of his sons. They executed many paintings of nocturnes as well as of religious and genre subjects. Of the sons, **Leandro** was probably the most gifted. He was well known for his numerous portraits in the style of TINTORETTO.   EDWARD J. SULLIVAN

Bibliography: Forster, Kurt, *Mannerist Painting: The Sixteenth Century* (1970); Freedberg, Sydney, *Painting in Italy, 1500–1600* (1970); Hauser, Arnold, *Mannerism: The Crisis of the Renaissance and the Origin of Modern Art*, 2 vols. (1965); Shearman, John K. G., *Mannerism* (1967); Würtenberger, Franzsepp, *Mannerism: The European Style of the Sixteenth Century* (1963).

See also: RENAISSANCE ART AND ARCHITECTURE.

Basse-Terre   [bahs'-tair']

Basse-Terre (1982 pop., 13,656) is a seaport town on the southwest coast of Basse-Terre Island and is the capital of the French overseas department of Guadeloupe in the eastern Caribbean Sea. It was first occupied by the French in 1643. The present economy is based mainly on sugar and tourism.

basset hound

The basset hound is a long-bodied, heavy-boned breed of hound that stands 28–35 cm (11–14 in) at the shoulder and weighs 18–27 kg (40–60 lb). Its long, soft, drooping ears, wrinkled brow, and short legs give it a distinctively wistful appearance. The smooth coat is accepted in any color and markings at breed competitions; for such shows, the dew claws may be removed.

The breed is an old one and has been known for centuries in continental Europe, particularly in France and the Low Countries. Having better scenting ability than any breed except the bloodhound, it was used by royalty as a slow-working, steady trailer of game. Because it is low-slung, the basset hound is particularly good in rough, dense terrain. The breed has been known throughout the United States since the late 19th century.   JOHN MANDEVILLE

Bibliography: Braun, M., *The New Complete Basset Hound*, 4th ed. (1979); Foy, M., and Nicholas, A. K., *The Basset Hound* (1985).

The basset hound, known for its melancholy expression, was bred to slowly trail rabbits and hares.

basso continuo: SEE FIGURED BASS.

bassoon   [buh-soon']

The bassoon is a double-reed woodwind, the bass of the OBOE family. Its normal range is from B flat below the bass staff to the *D* in the second octave above middle C. The tube, 2.79 m (9 ft 2 in) long, is bent to make a height of 1.22 m (4 ft) and consists of a metal crook on which the reed is placed and four sections of maple or pearwood: the tenor, the butt, the bass, and the bell.

In the mid-17th century the woodwind makers in the court of Louis XIV created the sectional bassoon from the Renaissance double-bored curtal, and its use immediately spread rapidly from Jean Baptiste LULLY's orchestra throughout Western orchestras as the proper woodwind bass for ensembles. The four-keyed bassoon was standard in Wolfgang Amadeus Mozart's time, but by the time of Ludwig van Beethoven a six- or eight-keyed bassoon was in use. Classical composers exploited the bassoon for effective tenor-range solos and for humorous effects.

Strong national differences in bassoons emerged in the second quarter of the 19th century. The French, willing to humor certain difficult tones, applied various mechanical improvements that made the instrument facile but preserved its highly

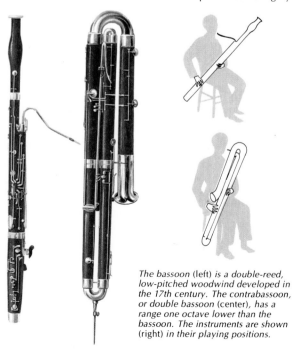

The bassoon (left) is a double-reed, low-pitched woodwind developed in the 17th century. The contrabassoon, or double bassoon (center), has a range one octave lower than the bassoon. The instruments are shown (right) in their playing positions.

individual tone quality. The Germans made (c.1830) radical changes, sacrificing tone quality for an instrument evenly effective (or ineffective) in all ranges and at all dynamic levels. After two generations of diligent development, a German family of instrument makers produced what became the basic German bassoon of today. It performed efficiently but produced a warm, rich tone, noticeably different from that of the French. The German bassoon is used in America and England and increasingly in other European countries.

ROBERT A. WARNER

Bibliography: Baines, Anthony, *Woodwind Instruments and Their History*, rev. ed. (1965); Carse, Adam, *Musical Wind Instruments*, 2d ed. (1939; repr. 1965); Jansen, W., *The Bassoon: Its History, Construction, Makers, Players, and Music*, 5 vols. (1978); Joppig, Gunther, *Oboe and the Bassoon* (1988).

See also: WIND INSTRUMENTS.

basswood: see LINDEN.

bastard toadflax

Bastard toadflax is the common name of the plant genus *Comandra*, in the sandalwood family, Santalaceae. *C. umbelata* is found in dry woods and fields of most of the eastern United States and west to Michigan. It reaches a height of up to 46 cm (18 in), has small, alternate, elliptical leaves and small white flowers borne in a terminal cluster, and is sometimes semiparasitic on the roots of other plants.

Bastien-Lepage, Jules   [bahs-tee-an'-luh-pahzh', zhuel]

Jules Bastien-Lepage, b. Damvillers, France, Nov. 1, 1848, d. Dec. 10, 1884, achieved fame in the 1870s and 1880s with paintings of country life and portraits of such personalities as the actress Sarah Bernhardt. After studying drawing as a young man, Bastien-Lepage entered the postal service but gave this up to be an artist. He studied under Alexandre Cabanel and exhibited at the Paris salon from 1870, trying allegorical subjects and fan paintings; but success came only when he turned to rustic subjects. His first essay of this kind was purchased by the French state in 1874. As his reputation grew, Bastien-Lepage blended into his detailed technique a lighter range of tones and a variety of brushstrokes suggestive of impressionism and took on the role of official painter of the peasants of his native Meuse region.

MARK ROSKILL

Bastille   [bah-steel']

A fortress and prison in Paris, the Bastille was a symbol of royal absolutism before the French Revolution. Begun in 1370, it was originally intended to augment the city's defenses. By the 17th century it was being used as a prison and was rumored to contain hundreds of political prisoners. Voltaire and the Marquis de Sade were among its most famous prisoners.

On July 14, 1789, at the beginning of the French Revolution, a mob gathered outside the Bastille, demanding the munitions that were stored within. The commander, the Marquis de Launay, refused to surrender, and the building was then stormed. Ironically, only seven prisoners were found inside. The Bastille was demolished soon after.

July 14, Bastille Day, has been set aside since 1880 as the French national holiday. As with the American Independence Day, or Fourth of July, the holiday is celebrated with the setting off of firecrackers and with parades and other festivity.

Basutoland: see LESOTHO.

bat

The bat is a winged MAMMAL with the ability to fly. Its ability to maintain sustained flight, unique among mammals, results from the modification of handlike forelimbs into wings. Bats belong to the order Chiroptera and are divided into two suborders: the Megachiroptera (megabats) and the Microchiroptera (microbats). Microbats detect their prey using ECHOLOCATION;

most megabats cannot echolocate but have highly developed eyesight. Bats are nocturnal or active at twilight (crepuscular). They are mainly tropical in distribution.

It has been suggested that megabats and microbats are less closely related than once believed. The fossil record suggests that megabats may be of much more recent origin than microbats. Researchers have shown that some megabats have the binocular vision associated with primates. Most bats in this group have a claw on the second finger and an unspecialized shoulder girdle. Their average weight is more than 100 g (3.5 oz). The largest megabat, *Pteropus vampyrus*, weighs up to 899 g (31.7 oz) and has a wingspan of 170 cm (67 in). On the other hand, microbats have no claw on the second finger. Their average weight is less than 30 g (1.058 oz) as adults. The smallest microbat, *Craseonycteris thonglongyai*, weighs from 1.8 to 2.0 g (0.063 to 0.071 oz) and has a wingspan of about 16 cm (6.3 in).

Nearly two-thirds of the 950 species of bats feed mainly on insects, and all insectivorous bats are microbats. Other bats eat fruit, nectar, and pollen; a few eat blood, fish, or other mammals. Fruit eaters and nectar and pollen feeders may be either megabats of the family Pteropodidae of the Old World tropics, or microbats of the family Phyllostomidae of the New World tropics. In other families of microbats, such as the Vespertilionidae and the Noctilionidae, bats are fish eaters. In India, Southeast Asia, Australia, and South America, several species in two families of microbats, the Megadermatidae and the Phyllostomidae, are carnivorous, feeding on birds, small mammals, and reptiles.

The three species of vampires (blood-feeding microbats) all are found in the New World tropics. Vampires had been considered a separate family (Desmodontidae) but are now usually treated as part of the family Phyllostomatidae. Vampires feed on blood obtained from mammals or birds. They use their sharp, highly modified teeth to make a shallow wound and secrete an anticoagulant in their saliva to inhibit clotting of the blood. The vampire's bite is painful but not usually dangerous, though the saliva may transmit certain diseases.

Bats roost in caves, hollow trees, foliage, crevices in rocks, and in spaces under the bark of trees. Three species in two families, one from Madagascar (Myzopodidae) and two from South America (Thyropteridae), have adhesive disks on their wrists and ankles, adaptations that facilitate moving and roosting on smooth surfaces. Several phyllostomids make tents out of the leaves of some plants, and some flat-headed vespertilionids in Southeast Asia roost in the hollow stems of bamboo, having entered the stems through holes made by wood-boring beetles. Species that roost in caves and trees often form huge colonies. Some caves in the American Southwest harbor millions of Mexican free-tailed bats (Molossidae) every summer. Many bats throughout the world roost in buildings and are often a considerable nuisance.

Bats have low rates of reproduction. Most species produce one or two young in a litter; bats of temperate areas have one litter a year, and those in tropical regions may have two. Some tropical bats are polyoestrous and annually produce more than two litters. Some species that hibernate have unusual reproductive cycles. Mating takes place in fall, and the females store sperm in their reproductive tracts during winter; ovulation and fertilization occur in spring. The gestation period for most of these species is about 40–70 days and for some up to 100 days. In the vampire bat the gestation could be as much as 8 months.

Although there is little information about the mating behavior of bats, it is known that some species mate promiscuously and that others form harems involving one male and several females. Female African hammer-headed bats select a mate from congregations of singing males.

Newborn bats are large, weighing from 15–30 percent of their mother's postpartum weight. Young are usually born rump first or feet first, presumably to minimize the chances of tangling the wings in birth canals. Baby bats are nursed from pectoral mammary glands by their mothers, who may move them from one roost to another. Some young bats first fly at about the age of three weeks, a time corresponding to the re-

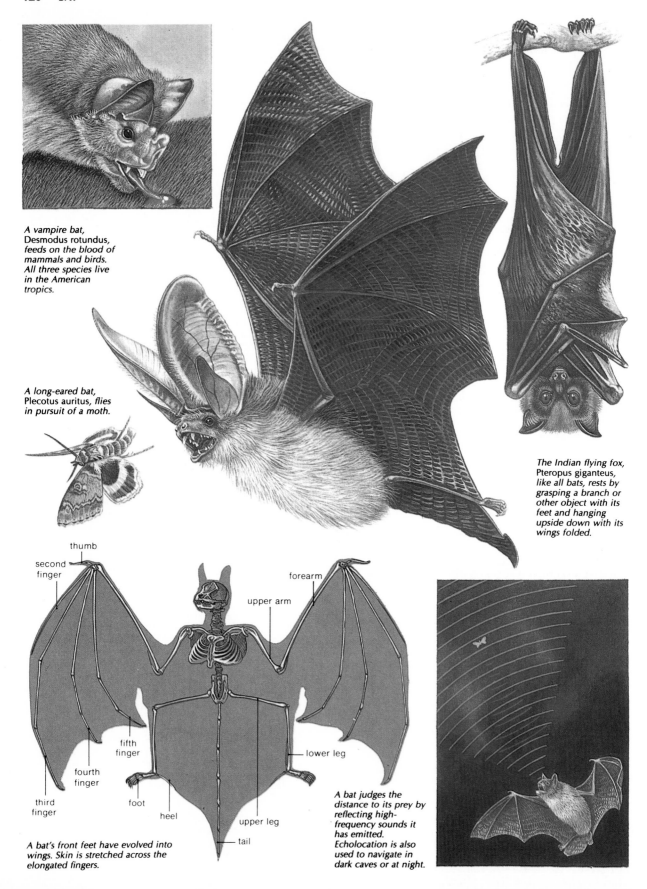

A vampire bat, Desmodus rotundus, feeds on the blood of mammals and birds. All three species live in the American tropics.

A long-eared bat, Plecotus auritus, flies in pursuit of a moth.

The Indian flying fox, Pteropus giganteus, like all bats, rests by grasping a branch or other object with its feet and hanging upside down with its wings folded.

thumb

second finger

forearm

upper arm

third finger

fourth finger

fifth finger

foot

heel

upper leg

lower leg

tail

A bat's front feet have evolved into wings. Skin is stretched across the elongated fingers.

A bat judges the distance to its prey by reflecting high-frequency sounds it has emitted. Echolocation is also used to navigate in dark caves or at night.

placement of milk teeth by permanent teeth and the initiation of weaning.

Parasites excepted, few predators exclusively feed on bats. Occasionally many animals, including hawks, owls, mice, skunks, foxes, and snakes, will eat bats. Bat hawks in Africa and New Guinea appear to eat only bats, and carnivorous bats probably also prey upon other bats. Mortality among bats is usually accidental or associated with human activity. Some temperate species are remarkably long-lived; little brown bats have been recorded as living 30 years, but 10 years is probably more common in that species. Hibernation by temperate species may contribute to their longevity, but many bats fail to survive their first winter.

In temperate areas, bats avoid winter conditions by migrating or by hibernating. Migration, which also occurs in tropical species, may involve long flights up to 1,600 km (1,000 mi) or shorter movements to places of hibernation. The torpor and hibernation of bats differ physiologically from that of other heterothermic mammals such as ground squirrels, at least in the number of times the animals arouse from torpor during the winter. All the Microchiroptera that have been studied and several species of dog-faced bats (*Rousettus*-Megachiroptera) use echolocation to orient themselves. Bats are not blind, however, and their eyes and sense of smell are well developed. Vocalizations, visual signals, and smell play important roles in the social lives of bats, which are among the most gregarious of the Mammalia.   M. B. FENTON

Bibliography: Barbour, R. W., and Davis, W. H., *Bats of America* (1969; repr. 1979); Hill, J. A., and Smith, J. D., *Bats: A Natural History* (1984); Leen, Nina, and Novick, Alvin, *The World of Bats* (1970); Yalden, D. W., and Morris, P. A., *The Lives of Bats* (1976).

See also: SHREW.

Bataan   [buh-tahn']

Bataan, a province of the Philippines, is a mountainous peninsula on the western side of Manila Bay. The capital of the province, Balanga, is located on the eastern coastal plain. The northwest coast includes Subic Bay, which is noted for its excellent anchorage.

In World War II, American and Filipino armies retreated from Manila to the Bataan Peninsula and held out for three months before surrendering to the Japanese on Apr. 9, 1942. The prisoners' forced march to captivity is known as the Bataan Death March because harsh treatment and starvation caused the deaths of nearly 10,000 men.

Bataille, Henry   [bah-ty']

Henry Bataille, b. Apr. 4, 1872, d. Mar. 2, 1922, a French dramatist, wrote plays exploiting sexual and scandalous themes such as *Maman Colibri* (1904), the story of a middle-aged woman's affair with a young man. Very well received and popular when first staged, and considered daring, his plays now seem dated because of their sentimentality. As a theorist of subconscious motivation, however, he influenced later playwrights.   ROBIN BUSS

Batak   [bah'-tahk]

The Batak are an Indonesian people who live on the rolling plateaus of north-central Sumatra, Indonesia. According to legend, they are descended from Si Radja Batak, a child of supernatural parents who lived on a holy mountain near Lake Toba. Although the approximately 3 million Batak people are divided into subgroups (of which the Toba is the largest), they share basically the same culture and language. Their native language, belonging to the Malayo-Polynesian linguistic family, is written in an Indian-derived script.

The Batak are predominately farmers who raise rice, maize, sweet potatoes, tobacco, and sugarcane. Genealogical descent is traced through the male line, and the nuclear family is the most important social and economic unit. Polygamy is practiced only among the most important families of the community, and divorce is rare. Batak handicrafts include ivory and wood carving, metalwork, and the weaving of tie-dye-patterned fabric. Traditional Toba Batak houses are distinguished by their high, saddle-shaped roofs decorated with carved water-buffalo horns.

The Toba Batak are Christians, although some subgroups (the Mandailing) are Muslims, and others (the Karo) worship the spirits of their deceased ancestors. Today the Batak region is part of the province of North Sumatra.   DONN V. HART

Bibliography: Koentjaraningrat, R., *Introduction to the Peoples and Cultures of Indonesia and Malaya* (1975) and *Villages in Indonesia* (1967).

Bates, Katharine Lee

Katharine Lee Bates, b. Falmouth, Mass., Aug. 12, 1859, d. Mar. 28, 1929, wrote the poem "America the Beautiful" that was later set to Samuel A. Ward's music. She was moved to write what became the unofficial national anthem of the United States after climbing Pikes Peak. Bates was professor of English at Wellesley College from 1891 to 1925. In addition to poetry, she wrote critical works and children's books.

Bates College

Established in 1864 by the Freewill Baptist Church, Bates College (enrollment: 1,435; library: 436,000 volumes) is a private 4-year liberal arts college in Lewiston, Maine. It was the first coeducational college in New England. Bates has a 5-year engineering program in affiliation with Columbia University and Rensselaer Polytechnic Institute.

Bateson, Gregory   [bayt'-suhn]

The British-born psychological anthropologist Gregory Bateson, b. May 9, 1904, d. July 4, 1980, was noted for his exploration of the social forces that both bind and divide individuals and groups. Using a communications model, he devised a method, termed the *double-bind theory*, of understanding social and cultural factors underlying schizophrenia. He was considered a pioneer in the areas of proxemics (spatial interactions), kinesics (communication by body motion), and photographic research techniques. Bateson's book *Naven* (1958) concerns his anthropological fieldwork in New Guinea in the 1930s. Bateson was married to the anthropologist Margaret Mead from 1936 to 1950.

Bibliography: Bateson, Mary C., *With a Daughter's Eye* (1984); Lipset, David, *Gregory Bateson* (1980).

batfish

Batfish are bottom-dwelling marine fish that live in shallow to deep marine waters in the tropics and subtropics. They are about 20 cm (8 in) long, have a wide, flattened body, and walk over the sea bottom, using highly modified pectoral fins that extend like arms at an angle from the head. The skin has small, bony prominences. Batfish can forcefully eject water from their small, circular gill openings and propel themselves away when danger threatens. Like their ANGLERFISH relatives, they possess an appendage that can be extended from the forehead. It is doubtful, however, whether this functions as a lure, for the batfish has a small mouth and only eats small invertebrates. About 55 species belong to the 9 genera of the family Ogcocephalidae.

Bibliography: Migdalski, Edward C., and Fichter, George S., *The Fresh and Saltwater Fishes of the World* (1976).

Bath   (England)   [bahth]

Bath is a city in Avon County, England, on steep slopes by the River Avon. It has a population of 84,200 (1982 est.). Hot mineral springs (49° C/120° F) attracted the Romans, who called the place Aquae Sulis, dedicated to Sul (Minerva). Bath contains Britain's finest Roman ruins. It became a fashionable spa in the 18th century, when much of the town was rebuilt in the Palladian style and extended with squares and crescents lined with limestone buildings designed by John Wood the Elder along with his son. The covered Pulteney Bridge (1769–74), built in the Venetian style, and the 16th-century Abbey Church, in the Late Perpendicular style, are other architectural landmarks. Bath is the site of the annual Bath Festival (June).

Bath (Maine) [bath]

Bath, the seat of Sagadahoc County, is a city in southwestern Maine with a population of 9,799 (1990). The shipbuilding industry there began in 1762 when the *Earl of Bute* was launched. The Bath Iron Works (1833) is the city's main economic asset and since 1889 regularly has built ships, including fishing, yachting, and naval vessels. Incorporated as a city in 1847, Bath has a manager-council form of government.

bath

The custom of building special rooms for bathing dates from prehistoric times. Bathing was important not only for cleanliness but also as a social activity and a religious ritual. Public baths achieved their most elaborate form in Imperial Rome.

Bathrooms were incorporated in the palaces and urban houses of many ancient civilizations. In the Hittite capital of Hattusa in Anatolia (*c.*1400 BC), houses contained paved washroom areas with clay tubs, some with built-in seats. The palaces of Knossos and Phaistos, Crete, and of the mainland Greek cities of Pylos and Tiryns (*c.*1700–1400 BC), had bathrooms, complete with water supply and drainage. Later Greek vase paintings depict showers.

Palaces, monasteries, and the houses of the wealthy in India as early as 200 BC had bathhouses. Each bathhouse contained a dressing room, a steam room with stone benches grouped around a fireplace, a cool basement room for relaxing, and a swimming pool for finishing the bath.

From the 3d century BC, wealthy Romans included elaborate baths in their town houses and country villas. These usually comprised a dressing room, separate rooms for damp and dry heat, and warm and cold tubs. The whole building was heated by a hypocaust—a furnace with flues that channeled hot air through the walls and under the floors. The furnace heated the boiler that supplied hot water. Imperial Rome refined the system in its vast public baths, or thermae, such as the Baths of Caracalla (see CARACALLA, BATHS OF). Served by great reservoirs that were supplied by aqueducts, the Baths of Caracalla had a system of hypocausts, dressing rooms (*apodyteria*), warm rooms (*tepidaria*), hot baths (*calidaria*), steam rooms (*sudatoria* or *laconica*), recreation rooms (*palaestrae*) where the bathers exercised, and cold baths (*frigidaria*).

The public bath (*hammam*) was of special importance in the Islamic empire. The Muslim bathhouse included a dressing room, cold bath, and warm bath clustered around a domed, central steam chamber. All were heated by a furnace with a system of flues, similar to the Roman hypocaust. The hammam survives today in Muslim countries, and in Europe it developed into the Turkish bath.

After a lengthy period of disuse in Europe, public baths were revived with the resurgence of the cities in the 11th and 12th centuries. In private homes, bathing was done in wooden tubs set up in bedrooms. Henry III of England (1217–72) installed hot and cold running water in a bathhouse in his palace at Westminster. The hot water was supplied by tanks filled from pots heated in a furnace.

From the Middle Ages to the 19th century, little progress was made in home bathing equipment. Where baths existed, they were portable tubs set up in a warm place and filled with hot water. In the mid-19th century permanent tubs were installed in bedrooms; cold water was piped in, but the tubs had to be emptied by hand. Shower water was supplied by a cylindrical tank suspended above the tub on iron legs; water was pumped into the tank from a bucket. Some baths were set in a hollow metal case filled with water that was heated by a small furnace; the heated water warmed the cold water in the tub. The later gas heater warmed the water as it ran into the tub. It was succeeded by central hot-water heaters.

Spas with hot springs were widely used for medicinal baths in ancient Greece and Rome, and many Roman watering places have survived into the modern era. Bath in England,

A fine example of a Roman medicinal bath survives in Bath, England. The Romans built health spas at the sites of hot mineral springs while occupying the area in the 1st century AD. Today, Bath is still known as a fashionable spa and resort city.

Baden-Baden in Germany, Aix-les-Bains in France, and Spa in Belgium underwent a revival in the 18th century and are still popular today. Natural hot springs are also exploited in Japan, where the hot water is channeled into a large central pool surrounded by steps on which the bathers sit. Notable spas in the United States are White Sulphur Springs, W.Va.; Hot Springs, Ark.; and Warm Springs, Ga.

The type of bathhouse known as a Finnish sauna, in which steam is produced by throwing water on heated stones, has been adopted by Western Europe and the United States. It is often used with swimming pools: a plunge in the pool substitutes for the Finnish custom of dashing from steamy sauna into a cold stream or snowbank.   FRANCES GIES

Bibliography: Cowan, Thomas, *Beyond the Bath: A Dreamer's Guide* (1983); J. L. Mott's Iron Works, *Mott's Illustrated Catalog of Victorian Plumbing Fixtures for Bathrooms and Kitchens* (1987); Mazzurco, Philip, *Bath Design* (1986); Wright, L., *Clean and Decent: The Fascinating History of the Bathroom and the W. C.* (1967; repr. 1984).

batholith [bath'-oh-lith]

A batholith is a large mass of plutonic rocks that cover areas of more than 100 km² (39 mi²) where exposed at the Earth's surface. Although they are composed of a wide variety of rocks, most are in the diorite-to-granite range. Some batholiths in the Sierra Nevada, Alaska, and British Columbia cover thousands of square kilometers. They are often composite, comprising several phases formed at different times. Most batholithic rocks probably form by melting or transformation of crustal or upper-mantle rocks in the lower zones of mountain belts. These processes may be accompanied by emplacement of ore deposits, many of which are located in or near batholiths.   WILLIAM D. ROMEY

Bibliography: Hyndman, D. W., *Petrology of Igneous and Metamorphic Rocks,* 2d ed. (1985).

Báthory (family) [bah'-toh-ree]

The Báthorys were a prominent Hungarian family who played a significant role in east central European history. Stemming from the Gutkeled clan, they emerged to relative prominence in the 13th century, when they assumed the name of one of their estates (Bátor means "valiant"). They reached the climax of their power in the 16th century, only to die out in 1658.

The most prominent family member was **Stephen Báthory**, b. Sept. 27, 1533, d. Dec. 12, 1586, who succeeded (1571) JOHN II (John Sigismund Zápolya) as prince of Transylvania and was elected (1575) king of Poland. Other Báthory princes of Transylvania included Christopher (r. 1576–81), Christopher's son Sigismund (r. 1581–98, 1601–02), Christopher's nephew Andrew (r. 1599), and Andrew's nephew Gabriel (r. 1608–13).

Many other Báthorys also held high civil, judicial, and ecclesiastical posts in Hungary. Thus, **István**, d. 1493, became the country's chief justice (1471–93) and the governor (*vajda*) of Transylvania (1479–93). **Miklós**, d. Feb. 24, 1506, the Bishop of Vác, was a noted humanist scholar. Intermarriage among the Báthorys also produced a few "evil geniuses." The most notorious was the sadistic **Erzsébet (Elizabeth) Báthory**, b. 1560, d. Aug. 21, 1614, who sought rejuvenation by bathing in the blood of young virgins.   S. B. VARDY

Bathsheba

In the Bible, Bathsheba was the beautiful wife of Uriah, one of King David's officers. DAVID seduced Bathsheba, had Uriah killed, and then married her (2 Sam. 11–12).

Bathurst   (Gambia):   see BANJUL.

Bathurst   (New Brunswick)   [bath'-urst]

Bathurst (1991 pop., 14,409) is the seat of Gloucester County in northeastern New Brunswick, Canada, at the mouth of the Nepisiguit River on Chaleur Bay. Lumbering, fishing, and mining are the area's main industries. Founded (1652) by trader Nicholas Denys, it was named Nepisiguit, then St. Peters, then renamed (1826) for colonial secretary Earl Bathurst.

bathyal zone   [ba'-thee-uhl]

The bathyal zone of the ocean extends from the edge of the continental slope, in 100–300 m (330–1,000 ft) of water, to the 4° C (40° F) ISOTHERM (the water temperature prevalent at depths of 1,000–4,000 m (3,300–13,000 ft). This zone extends into the NERITIC ZONE at the upper level and merges with the ABYSSAL ZONE at the lower level.

Conditions in the bathyal zone are more variable than in the abyssal zone, owing to proximity to the ocean's surface, where wave and current energy is higher, and to continental margins, which supply sediments that dilute or overwhelm the pelagic deposits.   HAROLD R. WANLESS

Bibliography: Bendavid-Val, Leah, ed., *Realm of the Sea* (1991).

bathyscaphe   [ba'-thi-skaf]

The bathyscaphe, a pioneering form of submersible craft, was conceived by French scientist Auguste PICCARD for the purpose of deep-sea exploration. The word is derived from the Greek *bathos,* meaning "deep," and *scaphos,* meaning "ship." Piccard's original craft, the *FNRS 2,* was completed in 1948. It was subsequently modified by others in 1952 and renamed the *FNRS 3.* Piccard and his son Jacques then developed an improved craft, the *Trieste,* in 1953. The *FNRS 3* designers produced a final bathyscaphe, *Archimède,* in 1961.

The bathyscaphes were essentially seagoing balloons. They consisted of a compressible gasoline-filled tank and a smaller, pressure-resistant sphere that could hold a crew of two. The tank provided buoyancy, because gasoline is much lighter but more compressible than water. The craft were equipped with air-filled ballast tanks that would open to fill with water to begin a descent. They also carried iron shot that could be released so as to control the descent and then enable the craft to rise again. Small motor-driven propellers provided a limited degree of maneuverability.

All of the bathyscaphes achieved notable descents in various locations. The most remarkable dive set an enduring world record. It was made on Jan. 23, 1960, by the *Trieste* after its purchase by the U.S. Navy. On that day Jacques Piccard and

The crew of the bathyscaphe Archimède *paddles out to the submersible from the mother ship. Hidden below the surface is the metal sphere for housing the crew. It is incorporated in the base of the vessel.*

navy lieutenant Donald Walsh descended 10,912 m (35,800 ft) into the Challenger Deep of the MARIANAS TRENCH of the Pacific Ocean (see OCEANOGRAPHY).   HILBERT SCHENCK

Bibliography: Gaines, R., *The Explorers of the Undersea World* (1994).

bathysphere   [ba'-thi-sfeer]

The bathysphere was the first modern system designed for the purpose of deep-sea exploration. Developed by American naturalist William BEEBE and engineer Otis Barton in the early 1930s, it consisted of a steel sphere with windows of fused quartz and equipped with searchlights, an oxygen supply, and a telephone. The sphere had to be lowered and raised by cable from a ship, and no rescue was possible if the cable broke. The deepest descent made by Beebe and Barton, in 1934, was to 923 m (3,028 ft). Later versions of the bathysphere have been called benthoscopes.

batik   [buh-teek']

Batik is a wax-resist dyeing process originally used by the Javanese, who are world famous for their colorfully printed fabrics. The fabrics colored in this way are also called batiks. The technique involves applying molten wax to those areas of the

An Indonesian woman uses a tjanting pen during the production of a batik-printed fabric in a factory in the town of Yogyakarta, Java.

cloth that are to remain undyed. When the waxed fabric is submerged in a dye bath, the unwaxed areas are colored, and the wax-coated areas repel or resist coloring.

Traditional batiks are made in the following manner: (1) the fabric, usually cotton, is washed and dried several times; (2) a diluted starch solution is washed in as a sizing; (3) the fabric is beaten to smooth it out and to prepare the fibers for dyeing; (4) the design is drawn on the fabric; (5) following the design, the wax pattern is drawn on the fabric with a spouted applicator called a *tjanting,* or printed on with a copper stamp called a *tjap;* (6) the fabric is dyed; (7) when dry, the fabric is either scraped or boiled to remove the wax. The waxing and dyeing process is repeated for each color in the finished batik.

The Javanese have been making batiks for about a thousand years. Wax-resist printing was also known to the ancient Egyptians and early Chinese. In recent years the technique has been adopted by artisans the world over, and many innovative contemporary designs have evolved.   MARK DITTRICK

Bibliography: Kitley, Philip, *Modern Techniques in Batik Art* (1987); Spee, Miep, *Traditional and Modern Batik* (1985).

Batista, Fulgencio   [bah-tees'-tah, ful-hen'-see-oh]

Fulgencio Batista y Zaldívar, b. Jan. 16, 1901, d. Aug. 6, 1973, was the most powerful political figure in Cuba from 1933 to 1944 and again from 1952 to 1959, when his government was overthrown by Fidel CASTRO. He was an army sergeant when he participated in the ouster of the dictator Gerardo Machado and then led the coup that overthrew the provisional government of Carlos Manuel de Céspedes in 1933. Made army chief of staff, he governed through a succession of puppet presidents until 1940, when he was elected in his own right. At the end of his term in 1944, he retired to Florida.

In 1952, Batista again became chief executive in a bloodless coup, and he won the presidential elections of 1954 and 1958. He became more repressive and more inclined to self-enrichment over the years, and dissent grew. One of his opponents, Fidel Castro, organized a guerrilla movement in 1956 and began to attract international attention. When the United States canceled arms sales to Batista, his regime collapsed. On Jan. 1, 1959, Batista fled Cuba; he settled in Spain.

Batlle y Ordóñez, José   [baht'-yay ee or-dohn'-yays]

As president of Uruguay (1903–07, 1911–15), José Batlle y Ordóñez, b. May 21, 1856, d. Oct. 20, 1929, promoted the adoption of a new constitution that stabilized Uruguay's government. Batlle founded the newspaper *El Día* in 1886 and went on to work for reform as leader of the Colorado party. During his second administration, he enacted much social-welfare legislation, inaugurated labor reforms, and nationalized public utilities and financial institutions. His constitutional proposals called for a collective executive, but he accepted modification to divide executive power between the president and an administrative council. His constitution was in effect from 1919 to 1933.

Bibliography: Vanger, Milton T., *The Model Country* (1980).

Baton Rouge   [bat'-uhn roozh']

Baton Rouge is the capital of Louisiana and the seat of East Baton Rouge Parish. The city has a population of 219,531 (1990), and the metropolitan area, 528,264. A port at the head of deepwater navigation on the Mississippi River, it is situated in the southeastern part of the state. The climate is hot and humid, with an average mean temperature of 22° C (71° F) and ample rainfall. Industrial growth began when an oil refinery was established in 1909. Many industries were attracted to the area because of ocean and river transportation, the proximity of oil fields, and the abundance of natural gas. Dock facilities expanded after the construction of the Port Allen–Morgan City Cutoff Canal.

Originally settled by the French, the area was ceded to the British in 1763. During the American Revolution the Spanish wrested the city from the British, but they ceded it to France in 1800. Baton Rouge was sold to the United States as part of the Louisiana Purchase in 1803. Union forces captured the city in 1862 and held it until the end of the Civil War. The capital, which had been moved during the war, was restored permanently to Baton Rouge in 1882.

Bibliography: Meyers, Rose, *A History of Baton Rouge* (1976).

Batoni, Pompeo Girolamo   [bah-toh'-nee, pohm-pay'-oh jee-roh'-lah-moh]

Pompeo Girolamo Batoni, b. Jan. 25, 1708, d. Feb. 4, 1787, was one of the most famous Italian painters of his time. After settling in Rome in 1727, he attracted an international clientele with his drawings of ancient Roman and Renaissance monuments. Batoni's religious, historical, and mythological compositions were praised by his contemporaries, who applauded the sensuousness and grace with which he infused his classically derived style. His special talent, however, lay in portraiture. Wealthy tourists, most of whom were Englishmen on the Grand Tour, were Batoni's most enthusiastic patrons. Batoni liked to show his subjects amid ancient ruins, backgrounds that became highly fashionable after the contemporary rediscovery of POMPEII. This setting was meant to suggest the erudition of the sitter and the neoclassical ideals of the artist. (See NEOCLASSICISM, art.) In some portraits, however, the viewer is struck more by the elegant draftsmanship and ravishing color than by any intellectual content. Batoni's mythological paintings, for example, *The Education of Achilles* (1746; Uffizi Gallery, Florence), are also noted for their charm rather than archaeological qualities.   LESLIE JONES

Bibliography: Held, Julius S., and Posner, Donald, *Seventeenth and Eighteenth Century Art* (1972).

battalion

A battalion is a basic unit of military organization that first appeared at the end of the 16th century as the lowest tactical unit of infantry and cavalry. Today it comprises a headquarters and two or more companies, ranging from several hundred to 1,000 men. Battalions of different kinds—artillery, infantry, tank, and others—are combined in varying proportions to form a division. During World War II the U.S. infantry battalion consisted of a headquarters company, three rifle companies, and a heavy-weapons company. In the 1950s the U.S. infantry battalion was eliminated in favor of "battle groups," but in the 1960s the battalion was reinstated.

Battambang   [bat'-uhm-bang]

Battambang (1987 est. pop., 45,000) is the capital of the Battambang province in western Cambodia (Kampuchea) and one of the most important cities in the country. Located on the Sangker River, Battambang is the market center for a rice-growing area. The city was acquired by Siam (Thailand) in 1794, and it was returned (1907) to Cambodia, only to be taken again (1941) by Thailand. Since 1946, Battambang has been a part of Cambodia.   ASHOK K. DUTT

Battani, al-   [bat-tah'-nee, al]

One of the greatest medieval Muslim astronomers, al-Battani (also known as Albategnius), c.858–929, was instrumental in transmitting Greek planetary theory to medieval Europe. His tables of planetary motion, based on the standard GEOCENTRIC WORLD SYSTEM, depended in part on his own observations made at al-Raqqa on the Euphrates.   STEVEN J. DICK

battered women

A battered woman is the victim of physical (and psychological) violence inflicted by her husband or boyfriend. Wife beating, an ages-old form of domestic violence that may stem in part from regarding the wife as a piece of property, often occurs along with another form of domestic battering, CHILD ABUSE. Both have gained increasing attention in recent decades through women's studies. The extent of such abuse is not known, but spouse abuse happens in all classes of society. Experts estimate that 3 to 4 million women in the United States are beaten by spouses, and over 1,000 are slain annually.

Why do women remain with men who repeatedly assault them? Researchers have found that the woman may initially feel guilt for somehow "provoking punishment" and, as battering continues and strong ties nonetheless persist, may feel both vulnerable and dependent. Financial dependency is certainly a factor, especially when the woman has small children.

With greater recognition of wife-assault as a social problem have come new approaches to helping the battered woman. Support groups have proliferated, as have shelters for battered women and their young children. In the 1980s, studies convinced many law-enforcement officials that police action reduces family assaults. Numerous jurisdictions now require arrests in cases of probable wife beating, whether or not the victim is willing to sign a complaint.

Bibliography: Gillespie, C. K., *Justifiable Homicide: Battered Women, Self-Defense, and the Law* (1989); Hyman, K. J., *Protection from Abuse* (1986); Warrior, B., ed., *Battered Women's Directory*, 10th ed. (1989).

battering ram

One of the most ancient of siege machines, the battering ram was a device used to break down the walls of fortified sites. The earliest ram was a metal-tipped wooden beam carried by a group of men who swung it by hand against a wall. Later beams were suspended by ropes from a wheeled wooden framework. A ram depicted on a clay tablet found in the ruins of Nineveh (7th century BC) had wheels and an armor of hides to protect the men who worked it from enemy arrows. Similar rams were used in Europe throughout the Middle Ages. After the 15th century, however, when gunpowder was introduced into warfare, ARTILLERY rendered the ram obsolete and transformed FORTIFICATION and siege tactics.

battery

A conventional battery is a device, usually portable, for generating electricity through an electrochemical reaction. Such a reaction involves the transfer of electrons between two electrodes that are immersed in an ion-conducting medium, the electrolyte (see ELECTROCHEMISTRY). The negative electrode, or anode, loses electrons; the positive electrode, or cathode, gains them (see OXIDATION AND REDUCTION). When the electrodes are connected by an external circuit to a light bulb, the gears of a watch, or another such "load," the circuit is complete and an electric current is generated. The electrolyte is typically a liquid or paste, but solid-electrolyte batteries using a conductive polymer have been produced. A battery unit is often referred to as a "cell."

Cell voltage—the free energy or potential difference between the reactants and the products—is a characteristic of the particular electrochemical reaction. For example, the open-circuit voltage of a single alkaline cell is approximately 1.5 volts. A 9-volt alkaline battery must be composed of at least 6 cells in series (1.5 volts/cells × 6) in order to yield 9 volts.

The first electrochemical battery was documented by Alessandro VOLTA in a letter to the Royal Society of London in 1800. The earliest major market for batteries was in telegraph systems in the 1830s. By the 1870s the introduction of electric bell circuits created a more widespread consumer application. Flashlights came into use about 1900, by which time producers in the United States were turning out more than 2 million batteries annually. Domestic radio receivers in the 1920s and, more recently, the development of solid-state microelectronic technology, provided further impetus for the growth of battery technology. In the 1980s it was estimated that per-capita battery consumption among industrialized countries ranged from 8 to 15 batteries annually.

Batteries are typically grouped into two categories: primary and secondary. A primary battery, once expended, cannot be easily recharged. Common examples include zinc-carbon, alkaline, and lithium types. A secondary, or storage, battery, is capable of being recharged and can be reused many times. Common examples include lead-acid car batteries and nickel-cadmium batteries for small electronics.

Other types of self-contained power supplies may also be categorized as batteries. For example, radiation energy conversion devices—solar and nuclear cells—are non-electrochemical batteries. (Fuel cells, by distinction, are supplied with reactants from an outside source during their operation and are therefore not classed as batteries.)

Primary Batteries. Zinc has been the most common anode material because of its good electrochemical properties, availability, and low cost. Cell voltage is nominally 1.5 volts. Both the zinc-carbon and the alkaline batteries discussed here are manufactured as "dry" cells, because the electrolyte is immobilized as a paste or is contained in a porous separator.

The zinc-carbon, or Leclanche cell, was the only widely available system until about 1940. Through the early 1980s it was still a popular, low-cost battery used in applications such as flashlights, radios, and toys. The alkaline battery is a variant of the standard Leclanche that uses the same basic electrode chemistries but a different electrolyte. It is somewhat more expensive but provides improved low-temperature performance, power, and shelf life. Uses include powering tape recorders, calculators, radios, and television sets.

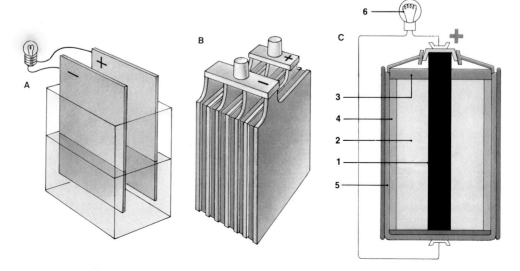

A laboratory cell (A) consists of an anode (−) and a cathode (+) immersed in an electrolyte. Current flowing through the connecting wire lights the bulb. The storage battery (B) has several positive and negative electrodes separated by porous insulators. The dry cell (C) consists of a carbon electrode (1), the cathode mix of manganese dioxide and carbon granules (2), an insulating cap (3), electrolyte paste (4), and a zinc anode (5). The light bulb (6) connects the anode and cathode terminals.

Lithium anode systems operating from 2.6 to 3.6 volts offer greater energy than zinc. They operate over a wide temperature range and possess high reliability and long shelf life, but they are expensive and not as readily available as zinc batteries. Applications include military radios, watches, cardiac pacemakers, and memory backup in computers when the main power is switched off.

A reserve battery is stored with one of its key components isolated and thus has an excellent shelf life because the active components cannot react with one another during storage. For example, the reserve thermal batteries used by the military are thermally activated: all components are in place during storage, but the electrolyte is not conductive and is incapable of supporting discharge until it is heated to become a liquid.

Secondary Batteries.   While the capability to recharge is attractive, secondary batteries generally suffer poorer energy density and charge retention than primaries. The lead-acid battery, a 2-volt cell, is in widespread use, mainly for automobile starting, ignition, and lighting systems. It has been improved virtually to the limits of the technology since its development in 1859. Other lead-acid applications include powering electric vehicles and providing standby power.

Nickel-cadmium, a 1.2-volt cell, has existed since 1909 for industrial applications. Improvements since 1950 have led to consumer applications in devices requiring high power, such as hand tools, toys, automatic cameras, and camcorders. Many of these devices can accept either nickel-cadmium or alkaline batteries, although the lower voltage of the nickel-cadmium sometimes compromises performance.

The lithium-ion cells that were developed in the mid-1990s offered improvements over the older technologies, particularly in the higher voltages they generate.

Radiation Batteries.   Solar cells convert sunlight, or photon radiation, into electricity via the photovoltaic effect that occurs in semiconducting materials. The sunlight interacts with the semiconductor to produce a negatively charged particle (electron) and a positively charged particle (hole) that move freely through the material, thereby producing electricity. Although the photovoltaic effect has been known since 1839, SOLAR CELLS using silicon as the semiconductor have been reported only since 1954. The first applications were in spacecraft. Today, solar cells are used in applications varying from large building power systems to hand-held calculators.

Nuclear energy is converted directly into electrical power in nuclear batteries. These batteries can provide very low currents for very long periods. The concept was described as early as 1913 and capitalizes on the energy released by the spontaneous disintegration of a radioactive isotope. The useful life of the battery is limited only by the half-life of the isotope. Beta radiation, from isotopes having half-lives from one to 25 years, is most commonly used. Several methods are available to convert the nuclear energy to electrical energy. In the Radioisotope Thermoelectric Generator, which has been utilized in NASA space missions, the principle of operation is to use the heat created by the radioactive material to produce a current flow across a dissimilar metal junction (see THERMOELECTRICITY).

WENDY R. CIESLAK

Bibliography: Hu, C., and White, R. M., *Solar Cells: From Basics to Advanced Systems* (1983); Linden, D., ed., *Handbook of Batteries and Fuel Cells* (1984); Tuck, Clive D., *Modern Battery Technology* (1991); Vincent, C. A., *Modern Batteries* (1984).

Battle, Kathleen

Soprano Kathleen Battle, b. Portsmouth, Ohio, Aug. 13, 1948, made her formal debut in 1972 at the Spoleto Festival in Italy. In 1977 she was signed by New York's Metropolitan Opera. She quickly became a reigning opera star—singing such lyric soprano roles as Pamina in Mozart's *The Magic Flute* and Sophie in Strauss's *Der Rosenkavalier*—as well as a much-admired recitalist. Battle's Met contract was canceled in 1994, however, because officials claimed that her demands for special treatment were "unprofessional" and jeopardized the quality of the performances in which she sang.

Battle-Axe culture

The Battle-Axe culture is one of a group of Late Neolithic and Chalcolithic cultures of the north European plain and Denmark. The culture, named for the distinctive shaft-hole axes of polished stone used by these people, appears to have invaded Europe from the steppes of southern Russia. It mixed with the native European cultures, among them the BEAKER CULTURE of central and northwestern Europe.

The cultural complex as a whole is sometimes called the Single-Grave Corded Ware culture, because these intruders into northern Europe brought with them the practice of single-inhumation burial under a barrow, or earthen mound. People of the Battle-Axe culture are also credited with introducing copper metallurgy and, according to some scholars, the wheel into northern Europe. It has also been suggested that they may have been among the first speakers of any Indo-European language in Europe.

LLOYD R. LAING

Bibliography: Champion, T., *Prehistoric Europe* (1984); Coles, J., and Harding, A., *The Bronze Age in Europe* (1979); Gregg, S. A., *Foragers and Farmers: Population Interaction and Agricultural Expansion in Prehistoric Europe* (1988); Wenke, R. J., *Patterns in Prehistory* (1980).

See also: EUROPEAN PREHISTORY.

Battle Creek

Battle Creek (1990 pop., 53,540) is a city in south central Michigan. Settled in 1831 and incorporated in 1850, it gained prominence when W. K. KELLOGG and C. W. Post set up ready-to-eat cereal factories. With the addition of a Ralston Purina plant, it became the world's breakfast-cereal center.

battleship

The battleship, an armored fighting ship of the largest and most powerful class, emerged in the 1870s as a separate and distinct class. It could defeat anything else afloat, and it dominated naval warfare for seven decades until World War II, during which the biggest battleships of all were built. Its name is derived from the line-of-battle ship in the time of sailing vessels, when ships went into combat in a line-ahead (column) formation.

The battleship was developed in the mid-19th century when armor was applied to the hulls of warships—a step taken in response to the introduction of shell-firing cannon. Designers experimented with various armament and protection methods. At first, mixed armament was used. French battleships, in particular, resembled floating castles from which turreted guns of all sizes jutted out in every direction. Early battleship design culminated after 1900 in the creation of the dreadnought battleship. On the dreadnought, major secondary armament was dispensed with to make room for larger guns. It carried a uniform main battery of the largest guns that could be mounted.

Battleship strength was considered a major component of national power, and naval nations expended enormous efforts to build the most powerful vessels possible. The result was continuous development. Larger and faster battleships were built, with improved armor protection and increased offensive power. The general trend was toward larger guns, fewer in

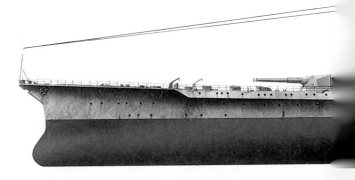

The battleship served as the key vessel in naval warfare for about a century ending during World War II. The French *Gloire*, often called the first battleship, was designed by S. H. L. Dupuy de Lôme at Toulon. It was the first fully seagoing ironclad ship. The *Gloire* (1859) was 78 m (255.7 ft) long, weighed 5,620 tons, and was armed with 36 164-mm (6.45 in) guns. It cruised at 13.5 knots (25 km/h; 15.5 mph), driven by a 900-horsepower engine and 3 fore- and aft-rigged masts. Technology for building all-metal ships was not available until the last decade of the 19th century. The *Oregon* (1893), among the earliest U.S. battleships, was used during the Spanish-American War (1898). The British *Dreadnought* heralded the era of modern, big-gun battleships. Built in record time (a year and a day) at Portsmouth Dockyard, it carried 10 305-mm (12-in) guns, 24 76-mm (3-in) guns, and 5 torpedo tubes. It was 160 m (526 ft) long, powered by a 25,000-horsepower engine, with armor plate 28 cm (11 in) thick at the waterline. The *Dreadnought* was manned by a crew of 800. It weighed 22,000 tons, and it cruised at 21.5 knots (39.5 km/h; 24.7 mph). The Japanese battleship *Yamato* was the largest ever built. It was 263 m (862 ft) long, weighed more than 72,000 tons, was powered by a 150,000-horsepower engine, and carried a crew of about 2,500 men. Armament included 9 457-mm (18-in) guns, 12 155-mm (6.1-in) guns, 12 25-mm (0.98 in) antiaircraft guns, 8 609-mm (24-in) torpedo tubes, 7 aircraft, and 2 launching catapults amidship. It cruised at 27 knots (50 km/h; 31 mph). The *Yamato* was sunk in April 1945, at the conclusion of the battleship era.

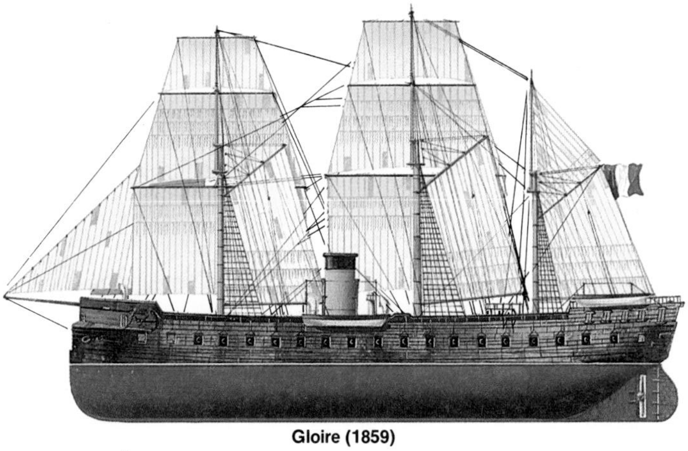

Gloire (1859)

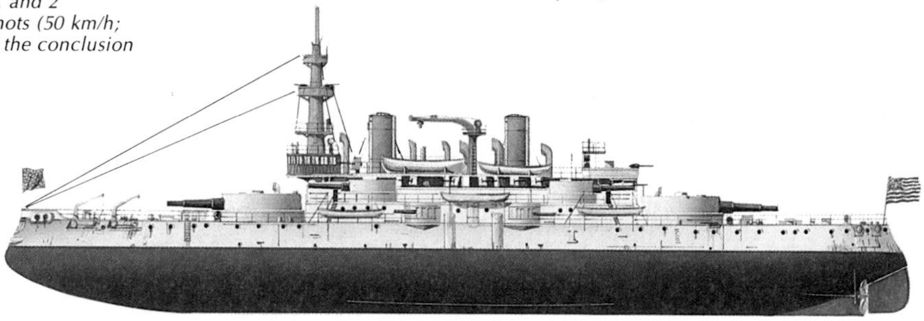

Oregon (1893)

Dreadnought (1906)

Yamato (1940)

number and mounted in larger turrets. Designers sought the greatest destructive power while conserving weight.

The British ship DREADNOUGHT, which put to sea in 1906, displaced some 22,000 tons at full load, had a speed of 21 knots, and mounted ten 12-in guns in five turrets. The British *Queen Elizabeth* class, launched in World War I, displaced some 33,000 tons at full load, could make about 25 knots, and mounted eight 15-in guns in four turrets. Development reached its peak in World War II with the American *Iowa* class and the Japanese *Yamatos*. The *Iowa*, fully loaded, displaced some 56,000 tons, mounted nine 16-in guns, and could make 33 knots. *Yamato*, although slower with a maximum speed of 27 knots, displaced nearly 73,000 tons, making it the largest battleship ever built.

All U.S. battleships were decommissioned in 1958 as the development of long-range missiles threatened even the most powerful ships. The *New Jersey* returned to service briefly during the Vietnam War as a specialized land-bombardment vessel. In 1981, Congress appropriated funds for the recommissioning of the *New Jersey* and three other battleships as part of a general naval buildup. During the Persian Gulf War (1991), the *Wisconsin* and the *Missouri* were used to shell hardened targets in Kuwait, firing cruise missiles as well as guns. The *New Jersey* was decommissioned in 1991, and both the *Missouri* and the *Wisconsin* were decommissioned in 1992 as a result of a reduction in military budgets. The *Iowa* had been decommissioned in 1990 following an explosion in one of her gun turrets.   JOHN F. GUILMARTIN

Bibliography: Breyer, S., *Battleships and Battlecruisers* (1973; repr. 1980); Friedman, N., *Battleship Design and Development, 1904–45* (1979); Jordan, J., *An Illustrated Guide to Battleships and Battlecruisers* (1985); Muir, Malcolm, *The Iowa Class Battleships* (1987); Patton, John H., *U.S.S.* Wisconsin, *Battleships, and Seamen* (1989); Preston, Anthony, *Battleships* (1989); Sturton, Ian, ed., *Conway's All the World's Battleships: 1906 to the Present* (1988).

See also: AIRCRAFT CARRIER; NAVAL VESSELS; SHIP.

Batu Khan   [bah′-too kahn]

Batu Khan, d. 1255, was a MONGOL leader who founded the Khanate of the GOLDEN HORDE. A grandson of Genghis Khan, he received from his father, Juchi (d. 1227), all the Mongol-claimed territories west of the Volga River and was given responsibility for the invasion of Europe. Batu moved west from Siberia in 1236, and by 1241 he had overrun most of Russia, Poland, and Hungary. This threat to Europe was terminated in 1242 when Batu withdrew to take part in the election of a successor to the Khan Ogadai, who had died in December 1241. He returned to southern Russia, however, and established the state of the Golden Horde in 1243.   RICHARD BUTWELL

Bibliography: Morgan, David, *The Mongols* (1987); Sokol, Edward, *The Mongol Invasion of Russia* (1987).

Batumi   [bah-too′-mee]

Batumi is the capital of the Adzhar autonomous republic, an enclave within the Caucasian republic of Georgia. It is a port on the southeast coast of the Black Sea and has a population of 136,000 (1989). The name *Batumi* is probably derived from the Greek word *bathos* meaning "deep" (for a deep harbor), used at the time the ancient Greeks had colonies along the Black Sea coast. The city has a warm, humid, subtropical climate, with an annual precipitation of about 2,500 mm (100 in). It is at the end of an oil pipeline from BAKU, has a refinery, and is known mainly as an oil export terminal. Other important exports include citrus fruits and manganese. It also is a center of tea plantations in the area. The city passed from Turkey to Russia in 1878, and it became the capital of a separate region for the Adzhar people in 1921.

Baty, Gaston   [bah-tee′]

Gaston Baty, 1885–1952, was a French theatrical producer whose innovative approach to lighting and decor brought him fame in Paris between the world wars. From 1930 he ran a theater in Montparnasse, where he staged such productions as

Brecht's *Threepenny Opera* (1930), an adaptation of Dostoyevsky's *Crime and Punishment* (1932), and his own *Dulcinée* (1938). His other writings include a history of theater and two works on puppetry.

Baudelaire, Charles   [bohd-lair′]

Charles Pierre Baudelaire, a 19th-century French poet, is caricatured in this cartoon drawn shortly after his trial in 1857. That year Baudelaire had published The Flowers of Evil, *a collection of sensual poems. He and his publisher were arrested and brought to trial on charges of offending public morality. The poet was found guilty and forced to delete six of the poems.*

The French poet and author of *The Flowers of Evil* (1857; various Eng. translations), Charles Baudelaire, b. Apr. 9, 1821, d. Aug. 31, 1867, significantly influenced modern poetry. Following the death of his father in 1827, his mother was remarried a year later to a young military officer, Jacques Aupick. In addition to the extraordinary influence exerted by his mother, Baudelaire's life and poetry were marked by the three women with whom he had liaisons: his first mistress, the mulatto Jeanne Duval, known as the Black Venus; the woman whom Baudelaire loved platonically, Madame Sabatier, the White Venus; and the well-known actress Marie Daubrun, or the Green-eyed Venus.

Baudelaire received the *baccalauréat* degree in 1839. In 1841 he was sent on a long ocean voyage, bound for Calcutta. The trip, however, was interrupted, and he returned to Paris. Shortly thereafter he settled into a fashionable apartment on Île Saint-Louis and led a leisurely, luxurious life made possible by his inheritance. At this time he began composing poems, some of which would find their way into *The Flowers of Evil*. It is said that Baudelaire contracted syphilis as a young man and that his involvement with drugs—opium and hashish—was initially for medical reasons. Later he was attracted by what he conceived to be the aesthetic potential of the "artificial paradises."

His first success as a writer was achieved in art criticism, in which he excelled. After publication of *The Flowers of Evil* and the trial that resulted in his condemnation for immorality, Baudelaire's reputation as a gifted and original poet was established, at least among literary persons. In 1864, Baudelaire left the French capital to take up residence in Belgium, where he remained, in spite of his antipathy for most of what he found around him and his increasingly poor health, until his condition worsened in early 1866. Suffering from paralysis and brain damage, he was returned to a clinic in Paris, where he died after slightly more than a year's illness.

Probably more than any other poet Baudelaire shaped modern poetry, which was derived in large measure from *The Flowers of Evil*. The Parnassians, symbolists, and surrealists all considered themselves direct heirs to Baudelaire's poetic legacy, which propounded the theory of *"correspondances"* and emphasized the importance and the role of imagery as a vehicle for poetic themes. In his poetry Baudelaire probed with candor humankind's depravity, propensity for evil, and suffering and solitude in a bleak and boring world. He tended to cast his ideas in exquisitely wrought, classical form. Insisting on the wretchedness of the human condition and the ugliness of urban life, he extracted a curious beauty from his material in a manner that revolutionized French poetry.

In addition to *The Flowers of Evil,* upon which his reputation justifiably rests, Baudelaire's work includes a group of fifty prose poems known as *Little Prose Poems* or *Spleen de Paris* (1869; Eng. trans., 1946); art criticism; a work on drugs, *Paradis Artificiels* (Artificial Paradises, 1860); a volume of intimate reflections, *Journaux Intimes;* and other writings. He also disseminated in France, through translations, the prose works of Edgar Allan Poe.   ROBERT T. CARGO

Bibliography: Baudelaire, Charles, *Art in Paris, 1845–1862—Salons and Other Exhibitions,* trans. and ed. by J. Mayne (1965), *Complete Verse,* trans. and ed. by F. Scarfe (1985), *Flowers of Evil: An Anthology of Translations,* ed. by M. and J. Mathews, rev. ed. (1962), *Intimate Journals,* trans. by Christopher Isherwood (1947; repr. 1985), *The Painter of Modern Life and Other Essays,* trans. and ed. by Jonathan Mayne (1964), and *Selected Letters,* trans. and ed. by Rosemary Lloyd (1986); Burton, Richard, *Baudelaire and the Second Republic* (1992); Hyslop, Lois, *Charles Baudelaire Revisited* (1992); Lloyd, Rosemary, *Baudelaire's Literary Criticism* (1981); Pichois, Claude, *Baudelaire,* trans. by G. Robb (1990); Sartre, J.-P., *Baudelaire,* trans. by M. Turnell (1950; repr. 1970); Starkie, Enid, *Baudelaire,* rev. ed. (1957; repr. 1988); Turnell, Martin, *Baudelaire: A Study of His Poetry* (1953; repr. 1972).

Baudouin I, King of the Belgians   [boh-dwan']

Baudouin I, b. Sept. 7, 1930, d. July 31, 1993, was king of the Belgians from 1951 until his death. Succeeding to the throne on the abdication of his father King LEOPOLD III, Baudouin married a Spanish noblewoman, Fabiola de Mora y Aragón, in 1960. A tactful mediator, he frequently helped to shore up Belgium's fragile unity in his role as sovereign. Baudouin was succeeded by his brother, Albert II.

Bauer, Harold

Harold Bauer, b. England, Apr. 28, 1873, d. Mar. 12, 1951, was a world-renowned pianist. Bauer was widely known in Europe and the United States as an interpreter of J. S. Bach, Johannes Brahms, Ludwig van Beethoven, and particulary Robert Schumann, whose music he edited. He was also an early advocate of the modern piano repertoire, introducing the music of Claude Debussy and Maurice Ravel to English audiences. He made his American debut in 1900 with the Boston Symphony Orchestra and later performed with other major orchestras. He became an American citizen in 1921.   ELLA MALIN

Baugh, Sammy   [baw]

The American football player Sammy Baugh, b. Temple, Tex., Mar. 17, 1914, was an outstanding all-around college and professional back for nearly 20 years and the holder of many records upon his retirement from the National Football League (NFL) in 1952. Baugh was an all-American tailback for Texas Christian University in the mid-1930s. In 1937 he joined the Washington Redskins, for whom he would play all 16 of his professional seasons. Switching from tailback to quarterback halfway through his professional career, "Slingin' Sammy" set many NFL passing records, including a completion percentage of 70.33 in 1945 that still stands. His season punting average (51.4 yd/47.0 m) also remains a record. In 1943 he led the league in passing, punting, and interceptions.

Bauhaus   [bow'-hows]

The Bauhaus (full name *staatliches Bauhaus,* "state building house") was the most famous school of architecture and design of the 20th century. Founded by Walter GROPIUS at Weimar, Germany, in 1919, the Bauhaus was originally a combined school of fine art and school of arts and crafts. In his opening manifesto, Gropius issued a call for the unification of all the creative arts under the leadership of architecture. He declared that a mastery of materials and techniques was essential

Bauhaus Staircase, painted in 1932 by Oskar Schlemmer, depicts students on the staircase at the Bauhaus in Dessau. (Museum of Modern Art, New York. Gift of Philip C. Johnson.)

for all creative design. Each course was to be taught by both an expert craftsman and a master artist.

The preliminary course, organized by Johannes Itten, introduced students to rudiments of design, freed from historic associations: size, shape, line, color, pattern, texture, rhythm, and density. This course has become the foundation for design education in many countries. It was followed in the curriculum by advanced work with form and materials, including workshops in stone, wood, metal, pottery, glass, painting, and textiles. Industrial design became a major focus.

Teachers appointed in the early years included Lyonel FEININGER, Gerhard Marcks, Johannes Itten, and Adolf Meyer (1919); Georg Muche (1920); Paul KLEE and Oskar SCHLEMMER (1921); Wassily KANDINSKY (1922); and László MOHOLY-NAGY (1923). From the beginning, the newness of the concepts developed at the Bauhaus and the liberal beliefs of many of the people associated with it aroused strong opposition.

In 1925 political pressures forced the removal of the school from Weimar to Dessau, where Gropius designed a new complex of buildings for it, including classrooms, shops, offices, and dwellings for faculty and students.

This group of buildings in Dessau came to symbolize the Bauhaus to the rest of the world. Although Gropius repeatedly insisted that it was never his intention to codify a Bauhaus style or dogma, the need for a new architectural image appro-

Gunta Stölzl's intricately patterned wall hanging was made about 1927–28 in the weaving workshop at Dessau. (Bauhaus-Archiv, Darmstadt; on permanent loan from the Carpet Association, Wuppertal.)

The faculty of the Dessau Bauhaus appears in this 1926 photograph. Members included (left to right) Josef Albers (glass), Hinnerk Scheper (wall painting), Georg Muche (weaving), László Moholy-Nagy (metal workshop), Herbert Bayer (printing workshop), Joost Schmidt (sculpture), Walter Gropius (director), Marcel Breuer (cabinetmaking), Wassily Kandinsky (general art education), Paul Klee (general art education), Lyonel Feininger (graphic arts), Gunta Stözl (weaving), and Oskar Schlemmer (theater and sculpture).

priate to a technological age caused the Bauhaus to be adopted as a model for what came to be known as the INTERNATIONAL STYLE or, more generally, modern architecture.

Gropius left the Bauhaus for private practice in 1928 and was succeeded as director by Hannes Meyer. Strong political pressures continued. Ludwig MIES VAN DER ROHE took over as director in 1930, moved the school to Berlin in 1932, and finally closed and disbanded it under pressure from the Nazis in 1933.

Among the former students who became important teachers at the Bauhaus were Josef ALBERS, Marcel BREUER, and Herbert Bayer. The Bauhaus became influential around the world as a result of the continued active teaching and designing by former faculty and students, including many Americans. In the United States, Gropius became dean of the School of Architecture at Harvard University, Mies van der Rohe became dean of architecture at Illinois Institute of Technology, and Moholy-Nagy founded the New Bauhaus in Chicago.

The work and principles of the Bauhaus have been further disseminated by many publications and exhibitions that have circulated internationally. A major Bauhaus Archive, founded at Darmstadt in 1961, was moved in the 1970s to Berlin. Another Bauhaus Archive is kept at Harvard University. The design philosophy of the Bauhaus continues pervasive to the present day.　　　　　　　　　　　　　　RON WIEDENHOEFT

Bibliography: Bayer, Herbert, et al., eds., *Bauhaus: 1919–1928* (1938; repr. 1972); Franciscono, Marcel, *Walter Gropius and the Creation of the Bauhaus in Weimar* (1971); Marzona, E., and Fricke, R., eds., *Bauhaus Photography* (1985); Naylor, Gillian, *The Bauhaus Reassessed* (1985); Wingler, Hans, *The Bauhaus* (1969).

Baum, L. Frank

Lyman Frank Baum, b. Chittenango, N.Y., May 15, 1856, d. May 6, 1919, was an American author who wrote 14 books about the magical land of Oz. The first and best known was *The Wonderful Wizard of Oz* (1900; film, 1939). Baum began his career as a newspaperman and was an editor of a trade magazine for store-window decorators. His first book was the highly successful *Father Goose: His Book* (1899). Altogether he wrote more than 60 popular books, mainly for children.

See also: WIZARD OF OZ, THE.

Baum, William W.

Cardinal William Wakefield Baum, b. Dallas, Tex., Nov. 21, 1926, is a specialist in interfaith relations. After studies in St. Louis, Mo., and Rome, Baum was ordained in 1951 and served as a priest in the diocese of Kansas City, Mo. He was bishop Springfield–Cape Girardeau, Mo., from 1970 to 1973 and archbishop of Washington, D.C., from 1973 to 1980. Since then he has been prefect of the Vatican's Congregation for Catholic Education. As executive director (1964–69) of the U.S. bishop's commission on ecumenical and interreligious affairs, Baum won widespread recognition for his activities in behalf of closer relations between faiths. He was made a cardinal in 1976.

Baumeister, Willi

Willi Baumeister, b. Jan. 22, 1889, d. Aug. 31, 1955, was a German abstract painter associated with the school of CONSTRUCTIVISM that included Oskar SCHLEMMER and Fernand LÉGER. A student of Adolf Hoelzel, Baumeister taught in Frankfurt am Main from 1928 to 1933, when he was dismissed by the Nazis in their drive against "degenerate" art. Influenced by Paul Klee and Joan Miró, Baumeister began about 1937 to include ideograms and organic shapes in his work.

Bibliography: Rickey, G., *Constructivism: Origins and Evolution* (1967).

Baumgarten, Alexander Gottlieb

Alexander Gottlieb Baumgarten, b. July 17, 1714, d. May 26, 1762, a German philosopher, was a leading figure in the 18th-century German ENLIGHTENMENT, or *Aufklärung*. Baumgarten is usually considered a follower of Gottfried Leibniz and Christian Wolff, although he differed with each of them on several important points. His most important contribution to philosophy was in the area of aesthetics, a term that he introduced in his *Reflections on Poetry* (1735; Eng. trans., 1954). In this and in his two-volume *Aesthetica* (1750–58), he expounded several original theories of aesthetics and a theory of knowledge. These and other works were widely read in German universities for their style and content. They heavily influenced KANT and his theory of the nature and function of sensibility in the growth of knowledge.　　　　　　　　　　　J. T. MOORE

Baur, Ferdinand Christian

Ferdinand Christian Baur, b. June 21, 1792, d. Dec. 2, 1860, was a German theologian who founded the Tübingen school of New Testament interpretation. He received his education at Tübingen University, where, from 1826 to his death, he was professor of ecclesiastical and doctrinal history.

Baur applied the philosophy of Hegel to New Testament interpretation. He was thus an early advocate of the historical or scientific study of the Bible. In 1845 he published a book on St. Paul, in which he applied the Hegelian principle to the history of early Christianity: Primitive Jewish (Petrine) Christianity, represented by the Gospel of St. Matthew, was the original force or thesis; Pauline Christianity was the antithesis or reaction against Peter-Matthew; and early Catholic Christianity, which brought these two forces together, was the synthesis. In the process, Baur rejected the traditional attribution of a number of Epistles to Paul. He held that Paul was the author only of Galatians, the two Epistles to the Corinthians, and most of Romans. Later Baur wrote extensively on historical theology.　　　　　　　　FREDERICK A. NORWOOD

Bibliography: Fitzer, Joseph, *Moehler and Baur in Controversy* (1974); Grant, Robert M., *The Bible in the Church* (1954).

bauxite [bawks'-yt]

Bauxite, the principal ore of aluminum, is a rock mixture consisting mostly of several hydrous aluminum oxide minerals,

Bauxite, the main source of aluminum, is a white to reddish, claylike mixture of aluminum oxide minerals. Distinctive rounded lumps of more darkly colored iron minerals, which are usually found embedded in bauxite, are clearly seen in this photograph of an Arkansas sample.

including boehmite, AlO(OH); diaspore, HAlO$_2$; gibbsite, Al(OH)$_3$; and impurities such as QUARTZ, CLAY MINERALS, and iron hydroxides.

The nature of the rock makes the individual minerals difficult to distinguish. Boehmite occurs in microscopic plates (ORTHORHOMBIC SYSTEM) as well as in pea-shaped aggregates called pisolites. Diaspore, identical in chemical composition with boehmite but structured differently, occurs in EMERY deposits and in bauxite and LATERITE. It forms thin whitish, grayish, or colorless platy or elongated crystals, as well as scales and cleavable, foliated masses. Its hardness is 6^1/$_2$–7, its luster is brilliant or vitreous pearly, and its specific gravity is 3.3–3.5. Gibbsite forms white or gray six-sided tabular crystals (MONOCLINIC SYSTEM) with one perfect cleavage. Often the chief mineral of bauxite or laterite deposits, it also occurs in low-temperature hydrothermal veins. Its hardness is 2^1/$_2$ to 3^1/$_2$, its luster is pearly or vitreous, and its specific gravity is 2.3 to 2.4.

Laterite, the principal type of bauxite deposit, contains pisolites ranging in size from that of buckshot up to 25 cm (10 in) in diameter. A mottled material that is white or gray when pure, it is colored pink, yellow, red, or brown by small amounts of iron. Lateritic bauxites result from WEATHERING of aluminum-rich rocks and clays in subtropical to TROPICAL CLIMATES. The world's leading producers of bauxite are Australia, Guinea, Jamaica, and Brazil.

See also: ORE DEPOSITS.

Bavaria

Bavaria (German: Bayern) is a state, or *land,* in south central Germany. Covering 70,553 km^2 (27,241 mi^2), and with

The southern German state of Bavaria jealously guards its regional traditions and keeps to its own ways in politics, culture, and life-style. It has its own dominant political party, the Christian Social Union (CSU), which is allied at the national level with the Christian Democratic Union (CDU). Bavaria is famous for its beer and its ornate 18th-century rococo churches.

11,221,000 inhabitants (1990), it is the largest German state in area and the second largest (after North Rhine-Westphalia) in population. Munich, its capital, is Germany's third largest city.

Bavaria encompasses four natural regions: the Franconian Jura, the Bohemian Forest, the Alpine Foreland (Bavarian Plateau), and the Bavarian Alps. Zugspitze, 2,963 m (9,721 ft), is the highest point. Elevations in the Alpine Foreland usually are between 400 and 1,000 m (1,300 and 3,281 ft); the lowest elevations, 200–400 m (656–1,312 ft), are in the Inn and Danube valleys. Temperatures vary according to elevation, with a January mean of about −2° C (28° F) and a July mean of 18° C (65° F). Annual precipitation averages 760 mm (30 in). The DANUBE RIVER, flowing generally eastward, is the main waterway; the INN and the MAIN are of lesser importance.

In addition to Munich, the main population centers are NUREMBERG (467,400; 1987), AUGSBURG (246,000; 1987), and WÜRZBURG (127,100; 1987). In 1987, Bavaria was 67% Roman Catholic and 24% Protestant. The southern part of the state is by tradition a solidly Catholic region.

The agricultural sector of the economy is characterized by small and fragmented farms. Major industries include automobile and textile manufacturing, and brewing; tourism is also an important source of income, especially in the Alpine region. Munich is a high-fashion center, and during the 1980s the Munich area experienced a significant development of high-tech industry.

The region was conquered by the Romans, overrun by Germanic peoples, and incorporated (788) into Charlemagne's empire. One of the five stem duchies of medieval Germany, it was ruled by the WELFS and later (1180–1918) the WITTELSBACHS. Duke MAXIMILIAN was a leading Catholic figure in the THIRTY YEARS' WAR (1618–48) and was awarded the rank of elector. During the War of the AUSTRIAN SUCCESSION (1740–48), Elector Charles Albert became Holy Roman Emperor CHARLES VII, but Bavaria suffered greatly in the fighting in this and other 18th-century wars.

Proclaimed a kingdom under French auspices in 1806, Bavaria kept this status by joining the anti-French coalition in the final defeat (1814–15) of NAPOLEON I. The 19th-century Bavarian kings, particularly LOUIS I and LOUIS II, were notable for their patronage of the arts, but their political influence declined both within and outside Bavaria. Allied with Austria until its defeat by Prussia in the SEVEN WEEKS' WAR (1866), Bavaria then switched its allegiance to Prussia, fought in the FRANCO-PRUSSIAN WAR (1870–71), and became part of the German Empire in 1871.

At the end of World War I the Bavarian monarchy was overthrown and a socialist republic established (1919) by Kurt EISNER. This regime was soon suppressed by the forces of the newly established Weimar Republic, in which Bavaria was incorporated as a state. The National Socialist party originated in Bavaria and made its first attempt to seize power there in the abortive MUNICH PUTSCH of 1923. After World War II, Bavaria was in the U.S. zone of occupation and subsequently (1949–90) part of West Germany.　　　　BRUCE L. LA ROSE

Bavarian Succession, War of the

The War of the Bavarian Succession (1778–79) was a conflict between Austria and Prussia in which little fighting took place. When the direct line of WITTELSBACHS ended in 1777 with Elector Maximilian Joseph, Holy Roman Emperor JOSEPH II signed a treaty with his successor, the Elector Palatine Charles Theodore, by which Lower Bavaria was ceded to Austria. Charles Theodore's heir presumptive, Charles, duke of Zweibrücken, immediately protested the cession, supported by FREDERICK II of Prussia, who declared war on Austria on July 3, 1778. The question was resolved by the Congress of Teschen (May 13, 1779). Austria received the Inn district, only a fraction of the territory it had claimed.

Bax, Sir Arnold

Sir Arnold Bax, b. Nov. 8, 1883, d. Oct. 3, 1953, was an eminent English composer. He studied composition at the Royal

Academy of Music with Frederick Corder. Bax was interested in ancient Irish folklore, and many of his works were inspired by Celtic legend. Knighted in 1937, he succeeded Sir Walford Davies as Master of the King's (now Queen's) Music in 1941. He was an excellent pianist with an extraordinary ability to reduce orchestral scores at the keyboard, but he was reluctant to play in public and did not conduct his own compositions.

Bax was a prolific composer. His style, rooted in neoromanticism, has elaborate chromatic harmonies combined with free counterpoint. His compositions include ballets, seven symphonies, symphonic poems, instrumental works, vocal and choral works, chamber music, settings of folk songs, and film music. His autobiography, *Farewell My Youth*, was published in 1943.   ROBERT M. CAMMAROTA

Bibliography: Foreman, L., ed., *Bax: A Composer and His Times* (1984); Hull, Robert H., *A Handbook on Arnold Bax's Symphonies* (1933); Parlett, Graham, comp., *Arnold Bax: A Catalog of His Music* (1972); Pirie, Peter J., *Twentieth Century British Music: A Collector's Guide* (1980); Young, Percy M., *A History of British Music* (1967).

Baxter, Richard

Richard Baxter, b. Nov. 12, 1615, d. Dec. 8, 1691, was an English Puritan clergyman. Ordained in 1638, he served (1641–60) in the parish of Kidderminster, where he effected major moral reforms. A supporter of Parliament during the Civil War, he was nonetheless a monarchist and, after the Restoration (1660) of Charles II, sought a compromise that would allow moderate Puritans to remain within the Church of England. The Clarendon Code, however, forced his withdrawal from the church as a NONCONFORMIST. In 1685 he was imprisoned for 18 months for libeling the Church of England. Baxter's many writings include *The Saints' Everlasting Rest* (1650), a devotional classic.   JAMES D. NELSON

Bibliography: Keeble, N. H., *Richard Baxter* (1982); Nuttall, Geoffrey F., *Richard Baxter* (1965).

bay: see GULF AND BAY.

Bay City

Bay City (1990 pop., 38,936), the seat of Bay County, is in east central Michigan on the Saginaw River. Incorporated in 1865, it was a consolidation of smaller villages. A principal market for the state's rich farmlands, Bay City has a deepwater harbor used by ships coming from the Great Lakes and from the Atlantic Ocean via the St. Lawrence Seaway. Although the city originally thrived on the vast local timber stands, its economy is now based on electrical equipment and automobile-parts manufacturing, beet-sugar refining, and shipbuilding.

bay leaf

Bay, or sweet laurel, a flavoring agent, is the leaf of the true laurel, *Laurus nobilis*, an evergreen tree native to the Mediterranean. Bay leaves were the laurels used for heroic Greek and Roman wreaths. Whole or ground bay leaf is used to season meats, potatoes, stews, sauces, fish, pickles, and vinegars.

West Indian bay, *Pimenta racemosa*, is a myrtle used to aromatize BAY RUM and other toiletries.   ARTHUR O. TUCKER

Bay of Pigs invasion

The Bay of Pigs invasion of April 1961 was an unsuccessful attempt by about 1,500 Cuban exiles, organized and financed by the U.S. Central Intelligence Agency (CIA), to topple the revolutionary regime of Fidel Castro in Cuba. In March 1960, President Dwight D. Eisenhower approved a CIA plan to train the exiles for an invasion of Cuba, and by autumn they were receiving military instruction in Guatemala. When John Fitzgerald Kennedy succeeded Eisenhower in January 1961, he allowed the preparations to proceed.

The exiles landed at the Bay of Pigs, on Cuba's southwestern coast, on Apr. 17, 1961. The operation was a disaster. News of the attack had leaked out in advance, and Kennedy had decided not to permit U.S. air support for the invaders. A general uprising, which the CIA had believed would be sparked by the landing, failed to materialize. Castro's forces blocked the exiles from moving inland, and by April 19 they had been crushed. The 1,200 survivors were captured. In December 1962, Castro released the prisoners in exchange for $53 million worth of U.S. drugs and food.

Bibliography: Higgins, Trumbull, *The Perfect Failure* (1987); Larson, David L., *The Cuban Crisis of 1962*, 2d ed. (1986); Wyden, Peter, *Bay of Pigs: The Untold Story* (1980).

Bay Psalm Book

The Bay Psalm Book, the name commonly applied to *The Whole Booke of Psalmes Faithfully Translated into English Metre* (1640), is considered the first book printed in Britain's American colonies. The translators were the Puritan clergymen Richard Mather, John Eliot, and Thomas Weld, their dual purpose being to have on hand a version of the Psalms more accurate than that in the King James Bible and to have verse renderings readily convertible to hymns. Of the 1,700 copies produced by printer Stephen DAY in Cambridge, Mass., fewer than a dozen survive.

Bibliography: Eames, Wilberforce, *The Bay Psalm Book* (1978); Haraszti, Zoltan, *Enigma of the Bay Psalm Book* (1956).

bay rum

Bay rum, a popular face lotion for men, is made from a combination of bay oil, citrus and spice oils, alcohol, and water. It was first made in the West Indies, where it was prepared by boiling the leaves of the West Indian bay, *Pimenta racemosa*, in white rum and collecting the distillate.

Bayard   (family)

The Bayards, an American family descended from French Huguenot refugees, have been prominent in U.S. public affairs from the 18th to the 20th century. **John Bubenheim Bayard**, b. Aug. 11, 1738, d. Jan. 7, 1807, a substantial Philadelphia merchant, presided as speaker of the Pennsylvania Assembly in 1777 and 1778. His nephew **James Asheton Bayard**, b. July 28, 1767, d. Aug. 6, 1815, a noted constitutional lawyer and leading Federalist, represented Delaware in the House of Representatives (1797–1803) and Senate (1805–13). He helped negotiate the Treaty of Ghent (1814; see GHENT, TREATY OF), which ended the War of 1812.

His sons, **James Asheton Bayard**, b. Nov. 15, 1799, d. June 13, 1880, and **Richard Henry Bayard**, b. Sept. 26, 1796, d. Mar. 4, 1868, also served as senators from Delaware, the former as a Democrat-turned-Republican (1851–64, 1867–69), the latter as a Whig (1836–39, 1841–45). **Thomas Francis Bayard**, b. Oct. 29, 1828, d. Sept. 28, 1898, son of the younger James Bayard, was a Democratic senator from Delaware (1869–85), secretary of state (1885–89) during President Grover Cleveland's first term, and U.S. ambassador to Britain (1893–97) in Cleveland's second term. His son, **Thomas Francis Bayard**, b. June 4, 1868, d. July 12, 1942, was another Democratic senator from Delaware (1922–29).

Bibliography: Borden, Morton, *The Federalism of James A. Bayard* (1954); Donnan, Elizabeth, ed., *The Papers of James A. Bayard, 1796–1815* (1915; repr. 1971); Tansill, Charles C., *Foreign Policy of Thomas F. Bayard, 1885–1897* (1940; repr. 1969).

Bayard, Hippolyte   [bah-yahr', ee-poh-leet']

Hippolyte Bayard, b. Jan. 20, 1807, d. 1887, a French clerk, independently invented a method of photography between 1837 and 1839. He exhibited his photographs a month before the details of L. J. M. Daguerre's more celebrated invention were revealed in August 1839. Government sponsorship of Daguerre, however, obscured the work of Bayard. His was at first a negative process, like the CALOTYPE, but it also could produce a direct positive on paper. With Gustave Le Gray, Charles Nègre, and others, Bayard photographed historic monuments during the 1850s for the government. His intimate views of his surroundings won him his place among French primitive photographers.   PETER GALASSI

bayberry

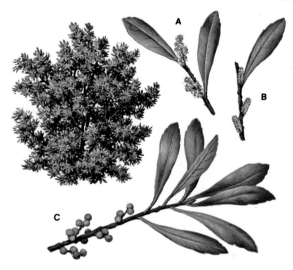

The common bayberry shrub, M. pensylvanica, *has elongated, toothed leaves and tiny male flowers (A) as well as female catkins (B). The shrub has a fragrant odor because of a resinous wax that coats the gray berries (C). This wax is used to make bayberry candles.*

The common bayberry, *Myrica pensylvanica,* an aromatic shrub of the bayberry family, Myricaceae, is found from Nova Scotia to New Jersey. Deciduous or semievergreen, it grows to a height of 3 m (9 ft). The aromatic, dull-green leaves are up to 10 cm (4 in) long, and small, grayishwhite fruits appear in winter. Bayberries are grown for their foliage and fruits. Aromatic wax is extracted from their fruits for making candles, as it is from the taller, less hardy wax myrtle, *M. cerifera,* of the southern United States. Both species are also known as candleberry. California bayberry, *M. californica,* an evergreen shrub or tree with reddish purple fruit, grows up to 11 m (35 ft) in height.

Bayeux Tapestry   [bah-yu']

The Bayeux Tapestry, actually an embroidery, depicts in 72 scenes the Norman conquest of England by WILLIAM I (William the Conqueror) in 1066. The embroidery, which may date from the 11th century, is an important historical and cultural document. It is executed in colored worsteds on linen and measures 70 m by 51 cm (230 ft by 20 in).

The central part of the work contains scenes beginning with the English king HAROLD II's visit to Bosham and ending with

This scene from the Bayeux Tapestry shows an incident in the Battle of Hastings: William the Conqueror (center), to quell a rumor that he has been killed, raises his helmet to let his men know that he is still with them. (Musée de la Reine Mathilde, Bayeux.)

the English fleeing in the Battle of HASTINGS. The decorative borders above and below the main narrative feature animals and scenes from fable. The embroidery has been partially restored and may contain portions not entirely faithful to the original. Although traditionally attributed to Matilda, wife of William the Conqueror, the work is now thought to be somewhat later in origin. It may have been commissioned by Odo, William's half brother and bishop of Bayeux. It is housed in the Musée de la Reine Mathilde, Bayeux, France.

Bibliography: Bernstein, D. J., *The Mystery of the Bayeux Tapestry* (1987); Fowke, Frank, *The Bayeux Tapestry* (1913; repr. 1972).

Bayezid I, Sultan of the Ottoman Empire
[by-yuh-zeed']

Bayezid I, b. 1354, Ottoman sultan (1389–1402), established the first centralized Ottoman Turkish administration. His initial campaigns included a blockade (1391–98) of Constantinople (held by Byzantine emperor MANUEL II), an invasion of Hungary (1395), and destruction of a crusade against him by Holy Roman Emperor SIGISMUND at Nicopol in 1396. Later, however, he clashed with TIMUR in Anatolia. Defeated near Ankara in July 1402, Bayezid died a captive in March 1403.

Bayezid II, Sultan of the Ottoman Empire

The Ottoman sultan Bayezid II, b. 1448, d. 1512, was the son and successor of MEHMED II. Reigning from 1481, he consolidated the conquests of his father and laid the bases for new expansion into the Arab world and central Europe. Bayezid was preoccupied (1481–95) by the revolt of his brother Jem Sultan in alliance with the MAMELUKES of Egypt and the papacy. He hoped to maintain peace so that he could concentrate on establishing regular administrative and tax systems, but he was forced into a war (1499–1502) with Venice, which feared Ottoman expansion toward its sea lanes in the Adriatic and Aegean. Venice eventually made peace on terms advantageous to the Turks. Bayezid failed to suppress revolts by nomadic Turkoman tribes in eastern Anatolia despite their connection with the heterodox Safavids, who were then conquering Iran. He left this problem to his son SELIM I, who deposed him shortly before his death.   STANFORD J. SHAW

Bayle, Pierre   [bayl]

Pierre Bayle, b. Nov. 18, 1647, d. Dec. 18, 1705, was a French rationalistic philosopher and skeptical writer important in the early development of the ENLIGHTENMENT. Born of Calvinist parents, he was trained by the Jesuits and converted to Roman Catholicism in 1669. The next year he returned to Protestantism. From 1675 to 1681 he taught philosophy at the Protestant academy of Sedan; after 1681 he taught at the University of Rotterdam. He was forced to retire in 1693 when he was accused of being an atheist. Between 1692 and 1702 he wrote the *Dictionnaire historique et critique* (Historical and Critical Dictionary), a compendium of critically annotated biographies that provided a model for the later French Encyclopedists. It was also a source for much of VOLTAIRE's thinking. Although he was a man of immense erudition, Bayle lacked conviction. He held that the only certainty is that everything is uncertain. Called by Voltaire "the greatest master of the art of reasoning," Bayle will be remembered for his dialectical skill, the accuracy of his work, and his encyclopedic knowledge.   JOHN P. DOYLE

Bibliography: Labrousse, E., *Bayle* (1983); Mason, H. T., *Pierre Bayle and Voltaire* (1963).

Bayliss, Sir William   [bay'-lis]

Sir William Maddock Bayliss, b. May 2, 1860, d. Aug. 27, 1924, was an English physiologist who, with physiologist Ernest STARLING, discovered (1902) secretin, an intestinal hormone that stimulates the release of pancreatic juice for digestion. They also discovered the peristaltic wave while studying how the intestinal tract is coordinated with the nervous system (see PERISTALSIS). Bayliss began the use of saline injections to treat surgical shock during World War I, thus saving many lives. From 1888 until his death he was associated with the department of physiology at University College in London. He was awarded the Copley Medal in 1919.

Bibliography: Bynum, W. F., and Porter, R., eds., *Encyclopedia of the History of Medicine* (1994).

Baylor, Elgin

The American basketball star and Hall of Fame member Elgin Baylor, b. Washington, D.C., Sept. 16, 1934, was one of the sport's greatest players. Baylor graduated an All-American from Seattle University in 1958 and was Rookie of the Year with the Minneapolis (later Los Angeles) Lakers of the National Basketball Association (NBA), for whom he played his entire career (1958–72). While in the NBA the 6-ft 5-in (1-m 96-cm) forward scored 23,149 points for a per-game average of 27.4 (4th best) and averaged 13.5 rebounds per game. He was a first-team all-NBA selection ten times (unsurpassed) before a recurring knee injury prematurely ended his career. Baylor once scored 71 points in a game—only two other NBA players ever scored more; he also once scored 61 points in a play-off game.

Baylor University

Established in 1845 and affiliated with the Texas Baptist General Convention, Baylor University (enrollment: 11,810; library: 1,392,721 volumes) is a private coeducational liberal arts institution in Waco, Tex. It has programs in the college of arts and sciences and schools of law, music, nursing, business, and education.

bayonet

The bayonet is a short sword or dagger attached to the muzzle of a rifle. First used by European armies in the 17th century, it proved useful as an additional infantry weapon for close combat, and it eliminated the need for a separate corps of pikemen. In its original form the bayonet was inserted into the muzzle itself, thus preventing the weapon from being fired. Later bayonets were clipped onto the side of the muzzle so that they could easily be removed and used as daggers in hand-to-hand fighting.

Bayonne (France) [bah-yuhn']

Bayonne is a city in Gascony in southwestern France. It is located in Pyrénées-Atlantique department on the Adour and Nive rivers. Situated near the Bay of Biscay, it is an active port and has a population of 40,051 (1990). In the 1st century BC, Bayonne, called Lapurdum by the Romans, was already a town of some importance. Until the 10th century it was successively invaded by Visigoths, Basques, Arabs, and Normans. It passed to the English in 1154, when the husband of Eleanor of Aquitaine succeeded to the English crown as Henry II. The French reclaimed Bayonne in 1451. Famous in the 16th and 17th centuries for the manufacture of cutlery and armaments, Bayonne is the site where Napoleon I forced Charles IV and Ferdinand VII of Spain to abdicate in 1808. The painter Léon Bonnat left his art collection to Bayonne, his native city, in 1922.

Bayonne (New Jersey) [bay-ohn']

Bayonne is a city in Hudson County in northeastern New Jersey with a population of 61,444 (1990). It lies on a peninsula between Upper New York Bay and Newark Bay and is connected to Staten Island by a bridge over the Kill van Kull. Lying within the jurisdiction of the Port Authority of New York and New Jersey, Bayonne has extensive docks and shipyards and is the home of a U.S. Navy supply depot. It is the eastern terminus for many oil pipeline systems, including the Big Inch, and is also an important manufacturing center for paint, radiators, electric motors, and chemicals. Settled in 1646 by Dutch traders and originally known as Konstapel's Hoeck (later Constable Hook), Bayonne consolidated with three other

villages in 1869. It served as an embarkation point and shipping center during both world wars. The city government consists of a mayor and a council.

bayou: see SWAMP, MARSH, AND BOG.

Bayreuth [by'-royt]

Bayreuth is a city in Bavaria, Germany. The capital of Upper Franconia, it is on the Roter Main River, northeast of Nuremberg, and has a population of 70,933 (1989 est.). It produces textiles, metals, and machinery, and the summer music festival is also important to Bayreuth's economy. First noted in the mid-12th century, Bayreuth was ruled by various branches of the Hohenzollerns from 1248. In 1603 the margraves of Brandenburg-Kulmbach made the city their residence. Bayreuth was ceded to Prussia in 1791 and to Bavaria in 1810. Richard WAGNER settled there in 1872, when construction was started on the Festspielhaus (Festival Theater), built to his specifications. His operas are performed in the theater every summer, drawing crowds from all over the world. Both Wagner and Franz Liszt are buried in Bayreuth.

Bayreuth Wagner Festival

On a hill above Bayreuth stands the Festspielhaus, the festival theater that has brought this German town international fame. Richard WAGNER, the celebrated German composer, chose this Franconian community as the site for an auditorium removed from urban bustle and capable of housing his *Ring of the Nibelung*, for he felt that no existing structure in Europe had the necessary technical resources.

As early as 1864 the composer had discussed with his patron, King LOUIS II (Ludwig) of Bavaria, the possibility of building an innovative theater in Munich, with Gottfried SEMPER as the architect. The project failed when Wagner, meddling in Bavarian political affairs, was obliged to leave the country temporarily. While at work on the *Ring* in Switzerland, he made an arrangement with the king through which, in exchange for Louis's financial help, the four music-dramas of the *Ring* were to have their world premieres at Munich's Bavarian National Theater. *Das Rheingold* (1868) and *Die Walküre* (1869) were in fact first mounted there. Then Wagner persuaded the king to release him from this obligation, and *Siegfried* and *Götterdämmerung* were first performed at Bayreuth.

The cornerstone was laid in 1872, and Semper's sketches for the proposed Munich auditorium (never built) were adapted to Bayreuth by Carl Brandt and Otto Brückwald. Featured were two devices revolutionary for the time—a fan-shaped stadium interior and a covered orchestra pit. Three cycles of the complete *Ring* opened the Festspielhaus in August 1876 to an invited audience of musical and social notables. Wagner's *Parsifal* was first performed there in 1882.

Festivals at Bayreuth, continuing initially under the direction of Wagner's widow, Cosima, were interrupted by World War I and at greater length by World War II. The theater was reopened in 1951 under the artistic guidance of the composer's eldest grandson, Wieland. Since his death in 1966, it has been administered by Wieland's brother, Wolfgang.

In the post–World War II years, Bayreuth came to be identified with a spare, nontraditional type of staging, usually dimly lighted. Sometimes called Bayreuth staging, it has made its mark throughout the operatic world, and not only in works by Wagner. The importance of this movement has ebbed in recent times in favor of a modified return to realism in scenic production. ROBERT LAWRENCE

Bibliography: Mayer, Hans, *Richard Wagner at Bayreuth* (1976); Skelton, Geoffrey, *Wagner at Bayreuth*, rev. ed. (1976; repr. 1982).

Bazelon, David L. [baz'-uh-lahn]

As a judge (1949–86) and chief judge (1962–78) of the U.S. Court of Appeals for the District of Columbia, David Lionel Bazelon, b. Superior, Wis., Sept. 3, 1909, d. Feb. 19, 1993, wrote landmark decisions expanding the rights of individuals and of criminal defendants. In *Durham* v. *United States* (1954)

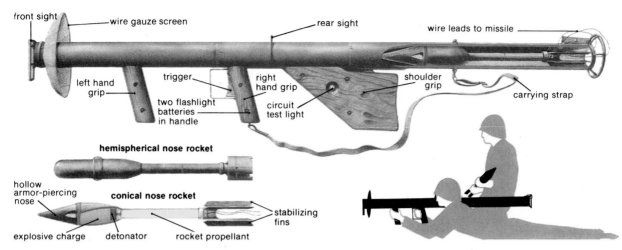

A bazooka was a portable, electrically fired rocket launcher operated by two soldiers. One soldier loaded the missile into the launcher; the other held, aimed, and fired it. The original World War II M1A1 launcher consisted of a long open tube with front and rear sights, two hand grips, a shoulder grip, two flashlight batteries, wire leads for plugging the missile into the electric firing circuit, a firing trigger, and a front-end screen to protect the firer from the rocket blast. The 2.36-caliber missile consisted of an armor-piercing hollow conical, or hemispherical, metal nose; an explosive charge; a detonator; a tube of solid rocket propellant; and stabilizer fins.

he rejected the longstanding M'Naghton rule limiting pleas of insanity to the single test of an inability to tell right from wrong (see INSANITY, LEGAL) and applied his own, so-called Durham rule whereby a defendant could plead insanity if his or her act could be shown to have been "the product of mental disease or mental defect." A judicial activist of liberal bent, he frequently questioned the status quo. *Questioning Authority* (1988) is a collection of his judicial writings.

Bazille, Frédéric   [bah-zee']

Frédéric Bazille, b. Dec. 6, 1841, d. Nov. 28, 1870, a French impressionist painter, was a contemporary and close friend of Claude Monet and Pierre Auguste Renoir. In the mid-1860s he painted outdoors alongside Monet and approximated his style. Bazille, however, remained closer to the academic tradition in making preparatory sketches and studies for his larger works, which were, furthermore, often retouched in the studio. His early death in combat in the Franco-Prussian War prevented him from developing the full impressionist style of the 1870s.   MARIAN BURLEIGH-MOTLEY

Bibliography: Denvir, B., *Impressionism* (1991); Rewald, J., *The History of Impressionism*, 4th rev. ed. (1990).

Bazin, André

André Bazin, b. Apr. 18, 1918, d. Nov. 11, 1958, was a French film critic and editor whose studies of deep-focus techniques, film aesthetics, Jean Renoir, and the American film influenced the directors and critics of the French New Wave. In 1947 he helped found and edit the film journal *La Revue du Cinéma*, later called *Cahiers du Cinéma*.

Baziotes, William   [baz-ee-oh'-teez]

William Baziotes, b. Pittsburgh, Pa., June 11, 1912, d. June 5, 1963, a painter, helped establish the school of ABSTRACT EXPRESSIONISM in New York in the 1940s. Like his contemporaries in the group, Baziotes was influenced in the early 1940s by both cubism and surrealism and evolved a style in which the subject was "found" during the act of painting, rather than being predetermined. His subjects are highly personal, sometimes conjuring up an underwater world inhabited by strange organisms. Often the subject Baziotes found is identified in the title of the work, for example, *Dwarf* (1947; Museum of Modern Art, New York).   MARIAN BURLEIGH-MOTLEY

Bibliography: Sandler, Irving, *The Triumph of American Painting: A History of Abstract Expressionism* (1970); Tuchman, Maurice, *The New York School*, rev. ed. (1970) and *The Spiritual in Art* (1986).

bazooka

The bazooka, a lightweight rocket launcher, was the first artillery weapon to use ROCKETS as offensive missiles. An American invention, it was first used in battle against German tanks in North Africa in 1943. An improved version was used in the Korean War. The name *bazooka* derived from the weapon's resemblance to a musical prop of the American comedian Bob Burns in the early 1940s. The launcher could be held, loaded, and fired by only two men, and it proved effective against heavily armored vehicles and emplacements. Modern light antitank weapons (LAW) can be carried by one person, have shorter tubes, and are no longer called bazookas.

BBC: see BRITISH BROADCASTING CORPORATION.

Beach, Amy Marcy

Amy Marcy Beach (known as Mrs. H. H. A. Beach), b. Amy Marcy Cheney in Henniker, N.H., Sept. 5, 1867, d. Dec. 27, 1944, was a pianist and the first American woman to gain a reputation as a composer of large-scale orchestral works. Musically precocious and mainly self-taught, she made her debut as a pianist in Boston in 1883. Her first large work, a mass, was premiered there in 1892. Beach appeared widely in the United States and Europe as a concert performer. She was the cofounder (1926) and first president of the Association of American Women Composers. She wrote mainly in the tradition of late romantics such as Brahms, although her chamber compositions sometimes exhibit an acerbic quality. Her many works include a one-act opera, *Cabildo* (1932), a symphony, a piano concerto, cantatas and anthems, solo piano works, and over 150 songs. Many of these have been recorded.

Bibliography: Ammer, Christine, *Unsung: A History of Women in American Music* (1980); Boetschius, Percy, *Mrs. H. H. A. Beach* (1906).

beach and coast

The coast is a zone of varying width, extending landward from the shoreline to the limit of marine influence—the head of an ESTUARY (landward limit of the influence of TIDES), the crest of a range of hills or mountains, or the solid ground that lies behind coastal SAND DUNES, LAGOONS, and marshes. The coasts attract human habitation. At present about two-thirds of the world's population lives within a narrow coastal belt that extends landward from the ocean's edge. In the United States, for example, the states that front on the oceans or Great Lakes contain a large proportion of the total population and many of the largest cities.

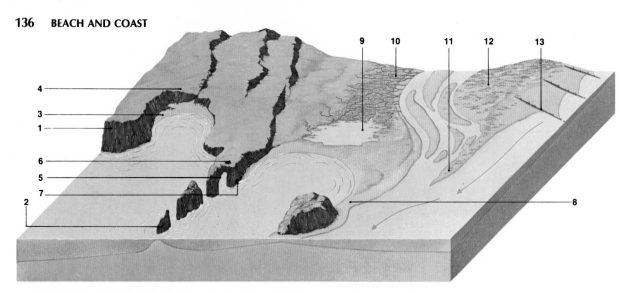

A number of characteristic coastline features are shaped by water and wind erosion and by rock and sediment deposition. Among these are promontories, or headlands (1); isolated rock pillars resulting from headland erosion, or sea stacks (2); bayhead beaches between headlands (3); cliffs (4); natural arches eroded in headlands (5); water-eroded tunnels, or blowholes, with both cliff-top and sea-level entrances (6); caves (7); island and mainland sand connections, or tombolos (8); lagoons (9); salt marshes (10); sand barriers deposited across a river mouth, or sand spits (11); sand dunes (12); and accumulations of sand behind low walls, or groins (13), built to prevent beach sand loss.

Beaches. Beaches are the most prevalent natural feature of the coastal zone. They are accumulations of loose sand, gravel, or boulders that are shaped by WATER WAVES and currents acting on the shore.

Along many lowland coasts, beaches occur as barrier islands that parallel the coast and are separated from it by a lagoon or bay. Barrier islands extend almost the entire length of the East and Gulf coasts of the United States. Along other stretches of coast, beaches are backed by eroding cliffs, or they may be totally absent, with high rocky cliffs facing the waves directly. The erosion of rocky cliffs forms SEA CAVES, SEA STACKS, and natural arches.

Beaches are a natural habitat for plants and animals, providing breeding and nesting grounds for seals, turtles, birds, and some fish. If the beaches are not overfished, clams and crabs are plentiful, particularly the beach clam, *Donax gouldii.*

In some areas beach sand has been mined for valuable minerals, including diamonds in South Africa, gold in Alaska, and platinum, zircon, and magnetite elsewhere.

Beach Sand. Most familiar are the beaches consisting of light-colored QUARTZ and FELDSPAR sand grains, derived originally from the WEATHERING and erosion of rocks such as GRANITE. Some beach sand comes directly from the erosion of sea cliffs, but most of it is created by the action of rivers flowing to the sea. Another source is the offshore sea bottom. Usually, however, sand moves from the beach to deeper waters, thus causing a loss rather than a gain. In some areas, an offshore loss occurs when beach sand is trapped in shallow SUBMARINE CANYONS; elsewhere, beach sand is lost when it is blown inland to form sand dunes.

Most beach sand contains fragments of clam shells, smoothed and rounded until they are the size of sand grains. In the tropics, especially near CORAL REEFS, beaches may consist almost entirely of shell and coral fragments. Beaches on volcanic islands such as Tahiti are made up of black sand, the result of disintegrating volcanic rock. They may also consist of SEDIMENT coarser than sand; shingle beaches composed of small flat stones are common on the coast of England. Some beaches contain cobbles and boulders, particularly where large, breaking waves strike the beach.

Waves and Currents. Waves and coastal currents help create and shape beaches, as well as moving marine sediment in the coastal zone. Waves breaking at an angle to the shoreline generate a longshore current that flows parallel to the coastline. This current is fastest between the waves and the shoreline. Together with the waves that stir beach sand into motion, the current causes sand to move along the coastline as LONGSHORE DRIFT and builds SPITS across the mouths of rivers and bays.

When waves break with their crests parallel to the shoreline they commonly produce a nearshore circulatory system consisting mainly of rip currents (sometimes called riptides)—powerful currents that flow seaward to the points at which the waves break. A hazard to bathers, they can sweep even the strongest swimmer out to sea. Because they are narrow, however, they can be escaped by swimming parallel to the shoreline before attempting to return to the beach.

By eroding sand from the beach, evenly spaced rip currents form embayments separated by cusps, which give the beach a scalloped appearance. When a storm occurs, beach erosion and property damage may be greatest in these embayments.

Beach sand is kept constantly moving by waves and currents. Some of it is swept upward toward the land by the uprush of the waves (swash) and deposited in the backshore zone, or BERM. The slope of the beach face, where the swash occurs, depends on the particle size of beach sand. The coarser the sand, the steeper the beach face. Very fine sand beaches slope at about 1°, coarse sand beaches at 9°, and cobble beaches up to 25°. Some beach material is carried offshore and deposited on BARS. Between the bar and the beach face may be a longshore trough where longshore currents flow parallel to the coast.

During storms, large waves erode sand from the beach face and berm, transferring it to offshore bars. Severe storms may result in total destruction of the berm, allowing waves to wash directly against sand dunes, seacliffs, or other parts of the shore. Under such conditions, homes, hotels, and highways built too close to the beach may be undermined by wave erosion and lost. When smaller waves return after a storm, sand moves ashore again, and the berm begins to grow, until the next storm, when once again it acts as a buffer.

Large-Scale Changes. Besides the growth and destruction of beaches and other shore features, coastlines are also subject to changes on a larger scale. These may come about through changes in water level—which, if worldwide, are called eustatic changes—or through the rising or sinking of the land itself. Uplifted coasts are known as coasts of emergence; they often take the form of long, straight shorelines with former seaside cliffs or beaches now some distance from the shore. Sinking coasts are known as coasts of submergence, or drowned coasts. When the sea enters and floods former river valleys along such coasts, the shoreline takes the form of branching bays; Chesapeake Bay is an example.

PAUL D. KOMAR

Bibliography: Bird, E. C., ed., *Geomorphology of Changing Coastlines* (1986); Bowden, K. F., *The Physical Oceanography of Coastal Waters* (1984); Komar, P. D., ed., *Handbook of Coastal Processes and Erosion* (1983); Nummedal, Dag, et al., eds., *Sea-Level Fluctuations and Coastal Evolution* (1987); Schwartz, M. L., ed., *The Encyclopedia of Beaches and Coastal Environments* (1982); Trenhaile, A. S., *The Geomorphology of Rock Coasts* (1987).

See also: COASTAL PROTECTION; LITTORAL ZONE; OCEAN AND SEA.

Beach Boys

The Beach Boys, a vocal-instrumental group from Los Angeles, gained national fame in the 1960s, popularizing a type of rock known as ''surf music.'' Filled with trademark vocal harmonies, such songs as ''Surfin' U.S.A.'' (1963), ''Fun, Fun, Fun'' (1964), and ''California Girls'' (1965) became instant hits. In the 1980s their annual July 4 concerts at the Washington Monument drew upward of 500,000 people. The members, all vocalists, are: Brian Wilson, b. June 20, 1942, who plays piano and wrote, arranged, and produced most of the music; Carl Wilson, b. Dec. 21, 1946, who plays guitar; Mike Love, b. Mar. 15, 1941; Al Jardine, b. Sept. 3, 1942, who plays guitar; and Bruce Johnston, b. June 24, 1944, who plays keyboards. Drummer Dennis Wilson, b. Dec. 4, 1944, died in a drowning accident on Dec. 28, 1983.

beacon

A beacon is a signaling device used to guide ships or aircraft or to warn them of navigational hazards. It is visible from a distance by day and is sometimes lighted at night. Early beacons were bonfires lighted on hills and beaches.

Navigational beacons are often situated in towers or on hills, islands, rocks, reefs, or shoals for the purpose of marking channels or warning against dangerous spots. Beacons with rotating lights mark airports at night or when visibility is poor. RADAR beacons are used to guide aircraft; when they are triggered by a signal from the aircraft they return a pulse that enables the plane to determine its position. Radio beacons send out a regular, characteristic signal that is used by both ships and planes to determine their location.   FRANCES GIES

Beaconsfield, Benjamin Disraeli, 1st Earl of:
see DISRAELI, BENJAMIN.

Beadle, George W.

George Wells Beadle, an American geneticist, shared the 1958 Nobel Prize for medicine or physiology for his role in determining that genes act to influence the chemical mechanisms of cells.

George Wells Beadle, b. Wahoo, Nebr., Oct. 22, 1903, d. June 9, 1989, was a pioneer in chemical genetics. In early work with the fruit fly, *Drosophila*, Beadle found that certain genes on certain chromosomes were responsible for specific biochemical reactions. In 1941, working with Edward L. TATUM, he began studying X-ray and ultraviolet-induced mutations in the bread mold *Neurospora*. They found that all biochemical reactions are controlled by genes, each gene being responsible for the synthesis of a particular enzyme that catalyzes, or brings about, a particular step in a series of biochemical reactions. This is referred to as ''one gene—one enzyme.'' They also found that an alteration in a gene—a mutation—blocks the biochemical reactions. For their discovery that genes act by regulating specific chemical processes, Beadle and Tatum were awarded part of the 1958 Nobel Prize for physiology or medicine. Beadle had a distinguished academic career and was president of the University of Chicago from 1961 to 1968. He also served on the council of the National Academy of Sciences from 1969 to 1972 and was the recipient of numerous honors. He coauthored *The Language of Life* (1966) with Muriel Beadle, his wife.

Bibliography: Szekely, Maria, *From DNA to Protein* (1980); Wasson, Tyler, *Nobel Prize Winners* (1987).

beads and beadwork

Beads, small objects usually pierced for stringing or for joining to another material, have been used for decoration and for other purposes in cultures throughout the world. Commonly used bead materials include shell, bone, wood, seeds, nuts, stone, ivory, metal, glass, and, more recently, plastic. In some cultures favorite materials include exotic resources such as porcupine and bird quills, coral, coal, basketry, and animal or human teeth.

FORMS OF BEADS

Beads generally range from about 1 mm (0.04 in) to as much as about 7.6 cm (3 in) in diameter. Although usually spherical, they are sometimes ovoid, tubular, cube-shaped, or even flat. Often the surface is carved or painted with a variety of designs ranging from abstract geometric patterns to animal or plant forms and symbols.

Manufacture. Techniques of bead manufacture vary with the material used. In most primitive cultures, beads made of shells, nuts, or seeds are ground into rounded form, after which a hole is drilled through the bead. Beads of ivory, wood, or stone are first carved into the desired form and then drilled. Some materials, such as glass, metal, and faïence, are cast into any of several shapes around a central core, which eliminates the labor of drilling. Beads formed of clay or stone are sometimes overlaid with an enamel or metal coating; gold beads are usually made in this way.

Uses. Beads are used in many ways, among which the making of jewelry and other kinds of ornamentation is primary. Primitive peoples often lavishly adorn their bodies with beads at the neck, waist, ankle, knee, and wrist; holes are sometimes pierced through the nose, ears, or lips in order to attach beads to the body. The Huichol Indians of Mexico fasten beads to the ears of their pets for decoration and protection.

In certain cultures, beads serve an additional function involving superstition or magic. Their possession is thought to bring good luck, to ward off evil, or to attract the attention of a deity. When strung together, beads are used in some religions to help the faithful count their prayers (see ROSARY).

Beads served an important function among certain Native American tribes of the East Coast. Shell beads, or WAMPUM, were strung together and exchanged as gifts during ceremonial occasions. Glass beads were introduced around 1700 by European explorers, who witnessed wampum exchanges and mistakenly assumed that the beads were a form of currency. Because wampum is hard to make, Native Americans highly valued the glass beads.

Most New World traders took large quantities of beads with them for the purpose of initiating good relations and barter. When beads were first introduced into North America, a single bead sometimes had the equivalent value of a beaver fur. This value eventually declined greatly as the supply of trade beads increased in most areas.

MAKERS OF BEADS

Beads have been in use since prehistoric times. Because they were readily transported and usually highly valued, they were natural objects of trade. This often poses a problem of identification for the archaeologist, because beads are often discovered thousands of kilometers from their point of origin.

A young Masai woman from Kenya wears an elaborate collection of bead collars, an ornament for which her tribe is noted. Among the Masai, a nomadic cattle-herding tribe of East Africa, fine beadwork is worn by both men and women.

Old World. From as early as 4000 BC, ancient Egypt was a major source of beads, as were the later cultures of Phoenicia, Babylon, Crete, Greece, and Rome. Glass beads were known in ancient China and India. With the perfection of glassmaking techniques in Italy in the 13th century, the island of Murano in Venice became a major European source of glass beads, followed later by Poland, Czechoslovakia, and France. Their products spread throughout the world.

New World. In the ancient Americas, the Olmec of Mexico and Guatemala produced magnificent jade beads as early as 2000 BC. Later the Maya of the same region created some of the largest beads known. The Chorotegan Indians of Costa Rica and Panama are noted for their thin disks of deep-green jadeite, but the real masters of bead production in pre-Columbian America were the Tairona of Colombia and the inhabitants of the tiny island of La Tolita in Ecuador. Working in carnelian, crystal, jasper, and gold, they turned out vast quantities of tiny, artistically worked beads between AD 1000 and 1500. In North America, the prehistoric Indians of the Southwest made beads of clay, shell, and stone; their turquoise *heishi* beads are among the smallest known.

Among contemporary Central and South American peoples, the Huichol of Mexico use beads extensively in costumes and ritual paraphernalia, notably their gourd offering-bowls, in which glass beads are impressed in colorful designs. The Guaymí and Chocó of Panama and northern Colombia make elaborate beaded collars and costume ornaments; the Wapishana and Makushí of the Guianas weave beautiful beaded skirts worn by the women.

Africa and Other Areas. Although beads were familiar to prehistoric peoples in Africa, it was only after the arrival of European and Mediterranean traders that their use spread widely throughout the continent. The Zulu, Masai, Yoruba, Bambara, Ndebele, and the peoples of the Cameroon grasslands are among those who have traditionally made great use of beads.

Skirts, body ornaments, headdresses, and weapons are profusely decorated with beads. Religious objects such as masks and figures of deities are also heavily adorned with colorful beaded ornaments obtained from traders. Among the Melanesians and New Guinean tribes in Oceania, shell beads were most commonly used. Philippine natives were also active bead producers, as were, to a lesser extent, the people of Borneo and Indonesia.

BEADWORK

Beadwork is the technique of embroidering beads on a surface. The most common method involves attaching single beads to a ground material by means of a thread or thin fiber. In the so-called lazy stitch, entire rows of beads are attached at the same time; in another technique, beads are interwoven into textiles as the weaving proceeds on the loom. Today beadwork is frequently machine-made.

In Europe, beading reached its greatest popularity in 16th-century England, during the reign of Queen Elizabeth I, when almost everything worn or displayed included some beadwork decoration. This fad declined during the 18th century, but by the Victorian era, it was once again extremely popular. Purses, containers, costumes, and home objects were profusely ornamented with tiny glass, pearl, or metal beads in many colors and shapes. Designs varied from geometric patterns, which were most common, to floral patterns and representational scenes.

Among tribal peoples, the use of beadwork was traditionally widespread. Solidly beaded objects were produced by many Indian tribes of North America, particularly the Crow, Blackfoot, and Sioux. These groups decorated their dwellings, costumes, and horse gear with colorful and highly valued beaded decorations. It was common for a Plains Indian woman to carry a weight of about 4.5 kg (10 lb) of glass beads on the upper portion of her buckskin dress; Seminole women in Florida displayed similar quantities of beads in their lengthy necklaces. The Mixe women of Oaxaca, Mexico, traditionally wear heirloom necklaces of beadwork often weighing more than 1.5 kg (3.5 lb).   FREDERICK J. DOCKSTADER

Bibliography: Dubin, Lois S., *The History of Beads* (1987); Orchard, William C., *Beads and Beadwork of the North American Indians*, rev. ed. (1985); Tanner, Clara Lee, *Southwest Indian Craft Arts* (1968); Van Der Sleer, W. G., *A Handbook on Beads* (1973); Wildschut, William, *Crow Indian Beadwork*, rev. ed. (1985).

beagle

The beagle is a small breed of hound with the general appearance of a miniature foxhound. The true origins of the beagle are unknown. It has long been used in France and the British Isles as a pack hound to hunt rabbits by scent. For show purposes, beagles are divided into varieties by size; the first stands up to 33 cm (13 in) at the shoulder, the second 33–38 cm (13–15 in). The ears are long and rounded at the tip, and the slightly curved tail is carried gaily. The close, hard coat may be of any hound color. The breed was well known in the United States by the mid-19th century. The National Beagle Club, formed in 1888, held its first field trial at that

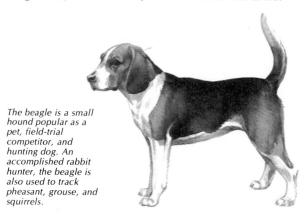

The beagle is a small hound popular as a pet, field-trial competitor, and hunting dog. An accomplished rabbit hunter, the beagle is also used to track pheasant, grouse, and squirrels.

time; more than 3,000 such trials, licensed by the American Kennel Club, are now held annually. The dog's small size, clean habits, and gentle and affectionate personality have made it for many years one of the ten most popular breeds in the United States.   JOHN D. MANDEVILLE

Bibliography: Berndt, Robert J., *Your Beagle* (1975); Nicholas, A. K., and Foy, M., *The Beagle* (1982).

Beagle, H. M. S.:   see DARWIN, CHARLES.

Beaker culture

The Beaker culture is a name given to a group of communities responsible for the spread of copper metallurgy in Europe in the 3d millennium BC. It is named for its most distinctive product, a pottery drinking vessel decorated with zones of linear ornament produced by whipcord impressions made on the clay surface. What was formerly believed to constitute a single culture is now seen to represent at least two separate but broadly contemporary groups. The earlier, distinguished by beakers with all-over cord ornament, originated in Central Europe, probably in the Lower Rhine basin, where the beakers evolved out of local so-called Corded-Ware traditions. It spread to Holland and Britain, where similar cord-ornamented beakers of around 3000 BC have been found.

The second major Beaker tradition probably originated in Iberia. The vessels of these southern Beaker people are distinguished by their bell-shaped profile. The Bell-Beaker or Maritime-Beaker culture, as it is sometimes called, developed out of the local culture represented at Villa Nova de São Pedro in Portugal, from which the Beaker people adopted copper metallurgy. Radiocarbon dating suggests that this happened around 2500 BC. From Iberia Bell-Beaker culture spread to France, Britain, and ultimately to Germany and the Low Countries. A fusion of traditions resulted in northwest Europe, Beaker people being influenced by the BATTLE-AXE CULTURE, through which they were introduced to single-grave burial. In Britain the Beaker people are associated with some major ritual monuments, including AVEBURY.   LLOYD R. LAING

Bibliography: Champion, T., et al., *Prehistoric Europe* (1984); Hawkes, Jacquetta, ed., *Atlas of Ancient Archaeology* (1974); Hyndman, Michael, *People before History: The Age of Metal* (1974).

Beale, Edward Fitzgerald

Edward Fitzgerald Beale, b. District of Columbia, Feb. 4, 1822, d. Apr. 22, 1893, was an American courier and explorer in the West. A naval officer, he served under Commodore Robert Stockton in California during the Mexican War. With Kit CAR-SON, he carried word of Stephen Kearny's engagement at San Pasqual (Dec. 6, 1846) through enemy lines to Stockton. Beale crossed the continent six times as a dispatch carrier. In 1848 he brought the first official news of the California gold discovery to the East. After leaving the navy in 1851, Beale was an Indian agent and a Western surveyor. In the latter capacity he persuaded the government to import camels for use on an 1857 expedition in the Southwest. He later served (1876–77) as U.S. minister to Austria-Hungary.

Bibliography: Faulk, Odie B., *The U.S. Camel Corps* (1976); Lesley, L. B., ed., *Uncle Sam's Camels* (1920).

Beamon, Bob

American track-and-field star Robert Beamon, b. New York City, Aug. 29, 1946, set, at the 1968 Olympics in Mexico City, a world record in the long jump that most experts consider the greatest single performance in track history. His jump of 8.90 m (29 ft 2$^{1}/_{2}$ in) exceeded the previous record by 55 cm (21$^{1}/_{2}$ in), and stood until Mike Powell jumped 8.95 m (29 ft 4$^{1}/_{2}$ in) at the 1991 World Championships in Tokyo.

bean

Bean is the common name for several leguminous plants, family Leguminosae, and their seeds and for several other unrelated species. Many beans are exceptionally good sources of vegetable protein and are important food staples. The name *bean* was originally applied to the broad bean, *Vicia faba*, also known as the Scotch, or Windsor, bean. This bean is still widely grown in Europe but is little known in the United States.

The best known bean plant of the New World is the common, snap, or kidney bean, *Phaseolus vulgaris*. Indigenous to Central America, it was widely disseminated in North and South America before European exploration, and distinct types had been developed. Forms include snap beans, which are consumed as the immature pods; green shell beans, which are eaten as full-size, immature beans removed from the pods; and dry shell, or kidney beans, which are used in the mature, dry form. String, stringless, and wax beans are varieties of the snap bean. Dry bean types include pinto, navy, Great Northern, red kidney, and pink beans.

The plants are annuals with a determinate (bush-type) or indeterminate (twining or pole-type) growth habit. The leaves have three leaflets; the flowers are of many colors; and the fruit is a legume, or pod, containing several white, red, or dark seeds. The pod may be round, oval, or flat in shape, and green, yellow, or red in color.

Snap beans are grown in every part of the United States,

Beans, P. vulgaris, are among the world's most important food crops. Shown (left to right) *are the snap bean bush; flowers; green and yellow (or wax) snap beans, which are harvested when the pods are immature and soft; and the leaves and immature and mature pods of the shell, or horticultural, bean. The shell bean is harvested when the pod is hard and mature and the bean is dry with a somewhat nutty taste.*

but commercial production for canning and freezing is highest in Wisconsin, Oregon, and New York, whereas production for fresh consumption is greatest in Florida, California, and New York. Dry-bean production is highest in Michigan, California, and Idaho.

The winged bean, *Psophocarpus tetragonolobus,* found in New Guinea and Southeast Asia, gained increased attention in the late 1970s and 1980s as a possible important food source for the future. Its cultivation is spreading. Almost all parts of the plant are highly nutritious, rich in protein and vitamins.

Other beans include the CAROB, CHICK-PEA, COWPEA, LIMA BEAN, and SOYBEAN (see also PULSE CROPS).   DONALD N. MAYNARD

Bibliography: Salunkhe, D. K., and Kadam, S. S., *Handbook of World Food Legumes* (1989).

Bean, Alan

American astronaut Alan LaVern Bean, b. Wheeler, Tex., Mar. 15, 1932, the fourth man to walk on the Moon, was a navy test pilot when selected as an astronaut in 1963. On his first spaceflight he served as lunar module pilot of APOLLO *12,* the second manned lunar landing, and, along with commander Charles CONRAD, set up the first lunar surface experiment package. In 1973, Bean, Owen GARRIOT, and Jack LOUSMA set a 59-day record for a single spaceflight on the SKYLAB *3* mission. Retiring from the navy in 1975, Bean became head of astronaut operations and training until retiring from NASA in 1981. He is a painter of space activities.   DAVID DOOLING

Bean, Roy

"Judge" Roy Bean, b. *c.*1825, d. Mar. 15, 1903, was a colorful justice of the peace on the American frontier, who dubbed himself "The Law West of Pecos." Born in Kentucky, he was a cattle rustler in Mexico and a Confederate irregular before settling in Texas. In 1882, Bean opened a saloon in the railroad construction camp of Vinegaroon, Tex. He renamed the settlement Langtry (for Lillie LANGTRY) and made himself justice of the peace. Holding court in his bar, he rendered sometimes shrewd, sometimes arbitrary decisions. Bean is also remembered for staging (1896) an illegal heavyweight championship fight on a sandbar in the Rio Grande.

Bibliography: Sonnichsen, C. L., *Roy Bean* (1943; repr. 1991).

bear

Bears are heavyset mammals that constitute the family Ursidae in the order Carnivora. Most bears live in Europe, Asia, and North America; the only South American species is the spectacled bear. Bears usually inhabit rough, forested lands that provide food and cover; polar bears, however, frequent the treeless, icy wastes of the Arctic.

Bears have a massive, long-snouted head and a stumpy tail. Short, thick legs end in large, five-toed feet, and each toe is armed with a long, heavy claw. The powerful jaws are lined with wide, flat-topped molars for grinding food; bears also have four long canine, or eye, teeth. Most have loose skin and long, shaggy fur. They have an excellent sense of smell but poor vision and hearing.

Types.   Seven genera and about nine species of bear exist. American black bears, *Euarctos americanus,* are about 1.5–1.8 m (5–6 ft) long and weigh 90–150 kg (200–330 lb). They once lived throughout most of North America, but hunting and agriculture drove them into heavily forested areas, where about 80,000 survive. Brown individuals, called cinnamon bears, often are born into the same litter as black cubs.

Brown bears, *Ursus arctos,* include the largest of the land carnivores, the Alaska brown bears, or kodiak bears, which may reach a length of 3 m (10 ft) and weigh up to 780 kg (1,700 lb). They live on the shores and islands of Alaska. The European brown bear was once common throughout the continent but is now found only in mountainous areas of Russia, Scandinavia, and southern Europe. It may be 1.8 m (6 ft) long and weigh 230 kg (500 lb). The smaller Asiatic brown bears include the tan-colored Syrian bear and the snow bear of the

Himalayas. Grizzly bears are closely related to the Alaska brown bears. They may be 2.8 m (9 ft) long and weigh 410 kg (900 lb). Their name is derived from the whitish tips of their brown fur. Grizzlies once roamed from Mexico to Alaska but today are found only in a few national parks in the American West. Some authorities recognize the grizzly and the Alaska brown bear as two species distinct from *U. arctos,* which includes the brown bears of the Old World.

Polar bears, *Thalarctos maritimus,* are inhabitants of the Arctic, although they are sometimes found some 1,200 km (750 mi) south of the Arctic Circle, where they raid garbage dumps. They may be 3.3 m (11 ft) long and weigh more than 680 kg (1,500 lb). Their white fur provides excellent camouflage in the snowy environment. Polar bears have fur on the soles of their feet that keeps them from slipping on ice.

Asiatic black bears, *Selenarctos thibetanus,* are also called moon bears because of a white, crescent-shaped mark between the front legs. These bears are about 1.6 m (5 ft) long and weigh 114 kg (250 lb). They live in central Asian forests and brushlands.

Sloth bears, *Melursus ursinus,* are so called because they move very slowly. These black, white-marked bears are about 1.6 m (5 ft) long and weigh 100 kg (220 lb) or more. They are nocturnal animals of tropical and subtropical India and Sri Lanka.

Spectacled bears, *Tremarctos ornatus,* live in cool, high forests of the Andes. They grow to be 1.8 m (6 ft) long and to weigh 114 kg (250 lb). This blackish-brown bear is named for the rim of white fur around its eyes.

Sun bears, or Malay bears, *Helarctos malayanus,* are the smallest bears. They get their name from the patch of yellowish fur on the black chest. Nocturnal feeders of east Asian forests, they weigh about 36 kg (80 lb) and are 0.9–1.2 m (3–4 ft) long.

Characteristics.   Bears are solitary animals. The breeding season is in summer, after which each individual prepares for winter. This is especially important for the pregnant female, whose cubs will be born during the winter. All bears eat heavily during summer and autumn to store fat for winter.

A bear's winter sleep is not true HIBERNATION, since the body temperature remains high and the animal emerges from the den to walk about on mild winter days. The female gives birth to from 1 to 4 cubs at a time, with a litter every 2 years. The cubs stay with their mother for a year or two, and she defends them against all intruders, including humans and sometimes cannibalistic male bears. Like humans but unlike most other animals, bears are plantigrade—that is, they walk with the sole and five toes of each foot almost flat on the ground. Most animals walk on their toes. Bears look clumsy, but they can run up to 40 km (25 m) per hour. Many of them are powerful swimmers, and most bears can climb trees.

Of all bears, the polar bear is the strictest carnivore. It eats seals, walrus, fish, caribou, and beached whales but has been known to graze on grass and seaweed. The Alaska brown bear will eat almost anything, including deer, cattle, and fish. Other bears tend to be omnivorous, eating fruits, roots, berries, and other plant matter, either by choice or when meat and grubs are unavailable. Most bears are known to be fond of honey.

Bears and Humans.   Since prehistoric times, humans have hunted bears for their meat, bone, sinew, fur, and fat. Favorite ornaments of many primitive peoples are bear teeth and claws. The bear has been made the center of myths and legends by the Finno-Ugric peoples of northern Eurasia, the American Indians, and the Ainu of Japan. People today must often be reminded that all bears are short-tempered and dangerous; a bear can kill a human with one swipe of its paw.

As agriculture and urbanization have advanced, bear habitats have disappeared, and some species are now almost extinct. Overhunting has depleted stock in many areas.

EVERETT SENTMAN

Bibliography: Brown, Gary, *The Great Bear Almanac* (1993); Dufresne, Frank, *No Room for Bears* (1991); Stirling, Ian, ed., *Bears* (1993); Zager, Peter, ed., *Bears: Their Biology and Management* (1987).

polar bear

brown bear

black bear

grizzly bear

The polar bear, Thalarctos maritimus, *travels great distances along arctic coasts. Its white fur furnishes camouflage against snow and ice. The brown bear,* Ursus arctos, *inhabits Eurasia and North America. Eurasian brown bears are frequently seen in circuses as dancing bears. The American black bear,* E. americanus, *inhabits forests of North America and climbs trees easily. The fierce North American grizzly, a subspecies of the brown bear, is nearing extinction. Bears sleep through cold winters but maintain a normal metabolism and are not true hibernators.*

Bear, The

"The Bear" is a chapter of William FAULKNER's *Go Down, Moses* (1942), a novel, although some critics consider it simply a collection of related short stories. "The Bear" is often published separately because of its effective dramatization of the consequences of racism, betrayal of the land, and human failure in the context of a young man's initiation into his family history and the hunting tradition. The long fourth section of "The Bear," using the STREAM OF CONSCIOUSNESS technique, is the major link to the whole novel and cannot be fully comprehended when the story is published alone. "The Bear" was published in *The Saturday Evening Post* on May 9, 1942, simultaneous with release of the book.

Bear Flag Republic

The Bear Flag Republic was a short-lived political entity established (1846) in California during the MEXICAN WAR. A group of American trappers and traders living in the Sacramento

River valley resented Mexican rule of the area. Aroused by rumors of approaching war between the United States and Mexico and apparently encouraged by the presence of a U.S. government expedition led by John C. FRÉMONT, a small force of settlers captured the town of Sonoma in June 1846. Shortly afterward they announced the creation of a new republic, named for the grizzly bear on its makeshift flag, with Frémont as president. After a brief skirmish with Mexican troops, Frémont led the Bear Flaggers southward to the capital, Monterey, in July. They found, however, that Monterey had already been captured (July 7, 1846) by U.S. naval forces under John D. Sloat. California was claimed for the United States, and the brief republic ended.   ELLIOTT WEST

Bibliography: Bean, Walton, and Rawls, J. J., *California: An Interpretive History*, 5th ed. (1987).

bear grass

Bear grass, *Xerophyllum*, is a hardy perennial in the lily family Liliaceae. It is also commonly called turkey beard. Bear grass is native to North America. The principal species is *X. asphodeloides*, which is found in pine barrens from New Jersey to Georgia. Racemes of yellowish-white flowers are borne on 1.5-m (5-ft) stems from May to July. *X. tenax* is native to the Rocky Mountains and the Pacific Coast region.

bearberry

Bearberry, *Arctostaphylos uva-ursi*, is a creeping evergreen shrub in the heath family, Ericaceae. Native to North America and northern Europe and Asia, it is valued for its colorful foliage, which turns bronze in fall, and for its bright red berries. The small, leathery leaves are up to 2.54 cm (1 in) long, and the flowers are white or pink. A hardy plant, it makes an excellent ground cover in sunny locations on sandy soils. Black bearberry, *A. alpina,* is named for its black fruit, or berry.

Beard, Charles A.

Charles Austin Beard, b. near Knightstown, Ind., Nov. 27, 1874, d. Sept. 1, 1948, was a controversial American historian and political scientist who encouraged a generation of Americans to reexamine their country's history. Raised in rural Indiana, he studied at DePauw and Oxford before receiving (1904) his doctorate from Columbia. His nearly 60 books, many written with the help of his wife or other collaborators, reflected the problems of a nation undergoing industrialization and helped shape the American progressive movement. Beard revolutionized American history in 1913 with the publication of *An Economic Interpretation of the Constitution*. His thesis that the Constitution furthered the interests of the property-owning classes challenged the conventional wisdom about the Founding Fathers.

Controversy seemed to follow Beard. In 1917 he resigned his teaching post at Columbia to protest the firing of two of his colleagues who opposed American entry into World War I. The following year, Beard helped create the New School for Social Research. With the aid of his wife, Mary (1876–1958), Beard offered the public a mature reinterpretation of the course of American history in *The Rise of American Civilization* (2 vols., 1927) and other works. He had long sympathized with reformers, but Franklin D. Roosevelt's New Deal troubled him. Fearing another war, Beard became a leading isolationist spokesman and made bitter personal attacks on Roosevelt. Until his death, Beard insisted that Roosevelt's foreign policy drove the Japanese to war.   JOEL COLTON

Bibliography: Beale, Howard K., *Charles A. Beard: An Appraisal* (1976); Borning, Bernard C., *The Political and Social Thought of Charles Beard* (1962); Hofstadter, Richard, *The Progressive Historians: Turner, Beard, Parrington* (1968; repr. 1979); Kennedy, T. C., *Charles A. Beard and American Foreign Policy* (1975); Martin, J. J., *Charles A. Beard: A Tribute* (1984); Nore, E., *Charles A. Beard* (1983).

bearded collie

The bearded collie is a breed of working dog related to the collie and the Old English sheepdog, which it resembles except for its shorter coat.

The bearded collie is a breed of dog that resembles a cross between the collie and the Old English sheepdog. The breed stands 51–56 cm (20–22 in) at the shoulder. The coat is longer than that of the collie but not as profuse as that of the Old English sheepdog, and it is usually a shade of slate or reddish tan, with white markings. Although an ancient breed, the bearded collie did not receive official recognition by the British until 1944 and by the American Kennel Club until 1978. Its antecedents are uncertain, but the collie, Old English sheepdog, and border collie are probably close relatives. In part, the breed's origins are obscure because the dog was valued by shepherds solely for its working ability. Intelligent and adaptable, it has grown steadily in popularity in the United States, although it is still relatively rare.   JOHN D. MANDEVILLE

Bibliography: Bishop, Ada, *All About the Collie* (1971; repr. 1989); Rieseberg, Barbara, and McKinney, B. J., *Beardie Basics,* rev. ed. (1984); Walkowitz, Chris, *The Bearded Collie* (1987).

Bearden, Romare

Romare Bearden, b. Charlotte, N.C., Sept. 2, 1914, d. Mar. 11, 1988, was a prominent Afro-American artist and collagist. Trained in the 1930s in New York City and, after army service in World War II, at the Sorbonne in Paris, Bearden established his basic collage approach with *The Prevalence of Ritual* (1964), a series of kaleidoscopic visions of black-American life. Interest in his work led Bearden into other artistic areas: covers for national magazines, posters, and stage sets, although his principal work continued to be collage art.

Beardsley, Aubrey

Aubrey Beardsley's The Ascension of St. Rose of Lima *(1896) displays the black masses, elongated figures, and elegant curved lines characteristic of his work. (Private collection.)*

Aubrey Vincent Beardsley, b. Aug. 21, 1872, d. Mar. 16, 1898, was a brilliant English illustrator of the late Victorian era. During his brief lifetime he produced an enormous quantity of drawings, mostly in black and white, that have been admired and emulated from his day to the present. His most notable efforts were the highly original illustrations for Oscar Wilde's Symbolist drama, *Salome* (1894), which are early and definative examples of the ART NOUVEAU style. Like many of his other illustrations, they engendered a feeling of decadence that both fascinated and shocked the society of his day.

As a child, Beardsley gave piano recitals at the Royal Pavilion at Brighton. That wildly exotic Regency summer palace undoubtedly left a vivid impression on him. Although Beardsley's education ended with secondary school, he was unusually knowledgeable in literature and art. His drawings were seen by the Pre-Raphaelite painter Sir Edward Burne-Jones, who advised Beardsley to study with the artist Frederick Brown at the Westminister School of Art in London. Japanese prints and the related works of James McNeill Whistler, as well as 15th-century Italian paintings, were important in the development of Beardsley's style.

Still not 20 years of age, Beardsley was asked by the publisher J. M. Dent to illustrate an edition of Sir Thomas Malory's *Morte Darthur* (1894). This was the first of many such commissions, which included lavish (and scandalous) special editions of *Volpone* (1898), *Lysistrata* (1896), and *The Rape of the Lock* (1896), as well as his original, erotic tale *Under the Hill*, published posthumously in 1907.

At the age of 22, he became art editor (1894) of the avant-garde London magazine *The Yellow Book* and was a major contributor (1896–98) to *The Savoy*, its even more advanced successor, until his untimely death at the age of 25.

Bibliography: Brophy, B., *Black and White: A Portrait of Aubrey Beardsley* (1970); Clark, K., *The Best of Aubrey Beardsley* (1978); Heyd, M., *Aubrey Beardsley* (1986); Hofstatter, H., *Aubrey Beardsley* (1980); Wilson, S., *Beardsley* (1976; repr. 1983); Weintraub, S., *Aubrey Beardsley: Imp of the Perverse* (1976).

beardtongue

The beardtongue P. hartwegii, *orginally from Mexico, produces bright-red flowers and is grown in flower beds or borders. One of its five stamens appears to have a beard and a tongue.*

Beardtongue, *Penstemon*, is a large perennial herb or shrub in the figwort family, Scrophulariaceae. Most of the approximately 250 species are native to North America. Leaves are opposite one another, and flowers are blue, purple, scarlet, yellow, or white. Beardtongues are dwarf shrubs and are often used for flower borders and rock gardens. A showy garden variety *P. gloxinioides*, has many flower shades and, like the geranium, can be used as a tender bedding perennial.

beardworm

The beardworm is any of about 10 species of wormlike marine invertebrates, in the phylum POGONOPHORA. These large animals reach a length of 10–85 cm (4–34 in) and are found in the ocean at depths of more than 1,000 m (3,300 ft), buried in the sea bottom and in chitinous tubes they construct around themselves. The name *beardworm* is derived from a threadlike mass of tentacles at the front of a long trunk, or proboscis. The tentacles, hollow with secondary branches, or pinnules, supplied with capillaries, probably have a respiratory and digestive function. Water enters a tentacle pore at the outer end and exits by a pore at the inner end. Microorganisms are possibly trapped inside the tentacles. The hind region, the opisthosoma, has bristles that may aid in burrowing and in anchoring in the tube.

bearing

A bearing is a structure that supports a rotating part of a machine, such as a shaft, axle, spindle, or wheel. Bearings also serve to reduce the FRICTION between the parts; this ability, whether the machine is a prime mover (an initial source of motive power) or a device driven externally, depends on adequate LUBRICATION as well as on the friction-reducing properties of the bearings themselves, the latter depending in turn on the material of which the bearing is composed.

Four principal types of bearings are used. In order of invention and development, they are the plain bearing, ball bearing, roller bearing, and fluid film bearing.

The Plain Bearing. The plain bearing—known more fully as the plain cylindrical journal bearing—was presumably invented at the same time as the wheel. An example of an early plain bearing is a chariot wheel rotating on its axle, a device in use in ancient Rome. Although it is not known what materials were used, scholars speculate that bronze and iron were the main constituents of bearings because both metals were used by the Romans.

Not all combinations of metals are compatible for bearings. Similar metals are not compatible and will quickly wear because of friction. In most machinery with rotating parts, shafts transmitting the power are made from steel. The sleeve, or lining, within which the shaft rotates—called the *bushing*—should be of a softer material than the *journal*, which is the section of the shaft that is supported by and turns within the bushing. Materials used for bushings include bronze, phosphor bronze, cast iron, hardened aluminum alloys, and some synthetic materials.

Babbit metal, or white metal, is often used for bearings, for example, in automobiles. This alloy is made of tin, copper, and antimony, and lead is sometimes included to strengthen the alloy.

Ball Bearings. Ball bearings, along with roller bearings, constitute a class that may be termed *antifriction bearings*, or rolling bearings. The development of rolling bearings must have begun soon after it was noticed by prehistoric humans that it is much easier to roll a rounded surface over another surface than to slide it. A ball bearing has three main elements: an inner grooved ring, or race, an outer race, and steel balls between the races spaced equidistant from one another in a *cage* made from some other material. The inner race is fastened to the shaft to be supported, and the outer race is secured to the stationary part of the machine.

Ball bearings should be lubricated, but only lightly, because they are most effective when the balls roll freely. The ordinary ball bearing serves when the load is in the radial direction, that is, perpendicular to the axis of the shaft. When thrust, or axial, loads are considerable, bearings called thrust bearings, which are designed to take thrust only, are used. When both radial and axial loading exist, specially designed double-purpose bearings are used.

Roller Bearings. The roller bearing, the other type of antifriction bearing, probably dates from the wheel, a device to which it is closely related. They both may have evolved from the discovery that heavy weights can be moved more easily if rollers made from cylindrical sections of tree trunks are placed between the weight and the ground. In addition to the basic type of roller bearing, which has cylindrical parallel rollers, common types include those fitted with tapered rollers and thin, parallel rollers (needle roller bearings).

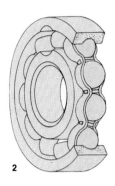

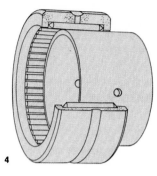

Bearings, designed to reduce friction between moving parts, comprise either three or four basic elements: an inner ring, or race; rolling elements (balls or rollers); a cage to hold the rolling elements; and an outer race. Ball bearings (1,2) are the simplest type. Roller bearings (3,4) produce even less friction than ball bearings. Some types (4) are designed to allow movement along the axle.

The roller bearing is better suited to heavy loads than the ball bearing, because contact is made along the entire line between the roller and the race, instead of point contact between the ball bearings and the races. In *tapered roller bearings*, both the races and the rollers are tapered; as a result, these bearings are capable of withstanding both radial and axial loads.

Fluid Film Bearings. In this type of bearing, friction between two surfaces is reduced by the presence of a film of fluid—oil, water, gas, or air—between them.   IAN BRADLEY

Bibliography: Eschmann, et al., *Ball and Roller Bearings* (1985); Houghton, P. S., *Ball and Roller Bearings* (1976); Society of Automotive Engineers, *Bearing Technology* (1985); Wilcock, D. F., and Booser, E. R., *Bearing Design and Application* (1957).

Béarn   [bay-ahrn']

Béarn is a historic region and former province in southwestern France, bounded on the south by the Pyrenees and on the west by the Bay of Biscay. Its capital was Orthez from the Middle Ages until 1460 and PAU thereafter. Part of the Roman province of Aquitania, Béarn was conquered by the Basques in the 6th century, became a viscounty of AQUITAINE in the 9th century, and a virtually independent principality in the 11th century. In the 15th century, Béarn came under the kings of NAVARRE and became part of France when Henry of Navarre was crowned Henry IV in 1589. Today it forms part of the Pyrénées-Atlantiques department.

beast epic: SEE ALLEGORY; FABLE; REYNARD THE FOX.

beat generation

A loosely knit group of American writers who became exiles within their own culture, the Beats were a clamorous bohemian reaction to the so-called silent generation of the 1950s. They had a marked influence on contemporary American literature and on the youth movement of the 1960s. The Beats became prominent around 1956, in New York City and then in San Francisco. The group included novelists Jack KEROUAC, William S. BURROUGHS, and John Clellon Holmes; and the poets Allen GINSBERG, Gregory CORSO, Lawrence FERLINGHETTI, Gary SNYDER, Michael McClure, and Philip Whalen. Kerouac coined the term, giving it a range of meanings from "beat down" to "beatific." The first Beat work is considered to be Holmes's pulsating, jazz-oriented novel *Go* (1952), but the masterpieces of the movement remain Kerouac's *On the Road* (1957) and Ginsberg's "Howl" (1956). The Beats rejected conventional consumer society and created their literature around an unconventional life-style of Zen Buddhism, drugs, jazz, and a heightened respect for the individual over the mass.

Bibliography: Cook, Bruce, *Beat Generation* (1971; repr. 1983); McClure, M., *Scratching the Beat Surface* (1982); McNally, Dennis, *Desolate Angel: Jack Kerouac, the Beat Generation, and America* (1979); Tytell, J., *Naked Angels: The Lives and Literature of the Beat Generation* (1976; repr. 1986).

beatification: SEE CANONIZATION.

beatitude   [bee-at'-i-tood]

A beatitude is a declaration of happiness or promised blessing because of some virtue or good deed. The most famous beatitudes are the blessings preached by Jesus in the Sermon on the Mount (Matt. 5). They describe the qualities of Christian perfection and promise future blessings rather than current rewards.

Bibliography: Fitch, William, *The Beatitudes of Jesus* (1961).

Beatles, The

The English rock music group The Beatles gave the 1960s its characteristic musical flavor and had a profound influence on the course of popular music, equaled by few performers. The guitarists John Winston Lennon, b. Oct. 9, 1940; Paul James McCartney, b. June 18, 1942; and George Harrison, b. Feb. 25, 1943; and the drummer Ringo Starr, b. Richard Starkey, July 7, 1940, were all born and raised in Liverpool. Lennon and McCartney had played together in a group called The Quarrymen. With Harrison, they formed their own group, The Silver Beatles, in 1959, and Starr joined them in 1962. As The Beatles, they developed a local following in Liverpool clubs, and their first recordings, "Love Me Do" (1962) and "Please Please Me" (1963), quickly made them Britain's top rock group. Their early music was influenced by the American rock singers Chuck Berry and Elvis Presley, but they infused a hackneyed musical form with freshness, vitality, and wit.

The Beatles (left to right, Paul McCartney, George Harrison, Ringo Starr, and John Lennon) entered American homes in February 1964 via Ed Sullivan's popular television program. Their hair and clothing styles influenced a generation of young people, and their music revolutionized rock and roll during the sixties.

The release of "I Want to Hold Your Hand" in 1964 marked the beginning of the phenomenon known as "Beatlemania" in the United States. The Beatles' first U.S. tour aroused universal mob adulation. Their concerts were scenes of mass worship, and their records sold in the millions. Their films, the innovative *A Hard Day's Night* (1964) and *Help* (1965), were received enthusiastically by a wide audience.

Composing their own material (Lennon and McCartney were the major creative forces), The Beatles established the precedent for other rock groups to play their own music. Experimenting with new musical forms, they produced an extraordinary variety of songs: the childishly simple "Yellow Submarine"; the bitter social commentary of "Eleanor Rigby"; parodies of earlier pop styles; new electronic sounds; and compositions that were scored for cellos, violins, trumpets, and sitars, as well as for conventional guitars and drums. Some enthusiasts cite the albums *Rubber Soul* (1965) and *Revolver* (1966) as the apex of Beatle art, although *Sergeant Pepper's Lonely Hearts Club Band* (1967), perhaps the first rock album designed thematically as a single musical entity, is more generally considered their triumph. The group disbanded in 1970, after the release of their final album, *Let It Be*, to pursue individual careers. On Dec. 8, 1980, John Lennon was fatally shot in New York City. In 1991, Paul McCartney's classical composition *Liverpool Oratorio* was performed to some acclaim in Britain and the United States.

Bibliography: *The Beatles Complete,* 2 vols. (1981; repr. 1987); Giuliano, G., *The Beatles: A Celebration* (1986); Martin, G., *All You Need Is Ears* (1982); Neises, Charles, *The Beatles Reader* (1984).

Beaton, Sir Cecil

The English designer and photographer Sir Cecil Beaton, b. Jan. 14, 1904, d. Jan. 18, 1980, is best known for his photographs of such notables as Greta Garbo, Edith Sitwell, and the British royal family, many of which appear in *Cecil Beaton's Scrapbook* (1937). Selections from Beaton's diaries were published in *Memoirs of the 40s* (1973). Beaton won a Tony Award (1957) for the period costumes in the stage production of *My Fair Lady* and an Academy Award (1958) for those in the film *Gigi*. He also designed for the Comédie Française and New York's Metropolitan Opera. He was knighted in 1972.

Bibliography: Mellor, D., ed., *Cecil Beaton* (1986); Strong, R., *Cecil Beaton: The Royal Portraits* (1988); Vickers, H., *Cecil Beaton* (1986).

Beatrice   [bay-ah-tree'-chay]

Beatrice Portinari, b. 1266, d. June 8, 1290, is believed to have been the Florentine woman who inspired such devotion in the poet DANTE ALIGHIERI that he composed *The New Life* (c.1293; Eng. trans., 1969) in her honor. In Dante's *Divine Comedy* (c.1310–21), Beatrice, symbolizing spiritual grace, is Dante's guide through Paradise. The poet's idealization of Beatrice, with whom he was barely acquainted, exemplifies the tradition of COURTLY LOVE.

Bibliography: Williams, Charles, *The Figure of Beatrice: A Study in Dante* (1961; repr. 1973).

Beatrice, Queen of the Netherlands

Beatrice, b. Jan. 31, 1938, succeeded to the throne of the Netherlands on Apr. 30, 1980, on the abdication of her mother, Queen JULIANA. In 1961 she earned a doctorate in law at the University of Leiden. Her marriage (1966) to Prince Claus von Amsberg, a German diplomat, aroused some initial opposition. The eldest of their three sons, Prince Willem Alexander, is heir presumptive to the throne.

Beattie, Ann   [bee'-tee]

Ann Beattie, b. Washington, D.C., Sept. 8, 1947, is a writer whose books portray the lives of her contemporaries with close attention to the details of everyday life. *Distortions* (1976), *Where You'll Find Me* (1986), and *What Was Mine* (1991) are collections of stories, many of which first appeared in the *New Yorker*. Her novels include *Chilly Scenes of Winter* (1976), *Falling in Place* (1980), and *Love Always* (1985).

Beattie, James

James Beattie, b. Nov. 5, 1735, d. Aug. 18, 1803, was a Scottish poet, philosopher, and essayist. His *Essay on the Nature and Immutability of Truth* (1770) attacks the skeptical philosophy of David Hume. Beattie's long poem in Spenserian stanzas, *The Minstrel* (1771–74), concerns the growth of the poet's mind and influenced the verse of Lord Byron.

Beatty, Warren   [bay'-tee]

Warren Beatty, b. Richmond, Va., Mar. 30, 1937, was known to Hollywood as the hottest playboy of the 1960s after he made his screen debut in *Splendor in the Grass* (1961). His desire to be taken seriously and his tenacious ambition, however, won him critical acclaim first as an actor, then as a producer, screenwriter, and director with such films as *Bonnie and Clyde* (1967), *Shampoo* (1975), *Heaven Can Wait* (1978), *Reds* (1981), for which he won an Academy Award for best director, *Dick Tracy* (1990), and *Bugsy* (1991).

Beaubourg   [boh-boorg']

The Centre National d'Art et de Culture Georges Pompidou is a museum for art and culture located in the Beaubourg district of Paris. President Pompidou conceived (1969) the idea for Beaubourg, as the center is also known. It was completed

The Beaubourg, a cultural center and museum in Paris, is noted for the controversial industrial nature of its design. Completed in 1978, it houses a modern art museum, a reference library, and research centers for industrial design, music, and acoustics.

(1978) by the architects Renzo Piano of Italy and Richard Rogers of England and by the engineering firm of Ove Arup and Partners of England. The structure forms a huge transparent box 167.6 m (550 ft) long, 59.1 m (194 ft) wide, and 42 m (138 ft) high. Its exposed frame of tubular steel columns carries trusses spanning the width of the building. External mechanical systems—elevators painted red; escalators in clear plastic tunnels; and giant tubes for air (painted blue), water (green), and electricity (yellow)—all are placed outside the main columns and supported by 7.9-m (26-ft) cantilevers of cast steel. Considerable controversy arose over the assertive industrial style of the Pompidou Center, which is set amid more traditionally styled buildings in the heart of an old section of Paris.

LELAND M. ROTH

Bibliography: Danto, Eloise, *Museums of Paris* (1987).

Beaufort   (city)   [bue'-furt]

Founded in 1710, Beaufort (1990 pop., 9,576) is the second-oldest city in South Carolina and the seat of Beaufort

County. Located on Port Royal Island, the city has an excellent natural harbor and was a prosperous port before the Civil War. The major industries are seafood processing, the canning of truck-farm produce, lumbering, and tourism.

Beaufort   (family)

Beaufort was the name of a prominent 15th-century English family that was descended from JOHN OF GAUNT and his mistress Catherine Swynford. Although legitimized in 1396, they were barred from succession to the throne, which from 1399 to 1461 was occupied by their cousins of the house of LANCASTER. **Henry Beaufort**, *c*.1377–1447, bishop of Winchester from 1404 and cardinal from 1426, was a dominant political figure during the reign of HENRY VI. His nephew, **Edmund Beaufort**, *c*.1407–1455, and the latter's son **Henry**, 1436–64, both dukes of Somerset, were the leaders of the Lancastrian party during the Wars of the ROSES. The last of the line was Edmund's niece, **Margaret Beaufort**, 1443–1509, whose second marriage (1455) was to Edmund Tudor, earl of Richmond and half-brother to Henry VI. Their son became king as HENRY VII after overthrowing Richard III in 1485.   GEORGE HOLMES

Bibliography: Keen, M. H., *England in the Later Middle Ages* (1973).

Beaufort scale

The Beaufort scale was long in use as a system for estimating wind speeds. It was introduced in 1806 by Adm. Sir Francis Beaufort (1774–1857) of the British navy to describe wind effects on a fully rigged man-of-war sailing vessel, and it was later extended to include descriptions of effects on land features as well. Today the accepted international practice is to report wind speed in knots (1 knot equals 1 nautical mile, or about 1.85 km/1.15 mi, per hour).

The Beaufort scale is divided into a series of values, from 0 for calm winds to 12 and above for hurricanes. Each value represents a specific range and classification of wind speeds with accompanying descriptions of the effects on surface features, as follows: 0 (calm), 0-1 knot—smoke rises vertically, and the sea is mirror smooth; 1 (light air), 1–3 knots—smoke shows the direction of the wind; 2 (light breeze), 4–6 knots—wind is felt on the face and leaves rustle in the trees; 3 (gentle breeze), 7–10 knots—wind extends a light flag; 4 (moderate breeze), 11–16 knots—loose paper blows around, and fairly frequent whitecaps occur; 5 (fresh breeze), 17–21 knots—small trees sway; 6 (strong breeze), 22–27 knots—wind causes whistling in telephone wires and some spray on the sea surface; 7 (moderate gale), 28–33 knots—large trees sway; 8 (fresh gale), 34–40 knots—twigs break from trees, and long streaks of foam appear on the ocean; 9 (strong gale), 41–47 knots—branches break from trees; 10 (whole gale) 48–55 knots—trees are uprooted, and the sea takes on a white appearance; 11 (storm), 56–63 knots—widespread damage; 12 (hurricane), 64 knots and higher—structural damage on land and storm waves at sea.   ROGER A. PIELKE

Beaufort Sea   [boh'-furt]

The Beaufort Sea, part of the Arctic Ocean, lies north of Alaska and the northern coast of Canada and west of Canada's Arctic Archipelago. It has no physically defined boundaries. The surface area is about 476,560 km² (184,000 mi²). It has an average depth of 1,004 m (3,293 ft) and a maximum of 4,682 m (15,360 ft). The sea contains only a few small islands near the coasts. Ice covers the sea for most of the year.

The sea has not been fully explored. In the 1950s, scientific studies were begun by icebreakers, atomic submarines, aircraft, and drifting stations. Eskimos inhabiting the shore fish and hunt furbearing animals. The northern terminus of the Alaska oil pipeline is at PRUDHOE BAY, an inlet of the Beaufort Sea. The sea was named for Sir Francis Beaufort, a British hydrographer in the early 19th century.

Beauharnais   [boh-ahr-nay']   (family)

The Beauharnais were a French family who achieved prominence after the marriage (1796) of JOSEPHINE Tascher de La Pa-

gerie, the widow of Alexandre, vicomte de Beauharnais (1760–94), to NAPOLEON I. One of Josephine's children by Alexandre was **Eugène de Beauharnais**, b. Sept. 3, 1781, d. Feb. 21, 1824, who governed (1805–14) Italy as Napoleon's viceroy and was an important French commander in the latter stages of the Napoleonic Wars. His sister, **Hortense de Beauharnais**, b. Apr. 10, 1783, d. Oct. 5, 1837, married (1802) Napoleon's brother Louis BONAPARTE, who was king of Holland (1806–10). Before she separated from Louis in 1810, Hortense bore three sons, although it was suspected that Louis was not the father of the third, the future NAPOLEON III. She was also the mother of the illegitimate duc de Morny (1811–65), who was Napoleon III's advisor.

Beaumarchais, Pierre Caron de   [boh-mahr-shay']

Pierre Augustin Caron de Beaumarchais, an 18th-century dramatist and adventurer, is the subject of this portrait by Jean Marc Nattier. Beaumarchais, who aided the American colonists in their rebellion against British rule, was also the author of The Marriage of Figaro, *a play that satirized the injustices of 18th-century French society and enjoyed great popularity in the period before the French Revolution.*

The colorful French dramatist Pierre Augustin Caron, b. Paris, Jan. 24, 1732, d. May 18, 1799, who took the name of Beaumarchais in 1757, is chiefly remembered for two comic plays, The BARBER OF SEVILLE (1775) and The MARRIAGE OF FIGARO (1784). The popular character Figaro, who appears in both plays, became a byword for clever and resourceful versatility. *The Marriage of Figaro,* considered subversive because of its criticisms of the established order, created a sensation when it was first performed in Paris and was adapted for the operatic stage by Wolfgang Amadeus Mozart two years later in Vienna. Rossini's operatic version of *The Barber of Seville* dates from 1816.

In addition to a kaleidoscopic career as a playwright, Beaumarchais was also a watchmaker, music teacher to the daughters of Louis XV, court official, civil servant, secret envoy, and businessman. Always an activist, he pursued careers as a pamphleteer and gunrunner and created, in 1777, the first society for the protection of dramatists' rights, La Société des Auteurs Dramatiques. He also edited the works of Voltaire. Beaumarchais is remembered for his enthusiastic support of the American Revolution, during the early months of which he supplied the rebels with vast amounts of weapons and ammunition.

After the outbreak of the French Revolution, Beaumarchais was alternately lauded and imprisoned, but he was finally accepted by the new regime.

Bibliography: Grendel, F., *Beaumarchais: A Biography* (1977); Shewmake, Antoinette, ed., *For the Good of Mankind* (1987).

Beaumont   [boh'-mahnt]

Beaumont is a city and major oil center on the Neches River in southeastern Texas. It is the seat of Jefferson County and has a population of 114,323 (1990). Heavily industrialized, with oil refining, shipbuilding, and petrochemical manufacturing, Beaumont is also the processing center for the surrounding area. The city was founded in 1835. The discovery of oil at Spindletop Field in 1901 and the completion of a channel to the Gulf of Mexico in 1916 spurred industrialization.

Beaumont, Francis, and Fletcher, John
[boh'-mahnt]

The most popular of all Jacobean dramatists, surpassing even Shakespeare in public esteem at that time, were Francis Beaumont, c.1584–1616, and John Fletcher, 1579–1625. Their collaboration began about 1606 and produced ten plays before it ended with Beaumont's retirement in 1612–13. Jointly and separately they wrote about 54 works.

So popular and influential were their best works, like the comedies *The Woman Hater* (1606) and *The Coxcomb* (1608–10), the fine examples of romantic tragicomedy *Philaster* (1608–10) and *A King and No King* (1611), and the joint tragedy *A Maid's Tragedy* (1608–11), that their names became indissolubly linked. Beaumont was considered best at constructing plots and at humor, and Fletcher excelled in presenting pathos and in verbal invention. Fletcher, however, wrote about 15 plays alone, including the pastoral *The Faithful Shepherdess* (1608–09), the tragedies *Valentinian* (1610–14) and *Bonduca* (1609–14), and the classic comedy *The Wild Goose Chase* (c.1621). Later he worked in collaboration with Philip MASSINGER, Samuel Rowley (d. 1633?), Nathan Field (1587–1619), and even with Shakespeare on *The Two Noble Kinsmen* and *Henry VIII* in 1613.

The so-called Beaumont and Fletcher plays were lauded for their authentic portrayal of manners and the gentlemanly ideals of wit and sensibility. They now seem highly artificial. Plots are managed effectively but theatrically, with sudden conversions and reversals of fortune, implausible motivation, and an often coarse strain of sensuality that undercuts such lofty sentiments as love and honor. The true decadence of Jacobean literature begins with Beaumont and Fletcher, who influenced the ribald comedies and the heroic tragedies of later Restoration drama.   FREDSON BOWERS

Bibliography: Appleton, William, *Beaumont and Fletcher: A Critical Study* (1956; repr. 1974); Wilson, John H., *Influence of Beaumont and Fletcher on the Restoration Stage* (1928; repr. 1969).

Beaumont, William

William Beaumont, b. Lebanon, Conn., Nov. 21, 1785, d. Apr. 25, 1853, was an American surgeon who contributed significantly to the knowledge of stomach functions. In 1822, Beaumont operated on a gunshot victim, Alexis St. Martin. Although St. Martin fully recovered, the wound failed to heal, leaving a small window that exposed the stomach. Beaumont took advantage of the situation and, over a period of several years, made observations and experiments that demonstrated the function of gastric juices.

Bibliography: Beaumont, William, *The Career of William Beaumont and the Reception of His Discovery: An Original Anthology,* ed. by Bernard I. Cohen (1980); Burns, Virginia, *William Beaumont: Frontier Doctor* (1978); Earle, Scott, ed., *Surgery in America from the Colonial Era to the Twentieth Century* (1965).

Beauneveu, André   [boh-nuh-vu']

André Beauneveu, c.1330–c.1402, was an important Franco-Flemish painter, sculptor, and architect. His works are mostly lost today, but he was well known in his own time. The historian Jean Froissart, his contemporary, praised him highly. Beauneveu executed commissions for many wealthy and influential patrons, including Charles V of France, who commissioned him to make four sculptures for the royal tomb in the crypt of SAINT-DENIS, Paris.

In 1386, Beauneveu went to Bourges as artistic advisor to Jean, duc de Berry. He painted 24 miniatures of apostles and prophets at the beginning of the Duke's Psalter (c.1380–85; Bibliothèque Nationale, Paris).   TANIA BAYARD

Beauregard, P. G. T.   [boh'-ruh-gahrd]

Pierre Gustave Toutant Beauregard, b. New Orleans, La., May 28, 1818, d. Feb. 20, 1893, was a leading Confederate general during the U.S. Civil War.

A member of a prominent Louisiana family, he graduated (1838) from West Point and fought in the Mexican War. In April 1861, Beauregard commanded Confederate troops at Charleston, where he initiated the bombardment of FORT SUMTER. He also played a major role in the first Battle of BULL RUN on July 21, 1861.

In April 1862, Beauregard took command on the western front, but illness soon forced him to retire. He later defended the south Atlantic coast. In 1864 he fought in Virginia and then commanded troops in Alabama, Mississippi, and Tennessee. After 1865, Beauregard was active in the railroad industry, managed the Louisiana state lottery, and defended his military reputation. Historians describe him as an able general.   RICHARD M. MCMURRY

Bibliography: Williams, T. Harry, *P. G. T. Beauregard: Napoleon in Gray* (1955).

Beauty and the Beast

Beauty and the Beast is a popular fairy tale that was first published in a collection of stories by Mme de Villeneuve in 1740–41. It is a heavily didactic tale of the value of solid virtues over base appearances. As the youngest and most beautiful daughter of a wealthy merchant, Beauty is loyal, persevering, and, unlike her proud sisters, willing to sacrifice herself for her father after he loses his money. When the father stumbles into a beast's lair, the Beast demands Beauty in exchange for not killing him and then falls in love with Beauty. When she finally consents to marry him, he is revealed to be a prince. The story was translated into a notably poetic film, *La Belle et la bête*, by the French director Jean Cocteau in 1946.   CHARLOTTE D. SOLOMON

beauty bush

Beauty bush, *Kolkwitzia amabilis*, is a hardy deciduous shrub in the honeysuckle family, Caprifoliaceae. It is native to China and grows up to 4.5 m (15 ft) high in temperate regions. Leaves are ovate, up to 7.5 cm (3 in) long. Both the young leaves and branches are hairy when young. Its bell-shaped flowers are soft pink with a yellow throat. The flower stalk and sepals are covered with white, bristly hairs.

The beauty bush, K. amabilis, *produces abundant clusters of small flowers in early spring. It is a member of the honeysuckle family and is native to China. It is propagated by cuttings.*

beauty leaf

Beauty leaf, *Calophyllum,* are about 100 species of tropical trees and shrubs in the garcinia family, Guttiferae. Their dark green, glossy leaves have a handsome pattern of fine lateral veins converging at a prominent central vein. Beauty leaf trees have fragrant, white flowers and fruit containing oily seeds, used medicinally or for lamp fuel. Species include the Alexandrian laurel, *C. ionophyllum,* of oceanic Asia and the maria, *C. braziliense,* of South America.

Beauvoir, Simone de   [boh-vwahr', see-muhn']

Simone de Beauvoir, French essayist and novelist, was a leading feminist and a proponent of existentialism. Her philosophical view closely resembled that of Jean Paul Sartre, a lifelong associate. The existential dilemma is the central theme of her works, but her perspective ranges from the autobiographical to the historical.

Simone de Beauvoir, b. Paris, Jan. 9, 1908, d. Apr. 14, 1986, was a French writer and feminist. A disciple and consort of Jean Paul SARTRE, she played a leading part in the existentialist movement. After receiving a degree in philosophy from the Sorbonne in 1929, Beauvoir was a teacher before she turned to fiction with *She Came to Stay* (1943; Eng. trans., 1949), a novel illustrating the existentialist idea of freedom through an autonomous act. She further elaborated on this philosophy in *The Blood of Others* (1945; Eng. trans., 1948), *All Men Are Mortal* (1946; Eng. trans., 1955), and *The Mandarins* (1954; Eng. trans., 1956), a fictionalized account of Jean Paul Sartre and his existentialist circle, for which she won the Prix Goncourt. Her most important nonfictional work is The SECOND SEX (1949; Eng. trans., 1953), a comprehensive study of the secondary role of women in society. The book is widely credited with inspiring the women's liberation movements—both in Europe and the United States—that began in the late 1960s.

Beauvoir later published a distinguished series of autobiographical volumes—*Memoirs of a Dutiful Daughter* (1958; Eng. trans., 1959), *The Prime of Life* (1960; Eng. trans., 1962), *The Force of Circumstance* (1963; Eng. trans., 1965)—which describe her own life and that of her contemporaries from her early twenties on. She continued in a similar vein in *A Very Easy Death* (1964; Eng. trans., 1966), about her mother's last days; *The Coming of Age* (1970; Eng. trans., 1972), in which she comes to grips with approaching old age; and *All Said and Done* (1972; Eng. trans., 1974). In their entirety, Simone de Beauvoir's works form an inestimable intellectual history of contemporary France.

Bibliography: Cottrell, R. D., *Simone de Beauvoir* (1975); Evans, M., *Simone de Beauvoir: A Feminist Mandarin* (1985); Leighton, J., *Simone de Beauvoir on Women* (1975); Madsen, A., *Hearts and Minds: The Common Journey of Simone de Beauvoir and Jean-Paul Sartre* (1977).

Beaux, Cecilia   [boh]

Cecilia Beaux, b. *c.*1855, d. Sept. 17, 1942, was a leading portrait painter in New York at the turn of the century. She studied with William Sartrain in Philadelphia and with William

Bouguereau and Tony Robert-Fleury at the Académie Julian in Paris. Her elegant, boldly brushed portraits can be compared stylistically with those of John Singer Sargent, but she rarely flattered her sitters. These included prominent figures in government, finance, and the arts, but her strongest works are portraits of family members and friends, such as *Ernesta Drinker* (1911; Metropolitan Museum of Art, New York City).

beaver

(Above) *A common beaver,* C. canadensis *is an aquatic rodent that ranges throughout most of North America. Its flattened tail and webbed hind feet are used for swimming. When in danger, a beaver will slap the water with its tail as it dives, warning other beavers.*

(Below) *A beaver (left)* constructs a dam of wood and mud in order to form a protective impoundment. Another beaver gnaws a birch tree (far right) *growing near the shore. In the pond, beavers build a lodge of branches* (center), *which has two underwater entrances and a vent for air in the dome. Beaver parents shelter their young inside the lodge and bring them food from a nearby woodpile. Besides building dams and lodges, beavers dig canals.*

building the dam

Beavers are large, aquatic, partly nocturnal rodents belonging to the family Castoridae. There are two species: *Castor fiber* is the Old World beaver, now found mainly in France, Germany, Poland, Russia, and Scandinavia. *C. canadensis* is the North American beaver, which lives in woodlands from northern Mexico to Alaska and Canada. Once overtrapped for its fur until it was confined to a far western habitat, this beaver has now returned to eastern regions.

Beavers are thickset and heavy, about 1.2 m (4 ft) long, including a 30-cm (1-ft) paddle-shaped tail; they weigh as much as 32 kg (70 lb). Their legs are short and their hind feet large and webbed. They use their forepaws like hands. A pair of anal musk glands, or castors, produce castoreum, used in making perfume. Dense brown to tan underfur is covered by coarse guard hairs. Chisellike front teeth enable the beaver to gnaw down trees used for building dams, island lodges, and canals. Beavers float small trees and branches through canals to the stream where they are building. The lodge has underwater entrances to keep out predators, with a large dry room inside that is used as a nursery and haven.

Beavers feed on marsh grasses, roots, barks, and twigs. They mate in January–February, and one to eight young are born in April–May. Beavers reach maturity in 2–3 years and live about 16 years.

EVERETT SENTMAN

Bibliography: Hilfiker, Earl L., *Beavers, Water, Wildlife and History* (1991); Ryden, Hope, *Lily Pond: Four Years with a Family of Beavers* (1989).

Beaver College

Established as a seminary by the Methodist Episcopal Church, Beaver College (1853; enrollment: 2,293; library: 119,000 volumes) is now affiliated with the United Presbyterian church, but it is nonsectarian. It is a 4-year coeducational liberal arts college in Glenside, Pa., with some master's programs.

Beaverbrook, Max Aitken, 1st Baron

William Maxwell Aitken, Lord Beaverbrook, b. May 25, 1879, d. June 9, 1964, was a British newspaper proprietor who exercised great influence on public policy. Born in Canada, he made a fortune as a financier before moving to England in 1910. There he acquired the *Daily Express* (1916) and the *Evening Standard* (1923) and founded the *Sunday Express* (1918).

Elected to Parliament in 1910 and created a peer in 1917, he was a close associate of Conservative leader Andrew Bonar Law. He was minister of information in the last year (1918) of World War I. Later he identified himself with a crusade for free trade within the British Empire and with a plan for close ties with the Commonwealth countries.

During World War II, Beaverbrook was brought into the war cabinet by his close friend Prime Minister Winston CHURCHILL. As minister of aircraft production (1940–41) during the Battle of Britain, he showed drive, irrepressible energy, and a knack for improvisation. As Churchill recorded, "This was his hour." Beaverbrook was minister of supply (1941–42), briefly minister of production (1942), and lord privy seal (1943–45).

DAVID DILKS

Bibliography: Cockett, Richard, ed., *My Dear Max: The Letters of Brenden Bracken to Lord Beaverbrook, 1925–1958* (1990); Taylor, A. J. P., *Beaverbrook* (1972); Young, Kenneth, *Churchill and Beaverbrook* (1967).

Bebel, August   [bay'-buhl]

August Bebel, b. Feb. 22, 1840, d. Aug. 13, 1913, was co-founder of the German Social Democratic party and a major figure in the Socialist International. The son of a Prussian non-commissioned officer, he was orphaned at an early age and became a woodturner, one of the few socialist leaders who was a worker. Wilhelm LIEBKNECHT brought him to Marxism, and together they founded at Eisenach in 1869 the Social Democratic Workers party, which amalgamated with the followers of Ferdinand Lassalle at Gotha in 1875.

A member of the Reichstag from 1867, Bebel, with Liebknecht, voted against credits for the Franco-Prussian War in 1870 and was imprisoned for high treason in 1872–74. Otto von Bismarck attributed his enmity to socialism to Bebel's support of the Commune of Paris. As chief leader of the German Social Democrats, Bebel opposed both the interference

by Karl MARX and Friedrich ENGELS and the revisionism of Eduard BERNSTEIN. He worked for concrete social benefits, and in his *Women under Socialism* (1883) he expressed support for the emancipation of women. Before his death Bebel was the leader of the largest Marxist party in the world. His autobiography, *My Life*, appeared in English in 1912.

FREDERIC B. M. HOLLYDAY

Bibliography: Roth, Guenther, *The Social Democrats in Imperial Germany* (1963).

Bebey, Francis

Francis Bebey, b. July 15, 1929, a Cameroonian writer and musician, won the Grand Prix Littéraire de l'Afrique Noire for his first novel, *Agatha Moudio's Son* (1967; Eng. trans., 1971). From 1957 to 1961 Bebey worked as a radio journalist, and from 1961 to 1974 he was employed by UNESCO. His other works include a book on African broadcasting, several short stories, the study *African Music: A People's Art* (1969; Eng. trans., 1975), and the novels *The Ashanti Doll* (1973; Eng. trans., 1977) and *King Albert* (Eng. trans., 1981).

bebop

The black JAZZ movement known as bebop (or rebop or bop) flourished in the decade 1940–50. At that time, a few black jazz artists, increasingly bored and restricted by the elaborately scored and arranged music of the large dance bands in which they played, turned to small groups using loosely constructed scores, or no scores at all. The bop group usually comprised a saxophone, a trumpet, a piano, a string bass, and drums; and bop styles featured extended harmonies that were reminiscent of avant-garde classical music. Bebop emphasized faster tempos than were usual in jazz, uneven phrasing, and ensemble passages played in unison rather than in conventional harmonies. The piano supplied chordal punctuations, and the string bass assumed a new importance as the center of the rhythm section. The guitarist Charlie CHRISTIAN, the trumpeter Dizzy GILLESPIE, the saxophonist Charlie PARKER, and the pianist Thelonious MONK (whose beret and horn-rimmed glasses became symbols of the movement) were major figures in bop. In the late 1940s a softer, more subtle brand of bop, or "cool jazz," was played by musicians like Miles DAVIS and Gerry MULLIGAN. Bop did not continue as a coherent movement beyond the early 1950s, but its idioms colored all branches of later jazz.

ROGER BAILEY

Bibliography: Collier, J. L., *The Making of Jazz* (1978); Dance, S., ed., *Jazz Era: The Forties* (1961; repr. 1987); Gitler, I., *Swing to Bop* (1985); Williams, M. T., *The Jazz Tradition*, rev. ed. (1983).

becard   [bay-kahrd']

The becard is any bird of the genus *Pachyramphus* or *Platypsaris* in the COTINGA family, Cotingidae; 16 species are represented by numerous subspecies in tropical and subtropical

The rose-throated becard, Platypsaris aglaiae, *is a small, 16-cm-long (6.5-in) woodland bird. It is the only member of the colorful family Cotingidae found in the United States. The male is at left.*

America. Becards are relatively inconspicuous, small, big-headed, and stout-billed; they are brownish, grayish, or greenish, and resemble flycatchers. In southern Arizona the northernmost cotinga, the rose-throated becard, is found. The males are gray with a pink throat; females are brown. The diet includes fruits and insects. The pendant, globular nest has side entrances.

WILLIAM A. LUNK

Beccafumi, Domenico   [bek-kah-foo'-mee, doh-may'-nee-koh]

Domenico di Pace, called Beccafumi, b. *c.*1485, d. May 1551, was an Italian Mannerist painter of the Sienese school. His early works show the influence of Sodoma, Raphael, and Michelangelo. Later, however, he developed a more personal style. In paintings such as *The Fall of the Rebel Angels* (*c.*1525; Pinacoteca, Siena) and *The Birth of the Virgin* (*c.*1543; Accademia Siena) the figures are elongated, the vivid colors are suffused with glowing light, and dramatic perspective effects are achieved. These works have an emotionally charged quality that is characteristic of MANNERISM. Beccafumi was a sculptor and architect as well as a painter. Most of his work was done in Siena, and his many commissions there included a number of floor mosaics for the cathedral.   TANIA BAYARD

Bibliography: Freedberg, Sydney J., *Painting in Italy: 1500–1600* (1971).

Beccaria, Cesare Bonesana   [bek-kah-ree'-ah, chay'-zah-ray boh-nay-zah'-nah]

Cesare Bonesana Beccaria, b. Mar. 15, 1738, d. Nov. 28, 1794, was an Italian criminologist and economist. His *Dei delitti e delle pene* (Essay on Crimes and Punishments, 1764) is one of the most influential treatises on criminal justice ever written. He held that punishment should not exceed what was necessary to maintain public order. He opposed capital punishment, torture, and secret proceedings. The 19th-century English reformer Jeremy BENTHAM took up Beccaria's ideas, and they influenced the penal laws of a number of European countries. Beccaria also wrote on economics, anticipating some of the ideas of Adam SMITH and Thomas MALTHUS. From 1771 until his death he served as a public official in Milan.

Bibliography: Maestro, Marcello, *Cesare Beccaria and the Origins of Penal Reform* (1972) and *Voltaire and Beccaria as Reformers in Criminal Law* (1942; repr. 1972); Phillipson, Coleman, *Three Criminal Law Reformers: Beccaria, Bentham, Romilly* (1923).

Becher, Johannes R.   [besh'-ur]

Johannes Robert Becher, b. May 22, 1891, d. Oct. 11, 1958, was German EXPRESSIONISM's most identifiably orthodox Communist poet. He was a member of the rebellious Spartakus Group, and his early experimentation with form gave way to a strict SOCIALIST REALISM. His most famous expressionist poem was "An Europa" (To Europe, 1916). He joined the German Communist party in 1919. In 1933 the Nazis forced Becher into exile, and in 1935 he settled in Moscow as editor of *Internationale Literatur, Deutsche Blätter*. After the war he was appointed cultural commissar of poetry in East Germany and demanded strict socialist dogma from writers. His own Marxist works include *Heimkehr* (Homecoming, 1946) and *Neue deutsche Volkslieder* (New German Folk Songs, 1950).

SOL GITTLEMAN

Bechet, Sidney   [beh-shay']

The jazz clarinetist and soprano saxophonist Sidney Bechet, b. New Orleans, May 14, 1897, d. May 14, 1959, began playing clarinet as a child and by the time he was 17 had performed with every major New Orleans jazz band. The first JAZZ musician to make serious use of the soprano saxophone, Bechet was famous as the creator of long, fluid, intensely melodic improvisations and for his unique vibrato tone, which made everything he played recognizably his own. Highly acclaimed in Europe, Bechet lived in France from 1928 until his death.

Bibliography: Bechet, Sidney, *Treat It Gentle* (1960; repr. 1978); Schuller, Gunther, *Early Jazz* (1968).

Bechuanaland: see BOTSWANA.

Beckenbauer, Franz

The West German soccer player Franz Beckenbauer, b. Sept. 11, 1945, became one of the world's best during the 1960s and '70s, revolutionizing the sweeper-back position by constantly attacking. Beckenbauer captained the winning West German World Cup team in 1974 and was European player of the year twice (1972, 1976) before starting a new soccer career in the United States with the North American Soccer League's New York Cosmos (1977–80, 1983). He won the NASL's Most Valuable Player award in 1977 and led the Cosmos to 3 NASL championships (1977–78, 1980). Beckenbauer soon began to coach; he led West Germany to the 1990 World Cup.

Becker, Boris

West German tennis star Boris Becker, b. Nov. 22, 1967, was the surprise 17-year-old winner of Wimbledon in 1985, a tournament he won in 1986 and 1989, as well. His fourth Grand Slam title was the U.S. Open of 1989, the year of his number-one world ranking. In both 1988 and 1989, Becker led West Germany to victory in the Davis Cup. He is a strong, sometimes acrobatic serve-and-volley player.

Becker, Carl

Carl Lotus Becker, b. Blackhawk County, Iowa, Sept. 7, 1873, d. Apr. 10, 1945, was an American historian who taught at Cornell University from 1917 to 1945. Regarding historical facts as present images, he argued that all historical knowledge is basically subjective. Becker studied the ideas of the American and French revolutions in *The Declaration of Independence* (1922) and *The Heavenly City of the Eighteenth Century Philosophers* (1932).

Bibliography: Smith, Charlotte W., *Carl Becker: On History and the Climate of Opinion* (1973).

Becket, Saint Thomas

Thomas Becket, b. *c.*1118, the chancellor of England under HENRY II and archbishop of Canterbury, became a famous martyr when he was murdered in his own cathedral on Dec. 29, 1170.

As a young man, Becket had joined the household of Archbishop Theobald of Canterbury and lived the life of an ambitious young cleric. He made contacts with patrons and was later recommended to Henry II, who appointed him chancellor in 1154. Becket's skill as an administrator, his charm, and his initiative created strong bonds of affection and reliance between the two men. His ambition showed itself in his building projects, and he was lavish in his hospitality.

When Theobald died in 1161, the king forced Becket's nomination and appointment as the archbishop of Canterbury. It was clear that the king hoped to rely on his close ties with Becket to bring the church into submission with the rest of his realm. But when Becket became archbishop he devoted himself to the task of being leader of the church in England with the same energy he had shown in earlier tasks. Soon the former friends were clashing as each sought to do his duty.

A critical break came in the disputes over the Constitutions of Clarendon (1164), which specified the extent of state control over the church and the clergy and the competence of church courts. Under pressure, Becket at first submitted, but then he recanted. This led to a fierce battle, and Becket was exiled for six years. He spent the time in France. Appeal was made to Pope Alexander III to moderate the intransigent stance on both sides.

Meanwhile, Henry grew worried about who would succeed him and arranged for his son Henry to be crowned in 1170 by the archbishop of York while Becket was still in exile. This was a clear violation of the rights of Canterbury to preside over the coronation. Eventually Henry had to yield, and a reconciliation with Becket was arranged.

Becket then began to press charges against those who had

Thomas Becket, archbishop of Canterbury, was slain by four of King Henry II's knights in Canterbury Cathedral. At odds with Becket over a succession of church-state issues, the king is reputed to have exclaimed, in a fit of temper, "Who will rid me of this turbulent priest?" His knights took him at his word. This fresco depicting the murder dates from shortly after the event. (SS. Giovanni e Paolo, Spoleto, Italy.)

violated his rights. A mixture of jealousy on the part of some of the bishops, the king's rash temper, and the resentment and impetuosity of four knights led to the decision of the knights to kill Becket under the mistaken supposition that this was what Henry wanted. The murder shocked all Europe. Henry faced excommunication and was forced to do penance.

Thomas was canonized in 1173. His tomb at Canterbury became a shrine that was often visited by pilgrims such as those portrayed in *The Canterbury Tales* of Geoffrey Chaucer. The shrine was destroyed by order of Henry VIII during the Reformation. Feast day: Dec. 29.   THOMAS E. MORRISSEY

Bibliography: Barlow, Frank, *Thomas Becket* (1986); Duggan, Anne, *Thomas Becket: A Textual History of His Letters* (1980); Jones, Thomas M., *The Becket Controversy* (1970); Knowles, David, *Thomas Becket* (1971); Smalley, Beryl, *The Becket Conflict and the Schools* (1973).

Beckett, Samuel

The Irish-born playwright and novelist Samuel Beckett, b. Dublin, Apr. 13, 1906, d. Dec. 22, 1989, is best known for the absurdist drama WAITING FOR GODOT (1952; Eng. trans., 1954). First performed in Paris on Jan. 5, 1953, the play received worldwide acclaim and became the first of a series of critical successes, some of them written earlier.

Life. Beckett came from a Protestant Anglo-Irish family, but much of his work was first written in French. After graduating with a degree in Romance languages from Trinity College, Dublin, Beckett spent two years (1928–30) in Paris as an ex-

Samuel Beckett, Irish playwright and novelist, wrote most of his works in French and translated many of them into English himself. A Nobel laureate in 1969, Beckett is best known for Waiting for Godot *(1952), a play in which two tramps wait for a mysterious authority, whose real identity is never revealed.*

change lecturer. Here he met James JOYCE and became a member of his circle. In 1930, Beckett returned to Trinity as a lecturer. The academic life did not agree with him, however, and he left after only four terms to become a free-lance writer. He traveled in Europe and England, settling finally in Paris, his intermittent home since 1937.

Writings. Beckett's entire literary output, the narrative prose as well as the dramatic works, reduces basic existential problems to their most essential features. His concerns are fundamental, but never simplistic—the evanescence of life; time and eternity; the individual's sense of loneliness and alienation as a result of the impossibility of establishing genuine communication and contact with others; the mystery of self.

Beckett's major early works constitute a trilogy of interior monologues: *Molloy* (1951; Eng. trans., 1955), *Malone Dies* (1951; Eng. trans., 1956), and *The Unnameable* (1953; Eng. trans., 1958). Here Beckett explores the paradox of the self that can never know itself; in the very act of observing itself the self splits in two, an observing consciousness and an object that is being observed. The self perceives itself as a stream of words, a narration. Each time it tries to catch up with itself, it merely turns into another story, thus putting before the reader a succession of storytellers. Beckett's other prose works also view in various ways the entrapment and anguish of the individual in increasingly grotesque situations and the self's quest for identity from within. These include *Murphy* (1938; Eng. trans., 1957); *Watt* (1953), his last novel in English; and, *Stories and Texts for Nothing* (1955; Eng. trans., 1967), a collection of short stories.

Among his principal plays, pioneering works in the THEATER OF THE ABSURD, are *Endgame* (1957; Eng. trans., 1958), *Krapp's Last Tape* (1959), *Happy Days* (1961), *Play* (1964), *Not I* (1973), *That Time* (1976), and *Footfalls* (1976). He has also written radio and television plays. In his later stage and television plays, Beckett's style is so concise that each work is ultimately reduced to a compressed, immensely powerful image.

Beckett received the Nobel Prize for literature in 1969. The 16-volume *Collected Works* were published in 1970.

MARTIN ESSLIN

Bibliography: Acheson, J., and Arthur, K., *Beckett's Later Fiction and Drama* (1987); Bloom, H., intro., *Samuel Beckett* (1986) and *Samuel Beckett's "Waiting for Godot"* (1987); Brater, E., *Beyond Minimalism: Beckett's Late Style in the Theatre* (1987) and, as ed., *Beckett at 80* (1986); Cohn, R., *Back to Beckett* (1974) and *Just Play: Beckett's Theatre* (1980); Esslin, M., *Samuel Beckett: A Collection of Critical Essays* (1975); Gontarski, S. E., ed., *On Beckett* (1986); Harvey, L. E., *Samuel Beckett* (1970); Kenner, H., *Samuel Beckett* (1974); Mercier, V., *Beckett/Beckett* (1977); O'Brien, Eoin, *The Beckett Country* (1986); Rabinovitz, R., *The Development of Samuel Beckett's Fiction* (1984).

Beckford, William

William Beckford, b. 1760, d. 1844, was an English writer famous for his oriental tale *The History of the Caliph Vathek* and for his eccentric life. Born to great wealth, he early scandalized society with his enthusiasm for a young boy and his liaison with Louisa Beckford, his cousin's wife, with whom he dabbled in black magic. *Vathek*, which was originally written in French, was published in English in 1786; it describes a sadistic caliph's descent through vice into hell. After traveling in Europe and writing *Recollections of an Excursion to the Monasteries of Alcobaça and Batalha*, Beckford returned to England, where, ostracized from society, he built a fantastic Gothic structure, Fonthill Abbey, in 1796. His other writings include burlesques of contemporary sentimental fiction.

JANET M. TODD

Bibliography: Gemmett, Robert J., *William Beckford* (1977); Oliver, J. W., *The Life of William Beckford* (1932; repr. 1984).

Beckmann, Max

The German painter and printmaker Max Beckmann, b. Feb. 12, 1884, d. Dec. 27, 1950, was one of the major expressionist artists of the 20th century. Beckmann studied art at the conservative Weimar Academy and in 1906 exhibited with the impressionist-dominated Berlin Secession. In 1910 he was

In Self-Portrait with Red Scarf *(1917), the German expressionist Max Beckmann suggests the psychological disturbance brought about by war. Beckmann was deeply affected by his experiences as a medical corpsman during World War I. (Staatsgalerie, Stuttgart.)*

elected to its board. He defended realism against expressionism in a published exchange with the Blaue Reiter artist Franz MARC in 1912. His early paintings were influenced by the styles of Eugène Delacroix and El Greco. Only after World War I did Beckmann's art become a psychological, expressionistic statement charged with highly personal, symbolic imagery.

During World War I he served in the medical corps but was released after suffering a nervous breakdown. His experiences in the battlefield surgery tent supplied many of the images of physical torture that later appeared in his art as the metaphor for an anguished emotional life. His painting entitled *The Night* (1918–19; Kunstsammlung Nordrhein-Westfalen, Düsseldorf), a ghastly depiction of a gang of thugs ravaging a tenement dwelling, expresses a symbolic synthesis of the psychological brutality of the time. In 1925, Beckmann joined the faculty of the Frankfurt Art Institute, where he remained until discharged by the Nazis in 1933. He moved to Berlin and completed the well-known *Departure* (1932–33; Museum of Modern Art, New York), the first of his large-scale triptychs. It can be interpreted both as a description of escape from Nazi oppression and as an allegory of spiritual freedom. After Beckmann's work was included in the Nazi-organized Degenerate Art Exhibition of 1937, he emigrated to Amsterdam. Many of his most powerful works date from this time.

Beckmann taught at Washington University, St. Louis (1947–49), and at the Brooklyn Museum School, New York (1949–50).

IDA K. RIGBY

Bibliography: Fischer, Friedhelm W., *Max Beckmann* (1973); Kessler, Charles S., *Max Beckmann's Triptychs* (1970); Schultz-Hoffman, Carla, and Weiss, Julia C., *Max Beckmann: A Retrospective* (1984).

See also: GERMAN ART AND ARCHITECTURE.

Becque, Henry François   [bek]

A French dramatist and critic, Henry François Becque, b. Apr. 18, 1837, d. May 12, 1899, established the vogue for naturalistic drama in France at the end of the 19th century. He is best known for two ironic comedies, *Les Corbeaux* (The Vultures, 1882) and *The Woman of Paris* (1885; Eng. trans., 1943).

STUART E. BAKER

Bécquer, Gustavo Adolfo   [bay-kair']

Gustavo Adolfo Bécquer, b. Feb. 17, 1836, originally named Gustavo Adolfo Domínguez Bastida, was an important Spanish poet, influenced by the poetry of romanticism. The poetry in *Symphony of Love* (1860; Eng. trans., 1974) concerns the typical romantic themes of melancholy and death. Sickly all his life, he died of pneumonia and hepatitis on Dec. 22, 1870. He also wrote short stories and romantic tales.

Becquerel, Antoine Henri [be-krel']

The French physicist Antoine Henri Becquerel, b. Dec. 15, 1852, d. Aug. 25, 1908, is known for his discovery of RADIOAC-TIVITY (1896), for which he shared the 1903 Nobel Prize for physics with Marie and Pierre CURIE. Among a variety of luminescent crystals, Becquerel found that only those containing uranium emitted radiation naturally. This significant discovery opened the way to nuclear physics. He subsequently discovered that the radiations of radium comprise electrons, and he was the first to supply experimental evidence of the phenomenon of radioactive transformation. He was elected to the Academy of Sciences (1889) and appointed professor of physics at the Museum of Natural History (1892) and the École Polytechnique (1895). E. ROBERT PAUL

Bibliography: Jones, Bessie Z., ed., *The Golden Age of Science: Thirty Portraits of the Giants of 19th Century Science* (1966); McGowen, Tom, *Radioactivity: From the Curies to the Atomic Age* (1986).

bed

A bed is a piece of furniture on which persons sleep or rest. Although the bed, in one form or another, has been in use since ancient times, it has served as a common article of furniture in the Western world only during the last three or four centuries. Japanese tradition favors the *futon*, a soft mat stored away during the day. String hammocks are common sleeping equipment in Africa and Asia.

Throughout history, most people slept on the ground, on straw mats, or on skins, with a round of wood or a cloak or blanket for a pillow. In some cultures heated platforms served for sleeping at night and for other activities during the day. From the earliest civilizations, however, the privileged have slept on beds, often made or decorated with precious materials and sometimes used, like thrones, for holding court.

During Roman times, rough, wooden shelf beds were used by the commoners. The rich used reclining couches (on which they also slept) in place of chairs at meals, and in the imperial era these were of such massive proportions that six people could recline and eat on one bed.

After the dissolution of the Roman Empire, beds vanished from common use and began to appear again in aristocratic houses only in the late Middle Ages. In northern Europe many were built into the walls, often next to a fireplace, so that they might be closed within doors or curtains to provide a warm and relatively private resting place. Beds were often built into corners, or completely surrounded by richly decorated wood to form the ''box'' bed.

The Elizabethan era saw the bed's emergence as a royal monument. Beds, both in England and on the continent, assumed massive proportions and were heavily decorated with carving and costly fabrics. Much of a court's business might be conducted around the royal bed. In middle-class households, beds became the most valued object of furniture.

As the bed became common in most households, bed frames became lighter and less ornate. Metal bedsteads, first manufactured commercially in England, became popular late in the 19th century. Eventually, double innerspring mattresses on legs were often used without any bed frame. The contemporary era has also brought the sofa bed—a couch containing a hidden, folded mattress—along with the newer water-filled mattress and a reversion to platform types. WILLIAM C. KETCHUM, JR.

Bibliography: Fitzgerald, O. P., *Three Centuries of American Furniture* (1981); Lucie-Smith, Edward, *Furniture: A Concise History* (1985).

bed-wetting

Bed-wetting, or enuresis, is involuntary urination that usually occurs during sleep. It is common in children up to age 5, and about 15 percent of older children aged 5 to 13 also have bed-wetting episodes. The precise cause is unknown, but it may be due to delayed development of bladder capacity, constipation, or disease, such as urinary tract infection, kidney disease, or diabetes mellitus. Emotionally stressful events, such as hospitalization or loss of a parent, may contribute to enuresis. In most cases children outgrow the problem, but persistent cases require a physical examination in case there is an underlying medical problem.

Enuresis not caused by a physical problem can be halted with effective behavior-modification therapies. Another technique uses a battery-operated urinary alarm that is set off by wetting; eventually the child learns to waken before the alarm. In rare cases the drug imipramine is prescribed.

Bibliography: Welford, H., *Toilet Training and Bed Wetting* (1988).

bedbug

The bedbug, C. lectularius, can ingest its body weight in human blood during a five-minute feeding. Engorged, it may survive for months without another feeding.

Bedbugs, family Cimicidae, order Hemiptera, are flat, broadly oval, wingless bugs about 0.6 cm (0.24 in) in length that feed by sucking blood from birds and mammals. The common bedbug that attacks humans is *Cimex lectularius*, which is often a pest in houses, hotels, military barracks, and other living quarters; it also attacks animals. This insect is usually nocturnal, hiding in cracks and crevices during the day. The adults may live several months and can survive long periods without food. Bedbugs inflict irritating bites; they are not known to cause disease. DONALD J. BORROR

Bede, Saint [beed]

An English Benedictine scholar, the Venerable Bede, b. *c.*672, d. May 27, 735, was one of the most learned men of his time. He wrote on practically every area of knowledge, including grammar, orthography, metrics, figures of speech, chronology, theology, and history. He also composed a summary of the works of Roman naturalists. His most important work is the *Ecclesiastical History of the English People* (completed 731), still considered an important source for early English history. As a historian he is noted for his reliability and perception. On his deathbed he reputedly dictated a translation of the Gospel of St. John into English. He was declared venerable by the Council of Aachen in 836, and he was canonized and formally recognized as a doctor of the church in 1899. Feast day: May 27. DAVID HARRY MILLER

Bibliography: Brown, George H., *Bede the Venerable* (1987); Duckett, E. S., *Anglo-Saxon Saints and Scholars* (1947; repr. 1967); Hunter Blair, P., *The World of Bede* (1971); Hurst, D., *The Venerable Bede: Commentary on the Catholic Epistles* (1985).

Bedford

Bedford (1981 est. pop., 74,500) is the county town of Bedfordshire in south central England, on the River Ouse about 70 km (43 mi) north of London. A quiet residential community, Bedford also has diversified industries producing farm implements, diesel engines, and transistors.

The site of a Saxon victory over the Britons in 571, the town is also associated with John BUNYAN, who preached and taught while imprisoned there in the 17th century.

Bedfordshire

Bedfordshire, also called Bedford (1984 est. pop., 515,700), is a county in the southern Midlands of England. It covers 1,235 km² (477 mi²). Bedford is the county town. Drained by the Great Ouse River, the landscape of Bedford is level except in the south, where a spur of the Chiltern Hills is found. Agriculture is the primary economic activity, supplying wheat, vegetables, and dairy products to nearby London. Diversified manufacturing takes place in Bedford and Luton. Woburn Abbey (built 1747), the home of the dukes of Bedford, is a famous tourist attraction.

Bedfordshire was settled by the Romans, then the Anglo-Saxons, and, by 1016, the Danes. Because of a large influx of Protestant refugees from the Continent during the 17th century, Bedford was a center of opposition to King Charles I during the ENGLISH CIVIL WAR.

Bédier, Joseph   [bay-dee-ay']

Joseph Bédier, b. Jan. 28, 1864, d. Aug. 29, 1938, was a French scholar whose illustrated history of French literature, written with Paul Hazard, is still a standard work of reference. A medievalist, he published studies of the origins of early epic and narrative poetry in French and produced a modern version of the Tristan and Isolde legend in 1900.   ROBIN BUSS

Bedlam

Bedlam is a popular name for Bethlehem Royal Hospital, London, which, as the Hospital of St. Mary of Bethlehem, became England's first hospital for the mentally ill about 1400. The word has come to mean "a confused uproar."

Bedlington terrier

The Bedlington terrier was developed by workers in northern England as a ratter and fighting dog. Its coat gives it a lamblike appearance.

The Bedlington terrier is a medium-sized, graceful breed of dog with a rounded head, hanging ears, a convex curve to the back, and a distinctive curly coat that makes it look like a lamb. The dog stands 39.4–42 cm (15.5–16.5 in) at the shoulder and weighs 7.7–10.4 kg (17–23 lb). The triangular ears are tasseled at the tip, and the tail tapers to a point; it is carried low. The soft but crisp cast, usually light gray, comes in a broad range of shades approaching blue in darkness and just off-white in lightness. Sandy, liver, blue and tan, sandy and tan, and liver and tan are also seen. At ease, the dog appears mild and gentle. When aroused, it is alert and full of energy. It is generally agreed that the Bedlington originated in the mining area of that name in the county of Northumberland, England, in the early 19th century. It was used to hunt badgers and catch rats and as a fighting dog but then became popular as a household pet. It has an obedient disposition and a unique lightness of movement.

Bibliography: Young, Elinore, *How to Raise and Train a Bedlington Terrier* (1966).

Bedloe's Island: see STATUE OF LIBERTY.

Bedny, Demian   [byed-nyee', dyim-yahn']

Demian Bedny is the pseudonym of E. A. Pridvorov, b. Apr. 13, 1883, d. May 25, 1945, a Russian poet of peasant birth famous for his fables and folk poems on propagandistic Soviet themes. His poems appeared regularly in *Pravda*, and he was one of the favorite poets of Vladimir Lenin. His satirical "Heroes" (1936) poked fun at Russian historical figures.
                R. D. SYLVESTER

Bedouin   [bed'-oo-in]

The Bedouin (Arabic: *badawi*, "desert dweller") are Arabic-speaking pastoral nomads in the Middle East and North Africa. The Bedouin are estimated to comprise one-tenth of the population of the Middle East (see ARABS). They are mainly associated with camel herding in desert areas, although many Bedouin in more favorable grazing areas also tend sheep, goats, or cattle.

Bedouin society is generally organized into patrilineal corporate groups, varying in size from 50 to several hundred members. In the cooler, rainy season, Bedouin typically migrate in small groups into the desert with their animals. In the hot, dry season they congregate in larger groups around water sources on the desert margins, especially in the vicinity of towns and markets. Some groups make annual migrations of as far as 1,000 km (620 mi) in each direction.

Many Bedouin tribes are formed into large confederacies, some of which have played an important role in the history of the Middle East. Converted to Islam in the 7th century, the Bedouin formed the armies that facilitated the expansion of Islam through North Africa and into Central Asia. In recent years the accelerating economic development in most Arab countries has made the Bedouin way of life increasingly sedentary.   BRIAN SPOONER

Bibliography: Abu-Lughod, Lila, *Veiled Sentiments* (1987); Chatty, Dawn, *From Camel to Trucks: The Bedouin in the Modern World* (1985); Eastip, Wayne, *Bedouin* (1985); Johnson, Alex R., *Living among the Bedouin Arabs* (1985); Marx, E., and Shmueli, A., eds., *The Changing Bedouin* (1983); Murray, G. W., *Sons of Ishmael: A Study of the Egyptian Bedouin* (1935; repr. 1977); Raswan, Carl, *Black Tents of Arabia* (1947; repr. 1977).

bedsore

A bedsore is an ulcer of the skin suffered by a bedridden patient who is unable to change position for a long period of time. Constant pressure on the skin and tissue cuts off the blood supply to a particular location, causing the skin to redden and later take on a bluish discoloration. Eventually, the tissue dies and the skin sloughs off. An untreated bedsore may ulcerate and penetrate to the bone.

bedstraw

Bedstraw, *Galium*, is a slender herb in the madder family, Rubiaceae. Bedstraw plants produce stalkless leaves in whorls and abundant clusters of tiny white or yellow flowers. Once used in making mattresses, today bedstraw is grown mainly in rock gardens, where it produces a light airy effect. One of the best-known species in the United States is *G. mollugo*, also known as wild madder, great or white bedstraw, or false-baby's-breath. Yellow bedstraw, *G. verum*, sometimes appears as a weed in the eastern United States.

bee

Bees are any of 20,000 species of insects belonging to the superfamily Apoidea and the order Hymenoptera, including such important pollinators of plants as the bumblebees; the yellow-faced, or plasterer, bees; the mining, or burrower, bees; and the economically important honeybees of the genus *Apis*, the only domesticated insects besides the silkworm. Honeybees are known for the honey and wax they produce and their ability to communicate with one another through dancelike postures (the so-called dance language).

Only 500 species of bees are social; these include the bumblebees, the tropical stingless bees, and the honeybees. They form colonies of from several hundred to 80,000 individuals, organized in rigid caste systems, and secrete wax from which they build their nests.

Most other species of bees either are solitary—secreting no wax and nesting in the ground, hollow plant stems, or similar niches—or, like the cuckoo bees, are parasitic in the nests of others. The solitary bees, named for the material or method they use to construct nests for their young, include the plasterer, burrower, mining, mason, and leaf-cutter bees.

A worker honeybee, Apis mellifera, *sucks flower nectar with its tonguelike glossa and stores the nectar in its honey stomach. The bee regurgitates the honey and either stores it in cells or feeds drones, larvae, and the queen. The worker bee carries pollen in a pollen basket located on its hind legs and scrapes the pollen off with its foreleg bristles. The bee has no true heart or lungs; instead, a blood vessel and several air sacs extend the length of its body. Most of its thorax consists of muscles that operate the hind and fore wings. A worker bee does not lay eggs and so has ovaries (not shown) that are useless and extremely small.*

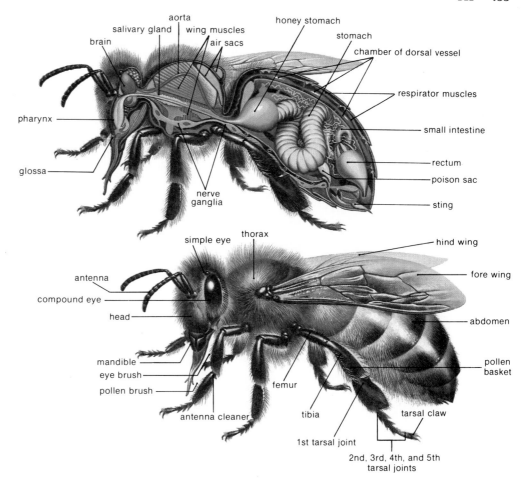

BEES AND WASPS

Bees belong to the same order as wasps. Like wasps, bees have mouth parts adapted for both chewing and sucking, but the bee's tongue is longer than the wasp's and better suited for gathering nectar from a greater variety of flowers. As adults, bees and almost all wasps feed only on nectar or honey; young wasps are fed only insects and spiders, whereas young bees are fed only nectar and pollen. Nectar is a sugary substance produced at the base of petals in many flowers and made into honey by bees.

Some wasplike bees swallow pollen and nectar, which they regurgitate into the cells in which they lay their eggs. Most bees, however, are distinguished from wasps by modifications that enable them to collect pollen. Bees have branched and feathery (plumose) body hairs. Females have brushes on their legs, and they use these brushes to remove pollen that sticks to the body hairs. The pollen is then stored under the abdomen or on the broadened hind legs. The parasitic cuckoo bees, however, can be distinguished from wasps only by the presence of the branched hairs characteristic of bees.

THE BEE FAMILIES

The Apoidea are subdivided into several families on the basis of how their wings are veined, and other criteria. Most of the 20,000 species are solitary bees. The queen constructs her own nest of one or more brood cells. She then stocks the cells with pollen and nectar to provide food for the larvae and deposits her eggs just before sealing the cell.

Some species are gregarious and place their nests in close proximity to each other. When such bees share a common entrance, a division of labor may be observed—for example, one bee may guard the entrance against parasites or predators. Bees are considered truly social when there is a single queen, when a worker caste of nonreproductive females

shares in the construction of the nest and other duties, and when the larvae are fed gradually.

Halictidae and Andrenidae. The family Halictidae constitutes 60 to 70 percent of the Apoidea, and the family Andrenidae another 20 percent. Queens of these families dig simple or branched tunnels in the ground and construct cells of firmly tamped earth, lined with waterproof secretions from the salivary glands to maintain the humidity required by the larvae. Those that do not secrete such linings have larvae that spin cocoons. A mass of pollen mixed with nectar is placed in the cell; the shape of this mass varies among species. In all species, however, minimal contact occurs between the mass and the cell wall and serves to deter the growth of mold. One species makes its pollen ball with a tripod of three short legs.

An egg is laid in each cell, and the tunnel is filled with loose dirt. The hatched larva uses the pollen as food, then pupates and transforms into an adult—a complete metamorphosis—and finally digs itself out of the tunnel.

In four species of Halictidae, the brood cells are not capped but are left open for removal of larval skins, dead larvae, and feces. This represents another step in the evolution toward more complex social behavior for which a mathematical genetic model has been formulated.

Halictidae are especially important because they include both the solitary and the truly social. The females that are produced in the fall eat only nectar before hibernating; but when they emerge in the spring they eat pollen, which stimulates ovarian development, and they undertake nesting.

One halactid, the alkali bee, *Nomia melandri*, nests in communities of thousands of individuals with almost 2,700 nests per square meter (250 per square foot). Eighty of these bees are equal to a small colony of honeybees in pollinating alfalfa blooms, and so farmers often establish alkali bees near alfalfa fields. A hectare of such nests is equal to almost 125 colonies

Life in a honeybee hive centers around the queen bee (A). The queen is constantly encircled by workers, who tend to all her needs. Royal birth chambers (B) are the largest of three types of cells in a hive; the other two cells house worker larvae (C) and drone larvae (D). Household workers secrete wax to build new cells (E). Foraging workers fly back to the hive loaded with pollen carried on their hind legs (F) and with nectar stored in their stomachs. Household workers receive and store pollen (G) and honey from the foragers. An intruding moth (H) is attacked by workers, but only a queen of the hive attacks and tries to sting to death an intruding queen from another colony (I). In hot weather, workers fan the air with their wings to keep the hive at a comfortable temperature (J); in the winter, bees huddle together for warmth (K). A queen bee (bottom) lays one egg in a cell (1), and the hatched larva (2) is fed royal jelly, a protein-rich food made by workers, or bee-bread, which is a mixture of pollen and honey. When the larva begins to pupate (3), workers seal its cell with wax. A mature bee (4) breaks open the cap of its cell, which is used to store pollen (5) or honey (6).

of honeybees (1 acre = 50 colonies). The males of some species, on the other hand, stake out a territory and chase away all bees except females of their own species.

Megachilidae. The family Megachilidae includes the shiny, bluish-green mason bees (*Osmia*), which construct small cells in clusters of 10 to 30 under stones, in decaying wood, in empty snail shells, or in the deserted burrows of other bees. The leaf-cutting bees (*Megachile*) make cells by finding a niche in wood, under loose bark, or in the ground and lining it with neatly cut leaves. Oblong pieces of leaves are used for the sides, and circular pieces for the ends.

Xylocopidae. The large carpenter bees of the family Xylocopidae look like dark, shiny bumblebees without hair on the abdomen. They alarm anxious homeowners, sometimes with good reason, with their habit of digging burrows in wood porches and in barns. The excavations may be 1 m (3 ft) long and are often reused in successive years.

Bombidae. Bumblebees (Bombidae) leave their nest in the autumn, and the fertilized queens hibernate in some protected place during the winter. In the spring each queen builds a nest of moss or grass, preferably in a deserted rodent nest. From scales secreted by abdominal glands, she makes a honeypot of wax and then makes a cell and half fills it with pollen before depositing her eggs in it. The queen covers the eggs with a layer of wax and sits on them like a brooding hen, sipping honey from her pot. After the larvae hatch, they eat the pollen and grow, then spin cocoons in which to pupate. When the workers emerge, they cut away the upper half of the cells, and the remainder is used as a receptacle for nectar.

Bumblebee populations vary from year to year, depending on environmental factors; but one typical nest collected in Wisconsin contained one queen, 515 adult workers, 117 worker and 119 queen pupae, 101 larvae, 308 eggs contained in 18 cells on cylinders of pollen, and 709 empty worker cells filled with honey.

The larger workers maintain the covering over the nest and collect food, and the smaller ones care for the young larvae and do the inside work.

Only males are produced late in the summer, and female larvae literally may be jettisoned to control the population. When workers lay eggs, the queen may chase the workers away and eat the eggs; but if the queen dies or is removed, one of the larger workers will take her place within four hours or less. The difference in size of workers is dependent upon the amount of food they have available to eat when they are larvae.

Bumblebees are superior to other bees in pollinating red clover, since they have a tongue that is 2.5 mm (0.1 in) longer than that of honeybees. Artificial methods of rearing bumblebees have been successful, but a better technique may be to encourage natural populations by providing forage plants that bloom eight to nine weeks prior to red clover, so that the colonies have abundant food on which to rear brood.

Meliponidae. The stingless bees (Meliponidae) have acquired many methods of defense to replace their long-lost stinging apparatus. Several hundred species exist in the tropics and subtropics, with colonies ranging in size from a few hundred to 80,000 individuals.

The colonies nest in cavities and build walls, cells, and honeypots of cerumen, which is a mixture of resin, wax, and sometimes mud. If the nest is in the open, the walls are as much as 20 cm (8 in) thick, with many separate layers for insulation and protection. The small entrance hole may be guarded by a single bee. As among solitary bees, the brood cell is sealed after the egg is laid on stored food. Observers report that the queen eats both the food stored in brood cells and the unfertilized eggs, laid by workers, that would develop into males.

To establish a new nest, the workers select a site and seal all cracks with material brought from the parent colony. Honey and pollen are transferred, and males follow the workers to the new nest. When all is ready, a virgin queen flies from the old nest to the new one and soon makes a mating flight.

Before the introduction of honeybees from Europe, the only honey and wax available in South and Central America was that produced by stingless bees. The wax was used for casting gold ornaments, and the honey for alcoholic beverages used on ceremonial occasions. These bees are still being cultivated in various parts of the world.

Apidae. The family Apidae, which includes honeybees, no longer uses honeypots that could be damaged by exposure to the elements. Instead, honey and pollen are stored, and

American carpenter bee
(*Xylocopa virginica*)

leaf-cutter bee
(*Megachile latimanus*)

Halictid mining bee
(*Augochloropsis metallica*)

mason bee
(*Chalicodoma muraria*)

A female solitary bee constructs her own nest without help from other members of her species. Four main types of solitary bee are named according to how each builds its nest, which contains eggs, larvae, and pollen. The American carpenter bee, X. virginica, tunnels into wood and lays her eggs on a bed of pollen. She builds walls of sawdust and saliva between each egg. The leaf cutter bee, M. latimanus, also tunnels into wood and lines its nest with neatly cut pieces of leaves. The halictid mining bee, A. metallica, shares a common entrance into an underground nest with other females, although each has her own eggs and larvae. The mason bee, C. muraria, builds a globe of cemented earth; some species lay eggs inside snail shells.

brood is reared, in vertical combs with a layer of cells on each face. Of the four species of honeybees in this family, three occur only in Asia: *Apis dorsata*, the giant Indian bee, which builds a single comb as large as 1.5 m (5 ft) wide and 1 m (3 ft) long attached to rocks, trees, or buildings; *A. florea*, with a single comb about 8 to 12 cm (3 to 5 in) across; and *A. indica*, the Oriental hive bee, with nests of several combs sheltered in crevices of rocks or hollows of trees.

A. mellifera, the western honeybee or hivebee, also builds its nest of many combs in sheltered places and is found in the United States, Europe, Anatolia, and Africa. Colonies kept in hives yield an average of 23 kg (50 pounds) of honey.

Numerous geographic races have arisen as a result of natural selection. The brown or black German bees were imported from Europe to America by the early colonists. The Italian race was imported to Long Island in 1860; it is now the most common commercial variety, with Caucasians the second most popular. The so-called killer bees, of African origin and accidentally released in South America in the mid-1950s, are more aggressive and likely to sting intruders. They are also more inclined to swarm and are unsuitable for commercial beekeeping. (See BEE, KILLER.)

Unlike other bees, honeybees do not hibernate during cold weather. They last out the rigors of northern winters by feeding on stored supplies and sharing their body heat, clustering together in dense packs.

Socialization is most advanced in the Apidae. As new, young queens are about to emerge in an established hive, half of the colony leaves with the old queen and clusters on a nearby bush or tree while scout bees search for a new home. When the scouts appear to agree on a new location, the swarm departs. At the old nest, meanwhile, the first queen to emerge disposes of the other queens (by stinging them) before they have a chance to emerge. Within a few days, the virgin queen will fly to where drones assemble, and mate with 6 to 12 drones. The sperm from these drones is stored in a sac (spermatheca) and used during her egg-laying life of from two to five years or a maximum of nine.

Honeybees are subject to various diseases and parasites, including the bee mite, *Acarapis woodi,* which weakens bees and reduces their honeymaking and pollinating abilities. Legislation enacted in the United States in 1922 to regulate importation of honeybees was thought to have prevented this infestation, which has caused serious losses in other countries, but in 1984 the mite was found in New York, Florida, Texas, Louisiana, and South Dakota. As a result, more than 150 million honeybees were destroyed by beekeepers to prevent further spread of the mite.

DRONES AND WORKERS

Drones develop by parthenogenesis from unfertilized eggs that the queen produces by withholding sperm from the eggs laid in large drone cells. Drones lack stings and the structures needed for pollen collection; in the autumn they are ejected by the colony to starve, unless the colony is queenless. New drones are produced in the spring for mating.

Both queens and workers are produced from fertilized eggs. Queen larvae are reared in special peanut-shaped cells and fed more of the pharyngeal gland secretions of the nurse bees (bee milk or royal jelly) than the worker larvae are. The precise mechanism for this caste differentiation is still uncertain. Although workers are similar in appearance and behavior to other female bees, they lack the structures for mating. When no queen is present to inhibit the development of their ovaries, however, workers eventually begin to lay eggs that develop into drones.

PHEROMONES

The integrity of the colony is maintained by chemical secretions, or PHEROMONES. Workers secrete pheromones from the so-called Nasanov gland at the tip of the abdomen when they cluster, enter a new nesting site, or mark a source of nectar or water. The colony scent is recognizable by bees of the same colony because of its unique combination of components derived from the colony's particular collections of nectar and pollen.

When queens fly to mate, a mandibular-gland pheromone attracts the drones. The same gland produces another phero-

The social order of a honeybee hive consists of three castes: infertile female workers (A), male drones (B), and a queen (C). About 50,000 workers occupy a hive and perform such chores as building cells; feeding larvae, drones, and the queen; and scouting for flowers that might be pollen sources. Male drones number about 1,000 and are completely cared for by workers; their sole task is to fertilize a virgin queen, after which they are turned out of the hive and die of starvation. Only one queen lives in a hive, and her sole function is to lay her eggs, which ensure the existence of her colony.

A scout honeybee, once she finds a distant source of nectar, returns to her hive and performs a wag-tail dance that informs other bees of the nectar's location. First she faces the Sun's direction (vertical line) as she saw it while she flew toward the food; then she makes a figure-eight pattern. She wag-tails (diagonal line) down the center line of the pattern, showing the bees the direction of the food source with respect to the Sun's direction. Her dance also indicates how close the food is to the hive and how plentiful it is. Another form of dance is used to indicate food sources closer to the hive.

mone, called queen substance, which workers lick from the queen's body and pass along as they exchange food with one another. The eaten pheromone inhibits the ovaries of workers; when the queen's secretion is inadequate, the colony produces queen cells to supersede her.

The mandibular glands of workers produce an alarm odor, which serves to alert the colony when it is disturbed. Workers also produce a sting odor, which is released at the site of the sting and serves to direct other bees to the sting area. Stingless bees bite leaves at intervals along their flight path to provide a scent trail of mandibular secretions.

DANCE LANGUAGE

The ability of honeybees to communicate direction and distance from the hive to nectar sources through dance ''language'' has received widespread attention. In 1973, Karl von FRISCH received a Nobel Prize for deciphering the language, which consists of two basic dances: a dance in a circle, for indicating sources without reference to specific distance or direction; and a tail-wagging dance in which the exact distance is indicated by a number of straight runs with abdominal wagging—the fewer runs per minute, the farther away the source. Wing vibrations produce sounds at the same rate as the tail wagging and are detected by organs in the legs of other bees. Researchers have developed a robot ''bee'' that can communicate with other bees in this way (see ANIMAL COMMUNICATION).

The various species of *Apis*, and races of *A. mellifera*, indicate a particular distance by a different dance tempo. This may lead the individuals in colonies with a mixture of races to misunderstand messages about the distance to a feeding site. Stingless bees communicate only by sounds.

The direction, or azimuth, to the food source is indicated by the angle of the wagging dance to the Sun. That is, bees use the Sun as a compass, orienting the dance angle to the plane of polarization of the sunlight. Even when the Sun is obscured by clouds, bees can detect its position from the light in brighter patches of the sky. Ultraviolet designs in flowers serve as nectar guides to blooms in areas as small as 4 m^2 (43 ft^2).

Honeybees also have a little-understood, built-in clock that appears to be synchronized with the store of nectar in flowers. Hence, honeybees making the rounds of flowers in search of nectar always seem to be at the right place at the right time.

TOGE S. K. JOHANSSON

Bibliography: Goodman, L. J., and Fisher, R. C., eds., *The Behaviour and Physiology of Bees* (1991); Gould, J. L. and C. G., *The Honey Bee* (1988); Hubbell, S., *A Book of Bees* (1988); Michener, C. D., et al., *The Bee Genera of North and Central America* (1994); O'Toole, C., and Raw, A., *Bees of the World* (1992); Seeley, T. D., *Honeybee Ecology* (1985); Winston, M., *The Biology of the Honeybee* (1987) and *Killer Bees* (1992).

bee, killer

Killer bees, so-called because they are known to fatally attack humans and other animals, are a hybrid between the African honeybee, *Apis mellifera scutellata*, accidentally released in Brazil in 1956, and wild bees. Killer bees are aggressive and often attack in swarms. In comparison to domestic honeybees, killer bees are inefficient pollinators and produce limited quantities of honey. Now established in most of tropical America, killer bees are moving northward. They reached northern Mexico by the late 1980s and crossed into the southwestern United States in the 1990s, despite efforts to halt or control them. They pose an agricultural threat by interfering with the pollination of crops by domestic bees.

bee balm

Bee balm, bergamot, and horsemint are the common names applied to 12 North American species of the genus *Monarda* of the MINT family, Labiatae. The bee balm's red, rose, lavender, or white flowers attract bees, and the red flowers also attract hummingbirds. The American Indians used bee balm leaves to make tea, and the American colonists drank a tea made from one species, *M. didyma*, which they called Oswego tea. Some species have a thymelike flavor, and in Mexico a type of bee balm substitutes for oregano.

The carmine, or Nubian, bee eater, Merops nubicus, of central Africa, catches insects (especially bees and wasps) in flight. It is about 35 cm (14 in) long.

bee eater

The bee eater is any of 24 species of birds in the family Meropidae, order Coraciiformes, whose diet consists of bees, wasps, and other insects. Common to tropical regions, they have slim bodies with curved beaks. Bee eaters range from 15 to 36 cm (6 to 14 in) in length and have a variety of bright plumage colors. African bee eaters are brilliant green or blue-green, with wing and tail feathers of bright colors. Most species have a wide band of black from the beak through the eye, with wing tips also black. Bee eaters nest in burrows; some species live in colonies. Both male and female help incubate the eggs and care for the young.

Bee Gees, The

The Bee Gees is a British-Australian rock music group formed in 1963 by the Gibb brothers Barry, b. Sept. 1, 1947, and twins Robin and Maurice, b. Dec. 22, 1949. Distinguished by Robin's poignant, quavering vocal style and by their penchant for luxurious orchestration, the Bee Gees made several hit records in the late 1960s, including ''Massachusetts'' and ''I Gotta Get a Message to You.'' Then, after a period of relatively unsuccessful recordings, they returned to rock stardom in 1975 with the song ''Jive Talkin','' featuring a strong, incessant beat that helped usher in the disco-music fad. Their string of hits over the next few years included songs for the best-selling movie soundtrack *Saturday Night Fever* (1977).

Beebe, Charles W. [bee'-bee]

The American naturalist Charles William Beebe, b. Brooklyn, N.Y., 1877, d. June 4, 1962, was the curator of birds for the New York Zoological Society from 1899 to 1952 and head of its Department of Tropical Research from 1916 to 1952. Beebe gained broad professional recognition with his monumental study *Monograph of the Pheasants* (1918–22). In 1929 he established Nonsuch Station in Bermuda as a center for tropical ocean research and made many ocean descents. In 1934 he set a world record when he made a dive to a depth of 923 m (3,028 ft), where he observed and accurately described many previously unknown abyssal fish. In addition to numerous scientific papers, Beebe wrote many popular books describing his work and adventures.

beech

Beeches, *Fagus*, are hardwood deciduous trees belonging to the beech family, Fagaceae. About ten species grow in the north temperate zone of North America and Eurasia. Beeches

Beeches are common forest trees and an important source of commercial wood. Shown are the American beech, F. grandifolia (left), and its close relative, the European beech, F. sylvatica (right). A seed case (center) contains two or three edible seeds, which are sometimes used as food for livestock.

are characterized by a smooth, thin gray bark, which makes them a popular choice for ornamental planting. The slender, slightly zigzag twigs have very long, narrow, shiny brown buds covered with many scales. The short-stalked leaves alternate in the two rows; they are elliptic or ovate, long-pointed, coarsely saw-toothed, and have many straight veins. The fruit, which is a hard spiny burr containing two or three triangular, edible nuts, matures and splits open in the autumn.

The American beech, *F. grandifolia*, is the only species of beech native to the United States. Although it is now confined to the eastern United States, it once extended as far west as California and probably flourished over most of North America before the glacial period. This species is a major component of the northern hardwood forests of the United States, and grows where moisture is fairly abundant in the upper soil. The largest specimens, which are found in the Ohio and lower Mississippi River valleys, reach more than 36 m (120 ft) in height and 1.2 m (4 ft) in diameter. Within its wide range in eastern North America, the beech is associated with many other trees. Its wood, moderately hard and strong, is used for boxes because it does not impart any odor. It is also used for flooring and furniture and in papermaking.

The European beech, *F. sylvatica*, a major forest tree of central Europe, is much like the American beech but has a more ovate shape and shinier leaves that turn reddish brown, instead of yellow, in the fall. The leaves may remain attached to the twigs throughout the winter. European beech is used for furniture and firewood. It was the wood used in Gutenberg's printing blocks. About 45 varieties of European beech exist, several of which are grown as landscape trees in North America. Varieties found in the United States have bronzed foliage and are commonly called copper beeches.

Beech is thin-barked and very sensitive to fire, sunscald, and flooding. It is, however, tolerant of salt and not readily injured by ice accumulation. Long frost cracks in the bark are common in the north. The tree is attacked by many rot fungi. Scale insects often introduce the fungus that causes *Nectria* canker, the disease most affecting the beech. Fungus and insects have combined to kill a large number of beeches in northeastern North America.

Bibliography: Grimm, W. C., *The Illustrated Book of Trees* (1983); Harlow, W. M., and Harrar, E. S., *Textbook of Dendrology*, 6th ed. (1979); Hillier, H. G., *Hillier's Colour Dictionary of Trees and Shrubs* (1981).

Beecham, Sir Thomas

Sir Thomas Beecham, b. Apr. 29, 1879, d. Mar. 8, 1961, was one of the century's most celebrated conductors. His father was a baronet, and Beecham succeeded to the title in 1916. He studied at Oxford, but not formally in the music school. A wrist injury in 1904 ended plans to be a concert pianist; he made his first important conducting appearance in 1906, lead-

ing the New Symphony Orchestra he had founded that year. Beecham's symphonic concerts given around this time included new works by Richard Strauss and Frederick Delius, whom Beecham championed. As an operatic impresario, Beecham produced more than 60 works that were new to Britain. He introduced (1911) Russian ballet to London. In 1923 he retired for three years, only to reemerge with an impressive performance of Handel's *Messiah*.

Beecham made his American debut in 1928; in 1932 he founded the London Philharmonic Orchestra; he became artistic director of Covent Garden Opera in 1933. During World War II he conducted both opera and symphony in America. In 1947 he formed another orchestra, the Royal Philharmonic. A prolific recording artist who is credited with starting a Mozart cult in England, Beecham was notable not only for the vividness of his interpretations but also for his service to British music and musicians. He was also the author of an autobiography, *A Mingled Chime* (1943; repr. 1976), and of a biography of Frederick Delius (1958).   STEPHANIE VON BUCHAU

Bibliography: Cardus, Neville, *Sir Thomas Beecham* (1961); Gray, M. H., *Beecham: A Centenary Discography* (1980); Proctor-Gregg, Humphrey, *Beecham Remembered* (1976).

Beecher   (family)

The Beecher family was a 19th-century American family that made significant contributions to the religious and cultural life of the United States.

Lyman Beecher, b. New Haven, Conn., Oct. 12, 1775, d. Jan. 10, 1863, a Presbyterian minister, was one of the most representative figures of American religion during his time. He served three congregations (1799–1832) before becoming the president and a theological professor of Lane Theological Seminary in Cincinnati, Ohio (1832–52). In his first pastorate he campaigned against dueling, in his second against drink, in his third against Unitarianism, and at Lane against slavery. Throughout his career he promoted revivalism. Perhaps his most influential publication was *A Plea for the West* (1832), which praised the potential of the frontier while warning of the dangers of Roman Catholicism. Not the least of his gifts to American religion were his 13 children, who included the novelist Harriet Beecher STOWE, the educator Catharine, and four sons who followed in their father's footsteps to achieve national reputations as clergymen and educators: Edward (1803–95), Henry Ward, Charles (1815–1900), and Thomas Kinnicut (1824–1900).

Henry Ward Beecher, b. Litchfield, Conn., June 24, 1813, d. Mar. 8, 1887, the most conspicuous of the brothers, was noted for his eloquence and ability to reflect virtues of the common person. After serving two Presbyterian churches in Indiana for a decade, he moved in 1847 to the Plymouth Congregational Church in Brooklyn, N.Y. Here his appealing messages and sincere moral earnestness made him a national figure. Beecher's popularity continued during a sensational adultery trial in 1875, arising from an alleged affair with Mrs. Theodore Tilton. His congregation backed him throughout the trial, which ended with a hung jury.

Henry Ward Beecher influenced 19th-century life through his ability to articulate the standard values of most middle-class American citizens. Although not an exponent of original ideas, he brilliantly articulated his convictions. As his liberalism grew, he was among the few clergymen to abandon notions about miracles, future punishment, and Christ's divinity and support Charles Darwin's theory of evolution.

Eldest of the children, **Catharine Esther Beecher**, b. East Hampton, N.Y., Sept. 6, 1800, d. May 12, 1878, was an early advocate of education for women in the homemaking profession. She started a girls' school in Hartford, Conn., in 1823 and a similar school in the 1830s in Cincinnati, Ohio. She promoted the need for education for women by founding the American Women's Educational Association. Catharine was strongly opposed to the women's suffrage movement.

Bibliography: Beecher, Lyman, *Autobiography,* ed. by Charles Beecher, 2 vols. (1864; repr. 1976); Caskey, Marie, *Chariot of Fire: Religion and the Beecher Family* (1978); Clark, Clifford E., Jr., *Henry Ward Beecher* (1978); Rugoff, Milton, *The Beechers* (1981); Sklar, K. K., *Catherine Beecher* (1973).

beef: SEE MEAT AND MEAT PACKING.

beefeaters

Beefeaters is the popular name for the Yeomen of the Guard, who act as ceremonial escorts for the British sovereign on state occasions. Established in 1485, the Yeomen wear picturesque Tudor costumes of red and gold. The name *beefeater* probably dates from 1669, when Cosimo, grand duke of Tuscany, described these guards as "great eaters of beef." The Yeoman Warders of the Tower of London, who wear a similar uniform, are also often called beefeaters.

beefwood: SEE CASUARINA.

beekeeping

Beekeeping, or apiculture, is the cultivation of colonies of honeybees. Commercial beekeeping includes the production of HONEY and beeswax, the breeding of bees for sale, and the rental of bees for pollinating crops. Beekeeping in most of the world means cultivating the western honeybee, *Apis mellifera* (see BEE). The aggressive killer bee, a relative of the African honeybee, *A. mellifera scutellata,* however, is unsuitable for commercial beekeeping (see BEE, KILLER). In parts of Asia the eastern honeybee, *A. indica,* is cultivated, as is, on an experimental basis, the giant honeybee, *A. dorsata.*

Modern beekeeping is based on the ancient Greek technique of creating a so-called bee space. The hive comprised a basket containing a series of parallel wooden bars separated by a distance equal to that between honeycombs naturally built by bees. That distance is 6.350–9.525 mm (0.25–0.375 in), and any departure from this range results in the space being filled with comb or propolis. A honeycomb is a mass of hexagonal cells in the nest that contain brood and honey.

A beehive based on the ancient principle was developed (1851) in the United States by Lorenzo Lorraine Langstroth. The typical beehive today comprises a bottom board and several boxes containing movable frames and a cover. Each frame is furnished with a beeswax foundation imprinted with the hexagonal shapes of cell bottoms. The bees are guided by the imprinted cells in building their honeycombs.

THE POLLINATOR INDUSTRY

The world's annual production of more than 1,000,000 metric tons (1,102,000 U.S. tons) of honey could be replaced with other sugar products, but the services of honeybees as pollinators of some 90 crops would be lost. Mixed farming as practiced on small family farms has given way to more effi-

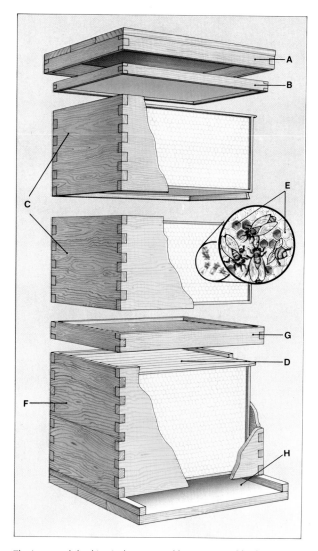

The Langstroth beehive is the type used by commercial beekeepers. A weatherproof outer cover (A) and inner cover (B) rest atop removable wooden boxes, or supers (C), that are vertically stacked. Each super has several removable frames (D) that contain wax imprinted with hexagonal shapes that serve as foundations for the wax cells (E) built by the bees. The hive usually contains two supers separated from the hive body, or brood chamber (F), by a queen excluder (G), which prevents the large queen bee, but not the smaller worker bees, from passing. The queen, therefore, lays her eggs in the brood chamber, which is also fitted with frames; workers tend to these eggs and can then move to the supers above to fill the cells with honey for storage. The hive body rests on a bottom board that includes the entrance (H) to the hive. Beekeepers can collect honey by removing full frames from the supers, without disturbing the brood chamber.

cient single-crop agribusiness, leaving little or no waste land where bees can find nesting sites or weeds that supply nectar and pollen. The use of pesticides to control harmful insects has also reduced the population of beneficial insects such as pollinators. Thus, fruit and seed growers contract with beekeepers to move honeybee colonies onto the farms. This ensures income to the beekeeper during years when honey production fails. The moving, however, increases the risk of spreading American foulbrood, a virulent disease of bees, so some beekeepers routinely feed antibiotics to avoid losses.

In North America new colonies are established with packages of bees, each container weighing 0.9 to 2.26 kg (2 to 5 lb), or small colonies called *nuclei,* shipped from breeders in the southern states. It is unlikely that a crop can be harvested from these colonies in the first season, because a hive requires 40.82 kg (90 lb) of honey for overwintering.

TOGE S. K. JOHANSSON

Bibliography: Goodman, L. J., and Fisher, R. C., eds., *The Behavior and Physiology of Bees* (1991); Graham, J. M., ed., *The Hive and the Honey Bee* (1992); Hubbell, S., *A Book of Bees* (1989); Morse, R., and Flottum, K., eds., *The ABC and XYZ of Bee Culture* (1990); Whynott, D., *Following the Bloom* (1992).

Beelzebub: see SATAN.

Beene, Geoffrey: see FASHION DESIGN.

beer

Beer is a beverage obtained by the YEAST-caused fermentation of a malted cereal, usually barley MALT, to which HOPS and water have been added. Among the earliest records of its use is a Mesopotamian tablet inscribed with a cuneiform recipe for the ''wine of the grain.'' The origin of beer brewing, however, has not been determined; nor is it known whether bread or beer was invented first.

The Mesopotamians and the Egyptians are thought to have been the first to render barley more suitable for brewing by malting, a process in which the barley grains are germinated, developing the enzymes that transform starch into fermentable sugars. The Greeks brewed beer from unmalted grains until they learned malting from the Egyptians. No conclusive evidence exists of beer brewing in Britain prior to the Roman occupation. The Germanic and Celtic tribes, however, made MEAD, brewed from corn and honey. The term *beer* did not come into common use until the Celtic word *beor* was applied to the malt brew produced in the monasteries of North Gaul. It is thought that hops, which have a preservative and aromatic effect on beer, were first used by Gallic monks.

BREWING

The centuries-old technique of brewing involves four steps: (1) mashing, the infusion of malt, water, and crushed cereal grains at temperatures that encourage the complete conversion of the cereal starch into sugars; (2) boiling, the concentration of the resulting ''wort,'' and the addition of hops; (3) fer-

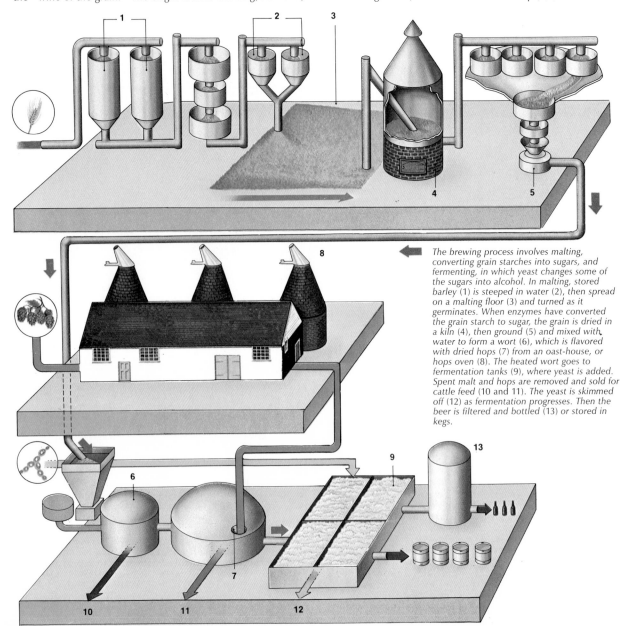

The brewing process involves malting, converting grain starches into sugars, and fermenting, in which yeast changes some of the sugars into alcohol. In malting, stored barley (1) is steeped in water (2), then spread on a malting floor (3) and turned as it germinates. When enzymes have converted the grain starch to sugar, the grain is dried in a kiln (4), then ground (5) and mixed with water to form a wort (6), which is flavored with dried hops (7) from an oast-house, or hops oven (8). The heated wort goes to fermentation tanks (9), where yeast is added. Spent malt and hops are removed and sold for cattle feed (10 and 11). The yeast is skimmed off (12) as fermentation progresses. Then the beer is filtered and bottled (13) or stored in kegs.

mentation, the addition of yeast to the wort, resulting in the production of alcohol and carbon dioxide gas, by-products of the action of yeast on sugar; (4) aging, in which proteins settle out of beer or are "digested" by enzymatic action. The aging process may last from 2 to 24 weeks. The carbonation that occurs during fermentation is now drawn off and forced back into the brew during bottling. The uniform clarity of modern beers results from filtration systems that use such agents as cellulose and diatomaceous earth. Additives are frequently used to stabilize foam and to maintain freshness, although they are less commonly used by European brewers. With few exceptions bottled and canned beer is PASTEURIZED in the container, in order to ensure that the yeast that may have passed through the filters is incapable of continued fermentation. Genuine draft beer is not pasteurized and must be stored at low temperature.

TYPES OF BREWED BEVERAGES

Most beer produced in the United States is lager—a pale, medium-hop-flavored beer that is kept for several months at a temperature of about 0.5° C (33° F) in order to mellow. It averages 3.3 to 3.4 percent alcohol by weight and is high in carbonation. European lagers—Pilsner is an example—are stored for a longer time and have a higher alcohol content.

Few dark beers are brewed in the United States with the exception of the seasonal bock, a dark-brown beer that owes its color to a roasting of the malt and is heavier and richer in taste than lager. Stout, a very dark beer, is brewed with a combination of roasted and regular malt and has a strong hop taste. Another dark beer, porter, was originally a mixture of ALE and beer and is today a sweet, malty brew, with a 6 to 7 percent alcohol content. Malt liquor is a beer made from a high percentage of fermentable sugars that are largely derived from malt. The resulting beverage has a higher alcohol content (5 to 9 percent by weight) than regular beer. The flavor is mildly fruity and spicy, without a hint of hops.

Low-calorie, or light, beers are made either by reducing the amount of grain used to make the brew or by adding an enzyme to reduce the starch content of the beer. They are lower in alcohol content (2.5 to 2.7 percent) than regular beer.

Many other fermented beerlike beverages are produced. In Japan steamed rice is hydrolyzed and fermented into SAKE. Kvass, a type of Russian beer, is brewed from barley-rye malt and fruits. In many tropical areas palm toddy is made from the sugary sap of coconut or palm trees. It is not intoxicating when fresh, but becomes so in a few hours.

BEER CONSUMPTION

Although ALCOHOL CONSUMPTION, in general, dropped throughout the 1980s and early 1990s, beer consumption showed slight gains. Low-alcohol beer grew in popularity, as did the more distinctive—and more expensive—imported beers. In response some U.S. brewers are now producing European-style beers, most of them intended only for local consumption.

Worldwide Germany boasts the highest per capita consumption of beer, as it has for many years.   JOHN H. PORTER

Bibliography: Jackson, Michael, *The New World Guide to Beer* 1990; Porter, John H., *All about Beer* (1974).

Beerbohm, Sir Max   [beer'-bawm]

Max Beerbohm, b. Aug. 24, 1872, d. May 19, 1956, was an English caricaturist, critic, and essayist. In the Edwardian age he was known as a dandy and wit.

Educated at Charterhouse and Oxford, where he contributed to *The Yellow Book* and associated with Oscar WILDE and his circle, he became a freelance writer and caricaturist in 1894. *The Works of Max Beerbohm* (1896), a book of essays and articles, and the fable *The Happy Hypocrite* (1897) earned him admission into the highest literary and social circles. He succeeded George Bernard SHAW in 1898 as drama critic for the *Saturday Review*, for which he produced a significant body of commentary on the intellectual and social life of the Edwardian period. He published further selections of characteristic essays in *More* (1899) and *Yet Again* (1909). His masterpiece, *Zuleika Dobson, or An Oxford Love Story* (1911), is his only full-length novel, a comic fantasy inspired by his experi-

ence of Oxford. In 1910 he settled in Italy, where he wrote the parodies in *A Christmas Garland* (1912) and the essays published in *And Even Now* (1920). He also continued to exhibit and publish caricatures of leading personalities of the age, including *Rossetti and His Circle* (1922), on which much of his present reputation rests. From 1935 he made occasional (and popular) radio broadcasts, collected in *Mainly on the Air* (1958). He was knighted in 1939.   RICHARD M. FORD

Bibliography: Behrman, S. N., *Portrait of Max* (1962); Danson, Lawrence, *Max Beerbohm and the Act of Writing* (1989); Viscusi, Robert, *Max Beerbohm* (1986).

Beersheba

Beersheba (Hebrew: Be'er Sheva; Arabic: 'Bir es Saba) is the capital of the Southern District of Israel. It is located at the northern edge of the Negev, about 89 km (55 mi) southwest of Jerusalem, and has a population of 113,800 (1990 est.). Chemicals and glass are manufactured; potash is produced nearby.

Named in biblical times, Beersheba is usually interpreted as "well of the pledge," denoting a well supposedly dug there by Abraham about 4,000 years ago. As ancient Palestine's southernmost city, it was on a major caravan route and was also an important religious sanctuary (notably for JACOB and ELIJAH). Beersheba was the site of a British victory over the Turks in 1917. The city, with its ancient Arab and modern Jewish sectors, has a thriving artists' colony and is a resettlement center for many immigrant Russian Jews. The Negev Museum, the Negev Institute for Arid Zone Research, and the Ben Gurion University of the Negev, founded in 1965, are in Beersheba.

Beery, Wallace

Wallace Beery, b. Apr. 1, 1886, d. Apr. 15, 1949, was a Hollywood star for 30 years, first in early silent films as a female impersonator and slapstick villain and then in talkies as a slow-thinking but reliable tough guy. Among his many credits are *Richard the Lionhearted* (1923), *The Lost World* (1925), *The Big House* (1930), *Min and Bill* (1930), *The Champ* (1931; Academy Award), *Grand Hotel* (1932), *The Bowery* (1933), *Tugboat Annie* (1933), *Treasure Island* (1934), *Ah, Wilderness!* (1935), and *Barbary Coast Gent* (1944).   LESLIE HALLIWELL

beet

A group of vegetables grown primarily for their edible roots and leaves, the beet group, *Beta vulgaris*, also includes Swiss chard, the SUGAR BEET, and mangle beet, which is used for

The beet, Beta vulgaris (left and middle), and swiss chard, B. vulgaris cicla (right), are closely related. The beet's root is edible, as are its young leaves. The edible portion of the chard is its leaves.

cattle feed. All are members of the goosefoot family, Chenopodiaceae.

Originating in the coastal regions of Europe, Africa, and the Near East, beets were first grown for their leafy tops; they began to be cultivated as a root vegetable sometime in the early Christian Era.

The plant is a biennial, usually grown as an annual. During its first year, it develops a rosette of long-petioled leaves and fleshy red roots. A tall flower stalk bearing inconspicuous flowers develops during the second year and produces a multiseeded fruit. A 3- to 4-week exposure to less than 5° C (41° F) causes the plant to flower as an annual.

Yields and quality are highest when beets are grown in moderate summer temperatures. They are usually seeded directly into rows and harvested when the roots reach a diameter of 2.54 to 4 cm (1 to 1.6 in). If allowed to grow much larger, they become tough and woody.

Swiss chard is grown only for its leaves, which are large and fleshy and can be eaten like spinach.

Flat-rooted beets include Crosby's Egyptian and Early Wonder; the Detroit Dark Red and Ruby Queen have round roots. Carrot-rooted types are also available. Green Top was developed for use as a leaf producer.   DONALD N. MAYNARD

See also: GARDENING; VEGETABLE.

Beethoven, Ludwig van   [bay'-toh-ven]

The culmination of the classical period is reached in the music of Ludwig van Beethoven. Although he began to grow deaf about 1800, he continued to compose and produce superlative music, including the Ninth Symphony and Missa Solemnis. A musical innovator, Beethoven produced works of an unsurpassed depth and emotional intensity.

Ludwig van Beethoven, one of the greatest masters of music, is particularly admired for his instrumental works, including symphonies, concertos, sonatas, and chamber music.
Early Life. Beethoven was born in the provincial court city of Bonn, Germany, probably on Dec. 16, 1770. His grandfather, also Ludwig, and his father, Johann, were both musicians in the service of, successively, the prince electors Max Friedrich and Max Franz. Beethoven's own talent was such that at the age of 12 he was already an assistant to the organist Christian Gottlob Neefe, with whom he studied. Attempts to establish him as a prodigy in the mold of MOZART had little success, however.

In 1787 Beethoven was sent to Vienna, but his mother fell ill, and he had to return to Bonn almost immediately. She died a few months later, and in 1789 Beethoven himself requested that his alcoholic father be retired, a move that left him responsible for his younger brothers Caspar Carl and Nikolaus Johann. Beethoven left Bonn for Vienna a second time in November of 1792, in order to study with Franz Josef HAYDN.

In 1794 French forces occupied the Rhineland; consequently, Beethoven's ties with and support from the Bonn court came to an end. His father had died a month after his departure from Bonn, and in 1794 and 1795 his two brothers joined him in Vienna. He remained there the rest of his life, leaving only for long summer holidays in the surrounding countryside and, in his early years, for occasional concerts in nearby cities. His only extended journey was to Prague, Dresden, and Berlin in 1796.

Beethoven never held an official position in Vienna. He supported himself by giving concerts, by teaching piano, and increasingly through the sale of his compositions. Members of the Viennese aristocracy were his steady patrons, and in 1809 three of them—Prince Kinsky, Prince Lobkowitz, and Archduke Rudolph—even guaranteed him a yearly income with the sole condition that he remain in Vienna.
Viennese Career. The last 30 years of Beethoven's life were shaped by a series of personal crises, the first of which was the onset of deafness. The early symptoms, noticeable to the composer already before 1800, affected him socially more than musically. His reactions—despair, resignation, and defiance—are conveyed in letters to two friends in 1801 and in a document—half letter and half will—addressed to his brothers in late 1802 and now known as the "Heiligenstadt testament." Resolving finally to "seize fate by the throat," he emerged from the crisis with a series of triumphant works that mark the beginning of a new period in his stylistic development.

A second crisis a decade later was the breaking off of a relationship with an unnamed lady (probably Antonie Brentano, the wife of a friend) known to us as the "Immortal Beloved," as Beethoven addressed her in a series of letters in July 1812. This was apparently the most serious of several such relationships with women who were in some way out of his reach, and its traumatic conclusion was followed by a lengthy period of resignation and reduced musical activity.

During this time Beethoven's deafness advanced to the stage that he could no longer perform publicly, and he required a slate or little notebooks (now known as "conversation books") to communicate with visitors. The death of his brother Caspar Carl in 1815 led to a 5-year legal struggle for custody of Caspar's son Karl, then 9 years old, in whom Beethoven saw a last chance for the domestic life that had otherwise eluded him. His possessiveness of Karl provoked a final crisis in the summer of 1826, when the young man attempted suicide. Shortly thereafter, Beethoven's health began to fail, and he died on Mar. 26, 1827 in Vienna.
Beethoven's Music. Traditionally Beethoven's works are grouped into early, middle, and late periods. The early works, up to about 1802, show a progressive mastery of the high classical style of Haydn and Mozart. Beethoven's formal studies in counterpoint (with Haydn and Johann ALBRECHTSBERGER), beginning in 1792, and his private study of the best new music of the time, particularly Haydn's symphonies, improved his treatment of both form and texture. During this period he wrote primarily for the PIANO and for chamber ensembles dominated by the piano. He approached the less familiar genres of quartet, symphony, oratorio, and opera with great caution, perhaps fearing comparison with Haydn and Mozart in these areas. His first six string quartets, op. 18, date from 1798–1800, the first symphony from 1800 and the second from 1801–02. He wrote a ballet, *The Creatures of Prometheus*, in 1800–01 and an oratorio, *Christ on the Mount of Olives*, in 1802–03.

A general growth in the proportions and rhetorical power of Beethoven's works in the period 1798–1802 culminates in the highly dramatic compositions that mark the beginning of the middle period in 1803. The earliest of these—the Third Symphony (*Eroica*, 1803), the opera *Fidelio* (1803–05), and the *Waldstein* (1804) and *Appassionata* (1804) sonatas—have a heroic cast that seems to respond to the initial fears provoked by Beethoven's deafness. In the works composed from about 1806 until 1812, this heroic character alternates with an Olympian serenity. The characteristic symphonic and chamber works from this period are the Fourth (1806), Fifth (1805–07), and Sixth (1807–08) symphonies; the Fourth (1805–06) and Fifth (*Emperor*, 1809) piano concertos; the Violin Concerto (1806); the *Rasumovsky* quartets (1806); the piano trios, op. 70 (1808) and op. 97 (*Archduke*, 1811); the *Coriolanus* Overture (1807); and the incidental music for Goethe's drama *Egmont* (1810).

This monumental middle-period style began to lose its attraction for Beethoven after 1812, the year of the Seventh and Eighth symphonies. The years 1813 and 1814 are not rich in impressive new works, and beginning in 1815 his music became generally less dramatic and more introspective. The first group of works in this new, late-period style includes the song cycle *An die ferne Geliebte*, op. 98 (To the Distant Beloved, 1816); the piano sonata, op. 101 (1816); and the two sonatas for cello and piano, op. 102 (1815). In these works and in a larger group of late sonatas, op. 109, 110, and 111 (1820–22), and string quartets, op. 127, 130, 131, 132, and 135 (1824–26), Beethoven relied less on the classical three- or four-movement format, dominated by a dramatic first movement in sonata form, and more on the juxtaposition of movements (from two to seven) of widely differing style and character. In particular, he favored variation and fugal procedures in which the hidden implications of his themes emerge gradually. Occasionally he reverted to elements of the heroic middle-period style, as, for example, in the *Hammerklavier* Sonata, op. 106 (1817-18); the *Missa Solemnis* (1818–23); and the Ninth (*Choral*) Symphony (completed 1823). Even these works, however, are colored by a new immediacy of expression. As Beethoven grew more isolated, from both his physical surroundings and the popular stylistic tendencies of the day, his music tended increasingly to expressive extremes. Passages of sublime contemplation join with simple folk melodies, impassioned recitatives, and abstract archaisms in a wholly personal synthesis.

Beethoven's Importance. Beethoven's music has never lost its central place in the concert repertory. Some works had an immediate and specific impact on the next generation of composers. The influence of the popular Seventh Symphony, for example, can be heard in Schubert's *Great* Symphony in C Major, Mendelssohn's *Italian* Symphony, Berlioz's *Harold in Italy*, and Wagner's Symphony in C. The influence of the Ninth Symphony was even more far-reaching; its special character had a profound effect on Bruckner and Brahms, and its combination of instrumental and choral forces prompted a series of hybrid symphonic works, from Berlioz to Mahler. The highly expressive quality of all Beethoven's music inspired poetic interpretations and encouraged a century of romantic instrumental works with programmatic overtones. Beethoven himself became a powerful symbol, the prototype of the modern artist-hero as opposed to the artist-craftsman of prerevolutionary Europe. His fierce independence and his painfully achieved artistic triumph over personal adversity, especially in the dramatically conceived works of the middle period, made him a model for those later composers such as Wagner who sought to teach or preach through art. At the same time, his fidelity to classical principles of composition, that is, his use of large-scale structure rather than local thematic events to achieve his most profound effects, has made his works the single most important source for the various systems of analysis developed by modern theorists and pedagogues.

DOUGLAS JOHNSON

Bibliography: Arnold, Denis, and Fortune, Nigel, eds., *Beethoven Reader* (1971); Comini, Alessandra, *The Changing Image of Beethoven* (1987); Crabbe, John, *Beethoven's Empire of the Mind* (1987); Hamburger, Michael, ed. and trans., *Beethoven: Letters, Journals, and Conversations* (1984); Johnson, Douglas, et al., *The Beethoven Sketchbooks* (1985); Kerman, Joseph, and Tyson, Alan, *The New Grove Beethoven* (1983); Matthews, Denis, *Beethoven* (1985); Rosen, Charles, *The Classical Style* (1971); Solomon, Maynard, *Beethoven* (1977); Thayer, A. W., *The Life of Ludwig van Beethoven*, rev. ed. by E. Forbes, 2 vols. (1964); Wegeler, F., and Ries, F., *Beethoven Remembered*, trans. by Frederick Noonan (1987).

beetle

A beetle is an insect of the order Coleoptera, the largest order in the animal kingdom, with over 250,000 species, about 28,000 of which occur in North America alone. Beetles are one of the most common insects and exist in every variety of habitat except the oceans and polar regions. The order Coleoptera has three suborders: Archostemata, Adephaga, and Polyphaga. In the suborder Polyphaga is found one of the largest families of beetles, Scarabaeidae. Nearly 1,300 species of it occur in North America. The members of this group are commonly referred to as scarab beetles. One member, the DUNG BEETLE, *Scarabaeus sacer*, was important to the ancient

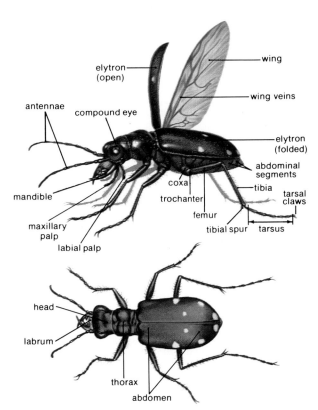

The tiger beetle, Cicindela hybrida, *has outer structures common to all beetles. Mandibles, labial palps, and maxillary palps, located on the head, are jaws used for biting. The beetle's compound eyes contain thousands of single lenses, or ommatidia. Its wings and elytra are attached to the thorax. Elytra are shieldlike wing cases that cover the fragile hind wings and the abdomen when the beetle is not in flight. The elytra can vary in color from shiny brown or black in some species of beetle to iridescent green in others, and it usually can have patterns of spots, stripes, and more complicated shapes.*

Egyptians, who considered it a symbol of resurrection. Other beetles common to this family are the June or May beetle (or JUNE BUG), the chafers, the rhinoceros beetle, the elephant beetle, and the Hercules beetle. Many family members, both larvae and adult, have done damage to cultivated crops.

Two insects not commonly known as beetles are the FIREFLY, or lightning bug, and the GLOWWORM; both are luminescent, but in the case of the glowworm the adult male is not.

Structure. Beetles differ from other insects in that the front wings, or elytra (singular, elytron), lack veins and nearly always meet in a straight line down the middle of the back. These wings are not used for flight. (The name Coleoptera is derived from Greek words meaning "sheath-wing.")

Viewed ventrally, the beetle's three body-parts—head, thorax, and abdomen—are readily distinguished. The head bears the mouthparts, antennae, and eyes. The three pairs of legs are attached to the thorax, and the segmented abdomen is behind the last pair of legs. Viewed dorsally, the head is obvious, but what appears to be the thorax is only the pronotum, the dorsal plate of the prothorax. The elytra overlie the membranous hind wings and usually conceal the abdomen.

All beetles have chewing mouthparts, although some, such as WEEVILS, have a much-elongated head, as though it were adapted for sucking. Each antenna of a beetle generally consists of 11 segments, although some have fewer segments or, rarely, more. The form of the antennae varies considerably: some antennae are threadlike; others have triangular-shaped segments; and still others are club-shaped.

Natural History. Beetles have complete METAMORPHOSIS. Each individual starts as an egg, hatches into a larva, becomes a pupa, and emerges as an adult. Beetles occur in almost every type of habitat in which insects are common. More species of beetles feed on living plants than on any other type of food. No part of a plant is free from attack by beetles; they feed on foliage, roots, flowers, seed, and fruits, and mine within wood. Some beetles feed on other animals, nearly always small, and often other insects. Still others feed on dead plant or animal material.

Economic Importance. Many species of beetles feed on the leaves of a number of garden crops, flowers, trees, and shrubs. Some of the worst insect pests are the spotted cucumber beetle and the JAPANESE BEETLE. Larvae and adults of both species are injurious, the larvae feeding in the ground, usually on roots, and the adults feeding on leaves. For sheer destructiveness, few insects can match certain species of BARK BEETLES. The bark beetle can build up tremendous populations in conifers (and other trees such as elms), resulting in the loss of millions of board feet of timber.

Some beetles transmit viral, bacterial, or fungal agents that cause plant disease. For example, the American elm tree has been greatly reduced in numbers because of the fungus transmitted by the bark beetle. This fungus is responsible for the condition commonly known as the Dutch elm disease.

Beetles may damage a wide variety of stored materials: dry, stored wood; fabrics made of animal materials; and stored food, such as meats, flour, meal, cereal, grains, and cheeses. The amount of food eaten by the beetles is generally insignificant; the chief problem is the difficulty of ensuring a pure, uncontaminated product for commerce.

Some of the most beneficial beetles are those that feed on other insects or on pest plants. Various species of LADYBUG beetles are important in controlling APHIDS and scale insects. In other cases injurious plants have been controlled by the introduction of a beetle that feeds on it. A good example is the control of the alligator weed by the alligator weed flea beetle in the waterways of the southeastern United States.

RICHARD E. WHITE

Bibliography: Arnett, R. H., Jr., *How to Know the Beetles* (1980); Crowson, R. A., *The Biology of Coleoptera* (1981); Evans, M. E., *The Life of Beetles* (1975).

See also: WATER BEETLE.

(Opposite page) *A selection of beetles reveals many shapes, colors, and sizes. The bar next to each beetle indicates the insect's length. The* **cetonid beetle**, *Eupoecila australasiae, a large Australian beetle, uses fecal matter to build its larval cocoon. The* **striped blister beetle**, *Epicauta vittata, of central and northeastern United States and eastern Canada, secretes an oily, poisonous fluid from its leg joints when threatened, giving it the nickname of oil beetle. The* **fiery searcher ground beetle**, *Calosoma scrutator, of the United States and Canada, runs quickly with its long legs. The* **stag beetle**, *Lucanus cervus, native to Great Britain, is the largest European beetle, measuring 50 mm (2 in). The male's jaws resemble antlers. The* **Goliath beetle**, *Goliathus meleagris, a giant flower beetle of Africa, grips and hangs from tree branches by its powerful forelegs. The* **Colorado potato beetle**, *Leptinotarsa decemlineata, a major food-crop pest, destroys leaves of potatoes and eggplants. The* **two-lined collops**, *Collops vittatus, of the United States and Canada, is a soft-winged flower beetle that preys on the corn leaf aphid, larva of the alfalfa weevil, and other agricultural pests. The* **golden spider beetle**, *Niptus hololeucus, of North America, Europe, and Asia, has a body resembling that of a spider. The* **sweet potato snout weevil**, *Cylas formicarias elegantulus, of the southern United States, produces larvae that feed on sweet-potato crops. The* **carrion beetle**, *Nicrophorus marginatus, of Canada and the western United States, buries carcasses of small animals as food for its larvae. Two species of* **tortoise beetle**, *Tauroma casta and Omaspides bistriata, of Central and South America, protect their eggs by secreting a fluid that hardens into a case and shields their larvae under their bodies. The* **two-spotted ladybug**, *Adalia bipunctata, is a familiar beetle of North America and Europe that is known by its brightly patterned back. The European* **hero longhorn beetle**, *Cerambyx cordo, like other members of the longhorn family, has long, segmented antennae. The* **click beetle**, *Chalcolepidus lacordairei, native to Mexico, can right itself by snapping its body into the air with a click and flipping over. The* **scavenger beetle**, *Eudicella morgani, of West Africa, feeds on rotting plant and animal matter, converting the waste into rich compost. The* **pleasing fungus beetle**, *Aphorista vittata, of eastern North America, hatches larvae that feed on mushrooms and other fungi. The* **Japanese beetle**, *Popillia japonica, a scarab beetle common to the United States and Japan, is a major pest, destroying fruits and leaves. The* **firefly**, *Photuris pennsylvanica, a common beetle of the eastern United States, flies in early summer evenings and emits a bright light. The* **hickory bark beetle**, *Scolytus quadrispinosus, native to the eastern United States, bores into hickory, butternut, and pecan trees. The* **diving beetle**, *Cybister marginalis, of Central Europe, swims underwater, holding air in a pocket between its back and wings. The* **giant longhorn beetle**, *Macrodontia cervicornis, of tropical south Brazil, bores through wood and lays its eggs inside a tree.*

The Japanese beetle, Popillia japonica, lays its eggs in August. The eggs develop into larvae during the fall and winter months. By June, a larva has developed into a pupa, which begins to look like an adult beetle. In July, a mature beetle emerges from its underground nest.

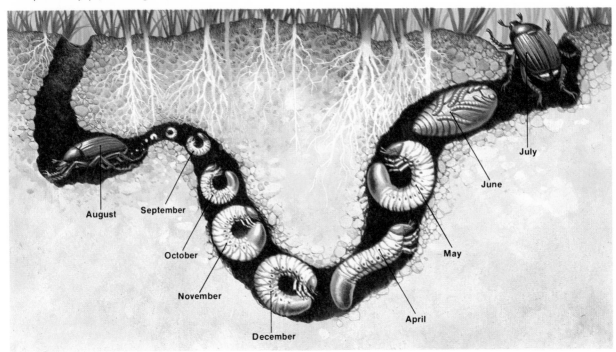

August September October November December April May June July

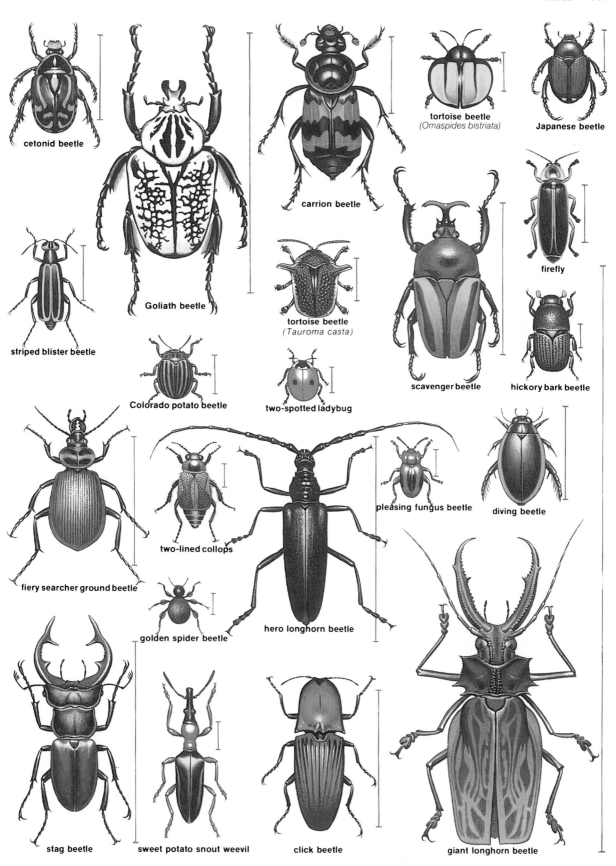

cetonid beetle

Goliath beetle

striped blister beetle

Colorado potato beetle

two-spotted ladybug

carrion beetle

tortoise beetle
(*Tauroma casta*)

tortoise beetle
(*Omaspides bistriata*)

Japanese beetle

scavenger beetle

firefly

hickory bark beetle

fiery searcher ground beetle

two-lined collops

golden spider beetle

hero longhorn beetle

pleasing fungus beetle

diving beetle

stag beetle

sweet potato snout weevil

click beetle

giant longhorn beetle

Beets, Nicolaas   [bayts]

Nicolaas Beets, b. Sept. 13, 1814, d. Mar. 13, 1903, was an important Dutch poet and prose writer and, after 1874, a professor of theology at Utrecht. While a student in Leiden, he published (1839) under the pseudonym Hildebrand the first version of his *Camera Obscura* (completed 1854), a remarkable collection of stories and essays filled with keen observations, insight into character, and humorous episodes. Beets also wrote poetry and helped introduce the works of Lord Byron into the Netherlands.   R. P. MEIJER

Beggar's Opera, The

The Beggar's Opera (1728), written by John GAY with a musical score by John Pepusch, is one of the earliest and most important examples of ballad opera, in which spoken dialogue is interspersed with ballads and folk tunes. The work burlesqued the form of the then-popular Italian opera and also satirized the hypocrisy and vice of London high society and Whig politics.

The plot of the opera, set among the thieves and prostitutes of London's lowest classes, revolves around the rivalry of the rakish Captain Macheath, a highwayman, and Jeremy Peachum, a fence. The characters are thinly veiled representations of Robert Walpole and members of his Whig administration. The premiere of the work was on Jan. 29, 1728, at Lincoln's Inn Fields, and the next year Gay wrote a sequel, *Polly*. *The Threepenny Opera* (1928), by Bertolt Brecht and Kurt Weill, was based on *The Beggar's Opera*.

Bibliography: Kidson, Frank, *The Beggar's Opera: Its Predecessors and Successors* (1922; repr. 1969); Schultz, William E., *The Beggar's Opera: Its Content, History and Influence* (1923; repr. 1967).

Begin, Menachem   [bay'-gin, me-nah'-kem]

Menachem Begin, prime minister of Israel (1977–83), became a Zionist while at the University of Warsaw in the 1930s. During World War II he was deported to a Soviet labor camp and from there made his way to Palestine in 1942. From 1943 to 1948 he commanded the Irgun Zvai Leumi guerrillas fighting against the British in Palestine. Begin described his early life in The Revolt *(1951; Eng. trans., 1964) and* White Nights *(1953; Eng. trans., 1957).*

Menachem Begin, b. Russia, Aug. 16 (N.S.), 1913, d. Mar. 9, 1992, was prime minister of Israel from 1977 to 1983. In Palestine from 1942, he led the Irgun Zvai Leumi guerrilla movement against the British and in 1948 became head of the right-wing Herut party. Herut was the leading element in the Likud coalition that won the 1977 elections, and Begin formed a government. In 1977, Begin and Egyptian president Anwar al-Sadat began peace talks culminating in a treaty signed on Mar. 26, 1979. The two men received the 1978 Nobel Peace Prize. Rejecting further compromises with the Arabs, Begin promoted Jewish settlement of territory taken by Israel from Jordan, formally annexed (1981) the Golan Heights taken from Syria, and authorized the Israeli invasion of Lebanon in 1982. He resigned on Sept. 16, 1983, and went into seclusion; he was succeeded by his foreign minister, Yitzhak SHAMIR.

Bibliography: Perlmutter, A., *The Life and Times of Menachem Begin* (1987); Silver, E., *Begin* (1984); Sofer, J., *Begin* (1988).

begonia

Begonias, genus *Begonia,* are a large group of succulent herbs, shrubs, and vines that are commonly grown as ornamentals. The genus, which belongs to the family Begoniaceae, includes more than 1,000 species; they are chiefly found in Central and South America, although a few are native to other tropical and subtropical regions. No indigenous species occur in the United States, but a number of species are native to Mexico. Most begonias are annual or perennial herbs with jointed stems; alternate, simple, palmately veined, and sometimes lobed leaves; and unisexual flowers.

Begonias are universally used as houseplants because of their ease in culture and wide variety. Among the more than 10,000 horticultural varieties and hybrids that are commonly

The begonia is named for the 17th-century French administrator and amateur botanist Michel Bégon. The tuberous-rooted begonia, B. tuberhybrida (left), *yields roselike flowers in summer. The wax begonia,* B. semperflorens (right), *blooms continuously.*

grown are many with outstanding and unusual foliage. Many also have large, showy, long-lasting flowers that vary in color from white through pink to red and yellow. Because they are susceptible to frost damage, they are usually used as summer bedding plants in the north, being set out after the danger of frost is past and taken indoors in the fall.

The cultivated begonias are commonly divided into three general groups by rootstock: those with fibrous, rhizomatous, and tuberous roots. Among the common fibrous-rooted species are the angel-wing begonia, *Begonia coccinea,* and the wax begonia, *B. semperflorens.* The rhizomatous-rooted begonias include the beefsteak begonia, *B. feastii,* and the rex begonia, *B. rex-cultorum.* A widely cultivated species of tuberous begonia, *B. tuberhybrida,* is probably the result of hybridization among several Andean species.   JOHN EBINGER

Bibliography: Catterall, E., *Growing Begonias* (1984); Thompson, M. L. and E. J., *Begonias* (1979).

Beham   (family)   [bay'-uhm]

The brothers Hans Sebald Beham and Bartel Beham were 16th-century German artists who, with George Pencz and others, formed the *Kleinmeister* ("Little Masters") printmaking group. The group issued numerous editions of prints, often in small formats, on a vast range of subjects and widely popularized Renaissance forms outside Italy.

Hans Sebald Beham, 1500–50, produced about 1,500 engravings, etchings, and woodcuts. His early works are characterized by exaggerated imitation of Albrecht Dürer's sculpturesque style in the graphic arts. In 1525, Hans Sebald and Bartel were expelled from Nuremberg for religious and political freethinking. Although Hans Sebald returned briefly to Nuremberg in 1531 to complete the *Planets* engraving series, he settled in Frankfurt in 1532, associating with the publisher Christian Egenolff. A technical virtuoso, he assimilated such disparate sources as popular prints and Italian classical works. Hans Sebald created the first pure genre pieces (scenes of daily life) in German art.

Bartel (or Barthel) **Beham**, 1502–40, a painter as well as an engraver, studied with his brother. He was particularly influenced by Dürer's later works. About 1527, Bartel settled in Munich, where he served (1530–40) as court painter to Duke William IV of Bavaria. The style of his mature portraits, such as *Portrait of Chancellor Leonhard von Eyck* (1527; Metropolitan Museum, New York City), was strongly influenced by Italian art. Even when using Mannerist devices, as in *The Testing of the True Cross* (1530; Alte Pinakotheck, Munich), he never forsook a vigorous realism.   MARCUS BURKE

Bibliography: Hollstein, F. W. H., *German Engravings, Etchings, and Woodcuts*, vols. 2 and 3 (n.d.); Von der Osten, Gert, and Vey, Horst, *Painting and Sculpture in Germany and the Netherlands, 1500 to 1600* (1969).

Behan, Brendan   [bee'-uhn]

The Irish writer Brendan Behan, b. Dublin, Feb. 9, 1923, d. Mar. 20, 1964, is equally well known for the sardonic humor of his plays and for the raucous life he led in the bars of Dublin and New York.

A street-wise youngster, Behan grew up in the slums of Dublin and at the age of 14 joined the outlawed Irish Republican Army (IRA). This earned him 3 years (1939–42) in a reformatory, an experience he described in his sentimental autobiography *Borstal Boy* (1958). Shortly after his release in 1942 he was sentenced to 14 years' imprisonment for political offenses. He was freed (1946) under a general amnesty. His prison experiences form the background of *The Quare Fellow*, his first play, which was performed in an avant-garde club in 1954 and opened in London in 1956. Set in an Irish prison just before a hanging, the play is compassionate yet macabre in its incisive gallows humor and colorful dialogue. Behan's second play, *The Hostage* (1958), also derived from his real-life experiences, is a lighter comedy concerning an Englishman held by the IRA in a Dublin brothel. Behan also wrote some frankly commercial books—*Brendan Behan's Ireland: An Irish Sketchbook* (1962) and *Brendan Behan's New York* (1964)—exploiting his own notoriety to pay for his style of life. A novel, *The Scarperer* (1964), and *Confessions of an Irish Rebel* (1965) were published posthumously.

The celebrated Irish revolutionary and playwright Brendan Behan dances a jig after a performance of his play The Hostage. *Behan developed his earthy, boisterous style of writing while incarcerated in English prisons. His satirical plays, which mock British authorities, were based on the experiences he had with the Irish Republican Army.*

At his best, Behan was an excellent portrayer of character. His dramatic dialogue, pervaded with a mixture of humor and sensuality, was constructed with great skill.

Bibliography: Behan, Dominic, *My Brother Brendan* (1965); Boyle, Ted E., *Brendan Behan* (1969); Mikhail, E. H., ed., *Brendan Behan*, 2 vols. (1982).

Behar: see BIHAR.

behavior modification

Behavior modification, sometimes called behavior therapy or applied behavior analysis, is the application of experimental findings from psychological research to the development and use of techniques for changing human behavior. It has been used to treat phobias, alcoholism, overeating, smoking, sexual deviance, and mental disorders, including schizophrenia and catatonia. Behavior-modification techniques have also been used in toilet training and in improving children's classroom behavior and even their academic performance. In the late 1950s and early '60s the approach became a movement in the United States, South Africa, and England, largely as a reaction to the perceived failure of clinical models of psychotherapy.

Behavior modification grew out of the work of B. F. SKINNER and of certain aspects of LEARNING THEORY and has progressed to specific behavior methodologies. Thus it is not characterized by any one theory of behavior or even by an underlying concept of human nature. Lack of a central theory has led to a blurring of the meaning of the term, but behavior modification is generally regarded as encompassing three basic techniques: desensitization, aversion therapy, and operant CONDITIONING.

Desensitization involves the use of classical conditioning methods in treating phobias, for example, by gradually relaxing the anxiety related to specific stimuli. Aversion therapy is also an application of classical conditioning methods. In it, socially undesirable behavior, such as uncontrolled drinking, is linked with a punishing response; in this case nausea and vomiting are induced by means of drugs that cause the patient to react physiologically to alcohol. Operant conditioning uses reinforcement to increase the frequency of desirable behavior, and punishment to decrease the frequency of undesirable behavior. For example, if each verbalization by an autistic child is followed promptly by the presentation of food, the child may increase the number of verbalizations. Desensitization and aversion techniques are used in a clinical environment, whereas operant conditioning may be, and frequently is, undertaken in a normal school, home, or work environment.

Behavior modification has evoked criticism ranging from the theoretical to the ethical. Some psychologists have charged that because only symptoms are treated, it is likely that one symptom may be substituted for another, with no improvement in the underlying cause of the disorder. Others have asserted that behavior-modification techniques can be used to treat only a few types of discrete behaviors, not general or diffuse behaviors. Some nonpsychologists view behavior modification as being manipulative and dehumanizing, fearing that behavior-modification techniques may be used to abridge human freedoms and thus lead to greater social control.   HELEN ALTMAN KLEIN

Bibliography: Craighead, W. Edward, et al., *Behavior Modification*, 2d ed. (1980); Garfield, Sol L., and Bergin, Allen E., eds., *Handbook of Psychotherapy and Behavior Change* (1986); Kazdin, Alan E., *History of Behavior Modification* (1978).

See also: PSYCHOPATHOLOGY, TREATMENT OF.

behavioral genetics

Behavioral genetics is the study of organisms by means of both behavioral and genetic analysis. Genetic analysis describes the genetic architecture of each species and is used to study the individual differences in the expression of a trait, in this case behavior. Behavior-genetic analysis is a method to determine how much a particular behavior trait is genetically influenced.

As researchers attempted to determine how much a behavior pattern is influenced by HEREDITY and how much by environment, what is known as the "nature-nurture controversy" developed. Some scientists believe that certain behaviors are determined mainly by genetic inheritance from parents (the nature theory). Others contend that the environment in which a child is brought up determines the amount of intelligence expressed (the nurture theory).

The concept known as norm of reaction takes a moderate position between these two extremes in the nature-nurture controversy. According to this concept, each unique genotype—the genetic makeup of the individual—can develop into various phenotypes—the traits that are actually expressed. The phenotypic expression of a genotype depends on the environment in which the genotype develops. Conversely, each environment can foster several different phenotypes, depending on the genotypes affected. Thus the interaction of heredity and environment is intimately involved in the development of every plant and animal.

Research. In the late 19th century the English scientist Francis GALTON introduced the method of comparing the traits both of identical human twins and of fraternal twins who were raised in the same environment and in different environments. Such traits as height, weight, and intelligence have been examined in studies of twins to determine whether environmental or genetic factors are most influential.

In the 1930s, '40s, and '50s the American scientist Franz Kallmann used the twin method to study SCHIZOPHRENIA. These twin studies and also the adoption studies of Leonard Heston and David Rosenthal in the 1960s seemed to indicate that schizophrenia is a behavior that is largely inherited. In adoption studies, children being brought up by normal foster parents were observed for the incidence of schizophrenia. One or both of the biological parents of some of the children were known by the researchers but not by the foster parents to be schizophrenic, and the other children's biological parents were considered normal. More of the children having biological parents who were schizophrenic developed the disorder than did children of normal biological parents.

Researchers have not been able to reconcile generally accepted ethical limitations on human studies with the kinds of observations necessary for rigorous experimental designs. For example, in certain studies some families would have to be purposely misinformed about their genetic makeup in order to control the psychological effects of knowing that an individual is genetically normal or abnormal.

Animal research is often conducted to see whether various behaviors, such as learning and courtship, are genetically induced. In one method, animals are selectively bred from a free-mating population, and the behavior patterns of several divergent lines are studied. In another method, the behavior is studied among several different lines of highly inbred animals, meaning those in which at least 60 generations of siblings were mated with one another.

Undoubtedly, the most fruitful source of knowledge concerning relations among heredity, environment, and behavior has been research on inborn errors of metabolism and chromosomal anomalies. In the case of the metabolic error called phenylketonuria (PKU), afflicted individuals inherit a gene mutation causing a deficiency of the mammalian liver enzyme phenylalanine hydroxylase, necessary for the metabolism of the amino acid phenylalanine, which is commonly found in milk. PKU patients eating a normal human diet accumulate phenylalanine in the blood and spinal fluid, a condition that contributes to mental retardation. With proper environmental controls, including a rigorous diet excluding milk products during early childhood, normal intelligence can develop. The chromosomal anomaly known as Down's syndrome is a condition also leading to mental retardation. This disorder occurs when an extra chromosome is attached to a normal pair of the human complement of chromosomes.

IQ. Great interest and controversy concerning the relation between heredity and test scores for intelligence quotient (IQ)

developed during the 1960s and '70s. In spite of extreme viewpoints, most researchers agree that the relation among heredity, environment, and intelligence is not simple. It is unlikely that a strong general relationship exists causally among these three factors.

The American scientist Gordon Harrington demonstrated that the bias characteristic of a particular IQ test is related to the psychological technique or theory used to construct the test and also to the composition of the populations used to standardize the test. In 1980 a furor broke out when it was discovered that the English psychologist Cyril BURT had falsified data from the studies of twins used to support his claim that IQ was about 80 percent causally determined by heredity. The heated debates on how much IQ is determined by heredity and how much by environment—part of the overall nature-nurture controversy—has stimulated scientists to develop increasingly rigorous methods for behavior-genetic analysis.

JERRY HIRSCH

Bibliography: Chase, Allan, *The Legacy of Malthus: The Social Cost of Scientific Racism* (1980); Ehrman, Lee, and Parsons, Peter, *The Genetics of Behavior* (1976); Fuller, J. L., and Simmel, E. L., eds., *Perspectives in Behavior Genetics* (1986); Gould, Stephen Jay, *The Mismeasure of Man* (1981); Hay, D. A., *Essentials of Behaviour Genetics* (1985); Hirsch, Jerry, and McGuire, T. J., eds., *Behavior-Genetic Analysis* (1982); Lockhard, Joan S., ed., *The Evolution of Human Social Behavior* (1980); Sakai, Toshiaki, and Tsuboi, Takayuka, eds., *Genetic Aspects of Human Behavior* (1985).

See also: ANIMAL BEHAVIOR; ETHOLOGY; SOCIOBIOLOGY.

behavioral sciences

Behavioral sciences are academic disciplines that deal with human activities and generalize about behavior in society. Of recent origin compared with the physical sciences and humanities, the behavioral sciences—ANTHROPOLOGY, PSYCHOLOGY, and SOCIOLOGY—frequently overlap those other disciplines from which they emerged. At first scorned as pseudoscientific, they are now generally accepted.

behaviorism

Behaviorism is the movement and school of PSYCHOLOGY that defines psychology as the science of the study of the behavior of humans and animals. Prominent behaviorists have included Edward C. TOLMAN, Clark HULL, and B. F. SKINNER.

History. Prior to the founding of psychology as a science in the last quarter of the 19th century, it was considered part of philosophy and defined as the introspective study of the mind. The founders continued this view but introduced experimental methods. They also defined psychology more narrowly as the scientific study of consciousness, especially of its contents. They adhered to mentalism, the study of the mind.

Developments soon led psychologists to become unhappy with mentalism. For mentalists the central method of psychology was introspection, the precise description of conscious events. The notion of the human mind's uniqueness, however, was destroyed for scientists as they absorbed the meaning of evolution. Psychologists then ran into difficulty when they sought to investigate the minds of animals, which cannot introspect. The same difficulty confronted those who wished to study children or the insane. Lacking introspective reports from their subjects in these cases, they were limited to observing behavior and inferring mental events from behavior.

Especially important were the studies of the psychologist Edward L. THORNDIKE, whose pioneering studies of LEARNING dispensed with introspection and reference to mind. In the 1890s psychologists developed mental tests, such as INTELLIGENCE tests, that produced objective data about people without collecting introspective reports. Testing became especially popular in the United States, where psychologists were eager to develop psychology as an applied science capable of solving personal and social problems and serving the needs of business, industry, and education. They naturally focused on behavior instead of consciousness.

Finally, around the turn of the century, mentalism began experiencing controversies that to some psychologists impugned its validity. For example, introspective psychology seemed unable to decide if all conscious experiences were sensations and images (memories of sensations), or if "imageless thoughts" also inhabited consciousness. One response was an American movement called functionalism, concerned with how the mind works rather than its contents. The functionalists were eclectic and used nonintrospective methods such as testing, but they remained mentalists who regarded psychology as the study of mind defined as conscious experience.

The existing dissatisfaction with mentalism was distilled in the founding manifesto of behaviorism, "Psychology as the Behaviorists View It," by John B. WATSON, published in the American journal *Psychology Review* in 1913. Watson was trained at the University of Chicago by the leader of functionalism, James Rowland ANGELL. While at graduate school, Watson became discontented with mentalism. He disliked serving as an introspective subject and felt that mentalism excluded, or at least looked down on, his own specialty of animal psychology. Leaving for Johns Hopkins University in 1905, he began to develop a new point of view, first for animal psychology and then, in the 1913 paper, for psychology as a whole. Watson boldly defined psychology as behaviorism, a "purely objective branch of natural science" whose goal was "the prediction and control of behavior." Central to his indictment of mentalism was his claim that introspection was not a scientific method, because it rested on data known only to the observer. While disagreeing with his rhetorical excesses, most psychologists admitted that Watson's stance was correct. Over the next decade or two, behaviorism became the central movement in psychology.

Varieties of Behaviorism. From its inception, however, psychologists found it difficult to define behaviorism. Watson's manifesto was effective propaganda but poor conceptual analysis. Beyond defining the subject matter of psychology as behavior, consensus was elusive. Two problems were paramount. The first, less discussed, was the difficulty of defining behavior itself. To say it meant anything an organism did was far too broad. "Molecular" behaviorists wanted to define it as specific muscle movements, while "molar" behaviorists defined it as meaningful actions. The second problem was how to treat the traditional concepts of mind and consciousness. This was more openly discussed, and it led to the formation of different schools within the movement. The two most commonly identified are methodological behaviorism and radical behaviorism.

Methodological behaviorists were more numerous and included the leading theorists of the 1930s and 1940s, Tolman and Hull, whose followers were influential into the 1960s. While rejecting the scientific study of consciousness, they permitted reference to inner states of the organism, provided the states were properly defined. For example, the learning theorist Hull said that when an organism learns something it acquires a habit, an inner but nonconscious state inferred from behavior by the psychologist. Especially after the mid-1930s, methodologists were heavily influenced by the philosophical movement called LOGICAL POSITIVISM led by Rudolf CARNAP. The positivists tried to define mental states as states of the body and their characteristic behavioral expressions.

Radical behaviorism was developed by B. F. Skinner. Influenced by the POSITIVISM of Auguste COMTE and Ernst MACH, he argued that exclusion of consciousness, or private events, from psychology was a mistake. It resulted in an incomplete science of behavior, since behavior is influenced by private stimuli such as headaches and private events such as conscious thoughts. At the same time, Skinner rejected the use of inferred organismic states. He held that private conscious stimuli and events were part of the natural world, even if observed by an audience of one, whereas inferred states were observed by no one, even their supposed possessor. Skinner regarded them as mythical. Radical behaviorism thus reverses the methodological behaviorist scheme, which excludes consciousness but includes inferred states.

A third school, strict behaviorism, was proposed by Watson's student Karl LASHLEY. Watson always emphasized the study of the nervous system, and Lashley—influenced also by Ivan PAVLOV—developed this emphasis into a programmatic view of psychology. He argued that psychologists should explain both conscious events and behaviors as the result of processes in the nervous system. Thus, learning was to be explained by discovering how the brain and nervous system change as a result of experience. Lashley set out in search of the hypothetical unit of memory storage, the engram. Because of the limited technology of his time Lashley failed in his quest, and strict behaviorism remained a tiny movement.

Behaviorism Today. In the 1960s a new movement developed called COGNITIVE PSYCHOLOGY. Disdainful of behaviorism, cognitive psychologists said they were returning to mentalism. In fact, cognitive psychology remains a form of methodological behaviorism because it studies behavior, not consciousness, and employs the strategy of inferring nonconscious mental processes from behavior. Radical behaviorism survived the death of Skinner and remains a healthy, if isolated movement within psychology. Lashley's strict behaviorism, without the name, is returning to psychology as modern techniques reveal the operations of the brain and nervous system in perception, learning, memory, and even thought. THOMAS H. LEAHEY

Bibliography: Buckley, K., *Mechanical Man: John B. Watson and the Beginnings of Behaviorism* (1984); Kosslyn, Stephen, and Koenig, Olivier, *Wet Mind* (1992); Leahey, Thomas H., *A History of Psychology*, 3d ed. (1992); O'Donnell, John M., *The Origins of Behaviorism* (1985); Rachlin, Howard, *An Introduction to Modern Behaviorism* (1991); Skinner, B. F., *About Behaviorism* (1974); Smith, Laurence D., *Behaviorism and Logical Positivism* (1986); Teichmann, Jenny, *Philosophy and the Mind* (1988); Zuriff, Gerald, *Behaviorism* (1985).

beheading

Beheading is a form of CAPITAL PUNISHMENT. Practiced in ancient Greece and Rome and later in other parts of Europe, Asia, and the Middle East, execution by decapitation was usually reserved for offenders of high rank or for notorious criminals. It was originally carried out with an ax, later with a sword, and, in France from the late 18th century until capital punishment was abolished there in 1981, with the GUILLOTINE. JOHN THE BAPTIST was an early victim of the practice. Later, death by beheading claimed such other notable figures as Anne BOLEYN, MARY, QUEEN OF SCOTS, Sir Walter RALEIGH, LOUIS XVI of France, and his wife, MARIE ANTOINETTE.

Beheading has died out in Europe, but it continues to be employed as a punishment in some Muslim countries, along with a variety of mutilations. It was also widespread in China until recent times.

Behistun [bay-his-toon']

The village and imposing cliff of classical Behistun, modern Bisutun or Bisitun, lie beside the ancient highway between Babylon and the Median capital Ecbatana (modern Hamadan) near Kermanshah in western Iran. High on the precipitous rock face are carved the famous bas-relief and trilingual inscription of the Achaemenid king DARIUS I (522–486 BC), the study of which was instrumental in the decipherment of CUNEIFORM script.

The inscription, in Old Persian, Babylonian, and Elamite, is the official monument of Darius, who gained a decisive victory near Behistun in 521 BC. The text includes an autobiographical account of events leading up to the battle, together with a list of satrapies, or provinces, of the empire. Above the inscription, in prominent relief, stands Darius attended by bow and spear warriors. His foot is placed on the prostrate and supplicating figure of his defeated enemy Gaumata, pretender to the Persian throne in 522 BC. Behind him stand nine other captive rebel leaders. The winged god Ahura Mazda hovers above, acknowledging the king's salute.

The dangerous task of copying the inscription on the cliff face was first undertaken in 1835 by Sir Henry Creswicke RAWLINSON. Further work on the text enabled Rawlinson to interpret the Old Persian section, thereby facilitating the decipherment of Babylonian and Elamite. KATE FIELDEN

Bibliography: Ceram, C. W., *Gods, Graves, and Scholars* (1951); Curtis, J., *Ancient Persia* (1990); Hole, F., *The Archaeology of Western Iran* (1987); Olmstead, A. T., *History of the Persian Empire* (1948).

Behn, Aphra [bayn, af'-ruh]

Aphra Behn, b. July 1640, d. Apr. 16, 1689, an English drama-tist, novelist, and poet, was the first woman to write profes-sionally for the English stage. Her famous novel *Oroonoko, or the History of the Royal Slave* (c.1688), a romantic fiction with realistic details about the oppression and rebellion of slaves brought to the New World, is set in Suriname, where Behn is believed to have lived in her youth.

Details of her life and career are open to question. After marriage (c.1664) to a Dutch-born merchant named Behn, she claimed to be a spy (c.1666) for Charles II in Antwerp during the Anglo–Dutch Wars. She signed her secret dispatches "As-trea," which is the pen name that appears on her early poetry. She returned to England penniless and may have spent time in debtors' prison. Between 1670 and 1689 she wrote approxi-mately 15 theatrically successful plays noted for their intrigue and bawdiness. The best of these was *The Rover, or the Ban-ished Cavaliers* (2 parts, 1677 and 1681). Her colorful life in-cluded friendship with such writers as John Dryden.

W. L. GODSHALK

Bibliography: Duffy, M., The *Passionate Shepherdess* (1989); Fraser, A., *The Weaker Yessel* (1984); Link, F. M., *Aphra Behn* (1968); Wood-cock, George, *The Incomparable Aphra* (1948; repr. 1989).

Behrens, Peter [bay'-ruhns, pay'-ter]

Peter Behrens, b. Hamburg, Apr. 14, 1868, d. Feb. 27, 1940, was a German architect, industrial designer, and educator who strongly influenced the development of modern European architecture. The architects who worked at Behrens's office early in their careers included Le Corbusier, Walter Gropius, and Ludwig Mies van der Rohe.

Behrens at first studied painting and worked in Munich dur-ing the 1890s. In 1899 he joined the Darmstadt artists' colony, where he designed his own house and its furnishings. In 1903 he was appointed director of the School of Applied Arts in Düsseldorf, and four years later he became artistic advisor for the German General Electric Company (AEG) in Berlin.

Behrens's association with AEG marked a turning point in industrial design. In addition to designing factories and show-rooms, Behrens also designed the company's stationery, cata-logs, packaging, and lighting equipment. His turbine factory (1909) was remarkable for its clarity and monumentality. His other building designs include the German Embassy in Saint Petersburg (1911–12); offices of the Höchst Dyeworks near Frankfurt (1920–24); and an apartment block for the housing exhibition at Stuttgart-Weissenhof (1927).

Behrens also held positions as professor of architecture at the Düsseldorf Akadamie (1921) and director of the School of Architecture of the Academy in Vienna (1922–27). In 1936 he became head of the architecture section of the Prussian Acad-emy of Arts in Berlin.

RONALD WIEDENHOEFT

Bibliography: Buddensieg, Tilmann, *Industriekulture* (1984); Hatje, Gerd, ed., *Encyclopedia of Modern Architecture* (1964); Hitchcock, Henry-Russell, *Architecture: Nineteenth and Twentieth Centuries*, 2d ed. (1963).

Behring, Emil Adolf von

Emil Adolf von Behring, b. Mar. 15, 1854, d. Mar. 31, 1917, was a German bacteriologist and a pioneer in IMMUNOLOGY. When Behring injected experimental animals with dead or weakened toxin from diphtheria bacteria, he discovered that the animals reacted by producing a neutralizing agent, an an-titoxin, that made them immune. Behring obtained the same results with tetanus toxin and found that surplus tetanus anti-toxin could be administered to other animals, to make them immune to tetanus.

In 1891 diphtheria antitoxin was administered to a human for the first time. Behring and Paul EHRLICH share the credit for this achievement. Behring was awarded (1901) the first Nobel Prize for medicine.

Bibliography: Singer, Charles, *A History of Biology to about the Year 1900*, 3d ed. (1959; repr. 1989); Sourkes, Theodore L., *Nobel Prize Win-ners in Medicine and Physiology, 1901–1965* (1967).

Behrman, S. N. [bair'-muhn]

Samuel Nathaniel Behrman, b. Worcester, Mass., June 9, 1893, d. Sept. 9, 1973, was an American playwright whose comedies are distinguished by their sophisticated wit and pi-quant social comment. His first successful comedy, *The Sec-ond Man* (1927), was followed by several other hits, including *Biography* (1932), *Rain from Heaven* (1934), *End of Summer* (1936), and *No Time for Comedy* (1939). His other works in-clude *Portrait of Max* (1960), a memoir of Sir Max Beerbohm.

Bibliography: Reed, Kenneth, *S. N. Behrman* (1975).

Beida [bay'-duh]

Beida (al-Bayda) is a city 32 km (20 mi) from the Mediterra-nean coast of Cyrenaica province in northeastern Libya. It lies in the foothills of the Jabal al-Akhdar at an elevation of 610 m (2,000 ft) and has a population of 67,120 (1984). Built on a site holy to Muslims, the modern city dates from the late 1950s, when King Idris planned to establish his capital there.

Beiderbecke, Bix [by'-dur-bek]

The cornetist, pianist, and composer Leon Bismarck "Bix" Beiderbecke, b. Davenport, Iowa, Mar. 10, 1903, d. Aug. 7, 1931, is considered the greatest white jazz artist of the 1920s, and his career had a profound influence on later jazz instru-mentalists. A self-taught cornetist, as a youth he played with the informal jazz groups that performed in small Chicago clubs. He became known for the recordings he made in 1924 with the Wolverines, a white jazz combo that would later in-clude a famous Beiderbecke disciple, Jimmy McPartland. In 1924, Beiderbecke also began a long collaboration with the saxophonist Frankie Trumbauer. From 1927 until his death, Beiderbecke played with popular orchestras, most notably with Paul Whiteman's band.

Beiderbecke's playing was distinguished by its warm, re-laxed tone, quite different from the intensely dramatic style of his only peer, Louis Armstrong. Beiderbecke's rendition of "Singin' the Blues" is a jazz classic; his piano composition "In a Mist" shows a musical awareness that was far ahead of the jazz conventions of his time.

DELMER ROGERS

Bibliography: Baker, Dorothy, *Young Man with a Horn* (1938); Berton, Ralph, *Remembering Bix: A Memoir of the Jazz Age* (1973); Burnett, James, *Bix Beiderbecke* (1961); Shapiro, Nat, and Hentoff, Nat, *Hear Me Talkin' to Ya* (1955; repr. 1966); Sudhalter, Richard M., and Evans, Philip R., *Bix: Man and Legend* (1974).

Beijerinck, Martinus Willem [by'-ur-ink]

Martinus Willem Beijerinck, 1851–1931, a Dutch botanist, was the first to recognize the existence of VIRUSES. While attempt-ing to discover the cause of tobacco mosaic disease, he isolat-ed a "living" fluid that contained no bacteria known at that time. In 1898, Beijerinck concluded that he had found a new type of infective agent, which he called a virus.

Beijing (Peking) [bay-jing']

Beijing (1989 est. pop., 6,800,000), the capital of the People's Republic of China, is located at the northwestern border of the North China Plain about 145 km (90 mi) from the Bo Hai (Po Hai), or Gulf of Zhili (Chihli). With a metropolitan area population of 10,819,407 (1990), it is the second most popu-lous urban area in China, after SHANGHAI. Greater Beijing cov-ers an area of about 16,800 km² (6,500 mi²), about two-thirds of which is hilly, especially in the northwest, where the Dai-hang (Taihang) Mountains exceed 1,000 m (3,300 ft) in eleva-tion. The remaining third is alluvial lowland to the southeast. The major rivers passing through the city are the Yongding (Yungting), the main branch of the Hai River system, and the Chaobai (Ch'ao-pai). Beijing is the northern terminus of the Grand Canal.

Contemporary City. The municipality of Beijing, like those of Shanghai and Tianjin (Tientsin), has a political status equiva-lent to that of a province and is under the direct administra-tion of the central government. The city is divided into nine

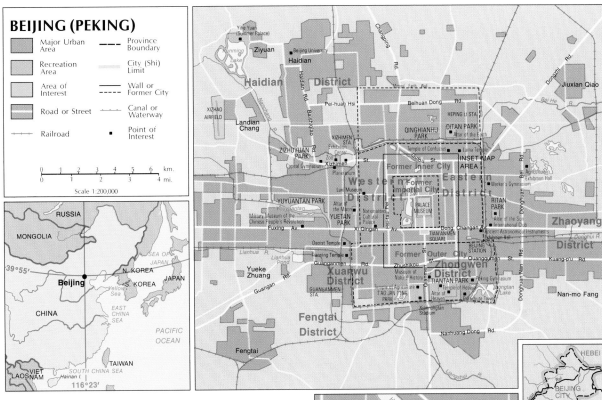

BEIJING (PEKING)

▨ Major Urban Area	--- Province Boundary
▨ Recreation Area	▨ City (Shi) Limit
▨ Area of Interest	— Wall or Former City
▨ Road or Street	┈ Canal or Waterway
┼ Railroad	■ Point of Interest

Scale 1:200,000

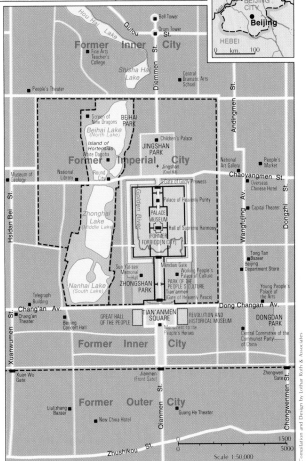

urban districts. Modern Beijing is a cosmopolitan city, with more ethnic diversity than most other large Chinese urban centers. In addition to the majority Han Chinese, Huis, Mongols, and members of other minority groups live in Beijing.

The core of Beijing consists of the old walled cities, the oldest of which is the Inner, or Tatar, City. It contains such landmarks as the Temple of Confucius, the Hall of Classics, and the Bell and Drum towers. Within this city lies the Imperial City, once restricted to members of the court and government officials. To the south lies the FORBIDDEN CITY, with its imperial palaces and the Hall of Supreme Harmony. Once accessible only to the imperial family and its staff, the palace is now the public Palace Museum. The Tiananmen (T'ien-an Men, or Gate of Heavenly Peace) Square marks the southern exit from the Forbidden City, leading to the Great Hall of the People, which is used for formal diplomatic receptions, and the Revolutionary and Historical Museum. The Old Legation Quarter, a scene of much fighting during the BOXER UPRISING, is also located south of the Forbidden City. Still farther south is the Outer, or Chinese, City, where the Chinese were herded when the Manchu assumed power. It is now an area of many government and business buildings. In the southern part of the Outer City stand the Temple of Heaven and the Temple of Agriculture. Outside the walls and surrounding the old cities lie the modern industrial quarters and the rural suburbs.

Modern industries have developed rapidly in Beijing since 1949. The city now has a wide range of industries manufacturing iron and steel, cement, machinery, chemicals, electronics, textiles, petrochemicals, motor vehicles, and processed foods. Beijing is also one of the leading centers of printing and publishing in China. Traditional handicraft articles, such as rugs, ivory and jade carvings, and cloisonné, are among the city's well-known exports.

As the national capital, Beijing is the focal point of communications and transportation in China. Railroads radiate to all major provincial capitals and industrial cities. The same pattern exists for air services. Water transportation, however, is not as well developed as in other major Chinese cities. An underground rapid transit system completed in 1988 moves people within the city limits.

Compilation and Design by Lothar Roth & Associates

(Left) *In the heart of Beijing is the former Forbidden City. Built between 1407 and 1421, it was the center of imperial power for more than 500 years. Today, it is open to the public as the Palace Museum and contains a magnificent collection of Chinese art.*

(Below) *The wide avenues of downtown Beijing are thronged with bicycles and buses, which remain the principal means of transportation. Cars are relatively rare. A subway system was completed in 1988.*

Beijing is China's leading center of learning and culture. BEIJING UNIVERSITY and Qinghua (Tsinghua) University (1911) are the two most respected in China. The National Library of Beijing houses a collection of 11 million volumes. More than 50 other major institutions of research and education are located in Beijing. The Palace Museum has the largest and most varied collection of cultural items of all museums in the country. The BEIJING OPERA enjoys an international reputation. The city is rich in historical sites, relics, scenic spots, and tourist attractions. The Ming Tombs are about 50 km (30 mi) northwest of the city. The Summer Palace, the Beihai (Pei-hai) Park, the Marco Polo Bridge, the Museum of Natural History, the Beijing Exhibition Center, the National Art Gallery, the Beijing Zoo, and many restaurants are frequented by both residents and tourists, although tourism declined after the government repression of prodemocracy demonstrators in Tiananmen Square in June 1989.

History. The name *Beijing* means "northern capital," and the city has had a long history. It was the capital of the Yen Kingdom during the Spring and Autumn period (722–481 BC) and until China was united in 221 BC by Shi Huangdi (Shih Huang-ti), first emperor of the Qin (Ch'in) dynasty. It served as the second capital of the Liao dynasty and the capital (1126–1234) of the succeeding Jin (Chin) dynasty, as well as that of the Yuan (1279–1368), Ming (1368–1644), and Qing (Ch'ing; 1644–1911) dynasties. The Boxer Uprising (1900) started in Beijing as an attempt to ward off colonial influences in the city. Subsequently the intellectual May Fourth Movement (1919–21) arose in Beijing and spread to the rest of the country. The second Sino-Japanese War (1937–45), during which Japan attempted to conquer China, began with a clash at the Marco Polo Bridge. From 1928 to 1949, while the capital was elsewhere, Beijing was known as Beiping (Peiping, or "northern peace"). In 1949, with the establishment of the People's Republic of China, the city again became the capital and resumed its old name.   JAMES CHAN

Bibliography: Greene, F., *Beijing* (1978); Morrison, H., *A Photographer in Old Peking* (1986); Sachen, Z., *Beijing—Old and New* (1986); Yi, W., et al., *Daily Life in the Forbidden City* (1989).

Beijing Opera

Beijing (Peking) Opera, a recent branch of the Chinese dramatic tradition that first appeared in China during the 11th century (Song, or Sung, dynasty), achieved maturity and acceptance by the theatergoing public of China's capital about the mid-19th century. It has, therefore, been designated the "theater of the capital" (*jinxi; ching-hsi*) and has acquired the prominence of a national style, although the genre originated in Hubei (Hopei) and Anhui (Anhwei) provinces.

Music in Beijing Opera is based on fixed rhythmic patterns and two families of melody: *xibi* (*hsi-p'i*) and *erhuang* (*erhuang*). Depending on the content and mood of the scene, the sex, age, and personality of a character, and tempo and meter, these melodic limitations are expanded to include diverse variations. The most important orchestral instruments are several types of bowed and plucked lutes. These are supported by a range of percussion instruments—gongs, cymbals, clappers, and drums—and occasionally, by reeds and flutes. Additional instruments vary with the troup and the opera.

The dramatic presentation consists of a sequence of arias and recitations. The recitations vary from unaccompanied, spoken delivery to several styles of musically expressive recitative. The verse structure of an aria is a sequence of rhymed couplets; arias are categorized according to rhythmic and dramatic features, such as lyric, narrative, animated, declamatory, dramatic, or interjective. Similarly, all character roles are designated as variants of one of four types: male, or *sheng*; female, or *dan* (*tan*); aggressive male with painted face, or *jing* (*ching*); and comic, or *zhou* (*chou*).

Beijing Opera has been based on episodes from traditional historical novels, such as *The Romance of the Three Kingdoms* and *The Water Margin,* and on Buddhist tales, such as *The White Snake* and *Travels to the West.* In modern Beijing Opera many conventions have been largely abandoned, and there are more revolutionary and contemporary themes.

ALAN L. KAGAN

Bibliography: Crump, J. I., and Malm, W. P., eds., *Chinese and Japanese Music-Dramas* (1975); Scott, A. C., *The Classical Theatre of China* (1957).

Beijing University

Founded in 1952, Beijing University (enrollment: 15,000; library: 3,700 volumes) incorporates the older Beijing (1898), Qinghun (Tsinghun; 1928), and Yanjing (Yenching; 1919) universities. A coeducational institution in Beijing, China, it has faculties of humanities, social sciences, sciences, and the languages and literatures of China, Russia, and the West.

Being and Nothingness

Being and Nothingness (1943; Eng. trans., 1956) is Jean Paul SARTRE's monumental philosophical treatise. In it Sartre presents the main tenets of his existentialist thought. Influenced by Martin Heidegger and Edmund Husserl, as the subtitle, ''An Essay in Phenomenological Ontology,'' makes clear, Sartre delves into the nature of existence, rejects the supernatural as well as any preconceived notion of humanity or morality, and argues that existence is pointless, ''contingent,'' and absurd. Each object simply is and has a ''being-in-itself,'' and, by virtue of their abundance, all objects encroach upon people. The human being is distinguished from the rest of the universe by consciousness, ''being-for-itself,'' and by the freedom to form an identity. The artistic and creative use of this freedom is the central value in existentialism. In *Being and Nothingness*, Sartre also investigates the questions of time, reality and appearances, bad faith, responsibility, and the limits of freedom.   JOSEPH REITER

Bibliography: Catalano, Joseph S., *Commentary on Sartre's ''Being and Nothingness''* (1974; repr. 1987); Hartmann, Klaus, *Sartre's Ontology: A Study of ''Being and Nothingness'' in the Light of Hegel's Logic* (1966); Lacapra, Dominick, *A Preface to Sartre* (1978; repr. 1987).

Being and Time

In *Being and Time* (1927; Eng. trans., 1962), the German philosopher Martin HEIDEGGER used the method of PHENOMENOLOGY developed by his teacher Edmund Husserl—namely, to establish universal truths by examining the essential structures of experience—and applied it to the problem of human existence. Human beings, he says, are thrown into a world that has no meaning by itself; this he calls *Dasein* (''being there''). It is the human task to give meaning to the world by achieving authentic existence, one that transcends bondage to the facts of everyday life, which blinds people to their true selves. Authenticity involves consciousness of time, which for humans is the process of emerging from nothing and moving toward the nothingness of death. Acceptance of this destiny confers freedom on the individual and gives meaning to one's life. One of the basic texts of EXISTENTIALISM, *Being and Time* exerted a wide influence on European thought in the 20th century.

Beira   [bay-i'-rah]

Beira (formerly Sofala), a port and former resort in east central Mozambique and one of the largest cities of the country, lies on the Mozambique Channel of the Indian Ocean. The population is 291,604 (1989 est.). From 1975 to 1990 port activities were virtually halted by civil war in Rhodesia (now Zimbabwe) and by the activities of Mozambican rebels. The port facilities were rebuilt in the early 1990s with international aid, and Beira now handles one-third of Zimbabwe's foreign trade and copper exports from Zambia.

Beira was founded in 1891 by the Mozambique Company of Portugal on the site of an Arab settlement dating back to the 10th century. The rehabilitation of the road, railroad, and pipeline linking Beira to Zimbabwe (the Beira corridor) is a major priority for neighboring nations seeking to reduce their economic dependence on South Africa. In 1990 a limited cease-fire accord halted fighting along the corridor, which is guarded by troops from Zimbabwe and has become a haven for refugees.

Beirut   [bay-root']

Beirut is the capital and largest city of Lebanon, located on a promontory extending seaward from the Lebanon Mountains, about midway along the country's Mediterranean coastline. Its population is about 200,000 (1989 est.). Most of the people of Beirut are Arabs. Approximately two-thirds are Christian, and one-third are Muslim. Many of them, especially the Christians, are strongly influenced by French and Western European culture. Between 1975 and 1990, however, Beirut became known chiefly as one of the principal battlegrounds of the Middle East. Armed militias frequently clashed along the ''Green Line'' separating Muslim West Beirut from Christian East Beirut, and the violence devastated Beirut's once-flourishing economy, disrupted normal life and essential services, and caused much of the population to leave the city.

Contemporary City. The older part of present-day Beirut centers on a square known as the Place des Martyrs. New residential areas lie to the west in Ras Beirut. The city has numerous mosques and Christian churches and a number of educational institutions. The medical school of the AMERICAN UNIVERSITY OF BEIRUT is particularly well known.

Traditionally, Beirut's economy was dependent on regional commerce and industry; tourism was also important. Long the most important port on the eastern Mediterranean and a hub of trade for all of southwest Asia, Beirut was a major international banking center and was considered the most cosmopolitan city in the Middle East. Its port reopened in 1991.

History. An ancient Phoenician settlement known as Berytus, Beirut traces its history to the 15th century BC. It was a great

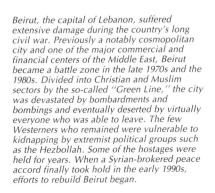

Beirut, the capital of Lebanon, suffered extensive damage during the country's long civil war. Previously a notably cosmopolitan city and one of the major commercial and financial centers of the Middle East, Beirut became a battle zone in the late 1970s and the 1980s. Divided into Christian and Muslim sectors by the so-called ''Green Line,'' the city was devastated by bombardments and bombings and eventually deserted by virtually everyone who was able to leave. The few Westerners who remained were vulnerable to kidnapping by extremist political groups such as the Hezbollah. Some of the hostages were held for years. When a Syrian-brokered peace accord finally took hold in the early 1990s, efforts to rebuild Beirut began.

seat of learning during the Roman Empire. An earthquake in 551 destroyed the city, but it was rebuilt. Ruled successively by the Crusaders, the Mamelukes, and the Ottoman Turks, Beirut emerged in the 19th century as a major Middle Eastern port with close ties to the West and was an early center of Arab nationalism. It became the capital of Lebanon in 1920. In the mid- and late 1970s, Beirut was damaged by fighting between Lebanese Christians and Muslims, and as a stronghold of the anti-Israeli Palestine Liberation Organization (PLO), it was subjected to air attacks by Israel. Large areas of Beirut were destroyed when the Israeli army occupied part of the city and expelled the PLO in 1982. The Israelis withdrew from Beirut in September 1983. In October, more than 230 American and 50 French members of an international peacekeeping force stationed in the city were killed when terrorists bombed their headquarters. Syrian peacekeeping forces arrived in Beirut in 1987. The Lebanese army, with Syrian support, gained control of Beirut late in 1990, and the enormous task of rebuilding the war-torn city was begun.   W. A. BLADEN

Bibliography: Ajami, Fouad, *Beirut: City of Regrets* (1988); Fawaz, Leila T., *Merchants and Migrants in 19th Century Beirut* (1983); Khuri, Fuad I., *From Village to Suburb* (1975).

Beisan: see BETH-SHAN.

Beissel, Johann Conrad   [by'-suhl]

Johann Conrad Beissel, b. April 1690, d. July 6, 1768, was a German-American religious leader who founded the Seventh-Day Baptist community at EPHRATA, Pa. After emigrating from Germany to Pennsylvania in 1720, he assisted Peter Becker, the leader of a group of radical pietist BRETHREN, or Dunkers, in Germantown.

An ascetic, Beissel formed (1732) a semimonastic community at Ephrata. There he and his followers lived a communal, celibate life and attempted to recapture the spirit of early Christianity. The Ephrata press, one of the earliest in America, became well known. Popular publications included *The Martyrs' Mirror* (1761), an account of the persecution of Mennonites in Europe, and *Turtel-Taube* (1747), a collection containing many hymns written by Beissel. At its height about 1750, the Ephrata community numbered several hundred members and was a cultural center for Pennsylvania Germans. Its influence lasted into the 19th century.

Bibliography: Klein, W., *Johann Conrad Beissel* (1942; repr. 1972).

Beja   [bay'-juh]

Beja (Arabic: Bujah) is the name given to a number of pastoral nomadic tribes inhabiting the arid country bordering the western shore of the Red Sea, from southeastern Egypt through Sudan into northern Ethiopia (Eritrea). The principal modern Beja tribes are the Ababada, Bisharin, Hadendoa, Amarar, and Beni 'Amer, with a combined population of more than 300,000. These tribes probably include descendants of the earliest inhabitants of the area. In the 6th century the Beja became Christians, but they converted to Islam in the 13th century. Most speak a Hamitic language (To Bedawi), but some speak Tigre. The Ababada now speak Arabic—a sign of the increasing Arabization that has affected all pre-Islamic tribal populations of the Middle East. Beja economy is primarily based on camel and goat herding, and the Beja have preserved a number of pre-Islamic rituals associated with their pastoral mode of subsistence. The society is stratified, and the relationship between classes is ritualized.   BRIAN SPOONER

Bibliography: Paul, Andrew, *A History of the Beja Tribes of the Sudan* (1954; repr. 1971).

Béjart, Madeleine   [bay-zhar']

Madeleine Béjart, baptized Jan. 8, 1618, d. Feb. 17, 1672, was the leader of a family of French actors who served as the basis of Molière's first company, the Illustre Théâtre. It was reputedly under her influence that Molière entered the theater, and she remained with him until her death, a year before his, creating such roles as Dorine in *Tartuffe* and Frosine in *The Miser*. Her daughter, Armande, became Molière's wife and played many of his heroines.   HARRY C. CARLSON

Bibliography: Bulgakov, M., *The Life of Monsieur de Molière* (1986); Chatfield-Taylor, H. C., *Molière* (1907; repr. 1973).

Béjart, Maurice   [bay-zhar']

Maurice Béjart, b. Maurice Berger in France, Jan. 1, 1927, is a choreographer whose interest lies in making ballet accessible to a wider public. His productions are lavish, often more spectacle than dance, and include elements of many dance styles. His own dancing career was eclectic. He cofounded (1953) Les Ballets de l'Étoile (later Ballet-Théâtre de Paris). In 1959 his choreography to Igor Stravinsky's *Le Sacre du printemps*, commissioned for the Théâtre Royal de la Monnaie in Brussels, was so well received that Béjart started a company, known as Les Ballets du XXᵐᵉ Siècle, based at that theater. He moved his company from Brussels to Lausanne, Switzerland, in 1987, renaming it Béjart Ballet Lausanne.

Among Béjart's more popular works are *Boléro* (1960), *Nijinsky, Clown de Dieu* (1971), and *Ninth Symphony* (1964). He likes the company to perform in such large spaces as sports arenas; the crowds are usually enthusiastic, even if critical reaction is mixed. In 1970, Béjart founded MUDRA (an acronym of his own invention) in Brussels as a training school for his company. Characteristic of Béjart's spectacular mixed-media later works are *Héliogabale, Molière Imaginaire*, and the controversial *Notre Faust* (Our Faust), all created in 1976. *Don Giovanni* (1980); *Le Martyre de Saint-Sebastien* (1988), with onstage orchestra, chorus, and solo singers as well as dancers; *Ring um den Ring* (1990); and *La Tour* (1991) are more recent works.   MICHAEL ROBERTSON

Bibliography: Gruen, John, *The Private World of Ballet* (1976); Stengele, Roger, *Who's Béjart?* (1972).

Békésy, Georg von

The studies of Hungarian-American physicist and physiologist Georg von Békésy, b. June 3, 1899, d. June 13, 1972, yielded essential new insights into human hearing and other sensory processes. Upon earning a Ph.D. in physics from the University of Budapest in 1923, Békésy began examining telephone communications problems. This in turn led him to investigate and determine the mechanics of the cochlea of the inner ear. His sensory studies, continued in the United States after 1947, brought him the 1961 Nobel Prize for physiology or medicine.

Bekhterev, Vladimir Mikhailovich   [bek'-tir-ef]

Vladimir Mikhailovich Bekhterev, b. Jan. 1, 1857, d. Dec. 24, 1927, was a Russian psychiatrist who founded the science of reflexology, the experimental study of reflexes. He also had a strong influence on the development of BEHAVIORISM. Bekhterev founded (1884) one of the first experimental psychology laboratories and wrote extensively on the central nervous system.   JOHN McLEISH

Bibliography: McLeish, John, *Soviet Psychology* (1975).

Bel and the Dragon

In some editions of the Bible, Bel and the Dragon is the name given to chapter 14 of DANIEL. Excluded from the Hebrew Bible, the chapter appears in the Protestant APOCRYPHA. Bel was a huge idol believed to consume great amounts of food and drink. When Daniel exposed the fraud, the Persian king Cyrus destroyed the statue. Daniel also poisoned a dragon that was worshiped as a god and was thereupon thrown to the lions, but he miraculously survived for six days. These popular stories were probably written around 130 BC.

bel canto   [bel kahn'-toh]

The Italian style of bel canto ("beautiful song") singing spread all across 18th-century Europe, except for France; it placed great value on breath control, agility, dynamic flexibility, beauty of sound, and virtuosic brilliance. Stemming from the *opera seria*, in which it was a weapon in the duel between CASTRATI and female singers, it became simply a vehicle for display, sharply dividing the musical elements of OPERA from the dramatic. Following an era of declamatory singing that was more functional than beautiful, bel canto was enthusiastically received by audiences until the reform period of the late 18th century. Since both virtuosity and lyric beauty are now esteemed, the principles of bel canto continue as part of the modern singer's training.   ELWYN A. WIENANDT

Bibliography: Duey, Phillip A., *Bel Canto and Its Golden Age* (1951; repr. 1980); Grout, Donald J., *Short History of Opera*, 3d ed. (1987).

Bel Geddes, Norman   [bel ged'-eez]

Norman Bel Geddes, b. Norman Melancton Geddes in Adrian, Mich., Apr. 27, 1893, d. May 8, 1958, was one of the most visionary of American scene designers. Many of his designs comprised mood-evoking, multilevel, abstract constructions that combined the lighting techniques of Adolphe Appia with the grandeur of Edward Gordon Craig. His design for an adaptation and production of Dante's *Divine Comedy* comprised a crater of concentric levels whose appearance was altered by light. Envisioned for Madison Square Garden, it, like many of his projects, was never realized. His most spectacular setting was the transformation of New York's Century Theatre into a Gothic cathedral for Max REINHARDT's production of *The Miracle* (1924). Over the years he proposed, but never built, theaters-in-the-round, a nonproscenium theater, and various mechanized stage devices. He designed General Motor's Futurama for the 1939 World's Fair and by the 1940s was concentrating on industrial design. His daughter, the actress Barbara Bel Geddes, b. New York City, Oct. 31, 1922, gained celebrity as Miss Ellie (1978–84, 1985–90) in the long-running television series "Dallas" (1978–91).   ARNOLD ARONSON

Belafonte, Harry   [bel-uh-fahn'-tay]

Harold George Belafonte, Jr., b. New York City, Mar. 1, 1927, became internationally famous as a singer of Jamaican calypso and other folk music. Born of West Indian parents, he spent part of his youth in the United States and part in Jamaica. He worked as a jazz singer in the late 1940s and became part of the Greenwich Village folk revival in the 1950s. His West Indian records include "Jamaica Farewell" (1956) and "Island in the Sun" (1957). He continues to perform.

Bibliography: Fogelson, G., *Harry Belafonte*, rev. ed. (1991); Shaw, Arnold, *Belafonte: An Unauthorized Biography* (1960).

Bélanger, François Joseph   [bay-lahn-zhay']

François Joseph Bélanger, b. 1744, d. May 1, 1818, was one of the foremost French architects and decorators in the neoclassic Louis XVI style. Of his work, only the beautifully proportioned Bagatelle Pavilion (1777), built for his patron and protector, the comte d'Artois, at Neuilly-sur-Seine and the chastely rich interiors (1777–84) of the Château des Maisons (both near Paris) survive intact. Bélanger's renowned *folies* (garden structures) and his elegant Parisian *hôtels* (private houses) have all been demolished or much altered.

Bibliography: Braham, Allan, *The Architecture of the French Enlightenment* (1980).

Belarus   [bel-ah-roos']

Belarus (Byelarus, Belorussia, White Russia) is a landlocked country in Eastern Europe, bordered in the north and east by Russia, in the south by Ukraine, in the west by Poland, and in the northwest by Lithuania and Latvia. MINSK is the capital. Until it achieved independence in 1991, Belarus was the Belorussian Soviet Socialist Republic within the USSR.

LAND AND RESOURCES

Most of Belarus is a flat plain, with little variation in relief. The elevation is generally higher in the north, and a chain of hills runs through the central portion of the country. Marshy lowlands cover the southern region of Polesye (the PRIPET

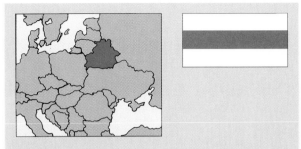

BELARUS

LAND. Area: 207,600 km² (80,155 mi²). Capital and largest city: Minsk (1991 est.): 1,633,600.

PEOPLE. Population (1992 est.): 10,390,000; density: 50 persons per km² (129.6 per mi²). Ethnic composition (1989): Belorussians (77.9%); Russians (13.2%); Poles (4.1%); Ukrainians (2.9%); Jews (1.1%).

EDUCATION AND HEALTH. Institutions of higher learning (1990): 33, plus 145 technical colleges. Hospital beds (1989): 138,300. Physicians (1989): 41,400.

ECONOMY. Principal products: agriculture—livestock, dairy products, flax, hemp, tobacco, potatoes, grain; manufacturing and industry—wood products, paper, textiles, food products, chemicals, motor vehicles, agricultural machinery, electrical equipment, leather products, machine tools; mining and extraction—crude oil, natural gas, peat. Currency: ruble.

GOVERNMENT. Type: republic. Legislature: Supreme Soviet. Administrative subdivisions: 6 regions (oblasts).

COMMUNICATIONS. Railroads (1990): 5,590 km (3,473 mi) total. Roads (1990): 92,200 km (57,290 mi) total.

MARSHES) in the basin of the Pripyat River. The major rivers drain either westward into the Baltic Sea (the Western DVINA and NEMAN) or southward into the Black Sea (the DNEPR, with its main tributaries, the Berezina and the Pripyat). Numerous streams and lakes are a prominent feature of the landscape, and a network of canals links the navigable waterways. About one-third of the country is covered with forests, mostly coniferous and birch. There is a rich variety of wildlife, including such rare animals as the European bison in the primal forest

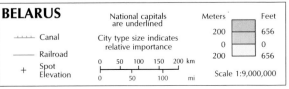

BELARUS

National capitals are underlined

┄┄┄ Canal

City type size indicates relative importance

──── Railroad

╋ Spot Elevation

Meters	Feet
200	656
0	0
200	656

0 50 100 150 200 km
0   50   100   mi

Scale 1:9,000,000

Minsk, the capital of Belarus and of the Commonwealth of Independent States, is situated on the Svisloch River (foreground). It is Belarus's main manufacturing center and accounts for one-third of the country's industrial output. Historically Minsk was one of the principal centers of East European Jewry. In 1897, Jews constituted more than half of the city's population. A large part of the Jewish community perished during the Holocaust.

reserve of Belaya Vezha (Białowieża) that straddles the Belorussian-Polish border.

Belarus was long thought to be poor in minerals, its natural resources limited to peat, gravel, sands, and clays. Recent surveys, however, have uncovered major deposits of coal, shale, oil, and potassium salts. Limestone, dolomite, and other building materials are also present. The soils are generally poor, and much of the land has been contaminated by radioactivity from the CHERNOBYL nuclear accident of 1986.

The climate is moderately continental. The temperature averages −6° C (21° F) in January and 18° C (64° F) in July. Average annual precipitation is 550–700 mm (22–28 in).

PEOPLE
More than three-fourths of the population consists of ethnic Belorussians. As a branch of the East Slavs, mostly Eastern Orthodox in religion, the Belorussians are linguistically and culturally closely related to the Russians and Ukrainians. They have traditionally been an overwhelmingly rural people, and only since the 1980s have a majority of them resided in cities. The Russians, who form 13% of the population, are much more highly urbanized, and the Russian language has long predominated in the cities and governmental institutions. The official use of Belorussian has increased, however, since 1990, when it was declared the country's official language.

Education and Health Care. Near universal literacy was achieved in Belarus by the 1950s. Ten-year primary and secondary education is free and compulsory; higher education is free, and entrance is by examination. In higher and specialized secondary education the Russian language predominates.

Medical services made dramatic advances in Belarus during the 20th century and have been free since the early Soviet period. The quality of medical care has declined since the 1970s, however, reflected in rising infant mortality and lowered life expectancy. The impact of the Chernobyl nuclear disaster on public health was undoubtedly severe.

Major cities, in addition to Minsk, are the administrative centers: BREST, Gomel' (Homel), Grodno (Hrodna), Mogilev (Mahilioŭ), and Vitebsk (Vitsebsk).

Culture. Belarus possesses a rich folklore and a legacy of literature, art, and architecture from the Kievan and Lithuanian periods. The 18th and 19th centuries were a time of Polish and Russian cultural ascendancy. A Belorussian literary rebirth began at the turn of the 20th century, and native cultural life was vibrant in the 1920s. Beginning in the 1930s Soviet policy favored the Russian language and culture; only in the late 1980s did Belorussian cultural life experience a revival.

ECONOMY
Until independence Belarus was fully integrated into the centrally planned Soviet economy, in which resource allocations, production targets, and monetary policy were determined in Moscow. The economic difficulties that beset the USSR in the 1980s were reflected in Belarus and intensified after independence. Movement toward a free-market system has been slow and largely limited to the service sector. Most industry continues to be under state management and agriculture remains collectivized.

Agriculture. Livestock (cattle, hogs, sheep, and goats) accounts for more than half the value of agricultural output in Belarus. The country's chief crops are fodder and potatoes, followed by cereal grains (mainly rye, barley, and oats) and sugar beets. Flax and hemp are also important.

Industry. Traditionally an agricultural land, Belarus experienced major industrialization only after World War II. The country long specialized in such light industries as food processing, woodworking, and textiles; newer industries include chemicals, oil refining, instrument making, and electronics. Important products include trucks, tractors, and agricultural machinery, as well as consumer goods such as sewing machines, pianos, and watches.

GOVERNMENT
During the Soviet period, the Communist party of Belarus was entirely subordinated to the central party organs in Moscow. The government of the Belorussian SSR in turn strictly implemented party policy directives. The first free and partly contested elections in Belarus were held in March 1990. The newly elected parliament, though still dominated by Communist deputies, gradually asserted greater autonomy from Moscow, and in the wake of the failed Soviet coup of August 1991, declared Belarus's independence. The activities of the Communist party were then suspended, but the development of a multiparty system proceeded slowly, and former Communists maintained their leading positions in government.

The new constitution, adopted in March 1994, provides for a popularly elected president who serves for a maximum of two five-year terms. The president is head of state and commander in chief of the armed forces. The unicameral legislature (the Supreme Soviet) has 260 members. In the first presidential election (June–July 1994) the two main candidates were then prime minister Vyacheslav Kebich and a former factory manager, Aleksandr Lukashenko, who ran on an anticorruption platform. Lukashenko won by a landslide, receiving more than 80% of the vote.

HISTORY

Beginning in the 6th century the territory of modern Belarus was settled by East Slavic tribes, the ancestors of the Belorussians. In the 9th and 10th centuries several principalities emerged, the most important being centered around Polotsk (Polatsk). Through dynastic links they came to be part of Kievan Rus' and were converted to Orthodox Christianity.

After the disintegration of Kievan Rus' in the 13th century, the Belorussian lands were incorporated into the expanding Grand Duchy of Lithuania. At first the Belorussians exerted a strong religious and cultural influence on the pagan Lithuanians; after the dynastic union of Lithuania and Poland in 1386, however, the Lithuanians converted to Latin Christianity, and the position of the Orthodox Belorussians began to decline. The Belorussian bishops accepted union with Rome in 1596. Most of the population adhered to the EASTERN RITE (Uniate) church, but the nobility largely adopted Latin Rite Catholicism along with the Polish language and culture.

In the Partitions of Poland (1772, 1793, and 1795; see PO-LAND, PARTITIONS OF), Belarus was annexed to the Russian Empire. In the 19th century the Russians and Poles competed for the loyalty of the Belorussian (largely peasant) masses. Only in the late 19th century, after a peasant revolt led by Kastus Kalinouski (Konstantin Kalinovsky) in 1863, did a distinct Belorussian national awareness begin to develop. This was further stimulated by a literary revival, exemplified by the works of the Belorussian poets Yakub Kolas and Yanka Kupala.

An independent Belarus was proclaimed (March 1918) after the collapse of the Russian Empire. After the POLISH-SOVIET WAR of 1920, however, western Belarus was occupied by Poland, and the eastern regions became the Belorussian SSR, part of the Soviet Union. In 1939, at the beginning of World War II, the western territories were also annexed by the USSR. As a principal theater of the war, Belarus suffered enormous devastation and lost one-quarter of its population.

Postwar reconstruction was followed by a period of considerable economic development and rapid industrialization. The reforms begun by Soviet leader Mikhail GORBACHEV in the mid-1980s stimulated a national revival, including the formation of a mass popular movement called Adradzhenne (Rebirth) in 1989, and unrest among Belorussian workers contributed to the economic crisis that hastened the end of the USSR. When the COMMONWEALTH OF INDEPENDENT STATES was formed by the former Soviet republics in December 1991, Minsk became its capital.   LUBOMYR HAJDA

Bibliography: Kipel, Viaut and Zora, eds., *Byelorussian Statehood: Reader and Bibliography* (1988); Lubachko, Ivan, *Belorussia under Soviet Rule* (1972); Vakar, Nicholas, *Belorussia* (1956).

Belasco, David

David Belasco was the first American theatrical producer to enjoy a widespread following. His stage productions were notable for their use of lavish settings, realistic props, and innovative special effects.

The American producer and playwright David Belasco, b. San Francisco, July 25, 1853, d. May 14, 1931, was an outstanding theatrical personality of his time. He is notable for his exotic productions, which became world renowned for their innovative scenic realism and lavishness; for his rivalry with and defeat of the Klaw-Erlanger theater syndicate; for his encouragement of American playwrights, whose dramas he performed in his theaters; for his discovery and training of such stars as Mrs. Leslie Carter, David Warfield, and Ina Claire; and for the popular, sentimental, and melodramatic plays he authored, coauthored, or adapted.

Belasco's early education in a Roman Catholic monastery influenced his austere mode of dress and helped earn him the soubriquet Bishop of Broadway. Acting from childhood on, he managed San Francisco theaters from 1873 to 1879. With James A. Herne, his first important collaborator, he wrote the popular melodrama *Hearts of Oak* (1879).

In 1880 he went to New York City, where he spent most of his life. For several years he was stage manager of the Madison Square Theater, for which he wrote plays, achieving popularity with *May Blossom* (1884), a Civil War love story. It was followed by *Lord Chumbley* (1888), a domestic drama featuring a comic Englishman; *The Girl I Left behind Me* (1893), a popular Indian melodrama written with Franklyn Fyles; and *The Heart of Maryland* (1895), a Civil War drama.

The most enduring of Belasco's plays, however, are *Madame Butterfly* (1900) and *The Girl of the Golden West* (1905), immortalized in Puccini's operas; *Du Barry* (1901), an episodic historical extravaganza; *The Darling of the Gods* (1902), an exotic romance written with John Luther Long; *Adrea* (1904, also with Long), a romantic 5th-century melodrama; and *The Return of Peter Grimm* (1911), a work of whimsy that turned out to be Belasco's last significant play. Thereafter he continued to write and adapt plays but devoted most of his efforts to production and management. He wrote an autobiography, *The Theatre through Its Stage Door* (1919).   MYRON MATLAW

Bibliography: Marker, Lise-Lone, *David Belasco: Naturalism in the American Theatre* (1975); Timberlake, Craig, *Life and Work of David Belasco, the Bishop of Broadway* (1954).

Belaúnde Terry, Fernando   [bay-lah-oon'-day ter'-ree]

Fernando Belaúnde Terry, b. Oct. 7, 1912, is an architect and urban planner who served as president of Peru from 1963 to 1968 and again from 1980 to 1985. During his first 5-year term he initiated social and land reforms and built highways across the Andes. Removed from office by a military junta, he lived in exile until 1976. During his second term he was preoccupied by efforts to contain a rebellion by the leftist *Sendero Luminoso* (Shining Path) guerrilla movement.

Belcher, Jonathan

Jonathan Belcher, b. Cambridge, Mass., Jan. 8, 1682, d. Aug. 31, 1757, was an American colonial governor. He graduated from Harvard in 1699 and spent several years in England before succeeding as a merchant in Boston. In 1718 he was elected to the first of eight one-year terms on the Massachusetts Council. His appointment as governor of Massachusetts and New Hampshire, which he obtained by journeying to London in 1730, was terminated by the British crown in 1741 as a result of irreconcilable differences between the crown and the colonists. As governor of New Jersey from 1747 until his death, he enlarged the College of New Jersey (Princeton), to which he bequeathed his library.

Belém   [bay-laym']

Belém, the capital of Brazil's Pará state, is the largest city in the Amazon Basin, with a population of 1,116,578 (1985). Belém is situated on the Pará River, a tributary of the Amazon, 145 km (90 mi) from the Atlantic Ocean. The climate is hot and rainy.

The city's recent growth has been stimulated by improved transportation connections. The Belém-Brasília Highway runs

2,350 km (1,460 mi) in an almost straight north-south line between the two cities. Long an important port, Belém now has an international airport, northern Brazil's largest.

As the major commercial center of the Amazon Basin, Belém exports nuts, jute, and black pepper. Livestock graze on Marajó island, the largest river island in the world. A wide variety of native handicrafts is available in the local market. A state university, several newspapers, and the large, white marble Paz Theater serve the educational and cultural needs of the people.

Belém, founded by the Portuguese in 1616, was the focus of several economic booms thereafter.   JAMES N. SNADEN

Belfast

Belfast is the seat of County Antrim in eastern Northern Ireland and the capital city of Northern Ireland. It is located on the Lagan River at the head of Belfast Lough in a valley between the Hills of Down and the Antrim Plateau. This port and industrial city is one of the world's largest shipbuilding centers. It is also the center of the Irish linen industry. Belfast has a population of 295,100 (1990 est.).

Queens University, Belfast, was founded in 1845. Other institutions of note include the Linen Hall Library (1788), the Botanic Gardens, the Grand Opera House, and the Ulster Folk Museum, which contains exhibits that illustrate life in Ireland before the Industrial Revolution. Stormont, on the outskirts of the city, is the site of the Parliament building.

First settled about 1177 around an ancient fort, Belfast was incorporated in the 17th century by James I of England. The English brought in Protestant settlers, and the city grew as Huguenot refugees, who arrived in the late 17th century, improved the linen-weaving industry.

In the 1790s, Belfast was a center of agitation for Irish independence (see UNITED IRISHMEN). Later, however, the city's Protestant majority became strongly unionist (favoring continued union with Britain). In 1920, Belfast became the capital of the self-governing British province of Northern Ireland. Belfast was much affected by the renewed Protestant-Catholic strife in the province in the late 1960s and 1970s. Since that time, although tensions between the Protestant and Catholic communities remain, much new housing has been built and the economy has improved.

Bibliography: Burton, Frank, *The Politics of Legitimacy: Struggles in a Belfast Community* (1978); Johnstone, Robert, *Belfast* (1991).

Belfort Gap

The Belfort Gap, also called Burgundy Gate, in eastern France, is a passage about 24 km (15 mi) wide between the Vosges and the Jura mountains. It is a strategic link between the Rhine Valley and the Paris Basin.

Belgian Congo: see ZAIRE.

Belgian horse

The Belgian horse, descendant of the medieval battle horse of western Europe, is one of the largest breeds of draft horse.

The Belgian is one of the most handsome and powerful of draft horses. Its coloration is usually sorrel, chestnut, or roan, with a flaxen mane, tail, and fetlocks. There may be a white blaze on the nose. The Belgian is among the heaviest of draft horses; it may weigh 1,000 kg (2,200 lb) and stand 17 hands (173 cm/68 in) at the shoulder. It is wide through the chest and more massive than other draft horses, although some may stand taller.   EVERETT SENTMAN

British troops patrol the streets in a Roman Catholic section of Belfast. A resurgence of sectarian violence in the early 1990s led to reinforcement of the British Army units in Northern Ireland.

Belgian literature

Maurice Maeterlinck, a Belgian essayist and dramatist, won international acclaim for The Blue Bird *(1908), a play about two children's search for happiness. In addition to the fictional works for which he received a Nobel Prize in 1911, Maeterlinck published several tracts concerning social organization in insect colonies.*

Because Belgium is a bilingual country whose independence dates only from 1830, its literature is written in both Flemish and French. In the southern part of Belgium, mainly French and Walloon, a French dialect, are spoken and written; in the northern part the prevailing language is Flemish, or Southern Netherlandic (see DUTCH AND FLEMISH LITERATURE).

An early French poem, the 9th-century *Cantilène de Sainte Eulalie,* shows some evidence of Walloon, and the verse tale *Aucassin et Nicolette* may have been written in the Belgian province of Hainaut during the first half of the 13th century. Belgian literature did not begin to assert itself, however, until the Burgundians gained control of the Belgian provinces in the 14th century. Jean FROISSART and Philippe de Commynes, who were among the most famous of the 14th- and 15th-century chroniclers, were from Flanders or Hainaut.

Until the 19th century, Belgian writing in French remained minor, although in the 18th century the Brussels-born prince Charles Joseph de Ligne wrote letters and memoirs that are a remarkable chronicle of his society and times. The first noteworthy Belgian writing in French after independence was Charles de Coster's *The Legend of the Glorious Adventures of Till Eulenspiegel* (1867; Eng. trans., 1918), which achieved international renown. In this epic novel, the rogue hero symbolizes Flanders in its struggle against Spanish domination and bigotry.

A genuine Belgian literary renaissance occurred in the early 1880s, when Belgian authors writing in French rallied around the review *La Jeune Belgique* (Young Belgium), founded in 1881. Walloon regionalist novels appeared in the late 19th century but were overshadowed by poetry. Georges Rodenbach wrote poetry before writing his novel, *Bruges-la-morte* (Bruges the Dead, 1892). The poet Albert Giraud adopted the style of the PARNASSIANS. The most famous Belgian writer of the time, however, was Maurice MAETERLINCK, whose works attracted wide attention as an expression of symbolism and antinaturalism. Nearly as well known is Émile VERHAEREN, a poet who derived his inspiration and images from Walt Whitman, the common people, and industrialization.

A successor of Maeterlinck, Albert Mockel, founded the symbolist periodical *La Wallonie;* Max Elskamp contributed poetry illustrated with woodcuts to *La Jeune Belgique;* and Charles Van Lerberghe wrote a long symbolist poem, *Chanson d'Eve* (Song of Eve, 1904). Despite the symbolist movement, realism remained an important influence in Belgian writing, represented by the novelists Camile Lemonnier and Georges Eekhoud.

After World War I, some Belgian poets came briefly under the influence of DADA and SURREALISM but soon adopted a combination of modern and traditional styles. Two gifted lyric poets of the period were Émile Cammaerts and Marcel Thiry. The novelists Marie Gevers and Olivier Degée, who wrote un-der the name of Jean Tousseul, created detailed portraits of Flemish country life and the simplicity of the people.

Starting with the novelist Charles Plisnier, the first non-Frenchman to win the Goncourt Prize, and increasingly after World War II, Belgians who gained renown writing in French achieved equal reputations in France. Among such authors were the surrealist poet Henri Michaux, the playwrights Fernand CROMMELYNCK and Michel de GHELDERODE, the internationally famous writer of psychological mystery stories Georges SIMENON, and the feminist writer Françoise MALLET-JORIS.

DAVID I. GROSSVOGEL

Bibliography: Holmes, James S., trans., *A Quarter Century of Poetry from Belgium* (1970); Mallinson, Vernon, *Modern Belgian Literature 1830–1960* (1966); Wilhelm, J. J., ed., *Anthology of Belgian Symbolist Poets* (1992); Willinger, David, *Belgian Plays: An Anthology of Contemporary Belgian Plays, 1970–82* (1984).

See also: FRENCH LITERATURE; WALLOONS.

Belgian Malinois   [mal-in-wah']

The Belgian Malinois is a large breed of herding dog. Ideally, males stand 61 to 66 cm (24 to 26 in) at the shoulders, and females 55.9 to 61 cm (22 to 24 in). The well-muscled, deep-chested body and the legs approximate a square in outline. The head and neck are carried proudly, and the triangular ears are stiffly erect. The long tail is held low except when the dog is in action.

The Belgian Malinois has a straight outercoat that is short, especially around the head and lower legs; the undercoat is dense. The color is fawn to mahogany, with a black face mask and ears. White toetips and a small white chest spot are permitted in show animals.

In most countries the Malinois, the BELGIAN SHEEPDOG, and the BELGIAN TERVUREN are considered different varieties of the same breed. In the United States, however, the American Kennel Club has recognized them as different breeds since 1959, and separate show classification was provided for the Malinois in 1965. Such dogs were in use by sheep raisers in Europe for centuries. As the industry declined in Belgium in the late 19th century, dog fanciers began to pay closer attention to the dog varieties that had developed in different regions.

Recognition of the Malinois as a distinct variety dates back to 1898. All of the breeds are alert workers, easily trained and readily adapted for guard duty and police work. They make good household companions.

JOHN MANDEVILLE

Bibliography: American Kennel Club, *The Complete Dog Book,* 18th ed. (1992).

The Belgian Malinois is used in Europe to herd sheep. Its coat is shorter than that of other Belgian sheepherding dogs.

Belgian sheepdog

The Belgian sheepdog, also known as the Groenendael, is a herding breed. It was used during World War I to deliver messages behind the lines.

The Belgian sheepdog is a large breed of herding dog that in general appearance resembles the Belgian Malinois and Belgian Tervuren. In most countries these are not recognized as distinct breeds, but the American Kennel Club gave them separate status in 1959. The Belgian sheepdog differs only in the length and color of its coat. The harsh, straight outercoat is long and abundant; the undercoat is dense. The hair must be black for show purposes, but some white is permitted: a small to moderate patch on the chest, frost on the muzzle, and white on the tips of the hind toes (on front toes, this is a fault).

JOHN MANDEVILLE

Bibliography: American Kennel Club, *The Complete Dog Book,* 18th ed. (1992).

Belgian Tervuren   [tuh-vurn']

The Belgian Tervuren, a longhaired herding dog, differs from the Belgian sheepdog mainly in the color of its coat.

The Belgian Tervuren is a large breed of herding dog that resembles the Belgian Malinois and Belgian sheepdog and is recognized as a distinct breed only by the American Kennel Club, since 1959. It differs from the Malinois in having a long coat and from the black sheepdog in its fawn to mahogany color. Like the Malinois, it has a black face mask and ears.

JOHN MANDEVILLE

Bibliography: American Kennel Club, *The Complete Dog Book,* 18th ed. (1992).

Belgium

Belgium is a constitutional monarchy in northwestern Europe. One of the Low Countries, it is bounded by the North Sea on the west, by France on the west and south, by the Netherlands on the north, and by Germany and Luxembourg on the east. Officially called the Kingdom of Belgium (Koninkrijk België in Dutch and Royaume de Belgique in French), Belgium is one of the smallest countries in Europe. Its territory includes the tiny exclave of Baarle-Hertog on the other side of the Dutch border, which is completely surrounded by territory of the Netherlands. Belgium's capital city, BRUSSELS, has a total population in its metropolitan area of 960,324 (1991 est.). ANTWERP, the second-largest urban area, has a population of 467,875 (1991 est.). The country is divided into nine provinces: Antwerp, Brabant, East Flanders, Hainaut, Liège, Limburg, Luxembourg, Namur, and West Flanders.

A very densely populated country, Belgium is situated at the center of a major urban and economic axis that encompasses much of western Europe. Modern agricultural practices, a vibrant economy, and an advanced social welfare system provide a high standard of living for its people. The country's name is derived from the Belgae, a Celtic people who inhabited the area in ancient times. Historically associated with the Netherlands, Belgium became a separate entity in the 17th century but did not become independent until 1830. Belgium was a founding member of the European Community (EC). Most of the EC's governing institutions are located in Brussels, as are the headquarters of the North Atlantic Treaty Organization (NATO), the Customs Cooperation Council, and other international bodies.

KINGDOM OF BELGIUM

LAND. Area: 30,519 km² (11,783 mi²). Capital and largest city: Brussels (1991 est. pop., 960,324).

PEOPLE. Population (1993 est.): 10,040,939; density: 329.0 persons per km² (852.1 per mi²). Distribution (1991): 95% urban, 5% rural. Annual growth (1993): 0.23%. Official languages: Dutch, French, German. Major religion: Roman Catholicism.

EDUCATION AND HEALTH. Literacy (1988): 100% of adult population. Universities (1991): 7. Hospital beds (1988): 91,170. Physicians (1988): 31,178. Life expectancy (1993): women—80.2; men—73.4. Infant mortality (1993): 7.4 per 1,000 live births.

ECONOMY. GNP (1992): $177.9 billion; $17,800 per capita. Labor distribution (1989): agriculture—2.5%; mining and manufacturing—18.8%; construction—5.4%; public utilities—1.0%; transportation and communications—6.1%; trade—16.5%; finance—7.6%; services—31.7%; other—10.4%. Foreign trade (Belgium–Luxembourg, 1991): imports—$121 billion; exports—$118 billion; principal trade partners (1990)—Germany, France, Netherlands, United Kingdom. Currency: 1 Belgian franc = 100 centimes.

GOVERNMENT. Type: constitutional monarchy. Legislature: Parliament. Political subdivisions: 9 provinces, 3 federal regions.

COMMUNICATIONS. Railroads (1990): 3,667 km (2,279 mi) total. Roads (1988): 128,345 km (79,750 mi) total. Major ports: 5. Major airfields: 5.

Belgium is located at the crossroads of Latin and Germanic Europe. The northern part of the country, loosely referred to as FLANDERS (Vlaanderen), has a predominantly Dutch (Flemish)-speaking population; in the southern region, known as Wallonia (Wallonie), the principal language is French. From these two peoples Belgium has derived a rich cultural heritage, as well as a tradition of sectional antagonism that is still very much a feature of its national life.

LAND AND RESOURCES

Belgium includes three major geographic zones. The northern lowlands rise from the polders along the shoreline. The polders are land reclaimed from the sea and adjacent estuaries by an elaborate system of dikes and drains that lie approximately at sea level. At 50 m (164 ft) the lowlands give way to the central low plateaus that rise gently to 350 m (1,148 ft) at the edge of the ARDENNES region. The southern hills zone comprises the high plateau of the Ardennes and Belgian Lorraine. The highest elevation in the country is Botrange peak (694 m/2,277 ft) in the upper Ardennes.

Soils and Drainage. Sea clay and peat bog dominate the soils of the polders, with the clays exceptionally fertile after drainage and desalination. The sands and clays of the interior lowlands are less suitable for agriculture and require heavy concentrations of humus and fertilizers. The SCHELDT (Schelde) River, with its tributaries, the Leie, Dender, Senne, Dijle, Demer, and Nete, drains northward off the plateaus and passes through Antwerp before emptying into the North Sea on the Dutch coast.

A deep layer of alluvium stretches from the edge of the plains to the Sambre-Meuse furrow that divides the central low plateaus from the southern hills. This is the most fertile region of the country. The Sambre River flows northeast from France to join the MEUSE (Maas) River at NAMUR. The Meuse then drains northward into the Netherlands, where it empties into the Rhine delta. The soils of the Ardennes are generally infertile, poorly drained, and not conducive to widespread agriculture. The high Ardennes serves as an important watershed between the Meuse and Moselle rivers.

Climate. Belgium has a northern maritime climate, with abundant precipitation, mild winters, and cool summers. Lowland Belgium is influenced by a combination of tropical and polar air masses that produce variable weather patterns—shifting winds, summer thunderstorms, winter drizzle, and overcast skies. The interior has more extreme summers and winters; the uplands have severe frost and a greater amount of cold and rain during the winter months. Temperatures average 17° C (63° F) in July and 2° C (35° F) in January. Precipitation averages 510–760 mm (20–30 in) a year north of the Sambre and Meuse rivers and may reach 1,300 mm (51 in) a year in the southern hills.

Flora and Fauna. Although evidence of undisturbed natural vegetation is rare in Belgium, more than 20% of the country is covered by moors and forests. About 60% of the productive forests are composed of deciduous species such as oak, beech, ash, and poplar; the remainder are coniferous, including spruce, larch, and various types of pine. The majority of the country's mixed forest is located in the Ardennes. Wildlife has been greatly reduced in the 20th century, and both government and private organizations are tackling the issues of conservation and preservation.

Natural Resources. Benefiting from the rich coal reserves in the Sambre–Meuse area, Belgium was one of the first coun-

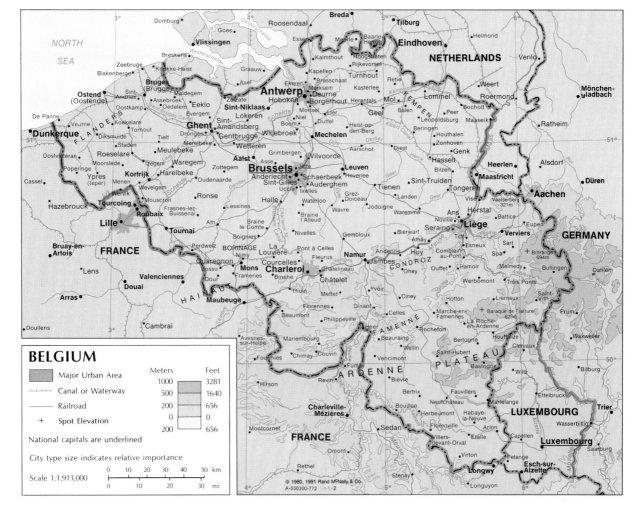

BELGIUM

	Major Urban Area	Meters	Feet
		1000	3281
+⧓⧓⧓+	Canal or Waterway	500	1640
——	Railroad	200	656
+	Spot Elevation	0	0
		200	656

National capitals are underlined

City type size indicates relative importance

Scale 1:1,913,000

0 10 20 30 40 50 km

0 10 20 30 mi

© 1980, 1991 Rand McNally & Co.
A-550300-772 -1-1-2

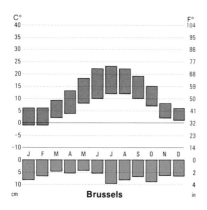

(Above) *Bars indicate monthly ranges of temperatures* (red) *and precipitation* (blue) *of Brussels, the capital of Belgium. Brussels has a marine west coast climate.* (Right) *The Bocq River, near Ciney, drains portions of the Condroz, a plateau in the Ardennes foothills that yields harvests of wheat, winter rye, barley, and potatoes.*

tries to begin industrialization in the early 19th century. Somewhat later, additional coal deposits were found in the Campine region of northeastern Belgium. In the late 20th century the coal-mining industry declined sharply because of the exhaustion of coal reserves, especially in the Sambre–Meuse valley, aggravated by high production costs and competition from cheap imported coal. Chalk and limestone are important mineral resources, along with glass sands, china clay, slate, and stone such as *petit granit*, marble, and porphyry. Water resources are becoming increasingly critical as Belgium struggles to satisfy the rising demands of cities and industries. A regional imbalance between supply and demand is growing: most of Belgium's groundwater originates in the southern half of the country, while urban and industrial users are concentrated in the north.

PEOPLE

Belgium's ancient Celtic–Germanic roots have been augmented by Roman, Frankish, Burgundian, Spanish, Austrian, and French cultural influences. The country's linguistic diversity has resulted from this mixture of peoples. Today, immigrant guest workers found in the cities include Italians, Turks, Moroccans, and Spaniards. In general, immigrants from EC countries constitute the majority of immigrants except in Brussels, where about half the newcomers are of non-European origin.

Language. Belgium has three official languages: Dutch, French, and German. Dutch is spoken by 57% of the population, French by 42%, and German by 0.6%. Most of the German-speaking community is concentrated in the Eastern Cantons of Liège province, a narrow area along the German border from around Eupen in the north to Saint Vith in the south.

For many years the Flemish and WALLOON (French-speaking) communities were in conflict over whether French or Dutch should be used in the schools, in the courts, for business, and for administration. French, being the language of the upper classes, had traditionally been dominant, a situation greatly resented by Dutch-speakers. In 1966 the country was divided into four linguistic areas. Dutch, which in Belgium includes the Flemish, Brabant, and Limburg dialects, became the official language north of a line running from east to west just south of Brussels. French, which in Belgium includes the Picardic, Walloon, and Lorraine dialects, became official south of the line. German became official in the Eastern Cantons, and the Brussels area was designated as bilingual. Each of the three language communities has autonomy in its own linguistic region over cultural affairs, language use, local social issues, and in national and international cultural relations.

Religion. Religious freedom was established by the constitution in 1831. The five officially recognized religions—those with clergy paid in part by the state—are Roman Catholicism, Protestantism, Anglicanism, Judaism, and Islam. It is estimated that about 70% of the population is Roman Catholic; Muslims, Jews, and Protestants make up a little over 10%; the remainder have no religious affiliation. The fastest-growing religion is Sunnite Islam. Most Muslims are urban-based migrant workers from Turkey and North Africa. Jews constitute less than one-half of one percent of the population and live mostly in Brussels and Antwerp.

Historically, religion has been a source of social division in Belgium. Profound disagreement has existed within the Catholic community about the appropriate relationship between church and state. Disagreement also exists between Catholics and non-Catholics, especially over Catholicism's social influence. In the 1950s, tensions flared over the issue of whether and to what extent the government should subsidize religious schools. An elaborate compromise was arranged, but strong differences of opinion persist.

Demography. Belgium is a highly urbanized country. The spatial distribution of people is very uneven, with the greatest densities found in the Antwerp–Brussels–Ghent central triangle. Flanders has a population density twice that of Wallonia. Some 135 cities account for more than 90% of the population. The largest cities, in addition to Brussels and Antwerp, are GHENT, CHARLEROI, and LIÈGE. The Ardennes region has no large city. The population density of Belgium is one of the highest in the world. Brabant, which includes Brussels, is the most densely populated province, and Luxembourg is the most sparsely populated. Since 1970, Belgium has experienced zero population growth. The birth- and death rates currently balance each other out at 12 per 1,000, and the balance between in- and out-migration is about equal. The population is aging as a result of falling birthrates, smaller families, and a longer life expectancy.

Health and Education. Education is compulsory for all children aged 6 to 18. Official (public) schools are operated by the government; most of the free (private) schools are affiliated with the Catholic church. Many children attend nursery schools beginning at age 2½. The largest universities are the state institutions at Ghent and Liège and the French- and Dutch-speaking universities at LOUVAIN and Brussels. Virtually the entire population is literate, and many are multilingual.

Nearly all Belgians are covered by national health insurance. The social security system also covers work accidents, unemployment, premature death, occupational diseases, invalidism, and retirement pensions.

CULTURE

Beginning in the 15th century, Belgium played a prominent role in the cultural life of Europe, especially in the visual arts and music. Painters such as Jan van EYCK and Rogier van der WEYDEN were chief among the early great masters of Northern Renaissance art. The tradition was continued in the 16th century by Peter BRUEGEL the Elder, who led the way for later painters of the Netherlands by choosing to focus on scenes from daily life. In the 17th century a more courtly and Italianate style was favored by Peter Paul RUBENS and Anthony VAN DYCK. The golden age of Flemish painting came to an end with the death of Rubens in 1640, but modern Belgium has also produced some outstanding painters, notably James ENSOR and René MAGRITTE. (See FLEMISH ART AND ARCHITECTURE.)

If the great centers of early Belgian painting were in Flanders, 15th-century Wallonia, especially Hainaut, was distinguished for the musical contributions of such composers as Gilles BINCHOIS, Guillaume DUFAY, JOSQUIN DES PREZ, and Jean d'OKEGHEM and others of the Burgundian School (see RENAISSANCE MUSIC). In the following century Flanders came to the fore with Adrian WILLAERT and Roland de LASSUS and others. Later Belgian composers included André GRÉTRY, César FRANCK, and the 20th-century master Jean Absil.

Belgium's literary heritage has been influenced by the country's linguistic divisions. French and Flemish literature have existed side by side since the Middle Ages, with matters complicated by the frequent use of the French language by Flemish authors prior to the 19th century. French became the preferred means of expression during the 16th century, and for a long time Flemish was neglected as a literary tongue. In the 19th century it was revived by such writers as the novelist Hendrik CONSCIENCE and the poet Guido GEZELLE. Twentieth-century Belgian writers in French include the poet, dramatist, and essayist Maurice MAETERLINCK, who won the Nobel Prize for literature in 1911, and the popular detective novelist Georges SIMENON. (See BELGIAN LITERATURE.)

Separate cultural councils have been established for the Dutch, French, and German linguistic regions. Belgium's impressive historical and architectural monuments attract tourists from around the world. Medieval castles and cathedrals, and guildhalls, municipal buildings, and fortifications dating from the 13th to the 17th century contrast dramatically with more contemporary structures. Biannually Belgium hosts the Europalia, a high-profile, months-long tribute to the visual and performing arts of one of the neighboring European countries. Another attraction is the prestigious Queen Elizabeth of Belgium International Music Competition. The film industry, sporting clubs, choirs, theatrical companies, and many other cultural, political, and social organizations add to Belgium's diverse artistic and cultural life.

ECONOMY

Belgium has a highly developed economy based on trade, industry, and services. The country's location near one of Europe's major trading arteries, the Rhine–Meuse–Scheldt delta, its dense network of railroads, highways, and navigable waterways, and the presence of EC and NATO headquarters have helped the Belgians develop a strong and diversified economic base. With the decline of mining and other traditional industries, the service sector has come to dominate the Belgian economy, today employing nearly 60% of the work force.

Agriculture. Belgian agriculture has undergone significant changes since the 1960s. Mechanization, soil fertilization, and greater intensification of agricultural production have resulted in higher yields per hectare, but not without an increase in ground- and surface water pollution. The farming sector provides more than 80% of Belgium's domestic food needs. Livestock raising and dairy farming are the leading agricultural activities of the Ardennes and Campine regions. Much land in the eastern and central regions is devoted to fodder, sugar beets, and potatoes. Wheat, barley, and oats are grown extensively, and Belgium is noted for its flowers and endives. High quality hops are used to produce a great array of outstanding beers.

Manufacturing and Mining. Technological advances and increased international competition have forced profound changes in Belgian industry. The manufacturing sector now accounts for less than 25% of total economic activity. Much of Belgium's manufacturing involves the processing of imported raw materials, especially textiles. Metallurgy, textiles, glass, mechanical engineering, chemicals, and food processing are concentrated around the major cities and form the backbone of modern Belgian industry. The mining sector has declined in importance since the 1950s; many coal mines have been closed or abandoned because they are no longer economically viable.

Forestry and Fishing. Roundwood production from the forests of the Ardennes supports a modest timber industry, of which paper products are the major component. However, about 50% of the timber needed for the country's paper and other industries is imported. Belgium does not have an important fishing industry. OSTEND and Zeebrugge are the principal fishing harbors, accounting for more than 90% of the total catch. Sole and halibut are the country's principal commercial fish.

Energy. Seven nuclear power stations generate about 80% of Belgium's total electricity consumption, making Belgium one of the world's most nuclear power–dependent countries. Natural gas imported from the Netherlands, Norway, and Algeria has taken the place of domestically produced coal gas. The reduction of petroleum imports has been a major energy policy objective of both Belgium and the European Community.

Encircled by an arm of the Leie River, 's Gravensteen, the castle of the counts of Flanders, is one of the major historic monuments of the Belgian city of Ghent. Originally built in the 9th century, reconstructed and enlarged by Philip of Alsace in 1180, and restored in the early 20th century, 's Gravensteen is one of the finest surviving examples of a medieval moated fortress.

(Left) *Tournai's cathedral of Notre Dame, built between 1140 and 1213, is one of Europe's finest cruciform basilicas. Tournai, in western Belgium near the French border, was a medieval crafts center noted for tapestry weaving and the production of copperware.*

(Below) *Traditional Flemish houses line one of Bruges's picturesque canals. In the background is the city's famous belfry, with its carillon of 47 bells. A major Flemish port and trading center in the Middle Ages, Bruges is now the capital of the Belgian province of West Flanders.*

The Belgian government is also pursuing solar, biomass, and geothermal energy alternatives, as well as the liquefaction and gasification of combustible solids. Belgium's power systems are linked to those in France, Germany, the Netherlands, and Luxembourg.

Transport and Communication. Belgium's central geographic position in western Europe has facilitated the development of one of the region's densest transport networks. Many Belgian cities are linked by a highly interdependent river and canal system that is focused on the port of Antwerp. The railroad system generally parallels the waterways, with major lines radiating from Brussels. High-speed rail lines are planned to connect Belgium with France, Germany, and the Netherlands. Major national and international highways cross the country, primarily from southwest to northeast. Belgium's domestic air network is negligible. The national airline, SABENA, based in Brussels, connects Belgium with some 50 European and overseas cities. Telecommunications facilities extend to all parts of the country.

Trade. The Belgian economy is extremely open and is fully integrated with the economies of surrounding countries. Few natural resources and a small domestic market mean that Belgium must depend heavily on foreign trade. The majority of trade today is with other members of the EC. The Belgium Luxembourg Economic Union (BLEU) accounts for more than 3% of world exports, making the union a sizable commercial power despite the small size of the two countries. Brussels has became a key European financial center, with trade in services playing a vital role in the Belgian economy.

GOVERNMENT AND POLITICS

Belgium is a parliamentary democracy with a constitutional hereditary monarchy. Legislative power is exercised by a 212-member Chamber of Representatives and a 184-member senate. The king and his elected ministers oversee the executive branch of the government and appoint members of the judiciary. Parliamentary representatives must be at least 25 years old, and senators must be at least 40 years old. Universal suffrage exists for all citizens 18 years or older, and voting is compulsory. The king and his ministers promulgate royal decrees. Although the king cannot act unilaterally, traditionally he has had considerable moral authority. The current king, ALBERT II, succeeded to the throne on the death of his brother, BAUDOUIN I, in 1993. Disputes that arise from administering the laws are settled by the judiciary branch of government. The Court of Cassation is the country's highest court. Appeals regarding decisions made by lower courts are heard in five regional tribunals. Labor disputes, commercial issues, jurisdictional disputes, and military justice are each handled by special courts.

The Language Areas. The governmental system set up by the Belgian Constitution of 1831, which vested most powers in the central government, was modified by the division of the country into linguistic areas in the 1960s. Constitutional revisions in the 1970s and '80s resulted in the establishment of a quasi-federal governmental structure based on the three official linguistic communities. As a further complication, the capital of the Dutch-speaking area is Brussels, which itself constitutes a fourth (bilingual) language area. Members of the national parliament are assigned to community and regional councils depending on their language and place of origin. These councils, together with their executives, acquired a considerable degree of influence over regional and national affairs during the 1980s and early 1990s. Negotiations aimed at converting to a fully federal system were under way in 1993.

Provincial and Local Government. Belgium's provinces and local municipalities have limited autonomy in matters of provincial and local interest. Each of the nine provinces has a provincial council. These councils act as representative assemblies for the provinces, and their members are elected at the same time as the members of the national Senate and Chamber of Representatives. Each province also has a governor who represents national interests and is appointed by the central government. Prior to 1977, Belgium had more than 2,500 municipalities. A major restructuring in that year reduced their number to 589. Municipal councils deal with all matters pertaining to the government of Belgium's cities and towns, including budgets and taxes.

Political Parties. Belgian politics is dominated by three major groupings: the Christian Democrats, the Socialists, and the Liberals. Each of these is divided into separate parties organized along linguistic lines. In Flanders, the leading party is the Dutch-speaking Christian Democratic party (CVP); in Wallonia, the French-speaking Socialists (PS) are predominant. Other important political groups include the environmentalist parties (ECOLO in Wallonia and AGALEV in Flanders); the Vlaams Blok (Flemish Bloc), a Flemish national party; the Volksunie (VU) of Flanders, which is also concerned with Flemish autonomy; and the Democratic Front of Brussels Francophones (FDF), which defends the interests of the French-speaking community. Belgium's government is usually a coalition of two or more of the major political parties. In 1992, Jean-Luc Dehaene of the CVP became prime minister, replacing Wilfried Martens (CVP), who had led the country for most of the previous 13 years.

Belgium in the EC. In the 1950s, Belgium was a founding member of the European Coal and Steel Community, the European Economic Community, and the European Atomic Energy Community. Eventually, these were grouped together under a single name, the EUROPEAN COMMUNITY, with Brussels as its primary administrative center. Belgium has been a consistent proponent of European integration and has developed far-reaching economic and political relationships with its Community partners. Brussels's role as the "capital of Europe" has had a significant impact on local and national life. The EC institutions have come to play an increasingly important role in the economy, and most Belgians see their future as being closely tied to that of the Community.

HISTORY

The area now known as Belgium was part of GAUL in ancient times and belonged to the Roman Empire from the 1st century BC to the 5th century AD, when it was conquered by the Franks. It remained under Frankish rule and in the 8th century became part of the empire of Charlemagne. When Charlemagne's realm was divided among his heirs, the central area containing Belgium went to LOTHAIR and was called LOTHARINGIA.

From the 9th to the 12th century the area was divided into separate principalities, dukedoms, and bishoprics. The county of Flanders, the duchy of BRABANT and Limburg, and the bishopric of Liège generally were unified despite geopolitical fragmentation and language differences between north and south. During the 12th and 13th centuries, communes (free cities) arose in the north, and towns such as Ghent and BRUGES developed as centers of trade and industry. Flanders, a center of the wool trade, played a key role in the economic and urban development of medieval and Renaissance Europe. The dukes of BURGUNDY ruled the Low Countries in the 14th and 15th centuries and made Brussels their capital.

The Spanish Netherlands. In the late 15th century the Burgundian territories came under the rule of the Habsburg emperor Maximilian I. When his grandson Charles V abdicated in 1555, sovereignty over the Low Countries (Netherlands) passed to Charles's son, PHILIP II of Spain. At the same time the Protestant Reformation spread into the area, and Philip's attempt to suppress Protestantism led to a revolt against Spain in 1568. In the course of the long war that followed (see DUTCH REVOLT), the seven northern provinces broke free of Habsburg rule to form the Dutch Republic (the present Kingdom of the Netherlands); the southern provinces (corresponding to modern Belgium and Luxembourg) remained under Spain and became known as the Spanish Netherlands. The boundary between the two halves of the Low Countries became fixed during the 17th century, during which time the Spanish Netherlands was repeatedly invaded by the armies of France and other countries at war with Spain. The wars and religious intolerance induced many Belgians, especially Protestants, to migrate to the north.

The Austrian Netherlands. At the conclusion of the War of the Spanish Succession (1700–13), which marked the end of Habsburg rule in Spain, the southern Netherlands was transferred to the Habsburgs of Austria, who held it until 1794. During most of the Austrian period Belgium enjoyed considerable autonomy. The estates (representative assemblies) of the various provinces controlled taxation, and there was no interference with local institutions. After 1763 peaceful conditions prevailed, and Belgian economy began to revive. Agriculture flourished, and the foundations were laid for the industrial development that took place in the period that followed. In the 1780s, however, the Habsburg emperor Joseph II aroused strong opposition among the Belgians by revoking their traditional system of self-government. In 1789, inspired by the French Revolution, they rebelled against the Austrians. Habsburg rule was restored in 1790 but ended in 1794 when Belgium was annexed by the new French Republic.

French and Dutch Rule. The period of French domination proved significant for the later linguistic evolution of Belgium because of French efforts to impose their language throughout the annexed area. The country remained part of France until the defeat of Napoleon I in 1815. The disintegration of Napoleon's empire left Belgium at the mercy of the great powers. At the Congress of Vienna (1815), Belgium was joined with the Netherlands to form one country under the Dutch king, WILLIAM I. The new united Netherlands was to serve as a barrier against further French expansion. The union brought prosperity and the development of industry and infrastructure (roads, canals, and ports) to Belgium. However, linguistic and religious differences, together with a Dutch lack of attention to Belgium local interests, provoked opposition to William's

Flags representing the member nations of the European Community (EC) stand in front of EC headquarters in Brussels. Because it is the site of many of the EC's governing institutions, the Belgian capital city is sometimes known as the "capital of Europe."

regime. In October 1830 the Belgians staged a revolt and declared their independence. Before the Dutch could put down the rebellion, France and Britain intervened and recognized Belgium as a nation.

Belgian Independence. In 1831, Prince Leopold of Saxe Coburg was elected king of the Belgians as LEOPOLD I, but William I of the Netherlands did not finally accept Belgium's independence until 1839, when the Grand Duchy of Luxembourg was also recognized as a separate country.

In the mid-19th century the Catholic and Liberal parties dominated Belgian political life. During the Liberal government of Charles Rogier (1857–67) a system similar to Britain's became established, in which the ministry in power represented the party that held a majority of seats in parliament.

Industrialization proceeded rapidly under Leopold I. From the 1830s to the 1870s heavy industry developed, especially in Wallonia. This growth was supported by an expanding rail transportation network and readily available capital and labor. Flanders remained a largely agricultural region, except for the port of Antwerp and the areas around Ghent devoted to textile production.

Although more than 50% of Belgium's population was Dutch-speaking in the 19th century, French was the language of business, government, and high society. As each group strove to advance its own cultural and economic interests, tensions developed that gave rise to the Flemish movement. In 1856 the government appointed a commission to investigate Flemish grievances, but it was not until 1898 that Dutch was declared an official language on a par with French.

Leopold II and the Congo. Under LEOPOLD II, who succeeded his father in 1865, Belgium became a colonial power. The king sponsored Henry Morton STANLEY's expedition to explore the Congo (Zaire) in 1879 and in 1885 got the European powers to recognize him as personal sovereign of the Congo Free State. Leopold's venture helped start the "scramble for Africa," in which almost the entire continent was subjected to European rule. Reports of exploitation and mistreatment of Congolese laborers aroused indignation in the early 1900s, and in 1908 the Belgian parliament forced Leopold to cede the Congo Free State to Belgium. The Belgian Congo provided Belgium with supplies of rubber, ivory, and other products and helped the country to develop an export economy.

Belgium in the 20th Century. Germany's violation of Belgian neutrality in 1914 was the event that brought Great Britain into World War I and remained one of the main grievances of the Allies against the Germans. The Belgian king, ALBERT I, was a popular hero. Occupation of the country by German troops during the war despoiled the country's mines, fields, and factories. In compensation the postwar Treaty of Versailles awarded Belgium the Eastern Cantons on its German border, along with Germany's East African colony, Ruanda-Urundi.

Belgium was again occupied by the Germans during World War II and suffered severe damage. This time the government fled into exile, while the king, LEOPOLD III, was taken prisoner and deported to Germany. When the country was liberated in 1944, Leopold's brother Charles was appointed regent. The "royal question" was constitutionally settled by a popular referendum in 1950 that voted in favor of Leopold's return. Opposition to Leopold persisted, however, and in 1951 he abdicated in favor of his son, Baudouin.

Belgium played an active role in European recovery after the war, supporting NATO and the movement for European unity. In the post–World War II period the Belgian Congo became the leading African producer of cobalt, diamonds, tin, tungsten, and zinc and the second-largest producer of copper. These strategic resources helped fuel Belgium's postwar economic recovery. At the same time the Congolese began to push for independence, and political unrest spread through the colony. Intervention by United Nations peacekeeping troops in 1960 forced the withdrawal of the Belgian military and led to the establishment of an independent Congo. Ruanda and Urundi became independent in 1962. In the 1960s and '70s, Belgium was further preoccupied with the conflict between the Dutch- and French-speaking sectors of the population, which at times seemed to threaten the nation's continued exis-

tence. A breakup was averted, but the issue remains potentially volatile. Industrial decline, high unemployment, and growing budget deficits have plagued Belgium since the mid-1970s. The country continues its efforts to restructure the economy, control urban expansion, pursue urban renewal, and maintain economic growth. ALEXANDER B. MURPHY

Bibliography:
GENERAL: Belgium Information and Documentation Institute, *Atlas of Belgium* (1985); Riley, Raymond, *Belgium* (1976); Wickman, Stephen, *Belgium: A Country Study,* 2d ed. (1985).
ECONOMICS AND POLITICS: De Brabander, Guido, *Regional Specialization, Employment, and Economic Growth in Belgium, 1846–1970* (1981); Fitzmaurice, John, *The Politics of Belgium: Crisis and Compromise in a Plural Society,* 2d ed. (1988); Senelle, Robert, *The Political, Economic, and Social Structures of Belgium* (1970).
HISTORY: Clough, Shephard B., *History of the Flemish Movement in Belgium* (1968); De Meeus, A., *History of the Belgians* (Eng. trans., 1962); Dhondt, Jan, *The Industrial Revolution in Belgium and Holland: 1700–1914* (1970); Kossman, E. H., *The Low Countries: 1780–1940* (1978).
PEOPLE AND SOCIETY: Boudart, Maria, et al., eds., *Modern Belgium* (1990); Lijphart, Arend, ed., *Conflict and Coexistence in Belgium* (1981); McRae, Kenneth, *Conflict and Compromise in Multilingual Societies: Belgium* (1986); Murphy, Alexander B., *The Regional Dynamics of Language Differentiation in Belgium* (1988).

See also: LOW COUNTRIES, HISTORY OF THE.

Belgrade

Belgrade (Serbian: Beograd) is the capital of Yugoslavia and of its constituent republic, Serbia, and has a population of 1,553,854 (1991 est.). It is located on the Sava River at its junction with the Danube. The name *Belgrade* means "white fortress" and was given to the medieval castle built on the steep bluff overlooking the rivers. Belgrade is by far the largest city on the Danube between Budapest and the Black Sea. An important river port, it is also the chief rail center in eastern Yugoslavia and is linked by highway with Zagreb, Croatia.

Situated on bluffs rising 60–90 m (200–300 ft) above the river, Belgrade occupies an ancient stronghold. The Romans established their frontier fort of Singidinum there, and the Serbs a fortress that became the capital of the small state of Serbia during the Middle Ages. The 20th-century growth of the city resulted largely from its position as capital of the larger Yugoslav state in existence from 1918 to 1991.

South of the city the land rises toward the forested mountains of Serbia, and to the north, beyond the Danube, lies the level plain of Hungary. The river banks opposite the bluff are marshy and have been sparsely developed. The tongue of land between the Danube and its tributary, however, rises somewhat higher and since World War II has been developed as Novi Beograd, a residential suburb in which the president's office and most government buildings are located.

Belgrade is a Serb city, and its prevailing religion is Eastern Orthodox Christianity. Its rapid growth in the present century stems from a vigorous migration from rural Serbia. The ancient fortress, the Kalemegdan, still stands. It is still basically medieval, although remodeled by the Turks, and it contains a military museum.

The southern part of the city is the business district, with the former royal palace and the Skupstina ("parliament house"). Residential suburbs stretch to the southeast, south, and southwest. Industrial districts lie mainly along the Danube and Sava. Manufacturing industries include engineering, metalworking, textiles, and food processing.

Belgrade has a university (1863), a surviving Turkish mosque, a 19th-century Orthodox cathedral, and an important ethnic and folklore museum. It also contains a number of parks and open spaces. The most important historic building is the Kalemegdan.

The Roman settlement was destroyed by a succession of barbarian invaders, and the site was later occupied by the white fortress of the Slavs. In 1500 the city became the capital of Serbia, but it was captured by the Turks soon afterward. Thereafter it was the scene of continuous fighting between the Turks and Austrians, who captured and lost it three times. Although incorporated by Austria into the revived Serbian state,

Belgrade, the capital of Serbia and the reduced state of Yugoslavia, is a port city at the confluence of the Danube and Sava rivers. Turkish influences resulting from centuries of Ottoman rule are still discernible in the older parts of the city. In the early 1990s, Belgrade's economy was affected by a UN-imposed embargo against Serbia.

it housed a Turkish garrison until 1867, when Serb nationalists finally drove the garrison out.

Belgrade became the capital of Yugoslavia in 1918. After the breakup of six-republic Yugoslavia in 1991–92, it became the capital of a smaller Yugoslavia comprising Serbia and Montenegro. NORMAN J. G. POUNDS

Belgrano, Manuel

Manuel Belgrano, b. June 3, 1770, d. June 20, 1820, was one of the leaders of the struggle for Argentinian independence. As secretary of the Buenos Aires merchants' guild, he was a prominent advocate of economic and educational reforms. Despite his lack of military training, he distinguished himself in the 1806–07 campaign to repel the British invasion of Buenos Aires. Joining the revolution of May 1810, he became a member of the patriot junta and, as a general of its forces, defeated the Spanish royalists in early clashes in Paraguay, Chile, Peru, and Uruguay. Routed at the battles of Vilcapugio and Ayohuma in 1813, Belgrano was replaced by José de SAN MARTÍN. Belgrano journeyed to Spain to negotiate independence in 1815, but his efforts failed. He returned to South America, where he commanded troops in Peru and Argentina from 1816 to 1819.

Bibliography: Kirkpatrick, F. A., *A History of the Argentine Republic* (1931; repr. 1969); Rock, David, *Argentina, 1516–1987: From Spanish Colonization to Alfonsín* (1987).

Belinsky, Vissarion Grigorievich [bi-leen'-skee, vis-sur-yohn' gri-gor'-yuh-vich]

Vissarion Grigorievich Belinsky, b. July 12 (June 30, O.S.), 1811, d. June 7 (May 26, O.S.), 1848, the foremost Russian literary critic of his day and a leader of the progressive intelligentsia, was instrumental in defining the aims of Russian literary naturalism. Expelled from Moscow University as a radical, Belinsky turned to journalism and literary criticism in 1833, working first in Moscow, then, from 1839, in Saint Petersburg. *Literary Reveries* (1834), in which he surveyed the previous two centuries of Russian literature, established his reputation. He became even more widely known for his annual surveys of Russian literature (1840–47) and essays on major figures of Russian and world literature, in which he attempted to synthesize German idealist aesthetics with a conception of literature as an organ of social progress. As a revolutionary, he felt that literature should, if necessary, sacrifice artistic excellence to social values. Belinsky's approach to criticism, if not his learning, was subsequently used in the service of Soviet socialist realism.

Bibliography: Bowman, Herbert E., *Vissarion Belinski, 1811–1848: A Study in the Origins of Social Criticism in Russia* (1954; repr. 1969); Terras, Victor, *Belinskij and Russian Literary Criticism: The Heritage of Organic Aesthetics* (1974).

Belisarius [bel-i-sair'-ee-uhs]

Belisarius, b. *c*.505, d. March 565, was a brilliant general responsible for many of the successes of the Byzantine emperor JUSTINIAN I. After victories against the Persians (527–31), he helped suppress the Nika Riot in Constantinople (532) and won North Africa from the Vandals in 533. His next campaign, in 535, was against the Ostrogoths in Italy; after initial successes he was recalled in disfavor in 540. His final campaigns in Italy (544–48) were unsuccessful because Justinian failed to supply enough troops. Despite his loyalty Belisarius was always distrusted by the emperor. C. M. BRAND

Bibliography: Downey, Glanville, *Belisarius* (1960) and *Constantinople in the Age of Justinian* (1981).

Beliveau, Jean [bel-ee-voh']

Jean Beliveau, b. Trois-Rivières, Quebec, Aug. 31, 1931, is a former hockey player who, as a star from 1953 to 1971 with the Montreal Canadiens, became the highest-scoring center in National Hockey League history. The rugged Beliveau, who was 1.9 m (6 ft 3 in) tall and weighed 93 kg (205 lb), scored 1,219 points on 507 goals and 712 assists. While leading his team to the playoffs 16 consecutive times and to 10 Stanley Cup championships, he also set the NHL record for the most points scored in postseason games—176; 79 goals and 97 assists. In 1956 and again in 1964, Beliveau was named the league's most valuable player and was chosen to the NHL all-star team 10 times. He was named to the Hockey Hall of Fame in 1972, the year after he retired.

Belize [buh-leez']

Belize is the northernmost nation of Central America. It is bordered by Mexico on the north, Guatemala on the south and west, and the Caribbean Sea on the east. BELMOPAN, a small inland town protected from the fury of tropical storms, became the capital in 1970, replacing the coastal BELIZE CITY, which is the nation's largest urban center.

Known as British Honduras until 1973, the former British colony achieved self-government in 1964. On Sept. 21, 1981, Belize was granted independence as a member of the Commonwealth, ending more than 300 years of colonial presence on the American mainland. The chief of state is a governor-general named by the British monarch on advice of the Belize government, which is headed by a prime minister. The bicameral legislature, the National Assembly, comprises an appointed Senate and an elected House of Representatives.

LAND AND PEOPLE

The coast of Belize is swampy and lined with lagoons; numerous reefs and cays, or low islands, lie off the coast. Most of the interior is low-lying savanna, much of which was originally covered by hardwood forests. Several short and turbulent rivers flow through Belize. In the south are the Maya Mountains. The average mean rainfall is 2,070 mm (81.5 in), and the temperature range is 16° C–32° C (60° F–90° F). The population consists of 40% Creoles (mixed European/African), 33% mestizos (mixed Maya Indian/Spanish), 8% Caribs (descendants of Carib Indians deported from St. Vincent in 1797), 7% pure Maya, and a scattering of Asians, Portuguese, and other Europeans. The Caribs had already mixed extensively with people of African descent and today are visually indistinguishable from the Creoles.

In 1988 school enrollment was 85–90% of all those of primary- and secondary-school age. The University College of Belize was established in 1986, and there is also an extramural branch of the University of the West Indies.

ECONOMY

During the 19th and early 20th centuries the economy was based on exploitation of the country's hardwood forests, largely exhausted today. The economy is now primarily agricultural, although only 5% of the land is under cultivation. The principal cash crops are sugarcane (44% of exports), citrus fruits (20% of exports), and bananas (9% of exports). Rice, kidney beans, and corn are the major domestic crops. The government is encouraging growing of cocoa, coconuts, and soybeans as well as dairy farming and beekeeping.

HISTORY AND GOVERNMENT

During most of the colonial period, Spain claimed sovereignty over Belize. However, from the mid-17th century, British freebooters settled in the area, using it as a base for privateer operations in the West Indies. It was not recognized as a British colony until 1862.

Meanwhile, Guatemala had assumed Spain's traditional claim to sovereignty over Belize. Although in 1859 it had agreed with Britain to cede sovereignty in return for the construction of a road from Guatemala City to Belize, that road was never constructed, and in 1940, Guatemala resumed its claims. As self-government was established and independence approached, there were lengthy negotiations between Guatemala and Britain involving possible cession of part of Belize to Guatemala. At one point the United States offered its "good offices" to try to bring about a settlement. In the meantime

BELIZE

LAND. Area: 22,965 km² (8,867 mi²). Capital: Belmopan (1990 pop., 5,256). Largest city: Belize City (1990 pop., 43,621).

PEOPLE. Population (1991): 192,000; density (1991): 8.4 persons per km² (21.7 per mi²). Distribution (1990): 51.6% urban, 48.4% rural. Annual growth (1991): 3.6%. Official language: English. Major religions: Roman Catholicism, Methodism, Anglicanism.

EDUCATION AND HEALTH. Literacy (1991): 93% of adult population. Universities (1991): 1. Hospital beds (1990): 525. Physicians (1990): 94. Life expectancy (1991): women—72; men—67. Infant mortality (1991): 35 per 1,000 live births.

ECONOMY. GNP (1989): $294 million; $1,600 per capita. Labor distribution (1985): agriculture—30%; services—16%; government—15.4%; commerce—11.2%; manufacturing—10.3%. Foreign trade (1990 est.): imports—$204 million; exports—$108 million; principal trade partners—United States, United Kingdom, Trinidad and Tobago, Canada, Mexico, Netherlands Antilles. Currency: 1 Belizean dollar = 100 cents.

GOVERNMENT. Type: independent state within Commonwealth of Nations. Legislature: National Assembly. Political subdivisions: 6 districts.

COMMUNICATIONS. Railroads: none. Roads (1985): 3,001 km (1,865 mi) total. Major ports: 2. Major airfields: 3.

the British stationed a battalion of troops and a detachment of fighter aircraft to guarantee Belizean sovereignty. In the early 1990s a 1,500-man British garrison remained in the country, costing Belize 15% of its GDP.

No formal agreement among Guatemala, Britain, and Belize was ever signed. However, the 1985 Guatemalan constitution gave up that country's unconditional claim to Belize. The government of Marcos Vinici Cerezo Arévalo, the first civilian

Ambergris Caye, among the largest of Belize's chain of coastal Caribbean islands, caters to affluent European and North American snorkelers. With its fishing village of San Pedro, miles of white beaches, and several new hotels, the island appeals to an increasingly diverse clientele. It can be reached by boat or plane from Belize City. Although still rudimentary by Caribbean standards, tourism was Belize's fastest-growing industry in the early 1990s.

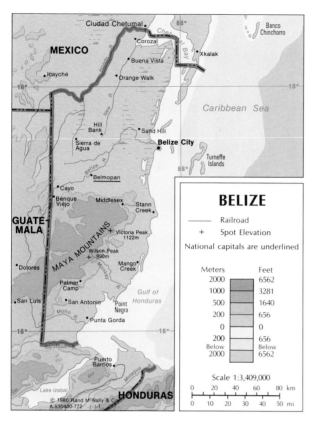

government in Guatemala in many years, finally officially recognized the independence of Belize in 1991, in return for a limitation of Belize's Caribbean offshore boundaries and a grant to Guatemala of access to the sea through its territory.

The drive for Belize to emerge from colonial status began soon after World War II, as part of a general movement in the British colonies in and around the Caribbean Sea. The lead was taken by the People's United Party (PUP), led by George Price, which was established in 1951. Some limited self-government was granted in 1954, and the PUP won eight of the nine elective seats in the Legislative Assembly in that year. Three years later it won all nine.

Under a new constitution that raised to 18 the number of elective seats, the PUP won all 18 in 1961 elections, and George Price became first minister. The year after the British granted Belize full internal self-government in 1964, Price assumed the title of premier.

The problem of Guatemala's claims on the country delayed the achievement of full independence by Belize. In 1981, however, the British and the government of Belize decided not to await the resolution of the Guatemalan question before Belize would become independent. With the proclamation of independence in September 1981, George Price became prime minister.

In the first postindependence election, in 1984, the People's United Party lost for the first time. The victor was the United Democratic Party, headed by Manuel Esquivel, who became prime minister. However, the Esquivel government's development policies, which the opposition claimed favored mainly foreigners and involved the selling of citizenship to Hong Kong Chinese, lost the UDP government some popularity. As a consequence, in the September 1989 election the United Democratic Party got only 49% of the votes. George Price became prime minister again. Following close elections in 1993, the UDP, with Esquivel still at its head, returned to power.   ROBERT J. ALEXANDER

Bibliography: Barry, Tom, *Belize* (1990); Bolland, O. Nigel, *Belize: A New Nation in Central America* (1986).

Belize City

Belize City (1990 pop., 43,621) is the main seaport of Belize and is located on the Caribbean coast, at the mouth of the Belize River. Fish packing and lumber milling are important activities. Formerly the capital of the country, Belize City was devastated by hurricane Hattie and an accompanying tidal wave on Oct. 31, 1961. As a result of that disaster, the capital was moved 80 km (50 mi) inland to Belmopan in 1970.

Belknap, William Worth   [bel'-nap]

William Belknap, b. Newburgh, N.Y., Sept. 22, 1829, d. Oct. 13, 1890, U.S. secretary of war (1869–76), was at the center of one of the scandals that shook President Ulysses S. GRANT's administration. A lawyer, he was a Union officer in the Civil War and an internal revenue collector in Iowa before his appointment to the cabinet in 1869. In 1876 impeachment proceedings were initiated against Belknap, who was accused of accepting bribes from trading-post agents on the Indian reservations. He resigned and later resumed private law practice.

bell

A bell is a hollow vessel that when struck produces a sound through the vibration of its mass. Made most often of metal, but also of clay, wood, or glass, bells are found in two basic forms. Most familiar, and exemplified by the church-tower bell, is the open, or cup-shaped, bell—although its size and shape vary extremely. The crotal, or closed, bell is spherical, with a long slot crossing its belly. It is usually small enough to be worn, either by a person or an animal (as in the sleigh bells worn by horses). A crotal produces sound when movement causes loose pellets enclosed inside the sphere to hit the bell sides. Bells differ from GONGS in terms of the region that produces maximum sound: in a bell, it is at the rim; in a gong, at the instrument's center.

Open bells are sounded either by means of a clapper, a rod or ball suspended inside the instrument, or, as in some large Buddhist bells, by striking the outside of the bell with a rod or

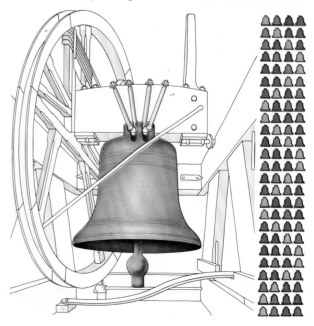

Change ringing is a traditional English practice of ringing church bells by teams, of which each member pulls the rope controlling one bell. The number of available changes (variations in the order of pulling) depends on the number of bells used. A set of changes is called a peal. The permutations of change ringing are illustrated with a peal of four color-coded bells in a sequence of a Singles, or Minimus, ring using the introductory Plain Bob method, which has 24 possible changes.

(Above, left) This early Irish iron-bronze bell (20 cm/7.9 in high) is one of several said to have belonged to Saint Patrick. (Above, center) The gold crotal bell (2.9 cm/1.1 in high) is a product of the goldworking art of the Mexican Mixtec. It dates from the 16th century. (Above, right) A 13.3-cm (5.2-in) handbell made (1535) by the famous German goldsmith Wenzel Jamnitzer is of gold and silver, with an encrustation of minutely realistic ornament. (Right) The Iranian bronze chariot bell—another example of a crotal design—dates from the 9th century BC.

hammer. Large open, western bells may be sounded by moving the bell itself, causing its clapper to hit the inner rim on opposite sides as the bell swings back and forth; or, the clapper may be pulled against one side of a stationary bell, a mode of sounding used in chimes and carillons.

Bronze CASTING, or bell founding, is the principal method of producing open bells. As early as the 11th century BC, the Chinese were making large, barrel-shaped brass bells with ornate designs cast on their outer surfaces. Bell founding in ancient western civilizations never reached the technical height of the Chinese; the Romans, for example, produced mainly "tintinabula," small bells that could be worn on a finger. Such as it was, the art of casting was lost to early medieval Europe, and until bell founding was rediscovered sometime in the 8th century, European bells were made of hammered and riveted iron plates.

The shape of the open bell evolved slowly over time, as more came to be known about the complexities of producing

The world's largest bell is the Tsar Bell in Moscow's Kremlin. Cast in 1733–35, it was damaged in a fire before it could be hung or rung. It measures 6.9 m (22.6 ft) across the mouth, is 6 m (19.7 ft) high, and weighs more than 180,000 kg (400,000 lb). This photograph of the bell, which stands at the foot of the Bell Tower of Ivan the Great in the Kremlin, was taken in the 1880s.

sound from resonant bronze. Early European cast bells had rounded walls of a uniform thickness. The bell rim was reinforced with an inner collar to protect it from cracking under the blows of the clapper. This reinforced rim became the sound bow, the region of the bell that determines its tone. The complex sound produced by a struck bell can be altered by shaving small amounts of metal from the bell's inner wall.

The sound produced by a large bell contains a number of partials, or overtones. The sound fades away relatively slowly, with the highest partials disappearing first. The lowest lasts longest and was called the "hum note" by early bell founders. The bell's main pitch is usually an octave above the hum note.

Sets of bells less than two octaves in range are called chimes. Once played by hand but now usually mechanized, they are used principally for signaling the time. Chimes are tuned to major scales. Russian chimes, the stationary *zvon*, are hand rung in a series of repetitive rhythmic patterns. Carillons, which can play much more complex music than chimes, are sets of tuned bells with a range of up to six octaves. Numbering at least twenty bells, they are operated from a keyboard. Change ringing, ringing a set of bells in a predetermined order so as to sound every possible variation, is an art practiced primarily in England. Small handbells are often played by bell choirs, which have become popular in some U.S. churches.

In the modern orchestra, bells are impractical because of their size and weight. Tubular bells, tuned tubes of various lengths but all of one diameter, are used instead.

Among the bells known the world over are the great bell of the Cathedral of Notre Dame, Paris; Big Ben in the Clock

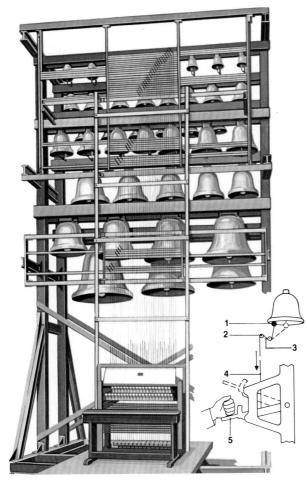

Alexander Graham Bell placed the call that formally inaugurated telephone service between New York City and Chicago in 1892. The Scottish-American scientist received the first patent on the telephone in 1876, but his claim to its invention was not legally recognized until a Supreme Court ruling decided the issue in 1893.

A carillon is a set of bells, usually in a tower, on which tunes are played either by heavy manual and pedal keyboards or mechanically, using clockwork or an electrically controlled pneumatic mechanism. The sketch illustrates the construction of a manually operated carillon: clapper (1), roller (2), crank (3), wire (4), and keyboard (5). New York City's Riverside Church and the University of Chicago Chapel have the world's largest carillons.

Tower of the British Houses of Parliament, Westminster, London; bells of St. Peter's in Vatican City; and, although it does not ring any longer, the Liberty Bell in Independence Hall, Philadelphia.   ELWYN A. WIENANDT

Bibliography: Cockett, M., *Bells in Our Lives* (1985); Jones, R. H., *About Bells and Bellringing* (1985); Price, P., *Bells and Man* (1983); Rossing, T. D., ed., *Acoustics of Bells* (1984).

Bell, Alexander Graham

Alexander Graham Bell, b. Scotland, Mar. 3, 1847, d. Aug. 2, 1922, was the inventor of the TELEPHONE and a number of other devices. In addition to his own great drive and energy, a number of external factors aided him in his work on the telephone, an invention that was to revolutionize the field of communications almost immediately. Born into a family deeply interested in the areas of speech and deafness, he was trained by his father and grandfather in public speaking and in teaching the deaf to speak. He taught and experimented along these lines, and he also studied anatomy and physiology, which provided him with a biological basis for his great invention. He was also trained in the field of music.

After Bell's two brothers died of tuberculosis, and he was threatened by the disease, his family moved in 1870 to a more healthful location in Ontario, Canada—his father sacrificing a successful career in London in the process. There, Bell and his father continued their work along the same lines, but during the next few years Bell's own work necessitated a move to the United States. He became a professor of vocal physiology at Boston University.

At this time, he was already nurturing the idea of transmitting speech by electrical means. An increasing interest in electricity led him to try to develop a harmonic TELEGRAPH, which would make it possible to transmit several telegraph messages over the same line. In 1875 he discovered the principle that made the telephone possible. The basic patent, granted Mar. 7, 1876, was later challenged many times, but his priority was always upheld. On Mar. 10, 1876, Bell transmitted the first message ever sent by telephone—"Mr. Watson, come here, I want you"—to his assistant, who was linked by wire and receiver to the sending device in Bell's office.

In 1877, Bell married Mabel Hubbard, who was deaf (as was his mother), and in 1882 he became a U.S. citizen. Bell was active in many fields and invented a number of other devices, including one that could transmit speech via light waves. He had much to do with the founding (1880) of the important magazine *Science*, was president of the National Geographic Society from 1898 to 1904, and was made a regent of the Smithsonian Institution in 1898. After 1895 his technical interests turned to aviation. He invented the tetrahedral kite, and under his patronage a group called the Aerial Experiment Association was formed in 1907. The group developed the HYDROFOIL, a new form of speedboat that in 1919 set a world speed record of 114.04 km/h (70.86 mph). The hydrofoil principle is still in use today.   HAL HELLMAN

Bibliography: Costain, Thomas B., *Chord of Steel: The Story of the Invention of the Telephone* (1960); Eber, Dorothy, *Genius at Work: Images of Alexander Graham Bell* (1982); MacKenzie, Catherine D., *Alexander Graham Bell* (1928; repr. 1971); Stevenson, Orlando J., *The Talking Wire* (1947).

Bell, Andrew

Andrew Bell, b. Mar. 27, 1753, d. Jan. 27, 1832, was a Scottish clergyman and one of the inventors of the monitorial system of teaching. In 1789 he became superintendent of a school in India for the orphaned children of European soldiers. Because teachers were scarce, Bell devised a system in which he taught the more able students and they each taught 25 to 30 other pupils.

Bell's monitorial system, modified by Joseph LANCASTER, was widely used in England and in the United States in the early 1800s. In 1811, Bell, having returned to England in 1796 for health reasons, became superintendent of the National Society for Promoting the Education of the Poor in the Principles of the Established Church.

Bibliography: Meiklejohn, John Miller Dow, *An Old Educational Reformer: Dr. Andrew Bell* (1881); Sturt, Mary, *The Education of the People* (1967).

Bell, Bert

De Benneville "Bert" Bell, b. Philadelphia, Feb. 25, 1895, d. Oct. 11, 1959, played a major role in the development of the National Football League, first as a team official and later as commissioner (1946–59). He was co-owner of the first Philadelphia Eagles franchise in 1933 and coached the team from 1936 to 1940, after which he joined the Pittsburgh Steelers in 1941. Bell was instrumental in balancing the talent on professional teams by proposing the draft of college players in 1935. As NFL commissioner he guided the game's growth through the early television era, helping defend the NFL against the rival All-American Football Conference.

Bell, Clive

The English art and literary critic Clive Bell, b. Sept. 16, 1881, d. Sept. 18, 1964, figured prominently in the BLOOMSBURY GROUP. Educated at Cambridge, he married (1907) Vanessa Stephen, a painter who was a daughter of the editor Sir Leslie Stephen and the sister of the writer Virginia Woolf. Some of Bell's most admired criticism is found in *Art* (1914), in which he expounded on his theory of "significant form," and in *Since Cézanne* (1922), in which he particularly championed modernism in art. His other writings include *Proust* (1929) and *Old Friends* (1956). Quentin Bell, his son, wrote about his parents in *Bloomsbury* (1968).

Bell, Daniel

Daniel Bell, b. New York City, May 10, 1919, is an American sociologist, journalist, and educator whose book *The End of Ideology* (1960; rev. ed. 1988) has exerted wide influence. He was originally a socialist radical but moved away from the left during the 1950s. In *The End of Ideology* he rejected the "isms" of the 1930s and '40s—especially communism and socialism—as bankrupt and outmoded.

Bell taught sociology at Columbia from 1959 to 1969 and after that at Harvard, where in 1980 he became Henry Ford II professor of social sciences. His other books include *The Reforming of General Education* (1966), *The Coming of Post-Industrial Society* (1973), *The Cultural Contradictions of Capitalism* (1976), *The Winding Passage* (1980), and *The Social Sciences since World War II* (1981).

Bell, Gertrude

Gertrude Bell, b. July 14, 1868, d. July 12, 1926, was an English traveler, author, and archaeologist. After graduating from Oxford University in 1888, she traveled and studied in the Middle East. During World War I, she was a British intelligence agent in Cairo and Basra, the Turkish province that later became part of Iraq. In 1921 she headed the group that chose Faisal I as first king of the newly independent Iraq. Among her books are *Amurath to Amurath* (1911) and *The Palace and Mosque of Ukhaidir* (1914).

Bibliography: Goodman, S., *Gertrude Bell* (1985); Winstone, H. V. F., *Gertrude Bell* (1978).

Bell, John

John Bell, b. near Nashville, Tenn., Feb. 15, 1797, d. Sept. 10, 1869, was a leader of the Whig party in Tennessee. An influential lawyer, he sat in the U.S. House of Representatives, from 1827 to 1841. He was originally a Jacksonian Democrat, but he aligned with the Whigs in opposing Andrew JACKSON's successful campaign against the BANK OF THE UNITED STATES. Bell served as secretary of war (1841) under President William Henry Harrison. He then went to the Senate (1847–59), where he led conservative Southerners who opposed secession. In 1860, Bell was the presidential candidate of the CONSTITUTIONAL UNION PARTY, which sought to hold the Union together until North-South hostility ebbed. He carried only Tennessee, Kentucky, and Virginia. After Tennessee's secession on May 7, 1861, Bell retired from public life.

Bibliography: Parks, Joseph H., *John Bell of Tennessee* (1950).

Bell, John Stuart

Irish physicist John Stuart Bell, b. July 28, 1928, d. Oct. 1, 1990, is best known for BELL'S THEOREM, or Bell's inequality, a work of mathematical logic that has further defined the implications of QUANTUM MECHANICS for the nature of the universe. A graduate of Queen's University, Belfast, Bell gained a doctorate in physics at the University of Birmingham in 1956. While working at the Atomic Energy Research Establishment in Harwell (1949–60) he became a consultant with CERN, the European Organization for Nuclear Research, on the construction of its first particle accelerator. In 1960 he joined the staff of CERN and remained there until his death.

Bibliography: Bernstein, Jeremy, *Quantum Profiles* (1991).

Bell Jar, The: see PLATH, SYLVIA.

bell magpie

The bell magpie family of birds, Cracticidae (order Passeriformes, suborder Passeres), is found in Australia, New Guinea, and adjacent islands. It includes the butcher birds, *Cracticus* (4 species); the currawongs, *Strepera* (3 species); and the bell magpie, *Gymnorhina* (1 species); authorities disagree on these species numbers, however. The name derives from their magpielike markings and their usually loud, metallic notes. Cracticids are 25.4–58.4 cm (10–23 in) long, are mostly black and white, and have stout, usually hooked bills. Gregarious, they nest high in trees, building a lined, open cup of twigs in which 2 to 5 eggs are laid. They feed mostly on the ground, taking fruits as well as small mammals, reptiles, and insects. The name *butcher bird* refers to their habit of impaling prey on thorns or wedging it in branches, either to aid in tearing the food apart or to store it.   ROBERT J. RAIKOW

Bibliography: Beehler, Bruce, et al., *Birds of New Guinea* (1986); Pizzey, Graham, *A Field Guide to the Birds of Australia* (1988).

Bella, Stefano della

Stefano della Bella, b. May 18, 1610, d. July 12, 1664, was an Italian engraver. His early work was modeled after that of Jacques Callot, whose own teacher, Remigio Cantagallina, was della Bella's first master. The same elegantly attenuated figures found in Callot's etchings are also typical of the style of della Bella. After a Roman sojourn, della Bella moved to Paris, where he lived from 1639 to 1649. Thereafter, his work consisted mainly of scenes of festivals, theatrical presentations, tournaments, and battles, all sketched in the open air.   THOMAS W. SOKOLOWSKI

Bibliography: Massar, P. D., *Presenting Stefano Della Bella* (1971).

Bella Coola   [bel'-uh koo'-luh]

The Bella Coola are a North American Indian tribe of the central coast of British Columbia, Canada. They lived on the upper reaches of Burke and Dean channels, North and South Bentinck Arms, and the lower Bella Coola River when encountered by (1793) overland explorer Alexander Mackenzie.

Traditionally, the Bella Coola spoke a Coast Salish language that became distinct from other Salish languages several thousand years ago. They lived in relative isolation.

Bella Coola winter villages were small and were occupied by single local groups whose members were usually related to one another and not by tribes composed of several local groups like most of their coastal neighbors. A Bella Coola specialty, apparently reflecting scarcity of level beaches along the steep-walled channels, were the pile dwellings they built that so impressed Mackenzie. In the 19th century the Bella Coola population diminished from an estimated 5,000 to 1,000. In 1988 there were again about 1,000 members of the tribe living at the village of Bella Coola, in the vicinity of their ancestral lands.   PHILIP DRUCKER

Bibliography: McIlwraith, T. F., *The Bella Coola Indians*, 2 vols. (1948).

belladonna

Belladonna, Atropa belladonna, also known as deadly nightshade, produces bell-like flowers and a black berry that yields purple juice. All parts of the plant are poisonous if eaten. The plant was called belladonna, Italian for "beautiful lady," because women used it as a cosmetic to dilate their pupils.

Belladonna, or deadly nightshade, *Atropa belladonna*, is a poisonous plant of the potato family, Solanaceae. Native to Europe and Anatolia, it is grown extensively in North America. Belladonna is a herbaceous perennial that grows from a creeping rootstock to a height of 1.5 m (5 ft). The oval leaves have smooth edges and are positioned singly along the stem; the solitary, purplish flowers are bell-shaped, about 2.5 cm (1 in) long, and upon maturity produce a brownish or blackish berry about the size of a cherry. All parts of the plant contain poisonous chemicals, called alkaloids, but the berries are most often responsible for poisoning in humans, especially children. The leaves and roots contain atropine, which is used as an antispasmodic in treating asthma and hyperacidity.

CHARLES H. STYER

See also: MEDICINAL PLANTS.

Bellamy, Edward

The writer Edward Bellamy, b. Chicopee Falls, Mass., Mar. 26, 1850, d. May 22, 1898, is best known for his novel *Looking Backward, 2000–1887* (1888), a critique of American capitalism. Bellamy depicts the utopian society of the year 2000, what he called a "cooperative commonwealth" in which competitive capitalism is dead. To a man miraculously transported into the future, Bellamy believed, the injustices of the 19th century would be apparent. The book inspired interest in socialism and led to the formation of Nationalist clubs, based on Bellamy's theories, that advocated the nationalization of public services.

Bibliography: Bowman, Sylvia E., *Edward Bellamy* (1986) and *The Year 2000: Edward Bellamy* (1958; repr. 1979); Morgan, Arthur E., *Edward Bellamy* (1944; repr. 1974); Thomas, John L., "Introduction," in Edward Bellamy's *Looking Backward* (1967).

Bellarmine, Saint Robert   [bel'-ahr-myn]

Robert Bellarmine, b. Oct. 4, 1542, d. Sept. 17, 1621, an Italian Roman Catholic theologian and cardinal, earned his fame as a controversial writer during the COUNTER-REFORMATION. He was originally named Roberto Francesco Romolo Bellarmino. In 1560 he became a Jesuit and served on the faculties of the University of Louvain (Belgium) and the Collegium Romanum (Rome). He spent his life in theological debate and scholarly work. Among his publications is *Controversies*, a 3-volume work opposing the Protestant Reformation. It contains his lectures on controverted doctrines, which he dealt with dispassionately and intellectually. He proved a formidable opponent of defenders of Protestantism, including Lancelot Andrewes.

Bellarmine got into trouble over his teaching on indirect papal power, by which he meant that the use of temporal or political power is permitted only when the spiritual power of the pope is threatened. The first volume of the *Controversies* was almost placed on the Index, despite his usual ULTRAMONTANISM, or strongly papal point of view. He was proclaimed a saint in 1930 and a Doctor of the Church in 1931. Feast day: May 17 (formerly May 13).

FREDERICK A. NORWOOD

Bibliography: Brodrick, James, *The Life and Works of Blessed Robert Cardinal Bellarmine*, 2 vols., rev. ed. (1966); Ryan, E. A., *The Historical Scholarship of Saint Bellarmine* (1936).

bellbird

Bellbird is the common name of four species of COTINGAS belonging to the Cotingidae family. They occur in the mountains of Central America and northern South America. An Australian flycatcher and a New Zealand honeyeater are also sometimes called bellbirds. Best known of the American species is the bearded bellbird, *Procnias averano*, which is native to Trinidad. About the size of a blue jay, it is a pale-gray bird with black wings and a mass of fleshy wattles hanging from the throat. All four bellbirds are fruit-eaters and have loud bell-like calls.

GEORGE J. WALLACE

Belleau Wood   [bel'-oh]

Belleau Wood (French: Bois de Belleau) is an area of dense tree-growth and large boulders just south of Belleau village in the Aisne department of northern France. It was the scene of an important World War I battle in which U.S. troops stopped the German advance, June 6–25, 1918. It was renamed Bois de la Brigade Marine to honor the 4th Marine brigade of the U.S. 2d Army division, and a U.S. war memorial is located in the woods 8 km (5 mi) northwest of Château-Thierry.

Bibliography: Suskind, Richard, *Battle of Belleau Wood* (1969).

Bellerophon   [buh-lair'-uh-fahn]

In Greek mythology, Bellerophon was a descendant of Sisyphus, the founder of Corinth. While he was visiting King Proetus in Argos, the king's wife Stheneboea, or Anteia, tried to seduce Bellerophon, but he refused her advances. Angered, the queen accused Bellerophon of improper conduct. King Proetus then sent Bellerophon with a message to his father-in-law, Iobates of Lycia; the message was to kill the bearer of the note. Upon Bellerophon's arrival, Iobates imposed a series of tests on him, each designed to kill him. First, he was asked to subdue the chimera, a lion-goat-serpent monster, but Bellerophon killed it with the aid of the winged horse PEGASUS. Next, he encountered a wild tribe called the Solymi, but defeated it. These tests were followed by several other difficult missions, all of which he accomplished. Impressed by Bellerophon's invincibility, Iobates allowed him to marry his daughter Philonoe; they had three children, one of whom, Laodamia, was loved by Zeus. Later, Bellerophon tried to ride to Mount Olympus on Pegasus, but Zeus caused Pegasus to throw off Bellerophon, who was lamed. In the *Iliad*, Homer says that Bellerophon then "wandered away, shunning the paths of men."

ROBERT E. WOLVERTON

belles lettres   [bel let'-ruh]

The term *belles lettres* (French: "fine letters") now denotes literary studies, the aesthetics of literature, and perhaps even light literature as long as it is elegant and urbane in style. The essay is the ideal vehicle for the belletrist. Originally the term was applied to such matters as grammar, rhetoric, and poetry and was the equivalent of *humaniores litterae* (Latin: "the more humane letters"). Jonathan Swift seems to have been the first person to use the term in English literature, in *The Tatler* (no. 230, 1710).

J. A. CUDDON

bellflower

The bellflower, C. elatines garganica, a plant that is native to Italy, produces star-shaped flowers in great abundance.

Bellflowers constitute a divergent genus, *Campanula*, of flowering herbaceous plants of the Campanulaceae family. They produce bell- or wheel-shaped, usually blue flowers. The blue varieties are called bluebells. Bellflowers vary greatly in size. *C. caespitosa* is a tiny plant that is commonly used in rock gardens. *C. pyramidalis* is a garden perennial that grows to heights of 1.5 m (5 ft) or more.

A few bellflowers bloom in May, but most bloom in June and July, and some last into August. Many bellflowers are perennials, although some are annuals or biennials. The wide diversity of types in the genus makes some species of this flower adaptable to almost every flower garden.

Some desirable species are *C. carpatica*, tussock bellflower, which grows to 45.7 cm (18 in) in height and has upright blue-lilac bells; *C. elatines garganica*, a trailing plant that spreads into broad tufts, and whose flowers are wide blue bells with five petal-like points; *C. glomerata*, which produces closely clustered, blue, funnel-shaped flowers; *C. persicifolia*, peach-leaved harebell, which grows to a height of 60 to 90 cm (2 to 3 ft) and produces violet blue, bell-like flowers in June and July; and *C. rotundifolia*, bluebell or common harebell, a compact plant that sends up thin stems bearing blue, bell-shaped flowers. One species, *C. rapunculus*, rampion, is sometimes used as a vegetable.

Belli, G. G.   [bel'-lee]

Giuseppe Belli, b. Sept. 10, 1791, d. Dec. 21, 1863, was one of Italy's most prolific poets. His verse, consisting of more than 2,000 sonnets written in Roman dialect, was partly inspired by the example of Carlo PORTA. Composed mainly after 1830 and published posthumously, his poems exhibit humor, irony, and compassion.   SERGIO PACIFICI

Bibliography: Belli, Giuseppe G., *The Roman Sonnets of G. G. Belli*, trans. by Harold Norse (1974).

Belli, Melvin   [bel'-y]

Melvin Mouron Belli, b. Sonora, Calif., July 29, 1907, became one of the most successful U.S. trial lawyers of the 1960s and '70s. Known for his flamboyant courtroom tactics, he appeared for the defense in well over 100 murder trials, and his success in winning large settlements in personal injury and medical malpractice cases earned him the title "King of Torts." He defended (1964) Jack Ruby, the killer of President John F. Kennedy's assassin, Lee Harvey OSWALD. Belli has written numerous legal works for both popular and professional audiences. He published his autobiography, *Melvin Belli: My Life on Trial*, in 1976 and *The Belli Files* in 1983.

Bellingshausen, Fabian Gottlieb von   [bel'-ingz-how-zen, fahb'-yahn gawt'-leeb fuhn]

Fabian Gottlieb von Bellingshausen, b. Sept. 20 (N.S.), 1778, d. Jan. 24 (N.S.), 1852, a Russian naval officer and scientist, commanded the 1819–21 Russian expedition to Antarctica that was the first to circumnavigate that continent. The Russians claim that he actually discovered the continent during this voyage on the *Vostok* because he sighted Alexander I Land (which later proved to be an island) within the Antarctic Circle on Jan. 29 (N.S.), 1821. He probably sighted the mainland on Jan. 28 (N.S.), 1820, but Bellingshausen himself was cautious in his claims. He was later military governor of Kronstadt, Russia.

Bellini   (family)   [bel-lee'-nee]

Jacopo Bellini, 1400–70, and his sons Gentile, c.1429–1507, and Giovanni, c.1430–1516, were central figures in the development of drawing and painting in Renaissance Venice.

Jacopo Bellini. As a young artist Jacopo was exposed first to the elaborate, colorful Venetian Gothic style. He is also assumed to have been in Florence briefly in the 1420s. His daughter Nicolosia married (1453) the Paduan painter Andrea Mantegna.

Jacopo's few surviving paintings are strongly Gothic in style. Some of his drawings (collected in two large books, one in the Louvre and the other in the British Museum), however, are characterized by the use of one-point perspective. Others depict convincingly articulated figures in landscapes and in complicated architectural settings, as, for example, in *The Flagellation* (c.1450) in the Louvre volume. These drawing books were workshop tools, consulted and probably added to by the members of Jacopo's shop, most notably by his two sons. Jacopo received many important commissions for religious works in Venice and in Padua. In 1441 his skill as a portraitist was recognized when he won the contest in competition with Pisanello to paint the portrait (lost) of Lionello d'Este, ruler of Ferrara.

Gentile Bellini. Gentile's early training was in his father's shop, where he helped on several of the important commissions given to Jacopo in the 1460s. After this period of apprenticeship he quickly became one of the most highly regarded painters in Venice. In 1469 he was made a *Cavaliere* of Venice and a Palatine Count by Holy Roman Emperor Frederick III, and in 1479 he was sent by the Venetian senate to Constantinople at the request of Sultan Mehmed II, whose portrait he painted (1480; National Gallery, London).

Gentile was particularly successful in the creation of the extended narrative cycles commissioned by religious confraternities in Venice for their meeting houses. Typical are the scenes depicting miracles of the true cross, painted in 1496–1501 for the Confraternity of St. John the Evangelist (Accademia Gallery, Venice). Many of his religious narrative paintings incorporate portraits of contemporary Venetians.

Gentile's paintings show the spatial sophistication and adept naturalistic description typical of the more advanced compositions in Jacopo's drawing books. His style does not convey great emotional depth but instead relies on straightforward, incisive, and dignified representation.

Giovanni Bellini. Giovanni Bellini's earliest years as a painter were also spent as an apprentice and assistant to Jacopo Bellini. Giovanni's work is in many ways similar to Gentile's, but Giovanni's achievements far surpass those of his father and his brother.

Appointed painter to the Venetian Republic in 1483, he remained the outstanding painter in Venice until his death in 1516. As Albrecht Dürer commented in a letter written during his visit to the city in 1506, "he is very old, and still he is the best painter of them all." His most famous pupils in his later years were Giorgione and Titian, who also influenced the style of Giovanni's late paintings.

In his official capacity Giovanni was required to paint the doge's portrait and numerous votive images; many other patrons commissioned portraits from him as well. He worked

The Transfiguration *(c.1480)* illustrates Giovanni Bellini's masterly use of color and glaze techniques to create luminous atmospheric effects. One of the great masters of the Renaissance, Bellini combined landscape and figure painting in many of his religious works, always achieving a serene monumentality. Both his father and brother were painters, although of lesser stature. (Museo di Capodimonte, Naples.)

with Gentile on some of the large narrative cycles, painted numerous devotional images, and created an important group of large altarpieces. His most sympathetic theme was the Virgin and Child, to which he brought an amazing range of subtly differentiated interpretations, as in *The Madonna with the Greek Inscription* (1470s; Brera Gallery, Milan) and *The Madonna of the Trees* (1487; Accademia Gallery, Venice). To what degree Giovanni was attracted to secular subject matter is not entirely clear, but two major works of this kind survive: the handsome *Feast of the Gods* (National Gallery, Washington), begun late in his career (1514) for Alfonso d'Este, ruler of Ferrara, and later finished and somewhat amended by Titian; and *Toilet of Venus*, also known as *Venus with Mirror* (1515; Kunsthistorisches Vienna Museum), Giovanni's only known female nude.

Giovanni is also associated with the gradual adoption of oil painting in preference to tempera that occurred in the later 15th and the early 16th centuries. The nature of his painting materials is not yet fully understood, although he became more and more skilled in the use of glazes (transparent paint layers).

Giovanni's late works, such as the San Zaccaria altarpiece, or *Enthroned Madonna with Four Saints* (1505; San Zaccaria, Venice), are in the spirit of the High Renaissance.

JULIA KEYDEL

Bibliography: Berenson, Bernard, *Italian Pictures of the Renaissance: The Venetian School*, vol. 1 (1957); Dussler, Luitpold, *Giovanni Bellini* (1949; repr. 1984); Fry, Roger, *Giovanni Bellini* (1899); Hendy, Philip, and Goldscheider, Ludwig, *Giovanni Bellini* (1945); Meiss, Millard, *Giovanni Bellini's St. Francis in the Frick Collection* (1964); Palucchini, Rodolfo, *Giovanni Bellini* (1959; Eng. trans., 1963); Robertson, Giles, *Giovanni Bellini* (1968; repr. 1980); Tietze, Hans, and Tietze-Conrat, Erika, *The Drawings of the Venetian Painters of the 15th and 16th Centuries* (1944); Walker, John, *Bellini and Titian at Ferrar* (1956); Wind, Edgar, *Bellini's Feast of the Gods* (1948).

Bellini, Vincenzo   [bel-lee'-nee, veen-chayn'-tsoh]

Vincenzo Bellini, b. Catania, Nov. 3, 1801, d. Sept. 23, 1835, was one of the greatest Italian composers of opera in the 19th-century style known as BEL CANTO. He was first trained by his father and grandfather, both organists, and then sponsored by a Sicilian nobleman in study at the conservatory at Naples. His first opera, produced there in 1825, attracted the interest of Domenico Barbaja, Italy's most influential impressario, who launched him on his meteoric career.

In 1825–26, Bellini wrote *Bianca e Fernando* in Naples for Barbaja, who gave him a commission for Milan's La Scala the following year. The result, *Il Cirata*, caused a sensation and won Bellini international fame. The first of Bellini's operas composed with the great singers of the day in mind, it also challenged ROSSINI's style of vocal brilliance with a new lyricism and simplicity that became Bellini's hallmark. Despite fluctuations, he consolidated this new style in his eight remaining operas. *I Capuletti ed i Montecchi* (Venice, 1830), freely based on Shakespeare's *Romeo and Juliet*, won success for the soprano Giuditta Pasta in the female "trouser" role of

Romeo. With *La Sonnambula* (Milan, 1831), Bellini created a lead part that was to be among the most popular soprano roles for decades. Norma (Milan, 1831), while not initially a success, became Bellini's most admired work, its title role still one of the supreme tests for the dramatic soprano. His last opera, *I Puritani*, for the Italian Theater in Paris (1835), is perhaps his most artful score and contains one of the classic mad scenes in all opera.

By that time, Bellini was the idol of Paris, an admired friend of its leading musicians and artists. But at this pinnacle, not yet 34 years old, Bellini suddenly became ill and died; he was buried in Paris's Père Lachaise cemetery.

Although never more than adequate as a harmonist or orchestrator, Bellini was a master of vocal subtlety and melodic beauty. His operas have received renewed acclaim through revivals and recordings in recent decades, notably those featuring Maria Callas, Beverly Sills, and Joan Sutherland.

JOHN W. BARKER

Bibliography: Einstein, Alfred, *Music in the Romantic Era* (1947); Grout, Donald J., *A Short History of Opera*, 3d ed. (1987); Orrey, Leslie, *Bellini* (1978); Porter, Andrew, et al., *The New Grove Masters of Italian Opera* (1983); Weinstock, Herbert, *Vincenzo Bellini* (1971).

Bellman, Carl Michael

The Swedish poet Carl Michael Bellman, b. Feb. 4, 1740, d. Feb. 11, 1795, was a favorite of King Gustav III. His career at the national bank was interrupted when he fled to Norway to escape creditors. Bellman later held several nominal positions, among them court secretary. His early religious poetry soon gave way to such popular parodies of biblical verses set to music as *Fredmans Sånger* (The Songs of Fredman, 1791). In *Fredmans Epistlar* (The Epistles of Fredman, 1790), which contains songs still greatly loved in Sweden, Bellman describes the colorful, bohemian, Bacchic existence of Stockholm's middle class and low life.

Bibliography: Van Loon, Hendrik W., and Castagnetta, Grace, *The Last of the Troubadors* (1939).

Bello, Andrés

Andrés Bello, b. Nov. 29, 1781, d. Oct. 5, 1865, was a prominent Venezuelan poet, philologist, and philosopher. In 1810, he left Venezuela to live in England and in 1829 went to Chile, where he taught at the University of Chile in 1843. He is considered one of the foremost Latin-American intellectual leaders and patriots during the period in which Latin-American countries achieved independence from Spain.

Bello's principal poetical works, such as "Alocución a la poesía" (Allocution to Poetry, 1823) and "Silva a la agricultura de la zona tórrida" (Ode to the Agriculture of the Torrid Zone, 1826), suggested the concept of literary Americanism that subsequently became a vital force in Latin-American literature. His *Principios del derecho de gentes* (Principles of International Law, 1847) and his Chilean Civil Code (1855) were influential in the formulation of several national civil codes in Spanish America. Of his three principal works on the Spanish language, *Gramática de la lengua castellana* (Grammar of the Castilian Languages, 1847) is the most monumental.

KEITH ELLIS

Bibliography: Burr, Robert N., *By Reason or Force: Chile and the Balancing of Power in South America, 1830–1905* (1967; repr. 1974); Caldera, Rafael, *Andrés Bello: Philosopher, Poet, Philologist, Educator, Legislator, Statesman*, trans. by John Street (1977); Collier, Simon, *Ideas and Politics of Chilean Independence, 1808–1833* (1967).

Belloc, Hilaire   [bel'-uhk]

Hilaire Belloc, b. July 27, 1870, d. July 16, 1953, was renowned during his lifetime as a Roman Catholic polemicist, historian, biographer, essayist, travel writer, poet, and novelist. Born in France and married to an American, he became a British subject in 1902. From 1906 to 1910 he was a Liberal member of Parliament from Salford. Belloc is remembered today for a few lyric poems and, most of all, for such light comic verse as *The Bad Child's Book of Beasts* (1896) and *Cautionary Tales*

(1908). In *The Servile State* (1912) he attacked both capitalism and socialism, favoring the Middle Ages as the most enlightened period of Western culture. His *History of England* (1925–31), not a history at all, searches out the roots of English culture in the Latin and Christian traditions. *The Postmaster General* (1932) is considered the best of his light novels, and his *Cromwell* (1934) is still read for the liveliness of its attack on the statesman. Together with his friend G. K. Chesterton, Belloc remains a major figure in the English Catholic literary tradition.

MARTIN SEYMOUR-SMITH

Bibliography: Baybrooke, Patrick, *Some Thoughts on Hilaire Belloc: Ten Studies* (1969; repr. 1973); Haynes, Renée, *Hilaire Belloc* (1953); Lowndes, Marie A., *The Young Hilaire Belloc* (1956); Morton, John B., *Hilaire Belloc: A Memoir* (1955; repr. 1984); Spaeight, Robert, *The Life of Hilaire Belloc* (1957); Wilson, A. N., *Hilaire Belloc* (1984).

Bellotto, Bernardo

Bernardo Bellotto, b. Jan. 30, 1721, was a Venetian painter of city scenes that have an almost photographic immediacy. The nephew of the renowned painter Canaletto, Bellotto sometimes added "Canaletto" to his signature on a painting, thereby creating confusion as to the true identity of the artist. Most of his paintings, however, can be distinguished by a cool, almost gray tonality, which is especially evident in the work he did after 1747, when he was appointed court painter at Dresden and left Venice.

Although Bellotto did numerous paintings of aristocratic country houses, such as his view of the Schlosshof Summer Palace (1760; Staatliche Kunstsammlungen, Gemäldegalerie, Dresden), his most famous works are the series of large canvases depicting the city and environs of Dresden. In *The Market-Place, Pirna* (1753; Kunsthistorisches Museum, Vienna), for example, his presentation of urban life, if less magical than that of Canaletto's Venice, is remarkable for its directness and clarity. In 1770, Bellotto came under the patronage of King Stanisław II of Poland, for whom he painted a superb series of views of Warsaw (National Museum, Warsaw). Bellotto died in Warsaw on Nov. 17, 1780.

LESLIE JONES

Bibliography: Kozakiewicz, Stefan, *Bernardo Bellotto*, 2 vols. (1972).

Bellow, Saul

Saul Bellow, one of the major American literary figures of the 20th century and a Nobel Prize winner, explores the resiliency of the human spirit in his novels and stories. The appeal of Bellow's protagonists lies in their blend of humor, nerve, and compassion.

The American writer Saul Bellow, b. Lachine, Quebec, June 10, 1915, won the Nobel Prize for literature in 1976 and also received the National Book Award three times—for The Adventures of Augie March in 1953, *Herzog* in 1965, and *Mr. Sammler's Planet* in 1970.
Life. The son of Russian emigré parents who moved from Canada to Chicago when he was nine years old, Bellow had a rough-and-tumble adolescence among the Jewish minority in a Polish neighborhood on Chicago's West Side. He won a scholarship to the University of Chicago but transferred to

Northwestern University, from which he graduated in 1937. He taught (1938–42) at the Pestalozzi-Froebel Teacher's College and briefly at several universities in subsequent years. Since 1962 he has been a professor at the University of Chicago and a fellow (chairman, 1970–76) of its Committee on Social Thought.

Writings. Bellow's first published story, "Two Morning Monologues," appeared in 1941 in the *Partisan Review.* Bellow won his first large popular audience with *The Adventures of Augie March* (1953), a boisterous, picaresque narrative filled with the popular idiom of Chicago's streets. Described as a modern urban *Adventures of Huckleberry Finn,* the novel narrates the growth and education of a young Chicagoan. Four of Bellow's early novels—*Dangling Man* (1944), *The Victim* (1947), *Seize the Day* (1956), and *Henderson the Rain King* (1959)—portray the moral and psychological dilemmas of protagonists caught in moments of crisis that force them to examine their lives and face the truths of their identities. Later works include the novels *Herzog* (1964), *Mr. Sammler's Planet* (1969), *Humboldt's Gift* (1975; Pulitzer Prize, 1976), *The Dean's December* (1982), and *More Die of Heartbreak* (1987); the stories in *Mosby's Memoirs* (1968) and *Him with His Foot in His Mouth and Other Stories* (1984); a play, *The Last Analysis* (1964); and an account of his experiences in Israel, *To Jerusalem and Back* (1976).

Bellow has often spoken out against the purely formal experimentation of much modern fiction. A humanist who argues strongly against the prevalent philosophy of his age, which he considers nihilistic, Bellow pits his characters against the temptations of absurdity. "Choose dignity," insists a spokesman in *The Victim.* The narrator of *Herzog* (The Viking Press, 1964) agrees, adding: "The canned sauerkraut of Spengler's 'Prussian Socialism,' the commonplaces of the Wasteland outlook, the cheap mental stimulants of Alienation, the cant and rant of pipsqueaks about Inauthenticity and Forlornness. I can't accept this foolish dreariness. We are talking about the whole life of mankind. The subject is too great, too deep for such weakness, cowardice—too deep, too great. . . ."
                                        JEROME KLINKOWITZ

Bibliography: Clayton, John J., *Saul Bellow: In Defense of Man,* 2d ed. (1979); Cohen, Sarah, *Saul Bellow's Enigmatic Laughter* (1975); Dutton, Robert R., *Saul Bellow,* rev. ed. (1982); Fuchs, Daniel, *Saul Bellow: Vision and Revision* (1983); Goldman, L. H., *Saul Bellow's Moral Vision* (1983); Tanner, Tony, *Saul Bellow* (1965; repr. 1978); Wilson, Jonathan, *On Bellow's Planet* (1985).

bellows

A bellows is a device used to produce a stream of air. It is essentially an air PUMP. A simple manual bellows consists of two boards, often heart- or pear-shaped, surrounded by an airtight pleated leather bag having a nozzle at the narrow end and handles at the other end. The handles are used to bring the boards together or to separate them, with a leather strip at the narrow end acting as a hinge; air is sucked in as the boards are pulled apart and expelled as the boards are brought together. One of the boards has a hole covered on the inside with a leather flap that acts as a valve. The valve permits air to enter the bellows through the hole when the handles are pulled apart, but seals the hole when the bellows is compressed, so that the air taken in cannot escape back out through the valve but must pass out through the nozzle in a stream, which can be directed at a particular point. The force with which the air is expelled depends on the force exerted on the handles.

Bellows, often ornately decorated, are used today to help start fires in fireplaces. They also supply the air for reed organs and are used by blacksmiths to intensify the heat in their furnaces.
                                        R. J. DE CRISTOFORO

Bellows, George

George Wesley Bellows, b. Columbus, Ohio, Aug. 12, 1882, d. July 8, 1925, is probably the best-known member of the group of American painters dubbed the ASHCAN SCHOOL for their honest and vivid depiction of seedy urban locales and their inhabitants. He revealed something of his physical ruggedness—he was an outstanding athlete at Ohio State University—and socialist learnings in what he chose to paint: fight scenes and other athletic events, as well as energetic people moving purposefully through their urban or rural environment.

Until about 1920 Bellows worked in the bold and vigorous style inherited from his teacher Robert HENRI, through which he conveyed the gusto of his subjects. His *Stag at Sharkey's*

Both Members of This Club (1909) is one of a series of dramatic boxing paintings by the American painter and graphic artist George Bellows. A member of the Ashcan school and one of the organizers of the Armory Show, Bellows is known for his uncompromising realism in paintings of urban New York, as well as in landscapes, figure compositions, and portraits. (National Gallery of Art, Washington, D.C.; Gift of Chester Dale.)

(1909; Cleveland Museum of Art) is an unforgettable scene: a brutal prizefight in the back room of a saloon. In *Forty-Two Kids* (1907; Corcoran Gallery of Art, Washington, D.C.), a painting of slum children swimming among the rotting wharves along Manhattan's East River, Bellows achieves both social realism and a lively outdoor scene, without sentimentality. His portraits are much admired for their combination of cool observation and sympathetic treatment of the subject. Bellows took up lithography in 1916 and raised the status of that medium, previously considered only a commercial process in the United States.

Bibliography: Doezema, Marianne, *George Bellows and Urban America* (1992); Mason, Lauris, and Ludman, Joan, *The Lithographs of George Bellows* (1977); Quick, Michael, et al., *The Paintings of George Bellows* (1992).

bells of Ireland

Bells of Ireland is an annual herb, *Moluccella laevis,* of the mint family, Labiatae. Also called molucca balm, it is native from the Mediterranean region to northern India. Its whorls of fragrant white flowers in green, cuplike calyxes are often used in fresh flower arrangements or, when dried, in winter arrangements.

Bell's theorem

In theoretical physics, Bell's theorem is a mathematical result that follows from the long-held assumption that the properties of a subatomic object, such as an electron, are independent of measurements made on any other physical system. This so-called local reality condition was first stated by Albert Einstein and coworkers in 1935.

In 1964, John Bell, a theoretical physicist from Northern Ireland, who was on the staff at CERN, in Geneva, extended the Einstein assumption when he envisioned a system containing two spinning particles (1 and 2), which begin with zero total spin and then separate. He calculated the expected results, assuming Einstein's local-reality condition, of a series of measurements done on such correlated pairs, in which the spin projection of particle 1 is measured along some direction while that of particle 2 is measured along a different direction. Thus the experimenter might choose three directions, A, B, C, in a plane, and measure the fraction of time that the spin of particle 1 lies in direction A, while that of particle 2 lies in direction B, and similarly for pairs A, C and B, C.

Bell showed that any theory incorporating Einstein's local-reality condition should lead to results in these three sets of measurements that satisfy a certain mathematical inequality —now called Bell's inequality. In QUANTUM MECHANICS, the local reality condition does not apply, so the predictions of quantum mechanics, for these experiments, would not lead to Bell's result. In subsequent tests Bell's inequality was not satisfied, indicating that Einstein's local-reality condition must be abandoned.   GERALD FEINBERG

Bibliography: Bell, John, *Speakable and Unspeakable in Quantum Mechanics* (1987); Herbert, Nick, *Quantum Reality* (1985).

Belluschi, Pietro   [bel-loos'-kee]

Pietro Belluschi, b. Ancona, Italy, Aug. 18, 1899, d. Feb. 14, 1994, was one of America's foremost regional architects. From 1927 to 1951, Belluschi practiced in Portland, Oreg., and came to dominate the developing architecture of the Pacific Northwest. His major commissions of this period reflect the INTERNATIONAL STYLE, culminating in the influential Equitable Saving and Loan Association Building (1948) in Portland, with its aluminum-clad structure flush with the exterior surface. Concurrently, his many small-scale domestic and religious designs, executed in wood, were inspired by indigenous vernacular structures. Between 1951 and 1965 he was dean of the School of Architecture and Planning at the Massachusetts Institute of Technology. Subsequently, he designed primarily in collaboration with other architects. Examples are the over-scaled Pan American World Airways Building (1963) in New York City (with Walter GROPIUS), the Juilliard School of Music

(1968) for New York's Lincoln Center, and the Bank of America (1969) and Symphony Hall (1980) in San Francisco.

Bibliography: Clausen, Meredith L., *Spiritual Space: the Religious Architecture of Pietro Belluschi* (1992).

belly dance

A Syrian dancer called Little Egypt introduced the belly dance to American audiences at the 1893 Chicago World's Fair. It is primarily a series of abdominal and pelvic gyrations. Its origins are probably Persian, and it is still popular in the Middle East, where the dancers use finger cymbals and wear costumes decorated with coins.

Belmondo, Jean Paul   [bel-mawn-doh']

Jean Paul Belmondo, b. Apr. 9, 1933, is a French film actor noted for his Bogart-like portrayals of unromantic heroes in films of the French NEW WAVE. His films include *Breathless* (1959), *That Man from Rio* (1964), *Pierrot le Fou* (1965), *Le Voleur* (1967), *Borsalino* (1970), *Stavisky* (1974), *L'Animal* (1977), *L'As des As* (1982), *Joyeuses Pâques* (1984), and *Itinéraire d'un enfant gâté* (1988).   LESLIE HALLIWELL

Belmont   (family)

The German-American financier **Auguste Belmont**, b. Dec. 2, 1816, d. Mar. 24, 1890, built one of the first banking fortunes in the United States. He settled in New York City in 1837 as an agent of the Rothschild bank in Frankfurt, Germany, and soon launched his own, highly successful banking house, August Belmont & Company. After his marriage to Caroline Perry, daughter of Commodore Matthew PERRY, in 1849, he became a leading figure in New York society. A Democrat and occasional diplomat, he used his European connections on behalf of the Union in the Civil War. He was an avid sportsman and introduced Thoroughbred horse racing into the United States. His son **Perry**, b. New York City, Feb. 28, 1850, d. May 25, 1947, was a lawyer, political writer, Democratic member of Congress from New York (1881–88), and minister to Spain (1888–89). Another son **August**, b. New York City, Feb. 15, 1853, d. Dec. 10, 1924, took over the family banking business. His son and grandson, both August, were also leading bankers.

Belmonte, Juan   [bel-mohn'-tay]

Juan Belmonte, b. Apr. 14, 1892, d. Apr. 2, 1962, was a Spaniard who revolutionized bullfighting by his graceful movements and by maintaining dangerous proximity to the animals he challenged. In a career that began in 1910 and ended in 1936, the slightly built Belmonte used cunning and quick moves to edge close to bulls, and this daring established the pattern for the great matadors who followed him. In becoming Spain's most popular sports hero, he fought as many as 109 bulls in a year (1919), killed more than 1,650 in his career, and was gored about 50 times. His autobiography was translated into English by the American writer Leslie Charteris as *Juan Belmonte, Killer of Bulls* (1937).

Belmopan   [bel-moh-pahn']

Belmopan (1990 pop., 5,256) has been the capital city of Belize (formerly British Honduras) since 1970. It is located at Roaring Creek on the Belize River, 80 km (50 mi) inland from the former capital, Belize City. The site for the new capital was chosen after hurricane Hattie and an accompanying tidal wave devastated Belize City on Oct. 31, 1961. A grant from Great Britain aided construction.

Belo Horizonte   [bel-ohr-ee-zohn'-tay]

Belo Horizonte is the capital of Brazil's leading mineral-producing state, Minas Gerais, and is located in eastern Brazil, 354 km (220 mi) north of Rio de Janeiro. It has a population of 2,048,861 (1991). Brazil's first modern planned city, Belo Horizonte has wide tree-lined avenues that were laid out like the spokes of a wheel in 1897 on a site near the geographic center of the state. Belo Horizonte is an important market for local crops and livestock and is a transportation center. Cotton from the São Francisco River valley keeps the city's many textile mills busy. Immense deposits of iron from nearby Itabira supply the steel mills. Industrial development has been rapid since 1950, and many factories have been built in the Cidade Industrial, about 16 km (10 mi) from the city's center.

The picturesque garden suburb of Pampuhla, site of the busy metropolitan airport, is noted for the magnificent buildings designed by the architect Oscar NIEMEYER, particularly the Chapel of São Francisco. Belo Horizonte is the site of the University of Minas Gerais (1927), Catholic University (1959), a music conservatory, and a ballet school.   JAMES N. SNADEN

Beloit College   [buh-loyt']

Established in 1846, Beloit College (enrollment: 1,000; library: 250,000 volumes) is a private 4-year liberal arts college for men and women in Beloit, Wis. In 1964 the college instituted the Beloit Plan, a nontraditional program based on trimesters, one of which was devoted to off-campus work-study. The school reverted to semesters in 1978 but retained many components of the Beloit Plan. In 1981, Beloit introduced moral obligation scholarships.

Belorussia: see BELARUS.

Belsen

Belsen (in full, Bergen-Belsen), a village in the German state of Lower Saxony, was the site of a concentration camp under Hitler. The camp was intended for Jews whom the Nazis wanted to exchange for Germans captured by the Allies. Large numbers, however, were either murdered in Belsen or died there from starvation or disease. When it was liberated in April 1945, 13,000 unburied corpses were found.

Belshazzar   [bel-shaz'-ur]

According to Babylonian sources, Belshazzar, crown prince of the Chaldean dynasty, was officially elevated (550 BC) to coregent by his father, King Nabonidus. The Chaldean dynasty ended when Babylon fell before Cyrus the Great in 539 BC. According to biblical sources, however, Belshazzar was the son of NEBUCHADNEZZAR. During a great banquet Belshazzar saw the original "handwriting on the wall," which only the prophet DANIEL could interpret (Dan. 5).

Belter, John Henry

John Henry Belter, b. Württemberg, Germany, 1804, d. 1863, was New York's most famous cabinetmaker in the Victorian era. His furniture is characterized by its curved shapes and elaborate carved ornament in rococo revival designs. Belter obtained five patents for processes related to the manufacture of laminated rosewood furniture between 1847 and 1858. Characteristic pieces are made of many layers of wood, comparable to plywood, that have been glued and steam-pressed in special iron molds into curving forms. Labeled pieces are rare, although similar furniture by other manufacturers is frequently called "Belter."   MARVIN D. SCHWARTZ

Bibliography: Bjerkoe, Ethel H. and John A., *The Cabinetmakers of America,* 2d ed. (1978).

beluga   (fish):   see STURGEON.

beluga   (whale)   [buh-loo'-guh]

The beluga, or white WHALE, *Delphinapterus leucas,* is a small whale of the Arctic Ocean and neighboring seas, sometimes venturing into estuaries. Together with the NARWHAL, it constitutes the family Monodontidae, order Cetacea. The male beluga ranges up to 4.5 m (15 ft) long and weighs about 1,500 kg (3,300 lb). The somewhat smaller female gives birth to a single young after a gestation period of 14 months and nurses it for several months thereafter; the young whale, black to bluish at birth, attains a creamy white color in about five years. Belugas feed on bottom-dwelling fish and other sea life, using echolocation to detect their prey. Traveling in small family groups and occasional large, migrating herds, they communicate by means of a great variety of squeals, trills, whistles, and clicks. Long exploited by natives of the Arctic region, belugas are now fished commercially under regulated limits.

belvedere   [bel'-vuh-deer]

The term *belvedere,* derived from the Italian, meaning "beautiful view," in architecture, indicates a towerlike structure, usually atop a larger building and affording a view. It may be small—in the form of a pavilion, cupola, turret, or GAZEBO—or large, in the form of a loggia or open gallery. The term is also applied to entire buildings, such as Johann Lucas von HILDEBRANDT's rococo Upper Belvedere (1714–16) and Lower Belvedere (1721–22) in Vienna, a sumptuous complex of two palaces connected by formal gardens and waterworks.

Bely, Andrei   [byel'-ee]

Andrei Bely is the pseudonym of the Russian writer Boris Nikolayevich Bugayev, b. Oct. 26, 1880, d. Jan. 8, 1934, who was one of the leading and most iconoclastic figures of Russian SYMBOLISM. He wrote poetry, plays, and criticism, but he is best remembered for his brilliant and innovative prose, which influenced the formal experiments of later Russian writers.

The son of a noted Russian mathematician, Bely studied mathematics, zoology, and philosophy at Moscow University before turning to literature. A friend and sometime rival of the poet Aleksandr Blok, he was influenced first by the mystical cosmology of Vladimir Soloviev and then by the oriental anthroposophy of Rudolf Steiner. The best of his early works are his four poetic "symphonies," especially the first of these, *The Northern Symphony* (1900), in which he sought to combine poetry, prose, music, and painting in one total work of art. Between 1898 and 1907 he worked on a monumental drama, *Antichrist,* but only fragments remain. His first collection of poems, *Gold in Azure,* appeared in 1904, when he also began collaborating on the literary journal *Vesy* (1904–09).

Bely is best known today for his monumental novels *The Silver Dove* (1908; Eng. trans., 1974); *Petersburg* (1912; Eng. trans., 1960, 1978), adapted into a play in 1925; and *Kotik Letayev* (1917; Eng. trans., 1971). Notable for its complex style and syntax, elaborate use of allusions, humor, and sophistication, his fiction has frequently been compared to that of James

The beluga, or white whale, D. leucas, ranges throughout the Arctic Ocean and northern seas into Hudson Bay, Canada.

Joyce. Bely also wrote numerous volumes of literary criticism, including a study of Gogol (1934), and several volumes of memoirs.

Bibliography: Alexandrov, V. E., *Andrei Bely* (1985); Elsworth, J. D., *Andrey Beli: A Critical Study of the Novels* (1984); Malmsted, J., *Andrey Bely* (1987); Maslenikov, O. A., *The Frenzied Poets* (1952); Mochulsky, K., *Andrei Bely*, trans. by N. Szalawitz (1976).

Belyayev, Pavel Ivanovich   [bil-yah'-yef, pah'-vel ee-vahn'-oh-vich]

The Soviet cosmonaut Pavel Ivanovich Belyayev, b. June 26, 1925, d. Jan. 10, 1970, was the crew commander of the 1965 VOSKHOD 2 flight during which copilot Aleksey LEONOV became the first man to walk in outer space. Belyayev, a Soviet Navy pilot who had flown several World War II combat missions against Japan, became a cosmonaut in March 1960. He was temporarily removed from flight status for medical reasons but was reinstated to command the *Voskhod 2* flight on Mar. 18–19, 1965. At the end of that flight, the spaceship's autopilot failed and Belyayev became the first cosmonaut to make a manually guided landing, setting the capsule down in a snow-filled pine forest in the Ural Mountains. In 1968, Belyayev confided to American astronauts that he had been chosen to command the USSR's first manned Moon flight in the ZOND program, but no manned flight was ever made.

JAMES OBERG

Belzóni, Giovanni Battista   [bel-tsoh'-nee]

Giovanni Battista Belzóni, b. Nov. 15, 1778, d. Dec. 3, 1823, was an Italian engineer and explorer and the first man in modern times to explore the interior of the second pyramid of Giza.

In 1803, after Napoleon's troops invaded Italy, he went to England and worked as a circus strong man. In 1815 he traveled to Egypt, hoping to interest the ruler, Mohammed Ali, in a waterwheel he had invented. The British consul-general Henry Salt commissioned him to oversee the removal of the huge bust of Ramses II from Thebes to the British Museum. He explored the tombs in the Valley of the Kings at Thebes, where he discovered that of the pharaoh Seti I in 1817. He also identified the ruined Red Sea port of Berenice in Egypt. He returned to England in 1819 and published a book on his discoveries in 1820.

Bibliography: Mayes, Stanley, *The Great Belzóni* (1959).

Bem, Józef

The Polish soldier and patriot Józef Bem, b. Mar. 14, 1794, d. Dec. 10, 1850, was a champion of liberal and nationalist causes in the first half of the 19th century. Bem distinguished himself in the abortive Polish insurrection of 1830–31 against Russian rule, and during the next two decades was a leader of the Polish community in exile. He was especially celebrated for his exploits during the REVOLUTIONS OF 1848, when he led the Vienna insurgents against the Austrian army and commanded Hungarian forces against the Austrians and Russians. After the defeat of the Hungarians Bem fled to Turkey and entered the service of the sultan. There he became a Muslim and, adopting the name Murad Pasha, was made governor of Aleppo.

Bemba   [bem'-buh]

The Bemba are a BANTU tribe inhabiting northeastern Zambia and parts of Zaire and Zimbabwe. They number more than 200,000 and speak Chibemba, now the lingua franca of Zambia. The Bemba have played an important part in Zambian politics, both in the British colonial and postcolonial periods, as trade union leaders, church founders, party politicians, and hereditary tribal rulers. They are closely akin to other central Bantu matrilineal peoples, such as the LUBA, LUNDA, Lala, Bisa, and Lamba. The Bemba were among the first to become mine workers on the Zambian copper belt.

Originating, according to legend, from one of the great empires in the upper Congo basin, either Luba or Lunda, the Bemba established their own highly stratified federation under a divine king, the Chitimukulu. In the 19th and early 20th centuries in northeastern Zambia, the Bemba state operated on a great scale, rivaled in size only by the Lunda kingdom of Kazembe on the Luapula River. Their past and present achievements in politics are all the more remarkable, given the poverty of their soil, the oppressive climate, the impermanence of their system of bush-fallow, or shifting cultivation (known as *citemene* or "cut garden" in Bemba), and the overall simplicity of their tools and techniques for fishing, hunting, and agriculture.

RICHARD P. WERBNER

Bibliography: Maxwell, Kevin B., *Bemba Myth and Ritual* (1983); Richards, Audrey, *Land, Labour and Diet in Northern Rhodesia: An Economic Study of the Bemba Tribe* (1939); Roberts, Andrew O., *A History of the Bemba* (1974).

Bembo, Pietro   [bem'-boh]

Pietro Bembo, b. May 20, 1470, d. Jan. 18, 1547, was an Italian poet, humanist, and churchman, and during his lifetime, the foremost figure of the Italian literary world. Born to a noble family, he received an extensive classical education and, an accomplished Latinist, was named (1512) secretary to Pope Leo X. He entered the church in 1522 and was made a cardinal in 1539. Bembo's first work of note was *Gli Asolani* (1505), prose dialogues on love set in a garden of the palace of Asolo. His great work, *Prose della volgar lingua* (Discussions of the Italian Language, 1525), was influential in establishing the Florentine dialect as the literary language of Italy, and constituted the first Italian grammar. Bembo's Italian poetry, much of it written in direct imitation of Petrarch, was published in the collection *Rime* (1530).

Bemelmans, Ludwig

Ludwig Bemelmans, b. Austria, Apr. 27, 1898, d. New York City, Oct. 1, 1962, was both an artist and the author and illustrator of a number of popular novels, travel books, and humorous essays, including the novels *Hotel Splendide* (1941) and *Dirty Eddie* (1947). His books for children, which have become classics, include the Madeline series of adventures (begun in 1939) and *Parsley* (1955)—all of them illustrated with his own slapdash but vivid watercolor pictures. Bemelmans was a naturalized U.S. citizen, and his work reflects a wide experience of cosmopolitan life in both Europe and America.

Bibliography: Smaridge, Norah, *Famous Author-Illustrators for Young People* (1973).

Bemis, Samuel Flagg   [bee'-mis]

Samuel Flagg Bemis, b. Worcester, Mass., Oct. 20, 1891, d. Sept. 26, 1973, was an American diplomatic historian and professor at Yale University from 1935 to 1960. His first major work was *Jay's Treaty* (1924). Bemis won two Pulitzer prizes, one in history for *Pinckney's Treaty* (1926) and one in biography for *John Quincy Adams and the Foundations of American Foreign Policy* (1949). His other works include *The Diplomacy of the American Revolution* (1935), *A Diplomatic History of the United States* (1936; 5th ed., 1965), and *John Quincy Adams and the Union* (1956).

ben Bella, Ahmed

Ahmed ben Bella, b. Dec. 15, 1918, was one of the chief organizers of the Algerian anti-French insurrection of November 1954. He became prime minister of independent Algeria in 1962 and was elected president the following year. In 1965, however, he was overthrown by his minister of defense, Col. Houari BOUMÉDIENNE (Abu Madyan), and was imprisoned. He was freed in July 1979 and formed an opposition movement in Paris in 1984. He returned to Algeria in 1990.

Bibliography: Merle, Robert, *Ahmed Ben Bella* (1965; Eng. trans., 1967); Ottaway, David and Marina, *Algeria: The Politics of a Socialist Revolution* (1970).

Ben-Gurion, David

David Ben-Gurion was one of the founders of the State of Israel and its first prime minister. For 15 years (1948–63) the dominant personality in Israeli politics, he established a strong Israeli army and created a sense of national unity among the diverse groups in the new state.

David Ben-Gurion was the first prime minister of ISRAEL and its leading personality during the first 15 years of the Jewish state. He was born on Oct. 16, 1886, in Russian Poland and originally named David Grün. From 1906, when he arrived in Palestine, until 1910 he was an agricultural laborer. To familiarize himself with the language and law of Palestine's Turkish rulers, he studied at the University of Constantinople in 1912 and became an Ottoman Turkish national to strengthen Jewish ties with the government. Nevertheless, during World War I he was banished by the Ottoman military authorities for subversive activities and fled to New York. When an American battalion of the Jewish Legion was formed under auspices of the British Army in 1918, Ben-Gurion joined. He became a corporal during service in the final Middle Eastern campaigns of the war.

After World War I, Ben-Gurion rose rapidly as a leader of the Zionist labor movement in Palestine. He was one of the founders of the Histadrut (General Federation of Jewish Labor in Palestine) in 1920 and its secretary-general from 1921 to 1935. He was also a founder (1930) of the Mapai (Labor) party. From 1935 to 1948 he was chairman of the World Zionist movement's Jewish Agency for Palestine.

At the end of World War II, Ben-Gurion led an activist campaign to establish a Jewish commonwealth in Palestine, which had been under British mandate since 1920. He escaped arrest when the British interned other members of the Jewish Agency executive during June 1946, because he was in Paris. When the British mandate was about to end in May 1948—with the first ARAB-ISRAELI WAR already taking place—Ben-Gurion urged an immediate declaration of independence for Israel on May 14, 1948. For the next 15 years Ben-Gurion was Israel's most renowned leader, serving as prime minister and defense minister until he retired in 1963—with an interval from December 1953 to February 1955, when he withdrew from politics to a kibbutz.

Ben-Gurion became impatient with controversy in the labor movement and announced his retirement from leadership of the Mapai party and as head of government in 1963. He and several of his associates left Mapai in 1965 to form a new labor party, Rafi (Israel Workers' List). When Rafi reunited with Mapai in 1968, Ben-Gurion refused to support the merger and formed another party. In 1970 he resigned from the Knesset and political activity, spending the remainder of his life at a desert kibbutz. He died on Dec. 1, 1973.

Ben-Gurion's major achievements were the establishment of Israel's armed forces and their development into one of the strongest military machines in the Middle East; defining defense and military policies that gave Israel the status of a Middle Eastern power; creating a sense of national identity and unity from diverse political factions and Jewish ethnic groups; and bringing together national and foreign resources that enabled Israel to more than quadruple its population during the first 15 years of its history.   DON PERETZ

Bibliography: Ben-Gurion, David, *Memoirs*, ed. by T. R. Bransten (1970); St. John, Robert, *Ben-Gurion*, rev. ed. (1971); Teveth, Shabtai, *Ben-Gurion* (1987) and *Ben-Gurion and the Palestinian Arabs* (1985).

Ben Nevis   [ben nee'-vis]

A peak in the Grampian Mountains of west central Scotland, Ben Nevis is the highest point in the British Isles (1,343 m/4,406 ft). It is composed mainly of volcanic rock, and the northeastern face offers difficult climbs.

Ben-Yehudah, Eliezer   [ben-yeh-hoo'-dah, el-ee-eh'-zur]

Eliezer Ben-Yehudah was the chosen name of Eliezer Yitshak Perelman, b. 1858, d. Dec. 16, 1922, who was a Lithuanian-born Zionist and linguist often called the father of modern Hebrew. He received both a secular and a traditional Jewish education. One of the first proponents of a national spiritual home for the Jewish people, he stated in 1879 that the Jewish people must have their own land that would serve as a focal point for world Jewish culture. Ben-Yehudah further advocated the revival of Hebrew as a spoken language in Palestine, where he moved in 1881. There he established several Hebrew periodicals through which he coined many new words and made Hebrew an effective means of communication among Jews. He founded the Hebrew Language Council, later called the Academy of Hebrew Language, and began publishing his most important work, the *Complete Dictionary of Ancient and Modern Hebrew* (17 vols., 1910–59).

LAWRENCE H. SCHIFFMAN

Bibliography: St. John, Robert, *The Tongue of the Prophets: The Life Story of Eliezer Ben-Yehudah* (1952; repr. 1972).

Ben-Zvi, Itzhak   [ben-tsvee', it'-sahk]

Itzhak Ben-Zvi, b. Dec. 6, 1884, d. Apr. 23, 1963, was an early Zionist leader who became the second president of Israel (1952–63). Born in the Ukraine and originally named Shimshelevitz, he went to Palestine in 1907, where he helped organize the Jewish defense organization, Ha-Shomer; edited the first Hebrew socialist newspaper, *Ahdut*; and became a leader of the Jewish labor movement. In 1931 he became chairman of the Jewish National Council and later served as its president from 1944 to 1948. Elected a Mapai (Labor) party member of the first Knesset, he was the only person chosen by that body to be president of Israel three times—in 1952, 1957, and 1962.   DON PERETZ

Benares: see VARANASI.

Benavente y Martínez, Jacinto   [bay-nah-vayn'-tay ee mar-tee'-nays, hah-ceen'-toh]

Jacinto Benavente, b. Aug. 12, 1866, d. July 14, 1954, was one of the most popular and prolific Spanish dramatists of the first half of the 20th century. Although his family wanted him to be a lawyer, he left the university to pursue his strong literary inclination. He dedicated his life to the theater, writing 172 plays. In many of them he satirized, without bitterness, the hypocrisy of the middle and upper classes, who, ironically, idolized him. In 1922 he was awarded the Nobel Prize for literature. A reformer of the Spanish theater of his time, Benavente introduced naturalness of speech and action, enhanced by masterful dialogue, a sense of rhythm, and an impeccable dramatic technique.   MARCELINO C. PEÑUELAS

Bibliography: Peñuelas, Marcelino C., *Jacinto Benavente*, trans. by Kay Engler (1968).

Bench, Johnny

Baseball player Johnny Lee Bench, b. Oklahoma City, Okla., Dec. 7, 1947, was the game's foremost catcher during the 1970s and one of the finest ever to have played. Spending his entire career (1967–83) with the Cincinnati Reds, Bench was voted National League (NL) Rookie of the Year (1968) and twice was named the NL Most Valuable Player (1970, 1972). Known for his fielding prowess as well as his slugging ability, he won 10 consecutive Gold Gloves (1968–77) as the NL's best defensive catcher. For his career, Bench had a .267 batting average, 2,048 hits, 1,376 runs batted in, and 389 home runs (325 as a catcher, the major league record).

Bibliography: Sabin, Louis, *Johnny Bench: King of Catchers* (1977).

bench mark

A bench mark is a disk, usually made of bronze, that serves as a permanent indicator of a precise elevation that has been determined by topographic SURVEYING. The disk is inscribed with the exact latitude and longitude of the location, the elevation above mean sea level, and the name of the agency that made the measurement; it is then embedded in a rock outcrop or affixed to a concrete post set in the ground. Bench marks are used as reference points by surveyors and engineers in fieldwork and aerial surveys.   JOSEPH S. WEISBERG

Bibliography: Brinker, R. C., and Wolf, P. R., *Elementary Surveying*, 7th ed. (1984).

Benchley, Robert

Robert Charles Benchley, b. Worcester, Mass., Sept. 15, 1889, d. Nov. 21, 1945, was a humorist, drama critic, and film actor. His whimsical sketches, collected under such titles as *Of All Things* (1921), *From Bed to Worse* (1934), *My Ten Years in a Quandary* (1936), *Inside Benchley* (1941), and *Benchley Beside Himself* (1943), are mostly about people confronted with the complex absurdities of modern life.

Bibliography: Yates, Norris W., *Robert Benchley* (1968).

Benda, Jiří Antonín   [ben'-dah, jeer'-zhee ahn'-toh-neen]

Jiří Antonín Benda, b. June 1722, d. Nov. 6, 1795, was a Bohemian composer influential in late-18th-century German opera. From 1742 to 1749 he was a violinist in Berlin and from 1750 to 1778 Kapellmeister (Master of the Chapel) at Gotha, Thuringia. Before 1775 he composed little. Suddenly, he began to produce musical stage works, employing a combination of spoken text and sung text (*singspeil*), or using a spoken text against an instrumental musical background (melodrama). Both, especially the melodrama, influenced Mozart and others and, through them, the future of German opera. Besides 11 stage works, Benda left church music, songs, symphonies, chamber music, and keyboard sonatas.   WILLIAM HAYS

Benda, Julien

Julien Benda, b. Dec. 26, 1867, d. June 7, 1956, French critic, essayist, and philosopher, was a champion of Cartesian thought in the early 20th century. Attacking romanticism and the intuitional philosophy of Henri BERGSON (*Le Bergsonisme*, 1912) as leading to error and intolerance, Benda insisted that reason alone must determine human action. In his *La Trahison des clercs* (1927; *Treason of the Intellectuals*, 1928), he confronts writers and thinkers who sacrifice truth and intellectual values for political considerations, and he condemns racial and national prejudices.   JOSEPH A. REITER

Bendix, Vincent

Vincent Bendix, b. Moline, Ill., Aug. 12, 1882, d. Mar. 27, 1945, an American inventor and industrialist, was associated with products ranging from self-starters to helicopters. As a young man he developed a drive mechanism that made possible the automobile self-starter. In 1912 he founded the Bendix Brake Company to produce automobile brakes. Over the years he launched other companies to produce airplane equipment, electronic gear, and home laundries; these companies eventually grew into the present Bendix International. Bendix also established the annual Bendix Transcontinental Air Race (1931) and the International Glider Meet, and was the donor of the Bendix Trophy.

Bendix, William

William Bendix, b. New York City, Jan. 14, 1906, d. Dec. 14, 1964, was a character actor with a strong Brooklyn accent famous for such film roles as the baseball hero of *The Babe Ruth Story* (1948) and the ordinary guy in *The Life of Riley* (film, 1949; television series, 1953–58). He also appeared in such films as *The Glass Key* (1942), *The Hairy Ape* (1944), *The Blue Dahlia* (1946), and *The Big Steal* (1949).   LESLIE HALLIWELL

bends

The bends is a syndrome caused by the rapid evolution of nitrogen gas bubbles from body fluids when an individual moves too quickly from a higher-pressure atmosphere to a lower-pressure atmosphere. It can develop in both divers and fliers. Fluids in the vicinity of large joints are especially susceptible to bubbling, which causes severe, sometimes incapacitating, pain in those areas. Other symptoms include nausea and abdominal pain; in severe cases, coma and death result. This happens because the amount of a gas that can dissolve in liquids is directly proportional to the amount and duration of pressure. Scuba divers therefore surface gradually to normal atmospheric pressure; otherwise nitrogen bubbles form in body fluids in a manner analogous to the fizzing that occurs when a bottle of carbonated beverage is uncapped. Caisson workers and others who spend long periods in high-pressure environments return to normal pressure in decompression chambers at staged intervals that may take hours, and experimental dives to real or simulated depths of several hundred meters require a return period lasting days.

Bibliography: Hills, B. A., *Decompression Sickness* (1977).

Bene Israel   [bay'-nee iz'-ree-uhl]

Bene Israel, which means Sons of Israel, denotes a Jewish community in India. Their origin is unknown. Some scholars believe that they fled from Yemen in the 7th century at the time of Muhammad. They appeared on the Konkan coast, about 42 km (26 mi) south of Bombay, speaking the Marathi language. They were oil pressers, farmers, artisans, soldiers, and civil servants. In the 19th century some became lawyers, physicians, architects, and writers. Eventually they assimilated with the Hindu civilization. They observe the Sabbath, circumcision, and some Jewish festivals and dietary rules.

A return to traditional Jewish life took place in the 19th century with the emigration of Jews from Baghdad to Bombay; the Sassoon family founded schools that introduced Hebrew instruction. The number of the Bene Israel, which in 1969 was approximately 12,000, has been declining. Thousands have emigrated to Israel.   NAHUM N. GLATZER

Bibliography: Strizower, Schifra, *The Bene Israel of Bombay* (1971); Timberg, T. A., ed., *Jews in India* (1986).

Benedetti, Mario

One of Uruguay's most popular authors, Mario Benedetti, b. Sept. 14, 1920, is also a leftist who has devoted much of his career to Cuba. Among his fictional works about Uruguayans are the short-story collections *Esta mañana* (This Morning, 1949) and *Montevideanos* (1959). His novel *The Truce* (1960; Eng. trans., 1969) is the only one among his numerous works to be translated. Works written in Cuba include *Cauderno Cubano* (Cuban Notebook, 1969) and the short-story collection *Con y sin nostalgia* (With and without Nostalgia, 1977).

Benedetto da Maiano: see MAIANO (family).

Benedict, Ruth

The American anthropologist Ruth Fulton Benedict, b. June 5, 1887, d. Sept. 17, 1948, was a pioneer in the study of how human personality is shaped by different cultures. She received her professional training from Franz BOAS at Columbia University. Benedict focused in her work on the religious beliefs and practices of various peoples, including the vision quest of the Plains Indians. In her popular book *Patterns of Culture* (1934) she wrote that a society's culture was simply "personality writ large."

During World War II, Benedict studied the culture of Japan for the U.S. government. For her book *The Chrysanthemum and the Sword* (1946) she is credited with having influenced American postwar policy toward Japan. A year before her death she served as president of the American Anthropological Association.   STEPHEN A. KOWALEWSKI

Bibliography: Benedict, Ruth, *An Anthropologist at Work*, ed. by Margaret Mead (1966; repr. 1977); Erikson, Erik H., *Ruth Fulton Benedict: A Memorial* (1949); Mead, Margaret, *Ruth Benedict* (1974); Modell, J. S., *Ruth Benedict* (1984).

Benedict, Saint

St. Benedict, 480–547, was an Italian monk who founded the BENEDICTINES. The rule that he wrote for his monks became a model monastic rule. The only source for his life is the second book of *The Dialogues* written by GREGORY I (the Great). After being a hermit for three years, Benedict gathered disciples around him, first at Subiaco and later at Monte Cassino. Recent scholarship has shown that many passages from the *Rule of Benedict* were copied from an older monastic rule known as the *Rule of the Master*, dating from the beginning of the 6th century. Benedict's rule, however, was more spiritual, more person-oriented, and less narrow in its approach. Feast day: July 11 (Western); March 14 (Eastern).

                                CYPRIAN DAVIS, O. S. B.

Bibliography: Chadwick, Owen, *Western Asceticism* (1958); De Waal, Esther, *Seeking God: The Way of Saint Benedict* (1984); Saint Gregory I, *Life and Miracles of Saint Benedict*, trans. by O. J. Zimmerman and B. R. Avery (1969); Maynard, Theodore, *Saint Benedict and His Monks* (1964); Von Matt, L., and Hilpisch, S., *Saint Benedict* (1961).

Saint Benedict, an Italian monk and founder of the Benedictines, receives Totila, king of Eastern Goths, in this fresco by Aretino.

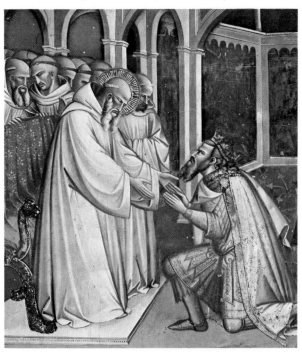

Benedict Biscop, Saint

Benedict Biscop, c.628–690, was a Northumbrian noble who left the service of King Oswy to become a Benedictine monk. He founded two monasteries, one at Wearmouth and the other at Jarrow. The books he collected in Rome and Gaul for the monastery libraries made possible the writings of the Venerable BEDE, his pupil. Feast day: Jan. 12.

Benedict the Black, Saint

Benedict, 1526–89, was a Sicilian freed slave of African ancestry. At first a hermit, he later became a lay brother and kitchen worker in the Franciscan priory at Palermo. Although he was illiterate, Benedict was chosen guardian of his community as well as novice master. He was canonized in 1807 and is sometimes called "the Moor." Feast day: Apr. 4.

Benedict XIII, "Antipope"

Benedict XIII, c.1328–1423, was "antipope" at Avignon from 1394 to 1417. A Spaniard, his name was Pedro de Luna. Appointed (1375) cardinal by Pope GREGORY XI, he took part in the controversial conclave that elected Gregory's successor and in the subsequent events of 1378 that brought about the Great SCHISM of the West. After the election of URBAN VI, he sided with the Avignon claimant, Clement VII, whom he succeeded as "antipope."

When he was elected in 1394, Benedict XIII swore that as pope he would work toward reunification of the two obediences, but he later resisted the pressure on him to abdicate. He argued that abdication was uncanonical. Pointing out that he was the only surviving cardinal from before the schism, he concluded that his vote was the only one that was certainly valid—and he would choose himself. His obstructive tactics, combined with those of the Roman claimant, Gregory XII, caused the cardinals to abandon both, summon the Council of Pisa (1409), and declare both deposed. The council then elected a third claimant to the papacy who took the name Alexander V. Union did not follow, however, until the Council of CONSTANCE (1416) formally declared Benedict deposed, and elected MARTIN V as the one papal claimant recognized by all. Benedict asserted his claims until his death.

                                THOMAS R. MORRISSEY

Bibliography: Glasfurd, A. L., *The Antipope (Peter de Luna 1342–1423): A Study in Obstinacy* (1965).

Benedict XV, Pope

Benedict XV, b. Nov. 21, 1854, d. Jan. 22, 1922, was pope from 1914 to 1922, succeeding PIUS X. His name was Giacomo della Chiesa, and he was born to an ancient aristocratic family in Genoa. He was created archbishop of Bologna in 1907 and cardinal in 1914, shortly before his election to the papacy. During World War I, Benedict won the good will of belligerents by his impartiality, his peace proposals, his charitable donations, and his prisoner-of-war services.

Bibliography: Peters, Walter H., *The Life of Benedict XV* (1959); Rope, Henry E. G., *Benedict XV: The Pope of Peace* (1941).

Benedictines

The Order of St. Benedict (O. S. B.) is the oldest order of monks in the West. There are both Roman Catholic and Anglican Benedictines, men and women who base their way of life on the rule written by St. BENEDICT.

Unlike other religious orders, the Benedictines are not a centralized organization. Each monastery is independent. A large monastery is an abbey headed by an abbot or an abbess. A small monastery is a priory headed by a prior or a prioress. Individual Benedictine houses are joined with others to form a congregation. The various congregations together form a confederation at the head of which is the abbot primate, first among equals of the various abbots. A few houses belong to no congregation and are directly subject to the abbot primate.

The Benedictine life is led within a community in the context of personal recollection and work, interspersed with the public recitation or singing of the Divine Office. Public worship is performed with solemnity and beauty. Work is essential; it can be manual, intellectual, or service-oriented. Each monastery may vary in its stress on prayer and its type of work without changing the basic orientation. The Benedictine habit is generally black, composed of tunic, belt, scapular, and hood, and a large flowing garment called the cowl for public worship. During the Middle Ages, the Benedictines were called the Black Monks.

Until the end of the 11th century, the Benedictines were the only monastic order in the West. They played important roles in apostolic activity, in education, and in the arts. Peter Abelard, the Venerable Bede, and Pope Gregory VII were Benedictines. CYPRIAN DAVIS, O. S. B.

Bibliography: Butler, Cuthbert, *Benedictine Monachism*, 2d ed. (1924; repr. 1961); Daly, Lowrie J., *Benedictine Monasticism* (1965; repr. 1970); Meisel, Anthony C., and Del Mastro, M. L., trans., *The Rule of St. Benedict* (1975); Mork, Wulston, *The Benedictine Way* (1987).

Beneš, Eduard   [beh-nesh']

Eduard Beneš, president of Czechoslovakia (1935–38 and 1945–48), developed the Little Entente alliance system in the interwar years. After the German seizure of the Sudetenland in 1938, Beneš went into exile. He later resumed office in Czechoslovakia after World War II but was ousted by the Communists in 1948.

Eduard Beneš, b. May 28, 1884, d. Sept. 3, 1948, was a prominent Czech statesman and—along with Tomáš MASARYK—one of the founders of Czechoslovakia. As a student and disciple of Masaryk, Beneš became an ardent spokesman for Czech nationalism. After the outbreak of World War I, he left Bohemia and, in cooperation with Masaryk and the Slovak leader Milan Štefanik, began to work for Czech and Slovak independence. With the collapse of Austria-Hungary and the founding of Czechoslovakia (1918) under Masaryk's presidency, Beneš became his country's foreign minister. He retained that post until 1935, when Masaryk retired and Beneš was elected president. During his tenure as foreign minister, Beneš became the prime architect of the Czechoslovak-Romanian-Yugoslav alliance (the so-called Little Entente, 1921) directed against Hungarian attempts to revise the 1920 peace settlement, as well as of Czechoslovakia's Francophile foreign policy.

Unable to prevent Germany's annexation of Bohemia's German-inhabited SUDETENLAND (September 1938), Beneš resigned as president and went into exile on Oct. 5, 1938. Returning (Apr. 3, 1945) after World War II at the head of the new Czechoslovak government, Beneš recognized the new dominant position of the USSR and tried to adjust to the situation by granting important concessions to the Czech Communist party (Košice Program, Apr. 5, 1945) and by agreeing to the Soviet annexation of Carpatho-Ruthenia (June 29, 1945). He was, however, unable to prevent a Communist takeover in 1948. Beneš resigned (June 7) and died three months later. He was an able and shrewd politician, but he lacked the lofty idealism and humanitarianism of his mentor, Tomáš Masaryk. S. B. VARDY

Bibliography: Crabitès, Pierre, *Beneš, Statesman of Central Europe* (1935); Craig, Gordon, and Gilbert, Felix, eds., *The Diplomats, 1919–1939* (1953); Kaplan, Karel, *The Short March: The Communist Take-Over of Power in Czechoslovakia, 1945–48* (1986); Mackenzie, Compton, *Dr. Beneš* (1946).

Benét, Stephen Vincent   [buh-nay']

The American writer Stephen Vincent Benét, b. Bethlehem, Pa., July 22, 1898, d. Mar. 13, 1943, the younger brother of William Rose Benét, is best known for *John Brown's Body* (1928), which won (1929) a Pulitzer Prize for poetry. Over 300 pages, the poem covers the Civil War from John BROWN's raid at Harpers Ferry, W.Va., to peace at Appomattox. It is not intended to be a eulogy of Brown—indeed his faults are clearly shown—but an epic narrative showing the fruitful diversity upon which modern America is built. The focus shifts from cabinet officers to frontiersmen, from battle scenes to domestic events. Benét invented stories dealing with men from various sections of the United States. His historical perspective, based on considerable reading, is not remarkably profound, but neither is it simplistic or partisan. He showed a gift for clear and rapid narration and an ability to bring a scene vividly to life by using image and metaphor.

Benét's other volumes of poetry include *Ballads and Poems, 1915–1930* (1931) and *The Burning City* (1936). He also wrote several novels, collections of short stories, and librettos for two short operas, *The Headless Horseman* (1937) and *The Devil and Daniel Webster* (1939). The latter was based on his famous 1937 short story. *Western Star*, a complete section of a projected epic poem dealing with the movement to the American West, was published posthumously in 1943 and was awarded a Pulitzer Prize for poetry in 1944. JAMES HART

Bibliography: Benét, William Rose, *Stephen Vincent Benét* (1943; repr. 1977); Deutsch, Babette, *Poetry in Our Time*, rev. ed. (1963); Fenton, Charles A., *Stephen Vincent Benét* (1958; repr. 1976); Stroud, Parry, *Stephen Vincent Benét* (1962).

Benét, William Rose

William Rose Benét, b. Brooklyn, N.Y., Feb. 2, 1886, d. May 4, 1950, the brother of Stephen Vincent Benét, was an American poet and editor. In 1924 he helped found the *Saturday Review of Literature*. His volumes of exotic verse include *Merchants from Cathay* (1913) and *The Great White Wall* (1916). His autobiographical poem *The Dust Which Is God* (1941) won a 1942 Pulitzer Prize for poetry. He was married to the American poet Elinor WYLIE, whose poems he collected and edited in 1932, and he coedited the *Oxford Anthology of Literature* (1938) and *The Reader's Encyclopedia* (1948).

Bengal   [ben-gawl']

Bengal is a historic region, now divided into the Indian state of West Bengal and the independent republic of BANGLADESH, that lies between the Himalayas in the north and the Bay of Bengal in the south. The region roughly approximates the area inhabited by the speakers of Bengali, the dominant language. The area is drained by the Ganges-Brahmaputra river system, which forms an extensive low-lying delta. Good soils are present throughout Bengal, except in the extreme north (the Himalaya fringe), thus making the region especially fertile for agriculture. Favorable climatic conditions have made Bengal the "rice bowl" of India and the world's only large-scale producer of jute. The delta area, however, is subject to flooding and resulting crop loss. Boiled rice and fish are the common Bengali diet. The temperature range is 10°–35° C (50°–95° F), and rainfall is generally heavy; the monsoonal rainfall occurs in the summer. Industries are primarily concentrated at the coal field locations around Asansol, near the port city of CALCUTTA, and at DACCA (Dhaka).

The Buddhist Pala dynasty established its rule over the area in the 8th century but in the 11th century gradually yielded control to the Hindu Sena dynasty. From about 1200 Bengal was ruled by Muslim princes, and in 1576 it became part of the Mogul Empire. In 1757, Robert CLIVE defeated the nawab (ruler) of Bengal at the Battle of Plassey (1757), signaling the beginning of British control. In 1905 the British viceroy Lord CURZON partitioned Bengal into two provinces. This arrangement, highly unpopular with the Hindu Bengalis, lasted until 1911. After independence in 1947, however, Bengal was again divided—into East Pakistan and West Bengal. East Pakistan seceded from Pakistan in 1971 and became the independent nation of Bangladesh. ASHOK K. DUTT

Bibliography: Baumer, R., ed., *Aspects of Bengali History and Society* (1975); Bose, S., *Agrarian Bengal* (1987); Inden, R. B., *Kinship in Bengali Culture* (1977); Marshall, P. G., *Bengal: The British Bridgehead* (1988); Risley, H. H., *Tribes and Castes of Bengal*, 2 vols. (1891; repr. 1981).

Bengal, Bay of

The Bay of Bengal is the northeastern section of the Indian Ocean and is bordered by India to the west and the Malay Peninsula to the east. Its southern boundary is formed by a line from the southern tip of Sri Lanka to the northern tip of Sumatra. It has an area of about 2,172,000 km² (839,000 mi²). Its salinity is reduced by the influx of water from many large rivers, including the Ganges, Irrawaddy, and Brahmaputra.

The bay is generally shallow, with an average depth of 790 m (2,600 ft). Its bottom is primarily a sedimentary plain marked, however, by deep canyons and the Indonesian Trench, which runs northward from Sumatra into the bay, as deep as 4,510 m (14,800 ft). Surface currents change seasonally, flowing clockwise in winter and east and north in summer. Cyclones occur generally at the end of the summer monsoon. Modern geophysical exploration has opened the possibility of exploiting vast mineral deposits on the seabed.

Bengali language: see INDO-IRANIAN LANGUAGES.

Bengel, J. A. [beng'-ul]

Johann Albrecht Bengel, b. June 24, 1687, d. Nov. 2, 1752, was a German Lutheran theologian and a New Testament scholar whose work marks the beginning of modern scientific studies of the Bible. While teaching (1713–41) at the theological school in Denkendorf, he produced the works for which he is remembered: a carefully prepared Greek text of the New Testament (1734) with the *Apparatus Criticus ad Novum Testamentum*, which is the basis for modern New Testament textual criticism; and the *Gnomon Novi Testamenti* (1742), an exegetical commentary.

Benghazi [ben-gah'-zee]

Benghazi is a city and major trading port in northeastern Libya. With a population of 446,250 (1988 est.), it is Libya's second largest city. It is situated on the northeastern shore of the Gulf of Sidra in a semiarid zone that supports some farming and little industry. The city grew after the discovery of oil to the south in the 1950s. It was founded in the 6th century BC as the Greek Euesperides; extensive Greek ruins are located to the northeast of the city. Libya was ruled by the Italians from 1912, and Benghazi was an Italian supply base during World War II, when it was severely damaged. After Libyan independence in 1951, it alternated with Tripoli as the capital. The University of Libya (1955) is in Benghazi.

Benguela [ben-gel'-uh]

Benguela (1983 est. pop., 155,000) is a port city and provincial capital on the Atlantic Ocean in western Angola. Founded in 1617, it became a base of Portuguese expansion in Africa and an important slave-trading port. For many years Benguela was the major rail terminus for minerals from inland Angola, Zaire, and Zambia. From 1975 to 1991, this lucrative traffic was disrupted by civil war and a guerrilla insurgency.

Beni Hasan [ben'-ee hah'-sahn]

Beni Hasan, a village about 25 km (16 mi) from Tell el-AMARNA, Egypt, is the site of 39 rock-cut tombs dating from the Middle Kingdom (c.2133–1786 BC). The tombs were built by provincial governors of the 11th and 12th dynasties and contain unique painted scenes. Among the more important tombs is that of Kheti, governor of the Antilope nome (province) during the 11th dynasty. It shows military scenes and an unusual depiction of wrestlers in various sequential positions. The tomb of Khnumhotep III, governor of the Antilope nome and of the entire Eastern Desert during the 12th dynasty, is the most magnificent. The entrance portico, with its polygonal columns supporting an architrave and cornice, has been called proto-Doric because of its affinities with Greek architecture. ROBERT S. BIANCHI

Benin [be-neen']

Benin is a small republic in West Africa known from 1960 to 1975 as the Republic of Dahomey. Located on the Bight of Benin in the Gulf of Guinea, it is bordered on the east by Nigeria, on the north by Niger and Burkina, and on the west by Togo. Formerly a French colony, Benin experienced extreme political instability after independence, partly because of the ethnic diversity of its population. The country's economy is heavily dependent on one crop: the palm kernel.

LAND AND RESOURCES

The southern coastline extends only 120 km (75 mi) from east to west and comprises sandy beaches backed by lagoons and swamps. Benin has no natural harbors; COTONOU is an artificial port made accessible to ships by two artificial jetties built out into the shallow coastal waters. Inland from the coastal

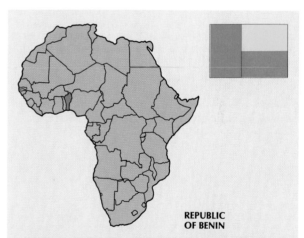

REPUBLIC OF BENIN

LAND. Area: 112,622 km² (43,484 mi²). Capital: Porto Novo (1984 est. pop., 167,000). Largest city: Cotonou (1984 est. pop., 478,000).

PEOPLE. Population (1990 est.): 4,673,964; density: 41.5 persons per km² (107.5 per mi²). Distribution (1985): 19% urban, 81% rural. Annual growth (1990): 33%. Official language: French. Major religions: traditional religions, Islam, Christianity.

EDUCATION AND HEALTH. Literacy (1991): 30% of adult population. Universities (1988): 1. Hospital beds (1982): 4,902. Physicians (1983): 238. Life expectancy (1990): women—52; men—48. Infant mortality (1990): 121 per 1,000 live births.

ECONOMY. GNP (1989): $1.75 billion; $380 per capita. Labor distribution (1988): agriculture—68%; public administration and services—25%; mining, manufacturing, utilities, and construction—7%. Foreign trade (1988): imports—$413 million; exports—$226 million; principal trade partners—France, Germany, Spain. Currency: 1 C.F.A. franc = 100 centimes.

GOVERNMENT. Type: republic. Legislature: National Assembly. Political subdivisions: 6 provinces.

COMMUNICATIONS. Railroads (1989): 635 km (395 mi) total. Roads (1986): 7,445 km (4,626 mi) total. Major ports: 1. Major airfields: 1.

zone, forming most of central and southern Benin, is a generally flat lowland area with some low hills and marshlands. In the northeast is a plateau region of savanna grasslands, and in the northwest are the Atakora Mountains, the highest peaks in the country, which rise to 641 m (2,102 ft). The principal river is the NIGER, which forms part of the northeastern border. The northern half of the nation drains toward the Niger River, the southern half directly into the Bight of Benin.

The climate in the south is hot and humid throughout the year; the average monthly temperature is around 27° C (80° F), and rainfall on the coast totals 1,300 mm (50 in) a year. The northern sections have a tropical wet-and-dry (savanna) type of climate. Temperatures here are high throughout the year, but the summer months (June–October) are usually wet and humid and the winter months relatively dry and with lower humidity. The vegetation reflects the differences in rainfall regimes and grades from a tropical rain forest over most of the south to savanna grasslands toward the north.

PEOPLE

The largest ethnic group are the FON, or Dahomeyans, who constitute about 25% of the total population and predominate in the south. Other ethnic groups in the south include the Adja and EWE, who are closely related to the Fon; the YORUBA; and the Aïzo, who are concentrated around Cotonou. In the north the principal ethnic groups are the Bariba in the northwest; the Somba in the northeast; and the FULANI, who have traditionally been nomadic herders. French is the official language. Fon and Yoruba are widely spoken in the south, and Bariba and Fulani are the principal languages in the north.

Benin's population is unevenly distributed. More than two-thirds of the people live in the south, where population densities are among the highest in West Africa. The northern half of the country is only sparsely settled. Medical facilities are limited, and life expectancy is low.

More than two-thirds of the population follow traditional (animist) religious beliefs; the remainder are Christians (mostly Roman Catholics) and Muslims. The school system is under government control and is free and compulsory. The only university is the National University of Benin.

Benin's presidential palace is located in Cotonou, the capital of the Atlantique district. Since the construction of an artificial deep-water harbor on the Gulf of Guinea, Cotonou has become the leading port and commercial center of Benin (formerly Dahomey).

ECONOMIC ACTIVITY

Benin is one of the poorest countries in West Africa. The economy is largely agricultural, and most of the labor force is engaged in subsistence farming. Palm kernels, grown mainly in the south, are the principal cash crop. Other cash crops are cotton, grown mainly in the north, and cocoa and coffee, grown mainly in the south. Millet and sorghum are the principal food crops in the north, and yams, cassava, corn, and peanuts in the south. Benin has no important manufacturing activities other than palm-oil processing. Limestone and small amounts of gold and petroleum are extracted.

The transportation system is poorly developed and comprises two short rail lines extending inland behind Cotonou and one extending inland as far as Parakou. A coastal highway links Benin with neighboring Nigeria and Togo. Benin sustains huge annual trade deficits that are relieved by infusions of monetary aid, especially from France.

GOVERNMENT

According to a new constitution approved by voters in December 1990, Benin has a multiparty, presidential system of government. Both the president and members of the legislature, the National Assembly, are directly elected by universal suffrage, and a president may serve only two five-year terms.

HISTORY

The kingdom of Dahomey, with its capital at Abomey, was preeminent in the region now known as Benin from the 17th to the early 19th century. It derived great wealth from trading slaves with Europeans along the coast, which was known as the Slave Coast. The French established a commercial agreement with the kingdom in 1851 and gradually consolidated their control of Dahomey until, in 1904, it was made a colony within French West Africa.

The independent nation of Dahomey was established on Aug. 1, 1960. For the first 12 years of independence it experienced great political instability, partly because of the ethnic diversity of its population. Periods of civilian and military rule alternated, and the political scene was dominated by three figures—Hubert Maga, Justin Ahomadegbé, and Sourou Apithy, each of whom represented a different part of the country. Such violence erupted during the 1970 elections, especially between north and south, that the three agreed to form a presidential council, with each serving two years in a rotating presidency. The council was overthrown in 1972 in a military coup led by Mathieu Kerekou, who formed the Military Council of the Revolution (CNR) to govern the country and adopted Marxism-Leninism as the national ideology. The "colonial" name of Dahomey was abandoned in 1975, when the country was renamed Benin, and much of the economy was placed under government control. In 1979, under a new constitution (adopted 1977), the CNR was dissolved and legislative elections were held. An economic crisis and popular protests led

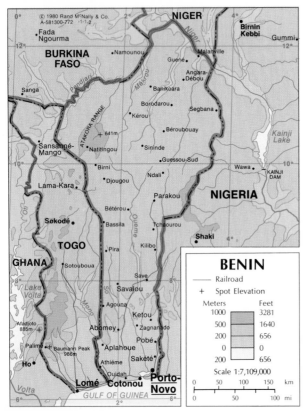

BENIN

Railroad

+ Spot Elevation

Meters	Feet
1000	3281
500	1640
200	656
0	0
200	656

Scale 1:7,109,000

0   50   100   150   km

0   50   100   mi

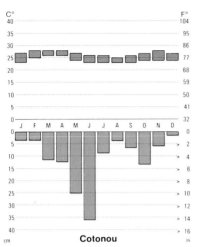

Bars indicate monthly ranges of temperatures (red) and precipitation (blue) of Cotonou, Benin. Benin has a tropical wet-dry climate.

Cotonou

to the abandonment of Marxism-Leninism as the official ideology in December 1989. Kerekou remained president of a transitional government created in 1990. When multiparty elections were held under a new constitution in March 1991, Kerekou became the first incumbent African president to be ousted in democratic elections. His successor, Nicephore Soglo, assumed office on April 4.   Reviewed by GODFREY UZOIGWE

Bibliography: Allen, C., and Radu, M., *Benin and the Congo* (1988); Diamond, S., *Dahomey* (1983); Manning, P., *Slavery, Colonialism, and Economic Growth in Dahomey, 1640–1960* (1982); Polyani, K., and Rotsfein, A., *Dahomey and the Slave Trade* (1966; repr. 1988); Ronen, D., *Dahomey* (1975).

Benin, Kingdom of

The Kingdom of Benin was an exceptionally vigorous West African state located in the rain-forest area of present-day southern Nigeria. In existence from probably the 12th to the 19th century, it is particularly famous for the many sculptures in brass, bronze, and ivory created by special guilds of artisans attached to the royal court (see AFRICAN ART).

Benin was a highly centralized kingdom ruled by a series of divine monarchs (*obas*). At the height of its power, it extended roughly from the Niger River in the west to Lagos in the

This figure of a horn player is one of the famous Benin bronzes. Although the lost-wax process used in creating these bronzes originated in Ife, Benin's artisans developed a distinctive style that was less naturalistic and more formal than that of Ife. The making of such sculptures virtually died out by 1700.

east. The first European to reach Benin, the Portuguese João Afonso de Aviero (in 1485), was greatly impressed by the wealth of the *oba*'s court and the orderly administration of the kingdom. By this time Benin was already a flourishing trading state with commercial colonies centered on the city of Benin, which had a population exceeding 100,000. The expansion of the kingdom, however, was facilitated by the introduction of European weapons. At Aviero's urging, some of the local EDO (Bini) princes were sent to Lisbon to study, and a Christian mission was established in the state. The links to Portugal did not last, and the power of the *obas* gradually declined, in part because of the anarchic conditions that resulted from the growth of the slave trade. The last of the line of independent rulers, Oba Ovonramwen (d. 1914), witnessed the conquest of his kingdom by a British force in 1897 and was sent into exile. *Obas* are still enthroned by the Edo in the traditional manner, however.   ROBERT R. GRIFFITH

Bibliography: Bradbury, R. E., *Benin Studies* (1973); Egharevba, J., *A Short History of Benin*, 4th ed. (1968); Elliot, K., *Benin* (1973); Pitt-Rivers, A., *Antique Works of Art from Benin* (1976); Ryder, A., *Benin and the Europeans, 1485–1897* (1969); Underwood, L., *Bronzes of West Africa*, 2d ed. (1968).

Benjamin

In the Bible, Benjamin was the youngest son of JACOB and the name of the smallest of Israel's twelve tribes. Because Jacob's favorite wife, RACHEL, died after Benjamin's birth, the boy was especially dear to his father and to his only full brother, JOSEPH. Thus Benjamin figures prominently in the Joseph narrative (Gen. 37–50). The name *Benjamin* may mean "son of the south" and refer to the Benjamite tribe's location. King Saul, Jeremiah, and Saint Paul were Benjamites.

Benjamin, Asher

Asher Benjamin, b. Greenfield, Mass., 1773, d. June 25, 1845, an important New England architect, was the author of *The Country Builder's Assistant* (1797), the first original book on architecture published in America. In his books, the proportions of the architectural orders, though based on English sources, were modified to facilitate their execution in wood and to satisfy American tastes. In Boston, Benjamin's important buildings include the Charles Street Meeting House (1807); the old West Church (1806; now a public library); and his personal residence at 9 West Cedar Street. The influence of Charles BULFINCH's FEDERAL STYLE is discernible in all of them. Benjamin's seven popular publications, in 44 editions, were responsible for the character of late colonial and early 19th-century architecture in America, especially for the popularization of the GREEK REVIVAL style.   SUSAN AND THOMAS SLADE

Bibliography: Benjamin, Asher, *The Works of Asher Benjamin*, 7 vols. (1806–43; repr. 1974); Cushing, George M., *Great Buildings and Sights of Boston* (1982); Hamlin, Talbot, *Greek Revival Architecture in America* (1944); Shand-Tucci, Douglass, *Built in Boston* (1988).

Benjamin, Judah P.

Judah Philip Benjamin was a Confederate cabinet officer and a close advisor of President Jefferson DAVIS. He was born in the West Indies on Aug. 6, 1811, but his family moved to North and then South Carolina, and he attended Yale. Moving to New Orleans, he became a nationally renowned lawyer and engaged in business. After holding minor public offices, he was elected (1852) to the U.S. Senate as a Whig.

As North-South tensions grew, Benjamin became a Democrat and an ardent defender of the South. In 1861 he favored secession and, after resigning from the Senate, was appointed attorney general in the Confederate cabinet. Later he became secretary of war (1861–62) and eventually secretary of state (1862–65).

A good administrator, Benjamin was the ablest member of the cabinet. His tenure as secretary of war, however, coincided with military disasters, and these defeats, coupled with anti-Semitism and jealousy of his influence with Davis, resulted in criticism of Benjamin. His advocacy of using slaves as soldiers also hurt his popularity. In 1865 he fled to Britain, where he won distinction as a lawyer. He died in Paris on May 5, 1884.   RICHARD M. MCMURRY

Bibliography: Evans, E., *Judah P. Benjamin* (1988); Meade, R. D., *Judah P. Benjamin* (1943; repr. 1975).

Benjamin, Walter

Walter Benjamin, b. July 15, 1892, d. Sept. 27, 1940, an influential literary and art critic, is recognized today as one of Germany's foremost aestheticians and cultural historians. A Jew, he was forced to emigrate to Paris in 1933, and fear of the Gestapo led to his suicide in Port Bou, Spain. In his cultural-historical philosophy, Benjamin seeks to maintain an uneasy tension between the dual influence of Marxism and Jewish theology. As an aesthetician, Benjamin was the first to recognize, in such essays as "Art in the Age of Mechanical Reproduction," that a technology that could reproduce art could also destroy it. He was the first German translator of Marcel Proust. His most important writings are collected in English in *Illuminations* (1961; Eng. trans., 1968), *Understanding Brecht* (1966; Eng. trans., 1973), and *Charles Baudelaire: A Lyric Poet in the Era of High Capitalism* (1955; Eng. trans., 1973).   MARILYN SIBLEY FRIES

Bibliography: Arendt, Hannah, *Men in Dark Times* (1968); Buck-Morss, Susan, *The Origin of Negative Dialectics: Theodor W. Adorno, Walter Benjamin, and the Frankfurt Institute* (1977).

Benjamin of Tudela   [too-day'-lah]

Benjamin of Tudela, a 12th-century Jewish rabbi from Navarre in Spain, was a noted traveler and explorer. His journeys, lasting 13 years, took him to countries in the Near East, to Persia, and to the frontiers of China. He described his travels in *Itinerary*, published in English in 1907.

Benn, Anthony Wedgwood

Anthony Wedgwood Benn, b. Apr. 3, 1925, was an unofficial leader of the left within the British Labour party. First elected to the House of Commons in 1950, he made sustained efforts to remain there when he inherited the title Viscount Stansgate. A 1963 bill made renunciation of titles possible, and he was reelected, serving in the cabinets of Harold Wilson and James Callaghan. Prominent in the bitter disputes that divided the Labour party in the 1980s, Benn made a bid to unseat party leader Neil Kinnock in 1988. His writings include *The New Politics* (1970) and *Writings on the Wall* (1984).

Benn, Gottfried

Gottfried Benn, b. May 2, 1886, d. July 7, 1956, was a German expressionist and sometimes nihilistic writer. In his early verse collections, *Morgue* (1912) and *Fleisch* (Flesh, 1917), Benn explores physical decay and the disintegration of self that recurs in his work. In his essay "Das moderne Ich" (The Modern I, 1919) he expresses the idea that concepts are being replaced by myths, but his notion that art is an alternative to NIHILISM is developed in *Nach dem Nihilismus* (After Nihilism, 1932).

In *Kunst und Macht* (Art and Might, 1934) Benn defended National Socialism. He reversed this position in the essay "Kunst und Drittes Reich" (Art and the Third Reich, 1941). His later works include *Statistische Gedichte* (Statistical Poems, 1948) and the posthumous collection *Primal Vision* (1958; Eng. trans., 1960).

Bibliography: Benn, Gottfried, *Selected Poems*, ed. by Friedrich Wodtke (1972); Ritchie, James M., *Gottfried Benn: The Unreconstructed Expressionist* (1972).

Bennett, Arnold

Enoch Arnold Bennett, b. May 27, 1867, d. Mar. 27, 1931, was a prolific and highly successful English writer of the Edwardian period best known for his realistic evocations of provincial life. Although neglected for a time, his deeply autobiographical and naturalistic novels are now enjoying a revival of critical and popular interest. (See EDWARDIAN LITERATURE.)

Arnold Bennett, an English novelist and critic, wrote an extremely popular series of novels set in the "Five Towns," a Midlands district known for its pottery manufacturing. Bennett's works are notable for their realistic treatment of working-class people in industrial England.

Bennett spent his early years in the industrial area of Staffordshire known as the Potteries, where he later set his best-known works. In 1889 he went to London, where he began a career as a writer and for a time worked as an editor. His first novel, the autobiographical *A Man from the North*, was published in 1898. This was followed by *Anna of the Five Towns* (1902) and the other four novels of his highly successful "Five Towns" series. The masterpiece of this series, *The Old Wives' Tale* (1908), is an exploration of the effects of time on female beauty. It includes much that is characteristic of Bennett's writings—the Potteries background, exhaustive naturalistic description, keen psychological insight, and verisimilitude. The trilogy that followed completed the series. In *Clayhanger* (1910), Bennett expressed distaste for his childhood environment (Methodism, provincialism, and ugliness), evoked his family life, and, with its sequels *Hilda Lessways* (1911) and *These Twain* (1916), explored the theme of the relationship between the sexes.

Bennett's other novels include *Riceyman Steps* (1923), a study of a miser; *Lord Raingo* (1926), with insights into political life; and *Imperial Palace* (1930), which in its frankness anticipates the modern approach to sexual themes. With his remarkable capacity for hard, disciplined work, Bennett also wrote innumerable short stories and such successful plays as *Milestones* (1912, with Edward Knoblock). He was an influential reviewer and the author of several nonfiction works, including *How to Live on 24 Hours a Day* (1907). His insightful memoirs were published as *The Journals of Arnold Bennett* (3 vols., 1932–33). He died of typhoid contracted from drinking polluted tapwater.   RICHARD FORD

Bibliography: Broomfield, O. R., *Arnold Bennett* (1984); Drabble, Margaret, *Arnold Bennett* (1974; repr. 1986); Pound, Reginald, *Arnold Bennett: A Biography* (1952; repr. 1986); Wain, John, *Arnold Bennett* (1967); Wright, W. F., *Arnold Bennett* (1971).

Bennett, Floyd

Floyd Bennett, b. near Warrensburg, N.Y., Oct. 25, 1890, d. Apr. 25, 1928, was an aviator for two of the Arctic expeditions of the 1920s and the first pilot to fly over the North Pole. He was awarded the Congressional Medal of Honor for his achievements. Bennett was an aviator and mechanic for the 1925 MacMillan expedition to the Arctic; and in 1926, with the explorer Richard E. BYRD in his crew as navigator, he piloted a plane nonstop from Spitsbergen to the North Pole and back. On a flight to rescue stranded flyers in the Gulf of St. Lawrence, he was stricken with pneumonia and died.

Bennett, James Gordon

James Gordon Bennett, b. Keith, Banffshire, Scotland, Sept. 1, 1795, d. New York City, June 1, 1872, was the founder of the *New York Herald*, the most influential U.S. newspaper of its day. Between 1835, when it began as a 4-page penny daily, and 1867, when control passed to Bennett's son, the *Herald* amassed a readership of 90,000. Its growth paralleled—as it helped to create—the rise of democracy in America.

After immigrating to the United States in 1819, Bennett wrote for various newspapers until his appointment (1827–28) as the *New York Enquirer*'s Washington correspondent brought him national recognition for his colorful sketches of the capital's personalities. When, at his urging, the *Enquirer* merged with the *New York Courier* in 1829, he became associate editor of the combined venture until 1832. In May 1835, Bennett, inspired by the success of Benjamin Day's *Sun*, founded the *Herald* with $500 capital. Within months the essentially one-man operation had printed the country's first stock exchange reports, extensively covered the great New York fire of December 1835, and made Bennett a reputation as a spirited iconoclast. Although the *Herald* was widely criticized for its sensationalism, it continued to prosper and innovate. Bennett pressured Congress to give his reporters free access to its sessions, established a fleet of dispatch boats off Sandy Hook, N.J., to speed European news to New York, and pioneered the regular use of the telegraph as a news-gathering tool. The *Herald*'s coverage of the Civil War, utilizing a corps of 63 correspondents, was highly regarded. In 1864 President Lincoln offered Bennett an ambassadorship to France, which he declined. At his death his pallbearers included such journalistic giants as Charles A. Dana and Horace Greeley.

Bibliography: Carlson, Oliver, *The Man Who Made News: James Gordon Bennett* (1942); Fermer, Douglas, *James Gordon Bennett and the New York Herald* (1986); Pray, Isaac C., *The Memoirs of James Gordon Bennett and His Times* (1855; repr. 1970); Seitz, Don C., *The James Gordon Bennetts, Father and Son* (1928; repr. 1974).

Bennett, James Gordon, Jr.

James Gordon Bennett, Jr., son of the founder of the New York Herald, *was known for his extravagance and capricious behavior. Bennett sponsored daring publicity stunts in order to boost circulation but was eventually eclipsed by his rivals, Joseph Pulitzer and William Randolph Hearst.*

James Gordon Bennett, Jr., b. New York City, May 10, 1841, d. May 14, 1918, was a newspaper publisher who in 1869 commissioned reporter Henry M. STANLEY to search for the Scottish missionary David Livingstone in Africa. Stanley found (1871) Livingstone, and his reports to Bennett's paper, the *New York Herald*, made journalistic history. Bennett inherited the management of the *Herald* from his father, James Gordon Bennett, in 1867. His editorial taste, like his father's, ran to the sensational; he was especially successful in organizing newsworthy events, such as the Stanley expedition, of which his paper could secure exclusive coverage. Among other ventures financed by Bennett were a search in 1875 for the Northwest Passage and the 1879–81 De Long expedition to the Arctic.

In 1867, Bennett founded the *Evening Telegram*, and in 1887 he established a Paris edition of the *Herald*, which by World War I had reached a circulation of 25,000. The parent paper, however, hurt by Bennett's neglect and competition from the new YELLOW JOURNALISM, had ceased to be a major force in newsgathering by the time of its owner's death. After 1877, as the result of a domestic scandal, Bennett lived mostly in France, where he figured prominently as a promoter of sports.

Bibliography: Crockett, Albert Stevens, *When James Gordon Bennett Was Caliph of Bagdad* (1926); Laney, Al, *Paris Herald: The Incredible Newspaper* (1947); O'Connor, Richard, *The Scandalous Mr. Bennett* (1962); Seitz, Don C., *The James Gordon Bennetts, Father and Son* (1928; repr. 1974); Villard, Oswald Garrison, *Some Newspapers and Newspaper-Men*, rev. ed. (1926).

Bennett, Michael

A director and choreographer of stage musicals, Michael Bennett, b. Buffalo, N.Y., Apr. 8, 1943, d. July 2, 1987, received wide acclaim for *Promises, Promises* (1968) and *Company* (1970), which preceded his four Tony Award-winning plays: *Follies* (1971); *Seesaw* (1973); *A Chorus Line* (1975), which also won a Pulitzer Prize for drama; and *Dreamgirls* (1981).

Bennett, Richard Bedford, Viscount Bennett

Richard B. Bennett, who became Conservative prime minister of Canada in 1930, attempted to battle the effects of the Depression of the 1930s by high tariffs and social reforms patterned on the New Deal in the United States. Such reforms, however, were introduced too late to save his government from defeat in the 1935 elections.

Richard Bedford Bennett, b. July 3, 1870, d. June 27, 1947, was prime minister of Canada from 1930 to 1935. He practiced law in New Brunswick before moving (1897) to Calgary, Alberta, where, in partnership with Sen. James A. Lougheed, he built a large legal firm. He was member of Parliament for Calgary from 1911 and was chosen leader of the Conservative party in 1927, following the resignation of Arthur MEIGHEN. When the Conservatives won the federal election of 1930, Bennett became prime minister.

His government wrestled with the economic problems of the Great Depression and established the Canadian central bank (the Bank of Canada), as well as a government radio broadcasting system. Nevertheless, Bennett failed to deal effectively with manifold problems. He was a private man, and after his government was defeated in 1935 he remained leader of the Conservatives for only three more years. He retired to England and was made a viscount in 1941.

P. B. WAITE

Bibliography: Watkins, Ernest, *R. B. Bennett: A Biography* (1963); Wilbur, J. R. H., *The Bennett Administration, 1930–1935* (1970) and *The Bennett New Deal: Fraud or Portent* (1968).

Bennett, Richard Rodney

Richard Rodney Bennett, b. Mar. 29, 1936, is a British composer whose work reflects many important changes in music in the last 30 years. He uses the 12-tone serial technique of Arnold SCHOENBERG and Anton von WEBERN with ease and naturalness. Bennett studied (1956–58) with Pierre BOULEZ in Paris and experimented with serial control of musical parameters other than pitch. He later composed more freely, but he also gave careful attention to rhythm. Among his many orchestral, vocal, and operatic works are the Concerto for Oboe (1969–70), written for Heinz Holliger, and *Spells* (1974–75), for soprano, chorus, and orchestra. The composer has also written many scores for motion pictures, including *Far From the Madding Crowd* (1967), *Murder on the Orient Express* (1974), and *Equus* (1977). He also achieved success as a concert pianist.

Bibliography: Palmer, C., and Foreman, L., eds., *British Music Now* (1975).

Bennett, William Sterndale

The pianist, conductor, and composer William Sterndale Bennett, b. Apr. 13, 1816, d. Feb. 1, 1875, was, in his time, one of England's most influential musicians. He studied in London at the Royal Academy of Music (1826–36) and in Leipzig with Felix Mendelssohn. In 1849, Bennett founded the London Bach Society, which brought the rediscovery of Bach's music to the British public. In 1854 he led the first performance in England of Bach's *St. Matthew Passion*. Bennett's compositions include church music, choral works, several overtures, a symphony, four piano concertos, and chamber music.

Benning, Fort: see FORT BENNING.

Bennington

Bennington is a town in the southwest corner of Vermont and the seat of Bennington County. It is on the Walloomsac River and has a population of 16,451 (1990). The economy is based on light manufacturing, agriculture, and tourism generated by nearby ski areas. Bennington College (1925) and several historic buildings, including the Old First Church (1806), are of interest. Bennington was settled in 1761 and named for Benning Wentworth, governor of New Hampshire. During the American Revolution, Vermonters under Seth Warner and New Hampshire militia under Gen. John Stark defeated a Hessian force near Bennington on Aug. 16, 1777. Part of the Saratoga Campaign, the battle is commemorated by a 93-m (306-ft) granite obelisk.

Bennington College

Established in 1925 as a private 4-year experimental liberal arts college for women, Bennington College (enrollment: 591; library: 100,000 volumes) in Bennington, Vt., is now coeducational. Emphasis is placed on the creative and performing arts, and students are encouraged to develop individual, independent programs reflecting their own interests and talents.

Benny, Jack

Jack Benny was the stage name of Benjamin Kubelsky, b. Chicago, Feb. 14, 1894, d. Dec. 26, 1974, a celebrated American comedian with a brilliant talent for self-ridicule. He was famous for his mean, skinflint image, superb comic timing, and deadpan silences. He began his career as a violinist before performing in vaudeville and film, where he appeared most notably in *To Be or Not To Be* (1942). He gained national fame on radio starting in 1932. Benny starred on television from 1950 to 1965.   FRANK MANCHEL

Bibliography: Benny, Mary Livingston, et al., *Jack Benny: A Biography* (1978); Fein, Irving A., *Jack Benny: An Intimate Biography* (1976).

Benois, Aleksandr Nikolayevich   [ben-wah', ul-yik-sahn'-dur nyik-ul-ly'-yeh-vich]

Aleksandr Benois, b. May 4 (N.S.), 1870, d. Feb. 9, 1950, was a painter, designer, and art critic who played a leading role in Russian artistic life in the early 20th century. A native of Saint Petersburg, Benois was a member of the group of young men who published *Mir iskusstva*, a journal of the arts. He is best known for his costumes and set designs, created first for the Imperial Theaters in Saint Petersburg and later for the BALLETS RUSSES DE SERGE DIAGHILEV. He was curator of paintings at the Hermitage from 1918 to 1926, the year he immigrated to Paris. As an artist and art historian, Benois was attracted to 18th- and early-19th-century Russian art and to prerevolutionary French culture, in both of which he saw elegance, grace, and the beauty of a vanished way of life.   ANN FARKAS

Bibliography: Benois, Aleksandr, *Reminiscences of the Russian Ballet* (1941; repr. 1977).

Benoit, Joan   [buh-noyt']

American Joan Benoit Samuelson, b. Portland, Maine, May 16, 1957, won the gold medal in the first Olympic women's marathon, at the 1984 Los Angeles Games, and received the 1985 Sullivan Award, given annually to the best U.S. amateur athlete. Benoit holds several U.S. road-racing records, including the American women's marathon record.

Benoît de Sainte-More   [ben-wah']

Benoît, fl. 12th century, was a French poet who wrote the influential medieval romance *Le Roman de Troie* (c.1160). Based on ancient sources, the work is noted for its romantic and rhetorical devices and for its version of the Troilus and Cressida story. He is frequently confused with and may be identical to another Benoît, a French author who wrote the historical verse narrative *Chronique des ducs de Normandie* (c.1175).   FRANCIS CARMODY

Bentham, Jeremy   [ben'-thuhm]

Jeremy Bentham, b. Feb. 15, 1748, d. June 6, 1832, was an English philosopher and social theorist. The son of a lawyer, he took a degree in law at Oxford in 1763 but never practiced, spending his life as a theorist and advocate of various reform causes. He was leader of the philosophical radicals, a group devoted to the cause of reform of the basic institutions of England. The group included James and John Stuart MILL.

Bentham's first book, *Fragment on Government* (1776), was a sustained criticism of Sir William BLACKSTONE, whose *Commentaries* was the basic document for the English legal system. In 1789, *An Introduction to the Principles of Morals and Legislation* appeared, the work for which Bentham is best known today. It contains a clear and rigorous statement of

The philosopher Jeremy Bentham believed that the fundamental principle of morality is "the greatest happiness of the greatest number." He is portrayed here by H. W. Pickersgill.

the principles of UTILITARIANISM, a doctrine whose antecedents Bentham had discovered in David HUME. Utilitarianism is the belief that the aim of the individual and the legislator in the conduct of society should be to achieve the greatest happiness for the greatest number. It became and remains a leading social and ethical theory. Bentham's utilitarianism was a form of HEDONISM; that is, he believed that right conduct was determined by the balance of pleasure over pain that a given act would produce for everyone involved. He believed that in principle pain and pleasure could be measured in strictly quantitative terms. This would mean that ethical and social decision-making could be reduced to a quasi-mathematical science. He proposed a "hedonistic calculus" that would enable moral decisions to be made on quantitative rather than impressionistic evidence. The fame of Bentham's reform principles spread widely. In 1792 he was made a citizen of France, and he maintained an active correspondence with leading citizens throughout Europe and the United States. His direct philosophical descendant was John Stuart Mill, who refined and elaborated many of Bentham's ideas.

When he died, Bentham's body was decapitated, embalmed, affixed with a wax replica of his head, and dressed in his customary clothes; it is still preserved in that condition at University College, London.   THOMAS K. HEARN, JR.

Bibliography: Harrison, Ross, *Bentham* (1983); Mack, Mary, *Jeremy Bentham* (1963); Sprigge, T. L., ed., *The Correspondences of Jeremy Bentham*, 3 vols. (1968-71).

benthonic zone   [ben-thahn'-ik]

The benthonic zone encompasses all marine bottom environments from high-tide level to the greatest depths. It is subdivided into three zones. The LITTORAL ZONE, from high-tide level to 200 m (660 ft) below the ocean surface, comprises the shore and nearshore areas and the CONTINENTAL SHELF bottom. Plants and filter- and bottom-feeding animals in this zone are subjected to variations in temperature and salinity, some wave or tidal influence, and, commonly, reworking or influx of bottom sediment. In the transitional BATHYAL ZONE, the environment is generally free of major temperature and salinity fluctuations and wave and tidal action, and the sea bottom is undisturbed, except for occasional DENSITY CURRENTS. The ABYSSAL ZONE, at the greatest ocean depths, generally 3,000 m (9,900 ft) or more, is characterized by uniform water temperature and salinity, little physical reworking of the bottom, and communities of organisms that are mainly carnivorous, eating organic detritus that rains down from above.

HAROLD R. WANLESS

Bibliography: Seibold, E., and Berger, W., *The Sea Floor* (1982).

See also: HYDROTHERMAL VENT; OCEAN AND SEA.

Bentinck   (family)   [ben'-tingk]

The Bentinck family was long prominent in British public life. Of Dutch origin, **William Bentinck, 1st earl of Portland**, b. July 7, 1649, d. Nov. 23, 1709, went to England in 1688 as chief advisor to William of Orange (William III of England). His great-grandson, **William Henry Cavendish Bentinck, 3d duke of Portland**, b. Apr. 14, 1738, d. Oct. 30, 1809, was twice prime minister (1783, 1807–09). The duke's son **Lord William Cavendish Bentinck**, b. Sept. 14, 1774, d. June 17, 1839, served as governor-general of Bengal (1827–33) and then of all India (1833–35). He initiated an extensive policy of Westernization, which included the abolition of SUTTEE. **Lord George Bentinck**, b. Feb. 27, 1802, d. Sept. 21, 1848, a cousin, led opposition to the repeal of the CORN LAWS in 1846.

Bibliography: Azariah, Isaiah, *Lord Bentinck and Indian Education, Crime, and the Status of Women* (1978); Rosselli, John, *Lord William Bentinck: The Making of a Liberal Imperialist, 1817–1839* (1974).

Bentley, Eric

The English-born writer Eric Bentley, b. Sept. 14, 1916, is one of the most important and influential American drama critics and theater scholars. Educated at Oxford and Yale universities, he was Brander Matthews professor of dramatic literature at Columbia University from 1953 to 1969. A tireless proponent of modern drama, Bentley was the first to translate into English and popularize the works of Bertolt Brecht. His most important books include *The Playwright as Thinker* (1946), *Bernard Shaw* (1947), *What Is Theatre?* (1956), and *The Life of the Drama* (1964).   COLETTE BROOKS

Bentley, Richard

Richard Bentley, b. Jan. 27, 1662, d. July 14, 1742, was an English philologist and critic. He became Master of Trinity College, Cambridge, in 1700. His editions of classical writers were marked by brilliant scholarship and changed many accepted opinions. He also published a celebrated exposure of literary forgery, *The Epistle of Phalaris* (1699), and a controversial 1732 edition of John Milton's *Paradise Lost*.   ROBIN BUSS

Benton, Thomas Hart   (painter)

The painter Thomas Hart Benton, b. Neosho, Mo., Apr. 15, 1889, d. Jan. 19, 1975, was an important exponent of regional-

Threshing Wheat (1939), by the American regionalist painter Thomas Hart Benton, demonstrates the artist's vivid rendering of subjects reflecting his rural midwestern background. (Sheldon Swope Art Gallery, Terre Haute, Ind.)

ism, or art based on depictions of rural scenes. Benton extolled in paint the virile, energetic American men and women who had tamed the frontier and built new cities; he showed them as lean, taut figures against stylized landscapes of farms and towns. His many mural cycles, such as *America Today* (1930–31; New School for Social Research, New York), were influenced by the Mexican muralists David Siqueiros, José Orozco, and Diego Rivera. His later murals, such as the powerful group (1936) for the Missouri State Capitol in Jefferson City, are characterized by increased vigor and even stronger linear emphasis, with the sinewy bodies caught up in swirling, colorful rhythms. Benton's later paintings reflected his growing preoccupation with mythological and biblical subjects, which he depicted in contemporary American terms.

ABRAHAM A. DAVIDSON

Bibliography: Benton, Thomas Hart, *An Artist in America,* 4th ed. (1983); Hurt, R. Douglas, and Daims, Mary K., eds., *Thomas Hart Benton: Artist, Writer, and Intellectual* (l989).

Benton, Thomas Hart   (political leader)

Thomas Hart Benton, b. Hillsboro, N.C., Mar. 14, 1782, d. Apr. 10, 1858, was a major American political figure in the Jacksonian era. He migrated to Tennessee, where he served (1809–11) in the state legislature, gained admission (1811) to the bar, and enlisted in the militia in the War of 1812. After being involved in a tavern brawl with Andrew JACKSON, Benton left Tennessee for St. Louis, where he edited the *St. Louis Enquirer* and won election (1821) to the U.S. Senate. As a senator, he supported western expansion, free land to settlers, and federally financed internal improvements.

Despite his earlier support of Henry Clay's presidential candidacy and his quarrel with Andrew Jackson, Benton in the 1830s became Jackson's strongest champion in the Senate. Benton advocated the abolition of bank-issued paper money and the establishment of a ''hard money'' system of federal coinage; he earned the nickname Old Bullion. He therefore supported Jackson's opposition to rechartering the Bank of the United States and defended both the removal of federal deposits and the Specie Circular of 1836, which stipulated that public lands be paid for only in hard currency.

Benton also supported Martin Van Buren's administration and the expansionist policies of the administration of James Polk. He was opposed, however, to the expansion of slavery and criticized the Democratic party's concessions to slaveholding interests. Refusing to support the COMPROMISE OF 1850, Benton lost his Senate seat. He served briefly (1853–55) as a U.S. representative but was voted out of office by Missourians offended by his antislavery position.

ALFRED A. CAVE

Bibliography: Chambers, W. B., *Old Bullion Benton: Senator from the New West* (1956; repr. 1970); Smith, E. B., *Magnificent Missourian: The Life of Thomas Hart Benton* (1958; repr. 1973).

Bentsen, Lloyd

Lloyd Millard Bentsen, Jr., b. Mission, Tex., Feb. 11, 1921, was named U.S. secretary of the Treasury (1993–   ) by President Bill Clinton. A three-term Texas congressman (1949–55) and four-term senator (1971–93), Bentsen was chairman of the Senate Finance Committee before being chosen as vice-presidential running mate by Michael Dukakis, the 1988 Democratic presidential nominee. Dukakis and Bentsen were decisively beaten by Republicans George Bush and Dan Quayle.

Benz, Karl

Karl Benz, b. Nov. 25, 1844, d. Apr. 4, 1929, was a German engineer and inventor who pioneered in the development of the internal-combustion engine and the automobile. He was trained in mechanical engineering and set up a workshop, where he improved the internal-combustion engine. In 1886 he obtained a patent for a vehicle that used a four-cycle engine he had designed and built the preceding year; this vehicle was the world's first practical automobile powered by an internal-combustion engine.

benzaldehyde   [ben-zal'-duh-hyd]

Benzaldehyde, C_6H_5CHO, is a clear liquid that becomes yellow with age. It is the artificial essential oil of almonds and has the characteristic odor of volatile almond oil. Benzaldehyde is the simplest aromatic ALDEHYDE and undergoes the reactions typical of aldehydes. It oxidizes in air to BENZOIC ACID, C_6H_5COOH. The compound is used in the manufacture of dyes, perfumes, and flavors.

benzedrine: see AMPHETAMINE.

benzene   [ben'-zeen]

Benzene, C_6H_6, is a clear, colorless, flammable liquid that is insoluble in water. Its boiling point is 80° C (176° F). In the past benzene was obtained from the distillation of coal in the absence of air. Today most benzene is made synthetically from petroleum products.

Benzene was isolated in 1825 by Michael FARADAY, but its structure remained a mystery for 40 years. The problem was perplexing because the C_6H_6 formula indicated a high degree of unsaturation, but benzene does not display the reactivity characteristic of such compounds.

In 1865, German chemist Friedrich August KEKULÉ VON STRADONITZ proposed that benzene is structurally a planar hexagon in which the six carbon atoms are joined by alternating single and double bonds. Because this simplistic structure could not account for all of the unique properties of benzene and its derivatives, German chemist Johannes Thiele suggested in 1899 that the bonds between carbon atoms exhibit RESONANCE. That is, each bond oscillates between being a double and a single bond, as seen below (see AROMATIC COMPOUNDS).

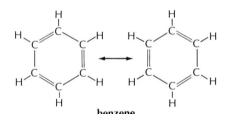

benzene

In modern chemistry, benzene is generally considered to have six identical carbon-carbon bonds, each intermediate between a single and a double bond. The carbon electrons are pictured as delocalized and existing as a cloud around the molecule. This arrangement is depicted as follows:

In the 1980s, however, some chemists questioned this model of benzene and suggested that Kekulé's original concept is more in accord with benzene's observed bonding energy.

Benzene is an excellent solvent. Its main use, however, is in the preparation of other compounds. The compounds prepared from benzene, in the order of quantity produced, are styrene, for polymerization; phenol; detergents; aniline, for dyes; and chlorine-containing compounds. Other uses include the production of pharmaceuticals, varnishes, and plastics. Inhalation or ingestion of benzene causes acute irritation of the mucous membrane, producing restlessness and convulsions and sometimes resulting in death from respiratory failure. Harmful amounts may be absorbed through the skin, causing leukemia and other cancers.

ELBERT H. HADLEY

Bibliography: Aksoy, M., ed., *Benzene Carcinogenicity* (1988); Mehlman, M. A., *Benzene: Scientific Update* (1985); Morrison, R. T., and Boyd, R. N., *Organic Chemistry,* 6th ed. (1992); VCH, *Benzene,* trans. by T. Russell (1992).

benzoic acid   [ben-zoh'-ik]

Benzoic acid is a colorless, almost tasteless, crystalline organic compound, C_6H_5COOH. Its melting point is 122° C, and it is slightly soluble in water. It is the simplest member of the series of aromatic CARBOXYLIC ACIDS. Benzoic acid occurs naturally and also in the form of various esters in some plants, most often in resins. As the sodium salt, it is used in small amounts as a preservative in foods such as sauces and as a mild antiseptic. Commercially prepared from toluene, benzoic acid serves as the starting point for the synthesis of many aromatic compounds.

Beowulf   [bay'-oh-wulf]

Beowulf (650?–750?), the most famous specimen of Old English literature, is an anonymous epic. The hero Beowulf rescues the Danes from the monster Grendel and his mother, and 50 years later dies saving his own people, the Geats, from a fire dragon. The poet captures the spirit of Germanic tribal life, notably the intense bond between the chief and his thanes. Although derived from Norse folklore and history, the poem fuses pagan and Christian elements, as in the character of Beowulf, reflecting the complexity of Anglo-Saxon culture after the coming of Christianity (AD 597). The verse follows the alliterative tradition, and the poet skillfully uses the metaphorical compounds known as *kennings* (for example, ''whale's road'' for *ocean*).   DAVID M. ZESMER

Bibliography: Bolton, W., *Beowulf* (1973; repr. 1982); Brodeur, A., *The Art of Beowulf* (1959; repr. 1969); Chambers, R., ed., *Beowulf*, 3d rev. ed. (1932; repr. 1959); Kiernan, K. S., *Beowulf and the Beowulf Manuscript* (1981); Klaeber, Fr., ed., *Beowulf*, 3d ed. (1936); Nicholson, L., ed., *Anthology of Beowulf Criticism* (1963); Ogilvy, J. D., and Baker, D. C., *Reading ''Beowulf''* (1983; repr. 1986).

bequest: see TRUST; WILL (law).

Bérain, Jean   [bay-ren']

Jean Bérain, b. June 1640, d. Jan. 20, 1711, was a French architect and decorator. His life coincided roughly with the reign of Louis XIV, and his work included some of the most beautiful classical designs associated with late Louis XIV style. Although not much is known about his architecture, a number of decorative prints have survived. The prints show that Bérain found inspiration in ancient Roman mural decoration, in which delicately rendered classical motifs are common. Bérain introduced interlacing and shell motifs that were lighter than most baroque designs, particularly those of his rival, Jules Hardouin Mansart. Bérain prints were the inspiration for much ornament of the period.   MARVIN D. SCHWARTZ

Bibliography: Kimball, F., *The Creation of the Rococo* (1943; repr. 1965).

Béranger, Pierre Jean de   [bay-rahn-zhay']

Pierre Jean de Béranger, b. Aug. 19, 1780, d. July 16, 1857, was acclaimed as the national poet of France during his lifetime. His poems and songs could be patriotic, witty, and gay, as well as satirical and biting. Many of his chansons, such as ''Le Roi d'Yvetot'' from *Chansons morales et autres* (1815), have become part of the French folk tradition.   JOSEPH A. REITER

Berbers

The name *Berbers* refers to the descendants of the pre-Arab populations of North Africa from the Egyptian frontier to the Atlantic and from the Mediterranean coast to the Niger. The term comes from the derogatory Greek word for non-Greek and was taken into both Latin and Arabic, yielding the English term *barbarian*. Berbers are Caucasoid, showing a fairly high incidence of blondness, and speak variations of a single language, Berber, which belongs to the Hamito-Semitic language family. They call themselves by some variant of the word *amazigh*, which means ''free man,'' and have no sense of community or ethnic unity beyond their tribal affiliations, which notably include the Kabyle of Algeria, the Riffians and Shluh of Morocco, and the TUAREG of the Sahara.

Nomadic Berbers of the Tuareg tribe are still dependent on the camel for food and transportation. The Berbers, a light-skinned Hamitic people, are thought to have been the original inhabitants of Mediterranean Africa.

Although their origins are unknown, Berber-speaking peoples are thought to have moved into North Africa, probably from the Near East, before 2000 BC. From *c*.600 BC, Berber lands were invaded by various groups, including Carthaginians, Romans, Vandals, and Turks. With the Arab conquest of North Africa in the second half of the 7th century, the Berbers converted to Islam. For a while they fought alongside the Arabs and extended the frontiers of Islam into Spain but later began to break away from both orthodox Islam and Arab hegemony. They chose a heresy known as Kharijism, which is still practiced in parts of Tunisia and Algeria. Many features of early pagan religion have also survived in Berber religious customs under the guise of orthodox Islam. Christianity disappeared among them in the 12th century, but Judaism, which made proselytes before Christianity, has survived to the present day.

The Arabs never completely reconquered the Berbers until the invasion by the Hilali tribes in the mid-11th century. Despite the appearance of two significant Berber dynasties, the ALMORAVIDS (1063–1147) and the ALMOHADS (1147–1269), the Berber tribes could never unite long enough to rid themselves of the conquerors. As a result, Berber history can only be followed as the history of individual tribes.

The Hilali invasion marked a turning point; from then on, Arab language and culture gradually predominated in the plains and the more accessible parts of North Africa, while Berber language and culture survived primarily in relatively inaccessible districts of the Aurès, Rif, and Atlas mountains. Islam was revived and revitalized among the Berbers in the 15th and 16th centuries by wandering pious men (*Marabouts*), who generally claimed to come from areas in south Morocco. Many whole tribes now claim descent from these men, and few were unaffected.

Berber speakers, who today number over 5 million, are distributed through Libya, Tunisia, Algeria, Morocco, Mauritania, and the western Sahara. Their density increases generally from east to west, but the Berber language is still retreating in favor of Arabic as the populations of the present nation-states become homogenized. The maintenance of Berber language and identity carries with it a number of social and cultural traits that conspicuously distinguish the Berbers from the surrounding Arabs. Despite great diversity, the Berbers generally are rural, both settled and nomadic, with an economy based on subsistence agriculture and animal husbandry. They are grouped territorially and governed in egalitarian districts run by councils, of which the head of each extended family is a member.

BRIAN SPOONER

Bibliography: Gellner, Ernest, and Michaud, Charles, eds., *Arabs and Berbers* (1972); Montagne, Robert, *The Berbers: Their Social and Political Organisation*, trans. by B. Seddon (1973).

Berchem, Nicolaes Pieterszoon [bair'-kem, nik'-oh-las peet'-ur-zohn]

Nicolaes Berchem, b. Haarlem, Netherlands, Oct. 1, 1620, d. Feb. 18, 1683, was a painter of Italianate pastoral and Arcadian landscapes. He was the son of Pieter CLAESZ, a still-life painter, but he developed his own style, influenced by the French landscape painter Claude Lorrain (1600–82), which reflects his sojourn in Italy (1642–46). Berchem worked in Haarlem and Amsterdam. He was a prolific painter and an accomplished etcher and often painted figures for the landscape painters Meindert HOBBEMA and Jacob van RUISDAEL.

CHARLES I. MINOTT

Bibliography: Rosenberg, Jakob, Slive, Seymour, and ter Kuile, E. H., *Dutch Art and Architecture, 1600–1800* (1966).

Berchtesgaden [bairk'-tes-gah-den]

Berchtesgaden (1989 est. pop., 7,644) is a town in the Bavarian Alps of southern Germany. Long noted for its salt mines, the town is now a center for tourism, noted as a market town and for its health spa. It is the site of Adolf Hitler's retreat, the "Eagle's Nest," on the Obersalzberg.

Berdyayev, Nikolai [byaird-yah'-yef, nyik'-oh-ly]

Nikolai Berdyayev, b. Mar. 6, 1874, d. Mar. 23, 1948, was a Russian Orthodox religious philosopher and one of the major spokesmen of contemporary Christian EXISTENTIALISM. He studied political economy at the University of Kiev, where he became a Marxist. His Marxist activities led in 1899 to a 3-year exile in Vologda. Together with an eminent group of Russian intellectuals, he later publicly renounced (1904–05) Marxist materialism in favor of philosophical idealism and Christianity. Expelled from Russia by the Communist government in 1922, he settled first in Berlin, then in Clamart, near Paris, where he died.

Berdyayev wrote numerous books, many of which have been translated into English—such as *Dream and Reality: An Essay in Autobiography* (1949; Eng. trans., 1950) and *The Destiny of Man* (1931; Eng. trans., 1937). He was also the editor of an influential Russian periodical, *Put' (The Way)*, and remained prominent in intellectual and theological dialogues between Eastern and Western Christians. The central idea of his thought was contained in his understanding of freedom. For Berdyayev, freedom is at the very heart of personal life; it is the condition for creativity, ultimately preparing a new world transformed into God's kingdom.

JOHN MEYENDORFF

Bibliography: Lowrie, Donald A., *Rebellious Prophet* (1960; repr. 1974); Vallon, Michael A., *Apostle of Freedom: Life and Teachings of Nicholas Berdyaev* (1958); Wernham, James C., *Two Russian Thinkers: An Essay in Berdyaev and Shestov* (1968); Wood, D. K., *Men against Time* (1982).

Berea College [buh-ree'-uh]

Established in 1855, Berea College (enrollment: 1,550; library: 260,000 volumes) is a private 4-year liberal arts college in Berea, Ky. The coeducational college charges minimal tuition. Instead, students, mainly from the Appalachian region, work at the college some hours per week to help to pay their room and board fees and to maintain the institution.

Beregovoi, Georgy T. [bair-eh-goh'-voy]

The Soviet cosmonaut Georgy Timofeyevich Beregovoi, b. Apr. 15, 1921, was a decorated Soviet air force test pilot who became the oldest man ever to be recruited into the cosmonaut corps, joining in 1964 at the age of 43. He was the single pilot of the four-day *Soyuz 3* mission launched on Oct. 26,

1968, the first manned SOYUZ flight following the death of the *Soyuz 1* pilot 18 months earlier. *Soyuz 3* conducted a series of maneuvers with an unmanned *Soyuz 2* companion spaceship. Beregovoi was later promoted to the rank of major general and became an administrator at the Soviet cosmonaut center near Moscow.

JAMES OBERG

Berengar of Tours [bair'-in-guhr, toor]

Berengar of Tours, *c*.1000–1088, was a French scholastic theologian, whose teaching about the EUCHARIST was the subject of much controversy. He seemed to deny the doctrine of the Real Presence, holding that the actual substance of the bread and wine could not change into the body and blood of Christ without undergoing a change in appearance. Treatises were written against him in all parts of Europe, and his teaching was condemned by several church synods and papal decisions. He recanted his doctrine and died at peace with the church, but the controversy he initiated forced a later clarification of Eucharistic doctrine.

DAVID HARRY MILLER

Berenice [bair-uh-ny'-see]

Berenice, b. AD 28, was the daughter of the Jewish king HEROD Agrippa I. In AD 65 she tried to ease Judeo-Roman tensions, but she later went to Rome, where she was courted, then rejected, by Emperor TITUS. This story forms the basis of a tragedy by the French dramatist Jean RACINE. Berenice's three earlier husbands included Polemon, king of Cilicia; she also had an incestuous relationship with her brother, Herod Agrippa II.

Berenson, Bernard

Bernard Berenson, b. Lithuania, June 26, 1865, d. Oct. 6, 1959, was a well-known American historian, connoisseur, and critic of Italian Renaissance art. He immigrated to Boston with his family in 1872. By 1887, when he graduated from Harvard, he had already attracted the attention of art collectors, including Isabella Stewart Gardner, for whom he later acquired Titian's *Rape of Europa* (Gardner Museum, Boston). From his first trip to Italy in 1887 until his death, he spent most of his life in or near Florence. Villa I Tatti at Settignano, which he and his wife, Mary, acquired after their marriage in 1900, houses Berenson's extensive library and art collection; it is today a center for the study of Italian art under the auspices of Harvard University.

Berenson is best known for his rigorous and sensitive studies of Italian artists. Among the most influential of his many publications are *Italian Painters of the Renaissance* (1952) and *Drawings of the Florentine Painters* (1938). He was concerned also with the methodology of art history and art criticism and wrote several books on that topic, including *Three Essays in Method* (1927) and *Aesthetics and History* (1948).

Bibliography: Berenson, Bernard, *The Bernard Berenson Treasury* (1962) and *The Passionate Sightseer: From the Diaries 1947–1956* (1988); Mariano, Nicky, *Forty Years with Berenson* (1966); Samuels, Ernest, *Bernard Berenson*, 2 vols. (1979, 1987).

Berg, Alban

Alban Berg, Arnold SCHOENBERG, and Anton von WEBERN constituted the so-called Second Viennese school (the first one being that of Haydn, Mozart, and Beethoven). These men worked together to create one of the 20th century's most far-reaching musical innovations, the method of composition known as the TWELVE-TONE SYSTEM. Linking the discoveries of Schoenberg to the techniques and forms of the past, Berg wrote music of great power and emotional appeal.

Berg was born on Feb. 9, 1885, in Vienna. Before he was 15 years old, he had written many songs and duets, becoming so engrossed in music that he neglected his other studies and failed his high school examinations. He finally graduated in 1904, however, and from shortly thereafter until 1910 studied with Schoenberg. He wrote songs, a piano sonata, a string quartet, and clarinet pieces. But his famous masterpiece was yet to come—the opera *Wozzeck*, which debuted in Berlin on Dec. 14, 1925. Berg wrote the text of the opera after a play

The Austrian composer Alban Berg, a friend and pupil of Arnold Schoenberg, used Schoenberg's twelve-tone system of composition and atonality but combined them with traditional forms. He is best known for his opera Wozzeck, which was first performed in Berlin in 1925.

by Georg BÜCHNER about a true-life criminal case; it is the sordid and tragic story of a poor soldier, Wozzeck, his girlfriend Marie, their child, and a strutting drum-major who seduces Marie. Berg's friend Schoenberg did not think he should choose such a vulgar, ordinary theme for an opera, but time has proved Berg right, for his powerful, emotional drama was a worldwide success. Its first U.S. performance took place in 1931 in Philadelphia, conducted by Leopold Stokowski, and it debuted at the Metropolitan Opera in 1959.

Berg's second opera, *Lulu* (text by the composer after plays by Frank WEDEKIND), fared less well, for the composer died (Dec. 24, 1935) before putting the finishing touches on the last act. The opera nevertheless was often performed, although Berg's widow, disliking the work's radical sexuality, suppressed the third act. After her death, however, the manuscript was released. The American premiere took place in Santa Fe, N.Mex., on July 28, 1979. Berg's other important works include Three Orchestral Pieces (1914), Chamber Concerto for piano, violin, and 13 wind instruments (1925), *Lyric Suite* for string quartet (1926), and a superb violin concerto, Berg's last completed composition.   DIKA NEWLIN

Bibliography: Berg, Alban, *Letters to His Wife*, trans. by Bernard Grun (1971); Carner, Mosco, *Alban Berg*, 2d rev. ed. (1983); Leibowitz, Rene, *Schoenberg and His School*, trans. by D. Newlin (1949; repr. 1975); Perle, George, *The Operas of Alban Berg*, 2 vols. (1980–84).

Bergamo   [bair'-gah-moh]

Bergamo is the capital city of Bergamo province in the Lombardy region of northern Italy and is located in the southern foothills of the Alps. It has a population of 119,427 (1985 est.). Bergamo is an agricultural market and a center for the manufacture of machinery, textiles, and cement. Ruled in turn by Gauls, Romans, and Lombard dukes, it became a free commune in the 12th century; it was later ruled by the Visconti of Milan from 1329 to 1428 and then by Venice until 1797. From 1815 to 1859 it was under Austrian control. Bergamo is divided into the upper old town and the lower new town. Its notable monuments include a 12th-century Romanesque cathedral, the baptistry (1340), and the Renaissance Colleoni Chapel (1470–76), decorated with Tiepolo frescoes. The composer Gaetano Donizetti was born there, and the city has the Donizetti Museum, as well as the Risorgimento Museum in a 14th-century castle.   DANIEL R. LESNICK

bergamot   [bur'-guh-maht]

The bergamot, *Citrus aurantium*, subspecies *begamia*, is a variety of citrus tree in the rue family, Rutaceae. It is grown primarily in Italy for the oil extracted from the aromatic rind of its small, pear-shaped fruit—a type of sour orange. Bergamot oil is used mainly in perfumes. Certain MINT plants of the *Monarda* genus, including BEE BALM, are sometimes called wild bergamots because their fragrance is similar to that of the fruit. The name is also given to several types of pear.

Berganza, Teresa   [bair-gahn'-thah]

The Spanish soprano Teresa Berganza, b. Madrid, Mar. 16, 1935, is best known for her operatic roles in the works of Wolfgang Amadeus Mozart and Gioacchino Rossini and for her recitals. She made her Metropolitan Opera debut (1967) in one of her most acclaimed roles, Cherubino in Mozart's *The Marriage of Figaro*. Although she specializes in the classical repertoire, her recitals also include the works of the romantic composers.

Bergen

Bergen is the seat of Hordaland County on the southwest coast of Norway, about 306 km (109 mi) west of Oslo. Located on a sheltered inlet of the North Sea, it is an important port and, with a population of 207,866 (1986 est.), is the country's third largest city. Bergen is heavily industrialized, manufacturing foodstuffs, textiles, and machinery, and building ships. Fish products are the main exports. Historical landmarks include Bergenhus fortress (1261), St. Mary's Church (12th century), and Rosencrantz Tower (1562). The city also has a university (1948), several museums, and National Theater (1850), and it was the birthplace of the composer Edvard Grieg and the violinist Ole Bull.

Founded in 1070 by King Olaf III, Bergen became a leading trade center and Norway's capital during the 12th and 13th centuries. It joined the HANSEATIC LEAGUE in the 14th century, and German merchants from the league developed trade monopolies there that lasted into the 18th century. Occupied during World War II by the Germans, the city suffered heavy damage during Allied bombings.

Bergen, Edgar, and McCarthy, Charlie

Edgar John Bergen, b. Chicago, Feb. 16, 1903, d. Sept. 30, 1978, an American ventriloquist, was the straight man for Charlie McCarthy, his brash, cheeky puppet. Bergen got the idea for the "magnificent splinter" while in high school in Chicago. Theodore Mack, a local carpenter, made the wisecracking dummy, who was later joined by another dummy, the stupid, literal-minded Mortimer Snerd.

The Bergen-McCarthy act moved from vaudeville in the 1920s to nightclubs before becoming a national sensation on radio. Charlie's strong characterization as an irreverent "timber wolf" overshadowed his master's low-keyed, comic timing and writing skills. The team also appeared in films and on television. The actress Candice Bergen, b. Beverly Hills, Calif., May 9, 1946, daughter of Edgar, made her film debut in 1966 in *The Group*.   FRANK MANCHEL

Bergen-Belsen: see BELSEN.

Berger, Thomas

Thomas Louis Berger, b. Cincinnati, Ohio, July 20, 1924, a prolific novelist, wrote a tetralogy that chronicles the exploits of a hulking German-American midwesterner named Carlo Reinhart (*Crazy in Berlin*, 1958; *Reinhart in Love*, 1962; *Vital Parts*, 1970; *Reinhart's Women*, 1981). Between these four, Berger published other novels, often replacing the tongue-in-cheek style of the quartet with much blacker humor. His best-known are *Little Big Man* (1964; film, 1970), the satire of Camelot *Authur Rex* (1978), *Neighbors* (1980; film, 1981), *The Feud* (1983), and *Being Invisible* (1987).

Berger, Victor L.

Victor Berger, b. Feb. 28, 1860, d. Aug. 7, 1929, was the first Socialist elected to the U.S. Congress. Born in Austria-Hungary, he emigrated (1878) to the United States and settled in Milwaukee, Wis. He was a founder of the American Socialist party. Berger first served in Congress from 1911 to 1913. Reelected in 1918, he was denied a seat because he had been convicted of sedition for opposing U.S. participation in World War I. Only when the conviction was overturned by the

Supreme Court was he permitted to take his seat, which he held from 1923 to 1929. His speeches and editorials are collected in *The Voice and Pen of Victor L. Berger* (1929).

Bibliography: Miller, Sally M., *Victor L. Berger and the Promise of Constructive Socialism, 1910–1920* (1973).

Bergius, Friedrich Karl Rudolf   [bair'-gee-us]

The German chemist Friedrich Bergius, b. Oct. 11, 1884, d. Mar. 30, 1949, was corecipient of the 1931 Nobel Prize for chemistry for his contributions to high-pressure methods applicable to industrial processes. He is noted for his work on the liquefaction of coal and on the transformation of wood into carbohydrates (sugars) usable as foodstuff for cattle. His coal liquefaction process, developed in 1913 but not applied until many years later, consists of combining coal with hydrogen in the presence of a catalyst and high pressure to yield motor fuels on an industrial scale.   HUGO ZAHND

Bergman, Hjalmar Fredrik Elgérus

Hjalmar Bergman, b. Sept. 19, 1883, d. Jan. 1, 1931, was a Swedish novelist, playwright, and scenarist for film and radio whose works are characterized by pessimism, brutal realism, and a taste for the grotesque. His best novel is probably *God's Orchid* (1919; Eng. trans., 1924).

Bergman, Ingmar

Ingmar Ernst Bergman, b. July 14, 1918, is a major Swedish filmmaker who for over 30 years has sustained a reputation as an artist of international stature. The son of a Lutheran pastor, Bergman attended Stockholm University and began his directing career in the theater, where he continues to work as extensively as he does in films. He wrote the screenplay for the director Alf Sjöberg's internationally acclaimed *Torment* in 1944, and the next year he directed his first film, *Crisis.*

The lighthearted *Smiles of a Summer Night* (1955) was the first of Bergman's films to arouse the interest of non-Swedish audiences. It was *The Seventh Seal* (1957), however, with its despairing philosophy and stark medieval imagery, that established him firmly as a filmmaker of extraordinary power and set the theme that was to characterize virtually all his subsequent work—the individual's quasi-religious search for faith in a context of anguished doubt. This theme is central to such varied films as *Wild Strawberries* (1957), *The Magician* (1958), *The Virgin Spring* (1960), and his "chamber" trilogy: *Through a Glass Darkly* (1961), *Winter Light* (1963), and *The Silence* (1963).

By the mid-1960s Bergman had assembled a team of actors who would appear in many of his subsequent films and plays, among them Max VON SYDOW and Liv ULLMANN. In 1966 he

Ingmar Bergman, a Swedish filmmaker, has been one of the most influential figures in contemporary cinema. Bergman's avant-garde works, which he often writes, directs, and produces, concern the themes of love and death, belief and doubt, purity and violation.

undertook a greater formal experimentation with *Persona,* a psychological study of two women that is considered one of his most important films. *Persona* was followed by the antiwar allegory *Shame* (1968), the realistic *Passion of Anna* (1969), and the intense yet dreamlike *Cries and Whispers* (1972). *Scenes from a Marriage,* a 6-part domestic drama originally made for Swedish television, was aired in the United States and other countries, introducing Bergman to a much larger public. *Autumn Sonata* (1978) featured Bergman's compatriot Ingrid Bergman. Two later films—*Fanny and Alexander* (1983), a brilliant vision of childhood in a theatrical family, and *After the Rehearsal* (1984), a richly symbolic portrait of an aging theater director—contain Bergman's autobiographical comments on theatrical life.   WILLIAM S. PECHTER

Bibliography: Bjorkman, Stig, et al., *Bergman on Bergman: Interviews* (1986); Cowie, P., *Ingmar Bergman* (1982); Gado, F., *The Passion of Ingmar Bergman* (1986); Marker, Lise-Lone and Frederick J., *Ingmar Bergman* (1982); Petrie, Vlada, ed., *Film and Dreams: An Approach to Bergman* (1981).

Bergman, Ingrid

Ingrid Bergman, b. Aug. 29, 1915, d. Aug. 29, 1982, was a popular stage and film actress in her native Sweden before going to Hollywood, where she made an English-language version of her Swedish hit *Intermezzo* (1939). Bergman was probably best known for her roles in *Casablanca* (1942); *For Whom the Bell Tolls* (1943); *Gaslight* (1944), for which she received her first Academy Award; *The Bells of St. Mary's* (1945); and two Alfred Hitchcock films, *Spellbound* (1945) and *Notorious* (1946). She returned to Europe after the scandalous publicity surrounding her affair with Italian director Roberto ROSSELLINI (whom she later married and divorced) during the filming of *Stromboli* (1950). But she returned to Hollywood and triumphed in *Anastasia* (1956), for which she received another Oscar. She received a third for her role in *Murder on the Orient Express* (1974). She also starred in Ingmar Bergman's *Autumn Sonata* (1978). Her last role was in the television film *A Woman Called Golda* (1981).

Bibliography: Bergman, I., and Burgess, A., *Ingrid Bergman: My Story* (1980); Leamer, L., *As Time Goes By: The Life of Ingrid Bergman* (1986); Quirk, L. J., *The Films of Ingrid Bergman* (1970; repr. 1975).

Bergman, Sir Torbern

Torbern Olof Bergman, b. Mar. 20, 1735, d. July 8, 1784, was a Swedish professor of chemistry and mineralogy at the University of Uppsala from 1767 to 1780. He developed analytical techniques, notably the blowpipe, advocated a chemical classification of minerals, and introduced laboratory instruction in beginning science courses.   RALPH GABLE

Bergmann, Gustav   [bairk'-mahn]

Gustav Bergmann, b. May 4, 1906, is an Austrian-American philosopher. As one of the younger members of the Vienna Circle, he grew up in the tradition of logical positivism. He began his career as a mathematician, and much of his early work was done in the areas of mathematics, philosophy of mathematics, and philosophy of science. About 1950 he began to stress the importance of metaphysics, an unusual viewpoint for a positivist. He published many of the essays from this period in his first book, *The Metaphysics of Logical Positivism* (1954). Other works include *Meaning and Existence* (1960) and *Realism* (1967).   E. D. KLEMKE

Bergonzi, Carlo   [bair-gohn'-tsee]

Carlo Bergonzi, b. July 13, 1924, is an Italian opera singer. Originally a baritone, he attended the conservatory in Parma, Italy, and in 1948 made his debut as Figaro in Rossini's *The Barber of Seville.* Three years later he emerged as a tenor, singing the title role in Umberto Giordano's *Andrea Chenier.* An engagement at La Scala soon followed. In 1956, Bergonzi appeared as Radames in Verdi's *Aïda* at the Metropolitan Opera, to which he returned frequently over the next 20 years.

Bergson, Henri

Henri Bergson, French philosopher, won the 1927 Nobel Prize for literature. He emphasized the value of intuition in scientific thinking and argued that reality is beyond rational understanding.

The French philosopher Henri Bergson, b. Oct. 18, 1859, d. Jan. 4, 1941, was internationally known for his concepts of inner duration, creative evolution, and the limits of human intelligence. After beginning his teaching career at Clermont-Ferrand in 1883, he joined (1900) the Collège de France, where his lectures enjoyed unparalleled success until his retirement in 1921. In 1918 he was accepted into the French Academy. During World War I he participated in diplomatic missions designed to bring the United States into the conflict. Afterward he participated in the League of Nations, presiding over the creation of the Committee for Intellectual Cooperation, later to become UNESCO. In his later years Bergson was forced by crippling arthritis into virtual seclusion. He was awarded the Nobel Prize for literature in 1927.

As a student, Bergson was tempted to pursue a career in mathematics; he was also a disciple of the mechanist Herbert SPENCER. But by the time of his doctoral thesis, *Time and Free Will* (1889), Bergson had rejected the primacy of mathematical and mechanical concepts. He pointed out that the flow of experienced duration cannot be measured and that human personalities, as they grow in duration, express themselves in acts that cannot be predicted. These key insights were expanded in *Matter and Memory* (1896) to include a theory of mind-body interrelations and in *An Introduction to Metaphysics* (1903), to include a theory of knowledge in which intuition (that which grasps the dynamic flux of duration) plays a central role. In *Creative Evolution* (1907), he applied his intuitive method to the problem of biological evolution, concluding that the expansive and creative thrust of life cannot be explained by Darwinian mechanism. In *The Two Sources of Morality and Religion* (1932), he described the Judeo-Christian tradition as a culminating point in human social evolution.

PETE A. Y. GUNTER

Bibliography: Čapek, Milic, *Bergson and Modern Physics* (1971); Douglas, Paul, *Bergson, Eliot, and American Literature* (1986); Kolakowski, Leszek, *Bergson* (1985).

Beria, Lavrenti Pavlovich   [bair′-ee-uh, luhv-ren′-tee pahv′-luh-vich]

Lavrenti Pavlovich Beria, b. Mar. 29, 1899, d. 1953, was head of the Soviet People's Commissariat for Internal Affairs (NKVD) from 1938 to 1953. A member of the Communist party from 1917, he was appointed (1921) head of the Transcaucasian section of the *Cheka* (the secret police). For 10 years Beria mercilessly purged the Georgian, Armenian, and Azerbaijan Communist parties of "nationalist deviationists." As deputy chairman of the Council of Ministers and a member of the Politburo from 1946, he supervised internal security, intelligence, and counterintelligence. After Joseph Stalin's death, members of the Politburo suspected that Beria was planning to establish a personal dictatorship and had him arrested on

June 26, 1953. On Dec. 23, 1953, it was officially announced that Beria had been sentenced to death and shot.

Bibliography: Wittlin, Tadeusz, *Commissar: The Life and Death of Lavrenty Pavlovich Beria* (1972).

beriberi   [bair′-ee-bair′-ee]

Beriberi is a NUTRITIONAL-DEFICIENCY DISEASE resulting from an insufficiency of thiamine, or vitamin B_1 (see VITAMINS AND MINERALS). It may result from an improper diet, as in parts of Asia where the main source of food is polished rice; from poor absorption of thiamine; from increased body requirements, for example, during pregnancy; and from poor utilization of thiamine, as in liver disease. Beriberi also occurs among chronic alcoholics. Symptoms include gastrointestinal disturbances, edema, inflammation and degeneration of nerves, and muscular weakness. Beriberi may lead to heart failure and, ultimately, death. Treatment consists of thiamine administration.

Bibliography: Chenault, A. A., *Nutrition and Health* (1984); Williams, R. R., *Toward the Conquest of Beriberi* (1961).

Bering, Vitus Jonassen   [bair′-ing, vee′-tuhs yoh′-nah-suhn]

Vitus Bering, a Danish explorer in the service of Russia, made two significant voyages along the coast of Siberia. Bering's death, as portrayed in this painting by C. J. L. Portman, occurred in 1741, when his ship was wrecked along the Commander Islands.

Vitus Jonassen Bering, b. 1681, d. Dec. 19, 1741, was a Danish navigator and explorer in Russian service, credited with discovering Alaska and the strait between it and Russia. He actually duplicated the discovery by Semyon Dezhnev, who sailed in 1648 but whose report lay unnoticed until the 18th century.

Bering was chosen to lead an expedition seeking a sea route around Siberia to China and surveying the possibility of expansion into the North American continent. From Kamchatka, Siberia, he explored (1728) the northeastern coast of Russia, sailing south through the strait later named for him. Bad weather prevented him from finding the coast of Alaska. A second expedition, launched in 1733, was overambitious, poorly organized, and underfinanced, but it mapped much of the Siberian coast. In 1741, Bering sailed again, reaching and exploring the southwest coast of Alaska and some of the Aleutian Islands. Misfortune plagued the two ships, which were separated and the crews of which were racked by scurvy. Bering's ship was wrecked, and he died on the island that today bears his name. A few survivors reached Russia to tell of their exploration.

Bibliography: Fisher, Raymond, *Bering's Voyages* (1977); Golder, F. A., *Bering's Voyages*, 2 vols. (1922–25); Lauridsen, Peter, *Vitus Bering* (1889; Eng. trans., 1969); Muller, G. F., *Bering's Voyages,* trans. by C. Urness (1986); Urness, C., *Bering's First Expedition* (1987).

Bering Land Bridge   [bair'-ing]

The Bering Land Bridge, or Beringia, is the great landmass that emerged in the Bering and Chukchi Seas following a drop in sea level at several times during the Quaternary Period (the last 2 million years). Archaeologists believe that the first humans to enter the New World used the ''bridge'' as they slowly migrated from what is now northeast Asia to northwestern North America. This migration presumably occurred during the last major phase of the Wisconsin glaciation, a period lasting from 30,000 to 10,000 years ago. At the end of the period the two continents were separated by the sea as the ice in the major continental ice sheets and other glaciers melted and caused a rise in sea level.

About 20,000 years ago the land bridge extended from Unalaska Island of the Aleutian chain on the southeast, northwestward to Cape Olyutorsky of the Koryak area north of the Kamchatka Peninsula, and from near the mouth of the Mackenzie River of Canada on the east to near the Kolyma and Indigirka rivers of eastern Siberia on the west.

Because much of the area was not glaciated, it supported Arctic vegetation, particularly dry grasslands or steppe, tundra, marsh vegetation, and boreal forests, which supplied adequate food for grazing animals. Such animals would have included the horse, the reindeer, and such Ice Age species as the mammoth, the mastodon, and the woolly rhinoceros. Birds and fish would have served as additional food sources for early American hunters.   JAMES B. GRIFFIN

Bibliography: Hopkins, D. M., ed., *The Bering Land Bridge* (1967); Snow, Dean, *The Archaeology of North America* (1976); West, Frederick, *The Archaeology of Beringia* (1981).

See also: NORTH AMERICAN ARCHAEOLOGY.

Bering Sea

The Bering Sea, an arm of the North Pacific Ocean, is bounded on the east by Alaska, on the south by the Aleutian Islands, and on the west by Siberia (Russian Asia) and the Kamchatka Peninsula. To the north, the Bering Strait leads to the Chukchi Sea of the Arctic Ocean. The sea extends 2,396 km (1,488 mi) east to west and 1,597 km (992 mi) north to south. Its area is about 2,300,000 km² (878,000 mi²). The greatest depth is 4,115 m (13,500 ft). Discovered (1648) by the Russian Semyon Dezhnev, the sea was named for Vitus BERING, a Danish explorer in the service of Russia in the early 18th century.

The largest islands are St. Lawrence, Nunivak, St. Matthew, and the Pribilof group, all of which are part of Alaska, and the Komandorskie Islands, which are Soviet territory. High winds and snow in winter and fog in summer create a climate with few clear days. Navigation is difficult, and ice closes the northern part of the sea from October to June. Herds of fur seals breed on the Pribilofs, and international friction over seal hunting was settled by agreement in 1911.

Bibliography: Hunt, William R., *Arctic Passage* (1975).

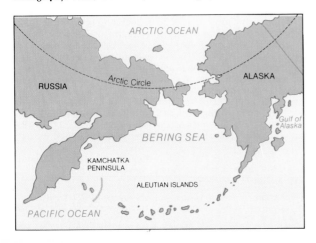

Bering Sea controversy

The Bering Sea controversy, a dispute between Canada and the United States, may be traced to the U.S. purchase of Alaska in 1867. The purchase included the offshore Pribilof Islands (in the Bering Sea), on which the world's largest herd of fur seals congregate each summer to breed. In 1870, Congress leased the islands to a U.S. company in return for a promise that the company's men would not slaughter more than 100,000 male seals a year, and only on land. This arrangement worked well for a decade, until Canadian schooners began to intercept the herd at sea, an enterprise known as pelagic sealing. American revenue cutters arrested Canadian ships far outside territorial waters in 1886–87 and again in 1889. An international arbitration on Aug. 15, 1893, led to the regulation of pelagic sealing but fined the United States $478,151 for interfering with Canadian sealers outside territorial waters. In 1911 the North Pacific Sealing Convention came into force, which restricted the area of pelagic sealing and awarded Japan revenues from the annual hunt. In 1957 it was replaced by a new convention.   ROBERT H. FERRELL

Bering Strait

The Bering Strait, which lies between Alaska and Siberia (Russian Asia), connects the Bering Sea with the Chukchi Sea of the Arctic Ocean. From Cape Prince of Wales in Alaska to Cape Dezhnev in Siberia, it is 89 km (55 mi) across, the shortest distance between the continents of North America and Asia. Big Diomede Island (Russia) and Little Diomede Island (United States) lie less than 5 km (3 mi) apart in the middle of the strait. The international date line runs between them.

Frozen over from October until June, the strait is between 30 and 52 m (100 and 170 ft) deep. Discovered (1648) by Semyon Dezhnev, it is named for Vitus BERING, who sighted the Diomede Islands on St. Diomede's Day, Aug. 16, 1728.

Berio, Luciano   [bair'-ee-oh]

The Italian composer Luciano Berio, b. Oct. 24, 1925, is a leading modernist whose works combine a natural lyricism with the more advanced techniques of electronic music. Berio's new compositions are always the subject of curiosity and intense critical scrutiny. He studied with Giorgio Ghedini at the conservatory in Milan and with Luigi Dallapiccola at the Berkshire Music Center in Tanglewood, Mass. In 1955 he founded, with Bruno MADERNA, the experimental electronic music laboratory at the Milan radio station. He also edited the journal *Incontri Musicale* (Musical Encounters), which discussed avant-garde music. Berio composes in a wide range of contemporary idioms. The *Sinfonia* (1968) for eight voices and orchestra is among his most successful pieces. His strong interest in folk music is reflected in his *Voci* (1984) for viola and orchestra, which was inspired by Sicilian work songs.

Bibliography: Machlis, Joseph, *Introduction to Contemporary Music*, 2d ed. (1979); Mellers, Wilfrid, *Caliban Reborn: Renewal in Twentieth Century Music* (1967; repr. 1979).

Berkeley   [bur'-klee]

Berkeley is a city in west central California, located on the northeastern shore of the San Francisco Bay. It has a population of 102,724 (1990). The city rises from sea level to an elevation of about 400 m (1,300 ft). The climate is temperate, with a mean yearly temperature of 14° C (57° F) and an average annual rainfall of 550 mm (22 in).

Site of the main campus of the University of California, the city is the location of the University Art Museum, a more than 7,000,000-volume library, and the Lawrence Berkeley Laboratory, an atomic research center. Other educational institutions include several divinity schools and Armstrong College. On the industrial shore, manufactures include processed food, metal products, pharmaceuticals, and chemicals. Granted (1820) to the Peralta family by the Spanish crown, the land was purchased and settled (1853) by Americans and called Ocean View. It was renamed Berkeley (for the philosopher George Berkeley) in 1866.

Berkeley, Busby [burk'-lee]

Busby Berkeley reviews chorus girls for one of his sumptuously choreographed film musicals. Berkeley's films, which were popular during the 1930s and '40s, are remembered for their precision dancing, their casts of hundreds, and their elaborate technical effects.

Busby Berkeley was the pseudonym of William Berkeley Enos, b. Los Angeles, Nov. 29, 1895, d. Mar. 14, 1976, a choreographer known for the grandiose spectacles he created in the Hollywood musical extravaganzas of the 1930s. From success on the Broadway stage, Berkeley took his dance-directing techniques to movies. The Berkeley trademark—kaleidoscopic patterns of massed dancers filmed from above—is most strikingly displayed in the Eddie Cantor vehicle *Whoopee* (1930) and in *42nd Street* (1933), the *Gold Diggers* series (1933, 1935, 1937, 1938), *Roman Scandals* (1933), *Footlight Parade* (1933), and *Babes in Arms* (1939). His lead dancer was Ruby Keeler.

WILLIAM S. PECHTER

Bibliography: Martin, Dave, and Pike, Bob, *The Genius of Busby Berkeley* (1973); Terry, Jim, and Thomas, Tony, *The Busby Berkeley Book* (1973).

Berkeley, George [bahr'-klee]

George Berkeley, b. Mar. 12, 1685, d. Jan. 14, 1753, was a leading advocate of EMPIRICISM in British philosophy. He studied divinity and later lectured at Trinity College, Dublin. He went to London to muster support for a venture to establish a college in Bermuda for colonists and Indians in America. Although his college never came to be, he spent three years in the colonies and was a stimulus to the development of higher education in America. In 1734 he was appointed bishop at Cloyne, in which office he devoted himself to the social and economic plight of Ireland.

Berkeley is the second of the three great British empiricists, the first being John LOCKE and the third David HUME. His most

George Berkeley, an 18th-century Anglo-Irish philosopher and Anglican bishop, is known as one of the three great British empiricists, with John Locke and David Hume.

characteristic philosophical doctrine is summarized in the Latin expression *esse est percipi*, "to be is to be perceived." This expresses a version of philosophical IDEALISM, the view that nothing can exist apart from minds and the contents of minds. To say that a material object exists, in this view, is to say that it is or can be seen, heard, or otherwise perceived by a mind.

Philosophers such as John Locke had adopted the view that human knowledge depends on the existence of material objects independent of minds or ideas. These objects causally produce ideas in our minds. Locke held that in some respects our ideas resemble objects in the material world, but some qualities that objects appear to have are not in the objects but depend upon our minds. That is, material objects possess in reality the measurable, quantitative qualities, such as size and weight, but their sense qualities, such as color, odor, and taste, depend upon the mind.

Against this view Berkeley held that all the qualities of the object depend upon the mind. Since objects have stable and regular existence, the mind they depend on must be divine rather than human. In Berkeley's view, therefore, the existence of a divine mind follows directly from the common-sense belief that physical objects exist when no one is perceiving them. Berkeley believed that the Lockean view gave a basis for skepticism and atheism. His arguments have been of continuing interest to philosophers.   THOMAS K. HEARN, JR.

Bibliography: Warnock, G. J., *Berkeley* (1953; repr. 1983).

Berkeley, Sir William [bahr'-klee]

Sir William Berkeley, b. 1606, d. July 9, 1677, served as royal governor of Virginia from 1642 until 1677, except during the period of the English Commonwealth (1652–60). Educated at Queen's College, Oxford, he served on the English privy council and made some reputation as a playwright before moving to Virginia. Berkeley was knighted by Charles I in 1639.

While governor of Virginia, Berkeley attempted, with scant success, to persuade the colonists to abandon their dependence on tobacco and diversify their economy. His advocacy of a relatively pacific Indian policy, in combination with provincial jealousy over the circle of men on whom he had bestowed patronage, led to the uprising against his administration known as BACON'S REBELLION (1676). Berkeley left office in 1677 and died shortly after returning to England.

RICHARD R. BEEMAN

Bibliography: Craven, Wesley Frank, *The Colonies in Transition, 1607–1689* (1949); Washburn, Wilcomb E., *The Governor and the Rebel: A History of Bacon's Rebellion in Virginia* (1957; repr. 1972); Wertenbaker, Thomas J., *Bacon's Rebellion* (1980).

berkelium [bur-kee'-lee-uhm or burk'-lee-uhm]

Berkelium is a chemical element, a metal of the ACTINIDE SERIES in Group IIIB of the periodic table. Its symbol is Bk, its atomic number 97, and its weight 247 (stablest isotope). Berkelium does not occur naturally. Glenn SEABORG, S. G. Thompson, and A. Ghiorso synthesized ^{243}Bk in 1949 by bombarding americium 241 with helium ions in a cyclotron at the University of California at Berkeley; the newly discovered element was named in honor of that city. The known isotopes, whose mass numbers range from 240 to 251, are radioactive; ^{247}Bk is the stablest isotope, with a half-life of about 1,400 years. Weighable amounts of ^{249}Bk, large enough to allow the study of the chemical properties of the element, are produced by prolonged neutron bombardment of curium 244 (derived from americium 243), followed by beta decay of curium 249. No practical applications of this element are known.

See also: TRANSURANIUM ELEMENTS.

Berkshire [bahrk'-sher]

Berkshire is a county in southern England, just west of London. It covers 1,259 km² (486 mi²), and the population is 715,300 (1984 est.) READING is the county town. A region of rolling hills and chalk downs, Berkshire is bisected by the River Thames and its tributaries. Barley, wheat, and oats are grown in the river valleys, and hog, poultry, and dairy farms are important to the local economy. Since World War II, industry has greatly increased, and a variety of light manufactures are produced at Reading and other towns. Two centers for nuclear research are located in the area. Berkshire is a major rail and road center. Tourists visit WINDSOR CASTLE and the famous racecourse at Ascot.

Berkshire Hills

The Berkshire Hills, an extension of the Green Mountains of Vermont, are a series of ridges that includes the Hoosac Range and Taconic Range (western Massachusetts) and the Litchfield Hills (Connecticut). Their average elevation is about 457 m (1,500 ft), and the highest point is Mount Greylock (1,064 m/3,491 ft). The area is a summer and winter resort.

Berkshire Music Festival

The Berkshire Music Festival, since 1984 officially called the Tanglewood Festival, is held each summer at the Tanglewood estate, near Lake Mahkeenac in Lenox, Berkshire County, Mass. The BOSTON SYMPHONY ORCHESTRA first performed there in 1937 under the leadership of famed conductor Serge Koussevitzky. Tanglewood then became the permanent summer home of the orchestra, and the location of its academy for advanced training in music, the Berkshire (now Tanglewood) Music Center. In 1938 a music shed was erected; designed by Eero Saarinen and Joseph Franz, the shed provides seating for over 5,000 patrons, with additional seating for many thousands more on the spacious lawns of the estate.

The festival is currently nine weeks in length, from late June through late August each year, and comprises weekend performances by the Boston Symphony, recitals by renowned soloists, and concerts by members of the music center.

Bibliography: Kupferberg, Herbert, *Tanglewood* (1976).

Berlage, Hendrik Petrus   [bair'-lah-ge, hen'-drik pay'-trus]

Hendrik Petrus Berlage, b. Feb. 21, 1856, d. Aug. 12, 1934, is considered the founder of modern Dutch architecture. Following his schooling in Zurich and a European tour, Berlage began his architectural career in his native Amsterdam in 1882. Within a decade his unique style had emerged, typified by the Amsterdam Bourse, or Exchange (1896–1903), a massive brick and stone edifice enclosing three arcaded courts roofed in glass and iron. His Gemeente (Municipal) Museum (1927–34) in The Hague, with its blocky forms and horizontal emphasis, reflects his admiration for Frank Lloyd WRIGHT.

Bibliography: Polano, Sergio, et al., *Hendrick Petrus Berlage: Complete Works* (1989).

See also: DUTCH ART AND ARCHITECTURE; MODERN ARCHITECTURE.

Berle, A. A.   [bur'-lee]

Adolf Augustus Berle, Jr., b. Boston, Jan. 29, 1895, d. Feb. 17, 1971, was an American economist, lawyer, and government official. He is chiefly remembered for being an original member of the Brain Trust, a group of scholarly advisors that President Franklin D. Roosevelt assembled to help set up the NEW DEAL in 1933. Berle's particular expertise was in drafting banking and securities legislation. He was professor of corporate law (1927–64) at Columbia University and served as assistant secretary of state (1938–44) for Latin America. He was also U.S. ambassador to Brazil (1945–46) and was a leading advisor on Latin American affairs during the Kennedy administration. In 1944, Berle helped found New York State's Liberal party, in which he was a leading figure for many years.

Berle, Milton   [burl]

Milton Berle is the stage name of Milton Berlinger, b. New York City, July 12, 1908, a popular American comedian who,

in 1948, became the first TV performer to gain a wide national following. As the star of "The Texaco Star Theater" (1948–53), Berle—known as "Mr. Television"—specialized in rapid-fire jokes and broad comedy routines. He began his career as a child comic and silent-screen actor before becoming a popular stage, radio, and nightclub comedian. *Milton Berle: An Autobiography* was published in 1974, and *B.S., I Love You,* a book of reminiscences, in 1988.   FRANK MANCHEL

Berlichingen, Götz von   [bair'-lik-in-gen]

Götz (or Gottfried) von Berlichingen, b. 1480, d. July 23, 1562, was a German knight famous for his exploits in the wars of the early 16th century. Götz served Emperor Charles V, fought against the Turks in Hungary, led rebel forces during the Peasants' War of 1524–26, and was frequently in trouble for acts of brigandage and private warfare. He was known as "Götz with the Iron Hand" because he lost his right hand as the result of a wound and thereafter used one made of iron. His autobiography, published in the 18th century, was the basis for Goethe's play *Götz von Berlichingen* (1773).

Berlin

Berlin, the capital and largest city of Germany, is located in the northeastern part of the country of the SPREE RIVER. Its population is 3,420,119 (1990 est.).

The most populous city on the European continent before World War II, Berlin lay in ruins at the time of Germany's defeat in 1945; it was divided among the four victorious powers: the United States, the USSR, Great Britain, and France, each of which had its own sector. Germany itself was also divided into zones of occupation, with Berlin, Germany's historic capital, in the middle of the Soviet zone. The hostility that developed in the postwar years between the Western Allies (the United States, Britain, and France) and the USSR had its effect on Germany and Berlin. In 1949 the three Western zones were united to form the Federal Republic of Germany (West Germany), and the Soviet zone became the German Democratic Republic (East Germany, or the GDR). At the same time, the three western sectors of Berlin were united to form West Berlin, and the Soviet sector became East Berlin, which in 1954 became the capital of the GDR. For the next four decades, West Berlin was a "stateless city." Although it was

One of Berlin's showplaces is the 18th-century Charlottenburg Palace. Opposite the palace is a statue of G. J. D. von Scharnhorst, reformer of the Prussian army during the period of the Napoleonic Wars.

(Left) *The Reichstag building was the meeting place of the German parliament under the imperial regime and the Weimar Republic. When it burned down in February 1933, Hitler blamed the Communists and used the event as an excuse to crack down on the opposition. The building was restored (minus its original dome) in the 1960s.*

(Below) *For many years Checkpoint Charlie was one of the main crossing points between East and West Berlin. When the Berlin Wall was demolished in 1989–90, this painful reminder of the city's past was removed as well.*

generally regarded as a part of West Germany and sent delegates to the West German parliament in Bonn, these delegates had only observer status—they could not vote.

When the division of Germany ended in 1990, the reunified city of Berlin was declared the capital of the newly enlarged Federal Republic, but according to a plan adopted in June 1991, the shift of government institutions from Bonn was scheduled to occur gradually, over a period of years.

Berlin is situated in the northern German lowlands in the area traditionally known as the Mark of BRANDENBURG. It covers an area of 886 km² (342 mi²) and has 23 districts, 12 from the former West Berlin, and 11 from the former East Berlin. In 1990, 2,147,540 people lived in the western part and 1,272,579 in the eastern part.

Economy. Western Berlin's manufactured products include electrical appliances, machinery, garments, optical goods, pharmaceuticals, and printed matter. In the 1980s it developed an important service industry and became a major convention city. Tourism is also important.

Berlin is an important center of scientific research, with some 180 research institutions, among them the Hahn-Meitner Institute for Nuclear Research, the Science Center Berlin, the Fritz Haber Institute, and the AKADEMIE DER WISSENSCHAFTEN.

The economy of eastern Berlin mirrors that of the former GDR in general: faltering industrial production and rising unemployment, caused by the difficult transition from a planned economy to a market system. Wages are 30 to 40 percent below western levels. Unemployment has hit women particularly hard. In eastern Berlin, as elsewhere in the GDR, nearly all women were employed outside the home, as opposed to about half in the western part of the city.

Transportation. Public transportation includes some 150 bus routes, a streetcar system in eastern Berlin, and an extensive subway (U-Bahn) and elevated train (S-Bahn) system. Berlin also has four long-distance railroad stations and three commercial airports (Tegel and Tempelhof in the west and Schönefeld in the east). An extensive network of canals also exists. The AVUS expressway crosses Berlin; highways from outside the city feed into the Berliner Ring, an expressway that encircles the city completely.

Government. Berlin is one of the 15 Lander (states) of the Federal Republic of Germany, and its executive body, called the Senat, exercises both state and municipal functions. The Senat consists of a governing mayor (Regierender Burgermeister) and 15 senators, each of whom is responsible for a particular government department. The senators, nominated by the governing mayor, must be approved by a majority of the Abgeordnetenhaus (House of Representatives), which is Berlin's parliament. The administrations of the city's 23 districts are responsible for implementing the laws and ordinances of the city under the supervision of the Senat.

Landmarks. The city's famous landmarks include the BRANDENBURG GATE and the tree-lined avenue leading up to it, called Unter den Linden. Nearby is the REICHSTAG building

(1894), home of Germany's old parliament, which was destroyed by fire in 1933, damaged in World War II, and restored in 1968. The bombed-out ruin of the Kaiser Wilhelm Memorial Church, left standing as a reminder of the destruction of war, dominates what was, before unification, the center of West Berlin; it stands at the beginning of the Kurfurstendamm, the main thoroughfare of the western part of the city. In the Tiergarten Park is the Victory Column (Siegessaule), constructed in 1873 to commemorate the Franco-Prussian War. Most famous of all is the BERLIN WALL, the hated symbol of the divided city. A few sections of it remain standing and are used as outdoor art galleries.

Cultural and Educational Institutions. Berlin has long been a cultural and educational center, noted for its State Opera, the BERLIN PHILHARMONIC ORCHESTRA, its museums and galleries, and its universities. The Humboldt University was founded (1809) as Friedrich Wilhelm University and became a model for universities around the world in the 19th century. The Free University of Berlin was founded in 1948.

History. Berlin and the neighboring town of Kölln were first mentioned in documents in the 13th century, but the city's rise to prominence was associated with the HOHENZOLLERN dynasty, which acquired the electorate of Brandenburg in 1415. Their gradually increasing power consolidated the status of Berlin as the capital of Brandenburg in the 16th century. FREDERICK WILLIAM (r. 1640–88), known as the Great Elector, induced artisans and merchants to settle in the city, added new districts, and laid out the central area, including the avenue Unter den Linden. The Jewish community was established in 1671, and large numbers of French Huguenots fleeing per-

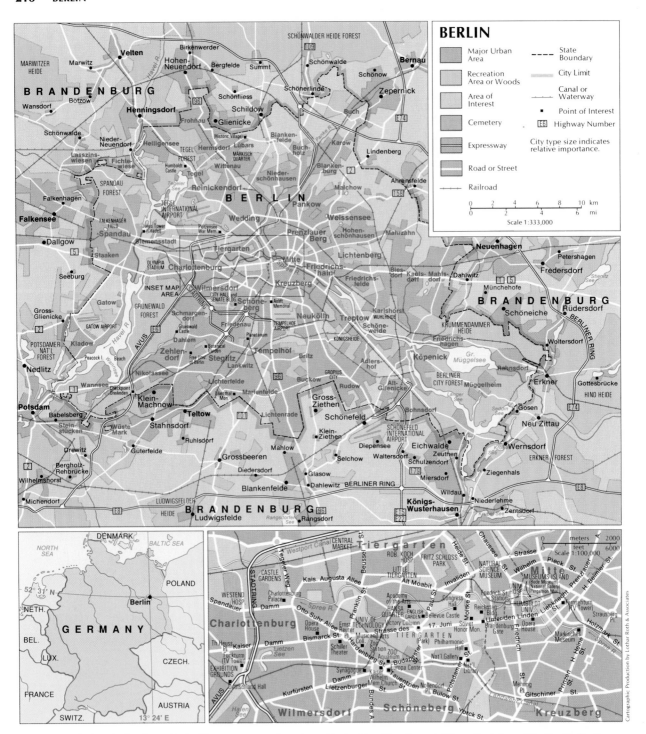

secution settled in Berlin. By 1720 the Huguenots constituted 20 percent of the city's population. Under FREDERICK I (r. 1688–1713), Berlin was united with Kölln and three other towns and became the capital of the new Kingdom of Prussia. Frederick built the city's elegant Charlottenburg Palace.

In the reign of Frederick II (the Great, r. 1740–86), Berlin emerged as a major European city. By 1781 it had 147,000 inhabitants and was known as "Athens on the Spree" because of its concentration of artists and scholars. It became the capital of Germany in 1871 and flourished in the age of imperial Germany (1871–1918) and the Weimar Republic (1919–33). Its scientific establishment boasted such luminaries as Robert

Koch, Max Planck, and Albert Einstein, while the Berlin theater was distinguished by the work of Gerhart Hauptmann, Max Reinhardt, and Bertolt Brecht. In the visual arts the city was the home of the Berlin Dada group. In 1920 the surrounding towns and villages merged with the city to form Greater Berlin, with a population of 4 million.

Berlin suffered great destruction during World War II, and the damage, especially in the east, took decades to repair. The life of the postwar city was marked by dramatic episodes such as the BERLIN AIRLIFT (1948–49), and the building of the Berlin Wall (1961), which practically cut off communication between the eastern and western sectors. When the GDR opened its borders in 1989, thousands of East Berliners thronged through openings in the Wall to the West. The emotional and highly publicized reunion that followed presaged the reunification of Germany that took place less than a year later.   SUSAN STEINER

Bibliography: Borneman, John, *After the Wall* (1991); Clelland, Doug, ed., *Berlin: An Architectural History* (1984); Darnton, Robert, *Berlin Journals* (1991); Otto, Friedrich, *Before the Deluge: A Portrait of Berlin in the Twenties* (1974; repr. 1986).

Berlin, Congress of

The Congress of Berlin convened on June 13, 1878, under the presidency of Germany's chancellor, Otto von BISMARCK, to restore the diplomatic balance of power following the RUSSO-TURKISH WAR of 1877–78. The Treaty of San Stefano (Mar. 3, 1878), which ended that war, had significantly increased Russian influence in the Balkans and thereby aroused the opposition of the other European powers. In addition to Germany, Austria-Hungary, Britain, France, Italy, Russia, and Turkey were represented at the Congress.

By the Treaty of Berlin (July 13, 1878), the San Stefano creation of Greater Bulgaria, an independent state supported by Russia, was replaced by a smaller Bulgaria under the suzerainty of the Ottoman sultan. Russia received southern Bessarabia from Romania and Kars, Ardahan, and Batum from Turkey. Serbia, Montenegro, and Romania acquired additional territory, along with full independence from the Ottoman Empire. Austria obtained the right to "occupy and administer" BOSNIA AND HERCEGOVINA but not the power to annex it from Turkey.   S. VICTOR PAPACOSMA

Bibliography: Medlicott, W. N., *The Congress of Berlin and After*, 2d ed. (1963).

Berlin, Free University of

The Free University of Berlin (enrollment: 55,000; library: 1,709,000 volumes) was founded (1948) in West Berlin by the non-Communist faculty and students of Friedrich Wilhelm University when Berlin was divided after World War II and Friedrich Wilhelm fell in the Communist zone. The Free University of Berlin is an independent coeducational institution with a full range of both scholarly and professional curricula.

Berlin, Irving

Irving Berlin, b. Tyumen, Russia, May 11, 1888, d. Sept. 22, 1989, dominated the world of American popular music for half a century. Of his 1,500 songs, for which he wrote both music and lyrics, several have become classics. Among them are "God Bless America," "White Christmas," "Easter Parade," "All Alone," and "Alexander's Ragtime Band." "White Christmas" won an Oscar in 1942. *Yip, Yip, Yaphank* (1918) and *This Is the Army* (1942), shows that he wrote and produced with all-soldier casts during the two world wars, earned

Irving Berlin, a Russian-born American composer-lyricist who specialized in developing musical scores for stage productions, entertained generations of Americans with such show tunes as "Oh, How I Hate to Get Up in the Morning" (1918) and "There's No Business Like Show Business" (1946). He was 101 when he died in 1989.

millions for war charities. For *This Is the Army* he was decorated with the Medal of Merit. Screen musicals with Berlin's songs include *Top Hat* (1935), *Easter Parade* (1948), *Blue Skies* (1946), and *White Christmas* (1954). Among his most successful Broadway musicals are the *Music Box Revues* (1921–24), *As Thousands Cheer* (1933), and *Annie Get Your Gun* (1946).
                                                    DAVID EWEN

Bibliography: Bergreen, Laurence, *As Thousands Cheer* (1990); Whitcomb, Ian, *Irving Berlin and Ragtime America* (1988); Woollcott, Alexander, *The Story of Irving Berlin* (1925; repr. 1982).

Berlin, Sir Isaiah

Isaiah Berlin, b. Riga, Latvia, June 6, 1909, is an important British philosopher and educator. Immigrating to Britain with his parents in 1920, he studied at Oxford University and taught there most of his life, serving as Chichele Professor of Social and Political Theory (1957–67) and president of Wolfson College (1966–75). He worked at the British Embassy in Washington, D.C., during World War II. His works include *Karl Marx: His Life and Environment*, 4th ed. (1978); *The Hedgehog and the Fox: An Essay on Tolstoy's View of History* (1953); *Historical Inevitability* (1954), a criticism of determinism in history; *Four Essays on Liberty* (1969); *Against the Current* (1979); *Personal Impressions* (1980); and *The Crooked Timber of Humanity* (1991). He was knighted in 1957.

Berlin Airlift

The Berlin Airlift was carried out from June 1948 to September 1949, when Britain and the United States flew more than 2 million tons of supplies to Berlin. The airlift was in response to a Soviet blockade of the city, precipitated by tension over the Western Allies' decision to unify the zones of Germany they had occupied following World War II.

Bibliography: Jackson, Bob, *The Berlin Airlift* (1988); Shlaim, Avi, *The United States and the Berlin Blockade, 1948–1949* (1983).

Berlin Philharmonic Orchestra

The Berlin Philharmonic Orchestra is considered one of the most accomplished in the world. It was founded in 1882 when 54 musicians seceded from Benjamin Bilse's Orchestra to play in a former roller-skating rink and were given the name Philharmonisches Orchester. Since then, the orchestra has always been associated with leading conductors. In 1887, Hans von BÜLOW became the permanent conductor, creating a model of symphonic interpretation. The composer Richard STRAUSS was in charge in the season 1894–95; next the Philharmonic was taken over by Arthur NIKISCH, who introduced the music of Anton Bruckner and Gustav Mahler to the repertoire. In 1922, Wilhelm FURTWÄNGLER succeeded Nikisch. From 1954 to 1989 Herbert von KARAJAN headed the orchestra; he was succeeded by Claudio ABBADO.   STEPHANIE VON BUCHAU

Berlin Wall

With the aim of preventing East Germans from seeking asylum in the West, the East German government in 1961 began constructing a system of concrete and barbed-wire barriers between East and West Berlin. This Berlin Wall endured for nearly 30 years, a symbol not only of the division of Germany but of the larger conflict between the Communist and non-Communist worlds. The wall ceased to be a barrier when East Germany ended restrictions on emigration in November 1989. The wall was largely dismantled in the year preceding the reunification of Germany.

Bibliography: Gelb, Norman, *The Berlin Wall* (1987); Merritt, R. L. and A. J., eds., *Living with the Wall* (1985).

Berlin Zoo

The Berlin Zoo is the oldest zoo in Germany. Located in West Berlin, it was opened in 1844. It leads all zoos worldwide in number of species, having more than 2,000 represented by more than 13,000 specimens. The zoo is noted for its arrangement of exhibits according to taxonomic classification.

Berliner, Emile   [bur'-li-nur, ay-meel']

The German-born American inventor and philanthropist Emile Berliner, b. May 20, 1851, d. Aug. 3, 1929, is generally credited with the invention of the telephone receiver (1877) and the disk recording system (1887), which he called the gramophone. This system, and the companies he helped found to exploit it, became the basis for the modern SOUND RECORDING industry. In his later years Berliner devoted himself to child health and nutrition, particularly to the promotion of milk pasteurization.   ROBERT LONG

Bibliography: Wile, Frederic William, *Emile Berliner* (1926; repr. 1974).

Berliner Ensemble   [bair-lee'-nur]

The Berliner Ensemble is a theater company founded in 1949 by Bertolt BRECHT. It was formed following the success that same year of his and Erich Engel's production of MOTHER COURAGE. Financed by the government of East Germany, it was managed for 22 years by Brecht's wife, actress Helene WEIGEL, with Brecht serving on the artistic advisory board. It acquired the 727-seat Theater am Schiffbauerdamm in 1954.

Mother Courage, *by Bertolt Brecht, was among the highly regarded plays included in the repertoire of the Berliner Ensemble. Founded in 1949, the Berliner Ensemble was administered as part of East Germany's Deutsches Theater until 1954 but later became independent.*

The ensemble's international reputation stems from the period of 1954–56, when its productions of *Mother Courage* and *The Caucasian Chalk Circle* were performed in the theater capitals of Paris and London. Ensemble productions are noted for their brilliant lighting, functional and starkly beautiful sets, direction, and casting of atypical heroes and heroines. After Brecht's death in 1956 the ensemble continued to flourish under his younger disciples, led by Manfred Wekwerth, but it declined after 1969. Although it has lost many of its best directors and actors, the Berliner Ensemble still affords the finest examples of Brecht's own production style.

Bibliography: Berlau, Ruth, *Living for Brecht* (1985; Eng. trans., 1987); Patterson, Michael, *German Theatre Today* (1978).

Berlinguer, Enrico   [bair-ling-gwayr', en-ree'-koh]

Enrico Berlinguer, b. May 25, 1922, d. June 11, 1984, a leader of the Italian Communist party, was a prominent advocate of the variant on traditional COMMUNISM called Eurocommunism. He joined the Communist party in 1943 and became a member of its executive in 1948. He entered the Italian Chamber of Deputies in 1968, became the party's assistant secretary in 1969, and was elected secretary general in 1972. As leader of the opposition party, Berlinguer worked for what he called a "historic compromise" between the Christian Democrats and the Communists.

Bibliography: Kertzer, D., *Comrades and Christians* (1980); Serfaty, S., and Gray, L., eds., *The Italian Communist Party* (1980).

Berlioz, Hector   [bair'-lee-ohz]

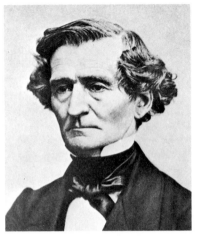

Hector Berlioz, the French romantic composer, conductor, and critic, is known for his delight in massive sounds produced by huge performing groups, as in his Requiem *(1837). Berlioz was a pioneer in the field of orchestration, and his 1844 treatise on the subject greatly influenced later composers.*

The French composer Louis Hector Berlioz, b. Dec. 11, 1803, d. Mar. 8, 1869, was one of the most important musical figures of the romantic era. His large-scale, brilliantly orchestrated compositions helped create the modern orchestra, and his musical ideas and innovations greatly influenced the development of 19th-century music.

Berlioz was sent to Paris by his father in 1821 to study medicine. Inspired by the operas of Christoph Willibald Gluck, he also studied music, first privately with the composer Jean François Lesueur and then in 1826 at the conservatory with Anton Reicha, a respected professor of counterpoint. After four ill-fated attempts, Berlioz received the prestigious Prix de Rome in 1830 with his cantata *Sardanapalus.* This permitted a sojourn in Rome at government expense.

That same year he was enthusiastically acclaimed for his first major work, the *Symphonie fantastique,* a musical description of the opium-induced reveries of a frustrated artist. It was inspired by Berlioz's intense adoration of the Irish actress Harriet Smithson (whom he married in 1833) and Thomas De Quincey's *Confessions of an English Opium Eater.* It is one of the most influential programmatic works of the 19th century. The symphony is in five movements instead of the classical four and is unified by Berlioz's novel use of a short, recurrent theme (*idée fixe*), which symbolizes the presence of the "loved one" and is heard throughout the composition.

For other ideas, Berlioz frequently turned to the works of Shakespeare and contemporary writers and poets. *Harold in Italy* (1834), best termed a symphony with viola solo, is based on Byron's *Childe Harold.* The *Damnation of Faust* (1846) is based on Goethe's poem, and Berlioz's song cycle *Les Nuits d'éte* stems from poems by Théophile Gautier.

The *Requiem* (1837), characteristic of Berlioz's grand musical conceptions, is an overwhelming work for large orchestra that includes 110 violins, an augmented brass section, 16 timpani, and more than 200 voices. Commissioned by the French government and well received, it did not compensate for the depressing rejections of his operas. *Benvenuto Cellini* (1838) was a total failure. *Les Troyens* (1856–59) was never performed in its entirety during Berlioz's lifetime.

Despite the support of such influential figures as Giacomo Meyerbeer, Berlioz's grand compositions—which required enormous choruses and orchestras vastly larger than the conventional 60-odd players—aroused mockery and misunderstanding in France.

In 1867, Berlioz returned in poor health from his last conducting tour in Russia. After a lengthy illness he died in Paris, having passed his last years in growing bitterness and loneliness after the deaths of his second wife, the singer Marie Recio, and his son Louis.

By his almost magical manipulation and understanding of individual instruments, Berlioz greatly increased the expressive capabilities of the orchestra, and his unorthodox musical structures and meters helped free composers from restrictive classical forms. Numerous French composers, among them Camille Saint-Saëns, Charles Gounod, and Paul Dukas, in addition to Wagner, Liszt, Gustav Mahler, and Richard Strauss, who revised Berlioz's treatise on instrumentation in 1905, are indebted to his vision.

Bibliography: Barzun, Jacques, *Berlioz and His Century* (1982); Berlioz, Hector, *Memoirs*, ed. and trans. by David Cairns (1969); Elliott, J. H., *Berlioz*, rev. ed. (1967); Holoman, D. K., *Berlioz* (1989); Primmer, Brian, *The Berlioz Style* (1973; repr. 1983); Rushton, Julian, *The Musical Language of Berlioz* (1984); Warrack, John, ed., *The New Grove Early Romantic Masters*, vol. 2 (1985).

Berlitz Schools of Languages   [bur-lits']

The Berlitz Schools of Languages pioneered the conversational approach to language teaching. The first Berlitz School was founded (1878) in Providence, R.I., by Maximilian D. Berlitz (1852–1921), a native of Germany. More than 320 Berlitz schools now exist in more than 30 countries throughout the world.   F. P. DINNEEN, S.J.

berm

The berm is the nearly horizontal portion of exposed beach that is formed by waves depositing their sand load as they dissipate on the beach. The size of the berm commonly varies with the season. It is largest in summer. Wave erosion reduces its size in winter, moving sand to the offshore bars. In summer, sand moves onshore again, and the berm becomes wider.
                                                                    PAUL D. KOMAR

Bibliography: Komar, P. D., *Beach Processes and Sedimentation* (1976); Bascom, W., *Waves and Beaches* (1980).

See also: BEACH AND COAST; WATER WAVES.

Berman, Eugene

Eugene Berman, b. Nov. 4, 1899, d. Dec. 14, 1972, was a Russian-American painter and scene designer of the neoromantic school that flourished in the 1920s in reaction against what was considered the dogmatic abstraction of the School of Paris. Berman's paintings are mostly dreamlike landscapes pervaded by an atmosphere of melancholy and strangeness reminiscent of Giorgio de Chirico's early works; they are usually peopled with brooding, sorrowful figures. Today Berman is remembered best for his outstanding designs for the ballet and opera, most notably the four commissioned by the Metropolitan Opera in New York: *Rigoletto* (1951), *La Forza del destino* (1952), *Don Giovanni* (1957), and *Otello* (1962).
                                                                    IRMA B. JAFFE

Bibliography: Aronson, Arnold, *American Set Design* (1985); Berman, Eugene, *Eugene Berman*, ed. by Julien Levy (1947).

Berman, Lazar

The Russian pianist Lazar Berman, b. 1930, has been likened to the great virtuoso pianist Vladimir Horowitz. He studied at the Central Music School in Moscow under Aleksandr Goldenweiser and at the Moscow Conservatory under Vladimir Sofronitsky. Before his U.S. debut in 1976, he toured Eastern Europe and the USSR and appeared in Belgium, Italy, and England. His repertoire includes Liszt, Chopin, and Beethoven in addition to the Russian masters.   ELLA A. MALIN

Bermuda

Bermuda is a self-governing British colony located in the Atlantic Ocean about 965 km (600 mi) east of Cape Hatteras. The colony has a population of 60,700 (1993 est.). It consists of a 35-km-long (22-mi) chain of more than 300 small islands with an area of 54 km² (21 mi²). The largest of the islands, Bermuda or Main Island, is 23 km (14 mi) long and is connected by bridges to the other important islands—Somerset, Boaz, Ireland, St. George's, and St. David's. Named after its

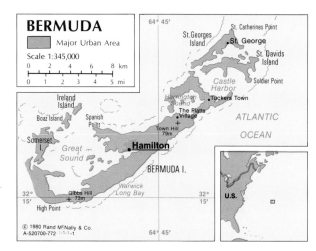

discoverer, Juan Bermudez, Bermuda has a mild climate and colonial charm that make it a major tourist resort.

The 20 inhabited islands of Bermuda are generally low, gently undulating limestone platforms covered with beautiful vegetation. Their coral origin has made the beaches famous and is evident in the distinctive pastel building materials used on the islands. The annual mean temperature is about 21° C (70° F), and rainfall averages 1,450 mm (57 in). The islands have no rivers or lakes, so the inhabitants depend on rain for water. Several hotels have their own desalinization plants, and houses are constructed with gutters and pipes leading from the roofs to underground tanks. More than half the people are descendants of slaves brought from Africa during the 18th century. The white population is mostly British, and English is the main language. The economy is tourist-oriented, with offshore banking and insurance growing industries in the 1990s. Commercial fishing and agriculture are of minor importance. Hamilton, the capital, and St. George are the major towns.

After its discovery in 1503, Bermuda remained unsettled until 1609, when British colonists landed there. It formally became a British colony in 1684. In 1815 the capital was transferred from St. George to Hamilton. The economy thrived as the tourist industry grew rapidly in the 20th century. Bermuda has exercised internal self-government since 1968; there is a directly elected 40-member House of Assembly. In 1973 the British military intervened when the governor was assassinated during civil disorders over independence, and subsequently racial tensions led to further unrest. After 1977, however, calm was restored as the government strove to eliminate racial discrimination. Thereafter, with black political power increasing, racial tensions tended to ease.   THOMAS D. BOSWELL

Bibliography: LaBrucherie, Roger A., *Images of Bermuda*, rev. ed. (1989); Tucker, Terry, *Bermuda Today and Yesterday*, 2d ed. (1979), and *Islands of Bermuda* (1970); Wilkinson, H. C., *The Adventures of Bermuda* (1976).

Bermuda Triangle

The Bermuda Triangle, also called the Devil's Triangle, is an area of the Atlantic Ocean off southeast Florida, where the disappearance of ships and airplanes on a number of occasions has led to speculation about unexplainable turbulences and other atmospheric disturbances. Violent storms and downward air currents frequently occur there, but studies have not revealed any significant peculiarities about the area in question.

Boundaries of the Bermuda Triangle have been formed by drawing an imaginary line from Melbourne, Fla., to Bermuda, to Puerto Rico, and back to Florida. These apparent boundaries vary widely, however, among writers trying to establish a Bermuda Triangle "mystery" by incorporating farther-ranging disappearances in their accounts.

Bibliography: Kusche, L. D., *The Bermuda Triangle: Mystery Solved* (1975).

Bern

Bern (also Berne) is the capital of Switzerland and of Bern canton. It is located in the northwestern part of the country on the Aare River, about 95 km (60 mi) southwest of Zurich. A commercial and administrative center with some industry, Bern has a population of 140,612 (1985 est.), most of which is German-speaking and Protestant. The city is the headquarters of several international organizations, and its industries include chemicals, machinery, textiles, and chocolate. The notable landmarks of the old section—the cathedral (begun 1421), city hall (1406–16), Nydegg Church (1494), and the famous Clock Tower (16th century)—attract many tourists. Several museums and a university (1834) are also located there.

Founded in 1191 by Berthold V, duke of Zähringen, Bern became an imperial free city in 1218 and grew quickly into a prospering trade center. After joining the Swiss Confederation in 1353, it began to acquire surrounding territories and, by the turn of the 18th century, held most of the Bernese Alps region. The French-speaking Jura region was added to the canton in 1815. In 1848, Bern became the capital of the Swiss Confederation.

Bernadette, Saint   [bur-nuh-det']

Bernadette Soubirous, b. Jan. 7, 1844, d. Apr. 16, 1879, was a French visionary who claimed to receive 18 apparitions of the Virgin Mary in a cave near Lourdes in 1858. According to Bernadette, the Virgin identified herself by saying: "I am the IMMACULATE CONCEPTION." A spring of water at the site of the apparitions has since attracted millions of pilgrims because of its reputed healing powers. Bernadette, after suffering a period of painful publicity, entered a convent at Nevers, France, where she remained until her death. She was canonized in 1933. Feast day: Feb. 18.

Bibliography: Christiani, Leon, *Saint Bernadette* (1981); Trouncer, Margaret, *Life of Saint Bernadette* (1958).

Bernadotte, Count Folke   [bair-nah-dawt', fawl'-ke]

Count Bernadotte, b. Jan. 2, 1895, was a Swedish diplomat and nephew of King Gustav V of Sweden. Active in the Swedish Red Cross, during World War II he arranged an exchange of injured British and German prisoners of war. In 1945 he carried to the Western Allies a German proposal for surrender that would have allowed Germany to continue the war against Russia. It was rejected. Bernadotte was chosen (May 20, 1948) to be United Nations mediator for Palestine. He was assassinated by Israeli extremists on Sept. 17, 1948.

Bibliography: Bernadotte Af Wisborg, Folke G., *To Jerusalem* (1951; repr. 1975); Hewins, Ralph, *The Life of Folke Bernadotte* (1950).

Bernadotte, Jean Baptiste Jules: see CHARLES XIV JOHN, KING OF SWEDEN.

Bernanos, Georges   [bair-nah-naws', zhawrzh]

Georges Bernanos, b. Feb. 20, 1888, d. July 5, 1948, was a French novelist, journalist, and polemicist best known for his novels, in which he called for a renewal of spirituality and sincerity in a materialistic world. His *Under the Sun of Satan* (1926; Eng. trans., 1949), *The Diary of a Country Priest* (1936; Eng. trans., 1937; film, 1951), and *The Open Mind* (1943; Eng. trans., 1945) present original and frightening visions of humankind lost in evil and boredom. In his polemical writings, such as *A Diary of My Times* (1938; Eng. trans., 1938) and *La France contre les robots* (France against the Robots, 1944), Bernanos decried the loss of freedom and honor in modern civilization. His last work, a play about the execution of a group of nuns during the French Revolution, *Dialogues des Carmélites* (1949; Eng. trans. as *The Fearless Heart*, 1952), was made into an opera by Francis POULENC in 1957.

Bibliography: Blumenthal, Gerda, *The Poetic Imagination of Georges Bernanos* (1965); Bush, William, *Georges Bernanos* (1975); Hebblethwaite, P., *Bernanos* (1965); Speaight, R., *Georges Bernanos* (1974).

Bernard, Claude   [bair-nar', klohd]

The French physiologist Claude Bernard, b. July 12, 1813, d. Feb. 10, 1878, is considered the founder of experimental physiology and experimental pharmacology. He believed that the body has mechanisms by which it seeks to maintain a stable internal environment despite changes in the external environment. In 1851, Bernard discovered that the nervous system, in response to internal cold, sends messages to the blood vessels to constrict in order to conserve body heat. Bernard found that most absorption and some digestion take place in the small intestine, that secretions of the pancreas play a role in fat digestion, and that the liver has an important glycogenic function. He also showed how the drug curare works in the body to produce its effect. His *Introduction to the Study of Experimental Medicine* (1865) is a science classic.

Bibliography: Olmstead, J. M. D. and E. H., *Claude Bernard and the Experimental Method in Medicine* (1952); Tarshis, Jerome, *Claude Bernard: Father of Experimental Medicine* (1968); Virtanen, Reino, *Claude Bernard and His Place in the History of Ideas* (1960).

Bernard, Jean Jacques

Jean Jacques Bernard, b. July 30, 1888, d. Sept. 12, 1972, the son of author Tristan Bernard, was a French dramatist. His plays, such as *Le Feu qui reprend mal* (The Fire Catches Badly, 1922) and *Le Printemps des autres* (Others' Springtime, 1924), reveal indirectly the subconscious hopes and fears of their characters, making use of psychoanalytic theories in a mode he called "drama of the unexpressed."

Bernard, Tristan

Tristan Bernard, b. Sept. 7, 1866, d. Dec. 7, 1947, a French dramatist, lawyer, journalist, and industrialist, is remembered for his comedies, farces, and vaudeville sketches, in which he gently satirized French bourgeois life at the turn of the 20th century. *L'Anglais tel qu'on le parle* (English As It Is Spoken, 1899) and *Le petit café* (The Small Café, 1911), prime examples of his numerous plays, are witty and humorous period pieces.   JOSEPH A. REITER

Bernard M. Baruch College: see NEW YORK, CITY UNIVERSITY OF

Bernard of Clairvaux, Saint   [bur-nard', klair-voh']

Bernard of Clairvaux, b. 1090, d. Aug. 20, 1153, was a French churchman, mystic, and doctor of the church. A major moral and spiritual leader of the Western Church in the 12th century, he became a Cistercian monk in 1113 and was chosen abbot of Clairvaux, a daughter house of Cîteaux, in 1115. Although Bernard did not reject the idea of rationalism in theology, he became the major opponent of rationalist theologians who, in his view, threatened religious orthodoxy. He attacked, and sought the condemnation of the teachings of, Peter ABELARD at the Council of Soissons (1121) and again at the Council of Sens (1140).

Bernard was a trusted advisor of popes and kings and a leading proponent of the Second CRUSADE. He also contributed heavily to the rules for the Order of the Knights TEMPLARS, which he hoped would become a model of Christian chivalry. He was active in papal affairs as early as 1130 and was instrumental in developing opinion in favor of Pope Innocent II and discrediting the antipope Anacletus II in the disputed election that followed the death (1130) of Honorius II. He denounced the political schemes of ARNOLD OF BRESCIA, an Italian monk and reformer, in Rome and produced a treatise on papal power in Christian society for Eugenius III in 1148.

His many writings, translated and collected in six volumes, reveal a solid grasp of biblical studies, spiritual theology, and philosophy. One of the most outstanding medieval works on mysticism is, in fact, his *De diligendo Deo*. He was canonized in 1174 and was formally recognized as a doctor of the church in 1830. Feast day: Aug. 20.   DAVID HARRY MILLER

Bibliography: Evans, G. R., *The Mind of St. Bernard of Clairvaux* (1983); James, Bruno Scott, *St. Bernard of Clairvaux: An Essay in Biography* (1957); Walker, Adrian, *St. Bernard of Clairvaux* (1960); Williams, Watkin, *St. Bernard of Clairvaux* (1935).

Bernardes, Diogo   [bur-nahr'-deesh, dee-oh'-goh]

Diogo Bernardes, c.1540–96, was a major poet of the Portuguese Renaissance. His lyrical pastoral verse, frequently set in his native Ponte da Barca, near the Lima River, shows the influence of his countryman Francisco de Sá de Miranda. Bernardes was second only to Luis de Camões in constructing Italianate verse forms. His devotional poems, *Várias rimas ao bom Jesus* (Poems on the Good Jesus), are among the finest Portuguese religious works.

Bibliography: Bell, A. F., *Portuguese Literature* (1922; repr. 1970); Vidigal, B., ed., *Oxford Book of Portuguese Verse*, 2d ed. (1953).

Bernart de Ventadorn   [bair-nahr' duh vahn-tah-dohrn']

Bernart de Ventadorn, fl. c.1150–90, is generally considered the greatest of the Provençal troubadour poets. His love lyrics, of which 40 survive, are remarkable for their clarity of style and mastery of form. The son of a servant at the castle of Ventadorn, he was encouraged by Viscount Eble and later joined the court of Eleanor of Aquitaine. At the end of his life, after serving the count of Toulouse, he retired to the monastery of Dalon.

See also: PROVENÇAL LITERATURE.

Bernese mountain dog   [bur-neez']

The Bernese mountain dog, a working breed, was used by the merchants of Berne to pull wagons loaded with goods to market.

The Bernese mountain dog is a rare working breed of substantial muscular build. The male stands 58.4–70 cm (23–27.5 in) at the shoulder, with females slightly smaller; the weight is 23–32 kg (50–70 lb). The soft, slightly wavy coat is solid black, with deep russet or tan markings on the forelegs and muzzle and over each eye. For show purposes, white markings on the feet, tail tip, muzzle, and chest are desirable.

More than 2,000 years ago Roman soldiers brought the breed's predecessors into Switzerland, where the Bernese was developed into an all-purpose draft animal by weavers in the canton of Berne. The breed was recognized by the American Kennel Club in 1937. Bernese are hardy and require minimal grooming.   JOHN D. MANDEVILLE

Bibliography: American Kennel Club, *The Complete Dog Book*, 17th ed. (1985).

Bernhard, Thomas

The Austrian novelist and playwright Thomas Bernhard, b. Feb. 10, 1931, d. Feb. 12, 1989, was the author of profoundly pessimistic works, many of them leavened by black humor. Bernhard is often compared with Franz Kafka and Samuel Beckett, both for his use of surrealist techniques and for his dense, headlong prose. His novels include *Gargoyle* (1967; Eng. trans., 1970), *The Lime Works* (1970; Eng. trans., 1973), *Correction* (1975; Eng. trans., 1979), *Concrete* (1982; Eng. trans., 1984), and *Woodcutter* (1984; Eng. trans., 1988). *Gathering Evidence*, an autobiography composed of five separate memoirs, was published in translation in 1986.

Bernhard of Lippe-Biesterfeld

Prince Bernhard of Lippe-Biesterfeld, b. Germany, June 29, 1911, is the consort of JULIANA, former queen of the Netherlands, and father of the present queen, BEATRICE. Married in 1937, Bernhard fought against the invading Germans in 1940 and was named commander of the Dutch resistance fighters who helped liberate the Netherlands in 1944–45. After Juliana became (1948) queen, he worked to encourage international trade. In 1976 he was implicated in a bribery scandal and resigned from his military and business positions.

Bernhardt, Sarah   [bair-nahr']

Sarah Bernhardt was the stage name of the French actress Sarah Henriette Rosine, b. Paris, Oct. 22, 1844, d. Mar. 26, 1923, whom many consider one of the greatest performers of all time. The illegitimate daughter of a Parisian courtesan, she began her training at the age of 13 and in 1862 made her debut at the Comédie Française in Jean Racine's *Iphigénie en Aulide*. She first came to notice in 1869 at the Théâtre de l'Odéon in François Coppée's *Le Passant* (The Passerby). After the Franco-Prussian War, during which she turned the Odéon into a military hospital, she became a star as the queen in Victor Hugo's *Ruy Blas*, as Doña Sol in his *Hernani*, and as Phèdre in Racine's classic drama. While at the Comédie Française she also had notable successes as Chérubin in Beaumarchais's *Marriage of Figaro* and in the title role of Racine's *Andromaque*. She made her London debut in 1879 in *Phèdre*. The following year she made her triumphant New York debut in *Adrienne Lecouvreur*, and during the next four decades she toured the United States nine times. In 1880, after years of quarreling with the conservative management of the Comédie Française, she left that theater.

Bernhardt had an extraordinarily beautiful voice, perfect diction, and an astonishing emotional range as a performer. Her slim figure and dark eyes made her especially suited for roles requiring seductiveness. She also excelled in expressing pain, tearful rage, and the throes of death. She herself managed several Paris theaters after 1893 and in 1899 reopened the Théâtre des Nations as the Théâtre Sarah Bernhardt, where she starred both in revivals and in new works. Her greatest performances there and elsewhere included lead

Sarah Bernhardt, the great stage actress of the 19th century, is shown as a teenager in this photograph taken about 1862, the year she joined the Comédie Française. She was also a poet, and wrote several plays in which she took leading roles.

roles in the plays *Fédora*, *Théodora*, and *La Tosca*, all written for her by Victorien SARDOU; *Lorenzaccio* by Alfred de MUSSET; *La Dame aux camélias* (The Lady of the Camelias) by DUMAS *fils*; *L'Aiglon* (The Eaglet) by Edmond ROSTAND; and *Hamlet*. She also painted, sculpted, and wrote poetry, a novel (*The Idol of Paris*, 1920; Eng. trans., 1921), and plays, including *L'Aveu* (The Confession, 1898) and *Un Coeur d'homme* (A Man's Heart, 1909). She performed all over Europe, North and South America, Australia, and Egypt. Her personal life was unconventional, and she was expert at creating and maintaining a fascinating public image. For instance, she was reputed to sleep in a coffin she carried with her. Even after her right leg was amputated in 1915 as a result of a fall, she continued to act. She published her autobiography, *Memories of My Life* (1907; Eng. trans., 1907), and *L'Art du théâtre* (Art of the Theater, 1923), a treatise on acting.   ANDREW J. KELLY

Bibliography: Agate, May, *Madame Sarah* (1945); Baring, Maurice, *Sarah Bernhardt* (1934); Richardson, Joanna, *Sarah Bernhardt and Her World* (1977); Salmon, Eric, ed., *Bernhardt and the Theatre of Her Time* (1984); Skinner, Cornelia Otis, *Madame Sarah* (1966); Taranow, Gerda, *Sarah Bernhardt: The Art within the Legend* (1972).

Bernini, Giovanni Lorenzo

Giovanni Lorenzo Bernini, b. Dec. 7, 1598, d. Nov. 28, 1680, was one of the most original, versatile, and prolific masters of Italian baroque art. Born in Naples, he was the son of the Florentine sculptor Pietro Bernini, who brought his family to Rome in 1605; except for a journey to Paris in 1665, the younger Bernini worked as an architect, painter, and sculptor in Rome for the rest of his life.

Sculpture and Painting. Bernini began work as a sculptor; his first surviving pieces, dating from 1615-17, are skillful but in his father's Mannerist style. With his subsequent works, *Neptune* and *Triton* (1620; Victoria and Albert Museum, London), and the three masterpieces in Rome's Villa Borghese—*Rape of Proserpina* (1621-22), *David* (1623), and *Apollo and Daphne* (1622-25)—he created a new form of sculpture, marked by the realism of its detail, its immediacy of expression, its presentation of a particular moment of action, and, above all, a concern for the perspective and reaction of the viewer. All of Bernini's sculpture displays these characteristics, as, for example, his dramatic and realistic portraits—*Scipione Borghese* (1632; Villa Borghese, Rome) and *Francesco I d'Este* (1650-51; Galleria Estense, Modena)—and the elaborate papal tombs, for Urban VIII (1628-47) and Alexander VII (1671-78) in Saint Peter's Basilica in Rome. In the Cornaro Chapel of the Church of Santa Maria della Vittoria in Rome, Bernini created his *Ecstasy of Saint Teresa* (1645-52), a complex, theatrical ensemble incorporating painting, sculpture, and architecture.

Giovanni Lorenzo Bernini's Self-Portrait (c.1623) is a painting of the artist as a young man. The portrait is one of the few authenticated paintings by Bernini, who is best known as a sculptor and architect. (Borghese Gallery, Rome.)

The Ecstasy of St. Teresa (1645-52) by Bernini portrays the saint at the moment of an ecstatic vision. Bernini combined sculpture, painting, and architecture in the life-size marble work in the Cornaro Chapel, Church of Santa Maria della Vittoria, Rome.

Little of Bernini's painting has survived, but his ideas on decoration, as carried out by other artists, for example, Giovanni Battista GAULLI in his opulent ceiling (1674-79) for the Church of the Gesù in Rome, were to influence all subsequent baroque and rococo monumental painting.

Architecture. In 1624 Bernini began work on the immense bronze baldachino, or canopy (finished 1633), for the high altar of Saint Peter's Basilica, directly over the saint's tomb; it is one of the richest monuments of baroque art. In the apse of the basilica, beyond the baldachino, Bernini and his assistants erected the gigantic Altar of the Chair, or Cathedra Petri (1657-66), enshrining the chair of Saint Peter in a spectacular composition that makes it the focal point of the church.

Bernini also built a number of more traditional structures. His churches include, among others, Santa Bibiana (1624-26), Rome, Santa Maria dell' Assunzione (1662-64), Ariccia, and the oval Sant' Andrea al Quirinale (1658-70), Rome. Among his secular buildings, the Palazzo Montecitorio (c.1650; completed by Carlo FONTANA) and the Palazzo Chigi-Odescalchi (1664-67) are outstanding. Bernini's fame from such works undoubtedly led to Louis XIV's invitation to come to Paris in 1665. Bernini's designs for the Louvre were never used, but they became so well known that they exerted considerable influence on later architects. Bernini also designed several fountains for Rome; the most impressive, and the largest, is the Fountain of the Four Rivers (1648-51) in the Piazza Navona.

In 1656, Bernini began his last and grandest project, the piazza fronting Saint Peter's Basilica. The piazza is laid out as an oval, rimmed with arcades of columns four deep, in the original plan running completely around the piazza; the central part of the colonnade was never built. Bernini subtly disguises the nonalignment of the central obelisk, the facade, and the nave, and provides a visual balance for Carlo MADERNO's awesome church facade by flanking it with clifflike trapezoidal walls. The effect is one of "the embracing arms of the church," in Bernini's words. Like all of Bernini's buildings, it had a lasting influence on European architecture.

DAVID CAST

Bibliography: Baldinucci, Filippo, *The Life of Bernini*, trans. by Catherine Engess (1966); Bauer, George C., *Bernini in Perspective* (1967); Borsi, Franco, *Bernini* (1985); Gould, Cecil, *Bernini in France: An Episode in Seventeenth-Century History* (1982); Lavin, Irving, *Bernini and the Crossing of Saint Peter's* (1968) and, as ed., *Gianlorenzo Bernini: New Aspects of His Art and Thought* (1985); Wallace, Robert, *The World of Bernini* (1970); Wittkower, Rodolf, *Gian Lorenzo Bernini, the Sculptor of the Roman Baroque*, 2d ed. (1966; repr. 1981).

Bernoulli, Daniel   [bur-noo'-lee]

The Dutch-born Swiss mathematician Daniel Bernoulli, b. Feb. 8, 1700, d. Mar. 17, 1782, was a son of Johann Bernoulli (1667–1748) and the nephew of Jacques BERNOULLI, both important mathematicians. In his youth he studied philosophy and logic; his great interest, however, was in mathematics and mechanics.

In 1725 he and his brother Nikolaus (1695–1726) were invited to work at the Saint Petersburg Academy of Sciences. These were the most fruitful years of Daniel Bernoulli's life, because of his collaboration with Leonhard EULER, who came to Saint Petersburg in 1727. In 1733, Daniel returned to Basel, where as a professor he taught botany and anatomy and later physiology and physics.

His most important work was in the field of hydrodynamics (FLUID MECHANICS). BERNOULLI'S LAW was published in *Hydrodynamica* (1738), his most important work. In this book he also gave a theoretical explanation of the pressure of a gas on the walls of a container. Assuming that the gas comprised a large number of small particles, moving randomly and in straight lines at high velocity, he suggested that the pressure was caused by the impact of the particles on the wall. He is therefore considered one of the founders of the kinetic theory of gases.

Bernoulli, Jacques

Jacques, or Jacob, Bernoulli, b. Dec. 27, 1654, d. Aug. 16, 1705, was the eldest child in a Swiss Protestant family of three generations of mathematicians. He taught mechanics at the University in Basel from 1683 and was appointed professor of mathematics in 1687.

Jacques and his brother Johann (1667–1748) studied Leibniz's work on differential calculus and ultimately helped lay the basis for the calculus of variations.

Jacques published many articles on infinite series and did pioneering work in the theory of probability. Bernoulli's theorem is named for him (see LARGE NUMBERS, LAW OF), and BERNOULLI'S LAW for his nephew Daniel.

Bernoulli's Law   [bur-noo'-leez]

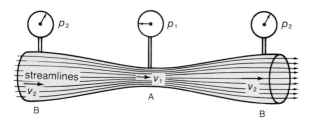

The diagram illustrates Bernoulli's law as applied to a fluid flowing through a horizontal pipe of varying diameter. The pressure (P_1) exerted by the fluid in the constricted section (A) is lower than the pressure (P_2) in the wider regions (B), as indicated by the pressure meter (top). Since the same volume of the fluid is passing through all sections of the pipe, the velocity of the fluid (V_1) in the constriction must be higher than the velocity (V_2) in the wider regions.

Bernoulli's law, first stated by Daniel BERNOULLI, expresses the relationship between pressure and velocity of moving fluids

(liquids or gases). As the speed of a fluid increases, the pressure inside the fluid, or exerted by the fluid, decreases. If water, for example, flows through a horizontal pipe of varying cross section, the water must flow faster in the narrower regions. The pressure on the water must be greater in the wider regions, because the walls of the pipe must exert a force to accelerate the water on its way to the constriction.

Bernoulli's law explains the lift, or upward force, that permits airplanes to fly. The upper surface of an airplane's wing is more curved than the lower; air, traveling across the wing, is made to travel faster, and thus its pressure on the upper surface is reduced. The relatively greater pressure from beneath supplies the lift. The effect is used in automotive carburetors and atomizers, in which air moving rapidly past a narrow opening creates a reduced pressure that sucks in liquid. The liquid is carried along by the stream in the form of a vapor or fine mist. The aspirator, commonly used by dentists to remove excess saliva from the mouth, uses a stream of water flowing in a constricted tube to create suction at the constriction. A side tube placed in the mouth collects the saliva.

See also: FLUID MECHANICS.

Bernoulli's theorem: see LARGE NUMBERS, LAW OF.

Bernstein, Carl, and Woodward, Bob

Bob Woodward (left) and Carl Bernstein (right), a team of investigative reporters with the Washington Post, *released the first stories of White House involvement in the 1972 break-in at the Democratic National Committee headquarters. Their book about the Watergate affair and its subsequent cover-up,* All the President's Men, *became a best-seller.*

Carl Bernstein, b. Washington, D.C., Feb. 14, 1944, and Robert Upshur Woodward, b. Geneva, Ill., Mar. 26, 1943, received national attention for their investigative reporting of the WATERGATE scandals for the *Washington Post*. The *Post* won (1973) the Pulitzer Prize for meritorious public service in journalism, with the "Woodstein" team receiving most of the credit. Bernstein and Woodward wrote ALL THE PRESIDENT'S MEN (1974; film, 1976) and *The Final Days* (1976).

Bernstein, who studied at the University of Maryland, worked on the *Washington Star* from 1960 to 1965 and on the *Post* from 1966 to 1976. Subsequently he was with ABC news. Woodward was educated at Yale, began his newspaper career with the *Montgomery* (Md.) *Sentinel* in 1970–71, and joined the *Post* in late 1971. Woodward's books include *The Brethren* (1979, with Scott Armstrong), and *Veil: The Secret Wars of the CIA 1981–87* (1987).

MICHAEL EMERY

Bernstein, Eduard   [bairn'-shtyn]

Eduard Bernstein, b. Jan. 6, 1850, d. Dec. 18, 1932, was a German socialist leader and theoretician. Compelled to live in exile for 23 years, many of them in England, he was influenced by the reform program of the FABIAN socialists and became critical of some of the ideas of Karl MARX. Among other things, he noted that the class struggle was not intensifying as Marx had predicted it would, that workers were not getting poorer, that the middle class was not shrinking, and that the collapse of capitalism did not appear to be imminent. He rejected violent revolution as impossible and undesirable. He argued that socialists should exploit concrete opportunities for betterment through the workers' increased power at the ballot box, through vigorous trade union activity, and through cooperation with other democratic forces. For this "Revisionism" he was bitterly attacked by orthodox Marxists such as V. I. LENIN, who held that the workers' liberation would come only with the violent overthrow of the existing order. Bernstein himself, on returning home, wrote *Evolutionary Socialism* (1899; Eng. trans., 1909) and served in the German Reichstag (1902–06, 1912–18, 1920–28).

Bibliography: Gay, Peter, *The Dilemma of Democratic Socialism: Eduard Bernstein's Challenge to Marx* (1952); Lichtheim, George, *Marxism: An Historical and Critical Study*, 2d ed. (1964).

Bernstein, Leonard   [burn'-styn]

Leonard Bernstein, b. Lawrence, Mass., Aug. 25, 1918, d. Oct. 14, 1990, was a well-known figure in contemporary American music. He studied composition with Randall Thompson and Walter Piston and conducting with Serge Koussevitzky. Conductor, composer, pianist, lecturer, television personality, and author, Bernstein was called a musical renaissance man. He was best known, however, as a conductor since his professional debut in 1943, when he replaced the indisposed Bruno Walter as the conductor of the NEW YORK PHILHARMONIC in a program that Bernstein directed without rehearsal. Later guest appearances with major American and European orchestras showed him to be one of the most talented conductors of his generation. He was the musical director of the New York City Center Orchestra from 1945 to 1947 and was musical director and conductor of the New York Philharmonic, the first American to hold this post, from 1958 to 1969, at which time he was named conductor laureate for life. He has conducted opera at La Scala, the Metropolitan Opera, and the Vienna State Opera. A dynamic personality with an acute musical intelligence and a large repertoire, Bernstein reached a large audience with his educational programs on television.

Bernstein pursued an impressive career as a composer of both serious and popular music. His major works include three symphonies: the *Jeremiah* (1944), *The Age of Anxiety* (1949), and the *Kaddish* (1963); three ballets, *Fancy Free* (1944), *Facsimile* (1946), and *Dybbuk* (1974); *Chichester Psalms* (1965), a choral work; and *Mass,* a theater piece that

The American conductor and composer Leonard Bernstein served as musical director of the New York Philharmonic from 1958 to 1969. His best-known works include the musical West Side Story (1957) and Mass, a "theater piece" commissioned for the opening (1971) of the Kennedy Center, Washington, D.C.

he wrote for the opening of the Kennedy Center for the Performing Arts in Washington, D.C., in 1971. He also composed music for the Broadway musicals *On the Town* (1944), *Wonderful Town* (1952), *Candide* (1956), and *West Side Story* (1957). *Candide* was successfully reprogrammed as an opera in 1982. Bernstein's other operas include *Trouble in Tahiti* (1952) and its sequel, *A Quiet Place* (1983). He was the author of *Young People's Concerts* (1970), a collection of his television talks, *The Unanswered Question* (1976), his Charles Eliot Norton lectures at Harvard, and *Findings* (1982).   DAVID EWEN

Bibliography: Ames, Evelyn, *A Wind from the West: Bernstein and the New York Philharmonic Abroad* (1970); Bernstein, Burton, *Family Matters: Sam, Jennie and the Kids* (1982); Briggs, John, *Leonard Bernstein: The Man, His Work and His World* (1961); Ewen, David, *Leonard Bernstein*, rev. ed. (1967); Gradenwitz, Peter, *Leonard Bernstein* (1987); Gruen, John, *The Private World of Leonard Bernstein* (1968); Peyser, Joan, *Bernstein: A Biography* (1987).

Berra, Yogi   [bair'-uh, yoh'-gee]

Lawrence Peter Berra, b. St. Louis, Mo., May 12, 1925, is a former baseball star known for his home-run hitting. As a star for the New York Yankees (1946–63), Berra was outstanding both as a hitter (.285 batting average, 358 home runs, 1,430 runs batted in) and catcher. He won the American League's Most Valuable Player Award three times—1951, 1954, and 1955—a salute to his ability as a leader of a team that won 14 pennants and 10 World Series while he played for them. He also played briefly for the New York Mets and managed both the Yankees and the Mets. During his long career, Berra became famous for his humorous, unpredictable comments. He is a member of the Hall of Fame.

Bibliography: Berra, Yogi, *Yogi: It Ain't Over* (1989); Pepe, Phil, *The Wit and Wisdom of Yogi Berra*, 2d, rev. ed. (1988).

Berruguete, Alonso   [bair-oo-gay'-tay]

Alonso Berruguete, c.1489–1561, was the foremost Spanish sculptor to bring Italian High Renaissance style to his country. Trained by his father, the court painter Pedro Berruguete, Alonso worked in Italy from about 1504 to 1517, where he may have been a pupil of Michelangelo, who mentioned Alonso in his letters. The direct influence of Michelangelo is revealed in Alonso's alabaster *Resurrection* (c.1517) in Valencia Cathedral. Perhaps because his work did not find favor with Emperor Charles V, Alonso worked largely for ecclesiastical patrons. He was much in demand after completing his altarpiece for the Church of San Benito, Valladolid (1527–32; now in Valladolid Museum); the tortuous, highly colored alabaster figures of this work make a strong, dramatic impression. Among other commissions, he completed (1537) an altarpiece for the Church of Santiago, Valladolid, and the dynamic alabaster *Transfiguration* (1543–48) for Toledo Cathedral, where, with Felipe Bigarny, he had worked (1539–43) on the walnut alabaster choir stalls. Berruguete's Mannerist paintings are not as impressive as his sculpture, which has an intense spiritual fervor that reveals Berruguete to be a true precursor of El Greco.   GIULIA BARTRUM

Bibliography: Kubler, George, *Art and Architecture in Spain and Portugal and Their American Dominions, 1500–1800* (1959); Smart, Alastair, *The Renaissance and Mannerism in Northern Europe and Spain* (1972).

Berruguete, Pedro

Pedro Berruguete, b. c.1450, d. Jan. 6, 1508, was Spain's first great Renaissance painter. His work combines Gothic Hispano-Flemish elements with influences from Piero della Francesca. He worked in Urbino, Italy, where he painted portraits of the court members, and in Spain, where he painted religious subjects for churches throughout Castile. His *Auto de Fé* (Prado, Madrid), from the church of Santo Tomás, Avila, is among his best-known works. His son Alonso was also a painter and an important sculptor.   EDWARD J. SULLIVAN

Bibliography: Smart, Alastair, *The Renaissance and Mannerism in Northern Europe and Spain* (1972).

Berry

Berry is a historical region in central France that roughly corresponds to the modern departments of Indre and Cher. Its capital was Bourges. The area was originally occupied by the Bituriges Cubi, a Celtic tribe mentioned in Caesar's *Gallic Wars*. Later, it was part of the Roman province of Aquitania. It became a duchy in 1360; Jean, duc de Berry (1340–1416), was an important patron of the arts. Berry was joined to the French crown in 1601.

berry

The berry is a simple fruit, formed by enlargement of the ovary of the pistil, that remains fleshy and succulent when mature and contains immersed seeds. According to botanical classification, such widely divergent crops as the BANANA, BLUEBERRY, CRANBERRY, CUCUMBER, CURRANT, GOOSEBERRY, GRAPE, PEPPER, SQUASH, TOMATO, WATERMELON, and the CITRUS FRUITS are true berries. In common usage, however, the term *berry* is loosely extended to include a wide group of perennial herbaceous and bush species that bear edible fruits, particularly aggregate fruits such as the BLACKBERRY, HUCKLEBERRY, MULBERRY, and STRAWBERRY; the ELDERBERRY, a drupe; and the SERVICEBERRY, a pome. Berry crops are generally adapted to a wide range of soil and climatic conditions, although some, such as the blueberry and cranberry, have specific soil requirements. The major necessity for growth and production is an adequate supply of soil moisture, since most species have shallow roots.

See also: FRUITS AND FRUIT CULTIVATION.

Berry, Chuck

Charles Edward Anderson Berry, b. Wentzville, Mo., Oct. 18, 1926, is a black American singer-songwriter-guitarist who has been one of the most important influences in the development of ROCK MUSIC. From 1955, the year of his first hit, "Maybellene," Berry's music has characteristically combined blues tunes with wry, country-influenced narratives describing teenage frustration, young love, and fast cars. Such Berry songs as "Roll Over, Beethoven"(1956), "Rock and Roll Music" (1957), "Sweet Little Sixteen" (1958), and "Johnny B. Goode" (1958) have become classics of the rock genre.

JONATHAN KAMIN

Bibliography: Berry, Chuck, *Chuck Berry* (1987); Miller, Jim, *The Rolling Stone Illustrated History of Rock & Roll* (1978).

Berry, Martha McChesney

Martha Berry, b. near Rome, Ga., Oct. 7, 1866, d. Feb. 27, 1942, was an American philanthropist and a pioneer of work-study educational programs. She opened the Mount Berry School on her Georgia plantation in 1902 with two teachers. Children paid for their tuition by working on the school farm or workshops. At the time of her death the Mount Berry Schools, including an accredited college, had 125 buildings, built and maintained by student labor. The 1,300 students could work in the mill, quarry, pastures, or farmlands on the 14,000-ha (35,000–acre) campus. Berry's work-study system was widely copied.

Bibliography: Byers, Tracy, *Martha Berry* (1932; repr. 1971).

Berry, Raymond

Raymond Emmett Berry, b. Corpus Christi, Tex., Feb. 27, 1933, enjoyed a highly regarded National Football League (NFL) career as a player and then as a coach. After playing for Southern Methodist University (Texas), Berry joined the Baltimore Colts in 1955 and played split end for them until 1967. During his career he caught 631 passes for 9,278 yd and 68 touchdowns. Neither big nor fast, Berry relied on his precise pass patterns and his great dexterity. He was inducted into the Hall of Fame in 1973. From 1968 to 1981 he was a receiving coach on various professional and college teams. In 1984, Berry was named head coach of the New England Patriots, leading them to the 1985–86 Super Bowl.

Berryman, John

John Berryman, an American poet, educator, and biographer, was awarded the Pulitzer Prize in 1964 for his 77 Dream Songs. *His reputation and his influence on modern poetry grew steadily until 1972, when Berryman took his own life.*

John Berryman, b. McAlester, Okla., Oct. 25, 1914, d. Jan. 7, 1972, is considered one of the finest American poets of his generation. Raised as a strict Roman Catholic, he continued throughout his life to be haunted by a religious conscience. His father committed suicide when the boy was only 12, and this also contributed to a lifelong sense of guilt and estrangement. In 1972, Berryman leaped to his death from a bridge over the Mississippi River at Minneapolis, Minn.

He began to publish in little magazines in the late 1930s, demonstrating his indebtedness to William Butler Yeats, then the most famous living poet. His fame grew considerably with *Homage to Mistress Bradstreet* (1956), innovative in form and daring in its psychological probings. Throughout the 1960s, almost until his death, he worked on *The Dream Songs* (1970), a long poem sequence combining a strict format (each song has three 6-line stanzas) with even more innovative techniques: voices mix with one another, and the language combines slang and literary references. His *77 Dream Songs* (1964) had already won the Pulitzer Prize for poetry.

Throughout his career, Berryman struggled with the problems of fame and the uncertain status of the poet in society. Berryman was often an explorer of tradition; he wrote a sonnet sequence (*Berryman's Sonnets*, 1967) about an adulterous affair, then withheld it from publication for some time. He was also, however, a dedicated experimentalist, striving to fulfill the charge of Ezra POUND to "make it new" and thus wrench poetry out of its 19th-century molds and force it into contact with the chaotic values of contemporary life. Berryman was also a critic (*The Freedom of the Poet*, 1974) and taught for several decades at various American universities. A book of poems, *Delusions* (1972), and a novel, *Recovery* (1973), appeared after his death.   CHARLES MOLESWORTH

Bibliography: Conarroe, Joel, *John Berryman: An Introduction to the Poetry* (1977); Haffenden, John, *The Life of John Berryman* (1984); Halliday, E. M., *John Berryman and the Thirties* (1987); Kelly, R. J., ed., *We Dream of Honour: John Berryman's Letters to His Mother* (1988); Thomas, Harry, ed., *Berryman's Understanding* (1988).

Berthelot, Marcelin   [bair-tuh-loh', mar-se-lan']

The French chemist Marcelin Berthelot, b. Oct. 25, 1827, d. Mar. 18, 1907, is known for his work on the synthesis of organic compounds, especially at high temperatures. This work led to the concept of total synthesis and the final overthrow of vitalism, the doctrine that the functions of living creatures cannot be reduced to physicochemical forces. Berthelot's research on the conversion of alcohols and acids to esters led to an understanding of equilibrium reactions. He developed a bomb CALORIMETER to study heat changes during chemical reactions. He also investigated explosives, plant chemistry, and the history of alchemy and chemistry.   AARON J. IHDE

Berthier, Louis Alexandre [bair-tee-ay', loo-ee' ahl-ek-sawnd']

Louis Alexandre Berthier, b. Nov. 20, 1753, d. June 1, 1815, was a French general who served as Napoleon I's valued chief of staff from 1796 to 1815. He gained military experience in the American Revolution and then fought in France and Italy, where he proclaimed (1798) the Roman Republic, and in Egypt, central Europe, and Russia. An indifferent commander, he had the gift of communicating Napoleon's instructions and was created (1809) prince of Wagram. After Napoleon's first abdication (1814) Berthier expressed his loyalty to Louis XVIII, but he died serving Napoleon during the Waterloo campaign.

Berthollet, Claude Louis, Comte de [bair-toh-lay', klohd]

Claude Louis Berthollet, b. Dec. 9, 1748, d. Nov. 6, 1822, was the first important French chemist to adopt Antoine LAVOISIER's theory of combustion. In a scientific controversy with Joseph PROUST, he held that the composition of each chemical substance is variable and depends on the amounts of reacting materials. Proust's view led to the law of constant composition, and Berthollet's pointed toward the law of mass action. Berthollet introduced chlorine as an industrial bleach and collaborated with Lavoisier in establishing modern chemical nomenclature. Berthollet was active in government work and became successively senator, officer of the Legion of Honor, and a member of the Chamber of Peers.   RALPH GABLE

Bertillon (family) [bair-tee-awn']

The French brothers **Jacques Bertillon,** b. Nov. 11, 1851, d. July 7, 1922, and **Alphonse Bertillon,** b. Apr. 23, 1853, d. Feb. 13, 1914, were noted for their introduction of statistical methods into various social fields.

Jacques Bertillon was trained as a physician but turned to demographic work, succeeding his father as head of the Paris bureau of vital statistics (1883–1913). His application of statistical methods to the study of social issues influenced the use of statistics in the social sciences as a whole. He also pioneered in the establishment of international statistical standards in demographic work.

Alphonse Bertillon, who served as chief of criminal identification in Paris from 1880 until his death, developed the so-called Bertillon system of criminal identification. His system involved taking a series of precise body measurements and a uniform sequence of photographs of criminal suspects. These photographic techniques continue to be employed in forensic science, although the use of body measurements as a means of lifelong identification was inadequate and has since been replaced by the use of FINGERPRINTS.

Bertoia, Harry [bair-toy'-uh]

The sculptor Harry Bertoia, b. Italy, Mar. 10, 1915, d. Nov. 6, 1978, worked with brass, bronze, nickel rods, and stainless steel, frequently using color in finishing these metals. His sculptures are usually either short, treelike forms or tall, fanlike groupings spreading out of a heavy base. Some are constructed of moving parts that, when activated, strike each other to produce pleasing sounds. Bertoia emigrated to the United States in 1930 and attended (1937–39) the Academy of Art of the Cranbrook Foundation in Michigan, where he subsequently taught (1939–43) metalworking techniques. One of his best-known works is the mass-produced Bertoia chair, a comfortable and utilitarian adaptation of the "butterfly" chair. Among his many public commissions is a large fountain (1967) for the Philadelphia Civic Center.

BARBARA CAVALIERE

Bibliography: Nelson, June Kompass, *Harry Bertoia: Sculptor* (1970).

Bertolucci, Bernardo [bair-toh-loo'-chee]

The Italian film director Bernardo Bertolucci, b. Mar. 16, 1940, was a prize-winning poet before he left (1961) college to assist poet-turned-film director Pier Paolo PASOLINI. Within three years the young Bertolucci had produced his first important film, the internationally acclaimed *Before the Revolution* (1964), a romantic portrait of politicized Italian youth. *The Spider's Strategem* (1970) and *The Conformist* (1970)—which is often ranked as Bertolucci's finest work—refer back to the period of Italian fascism. *Last Tango in Paris* (1972), with its heavily sexual plot and a superb performance by Marlon Brando, was Bertolucci's first popular hit. The film *1900* (1977), however, lost much of its epic sweep when its original 6-hour length was cut by one-third. Bertolucci's work during the 1980s was relatively unexciting until *The Last Emperor* (1987), a magnificent portrait of the unreal life of China's last emperor, P'u-yi, filmed in China. The work won nine Academy Awards, including two for director and screenwriter Bertolucci.

Bibliography: Kolker, Robert P., *Bernardo Bertolucci* (1985).

Bertrand, Marcel Alexandre [bair-trahn', mar-sel' ahl-ek-sawnd']

Marcel Alexandre Bertrand, b. July 2, 1847, d. Feb. 13, 1907, was a French geologist, best known for his research on the formation of the Alps. In *La Chaîne des Alpes et la formation du continent européen* (The Chain of the Alps and the Formation of the European Continent, 1887), he described the Alpine orogeny as a wave that had moved from north to south, gradually deforming the crust of southern Europe. He concluded that the Alps were composed of overturned folds and overthrust faults that were later modified by compression. The compression, he explained, detached great sheets of rock called nappes. Bertrand also developed the theory of the rock cycle, relating deposition of sedimentary rock to the deformation of the Earth's crust.

Bertrand de Born [ber-trahn' duh bawrn']

Bertrand de Born, b. c.1140, was a Provençal troubadour poet and soldier who excelled in describing military exploits. Although he sometimes wrote about love, the subject of most troubadour poetry, his main theme was the conflict between Henry II and his sons, in which Bertrand is said to have played an active part. He wrote two moving poems on the death of Prince Henry in 1183 and is mentioned in Dante's *Divine Comedy.* Bertrand died between 1208 and 1215 in a monastery.

Berwald, Franz [bair'-vahld]

Franz Berwald, b. July 23, 1796, d. Apr. 3, 1868, was Sweden's greatest 19th-century composer. After early training in Stockholm, he became active as a violinist (1812–29), going to Berlin and Vienna, but he returned to Sweden in 1842. He had great difficulty in securing recognition because contemporary Swedish taste was conservative (in 1849 he was denied an appointment at the University of Uppsala), and at times he had to make his living in other ways—at an orthopedic institute in Berlin (1835–41) and as manager of a glassworks in Ångermanland (1850–58). Finally, he was appointed (1867) to the conservatory in Stockholm. His compositions reveal the influence of MENDELSSOHN, SCHUMANN, and BERLIOZ, but his individuality is evident. His works are mostly instrumental and include four surviving symphonies, several concerti, and chamber works.   F. E. KIRBY

Bibliography: Layton, Robert, *Franz Berwald* (1959); Osborne, Charles, ed., *The Dictionary of Composers* (1981).

Berwick [bair'-ik]

Berwick (also called Berwickshire) was a sparsely populated county in southeastern Scotland until 1975, when it became part of the Borders administrative region. It was bounded by England on the southeast and the North Sea on the east. Duns was the county town. The Lammermuir Hills traverse the northern half of the area. The south is a fertile lowland, called the Merse, drained by the River TWEED. Agriculture is the main economic activity; sheep are raised in the northern hills, and grains, potatoes, and sugar beets are grown and cattle raised in the south. Wool-processing is the major industry, and fishing is important along the coast. Berwick was part of the Saxon kingdom of Northumbria, and it became part of Scotland in the 11th century.

Berwick, James Fitzjames, Duke of   [bair'-ik]

The duke of Berwick, b. Aug. 21, 1670, d. June 12, 1734, illegitimate son of JAMES II of England and Arabella Churchill (the duke of Marlborough's sister), fought at the Battle of the BOYNE (1690) in the unsuccessful effort to restore his father to the English throne and then became one of the leading commanders for LOUIS XIV of France during the War of the SPANISH SUCCESSION. Berwick revived the cause of the French contender PHILIP V in Spain at Almanza (1707), fought on France's eastern fronts, and returned to Spain to capture Barcelona (1714). Having served three crowns and become an English duke, French peer, and Spanish grandee, he died of a cannon shot in the War of the POLISH SUCCESSION.

A. LLOYD MOOTE

Bibliography: Petrie, Sir Charles, *The Marshal Duke of Berwick* (1953).

beryl   [bair'-ul]

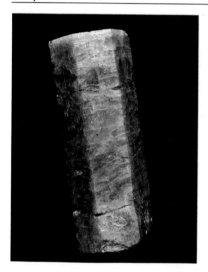

Beryl, an aluminum-beryllium silicate, is found as hexagonal crystals in various colors. In addition to being the chief ore for beryllium metal, beryl in its transparent form is a source of some of the major gemstones. Gem varieties include green emeralds, yellow heliodors, bluish-green aquamarines, and pink morganites.

Beryl, an aluminosilicate mineral (see SILICATE MINERALS), $Be_3 Al_2 Si_6 O_{18}$, is the principal ore of the rare element BERYLLIUM. Long prized as various gemstones, notably the deep-green EMERALD, the pale blue-green aquamarine, the pink morganite, and the golden heliodor, beryl is easily distinguished by its long, six-sided prismatic crystals (HEXAGONAL SYSTEM) but also forms compact to coarsely granular masses. The common material is whitish to green and is subtranslucent; gem material is transparent. Hardness is 7½–8, luster vitreous, and specific gravity 2.6–2.8.

Most beryl is found in PEGMATITE dikes, where large crystals are intergrown with quartz and feldspar, but the emerald variety also occurs in altered limestone and in various METAMORPHIC ROCKS. Crystal size ranges from tiny to enormous. A crystal weighing 200 tons was mined in Minas Gerais, Brazil, and crystals about 6 m (20 ft) long and 2 m (7 ft) across have been found in the Black Hills of South Dakota and in Albany, Maine. Common beryl has been mined for beryllium since 1925, notably in Brazil, where the largest deposits occur.

beryllium   [buh-ril'-ee-uhm]

Beryllium is a chemical element, one of the alkaline-earth metals in Group IIA of the periodic table. Its symbol is Be, its atomic number 4, and its atomic weight 9.0122. A steel gray metal, its properties are similar to those of aluminum and magnesium, except that its melting point, about 1,278° C, is high for a light metal. Chemically, beryllium differs markedly from the other alkaline-earth metals in that it forms compounds that are more covalent than ionic.

Beryllium is a rare element. Its concentration in the Earth's crust is approximately 6 ppm, and no rich deposits of it exist. It is produced from the mineral BERYL. (Emeralds and aquamarines are forms of beryl.) The element was discovered, in its oxide form, by the French chemist Louis Nicolas Vauquelin in 1798. The metal was first prepared in 1828 by Friedrich WÖHLER and Antoine Bussy, working independently.

In metallurgy, the specific applications of beryllium are based on its high ratio of strength to weight—it is lighter and yet much stronger than aluminum—and on its high melting point. In addition, it forms a strong oxide layer on its surface, which gives it a high corrosion resistance, as high as that of aluminum. The addition of traces of beryllium to alloys can greatly increase their corrosion resistance. However, the cost of beryllium, which is about 200 times that of aluminum, restricts its applications to a few special ones, such as in computer components, gyroscopes, and space technology.

The most important beryllium alloy is beryllium copper (up to 4% Be). This alloy is obtained by fusing beryllium oxide with copper, with carbon as a reducing agent. Beryllium copper is used in corrosion-resistant springs, electrical contacts—beryllium is a little less than half as conductive as copper—and, because of its hardness, in spark-proof tools. (Spark-proof hammers and wrenches are used in work with highly flammable materials.)

Beryllium is important in nuclear-reactor technology because it is an excellent neutron reflector and moderator. For this reason, and because of its strength and great resistance to heat, beryllium is employed as a cladding material for nuclear fuel elements. Beryllium, when bombarded with alpha radiation, emits a large number of neutrons. This was how the neutron was discovered in 1932.

The most important beryllium compound is beryllium oxide, BeO. It is used as a base material in ceramics and in special types of glass; in fluorescent tubes; and in nuclear reactors. Beryllium and its compounds are extremely toxic. Inhalation of dust particles or vapors containing beryllium may cause berylliosis, an inflammation of the lungs.

Berzelius, Jöns Jakob   [bur-zee'-lee-uhs, yuns yah'-kawp]

The Swedish chemist Jöns Jakob Berzelius, b. Aug. 20, 1779, d. Aug. 7, 1848, was one of the dominant figures in chemistry during the first half of the 19th century. His textbook, his system of chemical symbols, his dualistic electrochemical theory, his yearly review of chemical progress (1821–48), and his compilation of the first reasonably accurate atomic weight table, made him the ultimate chemical authority of his times. He introduced the use of filter paper into analytical chemistry and discovered several elements—selenium (1817), silicon (about 1824), and thorium (1829). He introduced many terms used in chemistry today. His increasingly entrenched scientific conservatism in later life impeded progress, however.

GEORGE B. KAUFFMAN

Besançon   [be-zahn-sohn']

Besançon is the capital city of Doubs department in eastern France. It is in the Franche-Comté region on the Doubs River east of Dijon and has a population of 119,194 (1990). It is most famous for its watchmaking and clockmaking, but other industries include paper and textile manufacturing. Besançon was an important Gallic town that was taken by Julius Caesar in 58 BC. Made a free imperial city in 1184 by Frederick Barbarossa, it remained so until 1674, when it became part of France. Principal buildings include the Cathedral of Saint-Jean (12th century) and many buildings in the Spanish Renaissance style. The Roman Grande Rue, where Victor HUGO was born, remains the principal street.

Besant, Annie [beez'-uhnt]

Annie Besant, b. Oct. 1, 1847, d. Sept. 30, 1933, was an English social reformer and theosophist. She married Frank Besant, an Anglican clergyman, in 1867 but separated from him five years later because of doctrinal differences. She joined the National Secular Society and with the atheist journalist Charles Bradlaugh crusaded for free thought, birth control, and women's rights. Besant was also a member of the socialistic FABIAN SOCIETY. A few years after her conversion (1889) to THEOSOPHY—a philosophical religious movement based on mystical insights—Besant went to India, which she made her home. She founded the Central Hindu College at Varanasi and was politically active. For many years, beginning in 1916, she campaigned for Indian home rule. She also traveled in Great Britain and the United States with KRISHNAMURTI, her adopted son whom she presented as a new messiah, a claim he later renounced. Besant wrote widely on theosophy and was president of the Theosophical Society from 1907 until her death.

Bibliography: Dinnage, Rosemary, *Annie Besant* (1987); Nethercot, Arthur H., *The First Five Lives of Annie Besant* (1960) and *The Last Four Lives of Annie Besant* (1963).

Bessarabia [bes-uh-ray'-bee-uh]

Bessarabia is a region in Eastern Europe that makes up the southwestern part of UKRAINE and the major part of MOLDOVA. Covering 44,421 km^2 (17,151 mi^2), it is bordered on the south by the Danube delta and Black Sea, on the west by the Moldavian region of Romania and the Prut River, and on the north and east by the Dnestr River. Kishinev, Bendery, and Beltsy are the main population centers. Its name is probably derived from the 14th-century Walachian dynasty of Basarab.

The area is made up mainly of the Beltsy and Budzhak steppes, parted by the Kodry Hills. The part that includes the Danube and Dnestr deltas, however, is a marshy lowland. Wheat, corn, wine, and tobacco are produced; cattle and sheep are raised. Bessarabia is inhabited by Moldavians, Ukrainians, and Russians. Its control has been disputed by Romania and Russia, and it has changed hands numerous times. From 1947 to 1991 it was part of the USSR.

Bessel, Friedrich [bes'-uhl]

Friedrich Wilhelm Bessel, b. July 22, 1784, d. Mar. 17, 1846, a German astronomer and mathematician, is best known for his determination of the first stellar PARALLAX, the earliest accurate method for measuring stellar distances. Bessel had little formal schooling but when, at the age of 26, he was appointed director of Frederick William III of Prussia's new Königsberg Observatory, he was granted the title of doctor by the University of Göttingen. Bessel remained at Königsberg for the rest of his life, and it was there that his monumental astrometrical program of determining the positions and proper motions of stars led to the discovery (1838) of the parallax of 61 Cygni. Bessel also worked out a method of mathematical analysis involving what is now known as the Bessel function, a still indispensable tool in physics and engineering.

Bibliography: Ley, Willy, *Watchers of the Skies* (1963); MacPhearson, Hector, *Makers of Astronomy* (1933); Pannekoek, Antonie, *A History of Astronomy* (1961).

Bessemer, Sir Henry [bes'-uh-mur]

The English inventor and industrialist Henry Bessemer, b. Jan. 19, 1813, d. Mar. 15, 1898, developed a process of steel manufacture that led to the production of a low-cost, high-quality steel and hastened the progress of the INDUSTRIAL REVOLUTION. Bessemer had already invented several industrial processes when, during the Crimean War (1853–56), he began to work on improving the iron used for casting cannon. By 1855 he had refined his process, essentially a method for blowing a blast of air through molten pig iron to oxidize its impurities. The heat of the oxidation raised the temperature of the iron and kept it in a molten state—hence the name of the famous paper Bessemer read to the British Association for the Advancement of Science in 1856: "The Manufacture of Iron without Fuel." Bessemer steel, made in his English works at Sheffield, was widely used in Europe. In America, Bessemer's patent was challenged by William KELLY, the discoverer of a similar process, although the two inventors eventually merged their companies. Bessemer was knighted in 1879.

Bibliography: Bessemer, Henry, *Sir Henry Bessemer: An Autobiography* (1905); Carr, J. C., and Taplin, W., *History of the British Steel Industry* (1962); Chaloner, W. H., *People and Industries* (1963).

See also: IRON AND STEEL INDUSTRY.

Best, Charles

Charles Herbert Best, b. West Pembroke, Maine, Feb. 27, 1899, d. Mar. 31, 1978, was an American-Canadian physiologist who, while still a medical student, worked with Sir Frederick G. BANTING on the isolation of the hormone insulin from the pancreas. Having successfully isolated insulin from the islets of Langerhans in the pancreas, they showed that it was effective in treating DIABETES mellitus. Banting was awarded part of the 1923 Nobel Prize for physiology or medicine for this work and, annoyed that Best had not also been honored, shared his part of the prize with Best. Best served as director of the Banting-Best Department of Medical Research and as head of the department of physiology at the University of Toronto.

Bibliography: Bliss, Michael, *The Discovery of Insulin* (1982).

Best, George

George Best, b. May 22, 1946, is a Northern Ireland–born soccer player who starred in England and later became one of the first notable players in the North American Soccer League. Best made his professional debut in 1963, when, at the age of 17, he played for Manchester United. He showed exceptional skill as a winger, and his talent and good looks made him a pop celebrity. Emotional problems and disagreements with his teams increased, however, and he joined (1976) the North American Soccer League, playing for two teams before his virtual retirement several years later.

Bibliography: Parkinson, Michael, *Best* (1975).

Best Friend of Charleston

The *Best Friend of Charleston* was the first commercial locomotive built in the United States. It pulled a passenger train from Charleston over the 9.7 km (6 mi) of completed line of the South Carolina Railroad on Christmas Day, 1830. The short trip by the $4,000, four-ton locomotive was the first scheduled run of a steam-powered railroad train in America. After several months of operation, the locomotive exploded when the engine's fireman tied down the safety valve of the boiler because the noise bothered him.   JOHN F. STOVER

Bibliography: Bruce, A. W., *The Steam Locomotive in America* (1952).

best-seller

A best-seller is a recently published book whose sales in bookstores are greater than those of other books in its class. Also considered best-sellers are regional and perennial best-sellers whose large sales continue over a period of years.

The systematic gathering of information on best-sellers began with the initial issue of *The Bookman*, a literary magazine, in February 1895. That issue carried "Books in Demand," a list compiled from bookstore sales in 16 cities throughout the United States. More cities were later added to the list, and a résumé called "Best Selling Books" was compiled. Beginning in 1899, *The Bookman* published a series of annual lists. Today, although publications such as the *New York Times Book Review* print weekly lists of best-sellers, *Publishers Weekly* alone cumulates this data on a yearly basis. Thus, over the course of a year, some 40 titles may appear in the journal's weekly lists, but only the top ten in sales are best-sellers.

In an effort to give precision to the term *best-seller*, Frank Luther MOTT, in his book *Golden Multitudes*, devised an original formula for determining a best-seller. His lists, covering the period 1662–1945 by decades, contained the names of books selling at least a number equal to 1 percent of the total population of the continental United States for the decade in which the book was published.

Until World War II, best-seller lists consisted solely of books published in hard cover. As a result of the rapid expansion of the paperback industry after the war, *Publishers Weekly* now contains two best-seller lists, one of hardcover books and the other of paperbacks. Only rarely does a hardcover book attain the status of a best-seller based on the requirement of 1 percent of the population, usually because the early appearance of its paperback edition cuts into its sales.

Leading any list of all-time best-selling or most widely distributed books is the Bible, with approximately 2.5 billion copies since 1816. The number of copies claimed for *Quotations from the Works of Mao Tse-tung* is 800 million; estimated copies of Noah Webster's *American Spelling Book* range from 50 to 100 million. Other titles with more than 20 million copies include *The Truth that Leads to Eternal Life*, published by Jehovah's Witnesses; *A Message to Garcia*, by Elbert Hubbard; *The World Almanac*; *In His Steps*, by C. M. Sheldon; the *Guinness Book of World Records*; *The Common Sense Book of Baby Care*, by Dr. Benjamin Spock, and Jacqueline Susann's *Valley of the Dolls*.

Bibliography: Bennett, J. O., *Much Loved Books* (1977); Bocca, G., *Best-Seller* (1981); Hackett, A. P., and Burke, J. H., *Eighty Years of Best Sellers* (1977); Sutherland, J., *Best Sellers* (1981).

Bester, Alfred

Alfred Bester, b. New York City, Dec. 18, 1913, d. Sept. 30, 1987, was an American writer best known for two classic science-fiction novels, *The Demolished Man* (1953) and *The Stars My Destination* (1957), which are characterized by high-speed action and a literate style. His other novels include *The Computer Connection* (1975) and *Golem 100* (1980), and his early stories are collected in *The Light Fantastic* (1976) and *Star Light, Star Bright* (1976).

Bibliography: Platt, Charles, *Dream Makers* (1987).

bestiary   [bes'-tee-air-ee]

The medieval bestiary was a collection of frequently marvelous descriptions of animals, plants, and inanimate objects such as magnets and diamonds. These descriptions were of particular interest to readers seeking explanations of the natural world, which was considered God's book and therefore an allegorical guide to the divine purpose. The basis for most medieval bestiaries, both prose and verse, was the 2d-century anonymous Greek Alexandrian work known as the *Physiologus* (Greek: *physiologos*, "naturalist"). Although fanciful or fabulous by objective standards, the bestiary differed from the fable or the BEAST EPIC in purporting to describe actual creatures rather than narrating typically human behavior in the guise of animal actors.   DONALD CHENEY

Bibliography: Elliott, T. J., ed., *Medieval Bestiary* (1971); McCulloch, Florence T., *Mediaeval Latin and French Bestiaries* (1962); Richard de Fournival, *Master Richard's "Bestiary of Love" and "Response,"* trans. by Jeanette Beer (1986); White, T. H., *The Bestiary* (1960).

beta decay   [bay'-tuh]

Beta decay is a spontaneous nuclear process that transforms some unstable radioactive atomic nuclei into others through electron emission, positron emission, or electron capture. The stability of a nucleus is determined by the number of neutrons and protons contained in the nucleus. Nuclei that have an equal number of neutrons and protons are the most stable, but most nuclei have an excess of either neutrons or protons. Such nuclei may be unstable or radioactive and may decay toward a condition of greater stability either by the emission of a negatively charged beta particle, known as an electron, or a positively charged beta particle, called a positron. A beta particle as such does not exist within the nucleus but is created at the moment of emission.

A nucleus that has too many neutrons for its stability decays by the emission of an electron. In this process a force known as weak interaction force (see FUNDAMENTAL INTERACTIONS) changes a neutron into a proton inside the nucleus, thereby increasing the charge or the number of protons by one. Similarly, a nucleus with an excess number of protons decays by the emission of a positron by changing a proton into a neutron, thereby decreasing the charge by one. The charge also decreases by one if the nucleus captures an orbital electron. The electron capture process competes with positron emission for those nuclei that have excess protons; that is, certain nuclei may decay by either mode. Each form of beta decay is always accompanied by the simultaneous emission of an antineutrino (see NEUTRINO).

The life of a radioactive nucleus is expressed in terms of a quantity known as a HALF-LIFE—that period of time during which the number of radioactive atoms diminishes by half. The half-life of each beta-emitting nucleus is different, ranging from a fraction of a second up to many years. Some beta emitters occur in nature, mostly among the uranium, thorium, and actinium groups. These elements have an excess of neutrons and hence decay by the emission of electrons. Most of these elements, however, are produced artificially by nuclear reactors. Some isotopes that decay by positron emission are carbon 11, oxygen 15, iron 52, and iodine 124. Produced by cyclotrons, they have short half-lives.

An extremely rare form of beta decay called double beta decay also occurs, in which two neutrons in a nucleus each simultaneously release an electron and an antineutrino. Interest was aroused in the mid-1980s by a report of evidence for neutrinoless double beta decay and the suggestion that the neutrinos had instead merged to form a new kind of particle called a majoron. This would imply that neutrinos do have mass; it would also violate the law of LEPTON conservation, which holds that the total number of leptons (light or weightless particles) entering into and emerging from an atomic reaction must be the same. Such an interpretation, however, remains to be confirmed.   R. R. ROY

Bibliography: Garcia, A., and Kielanowski, P., *The Beta Decay of Hyperons* (1985); Levi, B. G., "Two-Neutrino Double Beta-Decay Seen," *Physics Today*, December 1987; Wu, C. S., *Beta Decay* (1966).

Betancourt, Rómulo   [bet-ahn-koor', roh'-moo-loh]

Rómulo Betancourt, b. Feb. 22, 1908, d. Sept. 28, 1981, a Venezuelan lawyer, economist, and political leader, was twice president of Venezuela (1945–48, 1959–64). Founder of the leftist Acción Democrática party, he first came to power as president of the provisional government following a military coup in 1945. In a country of extremes in wealth and poverty, he brought about such reforms as an excess profits tax, including a 50 percent government tax on oil profits, and direct universal suffrage. Exiled ten years during the dictatorship of Martos Pérez Jiménez, Betancourt was elected president again. He was awarded a lifetime Senate seat in 1973.

Bibliography: Alexander, R. J., *Rómulo Betancourt and the Transformation of Venezuela* (1982).

betatron   [bayt'-uh-trahn]

The betatron is an electron ACCELERATOR that operates because a changing magnetic field produces an electric field. Part of the magnetic-field pattern supplies an accelerating electric field, and another part bends the electron on a circular orbit. As the field increases and the electrons accelerate, the field at the orbit keeps the orbit radius constant. Brought to a target just inside or outside of the orbit, the electrons produce X rays in a directed, intense beam. Betatrons are used in nuclear physics, medicine, and radiography. The first successful betatron was built in 1940 by Donald Kerst at the University of Illinois; he later built the largest betatron in existence, capable of accelerating electrons to 300 million electron volts (MeV). Betatrons have been commercially produced for use in the range between 10 and 100 MeV.   JOHN P. BLEWETT

betel [beet'-ul]

The betel palm, A. catechu, *is cultivated for its nuts, which grow in clusters; chewed as a mild stimulant, they stain the teeth black.*

Betel, or betel pepper, *Piper betle*, is a vine native to southern Asia. Many people of southern Asia and neighboring Pacific islands smear the fresh leaves of this plant with slaked (water-treated) lime and pieces of betel nut, which is the seed of the betel palm, *Areca catechu*. This mixture is chewed to obtain a mild stimulation and sense of well-being, produced by an alkaloid in the nut. The practice is not habit-forming, but it stains the saliva and teeth red or brown, and the nut may be carcinogenic. In veterinary medicine the nut is sometimes used for deworming. CHARLES H. STYER

Betelgeuse: see STAR.

Beth-shan

Beth-shan, or Beth-shean (modern Tell el-Husn), an imposing mound situated between the Jezreel and Jordan valleys in Palestine (present-day Israel), was a major Egyptian strategic stronghold, especially between the reigns of Seti I (1318–04 BC) and Rameses III (1198–66 BC).

Occupied almost continually since the mid-4th millennium BC, the site contains significant remains dating from the Late Bronze Age (c.1550–1200 BC). These include a mid-14th-century Canaanite-style courtyard and temple complex dedicated to the local Canaanite god Mekal. Superimposed on it is a later temple (c.1300–1150 BC) dedicated to the goddess Astarte. Its partly roofed forecourt and raised rear sanctuary are reminiscent in plan of small Egyptian shrines of the Amarna period. After the city was captured by the Israelites in the 10th century BC, two more temples were built; one is similar to the Phoenician-style temple of Jerusalem.

Of the later Beth-shan, little is well preserved. Under the Greek name Scythopolis, it was a town of some importance from the Hellenistic to the Byzantine period, when occupation moved off the mound itself and into the valley below. A fine Roman theater, seating up to 5,000 and dating from the Severan period (AD 193–235), has been excavated.

The site was excavated from 1921 to 1933 by archaeologists from the University of Pennsylvania under the directorship of Alan Rowe. Subsequent work has been undertaken by the Israel Department of Antiquities. JONATHAN N. TUBB

Bibliography: Fitzgerald, Gerald M., "Beth-Shean," in *Archaeology and Old Testament Study*, ed. by D. Winton Thomas (1967); Rowe, Alan, *Beth-shan*, vol. 2 (1940).

Bethany

Bethany was a biblical village at the foot of the Mount of Olives, about 3.2 km (2 mi) east of Jerusalem. The home of Lazarus, Mary, and Martha, Bethany is frequently mentioned in the New Testament. Jesus restored Lazarus to life there (John 11). The village is also associated with the final days and the Ascension of Christ. Today the West Bank town of El-Azariyeh, named in honor of Lazarus, occupies the site. The traditional locations of Lazarus' tomb and Simon the leper's house are there. DOUGLAS EZELL

Bethe, Hans [bay'-te]

The Alsatian-born American physicist Hans Albrecht Bethe, b. July 2, 1906, is known for his work in nuclear physics and its applications to astrophysics. He received his Ph.D. at the University of Munich in 1928 and spent the next five years teaching at German universities. When the Nazis came to power he went to England and then to the United States. By this time he had become noted for his studies of subatomic particle behavior in terms of quantum mechanics. Appointed a professor of physics at Cornell University in 1935, he retired from that position as professor emeritus in 1975.

In the United States Bethe became interested in investigating the source of energy of the Sun and other stars. By 1939 he had developed a promising answer to the problem posed by the large energy production of stars over long life spans. The solution involved the fusion, or binding, of hydrogen nuclei to form helium nuclei in the presence of a carbon catalyst. After developing a wave guide device for radar at the Massachusetts Institute of Technology, he went to Los Alamos, N.Mex., where he was chief of the theoretical division of the atomic bomb project.

After World War II, Bethe's research dealt with shock-wave theory, meson theory, and quantum mechanics. When President Truman ordered a crash program in 1950 to develop the hydrogen bomb, Bethe joined the effort with Edward Teller once the appropriate technological route for the program was determined. An advocate of nuclear energy, from 1956 to 1964 he served on the President's Science Advisory Committee. In 1958 he was head of a presidential study of disarmament, another effort in which he was deeply interested. He became an informal advisor on the subject to Presidents Eisenhower, Kennedy, and Johnson and helped negotiate the 1963 partial test ban treaty with the Soviet Union.

Bethe was awarded the 1967 Nobel Prize for physics for his contributions to nuclear theory and to the understanding of stellar processes. In later years he argued against the development of so-called defensive nuclear systems as being an exercise in futility. JAMES A. BOOTH

Bibliography: Bernstein, Jeremy, *Hans Bethe* (1980); Broad, W. J., "Rewriting the History of the H-Bomb," *Science*, Nov. 19, 1982; Weintraub, Pamela, ed., *The OMNI Interviews* (1984).

Bethel [beth'-uhl]

Bethel ("house of God") was an important biblical city in central Palestine, named by Jacob. Abraham built an altar nearby, and Jacob saw the famous ladder and received the name *Israel* there (Gen. 35). Bethel was briefly the site of the ark of the covenant. When the tribes of Israel split, Jeroboam I made Bethel and the city of Dan the northern kingdom's cultic rivals to Judah's Jerusalem.

Bethesda

Bethesda (1990 pop., 62,936) is an unincorporated residential suburb in central Maryland, outside of Washington, D.C. It is the site of the National Institutes of Health (1939) and the Naval Medical Center (1942). It was settled in the mid-1700s but remained a small village until the mid-1900s.

Bethlehem (Jordan/Israel)

Bethlehem (Hebrew: "house of bread" or "house of Lahm," a god) is a city in the Israeli-occupied West Bank territory, 10 km (6 mi) south of Jerusalem. The biblical city of David and birthplace of Jesus, it is a place of pilgrimage for both Christians and Jews. Its most famous shrine is the Church of the Nativity. The tomb of Rachel, Jacob's wife, is believed to be just north of the city. The story of Ruth took place in Bethlehem, and it was there that Samuel anointed David king of Israel.

The modern city, set on a hill overlooking the Dead Sea, has a population of about 20,000 (1984 est.) and is the center of trade for a fertile region that produces grains, olives, and wine. Industry is restricted to the production of religious artifacts and souvenirs for the pilgrim and tourist trade.

Bethlehem became part of Jordan after Britain's mandate of Palestine ended in 1948. During the Arab-Israeli war of 1967, Israeli troops took the city, which is part of the West Bank territory.

Bibliography: Harpur, Tom, *The Road to Bethlehem* (1977).

Bethlehem   (Pennsylvania)

Bethlehem, on both banks of the Lehigh River in eastern Pennsylvania, is world famous for its steel. Its population is 71,428 (1990). It is the site of Moravian College and of Lehigh University, whose annual Bach Festival in May is internationally acclaimed. The city was settled (1741) by Moravian missionaries. In 1829 the opening of the Lehigh Canal spurred industrialization, and by the 1850s the first ironworks was established, taking advantage of nearby sources of iron ore and coal. In 1904 several smaller iron and steel firms consolidated into the Bethlehem Steel Corp., a major U.S. steel producer and the main source of the city's prosperity. By the late 1980s, however, the U.S. steel industry was almost moribund, and Bethlehem Steel, faced with the possibility of bankruptcy, had shut down many of its operations.

Bethlen, Gábor, Prince of Transylvania
[bet'-len, gah'-bor]

Gábor Bethlen, b. 1580, d. Nov. 15, 1629, was the greatest ruling prince (r. 1613–29) of Transylvania and one of the greatest personalities in Hungarian history. A fervent Hungarian patriot and a devoted Protestant who saw his nation being torn between "two pagans" (the Roman Catholic Habsburg dynasty and the Muslim Turks), Bethlen came to regard the Turks as the lesser of two evils and generally pursued an anti-Habsburg policy. Although unable to attain his primary goal, the reunification of Hungary (including Transylvania), he made his capital city of Gyula-Fehérvár (Alba Julia) into a flourishing center of Hungarian culture and succeeded in making his principality influential in European politics.   S. B. VARDY

Bethlen, István, Count   [isht'-vahn]

Count István Bethlen, b. Oct. 8, 1874, d. 1947?, the scion of a distinguished Transylvanian-Hungarian family, was a dominant political figure in Hungary between the world wars. He played a significant role in establishing the counterrevolutionary regime (1920–44) of Admiral HORTHY, in which he served (1921–31) as prime minister. Dedicated to upholding Hungary's conservative social and political system and disliking communism and nazism equally, Bethlen, during World War II, became one of the leaders of the so-called Anglo-Saxon orientation in Hungarian politics, hoping to prevent Soviet occupation of Hungary. He is believed to have died in captivity in the USSR.   S. B. VARDY

Bibliography: Macartney, C. A., *October Fifteenth: A History of Modern Hungary 1929–1945*, 2 vols. (1956–57).

Bethmann-Hollweg, Theobald von
[bayt'mahn-hohl'-vayk, tay'-oh-bahld fuhn]

Theobald von Bethmann-Hollweg, b. Nov. 29, 1856, d. Jan. 2, 1921, became chancellor of the German Empire on July 14, 1909, after a distinguished career in the Prussian bureaucracy. Although he recognized the need for internal reforms, he lacked the decisiveness to challenge Emperor WILLIAM II, the army, and the governing class. His irresolute pessimism was shown in his failure to block the naval plans of Alfred von TIRPITZ and thus conciliate Britain. In 1914 he promoted military action according to the plan of Graf von SCHLIEFFEN, although Germany was unprepared diplomatically and economically for World War I.

Germany's swift declarations of war and Bethmann's admission that the invasion of Belgium was unjust helped brand his country as the aggressor in world opinion, even though he gained socialist support by portraying Russia as the attacker. Bethmann feared the might of the United States but voted, against his convictions, for unrestricted submarine warfare (which ultimately provoked U.S. entry into the war). His dismissal on July 14, 1917, resulting from a controversy over war aims with Generals HINDENBURG and LUDENDORFF, was welcomed by all sides in Germany.   FREDERIC B. M. HOLLYDAY

Bibliography: Jarausch, K. H., *The Enigmatic Chancellor: Bethmann-Hollweg and the Hubris of Imperial Germany* (1973).

Bethune, Mary McLeod   [buh-thoon']

Mary McLeod Bethune, an American educator, established a small school for black girls that grew into Bethune-Cookman College, Florida, where she served as president. Bethune, the founder of the National Council of Negro Women, was appointed a co-director of the National Youth Administration by Franklin D. Roosevelt. The painting is by Betsy G. Reyneau.

Mary McLeod Bethune, b. Mayesville, S.C., July 10, 1875, d. May 18, 1955, the youngest of 17 children of former slaves, became a leading black educator. As a child she attended the local free school and won a scholarship to continue her education, eventually graduating (1895) from Moody Bible Institute, Chicago. In 1904 she founded the Daytona Normal and Industrial Institute for Negro Girls in Daytona, Fla. Bethune continued to serve as its president after it became (1923) Bethune-Cookman College. She also served as head of several New Deal government agencies, founded (1935) the National Council of Negro Women, and was a vice-president of the National Association for the Advancement of Colored People.

Bibliography: Holt, Rackam, *Mary McLeod Bethune: A Biography* (1964); Meltzer, M., *Mary McLeod Bethune* (1988).

Beti, Mongo   [bay-tee', mohn-goh']

Mongo Beti is the pseudonym of the Cameroonian writer Alexandre Biyidi, b. June 30, 1932. Writing in French, Beti uses his satiric talent to denounce the effects of European colonialism in Africa. His third novel, *Mission to Kala* (1957; Eng. trans., 1958), which received the Sainte-Beuve Prize in 1957, established his reputation. Many of his other works have also been translated into English, including *Remember Ruben* (1980) and *Lament for an African Pol* (1985). Beti lives and teaches in France.   RICHARD K. PRIEBE

Betjeman, Sir John   [bet'-juh-muhn]

Sir John Betjeman, b. Aug. 28, 1906, d. May 19, 1984, England's poet laureate from 1972 until his death, became the nation's most popular poet with the appearance in 1958 of his best-selling *Collected Poems* (rev. ed., 1970). Betjeman is known for his nostalgic evocations of a bygone era and light satires on bad taste. He employs traditional meters, and his treatment of his subject matter—English "tennis-playing suburbia"—is ambiguous but sympathetic. He also advocated the virtues of Victorian architecture in such volumes as *Ghastly Good Taste* (1933; rev. ed., 1971). He was knighted in 1969. His autobiography in verse, *Summoned by Bells*, was published in 1960. Later works include *Church Poems* (1981) and *Uncollected Poems* (1982).   MARTIN SEYMOUR-SMITH

Bibliography: Delaney, Frank, *Betjeman Country* (1984); Denton, P., *Betjeman's London* (1989); Hiller, Bevis, *John Betjeman: A Life in Pictures* (1985); Press, John, *John Betjeman* (1975).

betony   [bet'-uh-nee]

Betony, *Stachys officinalis*, a perennial herb of the mint family, Labiatae, is native to Europe and Asia. The toothed leaves occur in pairs on stems up to 90 cm (3 ft) tall. The purplish or pinkish flowers grow in dense spikes. Physicians once considered betony a cure-all. The name woolly betony refers to the species *S. byzantina*.   CHARLES H. STYER

Betta   [bet'-uh]

Betta is the name of a genus of labyrinth fish, so classified because of their labyrinthine chamber above the gills, which enables them to breathe air. Twelve species of *Betta* occur in swampy, lowland freshwaters of southeast Asia, and one of them, *B. splendens*, is the famous SIAMESE FIGHTING FISH.

Bettelheim, Bruno   [bet'-ul-hym]

Bruno Bettelheim, b. Aug. 28, 1903, d. Mar. 13, 1990, was a naturalized American psychologist who applied the principles of psychoanalysis to the educational process, particularly in the creation of a therapeutic milieu for severely disturbed children. Born in Vienna, he received a doctorate in psychology and philosophy from the University of Vienna in 1938. After Germany's invasion (1938) of Austria, he was interned in Dachau and Buchenwald concentration camps. In 1939, however, he was allowed to emigrate to the United States. His analysis of his concentration-camp experiences, "Individual and Mass Behavior in Extreme Situations," was published in the *Journal of Abnormal and Social Psychology* in 1943.

In 1944, Bettelheim became director of the Sonia Shankman Orthogenic School of the University of Chicago, a post he held until his retirement in 1973. He described his efforts to rehabilitate emotionally disturbed children in *Love Is Not Enough* (1950), *Truants from Life* (1955), *The Empty Fortress* (1967), and *A Home for the Heart* (1974). Other works include *The Informed Heart* (1960), a further investigation of the behavior of concentration-camp internees; *The Children of the Dream* (1969), a study of kibbutz-raised Israeli children; *Freud and Man's Soul* (1983); and *A Good Enough Parent: A Book on Child Rearing* (1987). *The Uses of Enchantment* (1976), an analysis of the nature of fairy tales, won the National Book Award. Bettelheim died a suicide.   EDWARD A. WOLPERT

Better Business Bureau

A Better Business Bureau is a group of local organizations designed to protect business people and consumers from unethical business practices. The first bureau was set up in Minneapolis in 1912 through the efforts of business leaders disturbed by deceptive advertising techniques and selling abuses. Others were subsequently established throughout the United States, Canada, and Mexico, linked by the Council of Better Business Bureaus, located in New York City. The bureaus cooperate with public authorities to expose cheaters, encourage consumer education to reduce the ranks of the gullible, and promote high business and professional standards.

Betti, Enrico

The Italian mathematician Enrico Betti, b. Oct. 21, 1823, d. Aug. 11, 1892, is noted for his contributions to algebra and topology. Betti elaborated on the algebraic concept of Évariste Galois, making an important contribution to the transition from classical to modern algebra. He also published papers on the theory of functions, concentrating on elliptic functions. Influenced by his friend Bernhard Riemann, he did important work in theoretical physics.   THEODORE ALLEGRI

Betti, Ugo

Ugo Betti, b. Feb. 4, 1892, d. June 9, 1953, Italian playwright and poet, was born into a family of esteemed jurists, and he was a respected magistrate. His best plays, such as *Corruzione al Palazzo di Giustizia* (1944; *Corruption in the Palace of Justice*, 1962), reflect his deep concern with the idea of justice and how the law conflicts with ambitions and thirst for power. His work includes 26 plays and several volumes of poetry.   SERGIO PACIFICI

Bibliography: Licastro, Emanuele, *Ugo Betti: An Introduction* (1985).

Beuys, Joseph   [boys]

Joseph Beuys, b. May 12, 1921, d. Jan. 23, 1986, was an avant-garde German sculptor and performance artist. A combat pilot during World War II, he was shot down in the USSR and his life saved by Tatars who wrapped his near-frozen body in fat and felt cloth—substances that came to represent life-giving warmth in his art. Beuys studied and taught at the Academy of Art in Düsseldorf in the 1950s; by the 1960s he had become a major artistic voice in Europe. Although he produced many drawings and posters, it was his temporary installations—sculptures often made of odd collections of foods, dead animals, and bits of iron, or "actions" in which he figured—that excited an almost mythic power over those who saw them.

Bevan, Aneurin   [bev'-uhn, uh-ny'-rin]

Aneurin Bevan, b. Nov. 15, 1897, d. July 6, 1960, was a leading British Labour politician considered the founder of Britain's National Health Service, or "socialized medicine." A Welsh miner in his youth, he became a trade union officer and in 1929 was elected to Parliament. As minister of health (1945–51) in Clement R. Attlee's Labour government, Bevan in 1948 promoted the controversial legislation entitling the British people to free hospital, medical, and dental care. He later led the Labour party's left wing in advocating nuclear disarmament. From 1956 until his death, Bevan was Labour's foreign affairs spokesman.   DON M. CREGIER

Bibliography: Campbell, John, *Aneurin Bevan and the Mirage of British Socialism* (1987); Foot, Michael, *Aneurin Bevan: A Biography*, 2 vols. (1962–73); Krug, Mark M., *Aneurin Bevan, Cautious Rebel* (1961).

Beveridge, William Henry

William Henry Beveridge, b. Mar. 5, 1879, d. Mar. 16, 1963, was a social reformer who drew up the blueprint for Britain's welfare state at the end of World War II. He graduated from Oxford in 1902 and spent the next few years as a social worker in London. In 1909 he wrote *Unemployment: A Problem of Industry*. He was knighted for his services during World War I, administering manpower and food rationing.

The Beveridge Plan was drawn up during World War II by a government committee charged with finding ways to alleviate postwar poverty. Its proposals for a social insurance program covering illness, unemployment, old age, and death formed the basis for the social legislation subsequently adopted. In 1946, Beveridge was made a baron and thereafter took an active part in the House of Lords.

Bibliography: Beveridge, Janet P., *Beveridge and His Plan* (1954); Beveridge, William Henry, *Power and Influence* (1953); Harris, José, *William Beveridge* (1977); Williams, John and Tony, *Keynes, Beveridge, and Beyond* (1987).

Beverley

Beverley is a suburban town in Humberside county in northern England, about 6 km (4 mi) northwest of Hull. The population is 16,433 (1981). Its industries include automobile parts and leather manufacturing and some shipbuilding.

Beverley grew up around a monastery established in the 8th century. After Beverley received its first charter in 1129, it became an important market town. Until 1974 it was the county town of the East Riding of Yorkshire.

Beverley Minster, a Gothic church built between the 13th and 15th centuries, was famous as a place of sanctuary in medieval times.

Bevin, Ernest

A British trade unionist, Ernest Bevin, b. Mar. 9, 1881, d. Apr. 14, 1951, was minister of labour during World War II and foreign secretary in the immediate postwar years. As the organizer and general secretary (1922–40) of the huge Transport and General Workers' Union, Bevin dominated the trade union movement. He was therefore able, as minister of labour (1940–45) in the wartime coalition, to persuade the unions to adapt their aims to make the best use of manpower in the war effort. Becoming foreign secretary in the Labour government of 1945–51, Bevin favored close alignment with the United States and was instrumental in establishing the North Atlantic Treaty Organization in 1949.

Bibliography: Bullock, Alan, *Ernest Bevin,* 3 vols. (1960–84).

Bewick, Thomas   [bue'-ik]

Thomas Bewick, b. Aug. 12, 1753, d. Nov. 8, 1828, was a British engraver and illustrator. He was responsible for the 19th-century revival of wood engraving and the introduction of the technique of white-line engraving on wood, which made possible greater subtlety in the use of light and shade. Bewick learned his craft with a metal engraver in Newcastle. He was a keen, enthusiastic observer of nature, and his books and illustrations met with great success. His most important illustrated works are *A General History of Quadrupeds* (1790) and the two-volume *A History of British Birds* (1797, 1804).

Bibliography: Bain, Iain, *Thomas Bewick* (1981).

Beyazid: see BAYEZID.

Beyle, Henri: see STENDHAL.

Beyond Good and Evil

Friedrich NIETZSCHE's philosophical work *Beyond Good and Evil* (*Jenseits von Gut und Böse,* 1886; Eng. trans., 1907) is a series of 296 aphorisms and reflections that, like his THUS SPAKE ZARATHUSTRA, attack Western civilization and morality for their debilitating effect on the strong and willful. Traditional morality, which protects the weak and mediocre, must be surpassed to arrive at a *Herrenmoral* ("master, or superior, morality"), in which the strong will have achieved the evolutionary goal of humankind through their intellectual powers. Nietzsche's style is lyrical and relies heavily on irony.

JOSEPH A. REITER

Beza, Theodore   [bee'-zuh]

French theologian Theodore Beza, b. June 24, 1519, d. Oct. 13, 1605, was the successor of John Calvin as the leader of Reformed Protestantism. After a severe illness in 1548, Beza went to Geneva and professed the Protestant faith. Although he spent most of the rest of his life in Switzerland, he retained interest in French Protestantism, attending two gatherings of French Huguenots (1561, 1571) and writing a history of the Reformation in France (1580). His laudatory biography of Calvin appeared in the year of Calvin's death (1564). Beza published a critical edition of the Greek New Testament in 1565, based on 17 Greek manuscripts. It later influenced the translators of the King James Version of the Bible. Beza's *Tractationes Theologicae* (1570–82), with its emphasis on double

PREDESTINATION and the absolute character of God's decrees, moved beyond Calvin's thought toward the Protestant scholasticism of the 17th century.   MARK A. NOLL

Béziers

Béziers (1982 pop., 76,647), a city in southeastern France only 20 km (12 mi) from the Mediterranean coast, is located on a hill overlooking the Orb River at its junction with the Canal du Midi. Béziers is primarily a market for wines produced in the Languedoc region, but some chemicals and machinery used in the wine-producing industry are manufactured, and alcohol is distilled. Béziers is a transportation center, with both road and rail connections. After 120 BC the Romans established a colony there. In 1209, during the crusade against the ALBIGENSES, all residents of the town were massacred.

bezique   [buh-zeek']

Bezique is a card game for two that was the first to use melding as the principal means of scoring. It is played with two piquet (32-card) decks in which ace is high and 7 is low. The object of the game is to score points by declaring melds (certain combinations of cards) and by taking tricks that contain *brisques* (any ace or 10).

Bezique may be descended from the 15th-century French game of piquet, but most experts believe it was invented by a Swedish schoolmaster in the early 1800s. Although variations of the game (some involving three or four players and up to eight decks) are still played in parts of Europe, its popularity has been eclipsed by PINOCHLE, which is derived from bezique.

Bibliography: Hoyle, Edmund, *Hoyle's Card Games* (1979); Morehead, Albert H., ed., *Official Rules of Card Games* (1978); Scarne, John, *Scarne's Encyclopedia of Card Games* (1983).

Bhabha, Homi Jehangir   [bah'-bah, hoh'-mee juh-hahn-geer']

The Indian physicist Homi Jehangir Bhabha, b. Oct. 30, 1909, d. Jan. 24, 1966, was primarily responsible for inaugurating high-energy physics research and the peaceful use of atomic energy in India. He graduated (1930, 1935) from Cambridge and remained there until 1939, investigating cosmic rays and electron-positron pair production. During World War II, as professor at the Bangalore Institute of Science in India, Bhabha urged the national coordination of physics research; in 1945 he became the director of the new Tata Institute of Fundamental Research. He became chairman of India's Atomic Energy Commission in 1948 and secretary of the Department of Atomic Energy in 1962.   MICHAEL MEO

Bhagavad Gita   [bah'-guh-vuhd gee'-tah]

The Bhagavad Gita (Sanskrit, "The Lord's Song") is one of the most widely studied sacred writings of HINDUISM. Taken from book 6 of the Indian epic MAHABHARATA, the Bhagavad Gita, written as a poem, is KRISHNA's response to questions posed by Arjuna, a warrior prince, concerning his responsibility in good and evil as he is about to go into battle. Krishna, incarnated as Arjuna's charioteer, laid the cornerstone of Hindu philosophy by instructing Arjuna with the following principles: the world of matter and individual consciousness are grounded in the same spiritual reality; intuition can grasp the divine reality; human beings possess two natures, a divine self within a material being; and life is intended to lead people to unity with the divine spirit.   JANE COLVILLE BETTS

Bibliography: Minor, Robert N., ed., *Modern Indian Interpreters of the Bhagavad Gita* (1986); Nikhilananda, Swami, *The Bhagavad Gita* (1944).

bhakti   [bahk'-tee]

In Hinduism, *bhakti,* a Sanskrit word, means "devotion to God" or "love of God." *Bhakti* involves a surrender to God frequently intensified by the continuous repetition of his name. In the Bhagavad Gita, a religious classic of Hinduism, the discipline, or path (YOGA), of *bhakti* is one of three that are taught as methods of gaining liberation, the highest goal in many types of Hinduism. During what historians call the Bhakti period, from about the 8th century until the present, devotional movements within Hinduism have celebrated *bhakti* to the extent, in some cases, of viewing servitude to God as superior even to liberation as classically conceived. Devotion may involve symbols or images, or it may be the worship of God as all-pervading, formless spirit. KARL H. POTTER

bharata natyam [bah'-ruh-tuh naht'-yuhm]

A highly developed classical dance of India, bharata natyam is one of the oldest (as early as 1500 BC) documented dance forms in the world. It is a blend of pure lyric movement and pantomime drama. Modern performances sometimes last two hours without interruption. Rigid traditions govern every movement of the dance, which was first performed by temple dancers in southern India.

Bharhut [bah-root']

Bharhut, a village in Madya Pradesh state, north central India, is the site of an ancient Buddhist monastic retreat. Its principal stupa, or relic-shrine, has survived in the fragments of the stone railing with gates that originally surrounded it. Carved from a fine-grained reddish stone, c.150 BC, the rail and gates imitated the form and construction of wooden post-and-rail fences and portals. Each railing segment was made of three rails tenoned into uprights; each of the original four gates was carved to show a cluster of four poles. These were tied to form a pier at each side of the opening and supported the elaborate structure of a triple lintel. The faces of rails, uprights, and gates were elaborately carved with a rich variety of Buddhist symbols, floral motifs, heads of rajahs, and narrative references to key incidents in the Buddha's history. DIRAN KAVORK DOHANIAN

Bhartrihari [bahr-tree-hah'-ree]

Bhartrihari, fl. c.500, was a Sanskrit grammarian and philosopher best known for his *Vakyapadiya* (Treatise on Words and Sentences). The work deals with the philosophical problems of language and attempts to place it within the framework of metaphysics. Bhartrihari saw the Logos, or Word, as the one unifying principle. It is believed that this Bhartrihari was the lyric poet who wrote the three *shatakas* (centuries) of stanzas on love, worldly life, and renunciation. GAUTAM DASGUPTA

Bhavabhuti [bah-vuh-boo'-tee]

The Sanskrit writer Bhavabhuti, fl. c.700, was born in Vidarbha province of central India and flowered as a dramatist under the patronage of King Yashovarman of Kanauj. Known for his skillful characterization and handling of plot, he wrote elaborate verses that occasionally suffered from unwieldy syntax. Second only to Kalidasa in fame, Bhavabhuti wrote three major plays: *Malati and Madhava* (Eng. trans., 1913), frequently compared to *Romeo and Juliet* and based on a secular romance, *Mahavira-Carita* (Story of the Great Hero), and *Uttara-rama-Carita* (Later Story of Rama). GAUTAM DASGUPTA

Bhave, Acharya Vinoba [bah'-vay, vin'-oh-buh]

Acharya Vinoba Bhave, b. Sept. 11, 1895, d. Nov. 15, 1982, was an Indian ascetic and disciple of Mahatma Gandhi. A Brahmin, he joined Gandhi in 1916 and devoted his life to the movement of Sarvodaya, improving the lives of Indian villagers. The culmination of his work was his Bhoodan Yajna ("land gift") program of land reform, in which land would be donated by landowners for distribution to the landless Untouchables. He pursued this program from 1951 to 1956, and about 405,000 ha (1,000,000 acres) were actually distributed. The program was replaced with one combining village lands on a cooperative basis.

Bibliography: Diwakar, R. R., and Agrawal, M., eds., *Vinoba: The Spiritual Revolutionary* (1984); Narayan, S., *Vinoba: His Life and Work* (1970).

Bhil [beel]

The Bhil are a culturally varied tribal people numbering nearly 2.5 million and spread over the states of western and central India. Their history has been one of alternately friendly and hostile relations with Rajput, Mogul, and, later, British rulers; but their various uprisings against colonizing groups were mostly unsuccessful.

Although thought of as tribal and having the status of a Scheduled Tribe under the Indian constitution, the Bhil have not retained a distinct language and have adopted the kinship patterns and cultural practices of their dominant neighbors. Many follow the Rajput pattern, some have become Muslims, and some sections employ their own Brahmins in accordance with high-caste Hindu practices. Even where the Bhil have not been culturally assimilated, their way of life is highly influenced by the wider society. Groupings are internally ranked in the same way as castes, and their religion has incorporated Hindu gods, along with the worship of ancestors and nature spirits. Under British rule many gave up the traditional shifting cultivation and became settled agriculturists. Since then their notorious reputation for banditry has gradually declined. HILARY STANDING AND R. L. STIRRAT

Bibliography: Dhashi, S. M., *Bhils* (1971); Karve, Irawati, *The Bhils of Western Khandesh* (1961); Naik, T. B., *The Bhils* (1960).

Bhopal [boh-pahl']

Bhopal, the capital of Madhya Pradesh state in central India, is a rail, market, and industrial center with a population of 1,063,662 (1991). Leading industries include textile making, food processing, and the manufacture of electrical equipment. The older part of the city rises from the north shore of a large artificial lake up a steep ridge topped by the remains of an impressive fortress. Behind the fortress is a huge unfinished 19th-century mosque, the Taj-ul-Masjid.

The princely state of Bhopal was founded in the early 1700s by Dost Muhammad Khan, an Afghan who had served the Mogul emperor Aurangzeb. From 1818 until India gained independence, the city of Bhopal was the headquarters of Bhopal Agency, a group of nine princely states; it was the capital of Bhopal state until that state was incorporated into Madhya Pradesh in 1956. On Dec. 3, 1984, Bhopal was the scene of the worst industrial accident in history. Some 2,500 persons died and as many as 200,000 were injured when toxic methyl isocyanate gas leaked from a pesticide plant there. The tragedy raised serious questions about the safety of the chemical industry and the legal and moral responsibilities of multinational corporations operating in Third World countries.

Bhubaneswar [bu-vuh-naysh'-wur]

Bhubaneswar (1991 pop., 411,542), from 1948 the capital of Orissa state, east central India, has been developed since then into a model township and administrative center. Historically it was an important religious center noted for its Hindu temples that once numbered in the thousands and of which fewer than a hundred remain. The oldest among them, dedicated to Parashurameshvara, was built c.750. The Lingaraj, completed c.1000, is dedicated to Shiva Tribhuvaneshvar, "Lord of the Three Worlds," who is enshrined in the sanctum as a gigantic phallic column (lingam) and is the source, in this manifestation, of the name of the royal city.

The Hindu temples of Bhubaneswar are built of fine-cut stone and are closed over by corbeled vaults. The outer surfaces are often richly and delicately carved, with a splendid sense of proportion. Although they exhibit a variety of architectural effects, the temples are all organized around the simple relationship between a low, broad pavilion and a high tower, which rises directly over the icon in the innermost sanctum. Ancient Orissan architectural texts, which give precise directions for the design and construction of temples, designate the towers as mountains, as though to underscore the conception of them as replicas of those natural heights where the great gods of the Hindus were believed to dwell eternally. DIRAN KAVORK DOHANIAN

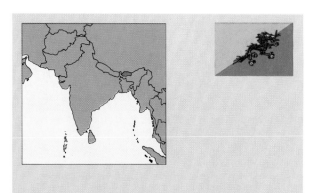

KINGDOM OF BHUTAN

LAND. Area: 47,000 km² (18,150 mi²). Capital and largest city: Thimphu (1985 est. pop., 20,000).

PEOPLE. Population (1987 est.): 1,472,911. Density (1987 est.): 31.3 persons per km² (81.2 per mi²). Distribution (1986): 95% rural, 5% urban. Annual growth (1978–86): 2%. Official language: Dzongkha. Major religions: Tibetan Buddhism, Hinduism.

EDUCATION AND HEALTH. Literacy (1986): 5%. Universities (1987): none. Hospital beds (1983): 831. Physicians (1983): 65. Life expectancy (1985): men—47.6; women—46.1. Infant mortality (1986): 139 per 1,000 live births.

ECONOMY. GNP (1985): $155.6 million; $140 per capita. Labor distribution (1986): agriculture—93%; commerce and services—4%; government and public authorities—2%; manufacturing—1%. Foreign trade (1985): imports—$69.4 million; exports—$15.1 million; principal trade partner—India. Currency: 1 ngultrum (Nu) = 100 chetrums.

GOVERNMENT. Type: monarchy. Legislature: National Assembly. Political subdivisions: 18 regions.

COMMUNICATIONS. Railroads (1987): none. Roads (1984): 2,050 km (1,274 mi) total. Major ports: none. Major airfields: 1.

Bhutan   [boo-tan']

Bhutan is an independent, landlocked kingdom located in Asia on the southern flanks of the eastern Himalayas. It is bordered on the south and east by Assam (India), on the west by Sikkim, and on the north and west by Tibet (China). The capital is THIMBU. The people are mainly of Tibetan origin, and the name *Bhutan* is derived from the Indian word *Bhotanta*, meaning "the edge of Tibet."

LAND

Bhutan is a mountainous land, located where the HIMALAYAS rise abruptly from the subtropical lowlands of the Ganges-Brahmaputra plains of northern India. In the south it includes a 16-km-wide (10-mi) zone of alluvial sands and gravels that are known as the Duars and are transitional between the lowlands of the Indian Plain and the mountain ranges of the Himalayas. North of the Duars is a 65–80-km-wide (40–50-mi) region occupied by the Inner Himalayas, which range in elevation between 1,500 m and 3,000 m (5,000 and 10,000 ft). The Inner Himalayas in Bhutan are dissected by a series of fertile north-south valleys where most of the population is concentrated. North of the Inner Himalayas are the Greater Himalayas, which occupy about one-third of Bhutan; they have an average elevation of more than 3,000 m (10,000 ft) and reach a high point on the Tibetan border of 7,554 m (24,784 ft).

The climate at low altitudes ranges from humid subtropical in the Duars and Inner Himalayas valleys below 1,050 m (3,500 ft) to a temperate zone with cool winters and hot summers at elevations between 1,050 and 2,250 m (3,000 and 7,500 ft). Most people live in this temperate zone. A cold zone suitable only for summer grazing lies between 2,250 m (7,500 ft) and the permanent snowline at 4,500 m (13,500 ft). The southern mountain slopes receive heavy summer rainfall of 5,100 to 7,600 mm (200 to 300 in) from winds of the summer monsoon moving in from the Bay of Bengal across the plains of northern India.

PEOPLE

The dominant ethnic group in Bhutan are the Bhutia, who constitute about 60% of the population and refer to themselves as the Drukpas ("dragon people"). The Bhutias are

Peasants in the fertile Paro Valley haul firewood past the local dzong, *a Buddhist monastery and administrative center. Paro, in west central Bhutan, is significant as a terminus of the nation's major highway.*

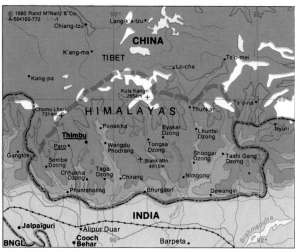

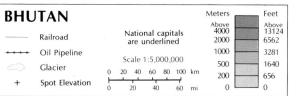

BHUTAN

———   Railroad

+‑+‑+‑+   Oil Pipeline

〜〜〜   Glacier

+   Spot Elevation

National capitals are underlined

Scale 1:5,000,000

0 20 40 60 80 100 km
0   20   40   60 mi

Meters	Feet
Above 4000	Above 13124
2000	6562
1000	3281
500	1640
200	656
0	0

related in language, religion, and customs to the people of Tibet and inhabit the middle reaches of the main north-south valleys in central Bhutan. The second-largest group are the Nepalese, who live mainly in the southwest foothills. In the early 1990s, the enforcement of a 1985 citizenship act requiring pre-1958 domicile in Bhutan made many Nepalese stateless and led to antigovernment protests and an exodus of Nepalese from Bhutan. Other groups include a few Assamese and frontier tribes in the east and a primitive people known to the Drukpa as Monpa, who engage in SLASH-AND-BURN AGRICULTURE in the east and southeast. Virtually all Bhutia practice a form of Buddhism of the Drukpa sect that is closely related to TIBETAN BUDDHISM; the Nepalese are Hindus.

ECONOMIC ACTIVITY

The economy of Bhutan is one of the world's least developed. Less than 10% of the land is cultivated, and about 95% of the labor force is engaged in largely subsistence agricultural activities. The principal food crop is rice, followed by maize (corn), other grains, and potatoes. Crops raised for export include cardamom (a spice), apples, and oranges. Animal husbandry is important; large numbers of yaks, cattle, sheep, pigs, goats, and poultry are raised in the valleys and on mountain pastures. Manufacturing activities focus mainly on such traditional handicrafts as papermaking, carved lacquer woodworking, and intricate metal and leather work. In 1961 the country embarked on a series of 5-year development plans financed mostly by India. Initial emphasis was on expanding education and health care and developing all-weather roads, hydroelectric-power facilities, and small-scale industries such as timber, mineral, and food and beverage processing. By the 1980s the focus had shifted to projects designed to make Bhutan economically self-sufficient. The Chuka hydroelectric installation, which became operational in 1986, provides power to western Bhutan and India.

Bhutan traditionally traded with Tibet. Since 1959, when the Tibetan border was closed, most trade has been with India; direct links with Nepal were established in 1986. Bhutan was opened to tourists in 1974; tourism soon surpassed the sale of stamps to collectors as the chief source of foreign exchange.

GOVERNMENT

Bhutan's head of state is a hereditary king with the title of Druk Gyalpo ("Dragon King"). Bhutan was an absolute monarchy from 1907 to 1969, but power is now, at least nominally, shared by the king, a council of ministers, and a national assembly (the Tsongdu). A majority of the assembly's members are elected by groups of village headmen; the remainder are appointed by the king or chosen by Bhutan's lamas. External affairs are governed by a 1949 Indo-Bhutan Treaty of Friendship, under which Bhutan agrees to seek, but not necessarily accept, the advice of India. Bhutan has no political parties.

HISTORY

Bhutanese links with Tibet date from at least the 7th century AD, and independence from Tibet dates from about 1630, when a dissenting Tibetan lama made himself the first dharma raja, or spiritual leader, of Bhutan. Under subsequent dharma rajas, a deb raja, or temporal ruler, was appointed to administer the country, but in time real power was held by the provincial governors. British interests, which became Indian interests after India became independent in 1947, date from 1774, when a treaty was concluded with the East India Company. In 1865 the British government agreed to support Bhutan financially, and under the 1910 Treaty of Punakha, Bhutan agreed to be guided in foreign affairs by British India. Sir Ugyen Wangchuk, the most powerful of the provincial governors, assumed control of the government in 1907 and was elected the first hereditary maharaja (later king) of Bhutan. The present king is Jigme Singye Wangchuk, the fourth in the line, who succeeded to the throne on July 24, 1972, on the death of his father, Jigme Dorji Wangchuk. In 1988 his eight-year-old son was named crown prince.   RHOADS MURPHEY

Bibliography: Edmunds, T. O., *Bhutan* (1989); Karan, P., *Bhutan* (1987; repr. 1990); Pommaret, F., *Introduction to Bhutan* (1991); Rose, L., *The Politics of Bhutan* (1977).

Bhutto   (family)   [boo'-toh]

Zulfikar Ali Bhutto, b. Jan. 5, 1928, d. Apr. 4, 1979, headed the government of Pakistan from 1971 to 1977. A wealthy lawyer who held several cabinet posts under Muhammad AYUB KHAN, he formed the opposition Pakistan People's party (PPP) in 1967. The PPP received a majority vote in West Pakistan in the 1970 election but not a legislative majority. Voiding the election helped spark the civil war in which East Pakistan gained independence as Bangladesh. Bhutto became president in 1971, after the war, and prime minister under a new constitution in 1973. Although he restored civil liberties, his land redistribution and nationalization policies aroused opposition. Overthrown in a July 1977 military coup led by Muhammad ZIA UL-HAQ, Bhutto was tried for ordering the murder of a political opponent and later hanged. His wife, **Nusrat Bhutto**, b. 1934, and his daughter, **Benazir Bhutto**, b. June 21, 1953, assumed leadership of the PPP. Benazir was under house arrest from 1981 to 1984 and in exile from 1984 to 1986. In December 1988, after Zia's death and elections in which the PPP won a plurality of seats (one of them held by her mother), she became prime minister and the first woman to head a modern Muslim state. She accomplished little and was dismissed by the president on Aug. 6, 1990. Her PPP decisively lost the 1990 elections, but she returned as prime minister after a narrow PPP electoral victory in October 1993.

Bibliography: Bhutto, Benazir, *Daughter of Destiny* (1989); Burki, Shahid Javed, *Pakistan under Bhutto* (1979).

Biafra   [bee-af'-ruh]

Biafra was the name taken by a secessionist state created in the southeastern section of Nigeria, West Africa, in May 1967. Biafra's boundaries during its brief existence were the Gulf of Guinea to the south, Cameroon to the east, the Niger River to the west, and the former Northern Region, making its area about 113,960 km^2 (44,000 mi^2). The state was created by the IBO and led by Lt. Col. Chukwuemeka Odumegwu OJUKWU. When Nigeria sought to reclaim the territory, a devastating civil war ensued. The Biafran capital of Enugu fell to federal troops in October 1967, and by April 1968 the federal army had reconquered most of the territory. The rebellion continued until January 1970. Severe malnutrition resulted in the death of perhaps 1 million of the civilian population.

The region is now divided among several Nigerian states. Tropical rain forests, which provide timber, are found inland. Long a source of agricultural products, the area has extensive oil and coal reserves and an expanding industrial sector.

Bibliography: Ekwe-Ekwe, H., *The Biafra War* (1991); Jacobs, D., *The Brutality of Nations* (1987).

Bialik, Hayyim Nahman   [bee- yah'-lik, hy'-im nah'-muhn]

The Ukrainian-born Hayyim Nahman Bialik, b. Jan. 9, 1873, d. July 4, 1934, was one of the most influential figures in modern Hebrew literature. After receiving a traditional Jewish education and working briefly as a merchant and a teacher, he began to write in the 1890s, when he became part of a literary circle in Odessa that included his mentor, ACHAD HA-AM.

Bialik initially achieved fame with such searing poems as "The City of Slaughter" (1903; Eng. trans., 1934), which recounts the horrors of the pogroms and the passivity of its Jewish victims. Imbued with the ideas of the Hebrew enlightenment (*Haskalah*), Bialik also edited and published pamphlets in Odessa and later in Warsaw and Germany. His often anguished writings, in both Hebrew and Yiddish, fuse traditional Jewish themes with an overpowering lyricism and majesty. His poetry in particular treats the conflicts between the Jewish past and the modern world and, in his later works, the Zionist ideal of founding a homeland in Palestine, where Bialik himself settled in 1924. He also translated works by Shakespeare, Cervantes, Heine, and others into Hebrew.

Bibliography: Aberbach, David, *Bialik* (1989); Mintz, Alan, *Hurban: Responses to Catastrophe in Hebrew Literature* (1984).

Biarritz   [bee-ah-reets']

Biarritz (1982 pop., 26,579) is a town in southwestern France, on the Bay of Biscay near the Spanish border. Endowed with fine beaches, a mild climate, and mineral waters, the town has been a fashionable resort since it was visited by Napoleon III and Empress Eugénie in 1854. The indigenous population of Biarritz is Basque.

biathlon   [by-ath'-luhn]

The biathlon is a relatively new sports event that combines two athletic skills. The summer biathlon consists of a 4,000-m (2½-mi) run and a 300-m (328-yd) swim. The Modern Pentathlon Association of Great Britain introduced this combination in 1968 to help future pentathlon contestants develop these skills early so they could later concentrate on fencing, riding, and shooting, the three other pentathlon skills. Senior men then adopted the biathlon as a separate event.

The winter biathlon combines a 20-km (12.4-mi) cross-country ski race with a series of pauses for shooting. This biathlon is a direct descendant of the World War II military ski patrol and had its Olympic debut at Squaw Valley, Calif., in 1960. The participants must carry a single-shot rifle and stop four times at roughly 4-km (2.5-mi) intervals and fire five shots at each stop. At the first and third stops they shoot from a prone position at a target that is 25 cm (9.8 in) in circumference and has a 12.5-cm (4.9-in) bull's-eye. At the second and fourth stops they shoot from a standing position at a 50-cm (19.7-in) target with a 35-cm (13.8-in) bull's-eye. The distances to the targets vary between 100 and 250 m (109 and 274 ft), with the greater distances used for the prone position. For each failure to hit the target, 2 min are added to the contestant's time, and for each shot in the outer ring, 1 min is added. The biathlon relay, for four men each traversing 7.5 km (4.7 mi), has slightly different rules and was introduced as an Olympic sport in 1968. At the 1980 Olympics a 10-km (6.2-mi) individual event was added to the agenda.

Biber, Heinrich Ignaz Franz von   [bee'-bur]

Heinrich Biber, b. Aug. 12, 1644, d. May 3, 1704, was a Bohemian violinist and composer. He is believed to have been a pupil of the Austrian composer Johann Heinrich Schmelzer. Biber spent the greater part of his life as a musician at the court of the archbishop of Salzburg and helped popularize *scordatura* (the abnormal tuning of a violin in order to create special effects). His 15 *Mystery* sonatas (c.1676) were important seminal works in the development of the sonata form. These sonatas and Biber's *Passacaglia in G Minor* for solo violin are still in the repertoire. He also composed 3 operas. Biber's compositions require that the performer possess the skill that made Biber the foremost violin virtuoso of the late 17th century.

Bibiena   (family):   see GALLI DA BIBIENA   (family).

Bible

The word *Bible* is derived from the Greek *biblia*, meaning "books," and refers to the sacred writings of Judaism and Christianity. The Bible consists of two parts. The first part, called the Old Testament by Christians, consists of the sacred writings of the Jewish people and was written originally in Hebrew, except for some portions in Aramaic. The second part, called the New Testament, was composed in Greek and records the story of Jesus and the beginnings of Christianity. Translated in whole or in part into more than 1,500 languages, the Bible is the most widely distributed book in the world. Its influence on history and culture, including literature and the other arts, is incalculable.

THE OLD TESTAMENT
Major Themes and Characteristics. The Hebrew Bible, written over a period of more than 500 years, consists of many types of literature and reflects varying points of view. It is essentially religious, but, unlike most ancient religious books, the Old Testament is characterized by a strong sense of history; even laws and exhortations are woven into the various narratives.

The themes are the uniqueness and glory of GOD (Yahweh), the COVENANTS he made with Israel, the Law, God's control of history and Israel's special destiny, God's revelation through the PROPHETS, the nature of humanity, corporate and individual sin and its remedy, and the true worship of God.

The Hebrews believed that their religion was founded on covenants that God offered them and that they had accepted. Yahweh had agreed to make them his specially chosen people and to protect them, but only if they obeyed his Law. Covenants were made with NOAH that embraced all humankind, and with ABRAHAM and his descendants; but the most important covenant was revealed to MOSES. Later, after the division of the JEWS into two kingdoms—JUDAH and ISRAEL—the people of Judah believed that a special covenant had also been made with King DAVID and his royal descendants.

Yahweh was different from all other deities. Israel was forbidden to worship any other god, and the Mosaic religion perhaps implied that no other existed, although this was not specifically emphasized until the time of the exile during the Babylonian Captivity (587–37 BC). Other gods personified natural forces or tribes and nations, but Yahweh was supreme over everything. Because he controlled history, he could use Assyria or Babylonia to punish a rebellious Israel. Plentiful crops depended on his will alone and not on the magical rites by which the Baals of Canaan were worshiped. The concept of the Book of LEVITICUS was that the Hebrews were to be a holy people, separated from all defilement.

Many laws in the Pentateuch, or TORAH, the first five books, were not different from those of surrounding nations. There were some unique commandments given, however, without

This 11th-century Byzantine manuscript illustration depicts one of the great events of the Old Testament: Moses receiving the Law, or Torah, from God on Mount Sinai while the people of Israel watch in awe. The hands of Moses are covered out of respect for the holiness of the Law.

specific rewards and punishments; most important were the TEN COMMANDMENTS, which have a high ethical content. The TORAH (Law) was a complete religious and civil law for the whole nation. It prescribed sacrifices and festivals similar to those of other nations, but the emphasis was on morality. Yahweh was a God of justice. All sin and injustice was an offense against him; and repentance could bring forgiveness.

In the Book of JOSHUA, Yahweh is a God of war who commands the slaughter of the Canaanites, but the Hebrew religion gradually outgrew such a concept, as can be seen in the books of JEREMIAH and JONAH. The prophets saw history as an interaction between the living God and his people, and its outcome depended on their obedience. Israel was destined to be a light to the nations, but it always had a special place in God's purpose and love, and the Hebrews always struggled with the two concepts of God's impartial justice and his love toward Israel. Late in the biblical period, writers of APOCALYPTIC LITERATURE, unlike the earlier prophets, despaired of the normal forces of history and believed that God would put an end to the present age, bringing in a miraculous reign of righteousness.

These themes were not systematized into a theology but

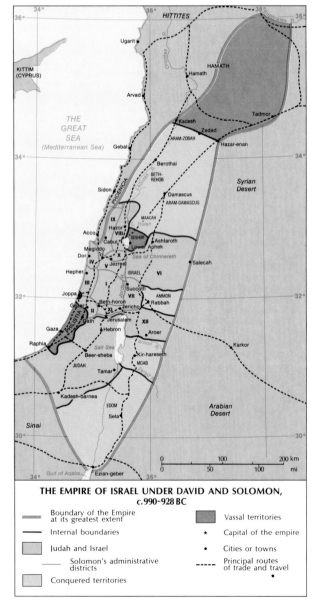

THE EMPIRE OF ISRAEL UNDER DAVID AND SOLOMON, c. 990–928 BC

▰▰▰ Boundary of the Empire at its greatest extent		▨ Vassal territories
▬▬ Internal boundaries		★ Capital of the empire
▨ Judah and Israel		• Cities or towns
▬ Solomon's administrative districts		---- Principal routes of trade and travel
▨ Conquered territories		•

can be discerned from the literature as a whole, which expresses the hopes, fears, laments, thanksgivings, and even the doubts of the Hebrews. Thus the Book of JOB criticizes the popular, facile doctrine of reward and punishment, and the Book of ECCLESIASTES often approaches skepticism.

The Canon. The canon, or officially accepted list of books in the Hebrew Bible, consists of 24 books according to Jewish reckoning and is divided into three parts: the Law, the Prophets, and the Writings. The Law (Torah), often called the Pentateuch, comprises five books, GENESIS through DEUTERONOMY. The Prophets (Neví im) are divided into three parts: the earlier prophets (Joshua, JUDGES, 1 and 2 SAMUEL, and 1 and 2 KINGS); the later prophets (ISAIAH, Jeremiah, and EZEKIEL); and twelve books called the Minor Prophets because of their brevity. The 11 Writings (Ketuvim) include three poetic books (PSALMS, PROVERBS, and Job); the five scrolls (SONG OF SOLOMON, RUTH, LAMENTATIONS, Ecclesiastes, and ESTHER); an apocalyptic work, DANIEL; and EZRA-NEHEMIAH and 1 and 2 CHRONICLES.

Christian Bibles arrange the books differently. The Law, or Pentateuch, comes first, then all the historical books. These are followed by the poetical, or wisdom, books and finally the prophetic books. Thus Ruth, Chronicles, Ezra, Nehemiah, and Esther appear in the second group and Daniel and Lamentations in the fourth.

The Jews never ceased writing religious books. Several books composed in Hebrew or Greek after 300 BC are part of the SEPTUAGINT, or Old Greek version, and were regarded as Scripture by many Christians. Roman Catholics and the Orthodox include these books, called APOCRYPHA or deuterocanonical books, in the Bible. Protestants omit them or print them as an appendix to the Bible.

Divisions of the Old Testament. The following discussion uses the Christian classification of books.

Pentateuch. Genesis recounts the creation of the universe and the first human beings, the traditions of the DELUGE, and the stories of the patriarchs down to the sojourn of the Hebrews in Egypt and the deaths of JACOB and JOSEPH. EXODUS tells how Moses led the people from Egypt and received the covenant and Law on Mount Sinai. Leviticus is largely a legal code; NUMBERS continues the story of migration toward the Promised Land. Deuteronomy partly repeats the narrative, recording other laws, and concludes with the death of Moses. It teaches a strict doctrine of corporate reward and punishment.

The Pentateuch is based on four principal sources. The oldest, J, was perhaps written in Judah, the southern kingdom, about 950 BC. Between 900 and 750, another version from Israel, the northern kingdom, was woven in; this is called EPHRAIM (E). In the 7th century BC, Deuteronomy, or most of it (D), was compiled. About 550 BC, during the exile, the final edition of the Torah added a priestly source (P), some parts of which are very old.

Historical Books. Joshua tells of a thorough conquest of Canaan, but Judges contains traditions of the Hebrew tribes in the period before the monarchy that reveal the conquest as partial. The books of Samuel are about the founding of the monarchy under SAUL and David and contain a magnificent early source for the life of David, probably written about 961–22 BC. All the above books have been extensively edited by writers who shared the theology of the D source.

Ezra and Nehemiah were composed after the exile, when these two leaders restored Judaism in Palestine, and Nehemiah's own memoirs make up much of the latter book. The two Books of Chronicles cover Hebrew history from Ezra's priestly point of view but contain some valuable earlier traditions. Ruth is the story of a foreign woman who became loyal to Israel and was the ancestor of David. Esther is a tale of a Jewish queen of Persia who saved her people from persecution.

Poetical, or Wisdom, Books. Job contains some of the finest poetry in the Bible. Its themes are the problems of suffering and of man's standing before God. The Psalms were essentially composed for temple worship, although some may be pieces of individual devotion. Many are ascribed to David, but some come from an earlier period. Proverbs comprises several collections of ancient wisdom. Parts of Ecclesiastes are skeptical, but other sections express conventional wisdom. The Song of Solomon is a collection of love poems.

The Prophets. The great prophets of the 8th century BC were AMOS, HOSEA, Isaiah, and MICAH. They proclaimed God's holiness and his judgment on the idol worship and moral abuses of the Hebrew kingdoms, and called the people back to loyalty to the covenant. Jeremiah, the greatest prophet of the 7th century BC, was unique in recording his inner spiritual struggles and in promising a new covenant. Like Isaiah, he opposed military alliances with foreign nations and resistance to the Babylonian invasion. ZEPHANIAH and perhaps HABAKKUK belong to the same century. NAHUM gloats over the destruction (612 BC) of Nineveh. The most significant prophets during the period of Babylonian exile were the Ezekiel and the unknown authors of chapters 40–55 and 56–66 of Isaiah, who encouraged the return of the Jews to the Holy Land and promised a glorious national life. Lamentations reflects the miseries of the exile.

The remaining prophets followed the exile. OBADIAH is strongly nationalistic; JONAH expresses God's concern for Gentiles as well as Jews. HAGGAI and ZECHARIAH 1–8 reflect the rebuilding of a small temple in Jerusalem. JOEL, Zachariah 9–14, and MALACHI combine the themes of judgment and restoration and have apocalyptic elements. Daniel is an apocalypse from the Maccabean period (*c.*164 BC) and promises God's help to the Jews in time of persecution.

THE NEW TESTAMENT

Major Themes and Characteristics. Covenant and law are central in the Old Testament, and JESUS CHRIST is central in the New Testament. The dominant theme is the interpretation of Jesus' nature as CHRIST or MESSIAH (the anointed one), Son of man, Son of God, Lord, and Prophet. This was a complete reinterpretation of the Jewish hope for an anointed king descended from David. Perhaps before Jesus' death, his disciples had already acclaimed him as Messiah, but they became convinced of this from experiences that proved to them he

Saint Matthew is shown writing his Gospel, the first book of the New Testament. This illustration appears in the Sainte-Chapelle Gospel Book, a German manuscript of the early 11th century.

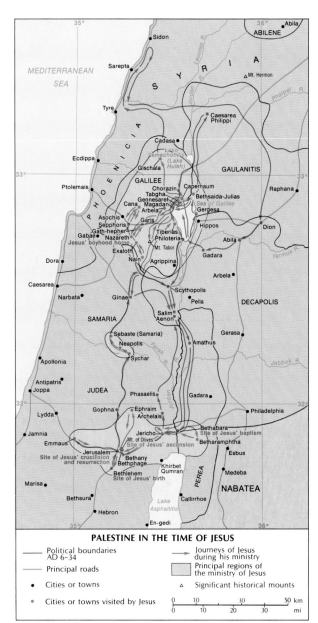

PALESTINE IN THE TIME OF JESUS

—— Political boundaries AD 6–34	→ Journeys of Jesus during his ministry
—— Principal roads	▢ Principal regions of the ministry of Jesus
• Cities or towns	△ Significant historical mounts
• Cities or towns visited by Jesus	0 10 30 50 km 0 10 20 30 mi

was again alive. Thus the RESURRECTION is the second major theme. The Messiah now came to mean, not a conquering, successful king, but a crucified Lord whose unique relationship to God could be suggested only partially by the titles applied to him.

In explaining and defending their faith, the disciples of Jesus found passages in the Old Testament that they believed were prophecies of his death, resurrection, and nature (for example, Psalm 110:1, Isaiah 53; Daniel 7:13–14). They also preserved Jesus' sayings and the stories of his life, which they interpreted in light of their faith. Jesus had proclaimed the gospel ("good news") of the coming reign, or kingdom, of God and carried on a ministry of teaching, forgiveness, and healing. Although much of his teaching agreed with that of other Jews, his more radical and prophetic sayings made enemies. The high priest and his associates feared Jesus as a threat to the established order, and the Roman governor Pontius PILATE was persuaded to have Jesus crucified. Thus, the gospel tradition contains both the message of Jesus and the proclamation of his divine nature.

Other new experiences of ecstasy and prophecy were inter-

BOOKS OF THE BIBLE

Christian Bible				Hebrew Bible	
OLD TESTAMENT		*The Prophetical Books*		*The Law (Torah)*	
The Pentateuch		Isaiah	Obadiah	Genesis	Numbers
Genesis		Jeremiah	Jonah	Exodus	Deuteronomy
Exodus		Lamentations	Micah	Leviticus	
Leviticus		Baruch*	Nahum		
Numbers		Ezekiel	Habakkuk	*The Prophets (Neví im)*	
Deuteronomy		Daniel	Zephaniah	(Early Prophets)	
		Hosea	Haggai	Joshua	Joel
The Historical Books		Joel	Zechariah	Judges	Amos
Joshua	2 Chronicles	Amos	Malachi	1 Samuel	Obadiah
Judges	Ezra			2 Samuel	Jonah
Ruth	Nehemiah	**NEW TESTAMENT**		1 Kings	Micah
1 Samuel	Tobit*			2 Kings	Nahum
2 Samuel	Judith*	Matthew	1 Timothy	(Later Prophets)	Habakkuk
1 Kings	Esther	Mark	2 Timothy	Isaiah	Zephaniah
2 Kings	1 Maccabees*	Luke	Titus	Jeremiah	Haggai
1 Chronicles	2 Maccabees*	John	Philemon	Ezekiel	Zechariah
		The Acts	Hebrews	Hosea	Malachi
The Poetical or Wisdom Books		Romans	James		
Job		1 Corinthians	1 Peter	*The Writings (Ketuvim)*	
Psalms		2 Corinthians	2 Peter	Psalms	Esther
Proverbs		Galatians	1 John	Proverbs	Daniel
Ecclesiastes		Ephesians	2 John	Job	Ezra
Song of Solomon (Songs)		Philippians	3 John	Song of Songs	Nehemiah
Wisdom*		Colossians	Jude	Ruth	1 Chronicles
Sirach*		1 Thessalonians	Revelation	Lamentations	2 Chronicles
		2 Thessalonians		Ecclesiastes	

* Roman Catholics include these books in the canon and refer to them as deuterocanonical; Protestants sometimes place them in an appendix with other Apocrypha.

preted as gifts of the HOLY SPIRIT. Indeed, most books of the New Testament ponder the relation of the old and the new. Christians, and Jesus himself, believed in the same God as other Jews and recognized the authority of the Old Testament. Yet Jesus had made radical statements that undermined the separateness of Judaism and led logically to the admission of Gentiles into the community. Thus, there emerged a CHURCH embracing Jews and non-Jews that was interpreted as based on a new covenant inaugurated by Jesus. PAUL, the greatest apostle of the Gentile mission, defended his policies by teaching that the basis for acceptance by God is faith in Jesus Christ; yet Paul did not wish to break continuity with the old religion.

The New Testament contains a strong apocalyptic element. Jesus' parables and sayings regarding the coming reign of God are enigmatic, and it is not certain that he expected the early end of the world; but many original Christians believed that they were living in the last age. Nevertheless, much of the moral teaching of the New Testament is aimed at everyday life in this world, and Christian behavior is a constant theme. The New Testament reflects other concerns of community life, including public worship and church organization, but equal emphasis is placed on individual PRAYER and communion with God.

The New Testament covers a much shorter period of time than the Old Testament, and its interests are fewer and more intense. This is partly because Christians had access to the Old Testament and other Jewish books. The New Testament was written concisely. Almost no attempt was made to imitate the fashionable literature of the time; yet the writings have great rhetorical power. Natural science had little influence. The outlook is not unscientific but prescientific; these are writings of faith, not speculation.

The Canon. The process by which the canon of the New Testament was formed began in the 2d century, probably with a collection of ten letters of Paul. Toward the end of that century, IRENAEUS argued for the unique authority of the portion of the Canon called the Gospels. Acceptance of the other books came gradually. The church in Egypt used more than the present 27 books, and the Syriac-speaking churches fewer. The question of an official canon became urgent during the 4th century. It was mainly through the influence of ATHANASIUS, bishop of Alexandria, and because JEROME included the 27 books in his Latin version of the Bible called

the Vulgate, that the present canon came to be accepted.

Divisions of the New Testament. The New Testament consists of four Gospels, the ACTS OF THE APOSTLES, collections of Epistles, and the Book of REVELATION.

The Gospels. Originally *gospel* meant "good news" (Greek *evangelion*). The term was later applied to books embodying this message. These are not biographies but proclamations of the good news in story form. Although all dates for New Testament books are debated, prevailing opinion dates MARK AD 68–72, LUKE and MATTHEW c.85, and JOHN 95–100. The first three, called synoptic because they can be compared side by side, have a complicated literary relationship with each other. Probably Matthew and Luke used Mark and a lost document called Q (German *Quelle*, "source"), consisting mainly of Jesus' sayings. The parables—short illustrative stories told by Jesus, usually reflecting daily life—are prominent in the synoptics. The Gospel of John differs from the others in structure and reflects the theological development of the first century, but it contains traditions independent of the synoptics.

The Acts. The Acts of the Apostles was evidently written by Luke as a sequel to his Gospel. It recounts the traditions of the earliest churches in Palestine and gives the details of Paul's missionary journeys.

The Epistles. Two kinds of Epistles are attributed to St. Paul in the New Testament. Nine of them (ten, if EPHESIANS is included) are letters addressed by Paul to specific churches and deal mainly with problems of faith, morals, and community life. These letters disclose Paul's interpretation of Christianity and his methods of dealing with pastoral problems. The remainder are not actual letters; rather they are writings in letter form, intended for the whole church or large parts of it. Thus, the pastoral Epistles—1 and 2 TIMOTHY and TITUS—written in Paul's name, contain directions for church leaders and warn against errors in doctrine and behavior. HEBREWS is a carefully constructed sermon by an unknown author and interprets Christ as high priest and urges fidelity in time of persecution.

The general, or catholic, Epistles are so called because they are directed to the church as a whole. The Epistle of JAMES emphasizes the importance of good deeds against an empty type of belief that involves no right action. The first Epistle of PETER proclaims joy in the face of persecution and is addressed particularly to churches with newly baptized members. The Epistles of JOHN resemble the fourth Gospel. St.

John teaches the intimate relationship between love of the brotherhood and the true doctrine about Christ; he also attacks division within the church.

Revelation. The Book of REVELATION was probably written to encourage Christians to be faithful during a persecution under Domitian (AD 81–96). It portrays the future through many symbols, and the prophet expects God's judgment on the Roman Empire, a 1,000-year reign of Christ, and a new heaven and a new Earth.

VERSIONS OF THE BIBLE

Several Aramaic targums (free translations or paraphrases) of the Old Testament exist; some of them may be older than the Christian Era. The Greek Septuagint, whose canon was not strictly defined, was gradually produced during the last three centuries BC. An Old Latin version of both Testaments was revised by Jerome, producing the Vulgate. Ancient versions exist in Syriac, Coptic, Armenian, and other languages.

During the Middle Ages, parts of the Bible were put into Anglo-Saxon and Middle English. The first English versions of the entire Bible were made (1380–93) by John WYCLIFFE and his associates who used the Latin text. The REFORMATION gave further impulse to translations into modern languages, notably that of Martin LUTHER in German and William TYNDALE in English. Among later versions are the following: Miles COVERDALE's Bible (1535), Matthew's Bible (1537), the Great Bible (1539), Geneva Bible (1560), Rheims-Douai Bible (1582, 1609), King James, or Authorized, Version (1611), English Revised Version (1881–85), American Standard Version (1946–57), New English Bible (1961–70), Jerusalem Bible (1966), New American Bible (1970), Today's English Version (1966–76), and the Revised Standard Version (1946–1971).

INTERPRETATION AND STUDY OF THE BIBLE

Ancient Interpretations. Ancient Jews and Christians believed their Scriptures to be inspired by God and intended to guide all generations. The interpretative method called MIDRASH sought to make the biblical message relevant to the actual needs of the community, to remove obscurities and contradictions, to find fulfillments of prophecies, and to answer questions not raised in the Bible by discovering allegorical meanings. This process is seen in the DEAD SEA SCROLLS, the paraphrases, or targums, of the Old Testament, and the writings of the philosopher PHILO; and it has influenced New Testament theology. The RABBIS used midrash to settle legal problems; it appears in the TALMUD as well as in the Midrashim, or homiletical commentaries.

Christians were influenced both by Jewish tradition and by philosophers who explained Greek myths as allegories. The Alexandrian scholar ORIGEN distinguished literal and allegorical meanings in the Old Testament, and his followers found three or four ways to interpret a specific text. The school of Antioch, represented by commentators such as THEODORE OF MOPSUESTIA and the great preacher John CHRYSOSTOM, insisted on the natural and literal meaning of Scripture. During the period of the Middle Ages the allegorical method largely prevailed.

Modern Study. During the RENAISSANCE, a revival of the study of Greek and Latin classics occurred that led Christian scholars to study Hebrew. Literary and historical criticism, which had been carried on in ancient times, now received a new impetus. Although the allegorical method never died out in Catholicism and Protestantism, the new learning influenced the study of the Bible, and in the 18th century the techniques of classical studies began to be employed systematically. Improved dictionaries and grammars were part of this process.

Textual criticism is an important part of biblical interpretation. This is the comparison of manuscripts of the Bible in the original languages and versions, including quotations by ancient authors, to determine as nearly as possible the original wording. Literary criticism is the study of the document itself in comparison with other books—biblical and nonbiblical—to disclose the method, style, and purpose of the author; his identity; the written and oral sources he used; and the date and place of the writing. This has led to theories regarding sources of the Pentateuch and the Gospels, the dating of Paul's letters, and the distinctions between parts of Isaiah.

Form criticism studies the oral tradition behind a document. Every oral tradition is modified by the life situations in which it is transmitted, and the stages of change can often be discerned, as in the stories of Abraham and SARAH. One may classify the Psalms according to their probable uses in worship. In the parables of Jesus, the original purpose can be distinguished from the church's interpretations and modifications. Form critics believe that the elements in Jesus' teaching that do not match the interests of Judaism or of the early church reflect his specific point of view.

Redaction criticism, the study of editing, assumes that the authors of biblical books had a definite theology and purpose and were not mere collectors of traditions. Thus the traits of the writer of a book or a source can be distinguished from those of the materials by observing style and editorial method. Both form and redaction criticism involve the individual judgments of scholars; perfect agreement cannot be expected.

Historical criticism, which is the method of all serious historians, applies all these disciplines to the Bible and takes into account all historical evidence available, in both written documents and archaeological discoveries. Thus Ugaritic, Babylonian, Assyrian, Egyptian, Persian, and other records used with the Bible, aid in reconstructing the course of Hebrew history. New Testament history and the development of early Christian theology are illuminated by studying the documents of the Jewish and Greco-Roman religions and Christian writings outside the New Testament.   SHERMAN E. JOHNSON

Bibliography:
    OLD TESTAMENT: Anderson, Bernhard W., *Understanding the Old Testament*, 4th ed. (1986); Coats, George W., and Long, Burke O., eds., *Canon and Authority* (1977); McKenzie, John L., *The Two-Edged Sword* (1956); Sanders, James A., *Torah and Canon* (1972); Von Rad, Gerhard, *Old Testament Theology*, 2 vols. (1962).
    NEW TESTAMENT: Grant, Robert M., *The Formation of the New Testament* (1966); Kee, Howard C., et al., *Understanding the New Testament*, 4th ed. (1983); Moule, C. F. D., *The Birth of the New Testament*, rev. ed. (1981); Robinson, James M., and Koester, Helmut, *Trajectories through Early Christianity* (1971).
    HISTORY AND CRITICISM: Alter, Robert, and Kermode, Frank, eds., *The Literary Guide to the Bible* (1987); Bruce, F. F., *History of the Bible in English*, 3d ed. (1978); Dodd, C. H., *The Bible Today* (1946); Friedman, Richard E., *Who Wrote the Bible?* (1987); Grant, Robert M., and Tracy, David, *A Short History of the Interpretation of the Bible*, 2d ed., rev. and enl. (1984); Koch, Klaus, *The Growth of Biblical Tradition* (1969); Perrin, Norman, *What Is Redaction Criticism?* (1969).

Bible societies

Bible societies are organizations formed for translating and distributing the BIBLE. The model for most Bible societies, the British and Foreign Bible Society, was founded in 1804. Its purpose was to supply inexpensive Bibles or portions of the Bible, "without note or comment" in the languages of the areas where British missionaries were working. Although a short-lived Catholic Bible Society was begun in Regensburg in 1805, which printed a German New Testament with Psalms, Bible societies have been essentially Protestant enterprises. By the mid-19th century, they existed as far north as Scandinavia, in Russia to the east, and in North America. The American Bible Society, an ecumenical venture, was founded in 1816.

The expansion of the work of the various societies, and the creation of new national societies brought about duplication of effort, especially in the support of translators and in distribution. Hence, 20 societies joined in 1946 to form the United Bible Societies. One of the best-known Bible societies is Gideons International, which places a copy of the Bible in hotel and motel rooms.   PAUL MERRITT BASSETT

biblical archaeology

The term *biblical archaeology* refers to archaeological investigations that serve to clarify, enlighten, and enhance the biblical record. Its development, from the 19th century, has been largely tied to the history of research and excavation in ancient Palestine.

The American clergyman and biblical scholar Edward Robinson played a fundamental role in recognizing that an acquaintance with the Holy Land was essential to an understanding of biblical literature. After traveling in Sinai and Palestine, he published *Biblical Researches in Palestine* (1841), which inspired many other scholars to follow his lead. The British founded the Palestine Exploration Fund (PEF) in 1865, and in 1867 the first PEF expedition was sent to Jerusalem to search for specific biblical sites, among them the location of Solomon's temple.

Pioneering excavations were undertaken in 1890 by Flinders PETRIE at Tell el-Hesi, 26 km (16 mi) east of Gaza. His development of a relative scale of dating based on changes in pottery at successive levels of excavation was of immense importance for biblical archaeology, since sites in Palestine have yielded relatively few historical monuments or records. A notable exception is the site of QUMRAN on the Dead Sea, where the first of the important Hebrew and Aramaic manuscripts known as the DEAD SEA SCROLLS were discovered (1947).

By the early 1900s, American, German, and French archaeological teams also began excavations in Palestine, directed primarily toward those cities mentioned in the Bible. Pre-World War I excavations included work at GEZER, JERICHO, MEGIDDO, Ta'anach, Samaria, and Beth-shemesh. William Foxwell Albright directed the American School of Oriental Research in Jerusalem (founded 1910) in 1920–29 and 1933–36. His excavations at Tell Beit Mirsim (1926–32) supplied the framework for establishing the chronology of ancient Palestine based on ceramic typology, which is still used today with only minor changes. The Palestine Department of Antiquities, established in 1918, played a major role in archaeological research until the state of Israel was formed in 1948. Since then, Israeli archaeologists have conducted several important excavations, including Yigael Yadin's work at HAZOR (1955–58 and 1968–70) and at MASADA (1963–65), Yohanon Aharoni and Ruth Amiran's work at Arad (1962–67), and Yigal Shiloh's finds at the City of David in Jerusalem (1978–85).

Although biblical archaeology concentrates on excavating and interpreting biblical sites, archaeological material of either the pre- or post-biblical era is often uncovered as well. For example, the excavations of the American archaeologist James Pritchard at Gibeon, in addition to revealing the rock-cut water system mentioned in 2 Samuel, produced important pottery from a Bronze Age cemetery. Excavation at the important biblical site of Jericho has revealed little of significance dating from later than the 2d millennium BC, but has been invaluable for the study of early Palestine.

An important function of biblical archaeology has been to describe a setting in which the stories of the Old and New Testaments achieve a new and vivid meaning. Inevitably, however, more problems have been discovered than have been resolved. The question of the nature and date of the

Masada, an ancient Hebrew fortress located on a rocky plateau above the Dead Sea, was the site of archaeological excavation by Yigael Yadin in the early 1960s, in which architectural remains associated with Herod the Great were unearthed. Masada was held unsuccessfully by Zealot Jews against a Roman legion between AD 66 and 73.

Exodus and the manner of the conquest of Palestine by the Israelites is still open to debate, despite the large number of excavated sites. Since the Israelites left no characteristic artifacts during the early years of their settlement, it is virtually impossible to determine whether the destruction of a site in the 13th century BC was the work of the Israelites or the Egyptians. Sometimes the archaeological evidence seems to contradict the biblical record. Thus, although the city of Ai is recorded as having been captured by Joshua, no remains dating from the appropriate period were found during its excavation, which suggests that the site was unoccupied at the time of the supposed conquest.   JONATHAN N. TUBB

Bibliography: Dever, William G., *Archaeology and Biblical Studies* (1974); Kenyon, Kathleen M., *Archaeology in the Holy Land*, 4th ed. (1979); Millard, A. R., *Treasures from Bible Times* (1985); Negev, Avrahem, ed., *Archaeological Encyclopedia of the Holy Land* (1974; repr. 1980); Paul, Shalom, and Dever, William, eds., *Biblical Archaeology* (1973); Thomas, W. D., *Archaeology and Old Testament Study* (1967); Wright, G. E., *Biblical Archaeology*, rev. ed. (1963).

bibliography   [bib-lee-ah'-gruh-fee]

Bibliography, in the broad sense, is the science or study concerned with describing and giving information about writings or publications. Such information may include the author, full title, publisher, place and date of publication, number of pages, and size of the book. Depending on the intended use, it may include an abstract, or at least an indication, of the book's general content; it may also contain a detailed physical description, such as the characteristics of the binding, the typeface, illustrations, and collation of the book—in short, any and all peculiarities that may serve to distinguish one book from another.

More commonly, however, the word *bibliography* is used to denote a list of books compiled for a specific purpose. Such a bibliography—examples of which may be found affixed to many articles in this encyclopedia—may list books on the same subject, or related subjects, by the same author, or of the same period, or it may list books consulted in preparing a report, book, or thesis. A bibliography is said to be systematic if the entries are arranged in some sort of order designed to enhance usefulness. An enumerative bibliography is

This Dead Sea scroll fragment of the Book of Isaiah dates from the 2d to the 1st century BC and is one of the oldest known biblical manuscripts. The scrolls, found between 1947 and 1956 in caves near the ancient Essene monastery Qumran, are in the Israel Museum in Jerusalem.

usually arranged in an alphabetical or a chronological order without any attempt at classification. A critical bibliography contains evaluations and comparisons of the items listed.

Bibliography: Besterman, T., *The Beginnings of Systematic Bibliography,* 2d ed. (1936; repr. 1966), and *World Bibliography of Bibliographies,* 5 vols., 4th ed. (1963); Bowers, F., *Principles of Bibliographic Description* (1986); Downs, R. B., *American Library Resources: A Bibliographic Guide,* ed. by Lee Ash (1972; supplement 1981); Harmon, R. B., *Elements of Bibliography* (1981); Krummel, D., *Bibliographies* (1984); Stokes, R., ed., *Esdaile's Manual of Bibliography,* rev. ed. (1981).

Bibliothèque Nationale   [beeb-lee-oh-tek' nah-see-oh-nahl']

The Bibliothèque Nationale de France, the national library of France, is the oldest of the European national libraries, with a continuous history dating from the reign of Louis XI (1461–83). Its growth was actively encouraged during the reign of Francis I (1515–47) when it received legal deposit privileges, the first such granted in Europe. It was known as the Royal Library until the French Revolution, when it acquired by appropriation some of its rarest items. Current holdings total more than 21 million items, including 9 million books and pamphlets, 800,000 maps, and 180,000 manuscripts. The library, in Paris, has numerous sections, such as printed books, manuscripts, prints, medals, maps, music, and the Bibliothèque de L' Arsenal.   COLIN STEELE

Bibliography: Esdaile, Arundell J. K., *National Libraries of the World,* 2d ed. (1957).

bicameral system: see LEGISLATURE.

bicarbonate of soda: see SODA.

Bicentennial, Australian

In 1988, Australia celebrated the 200th anniversary of European settlement. The year-long celebration began on Jan. 26, 1988, when "tall ships" from all over the world sailed into Sydney harbor. Leading them were 11 square-rigger sailing ships that had reenacted the 8-month-long voyage from England of the first convict fleet. Among the more than 3,000 bicentennial events were the opening of the new Parliament House in Canberra and World Expo 88 in Brisbane, a 6-month world's fair with the theme "Leisure in the Age of Technology." The activities were coordinated by the Australian Bicentennial Authority.

Bicentennial, U.S.

The Bicentennial marking the 200th anniversary of America's independence was celebrated on July 4, 1976, with enormous enthusiasm and unprecedented fanfare. Millions of people in the United States turned out for parades, picnics, regattas, fireworks displays, reenactments of historical events, rodeos, concerts, and formal ceremonies honoring the nation's past.

Although the most spectacular celebrations took place on July 4, Bicentennial events occurred throughout the year.

In Washington, D.C., a special American Revolution Bicentennial Administration was set up (1973) to coordinate activities on a national scale. The states set up their own Bicentennial commissions to organize activities, and a Bicentennial Council of the Thirteen Original States was formed.

The Freedom Train. Events were initiated also by unofficial groups. In 1975, the American Freedom Train, funded with $5.6 million in corporate donations, began a 22-month cross-country trip stopping at 80 cities. It displayed a wide assortment of Americana that included George Washington's copy of the Declaration of Independence.

Partly as a result of the Bicentennial, there was a surge of national interest in the Revolutionary period. In April 1976, about 150,000 spectators in Massachusetts watched a reenactment of Paul Revere's ride and Minutemen routing British Redcoats on the Lexington Green. Then in June 1976 the na-

tional Bicentennial wagon-train pilgrimage began, with Pennsylvania's Bicentennial Commission sponsoring an official wagon from each state. Reversing the route taken by the 19th-century pioneers, the 60 official wagons headed eastward rather than westward and converged on Valley Forge, Pa., in early July.

The Cities Celebrate. In Philadelphia, about 200 events were scheduled, including a July 4 reenactment of the signing of the Declaration of Independence. In Boston, a crowd of about 400,000 assembled along the Charles River to hear a Boston Pops concert. In Washington, D.C.'s weeklong celebration, 30 metric tons (33.5 U.S. tons) of fireworks were set off. In New Orleans, entertainers performed at the Superdome.

The Tall Ships. By far the most publicized event was the gathering in New York harbor of 212 sailing ships from 34 countries. An unprecedented collection of the world's last great sailing vessels, the flotilla of "tall ships" was led by the U.S. Coast Guard training ship *Eagle.* The longest was the 114-m (374-ft) Russian bark *Kruzenshtern,* built in 1926 and used to train naval cadets. The oldest was the American barkentine *Gazela Primeiro,* built in 1883 as a fishing vessel and now the property of Philadelphia's Maritime Museum. After gliding past an honor guard of warships in New York harbor, where the largest national flag ever raised hung from the Verrazano-Narrows Bridge, the ships sailed up the Hudson River to the George Washington Bridge and then back down. Crowds in New York City were estimated at more than 6 million. After leaving New York, the ships headed for a dozen other cities, including Boston, Miami, Chicago, and Los Angeles.

Bicentennial of the Constitution. In 1987, Americans celebrated the 200th birthday of the U.S. Constitution. The chairman of the official bicentennial committee was Warren E. Burger, former chief justice of the United States. The occasion prompted numerous publications, seminars, debates, and televised commemorations, a major aim of which was to encourage Americans to study their Constitution.

Bibliography: American Revolution Bicentennial Administration, *The Bicentennial of the United States of America: A Final Report to the People,* 5 vols. (1977); Clark, Hyla M., *The Tall Ships* (1976); Mees, Charles L., Jr., *The Genius of the People* (1988); Nevins, Jane, *Turning 200: The Bicentennial of the U.S. Constitution* (1988).

bichir   [bich'-ur]

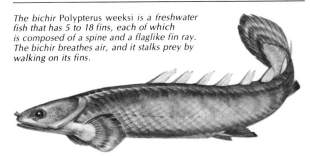

The bichir Polypterus weeksi is a freshwater fish that has 5 to 18 fins, each of which is composed of a spine and a flaglike fin ray. The bichir breathes air, and it stalks prey by walking on its fins.

Bichirs are primitive, air-breathing fish that live at the edges of rivers and lakes in tropical Africa. The slender body is up to 1 m (39 in) long. The bony skeleton contains much cartilage, and the intestine has the spiral ridge of mucous membrane that cartilaginous fish such as sharks have. The body is armored with hard, ganoid scales, and the area below the mouth is plated. The lunglike swim bladder is paired; in addition to gills, the bichir have spiracles, or openings, behind the eyes. Separate, flaglike finlets extend down the back from midbody to rounded tail, and the muscular pectoral fins are used for walking underwater. Bichirs stalk their prey of small fish and other aquatic animals. They rise to the surface to gulp air, which they require.

The 10 bichir species, genus *Polypterus,* with the reedfish, comprise the family Polypteridae. They, the PADDLEFISH, and the STURGEON are remaining representatives of a group of fish that flourished from Devonian to Triassic times.

bichon frise   [bee-shohn'-freez]

The bichon frise is one of the probable ancestors of the toy poodle. Francisco Goya depicted the dog in paintings of Spanish courts.

(Above) *The first foot-pedaled bicycle was built in 1839 by Kirkpatrick Macmillan, a Scotsman. It consisted of two wheels and a crossbar and used stirrup pedals, cranks, and drive rods to turn the rear wheels.*

The bichon frise, or "curly lapdog," is a small, nonsporting breed of dog. Of the four varieties, the Maltese is the most widely known. The dog stands 20–30 cm (8–12 in) at the shoulder. Both ears and tail, which is curved to lie on the back, are covered with long hair. The thick, silky coat, loosely curled, is solid white with cream, apricot, or gray sometimes seen on the ears. Bred centuries ago in Spain and the Mediterranean countries, the dog became a favorite with royalty and appears in Francisco Goya's court paintings. The breed was officially recognized by the French Kennel Club in 1934 and the American Kennel Club in 1972. Intelligent, sturdy, and lively, the bichon has gained increasing popularity in the United States.

Bibliography: American Kennel Club, *The Complete Dog Book,* 15th ed. (1975).

(Left) *The pennyfarthing bicycle, c.1872, was so named because its giant front wheel and minuscule rear wheel resembled the two British coins in proportion. Both wheels were of rubber-rimmed metal.*

Bickerdyke, Mary Ann

Mary Ann Bickerdyke, b. July 19, 1817, d. Nov. 8, 1901, was a Union nurse during the U.S. Civil War. Often called Mother Bickerdyke, she was beloved by the soldiers and respected by the generals. After the war she petitioned the federal government for pensions for Civil War veterans and nurses and was active in charitable causes.

bicycle

A bicycle is a two-wheeled vehicle propelled by its rider. The most energy-efficient means of transportation, the bicycle is used throughout the world. Particularly in developing countries—most notably in China, where some 300 million bicycles are on the road—the vehicle has been a common form of local transportation for many years.

History. The first step toward the development of the bicycle was the invention of the *célérifère,* or wooden horse, probably in France in the 1790s. Because its front wheel was fixed, this vehicle could not be steered, and the rider propelled it by pushing his or her feet along the ground. An important advance was made by the German baron Karl von Drais in 1817, when he introduced a steerable front wheel, creating the *draisienne,* or dandy horse. In 1839, Kirkpatrick Macmillan, a Scottish blacksmith, made the first machine with pedals, which were attached to and drove the rear wheel by means of cranks. On the velocipede, a French invention of 1852, the front wheel was pedal driven and revolved once with each revolution of the pedals. The speed of the machine was dependent on the size of the front wheel: the larger the wheel, the faster the bicycle. The front wheel of the high-wheel, or pennyfarthing—used from the 1870s—reached diameters of 1.5 m (5 ft) and more, while the back wheel might be only one-quarter that size. With its seat mounted over the huge front wheel, the high-wheel was dangerously unstable, and its use on poor roads led to many bicycling accidents.

An English "safety bicycle," with a chain and sprocket driving the rear wheel, was introduced by H. J. Lawson in 1879. In 1885 a safety model designed by J. K. Starley, which had wheels of equal size, became the basic model for the modern bicycle. Succeeding years saw the addition of pneumatic tires

(Above) *In 1901 the Raleigh Cycle Co. introduced its All Steel Safety Bicycle. The use of a new brazing process and pressed, instead of cast, brackets produced a strong, lightweight frame.*

The popularity of the mountain bike has skyrocketed since the mid-1980s. Riders have found that its sturdy build, 18 to 21 gears, and fat, treaded tires perform well in both the rough terrain off the road and the potholed streets of big cities.

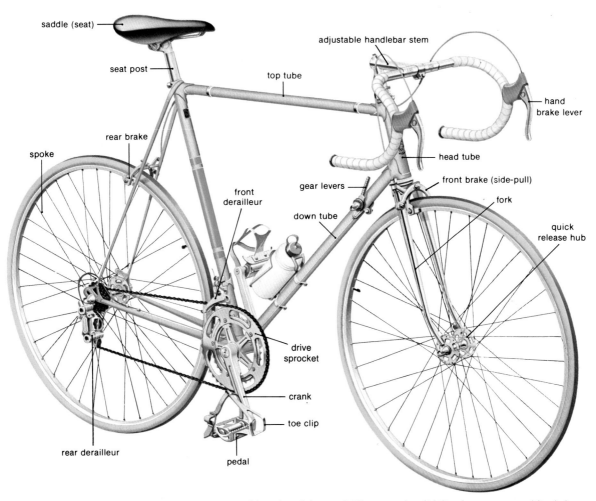

saddle (seat)

seat post

top tube

adjustable handlebar stem

hand brake lever

rear brake

spoke

head tube

front derailleur

gear levers

front brake (side-pull)

down tube

fork

quick release hub

drive sprocket

crank

toe clip

rear derailleur

pedal

(Above) *The modern racing bicycle is precision engineered for safety, lightness, rigidity, strength, reliability, fast response, and fine balance. The turned-down handlebars ensure more efficient riding posture, comfort, better use of muscle power, and better weight distribution.*

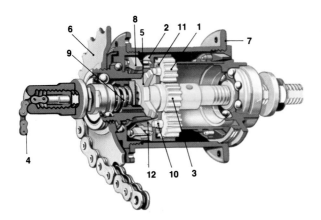

(Above) *A Sturmey Archer 3-speed hub gear changes speed ratios by means of four caged planet gears (1) and an outer ring (2) that revolve around a central fixed, or sun, gear (3). In medium gear (above), a cable (4) is used to move a clutch (5) so that a chain-driven sprocket (6) engages the gear ring directly and turns the rear wheel hub (7) via the ring pawls (8). In high gear, a spring (9) moves the clutch arms inward to engage the pinions (10), which allows the planet cage (11) to drive the gear ring and hub. In low gear, the clutch is in its outer position, so that the gear ring turns the planet cage, which then drives the hub by means of the cage pawl (12).*

(Right) *To change speed ratios in a derailleur gear system, the chain drive is moved over a range of sprocket sizes. The highest speed is obtained by using the smallest sprocket (A). A low speed results from the use of a large sprocket (B). The chain (1) is moved by means of a hinged parallelogram (2) and two jockey wheels (3, 4). When the position of the parallelogram is changed by means of a gear-shift cable, the chain lifts to another sprocket and the jockey wheels move to take up or release slack chain. A quick-release wheel hub (5) allows removal of the wheel from the bicycle frame (6) without the use of tools.*

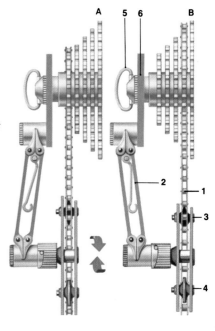

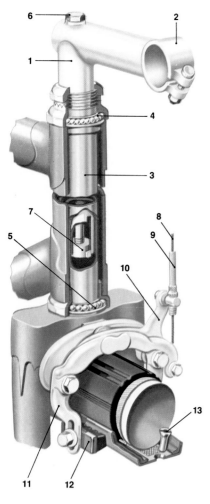

(Left) *The handlebar stem (1), with a clamp (2) that holds the handlebars in place, is supported within the frame of the bicycle by a head set (3) mounted on ball bearings (4, 5). The handlebar stem is held inside the head set by an expander bolt (6) and a tapered wedge nut (7). In a sidepull brake, the brake cable (8) and its casing (9) are attached to inner and outer calipers (10, 11) that hold rubber brake shoes (12). When the cable is pulled by compressing the brake lever, the shoes are forced against the wheel and stop its rotation. Spoke nipples (13, shown here in a raised position) attach the spokes of the wheel to the wheel rim.*

rials, including aluminum, titanium, and carbon fiber, that combine great strength with light weight. New techniques have been developed for strengthening the tube joints, or "butts." Narrower, higher-pressure tires have replaced the heavy "balloon" tires of yesteryear. The now-standard 10- to 18-speed adult touring bike, designed for speed, efficiency, and ease of handling, is a far cry from the machine that was once the basic U.S. bicycle (and which was essentially a vehicle for children)—heavy, ungeared, and with an inefficient coaster brake.

A proliferation of new ideas has produced several innovations in bicycle components. For instance, indexed shifting levers greatly improve the gear-shifting motion. And an automatic transmission is being developed that uses a computer placed under the seat and a speed sensor on the rear-wheel hub. This component allows the biker to pedal at a steady pace, no matter what the terrain, without the bother of manually changing gears.

The bicycle's power system, until now essentially simply a geared chain-and-sprocket, may receive an efficiency boost from a new design that uses a cam instead of a crankshaft. As the pedal turns the cam, oscillators pull chains attached to each wheel. Another design uses a pedal-attached spring and a steel cable to turn the wheels. Both systems reportedly provide greater power with less pedaling effort.

The mountain, or all-terrain bike, equipped with an 18- or 21-speed gear, was originally designed for off-road use. But its durable frame and fat tires have made it popular for cummuting over potholed, sewer-grated city streets. Recently, the hybrid bike, a cross between the sturdy mountain bike and the lightweight touring bike, has gained popularity. Pedaling is easier than on a mountain bike because the wheel diameter of the hybrid is larger and the tires are thinner. However, the wide saddle, upright handlebars, and the low gearing, similar to those of a mountain bike, make steep inclines easier to negotiate.

Wheel sizes are also changing. Smaller wheels lower the bicycle's center of gravity, making it slightly easier to stay upright. The English small-wheeled bicycle, designed by Alexander Moulton in 1962, is an example. Moulton also engineered a folding bike that incorporates a totally new frame construction. In addition, it features a suspension spring in its front fork that can be adjusted to accommodate the weights of different riders and has a seat that—when moved up or down—allows the bicycle to be used by people of greatly differing heights.

Lower and longer bicycle wheelbases provide greater stability. A relatively new design, the recumbent bicycle, is longer than a conventional vehicle by at least one-third, has a small front wheel, and is characterized by its rider's position. Instead of sitting up over the pedals, a recumbent rider sits slightly reclined in a high-backed seat. For riders accustomed to it, the position is far more comfortable than that on a conventional bike and offers greater pedaling efficiency.

KEITH KINGBAY

Bibliography: *Bicycling Magazine* Editors, *Complete Guide to Bicycle Maintenance and Repair* (1990); Cuthbertson, Tom, *Anybody's Bike Book* (1988); Langley, James, *The New Bike Book* (1990); Sloane, Eugene A., *The Complete Book of Bicycling* (1988).

See also: CYCLING.

bicycle, motorized: see MOPED.

Bidault, Georges   [bee-doh']

Georges Bidault, b. Oct. 5, 1899, d. Jan. 27, 1983, was a French political figure during and after World War II. In the war he served in the underground, becoming chairman of the National Council of Resistance in 1943. He was foreign minister in Charles DE GAULLE's provisional government (1944–46) and in the first postwar government (1947–48). He was a member of parliament for the years 1947–62, serving several times as foreign minister and as premier in 1949–50. In the ALGERIAN WAR, Bidault led resistance to Algerian independence, cooperating with the terrorist Secret Army Organization in

(in the 1880s), two- and three-speed hub gears (in the 1890s), and derailleur gears, which were invented in 1899. The development of the internal-combustion engine led to attempts to motorize the bicycle. Gottlieb Daimler developed the MOTORCYCLE in 1885.

The addition of the derailleur was the last major advance in bicycle technology until, beginning in the 1970s, the upsurge of enthusiasm for the vehicle and its energy-saving potential attracted the interest of designers and engineers. They have developed aerodynamically improved models using unconventional frame shapes and plastic enclosures, or "fairings," and have found ways to provide greater stability—primarily by adding a third wheel, as on a tricycle.

The Modern Bicycle. Most American bicycles are equipped with either an internally geared multispeed hub or a derailleur gear system. Similar to an automobile TRANSMISSION, the multispeed hub, which usually accommodates three speeds, allows the gear ratio to be changed so that the force exerted by the rider can match the force needed to pedal the bicycle under particular conditions.

The derailleur system, developed in 1899, is a more sophisticated gearshift. It is a simple device that allows the bicycle chain to be shifted among sprockets of different sizes on front and rear hubs, thereby permitting several gear ratios, or speeds. The chain is "derailed" by means of a lever and cable that move the main mechanism sideways and realign the parts. The long arm and springs of the derailleur on the rear wheel keep the chain under the proper tension as the circumference of the sprockets changes.

The tubing that constitutes the major portion of the bicycle frame is made today from one of a variety of space-age mate-

1962. When the movement collapsed after de Gaulle agreed to an independent Algeria, Bidault was charged with plotting against the security of the French state. He lived in exile from 1963 to 1967, returning to France in 1968.

Biddle, John

John Biddle, b. 1615, d. Sept. 22, 1662, was an English Unitarian who was imprisoned repeatedly for his religious beliefs. His study of the Bible convinced him that the doctrine of the TRINITY as commonly believed was incorrect. Biddle's publications on the subject, beginning in 1647 with *Twelve Arguments Drawn Out of Scripture*, angered many, and for much of the latter part of his life he was either in jail or in exile. His views, however, did find support among a gradually increasing number of people. It was from this group that the first English-speaking Unitarian church sprang.   CONRAD WRIGHT

Bibliography: Wilbur, Earl M., *A History of Unitarianism* (1965).

Biddle, Nicholas

The American financier Nicholas Biddle was born in Philadelphia on Jan. 8, 1786, and educated at the University of Pennsylvania and the College of New Jersey (now Princeton University). A precocious student, he completed his college education at the age of 15 and embarked on a literary career that included preparation, from the explorers' notes, of the *History of the Expedition Under the Command of Captains Lewis and Clark* (1814) and the editorship (1812) of *Port Folio*, the nation's first literary magazine.

Abandoning literature for the law and public service, Biddle served in the Pennsylvania House of Representatives (1810–11), the Pennsylvania Senate (1814–17), and as a federal appointee to the board of directors of the Second BANK OF THE UNITED STATES. In 1823 he was named president of the Bank of the United States, an office he held until the expiration of the bank's charter in 1836. Under Biddle's direction, the bank's influence was used to stablize the currency and restrain excessive note issues of state-chartered banks.

Although skilled as a banker, Biddle proved an inept politician. Alarmed by President Andrew JACKSON's opposition to recharter, he made alliances with Jackson's political enemies and sought to force an early rechartering of the bank in 1832. Jackson vetoed the recharter bill and after his reelection in 1832 removed all federal deposits from the bank. After expiration of the federal charter, the Bank of the United States operated under a charter from Pennsylvania. Biddle continued as president until his involvement in unsound speculative banking practices led to his resignation in 1839. He died in retirement on Feb. 27, 1844.   ALFRED A. CAVE

Bibliography: Govan, Thomas P., *Nicholas Biddle: Nationalist and Public Banker* (1959; repr. 1975); Taylor, George R., ed., *Jackson Versus Biddle's Bank*, 2d ed. (1972).

Biedermeier   [bee'-dur-my-ur]

Biedermeier is a style in furniture design, painting, and literature dominant mainly in Germany and Austria from about 1800 to 1848. The name derives from the poet Ludwig Eichrodt's satiric figure of Gottlieb ''Papa'' Biedermeier, who became a symbol of the staid, philistine middle classes. The period coincided broadly with the politically conservative restoration period in Germany and Austria and was characterized by a smug satisfaction with the status quo, aversion to innovation, avoidance of all extremes, especially political and religious, and a love for detail, even trivia. The best of the Biedermeier furniture designs, noted for comfort as well as relative inexpensiveness, were created between 1820 and 1830. This well-made, functional furniture, sensitive in form to the glistening mahogany or lighter woods employed, was modeled on GrecoRoman designs and is currently popular with collectors. The rooms were intimate in scale, often decorated with striped wallpaper and carpets, with muslin curtains over the windows. Biedermeier painting was characterized by a meticulous attention to detail and a preference for humor-

The governors of an Amsterdam leper hospital, posed in a stilted variant of traditional Dutch group portraiture, were painted (c.1835) by Jan Adam Kruseman in the Biedermeyer style, which is marked by sentimentality, lush color, and a love for the trappings of 19th-century bourgeois life. (Rijkmuseum, Amsterdam.)

ous genre scenes and sunny landscapes. Representative painters include the Dane Christen Købke, the Austrian Ferdinand WALDMÜLLER, and the Germans Karl Blechen, Franz Krüger, Carl Spitzweg, and Moritz von SCHWIND. Although the scope of such writers as the German poet Annette DROSTE-HÜLSHOFF, the Austrian playwright Franz GRILLPARZER, and the Hungarian poet Nikolaus Lenau is wider than that of their counterparts in the fine arts, they are also considered part of the Biedermeier movement.

Bibliography: Boeschenstein, Hermann, *German Literature of the 19th Century* (1969); Himmelheber, Georg, *Biedermeier Furniture* (1975); Wilkie, Angus, *Biedermeyer* (1987).

Bienville, Jean Baptiste Le Moyne, Sieur de
[bee-an-veel']

Jean Baptiste Le Moyne, sieur de Bienville, b. Feb. 23, 1680, d. Mar. 7, 1767, was a French-Canadian explorer and administrator who founded Mobile, Ala., and New Orleans, La. The son of the sieur de LONGUEUIL and the brother of the sieur d'IBERVILLE, he earned military plaudits in the French naval campaigns against the English in the North Atlantic and Hudson Bay from 1695 to 1698. He took part in Iberville's expedition to the mouth of the Mississippi in 1698–99 and in 1700 explored up the Red River as far as Natchitoches (La.). French control of the area was assured by alliances with the Indians.

Assuming command of the Louisiana colony in 1701, Bienville constructed (1702) a fort at 26-Mile Bluff on Mobile Bay; in 1710 the fort was moved to the present site of Mobile on the lower part of the bay. Superseded by the sieur de CADILLAC in 1712, Bienville was restored (1717) to the governorship under the MISSISSIPPI SCHEME and founded New Orleans in 1718. The collapse of the Mississippi scheme and quarrels with other colonial administrators resulted in his recall in 1725. His reappointment in 1732 was greeted with rejoicing among the New Orleans settlers. Indian wars occupied his time, however, and he never achieved the brilliance for which his supporters had hoped. He left Louisiana in 1743.

Known as a fair-minded man to those who admired him, Bienville was attacked unmercifully by his enemies. A key figure in the establishment of French dominion on the Gulf of Mexico, he is still regarded as the founding father of New Orleans.   JACK D. L. HOLMES

Bibliography: Chambers, Henry E., *A History of Louisiana*, vol. 1 (1925); Gayarré, C. E. A., *History of Louisiana*, vol. 1 (1903); King, Grace, *Jean Baptiste Le Moyne, Sieur de Bienville* (1892; repr. 1972); Leavitt, Mel, *A Short History of New Orleans* (1982); McDermott, John F., ed., *The French in the Mississippi Valley* (1965).

Albert Bierstadt's Sunrise, Yosemite Valley (n.d.) *captures the grandeur and ruggedness of the American frontier. Bierstadt emphasized the spectacular beauty of the western landscape by combining a panoramic view with dramatic atmospheric and lighting effects on a large canvas. (Amon Carter Museum of Western Art, Fort Worth, Tex.)*

Bierce, Ambrose   [beers]

Ambrose Bierce, b. June 24, 1842, was an American author and journalist whose cynical wit and macabre stories about warfare, horror, and death earned him the nickname Bitter Bierce. His fascination with the grotesque probably originated in the Civil War, during which he fought at Shiloh and Chickamauga and was wounded at the battle of Kennesaw Mountain. Several memorable stories, including "An Occurrence at Owl Creek Bridge" and "Chickamauga," were derived from these war experiences.

Bierce left the army in 1865 and, traveling westward, was soon contributing articles to the San Francisco *News Letter*, a publication of which he became editor in 1868. His first story, "The Haunted Valley," appeared in 1871, the same year he married Mary Ellen Day, a marriage that was to prove unhappy. With her, he went to England, where his first three books were published: *The Fiend's Delight, Nuggets and Dust Panned Out in California* (both 1872), and *Cobwebs from an Empty Skull* (1874). Returning to the United States, Bierce worked for several San Francisco newspapers and in 1891 brought out the first of three works for which he is best known today, *In the Midst of Life*. The other two are *Can Such Things Be?* (1893), another collection of stories, and *The Devil's Dictionary* (1906), a book of mordant and ironic definitions. He moved to Washington, D.C., in 1896 to continue his journalistic career. In 1913, restless with life in the United States, he went to Mexico to report on Pancho Villa's revolution, and was never heard from again. He may have died in the siege of Ojinaga in January 1914.   ROBERT D. ARNER

Bibliography: Berkove, Laurence I., *Ambrose Bierce* (1978); Davidson, Cathy N., *The Experimental Fictions of Ambrose Bierce: Structuring the Ineffable* (1984); Decastro, Adolph, *Ambrose Bierce* (1929; repr. 1974); Grenander, M. E., *Ambrose Bierce* (1971); Saunders, Richard, *Ambrose Bierce: The Making of a Misanthrope* (1984).

Bierstadt, Albert   [beer'-stat]

The landscape painter Albert Bierstadt, b. Jan. 7, 1830, d. Feb. 18, 1902, was the first artist of distinction to take as his subject the vastness of the mountains of western North America. Born in Germany, Bierstadt emigrated to the United States with his parents in 1832. After his early works were exhibited in Bos-

ton, he traveled (1853) to Germany to study painting for three years at the Düsseldorf Akademie. In 1857 he returned to the United States and painted throughout the northeast; in 1858 he made the first of several trips to the West. From sketches and oil studies done from nature (admirable works in themselves), he painted in his New York studio the huge, carefully detailed panoramic views of Western scenery that made him one of America's most admired painters in the 1860s and '70s. His approach to landscape was a romantic one, emphasizing and sometimes exaggerating the spectacular landforms and atmospheric effects he had seen on his travels, as in his dramatic *The Rocky Mountains* (1863; Metropolitan Museum, New York).   DAVID TATHAM

Bibliography: Hendricks, Gordon, *Albert Bierstadt* (1973); Novak, Barbara, *Nature and Culture* (1980); Weber, Bruce, and Gerdts, W. H., *In Nature's Ways* (1987).

big bang theory

The big bang theory of COSMOLOGY assumes that the universe began from a singular state of infinite density. This theory was implicit in the complete solution of Albert Einstein's equations, obtained by Aleksandr FRIEDMANN in 1922. In 1927, Georges LEMAÎTRE used these equations to devise a cosmological theory incorporating the concept that the universe is expanding from an explosive moment of creation.

The term *big bang*, as a name for the initial cataclysmic event, was coined (1946) by George GAMOW, who with R. A. Alpher envisaged a high-temperature state in the beginning and elaborated the theory to include a theory of element synthesis and BACKGROUND RADIATION. In the light of the evidence currently available, including the discovery of the background radiation, this theory appears to best account for the evolution of the universe. In the later 20th century the theory was elaborated by the so-called INFLATIONARY THEORY, which seeks to account for the physical events taking place in the very first moments. The steady-state theory, which postulates the continuous creation of matter and a universe with no beginning or end, still has adherents.   HONG-YEE CHIU

Bibliography: Gribbin, John, *The Omega Point* (1987); Hawking, Stephen, *A Brief History of Time* (1988); Silk, Joseph, *The Big Bang* (1980); Trefil, James, *Space, Time, Infinity* (1985).

Big Bend National Park

Big Bend National Park is in southwestern Texas along the U.S.-Mexico border inside a huge bend of the Rio Grande, which forms the park's southern boundary and for which it is named. Most of the park's 2,866 km^2 (1,106 mi^2) is desert. The Chisos Mountains, in the south, are forested; Emory Peak, the highest point, reaches 2,388 m (7,835 ft). Three beautiful canyons—the Boquillas, Mariscal, and Santa Elena—were formed by the Rio Grande and are about 460 m (1,500 ft) high. More than 1,000 plant species are found, some of them unique to the park. Big Bend became a national park in 1944.

Big Bertha: see ARTILLERY.

Big Dipper

The Big Dipper, also known to the British as the Plough, Charlie's Wain, or the Wagon, is a group of seven bright stars that forms part of the constellation Ursa Major, the Great Bear. The stars of the Big Dipper are circumpolar and can be seen from northern latitudes all night every clear night. The group can never be seen from southern latitudes.

The seven stars that form the Big Dipper, starting from the end of the bowl and moving toward the handle, are Dubhe, Merak, Phecda, Megrez, Alioth, Mizar, and Alkaid. Mizar, at the bend in the handle, is a naked-eye double star; an ancient test of eyesight involved the subject's ability to locate Alcor, the faint companion star of Mizar.

The nightly appearance of the Big Dipper and the relative ease of locating the group make it a particularly useful guidepost for finding other stars and constellations. The first two stars in the bowl are called the Pointers; Polaris, the North Star, is easily located by drawing an imaginary line from Merak to Dubhe and extending it about five times their separation length. Extending the line in the opposite direction locates the bright star Regulus in the constellation Leo, the Lion.

The star Arcturus, in the constellation Boötes, can be found by extending the handle of the Big Dipper away from the bowl in an arc; a continuation of this arc past Arcturus will pass through the bright star Spica that is in the constellation Virgo, the Virgin.

The five central stars of the Big Dipper are part of an associated group that also includes stars from other parts of the sky. These stars form an open cluster. Approximately 75 light-years away, it is the nearest open cluster to Earth.

bigamy

Bigamy is the crime committed when a person—man or woman—who is legally married and undivorced, and whose spouse is living, contracts a marriage with a second person. Bigamy, which literally means ''second marriage,'' is a crime only in monogamous societies. In some countries POLYGAMY, or plural marriage, is legal.

Although bigamy is a crime in the United States, the U.S. federal system complicates the bases for prosecution. Each state is in part free to make its own determinations as to the legal effect of divorces granted in other states. A notable reinforcement of this principle was the 1945 Supreme Court ruling in *Williams* v. *North Carolina* that a Nevada divorce did not have to be recognized in North Carolina because the parties had not established legal domicile in Nevada under North Carolina law. Another matter of differing jurisdictions concerns the unexplained absence of spouses; many, but not all, courts consider a spouse dead if missing for seven years or more.

Bibliography: Deer, John, *Bigamy, Polygamy and Polyandry: A Comprehensive Bibliography* (1986).

Bigelow, John

John Bigelow, b. Malden, N.Y., Nov. 25, 1817, d. Dec. 19, 1911, was an American diplomat and writer. After a brief career as a lawyer, he became (1848) part owner and editor, with William

Cullen BRYANT, of the *New York Evening Post*; for a dozen years thereafter, he wrote editorials vigorously supporting free trade and denouncing slavery. In 1861 he went to Paris as consul general and in 1865–66 served as the U.S. minister to France. While in France, Bigelow was instrumental in generating support for the Union cause and in discouraging NAPOLEON III from undertaking an imperial expedition to Mexico.

In the latter half of his life, Bigelow produced a valuable analysis of French relations with the Confederate navy (1888), biographies of Édouard Laboulaye (1889) and Samuel TILDEN (1895), and two books reflecting his devotion to the philosophy of the Swedish theologian Emanuel von SWEDENBORG. He also edited the works of Benjamin FRANKLIN in ten volumes (1887–88); his *Life of Benjamin Franklin* (1874) is a version of the famous *Autobiography* that Bigelow had edited from a manuscript discovered in 1868. His own autobiography *Retrospections of an Active Life*, was published in five volumes from 1909 to 1913.

Bibliography: Clapp, Margaret A., *Forgotten First Citizen: John Bigelow* (1947; repr. 1968).

bigeye

The bigeyes, or catalufas, of the family Priacanthidae, are common reef fish in all tropical oceans. They have large eyes and are usually red in color, both characteristics suggesting nocturnal habits, but in fact they do some feeding during the day. Bigeyes have oblique mouths with small conical teeth and projecting lower jaws. They are carnivorous, eating crustaceans, small fish, and worms. Their maximum sizes range from 30 to 60 cm (12 to 24 in), depending on the species.

C. P. IDYLL

Biggers, Earl Derr

Earl Derr Biggers, b. Warren, Ohio, Aug. 26, 1884, d. Apr. 5, 1933, was the American mystery novelist and playwright who created the amiable and aphoristic sleuth Charlie Chan. Although Chan appeared in only six of Biggers's novels, including *The Chinese Parrot* (1926) and *Charlie Chan Carries On* (1930), more than 40 Charlie Chan films were made between 1926 and the early 1950s; the title role was usually played by Warner Oland or Sidney Toler. Biggers also wrote the popular novel *Seven Keys to Baldpate* (1913).

Biggs, E. Power

Edward George Power Biggs, b. Mar. 29, 1906, d. Mar. 10, 1977, was one of the most celebrated organists of his generation and did much to popularize the organ and its literature. Of English birth, he graduated from the Royal Academy of Music in London before becoming an American citizen in 1937. From 1942 to 1958, Biggs gave weekly recitals over CBS radio from Harvard's Busch-Reisinger Museum. During this time he played the complete organ works of J. S. Bach, as well as much other music from the 16th to the 20th century and many specially commissioned works by contemporary American composers. He toured widely in both Europe and the United States and recorded extensively.

bighorn

The bighorn, or bighorn sheep, *Ovis canadensis*, is of the family Bovidae in the order Artiodactyla. It is a wild sheep with a silky coat similar to that of a deer, varying from brown to buff. The male bighorn, or ram, may be as much as 150 cm (5 ft) long, about 100 cm (40 in) high at the shoulder, and weigh 157 kg (350 lb); females are smaller. The muzzle is narrow. Despite its bulk, the bighorn can negotiate mountainous terrain, aided by its sharp cloven hooves with flexible pads. The ram carries a majestic set of curving horns about 45 cm (18 in) in circumference at the base and up to 120 cm (4 ft) long; the female's horns are smaller. The largest bighorns are the Rocky Mountain bighorn and the California bighorns from Canada. Bighorns are characterized by their short ears and large horns. They eat grasses, flowers, young plants, and even cacti.

Bighorn sheep maneuver skillfully along rocky mountain ledges. Rams with the largest horns generally dominate other males in competition for ewes during the mating season.

The bighorn was once numerous from the mountains of southern Canada to northern Mexico; disease, food scarcity, and overhunting, however, have reduced the bighorn population. Today, they are found only in remote mountain areas and national parks in the United States.   EVERETT SENTMAN

bight: see GULF AND BAY.

bignonia

The genus *Bignonia* is represented by a single species, *B. capreolata,* a woody vine native to southeastern North America. This genus lends its name to the family Bignoniaceae, a group of trees and woody vines that grow in subtropical and tropical areas. Both the CATALPA tree and the TRUMPET TREE are members of the Bignoniaceae.

Bihar   [bee-hahr']

Bihar is a state in northeastern India bordered by Nepal on the north and West Bengal state on the east. Bihar covers 173,876 km² (67,134 mi²), and the population is 69,914,734 (1981). Patna is the capital. The Ganges River flows through the northern half of Bihar. The southern half of the state is dominated by the Chota Nagpur plateau, with an average elevation of about 600 m (2,000 ft). Bihar is one of India's most densely populated states, with 402 persons per km² (1,041 per mi²). The majority of the population, which is concentrated on the river plain, is engaged in agriculture. Rice is the leading crop, but grains, beans, sugar, and jute are also grown. Bihar is most important for its mineral wealth. The Chota Nagpur is the richest mineral source in India and produces coal, copper, phosphate, bauxite, mica, and iron ore. Bihar was the center of the Magadha kingdom (6th century BC–8th century AD). The Buddha spent his early life in Bihar, and he is said to have received enlightenment at BODH GAYA. Bihar came under British control in 1765.

Bihzad, Kamal al-Din   [be-zahd' kah-mahl' ahl-deen']

Kamal al-Din Bihzad, *c.*1450–1536, was a renowned master of Persian miniature painting. Bihzad flourished in the unique cultural environment of the court of Sultan Husayn Mirza Bayqara (1470–1506) of Herat. About two years after the death of the Mirza, Bihzad found a new patron in Shah Ismail, who founded the Safavid dynasty of Iran and made Tabriz his capital. There Bihzad worked as the head of the imperial library, training many eminent artists. Bihzad's miniatures are noted for the expressive gestures and poses of the figures, and his arrangement of groups shows a keen understanding of spatial relationships. Touches of bright red and the fre-

quent use of subtle tones of brown are characteristic of his paintings. The copy of the *Bustan* manuscript in the Egyptian Library, Cairo, bears Bihzad's signature. Also attributed to him are miniatures in Nizami's *Khamsa* in the British Museum, in Mir Ali Shir Nawai's *Khamsa* in the Bodleian Library, Oxford, and in the Gulistan Palace Library, Tehran.

S. A. A. RIZVI

Bibliography: Arnold, Thomas W., *Painting in Islam* (1965); Gray, Basil, *Persian Painting* (1930; repr. 1977); Martin, F. R., *The Miniature Painting and Painters of Persia, India and Turkey* (1912; repr. 1972).

See also: PERSIAN ART AND ARCHITECTURE.

Bikila, Abebe   [bee-kee'-lah, ah-bay'-bay]

Abebe Bikila, b. Aug. 7, 1932, d. Oct. 25, 1973, was an Ethiopian runner who twice won the Olympic marathon. A frail-looking member of Emperor Haile Selassie's personal guard, Bikila was an unknown at the Rome Olympics in 1960, but he won the marathon, running barefoot. His hope of duplicating the feat in 1964 suffered a severe setback when he underwent an appendicitis operation about a month before the Tokyo Olympics. He recuperated, however, to become the only person to win the race twice, until Waldemar Cierpinski of East Germany won in 1976 and 1980. A knee injury kept Bikila from repeating in 1968, and the next year an automobile accident paralyzed him from the waist down.

Bikini   [bi-kee'-nee]

Bikini Island is an atoll in the Pacific Ocean in the Ralik (Sunset) chain of the MARSHALL ISLANDS. It has an area of 5 km² (2 mi²). Part of the U.S.-administered Trust Territory of the Pacific Islands, it was the site of nuclear and thermonuclear weapons tests from 1947 to 1958. Bikini's three dozen coral islets rise little above sea level and encircle a large lagoon. The Micronesian inhabitants, who numbered about 200 before the United States relocated them after World War II, ate fish, shellfish, bananas, and coconuts.

Between 1946 and 1958, 23 nuclear devices were exploded at Bikini Island. In 1968 the United States declared Bikini habitable and started bringing the Bikinians back to their homes; however, in 1978 the islanders were removed again when STRONTIUM 90 in their bodies reached dangerous levels. The islands are expected to be off limits for many years.

Bilbao   [beel-bah'-oh]

Bilbao, also called Belvoa, a port city on the Nervión River near the Bay of Biscay in northern Spain, is the capital of Vizcaya (Biscay) Province. With a population of 433,030 (1981), it is the most populous city in the Basque provinces. Set in a region of rich iron mines, it has heavy metallurgical and chemical industries. The port, one of Spain's most important, serves both oceangoing and coastal vessels and has shipbuilding and fishing industries.

Probably settled much earlier, by 1300 the site was inhabited by a seafaring people who exported high-quality iron products fashioned from ore mined along the river bank. The city flourished anew during the 15th and 16th centuries because of a thriving wool trade between Castile and Flanders. In the 18th century Bilbao became the chief port for commerce between Spain and its American colonies. Bilbao was invaded by the French in 1795 and in 1808. Three efforts by the Carlists during the 19th century to besiege the city were unsuccessful. Bilbao was the headquarters of the short-lived Basque autonomous government in 1936–37.

Architectural monuments in Bilbao include the Gothic cathedral of Santiago and the Plaza Nueva. The city has mining and engineering schools.

Bilbo, Theodore Gilmore

Theodore Gilmore Bilbo, b. Pearl River County, Miss., Oct. 13, 1877, d. Aug. 21, 1947, was a Southern populist political leader. He served two terms (1916–20, 1928–32) as governor of Mississippi. As a Democratic U.S. senator (1935–47), Bilbo urged deportation of all black Americans to Africa. In 1947 he was barred from taking his seat for a third term in the Senate as a result of charges that he had used intimidation against black voters and had accepted bribes.

Bibliography: Green, A. Wigfall, *The Man Bilbo* (1963; repr. 1978); Morgan, Chester M., *Redneck Liberal* (1985).

Bilderdijk, Willem [bil'-dur-dik, vil'-uhm]

Willem Bilderdijk, b. Sept. 7, 1756, d. Dec. 18, 1831, was a Dutch poet whose work expresses both the antiquarian romanticism of the Gothic revival and its author's monarchist sympathies. Educated at Leiden, Bilderdijk practiced law at The Hague until 1795, when he exiled himself for more than a decade to protest the new Dutch republic. His *Geschiedenis des Vaderlands* (History of the Fatherland, 1832–51) defends his antirepublican position. Bilderdijk's *Gebed* (Prayer, 1796) strongly influenced later religious lyrics, and his 1803 translation of OSSIAN introduced early romantic sentiment to the Netherlands. He also wrote *De Kunst der Poëzy* (The Art of Poetry, 1809), a defense of personal emotion in poetry, and the unfinished epic *De Ondergang der Eerste Wareld* (The Destruction of the First World, begun in 1809–10).

Bibliography: Meijer, R. P., *Literature of the Low Countries* (1971; repr. 1978).

bildungsroman [bil'-dungz-roh-mahn']

A *bildungsroman* (German: "education novel") is a novel about the development and maturation of a youthful hero or heroine. The form was especially popular between 1790 and 1860. The earliest example is Christoph Martin WIELAND's *Agathon* (1766–67; *The History of Agathon,* 1904). Other notable examples include GOETHE's *Wilhelm Meister's Youth* (1796; Eng. trans., 1826) and Thomas MANN's *Joseph and His Brothers* (1933-42; Eng. trans., 1934-45) and *The Magic Mountain* (1924; Eng. trans., 1927). Perhaps the chief examples in English are Charles DICKENS's *David Copperfield* (1849-50) and James JOYCE's *A Portrait of the Artist as a Young Man* (1916).

J. A. CUDDON

bile: see GALLBLADDER; LIVER.

bilharziasis: see SCHISTOSOMIASIS.

bilingual education

Bilingual education provides for instruction to students in two languages: the native language of the student, if that differs from the language of the host country, and the language of the host country.

Some educators argue that the aim of bilingual education should be the assimilation of a child into the regular school system and, eventually, into the host society. Others hold that this form of bilingual education belittles a child's cultural heritage and that, therefore, all courses should be taught in two languages, thus fostering biculturalism.

In the United States, these philosophies have yielded two basic types of programs designed to integrate non-English-speaking children with speakers of English. In the transition program, students are gradually led from exclusive use of their native language to full use of English. In the maintenance program, the native language is used simultaneously with English; as a result, students develop reading and speaking fluency in both languages.

The U.S. government appropriates yearly funds for bilingual education and also supplies policy guidelines for such programs. In the mid-1990s, when there were about 2.8 million students whose home language was not English, the Department of Education, having previously relaxed strict federal guidelines, allowed local school boards to try a variety of bilingual approaches. Many of the students in these programs are originally Spanish-speaking; an increasing number of them speak Asian languages.

Bibliography: Dodson, C. J., *Bilingual Education* (1985).

Bill, Max

Max Bill, b. Dec. 22, 1908, d. Dec. 9, 1994, was the leading Swiss exponent of the theories of concrete, as opposed to abstract, art. His studies (1927–29) with the artist Josef ALBERS at the Bauhaus in Germany determined the style and content of all his subsequent work as a painter, sculptor, architect, industrial designer, and writer. His paintings deal exclusively with the interaction of color, and his geometric sculpture is based on relativistic physics. Bill was a member of the Swiss Parliament from 1967 to 1971.

Bibliography: Huttinger, Eduard, *Max Bill* (1978).

bill of exchange

A bill of exchange is a negotiable written order for payment of a specified sum to a designated person. Bills of exchange are commonly used in international trade. The person receiving a shipment of goods must pay the sum specified in the bill to take title to the goods. Bills of exchange are often purchased by banks at a discount, and they may pass through several hands before redemption. The modern bill of exchange originated during the 13th century among the Lombards of northern Italy, who were active international traders. It is sometimes called a bank draft.

bill of health

A bill of health is a statement carried by a ship. It indicates the state of public health in the last port from which the ship sailed and the health of the vessel's passengers and crew. If the latter show no evidence of contagious disease, the ship is said to have a "clean bill of health." The term has come into general usage to mean that a person has been cleared of all question about his or her associations or past actions; for example, "He was given a clean bill of health by the investigators."

bill of lading

A bill of lading is a contract between a shipper of goods and a carrier that acknowledges the receipt of certain goods from a shipper and agrees to transport and deliver them to the designated destination at a specified time. A copy of the bill of lading is sent to the buyer, thereby establishing ownership. The bill of lading also explains the liability assumed by the carrier when it contracts to carry the goods. The carrier is responsible for any loss or damage occurring through negligence, or for delaying the shipment for an unreasonable length of time. The carrier, however, is not liable for loss or delay caused by an act of God, that is, an unavoidable natural accident, or by civil disturbances or strikes.

The bill of lading was originally an ocean freight document. The master of a ship acknowledged the receipt of certain merchandise that was in good condition and promised to deliver it to the consignee, or buyer, named in the bill. In the 19th century, however, the seagoing bill of lading also became a railroad document.

bill of rights

The first ten amendments to the U.S. CONSTITUTION are called the Bill of Rights because they provide basic legal protection for individual rights. The term is also applied to the English Bill of Rights of 1689, to similar guarantees in the constitutions of the American states, and to the Canadian Charter of Rights and Freedoms.

The first American use of the term was in 1774 when the First Continental Congress adopted the Declaration and Resolves, which was popularly termed the Bill of Rights because it was an American equivalent of the English Bill of Rights. Two years later came the Virginia Declaration of Rights, which contained the first guarantees for individual rights in a legally enforceable constitution. The distinctive feature of the provisions in American bills of rights is that they are enforced by the courts; statutes and other governmental acts that conflict with them may be ruled void if their constitutionality is appropriately challenged.

The Bill of Rights, comprising the first ten amendments to the Constitution of the United States, remains on display in the National Archives in Washington, D.C. The document, which defines certain inviolable liberties of American citizens, was adopted in 1791.

U.S. BILL OF RIGHTS

Adoption. From the time they first settled in Virginia and Massachusetts, the American colonists relied upon the rights enjoyed by Englishmen. The struggle for independence, however, demonstrated to them that rights not specified and codified in constitutional documents were insecure. The result was a movement, as soon as independence was declared, to adopt binding constitutions that limited governmental powers and protected individual rights. Seven of the thirteen states adopted constitutions that included specific bills of rights; the other states included specific guarantees of individual rights in various provisions contained throughout their constitutional texts. The first state bill of rights was the Virginia Declaration of Rights, adopted as part of the state's first constitution on June 12, 1776. Virginia's declaration, drafted mainly by George MASON, served as the model both for similar state documents and for the U.S. Bill of Rights. It provided guarantees for most of the rights secured in the latter document.

The U.S. Constitution contains protection for some individual rights in the body of its text, notably the rights to HABEAS CORPUS and jury trial and against bills of ATTAINDER and ex post facto laws. As originally drafted in 1787 by the Philadelphia Convention, however, no federal bill of rights was included. A motion by George Mason to add such a bill was overwhelmingly defeated.

The failure of the Constitution to include a bill of rights gave rise to widespread popular dissatisfaction. The people refused to accept the Federalist claim that a bill of rights was

not necessary, since the powers delegated to the new government did not include authority over individual rights. As Chief Justice Earl WARREN later wrote, "Our people wanted explicit assurances. The Bill of Rights was the result."

The popular demand for a bill of rights found practical expression in the state conventions that ratified the Constitution. The ratifying conventions of six states submitted, along with their instruments of ratification, proposed amendments protecting individual rights. These recommended amendments covered virtually all the rights that were later protected in the U.S. Bill of Rights. The action of the ratifying conventions made the movement for a federal bill of rights irresistible. Ratification would probably not have been secured had not the Federalists agreed to the amendments and promised to secure their adoption.

In the 1st Congress under the new Constitution, James MADISON led the movement to make good these promises. He drafted the amendments that became the U.S. Bill of Rights and was the floor leader in the House debate on their adoption. The Madison amendments were put together from the various proposals emanating from the state conventions. In introducing the amendments in the House of Representatives on June 8, 1789, Madison urged the need for a bill of rights to "provide those securities for liberty . . . and expressly declare the great rights of mankind." The purpose was to limit and qualify power, guard against legislative and executive abuses, and protect the minority against the majority.

The Congressional debate on Madison's amendments produced stylistic and substantive changes. The most important of the former was adoption of the amendments as a series of separate articles to be added at the end of the Constitution, rather than as insertions into its body, as Madison had proposed. Four of Madison's amendments were eliminated during the Congressional debate; the most important of them was a prohibition against state violations of the rights of conscience, freedom of the press, and jury trial. Elimination of that amendment made the Bill of Rights as adopted applicable only to the federal government; its prohibitions did not impose limitations on the states.

Congress voted in September 1789 to submit 12 amendments for ratification by the states. The first two, dealing with congressional size and compensation, failed. The other ten (renumbered to reflect the nonratification of the first two) were ratified by the required ten state legislatures, with Virginia the last to ratify, on Dec. 15, 1791. September 25—the day on which Congressional approval was completed—is celebrated as the anniversary of the federal Bill of Rights.

Summary. The most important rights protected by the U.S. Bill of Rights are contained in the 1ST AMENDMENT. It provides that Congress shall make no law respecting an establishment of religion or prohibiting its free exercise, or abridging freedom of speech or press or the right to assemble and petition for redress of grievances. These rights are the core rights protected by the system of ordered liberty established by the Bill of Rights. Under the 1st Amendment, the domain of "liberty," withdrawn from federal encroachment, was enlarged to include liberty of mind and beliefs.

The 2d and 3d amendments reflect the colonists' hostility toward standing armies; they guarantee the people's right to bear arms and limit the quartering of soldiers in private homes. The 4th AMENDMENT is aimed at the abuses the colonists had suffered from writs of assistance and general warrants; it secures the people against unreasonable searches and seizures and requires warrants to be specific and issued only upon probable cause.

The 5TH AMENDMENT requires grand jury indictments in major criminal prosecutions and prohibits trying a person twice on the same charge or requiring that person to testify against himself or herself; it forbids taking of private property for public use without just compensation and forbids deprivation of life, liberty, and property without due process of law. The due process concept was a major step forward; since then, due process has served as the principal constitutional tool for the protection of rights not defined in the Bill of Rights.

The 6TH AMENDMENT protects criminal defendants; it guarantees the accused a speedy public trial by jury and the rights to be informed of the accusation, to be confronted with the witnesses against the accused, to use compulsory process to secure witnesses, and to have the assistance of counsel.

The 7th AMENDMENT guarantees jury trials in civil cases; the 8th prohibits excessive bail or fines or cruel and unusual punishments; the 9th provides that the enumeration of rights in the Constitution does not deny others retained by the people; and the 10th states the doctrine of reserved powers—that all powers not delegated to the United States are reserved to the states or the people.

From the perspective of two centuries, it can be said that Madison chose well among the pyramid of proposals in the state-recommended amendments. He included all the great rights appropriate for constitutional protection (except equal protection, not even thought of as a basic right at the time). The U.S. Bill of Rights contains the classic inventory of individual rights, and it has served as the standard for all subsequent attempts to safeguard human rights.

ENGLISH BILL OF RIGHTS

The English Bill of Rights of 1689 bore the technical title "Act declaring the rights and liberties of the subject and settling the succession of the crown." It was the culmination of the so-called GLORIOUS REVOLUTION of 1688, which forced JAMES II to vacate the throne. From James's flight until February 1689, when WILLIAM III and MARY II accepted the crown, England had no legal government. Not only was there no king, but no Parliament, since Parliament had been dissolved in July 1688. Without a king it was impossible to assemble a lawfully constituted Parliament, and without Parliament a legal solution of the problem posed by James's flight also seemed impossible.

The dilemma was resolved by extralegal methods. William called an assembly of the peers, members of the Commons, and the magistrates of London, using as precedent an assembly called under Charles II. The assembly called by William advised him to summon a convention Parliament. It met on Jan. 22, 1689, and soon thereafter passed a resolution announcing that James II had abdicated and that the throne was thereby vacant. After the crown was settled on William and Mary, the convention passed an act declaring itself to be a Parliament.

The throne was offered to William and Mary, subject to the conditions laid down in an instrument known as the Declaration of Right, drawn up by a committee of the convention. After that body had declared itself a Parliament, it turned its declaration into a regular act of the legislature, enacted as a statute in 1689. Hence, the name Bill of Rights results from the introduction of the original declaration as a bill—the first step in enactment of a statute—in the new Parliament.

The 1689 Bill of Rights served notice on the king that royal efforts to dominate Parliament must henceforth cease. It declared that the election of members of Parliament ought to be free; that freedom of speech and debates in Parliament ought not to be questioned in any court or other place; and that Parliament ought to be held frequently (a provision made more specific by the 1694 Triennial Act, which required parliamentary elections every three years).

In addition, the Bill of Rights specifically condemned the abuses of the parliamentary prerogative by James II. It declared "that the pretended power of suspending of laws or the execution of laws by regal authority without consent of the Parliament is illegal." A similar provision outlawed the dispensing power "as it hath been assumed and exercised of late." Another royal abuse was corrected in a provision prohibiting the raising or keeping of an army in time of peace "unless it be with consent of Parliament." A statement of the right of the people to bear arms was included, as well as a complaint against the quartering of soldiers.

Those sections of the Bill of Rights that deal with perversions of justice are of particular interest, for they served as the models for similar provisions in the American Bill of Rights. These sections provide that "excessive bail ought not to be required, nor excessive fines imposed, nor cruel and unusual punishments inflicted" (the direct ancestor of the 8th Amendment to the Federal Constitution); that jurors should be duly impaneled; and that grants and promises of fines and forfeitures by particular persons before conviction are illegal.

FRENCH DECLARATION OF THE RIGHTS OF MAN

The French Declaration of the Rights of Man and of the Citizen was adopted by the Constituent Assembly in August 1789. It was intended as a statement of the basic philosophical principles that inspired the FRENCH REVOLUTION. Among the important principles declared by its 17 articles were freedom and equality; popular sovereignty and the general will; representative government; punishment only for legally defined offenses; free communication of thought and opinion; taxation only by popular consent; separation of powers; and the right to private property and just compensation.

Although the French declaration was the contemporary counterpart of the U.S. Bill of Rights, crucial differences exist between the two documents that illustrate the basic dissimilarity between American and French constitutional thinking. The French declaration does not lay down practical rules, only general principles deemed fundamental to humankind and hence universally applicable. Madison had also included some general principles in his proposed amendments, but they were eliminated during the Congressional debates. What was left in the ten amendments ratified in the United States was specific protection for the basic rights of free expression and association, the rights to privacy and due process, and freedom from arbitrary restraint and trial and cruel and unusual punishments. The provisions protecting them were set forth as legal rules, enforceable as such by the courts. Nothing like this is contained in the French Declaration, which was drafted only in terms of the general rights people should have. The French document does not contain mandatory inhibitions that must be respected by the government, nor does it descend to the level of practical enforcement through specific provision for the basic rights of defendants and others dealing with law-enforcement officials.

CANADIAN BILL OF RIGHTS

In 1960 the Canadian Parliament adopted an Act for the Recognition and Protection of Human Rights and Fundamental Freedoms. Whereas this document served successfully as a bill of rights, it did not have a constitutional guarantee beyond the power of the legislature itself. Enacted as a statute, it was subject to alteration or repeal by act of Parliament alone, without any need for constitutional amendment.

After years of debate the Canadian government agreed to extend a constitutional guarantee to a bill of rights when, in 1982, a Charter of Rights and Freedoms was entrenched in the Constitution. The Charter of Rights and Freedoms recognizes the supremacy of God and the rule of law. It recognizes the right of the individual not to be deprived of life, liberty, security of the person, and property except by due process of law; freedom of religion, of speech, and of the press and other media of communication; and freedom of peaceful assembly and association. Equality before and under the law is guaranteed without discrimination based on race, national or ethnic origin, color, religion, sex, age, or mental or physical disability. The charter prohibits arbitrary detention and imprisonment, cruel and unusual punishment, denial of habeas corpus, denial of counsel or self-incrimination, denial of innocence until proved guilty, and denial of bail. French and English are specified as official languages.

While the charter has a constitutional guarantee, Parliament and the provincial legislatures have limited power to pass laws that might conflict with certain charter rights. The body passing the law must include a clause that specifically states it is doing so "notwithstanding" the charter. The clause, unless reenacted, expires after five years.   BERNARD SCHWARTZ

Bibliography: Dumbauld, Edward, *The Bill of Rights and What It Means Today* (1957; repr. 1979); Kukla, Jon, ed., *The Bill of Rights* (1987); Rutland, Robert A., *The Birth of the Bill of Rights* (1983); Schwartz, Bernard, *Roots of the Bill of Rights*, 5 vols. (1981).

Billaud-Varenne, Jean Nicolas [bee-oh'-vah-ren', zhawn nee-koh-lah']

A French lawyer, writer, and revolutionary, Jean Nicolas Billaud-Varenne, b. Apr. 23, 1756, d. June 3, 1819, led the National Convention of September 1792 in declaring France a republic and was a member (September 1793–July 1794) of the Committee of Public Safety. A fervent left-wing Jacobin, he helped proscribe the Girondist moderates and then overthrew Georges DANTON. Eventually, he also turned on Maximilien ROBESPIERRE and helped secure his downfall in the Thermidorian Reaction of July 1794. Subsequently, with his associate Jean Marie Collet d'Herbois, he was deported to French Guiana, where he became a farmer. Billaud-Varenne refused Napoleon I's amnesty of 1800 and died in Haiti.

Bibliography: Bouloiseau, Marc, *The Jacobin Republic 1792–1794*, trans. by J. Mandelbaum (1984); Brinton, Crane, *The Jacobins* (1930; repr. 1961); Woloch, I., *Jacobin Legacy* (1960).

billiards

All billiards games are played on a rectangular, slate-topped table twice as long as it is wide and covered with a felt cloth. The playing area is surrounded by rubber cushions, or rails. Two basic types of billiards exist: pocket billiards, also called pool, on a table with six pockets (see diagram), and carom billiards, usually on a table with no pockets.

Pocket Billiards. Pocket billiards requires cue sticks, a white cue ball, and, in the United States, 15 object balls numbered 1–15 (1–8, solid; 9–15, striped).

The most popular U.S. pocket billiards game, called 14.1 continuous or straight pool, is for 2 players only. The game begins with the 15 object balls racked unordered in a triangle (see diagram). The player who begins, or breaks, strokes the cue ball and must drive 2 or more object balls to a cushion or at least 1 object ball into a pocket. After that, each player attempts to make a continuous run of balls, in any order, until only 1 object ball remains on the table. The 14 balls are then racked again, with a space left at the head of the triangle. The player who pocketed the 14th ball now attempts to pocket the 15th and scatter the racked balls. Before each shot a player must call the shot, that is, identify ball and pocket. Each turn taken is called an inning. One point is scored for each successful shot, and a game is usually set to 150 points.

Another pocket billiards game is rotation, in which the object balls are racked in order—the number 1 ball at the apex of the triangle and so on. Each ball must be pocketed in order and is worth its face value. The player or team to reach 61 points or more wins.

A variation of rotation is nine ball, which, from the early 1980s, rivaled straight pool in U.S. popularity. Only balls 1–9 are used, racked in a diamond with the number 9 ball in the center and the 1 ball at the apex. On all shots the cue ball must first strike the lowest-numbered ball on the table; the player who pockets the 9 ball wins.

Eight ball, the game most played on coin-operated tables, begins with the number 8 ball racked in the center of the triangle. After the break, 1 player (or team) shoots only at balls 1–7 (solids), the other player only at 9–15 (stripes). After a player pockets an entire group, the 8 ball must be pocketed.

In Great Britain snooker is the most popular billiards game. It uses 21 object balls: 15 red (worth 1 point each) and 1 each of yellow (2), green (3), brown (4), blue (5), pink (6), and black (7). A player must first pocket a red ball, then a "colored" one, then a red, and so on. Each colored ball is respotted on the table, however, until all the reds are off; then the colored balls must be pocketed in ascending order. The play-

A snooker player prepares to make a shot. Although billiard games have been a popular pastime for centuries, the introduction of slate-topped tables and rubber side cushions in the mid-1800s stimulated the development of billiards as a competitive game.

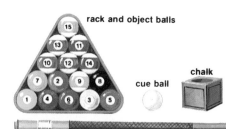

rack and object balls

cue ball

chalk

The term billiards *generally applies to two basic types of game: pocket billiards and carom billiards. In the former, of which three variations are shown below, a player using a cue strikes the single cue ball into one or more object balls to sink them into the table's pockets. Straight pool and rotation, played mostly in the United States, employ 15 object balls (left and below left). Snooker (below center), played mostly in Britain, uses 21 smaller object balls that must be sunk in a partially predetermined sequence; a player is snookered when the path from the cue ball to a playable object ball is obstructed by another object ball. English billiards (below right) uses only 2 object balls and is really a combination of pocket and carom billiards: players score by hitting the cue ball into both object balls or by sinking one or more balls.*

cue

**pocket billiards
(pool)**

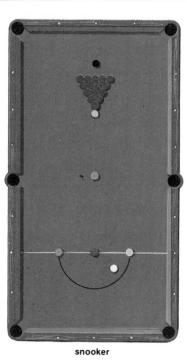

snooker

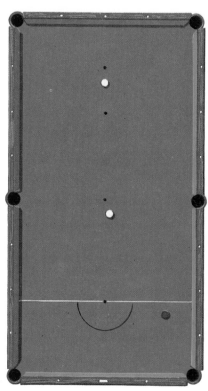

English billiards

er with the most points wins.

Carom Billiards. The most popular form of carom billiards is three-rail billiards, played with two white balls and one red on a pocketless table. To score a point a player must stroke the cue ball (one of the white balls), and it must hit one of the other balls and at least three cushions before hitting the second ball. The cue ball may also strike the other two simultaneously as long as it has already hit at least three rails. Games are usually played to 50 points.

In straight-rail billiards the cue ball must strike the other two but not necessarily any rails. English billiards is played on a somewhat larger table, with pockets, and with some rule variations (see diagram).

History. Billiards is of unknown origin, but the game was played in 16th-century England. The word *billiards* is derived from the Old French *billart,* "curved stick." The Billiard Congress of America, in Iowa City, Iowa, sanctions U.S. play. The greatest U.S. players were Willie HOPPE (three-rail) and Willie MOSCONI (straight pool).

Bibliography: Byrne, Robert, *Byrne's Standard Book of Pool and Billiards* (1987); Hoppe, Willie, *Billiards As It Should Be Played* (1941; repr. 1977); Mosconi, Willie, *Winning Pocket Billiards* (1965).

Billings

Billings, the seat of Yellowstone County, is a city in south central Montana with a population of 81,151 (1990). Located on the Yellowstone River, it lies about 975 m (3,200 ft) above sea level. The economy is highly diversified, ranging from the growing of sugar beets and truck crops to the raising of cattle and sheep to oil refining, meat-packing, and flour milling. Grasshopper Glacier, with millions of grasshoppers frozen in its ice, lies nearby in Custer National Forest, for which the city is headquarters. Established in 1882 (incorporated 1885) by the Northern Pacific Railway, Billings was named for the company president Frederick Billings.

Billings, Josh

Josh Billings was the pen name of Henry Wheeler Shaw, b. Lanesboro, Mass., Apr. 21, 1818, d. Oct. 14, 1885, a comic writer who gained fame with his "Essa on the Muel" (1864). His humor depended chiefly on misspellings, bad grammar, and crackerbox philosophy. From 1869 to 1879 he published *Josh Billings' Farmer's Alminax,* a burlesque of *The Old Farmer's Almanac. Everybody's Friend* (1874) is one of the compilations of his newspaper writings.   ROBERT D. ARNER

Bibliography: Kesterson, David B., *Josh Billings* (1974).

Billings, William

William Billings, b. Boston, Oct. 7, 1746, d. Sept. 26, 1800, best known for his hymns and anthems, was one of the first important native-born American composers. Uneducated and a tanner by trade for most of his life, he was ardently devoted to choral singing. He taught himself the rudiments of music and compensated for his lack of a thorough music education by enthusiasm and a wealth of original ideas; his music is unsophisticated, but it remains fresh and vital.

With the spread of singing schools and the rise of the evangelical movement in New England, Billings found a ready market for his folklike hymn compositions. At the age of 24 he published his first collection of hymns, *The New England Psalm Singer* (1770), with a frontispiece engraved by Paul Revere. This contained what Billings subsequently described as ''fuging tunes,'' that is, pieces in simple fugal, or imitative, style ''with each part striving for mastery.'' His later collections include *The Singing Master's Assistant* (1778), *Music in Miniature* (1779), *The Psalm Singer's Amusement* (1781), and others. Some of his anthems became popular, particularly ''Chester'' (as a patriotic song during the Revolutionary War) and ''The Rose of Sharon.''

Humor combined with solemnity characterizes much of Billings's music, which has fascinated many 20th-century American composers. Henry Cowell, for example, has written a series of ''fuging tunes'' for orchestra. Billings is the second American composer—Scott Joplin was the first—whose complete works are being collected in a modern edition.

Bibliography: Barbour, J. Murray, *The Church Music of William Billings* (1960; repr. 1972); Daniel, Ralph T., *The Anthem in New England before 1800* (1966); McKay, David P., and Crawford, Richard, *William Billings of Boston* (1975); Nathan, Hans, *William Billings* (1976).

Billy Budd

Billy Budd, Foretopman (written 1888–91, published 1924; film, 1962), a short novel, may be viewed as either Herman MELVILLE's final testimonial of faith or his ironic farewell to humankind. The allegorical drama of innocence (Billy) falsely accused by depraved evil (Claggart) before an intelligent but feeling authority (Captain Vere) is enacted entirely at sea, aboard a British man-of-war in wartime (1797) with the fear of mutiny in the air. When jealous Claggart lies and tongue-tied Billy strikes him dead, Vere must hang the angelic killer to assure the obedient well-being of society (the puzzled crew). In enigmatic, partly archaic, highly imagistic prose, Melville's ''inside narrative'' is deliberately unshapely, like life itself. Benjamin BRITTEN based his opera *Billy Budd* (1951) on the novel.   ROBERT L. GALE

Billy the Kid

Billy the Kid was one of several aliases of William H. Bonney, b. New York City, Nov. 23, 1859, a New Mexico outlaw whose short, bloody career became a legend. By the age of 18 he had been charged with 12 murders. While working as a cowhand in the Pecos Valley, he turned to cattle rustling. After the gang he led killed a sheriff and a deputy, he was captured and sentenced to death. He escaped from jail, killing two guards, but was trapped and shot to death on July 13, 1881.

A ballet based on his life, with music by Aaron Copland, was first performed in Chicago in 1938.

Bibliography: Garrett, Pat, *The Life of Billy the Kid* (1882; repr. 1977); Tatum, Stephen, *Inventing Billy the Kid* (1982); Tuska, Jon, *Billy the Kid* (1986); Utley, Robert M., *Billy the Kid* (1989).

Biloxi   [buh-lahk'-see]

Biloxi, a city in southeastern Mississippi with a population of 49,319 (1990), is located on a narrow peninsula on the Gulf of Mexico between Biloxi Bay and Mississippi Sound. A large fishing fleet operates out of the port, making seafood—mainly shrimp and oysters—the main industry. Boatbuilding, fertilizer production, and tourism are also economically important. Nearby are Keesler Air Force Base and a veterans' hospital.

In 1699 the first white settlement in the lower Mississippi Valley was established across Biloxi Bay at Old Biloxi (now Ocean Springs). Fort Louis, founded in 1719 on the site of present-day Biloxi, served (1720–22) as the capital of French colonial Louisiana. Biloxi suffered considerable damage in 1969 from hurricane Camille. Beauvoir, the home of Jefferson DAVIS, is located in the city. Deer Island, one of the nearby coastal islands, is noted for legends of buried pirate treasure.

binary number   [by'-nair-ee]

A binary number is a number written in BASE two. This means that each position in a numeral represents a particular power of two. In the more common DECIMAL system, powers of ten are used. Binary numbers are important because of their application in computers. A positive integer is represented in base two by a string of 0s and 1s, for example, 1101001. Each digit represents a place value: the first (reading from right to left) represents the number of units; the second represents the number of twos; the third, the number of fours (= 2^2); the fourth, the number of eights (= 2^3), and so forth. For comparison, note that the first four decimal places represent, respectively, the number of units (10^0), tens (10^1), hundreds (10^2), and thousands (10^3). Thus

$$
\begin{aligned}
1 \text{ (base 2)} &= 1 \text{ (base 10)} \\
10 \text{ (base 2)} &= (1 \times 2) + (0 \times 1) = 2 \text{ (base 10)} \\
11 \text{ (base 2)} &= (1 \times 2) + (1 \times 1) = 3 \text{ (base 10)} \\
100 \text{ (base 2)} &= (1 \times 2^2) + (0 \times 2) + (0 \times 1) \\
&= 4 \text{ (base 10)} \\
1101001 \text{ (base 2)} &= (1 \times 2^6) + (1 \times 2^5) + (0 \times 2^4) + \\
&\quad (1 \times 2^3) + (0 \times 2^2) + (0 \times 2) + (1 \times 1) \\
&= 105 \text{ (base 10)}
\end{aligned}
$$

The arithmetic operations for binary numbers are simple. For example, consider the addition of 1101001 and 1101110:

```
   11 1
  1101001
  1101110
  --------
 11010111
```

(Note that $1 + 1 = 10$ in any column.)

Electronic devices lend themselves to the use of binary numbers because on/off, or go/no-go circuits are involved. In modern computers and calculators, two-state devices are employed to represent the binary digits 0 and 1. One of the states represents 0; the other state represents 1.

WILLIAM W. ADAMS

Bibliography: Bartee, Thomas C., *Digital Computer Fundamentals*, 6th ed. (1985); Scott, N. R., *Computer Number Systems and Arithmetic* (1985); Wicks, Keith, *Working with Computers* (1986).

binary stars

Binary stars are pairs of stars that, because of their mutual gravitational attraction, orbit around a common center of mass. If a group of three or more stars revolve around one another, it is called a multiple system. It is believed that approximately 50 percent of all stars belong to binary or multiple systems.

Types. Systems with individual components that can be seen separately by telescope are called visual binaries or visual multiples. William Herschel recognized in 1803 that the components of these systems revolve around each other in the same way that the Earth and the Moon do. The periods of visual binaries are very long—sometimes several hundred years. Herschel's discovery of their orbit was the result of many years spent in making precise measurements of the positions of the components.

A binary system in which an apparent variability in the brightness of the stars exists is called an eclipsing binary. In 1782, John Goodricke observed such periodic changes in the brightness of the star ALGOL (β Persei); about every 69 hours the star showed a sharp drop in brightness. Goodricke correctly speculated that this minimum was caused when one component of a binary periodically eclipsed the other, much brighter member of the system as seen from the Earth. Such a system is also called an eclipsing VARIABLE STAR, as opposed to a physical variable, in which the brightness changes because of changes inside the star. An eclipsing binary may or may not also be a visual binary.

A binary with components that are so close together that it is known to be a binary only by its spectrum is called a spec-

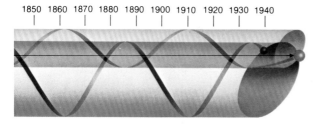

1850 1860 1870 1880 1890 1900 1910 1920 1930 1940

Binary stars move so that a line between their centers always passes through their common center of gravity. This common center is called the barycenter. The more massive star remains closer to the barycenter, has a smaller elliptical orbit, and moves more slowly than the smaller star. The diagram depicts the 100-year space motion of the binary stars Sirius A (red) and Sirius B (blue). The barycenter moves in a straight line in space, whereas each star describes a wavy path, or elliptical helix, around it. The more massive star, Sirius A, travels in the smaller helical path.

troscopic binary. When the components orbit one another in a plane almost parallel to the line of sight from the Earth, they move periodically toward and away from the Earth. Because of the DOPPLER EFFECT, their line-of-sight, or radial, velocities can be measured from the Doppler shifts of the spectral lines. That Goodricke was right in supposing that Algol is an eclipsing binary was proved by German astronomers H. K. Vogel and Julius Scheiner in 1889 when they discovered periodic Doppler shifts in the lines of Algol's spectrum.

Significance to Astronomy. The study of binary stars has been of great importance in stellar astronomy. The study of close binaries furnished most of the information necessary for establishing the theories of stellar interiors and composition, STELLAR EVOLUTION, X-ray binaries, and possible BLACK HOLES. The first direct measurements of stellar masses were made possible by the determination of the orbits of a small number of visual binaries that have measurable parallaxes. Geometric techniques were developed to derive the true orbit from the apparent orbit, which is the orbit actually seen and is the projection of the true orbit onto the celestial plane. From the dimensions of the orbits the masses of the components can be computed by using the third of KEPLER'S LAWS.

Far more interesting results were obtained from close binaries that are both spectroscopic and eclipsing binaries. From the velocity curve—that is, the radial velocity plotted against time—the binary's orbit can be determined, except for the inclination of the orbital plane to the celestial plane. This inclination can be deduced, however, from the light curve of the binary—that is, the graph of the brightness against time. Moreover, from the sizes of the minima on the light curve the sizes of the system's two components can be derived.

Transference of Mass. During the 1950s the results of the observation of the light curves and spectra of many close binaries became available, and from them the masses, sizes, and temperatures of the components could be determined. It was known that in heavier stars the fusion of hydrogen is faster and that, consequently, the evolution of heavier stars is much

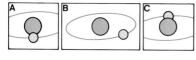

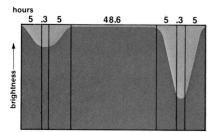

hours

Algol, a double star system in the Perseus constellation, varies from maximum to minimum brightness every 69 hours. (A) When the bright star passes in front of the dim star, a slight drop in brightness is observed. (B) Maximum brightness results when neither star is eclipsed. (C) Minimum brightness occurs when the dim star covers the bright one.

faster than that of lighter stars. In many binary systems, however, such as Algol, the lighter star was found to be in a more evolved stage even though the evolution of both stars should have started at the same time. This apparent paradox was resolved by assuming that during their evolution the heavier star expanded to fill its so-called Roche's lobe, or sphere of gravitational influence (see ROCHE'S LIMIT). Its matter entered the gravity field of the lighter star, and matter transferred onto the lighter star until their mass ratio was reversed. Such binaries are called semidetached. In some systems, called contact binaries, both stars fill their Roche's lobe, and the transfer of mass becomes more complex. Astronomers speculate that some systems may even coalesce.

In X-ray binaries (see X-RAY ASTRONOMY) the smaller component is a compact object: a WHITE DWARF, as in SIRIUS; a NEUTRON STAR; or possibly even a black hole. The X-radiation is produced by the impact of matter on the compact object. In some systems, a periodicity in X-ray intensity is observed as the X-ray source is eclipsed by its companion. In 1986 astronomers announced the determination of a system with an orbital period of 11 minutes—the shortest yet found—that may consist of two compact stars, a white dwarf and a neutron star. Hope was expressed that it might prove useful in the search for GRAVITATIONAL WAVES.   STEVEN J. DICK

Bibliography: Boss, A. P., "The Genesis of Binary Stars," *Astronomy,* June 1991; Crosswell, Ken, "Contact Binaries," *Astronomy,* December 1982, and "When Stars Coalesce," *Astronomy,* May 1985; Heintz, W. D., *Double Stars* (1978); Ibanoglu, Cafer, ed., *Active Close Binaries* (1990); Terrell, Dirk, et al., *Binary Stars: A Pictorial Atlas* (1992).

Binchois, Gilles   [ban-shwah', zheel

Gilles Binchois, c.1400–60, was one of the finest composers of the early 15th century. Most of his life was spent in Mons, in what is now Belgium. After a brief career as a soldier, he took priestly vows; about 1424 he was employed by William de la Pole, earl of Suffolk. From 1430 on he was at the court of Burgundy during its most brilliant epoch. Binchois wrote some sacred music, but his masterpieces are his 50 or more secular French chansons for solo voice and two instruments. The voice carries the melodic line, the lowest instrument establishes a feeling of key, and the middle instrument fills in the other essential notes in the chord, all characteristics that are remarkably advanced for the time.   WILLIAM HAYS

Bibliography: Gleason, H., and Becker, W., *Music in the Middle Ages and Renaissance,* 3d ed. (1988).

Bindesbøll, Michael Gottlieb Birkner   [bayn'-uhs-burl]

Michael Gottlieb Birkner Bindesbøll, b. Sept. 5, 1800, d. July 14, 1856, was a leading Danish architect of the mid-19th century noted for his imaginative interpretations of the neoclassic revival style, which he had absorbed during his extensive European travels. His innovative neoclassicism is evident in the Thorvaldsen Museum (1839–48) in Copenhagen, built to house the sculptures of Bertel THORVALDSEN. He also worked in other traditional styles and was one of the first Scandinavian architects to draw inspiration from the native tradition of building with wood.   MARION JOHN NELSON

Bibliography: Faber, Tobias, *A History of Danish Architecture* (1963).

binding energy

The nucleus of an atom is composed of neutrons and protons bound together by the strong nuclear force, the strongest of the FUNDAMENTAL INTERACTIONS of matter. The total binding energy of a nucleus is the energy required to separate it into its constituent neutrons and protons. Conversely, when particles form nuclei, energy equal to the binding energy is released. Nuclear binding energies are typically a million times greater than the electromagnetic energies binding electrons to an atomic nucleus or binding atoms together in molecules.

According to Einstein's relation $E = mc^2$, in which c is the speed of light, energy is equivalent to mass. Thus when energy is given off in the formation of a nucleus, the mass of the nucleus decreases compared to the sum of the masses of the free neutrons and protons from which it is formed. For example, when a neutron and proton combine to form a deuteron—the nucleus of a deuterium (heavy hydrogen) atom—a gamma ray is emitted, carrying away energy. The same amount of energy would have to be supplied from the outside in order to separate a deuteron again into a neutron and proton. Accordingly, the mass of a deuteron is less than the combined masses of a neutron and proton by about 0.1 percent. This amount, multiplied by c^2, is equivalent to the deuteron's binding energy.

In any nuclear reaction, energy is either absorbed or released. The most stable atoms are those with the highest binding energy per particle in the nucleus. This average nuclear binding energy is greatest for elements of medium weight—around iron, in the PERIODIC TABLE. In general, when light nuclei combine (fusion reactions) and when heavy, unstable nuclei divide (fission reactions), energy is released. The energy released corresponds to changes in binding energy of the nuclear particles, or conversion of a small fraction (about 0.1 to 1 percent) of the mass of the nuclear particles into other forms of energy.   WILLIAM J. KNOX

Bibliography: Krane, Kenneth S., *Introductory Nuclear Physics* (1987); McPhee, John, *The Curve of Binding Energy* (1974); Yarwood, John, *Atomic and Nuclear Physics* (1981).

See also: ATOMIC NUCLEUS; MASS DEFECT; NUCLEAR PHYSICS.

bindweed

Field bindweed, Convolvulus arvensis, *is often found entwined around the stems of cultivated crop plants.*

Bindweeds include about 250 species of twining vines of the genera *Convolvulus* and *Calystegia* of the morning glory family, Convolvulaceae. They are often grown on trellises or fences to display their heart- or arrow-shaped leaves and funnel-shaped white, pink, or blue flowers. Some species are troublesome weeds, especially the hedge bindweed, *Calystegia sepium*. The hedge bindweed has been used medicinally for its purgative action.   CHARLES H. STYER

Bibliography: Beckett, K. A., *Climbing Plants* (1983).

Binet, Alfred   [bee-nay']

Alfred Binet, b. July 8, 1857, d. Oct. 18, 1911, is famous as the author of the first test of individual INTELLIGENCE. He worked at the Sorbonne in Paris and became director of its psychologi-

Alfred Binet, a French psychologist and the founder of the journal L'Année Psychologique, is best remembered for his pioneering studies of human intelligence. In 1905, Binet and a colleague devised the series of intelligence measurements that eventually formed the basis for intelligence quotient, or IQ, testing.

cal laboratory in 1894. Binet rejected the German approach then dominating psychology—experiments on elementary sensations or reaction times—and began to study the higher mental processes, carrying out detailed observations of their development in his two daughters. His first book on reasoning appeared in 1886. In 1895 he founded and became one of the editors of *L'Année Psychologique*, which soon was the leading French psychological journal.

When the Ministry of Public Instruction requested a method of selecting those children who were too dull to be educated in ordinary schools, Binet and Théodore Simon produced (1905) a series of graded tasks typical of the intellectual development of children of different ages. In 1908 and 1911 this scale was extended, and the tasks were assigned to the age level at which average children could manage them. This test formed the basis for the STANFORD-BINET TESTS.

PHILIP E. VERNON

Bibliography: Wolf, Theta Holmes, *Alfred Binet* (1973).

Binford, Lewis R.

The American archaeologist Lewis Robert Binford, b. Norfolk, Va., Nov. 21, 1930, is best known as the pioneer of a movement termed the "new archaeology," begun by him and others in the 1960s. Binford has argued that archaeological research should be directed not only at reconstructing past events but also at determining the processes responsible for them. The approach he advocates involves the formulation of hypotheses to be tested by archaeological investigation. Many of Binford's ideas have been incorporated in the theory and methodology of modern archaeology and can be found in the book he coedited, *New Perspectives in Archaeology* (1968). Among his other works is *In Pursuit of the Past* (1983).

Bing, Sir Rudolf

Sir Rudolf Bing, b. Vienna, Jan. 9, 1902, was general manager and artistic director of New York's Metropolitan Opera from 1950 to 1972. He received his early training and experience in music and art at the University of Vienna. From 1927 to 1933, Bing worked in Germany, providing municipal and state opera houses with artists and other personnel. From 1934 to 1949, except for the war years, he organized and headed the Glyndebourne Opera Festival and from 1947 to 1949, the newly created Edinburgh Festival of Music and Drama. He became a British subject in 1946 and was knighted ten years later. At the Metropolitan Opera Bing made opening-night seats available to the general public, lengthened the subscription season, had old productions restaged and redesigned by theater directors and such artists as Marc Chagall and Eugene Berman, and revitalized the corps de ballet. More operas were sung in English than ever before, and opera was televised from the studio and the stage.   ELLA A. MALIN

Bibliography: Bing, Rudolf, *Five Thousand Nights at the Opera* (1972).

Bingham   (family)

Three generations of the Bingham family were prominent in Protestant missionary work, Bible translation, and overseas exploration. **Hiram Bingham,** b. Bennington, Vt., Oct. 30, 1789, d. Nov. 11, 1869, prepared for the ministry at Andover Theological Seminary. The American Board of Boston (Congregationalist) sent him to the Sandwich Islands (Hawaii) in 1819. The first Protestant missionary to the islands, he organized the Hawaiian Clerical Association, converted Queen Kaahumanu, and contributed to the Hawaiian translation of the Bible. One of his sons, another **Hiram Bingham,** 1831–1908, also trained at Andover and went as a missionary to Micronesia, arriving (1857) at Apaiang in the Gilbert Islands. He founded churches and translated the Bible into Gilbertese.

His son, a third **Hiram Bingham,** b. Honolulu, Hawaii, Nov. 19, 1875, d. June 6, 1956, was an explorer, historian, and statesman. He taught Latin American history at Yale University from 1907 to 1924. In 1908–09 he undertook field trips to South America in order to elucidate ancient Spanish trade routes between Buenos Aires and Lima. He led the Yale University Peruvian Expeditions, cosponsored by the National Geographic Society, in 1911–12 and 1914–15. In 1912, Bingham located the ancient Inca cities of MACHU PICCHU and Vitcos, his most famous discoveries, high in the Peruvian Andes. These lost cities had been forgotten for nearly 400 years. Bingham found the cities in nearly perfect condition, preserved in almost the same state as when they were abandoned at the time of the Spanish conquest in 1532–33.

Bingham's later interests turned to politics. He served as lieutenant governor of Connecticut in 1923–24, as governor in 1924–25, and as a U.S. senator in 1925–33. Among his books recounting his adventures are *Inca Land* (1922) and *Lost City of the Incas* (1948; repr. 1963).   JOHN F. PIPER, JR.

Bibliography: Fagan, Brian, *Elusive Treasure* (1977).

Bingham, George Caleb

The American frontier artist George Caleb Bingham painted Fur Traders Descending the Missouri *in 1845, revealing his characteristic combination of humor, tranquillity, and clarity. (Courtesy of the Metropolitan Museum of Art, New York; Morris K. Jessup Fund, 1933.)*

George Caleb Bingham, b. Mar. 20, 1811, d. July 7, 1879, was a major painter of American life in the newly settled Missouri River region in the years before the Civil War. A native of Virginia, he moved as a child to Missouri, which then remained his home. He studied briefly at the Pennsylvania Academy of the Fine Arts in 1837, and he painted portraits in Washington, D.C., between 1840 and 1844. Returning to Missouri, he spent the next 12 years creating the pictures of riverboatmen, farmers, and other sturdy citizens that brought him lasting fame.

Among the best known of these is *Fur Traders Descending the Missouri* (1845; Metropolitan Museum, New York).

Several of Bingham's works from this period portray the democratic political processes of the frontier, as in *The County Election* (1852; City Art Museum, St. Louis). At his best, as in these paintings and in the many figure drawings that served as sources for them, he imbued commonplace people and events with dignity and a sense of well-being. In 1856 he went abroad for the first time to study at the Düsseldorf Akademie in Germany; as a result, Bingham lost some of the simplicity and earnestness that made his earlier works such convincing images of American life. In 1978, Bingham's *The Jolly Flatboatmen,* one of four versions, sold at auction for $980,000, an all-time record for a painting by an American.

DAVID TATHAM

Bibliography: Bloch, E. Maurice, *The Paintings of George Caleb Bingham* (1986); Christ-Janner, Albert, *George Caleb Bingham* (1975).

Binghamton

Binghamton, the seat of Broome County, is a city in south central New York with a population of 53,008 (1990). Located at the confluence of the Susquehanna and Chenango rivers, just north of the Pennsylvania border, Binghamton, Endicott, and Johnson City form the Triple Cities. The economy is extremely diversified, with major manufactures of aircraft parts, small boats, photo supplies, electronics equipment, and computers. Dairy, poultry, and livestock also support the economy. Settled in 1787 as Chenango Point, it was later renamed for William Bingham, a local landowner. The linking (1837) of the Chenango and Erie canals and the arrival in 1848 of the Erie Railroad aided Binghamton's growth, and it was incorporated as a city in 1867.

bingo

Bingo is a game in which each player's chances depend on numbers drawn at random; in this sense, it is a lottery. Perhaps because of its simplicity, bingo is a favorite pastime in the United States and many other countries.

Bingo cards bear a printed design of five rows of five squares each, or 25 squares in all. The letters B-I-N-G-O appear above this grid, with a letter heading each vertical column. A number from 1 to 75 appears in every square except the center one, which is a free play. Corresponding to the letters and numbers on the cards are 75 bingo balls. On each ball is printed a number and a letter of the word *bingo.* From a bowl or box of metal, wood, or plastic, a caller chooses at random one ball at a time and announces the letter and number appearing on the ball. The players with these numbers on their cards place markers on the numbers. As soon as five numbers are covered in a straight line—vertically, horizontally, or diagonally—the player with the numbers calls out "Bingo!" Each player with bingo wins a prize; a big prize, or jackpot, is usually awarded to the player who first covers an entire card. At the end of each game, players clear their cards of markers and, before starting the next game, either keep the cards or exchange them.

Bingo games are usually run by religious or charitable organizations. In some U.S. states bingo is legalized, in some it is banned, and in the others each community decides for itself. Detractors claim that bingo is a form of gambling or that little money actually reaches the sponsors or both.

Bibliography: Rudinger, Joel, *How to Bingo 75 Ways: A Complete Guide to American Bingo Patterns* (1976).

binoculars

Binoculars consist of a pair of parallel telescopes, hinge-mounted to allow the eyepieces to be brought to a suitable interocular distance for the user. The optical trains of the telescopes, which produce real, erect images, are folded by prisms to permit the use of large objectives and to reduce the physical size of the binoculars. A common focus control adjusts both telescopes for object distance, and one eyepiece

Binoculars with 7 × 50 specifications magnify an image by a factor of 7 and have a 50-mm (2-in) aperture. Shown are objective lens (1); prism mounting (2); reversing porro prism (3); light path (4); fixed eyepiece (5); hinge (6); center focusing barrel (7), which adjusts the focus of both lenses simultaneously; and adjustable eyepiece (8), for finely balancing possible differences in the viewer's eyes.

has a differential focus control calibrated in diopters (the reciprocal of the length in meters) to compensate for vision errors of the user. Lenses are coated to reduce scattered light.

Binoculars are specified, for example, as 7 × 50, the first figure giving angular magnification and the second the objective lens diameter in millimeters. The field of view may range from about 2° to 10°, according to design, with inexpensive large-field versions sometimes showing peripheral optical aberrations. In binoculars for night use, the so-called exit pupil (the size of the entering image at the eyepiece) is large to match darkness-adapted eyes. Field glasses, including the small opera glasses, have Galilean telescopes that yield virtual images. Specification 7 × 50 will show Jupiter's large satellites and 10th-magnitude stars under good conditions.

DAVID S. EVANS

Bibliography: American Institute of Physics, *The Binoculars* (1975); Morris, Kendall, "Binoculars for Astronomy," *Astronomy*, December 1986; Schwalberg, Bob, "A Buyer's Guide to Binoculars," *Popular Photography*, June 1987.

binomial distribution

In statistics the so-called binomial DISTRIBUTION is the PROBABILITY distribution of the various possible number of times that a particular event will occur in a sequence of trials. If the event has a given probability of occurring during any one trial, the binomial distribution states that the probability of the event occurring a certain exact number of times in a sequence of trials corresponds to values of the binomial coefficients in the BINOMIAL THEOREM.

For example, if a coin is tossed n times, then the likelihood of obtaining 0, 1, 2, . . ., and n heads will be given by the terms in the expansion of $(p + q)^n$ using the binomial theorem, where p is the probability an event (in this case, heads) will occur and $q = 1 - p$ is the probability it will not occur (here, $p = q = \frac{1}{2}$). If a coin is tossed four times, then

$$(p + q)^4 = p^4 + 4p^3q + 6p^2q^2 + 4pq^3 + q^4$$

and the likelihood of obtaining 0, 1, 2, 3, and 4 heads will be, respectively, $\frac{1}{16}$, $\frac{4}{16}$, $\frac{6}{16}$, $\frac{4}{16}$, and $\frac{1}{16}$. Thus one is likely to obtain 3 heads in 4 tosses in 4 out of 16 experiments.

Other situations in which binomial distributions arise are games of chance, genetics, public-opinion surveys, medical research, and insurance. In certain limiting cases the binomial distribution approaches the NORMAL DISTRIBUTION and the POISSON DISTRIBUTION.

DAVID S. MOORE

Bibliography: Anderson, D. R., et al., *Statistics* (1986); Hogg, R. V., and Tanis, E. A., *Probability and Statistical Inference*, 3d ed. (1988); Moore, David S., *Statistics*, 2d ed. (1985).

binomial theorem

A binomial is a mathematical expression that has two terms, such as $a + b$ or $2x + 3y$. A binomial is a special case of a polynomial, or expression containing any number of terms. Calculations involving binomials often include raising them to a power, as in the expression $(a + b)^n$, where n is an EXPONENT. The binomial theorem indicates how $(a + b)^n$ can be calculated as a polynomial—called the expansion of $(a + b)^n$ —in a and b, where n is a natural number (1, 2, 3, . . .).

The polynomial equal to $(a + b)^n$ has $n + 1$ terms, beginning with a^n and ending with b^n. The exponents of a decrease by 1 with successive terms after a^n, and the exponents of b increase by 1 until b^n is reached. Furthermore,

the coefficient of $a^{n-1}b$ is $\dfrac{n}{1}$

the coefficient of $a^{n-2}b^2$ is $\dfrac{n(n-1)}{1 \times 2}$

the coefficient of $a^{n-3}b^3$ is $\dfrac{n(n-1)(n-2)}{1 \times 2 \times 3}$

In general, the coefficient of $a^{n-m}b^m$ is

$$\frac{n(n-1)(n-2)\ldots(n-m+1)}{1 \times 2 \times 3 \times 4 \times \ldots \times m}$$

where the ellipses (. . .) indicate that factors are written following the same pattern until $n - m + 1$ is reached in the numerator and m is reached in the denominator. The coefficients in the expansion of $(a + b)^n$ are called binomial coefficients.

Thus, for example,

$$(a + b)^1 = a + b$$
$$(a + b)^2 = a^2 + 2ab + b^2$$
$$(a + b)^3 = a^3 + 3a^2b + 3ab^2 + b^3$$

and the coefficient of a^3b^7 in the expansion of $(a + b)^{10}$ is

$$\frac{10 \times 9 \times 8 \times 7 \times 6 \times 5 \times 4}{1 \times 2 \times 3 \times 4 \times 5 \times 6 \times 7} = 120$$

ROY DUBISCH

Bibliography: Groza, V. S., *Elementary Algebra*, 4th ed. (1986); Steffensen, A. R., and Johnson, L., *Introductory Algebra*, 3d ed. (1987).

biochemistry

Biochemistry is the study of the chemistry of living organisms. It includes knowledge of the structure and function of the molecules found in the biological world, and understanding of the precise pathways by which these molecules are synthesized and degraded. In more recent years, with the development of powerful scientific instruments, biochemistry has also come to include the development of ways to synthesize molecules that duplicate those of living systems, and molecules that can perform entirely new functions.

FOUNDATIONS

The foundations of modern biochemistry were laid in the 18th century by such figures as the British scientist Joseph PRIESTLEY, who discovered oxygen in 1770; the French chemist Antoine Laurent LAVOISIER, who showed that animals needed oxygen and that respiration involved the oxidation of substances; and the Swedish chemist Carl Wilhelm SCHEELE, who isolated citric, lactic, and uric acid from biological sources.

Throughout the century that followed Priestley's discovery, however, biochemistry was considered simply as an aspect of other sciences as applied to living organisms. Thus thermodynamics, the study of the relationships of heat to work and energy, was applied to BIOLOGY by the German scientists Julius Mayer (1814–78) and Hermann HELMHOLTZ. Also, in the hands of the French physiologist Claude BERNARD, physiology soon became the study of chemical pathways in the living organism, that is, METABOLISM.

The philosophical problem that occupied much of the 19th century, with respect to living organisms, was that of vitalism. At issue was whether organisms have capabilities derived not only from chemical and physical properties but also from an unknown and perhaps unknowable *elan vital,* or "vital force." The importance of this debate rested on the fact that if the vitalists were correct, biology and biochemistry could go only so far and no farther in scientific exploration. The first important blow against vitalism was struck in 1828 by the German chemist Friedrich WÖHLER when he synthesized urea, a substance previously known to be made only by living organisms. The vitalist question, however, was not yet settled. In France, Louis PASTEUR's work in the field of bacteriology led him to the conclusion not only that spontaneous generation—the generation of life from nonliving matter—was impossible, but also that all biological functions, such as fermentation, depended on the presence of living organisms. This was still a form of vitalism, although on a much higher scientific level than the older, naive speculations. Pasteur was opposed in his view by the German chemist Justus von LIEBIG, but the issue was not settled until 1897, when another chemist, Eduard BUCHNER, showed clearly that glucose could be fermented by a nonliving process in the laboratory.

During the first third of the 20th century, the burgeoning of ORGANIC CHEMISTRY put biochemistry on a sound scientific footing. Hundreds of hitherto unknown materials were now being isolated from living organisms, and their chemical structures and their functions in metabolic pathways were being determined. Preeminent in this field was the work of the German biochemist Emil FISCHER and his students, along with the investigations of the German biologist Peter Michaelis (1900–) and many others into the dynamics of ENZYME action. Not until the American biochemist James B. SUMNER crystallized the enzyme urease in 1926, however, and showed that it and, by inference, all enzymes are simply PROTEINS, was the last vestige of vitalism laid to rest.

MAJOR DEVELOPMENTS
A new era in biochemistry began with the introduction of the use of ISOTOPES by the German Rudolf Schoenheimer (1898–1941) and the American David Rittenberg (1906–). Scientists could now follow individual substances in living tissues by tagging one or more of their atoms or molecules and following them as they were incorporated into larger molecules,

The laboratory of the biochemist Justus von Liebig, shown as it appeared in 1842, was established in Giessen, Germany. It was the first specifically designed both to teach students the latest chemical techniques and to develop their skills in practical experimental work, including physiologically oriented studies.

modified, broken down into simpler molecules, and finally excreted. Through the use of isotopes, most of the major pathways of metabolism have since been revealed, including the biochemical cycles—self-renewing reaction sequences in which the last product formed becomes part of the first reaction in the sequence. This concept first appeared in 1933, when the German-English scientist Sir Hans Adolf KREBS and coworkers proposed the urea cycle. Many biochemical cycles have since been determined; perhaps the most famous is the tricarboxylic acid cycle (see KREBS CYCLE).

Protein Structure. Other advances in technology enabled scientists to make similar critical discoveries that are central to biochemical knowledge today. Proteins, for example, are of basic importance to biochemists because they are essential to the structure and function of all living organisms. In the early 20th century, Fischer and his colleagues had already shown that proteins are polymers of AMINO ACIDS linked together in a linear manner by PEPTIDE bonds. Following Sumner's proof that enzymes are proteins, biochemists began to try to unravel the structure of these molecules in order to synthesize them. This was facilitated in 1941 by the development of partition CHROMATOGRAPHY, a method of separating similar molecules by moving a mixture of them over a long column or strip of material that adsorbs the molecules at different rates. The amino acids in a milk protein were established in this way in 1949, and in 1953 the English biochemist Frederick SANGER was able to determine the structure of the protein INSULIN. Automated instruments can now determine the amino acids and their order in giant proteins within a matter of hours.

The activity of proteins was found to be determined not only by their composition but also by their three-dimensional configuration, and in the early 1950s the American chemist Linus PAULING showed that proteins have a basically helical structure. This knowledge provided the groundwork for understanding, in chemical and molecular terms, how enzymes work—a matter of crucial importance, because enzymes direct the synthesis of all the other components of biological organisms. The overriding question then became: what mechanism, in turn, determines the structure of these crucial proteins? Whatever the mechanism, it would be the one that enables life forms to pass on their characteristics from generation to generation.

Protein Synthesis. In 1944 the Canadian-American bacteriologist Oswald T. AVERY and coworkers had already shown that the NUCLEIC ACID called DNA was the material in the CELL that is responsible for inducing heritable changes in almost all living organisms, and that it is contained in chromosomes. In 1952, American scientist Paul Zamecnik further showed that proteins are synthesized on ribosomes, which are cellular structures made of protein and another nucleic acid called RNA. Shortly thereafter, Zamecnik and another American, Mahlon Hoagland, found that another form of RNA activates amino acids so that they can be polymerized into proteins on the ribosomes. The race was now on to tie this information together, and the key to the problem was to find how genetic information is stored on the DNA molecule.

This key was provided in 1953 by the joint efforts of the American biologist James D. WATSON and the English biochemist Francis CRICK. Basing their work on X-ray data provided by Maurice WILKINS and Rosalind FRANKLIN, as well as Pauling's research, they showed that the DNA molecule is a double helix in which each single helix is the complement of the other. DNA was found to direct the synthesis of RNA copies, which translocate to the ribosomes. There, given a supply of activated amino acids, RNA governs the production of proteins—including the enzymes that synthesize the other cellular components. Thus all the information needed to build a biological organism is ultimately found in the DNA molecule. Determination of the form in which this information is stored—the GENETIC CODE—has been a major achievement of biochemical research. Rapid methods now exist for the synthesis of proteins from amino acids.

Biological Membranes. The development of radioactively labeled high-potency antibodies to many proteins has enabled biochemists to detect, with some accuracy, amounts of cellular constituents measuring no more than billionths of a gram. Such techniques are needed to explore the complex chemistry of cell membranes (see MEMBRANE CHEMISTRY). These highly reactive structures are engaged in actively moving materials in and out of the areas they enclose, conducting messages, and performing other vital functions that provide energy to the organism and protect it against drugs and toxins. The study of cell membranes is one of the major fields of current biochemical research.

THE BIOCHEMISTRY OF DISEASE

Another major field of study is the biochemistry of disease. Early in the 20th century, certain inherited illnesses had already been defined as inborn errors of metabolism. (In more modern terms, they are diseases involving defective enzymes.) In the 1940s, American geneticists George W. BEADLE and Edward L. TATUM then postulated that each gene in a chromosome codes for one particular enzyme, and that the relative amounts and activities of the enzymes determine all other heritable characteristics of an organism. This postulate remains a cornerstone of modern biochemical thinking, although it has since been restated in a much more complex manner. Illnesses are known in which a change in a single molecule, in the DNA of one chromosome, results in the substitution of a single amino acid out of many hundreds in a protein, leading in turn to a life-threatening malfunction in the affected individual.

Immunology. Research in the 1960s and 1970s has also provided a solid chemical basis for work in IMMUNOLOGY. The mammalian organism fends off disease by means of two major mechanisms. One is the deployment of special cells—the leukocytes and macrophages (see BLOOD)—to ingest invading organisms. The other is the production of antibodies (see ANTIBODY) that can attach to the invader and destroy it, in association with a group of proteins in the blood. Biochemists, in careful studies of antibody structure, have found invariant and variable regions on these proteins. The invariant regions determine the biological properties of the antibody, and the variable ones determine with which ANTIGEN the antibody will combine. Future advances in medicine will depend in great part on further knowledge of the chemistry of antibodies and related compounds.

Hormones. Also of great importance is the biochemical study of HORMONES. Endocrine hormones are chemicals secreted into the bloodstream by glands; carried to their target cells, they can drastically influence the metabolism of those cells. In general, a gland secretes a hormone in response to a stimulus from elsewhere. For example, nerve processes leading to the portion of the brain called the hypothalamus secrete NEUROTRANSMITTERS (chemicals related to the amino acids) that cause the hypothalamus, in turn, to secrete one of several so-called releasing hormones. These hormones travel directly to the an-

In an application of the techniques of modern biochemistry, a glass capillary is maneuvered into position for the microinjection of DNA or RNA molecules into a variety of tissue-culture cell.

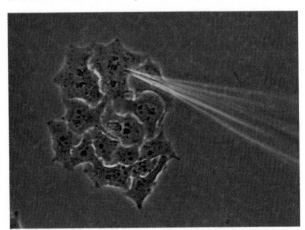

A technician places genetically manipulated cells in a medium where they can secrete a desired enzyme. By such means, biochemists now produce several enzymes in quantity for science and industry.

terior pituitary gland and cause the release of other hormones called trophic hormones. The latter then travel to appropriate glands where they can combine with receptors for a particular hormone. (Many of these receptors are on the outer membrane of the cell and show strong chemical relationships to antibody structure.) Such hormone-receptor combinations enter the cell and initiate metabolic changes that are under active investigation in many laboratories. From the foregoing it is evident that an "endocrine" disease can be due to defects at many levels, from the interaction of nervous tissue with the hypothalamus to abnormal responses deep within the cell. Such defects are known clinically, and in many cases the biochemical defects are now also known.

Cancer Research. One of the leading areas of biochemical research in medicine is that of CANCER. Contemporary research indicates that many and perhaps all cancers result from chemical changes in the nucleic acids. Many cancer-producing chemicals do so by adding or subtracting portions of individual bases in the DNA molecule. Of great interest today are the areas of DNA called proto-oncogenes (from Greek words meaning "antecedent tumor genes"). Many of these areas are thought to play a role in activating normal growth hormones. In laboratory studies, animal proto-oncogenes have been broken off from their chromosome, altered somewhat chemically, and introduced into certain viruses called RETROVIRUSES. The resulting molecules, called ONCOGENES, are responsible for cancer production by one class of viruses; biochemistry made it possible to understand the mechanism of this process.

Genetic Engineering. Perhaps the most dramatic development arising from advances in biochemical research has been that of GENETIC ENGINEERING. Using techniques that capitalize on current knowledge of protein and nucleic-acid metabolism and on advances in endocrinology, microbiology, and many other biological sciences, researchers can now introduce synthetic strands of DNA into bacteria and cause them to produce large amounts of specifically desired proteins. For example, human insulin and INTERFERON are now made in quantity in this manner, and a host of other biochemicals are in the process of similar synthesis—including modified proteins never before known.

Thus biochemistry, while increasingly important in modern society as a separate field of research, is also blending more and more with other biological disciplines. The growth of such new areas of study as cell biology and molecular biology reflects this integration. Increasingly, current problems in the biological sciences are being solved by team efforts of scientists from many disciplines who have mastered their once-separate fields.   AARON D. FREEDMAN, M.D.

Bibliography: Briggs, T., and Chandler, A. M., eds., *Biochemistry* (1987); Hill, H. W., and Feigl, D. M., *Chemistry and Life*, 3d ed. (1987); Wilson, Keith, and Goulding, K. H., *A Biologist's Guide to Principles and Techniques of Practical Biochemistry*, 3d ed. (1986).

biofeedback

Biofeedback is a method for learned control of physiological responses of the body. These responses can be either in the voluntary system, such as skeletal musculature, or in the involuntary, or autonomic, NERVOUS SYSTEM, such as heart rate, vascular responses (frequently indirectly measured as temperature), and sympathetic discharges (measured by the electrical skin response).

The experimental data to support the feasibility of such learned controls first appeared in the 1950s with the work of psychologists such as Neal E. MILLER. They increased in the 1960s, mostly through animal studies, although some experiments with humans were also performed. Next came a joint endeavor between experimental psychology and physiology. It became clear that certain dramatic gains could be achieved by using psychological techniques on patients with medical problems. Autonomic and disease specificity and the patient's psychological state must be considered before treatment can begin. For example, learning to relax certain muscles may be somewhat useful in many disorders but may not be the most effective treatment. An anxious patient with tachycardia (rapid heartbeat) benefits much more by learning to slow his or her heart rate rather then by relaxing muscles.

Biofeedback can be used to control certain biological responses that cause health problems, such as headaches, chronically taut muscles from accidents or sports injuries, asthma, high blood pressure, and heart arrhythmias. It is often used instead of, or as a complement to, drugs in pain control.

The training methods are relatively simple, although they require complex and precise instrumentation. After the desired mode of treatment has been determined for a given disorder, the patient is connected to a computer or an equivalent instrument by a polygraph, and the response is presented back to the patient in either a binary or an analog fashion. In the binary approach a threshold is set, and whenever the patient crosses that threshold, a light or music indicates that the patient is succeeding. In the analog approach the patient monitors the actual numbers in electrical units that represent bodily states such as heart rate, temperature, or vasculature. The two techniques can be combined. Initially the criteria are made easy by the therapist, and as the patient succeeds, the task is made more difficult. Ultimately the patient should become his or her own therapist and eventually control specific body functions without the use of instrumentation.

B. M. SHMAVONIAN

Bibliography: Benjamin, John V., *Biofeedback* (1989); Green, Elmer and Alyce, *Beyond Biofeedback* (1989); Hatch, J. P., et al., eds., *Biofeedback: Studies in Clinical Efficacy* (1987); Marcer, Donald, *Biofeedback and Related Therapies in Clinical Practice* (1986); Richter-Heinrich, E., and Miller, N. E., *Biofeedback* (1982).

biography

The word *biography* (Greek, "record of a life") may be used to refer to the record of the life of anything: an insect, a geological process, or an organization, for example. Usually, however, it refers to literary works that tell the story of an individual human life. Although it is occasionally used as a means of flattery (as of kings) or advertising (as campaign biographies), biography is normally considered a factual genre; because it is a branch of history, truth and accuracy are held to be its primary objectives. AUTOBIOGRAPHY, a closely related genre, is biography written by the subject.

The genre of biography has had a long and varied history. It began 5,000 years ago, when Egyptian kings left records of their deeds and wealth in their tombs. Although the form of these earliest records is autobiographical, it is believed that they were written for the kings rather than by them. By 1400 BC, Assyrian and Babylonian kings regularly had their deeds recorded and celebrated, but these first biographies were highly selective; their object was glorification, rather than truth or candor.

The ancient Greeks produced more sophisticated biographies, but they were concerned primarily with ideal types and with the mature person rather than with the full history of the formative process. In China SSU-MA CH'IEN began the writing of biography in the 2d century BC. The real antecedents of modern biography are the works of such Roman writers as SUETONIUS (*The Lives of the Caesars*; Eng. trans., 1606) and TACITUS (*Annals*; Eng. trans., 1869–72), which present striking portraits of individuals, and especially PLUTARCH (*The Lives of the Noble Grecians and Romans*, 1st century; Eng. trans., 1579), the greatest and most influential ancient biographer. Plutarch paired his subjects—one Greek, one Roman—and included the whole of their lives. He demonstrated the interconnections among history, personality, and career and used illuminating personal and particular detail.

Plutarch had a major influence on the form and nature of biography for the next several centuries, but his influence was not felt directly in England and Europe until the Renaissance. The few biographies written during the Middle Ages were either chronicles, or *res gestae* ("things done"), which described the deeds and events in the reign of a king and were closer to history than to biography, or spiritual biographies, usually the lives of saints or martyrs. These often treated lives as exempla (models to be followed or avoided), seldom examining them outside of a spiritual or didactic context. In the Renaissance, however, which saw the rise of humanism and growing secular interest in all things human and worldly, both biography and autobiography began to flourish and assumed forms much like their modern counterparts. Writers became interested in what made persons unique rather than examples or ideal types.

Benvenuto CELLINI and PETRARCH wrote autobiographies, BOCCACCIO and ERASMUS produced biographies, and Giorgio VASARI's *Lives of the Most Eminent Italian Painters, Sculptors, and Architects* (1500; Eng. trans., 1912–14) is still an important source of information about major Renaissance artists. In England major biographies were written by Thomas MORE (*The History of Richard III*, c.1513), William Roper (*The Life of Sir Thomas More*, 1636), and George Cavendish (*The Life of Cardinal Wolsey*, 1641).

In the late Renaissance and early 18th century biography and autobiography continued to grow in importance and popularity. Such religious movements as Puritanism encouraged self-study, and philosophers encouraged empiricism, the close study of particulars and the physical world. The 17th and 18th centuries were the great ages of journals, diaries, and memoirs (political, military, and erotic). This period also saw the growth of newspapers and magazines and the rise of the novel, as the lives of ordinary people began to be considered subjects worthy of treatment by major authors. The greatest English diarists of the age were James BOSWELL, John EVELYN, and Samuel PEPYS. The major biographers included Izaak WALTON (*Lives*; 1670, 1678), John AUBREY (*Brief Lives*, 1813), Roger North (*The Lives of the North*, 1740–44), and Samuel JOHNSON (*Lives of the Poets*, 1778).

Toward the end of the 18th century, James Boswell published his monumental LIFE OF SAMUEL JOHNSON (1791), generally considered the greatest biography ever written. Boswell had a close personal relationship with Johnson and made use of particular detail and personal anecdote, along with Johnson's own letters and private meditations. His treatment shocked readers at first, because he tried to show Johnson "warts and all," but his re-creation of Johnson's famous conversations comes as close to capturing and fully reproducing in prose another person as any biographer is ever likely to do.

The Life of Johnson called yet more serious attention to the possibilities of the genre and expanded people's ideas about its potential. The 19th and 20th centuries have seen further expansion of the concept of biography and experimentation with the methods of the biographer.

In 19th-century England a large number of literary biographies were written, including Elizabeth GASKELL's *Life of Charlotte Brontë* (1857), John Gibson Lockhart's *Life of Sir Walter Scott* (1837–38), and William Froude's *Thomas Carlyle* (1882–84). CARLYLE wrote the biography of "heroes" (*Frederick the Great*, 1858–65), and others turned to more scholarly and scientific biography. By the end of the century, Sigmund FREUD had written the first formally psychological study of a historical figure (*Leonardo Da Vinci,* 1910); so-called psycho-biographies have more recently been written by such authors as Eric ERIKSON (*Young Man Luther,* 1958).

Early in the 20th century Lytton STRACHEY (*Eminent Victorians,* 1918) popularized reductive biography, treating his subjects with humor and often cynicism. The turn of the century also saw the emergence of several biographical dictionaries, such as the *Dictionary of National Biography* (DNB), which began in 1882 under editorship of Leslie Stephen and still continues. More recently, such scholars as Richard Ellman (*James Joyce,* 1959; rev. ed., 1982), Leon Edel (*The Life of Henry James,* 5 vols., 1953–72), Edgar Johnson (*Charles Dickens,* 2 vols., 1952; rev. ed., 1978), and Deirdre Bair (*Samuel Beckett: A Biography,* 1978) have produced extended treatments of major literary figures that discuss the relation between historical events and individual personality and achievements. Many recent studies have been much franker about sexual behavior than would have been possible a few decades ago. This aspect forms an integral part of David Garrow's Pulitzer Prize–winning study of Martin Luther King, Jr., *Bearing the Cross* (1986). Interest in theories of biography has also increased substantially. Recently developed forms, such as taped oral reminiscences and filmed biographies, are flourishing; the art of biography has seldom been more varied and popular than it is today.   WILLIAM R. SIEBENSCHUH

Bibliography: Clifford, James L., ed., *Biography as an Art* (1962); Edel, Leon, *Writing Lives* (1984; repr. 1987); Empson, W., *Using Biography* (1985); Friedson, A. M., ed., *New Directions in Biography* (1982); Garraty, John, *The Nature of Biography* (1957); Hoberman, Ruth, *Modernizing Lives* (1986); Kendall, Paul, *The Art of Biography* (1965; repr. 1985); Nicolson, Harold, *The Development of English Biography* (1928); Pachter, M., ed., *Telling Lives* (1981); Siebenschuh, W. R., *Fictional Techniques and Factual Works* (1983).

Bioko

Bioko (formerly Fernando Po) is a volcanic island located in the Bight of Biafra about 40 km (25 mi) west of the Cameroon coast. The area is 2,017 km² (779 mi²), and the population is 57,190 (1983). The island, comprising two of the seven provinces of Equatorial Guinea, contains the nation's capital, MALABO. Cacao plantations are the mainstay of the economy. The island was known as Fernando Po until 1973, when it was renamed Macías Nguema Biyogo for the country's president. The present name was adopted after the overthrow of Macías Nguema in 1979.

biological clock

A biological clock is a self-sustained internal timing mechanism that controls cyclic patterns, or rhythms, of a living organism. By providing temporal information, such as the time of day, month, or season, nearly all organisms are adapted to events in both their internal or external environments. The products of this internal timing are physiological or behavioral events that, over time, vary in intensity. Such time-dependent variability is expressed as a rhythm, or oscillation, with a frequency equal to that of the underlying biological clock. Rhythms that occur more than once a day are called ultradian rhythms; once a day, circadian; once a lunar day (24.8 hr), lunar; and once a year, circannual.

Ultradian Rhythms. In some cases the frequency of an oscillation may be high, or conversely, the period of the oscillation may be brief. Certain rhythms of the BRAIN associated with sleep can occur with a frequency of approximately seven cycles per second. Another ultradian rhythm is the release of luteinizing hormone from the PITUITARY GLANDS of male mammals. This chemical, which helps maintain reproductive activity of the testes, is released from the pituitary of males in pulses approximately 1 to 2 hours apart throughout the day.

Circadian Rhythms. Circadian rhythms are intermediate-length rhythms corresponding to the solar day (24 hours). These are the most pervasive rhythms, regulating the temporal spacing and organization of many events for every day in the lives of most living organisms.

The *Gonyaulax* is an ocean-dwelling, single-celled alga. When placed under constant environmental conditions (for example, constant darkness), its biological clock generates a rhythm approximating 24 hours. Without light-dark cues the circadian rhythm is said to persist in a free-running fashion, the rhythm assuming the natural period generated by the internal clock. Such free-running rhythms are easily demonstrated in plants or animals under laboratory conditions.

It is more natural for circadian rhythms to be synchronized to an external time-giving stimulus than to exist in the free-running state. In theory, external time-giving stimuli may be any rhythmically occurring events, for example, temperature, barometric pressure, gravitational change, or other cues that impinge on the organism. In reality, however, only one external stimulus is important for most organisms: the daily light-dark cycle determined by the Earth's rotation. The 24-hour light-dark solar day acts as an external oscillation that entrains, or synchronizes, the internal—circadian—clock to 24 hours. Events generated according to this clock become regulated so that they always occur at specific times of day.

Entrainment occurs when light interacts with the "phase response curve," which is a product of circadian-clock function. For example, a 15-minute pulse of light shown to a free-running organism, usually in constant darkness, will alter the measured circadian rhythm. The extent to which the light pulse alters the rhythm, however, is not the same at different times of the day. Numerous experiments show clearly that the circadian rhythms of organisms are affected only when the pulse occurs during the expected nighttime. Under normal day-night light conditions, such rhythmic behavior as eating and sleeping are regulated by an internal clock in harmony with the environment. Rhythmic physiological responses, such as body temperature, are also controlled in this way.

Jet air travel often illustrates the similarity of the circadian clock in humans and other species. For example, one-eighth of the solar day is 3 hours and represents the time difference between clocks in New York and San Francisco. A person who flies nonstop from New York to San Francisco will experience a 3-hour phase difference between body time and local time. The body of the displaced traveler will continue to function 3 hours in advance of local time. Several days of exposure are required for the circadian clock to become synchronized to the San Francisco photoperiod. Meanwhile, the traveler usually feels jet lag, a general feeling of discomfort caused by rhythms derived from the body's circadian clock being out of synchrony with the new local time and by the body's attempt to entrain to that time.

Lunar Rhythms. Lunar rhythms are exemplified by the patterning of locomotor activity in fiddler crabs that, under constant laboratory conditions, exhibit an activity rhythm of 24 hours, 50 minutes—the lunar day. The rhythmic patterning of the crabs' activity is synchronized with daily low tides caused by the gravitational effects of the Moon, although the laboratory has no water movements or lunar light. Many tidal invertebrates are synchronized with lunar rhythms; changing water level is a major ecological variable.

Circannual Rhythms. Many physiological or behavioral events recur annually in wild animals. The circannual rhythm theoretically consists of a series of stages called interval timers. Each stage requires a fixed amount of time and leads to the next stage. For instance, the golden-mantled ground squirrel, *Citellus lateralis,* shows a yearly cycle of weight gain in the summer and fall and weight loss during winter hibernation and springtime breeding season. The weight increases during summer and fall may possibly occur only if the squirrel has already been through a sequence of interval timers. Over the course of a year, several timers may operate in a pattern.

In human beings, circannual rhythms of some form are involved in the seasonal changes in behavior observed in many individuals, apparently in response to the difference in light levels at different times of year. The most striking examples are those persons who suffer from seasonal affective disorder (SAD), which is often marked by prolonged periods of deep depression that generally occur in the fall or winter. The mechanisms causing SAD are as yet not well understood.

In many species of animals evidence exists for a hierarchical organization of the circadian system. Neuroanatomists have established a nerve pathway from the eye to a region of the hypothalamus, the suprachiasmatic nuclei; this pathway allows light to exert internal synchronization. This region of the brain has been shown to be necessary for rhythmicity and entrainment of several forms of behavior. The suprachiasmatic nuclei also seems to be responsible for the circadian neural signal for ovulation in the hamster. When the nuclei are destroyed, the rhythmic release of ACTH, an activating hormone from the pituitary, stops. Thus these nuclei appear to be at or near the top of the hierarchical control of bodily circadian rhythms, and they may be the site of the predominant circadian clock in mammals, acting as a pacemaker for other body clocks.

LAWRENCE P. MORIN

Bibliography: Gwinner, E., *Circannual Rhythms* (1986); Moore-Ede, M. C., et al., *The Clocks That Time Us: Physiology of the Circadian Timing System* (1984); Rose, K. J., *The Organic Clock* (1988); Saunders, David S., *Insect Clocks*, 2d ed. (1982); Sweeney, B. M., *Rhythmic Phenomena in Plants*, 2d ed. (1987).

biological equilibrium

All living things are constantly interacting with and opposing gravity. Three biological systems integrate to keep vertebrates oriented to the balanced and upright position: (1) the vestibular system—organs in the inner ear that act like a carpenter's level; (2) vision—information from the eyes about the position of the horizon constantly feeds to the brain; and (3) proprioception—the brain's knowledge of the position of the body parts without the help of the external senses.

Vestibular System. This system is composed of two closely related organs in the inner ear that have two separate functions: gravitational orientation and orientation to movement through space. The saccule and utricle, two saclike structures, provide orientation to gravity. These organs contain small granules embedded in a gelatinous material. Nerves respond to changes in the position of these granules in respect to gravity. The brain knows which way is down by sensing the position of the granules in the ear.

For movement through space there are three semicircular canals that are oriented at right angles to one another. These canals are filled with a fluid that flows through the canals when the head moves. The flow of liquid is sensed by small hairs that "feel" the flow and constantly update the brain. The brain processes the data and utilizes the information for many uses in balance and orientation. This system coordinates with the visual system so the eyes can continue tracking even when the head is moving. The two systems can be intentionally confused by spinning the head in one direction for a number of revolutions to produce dizziness. When the fluids in the ear stop flowing, the dizziness disappears.

Visual System. The brain uses the horizon as a reference to gravity. The eyes send signals to the brain to help it find the perpendicular to gravity and the position of the head while viewing the horizon. This helps the brain find the direction of the gravitational pull. As mentioned above, the visual system works closely with the vestibular system so that the eyes can keep tracking in a stable pattern even though they are moving through space. These two systems together let us continue reading even as we rock our heads from side to side.

Proprioception. This special sense, found in all muscles, tells the brain where the muscles are in space in relation to the rest of the body. It is best demonstrated by the ability to touch the tip of the nose with the tip of any finger even though the eyes are closed. This sense automatically coordinates with the vestibular and visual senses to keep us upright.

Integration of these three systems occurs primarily in the vestibular nuclei, located near the inner ear, and the cerebellum. The three systems are redundant, so that if one system fails, an upright position can be maintained by using the information supplied by the other two. For example, a blind person can function well if the proprioceptive and vestibular systems are intact. However, a disruption of the vestibular system may cause a mixup in the brain's gravity and motion detectors. Problems such as viral or bacterial infection, a blow to the head, alcohol, some medications, and certain diseases like diabetes or multiple sclerosis may cause brief or chronic attacks of dizziness, nausea, and balance problems.

LOUIS D. LOWRY, M. D.

Bibliography: Dublin, W. B., *Fundamentals of Vestibular Pathology* (1987); Pippard, Brian, *Response and Stability* (1985); Rademaker, G. G., *The Physiology of Standing* (1981).

biological locomotion

Biological locomotion is the process by which living organisms actively propel themselves. They use CHEMICAL ENERGY to generate mechanical forces, which they apply to their surroundings in order to drive themselves along. The biological devices for generating locomotor forces are few in kind but are used by a wide variety of species. The four basic devices are: bacterial flagella, cilia and flagella of higher (eukaryotic) cells, pseudopodia (amoeboid movement), and muscle.

Bacterial Flagella. Bacteria use a rotary propeller for swimming. The bacterial flagellum is a thin spiral filament, attached to a motor mounted in the wall of the bacterium; some bacteria have many flagella, some only one. Each motor runs on chemical fuel within the bacterium and rotates at about 50 revolutions each second. From time to time, with a frequency influenced by light, warmth, and nutrients, the flagellar motors reverse, which causes the bacterium to tumble and swim off along a new course.

Cilia and Flagella of Higher Cells. Many of the more advanced cells propel themselves by means of cilia (lashes) or flagella (whips). These organelles have a similar structure and are quite different from bacterial flagella. They contain a characteristic arrangement of 20 long, parallel microtubules, or hollow rods of the protein tubulin. Bending is caused by the relative sliding of these rods. The sliding force is exerted through rows of "arms," which comprise dynein (another protein) and project from one pair of rods toward the next. The dynein converts the chemical energy of adenosine triphosphate (ATP) into a mechanical tug. There is a cyclical rhythm, such that waves of bending propagate down the cilium or flagellum. The sinuous thrashing of a flagellum, like the wriggling of an eel, can drive a cell along. The sperm of almost all animals, including humans, and the spermatozoids of some algae, fungi, mosses, and ferns swim in this way, as do many protozoa, such as *Euglena*. Other protozoa, such as *Paramecium*, have, instead of one or a few flagella, a whole field of small cilia on their surface. Coordinated waves of bending pass over these, giving the appearance of wind over a field of wheat, and propel the creature as though by the beating of ranks of oars. A few multicellular animals—some mollusks and small flatworms—also crawl by means of cilia. In higher animals, cilia commonly serve to set up currents in the surrounding medium. Cilia in the wall of the trachea, for example, sweep mucus up out of the lungs.

Pseudopodia. Instead of using some permanent organ for propulsion, a cell may put out temporary protrusions, called pseudopodia ("false feet"); the tip of the advancing pseudopodium sticks to the substratum, and the cell contents flow forward toward the point of attachment. The process is typified by the amoeba, in which the cell contents, or cytoplasm, constantly and cyclically stream from the rear end of the cell down the middle of the pseudopodium toward its tip. Pseudopodial locomotion is common. Human white blood cells, for example, migrate through the tissues in this way, as do many types of cell in the embryo. In most cases no such orderly cytoplasmic streaming has been observed as in the amoeba, but some type of cytoplasmic movement must occur, and some internal machinery must be present to provide the motive power. This machinery appears to be of a standard type regardless of the organism. The fuel is ATP, and the force is most probably generated by the relative sliding of protein filaments. Notable among these proteins are actin and myosin, indicating close similarities with muscle.

Muscle. In multicellular animals certain cells are specialized for converting chemical energy into mechanical work. The

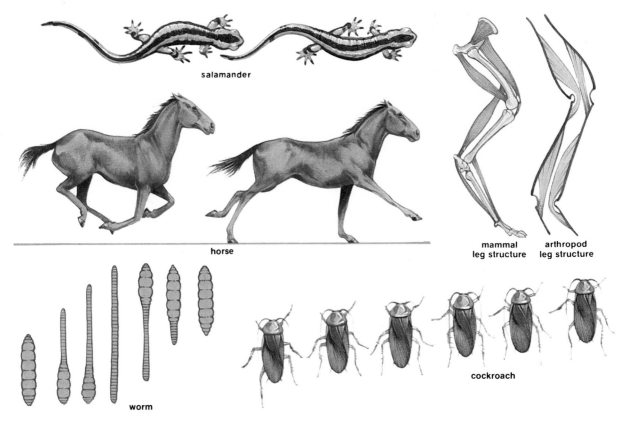

salamander

horse

mammal
leg structure

arthropod
leg structure

cockroach

worm

An animal's method of locomotion depends on its body structure and size. The internal skeletons of all vertebrates are moved by attached striated muscles. The leg of a fast-running mammal consists of a short upper section with thick muscles for power and a lower section with thin muscles for rapid motion. A horse may have five different gaits, depending on the sequence in which the leg muscles are used. The fastest of these is the gallop, where only two hooves touch the ground at one time. A salamander generally moves by undulating its tail and body to extend the reach of its short legs. Arthropods such as insects and spiders have a protective outer covering, or exoskeleton, that also serves for muscle attachment. A cockroach moves its six legs in a symmetrical, coordinated pattern, most commonly moving two legs on one side and one on the other while maintaining a tripod balance with the other three. Annelids have flexible, fluid-filled bodies with no skeleton. An earthworm moves from a contracted position by fully extending its body, anchoring to a new site, and pulling its body forward.

molecular mechanism again involves sliding filaments of actin and myosin and uses ATP as a fuel (SEE MUSCLE CONTRACTION). Muscle cells can pull, but not push. The endless varieties of animal locomotion are, for the most part, merely different ways of harnessing and applying this force of contraction.

The vertebrates have a hard internal skeleton that furnishes a system of braces, levers, and pivots through which the muscular forces can be brought to bear. The arthropods (insects, spiders, crustaceans, millipedes, and the like) are encased in a hard, hinged cuticle (the exoskeleton) that serves a similar purpose. Echinoderms (starfish and sea urchins, for example) likewise have a skeleton of sorts. The soft-bodied invertebrates, by contrast, typically produce forces of extension from the muscular contractions by squeezing or otherwise deforming the fluid-filled compartments of their bodies.

Soft-Bodied Invertebrates. The bodies of annelids, such as earthworms and leeches, are divided into segments, each of fixed volume but variable shape. The body wall contains two antagonistic sets of muscles: the circular muscles constrict and thus elongate the segment, and the longitudinal muscles tug it back into a shorter, squatter shape. Such animals can thus crawl by rhythmically lengthening and shortening the segments of the body, using a variety of means to get a grip on the surroundings. The earthworm braces itself with its shortened, thickened segments against the sides of its burrow while the thin, elongated segments advance. The leech has a sucker at each end and attaches to the substratum alternately at the front and at the rear. The leech can also swim like an eel, by undulations of its body, contracting the longitudinal muscles along its back and its belly in alternation. Many flatworms and roundworms move by similar means.

Jellyfish swim by rhythmically contracting their bell. Squid and octopuses use jet propulsion, squirting out water from the mantle cavity through a funnel. The scallop swims by clapping the two parts of its shell together. Some other bivalves, for example, the piddock *Pholas*, use their shells for grinding through rock, others burrow through mud by thrusting out a long, tongue-shaped "foot." Slugs and snails creep on a single flat foot, along which pass slow ripples of muscular contraction. They lift each region of the sole in turn off the ground, move it forward, and put it down again.

Arthropods. Arthropods, with their jointed limbs, primarily move in ways that have familiar counterparts among the vertebrates. The principles of walking are the same for a millipede as for a horse, except that the millipede has a larger number of legs to coordinate: the phase of movement of each stepping appear to pass along the body. Many of the locomotor peculiarities of insects depend on their small weight: some can walk upside down, supported by adhesive pads on their feet; others walk on water, supported by the surface tension. Many insects can swim submerged or half-submerged. Most crustaceans walk on the ocean bottom; some swim by rowing with their legs. The jumping fleas have a specialized, internal elastic ligament to catapult them into the air. In dipteran flies, the hind pair of wings have become modified into little clubs on stalks, called halteres, which vibrate up and down and serve as alternating GYROSCOPES to stabilize the flight.

Vertebrates. Most fish swim by waving the tail from side to side, with relatively little body undulation. As the tailfin is swept toward the midline, it is inclined at an angle to the

A snake commonly moves by pushing various segments of its body against the raised surfaces of its surroundings; the rest of the body follows the same path as the head. Undulation of the rear part of the body, especially the tail fin, propels most fishes through the water. Cephalopod mollusks, such as squids and octopuses, swim by jet propulsion, ejecting water through a funnel-shaped siphon. In propulsive flight, a bird's wings move to produce lift and forward thrust on the downbeat and supply lift on the upbeat.

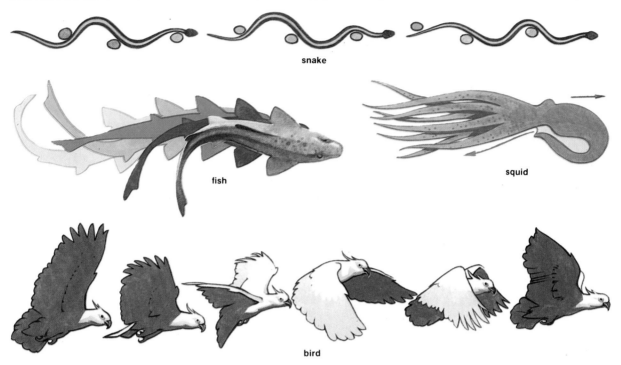

snake

fish

squid

bird

body axis so that the reaction of the water against it has a component propelling the fish forward. In a similar way a boat may be sculled along with a single oar over the stern. The fins other than the tail usually serve only for stabilization and steering. Some amphibians, such as the newt, and some reptiles, such as the crocodile, also swim by sinuous motion of the tail. Whales beat the tailfin up and down, not from side to side. Long, thin fish and reptiles, such as eels and snakes, swim by undulating the whole body; the waves of bending pass tailward so that the water exerts a net forward reaction on the animal. Tailless amphibians such as the frog, reptiles such as the turtle, birds, and most mammals use their limbs as paddles or flippers in swimming.

The walk is the standard slow gait of land animals with legs; body stability is maintained throughout the cycle of movements. Thus, four-legged animals, when walking slowly, raise only one leg off the ground at a time. As the pace quickens, static points of support become less necessary, and two or more legs may be off the ground together, until in the gallop the animal loses contact with the ground entirely at times. Various four-limbed animals, from lizards to bears, can walk or run on their two hind legs; others hop. The kangaroo, however, uses its tail as a fifth point of support when walking slowly.

The spider monkey swinging through the trees uses its prehensile tail as a fifth limb; the great apes swing from branch to branch with their arms. The chameleon, an oddity among reptiles, has opposable digits for gripping the twigs along which it walks. The gecko can walk up walls and across ceilings because of suction-adhesive pads on its feet.

Some reptiles are specialized for burrowing, with limbs much reduced or absent: the amphisbaena drives itself through the soil in the manner of an earthworm; skinks and slowworms undulate through sand or soft earth as eels do through water. Snakes slither overland by the same means: waves of bending pass backward along the body, exerting a thrust against vertical projections in the surroundings. In a smooth, straight tube a snake can advance by throwing parts of its body into concertina folds that brace it against the sides of the tube. Boas and vipers can also creep along with their bodies straight by waves of muscular contraction passing along the belly, in the style of the earthworm.

The principles of flight are similar for birds, bats, and insects, allowing for differences of scale. The lift and drag exerted by the airflow over a wing increase as the square of its speed and in proportion to its surface area, and the lift must balance the weight of the animal. Whereas the insect wing is essentially just a plate of cuticle attached to the body by a hinge, the wing of a bird contains muscles for adjusting its angle of attack, the flexure of its joints, and the set of its feathers. In normal rapid flight the leading edge of the bird's wing is twisted downward in the vigorous downbeat, which thus supplies forward propulsion and lift. In the more passive upbeat the tilt is reversed, and the wing, like that of an airplane, supplies lift as it cuts through the air, but no forward propulsion; the wings function in the same way in gliding. The wing movements are somewhat different at takeoff, when there is no forward momentum to furnish lift during the upbeat. It is difficult for the largest birds to get airborne from level ground when there is no wind; and sustained hovering in still air is energetically impossible for them, although it is commonplace among small birds and bats and insects. The so-called flying fish, flying dragon (a lizard), and flying squirrels, for example, can glide, but not fly.

Neural Control. The nervous system coordinates movement. Each of the 40-odd muscles of a bird's wing, for example, must be brought into play, with precisely controlled timing and intensity, by commands sent through the peripheral nerves from the spinal cord and the brain. The basic rules of limb coordination are built into the internal wiring of neural connections in the spinal cord; walking, of sorts, is possible in many vertebrates even after the brain has been destroyed. The brain sets spinal locomotor rhythms into action and modulates them.

The first movements of the embryo of a typical four-limbed vertebrate are sinuous flexions of the trunk, reminiscent of the swimming movements of the ancestral fish; later it begins to wave its growing limbs about haphazardly, just as a baby kicks in the womb. Eventually, as the hierarchy of nerve connections develops, these movements come under the coordinate control manifest in locomotion.   JULIAN LEWIS

Bibliography: Alexander, R. McNeill, *Locomotion of Animals* (1982); Braune, W., and Fischer, O., *The Human Gait* (1987); Elder, H. Y., and Trueman, E. R., eds., *Aspects of Animal Movement* (1980); Grillner, Sten, ed., *The Neurobiology of Vertebrate Locomotion* (1986); Hay, James G., et al., *The Anatomical and Mechanical Bases of Human Motion* (1982); Tricker, R. A. and B. J., *The Science of Movement* (1967); University of Pennsylvania, *Animal Locomotion: The Muybridge Work at the University of Pennsylvania* (1888; repr. 1973).

biological warfare:

see CHEMICAL AND BIOLOGICAL WARFARE.

biology

Biology is the science of living systems. It is inherently interdisciplinary, requiring knowledge of the physical sciences and mathematics, although specialties may be oriented toward a group of organisms or a level of organization. BOTANY is concerned with plant life, ZOOLOGY with animal life, algology with algae, MYCOLOGY with fungi, MICROBIOLOGY with microorganisms such as protozoa and bacteria, CYTOLOGY with cells, and so on. All biological specialties, however, are concerned with life and its characteristics. These characteristics include cellular organization, METABOLISM, response to stimuli, development and growth, and reproduction. Furthermore, the information needed to control the expression of such characteristics is contained within each organism.

FUNDAMENTAL DISCIPLINES

Life is divided into many levels of organization—atoms, molecules, cells, tissues, organs, organ systems, organisms, and populations. The basic disciplines of biology may study life at one or more of these levels.

Taxonomy attempts to arrange organisms in natural groups based on common features. It is concerned with the identification, naming, and classification of organisms (see CLASSIFICATION, BIOLOGICAL). The seven major taxonomic categories, or taxa, used in classification are kingdom, phylum, class, order, family, genus, and species. Early systems used only two kingdoms, plant and animal, whereas most modern systems use five: MONERA (BACTERIA and BLUE-GREEN ALGAE), PROTISTA (PROTOZOA and the other ALGAE), FUNGI, PLANT, and ANIMAL.

The discipline of ECOLOGY is concerned with the interrelationships of organisms, both among themselves and between them and their environment. Studies of the energy flow through communities of organisms and the environment (the ecosystem approach) are especially valuable in assessing the effects of human activities. An ecologist must be knowledgeable in other disciplines of biology.

Organisms respond to stimuli from other organisms and from the environment; behaviorists are concerned with these responses. Most of them study animals—as individuals, groups, or entire species—in describing ANIMAL BEHAVIOR patterns. These patterns include ANIMAL MIGRATION, courtship and mating, social organization, TERRITORIALITY, INSTINCT, and learning. When humans are included, biology overlaps with psychology and sociology. Growth and orientation responses of plants can also be studied in the discipline of behavior, although they are traditionally considered as belonging under development and PHYSIOLOGY, respectively.

Descriptive and comparative EMBRYOLOGY are the classic areas of DEVELOPMENT studies, although postembryological development, particularly the aging process, is also examined. The biochemical and biophysical mechanisms that control normal development are of particular interest when they are related to birth defects, cancer, and other abnormalities.

Inheritance of physical and biochemical characteristics, and the variations that appear from generation to generation, are the general subjects of GENETICS. The emphasis may be on improving domestic plants and animals through controlled breeding, or it may be on the more fundamental questions of molecular and cellular mechanisms of HEREDITY.

A branch of biology growing in importance since the 1940s, molecular biology essentially developed out of genetics and

BIOCHEMISTRY. It seeks to explain biological events by studying the molecules within cells, with a special emphasis on the molecular basis of genetics—nucleic acids in particular—and its relationship to energy cycling and replication. EVOLUTION, including the appearance of new species, the modification of existing species, and the characteristics of extinct ones, is based on genetic principles. Information about the structure and distribution of fossils that is provided by paleontologists is essential to understanding these changes.

Morphology (from the Greek, meaning "form study") traditionally has examined the ANATOMY of all organisms. The middle levels of biological organization—cells, tissues, and organs—are the usual topics, with comparisons drawn among organisms to help establish taxonomic and evolutionary relationships.

As important as the form of an organism are its functions. Physiology is concerned with the life processes of entire organisms as well as those of cells, tissues, and organs. Metabolism and hormonal controls are some of the special interests of this discipline.

HISTORY OF BIOLOGY

The oldest surviving archaeological records that indicate some rudimentary human knowledge of biological principles date from the Mesolithic Period. During the NEOLITHIC PERIOD, which began about 10,000 years ago, various human groups developed agriculture and the medicinal use of plants. In ancient Egypt, for example, a number of herbs were being used medicinally and for embalming.

Early Development. As a science, however, biology did not develop until the last few centuries BC. Although HIPPOCRATES, known as the father of medicine, influenced the development of medicine apart from its role in religion, it was ARISTOTLE, a student of Plato, who established observation and analysis as the basic tools of biology. Of particular importance were Aristotle's observations of reproduction and his concepts for a classification system.

As the center of learning shifted from Greece to Rome and then to Alexandria, so did the study of biology. From the 3d century BC to the 2d century AD, studies primarily focused on agriculture and medicine. The Arabs dominated the study of biology during the Middle Ages and applied their knowledge of the Greeks' discoveries to medicine.

The Renaissance was a period of rapid advances, especially in Italy, France, and Spain, where Greek culture was being rediscovered. In the 15th and 16th centuries, Leonardo da Vinci and Michelangelo became skilled anatomists through their search for perfection in art. Andreas VESALIUS initiated the use of dissection as a teaching aid. His books, *Fabrica* (1543) and *Fabrica*, 2d ed. (1550), contained detailed anatomical illustrations that became standards. In the 17th century, William HARVEY introduced the use of experimentation in his studies of the human circulatory system. His work marked the beginning of mammalian physiology.

Scientific Societies and Journals. Lack of communication was a problem for early biologists. To overcome this, scientific societies were organized. The first were in Europe, beginning with the Academy of the Lynx (Rome, 1603).

The Boston Philosophical Society, founded in 1683, was probably the first such society to be organized in colonial America. Later, specialized groups, principally of physicians, organized themselves, among them the American Association for the Advancement of Science (AAAS), founded in 1848. Much later, in 1951, the American Institute of Biological Science (AIBS) was formed as an alliance of the major biological societies in the United States.

The first journals to present scientific discoveries were published in Europe starting in 1665; they were the *Journal des Savants*, in France, and *Philosophical Transactions* of the Royal Society, in London. Over the years numerous other journals have been established, so that today nearly all societies record their transactions and discoveries.

Development and Early Use of the Microscope. Before 1300 optical lenses were unknown, except for crude spectacles used for reading. Modern optics began with the invention of the MICROSCOPE by Galileo Galilei about 1610. Microscopy originated in 1625 when the Italian Francesco Stelluti published his drawings of a honeybee magnified 10 times.

The 17th century produced five microscopists whose works are considered classics: Marcello MALPIGHI (Italy), Antoni van LEEUWENHOEK and Jan SWAMMERDAM (Holland), and Robert HOOKE and Nehemiah GREW (England). Notable among their achievements were Malpighi's description of lung capillaries and kidney corpuscles and Hooke's *Micrographia*, in which the term *cell* was first used.

Basis for Modern Systematics. Consistent terminology and nomenclature were unknown in early biological studies, although Aristotle regularly described organisms by *genos* and *eidoes* (genus and species). Sir Isaac NEWTON's *Principia* (1687) describes a rigid universe with an equally rigid classification system. This was a typical approach of the period. The leading botanical classification was that used in describing the medicinal values of plants.

Modern nomenclature based on a practical binomial system originated with Karl von Linné (Latinized to Carolus LINNAEUS). In addition to arranging plants and animals into genus and species based on structure, he introduced the categories of class and order. Jean Baptiste LAMARCK based his system on function, since this accommodated his view of the inheritance of acquired characteristics. In 1817, Georges, Baron CUVIER, became the first to divide the entire animal kingdom into subgroups, for example, Vertebrata, Mollusca, Articulata, and Radiata.

Explorations and Explorers. During the 18th and 19th centuries numerous important biological expeditions were organized. Three of these, all British, made outstanding contributions to biology. Sir Joseph BANKS, on Captain Cook's ship *Endeavor*, explored (1768–71) the South Seas, collecting plants and animals of Australia. Robert BROWN, a student of Banks, visited Australia from 1801 to 1805 on the *Investigator* and re-

(Right) *Antoni van Leeuwenhoek, a Dutch linen draper, ground more than 400 lenses for microscopes of his own design. He was the first to observe and describe many microorganisms, including bacteria and protozoa, his "little animalcules," and to accurately describe red blood cells.*

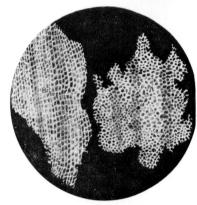

(Left) *Robert Hooke coined the word* cell *in 1665 to describe the minute compartments he saw in cork tissue. This drawing of magnified tissue is from his book* Micrographia.

Andreas Vesalius revolutionized the study of anatomy and medicine with the first anatomy text based on the dissection of the human body. The detailed illustrations, including the magnificent title page (below), are attributed to the Flemish artist Jan Stephan von Calcar.

turned with more than 4,000 plant specimens. On perhaps the most famous voyage, Charles DARWIN circumnavigated (1831–36) the globe on the *Beagle.* His observations of birds, reptiles, and flowering plants in the Galápagos Islands in 1835 laid the foundation for his theories on evolution, later published in *On the Origin of Species* (1859).

The Discovery of Microorganisms. Arguments about the spontaneous generation of organisms had been going on since the time of Aristotle, and various inconclusive experiments had been conducted. Louis PASTEUR clearly demonstrated in 1864 that no organisms emerged from his heat-sterilized growth medium as long as the medium remained in sealed flasks, thereby disproving spontaneous generation. Based on Edward JENNER's studies of smallpox, Pasteur later developed a vaccine for anthrax and in 1885 became the first to successfully treat a human bitten by a rabid dog.

Beginning in 1876, Robert KOCH developed pure-culture techniques for microorganisms. His work verified the germ theory of disease. One of his students, Paul EHRLICH, developed chemotherapy and in 1909 devised a chemical cure for syphilis.

The value of ANTIBIOTICS became evident when Sir Alexander FLEMING discovered penicillin in 1928. An intensive search, between 1940 and 1960, for other antibiotics resulted in the development of several dozen that were used extensively. Although antibiotics have not been the panacea once anticipated, their use has resulted in a decreased incidence of most infectious diseases.

The Role of the Cell. Following Hooke's use of the term *cell*, biologists gradually came to recognize this unit as common throughout living systems. The cell theory was published in 1839 by Matthias Schleiden (see SCHWANN, THEODOR, AND SCHLEIDEN, MATTHIAS JAKOB), a plant anatomist. Schleiden saw cells as the basic unit of organization and perceived each as having a double life, one "pertaining to its own development" and the other "as an integral part of a plant."

Charles Darwin (left) *based much of his theory of evolution on observations of animals made while he was a naturalist aboard the* Beagle *from 1831 to 1836.*

(Below) *Louis Pasteur's pioneering work in microbiology laid the foundation for modern medical research. He substantiated the belief that microbes cause disease. He developed the technique of vaccination to combat infection.*

(Left) *Paul Ehrlich added a new dimension to the study of immunology with his search for a "magic bullet," a chemical agent for the treatment of disease. Chief among his discoveries was Salvarsan, the first cure for syphilis.*

Schwann, an animal histologist, noticed that not all parts of an organism consist of cells. He added to the theory in 1840 by establishing that these parts are at least "cell products." Between 1868 and 1898 the cell theory was enlarged as substructures of the cell—for example, plastids and mitochondria—were observed and described.

Basic Life Functions. Until the 17th century it was believed that plants took in food, preformed, from the soil. Jan Baptista van HELMONT, the first experimental physiologist, around 1640 concluded that water is the only soil component required for plant growth. Stephen HALES showed (1727) that air held the additional ingredient for food synthesis. In 1779, Ingenhousz identified this as carbon dioxide.

The study of PHOTOSYNTHESIS began with a demonstration by Julius von Sachs and Nathanael Pringsheïm in the mid-19th century that light is the energy source of green plants. Vernon Herbert Blackman showed (1905) that not all parts of this process require sunlight. Results of work done during the 1920s and '30s proved that chloroplasts produce oxygen. Subsequently, it was shown that the light-dependent reactions cause two types of high-energy molecules to be formed that use the energy from light.

The route of carbon dioxide in photosynthesis was worked out by Melvin CALVIN in the early 1950s, using the radioisotope carbon-14. His results proved Blackman correct: there exist two distinct but closely coordinated sets of chloroplast reactions, one light-dependent and the other light-independent. High-energy products of the light-dependent reactions are required for incorporation of carbon dioxide into sugars in the light-independent reactions.

The earliest demonstration of *ferments* (the word ENZYME was not coined until 1878) in pancreatic juice was made by Claude BERNARD in France. Bernard also experimentally determined numerous functions of the liver as well as the influence of vasomotor nerves on blood pressure.

In the 1930s, Otto WARBURG discovered a series of cellular enzymes that start the process of glucose breakdown to produce energy for biological activity. When Hans KREBS demonstrated (1950s) an additional series of enzyme reactions (the citric acid cycle) that completes the oxidation process, the general respiration scheme of cells became known.

Chemical synchronization of body functions without direct control by the nervous system was discovered in 1905 by Sir William M. BAYLISS and Ernest Henry STARLING (the first to use the term *hormone*). Steroids were discovered in 1935.

Continuity in Living Systems. The early biologists known as preformationists believed that animals exist preformed, either in sperm (the animalculist's view) or in the egg (the ovist's belief). Embryology actually began when Karl Ernst von BAER,

Theodor Schwann extended botanist Matthias Schleiden's work on the cell theory—a central concept of modern biology—to include animals, illustrating his claim with a drawing (below) *in which he showed the similarities between plant and animal cells.*

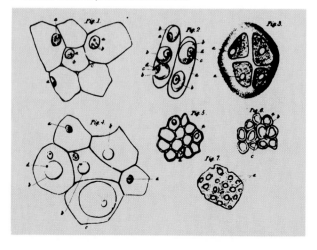

(Left) *Claude Bernard, shown experimenting on a rabbit, was a central figure in the development of experimental medicine.*

Experiments with peas in the garden of his monastery led the Austrian monk Gregor Mendel (right) to formulate the basic principles of heredity. Mendel's mathematical interpretation of his data became the basis for modern genetic research.

using the microscope, observed that no preformed embryos exist. Modern interpretations of developmental control in embryogenesis can be traced to Hans SPEMANN's discovery in 1915 of an ''organizer'' area in frog embryos. More recent research has shown the importance of other factors, such as chemical gradients.

Genetics, the study of heredity, began with the work of Gregor Johann MENDEL, who published his findings in 1866. Mendel's extensive experiments with garden peas led him to conclude that the inheritance of each characteristic is controlled by a pair of physical units, or genes. These units, one from each parent (the law of segregation), were passed on to offspring, apparently independent of the distribution of any other pairs (the law of independent assortment). The gene concept was amplified by the rediscovery and confirmation of Mendel's work in 1900 by Hugo De VRIES in Holland, Karl Erich Correns in Germany, and Gustav Tschermak von Seysenegg in Austria. De Vries's mutation theory became the foundation of modern genetics.

The chromosome theory is based on the speculations of Pierre Paul ROUX in 1883 that cell nuclei contain linear arrangements of beadlike components that replicate (produce exact copies) during cell division. Many important contributions were made early in the 20th century by the American Thomas Hunt MORGAN. These included sex-linked inheritance and the association with gene theory of the crossing over of chromosomes.

The discovery by Geoffrey Hardy and Wilhelm Weinberg of the equilibrium relationship that exists between frequency of alleles (a term originated by William Bateson in 1909 for alternate forms of a gene) in a population led to formulation of the law bearing their names. The role of genetics in evolution was publicized in 1937 by Theodosius DOBZHANSKY's *Genetics and the Origin of Species.*

Molecular biology, the most recent branch of biology, began early in the 20th century with Archibald Garrod's work on the biochemical genetics of various diseases. The concept of one gene producing one enzyme was established in 1941 by George W. BEADLE and Edward L. TATUM. The work on protein synthesis by Jacques MONOD and François JACOB and others in 1961 has modified the one gene–one enzyme concept to one gene–one protein. Essential to the understanding of PROTEIN SYNTHESIS were the advances made in the 1940s and '50s in understanding the role and structure of nucleic acids. The structural model proposed in 1953 by James D. WATSON and F. H. C. CRICK is a landmark in biology. It has given biologists a feasible way to explain the storage and precise transmission of genetic information from one generation to the next (see GENETIC CODE). Knowledge of biological processes at the molecular level has also enabled scientists to develop techniques for the direct manipulation of genetic information, a field now called GENETIC ENGINEERING.

UNITY OF LIVING SYSTEMS

Despite the astounding diversity of organisms that have been discovered, an equally astounding degree of unity of structure and function has been discerned. The structure of flagella is essentially the same in all cells having nuclei. The molecules involved in growth and metabolism are remarkably similar, and often they are constructed of identical subunits. Furthermore, enzymes, the catalysts of biological chemistry, are now known to act similarly in all organisms. Phenomena such as cell division and the transmission of the genetic code also appear to be universal.

LARRY A. GIESMANN

Bibliography: Angros, Robert, and Stanciu, George, *The New Biology* (1987); Antébi, Elizabeth, and Fishlock, David, *Biotechnology* (1987); Asimov, Isaac, *A Short History of Biology* (1964; repr. 1980); Darnell, James, et al., *Molecular Cell Biology* (1986); Ehrlich, Paul, *The Machinery of Nature* (1987); Gardner, Eldon J., *History of Biology*, 3d ed. (1972); Lanham, U. N., *The Origins of Modern Biology* (1968); Maynard Smith, John, *The Problems of Biology* (1986); Mayr, Ernst, *The Growth of Biological Thought* (1982); Medawar, P. B. and J. S., *Life Science* (1978); Pauley, Philip, *Controlling Life* (1987); Watson, J. D., et al., *Molecular Biology of the Gene*, 2 vols., 4th ed. (1987).

In 1953, James D. Watson (left) and Francis H. C. Crick (right) constructed this molecular model of deoxyribonucleic acid (DNA), the storehouse of genetic information. Watson and Crick shared the 1962 Nobel Prize for physiology or medicine with Maurice Wilkins, whose X-ray diffraction studies enable them to break the genetic code.

bioluminescence [by'-oh-loom-i-nes'-ens]

Bioluminescence, or "living" light, is the light produced by some living organisms. FIREFLIES and GLOWWORMS—larval and some adult forms of certain beetles and gnats—are the most familiar light-emitting organisms, but other groups of organisms—bacteria, crustaceans, fish, fungi, jellyfish, mollusks, Protozoa, sponges, and worms—also have species that emit light. The only groups that do not are the mammals, birds, reptiles, amphibians, and leafy plants.

Nature. Bioluminescence is produced by basically the same kind of reaction in most organisms. The light is emitted when oxygen combines with a substance in the organism called luciferin in the presence of an enzyme called luciferase. The composition of these substances varies somewhat from organism to organism and has not been determined in all cases. Other substances also take part in the reaction in some organisms, and the light emitted ranges from the yellow green of the firefly to blue, blue green, green, and red. Living light is often called cold light, because almost no energy is lost as heat in the reaction. It compares favorably in heat-loss efficiency with that of modern fluorescent lamps, whereas most of the energy used by an electric light bulb produces heat rather than light.

Although bioluminescence is produced by organisms, the process is a chemical one that can be carried out in the laboratory as well. Bioluminescence is therefore a special type of chemiluminescence, in which the energy of a substance is first increased by a chemical reaction, then returned to its original level when the substance emits the added energy as light. The enzyme luciferase promotes the energy-increasing reaction of oxygen with luciferin. In 1986 scientists produced bioluminescent tobacco plants by inserting the luciferase gene into the genetic material of the plants.

Function. In some cases the role played by bioluminescence in the life of an organism seems obvious. The flashing of light-producing organs on the abdomen of the firefly, for example, serves to bring the males and females together. Similarly, female marine fireworms appear at the surface of the sea during the mating season and glow. Males attracted from the deeper waters join the females in a mating dance, and both sexes release their reproductive cells into the water.

Many deep-sea fish have bulblike organs on their bodies, called photophores, that may also attract mates or prey, or illuminate the search for them in the perpetual darkness. Some ANGLERFISH, for example, have a photophore on the tip of a long ray and dangle it in front of their mouth as a lure. Other luminescent fish use their light displays to escape being eaten, flashing on and off as they zigzag through the water to confuse the pursuing animal. Some mollusks emit luminescent clouds for the same survival purpose.

Many light-emitting deep-sea species, however, are also blind, in which case the light seems to have no function. Neither has any purpose been discovered for the glowing of

The flashing pattern of the bioluminescent abdomen of this firefly of the genus Luciola *is species-specific.*

These glowing corals, which live on the Great Barrier Reef off the eastern coast of Australia, are an example of organisms that serve as light sources in some marine environments.

bacteria and fungi. Bioluminescence appeared independently in the evolution of many kinds of organisms, and it may be no more than an accident of changing body chemistry that, in some cases, further evolved to serve a useful function.

Kinds of Displays. Such organisms as bacteria and fungi emit a steady light; others, such as brittle stars and jellyfish, emit light only when stimulated. The light displays of some animal species are highly colorful. For example, the railroad worm, the larva of the beetle *Phrixothrix*, is so named because it has a pair of rows of green lights along the sides of its body and a pair of red spots at the head. Some shrimp have accessory lenses, reflectors, and color filters, so that the entire assembly looks like a multicolored lantern.

Luminous single-celled organisms called dinoflagellates are the most common cause of brilliant displays of light seen in the ocean. One species, *Noctiluca miliaris,* may tint the sea-surface pink in the daytime and light it up at night. A ship plowing through tropic seas may produce a wake that glows eerily as millions of these organisms light up. (Another source of light in tropic oceans is the luminous jellyfish *Pelagia noctiluca*.) On land the equally eerie glow known as fox fire, sometimes seen on decaying wood, is produced by luminescent fungi.

In some animal species the glow is produced by luminescent bacteria rather than by the animals themselves. (The most common luminescent bacteria are those responsible for the glow on decaying fish or meat.) For example, the East Indian fishes *Anomalops katoptron* and *Photoblepharon palpbebratus* have light organs under their eyes in which bacteria live and emit light continuously. The former fish can rotate this organ to shut out the light, and the latter has a black membrane that can be drawn over the organ. An unsolved mystery is how the bacteria first collect in the light organ.

Some organisms can produce an amazing amount of light. Lanterns made of fireflies are used in a number of countries, and a flask containing a pure culture of *Photobacterium phosphoreum* gives off enough light to illuminate an object several meters away.   Reviewed by LAWRENCE J. CROCKETT

Bibliography: Deluca, Marlene, and McElroy, William, eds., *Bioluminescence and Chemiluminescence* (1981); Herring, Peter J., ed., *Bioluminescence in Action* (1979); Johnson, Frank H., *Luminescence, Narcosis, and Life in the Deep Sea* (1987).

biomass: SEE SYNTHETIC FUELS.

biome [by'-ohm]

Biomes are the largest recognizable terrestrial components, or units, of the BIOSPHERE (the entire surface of the Earth.

BIOME DISTRIBUTION

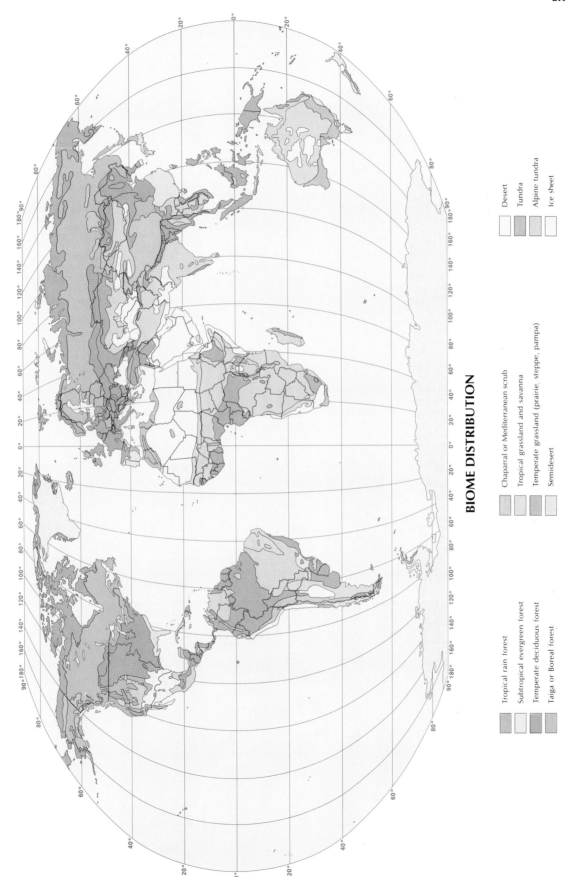

Tropical rain forest

Subtropical evergreen forest

Temperate deciduous forest

Taiga or Boreal forest

Chaparral or Mediterranean scrub

Tropical grassland and savanna

Temperate grassland (prairie, steppe, pampa)

Semidesert

Desert

Tundra

Alpine tundra

Ice sheet

A biome encompasses large geographic regions that contain characteristic vegetation and animals. Major biomes include tropical rain forests, temperate deciduous forests, taigas, savannas, deserts, and tundras. Each biome has a certain type of climate and soil to which plants and animals adapt for their survival. A temperate deciduous forest contains elm, maple, oak, and beech trees and is the home of such animals as deer, chipmunks, squirrels, and songbirds. In contrast, a southwestern United States desert has shrubs, cacti, lizards, snakes, and coyotes.

occupied by life). They are distinguished from one another by vegetation and climate. The dominant vegetation, or flora, in each biome supports a collection of animal life, or fauna, characteristic of that particular biome. The biota (plants and animals) each kind of biome have similar characteristics worldwide. Biomes comprise smaller units called HABITATS.

CLIMATE is the primary feature that distinguishes one biome from another. For example, the climate in a tropical rain forest differs dramatically from that of coniferous forests of the U.S. West. The tropical rain forest always has ample water, and its daily temperatures are nearly perfect for plant growth. The coniferous forest typically must tolerate drought in summer and very cold weather in winter. Thus, different types of flora and fauna have evolved in each biome, eventually filling the ecological niches. For example, the climate of the northern tundra is frigid most of the year, and the growing season is cool and wet. The flora and fauna, however, have adapted to survive these rigorous conditions. The treeless tundra flora of the Arctic region is mostly low-growing perennials. The low stature of the plants is an adaptation to the harsh, drying winds that wear away the tall plants, as well as to such other conditions as soil moisture and nutrients.

Similar biomes often are found at the same latitude. This is apparent in the tundra and the northern coniferous boreal forest, or taiga. In addition to latitudinal similarities, altitudinal similarities exist as well. As one ascends a tall mountain the temperature becomes cooler, the air thinner, and the winters longer and more severe (even tall mountains near the equator are snow-capped). Therefore, several different climates often exist on one mountain (see MOUNTAIN LIFE). For example, Mount Washington in the White Mountains of New Hampshire has three different biomes, in order of increasing altitude: temperate deciduous forest biome mantles the foothills and lower slopes, boreal forest, and tundra.

The distribution of the world's major biomes is shown on the accompanying map. A map of the world's major climatic zones would in general correspond fairly closely to the divisions seen there, although the names of the climatic zones vary somewhat. Thus the "tropical rain forest" biome includes the "tropical wet" climatic zone along with the "monsoon" climates of the eastern coasts of India and Southeast Asia. The "tropical grassland and savanna" biome corresponds to the "tropical wet-dry" climate, and so on.   STEPHEN FAUER

Bibliography: Brown, J., and Gibson, A., *Biogeography* (1983); Cox, C., and Moore, P., *Biogeography,* 4th ed. (1985); Pielou, E., *Biogeography* (1979; repr. 1992); Walter, H., and Breckle, S., *Ecological Systems of the World,* 2 vols. (1985–86); Whittaker, R., *Communities and Ecosystems,* 2d ed. (1975).

See also: CHAPARRAL; DESERT; FORESTS AND FORESTRY; GRASSLANDS; SAVANNA; TAIGA; TUNDRA.

biomedical engineering

Biomedical engineering is an interdisciplinary field that uses engineering, physics, and chemistry to develop instruments, machines, and methods for studying and treating living organisms. Biomedical engineering as a distinct profession is only about 20 years old. It is still so specialized that few universities offer graduate-level training in the field, and even fewer have undergraduate programs. Therefore biomedical engineers usually start out in a related field such as medicine or engineering. With the emphasis in medicine on electronic devices, a useful background for a biomedical engineer is electronic engineering.

See also: ARTIFICIAL LIMBS; ARTIFICIAL ORGANS; BIOTECHNOLOGY; ELECTROCARDIOGRAPH; ELECTROENCEPHALOGRAPH; HEART, ARTIFICIAL; KIDNEY, ARTIFICIAL; PACEMAKER, ARTIFICIAL; RADIOLOGY.

bionics   [by-ahn'-iks]

Bionics is the study of the properties of biologic systems that may be applied to the solution of engineering problems. Areas of study range from propulsion (in fish and birds especially) to energy conversion. Bionics is closely linked to the field of study once known as CYBERNETICS—that is, the comparative analysis of communication, control, and information systems in living organisms and machines.

Bionic studies may be physiological, biochemical, biophysical, or biomechanical, and the applications usually involve a great deal of mathematics, physics, and electronic engineering. The field is related to so-called general-systems theory and owes much to such scientists as the Russian-American Nicholas Rashevsky, who developed the first mathematical analyses of various functions of the central nervous system. The nervous systems of organisms have since been studied by many physicists and engineers interested in bionics. For example, the encoding processes of the visual system have been intensively studied, with resulting improvements in the design of cameras, television, and optical-recognition systems. Auditory systems have also been studied. Such research has influenced the development of radio transmitters and receivers. Similar research in muscular and other systems concerned with propulsion has influenced the design of submarines and ships. Studies of bird flight have been used in aircraft design. Studies of respiratory, circulatory, and digestive systems have also been used to improve the performance of electronic control systems.

Another aspect of bionics is the transplantation of artificial organs. A similar application is the use of artificial limbs. Electrically controlled arms and legs have been developed, which work on principles of pattern recognition. That is, move-

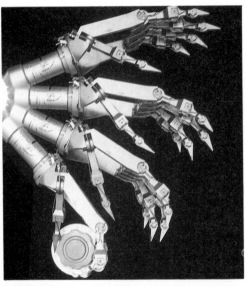

Bionics uses knowledge of living systems to create analogous mechanical devices. A metal hand, hinged at the wrist and knuckles, having an opposable thumb, and controlled by a computer, can easily manipulate a combination lock.

ments of the artificial limbs are controlled through the detection of electrical-field patterns in muscle tissue, usually measured at many sites on the surface of the skin. Other research activities that may be said to come within the field of bionics are the development of aids that permit the blind to "see" by nerve pathways other than the diseased pathways and the development of hearing aids. Apart from the senses and internal systems, social and behavioral systems related to tracking and interception have been studied. The principles learned have aided in developing homing systems for missiles.

Bionics has become a powerful engineering force in recent years; this is largely a result of making explicit ideas that were always implicit in engineering. Now these ideas are being systematically used in mathematical and computer techniques that have enormously multiplied the effectiveness of biological engineering.   F. H. GEORGE

Bibliography: Dario, P., et al., eds., *Robots and Biological Systems: Towards a New Bionics* (1993).

biopharmaceuticals

Biopharmaceuticals are drugs that duplicate the actions of naturally occurring compounds in the body. They can act directly on abnormal cells through a biochemical interaction with a specific component of the cells, by stimulating specific cells to attack abnormal ones, or by taking over the functions of compounds that are absent or deficient. The advantage of biopharmaceuticals is that their actions are very specific, thus avoiding many problems of side effects.

The biopharmaceutical industry began in the mid-1970s as an outgrowth of recombinant-DNA technology (see GENETIC ENGINEERING). Biopharmaceuticals are produced by CLONING, by extraction and purification of natural substances, or by the chemical synthesis of proteins. One of the chief applications of these drugs is in cancer treatment. INTERFERON—the first successful drug to be genetically engineered—inhibits certain types of cancer cells and some viruses. Cellular hormones known as interleukins, lymphotoxins, and tumor necrosis factor may also treat cancers and immune deficiency diseases. Monoclonal ANTIBODIES can destroy cancer cells or deliver toxins or radioisotopes to such cells. Many other conditions may also benefit from biopharmaceutical research. For example, a bioengineered hormone has proved effective in preventing paralysis after spinal-cord injuries in animal studies, and genetically engineered insulin will replace insulin extracted from animal tissues. Biopharmaceuticals are also being developed for use as diagnostic agents and treatments for emphysema, ulcers, atherosclerosis, viral infections, allergies, and MULTIPLE SCLEROSIS.   Reviewed by ROLLAND I. POUST

Bibliography: Weinstock, C. P., "Medicines from the Body," *FDA Consumer* (April 1987); Wiley, R. A., and Rich, D. H., "Peptodomimetics Derived from Natural Sources," *Medicinal Research Reviews*, vol. 13 (1993).

biophysics

Biophysics is a branch of physics concerned with living organisms. The goal of biophysics is to explain biological events in terms of physical laws and principles. Biophysics uses the tools and concepts of the physicist to define and approach biological problems. The science of biophysics is related to physics as the science of BIOCHEMISTRY is related to chemistry. They both interrelate the physical and biological sciences. During the 19th century those engaged in what today would be called biophysics were studying the molecular and thermodynamic processes related to METABOLISM and MUSCLE contraction. The results of these studies indicated that living things function according to the laws of physics and that no evidence existed for the presence of so-called vital forces unique to life. In addition the measurements helped to establish in biology what had already become one of the most powerful laws in physics—the law of conservation of energy.

In this century the development of such biophysical tools as X-ray diffraction has contributed to knowledge of the structure of such important molecules as proteins and DNA. Advances in electronics have permitted a better understanding of how nerve cells function. Biophysicists' studies of osmotic pressure and diffusion have contributed much to understanding how cell membranes regulate the passage of various substances to and from the environment. Studies of muscles, heat generation, and cell motility have contributed to molecular-level understanding of muscle contraction. The development of biophysics as a major discipline within biology came after World War II, when a significant number of physicists moved into the field of biology.   DAVID L. WILSON

Bibliography: Cerdonio, M., and Noble, R. W., *Introductory Biophysics* (1986); Mielczarek, E., et al., eds., *Biological Physics* (1993).

biopotential

The cells of many biological organs generate an electric potential called "biopotential" that may result in the flow of electric current. Electrical impulses may arise spontaneously or from stimulation; once initiated, they can propagate and excite adjacent cells. Nerve and muscle constitute the largest class of excitable tissue, and their electrical behavior is similar. Nearly all sensory, motor, and regulatory functions of the nervous system depend on some form of bioelectric signal to carry out their functions.

Bioelectricity originates in cell membranes as a result of the behavior of such common ions in organisms as sodium and potassium. Electrochemical processes result in the accumulation of opposite charges on the inside and outside of the membrane, which in effect constitutes an electric battery. Cell membranes are virtual insulators except for the presence of specific ion channels that are gated; the permeability of an ion simply reflects the availabiliy of open-gated channels for that ion.

Nerve Cell Membrane. The nerve cell, particularly its axon, has the specific function to conduct electrical signals (action potentials); these may convey information or control muscles. Bioelectricity in the axon results from the difference in the concentration of ions inside and outside its membrane and to the ion-selective permeability of the membrane. The most important ions are those of sodium and potassium; for example, the ratio of the outer sodium-ion concentration to the inner is about 10 to 1 and that of potassium is 1 to 35. The membrane at rest is highly permeable to potassium (while having only a very low degree of permeability to sodium); therefore, potassium readily diffuses outward (from high concentration to low concentration). A net efflux of positive charge results, whereby the outside surface of the membrane acquires a net positive charge while an equivalent negative

polarized membrane
resting potential | repolarized membrane
refractory phase | depolarized membrane
action potential | membrane about
to be polarized

Biopotential is a cell's ability to transmit electrical impulses resulting from ion flow across its membrane. A resting membrane is polarized when a greater-than-normal ratio of sodium to potassium ions is outside the membrane and of potassium to sodium ions inside the cytoplasm. As an impulse passes through, the membrane allows sodium ions into the cell and potassium ions out. This creates an action potential that depolarizes the membrane and affects the region just ahead of the electrical impulse, which becomes depolarized as the wave passes. After depolarization, sodium and potassium ions flow back, repolarizing the membrane.

charge is left at the inner membrane surface. Ionic forces limit the net charge accumulation and at equilibrium an associated transmembrane voltage, or "resting potential," of about -85 (mV) (inside relative to outside) results. Because the cell membrane is only 75 angstroms (Å) thick, this constitutes a powerful electric field—about 10 million volts a meter. Thus far, however, no electric current has occurred in the surrounding (extracellular) medium. Currents flow when membranes are depolarized and an action potential is propagating along excitable tissue; such currents can be detected by electrodes lying within or at the surface of the surrounding tissue as in electroneurography.

NERVE IMPULSE

Depolarization, or activation, occurs when the membrane's permeability to sodium suddenly rises to several hundred times its resting value. This rapid change may be the result of a signal from a sensory receptor or another nerve cell. The signal raises the transmembrane potential beyond a threshold value, and the relatively high sodium permeability results in an inward diffusion of sodium and a reversal of the resting potential. Now a net positive intracellular charge (negative extracellular charge) of +50 mV exists on the membrane.

This change in transmembrane potential (or action potential) sets up currents that depolarize the adjoining, resting membrane—a process that when continually repeated creates a wave of depolarization. If the axon is stimulated at any point, the action potential will propagate over the entire length of the nerve fiber. Once initiated, the action potential has a stereotyped shape and therefore an essentially fixed amplitude —an "all or none" response to a stimulus. The propagation of each impulse is followed by the absolute refractory period during which the fiber cannot transmit an impulse. Full excitability returns upon complete membrane repolarization.

Transmission among Nerve Cells. Communication among adjacent nerve cells occurs at points called synapses. Here, a chemical transmitter substance (produced by the neuron) is released from the cell on one side of the synapse and diffuses across the synaptic cleft (a distance of some 200 Å) to the active cell on the other side (the postsynaptic cell). The result is a modification of membrane permeability. Depending on the transmitter released, it either depolarizes the membrane and excites a postsynaptic signal or hyperpolarizes it and inhibits further transmission. When the impulses are carried by motor neurons and communicated to a target muscle at a synaptic, neuromuscular junction, the muscle is always excited. At this synapse the transmitter is ACETYLCHOLINE, which depolarizes the muscle "endplate" region by increasing the sodium and potassium permeability. This, in turn, initiates an action potential that propagates along the muscle fibers by the same mechanism described above. The excitation is also conducted into the fibers and triggers MUSCLE CONTRACTION.

Muscle. Cardiac muscle cells, for example, are bounded by a plasma membrane similar to that of nerves. These cells propagate action potentials in essentially the same way. The only significant difference is the 200–300 millisecond (msec) duration of the cardiac action potential. Each cardiac cell, however, is connected to its neighboring cells. Consequently excitation, once initiated, spreads electrically to all the cells in the heart. Such intercellular transmission also occurs among smooth muscle cells.

Fish. Electric fish generate biopotential through their electric organ, which comprises specialized compartments so arranged as to promote the production of electricity (see ELECTRIC FISH). Some fish also exhibit another bioelectrical phenomenon, BIOLUMINESCENCE. Energy is developed through biochemical reactions on the luminescent enzyme, which, through neural stimulation, is transported across the cell membrane or is secreted.

ROBERT PLONSEY

Bibliography: Brown, A. G., *Nerve Cells and Nervous Systems* (1991); Junge, D., *Nerve and Muscle Excitation* (1992); Malmivuo, Jaakko, and Plonsey, Robert, *Bioelectromagnetism* (1994); Marino, Andrew A., *Modern Bioelectricity* (1987); Nuñez, Paul L., *Electric Fields of the Brain* (1984); Plonsey, Robert, and Barr, R. C., *Bioelectricity* (1988).

See also: BRAIN; NERVOUS SYSTEM; NEUROPHYSIOLOGY.

biopsy

A biopsy is a procedure for removing for examination a small sample of tissue from a living organism. The specimen, obtained with surgical instruments, is prepared for microscopic or biochemical testing. A biopsy may also be performed, without surgical incision, by using needles or punches. Although a variety of diagnostic information can be obtained from tissue thus examined, recognition of the typical pattern of cell disruption under the microscope is the standard method for diagnosing cancer.

Bibliography: Nguyen, G.-K., *Essentials of Aspiration Biopsy Cytology* (1991); Ranzy, I., *Clinical Cytopathology and Aspiration Biopsy* (1990).

biorhythm: see BIOLOGICAL CLOCK.

Biosatellite

Three Biosatellites were launched by NASA in the 1960s to investigate the effects of weightlessness, cosmic rays, and the absence of the diurnal cycle on various living organisms, and to return their experiment capsules to the Earth by parachute. The failure of a retrorocket on *Biosatellite 1*, launched Dec. 14, 1966, resulted in the loss of its capsule, but the duplicate *Biosatellite 2*, launched Sept. 7, 1967, for an orbital mission of 45 hours, was a success. Among the organisms aboard were bacteria, bread molds, flour beetles, flowering plants, wasps and their larvae, fruit flies, wheat seeds, pepper plants, frog eggs, and amoebas. *Biosatellite 3*, launched June 28, 1969, carried a pigtail monkey. Its planned 30-day mission was terminated after nine days when the monkey was observed to be dying, but the capsule was successfully recovered.

biosensor

Biological sensors, or biosensors, are electronic devices designed to provide data on biochemical processes taking place in the body. Such data can be used for medical purposes as well as in basic research. Essentially a biosensor couples a tiny electronic transducer with a membrane in which a biological receptor such as an enzyme has been embedded. When the receptor detects a change in concentration of the chemical it was selected to monitor, the transducer converts this datum into an electrical signal that is relayed to an external receiver. In advanced biosensors the transducer can be a computer chip that itself analyzes data—for example, concentrations of ions in the blood—before relaying the results. Such a device is known as a chemical field effect transistor, or chem-FET.

Bibliography: Blum, L., and Coulet, P., eds., *Biosensor Principles and Applications* (1991); Buerk, D., *Biosensors: Theory and Applications* (1993).

biosphere

The Earth's biosphere, the zone capable of supporting and sustaining LIFE, is a thin envelope extending 8 to 10 km (5 to 6 mi) above the planet's surface and a few meters below it into the soil. Earth organisms owe their existence to the Sun's energy and its interactions with the elements and compounds of the biosphere. The Earth's average air temperature permits reactions essential to life to take place. Patterns of growth in various areas of the Earth are determined by such things as water, light, altitude, and soil composition. Different patterns form large units called BIOMES.

ENERGY FLOW

The atmosphere of the Earth selectively reflects, dissipates, and distributes the Sun's energy. It also prevents primary COSMIC RAYS and excessive ULTRAVIOLET LIGHT from reaching the surface, while allowing heat and light energy to penetrate. Land and water absorb heat during the day and slowly release it at night. By retaining some of this heat the atmosphere slows down the cooling off of the surface. Because the Earth also has hot and cold spots, it heats up and cools off unevenly. These differences cause CONVECTION currents that determine the patterns of rainfall and wind. The energy balance necessary to maintain life results from a transfer of energy from areas of excess to areas of deficient heat. The motion of the oceans also transports energy. This energy transfer is needed to equilibrate temperature extremes and provide hospitable environments.

In order for life to be maintained, however, some of this energy must also be converted into food. By means of PHOTOSYNTHESIS, plants convert light energy into a primary food source for animals. In addition to the elemental compounds needed for photosynthesis, many other raw materials cycled in the biosphere are required in the energy transformation and life-maintenance process.

CYCLING OF MATTER

Among the most important substances for life are water, carbon, nitrogen, oxygen, phosphorus, and sulfur. The principal components of organic matter are carbon, hydrogen, and oxygen. Nitrogen, phosphorus, and sulfur are important, because they interact with the carbon-hydrogen-oxygen matrix. These substances are components of natural cycles that have geological as well as biological components.

WATER, an integral part of all natural cycles, can dissolve many different substances. This is important both in cells and the environment. When water moves through the HYDRO-LOGIC CYCLE, it transfers many dissolved substances with it.

Carbon is available for life processes as carbon dioxide and as organic carbon. The two major carbon reservoirs are the oceans and the atmosphere. Carbon is converted into organic compounds through photosynthesis. This occurs in plants, macroalgae, and phytoplankton (see PLANKTON). Carbon is then returned to the atmosphere through direct diffusion at the air-water interface, combustion of fossil fuels such as oil and coal, and respiration (see RESPIRATORY SYSTEM).

Nitrogen, the key component in all PROTEINS, is crucial to life, but gaseous nitrogen, although common in the atmosphere, is not available to most organisms in this form. Nitrogen is instead most readily assimilated by plants as nitrates (NO_3), into which it is converted by a bacterial process in the soil. The largest amounts of nitrogen are stored in crustal rocks (see NITRATE MINERALS) and the atmosphere. Decaying organic matter is the next largest reservoir of nitrogen and the most easily exploited by plants.

Oxygen cycles in three common forms: water, gaseous oxygen, and carbon dioxide. Crustal rocks also contain a great oxygen reservoir, as do the oceans, groundwater, and the atmosphere. Thus the hydrologic and carbon dioxide cycles are also fundamental components of the oxygen cycles.

Phosphorus is important to organisms because it is directly involved in the biochemical transfer of energy. Available to plants as phosphates through erosion of sedimentary rocks, it is cycled either by biological decomposition or by washing into the oceans, where it is reincorporated into marine sediments. Because this cyclic process is not fast, and because people use great amounts of phosphorus for fertilizers, the supply of phosphorus is limited.

Sulfur is found in the oceans, crustal rock, groundwater, the atmosphere, and the soil. Plants use it in its sulfate form and incorporate it into proteins. Animals obtain sulfur by eating plants or other animals that have eaten plants.

THE HUMAN ROLE

As the Earth evolved, the biosphere became a system that has been relatively balanced for millions of years. Since the Industrial Revolution, however, human technology has come to threaten this global balance. Pollution has led to deterioration of the atmosphere, oceans, and land surfaces (see POLLUTION, ENVIRONMENTAL) at increasing rates. Mineral resources are being depleted, as are the world's forests—which are also showing the effects of ACID RAIN. The possibility exists that the biosphere as a whole may be altered dramatically in coming years through the GREENHOUSE EFFECT. For all these reasons concerned scientists are urging long-scale planning and immediate measures to meet these threats.   STEPHEN FAUER

Bibliography: Boyden, S., ed., *Biohistory* (1992); Bradbury, I., *The Biosphere* (1991); Budyko, M., *The Evolution of the Biosphere* (1986); Margulis, L., and Olendzenski, L., *Environmental Evolution* (1992); Wallace, R., and King, J., *Biosphere: The Realm of Life*, 2d ed. (1987).

See also: CONSERVATION; ECOLOGY; ENVIRONMENT; GAIA HYPOTHESIS.

Biosphere II

Biosphere II is a privately funded research effort to test the feasibility of creating a self-contained environment able to sustain human life. The greenhouselike dome near Tucson, Ariz., supposedly resembles Earth—"Biosphere I"—in that, in theory, all raw materials and wastes are recyclable by the life in the structure. When researchers first stayed in the dome (1991–93) the project's value was questioned, because pure oxygen had to be pumped in and a carbon dioxide removal machine installed. Under a new management team, a second crew occupied the dome for six months in 1994.

Biot, Jean Baptiste   [bee-oh']

The French physicist Jean Baptiste Biot, b. Apr. 21, 1774, d. Feb. 3, 1862, did his most important work in optics. Early in his career he investigated chromatic polarization. He interpreted his findings in terms of the corpuscular theory of light and extended that theory. Discouraged when the wave theory won acceptance, he temporarily abandoned optics. When he returned to the subject, he followed up earlier work on the rotation of the plane of polarization as polarized light is passed through certain crystals and liquids. This line of investigation was continued by Louis PASTEUR, who acknowledged Biot's pioneering achievement.   ROBERT SILLIMAN

biotechnology

Biotechnology is a general category of all the studies and techniques that combine the ideas and needs of biology and medicine with engineering. Universities offer specialized programs in BIOMEDICAL ENGINEERING (bioengineering), BIOPHYSICS, engineering psychology, and other interdisciplinary fields that together constitute the realm of biotechnology. The word is now often used to signify the field of GENETIC ENGINEERING.

Bibliography: Steinberg, M. L., and Cosloy, S., *The Facts on File Dictionary of Biotechnology and Genetic Engineering* (1994).

See also: BIONICS; CYBERNETICS.

biotite: see MICA.

bipolar disorder

Bipolar disorder is a medical disorder with strong psychological impacts. It was once known as manic-depressive psychosis. Three basic forms of the disorder are observed: one in which the resulting dominant psychological state is DEPRESSION, one in which the dominant state is a highly elevated mood, and one in which these states frequently alternate. In all three forms at least one manic state occurs. The mood changes are also far more severe than in other disorders involving mood swings. In the manic phase a person is inappropriately optimistic and grossly overestimates his or her positive attributes, shows speeded movement and speech, undergoes intellectual disorganization, and has pathologically bad judgment. In the depressive phase a person exhibits slowed speech and movements in addition to depression. In either phase it is not unusual for hallucinations, delusions, or both to occur.

Bipolar disorder develops at least once in about 0.5 to 1 percent of the population. The first episode usually takes place in persons in their twenties, and it occurs equally in both sexes. Its causes are unknown but may be rooted in some genetic defect. Stressful life experiences may be contributing factors but do not seem to trigger its onset. In some 15 to 20 percent of people with untreated mood disorders, the condition may be fatal. Lithium salts (see LITHIUM, drug) are a common medical treatment, but side effects of this drug can be severe. Newer drugs such as Prozac and Anaframil have also shown promise. Even without treatment perhaps 85 percent of the persons with the disorder survive, but without treatment most of them will not be fully functional.   LOREN J. CHAPMAN

Bibliography: Caramagno, T. C., *The Flight of the Mind* (1992); Goodwin, F., and Jamison, K., *Manic-Depressive Illness* (1990); Schou, M., *Lithium Treatment of Manic-Depressive Illness*, 5th ed. (1993).

The paper, or white, birch, B. papyrifera (left), grows to more than 30 m (100 ft) tall. The European birch, B. pendula (right), is one of the northernmost of all trees and among the few trees native to Iceland. It is about half as tall as the paper birch. Birches have pendulous male flowers (catkins) and conelike female flowers.

birch

The birches, *Betula,* are deciduous hardwood trees and shrubs that belong to the birch family, Betulaceae. Birch trees and shrubs comprise 50 or more species that are widely distributed throughout arctic regions and cooler parts of the Northern Hemisphere. Several tree species are found in the United States and Canada. The Old World species grow in south and southeastern Europe, Anatolia, the Himalayas, and China.

Birch trees are characterized by a smooth bark that often peels off in thin, papery layers and becomes thick, deeply furrowed, and scaly. Numerous minute male and female flowers are borne each spring on different hanging catkins of the same tree. The solitary erect fruits are conelike and are composed of many minute two-winged nutlets that mature in summer and are shed in fall and early winter.

Birches have attractive foliage and bark and are often used as landscape plants. Among the favorites for planting are the European white birch, *B. pendula,* and its varieties, which have been in cultivation for centuries. A borer insect can cause considerable damage to this species.

The yellow birch, *B. alleghaniensis,* is the most valuable American birch in number, size, and usefulness. Members of this species reach heights of 30 m (100 ft) and diameters of 1.2 m (4 ft), and many live to be more than 300 years old. The yellow birch grows as far south as Georgia, but it flourishes most in the cool, moist, northern soils at high elevations of the eastern mountains. The root system is typically shallow.

The sweet birch, *B. lenta,* also known as the black, or cherry, birch, is found from near sea level in New England, through New York and Pennsylvania, and southwestward into the Southern Appalachians. The young twigs and bark are the major source of oil of wintergreen. Sweet birch's main enemies are a group of fungi, *Nectria,* and heartrots.

River birch, *B. nigra,* is a native of riverbanks, lake shores, and swampy areas throughout the eastern United States. The only southern birch, it is widely distributed along rivers there.

The paper, or white, birch, *B. papyrifera,* is a tree of cold climates. It is primarily a Canadian species and is transcontinental in range. The bark was used by the Indians for utensils, canoes, and wigwam covers. (It is also readily flammable and good for starting fires.) Valuable as a landscaping tree, it is susceptible to the bronze birch borer.

Gray birch, *B. populifolia,* a small, graceful tree, grows mainly in New York and New England but ranges from Nova Scotia, Canada, and southward through Delaware.

Several species of birches form vast forests in far north countries. Dwarfed species grow on mountain slopes or near the timberline. The resin birch, *B. glandulosa,* a shrub common to peat bogs and high mountains in the northern United States and Canada, is suitable for sheep and cattle to browse. The ground birch, *B. nana,* is a favorite food of Alaskan caribou.

bird

Birds, class Aves, are warm-blooded, egg-laying vertebrate animals covered with FEATHERS and possessing forelimbs modified as wings. Among all the vertebrates they are thus the class most strongly adapted for flying, although not all flying vertebrates are birds. BATS are mammals, and the long-extinct pterosaurs (see PTERYODACTYLS) were reptiles. All modern birds are descended from flying ancestors, but a few families, such as OSTRICHES, EMUS, and RHEAS, and some species of otherwise flying families—for example, some GREBES and CORMORANTS—have lost the capacity for aerial flight. Other birds, such as PENGUINS have become fully adapted to flying in another, much denser medium—water.

In addition to feathers and wings birds have other adaptations for flight: a wide keel on the sternum (breastbone) where the large wing muscles are attached, a system of air spaces and sacs throughout the body and bones to decrease the total weight, and various bone fusions and reductions that strengthen and streamline the body.

With more than 8,700 living species, birds have colonized all parts of the world and are found in virtually all habitats: from the icy shores of Antarctica to the hottest parts of the tropics, and from mountains, deserts, plains, and forests to open oceans and densely urbanized areas. Birds range in size from the tiny bee HUMMINGBIRD, *Mellisuga helenae,* of Cuba, with an overall length (including bill and tail) of 6 cm (2.5 in), to the wandering ALBATROSS, *Diomedea exulans,* with a wingspan of over 3.5 m (11.5 ft), and the trumpeter SWAN, *Olor buccinator,* which may weigh up to 17 kg (38 lb).

Birds that have adapted to a life spent wholly on the ground can grow much larger than those that fly. (One fossil of the condorlike *Teratornis* had a wingspread of about 7.6 m (25 ft), but it would have been relatively light compared with its size.) The ostrich, *Struthio camelus,* the largest and heaviest of all living birds, stands almost 2.4 m (8 ft) high and weighs up to 160 kg (350 lb). Several extinct flightless species were even larger. A New Zealand MOA, *Dinornis maximus,* and a Madagascar elephant bird, *Aepyornis titan,* both stood about 3 m (10 ft) tall. The predatory terror cranes, *Diatryma,* of the Eocene were not much shorter.

EVOLUTION

An ongoing argument among various paleontologists concerns the possible descent of birds from the DINOSAURS. A clear evolutionary line of fossils that might settle this controversy has not yet been established. The most familiar fossil bird is the pigeon-size ARCHAEOPTERYX, which lived about 150 million years ago, but the birdlike *Protoavis,* the incomplete skeletal remains of which were discovered in 1986, may have lived about 75 million years earlier. Like *Archaeopteryx,* the *Protoavis* fossil is reptilelike in many ways, confirming the theory that birds are indeed the offspring of reptilian ancestors, but

Archaeopteryx was a *primitive bird with reptilian features, teeth, and clawed wings. It lived during the late Jurassic Period and had a skeletal structure resembling that of a meat-eating dinosaur. Archaeopteryx was possibly capable of weak flight or at least gliding. It also could climb trees by using the claws on its wings.*

(Left) Hesperornis, *an extinct aquatic bird, existed during the Late Cretaceous Period. It has a torpedo-shaped body, webbed feet for swimming, and reptilelike teeth.* (Center) Ichthyornis, *a seabird of the Cretaceous Period, resembled more closely a modern bird than other prehistoric species.* (Right) Diatryma *was a flightless predatory bird that measured up to 2 m (7 ft) in height and existed during the Eocene Period.*

whether or not those ancestors were also dinosaurs is unknown. Both fossil bird species had well-developed wings, and *Archaeopteryx* had other characteristics of modern birds: a birdlike fused pelvis, a furcula ("wish-bone"), and a grasping opposable hallux (hind toe). Lacking a keel on its sternum, *Archaeopteryx* could not fly, although it was able to glide. *Protoavis* had a keel, and scientists believe that it could fly.

One reason why the record of bird evolution is sparse is that, because of their mainly delicate bones, birds have left few fossilized remains. Most of the fossils are of the larger and heavier-boned species, especially seabirds and flightless birds such as ostriches. After *Archaeopteryx*, the next fossil birds to appear are from the Cretaceous Period, some 30 million years later. By then birds had become strong fliers and had begun to move into many environments. Some 35 species are known from the Cretaceous Period of Europe, North and South America, and Australia. Birds continued to evolve, and by Pliocene times most modern genera had formed. During the Pleistocene most of the modern species developed.

CLASSIFICATION
Birds are formally classified as members of the class Aves, subphylum Vertebrata, phylum Chordata, kingdom Animalia. They have feathers, scaly legs, and no teeth (except in a few early fossil forms), with well-developed air-breathing lungs and a four-chambered heart. They maintain a constant body temperature of about 41° C (106° F). Birds reproduce by laying comparatively large, hard-shelled eggs.

The class Aves is generally divided into 32 orders, of which three are known only from fossil forms. By far the largest order is PASSERIFORMES, which comprises more than 5,000 species, a large majority of the birds of the world. These passerines are the most highly evolved members of the class and are characterized by a specialized "perching" foot structure. They are generally divided into six suborders, based largely on the structure of the syrinx (vocal apparatus).

One of the most lasting controversies in bird taxonomy has been the classification of the passerines into families. Some systems divide the passerines into as many as 60 or more families.

EXTINCT AND ENDANGERED BIRDS
All forms of life follow the same pattern. Species develop, then flourish, and eventually become extinct. The rate of this natural process varies greatly and is strongly tied to geological, climatic, and biological changes in the environment. During the Pleistocene Period the dramatic changes in temperature and rainfall and the advancing and melting back of ice sheets resulted in an especially high rate of extinction, perhaps 25 percent for birds during the approximately 2.5 million years of this epoch.

The life expectancy of an avian species is estimated to have been 1.5 million years at the beginning of the Pleistocene but only 0.04 million years at the end, approximately 10,000 years ago. Since 1680 (about when bird records began) that expectancy has dropped to 16,000 years, demonstrating the

The 27 Orders of Living Birds

Psittaciformes
gray parrot

Coliiformes
blue-naped mousebird

Apodiformes
ruby-throated hummingbird

Passeriformes
blue jay

Coraciiformes
carmine bee-eater

Gruiformes
crowned crane

Rheiformes
common rhea

Tinamiformes
variegated tinamou

Columbiformes
victoria crested pigeon

Casuariiformes
Australian cassowary

Anseriformes
wood duck

Falconiformes
bald eagle

Apterygiformes
brown kiwi

T. BOYER

Piciformes
keel-billed toucan

Trogoniformes
collared trogon

Cuculiformes
white-eared turaco

Procellariiformes
gray-headed albatross

Caprimulgiformes
common nighthawk

Struthioniformes
ostrich

Strigiformes
snowy owl

Ciconiiformes
black-crowned night heron

Charadriiformes
ruddy turnstone

Pelecaniformes
great frigate bird

Galliformes
Amherst's pheasant

Sphenisciformes
king penguin

...viiformes
...ctic loon

Podicipediformes
western grebe

(Right) *The flight of a male mallard duck,* Anas platyrhynchos, *involves a semicircular wing motion with two basic movements, the downward and upward strokes. The downstroke, with twisting of the primary feathers at the wing tips, supplies downward and forward thrust, while the upstroke supplies upward and forward thrust.*

(Below) *The skeleton of a domestic pigeon,* Columba livia, *reveals a large breastbone, which supports the muscles that power the bird's wings. The rearward portion of the spinal column is fused to furnish solid anchorage for musculature. The wing bones of the pigeon are similar in structure to those of the arm of a human being.*

(Below) *The large pectoral muscles of a bird pull the wings down during flight. On the upstroke, the supracoracoideus muscles, aided by a tendon riding over a bone, pull the wings up enabling the bird to fly.*

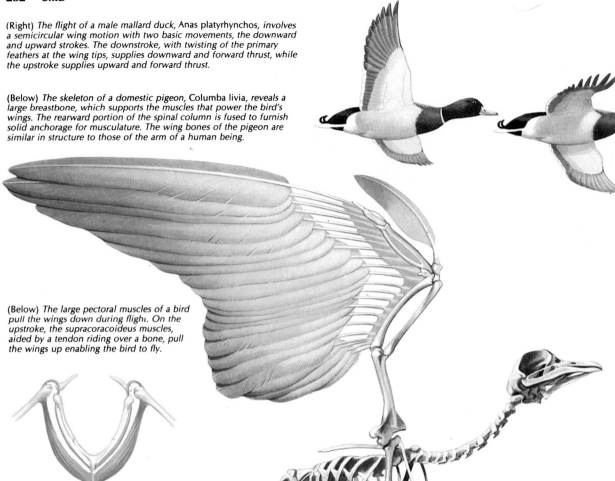

(Below) *A cross-section of a bird's wing bone reveals a hollow cavity crisscrossed with struts that strengthen the bone as well as maintain flexibility. The air cavities make the bone extremely light.*

adverse effects humans have had on the natural environment. Approximately 85 species and 50 distinct subspecies have become extinct in the last 300 years, over half of which vanished during the 1800s and another 30 percent since 1900. More than 90 percent of these historic extinctions have been of island forms, which are particularly vulnerable to human interference.

Extinction, of course, is still partly caused by natural circumstances such as changes in climate and volcanic eruptions, but the most important modern causes are those of humans. These include destruction of habitat (the single greatest); introduction of predaceous human symbionts such as cats, rats, dogs, pigs, and goats; introduction of diseases, for example, avian malaria in the Hawaiian islands; introduction of competitors, for example, foreign GAME BIRDS; environmental poisoning, for example, pesticides and other chemicals; and direct hunting. Although concern about extinctions has increased, and although worldwide efforts are being made to save as many species as possible, human self-interest and local apathy about endangered species will probably continue to cause many birds to become extinct.

STRUCTURE AND FUNCTION

Feathers. Essentially aerial, warm-blooded creatures, birds have been limited in body size and weight by the physical laws governing heat conservation and flight. Thus all flying species are small to medium-sized, compared to mammals.

Feathers serve as a versatile covering for the avian body. They form a smooth surface that reduces friction with the air; furnish flexible but strong structures for powered flight (wings) and steering (tail); act as superb insulation to conserve body heat; and are relatively waterproof, to protect the body. Feathers grow from pits in the skin called follicles. Feather follicles have muscles and nerves that serve to control the feather's position, and it is through the follicles that the feathers receive the blood necessary to growth. The follicles of most feathers are not randomly positioned in the skin but rather are in organized groups (tracts or pterylae) with bare spaces (apteria) between. Fully grown feathers are lifeless structures composed of keratin (a protein also found in scales and hair). All feathers are replaced periodically, usually once or twice a year, by molting, or the loss of old feathers and growth of new ones.

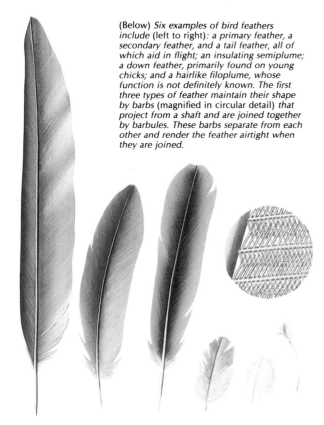

(Below) *Six examples of bird feathers include* (left to right): *a primary feather, a secondary feather, and a tail feather, all of which aid in flight; an insulating semiplume; a down feather, primarily found on young chicks; and a hairlike filoplume, whose function is not definitely known. The first three types of feather maintain their shape by barbs* (magnified in circular detail) *that project from a shaft and are joined together by barbules. These barbs separate from each other and render the feather airtight when they are joined.*

Typical feathers are called contour feathers; they consist of a base (calamus), a central tapering shaft (rachis), and a paired series of thin barbs on either side of the shaft that form the vane. Barbs have a system of interlocking hooks that give flexibility, strength, and substance to the feather. If a vane becomes disarranged, it can be "zipped up" again by being drawn through the bird's bill.

Most of the feathers visible on an adult bird are contour feathers, ranging in size from the large flight feathers on the wing (remiges) and tail (rectrices) to the tiny feathers covering the face.

Other types of feathers include downs (with little or no shaft) for insulation; filoplumes (hairlike feathers) that may be sensory in function; and bristles (with stiff shafts but little or no vane) with several functions, including serving as eyelashes or as filters over the nostrils.

Feathers may be dull or brightly colored, and plain or with complex patterns. Colors, sometimes bright, are also present in unfeathered parts such as bills, legs, wattles, and bare areas of the skin (usually on the head). Birds manufacture their own melanins (brown and black pigments) and porphyrins (some red and green pigments), but most of the carotenoids (red, orange, and yellow pigments) are derived from their food. The blues in birds do not come from pigments but from the internal structure of their feathers, which reflects the blue component of light while the other colors in the spectrum are absorbed by melanins. Greens are usually the result of yellow pigment and structural blue. The many iridescent colors of birds are also largely structural.

Most of the nonfeathered parts of a bird's body are protected by a hard layer of keratin. Beaks are covered by a horny rhamphotheca, which may be divided into plates. The legs and feet are covered by scales. The tip of each toe has a claw, varying in size and shape according to the habits of the bird; in predaceous species, for example, this claw is strong and hooked.

Wings. The structure of the wing is highly modified from the general vertebrate forelimb. The upper arm bone (humerus) and forearm bones (radius and ulna) are elongated. The wrist and hand bones (carpals and metacarpals) are much reduced and fused together into a structure that will support the main flight feathers, the primaries. Three digits are retained; two digits and all claws (except in a few species) are lost. The remaining flight feathers, the secondaries, are supported by the rear edge of the ulna. On both the upper and under sides of the wing, the skin and bases of the remiges are covered by overlapping rows of small feathers, the coverts.

Legs. The structure of the leg is also much modified. The upper leg bone (femur) is present, although this thigh is not apparent in many living birds, being hidden by the body feathering. The lower leg ("drumstick") is long and composed of a strong tibiotarsus and a thinner, sometimes splinterlike fibula. Both the upper and lower legs are well muscled and covered by skin and feathers. The true foot of birds consists of a long, scale-covered tarsometatarsus, ending in a variable number of toes—two in ostriches, three in such birds as emus and CASSOWARIES, some SHOREBIRDS, and some WOODPECKERS; and four in most species. Superficially, the scaly upper part of the foot resembles a leg, and the word *foot* is generally, if incorrectly, applied to the toes only.

Internal Structure. The remainder of the musculoskeletal system is similarly specialized. The skull has a relatively large cranium, and, unlike mammals, both the upper and lower jaws (the bony cores of the upper and lower bills) move when a bird opens its mouth. The large eye has a strengthening ring of bony plates within it. The number of vertebrae varies from 39 to 63 (the larger number in long-necked species), with many in the trunk fused to each other and to other bony elements to form a rigid central framework for flight. Many of the major bones, especially in the wing, are filled not with marrow but with air sacs. The muscles that power the wings, especially on the downstroke, are enormously developed, with an accompanying specialized breastbone, the keeled sternum, to serve as a strong attachment for them.

Other internal anatomical systems of birds are similarly adapted for flight. The respiratory system has not only a pair of lungs but also a complex system of air sacs that branch out from the lungs into certain bones and many parts of the body cavity. Birds also have a proportionately larger heart than mammals, and its beat varies between 60 and 70 a minute in the ostrich to over 1,000 a minute in the hummingbirds. Some birds also have an enlargement of the esophagus (a crop) for temporary storage of undigested food. In many birds, part of the stomach (the gizzard) is enlarged and well muscled for grinding food, which compensates for the lack of teeth and strong jaws: birds swallow grit and small stones that remain in the gizzard to grind hard food.

The reproductive system is completely internal. Males have paired testes that are enlarged and functional only during the breeding season. Most female birds have only a seasonally functional left ovary and oviduct. The oviduct is complex, with glands that lay down albumen (egg white), membranes, and a shell as the fertilized egg (with yolk) passes down it. Fertilization is internal, with copulation an awkward procedure that usually lasts only a few seconds. The male stands on the back of the female and, by bending and twisting the posterior ends of their bodies, the cloacas (the sole posterior openings) are pressed together, and the sperm passes into the female. Only a few species have a male insertion organ.

The cloaca is the end of both the digestive and urinary tracts and thus voids feces and urine together. It also receives and discharges reproductive products from the gonads. Birds lack a urinary bladder to collect metabolic wastes from the paired kidneys. Some, notably seabirds that drink only salt water, have a specialized salt-excreting gland in their heads.

Birds have a unique oil gland (used for feather maintenance) that lies in the skin above the base of the tail. Unlike mammals, they lack sweat glands, so body cooling is largely accomplished by panting. Some species, such as gannets, lose excess heat by fluttering a throat pouch at the base of the bill, others lose heat through their legs and feet, but most simply avoid overheating by seeking shade. In cold weather heat is

normally conserved by a layer of body fat (especially in water birds) and by fluffing the plumage to increase insulation. Some exceptional birds, such as hummingbirds, SWIFTS, and GOATSUCKERS, may become torpid when it is cold.

Senses. Birds, as a class, have the best vision of all animals. Their eyes are relatively large, sometimes weighing more than the brain, and have exceptionally acute resolution. In most birds the eyes have limited mobility, and in OWLS they are immovably set in the skull. Increased mobility of the head upon the neck compensates for this—up to 270° of arc in some owls, but not 360° as is commonly believed. Predatory species have binocular vision, most other birds have partially binocular vision, and monocular vision is found in certain penguins. Color perception in birds is excellent, as might be deduced from the varied colors of the birds themselves.

Hearing is acute, especially in nocturnal birds; but only a few species, such as KIWIS, HONEY GUIDES, and certain VULTURES, have a highly developed sense of smell. In general, the sense of taste is also poorly developed.

REPRODUCTION BEHAVIOR AND COURTSHIP

Birds have a wide variety of behavioral systems for reproduction. Some species are solitary nesters; others breed communally, the assemblies ranging from small, loosely organized groups to closely packed colonies of thousands of pairs. Most species are monogamous (one male and one female in the breeding unit), but some are polygynous (one male, several females), a few are polyandrous (one female, several males), and a small number may be promiscuous (copulation takes place with any member of the opposite sex, without a true pair bond being formed).

The duration of the pair bond is highly variable. In some species, such as prairie chickens, *Tympanuchus,* and some

(Below) *A sparrow's external anatomy is representative of passerine birds, which constitute the largest bird family. The auricular region consists of an ear opening that is covered by feathers. The lore is a space between the beak and eye, and the malar region refers to the cheek of the bird.* (Right) *Several types of feathers aid a passerine bird in flight. Covert feathers are body-contour feathers that cover the quills of the larger primary, secondary, and tail feathers. Coverts also mold the wings and tails into smooth, aerodynamic surfaces.*

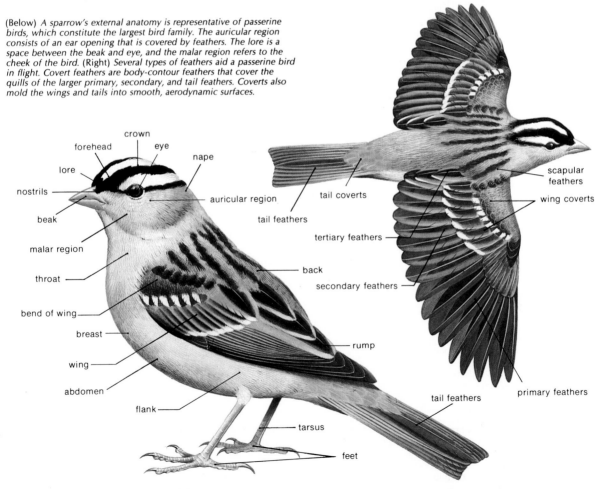

crown
forehead
eye
nape
lore
nostrils
auricular region
beak
malar region
throat
bend of wing
breast
wing
abdomen
flank
tarsus
feet
back
rump

tail coverts
tail feathers
tertiary feathers
secondary feathers
scapular feathers
wing coverts
primary feathers
tail feathers

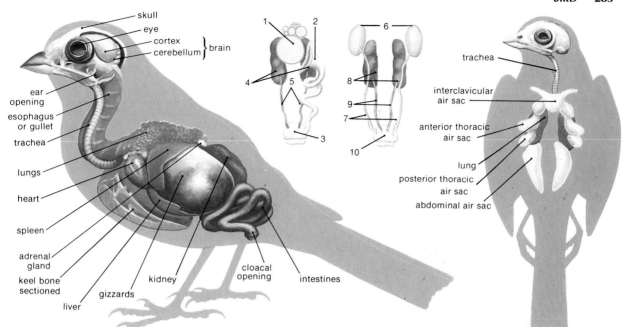

skull
eye
cortex
cerebellum } brain
ear opening
esophagus or gullet
trachea
lungs
heart
spleen
adrenal gland
keel bone sectioned
liver
gizzards
kidney
cloacal opening
intestines

1 2
4 5
3

6
8
9
7
10

trachea
interclavicular air sac
anterior thoracic air sac
lung
posterior thoracic air sac
abdominal air sac

The principal anatomical features of a bird are labeled above. The female urogenital system (numbered parts) *includes an ovary (1), where eggs are produced; one oviduct (2); and a cloaca (3), which acts as a passage for waste and reproductive materials. Kidneys (4) are connected by ureters (5) to the cloaca. The male urogenital sys,em includes testes (6), vas deferens (7), kidneys (8), ureters (9), and cloaca (10). The respiratory system* (above right) *includes lungs that connect to air sacs, which extend into various parts of the body.*

BIRDS OF PARADISE, the male and female meet only for copulation and the females carry out all the nesting duties alone. In others the sexes may remain together only until the nest has been completed and incubation has begun. This period may last for weeks or months, as with most ducks, or for only a few days, as with ruby-throated hummingbirds, *Archilochus colubris,* in which the female then attends the nest and the young alone; or spotted SANDPIPERS, *Actitis macularia,* in which the male is left with the nest and eggs. Most birds remain with their mates throughout the breeding season, until the young are completely raised. Many of these pairs stay together only during a single nesting season, but individuals of some species mate for life, usually remaining together year-round.

The process by which a pair bond is formed is also extremely variable, taking from a few minutes to several months to accomplish. Courtship may be simple, but more often it is relatively elaborate, usually with the male going through a series of activities to attract a female and then establishing a relationship that will allow copulation. Courtship displays may involve stereotyped posturing, specialized movements such as ritualized flights and "dancing," and specific vocalizations by one or both sexes. For any given species, the plumage pattern in combination with the detailed courtship procedures are unique, thus ensuring that pairing birds will be of the same species. Occasionally a bird will mate with the wrong species; the resulting offspring, if any, are usually sterile or maladapted to the way of life of either parent species.

During the breeding season most birds acquire a territory, an area defended by one or both members of the pair. Breeding territories are of four general types: (1) a space large enough to serve the pair and all their needs—courtship and mating, a nest site, and sufficient foraging grounds for both adults and young; (2) an area where all the breeding activities take place but one that is not large enough to supply all the necessary food; (3) a small space, usually just large enough for the nest and its immediate surroundings (normally found only in colonial breeders); and (4) a display ground employed by males, singly or in groups, to attract and mate with fe-

(Below) *A hawk can see up to eight times more sharply than a human, as illustrated here in the two views of a mouse. The eye of most birds is somewhat flattened, with a bulging lens and cornea. Rods, important for keen night vision, and cones, by which the bird perceives detail and color, line the retinal surface.*

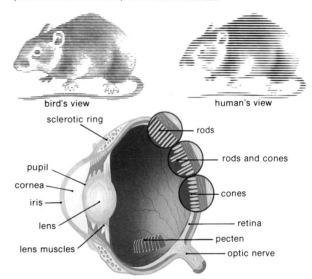

bird's view
human's view

sclerotic ring
rods
rods and cones
pupil
cornea
iris
lens
cones
retina
pecten
lens muscles
optic nerve

(Below) *A woodcock, whose eyes are located on the sides of its head, has a narrow overlapping field of vision both in front and behind, producing limited depth perception. An owl has eyes placed in front and has a wide overlapping field and good depth perception.*

woodcock   **owl**

The courtship behavior of birds varies widely among species. (Left) The male great frigate bird, Fregata minor, puffs out his brightly hued throat sac in order to attract a female that flies overhead.

(Right) A pair of great crested grebes, P. bodiceps cristatus, performs a courtship ritual, known as a penguin dance, in which the couple rises out of the water and presents to each other nesting materials.

(Left) A male European kingfisher, Alcedo atthis, feeds a female with a fish, presented head first, after which the two birds mate.

males. Territorial defense seldom involves actual fighting; instead it is usually accomplished by threat displays, vocalizing, and chasing. Not all territories are used for breeding. Some species defend individual spaces for night roosts, and others establish territories on the wintering grounds.

Birds' nests may be built by either sex, or cooperatively, and may be placed in a variety of locations: on or under the ground, in holes in trees or crevices in rocks, or in trees, shrubs, and other kinds of vegetation. They are usually well camouflaged or hidden from predators or are built in places difficult to reach. Some species build no nest at all, either laying their eggs directly on the gound or in other species' nests to be cared for by the unwitting foster parents.

Nests may take many shapes: simple platforms; open cups; single rounded balls with an internal cavity; woven slings suspended from the tip of a branch or large leaf; or communal nests of huge masses of plant materials, with many egg cavities. They may be constructed of mud, stones, parts of plants (sticks, twigs, leaves, grass, rootlets, bark, or lichens), and animal products (hair, feathers, spiderwebs, snakeskin or shells). The materials may be simply piled up or more complexly woven, sewn, glued, or felted. Some birds, notably swifts, use their sticky saliva either to glue materials to a substrate or to form the entire nest.

Probably the most unusual nests are built by megapodes. They are massive, mounded excavations in sand or soil, with the eggs incubated either by subterranean volcanic heat or by the heat of decaying vegetation buried by the male parent. All other birds that build their own nests incubate by their own body heat.

As a class, birds lay from 1 to about 20 eggs for each nest and may have more than one nest each season. The eggs hatch in 11 to 80 days. Those that hatch quickly usually produce naked, helpless (altricial) young that require long periods of parental feeding and care before they become independent. Species with long incubation periods normally produce down-covered young that can move about soon after hatching and find some of their own food (precocial). The period of time required for young to become independent is variable—from no time at all in megapodes (the newly-hatched young receive no parental care and can fly within hours of burrowing up out of the nest), to more than six months in the larger albatrosses, and probably more than a year in CONDORS.

The average breeding schedule for an American ROBIN, Turdus migratorius, is typical for many songbirds. The nest takes from 2 to 20 days to build; 4 eggs are generally laid, normally 1 a day; the clutch is incubated primarily by the female, for about 13 days; and the altricial young are fed and brooded by both parents for an average of 15 days. When they leave the nest, the fledglings have almost reached their adult body size and are fully covered by feathers, but their wings and tails are still growing, and so they fly poorly and must be cared for

A male American robin, Turdus migratorius, claims territory (heavy broken lin and attacks another male trespasses the boundaries. springtime song primarily serves to warn other male away from his domain.

(Above) *Six types of nest illustrate the wide range of materials used by birds. The tailorbird,* Orthotomus sutorius (left), *sews together leaves with plant fibers and builds a nest inside. The osprey,* Pandion haliaetus (center), *constructs a nest of twigs on top of a tree or in other high places. The penduline tit,* Remiz pendulinus (right), *nests in such trees as the willow, whose branches hang over water. The tit weaves a basketlike nest with prominent entrance, using such materials as plant fibers, grass, roots, seed hairs, and animal fur.*

(Above) *A killdeer,* Charadrius vociferus, *like other birds of the plover family, lays its eggs on a rudely constructed nest (left) of pebbles. The cactus wren,* Campylorhynchus brunneicapillus, *protects its eggs from predators by building a nest (center) on top of a cactus. The ruby-throated hummingbird,* Archilochus colubris, *builds a tiny, bowllike nest (right) of plant fiber, lichen, and spider webs, in which its two chicks are raised.*

and fed by the parents for about another 2 weeks. Because robins normally have two or three broods a year, when the first nest fledges, usually the male parent accompanies the youngsters; the female builds the next nest, or repairs the old one, lays the next clutch of eggs, and incubates them. By the time the first fledglings are in full plumage and have learned to find their own food, the second clutch is ready to hatch, and the male is free to assist the female again at the nest.

NUTRITION

Birds have many behavioral and morphological adaptations to exploit a broad variety of food types. Some species are specialists, concentrating on a single kind of food; most are more general, taking several types and often capitalizing on local or seasonal abundances; and a few birds are wide-ranging in their tastes.

Most small birds are insectivorous. They search the ground, vegetation, and cracks and crevices in bark or rocks for insects, but some, such as SWALLOWS, swifts, and goatsuckers, catch aerial forms on the wing, and others, such as FLYCATCHERS, fly out from a perch to catch one insect at a time (hawking). Many birds are vegetarians most of the year, feeding on

An altricial chick, such as a one-day-old ruby-throated hummingbird (top), is blind, helpless, and often naked. It instinctively opens its mouth in order to be fed by its parents. In contrast, a precocial chick, such as a killdeer (bottom), is born with down feathers and can take care of its own needs from the first day.

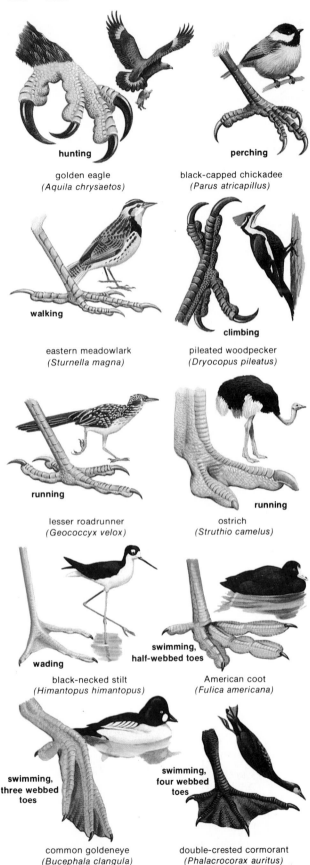

hunting

golden eagle
(Aquila chrysaetos)

perching

black-capped chickadee
(Parus atricapillus)

walking

eastern meadowlark
(Sturnella magna)

climbing

pileated woodpecker
(Dryocopus pileatus)

running

lesser roadrunner
(Geococcyx velox)

running

ostrich
(Struthio camelus)

wading

black-necked stilt
(Himantopus himantopus)

swimming,
half-webbed toes

American coot
(Fulica americana)

swimming,
three webbed
toes

common goldeneye
(Bucephala clangula)

swimming,
four webbed
toes

double-crested cormorant
(Phalacrocorax auritus)

(Left) *The feet of birds serve a variety of functions. A hunting bird, the golden eagle, has curved, sharp talons, which grip and pierce its prey. The black-capped chickadee, a songbird, has perching feet for clasping branches. The walking feet of the eastern meadowlark have three long toes in front and one long toe in back used to balance the bird. The pileated woodpecker has two toes in front and two toes in back, which serve as braces while the bird pecks at trees. Running birds have variously shaped feet; the roadrunner has long, flat toes, and the ostrich has only two long toes. The black-necked stilt, a wading bird, has long legs and widely spaced toes. The feet of swimming birds range from the partially webbed feet of the American coot to the three webbed toes of the common goldeneye and the four webbed toes of the double-crested cormorant.*

seeds and fruits, leaves and buds, and nectar and sap, but even these often feed insects to their nestlings. Some species specialize in digging for their food. Woodpeckers drill into trees for ants and insect larvae; LYREBIRDS (*Menura*) and many gamebirds scratch in the ground for terrestrial invertebrates; and shorebirds probe sand and mud with their bills for small aquatic and marine life.

A few species follow other animals, seizing insects as they are flushed. Cattle egrets, *Bubulcus ibis*, for example, accompany large ungulates, and troops of mixed species follow army ants in the New World tropics. Gulls even follow plows, and the African honey guides lead certain mammals, including humans, to bee trees. Fish are captured from near the surface by TERNS, HERONS, and KINGFISHERS, and from deep water by diving MERGANSERS and GANNETS. Penguins and ANHINGAS actively chase fish under water.

Minute water life, such as algae, diatoms, and invertebrates, is filtered out by the specialized lamellae ("strainers") on the bills of FLAMINGOS and some DUCKS. Large animals, including other birds, are captured by HAWKS and owls, and carrion is eaten by a variety of scavengers such as vultures, CROWS, some gulls, and STORKS.

MIGRATION

Birds have been able to colonize so much of the world, including the most isolated islands, because they have wings. They can quickly move into a region when it is hospitable and move out again when conditions deteriorate. Most of the extremely cold or dry parts of the world contain a few resident species of birds that are specially adapted to the severe conditions; they can withstand the temperature extremes and find sufficient food to remain there permanently. In summer, however, or after rains in a desert region when food is abundant, migratory species move in to take advantage of this resource, and they usually breed there as well. Birds that move back and forth in a regular seasonal manner are termed *migratory*, whether they fly north-south in response to temperature and daylength changes; move up and down mountains (altitudinal migrants); or come to land seasonally to breed, as do many seabirds. Species that move without a regular schedule—usually desert birds responding to rainfall whenever and wherever it occurs—are called nomads.

Migrations can involve short distances, as in altitudinal migrants, or long ones. One famous long-distance migrant is the Arctic tern, *Sterna paradisaea*, which flies each year from the Arctic to the Antarctic and back. Less well-known, but perhaps more impressive, are the small landbirds that make nonstop flights over long stretches of open ocean, such as the warblers that fly from the coast of New England to South America. Long-distance migrants carry fuel as fat deposits in their bodies and usually make stops to feed along the route.

Precisely how birds know when and where to migrate has been intensively studied for decades. Although many questions remain, it is now known that changes in daylength, and perhaps in temperature and rainfall in some regions, can serve as a stimulus.

It is also known that birds use several navigational aids— star patterns, the sun, topographic features on the ground below, and perhaps the Earth's magnetic grid. Weather also affects the particular time a migratory flight is begun and how long the flight lasts before the bird comes down to rest and feed. Like so many other behavioral patterns the urge and ability to migrate is apparently innate, or instinctive, to migratory species.

(Right) *The bald eagle, a hunting bird, has a bill designed to tear apart flesh. The yellow-bellied sapsucker, a woodpecker, has a long bill used to hammer into wood. The black-crowned night heron, a waterbird, has a long, sharp bill to spear fish. The prising bill of an American oystercatcher is used to force open clam shells. Most songbirds, such as the common redpoll, have bills shaped to crack open seeds. The red crossbill's peak is adapted to picking seeds out of pine cones. A slender probing bill of the common snipe is used to pull insects and worms out of trees and soil. The common nighthawk, an insect eater, has a gaping bill to catch insects during flight. The bent beak of a flamingo has teethlike edges used to filter mud and water while the bird eats small plants and animals. A roseate spoonbill's beak is shaped like a shovel to sift aquatic animals from mud bottoms.*

VOCALIZATIONS

Virtually all birds make sounds. They may be nonvocal, as in the whistling of the wings of WOODCOCK, the drumming of woodpeckers, or the bill-clattering of storks, but in most species they are vocalizations, serving a variety of functions. Many vocalizations, particularly the often musical BIRDSONGS of passerines, help to establish and defend territories and attract mates. Quiet "location notes" are used to keep a flock together, as on a migratory flight, or to keep track of a mate. The begging calls of young stimulate their parents to feed them. Alarm calls signal danger and are usually recognized as such by many other species in the vicinity. Other calls may announce the finding of food or may bring a flock together to roost. A few species such as OILBIRDS, *Steatornis*, use calls for ECHOLOCATION in a dark cave, like bats.

Bird vocalizations roughly approximate a language. The different sounds have different meanings, and the way they are produced or uttered will identify the species, and sometimes the individual. Although the sounds a bird can make are largely determined genetically, in many species the typical sequences of notes may be at least partially learned. Some species have even developed local dialects in their songs. Some birds, such as MOCKINGBIRDS, mynas, lyrebirds, and PARROTS, are also accomplished mimics, singing not only their own species' song but imitating sounds they hear around them—other birds' songs, creaking windmills, or human speech.

IMPORTANCE OF BIRDS

Birds are important to humans in many ways. Professional study of birds has led to the formulation of many modern principles in biology, ethology (animal behavior), and ecology. The eggs and meat of domestic forms such as CHICKENS, DUCKS, and TURKEYS are widely used as food staples, and the serious harvest of game species is also significant. Feathers have long been used for decoration as well as for clothing and warmth. Pigeons have been used to carry messages and

The European white stork, Ciconia ciconia, migrates to Europe in summer and to Africa in winter. The western population, which inhabits the Iberian peninsula, flies over the Gibraltar Strait and southward. The larger group of storks, which range throughout eastern Europe, migrate by way of Turkey and the Arabian peninsula to Africa.

tearing

bald eagle
(Haliaeetus leucocephalus)

hammering

yellow-bellied sapsucker
(Sphyrapicus varius)

spearing

black-crowned night heron
(Nycticorax nycticorax)

prising

American oystercatcher
(Haematopus bachmani)

cracking

common redpoll
(Acanthis flammea)

picking

red crossbill
(Loxia curvirostra)

probing

common snipe
(Gallinago gallinago)

gaping

common nighthawk
(Chordeiles minor)

filtering

American flamingo
(Pheonicopterus ruber)

shoveling

roseate spoonbill
(Ajaia ajaja)

lightweight supplies. In agriculture, birds' droppings (GUANO) are a rich fertilizer. On the negative side some bird species can be serious agricultural pests, and some birds may carry diseases. Birds have occasionally been hazardous to aircraft, and huge winter roosts of blackbirds and starlings can be a smelly nuisance.

The most important impact of birds, however, is the role they play in the world's environments. Birds form a major component of all ecosystems and, as such, are vitally important to all forms of life on Earth.   MARY H. CLENCH

Bibliography: Austin, O. L., Jr., *Birds of the World* (1983); Flegg, Jim, *Birdlife: Insights into the Daily Lives of Birds* (1987); Gill, F. B., *Ornithology* (1988); Mead, Christopher, *Bird Migration* (1983); Simms, Eric, *The Natural History of Birds* (1982); Stokes, D. W., *A Guide to Bird Behavior* (1983); Terres, J. K., *How Birds Fly* (1987); Welty, Carl, *The Life of Birds,* 3d ed. (1982).

Bird, Larry

Basketball star Larry Joe Bird, b. French Lick, Ind., Dec. 7, 1956, was College Player of the Year at Indiana State University before joining (1979) the Boston Celtics of the National Basketball Association. Bird, a 6-ft 9-in (2-m 6-cm) forward, was Rookie of the Year (1980), the NBA's Most Valuable Player in 1984–86, and a perennial first-team All-NBA selection. Over 13 years, he averaged 24.2 points, 10 rebounds, and 6 assists per game, and led the Celtics to three championships (1981, 1984, 1986). He retired after playing in the 1992 Olympics.

Bird, Robert Montgomery

The American playwright and novelist Robert Montgomery Bird, b. New Castle, Del., Feb. 5, 1806, d. Jan. 23, 1854, was also a medical doctor who taught (1841–43) at the Pennsylvania Medical College. His earliest plays were farces, but he soon began to write the romantic tragedies for which he is best known. *The Gladiator* (1831) and *The Broker of Bogata* (1834) were written for the American actor Edwin FORREST, with whom Bird had a productive but stormy relationship. When their collaboration ended, Bird turned to journalism and politics. Later he wrote novels, among them *The Hawks of Hawk-Hollow* (1835) and *Nick of the Woods* (1837).

JAMES HART

Bibliography: Dahl, Curtis, *Robert Montgomery Bird* (1963).

bird of paradise

The magnificent bird of paradise, Diphyllodes magnificus, of the forests of New Guinea, has sickle-shaped feathers extending from its tail. Excluding these, the bird is about 18 cm (7 in) long.

Bird of paradise is the common name for about 42 species of colorful passerine birds common to New Guinea, nearby islands, and northeast Australia. They live mainly on insects and fruit. Noted for their bright plumage and long tail, or wires,

they are sexually dimorphic and usually polygamous. During the breeding season the male usually shows full expression of its plumage to the female, who is drab in color; the male's courtship ritual usually includes fluffing out its feathers, prancing, and bowing. The female incubates the eggs.

The greater bird of paradise, *Paradisaea apoda*, is found in New Guinea and the Aru Islands of Indonesia. The male, in full plumage, has a black breast, yellow head and nape, and chestnut tail, wingfeathers, and belly. Its long feathers, separated by barbs, are bright orange-yellow, with red shade near the extremities; the bird can gracefully curve these feathers or press them to its body. The hen has no long feathers and is dull in color. The scarlet red king bird of paradise, *Cicinnurus regius*, is the smallest in the family. It is only 15 cm (6 in) long, with blue legs, green plumes, and white underparts.

Bibliography: Gilliard, E. Thomas, *Birds of Paradise and Bower Birds* (1969).

bird-of-paradise flower

The bird-of-paradise flower, which may be up to 20 cm (8 in) long, is often grown in greenhouses by florists because of its bright colors and striking shape.

The bird-of-paradise flower, *Strelitzia reginae*, is a perennial herbaceous plant belonging to the banana family, Musaceae. This plant has oddly shaped flowers, which are blue and orange and resemble a bird in flight. Bird-of-paradise flowers are native to South Africa.

bird sanctuary: see WILDLIFE REFUGE.

bird-watching

Bird-watching is a hobby that combines the joy of discovery, scientific curiosity, and aesthetic appreciation. Binoculars, a field guide for identification, and patience are necessary. Telescopes and cameras are also useful. With feeding stations, a bird bath, and plants that supply food and shelter to entice birds, bird-watching can be a backyard avocation. The field enthusiast has a choice of local, regional, state, and national organizations, such as the National AUDUBON SOCIETY. Data on bird migration, dispersal, age, and behavior are collected by birdbanders, who must be licensed by the U.S. Fish and Wildlife Service.

Bibliography: Peterson, Roger Tory, *Peterson's First Guide to Birds* (1986); Socha, Laura O'Biso, *A Bird Watcher's Handbook* (1987).

bird's nest fungus

Bird's nest fungus, order Nidulariales, is an easily recognized fungus that grows in open fields and on rotting wood. A hollow, nestlike fruiting body, the basidiocarp, contains peridioles, which resemble eggs and carry the spores when they disperse. The protective membrane ruptures and the peridioles are splashed out of the basidiocarp by rain. Bird's nest fungus measures up to 1.3 cm (0.5 in) in height. Common species are *Crucibulum vulgare* and *Cyathus striatus*.

birds of prey

Birds of prey are HAWKS and their relatives in the order Falconiformes, and OWLS in the order Strigiformes. These orders are not closely related; instead, they share such feeding adaptations as a strong, hooked bill and long, sharply curved talons. In general the falconiformes feed during daylight hours, the owls at night. Therefore, the two groups are often referred to, respectively, as "diurnal birds of prey" and "nocturnal birds of prey."

The order Falconiformes includes several families. The family Accipitridae (more than 200 species) includes hawks, EAGLES, kites, and harriers. Although woodland hawks, *Accipiter*, have rounded wings that provide great maneuverability, they seldom soar; rather, they specialize in preying on other birds. Larger hawks of open areas have broad wings with extensive slotting between the primary feathers. Those birds spend much of their time soaring in updrafts, searching for small mammals and reptiles. The red-tailed hawk (*Buteo jamaicensis*) and the golden eagles (*Aquila chrysaetos*) are well-known examples in North America. Most birds of prey take a variety of species; some, however, are highly specialized. The Everglade kite, *Rostrhamus sociabilis*, eats only snails, removing them from their shells with its pointed upper mandible. The bat hawk of Africa, *Machaerhamphus alcinus*, captures and swallows bats in flight.

The sole member of the family Pandionidae, the widespread, fish-eating OSPREY, *Pandion haliaetus*, has spiny scales on its feet that form a rough surface useful for gripping slippery prey. Ospreys dive to the water and extend their legs just before hitting the surface, often submerging completely while grasping their prey.

The family Falconidae (about 60 species) includes the true FALCONS and their relatives. The more primitive species are forest dwellers. Typical falcons are swift-flying birds of open country, with long, pointed wings. The 15-cm (6-in) long Philippine falconet, *Microhierax erythrogonys*, feeds on insects, although most falcons take vertebrate prey, especially birds, which they capture in flight. On the plains of Africa lives the unique secretary bird, *Sagittarius serpentarius*, sole member of the family Sagittariidae. Moving about the grasslands on its remarkably long legs, this 1-m (3-ft) high hawk preys on snakes, which it beats to death with its feet.

VULTURES feed on carrion. The Old World vultures are a subfamily of the Accipitridae, whereas the New World vultures are a separate family, the Cathartidae, that evolved such feeding specialization independently.

The owls, order Strigiformes, differ from hawks, particularly in having a facial disk of stiffened feathers and soft plumage that muffles the sound of their flight. They also tend to swallow their prey whole rather than tear it into pieces, as hawks often do. Owls have a keen sense of hearing and acute eyesight, which are useful in pinpointing prey in the relative darkness in which many species commonly hunt. They are classified as typical owls belonging to the family Strigidae (more than 120 species), or as barn owls belonging to the family Tytonidae (11 species), although the differences between the two families are minor, and they are sometimes considered one family.   ROBERT J. RAIKOW

Bibliography: Bent, Arthur C., *Life Histories of North American Birds of Prey*, 2 vols. (1958); Cade, Tom, *The Falcons of the World* (1982); Ford, Emma, *Birds of Prey* (1982); Newton, Ian, *Population Ecology of Raptors* (1979); Weick, Friedhelm, and Brown, Leslie, *Birds of Prey of the World* (1980).

Birdseye, Clarence

The founder of the FROZEN FOOD industry, Clarence Birdseye, b. Brooklyn, N.Y., Dec. 9, 1886, d. Oct. 7, 1956, evolved a method for quick-freezing food in the early 1920s. His frozen fish, packaged in small, compact boxes, was introduced by 1925. The company he founded to manufacture his products was sold four years later for more than $20 million and became the General Foods Corp. Throughout the remainder of his life, Birdseye continued to invent. When he died, he owned about 300 patents, including one for a dehydrating technique that reduced drying time for most foods from 18 hours to about 90 minutes.

See also: FOOD PRESERVATION.

birdsong

Any sounds produced by birds may be called songs, including a wide range of alarm, flocking, and other calls. Most biologists, however, use the term *birdsong* to refer to the complex sound patterns produced principally by the most recently evolved order of birds—the perching, or passerine, birds. Many birdsongs have rhythms that are pleasing tones familiar to the human ear, but the sounds of birds are usually modulated so rapidly that no comparisons can be made with musical notes and scales. In fact individual song structures are less significant than the Darwinian, or adaptive, aspects of birdsong.

The songs of perching birds are concerned with the breeding season and mating behavior. For most of the 5,000 species of songbirds this means a male holds territory and acquires a single female, although many exceptions exist to the monogamy rule. Birdsong is heard primarily from the males, each perched somewhere in his territory, and is related to hormonal secretions. The song identifies the species among other species in the same area and, sometimes, the individual singer relative to its neighbors of the same species. These facts have been shown by playback of recorded song.

SOUND PRODUCTION
Songbirds produce sounds in the syrinx at the junction of the windpipe and the bronchi branching to the lungs. Because two bronchi exist, at least two independent sources of sound are possible. It appears that the left side produces more sound than the right. This is reflected also in larger song-control areas in the left side of the brain. Passerines have at least four and sometimes as many as eight pairs of muscles controlling the movements of the cartilage-supported syrinx, in which thin vibrating tympaniform membranes are assumed to generate sound.

Although some species sing only a single sound over and over, in extreme cases individual sounds may number in the hundreds or more. This is true of the American mimic thrushes, including the mockingbird. These repertoires of sounds may be clustered into discrete songs, as exhibited by garden sparrows and warblers, or may be sung in a continu-

Birds of prey belong to either of two orders. Strigiformes, such as the brown fish owl, Ketupa zeylonensis (left), are nocturnal predators that feed primarily on insects, reptiles, and small mammals. Falconiformes are daytime predators and include the golden eagle, Aquila chrysaetos (below), one of the few species that hunt prey as large as chamois and roe deer.

ous string, as exhibited by mockingbirds. The sequences are often highly predictable but not necessarily fixed.

LEARNING

Young birds develop song repertoires in much the same way that humans learn to speak. The young copy the sounds of their parents or other members of their species. After a certain age, however, copying becomes difficult or even impossible. This age may be three months for the white-crowned sparrow; others may retain their copying capability into their first, or possibly second, breeding season.

Although part of the restriction on learning is social, the evidence suggests that the nervous system of the birds is tuned to accept only sounds with certain characteristic features. Swamp sparrows will copy recorded sounds taken from songs of their own species but will not copy sounds taken from songs of their close relative, the song sparrow. Other birds—including the mockingbird, lyrebird, starling, and myna—mimic the sounds of other species.

Repertoires among species that copy only the songs of their species may be remarkably similar among different birds. Often such similarities are locally distributed and are called a dialect. Not all species develop songs primarily through copying adults; some do so through the related process of improvisation.

DUETTING

Particularly common among tropical songbirds, especially mates, is the habit of duetting. One member begins, and the other replies with remarkably precise timing. Examples are the African shrike, New World wren, and Asian jay. The sounds used by each partner are often highly predictable, although the birds may use different sounds in different duets. Duetting among tropical birds seems to be associated with long tenure of territory through the season and with long, perhaps life-long, pair bonds.   R. E. LEMON

Bibliography: Borror, Donald J., *Bird Song and Bird Behavior* (1971); Hartshorne, Charles, *Born to Sing* (1973); Jellis, Rosemary, *Bird Sounds and Their Meaning* (1984); Thielcke, Gerhard, *Bird Sounds*, trans. by John Drury (1976); Walton, R. K., and Lawson, R. W., *Birding by Ear* (1990).

See also: ANIMAL BEHAVIOR; ANIMAL COMMUNICATION; BIRD.

Birkenhead, F. E. Smith, 1st Earl of

Frederick Edwin Smith, 1st earl of Birkenhead, b. July 12, 1872, d. Sept. 30, 1930, was a colorful British lawyer and politician. He commanded large fees as a barrister and, after entering Parliament in 1906, was a leader of the Conservative social reformers. In 1912–14 he was a leading opponent of the Third Home Rule bill for Ireland, but in 1921 he helped draft the treaty establishing the Irish Free State. Between 1915 and 1922, Smith was successively solicitor general, attorney general, and (as a peer, created 1919) lord chancellor in Herbert Asquith's and David Lloyd George's coalition governments. Birkenhead served (1924–28) as secretary for India in Stanley Baldwin's Conservative cabinet.   DON M. CREGIER

Bibliography: Birkenhead, 2d Earl of, *F. E.: The Life of F. E. Smith, First Earl of Birkenhead, by his Son* (1959); Campbell, John, *F. E. Smith: First Earl of Birkenhead* (1984).

Birkhoff, George David

One of the first great American-born mathematicians, George David Birkhoff, b. Overisel, Mass., Mar. 21, 1884, d. Nov. 12, 1944, made important contributions to differential equations, the theory of map coloring (an important aspect of topology), and the restricted three-body problem of classical mechanics. He published his first mathematical work at the age of 18 and received his Ph.D. degree at the age of 23.

Birkhoff taught at the University of Wisconsin, Princeton University, and Harvard University; many of the most productive American mathematicians of the mid-20th century studied or worked under his direction at some time in their careers. Birkhoff was president of the American Mathematical Society (1925) and of the American Association for the Advancement of Science (1937).   H. HOWARD FRISINGER

birling

Birling, also known as logrolling, is a sport in which two contestants wearing spiked boots stand near the opposite ends of a large floating log and attempt to dislodge each other into the water by spinning, stopping, or reversing the log. As a sport, birling dates back to about 1840, when it was played in lumberjack camps in Maine; it soon spread across the United States and into Canada. Public competition began in 1888, and ten years later the first world championship was held in Omaha, Nebr., sponsored by the Lumberman's Association of America.

Lumberjacks had to learn dexterity while walking over floating logs to unjam pileups. This skill was put to use in birling. As a free-time sport, rules were devised, defining a fall as the moment when one opponent dislodges another. Generally, two falls out of three win a match. Trick riding and racing on logs were other diversions in a sport that has dwindled in popularity in the 20th century.

Birmingham   (Alabama)   [bir'-ming-ham']

Birmingham, a city in north central Alabama, is the state's largest and most industrialized city and the seat of Jefferson County. The city proper has a population of 265,968 (1990), and the population of the metropolitan area is 907,810. Birmingham—along with its neighboring industrial city, Bessemer—is the largest iron and steel producer of the South and a commercial and shipping center with a port on the Locust Fork of the Black Warrior River.

Often referred to as the heart of the new South, Birmingham is a growing educational and cultural center. It is the site of the University of Alabama in Birmingham and also of Samford University, Birmingham-Southern College, and several other colleges. A large cultural complex was completed in 1974.

Also located there are the Birmingham Museum of Art, Birmingham Botanical Gardens, Birmingham Zoo (the largest in the Southeast), and Arlington, an antebellum home that housed Union troops during the Civil War. A 17-m (55-ft) cast-iron statue of Vulcan, the Roman god of the forge, overlooks the city from atop Red Mountain.

Iron ore from Red Mountain was first smelted in the early 1860s, after the ore's industrial value was proved. Two railroads converged on the site in 1870. Their junction determined the location of the village that was founded by the Elyton Land Company in 1871. The town was named Birmingham for England's great steel center. For many years the hematitic iron ore, coal, and limestone that fed the city's large steel mills were mined within the area. Local mining eventually declined, and the economy diversified; but since 1974 coal mining has increased.

Birmingham has made much progress toward racial harmony since 1963, when Dr. Martin Luther King, Jr., led civil rights demonstrators through the city.

Birmingham   (England)   [bir'-ming-uhm]

Birmingham, with a population of 993,700 (1988 est.), is the second largest city in the United Kingdom and a major industrial center located in the West Midlands region of England. Situated on fairly high ground averaging about 130 m (425 ft) above sea level, it developed despite its location away from any significant river. The metropolis is enclosed by a ring of industrial towns, for which the central city serves as the commercial and financial center. Following the reorganization of British local government effected in 1974, Birmingham was absorbed into the metropolitan county of West Midlands.

Birmingham's development from a small town in the Middle Ages resulted from the discovery nearby of both coal and iron. The city first acquired a reputation for small hardware goods, known as Birmingham ware, and in the 18th century pioneered in the development of the steam engine. At that time Birmingham was linked by canal with the nation's chief ports. It grew rapidly during the Industrial Revolution and became one of the foremost manufacturing cities in Britain.

Moreover, its central location in the Midlands contributed to its development as a major highway and rail center. The importance of the metal industries has declined in the 20th century—iron and steel are no longer made in the area—but light industries and automobile manufacturing have expanded.

Birmingham has a rich cultural life centered on a university, an art museum, and the City of Birmingham Symphony Orchestra, vitalized in the 1980s by its conductor, Simon Rattle.

Birmingham's early prosperity owed much to its status as an unincorporated borough. Free of the guild restrictions that inhibited growth elsewhere, it attracted entrepreneurs in both industry and science. The Lunar Society, composed of local scientists destined to become world famous, such as James WATT, Matthew BOULTON, and Joseph PRIESTLEY, became an important forum for philosophical and scientific inquiry in the 18th century. Politically progressive, the city in the 19th century played an important part in the development of parliamentary democracy. The notable national political leaders Joseph CHAMBERLAIN and his sons Sir Austen and Neville are identified with Birmingham.   NORMAN J. G. POUNDS

Birmingham, University of

Founded in 1880 as the Mason Science College and incorporated in its present form in 1900, the University of Birmingham (enrollment: 9,016; library: 1,500,000 volumes) is a coeducational institution in Birmingham, England. It has faculties of arts, science, engineering, medicine and dentistry, commerce and social science, law, and education. Undergraduate and graduate degrees are granted in all programs. The Shakespeare Institute, the Barber Institute of Fine Arts, and a hospital are associated with the university, and the papers of Joseph, Sir Austen, and Neville Chamberlain and John Galsworthy's manuscripts are housed in its library.

Birney, Earle

Alfred Earle Birney, b. Calgary, Alberta, May 13, 1904, is a Canadian writer whose work concerns the differences between rural and urban life. His poetry includes *David and Other Poems* (1942), *Now Is Time* (1945), *Trial of a City* (1952), *Collected Poems* (1975), and *One Muddy Hand* (1986). He also has written two novels—*Turvey* (1949) and *Down the Long Table* (1955)—and literary criticism.

Birney, James Gillespie

James Gillespie Birney, b. Feb. 4, 1792, d. Nov. 25, 1875, was an American abolitionist. The son of wealthy slaveowning parents, Birney was educated at Princeton and became a lawyer in his birthplace, Danville, Ky. In 1818 he moved to Alabama. He first attempted to alleviate slavery's worst features by supporting the AMERICAN COLONIZATION SOCIETY. Frustrated in this effort, he sold his Alabama plantation, freed his slaves, and returned (1834) to Danville, where he attempted without success to persuade other planters to follow his example. He then went to Cincinnati, Ohio, where for two years he braved harassing mobs while publishing an antislavery newspaper, *The Philanthropist*. Birney developed a national reputation, and in 1840 and 1844 he was the presidential candidate of the abolitionist LIBERTY PARTY.   JAMES BREWER STEWART

Bibliography: Fladeland, Betty, *James G. Birney* (1955).

birth: see PREGNANCY AND BIRTH; REPRODUCTIVE SYSTEM, HUMAN.

birth control

The practice of birth control prevents conception, thus limiting reproduction. The term *birth control*, coined by Margaret SANGER in 1914, usually refers specifically to methods of contraception, including STERILIZATION. The terms *family planning* and *planned parenthood* have a broader application.

METHODS OF BIRTH CONTROL
Attempts to control fertility have been going on for thousands of years. Some ancient methods, though crude, were based

on sound ideas. For example, women were advised to put honey, olive oil, or oil of cedar in their vaginas. The stickiness of these substances was thought to slow the movement of sperm into the uterus. Wads of soft wool soaked in lemon juice or vinegar were used as tampons, in the belief that they would make the vagina sufficiently acidic to kill the sperm. The Talmud mentions using a piece of sponge to block the cervix, the entrance to the uterus.

Sperm Blockage. Several modern methods of birth control involve creating a barrier between the sperm and the egg cell through use of a chemical foam, a cream, or a suppository. Each contains a chemical, or spermicide, that stops sperm but is not harmful to vaginal tissue. Each must be inserted shortly before coitus. Foams are squirted from aerosol containers with nozzles or from applicators that dispense the correct amount of foam and spread it over the cervix; creams and jellies are squeezed from tubes and held in place by a diaphragm or other device; and suppositories—small waxy pellets melted by body heat—are inserted by hand.

More effective at keeping sperm and egg apart are mechanical barriers such as the diaphragm and cervical cap (both used with a spermicide), the sponge, and the condom. A diaphragm is a shallow rubber cup that is coated with a spermicide and positioned over the cervix before intercourse. Size is important; women need to have a pelvic examination and get a prescription for the proper diaphragm. The cervical cap, less than half the size but used in the same way, has been available worldwide for decades. It was not popular in the United States, however, and in 1977 it failed to gain approval by the Food and Drug Administration (FDA); in 1988, the FDA again permitted its sale. The contraceptive sponge, which keeps its spermicidal potency for 48 hours after being inserted in the vagina, was approved in 1983. Like the diaphragm and cervical cap, the sponge has an estimated effectiveness rate of about 85%. The devices only rarely produce side effects such as irritation and allergic reactions and, very rarely, infections.

The condom, a rubber sheath, is rolled onto the erect penis so that sperm, when ejaculated, is trapped, but care must be taken so that the condom does not break or slip off. A fresh condom should be used for each sexual act. Condoms also help protect against the spread of VENEREAL DISEASES, and, unlike other barrier devices, condoms made of latex do provide some protection against AIDS (see AIDS).

Altering Body Functions. Even in ancient times, attempts were made to find a medicine that would prevent a woman's body from producing a baby. Only within the last century, however, have methods been developed that successfully interrupt the complex reproductive system of a woman's body.

The first attempt, made in the 19th century, was based on a legend that camel drivers about to go on long journeys in the desert put pebbles in the wombs of female camels to keep them from becoming pregnant. Researchers tried to find something that would work similarly in a woman's cervix. The earliest such objects were made of metal and were held in by prongs. Later, wire rings were placed beyond the cervix, in the uterus itself, thus giving rise to the term *intrauterine device*, or IUD. IUDs appear to work by altering the necessary environment in the uterus for the fertilized egg. It was only with the introduction of modern plastics such as polyethylene, however, that IUDs became widely accepted. Their pliability led to simpler insertion techniques, and they could be left in place until pregnancy was desired unless a problem arose with their use. Copper-containing IUDs, and those that slowly released the hormone progesterone, had to be replaced periodically.

Some users of IUDs, however, complained increasingly of the side effects of the devices. The most common problem was bleeding, and the devices could also cause uterine infection. More dangerous was the possible inducement of pelvic inflammatory disease (see UROGENITAL DISEASES), an infection that may lead to blockage of the Fallopian tubes and eventual sterility or an ectopic pregnancy. Studies in the 1980s confirmed this link with the increased risk of infertility even in the absence of apparent infections, especially with plastic IUDs. The A. H. Robins Company, in particular, was ordered in

1987 to set aside nearly $2.5 billion to pay the many thousands of claims filed against it by women injured through use of its Dalkon Shield. By that time only a single, progesterone-releasing IUD remained on the U.S. market, but a copper IUD later became available and other steroid-releasing devices were being planned for issue.

The birth control pill, taken once a day, is the most popular birth-control method among American women. Oral contraceptives are similar in composition to natural hormones, and most pills prevent ovaries from producing eggs. Use of the pill does not prevent MENSTRUATION, however, and usage may even cause periods to be more regular, with fewer cramps and less blood loss. The pill may also protect against such relatively common ailments as iron deficiency anemia (from heavy bleeding), pelvic inflammatory disease, and some benign breast disorders. Long-term statistical studies also point to a lower incidence of ovarian and uterine cancer among women who use the pill. Other studies, however, have linked its use with the increased occurrence of breast cancer. Ongoing studies by such organizations as the American Cancer Society continue to study a possible breast cancer link.

For some users the pill can have undesirable and sometimes serious side effects such as weight gain, nausea, hypertension, or the formation of blood clots or noncancerous liver tumors. The risk of such effects increases for women above the age of 35 who smoke. Pills are obtainable only by prescription and after a review of a woman's medical history and check of her physical condition.

In 1991 the FDA approved the use of Norplant, a long-lasting contraceptive that is implanted under the skin on the inside of a woman's upper arm. The implant consists of six matchstick-size flexible tubes that contain a synthetic hormone called progestin. Released slowly and steadily over a five-year period, this drug inhibits ovulation and thickens cervical mucus, preventing sperm from reaching eggs. The FDA approved the use of Depo-Provera in 1992. This injectable contraceptive contains a synthetic version of the hormone progesterone and is given four times a year.

Avoiding Intercourse. The time to avoid sex, when conception is not desired, is about midway in a woman's menstrual cycle; this was not discovered until the 1930s, when studies established that an egg is released (ovulation) from an ovary about once a month, usually about 14 days before the next menstrual flow. Conception may occur if the egg is fertilized during the next 24 hours or so or if intercourse happens a day or two before or after the egg is released, because live sperm can still be present. Therefore, the days just before, during, and immediately following the ovulation are considered unsafe for unprotected intercourse; other days in the cycle are considered safe. The avoidance of intercourse around ovulation, the rhythm method, is the only birth control method approved by the Roman Catholic church.

Maintenance of calendar records of menstrual cycles has proved unreliable, because cycles may vary due to fatigue, illness, or physical or emotional stress. A woman's body temperature, however, rises slightly during ovulation and remains high until just before the next flow begins. Immediately preceding the release of the egg, the mucus in the vagina becomes clear and the flow is heavier. As the quantity of mucus is reduced, it becomes cloudy and viscous and may disappear. These signals can help a woman determine when she must avoid intercourse to prevent pregnancy.

Permanent Contraception. Couples who wish to have no more children or none at all may choose sterilization of the man or of the woman instead of the prolonged use of temporary methods. Sterilization blocks or separates the tubes that carry the sperm or the eggs to the reproductive system. The man is still capable of ejaculating, but his semen no longer contains sperm. The woman continues to menstruate and an egg is released each month, but it does not reach her uterus. Neither operation affects hormone production, male or female characteristics, sex drive, or orgasm. Tubes may be separated by surgically cutting them, they may be blocked with clips or bands, or they may be sealed using an electric current. The man's operation, or VASECTOMY, is simpler and is usually performed in a doctor's office or a clinic. The operation for women is usually performed in a hospital or an outpatient surgical center and may require a stay of only a few hours. Some soreness and discomfort may be expected after surgery, occasionally with swelling, bleeding, or infection; the risk of serious complication is slight. In the 1980s sterilization became the preferred method among U.S. couples desiring no further children.

Although considered irreversible in most cases, prospects for reversing sterilization for women and men exist when there is relatively little damage to their tubes. It is estimated that as many as 60 percent of reversals are successful (success is measured by a pregnancy). Many individuals, however, may not even be candidates for an attempt at reversal, especially women who have undergone electrocauterization or surgical cutting of their tubes.

New or Experimental Contraceptives. Several new drugs and devices are being tested in the United States. The controversial French pill RU 486 is undergoing trials as a ''morning-after'' pill, to prevent pregnancy. A capsule implanted beneath the skin of the upper arm of the woman that releases the synthetic hormone levonorgestrel over a period of five years is still being tested in the United States, despite its use in other countries and approval by the World Health Organization in 1985 for distribution by United Nations agencies.

Vaccination is a contraceptive approach that has been successful in animals and is undergoing human trials. One vaccine delivers antibodies against a hormone that plays a crucial role in pregnancy. A second works against a hormone in the matrix surrounding the egg, by blocking sperm. Male and unisex oral contraceptives are currently in research.

SOCIAL ISSUES

Birth control, or limiting reproduction, has become an issue of major importance in the contemporary world because of the problems posed by POPULATION growth. Until relatively recently most cultures encouraged such growth. The English economist Thomas MALTHUS (1766–1834) was the first to propose that the population of the world was increasing at a faster rate than its means of support, but 19th-century reformers who in response advocated birth control met bitter opposition from churches and physicians. The American Charles Knowlton, author of a treatise on contraception entitled *The Fruits of Philosophy* (1832), was prosecuted for obscenity, and similar charges were brought against Annie BESANT and Charles Bradlaugh, who distributed the book in Britain.

Nonetheless, the movement persisted, gathering strength at the end of the century from the women's rights movement. In Britain and continental Europe, Malthusian leagues were formed, and the Dutch league opened the first birth control clinic in 1881. An English clinic was started by Dr. Marie Stopes (1882–1958) in 1921. In the United States, Margaret Sanger's first clinic (1916) was closed by the police, but Sanger opened another in 1923. Her National Birth Control League, founded in 1915, became the Planned Parenthood Federation of America in 1942 and then, in 1963, the Planned Parenthood–World Population organization.

In GRISWOLD V. CONNECTICUT (1965) the U.S. Supreme Court struck down the last state statute banning contraceptive use for married couples, and in 1972 the Court struck down remaining legal restrictions on birth control for single people. The federal government began systematically to fund family-planning programs in 1965. Contraceptive assistance was provided to minors without parental consent until Congress ruled in 1981 that public health-service clinics receiving federal funds must notify parents of minors for whom contraceptives have been prescribed. Suits challenging the regulation have been upheld; the government has announced plans to appeal.

Despite the wide availability of contraceptives and birth control information, the rate of childbirth among unmarried teenage girls in the United States rose in the 1970s and 1980s. A major focus of current concern, therefore, is the improvement of SEX EDUCATION for adolescents.

Other countries where the birth control movement has been notably successful include Sweden, the Netherlands, and Britain, where family planning associations early received government support; Japan, which has markedly reduced its birthrate since enacting facilitating legislation in 1952; and the Communist countries, which after some fluctuations in policy, now provide extensive contraceptive and abortion services to their inhabitants. Many of the less developed countries are now promoting birth control programs, supported by technical, educational, and financial assistance from various United Nations agencies and the International Planned Parenthood Federation. A series of World Population Conferences has sought to strengthen the focus on population control as a major international issue.

At present the strongest opposition to birth control in the Western world comes from the Roman Catholic church, which continues to ban the use of all methods except periodic abstinence. In Third World countries resistance to birth control programs has arisen from both religious and political motives. In India, for example, a country whose population is increasing at a net rate of 10–13 million a year, the traditional Hindu emphasis on fertility has impeded the success of the birth control movement. Some Third World countries continue to encourage population growth for internal economic reasons, and a few radical spokespersons have alleged that the international birth control movement is attempting to curtail the population growth of Third World countries for racist reasons. A similar argument has been heard within the United States with regard to ethnic minorities; the latter, however, voluntarily seek family planning in an equal proportion to nonminorities. Most informed individuals and governments acknowledge that the health benefits of regulating fertility and slowing the natural expansion of the world's population are matters of critical importance.   LOUISE B. TYRER, M.D.

Bibliography: Belcastro, P. A., *The Birth Control Book* (1986); Bullough, Vern L., and Bullough, Bonnie, *Contraception: A Guide to Birth Control Methods* (1990); Djerassi, Carl, *The Politics of Contraception* (1981); Filshie, Marchs, and Guillebaud, John, *Contraception: Science and Practice* (1989); Gordon, Linda, *Woman's Body, Woman's Right: A Social History of Birth Control in America* (1976); Kennedy, D. M., *Birth Control in America: The Career of Margaret Sanger* (1970); Knight, James W., and Callahan, Joan C., *Preventing Birth: Contemporary Methods and Related Moral Controversies* (1989); Zatuchni, G. I., et al., *Male Contraception* (1986).

See also: FERTILITY, HUMAN; REPRODUCTIVE SYSTEM, HUMAN.

birth defects

Birth defects, or congenital malformations, are the faulty formation of structures or body parts present at birth. Sporadic, hereditary, or acquired defects may be immediately observed or may become manifest later in life; they may be visible on the body surface or present internally.

Birth defects may be life threatening and require surgical correction, or they may interfere with function or appearance. It is estimated that about 3% of all children are born with major defects; minor defects or variations are estimated to occur in 10% to 15% of births. Malformations may be single or multiple. Multiple malformations that occur in a regular recognizable pattern are referred to as syndromes—for example, the FETAL ALCOHOL SYNDROME sometimes observed in infants of mothers who drank heavily when pregnant. Birth defects may result from the action of genes, chromosomes, or the environment on the developing fetus, but often the cause cannot be determined.

Inherited Defects. Abnormal genes cause a significant number of different birth defects. Some can be identified as a single-gene disorder that is inherited in a simple Mendelian mode, that is, either a dominant or a recessive pattern. For example, lobster claw deformity of the hands and feet (split hands or feet) is inherited and results from the effect of a single dominant gene. A person who has this deformity runs a 50% risk (1 in 2) of bearing offspring who will inherit the gene and will therefore also be affected.

Autosomal recessive inheritance and X-linked recessive inheritance account for the other forms of single-gene inheritance that cause birth defects. In cases of autosomal recessive inheritance, both parents are normal but each carries a silent, or recessive, gene that, if matched in an offspring, causes

the birth defect. Because both parents are so-called carriers (heterozygotes) of the same abnormal gene, they run a 25% risk (1 in 4) of having a child with the birth defect caused by that particular gene. Examples of birth defects inherited in this autosomal recessive manner are TAY-SACHS DISEASE and SICKLE-CELL ANEMIA (see GENETIC DISEASES).

In cases of X-linked recessive inheritance the abnormal gene is located on the X chromosome. The normal mother has two X chromosomes, one of which carries the gene for the abnormal condition; but if her son inherits her X chromosome with the abnormal gene, he will be affected with the condition. HEMOPHILIA is inherited in this manner.

Multifactorial Defects. Many common birth defects do not occur in a pattern that indicates simple Mendelian inheritance. They seem to result from an interaction of genes and the environment, including the intrauterine environment, and each factor includes a number of different hereditary and environmental influences; hence, these defects are called multifactorial. Among them are congenital heart disease; neural tube defects, including SPINA BIFIDA, myelomeningocele, and anencephaly; and CLUBFOOT, CLEFT LIP AND PALATE, and dislocated hips.

Chromosome Number. An increase or decrease in the total chromosome material can cause birth defects. For example, the additional chromosome material in DOWN'S SYNDROME (mongolism) caused by an extra chromosome, number 21, is responsible for the characteristic mental retardation, short stature, and facial appearance. The gain or loss of chromosome material may involve a partial or entire chromosome. The specific birth defects that occur depend on the chromosome involved as well as on the amount of loss or gain.

Environmental Factors. Environmental causes of birth defects include teratogenic (literally, "monster-making") agents and physical abnormalities in the mother's uterus. Certain medications and chemicals as well as alcohol have been suggested as causes of birth defects. It is difficult to establish definitive proof of a drug's teratogenic action, and most available information is based on available animal studies and case reports of malformed children whose mothers all took a certain medication (see THALIDOMIDE). Nutritional deficiencies and medical illnesses such as diabetes in the mother can also be viewed as contributing to an increase in malformations. Recent studies suggest that some substances, such as alcohol and heroin, may also cause genetic mutations or other alterations to sperm, possibly leading to birth defects.

Prenatal Detection. Currently, birth defects due to chromosome abnormalities, some inborn errors of metabolism, and a very few other disorders, including spina bifida and anencephaly, may be detected in the fourth month of pregnancy by a procedure known as AMNIOCENTESIS. This consists of withdrawing a small amount of amniotic fluid and analyzing it for the specific defect for which the pregnancy is at risk. Another procedure used to detect chromosomal problems, called chorionic villi sampling (CVS), involves the use of a catheter to withdraw a sample of the chorionic villi, a tissue that surrounds the fetal sac. Preconception and prenatal genetic counseling is now widely available in the United States for parents to learn their risks of producing a baby with a birth defect (see GENETIC TESTING).   MARYLOU BUYSE

Bibliography: Garell, Dale C., and Snyder, Solomon H., eds., *Birth Defects* (1989); Jones, Kenneth L., *Smith's Recognizable Patterns of Human Malformation*, 4th ed. (1988); Pergaud, T. V., *Environmental Causes of Human Birth Defects* (1990).

Birth of Tragedy, The

The Birth of Tragedy from The Spirit of Music (1872; Eng. trans., 1910) was the first work of Friedrich Wilhelm NIETZSCHE, the German philosopher and spokesman for nihilism. In this revolutionary examination of the background of Greek tragedy Nietzsche sees tragedy as a conflict between Apollonian and Dionysian principles. The Apollonian element reflects the lucidity, tranquillity, and intellectual detachment of the Greek god Apollo; the Dionysian element expresses the dark, passionate, even frenzied qualities of the Greek god Dionysus.   JANE COLVILLE BETTS

Birth of Venus, The: see BOTTICELLI, SANDRO.

birthmark

A birthmark is an abnormal growth or discoloration of the skin that is present at birth or that appears soon after. A MOLE is a usually benign growth, either flat or raised, with an excess amount of pigmentation that ranges from light brown to black. A hemangioma is a flat, reddish area of skin resulting from the abnormal growth of blood vessels close to the skin's surface; the two most common types are port wine stains, involving small blood vessels, and strawberry marks, involving capillaries.

birthrate: see POPULATION.

birthstone

Birthstones are gems that are symbolically associated with the month or zodiacal sign of one's birth and are believed by some to bring their owners good health or good fortune.

In the Old Testament description of the garments to be made for Aaron, the High Priest (Exod. 28:17–21), the breastplate is to carry four rows of three gemstones each; each stone represents one of the twelve tribes of Israel. Various translations of the Bible offer different lists of these stones, and, in any case, what the ancient Jews meant by sardius (in the King James version) was a red stone that might have been ruby, garnet, or carnelian. Topaz could refer equally to topaz quartz or to citrine. Other stones, as well, were identified only by color, so that sapphire and lapis lazuli were often confused, as were emerald with other green stones and diamond with white sapphire or white topaz.

The New Testament names the foundation stones of the New Jerusalem (Rev. 21:19–21), and although the order of the names is not the same as that in the Old Testament, and the list does not include all of the same names, the New Testament list is believed to derive from the description of the stones in Aaron's breastplate.

Breastplate Stones (Old Testament)	Probable Identity	Foundation Stones (New Testament)
Carnelian (sardius)	Red jasper	Jasper
Chrysolite	Serpentine	Sapphire
Emerald	Green feldspar	Chalcedony
Ruby	Garnet	Emerald
Lapis lazuli	Lapis lazuli	Sardonyx
Onyx	Onyx	Sardius (carnelian)
Sapphire	Brown agate	Chrysolite
Agate	Banded agate	Beryl
Amethyst	Amethyst	Topaz
Topaz	Yellow jasper	Chrysoprase
Beryl	Malachite	Jacinth
Jasper	Jade	Amethyst

The gems that have traditionally been used as birthstones are listed below. It may be noted that this list and the New Testament list of foundation stones parallel one another, if the cycle of months is begun with March. The American National Association of Jewelers adopted their own list in 1912, and today many synthetic stones are also used as birthstones.

The stones have long been associated with particular kinds of luck or talent. The wearer of the blood-red garnet, for example, may be sure of fidelity in love. The purple amethyst is Saint Valentine's stone and in addition protects its owner from drunkenness. The aquamarine imparts courage; the diamond, happiness; and the emerald, Venus's stone, love.

Garnet

Amethyst

Aquamarine

Diamond

Emerald

Pearl

Ruby

Peridot

Sapphire

Opal

Topaz

Turquoise

Traditional Birthstones	Jewelers' List (1912)	Synthetic Material	Month
Garnet	Garnet	Dark-red corundum	January
Amethyst	Amethyst	Purple corundum	February
Jasper; bloodstone	Bloodstone; aquamarine	Light-blue spinel	March
Diamond; sapphire	Diamond	Colorless spinel or corundum	April
Emerald; agate	Emerald	Emerald or green spinel	May
Agate; emerald	Pearl; alexandrite	Cultured pearl	June
Onyx; turquoise	Ruby	Red corundum	July
Sardonyx; carnelian	Sardonyx; peridot	Green spinel	August
Chrysolite	Sapphire	Blue spinel or corundum	September
Beryl; opal	Opal; tourmaline	Pink spinel or corundum	October
Topaz	Topaz; citrine	Yellow corundum	November
Ruby	Turquoise; zircon	Medium-blue spinel	December

Bibliography: Kunz, G. F., *The Mystical Lore of Precious Stones*, 2 vols. (1986); Zucker, B., *Gems and Jewels: A Connoisseur's Guide* (1984).

Birtwistle, Harrison

Harrison Birtwistle, b. July 15, 1934, is an English composer whose works concern such basic themes of existence as the brevity of life, rebirth, eternal return, and the inevitability of death. His style shows a fascination with the fundamental elements of music, such as speech inflection, single tones, repeated tones, unisons, and octaves. Birtwistle's best-known works include *Refrains and Choruses* (1957) for wind quintet and the chamber opera *Punch and Judy* (1966–67), a grotesque ritual drama. His opera *Orpheus* (1976) concerns basic problems of creativity.   DIKA NEWLIN

Bisayan   [bi-sy'-uhn]

The Bisayan (Visayan) Filipinos, the largest cultural-linguistic group in the Philippines, occupy the central islands (principally Negros, Cebu, Leyte, Samar, and Panay) of the archipelago. The population of the Philippines is 61,500,000 (1986 est.), of which more than 40 percent are Bisayan. They share the physical features of other Filipinos, with brown skin, straight black hair, slender build, and sparse body hair. Their languages belong to the Malayo-Polynesian linguistic family.

Before the European discovery of the Philippines in the 16th century the Bisayan people had lively trade contacts with other Southeast Asians and with the Chinese. With the coming of Spanish colonial rule (1521–1898) most lowland Filipinos were converted to Catholicism. The economic development of the Bisayan region was expanded during the American period (1898–1946) through the introduction of such commercial crops as sugarcane. Since the Philippines gained independence in 1946, persons of Bisayan descent have played a major role in the national government.

Most Bisayan are village-dwelling farmers whose raised houses are either clustered together or scattered among their fields of rice and maize. Genealogical descent is traced through both parents, and the nuclear family is the primary social group. Many Bisayan still retain some of their pre-Hispanic beliefs regarding environmental spirits, which are often blamed for misfortunes.   DONN V. HART

Bibliography: Hart, Donn V., "Christian Filipinos," in *Ethnic Groups of Insular Southeast Asia*, vol. 2, ed. by Frank M. Le Bar (1975).

Biscay, Bay of

The Bay of Biscay (derived from the Spanish name, Vizcaya) is a triangular extension of the North Atlantic Ocean along the west coast of France between Brittany and the northern coast of Spain. It has an area of 223,000 km^2 (86,000 mi^2) and a maximum depth of 4,732 m (15,525 ft). Its western waters are important shipping routes from Europe to the Strait of Gibraltar. The principal ports on its shores—La Rochelle, Nantes, Brest, Bilbao, and Gijon—are unable to accommodate large ships and are primarily fishing ports. Seas are often rough.

bishop

A bishop (from the Greek word meaning "overseer" or "superintendent") is a member of the highest ranking order of the Christian ministry (see MINISTRY, CHRISTIAN). The word was first applied to the elders, or presbyters, of local churches in the New Testament. By the 2d century the office of bishop had become distinct from and superior to the office of elder.

Bishop, Elizabeth

Elizabeth Bishop, b. Worcester, Mass., Feb. 8, 1911, d. Oct. 6, 1979, was a poet whose work is distinguished by its meticulous attention to the particulars of experience. Her close examinations of nature have much in common with those of Marianne Moore. After graduation (1934) from Vassar College, Bishop traveled (1935–37) in Europe and North Africa; she lived briefly in both Mexico and Key West, Fla., before a long stay, 1951–1969, in Brazil, after which she taught writing at Harvard. She won recognition with her collection *North and South* (1946), and an expanded volume, *Poems: North and South—A Cold Spring* (1955), won the Pulitzer Prize for poetry in 1956. *Questions of Travel* (1965) secured her place in American letters. Her *Collected Poems* appeared in 1969 (National Book Award, 1970), followed by *Geography III* (1976), which won the National Book Critics' Circle Award.

Bibliography: Kaufelt, Lynn, *Key West Writers and Their Houses* (1986); Motion, A., *Elizabeth Bishop* (1986); Schwartz, L., and Estess, S. P., *Elizabeth Bishop and Her Art* (1982); Stevenson, A., *Elizabeth Bishop* (1976).

Bishop, Sir Henry Rowley

Sir Henry Rowley Bishop, b. Nov. 18, 1786, d. Apr. 30, 1855, was an English composer and conductor best known for his stage works. He wrote oratorios, glees, cantatas, operettas, and about 88 operas, and he adapted the operas of continental composers for the London stage. A founding director of the London Philharmonic Society (1813), Bishop conducted many of its concerts. His masque *Fortunate Isles* (1840) honored the marriage of Queen Victoria, by whom he was knighted in 1842. Bishop's "Lo, Here the Gentle Lark" and "Home, Sweet Home" (from his opera *Clari* of 1823) were beloved by Victorian audiences.

Bibliography: Blom, Eric, *Music in England* (1977); Northcott, Richard, *The Life of Sir Henry R. Bishop* (1920).

Bishop, Isabel

The American artist Isabel Bishop, b. Cincinnati, Ohio, Mar. 3, 1902, d. Feb. 19, 1988, was best known for her colorful paintings of working women strolling through New York City's Union Square, which reveal the influence of the ASHCAN SCHOOL of painters on her work. She studied at the New York School of Applied Design for Women and at the Art Students League. Typical of her work is the vivid *Subway Scene* (1957–58; Whitney Museum of American Art, New York City).

Bibliography: Lunde, Karl, *Isabel Bishop* (1975); Newsom, P. P. "Isabel Bishop," *American Artist*, September 1985.

Bishop, Isabella Lucy

Isabella Bishop, b. Oct. 15, 1831, d. Oct. 7, 1904, was an English explorer and travel writer. In 1892 she became the first woman member of the Royal Geographical Society. Her travels took her to North America, Central and Southeast Asia, China, Japan, and North Africa and were recorded in such books as *The English Woman in America* (1856), *A Lady's Life in the Rocky Mountains* (1879), *Journeys in Persia and Kurdistan* (1891), and *Chinese Pictures* (1900).   ROBIN BUSS

Bishop, Jim

James Alonzo Bishop, b. Jersey City, N.J., Nov. 21, 1907, d. July 26, 1987, was a writer and editor known for his novelistic reconstructions of significant dates in history, such as *The Day Lincoln Was Shot* (1955). A reporter for the *New York Daily News* (1929) and an editor and feature writer on the *New York Daily Mirror* (1930–43), Bishop held editorial posts at *Collier's* and *Liberty* magazines from 1943 to 1947. He then turned to historical writing and television commentary.

A 1966 television report moderated by Bishop, which reexamined the findings of the Warren Commission, led to one of his most popular reconstructions, *The Day Kennedy Was Shot* (1968). Other books in this genre include *The Day Christ Died* (1957) and *The Days of Martin Luther King, Jr.* (1971). His autobiography is *A Bishop's Confession* (1981).

Bishop, John Peale

John Peale Bishop, b. Charles Town, W.Va., May 21, 1892, d. Apr. 4, 1944, was a writer principally known for his two volumes of poetry, *Now with His Love* (1933) and *Minute Particulars* (1936). He also wrote essays on Ernest Hemingway and Thomas Wolfe, the novel *Act of Darkness* (1935), and the collection of stories *Many Thousands Gone* (1931). Bishop published *Collected Essays* and *Collected Poems* in 1948.

Bibliography: White, Robert L., *John Peale Bishop* (1966); Young, T. D., and Hindle, J. J., eds., *The Republic of Letters in America* (1981).

bishop's-cap

Bishop's-caps, *Mitella*, are about 12 species of delicate but hardy woodland herbs of North America and northeastern Asia belonging to the family Saxifragaceae. Their leaves are heart shaped and produce small white or greenish flowers whose shape gives the plants their name. These plants are often transplanted into wild flower gardens. The most popular species for this purpose is *M. diphylla*, which produces white flowers in a slender raceme up to 20 cm (8 in) long. Two species of star cactus, *Astrophytum*, are also bishop's-caps.

Bishops' Wars

The Bishops' Wars, in English and Scottish history, resulted from the attempt of King CHARLES I to impose (1637) the Anglican prayer book and enforce rule by bishops in Scotland, the population of which was predominantly Presbyterian. In 1638 the Scots vowed in the National Covenant to restore Presbyterianism (see COVENANTERS), and an assembly of the Scottish church formally ended rule by bishops. Charles led an English army into Scotland in 1639, but his own military weakness forced him to accept the Treaty of Berwick recognizing Scottish demands. In 1640, Charles called the Short Parliament to raise money for a new war. Although it refused to grant him the funds, he challenged the Scots anyway. They promptly invaded and occupied much of northern England. By the Treaty of Ripon (October 1640) Charles agreed that the Scottish army would remain on English soil and receive payments until a final peace was concluded. To obtain the funds with which to pay the Scots the king had to convene the LONG PARLIAMENT, thus setting in motion the events that led to the ENGLISH CIVIL WAR.

Bibliography: Mathew, David, *Scotland under Charles I* (1955; repr. 1977); Mullan, D., *The Episcopacy in Scotland* (1986); Wedgwood, C. V., *The Great Rebellion: The King's Peace, 1637–1641* (1955).

Bismarck

Bismarck is the capital city of North Dakota. Situated on the Missouri River in the south central part of the state, it has a population of 49,256 (1990) and is the seat of Burleigh County. Bismarck serves as a trade and shipping point for an area of large mechanized farms. It is the administrative center for the nearby Williston oil reserves and has a livestock market and some manufacturing. The city is modern and spacious, and its state capitol building, the Skyscraper of the Prairies (built 1932), is a striking landmark. Also of interest at the capitol is the North Dakota State Museum. Because of its site on a natural ford of the Missouri River, Bismarck served as an early steamboat port. The city grew when the railroad arrived in 1873. Bismarck became the capital of the Dakota Territory in 1883 and the capital of North Dakota six years later. It was named for German chancellor Otto von Bismarck in the hope of encouraging German investment in the railroad.

Bismarck, Otto von   [biz'-mahrk]

The Prussian statesman Otto von Bismarck, sometimes called the "Iron Chancellor," was the architect of German unification and the arbiter of European power politics in the second half of the 19th century.

Early Life. Bismarck was born at Schönhausen in Brandenburg on Apr. 1, 1815. His father came of the old Prussian nobility, his mother from the upper bourgeoisie. Distaste for the study of law and bureaucracy caused Bismarck to turn to management of the family estates in Brandenburg. There he was converted to the fundamentalist views of the Lutheran pietists.

During the Revolutions of 1848, Bismarck gained political notice in Prussia as an extreme reactionary who supported suppression of revolt and continued Austrian leadership in Germany. As Prussian minister to the German Confederation in Frankfurt (1851–59), he adopted the independent line of *realpolitik*, backing a policy based on Prussian interests, without regard for ideology, or humanitarianism. He now supported the Zollverein against Austria, favored cooperation with NAPOLEON III of France, and opposed intervention in the internal affairs of other states in the interest of legitimate sovereigns. After briefly representing Prussia at Saint Petersburg and Paris he was summoned home to become (Sept. 22, 1862) minister president and foreign minister for the Prussian king (later German emperor) WILLIAM I.

Unification. After proclaiming the policy of "iron and blood," Bismarck defied the Prussian Chamber of Deputies, which was locked in a constitutional conflict with the king, by implementing army reforms, administering without an approved budget, and following an independent foreign policy. His diplomacy brought victorious wars with Denmark (over SCHLES-

Otto von Bismarck brought about the unification of Germany through a policy of "blood and iron" and directed the affairs of the new German Empire from 1871 to 1890. In this 1889 cartoon, Bismarck is pictured as being outraged to find a civilian in his military cabinet.

WIG-HOLSTEIN, 1864) and Austria (the SEVEN WEEKS' WAR of 1866), as a result of which the chamber passed an indemnity bill (in effect forgiving Bismarck's constitutional transgressions) and voted past budgets. With Austria excluded by force from Germany the North German Confederation was formed (July 14, 1867) under Prussian control. Under the constitution of the new state the Prussian king retained control of the army and policy-making, and the chancellor (Bismarck) was responsible only to him. The Bundesrat (federal council) represented the interests of the separate states, while in the parliament, or REICHSTAG, universal adult male suffrage (which Bismarck had discussed with the socialist Ferdinand LASSALLE) was instituted.

In 1870, Bismarck's backing of a Hohenzollern prince as candidate for the Spanish throne, coupled with his inflammatory editing of the Ems Dispatch (a message from William I to Napoleon III), had the desired effect of provoking France into the FRANCO-PRUSSIAN WAR. France was rapidly defeated, the German Empire (including the southern German states) was proclaimed at Versailles on Jan. 18, 1871, and Bismarck was named prince and German chancellor. The 1867 constitution was retained, and Bismarck also maintained civilian control over the army with William. He was thus able to block preventive war in the following years.

Imperial Chancellor. Bismarck's foreign policy was now directed at maintaining and strengthening the power of the German Empire, which he saw as satiated territorially. Its security was ensured by marshaling its political and diplomatic resources in Europe and by isolating France diplomatically. When the Three Emperors' League (1873) with Russia and Austria disintegrated as a result of rivalry in the Balkans, Bismarck sought to mediate as an "honest broker" at the Congress of Berlin (1878; see BERLIN, CONGRESS OF). Increasing Russian hostility brought—against William's wishes—the Dual Alliance with Austria (1879), which became the TRIPLE ALLIANCE when Italy joined it in 1882. Bismarck, however, sought to tie Russia to this alliance by reviving the Three Emperors' League (1881–87) and through the Reinsurance Treaty (1887–90). He also gained British cooperation.

Domestically in alliance with the National Liberals from 1867 to 1877, Bismarck extended the powers of the imperial government, adopted laissez-faire economic policies, and fought the political power of the Roman Catholic church in the KULTURKAMPF. The growth of the Catholic Center party and the challenges created by an economic depression (1873–96) brought a break with the liberals and the abandonment of laissez-faire. With Conservative, intermittent Center, and some remnants of National Liberal support, he embarked upon a policy of protective tariffs, suppression of the Social Democrats under August BEBEL, and pioneering social welfare measures, including insurance against illness, accident, and old age. Increasing socialist strength and the desire of the new emperor, WILLIAM II, to conciliate his people brought Bismarck's dismissal on Mar. 18, 1890. Until his death on July 30, 1898, he devoted his time to attacking his successors and dictating his savage reminiscences (1898; trans. by A. J. Butler as *Bismarck, the Man and the Statesman*, 1898).

Bismarck unified Germany and maintained European peace for a generation, but he also perpetuated the obsolete dominance of the Prussian landed aristocracy (JUNKERS) and upper middle class, as well as a tradition of intolerance of partisan and personal dissent. Under William II, Bismarck's alliance system (with crucial modifications) contributed to World War I and the collapse of the German Empire.

FREDERIC B. M. HOLLYDAY

Bibliography: Crankshaw, Edward, *Bismarck* (1981); Eyck, Erich, *Bismarck and the German Empire*, 3d ed. (1968); Gall, Lothar, *Bismarck*, 2 vols. (1986); Hollyday, Frederic B. M., *Bismarck* (1970); Stern, Fritz, *Gold and Iron: Bismarck, Bleichroder and the Building of the German Empire* (1977).

See also: GERMANY, HISTORY OF.

Bismarck Archipelago

The Bismarck Archipelago is an island group in the southwest Pacific that comprises three districts of PAPUA NEW GUINEA. The group includes NEW BRITAIN (the largest island), NEW IRELAND, and Lavongai and such smaller groups as the ADMIRALTY, Duke of York, and Vitu islands. The total area is about 49,700 km^2 (19,200 mi^2), and the highest mountains reach 2,300 m (7,546 ft). The population is estimated at 314,308 (1980). Discovered in 1616, the islands were annexed by Germany in 1884 and named for the German chancellor Otto von Bismarck.

The major islands are volcanic and mountainous, but about 100 small ones are low coral atolls. They are hot and humid. Coconut and cacao trees produce commercial crops, but the people, mostly MELANESIANS, subsist on rice, bananas, root crops, and fish. Pearls are found, and gold and copper are mined. Rabaul (1980 pop., 14,973), on New Britain, is the main town.

Germany held the islands from 1884 to 1914. In 1920 the League of Nations mandated them to Australia. They were occupied by Japan during World War II, after which Australia administered them as part of the Trust Territory of New Guinea until 1975; at that time Papua New Guinea became independent.

bismuth   [biz'-muhth]

The chemical element bismuth is a soft, brittle, highly lustrous metal belonging to the same group in the periodic table as arsenic, Group VA. Its symbol is Bi, its atomic number is 83, and its atomic weight is 208.9806. The discoverer of the element is unknown, as is the origin of its name. No record exists of its use in ancient times, but Europeans had become aware of its existence by the Middle Ages.

The average abundance of bismuth in the Earth's crust is about 0.00002%. It is most commonly found as an oxide, sulfide, or carbonate in silver, lead, zinc, and tin mineral deposits. The metal is a by-product of the smelting of these ores.

Bismuth metal has a melting point of 271° C (520° F) and a boiling point of 1,560° C (2,840° F). On freezing, molten bismuth expands 3.3% by volume, a property shared by only one other element, gallium. Bismuth forms compounds in the +3 and +5 oxidation states; the +3 state is the more stable of the two. The metal dissolves in nitric acid to form Bi(NO$_3$)$_3$, which on controlled hydrolysis produces bismuth subnitrate, BiO(NO$_3$). Other mixed oxide salts of bismuth are similarly named.

The very low toxicity of ordinary bismuth salts permits their use in the cosmetic and pharmaceutical industries. An important application is the use of the complex salt bismuth phosphomolybdate as an industrial catalyst in the synthesis of acrylonitrile, an intermediate product in the manufacture of acrylic fibers and various plastic products.   PHILIP C. KELLER

Bibliography: Cotton, F. A., and Wilkinson, Geoffrey, *Advanced Inorganic Chemistry* (1980).

bison   [by'-suhn]

The massive American bison, B. bison, is aggressive and easily angered. Before combat, a bull competes with other bulls in roaring the loudest.

A bison is either of two existing species of the wild cattle genus *Bison*. One, commonly but incorrectly known as the buffalo, is the American bison. The other, the European species, is the wisent.

The bull of the American buffalo, *Bison bison*, may weigh more than 900 kg (about 2,000 lb) and stand more than 1.9 m (6 ft) high. The massive head and forequarters are covered with long hair, and the body slims down toward the hindquarters, which are covered with shorter hair. The female of the species is somewhat smaller. Both sexes have horns, but those of the male are more massive. During the breeding season, July and August, bulls leave their bachelor groups and mingle with the cow-calf herds. The strongest bulls tend individual cows until copulation is completed. A single calf is born after a gestation period of nine months.

The bison was a principal resource of the Plains Indians, furnishing them with food, skins for shelter and boats, bones for tools and utensils, and "buffalo chips" (dung) for fuel.

Few wild animals have undergone a more devastating encounter with humans than the bison. The grasslands from the Mississippi River to the Rocky Mountains were the home of 30 million prairie bison when white settlers first arrived. These numbers were reduced to about 500 near the end of the last century, and then slowly increased to an estimated 35 to 50 thousand on refuges and ranches today.

The European bison, *Bison bonasus*, known as the wisent, may weigh up to 1,000 kg (about 2,200 lb) and stand more than 2 m (6 ft 1 in) high. In comparison with the American bison, the wisent has longer legs and a smaller head with longer horns. Lacking the shaggy coat of the American bison, the wisent appears more oxlike.

The wisent inhabits woodlands and feeds on grasses, ferns, leaves, and tree bark. At one time the wisent ranged from western Europe to Siberia. The destruction of the forests led to the decline of the bison population in Europe. On the verge of extinction in the early 1900s, the wisent is no longer endangered; captive breeding has been successfully used to increase the dwindling population. Herds of wild wisent composed of approximately 1,500 individuals now live in Poland and Belarus.   HARVEY L. GUNDERSON

Bissau [bi-sow']

Bissau (1988 est. pop., 125,000) is the chief port and capital of Guinea-Bissau, on the west coast of Africa. It was established by the Portuguese in 1687 as a fortified post.

Bisson, Louis and Auguste [bee-sohn']

Louis Auguste Bisson, 1814–76, and **Auguste Rosalie Bisson**, 1820–1900, were brothers and partners in photography in Paris. There, in 1841, they opened a studio for portrait DAGUERREOTYPES. By the end of that decade their studio had become a popular meeting place for prominent artists and authors, whose portraits were among the thousands made by the Bissons. The brothers also daguerreotyped all the members of the National Assembly—over 900 portraits, which were lithographed and distributed throughout France.

From 1851, the Bissons used F. S. ARCHER's new collodion process, rather than daguerreotypes, to make landscape and architectural photographs, for which they became famous. Official photographers for Napoleon III, they accompanied him on a trip to the Alps in 1860 during which Auguste made the first photographs from the summit of Mont Blanc.
                                        PETER GALASSI

Bisutun: see BEHISTUN.

bit, computer

The word *bit* is an abbreviation for binary digit, one of the two digits (0 or 1) used in a system of BINARY NUMBERS. Since components of digital computers typically are two-state devices, the bit is the elementary unit of information stored by a COMPUTER. Computers represent all data, including numbers and alphabetic text, as sequences of bits. A sequence of eight bits is called a BYTE.   SUSAN OWICKI AND ELLIOTT ORGANICK

Bithynia [bi-thin'-ee-uh]

Bithynia was a region of northwest Anatolia bordering on the present-day Sea of Marmara, the Bosporus, and adjacent Black Sea coastlands. So situated, it occupied a strategic position as a passage area between Europe and inner Anatolia. It was dominated by the Sangarius River and its tributaries, which both watered the fertile agricultural lands and made possible easy communications. One of the immigrating tribal groups in the early first millennium BC, the Indo-European Thracian Bithynians, gave their name to the territory.

Never much affected by Phrygian or Persian rule, Bithynia survived into Hellenistic times ruled by a local dynasty. Between 279 and 74 BC Bithynia stabilized itself internally while shifting alliances and warring with powerful neighbors—for example, PERGAMUM. King Nicomedes I (r. 279–250 BC) invited the warlike Celts, who subsequently were settled in GALATIA, into Anatolia as mercenary allies, thereby inciting turbulent conditions in the country for many years thereafter. When Nicomedes IV died in 74 BC, he willed Bithynia to Rome. This led to the Third Mithradatic War (74–63) when MITHRADATES VI of PONTUS attempted unsuccessfully to prevent the Roman annexation of Bithynia. POMPEY THE GREAT organized Bithynia and Pontus into a single Roman province c.65–63 BC. PLINY THE YOUNGER, who was special commissioner there (AD 111–13), reported to Emperor Trajan that many Christians were in Bithynia.   LOUIS L. ORLIN

Bibliography: Magie, David, *Roman Rule in Asia Minor*, 2 vols. (1950; repr. 1975).

Bitola [bee'-toh-luh]

Bitola (1991 pop., 122,173), a city in the former Yugoslav republic of Macedonia, is situated in the extreme south, close to the border with Greece. A market center for the adjacent fertile plain, Bitola is also an industrial city. The site of the ancient Heraclea Lyncestis, founded by Philip II of Macedonia (r. 359–336 BC), is nearby. First mentioned in the 10th century, Bitola was a major commercial center during the period (1382–1913) of Turkish rule. It was badly damaged during World War I but retains some of its Muslim heritage.

bittern

The bittern is any of 12 species of wading birds closely related to the herons but generally with shorter legs, necks, and bills. Many have brownish bodies with dark, longitudinal stripes that blend with the tall grasses of their marshland habitat. They feed on small aquatic animals and nest on the ground; three to six eggs are laid. The American bittern, *Botaurus lentiginosus*, when approached, may stand upright with its bill pointed to the sky, using its coloration for concealment. At such times its neck may undulate in imitation of windblown grass. It is about 75 cm (30 in) long, the size varying somewhat but averaging a little smaller than the similarly marked great bittern, *B. stellaris*, of the Old World. Quite different in size and plumage is the boldly patterned least bittern, *Ixobrychus exilis*, of the Americas, 30 cm (12 in) long, black above and

The American bittern, B. lentiginosus (left), is twice the size of the least bittern, I. exilis (right). They are the only bitterns found in the United States. The American bittern has an explosive mating cry that may be heard 1 km (0.6 mi) away. Because of its loud call, it is also known as "thunder pumper" or "stake driver."

light below, with conspicuous buff wing-patches. Its Old World equivalent is the little bittern, *I. minutus*. Bitterns are classified in the family Ardeidae, order Ciconiiformes.

WILLIAM F. SANDFORD

bitterroot

Bitterroot, *Lewisia rediviva*, is a herbaceous perennial plant in the family Portulacaceae with a fleshy edible root, a rosette of leaves, and short-stalked white or rose flowers. The bitterroot grows in the gravelly foothills of the Rockies and other western mountains of the United States. It is the state flower of Montana.

JANE PHILPOTT

bitters

Bitters are alcoholic extracts of bitter roots and barks flavored with herbs and spices. They are often used to give a finishing touch to dry drinks such as aquavit or to cocktails. They are considered aids to digestion by stimulating the secretion of various digestive juices. The bitter taste is supplied by orange peel, gentian root, rhubarb root, cinchona, quinine, and quassia, and the flavor is supplied by caraway, anise, juniper, chamomile, cloves, and other herbs and spices. The best-known bitters are angostura aromatic bitters, created in the 1820s as an appetite enhancer and general cure-all by a German physician in the army of Simón Bolívar. He blended his first batch in the city of Angostura (now Ciudad Bolívar), Venezuela.

ARTHUR O. TUCKER

bittersweet

Bittersweet is the common name for two species of *Celastrus* in the small woody plant family Celastraceae, as well as for *Solanum dulcamara* in the very large and economically important, mostly herbaceous plant family Solanaceae. Both species of *Celastrus* are climbing, deciduous, woody vines best known for their clusters of small colorful fruit. The dull-orange fruit consists of capsules that split open after a frost, exposing scarlet, flesh-coated seeds. *Celastrus scandens* grows in moist thickets and along the streams of eastern North America. Although *Celastrus orbiculatus* is native to eastern Asia and has not been cultivated in North America, it has been naturalized from Massachusetts southward. The stems of both species of *Celastrus* bearing the showy, orange fruit with red seeds are frequently used in dried arrangements in winter. The European red-berried bittersweet, *Solanum dulcamara*, is a perennial vine that is woody only near the ground. Its pale violet, blue, or white flowers are similar to those of the potato and eggplant, which are also members of the genus *Solanum*. This bittersweet has a red, tomatolike berry that, like other parts of the plant, is poisonous. *Solanum dulcamara* is not usable for dried arrangements.

JANE PHILPOTT

The European red-berried bittersweet, S. dulcamara, *is a poisonous member of the nightshade family. Naturalists who dared taste the toxic berry found it to be sweet, then extremely bitter.*

bitumen [bi-too'-min]

In geology and industry, bitumen is a common term applied to various mixtures of naturally occurring solid or liquid hydrocarbons, excluding coal. Historically, however, the term is most often applied to the asphalts (see TAR, PITCH, AND ASPHALT). The residues obtained from the refining of petroleum may also be called bitumen, particularly those soluble in carbon disulfide. Bituminous rock, or rock asphalt, is mined commercially and used for paving, roofing, and the production of varnishes, paints, and stains.

bituminous coal [bi-too'-min-uhs]

Bituminous COAL, or "soft coal," is the most common kind of coal, midway between lignite and anthracite in degree of metamorphic change from the original plant materials. Technically defined as exceeding 6,040 cal/g (11,000 Btu/lb) in heating value, bituminous coal contains less than 86 percent "fixed" carbon, calculated on a dry basis. In the United States bituminous coal is mined in the interior basins and Appalachian Basin and is used mostly for producing COKE, essential for reduction of iron ore, and for generating electrical power (unless prohibited because of sulfur content or other impurities).

JAMES M. SCHOPF

bivalve

Bivalves are members of a large class of invertebrate animals in the phylum Mollusca (known as the class Bivalvia or Pelecypoda, which means "hatchet-foot"). Representative bivalves include CLAMS, MUSSELS, OYSTERS, and SCALLOPS. They have a flattened body enclosed by two shells, or valves, hinged in the back, as well as a strong muscular foot for digging. The head is either reduced in size or is missing altogether.

Bivalves are mostly sedentary filter feeders and are found in marine environments in shallow water and intertidal zones. A few live in fresh water, and some live attached to rocks or other objects by means of strong threads called byssus threads. Still other bivalves, such as the scallop, are capable of swimming relatively fast. Most bivalves are divided into separate sexes, although some are hermaphroditic. Edible bivalves such as clams, oysters, scallops, and mussels are valuable commercially and are "farmed."

S. C. REINGOLD

Bibliography: Purchon, R. D., *The Biology of the Mollusca*, 2d ed. (1977); Quayle, D. B., and Newkirk, C. F., *Farming Bivalve Molluscs* (1989); Vokes, Harold E., *Genera of the Bivalvia*, rev. ed. (1987).

Bizerte [bi-zur'-tee]

Bizerte (Binzerte, Banzart) is the fourth-largest city in Tunisia and the northernmost town in Africa. A port city located in the Northern Tell region at Cap Blanc on the Mediterranean coast, it is about 72 km (45 mi) northwest of Tunis. Its large harbor consists of an outer Mediterranean harbor protected by breakwaters, the Bay of Sebra, and Lake Bizerte. The city has a population of 94,509 (1984). Iron ore, phosphates, lead, and zinc—mined to the southwest of the city—are processed in Bizerte for export. Oil refineries, cement plants, and steel mills are located in the city, and fishing and fish canning are also important.

Bizerte was the site of the ancient city Hippo Zarytus, 65 km (40 mi) northwest of the Phoenician city of Carthage. Bizerte was taken by the Arabs in the 7th century. The French took control in 1881, restored the harbor in 1895, and established a large naval base there. The base remained until 1963.

Bizet, Georges [bee-zay']

Georges Bizet, b. Oct. 25, 1838, d. June 3, 1875, was a great French composer best known for his opera CARMEN. His parents were musicians, and he showed musical talent at an early age. Shortly before his tenth birthday Bizet entered the Paris Conservatory, where he studied theory with Pierre

Georges Bizet, a 19th-century French composer, is best known for his popular operatic masterpiece Carmen. Bizet composed several operas, a symphony, and many other musical works.

Joseph Guillaume Zimmerman and, occasionally, with Charles Gounod and composition with Jacques Halévy. His earliest known compositions were written at the age of 12; his first published works date from 1854. In 1857, Bizet's cantata *Clovis et Clotilde* won the Prix de Rome. In December of that year he went to Rome, where he remained until July 1860. Despite the financial security of these years, Bizet began to have doubts about his talent. He was also afflicted by chronic throat trouble, which he endured for the rest of his life. He completed only three compositions between 1857 and 1860.

Bizet's first important opera, *The Pearl Fishers*, was performed without success in 1863. In 1867 he was engaged to Geneviève Halévy, the daughter of his former teacher. They married in 1869 and had a son, Jacques.

Late in 1867, Bizet's new opera, *The Fair Maid of Perth,* was successful but had only 18 performances. Another opera, *Djamileh*, failed in 1872, as did the production of Alphonse DAUDET's drama *L'Arlésienne* (The Girl from Arles), with music by Bizet. His masterpiece, *Carmen*, composed in 1873–74 and produced in 1875, was poorly received, although it ran for 48 performances. Bizet's depression was renewed by the disappointment, and his throat ailment was aggravated. He died a few hours after the 31st performance of *Carmen*.

Besides operas, Bizet wrote piano pieces, songs, orchestral music, and choral music. His fame, however, rests predominantly on *Carmen*, an early Symphony in C Major, the music to *L'Arlésienne*, and a suite for piano duet, *Jeux d'enfants* (Children's Games). He projected or began many works but completed few and even destroyed some. His style incorporates long melodic lines influenced by Gounod and classical form inspired by Mozart and Beethoven.   WILLIAM HAYS

Bibliography: Cooper, M., *Georges Bizet* (1938; repr. 1971); Curtiss, M. S., *Bizet and His World* (1958; repr. 1977); Dean, Winton, *Bizet*, rev. ed. (1975), and *Introduction to the Music of Bizet* (1976).

Bjerknes, Vilhelm and Jacob   [byairk'-nes]

Vilhelm Frimann Koren Bjerknes, b. Mar. 14, 1862, d. Apr. 9, 1951, was a Norwegian physicist and meteorologist who helped found modern METEOROLOGY. In 1897, Bjerknes propounded the circulation theorems of hydrodynamics that enabled him to explain the large-scale movement of air masses. While an assistant (1891–95) to Heinrich Hertz in Bonn, he produced a fundamental study of electrical resonance that was important in the later development of radio. As professor of geophysics at the University of Leipzig from 1912 to 1917, he organized and directed the Leipzig Geophysical Institute. Bjerknes founded (1917) a similar institute in Bergen. Four years later, he published his classic work, *On the Dynamics of the Circular Vortex with Applications to the Atmosphere and to Atmospheric Vortex and Wave Motion.*

Bjerknes's son, the Norwegian-American meteorologist **Jacob Aall Bonnevie Bjerknes**, b. Nov. 2, 1897, d. July 7, 1975, served as meteorologist and then superintendent of the

Weather Forecasting Center at the Meteorological Observatory in Bergen. It was during this period (1918–31) that he organized, with his father's help, a network of weather stations throughout Norway. With data produced by this network, he worked out the theory that the ATMOSPHERE comprises tropical and polar AIR MASSES separated by distinct boundaries, which he called FRONTS. Wave disturbances in these fronts give rise to cyclones. Immigrating to the United States in 1939, Bjerknes contributed significantly to the war effort by training meteorologists for the aviation programs of the U.S. armed forces.   ROBERT C. FITE

See also: CYCLONE AND ANTICYCLONE.

Björling, Jussi   [byur'-ling, yoo'-see]

The Swedish opera singer Jussi Björling, b. Feb. 2, 1911, d. Sept. 9, 1960, was one of the finest lyric tenors of the century. At the age of six he toured the world as part of a vocal quartet. Björling studied at the Royal Opera School in Stockholm and debuted (1930) at Stockholm's Royal Opera as Ottavio in Mozart's *Don Giovanni*. International fame followed his appearance at Covent Garden Opera in London (1936) and the Salzburg Festival (1937). Björling's first American opera appearance (1937) was in Chicago; he went (1938) to the Metropolitan Opera in New York, where his last performance took place on Dec. 2, 1959. Blessed with a lyric tenor voice of great tonal beauty, Björling was outstanding in Mozart, and in the French and Italian repertoires. Fortunately for posterity, he made a large number of recordings.   STEPHANIE VON BUCHAU

Bjørnson, Bjørnstjerne   [byurn'-sohn, byurn'-styair-ne]

Bjørnstjerne Martinus Bjørnson, b. Dec. 8, 1832, d. Apr. 26, 1910, was a dominant Norwegian literary and political figure from 1860 until his death. A novelist, poet, playwright, theater director, and political activist, he gained an early reputation in Scandinavia for his idyllic and realistic depictions of Norwegian rural life. *Synnøve Solbakken* (Sunny Hill), considered the first major Norwegian novel, was published in 1857 and was translated into English as *Trust and Trial* (1858), *Love and Life in Norway* (1870), and *Sunny Hill* (1932). The novel was followed by *Arne* (1858; Eng. trans., 1866) and *The Happy Boy* (1860; Eng. trans., 1869). Inspired by Scandinavian sagas, these tales of rural life display Bjørnson's national pride and possess a combination of simple lyrical language and a sense of dramatic structure. In addition, for the years 1857–59, Bjørnson replaced Henrik Ibsen as artistic director at the Bergen theater.

In the years immediately following Bjørnson was active in political battles, one of which was his opposition to the amalgamation of Norway and Sweden. At this time he wrote *Sigurd Slembe* (1862; Eng. trans., 1888), a trilogy of sagalike dramas. While director of the Christiana Theatre (and here,

Bjørnstjerne Bjørnson, a 19th-century dramatist and novelist, is one of Norway's most noted public figures. In his writings, Bjørnson extols the virtues of Norwegian culture and examines international social issues. His poem "Ja vi elsker dette landet" ("Yes, We Love This Country") is used as Norway's national anthem.

again, he took over from Ibsen), he published poetry both epic in scope and characterized by a fine sense of detail, including *Poems and Songs* (1870; Eng. trans., 1915) and the epic *Arnljot Gelline* (1870; Eng. trans., 1917).

Bjørnson achieved an international reputation with dramas that debated social and political problems, notably *The Editor* (1874; Eng. trans., 1914) and *The Bankrupt* (1875; Eng. trans., 1914), and with dramas concerning religious questions, including the two-part work *Beyond Our Power* and *Beyond Human Might* (1883 and 1895; Eng. trans., 1913 and 1914).

Bjørnson's plays influenced the development of the drama of social realism. His commitment to the ideals of humanism made him a tireless and increasingly influential spokesman for the rights of individuals and minorities throughout Europe. In 1903 he received the Nobel Prize for literature. Often called Norway's national poet, Bjørnson wrote the words of the Norwegian national anthem.   KJETIL A. FLATIN

Bibliography: Brandes, Georg, *Henrik Ibsen, Bjørnstjerne Bjørnson: Critical Studies* (1899; repr. 1964); Larson, Harold, *Bjørnstjerne Bjørnson: A Study in Norwegian Nationalism* (1944).

Bjørnvig, Thorkild   [byurn'-vig, thor'-kild]

Thorkild Bjørnvig, b. Feb. 2, 1918, is a prominent Danish poet and essayist. His first book, *Stjaernen bag Gavlen* (The Star Behind the Gable, 1947) established him as one of Denmark's foremost poets. His later works include *Delfinen* (The Dolphin, 1975), *Stoffets Krystalhav* (The Crystal Sea of Matter, 1975), and *The Pact: My Friendship with Isak Dinesen* (1974; Eng. trans., 1983).

BL Lacertae objects   [luh-sur'-tee]

BL Lacertae objects, or Lacertids, are active galaxies with sharp, brilliant nuclei and fuzzy halos. They are named for their prototype, BL Lacertae. These objects emit energy mostly in the infrared, but also at optical and radio wavelengths. Rapid variations in intensity at all these wavelengths indicate powerful but compact sources of energy. At least 30 BL Lacertaes have been identified to date. In every case the energies radiated are far greater than normal for galaxies, to the extent that they are similar to RADIO GALAXIES, SEYFERT GALAXIES, and QUASARS.   JOHN B. IRWIN

See also: RADIO ASTRONOMY.

Black, Davidson

Davidson Black, b. Toronto, July 25, 1884, d. Mar. 15, 1934, a Canadian physician and paleontologist, was responsible for the identification of the fossil known as PEKING MAN. Educated at the University of Toronto and the University of Manchester, England, he went (1918) to China and became professor of neurology and embryology at Peking Union Medical College. Black proposed in 1927 that a fossil tooth found at CHOU-K'OU-TIEN belonged to a previously unknown species of early man, which he named *Sinanthropus pekinensis*. He later noted the affinity between the Peking man fossils and those of JAVA MAN, both of which were later classified within the same extinct hominid group HOMO ERECTUS.

Black, Harold

Harold Stephen Black, b. Leominster, Mass., Apr. 14, 1898, d. Dec. 11, 1983, was a U.S. electrical engineer best known for his invention of the negative feedback AMPLIFIER, which makes use of the FEEDBACK of a signal from the output to the input of a device. This invention made high-fidelity amplification possible in telephone, radio, and telegraph systems. Black also pioneered the carrier telephone apparatus, which can carry several conversations on a single pair of wires. He spent most of his career with Bell Telephone Laboratories.

Black, Hugo L.

Hugo LaFayette Black, b. Clay County, Ala., Feb. 27, 1886, d. Sept. 25, 1971, served 34 years as a justice of the U.S. Supreme Court. A successful Birmingham lawyer, he was elected as a Democrat to the U.S. Senate in 1926. During the 1930s he vigorously supported the NEW DEAL. Black's investigations of merchant marine subsidies and the public utilities lobby gained him wide public attention. In 1937, President Franklin Roosevelt named him to the Supreme Court, where, as a liberal, activist justice, he became known as a dedicated protector of the Constitution and the Bill of Rights, particularly in opposing any restriction of free speech or publication.

Bibliography: Black, Hugo L. and Elizabeth M., *Justice and Mrs. Black* (1986); Black, Hugo, Jr., *My Father: A Remembrance* (1975); Hamilton, Virginia, ed., *Hugo Black and the Bill of Rights* (1978) and *Hugo Black: The Alabama Years* (1982); Magee, James, *Mr. Justice Black: Absolutist on the Court* (1980).

Black, Jeremiah Sullivan

Jeremiah Sullivan Black, b. near Stony Creek, Pa., Jan. 10, 1810, d. Aug. 19, 1883, was a U.S. cabinet officer under President James BUCHANAN. After an academy education, he studied law and entered practice in Somerset, Pa. He served as a Pennsylvania district judge from 1842 to 1851 and thereafter on the state supreme court until his appointment as U.S. attorney general in March 1857. Black was named secretary of state in December 1860, at the beginning of the secession crisis. Although he believed that the federal government could not coerce a seceding state, he nevertheless urged Buchanan to enforce federal laws and protect federal property in the South. After his retirement from the cabinet in March 1861, Black built up an extensive law practice.   EDWIN A. MILES

Bibliography: Brigance, William N., *Jeremiah Sullivan Black: A Defender of the Constitution and the Ten Commandments* (1934).

Black, Joseph

The Scottish chemist Joseph Black, b. Apr. 16, 1728, d. Dec. 6, 1799, performed early quantitative experiments and was among the first to emphasize the importance of such experiments to chemists. He showed that carbon dioxide differs from ordinary air, and his studies of specific heat and latent heat furnished a basis for Antoine Laurent LAVOISIER's caloric theory of heat. He taught at the universities of Glasgow and Edinburgh.   RALPH GABLE

Bibliography: Ramsay, W., *Life and Letters of Joseph Black, M.D.* (1918).

Black, Max

The analytic and linguistic philosopher Max Black, b. Russia, Feb. 24, 1909, d. Aug. 27, 1988, studied and taught in England before going (1940) to the United States. He taught first at the University of Illinois (1940–46) and then at Cornell. Black's wide-ranging philosophical writings—including *Language and Philosophy* (1949) and *The Labyrinth of Language* (1968)—reveal a commitment to the clarification of meaning. He urged close attention to the multiplicity of ordinary uses of words and denied that language is a mirror of reality.

black American literature

Black American literature, as defined by many contemporary literary critics, is the literature produced in the United States (or in exile therefrom) by blacks about blacks and is most often associated with works having a strong didactic flavor. As such, the term would exclude such black writers as the poet Phillis WHEATLEY and the contemporary novelist Frank YERBY.

Black American literature can be said to have begun with the slave narratives and folktales that were transmitted orally during the period of the "peculiar institution" and later dictated and written down. These narratives, chronicling the harsh treatment experienced by enslaved blacks, form part of the centuries-long, worldwide tradition of oral literature and today serve as an important source for American historians. In a more sophisticated vein, the escaped slave and prominent abolitionist Frederick DOUGLASS inaugurated the tradition of black autobiographical writing with the publication of his *Narrative of the Life of Frederick Douglass* in 1845.

The first published work of black American fiction was William Wells Brown's abolitionist novel *Clotel; or, the President's Daughter* (1853). A generation later Charles W. Chesnutt's short story "The Goophered Grapevine" (1887) appeared in the prestigious *Atlantic Monthly*. This led to the publication of two volumes of short stories by Chesnutt, *The Conjure Woman and Other Tales* and *The Wife of His Youth*, in 1899. Even though the three novels that followed struck themes that have persisted in black literature, Chesnutt is best remembered for the artistry and insight he brought in his short stories to the complexities of slavery. At the same time, Paul Laurence Dunbar was experimenting with the use of black folk material in his lyric poetry.

The support of white patrons of the arts, the countrywide acceptance of JAZZ, the mass migration of Southern American, Caribbean, and African blacks to Harlem during and after World War I, and the fruitful mix of attitudes and cultures thereby produced all combined to bring about the literary flowering known as the HARLEM RENAISSANCE (1920–30). An additional driving force was supplied by the determination of the NAACP, especially under the leadership of W. E. B. DU BOIS, himself the author of *The Souls of Black Folks* (1903), to improve the lot of blacks in America. Alain LOCKE, a Harvard Ph.D., Rhodes scholar, and editor of a book of essays called *The New Negro* (1925), spoke for this movement when he articulated the responsibility of the black to become a "collaborator and participant in American civilization."

This injunction was echoed in the works of the outstanding Renaissance writers, among whom were the Jamaican poet and novelist Claude McKay; the poet and short-story writer Langston Hughes; Jean Toomer, author of the fragile miscellany *Cane* (1923); and the lyric poet Countee Cullen. What these different writers shared was a felt need to trace the injustices perpetrated against blacks and the desire to give expression to the character of black life.

The versatility of the Harlem group was matched in the decade of the Great Depression by Richard Wright, whose novel *Native Son* (1940) constituted a bitter indictment of the inequities that continued to dash black aspirations in the period between the two world wars. Wright's autobiography *Black Boy* (1945), the short stories in *Uncle Tom's Children* (1938), and his 1953 novel *The Outsider* cast a searching light on the racial and political conditions that led some blacks, at least for a time, to embrace the Communist party.

Ralph ELLISON's *Invisible Man* (1952) is the odyssey of a Southern youth's search for self and acceptance. Incorporating the folk, the classical, and the mythic, the book is considered a landmark. In a more traditional mold, Gwendolyn BROOKS and Lorraine HANSBERRY reflected the American black urban experience in highly regarded poetry and plays. Also in the 1950s and early 1960s, James BALDWIN began to pursue the themes of the son's search for acceptance by a father, of homosexuality, and of race relations in his novels *Go Tell It on the Mountain* (1953), *Giovanni's Room* (1956), and *Another Country* (1962), as well as in plays and essays. Baldwin's 1963 nonfictional investigation into the status of U.S. blacks, *The Fire Next Time*, galvanized white America.

Baldwin's work served as a transition to the revolutionary sixties when both MALCOLM X and Martin Luther KING, Jr., before their assassinations, brought a new dimension to speechmaking and political writing through an electrifying blend of moral fervor and rhetorical richness. The new black nationalist awareness was reflected by LeRoi Jones (later Imamu Amiri BARAKA), who stressed the didactic mission of black writers in his intense, frightening plays and essays. A writer of myriad talents, Jones moved from the status of middle-class intellectual as a Howard University undergraduate to political activism. His literary reputation at this time was matched only by that of the BLACK PANTHER minister of information, Eldridge CLEAVER, whose autobiographical *Soul on Ice* (1968) and later poetry interpreted the radicalizing black prison experience.

The growing interest in the black historical experience among both blacks and whites created an enormous audience for the televised dramatizations (1977, 1979) of *Roots*, Alex HALEY's fictional exploration of the generations of a black family from its enslavement in Africa. The growing number of plays by black writers—most notably the dramas of August WILSON, which have all received major productions—have interpreted aspects of black American life for a broad audience. The imaginative use of autobiographical material has characterized the work of novelists Toni MORRISON, Maya ANGELOU, and Alice WALKER, and the popular poet Nikki GIOVANNI. Other important novelists include Ernest J. GAINES, Ishmael REED, and Gloria Naylor (*The Women of Brewster Place*, 1982). From outside the American landscape, Jamaica Kincaid creates visions of an almost idyllic childhood in her Caribbean birthplace (*Lucy*, 1990). John Edgar Wideman transforms the bitter facts of black urban ghetto life into searing fiction (as in *Philadelphia Fire*, 1990).   CECILIA HODGES DREWRY

Bibliography: Bontemps, A., *American Negro Poetry*, rev. ed. (1974); Davis, C. T., *Black is the Color of the Cosmos* (1989); Gates, H. L., et al., eds., *The Norton Anthology of Afro-American Literature* (1990); Jackson, B., *A History of Afro-American Literature*, vol. 1 (1984); Johnson, C., *Being and Race: Black Writing Since 1970* (1990); Willis, S., *Specifying: Black Women Writing the American Experience* (1987).

black Americans

Black Americans are those persons in the United States who trace their ancestry to members of the Negroid race in Africa. They have at various times in United States history been referred to as African, colored, Negro, Afro-American, and African American, as well as black. The vast majority of black Americans are descendants of people forcibly removed to North America as slaves. The black American population also includes more recent immigrants from black Africa, the West Indies, and Latin America.

The black population of the United States has grown from three-quarters of a million in 1790 to nearly 30 million in 1990. As a percentage of the total population, blacks declined from 19.3 in 1790 to 9.7 in 1930. A modest percentage increase has occurred since that time.

Exactly what portion of the black American population is of solely African ancestry is not known. Over the past 300 and more years in the United States, considerable racial mixture has taken place between persons of African descent and those with other racial backgrounds, mainly of white European or American Indian ancestry.

Physical differences among black Americans are probably roughly equivalent in degree to those among members of other racial groups in the United States. Shades of skin color range from dark brown to ivory. In body type black Americans range from short and stocky to tall and lean. Nose shapes vary from aquiline to extremely broad and flat; hair color from medium brown to brown black; and hair texture from tightly curled to limp and straight.

Historically, the predominant attitude toward racial group membership in the United States has been that persons having any black African ancestry are considered to be black. In some parts of the United States, especially in the antebellum South, laws were written to define racial group membership

BLACK POPULATION

Year	Slave	Free	Total	% of U.S. Population
1790	697,681	59,527	757,208	19.3
1800	893,602	108,435	1,002,037	18.9
1810	1,191,362	186,466	1,377,808	19.0
1820	1,538,022	233,634	1,771,656	18.4
1840	2,487,355	386,293	2,873,648	16.1
1860	3,953,760	488,070	4,441,830	14.1
1880			6,580,793	13.1
1900			8,833,994	11.6
1920			10,463,131	9.9
1940			12,866,000	9.8
1960			18,871,831	10.5
1980			26,488,219	11.7
1990			29,986,060	12.1

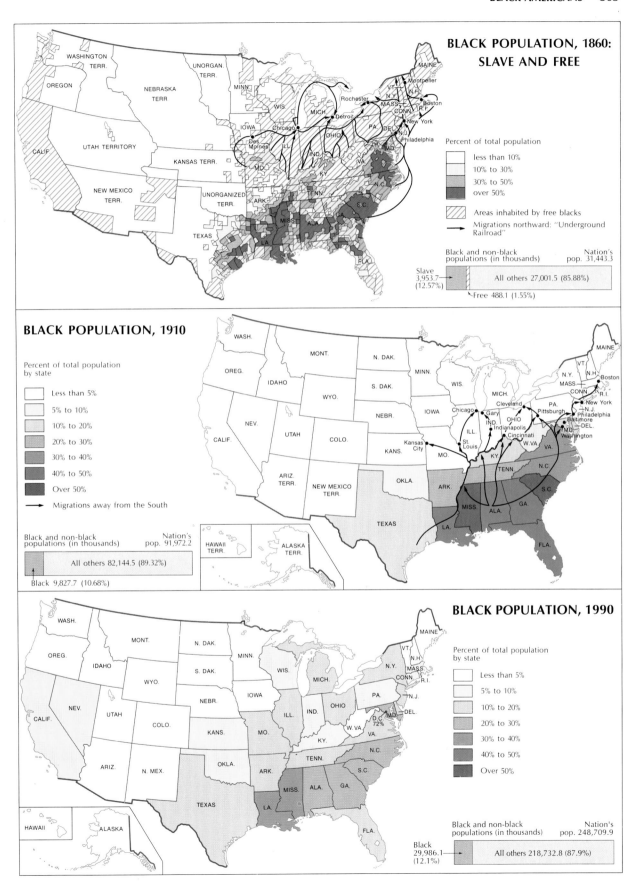

BLACK POPULATION, 1860:
SLAVE AND FREE

Percent of total population

less than 10%
10% to 30%
30% to 50%
over 50%

Areas inhabited by free blacks

Migrations northward: "Underground
Railroad"

Black and non-black   Nation's
populations (in thousands)   pop. 31,443.3

Slave
3,953.7   All others 27,001.5 (85.88%)
(12.57%)
Free 488.1 (1.55%)

BLACK POPULATION, 1910

Percent of total population
by state

Less than 5%
5% to 10%
10% to 20%
20% to 30%
30% to 40%
40% to 50%
Over 50%

Migrations away from the South

Black and non-black   Nation's
populations (in thousands)   pop. 91,972.2

All others 82,144.5 (89.32%)

Black 9,827.7 (10.68%)

BLACK POPULATION, 1990

Percent of total population
by state

Less than 5%
5% to 10%
10% to 20%
20% to 30%
30% to 40%
40% to 50%
Over 50%

Black and non-black   Nation's
populations (in thousands)   pop. 248,709.9

Black
29,986.1   All others 218,732.8 (87.9%)
(12.1%)

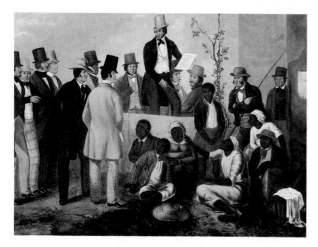

Black families were often broken up when sold at auction to slave buyers. Slavery developed in America largely because the South's plantation-based agricultural system demanded a vast supply of inexpensive, manageable labor. (Chicago Historical Society.)

in this way, generally to the detriment of those who were not Caucasian. It is important to note, however, that ancestry and physical characteristics are only part of what has set black Americans apart as a distinct group. The concept of race, as it applies to the black minority in the United States, is as much a social and political concept as a biological one.

BLACKS UNDER SLAVERY: 1600–1865

The first Africans in the New World arrived with Spanish and Portuguese explorers and settlers. By 1600 an estimated 275,000 Africans, both free and slave, were in Central and South America and the Caribbean area. Africans first arrived in the area that became the United States in 1619, when a handful of captives were sold by the captain of a Dutch man-of-war to settlers at JAMESTOWN. Others were brought in increasing numbers to fill the desire for labor in a country where land was plentiful and labor scarce. By the end of the 17th century, approximately 1,300,000 Africans had landed in the New World. From 1701 to 1810 the number reached 6,000,000, with another 1,800,000 arriving after 1810. Some Africans were brought directly to the English colonies in North America. Others landed as slaves in the West Indies and were later resold and shipped to the mainland.

Slavery in America. The earliest African arrivals were viewed in the same way as indentured servants from Europe. This similarity did not long continue. By the latter half of the 17th century, clear differences existed in the treatment of black and white servants. A 1662 Virginia law assumed Africans would remain servants for life, and a 1667 act declared that "Baptisme doth not alter the condition of the person as to his bondage or freedome." By 1740 the SLAVERY system in colonial America was fully developed. A Virginia law in that year declared slaves to be "chattel personal in the hands of their owners and possessors . . . for all intents, construction, and purpose whatsoever."

The principle by which persons of African ancestry were considered the personal property of others prevailed in North America for more than two-thirds of the three and a half centuries since the first Africans arrived there. Its influences increased even though the English colonies won independence and articulated national ideals directly in opposition to slavery. In spite of numerous ideological conflicts, however, the slavery system was maintained in the United States until 1865, and widespread antiblack attitudes nurtured by slavery continued thereafter.

Prior to the American Revolution, slavery existed in all the colonies. The ideals of the Revolution and the limited profitability of slavery in the North resulted in its abandonment in northern states during the last quarter of the 18th century. At the same time the strength of slavery increased in the South,

with the continuing demand for cheap labor by the tobacco growers and cotton farmers of the Southern states. By 1850, 92 percent of all American blacks were concentrated in the South, and of this group approximately 95 percent were slaves.

Life on the plantations was hard, and no consideration was given to the cultural traditions of blacks. In the slave market men were separated from their wives, and frequently children were taken from their mothers. Family and tribal links were thus almost immediately cut. Fifty percent of the slaves were owned by 10 percent of the 385,000 slave owners. This concentration within a limited number of agricultural units had important consequences for the lives of most blacks.

Under the plantation system gang labor was the typical form of employment. Overseers were harsh as a matter of general practice, and brutality was common. Punishment was meted out at the absolute discretion of the owner or the owner's agent. Slaves could own no property unless sanctioned by a slave master, and rape of a female slave was not considered a crime except as it represented trespassing on another's property. Slaves could not present evidence in court against whites. Housing, food, and clothing were of poor quality and seldom exceeded what was considered minimally necessary to maintain the desired level of work. Owners reinforced submissive behavior not so much by positive rewards as by severe punishment of those who did not conform. In most of the South it was illegal to teach a black to read or write.

Opposition by Blacks. All Southern states passed slave codes intended to control slaves and prevent any expression of opposition. Outbreaks of opposition did occur, however, including the Prosser and Bowler Revolt of 1800, the revolt led by Denmark VESEY in 1822, Nat TURNER's rebellion in 1831, and numbers of smaller uprisings. As a result, the substance and the enforcement of repressive laws against blacks became more severe. Blacks were forbidden to carry arms or to gather in numbers except in the presence of a white person.

Free blacks, whether living in the North or South, were confronted with attitudes and actions that differed little from those facing Southern black slaves. Discrimination existed in most social and economic activities as well as in voting and education. In 1857 the DRED SCOTT V. SANDFORD case of the U.S. Supreme Court placed the authority of the Constitution behind decisions made by states in the treatment of blacks. The Dred Scott decision was that black Americans, even if

Nat Turner exhorts a group of his fellow slaves during their abortive insurrection in 1831. This Virginia rebellion ended in the execution of Turner and 16 others. Southern state legislatures thereafter enacted harsh codes of laws regulating the conduct of slaves.

This cover from an 1845 songsheet pays homage to Frederick Douglass, a former slave who became a leader of the abolitionist movement. Douglass, a gifted orator and pamphleteer, spoke out against slavery during his popular lecture tours in the Northern states.

free, were not intended to be included under the word *citizen* as defined in the Declaration of Independence and could, therefore, claim none of the rights and privileges provided for in that document.

Blacks responded to their treatment under slavery in a variety of ways. In addition to such persons as Prosser, Vesey, and Turner, who openly opposed the slave system, thousands of blacks escaped from slavery and moved to the northern United States or to Canada. Others sought ways to retain some sense of individuality and some vestige of their African heritage under difficult circumstances. Still others accepted the images of themselves that white America sought to project onto them. The result in some cases was the "Uncle Tom" or "Sambo" personality, the black who accepted his or her lowly position as evidence that whites were superior to blacks.

In spite of the absence of legal status and the adverse effects of the domestic slave trade, the black family retained its traditional role in ordering the relations between adults and children. Much religious activity among slaves reflected the influences of African religious practices and served as a means by which slaves could develop and promote views of themselves different from those held by the slave owner. Outside the South, blacks established separate churches and, eventually, denominations within Protestantism, including many black Baptist churches. Another early denominational effort was the African Methodist Episcopal Church, initially called the Free African Society, which was founded (1787) in Philadelphia by Richard ALLEN.

Civil War. The issue of slavery appeared in national politics from the start of the nation. In 1820 it was the subject of the MISSOURI COMPROMISE, a measure enacted by Congress to prohibit slavery north of the state of Missouri. In the 1850s the slavery issue further divided the nation along regional lines. For the most part, however, both proslavery and antislavery positions included antiblack attitudes. Except for the ABOLITIONISTS, most Northern opinion was more concerned with the dangers slavery posed to free labor than with the moral issue of the restrictions on the human rights of those held as slaves.

When the South seceded (1860–61) because of the dangers to slavery it perceived in Lincoln's election, the North declared that it was not slavery but the act of secession that precipitated the CIVIL WAR. President Lincoln supported a Constitutional amendment that would have given federal protection to slavery in the Southern states. On his order slaves who escaped into the Union lines were returned to their owners by federal troops early in the war.

Later, as the cost of the war in men and materials and national support for the abolitionists' position grew, President Lincoln shifted his position. In 1862 his EMANCIPATION PROCLAMATION declared slaves to be free if the areas in which they were held were still in revolt against the Union on Jan. 1, 1863. Slaves within the Union and in areas of the Confederacy under Union control, however, were initially excluded from the provisions of the proclamation. Thus at its inception, the proclamation functioned principally as military propaganda: slaves were declared free only in those areas where no real authority existed to free them. In those areas under federal authority, no action was taken. Nevertheless, the Emancipation Proclamation represented a point of no return on the issue of slavery.

As the war moved into various parts of the South, activities by blacks demonstrated the falsehood of the Southern claim of a satisfied slave population. Information and provisions were turned over to the Union troops, and slaves fled into the lines of approaching Union armies in such numbers as to create logistical problems. Letters and diaries of slave owners and their families contain frequent references to increased difficulty in controlling slaves as the fighting neared.

Beginning in 1862, provisions were made for enlisting blacks into the Union army. They were organized into all-

(Below) The 54th Massachusetts Colored Regiment, one of many black units serving in the Union army after the Emancipation Proclamation, led the charge against Confederate positions at Fort Wagner, S.C., in July 1863. (Library of Congress, Washington, D.C.)

(Above) This cartoon advertised the antics of "Daddy" Dan Rice, a white performer who introduced the character of Jim Crow, a caricature of black entertainers, in the white minstrel shows of the 1830s.

black units referred to as the U.S. Colored Troops. Of the 209,000 blacks who entered service, 93,000 came from the area of the Confederacy. Units composed of soldiers from this area included the 1st and 3d Louisiana Native Guard and the 1st South Carolina Volunteers. The Confederacy at first refused to recognize blacks as soldiers. Unlike other Union troops who were captured, black soldiers were at first not allowed to surrender. Many were shot. The most infamous of such occurrences was at Fort Pillow, which fell to Confederate troops under Gen. Nathan B. FORREST (later a founder of the KU KLUX KLAN).

Blacks took part in more than 200 battles and skirmishes. In all, 68,178 died in battle or as the result of wounds or disease during the war. Lower pay for blacks and other forms of discrimination were common. In spiteof this, desertion among blacks was more than 50 percent lower than for the Union army as a whole.

RECONSTRUCTION AND ITS AFTERMATH: 1865–1915
During the period of RECONSTRUCTION (1865–77), Union policy evolved to embrace the total abolition of slavery, as provided in the 13th Amendment to the Constitution, passed in 1865. Government policy also moved toward equality of rights for blacks as reflected in the 14th Amendment (1868) and 15th Amendment (1870) and in related legislation. Opposition to equal rights for blacks was almost universal in the South and nearly so in the North, however. Passage of the 14th and 15th amendments had been primarily motivated by the desire of the Republican party to maintain political control in the former Confederacy.

Participation by Blacks. Blacks took an active part in all aspects of public life during Reconstruction. They voted in large numbers and were active in the conventions that formulated new state constitutions in the South. Many held political office at the local and state levels; 14 were elected to the U.S. House of Representatives, and two were elected to the U.S. Senate. Blacks pressed for and helped to establish systems of public education where none had previously existed. They established private schools and colleges with the assistance of the FREEDMEN'S BUREAU, a federal agency, and Northern church groups. Legislation backed by federal troops made access to public accommodations possible. Many former slaves hoped that confiscated land of Confederate officials or land owned by the federal government might be divided into family farms and distributed among them. This was not done, however, and only a small number of blacks were able to purchase land, leaving the vast majority of Southern blacks economically dependent on former slave owners.

Opposition by Whites. The major attack on the rights of blacks came from Southern whites, many of whom insisted that federal policies under Reconstruction were oppressive and vindictive. High among their complaints was the erroneous claim that state governments were controlled by blacks. Many sought to remove blacks from participation in policies and to restore, as closely as possible, conditions that existed before the war. As the federal government restored suffrage to former Confederates, a variety of legal and extralegal means were used to accomplish these goals. The illegal activities of the Ku Klux Klan and similar organizations founded in the late 1860s, coupled with waning interest in the North in protecting the rights of black citizens, resulted in the gradual return of control of state governments into the hands of the Democratic party. This was effectively accomplished by 1877, when all federal troops were withdrawn from the South, and Reconstruction was officially ended. White rule of the Southern states was fully restored, and the rights of black citizens were once again in jeopardy.

The Southern Race System. As Reconstruction ended, an extremely difficult period began for black citizens. For protection of their civil rights, blacks were forced to rely on state governments controlled by persons who openly opposed the existence of those rights. The federal government increasingly withdrew from issues concerning the rights of blacks, and the executive and judicial branches tended to support the Southern white position. The disfranchisement of blacks that had begun in the South with illegal harassment and violence soon after the war was almost completed by the early years of the 20th century. Many Southern states instituted POLL TAXES, literacy tests, and the so-called GRANDFATHER CLAUSE as a means of removing blacks from voting while allowing white suffrage to continue. The success of these efforts is attested to by the decline in registered black voters in Alabama from 181,471 in 1900 to 3,000 as a result of constitutional changes effected in 1901. Similar action in Louisiana reduced registered blacks from 130,334 in 1896 to 1,342 in 1904.

The radical curtailment of black voting rights in the South facilitated the institutionalized separation of blacks from whites in various aspects of everyday life. Blacks were excluded from participation on juries and were refused service in hotels, restaurants, and amusement parks. They were forced to occupy separate sections in vehicles of public transportation and in public gathering places, and separate educational systems were provided for each race. By the outbreak of World War I, so-called JIM CROW LAWS that legalized segregation of blacks and whites existed throughout the South. Jim Crow existed in other parts of the United States as well, either by law as in the South or by local practice.

The judicial stamp of approval for Jim Crow came in 1896 with the case of PLESSY V. FERGUSON, whereby the U.S. Supreme Court declared constitutional a Louisiana law requiring separation by race on railroad coaches. The court held that

(Left) *W. E. B. Du Bois, a black sociologist and author, was one of the founders of the NAACP. In* The Souls of Black Folk *(1903), Du Bois opposed Booker T. Washington's strategy of accommodation.*

(Right) *George Washington Carver, an educator and botanist, instructs a class in his laboratory at Tuskegee Institute in Alabama. Carver's agricultural research led to the development of important new products derived from such crops as peanuts, sweet potatoes, and soybeans.*

enforcing such separation was a legitimate use of the police power of the states so long as equal facilities were provided. Such facilities for blacks were invariably inferior to those for whites, however. This inequality was perhaps most devastating in the area of education. As late as the start of World War II certain Southern school districts did not provide 12 years of public education for blacks. In addition, blacks frequently suffered discrimination in the distribution of tax moneys for support of schools. Publicly supported colleges in the South were likewise few and of poor quality.

The powerlessness of blacks during the post-Reconstruction period is exemplified in the high incidence of lynchings (3,402) that occurred between 1882 and 1938. The several attempts to secure passage of a federal antilynching bill during this period were all unsuccessful. In spite of efforts by Southern whites to suppress blacks politically and to deny them social equality, the activities and efforts of blacks after Reconstruction to improve their economic condition and exercise their political rights met with some measure of success. In 1870, 80 percent of the black population over 10 years of age was illiterate; by 1900 illiteracy among blacks was reduced by almost 50 percent. Farm ownership, although still low, increased significantly; by 1901 about 25 percent of black farmers in the South owned their own land. Seven blacks were elected to the U.S. House of Representatives for a cumulative total of 13 terms between 1877 and 1901, and Jim Crow legislation was challenged in the courts, albeit unsuccessfully.

A variety of organizations sought to advance the rights of blacks, best known among them being the NATIONAL ASSOCIATION FOR THE ADVANCEMENT OF COLORED PEOPLE (NAACP), founded 1909. One of its founders, William E. B. Du Bois, was the leading spokesperson for full and immediate rights for blacks. In spite of his and other efforts directed toward full racial equality for blacks during this period, historians have generally focused on the accommodation of blacks to post-Reconstruction racism. The accommodation espoused by some blacks was symbolized in the activities of the black educator Booker T. Washington, who cautioned blacks to be patient and to work hard toward attaining economic equality before striving for civil rights. His ideas fitted well with the views of many conservative whites but were opposed by many black leaders, among them Du Bois.

PERIOD OF TRANSITION: 1915-45

World War I was a turning point in black American history. The trickle of blacks moving out of the South after 1877 increased enormously as war industries and the decline of European immigration combined to produce demands for labor in Northern cities. The coming together of large numbers of blacks in urban areas, the exposure of some blacks to European whites who did not hold the same racial attitude as American whites, and war propaganda to "make the world safe for democracy" combined to raise the hopes, dreams, and aspirations of blacks. Segregationists countered this optimism with an upsurge of lynchings, riots, and other antiblack violence after World War I, however. The Ku Klux Klan was revived and gained impetus in Northern as well as Southern states during the 1920s. These actions blunted the efforts of blacks in politics, but the changing attitudes among blacks found other forms of expression. During the 1920s notable productions of black literature, music, and art took place, and race consciousness increased. The latter is reflected in the writings of the influential black leader Marcus GARVEY, founder of the Universal Negro Improvement Association and an ardent proponent of BLACK NATIONALISM.

In the 1930s blacks initially were less affected by the Depression than whites because the economy of the black community was already depressed. Before long, however, the worsening economic conditions hit blacks, as the group at the low end of the economic scale, the hardest. Reforms attempted by the New Deal almost exclusively concerned economic matters. No attack was made on problems suffered by blacks because of their racial minority group status. In New Deal efforts to aid the poor, however, blacks encountered the first assistance from government since Reconstruction. Frank-

Marcus Garvey defended the cultural achievements of blacks and attracted a considerable following of black Americans between 1916 and 1922 by encouraging them to found a sovereign nation in Africa.

lin D. Roosevelt's sensitivity to the existence of racism, coupled with growing disaffection with the Republican party, caused more and more voting blacks to support the Democratic party. This was often an uncomfortable decision for blacks, because under the seniority practices followed by Congress, control by Democrats placed avowed segregationists in major positions of legislative leadership. The shift continued, however, and since the New Deal period blacks have increasingly voted for Democrats.

With the outbreak of World War II, wholehearted black support was given to the war effort with the hope that the fight against Nazi racism would weaken racism in the United States. Of the 891,000 blacks who joined the military, approximately half a million served overseas. Black combat units included the 92d and 93d divisions and a small group of air force pilots. As in World War I the majority of blacks were organized into service units, and many were never trained in the use of basic weapons. In an attempt to encourage and improve job training for minority group workers in war industries, President Roosevelt established a national Fair Employment Practices Committee. The war ended, however, with no major attack on discrimination in employment and in labor unions, and Jim Crow practices persisted in many parts of both the North and the South.

THE CIVIL RIGHTS MOVEMENT

Many things influenced the changes in U.S. race relations after World War II. The anti-Nazi propaganda generated during the war increased the realization by many Americans of the conflict between ideals and the reality of racism in their own country. The concentration of large numbers of blacks in cities of the North and West increased their potential for political influence. It also projected the problems related to race as national rather than regional. The establishment of the United Nations headquarters in the United States made American racial inequality more visible to a world in which the United States sought to give leadership during the Cold War with the USSR. The growth of a white minority willing to speak out against racism provided allies for blacks. Most important in altering race relations in the United States, however, were the actions of blacks themselves.

Legal Action Against Racism. The first major attack by blacks on racism was through the courts. In a series of cases involving professional and graduate education, the Supreme Court required admission of blacks to formerly all-white institutions when separate facilities for blacks were clearly not equal. The major legal breakthrough came in 1954. In the case of BROWN V. BOARD OF EDUCATION OF TOPEKA, KANSAS, the Supreme Court held that separate facilities are, by their very nature, unequal. In spite of this decision, more than a decade passed before

(Right) *Federal troops escort black students home after class at Central High School in Little Rock, Ark. When Gov. Orval Faubus refused to allow blacks to attend the all-white school, President Eisenhower dispatched units of the U.S. Army to ensure Little Rock's compliance with a 1957 Supreme Court order to integrate.*

(Left) *Dr. Martin Luther King, Jr., the most prominent civil rights leader of the 20th century, addressed a vast crowd of supporters at a 1957 rally in Washington, D.C. In recognition of his leadership, his belief in the Gandhian principles of nonviolent protest, and his personal courage, Dr. King was awarded the Nobel Peace Prize in 1964. Four years later, he was assassinated.*

significant school integration took place in the South. In the North, where segregated schools resulted from segregated housing patterns and from manipulation of school attendance boundaries, separation of races in public schools increased after 1954. A second major breakthrough in the fight against segregation grew out of the Montgomery, Ala., bus boycott in 1955. The boycott began when Rosa Parks, a black woman, refused to give up her seat on the bus to a white person. Her arrest resulted in a series of meetings of blacks in Montgomery and a boycott of buses on which racial segregation was practiced. The boycott, which lasted for more than a year, was almost 100 percent effective. Before the courts declared unconstitutional Montgomery's law requiring segregation on buses, Martin Luther KING, Jr., a Baptist minister, had risen to national prominence and had articulated a strategy of nonviolent direct action in the movement for CIVIL RIGHTS.

Nonviolent Direct Action. Nonviolent direct action, born in the boycott, was taken up by blacks and white supporters throughout the country. It was applied at sit-ins and freedom rides, aimed at ending segregation in public places, and also at protest demonstrations of all kinds. Among these activities were the march on Washington of Aug. 28, 1963, in which more than 200,000 blacks and whites protested continued segregation and discrimination, and large-scale demonstrations in Birmingham, Ala. (April 1963), and Selma, Ala. (March 1965). These civil rights activities were directed by long-established groups such as the NAACP and CORE (the CONGRESS OF RACIAL EQUALITY, founded 1942), by newly formed national groups such as the SOUTHERN CHRISTIAN LEADERSHIP CONFERENCE and SNCC (the Student Non-violent Coordinating Committee), and by such local groups as the Dallas County (Ala.) Voters League and the Princeton (N.J.) Association for Human Rights.

The response of segregationists to the demonstrations was to blame outside agitators for causing the trouble. Many law officials took strong, often brutal measures to halt demonstrations or else refused to protect the right of demonstrators to protest peacefully.

Violence against black and white civil rights activists was commonplace. Three civil rights workers were brutally murdered in Philadelphia, Miss., in 1964; four black children were murdered in the bombing of 16th Street Baptist Church in Birmingham in 1963; and dozens of black churches throughout the South were burned or bombed. Two whites and one black were murdered during the 1965 demonstrations in Selma, Ala. In 1968, Martin Luther King, Jr., the recognized leader of the civil rights movement, was assassinated.

The federal response to the violent reaction of segregationists was the passage of several new laws, the most important of which were enacted in 1964 and 1965. The CIVIL RIGHTS ACT (1964) undermined the remaining structure of Jim Crow laws and provided federal protection in the exercise of civil rights. The Voting Rights Act (1965) provided for federal action to put an end to actions by local governments and individuals that interfered with the right of blacks to register and vote. Both these laws were upheld in challenges before the U.S. Supreme Court. (See INTEGRATION, RACIAL.)

Urban Unrest and Militant Protest. During the middle and late 1960s, black leadership spoke increasingly of the limits of political successes, of the absence of accompanying economic change, and of the relationship between problems of race at home and affairs in which the United States was engaged abroad. Opposition also grew to the strategy of nonviolent resistance as its failure to alter significantly the lives of ghetto dwellers was perceived by some blacks. Unrest among urban blacks resulted in a series of riots beginning in the Watts section of Los Angeles in 1965. Attacks were mainly against white property and symbols of white authority in the ghetto.

When Martin Luther King, Jr., was assassinated in 1968, a new wave of riots spread across the country. A report by the National Advisory Commission on Civil Disorders, appointed by President Lyndon Johnson, identified more than 150 riots between 1965 and 1968. In 1967 alone, 83 people were killed (most of them black), 1,800 were injured, and property valued at more than $100 million was destroyed. (See RACE RIOTS.)

The growing black consciousness movement and the aggressive civil rights activism of the late 1960s resulted in what some have termed the white backlash. White supporters of moderate black organizations and activities declined. Harassment of some activists, especially the BLACK PANTHER PARTY and BLACK MUSLIMS, became common. Federal programs beneficial to poor ghetto youth were cut back, and the direction taken by the Supreme Court weakened the base for progress set under Chief Justice Earl WARREN. Evidence began to leak out that the FBI had sought to discredit and destroy Martin Luther King, Jr., as a leader and had participated in efforts to reduce the effectiveness of some black organizations.

Black Pride. The riots, the white backlash, and new developments within the black community during the late 1960s brought to an end one phase of the civil rights movement. The chief characteristic of the black experience in the 1970s and early 1980s was the development of black consciousness and black pride. These values found renewed vigor as increasing numbers of blacks came to believe that the key to dealing with problems of race in the United States was the way they felt about themselves as individuals and as a group.

The concept of black pride had been earlier articulated in such slogans as *black is beautiful* and *black power*. The latter term, introduced (1966) by Stokely Carmichael, the chairman at that time of SNCC, became the rallying cry for the more radical civil rights activists of the latter half of the 1960s. It found organizational expression in the Black Panther party, the Organization of Afro-American Unity, the Black Muslims, and other groups. Leading spokespersons of the concept of racial pride included MALCOLM X, Imamu Amiri BARAKA (formerly LeRoi Jones), Ron Karenga, and Huey Newton. This concept frightened some whites who perceived it as racism.

Black Political Activity. Beginning in the 1960s many blacks focused on political activity as a means of obtaining justice, equality of opportunity, and full political participation. During this Second Reconstruction, as the period has been called, a rapid increase occurred in the number of black registered voters, particularly in the South, followed by a marked increase in the number of black elected officials. Even before the passage of the Voting Rights Act of 1965, black voters were influen-

tial in some Northern states, as in the election to the presidency of Democrat John Kennedy in 1960. In the presidential election of 1976 widespread black support for the Democratic candidate Jimmy Carter produced critical parts of his majorities in several Northern and Southern states.

In 1984 the Rev. Jesse JACKSON, a civil rights activist in the 1960s, first campaigned in the primaries for the Democratic-party presidential nomination. He won over 3 million primary votes (and about 75% of the black vote) but fell far short of winning enough convention delegates to gain the nomination. In 1988 his second failure to win the nomination was a history-making event—he ran second in the primary season, winning 6.6 million votes and about 30% of the delegates to become the first "serious" black contender for the presidency. Jackson attracted 92% of the black vote and 12% of the white. He addressed issues of interest to a wide public, did much to register new voters, and secured himself a prominent place in national politics. In 1992, L. Douglas WILDER of Virginia, the first elected black governor in the United States, ran unsuccessfully for the Democratic presidential nomination.

A steady increase in black elected officials has taken place at all levels of government since the 1960s. In 1967, Thurgood MARSHALL became the first black Supreme Court justice. In the same year, Edward W. BROOKE of Massachusetts became the first black member of the U.S. Senate since Reconstruction. In 1993, Carol Moseley BRAUN became the first black woman U.S. senator. In the mid-1970s, 17 blacks served in the House of Representatives, among them, Shirley CHISHOLM, Barbara JORDAN, and Andrew YOUNG; by the mid-1990s the number was 38.

From the mid-'60s through the mid-1990s, black mayors of major cities included Tom BRADLEY in Los Angeles; Kenneth Gibson and Sharpe James in Newark, N.J.; Richard Hatcher in Gary, Ind.; Maynard Jackson in Atlanta, Ga.; Ernest Morial in New Orleans, La.; Carl Stokes in Cleveland, Ohio; Walter WASHINGTON and Sharon Pratt Kelly in Washington, D.C.; Coleman Young in Detroit; Harold WASHINGTON in Chicago; Wilson Goode in Philadelphia; and David DINKINS in New York.

Blacks began to fill major appointive positions in force in the administration of President Jimmy Carter, when Patricia Roberts HARRIS became the first black woman cabinet member as secretary of housing and urban development.

BLACK AMERICAN CULTURE TODAY

Blacks in the United States today are mainly an urban people. Their shift from the rural South to cities of the North and West during the 20th century constitutes one of the major migrations of people in U.S. history. This enormous shift of population has put severe strains on the fabric and social structure within both the old and new communities of migrating blacks. If one adds to this the problems of low income, high unemployment, poor education, and other problems related to racial discrimination, it could be said that the black community in the 20th century has existed in a perpetual state of crisis. The black community, however, has developed a number of distinctive cultural features that black Americans increasingly look upon with pride. Many of these features reflect the influence of cultural traditions that originated in Africa; others reflect the uniqueness of the black American in the United States. The unique features of black American culture are most noticeable in music, art and literature, and religion. They may also exist in speech, extended family arrangements, dress, and other features of life-style. Whether African ancestry or survival in the hostile environment of slavery and Jim Crow was more important in shaping cultural patterns of black American life is a question that requires further study.

Music and the Arts. Black American traditions in music reflect the mingling of African roots with the American experience. BLUES and spirituals (see GOSPEL MUSIC) can be traced back to the African call-and-response chant, in which a solo verse line is alternated with a choral response of a short phrase or word. They also reflect the personal experiences of blacks and the difficult adjustments demanded in the American environment. The writings of James Weldon JOHNSON and the American and European tours of the Fisk University Jubilee Singers brought black religious folk music to the nonblack com-

Malcolm X, a fiery orator, was a prominent member of the Black Muslims until 1963, when he formed an independent black nationalist organization, the Muslim Mosque, Inc. Following a pilgrimage to Mecca in 1964, Malcolm X moderated his separatist beliefs, conceding the possibility of forging a brotherhood between blacks and whites. He was assassinated while addressing a rally in New York City on Feb. 21, 1965.

W. C. Handy, who wrote such classic compositions as ''Memphis Blues'' (1911) and ''St. Louis Blues'' (1914), is generally regarded as the originator of the musical genre known as the blues. Handy formed his own publishing house to print his compositions and, although blind, led an orchestra for nearly 20 years.

don Johnson; writers Claude McKAY and Jean TOOMER; painters Aaron Douglas (1899–1979) and Laura Wheeler (1887–1948); sculptor Meta Warrick (1877–1967), and, in music, Paul Robeson, Ethel WATERS, Harry T. Burleigh (1866–1949), and Nathaniel Dett (1882–1943). The work of the Harlem Renaissance and writers such as Richard WRIGHT reflected the growing race consciousness among blacks and their opposition to the segregation encountered in all forms of life. These themes continue to be important in the work of such writers as James BALDWIN, Gwendolyn BROOKS, Ralph ELLISON, Douglas Turner WARD, John A. WILLIAMS, Alice WALKER, and the 1993 Nobel Prize winner, Toni MORRISON. Meanwhile Spike Lee has projected urban black consciousness onto the screen.

Religion. Religion has traditionally been important to black American life. The first major denomination among blacks, the African Methodist Episcopal Church, grew from the church established by Richard Allen in Philadelphia in 1787. Others were created or derived from white denominational groups. Slave churches existed prior to the Civil War, often without denominational attachments and usually under the watchful eye of slave owners. Because of the religious connections of leaders of some slave revolts, these uprisings resulted in stricter controls of religious activity. With Emancipation, most former slaves joined Baptist or Methodist churches. These remain today as the church groups with the largest black memberships. Smaller numbers belong to other denominations and to independent churches of varying sizes. Among non-Christian religious groups that have attracted sizable followings are the Peace Mission of Father DIVINE and the Nation of Islam, often referred to as the Black Muslims. Both are urban in origin and date from the 1930s. The Peace Mission is strongly integrationist in teachings, a concept opposed by the Nation of Islam during most of its history. In recent years the racial character of leadership and members of the Peace Mission have become increasingly white. In 1985 the main Black Muslim group was unified with the Muslim community worldwide.

Black ministers prominent in politics during the post–World War II period include Adam Clayton POWELL, Jr., Martin Luther KING, Jr., Jesse Jackson, and Andrew Young.

The Family. The black family through much of U.S. history has borne the strain of slavery and Jim Crow. These institutions limited the opportunity for the black male to fulfill his traditional role of head of household and protector of and provider for his family. Because women were often able to

munity. Bessie SMITH and W. C. HANDY stand out as major figures in the development of this form of music. JAZZ, a direct descendant of blues, developed among blacks in New Orleans and spread with their migration. By 1920 it was popular throughout the country. The enduring popularity of Louis ARMSTRONG and Duke ELLINGTON over several decades attests to its continuing attraction. The influence of jazz on other forms of music is clearly recognized. In 1984, Michael JACKSON dominated the popular music world as no other person had done by winning an unprecedented eight Grammy Awards.

Among a number of concert musicians, Paul ROBESON, Marian ANDERSON, and Leontyne PRICE had impressive careers.

BLACK AMERICAN LITERATURE and art were slower to develop than was black music. Early artists and writers who were black dealt with themes that, in selection and approach, were indistinguishable from the works of whites. By the 1920s centers of artistic activity had developed, the best known being in New York. The HARLEM RENAISSANCE, as this artistic outpouring was known, produced outstanding figures. Among them were poets Langston HUGHES, Countee CULLEN, and James Wel-

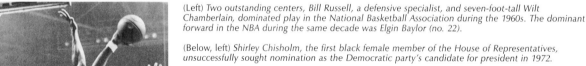

(Left) Two outstanding centers, Bill Russell, a defensive specialist, and seven-foot-tall Wilt Chamberlain, dominated play in the National Basketball Association during the 1960s. The dominant forward in the NBA during the same decade was Elgin Baylor (no. 22).

(Below, left) Shirley Chisholm, the first black female member of the House of Representatives, unsuccessfully sought nomination as the Democratic party's candidate for president in 1972.

(Below, right) Jesse Jackson was hailed at the Democratic national convention in Atlanta in 1988 after he ran a strong second in the race for the presidential nomination. He had also campaigned for the nomination in 1984, but in 1988 he doubled his electoral support.

find domestic employment when no jobs were available to black men, women often provided more dependable and regular incomes. Statistically, black women are more frequently the head of families than is the case in nonblack families. In addition to problems of unemployment, urbanization produced strains of overcrowding, weakening of the extended family concept, and alienation. Nevertheless, relations among family members have traditionally been close. Many first- and second-generation city-dwelling blacks continue to think of home as the Southern place from which the family came.

Education. Until the post–World War II period, most blacks seeking higher education attended private BLACK COLLEGES located mainly in the South. Most of these had been started in the years immediately following the Civil War as a joint effort of blacks, Northern church groups, and the Freedmen's Bureau. Among these were Fisk University, Atlanta University, Talladega College, Morehouse College, and Spelman College. Late in the 19th century Tuskegee Institute was founded by Booker T. Washington, and a number of colleges were established by black church groups. In the 1940s some improvement was made in publicly supported institutions of higher education for blacks, and for the first time black students began to appear in colleges that had previously been all white. In the 1970s the percentage of blacks attending college increased markedly, but in the 1980s blacks lost ground.

Although desegregation of the public schools in the South proceeded slowly for the first decade after the *Brown* v. *Board of Education* decision, by 1969 school districts in every state were at least in token compliance with the 1954 ruling. By that time all forms of de jure segregation had been struck down by the courts. De facto school segregation continued, however, in large part because the communities the schools served were segregated in their residential patterns. This was particularly true in large urban areas and more prevalent in the North than in the South. One method adopted to overcome such segregation was to bus children across school district lines in order to achieve racial balance in the schools. This caused major controversy in the early 1970s and led to instances of violent opposition (see BUSING, SCHOOL). The overwhelming majority of black children now attend legally integrated schools. Many of these institutions, however, are attended exclusively or overwhelmingly by minority students. In other cases, blacks in so-called integrated schools may have little contact with whites because of various forms of grouping that intentionally or unintentionally maintain a kind of separation of the races.

The Press and Sports. The black press is another of the institutions strongly influenced by urbanization. The major black papers, magazines, and radio stations exist because racial concentration in urban areas makes them a necessary and profitable activity. Among the oldest and most prominent black newspapers are the *Baltimore Afro-American* (founded 1892), the *Chicago Daily Defender* (1905), the *New York Amsterdam News* (1909), and the *Atlanta Daily World* (1928). During the past few decades a score or more new publications, mostly magazines, have appeared. Among the most successful are *Jet* and *Ebony*, both published by Johnson Publications of Chicago.

In recent years the one area in which blacks and whites have most successfully competed on a basis of equality is sports. Before the 1940s competition seldom existed across racial lines except in boxing and track. It was not until Jackie ROBINSON was hired by the Brooklyn Dodgers baseball team in 1947 that major changes began to occur. Today blacks appear in disproportionately large numbers in the college and professional team sports of basketball, baseball, and football, and in boxing and track. The proportion of blacks is even greater among those athletes classed in the superstar category. Outstanding sports players include boxing champions Joe LOUIS and Muhammad ALI; track stars Jesse OWENS and Carl LEWIS; Jim BROWN and O. J. SIMPSON in football; Wilt CHAMBERLAIN, Bill RUSSELL, and Kareem ABDUL-JABBAR in basketball; and baseball players Willie MAYS, Henry AARON, Frank ROBINSON, and Reggie JACKSON. Nonplaying leadership roles for blacks have been much slower to open up. There have been fewer

than a dozen coaches and managers of major professional teams. These have included Bill Russell and K. C. Jones of basketball and Frank Robinson of baseball. In college ranks, John Thompson coached Georgetown University to the 1984 NCAA basketball title and then coached the U.S. team at the 1988 Olympics in Seoul; Lawrence Ellis, of Princeton University, coached the U.S. track and field team at the 1984 Olympics in Los Angeles. In 1989 former major league baseball player Bill White was named president of the National League, the first black to head a major U.S. sports league.

Other Contributions; Recent Concerns. Black Americans have also made significant contributions in many other fields, despite the patterns of prejudice and inequality that historically have restricted their opportunities. Charles Drew's work in hematology leading to the establishment of the American Red Cross blood bank and Ralph BUNCHE's appointment as undersecretary of the United Nations in 1950 are examples. The first black American in space was Air Force Lt. Col. Guion S. BLUFORD, who took part in a 1983 Space Shuttle flight.

In the 1980s the median income of blacks still remained significantly below that of whites. Although modest economic gains have been made, large numbers of blacks continue to live in poverty. Many blacks share concern that actions taken by the administration of President Ronald Reagan—withdrawing funds from programs to aid the poor and reducing support for affirmative action—have seriously harmed their communities. Perceived indifference on the part of the administration of President George Bush sustained resentments. On Apr. 30, 1992, south-central Los Angeles exploded in a fiery riot and demonstrations erupted in other cities after a California jury failed to convict four Los Angeles policemen charged with using excessive force in the videotaped beating-arrest of a black motorist, Rodney King.   HENRY DREWRY

Bibliography: Aptheker, Herbert, *Afro-American History* (1971); Clark, K. B., *Dark Ghetto* (1965); Du Bois, W. E. B., *Black Reconstruction in America, 1860–1880* (1935; repr. 1976); Franklin, John Hope, *From Slavery to Freedom*, 6th ed. (1987), and, as ed. with August Meier, *Black Leaders of the Twentieth Century* (1983); Frazier, E. Franklin, *The Negro Church in America*, rev. ed. (1974); Gutman, H. G., *The Black Family in Slavery and Freedom, 1750–1925* (1976); Hacker, Andrew, *Two Nations: Black and White, Separate, Hostile, Unequal* (1991); Hughes, Langston, *Fight for Freedom* (1962); Jones, Jacqueline, *Labor of Love, Labor of Sorrow: Black Women, Work, and the Family from Slavery to the Present* (1985); Lemann, Nicholas, *The Promised Land* (1991); Levine, Lawrence W., *Black Culture and Black Consciousness* (1977); Lincoln, C. E., and Mamiya, L. H., *The Black Church in the African-American Experience* (1990); Myrdal, Gunnar, et al., *An American Dilemma*, 2 vols., rev. ed. (1962; repr. 1975); Woodward, C. Vann, *American Counterpoint: Slavery and Racism in the North-South Dialogue* (1983) and *The Strange Career of Jim Crow*, 3d rev. ed. (1974).

Black Beauty

Anna SEWELL's *Black Beauty* (1877), a children's classic, is the sentimental, imaginary autobiography of a horse. Originally a gentleman's mount, Black Beauty is mistreated by a careless groom and breaks a leg. No longer useful, he receives harsher and harsher treatment until he is at last rescued by a kind woman. Intended by Sewell as an argument for the humane treatment of animals, the book has been called "the *Uncle Tom's Cabin* of animal stories." *Black Beauty* has been made into a film several times.   CHARLOTTE D. SOLOMON

black codes

Black codes were legal enactments governing the behavior and status of blacks in American states before the 14TH AMENDMENT (1868) to the Constitution made such discriminatory legislation unconstitutional. Before the Civil War the term usually referred to laws regulating free blacks; those governing slaves were usually called slave codes. After the Civil War, the Southern state governments set up by President Andrew JOHNSON passed new black codes to control the newly freed ex-slaves. Based largely on the old black codes, the new laws gave the ex-slaves some basic rights, but they also discriminated against them. In no state with such a code could a black testify in court unless he was party to a legal action; in most states, blacks were forbidden to bear arms or meet in un-supervised groups; in many they were made liable to criminal punishment for breaking labor contracts, instead of being subject to civil penalties as whites were. Usually punishments for crimes were different from those for whites. Stiff, discriminatory vagrancy laws were passed, and it was made easy to force black children into apprenticeships—virtual slavery—to whites.

The passage of these laws alienated most Northern whites, leading to a new program of RECONSTRUCTION and to passage of the 14th Amendment, which guarantees equality before the law to all persons in the United States.   MICHAEL LES BENEDICT

Bibliography: Finkelman, Paul, ed., *Race and Law before Emancipation* (1992); Wilson, T. B., *The Black Codes of the South* (1965).

black colleges

Black colleges and universities are institutions in the U.S. system of higher education that were founded for the post–high school instruction of blacks. They are a source of pride among African Americans, having produced many of the teachers, ministers, physicians, lawyers, and others who provide leadership as well as education, health care, and legal and technical services to the black community.

In 1991, 105 U.S. institutions were classified as traditional or historic black colleges, most of them in the South; 51 were public institutions, and 54 schools were private. A number of other institutions, however, were predominantly black—mostly two-year urban institutions, many established in the 1970s. In 1964 more than 51% of all blacks in college attended historic black colleges; in 1991 that figure was 16.4%.
History. Although repeated efforts were made before the Civil War to found institutions of higher learning for blacks, most black colleges and universities were established after that conflict. In cooperation with the FREEDMEN'S BUREAU and in the face of beatings, murder, and arson by Southern white terrorists, the large black and Northern white church groups—the Methodists, Baptists, Presbyterians, and Congregationalists—founded literally hundreds of colleges and universities in the South for blacks. At first, black colleges enrolled elementary and secondary students, but their names indicated the purpose their founders hoped they would serve. Because racial segregation was legalized in the South during the late 19th century, and because Northern white colleges were reluctant to enroll blacks, these schools became the chief source of higher learning for African Americans until the 1960s.

In academic programs, black colleges and universities reflect their origins. Some, such as Tuskegee Institute in Alabama and Hampton Institute in Virginia (both now universities), began as vocational training schools. Because they were successful in attracting white financial support, Tuskegee and Hampton became models for incorporating an industrial education curriculum in other black institutions, which became agricultural and mechanical or technical schools. Others, such as Talladega (Alabama), Spelman (Georgia), and Tougaloo (Mississippi), were founded upon, or adopted, a liberal arts curriculum. In the early 20th century, which of these academic programs—industrial or classical—would best serve the needs of blacks was a matter of debate. The chief disputants were Booker T. WASHINGTON and W. E. B. DU BOIS.
Special Aspects. Black colleges and universities tend to be more involved in service activities than other colleges. Miles College in Alabama, Fisk University, Tuskegee, and Xavier University in Louisiana, for example, have conducted workshops on issues of importance to blacks, extended help to preschool ghetto children and high school dropouts, offered retraining programs, and provided neighborhood and family counseling services. Teams from Howard University and Meharry medical and dental schools have provided health-care services to impoverished rural and urban areas. Morgan State College in Maryland participates in student exchange programs with white higher educational institutions and has offered work-study programs with American industry. Others have developed special admissions and academic programs for educationally disadvantaged youths.

A number of problems hamper black institutions of higher education in fulfilling their educational mission. Today, despite enrollment surges at some black schools, most black undergraduates attend predominantly white colleges and universities. The schools also face problems of institutional poverty, including generally lesser salaries for black college faculty and administrators, small endowments, low alumni support, and minimal state funding for the public institutions. In many cases physical facilities need upgrading and modernizing.

Black colleges also confront additional problems and new opportunities. Desegregation threatens some of them with extinction or with consolidation with rival white institutions. They are also seeking a new definition of black education. Some educators argue that only black colleges can truly impart self-confidence and pride to black youths and educate them for liberation and black nationhood. Others argue that the challenge of the future lies in training black students to rebuild a broadly based coalition of different racial and ethnic groups to combat racial tribalism.   MONROE H. LITTLE

Bibliography: Aldridge, Daniel W., Jr., *The Aldridge Historically Black College Guide* (1983); Ballard, Alan B., *The Education of Black Folk* (1973); Bowman, J. Wilson, *America's Black Colleges*, ed. by R. Rolle-Whatley (1992); Bullock, Henry A., *A History of Negro Education in the South from 1619 to the Present* (1967); Du Bois, W. E. B., *The Education of Black People: Ten Critiques, 1906 to 1960,* ed. by Herbert Aptheker (1973); Wilson, Erlene B., *The One Hundred Best Colleges for African-American Students* (1993).

Black Death: see BUBONIC PLAGUE.

black dwarf

A black dwarf is the final phase in the STELLAR EVOLUTION of a WHITE DWARF. Such stars have exhausted their nuclear energy sources, so any light they produce is from gravitational contraction. The cold hulks that remain when this energy is expended are called black dwarfs. Because they are dark and distant, none has yet been found.   R. H. GARSTANG

black English: see SOCIOLINGUISTICS.

black-eyed Susan

Black-eyed Susan, also called yellow daisy, *Rudbeckia hirta,* is a name commonly given a wild flowering plant belonging to the composite family, Compositae. Native to southern Canada and the eastern United States, it is an annual, biennial, or short-lived perennial that is sometimes a bothersome weed but is also cultivated. It grows to about 1 m (3 ft) high and bears

The black-eyed Susan vine, T. alata, a twining plant with arrowhead-shaped leaves, can be trained to climb a trellis or be displayed in a hanging basket.

heads of orange yellow ray flowers around a purple brown disk or cone. The black-eyed Susan is the state flower of Maryland. The name *black-eyed Susan* is also given to clock vine, *Thunbergia alata;* treasure flower, *Gazania splendens;* and coneflower, *Rudbeckia lacinata.*

Black Forest

The Black Forest (German: Schwarzwald) is a mountainous region in Baden-Württemberg, in southwestern Germany. Its highest peak is Feldberg (1,493 m/4,898 ft). It has an area of about 6,009 km² (2,320 mi²) and is about 161 km (100 mi) long from north to south. The Black Forest lies east of the upper Rhine. The valleys are fertile and make good pastureland as well as providing good soil for grape vineyards, but forested regions are now showing serious effects of ACID RAIN. Lumbering, woodworking, and the manufacture of toys and cuckoo clocks are the main industries. Winter sports facilities and mineral springs attract tourists to the area.

Black Friday

In U.S. history, Black Friday is the name given to Sept. 24, 1869, the day when a panic on Wall Street caused the financial ruin of thousands of investors. Two speculators, Jay GOULD and James FISK, had attempted to corner the gold market. To prevent that from happening, the U.S. Treasury released its gold on the market. The sudden glut of gold not only brought down its price but collapsed the entire stock market as well. The name *Black Friday* is sometimes applied also to Sept. 19, 1873, when the failure of Jay COOKE's banking house led to another financial panic.

Black Hand

Black Hand was the name given early in the 20th century to a probably nonexistent organization believed responsible for crime in the Italian community in the United States. Many victims of extortion received letters marked with a black hand, but it is believed now that the symbol was used as a technique to inspire terror rather than to represent a specific organization. Although some Italian immigrants had ties to the MAFIA and to other Old World criminal societies, organized crime was not highly developed in the United States at that time.

Bibliography: Pitkin, Thomas Monroe, and Cordasco, Francesco, *The Black Hand: A Chapter in Ethnic Crime* (1977).

Black Hawk War

The Black Hawk War (1832) was the last major Indian-white conflict east of the Mississippi River. In 1804 representatives of the SAUK and FOX tribes signed a treaty abandoning all claims to land in Illinois. Although expected to remove to Iowa, they were permitted to remain east of the Mississippi until their former lands were sold. The Sauk leader, Black Hawk (1767–1838), opposed the treaty and rose to prominence when he fought for the British during the WAR OF 1812.

When the Indians were finally ordered into Iowa in 1828, Black Hawk sought in vain to create an anti-American alliance with the Winnebago, Potawatomi, and Kickapoo. In 1829, 1830, and 1831, Black Hawk's band returned across the Mississippi for spring planting, frightening the whites. When the Indians returned in 1832, a military force was organized to repulse them.

For 15 weeks Black Hawk was pursued into Wisconsin and then westward toward the Mississippi. He received no substantial support from other tribes, some of which even aided in his pursuit. On Aug. 3, 1832, the remnants of his band were attacked as they attempted to flee across the river and were virtually annihilated. Black Hawk escaped but soon surrendered. Imprisoned for a short time, he later settled in a Sauk village on the Des Moines River.   LAWRENCE C. KELLY

Bibliography: Black Hawk, *Black Hawk: An Autobiography,* ed. by Donald Jackson (1833; repr. 1964); Eckert, A. W., *Twilight of Empire* (1988); Gurko, Miriam, *Indian America: The Black Hawk War* (1970); Hagan, William T., *The Sac and Fox Indians* (1958).

Black Hills

The Black Hills are a group of eroded mountains in western South Dakota and eastern Wyoming. The name is derived from the dark pine trees that cover the slopes. The Black Hills extend over an area of about 15,540 km² (6,000 mi²). Harney Peak (2,207 m/7,242 ft) is the highest summit. A tourist attraction, the region contains Wind Cave National Park, Mount Rushmore National Memorial, and the Homestake Mine—the largest gold mine in the United States.

black hole

A black hole is a theorized celestial body whose surface gravity is so strong that no light can escape from within it. Although black holes have been of intense scientific interest only in the later 20th century, the concept goes back to the French mathematician Pierre Simon de LAPLACE. In a 1798 treatise Laplace agreed with Isaac Newton that light is composed of particles. He reasoned that if enough mass were added to a star like the Sun, the gravitational force of the star eventually would become so great that its escape velocity would equal the velocity of light. At that point, light particles would not be able to leave the surface of the star, and it would "blink out" and become an invisible black star.

More than a century later, Albert Einstein, in his special theory of relativity, maintained that nothing can move faster than light. This means that Laplace's black stars are also black holes, because if light cannot escape, all other matter must be trapped as well. The surface of a black hole thus acts like a one-way membrane: material may fall into a black hole, but no information or energy can come out of a black hole. The detailed properties of black holes are studied by using Einstein's general theory of relativity and gravitation.

In 1917 a German astrophysicist, Karl SCHWARZSCHILD, used Einstein's theory to calculate that if any star were compressed to a size smaller than a certain critical radius—now called the SCHWARZSCHILD RADIUS in his honor—the density would become so high and the gravitational force so great that the star would become a black hole. The spherical surface about the star at the Schwarzschild radius is called the "event horizon." It marks the outer surface of the black hole at which the escape velocity just equals the velocity of light. Further calculations revealed to Schwarzschild that the critical radius of a black hole is proportional to its mass. For the Sun, this radius is about 3 km (about 2 mi). To find the Schwarzschild radius of any other object, one divides the mass of that object by the mass of the Sun and then multiplies by 3 km.

If a star more massive than the Sun undergoes gravitational collapse at the end of its evolution, it will form either a WHITE DWARF, a NEUTRON STAR, or—according to theory—a black hole, depending primarily on its mass (see STELLAR EVOLUTION). If this collapse process is nonspherical, perhaps because the star is flattened at the poles, then theoretical GRAVITATIONAL WAVES could be given off just before the black hole is formed. Attempts are being made to detect such waves, and supercomputers are being used to determine black-hole behaviors.

The only other way to identify a black hole would be through its interactions with other matter. For example, if the black hole is formed in a binary star system, gas from the normal star may later flow toward the black hole. As the gas falls toward the hole, its molecules increase in speed and approach the speed of light. The molecules begin to bunch up and collide, heating them to temperatures at which X rays are emitted. Such X rays have been detected in eclipsing binary star systems in which the X-ray source is not visible. The X-ray nova V404 Cygni 1s the most likely black-hole candidate of this kind thus far. The Hubble Space Telescope has also photographed, in the center of galaxy M87, a disk of dust and gas rapidly rotating around what is probably a black hole.

Black holes, if they exist, could come in a great range of sizes. The English physicist Stephen HAWKING has speculated that tiny black holes with masses no larger than that of a large mountain are possible. Such black holes, in the size range of elementary particles, would have been formed only under the extreme conditions that COSMOLOGY theories indicate ex-

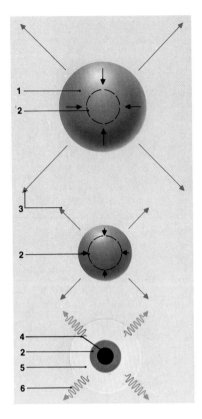

(Left) *As a massive star* (1) *collapses, its density and surface gravity increase. Below a critical volume* (2), *or event horizon, gravitational forces become too strong for light to escape. The energy* (3), *or frequency, of emitted light also decreases as gravitational fields increase. When the black hole forms* (4), *incoming particles* (5) *become hot because of high-speed collisions, and X rays* (6) *are given off outside the event horizon.* (Above) *Envisioned in the model of a black hole are a blue supergiant star and an invisible black hole in close orbit about each other. Gas particles are thought to stream from the supergiant* (left) *to the black hole* (right), *the tiny hole in the center of the accretion disk. The disk is formed by particles orbiting the black hole. Matter close to the event horizon revolves more rapidly than that farther out. The friction between adjacent gas streams heats the gas and causes it to spiral into the black hole.*

isted in the very first moments of the universe (see INFLATION-ARY THEORY). On the other hand, gigantic black holes may lie at the center of galaxies. Some astronomers suggest that such black holes may be linked to the differences that exist between galaxies, ranging from normal ones such as our own to the highly active galaxies called radio galaxies and quasars (see EX-TRAGALACTIC SYSTEMS).

Various speculations have been made as to the permanence or instability of black holes themselves. Laws of physics suggest that black holes would emit particles and shrink with time. According to Hawking, their temperatures would rise as they shrank, and they might finally evaporate with an enormous burst of energy. Other theorists suggest that certain factors would halt this process along the way. Some theorists have even suggested the existence of so-called white holes in which matter would flow through a completely collapsed black hole—a singularity, or body of zero radius and infinite density —into another universe. This notion is quite speculative.

A popular misconception is that black holes act like cosmic vacuum cleaners, sucking up everything within reach. In fact the gravitational attraction of a black hole would be no stronger than that of a normal star of the same mass. Thus, if the Sun could collapse to form a black hole (it cannot, how-ever, and will instead end as a white dwarf), the Earth would continue to orbit just as it does now.   LARRY SMARR

Bibliography: Chaisson, Eric, *Relatively Speaking* (1988); Folger, Tim, "The Ultimate Vanishing," *Discover*, October 1993; Greenstein, George, *Frozen Star* (1984); Gribbin, John, *Unveiling the Edge of Time* (1992); Kafatas, Minas, *Supermassive Black Holes* (1988); Price, R. H., and Thorne, K. S., "The Membrane Paradigm for Black Holes," *Scientific American*, April 1988; Wald, R. M., *Space, Time, and Gravity*, 2d ed. (1992).

See also: GRAVITATIONAL COLLAPSE.

Black Hole of Calcutta

On June 20, 1756, the British garrison in the Indian city of Cal-cutta was captured by the nawab (ruler) of Bengal and im-prisoned for the night in a small room known as the Black Hole. Most of the prisoners (123 out of 146, according to the original British account; 43 out of 64, by recent Indian re-search) stifled to death. The incident became a cause célèbre in British imperial history, but details remain debatable.

black humor

Black humor is a mordant, aggressive, iconoclastic type of com-edy, sometimes called "comedy of the absurd" or "tragic farce." The term *black humor* was apparently first used in its modern sense by André BRETON, the French surrealist poet and critic, in his *Anthologie de l'humour noir* (Anthology of Black Humor), first published in 1940.

Proponents of black humor contend that themes formerly appropriate to tragedy are now the proper province of their humor. In Samuel BECKETT's play *Waiting for Godot* (1952), theological and philosophical concerns mingle freely with old jokes and music-hall and vaudeville routines.

The prevailing tone in black humor is ironic and ambivalent. Fundamental values and assumptions are questioned or turned upside down. Reason and the power of reason to uncover truth are attacked. Both language and logic are disturbed, as in Eugène IONESCO's play *The Bald Soprano* (1953), which at-tacks the clichés of ordinary social discourse. The intense ba-nality and absurdity of the dialogue call attention to a world gone mad. The general effect of black humor is, in Peter HANDKE's phrase, to "offend the audience," leaving it puzzled and disoriented.   MAURICE CHARNEY

Black Kettle

Chief Black Kettle, d. 1868, a leader of the southern CHEYENNE Indians in Colorado, is remembered mainly in connection with the SAND CREEK MASSACRE of 1864, in which Colorado militia-men under Col. John M. Chivington attacked a peaceful encampment of his people. The surprise attack, during which hundreds of Cheyenne warriors, women, and children were killed, occurred after Black Kettle had agreed to an armi-stice with the U.S. Army. Despite this, Black Kettle continued to negotiate with the U.S. government until Nov. 27, 1868, when U.S. troops under Gen. George Custer attacked his camp on the Washita River in Oklahoma, again without warning. Black Kettle was killed.   GENE WELTFISH

Bibliography: Hoig, Stan, *The Battle of the Washita* (1976).

black light: see ULTRAVIOLET LIGHT.

black lung

Black lung is a disease of the lung caused by breathing fine particles of coal dust over a period of years; it is an occupational disease of coal miners and coal loaders.

The disease is a form of pneumoconiosis, which is a general term for lung disease caused by breathing dust in such occupations as stone-cutting, sandblasting, and knife-grinding as well as coal mining. The accumulation of dust in the lungs can cause scarring and eventual breakdown of the air sacs, or alveoli, where gas exchange takes place. Common complications are EMPHYSEMA and increased susceptibility to respiratory infections, especially tuberculosis. Extensive scarring may stiffen the lung tissue and decrease its ability to absorb oxygen from the air; this forces the heart to work harder and increases the risk of death from heart failure. Recent studies suggest that much of the lung damage from coal dust is caused by toxic chemicals in the particles, as well as by direct physical abrasion of lung tissue. No cure is known for the disease, and the lung damage is permanent.

The knowledge that black lung was directly related to dust levels in coal mines led to improved conditions and a significantly reduced incidence of the disease early in the 20th century. The efforts of coal miners' unions, perhaps more than the work of any other group, brought about improvements in occupational safety. However, the introduction of machine-cutting of coal, which raises more dust than pick-and-shovel methods, soon caused the incidence to rise again. Federal legislation enforced by the Bureau of Mines now limits the permissible level of dust in coal mines.   PETER L. PETRAKIS

Bibliography: Barth, P. S., *The Tragedy of Black Lung* (1987); Morgan, W. K., and Seaton, A., *Occupational Lung Diseases* (1975); Zahorski, Withold, ed., *Coal Workers' Pneumoconiosis* (1974).

black market

A black market involves trade that violates government laws regulating prices or forbidding trade in certain goods. Black markets are common in wartime when consumer goods are scarce and in many Third World and Communist countries without convertible currencies. The black marketeer characteristically charges prices that exceed those established by the government.

Black Mass

The Black Mass, usually connected with Satanic cults, is a parody of the MASS. It is celebrated with blasphemous intention in honor of the devil instead of God. The rituals and symbols of the Mass are inverted. For example, the Lord's Prayer is recited backward, and the cross is suspended upside down. Generally, a particle of the Communion bread consecrated at a valid Mass is desecrated.

Black Mountain school of poetry

The Black Mountain school of poetry was a group of poets connected with Black Mountain College, in North Carolina, an experimental community of students, teachers, writers, painters, musicians, and dancers, active from 1933 to 1956. The Black Mountain poets were Charles OLSON, Robert CREELEY, who edited *The Black Mountain Review* from 1954 to 1957, and Robert DUNCAN. All relied on personal forms of poetic expression to express deep feeling; this was in reaction to the objectivity valued by the then-dominant New Critics. Juxtaposing the historical and the familiar, violating continuity, experimenting with Olson's ideas on projective verse, these poets began to change the rigid view of how a poem should

read and look. Among their students at Black Mountain who became poets and continued their ideas were Joel Oppenheimer, John Wieners, Ed Dorn, Jonathan Williams, and Michael Rumaker.   JOHN TYTELL

Bibliography: Duberman, Martin, *Black Mountain: An Exploration in Community* (1972).

Black Mountains

The Black Mountains, unglaciated peaks in western North Carolina, are the highest range of the Appalachian mountain system. Mount MITCHELL (2,037 m/6,684 ft) is the highest peak in the United States east of the Mississippi River. A spur of the BLUE RIDGE MOUNTAINS, the range runs north and south for 32 km (20 mi).

Black Muslims

Elijah Muhammad, the organizational and spiritual leader of the Nation of Islam (Black Muslim) sect, preached a doctrine of separatism and economic independence for blacks. The Muslims have taken a markedly different course since his death in 1975.

Black Muslims is a widely used name for the adherents of an American black nationalist religious movement whose self-designation changed in 1976 from "The Lost-Found Nation of Islam" to "The World Community of Islam in the West." By 1980 the group had become the "American Muslim Mission." The movement traces its beginnings to the enigmatic figure of Wallace D. Fard (Wali Farad), known as "Prophet Fard," "The Great Mahdi" or "The Savior," who attracted 8,000 followers in the short period between his appearance in Detroit in 1930 and his disappearance in June 1934.

The movement, with its headquarters in Chicago, gained ground significantly under Fard's successor, Elijah MUHAMMAD, who exercised strong leadership until his death in 1975, when Black Muslims numbered between 150,000 and 200,000. He saw himself as the "prophet and apostle of Allah," claiming that God had appeared in the figure of Fard. Preaching an antiintegrationist message, Elijah Muhammad frequently voiced warnings about "the human beast the people or race known as the white." He called "every Black Man in America [to] be reunited with his own" and urged a sense of black self-reliance and separation from the white society, even economically. One of the best-known Black Muslim ministers during this period was MALCOLM X, converted while he was in prison in 1947, who broke with the movement in March 1964 and was assassinated 11 months later.

A radically different phase began under Elijah Muhammad's son and successor, Warith Deen (or Wallace D.) Muhammad. He called for a new sense of patriotism, urging blacks to "identify with the land and flag." Advocating the "religious unification of the world's Muslims," W. D. Muhammad abandoned unorthodox notions and expressions that had presented obstacles for many other Muslims' recognition of this movement as being authentically Islamic. In May 1985 he announced the dissolution of the American Muslim Mission to unify its members with the worldwide Muslim community.

A splinter group led by Louis Farrakhan, however, retains the earlier separatist principles and the name *Nation of Islam*. Its racial, often anti-Semitic comments have offended many blacks as well as whites, although its successful work with youth in inner-city black communities and its willingness to cooperate with other groups in behalf of black youth have been admired even by critics.   WILLEM A. BIJLEFELD

Bibliography: Lomax, L. E., *When the Word Is Given: A Report on Elijah Muhammad, Malcolm X, and the Black Muslim World* (1963; repr. 1979); Marsh, Clifton E., *From Black Muslims to Muslims: The Transition from Separatism to Islam, 1930–1980* (1984); Muhammad, Elijah, *Message to the Blackman in America* (1965); Shalaby, Ibrahim, *Education of a Black Muslim* (1980).

black nationalism

Black nationalism is the name given to revitalization movements among black Americans, emphasizing their African origins and identity, their pride in being black, their desire to control their own communities, and sometimes the desire to establish a black nation in Africa or some part of the United States. The exact origins of black nationalist movements are lost in the largely unwritten history of blacks in early America, but it is clear that such movements began as protests against the brutal and dehumanizing conditions of SLAVERY. A few records indicate that early African protest against slavery conditions had overtones of black nationalism.

Organized black nationalist movements appear to have begun with Paul Cuffe (1759–1817), a black sea captain. Between 1811 and 1815 he made the first attempt to establish a black American colony in Africa, transporting several dozen people to Africa. Early in the 20th century W. E. B. DU BOIS developed a sophisticated rationale for a Pan-African movement that would join blacks in America and Africa. But not until after 1910 did a mass movement emerge with black nationalism as its central theme. The leader of this new movement, Marcus GARVEY, recruited thousands into his Universal Negro Improvement Association (UNIA). Its goals included a black nation oriented toward Africa but controlled by black Americans. The UNIA developed the first major black capitalist enterprises, including restaurants, grocery stores, hotels, and a steamship line. Because of antagonism from whites and mismanagement at the top, this movement failed, but it was soon followed by a number of Africa-oriented movements, the most important of which was the Nation of Islam, known inaccurately as the Black Muslims.

The Nation of Islam grew under the leadership of Elijah MUHAMMAD from the mid-1930s to the mid-1970s. Along with Islamic and Christian ideas it emphasized black pride, the central role of the male in the family, the importance of economic self-sufficiency, and a way of life that was often equated with middle-class morality. It exchanged the goal of a separate nation outside the United States for one of independence and autonomy within it. Perhaps its best-known leader was MALCOLM X. An offshoot "Nation of Islam" led by Louis Farrakhan upholds these separatist ideas.

By the late 1960s many themes of black nationalism had become part of the lifestyle of ordinary black Americans, particularly young people. These ideas persist today in colleges and universities, many of which have developed courses in black studies.   JOE R. FEAGIN

Bibliography: Draper, Theodore, *The Rediscovery of Black Nationalism* (1970); Essien-Udom, E. U., *Black Nationalism* (1962); Helmreich, W. B., *Afro-Americans and Africa: Black Nationalism at the Crossroads* (1977); Moses, W. J., *The Golden Age of Black Nationalism* (1988).

Black Panther party

The Black Panther party was a militant organization of blacks founded in Oakland, Calif., in 1966 by Huey P. Newton and Bobby G. Seale. Panther leaders called upon blacks to arm themselves for a struggle against their oppressors and collected small arsenals. At the same time the party provided free breakfasts, financed by donations from local merchants and wealthy sympathizers, for children in some ghetto areas. It also opened schools and medical clinics.

Several armed clashes with the police occurred. Huey Newton was found guilty of killing an Oakland policeman in 1967, but the conviction was reversed on appeal. He was charged with murder in a street brawl in 1974 and fled to Cuba. Seale and other Panther leaders were accused of torturing and murdering a former Panther whom they suspected of being a police informer, but the jury failed to reach a verdict. Another leader, Eldridge CLEAVER, fled abroad to avoid imprisonment for parole violation; he later returned, abandoned radicalism, and became a proselytizer for Christianity.

The Panthers lost a leader in 1969 when Chicago police made an early-morning raid on a Panther residence and killed Fred Hampton in his bed. The movement declined after quarrels among its leaders increased and as black radicalism waned in the 1970s. Two former Black Panthers were implicated in the Brink's robbery incident in New York in 1981.

Bibliography: Anthony, Earl, *Spitting in the Wind* (1990); Brown, Elaine, *A Taste of Power: A Black Woman's Story* (1993); Heath, G. Louis, ed., *Black Panther Leaders Speak* (1976); Marine, Gene, *Black Panthers* (1969); Moor, Gilbert, *Rage* (1993).

Black Prince, the: see EDWARD, THE BLACK PRINCE.

Black Sea

The Black Sea, in the southeastern corner of Europe, is bordered on the north and the east by Ukraine, Russia, and Georgia, on the south by Turkey, and on the west by Bulgaria and Romania. It is linked with the Atlantic Ocean through the BOSPORUS, the Sea of MARMARA, the DARDANELLES, the Aegean Sea, and the Mediterranean Sea; and with the North Sea by the Rhine-Danube Canal. The Crimean peninsula extends into it from the north, and the small Sea of AZOV is connected to it by the narrow Kerch Strait to the east of the CRIMEA. The Black Sea has an area of 420,300 km² (162,280 mi²) and a maximum depth of 2,210 m (7,250 ft). The Turks named it Karadeniz ("black sea") because storms tend to arise in it unpredictably. It has been economically important as a trade route, tourist attraction, and fishing area, but its fisheries have declined because of overfishing and the effects of toxic waste. ODESSA (Ukraine), SEVASTOPOL (Crimea), BATUMI (Georgia), Novorossiisk (Russia), CONSTANTA (Romania), VARNA and BURGAS (Bulgaria), and Zonguldak, TRABZON, and SINOP (Turkey) are the major ports. On the east, the Black Sea is bordered by the CAUCASUS MOUNTAINS and on the south by the Pontic range; neither area has much of a coastal lowland. The western coast is much less steep, except where the Istranca and Balkan ranges meet the sea. The Crimean Mountains are the only cliffs on the generally flat north coast.

The Black Sea is a remnant of the Tethys Sea, which split off from the Mediterranean about 40 million years ago. The present-day sea may be divided into three concentric submarine relief zones. The outer ring, about 25% of the area, is in a shallow shelf zone less than 100–110 m (330–360 ft) deep. The second zone comprises the slopes that lead to the third zone, the central depths. This central area is a featureless plain covering about a third of the total area. An underwater mountain range lies off the coast of Turkey between Sinop and Samsun.

The sea's salinity, which averages 22 parts per thousand, is about half that of the oceans and is much reduced where the principal tributaries—the DANUBE, DNESTR, Bug, and DNEPR rivers—enter in the northwest. Wind-driven currents run counterclockwise, and tides are of little importance.

Marine life reflects the unusual layering of the waters. Below 155 m (510 ft) in the center and 310 m (1,020 ft) near the shores, hydrogen sulfide permeates the water and oxygen is sparse; this lower layer of water cannot support life. Oysters, mollusks, and fish live above this level and are taken commercially. Water plants of the genus *Phyllophora* grow in the northwest section. Marine life has been severely damaged by pollution from oil tankers and industries.

The ancient Greeks founded colonies on the coast of the Black Sea, which was known in ancient times as Pontus Euxinus (Greek for ''hospitable sea''). After the fall of the Byzantine Empire in 1453, the Turks took control of the sea and held it until the late 18th century, when they were driven from their holdings on the northern shore by Russia. Russian attempts to dominate the sea were frustrated by a series of setbacks, including defeat in the CRIMEAN WAR (1853–56). Several international treaties have attempted to guarantee freedom of passage on the sea. Commercial shipping has been unrestricted since 1829, but the Montreux Convention of 1936 restricted the passage of warships of nations that do not border the sea.   IRA M. SHESKIN

Bibliography: Setlowe, Richard, *The Black Sea* (1991); Tolmazin, D., *Changing Coastal Oceanography of the Black Sea* (1985).

black-and-tan coonhound

The black-and-tan coonhound is the only one of six well-developed American coonhounds recognized as a separate breed by the American Kennel Club. The other five breeds, all closely related to the black-and-tan and registered by the United Kennel Club of Great Britain, are the redbone, the English coonhound, the bluetick, the treeing walker, and the

The black-and-tan coonhound, originally bred in the United States, is a hunting dog that trails by scent. It pursues raccoons, opossums, and larger wild game, trees them, and barks to call the hunter.

plott. As their name suggests, coonhounds were developed to hunt raccoons, although various breeds have been used to hunt opossums, mountain lions, and bears.

The black-and-tan was developed by crossing bloodhounds and foxhounds. The breed, which was officially recognized by the American Kennel Club in 1945, resembles the bloodhound. It stands up to 69 cm (27 in) high at the shoulder, weighs 32–38 kg (70–85 lb), and has pendulous ears and an erect sickle tail. The coat is short, dense, and black, with tan markings on the chest, legs, and muzzle and above the eyes. Black-and-tans trail like bloodhounds: by scent, nose close to the ground, and sounding off with a deep bellow when the quarry has been treed.

Black and Tans

The Black and Tans, named for their khaki uniforms with black caps and black armbands, were a group of former soldiers recruited by the British government to help the Royal Irish Constabulary put down the Irish nationalist rebellion in 1920. Numbering between 6,000 and 7,000, they were rough men who used brutal methods in retaliation against the terrorist tactics of the IRISH REPUBLICAN ARMY. Herbert Asquith, prime minister of Britain from 1908 to 1916, said: ''Things are being done in Ireland which would disgrace the blackest annals of the lowest despotism in Europe.'' The Black and Tans served until the creation of the Irish Free State by the treaty of Dec. 6, 1921.

See also: IRELAND, HISTORY OF.

black widow

The venomous bite of the black widow spider, Latrodectus mactans, *causes muscle spasms and breathing difficulty in humans and may be fatal. The female is distinguished by a red hourglass marking on its underside.*

The black widow, *Latrodectus mactans*, is a poisonous spider of the family Theridiidae, order Araneida. The female, about 1.3 cm (0.5 in) long, is glossy black, densely clothed with microscopic hairs, and marked with a characteristic red hourglass on the underside of the abdomen. The male, which is rarely seen, is smaller than the female and has four pairs of red marks along the sides of the abdomen. The black widow is found worldwide in the warmer regions in every state in the United States except Alaska and Hawaii; it lives in a variety of natural and domestic habitats. Generally, the females are not aggressive unless agitated, although they are prone to bite when guarding an egg sac. This spider is venomous, and its bite can be fatal.

The diet of the black widow consists of insects, spiders, and centipedes captured with its web. After mating, the female may ensnare and feed upon her mate—hence the name *black widow.*

Bibliography: Crompton, John, *The Spider* (1987); Thorp, R. W., and Woodson, W. D., *The Black Widow Spider* (1976).

Blackbeard

Blackbeard was the nickname of an English pirate, Edward Teach (or Thatch), who attacked ships in the Caribbean and along the Atlantic coast of North America from 1716 to 1718. He apparently turned to piracy after a career as a privateer during the War of the Spanish Succession (1701–13). Operating from a base in North Carolina (with whose governor he shared his booty), Blackbeard terrorized the coastal settlements of Virginia and the Carolinas. He was finally killed on Nov. 22, 1718, during an engagement with a force sent from Virginia.

Bibliography: Lee, Robert, *Blackbeard the Pirate* (1984).

blackberry

The blackberry, genus Rubus, *a bramble related to the raspberry and dewberry, produces thorny, climbing branches and delicate flowers. Its fruit is used to make pies, jellies, jams, and preserves. Illustrated is the Darrow variety, popular in the northeastern United States.*

The blackberry is a trailing-to-erect bramble, usually spiny, in the genus *Rubus* of the Rosaceae (rose) family. Blackberries occur throughout the world, with the exception of dry desert regions, but the greatest number are in the Northern Hemisphere. Commercial production is largely limited to the United States, where the principal producers are Oregon, Texas, Oklahoma, and Arkansas. Important types are Thornless Evergreen, Marion, Boysen, Olallie, Cherokee, Comanche, Cheyenne, Humble and Darrow. Loganberry is a trailing type with purplish fruit that is different in many respects from other blackberries; most taxonomists consider it a true and separate species. J. N. MOORE

See also: BERRY; FRUITS AND FRUIT CULTIVATION.

blackbird

Blackbird is the common name for about 25 species of birds of the New World family Icteridae, which also includes orioles and bobolinks, and for several unrelated Old World birds of the THRUSH family, Turdidae. American blackbirds range from 20 to 28 cm (8 to 11 in) long and have pointed bills and rounded tails. Males are typically black, and some have markings in bright colors. Females may be brown, grayish, or mottled. The red-winged blackbird *Agelaius phoeniceus* male has flashing-red shoulder patches, for example, and the female is brown and striped; they are abundantly distributed over the marshes and upland fields of most of North America. Many blackbirds are gregarious and nest in colonies; 2 to 7 eggs are laid. They feed on insects, seeds, and grain. The common blackbird of the Old World resembles the duller species of American blackbirds but is actually a thrush related to the American robin. WILLIAM F. SANDFORD

blackbody radiation

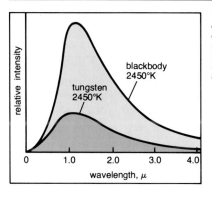

The spectral distribution of energy emitted by a tungsten filament is compared with energy from an ideal blackbody at the same temperature.

A blackbody is an object that absorbs all the energy that falls upon it. Because it reflects no light, it would appear black to an observer. (No perfect blackbody exists in nature, but surfaces coated with carbon black or soot absorb 97 percent of incident energy.) A blackbody is also a perfect emitter. At any specified temperature, a blackbody emits, in each part of the electromagnetic spectrum, the maximum energy obtainable from any radiator because of its temperature alone. Such emitted energy has characteristic energy distribution properties and is called blackbody radiation. Comparison of radiation emitted by real objects with that of a theoretically ideal blackbody can give information about the thermodynamic properties of materials. Also, the ability to accurately explain blackbody radiation enables scientists to test the validity of physical laws.

Toward the end of the 19th century, intensive studies were made to correlate the energy and spectral distribution of blackbody radiation. In 1879, Josef Stefan discovered through experimentation that the radiant energy is proportional to the

Blackbirds are among the most populous of all birds, with some winter flocks numbering in the millions. (Left to right, with male in foreground): the yellow-headed blackbird, Xanthocephalus xanthocephalus, *the only North American bird with a yellow head and a black body; the red-winged blackbird,* Agelaius phoeniceus; *and the brewer's blackbird,* Euphagus cyanocephalus.

fourth power of absolute temperature. The same conclusion was reached in 1884 by another Austrian physicist, Ludwig BOLTZMANN, from theoretical considerations. The combined Stefan-Boltzmann law states the proportionality of energy and temperature as $E = \sigma T^4$. In this equation, σ is the Stefan-Boltzmann constant; the constant has a value of 5.67×10^{-5} erg/sec$\cdot$cm$^2\cdot$deg^4.

Physicists encountered a major difficulty, however, when they tried to calculate the energy radiated from a blackbody at a single, specified wavelength λ. The classical methods of physics—the laws of motion of particles, and MAXWELL'S EQUATIONS for electromagnetic waves—proved unsatisfactory. For example, in 1896 the German physicist Wilhelm WIEN derived an expression for calculating blackbody radiation at a specific wavelength. His radiation law matched experimental observations closely, but not when large values of λ were involved. Another equation, developed by the English physicist Lord RAYLEIGH and modified by another English scientist, James JEANS, was accurate for large wavelengths but failed for short wavelengths. Their law, in fact, predicted that as λ approached zero, blackbody energy would become infinite—an impossibility that became known as the "ultraviolet catastrophe."

Resolution of these problems came with the development of QUANTUM MECHANICS. The German physicist Max PLANCK, in 1900, used experimental results to develop an expression that is accurate for all wavelengths. Shortly thereafter he derived it from theoretical considerations as well. He did so, however, only by assuming that energy is not continuous but instead exists in discrete "bundles" that were later named quanta. The size of a quantum is determined by a constant, h, called PLANCK'S CONSTANT. Planck tried to justify his law on classical grounds, but the appearance of h in Albert EINSTEIN's photoelectric theory in 1905 established the quantum hypothesis and began a new era in physics.

Bibliography: Ingram, D. J., *Radiation and Quantum Physics* (1974); Kuhn, Thomas S., *Black-Body Theory and the Quantum Discontinuity* (1978); Reimann, Arnold L., *Physics: Mechanics and Heat* (1971); Resnick, Robert, and Halliday, David, *Basic Concepts in Relativity and Early Quantum Theory*, 2d ed. (1985).

See also: PHOTOELECTRIC EFFECT; THERMODYNAMICS.

Blackett, Patrick Maynard Stuart, Baron Blackett   [blak'-it]

Patrick, Lord Blackett, b. Nov. 18, 1897, d. July 13, 1974, was an English physicist known for his research utilizing the Wilson CLOUD CHAMBER, for which he received the 1948 Nobel Prize for physics. A graduate of Cambridge University, he served as a professor of physics at the University of London and at Manchester University.

In 1937, Blackett devised a process for photographing, with the help of GEIGER COUNTERS, cosmic rays traversing a Wilson cloud chamber. He also identified positron-electron pairs formed from secondary cosmic rays interacting with matter in particular regions of the cloud chamber. Blackett worked on radar and the atomic bomb during World War II and later investigated rock magnetism as a clue to the origin of the magnetic fields of the Earth, Sun, and stars.   RAYMOND J. SEEGER

Bibliography: Lovell, Bernard, *P. M. S. Blackett* (1976); Oxbury, H. F., *Great Britons* (1985).

Blackfoot

The Blackfoot Indians of North America inhabited much of Montana and parts of neighboring Canadian provinces in the early 19th century. Traditionally a loose confederation of Algonquian-speaking peoples of the Great Plains, they are divided into three main tribes: the Blackfeet (Siksika), the Piegan (Pikuni), and the Blood (Kainah).

Blackfoot Indians used the conical skin tent, or tepee, for shelter and relied on buffalo, antelope, moose, and deer for food and skins. They hunted and fought on horseback and practiced horse stealing from their enemies, seen as an emblem of prowess and prestige. Horses were counted as wealth

and offered in marriage to the bride's family. The taking of multiple wives was prevalent and insured a livelihood for women in a society whose male population was often reduced greatly in intertribal warfare. The SUN DANCE was an important tribal ritual led by an aged medicine woman who also presided in the sweat lodge ceremony and the buffalo tongue ceremony, a sacramental ritual still practiced by the Blood. An estimated 15,000 Blackfeet now live in Canada; in the United States they number about 10,000. Many engage in ranching.   BEA MEDICINE

Bibliography: Ewers, John C., *The Blackfeet* (1958; repr. 1985); Wissler, Clark, *A Blackfoot Sourcebook* (1986).

blackjack

Blackjack, also known as twenty-one, is among the most widely played card games. The French know it as *vingt-et-un* ("21"), which the English sometimes corrupt to Van John. Any number of persons may play, although five to nine is the preferred range. There may be a permanent dealer, or the deal may pass from player to player. Using one to six 52-card decks shuffled together, the dealer begins by giving one card face down to each player, including himself or herself, in clockwise order. Next, each player is dealt another card face down and the dealer a second card face up. Each player, in turn, may then request a "hit," that is, an additional card dealt face up; this may be done as often as the player wishes. The object is to amass cards that total 21 or as close to that number as possible without exceeding 21. Aces count 1 or 11, at the holder's discretion. Face cards and 10s count 10, and all other cards count their numerical value. A player loses automatically if his or her cards total more than 21. Bets are placed before each new hand is dealt. If a player's first two cards total 21, that player is said to have a natural, or a blackjack, and wins immediately unless the dealer also has a natural. In that case, they tie. A player may stop taking additional cards at any point; the dealer must "hit" if his or her total count is below 17, and must stop if it is 17 or more.

Bibliography: Allen, J. E., *The Basics of Blackjack* (1984).

blacklist

A blacklist is a list of persons or companies that are to be boycotted or discriminated against. Governments in wartime have compiled blacklists of firms in other countries suspected of dealing with the enemy. Arab countries in the 1970s drew up a blacklist of U.S. firms that did business with Israel. Blacklists have been used by employers against suspected union organizers and by unions against employers. In the 1950s, motion picture companies and radio and TV broadcasters placed workers accused of pro-Communist sympathies on a blacklist that denied many employment for a number of years.

Bibliography: Faaland, Just, *Essays in the Theory of Trade Discrimination* (1964); Navasky, Victor, *Naming Names* (1981); Teslik, K. L., *Congress, the Executive Branch, and Special Interests: The American Response to the Boycott of Israel* (1982); Wolman, Leo, *Boycott in American Trade Unions* (1916; repr. 1971).

blackmail

Blackmail is the exacting of money from someone by threat. In common usage it means taking money in exchange for not revealing information about a person's illegal or immoral conduct. The victim may also be forced to pay by giving information of a confidential nature. The term *extortion* is often used in connection with blackmail; in the strict sense, however, extortion is the demanding or taking of payment by a public official in return for performing favors.

Blackmore, Richard Doddridge

Richard Doddridge Blackmore, b. June 7, 1825, d. Jan. 20, 1900, was an English novelist and poet best known for his historical romance *Lorna Doone* (1869), set in the wild country of Exmoor. His volumes of poetry and his other novels, such as *The Maid of Sker* (1872), were less popular.

Bibliography: Burris, Q. G., *Richard Blackmore* (1930; repr. 1970).

Blackmun, Harry A.

Harry Andrew Blackmun, b. Nashville, Ill., Nov. 12, 1908, was a justice of the U.S. Supreme Court from 1970 to 1994. A graduate of Harvard Law School, he taught at St. Paul College of Law and the University of Minnesota Law School. In 1959 he was appointed to the U.S. Court of Appeals for the Eighth Circuit. Named to the high court by President Nixon, Blackmun emerged as a centrist (some characterized him as a left-leaning moderate). He took generally conservative stands on criminal law, although he moderated his view on death-penalty cases. In 1976 he held that capital punishment was constitutional, in 1987 he dissented when the Court rejected a racial challenge to the death penalty, and in 1994 he denounced capital punishment altogether. Blackmun's positions in affirmative-action cases were liberal. He wrote the ROE V. WADE decision (1973), which held state laws prohibiting abortion illegal.

blackout, electrical

The term *electrical blackout* refers to a power failure caused either by a planned interruption—such as the limiting of loads during power shortages by rotating power shutoffs through several areas—or by an accidental failure caused by a storm, a failure of generating or transmission equipment, or human error. In general, the pattern of such disturbances starts with the loss of some power-system element followed by the rapid development of unstable or overload conditions, resulting in the automatic disconnection of other generating or transmission elements and a cascading, widespread loss of electrical service. A *brownout* is a curtailment, or reduction, of power.

Major Occurrences. A blackout that attracted great attention occurred on the evening of Nov. 9, 1965, when a massive power failure cascaded across much of the northeastern United States and parts of eastern Canada. The chain of events was initiated by a relay with too low a setting, which operated to disconnect a transmission line at the Ontario Hydroelectric Commission's generating plant at Niagara Falls. Some 30 million people were affected, and the incident precipitated a comprehensive investigation of electric-utility system design.

Among blackouts affecting large areas and millions of people were a failure in parts of Pennsylvania, New Jersey, Maryland, and Delaware in June 1967 that involved some 9,300 megawatts of electrical load and 13 million people, and several affecting eastern Florida and involving as much as 1,500 megawatts of load and a million people. On July 13, 1977, the New York City area was blacked out following transmission line losses caused by storms. About 9 million people were affected and—unlike the 1965 blackout—this one was accompanied by extensive looting and vandalism. Power was off in some areas for more than 24 hours.

In August 1990 a fire at a New York City electrical substation caused a blackout of lower Manhattan, including the Wall Street area. Although emergency generators kept computers from wiping out, trading on most exchanges ceased, and operations were not fully restored for several days. The cost in lost trades was estimated in the tens of millions of dollars. Financial centers are particularly vulnerable to power outages.

Effects and Prevention. Serious blackouts cause losses of industrial production, disturbances to commercial activities, traffic and transportation problems, disruption of municipal services, and severe personal inconvenience to people.

Preventive measures include careful design and operation of power networks; the interconnection of power networks to improve stability; monitoring of generating reserve needs and emergency load-shedding arrangements; and standby power for emergency needs.   ROBERT B. BOYD

See also: POWER, GENERATION AND TRANSMISSION OF.

Blackpool

Blackpool (1991 pop., 150,100) is a resort city in Lancashire in northwestern England, on the coast of the Irish Sea, about 45 km (28 mi) north of Liverpool. Tourism is the economic mainstay because of amusement parks and a large beach, but there is some light manufacturing. A small hamlet until the 19th century, Blackpool grew rapidly when the railroad arrived (1846) and its beach was transformed into a popular resort.

Blackshirts

Blackshirts was the name of the paramilitary action squads of the Italian Fascist party, organized in 1919. These squads, whose uniforms included black shirts, broke up strikes and made other violent attacks on the opponents of fascism. They staged the March on Rome (1922) that brought Benito MUSSOLINI to power. Members of the German SS (*Schutzstaffel*), the Nazi party's paramilitary corps, were called Blackshirts.

blacksmith

A blacksmith is an artisan who shapes and welds iron to produce horseshoes and to make or repair hardware, tools, utensils, and other objects. He begins his work by heating a piece of iron in a furnace, or FORGE, and by means of a BELLOWS forces air into the forge to increase its temperature. When the iron is white hot, it is placed on a heavy iron block, called an anvil, where it is hammered into the desired shape. The term *blacksmith* describes a worker in metal, or smith, who shapes black metal, or iron, as distinguished from a tinsmith, who works with white metal, or tin. The early importance of the blacksmith as a maker of tools and weapons was evident in his deification in ancient mythologies; the Roman god Vulcan, for example, was a blacksmith. Until the Industrial Revolution, nearly all forging was done by blacksmiths. While shoeing horses, they gained a working knowledge of horse diseases and their treatment and thus often served as veterinarians. The development of the automobile and machine forging has greatly reduced the number of blacksmiths.

Bibliography: Andrews, J., *Edge of the Anvil,* rev. ed. (1991); Harris, D., and Heer, B., *Basic Blacksmithing* (1993); McNaughton, P. R., *The Mande Blacksmiths* (1988); Reichelt, R., *Heartland Blacksmiths* (1988).

Blackstone, Sir William

William Blackstone, b. July 10, 1723, d. Feb. 14, 1780, an English lawyer, was the author of *Commentaries on the Laws of England,* the first comprehensive treatment of the English law and constitution. After studying at Oxford, Blackstone read law at the Middle Temple and in 1746 began to practice at Westminster. A poor speaker, he was considered deficient in the talents appropriate to an advocate, and he made little headway in his profession. After seven years he returned to teach at Oxford, where in 1753 he introduced courses in English law. Until then, COMMON LAW had been taught only at the INNS OF COURT. When the university was given an endowment for the study of common law, Blackstone became the first Vinerian professor. In 1761 he was elected to Parliament.

Blackstone's *Commentaries,* a collection of his Oxford lectures, was published in 1765–69. Remarkable for their style, as well as for the way they dealt with a complex subject as a lucid and organic whole, they were widely used in England and abroad until the end of the 19th century. They came under some criticism, notably from the 19th-century legal reformer Jeremy BENTHAM, who contended that Blackstone smugly viewed English law as beyond improvement and that he did not properly understand the social elements underlying legal systems. For many years, however, the *Commentaries* were the dominant influence on the development of U.S. law.

Blackstone was offered the post of solicitor general in 1770 but declined, accepting instead a judgeship of the Court of Common Pleas, which he held until his death.

Bibliography: Boorstin, Daniel J., *Mysterious Science of the Law* (1941; repr. 1961); Holdsworth, William, *A History of English Law,* vol. 12, 7th ed. (1956); Lind, Louise, *William Blackstone* (1993); Lockmiller, David A., *Sir William Blackstone* (1938).

Blackwell   (family)

The Blackwells were a U.S. family that included pioneering, professional women who were advocates of women's rights.

Elizabeth Blackwell, b. Feb. 3, 1821, d. May 31, 1910, was the first woman to obtain (1849) a medical degree from a U.S. medical school, Geneva Medical College. Confronting prejudice when she sought a hospital post, Blackwell opened (1857) the New York Infirmary for Women and Children. She later went (1869) to England, her birthplace, where she helped found the London School of Medicine for Women. Her younger brother, Henry Brown Blackwell, b. May 4, 1825, d. Sept. 7, 1909, was a speaker for women's suffrage. He married feminist Lucy STONE and with her edited the *Woman's Journal* from 1872. Their daughter, Alice Stone Blackwell, b. Sept. 14, 1857, d. Mar. 15, 1950, also edited the journal from 1881 to 1916 and wrote a biography of her mother (1930).

Antoinette Louisa Brown Blackwell, b. May 20, 1825, d. Nov. 5, 1921, the wife of Henry and Elizabeth Blackwell's brother, Samuel, was the first woman to be ordained a minister in the United States. After graduating from Oberlin College (1847) and from its theological seminary (1850), she was refused ordination because of her sex. In 1853 she was ordained pastor of the Congregational Church in South Butler, N.Y., but she resigned four years later and became a Unitarian. She was an advocate of abolition, prohibition, and women's rights. Her writings include *Shadows of Our Social System* (1855) and *The Making of the Universe* (1914).

Bibliography: Cazden, Elizabeth, *Antoinette Brown Blackwell: A Biography* (1983); Hays, Eleanor Rice, *Those Extraordinary Blackwells* (1967); Lasser, Carol, and Merrill, M. D., eds., *Friends and Sisters: Letters between Lucy Stone and Antoinette Brown Blackwell, 1846–93* (1987); Ross, Ishbel, *Child of Destiny* (1950); Wilson, Dorothy C., *Lone Woman: The Story of Elizabeth Blackwell* (1970).

bladder, urinary

The urinary bladder is a hollow sac for the storage and release of urine. When the bladder is filled with urine brought to it from the kidneys by tubes called ureters, pressure on sensory nerve endings in the bladder wall causes a desire to micturate. Micturition, the passing of urine from the bladder into the urethra and out of the body, begins with the voluntary or involuntary relaxation of circular muscles, or sphincters, that surround the urethra at the point where it joins the bladder. Urine is then propelled from the body by reflex contraction of muscles in the bladder wall.   PETER L. PETRAKIS

Bibliography: Sturdy, David, *Outline of Urology*, 2d ed. (1986).

bladdernut

The bladdernut, *Staphylea*, is any of several ornamental shrubs or small trees of the family Staphyleaceae. These plants are found in temperate regions of the Northern Hemisphere. Their white flowers are produced in nodding clusters. The name *bladdernut* is derived from its inflated, bladderlike fruits. The American bladdernut, *S. trifolia*, is an upright shrub that grows to 4.5 m (15 ft) tall and is found from Quebec to Georgia. The European bladdernut, *S. pinnata*, has longer flower clusters and smaller fruit than the American bladdernut.

bladderwort

Bladderwort is the common name for small aquatic or terrestrial carnivorous plants belonging to the genus *Utricularia* of the bladderwort family, Lentibulariaceae. They get their name from the bladderlike structures on their stems and leaves; these bladders serve as traps for insects and larvae and also help to keep aquatic forms afloat. Species of bladderworts grow throughout the world. Most are aquatic, but some tropical species are terrestrial or grow on other plants and have beautiful orchidlike flowers. The flowers of aquatic forms are inconspicuous and float on the surface of the water; the extensive roots may be up to 1 m (3 ft) long.

The bladder of the bladderwort is a sac that has an opening, or trapdoor, and a trigger mechanism to open the door. Aquatic insects or larvae trip the trigger mechanism, causing the trapdoor to open and allowing the prey to be swept into the bladder in a stream of water. The trapdoor subsequently

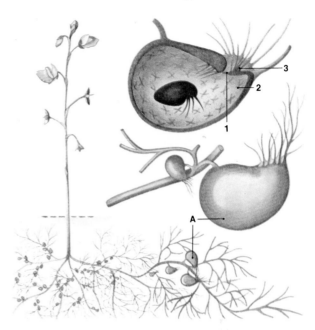

Bladderwort, Utricularia, is an insectivorous plant that lives in slow-flowing streams or ponds. Underwater leaves are modified to form bladders (A). The trapdoor (1) is normally closed, and miniscule glands (2) constantly remove water, keeping the inside at a reduced pressure. A tiny animal touching a trigger hair (3) is carried into the bladder by an inrush of water. It cannot force open the trapdoor and suffocates in less than a day. Its body decays and is absorbed by the bladder lining.

closes. The bladderwort has digestive enzymes in the bladder that degrade the trapped material and allow the plant to use it for nutrients. Mosquito larvae are among the most common insects caught by bladderworts, and hence some observers maintain that these plants play an important part in mosquito control in certain areas.

blade tool: see PALEOLITHIC PERIOD.

Blaine, James Gillespie

The most popular Republican of his time, James Gillespie Blaine served as U.S. congressman, senator, secretary of state, and presidential candidate. He was an important architect of his party's electoral success during the 1880s and '90s.

Blaine was born on Jan. 31, 1830, in West Brownsville, Pa. After teaching for several years, he became a journalist in Maine in 1854 after his marriage to Harriet Stanwood. He went into Republican politics in the 1850s and served in the state legislature between 1859 and 1862. From 1863 to 1876 he sat in the U.S. House of Representatives, serving as speaker (1869–75). Blaine was moderate on Reconstruction issues. He led the Half-Breed faction of the Republicans in a feud with the Stalwart faction of Roscoe CONKLING, and the opposition of the Stalwarts helped to deny him presidential nominations in 1876 and 1880.

As a leading contender for his party's nomination in 1876, Blaine became embroiled in charges of corruption relating to an Arkansas railroad and the "Mulligan Letters" that bore on his involvement. Whatever his actual role, the episode made him unacceptable to reformers of the day. This blow to his reputation probably cost him the nomination in 1876 and hurt his chances again in 1880. President James A. GARFIELD named him secretary of state in 1881, but Garfield's term in office was too brief to allow Blaine to develop a foreign policy. In the months of his secretaryship he gave evidence of his interest in an isthmian canal, Pan-Americanism, and reciprocal trade. After Garfield was assassinated, Blaine resigned.

In 1884 the Republicans at last selected Blaine as their presidential candidate to run against the Democrat Grover

James G. Blaine was a leading Republican politician of the late 19th century. Although expected to win the 1884 presidential election, he was defeated by Grover Cleveland.

CLEVELAND. Some Republicans bolted, old scandals were aired, and both parties threw mud. Blaine was narrowly defeated, but he had run better than his party and had laid the basis for the party's success four years later. By now he was the preeminent spokesman for a protective tariff, helping to make that issue a central part of Republican doctrine. He was not a candidate in 1888 but supported Benjamin HARRISON, who made him secretary of state again in 1889.

Among the diplomatic problems that Blaine confronted were disputes with Great Britain over seals in Alaska and fishing in Canada. He convened the first Pan-American conference in 1889, looked toward the annexation of Hawaii, and succeeded in getting reciprocal trade provisions included in the McKinley Tariff of 1890. By 1892 his relations with Harrison had deteriorated, and he resigned on June 4, 1892. An abortive campaign to nominate him at the Republican convention failed. He died on Jan. 27, 1893.

The most charismatic politician of the Gilded Age, Blaine provoked extreme reactions for and against himself. He was a farsighted diplomat and a party leader whose advocacy of the tariff was a key to Republican dominance after 1894. Although he never became president, his impact on his time was larger and more enduring than that of the two presidents with whom he worked.   LEWIS L. GOULD

Bibliography: Morgan, H. Wayne, *From Hayes to McKinley: National Party Politics, 1877–1896* (1969); Muzzey, David S., *James G. Blaine: A Political Idol of Other Days* (1934; repr. 1965); Tutorow, Norman E., *James Gillespie Blaine and the Presidency* (1989).

Blair   (family)

Two generations of the Blair family were active in American politics during the 19th century. **Francis Preston Blair**, b. Abingdon, Va., Apr. 12, 1791, d. Oct. 18, 1876, was the son of James Blair, attorney general of Kentucky (1796–1816). Francis Preston Blair became a prominent Jacksonian newspaper editor in Kentucky and was brought to Washington by Amos KENDALL to edit the *Washington Globe*, the semiofficial Democratic organ. Because of his antislavery views he later joined the Republican party and organized the abortive Hampton Roads peace conference (Feb. 3, 1865).

His son **Francis Preston Blair, Jr.**, b. Lexington, Ky., Feb. 19, 1821, d. July 9, 1875, practiced law in St. Louis and was instrumental in keeping Missouri in the union. During the Civil War he held a command under Gen. William T. Sherman. Another son, **Montgomery Blair**, b. Franklin County, Ky., May 10, 1813, d. July 27, 1883, acted as counsel in the Dred Scott case (see DRED SCOTT V. SANDFORD). As postmaster general under Lincoln, he introduced postal money orders and free urban mail delivery. Critical of radical RECONSTRUCTION, Montgomery Blair and his brother and father became Democrats after the Civil War.   HARRY AMMON

Bibliography: Smith, E. B., *Francis Preston Blair* (1980); Smith, W. E., *The Francis Preston Blair Family in Politics*, 2 vols. (1933; repr. 1969).

Blair, Bonnie

Speed skater Bonnie Blair, b. Mar. 18, 1964, Cornwall, N.Y., is the only American woman to have won five gold medals in Olympic competitions. The youngest member of a speed-skating family, she has been skating since age two. In the 1988 Calgary Winter Olympics, Blair won the 500-m race with a world-record skate. She retained her 500-m title and won the 1,000-m race, at the 1992 Albertville Olympics. Blair repeated her 1992 victories at the 1994 Olympics in Lillehammer. She retired from competition after the 1994 season.

Blair, James

James Blair, b. 1656, d. Apr. 18, 1743, was a missionary of the Church of England to colonial Virginia and the founder and first president of William and Mary College, Williamsburg, Va. In 1689 he became the designated commissary, or deputy, of the bishop of London, with authority to supervise the American clergy. He returned to England in 1691 to request the chartering of a college to ensure a learned ministry. When founded in 1693, the college was named for the reigning monarchs. Blair's interests later turned to political concerns; from 1694 he was a member of the governor's council.

Blair, Tony

Anthony Charles Lynton Blair, b. May 6, 1953, was elected leader of Britain's opposition Labour party in July 1994 after the untimely death of John SMITH. Oxford-educated and a lawyer, Blair entered Parliament at age 30 in 1983 and rose rapidly. A moderate, he positioned himself to appeal to consituencies outside Labour's traditional strongholds.

Blais, Marie Claire   [blay]

Marie Claire Blais, b. Quebec City, Oct. 5, 1939, is a French Canadian author. A writer of drama, fiction, and poetry, she is best known for such novels as *A Season in the Life of Emmanuel* (1965)—with an introduction by Edmund Wilson, who was a great admirer—*Deaf to the City*(1981), and *Nights in the Underground* (1982). These works, peopled with beautiful idiots, devout prostitutes, and wolfish lovers, have the hauntingly ambiguous qualities that characterize Blais's evil yet compassionate world.   MARY JANE EDWARDS

Blake, Edward

Edward Blake, b. Adelaide township, Upper Canada (now Ontario), Oct. 13, 1833, d. Mar. 1, 1912, was a Canadian political leader who served as premier of Ontario (1871–72), federal minister of justice (1875–77), and national leader of the Liberal party (1880–87). Although expert in constitutional law, he failed to inspire party loyalty and led the Liberals to defeat in two elections (1882, 1887). He later sat (1892–1907) in the British parliament as an Irish nationalist.

Blake, Eubie

Once a ragtime pianist, James Hubert "Eubie" Blake, b. Baltimore, Md., Feb. 7, 1883, d. Feb. 12, 1983, had a long career in popular music, primarily as a composer. Together with his long-time vaudeville partner, the songwriter Noble Sissle, Blake wrote the trend-setting musical *Shuffle Along* (1921), which became the most successful black show on Broadway, running for 504 performances. Two of his show tunes, "Memories of You" and "I'm Just Wild about Harry," became standards. Although he continued to work intermittently for many years, he was not "rediscovered" until 1969, when John Hammond produced the album *The Eighty-Six Years of Eubie Blake*. Blake later founded a record company and made a biographical film.   ROGER BAILEY

Blake, Eugene Carson

A Presbyterian minister and world church leader, Eugene Carson Blake, b. St. Louis, Mo., Nov. 7, 1906, d. July 31, 1985, was president of the U.S. National Council of Churches (1954–57)

and general secretary of the World Council of Churches (1966–72). Educated at Princeton University, New College, Edinburgh, and Princeton Theological Seminary, Blake ministered to congregations in New York City, Albany, N.Y., and Pasadena, Calif., between 1932 and 1950 and was stated clerk of the general assembly, first of the Presbyterian Church in the U.S.A. (1951–58), and later of the United Presbyterian Church (1958–66), formed by a merger of the former with the United Presbyterian Church of North America. With Episcopal bishop James A. PIKE, he sponsored the Blake-Pike proposals (1960) for a union of U.S. Protestant churches.

Blake, Peter   (architect)

Peter Jost Blake, b. Germany, Sept. 20, 1920, is a prolific American architect and writer. His books—which include *Master Builders* (1960), *God's Own Junkyard* (1964), and *Form Follows Fiasco* (1977)—as well as the editorship of *Architectural Forum* (1964–72) and *Architecture Plus* (1972–75), gave Blake a forum for his witty and perceptive architectural criticism. He has designed many buildings, basically in the INTERNATIONAL STYLE, and was chair (1979–86) of the architecture department of the Catholic University of America.   C. RAY SMITH

Blake, Peter   (painter)

Peter Thomas Blake, b. June 25, 1932, emerged in the mid-1950s as one of the pioneer group in English POP ART. Working in assemblage, collage, and from photographs, he takes his subject matter from the popular culture of both Britain and the United States, painting, for example, a portrait of Elvis Presley. More frequently than other pop artists, however, he turns to the past, usually the 1930s and '40s, for some of his subjects, treating them with humor and nostalgia. Blake is a realist artist who depicts with painstaking accuracy the objects he enjoys. His work is represented in the Tate Gallery, London, and in many avant-garde collections.   MARIAN BURLEIGH-MOTLEY

Bibliography: Compton, Michael, *Pop Art* (1970).

Blake, Robert

Robert Blake, b. 1599, d. Aug. 7, 1657, one of England's greatest admirals, established the naval supremacy of Oliver Cromwell's Commonwealth over the Dutch and Spanish. He earned his first laurels by resolute defense of Lyme and Taunton for the parliamentarians in the ENGLISH CIVIL WAR. Entrusted with the demoralized parliamentarian navy in 1649, he nevertheless destroyed the royalist fleet. The first ANGLO-DUTCH WAR (1652–54) consisted largely of his victories over the ably led Dutch fleets. In 1655, Blake ravaged the strongholds of the Barbary pirates, and in the winter of 1656–57 he blockaded the entire Spanish coast. His last naval action was to destroy a Spanish fleet at Tenerife, Canary Islands, in 1657.

Bibliography: Baumber, Michael, *General-at-Sea* (1990); Raine, Kathleen J., *Blake and England* (1960; repr. 1980).

Blake, Toe

As a hockey player and coach, Hector "Toe" Blake, b. Victoria Mines, Ontario, Aug. 21, 1912, has been associated with 11 Stanley Cup championship teams. As a left wing who played alongside the great Maurice Richard on the Montreal Canadiens (1936–48), Blake earned Hall of Fame recognition. He retired as a player with 235 goals, 292 assists, and trophies for 3 Stanley Cup championships. He then served for 13 years as the Canadiens' coach, during which period the team won 8 Stanley Cups, including 5 (1956–60) in a row. He retired after the 1967–68 season.

Blake, William

William Blake, a visionary English poet and painter who was a precursor of English ROMANTICISM, combined the vocations of engraver, painter, and poet. He was born on Nov. 28, 1757, the son of a London hosier. Blake spent all of his relatively quiet life in London except for a stay at Felpham, on the southern coast of England, from 1800 to 1803. At Felpham he evicted

William Blake's watercolor The Beating of Achan *(c.1800) illustrates what Blake called the "cruelties of Moral Law." The first of the great English romantic poets, Blake proclaimed the primacy of imagination and freedom over reason and law. (Tate Gallery, London.)*

from his garden a drunken soldier who then accused him of making treasonous remarks, but a jury acquitted him of the charge. This incident figures in some of Blake's poems.

Life and Works. Educated at home, Blake was sent at age ten to a drawing school. Later he was apprenticed to the engraver James Basire. From sketching frequently at Westminster Abbey, he developed an interest in the Gothic style, which he combined with a taste for the art of Raphael, Michelangelo, and Dürer. He exhibited his first artwork in 1780, married Catherine Boucher in 1782, and published his first poems, *Poetical Sketches*, in 1783. He quickly withdrew them from circulation, however, apparently offended by the condescending preface written by a patron. This volume contained the only poems Blake published by conventional means. Although book 1 of an unfinished poem called *The French Revolution* (1791) was set up in type, it was never issued.

Blake produced and published his other works himself, except those which remained in manuscript at his death, by using his own unique method of engraving both illustration and text on copper plates and coloring the printed volumes by hand. He executed numerous engravings for books by others as well as watercolors and other kinds of paintings. Blake gave only one private exhibition, for which he wrote an interesting *Descriptive Catalogue* (1809), but the show was a failure and received severe criticism. Some of the major works exhibited at it have since been lost.

The earliest of Blake's well-known works is SONGS OF INNOCENCE (1789), a series of lyrics in the deceptively simple form of children's poems. He reprinted them in 1794, adding a complementary series of *Songs of Experience*. Blake wrote, but never published, a number of additional short poems, including the cryptic "Mental Traveller" and an unfinished poem on the acts of Jesus entitled "The Everlasting Gospel." For the most part, though, he concentrated on producing longer engraved works, most of which have powerful and astonishing illustrations and designs and form a huge, original cosmic drama of titanic powers who war among themselves, with their wives, and with views of reality different from their own. The best known of these so-called Prophetic Books (a title assigned to them by their early critics) are *Milton* (c.1802–08) and *Jerusalem* (c.1804–20), both engraved, and the unfinished *Vala; or, The Four Zoas,* written about the same time and discovered in manuscript only in 1893.

Before doing these, Blake executed a number of so-called minor prophecies, which extend the concepts of innocence and experience, as in *Tiriel* (c.1789, unengraved) and *The Book of Thel* (1789). Blake followed these with *Visions of the Daughters of Albion* (1793), in which he offers radical views on sex, religion, and politics. Other works look forward to the later prophecies by introducing his "giant forms" in symbolical and historical poems heavily influenced by the Bible. The most notable of these are *America* (1793), *Europe* (1794), and the books of *Urizen* (1794), *Ahania* (1795), and *Los* (1795). *The Marriage of Heaven and Hell* (c.1792), a work that combines prose and verse, story, proverb, and argument, is especially important for understanding Blake's corpus.

Blake left no poetry written after about 1818, but he remained active as an engraver and artist. Among his greatest works of this later period are the illustrations for Dante's Divine Comedy, the Book of Job, and Thornton's translation of Vergil, the last a set of charming woodcuts. After his death on Aug. 12, 1827, and that of his wife four years later, Blake's works were dispersed, and some may have been destroyed.

Influence. Blake's work was not well known in his lifetime, but his influence is apparent in the work of several painters who knew him when he was an old man, particularly Samuel Palmer. He also influenced the Pre-Raphaelite painters of the 19th century, and his first editor was W. B. Yeats, who knew much of his poetry by heart. James Joyce, D. H. Lawrence, and Joyce Cary, among others, found inspiration in his writings, and he has had considerable influence on modern literary criticism through the work of Northrop Frye. Today Blake is one of the most frequently discussed poets. Of those who actually knew Blake, Palmer left the most interesting estimate of him: "In him you saw the Maker, the Inventor. . .He was energy itself and shed around him a kindling influence, an atmosphere of life, full of the idea. . . . He was a man without a mask."

HAZARD ADAMS

Bibliography: Adam, Hazard, et al., *Critical Essays on William Blake* (1991); Bindman, David, *The Complete Graphic Works of William Blake* (1986); De Luca, V. A., *Words of Eternity* (1991); Erdman, David, *Blake: Prophet against Empire,* rev. ed. (1969; repr. 1991); Essick, Robert N., *William Blake, Printmaker* (1980); Frye, Northrop, *Fearful Symmetry: A Study of William Blake* (1947); Keynes, Geoffrey, ed., *Complete Portraiture of William and Catherine Blake* (1977).

Blakelock, Ralph Albert   [blayk'-lahk]

Ralph Blakelock's vision of the American wilderness charges his nocturnal landscapes with romantic melancholy. In Moonlight *(c.1885), the primeval forest is silhouetted in a delicate pattern against the pale sky. (Brooklyn Museum of Art, New York.)*

The American painter Ralph Albert Blakelock, b. New York City, Oct. 15, 1847, d. Aug. 9, 1919, broke from the long-established realism of the Hudson River school by creating landscapes of the imagination in which poetic mood was paramount. Blakelock was largely self taught as a painter. He was deeply influenced by travels in the American West between 1869 and 1872, and he developed his highly personal style in response to the land and the life of that region. Indian motifs appear often in his work, but they are not of specific tribes or settings.

Blakelock's works are characterized by dark colors, broadly defined forms that show little pictorial detail, and richly textured surfaces. He often painted moonlit scenes with the foliage of trees silhouetted against a shimmering sky, as in *Moonlight Sonata* (c.1883–88; Museum of Fine Arts, Boston). He persisted in his subjective style despite critical hostility and poor sales. The years of discouragement finally brought on a mental collapse in 1899, and he was confined to asylums until his death. Ironically, his work suddenly achieved recognition in 1900, although neither Blakelock nor his family gained materially from this belated and deserved fame.   DAVID TATHAM

Bibliography: Gebhard, David, *Ralph A. Blakelock* (1969).

Blanc, Louis   [blahn]

Louis Blanc, b. Oct. 29, 1811, d. Dec. 6, 1882, was a Parisian journalist and one of the most influential of the early French socialists. France's salvation, he believed, lay in establishing a democratic republic and organizing *ateliers sociaux,* producer cooperatives that would guarantee the right to work to every citizen. His analyses and proposals, expressed in clear, forceful language, were easily grasped, and his writings—of which *Organization of Labor* (1840) was the most influential—implanted socialist ideas among French workers, raised their political consciousness, and shaped their demands in the REVOLUTIONS OF 1848.

In February 1848, after the overthrow of King Louis Philippe, Blanc became a member of the provisional government of the Second Republic. He organized the Luxembourg Commission, a labor parliament in which he and his followers discussed radical economic and social reforms but had no real power. Nonetheless, Blanc became the personification of conservatives' fears, and after the workers' insurrection of June 1848, he fled to England to avoid prosecution.

He returned to Paris and to political life in 1870 but never again played so important a role.   DAVID H. PINKNEY

Bibliography: Loubère, Leo, *Louis Blanc: His Life and His Contribution to the Rise of Jacobin-Socialism* (1961; repr. 1980).

Blanc, Mont

Mont Blanc, the highest peak in the Alps, is located in the Haute-Savoie department of southeastern France on the French-Italian border. It is part of the 48-km-long (30-mi) Alpine massif also known as Mont Blanc. The highest peak in Europe except for Mount Elbrus in the Caucasus, it has an elevation of 4,807 m (15,771 ft). The northwest, or French, side of the massif slopes moderately and has many glaciers, including the Mer de Glace. The massif drops steeply on the Italian side. The first ascent was made in 1786, and today numerous routes are used to reach the summit. One of the longest vehicular tunnels in the world, the 12-km (7.5-mi) Mont Blanc tunnel, passes through the mountain from Chamonix-Mont Blanc, France, to Courmayeur, Italy. It was opened in 1965. Two observatories are located on Mont Blanc for glacier study, and nearby are many resort hotels.

Blanchard, Doc

Felix "Doc" Blanchard, Jr., b. McColl, S.C., Dec. 11, 1924, achieved fame as a football player for the U.S. Military Academy (West Point). A fullback, he was the power-running "Mr. Inside" who complemented breakaway threat Glenn DAVIS, "Mr. Outside," as West Point went undefeated in 3 consecutive seasons (1944–46). Blanchard scored 38 touchdowns during that time. In 1945 he won the Heisman Trophy as the best college football player in the country and the Sullivan Award as the best amateur athlete. Blanchard rose to the rank of colonel before retiring from the army in 1971.

Blanchard, Jean

Jean Pierre François Blanchard, b. July 4, 1753, d. Mar. 7, 1809, a French aeronaut, is best known for his many pioneering BALLOON flights. On Jan. 7, 1785, Blanchard, along with Dr. John Jeffries, an American physician, made the first flight over the English Channel. He was credited with numerous firsts, including the first balloon flights in the United States, Germany, and the Netherlands. In addition to his balloon flights, Blanchard attempted to develop manually powered airplanes and helicopters, but was unsuccessful. In 1785 he lowered small animals from balloons via parachutes to entertain watching crowds, foreshadowing the epic parachute descent of André GARNERIN during the next decade.

RICHARD P. HALLION

Blanche of Castile

Blanche of Castile, b. 1188, d. Nov. 12, 1252, was the queen consort of LOUIS VIII of France and twice regent for their son LOUIS IX. The daughter of Alfonso VIII of Castile, she married Louis in 1200. As regent during the minority (1226–34) of Louis IX, she defeated a major baronial rebellion in 1226 and repelled an English attack in 1230. Blanche remained influential after Louis came of age and became regent again in 1248, during her son's absence on crusade.

Bland-Allison Act

The Bland-Allison Act of 1878 remonetized silver on a limited basis in the United States. It was named for its two sponsors, Rep. Richard P. Bland of Missouri and Sen. William Allison of Iowa. The law, passed over the veto of President Rutherford B. Hayes, authorized the government to purchase between $2 million and $4 million worth of silver monthly for coinage. It pegged the price of silver at one-sixteenth that of gold. The act was a compromise between the FREE SILVER radicals, who wanted unlimited coinage of silver, and the more conservative advocates of a strict gold standard. The Bland-Allison Act was replaced in 1890 by the Sherman Silver Purchase Act, which allowed increased coinage of silver.

Blanda, George

Placekicker and quarterback George Frederick Blanda, b. Youngwood, Pa., Sept. 17, 1927, scored more points—2,002—than any player in professional football history. Blanda's career, with 4 teams, continued past his 48th birthday: Chicago Bears (1949, 1950–58), Baltimore Colts (1950), Houston Oilers (1960–66), and Oakland Raiders (1967–75). His teams won league titles in 1960, 1961, and 1967. Blanda's scoring comprised 9 touchdowns (54 points), 335 field goals (1,005 points), and 943 points after touchdowns, the last still a record. His other all-time records include 68 passes attempted in a single game and 340 games played. He was elected to the Hall of Fame in 1981.

blank verse

Blank verse is unrhymed iambic PENTAMETER verse, each line composed of ten syllables of alternating stress or accent. A versatile medium, blank verse was modeled after classical Greek and Roman poetry. It has been utilized in English and continental verse drama and narrative poetry since the 16th century.

Henry Howard, Earl of SURREY, brought blank verse from Italy to England with his partial translation of Vergil's *Aeneid* (c.1550). MARLOWE used blank verse to good effect in his plays, but SHAKESPEARE was the first English master of the form. His sure-handed use of metrical variations, runover lines, and feminine endings in such works as *Hamlet* (c.1600) and *The Tempest* (c.1611) made blank verse even more flexible. In the

hands of lesser poets and dramatists who imitated Shakespeare's innovations, the form degenerated, until Milton restored it to its former promise in poems such as his epic masterpiece, *Paradise Lost* (1667).

Later examples of blank verse include Keat's *Hyperion* (1820), Tennyson's *Idylls of the King* (1888), and T.S. Eliot's verse plays (in part).

See also: VERSIFICATION.

Blankers-Koen, Fanny

Francina "Fanny" Blankers-Koen, b. Apr. 26, 1918, is a former Dutch track star who won four gold medals in the 1948 Olympic Games at age 30 after her career had seemingly been cut short by World War II. She began competing when she was 17, but after the Germans overran Holland her competition was restricted. Nevertheless, she became a world-class competitor in the 100-meter sprint, the 80-meter hurdles (tying world records in both events), the high jump, and the long jump. In the 1948 games, Blankers-Koen, then the mother of two, won the 100- and 200-meter sprints and the hurdles, and led her team to a 400-meter relay victory. Between 1938 and 1951 she set world records in seven individual events.

blanket flower

Blanket flower, *Gaillardia*, is the common name for several species of plants in the sunflower family, Compositae. The annuals and herbaceous perennials have large yellow or purple flower heads and grow in open fields in North and South America. Numerous cultivated varieties are commonly used in gardens.

JANE PHILPOTT

Blanquart-Evrard, Louis Désirée   [blahn-kahrt'-ay-vrahr', loo-ee' day-zee-ray']

Louis Désirée Blanquart-Evrard, 1802–72, was a French photographer and entrepreneur. In the late 1840s he improved the English CALOTYPE photograph and popularized the process in France. He invented the ALBUMEN PRINT in 1850. The following year in Lille, he opened an establishment for mass-producing photographic prints, the first of its kind in France. The firm issued editions of photographs by Maxime DU CAMP, Charles NÈGRE, Henri Le Secq, and others and pioneered the use of original photographs for book illustration.

PETER GALASSI

Blanqui, Louis Auguste   [blahn-kee']

Louis Auguste Blanqui, b. Feb. 1, 1805, d. Jan. 1, 1881, was a French revolutionist who was prominent in European radical movements of the 19th century. Although he spent nearly half his life in prison, Blanqui became a symbol to many in the worker's movement. He maintained that the workers needed to be led by a small, dedicated minority and that a successful revolution would have to establish a temporary dictatorship in order to carry out the necessary transformation of society—views that were later adopted by Vladimir Ilich Lenin and the Soviet Communists.

Blanqui studied law and medicine, but became increasingly involved in politics, fighting in the Revolution of 1830. Disenchanted with the new government, Blanqui organized secret republican societies and was twice imprisoned (1831, 1836) for this activity. He was imprisoned for 9 years after leading an armed assault on the city hall in Paris in 1839. Released in 1848, he served (1849–59) another prison term for his activities during the REVOLUTION OF 1848.

Sentenced once again in 1861, Blanqui escaped prison to Belgium in 1865, where he studied, wrote essays (collected in the important *Critique sociale*, 1885), and plotted future insurrections. He returned to Paris in 1870, leading his followers in two efforts to overthrow the government in the space of three months. Imprisoned again in 1871–79, he could not take part in the great uprising known as the COMMUNE OF PARIS in 1871, although he was elected its president. While still in prison, Blanqui was elected (1879) deputy for Bordeaux. He was freed, but the government declared his election invalid. Blanqui continued his revolutionary campaigning until his death.

Bibliography: Bernstein, Samuel, *Auguste Blanqui and the Art of Insurrection* (1971); Spitzer, Alan B., *The Revolutionary Theories of Louis Auguste Blanqui* (1957; repr. 1971); Stewart, Neil, *Blanqui* (1939).

Blantyre   [blan-tyr']

Blantyre is a city in southern Malawi, southeastern Africa, with a population of 333,800 (1984 est.). It is the administrative center for the region as well as a chief trade and industrial center, processing tobacco, tung oil, and timber. In 1956 the city was combined with Limbe to form the largest urban area in Malawi. Blantyre's high altitude (1,039 m/3,409 ft) has a moderating effect on its climate.

Blarney stone

Built into the southern wall of Blarney Castle, in County Cork, Ireland, the Blarney stone is supposed to endow those who kiss it with the gift of eloquence. According to legend, the castle was once saved from attack through flattery and cajolery; hence, the power of the stone, and the word *blarney*.

Blasco-Ibáñez, Vicente   [blahs'-koh-ee-bahn'-yayth, vee-thayn'-tay]

Vicente Blasco-Ibáñez, b. Jan. 29, 1867, d. Jan. 28, 1928, was a Spanish novelist best known for his naturalistic novels. His early works, notably *The Cabin* (1898; Eng. trans., 1917) and *Reeds and Mud* (1902; Eng. trans., 1928), were praised for dramatically depicting the lives of farmers and fishermen in his native Valencia. His later works grew increasingly didactic, and he gained a worldwide readership at the expense of critical acclaim. *The Four Horsemen of the Apocalypse* (1916; Eng. trans., 1918), a World War I spy novel, was his most popular work.

Blashfield, Edwin Howland

Edwin Howland Blashfield, b. New York City, Dec. 15, 1848, d. Oct. 12, 1936, was an American painter of eclectic allegorical murals for public buildings. In 1867 he went to Paris, where he studied with the French painter Léon Bonnat; he subsequently exhibited his easel paintings in Paris and London. Blashfield returned to the United States in 1881, working as a portraitist in New York City. He was given his first mural commissions for the WORLD'S COLUMBIAN EXPOSITION OF 1893 in Chicago. Thereafter, he painted murals for state capitals and courthouses and for the Library of Congress.

Bibliography: Blashfield, Edwin Howland, *The Works of Edwin Howland Blashfield* (1937).

Blatch, Harriot Eaton Stanton

Harriot Eaton Stanton Blatch, b. Seneca Falls, N.Y., Jan. 20, 1856, d. Nov. 20, 1940, was a leading women's rights activist. A daughter of suffragist Elizabeth Cady Stanton and a graduate (1878) of Vassar College, she assisted in the compilation of *The History of Woman Suffrage* (1881; repr. 1971). Blatch lived for 20 years in England, where the militant women's suffrage movement inspired her. After returning to the United States, she formed (1907) the Equality League of Self-Supporting Women (later the Women's Political Union), which initiated the drive to achieve the vote in New York State. The group subsequently shifted attention to the struggle for a federal suffrage amendment and joined the National Woman's party. An administrator for wartime agencies, Blatch wrote *Mobilizing Woman Power* (1918; repr. 1974), urging American women to support the war effort. After World War I she continued to work for women's rights and other liberal causes. Her autobiography, *Challenging Years*, written with Alma Lutz, was published in 1940 (repr. 1976).

BARBARA CUNNINGHAM

blast furnace

The blast furnace is a device in which sufficient heat is generated to reduce iron ore to a relatively pure molten metal. It was first developed in a crude form during the Middle Ages, but significant improvements in blast-furnace structure and practice during the 20th century have resulted in great increases in the production of iron.

The modern blast furnace is essentially a giant stove lined with firebrick, with a stack more than 30 m (100 ft) in height and 12 m (40 ft) in diameter at the hearth. Iron ore, COKE, and limestone are introduced at the top of the vertical stack. As they descend, these ingredients are met by a rising volume of hot gas formed by combustion of the coke with preheated air blown in under pressure through openings called tuyeres, located at the base of the stack. The burning of the coke produces carbon monoxide and reduces the iron oxide to iron. The limestone removes impurities by combining with them and forming a molten mass, called slag, that is lighter than iron. The slag is drained off at intervals through an opening in the furnace located a short distance above the tapping hole where the iron itself is drawn off.

For efficient use, a blast furnace must operate continuously. A single furnace can produce as much as 10,000 tons of molten iron per day.   WILLIAM T. HOGAN

Bibliography: Szekely, Julian, ed., *Blast Furnace Technology* (1978).

See also: IRON AND STEEL INDUSTRY.

blasting: see DEMOLITION.

blastoid

Blastoids are fossils of an extinct group of ECHINODERMS (marine invertebrates) that resembled certain modern CRINOIDS. They have been found in rocks spanning the geologic time interval from the SILURIAN to the PERMIAN. They lived in warm, shallow, tropical seas, rooted to the seafloor by a long stem that culminated in a round, calcium-carbonate–plated cup (theca), which housed most of the animal's soft parts. Five food grooves radiated from the mouth, centrally located on the upper thecal surface, and numerous small arms lining the sides of the grooves captured food from the water around the animal.   WILLIAM B. N. BERRY

Bibliography: Moore, Raymond, et al., *Invertebrate Fossils* (1952).

See also: FOSSIL RECORD.

Blaue Reiter, Der   [blow-e ry'-tur, dayr]

Der Blaue Reiter (German for "the blue rider") was a group of artists, formed in Munich in December 1911, that significantly influenced the early development of MODERN ART. The group's cofounders, Wassily KANDINSKY and Franz MARC, sought to

Franz Marc's The Blue Horse (1912) *typifies the Blaue Reiter group's use of brilliant color, especially blue. Marc and Wassily Kandinsky were the cofounders of the group, which included August Macke and Heinrich Campendonck. (Saarland Museum, Saarbrücken.)*

evolve an art that reflected in its expressionistically oriented forms and colors a new, more abstract conception of the universe revealed by physics, mathematics, and mystical spirituality. Their emphasis on the evocative role of color, line, and composition reflected such diverse sources as the romantic color theory of Goethe and Philipp Runge, ART NOUVEAU, the Orphic theories of Robert DELAUNAY, and the theosophy of Rudolf STEINER. The group took its name from a painting by Kandinsky, *Le cavalier bleu.*

To promote artistic freedom and provide a forum for presenting new forms, Der Blaue Reiter held two exhibitions in Munich, one in the winter of 1911 and one in the spring of 1912; both were summaries of French, German, Russian, and Swiss avant-garde movements with no stylistic common denominator. As part of their educational mission, they published (1911) *Der Blaue Reiter Almanac,* with essays by artists and critics surveying art, literature, theater, and music. A final Blaue Reiter exhibition was held in Berlin in late 1913.

With the outbreak of World War I, the association dissolved. Kandinsky returned temporarily to Russia; Marc died in combat. In 1924 a successor group composed of Alexey JAWLENSKY, Kandinsky, Paul Klee, and Lyonel FEININGER joined to exhibit *Die Blaue Vier* ("The Blue Four"). A large collection of paintings and memorabilia of Der Blaue Reiter is in the Lenbachhaus, Munich.   IDA K. RIGBY

Bibliography: T. Lankheit, Klaus, ed., *The Blaue Reiter Almanac* (1974); Miesl, Victor, ed., *Voices of German Expressionism* (1974); Raabe, P., ed., *The Era of German Expressionism,* trans. by J. M. Ritchie (1986); Roethel, Hans Konrad, *The Blue Rider* (1971).

Blavatsky, Helena Petrovna   [bluh-vat'-skee, hel-ay'-nuh pet-rohv'-nuh]

Madame Helena Petrovna Blavatsky, b. Russia, Aug. 12, 1831, d. May 8, 1891, was the principal founder of the Theosophical movement. The daughter of a German named Hahn, she was briefly married to one Nicephore Blavatsky. Traveling extensively in Asia, she met spiritual teachers who, she claimed, taught her the mysteries of the occult and chose her to spread the teachings of THEOSOPHY. Taking citizenship in the United States, Blavatsky became an outspoken defender of SPIRITUALISM, challenging both religious dogma and scientific materialism. The Theosophical movement that she and her collaborators founded (1875) in New York was organized to promote universal brotherhood; to study all great religions, philosophies, and sciences; and to investigate the unexplained laws of nature and the psychic powers of human beings. Blavatsky's philosophical writings have been investigated with renewed interest during the second half of the 20th century. Her major works are *Isis Unveiled,* 2 vols. (1877); *The Secret Doctrine* (1888); *The Key to Theosophy* and *The Voice of Silence* (both 1889).

Bibliography: Ryan, Charles J., *H. P. Blavatsky and the Theosophical Movement* (1978).

blazing star

Blazing star is the common name for plants in three different families, but only *Mentzelia laevicaulis,* in the family Loasaceae, has gaudy, star-shaped, blazing-yellow flowers. *Chamaelirium luteum,* family Liliaceae, and about 40 species of *Liatris,* family Compositae, have spikes of small flowers that are either yellowish white or rose purple.   JANE PHILPOTT

bleaches and brighteners

Bleaches and brighteners are chemical substances used to enhance the appearance of certain materials, specifically their whiteness. Paper, textiles, and flour are bleached industrially on a large scale. Brighteners are applied industrially to whiten paper, textiles, and plastics. Both bleaches and brighteners play an important role in home laundry: bleaches remove stains, and brighteners enhance the whiteness of washed fabrics.

Bleaches remove unwanted colored substances by transforming them into colorless materials. They do so either by OXIDATION or by reduction. The most common oxidizing bleaches are chlorine or peroxide, each in various chemical combinations. Chlorine gas, sodium hypochlorite, and sodium chlorite are important chlorine bleaches. Hydrogen peroxide, sodium perborate, sodium percarbonate, and sodium peroxydisulfate are examples of peroxide, or oxygen, bleaches. Less common in household use but important in the bleaching of wood pulp are reducing bleaches, such as gaseous sulfur dioxide, sodium hydrosulfite, and sodium sulfite.

Color in organic materials is the result of light absorption by certain chemical configurations, called chromophores, in the molecule. Carbon-carbon double bonds and carbon-oxygen double bonds are examples of chromophores. Oxidizing bleaches break up chromophores; reducing bleaches convert double bonds into single bonds. In both cases, the end products are colorless.

Brighteners—also called optical bleaches or fluorescent whitening agents (FWAs)—are complex organic molecules similar in structure to chemical dyes. FWAs absorb radiation in the invisible near-ultraviolet region of the spectrum and reemit it in the blue region of the visible spectrum. When FWAs are applied to fabric of yellowish, off-white appearance, the added blue light contributes to a whiter appearance. Since 1940, FWAs have been present in almost all U.S. laundry detergents. During washing, FWAs are taken up by fabric. Cotton fabrics readily take up FWAs; synthetic fabrics do not. In the latter, FWAs are often incorporated into the melted synthetic resin before it is spun into yarn. As a result of this process, called mass whitening, FWAs form an integral part of the synthetic fabric structure.   ARNO CAHN

Bibliography: Cutler, W. Gale, and Davies, R. C., eds., *Detergency: Theory and Test Methods* (1975).

bleeding heart

The common bleeding heart, D. spectabilis, *which has divided leaves, yields rows of heart-shaped flowers that hang from slender branches.*

The common bleeding heart, *Dicentra spectabilis*, is a hardy spring-flowering perennial popular for its graceful form and beautiful blooms. Its outer petals are rosy red (rarely white) and heart shaped, thus suggesting its name, and the inner petals are white. The bleeding heart grows to a height of 0.6 m (2 ft). The plant remains in bloom for about six weeks, thriving in partial shade and with an adequate supply of moisture. It is a member of the family Fumariaceae.

Blenheim, Battle of   [blen'-hym]

The Battle of Blenheim, fought on Aug. 13, 1704, at the village of Blenheim on the Danube River in Bavaria, was a major victory for the English and Austrian forces (under the duke of MARLBOROUGH and EUGENE OF SAVOY) over the French and Bavarians in the War of the SPANISH SUCCESSION. Marlborough was rewarded by the English Parliament with Blenheim Palace.

Blenheim Palace   [blen'-uhm]

Blenheim, in Woodstock Park near Oxford, is a large English baroque palace designed by Nicholas HAWKSMOOR and Sir John VANBRUGH for John Churchill, duke of MARLBOROUGH. Named for the site of Marlborough's 1704 victory in Europe, Blenheim was a public gift to the duke. The vast North Court, flanked by two service courts, is dominated by the tall pillared entrance to the central block and by the fantastic ornaments of the four corner towers.

Foundations were laid in 1705, but financial problems and disputes, especially between Vanbrugh and the duchess, held up completion until 1727. The original formal gardens were replaced in the 1760s with an extensive and picturesque "English" park by "Capability" BROWN. In this century, however, the east and west formal parterres were restored.

DAVID CAST

Bibliography: Downes, Kerry, *Vanbrugh* (1977); Green, David, *Blenheim Palace* (1951); Huseboe, Arthur P., *Sir John Vanbrugh* (1976); Montgomery-Massingherd, Hugh, *Blenheim Revisited* (1985); Sitwell, Sacheverell, *Great Houses of Europe* (n.d.).

Blennerhassett, Harman   [blen-ur-has'-et]

Harman Blennerhassett, b. Oct. 8, 1765, d. Feb. 2, 1831, a wealthy American landowner on the Ohio-Virginia border, provided financial backing to Aaron BURR in his apparent scheme to invade Mexico and detach the western states from the Union. Arrested with Burr in 1807, Blennerhassett was indicted for treason but never brought to trial.

blenny   [blen'-ee]

A tompot blenny, Blennius gattorugine, *is a small, elongated fish of the Mediterranean Sea. It is scaleless and has a crest on its head.*

Blenny is the common name for perchlike fish of the suborder Blennioidei that are found primarily in marine waters. The suborder contains several families: the most well-known include the blenny family, Blennidae; the CLINID family, Clinidae; the GUNNEL family, Pholidae; the PRICKLEBACK family, Stichaeidae; and the wolffish family, Anarhichadidae, which is discussed below. Some fish in unrelated families are also known as blennies.

The family Blennidae can be divided into two major subfamilies, based largely on diet and teeth arrangement. The Blenniae feed chiefly on bristle worms, crustaceans, and mollusks and have special teeth for tearing and chewing. The Sal-

ariinae, on the other hand, have sharp, movable teeth that they use to scrape algae from rocks.

The most distinctive physical characteristics of blennies (Blennidae) are branching tentacles on the heads of some species. Others have a lobe of skin, or comb, that is shaped like a helmet. Many species can change color rapidly, adopting up to six different color phases for camouflage or to threaten rivals during courtship (see ANIMAL COMMUNICATION). During the spawning season, the male Caneva's blenny (*Blennius canevae*) assumes a striking, masked pattern: the top of the head and bridge of the nose become black, the cheeks become bright yellow, and the throat becomes orange red (see COLORATION, BIOLOGICAL).

In aquariums, blennies are alert and appear to be intelligent. Scientists have shown that blennies can be taught to come for food at certain places, to distinguish objects by their color, brightness, shape, or size, and even to tell the difference between such letters as U and E, and W and L.

Vision is the blenny's most important sense; it is essential to obtaining food. Many other fish, however, rely on their sense of smell or on their ability to sense vibration. Skin divers have reported that blennies on the rocky coast of the Mediterranean swim toward moving objects, half leaping along the bottom on their fins; then, supported by their fins, they observe the objects closely.

Several species of blennies are amphibious. *Lophalticus kirkii*, from the Red Sea and from Africa's east coast, leaves the water to feed on algae-covered rocks. These blennies are protected from the rough, rocky surface by their horny skins and by a secretion of slime on the skin. Amphibious blennies also have a larger-than-normal thyroid gland. When injected with an extract of thyroid, species that ordinarily spend their entire lives in water become amphibious, breathing air for as much as eight hours at a time.

Unlike many blennies, members of the wolffish family are large fish. The spotted wolffish grows to lengths of 1.8 m (6 ft). Wolffishes will attack anything in their path; often dragged up in the nets of cod fishers, they are capable of piercing a fisher's boot with their sharp teeth.

Bibliography: Axelrod, H. R., and Burgess, W., *Marine Fishes* (1979); Migdalski, E. C., and Fichter, G. S., *Fresh and Salt Water Fishes of the World* (1976); Nelson, J. S., *Fishes of the World*, 2d ed. (1984).

Blepharisma   [blef-uh-riz'-muh]

Blepharisma is a densely ciliated rose red protozoan with a terminal contractile vacuole for water and waste elimination. Many species are found in both fresh and salt water and in decaying vegetation. Two substances that one species of blepharisma secretes in order to reciprocally stimulate the opposite mating type have been isolated and chemically identified. Blepharisma is used in photosensitivity experiments.

J. F. McCLELLAN

blepharitis   [blef-uh-ry'-tis]

Blepharitis is an inflammation of the eyelid margins caused either by bacteria (usually staphylococcus), certain viruses, seborrheic dermatitis (dandruff), or by allergic reactions to certain eye medications or cosmetics. Although generally not a threat to vision, blepharitis can lead to lid scarring, which turns the eyelashes inward so that they rub against the cornea.

THOMAS P. MATTINGLY AND MELVIN L. RUBIN

Blériot, Louis   [blayr-ee-oh']

Louis Blériot, b. July 1, 1872, d. Aug. 2, 1936, is best remembered for his pioneering 39.7-km (23.5-mi) flight across the English Channel on July 25, 1909. He flew a No. XI tractor monoplane of his own design. For accomplishing this feat, he won the £1,000 prize put up by the *Daily Mail*, a London newspaper. Its significance, however, was far greater than this; the flight proved that Britain could be reached by airplane from the European continent.

Blériot had experimented with various configurations before settling on the layout of the No. XI, a monoplane with a wheeled landing gear and externally braced wing. Variations of this design were used throughout the world before and during World War I. During the war, Blériot helped create the SPAD concern, a company responsible for many of the finest French fighters.   RICHARD P. HALLION

See also: SPAD.

blesbok   [bles'-bahk]

The blesbok, D. philippsi, is an antelope common to the southern African grasslands. Blesbok, an Afrikaans word, refers to the blaze of white on its face.

The blesbok, or blesbuck, *Damaliscus dorcas philippsi*, is an antelope, in the family Bovidae, order Artiodactyla. It is about 140 cm (55 in) long and 85 cm (34 in) high at the shoulders, with a sloping back. The blesbok weighs about 113.5 kg (250 lb) and has a soft, reddish brown coat, a brown rump, and dark-brown legs. Both sexes have backward-curved, lyre-shaped horns. Blesboks are native to arid grasslands of southern Africa and are one of the fastest antelope in Africa, running low off the ground. They have been semidomesticated in nature preserves and are also raised for their highly prized meat and trophy heads.   EVERETT SENTMAN

Bleuler, Eugen   [bloy'-lur, oy'-gen]

Eugen Bleuler, b. Apr. 30, 1857, d. July 15, 1939, was a Swiss psychiatrist who introduced the term SCHIZOPHRENIA to refer to a group of related mental disorders. He was among the first to describe the symptoms of schizophrenia carefully and among the first to believe that these disorders are curable.

Blicher, Steen Steensen   [blee'-kur, stin stin'-sen]

The Danish writer Steen Steensen Blicher, b. Oct. 11, 1782, d. Mar. 26, 1848, a poor country parson when he began his literary endeavors (as a poet), developed into one of the finest prose writers in the Danish language. The most celebrated of his stories—really an amalgam of tales—is ''The Knitting Room'' (1842; partial Eng. trans., 1896), written in the Jutland dialect and brimming with verse and anecdotes. Among his other tales are ''The Journal of a Parish Clerk'' (1824), ''The Robber's Den'' (1827), ''Alas, How Changed!'' (1828), ''The Parson at Vejlbye'' (1829), and ''Marie'' (1836). These are included in a collection of his writings, *Twelve Stories,* published in English translation in 1945. Blicher's writings are strongly pessimistic, his main theme being that people's hopes are rarely realized.   HALLBERG HALLMUNDSSON

Bligh, William   [bly]

A British naval officer and colonial governor, William Bligh, b. Sept. 9, 1754, d. Dec. 7, 1817, is remembered chiefly in connection with the mutiny on the BOUNTY, only one incident in an unusually adventurous career. Bligh first saw service as the sailing master on Capt. James COOK's last voyage (1776–80). Given command of the H.M.S. *Bounty*, he was commissioned (1787) to sail to Tahiti and pick up a cargo of breadfruit trees for the Indies. Harsh treatment of his crew resulted in the mutiny in April 1789. Bligh and 18 loyal crew members were set adrift in an open boat and by skillful seamanship navigated more than 5,800 km (3,600 mi) to Timor. En route, Bligh charted part of the northeast coast of New Holland (Australia).

After two more voyages to the South Pacific and service under Horatio NELSON in the wars with France, Bligh was appointed (1805) the governor of New South Wales. Vigorous attempts to combat corruption and maintain law and order made him extremely unpopular in the colony. An army mutiny occurred in 1808, and the mutineers sent Bligh back to England in 1810. They were punished, and he died a vice-admiral.   E. J. TAPP

Bibliography: Hawkey, Arthur, *Bligh's Other Mutiny* (1975); Kennedy, Gavin, *Bligh* (1978); Mackaness, George, *The Life of Vice-Admiral William Bligh* (1951).

blight: see DISEASES, PLANT.

blimp: see AIRSHIP.

blind, education of the

Programs for educating blind and visually impaired children exist in countries all around the world. Outside the United States, blind children are usually educated in special schools. Until the beginning of the 20th century, residential schools in the United States provided education for visually handicapped children. Three such schools, founded in the 1830s and still serving blind children, are the Perkins School for the Blind, in Watertown, Mass.; the New York Institute for Special Education, in the Bronx, N.Y.; and the Overbrook School for the Blind, in Philadelphia. In the late 1980s over 50 residential schools served approximately 10 percent of the visually handicapped U.S. school-age population. The majority of these children are multiply handicapped.

A growing realization of the need to integrate visually handicapped people into society, as well as recognition of the importance of family life for their adequate emotional and social growth and development, resulted in the establishment of public day-school programs. In the late 1980s approximately 84 percent of visually handicapped school-age children attended their neighborhood schools. The four major special types of educational programs that now exist in public schools serving blind and visually handicapped children are a special self-contained classroom or special class, a resource room for the students, a visiting teacher but with the child in regular classes the majority of the time, and a teacher consultant program. All of these programs enable the teacher of visually handicapped children to work with the regular classroom teachers.

If a child is identified as legally blind, he or she is entitled to special U.S. federal funds to help defray the cost of education. (For the U.S. definition of legally blind, see BLINDNESS.) If peripheral vision is reduced to an angle of 20 degrees or less, it is considered equivalent to legal blindness and is described as ''tunnel vision.'' Many states have adopted a more liberal definition of visual handicap for educational purposes; this entitles students to receive specialized services from a teacher of blind and visually impaired children. An example of such a definition is: ''visual impairment which, even with correction, adversely affects a pupil's educational performance.''

In the late 1980s there were approximately 40,800 legally

blind students in the United States. Only 5,200 of these children read by the BRAILLE SYSTEM. The rest use taped materials, regular or large-print books, optical, nonoptical, and/or electronic vision-enhancement devices such as magnifiers and telescopes. These children need specialized instruction in listening skills and the use of their vision in order to obtain maximum visual efficiency. Statistics on the numbers of visually impaired or low-vision children are difficult to acquire, but two commonly accepted ratios are that one in 2,500 children is legally blind (National Society to Prevent Blindness) and one in 1,600 children has a visual disability severe enough to require special education services (American Printing House for the Blind).

New technical devices such as the talking calculator and the optacon, which creates a tactile display allowing inkprint to be felt by touch, have helped visually handicapped children at school, at home, and in the community. Additional educational and vocational devices, such as speech-output computer add-ons, continue to be used and developed.

At the end of World War II, when many war-blinded veterans returned home, orientation and mobility became an important part of a blind person's training. It was recognized that with proper training in the use of the long cane, blind people could be more independent and travel by themselves. This type of training is now available to many blind children. Blind people between the ages of 16 and 55 in good physical and emotional health are candidates for GUIDE DOGS. Not all people, however, are suited to them, nor do all want them.

In 1975 the U.S. government passed legislation that guaranteed a free and appropriate education for all handicapped children in the least restrictive learning environment. They were to be given an appropriate education in their neighborhood public schools when the special support staff and facilities are available. More than a decade after the act's passage, however, because of inadequate funding and a tremendous shortage of special-education teachers, many blind and visually impaired children still do not receive the needed specialized instruction. In addition, in 1986 the U.S. Congress extended mandatory special-education services downward from age 6 to age 3 by 1990. Although many felt that this was a badly needed law, it probably means that the specialized teacher shortage will become even more dramatic.

SUSAN JAY SPUNGIN

Bibliography: Barraga, Natalie, *Visual Handicaps and Learning*, rev. ed. (1983); Ferrell, Kay, *Reach Out and Teach* (1985); Liscio, Mary Ann, *A Guide to Colleges for Visually Impaired Students* (1986); Scholl, Geraldine, ed., *Foundations of Education for Blind and Visually Handicapped Children and Youth: Theory and Practice* (1986); Spungin, Susan Jay, *Guidelines for Public School Programs Serving Visually Handicapped Children*, 2d ed. (1981); Swallow, Rose-Marie, and Huebner, Kathleen Mary, eds., *How to Thrive, Not Just Survive: A Guide to Developing Independent Life Skills for Blind and Visually Impaired Children and Youths* (1987).

blind snake

The blind snakes (family Typhlopidae, about 200 species) and the unrelated slender blind snakes (family Leptotyphlopidae, about 40 species) are so called because their eyes are vestigial and covered by head scales, as an evolutionary result of their burrowing habits. Found worldwide, they are rarely seen because of their small size (usually less than 20 cm/8 in long) and underground life. They possess smooth scales, cylindrical bodies, blunt, rounded heads, short, rounded tails, and (in the typhlopids) only the remnants of the pelvic girdle. The typhlopids have no teeth in their lower jaw, whereas the leptotyphlopids have no teeth in their upper jaw. The snakes feed on ants and termites and their larvae.

JONATHAN CAMPBELL

Bibliography: Mehrtens, J. M., *Living Snakes of the World* (1987).

blindfish

Blindfish are any of several unrelated species of sightless cave-dwelling fish comprising three families, Brotulidae, Amblyopsidae, and Characidae. Brotulids, for example, include the genera *Lucifuga* and *Stygicola*, which inhabit freshwater caves in Cuba, and *Typhlias*, found in freshwater caves in Yucatán, Mexico. Most other brotulids are marine, and blindfish evolved from forms that invaded the limestone caverns in these two areas. The freshwater *Astyamax mexicanus* of the family Characidae, which also inhabits caves in Mexico, is eyeless and is potentially dangerous as a biter. Three species belong to the family Amblyopsidae and live in limestone caves along the Atlantic coast of the Americas. Young fish have eyes and skin pigment that degenerate with age.

blindness

The term *blindness* implies total or partial loss of vision involving both eyes. The exact level of vision defined as blindness, however, varies in different countries because of differing legal or social requirements. In the United States, blindness is defined as unimprovable vision of 20/200 (6/60) or worse. This means that an individual is generally considered blind who, even with the use of ordinary eyeglasses, can see no better at 20 ft (6 m) than a person with normal vision can see at 200 ft (60 m). On the other hand, the World Health Organization (WHO) Program Advisory Group on the Prevention of Blindness lists the vision level suggested as blindness as a visual acuity of less than 10/200 (3/60), which is twice as low as the U.S. definition. The WHO level of visual acuity is also described as the inability to count fingers in daylight at a distance of 10 ft (3 m), because in many regions a great number of people cannot receive formal eye examinations but may be tested by unspecialized personnel.

From data available in the 1980s, the number of persons worldwide who have a visual acuity of less than 10/200 is estimated as 28 million. This level of handicap precludes an individual from functioning effectively in the community without special assistance and rehabilitation (see BLIND, EDUCATION OF THE). Were the definition of blindness instead taken as 20/200, as is done in a number of industrialized countries besides the United States, the total number of blind persons in the world would be about 42 million.

The prevalence and causes of blindness vary according to the geographical location and economic status of a region. Thus in developing countries in tropical areas, the number of blind persons may reach at least 21 million (using the WHO definition). This high figure is due to the massive prevalence of such eye diseases as TRACHOMA, onchocerciasis (RIVER BLINDNESS), and the NUTRITION-DEFICIENCY DISEASES keratomalacia and xerophthalmia. In addition, few eye doctors are present in such regions to treat CATARACT or accidental eye injuries. In other developing countries where eye care is not easily available and the presence of untreated cataract and undetected GLAUCOMA is also critical, the number of blind persons may

A blind student touches a relief globe to learn about the Earth's major geophysical features. Many teaching aids using the tactile senses have been developed for educating the blind.

reach as many as 5.5 million.

In developed countries with advanced medical services, on the other hand, most curable blindness is treated. Thus although many persons may have vision problems, the exact number of blind individuals may be less than 2 million. The main causes of blindness in such countries are age-related cataract, glaucoma, DIABETES, and macular degeneration (see EYE DISEASES). In the United States about 1 million cataracts are removed each year and vision improved with either an intraocular plastic lens, a contact corneal lens, or a cataract glass. Several million Americans are also being treated for glaucoma, which if caught in its early stages can usually be dealt with by medication or surgery.   PAUL HENKIND, M.D.

Bibliography: Dobree, J. H., and Boulter, Eric, *Blindness and Visual Handicap: The Facts* (1982); Henkind, Paul, et al., *Compendium of Ophthalmology* (1983); Kirchner, Corinne, *Data on Blindness and Visual Impairment in the U.S.A.* (1985); Koestler, Frances, *The Unseen Minority: A Social History of Blindness in the United States* (1976); Kupfer, Carl, ed., *World Blindness and Its Prevention* (1988); Naumann, G. O., and Apple, D. J., *Pathology of the Eye* (1986); Sardegna, Jill, and Paul, T. O., *Encyclopedia of Blindness and Visual Impairment* (1990); Vaughan, C. E., *The Struggle of Blind People for Self-Determination* (1993).

blink microscope

The blink microscope, or blink comparator, is used for detecting changes between astronomical photographic plates of the same sky area taken at different times. Dual optical trains bring the images from the negative photographic plates to a common eyepiece, but only one image can be seen at a time, the images being alternated rapidly either by a manually controlled flip mirror or by alternate illumination of the plates. Any differences between the two, due to variability of the brightness of a star (different image size), or a shift in position, attract the eye of the operator as a blinking in and out or a shift back and forth. The plates must be very well matched in image quality and exposure characteristics for best results. The blink microscope is used to discover variable stars in dense star fields and to detect stars with high proper motion, whose positions shift noticeably, as well as small planetary objects in the solar system.   DAVID S. EVANS

Blish, James

James Blish, b. East Orange, N.J., May 23, 1921, d. July 29, 1975, was an American science fiction writer who wrote two highly respected tetralogies. The first, *Cities in Flight* (1970), concerned the results of longevity and easy mass space travel. The second and more highly regarded loosely unites four novels with theological themes: *A Case of Conscience* (1958), which won a 1959 Hugo Award; *Doctor Mirabilis* (1964), on the life of Roger Bacon; *Black Easter* (1968); and *The Day after Judgment* (1970). Under the pseudonym William Atheling, Jr., Blish published two volumes of criticism, *The Issue at Hand* (1964) and *More Issues at Hand* (1970).

Bliss, Sir Arthur

The English composer Arthur Edward Drummond Bliss, b. Aug. 2, 1891, d. Mar. 27, 1975, was known for his experimental as well as his conventional musical compositions. He studied at Pembroke College, Cambridge, and at the Royal College of Music in London with Gustav Holst and Ralph Vaughan Williams. Bliss was director of music at the BBC in the early 1940s and Master of the Queen's Music in 1953. He wrote the score for the film adaptation (1936) of H. G. Wells's *The Shape of Things to Come,* and his ballet *Checkmate* (1937) has been a lasting success.

His works of the early 1920s, such as *Rhapsody and Rout* (1918–19) and *Colour Symphony* (1922) were considered avant-garde. Bliss's later works, which include Piano Concerto (1938) and the quintets for oboe and strings and clarinet and strings, are classical in form. He also wrote an opera for television, *Tobias and the Angel* (1960). Bliss was knighted in 1950. His autobiography was published in 1970.

blitzkrieg

Blitzkrieg (German: "lightning war") is a method of fast-moving, air-and-land warfare first used extensively during World War II. German armies invading Poland in 1939 used tanks, armored trucks, self-propelled guns, and dive bombers to break through opposing forces and penetrate far behind their lines. During the invasion of the Low Countries and France in 1940, the German armored columns again used these tactics to shock and disorganize the defenders. On the Allied side, U.S. Gen. George S. PATTON exhibited (1944) particular skill in mobile warfare in Europe.

In a blitzkrieg, tanks and troop-transport vehicles were concentrated, and massive attacks by dive bombers were conducted on enemy front-line positions. When these forces had broken through, they continued deep into enemy territory, encircling and cutting off the enemy. The techniques were first developed by the German army late in World War I in an effort to overcome static trench warfare, but the Germans lacked the mobility to succeed. Between the wars, armored tactics were further developed by Basil LIDDELL HART and J. F. C. Fuller in Britain, Charles DE GAULLE in France, and Heinz GUDERIAN in Germany. Made chief of German mobile troops in 1938, Guderian led the drive across France in 1940.

Bibliography: Corum, J. S., *The Roots of Blitzkrieg* (1992); Perrett, Bryan, *A History of Blitzkrieg* (1983).

Blitzstein, Marc [blit'-styn]

The American composer Marc Blitzstein, b. Philadelphia, Mar. 2, 1905, d. Jan. 22, 1964, was the foremost musical spokesman of the left-wing theater of the 1930s. *The Cradle Will Rock* (1937), a satire on capitalism for which he wrote both libretto and songs, provoked an uproar, and its first public performance was banned. An opera, *Regina* (1949), is perhaps his most important work. Blitzstein was murdered while vacationing in Martinique.   DAVID EWEN

Blixen, Karen: see DINESEN, ISAK.

blizzard

Blizzard is a North American name for a violent, bitterly cold WIND accompanied by blowing snow whipped up from the ground. Freezing temperatures, high wind speeds, low visibility, and drifting snow create hazardous conditions. A similar wind in Russia is called a *buran.* Most blizzards occur in a cold wave that follows the passage of a cold FRONT in a mid-latitude cyclonic storm (see CYCLONE AND ANTICYCLONE). The term *blizzard* also refers to blowing snow in polar regions. In the Great Plains some winter dust storms are sometimes called black blizzards.   HOWARD J. CRITCHFIELD

Bibliography: Atkinson, B., and Gadd, A., *Weather* (1987); Eagleman, J., *Severe and Unusual Weather* (1982); Lampton, C., *Blizzard* (1992).

Bloch, Ernest

The major Swiss-American composer and teacher Ernest Bloch, b. Geneva, July 24, 1880, d. July 15, 1959, is known for his efforts to establish a specifically Jewish style in music. After studies abroad, he conducted and taught in Switzerland. In 1916 he came to the United States on tour but remained, first as a teacher at the Mannes School in New York and then as director of the Cleveland Institute of Music (1920) and the San Francisco Conservatory (1925). Although he retired in 1930 and returned to Switzerland to devote himself to composition, he came back to the United States in 1938, teaching in the summers at Berkeley from 1943 on. Although his Jewish works, which employ features of Eastern music, are best known, he composed many other works, all characterized by strong expression. Among his compositions are *Trois poèmes juifs, Schelomo,* several concerti, five string quartets, and a number of pieces for chorus and orchestra.   F. E. KIRBY

Bibliography: Bloch, S., and Heskes, I., *Ernest Bloch, Creative Spirit* (1976); Strassburg, Robert, *Ernest Bloch* (1977).

Bloch, Ernst

Ernst Bloch, b. July 8, 1885, d. Aug. 3, 1977, was a German Marxist philosopher. After studying at the University of Leipzig, he left (1933) Nazi Germany for Switzerland and then the United States. He returned to East Germany in 1948 and was a professor at Leipzig until 1957. Branded a revisionist, he applied for asylum in West Germany in 1961 and became a professor at Tübingen. Bloch's major work, *Das Prinzip Hoffnung* (The Hope Principle, 3 vols., 1954–59), attempts to formulate an optimistic Marxist philosophy of progress and political salvation with strong Judeo-Christian elements.

Bloch, Felix

The Swiss-born American physicist Felix Bloch, b. Oct. 23, 1905, d. Sept. 10, 1983, is noted for his determination of the magnetic moment of the neutron. During World War II he worked on the Manhattan Project, and during 1944–45 he investigated countermeasures to radar. Returning to Stanford University, he developed magnetic resonance spectroscopy, used in determining molecular structure and composition; NUCLEAR MAGNETIC RESONANCE IMAGING has also become an important medical technique. Bloch shared the 1952 Nobel Prize for physics with Edward Mills PURCELL.   JAMES A. BOOTH

Bloch, Konrad

Konrad Emil Bloch, b. Jan. 21, 1912, is a German-born American biochemist. He traced many of the metabolic changes that occur in the body's fats and carbohydrates as acetic acid is converted into cholesterol, a chemical essential to the production of bile acids and some hormones. For this, Bloch, with Feodor Lynen, was awarded the 1964 Nobel Prize for physiology or medicine.

Bloch, Marc

Marc Bloch, b. July 6, 1886, d. June 16, 1944, was an influential French social historian who was executed by the Germans while serving in the French Resistance during World War II. In a series of studies, including *French Rural History* (1931; Eng. trans., 1966) and *Feudal Society* (2 vols., 1939–40; Eng. trans., 1961), Bloch provided a model for a new kind of history. He turned away from the narration of political events to explore social structures in their broadest sense—the interrelation of material and economic factors, social institutions, and dominant mentalities in a historical context. In 1929, Bloch cofounded the journal *Annales d'histoire économique et sociale* (Annals of Economic and Social History), which became an influential international forum for the new social history.

GEORG G. IGGERS

Bibliography: Fink, Carole, *Marc Bloch: A Life in History* (1989).

Block, Adriaen

Adriaen Block was a 17th-century Dutch mariner who in 1613 was commissioned by Dutch merchants to explore the regions of North America discovered by Henry Hudson. He sailed up the Hudson to Albany and then explored (1614) Long Island Sound, discovering the Connecticut River and going as far north as 42° 30' on Massachusetts Bay. The first detailed map of the southern New England coast, the so-called Figurative Map (1616), was based on his data. As a result of Block's explorations the New Netherland Company, forerunner of the Dutch West India Company, was created. Block Island was named for him.

Block, Herbert Lawrence: see HERBLOCK.

block printing

Printing with wood blocks is the earliest technique known for producing multiple images or designs on fabric, paper, or other printable material. It is a relief-printing technique, so called because part of the block's surface is cut away, or excised, leaving in relief only the desired design. When ink or other coloring matter is applied to the block, only the areas left in relief receive it; and when the block is pressed against the surface of the material being printed, only the ink-bearing relief areas make an impression. Block printing is the forerunner of modern LETTERPRESS printing.

Blocks may have been used to print textiles in India as early as 400 BC. Books were block printed in China in about the 9th century AD, as was the paper money in Kublai Khan's 13th-century Mongol empire. The earliest example of block-printed cloth from Egypt dates back to the 9th century, but the technique was probably practiced there much earlier.

Block printing in Europe seems to have started in Italy in the 13th century. During the 14th century the technique was used in Germany for illuminating manuscripts, and that country became a major center for block-printed textiles a century later. Some books were also block printed at this time, but the invention of movable type by Gutenberg about 1450 ended the use of blocks for all but the printing of textiles.

During the last half of the 18th century sizable block-printing industries were established in Europe. The first commercial block-printing enterprise in the New World was established in Philadelphia in 1772, and the technique remained important until well into the 20th century. Block printing today is fairly rare, having been almost entirely replaced by SILK-SCREEN PRINTING.   MARK DITTRICK

See also: GRAPHIC ARTS; WOODCUTS AND WOOD ENGRAVINGS.

block and tackle: see PULLEY.

blockade

In international law, a blockade is the use of warships and planes to prevent ships from transporting arms, munitions, and other goods to an enemy's ports. The Declaration of Paris in 1856 established rules of maritime warfare that are still generally recognized: a blockade must be announced to all nations affected, and it must be enforced in order to be binding.

The development of long-range coast artillery, mines, submarines, and, later, aircraft has minimized 20th-century use of the kind of close blockade that Britain maintained against the French coast during the Napoleonic Wars—itself in retaliation against Napoleon's CONTINENTAL SYSTEM. Thus the long-range blockade—one carried out well beyond the enemy coast—was used by Britain against Germany in both world wars. At the outset of World War I, the British mined the North Sea, and their warships patrolled the sea lanes to stop and search neutral ships for CONTRABAND, which they regarded as anything that might aid the German war effort. Germany struck back with mines and submarines to sink merchant ships approaching the British Isles. The United States vigorously protested against British violations of neutral rights, but it was Germany's sinking of such as the LUSITANIA that finally caused the United States to enter the war against Germany in 1917.

A pacific blockade is one used in time of peace to coerce a country into fulfilling some agreement or obligation. In 1902, Germany, Britain, and Italy instituted a pacific blockade against Venezuela, which had defaulted on its debts. During the CUBAN MISSILE CRISIS of 1962 the United States established a blockade to prevent Soviet vessels from carrying missiles to Cuba. In 1990 the United States and its allies imposed a blockade of Iraq to enforce the United Nations trade embargo on that country. The intention was to force Iraq's withdrawal from Kuwait, which it had invaded in August.

Bloemfontein   [bloom'-fahn-tayn]

Bloemfontein is the capital of the Orange Free State and the judicial capital of South Africa. The city lies at an elevation of more than 1,300 m (4,500 ft) and has a population of 104,381 (1985). Established in 1854 as the capital of the Orange Free State Republic, it grew rapidly in the late 19th century following the discovery both of diamonds near Kimberley and of gold on the Witwatersrand. Bloemfontein ("fountain of flowers") is an important railroad junction and an agricultural and commercial center and is known for its stately streets, university, and public buildings. The clear atmospheric conditions have resulted in the founding of two observatories.

ALAN C. G. BEST

Blois, Château de [blwah]

The Château de Blois is adjacent to the French town of Blois, capital of the department of Loire-et-Cher, about 146 km (91 mi) southwest of Paris. It is one of the first châteaus that Francis I rebuilt on assuming the throne in 1515 and one of the first in which Italian Renaissance architectural elements were introduced. Thus the château incorporates features of French architecture from the 13th through the 17th century, from late French Gothic to early baroque.

Since the Middle Ages, Blois had been the residence of powerful counts. In the 14th century it became the seat of Louis, duc d'Orléans, whose grandson came to the throne as Louis XII. His heirs made Blois the virtual second capital of France through the 16th century.

The main hall of the château survives from the 13th century; the Charles d'Orléans Gallery is of the mid-15th century; both the Chapelle Saint–Calais and the Louis XII wing (1498–1503) exemplify the transition from Flamboyant Gothic to French Renaissance; a new court facade and the northwest facade were built in 1515–24 for Francis I. The most notable of Francis's additions is the spiral staircase of five stories (part of the new court facade), in an open octagonal case of carved stone. In 1635–38, François MANSART built a new wing for Gaston de France, duc d'Orléans, brother of Louis XIII.

LELAND M. ROTH

Bibliography: Blunt, Anthony F., *Art and Architecture in France, 1500–1700*, rev. ed. (1954; repr. 1977).

Blok, Aleksandr Aleksandrovich [blawk, ul-yek-sahn'-dur ul-yek-sahn'-droh-vich]

Aleksandr Aleksandrovich Blok, b. Nov. 28 (N.S.), 1880, d. Aug. 7, 1921, is generally considered the foremost poet of Russian symbolism. He epitomizes Russia's majestic prerevolutionary poetic tradition. Blok electrified his generation with his poetry and fascinated it with his life, itself a kind of tragic, lyrical drama inseparable from his personal, almost confessional, verse. His early poetry, such as the *Verses about the Fair Lady* (written 1901–02; published 1904), reflects the idealistic, mystical philosophy of Vladimir SOLOVIEV, with its exaltation of Divine Wisdom (Greek *Sophia*). His subsequent plunge into Dionysian carnality and inebriate self-destructiveness appears in "The Unknown Woman" (1906) and in the cycles *The City* (1904–08) and *The Mask of Snow* (1907). Here Divine Sophia, contaminated by life, becomes a mysterious prostitute. Blok's next phase gave rise to an ambivalent, apocalyptic evocation of a new "lady," his "beggared" and "fatal" Russia, land of high destiny, presented in the cycle "My Native Land" (1907–16).

From this thematic perspective, Blok's poetry is a chronicle of his compulsive efforts to escape his isolated and sometimes despairing individualism. He attempts self-deliverance by falling in love (a favorite image), that is, by cherishing a series of ideals greater than himself, feminine in essence and capable of rendering mundane, earthy life miraculous. Blok's eroticism, sometimes sublimated and sometimes explicit, and his passionate sincerity give great vitality to his verse, but its beauty lies in the "music" that he heard in the life around him and translated into rich, rhythmic intonations that are distinctly his own. After initially accepting the Communist revolution in his epic poem *The Twelve* (1918; Eng. trans., 1920), Blok slipped into depression and then into a physical and spiritual decline that ended in his death.

KENNETH N. BROSTROM

Bibliography: Erlich, Victor, *The Double Image* (1964); Kemble, Robin, *Alexander Blok: A Study in Rhythm and Metre* (1965); Kisch, Cecil, *Alexander Blok* (1960); Pyman, Avril, *Aleksandr Blok: A Biography*, 2 vols. (1979, 1980); Reeve, Franklin, *Aleksandr Blok* (1962; repr. 1980).

Blondel, Maurice [blawn-del', moh-rees']

The French Catholic philosopher Maurice Édouard Blondel, b. Nov. 2, 1861, d. June 4, 1949, held that philosophy should be based on action rather than on pure thought. Early in his career he was influenced by the idea of John Henry NEWMAN that belief springs from volition as well as from logical demonstration. Blondel taught at the universities of Montauban and Lille before taking a position in 1896 at Aix-en-Provence, where he remained for the rest of his life.

The basis for Blondel's later philosophy is developed in his book on action (1893). Philosophy, he explained, must turn to the whole man for its explanations—to actual experience in all its richness. The key to this experience is that individuals must act and cannot keep from questioning the meaning of their actions. This question of meaning cannot be avoided and must find a positive solution through the recognition that action is always incomplete. The permanent gap between action and its realization creates human discontent and impels them to ever wider spheres of action. Even the most expansive acts—those aiming at the good of humankind—cannot still human restless discontent, however. Only God's grace, already present in human imperfect strivings, can achieve this fulfillment. Blondel's position is restated, with fewer anti-intellectual implications, in *Thought, Being and Action* (1934–37). Among the translations of his works are *The Letter on Apologetics, and History and Dogma* (1965) and *Pierre Teilhard de Chardin, Maurice Blondel, Correspondence* (1967).

PETE A. Y. GUNTER

Blondel de Nesle [blawn-del' duh nel']

Blondel de Nesle, fl. late 12th century, was a French trouvère (see MINSTRELS, MINNESINGERS, AND TROUBADOURS) and a favorite of England's King Richard I, or Richard the Lion-Hearted. He composed about 20 poems, some of which survive with music in the Chansonnier Cangé. According to an apocryphal story, he was responsible for rescuing Richard the Lion-Hearted from captivity in Austria. Appearing before Richard's prison window, the troubador sang a strophe of a song; Richard made known his location by responding with the second strophe.

ELWYN A. WIENANDT

blood

Blood is the essential red fluid that is pumped by the HEART through the CIRCULATORY SYSTEM of humans and all higher animals. It is complex in its composition and in its functions. Blood has two main constituents. The cells, or corpuscles, comprise about 45 percent, and the liquid portion, or PLASMA, in which the cells are suspended comprises 55 percent. The blood cells comprise three main types: red blood cells, or erythrocytes; white blood cells, or leukocytes, which in turn are of many different types; and platelets, or thrombocytes. Each type of cell has its own individual functions in the body. The plasma is a complex colorless solution, about 90 percent WATER, that carries different ions and molecules including PROTEINS, ENZYMES, HORMONES, nutrients, waste materials such as UREA, and fibrinogen, the protein that aids in clotting.

RED BLOOD CELLS

The red blood cells are tiny, round, biconcave disks, averaging about 7.5 microns (0.003 in) in diameter. A normal 76.5-kg (170-lb) man has about 5 l (5.3 qt) of blood in his body, containing more than 25 trillion (25×10^{12}) red cells. Because the normal life span of red cells in the circulation is only about 120 days, more than 200 billion cells are normally destroyed each day by the spleen and must be replaced. Red blood cells, as well as most white cells and platelets, are made by the BONE marrow. Large numbers of primitive red cells, or erythroblasts, grow here and divide repeatedly, each primitive cell normally producing 16 mature red cells. The maturing cells lose their nucleus before leaving the marrow, making the red blood cells the most numerous nonnucleated cells.

The main function of the red blood cells is to transport OXYGEN from the LUNGS to the tissues (see RESPIRATORY SYSTEM). Oxidation of various food substances to supply most of the

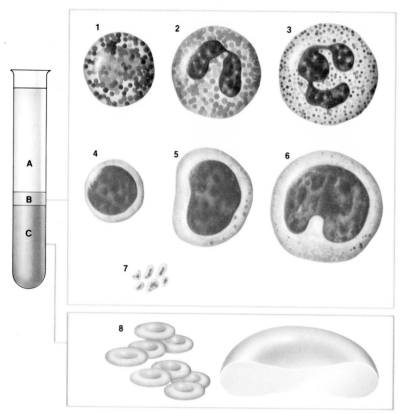

Blood is a tissue comprising two main components: a plasma fluid (A) and freely moving blood cells, which are white (B) or red (C). Plasma, comprising 90% water, does not have cells but contains proteins and salts that buffer substances traveling through the blood vessels. White blood cells include three types of granulocytes, which are basophils (1), eosinophils (2), and neutrophils (3); small and large lymphocytes (4, 5); and monocytes (6). White blood cells defend the body against infection by engulfing the invading bacteria and by healing wounds. Platelets (7) are cell fragments that catalyze blood clotting. Red blood cells (8), which have no nuclei, are shaped like indented disks. These cells contain hemoglobin, protein that transports oxygen to body tissues.

energy requirements of the body results in CARBON DIOXIDE, one of the chief waste products, and red blood cells carry it to the lungs for release and to pick up more oxygen.

The substance in the red blood cells that is largely responsible for their ability to carry oxygen and carbon dioxide is HEMOGLOBIN, the material that gives the cells their red color. It is a protein complex comprising many linked AMINO ACIDS, and occupies almost the entire volume of a red blood cell. Essential to its structure and function is iron.

The red blood cell depends on its cell wall to protect it against the turbulent racing through kilometers of blood vessels. This cell wall has sufficient pliability to prevent prompt traumatic destruction but sufficient rigidity to maintain, under most circumstances, the normal disk shape of the cell.

BLOOD TYPING

The cell wall contains many antigenic proteins, which determine the blood type. Among these proteins are the ANTIGENS A and B, the major blood group factors. Blood containing the antigen A is called group A. Blood with antigen B is group B. Blood with both antigens is called AB, and blood with neither is called group O. Normally, the plasma of every person contains an antibody against the A or B antigen missing from the cell wall. In typing the blood, the antigens in the red cells are determined by mixing them with known typing serums. The ANTIBODIES in the serum or plasma are determined by mixing it with cells of known A or B type. Such typing is necessary in preparation for blood transfusion. Antigens of the various Rh and Hr types, M and N, S and s̄, Kell, Duffy, and many others also exist in the red blood cell. All, like the A and B antigens, are inherited. When the red-cell antigens are determined, they show so many different combinations as to make a person's blood type almost as individual as a fingerprint.

Antibodies against antigens other than A and B do not normally occur in the plasma. They may appear after transfusion, however, and may cause transfusion reactions and destruction of red blood cells or hemolytic disease of the newborn (erythroblastosis fetalis).

The remainder of the red blood cell is the stroma, which

contains a complex series of enzymes that derive energy from the SUGAR in the plasma. It also acts as a chemical pump to keep out the SODIUM, an excess of which would cause so much water to enter the cell that it would burst.

WHITE BLOOD CELLS

The leukocytes, or white blood cells, are of three types, all involved in defending the body against foreign organisms. The granulocytes comprise three types: neutrophils, eosinophils, and basophils, with neutrophils the most abundant. Neutrophils seek out bacteria and phagocytize, or engulf, them. The lymphocytes' chief function is to migrate into the connective tissue and build antibodies against BACTERIA and VIRUSES. Leukocytes are almost colorless, considerably larger than red cells, have a nucleus, and are much less numerous; only one or two exist for every 1,000 red cells. The number increases in the presence of infection. Monocytes, representing only 4 to 8 percent of white cells, attack organisms not destroyed by granulocytes and leukocytes.

The granulocytes, accounting for about 70 percent of all white blood cells, are formed in the bone marrow, where they mature from the primitive myeloblast, divide several times, and eventually become granulated cells with multilobed nuclei.

The lymphocytes, on the other hand, are produced primarily by the lymphoid tissues of the body—the SPLEEN and lymph nodes. They are usually smaller than the granulocytes and have a round or oval nucleus. Monocytes are believed to originate from lymphocytes. Just as the oxygen-carrying function of red cells is necessary for survival, so do normal numbers of functioning leukocytes protect against infection (see also LYMPHATIC SYSTEM).

PLATELETS

Platelets, or thrombocytes, are tiny bits of cytoplasm, much smaller than the red blood cells but lacking a nucleus. They are round or biconcave disks and are normally about 30 to 40 times more numerous than the white blood cells. They are produced as broken fragments of the cytoplasm of the giant cells of the bone marrow—the megakaryocytes. The platelets' primary function is to stop bleeding. When tissue is damaged, the platelets aggregate in clumps as part of the clotting process described below.

PLASMA

The plasma is more than 90 percent water and contains a large number of substances, many essential to life. Its major solute is a mixture of proteins. The most abundant plasma protein is ALBUMIN. This material is normally kept inside the blood vessels. Its ability to attract water keeps a large portion of the body water in the blood. When the plasma albumin concentration becomes dangerously low, because of disease, free water collects in the tissues outside the blood vessels, producing a swelling known as EDEMA.

The GLOBULINS are even larger protein molecules than albumin and are of many chemical structures and functions. The antibodies, produced by lymphocytes, are globulins and are carried throughout the body, where many of them fight bacterial or viral invasion. Other antibodies are related to the blood groups. One plasma globulin, transferrin, binds free iron, making it possible for the blood to pick up iron absorbed from food in the intestines and carry it to the bone marrow, where it is used for the production of hemoglobin. Haptoglobin ties up the free hemoglobin released by the destruction of red blood cells.

An important function of plasma is to transport nutrients to the tissues. Glucose, absorbed from the bowels, constitutes a major source of body energy. Some of the plasma proteins and fats, for example, lipids, are also used by the tissues for cell growth and energy. Minerals essential to body function, although present only in trace amounts, are important elements of the plasma. The calcium ion, for example, is essential to the building of bone, as is phosphorus. Calcium is also essential to the clotting of blood. Copper, although toxic in more than trace concentrations, is also a necessary component of the plasma.

BLOOD CLOTTING

The clotting process was long thought to be intrinsic to the bloodstream, but by the late 1980s researchers determined that the molecule initiating the process—a protein called tissue factor—is in fact tightly bound to the membranes of most cells outside the bloodstream. Blood coming into contact with these membranes sets off a cascading sequence of reactions involving various blood proteins called factors. Thus a molecule of factor VII coming into contact with tissue factor is converted to an active form that in turn converts ten molecules of factor X into thromboplastin, with the help of calcium ions. Thromboplastin in turn binds to factor Va, which then binds to a circulating protein called prothrombin to form two million molecules of the clotting enzyme thrombin. Thrombin acts as a catalyst to convert soluble fibrinogen to billions of molecules of the insoluble protein fibrin, the basis of the final clot. The clot is made firm by fibrin-stabilizing factor XIII, reinforced by blood platelets, which attach to the fibrin, contract, and pull the clot together.

Because minor injuries often occur, the clotting process is almost constantly taking place somewhere in the body. It must be terminated quickly, however, or blood would clot everywhere and death would ensue. To prevent this from happening, plasma proteins known as fibrinolysins, or plasmins, dissolve old clots in the bloodstream.

BLOOD DISEASES

Anemia. Anemia is a deficiency of hemoglobin in the blood, and anemias are generally classified as caused by blood loss, abnormal destruction of the red cells, and inadequate red cell formation by the bone marrow. Anemia caused by acute or chronic blood loss, or abnormal bleeding, results from the inability of the bone marrow to make new cells as fast as they are needed. In acute, or massive, bleeding, the red blood cells and their hemoglobin are normal but are not abundant. Chronic, usually slow bleeding leads to a deficiency in iron stores needed for hemoglobin. This deficiency results in red blood cells that are both smaller and paler than they are normally.

Abnormal destruction of red cells (the hemolytic anemias) leads to a shorter than normal red cell survival. For example, in the hereditary disease SICKLE-CELL ANEMIA the hemoglobin is built erroneously. Another hereditary hemolytic anemia is familial spherocytosis. In this disorder, the fault is in the struc-

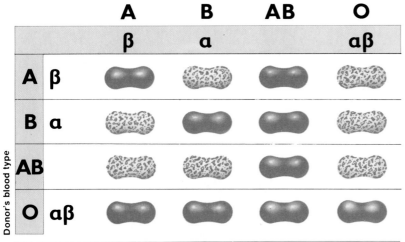

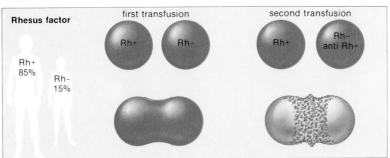

The chart representing two blood-typing systems, ABO (top) and Rh (bottom), illustrates blood compatibility between donor and recipient, as shown by solid red blood cells, and incompatibility, as shown by fragmented red blood cells. Compatibility of blood types is based on whether specific antigens are present or absent on the surface of a person's red blood cells, and also whether specific antibodies are present or absent in the plasma. For example, a person might have type A blood, with A antigens and β antibodies. Type B blood contains B antigens and δ antibodies, type AB has A and B antigens and no antibodies, and type O has no antigens and α and β antibodies. A patient who needs a blood transfusion must receive a donor's blood that is compatible with the patient's blood. A type A recipient can receive blood from a type A donor; if a type A recipient receives blood from a type B donor, however, the recipient's β antibodies attack the donor's blood and cause the blood to clump and disintegrate. The clumped blood clogs arteries. The Rh system involves the Rhesus factor, found on the surface of red blood cells of 85 percent of the world's population. Blood that lacks the Rhesus factor, or Rh− blood, normally does not have antibodies against the Rhesus factor. If an Rh− person receives Rh+ blood in a transfusion, however, antibodies may be created. If the Rh− person receives a second transfusion of Rh+ blood, the antibodies will attack and clump the Rh+ blood, causing severe problems. Typing the Rhesus factor is especially important for a pregnant mother with Rh− blood who bears an Rh+ child.

ture of the red-cell membrane, which is not large enough for the volume of the cell. Such cells break more readily in circulation. Not all hemolytic anemias are congenital. In autoimmune hemolytic anemia, the person manufactures antibodies that attack and destroy the red cells. The blood of persons with this disease often shows spherocytes, and the disease resembles familial spherocytosis.

Anemias caused by bone-marrow failure include aplastic anemia, in which the bone marrow lacks adequate numbers of some or all types of blood cells, and pernicious anemia, in which the stomach fails to produce "intrinsic factor." This factor is necessary for the normal absorption of vitamin B-12 from the intestines, and vitamin B-12 in turn is essential for normal bone marrow function.

In some persons, the concentration of red cells and of hemoglobin in the blood may be abnormally increased, rather than decreased, resulting in POLYCYTHEMIA. This is usually caused by an increased production of red cells, but in some persons it may be caused by a decreased volume of plasma.

Neutropenia. Deficiency of circulating granulocytes, with poor resistance to infection, may occur in many diseases. (In general, if fewer than 500 neutrophiles exist for every cubic millimeter of blood, the chance of severe infection is greatly increased.) One common cause is the use of X rays and toxic drugs to treat many malignant diseases.

Leukemia. A great increase in abnormal leukocytes may occur for unknown reasons, resulting in the diseases known as the LEUKEMIAS. These range from the chronic lymphocytic leukemia, in which a person may live for many years, to devastating acute leukemia, often causing death within months.

Thrombocytopenia. The number of platelets can severely decrease, with danger of bleeding. Perhaps the most common cause of platelet deficiency, or thrombocytopenia, is an autoimmune disease related to autoimmune hemolytic anemia. The difference is that, in these cases, the body produces antibodies that attack only the platelets. Platelet deficiency is also found in such diseases as aplastic anemia, in which some or all the normal bone marrow cells are decreased. Severe platelet deficiency may also occur in the severe bone-marrow depression of acute leukemia and of its treatment.

Hemophilia. Deficiencies of one or more of the plasma coagulation factors may also cause abnormal bleeding. The existence of many of the clotting factors was recognized only when persons were found who lacked such a factor. The best known such bleeding disorder is HEMOPHILIA, in which a hereditary deficiency of factor VIII, or "antihemophilic globulin," exists. This disorder is inherited as a sex-linked characteristic and occurs almost exclusively in males.

Thromboembolic Disease. More common than abnormal bleeding, however, is abnormal clotting in the blood vessels, known as thromboembolic disease. Such a tendency may be caused by an excess of one or more of the plasma clotting factors, or at times to a deficiency of one of the fibrinolytic factors. This group of disorders is one of the most common causes of death in middle-aged and elderly persons.

BLOOD SUBSTITUTES

Researchers seek to develop blood substitutes to increase supplies and also to avoid transfusion problems caused by contaminants. Synthetic plasma substitutes such as dextran serve to raise blood-fluid levels, but the further need is for substances that can supply oxygen to tissues. So-called "white bloods" can perform this function temporarily. These fluids, called perfluorocarbons, or PFCs, are problematic in that they tend to form circulation-blocking globules, but researchers are working to surmount this difficulty. Another attempted approach is to reconstitute hemoglobin molecules from dead red blood cells, but such efforts are still in the trial stage. Scientists are also working to produce hemoglobin in limitless quantities through genetic engineering, once the responsible gene is isolated.   PAUL G. HATTERSLEY, M.D.

Bibliography: Callender, S. T., *Blood Disorders* (1986); Golde, D. W., and Gasson, J. C., "Hormones that Stimulate the Growth of Blood Cells," *Scientific American*, July 1988; Jandl, James, *Blood* (1987); Matthias, F. R., *Blood Coagulation Disorders* (1987); Weiss, Leon, *The Blood Cells and Hematopoietic Tissues*, 2d ed. (1984).

blood bank

A blood bank is a facility at which blood is collected, stored, and processed for later use in BLOOD TRANSFUSIONS. Although such transfusions were already being practiced in the early 19th century, the emergence of blood banks had to await the development of solutions to keep blood from coagulating, of adequate means of refrigeration, and of sterile methods of storage. Thus the first U.S. blood bank was not formed until 1937, at Cook County Hospital in Chicago. Most blood today is collected at regional and community centers that then provide it to regional hospitals, although some large hospitals collect a portion of their supply on their own. Regional and community blood centers are operated mainly by the RED CROSS and by institutional members of the American Association of Blood Banks. Many commercial blood banks exist.

Collection of whole blood involves the screening of prospective donors to ensure that the donation will not be harmful either to them (because of blood loss) or to the eventual recipients (because of transmission of diseases). Almost all transfused blood today is obtained from volunteer donors, who have proved less likely to have transmissible diseases than are paid donors. The maximum frequency of donation—five times a year, or one unit of 480 ml (about 1 pint) every eight weeks—is related to the body's ability to replenish iron lost in the red cells of the donated blood. The blood is collected into sterile bags, along with samples for testing. The bags contain an anticoagulant and a nutritive solution that permits blood storage for up to five weeks under controlled refrigeration at temperatures of 1°–6° C (33.8°–42.8° F). In some instances the blood is collected into a bag whose tubing is integrally attached to other bags, so that blood components can be prepared without risk of contamination.

The blood bank must determine the blood type in terms of ABO categories, Rh factors, and so forth (see Blood Typing under BLOOD). All donated units must also be tested for antibodies to infectious diseases, such as AIDS and some forms of hepatitis, that would be transmissible to the recipient (see BLOOD TESTS). Blood type and a unique bar code number are then prominently displayed on the label of the unit.

Most units of blood are separated into components by blood banks, the most common components being packed red cells, platelet concentrates, plasma, and Factor VIII-containing cryoprecipitate (see HEMOPHILIA). The use of packed red cells for correction of ANEMIA avoids administration of unnecessary plasma to patients, thereby enhancing the effectiveness and safety of transfusions. Platelet transfusions are required for patients who are deficient in platelets and therefore have a tendency to bleed. Plasma transfusions, often in the form of fresh frozen plasma, find greatest use correcting deficiencies of plasma clotting factors, whereas cryoprecipitate is important for the treatment of patients with hemophilia A.

In addition to conventional blood collection, many blood banks collect plasma and some components by a process called plasmapheresis, in which red cells of the collected blood are returned to the donor after the plasma is separated. Because the donor's red-cell volume is maintained, and because plasma is reconstituted much more rapidly than are red cells, plasmapheresis can be practiced substantially more often than whole-blood donation. Most commercial blood banks are plasmapheresis centers of this type.

Blood banks also collect blood for autologous transfusion—that is, collection of blood from a patient in advance of an anticipated transfusion (usually a surgical procedure), with subsequent transfusion of the unit during the operation. This process eliminates the risk of transfusion-transmitted disease and also facilitates blood provision for patients with rare blood types. No age restrictions or minimum time intervals between donations are involved. Because of concerns about AIDS, the practice of autologous transfusion increased more than tenfold during the 1980s.   HAROLD A. OBERMAN, M.D.

Bibliography: Harmening, Denise, ed., *Modern Blood Banking and Transfusion Practices*, 2d ed. (1989); Holland, Paul, ed., *Standards for Blood Banks and Transfusion Services* (1987); U.S. Office of Technology Assessment, *Blood Policy and Technology* (1985).

blood pressure

Blood pressure is the pressure, or tension, of the blood within the arteries of the CIRCULATORY SYSTEM. The pressure is caused by the pumping of blood from the heart, the resistance of the arterioles, and the elasticity of the arterial walls.

Arterial blood pressure is conventionally written as systolic pressure over diastolic pressure. Systolic pressure is the maximum blood pressure that occurs during the contraction, or systole, of the heart; diastolic pressure is the minimum pressure measured during diastole, or the resting period.

The normal blood pressure varies widely among species of animals, within a given species, and with an individual. The average pressure in the brachial artery of a young human adult at rest, for example, is in the range of 120/80 mm of mercury (Hg). For a giraffe, systolic pressures as high as 260 mm Hg are required to supply the brain with blood.

Much controversy exists about what constitutes normal and elevated blood-pressure levels (HYPERTENSION) in humans. The upper normal limit of blood pressure in the adult under the age of 50 is considered to be 150/90 mm Hg. Blood pressures normally rise with age, mostly because of decreased elasticity of the arteries. Physical activity and emotional stress can temporarily increase blood pressure.   JOHN M. WELLER, M.D.

Bibliography: Fung, Y. C., *Biodynamics: Circulation* (1984).

blood tests

Tests of a patient's blood, when used along with physical examination and medical history data, are a major source of the information needed for diagnosis and treatment of disease. The tests may be broadly grouped as chemical, immunological, hematological, microbiological, or immunohematological, according to the kinds of analysis performed.

Chemical laboratories perform the greatest variety of blood tests, including assays of organ function. Among the tests of liver function, for example, are those which assess liver damage (including transaminase tests) and those which indicate abnormal liver metabolism (such as tests for bilirubin, a bile pigment). Other tests are used for monitoring drug treatments and for toxicological studies, including the identification of drugs of abuse; some must be performed quite rapidly, such as the enzyme tests used for diagnosis of heart attacks.

An IMMUNOLOGY laboratory performs blood tests that are based upon the reactions of antigens and antibodies (see ANTIBODY; ANTIGEN). These include tests for various infectious diseases, such as hepatitis and AIDS; tests for autoimmune diseases, such as rheumatoid arthritis; and tests for endocrine abnormalities. These tests may be performed through examinations of antigen-antibody reactions in the laboratory, or through the use of radioisotopes.

Hematological studies define characteristics of the cellular constituents of blood. The most common procedure is to perform a complete blood count (CBC) of the number of red blood cells, white blood cells, and platelets per unit volume of blood, along with a microscopic examination of the cells (see BLOOD). A hematocrit test is also performed, indicating the percentage of whole blood that comprises these cellular elements. Tests for abnormalities of blood coagulation assume great importance in support of surgical procedures or in the management of patients with a tendency to bleed.

Microbiology laboratories also perform a small number of blood tests, particularly those which require the culturing of blood for infective agents. Antibodies to various infectious diseases are also determined in such laboratories.

Finally, an immunohematology laboratory, or BLOOD BANK, performs blood-typing and antibody determinations that are needed in order to establish donor-recipient blood compatibility prior to transfusions (see BLOOD TRANSFUSION). Other blood tests performed in such a laboratory may include paternity testing and HLA (histocompatibility locus antigen) testing, the latter being of extreme importance in organ transplantations.   HAROLD A. OBERMAN, M.D.

Bibliography: Darovic, G. O., *Hemodynamic Monitoring* (1987); Hall, Roger, and Malia, R. G., *Medical Laboratory Haematology* (1984).

blood transfusion

Blood transfusions involve the intravenous administration of blood from a donor to a patient. Use of human blood for transfusion has been practiced since the early 19th century; however, knowledge of blood-group antigens and their corresponding antibodies—prerequisites for safe transfusion—has been available only since 1900. Blood is now mainly transfused in the form of its components rather than as whole blood; a donated unit is separated into its cellular and plasma components and transfused according to the patient's clinical requirements. In this way the donation of blood from a single donor can provide for the needs of several patients.

The safety and effectiveness of blood transfusion relates, in large measure, to careful donor selection and to pretransfusion testing (see BLOOD BANK; BLOOD TESTS). Such testing for the compatibility of blood-group antigens and antibodies between donor and patient ensures optimum survival of the transfused red cells of the blood. Pretransfusion tests also assess the presence of transmissible diseases in the donor's blood. Before apparently compatible units are transfused, a major crossmatch is also performed wherein red cells of the donor are matched with plasma of the patient.

There is no true artificial substitute for blood. Some experimental solutions can transport oxygen to the tissues temporarily, in a manner somewhat comparable to the performance of red cells (see BLOOD), but they have not proven acceptable as real substitutes.   HAROLD A. OBERMAN, M.D.

Bibliography: Brozovic, B. and M., *Manual of Clinical Blood Transfusion* (1986); Moore, S. B., ed., *Transfusion-Transmitted Diseases* (1987).

blood typing: see BLOOD.

blood vessels: see ARTERY; CAPILLARY; CIRCULATORY SYSTEM; VEIN.

bloodhound

The bloodhound is an ancient breed of dog renowned for its scenting powers. The breed reached its present state in England and the United States during the last century. Bloodhounds are strong, reaching 68.5 cm (27 in) in height and more than 50 kg (110 lb) in weight. The breed's wrinkled face and extremely long ears are its trademarks. Bloodhounds may be black and tan, red and tan, or red.

Bibliography: Brey, Catherine F., *The Complete Bloodhound* (1978).

The bloodhound, whose name means "blooded" or "purebred," trails animals and humans by scent; it will not harm the person it is trailing.

bloodroot

Bloodroot, *Sanguinaria canadensis*, is a showy, early flowering plant in the family Papaveraceae. Found in the open woodlands of eastern and midwestern North America, the bloodroot has a single, symmetrical, white flower appearing on a leafless stem enfolded by one large, deep-lobed leaf on a separate stalk. Both the leafstalk and flower stalk grow from a perennial, underground rhizome that produces orange red sap. The generic name is derived from the Latin, *sanguis*, meaning "blood," although the POPPY family, of which bloodroot is a member, is generally characterized by its milky or colored juice.   JANE PHILPOTT

bloodstone

Bloodstone is dark-green CHALCEDONY spotted red with HEMATITE. It is the birthstone for March. In the Middle Ages it was highly prized and used in religious statues, particularly scenes of the crucifixion. Also called heliotrope for the reddish reflections given off by water containing the stone, bloodstone supposedly had the power to cause thunderstorms.

Bloody Assizes: see JEFFREYS, GEORGE JEFFREYS, 1ST BARON.

bloom, algal

A sudden, heavy growth of algae is generally described as an algal bloom. It is a condition in which the population of algal cells, such as marine PHYTOPLANKTON, has reached such dense proportions as to discolor the water green, brown, yellow, or red, depending on the pigment composition of the particular algae causing the bloom (see RED TIDE).

Blooms comprising large diatoms may have algal concentrations of greater than one million cells a liter (quart); small plant flagellates may have bloom concentrations of greater than one billion cells a liter. Such dense accumulations of phytoplankton occur most often when nutrients are available, in calm waters and in the presence of bright sunlight. Algal blooms are known to occur in lakes, particularly where agricultural fertilizer or sewage has enriched the lake water. In the oceans, algal blooms occur where nutrient-rich deep water is brought to the surface by ocean currents, a condition that occurs in many coastal regions or along certain major currents, such as the Peru Current. Because algal blooms tend eventually to exhaust their nutrient supply and then die, the period of bloom decline is often followed by a period of oxygen depletion caused by the excessive oxygen requirement of the decaying phytoplankton.   TIMOTHY R. PARSONS

Bloom, Harold

Harold Bloom, b. New York City, July 11, 1930, is a Yale professor of English who has written extensively about the romantic tradition in English and American poetry. In such works as *The Anxiety of Influence* (1973), *A Map of Misreading* (1974), *Poetry and Repression* (1976), and *Agon: Towards a Theory of Revisionism* (1982), Bloom developed a theory that "strong poets" such as William Butler Yeats and Wallace Stevens inevitably "misread" or reinterpret the works of their predecessors and "become great only by striving against an earlier greatness." Bloom is also a scholar of Hebrew literature. In *The Book of J* (1990), he presents evidence for his theory that J, the earliest of the four putative sources for the biblical Pentateuch, was actually a woman.

Bloomer, Amelia Jenks

Amelia Jenks Bloomer, b. Homer, N.Y., May 27, 1818, d. Dec. 30, 1894, founded in 1849 the *Lily*, probably the first American magazine edited by and for women. It treated such subjects as temperance, morality, and women's suffrage and also publicized "bloomers," an outfit comprising a short skirt and baggy trousers, which at that time symbolized radical feminism.

Bloomfield, Leonard

Leonard Bloomfield, b. Chicago, Apr. 1, 1887, d. Apr. 18, 1949, was one of the most respected linguists of the first half of the 20th century. His book *Language* (1933) was for years the standard summary of the dominant approach being taken toward linguistics in North America.

After teaching at three universities—Illinois, Ohio State, and Chicago—Bloomfield served as professor of linguistics at Yale from 1940 until his death. His initial specialty was a comparative study of Indo-European languages, particularly Germanic languages. He undertook pioneering studies of the Malayo-Polynesian languages, notably Tagalog; investigated American Indian languages, particularly those of the Algonquian family; and published articles and books in a broad spectrum of linguistics, including phonetics, historical linguistics, semantics, and the teaching of foreign languages.

Bloomfield believed that linguistics should be an autonomous, empirical science and that language should be studied in isolation from nonlinguistic influences. Although he espoused behaviorist principles, he refused to subordinate the study of language to any set psychological premise.

His masterpiece, *Language*, deals with, among other subjects, descriptive phonology and grammar, and language change. Bloomfield's descriptive method starts by identifying the smallest units of speech (phonemes) by minimal pairs. It then establishes a morphology, or system of word-forming elements, by which the relationship among the minimal meaningful linguistic units (morphemes) can be distinguished and classified. Finally, by distinguishing various construction types, it examines how syntax is effected.

Later linguists have argued that Bloomfield's approach is simply a taxonomic examination of surface structures and thus ignores the deep structures that may be universal in language. Despite the unresolved debate between Bloomfieldians and those who question his empirical approach, Bloomfield's studies have made a lasting impact upon linguistic study.
                                              F. P. DINNEEN, S.J.

Bibliography: Hall, Robert A., Jr., *Leonard Bloomfield* (1987); Hockett, C., ed., *A Leonard Bloomfield Anthology* (1970; repr. 1987).

Bloomington   (Illinois)

The seat of McLean County, Ill., Bloomington (1990 pop., 51,972) is situated in a rich farming region. Its economy is based on farming (corn, hybrid seed corn) and livestock raising. The city is the site of Illinois Wesleyan University.

Bloomington   (Indiana)

Bloomington (1990 pop., 60,633) is a city in south central Indiana and the seat of Monroe County. Bloomington is a limestone-quarrying center, and its manufactures include electronic equipment, electrical appliances, and elevators. Indiana University was established there in 1820, about two years after the city was settled. Nearby Lake Monroe attracts tourists.

Bloomsbury group

The Bloomsbury group was a literary, artistic, and intellectual circle of friends who met at one another's homes in and around the Bloomsbury area of London in the early decades of the 20th century. At its core were the sisters Vanessa Bell and Virginia WOOLF, daughters of Sir Leslie STEPHEN. It also included E. M. FORSTER, the novelist; Roger FRY, the artist and critic; John Maynard KEYNES, the influential economist; Victoria SACKVILLE-WEST, the poet and writer; Lytton STRACHEY, the biographer; Clive Bell, the art critic; and Duncan Grant, the artist. Used initially to ridicule an apparently exclusive and pretentious group, the term *Bloomsbury* was later accepted by the group as its legitimate name.

The circle's meetings, begun in 1904, were a continuation of friendships formed at Cambridge University. Members started thinking of the group as a cohesive unit between 1911 and 1914, and they maintained close contact through the 1920s and '30s. Under the influence of G. E. Moore's *Princip-*

ia Ethica (1903), they held in common a belief in the paramount importance of good taste, personal relationships, and the pursuit of knowledge. They discussed nearly every subject except politics and business. Although not a distinct literary school, the Bloomsbury group had a profound influence on English cultural life.   RICHARD FORD

Bibliography: Bell, Quentin, *Bloomsbury* (1968); Dowling, David, *Bloomsbury Aesthetics and the Novels of Forster and Woolf* (1985); Partridge, Frances, *Love in Bloomsbury* (1981); Rosenbaum, S. P., ed., *Bloomsbury Group: A Collection of Memoirs, Commentary, and Criticism* (1975) and *Victorian Bloomsbury* (1987); Shone, Richard, *Bloomsbury Portraits* (1976).

Blount, William   [bluhnt]

William Blount, b. Bertie County, N.C., Mar. 26, 1749, d. Mar. 21, 1800, fought in the American Revolution, was a delegate to Congress (1782–83, 1786–87) and the Constitutional Convention (1787), and served as governor of Tennessee territory (1790–96) before being elected (1796) a U.S. senator from the new state of Tennessee. He became involved, however, in a British plan to seize Florida and Louisiana from Spain, and in 1797 the Senate voted to expel him.

Blow, John

John Blow, b. February 1649, d. Oct. 1, 1708, was an outstanding English musician of the late 17th century. He was the organist for Westminster Abbey from 1668 to 1679 and again from 1695 to 1708. From 1679 to 1695 he was succeeded by his most famous pupil, Henry PURCELL. In 1699 he became the first Composer for the Chapel Royal. Blow wrote an enormous quantity of music, mostly English choral anthems, services, and occasional music. His masque *Venus and Adonis* is the earliest example of true English opera.   WILLIAM HAYS

Bibliography: Shaw, H. Watkins, *John Blow, Doctor of Music: A Biography* (1943).

blowfly

The blowflies comprise the bluebottles and greenbottles in the family Calliphoridae, insect order Diptera. The adults of most species are generally metallic blue, green, or green black in color. The blowflies lay their eggs on dead animals, in open wounds, and sometimes on healthy animals. The larvae, or maggots, then live on the tissue and can cause extensive damage. They are parasites of humans and animals.

Bibliography: Hall, D. G., *Blowflies of North America* (1948).

blowgun

A blowgun is a weapon used in the past in Europe and Mesoamerica and today by primitive peoples in Africa, South America, and Asia, primarily for hunting wild game. A bamboo, cane, or reed barrel with a smooth bore is fitted with a mouthpiece. Darts, which are often daubed with poison and have a soft pith butt, are ejected through the blowgun when the hunter exhales sharply. Blowguns vary from 0.5 to 7 m (1.5 to 23 ft) in length.   DONN V. HART

blowtorch

A blowtorch is a burner that combines a gaseous fuel with a jet of air, or oxygen, in order to obtain a hotter flame. According to the type of fuel used and the complexity of the burner, blowtorches can be used for a large number of industrial operations: BRAZING, GLASSBLOWING, WELDING AND SOLDERING, cutting, and flame-hardening metal.

The smallest type of blowtorch is the portable burner used by plumbers and mechanics to thaw frozen pipes or to melt soldering lead. Here, a two-compartment container holds the fuel and air under pressure. The mixture of the two gases occurs in a chamber in the container and is controlled by valves. The flame emerges through a nozzle at the top of the container.

Other types of blowtorch use separate cylinders for each gas, connected to the torch by flexible hoses. Oxyacetylene

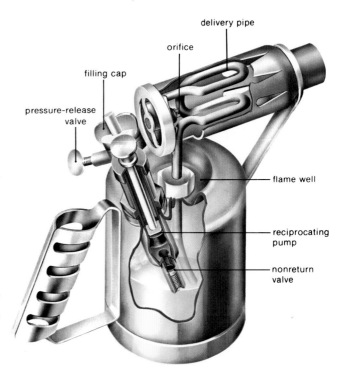

A blowtorch is lighted in several stages. Pressurized by the reciprocating pump, liquid paraffin fuel is driven into the delivery pipe. The flame well is filled with denatured alcohol and lighted. Heat from the flame well vaporizes the liquid paraffin in the delivery pipe. The vaporized paraffin is forced out of the orifice of the delivery pipe, which further decomposes it and mixes it with air. Heat from the flame well causes the vaporized paraffin to ignite, which heats the delivery pipe still more. Additional paraffin vaporizes, fueling the flame jet at the orifice. Most intense burning is achieved by pumping, which drives more liquid paraffin into the system.

torches, which use mixtures of ACETYLENE gas and oxygen, can reach temperatures of 3,315.5° C (about 6,000° F). This very hot flame is used to melt metal edges, which are then fused together in the process known as fusion welding. In metal cutting a jet of pure oxygen in the center of the acetylene flame oxidizes the white-hot metal, leaving a narrow, clean-edged cut. Different proportions of oxygen to acetylene create different flame intensities. An excess of acetylene produces a reducing, or carburizing, flame, which is used to weld nickel, some steel alloys, and certain nonferrous metals. An excess of oxygen is used to weld brass and bronze. A neutral flame, using an equal mixture of oxygen and acetylene, has the widest application and is most commonly used. Other, lower-temperature blowtorches burn an oxygen-hydrogen mixture, which is used for sheet-metal welding, or air-acetylene, which is used for lead welding and low-temperature brazing and soldering.

Blücher, Gebhard Leberecht von   [blue'-kur, gep'-hart lay'-buh-rekt fuhn]

Gebhard Leberecht von Blücher was a Prussian general known for his daring exploits against NAPOLEON I, for which he was affectionately called Marshal Forward. Born a Swedish subject at Rostock, Mecklenburg, on Dec. 16, 1742, he enlisted in the Swedish cavalry at age 14 but later joined (1760) the Prussian hussars. Although rough and uneducated, he collaborated with more sophisticated colleagues like General von SCHARNHORST in reforming the Prussian army after its disastrous defeat (1806) by the French at Jena.

Returning from retirement in 1813, Blücher fought at Leipzig and spearheaded the drive to Paris in 1814, for which he was created Fürst ("Prince") von Wahlstatt. On June 16, 1815, he was beaten by Napoleon at Ligny, but although severely wounded, he countermanded his chief of staff's order to retreat and daringly marched to join the duke of WELLINGTON near Waterloo. Arriving at dusk on June 18, he attacked Napoleon's flank just in time to save the decisive victory. Blücher died on Sept. 12, 1819, in Silesia.   ENNO E. KRAEHE

Bibliography: Bowden, Scott, *Armies at Waterloo* (1983); Henderson, E. F., *Blücher and the Uprising of Prussia against Napoleon* (1911; repr. 1973); Parkinson, Roger, *The Hussar General* (1975).

See also: NAPOLEONIC WARS; WATERLOO, BATTLE OF.

blue baby

A blue baby is an infant with cyanosis, a bluish coloration of the skin resulting from incomplete oxygenation of the blood in the arteries. The cyanosis commonly occurs in a congenital disease called patent, or open, ductus arteriosus.

The ductus arteriosus is a shunt between the pulmonary artery and the aorta. In the fetus it diverts venous blood away from the nonfunctioning lungs to the aorta and eventually into the placental circulation, where gas exchange occurs between fetal and maternal blood. After birth, the shunt normally closes, causing venous blood to be carried through the baby's pulmonary artery to the lungs for gas exchange. In some babies, however, the duct fails to close, causing oxygen-deficient venous blood to mix with arterial blood in the aorta and be sent throughout the body. The result is a chronic deficiency of oxygen in the blood.

Cyanosis is also seen in a congenital condition called the *tetrology* of Fallot, in which a hole in the wall between the right and left ventricles of the heart allows venous and arterial blood to mix. Surgical correction of these circulatory defects is necessary and is highly successful. Without treatment, the average blue baby lives only until the age of 12 years.

PETER L. PETRAKIS

Bibliography: Avery, G. B., *Neonatology*, 3d ed. (1987); Billig, Donal, and Kreidberg, Marshall, *The Management of Neonates and Infants with Congenital Heart Disease* (1973); Filston, H. C., and Izant, Robert, Jr., *The Surgical Neonate*, 2d ed. (1985).

Blue Cross

Blue Cross is a privately operated nonprofit U.S. insurance plan that pays part of the costs of hospital services. Physicians' charges are covered by a companion plan called BLUE SHIELD. Blue Cross is organized nationally, with a separate plan for each state and for many communities as well. In each case, Blue Cross contracts with individual hospitals to provide medical services to its membership. Most people subscribe through their place of employment, because the cost is lower for groups. The idea originated in 1929 with a single hospital contract that covered a group of teachers.

blue-eyed grass

Blue-eyed grass, *Sisyrinchium*, is the common name for several species of plants in the iris family, Iridaceae. The small perennials have fibrous roots, stiff, grasslike leaves, and flat stems bearing clusters of purplish blue symmetrical flowers. Eastern U.S. species grow mainly in open fields; those in the West grow mainly on wet, grassy slopes.   JANE PHILPOTT

blue-green algae

The blue-green algae, phylum Cyanophyta, and the closely related BACTERIA, constitute the kingdom Monera in the five-kingdom classification system. The essential feature of the blue-green algae, which scientists also call the Cyanobacteria, is that although their cellular structure is like that of bacteria, they carry out PHOTOSYNTHESIS in a fashion similar to algae and green plants. While the photosynthetic machinery of other algae and green plants is contained in tiny organelles called chloroplasts, blue-green algae contain no such bodies.

Blue-green algae, like bacteria, have no distinct nucleus and, like plants, are photosynthetic organisms. Some forms are unicellular; others are colonial or filamentous; known reproduction is asexual and occurs by cell division, fragmentation, or spore formation. Chroococcus is unicellular but forms temporary colonies when cell walls fail to separate promptly after cell division. Oscillatoria is filamentous, and Rivularia grows in gelatinous colonies attached to moist rocks; both reproduce by fragmentation. Anabaena is a filamentous alga that can fix nitrogen, and Dermocarpa, which may grow in colonies on other algae, reproduces by spore formation.

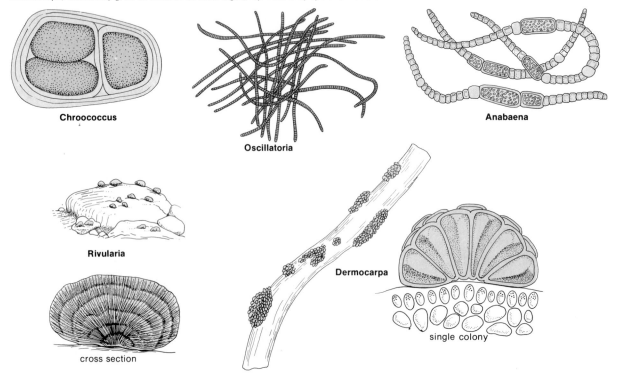

Chroococcus

Oscillatoria

Anabaena

Rivularia

cross section

Dermocarpa

single colony

Their photosynthetic apparatus is embedded in lamellalike membranes throughout the cell. The characteristic blue-green color of these microorganisms results from the presence of two pigments that serve to capture light energy. One of these is CHLOROPHYLL, which is green and is found in all photosynthetic organisms; the other is phycocyanin, which is blue and is peculiar to blue-green algae. The light energy is converted by the cell to chemical energy in the form of ATP that is used by the cell to carry out its essential activities.

The other major class of pigments present in the blue-green algae are the carotenoids. These are hydrocarbonlike pigments, similar in structure to vitamin A and found in all photosynthetic organisms.

Blue-green algae grow in a wide variety of aquatic and terrestrial habitats. They occur either as individual cells, as chains, or as filaments. The smallest blue-green algae are about 0.5–2.0 micrometers (1 micrometer = one-millionth of a meter) in diameter, and the largest may contain cells with a diameter of 60 micrometers. Blue-green algae reproduce through cell division, fragmentation of filaments, and spore formation. During their life cycle, specialized cells called heterocysts and akinetes are formed. The heterocysts convert atmospheric nitrogen to nitrates and are a source of nitrogen for the other cells. The akinetes are resistant cells that allow the organism to withstand extreme environmental conditions.

Unlike most bacteria, which swim by means of whiplike flagella, some blue-green algae glide over surfaces. The mechanism of this motility is unknown, and no organelles have been shown to play a part in the movement. This sort of motility is consistent with discoveries of blue-green algae attached to and growing on solid surfaces. Species that live in open waters usually contain gas vacuoles within their cells. These vacuoles function as flotation organelles, allowing the organisms to rise and fall in response to changing light intensities.

Nutritionally self-sufficient organisms, blue-green algae are ecologically important. Species that obtain their nitrogen from the atmosphere make nitrogen readily available to other organisms (see NITROGEN CYCLE); in parts of Southeast Asia many farmers use nitrogen-fixing blue-green algae in place of nitrogen fertilizers to enrich rice paddies. Some nitrogen-fixing blue-green algae live symbiotically in a mutually beneficial relationship with fungi as LICHENS. Most nutrients that limit the growth of blue-green algae are usually inorganic, and pollution of fresh water with inorganic phosphate is likely to result in blooms of blue-green algae. These organisms are able to reproduce in a short period of time, particularly in stagnant waters, often resulting in noxious odors and compounds that are toxic to fish.

Since blue-green algae were probably the first oxygen-evolving organisms, they are believed to have played a role in the initial conversion of the Earth's atmosphere from anaerobic to aerobic.   MARTIN DWORKIN

Bibliography: Bold, H., and Wynne, M. J., *Introduction to the Algae,* 2d ed. (1985).

See also: ANABAENA; CLASSIFICATION, BIOLOGICAL; NOSTOC; PLANKTON.

Blue Grotto

The Blue Grotto (Italian: Grotta Azzura) is a natural limestone cavern on the north shore of the Italian island of CAPRI, in the Bay of Naples. Accessible only by boat, the grotto is about 53 m (175 ft) long and 15 m (50 ft) high. Sunlight enters through the water and reflects a dazzling blue light inside.

blue jay

The blue jay, *Cyanocitta cristata*, is a perching bird of the crow family, Corvidae, and is common in southern Canada and the United States east of the Rocky mountains. The adult jay is nearly 30 cm (12 in) long. It has a prominent crest and is bright blue above, with white and black markings and a narrow black collar, and mostly white below. A handsome, noisy bird, the jay is sometimes resented by humans for its aggressiveness in driving other birds away. It feeds on insects,

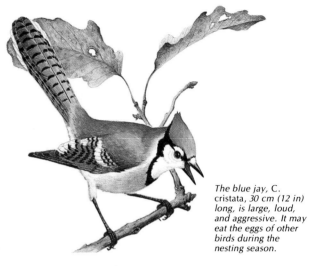

The blue jay, C. cristata, 30 cm (12 in) long, is large, loud, and aggressive. It may eat the eggs of other birds during the nesting season.

nuts, and seeds but also, sometimes, on eggs or even nestlings.   WILLIAM F. SANDFORD

blue laws

Blue laws are statutes or ordinances regulating the conduct of persons, particularly on Sunday. Such laws are now also referred to as *Sunday legislation* and relate to work and commerce. The term *blue laws* may stem from a book by Samuel A. Peters, *General History of Connecticut* (1781), which listed the Sabbath regulations of New Haven; it was printed on blue paper. It may derive from the old definition of *blue* as "puritanical." In any case, the American colonies had statutes prohibiting drunkenness and sexual misconduct, as well as work, play, or travel, on Sunday. The church-attendance law in Virginia authorized the militia to force all persons to attend Anglican services.

Although the sale of liquor on Sundays is still commonly restricted by U.S. states, other kinds of retail commerce on Sunday is now less frequently regulated. Courts in some states (Connecticut and New York, for example) have ruled that bans on Sunday commerce are unconstitutional. Some jurisdictions maintain Sunday restrictions by local option. Arguments for Sunday restrictions are now more often secular than religious.

Bibliography: Laband, David N., and Heinbuch, Deborah, *Blue Laws: The History, Politics, and Economics of Sunday Closing Laws* (1987).

Blue Ridge Mountains

The Blue Ridge Mountains of the APPALACHIAN MOUNTAIN system extend about 990 km (615 mi) from southern Pennsylvania to northern Georgia. Their greatest width, 112 km (70 mi), is in North Carolina. Average elevation ranges from 609 to 1,219 m (2,000 to 4,000 ft), but many peaks exceed 1,524 m (5,000 ft). The POTOMAC, JAMES, and Roanoke rivers cut gaps in the mountains. Mixed hardwood forests cover the ridges, and mineral resources are few. The mountains are a scenic recreation area, traversed by motor parkways and foot trails. In remote valleys descendants of 18th-century settlers retain archaic customs and patterns of speech.

Blue Shield

Blue Shield is a privately operated nonprofit U.S. insurance plan that pays part of the costs of services performed by physicians in hospitals and elsewhere. Charges for other medical services performed in hospitals are covered by a companion plan called BLUE CROSS. Blue Shield is organized nationally, with a separate plan for each state and for many communities as well. In each case, Blue Shield contracts with individual physicians to provide medical services. Most people subscribe to Blue Shield as members of groups. The idea originated in 1939, ten years after Blue Cross began.

Bluebeard

The story of Bluebeard appears in the folklore of many countries, but the name *Bluebeard* usually refers to the monstrous protagonist of the fairy tale by that name, written by the French author Charles Perrault in 1697. In the tale, the young wife of a blue-bearded chevalier is forbidden to open a certain room in their castle. Eventually overcome by curiosity, however, she enters the room only to find the slain bodies of her husband's former wives. When Bluebeard discovers his wife's transgression, he prepares to kill her, too, but she is saved by the arrival of her brothers, who slay the chevalier.

bluebell

The English bluebell, Endymion nonscriptus, *is a bulbous European woodland lily that flowers early (April to June). It is 0.5 m (1.5 ft) in height.*

The bluebell is any of several different plant species of the genus *Campanula* and especially *C. rotundifolia.* California bluebell is *Phacelia campanularia;* English bluebell, *Endymion nonscriptus;* Spanish bluebell, *E. hispanicus;* and Virginia bluebell, *Mertensia virginica.*

blueberry

Blueberry is the common name of various deciduous shrubs of the genus *Vaccinium* in the heath family, Ericaceae. About 24 recognized species of blueberries exist, varying from shrubs less than 0.3 m (1 ft) tall to large bushes more than 5 m (16 ft) in height, and differing in habitat from marshy bogs to dry upland mineral soils. The sweet-tasting berry con-

The highbush blueberry, V. corymbosum, *native to North America, produces an array of small, bell-like flowers and clusters of sweet, fleshy fruit. Like their wild relatives and the closely related cranberry, cultivated blueberries grow best in peaty or sandy, acidic soil.*

tains 40 to 50 small, soft seeds and often has a powdery coating. Most blueberry species are indigenous to eastern North America, and commercial culture of the crop is largely limited to that area. The berries have been used since early days, but the cultivated blueberry industry has developed entirely in the 20th century. Among the leading states in blueberry production are Michigan, New Jersey, and North Carolina, where horticultural varieties of the highbush blueberry, *V. corymbosum,* are grown. Major types grown are Jersey, Bluecrop, Collins, and Coville. The rabbiteye blueberry, *V. ashei,* which can tolerate higher summer temperatures than highbush blueberries, is cultivated solely in the southern United States. Lowbush blueberries are harvested commercially from natural stands in Maine and eastern Canadian provinces. Many blueberry species are erroneously called HUCKLEBERRIES, which are closely related plants.   J. N. MOORE

bluebird

Bluebird is the common name for three species of North American perching birds comprising the genus *Sialia* in the thrush family, Turdidae. With a length of 18 cm (7 in), the eastern bluebird, *S. sialis,* is smaller than the related American ROBIN; the male is bright blue above with rusty red breast and

Bluebirds include (left to right, all male) *the eastern,* S. sialis, *the western,* S. mexicana, *and the mountain bluebird,* S. currucoides. *They are popular perching birds that are welcome in rural areas because they eat grasshoppers, caterpillars, and other cropland pests.*

white belly, and the female is similar but duller. The bird feeds on insects and fruits; it has a warbling song. Four to six eggs are laid in a loose nest of grass and stems, usually twice each brooding season. The bird nests from the Gulf states and Florida north to southern Canada, east of the Rocky Mountains, retreating from northerly limits of its range in winter and returning in early spring. Its declining population in some areas may be due in part to competition with house sparrows and starlings for tree-cavity nesting sites. Species found in the western United States are the pale blue–breasted mountain bluebird, *S. currucoides*, and the western bluebird, *S. mexicana*, which is blue on the throat.

WILLIAM F. SANDFORD

bluefish

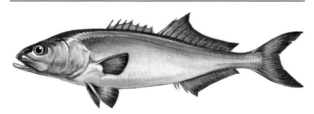

The bluefish, P. saltatrix, hunts in schools that may extend up to 7 km (4 mi) in length. It is a vicious predator, and the gluttonous abandon with which it destroys its prey causes some to call it the sea piranha. It is a favorite target of anglers, both in boats and in the surf.

Bluefish, *Pomatomus saltatrix*, are the only species of the family Pomatomidae, are voracious predators and hard-fighting game fish. They are found in most tropical and temperate waters of the world except parts of the Pacific Ocean, and they sometimes enter bays and estuaries. The fish have stout bodies that may reach a length of more than 1.1 m (45 in) and a weight of nearly 12 kg (more than 25 lb), but larger fish have been recorded. The back of the bluefish is deep blue, tinged with green, and its belly is silvery. The teeth are strong and sharp, and the fish has two dorsal fins and a forked tail.

Bluefish swim in schools, actively pursuing prey and, reputedly, sometimes killing more than they can consume. Dead or disabled menhaden and similar small fish sometimes strew the water in the wake of a school of bluefish. As commercial and game fish, bluefish have an excellent flavor. They are classified in the order Perciformes.

C. P. IDYLL

bluegrass

Bluegrass, *Poa*, is the common name for many lawn grasses belonging to the family Gramineae. Bluegrass was widespread throughout Europe for hundreds of years before seeds were brought to the United States. One species, *P. pratensis*, was first called June grass and later became known as Kentucky bluegrass. More than 18 million kg (40 million lb) of bluegrass seed are planted each year for lawns in the United States. A number of improved varieties are available. Bluegrass grows best in cooler climates; it is less common in the Gulf states and absent from arid regions.

Bibliography: Harrington, H. D., *How to Identify Grasses and Grass-like Plants* (1977); Pohl, Richard W., *How to Know the Grasses*, 3d ed. (1978).

bluegrass music

The Scots-Irish traditional music of the southern Appalachian Mountains evolved into a newer form that, since the early 1950s, has been known as bluegrass music. Bluegrass uses traditional mountain dance-group instrumentation, usually featuring unamplified mandolin, banjo, and fiddle, but as developed by Bill Monroe and his Bluegrass Boys it also has a hard, fast drive and a high-pitched, emotional singing style.

Monroe, a mandolin player born in Rosine, Ky., in 1911, and the Bluegrass Boys began to play regularly on the "Grand Ole Opry" radio program in Nashville, Tenn., in 1939. The band has included such seminal musicians as banjoist Earl

Scruggs, of the famous duo FLATT AND SCRUGGS.

Although as a distinct style bluegrass is relatively new—compared, for example, with the more traditional aspects of COUNTRY AND WESTERN MUSIC—it has come to symbolize an older, more rural America and has attracted many young urban musicians, some of whom use its hard-driving instrumental techniques as a backing in soft rock and country rock. Notable among these are such eclectic pop-music groups as Seldom Scene and New Grass Revival.

Bibliography: Artis, Bob, *Bluegrass* (1975); Cantwell, Robert, *Bluegrass Breakdown* (1984); Guptill, David, *Themes and Variations for Bluegrass Banjo* (1984); Rosenberg, Neil V., *Bluegrass: A History* (1985).

blueprint

A blueprint is a reproduction of a map, architect's plan, or mechanical drawing, although the reproduction may not be a print that is blue in color. Originally the term meant that the drawing was made by a wet process that involved the reaction of a chemically treated paper that produced white lines on a blue background. In making a true blueprint, the original drawing, done on a translucent paper or film, is placed face up, over the light-sensitive side of blueprint paper, and then exposed to a bright light. After the appropriate exposure time, the blueprint paper is removed and washed in water to remove some of the chemicals. The lines will appear white. The print is then washed in a mild solution of potassium dichromate and water, which makes the blue background darker and the white lines more prominent. The print is then again washed in water until no trace of the potassium dichromate can be seen. The final step is a drying process; usually the wet print is placed on a dryer belt or hung on a line. This process produces a true blueprint, but it is time-consuming and some shrinkage occurs.

A related process called the Diazo process also produces what is commonly called a blueprint. The two basic types are Diazo-moist printing and a Diazo-dry process; both types are basically similar to the blueprint process. They require only two steps, however. Diazo-moist printing gives a white or light background, with the lines in red, blue, brown, or black, depending on the type of paper used. The print will be slightly damp but dries in a few seconds. The Diazo-dry print is made in basically the same way but uses specially prepared paper. The Diazo paper is first exposed to light and is then run through a developer that uses ammonia fumes to bring out the lines on the print. This type of print is returned from the machine dry and ready for use and is perhaps the most commonly used type.

RALPH M. COLEMAN

Bibliography: Hoffman, E., *Print Reading and Sketching Fundamentals* (1986); Jensen, C. H., and Hines, R. D., *Interpreting Engineering Drawings*, 3d ed. (1984); Nelson, J., *How to Read and Understand Blueprints* (1982).

blues

The blues is a distinctive black-American song form, important not only in its own right but because it was a major element in the evolution of JAZZ. Music with the melodic and structural qualities that came to characterize the blues began to emerge late in the 19th century, and was sung and played by rural musicians.

Blues Form. The most distinctive melodic characteristic of the blues is the use of microtones (intervals smaller than a half-step), commonly called bent pitches. Although these pitch inflections may occur on any tone, they are used most often on the third and seventh notes of the scale—the "blue notes" that give the blues their poignant character. Most scholars believe that the practice of bending pitches was carried over from African melodic practice. In the United States, bent pitches were frequently used in field hollers, shouts, and street cries—all ancestors of the blues.

As the blues became formalized, a consistent rhythmic and vocal progression developed. Although many blues are based on an 8-bar pattern, the 12-bar blues became the most common type. The classic 12-bar pattern consists of three vocal lines, each of four bars, with a musical accompaniment that echoes, answers, and completes the vocal part. This characterizing "call and response" pattern has also been derived from African vocal forms; it provided the opportunity for a great range of instrumental improvisation.

Country Blues. The earliest blues, country blues, were a product of the 19th-century black rural experience, especially after emancipation. Itinerant performers traveled from one black community to another, playing the guitar while singing about the loss of love, the pain of poverty, the burden of hard work. Like much folk expression, many songs spoke of the delights and torments of sex.

Early country blues still may be heard on records made by LEADBELLY, Blind Lemon Jefferson, and others. Jelly Roll MORTON wrote his "New Orleans Blues" in 1902. Among the earliest blues published as sheet music were those of W. C. HANDY. They included "Memphis Blues" (1912) and "The St. Louis Blues" (1914).

City Blues. Stimulated by the recording industry, city blues flourished in the 1920s. Singers were often accompanied by a piano and other instruments. The opportunity for responsive improvisation during the instrumental interludes attracted some of the most respected jazz musicians. "Race records," produced for sale in black communities, were hugely successful. Mamie Smith, a New York vaudeville singer, made the first blues recording in 1920. Soon the best known was Bessie SMITH, "Empress of the Blues." The blues flourished as dance music in small dance halls, barrooms, and juke joints. BOOGIE-WOOGIE piano, an outgrowth of the blues, was developed in a dance context.

After World War II, RHYTHM AND BLUES recordings became commercially successful. Many of the earliest ROCK MUSIC hits were simply re-recordings ("covers") by white musicians of pieces that previously had been recorded as rhythm-and-blues numbers by black performers.   DONALD J. IVEY

Bibliography: Baraka, Amiri, *Blues People* (1963; repr. 1987); Evans, D., *Big Road Blues* (1981); Finn, J., *The Bluesman* (1984); Hatch, D., and Millword, S., *From Blues to Rock* (1987).

bluestem

Bluestem is the common name for about 300 species of perennial grasses in the genera *Andropogon* and *Schizachyrium* in the grass family, Gramineae. Big bluestem, *A. gerardii*, is a robust, pasturable bunch grass native to the tall-grass prairies of the United States. Little bluestem, *S. scoparius*, which is the state grass of Nebraska, occurs in the Great Plains.

JANE PHILPOTT

bluethroat

The bluethroat, *Luscinia*, or *Erithacus*, *svecicus*, is a small (12 cm/4.7 in) Eurasian THRUSH, belonging to the Turdidae family of birds, that now occurs as a summer resident in parts of northwest Alaska. The male has a bright-blue, red-spotted throat patch. Bluethroats lurk and feed in the underbrush except when the males mount a perch to sing.

GEORGE J. WALLACE

The bluethroat, L. svecicus, a relative of the nightingale, is an Old World bird that summers in northwest Alaska.

Bluford, Guion S.

Guion "Guy" Stewart Bluford, Jr., b. Philadelphia, Nov. 22, 1942, became the first black U.S. astronaut when he flew on the eighth SPACE SHUTTLE mission in 1983. (The first black in space was the Cuban cosmonaut Arnaldo Tamayo Méndez, who flew in *Soyuz 38* on Sept. 18–26, 1980.) Bluford graduated from The Pennsylvania State University in 1964, fought as an air force pilot in Vietnam, and earned a Ph.D. in aerospace engineering from the Air Force Institute of Technology before being selected as an astronaut in 1979. He served as a mission specialist on the second flight of the space shuttle *Challenger* (Aug. 30–Sept. 5, 1983).

Blum, Léon   [bluem′, lay-ohn′]

Léon Blum led France's Socialist party during the 1920s and '30s. As head of the Popular Front government (1936–37), he nationalized major industries and introduced social reforms that gave new protection to French workers but earned him the undying hostility of his country's business leaders.

Léon Blum, b. Apr. 9, 1872, d. Mar. 30, 1950, was both the first socialist and the first Jew to serve as premier of France. A literary critic, he became involved in socialist politics during the DREYFUS AFFAIR and was increasingly active after the assassination (1914) of Jean JAURÈS. In 1920, when the Communist faction prevailed at the Socialist party congress, Blum left the meeting with his followers. They formed a minority socialist group, and Blum founded the daily paper *Le Populaire*.

In June 1936, Blum became premier, presiding over the Popular Front coalition of Socialists, Communists, and liberals. He responded to worker unrest with such reforms as paid vacations, collective bargaining, and the 40-hr work week. His reforms were accompanied by inadequate economic measures, however, and they were thus more spectacular than effective. Hated by the right, he also lost leftist support as a result of his noninterventionist policy in the SPANISH CIVIL WAR. He resigned in June 1937, recovering office only for a few months in 1938. During World War II he was arrested (1940) by the VICHY GOVERNMENT and tried (1942) at Riom. He defended himself so brilliantly that the trial was suspended, but he remained in custody until 1945. In 1946 he served briefly as interim premier, playing a key role in the establishment of the Fourth Republic.   P. M. EWY

Bibliography: Colton, Joel, *Léon Blum* (1974; repr. 1987).

Blumberg, Baruch S.   [bloom′-burg]

Baruch S. Blumberg, b. New York City, July 28, 1925, a physician and biochemist who discovered the hepatitis B antigen, was a corecipient of the 1976 Nobel Prize for physiology or medicine for his part in "discoveries concerning new mechanisms for the origin and dissemination of infectious diseases." His work paved the way for programs to screen blood donors as well as later work on hepatitis B vaccines.

Blume, Judy

Judy Blume, b. Elizabeth, N.J., Feb. 12, 1938, an American writer of romantic books for young people, has earned a reputation for dealing candidly with problems of early adolescence that traditional children's literature ignores. Her books include *Are You There God? It's Me, Margaret* (1970), *It's Not the End of the World* (1972), *Superfudge* (1980), *Just as Long as We're Together* (1987), and *Fudge-o-Mania* (1990).

Blume, Peter

Peter Blume's Light of the World *(1932) is an example of magic realism, an American art movement closely related to surrealism. Blume's works combine realistic detail with surrealistic imagery and elements of fantasy. (Whitney Museum of American Art, New York.)*

Peter Blume, b. Oct. 27, 1906, d. Nov. 30, 1992, was a prominent member of the group of American surrealist painters called magic realists. Born in Russia, he emigrated to the United States in 1911.

Blume's typical mixture of the prosaic and the fantastic, conveying social comment with irony, is evident in *South of Scranton* (1931; Metropolitan Museum, New York), one of the earliest American surrealist paintings. Blume's *The Eternal City* (1934–37; Museum of Modern Art, New York) portrays Mussolini as a green jack-in-the-box in a nightmarish Rome; it was rejected as "too inflammatory" for the Corcoran Gallery (Washington, D.C.) 1939 Biennial Exhibition.

Bibliography: Miller, D. C., and Barr, A. H., Jr., eds., *American Realists and Magic Realists* (1943; repr. 1970); Rose, B., *American Art since 1900,* 2d ed. (1975).

Blumenbach, Johann Friedrich   [bloom'-en-bahk]

Johann Friedrich Blumenbach, b. May 11, 1752, d. Jan. 22, 1840, was a German anatomist, physiologist, and naturalist often considered the father of physical anthropology. Professor of medicine at the University of Göttingen from 1776, he developed an important collection of 60 human skulls that formed the basis for his research into variations within the human species. His major theoretical contribution was his division of humankind into five races—Caucasian, Mongolian, Ethiopian, American, and Malay—from which later systems of racial classification were developed. Blumenbach's major works include *Collectio craniorum diversarum gentium illustrata* (Illustrated Collection of Diverse Types of Crania, 1790–1828), which describes and measures the skull collection, and *On the Natural Variety of Mankind* (1795; Eng. trans., 1865).

Blundell, Sir Denis   [bluhn'-duhl]

Edward Denis Blundell, b. Wellington, New Zealand, May 29, 1907, served as governor-general of New Zealand from 1972 to 1977. He graduated from Cambridge University in England and practiced law in Wellington from 1930 to 1968. In 1968–72 he was ambassador to Ireland as well as New Zealand's chief representative in the United Kingdom.

Blunden, Edmund Charles   [bluhn'-duhn]

Edmund Charles Blunden, b. Nov. 1, 1896, d. Jan. 20, 1974, was an English poet whose verse, particularly his *Poems* (1914) and *Pastorals: A Book of Verses* (1916), reflected his love of the English countryside and his experiences in World War I. His prose works include his antiwar autobiography *Undertones of War* (1928) and critical studies of Charles Lamb, Leigh Hunt, Thomas Hardy, and Percy Bysshe Shelley.   ROBIN BUSS

Blunt, Wilfrid Scawen

Wilfrid Scawen Blunt, b. Aug. 17, 1840, d. Sept. 12, 1922, was an English poet and Arabist. After serving in the diplomatic corps he wrote passionately against British imperialism in India, Ireland, and Egypt. His poetry includes *The Love Sonnets of Proteus* (1880) and *The Wind and the Whirlwind* (1883), a verse novel, and translations from the Arabic. He also wrote political and travel books about the Arab world.   ROBIN BUSS

Bluntschli, Johann Kaspar

Johann Kaspar Bluntschli, b. Mar. 7, 1808, d. Oct. 21, 1881, was a Swiss jurist, educator, and writer whose work became the basis of much international law. His comprehensive book *Das moderne Kriegsrecht* (The Modern Law of War, 1866) contributed significantly to the codification of the laws of war at the HAGUE CONFERENCES of 1899 and 1907. His other major works, *Das moderne Völkerrecht* (Modern International Law, 1868) and *Lehr vom modernen Staat* (Lessons of the Modern State, 1875–76), were also highly influential. Bluntschli studied law at Zurich, Bonn, and Berlin and taught at Zurich, Munich, and Heidelberg. In 1873 he cofounded the Institute of International Law, now in Switzerland.

Bly, Nellie

Nellie Bly, the first American woman journalist to achieve international fame, often obtained her stories at a considerable personal risk. Her best-known exploit, an attempt to travel around the world in record time, captured the nation's interest and boosted her newspaper's circulation.

Nellie Bly was the pen name of Elizabeth Cochran, b. May 5, 1867, d. Jan. 27, 1922, an American journalist whose exposés and daring exploits made her a prototype of the star woman reporter. Cochran took her pen name from a Stephen Foster song after she began work for the *Pittsburgh Dispatch* in the early 1880s, writing about such subjects as divorce and slum life. In 1887 she became famous overnight when, as a reporter for the *New York World,* Bly faked insanity to get inside an asylum to write an exposé of its dismal conditions. Her reports were published in *Ten Days in a Mad House* (1887). Her most publicized feat was beating the time of Phileas Fogg, Jules Verne's imaginary hero, for an around-the-world trip. She recorded her adventures in *Nellie Bly's Book: Around the*

World in 72 Days (1890; repr. 1992). Starting on Nov. 14, 1889, she returned to New York on Jan. 26, 1890, setting a record of 72 days, 6 hours, 11 minutes. In 1895 she married Robert Seaman, a wealthy businessman.   DONALD H. JOHNSTON

Bibliography: Rittenhouse, Mignon, *The Amazing Nellie Bly* (1956; repr. 1977).

Bly, Robert

Robert Bly, b. Madison, Minn., Dec. 23, 1926, is an American poet, editor, and a prolific translator of foreign poetry. *The Fifties* (later *The Sixties* and *The Seventies*), a literary magazine that he founded (1958) and edits, has exerted considerable influence on contemporary poetry by publishing his translations and much unconventional poetry. Bly's earlier poetry, published in such collections as *The Light around the Body* (1967; National Book Award for Poetry, 1968), is evocative of his native Minnesota. Later works include more poetry (much of it reprinted in *Selected Poems*, 1986) and literary works such as his *The Eight Stages of Translation* (1986). Bly became more widely known with the publication of *Iron John* (1990), a best-selling book that specifies the need for young men to find mentors, "male mothers," to initiate them into true manhood. The title comes from a Grimm fairy tale.

Blythe, David Gilmour

David Gilmour Blythe, b. East Liverpool, Ohio, 1815, d. 1865, was an American genre painter (see GENRE PAINTING) best known for such satirical studies of everyday life in Pittsburgh as *The Post Office* (c.1860; Museum of Art, Carnegie Institute, Pittsburgh). Blythe also worked as an artist during the Civil War, producing many outstanding war scenes.

Bibliography: Miller, Dorothy C., *The Life and Works of David G. Blythe* (1950).

BMEWS

The Ballistic Missile Early Warning System (BMEWS) comprises a small but geographically widely dispersed chain of very large radars for the detection of a ballistic missile attack on North America from the general direction (over the North Pole) of the former Soviet Union. Site I is in Thule, Greenland; site II, in Clear, Alaska; and site III, in Fylingdales Moor on the east coast of England.

In operation since 1962, the RADAR installations, in conjunction with large computer systems, can measure the position and velocity of a passing missile and calculate its launch site, trajectory, impact point, and impact time. Radar information is automatically transmitted to the North American Aerospace Defense Command and other centers. The Fylingdales site also supplies early warning service to the United Kingdom.

In 1985 the United States embarked on a program to replace the original installations with large phased array radar systems. Phased arrays use banks of thousands of solid-state modules, rather than antennas, to pick up signals. They can detect and track targets at a range of 3,000 nautical miles (5,560 km/3,455 mi). Phased arrays were also built at four U.S. Air Force bases to cover each of the four quarters of the United States. Over-the-horizon (OTH) radar, designed to detect incoming enemy bombers, was added on the East and West Coasts, although in 1991 the West Coast facility was mothballed.   R. T. PRETTY

See also: MILITARY WARNING AND DETECTION SYSTEMS.

B'nai B'rith

B'nai B'rith, which means "sons of the covenant," is the oldest and largest American Jewish service organization. Founded on Oct. 13, 1843, as Bundes Bruder by 12 German Jews in New York, B'nai B'rith had as its purpose "to unite Israelites in the work of protecting their highest interests and those of humanity." The organization is open to all branches of JUDAISM and operates lodges from Romania to Ireland. Dedicated to philanthropy, B'nai B'rith has offered assistance in such calamities as the Johnstown and Galveston floods, the Chicago fire, the San Francisco earthquake, the Kishinev Massacre, and both world wars. Among its other projects are orphanages, hospitals, libraries, vocational-training programs, and Hillel religious facilities at colleges in the United States, as well as programs for agricultural development and refugee assimilation in Israel. B'nai B'rith established the Anti-Defamation League, America's principal watchdog against anti-Semitism, in 1913, and enjoys observer status at the United Nations.
          SAUL S. FRIEDMAN

Bo Ju'-yi   (Po Chü-i)   [boh joo-ee]

One of the Tang poets who gained a considerable literary reputation during his lifetime, Bo Ju'-yi, or Bai Ju'-yi (772–846), remains popular today. With friend Yuan Zhen (Yüan Chen), a rival poet, he instituted many literary reforms. One of these was the use of everyday language to write poetry of social protest. Popular among his long poems are *Song of the Everlasting Sorrow* (806; Eng. trans., 1918) and *The Lute Song* (816; Eng. trans., 1918).   ANGELA JUNG PALANDRI

bo tree

The bo tree, *Ficus religiosa*, is a large, long-lived tree belonging to the mulberry family, Moraceae. It grows up to 30 m (100 ft) tall and is native from India to Southeast Asia. Its shining, pendulous leaves are heart-shaped, with long terminal points. The long leaf tips distinguish the bo tree from the 800 other species of FIGS. Bo trees are widely planted in the tropics and subtropics. According to tradition, Gautama Buddha attained perfect knowledge while meditating under a bo tree in BODH GAYA in northeast India. A descendant of this bo tree allegedly grows in ANURADHAPURA, Sri Lanka. Bo trees, sometimes known as bodhi or pipal trees, are sacred to Hindus and Buddhists.   JANE PHILPOTT

boa   [boh'-uh]

The boa constrictor, C. constrictor, is a New World snake that grows up to 3.7 m (12 ft) long. It kills rodents and other small animals by striking and coiling around its victim with incredibly fast movements. Once wrapped around its prey, the boa constrictor tightens its coils, preventing the animal from breathing. It then swallows its meal whole.

Boa is the common name for about 6 genera and 50 species of SNAKES that constitute the family Boidae. Closely related to PYTHONS, the family includes the largest of all snakes, the water-dwelling ANACONDA of South America. Among other boas are the smaller sand boas, *Eryx*, and the woodsnakes, *Tropidolphus* and related genera. The typical boa genera are ground or tree dwellers of tropical America—as are the woodsnakes—and the island of Madagascar, whereas the sand boas are semi-desert burrowing snakes of northern Africa and southern Asia. The two North American boas—the rosy and the rubber boa—resemble the sand boas.

All boas are nonpoisonous and kill by constriction; unlike the pythons, they bear live young. They are primitive snakes with anatomical features that reflect their lizard ancestry, such as bony vestiges of hind limbs that terminate in external claws, and the presence—except in the woodsnakes—of two functional lungs. Most boas are active at night and have pits along their lips that are sensitive to the heat of prey. The snakes are usually handsomely marked and often iridescent, the most striking being the rainbow boa, *Epicrates cenchis.* The species best known as "boa" is the boa constrictor, *Constrictor constrictor,* which ranges from Mexico to Argentina and the West Indies. The snake grows up to 3.7 m (12 ft) long, but a 5.6-m (18.5-ft) specimen is on record.

Boabdil   [boh-ahb-deel']

Boabdil was the name the Spanish gave to Abu Abdallah Muhammad, d. c.1527, the last Moorish ruler of the kingdom of GRANADA. He overthrew his father to become sultan as Muhammad XI in 1482. Civil war ensued, and the Spanish monarchs FERDINAND II of Aragon and ISABELLA I of Castile took advantage of it to attack Granada. The city of Granada finally fell to the Christians in 1492, and Boabdil fled to Morocco. He was the last Moorish ruler in Spain.

Bibliography: Hilgarth, J. N., *The Spanish Kingdoms, 1250–1516* (1976); Kamen, Henry, *Spain, 1469 to 1714* (1983).

Boadicea   [boh-ad-i-see'-uh]

Boadicea, or Boudicca, d. AD 61?, was a queen of the British Iceni tribe. When her husband, Prasutagas, died (AD 60), he left his property to be divided among his daughters and the Roman emperor. The Romans, however, seized his whole kingdom (in present-day Norfolk), provoking Boadicea to raise a rebellion. Her army sacked several cities before the Romans regained control. Boadicea probably killed herself with poison.

boar: see PIG.

boarfish

Boarfish, family Caproidae, are deep-bodied, small, red FISH living in marine waters 1,000–6,000 m (3,300–20,000 ft) deep and often near irregular bottom features. They reach 150 to 200 mm (6 to 8 in) in length and have small mouths that can be protruded. Their diet almost entirely comprises small crustaceans. Boarfish are found in the temperate and tropical regions of the Atlantic, Pacific, and Indian oceans. They are sometimes caught in large numbers in trawls but have no commercial value.

Boas, Franz   [boh'-az]

Franz Boas, b. July 9, 1858, d. Dec. 21, 1942, was a German-American anthropologist who is generally considered the father of American anthropology. Educated in Germany, he received (1881) his doctorate in physics from the University of Kiel, where he also studied geography and mathematics. On a scientific expedition to Baffin Island (1883–84), he became interested in Eskimo culture and thereafter devoted his career to anthropology. In 1886, Boas began fieldwork among the KWAKIUTL and other Indians of the northwest Pacific coast. He served (1896–1905) as curator of ethnology at the American Museum of Natural History, New York, and became (1899) Columbia University's first professor of anthropology, a position he held until his death.

A prolific scholar, Boas published hundreds of articles and books on physical anthropology, linguistics, and North American archaeology and ethnology. He trained some of America's best-known anthropologists, including Ruth BENEDICT, Alfred L. KROEBER, Robert H. Lowie, and Margaret MEAD. His impact on American anthropology, in particular on its methodology, was immense. Opposed to the armchair theorizing that had previously dominated the field, Boas encouraged an empirical approach to ethnology based on meticulous observation and quantification of data; many scholars later criticized him, however, for collecting masses of facts without attempting to reveal the significance of the data. His best-known books include *The Mind of Primitive Man* (1911; rev. ed., 1963; repr. 1966); *Primitive Art* (1927; 2d ed., 1955; repr. 1962), and *Race, Language, and Culture* (1940; repr. 1968).

Franz Boas (top, far right), *anthropologist, ethnologist, and linguist, appears here with a Kwakiutl Indian family. Boas, who had a profound influence on anthropology in the United States, promoted an empirical approach to the analysis of differing cultures.*

Bibliography: Boas, Franz, *Ethnography of Franz Boas,* ed. by Ronald P. Rohner (1969); Herskovitz, Melville J., *Franz Boas* (1953; repr. 1973); Kroeber, Alfred L., *Franz Boas* (1943); Stocking, George W., Jr., *A Franz Boas Reader* (1982).

boat and boating

Old-time sailors define a boat as a vessel capable of being carried aboard a ship. Many large vessels, however, are also called boats: tug boats, ferry boats, fireboats, and so forth. In the most general sense a boat is a comparatively small, often open vessel propelled by oars, paddles, sails, or a motor and designed and outfitted for any number of functions—from the simple short-haul transport a rowboat provides, to the highly specialized activities of a Coast Guard rescue boat.

This article deals with small boats and yachts, both power and sail, and with special small boat types such as CANOES. The history of larger vessels, both sail- and engine-powered, as well as modern construction methods will be found under SHIP. Separate articles describe special types of craft (for example, BARGE; GONDOLA; PT BOAT). NAVAL VESSELS treats the development of ships used for war as well as modern naval ship types.

EARLY BOAT DEVELOPMENT

Anthropologists assume that hollowed-out logs were the earliest form of boat. Indeed, many societies still use this type, often with sails and a stabilizing outrigger—a spar-attached length of wood riding parallel to the length of the boat. The famous Malay outrigger sailing canoe is an example of such a boat.

Other early types of boat construction included vessels made of tied bundles of reeds or grass, known to have been used in Sardinia, India, Egypt, and Mexico, on Lake Titicaca in South America, and by early American settlers in California. Another primitive form of boat construction, animal skins stretched over a wooden frame, can still be seen in the Eskimo kayak and the Irish coracle (curragh). The Maine canoe, painted canvas over spruce ribs, was developed in the 1890s using the basic design of the North American Indian canoe, a vessel made of birch bark sewn over a wood framework. Today, high-strength plastics are used to make the same canoe shape.

Although different societies developed similar types of boats, such conditions as the availability of tools and materials or the kinds of water to be traveled—as well as the

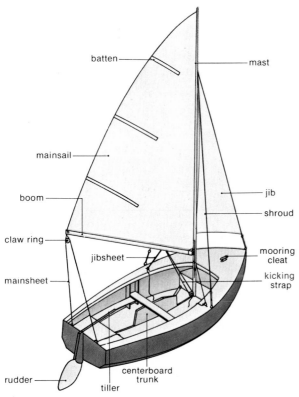

The Marconi-rigged sloop is one of the most popular of the small sailing craft. The mainsail and the jib are both attached to the single mast, which is positioned toward the bow of the boat. Battens, small pieces of wood or plastic, are inserted into pockets in the mainsail, and serve to keep the sail's edge from curling. Rigging ropes, or lines, adjust the sails and support the mast. The ropes used to control the mainsail and jib are called sheets and are attached by claw rings. Lines running from the mast to the sides of the boat are called shrouds. The centerboard can be lowered through a slot in the bottom and prevents the boat's sideslipping in the water.

requirements of fisherman or traders—were of great importance in the growth of maritime technology. American Indians, living mostly inland, never needed to use sails. Pacific islanders, surrounded by ocean, constructed sails from tree-bark mats or plaited strips of wood and were able to travel thousands of miles. They learned to navigate by weather signs, such as cloud banks over distant islands, and by the stars and ocean currents. Variations of multihulled boats, propelled by paddles and sails, were developed by the Micronesians and Polynesians. Micronesian outriggers, and those of Ceylon and Malaya, were extremely fast. Many Tahitian craft measured 20 m (65 ft) or more—as long as a large modern power cruiser. (One canoe that Capt. James Cook measured on his visit to Tahiti in 1769 was longer than his own ship, the *Endeavour.*) Pacific islanders cut planks with adzes and used lashings of a rope made from vegetable fibers and a caulking of breadfruit sap to hold their boats together.

Ancient Egyptian carvings reveal that the stones used to build the pyramids were transported by boat. Egyptian wall painters and pottery makers depicted sail and paddle boats on their ceramics. By perhaps 3000 BC, Egyptian sailors were voyaging as far as Crete, a round-trip of about 950 km (about 600 mi). They brought back cedar wood, for Egypt even then possessed few trees from which to construct boats. Egyptian nautical development occurred along with the invention of woven cloth for sails and twisted rope for rigging. A modern sailor, looking at rope made thousands of years ago and preserved in the dry air of the pharaohs' tombs, might well be amazed to realize that this ancient rope is constructed in a way still used today—three strands in a right-hand twist.

Paddles, oars, and single large sails were early forms of propulsion. At least one ancient method of arranging mast, spar, and sail, the lateen rig—a triangular sail set obliquely on a short mast—can still be seen on many Mediterranean and Middle Eastern craft.

Although Cretan and Phoenician mariners have left far fewer permanent records than did the Egyptians, historical evidence of long and difficult voyages made by these civilizations indicates a high level of seamanship and, presumably, a well-developed knowledge of boat building.

The vessels known from Greek and Roman times belong rather to the ship category and are therefore discussed there.

The northern European path of nautical development, meanwhile, had been along different lines. The Scandinavians made open boats, both of hollowed out logs and planked lumber, long before the Roman conquest of Britain. The Nydam boat, now preserved at Kiel, was about 25 m (82 ft) long and is made of planks fitted clinker style (each plank overlapping the one beneath it), rather than carvel-built, with the planks fitted edge to edge. There are 14 pairs of oars and a rudder, but no sail. Coins found near the Nydam boat date it as between AD 69 and 217. Scandinavian boats began using sails only about AD 600. By the 3d century AD the Jutes, Angles, and Saxons were raiding across the North Sea to England. Still more centuries passed before the Vikings crossed the Atlantic to Iceland, Greenland, and America in open boats with woolen sails.

Throughout the succeeding centuries, boat types and boat construction evolved slowly, sometimes spurred by occupations such as smuggling that required fast, maneuverable vessels, sometimes making rapid strides as new materials for sails and rope entered commerce. The basic carvel and clinker methods of constructing the hull were augmented by a variation on the carvel style, using two layers of planks set in opposing diagonal directions. Hull shapes were refined, and the addition of movable centerboards, or leeboards attached to the sides of the boat, reduced sideway slippage. The development of fore-and-aft sails enabled a boat to sail "into the wind," if not directly, at least by making a series of slanting "tacks."

By the late 19th century, almost every possible rowboat and sailboat design had been tried. It was not until the 1890s that the first gasoline engine–powered boat, fathered by the German inventors Gustav Daimler and Karl Benz, became commercially feasible. Eventually, power boats would outnumber sailboats by nine to one.

SMALL BOAT TYPES

In the 19th century each boat was made by hand, and ownership of a sailing yacht or other pleasure boat was restricted to the rich. The advent of aluminum and glass-reinforced plastic (fiberglass) as construction materials, however, introduced the advantages of mass production to the boat-building industry, and for the first time boat owning became a possibility for large numbers of people. As a result, the numbers of available boat styles, sizes, and types multiplied. Today the spectrum of small boat types begins with the smallest dinghies, prams (small ships' boats), and flat-bottom rowboats. Some can even fold to be carried overland and thus compete with a whole range of inflatable rubber boats, once used as emergency life-rafts but now popular for rowing, outboarding, and even sailing. Boating enthusiasts also use HOUSEBOATS, canoes, racing shells, punts, and rubber or aluminum rafts. A houseboat is a broad-beamed vessel that furnishes the maximum living space. Although some are surprisingly fast and maneuverable, they are suited primarily to inland waters. Racing shells are long, narrow craft that are propelled by one to eight rowers using long oars known as sculls or sweeps. The punt is a shallow draft boat with blunt ends that is usually propelled by poling. Large rafts, which may be powered by small outboard motors, are popular for river excursions.

Sailboats vary in size from light sailboards easily carried atop a car to cruising yachts—some only a little roomier than a station wagon—that can sail around the world. Such technical developments as aluminum masts and booms, stainless-steel rigging, nylon and dacron rope, and sails made of syn-

The rich variety of powered pleasure boats includes the cabin cruiser (top), made in numerous sizes and styles, and the houseboat (bottom), a capacious, flat-bottomed craft designed for touring inland waterways. Many houseboats provide permanent homes for their owners.

thetic materials have further expanded the field of recreational boating by making it easier to handle boats under sail and to maintain them in dock. The once-laborious process of sail handling is now mechanized with electrically powered winches that hoist, lower, and control the sails. Many small racing boats are manufactured to conform to various class measurement rules. There are as many as 600 recognized classes.

Along with the perfection of synthetic construction materials, the development of the outboard motor has created another major change in pleasure boating. The motor is light, comparatively inexpensive, and capable of being attached to a wide variety of craft, from simple rowboats to small cruising sailboats and catamarans. Boating competition has led to ever more powerful outboard engines (up to 200 hp in standard boats and reaching 900 hp in craft built for high-speed racing) and to increased reliability. The modified V-bottom hull, developed for offshore power-boat racing, is now the dominant hull design for fast open boats, cruisers, and sport-fishing boats. In addition to increasing the number of pleasure-boating enthusiasts, the outboard motor has become a significant source of marine mobility in remote frontier areas and on the waters of developing countries.

Larger MOTORBOATS include cabin cruisers, ranging in size up to around 10 m (35 ft) and equipped with an inboard motor and living accommodations that often include bunks for up to six people, a galley (kitchen), and such other amenities as a shower. Some are outfitted for fishing, with a control station (called a flying bridge) built above the main cabin for better visibility. Above 10 m, cabin cruisers are more properly called motor yachts; many carry such sophisticated navigational and power equipment that they can operate like large transocean ships.

RECREATIONAL BOATING
By the late 1980s, over 17 million recreational boats were registered with the U.S. Coast Guard. About 50 percent of the recreational boats in the United States are outboard powered, 12 percent have inboard motors, and about 9 percent are

sail-powered boats. Thousands of law-enforcement officers of various jurisdictions administer U.S. waterways. The volunteer-staffed United States Power Squadrons teach boating to more than 50,000 adults a year in 400 locations across the country, and the Coast Guard auxiliary instructs an almost equal number. Hundreds of sailing schools, state and local boating education programs, and specialized schools provide beginning through advanced courses. As proof of the popularity of boating, one book—*Chapman Piloting, Seamanship and Small Boat Handling,* first published in 1917—has sold several million copies.

Most of the thousands of boating enthusiasts simply enjoy spending recreational time on the water. A smaller group compete in the thousands of races held every year, and for the most important of these races, naval architects design craft incorporating the most advanced computer-generated shapes and the latest in experimental materials. In sailboating competition, catamarans and trimarans (improving on the Pacific Island multihulls) can approach speeds of 26 knots (48 km/h; 30 mph). While monohulls tend to dominate the sailboat world, *Stars and Stripes,* a catamaran, defeated the New Zealand monohull yacht *New Zealand* to win the 1988 AMERICA'S CUP—the most important sailing race.

Sailboating competition is often a well-organized sport, especially at the 1,200 yacht clubs in the United States. A racer may start at the club level and advance to interclub, regional, and—in the United States—the North America Yacht Racing Union's national championships. On the world level the International Yacht Racing Union is the governing body. Men, women, and juniors compete at their own levels and in varying combinations. The pinnacle of small-craft sailing competition is the Olympic Games.

Separate from clubs and regional associations are the organizations for boats of particular classes. These are known as one-designs because the boats in a given class are all of the same design and size, and they race without handicap or time allowance—that is, the first boat to cross the finish line is the winner. Some of the most popular of the hundreds of one-design classes are the Sunfish, Hobie Cats, Lasers, Stars, Snipes, and Lightnings. Some classes are commercially controlled, and others are run by the owners' organization.

Handicap racing allows for boats of differing sizes and designs to race against one another, with time allowances based on a rating derived from a boat's measurements in conjunction with the finishing times. The first boat to the finish line is not necessarily the winner. Most ocean races are run on a handicap basis. Some of the best known are the Bermuda Race, the Honolulu Race, and the Southern Ocean Racing Conference, as well as the Chicago-to-Mackinac (Island) race on Lake Michigan and the Detroit-to-Mackinac race on Lake Huron. Distances range from 480 to 3,200 km (300 to 2,000

A sleek 900-hp Bertram powerboat almost leaves the water during a race. To eliminate the slowing effect of water resistance, competition powerboats have been designed so that at high speeds most of the hull rides above the surface of the water.

mi), and occasionally special races across the Atlantic and even around the world are held. Boats for these races range from 10 to 24 m (35 to 80 ft).

Among the most famous American racing sailboats are *Brilliant*, the schooner that had the fastest elapsed time in the 1936 Bermuda Race (114 hr, 54 min, 32 sec; in corrected time, however, *Brilliant* placed second) and is still sailing out of Mystic seaport; *Finisterre*, the broad-beamed yawl that won the Bermuda Race three times in succession—in 1956, 1958, and 1960; and *Courageous*, the U.S. 12-meter boat that successfully defended the America's Cup in 1974 and 1977.

Offshore powerboat racing is a special development that began in the 1960s, and a good proportion of the powerboat racing in American waters is done by professionals. A major power-boat competition in the United States is the Gold Cup series, dominated by high-powered hydroplanes that average 130 to 160 km/h (80 to 100 mph). Not nearly so fast, but involving a high level of seamanship, is the type of powerboat race called ''Predicted Log Racing,'' where amateur skippers predict the time it will take their cruisers to cover a given route—taking into consideration winds, currents, and navigational hazards.
JOHN R. WHITING

Bibliography: Anderson, Romola and R. C., *The Sailing Ship: 6,000 Years of History* (1963); Bartlett, M., and Fishman, J. A., eds., *The Sailing Book* (1982); Blandford, P., *The Illustrated History of the Small Boat* (1974); Bottomley, Tom, *Boatman's Handbook,* 2d ed. (1988); Gardiner, Robert, and Greenhill, Basil, eds., *Sail's Last Century* (1993); Gerr, Dave, *The Nature of Boats* (1992); Greenhill, Basil, *The Archaeology of the Boat* (1976); Heyerdahl, Thor, *Early Man and the Ocean* (1978); Maloney, E. S., *Chapman Piloting, Seamanship, and Small Boat Handling,* 60th ed. (1991); Time-Life Books, *The Boat* (1975) and *The Classic Boat* (1977); Watts, Alan, *Wind and Sailing Boats* (1987); West, Gordon, *Boatowner's Guide to Marine Electronics* (1993); Whiting, John R., *On Deck* (1985).

(Above) Courageous *passes* Enterprise *in the trials for the 1977 America's Cup. Piloted by magnate Ted Turner,* Courageous *went on to a 4-race sweep in the 23d successful U.S. defense of the Cup.*

(Below) *With her striped spinnaker leading the way,* Australia II *speeds to victory in the 1983 America's Cup. Australia's win ended the 132-year possession of the Cup by the United States.*

bobcat

The bobcat, F. rufus, derives its name from its bobbed (stubby) tail. Small and fierce, the bobcat can leap onto the back of a young deer and kill it.

The bobcat, *Felis rufus*, is a mammal in the cat family, Felidae, order Carnivora. It is also known as the wildcat and bay lynx. The bobcat is about 71 cm (28 in) long and has a short tail. Large males may weigh 11 kg (24 lb). The long, soft fur is pale brown with blackish splotches. The face is much like that of the domestic cat, but larger. The legs are long and heavy, and the large paws are furred. Bobcats live in forests and on plains from southern Canada to northern Mexico. They eat rodents and rabbits.
EVERETT SENTMAN

bobolink [bahb'-oh-link]

The bobolink is a songbird of the American blackbird family. It nests in the grassy fields of the northern United States and

The male bobolink, D. oryzivorus *(left), has different colored plumage from the female's only during the summer breeding season. It is light above and dark below, which is why it is nicknamed "skunkbird."*

southern Canada, east of the Rocky Mountains, and migrates to Argentina. Its name is derived from one of its melodious songs. The bird is about 18 cm (7 in) long. In winter both sexes are buff-brown, with buff and black stripes, but in the breeding season the male has a mainly black body with white shoulders and rump and a yellowish nape. The rough nest of grass and weeds is placed on the ground. The bobolink is also called the reedbird—and sometimes ricebird, because it settled on rice fields that used to lie along its migratory path in the southern United States and fed on them, sometimes doing serious damage. The bobolink, *Dolichonyx oryzivorus,* is classified in the family Icteridae, order Passeriformes.

WILLIAM F. SANDFORD

bobsledding

Bobsledding is a fast and dangerous winter sport in which two or four persons maneuver a bobsled down a winding ice track. Most bobruns are in the Alps or at Winter Olympic sites. One of the greatest bobsledders was Eugenio Monti, an Italian who piloted 11 crews to world championships between 1957 and 1968. Most European countries hold national championships; international competitions are controlled by the International Bobsled Federation. The first four-man world championship took place at the 1924 Olympics. Two-man championships began in 1931 and were added to the Olympic program in 1932. St. Moritz was the home of the first bobsled (1888), the first organized competitive bobsled meet (1898), and the first designed bobrun (1902).

Modern bobsleds are sleek, streamlined, aluminum and steel vehicles that travel up to 145 km/h (90 mph). Their length may not exceed 3.8 m, or 12.5 ft (2.7 m, or 8.9 ft, for two-person boblets), and total weight, including crew, may not exceed 630 kg, or 1,389 lb (375 kg and 827 lb, for boblets). International courses are at least 1,500 m (4,920 ft) long with at least 15 banked turns, some more than 6 m (19 ft) high. Championship matches usually include four heats, and the team with the lowest composite time wins.

The driver steers with either a rope or a wheel. The second and third person push off and join the braker in bobbing backward and forward on straightaways to increase momentum.

bobwhite

The bobwhite, a game bird, is a QUAIL found throughout most of the United States east of the Rocky Mountains and south to Central America. The name is derived from its characteristic mating call. Relatively small (25 cm/10 in), it is plump bodied, chestnut-brown on the back, and pale but heavily

streaked and spotted below. The throat and eyebrow stripes are boldly white in the male and buffy in the female. The plumage blends well with the bird's habitat of overgrown fields and woodland openings. The nest is built on the ground, and 12 to 15 eggs are laid. Between breeding seasons, bobwhites gather into groups, called coveys, of up to 20 birds and establish territories that they defend against other coveys; they sleep in a circle with tails pointed inward so that they can flee separately in all directions if disturbed. They feed on insects and weed seeds. The bobwhite is classified as *Colinus virginianus,* family Phasianidae (which includes the pheasants and partridges), order Galliformes.   WILLIAM F. SANDFORD

Bobwhites, C virginianus *(male at left), are usually monogamous. Members of a family roost together in a circle, heads pointing outward, and at the first sign of danger fly off in all directions.*

Boccaccio, Giovanni   [boh-kah'-choh]

Giovanni Boccaccio, b. 1313, d. Dec. 21, 1375, best known as the author of the DECAMERON, is generally considered the father of Italian prose style, the creator of the novella (see NOVELLA AND NOVELETTE) and the psychological NOVEL, and the renovator of the ancient EPIC in the vernacular. He was also, with PETRARCH, one of the first Renaissance humanists.

Neapolitan Period. In 1327, Boccaccio's father, who held important positions in the Bardi bank, apprenticed him to the banking trade in Naples. Boccaccio, however, preferred the aristocratic and intellectual circles of the Neapolitan court of King Robert of Anjou, where men of learning and taste gathered. In this courtly and stylized atmosphere, he created the mythical Fiammetta, a lady who dominated his prose and poetry. She is traditionally but questionably identified as Maria d'Aquino, daughter of King Robert. During this Neapolitan period (c.1327–41) Boccaccio composed his first literary works: the pastoral allegory *La caccia di Diana* (Diana's Hunt, 1334?); the heroic version of the Troilus and Cressida myth, *Filostrato* (1335?; Eng. trans., 1973), which influenced Chaucer and Shakespeare; the prose romance *The Most Pleasant and Delectable Questions of Love* (1336–38?; Eng. trans., 1566; repr. 1927); the epic poems in octava rima, *The Book of Theseus* (1339–41?; Eng. trans., 1974); and numerous short lyrics.

Life in Florence. In 1341, for family reasons, Boccaccio returned to the mercantile world of Florence where he discovered that Florence, unlike Naples, had a vital artistic and intellectual community that followed the style of DANTE and the allegorical-didactic literary tradition. Under this influence he began composing his finest works: the allegorical *Commedia delle ninfe fiorentine* (Comedy of the Florentine Nymphs, 1341–42); a dream vision, *L'amorosa visione* (The Amorous Vision; 1342–43); a psychological novel, *Amorous Fiametta* (1343–44; Eng. trans., 1587; repr. 1976); and the mythological pastoral *The Nymph of Fiesole* (1344–46; Eng. trans., 1960).

Giovanni Boccaccio, a 14th-century Italian poet and scholar, appears as a Roman laureate in this engraving. Boccaccio, a leading writer of the early Renaissance, is best known for the Decameron, *a collection of lively, humorous tales set against the background of plague-stricken Italy.*

The Decameron. The specter of the bubonic plague of 1348 concluded this productive phase in his life, but also serves as the basis for Boccaccio's masterpiece of 100 tales, *Decameron* (1348–53; Eng. trans., 1955). Rich in authentic and literary details, the tales mark a breakthrough in Italian prose style.

About 1350 he became deeply involved in the political affairs of the Florentine Commune, undertaking various ambassadorial missions. In the same year he met Petrarch for the first time, beginning a friendship that endured until Petrarch's death in 1374. With Petrarch's encouragement, Boccaccio developed the humanistic interests always evident in his works and in his translation of Livy: the search for ancient manuscripts; the study of Greek and, in the process, the establishment of a chair in Greek at the Florentine Studio in 1359; and the scholarly study of classical history, literature, and mythology. Except for the later misogynistic satire, *Il Corbaccio* (1365; Eng. trans., 1975), and some late poetry, his writing of imaginative literature ceased. He turned instead to critical studies: a cultural geography, *De montibus* (concerning mountains, c.1355–74); the biographical *Fates of Illustrious Men* (c. 1355–74; Eng. trans., 1965) and *Concerning Famous Women* (c.1360–74; Eng. trans., 1963); and the encyclopedic *On the Genealogy of the Gentile Gods* (c. 1350–60; Eng. trans., 1930). The *Genealogia* was particularly important as a mythological sourcebook as well as for its vigorous defense of poetry.

Spiritual Crisis. In 1362, following a visit from the fanatical monk Gioacchino Ciani, who urged him to renounce secular studies and embrace religion, Boccaccio underwent a profound spiritual crisis. He seriously considered burning the *Decameron* together with his other works, but was dissuaded by Petrarch. Having retired to Certaldo in 1363, Boccaccio remained active in Florentine politics and completed his affectionate biography of Dante, *Trattatello in laude di Dante* (Little Tractate in Praise of Dante, 1372). In 1373, by invitation of the Florentine Commune, he delivered public readings of Dante's *Divine Comedy* and is said to have met Chaucer in Florence the same year.   CHRISTOPHER KLEINHENZ

Bibliography: Branca, Vittore, *Boccaccio*, trans. by Richard Monges, ed. and trans. by Dennis J. McAuliffe (1976); Carswell, Catherine M., *The Tranquil Heart* (1937; repr. 1976); Chubb, Thomas C., *The Life of Giovanni Boccaccio* (1930; repr. 1973); Cottino-Jones, Margo, *Order from Chaos* (1983); MacManus, Francis, *Boccaccio* (1947).

Boccherini, Luigi   [boh-kay-ree'-nee]

Luigi Boccherini, b. Feb. 19, 1743, d. May 28, 1805, was an Italian composer and cellist, who exemplified the classical style in Italy and Spain. During an era when Austria and Germany dominated European musical life, Boccherini's chamber music was often considered the equal of Haydn's. As a boy he studied in Rome, then played in bands and orchestras in his home-

town. For several years he toured in France, where he was enthusiastically received, and then in Spain, where he was named composer to Don Luis, brother of King Carlos III. He later spent some years in Germany, and was named Kammerkomponist ("chamber composer") to King Frederick William II of Prussia. His last years were spent in Spain, some of them in the service of Lucien Bonaparte, but poor health necessitated his giving up playing the cello. He sank into abject poverty and died in Madrid.

Boccherini was at his finest in chamber music, which includes many duos, trios, quartets, quintets, sextets, and octets, mostly for stringed instruments. His cello concertos are an important part of the repertory for that instrument, and his orchestral symphonies are sometimes performed. He also wrote a number of operas and choral works, most of which have never been published.   FARLEY K. HUTCHINS

Bibliography: Gerard, Yves, ed., *Thematic, Bibliographical, and Critical Catalogue of the Works of Luigi Boccherini*, trans. by Andreas Mayor (1969).

boccie   [bah'-chee]

Boccie is a bowling game that originated in Italy and is still associated with Italians or those of Italian descent in the United States, Australia, South America, and elsewhere. It is a game in which two to four players lob or roll hard balls (wood or a composite) 11 cm (4.5 in) in diameter at a smaller (7.0 cm/2.75 in) target ball. The object of the game is to get a ball closer to the target than the opposition does. Each side is allowed four attempts. After all balls are played, a team scores one point for each of its balls nearer the target than the opposition's closest one. (See also LAWN BOWLS.)

Boccioni, Umberto   [boh-choh'-nee]

Umberto Boccioni, b. Oct. 19, 1882, d. Aug. 16, 1916, was an Italian futurist painter and sculptor and a leading theoretician of the futurist movement. In 1898 he moved to Rome, where he met Giacomo BALLA and Gino SEVERINI, both of whom later became fellow futurists. Balla's neoimpressionist style influenced Boccioni's early work. This influence was enhanced by the paintings of Georges Seurat and Paul Signac, which Boccioni saw in Paris in 1902. During the years 1902–04, he traveled throughout Europe and Russia, where he acquainted himself with the latest movements in art. Returning to Italy in 1905, Boccioni joined (1909) Filippo Tommaso MARINETTI, the founder of Italian FUTURISM, and painted his first major futurist work, *Riot in the Gallery* (1909; Jesi Collection, Milan). He was a coauthor with Marinetti and the painters Carlo CARRÀ, Luigi Russolo, Balla, and Severini of the *Technical-Manifesto of Futurist Painters* (1910) and became active in the move-

Umberto Boccioni's Unique Forms of Continuity in Space *(1913) is an expression of an object's movement through space. The bronze figure is typical of futurist sculpture. (Private collection, Milan.)*

ment throughout Europe. On a trip to Paris in 1911, Boccioni first encountered the cubists. Subsequently, his style showed a strong cubist influence, which became apparent in his growing interest in the intensive analysis of form. By 1912 he had developed an interest in sculpture, publishing the *Technical Manifesto of Futurist Sculpture* that year.

Boccioni's stylistic evolution led from NEOIMPRESSIONISM to an idiom influenced by CUBISM and the theories of universal dynamism. In an attempt to capture a material world in flux and resolve the contrast between the world of external appearances and that of the internal spirit, Boccioni gradually moved toward greater abstraction. His paintings, such as *The City Rises* (1910; Museum of Modern Art, New York), and sculpture, for example, *Unique Forms of Continuity in Space* (1913), are characterized by the fusion of the object and its environment.

Boccioni was perhaps the most gifted of the futurist artists, and his work was influential in the development of other abstract styles.   MAGDALENA DABROWSKI

Bibliography: Golding, John, *Boccioni's Unique Forms of Continuity of Space* (1972; repr. 1985); Lista, Giovanni, *Futurism* (1986); Martin, Marianne W., *Futurist Art and Theory 1909–1915* (1968); Taylor, Joshua, *Futurism* (1961); Tisdall, Caroline, and Bozzolla, Angelo, *Futurism* (1978).

Bochum   [boh'-kum]

Bochum (1989 est. pop., 390,100) is a city in the state of North Rhine–Westphalia in western Germany. Located in the industrial Ruhr valley, it is a commercial and manufacturing center that produces automobiles, chemicals, and electrical equipment. It also has metallurgical industries.

First chartered in 1298 and 1321, it went to the duchy of Cleves in 1461 and to Brandenburg in 1609. In the 19th century the coal, iron, and steel industries were developed. Mining was the chief industry until the late 1950s, when mines closed down and the economy shifted. Bochum's center, almost totally destroyed in World War II, was rebuilt after 1946. The priory church (1599) is the only historic building remaining. Bochum has a university, an institute for space research, and a geological and mining museum.

Bock, Jerry, and Harnick, Sheldon

Jerry Bock, composer, b. New Haven, Conn., Nov. 23, 1928, and Sheldon Harnick, lyricist, b. Chicago, Apr. 30, 1924, wrote the score for the enormously popular *Fiddler on the Roof,* which had one of the longest continuous performance runs in Broadway theater history (3,242). Their first musical was *Mr. Wonderful* in 1956. *Fiorello!* won the Pulitzer Prize for drama in 1960. Later collaborations include *The Apple Tree* (1966) and *The Rothchilds* (1970).   DAVID EWEN

Böcklin, Arnold   [burk'-lin]

The Swiss artist Arnold Böcklin, b. Oct. 16, 1827, d. Jan. 16, 1901, was a precursor of the international symbolist movement. Steeped in classical mythology, Böcklin's art strove to reestablish a sense of the living presence of the pagan gods and to capture the atmosphere of dreams. His popular *Island of the Dead* (1880; The Metropolitan Museum of Art, New York City, one of five versions) owes much of its appeal to a combination of classical motifs with dream imagery. Aspects of Böcklin's art prefigure SURREALISM; the metaphysical modern painter Giorgio de CHIRICO began as an imitator of Böcklin.

Böcklin was trained in Basel and at the Dusseldorf Akademie but lived most of his life after 1850 in Rome and Florence. About 1856 he shifted his emphasis from landscapes to figural subjects, including many portraits. Böcklin's closest associates were Anselm FEUERBACH and Franz von Lenbach, artists who were known with him as the "German-Romans." Earlier German art also played a large part in Böcklin's synthesis. His *Self-Portrait with Death Playing a Violin* (1872; Nationalgalerie, Berlin) was inspired by a portrait then attributed to Hans Holbein the Younger. *War* (1896; Staatliche Kunstsammlungen, Dresden) was based on Albrecht Dürer's *Apocalypse* woodcuts. *Vanitas* symbols, or reminders of death, were a fre-

Arnold Böcklin's Self-Portrait with Death Playing a Violin *(1872) is one of his many allegorical canvases on the subject of death. The Swiss artist's works exerted a powerful influence on the metaphysical and surrealist painters of the 20th century. (Nationalgalerie, Berlin.)*

quent feature in Böcklin's art, and yet his work also exhibits humor. In his later years Böcklin was much occupied with plans for a flying machine, although he continued to paint.
JEFFERY HOWE

Bibliography: Fuchs, Ernest, *Böcklin* (1976).

See also: SYMBOLISM (art).

Bocskay, István, Prince of Transylvania
[bawch'-koy, isht'-vahn]

István Bocskay, b. Jan. 1, 1557, d. Dec. 29, 1606, prince of Transylvania (1605–06), was also the elected "ruling prince" of Hungary (1605–06). Although initially a supporter of the anti-Turkish and pro-Habsburg faction in Transylvania, Bocskay turned against Vienna because of Habsburg insensitivity and persecution of Hungarian Protestants. In 1604, with Turkish help, he launched a war of liberation, which ended in the Peace of Vienna (June 23, 1606). By this treaty Holy Roman Emperor RUDOLF II, as king of Hungary, guaranteed the rights of the Hungarian estates as well as religious freedom to the Protestants.   S. B. VARDY

Bode, Johann Elert   [boh'-de]

The German astronomer Johann Elert Bode, b. Jan. 19, 1747, d. Nov. 23, 1826, is best known for his role in publicizing the TITIUS-BODE LAW, which demonstrated a nearly geometric progression in the distances between the planets known at that time. Almost entirely self-educated, Bode was brought to the observatory of the Berlin Academy in 1772 by Johann Lambert. For 50 years he performed the calculations for the famous almanac *Astronomisches Jahrbuch*, published star catalogs unsurpassed in their time, and from 1786 served as director of the observatory.

Bodenheim, Maxwell   [boh'-den-hym]

The poet and novelist Maxwell Bodenheim, b. Hermanville, Miss., May 26, 1893, d. Feb. 6, 1954, was one of the foremost literary bohemians of the 1920s. Beginning with *Minna and Myself* (1918), six volumes of Bodenheim's poetry were published in six years. His poems, often in free verse, show the influence of imagism and of Carl Sandburg. He wrote several plays and novels in which he included both the iconoclastic hedonism of the jazz age and sympathy for the working classes. His incomplete autobiography, *My Life and Loves in Greenwich Village* (1954), was published after Bodenheim and his third wife were murdered in their New York apartment.   JAMES HART

Bode's law: see TITIUS-BODE LAW.

Bodh Gaya   [buhd gah'-yah]

Bodh Gaya, also Buddh Gaya, a village in Bihar state, northeast India, is the Buddhist site where, according to tradition, Prince Siddhartha (Gautama Buddha) attained enlightenment under the sacred pipal tree (the bodhi tree). Architectural remains include a fragment of a stupa railing (1st century BC) and restored shrines of the Pala dynasty (AD 750–1200).

Bodhidharma   [boh-dee-dahr'-muh]

Bodhidharma was a 6th-century Indian Buddhist monk who founded a meditation school of Buddhism called Ch'an that later developed into ZEN BUDDHISM. Although many accounts of his life are legendary, he was a historical person. Bodhidharma held that more than good deeds are necessary for salvation and that meditation is the fulfillment of Buddha's precepts. After traveling to China, he is said to have spent nine years in meditation, staring at the wall of a cave.

bodhisattva   [boh-dee-saht'-vuh]

In BUDDHISM, the name *bodhisattva* is given to anyone destined for Buddhahood. In the Theravada school, the term is generally reserved for the BUDDHA Gautama in the period before his enlightenment, and for the Buddha of the future, Metteya. In Mahayana Buddhism, the concept takes on central importance, and refers more generally to anyone who, by means of vows and practices, has undertaken to achieve complete enlightenment, but who then refrains from entering final NIRVANA and remains in this world to assist other sentient creatures to that goal. As such, these compassionate bodhisattvas are opposed to the *arhats* (perfected ones) of the Theravada, who attain enlightenment and enter nirvana for themselves alone. At a more mythological level, the Mahayana also recognizes many individual "celestial bodhisattvas" who became popular figures in legend and cult. Among them are Avalokitesvara (Kuan-yin in China), Manjusri, Khitigarbha (Jizo in Japan), and Mahasthamaprapta.
JOSEPH M. KITAGAWA AND JOHN S. STRONG

Bodin, Jean

Jean Bodin, b. c.1530, d. June 1596, was a French philosopher, statesman, and jurist. He taught and practiced law in Toulouse until he went to Paris at the age of 40. There he joined the *politique* party and became a prominent figure in the entourage of François de Valois, the youngest son of CATHERINE DE MÉDICIS. In 1576, Bodin opposed a suppression of the HUGUENOTS and in so doing fell from royal favor. He was demoted to a relatively minor post at Laon, where he wrote the Latin version of his *Six Books of the Republic* (1566; modern ed., 1962), considered a major work on political theory.

Bodin defined the republic as "the lawful government of many families, and of what is common to them, with sovereign power." Sovereignty is necessary in every political community; it is limited only by God and NATURAL LAW. Although the family is the basic natural community, political power is exercised through governments, which fall into one of three categories: monarchy, aristocracy, or democracy. He preferred a monarch with absolute power to command the subjects,

even to the point of determining their religion. At the same time, he held that the monarch should be moderate and just in the use of that power. In the extreme case of tyranny, rebellion might be justified. Bodin was one of the most learned men of his age. His theories and definitions influenced subsequent political thought.   JOHN P. DOYLE

Bibliography: Franklin, Julian, *Jean Bodin and the Rise of Absolutist Theory* (1973); King, Preston, *The Ideology of Order: A Comparative Analysis of Jean Bodin and Thomas Hobbes* (1974); Mayer, J. P., ed., *Fundamental Studies of Jean Bodin* (1979).

Bodleian Library   [bahd'-lee-uhn or bahd-lee'-uhn]

The Bodleian Library at Oxford University was the first public library in Europe and is the second largest in England. Funded by Sir Thomas Bodley (1545–1613), a scholar-diplomat, the library opened Nov. 8, 1602, to replace the Oxford library that had been virtually destroyed in the 1550s. Entitled to receive a free copy of every new book published in England, the Bodleian today contains in excess of 5 million books and about 135,000 manuscripts, including many rare items in both categories. Its collections in English history, early printing, biblical and Arabic material, and Shakespeare are especially notable.

Bibliography: Hassall, W. O., *Treasures from the Bodleian Library* (1976); Philip, Ian, *The Bodleian Library in the 17th and 18th Centuries* (1983).

Bodmer, Karl   [bohd'-mur]

The Swiss artist Karl Bodmer, b. Feb. 6, 1809, d. Oct. 30, 1893, was an early painter of the American West. As the expedition's documentary artist, Bodmer accompanied the German naturalist Prince Maximilian of Wied-Neuwied on his 13-month journey of 1833–34 along the Missouri River. Bodmer produced dozens of superb drawings and watercolors of the Indian tribes they encountered, as well as of landscapes and animals. Of these, 82 were reproduced as aquatints in the account of the expedition published in Europe in 1839. Bodmer settled in Barbizon, France, where he continued to paint until his death.

Bibliography: Bodmer, Karl, *Karl Bodmer's America,* ed. by David Hunt, et al. (1984); *People of the First Man* (1976); Ewers, John Canfield, *Early White Influence upon Plains Indian Painting: George Catlin and Carl Bodmer among the Mandan Indians* (1957; repr. 1971).

Bodoni, Giambattista   [boh-doh'-nee, jahm-bah-tees'-tah]

Giambattista Bodoni, b. Feb. 26, 1740, d. Nov. 30, 1813, was an Italian printer whose beautiful editions are among the best examples of Italian typography. At the age of 18 he entered the Stamperia di Propagando of the Holy See, where he studied oriental languages and literature. His abilities were quickly recognized, and he was named head of a ducal press in 1768. Bodoni improved on existing TYPEFACES to emphasize the difference between thick and thin strokes, and his brilliant typography was soon emulated throughout Europe. His finest work is his *Manuale tipografico* (Inventory of Types), published as a partial edition in 1788 and issued complete by his widow after his death.   M. C. FAIRLEY

Bibliography: Gray, Nicolete, *History of Lettering* (1987); Steinberg, Sigfrid H., *Five Hundred Years of Printing* (1956; rev. ed., 1961).

body language: see NONVERBAL COMMUNICATION.

body marking

The body-marking techniques of tattooing, scarification, and painting have been used in a vast range of cultures, both ancient and contemporary, for decoration and for communicative purposes. The markings may give information about group membership, rank, and status. Body painting may also indicate the particular social role one is playing at a given

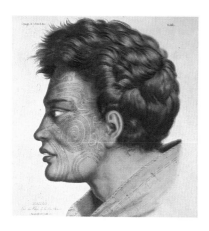

This 19th-century drawing by a crew member of the French expeditionary ship Astrolabe *portrays an* ariki, *or chief, of the* Maori, *a Polynesian people native to New Zealand. The chief's elaborate facial tattoos were made by puncturing the skin and applying vegetable dyes to the wounds.*

time and express social and religious values.

Tattooing, the introduction of pigment through punctures in the skin to create patterns, was practiced in ancient Egypt. Some of the most elaborate tattoos have been found among the cultures of Oceania—for example, the MAORI of New Zealand tattoo complex spiral designs on the face and buttocks. Traditionally, fine tattoos have been to them a sign of good breeding. In contemporary Japan full-body tattoos are flaunted by the *yakuza* (organized gangsters).

The word *tattoo* is derived from a Tahitian term. Sailors showed an early interest in the tattoos of the Pacific, and the practice of tattooing has persisted among seamen. Tattooing techniques vary widely—for example, the Eskimo use bone needles to draw soot-covered thread through the skin; the Japanese use fine metal needles and colored pigments.

Scarring, or cicatrization, is most common in the cultures of Africa, Australia, and Melanesia. In the initiation rites of boys among the Nuer of the Sudan, six cuts are made across the forehead and remain for life as scars. Finer tattoolike patterns are chiseled onto the faces of young female initiates of the Kaoka-speakers of the Solomon Islands. In each case the practice serves to mark a new stage of life. In some African and Australian societies raised weals, or keloids, are created by rubbing irritants into a wound.

Body painting is most commonly practiced for participation in ceremonies, feasting, and dancing. Among the people of Mount Hagen, New Guinea, it is used as part of a complex of personal decoration that may express the prestige and unity of a clan, individual health and wealth, and also may reflect links with the ancestors. Painting for war is also widespread; in this case body-marking symbolizes radical change in the pattern of social relations.   CHRISTIAN CLERK

Bibliography: Field, Henry, *Body-Marking in Southwestern Asia* (1958); Faris, James C., *Nuba Personal Art* (1972); Hambly, Wilfred D., *The History of Tattooing and Its Significance* (1925; repr. 1975); Richie, Donald, and Buruma, Ian, *The Japanese Tattoo* (1980).

body snatching

The stealing of corpses from newly closed graves, known as body snatching, became a pursuit for criminals in Britain during the 18th and early 19th centuries. The crime was profitable because medical schools needed cadavers for use in teaching anatomy. At the time, laws did not permit the schools to acquire unclaimed bodies from the public morgues. Two notorious body snatchers in Scotland were William Burke and William Hare, who turned to murder in order to augment their supply.

body temperature

Body temperature reflects the level of heat energy in an animal's body and is the consequence of the balance between heat produced from METABOLISM and the exchange of heat with the surrounding environment. The continuance and activity of life processes are profoundly influenced by temperature. Usually animal life is feasible only within a relatively narrow range of temperatures: the lower limit is just about freezing, 0° C (32° F), whereas the upper limit is about 45° C (113° F), the temperature at which cell structures begin to degenerate. With special preparation, however, it is possible to freeze and store animal cells and tissues at extremely low temperatures.

Birds and mammals are warm-blooded homeotherms—that is, they have effective regulatory mechanisms for maintaining their relatively high body core temperatures within narrow limits, despite large variations in surrounding (ambient) temperature. Homeotherms can maintain a temperature difference between their body core and the environment because of their fast metabolic rates—a kind of metabolism called tachymetabolism—and their effective thermal insulation. In contrast, the so-called cold-blooded animals—the temperature conformers, or poikilotherms—lack effective temperature regulation. Their temperature, metabolism, and activity vary in proportion to ambient temperature and, because of their slow metabolic rates (bradymetabolism) at rest, they have difficulty maintaining core temperature much above ambient temperature. Some poikilotherms may at times exhibit a kind of homeothermy, maintaining their body temperatures at more or less constant levels by adjustments of their behavioral and activity patterns. This form of thermal regulation is callled ectothermic ("outer-heated") and depends on uptake of heat from the environment. On the other hand, the true homeothermic animals are endothermic ("inner-heated") and depend largely on their fast and controlled rates of heat production. The effectiveness of ectothermy is evident in lizards, which maintain their body temperature by movement in or out of shade, by orientation of their bodies in relation to solar radiation, and by postures that control conduction of heat to and from the ground contact surface. After sunset, the lizards burrow, seeking warmer temperatures, but usually insufficient soil warmth is available and their body temperatures fall. The preferred temperatures are reachieved in the morning when the lizards leave their burrows to bask in the sun.

Temperatures in homeotherms are not uniform; core temperatures vary among different species. Spatial and temporal variations also occur within the body of a given species. That is, the temperature of the inner organs, including the brain, varies by 1° to 2° C (1.8°–3.6° F), and there may be gradients of a few degrees within and between organs. Skin temperatures are often 10° to 20° C (18°–36° F) below core temperature, or less, depending on ambient temperature and the capacity of the surface covering of feathers, hair, or clothing to slow the rate of heat flow from the body. In species active during the day, maximal temperatures are usually found in the afternoon and minimal values in the morning, before the start of the day's activities. In nocturnal species, the diurnal pattern is reversed.

BODY CORE TEMPERATURES IN SOME BIRDS AND MAMMALS

	Temperature (°C)	(°F)		Temperature (°C)	(°F)
Sparrow	43.5	110.3	Pig	38.6	101.5
Pigeon	42.2	108.0	Dog	38.2	100.8
Duck	42.1	107.8	Mouse	37.9	100.2
Chicken	41.9	107.4	Polar bear	37.6	99.7
Magpie	41.8	107.2	Human	37.0	98.6
Turkey	41.2	106.2	Opossum*	34.7	94.5
Sheep	39.0	102.2	Echidna†	28.1	72.6
Cattle	38.6	101.5			

*marsupial   †monotreme

An elevation in core temperature of homeotherms above the normal range is called hyperthermia, while a corresponding decrease is hypothermia. Hyperthermia or hypothermia can be brought about by extremes in the environment or an inability of the animal to avoid or compensate for a thermally stressful situation. Internal core temperatures are readily measurable by means of natural body orifices, such as the rectum, vagina, mouth, or aural opening, and have become generally accepted clinical indices of the physiological well-being of humans and other homeothermic animals. FEVER is a hyperthermia involving a change in the thermal regulatory system and is usually induced by toxins from bacterial infection. HIBERNATION is a special, controlled form of hypothermia exhibited by some small mammals, such as some ground squirrels, chipmunks, hedgehogs, and bats. For most of the year, hibernators act as normal homeotherms; during the winter, however, when food is scarce, the control mechanism for homeothermy changes and the hibernators become poikilothermic, with a markedly reduced metabolism and a body temperature that follows the temperature of the environment. Temperature control is maintained, however: if body temperature falls too low, arousal occurs and tachymetabolic heat production mechanisms are activated to prevent freezing.

A negative FEEDBACK control system integrated in the central nervous system regulates the temperature of homeotherms. Warm and cold thermoreceptors in the core and periphery, particularly the skin, initiate electrical impulse discharges along nerves that lead to the central control system in the brain. When incoming signals from the warm receptors predominate over signals from the cold receptors, the heat-loss motor mechanisms are enhanced. Such mechanisms include increased blood flow to the skin, sweating, and panting. Similarly, when the signals from the cold receptors prevail, the body heat-conserving or heat-producing mechanisms are activated. Blood flow is reduced to the skin (vasoconstriction), and a fluffing out of feathers and hair occurs to increase entrapment of air and thus provide more thermal insulation. Heat production is increased by shivering and other such metabolic reactions. Conscious awareness of thermal discomfort usually exists, as well, invoking behavioral responses such that the animal will seek a more comfortable thermal environment.   B. A. YOUNG

Bibliography: Cossins, A. R., and Bowler, K., *Temperature Biology of Animals* (1987); Hales, J. R. S., ed., *Thermal Physiology* (1984); Houdas, Y., and Ring, E. F., eds., *Human Body Temperature* (1982); Precht, H., et al., *Temperature and Life* (1973); Stanier, M. W., et al., *Energy Balance and Temperature Regulation* (1984).

Boehler, Peter   [bur'-lur]

Peter Boehler, b. Dec. 31, 1712, d. Apr. 27, 1775, was a German bishop and missionary of the Moravian Church in America. Boehler left his native Germany to minister to the black slaves and a group of Moravians in Savannah, Ga. He later led (1740) the migration of the Georgia Moravians to Pennsylvania, where he founded Nazareth and Bethlehem. After serving in England as superintendent of the Moravians from 1747 to 1753, he returned to America as a bishop and continued his work of establishing new Moravian communities.

Bibliography: Lockwood, J. P., *Memorials of the Life of Peter Boehler* (1868).

Boehm, Martin   [baym]

Martin Boehm, b. Nov. 30, 1725, d. Mar. 23, 1812, was one of the founders of the Church of the United Brethren in Christ. Born in Lancaster County, Pa., the son of German immigrants, he began his career as an itinerant preacher and revivalist. Boehm knew both English and German, but most frequently preached in German. He was selected a bishop by the Mennonites in 1759, but they later excluded him because he departed from traditional Mennonite customs. He was an early associate of Francis ASBURY and shared with Philip OTTERBEIN in the organization of the United Brethren. In 1800, Boehm and Otterbein were chosen the first bishops of that denomination.   JOHN F. PIPER, JR.

Boehme, Jakob: see BÖHME, JAKOB.

Boeing, William Edward   [boh'-ing]

William Edward Boeing, b. Detroit, Oct. 1, 1881, d. Sept. 28, 1956, was a pioneer in the U.S. aircraft industry. After study-

ing at Yale University's Sheffield Scientific School, he entered his father's lumber business in Seattle. In 1916 he switched to the manufacture of airplanes by founding the Pacific Aero Products Company, which later became the Boeing Airplane Company. He helped design the company's first plane, a two-seat seaplane for the U.S. Navy, the forerunner of a long line of military and commercial aircraft. In 1927 he also founded Boeing Air Transport, which, through a merger, later became United Air Lines.

Bibliography: Taylor, M. J., ed., *Planemakers: Boeing* (1982).

Boeotia   [bee-oh'-shuh]

Boeotia is the name of a region of about 2,580 km² (1,100 mi²) in ancient Greece; it lay north of Attica and the Corinthian Gulf. To the north and south of its rich plains, where the important cities of THEBES and ORCHOMENUS were located, the terrain is rough and rocky. Inhabited from Neolithic times, and the site of an important Bronze Age settlement, the area was settled by Thessalians at the time of the Trojan War. Largely agricultural in character and dominated politically by Thebes, Boeotia was the site of major battles between rival Greek city-states (Plataea, Leuctra, Coronea, and Chaeronea). The Boeotian League was formed in the 7th century BC and was controlled with only brief interruption by Thebes. Boeotia was the homeland of several poets, of whom PINDAR and HESIOD are the foremost.

Boer War: see SOUTH AFRICAN WAR.

Boerhaave, Hermann   [boor'-hah-ve]

The Dutch physician Hermann Boerhaave, b. Dec. 31, 1668, d. Sept. 23, 1738, is considered the founder of clinical teaching. At the University of Leiden in the early 18th century, he introduced the practice of teaching medical students at patients' bedsides. Boerhaave was the first to isolate urea; to describe the sweat glands, publishing an anatomy book on glands; and to establish that smallpox is spread only by contact.

Bibliography: Lindeboom, G. A., *Herman Boerhaave* (1968).

Boers: see AFRIKANERS.

Boethius, Anicius Manlius Severinus   [boh-ee'-thee-uhs]

Boethius, c.480–c.524, was a philosopher and statesman who was descended from an ancient Roman family. Orphaned at an early age, he received a classical education in Latin and Greek. A friend and advisor of Theodoric, king of the Ostrogoths who occupied Italy, he became a Roman consul in 510 and *magister officiorum* (''master of the Palace'') in 522. Unjustly charged with treason in his relations with Pope John I, he was executed by Theodoric.

During his imprisonment at Ticinum (Pavia), Boethius composed the classic *On the Consolation of Philosophy*. Seeing the ancient civilization crumbling around him, he translated most of Aristotle's treatises on logic into Latin, commented on some of them, wrote brief treatises on logic, summarized Euclid's *Geometry* and the *Arithmetic* and *Music* of Nicomachus of Gerasa, and composed five important theological treatises. These became the major source of early medieval education in the liberal arts and the most succinct presentations of Christian Greek theology on the Trinity, the incarnation, and the creed. He has been justly called ''the last of the Romans, the first of the Scholastics.''   JAMES A. WEISHEIPL

Bibliography: Barrett, Helen M., *Boethius* (1940); Lerer, Seth, *Boethius and Dialogue* (1985).

Boffrand, Germain   [baw-frahn']

Gabrie Germain Boffrand, b. May 7, 1667, d. Mar. 18, 1754, was a prolific French architect whose career spanned the period of transition from the baroque to the rococo. He went to Paris in 1681, where he first studied sculpture with François Girardon. About 1685 he joined the architectural workshop of JULES HARDOUIN MANSART, with whom he worked at VERSAILLES and the Place Vendôme in Paris. During Boffrand's long career, he traveled to Lorraine, Bavaria, and other parts of modern Germany, where he exerted a strong influence, particularly on Johann Balthasar Neumann's Würzburg Residenz. His early work resembles François Mansart's in its bold and simple classicism. The grandeur of the style of Louis XIV, however, gradually gave way to the flamboyant rococo style associated with Louis XV. Boffrand designed several private houses in Paris, including the Hôtel Seignelay (1718), and several châteaus, such as the Château d'Haroué (1712–13) in Lorraine. The interior decoration of the Hôtel de Soubise (1732–37) in Paris is his best-known work. He published the treatise *Livre d'Architecture* (1745), which established the tenets of 18th-century French classicism.   MARVIN D. SCHWARTZ

Bibliography: Norberg-Schulz, Christian, *Late Baroque and Rococo Architecture* (1974; repr. 1985).

bog: see SWAMP, MARSH, AND BOG.

bog iron ore: see LIMONITE.

bog rosemary

Bog rosemary, *Andromeda*, refers to two species of plants in the family Ericaceae. Native to peat bogs in North America, Europe, and Asia, the low evergreen shrubs have leathery leaves and pink to white flowers in nodding, terminal groups. They are not the rosemary used in perfume and seasoning but are grown in rock gardens and are used as border plants.
JANE PHILPOTT

bog turtle

The bog turtle, *Clemmys muhlenbergi*, family Emydidae, often called Muhlenberg's turtle, is a small species, usually less than 10 cm (4 in) in length, with a dark carapace (upper shell) and orange (occasionally yellow) blotches on the side of the head. It is one of the rarest turtles in North America, living only in sphagnum bogs and swamps in several scattered populations from New York to North Carolina. Formerly popular as a pet, it has been designated an endangered species because of habitat destruction.   JONATHAN CAMPBELL

Bogalusa   [boh-guh-loo'-suh]

Bogalusa (1990 pop., 14,280) is a logging city in Washington Parish in southeastern Louisiana. It is located at the northern terminus of the Pearl River Navigation Canal. Bogalusa has developed into a major production center of lumber, paper, and tung oil.

Bogan, Louise   [boh'-guhn]

A distinguished American poet and critic, Louise Bogan, b. Livermore, Maine, Aug. 11, 1897, d. Feb. 4, 1970, was poetry critic for the *New Yorker* magazine from 1931 to 1968. In 1945 she held the chair in poetry at the Library of Congress. Her criticism is collected in *Selected Criticism: Prose, Poetry* (1955) and *A Poet's Alphabet* (1970). For *Collected Poems, 1923–53* (1954) she shared the 1954 Bollingen Prize in Poetry with Léonie Adams. A larger volume of poems, *The Blue Estuaries*, appeared in 1969. Her lyrical style was well suited to her themes: the limitations of love and the consolations of art. *What the Woman Lived* (1974) is a posthumous collection of letters.

Bibliography: Frank, E., *Louise Bogan* (1985).

Bogarde, Dirk   [boh'-gard]

The Anglo-Dutch actor Dirk Bogarde, b. Mar. 28, 1921, had a disastrous career in Hollywood before blossoming as an international actor. He has appeared in more than 60 films, including *Victim* (1961), *The Servant* (1963), *Darling* (1965), *The Damned* (1969), *Justine* (1969), *Death in Venice* (1971), *The Night Porter* (1974), *Despair* (1978), and *Daddy Nostalgia* (1990). In the late 1970s he began writing and has published autobiographical volumes and novels.   LESLIE HALLIWELL

Bogardus, James

James Bogardus, b. Catskill, N.Y., Mar. 14, 1800, d. Apr. 13, 1874, an American engineer and inventor, is considered the originator of the cast-iron building facade in the United States. Made of separate components, these facades, which could be shipped anywhere and assembled, were the forerunners of prefabricated building parts and of the steel-frame construction used in skyscrapers. The craze for CAST-IRON ARCHITECTURE came about because iron was fire-resistant, could be cast in any shape, was comparatively cheap, and could be substituted for load-bearing masonry walls.

Bogardus patented designs for buildings made entirely of iron and glass. Among his best-known works were designs (1853; rejected) for the New York Crystal Palace exhibition; his own 5-story cast-iron foundry in New York (1848–49); and the Harper and Brothers Building in New York (1854).
RON WIEDENHOEFT

Bibliography: Bogardus, James, *Origins of Cast Iron Architecture in America* (1856; repr. 1970); Condit, Carl W., *American Building* (1968).

Bogart, Humphrey

The American actor Humphrey Bogart, shown in a scene from Across the Pacific *(1942), began his motion-picture career in 1936 in* The Petrified Forest. *Despite a box-office image that typecast him as a rugged antihero, Bogart was one of the most versatile actors of his time. He won an Academy Award for his portrayal of the seedy riverboat pilot in* The African Queen *(1951).*

The film star Humphrey De Forest Bogart, b. New York City, Dec. 25, 1899, d. Jan. 14, 1957, was one of Hollywood's greatest box-office attractions. He had an early career on the Broadway stage until his performance as Duke Mantee in *The Petrified Forest* (1936) catapulted him onto the screen in a film version of the play. In a string of successful films that followed, he generally played hard-boiled detectives and other cynical but moral characters. Some of his most popular films were *The Maltese Falcon* (1941); *Casablanca* (1942), with Ingrid Bergman; *The Big Sleep* (1946), costarring his wife, Lauren Bacall; *The Treasure of Sierra Madre* (1948); and the film that won him an Academy Award, *The African Queen* (1951), with Katharine Hepburn.

Bibliography: Barbour, Alan D., *Humphrey Bogart* (1973); Hepburn, Katharine, *The Making of "The African Queen"* (1987); McCarty, Clifford, *Bogey: The Films of Humphrey Bogart* (1965); Pettigrew, Terence, *The Bogart File* (1981).

Boğazköy   [boh-ahz-ku'-ee]

Boğazköy, a village in north central Turkey about 200 km (125 mi) east of Ankara, adjoins the ancient settlement of Hattuša, renowned capital of the HITTITES. First inhabited in the late 3d millennium BC, this Anatolian settlement subsequently became the site of an Assyrian merchant colony. It was destroyed c.1720 BC and reoccupied during the next century, after which it became the center of Hittite rule (c.1600–c.1200 BC).

Hattuša covered some 166 ha (410 acres) at the height of the Hittite period. Major monuments include the citadel with its royal and administrative buildings, five temple complexes, and the massive defensive enclosure wall with its famous lion, sphinx, and so-called king's gates. The 13th-century BC rock sanctuary of Yazilikaya, containing reliefs of deities and kings, is located 2 km (1.2 mi) northeast of Boğazköy. Formal excavations at the site were directed by Hugo Winckler of the German Orient Society in 1906–07 and 1911–12, and under Kurt Bittel in 1931–39; fieldwork was resumed in 1952. Boğazköy's royal archives, containing thousands of cuneiform tablets, are a major source of information about Hittite history and culture.   LOUISE ALPERS BORDAZ

Bibliography: Bittel, Kurt, *Hattusha: The Capital of the Hittites* (1970).

Bogomils [bohhg'-uh-meelz]

The Bogomils (a Slavic word meaning "pleasing to God") were members of a medieval religious sect that adopted the principles of MANICHAEISM and DUALISM, professing that good and evil are the two equally divine principles in the life of the world. The Bogomils were particularly numerous in 8th-century Bulgaria, where they were also known as Messalians or PAULICIANS. They believed in the possibility of a perfect life, which required abstention from sexual contacts, meat, and wine. In their view, however, such a life was accessible to only a few, who were then entitled to leadership over the sinners. They rejected the hierarchy and sacraments of the Christian church and were intermittently persecuted by civil authorities. During the 11th century, they spread to Italy and France, where they were known as Cathari ("the pure ones"), or ALBIGENSES. In the late Middle Ages, their major center was located in Bosnia. After the Turkish conquest of the Balkans, most Bogomils adopted Islam.   JOHN MEYENDORFF

Bogotá [boh-goh-tah']

Bogotá, founded in 1538 as Santa Fe de Bogotá, is the capital of Colombia. It is situated more than 2,590 m (8,500 ft) above sea level at the eastern edge of the Basin of Cundinamarca and is near the geographical center of Colombia. The largest city in the country and one of the fastest growing in Latin America, Bogotá has a population of 4,819,696 (1990 est.). Although located at an equatorial latitude, the high altitude

Bogotá is situated at the western edge of the Andean mountain Monserrate. It is the capital and the largest city of Colombia. Until the establishment of airline service in 1922, Bogotá was isolated by its mountainous surroundings and has only recently developed into a commercial center.

moderates its climate. Average annual temperature is about 14° C (58° F), and the climate changes little through the year. Relatively inaccessible until recently, Bogotá is now easily reached both by air and by the national highway system.

Bogotá is sometimes known as the Athens of America, and it has long been one of the hemisphere's centers for writers, intellectuals, and artists. Its university was founded in 1572. In addition to supporting many newspapers and literary journals, Bogotá has a thriving book-publishing industry. The mixture of colonial architecture and modernistic structures gives the city a strikingly cosmopolitan appearance. Since it is the seat of national government, its daily life is highly political. The city has autonomous status and is governed by a mayor appointed by the president. Bogotá is less dominant in the country's economy than many Latin American capitals. Though less important than MEDELLÍN and BARRANQUILLA, however, Bogotá nonetheless generates more than one-third of Colombian economic output.

Bogotá had, by the end of the 16th century, already become a major cultural center of the Spanish colonies in the New World. In 1717 it became the capital of the viceroyalty of NEW GRANADA. Following independence (1819), it was the capital of Gran Colombia (composed of what are now Venezuela, Colombia, Panama, and Ecuador) and with the 1830 dissolution of the federation became the Colombian capital. The single most dramatic event in recent years was the Apr. 9, 1948, *bogotazo*, when the assassination of liberal leader Jorge Gaitán precipitated 24 hours of violence, causing great destruction. Although the fury of this outbreak has never been repeated, political confrontations are common.   JOHN D. MARTZ

Bohan, Marc: see FASHION DESIGN.

Bohème, La [boh-em', lah]

Of all Giacomo PUCCINI's operas, none has surpassed the appeal of *La Bohème*—first given at the Teatro Regio, Turin, on Feb. 1, 1896, under Arturo Toscanini. The opera is in four acts, with a libretto by Luigi Illica and Giuseppe Giacosa based on the novel by Henri Murger, *Scènes de la Vie de Bohème*. Set in the Latin Quarter of Paris about 1830, it features the tragic love story of the poet Rodolfo and Mimi, a consumptive seamstress. *La Bohème* is one of the best-known examples of VERISMO, or operatic realism. Although a comparative failure at its first performance, after its third presentation, in Palermo (1896), its true merits were recognized. The American premiere took place in Los Angeles on Oct. 14, 1897, and it was first performed at the Metropolitan Opera on May 16, 1898.   ROBERT LAWRENCE

Bohemia

Bohemia (Czech: Cechy) is a former kingdom of central Europe; today Bohemia and the neighboring territory of MORAVIA form the Czech Republic, which was part of Czechoslovakia until the end of 1992. Bohemia, divided administratively into six regions, contains about three-quarters of the republic's population and is its most industrialized region. PRAGUE (Praha), the principal city, is the capital of the Czech Republic. Geographically, Bohemia comprises lowlands drained by the Elbe (Labe) River that are surrounded by four ranges of mountains and hills: the Ore Mountains (Krušné Hory) to the northwest, the SUDETEN MOUNTAINS (Sudety) to the northeast, the Šumava and Bohemian Forest to the southwest, and the Bohemian-Moravian Uplands to the southeast. The northernmost part of Bohemia was traditionally called SUDETENLAND.

The name *Bohemia* is derived from that of the Boii, a Celtic people who inhabited the area in Roman times. The Slavic Czechs appear to have settled there by the 6th century, and in the 7th century they founded a short-lived state under Samo, a ruler of Frankish origin. The Czech PREMYSL dynasty was established in the region by the 9th century, when Christianity was introduced. In the period that followed, Bohemia developed close ties with neighboring German states and was drawn into the orbit of the Holy Roman Empire. In 1198 the

The map indicates the boundaries of Bohemia, the western part of the Czech Republic. When the Habsburg empire collapsed after World War I, Bohemia joined Moravia, Slovakia, and portions of Silesia to form the Czechoslovak republic. The Czech Republic separated from Slovakia at the end of 1992.

Premsyl prince Ottokar I was granted the hereditary title king of Bohemia by Emperor Henry VI. Early in the 14th century the crown passed to the house of Luxemburg, and in 1355 the Luxemburg king Charles I of Bohemia became Holy Roman Emperor CHARLES IV. Under Charles, Prague became an important European cultural center, and the prestige of the Bohemian monarchy was greatly enhanced. In the 15th century the HUSSITES, a native Czech religious reform party, were able for a time to challenge the entrenched power of the Catholic church. Beginning in 1526, Bohemia was ruled by the Austrian HABSBURGS, and its history belongs to that of Austria from the mid-17th century until the establishment of Czechoslovakia in 1918. Bohemia survived as a province of Czechoslovakia until 1949, when it was divided into regions. It remained part of Czechoslovakia until 1992.

Bohemond I, Prince of Antioch   [boh'-uh-muhnd, an'-tee-ahk]

Bohemond I, b. c.1058, was a distinguished Norman leader of the First CRUSADE, who founded the principality of ANTIOCH. A son of ROBERT GUISCARD, duke of Apulia (in southern Italy), Bohemond cooperated in his father's campaign (1081–85) against the Byzantines. Deprived of the ducal inheritance in favor of a stepbrother, he joined the First Crusade in 1096 and claimed Antioch in 1098. Exhausted by its defense against Turks and Byzantines, he returned to Italy in 1104 to organize an anti-Byzantine crusade. He was defeated, however, by the Byzantine emperor ALEXIUS I in 1108 and died in retirement in Italy on Mar. 7, 1111.   C. M. BRAND

Bohlen, Charles Eustis   [boh'-luhn]

Charles E. Bohlen, b. Clayton, N.Y., Aug. 30, 1904, d. Jan. 1, 1974, was an American diplomat who was a recognized expert on the USSR for more than 30 years. Bohlen entered the foreign service in 1929 and played an active role in formulating U.S. policy toward the USSR from 1934, when he was first assigned to Moscow as a consular official. During World War II, Bohlen served as Russian interpreter to Presidents Roosevelt and Truman at the Teheran, Yalta, and Potsdam conferences. He was later ambassador to the USSR (1953–57), the Philippines (1957–59), and France (1962–68).

Bibliography: Bohlen, Charles E., *Witness to History* (1973).

Böhm, Gottfried   [burm]

Gottfried Böhm, b. Jan. 23, 1920, a postmodern German architect, was the winner of the 1986 Pritzker Prize. The son of Dominikus Böhm, a distinguished church architect, he has himself designed many religious buildings, including Saint Albert's church in Saarbrücken (1952–54) and a pilgrimage church complex at Neviges, near Düsseldorf (1964). A later example of his work is Zueblin House (1984), an office build-

ing outside Stuttgart. Böhm's style, while influenced by historic forms, is at the same time idiosyncratic and boldly innovational.

Böhm, Karl

The Austrian musician Karl Böhm, b. Aug. 28, 1894, d. Aug. 14, 1981, was one of the most notable opera conductors of the 20th century. Conductor of the Munich State Opera (1921–27) and general music director in Darmstadt (1927–31), Hamburg (1931–34), and Dresden (1934–42), Böhm was twice director of the Vienna State Opera (1943–45, 1954–56); in 1955 he reopened the reconstructed opera house with a historic performance of Beethoven's *Fidelio*. For more than 25 years, Böhm was the principal conductor of the Salzburg Festival, where he was best known for his Mozart and Richard Strauss performances. He was also admired for his interpretation of Wagner.   STEPHANIE VON BUCHAU

Böhme, Jakob   [burm'-eh]

Jakob Böhme (or Boehme), b. 1575, d. Nov. 17, 1624, was a German Protestant mystical writer who profoundly influenced a number of philosophers and theologians, including G. W. F. HEGEL and F. W. J. SCHELLING. Born of peasant stock, he received an elementary education and became a master shoemaker. At the age of 36 he abandoned his trade and began his mystical writings, supporting himself by making and selling woolen gloves.

Writings by an untrained layman, however, attracted scrutiny by church and state, and this led to charges against Böhme. Forbidden to write after his *Aurora, Oder die Morgenröte im Aufgang* (Aurora, or the Rising of the Dawn, 1612), he broke his silence in 1623 with *Der Weg zu Christo* (The Way to Christ), a devotional work. He was under prosecution at the time of his death.

Böhme's works describe his mystical vision. He held that God is the substance that underlies the universe. Böhme identified God as Abyss (*Ungrund*) and Primal Foundation (*Urgrund*), representing a polarity of all and nothing that underlies the polar tensions in all reality. This abiding succession described by Böhme was later popularized in the dialectic of Hegel.   JAMES D. NELSON

Bibliography: Hartmann, F., *Life of Jacob Boehme* (1985); Walsh, D., *The Mysticism of Innerworldly Fulfillment* (1983).

Bohr, Aage Niels   [bor, aw'-ge neels]

Aage Niels Bohr, b. June 19, 1922, one of the six sons of famous Danish physicist Niels Bohr, shared a Nobel Prize in 1975 for discovering the asymmetry of atomic nuclei. Bohr served as director of the Niels Bohr Institute in Copenhagen from 1962 to 1975. His many honors include the 1969 Atoms for Peace Award.   CARL ZAPFFE

Bohr, Niels

Niels Henrik David Bohr was one of the most important theoretical physicists of the 20th century. Through his own work and through his influence on younger physicists, he played a major role in formulating and interpreting QUANTUM MECHANICS, the theory used to describe atomic and subatomic phenomena.

Bohr was born in Copenhagen on Oct. 7, 1885. His father was a professor of physiology. Bohr's training took place at the University of Copenhagen, where he received a doctorate in 1911 and presented a thesis in which he studied the electron theory of the structure of metals.

In 1911, Bohr went to Cambridge, England, to work with J. J. Thomson, then the leading atomic theorist. This collaboration did not work well, and after a few months Bohr made the happy decision to move to Manchester, England, to work with Ernest Rutherford. Rutherford had recently formulated the nuclear model of the atom, and Bohr used this theory in his own work, the application of quantum ideas to atomic structure and spectra.

Niels Bohr, a Danish physicist, founded the modern quantum theory of matter. He is best known for his investigations of atomic structure and radiation, for which he won the 1922 Nobel Prize for physics. This photograph was taken in 1925.

This work was carried out in Manchester and also Copenhagen, to which Bohr returned in 1912 to be married. In Copenhagen Bohr wrote three major papers in which he laid the foundation of a quantum theory of atoms. In this work, Bohr pointed out that atoms could not be described solely through the application of the concepts of classical physics. He proposed that an electron in an atom ordinarily resides in one of a discrete number of possible orbits, called stationary states, and each state corresponds to an angular momentum that is an integer multiple of Planck's constant divided by 2π. Applying this assumption to the hydrogen atom, Bohr calculated the energies of the stationary states and showed that the known frequencies of light emitted by hydrogen could be expressed as the difference between two such energies. This implied that the electron (and hence atom) emits radiation only when jumping from one stationary state to another.

The success of these calculations did much to convince physicists of the importance of quantum ideas, and Bohr was awarded the Nobel Prize in physics in 1922. He had already, in 1920, been named the director of the new Institute for Theoretical Physics in Copenhagen. In the 1920s, Bohr, through his teaching and through discussions with Albert Einstein and others, displayed leadership in the quest to understand the meaning of quantum mechanics. His contributions to the formulation of Heisenberg's UNCERTAINTY PRINCIPLE were especially important. As a result the way in which quantum mechanics is understood by most physicists is called the Copenhagen interpretation.

In the late 1930s, Bohr's interest turned to nuclear physics, and he formulated the "liquid drop" model of the nucleus. With the aid of this model, Bohr realized, soon after the discovery of uranium fission, that it was the isotope U-235 that was fissioned by slow neutrons. This discovery was instrumental in the development of the atomic bomb. In 1943, Bohr escaped from occupied Denmark, and for the remainder of World War II he worked in the United States, contributing to the atomic bomb project. After the war he returned to his homeland and spoke out periodically about the need for responsible nuclear policy. Bohr died in Denmark on Nov. 18, 1962. GERALD FEINBERG

Bibliography: Bohr, Niels, *Niels Bohr Collected Works*, 6 vols. (1973–85); Moore, Ruth E., *Niels Bohr: The Man, His Science, and the World They Changed* (1966).

Bohr magneton

The Bohr magneton is the fundamental unit for the intrinsic MAGNETIC MOMENT of the electron, that is, the unit of intensity of the magnetic field resulting from the orbital motion of an electron about the nucleus of an atom. The magnitude of the Bohr magneton, 9.274×10^{-24} ampere-meter^2, may be calculated from its definition in terms of other physical constants, $\mu_B = eh/4\pi m$, in which e is the charge of the electron, h is PLANCK'S CONSTANT, and m is the mass of the electron.

Boiardo, Matteo Maria [boy-ahr'-doh, mah-tay'-oh mah-ree'-ah]

Matteo Maria Boiardo, b. *c.*1440, d. Dec. 19, 1494, was an Italian poet and diplomat. As a classical humanist he translated Herodotus, Xenophon, and Apuleius. The poetry of his *Canzoniere* (1499) was written for Antonia Caprara in the tradition of Petrarch. The characters of his unfinished epic *Orlando innamorato* (1483) are derived from the French epic of *Roland*, yet love rather than battle is its central theme. ARIOSTO wrote the incomparable sequel in his ORLANDO FURIOSO (1532).

OSCAR BÜDEL

Boieldieu, François Adrien [bwahl-dee-oo', frahn-swah' ah-dree-an']

François Adrien Boieldieu, b. Dec. 16, 1775, d. Oct. 8, 1834, was a composer of French comic operas. The great success of his opera *Le Calife de Bagdad* (1800) helped win him the post of music director to Tsar Alexander I, a position he held from 1803 to 1811. On his return to Paris, Boieldieu found a public eager for the light, melodious, and elegant music and romantic fantasy of his *Jean de Paris* (1812). His masterpiece and most popular work, *La Dame Blanche* (1825), based on stories by Sir Walter Scott, received 1,000 performances in Paris alone in 37 years. Besides 40 operas, Boieldieu wrote songs and composed for the piano. JOHN WALTER HILL

boil

A boil is a painful, swollen ABSCESS of the skin. It is usually caused by the bacteria *Staphylococcus aureus*, which enters a hair follicle or an oil gland duct. Although the boil feels hard to the touch, it is actually filled with pus. The accumulation of pus puts pressure on adjacent nerves and causes inflammation. Boils occur in areas that are frequently chafed, such as the neck, face, ear, and extremities; but they may occur anywhere on the body. A STY is a boil located at the hair follicle of an eyelash, and a CARBUNCLE is a group of adjoining boils. Treatment of a small boil consists of keeping the area clean, avoiding irritation, and applying antibiotic ointments. Large boils, particularly on the face, can cause blood poisoning, or SEPTICEMIA. They must be treated medically by draining the boil of pus and applying antibiotics.

Boileau-Despréaux, Nicolas [bwah-loh'-day-pray-oh', nik-oh-lah']

Nicolas Boileau, b. Nov. 1, 1636, d. Mar. 11, 1711, known as Despréaux, was a French poet and essayist whose critical verse treatise *L'Art poétique* (The Art of Poetry, 1674) contributed to the formulation of French CLASSICISM. Boileau had many friends in high positions, but he also made many enemies as a result of a series of biting satires published between 1666 and 1711. He burlesqued the clergy in the mock epic *Le Lutrin* (The Lectern, 1683) but softened his satire in a number of *Épîtres* (Epistles), produced between 1675 and 1698.

Bibliography: Bray, R., *Boileau* (1942); Pocock, Gordon, *Boileau and the Nature of Neoclassicism* (1980).

boiler

A boiler is an apparatus that converts water to steam, at a pressure above the surroundings, using an internal source of heat. Boilers are used to produce steam for operating steam turbines both in electrical generating plants and on board ships and to supply steam for industrial processes. The source of heat can be either the combustion of a fossil fuel (coal, oil, or natural gas) or the nuclear fission of a radioactive substance such as uranium-235.

Fossil-fuel boilers contain a combustion chamber or furnace in which the fuel is burned, a means of transferring the heat from the hot combustion gases to the water, and a way of containing the water and steam. In the water-tube boiler the furnace walls are lined with heat-absorbing alloy steel tubes through which water flows. In absorbing heat from the com-

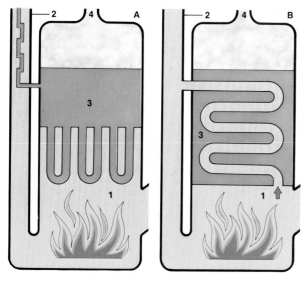

In the water-tube boiler (A), water is led down through pipes into the combustion chamber or furnace (1). Water entering the system is preheated by entry through the smokestack (2). The fire-tube boiler (B) routes hot combustion gases through pipes that enter the main water chamber (3) before reaching the smokestack. In both cases, the steam generated is collected from a point (4) well above the boiling water, at the top of the main chambers.

bustion gases, the water is converted into steam. The water may be preheated and the steam superheated by passing it through tubes over which the combustion gases move on their way to the smokestack. Modern electrical generating stations use water-tube boilers with heights of up to 45 m (150 ft) and 2.8 m² (30 ft²) cross sections. Such boilers can produce up to 204,000 kg (450,000 lbs) of steam per hour, at pressures up to 34 megapascals (5,000 lbs per square inch) and at a maximum temperature of 566° C (1050° F). In one hour they can consume up to 91 tons (100 U.S. tons) of pulverized coal, or 64 tons (70 U.S. tons) of oil, or 56,000 m³ (2 million ft³) of natural gas.

The fire-tube boiler consists of a tank containing a furnace and tubes through which the combustion gases pass from the boiler to the smokestack. The tank is partially filled with water until the furnace and tubes are completely immersed. Heat from the combustion gases boils the water in contact with the tubes, and the steam gathers in the space above the water.

In a NUCLEAR REACTOR the water is pumped over plates made from the fissionable material, absorbing the heat produced by the nuclear reaction. For the same total amount of heat released the nuclear-reactor steam boiler is much smaller than the fossil-fuel boiler.

In 1698 the English inventor Thomas Savery was granted a patent for a steam-operated water pump that used a large kettle with a fire built under it to generate steam. A water-tube boiler was patented in 1766, but most early boilers were variations on the fire-tube design. The demand for greater steam pressures led to the development of the water-tube boiler, which is the type most commonly used today.

EUAN F. C. SOMERSCALES

boiling point

The boiling point is the temperature at which a liquid boils. Boiling is a thermodynamic phenomenon in which a liquid churns violently and releases vapor bubbles. The best-known boiling point is that of water, normally 100° C (212° F). A less-common liquid is liquid oxygen, which boils at −183° C (−297° F). At the boiling point the VAPOR PRESSURE of a liquid is equal to the local atmospheric pressure. Thus, the exact boiling temperature is a function of atmospheric conditions and altitude. The temperature of a boiling liquid remains at the boiling point, even if more than enough heat to maintain boiling is applied.

GARY S. SETTLES

Boilly, Louis Léopold   [bwah-yee']

Louis Léopold Boilly, b. July 5, 1761, d. Jan. 4, 1845, was a popular painter and engraver known for his genre and anecdotal paintings and portraits. Curious and technically adept, he was an untiring observer of the social scene in France. Typical works are *Arrival of the Coach* (1803; Louvre); *Impromptu Concert* (1790; Musée Hôtel Sandelin, Saint Omer); and *Studio of Isabey* (1798; Louvre), which revived the Dutch tradition of group portraits. He escaped execution during the French Revolution by painting a picture of Marat, now in the museum at Lille.   SUZANNE J. WILSON

Boise   [boy'-zee]

Boise is the capital and largest city in Idaho and the seat of Ada County. Located on the Boise River, it lies west of the Rocky Mountains at an altitude of 835 m (2,740 ft) and has a population of 125,738 (1990). Boise is a trade center for a large agricultural and livestock-raising region in southwestern Idaho and eastern Oregon. The main industries are meat-packing, food processing, wholesale trade and trucking, and manufacture of steel and lumber products. State and federal agencies are also major employers. Points of interest include Boise State University (1932), the state capital building, and Julia Davis Park, which contains an art gallery, a museum, pioneer buildings, and a zoo.

Boise was founded after the 1862 gold rush in Boise Basin, at the crossroads of the Oregon Trail and a primary mining route. Its development was aided by lumbering and agricultural activities, especially after implementation (1902) of the Boise Irrigation Project.

Boito, Arrigo   [boh-ee'-toh, ah-ree'-goh]

Arrigo Boito, b. Feb. 24, 1842, d. June 10, 1918, was an Italian poet and composer best known for his opera *Mefistofele* and his librettos for VERDI's operas *Otello* and *Falstaff*. *Mefistofele*, with a libretto by the composer, was first performed at La Scala in 1868 and later revised, in which version it has remained in the standard repertory. Boito began another opera but did not finish it. Although he wrote the libretto for Ponchielli's *La Gioconda*, his librettos for *Otello* and *Falstaff* are considered his masterpieces. Boito also made admirable translations of some of Richard Wagner's operas.

Bojer, Johan   [boy'-ur]

Johan Bojer, b. Mar. 6, 1872, d. July 3, 1959, was a Norwegian novelist who enjoyed great international popularity during the 1920s and '30s. His most important works include *The Power of a Lie* (1903; Eng. trans., 1908), *The Great Hunger* (1916; Eng. trans., 1918), *Last of the Vikings* (1921; Eng. trans., 1923), and *Folk by the Sea* (1929; Eng. trans., 1931). The latter two novels, in which Bojer describes the daily lives of Norwegian fishermen and farmers, are considered his best. *The Emigrants* (1924; Eng. trans., 1925) is about the Norwegian emigration to the United States.   KJETIL A. FLATIN

Bibliography: Beyer, Harald, *A History of Norwegian Literature* (1956); Gad, Carl, *Johan Bojer,* trans. by Elizabeth J. Macintire (1920; repr. 1974).

Bok, Bart Jan

The Dutch-born American astronomer Bart Jan Bok, b. Apr. 28, 1906, d. Aug. 5, 1983, was known for his research on the structure and dynamics of the Milky Way galaxy. A graduate (1932) of the University of Groningen, Holland, Bok was professor of astronomy at Harvard (1933–57), the Australian National University (1957–66), and the University of Arizona (1966–74) and was director (1966–70) of the Steward Observatory in Tucson, Ariz.   STEVEN J. DICK

Bok, Edward William

Edward William Bok, b. den Helder, the Netherlands, Oct. 9, 1863, d. Lake Wales, Fla., Jan. 9, 1930, an editor of the *Ladies' Home Journal*, was a significant figure in the development of the modern women's magazine.

Bok immigrated to New York City in 1870, and in 1886 he founded the Bok Syndicate Press, which distributed weekly articles by Henry Ward Beecher as well as a regular page of women's features. In 1889, Cyrus H. K. CURTIS made him editor of the *Journal*. Bok transformed the 6-year-old magazine into a potpourri of fiction, household hints, personal advice, and reader correspondence. Among its contributors were Grover Cleveland, Dwight L. Moody, Theodore Roosevelt, and Mark Twain. He monitored the *Journal*'s advertising and in 1892 banned patent medicine advertisements. The ensuing lawsuits led indirectly to the Food and Drug Act (1906).

Bok's autobiography, *The Americanization of Edward Bok* (1920), won a 1921 Pulitzer Prize for autobiography.

Bibliography: Hoff, Rhoda, ed., *America's Immigrants* (1967).

Bokassa, Jean Bedel   [boh-kah'-sah]

Jean Bedel Bokassa, b. Feb. 22, 1921, former army chief of staff, became president of the Central African Republic after staging (Dec. 31, 1965) a coup ousting his cousin, President David Dacko. In 1977 he crowned himself Emperor Bokassa I of the Central African Empire. Bokassa was overthrown in 1979 and sentenced to death in absentia in 1980 for crimes ranging from murder to embezzlement. After he voluntarily returned to the Central African Republic in 1986, he was retried and again sentenced to death; his sentence was commuted to 20 years hard labor in 1991. He was released in 1993.

Boker, George Henry   [boh'-kur]

An American poetic dramatist and diplomat, George Henry Boker, b. Philadelphia, Oct. 6, 1823, d. Jan. 2, 1890, wrote a number of popular blank-verse tragedies, the most famous being *Francesca da Rimini* (1855). Boker's poems about the Civil War are included in *Poems of the War* (1864).

Bolcom, William

William Elden Bolcom, b. Seattle, Wash., May 26, 1938, is a prolific and honored contemporary American composer. A graduate (1958) of the University of Washington, he has taught at the University of Michigan since 1973. His compositions range from symphonies to chamber works and electronic music; in 1988 his New Études for Piano, 1977–86, won a Pulitzer Prize. He may be best known, however, for his work in the ragtime revival and for his many recordings as a pianist and as an accompanist for both popular and classical singers. Like much of his other work, his opera *McTeague* (1992) is an eclectic mixture of musical idioms.

Boldini, Giovanni   [bohl-dee'-nee]

Giovanni Boldini, b. Dec. 31, 1842, d. Jan. 11, 1931, was an Italian portrait painter whose popularity in Paris, where he settled in 1872, was comparable to that of John Singer SARGENT in London. His most famous portrait is *James McNeill Whistler* (1897; Brooklyn Museum, New York). Boldini also produced numerous impressive landscapes.

Bibliography: Novotny, Fritz, *Painting and Sculpture in Europe 1780–1880* (1970; repr. 1992).

Boldrewood, Rolf: see BROWNE, THOMAS ALEXANDER.

Bolender, Todd   [boh'-len-dur]

Todd Bolender, b. Canton, Ohio, Feb. 17, 1919, is an American ballet dancer, choreographer, and company director. With New York City Ballet he created roles in key works by George Balanchine and Jerome Robbins. His own choreography, which includes *Mother Goose Suite*, has a simple, touching appeal. Since 1981 he has been artistic director of the State Ballet of Missouri, Kansas City.   TOBI TOBIAS

bolero   [boh-lair'-oh]

The bolero is a Spanish dance in moderate 3/4 time, with sharp turns, brilliant arm and hand movements, and stamping feet. It is also a Cuban song/dance form in slow to moderate 4/4 time, with lyrical love texts. The bolero is extremely popular in Latin America and is a standard international ballroom dance (sometimes misnamed rhumba).   THEODORE SOLÍS

Bolesław I, King of Poland   (Bolesław the Brave)
[boh'-les-lahv']

Bolesław I, b. c.966, d. 1025, was the first king of Poland. The son of Mieszko, the first Christian prince of that country, he began to rule on his father's death (992). In 1000 he obtained from Holy Roman Emperor OTTO III abolition of the tribute that Mieszko had agreed to pay and the creation of an independent Polish church administration, with a metropolitan at Gniezno.

Bolesław fought three wars against Otto's successor, HENRY II, and by the Treaty of Bautzen (1018) won recognition of Lusatia, Moravia, and Misnia (Meissen) as parts of Poland. He was crowned king shortly before his death.

boletus   [boh-lee'-tuhs]

Boletus is the common name for the club FUNGI belonging to the family Boletaceae in the class Basidiomycetes. The boletus is red to brown and umbrella-shaped with a cap usually 5–25 cm (2–10 in) across. It is widely distributed throughout North America and Europe. The edible *Boletus edulis,* also called cèpe, can be found in woods in the summer.

Boleyn, Anne   [boh-lin']

Anne Boleyn, b. 1507?, was the second wife of HENRY VIII of England and the mother of ELIZABETH I. Henry's infatuation with Anne—and his desire for a male heir—led him to divorce his first wife, CATHERINE OF ARAGON, a step that required breaking with the Roman Catholic church. Anne and Henry were married in January 1533, and Anne gave birth to Elizabeth in September. Henry soon lost interest in Anne, and finally in 1536, after the stillbirth of a boy, he had her arrested and tried for adultery. She was beheaded on May 19, 1536.

Bibliography: Ives, Eric W., *Anne Boleyn* (1987).

Bolger, Ray   [bohl'-jur]

Ray Bolger, b. Boston, Jan. 10, 1904, d. Jan. 16, 1987, was an American actor and dancer. His best-known stage role was in *Where's Charley?* (1948), in which he introduced what soon became his theme song, "Once in Love with Amy." He repeated this role for the movies in 1952 but is probably best remembered for his performance as the Scarecrow in the film *The Wizard of Oz* (1939).   LESLIE HALLIWELL

bolide: see METEOR AND METEORITE.

Bolingbroke, Henry St. John, 1st Viscount
[bahl'-ing-bruk]

Henry St. John, 1st Viscount Bolingbroke, b. Oct. 10, 1678, d. Dec. 12, 1751, was an English Tory minister during the reign of Queen ANNE and afterward an embittered spokesman for the opposition to Whig government. After serving (1704–08) as secretary at war, he became a secretary of state in 1710 and, with Robert HARLEY, helped negotiate (1713–14) the Treaty of Utrecht, which ended the War of the SPANISH SUCCESSION. Dismissed by GEORGE I in 1714, Bolingbroke fled to France and joined the JACOBITES. Permitted to return after 1723 but excluded from Parliament, he wrote against Sir Robert WALPOLE and the Whigs. His publications included *The Idea of a Patriot King* (1749), in which he upheld monarchy as a unifying power. A brilliant orator but also an unreliable self-seeker and a rake, he never regained his early influence.

Bibliography: Biddle, Sheila, *Bolingbroke and Harley* (1974); Hart, J., *Viscount Bolingbroke* (1965); Kramnick, Isaac, *Bolingbroke and His Circle* (1968; repr. 1992); Varey, Simon, ed., *Lord Bolingbroke* (1982).

See also: UTRECHT, PEACE OF.

Bolívar, Simón   [boh-leé-var, see-mohn']

Simón Bolívar, a brilliant general known as the Liberator, led the revolution against Spanish rule in northern South America in the early 19th century. His goal of uniting South America into one nation was never realized.

The Latin American revolutionary Simón Bolívar was the single most important person in the struggle against Spanish authority in what became known as the Bolivarian countries (Venezuela, Colombia, Ecuador, Peru, and Bolivia). He is called the ''Liberator.''

Born on July 24, 1783, to a wealthy landowning family in Caracas, Bolívar was educated largely by private tutors, most importantly Simón Rodríguez, from whom he became familiar with Enlightenment thought and especially the writings of Jean Jacques Rousseau. During a visit to Europe (1799-1802), he married a young Venezuelan woman who died after his return home.

During a second trip to Europe (1804) Bolívar vowed to fight for independence from Spain, emerging as a leader of the revolutionaries in 1810. He contributed to the July 5, 1811, declaration of independence in Venezuela and became a military leader. Soon driven from the country, he returned in 1813 to establish the second Venezuelan republic.

Later setbacks forced Bolívar to take refuge (1815) in Jamaica and later Haiti, but by 1817 he had again taken up arms on the mainland. He achieved a major victory in Colombia at the Battle of Boyacá on Aug. 7, 1819. That same year he convened the Angostura Congress to found Gran Colombia (a federation of present-day Venezuela, Colombia, Panama, and Ecuador), of which he became president. This action was formalized at Cúcuta in July 1821. A year later Bolívar met with Argentine José de SAN MARTÍN at Guayaquil, Ecuador, but this potentially momentous encounter ended inconclusively. Meanwhile, Antonio José de SUCRE had liberated Ecuador by his victory at Pichincha (May 1822), and subsequent victories in Peru—at Junín (August 1824) and Ayacucho (December 1824)—completed the ouster of the Spanish from the Bolivarian states.

By this time rival ambitions were producing outbursts of rebellion and defiance of Bolívar's authority. Eventually assuming dictatorial powers over Gran Colombia in 1828, he was still unable to create stability. The resulting problems, combined with a deterioration in his health, led to his disillusioned resignation in the spring of 1830. He died on December 17 of the same year. If ultimately unsuccessful in establishing liberal regimes committed to political liberties, he had nonetheless been the preeminent figure in the independence movement for the region.

Bolívar was an intellectual as well as a military and political figure, and his writings were often prophetic. His ''Jamaica Letter'' of 1815 acutely analyzed the traits and characteristics of Spanish-Americans, and the Angostura Discourse (1819) and the Bolivian constitution of 1826 outlined political ideals that retain their relevance. A lifetime of voluminous correspondence further enriched the literature on freedom, liberty, and forms of government. Bolívar also conceived the 1826 Congress of Panama, which is regarded as the first hemispheric diplomatic conference.   JOHN D. MARTZ

Bibliography: Bolívar, Simón, *Selected Writings of Bolívar*, comp. by V. Lecuna and ed. by H. A. Bierck, 2 vols. (1951); Bushnell, David, ed., *The Liberator, Simón Bolívar* (1970); Johnson, John H., *Bolívar and Spanish American Independence 1783–1830* (1968); Masur, Gerhard, *Simón Bolívar*, rev. ed. (1969); O'Leary, D., *Bolívar and the War of Independence*, trans. by R. McNerny (1970); Salcedo-Bastardo, J., *Bolívar* (1986); Trend, J., *Bolívar and the Independence of Spanish America* (1946); Wepman, D., *Bolívar* (1985).

Bolivia   [boh-liv'-ee-uh]

Bolivia is a landlocked country straddling the central Andes Mountains in west central South America. It is bounded on the north and east by Brazil, on the southeast by Paraguay, on the south by Argentina, and on the west by Chile and Peru. SUCRE is the judicial capital; LA PAZ is the administrative capital. Bolivia became a republic in 1825, when it gained independence from Spain. It is named for Simón Bolívar, the liberator of South America.

REPUBLIC OF BOLIVIA

LAND. Area: 1,098,581 km² (424,164 mi²). Capital (legal): Sucre (1985 est. pop., 86,609). Largest city and administrative capital: La Paz (1985 est. pop., 992,592).

PEOPLE. Population (1988 est.): 6,448,297; density: 5.9 persons per km² (15.2 per mi²). Distribution (1988): 49% urban, 51% rural. Annual growth (1987): 2.6%. Official languages: Spanish, Quechua, Aymará. Major religion: Roman Catholicism.

EDUCATION AND HEALTH. Literacy (1985): 63% of adult population. Universities (1986): 9. Hospital beds (1983): 10,789. Physicians (1984): 4,032. Life expectancy (1980–85): women—53.0; men—48.6. Infant mortality (1987): 110 per 1,000 live births.

ECONOMY. GDP (1987 est.): $3.87 billion; $610 per capita. Labor distribution (1983): agriculture—50%; services and utilities—26%; manufacturing—10%; mining—4%. Foreign trade (1985 est.): imports—$750 million; exports—$495 million; principal trade partners—United States, Argentina, Brazil, West Germany. Currency: 1 peso Boliviano=100 centavos.

GOVERNMENT. Type: republic. Legislature: Congress. Political subdivisions: 9 departments.

COMMUNICATIONS. Railroads (1986): 3,538 km (2,198 mi) total. Roads (1984): 40,987 km (25,468 mi) total. Major ports: none. Major airfields: 2.

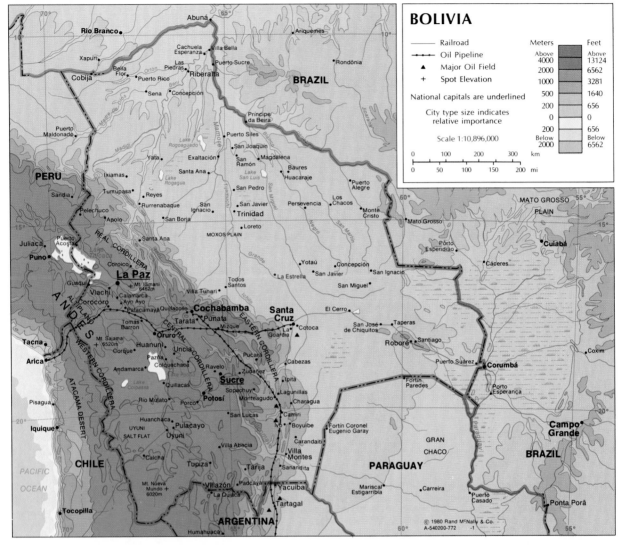

BOLIVIA

	Meters	Feet
Railroad	Above	Above
Oil Pipeline	4000	13124
▲ Major Oil Field	2000	6562
+ Spot Elevation	1000	3281
	500	1640
National capitals are underlined	200	656
City type size indicates	0	0
relative importance	200	656
	Below	Below
Scale 1:10,896,000	2000	6562

© 1980 Rand McNally & Co.
A-540200-772   -1

(Below) Lake Titicaca, the highest large navigable lake in the world, lies on Bolivia's western border with Peru. A succession of advanced pre-Columbian civilizations developed along its shores.

LAND AND RESOURCES

The southwestern quarter of Bolivia is dominated by the Andes Mountains, which reach their widest extent of 650 km (400 mi) in Bolivia and are divided into two great mountain chains, or cordilleras, separated by a broad upland plateau known as the Altiplano. The Western Cordillera forms Bolivia's eastern border with Chile; it rises to snowcapped peaks between 5,700 m (18,700 ft) and 6,500 m (21,300 ft) and reaches 7,014 m (23,012 ft) in Nevada de Ancohuma, which is the highest point in Bolivia. The Eastern Cordillera rises abruptly from the eastern Altiplano and is dominated by the snowcapped peaks of Illampu (6,485 m/21,231 ft) and Illimani (6,882 m/22,578 ft). North of COCHABAMBA, the Eastern Cordillera runs in a northwest-southeast direction and slopes northeastward toward the lowlands of the Amazon Basin; south of Cochabamba, the cordillera assumes a more north-south orientation and slopes eastward toward the CHACO. Narrow, steep-sided valleys, known as yungas, are deeply incised into these eastern slopes, the more notable being those in which the important towns of Cochabamba, Sucre, and Tiraja are located. Between the Western and Eastern cordilleras is the Altiplano, which has an average elevation of about 3,600 m (12,000 ft) and is one of the highest populated areas in the world. The Altiplano is about 840 km (520 mi) long and an average of 140 km (80 mi) wide and is dominated in northern Bolivia by Lake TITICACA, located on the Peruvian border and the world's highest navigable lake.

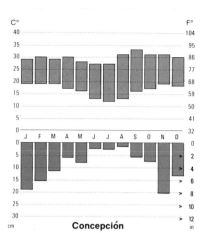

Concepción

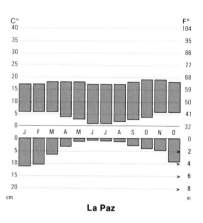

La Paz

Annual climate charts for two cities in Bolivia illustrate the types of climate in this South American country. Bars are used to indicate monthly ranges of temperatures (red) and precipitation (blue). *Concepción* (left), in the eastern lowlands, has a tropical wet-dry climate. La Paz (right), situated in the Andes at an elevation of 3,658 m (12,001 ft), has a cooler highland climate.

The remaining three-fourths of Bolivia lie east of the Andes and are occupied by the Eastern Lowlands, or llanos, which slope gradually eastward from elevations of about 450 m (1,500 ft) in the foothills of the eastern Andes to 200 m (650 ft) or less along the borders with Brazil, Paraguay, and Argentina.

The northern llanos, widely referred to as the Beni Plain, are drained by the Beni and Mamoré rivers and their tributaries and form part of the great Amazon River basin. The central and southern sections are drained by the Pilcomayo River and are part of South America's Chaco plain.

Climate. The climate of the Altiplano is cool and harsh all year because of the high altitude. Daytime temperatures often reach 15°–18° C (60s F), and nights frequently fall below freezing, especially during the winter (June–August) months. Rainfall totals 700 mm (28 in) on the shores of Lake Titicaca, which is so large and deep that it exerts a moderating marine effect on the climate of the northern Altiplano, to less than 125 mm (5 in) in the arid southern parts of the plateau. The yungas are considerably warmer because of their lower altitude. The northern yungas have a humid subtropical climate, characterized by a heavy annual rainfall of about 1,250 mm (50 in), a high humidity throughout the year, and a mean annual temperature of 23° C (73° F); rainfall, temperatures, and humidity diminish toward the south, and the southern yungas are considered to have the most pleasant climate in all Bolivia, with a rainfall of 450 mm (18 in) a year and a mean annual temperature of 20° C (68° F). The llanos have a hot and wet subtropical climate, with heavy summer rainfall in the north and a drier, more temperate climate toward the south.

Vegetation and Animal Life. The Altiplano is too high for tree growth and has only a thin vegetation cover. Extensive subtropical and tropical forests cover the Beni Plain and the lower slopes of the northern yungas and give way to savanna and scrub brush as rainfall diminishes toward the south. Bolivia's animal life varies greatly. Animals commonly found in the rain forest include the jaguar, capybara, toucan, and anaconda. The grasslands contain the rhea, puma, and deer. The llama, alpaca, vicuña, and chinchilla inhabit the highlands.

PEOPLE

The principal ethnic groups in Bolivia are Indians, who make up an estimated 55% of the total population; mestizos (of mixed Indian and European ancestry), who make up 25–30% of the total population; and people of European (primarily Spanish) origin, who make up 5–15% of the total population. The two largest Indian groups are the QUECHUA, who make up about 30% of the total population, and the AYMARA, who make up about 25% of the total population.

About 95% of the people are Roman Catholics. The state no longer supports Catholicism as an official religion, and many Indians combine traditional, pre-Christian symbolism with Catholic religious practices. Spanish is widely spoken in the cities and has traditionally been the language of the educated elite. Quechua and Aymara, together with other Indian languages, predominate in rural areas. Spanish, Quechua, and Aymara are all official languages.

Much of the population is concentrated in the 10% of Bolivia located on the cold and bleak Altiplano, which has been the center of Indian life since pre-Inca days. The warmer and potentially far more productive Eastern Lowlands remain sparsely settled despite official colonization efforts to relocate Indians from the Altiplano since the 1950s. About half of the population live in rural areas, mostly by subsistence farming. The largest urban centers are La Paz, SANTA CRUZ, Cochabamba, and Oruro.

Education is free and compulsory for all children aged 6–14, but many are not enrolled owing to lack of school facilities in certain rural areas. About 75% of the population are literate, and all illiterates between the ages of 15 and 50 are required to attend literacy classes. Spanish is the language of instruction in the schools, with the study of Quechua and Aymara made compulsory in 1979. Bolivia has nine universities.

La Paz, Bolivia's administrative capital and most populous city, is the highest major metropolis in the world (elevation 3,658 m/12,001 ft). The city's location, in a valley of the steep Cordillera Real, affords protection against the strong winds of the Andes.

(Above) *An experienced team of drillers prepares to extract ore from one of Bolivia's nationalized mines. Despite the nation's extensive mineral resources and the development of newly discovered petroleum deposits, Bolivia has one of the lowest per-capita incomes in South America.*

(Right) *Bolivian farmers on the Altiplano, or high plateau, till their fields by traditional methods. Because of the region's harsh climate and unproductive soils, only the most hardy varieties of crops are raised.*

Indian women of La Paz display their merchandise in the open-air market near the 18th-century Church of San Francisco. La Paz, which developed along trade routes between Pacific ports and the mining districts of the interior, is the center of Bolivia's commerce.

ECONOMIC ACTIVITIES

Mining and subsistence agriculture continue to dominate Bolivia's economy as they have since the 16th century, although efforts are being made to expand manufacturing, stimulate commercial agriculture, and otherwise diversify the economy. Mining employs less than 3% of the labor force and accounts for valuable export commodities; agriculture employs nearly half of the labor force but is practiced on a mainly subsistence basis and does not meet domestic food needs.

Mining. Bolivia is one of the world's largest producers of zinc and tin, the principal minerals mined there today. After 1870 tin replaced silver, which had been mined since the Spanish first discovered it at Potosí in 1545, as the principal mineral mined. It was replaced by zinc in the 1980s. Despite an aggressive program of privatization in the late 1980s and 1990s, Bolivia's principal mining companies, nationalized in 1952, remained state-owned.

Other important metals are antimony, tungsten, lead, copper, silver, and gold, most of which, together with the tin and zinc, are produced at high altitudes on the Altiplano. Major oil and natural gas deposits are located in the eastern llanos near Santa Cruz, and natural gas is now a major export. Iron ore discovered at El Mután will further diversify mining.

Agriculture. The principal farming area is along the shores of Lake Titicaca on the northern Altiplano, with crops of potatoes, corn, quinoa (a high-protein seed), wheat, barley, and oca (a tuber) supporting a large rural population. Malnutrition is widespread, and cultivable land is scarce; much of the better land is terraced, and the terraces, like the farming methods, date from pre-Inca times. Herds of sheep and llamas are raised on the drier, southern parts of the Altiplano, and irrigated agriculture is practiced in the south where fresh water is available. Other important farming areas are the fertile valleys surrounding the towns of Cochabamba, Sucre, and Tarija on the eastern slopes of the Andes, where large quantities of maize, wheat, and potatoes are produced. Potentially better farming lands are located in the eastern yungas and llanos, and continuing government-sponsored colonization efforts are relocating many poverty-stricken Indians from the Altiplano to the eastern regions. Coca (which local people chew and from which cocaine is extracted) is grown on about 75% of all farmland and is the nation's leading source of foreign exchange, although its export is illegal. Coffee, cacao, bananas, and sugarcane are grown in the yungas, and a variety of crops—including sugarcane, rice, citrus fruits, coffee, and cotton—are produced in the lowlands near Santa Cruz. Cattle ranching is the main activity on the Beni Plain and the Chaco.

Manufacturing. Manufacturing activities focus mainly on raw-material processing and the reduction of bulk in materials designed for export. There are numerous tin smelters on the Altiplano, an antimony smelter at Vinto, a zinc refinery, a bismuth refinery, and tungsten plants, and plans exist for a steel plant that will use the El Mután iron ores. Oil is refined at Santa Cruz and Cochabamba.

Trade and Transportation. Bolivia's principal exports are minerals and natural gas, which together accounted for some 70% of all legal exports in 1992. Food is the principal import. Bolivia has no outlet to the sea for foreign trade and is dependent on agreements with Chile and Peru for access to Pacific coast ports across lands lost by Bolivia to Chile in the War of the Pacific (1879–84). Access to the Atlantic Ocean is provided by a 1938 agreement with Paraguay that allows navigation on the Paraguay and Paraná rivers, by a 1974 agreement with Brazil that allows duty-free access to the Brazilian ports of Belém and Santos, and by a 1976 agreement with Argentina for free port facilities at Rosario. Bolivia is a member of the LATIN AMERICAN INTEGRATION ASSOCIATION and in 1978 was a signatory to the Amazon Cooperation Treaty. In recent years, Bolivia has been a leading recipient of overseas aid to South American nations, much of it earmarked to fight cocaine.

Bolivia's transportation network is poorly developed, and only since the 1950s have roads been built to link the llanos with the populated highlands. Railroads replaced mules and llamas in the late 19th century in transporting ores from the Altiplano to Pacific coast ports, but the first link between east and west was the highway built from Santa Cruz to Cochabamba in 1954. Other highways have since been built, and a railroad in the east now links Santa Cruz with Yacuiba and with Trinidad Beni. Pipelines carry oil and natural gas across the Andes from Santa Cruz to Arica (Chile) via Oruro and from Santa Cruz southward to Argentina via Choreti.

GOVERNMENT

Bolivia is, constitutionally, a republic. The constitution (often suspended) was promulgated in 1947 and provides for the election of a president every four years and a Congress consisting of a Senate and a Chamber of Deputies. For local administrative purposes Bolivia is divided into nine departments.

HISTORY

Between AD 600 and 900, Indians of Aymara origin were living at the southern end of Lake Titicaca, where they developed a highly advanced culture known as the TIAHUANACO. About 1400 the Quechua-speaking Incas invaded Bolivia from Peru and incorporated the highlands into the Inca Empire (see INCA). The Spanish conquered the country in 1538 and were not driven out until independence from Spain was achieved in 1825. Since independence, Bolivia has been plagued by numerous internal revolutions, and disastrous territorial losses have greatly reduced its original extent. In the War of the Pacific, Bolivia lost its Pacific seacoast and rich nitrate deposits in the Atacama Desert to Chile (see PACIFIC, WAR OF THE). In 1903 it lost the Acre Territory on the north to Brazil; and in the CHACO WAR (1928–35) large areas of the Chaco were lost to Paraguay.

The loss of the Chaco severely discredited the ruling class, and this, combined with discontent among the miners, led to the establishment in the 1940s of the leftist-oriented MNR (Movimiento Nacionalista Revolucionario), headed by Victor PAZ ESTENSSORO. The MNR seized power in 1943 and, with Maj. Gualberto Villaroel as president, urged the unionization of the tin miners and other reforms. When Villaroel was murdered in La Paz in 1946, Paz Estenssoro fled to Argentina; he was elected president in 1951 while still in exile but did not

assume office until the MNR again seized power from the governing military junta in 1952. Paz Estenssoro then instituted far-reaching social reforms, including the nationalization of the tin mines, introduction of universal suffrage, land reforms, and curtailment of the military. Hernán Siles Zuazo, a vice-president under Paz Estenssoro, served as president from 1956 to 1960, and Paz Estenssoro was reelected in 1960, only to be overthrown in a military coup in 1964 by Gen. René Barrientos Ortuño, who assumed the presidency and was elected president in 1966. Barrientos, a rightist, remained in office until 1969, when he was killed in a helicopter crash and was succeeded by Luis Adolfo Siles Salinas. Salinas was overthrown the same year and replaced by Gen. Ovando Candia, who was himself deposed in 1970 by Gen. Juan José Torres Gonzáles, a leftist. In 1971, Col. Hugo BANZER SUÁREZ, a rightist, overthrew Torres and assumed the presidency.

Elections in 1978 were deemed fraudulent, and the military took control until August 1979, when an interim civilian government was chosen by the Congress. Former president Siles Zuazo was reelected in July 1980, but he was prevented by the army from taking office until October 1982. In elections held a year early, in July 1985, no candidate won a majority. The election thus passed to the Congress, which chose Paz Estenssoro. The 1989 and 1993 elections also were inconclusive, but successful economic reforms under President Jaime Paz Zamora, led to the presidential succession of his planning minister, Gonzalo Sanchez de Lozada, in 1993.

RAY HENKEL

Bibliography: Godoy, Ricardo A., *Mining and Agriculture in Highland Bolivia* (1990); Klein, Herbert S., *Bolivia: The Evolution of a Multi-Ethnic Society* (1982); Malloy, J., and Gamarra, E., *Revolution and Reaction* (1987); Swaney, Deanna, and Strauss, Robert, *Bolivia*, 2d ed. (1993).

Böll, Heinrich   [burl]

Heinrich Böll, a leading German author of the postwar era, explored the fragmentation of modern German society in his satirical novels. Böll is among the few contemporary writers whose works have become popular in both Western and Communist countries. His memoir What's to Become of the Boy? *appeared in English translation in 1984.*

Heinrich Böll, b. Dec. 21, 1917, d. July 16, 1985, was one of the most significant and outspoken writers in postwar Germany. He served in World War II for six years, was four times wounded, and was taken prisoner of war. These experiences greatly influenced his writings. In 1947 he settled in Cologne, studied German literature, and began his career as a writer. In 1972 he received the Nobel Prize for literature.

Böll's early realistic works deal variously with the war and the immediate postwar years. *Wo warst du, Adam* (1951; *Adam, Where Art Thou?*, 1955) seeks to demythologize war and expose it as a plague. *Haus ohne Hüter* (1954; *Tomorrow and Yesterday*, 1957) describes the typical postwar situation of women and children whose husbands and fathers were lost in war. In *Billard um halbzehn* (1959; *Billiards at Half-past Nine*, 1962), Böll uses flashback and interior monologue to narrate the story of three generations of one family.

With greater distance from the war years, Böll's angry and bitter condemnation of society became increasingly directed at institutions whose restrictions demand conformity and denounce individuality. This theme is sounded in his popular novel *Ansichten eines Clowns* (1963; *The Clown*, 1965), which also questions the responsibilities of the artist vis-à-vis society. The dehumanization caused by institutions seems to be balanced by naive and natural characters, such as Leni, the lady in *Gruppenbild mit Dame* (1971; *Group Portrait with Lady*, 1973). Here, Böll presents a broad panorama of recent German history through the device of multiple narration. The novel's open-endedness suggests the possibility of a new social order; for the moralist and pacifist Böll, this is necessary.

Böll alienated himself from many sectors of German society by arguing for the just treatment of German terrorists of the 1970s. He was forcefully denounced by West Germany's extremely powerful conservative press. His novel *Die verlorene Ehre der Katharina Blum* (1974; *The Lost Honor of Katharina Blum*, 1975; film, 1975), can be seen in part as a reaction to this denunciation; it shows the destruction of an innocent human being by journalistic slander. The novel presents Böll's strongest attack against what he perceived as the most dangerous of modern Germany's hypocritical and immoral institutions. *Fürsorgliche Belagerung* (1979; *Safety Net*, 1982) took a satirical look at political terrorism and its impact on West German life.   MARILYN SIBLEY FRIES

Bibliography: Macpherson, Enid, *A Student's Guide to Böll* (1972); Reid, James H., *Heinrich Böll: Withdrawal and Re-emergence* (1973).

Bollandists   [bahl'-uhn-dists]

The Bollandists are a group of Belgian Jesuits who publish the *Acta Sanctorum*, a critical edition of the lives of the saints. Named after their first editor, Jean Bolland (1596–1665), they also publish a quarterly review, the *Analecta Bollandiana*.

Bollingen Prize in Poetry   [bahl'-ing-gen]

The Bollingen Prize in Poetry is given biennially to an American poet selected by Yale University Library for outstanding achievement. Philanthropist Paul Mellon established the funds for the Bollingen Foundation and the cash prize, which was first awarded in 1949 to Ezra Pound. Other recipients have included Marianne Moore (1952), W. H. Auden (1954), Robert Frost (1963), Robert Penn Warren (1967), W. S. Merwin (1979), and Stanley Kunitz (1987).

Bologna   [boh-lohn'-yah]

Bologna is the capital city of Bologna province and of the Emilia-Romagna region of north central Italy. It has a population of 442,307 (1985 est.) and is at the foot of the Apennine Mountains, north of Florence on the ancient Aemilian Way. Strategically located on the motor and rail axis running north-south through Italy, it is a major commercial center. At the southern extremity of the fertile Paduan plain, it has long thrived as an agricultural center. Since World War I, Bologna has developed important industry, including manufacture of railroad equipment, farm machinery, motorcycles, electric motors, and chemicals.

Originally Etruscan (Felsina), it was a Roman colony (Bononia) from 190 BC and a Byzantine colony from the 6th century AD. During the 12th century it became one of the first free communes of Italy and fought against the German emperors Frederick I Barbarossa (*c.*1123–90) and Frederick II (1194–1250). Conflict between the pro-papal Guelphs and pro-imperial Ghibellines divided the city and allowed domination by *signori* (lords)—the Pepoli, the Visconti of Milan, and the Bentivoglio—before papal rule was established in 1506. Bologna became part of united Italy in 1860. Throughout the Middle Ages the University of Bologna (founded late 11th century) had Europe's most esteemed law school (founded 1088), where Irnerius and Francesco Accursius taught and from which the European revival of Roman law spread.

Although heavily bombed in World War II, the city remains a veritable living museum of the Middle Ages and the Renaissance, with its many arcaded streets. Notable buildings include its two remaining family-military towers, the Gothic

Church of San Petronio (with a 15th-century doorway by Jacopo della Quercia), the 16th-century Fountain of Neptune, and the 13th- and 15th-century porticoed Palazzo Comunale (town hall).

Among Bologna's other structures are the churches of San Giacomo Maggiore (13th–15th century), of San Domenico (early 13th century), and of San Francesco (13th century), which was influenced by French Gothic, and the Podesta palace (13th–15th century). The Pinacoteca Nazionale (National Picture Gallery) is rich in works of the Bolognese primitive, Renaissance, and baroque schools.   DANIEL R. LESNICK

Bologna, Giovanni da

Giovanni da Bologna's Mercury (1564) is one of several versions by the artist on the theme of the god in flight. The graceful bronze work gives an impression of fleet movement and weightlessness. (Bargello, Florence.)

Giovanni da Bologna, also known as Jean Boulogne and Giambologna, b. Douai, France, 1529, d. Florence, Italy, 1608, was the first sculptor in Western history to break with the tradition of compositions having a single angle of view to which all others are subordinated. Intertwining complex groupings of figures in a continuous spiral, as in his *Rape of the Sabine Women* (1579–83; Loggia dei Lanzi, Florence), Giambologna requires the viewer to move around the sculpture from one vantage point to another. The often violent projection of arms and legs violates every principle of the sculpture of MICHELANGELO and the High Renaissance, and thus leads directly to MANNERISM. The new multiplicity of views points the way to the work of Giovanni BERNINI and the baroque period.

Giambologna received his early training in the workshop of Jacques Dubroeucq, a Flemish sculptor working in the Italian tradition. In 1554 he traveled to Rome, where for two years he studied ancient and contemporary monuments. The restrained majesty of the *Equestrian Statue of Cosimo I* (1594; Piazza della Signoria, Florence) shows the influence of the *Equestrian Statue of Marcus Aurelius* (c.161–80; Campidoglio, Rome). On his return from Rome, Giambologna visited Florence and gained the sponsorship of the MEDICI family. His first important work, the *Fountain of Neptune* (1563; Piazza Nettuno, Bologna), was submitted to a competition in Florence in 1560 but was commissioned, after modifications, by the city of Bologna, which accounts for the sculptor's Italianate name. Subsequent works include the elegant *Mercury* (1564; Museo Nazionale, Florence); the colossal *Appenine* (1577–81; in the garden of the Medici villa at Pratolino); and the dramatic *Samson and a Philistine* (c.1566–70; Victoria and Albert Museum, London).

Giovanni da Bologna maintained a large studio. Among his outstanding assistants were Antonio Susini and Pietro TACCA; the latter succeeded his master as sculptor to the Court of the Medici. JOHN TANCOCK

Bibliography: Avery, Charles, *Giambologna: The Complete Sculpture* (1987); Bazin, Germain, *The History of World Sculpture*, trans. by Madeline Jay (1968); Holderbaum, James, *The Sculptor Giovanni da Bologna* (1977); Pope-Hennessy, John, *Samson and a Philistine* (1954); Radcliffe, Anthony, *European Bronze Statuettes* (1966).

Bologna, University of

Founded in the 11th century, the University of Bologna (enrollment: 59,000; library: 900,000 volumes) in Bologna, Italy, is perhaps the oldest university in Europe. It is now a state institution with a full range of scholarly and professional programs.

bolometer   [buh-lahm'-uh-tur]

A bolometer is a sensitive type of electrical resistance THERMOMETER used to measure thermal radiation from a distant source in the infrared or microwave region of the spectrum. Changes in temperature are detectable to 0.0001° C. One of the first applications was to detect the heat of radiation from stars. Most present applications are in aerospace research.

The bolometer was invented in 1880 when the American astronomer and physicist S. P. LANGLEY used two thin strips of platinum foil, blackened to absorb radiation, as legs of a WHEATSTONE BRIDGE resistance circuit. One strip was exposed to the radiation and the other was covered, as a reference resistance. Platinum is still used today in the form of film or small diameter wire, as well as nickel and bismuth. The metal is usually mounted in a taut suspension under reduced pressure in hydrogen.

A THERMISTOR bolometer, using a semiconductor material whose resistance drops with temperature increase (negative temperature coefficient), has been applied as a horizon sensor for spacecraft. It distinguishes between the zero radiation from the black space background and the infrared radiation from the Earth. To make the device insensitive to daylight, an optical filter of pure germanium is used. FRANK J. OLIVER

Bolsheviks and Mensheviks   [bohl'-shev-iks, men'-shev-iks]

The Bolsheviks and Mensheviks emerged as rival factions within the Russian Social Democratic Labor party, a Marxist organization, at its 1903 congress in Brussels and London. The division stemmed from a dispute over party membership qualifications. The party's left wing, led by Vladimir Ilich LENIN, wanted a disciplined, centralized organization consisting only of activists. The moderates, led by Julius Martov, favored a more loosely organized mass party. Lenin's followers, who

gained a short-lived ascendancy in 1903, became known as *Bolsheviks* (majority), and Martov's backers were dubbed *Mensheviks* (minority).

Although the cause of the initial split seemed trivial, it reflected a basic difference of approach that became clearer as spokesmen for the two factions elaborated their views in the following years. The Mensheviks adhered to the belief of veteran revolutionary Georgy PLEKHANOV that a bourgeois-led, democratic revolution bringing Russia into the capitalist era would have to precede the socialist revolution. Lenin, on the other hand, argued that a revolution of workers and peasants, if properly led, could establish socialism in one stage. The two factions finally split into separate parties in 1912.

Because the Mensheviks believed in standing aside for the bourgeois revolution, they declined to seek power after Emperor NICOLAS II was overthrown in March (February, O.S.) 1917, although they did accept cabinet posts in the provisional government. The Bolsheviks, however, gained control of key workers' soviets (councils) and toppled the provisional government in November (October, O.S.) 1917. Lenin's regime suppressed the Mensheviks shortly after the beginning of the Civil War in 1918, but they were permitted occasional spurts of political activity until the spring of 1921, when all opposition parties were abolished.

Bibliography: Haimson, Leopold H., ed., *The Mensheviks* (1974) and *The Russian Marxists and the Origins of Bolshevism* (1955); McCauley, Martin, *Octobrists to Bolsheviks* (1984); Ulam, Adam B., *The Bolsheviks* (1955; repr. 1968).

See also: COMMUNISM; MARXISM; RUSSIAN REVOLUTIONS OF 1917; SOCIALISM.

Bolshoi Ballet   [bohl'-shoy or buhl-shoy']

The Bolshoi Ballet, the principal ballet company of Moscow, takes its name from the city's Bolshoi (or large) Theater, as distinct from its Maly (or small) Theater, which has its own ballet company. Today the Bolshoi Ballet dances regularly, not only at the Bolshoi, which it shares with the Bolshoi Opera, but also in the huge Palace of Congresses in the Kremlin. Ballet has been state supported in Moscow since 1776, although

Marius Liepa, as Bacchus, and Marina Kondratyeva, as a bacchante, perform in the ballet divertissement "Walpurgis night," choreographed by Mikhail Lavrovsky for Gounod's opera Faust, *at the Bolshoi Theater in Moscow. The Bolshoi Ballet, now the premier dance company of the Soviet Union and one of the most acclaimed in the world, is best known for its dynamic interpretations of classical ballets.*

the present building dates from 1856. During the 19th century the Moscow company was considered artistically inferior to the Maryinsky (now KIROV) Ballet in Saint Petersburg (now Leningrad), and its dancers were judged provincial by comparison. In 1869, Marius PETIPA's *Don Quixote* (music by Ludwig MINKUS) premiered at the Bolshoi, as did Wenzel Reisinger's *Swan Lake* in 1877; the latter, however, did not enjoy much success at first, despite Peter Ilich Tchaikovsky's melodious score. In 1900, Aleksandr Gorsky restaged Petipa's *Don Quixote*, initiating a series of reforms designed to make ballet more dramatically coherent. Gorsky, at the head of the Moscow company from 1900 until his death in 1924, had great influence on the development of Russian ballet.

The first important Soviet work, *The Red Poppy* (music by Reinhold GLIÈRE) was presented at the Bolshoi in 1927, but until well after World War II most of the significant developments in Russian ballet continued to emanate from Leningrad, including Vassily Vainonen's *Flame of Paris* (1932) and Aleksandr Lavrovsky's *Romeo and Juliet* (1940; music by Sergei Prokofiev). Only in 1944, when Lavrovsky and Galina ULANOVA, the Kirov's prima ballerina, were transferred from Leningrad to Moscow, did the Bolshoi achieve indisputable artistic distinction. In 1962, Maya PLISETSKAYA succeeded Ulanova as prima ballerina.

Yury GRIGOROVICH became the Bolshoi's chief choreographer and artistic director in 1964. His work, marked by spectacular athleticism, has proved extremely popular in Russia and Western Europe, especially *Spartacus* (1968; music by Aram Khatchaturian)and *Ivan the Terrible* (1975; music by Prokofiev). In the West, where the Bolshoi has been seen regularly since 1956, the company's greatest asset is generally considered to be the dancing of such stars as Ekaterina Maximova, Vladimir Vasiliev, Natalia Bessmertnova, Vyacheslav Gordeyev, and Ludmila Semenyaka.   DALE HARRIS

Bibliography: Demidov, Alexander, *The Russian Ballet, Past and Present* (1977); Doeser, Linda, *Ballet and Dance: The World's Major Companies* (1978); Grigorovich, Y., and Vanslov, V., *Bolshoi Ballet* (1984); Roslavleva, Natalia, *The Era of the Russian Ballet* (1966).

bolt: see NUTS AND BOLTS.

Bolt, Robert

Robert Bolt, b. Aug. 15, 1924, is an English dramatist and screenwriter who achieved international fame with his play on Sir Thomas More, *A Man for All Seasons* (1960), and his script for David Lean's films, *Lawrence of Arabia* (1962), *Dr. Zhivago* (1965), and *Ryan's Daughter* (1970). His other plays include *Flowering Cherry* (1957) and *Vivat! Vivat Regina!* (1970). Recent screenplays are *The Bounty* (1984) and *The Mission* (1986).   ROBIN BUSS

Bolton

Bolton (in full, Bolton-le-Moors) is a borough in Greater Manchester County (formerly Lancashire), in northwest England. It has a population of 262,300 (1982 est.). The River Croal divides the town into Great Bolton and Little Bolton. In the 18th and 19th centuries Bolton became a leading cotton-spinning center. As late as 1929, half the labor force was engaged in spinning, and textiles remain important to the economy. In 1769, Richard ARKWRIGHT developed spinning machinery while living in Bolton. The first spinning factory was established in 1780, and by 1791 Bolton was linked to the city of Manchester by canals. The home of Samuel CROMPTON, who invented the spinning mule in 1779, is now a museum.

Bolton, Herbert Eugene

Herbert Eugene Bolton, b. Wilton Township, Wis., July 20, 1870, d. Jan. 30, 1953, was a historian of the Spanish in the American West, and one of the pioneers in the discovery and opening of foreign archival material on American history. Most of his 50 years of teaching were spent at the University of California at Berkeley, during which time he served as chairman of the department of history (1919–40) and director of the famous Bancroft Library (1916–40). Bolton wrote or edited more than 25 books, including his study of Father KINO, *Rim of Christendom* (1936), and *Anza's California Expeditions, 1774–76* (5 vols., 1930). Dozens of his graduate students became distinguished historians in the fields of the American West or "Spanish Borderlands," a term that Bolton coined.   W. EUGENE HOLLON

Bibliography: Bannon, John Francis, *Herbert Eugene Bolton* (1978); Jacobs, W. R., et al., *Turner, Bolton, and Webb* (1979).

Boltwood, Bertram Borden

The American physicist Bertram Borden Boltwood, b. Amherst, Mass., July 27, 1870, d. Aug. 15, 1927, made fundamental contributions to the understanding of the process by which uranium decays. He developed a superior method for determining the half-life of radium and demonstrated that the ultimate degradation product of uranium and radium is lead. Reversing his procedure, he claimed that the Earth was a billion years old, in sharp contrast to prevailing views that it was far less than 100 million years old.   E. ROBERT PAUL

Boltzmann, Ludwig

The Austrian physicist Ludwig Boltzmann, b. Feb. 20, 1844, d. Sept. 5, 1906, developed, with J. W. GIBBS, the branch of physics known as statistical mechanics, which uses the laws of probability to describe how the properties of atoms determine the visible properties of matter. Boltzmann received his doctorate from the University of Vienna in 1867 and subsequently held professorships at the universities of Vienna, Graz, Munich, and Leipzig. During the 1870s he published a series of papers illustrating the application of the laws of probability to atomic motion in connection with the second law of THERMODYNAMICS, which involves energy exchange. He also obtained the so-called Maxwell-Boltzmann distribution, which states that the average amount of energy used for each direction of motion of an atom is the same. He was thus the first to develop the kinetic theory of gases. His work was opposed by many European physicists. Depressed and in poor health, Boltzmann committed suicide in 1906, shortly before the experimental studies of the French scientist Jean PERRIN verified much of his work.   SHELDON J. KOPPERL

Boltzmann constant

At any temperature above ABSOLUTE ZERO, atoms and molecules are in thermal motion. The KINETIC THEORY OF MATTER shows that the average kinetic energy of these particles is proportional to the temperature T (measured from absolute zero):

$$\frac{1}{2}m\bar{v}^2 = \frac{3}{2}k_B T$$

where m is the mass and $\bar{v}$ the velocity of the particles. The proportionality factor k_B relating the average kinetic energy to the temperature is the Boltzmann constant; its numerical value is 1.3805×10^{-23} joules/Kelvin.   DAVID W. OXTOBY

Bolyai, János   [bohl'-yoy]

The Hungarian mathematician János Bolyai, b. Dec. 15, 1802, d. Jan. 27, 1860, is best known for his development of NON-EUCLIDEAN GEOMETRY, a form of geometry that does not contain Euclid's axiom that only one line can be drawn parallel to a given line through a point not on the line.

By the time Bolyai was 13, he had mastered the calculus and other forms of analytical mathematics. Between 1820 and 1823 he prepared a treatise on a complete system of non-Euclidean geometry, which was published in 1832 with an essay by his father. Although Carl Friedrich GAUSS, Nikolai LOBACHEVSKY, and Saccheri had preceded him in this conceptual area, Bolyai was probably unaware of this at the time he wrote his treatise.

In addition to his work in geometry, Bolyai developed a rigorous geometric concept of complex numbers as ordered pairs of real numbers.   THEODORE H. ALLEGRI

Bolzano [bohl-tsah'-noh]

Bolzano (German: Bozen) is the capital city of Bolzano province in the Trentino–Alto Adige region of northern Italy. It is the center of the German-speaking part of the southern Tyrol and has a population of 101,515 (1986). Annual average rainfall is 717 mm (28.22 in). Located on the Isarco River northeast of its confluence with the Adige River, south of the Brenner Pass, Bolzano has been the chief commercial center of the area since the Middle Ages. Bolzano manufactures steel, aluminum, plastics, and textiles and has engineering and electrometallurgical industries. Historically under German and Austrian control, the city was ceded, with the rest of the southern Tyrol, by Austria to Italy after World War I. Badly damaged in World War II, the city still has its cathedral (14th–15th century) and a notable civic museum. Bolzano's spectacular Alpine scenery has also made the city a popular resort area.

DANIEL R. LESNICK

Bolzano, Bernhard

Bernhard Bolzano, b. Oct. 5, 1781, d. Dec. 18, 1848, was a Czech philosopher, mathematician, and theologian who made significant contributions to both mathematics and the theory of knowledge. A Roman Catholic priest, he was appointed (1805) to the chair of philosophy and religion at Prague. In 1819, however, Bolzano was suspended from his position because of pressure from the Austrian government, which opposed his pacifism and his expressed concerns with economic justice. Although some of his books had to be published outside Austria because of government censorship, he continued to write and to play an important role in the intellectual life of his country.

Among Bolzano's important works are *Rein analytischer Beweis* (Pure Analytical Proof, 1817), which contains an effort to free calculus successfully from the concept of the infinitesimal; *Wissenschaftslehre* (1837; Eng. trans. and abridgment, *Theory of Science*, 1972), an attempt at a complete theory of science and knowledge; and the posthumous *Paradoxien des Unendlichen* (1851; Eng. trans., *Paradoxes of the Infinite*, 1950). Bolzano's theories of mathematical infinity anticipated Georg CANTOR's theory of infinite sets (see SET THEORY). His distinction between psychology and logic influenced Edmund HUSSERL and later proponents of PHENOMENOLOGY.

PETE A. Y. GUNTER

Bibliography: Jarnik, V., *Bolzano and the Foundations of Mathematical Analysis* (1981).

bomb

A bomb is a container filled with an explosive, incendiary matter, or gas that can be dropped, hurled, or set in place to be detonated by an attached exploding device. It may range in design from a homemade device used by terrorists, assassins, or clandestine raiders to a sophisticated weapon of war.

The original bomb, an ancestor of the hand-thrown GRENADE, was a simple container filled with black powder (see GUNPOWDER), which was set off by a fuse lit by the thrower.

In the 16th century, the Dutch invented a more sophisticated version, the MORTAR bomb, a round iron container filled with black powder that was set off when a fuse was ignited by the detonation of a propelling charge in the base of the mortar tube. By varying the length of the fuse, the bomb's time of detonation could be adjusted; thus, a bomb could burst in air. These bombs were predecessors of the ARTILLERY shell fired from a field gun with rifled bore.

In the 20th century the aerial bomb became the most important adaptation of the weapon. Its construction is similar to that of the artillery shell. The conventional aerial bomb consists of an explosive or chemical agent in a container, one or several fuse-and-igniter mechanisms, and external fins for directional stability. Bombs dropped from high-performance aircraft have an advanced aerodynamic shape.

The ultimate category of bomb is that utilizing nuclear material as the explosive ingredients—the ATOMIC BOMB, HYDROGEN BOMB, and NEUTRON BOMB.

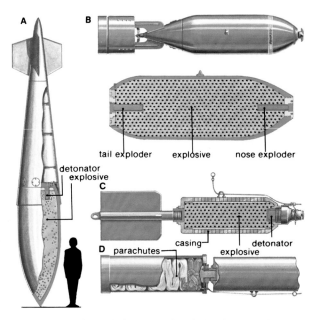

The 10-ton British Grand Slam, or Earthquake, bomb (A) was the heaviest bomb used in World War II. Designed to destroy underground factories, heavily armored buildings, and U-boat pens, it could penetrate the earth up to 30 m (110 ft). A modern American 227-kg (500-lb) high explosive bomb (B) is used for the destruction of open targets. Fragmentation bombs (C and D) are antipersonnel weapons whose casings are designed to burst into jagged fragments. Parachutes are used to control descent.

20th-Century Military Use. The advent of the airplane in warfare led to the development of new types of bombs. The first massive aerial bombing took place in 1915 when German zeppelins carrying more than two tons of bombs began dropping "terror from the skies" on the British Isles. In the early stages of World War I, airplane pilots had their hands full just flying, and bombing was relegated to observers who merely tossed small bombs over the side. Aircraft engineering advanced, however, so that by 1918 multiengine bombers had become a reality and 450-kg (1,000-lb) bombs were in production.

The next major step in the development of aerial bombing took place on July 21, 1921. Gen. Billy MITCHELL, a champion of military airpower, was finally allowed to test his theory that aircraft carrying bombs could sink major naval units, a theory that naval officials had considered ridiculous. On that date, in the first of three such demonstrations, the captured German dreadnought *Ostfriesland* was sunk in minutes by U.S. Army Air Corps bombers dropping 900-kg (2,000-lb) bombs. Warfare had been revolutionized; seapower was in jeopardy.

During World War II, aerial bombardment was perfected. Massive raids, first by Germany and then by the Allies, demonstrated the devastating power of the conventional aerial bomb. As aircraft size and performance increased, so did bomb size, ending in the 10-ton (9,900-kg/22,000-lb) British "Earthquake" bomb. Incendiary bombs containing thermite, a mixture of iron oxide, powdered aluminum, and magnesium, were dropped nightly by the thousands to cause fires. Other bombs were manufactured for exacting tasks; one of the most unusual was the Wallis "skipping bomb," used against German reservoir dams. Others, such as the British "Tall Boy," were designed to destroy massive concrete slabs. During the closing stages of the war, Germany sent more than 8,500 V-1 guided bombs flying across the English Channel to fall on England. A quantum jump in bomb manufacture and use occurred in 1945 when U.S. planes dropped atomic bombs to destroy two cities, HIROSHIMA (Aug. 6) and NAGASAKI (Aug. 9). The bombings led Japan to surrender and initiated a new era characterized by NUCLEAR STRATEGIES on which the survival of whole countries depended.

Along with the development of the high-yield nuclear weapons, new types of conventional bombs have also been developed. NAPALM, a petroleum-jelly incendiary mixture, is an ingredient used worldwide in tactical bombs. The fuel-air explosive bomb consists of an aerosol mixture of fuel and air in cloud form. When it is ignited in the air, its blast covers a very wide area, and for this reason the bomb has been used for clearing minefields, among its other functions. Cluster bombs, hundreds of miniature bomblets that are air-delivered in a single large bomb casing, are designed primarily as antipersonnel weapons.

Handmade Bombs. The ability to make amateur bombs has been central to the conduct of guerrilla and terrorist warfare. The development of plastic EXPLOSIVES during World War II has enabled terrorists to produce bombs that are difficult to detect (they have been smuggled aboard airplanes, for example) but that have tremendous explosive power. Letter and car bombs—plastic charges triggered to explode by the opening of an envelope or the turning of an ignition key—are fairly simple devices. More sophisticated handmade bombs —such as those responsible for the 1993 explosions in the Uffizi Gallery in Florence, Italy, and in New York City's World Trade Center skyscraper—may incorporate electronic timing and triggering devices.   RUSSELL J. PARKINSON

Bibliography: Crane, C. C., *Bombs, Cities, and Civilians: American Airpower Strategy in World War II* (1993); Graetzer, H. G., and Browning, L. M., *The Atomic Bomb* (1992); Hubbard, David G., *Winning Back the Sky* (1986); Kennett, Lee, *A History of Strategic Bombing* (1983); Stoffel, J., *Explosives and Homemade Bombs,* 2d ed. (1977); U. S. Office of Technology Assessment Staff, *Technology against Terrorism* (1992).

Bombay

Bombay, the capital of the western Indian state of Maharashtra and the largest metropolis in India, has developed into an industrial complex second only to Calcutta. Of all the Indian metropolises, it is the most cosmopolitan and has the greatest concentration of skyscrapers. Greater Bombay, comprising the island of Bombay (formerly Bombay City), Trombay, and part of Salsette, has a population of 9,909,547 (1991); the Bombay metropolitan area, including its suburbs, has a population of 12,571,720 (1991). The city has been designated the *Gateway of India* because it is India's major port of Western contact. The port is built around a harbor and handles the country's largest tonnage of foreign trade.

Greater Bombay is separated from the Indian mainland by the waters of Bassein Creek. The Arabian Sea lies to the west and south. The rock formations exposed in and around Bombay are of volcanic origin and are referred to as Deccan Trap. Alluvium cover is found in the lowlands.

Contemporary City. Greater Bombay, of which the southernmost part is the island of Bombay, was formed into a metropolitan municipal organization in 1957. About two-thirds of the population is concentrated on Bombay Island, which has an area of 67 km² (26 mi²). Bombay has one of the highest population densities in the world, in some areas reaching 580 persons per km² (1,500 per mi²). The city attracts a large number of migrants, particularly from the states of Maharashtra, Gujarat, and Madhya Pradesh. The principal languages spoken are Marathi, Gujarati, and Hindi. Of all India's large cities, Bombay offers the greatest religious diversity. More than half its population is Hindu; the rest is divided among PARSIS, Christians, Jains, Muslims, and others.

The surrounding Black Cotton Soils, India's greatest cotton-growing area, has made Bombay one of the largest cotton textile centers in the country, and the cotton textiles industry employs almost one-half of Bombay's factory workers. The rest are primarily employed in the production of silk, artificial fibers, chemicals, and glassware and in the dyeing, bleaching, and printing industries. The city is the home of one of the most successful business families of India, the Tatas. The University of Bombay, founded in 1857, the Atomic Research Institute, and the Haffkine Institute, a major center of research in medicine and allied sciences, are some of Bombay's seats of higher education.

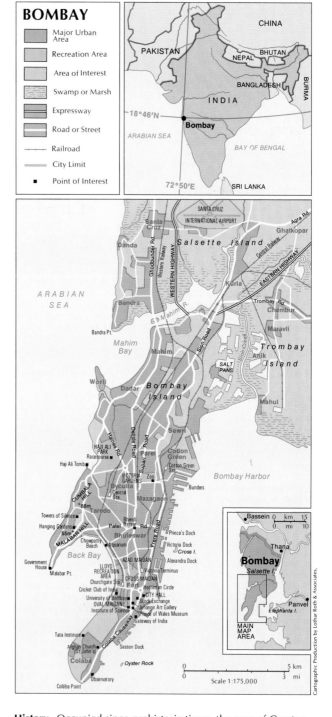

History. Occupied since prehistoric times, the area of Greater Bombay was ruled by the kingdom of Aparanta (north Konkan) in the 2d century and subsequently passed under the control of successive Indian dynasties. It formed part of the kingdom of Gujarat from 1348 to 1534, when the area was ceded to the Portuguese. In 1664 the British were granted control of the island of Bombay, and three years later they established a fort and a township there. Bombay became the headquarters of the East India Company in India from 1672 to 1858. In the 19th century, the seven islands of Girgaum (where the fort is located), Oldman's Island, Colaba, Mazagaon, Parel, Mahim, and Worli were joined and the alluvial lowlands drained, resulting in a single island. Landmarks of Western influence of the Victorian era include the Gateway of India, the Victoria Terminus, the Taj Mahal Hotel, the Rajabai Clock Tower, and the High Court.   ASHOK K. DUTT

Bibliography: Kaye, Myriam, *Bombay and Goa* (1988).

Bombois, Camille   [bohm-bwah', kah-meel']

Camille Bombois, b. Feb. 3, 1883, d. June 11, 1970, was a French primitive painter whose characteristic themes were populated street scenes. Totally self-taught, Bombois began sketching as a diversion at 16 years of age. By 1922 he was painting full time. That year he first displayed his work in an open-air exhibition, and an enthusiastic review by the poet Noël Bureau brought him to the attention of major collectors. In his paintings, such as *Before Entering the Ring* (1930–35; Museum of Modern Art, New York), Bombois emphasized the mass and solidity of his figures by reducing detail and sharpening contours with bright, local color.

Bona Dea   [boh'-nuh day'-uh]

In ancient Rome, Bona Dea ("the good goddess") was a deity worshipped by women in secret rites held in May and December. She was also known as Fauna.

bona fide   [bah'-nuh fyd or boh'-nuh fyd]

Bona fide (Latin: "in good faith") is a legal term that indicates an act was performed sincerely, without intent to deceive. A person who supposes that he or she has title to some property, and who is unaware that someone else has a better right to it, is a bona fide possessor.

Bonampak   [boh-nahm-pahk]

At Bonampak, Chiapas, Mexico, skillful Maya artists recorded the courtly and warlike world of the Maya nobility in paintings on stucco that cover the interior walls and vaulted ceilings of a small, three-chambered palace. Brought to modern attention in 1946 by American photographer Giles Healey, these Maya murals are the most complete indigenous paintings in the New World, and in their color, craft, and complexity, they are among the finest wall murals in the world. Several fine sculptures have also been found at Bonampak.

Commissioned at the end of the 8th century by the last known king of Bonampak, Chaan-muan (reigned AD 775?–792?), the paintings reveal the pageantry and bloodshed of noble life at the end of the Classic era (see MAYA). In Room 1, Chaan-muan presides over the presentation of a little heir to the throne and the ensuing festivities while other lords and regional governors look on. In Room 2 the king leads his warriors in battle and then directs the sacrifice of prisoners at dawn on the day Venus rose as Morning Star, an appropriate time for sacrifice in Mesoamerica. In Room 3, lords draw their own blood as the sacrifice continues. The paintings were not completed, and Bonampak was apparently abandoned as widespread warfare engulfed the region.

MARY ELLEN MILLER

Bibliography: Miller, Mary Ellen, *The Murals of Bonampak* (1986).

Bonaparte   (family)

The Bonapartes were a family of Corsican origin that rose to prominence as a result of the successes of Napoleon Bonaparte, who became (1804) Emperor NAPOLEON I of France.

Napoleon's father, **Carlo Maria Buonaparte**, b. Mar. 29, 1746, d. Feb. 24, 1785, was a minor Corsican nobleman. Initially he supported the Corsican independence movement of Pasquale PAOLI, but he transferred his allegiance to France after 1769. He was named a royal councilor but left little wealth to his widow and eight children when he died.

His widow, **Letizia Ramolino Bonaparte**, later called Madame Mère, b. c.1750, d. Feb. 2, 1836, was forced by Paoli to flee to France with her family in 1793. After her second son, Napoleon, became emperor, he gave her funds to maintain a household; yet her mode of life remained thrifty and unassuming. When Napoleon abdicated in 1814, she took up residence in Rome.

Her oldest son was **Joseph Bonaparte**, b. Jan. 7, 1768, d. July 28, 1844. He was a Corsican official until expelled with his family by Paoli. He accompanied (1796) Napoleon to Italy and was elected (1797) a Corsican representative to the Council of Five Hundred under the French DIRECTORY. Joseph served in various governmental positions until Napoleon named him (1806) king of Naples, in which position he introduced significant reforms. He was appointed king of Spain in 1808, but his authority was severely restricted, and he abandoned the country following the French defeat in the Battle of Vitoria (1813). In 1815 he fled to the United States and lived in Bordentown, N.J., until 1841.

The third son was **Lucien Bonaparte**, b. May 21, 1775, d. June 29, 1840. He, too, was elected to the Council of Five Hundred, and his role as council president on 18 Brumaire (Nov. 10, 1799) guaranteed the success of Napoleon's coup against the Directory. Lucien served as minister of the interior and then ambassador to Spain, but he was recalled in disgrace. In 1803 he married a commoner, against Napoleon's wishes, and was expelled from France. He was captured by a British ship while traveling to the United States and interned in England until Napoleon's abdication in 1814; thereafter he lived in Italy.

The fourth child of Carlo and Letizia was **Élisa Bonaparte**, b. Jan. 3, 1777, d. Aug. 6, 1820. She married (1797) Felix Bacciochi and was named by Napoleon princess of Piombino and Lucca (1805) and grand duchess of Tuscany (1809). She introduced significant reforms in her lands, but after Napoleon's abdication she moved to Bologna and later to Trieste.

Louis Bonaparte, b. Sept. 2, 1778, d. July 25, 1846, whom Napoleon made king of Holland, was the fifth child. He served on Napoleon's staff in the Italian and Egyptian campaigns and was forced to marry (1802) his stepsister, Hortense de Beauharnais (see BEAUHARNAIS family). Proclaimed king of Holland in 1806, Louis defied Napoleon's CONTINENTAL SYSTEM for the benefit of the Dutch until French troops invaded and annexed Holland in 1810; he abdicated and went to Rome.

The sixth child, **Pauline Bonaparte**, b. Oct. 29, 1780, d. June 9, 1825, was the most beautiful of the Bonaparte girls. In 1787 she married Gen. Charles Leclerc (1772–1802), who died while leading an expedition to suppress the revolution in HAITI. Napoleon then arranged her marriage (1803) to Camillo Borghese (1775–1832), a Roman nobleman. Pauline's scandalous conduct in Paris and her hostility toward Napoleon's second wife, Marie Louise, led to her dismissal from court in 1810. In 1814 she moved to Elba to share Napoleon's exile.

Pauline's younger sister, **Caroline Bonaparte**, b. Mar. 25, 1782, d. May 18, 1839, married Joachim MURAT in 1800. She became duchess of Berg and Cleves (1806) and then queen of Naples (1808). She counseled her husband to intrigue with Austria against Napoleon in 1813, but this did not save their throne after Napoleon's defeat. Expelled from Naples, she settled for a time in Trieste.

The youngest child in this generation was **Jérôme Bonaparte**, b. Nov. 15, 1784, d. June 24, 1860. Commissioned in the French Navy, he visited the United States, where he married (1803) Elizabeth Patterson of Baltimore. When Jérôme returned to France, Napoleon had the marriage annulled, and Jérôme married (1807) Catherine of Württemberg. Named king of Westphalia, Jérôme commanded an army in the invasion of Russia in 1812. After taking part in the Battle of Waterloo (1815), he fled France. He later returned and witnessed the establishment (1852) of the Second French Empire under his nephew NAPOLEON III.

Napoleon III, earlier known as Charles Louis Napoléon, was the son of Louis Bonaparte. He assumed the reign number III because his cousin, Napoleon I's son François Charles Joseph Bonaparte, b. Mar. 20, 1811, d. July 22, 1832, was considered by Bonapartists to have succeeded his father as **Napoleon II.** In fact, after 1815 he was a virtual prisoner in Austria. Another notable member of this generation was **Napoléon Joseph Charles Paul Bonaparte**, b. Sept. 9, 1822, d. Mar. 17, 1891, the son of Jérôme Bonaparte and Catherine of Württemberg.

Known as Prince Napoleon and nicknamed Plon-Plon, he married (1859) Marie Chlotilde, daughter of Victor Emmanuel II of Sardinia, and commanded French troops in the Italian war of liberation. After the death of Napoleon III's son (1879), he became the Bonapartist pretender to the throne.

Although the marriage of Jérôme Bonaparte and Elizabeth Patterson was annulled, their son, **Jerome Napoleon Bonaparte**, b. July 7, 1805, d. June 17, 1870, founded a line of the family in the United States. Its most prominent member was **Charles Joseph Bonaparte**, b. June 9, 1851, d. June 28, 1921, a grandson of Jerome. A lawyer, he served as secretary of the navy (1905–06) and attorney general (1906–09) under Theodore Roosevelt. In the latter capacity he handled many of the administration's antitrust suits.   DONALD D. HORWARD

Bibliography: Anderson, Robert G., *Those Quarrelsome Bonapartes* (1927); Aronson, Theo, *The Golden Bees: The Story of the Bonapartes* (1964); Delderfield, Ronald, *The Golden Millstones: Napoleon's Brothers and Sisters* (1965); Geer, Walter, *Napoleon and His Family: The Story of a Corsican Clan*, 3 vols. (1927–29); Macartney, Clarence, and Dorrance, Gordon, *The Bonapartes in America* (1939); Seward, Desmond, *Napoleon's Family* (1986); Stacton, David, *The Bonapartes* (1966).

Bonaventure, Saint   [bahn-uh-ven'-chur]

A scholastic theologian and philosopher, Bonaventure, b. c.1217, d. July 15, 1274, was known as the Seraphic Doctor. Though Italian (Tuscan) by birth, he studied philosophy and arts in Paris (1236–42). After he became a Franciscan in 1243, he studied theology under ALEXANDER OF HALES and taught at the University of Paris until Feb. 2, 1257, when he was elected minister general of his order. Although he was well acquainted with the philosophy of ARISTOTLE, he feared its use in Christian theology and preferred the more traditional philosophy of ST. AUGUSTINE, often opposed to the Aristotelian synthesis of St. Thomas AQUINAS. He successfully defended the rights of Mendicant orders to teach at the University of Paris, and he was mainly responsible for the Augustinian orientation of the Franciscans. He set forth his essentially Augustinian and mystical theory of Christian knowledge in his short *Itinerary of the Mind into God* (1259) and *Retracing the Arts to Theology* (1255–56). Created cardinal bishop of Albano by Gregory X on May 28, 1273, he played a prominent role at the Council of Lyons (1274), but resigned as minister general on account of illness. He was canonized on April 14, 1482, and declared a Doctor of the Church on March 14, 1587. Feast day: formerly July 14; now July 15.   JAMES A. WEISHEIPL

Bibliography: Bettoni, Efrem, *Saint Bonaventure*, trans. by Angelus Gambatese (1964); Gilson, Étienne, *The Philosophy of Saint Bonaventure* (1938); Ratzinger, Josef, *The Theology of History in St. Bonaventure* (1971); Reist, Thomas, *Saint Bonaventure as a Biblical Commentator* (1985).

bond

A bond, in finance, is a written promise to pay a specified sum of money on a fixed future date. Bonds are issued by business firms, state and local governments, sovereign states, and other organizations that need long-term funds at a specific rate of interest. As a form of debt financing, the issuance of bonds has been a long-standing means of supporting the development of cities and corporations.

Corporate bonds provide maximum safety to lenders while offering a steady income in the form of interest. Several kinds of corporate bonds are used. Mortgage, or secured, bonds are backed by specific company assets, such as land, buildings, machinery, or furniture. Debentures, on the other hand, have no specific asset pledged as security.

Municipal bonds can be divided into two main categories, general obligation bonds and revenue bonds. The security for the general obligation is the taxing power of the state or local government. Revenue bonds, on the other hand, are payable solely from revenues derived from projects financed by the bonds, such as airports and toll roads. Interest income from municipal bonds, unlike that from other securities, was exempt from federal income tax until the Tax Reform Act of 1986 affected municipal revenue bonds.

Until 1983, bonds were available to investors in two forms: bearer bonds and registered bonds. Bearer bonds, also known as coupon bonds, are payable to anyone who possesses them at the time payments are due. A U.S. Treasury ruling in 1982, aimed at reducing tax evasion, disallowed future issuance of bearer bonds. Now, all bonds are registered bonds, so named because the issuer must keep a record of ownership.

Bibliography: Darst, D. M., *The Complete Bond Book* (1975); Holt, R. L., *The Complete Book of Bonds* (1985).

Bond, Edward

Edward Bond, b. July 18, 1934, is a contemporary English playwright best known for his provocative, shocking themes. He first achieved international recognition with the play *Saved* (1965), banned in England for portraying the stoning of a baby. The play's eventual performance ended England's censorship of the stage. *Early Morning* (1968) is a historical fantasy that includes cannibalism and portrays Queen Victoria as a lesbian enamored of Florence Nightingale; *Narrow Road to the Deep North* (1968) is an Oriental fable in the style of Bertolt Brecht; *Lear* (1971) presents Shakespeare's king as an evil autocrat; and *Bingo* (1973) features a cynical Shakespeare in retirement. Bond's later plays include *Restoration* (1981), *Summer: A Play for Europe* (1982), and the three-play cycle *The War Plays* (1985). He has also written film scripts (*Blow-Up*, 1966; *Walkabout*, 1971) and libretti for ballets (*Orpheus*, 1982) and opera (*The English Cat*, 1983, with music by Hans Werner Henze).   MYRON MATLAW

Bibliography: Hirst, David, *Edward Bond* (1986); Scharine, Richard, *The Plays of Edward Bond* (1976).

Bond, Julian

Julian Bond, b. Nashville, Tenn., Jan. 14, 1940, is known for his advocacy of civil rights. At age 20 he cofounded the Student Nonviolent Coordinating Committee (SNCC). A Democratic member of the Georgia House of Representatives (1965–75), he was initially barred from taking his seat because of his public denunciations of the Vietnam War, but the Supreme Court ordered (1966) his admission. He served in the Georgia Senate from 1975 to 1987.

Bond, William Cranch

One of the earliest American astronomers of note, William Cranch Bond, b. Falmouth (now Portland), Maine, Sept. 9, 1789, d. Jan. 29, 1859, overcame a lack of formal education to be named first director of the HARVARD COLLEGE OBSERVATORY. In 1839, Bond transferred the equipment from his excellent private observatory to Harvard, where 8 years later a 15-in (38-cm) refractor, equal in size to the largest in the world, was installed. Bond then studied especially Saturn and the Orion Nebula and made some of the earliest astronomical photographs in collaboration with his son G. P. Bond, who succeeded him as observatory director.

bonderizing

Bonderizing is a method of coating steel with a phosphate solution to protect the metal against corrosion and to improve its adhesion to enamels, paints, and varnishes. The steel is immersed in the solution at a temperature of about 100° C (212° F), and the metal surface is converted to an insoluble crystalline phosphate coating.   MERLE C. NUTT

Bondi, Hermann   [bawn'-dee]

The Austrian-born English mathematician and astronomer Sir Hermann Bondi, b. Nov. 1, 1919, is a major proponent of the now generally discounted STEADY-STATE THEORY of the origin of the universe. A graduate of Trinity College, Cambridge, he was a professor at the University of London (1954–84) and chief scientist of the British Department of Energy (1977–80). He was knighted in 1973.   STEVEN J. DICK

bonding, chemical: see CHEMISTRY.

bone

Bone is a type of skeletal tissue. Bones are also organs made largely of this tissue and surrounded by a membrane called the periosteum. The study of bones is called osteology.

Bone tissue contains living cells embedded in a hard matrix. This matrix consists mostly of calcium phosphate (as hydroxylapatite) and other calcium minerals, held together by COLLAGEN (a protein) and other organic substances.

Two major types of bone tissue exist. Compact bone tissue has many rodlike Haversian systems, each containing many concentric cylindrical layers (lamellae) surrounding a central blood vessel. Between these layers the bone cells (osteocytes) lie within spaces called lacunae. Tiny pores (canaliculi) connect the osteocytes with one another and with the BLOOD vessel, allowing oxygen and nutrients to reach the cells.

Cancellous, or spongy, bone tissue has a loose network of rigid beams (trabeculae). The spaces between these trabeculae contain marrow, a blood-forming tissue. Young marrow is red because many new blood cells are forming. Older marrow becomes yellow with the deposition of fat cells.

Bone tissue renews itself throughout life, constantly tearing down and rebuilding its mineralized framework. Chemical factors secreted by immune-system cells apparently regulate the balance between bone resorption and formation. Bone-absorbing cells (osteoclasts) dissolve old tissue, and bone-forming cells (osteoblasts) deposit new tissue, changing into mature osteocytes as the tissue hardens; a protein called osteogenic growth factor (OsGF) induces production of the osteoblasts. New trabeculae and Haversian systems are mainly oriented parallel to the direction of greatest stress.

The single most important function of bones is the support of the softer tissues of the body. The action of voluntary MUSCLES on bones and JOINTS produces locomotion in vertebrates. A second important function is the protection of softer structures, especially those of the NERVOUS SYSTEM. A third is the production of blood cells in the marrow. Cells there called stem cells are the ultimate source of all types of blood cells; long sought, they were finally isolated in the late 1980s. Bones also store calcium salts, and bones in the middle EAR of higher animals conduct sound waves and make hearing possible.

Bones can be long, short (wrist bones), flat (many skull bones), irregular (vertebrae), or sesamoid (kneecap). Most limb bones are long and roughly cylindrical. The shaft (diaphysis) consists of compact bone surrounding an interior (the medullary cavity) or spongy bone and marrow. The ends (epiphyses) are mostly spongy bone tissue, capped by CARTILAGE at the joints. During youth, rapid growth occurs in the epiphyseal cartilage, which lies between the flared section of the bone (metaphysis) and the epiphysis.

Ossification is the formation of bone tissue. The clavicle (collarbone) and many skull bones are called dermal bones because they ossify directly within the CONNECTIVE TISSUE of the skin (intramembranous ossification). Most other bones are endochondral; that is, they first form as cartilage before ossifying. A protein hormone called cartilage induction factor (CIF) stimulates the production of cartilage.   ELI C. MINKOFF

Bibliography: Shipman, Pat, et al., *The Human Skeleton* (1985); Simmons, D. J., *Nutrition and Bone Development* (1989); Tavassoli, Mehdi, and Yoffey, J. M., *Bone Marrow* (1983); Vaughan, Janet M., *The Physiology of Bone,* 3d ed. (1981).

See also: LIGAMENT; SKELETON, HUMAN; TENDON.

bone diseases

Bone diseases most directly influence the ability to walk or to move any part of the body—hands, limbs, neck, and spine. They are related to JOINT disorders—ARTHRITIS, COLLAGEN DISEASE, DISLOCATION of joints, and RHEUMATISM. The medical specialty pertaining to bone disorders is ORTHOPEDICS.

FRACTURES are the most common bone disorders. They can occur because of an accident or be secondary to metabolic diseases. Fractures are life-threatening to aged people having the disease OSTEOPOROSIS, in which bones become brittle.

Birth Defects. Congenital bone diseases constitute a wide spectrum, ranging from the unimportant—for instance, mild bow legs—to severe lesions, such as SPINA BIFIDA, in which the lower end of the spine fails to develop properly and the baby is born with paralysis and misshapen vertebrae. Congenital diseases may have hormonal bases: for example, some girls suffering from fibrous DYSPLASIA, in which fibrous tissue replaces that of some bones, often resulting in bone deformity, physically mature so early that they are capable of pregnancy and childbirth at the age of seven. Congenital defects also may have genetic bases, as in families who have extra fingers or toes or in the disease osteogenesis imperfecta, in which children have such brittle bones that many are fractured. Disorders of growth include several kinds of dwarfism and gigantism (see ENDOCRINE SYSTEM, DISEASES OF THE). Bones may develop deformity as the result of known causes, such as the infection POLIOMYELITIS, or unknown or variable causes, such as curvature of the spine (SCOLIOSIS) or CLUBFOOT.

Infections. Infections of bone, called OSTEOMYELITIS, are usually caused by pus-producing bacteria, especially *Staphylococcus* and *Streptococcus*. Before the development of antibiotics, children frequently contracted this disease. Today bone infections are introduced primarily through fractures and during surgical operations. People infected with syphilis, tuberculosis, leprosy, or yaws are also susceptible to bone damage.

Metabolic Disorders. Metabolic abnormalities often involve defects in the storage of minerals, particularly calcium and phosphate ions, in bone. Diseases of the kidney can cause a metabolic imbalance of phosphate and calcium so that bone weakening occurs. Other metabolic bone diseases are osteoporosis, gout, OSTEOARTHRITIS, and PAGET'S DISEASE.

Nutritional Disorders. Nutritional deficiencies that result in bone damage include RICKETS in children and osteomalacia in adults, caused by a lack of vitamin D. In children, calcium and phosphate are poorly distributed on bones during development, resulting especially in deformity of the legs and

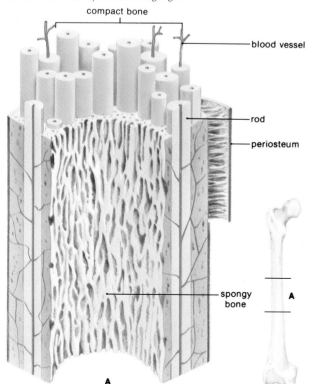

Bones are highly complex organs. This magnified cross section of a femur, or thighbone (A), shows a thin, fibrous outer covering called the periosteum. Bundles of rodlike Haversian systems containing blood vessels form a layer of compact bone, which provides strength and support and surrounds an inner layer of spongy bone. Marrow is found in the inner layer in the living organ.

compact bone

blood vessel

rod

periosteum

spongy bone

A

A

arms. In adults, bones of the spine, pelvis, and legs become demineralized and the bones weaken. SCURVY—caused by a lack of vitamin C—also affects bone tissues. A study in the late 1980s indicated that the mineral boron is nutritionally important, as well. Apparently, it reduces loss of the bone minerals calcium, phosphate, and magnesium and helps to maintain adequate blood levels of estrogen and testosterone, which play a role in bone health.

Toxic Diseases. The importance of toxic conditions of bones to public health became evident because of such tragedies as thalidomide-induced birth defects and radium poisoning. The drug THALIDOMIDE was given to pregnant women in Britain and Germany for use as a sleeping pill and to treat nausea. It caused an epidemic in which thousands of babies were born with deformed or missing limbs. Women employed during the 1920s as painters of luminescent clock dials were unwittingly exposed to radium from the paint as they licked their brushes. Many died, either from anemia or from bone cancer, alerting doctors to the dangers of radioactivity and subsequent radiation injury. Other types of toxic bone disease include fluoride and lead poisoning and overexposure to X rays.

Tumors. Bone tumors, although not common, are not rare; benign tumors are more common than malignant ones (sarcomas). Metastatic tumors—those which arise primarily in another tissue and spread by the blood to the skeleton, where they usually grow in many places at once—are very common in bones, although tumors originating in bones are not. The skeleton is second only to the lung as a site for metastases of CANCER. More fatalities and greater pain are associated with metastases of bone than with any other type of cancer.

Treatments. Treatments for bone diseases vary as widely as the causes. Physical disorders often require mechanical therapy—for instance, plaster casts for fractures and braces and splints for support. Drugs are used for metabolic problems and antibiotics for infections. Corrective surgery benefits many people having such diseases as scoliosis. Therapy can involve REHABILITATION MEDICINE, by which victims of injury, deformity, and amputation can learn how to function as normally as possible. Researchers are working on ways to replace bone for patients with birth defects and to speed healing of bone fractures. Specially treated coral has been used to repair fractures requiring bone grafts and to reconstruct facial bones destroyed by cancer. Still experimental are tiny beads of starch with a negative charge that are applied to the area of a fracture to promote the growth of new bone and a process to turn muscle into new bone.   JONATHAN COHEN, M.D.

Bibliography: Berry, C. L., ed., *Bone and Joint Disease* (1982); Castells, S., and Finberg, L., eds., *Metabolic Bone Diseases in Children* (1990); Martin, R. B., and Burr, D. B., *Structure, Function and Adaptation of Compact Bone* (1989); Stevenson, J. C., *New Techniques in Metabolic Bone Disease* (1990).

bonefish

The bonefish, or banana fish, is found in all tropical seas and is a sport fish for the light-tackle enthusiast. A member of the family Albulidae, order Elopiformes, it may reach 76 cm (30 in) in length and weigh as much as 10 kg (22 lb). Clams, snails, crabs, shrimp, and small fish are its principal foods.
                                                        ALFRED PERLMUTTER

Bonfils, Frederick G.   [bahn'-filz]

Frederick Gilmer Bonfils, b. Troy, Mo., Dec. 31, 1860, d. Feb. 2, 1933, was, with Harry H. Tammen, responsible for transforming the nearly bankrupt *Denver Post* into the most widely circulated newspaper in the mountain states and one of the most sensational U.S. newspapers. Before buying the *Post* in 1895, Bonfils had been discharged from West Point before graduating. He had been involved in a land fraud and convicted of conducting lotteries in Kansas and Missouri. Even after muckraking became less prevalent in the United States, the *Post* continued to print exposés—one caused an attempt on his life by a disgruntled lawyer—and established itself as an influential newspaper.   SAM KUCZUN

Bibliography: Hosokawa, Bill, *Thunder in the Rockies* (1976).

The bongo, B. eurycerus, a rare eland antelope, inhabits central west Africa. It has spirally twisted horns and unusual white markings.

bongo

The bongo, *Boocercus eurycerus*, is a large antelope that lives in dense, cool, humid mountain forests of central Africa from Kenya to Sierra Leone. It is classified in the family Bovidae, order Artiodactyla. The male stands about 140 cm (4.5 ft) tall at the shoulder, is about 180 cm (6 ft) long, and weighs up to 220 kg (485 lb); the female is smaller. Both sexes have backward-sloping, single-spiral horns that are usually a bit more than 80 cm (31 in) long. The ears are large, and a short mane runs from shoulder to rump. The bright reddish brown coat is marked with vertical white stripes on each side; white markings also appear on the face, breast, and legs. The tail tuft is maroon or black. Bongos travel in groups of up to about 20 individuals, rather than gathering in herds. They are shy, swift animals that browse on leaves and roots, rearing at times with forelegs against a tree to reach higher branches. They move farther up the mountain slopes during the dry season, then farther down the mountain during the rainy season.
                                                        EVERETT SENTMAN

Bibliography: Mochi, Ugo, and Carter, T. D., *Hoofed Mammals of the World* (1953; repr. 1971); Walker, Ernest P., et al., *Mammals of the World*, 2 vols., 4th ed. (1983).

Bonheur, Rosa   [bawn-ur']

Rosa Bonheur, b. Mar. 16, 1822, d. May 25, 1899, a highly acclaimed French painter and sculptor of animals, was one of the most unconventional artists of the 19th century. Bonheur studied with her father, the landscape painter Raymond Bonheur, and with Léon Cogniet. At an early age she began sketching animals at the Louvre and in sections of the Bois de Boulogne. She frequented slaughterhouses and butcher shops to study animal anatomy. In 1852 she received permission from the police prefect to wear male garb more suitable to her activities and to the outdoor life she preferred.

Her admiration for the novelist George SAND and her father's contacts with the St.-Simonians, who believed in equality of the sexes, encouraged Bonheur to pursue her career. She undertook enormous, complex canvases, such as *The Horse Fair* (1853; The Metropolitan Museum of Art, New York City), considered her masterpiece. Bonheur was a regular contributor to the Salon and won gold medals in 1848 and 1855. Her animal bronzes are less known than her paintings.

Bonheur's technical abilities and understanding of animal behavior often approach in quality the animal paintings of such 17th-century Dutch artists as Paulus POTTER. Her fame was comparable to that of the English animal painter Sir Edwin LANDSEER. Her companion in later years was the American artist Anna Klumpke, who wrote her biography.

Bibliography: Heller, N. G., *Women Artists* (1987); Shriver, R., *Rosa Bonheur* (1982); Stanton, T., ed., *Reminiscences of Rosa Bonheur* (1910; repr. 1976); Tufts, E., *Our Hidden Heritage* (1974).

The Horse Fair *(1853) is often considered Rosa Bonheur's masterpiece. Best known for her realistic and vigorous animal paintings, the unconventional Bonheur was the first woman to receive the French Legion of Honor. (Metropolitan Museum of Art, New York City.)*

Bonhoeffer, Dietrich   [bawn'-hur-fur, dee'-trik]

Dietrich Bonhoeffer, b. Feb. 4, 1906, was a German Lutheran pastor and theologian who was imprisoned at Buchenwald and executed on Apr. 9, 1945. His renown rests less on his achievements as a theologian than on his life, which illustrated his belief that Christian discipleship means costly involvement in modern secular society. Bonhoeffer studied theology at Berlin, but under the influence of Karl Barth he rebelled against the academic type of theology that he found there. The beginnings of his ministry coincided with the rise of the Nazi party in Germany, and Bonhoeffer joined the "Confessing church," those elements in the church opposed to Hitler. He taught theology first in Berlin and then in the unofficial seminaries of the Confessing church. He was on a lecture tour in the United States at the outbreak of World War II and immediately returned to Germany. Soon after, he joined a group of conspirators working for the overthrow of the regime. Arrested in 1943, he was hanged shortly before the downfall of Hitler. His best-known works are *The Cost of Discipleship* (Eng. trans., 1948) and *Letters and Papers from Prison* (Eng. trans., 1953).   John Macquarrie

Bibliography: Bethge, Eberhard, *Dietrich Bonhoeffer: Man of Vision, Man of Courage*, trans. by E. Mosbacher et al. (1970; repr. 1977); Fell, Ernst, *The Theology of Dietrich Bonhoeffer* (1985); Godsey, J. D., *The Theology of Dietrich Bonhoeffer* (1960).

Boniface, Saint   [bahn'-uh-fuhs]

Saint Boniface, originally named Wynfrith, b. c.673, d. June 5, 754, was an English monk and missionary who became known as the Apostle of Germany. As a young priest he went to Rome to obtain the approval of Pope Gregory II to act as missionary to Germany. The pope appointed him bishop in 722 with the responsibility of preaching the gospel throughout Germany. It was at this time that the pope gave him the name Boniface. In 732 he was promoted to archbishop, still without a fixed diocese. After being named papal legate for Germany by Pope Gregory III, he was asked to organize the dioceses of the church in German lands. Later, he was approached by the Carolingian rulers Pepin the Short and Carloman to preside over a series of reform synods for the Frankish church. About 745, his own diocese was finally fixed at Mainz. He resigned in 752 to return to missionary work and was killed by pagan Frisians. Feast day: June 5.   David Harry Miller

Boniface VIII, Pope

Boniface VIII, b. c.1235, was pope from 1294 to 1303. His name was Benedetto Gaetani. His pontificate was deeply marked by his quarrel with Philip IV of France, which began in 1296 over the question of royal taxation of the French church. In the bull *Clericis laicos* (1296), Boniface argued that taxing the church was grounds for excommunication. French threats of action against Italian banking houses forced Boniface to give way, and in *Et si de statu* (1297), he admitted the propriety of voluntary grants by churches to the state. The quarrel was renewed in 1301, when Philip trumped up charges of treason against Bernard Saisset, bishop of Pamiers, and demanded that the pope degrade the bishop from his clerical status so that he could be punished under secular law. Boniface thereupon revoked all previous concessions to Philip, and in *Ausculta, fili*, called for a council to meet in Rome to reform the government of France.

In the bull *Unam sanctam* (1302), Boniface set forth the most sweeping statement of papal political power ever released. Without mentioning Philip's name, Boniface declared that since the spiritual is greater than the temporal, secular authority must be subject to the spiritual. To oppose the authority of the pope would be to oppose God himself. This position marked the zenith of medieval papal claims.

Meanwhile Philip planned the abduction of the pope to France. On Sept. 7, 1303, Boniface was attacked in his residence at Anagni. The French could not make good their escape with the aged man; so they left him. The maltreatment he suffered at their hands, however, caused his death on Oct. 11, 1303, shortly after he returned to Rome.

David Harry Miller

Bibliography: Barraclough, Geoffrey, *The Medieval Papacy* (1968); Partner, Peter, *The Lands of St. Peter* (1972); Ullman, Walter, *The Growth of Papal Government in the Middle Ages*, 2d ed. (1962) and *A Short History of the Papacy in the Middle Ages* (1972); Wood, C. T., *Philip the Fair and Boniface VIII* (1967; repr. 1976).

Bonin Islands   [boh'-nin]

The Bonin Islands, which belong to Japan, lie about 800 km (500 mi) south of Tokyo. There are more than 25 islands, of which Chichi (formerly Peel Island) is the largest. They have an area of 104 km² (40 mi²) and a population of 2,010 (1980). The volcanic islands are mountainous, with an annual mean temperature of 23° C (73° F) and an average rainfall of

162 cm (64 in). Cedar, sandalwood, and ironwood trees are abundant. Fruit bats are the main native animal species. The people, mostly Japanese with some Taiwanese and Koreans, raise sugarcane, bananas, pineapples, and cacao.

Discovered by the Spanish in 1543, the Bonins were claimed by the United States (1823) and Britain (1825), but Japan annexed the islands in 1876. A military base during World War II, the Bonins were occupied by the United States in 1945. Japan's sovereignty over the islands was recognized in 1951, and the United States withdrew in 1968.

Bonington, Richard Parkes   [bahn'-ing-tuhn]

Richard Parkes Bonington, b. Oct. 25, 1801, d. Sept. 23, 1828, was a British painter who spent much of his short working life in France. There he was an important influence on the emergence of French romantic painting (see ROMANTICISM) during the 1820s, partly through his introduction of the English watercolor techniques developed by Thomas GIRTIN. Bonington also introduced new qualities of light, atmosphere, and color in his watercolor and oil landscapes that were painted directly from nature, for example, *Normandy Coast* (c.1824; Louvre, Paris). Such landscapes were important in the development of the painters of the BARBIZON SCHOOL.

Bonington's historical paintings were influenced by those of his friend Eugène DELACROIX, with whom he shared an interest in medieval history and English literature, especially the works of William Shakespeare and Sir Walter Scott. Both artists often illustrated scenes from the works of these authors. Bonington was highly influential and widely imitated during his lifetime. His landscapes and historical paintings were widely admired by the 19th-century romantic painters, including Delacroix, Théodore Géricault, and the members of the Barbizon school.

Bibliography: Hardie, Martin, *Water Colour Painting in Britain*, vol. 2 (1967); Shirley, Andrew, *Bonington* (1940); Wilton, Andrew, *British Watercolours, 1750–1850* (1977).

bonito   [buh-nee'-toh]

A bonito is any one of several open-sea fish closely related to the larger tuna and the smaller mackerel. They are found worldwide in warm and tropical waters but are more coastal in distribution than the tunas. Bonitos have torpedo-shaped bodies, streamlined fins, and large mouths with relatively large, conical teeth suitable for predation on other fish, squid, and shrimp. They weigh up to about 5.5 kg (12 lb) and grow to about 90 cm (3 ft) long. Bonitos lack the specialized heat-conserving vascular system of the tunas, and they must swim continuously not only to ventilate their gills but also because they lack an air bladder. Like tunas, they have two dorsal fins followed by finlets, as is the anal fin. They travel in large schools.

Bonitos are important game and commercial fish in Australia, Peru, Chile, the Pacific coast of Mexico, California, Brazil, the Mediterranean area, particularly the eastern end, and the Black Sea. They are usually canned and are considered good eating.

The classification of bonitos into species varies among authorities. Some list 4 or 5 different genera and about 8 spe-

The Atlantic bonito, Sarda sarda, *is a member of the mackerel family. It is caught commercially and for sport.*

cies; the genera include *Gymnosarda, Orcymopsis, Cybiosarda,* and *Sarda.* They belong in the family Scombridae, order Perciformes.   CAMM C. SWIFT

Bibliography: Migdalski, Edward C., and Fichter, George S., *Fresh and Saltwater Fishes of the World* (1976); Nelson, Joseph, *Fishes of the World,* 2d ed. (1984).

Bonn

Bonn was the capital of the Federal Republic of Germany from 1949 until the reunification of Germany in 1990. It lies on the west bank of the Rhine River in the Land, or state, of North Rhine-Westphalia, some 24 km (15 mi) south of Cologne, and has an area of 141 km^2 (55 mi^2). It is also situated at the junction of the northern plain and the hills of central Germany. About 10 km (6 mi) to the south, the Rhine emerges from its scenic gorge tract. The population is 276,500 (1987 est.).

Contemporary City. In 1949, when the three western-occupied zones of Germany were merged to form the Federal Republic, Bonn was chosen as a temporary federal capital because Berlin, which would have been preferable, was divided among the occupying powers and the eastern sector was under Soviet occupation. As a choice for the capital, Bonn had the advantage of seeming insignificant in comparison to Berlin, which implied that it was not considered a permanent capital. Bonn had previously been a market city, serving primarily the needs of the surrounding countryside. Its population before World War II had been only 100,400. It was, however, noted for book publishing, and it had some light metal industries. Among its historic buildings are a medieval cathedral and an 18th-century town hall. Bonn was the birthplace of Ludwig van Beethoven, and the house in which he was born is now preserved as a museum. The Beethovenhalle, a modern concert hall, was completed in 1959. Bonn also has a university that was founded in 1786, suppressed by the French when they occupied the Rhineland in 1794, and refounded in 1818 by the king of Prussia. It is housed in the Kurfürstliche Residenz (Electoral Castle), the former residence of archbishops of Cologne. A number of learned societies have headquarters in Bonn.

Today the city is dominated by governmental functions, most of which were expected to remain there for some time even after the formal return of the capital to Berlin in 1990. Government buildings, including the Bundeshaus, where the

The Münsterkerk, a Roman Catholic cathedral dating from the 12th century, stands in the center of Bonn's business district. Bonn, on the Rhine River, served as the capital of West Germany (the Federal Republic of Germany) from 1949 to 1990.

West German parliament met, the residences of the president and the chancellor, and the ministries of the Federal Republic, are grouped together close to the bank of the Rhine to the south of the city.

History. The earliest settlement, just before the Christian Era, was a Roman frontier fort known as Castra Bonnensia. Tradition has it that the saints Cassius and Florentinus were martyred on the site of the cathedral. The town was devastated by the Normans in the 9th century, and its later growth was inhibited by the proximity of Cologne and by Bonn's dependence on the archbishop of Cologne. In 1794, Bonn was incorporated into France, but in 1815, after the Napoleonic Wars, it was transferred to Prussia. It has grown rapidly since 1949. In 1969 its boundaries were redrawn to include Bad Godesberg and other suburban communities.

NORMAN J. G. POUNDS

Bibliography: Lutzeler, H., *Bonn: The Capital of West Germany in Photographs*, 3d rev. and enl. ed. (1985); *Michelin Green Guide to Germany*, 6th ed. (1984).

Bonnard, Pierre   [baw-nar']

Nude in the Bathtub (1937) is one of the intimate glimpses of everyday life that figured prominently in Pierre Bonnard's work. Bonnard, a master in manipulating color and light, was fascinated by twists of perspective. His work is characterized by simple composition and rich color. (Musée du Petit Palais, Paris.)

Pierre Bonnard, b. Oct. 3, 1867, d. Jan. 23, 1947, began his long painting career in Paris in the early 1890s. He was one of the first artists to use pure color in flat patterns enlivened by decorative linear arabesques in paintings, posters, and designs for stained-glass windows and books. Together with his friend Édouard VUILLARD and the other members of the group known as the NABIS (Hebrew for "prophets"), he helped establish a new, modern style of decoration that was important for the emergence of ART NOUVEAU in the late 1890s.

The paintings of Paul Gauguin and Claude Monet done in the late 1880s were the principal source for the new style of the Nabis. Bonnard, "the very Japanese Nabi," also drew on Japanese prints for his striking simplifications of form and his bold use of bright colors. In 1894, however, he turned to more somber colors and restricted his subject matter to intimate views of domestic life. When, around 1900, he again began to use bright hues, he adopted the impressionist broken brushstroke and abandoned the linear configurations of his earlier work.

Throughout the remainder of his career, Bonnard continued and expanded the impressionists' concern for depicting the personal environment of the artist. His naturalism, however, was merely a starting point for striking innovations in color and the construction of perspective. After 1920 intense colors dissolve forms yet celebrate the painter's sensuous delight in the lush southern French landscape and, above all, the beauty of the female nude.

Bonnard's entire stylistic evolution offers a transition from impressionism to a coloristic, abstract art. Critics now recognize the importance of Bonnard's contribution to the development of abstraction. During his lifetime, however, they often found his work old-fashioned, because of his commitment to figuration and the narrow scope of his themes. *Dining Room on the Garden* (1934–35; Guggenheim Museum, New York) is an excellent example of Bonnard's late style.

MARIAN BURLEIGH-MOTLEY

Bibliography: Babin, Alexander, *Pierre Bonnard* (1986); Fermigier, André, ed., *Pierre Bonnard*, trans. by Althea Schlenoff (1969); Ives, Colta, et al., *Pierre Bonnard: The Graphic Art* (1989); Newman, Sasha, et al., *Bonnard: The Late Paintings*, trans. by R. Le Fanu et al. (1984); Rewald, John, *Pierre Bonnard* (1948); Terrasse, Antoine, *Pierre Bonnard: Illustrator* (1989).

Bonnefoux, Jean Pierre   [bawn-foo']

Jean Pierre Bonnefoux (formerly Bonnefous), b. Bourg-en-Bresse, France, Apr. 9, 1943, is a ballet choreographer and artistic director of Indiana University's Ballet Department (1985–). He began his performing career with the Paris Opéra Ballet and was a principal dancer with the New York City Ballet (1970–81). As a dancer he performed in *Union Jack*, *Dances at a Gathering*, and *Who Cares?* His efforts as a choreographer include *Shadows*.   MICHAEL ROBERTSON

Bonnefoy, Yves   [bawn-fwah']

Yves Bonnefoy, b. June 24, 1923, is a French poet and critic whose work often concerns death and material transformation. His poetry includes the imagistic *On the Motion and Immobility of Douve* (1953; Eng. trans., 1967) and *Poèmes, 1947–75*. He has also written essays, many of which are on poetry and art, and studies of Arthur Rimbaud and Joan Miró.

Bonner Durchmusterung   [bawn'-ur doork'-moos-tur-ung]

The *Bonner Durchmusterung* (Bonn Observations of the Northern Skies) is one of the most important star catalogs. It was compiled at Bonn by Friederich W. A. Argelander over a period of about 25 years. Published in 1859–62 and 1863, it included about 324,000 stars and has since been extended (1886) by Edward Schönfeld and others to include 134,000 stars south of declination −23°.

Bonneville, Lake: see LAKE, GLACIAL.

Bonneville Salt Flats   [bahn'-uh-vil]

The Bonneville Salt Flats is a salt desert region located in Tooele County in northwestern Utah. Covering about 260 km² (100 mi²), it is the former bed of Lake Bonneville, which covered about 49,210 km² (19,000 mi²) during the Pleistocene Epoch. The flats, which are about 22.5 km (14 mi) long and 11.2 km (7 mi) wide, are covered with a smooth, white saltcrust formed by evaporation. They are flooded by high-ground runoff in winter, which smooths the salt surface, making them a favorite site for establishing automobile speed records.

Bonnie Prince Charlie: see STUART, CHARLES EDWARD.

Bononcini   (family)   [boh-nohn-chee'-nee]

A father and two sons of the Bononcini family were Italian musicians of the baroque period.

Giovanni Maria Bononcini, 1642–78, was a violinist and a composer of mostly ensemble music for strings. He is associated with the city of Bologna, where he directed music at the Basilica of San Petronio. He wrote an important theoretical treatise, *Musico prattico* (1673).

Giovanni Bononcini, 1670–1747, son of Giovanni Maria, was the most important composer of the family. He is best remembered as a rival of George Frideric HANDEL in the writing of operas for English audiences in London. He was active in Italy, Austria, Germany, England, and France as a composer and cellist. In addition to operas, he wrote cantatas, masses, oratorios, and instrumental works. He settled (1737) finally in Vienna where, reduced to poverty, he lived on a pension granted by Empress Maria Theresa.

Antonio Maria Bononcini, 1677–1726, was an opera composer whose *Camilla* (1696) is often wrongly attributed to his brother Giovanni.

Bibliography: Klenz, William, *Giovanni Maria Bononcini of Modena*, 2d ed. (1984); Lindgren, L., and Gianturco, C., eds., *Cantatas by Giovanni Bononcini* (1986).

bonsai   [bahn-sy']

Bonsai is the ancient Japanese art of dwarfing and shaping trees and other plants in small containers to obtain miniaturized versions of mature species. A given bonsai tree may be only 30 cm (1 ft) tall but otherwise be a replica of a tree in nature. In Japan, a densely populated country, the culture of such miniature plants is highly valued.

The art of bonsai originated perhaps more than 1,000 years ago in China. Early Japanese aristocrats showed a fondness for bonsai and contributed greatly to its development. A feudal lord in Sendai—the focus for bonsai art in Japan today—began to encourage the growing of bonsai in his territory in the 16th century. Bonsai culture was first popular in the United States among Japanese-Americans on the West Coast. Many servicemen returning from Japan after World War II brought with them an enthusiasm for the art form, which is now practiced throughout the United States. Bonsai can be classified according to their size as miniature, under 15 cm (6 in) tall; small, 15–30 cm (6–12 in); medium, 31–60 cm (12–24 in); and large, more than 60 cm. The shape of bonsai can be used to group them into five basic styles: formal upright, *chokkan*; informal upright, *moyogi*; slanting, *shakan*; semicascade, *han-kengai*; and cascade, *kengai*.

Bonsai are also classified according to the following arrangements of their trunks: (1) double-trunk style, *sokan*—two trunks form a common root system with one being dominant; (2) clump style, *kabubuki, kabudachi*—a clump of trunks grows closely together; (3) stump style, *korabuki*—the root forms an aboveground hump from which trunks arise; (4) raft, or straight-line, style, *ikadabuki*—branches grow in a straight line from a trunk laid on its side under the soil; (5) sinuous style, *ne-tsuranari*—like the raft style except that the underground stem twists around, causing the trunks to come up in a curved line.

The art of bonsai involves growing a plant under constant and proper care until it blends with the container in which it is planted in a natural and aesthetically pleasing manner. The size and shape of the container are chosen to enhance the plant's appearance. The plant must receive adequate sunshine, water, fertilizer, and suitable soil for healthy growth. Careful trimming, pruning, repotting, wiring, and other techniques are required to form the trees into desired shapes.

A bonsai tree is carefully shaped to remain small but still have the gnarled appearance of a large, weathered tree. After the taproot has been cut back, wires extending below the roots are wound about the trunk for support. Additional wires are used to shape the branches.

Almost all woody plants can be grown as bonsai. Evergreen species of juniper, pine, and spruce are frequently used because their needlelike leaves can be viewed throughout the year. Japanese white pine, *Pinus parviflora,* is well suited to bonsai culture. Deciduous plants that lose their leaves in winter such as azaleas, cherries, and maples are grown for their attractive flowers, fruits, and fall foliage. *Zelkova serrata,* a deciduous species, is a favorite bonsai subject. Witch hazel, *Hamamelis virginiana,* is one of the many American plants that make good bonsai specimens. Extensive collections of bonsai are housed at the Brooklyn Botanic Garden and Arboretum, New York, and at the United States National Arboretum, Washington, D.C.

Bibliography: Allen, Oliver E., *Gardening with the New Small Plants* (1987); Dante, Horst, *The Macmillan Book of Bonsai* (1986); Dunton, Darlene, *Complete Bonsai Handbook* (1978); Koreshoff, Deborah, *Bonsai* (1984); Young, Dorothy, *Bonsai* (1985).

Bontecou, Lee   [bahn'-te-koo]

Lee Bontecou, b. Providence, R.I., Jan. 15, 1931, became known in the early 1960s for her constructions and canvas and plastic reliefs. These works took their imagery from flowers, insects, fish, and the human face. The plastic cells of some of Bontecou's constructions possess an artificial air that often clashes disturbingly with their natural imagery. Some of her sculptural forms resemble those of genitalia and hint at the universal sexuality underlying all forms.   PHIL PATTON

Bontempelli, Massimo   [bohn-taym-pel'-lee, mahs'-see-moh]

Massimo Bontempelli, b. May 12, 1878, d. July 21, 1960, was an Italian writer who rejected 19th–century ideals and developed his own aesthetic theory, magical realism. He was most active about 1930 and exerted considerable influence on his generation. His best novel is *Vita e morte di Adria e dei suoi figli* (The Life and Death of Adria and Her Children, 1930).
                LOUIS KIBLER

Bontemps, Arna   [bohn'-tohm]

Arna Wendell Bontemps, b. Alexandria, La., Oct. 13, 1902, d. June 4, 1973, was an American writer whose poetry, stories, and children's literature have won critical acclaim since the 1930s for their deft handling of black dialect, generous humor, and realism. Among his best-known poems are "Nocturne at Bethesda," and "Reconnaissance." *The Old South* (1973), a collection of stories, contains the haunting "A Summer Tragedy." Of his three novels, the first, *God Sends Sunday* (1931), was staged in 1946 as *St. Louis Woman,* and the second, *Black Thunder* (1936), was a strong treatment of an abortive American slave rebellion. With Jack CONROY, he wrote *They Seek a City* (1945; rev. as *Anyplace But Here*, 1966), an account of the northward migration of blacks since Reconstruction.

Bonus Army

The Bonus Army was the popular name for a group of American World War I veterans who gathered in Washington, D.C., in 1932, demanding the immediate payment of a bonus due them in 1945. In May 1932 about 15,000 veterans, many of them unemployed and destitute, converged on Washington to pressure Congress into passing the bonus bill. The House passed such a bill on June 15, but it was defeated in the Senate. The marchers continued to camp at Anacostia Flats, Md. On July 28 a riot there led to an order by President Herbert Hoover to break up the camp. Federal troops under Gen. Douglas MACARTHUR dispersed the veterans with cavalry, infantry, tanks, and tear gas.

booby

Booby is the common name for six species of seabirds that make up the genus *Sula.* Boobies (together with gannets) make up the family Sulidae, order Pelecaniformes. They live along tropical and subtropical coasts except in the northern

Pacific area. They range in length from 65 to 100 cm (26 to 40 in) and are mostly white, with dark tails and brownish black on the wings. Two species have brown on the head and neck. The stout bill is conical and sharply pointed with a slight curve toward the tip; the nostrils are closed by overgrowth of the bill's horny sheath. The wings are long and pointed, and the tail is moderately long and wedge-shaped. The legs are short, with webbing between all four toes. The bare skin on the face and throat is usually brightly colored, as are the feet and bill. Boobies sleep on water and seldom come to land except to breed. Feeding—on fish and squid—is usually done near the shore. The birds soar over the water at heights of up to 30 m (100 ft), then fold their wings and dive into the water to grasp their prey in their bills. They nest in colonies, either using depressions in the ground or building stick nests in trees. Both sexes incubate the 1 to 3 pale blue eggs and care for the young.   ROBERT J. RAIKOW

Bibliography: Line, Les, *The Audubon Society Book of Water Birds* (1987).

boogie-woogie

Boogie-woogie is a JAZZ piano style characterized by sustained, rolling, eight-beats-to-the-bar riffs in the left hand. A fast, rhythmically intense version of blues guitar, it was played as dance music in honky-tonks and at rent parties—money-raising entertainments given by apartment tenants. The style did not reach wide popularity until the mid-1930s, when it was promoted by the jazz record producer John HAMMOND; after hearing a recording of "Honky Tonk Train Blues," Hammond sought out its composer, Meade Lux Lewis, who was working in a Chicago car wash. Lewis made many records for Hammond, as did Pine Top Smith and Albert Ammons. Hammond, Smith, and Ammons formed a boogie-woogie trio and played in Carnegie Hall at the height of the boogie-woogie craze of the late 1930s.

Bibliography: Collier, James L., *The Making of Jazz* (1978); Hentoff, Nat, and McCarthy, Albert, *Jazz* (1959; repr. 1974); Lyttleton, Humphrey, *The Best of Jazz II* (1983); Lyons, Les, *The Great Jazz Pianists* (1983).

boojum tree

The boojum tree, *Idria columnaris*, is a thorny deciduous tree belonging to the candlewood family, Fouquieriaceae. Native to Baja California, Mexico, it is rarely found north of 30° north latitude. When the tree is young, it has a swollen trunk that looks like an inverted carrot. Often hollow, the soft trunk produces branches that sometimes arch over and root at their tips. The tree grows up to 20 m (66 ft) high and resembles a spiny telephone pole. The small, oval leaves are wider at the end of the leaf; the greenish yellow flowers are borne at the top of the tree. The tree was named "boojum"—the mysterious monster in Lewis Carroll's *Hunting of the Snark*—because of its odd shape.

Bibliography: Humphrey, Robert R., *The Boojum and Its Home* (1974).

book

Books, ranging from ancient scrolls to today's mass-produced volumes, are an important storehouse of human knowledge. They originated in humanity's efforts to make permanent what oral tradition could not adequately preserve. This article discusses the history of books from their ancient origins to the present, focusing upon major developments in the art of bookmaking. Related information appears in the articles on BOOK ILLUSTRATION, LIBRARY, and PUBLISHING and in discussions of types of books such as ATLAS, BEST-SELLER, DICTIONARY, and ENCYCLOPEDIA. Technical information is presented under BOOKBINDING; LINOTYPE; PAPER; PRINTING; and TYPE AND TYPESETTING.
Origins. Although the ancient Mesopotamians developed writing on clay tablets, the genesis of the modern book can be traced to the PAPYRUS scrolls produced in Egypt. Much like the Torah scrolls still used in synagogues, these scrolls were unrolled as they were read. At first only single copies were made. The papyrus rolls varied in length; some of those con-

The Egyptian Book of the Dead (c.1300 BC), one of the first books, was written on papyrus and profusely illustrated. A collection of incantations and formulas written in linear hieroglyphics, these scrolls were funerary gifts buried with the deceased for use in the afterlife.

tained in the library at Alexandria might have been as long as 9 m (30 ft). The earliest books contained prayers, rituals, and incantations; laws and government records; medical and scientific observations; and epics previously passed down orally. The BOOK OF THE DEAD, which is often considered the first book despite the existence of earlier papyrus fragments, contained prayers and magic formulas to guide the dead in the afterlife.

By the 2d century BC, the Ptolemies of Egypt, jealous of their library at Alexandria, forbade the export of papyrus. The Romans, who replaced the Ptolemies as rulers of Egypt, continued to produce papyrus rolls, however, and by classical Roman times had developed book reproduction so rapidly that several hundred copies of the same work could be made in a relatively short time. Meanwhile, EUMENES II, ruler of the ancient Greek kingdom of Pergamum, encouraged the production of vellum, a material made from the dressed skin of goats, sheep, or calves, and compiled a library rivaling that of the Ptolemies. Protected between pairs of wooden boards and sewn together, bound volumes of vellum were the antecedents of books as they are known today, although the Chinese had at the time made books consisting of bamboo strips bound together with cord. Smooth, tough, and durable, vellum, for which the Latin name is still *pergamena* ("parchment"), forms an ideal writing material, although, in modern times, the high cost has limited its use to special purposes.
The Middle Ages. Bookbinding in the West originated with the gradual development of the *codex*—folded leaves or pages contained within two or more wooden tablets covered with a wax writing surface and held together by rings. By the 4th century these codices had largely replaced the scroll. The codex marked a revolutionary change from the rolled manuscript. Despite the cost of materials, great bibles and service books were produced, splendidly illuminated with pictures, decorated initials, and borders. Examples are the BOOK OF KELLS (8th century) and the Winchester Bible (pre–13th century).

Even so, few people could read during the Middle Ages, and virtually all the manuscripts, knowledge, and literature of the ancient world, as well as the Bible and the great texts of Christendom, were produced and preserved in monasteries. The great medieval scriptoria reflected the efforts of many monks working together, as well as the labors of theologians, skilled illuminators, and scribes. A remarkable number of copies of works, both secular and religious, were produced by hand copying.

By the 13th century the thrust of intellectual life had passed to the universities. Workshops developed, and professional scribes became the principal creators of books. More people could read, and many more books were privately owned. As the Middle Ages progressed, kings and rich laymen became patrons to the artists, who produced such richly illuminated

(Left) *The vellum manuscript of the Book of Kells (c.8th century) is the pinnacle of Celtic illumination and calligraphy. The page, with its intricate tracery, shows the symbols of the four Evangelists. (Trinity College, Dublin.)*

(Right) *The Très Riches Heures (c.1415), painted by the Limbourg brothers for their patron, the Duke of Berri, is considered the highest achievement of medieval manuscript illumination. This page is a miniature evocation of the month of February. (Musée Condé, Chantilly, France.)*

Greek and Roman classics and revolutionized printing by creating an entirely new space-saving italic type for use in the widespread production of pocket editions.

William CAXTON printed the first books in English in the late 15th century. He also combined scholarship with being a craftsman. About a third of the more than 100 books he printed were his own translations.

(Below) *The Gutenberg Bible (1450-55), the first book printed in Europe with movable type, is the masterpiece, in both design and craft, of Gutenberg's press. The text is set in a Gothic type that resembles the most elegant script of the time; the illuminations and initials were added by hand.*

works as the *Très Riches Heures of the Duc de Berry* (finished *c.*1416, published and translated in 1969). Medieval manuscripts were at first written in Romanesque script and later in Gothic. (See ILLUMINATED MANUSCRIPTS.)

By the 14th century, in Italy, the humanists were turning for inspiration to the ancient world and were developing a new handwriting. Their capital letters were taken from Roman lapidary (incised) inscriptions and their lower case from the minuscule (small letter) manuscripts of the school of Charlemagne. When early printers produced the classics, they cut types derived from these scripts, from which the roman type commonly used today is a direct descendant. Such manuscripts were often exquisitely illuminated. By the 15th century even more people could read, creating an urgent need for a less laborious method of book production—a need accentuated by the RENAISSANCE and the REFORMATION.

Development of Printing. The key to the invention of printing lay in movable type. This type might be set up in any order and mistakes corrected; after printing, the same type could be used again. Although similar printing had developed earlier in China and Korea, Johannes GUTENBERG (b. Mainz, Germany, *c.*1397) is generally credited with the introduction of printing in the West. The GUTENBERG BIBLE, occasionally called the Mazarin Bible (1450-55), was the first book to be printed in Europe and is still one of the most beautiful.

Printing now spread swiftly, as journeymen left masters and set up for themselves. Printed works appeared in Italy (1453), Basel (1466), France (1470), Hungary (1473), Spain (1473), Poland (1474), Bruges (1474), England (1476), Sweden (1483), and Mexico (1539).

Spread of Printing. Because printing needed organized commercial outlets to be successful, the powerful trading center of Venice became the focus of early printing. Nicolas Jenson (*c.*1420-1480), a Frenchman working in Venice, was the first important printer whose nationality was not German. Jenson developed a superior roman type that inspired many subsequent printers.

Jenson was primarily a craftsman, albeit of genius, but the Venetian printer Aldus MANUTIUS was a scholar devoted to printing meticulously accurate texts. He printed many of the

The vast amount of printing during the 15th century and later would have been impossible without paper, first produced in China as early as the 2d century BC. By the 15th century sufficient paper mills existed in France and England to supply the expanding demand of printers.

The first printed books, now called INCUNABULA, resembled the manuscripts that they were to supersede. The title page did not exist, but within a short time details of author, title, printer, place, and date were given in the final paragraph, known as the colophon. Many printers used a woodcut device for identification.

16th and 17th Centuries. During the 16th century, books developed into volumes similar to those produced today. They contained a title page and were well-edited, accurate texts made available to the public at a moderate price.

The cultural impact of books became more apparent as their distribution became widespread. Books disseminated political, religious, and philosophical ideas more widely and more rapidly. The printed word was largely responsible for spreading the ideas of the Reformation during the 16th century. Literary works reached increasingly larger audiences.

By the mid-16th century and into the 17th, the center of innovative book production moved from Italy to France and into the Low Countries. Families, often related by marriage, formed publishing dynasties that spanned several generations, and scholar-printers founded publishing houses in Leiden, Paris, and Antwerp.

18th-Century Developments. Significant strides in bookmaking were made during the 18th century. The French influence continued to be felt, particularly in masterful engravings that reflected aristocratic tastes. Intaglio engraving was vastly improved, and color printing was developed. Notable innovations in type were made by John BASKERVILLE and William CASLON in England and by Giambattista BODONI in Italy.

Writing began to provide a profitable living during the 18th century. Books were purchased by the public and not just the private patron, and novels, children's books, and the family magazine enjoyed wide circulation. The 18th century also saw the development of encyclopedias, dictionaries, and other reference books. At the end of the 18th century and into the 19th, almost everyone had an opportunity to read. The growth of democratic ideas, and their dissemination through the written word, created an increasing demand for books and newspapers. Earnest 19th-century reformers made numerous series of good books available, and devoted Christians distributed Bibles.

Mechanization of Printing. The Industrial Revolution had a profound effect on printing. The power-driven press of Friedrich Koenig (1774–1833), first used in 1811, raised the number of pages printed in an hour from 250 to 1,000. The rotary press, introduced in 1848, achieved 24,000, and today more than a million pages an hour are printed. Mechanical typesetting was first used in the 1860s in a limited form. The linotype was developed in 1884, the first punch-cutting machine in 1885. At the beginning of the 19th century, the paper industry began manufacturing its product mechanically rather than by hand. Another major 19th-century development was the creation of cloth binding.

The invention of photography by Louis DAGUERRE in 1839 had an enormous impact on all forms of pictorial reproduction and ultimately on the typesetting process itself. Among the processes made possible by photography were line engraving, rotogravure, and offset printing. The offset process remains an integral part of modern computerized printing. Despite technical advances, standards of design in book production had drastically declined by the middle of the 19th century. A movement for reform was mounted from outside the trade in the form of the Private Press Movement, which received its impetus from William MORRIS, a writer, artist, and leading figure in the ARTS AND CRAFTS MOVEMENT, who founded the KELMSCOTT PRESS in 1891. Morris's books were decorated with his brilliant designs for woodcut borders and initials and were produced with the finest materials. His work inspired the creation of other presses that produced high-quality books, and his influence extended beyond England to Germany and the United States.

The 20th Century. As the movement spread to the United States, special editions and books of remarkably high quality and aesthetic beauty were produced by publishers and their designers. Approximately 50,000 separate new titles are published each year in the United States alone. Although the quality of paper used in mass production remains a problem,

Itaq;, quas pueri miferimus ad te lucubrationes noftras ; numerare aliquas poffumus; quas adolefcentes, non poffumus : quo in confilio nobis diutius permanen dum effe non puto: nam ut interdum nó loqui moderati hominis eft; fic femper filere cum eo , quem diligas, perignaui: neq; Hercule; fi in officio permanfimus in prima aetate ; debemùs nunc , tanq inexercitati hiftriones , in fecundo , aut tertio actu corruiffe . praefertim cum aemulatio tuorum ftudiorum Angéle nos non excitare modo languentes poffit, fed etiam incendere;quippe , qui multa, et praeclara habuimus a te femper,habe múfq; quotidie et confuetudinis noftrae teftimonia , et doctrinae tuae. Quare fi cuti pueri fcriptiunculas noftras, quafi la ctentis ingenii acerbitatem , detulimus ad te; fic nunc deinceps etiam ad te adole fcentiae noftrae primos foetus deferemus; non quo me ipfe plus ames: nam iam id

(Left) Pietro Bembo's De Aetna (1495) was a publication of Aldus Manutius' Aldine Press. Generally credited with the introduction of both italics and small capitals, Manutius produced books noted equally for excellent editing and clear, readable typography.

(Right) This page from the Prologue of Chaucer's Canterbury Tales *is from* The Works of Geoffrey Chaucer (1896). *William Morris founded the Kelmscott Press in 1891 as part of the revolt against the inferior craftsmanship that resulted from mechanization and mass production.*

new, acid-free papers are now available, and many publishers have agreed to use them. (Most books produced over the past century have been printed on paper with an acid content that turns pages yellow and brittle.) Mass production, computerized printing, the development of relatively inexpensive paperback editions, book clubs, and public libraries have made more books available to more people than ever before.

In this age of mechanization, book collecting, which dates from the Ptolemies, is still prevalent. Collectors range from professional booksellers to bibliophiles who collect books for their literary value, their aesthetic appeal, or their monetary worth as an investment. For whatever reason—and despite the competition from television, movies, and other forms of entertainment—old books are still cherished, and new books are still produced, bought, and read.   ALAN G. THOMAS

Bibliography: Brook, G. L., *Books and Book-Collecting* (1980); Blumenthal, Joseph, *The Printed Book in America* (1989); Chappell, Warren, *A Short History of the Printed Word* (1970); Hollick, Richard, *Book Manufacturing* (1986); Johnson, Arthur, *The Practical Guide to Book Repair and Conservation* (1988); Kenyon, F. G., *Books and Readers in Ancient Greece and Rome*, 2d ed. (1951; repr. 1980); Levarie, Norma, *The Art and History of Books* (1968; repr. 1982); Martin, Douglas, *Book Design: A Practical Introduction* (1990); Matthews, Jack, *Memoirs of a Bookman* (1989); Wilson, Adrian, *The Design of Books* (1993); Winckler, P. A., ed., *Reader in the History of Books and Printing* (1978).

Book of Changes

The *Book of Changes* (*Yijing*, or *I Ching*) is one of the central texts of Confucianism and one of the earliest works of Chinese literature. It consists of 64 hexagrams, each of which is made up of six divided or undivided lines, possibly created at the end of the 2d millennium BC; a cryptic, partly unintelligible text, written at the beginning of the 1st millennium BC; and a treatise on the text, the *Ten Wings*, written at the end of the 1st millennium BC. Although rejected by the empiricist scholars of the Qing (Ch'ing) dynasty, the numerological aspects of the work have been reemphasized by Westerners interested in Eastern mysticism.   LENNART FRANTZELL

Bibliography: Wilhelm, H., *The Book of Changes in the Western Tradition* (1976); Wilhelm, R., *Lectures on the I Ching* (1986).

Book of Common Prayer

The order of worship of the Church of England and the other churches of the ANGLICAN COMMUNION is called the Book of Common Prayer. The first edition was published in 1549 during the English REFORMATION; Thomas CRANMER was chiefly responsible for its contents. His aim was to reform the medieval prayer books; he wanted to produce a book in English that would be true to the example of the early church, biblical in content and spirit, and an instrument for unity in the church and the nation. The new book contained daily offices of morning and evening prayer, baptism, and the Lord's Supper and offices for confirmation, marriage, churching of women, visitation of the sick, and burial; ordination rites were added in 1550. In 1552 a more Protestant version was produced, and in 1559, under Queen Elizabeth I, a new book, incorporating the features of the 1549 and 1552 editions, was authorized. Further revisions occurred in 1604 and 1662. In 1979 the Episcopal church in the United States adopted a new version that, while retaining many traditional texts, introduced the use of contemporary language for the first time. In the Church of England the 1662 prayer book is used, along with an Alternative Service Book adopted in 1980.

The prayer book, along with the King James version of the Bible, has long been regarded as part of the literary heritage of the English-speaking world.   JOHN E. BOOTY

Bibliography: Leuenberger, Samuel, *Archbishop Cranmer's Immortal Bequest* (1990).

Book of Concord

The Book of Concord is a collection of documents that gave voice to the teachings of LUTHERANISM several decades after the death of Martin LUTHER. After a period of disagreement, re-sponsible Lutheran parties gathered together the creedal or confessional writings from the half century after the writing of the AUGSBURG CONFESSION (1530) and collected them in one book (1580). It was accepted by both civil and religious leaders who embraced the Augsburg Confession. Although not all Lutheran churches since 1580 have been willing to measure all their teaching in light of it, the Book of Concord is a respected and studied document among the theologians and ministers of the Lutheran world.   MARTIN E. MARTY

Bibliography: Bente, F., *Historical Introduction to the Book of Concord* (1965).

Book of the Dead

The Book of the Dead is a compilation of more than 100 texts translated and collated from Egyptian papyri of the 18th and 19th dynasties. The handpainted originals are considered works of art. The texts, religious and poetic in spirit, are largely songs, hymns to the gods, and prayers to AMON-RE and OSIRIS. Committed to memory, these texts were supposed to aid the dead, giving the soul directions for the journey through the underworld and words or magic spells to protect it from its enemies. The book is thus a primary source for the major religious beliefs of ancient Egypt: immortality of the soul, resurrection of the body, descent into the underworld, spiritual rebirth for believers, and final judgment before Osiris. The *Papyrus of Nebseni* (British Museum) lists the commandments, or the negative confession, that each soul recited before the seat of judgment.   NORMA L. GOODRICH

Bibliography: Shafer, Byron, *Religion in Ancient Egypt* (1991).

Book of Hours

The Book of Hours is a prayer book developed in the late Middle Ages for the personal devotions of the laity. Such books are based on the BREVIARY, the official collection of texts used in the celebration of the DIVINE OFFICE, but are abbreviated for easier use by private individuals.

Although the contents vary from place to place and according to the tastes of individual patrons, a Book of Hours usually contains, in addition to the Hours of the Virgin—the core from which it receives its name—a liturgical calendar, penitential psalms, passages from the Gospel, the Office of the Dead, and the Litany of the Saints. The prayers are arranged according to the eight canonical hours of the liturgical day, as practiced during the Middle Ages.

In the 14th and 15th centuries the Book of Hours became the most popular type of private devotional book. One of the best known is the *Très Riches Heures* of the duc de Berry (Musée Condé, Chantilly, France). This exquisitely illustrated 15th-century manuscript, made for a great patron of the arts, is an example of the luxurious Books of Hours commissioned by wealthy noblemen and princes.   TANIA BAYARD

Bibliography: Pacht, Otto, *Book Illumination in the Middle Ages* (1987); Sutton, Anne F., and Visser-Fuchs, Livia, *The Hours of Richard III* (1990); Thomas, M., *The Golden Age* (1979).

book illustration

Book illustration was developed from the ILLUMINATED MANUSCRIPT, which it eventually replaced when the once hand-drawn elements began to be printed from woodcuts. The invention of movable type (c.1451) made it possible to produce books by mechanical means. The precedent for their design was set by the manner in which illuminated manuscripts had been organized and decorated. Pages were framed with ornamental designs, initials were embellished, and full pages were devoted to pictures at regular intervals. This was now done mechanically in relief printing, basically the same graphic process used for letterpress.

Woodcuts and Movable Type. Earlier in the 15th century (probably about 1420, although later according to some experts), another type of illustrated book, the block book, had appeared. Although they were bound as BOOKS, the pages of block books are in fact prints that joined text and illustra-

The Four Horsemen of the Apocalypse *(c.1496) by Albrecht Dürer conveys a vision of doomsday. By the turn of the 15th century, Dürer was producing woodcuts of unequaled virtuosity. (Metropolitan Museum of Art, New York. Gift of Junius S. Morgan, 1919.)*

Gustave Doré's wood engravings, such as this scene from Don Quixote *(1863) by Cervantes, extended the text into the realm of bizarre imagination. The engravings elicited an emotional response that would later be duplicated in illustrations for children's literature.*

tions, both of which were printed from the same block of wood. Not until about 1460 or slightly later were books printed that combined woodcut illustrations with a text set in movable type. The German printer Albrecht Pfister (*c.*1410–1465) of Bamberg is credited with being the first to do this; Pfister's edition of Ulrich Boner's *Edelstein* (*c.*1461) is widely accepted as the first illustrated book. *Der Edelstein's* text, however, was printed from movable type, and the illustrations were then printed separately on blank areas left on the pages. Eventually text and illustrations were printed simultaneously, a considerable technical improvement.

15th-Century Illustrated Books. By the late 15th century Germany had become the publishing center of Europe. In Nuremburg, Anton Koberger (*c.*1440–1513) brought out the best-known illustrated book of the age, Hartmann Schedel's *Die Weltchronik* (1493), employing such artists as Wilhelm Pleydenwurff (d. 1494), Michael Wolgemut (1434–1519), and the young Albrecht Dürer to design it. In 1498, Dürer produced his illustrated *Apocalypse* in German and Latin editions, using full-page illustrations without captions and with printed texts on the back.

In Italy, France, and other European countries, books with illustrations were current by the 1470s, but the masterpieces of the art did not come out until the 1490s, for example, Francesco Colonna's *Hypnerotomachia Poliphili* (The Strife of Love in a Dream, 1499), published in Venice by Aldus Manutius. In Germany such major 16th-century artists as Hans Burgkmair the Elder, Hans Baldung-Grien, Lucas Cranach the Elder, and Hans Holbein the Younger were responsible for magnificent illustrated books. During the first half of the century, woodcuts were the most popular medium for illustrations, until engraved metal plates began to be used in the 1540s. By the end of the century, woodcuts had become rare, and engraving had become the rule.

Engravings and Picture Books. An important creation of the 16th century was the picture book, with text subordinated to elaborate illustrations; the subject matter ranged from maps to botanical studies and human anatomy, as in Andreas Vesalius's monumental *De humani corporis fabrica* (Basel, 1543). Another important development was the elaboration of both the title page and frontispiece; these were given enhanced symbolic importance as visual commentaries on the book's contents.

In the 17th century such major artists as Peter Paul Rubens, Rembrandt, and Nicolas Poussin illustrated many books. In 1658, John Amos Comenius published his *Orbis sensualium pictus* (Nuremberg), the first picture book designed specifically for children. During the 18th century handy, sensible formats replaced cumbersome, if beautiful, massive tomes. Illustrations were smaller, and decorative cuts and details were emphasized. The most important and influential illustrated book of the period was Denis Diderot's *Encyclopédie* (Paris, 1751–72), whose 17 volumes of text were supplemented by 11 volumes of illustrations. French 18th-century books exerted great influence throughout the world. Major painters, including François Boucher and Jean Honoré Fragonard, made significant contributions, and other artists, such as the Cochin family, the Moreau family, Jean Baptiste Oudry, Bernard Picart (1673–1733), and Hubert François Gravelot, executed innumerable book illustrations.

In Italy, Giovanni Battista Piranesi recorded his versions of the grandeurs of ancient Rome in monumental prints that, in bound books, brought to the farthest corners of Europe powerfully influential impressions of the Eternal City. In Germany, Daniel Nikolaus Chodowiecki made witty illustrations for both classics and contemporary works. Britain's contribution was primarily in scientific and architectural books, profusely illustrated with plans, diagrams, and pictures.

Wood Engraving. In the late 18th century the Englishman Thomas BEWICK discovered the technique of wood engraving (see WOODCUTS AND WOOD ENGRAVINGS). Until the improvement of photomechanical processes in the late 19th century, wood engraving was the favorite medium for illustration.

The Lithograph. Lithography (invented in 1798) introduced an inexpensive process for book illustration, and lithographs began to be widely used. Among the most memorable illustrations in this medium are Eugène DELACROIX's treatments of scenes from Shakespeare's *Hamlet* and Goethe's *Faust*. The most famous French illustrator of the 19th century is probably the gifted and prolific Gustave DORÉ. His editions of Dante's *Divine Comedy*, Cervante's *Don Quixote*, and Milton's *Paradise Lost* are among the most universally admired ever done; the illustrations for *Contes drôlatiques* (*Droll Tales*) by Balzac (Paris, 1855) are considered Doré's masterpieces. In Britain, William MORRIS and his KELMSCOTT PRESS did much to revive the illustrated book. Morris's attempt to achieve harmony between letterpress and illustration had a great impact in Europe and America and was widely imitated.

The Livre de Peintre. The invention of photomechanical means of picture reproduction (perfected by the 1880s) led to mass production on a huge scale and to an inevitable decline in artistic quality. Illustrations were often excellent, but they were no longer original prints. In France the so-called *livre de peintre* (literally "painter's book") made its appearance. This is an illustrated book, completely designed by an artist, and issued in limited numbers. Pierre BONNARD's *livre* of Paul Verlaine's *Parallèlement* (Paris, 1900) is one of the most famous, but many other artists, such as Pablo PICASSO, Henri MATISSE, Georges ROUAULT, and Marc CHAGALL, have created them.

American Book Illustrators. Standards of book illustration in America have been high since the 19th century, with outstanding works by such artists as J. J. AUDUBON, Elihu VEDDER, Howard PYLE, and N. C. WYETH. Rockwell KENT did a remarkable series of woodcuts for *Moby-Dick* (1930). Leonard BASKIN has illustrated the poetry of Emily Dickinson, Hart Crane, Ted

(Below) Aubrey Beardsley made full use of the photomechanical processes developed during the late 19th century to reproduce and distribute his highly stylized artworks in books and periodicals. This leering Ali Baba was the cover illustration for The Forty Thieves.

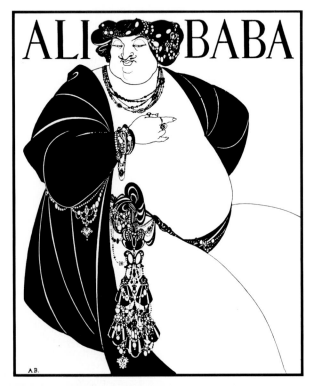

(Above) *Howard Pyle's illustrations, like Beardsley's, were assured a wide audience through photoengraving techniques.* The Flying Dutchman, *which first appeared in* Collier's Weekly *in 1900, is one of Pyle's illustrations for children. (Delaware Art Museum, Wilmington.)*

Hughes, Dante, and Homer. Some of the finest illustrated books of this century were created for children; Ludwig BEMELMANS, Maurice SENDAK, Edward GOREY, and Dr. SEUSS (Theodore Seuss Geisel) have carried on the imaginative 19th-century traditions of Sir John TENNIEL's classic illustrations for ALICE'S ADVENTURES IN WONDERLAND.   RAFAEL FERNANDEZ

Bibliography: Benesch, Otto, *Artistic and Intellectual Trends from Rubens to Daumier in Book Illustration* (1969); Bland, D. F., *A History of Book Illustration* (1969); Booth-Clibborn, Edward, ed., *American Illustration*, 3d ed. (1984) and *European Illustration*, 10th ed. (1984); Heck, J. G., *The Complete Encyclopedia of Illustration* (1979); Heller, Steven, *Innovators of American Illustration* (1986); Lacy, Lyn E., *Art and Design in Children's Picture Books* (1986); Ray, Gordon N., *The Illustrator and the Book in England from 1790–1914* (1976) and *The Art of the French Illustrated Book, 1700–1914* (1986).

Book of Kells

The large Irish ILLUMINATED MANUSCRIPT of the four Gospels known as the Book of Kells is one of the most famous of all medieval books. Now in the library of Trinity College, Dublin, it was probably begun by monks at the monastery of Iona and completed at the Irish monastery of Kells sometime between the mid-8th and the early 9th century. The gospels are written on thick vellum and lavishly illuminated with the rich ornamentation characteristic of Celtic art of this period. In addition to 31 full-page illustrations, fanciful figures and tightly interlaced bands, knots, and spirals of extraordinary intricacy and density occur throughout the book.   TANIA BAYARD

Bibliography: Alton, E. H., and Meyer, Peter, *The Book of Kells*, 3 vols. (1950–51); Henry, Françoise, *The Book of Kells* (1974).

book louse

Book lice, order Psocoptera, are wingless, soft-bodied insects a few millimeters in length that often live among papers or books. They feed on molds, cereals, fragments of dead insects, and other organic materials. They generally cause little damage but are frequently a nuisance. Winged members of this order are found outdoors on bark or foliage and are called bark lice. The psocopterans are not true LICE, which are members of another order, and they undergo an incomplete metamorphosis.   DONALD J. BORROR

Book of Mormon: see MORMONISM.

bookbinding

Bookbinding is the art and craft of fabricating protective covers, or bindings, for books and of restoring deteriorated volumes.

Folded pages between covers replaced the scroll form during the first five centuries of the Christian Era, and early

(Right) Hand bookbinding begins with multipage sections called signatures—groups of 8, 16, 32, or 64 pages in numerical order. The signatures are stacked into complete books in a sewing frame and sewn together by passing a thread through each section in turn and around vertical cords (1). The stitched book is trimmed on the three open sides and placed in a vise, where the back edge, or spine, is hammered into a more rigid rounded shape (2). The cords holding the sections together are laced through cardboards on each side (3), hammered flush, and glued down. The spine is reinforced with glued paper and gauze liners and with headbands, or thin fabric strips, sewn at the top and bottom (4). The boarded sections are held in place until the glue dries by cords tied tightly around protective wooden blocks (5). An outer cover of cloth or leather is glued to the boards (6), and endpapers are glued to the first and last pages of the book and to the covered board (7). The entire book is kept under pressure until the adhesives have set (8), at which point the book is completed (9).

This binding of the Codex Aureus manuscript of St. Emmeram is decorated with gold and inlaid with precious jewels. Dating from the 9th century AD, the volume used gold lettering on purple-stained sheets. (The Bayerische Staatsbibliothek, Munich, Germany.)

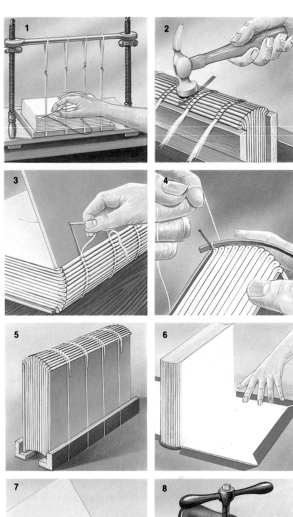

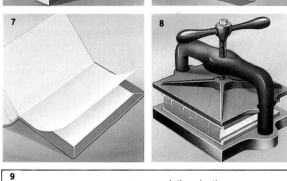

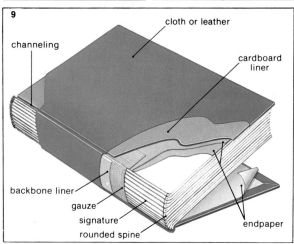

cloth or leather
channeling
cardboard liner
backbone liner
gauze
signature
rounded spine
endpaper

of Egyptian and Ethiopian Coptic bindings with wood covers, Roman codices, and Irish books indicate the adoption of this form across Europe. The folded groups of pages, or signatures, were sewn onto leather or vellum thongs or linen cords, the ends of which were laced into the cover boards. Between the 12th and 15th centuries bookbinding developed into a high craft, and covers were embellished with precious metals and jewels or blind-stamped leather.

After the process of printing from movable type was invented in the late 1440s, the volume of bookbinding work increased rapidly, leading to a deterioration in quality of materials and construction techniques. In 1825 a new technique, casebinding, was introduced, in which covers were prepared separately from the text block and glued on after the pages were sewn together. This easily mechanized operation is still used for most hardcover bindings. Since 1785 binders have experimented with glued rather than sewn bindings using rubber, gelatin, and now plastic adhesives. Glued bindings can be weak—for example, those of paperbacks that fall apart on the first reading—but they can also be stronger and more durable than the paper the book is printed on, depending on the adhesive used and the method of application.

Today the hand bookbinder is primarily involved with restoring deteriorated books, with binding small editions of well-printed texts, and with the design and construction of books as an art medium.

A restorer must be familiar with the style of design, technique, and materials used in different geographical areas during all periods of history and must know the chemistry of materials available today and methods of testing their durability and reversibility. Some people want a restored book to resemble the original as much as possible; others feel that what remains of the original binding should be preserved and that the restored parts should be clearly visible as new work.

The designer-binder uses single copies of a book to create works of visual art or high craft, calling attention to exceptional texts, examples of printing art, typographic design, and illustration. Some bookbinders design and develop binding forms, and for them the binding itself is a work of art.

RICHARD MINSKY

Bibliography: Cundall, Joseph, *On Bookbindings, Ancient and Modern* (1881; repr. 1977); Darley, Lionel S., *Introduction to Bookbinding* (1977); Watson, Aldren, *Hand Bookbinding* (1986).

bookkeeping

Bookkeeping is the systematic recording of the monetary value of business transactions in a book of accounts. It is the preliminary record-keeping stage of ACCOUNTING.

THE DOUBLE ENTRY SYSTEM

The double entry system of bookkeeping enables a business to know at any time the value of each item that is owned, how much of this value is owed to creditors, and how much belongs to the business clear of DEBT. It also indicates the portion of this debt-free ownership that is the result of the original investment in the company and the portion accruing from profits. One advantage of the double entry system is that its information is so nearly complete that it can be used as the basis for making business decisions. Another advantage is that errors are readily detected, since the system is based on two equations that must always balance. The term *asset* means anything of value that is owned. Assets may be tangible, as are furniture and property, or intangible, as are stocks and good will. Assets belong to their owner, regardless of who possesses them and regardless of whether they were purchased with borrowed money. All of a company's assets are either owed to someone else or are owned clear of debt.

LIABILITY is the amount that a business owes to another firm, to an individual, or to the government. The amount that is not owed to anyone else but is owned free of debt is called the owner's equity in the firm. Since everything that is owned is either owed or is free of debt, assets equal liabilities plus EQUITY. This is called the accounting equation.

Assets = **Liabilities** + **Equity**
(owned)   (owed)   (clear of debt)

Each of the assets and the liabilities and the equity is shown separately on a company's books and is called an account. An account has two sides, the left side (debit) and the right side (credit). One is the increase side; the other is the decrease side. All assets are increased on the debit side of the account, and any decrease in value is shown on the credit side.

Liabilities and equity, the other half of the equation, are increased and decreased in the opposite manner. Liabilities and equity are increased on the credit side and decreased on the debit side.

The owners' equity can be increased either by investing more money in the firm or by earning a profit. Equity is decreased by the owners' withdrawal of funds from the business or by losses of the firm. A separate type of equity account is used for each of these. The owners' investment is shown in an account called capital or, if there is one owner, proprietorship. The earnings of the company are put into an income account. Since both the capital and the income increase the owners' equity, capital and income accounts are increased on the credit side (the increase side of equity). Withdrawals and expenses (expenditures incurred without receiving an asset) are increased on the debit side, for each additional expense or withdrawal takes from the owners' equity.

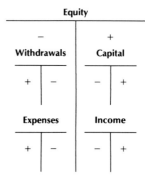

Every transaction, or change in the firm's values, affects two or more accounts, which will result in a debit and a credit of the same total amount. For example, if a new typewriter is purchased for cash, the asset account *office equipment* is increased by debiting, and the asset account *cash* is decreased by crediting. If the typewriter had been bought on credit, the office equipment account would have been increased by debiting, and the liability *accounts payable* would have been increased by crediting. If, instead of purchasing the typewriter, it had been rented, the expense account *rent expense* or *miscellaneous expense* would have been increased by debiting, and either the asset *cash* decreased by crediting or the liability *accounts payable* increased by crediting.

Thus, the same amount is always debited to one account and credited to another account. At all times, when the balances remaining in each of the accounts are added together, total debits will equal total credits. At the end of each month, or more often if desired, the record-keeping accuracy can be checked by making a trial balance: the total of all accounts having a debit balance must equal the total of all accounts having a credit balance. Thus, if the ABC Company has the following accounts, the trial balance will be as shown.

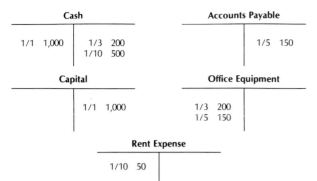

Cash				Accounts Payable	
1/1 1,000	1/3 200				1/5 150
	1/10 500				

Capital		Office Equipment	
	1/1 1,000	1/3 200	
		1/5 150	

Rent Expense
1/10 50

ABC COMPANY
Trial Balance Dec. 31, 19--

	Debit	Credit
Cash	$ 750	$
Office equipment	350	
Accounts payable		150
Capital		1,000
Rent expense	50	
Total	$1,150	$1,150

Ledgers. The book of accounts is known as a general ledger and usually has a separate page for each account. A separate book showing the name and balance owed for each account payable may be kept. This is called a subsidiary ledger; and the total of the balances owed as shown in the accounts-payable ledger would, of course, be identical to the balance of the accounts-payable account in the general ledger. A subsidiary ledger can also be kept for accounts receivable if the firm extends credit to its customers.

Journals. Transactions are not entered directly in the accounts. They are first recorded in a book known as a journal, sometimes called the book of original entry. Several kinds of journals are used.

The most common type is the general journal. In this, the title of the account to be debited is placed on the top line, with its amount shown in the debit column. The title of the account that is to be credited is shown below it, with its amount placed in the credit column. Below this may be a written explanation of the transaction. If more than one account is to be debited or credited, a separate line is used for each, always showing debits first and then credits below. The total of the debits column should always equal the total of the credits column on each general journal page.

GENERAL JOURNAL

Date	Account Title	Post	Debit	Credit
Jan. 1	Cash		1,000	
	Capital			1,000
	Owner's investment			
3	Office equipment		200	
	Cash			200
	Purchased typewriter			
5	Office equipment		150	
	Accounts payable			150
	Purchased typewriter from Z Co.			
10	Rent expense		50	
	Cash			50
	Rented typewriter			
			1,400	1,400

If a large portion of the firm's business concerns cash transactions, a separate cash journal can be used instead of the general journal for all those transactions affecting the cash account. All entries not affecting cash are made in the general journal.

CASH JOURNAL

Cash Disbursements				Cash Receipts		
Date	Acct. to Debit	Amount		Date	Acct. to Credit	Amount
1/3	Office Equipment	200		1/1	Capital	1,000
1/10	Rent expense	50				
1/31	Total-credit to cash	250		1/31	Total-Debit to cash	1,000

At the end of the month, or more frequently if desired, all journal entries are recorded in the ledger accounts. This is called posting. As each journal entry is recorded on the planned side of its account, a mark is placed in the post column of the journal to show that it has been recorded in the ledger. The date used in the ledger is the date on which it was first entered in the journal. The post column in the account is designed to show which page this entry was posted to in the ledger. If a cash journal is used, the monthly cash totals, rather than each entry, can be posted to the cash account.

FINANCIAL STATEMENTS
The principal financial statements used to determine the status of a company are the income and expense statement and the balance sheet. These may be made out annually, monthly, or at any desired time. Before preparing the financial statements, a trial balance is made to be certain that the debits equal credits.

XYZ COMPANY
Trial Balance
Dec. 31, 19--

	Debit	Credit
Cash	$10,000	$
Office supplies	2,000	
Office equipment	2,000	
Office equipment depreciation		500
Delivery truck	8,000	
Delivery truck depreciation		1,000
Accounts payable		2,000
Capital		10,000
Withdrawals	100	
Income		24,000
Rent expense	2,400	
Salary expense	12,000	
Miscellaneous expense	1,000	
Total	$37,500	$37,500

Adjusting Entries. In the above trial balance, the delivery truck and the office equipment are continually losing value as a result of age and use. This loss of value, called depreciation, must be calculated and recorded prior to preparing the statements. Several methods may be used to calculate depreciation. The simplest and most common method is to write off the original cost of the asset evenly over the period of its expected usefulness. If the delivery truck is expected to last eight years, it can be thought of as losing $1,000 in value each year because of depreciation. Depreciation takes from the value of the asset and increases the firm's expenses. The following depreciation entry will be made in the general journal and then posted:

Dec. 31 Depreciation expense..1,000
            Del. truck depreciation 1,000
                Recording 1 year's depreciation

Another expense that must be recorded before financial statements are prepared is the value of the office supplies that have been used. The used supplies are no longer owned and should be taken out of the asset account and recorded as an expense. To determine the used portion of office supplies, the value of the supplies currently on hand is subtracted from the total amount purchased, as shown in the office-supplies

XYZ COMPANY
Balance Sheet Dec. 31, 19--

Assets			Liabilities		
Cash		$10,000	Accounts payable		$ 2,000
Office supplies		200			
Office equipment	$2,000		*Equity*		
Less depreciation	1,000	1,000	Capital investment	$10,000	
Delivery truck	$8,000		Plus net income	5,300	
Less depreciation	2,000	6,000	Less withdrawals	100	
			Capital, Dec. 31		15,200
Total assets		$17,200	Total liabilities and equity		$17,200

account. If the firm has a current supplies inventory worth $200, the following entry will be made to take the used portion out and record it as an expense:

Dec. 31   Office supplies expense 1,800
                Office supplies 1,800
                      Inventory of supplies $200

The same type of entry is made for insurance, interest, and any other prepaid expense.

The following are some other entries that may need to be recorded: the allowance for bad debts if the firm extends credit, any government taxes or employee salaries that are owed but have not yet been recorded, and a merchandising firm's change in the inventory of items for sale.

After these entries are posted, it is often wise to make another trial balance to be certain that the debits and credits still balance.

Income and Expense Statement. The income and expense statement indicates the change in the owners' equity as a result of the firm's operation. It shows the net income, or net profit, that the firm has earned in the interval since financial statements were last prepared. The income and expense statement lists the total amounts of all the income and expense accounts as shown on the trial balance after the adjusting entries have been recorded.

XYZ COMPANY
Income and Expense Statement
For the Year Ending Dec. 31, 19--

Revenue		$24,000
Expenses:		
Rent expense	$ 2,400	
Salary expense	12,000	
Depreciation expense	1,500	
Office supplies expense	1,800	
Miscellaneous expense	1,000	18,700
Net Income		$ 5,300

If the total expenses had exceeded the total incomes during this period of time, the difference would have been a net loss.

Since the financial statements are prepared for the use of management rather than for the bookkeeping department, they contain no debit and credit columns.

Balance Sheet. The balance sheet is a statement of the total assets owned at a specified time, the value that the firm owes to others, and the value that is clear of debt. It is basically a statement of the accounting equation: assets equal liabilities plus equity.

All asset accounts are listed as shown on the trial balance, with any accumulated depreciation taking from the value of the asset. Usually, assets that can be readily converted into cash, known as current assets, are shown first.

All liability accounts are also recorded. The equity section states the owners' investment, as shown in the proprietorship or capital account, plus any net income earned. This net income is taken from the income and expense statement and is the excess of the revenue accounts over the expense accounts. If the income and expense statement had resulted in

a net loss, this would be deducted from the owners' investment. Any withdrawals made by the owners are deducted, since they take from their equity remaining in the firm.

The two sides of the balance sheet, assets and liabilities plus equity, must be in balance. Sometimes a worksheet is used to plan the adjusting entries, the income and expense statement, and the balance sheet.

CLOSING ENTRIES

Closing the books simply means transferring the balances of the three other types of equity accounts (income, expense, and withdrawals) into the capital account. Thus, closing entries affect only the equity accounts. After closing entries, the owners' capital or proprietorship account will show the balance indicated at the end of the equity section of the balance sheet. All other equity accounts will be at a zero balance, since their amounts have been transferred into capital.

Often the credit balances of the income accounts and the debit balances of the expense accounts are first transferred into a temporary account known as the income and expense summary. The balance of this account would then be the same as the net income or net loss shown on the income and expense statement. This balance is then taken out of the income and expense summary and transferred into capital.

The debit balance of the withdrawals account is transferred into capital by debiting and out of withdrawals by crediting.

GENERAL JOURNAL CLOSING ENTRIES

		Debit	Credit
Dec. 31	Income	24,000	
	Income and expense summary		24,000
	To transfer to summary		
31	Income and expense summary	18,700	
	Rent expense		2,400
	Salary expense		12,000
	Depreciation expense		1,500
	Office supplies expense		1,300
	Miscellaneous expense		1,000
	To transfer to summary		
31	Income and expense summary	5,300	
	Capital		5,300
	To transfer net income		
31	Capital	100	
	Withdrawals		100
	To transfer to capital		

These general journal closing entries are posted to the ledger accounts, and all zero-balance accounts are double ruled. Thus the books are now ready to begin the new accounting period.

MARY LEE DYER

Bibliography: Barnes, John, *How to Learn Basic Bookkeeping in Ten Easy Lessons* (1987); Dyer, Mary Lee, *Practical Bookkeeping for the Small Business* (1976); Palmer, Alfred, *Munro's Bookkeeping and Accountancy,* 23d ed. (1975).

Boole, George   [bool]

The English mathematician George Boole, b. Nov. 2, 1815, d. Dec. 8, 1864, is best known for his work in mathematical LOGIC. Born into the lower class, Boole was mainly self-educated. Despite his lack of an academic degree, he was appointed professor of mathematics at Queens College, Cork, Ireland, in 1849; he taught there for the rest of his life, gaining a reputation as a dedicated teacher.

Boole published about 50 papers on differential equations, difference equations, logic, and algebra. Much of his work on logic, algebra, and probability is contained in *An Investigation of the Laws of Thought on Which Are Founded the Mathematical Theories of Logic and Probabilities* (1854). Boole approached logic in a new way: he reduced it to a simple algebra, thereby incorporating logic into mathematics and giving the development of logic a new direction. Boole's two-valued, or binary, algebra is the simplest form of the more general Boolean algebra, which he developed, and has wide applications in computer design.   ARTHUR SCHLISSEL

Bibliography: Meschowski, Herbert, *Ways of Thought of Great Mathematicians* (1964); Smith, G. C., ed., *Boole–De Morgan Correspondence, 1842–1864* (1982).

Boolean algebra   [boo'-lee-uhn]

Boolean algebra was developed essentially as an algebra of LOGIC. Symbolism was introduced by George Boole to permit the basic principles of logic to be represented as an algebra of sets. (See SET THEORY.)

Denoting the universal set as 1 and the empty, or null, set as 0, Boole used $x \cdot y$ to represent the intersection of two sets, x and y, $x + y$ to represent their union, and $1 - x$ to represent the complement of the set x. To indicate that one set, x, was a subset of a second set, y, he wrote $x \cdot y = x$. Thus, common notation of set theory can be translated into algebraic language as follows:

$$x \cap y = x \cdot y$$
$$x \cup y = x + y$$
$$x \subseteq y \text{ if and only if } x \cdot y = x$$

Boolean algebra can be interpreted as an algebra of propositions, as well as an algebra of sets. Given propositions x and y, $x \cdot y$ represents the joint assertion of x or y or both, and $1 - x$ represents the denial of x.

Bibliography: Bukstein, E. J., *Practice Problems in Number Systems, Logic, and Boolean Algebra* (1986); Whitesitt, J. E., *Boolean Algebra and Its Applications* (1961).

boomerang

A boomerang is a curved throwing stick used principally by the Australian Aborigines, from whom the name is derived. The most well-known form is the returning boomerang, developed by Aboriginal groups in eastern and western Australia and used for hunting. It is deeply curved, some having a sharply angled bend, and measures 46–76 cm (18–30 in) in length and up to 340 g (12 oz) in weight. After being held by one end behind the thrower's head, the boomerang is swung rapidly over the head and thrust vertically downward before being released. It then sweeps upward and rotates horizontally in flight, often completing a circle up to 90 m (100 yd) wide followed by several smaller circles as it returns to the thrower. The form of boomerang used mainly for fighting is larger (61–91.4 cm/24–36 in long) and does not return. Crescent-shaped, with a shallow curve, it is sometimes thrown so that it ricochets off the ground to strike its quarry. Fighting boomerangs from western New South Wales and central Queensland were often beautifully decorated. Other forms of nonreturning boomerang were used by North American Indians of the Southwest, in southern India, and in ancient Egypt and India.   RONALD M. BERNDT

Bibliography: McCarthy, F. D., *Australian Aboriginal Decoration Art* (1958); Mason, Bernard S., *Boomerangs: How to Make and Throw Them* (1974); Ruhe, Benjamin, and Darnell, Eric, *Boomerang: How to Throw, Catch, and Make It* (1985).

boomslang

The boomslang, *Dispholidus typus*, is a South African tree snake. Although this species is a member of the predominantly harmless family Colubridae, it has rear fangs that are large and deeply grooved, and well-developed venom glands.

The African boomslang, D. typus, is about 1.5 m (5 ft) long, and is very dangerous. It is found in both open bush country and wooded areas.

It has caused human fatalities, among them the eminent American herpetologist Karl Patterson Schmidt. Boomslangs may be green, brown, or black. The diet of boomslangs consists of birds, bird eggs, frogs, and chameleons. The snakes lay 10 to 14 eggs.   JONATHAN A. CAMPBELL

Boone, Daniel   [boon]

Daniel Boone, b. Pennsylvania, Nov. 2, 1734, achieved fame as a frontiersman in the era of the American Revolution. As a youth he settled with his Quaker parents in western North Carolina.

Boone went as a wagoner on the expedition of Gen. Edward BRADDOCK to Fort Duquesne (1755), but he came into prominence much later for his explorations and hunting expeditions in the Kentucky region. He first visited that area in the winter of 1767–68, and on a second expedition from 1769 to 1771 he went through the Cumberland Gap.

When speculator Richard HENDERSON, who had organized the TRANSYLVANIA COMPANY, planned a settlement in Kentucky in 1775, Boone was the natural choice to blaze a trail. He marked out the WILDERNESS ROAD and founded the settlement of Boonesborough on the Kentucky River. In the Revolution Boone helped the Kentucky settlements as a hunter and as an Indian fighter. He was captured by the Shawnees in 1778, but he escaped and later traveled to the East to bring in more settlers.

Although Boone held public office in Kentucky (including serving in the Kentucky legislature), he first became well known in the East, and even in Europe, because of the account of his exploits given by John Filson in *The Discovery,*

Daniel Boone, one of America's most famous pioneers, has been the subject of many colorful legends. In this painting, the American artist George Caleb Bingham portrayed Boone leading his wife, daughter, and several other families through the Cumberland Gap into Kentucky.

Settlement, and Present State of Kentucke (1784). Boone then figured in Lord Byron's poem *Don Juan*. As a result, Boone was set apart from his fellow hunters and explorers, and a variety of myths were woven around his life.

Boone suffered major disappointments after the Revolution. The absence of proper land titles resulted in the loss of his Kentucky lands, and in the late 1790s he moved to what is now Missouri. When he died there on Sept. 26, 1820, he was the most famous of frontier heroes.   REGINALD HORSMAN

Bibliography: Bakeless, John, *Daniel Boone* (1939); Lofaro, Michael A., *The Life and Adventures of Daniel Boone* (1986).

Boötes   [boh-oh'-teez]

Boötes the Bear Keeper, or Herdsman, is a kite-shaped constellation prominent during summer in the Northern Hemisphere. Its brightest star, Arcturus, is the 4th brightest star in the heavens, a red giant of visual magnitude −0.06. It is found by following the curve of the handle of the Big Dipper. The constellation also contains several double stars and M 101, one of the brightest spiral galaxies; all are visible with a small telescope.

Booth   (family)

John Wilkes Booth, a popular actor of the 19th century, came from a distinguished family of Anglo-American actors. In 1865, Booth, a Confederate sympathizer, conspired to murder high-ranking government officials and personally assassinated President Abraham Lincoln.

The Booths were an Anglo-American family of stage tragedians who made significant contributions to the development of the American theater. The most famous member of the family, John Wilkes Booth, is notoriously remembered as the assassin of President Abraham Lincoln.

The family patriarch, **Junius Brutus Booth**, b. May 1, 1796, d. Nov. 30, 1852, made his London debut in 1813 and, with his portrayal of Richard III in 1817, became the chief rival of the celebrated Edmund KEAN. He came to America in 1821, where he helped to promote the tradition of tragic acting on the American stage. **Junius Brutus Booth, Jr.**, b. Dec. 22, 1821, d. Sept. 16, 1883, was the eldest of his ten children. Although himself an actor, Junius had a more profitable career as a theater manager.

Edwin Thomas Booth, b. Nov. 13, 1833, d. June 7, 1893, carried on his father's tradition by becoming the finest internationally known American tragedian of the 19th century. He debuted with his father at the age of 16. In 1854 he toured Australia with actress Laura Keene, and in 1861 he appeared in London, although without much success. This is probably because his acting style was more restrained and subtle than that to which audiences were accustomed. Edwin also managed (1863–67) New York's Winter Garden Theater, acted a

record 100 consecutive performances in the role of Hamlet, and built New York's Booth's Theater (still in use) after the Winter Garden burned down. His career ebbed after his brother assassinated Lincoln, but it revived again in the late 1800s. He helped to found The Players Club in 1888, which is still located on New York's Gramercy Park.

John Wilkes Booth, b. May 10, 1838, d. Apr. 26, 1865, was also a noted Shakespearean actor. Yet his wild and erratic behavior prevented him from achieving genuine acclaim as an actor. His advocacy of slavery and support of the Confederacy during the Civil War engendered a deep hatred in him for the newly elected President Lincoln.

A Confederate secret agent, Booth, along with select coconspirators, plotted throughout 1864–65 to abduct LIncoln, but their several attempts failed. Learning that the president was to attend a performance by Laura Keene in *Our American Cousin* at Washington, D.C.'s Ford Theatre (Good Friday, Apr. 14, 1865), Booth and his band hastily mapped out a plan to assassinate not only Lincoln but also Vice-President Andrew Johnson and Secretary of State William H. Seward, hoping to thus promote the South's victory in the war. Booth entered the unguarded presidential box during the third act of the play, shot Lincoln through the back of the head with a pistol, and then leaped down onto the stage, shouting "Sic semper tyrannis! The South is avenged!" He managed to escape to a waiting horse through a rear alley despite a broken left leg. Twelve days later Union troops surrounded Richard Garret's farm near Bowling Green, Va., where Booth was allegedly hiding in a barn. The troops set fire to the building, and Booth probably died during the ensuing gun battle or may even have shot himself. His body was never positively identified, leading to the persistent myth that he escaped his captors.   ANDREW KELLY

Bibliography: Clarke, Asia, *The Unlocked Book: A Memoir of John Wilkes Booth by His Sister* (1938); Kimmel, Stanley, *The Mad Booths of Maryland*, 2d ed. (1969); Ruggles, Eleanor, *Prince of Players* (1953); Samples, Gordon, *Lust for Fame* (1982); Shattuck, Charles H., *The Hamlet of Edwin Booth* (1969); Skinner, Otis, *The Last Tragedian* (1939); Winter, William, *Life and Art of Edwin Booth* (1894; repr. 1973).

Booth, Charles

Charles Booth, b. Mar. 30, 1840, d. Nov. 23, 1916, was an English social reformer who made important contributions to the study of poverty. A pioneer in the use of statistical methods of investigation, Booth, in his *Life and Labour of the People in London* (17 vols., 1891–1903), classified the city's population in terms of employment and income and sought to show that poverty is the source of vice.

Bibliography: Booth, Mary Macaulay, *Charles Booth: A Memoir* (1918); Fried, Albert, and Elman, Richard, eds., *Charles Booth's London* (1968).

Booth, John Wilkes: see BOOTH (family).

Booth, William

William Booth, b. Nottingham, England, Apr. 10, 1829, d. Aug. 20, 1912, was a fiery evangelist who brought the SALVATION ARMY into existence in 1865. Booth resolved as a young man to devote his life to waging war against sin and suffering. A minister of the Methodist New Connexion Church, he was forced to resign his post when he refused an order to give up his independent evangelical work. Booth began to preach to the poor in London's East End and formed the East London Revival Society, which later became the Christian Mission and then the Salvation Army. Headquarters were established on Whitechapel Road, and William Booth was named general and served in that capacity until his death. Despite many setbacks, the Salvation Army grew into an international organization now serving in 82 countries. Booth's eight children played a vigorous role in the Army's expansion, and two of them, Bramwell and Evangeline, eventually served as general.

Booth's interests included education, housing, employment, health, and the problems of poverty. In advance of his times,

William Booth, founder and first general of the Salvation Army, was an ardent evangelist who devoted his life to improving the condition of working-class people. He was especially concerned with such issues as alcoholism, legal aid for the poor, and rehabilitation for ex-convicts.

he realized that alcoholics must be aided rather than condemned. During his lifetime he saw his small band of followers swell to an army of thousands.

Bibliography: Bennett, David, *William Booth* (1994); Carpenter, Minnie L., *William Booth* (1986).

Boothia Peninsula   [boo'-thee-uh]

The Boothia Peninsula is a northern extension of the CANADIAN SHIELD and the North American mainland. Located in the Arctic portion of the Northwest Territories, Canada, it was discovered in 1829 by Sir James Clark Ross and named for his patron, Sir Felix Booth. Boothia Peninsula is the former location of the North Magnetic Pole, which by 1970 had migrated northward, to Bathurst Island.

bootlegging

Bootlegging is the illegal manufacture and transportation of alcoholic beverages. It may involve transporting them into a territory where their sale is banned, making them where their manufacture is illegal, or attempting to evade taxes on them. Bootlegging was widespread in the United States during the period of PROHIBITION (1920–33). Although the 18th Amendment to the U.S. Constitution prohibited the manufacture and sale of alcoholic beverages, demand for these products continued, and it remained a lucrative business. Rural distillers produced illegal beverages for bootlegging to urban markets, and in the cities thousands of small stills, breweries, and wineries appeared. Bootleggers also brought in illegal products from foreign suppliers. The law was so widely violated by the general public that officials were unable, and in some cases unwilling, to enforce it. The profits of the traffic attracted criminals, who soon took over much of it. After the repeal of the 18th Amendment by the 21st Amendment in 1933, organized crime turned to other pursuits. For a time, however, they supplied alcohol to customers in states that retained local prohibition laws.   K. AUSTIN KERR

Bibliography: Coffey, Thomas M., *The Long Thirst* (1976).

Bophuthatswana   [bah-poo-thaht-swah'-nah]

From 1977 to 1994, Bophuthatswana was an ''independent'' Bantu homeland in South Africa. Originally composed of 19 separate land parcels, the homeland was later consolidated into 7 areas in what are now the provinces of North West, Northern Transvaal, Pretoria/Witwatersrand/Vereeniging, and the Orange Free State. Bophuthatswana had a total area of 44,000 km² (16,988 mi²) and was the official homeland for the 2,500,000 TSWANA people, most of whom lived elsewhere.

On Dec. 6, 1977, Bophuthatswana was granted independence by South Africa. It had its own president and legislature but remained economically tied to South Africa. No other country recognized its independence. Bophuthatswana produced 30% of the world's platinum, had large deposits of other minerals, and was more successful than other homelands in attracting new industries, including a casino resort known as Sun City. But two-thirds of its employed inhabitants held jobs in white areas. On Mar. 10, 1994, under pressure from blacks wanting to reincorporate with South Africa, the government of Botswana collapsed, and South African troops moved in to restore order. On March 22, South Africa took control of the Ciskei homeland, whose ruler had also refused to participate in South Africa's scheduled April 1994 all-race elections. After the elections, all of the homelands were incorporated into South Africa.

Bopp, Franz

The German philologist Franz Bopp, b. Sept. 14, 1791, d. Oct. 3, 1837, was one of the founders of scientific comparative linguistics. After mastering classical languages and the history of Germanic languages, Bopp studied Sanskrit and demonstrated a relationship between Sanskrit inflection and that of other languages. His studies of the interrelationships among Indo-European languages were published in *Vergleichende Grammatik* (Comparative Grammar, 1833–52).   F. P. DINNEEN, S.J.

Bibliography: Sebeok, Thomas, ed., *Portraits of Linguists* (1967).

Bora-Bora

Bora-Bora is an island cluster in the Leeward Island group of the Society Islands of French Polynesia in the South Pacific Ocean. About 225 km (140 mi) northwest of Tahiti, the main island, also called Bora-Bora, is about 10 km (6 mi) long and 4 km (2.5 mi) wide.

borage   [bor'-ij]

Borage, an annual herb of the family Boraginaceae, is native to the Mediterranean region. The plant has a delicate cucumberlike flavor and odor, and its leaves have been brewed into tea for centuries. In medieval herbals, the tea was recommended as a source of courage and a purgative of melancholy. Borage's starlike blue flowers bloom throughout the summer, are a favorite of bees, and are often candied and used as a pastry garnish. Young leaves can be eaten raw or cooked.   ARTHUR O. TUCKER

Borah, William Edgar

William Edgar Borah, b. June 29, 1865, d. Jan. 19, 1940, one of the most powerful progressive Republicans of his era, served in the U.S. Senate from 1907 to 1940. A gifted orator, Borah, who was fiercely independent, cherished the values of 19th-century rural America. He distrusted the cities, big business, the great powers of Europe, and any concentration of power in private or public hands.

Born in Jasper Township, Ill., and educated in Kansas, Borah moved to Boise, Idaho, in 1890, where he established a large legal practice. In 1907 he unsuccessfully prosecuted Big Bill HAYWOOD for the murder of former Idaho governor Frank Steunenberg. Elected (1907) to the Senate by the Idaho legislature, he joined the supporters of President Theodore ROOSEVELT. He opposed much of Woodrow WILSON's program, however, voting against the Federal Reserve Act (1913), which he felt would give too much power to private bankers, and against the creation of the Federal Trade Commission (1914), fearing its domination by big business.

A nationalist, Borah endorsed U.S. entry into World War I, but he led the opposition to the Treaty of Versailles and its provision for a LEAGUE OF NATIONS, claiming that the world organization would be dominated by France and Britain and would infringe U.S. sovereignty. Instead, the senator sponsored the WASHINGTON CONFERENCE of 1921–22, which was to limit naval armament. As the chairman of the Senate Foreign Relations

Committee (1924–33), he also championed the outlawing of war by the KELLOGG–BRIAND PACT of 1928. Borah, who opposed imperialism, early recognized the force of nationalism in the underdeveloped world. He saw the Russian Revolutions of 1917 as a reflection of this and urged U.S. recognition of the Soviet Union. In the 1930s, Borah endorsed the New Deal laws that benefited the lower classes or were intended to tax wealth and curb corporate and financial power. He opposed, however, direct government intervention in the economy. On the eve of World War II, he voted against President Franklin D. ROOSEVELT's efforts to weaken the neutrality laws.

ELLIOT A. ROSEN

Bibliography: Ashby, LeRoy, *The Spearless Leader* (1972); Maddox, Robert, *William E. Borah and American Foreign Policy* (1969); McKenna, Marian, *Borah* (1961); Vinson, John, *William E. Borah and the Outlawry of War* (1957).

borane

Boranes, or boron hydrides, are highly reactive chemical compounds consisting mainly of BORON and hydrogen, although some derivatives are also called boranes. The lightest is diborane (B_2H_6), and others include pentaborane (B_5H_9 and B_5H_{11}) and decaborane ($B_{10}H_{14}$). Because their molecules do not have enough electrons to form normal covalent bonds, boranes exhibit unusual molecular structures. They decompose spontaneously and sometimes explosively on contact with air and in general are unstable compounds. Beginning with the work of German chemist Alfred Stock (1876–1946) in the 1910s, boranes have been investigated for potential uses—particularly, in recent years, as high-energy fuels. They are also now employed in silicone-rubber preparation and other polymerization processes. Diborane is decomposed thermally to form coatings of pure boron for scientific and technological devices, and to produce boranes of higher molecular weight. Boranes are extremely toxic but have a strong, disagreeable odor that warns of their presence.

borate minerals   [bohr'-ayt]

The borates comprise a large group of minerals characterized by the borate ion (BO_3^{3-}). All but a few of the more than 100 borates are very rare. Most are slightly soluble in water and occur in marine EVAPORITE deposits or in desert basins (PLAYAS). A few borosilicates, including TOURMALINE and dumortierite, occur in IGNEOUS or METAMORPHIC ROCKS.

The most common borate mineral, borax ($Na_2B_4O_7\cdot10H_2O$), was mined in ancient times from salt lakes in Tibet and Kashmir, where it was called tincal. Borax from deposits in DEATH VALLEY was transported by the famous 20-mule teams. At present, most of the world's boron is extracted from borax, kernite ($Na_2B_4O_7\cdot5H_2O$), and colemanite ($Ca_2B_6O_{11}\cdot5H_2O$) mined at Borax, Searles, and Kramer lakes in California. In arid climates, borax alters to powdery tincalconite by loss of five waters of hydration. Ulexite ($NaCaB_5O_9\cdot8H_2O$) is mined from lake deposits in Argentina.

ALAN M. GAINES

borax: see BORATE MINERALS; BORON.

Borchert, Wolfgang   [bor'-shairt]

Wolfgang Borchert, b. May 20, 1921, d. Nov. 20, 1947, was a German poet and short-story writer who expressed for an entire postwar generation the loneliness, despair, and absurdity of World War II. His collected stories, *An diesem Dienstag* (On This Tuesday, 1947); a volume of verse, *Laterne, Nacht und Sterne* (Lamp, Night, and Star, 1946); and a radio play about a returning soldier, *The Man Outside* (1947; Eng. trans., 1971), chronicle in a sober and terse style the sacrifice of innocent victims.

JOSEPH A. REITER

Borchgrevink, Carsten Egeberg   [bork'-gray-vingk, kar'-sten eg'-e-bairg]

Carsten Egeberg Borchgrevink, b. Dec. 1, 1864, d. Apr. 21, 1934, was a Norwegian explorer of the Antarctic. Sailing on the whaler *Antarctic* from Australia, he was in the first landing party to set foot on the Antarctic mainland at Cape Adare, Victoria Land, on Jan. 23, 1895. As commander of the British *Southern Cross* expedition (1898–1900), he went ashore at Cape Adare in February 1899 and, with nine men, was the first to spend a winter and following summer in Antarctica.

Bordeaux

Bordeaux is a port city in southwestern France and the capital of the department of Gironde. It has a population of 201,965 (1982). Bordeaux lies on the west bank of the Garonne River, 18 km (11 mi) above its junction with the Gironde and 97 km (60 mi) from the sea. The city is accessible to seagoing ships and is the chief port of the region of AQUITAINE. It is surrounded by a rich agricultural region that is noted primarily for its vineyards; Bordeaux wines, both red and white, have been famous since the Middle Ages and include Margaux, Médocs, Graves, and Sauternes. The Garonne is navigable above the city by river craft and is linked by the Canal du Midi with the Mediterranean.

Bordeaux was founded by the Gauls as Burdigala and later became a provincial headquarters for the Roman garrison. It survived the invasions of the early Middle Ages and was, from 1154 to 1453, the capital of the English-held province of Aquitaine and an important port for exporting wine to northern Europe. The city declined after it was reconquered by the French, but it began to prosper again in the 18th century. The University of Bordeaux was founded in 1441 and was reorganized along modern lines in the 19th century.

The appearance of the city is largely the result of the work of 18th-century planners and architects who laid out its wide streets and large squares and built its baroque churches. Behind this facade are traces of a Roman settlement as well as a cathedral and fragments of a town wall dating from the Middle Ages. This core is now partly enclosed by industrial suburbs built during the 19th and 20th centuries.

In the 18th century, Bordeaux became the chief port of France's colonial empire, but this role ended with the loss of the empire. Manufacturing industries expanded during the 19th century and were at first associated with imported tropical products such as those used in soap manufacture and the processing of oilseeds. Later, mechanical engineering, oil refining, and the manufacture of chemicals, especially fertilizers needed in the vineyards, were added.

NORMAN J. G. POUNDS

Borden, Gail

Gail Borden, b. near Norwich, N.Y., Nov. 9, 1801, d. Jan. 11, 1874, invented a process for condensing milk. A pioneer settler in Texas, he wished to develop methods of preserving food so that it would remain edible during the long pioneer wagon treks of the time. Bordon first developed a dehydrated meat biscuit, then in 1853 perfected a process for preserving milk by boiling and evaporating it in a closed container. His condensed milk was used by the U.S. Army during the Civil War, afterward becoming a popular staple, since it was safe and long lasting, unlike the raw milk then available. The New York Condensed Milk Company, founded by Borden in 1858, survives today as Borden's, Inc.

Borden, Lizzie

Lizzie A. Borden, b. Fall River, Mass., July 19, 1860, d. June 1, 1927, a Sunday school teacher living with her father and stepmother in Fall River, was charged with killing them with an ax on Aug. 4, 1892. Although she was tried and acquitted in 1893, a doubting public continued to believe in her guilt and immortalized its belief by repeating this verse:

Lizzie Borden took an ax
And gave her mother 40 whacks.
And when she saw what she had done,
She gave her father 41.

Bibliography: Porter, Edwin H., *The Fall River Tragedy* (1893; repr. 1985); Spiering, Frank, *Lizzie* (1984).

Borden, Sir Robert L.

Sir Robert L. Borden, Conservative prime minister of Canada from 1911 to 1920, sought to strengthen bonds within the British Empire while at the same time asserting Canada's independent status in international diplomacy. Borden's introduction (1917) of military conscription during World War I was opposed especially by the French Canadians.

Sir Robert Laird Borden, b. Nova Scotia, June 26, 1854, d. June 10, 1937, was a Canadian political leader who served as prime minister throughout World War I. He taught school for a time but found the law more attractive and rewarding. By 1896 his legal practice in Halifax was the most lucrative in the Maritime Provinces. At the instigation of Sir Charles TUPPER, Borden ran for election to Parliament from Halifax in 1896 and became leader of the Conservative opposition on the retirement of Tupper in 1901.

Scrupulously honest and highly intelligent, Borden did not have much of a taste, or perhaps a flair, for political life. He therefore found the vexations of politics hard to endure. Nonetheless, he vigorously attacked the Liberal government's policies of reciprocity with the United States and creation of a separate Canadian navy, and, rather to his surprise, he and his party won the election of 1911. Borden thus became prime minister.

When Canada entered World War I in August 1914, Borden's moral force was a great source of strength. His relationship with the French-Canadian population was poor, however. By 1917 he believed military conscription to be essential, and it was adopted despite French-Canadian opposition. With some electoral unscrupulousness, which doubtless seemed justified to him by the exigencies of war, Borden won the general election of December 1917 as head of a Union government that included Liberal members. He thus garnered the support of most English-speaking Liberals and increased the isolation of the French Canadians.

After the war, the government began to weaken. Borden's own interests were now on the larger world stage and on achieving recognition of Canada's separate role at the Paris Peace Conference (1919). He left domestic affairs, such as the Winnipeg general strike of 1919, to his lieutenants. Retiring in July 1920, Borden lived on as a highly regarded elder statesman and received numerous honors.   P. B. WAITE

Bibliography: Borden, Sir Robert Laird, *Letters to Limbo,* ed. by Henry Borden (1971); Brown, R. C., *Robert Laird Borden, 1854–1914,* vol. I (1975); English, John, *Borden: His Life and World* (1977); Wilson, H. A., *The Imperial Policy of Sir Robert Borden* (1966).

border collie

The border collie is a breed of dog renowned for its sheepherding ability. It stands about 46 cm (18 in) at the shoulder and weighs about 20 kg (45 lb). Resembling a collie but with a shorter, wavy coat and erect ears with tips forward, it is usually black or black and tan, with white markings on the muzzle, chest, feet, and tip of the tail.

The border collie, a working dog native to northern England, is considered one of the world's best herding dogs. It is used to drive sheep as well as cattle and other livestock.

The border collies originated centuries ago in the border country between England and Scotland. The breed is not recognized for show purposes in either the United States or Great Britain, but the dogs may compete in obedience trials. They are easily trained and make good companions.

JOHN MANDEVILLE

Bibliography: Larson, J. E., *The Versatile Border Collie* (1986).

border terrier

The border terrier, native to Great Britain, is a rugged working dog that was used in the hunting of foxes. Its coarse coat protects it from bad weather.

As the name implies, the border terrier was developed in the border country between England and Scotland, at least as early as the 18th century. The border terrier is a keen, lively breed of dog that stands somewhat more than 30 cm (1 ft) at the shoulder and weighs 6.7 kg (about 15 lb). It has an otter-like head, with a short, strong muzzle and closely folded ears. The coat is double; the outercoat is short, harsh, and straight, and the undercoat is dense. The color may be red, wheat, grizzle and tan, or black and tan. The moderately short tail is carried gaily. The border terrier was bred to help farmers and shepherds control the fox population. The dog had to be strong, tireless, big enough to follow hunters on horses but small enough to pursue the fox into hiding. The breed, recognized by the English Kennel Club in 1920, is still rare in the United States.   JOHN MANDEVILLE

borderline personality disorder

Borderline personality disorder is a fairly common behavioral disorder marked by self-image problems, strong mood shifts, and difficulty in maintaining relationships but dread of being alone. Usually this pattern is fully developed and persists by early adulthood. The mood swings, which last a few hours to a few days, include spells of depression, anxiety, and intense anger as well as feelings of boredom and emptiness. Overeating, substance abuse, and other impulsive, reckless actions are common, as are suicide threats or self-mutilation in more severe cases. The personal or family factors that may cause this disorder to develop are as yet insufficiently understood; it is addressed by various forms of psychotherapy.

Borders

Borders is one of Scotland's nine regions, created in 1975. It is located in southeastern Scotland, just south of Edinburgh and northwest of the border with England. Its area is 4,670 km² (1,803 mi²), and the population is 101,300 (1984 est.). The region includes the former BERWICK, PEEBLES, ROXBURGH, and SELKIRK counties, and part of Midlothian county. Sheep raising is important, and the main industries are wool processing and the production of Scottish tweed.

Bibliography: Douglas, George, *A History of the Border Counties* (1988); Tranter, Nigel G., *Portrait of the Border Country* (1972).

Bordes, François   [bohrd]

The French archaeologist François Bordes, b. Dec. 30, 1919, d. Apr. 30, 1981, was a renowned authority on the European Paleolithic Period, or Old Stone Age. His excavations at COMBE GRENAL and other cave sites in southwestern France helped in the reconstruction of a cultural sequence there that extends back more than 100,000 years ago. Noted for his research on Neanderthal culture (see NEANDERTHALERS), Bordes was also known for his flint-knapping (stone-toolmaking) skills and for his effort to systematize stone-tool typology. His writings include *The Old Stone Age* (1968) and *A Tale of Two Caves* (1972).   STEPHEN A. KOWALEWSKI

Bordet, Jules   [bohr-day']

The Belgian bacteriologist and immunologist Jules Jean Baptiste Vincent Bordet, b. June 13, 1870, d. Apr. 6, 1961, was awarded the 1919 Nobel Prize for physiology or medicine for his work in immunology. Bordet discovered that all normal mammalian blood serum contains complement, a substance that combines with an antigen-antibody complex to produce antibody-caused immunity. This "complement fixation" tells whether an antigen-antibody reaction has occurred and is the basis of several diagnostic tests, including the Wassermann test for syphilis (see VENEREAL DISEASE). In 1906, Bordet discovered the bacillus responsible for whooping cough and developed a vaccine for immunization against the disease.

Bibliography: Wasson, Tyler, ed., *Nobel Prize Winners* (1987).

Bordone, Paris   [bohr-doh'-nay]

The Venetian painter Paris Bordone, b. 1500, d. Jan. 19, 1571, was a follower of Titian, with whom he studied, and Giorgione. He specialized in portraits and large religious and secular scenes, often set in elaborate architectural perspectives. In his mature style he combined Mannerist qualities with Venetian opulence. One of his most important surviving works (many have been lost) is *The Fisherman Consigning a Ring to the Doge* (c.1533–35; Accademia, Venice).   TANIA BAYARD

bore: see TIDAL BORE.

boreal climate: see TAIGA CLIMATE.

Boreas   [bohr'-ee-uhs]

In Greek mythology, Boreas was a personification of the north wind, the son of Eos and Astraeus. When his wooing of the Athenian princess Oreithyia was unsuccessful, Boreas carried her away in a great gust of wind. Their twin sons, Calais and Zetes, called the Boreades, accompanied Jason and the Argonauts. Athens held the Boreasmos festival in honor of Boreas.

Borel, Émile   [bohr-el']

The French mathematician Félix Édouard Justin Émile Borel, b. Jan. 7, 1871, d. Feb. 3, 1956, created the first effective theory of the measure of sets of points. This work, along with that of two other French mathematicians, René Baire and Henri Lebesgue, marked the beginning of the modern theory of functions of a real variable. Borel was also the first to develop (1899) a systematic theory for a divergent series (a series of numbers whose sum does not approach a given number). In addition, he published (1921–27) papers on game theory and became the first to define games of strategy. After 1924, Borel became active in the French government. He received awards both for his government work and for his scientific accomplishments.   H. HOWARD FRISINGER

Borelli, Giovanni Alfonso   [boh-rel'-lee, joh-vahn'-nee ahl-fohn'-soh]

The Italian scientist Giovanni Alfonso Borelli, b. Jan. 28, 1608, d. Dec. 31, 1679, was the first to describe planetary motion around the Sun in terms of centrifugal and centripetal forces, describing centripetal force as the natural tendency of a body to move toward the object around which it revolves. His work was soon overshadowed, however, by the work of Sir Isaac Newton and others. Applying mechanics to biology, Borelli described bones as levers acted on by muscle force to produce motion. His description of the flight of birds was the first correct analysis of flight (see FLIGHT, HUMAN-POWERED).

Bibliography: Koyré, Alexandre, *The Astronomical Revolution* (1973); Magner, L. N., *History of the Life Sciences* (1979).

Borg, Björn

Björn Borg became a dominant figure in world tennis during the late 1970s. The Swedish athlete made his professional debut at the age of 14, and in 1976 he won the first of his five consecutive Wimbledon singles titles, an unsurpassed feat. In 1979–81, Borg and the U.S. star John McEnroe played several U.S. Open and Wimbledon finals that are considered among the best played and most exciting in the history of those important events. In 1982, Borg was ruled ineligible to compete in the major championships because he had not entered a specified minimum number of tournaments. Late that year he retired from competitive tennis.

Björn Borg, b. June 6, 1956, a Swedish tennis star who is primarily a baseline player with powerful strokes, magnificent speed, and great concentration, achieved international fame at an earlier age than any other man in the sport's history. In 1973, at age 17, he earned $62,500 in prize money. He won the French and Italian Open titles in 1974, and in 1975 he won the French Open a second time, gained the U.S. professional title, and led Sweden to its first Davis Cup victory. In all, Borg won 6 French Open titles and 5 consecutive Wimbledon championships (1976–80), gaining the world's number-one ranking for the years 1978–80. His 11 Grand Slam singles titles place him second on that all-time list, one behind Australia's Roy Emerson. Borg retired at age 26 in late 1982. In 1991 he failed in a comeback attempt.

Borges, Jorge Luis   [bohr'-hays, hor'-hay loo'-ees]

Jorge Luis Borges, b. Aug. 24, 1899, d. June 14, 1986, is the most important figure in Argentine literature and one of the major writers in world fiction. Relatively unknown in the early years of his career, he became an influential force in both

Perhaps the most important contemporary Latin American author, Jorge Luis Borges was a poet and short-story writer. His works have a dreamlike quality reminiscent of the writings of Franz Kafka. Like Kafka's, Borges's characters wander in a confused, labyrinthine world. But unlike Kafka's hero, K, the figures in Borges's stories seem not to know that their works and their beliefs are ultimately absurd.

European and American letters after sharing the Formentor Prize (International Publishers Prize) with Samuel Beckett in 1961.

Borges's ancestors fought in the Argentine wars for independence, and his grandmother was British. He grew up speaking and reading both Spanish and English. In 1914 his family moved to Europe, and until 1919, Borges went to school in Geneva, where he learned French, German, and Latin. Before returning to Argentina in 1921, he spent two years in Spain and began writing his highly experimental first poems.

Back in Argentina Borges and a group of friends interested in avant-garde poetry initiated a literary movement known as Ultraísmo and began publishing the journal *Proa*. His first book of poetry, *Fervor of Buenos Aires* (1923; Eng. trans., 1972), reflected those trends and has as its central theme the rediscovery of his own city, Buenos Aires. Other collections of poems followed, including *Luna de enfrente* (1925). Borges gradually abandoned his early experiments and cultivated more traditional forms, notably the sonnet, which he polished to perfection. His poems about his country, his city, his ancestors, and his favorite books and authors achieve an intense lyricism and a rare intimacy.

In 1938, Borges began working as a librarian in a modest library in suburban Buenos Aires. In 1955 he was appointed director of the National Library in the same city. He made his first trip to the United States in 1961, at the invitation of the University of Texas, where he lectured on Argentine literature. In 1967, Harvard University invited him to return to the United States as Norton professor of poetry. He made subsequent trips to the United States, Europe, and Israel.

Despite his great accomplishments as a poet, the international reputation Borges enjoys today rests on his short stories. In his first collection, *A Universal History of Infamy* (1935; Eng. trans., 1972), he reworked old plots and developed some of the main features of his concise style. With FicCIONES (1944; Eng. trans., 1962) and *The Aleph* (1949; Eng. trans., 1970) he established himself as a skilled artist of the genre. In *Dreamtigers* (1960; Eng. trans., 1962)—which also contains some of his best poetry—and *The Book of Imaginary Beings* (1957, 1967; Eng. trans., 1969), he further developed the terseness and transparency of his prose. Borges believed that philosophy and theology are no less fantastic than fiction itself. His plots often centered on philosophical and theological arguments, shedding new light on the limitations of human culture. Many of his best-known stories appear, translated, in *Labyrinths* (1962; rev. ed., 1970). The motif of the world as a labyrinth is one of Borges's favorites.

When Borges became blind in the late 1950s, he began to compose his poems by memorizing and then dictating them. His short stories lost the powerful quality of the first collec-

tions and became more straightforward, as in *Doctor Brodie's Report* (1970; Eng. trans., 1972) and *The Book of Sand* (1975; Eng. trans., 1977).   JAIME ALAZRAKI

Bibliography: Alazraki, Jaime, *Jorge Luis Borges* (1971); Alifano, Roberto, ed., *24 Conversations with Borges, 1981–1983* (1984); Barnstone, Willis, *Borges at 80: Conversations* (1982); Dunham, L., and Ivask, I., *The Cardinal Points of Borges* (1972); McMurray, George R., *Jorge Luis Borges* (1980); Newman, C., *Prose for Borges* (1974); Sturrock, John, *Paper Tigers: The Ideal Fictions of Jorge Luis Borges* (1978).

Borgese, Giuseppe Antonio   [bohr-jay'-say]

Giuseppe Antonio Borgese, b. Nov. 12, 1882, d. Dec. 4, 1952, was an Italian historian of aesthetics, as well as a poet and novelist. Self-exiled to the United States in 1931, he taught in several American universities, speaking out eloquently against Mussolini's Fascist policies. Aside from his critical essays, he produced an unusual novel, *Rubè* (1921), the story of a young, idealistic lawyer victimized by the confusing, squalid beliefs of his time.   SERGIO PACIFICI

Borgia   (family)   [bohr'-jah]

The Borgia (Spanish: Borja) were a noble family from Valencia, Spain, that contributed two popes and other political and church leaders to Renaissance Italy. The founder of the family's influence in Italy was **Alfonso de Borgia**, who became pope as CALLISTUS III in 1455. His nephew **Rodrigo** also became pope as ALEXANDER VI in 1492.

Rodrigo fathered several illegitimate children by his mistress Vannozza Cattani. His son **Cesare Borgia**, b. September 1475, was perhaps the most ruthless prince of the Italian Renaissance. He was the apparent model for Machiavelli's PRINCE. Created a cardinal by his father in 1493, Cesare renounced his ecclesiastical career in 1498 and was sent by his father to pacify the Romagna in the PAPAL STATES. Granted the title duke of Valentinois by the French king LOUIS XII, Cesare, now known as *il Valentino*, crushed many of the noble families of central Italy (including the MALATESTA of Rimini) in his quest to establish absolute power over the Romagna. With the death (1503) of Alexander VI, Cesare was imprisoned by the new pope, JULIUS II. Later he escaped to Spain, where he fought for the royal house of Navarre (into which he had married) until he was killed in a skirmish near Viana, Spain, on Mar. 12, 1507.

Cesare's sister, **Lucrezia Borgia**, b. Apr. 18, 1480, d. June 24, 1519, was renowned as a master of political intrigue as well as a patron of the arts. She was married three times: first, to Giovanni Sforza, lord of Pesaro, a marriage annulled by her father in 1497; second, to Alfonso (illegitimate son of Alfonso II of Naples), who was assassinated in Rome in 1500; and finally, to

Cesare Borgia, shown in this Giorgione painting, was one of the major princes of Renaissance Italy. Ambitious, sophisticated, and cruel in his rise to political power, he served as one of the models for Machiavelli's The Prince.

Alfonso d'Este, who became duke of Ferrara in 1505. Lucrezia then presided over a brilliant Renaissance court in Ferrara that included the poets Ludovico ARIOSTO and Pietro BEMBO and the painter TITIAN.

Other distant family members included St. Francis Borgia and **Stefano Borgia**, b. Dec. 3, 1731, d. Nov. 23, 1804, a cardinal and noted antiquarian.   BENJAMIN G. KOHL

Bibliography: Chambers, E. R., *Fall of the House of Borgia* (1974); Hansen, W. P., and Haney, J., eds., *Cesare Borgia* (1986); Mallet, Michael, *The Borgias*, rev. ed. (1975).

Borgia, Saint Francis   [bohr'-jah]

Saint Francis Borgia, b. Spain, Oct. 28, 1510, d. Rome, Sept. 30, 1572, the great-grandson of Pope Alexander VI, was duke of Gandia and the third superior general of the Jesuits. In 1528 he entered the service of Emperor Charles V; the next year he married Leonor de Castro, by whom he had eight sons. After his wife's death (1546), he pronounced his vows as a Jesuit and became a zealous churchman. He established many schools and colleges and was the advisor of St. IGNATIUS LOYOLA. His vigorous administration of the Jesuits and the austerity of his life won him canonization on Apr. 12, 1671. Feast day: Oct. 3 (formerly Oct. 10).   JOHN W. O'MALLEY

Borglum, Gutzon   [bohr'-gluhm, guht'-suhn]

Gutzon Borglum began work in 1927 on the sculptures of George Washington, Thomas Jefferson, Abraham Lincoln, and Theodore Roosevelt at the Mount Rushmore National Memorial in the Black Hills of South Dakota. Each of the heads stands 18.3 m (60 ft) high.

John Gutzon de la Mothe Borglum, b. Idaho, Mar. 25, 1871, d. Mar. 6, 1941, was an American sculptor who became famous for his gigantic Mount RUSHMORE National Memorial in South Dakota's Black Hills. Borglum began his art studies in San Francisco and completed them in Paris. There and in London he enjoyed early success as a muralist and an illustrator. His friendship with the French sculptor Auguste Rodin led him to concentrate on sculpture.

Borglum moved to New York in 1901, where he soon became popular as a sculptor of portraits and public monuments. Among these are the 12 stone apostles for New York's Cathedral of Saint John the Divine and the 6-ton marble head (1908) of Lincoln in the U.S. Capitol rotunda. The latter led to a commission (1916) for a colossal Confederate memorial to be carved in high relief on the flank of STONE MOUNTAIN near Atlanta, Ga. Financial controversies halted work in 1925 (resumed 1963; completed 1970).

Mount Rushmore was authorized as a national memorial by the U.S. Congress in 1929, although work had begun in 1927. Over the next 12 years, Borglum and his workmen, using pneumatic drills and dynamite, carved four immense (18 m/60 ft) heads out of the mountaintop—Washington (1930), Jefferson (1936), Lincoln (1937), and Theodore Roosevelt (1939).

Bibliography: Casey, R. J., and Borglum, Mary, *Give the Man Room: The Story of Gutzon Borglum* (1952); Fite, Gilbert C., *Mount Rushmore* (1952; repr. 1984); Price, Willadene, *Gutzon Borglum* (1961); Zeitner, June C., and Borglum, Lincoln, *Borglum's Unfinished Dream—Mount Rushmore* (1976).

Bori, Lucrezia   [boh'-ree, loo-kray'-zee-uh]

The Spanish opera singer Lucrezia Bori, b. Dec. 24, 1887, d. May 14, 1960, was one of the Metropolitan Opera's most beloved sopranos. She made her debut in 1908 in Rome and appeared at La Scala in 1910. Bori opened the Metropolitan in 1912 as Manon Lescaut; after a throat operation, she sang there from 1921 to her retirement in 1936. She was one of the first operatic artists to sing on radio and the first woman named to the Metropolitan's board of directors.

STEPHANIE VON BUCHAU

boric acid: see BORON.

Boring, E. G.

Edwin Garrigues Boring, b. Philadelphia, Oct. 23, 1886, d. July 1, 1968, was an American psychologist who taught at Cornell (1919–22) and Harvard (1922–57) universities and influenced the historical perspective of a generation of psychologists. His *History of Experimental Psychology* (1929) is considered one of the most important books on the subject.

Boris Godunov   (opera)   [bohr-ees' guh-doon-awf']

The best-known opera by the Russian composer Modest MUSSORGSKY, *Boris Godunov*, in four acts, was completed in 1869, twice revised, and first performed (in a truncated version) at the Maryinsky Theater, St. Petersburg, on Feb. 8, 1874. Mussorgsky himself wrote the libretto, based on a chronicle play by Aleksandr PUSHKIN and on Karamzin's *History of the Russian State*. *Boris* was edited and reorchestrated by Nikolai RIMSKY-KORSAKOV and, later, by Dmitry SHOSTAKOVICH. Today the opera is most often presented as Mussorgsky wrote it.

Boris is set during 1598–1605. Boris Godunov, regent of Russia and brother-in-law of the feeble Tsar Fyodor, has contrived the murder of the child Dmitry, rightful heir to the throne, so that he, Boris, would be tsar. The story begins with the death of Fyodor, upon which Boris, waiting for an expression of the people's will, retires to the monastery of Novodievich. His brutal police whip the populace into urging him toward the throne. He accepts, but at the coronation in the courtyard of the Kremlin, memories of the murdered heir oppress him.

A renegade monk, Grigory Otrepiev, decides to impersonate the dead child. Escaping across the border into Lithuania, Grigory openly calls himself Dmitry. Meanwhile Boris, a devoted father and a tortured man, tries to rule justly, but the land is plagued by famine, and his chief advisor, Prince Schuisky, is a wily intriguer. Plagued by guilt, Boris hallucinates and fancies that he sees the ghost of the murdered child. In Poland, the false Dmitry gains a fiancée, the ambitious Marina Mnishek. Leading an army, he advances against Moscow. The peasants revolt; and Boris, who dies distraught, leaves the empire to his young son, Fyodor, who can look only to an uncertain future.

Boris Godunov is the masterpiece of Russian national opera. In it, striking use is made of the chorus, which represents the Russian people; it is regarded by many as the real hero of the opera rather than Boris himself. The opera was first performed at the Metropolitan Opera on Mar. 19, 1913, with Adam Didur as Boris and conducted by Arturo Toscanini. The most notable performer of the role of Boris, however, has been the bass Fyodor CHALIAPIN.   ROBERT LAWRENCE

Boris Godunov   (play)

Boris Godunov (1825), a dramatic tragedy, largely in blank verse, by the Russian poet and playwright Alexander PUSHKIN, is considered one of the masterpieces of the Russian stage. Set in the period 1598–1605, the play deals in Shakespearean fashion with the right of Boris Godunov to rule as tsar after he had seized the Russian throne by murdering the crown prince, Dmitry, the younger brother of Fyodor I. Challenged by an imposter Dmitry, Boris is victorious on the battlefield and yet a failure with the people and his own conscience. Eventually, he succumbs to a heart attack, and his family, in their turn, to assassination. A model of poetic and dramatic conciseness, *Boris Godunov* also brought a forceful historical accuracy to the Russian stage for the first time. The play was translated (1868–74) into operatic form by Modest MUSSORGSKY.
EDWARD WASIOLEK

Bibliography: Bayley, John, *Pushkin* (1971); Cross, Samuel H., and Simmons, Ernest J., eds., *Centennial Essays for Pushkin* (1937; repr. 1967); Magarshack, David, *Pushkin: A Biography* (1967).

Boris Godunov, Tsar of Russia   [bohr-ees' guh-doon-awf']

Boris Fyodorovich Godunov, chief advisor to Tsar Fyodor I from 1584 to 1598, was tsar of Russia from 1598 to 1605. Born in Moscow about 1551, Godunov was a member of the Saburov-Godunov family of Mongol origin. After his sister married Fyodor, the son of IVAN IV, in 1580, Godunov was promoted to the rank of boyar. Fyodor, who became tsar in 1584, proved incapable of ruling effectively, and a dual regency of his uncle and Godunov was established. In 1586, Godunov became sole regent and Russia's new master in all but name. One of the most important events of Godunov's regency was the elevation of the Russian Orthodox church to the rank of patriarchate. When Fyodor died in 1598, Godunov was elected to the throne by a national assembly. During his brief reign several tragic events occurred, the most serious of which was a severe famine. In 1603 a claimant to the throne appeared, professing to be Tsarevich Dmitry, son of Ivan IV. (The real Dmitry had died in 1591.) Gaining support in Poland and playing upon Russia's social discontent, the pretender marched on Moscow. When the government's armies appeared on the point of victory, Godunov died suddenly on Apr. 23 (N.S.), 1605. A period of chaos ensued, the so-called TIME OF TROUBLES.   DONALD L. LAYTON

Bibliography: Emerson, C., *Boris Godunov* (1986); Graham, S., *Boris Godunof* (1970); Grey, Ian, *Boris Godunov* (1973); Platonov, S., *Boris Godunov, Tsar of Russia*, trans. by L. Rex Pyles (1973).

Boris I, Tsar of Bulgaria

Boris I, d. May 2, 907, who ruled Bulgaria from 852 to 889, converted his subjects to Christianity. Baptized by Byzantine rite in 864 or 865, he approached the pope with a proposal to establish an independent Bulgarian church with Roman rites. When the pope failed to respond, he turned back to Constantinople and in 870 achieved his goal of a Bulgarian archbishopric within the Byzantine fold. In 889, Boris abdicated in favor of his eldest son, Vladimir, but emerged (893) from monastic retirement to depose Vladimir and place a younger son, SIMEON I, on the throne. Boris was canonized by the Orthodox church.

Bibliography: Lang, David Marshall, *The Bulgarians* (1976).

Boris III, Tsar of Bulgaria

Boris III, b. Jan. 30, 1894, d. Aug. 28, 1943, succeeded to the throne on the abdication (1918) of his father, FERDINAND I. He

ruled constitutionally at first, but in 1935 set up a personal dictatorship. Boris allied with the Axis in World War II, but refused to declare war on the Soviet Union. He died mysteriously a few weeks after an angry meeting with Adolf Hitler.

Borlaug, Norman Ernest   [bohr'-lawg]

Norman Ernest Borlaug, b. Mar. 25, 1914, was one of the creators of the GREEN REVOLUTION in agriculture and is its most famous exponent. He won the Nobel Peace Prize in 1970 for his work in breeding the "miracle" wheat strains that greatly increased grain yields in Mexico and India. Born on an Iowa farm, Borlaug attended the University of Minnesota, earning a Ph.D. in plant pathology in 1941. In 1944 he headed a program in Mexico, funded by the Rockefeller Foundation, whose purpose was the development of improved grain strains. Within two decades he succeeded in breeding a strain of wheat that was capable of thriving in Mexico's varied climates and that has helped to make both Mexico and India self-sufficient in that crop. Honored by governments and institutions around the world, Borlaug serves as a consultant to various agricultural organizations.

Borman, Frank

The American astronaut Frank Borman, b. Gary, Ind., Mar. 14, 1928, commanded the first manned mission around the Moon. After graduation from the U.S. Military Academy, he was assigned to the U.S. Air Force. He was a test pilot when selected to become an astronaut in 1962. As commander of GEMINI 7 (1965), Borman and pilot James LOVELL set a 14-day endurance record. The mission was designed to exceed the length of a lunar landing mission and to serve as a rendezvous target for *Gemini 6*. During the 1968 APOLLO 8 mission, the first manned flight around the Moon, he and crew members Lovell and William ANDERS read from Genesis as part of a Christmas greeting to the world. Borman retired from NASA and the air force in 1970 and joined Eastern Airlines. He became president of the company in 1975, a post he held until his resignation (1986).   DAVID DOOLING

Bormann, Martin

Martin Bormann, b. June 17, 1900, d. 1945, was a German Nazi leader who exercised great power in the final years of World War II. A Nazi from 1925, he rose to the top of the party administration and, after the defection (1941) of Rudolf HESS, became Hitler's secretary and closest advisor. After Hitler's suicide (Apr. 30, 1945) Bormann vanished. Persistent speculation that he was alive in South America was more or less halted by the discovery (1972) of a skeleton identified as his in West Berlin.

Born, Max

The German theoretical physicist Max Born, b. Dec. 11, 1882, d. Jan. 5, 1970, was a pioneer in developing QUANTUM MECHANICS. He received his doctorate in 1907 from Göttingen, where he was influenced by the mathematicians David Hilbert, Felix Klein, and Hermann Minkowski. He remained there until 1915, when he accepted a position at the University of Berlin and became a colleague and friend of Max Planck and Albert Einstein. In 1921, Born was appointed director of the Physical Institute at Göttingen.

The years 1921 to 1933 were Born's most productive. In collaboration with his students and assistants Werner Heisenberg, Pascual Jordan, and Wolfgang Pauli, he attempted to develop a new quantum mechanics. When Heisenberg succeeded in 1925, Born and others were able to advance the theory, using more systematic and powerful mathematics. For Born's interpretation of the square of Schrödinger's wave function as the probability of an electron's position, and for his further clarification of the wave-particle duality, he was awarded the Nobel Prize for physics in 1954.

Born, of Jewish origins, lost his professorship with Hitler's rise to power, but he soon was appointed (1936) to a chair at the University of Edinburgh, which he held until 1953. Upon retirement to the countryside near Göttingen, he not only continued his scientific work but wrote and spoke frequently on the social responsibility of scientists.   LAWRENCE BADASH

Bibliography: Born, Max, *My Life and My Views* (1968).

Börne, Ludwig

Ludwig Börne, b. May 6, 1786, d. Feb. 12, 1837, was a powerful German essayist and, after Heinrich HEINE, a preeminent prose stylist. Born a Jew, he changed his name in 1818 on conversion to Christianity. As a writer he never wavered in opposing reactionary regimes in Germany. His *Briefe aus Paris* (Letters from Paris, 1832-34) led to Prince Metternich's ban on the group of writers known as Young Germany, and he left home in 1830 to live in Paris. Börne was hostile to Goethe, whom he regarded as representative of a past aesthetic age, preferring the present political epoch, in which literature had to further political and social progress.   G. W. FIELD

Borneo

The island of Borneo is in the Malay Archipelago, southeast of the Malay Peninsula and southwest of the Philippine Islands. The population is 10,184,443 (1984 est.). It is divided into four political regions: Kalimantan, the largest, is Indonesian; SABAH (North Borneo) and SARAWAK are part of Malaysia; and tiny BRUNEI, formerly a British protectorate, gained independence in 1984. Borneo, with a length of 1,336 km (830 mi) and a maximum width of about 965 km (600 mi), is the third largest island in the world; its area is more than 743,107 km² (286,914 mi²). Borneo is mountainous and thick with rain forest. In the northeast the mountains reach their greatest height; among these, Mount Kinabalu rises 4,101 m (13,455 ft). A long ridge of mountains also covers the central part of Borneo.

The climate is hot and wet, with monsoons occurring between October and March. Many rivers, most of which are navigable, drain the island. The soil is substandard, with rice the main crop; rubber and spices are exported. The population consists of non-Muslim Dayaks and Islamic Malays, as well as Chinese and Europeans.

Spain and Portugal established relations with Borneo in the 16th century, but the Dutch and British held power from the 17th to the 20th century. The Dutch controlled most of the island until 1949, when Indonesia became a sovereign state.

Bibliography: Hausen, Eric, *Stranger in the Forest: On Foot across Borneo* (1988); MacKinnon, John, *Borneo* (1975).

Bornholm

Bornholm is an island county of Denmark in the Baltic Sea near southern Sweden. A resort area, it covers 588 km² (227 mi²) and has a population of 47,200 (1985 est.).

Largely composed of volcanic rock and surrounded by rocks and islets, Bornholm consists of an undulating, rocky plain where granite and coal are found. The people fish, grow oats and hemp, and raise dairy cattle. Butter is a major product, as are handicrafts such as textiles and pottery.

A Viking possession in about AD 1000, Bornholm changed hands several times before it became part of Denmark in 1660. Remains of four 12th-century fortress churches and a 13th-century castle are there. Bornholm was occupied by the Germans during World War II and then briefly by the Soviets.

bornite   [bohr'-nyt]

Bornite is a common and widespread copper and iron SULFIDE MINERAL (Cu_5FeS_4) and a minor ore of copper. It forms brittle, granular, or compact masses that on fresh fractures are metallic and brassy. Upon exposure to moisture, bornite tarnishes to a purplish iridescence, for which reason it is commonly called peacock ore. Hardness is 3, streak pale grayish black, and specific gravity 5.0–5.1. Bornite occurs with CHALCOPYRITE and chalcocite, both more important as ores, in copper deposits that typically form as zones of contact metamorphism (see METAMORPHIC ROCK) and as sulfide ore veins.

Bornu: see KANEM-BORNU.

Borobudur   [boh-roh-boo-door']

Borobudur, located about 40 km (25 mi) from Jogjakarta in central Java, is the ruined site of a major Buddhist monument. It was built about AD 800 by a king of the powerful and wealthy Sailendra dynasty. Crowning a small hill, the great shrine is constructed of dark-gray volcanic stone and has no interior spaces. It rests on a square base 121 m (403 ft) on each side and consists of eight diminishing tiers of terraces

The Borobudur shrine in central Java, built about 800 by the Sailendra dynasty, is an outstanding example of Buddhist architecture. The enormous pyramidal monument is particularly noted for its series of wall reliefs illustrating scenes from the life of Buddha and his path toward spiritual enlightenment.

connected by stairways. A huge STUPA, or bell-shaped dome, rises over 30 m (100 ft) from the uppermost terrace.

The lower five terraces are square, each bounded by a roofless corridor, the walls of which are lined with intricately carved bands of narrative relief. These illustrate the progress of the Bodhisattva (the Buddha before his enlightenment)—a prototype of ideal royalty—in his striving for all-embracing compassion. Each terrace shows a phase of his development: the lower scenes are more mundane and contain moral lessons; the higher are more spiritual and are more severe and static in style. Also depicted are many common objects of secular life—buildings, ships, weapons, musical instruments, and utensils. A sense of opulence and tranquillity is conveyed through the gently rounded contours of the relief sculpture bearing the influence of Indian Gupta and post-Gupta art.

The upper three terraces are unwalled and circular, intended to represent the sphere of enlightenment. They carry 72 stupas, enclosed in stone latticework, that surround the colossal central stupa. All contain large, stonecut Buddha images. As a summary, in architecture, of Mahayana Buddhist doctrine, the central stupa symbolizes the axis of the world, source both of the universe created through mind and of enlightenment through total self-abnegation and compassion.

The site was restored by the Dutch in 1907–11. In 1975 the Indonesian government launched a restoration project following the discovery that extensive water seepage into the body of the monument threatened it with eventual collapse; the project was completed in 1983. In 1985 several stupas were damaged by bombs believed to have been planted by Muslim extremists.   PHILIP RAWSON

Bibliography: Dumarcay, Jacques, *Borobudur*, ed. by Michael Smithies (1986); Kempers, A. J., *Ageless Borobudur* (1979); Krom, N. J., *Borobudur*, 2 vols. (1927).

Borodin, Aleksandr   [bohr-oh-deen', uhl-yik-sahn'-dur]

Aleksandr Porfirevich Borodin, b. Saint Petersburg (now Leningrad), Nov. 12 (N.S.), 1833, d. Feb. 27 (N.S.), 1887, was a renowned Russian composer who was also a distinguished professor of chemistry. The illegitimate son of a Georgian prince named Gedeanov, he was registered at birth as a "son" of the prince's servant Porfiri Borodin. He was given an excellent education, spoke several languages, and learned in his early years to play the flute, the piano, and the cello. In his ninth year he wrote his first musical composition. He completed his medical studies in Russia and in 1859 went to Germany to specialize in chemistry. He returned to Saint Petersburg in 1862 and became a leading chemistry teacher at the Medico-Surgical Academy there.

The same year, Borodin met Mily BALAKIREV and joined the group known as The FIVE, which was dedicated to the creation of a new school of Russian music. Preoccupied with work in chemistry, Borodin never had enough time for composing; he joked that his musical friends wished he were chronically sick, since he worked in his laboratory when healthy and wrote music only when ill. He worked on his opera *Prince Igor* for 18 years but never finished it. This was done by Nikolai RIMSKY-KORSAKOV and Aleksandr GLAZUNOV.

Borodin was a staunch musical nationalist and consistently used Russian folk music in his work. On one of his many trips to Western Europe he met Franz Liszt, who became a close friend and musical advisor. In 1880 he wrote the popular symphonic poem *In the Steppes of Central Asia*, and in 1876 he completed his Symphony no. 2 in B Minor. The dance suite called Polovtsian Dances, from *Prince Igor*, was orchestrated by Rimsky-Korsakov at Borodin's request.

Borodin also wrote a number of chamber works, including several string quartets and the Trio in D Major for violin, cello, and piano. His exceptionally beautiful songs are popular in Russia and are beginning to be heard in concert in the West. The worldwide success of the musical *Kismet* (1953), the melodies of which are all derived from Borodin, led to a revival of interest in Borodin's works, which have been increasingly performed and recorded.   MILOS VELIMIROVIĆ

Bibliography: Abraham, Gerald E., *Borodin* (1927; repr. 1976); Dianin, Serge, *Borodin*, trans. by Robert Lord (1963; repr. 1980); Seroff, Victor I., *The Mighty Five* (1948); Zetlin, Mikhail, *The Five*, ed. and trans. by George Panin (1959; repr. 1975).

Borodino, Battle of: see NAPOLEONIC WARS.

boron   [bohr'-ahn]

Boron is a metalloid chemical element that exhibits properties significantly different from the other members of group IIIA. Its chemical symbol is B, atomic number 5, and atomic weight 10.811. Boron constitutes only 3 ppm of the Earth's crust. It is most commonly found in the BORATE MINERALS borax, $Na_2B_4O_7 \cdot 10H_2O$, and kernite, $Na_2B_4O_7 \cdot 4H_2O$. The element was first isolated by Sir Humphry Davy in 1807 and by Joseph Gay-Lussac and Louis Thénard in 1808.

Boron exists in an amorphous form as an extremely hard, blackish brown powder, and in three crystalline forms that look like metals. Crystalline boron is second only to diamond in hardness but is too brittle for use in metals.

Research suggests that boron may be nutritionally important. Apparently it helps to maintain appropriate body levels of minerals and hormones needed for bone health.

Uses. The low electrical conductivity of boron increases greatly as its temperature is raised. At certain temperatures, therefore, boron behaves as a SEMICONDUCTOR, and it is often added to germanium and silicon to increase their electrical conductivity. The use of cubic boron nitride as a high-temperature semiconductor is also being explored.

Small additions of boron to steel appreciably increase the hardness of the alloy. Boron is also used in the production of pure, strong metals to remove the oxygen and nitrogen dissolved in the metal or chemically bound to it, and it is used to absorb fast neutrons in nuclear reactors.

The most important boron compound is borax, which has been used in pottery glazes since the Middle Ages. Borax deposits were first found in Tibet, and borax was brought to Europe by the Arabs. It is still important in the ceramic industry. Borax combines with chromium, copper, manganese, cobalt, and nickel to form beautifully colored compounds. Borax beads were once used as a reagent in the detection of these elements. Borax is also important in the production of borosilicate glass, which has a high refractive index and is suitable for the manufacture of lenses. Other applications of borax include the impregnation of textiles and wood to make them fire resistant; softening water for laundry; and as a flux in brazing (dissolution of oxides). A weak base, borax is also used in buffer solutions and photographic developers.

Since boron is important in the calcium cycle of plants, borax or boric acid is often added to boron-poor soils as a fertilizer. Boric acid is obtained by the action of strong acids on borax and is used as a mild disinfectant. Although its toxicity is low, it is not completely harmless. Its use as a food preservative is prohibited in many countries.

Boron Chemistry. Boron has three valence electrons and forms covalent compounds almost exclusively. It generally forms planar, three-bonded compounds with 120° bond angles. These compounds have only six bonding electrons. The boron atom can attain a rare gas configuration, with eight bonding electrons, in reactions of molecules with free electron pairs, such as NH_3 or F^-:

$$NH_3 + BH_3 \rightarrow H_3NBH_3$$

$$K^+ + F^- + BF_3 \rightarrow K^+BF_4^-$$

Bibliography: Alekseev, N. V., et al., *Structural Chemistry of Boron and Silicon* (1986); Greenwood, N. N., *The Chemistry of Boron* (1975); Wells, A. F., *Structural Inorganic Chemistry*, 5th ed. (1983).

Bororo   [boh-roh'-roh]

The Bororo are a South American Indian people living in the Mato Grosso region of Brazil and in parts of eastern Bolivia. Their population is estimated at less than 1,000, and they are divided into an eastern and a western group. They speak either of two dialects of the Macro-Ge subfamily of South

American Indian languages. Originally a hunter-gatherer and fishing people, the Bororo later developed slash-and-burn horticultural methods and now grow maize, manioc, rice, and other tropical-forest crops. They live in small villages along riverbanks during the dry season and move to higher ground in the rainy season. Their settlements are circular in plan, with the houses grouped around a men's house and a central plaza. Kinship, residence, and clan membership are determined according to female ancestry. Traditionally each village had a chief whose authority was based on consensus and whose responsibilities were limited to organizational activities, such as planning hunting and fishing expeditions.

Bororo religion is governed by two complex sets of animalistic beliefs. The first centers around the SHAMAN, who is believed possessed by a spirit that enables him to cure supernaturally induced illness. The second involves the spirits of ordinary tribal ancestors, who are believed to commune with their descendants, imparting curative knowledge to those lacking special powers. The latter are thereby empowered to effect cures using traditional medicines and without resorting to the shamans.

LOUIS C. FARON

Bibliography: Steward, Julian, and Faron, Louis, *Native Peoples of South America* (1959).

borough

A borough is a unit of local goverment in Great Britain and in a few states in the United States. The term is derived from the Old English *burg* ("fortress"), applied in the 8th and 9th centuries to walled communities built in England in defense against Danish invaders. During the Middle Ages the boroughs developed into urban centers with special trade and tax privileges, and local autonomy was granted to them by royal charter. Beginning in the 13th century representatives of the boroughs were also summoned to Parliament. In the parlance of 19th-century parliamentary reformers, a *rotten borough* was one that remained a parliamentary constituency after most of its population had left, and a *pocket borough,* a constituency controlled by a powerful landowner. Both types were largely eliminated by the REFORM ACT of 1832.

In colonial America, boroughs were chartered by the governors and the crown and designated as election districts for representation to colonial legislatures. After the American Revolution, use of the term *borough* declined. Today the term is applied to some incorporated places in New Jersey, Pennsylvania, Connecticut, and Minnesota and to the five subdivisions of New York City.

RITA IMMERMANN

Borough, Stephen

Stephen Borough, b. Sept. 25, 1525, d. July 12, 1584, was an English navigator who made several voyages in search of the Northeast Passage. As master of the *Edward Bonaventure* in 1553, he was the first Englishman to sight and sail around the North Cape of Norway and to reach the White Sea. In 1556 he sailed as commander of the *Searchthrift* for the English merchants' Muscovy Company and reached the island of Novaya Zemlya. Probably the first Englishman to sail this far east, he was turned back at the Kara Sea by ice storms. His subsequent voyages were devoted to establishing trade between England and Russia.

Borowski, Tadeusz [buh-rawf'-skee]

The Polish writer Tadeusz Borowski, b. Nov. 12, 1922, d. July 3, 1951, is remembered for his short stories based on his experiences in the concentration camps of Auschwitz and Dachau during World War II. Not a Jew, he was sent to the camps as a political prisoner. A selection of his stories has been published in English under the title *This Way for the Gas, Ladies and Gentlemen* (1967). These stories are among the finest literary portraits of life in the Nazi death camps; their power lies in the fact that Borowski did not divide that monstrous world into victims and villains but instead showed, without editorial comment, the everyday weakness of human nature. Borowski committed suicide.

MICHAEL KANDEL

Borrelia: see RELAPSING FEVER.

Borromeo, Saint Charles   [bohr-roh-may'-oh]

Saint Charles Borromeo, b. Oct. 2, 1538, d. Nov. 3, 1584, was one of the most important figures of the COUNTER-REFORMATION. From childhood, his family intended him for a career in the church, and he held many important offices in Rome while his uncle, Pius IV, was pope. In April of 1566, he took up residence in Milan as archbishop and cardinal and achieved great fame there as a reformer of the church. He was considered a model bishop because he promoted the ideals of the recently adjourned Council of Trent (1545-63). He gave special attention to convocation and visitation of his clergy, to promoting the instruction of the laity in Christian doctrine, and to reorganizing the administration of the diocese. He was canonized on Nov. 1, 1610. Feast day: Nov. 4.

JOHN W. O'MALLEY

Bibliography: Yeo, Margaret, *Reformer: St. Charles Borromeo* (1938).

Borromini, Francesco   [bohr-roh-mee'-nee]

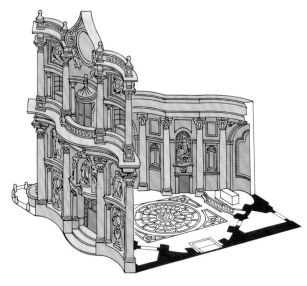

Francesco Borromini's Church of San Carlo alle Quattro Fontane (1638-67) in Rome, shown above in a cutaway drawing, could serve as a three-dimensional definition of baroque architecture, with its undulating facade, floor plan of interlocking ovals, and oval dome.

Francesco Borromini, b. Sept. 25, 1599, d. Aug. 2, 1667, was the first Roman high-BAROQUE architect to break with the classical concept of architecture as formulated in the era of Filippo Brunelleschi (1377-1466). In place of this principle of planning, which involved the multiplication of arithmetic units called modules, Borromini adopted geometric units.

The son of the architect Giovanni Domenico Castelli, Borromini settled in Rome about 1620 and began his career as a stonecarver, spending more than a decade working mainly in SAINT PETER'S BASILICA on coats of arms, decorative putti, festoons, and balustrades. In addition, the architect Carlo Maderno, a distant relative, employed him as a draftsman for Saint Peter's, for the Palazzo Barberini, and for the church and dome of Sant'Andrea della Valle. After Maderno's death, Borromini worked under Giovanni Bernini for 5 years.

In 1634, Borromini received his first commission, the monastery of SAN CARLO ALLE QUATTRO FONTANE (completed 1641; facade completed 1667). This project was characteristic of Borromini's lifelong concerns. Space and mass are molded through the variations of a principal motif, in this instance the triangle; each additional structure, including the very smallest detail, is subordinated to the key geometrical unit. Emphasizing the "skeleton" of the monastery, Borromini assimilated structural principles of GOTHIC ARCHITECTURE and simultaneously incorporated Mannerist features (see MANNER-ISM), many ideas from MICHELANGELO's architecture, and even severely classical elements from Andrea PALLADIO. In his late works Borromini increasingly stressed the blending of architecture and sculpture. Among his most outstanding projects are the Oratory of San Filippo Neri (1637–50), the Palazzo Falconieri (c.1640), Sant'lvo della Sapienza (1642–50), and the Collegio di Propaganda Fide (1646–67). DAVID CAST

Bibliography: Blunt, Anthony, *Borromini* (1979); Portoghesi, Paolo, *The Rome of Borromini*, trans. by Barbara Luigia La Penta (1968); Steinberg, Leo, *Borromini's San Carlo Alle Quattro Fontane* (1976).

Borrow, George Henry

George Henry Borrow, b. July 5, 1803, d. July 26, 1881, was an English writer, traveler, and translator best known for his eccentric, semiautobiographical books about Gypsy culture. He abandoned work in law and publishing to travel on the Continent (1833–40), serving in Russia and Spain as an agent for the British and Foreign Bible Society. Based on his wanderings and research, Borrow wrote *The Zincali* (1841), about the Gypsies in Spain; *The Bible in Spain* (1843), his most popular book; *Lavengro* (1851); and *Romany Rye* (1857). A prolific translator, Borrow knew some 30 languages.

Bibliography: Armstrong, Martin, *George Borrow* (1950; repr. 1974); Williams, David, *A World of His Own* (1982).

borzoi [bohr'-zoy]

The borzoi, or Russian wolfhound, was originally used to hunt wolves. Its name, which means "speed" in Russian, refers to the swiftness and agility of the breed. It is still used to hunt hares and foxes.

The borzoi, or Russian wolfhound, is a large, slender, lean-headed, long-coated breed of dog with a heavily feathered tail. Graceful and agile, it is primarily a running dog, with muscular legs and a strong neck and jaws. The male stands at least 71 cm (28 in) at the shoulder and weighs 34–47 kg (75–104 lb); the female stands at least 66 cm (26 in) high and weighs 7–9 kg (15–20 lb) less. The silky coat is flat, wavy, or curly, and may be a variety of colors.

The breed was developed from the greyhound and a collie-like dog by the 17th-century Russian aristocracy to course wolves and other game—that is, run them down by sight. The first borzoi was brought to the United States in 1889, and the breed was recognized under the name *borzoi* by the American Kennel Club in 1936. JOHN MANDEVILLE

Bibliography: McRae, Gail C., *Borzois* (1989).

Bosch, Carl [bawsh]

Carl Bosch, b. Aug. 27, 1874, d. Apr. 26, 1940, was the co-winner (with Friedrich Bergius) of the 1931 Nobel Prize for chemistry for his research in high-pressure synthesis. Bosch developed (1913) an industrial process for converting hydrogen and nitrogen into ammonia, which is an ingredient of fertilizers and explosives and was, until then, in short supply. The process was based on the laboratory work of Fritz HABER, and is known as the Haber-Bosch process.

Bosch, Hieronymus [hay-raw'-nee-mus]

Hieronymus, or Jerome, Bosch, b. c.1450, d. August 1516, spent his entire artistic career in the small Dutch town of 's Hertogenbosch, from which he derived his name. At the time of his death, Bosch was internationally celebrated as an eccentric painter of religious visions who dealt in particular with the torments of hell. His works were imitated throughout the 16th century, notably by Peter Bruegel the Elder.

Bosch was a member of the religious Brotherhood of Our Lady, for whom he painted several altarpieces for the Cathedral of Saint John, 's Hertogenbosch, all now lost. The artist probably never went far from home. None of Bosch's pictures are dated, although many are signed.

Bosch's most famous and unconventional picture is *The Garden of Earthly Delights* (c.1500; Prado, Madrid) which, like most of his other ambitious works, is a large, three-part altarpiece, called a triptych. This painting was probably made for the private enjoyment of a noble family. It is named for the luscious garden in the central panel, which is filled with cavorting nudes and giant birds and fruit. The triptych depicts the history of the world and the progression of sin. Beginning on the outside shutters with the creation of the world, the story progresses from Adam and Eve and original sin on the left panel to the torments of hell, a dark, icy, yet fiery nightmarish vision, on the right. The Garden of Delights in the center illustrates a world deeply engaged in sinful pleasures.

The subject of sin and its punishments was central to all of Bosch's art. Another famous triptych, the *Haywain* (c.1485–90; Prado, Madrid), contains a similar progression of sin, from Eden to hell, across its panels. In the central panel sin is represented through the metaphor of a large wagonload of hay for which a greedy world grasps. *The Seven Deadly Sins* (c.1485; Prado, Madrid) is a painted rectangle with a central image of the eye of God watching the world. The "Seven Deadly Sins," depicted through scenes of worldly transgression, are arranged around the circular shape. In the corners of the image appear the "Four Last Things" mentioned in late medieval spiritual handbooks: Deathbed, the Last Judgment, Heaven, and Hell, all of which are favorite themes of Bosch.

Bosch's belief in the pervasive evil of the world colored his paintings of more conventional religious subjects; the stories of Christ and the saints became images of torment by demons or mobs of mocking humans. Typical of these interpretations are the numerous images from Christ's passion, such as the half-length *Crowning with Thorns*, or *Christ Being Shown to the People* (c.1485; National Gallery, London).

Bosch's spiritual heroes were the saints who endured both physical and mental torment yet remained steadfast. Among the saints, his favorite was Saint Anthony, the subject of the triptych *The Temptation of Saint Anthony* (c.1500; Museo Nacional de Arte Antiga, Lisbon), which features physical punishment on the left, a Black Mass in the center, and the blandishments of food and sex on the right. Anthony's triumph over such trials is mirrored by those of other hermit saints and by the Passion of Christ, whose arrest and carrying of the cross adorn the exterior of the Lisbon altarpiece.

Bosch was preoccupied with themes of torment and the sinfulness of man, which replaced earlier, more optimistic visions of Christ and the Virgin with feelings of anxiety, fear, and guilt. His sources for such unusual images were the dark corners of the medieval imagination, the gargoyles and monsters of cathedral decoration, and the marginal illustrations of books and popular prints. LAWRENCE SILVER

Hieronymus Bosch's conception of the torments of Hell forms the right panel of his triptych The Garden of Earthly Delights (c.1500), one of many versions Bosch painted of this subject. Bosch created an allegory that carries the theme of temptation, sin, and punishment, beginning with the Fall of Man (left panel), a lush scene of life devoted to the sensual pleasures (central panel), and in the final panel, shown, the consequences of sin. (Prado, Madrid.)

Bibliography: Delevoy, Robert, *Bosch* (1991); Fraenger, Wilhelm, *Hieronymus Bosch,* trans. by H. Sebba (1983); Gibson, Walter, *Hieronymous Bosch,* rev. ed. (1985); Guillaud, Maurice and Jacqueline, *Bosch: The Garden of Earthly Delights* (1989); Luifert, Carl, *Bosch* (1989).

Bosch, Juan   [bawsh]

Juan Bosch Gaviõn, b. June 30, 1909, was president of the Dominican Republic in 1963. He lived in exile during the dictatorship (1930–61) of Rafael TRUJILLO. After Trujillo's assassination, the Partido Revolucionario Dominicano, which Bosch had helped establish (1939), introduced (September 1962) a constitution and sweeping reforms favoring workers and peasants. Bosch was elected president in the country's first free balloting since 1924. However, long-standing economic problems, conflict with Haiti, and opposition from conservative elements led to his overthrow in September 1963. When Bosch's supporters attempted to restore him in 1965, the United States intervened to restore the status quo. Bosch ran unsuccessfully for the presidency in 1966, 1982, 1986, and 1990.

Bosch, Robert   [bawsh]

Robert August Bosch, b. Sept. 23, 1861, d. Mar. 9, 1942, a German inventor, industrialist, and philanthropist, manufactured the first practical automotive IGNITION SYSTEM. His low-voltage magneto (1897), a type of alternator, was a much safer improvement over the open-flame hot-tube ignitions then in use. In 1903 his company introduced the high-voltage magneto. Until the 1930s, European automobile manufacturers relied exclusively on this system. Bosch was also involved in the development of spark plugs, windshield-wiper motors, starters, generators, and fuel-injection systems. In 1936 he founded the Robert Bosch Hospital in Stuttgart, an act characteristic of his renowned generosity.   DENNIS SIMANAITIS

Bosco, Saint John

Saint John Bosco, b. Turin, Italy, Aug. 16, 1815, d. Jan. 31, 1888, a pioneer in the field of vocational training in Italy, founded (1859) the Society of Saint Francis de Sales (Salesians), a community of Roman Catholic priests specializing in the education of boys. With Saint Maria Mazarello, he also founded the Salesian Sisters in 1872. Bosco was canonized in 1934. Feast day: Jan. 31.

Bose, Subhas Chandra   [bohz]

Subhas Chandra Bose, b. Jan. 23, 1897, d. Aug. 18, 1945, was an Indian nationalist who formed an Axis-sponsored Indian army during World War II. An early supporter of Mahatma Gandhi, Bose was president of the Bengal Congress party (1927–31) and of the national Congress party (1938–39). Imprisoned by the British, he escaped (1941) to Germany and later went to Japanese-held Singapore. In 1944 the army that he had formed advanced across Burma to India, where it was defeated. Bose died as a result of a plane crash in Taiwan.

Bosnia and Hercegovina   [bahz'-nee-uh, hur-tsuh-goh-vee'-nuh]

Bosnia and Hercegovina (often referred to as Bosnia), a Balkan country, was formerly one of the republics of YUGOSLAVIA. It declared its independence in the spring of 1992 and was immediately convulsed by civil war. The republic is bounded on the east by Serbia, on the south by Montenegro, and on the north and west by Croatia. Its capital is SARAJEVO.

LAND AND PEOPLE

The names *Bosnia* and *Hercegovina* (also spelled *Herzegovina*) refer to two separate regions: Bosnia (its name derived from the Bosna River) occupies the great majority of the republic's territory; Hercegovina is a much smaller area in the south, around the city of Mostar; its name derives from the German *Herzog* (''duke''), the title borne by its former rulers.

Most of Bosnia and Hercegovina is covered by the DINARIC ALPS. The Bosna, Drina, Una, and Vrbas rivers are tributaries of the SAVA, which forms part of the country's northern border. The Neretva River flows south into the Adriatic; near its

**BOSNIA AND
HERCEGOVINA**

LAND. Area: 51,129 km² (19,741 mi²). Capital and largest city: Sarajevo (1991 pop. 525,980).

PEOPLE. Population (1993 est.): 4,618,804; density: 90.3 persons per km² (223.9 per mi²). Distrib. (1981): 36% urban, 64% rural. Ann. growth (1991): 0.5%. Off. language: Serbo-Croatian. Maj. religions: Islam, Orthodox church, Roman Catholicism.

EDUCATION AND HEALTH. Literacy (1981): 86% of adult population. Universities (1992): 4. Hospital beds (1990): 19,858. Physicians (1989): 6,929. Life expectancy (1993): women—77.7; men—72.1. Infant mortality (1993): 13.2 per 1,000 live births.

ECONOMY. GNP (1990): $10.7 bill.; $2,454 per capita. Labor distrib. (1990): agri.—3.8%; manuf. and mining—48.3%; const.—7.3%; pub. util.—2.2%; transport and commun.—6.7%; trade—12.8%; finance—3.8%; other—15.1%. Foreign trade (1990): imports—$1.9 bill.; exports—$2 bill.; principal trade partners—other Yugoslav republics. Currency: 1 dinar = 100 para.

GOVERNMENT. Type: republic. Legislature: National Assembly. Political subdivisions: 100 districts.

COMMUNICATIONS. Railroads (1990): 1,039 km (646 mi). Roads (1991): 21,168 km (13,153 mi). Major ports: none. Major airfields: 1.

mouth is the republic's only outlet to the sea—about 20 km (12 mi) of coastline. In addition to Sarajevo and Mostar, other important towns include Banja Luka and Tuzla.

Bosnia and Hercegovina's three main population groups—the Muslims, the Orthodox Serbs, and the Roman Catholic Croats—are all South Slav peoples who speak Serbo-Croatian but differ in religion and culture. At the beginning of the 1992 war, 43.7% of the population were Muslim Slavs; 31.3% were Serbs, and 17.2% were Croats. The Croats were concentrated along the western border; the Muslims and Serbs were more widely dispersed throughout the republic.

ECONOMIC ACTIVITY

In normal times about half the workforce is employed in industry. The republic is a major producer of timber, and it contained about 60% of the former Yugoslavia's armaments industry. Its rivers are an abundant source of hydroelectric power. Bosnia's economy, however, was completely disrupted by the warfare that broke out after independence was declared.

HISTORY AND GOVERNMENT

Medieval Bosnia was nominally a banat (client state) of Hungary, but by the 13th century it enjoyed autonomy under its rulers, the bans. The most prominent of these was Turtko (r. 1353–91), who adopted the title king of Bosnia and Serbia. Hercegovina was established as a separate duchy in 1448. In the 14th and 15th centuries the BOGOMILS, a heretical Christian sect, were numerous in Bosnia. When the Ottoman Turks conquered the area in 1463, many of the Bogomils adopted Islam. During the Ottoman period the Bosnian nobles were Muslim and the peasantry Christian.

As Turkish power waned in the 19th century Bosnia's Muslim nobility repeatedly rebelled against the sultan; a general revolt in 1875–76 was supported by Serbia, which claimed Bosnia and Hercegovina as part of its territory. After the revolt had been quelled, the Congress of Berlin (1878) allowed Austria-Hungary to occupy the two provinces, which remained nominally part of the Ottoman Empire. Austria-Hungary's outright annexation of Bosnia-Hercegovina in 1908 further in-

creased tensions with Serbia, and the Bosnian Serbs agitated against Austrian rule. In June 1914, Gavrilo Princip, a Bosnian Serb, assassinated the Austrian archduke FRANZ FERDINAND in Sarajevo. The resulting conflict between Serbia and Austria-Hungary quickly escalated into World War I.

After the war Bosnia-Hercegovina was incorporated into the Kingdom of the Serbs, Croats, and Slovenes, which became Yugoslavia in 1929. During World War II the region was divided between Italy and the German puppet state of Croatia, and in 1945 it was reincorporated into Communist Yugoslavia as one of the country's six federal republics.

Croatia and Slovenia seceded from Yugoslavia in 1991, and Bosnia followed their example in March 1992. The Bosnian Serbs took up arms to resist this move and were backed by the Serb-led Yugoslav military, many of whose weapons factories are located in Bosnia. A bitter struggle ensued, in which the Serbs systematically expelled Muslims and Croats from the Serb-controlled areas—a policy known as "ethnic cleansing" —which eventually created an estimated 3 million refugees (see YUGOSLAV WAR). By the summer of 1992, Serbian forces held about two-thirds of the republic's territory and had proclaimed their own Serbian Republic of Bosnia and Hercegovina. Meanwhile, fighting had broken out between Muslims and Croats in the area around Mostar, where the Croats too created an enclave for themselves.

Beginning in the fall of 1992 the UN and the European Community, joined later by the United States and Russia, tried vainly to mediate a settlement that would satisfy all three parties. A series of cease-fires reduced the level of the fighting in early 1994; in March of that year the Muslims and Croats made peace, and Croatia agreed to form a federation with Bosnia. In the fall of 1994 the Bosnian Muslims and Croats mounted a joint offensive against the Serbs, but the Serbs soon regained the upper hand, and by December they were threatening the Muslim enclave of Bihać.

Bibliography: Malcolm, N., *Bosnia: A History* (1994).

boson   [bohs'-sahn]

Bosons, or gauge particles, in physics, are the FUNDAMENTAL PARTICLES that carry the FUNDAMENTAL INTERACTIONS of nature. They include the GLUON, PHOTON, W PARTICLES, Z particle, and hypothetical graviton. Most bosons have one unit of spin; gravitons would have two. The mathematics of bosons was worked out by Albert Einstein and Indian physicist Satyendra Nath Bose. The word *boson* derives from the latter's name.

Bosporus   [bahs'-pur-uhs]

The Bosporus, or Bosphorus, is a narrow strait between Europe and Asia connecting the BLACK SEA to the Sea of MARMARA, which in turn is connected by the Dardanelles to the Aegean, part of the Mediterranean Sea. ISTANBUL, Turkey, spreads out over both sides. Since ancient times the strait, with a maximum width of 3.7 km (2.3 mi) and 30 km (19 mi) long, has been strategic for trade and military purposes.

boss, political

In U.S. politics, a boss is a person who controls a political organization (called a machine) at the ward, city, county, or state level of government. Bosses are usually thought of as power-seekers who promote their own interests and those of their supporters by using fraudulent or corrupt means if necessary. Although bosses may be elected government officials, they also may hold no elective office and yet exercise power through informal party machinery.

The boss system flourished in the late 19th and early 20th centuries in both U.S. political parties. Its development coincided with the growth of the cities and the influx of European immigrants. Bosses were often of poor, foreign-born parentage, able to adapt their native codes of personal loyalty and individual help to the opportunities for political advancement afforded in America. Their political machines helped assimilate the immigrants into their new society by providing them with jobs, housing, clothing, food, money, and fuel in exchange for votes, and by introducing them to democratic ways. In large urban areas the machines balanced their slates of candidates to represent all ethnic groups. The bosses are also credited with building hospitals, parks, civic centers, and transportation arteries, although their motives for doing so were largely self-serving.

The most famous of the 19th-century city bosses was William Marcy TWEED in New York City. There the local Democratic machine, TAMMANY HALL, was later led by John Kelly, Richard CROKER, Charles Murphy, and, in the mid-20th century, Carmine De Sapio. Other 20th-century bosses have included Edward Crump of Memphis, James M. CURLEY of Boston, Richard J. DALEY of Chicago, Frank HAGUE of Jersey City, and Thomas J. PENDERGAST of Kansas City. The LONG family created a powerful political machine in Louisiana.

Various reforms have hastened the decline of the boss system. Among them are the direct primary, the merit system for public employment, public welfare programs, and competitive bidding for government contracts.　　　RITA J. IMMERMAN

Bibliography: Stone, Bruce, *Urban Bosses, Machines, and Progressive Reformers* (1972); Van Devander, C. W., *The Big Bosses* (1974).

Bosse, Abraham　[baws]

Abraham Bosse, b. 1602, d. Feb. 14, 1676, was a French engraver, etcher, and art theorist. In his many graphic works he depicted various aspects of French society during the reign of Louis XIV. His painstaking attention to detail makes these a valuable record of the life of the period. Bosse was a quarrelsome man who openly criticized the society in which he lived. He was a professor in the French Academy, but his personality and his unorthodox theories on perspective led to disagreements with his colleagues and to his eventual expulsion. He published many books on engraving, perspective, and art theory. One of the most important was *The Art of Graving and Etching* (1645; Eng. trans., 1662).　　　TANIA BAYARD

Bossuet, Jacques Bénigne　[baw-sue-ay']

Jacques Bénigne Bossuet, b. Sept. 27, 1627, d. Apr. 12, 1704, was a French Catholic orator and theologian who dominated Paris preaching for a decade (1659–69). While he was tutor to the dauphin (father of Louis XV) from 1671 to 1681, he wrote his trilogy on history, politics, and the knowledge of God. In addition to his scholarly writings, his meditations are considered classics of French devotional literature. He served conscientiously as bishop of Meaux after 1681, but theological controversy embittered his final years.　　　JAMES D. NELSON

Bibliography: Reynolds, Ernest E., *Bossuet* (1966).

Bossy, Mike

A Canadian professional ice hockey player, Michael Bossy, b. Montreal, Jan. 22, 1957, was one of the best right wings in the National Hockey League (NHL) during the early and mid-1980s. Bossy joined the NHL's New York Islanders in 1977–78, when he scored 53 goals and was NHL Rookie of the Year. In 1979 and again in 1981 he led the league in goals scored. Meanwhile, the Islanders were winning four consecutive Stanley Cups (1980–83), and in 1982 Bossy was Most Valuable Player in the play-offs. He retired in 1988 with 1,126 points on 573 goals and 553 assists.

Boston

Boston is the capital of Massachusetts and New England's largest city. The city is named for the English port in Lincolnshire. It is situated on a hilly peninsula, where the Mystic and Charles rivers flow into Massachusetts Bay. With one of the finest natural harbors in the United States, it is New England's most important seaport.

Reclamation of swampy tidal flats has more than doubled the size of Boston's original peninsula. The city has grown by annexation and reclamation to more than 35 times its colonial size. The city proper is small in area (130 km²/50 mi²) and has a population of 574,283 (1990). Included within the city limits are East Boston, Charlestown, Roxbury, Dorchester, Brighton, West Roxbury, Jamaica Plain, and Hyde Park. The metropolitan area, however, includes parts of at least 5 counties.

The Contemporary City. A 30-year decline in population in the core city was reversed between 1980 and 1990 as the population increased by 2%. In 1990 blacks constituted about 25% of the population. The Irish form the largest white ethnic group, and Italian and French Canadians are also numerous. South Boston remains an ethnic stronghold of the Irish, and Little Italy is found in the North End section. A Chinatown is adjacent to the Washington Street downtown shopping area. Hispanics make up 11% (1990) of Boston's population.

(Left) *Many of the skyscrapers in downtown Boston, the capital of Massachusetts, were erected during the 1960s as part of an urban renewal program.* (Below) *Boston's Old State House, the seat of British colonial government from 1748 to the beginning of the American Revolution, is a museum.*

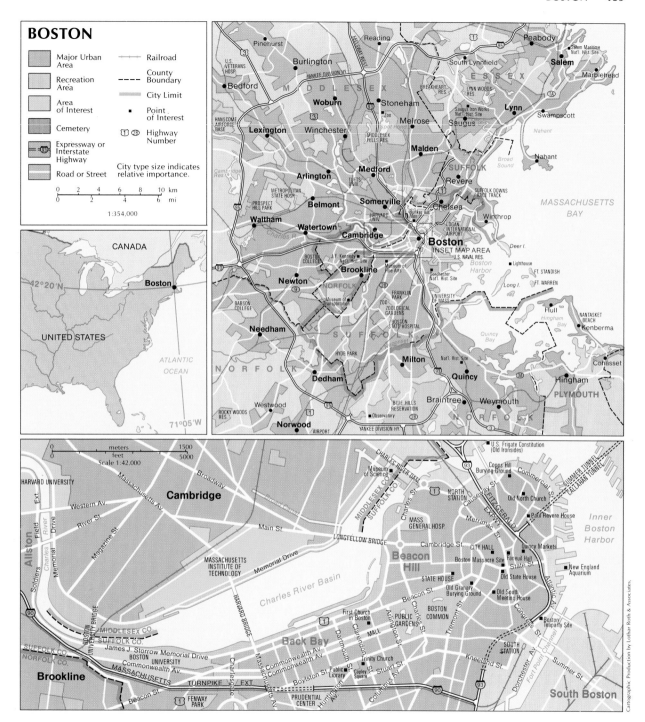

The city serves the New England region as a major financial and insurance center as well as an important industrial center. Small-scale and widely diversified industries characterize the manufacturing structure. In recent years research and development facilities, concentrating in sophisticated electronics, computers, and chemicals, have had a great impact on the industrial structure of the metropolitan area. Although on the decline, an important fishing fleet operates from the city. Boston has a significant tourist industry.

Cultural Institutions. Boston has been an educational and cultural center since 1635, when the first American public school, Boston Latin School, was established. More than 50 institutions of higher learning are found in the metropolitan area.

These include Northeastern University, Boston University, the University of Massachusetts at Boston, and the New England Conservatory of Music, in Boston proper; Harvard University and the Massachusetts Institute of Technology, in Cambridge; and Boston College in Chestnut Hill (Newton), Tufts University in Medford, and Wellesley College in Wellesley.

The Boston Public Library, the first free public library in the United States, opened in 1854. The Boston Museum of Fine Arts contains some of the nation's prime art holdings. The BOSTON SYMPHONY ORCHESTRA and the BOSTON POPS ORCHESTRA are important musical elements in the city.

Historic landmarks abound in the Boston area. Churches of significance include King's Chapel, Christ Church, Trinity

Episcopal Church, Holy Cross Cathedral (Roman Catholic), Saint Paul's Cathedral (Episcopal), and the first Christian Science church (1894). Other notable buildings include the Old State House, Paul REVERE's house, FANEUIL HALL, Old South Meeting House, and the Quincy Market.

History. In 1614, Capt. John SMITH mapped Boston Harbor, and in 1630 the settlement of Boston was established on the hilly peninsula. By 1700 the settlement's principal activities were shipbuilding, whaling, fishing, and trading. Bostonians were at the forefront of colonial resistance to England. In 1770, British troops and citizens clashed in the BOSTON MASSACRE, and three years later Bostonians dumped British tea into the harbor in the BOSTON TEA PARTY. After the war Boston developed a profitable trade with China; also manufacturing and other industry were becoming more important.

During the late 1830s and 1840s rails began to link the city to the New England hinterland. European immigrants, especially from Ireland, arrived to become a new supply of labor. Around 1830, Boston was also a center for the antislavery movement. By the late 19th century, the city had become the urban hub of an enormous suburban area.

In the 1960s an extensive renewal project for the decaying downtown area began, changing Boston's low skyline to one dominated by skyscrapers. The Prudential Center, Government Center, and the John Hancock Mutual Life Insurance Company building are among the most prominent of these landmarks. A later downtown project, Lafayette Place, which includes a shopping complex and a hotel, was completed in the mid-1980s. In the early 1990s a huge public-works project to clean up the polluted Boston Harbor got under way.

In 1974 a court-ordered busing plan for the desegregation of public schools was disrupted by violence and a boycott by white students. In September 1985 a federal judge returned control of the schools to the city's school committee, but racial divisions have persisted and the school system remains troubled. DANIEL GONSALVES

Bibliography: Bunting, William H., *Portrait of a Port* (1971); Durang, Charles F., *Boston: A Brief History* (1988); Formisano, Ronald P., *Boston against Busing* (1991); Formisano, Ronald P., and Burns, Constance K., eds., *Boston 1700–1980: The Evolution of Urban Politics* (1984); Handlin, Oscar, *Boston's Immigrants*, rev. ed. (1959); Jacobs, Donald M., ed., *Courage and Conscience: Black and White Abolitionists in Boston* (1993); Jones, H. M., and Zaban, B., *The Many Voices of Boston* (1975); Kennedy, Lawrence W., *Planning the City upon a Hill* (1992); Lyndon, Donlyn, *The City Observed* (1982); Rutman, Darret Bruce, *Winthrop's Boston* (1965; repr. 1972); Shand-Tucci, D., *Built in Boston* (1988); Vanderwarker, P., *Boston Then and Now* (1983).

Boston College

Established by the Jesuits in 1863, Boston College (enrollment: 14,557; library: 1,236,330 volumes) is a liberal arts university in Chestnut Hill, Mass. It has schools of law, management, nursing, and education and a graduate school of social work. The college offers cross-registration with several area schools.

Boston Globe

The *Boston Globe,* founded in 1872, is a distinguished daily morning and evening newspaper serving northeastern New England. Under the management of Charles H. Taylor, circulation rose in 13 years (1877–90) from 8,000 to 150,000. Under Taylor heirs, daily circulation reached 504,869 and Sunday circulation 811,409 in 1993, when the family-owned business was sold to *The New York Times.* ROY HALVERSON

Boston Latin School

Boston Latin School (enrollment: 2,300) was founded in 1635 and is the oldest public school in the United States. The 6-year college-preparatory curriculum is "centered in the humanities," and admission is open to all residents of Boston on the basis of an examination.

Boston Massacre

The Boston Massacre—the killing of five men by British soldiers on Mar. 5, 1770—was the culmination of civilian-military tensions that had been growing since royal troops first appeared in Massachusetts in October 1768. The soldiers were in Boston to keep order, but townspeople viewed them as potential oppressors, competitors for jobs, and threats to social mores. Brawls became common. Finally, a squad led by Capt. Thomas Preston fired into an unruly crowd in front of the Customs House, killing three men outright and mortally wounding two others.

All troops were immediately withdrawn from town. John ADAMS defended the soldiers at their trials (Oct. 24–30 and Nov. 27–Dec. 5, 1770). Preston and four men were acquitted; two soldiers were found guilty of manslaughter and released after being branded on the hand. The massacre served as anti-British propaganda for Boston radicals and heightened American fears of standing armies. LARRY R. GERLACH

Bibliography: Zobel, Hiller B., *The Boston Massacre* (1971).

Boston Pops Orchestra

Originating in 1885 as the Promenade Concerts, the Boston Pops Orchestra was organized by members of the Boston Symphony Orchestra to provide the people of Boston with music after the regular symphony season ended, a practice it continues today. The orchestra became known as the Boston "Pops" because its repertoire consisted mostly of the lighter and more popular classics. In 1930, Arthur FIEDLER was appointed permanent conductor, a position he held until his death in 1979. In January 1980, John Williams became conductor. In addition to presenting lighter classics, the Boston Pops performs show tunes, folk music, and popular songs from its large repertoire. These performances are frequently televised. ELLA A. MALIN

Boston Post Road

The Boston Post Road was the major land route between New York City and Boston during the 18th century and the first third of the 19th century. It extended from New York City through Westchester County, followed the shoreline of Long Island Sound to New Haven, Conn., and then split into three roads: the Upper Road, which was the original route, passing through Hartford, Springfield, and Worcester; the Middle Road, through Hartford, Uxbridge, and Dedham; and the Lower Road, through Westerly and Providence. The modern U.S. Highway 1 follows much of the route of the Lower Road.

Bibliography: Holbrook, Stephen H., *The Old Post Road* (1962).

Boston Symphony Orchestra

The Boston Symphony Orchestra was founded in 1881 by Henry Lee Higginson, a businessman and civic leader who supported it for 37 years. In 1918 it was incorporated. The first concert, on Oct. 22, 1881, was conducted by Sir George HENSCHEL. In 1900 the orchestra acquired its permanent home —Symphony Hall. Important conductors have been Serge KOUSSEVITZKY (1924–49), Charles MUNCH (1949–62), Erich LEINSDORF (1962–69), and Seiji OZAWA (1973–   ). In addition to its regular concert season, the Boston Symphony initiated (1885) the Promenade Concerts (now known as the Boston Pops), began a lasting association with the Berkshire Music Festival (later called Tanglewood Festival) in 1936, and became associated with the Berkshire Music Center 4 years later. The Boston Symphony Chamber Players, made up of first-chair players, was founded in 1964. ELLA A. MALIN

Bibliography: Baker-Carr, Janet, *Evening at Symphony* (1977); Howe, Mark A., and Burke, J. N., *The Boston Symphony Orchestra: 1881–1931*, rev. ed. (1931; repr. 1978); Vigeland, Carl A., *In Concert* (1991).

Boston Tea Party

The Boston Tea Party—the destruction of British tea on Dec. 16, 1773, by colonists ill-disguised as Indians—signaled American opposition to the Tea Act of May 1773 and renewed the dormant controversy between Britain and its American colonies. Although the act made available inexpensive tea because of marketing privileges granted by Parliament to the

The Boston Tea Party (Dec. 16, 1773), shown in this early engraving, was a raid by American patriots who, disguised as Indians, dumped crates of tea off British merchant ships to protest the Tea Act.

near bankrupt British East India Company, the colonists resented monopolization of the tea trade by selected merchants and payment of the sole tax remaining from the TOWNSHEND ACTS. Amid growing hostility, a band of Bostonians boarded three ships in Boston harbor during the night of the 16th and dumped into the water 342 chests of tea valued at £9,000. Similar tea parties soon occurred elsewhere in America. The British government responded to the latest colonial challenge to crown authority by passing the INTOLERABLE ACTS.

LARRY R. GERLACH

Bibliography: Fowler, W., and Coyle, W., eds., *The American Revolution* (1979); Labaree, B. W., *The Boston Tea Party* (1964; repr. 1979).

Boston terrier

The Boston terrier is a nonsporting breed of dog with a short, wide muzzle and erect, batlike ears. The dog stands 36–43 cm (14–17 in) at the shoulder and weighs 6–11 kg (13–25 lb); a weight exceeding 11 kg is not usually acceptable for show purposes. The head is square, the eyes are set wide apart, the body is terrierlike, and the tail should be short. The ears may be cropped for show. The smooth coat is black or, preferably, brindle, with white markings that ideally include the muzzle, blaze up the head between the eyes, collar, chest, all the front legs, and the rear legs below the hocks.

One of the few native U.S. breeds, the Boston terrier was the result of crossing an English bulldog with a white English terrier during the second half of the 19th century. It was variously known as the American bull terrier, the Boston bull, the Boston bulldog, and the Boston bull terrier before its name was fixed as the Boston terrier at the time of its recognition by the American Kennel Club in 1893. For many years, the breed

The Boston terrier was developed in the United States from the English bulldog and the white English terrier. It has a satiny black-and-white coat.

was the most popular in the United States; Tige, the dog of the comic strips' Buster Brown, was a Boston terrier.

JOHN MANDEVILLE

Bibliography: American Kennel Club, *The Complete Dog Book*, 17th ed. (1985); Huddleston, Arthur R., *The Boston Terrier* (1985).

Boston University

Established in 1839 by the Methodist Church, Boston University (enrollment: 24,279; library: 1,700,000 volumes) is an independent institution in Boston, Mass. Among its 15 schools and colleges are schools of medicine, law, and theology.

Bostonians, The

The Bostonians (1886), a novel by Henry JAMES, is a subtle study—initially unpopular because of its length and its irreverence—of various women associated with the feminist movement in post–Civil War Boston. Olive Chancellor is radical and neurotic; Miss Birdseye, superannuated, ridiculously ineffectual, but sweet; Mrs. Amariah Farrinder, militant; and Verena Tarrant, beautiful and incredibly eloquent. Into this group comes lawyer-writer Basil Ransom, Olive's reactionary cousin from Mississippi and a Confederate army veteran. James brilliantly shows Ransom challenging Olive's hold on pliant Verena in his effort to lure the latter from the lecture platform into matrimony.

ROBERT L. GALE

Boswell, James

James Boswell, an 18th-century biographer, essayist, and journal writer, appears in this portrait by Sir Joshua Reynolds. Boswell dedicated his Life of Samuel Johnson *(1791) to Reynolds.*

The Scottish writer James Boswell, b. Edinburgh, Oct. 29, 1740, d. May 19, 1795, known principally for his *Life of Samuel Johnson,* was also the author of a number of works in verse and prose, most notably the *Journal of a Tour to the Hebrides.* The 20th-century discovery of Boswell's journals and other private papers is one of the more important literary events of modern times.

Boswell was the son of Alexander Boswell, Lord Auchinleck, a Scottish judge. Like his father, the younger Boswell became a lawyer, and although a large portion of his time was spent as a practicing advocate in Scotland, what leisure he had was devoted to the literary life of London and to travel. Boswell's attempts to secure support for the Corsicans in their struggle for independence against the Genoese, and his *Account of Corsica* (1768), contributed significantly to his contemporary reputation.

In 1763, Boswell met the 54-year-old literary giant Samuel JOHNSON and established a relationship that continued until Johnson's death, in 1784. In 1773 the two toured the Hebrides and the Scottish highlands, and this journey constitutes the only extended period of time that Boswell spent in Johnson's company. Boswell's personal journal served as the basis for the much revised published version of the *Journal of a Tour to the Hebrides with Samuel Johnson, LL.D.* (1785). Some consider the *Journal* to be Boswell's true masterpiece, in part because it is based on continuous contact with Johnson.

The Life of Samuel Johnson (1791) is built on a host of materials (Boswell's journals and notes, the reminiscences of others, letters, and so on) and covers Johnson's entire life, a period of 75 years. In recent years the historical dimensions of the *Life* have been challenged, while at the same time there has been an increased appreciation of Boswell's artistic skill, and the recognition that, despite its shortcomings as biography, Boswell's life of Johnson remains one of the great books of British literature.

The Boswell papers—which record his times in London and on the continent, his meetings with such eminent friends of Johnson's as Edmund Burke, David Garrick, and Oliver Goldsmith, his search for a wife, his life as a lawyer, husband, and Scottish laird, and his struggles with drinking, gambling, and ill health—were found in the early 20th century. They were acquired by Yale University, which has published the edited papers in a series of volumes, beginning in 1950 with *Boswell's London Journal, 1762–63.* This record of Boswell's experience is a rich and extended one and serves to counter the caricatured impression of Boswell inherited from the 19th century, particularly through the comments of Thomas Babington Macaulay. As in the case of Johnson, Boswell is now studied as a significant writer rather than as a curious personality.   RICHARD B. SCHWARTZ

Bibliography: Abbott, Claude C., *Boswell* (1946; repr. 1985); Brady, Frank, *Boswell: The Later Years, 1769–1795* (1984); Clifford, James L., ed., *Twentieth Century Interpretations of Boswell's "Life of Johnson"* (1970); Dowling, William C., *The Boswellian Hero* (1979); Finlayson, Iain, *The Moth and the Candle* (1984); Pottle, Frederick A., *James Boswell: The Earlier Years, 1740–69,* 2d ed. (1984); Schwartz, Richard B., *Boswell's Johnson: A Preface to the "Life"* (1978).

botanical garden

A botanical garden is an area in which plants are grown primarily for scientific study or for viewing by the public. A garden solely for trees, shrubs, and vines is more exactly termed an arboretum. Some gardens are chiefly for scientific study; others emphasize ornamental displays and public education, and some are solely recreational areas. Many gardens maintain large herbaria, collections of dried plant specimens used as references for classifying unknown plants.

History. Some of the first botanical gardens were formal parks built as early as 2000 BC by the Assyrians. Most of the earliest gardens, however, were ancient Chinese and Egyptian temple gardens for raising fruit, vegetables, and medicinal herbs. The first record of such facilities is a description of the

Founded in 1759, Kew Gardens dates from an original botanical collection of the late 1600s. Formerly known as the Royal Botanic Gardens, the gardens became a government institution in 1841. This is one of three museums on the grounds near London.

temple garden at Karnak, built in 1500 BC. Better documented is Aristotle's herbal garden, built about 350 BC and directed by the noted botanist Theophrastus.

Stimulated by the reliance on herbal medicine in the 16th and 17th centuries, European medical schools founded botanical gardens devoted mainly to medicinal species. The gardens were used for training medical students, growing plants to make medicines, and conducting research. The first such gardens were in Italy—in Pisa around 1543 and Padua in 1545—and similar gardens were later founded in other major cities. The garden in Leiden, Holland (1587), is credited with starting the Dutch bulb industry.

Later Development. As the science of botany grew during the 18th and 19th centuries, the traditional herbal gardens gave way to gardens for the scientific study, commercial development, and display of wider varieties of plants. Botanical gardens then spread rapidly, with the founding of such famous gardens as those in Kew (near London, 1759; see KEW GARDENS), Uppsala (1787), Madrid (1788), Rio de Janeiro (1808), Leningrad (1843), Washington, D.C. (1850), St. Louis, Mo. (1859), the Arnold Arboretum in Cambridge, Mass. (1872), and New York City (1895). The Royal Botanic Gardens at Kew sent expeditions all over the world to find commercial species, and reputedly those efforts spread the cultivation of such plants as rubber, banana, tea, pineapple, coffee, cacao, and the quinine-yielding cinchona.

The United States today has over 300 botanical gardens. The most important are the BROOKLYN BOTANIC GARDEN AND ARBORETUM, the LONGWOOD GARDENS (near Kennett Square, Pa.), the UNITED STATES NATIONAL ARBORETUM (Washington, D.C.), the Arnold Arboretum, the Missouri Botanical Gardens (St. Louis), the New York Botanical Garden (New York City), the University of California Botanic Garden (Berkeley), the Holden Arboretum (Mentor, Ohio), and the Fairchild Tropical Garden (Miami). The Longwood Gardens, in cooperation with the U.S. National Gardens, in recent years has sent out botanical expeditions worldwide.

The foremost Canadian gardens include the Montreal Botanical Garden, with its special collections, and the Dominion Arboretum and Botanic Garden, Ottawa (1889), Canada's oldest botanical garden. Australia's well-designed Royal Botanic Gardens and National Herbarium emphasize plant species native to Australia.   P. VAN ROYEN

Bibliography: Hyams, E. S., and MacQuitty, W., *Great Botanical Gardens of the World* (1969); Prest, John, *The Garden of Eden: The Botanical Garden and the Re-Creation of Paradise* (1982); Wright, Tom, *Large Gardens and Parks: Maintenance, Management and Design* (1982); Wyman, Donald, *The Arboretums and Botanical Gardens of North America* (1969).

botany

Botany is the science concerned with the study of plants. Botany, microbiology, and zoology constitute the science of biology. Biologists recognize five kingdoms: MONERA (BACTERIA and BLUE-GREEN ALGAE), PROTISTA (one-celled organisms), FUNGI, PLANT, and ANIMAL. Of these, the monerans, the protists that contain chlorophyll, the fungi, and the plants are studied by botanists.

Subdivisions of Botany. The study of plants may be approached from many directions, each of which is a specialization involving an aspect of plant life, for example, classification, form and structure, life processes and functions, diseases, fossils, and heredity and variation.

Plant taxonomy is the study of plant classification, that is, the grouping of plants into species, genera, families, orders, classes, and divisions reflecting evolutionary, or family tree, relationships. Taxonomists provide internationally recognized scientific names for plants. As taxonomy has become more specialized, various branches of the discipline have appeared, including biosystematics, numerical taxonomy, cyto-taxonomy, and chemical taxonomy, which reflect different approaches to problems of classification.

Plant morphology is the study of the form and structure of plants. Morphologists may investigate plant life-cycles or internal structure (plant anatomy). Specialized branches of morphology are CYTOLOGY (study of cell structure and function), palynology (study of pollen and spores), and morphogenesis (study of how plants develop their form).

Plant physiology is the study of life processes of plants, for example, PHOTOSYNTHESIS and respiration, and of the functions of different tissues and organs. Many physiologists, working mainly with chemical processes in plants, might well be called biochemists.

Plant ecology is the study of how plants affect, and are affected by, their environment and of the structure and distribution of vegetation, or communities of plants.

Plant pathology is the study of plant diseases (see DISEASES, PLANT). *Paleobotany* is the study of the fossil record of plants. A developing science is paleoecology, which considers all fossil life and its environmental relationships. *Genetics* is the study of heredity and variation. The basic principles and processes of genetics are so similar in plants and animals that little distinction is made between them.

Some additional branches of botany are devoted to particular groups of plants. For example, bacteriology is the study of bacteria; mycology, the study of fungi; and phycology, the study of algae. Workers in these fields may be concerned with any aspect—taxonomy, morphology, physiology, ecology—of the group. Economic botany is concerned with those plants that are of economic importance, because of their usefulness (food, fiber, medicine) or because of the harm they do (weeds, poisionous plants). Ethnobotany is concerned with how primitive societies used plants.

These many facets of botany are not mutually exclusive. Each relies on one or more of the others. Plant pathologists, for example, are interested in taxonomy, morphology, physiology, ecology, and genetics of the disease-causing organisms they study.

History. People have always been interested in plants as sources of useful products or as troublemakers. In prehistoric societies some persons probably were more interested in plants than others, and perhaps it was these "primitive botanists" who discovered that seeds produce plants, that pieces of plants (cuttings) can grow into new plants, and that certain plant parts had healing properties.

The first written records of scientific botany are from the time of the ancient Greeks and Romans. It was among these people that some of the methods of science—observation,

description, deduction, and organization of knowledge—first appeared. THEOPHRASTUS, the "father of botany," wrote extensively about plants—their form, classification, and natural history—but only two of his works, *Historia plantarum* and *De causis plantarum*, survive. Pedanius DIOSCORIDES wrote *De materia medica*, a popular herbal that described plants, especially those useful in medicine. It combined fact with superstition. Several Roman authors also contributed to the first literature of botany. In spite of their imperfections, for 1,500 years these early works, especially those by Theophrastus and Dioscorides, were accepted in Europe without serious question.

During the 16th century, after the invention of the printing press, a number of herbals appeared that contained original rather than borrowed observations and that critically evaluated knowledge and authority from earlier times. Exploration of various parts of the world was making Europeans aware of a great variety of plants, and plants were again studied carefully.

Exploration of the invisible world began in the late 16th century when the compound microscope was invented. The pioneer microscopic studes that took place in the 17th century were the start of plant anatomy.

The age of botanical experimentation, a fundamental activity in science, began during the 17th century. Experimental plant physiology had its beginnings when water uptake of a tree was measured by Johannes Baptista van Helmont (1577–1644); the study was published in 1648. The work of Stephen HALES, considered the founder of plant physiology, led to studies of basic processes such as photosynthesis.

Other early physiologists studied the movement of water in plants, and in 1779 the chemist Joseph PRIESTLEY showed that plants produce oxygen in sunlight.

In 1753, Carolus LINNAEUS published *Species plantarum*, which described 6,000 species of plants and introduced the consistent use of binomials, two-word names of plants (for example, *Quercus alba* for white oak), a basis for the classification system in use today. The history of taxonomy since then has involved, primarily, efforts to make plant classification more nearly reflect evolutionary relationships and, secondarily, refining the rules for scientific names of plants.

Vast herbaria (collections of pressed, dried plants) have been built up as research facilities of importance in plant tax-

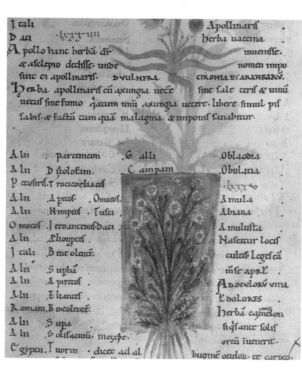

Herbals—early botanical books—often blended superstition with scientific fact in describing the medicinal qualities of plants. This illustration (left) from a 12th-century work depicts foxglove, a source of the cardiac stimulant digitalis, and camomile, still made into a tonic or a soothing tea.

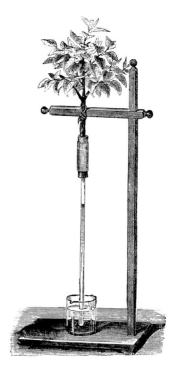

Stephen Hales, an early leader in experimental plant physiology, used this apparatus (right) to measure the rate at which sap flows upward through a plant. Hales determined that the loss of water vapor through a plant's leaves (transpiration) leads to the sap's continuous elevation.

Carolus Linnaeus, founder of the modern system of binomial nomenclature used for classifying plants and animals, spent 5 months in 1732 exploring Lapland and collecting plant specimens. Linnaeus returned with this Lapp outfit, complete with a native drum, as a memento of his trip.

centuries. The rediscovery in 1900 of Gregor Johann MENDEL's then 3-decade-old work on plant breeding completely reoriented research in genetics and led to the remarkable development of modern genetics.

Plant fossils have been known since early times, and some ancient Greek writers recognized that fossils are evidences of past life. This view was replaced in succeeding centuries, however, by fantastic or mystical explanations. Starting in the 15th century, fossils were directly observed and reasonably interpreted, but not until the late 19th century was the debate about the true nature of fossils essentially over. By the early 19th century, as the richness of the fossil record was gradually revealed and the great age of the Earth began to be understood, paleobotany had become well established as a science.

The beginnings of ecology were apparent in Theophrastus's writings on natural history, but ecology did not emerge as a unified science until the late 19th and early 20th centuries. Concern for the environment increased after 1950 and has made ecology one of the most talked-about specialties in biology. Although plant ecology is a logical subdivision of ecology and has its own history, philosophy, and methods, the concept of ecosystem (or total environment) has done much to bring plant and animal ecologies together.

Recent milestones in botany and biology include the following: the development of electron-microscopic techniques that allow scientists to observe the three-dimensional structure of living cells; the discovery of fossils of prokaryotes about 3.5 billion years old and the remains of unicellular eukaryotic algae about 1.4 billion years old; the development of radioactive isotopes for dating and tracing materials as they move in biological systems; the rapid expansion of genetic engineering and other areas of biotechnology; the elucidation of the structures of DNA and RNA and their role in protein synthesis; and the appearance of new ideas on the origin of life.

Botany and Other Sciences. Botany relies heavily on the physical sciences (chemistry, physics), the earth sciences (geology), and mathematics. It contributed to and borrows from zoology, especially entomology (the study of insects) as related to pollination and to transmission of plant diseases, and from anthropology. Knowledge of botany is basic to serious work in agriculture, horticulture, forestry, conservation, and other areas.   JOHN W. THIERET

onomy. Charles DARWIN's exposition of evolution in *On the Origin of Species* (1859) encouraged taxonomists to build evolutionary classifications, and it profoundly influenced botanical research.

Although plant taxonomy and morphology dominated botany during the 18th century and part of the 19th century, other botanical disciplines eventually matured or developed as the necessary tools and techniques appeared and were improved. Plant diseases have been known since ancient times, but the modern science of plant pathology did not begin to develop until the mid-19th century. The devastating potato blight in Ireland in the 1840s greatly stimulated the study of plant diseases.

Until 1900, plant genetics was concerned largely with practical hybridization and selection in plants, especially crops and ornamentals. Work in genetics had become important in agriculture. The mechanism of heredity and variation, however, was not understood until the late 19th and early 20th

Bibliography: Arber, Agnes, *Herbals, Their Origin and Evolution: A Chapter in the History of Botany, 1470–1670,* 2d ed. (1938; repr. 1970); Barden, J., and Halfacre, R. G., *Plant Science* (1987); Bigrami, K. S., et al., *Fundamentals of Botany* (1986); Cronquist, Arthur, *Basic Botany,* 2d ed. (1981); Glimn-Lacy, J., and Kaufman, P. B., *Botany Illustrated* (1984); Heiser, C. B., Jr., *Of Plants and People* (1985); Jensen, W. A., and Salisbury, F. B., *Botany: An Ecological Approach* (1972); Mantell, S. H., et al., *Principles of Plant Biotechnology* (1985); Morton, A. G., *History of Botanical Science* (1981); Scagel, R. F., et al., *Plants: An Evolutionary Survey* (1984); Stern, Kingsley, *Introductory Plant Biology,* 3d ed. (1985).

Botany Bay

Botany Bay is a small inlet of the South Pacific Ocean located south of Sydney, Australia. It is not quite 8 km (5 mi) wide. The shores of the bay were the site of the first landing (1770) in Australia by Capt. James COOK, and a monument commemorates the landing. The name *Botany Bay* is derived from the interest of Joseph BANKS, the botanist of the Cook expedition, in the area's variety of flowering shrubs and plants. A penal settlement established in 1788 was later removed, but the name was applied generally to Australian penal settlements.

Botero, Fernando   [boh-tay'-roh, fair-nahn'-doh]

Fernando Botero, b. Medellín, Columbia, Apr. 19, 1932, is a major South American painter. His renderings of suffering and labor are reminiscent of Goya and suggest the social criticism of South America's flourishing modernist literature. The fullness and thickness of Botero's figures reflect the influence of the cubists (especially Fernand Léger), Mexican muralists, and the pre-Columbian art of South America.   PHIL PATTON

Botanists who accompanied Capt. James Cook on his first expedition (1768–71) to the South Pacific collected samples and made drawings of new plants they found.

Botev, Khristo [baw'-tef, kris'-toh]

Khristo Botev, b. Jan. 5, 1848, d. May 20, 1876, was a Bulgarian patriot who fought for the liberation of Bulgaria from the Ottoman Turkish rule. He subjected all his activity, including his poetry, to this goal. He wrote only a few poems (*Pesni ustihove;* Songs and Verses, 1875), all in the style of folk songs, and dedicated them to the liberation struggle, thus becoming a legend and an inspiration to his countrymen. He was killed fighting against the Turks.   VASA D. MIHAILOVICH

botfly

Botflies are flies of several families of the order DIPTERA whose larvae are internal parasites of mammals. Adult botflies, which are rarely seen, look like fuzzy bees.

Adults of one botfly, the cattle grub, lay their eggs on cows' heels. The larvae migrate through the skin and connective tissue to just under the skin on the back, where they form a large swelling, or warble. Here they feed on secretions and cause irritation to the cow. When mature, the larvae wriggle from the warble and pupate on the ground. A botfly of tropical America causes warbles on people. This fly catches a mosquito or other biting fly and attaches an egg to it; the egg hatches when warmed as the mosquito bites its next victim. Sheep are infested by bot larvae that feed within their nasal cavity. Larvae of horse bots develop in the stomach and intestines of horses. Deer and rodents are also affected by larvae of botflies.   DAVID J. HORN

Botha, Louis [boh'-tah]

Louis Botha, b. Sept. 27, 1862, d. Aug. 27, 1919, was an Afrikaner soldier and political leader who was the first prime minister of the Union of South Africa. Botha had little formal schooling and grew up as a farmer. During the SOUTH AFRICAN WAR (1899–1902), he fought against the British and in 1900 assumed command of the Transvaal forces with the rank of commandant general. When the Boer armies were defeated in the field, he turned to guerrilla warfare. He led the Transvaal delegation at the peace conference held at Vereeniging (1902). In 1907, Botha, a moderate and now an advocate of Anglo-Boer reconciliation, assumed office as prime minister of the Transvaal. He took part in the deliberations that led to the formation of the Union of South Africa and in 1910 became its first prime minister. During World War I, he sent (1915) South African troops to occupy the German colony of South West Africa (NAMIBIA).   L. H. GANN

Bibliography: Buxton, Earl, *General Botha* (1924); Williams, Basil, *Botha, Smuts, and South Africa* (1948).

Botha, P. W.

P. W. Botha served as head of the South African government from 1978 to 1989. Under Botha, many public places were desegregated, blacks were allowed to hold jobs once reserved for whites and form their own trade unions, and the hated pass laws were suspended. These and other reforms left white political and economic dominance intact, however, and were accompanied by firm repression of dissent.

Pieter Willem Botha, b. Orange Free State, Jan. 12, 1916, succeeded B. Johannes VORSTER as prime minister of South Africa in 1978. In 1984, under a new constitution granting limited parliamentary representation to Coloureds and Asians, Botha became state president. His previous posts included deputy minister of the interior (1958–61), minister of community development, public works, and coloured affairs (1961–65), and minister of defence (1965–78). Under Botha, some APARTHEID legislation was eased or abolished. His reforms, however, failed to satisfy the demands of South African blacks. In 1986, after nearly two years of violent antigovernment protests in black townships and increasing international pressure to end apartheid, Botha imposed a nationwide state of emergency. In an effort to end South Africa's diplomatic isolation, Botha signed a tentative peace accord for Angola in 1988 that would also lead to independence for Namibia. He also, unexpectedly, met with black leader Nelson Mandela in 1989. A power struggle between Botha and F. W. DE KLERK, who had replaced Botha as National party leader in February 1989 after Botha suffered a stroke, led to Botha's resignation as president in August 1989. De Klerk succeeded him.

Bothe, Walther Wilhelm [boh'-teh]

The German physicist Walther Wilhelm Georg Bothe, b. Jan. 8, 1891, d. Feb. 8, 1957, received the 1954 Nobel Prize for physics for developing and applying the coincidence method. Using this method, Bothe and Hans Geiger demonstrated (1924) that the conservation of momentum and energy is valid in certain elementary processes and discredited the hypothesis that these physical properties are conserved only statistically. In 1929, Bothe and Werner Kolhorster demonstrated the existence of high-energy particles in cosmic radiation, and the following year Bothe, with H. Becker, detected a new radiation, which James Chadwick identified as the neutron. Bothe taught physics in Berlin and Giessen and directed the Max Planck Institute at Heidelberg, Germany, from 1934 until his death.
ROBERT PAUL

Bothnia, Gulf of [bahth'-nee-uh]

The Gulf of Bothnia (Swedish, Bottenviken; Finnish, Selkämeri) is a northern arm of the Baltic Sea extending 725 km (450 mi) between Sweden and Finland. It is nearly closed off by the Aland Islands. Because of its low salinity (0.3%) and shallowness (average depth 60 m/200 ft), it freezes for three to five months a year.

Bothwell, James Hepburn, 4th Earl of

James Hepburn, 4th earl of Bothwell, b. *c.*1536, d. Apr. 14, 1578, was the third husband of MARY, QUEEN OF SCOTS. During the Reformation era, he supported the Protestant faction in Scottish politics. Nonetheless, in 1565 he helped the Roman Catholic Mary put down the earl of Moray's rebellion. After the murder (which Bothwell probably arranged) of Mary's second husband, Lord DARNLEY, at Kirk-o'-Field on the night of Feb. 9–10, 1567, Bothwell made preparations to wed Mary himself. This he did on May 15 by Protestant rites. Soon after, a coalition of Protestant and Catholic nobles confronted the queen and Bothwell at Carberry Hill near Edinburgh. Bothwell fled; he died in Denmark.   CHARLES H. HAWS

Botswana [baht-swahn'-uh]

Botswana, a landlocked republic in southern Africa, is bordered by South Africa on the south, Namibia on the west and north, Zimbabwe on the east, and a small section of Zambia on the north. Formerly the British Protectorate of Bechuanaland, Botswana became independent on Sept. 30, 1966. The country is named for the Batswana (TSWANA), the largest population group. The capital is GABORONE.

LAND AND RESOURCES

Botswana is a semiarid, gently undulating plateau, with an average elevation of 900 m (3,000 ft), that rises to low hills in the extreme east. Tsodilo Hill (1,805 m/5,922 ft), in the northwestern corner of Botswana, is the highest point in the coun-

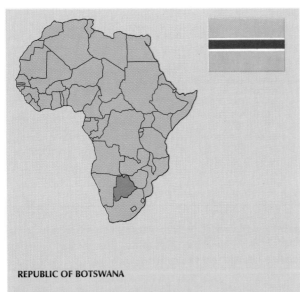

REPUBLIC OF BOTSWANA

LAND. Area: 582,000 km² (224,711 mi²). Capital and largest city: Gaborone (1991 pop., 133,791).

PEOPLE. Population (1994 est.): 1,400,000; density: 2.4 persons per km² (6.2 per mi²). Distribution (1994 est.): 26% urban, 74% rural. Annual growth (1994 est.): 2.7%. Official language: English. Major religions: traditional religions, Christianity.

EDUCATION AND HEALTH. Literacy (1990): 72% of adult population. Universities (1991): 1. Hospital beds (1990): 3,212. Physicians (1990): 240. Life expectancy (1994 est.): women—64; men—59. Infant mortality (1994 est.): 43 per 1,000 live births.

ECONOMY. GNP (1992): $3.8 billion; $2,800 per capita. Labor distribution (1990): agriculture—63%; industry, construction, and mining—11%; government and services—26%. Foreign trade (1991): imports—$1.7 billion; exports—$1.6 billion; principal trade partners—Switzerland, United Kingdom, South Africa, United States. Currency: 1 pula = 100 thebe.

GOVERNMENT. Type: republic. Legislature: National Assembly. Political subdivisions: 9 districts, 4 towns.

COMMUNICATIONS. Railroads (1992): 887 km (551 mi) total. Roads (1991): 19,204 km (11,933 mi) total. Major ports: none. Major airfields: 1.

try. The most important river is the Okavango, which brings large quantities of water from the highlands of Angola to the dry lands of Botswana; this river has no outlet to the sea, however, and flows into a huge, basinlike depression in the northern part of the plateau about 145 km (90 mi) from the Angola border, where its waters spread out to form the OKAVANGO SWAMP and ephemeral Ngami Lake. During the summer rainy season the Okavango Swamp resembles a lake, and its waters are drained southeastward by the Botletle River into Lake Xau and finally dry up in the Makgadikgadi salt pan. The Limpopo River forms part of the boundary with South Africa and with its tributaries drains the eastern sections of the nation; a small section in the north is drained by the Chobe River, a tributary of the Zambezi.

Most of Botswana has a semiarid climate, and the western and southern two-thirds of the country are part of the vast KALAHARI DESERT. Rainfall is light and ranges from about 635 mm (25 in) in the northeast to less than 250 mm (10 in) in the southwest. Precipitation is variable from year to year, and severe droughts are a frequent occurrence. Most rain falls in summer (October to April), when losses by evaporation are greatest. Summers are hot, with daytime highs reaching 38° C (100° F). Winters are cooler, and temperatures frequently fall below 0° C (32° F).

The natural vegetation reflects the shortage of water and varies from dry scrub and tree savanna in the better-watered northeast to sparse thornbush in parts of the Kalahari. Soils are generally sandy and saline, and most of those considered suitable for agriculture are too dry for cultivation. The country has substantial mineral deposits, including diamonds, copper, nickel, and coal.

PEOPLE

The Bantu-speaking Tswana tribes, the largest ethnic group, comprise eight related tribal groups and constitute about 95% of the total population. The largest tribe is the Bamangwato (about 34% of the total population); the others are the Bangwaketse, Bakwena, Batawana, Bakgatla, Bamalete, Baralong, and Batlokwa. Seven of the eight tribes live in eastern Botswana, and the Batawana live in the Okavango Swamp region. Other peoples include SAN (bushmen), who live mainly as hunters and gatherers in the Kalahari, and small numbers of Europeans, Asians, and other peoples.

Botswana is one of the world's most sparsely populated nations. About 90% of the people live along the eastern border; the Okavango region has approximately one person every 4 km² (1 every 10 mi²), while the Kalahari is virtually uninhab-

The Palace of the National Assembly, in Gaborone, has been the seat of Botswana's government since 1965, a year before the nation achieved its independence. In addition to the president and the National Assembly, Botswana's government includes the House of Chiefs, an advisory body representing the nation's eight major tribes.

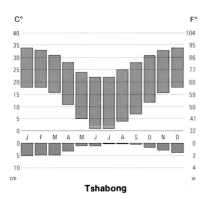

Tshabong

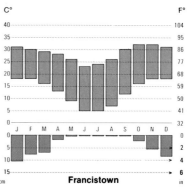

Francistown

Bars indicate monthly ranges of temperatures (red) and precipitation (blue) of Botswana's two types of climate. Tshabong, on the fringes of the Kalahari Desert, has a steppe climate. Francistown, in the east, has a tropical wet-dry climate.

ited. Although Botswana is predominantly rural, the percentage of urban residents more than tripled in the 15 years after independence, and the migration from rural to urban areas continues. The fastest-growing city is the capital, Gaborone. Other large population centers are Francistown, Selebi-Pikwe, Mochudi, Molepole, Lobatse, and Serowe.

Primary education was made free in 1980, and secondary education in 1988. About 95% of all primary-school-age children attend school, where most instruction is in Setswana, the national language. Health services are free for children under the age of 11, and health facilities increased after independence.

ECONOMIC ACTIVITY

At independence, Botswana was one of the world's poorest nations. Although development remains handicapped by the harsh, semiarid environment and the nation's landlocked location, the discovery of mineral reserves since the early 1970s has given the country one of the highest economic growth rates in the world. The diamond mines at Orapa and Jwaneng are among the world's largest, and diamonds provide 80% of export earnings. Another major export is copper-nickel matte, produced at Selebi-Pikwe. Coal reserves in eastern Botswana provide electricity, and gold, salt, and soda-ash are also mined. Other minerals await exploitation.

Pastoralism is the traditional way of life and remains the chief economic activity outside the mining sector, which employs only a small portion of the labor force. Cattle herds vary in size with climatic fluctuations and were drastically depleted by severe drought in 1981–87 and again in the early 1990s. Water shortages limit agriculture on even the small amount of land considered suitable for farming, although the government has invested much of its mineral revenues in rural development to lessen the need for imported foods. Maize (corn), sorghum, and millet are the principal crops. Manufacturing is limited to processing livestock products and to small-scale light industry at Gaborone and Francistown. Most imports come from South Africa, where thousands of Botswana citizens work. Domestic unemployment is high.

Transportation facilities have been expanded significantly since independence. Most vital is the railroad from Bulawayo, Zimbabwe, to Mafeking, South Africa. An international airport at Gaborone was completed in 1984, and a railroad across the Kalahari to the coast of Namibia has been proposed.

GOVERNMENT

Botswana is a multiparty democratic state. The constitution of 1966 provides for a president and a legislature of 32 members elected by universal suffrage and 4 members elected by the president. The government is advised by the House of Chiefs, consisting of the chiefs of the eight principal tribes and seven other members.

HISTORY

The Tswana are believed to have entered Botswana and subjugated the local San about the end of the 18th century. The 19th century was marked by devastating invasions by Zulus and Boers and by contact with British Christian missionaries. The Tswana, led by Khama III, chief of the Bamangwato tribe, asked for help against the Boers from the British, and in 1885 the British Protectorate of Bechuanaland was established. The British favored eventual incorporation of the land into South Af-

rica with the consent of the chiefs, but this policy was ended when apartheid was formally introduced into South Africa. Internal self-government was granted in 1965 and full independence on Sept. 30, 1966. Sir Seretse Khama was elected president and served until his death in 1980. His successor, former vice-president Quett Masiri, won reelection in 1984, 1989, and 1994. Botswana long advocated majority rule for all of southern Africa despite its economic dependence on South Africa. It refused to allow its territory to be used as a base for guerrilla operations against its neighbors but did grant asylum to political refugees, a fact that prompted raids into Botswana by South Africa in the mid-1980s. The ending of white minority rule in South Africa in 1994 was expected to spur economic growth throughout southern Africa.

ALAN C. G. BEST

Bibliography: Alverson, M., *Under the African Sun* (1987); Hesselberg, J., *The Third World in Transition: The Case of the Peasantry in Botswana* (1988); Hitchcock, R. R., and Smith, M., *Settlement in Botswana* (1982); Holm, J. D., and Molutsi, P. P., eds., *Democracy in Botswana* (1991); Lanting, F., *Okavango* (1994); Picard, L. A., *The Politics of Development in Botswana* (1987); Sillery, A., *Botswana: A Short Political History* (1974); Wylie, D., *A Little God* (1990).

Botta, Paul Émile   [baw-tah']

Paul Émile Botta, b. Dec. 6, 1802, d. Mar. 29, 1870, a French diplomat and archaeologist, is remembered chiefly for his discovery of the palace of the Assyrian king Sargon II at KHORSABAD in 1843. He also began (1842) excavations at Kuyunjik, the site of ancient Nineveh, while serving (1840–43) as consul in Mosul, Iraq. Botta initially mistook Khorsabad for Nineveh, and his work entitled *Monument de Ninive* (5 vols., 1849–50) in fact describes the former site. He later held consular posts in Jerusalem (1847–57) and in North Africa at Tripoli (1857–70).

Botticelli, Sandro   [bawt-tee-chel'-lee, sahn'-droh]

Sandro Botticelli, b. Florence, Italy, 1445, d. May 17, 1510, was one of the most influential painters of the Italian Renaissance. He did poorly in school, and his father apprenticed him to a goldsmith. Sometime in the early 1460s, however, Botticelli is said to have begun an apprenticeship with the painter Fra Filippo Lippi. By the late 1460s he was associated with the painter-sculptor Andrea del Verrocchio, in whose studio the young Leonardo da Vinci was also working at the same time.

Botticelli's early style is clearly based on those of Lippi and Verrocchio. His *Madonna and Child with Young Saint John and Two Angels* (c.1468; Accademia, Florence) indicates Botticelli's understanding of Lippi's ability to endow fleshy, firmly modeled figures with suavity and grace. Botticelli's *Fortitude* (1470; Uffizi, Florence), his first documented work, is an attempt to bring his youthful manner into line with that of Verrocchio, the most fashionable Florentine painter-sculptor of the time. By contrast with the earlier *Madonna, Fortitude*'s posture conveys the tension and her draperies the sharp contrast of light and dark that often characterize the work of an artist influenced by a painter-sculptor. Present here also are details of classical ornament and that precise attention to reflections and textures epitomized by the mature Botticelli.

The painter Sandro Botticelli, one of the most important and influential artists of the Florentine Renaissance, painted the Birth of Venus about 1485. The painting, one of Botticelli's large allegorical works, demonstrates his purity of line and color. (Uffizi, Florence.)

By the early 1470s Botticelli was in the orbit of the MEDICI, one of Europe's richest families and influential patrons of Renaissance art and learning. The *Adoration of the Magi* (Uffizi, Florence), dating from about 1475, is a form of homage to the Medici, containing portraits of the male family members under the guise of the Wise Men, their patron saints. Several of Botticelli's mythological pictures, such as *Primavera* (*c.*1478; Uffizi, Florence) and *Birth of Venus* (*c.*1485; Uffizi, Florence), were painted as allegories of the family, celebrating in Neoplatonic symbolism the beneficence and wisdom of Medici rule. Botticelli's most famous works, which define his style, are early examples of the Renaissance interest in large-scale representations of classical mythology. The *Madonna of the Magnificat* (*c.*1483–*c.*1485; Uffizi, Florence), one of the many versions of this widely imitated Botticelli type, also belongs to this period.

In 1481, Pope SIXTUS IV called Botticelli to Rome to assist in the decoration of the newly finished SISTINE CHAPEL. Under the direction of PERUGINO, who was in charge of the project, Botticelli was assigned *The Youth of Moses, The Punishment of Korah,* and *The Temptation of Christ*. Botticelli was thus acknowledged to be one of Italy's leading masters. The period from 1482 to about 1494 was the apogee of his career, during which he and his workshop produced numerous paintings of all types: mythologies, portraits, small-scale devotional pictures, and altarpieces, such as the *St. Barnabas Altarpiece* (*c.*1488; Uffizi, Florence).

The Medici family's expulsion from Florence in 1494 and the virtual theocracy subsequently established by the Dominican friar Girolamo SAVONAROLA, which ended with Savonarola's execution in 1498, caused serious upheavals in Botticelli's career. It is not known to what extent Botticelli subscribed to the gloomy teachings of Savonarola, but late paintings, such as the *Mystic Nativity* (1500; National Gallery, London) and the *Pietà* (1501; Alte Pinakothek, Munich), are marked by an unmistakably brooding, introverted tone. Bereft of his former patrons, Botticelli seems to have worked little until his death, and to have suffered extreme financial hardship. After 1500, moreover, Florentine painting began to move rapidly in new directions, following Leonardo's return to the city in 1501.

Botticelli's influence was deeply felt in Florentine painting of the 15th and 16th centuries. Through his most gifted pupil, Filippino LIPPI, son of his first teacher, his style survived into the next generation.

Too often overlooked are the traces of Botticelli's cool, elegant, attenuated forms in the work of such Mannerist painters as PONTORMO and BRONZINO, who kept this supremely Florentine aesthetic vigorous until the 1570s.   WILLIAM HOOD

Bibliography: Baldini, Umberto, *Primavera: The Restoration of Botticelli's Masterpiece* (1986); Clark, K., *The Drawings of Sandro Botticelli for Dante's Divine Comedy* (1976); Ettlinger, L. D. and H., *Botticelli* (1977; repr. 1985); Horne, Herbert P., *Botticelli: Painter of Florence* (1980); Levey, Michael, *Complete Paintings of Botticelli* (1986); Santi, Bruno, *Botticelli* (1981).

bottle

Bottles have been in use for as long as humans have had the skill to make them or to utilize natural shapes, such as hollow gourds or animal skins, as containers for liquids. Although pottery, wood, metal, and leather have been the most common bottle materials throughout most of history, the art of making GLASS bottles is also old.

The Egyptians made small molds of clay or earth, then coiled threads of molten glass around them. The glass threads were often of contrasting colors, and intricate patterns were worked into the surface. Egyptian techniques were continued by North African glassmakers and by the Greeks, but it was the discovery of GLASSBLOWING, about 50 BC, that first allowed widespread use of glass as a bottle material. Bottles could now be blown directly by hand and without a mold, or in a mold that shaped only the bottom half of the bottle. The upper parts of the bottle, including the neck and shoulder, were formed while the glass was still hot and soft by applying a shaping tool to the bottle as it rotated. After cork stoppers came into use in the 17th century, glass became the most widely used substance for bottles.

Early wine bottles were globular with a round base and had to be held in special stands or baskets. After about 1650 the base was made flatter to give better support, even though this shape was harder to blow than the round base. By about 1750 the bottle shape had been developed to its present form.

As the demand for glass bottles increased in the 19th century, more rapid means of production were sought. Entire bottles were blown into hinged molds, which could be opened for bottle removal. The first practical machines for blowing bottles were developed at the beginning of the 20th century. The invention of the individual section machine in the 1920s

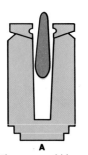 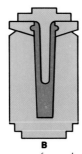  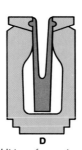 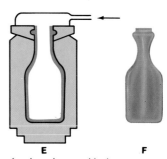

A   B   C   D   E   F

The press-and-blow machine process for producing bottles begins (A) with the addition of a precise amount of molten glass to a blank parison mold. A preliminary hollow bottle shape, or parison, is formed (B) by pressing the glass with a metal plunger. The complete parison (C) is lifted out and transferred to the blow mold (D), in which compressed air (E) is used to blow the glass into final bottle shape (F).

permitted the continuous blowing of bottles. In this machine a gob of glass is fed into a blank metal mold and the neck is formed with a metal plunger. The blank shape is transferred to a blow mold, where compressed air blows the glass into final shape.

Plastic bottles are manufactured in similar fashion, and have taken over many of the markets once served by glass. Unlike glass, however, the plastics used for containers of beverages and other liquids cannot be reused or recycled, and their indestructibility has created severe disposal problems.

ROBERT H. DOREMUS

Bibliography: Fike, Richard, *The Bottle Book* (1987); Sellari, C. D., *Official Guide to Bottles, Old and New* (1977).

See also: GLASSWARE, DECORATIVE.

bottle tree

The bottle tree is any of several species of trees in two closely related families. They are characterized by their bottleshaped trunks, which are wide and barrel-shaped from the base to varying heights and narrow abruptly just before branching. Species of *Brachychiton*, in the chocolate family, Sterculiaciae, are native to Australia and are grown as ornamentals in southern California and Florida. Species of *Adansonia*, in the bombax family, Bombacaceae, are native to Africa, Madagascar, and Australia. *Adansonia digitata*, also known as the BAOBAB, has a huge trunk. Its bark yields fibers, and its fruit pulp is the base of a drink similar to lemonade. JANE PHILPOTT

bottlebrush

The name *bottlebrush* refers to evergreen Australian shrubs, climbers, and small trees in four genera within the myrtle family, Myrtaceae. Colorful stamens that are longer than petals cause the spikes of their flowers to appear as bottle brushes. The many stamens are separate in flowers of *Callistemon* and *Metrosideros*; they are united in 5 bundles in flowers of *Melaleuca*. In *Calothamnus* the clusters are one-sided. Bottlebrushes are grown in the Gulf states and California.

JANE PHILPOTT

botulism [bah'-chuh-lizm]

Botulism is an acute illness resulting from a powerful toxin produced by food containing the bacillus *Clostridium botulinum*. The bacterium can only grow in an oxygen-free atmosphere (for example, in canned or preserved food). Improper processing fails to destroy the toxin; heating for 30 minutes at 80° C (176° F) is required. The toxin, which is not destroyed by gastrointestinal enzymes, is rapidly absorbed. Symptoms of poisoning, which appear 1 to 6 hours after ingestion, include disturbances in vision, speech, and swallowing. Botulism ultimately results in death from respiratory paralysis and suffocation. The mortality rate for botulism is high. Botulinus antiserum is used for treatment. PETER L. PETRAKIS

Bibliography: Lewis, George, ed., *Biomedical Aspects of Botulism* (1981); Smith, Louis, *Botulism* (1977).

Bouchardon, Edmé [boo-shar-dohn', ed-may']

Edmé Bouchardon, b. May 29, 1698, d. July 27, 1762, was a significant French 18th-century sculptor, whose work is characterized by a fusion of baroque vivacity and neoclassical serenity. Bouchardon was a pupil of Guillaume Coustou, and spent nine active years in Rome after winning the Prix de Rome in 1722. His two most notable, extant works are the large Fountain of the Four Seasons (1739–45) in the rue de Grenelle, Paris, and the life-sized marble *Cupid* (1739–50) in the Louvre. The elegant architectural forms of the great wall-fountain are nobly complemented by allegorical figures and reliefs. Bouchardon's most important public work was the equestrian statue (1749–63) of Louis XV in the Place Louis XV (now Place de la Concorde), which was destroyed during the French Revolution.

Bibliography: Dilke, E. F., *French Architecture and Sculpture of the 18th Century* (1900); Kalnein, Wend G., and Levey, Michael, *Art and Architecture of the Eighteenth Century in France* (1973); Souchal, Françoise, *French Sculptors of the 17th and 18th Centuries*, vol. 1 (1977).

Boucher, François [boo-shay', frahn-swah']

The art of François Boucher epitomized the refinement and glittering luxury of the court of Louis XV. The sensuality of Nude Lying on a Sofa *(1752) typifies Boucher's rococo style, and the intimate setting is characteristic of his "boudoir art." (Alte Pinakothek, Munich.)*

The French painter François Boucher, b. Sept. 29, 1703, d. May 20, 1770, was the leading exponent of the Louis XV rococo style. A favorite of Madame de Pompadour, he enjoyed considerable success during most of his lifetime. In 1735 he received his first commission for the Palace of Versailles; henceforth, he was consistently employed on the most important royal decorative projects of the mid-18th century. In 1765 he was appointed First Painter to the King. His work, however, was disliked by such critics as Denis Diderot.

Boucher first studied with his father, but his art was essentially influenced by his teacher, François Lemoyne. By about 1740 he had developed his mature style, which depends heavily on the use of pastel colors, on brilliant brushwork, and, frequently, on the outspoken eroticism of figures and compositions. His art was meant to please, charm, and seduce, and it succeeds admirably in works like the *Nude Lying on a Sofa*, also called *Mademoiselle O'Murphy* (1752; Alte Pinakothek, Munich). Boucher's vision went beyond the merely sensual, however. He used his extraordinary talent for flawless drafting and breathtaking brushwork to conjure up a world in which luxuriant nature creates a splendid setting for a goddess, as in *Triumph of Venus* (1740; National Museum, Stockhholm), or a mortal whose aura seems divine, as in *Marquise de Pompadour* (1759; Wallace Collection, London).

Boucher's production ranges from mythological subjects to portraiture, stylish genre, pastoral, and Oriental scenes. He was also active as a book illustrator, as a designer of tapestries and small porcelain sculptures, and as a painter of such religious works as the *Adoration of the Shepherds* (1750; Museum of Fine Arts, Lyon).

Boucher's art too often has been dismissed as merely pretty and superficial. Critics claim that he lacked the sensitivity and subtlety of a master such as Antoine WATTEAU; nonetheless, his work is an eloquent hymn to youth, beauty, and life.

DONALD POSNER

Bibliography: Goncourt, Edmond and Jules de, *French Eighteenth Century Painters*, 3 vols., trans. by R. Ironside (1880–83; trans. 1948); MacInnes, Ian, *Painter, King and Pompadour: François Boucher at the Court of Louis XV* (1965); Schwarz, Michael, *The Age of the Rococo*, trans. by Gerald Onn (1971); Soehner, Halldor, and Schönberger, Arno, *The Rococo Age, Art and Civilization of the Eighteenth Century* (1969).

Boucher de Perthes, Jacques   [boo-shay' duh pairt']

Jacques Boucher de Crèvecoeur de Perthes, b. Sept. 10, 1788, d. Aug. 5, 1868, was a French antiquarian and writer whose research was of great importance in proving that the human race was much older than had previously been thought.

Appointed (1825) director of the Abbeville customhouse, from 1837 on, Boucher de Perthes found stone artifacts in association with extinct animals in the Pleistocene gravel deposits of the Somme Valley. He published his findings in *De la Création: essai sur l'origine et la progression des êtres* ("On the Creation: Essay on the Origin and Development of Life," 5 vols., 1838–41), *De l'industrie primitive* ("On Primitive Industry," 1846), and *Antiquités celtiques et antédiluviennes* ("Antediluvian and Celtic Antiquities," 3 vols., 1847–64). He was among the first to use geological stratigraphy as an aid to assessing the age of humankind. Boucher de Perthes's views on the antiquity of humankind were at first disbelieved, but in 1858–59 several eminent geologists visited the Somme site and supported his conclusions.

Boucicault, Dion   [boo'-see-koh]

Dion Boucicault, b. Dec. 26, 1820?, d. Sept. 18, 1890, an Irish-American playwright and actor, was one of the most influential figures on the English-speaking stage during the last half of the 19th century. He went on the stage while still in his teens, and in 1841 his sparkling comedy *London Assurance* took London by storm. When later comedies proved less profitable, he turned to sentimental and melodramatic entertainments, of which he wrote more than a hundred, producing and acting the leading role in many of them. His rollicking Irish plays, *The Colleen Bawn* (1860) and *The Shaughraun* (1874), and their American counterpart, *Rip Van Winkle* (1865), are still successful today. He died in New York City.

ROBERT HOGAN

Bibliography: Hogan, Robert, *Dion Boucicault* (1969); Walsh, Townsend, *The Career of Dion Boucicault* (1915).

Boudicca: see BOADICEA.

Boudin, Eugène Louis   [boo-dan']

Eugène Louis Boudin, b. July 12, 1824, d. Aug. 8, 1898, was a noted French landscape and marine painter, probably the first artist to paint directly from nature in the open air. At the urging of the painter Jean François MILLET, Boudin studied (1850–53) in Paris, where he was deeply influenced by the work of Camille COROT. Upon his return to the Atlantic coast he produced a series of remarkable marine and sky pastel studies reminiscent of John CONSTABLE's similar sketches.

In 1858, Boudin met Claude MONET, then an 18-year-old art student, and persuaded the future impressionist to join him in painting out-of-doors, which profoundly affected Monet's entire career. Although Boudin was not an impressionist, being closer to Corot in his treatment of light and air, he exhibited with them in 1874; he reverted to the official Salon exhibitions the next year, however. His work was much admired by the painter Gustave COURBET and the poet and critic Charles BAUDELAIRE. The latter suggested around 1859 that Boudin people his landscapes with figures, which resulted in the characteristic beach scenes that made Boudin famous. Most of these depict the fashionable resorts at Trouville and Deauville; elegantly garbed vacationers, strolling or sitting, appear as bright accents against the windswept sea and sky, as in *On the Beach of Deauville* (1869; Musée d'Orsay, Paris). Boudin achieved considerable success during his lifetime and was awarded the Legion of Honor in 1892.

Bibliography: Aubry, Georges Jean, *Eugène Boudin*, trans. by Caroline Tisdall (1969); Aubry, Georges Jean, and Schmit, Robert, *Eugène Boudin*, trans. by Caroline Tisdall (1968); Selz, J., *Boudin* (1982).

Boudinot, Elias   [boo'-di-noh]

Elias Boudinot, b. Philadelphia, May 2, 1740, d. Oct. 24, 1821, was a prominent patriot during the American Revolution. Although he initially believed that "firm dependence in the mother country [was] essential," he was converted to the cause of independence and served twice (1777–78, 1781–84) in the Continental Congress. In 1782–83 he was president of that body. Boudinot helped bring about ratification by New Jersey of the U.S. Constitution and subsequently was a member of Congress (1789–95) and director of the U.S. mint (1795–1805). He was a founder and the first president (1816–21) of the American Bible Society.

Bibliography: Boyd, G. A., *Elias Boudinot* (1952); Gabriel, Ralph H., *Elias Boudinot* (1941); Perdue, T., ed., *Cherokee Editor* (1983).

Bougainville   [boo'-guhn-vil]

Bougainville, largest of the Solomon Islands, lies in the southwest Pacific and is, with neighboring islands, a district of Papua New Guinea. It has a population of 109,000 (1980) and an area of 10,049 km² (3,880 mi²). The highest point is Mount Balbi, 2,591 m (8,502 ft). The island was discovered (1768) by Louis Antoine de Bougainville.

A volcanic island, Bougainville is mountainous, with a heavily indented coast. In the hot, humid climate and rich soil, palms, rubber trees, cacao, and coffee grow well. Copra, rubber, tortoise shell, and copper are exported. The people, mostly Melanesian tribesmen, hunt, farm, and fish.

Germany gained control of Bougainville in 1898 and lost it in 1914 to Australia, which administered it until Japan took possession in 1942. After World War II it was part of a United Nations trust territory, which became Papua New Guinea.

Bougainville, Louis Antoine de   [boo-gan-veel']

Louis Antoine de Bougainville, b. Nov. 11, 1729, d. Aug. 31, 1811, was a French explorer in the Pacific who made the first French voyage around the world (1766–69). A naval officer, Bougainville took his frigate *La Boudeuse* to Tahiti, the Samoas, and other Pacific islands. His account of the voyage inspired a work by DIDEROT, *Supplément au voyage de Bougainville* (1769). The plant BOUGAINVILLEA is named after him. Bougainville also served in Canada during the French and Indian War (1754–63) and with the French fleet under Admiral de GRASSE in the American Revolution.

bougainvillea   [boo-guhn-vil'-ee-uh]

The bougainvillea, B. glabra, *is a flowering vine or shrub commonly grown in warm climates. Originally found growing along the Brazilian coast, it was named for the French explorer Louis A. de Bougainville.*

Bougainvillea, *Bougainvillea glabra*, is an evergreen vine or shrub belonging to the four-o'clock family, Nyctaginaceae. Native to South America, bougainvillea can be grown outdoors in any frost-free area. In the tropics bougainvillea plants are grown as pruned shrubs. In Florida and California they are used as showy flowering vines. The actual flowers are small and inconspicuous but have large, rose-colored bracts.

Bouguereau, Adolphe William   [boo-groh']

Adolphe William Bouguereau, b. Nov. 30, 1825, d. Aug. 19, 1905, had a long, successful career as an academic painter, exhibiting in the annual Paris Salons for more than 50 years. His paintings of religious, mythological, and genre subjects were carefully composed and painstakingly finished. Thus he opposed the admission of works by the impressionists to the Salon, because he believed that their paintings were no more than unfinished sketches. After a period of neglect following his death, Bouguereau's paintings were returned to view as part of a renewed interest in and reappraisal of academic painting and of École des Beaux-Arts works in general.

MARIAN BURLEIGH-MOTLEY

Bibliography: Boime, Albert, *The Academy and French Painting in the Nineteenth Century* (1971).

Boulanger, Georges   [boo-lahn-zhay']

Georges Boulanger, b. Apr. 29, 1837, d. Sept. 30, 1891, posed a major threat to the Third Republic in France. After military service in North Africa and the Franco-Prussian War (1870–71), he was appointed minister of war in 1886. He instituted reforms in weaponry and barrack conditions and became a popular national hero. He was dismissed in 1887, however, when leading republicans became frightened by his militant nationalism and political ambitions. Both Bonapartists and monarchists secretly worked with Boulanger in the hope of regaining power. They ran Boulanger in several parliamentary elections, supposedly without his permission; as a soldier on active duty, he was ineligible to run. The government, hoping to stem his success, retired him from the army in 1888, but this only freed him to campaign. In January 1889 he defeated a strong republican candidate in Paris. A coup d'état might have succeeded, but Boulanger waited, hoping to gain power legally through election. The republicans then charged him with treason, and he fled to Belgium. The Boulangist movement collapsed. Two years later, Boulanger committed suicide at his mistress's grave.

P. M. EWY

Bibliography: Irvine, W. D., *The Boulanger Affair Reconsidered: Royalism, Boulangism, and the Origins of the Radical Right in France* (1988).

Boulanger, Lili

Juliette Marie Olga Boulanger, b. Aug. 21, 1893, d. Mar. 15, 1918, was a French composer and the sister of the teacher Nadia Boulanger. She displayed precocious musical ability as a child. After studying at the Paris Conservatory under Paul Vidal in 1912, she won the Grand Prix de Rome in 1913 for her cantata *Faust et Hélène*, the first woman to gain this distinction. Acclaimed as a brilliant composer, she wrote orchestral works, chamber music, and songs.

CAROLYNN BAILEY

Bibliography: Rosenstiel, Léonie, *The Life and Works of Lili Boulanger* (1978).

Boulanger, Nadia

Nadia Boulanger, b. Sept. 16, 1887, d. Oct. 22, 1979, was a French composer, conductor, and teacher of a number of eminent 20th-century composers. Boulanger was educated at the Paris Conservatory, where she studied composition with Gabriel Fauré and organ with Charles Marie Widor. In 1908 she won second place in the Prix de Rome with her cantata *La Sirène*. Boulanger taught at the Paris Conservatory from 1909, at the École Normale de Musique from 1920 (she was appointed teacher of composition there in 1935), and at the American Conservatory in Fountainebleau from 1921, becoming its director in 1950. Meanwhile, she taught privately, and as her reputation as a teacher spread, young musicians from many countries traveled to Paris to study composition with her. Among her famous pupils were the composers Aaron Copland, Jean Françaix, Roy Harris, Walter Piston, and Virgil Thomson. Boulanger toured as a conductor, organist, and lecturer. She was a guest conductor of the Boston Symphony Orchestra in 1938 and of the New York Philharmonic in 1939; that year, she taught at Radcliffe and Wellesley colleges and at the Juilliard School. Boulanger was also a noted choral director and led a group she organized and trained. Among her works are orchestral pieces and songs.

Bibliography: Kendall, Alan, *Tender Tyrant: Nadia Boulanger* (1977); Monsaingeon, Bruno, *Mademoiselle*, trans. by R. Marsack (1985); Rosenstiel, Léonie, *Nadia Boulanger: A Life in Music* (1982).

Boulder

Boulder (1990 pop., 83,312) is a city in north central Colorado, located at an altitude of 1,629 m (5,343 ft). Settled by miners in 1858, it is the seat of Boulder County and the site of the University of Colorado, as well as many government-sponsored scientific environmental research facilities.

boulevard theater

The boulevard theaters (*théâtres du boulevard*) of Paris are mostly situated on or near the large boulevards of the Right Bank and cater to popular theatrical taste. They are roughly equivalent to New York's Broadway or London's West End. The term originated in the late 18th century when several theaters opened on the Boulevard du Temple, which shortly became known as the Boulevard du Crime because of the popularity of violent melodrama. Since the late 19th century their usual fare has been light comedy.

STUART E. BAKER

Boulez, Pierre   [boo-lez']

The French conductor and experimental composer Pierre Boulez, b. Mar. 26, 1925, is known for his carefully crafted, complex compositions, including *Pli selon pli*, a portrait of the poet Stéphane Mallarmé for voice and orchestra. Boulez studied with Olivier Messiaen and René Leibowitz, who introduced him to Arnold Schoenberg's twelve-tone system, which disregards traditional concepts of tonality, harmony, counterpoint, and thematic development. Boulez expanded this method to include not only pitch, as had been the case with Schoenberg, but also rhythm, dynamics, and timbre. This method is known as SERIAL MUSIC. Among his famous serial works are *Le Marteau sans maître* (The Hammer without a Master, 1953–54) and *Doubles, Rituel, Éclat/Multiples. Po-*

ésies pour pouvoir (*Poems for Power*) makes use of electronic sounds. Mallarmé's poetry also stimulated Boulez's *Improvisations on Mallarmé* (1959), a piece for voice and orchestra.

In 1970–71, Boulez served as principal guest conductor of the Cleveland Orchestra and from 1971 to 1975 as musical director of the BBC Symphony Orchestra in London. He has also conducted opera at the Bayreuth and Salzburg summer festivals. In 1971 he became musical director of the New York Philharmonic, succeeding Leonard Bernstein. His tenure there was marked by respect, if not always wild enthusiasm, partly because of his unflagging championship of avant-garde music, which disturbed subscription audiences. In 1976, Boulez left the Philharmonic to become director of the Institut de Recherche et de Coordination Acoustique/Musique in Paris, which explores new possibilities of electronic and computer-made music.   DAVID EWEN

Bibliography: Boulez, Pierre, *Boulez on Music Today* (1974) and *Notes of an Apprenticeship* (1968); Griffiths, P., *Boulez* (1979).

Boulle, André Charles   [bool]

André Charles Boulle, b. Nov. 11, 1642, d. Feb. 29, 1732, was a French cabinetmaker who developed the technique of decorating tortoiseshell and wood veneers with inlaid, delicately cut metals in classical designs. Boulle studied painting and sculpture before opening his Parisian shop in 1664. By 1672 he was *ébeniste du roi* (royal cabinetmaker) to Louis XIV and given lodgings in the Louvre. His designs were in such demand that Boulle also maintained shops near the Collège de Reims. When his technique was revived in the 19th century, it was called "Boulle" or "Buhl."   MARVIN D. SCHWARTZ

Bibliography: De Ricci, Seymour, *Louis XIV and Regency Furniture and Decoration* (1929).

Boullée, Étienne Louis   [boo-lay']

Étienne Louis Boullée, b. Feb. 12, 1728, d. Feb. 6, 1799, was a French architect and noted theorist of so-called visionary architecture. His monumental conceptions were thought megalomanic by his contemporaries, but they strongly influenced 19th-century architecture and are now considered brilliantly prophetic. Dissuaded by his architect father from becoming a painter, he studied the classical tradition under Jacques François Blondel and became a member of the Academy of Architecture in 1762. He contributed significantly to the antirococo movement of the 1760s, advocating classical stability and a return to basic geometric shapes. The extreme novelty and impracticality of his projects and plans led to his retirement from practice in 1774. Boullée then devoted the rest of his life to theoretical writing and fantastic projects. He remained a popular and influential teacher, even after the French Revolution. Two significant projects are those for a Newton memorial (1784) and a Municipal Palace of Justice (1792); both show his masterly handling of simple, massive forms and spaces.   SUZANNE J. WILSON

Bibliography: Lemagny, J. C., *Visionary Architects, Boullée, Ledoux, Lequeu* (1968); Rosenau, Helen, *Boullée and Visionary Architecture* (1976).

Boulogne-sur-Mer   [boo-lawn'-yuh-suer-mair']

Boulogne-sur-Mer (or Boulogne) is a seaport in northern France in Pas-de-Calais department. Located on the English Channel southwest of Calais, it is a center of boatbuilding, fishing, and foundries and has a population of 47,482 (1982 est.). The city, with passenger service to Dover and Folkestone, England, has a considerable English population. In Roman times it was called Bononia. Henry VIII of England captured the city after a six-week siege in 1544, but it was returned to France in 1550. In 1803–05, Napoleon I gathered an army near Boulogne to launch his intended invasion of England, which never materialized. The upper town is the older part of the city, surrounded by medieval ramparts and connected by a bridge to a 13th-century castle. The pilgrimage church of Notre Dame dates from 1827–66. The lower town is the commercial and industrial area around the port.

Boult, Sir Adrian Cedric   [bohlt]

Sir Adrian Boult, b. Apr. 8, 1889, d. Feb. 23, 1983, was a distinguished British symphony conductor. He received a music degree from Oxford and also studied in Leipzig. A champion of British music, Boult gave the first performances of Vaughan Williams's *Pastoral* Symphony and parts of Holst's *Planets*, with the Royal Philharmonic. His appointments included the Birmingham Orchestra (1924–30, 1959–60), the BBC Symphony Orchestra (1930–50), and the London Philharmonic Orchestra (1950–57). Boult, who taught for many years at the Royal College of Music, was knighted in 1937.

STEPHANIE VON BUCHAU

Bibliography: Boult, Adrian, *My Own Trumpet* (1973).

Boulton, Matthew   [bohl'-tuhn]

The partner of James WATT in the development and manufacture of the STEAM ENGINE, Matthew Boulton, b. Sept. 3, 1728, d. Aug. 18, 1809, was master of the famous Soho Iron Works in Birmingham, England, when he became (1775) Watt's financial backer and colleague. As a founder of the Lunar Society of Birmingham, whose members were active scientists and science-oriented industrialists, Boulton was a central figure during the early days of the Industrial Revolution.

Boumedienne, Houari   [boo-muh-dee-en', hoo-ar'-ee]

Houari Boumedienne, originally named Muhammad Boukharouba, b. Aug. 23, 1927, d. Dec. 27, 1978, was the second president of the Algerian republic. He was a leader of rebel forces during Algeria's war for independence, becoming minister of defense in 1962. In 1965 he succeeded President Ahmed BEN BELLA in a bloodless coup, serving 13 years until his death. Maintaining that modernization was not inconsistent with the precepts of Islam, Boumedienne pushed the industrialization of Algeria, based on the oil, steel, and chemical industries, and concentrated all political power in his own hands.

Bibliography: Ottaway, David and Marina, *Algeria* (1970); Quandt, William B., *Revolution and Political Leadership* (1969).

Bounty

The *Bounty* was an 18th-century British ship famous for the mutiny of its crew. Commanded by William BLIGH, the ship was en route from Tahiti to Jamaica with a cargo of breadfruit plants when the crew, led by master's mate Fletcher Christian, seized it on Apr. 28, 1789. Bligh and 18 crew members were set adrift in a small boat and, by brilliant seamanship, sailed 5,823 km (3,610 mi) to the island of Timor. Christian and some of the mutineers took refuge on PITCAIRN ISLAND.

Bibliography: Hough, Richard, *The Bounty,* 2d rev. ed. (1984); McKee, Alexander, *H.M.S. Bounty* (1961).

Bourassa, Henri   [boo-rah-sah']

Joseph Napoléon Henri Bourassa, b. Sept. 1, 1868, d. Aug. 31, 1952, was a French-Canadian political leader who sat in the Canadian House of Commons (1896–1907, 1925–35) and in the Quebec Legislative Assembly (1908–12). In 1910 he founded *Le Devoir*, a French-Canadian nationalist newspaper that is still published in Montreal; he was its editor until 1932. Bourassa was an outstanding orator and a prolific pamphleteer. His main policies were Canadian autonomy within the British Empire and integral biculturalism inside Canada. He opposed close imperial ties and condemned the introduction of military conscription in 1917 and 1942. He also spoke out to protect the interests of French Canadians outside Quebec.

ANDRÉE DÉSILETS

Bibliography: Murrow, Casey, *Henri Bourassa and French-Canadian Nationalism* (1968).

Bourbaki, Nicolas   [boor-bah-kee']

Nicolas Bourbaki is the pseudonym of an influential group of French mathematicians. The name was probably derived from the French general Charles D. S. Bourbaki (1816–97), whose statue stands in Nancy, where many members of the group have taught. The name "Nicolas" probably hints at the saint who offers a gift to the mathematical world. Since 1939 the group has been writing a survey of mathematics whose scope, purpose, and terminology are entirely different from other mathematical works. The axioms of Bourbaki are defined so as to be as broad as possible, in contrast to the systems of axioms of EUCLID, which characterize only Euclidean geometry, and of Giuseppe PEANO, which concern the theory of natural numbers. Numerous volumes by the group have thus far been published, concerning the foundations of analysis.

The work of Bourbaki has strongly affected the vocabulary of mathematics and has become widely known in mathematical circles because it is the first systematic survey of subjects that had previously been available only in widely scattered articles. The group has a constantly changing membership whose names are kept secret, but it is assumed that such famous mathematicians as E. Cartan, C. Chevalley, and A. Weil were among its founders.

Bourbon   (dynasty)   [boor-bohn']

The house of Bourbon was the ruling dynasty of France from 1589 to 1792 and again from 1814 to 1830; in Spain, where it ruled (with interruptions) from 1700 to 1931, the dynasty was recently restored to the throne in the person of JUAN CARLOS.

Robert of Clermont, 1256–1318, the sixth son of the French king LOUIS IX, married the heiress to the duchy of Bourbon and founded the dynasty. There were six subsequent dukes in the direct line before the title passed (1503) to the Montpensier branch of the family. It too became extinct when its representative, Charles, duc de BOURBON, died in 1527. The surviving collateral line was that of Vendôme, descending from Jacques de la Marche, d. 1361, constable of France, a grandson of Robert of Clermont. The first Bourbon king, HENRY IV, who succeeded to the throne when the VALOIS dynasty died out, was the son of Antoine de Vendôme, b. 1518, d. Oct. 26, 1562, king-consort of Navarre, himself eight generations removed from Louis IX. The junior Bourbon line of CONDÉ descended from Antoine's brother, Louis (1530–69).

From Henry IV descended the next four Bourbon kings of France—LOUIS XIII, LOUIS XIV, LOUIS XV, and LOUIS XVI, who was overthrown in the French Revolution. LOUIS XVII died during the Revolution without reigning. After the defeat (1814–15) of Napoleon, the restored Bourbons—LOUIS XVIII and CHARLES X—were brothers of Louis XVI. The next and last king of France, Louis-Philippe (r. 1830–48) was a member of the cadet branch of ORLÉANS. The direct Bourbon line in France died out in 1883 with Henri, comte de Chambord.

Louis XIV made one of his grandsons king of Spain as PHILIP V, thus establishing the Spanish Bourbon branch in 1700. Philip's successors were FERDINAND VI, CHARLES III, CHARLES IV, FERDINAND VII, ISABELLA II, ALFONSO XII, ALFONSO XIII, and the present king, Juan Carlos. In the 19th and 20th centuries the rule of the Spanish Bourbons suffered several schisms and interruptions. The CARLIST branch, founded by Don Carlos, 1788–1855, the brother of Ferdinand VII, was reunited to the main line on the death (1936) of Don Alfonso de Borbón.

Before becoming king of Spain, Charles III was duke of Parma and king of the Two Sicilies (Naples–Sicily). One set of his descendants ruled Parma, with interruptions, until 1859; Naples and Sicily passed to Charles's son FERDINAND I of the Two Sicilies, whose descendants held the throne until 1860.

J. H. M. SALMON

Bibliography: Acton, Harold, *The Bourbons of Naples* (1963); Petrie, Sir Charles, *The Spanish Royal House* (1958); Seward, Desmond, *The Bourbon Kings of France* (1976).

See also: FRANCE, HISTORY OF; NAPLES, KINGDOM OF; SPAIN, HISTORY OF.

Bourbon, Charles de Bourbon, Duc de

Charles, duc de Bourbon, b. Feb. 17, 1490, was constable of France under King FRANCIS I, whom he betrayed to serve Holy Roman Emperor CHARLES V in the ITALIAN WARS. He inherited his dukedom in 1503 and, made constable by Francis, played a significant role in the French victory at Marignano (September 1515). Harassed by Francis, who was jealous of his influence and vast estates, Bourbon entered imperial service in 1523. He fought in the Battle of Pavia (1525) and was killed attacking Rome on May 6, 1527.

Bourbon, Louis Henri de Bourbon-Condé, Duc de

The French nobleman Louis Henri de Bourbon-Condé, b. Aug. 18, 1692, d. Jan. 27, 1740, became duc de Bourbon on Louis XIV's death (1715) and head of the regency council under Philippe II, duc d'ORLÉANS. From 1723 to 1726 he was chief minister for LOUIS XV. To ensure a royal heir, Bourbon arranged that the sickly Louis marry (1725) the 21-year-old Maria Lesczcyńska, daughter of the deposed STANISŁAW II of Poland, rather than the Spanish child princess to whom he had been betrothed. This move troubled Franco-Spanish relations.

bourbon whiskey: see WHISKEY.

Bourbonnais   [boor-baw-nay']

Bourbonnais was one of the provinces of France before 1790. It was approximately the same area as the modern department of Allier and is located on the northern flank of the Massif Central. Bourbonnais is a transitional region geologically, and in the north crystalline rocks yield to recent sandy deposits. Its diverse agriculture is characterized by wheat, dairying, Charolais beef cattle, and pigs. Moulins (1982 pop., 25,159), a railroad junction on the Allier River and the traditional capital, is the administrative center of the department. Montluçon in the fertile Cher Valley is the major manufacturing center, having rubber and a variety of metallurgical industries.

TIMOTHY J. RICKARD

Bourdelle, Émile Antoine   [boor-del']

Émile Antoine Bourdelle, b. Oct. 30, 1861, d. Oct. 1, 1929, was a French sculptor and teacher. Chronologically and stylistically, his life and work span the 19th and 20th centuries. At the age of 15 he won a scholarship to the École des Beaux-Arts in Toulouse and later attended that academy in Paris. He became a member of Auguste RODIN's workshop, and carving figures for Rodin formed the most important part of his training. The two artists were close colleagues, although Bourdelle eventually broke away from Rodin's style.

Bourdelle, a native of southern France, was familiar with Romanesque sculpture and architecture, and he never lost the feel of the great, simple representations in those monuments. He hoped to produce a sculpture imbued with what he called the "ardent wisdom" of Romanesque and Gothic churches, which he valued more than the masterpieces of the Italian Renaissance. He did not hesitate to borrow motifs from the past. In 1910 the Paris SALON recognized his first great work, the bronze *Heracles, the Archer* (1909; Metropolitan Museum of Art, New York). Among Bourdelle's other important works are the Beethoven heads, a series of more than 60 studies, and the colossal *Virgin of Alsace* (1922; Niederbruck, Alsace).

Because Bourdelle believed in sculpture as the realization of an object, many critics consider him the predecessor of the cubist sculptors. A noted teacher, he influenced a number of artists who became members of the modern movement; among them were Henri MATISSE, Alberto GIACOMETTI, and VIEIRA DA SILVA.

ALBERT BOIME

Bibliography: Bourdelle, Émile Antoine, *Antoine Bourdelle, 1861–1929* (1961) and *Sculptures of Antoine Bourdelle* (1970); Jianou, Ionel, and Dufet, Michel, *Bourdelle*, trans. by Kathleen Muston and Bryan Richardson (1965).

Bourdon, Sébastien   [boor-dohn']

Sébastien Bourdon, b. Feb. 2, 1616, d. May 8, 1671, was a French painter. A highly eclectic artist, he never evolved a truly personal style. Bourdon worked in Rome from 1634 to 1637, coming under the influence of the circle of northern genre painters called the BAMBOCCIATI. In the next decade he departed from the depiction of anecdotal scenes of everyday life in favor of historical themes in a classical style modeled after that of Nicolas POUSSIN. He worked from 1652 to 1654 as court portrait painter to Queen Christina of Sweden. Even as court portraitist and a painter of historical subjects in a classical vein, however, he continued to excel in didactic illustrations of human behavior.   THOMAS W. SOKOLOWSKI

Bibliography: Blunt, Anthony, *Art and Architecture in France 1500–1700,* 3d ed. (1970).

Bourgeois, Louise   [boor-zhwah']

Louise Bourgeois, b. Dec. 25, 1911, is a French-born American sculptor. After studying art in Paris, she married the American art historian Robert Goldwater and settled (1938) in New York. In 1945 her work was displayed in a Whitney Museum annual exhibit, and she had her first one-woman show. Her earliest mature works—large, semifigurative, totemic sculptures—were carved in wood. After the early 1960s, when she worked in plaster and papiér-mâché, Bourgeois developed into a virtuoso stone carver. Her work in this medium has tended toward clustered, highly polished forms with a strongly phallic quality.   CARTER RATCLIFF

Bibliography: Baur, John, *Nature in Abstraction* (1958); Wye, Deborah, *Louise Bourgeois* (1982).

Bourgeois Gentleman, The   [boor-zhwah']

The Bourgeois Gentleman (1670; Eng. trans., 1675), a comedy by MOLIÈRE, was first performed at the court of France's Louis XIV. It satirically portrays Monsieur Jourdain, a dull-witted tradesman whose eagerness to appear a gentleman causes him to hire a host of pompous tutors who succeed only in making him look ridiculous. Because of his regard for the marchioness Dorimène, Jourdain loses his own level-headed, bourgeois wife and allows himself to be duped out of a fortune by the dissembling nobleman Dorante. The play is one of Molière's most popular thrusts at human vanity and pretension.

bourgeoisie   [boor-zhawh-zee']

Bourgeoisie is a French word originally denoting the class of people between the aristocracy and the peasants, or the middle class. In industrialized societies, the word has come to mean those who own the means of production. The distinction between the bourgeoisie (employers) and the proletariat (employees) is fundamental to MARXISM.

Bourget, Paul   [boor-zhay']

Paul Bourget, b. Sept. 2, 1852, d. Dec. 25, 1935, was a French writer whose psychological novels about leisure-class life resemble those of Henry James. Representative novels include *A Cruel Enigma* (1885; Eng. trans., 1887), *The Disciple* (1889; Eng. trans., 1898), and *The Night Cometh* (1915; Eng. trans., 1916). He also wrote plays, poetry, and critical essays.

Bibliography: Singer, Armand E., *Paul Bourget* (1976).

Bourguiba, Habib   [bur-gee'-buh, hah'-beeb]

Habib Bourguiba, b. Aug. 3, 1903, was the first president of the Tunisian republic. A founder (1934) of the Neo-Destour party, which aimed to secure Tunisian independence from France, Bourguiba was frequently imprisoned by the French. When France finally accepted Tunisian independence (March 1956), Bourguiba became prime minister. After the abolition of the monarchy on July 25, 1957, he was elected president. In 1987 the ailing Bourguiba was ousted by his prime minister, Zine el-Abidine Ben Ali.

Bourignon, Antoinette   [boor-een-yohn']

A Flemish mystic, Antoinette Bourignon, b. Jan. 13, 1616, d. Oct. 30, 1680, gathered a fanatical following and tried unsuc-

cessfully to found an ascetic order. Convinced that God chose her as a new Eve or Mary, the ''woman clothed with the sun'' of Revelation 12, she became estranged from organized Christianity in 1662 and taught a doctrine of the inner light and divine immediacy. Her extreme form of QUIETISM found some support in Scotland.

Bourjaily, Vance   [boor-jy'-lee]

Vance Bourjaily, b. Sept. 17, 1922, is an American novelist whose typical subject has been the moral and social rootlessness of his own generation. His most admired works are *The End of My Life* (1947), a war novel; *The Violated* (1958), a story of generational conflict; and *Now Playing at Canterbury* (1976), a contemporary version of Chaucer's tales. Later works include *A Game Men Play* (1980) and *Old Soldier* (1990).
          MARCUS KLEIN

Bourke-White, Margaret

This famous photograph (1950) by Margaret Bourke-White shows South African gold miners working 2 km (1.2 mi) beneath the Earth's surface. Photos by this pioneering photojournalist became a main feature in Life, *one of America's most prominent picture magazines.*

Margaret Bourke-White, b. June 14, 1906, d. Aug. 27, 1971, was a pioneer in PHOTOJOURNALISM. In 1929 her photographs were featured in the first issue of *Fortune* magazine. A year later she became the first foreigner admitted to the USSR to take motion pictures of industry and social conditions. In 1936 she joined the staff of *Life* magazine as one of its first four photographers; her method was to take many pictures in order to capture a single moment that conveyed the human drama of an event. Bourke-White collaborated with the writer Erskine CALDWELL, whom she later married, on a documentary book, *You Have Seen Their Faces* (1937), a powerful look at the plight of poverty-ridden Southern blacks. In 1941 she collaborated with Caldwell on a survey of life in America, *Say! Is This the U.S.A?*. During World War II she became the first woman to be accredited as a war photographer and to fly a combat mission. *Dear Fatherland, Rest Quietly* (1946) records her experiences as American troops liberated prisoners from German concentration camps.   ELIZABETH POLLOCK

Bibliography: Bourke-White, Margaret, *Portrait of Myself* (1963; repr. 1985); Brown, T. M., and Callahan, S., *Photographs of Margaret Bourke-White* (1972); Goldberg, V., *Margaret Bourke-White* (1986).

Bournemouth   [bohrn'-muhth]

Bournemouth (1988 est. pop., 154,800), a county borough in Dorset in southern England, is located at the mouth of the River Bourne on the English Channel, about 45 km (28 mi) southwest of Southampton. The mild climate and beautiful countryside, with its many parks and gardens and areas of pine woods and sandy heaths, make Bournemouth one of the most popular vacation and retirement centers in the country, as well as an important conference and convention center. Bournemouth grew up around a private summer residence built after 1810. The arrival of the railroad in 1870 spurred the city's growth.

Bournonville, August   [boor-nahn-veel']

August Bournonville, b. Aug. 21, 1805, d. Nov. 30, 1879, was one of the greatest choreographers of the romantic ballet and creator of the Danish ballet style. The son of a French dancer, he entered the Royal Danish Ballet (RDB) School in Copenhagen and made his debut at the age of eight. At the age of 15, Bournonville became a member of the RDB. In 1824 he went to Paris to study with Auguste VESTRIS and in 1826 joined the Paris Opéra Ballet, where he became a favorite partner of Marie TAGLIONI. Returning to Copenhagen in 1828, Bournonville was appointed choreographer, teacher, and, until 1848, first dancer of the RDB.

Bournonville's earliest surviving ballet is *La Sylphide* (1836), his own version of the ballet made famous by Taglioni in 1832. This and others of Bournonville's more than 50 ballets have survived through continuous performance in Denmark, just as his classroom exercises have been preserved in the school. Although deeply influenced by the ballets he had seen and danced in Paris, Bournonville created his own, typically Danish type of romanticism in which fantasy is contrasted with everyday characters and incidents, as in *Napoli* (1842), *Konservatoriet* (1849), and *Kermesse in Bruges* (1851). *La Sylphide* and excerpts from his other ballets (notably the *pas de deux* from *Flower Festival at Genzano*, 1858) are performed throughout the world.   DAVID VAUGHAN

Bibliography: Bournonville, Auguste, *My Theatre Life*, trans. by Patricia McAndrew (1979); Bruhn, E., and Moore, L., *Bournonville and Ballet Technique* (1961); Moore, L., *Bournonville's London Spring* (1966).

Boussingault, Jean Baptiste   [boo-san-goh', zhawn bah-teest']

Although he had a varied career as a mineralogist, geologist, and political figure, Jean Baptiste Joseph Diendonné Boussingault, b. Feb. 2, 1802, d. May 12, 1887, did his most important work in the field of agricultural chemistry. As professor of chemistry at the University of Lyon and at the Sorbonne, his research on the role of nitrogen as a plant nutrient opened the way for the use of inorganic fertilizers. Boussingault was also among the first to study the chemistry of foods.

Boutens, Pieter Cornelius   [bow'-tuhns, pee'-tur kor-nay'-lis]

Pieter Cornelius Boutens, b. Feb. 20, 1870, d. Mar. 14, 1943, was a Dutch poet whose work, originally modeled after *De Nieuwe Gids* (The New Guide) movement, soon acquired a distinct personality with *Stemmen* (Voices, 1907) and subsequent collections of mystically inspired and technically polished symbolist poetry. He also translated the classics and, in his *Beatrijs* (1908), modernized the medieval Beatrice legend.   THEO D'HAEN

Boutros-Ghali, Boutros   [boo'-truhs-gah'-lee]

In 1992 the Egyptian diplomat Boutros Boutros-Ghali, b. Nov. 14, 1922, became the first United Nations secretary-general from the Arab world and the first from Africa. The grandson of an Egyptian prime minister, Boutros Pasha Ghali, he received a law degree from Cairo University in 1946 and a doctorate from the Sorbonne in Paris in 1949, when he began a long association with Cairo University teaching international relations. A Coptic Christian with a Jewish wife, he began his diplomatic career in 1977 and became foreign minister in 1991.

Bouts, Dirk   [bowts]

Dirk Bouts, b. Haarlem, *c.*1415, d. May 1475, was a Dutch painter active in Flanders who is notable for his originality in depicting austere, emotionally intense figures and for his subtle uses of changing color and light in his landscape backgrounds. About 1448 he married a woman from Louvain, in Flanders, and moved there. Little else is known about his early years and influences; his paintings do, however, bear a strong stylistic resemblance to those of the contemporary

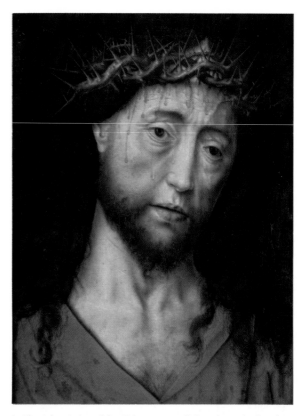

In Flemish painting of the 15th century, religious drama is played on realistic human terms. Ecce Homo (c.1460), by Dirk Bouts, portrays the patient suffering of Christ at the hands of his mocking tormentors. The ascetic, noble face furrowed with tears draws the spectator's sympathy and love. (Musée des Beaux-Arts, Dijon.)

Haarlem painter Albert van Ouwater. Although Bouts retained the Dutch concern for refined landscape, luminous atmosphere, and religiously sober, almost stiff, figures, in such early works as the *Lamentation* (c.1460; Louvre, Paris) and the Passion triptych (c.1450; Capilla Real, Cathedral, Granada) he succumbed to the widespread influence of the Flemish master Rogier van der Weyden, the official city painter of Brussels.

Bouts's masterpiece is the triptych of the *Last Supper*, executed from 1464 to 1467 for the Brotherhood of the Holy Sacrament (St. Pierre, Louvain). Like his contemporary triptychs of the martyred saints Erasmus (St. Pierre, Louvain) and Hippolytus (Cathedral, Bruges), Bouts's paintings at first suggest a taste for provincial naïveté, but further analysis reveals his distinctive ability to render controlled, intense emotions and to group well-drawn figures by a sensitive awareness of true perspective, rich colors, and modulated lighting.

Although the subject matter of Bouts's paintings may occasionally seem morbid, as in the two panels of the *Judgment of the Emperor Otho III, Execution of the Innocent Count* and *Ordeal by Fire* (1470–75; Palais des Beaux-Arts, Brussels), his exaggeratedly tall figures and solemn, placid spaces imbue his art with an immanent, elegant refinement that influenced painting in Louvain for several decades.   ALAN P. DARR

Bibliography: Eisler, Peter, *Early Netherlandish Painting* (1989); Friedländer, Max, *Dieric Bouts and Joos van Gent, Early Netherlandish Painting*, trans. by Heinz Norden, vol. 3 (1968).

Bouvier des Flandres

The Bouvier des Flandres originated in southwestern Flanders and northern France as a large herding and drover dog. The breed was nearly wiped out during World War I, in which it was used for guard duty and for carrying messages. A Belgian army veterinarian preserved some dogs, however, among which was the foundation sire of the modern Bouvier.

The Bouvier des Flandres, a large working dog, has a rough, weather-resistant coat and a sturdy demeanor. The breed was nearly annihilated during World War I because of heavy damage to major breeding areas.

The Bouvier is a large working breed with a rough coat, cropped ears, a noticeable beard, and a short, docked tail. The double coat is dense and profuse, and the outer coat is very coarse. Bouviers range in color from fawn to black, pepper and salt, gray, and brindle. They stand up to 70 cm (28 in) high) at the shoulder and weigh from 27 to 32 kg (60 to 70 lb). Bouviers are powerfully built, with deep chests, muscular thighs, and a short, powerful back. In Belgium no Bouvier can become a champion unless it is also certified in a work competition as a police, defense, or army dog.

Bibliography: Leggett, Gerene C., *How to Raise and Train a Bouvier des Flandres* (1965); McLean, Claire, *The Complete Bouvier des Flandres*, 2d ed. (1981).

Bouvines, Battle of   [boo-veen']

In the Battle of Bouvines on July 27, 1214, near Lille in France, PHILIP II of France defeated the English king JOHN and Holy Roman Emperor OTTO IV. This victory excluded the English from northern France and established the power of the French monarchy.

Bovet, Daniele   [boh-vay']

Daniele Bovet, b. Mar. 23, 1907, d. Apr. 8, 1992, a Swiss-Italian pharmacologist, developed the first antihistamine and pioneered in the development of muscle-relaxing drugs. He was awarded the 1957 Nobel Prize for physiology or medicine. After early work on the sulfa drugs, Bovet and his colleague A. M. Staub, in 1937, discovered the first antihistamine, which although itself too weak and toxic for human use was the basis for most antihistamines developed later. Turning his attention to the natural alkaloid curare, he developed synthetic curarelike muscle-relaxing compounds that could be used to supplement light anesthesia in surgery. Among his writings is *Curare and Curarelike Agents* (1959).

bovid   [boh'-vid]

Bovid is the collective name for hoofed mammals belonging to the family Bovidae, order Artiodactyla. The family comprises 49 genera and about 115 species. Bovids take diverse forms, but they all are herbivores, or eaters of plant material, and ruminants, or cud chewers. The food is swallowed, then brought up from the first compartment of the four-chambered stomach and chewed at leisure before being swallowed again to complete the digestion process.

Most bovids are native to the Old World, but both domesticated and wild species have been introduced into the New World. Among the bovids are the ANTELOPES; BANTENG; CATTLE; GAUR; GOATS; SHEEP, YAK; gayal; kouprey (see OX); and takin.

EVERETT SENTMAN

bow

The bow is an implement of wood and horsehair for setting in motion the strings of instruments in the VIOL and VIOLIN families. It is named after the archery bow, which at first it resembled. Originating in the East, the bow was first known in Europe in the 9th century. Its modern shape was established early in the 19th century by François Tourte (1747–1835), who used a pernambuco, or brazilwood, stick about 75 cm (30 in) long strung with 150 to 250 horsehairs for his violin bows. A screw mechanism tightens the hair of the bow so that the stick curves only slightly toward the hair. Violin and viola bows are longer and weigh less than cello and bass bows. Rosin is applied to the hairs to increase the friction between them and the strings.   ELWYN A. WIENANDT

Bow, Clara

Clara Gordon Bow, b. Brooklyn, N.Y., Aug. 25, 1905, d. Sept. 26, 1965, became known as Hollywood's "It Girl" for her portrayal of a carefree, wide-eyed flapper in the 1927 film *It*. She capitalized on her notoriety as a sex symbol in *Mantrap* (1926), *Wings* (1927), *The Fleet's In* (1928), and *Call Her Savage* (1932), but scandal in her private life led to the end of her career after *Hoopla* (1933).   LESLIE HALLIWELL

bow and arrow

The bow and arrow, in many variations, has been used by most civilizations. The first archery equipment, it is believed, was made from wood and hide; the earliest specific information, however, comes from Paleolithic knapped-flint arrowheads, and much later, cave paintings of bowmen. Assyrian archers (700 BC) were renowned for their excellent organization, strong bows, and iron-tipped arrows. The Persians (600 BC) added a new dimension to warfare with the use of mounted archers. The bow was a principal weapon in warfare until eclipsed by firearms in the 15th century; it is still the primary arm of primitive peoples today.

Types of Bows. Bows are constructed in three basic forms: a self-bow is made of one homogeneous piece of material; a built bow is made of joined pieces of the same material; and a composite bow is made of different materials. The best-known bow-form is the Welsh, or English, long-bow. As tall as a man, it revolutionized medieval warfare because it could fire heavy arrows with deadly accuracy at targets more than 180 m (600 ft) distant. It was so well designed that it remained in use, virtually unchanged, as a sporting bow until the 1930s.

A popular European variation was the crossbow, horizontally mounted in a stock (tiller), which was aimed and fired much like a rifle. Because of its mechanical advantage, the crossbow permitted smaller men to fire to greater ranges.

Most modern bows are of composite construction—the handle riser may be wood, aluminum, or magnesium, and the bow limbs are made of wood and fiberglass, sometimes with graphite or carbon as well.

Arrows and Arrow Releases. Arrows vary considerably in size, use, and construction. Generally, larger arrowheads are used for game hunting, and smaller, harder heads are used for military and sport purposes. Fletchings are added to the rear of the arrow shaft to give directional stability to the arrow's flight. At one time made of feathers (or occasionally hair or wood), fletchings are now normally plastic, although some hunters and indoor shooters sometimes still use feathers. Modern arrow shafts are almost always made of aluminum tubing, and with the plastic fletchings the result is uniform weight, flight characteristics, and performance. (See also ARCHERY.)   LANE ROGERS

Bibliography: Bear, Fred, *The Archer's Bible*, rev. ed. (1980); Bow & Arrow Magazine Staff, and Lewis, Jack, eds., *Archery Equipment Illustrated* (1984); Hamilton, T. M., *Native American Bows*, 2d ed. (1982).

Bowditch, Nathaniel   [bow'-dich]

The American sea captain, mathematician, and astronomer Nathaniel Bowditch, b. Mar. 26, 1773, d. Mar. 16, 1838, is best known for his works on navigation and for his annotated

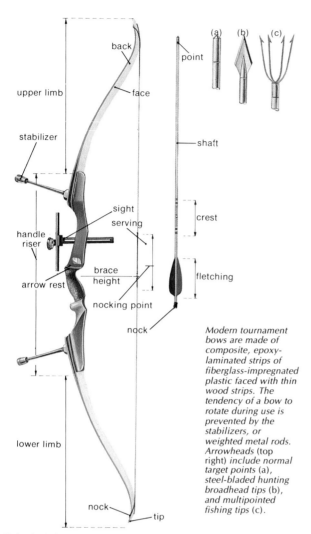

Modern tournament bows are made of composite, epoxy-laminated strips of fiberglass-impregnated plastic faced with thin wood strips. The tendency of a bow to rotate during use is prevented by the stabilizers, or weighted metal rods. Arrowheads (top right) include normal target points (a), steel-bladed hunting broadhead tips (b), and multipointed fishing tips (c).

(Below) *Aiming ease, power, and distance are achieved with modern crossbows, which use riflelike stocks and horizontal bowstrings.*

(Below) *A Mongolian draw (left) uses a ring-protected right thumb and index finger to pull the string. A Mediterranean draw (right) uses the right index finger and the next two fingers.*

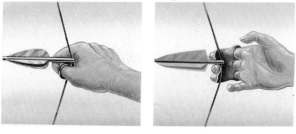

translation of Laplace's *Mécanique céleste* (*Celestial Mechanics*). After spending the first part of his life at sea, Bowditch entered (1804) the world of commerce and had notable success in the area of life insurance, where he served as an actuary. His articles on astronomy, mathematics, and physics made him well-known in scientific circles.

Bibliography: Berry, Robert E., *Yankee Stargazer* (1941); Reingold, Nathan, ed., *Science in Nineteenth Century America* (1964).

Bowdler, Thomas   [bowd'-lur]

The English editor Thomas Bowdler, b. July 11, 1754, d. Feb. 24, 1825, edited the *Family Shakespeare* (1818), removing "those words and expressions . . . which cannot with propriety be read aloud in a family." He also expurgated the *Old Testament* (1822) and Gibbons's *Decline and Fall of the Roman Empire* (1826). Although Bowdler's editions were popular, he was ridiculed by critics because of the extremes to which he went. "Bowdlerizing" now connotes expunging work to such a degree that the spirit of the original is lost.

ROBIN BUSS

Bibliography: Perrin, Noël, *Dr. Bowdler's Legacy* (1969).

Bowdoin, James   [boh'-duhn]

James Bowdoin, b. Aug. 7, 1726, d. Nov. 6, 1790, was a leader of resistance to British rule in Massachusetts before and during the American Revolution. A Boston merchant, he served (1779–80) as president of the Massachusetts Constitutional Convention. As governor (1785–87) of the state, he suppressed SHAYS'S REBELLION.

Bowdoin College   [boh'-duhn]

Established in 1794 in Brunswick, Maine, Bowdoin College (enrollment: 1,350; library: 750,000 volumes) is a private 4-year liberal arts institution for men and women. It has a cooperative engineering program with the Massachusetts Institute of Technology, the Columbia University School of Engineering, and the California Institute of Technology.

Bowell, Sir Mackenzie   [boh'-uhl]

Sir Mackenzie Bowell, b. Dec. 17, 1823, d. Dec. 10, 1917, was prime minister of Canada. Elected to the Canadian House of Commons as a Conservative in 1867, he later served (1892–1906) in the Canadian Senate. Bowell was chosen to succeed John S. THOMPSON as prime minister in 1894; but was unable to provide strong party leadership. After numerous cabinet resignations, he resigned in 1896.

Bowen, Elizabeth   [boh'-uhn]

Elizabeth Dorothea Cole Bowen, b. Dublin, Ireland, June 7, 1899, d. Feb. 22, 1973, was a writer of impeccable craftsmanship, whose hallmark was perceptive, delicate characterization. Bowen was raised among the Anglo-Irish gentry and wrote primarily about the upper middle class. Having already published *Encounters* (1923), a book of short stories, she established herself as a novelist with *The Hotel* (1927), in which she drew on her experiences as a governess to her young cousins during a stay at an Italian hotel. This was followed by *To the North* (1932); *The Cat Jumps* (1934), another collection of short stories; *The House in Paris* (1935); and *The Death of the Heart* (1938), a sensitive story of betrayed innocence that is considered one of her finest novels. After another volume of short fiction, *Ivy Gripped the Steps* (1946), Bowen published *The Heat of the Day* (1949), a spy novel. Like the stories in *Ivy*, this novel was based on her experiences during World War II as an air-raid warden and a member of the British Office of War Information. Among Bowen's later novels are *A World of Love* (1955), *The Little Girls* (1964), and *Eva Trout* (1969).

Bibliography: Blodgett, Harriet, *Patterns of Reality: Elizabeth Bowen's Novels* (1975); Glendinning, Victoria, *Elizabeth Bowen* (1978; repr. 1986); Kenney, E. J., *Elizabeth Bowen* (1975); Lee, Hermione, *Elizabeth Bowen: An Estimation* (1981).

Bowen, Ira Sprague   [boh'-uhn]

The astronomer Ira Sprague Bowen, b. Seneca Falls, N.Y., Dec. 21, 1898, d. Feb. 6, 1973, is known for his work in the field of spectroscopy. After graduation (1926) from California Institute of Technology, Bowen served there as professor from 1926 to 1945. He was director (1946–64) of Mount Wilson Observatory. Bowen demonstrated the presence of hydrogen and helium in nebulae and showed that spectroscopic evidence for a proposed new element in nebulae, called nebulium, could be better interpreted as due to oxygen and nitrogen under special conditions. This interpretation supported his theory that the universe was composed of the same elements as are found on Earth.   STEVEN J. DICK

Bowen, Norman Levi

The Canadian-American experimental petrologist Norman Levi Bowen, b. Kingston, Ontario, June 21, 1887, d. Sept. 11, 1956, showed how the experimental study of simplified chemical systems can be used to interpret the formation of the rocks that make up the Earth. He worked for many years at the Geophysical Laboratory of the Carnegie Institution of Washington, D.C., where he produced his best-known book, *The Evolution of the Igneous Rocks* (1928).

                    PETER B. LEAVENS

bowerbird

The tooth-billed bowerbird, Scenopoeetes dentirostris, *is named for its deeply notched bill. The bird, which is 23 cm (9 in) long, is found in the forested uplands of northeastern Australia. One of the plainer plumed bowerbirds, it builds a bower of the stage type.*

Bowerbirds are medium-sized birds known for the elaborate bowers, or display areas, that males build for courtship and mating. About 18 species, in the family Ptilonorhynchidae and closely related to birds of paradise, are found in New Guinea and Australia and on adjacent islands. Bowerbirds are often secretive in their habits, and many are restricted to cloud forests in mountainous regions. One species long thought extinct—the yellow-fronted gardener bowerbird, *Amblyornis flavifrons*—was sighted in 1981 in western New Guinea. The males in many species have ornate, colorful plumage. Those species with less ornate plumage typically built the most elaborate bowers to attract the females.

The species may be grouped by the type of bower constructed: maypole builders, avenue builders, stage builders, and those which build no bowers. The bowers may be large; the maypole of the golden bowerbird, *Prionodura newtoniana*, for example, may be up to 2.7 m (9 ft) high. Many are intricately designed with pillars, moss-covered floors, and roofs woven from vines. Some species use leaves or bark to apply a paint of saliva and ground bark or dirt to the inner walls of the bower. The bowers may also be decorated with snail shells or bright fruits that the male gathers. The female constructs the cup-shaped nest in a tree away from the bower and incubates the one to three eggs.   GARY D. SCHNELL

Bibliography: Gilliard, E. T., *Birds of Paradise and Bower Birds* (1969).

Bowery, The

The Bowery is a street in New York City's lower Manhattan, named *bouwerie* (''farm'') by early Dutch settlers because it led to the farm of Gov. Peter Stuyvesant. By the 1820s, when the Bowery had become New York's theatrical district, it was simultaneously deteriorating into a slum, as thousands of immigrants were packed into the area. It later became a skid row populated by derelicts.

bowfin   [boh'-fin]

The bowfin, *Amia calva*, is the sole surviving species of a fish family, Amiidae, that flourished during the Mesozoic and Cenozoic eras. It lives in the fresh waters of eastern North America. Bowfins are long bodied, with a long dorsal fin; using their air bladder as a lung, they can survive as long as one day out of the water. They feed on fish, frogs, and invertebrates. Once classified with the gar in the superorder Holostei of lower bony fishes, they are now placed by some authorities in the superorder Teleosti of higher bony fishes (see FISH).

                    EDWARD O. WILEY

Bowie, David   [boh'-wee]

David Bowie is the stage name of the British actor, singer, and songwriter David Robert Jones, b. Jan. 8, 1947. He gained fame in the early 1970s, combining his talents in rock music productions that often used science fiction themes, and starred himself in various androgynous personae. Following years of experimenting with his image and art, Bowie emerged in the 1980s as a versatile and powerful, if more conventional, musical showman. His film appearances include *The Man Who Fell to Earth* (1976), *Merry Christmas, Mr. Lawrence* (1983), and *Labyrinth* (1986). He has also starred on Broadway.   JONATHAN KAMIN

Bowie, James   [boo'-ee]

James Bowie, b. 1796, was a hero of the Texas Revolution. He early joined the revolutionary forces and was made commander, with William B. Travis, of the ALAMO in San Antonio (February 1836). He soon fell ill, leaving Travis in sole command during the siege by the Mexicans. He was killed when the Alamo fell on Mar. 6, 1836. He is credited with inventing the Bowie knife, a weapon widely used on the frontier.

Bibliography: Garst, Doris Shannon, *James Bowie and His Famous Knife* (1955).

Bowles, Chester

Chester Bowles, b. Springfield, Mass., Apr. 5, 1901, d. May 25, 1986, headed (1929–41) his own highly successful advertising firm before beginning a long career in public service during World War II. In 1943 he became director of the Office of Price Administration, and he served on the War Production Board (1943–46). Elected Democratic governor of Connecticut in 1948, he was the first to set up a State Commission on Civil Rights. Bowles was also a U.S. representative (1959–61), ambassador to India and Nepal (1951–53), and to India (1963–69). His writings include *Ambassador's Report* (1954).

Bowles, Jane Auer   [bohlz]

Jane Auer Bowles, b. New York City, Feb. 22, 1917, d. May 4, 1973, wrote eccentric, haunting fiction. In a novel, *Two Serious Ladies* (1943), a play, *In the Summer House* (1954), and a group of seven short stories, *Plain Pleasures* (1966), she proved an original, spare stylist whose wit and subtle insights could consistently surprise her readers. From 1947 she lived abroad, mostly in Tangier, with her husband Paul Bowles.

Bowles, Paul

The writer Paul Bowles, b. New York City, Dec. 30, 1910, first had a career as a composer. After studying with Virgil Thomson and Aaron Copland, he wrote opera, orchestral pieces, and film scores. In 1952, Bowles moved to Tangier, Morocco, and began to write novels and short stories that explore the harsh cultural incongruities between primitive and modern modes of life. These works include *The Sheltering Sky* (1949) and *Let It Come Down* (1952).

Bowles, Samuel, III

Samuel Bowles III, b. Springfield, Mass., Feb. 9, 1826, d. Jan. 16, 1878, became editor of the *Springfield Republican,* founded in 1844, when he persuaded his father, the publisher of the *Weekly Republican* (founded 1824), to produce a daily edition. He helped it to become one of the most widely circulated and comprehensive provincial newspapers in the United States. He was in the vanguard of a movement that directed the American press away from partisan reporting toward more in-dependent and objective news coverage. An early and ar-dent member of the Republican party, Bowles led an unsuc-cessful effort by the liberal Republicans, or "mugwumps," to oppose President Grant's reelection in 1872.

Bowles trained many news reporters who went on to fame in larger cities, thus creating for the *Republican* a reputation as a "school of journalism." SAM KUCZUN

Bibliography: Merriam, George S., *The Life and Times of Samuel Bowles,* 2 vols. (1885; repr. 1970).

bowling

Bowling, sometimes called tenpins, is an indoor game played on a polished wooden floor (or alley) by individuals or teams. Although most popular in the United States, where more than 60 million people actively participate, bowling is also, sometimes in different versions such as candle stick and duck pin bowling, well known around the world. (See also BOC-CIE; LAWN BOWLS; SKITTLES.)

Rules and Object. In the U.S. game, contestants roll balls, which have two or, commonly, three finger holes for gripping, toward ten 15-in. (38.1-cm) wooden pins. The pins are ar-ranged in triangular formation, with the headpin 60 ft (18.3 m) from a foul line. The balls, made of hard rubber or plastic, are 8.5 in. (21.6 cm) in diameter and must not weigh more than 16 lb (7.26 kg). The bowler, who rolls the ball underhand, has a runway at least 15 ft (4.57 m) long from which the ball may be released.

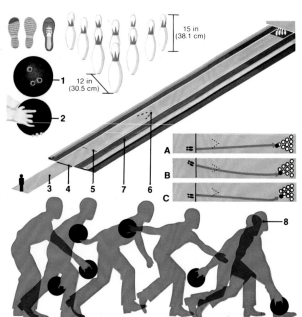

This illustration shows some of the techniques and equipment used in tenpin bowling. The ball used in competition is gripped with the thumb, middle finger, and ring finger (1, 2). The bowler takes a position on the alley behind the approach area (3), then moves forward and releases the ball before reaching the foul line (4). Two sets of guide marks (5, 6) aid in lining up the shot. If the delivery is made too far on either side, the ball will fall into a gutter (7). The paths of three common deliveries—the straight ball (A), the curve (B), and the hook (C)—are diagramed. A silhouette (8) demonstrates the proper form for a bowler during approach and at release of the ball.

BOWLERS OF THE YEAR

Year	Men	Year	Women
1948	Andy Varipapa	1948–49	Val Mikiel
1949	Connie Schwoegler	1950–55	Marion Ladewig
1950	Junie McMahon	1956	Sylvia Martin
1951	Lee Jouglard	1957	Anita Cantaline
1952	Steve Nagy	1958–59	Marion Ladewig
1953–54	Don Carter	1960	Sylvia Martin
1955	Steve Nagy	1961–62	Shirley Garms
1956	Bill Lillard	1963	Marion Ladewig
1957–58	Don Carter	1964	Laverne Carter
1959	Ed Lubanski	1965	Betty Kuczynski
1960	Don Carter	1966	Joy Abel
1961	Dick Weber	1967	Mildred Martorella
1962	Don Carter	1968–69	Dorothy Fothergill
1963	Dick Weber	1970	Mary Baker
1964	Billy Hardwick	1971	Paula Sperber
1965	Dick Weber	1972	Patty Costello
1966	Wayne Zahn	1973	Judy Cook
1967	Dave Davis	1974	Betty Morris
1968	Jim Stefanich	1975	Judy Cook Soutar
1969	Billy Hardwick	1976	Patty Costello
1970	Nelson Burton, Jr.	1977	Betty Morris
1971–72	Don Johnson	1978–81	Donna Adamek
1973	Don McCune	1982	Nikki Gianulias
1974–76	Earl Anthony	1983	Lisa Rathgeber
1977–79	Mark Roth	1984–85	Aleta Sill
1980	Wayne Webb	1986	Lisa Rathgeber Wagner
1981–83	Earl Anthony		
1984	Mark Roth	1987	Betty Morris
1985	Mike Aulby	1988	Lisa Wagner
1986	W.R. Williams, Jr.	1989	Robin Romeo
1987	Marshall Holman	1990	Tish Johnson
1988	Brian Voss	1991	Leanne Barrette
1989–90	Amleto Monacelli	1992	Tish Johnson
1991	David Ozio	1993	Lisa Wagner
1992	Dave Ferraro		
1993	W.R. Williams, Jr.		

A bowling game is divided into 10 frames; the object of the game is to knock down all of the pins on the first or, if necessary, the second of the 2 rolls allowed in each frame. Each pin that is knocked down counts as 1 point. Knocking down all the pins with the first ball is called a strike and is scored as 10 points plus a bonus determined by the total points gained in the next 2 rolls. If a bowler should continue to roll only strikes throughout the game (a total of 12 attempts, be-cause 2 bonus tries are allowed after the final strike), the re-sult would be a rare "perfect game" of 300 points. If 2 deliver-ies are needed to knock down all of the pins in a frame, the outcome is called a spare. A bowler is then awarded 10 points plus a bonus of the score on the next roll. If a spare is made in the final frame, one extra roll is allowed, and the number of pins on that roll is added to the score. For a novice bowler, a score of 120 or so is considered good. A regular participant considers an average of 160 to 180 quite good. Top profes-sionals average more than 200.

History. Objects used for a game similar to bowling, which date from 5200 BC, were found in the tomb of a young Egyptian boy. In the 3d and 4th centuries, bowling in Europe was a religious ceremony; participants tried to hit the pin, or *kegel* (hence the word *kegling* for bowling), in order to be judged free of sin. The game of ninepins was taken to America by Dutch colonists in the 17th century. The introduction of the tenth pin to the game is popularly believed to be the result of an effort to circumvent laws against ninepins, which had been passed because of widespread gambling in the 1800s. An outdoor game for most of its history, indoor bowling be-came popular in the mid-19th century.

Organization. The American Bowling Congress (ABC; 1895) is the men's governing body for tenpins. The ABC standardized rules and the scoring method, and it also organized the first U.S. national bowling tournament, in 1901. Each year the ABC sponsors nationals in singles, doubles, and five-man team competition for its members, whose number exceeds 5 mil-lion. The Women's International Bowling Congress (WIBC) was founded in 1916 and has grown to 3.5 million members. The Professional Bowlers Association was organized in 1958 to promote exhibitions and arrange major tournaments. Interest in bowling, particularly in the United States, had its major spurt after World War II.

The introduction of the first automatic pinsetter in Brooklyn, N.Y., in 1952 was responsible for much of this growing popularity. Previously, pins were set by hand by young boys, and bowling alleys, as the establishments were called, often had poor reputations. The modern game, however, promoted in part by competition on television, is a booming family sport. There is virtually no age limit for the active bowler.

Outstanding Participants. Don CARTER, named Bowler of the Year six times, was the greatest of the post–World War II stars and a legendary figure in modern bowling. Dick WEBER and more-current standouts, such as Don Johnson, Earl ANTHONY, and Mark Roth, are almost as impressive. Ned Day and Andy Varipapa—the latter known for his trick bowling—were the best of the old-time stars. The most successful woman bowler was Marion LADEWIG, named Woman Bowler of the Year nine times between 1950 and 1963.   GERALD S. COUZENS

Bibliography: Allen, G., and Ritger, D., *Encyclopedia of Bowling Instruction*, 3 vols. (1982); Anthony, E., and Dawson, T., *Earl Anthony's Championship Bowling* (1983); Martin, J. L., and Tandy, R. E., *Bowling*, 3d ed. (1986); Weber, Dick, *Champion's Guide to Bowling* (1979).

Bowman, Isaiah   [boh'-muhn]

Isaiah Bowman, b. Waterloo, Ontario, Dec. 26, 1878, d. Jan. 6, 1950, was an American geographer and educator. He taught at Yale University from 1905 to 1915, during which time he led two expeditions to South America.

From 1915 to 1935, Bowman was director of the American Geographical Society and from 1935 to 1948 president of The Johns Hopkins University. Active in national and international geographic organizations, he also held several governmental advisory posts and wrote numerous books on geography and international relations.

Bowman, Sir William

Sir William Bowman, b. July 20, 1816, d. Mar. 29, 1892, was an English physician and anatomist who made important discoveries about the kidney and the eye.

In studying the detailed structure of the kidney, he discovered the membranous sac, now known as Bowman's capsule, and determined the kidney's filtering function in the production of urine.

Bowman also discovered the basement membrane of the cornea (Bowman's membrane) and explained the function of several components of the eye.

Bowne, Borden Parker   [bown]

Borden Parker Bowne, b. Leonardville, N.J., Jan. 14, 1847, d. Apr. 1, 1910, was an American philosopher and advocate of PERSONALISM. Chairman of the philosophy department and first graduate dean at Boston University, he emphasized conscious experience as the starting point of reflection.

The key to reality, Bowne said, is the thinking self that interacts with other selves in a world where ethical achievement is a primary goal. Ethical achievement and interaction among selves are possible because finite selves are free, creative manifestations of an Infinite Self (God) whose purposive will orders reality. Bowne's major systematic work is *Personalism* (1908).   ROBERT M. BAIRD

box elder

Box elder, or ash-leaved maple, *Acer negundo*, family Aceraceae, is a small to medium-sized deciduous tree widely distributed in the United States and Canada. Growing up to 21.3 m (70 ft) tall, this compound-leaved maple is quick growing and drought resistant. Its soft wood is used for boxes, pulpwood, and inexpensive furniture.

Pollen from stamens (bottom left) *of the male box elder,* A. negundo, *fertilizes pistils* (center) *of the female, yielding winged fruit.*

box turtle

The box turtle is any member of the reptile genus *Terrapene*, family Emydidae, and is found in the eastern and central United States, northern Mexico, and the Yucatán. Box turtles are small, generally less than 18 cm (7 in); all are terrestrial except for the Coahuilan box turtle, *T. coahuila*, which lives along water courses and is semiaquatic. The turtles eat a variety of foods, including mushrooms, insects, earthworms, slugs, snails, and blackberries. Both lobes of their lower shells have a common hinge that enables the turtles to close their shells tightly. Instances of box turtles living 40 to 50 years have been recorded, and a few exceptional individuals may live more than 100 years.

The eastern box turtle, *T. carolina*, ranges over much of the eastern United States. It is essentially a woodland species. The ornate box turtle, *T. ornata*, another common species, prefers more open regions and is found in the central United States from South Dakota to south Texas. It has a more flattened upper shell, or carapace, than the eastern box turtle.   JONATHAN CAMPBELL

Bibliography: Cobb, Jo, *A Complete Introduction to Turtles and Terrapins* (1987); Obst, Fritz J., *Turtles, Tortoises and Terrapins* (1986).

boxer

The boxer, a muscular dog, is named for its habit of boxing with its front paws during a fight. It is used as a guide dog for the blind and by police and security guards.

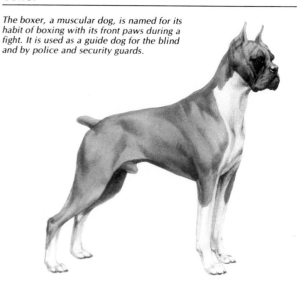

The boxer is a medium-size, compact but powerful dog with a distinctive head; cropped ears and a docked tail are required for show purposes. It combines courage and stamina with intelligence, fearlessness, agility, and strength. The boxer measures approximately 53.3 to 63.5 cm (21 to 25 in) high at the shoulder and weighs about 29.5 kg (65 lb) with little or no trace of fat. The short, shiny, smooth coat is red or fawn, of varying shades, or brindle with white markings on the feet, chest, and head.

First bred in Germany during the 19th century, the boxer is a relative of all the bulldog breeds. Virtually unknown before World War II, by the mid-1950s the breed was among the most popular. Although still well known, it is no longer as popular. As were all dogs of the bulldog family, the predecessors of the modern boxer were used for dog fighting and bull-baiting. When these sports were outlawed in the 19th century, the boxer was bred in Germany as a police dog.

Bibliography: Gordon, J. F., *All about the Boxer* (1988); McFadden, Billie, *The New Boxer* (1989); Meyer, Lorraine, *Your Boxer* (1973).

Boxer Uprising

The Boxer Uprising (also known as the Boxer Rebellion) was a violent movement by the Chinese people in 1898–1900 to rid their country of foreigners and foreign influences. It was spearheaded by militia units in the north called Yihequan (*I-ho Ch'üan*) (''righteous harmony fists''); this name resulted in the label *Boxers* in the foreign press.

Encouraged by Empress Dowager Cixi (Tz'u-hsi), the Boxers rampaged throughout the land, killing foreigners as well as Christian Chinese and other Chinese with ties to foreigners. The climax came when an international force of British, French, German, Japanese, Russian, and U.S. troops entered Beijing (Peking) in August 1900 to lift the siege of the foreign legations there. The imperial court fled to Xi'an (Sian). Under the subsequent protocol of September 1901, China was forced to pay a punitive indemnity and to yield to several new foreign demands, notably the right to station troops in Beijing at the legations and along the route to the sea.

Bibliography: Fairbank, J. K., *The Great Chinese Revolution* (1987); Purcell, V. W. W. S., *The Boxer Uprising: A Background Study* (1963).

boxfish

The boxfish, family Ostraciidae, is a marine fish so named because of the bony, armorlike carapace that encases its body. Because of the carapace, boxfishes swim slowly, and swimming movements are restricted to the back (caudal) and pectoral fins (they lack pelvic fins). Trunkfish and cowfish are

species of boxfish. The largest species of boxfish grow to lengths of about 50 cm (20 in).

Boxfishes inhabit tropical and subtropical coastal marine waters throughout the world, and some species are among the most beautifully colored of all fishes.   EDWARD O. WILEY

boxing

Boxing, often called ''the manly art of self-defense,'' is a sport in which two competitors try to hit each other with their glove-encased fists while trying to avoid each other's blows. The competition is divided into a specified number of rounds, usually 3 minutes long, with 1-minute rest periods between rounds.

Although amateur boxing is widespread, professional boxing has flourished on an even grander scale since the early 18th century.

Rules. Amateur fights consist of 3 or sometimes 5 rounds. Professional fights range from 4 to 15 rounds. The recognized length of championship fights is 12 rounds. In most countries, professional boxing is the more popular version, but the rules vary because there is no true governing body. Even in the United States, boxing regulations vary from state to state.

In all boxing, however, winners are determined either by a decision of the judges (who keep points or round victors on a scorecard as the fight progresses), the referee, or both. The winner also may be decided by a knockout, in which one rival is sent to the floor by a punch and cannot get up within 10 seconds. A doctor or referee can declare the boxer injured or defenseless even if there is no knockdown. A tied or even match is ruled a draw.

The boxing ring is actually a square, 12 to 20 ft (3.7 to 6.1 m) on each side and enclosed on each side by three or four ropes. Gloves have been worn by boxers as a general practice since 1892. Gloves are made of leather, have no finger holes except for the thumb, and weigh from 8 oz (227 g) for amateur bouts down to 6 oz (170 g) for professional and all title bouts.

Early History. Boxing originated when a person first lifted a fist against another in play. Different eras of the sport have been distinguished by the use or nonuse of fist coverings. The ancient Greeks believed fistfighting was one of the games played by the gods on Olympus; thus it became part of the Olympic Games in about 688 BC. Homer has a reference to boxing in the *Iliad*. During Roman times the sport began to thrive on a wide scale. Boxers fought with leather bands around their fists for protection and sometimes wore metal-filled, leather hand coverings called cesti, resulting in bloody, often duel-to-death, battles. Boxing diminished after

(Left) *Muhammad Ali scores with a left hook to the head of Joe Frazier during their 1975 bout, dubbed the ''Thrilla in Manila.'' The two heavyweights met three times; Frazier took a close decision in the first bout, and Ali won the next two.* (Below) *John L. Sullivan* (right) *met Jake Kilrain in 1889 to determine the world's heavyweight championship. The fight was staged at a secret ring site in Mississippi because bare-fisted prizefights were illegal in all 38 states. The grueling match, which Sullivan won by a knockout after 2 hr 16 min, was the last bare-knuckle title bout sanctioned by ring authorities.*

(Left to right) Jack Johnson, the first black fighter to hold the modern heavyweight championship, lost his crown in 1915 to Jess Willard in a match he claimed to have thrown. Jack Dempsey, a savage brawling champion, attracted the first million-dollar gate in the sport's history. Joe Louis, who held the championship from 1937 to 1949, defended his title 25 times, a record that still stands. Rocky Marciano, who won the title from "Jersey Joe" Walcott in 1952, was the only professional heavyweight champion to retire without a defeat.

the fall of Rome. It was revived in the 18th century in England and became especially popular during the championship reign of James Figg, who held the heavyweight title from 1719 through 1730. Boxing became a workingman's sport during the Industrial Revolution as prizefights attracted participants and spectators from the working class. Organization was minimal at first, and the bouts resembled street fights.

The second heavyweight champion, Jack Broughton of England, drew his own set of rules for his own fights, and these were recognized in 1743. They outlawed some of the gorier aspects that the sport had acquired, such as hitting below the beltline. Instead of a ring of spectators—hence, the name ring—Broughton insisted upon a squared-off area. His rules governed what is known as the "bareknuckle era."

Modern Era. In 1866 the marquess of Queensberry gave his support to a new set of rules, which were named in his honor. These rules limited the number of 3-minute rounds, eliminated gouging and wrestling, and made the use of gloves mandatory. Bareknuckle bouts did not cease immediately but did begin to decline. A new era dawned in 1892, when James J. CORBETT defeated the last of the great bare-fisted fighters, John L. SULLIVAN, under the new rules.

With the growing popularity of boxing, especially in the United States, weight classes other than the unlimited heavyweights emerged. These classes became popular as world championships were held at the new weights. Currently, there

are eight major professional divisions: flyweight (up to 112 lb/50.8 kg); bantamweight (118 lb/53.5 kg); featherweight (126 lb/57.2 kg); lightweight (135 lb/61.2 kg); welterweight (147 lb/66.7 kg); middleweight (160 lb/72.6 kg); light heavyweight (175 lb/79.4 kg); and heavyweight (unlimited). In recent years there has been some recognition of junior weights, or between-weights, such as junior lightweight and cruiserweight.

Because of its violent nature and its identification with betting, boxing has had a controversial history. Despite periodic efforts to outlaw the sport—including a condemnation by the American Medical Association in 1984—boxers are internationally famous, particularly heavyweight champions, most of whom, in this century, have come from the United States. Among the best heavyweights have been Muhammad ALI, Jack DEMPSEY, Jack JOHNSON, Joe LOUIS, Rocky MARCIANO, Gene TUNNEY, Corbett, and Sullivan. Outstanding champions in the lighter weights have included Benny Leonard, Mickey WALKER, Barney Ross, Henry ARMSTRONG, and Sugar Ray ROBINSON. Louis, Marciano, and Ali benefited greatly—both in popularity and financially—from the promotion of televised fights.

Asia and Latin America have produced many champions in recent years in the lower weights; Russia, Cuba, and Eastern Europe have done very well in the Olympics.   MICHAEL KATZ

Bibliography: Andre, S., and Fleisher, N., *A Pictorial History of Boxing*, rev. ed. (1993); Ashe, A. R., Jr., *A Hard Road to Glory—Boxing* (1993); Liebling, A. J., *A Neutral Corner* (1992) and *The Sweet Science* (1951; repr. 1991); Mullan, H., *Great Book of Boxing* (1990); Sammons, J. T., *Beyond the Ring* (1987); Suster, G., *Champions of the Ring* (1993).

HEAVYWEIGHT BOXING CHAMPIONS

1882–92	John L. Sullivan	1959–60	Ingemar Johansson
1892–97	James J. Corbett	1960–62	Floyd Patterson
1897–99	Bob Fitzsimmons	1962–64	Sonny Liston
1899–1905	James J. Jeffries	1964–67	Muhammad Ali
1905–06	Marvin Hart	1965–67	Ernie Terrell*
1906–08	Tommy Burns	1968–70	Jimmy Ellis*
1908–15	Jack Johnson	1968–73	Joe Frazier
1915–19	Jess Willard	1973–74	George Foreman
1919–26	Jack Dempsey	1974–78	Muhammad Ali
1926–28	Gene Tunney	1978	Leon Spinks*
1928–30	None	1978	Ken Norton+
1930–32	Max Schmeling	1978–79	Muhammad Ali*
1932–33	Jack Sharkey	1978–85	Larry Holmes
1933–34	Primo Carnera	1985–86	Michael Spinks
1934–35	Max Baer	1986–90	Mike Tyson
1935–37	James J. Braddock	1990	Buster Douglas
1937–49	Joe Louis	1990–92	Evander Holyfield
1949–51	Ezzard Charles	1992–93	Riddick Bowe
1951–52	Joe Walcott	1993–94	Evander Holyfield
1952–56	Rocky Marciano	1994	Michael Moorer
1956–59	Floyd Patterson	1994–	George Foreman

NOTE: Champions not universally recognized are designated * (World Boxing Association title) or + (World Boxing Council title). First, Holmes was WBC champion, then (1983) International Boxing Federation champion. From 1979 to the mid-1980s there were various titleholders, but Holmes, Spinks, and Tyson were considered by most experts to have the most legitimate claims to the championship.

Sugar Ray Robinson (left) won the middleweight championship on five different occasions. In 1938, Henry Armstrong (right) simultaneously held championships in three divisions—featherweight, lightweight, and middleweight—a feat not equaled before or since.

Boxing Day

Boxing Day is an English holiday that falls on the first weekday after Christmas. The name was derived from the boxed Christmas presents given by householders to their servants and to the providers of such services as postal delivery and trash collection—thanking them for their work.

boxwood

Boxwoods, *Buxus*, are any of several ornamental, evergreen shrubs or small trees in the box family, Buxaceae. They are used for hedges and in topiary gardens. The flowers are insignificant; the leaves are attractive, small, and leathery. The English use the term *box* rather than *boxwood*. Native to southern Europe, northern Africa, and western Asia, *Buxus sempervirens* was brought by early settlers from Europe to American colonial gardens. In the mid-19th century, *Buxus microphylla* was brought to America from Japan. The numerous varieties of the two species differ mainly in their size and hardiness during cold winters and warm summers. The wood's fine-grain, smooth texture and weight make it an ideal surface for wood engraving.   JANE PHILPOTT

The common boxwood, B. sempervirens, *a densely foliated, evergreen shrub used as hedging, is often pruned into ornamental shapes.*

Boy Scouts: see SCOUTING.

boyars   [boh-yahrz']

In medieval Russia the boyars formed the upper level of society and of state administration. A boyar council advised the grand prince of Kiev on all important matters of state. During the 15th and 16th centuries the boyars of Moscow formed a closed aristocratic caste that surrounded the throne, although IVAN IV made a determined effort to break their influence. During the so-called TIME OF TROUBLES (1605–13), the social and political importance of the boyars declined. PETER I abolished the rank of boyar and made state service the sole means of attaining a high position in the bureaucracy.

Boyce, William

William Boyce, b. 1710, d. Feb. 7, 1779, was an English composer and organist. He was influential in the transition from baroque to classical style and the compiler of a collection of English choral music that by itself would have ensured his fame. Boyce served as choir singer and then as organist in important London churches, including Oxford Chapel in Cavendish Square, St. Michael's in Cornhill, and the Chapel Royal. He was Master of the King's Music from 1755.

Troubled by increasing deafness after 1768, Boyce gave up most of his positions and devoted himself to compiling and publishing the volumes of *Cathedral Music,* a project originally begun by his teacher Maurice Greene. This collection was important in preserving the music of British composers of the preceding two centuries, in furnishing the repertory of English choirs, and in establishing the British choral tradition.

Boyce composed symphonies, chamber music, anthems, services, and music for the stage.   FARLEY K. HUTCHINS

boycott

A boycott is a concerted action to isolate economically or socially an individual, group, or nation in order to express disapproval or to coerce change. It takes its name from Charles Boycott, an English estate manager, whose rent-collection tactics in the 1880s so enraged Irish tenants that they refused to harvest crops for him. In the United States the boycott is most often used in labor disputes; businesses and consumers, however, also use it in efforts to reduce prices or to protest against a company or nation's policies.

Labor boycotts fall into two basic categories. A primary boycott puts pressure directly on the employer with whom a union is engaged in dispute. The most common form of primary boycott is the STRIKE. In a secondary boycott the pressure is on an employer or employees who are not immediate parties to a dispute. The secondary boycott is prohibited in the United States under the Labor-Management Relations Act. A boycott may be accompanied by a BLACKLIST of persons or companies to be discriminated against. A well-known modern boycott was the 7-year United Farm Workers' boycott of grapes and lettuce produced by California growers.

The boycott is also used in international relations and is often confused with an EMBARGO, which bans the export of goods to a foreign country. Examples of international boycotts are the refusal by Americans to buy British goods after the STAMP ACT of 1765, and the refusal of the Chinese to buy U.S. goods in 1905 because of U.S. immigration policies excluding Chinese. The Arab League's Special Bureau for Boycotting Israel maintains a list of foreign companies dealing with Israel with which Arab trade is forbidden.

The use of the boycott as a tactic in international affairs can be noneconomic. In 1980 the United States and other countries refused to participate in the Moscow Olympics in protest against the Soviet invasion of Afghanistan. The Soviet-bloc countries boycotted the 1984 Games in Los Angeles.

Bibliography: Shister, Joseph, et al., *Public Policy and Collective Bargaining* (1962; repr. 1982).

Boyd, Belle

Belle Boyd, b. Martinsburg, Va., May 9, 1843, d. June 11, 1900, was a Confederate spy in the U.S. Civil War who operated in the Shenandoah Valley of Virginia. Jailed twice but freed for lack of evidence, she went to England in 1864, reportedly to deliver messages to Confederate agents there. In 1866 she began acting, appearing in New York in 1868.

Boyd-Orr, John, 1st Baron Boyd-Orr of Brechin Mearn   [bree'-kin mahrn]

John Boyd-Orr, b. Sept. 23, 1880, d. June 25, 1971, was a British nutritionist, agricultural scientist, writer, and teacher. He wrote *Food, Health, and Income* (1936) and made important contributions to the science of nutrition and the management of world food supply problems. As the first director general of the United Nations Food and Agricultural Organization (1945–48), he formulated rationing programs to deal with famine after World War II, for which he won the Nobel Peace Prize in 1949. An advocate of world government, Boyd-Orr was president of the World Federalist Movement.

Boyden, Seth

A typical ingenious Yankee, Seth Boyden, b. Foxborough, Mass., Nov. 18, 1788, d. Mar. 31, 1870, was inventive in many areas. The son of a Massachusetts machine-shop operator, he devised machines for making nails and cutting files while still in his teens. In 1819 he adapted a European process for making patent leather and established the industry in America. In 1826, Boyden invented a method for casting steel; he also built locomotives and steam engines and equipped them with his automatic speed governor. Among his other contributions were a hat-forming machine and an imitation-gold alloy.

Boye, Karin

Karin Maria Boye, b. Oct. 26, 1900, d. Apr. 24, 1941, was one of the first well-known women poets in Sweden. Her early poems are characterized by disciplined simplicity and the influence of psychoanalytic theory. The richly symbolic collection of poems *För Trädets Skull* (For Love of the Tree, 1935) and the posthumous *De Sju Dödssynderna* (Seven Deadly Sins, 1941) are dominated by the central image of a regenerating green tree, signifying the reconciliation of life and death. Boye's best-known novel is *Kallocain* (1940; Eng. trans., 1966), a prophetic warning about life under totalitarianism. She commited suicide.   VIRPI ZUCK

Boyer, Charles   [bwah-yay']

A French screen actor known for his velvet voice, Charles Boyer, b. Aug. 28, 1899, d. Aug. 26, 1978, made his international reputation in the lushly romantic *Mayerling* (1936). He took the leads in such Hollywood films as *The Garden of Allah* (1936), *Tovarich* (1937), *Conquest* (1937), *Algiers* (1938), *Love Affair* (1939), *All This and Heaven Too* (1940), and *Gaslight* (1944). Two of his best roles were in the French films *The Earrings of Madame de . . .* (1952) and *Stavisky* (1974).

Boyer, Jean Pierre   [bwah-yay']

Jean Pierre Boyer, b. 1776, d. July 9, 1850, was president of the Haitian republic from 1818 to 1843. A free mulatto, he fought with Haitian revolutionary forces in 1792. After a period in France, he returned (1802) with the French army of Charles Leclerc and helped found (1807) the republic in the south. Succeeding Alexandre PÉTION as president, he gained control of northern Haiti in 1820 and conquered Santo Domingo in 1822. His dealings with France and his forced-labor practices cost him popularity, and he was overthrown in 1843.

Boyle, Kay

The American writer Kay Boyle, b. Saint Paul, Minn., Feb. 19, 1902, d. Dec. 27, 1992, was best known for her short stories, many of them written in France in the 1920s and '30s and in Germany, where Boyle was a journalist in the years following World War II. The collection *Fifty Stories* (1980) best summarizes her work over those years. Much of Boyle's writing reflects her political concerns; for example, the novel *The Underground Woman* (1975) draws on her experiences as a teacher at San Francisco State College during the 1960s, years of antiwar protests in which she participated. In 1968 she published the joint autobiography *Being Geniuses Together* (repr. 1984), which combines the Paris memoirs of the publisher Robert McAlmon with her own recollections of France between the wars. *Words That Must Somehow Be Said: The Selected Essays of Kay Boyle, 1927–84* was published in 1985.

Bibliography: Spanier, S. W., *Kay Boyle* (1986).

Boyle, Robert

The English natural philosopher and chemist Robert Boyle, b. Jan. 25, 1627, d. Dec. 30, 1691, made important contributions to experimental chemistry and is known for his ideal-GAS LAW, subsequently termed Boyle's law. Boyle was born into an affluent English aristocratic family and received a conventional gentleman's education. He became interested in medicine and the new science of Galileo and studied chemistry. Boyle was a founder and an influential fellow of the ROYAL SOCIETY, was continuously active in scientific affairs, and wrote prolifically on science, philosophy, and theology.

Boyle's earliest publication was on the physical properties of air, from which he derived his law that the volume of a given amount of a gas varies inversely with pressure. His work in chemistry was aimed at establishing it as a rational theoretical science on the basis of a mechanistic theory of matter. Boyle was a skillful experimenter who insisted that experimentation was an essential part of scientific proof, an approach that influenced Sir Isaac NEWTON and the methodology of many later scientists.   NICHOLAS H. CLULEE

Robert Boyle, a 17th-century English natural philosopher, developed the well-known theory of gases called Boyle's law (1662), which states that the volume of a gas varies inversely with pressure. Boyle's mechanistic theory of nature (based on particles and their motion) helped displace the older Aristotelian view.

Bibliography: Alexander, P., *Ideas, Qualities, and Corpuscles* (1985); Boas, M., *Robert Boyle and 17th-Century Chemistry* (1958; repr. 1968); Harwood, J., ed., *The Early Essays and Ethics of Robert Boyle* (1991).

Boyne, Battle of the

On July 11, 1690, on the banks of the River Boyne near Drogheda, in Ireland, the deposed Roman Catholic king JAMES II of England was defeated by the army of his Protestant successor, WILLIAM III.

Boys & Girls Clubs of America

The Boys & Girls Clubs of America (known as Boys Clubs of America until 1990) is a national (including Puerto Rico and the U.S. Virgin Islands) federation of clubs that provide after-school sports, recreations, vocational training, and job-finding skills to boys and girls primarily in urban areas. The movement began in 1860 with the founding of a club in Hartford, Conn., and in 1906 a national organization was formed. Today about 1,460 clubs exist, each with a professional staff. Total membership is about 1.8 million youths.

Boys Town

Boys Town, located near Omaha, Nebr., is a community for neglected, abused, and abandoned boys and (since 1979) girls. It was founded (1917) by Father Edward Joseph FLANAGAN, who started with five youngsters in an old, rented house and, over the years, built a 526-ha (1,300-acre) community that was incorporated as a village in 1936. Self-governing and nonsectarian, Boys Town is supported in part by voluntary contributions. The Omaha Boys Town cares for more than 500 boys and girls, who live in home settings and have available a range of educational facilities and health and counseling services. Boys Town also operates programs in several other states.

boysenberry

The boysenberry, *Rubus ursinus loganobaccus*, family Rosaceae, is a thorny, trailing shrub that is cultivated for its tart reddish black fruit. Closely related to the BLACKBERRY, though the fruit is slightly larger, it is grown primarily in the Pacific Coast region of the United States.

Bozeman Trail

First traveled by John M. Bozeman in 1863–65 as a shorter route to the gold fields in southwestern Montana, the Bozeman Trail followed the OREGON TRAIL from Julesburg, Colo., to southeastern Wyoming, where it branched northward around the Big Horn Mountains and west to Bozeman and Virginia City. The U.S. Army fortified the trail, but the Sioux Indians, under Chief RED CLOUD, fought this intrusion into their land, and in 1866 they annihilated a party of 82 soldiers under Capt. William J. Fetterman. Because of this resistance and a more direct route offered by the Union Pacific Railroad, the government had abandoned the trail by 1868.   ELLIOTT WEST

Bibliography: Hebard, G. R., and Brininstool, E. A., *The Bozeman Trail* (1922; repr. 1990); Murray, Robert A., *The Bozeman Trail* (1988).

Brabant, Duchy of   [brah-bahnt']

The Duchy of Brabant in the Low Countries was a wealthy agricultural and manufacturing province from the 11th to the 18th century, around which the modern country of BELGIUM was formed. It included the modern Belgian provinces of Brabant and Antwerp as well as the Dutch province of North Brabant.

The duchy was created in the early 12th century from the county of Leuven (French: Louvain) and thereafter expanded into the region lying between the Scheldt and Meuse rivers and extending to the south of Brussels. The powerful towns, in alliance with the nobility, won a charter of rights called the Joyous Entry (*Blijde Inkomst*) from the ruling house in 1356. In 1430 the duchy became a possession of the French ducal house of BURGUNDY. Under the Burgundian rulers, whose dynasty merged with the HABSBURGS in 1482, Brabant became the dominant province of the Netherlands. The DUTCH REVOLT against the Spanish Habsburgs in 1568 led to the loss of the northern Brabant to the Dutch Republic, while the south remained under Habsburg rule. In the 18th century, Brabant was the center of resistance to the Austrian Habsburgs, and in 1830 it led the revolt against the Dutch that produced an independent Belgium.   HERBERT H. ROWEN

brachiopod   [brak'-ee-oh-pahd]

Brachiopods are bivalved marine invertebrates that constitute a separate phylum, Brachiopoda. Brachiopods were prominent SHELLFISH in many continental-shelf sea environments for about 250 million years, from the Ordovician into the Permian. In the Cambrian, some were prominent in nearshore environments. Since the end of the Paleozoic, clams appear to have been the prominent marine benthic bivalved animal in environments previously inhabited by brachiopods. Today, brachiopods are found in many habitats in nearly all of the shelf seas. Brachiopod SHELLS—known as lamp shells because they resemble ancient Roman oil lamps—are frequently collected. In some places, brachiopods are used for food.

The two shells of a brachiopod, unlike those of a clam, are dissimilar. About two-thirds of the shell interior is occupied by a tentacle-bearing arm. This organ functions essentially as a pump, bringing in oxygenated water and food particles and generating currents that take away wastes. Most brachiopods are attached by a fleshy, muscular stalk to the sea floor for most, if not all, of their life. The body cavity is hollow, containing a rudimentary digestive system and some kidneylike organs. Brachiopods lack discrete respiratory and circulatory systems.

A brachiopod (A) is an ancient bivalve marine animal that still exists today. It has an inner structure (B) that includes a lophophore (1), with ciliated tentacles used for finding food; two shells (2); a digestive gland (3); a mouth (4); and a stalk (5), which grips rocks or burrows. The brachiopod genus Lingula (C), which resembles its fossil ancestor of 500 million years ago, burrows a hole in a mud flat. It contracts its stalk when alarmed (D).

All brachiopods, except for members of the genus *Lingula*, live on the sea floor. As bottom dwellers they are vulnerable to rapid rates of sedimentation and to predation. They have proved valuable as a means of dating rocks. Also, paleontologists working with Paleozoic rocks have used them to establish the depth of the ancient sea floor during different periods; different types appear to have been distributed in bands paralleling ancient shorelines, and the bands of particular types of brachiopods can be correlated with differing sea-floor depths.   WILLIAM B. N. BERRY

Bibliography: Rudwick, M. J., *Living and Fossil Brachiopods* (1970).

Brachiosaurus   [brak'-ee-oh-sohr-uhs]

One of the largest of the sauropod DINOSAURS, *Brachiosaurus* (Greek: *brachion*, "arm"; *sauros*, "lizard") was about 21 m (70 ft) long, 12 m (40 ft) high, and weighed an estimated 78 metric tons (more than 170,000 lb). It is believed to have been amphibious, seeking deep waters to avoid predators and to feed on water plants. Specimens were first found in Upper JURASSIC rocks in Colorado, and are now also known from Europe and Africa. As in other sauropods, the head was relatively small; the neck, however, was much longer and the tail was shorter than is usual in this suborder. The forelimbs were unusually long, as the name suggests. A spectacular articulated skeleton from Tanzania is on exhibit at the Berlin Museum.   WANN LANGSTON, JR.

Bibliography: Colbert, E. H., *Dinosaurs: An Illustrated History* (1986).

Brachiosaurus, one of the largest dinosaurs, lived from 140 to 165 million years ago. Much larger than the modern African elephant, this dinosaur measured about 21 m (70 ft) long and 12 m (40 ft) high. The Brachiosaurus probably lived mainly in water and fed on plants.

bracken

Bracken, also called brake, *Pteridium aquilinum*, family Polypodiaceae, is a terrestrial fern with coarse, triangular fronds. Distributed worldwide, bracken tolerates a wide variety of environmental conditions. It ranges in height from 1 m (3.3 ft) to more than 5 m (16.4 ft). The fronds are poisonous to livestock if consumed for long periods.

Bracken, John

John Bracken, b. Ellisville, Ontario, June 22, 1883, d. Mar. 18, 1969, was a Canadian politician who was premier of Manitoba from 1922 to 1943 and then leader of the national Progressive Conservative party until 1948. In Manitoba, where he headed the provincial Farmers' Progressive party, Bracken's administration was known for economy and for faithfulness to its rural supporters. Chosen national party leader at the Progressive Conservatives' 1943 convention, Bracken served in Canada's House of Commons from 1945 to 1949.

bracket fungus

The bracket fungus comprises about 1,000 species in the family Polyporacae; nearly 50 percent are of the genus *Polyporus*.

The basidiocarps, or fruiting bodies, are generally umbrella- or bracket-shaped. They may grow to 50 cm (20 in) or more in diameter and cause losses in forestry by spoiling or killing trees. *Merulius lacrymans*, a dry-rot fungus, attacks structural timbers and often causes great destruction to buildings.

Bracquemond, Félix   [brahk-mohn', fay-leeks']

Félix Braquemond, 1833-1914, was a French graphic artist who produced more than 900 prints in a variety of techniques. He is best known for his lively animal prints, although his etched portraits of notable fellow Parisians are of the same high quality. Bracquemond discovered (1856) the prints of the Japanese artist Hokusai and popularized them among such friends as Edgar Degas and Édouard Manet.

Bibliography: Weisberg, G. P., *The Etching Renaissance in France* (1971).

Bradbury, Ray

Ray Bradbury, a celebrated American writer of science fiction and fantasy, began his career by submitting stories to pulp magazines in the 1940s. Bradbury's works, several of which have been adapted for motion pictures, often comment on the dehumanizing influence of a machine-dominated society.

A science fiction writer, Ray Bradbury, b. Waukegan, Ill., Aug. 22, 1920, is recognized as an innovator in that genre. *The Martian Chronicles* (1950), *The Illustrated Man* (1951; film, 1969), and *Something Wicked This Way Comes* (1962; film, 1983) are classic evocations of one of his principal themes: the beautiful but dangerous power of the imagination. His

Fahrenheit 451 (1953; film, 1966) is essentially a novel of social criticism, and *Dandelion Wine* (1957) is a nostalgic return to a small American town in the 1920s. Bradbury's collected short stories were published in 1980. He has also written stage and screenplays, verse, and children's literature.

Bibliography: Mogen, David, *Ray Bradbury* (1986).

Braddock, Edward

Gen. Edward Braddock, b. 1695, d. July 13, 1755, was a British commander whose unexpected defeat near the Forks of the Ohio in 1755 raised doubts about the effectiveness of British regulars in American warfare. He had been an officer in the Coldstream Guards from 1710 to 1753; in 1754, after the outbreak of fighting between British colonists and the French, he was promoted to general and commander in chief for North America.

Proceeding to Virginia, Braddock approved a plan that involved four offensives, including an advance led by himself westward through mountainous wilderness to capture FORT DUQUESNE. Although hampered by colonial reluctance and inadequate Indian scouts, Braddock set his army of regulars and provincials in motion in June 1755. He was not the stupid Redcoat of later American tradition and did take precautions against surprise, but he lacked full appreciation of the intricacies of wilderness warfare. On July 9, 1755, only 13 km (8 mi) from the objective, Braddock's advance force suddenly encountered and was routed by a force from Fort Duquesne, the general himself receiving a mortal wound. Much of the blame for the bloody debacle rests on Braddock's subordinates, who failed to react properly when the fighting began.

DOUGLAS EDWARD LEACH

Bibliography: Kopperman, Paul E., *Braddock at the Monongahela* (1977); McCardell, Lee, *Ill-Starred General* (1958).

See also: FRENCH AND INDIAN WARS.

Bradford   (city)

Bradford (1984 est. pop., 464,400) is an industrial city in northern England just west of Leeds in West Yorkshire. A leading producer of woolen fabrics since the Middle Ages, the city now manufactures synthetic fabrics, machinery, and automobiles as well. A large, raw wool market is also located there. The 15th-century church of Saint Peter is well known, as is the University of Bradford (1966).

Bradford was an important market town during the Middle Ages, and in 1798 its growth was assured by the introduction of one of the first steam-powered mills in England, which was used in the textile industry.

Bradford   (family)

The Bradfords were a family of printers in colonial New York and Philadelphia. **William Bradford**, b. Leicestershire, England, May 20, 1663, d. New York City, May 23, 1752, the founder of the family interest, immigrated to Philadelphia in 1685, where he became Pennsylvania's first printer. He weathered intermittent governmental suppression until 1693, when he became crown printer in New York. There he printed the first record of American legislative proceedings (1695), New York colony's first paper currency (1709), and its first newspaper (1725).

His son, **Andrew Bradford**, b. Philadelphia, 1686, d. Nov. 24, 1742, learned the trade in his father's New York shop. In 1712 he established his own press in Philadelphia and, in 1719, Pennsylvania's first newspaper, the *American Weekly Mercury*, which rivaled Benjamin Franklin's *Gazette*. His short-lived *American Magazine* (1741) is considered the first colonial magazine.

Andrew's nephew, **William Bradford**, b. New York City, Jan. 19, 1721, d. Sept. 25, 1791, was known as the patriot printer. His *Pennsylvania Journal, or Weekly Advertiser* (founded 1742), criticized the 1765 Stamp Act and urged unification of the colonies. William also ran a bookstore, a coffee house, an insurance company, and a very successful press.

William's son, **Thomas Bradford**, b. Philadelphia, May 4,

1745, d. May 7, 1838, edited the *Pennsylvania Journal* with his father until 1778, when he assumed full control. He founded (1797) the *Merchants' Daily Advertiser*, an early financial bulletin. In 1798 its name became the *True American*, and it introduced the nation's first literary supplement.

Bibliography: Jones, Horatio, *Andrew Bradford, Founder of the Newspaper Press in the Middle States of America* (1869; repr. 1970); Levy, Leonard W., *The Legacy of Suppression: Freedom of Speech and Press in Early American History* (1960); Schlesinger, Arthur M., *Prelude to Independence: The Newspaper War on Britain* (1957); Wallace, John W., *An Old Philadelphian: Colonel William Bradford* (1884); Winterich, John T., *Early American Books and Printing* (1935); Wroth, Laurence C., *The Colonial Printer*, 2d ed. (1938).

Bradford, Gamaliel   [gam'-uh-leel]

Gamaliel Bradford, b. Boston, Oct. 9, 1863, d. Apr. 11, 1932, was a biographer and writer best known for his "psychographs," short, montagelike sketches of historical figures that sought to reveal their inner lives. *Types of American Character* (1895), *Lee, the American* (1912), *Portraits of Women* (1916), and *Damaged Souls* (1923) were representative of 11 such volumes. As a poet, novelist, and playwright, Bradford was less successful. *The Journal of Gamaliel Bradford* (1933), edited by Van Wyck Brooks, and Bradford's *Letters, 1918–1931* (1934) were published posthumously.   F. M. PAULSEN

Bradford, William

William Bradford, b. August 1590, d. May 9 or 19, 1657, was one of the leaders of the PILGRIMS who established PLYMOUTH COLONY. He was its governor for more than 30 years. His *History of Plymouth Plantation, 1620–1647*, first printed in full in 1856, is a minor classic, reflecting the unusual qualities of the man and the values of the small group of English separatists who became known as Pilgrims.

Bradford was born in Austerfield, Yorkshire, the son of a yeoman farmer. He was self-taught. As a young man, he joined Puritan groups that met illegally in nearby Scrooby and was a member of that congregation when it separated from the Church of England in 1606. Bradford was among the 125 Scrooby separatists who sought (1608) sanctuary in Holland.

When the congregation decided (1617) to seek refuge in America, Bradford took major responsibility for arranging the details of the emigration. The term *Pilgrim* is derived from his description of himself and his coreligionists as they left Holland (July 22, 1620) for Southampton, where they joined another group of English separatists on the MAYFLOWER. Bradford was one of about a dozen original Scrooby church members who sailed for America on the *Mayflower*.

When John CARVER, Plymouth Colony's first governor, died suddenly in April 1621, Bradford was unanimously elected to replace him. He was reelected 30 times. In 1640, Bradford and the group of original settlers known as the "old comers" turned over to the colony the proprietary rights to its lands, which had been granted (1630) to him by the Warwick Patent and then shared by him with the old comers.

During the period of his governorship, and especially during the first few years, Bradford provided the strong, steady leadership that kept the tiny community alive. He strove to sustain the religious ideals of the founders and to keep the colony's settlements compact and separate from the larger neighboring colonies.   OSCAR ZEICHNER

Bibliography: Bradford, William, *Of Plymouth Plantation, 1620–1647*, ed. by S. E. Morison (1952); Langdon, G. D., Jr., *Pilgrim Colony: A History of New Plymouth, 1620–1691* (1966); Smith, Bradford, *Bradford of Plymouth* (1951); Westbrook, Perry D., *William Bradford* (1978).

Bradlee, Benjamin C.

Benjamin Crowninshield Bradlee, b. Boston, Aug. 26, 1921, achieved prominence when the WASHINGTON POST, under his editorship, helped expose the Watergate scandals. He began his career as a reporter for the *Post* (1948–51). From 1953 to 1965 he was a European correspondent, Washington reporter, and Washington bureau chief for *Newsweek*. Bradlee returned to the *Post* in 1965 as managing editor and became executive editor in 1968. He wrote *That Special Grace* (1964) and *Conversations with Kennedy* (1975; repr. 1984).   MICHAEL EMERY

Bradley, A. C.

Andrew Cecil Bradley, b. Mar. 26, 1851, d. Sept. 2, 1935, was among the foremost Shakespearean critics of the early 20th century. The younger brother of the philosopher F. H. Bradley, he was professor of poetry (1901–06) at Oxford. His most famous work is *Shakespearean Tragedy* (1904). In his analysis Bradley asserted that tragic character was the crucial element of the drama. Tragic poetry expressed the redemptive value of each character's suffering. Yet Bradley has been criticized for analyzing the plays' characters as if they were actual people. His *Oxford Lectures on Poetry* (1909) influenced much subsequent literary criticism.   CHARLES CANTALUPO

Bibliography: Cooke, Katherine, *A. C. Bradley and His Influence in Twentieth-Century Shakespeare Criticism* (1972).

Bradley, Bill

William Warren Bradley, b. Crystal City, Mo., July 28, 1943, is a former basketball player who was elected Democratic senator from New Jersey in 1978. Bradley rose to fame as a 6-ft 5-in (1-m 96-cm) All-American forward at Princeton University (1961–65), where he became one of the highest scorers in collegiate history (2,503 points; 30.1 per game) and won the 1965 Sullivan Award as the nation's outstanding amateur athlete. He also captained the 1964 U.S. Olympic basketball team, which won a gold medal. Upon graduation Bradley attended Oxford for 2 years as a Rhodes scholar before playing professionally (1967–77) with the New York Knicks. He was inducted into the Hall of Fame in 1983. In the U.S. Senate Bradley gained national recognition as an energy and tax expert. Easily reelected in 1984, Bradley had an unexpectedly tough race for reelection in 1990, a setback attributed to voter displeasure over tax increases in New Jersey. He is the author of *Life on the Run* (1976) and *The Fair Tax* (1984).

Bibliography: McPhee, John, *A Sense of Where You Are*, 2d ed. (1978).

Bradley, F. H.

An English philosopher at Oxford, Francis Herbert Bradley, b. Jan. 30, 1846, d. Sept. 18, 1924, was the most famous metaphysician in the British school of absolute IDEALISM. He wrote many books on topics in metaphysics, logic, and ethics. Among these, *Appearance and Reality* (1893) was widely known and read. His *Collected Essays* was published in 1935.

Bradley's metaphysics begins with the notion of immediate experience. Thought and judgment require, however, that one pass beyond this, in that thought abstracts from experience, and such abstraction leads to contradictions. Since everything that a person says about the world is riddled with contradictions, it is mere appearance, not reality. Metaphysics therefore attempts to find a view that can satisfy the intellect and be true and thus self-consistent. This can only be found in the absolute. Although the absolute cannot be grasped by thought, it is not totally unknowable because various features of experience suggest what it must be like. The absolute is an "all-inclusive and super-relational experience," in which all experiences are transcended.   E. D. KLEMKE

Bibliography: Manser, Anthony, and Stock, Guy, eds., *The Philosophy of F. H. Bradley* (1984); Wollheim, Richard, *F. H. Bradley* (1959).

Bradley, James

James Bradley, b. March 1693, d. July 13, 1762, was an English astronomer known chiefly for his discovery of the ABERRATION of starlight and the NUTATION of the Earth. Bradley, a graduate of Balliol College, Oxford, was ordained a priest in 1719. His recognized talents in astronomy, however, led to his appointment two years later as Savilian professor at Oxford.

The importance of Bradley's work lies in the extreme accuracy of his observations of stellar positions. It was this work that led to his discovery, announced in 1729, that certain small changes in the positions of stars were due to the combined effect (which he called aberration) of the velocity of light and the orbital motion of the Earth. That discovery resulted in his later detection of the nutation, or nodding, of the Earth's axis. Bradley succeeded Edmund Halley in 1742 as Astronomer Royal and director of the Royal Greenwich Observatory. His work there on astrometry was of such accuracy as not only to provide the data for F. Bessel's star catalogue but to lay the cornerstone for 19th-century astronomy.

Bradley, Omar N.

Omar N. Bradley, a 5-star general and one of the most respected Allied commanders of World War II, led U.S. forces in the invasions of North Africa and Sicily, in the Normandy landings, and in the battle for Germany. He later served (1949–53) as chairman of the Joint Chiefs of Staff.

Omar Nelson Bradley, b. Clark, Mo., Feb. 12, 1893, d. Apr. 8, 1981, was one of the ablest U.S. generals of World War II. He graduated from West Point in 1915 and was commandant of the infantry school at Fort Benning, Ga., and leader of the 82d and 28th divisions before being named commander of the II Corps. In this last position he participated in the invasion of North Africa, his forces playing a pivotal role in the victory in Tunisia in May 1943 as well as the capture of Sicily in August.

Bradley possessed the respect and affection of common soldiers as well as superiors. He took part in the NORMANDY INVASION in June 1944, and his forces liberated Paris on August 25. Promoted to command of the million-man Twelfth Army Group, comprising the First, Third, Ninth, and Fifteenth armies, Bradley played a large part in helping to defeat the German forces in France, Belgium, Luxembourg, Germany, and Czechoslovakia. Gen. George C. Marshall called him "the finest army group commander in any nation's ground forces."

After World War II, Bradley served as head of the Veterans Administration (1945–47), Army Chief of Staff (1948–49), and chairman of the Joint Chiefs of Staff (1949–53). In the last capacity, he supported President Harry Truman in relieving Douglas MacArthur as supreme Allied commander in Korea. Bradley retired in 1953.   WARREN W. HASSLER, JR.

Bibliography: Bradley, Omar N., and Blair, C., A General's Life (1983).

Bradley, Pat

The professional golfer Patricia Ellen Bradley, b. Westford, Mass., Mar. 24, 1951, has won more money on the Ladies Professional Golf Association (LPGA) tour than any player—about $2.9 million. Bradley joined the LPGA in 1974. She won the women's U.S. Open in 1981 and had her best year in 1986, winning three of the four major tournaments—including the LPGA—earning $492,021, and winning the LPGA Player of the Year award.

Bradley, Tom

Thomas Bradley, b. Calvert, Tex., Dec. 29, 1917, became the first black mayor of Los Angeles in 1973. A former police officer, he practiced law before serving on the city council (1963–73). In 1989, Bradley, a liberal Democrat, was elected to an unprecedented fifth mayoral term. He ran unsuccessfully for the California governorship in 1982 and 1986.

Bradstreet, Anne

Anne Bradstreet, b. c.1612, d. Sept. 16, 1672, was an American Puritan poet whose The Tenth Muse Lately Sprung up in America (1650) was the first book of poems written in America. She was born in Northamptonshire, England, and went to America with her husband, Simon, about 1630.

The Tenth Muse was apparently published without her knowledge. Although she was embarrassed to see her "rambling brat" in print, she continued to write poetry. She turned from historical to domestic subjects and thereby created the unique idiom for which she is most admired today. Her Several Poems Compiled with Great Variety of Wit and Learning, which contains much of her best poetry, was published six years after her death.   ROBERT D. ARNER

Bibliography: Crowell, Pattie, and Stanford, Ann, Critical Essays on Anne Bradstreet (1983); Piercy, Josephine, Anne Bradstreet (1964).

Brady, Diamond Jim

James Buchanan "Diamond Jim" Brady, b. Aug. 12, 1856, d. Apr. 13, 1917, was a remarkably successful railway-equipment salesman and a Broadway celebrity. He acquired vice-presidencies or directorships in several firms, including the Standard Steel Car Company. He loved to eat gargantuan meals in expensive restaurants and to entertain lavishly. His nickname came from his collection of diamond jewelry, said to be worth $2 million.

Bibliography: Burke, John, Duet in Diamonds (1972).

Brady, Mathew B.

Gen. Ulysses S. Grant (seated third from left) poses at his field headquarters in this photograph by the studio of Mathew Brady, a pioneering American photographer of the 19th century. Brady and his assistants covered the battlefields of the Civil War, compiling a unique pictorial account of that conflict.

Mathew B. Brady, b. Warren County, N.Y., 1823, d. Jan. 16, 1896, was one of the first American photographic entrepreneurs. In 1844 he opened a daguerreotype studio in New York City; by 1860 he had two more (a second in New York City and another in Washington, D.C.) through which he maintained a thriving portrait business. In 1845 he began to make a series of portraits of famous Americans, which he published as The Gallery of Illustrious Americans (1850). He made more than one-third of the 100 known photographs of Abraham Lincoln. The U.S. Civil War offered new scope for Brady's ambition. At an expense that depleted his fortune, he outfitted perhaps as many as 20 photographers to cover all fronts. Their equipment was too cumbersome to capture action, but their thousands of pictures showed war in a new and brutal light. By the accepted convention of studio photography, Brady's name appeared on all the images. Among Brady's best Civil War photographers were Alexander GARDNER and Timothy H. O'SULLIVAN, both of whom left Brady's employ in 1863.   PETER GALASSI

Bibliography: Horan, James D., Mathew Brady: Historian with a Camera (1955); Kunhardt, D. M. and P. B., Mathew Brady and His World (1977); Meredith, Roy, Mr. Lincoln's Camera Man, 2d rev. ed. (1974).

Brady, Nicholas F.

Nicholas Frederick Brady, b. New York City, Apr. 11, 1930, became U.S. secretary of the treasury in 1988 under President

Ronald Reagan and continued in the post under George Bush. He proposed the Brady plan to alleviate Third World debt. A graduate of Yale (1952) and Harvard (1954), Brady had been a prominent Wall Street financier. He filled an unexpired U.S. Senate seat (1982) as a Republican from New Jersey and also headed a commission investigating the 1987 stock crash.

Braga   [brah'-gah]

Braga (1981 pop., 63,033) is the capital of Braga district and of Minho province in northwest Portugal. A historic city, Braga is a distribution center for the surrounding agricultural region and a center of light industry. Notable landmarks include a 12th-century cathedral with the tomb of Henry of Burgundy and the sanctuary of Bom Jesus do Monte (18th century).

Said to have been founded by the Carthaginians around 296 BC, Braga was called Bracara Augusta by the Romans. The city was taken by the Moors in 716 and recaptured in 1040 by Ferdinand I of Castile and León. Braga later served (1093–1147) as the residence of Portugal's royal court.

Bragança   [brah-gahn'-sah]

The house of Bragança was the ruling dynasty of Portugal from 1640 to 1910 and of Brazil from 1822 to 1889. In 1442, King John I of Portugal made his illegitimate son, Afonso, duke of Bragança. Afonso's descendants became the wealthiest noble landowners in Portugal. In the national revolution against Spanish rule in 1640, João, duke of Bragança, was crowned King JOHN IV. The dynasty ruled Portugal until the overthrow of Manuel II and the establishment of a republic in 1910. When Brazil became independent from Portugal in 1822, it became an empire under PEDRO I, son of the Portuguese king JOHN VI. Pedro's successor, PEDRO II, was overthrown in a republican revolution in 1889.   DANIEL R. HEADRICK

Bibliography: Gribble, Francis, *Royal House of Portugal* (1915; repr. 1970).

Bragg, Braxton

Braxton Bragg, b. Warren County, N.C., Mar. 22, 1817, d. Sept. 27, 1876, was a Confederate general in the U.S. Civil War. He graduated from West Point in 1837 and was an artillery officer until 1856, when he resigned to manage his Louisiana plantation. In 1861, Bragg volunteered for military duty. Sent to the western front, he replaced P. G. T. Beauregard as commander in June 1862. Until December 1863, he commanded the Western Confederate army, leading it several times to the brink of victory. For psychological reasons that may never be understood, he failed to grasp his opportunities, and the ultimate result was defeat. In 1864, Bragg became advisor to his friend President Jefferson Davis; he held several minor commands late in the war. After 1865 he was active in civil engineering and railroading.   RICHARD M. MCMURRY

Bibliography: McWhiney, Grady W., *Braxton Bragg and Confederate Defeat* (1969).

Bragg, Fort: see FORT BRAGG.

Bragg, Sir William H.

The English physicist Sir William Henry Bragg, b. July 2, 1862, d. Mar. 12, 1942, pioneered the determination of crystal structure by X-RAY DIFFRACTION methods, for which he and his son William Lawrence Bragg received the 1915 Nobel Prize for physics. After Wilhelm Roentgen discovered X rays in 1895, Bragg began a lifelong investigation of the nature of radiations, principally X rays but also alpha and beta particles and gamma rays.

After the discovery of the diffraction of X rays by crystals in 1912, Bragg and his son, William L., derived Bragg's law, which relates the wavelength of X rays to the glancing angle of reflection. In 1913 the elder Bragg built the first X-ray spectrometer, which he initially used to study X-ray spectral distributions. Within several years the Braggs were able to use this instrument and Bragg's law to derive the structure of crystals and show the exact positions of atoms. Subsequently, they demonstrated that the properties and behavior of a large variety of substances can be related to the position of their constituent atoms.

Bragg was appointed professor of physics at the University of Leeds (1908) and at University College, London (1915). He was named (1923) director of the Royal Institution. In London he analyzed organic crystals, making fundamental contributions to molecular biology.   E. ROBERT PAUL

Bibliography: Caroe, G. M., *William Henry Bragg* (1978).

Bragg, Sir William L.

The English physicist Sir William Lawrence Bragg, b. Adelaide, Australia, Mar. 31, 1890, d. July 1, 1971, was awarded the 1915 Nobel Prize for physics jointly with his father, William Henry Bragg, for their determination of the structures of crystals, using X-RAY DIFFRACTION methods. Building upon his collaboration with his father, the younger Bragg and his coworkers at the University of Manchester developed the field of modern crystallography. They extended their work to the determination of more and more complex structures, eventually including silicate mineralogy.

Bragg became director of the National Physical Laboratory in 1937 and was appointed professor of experimental physics at Cambridge in 1939. He was appointed professor of chemistry at the Royal Institution in 1953 and director a year later. While serving at these institutions his interests turned to metals and the crystallographic study of the complex nature of proteins.   E. ROBERT PAUL

Bragg's law: see X-RAY DIFFRACTION; X RAYS.

Bragi   [bray'-gee]

In Norse mythology, Bragi was the god of wisdom, poetry, and eloquence, whose song celebrated the deeds of warriors. His father was ODIN and his wife was Iduna, the goddess of youth.

Brahe, Tycho   [brah'-uh, tee'-koh]

Tycho Brahe, a 16th-century Dane, was the greatest observational astronomer in the era before the telescope. He built and operated improved instruments, using them to refine the accuracy of almost all astronomical measurements. His extraordinarily accurate observations led Johannes Kepler to posit elliptical orbits for the planets. (Royal Observatory, Edinburgh.)

The Danish astronomer Tycho Brahe made the most accurate astronomical observations in the era before the invention of the telescope. He was born at Knudstrup in Scania, Denmark, on Dec. 14, 1546, and raised by his uncle, Jorgen Brahe, who sent him in 1559 to Copenhagen to study law. The observation of a solar eclipse in 1560 turned his interest to observational astronomy and, contrary to his uncle's intentions, he studied the subject independently, using Ptolemy's *Almagest*. In 1563, Brahe observed the conjunction of Jupiter and Saturn, which clearly demonstrated to him the inaccuracy of the existing records of planetary positions. After the death of his uncle in 1565, Brahe decided to travel throughout Europe, and he studied science at several universities. He returned to Denmark in 1571 and installed a chemical laboratory in the castle of a relative at Heridsvad Abbey. There he observed (1572) a "new star" in the constellation of Cassiopeia. In his first work, *De Nova Stella* (1573), he established that his nova was a star beyond the Moon's orbit.

In order to keep Brahe from leaving the country, the king of Denmark, Frederick II, granted him in 1576 the island of Ven (formerly Hven), between Sweden and Denmark, together with a generous pension. There Brahe constructed his famous observatory, Uraniborg, where during the next 21 years he built his own instruments and carried out an extensive program of observations. His rights on Ven and his pension were withdrawn by Frederick's son, Christian IV, and he left Ven in 1597. In 1599 the emperor Rudolph II offered him the position of imperial mathematician of the Holy Roman Empire at his court in Prague. Some of Brahe's instruments were shipped to Prague, and in 1600 he was joined by a young and promising astronomer, Johann Kepler. Upon Brahe's death on Oct. 24, 1601, Kepler became his successor and inherited his large collection of astronomical observations, from which Kepler deduced his famous laws of planetary motion.

Despite the high precision of his measurements, Brahe was unable to detect any annual variation in the relative directions of the stars (see PARALLAX), which, he correctly assumed, should be visible if the Earth revolves around the Sun. Thus he rejected the Copernican system and believed that the Sun revolves around the Earth. He discarded the Ptolemaic system, however, because of its incompatibility with his observations of planetary motions, proposing instead a new model for planetary motion, the Tychonic system, according to which the Earth is the fixed center of the world, the Sun and Moon revolve around the Earth, and the other planets revolve around the Sun.

By proving that the nova of 1572 was a star, Brahe demonstrated a basic flaw in the Aristotelian world view of the immutability of the heavens. His observation of the comet of 1577 and five subsequent comets also convinced him that their orbits were far beyond the lunar orbit. This discovery, and the phenomenal accuracy of his observations of planetary positions, laid a firm basis for the breakthrough of the Copernican world view in the 17th century.

Bibliography: Christianson, Gale E., *This Wild Abyss* (1978); Dreyer, J. L. E., *Tycho Brahe: A Picture of Scientific Life and Work in the Sixteenth Century* (1890; repr. 1963); Jardine, Nicholas, *The Birth of History and Philosophy of Science: Kepler's "A Defense of Tychos against Ursus"* (1984).

See also: ASTRONOMY, HISTORY OF.

Brahm, Otto

Otto Brahm, b. Feb. 5, 1856, d. Nov. 28, 1912, was a German theater director who helped introduce NATURALISM to the modern German stage. He championed the movement first as a critic, then in 1890 as director of Die Freie Bühne, which introduced Ibsen, Strindberg, and Hauptmann to Berlin. In 1890 he aided Bruno Wille in forming the socialist-oriented Freie Volksbühne and in 1894 became director of the Deutsche Theater, which under his guidance became Germany's leading theater. It won fame for its realism and its acting ensemble. Max Reinhardt, a Brahm protégé, followed him as director in 1905.   MARVIN CARLSON

Bibliography: Gorelik, Mordecai, *New Theaters for Old* (1940; repr. 1975); Newmark, Maxim, *Otto Brahm, the Man and the Critic* (1938).

Brahma and Brahman

In HINDUISM, Brahma is frequently viewed as the creator or creative aspect of God, responsible for originating the world at the beginning of each endless cycle of existence recognized in classical Hinduism. Brahma is often depicted as an aspect of VISHNU or SHIVA, rarely as the supreme Godhead in his own right.

Brahman, the neuter form of Brahma, is the name given to the fundamental principle of the universe in the VEDANTA, the

teachings of the UPANISHADS, and philosophies stemming from them. The world came from Brahman and depends on it for existence.   KARL H. POTTER

Brahman cattle

The Brahman is a breed of cattle developed in the United States from cattle imported from India. It has a high tolerance to heat, insects, and disease.

Brahman cattle are a hybrid breed developed in the United States from strains of the native cattle of India, the humped ZEBU, *Bos indicus*, possibly crossed with European cattle, *Bos taurus*. The Brahman is distinguished by a massive hump on its shoulders and by its pendulous ears and loose throat skin. Brahman cattle yield heavy carcasses with a high percentage of lean meat. Since they are highly adaptable to hot, humid, and arid environments and are resistant to ticks and other insects that attack cattle, they are most numerous in the southeastern United States. Of several breeds of cattle with Brahman characteristics, the best-known is the Santa Gertrudis (Brahman cross-bred with Shorthorn cattle).   A. L. NEUMANN

Bibliography: Bishop, Denis and Dennis, *Cattle of the World* (1978); Rouse, John E., *World Cattle* (1972).

See also: CATTLE AND CATTLE RAISING.

Brahmanism: see HINDUISM.

Brahmaputra River   [brah-mah-poo'-truh]

The Brahmaputra River flows for 2,900 km (1,800 mi) through southwestern China (Tibet), India, and Bangladesh, draining an area of about 935,000 km² (361,000 mi²). It rises from a glacier in the Kailas Range of the Himalayas and flows eastward for 1,127 km (700 mi) across Tibet, where it is known as the Tsangpo. It crosses the Himalayas through gorges 7,150 m (23,458 ft) and 7,756 m (25,446 ft) deep and then flows south and west-southwest through the Assam Valley in northeastern India, where it is known as the Dihang. During the rainy season there, the river often floods to 8 km (5 mi) wide, rising 9–12 m (30–40 ft) and depositing sediment carried down from the mountains. The river flows south through Bangladesh and enters the complex and densely populated Ganges-Brahmaputra delta, where it becomes the Jamuna River and then empties into the Bay of Bengal. The Brahmaputra Valley in Assam has marshy jungle, teak forest, and commercial fisheries; rice, jute, tea, and sugarcane are grown there as well. The river is navigable by steamers and barges for almost 1,300 km (800 mi) to Dibrugarh, India. Navigation in the river's upper courses was impeded by the effects of a 1950 earthquake and disputes over division of the river's waters.

Brahmin

A Brahmin, or Brahman (properly *Brahmana*), is a member of the priestly class or CASTE in India. The Brahmins are one of four great classes recognized by classical Indian authorities, the others being the Kshatriyas, Vaishyas, and Shudras. The term has been maintained in the present-day naming of castes, among which those whose traditional occupation is or was priestcraft are so designated.   KARL H. POTTER

Brahmo Samaj   [brah'-moh sa-mahj']

Founded in Calcutta in 1828 by Rammohun ROY, the Brahmo Samaj, or Brahma Society, is a religious movement intended to restore the original purity of HINDUISM. It rejects certain aspects of traditional Hinduism such as the worship of idols, widow suicide, the doctrines of KARMA and TRANSMIGRATION OF SOULS, and to some extent the CASTE system. After Roy's death, the society was led by Debendranath Tagore. It eventually split into two factions, one led by Tagore, the other by Keshab Chander Sen. Since the 1870s the society has been less influential than it was formerly, but it has nevertheless remained important among intellectuals throughout India.

KARL H. POTTER

Bibliography: Sastri, S., *History of the Brahmo Samaj*, 2 vols. (1911–12).

Brahms, Johannes

Johannes Brahms, the composer of *A German Requiem*, four symphonies, four concertos, and many songs, piano pieces, and chamber works, was one of the seminal musical figures of the 19th century. Opera was the only major musical medium in which he did not write.

EARLY CAREER

Brahms was born in Hamburg, Germany, on May 7, 1833. He first studied music with his father, a double-bass player for the Hamburg opera; subsequently he studied composition with Eduard Marxsen. Brahms was a talented pianist, giving his first public recital at the age of 14, and making a living by playing in taverns and dance halls.

On a concert tour in 1853 as accompanist for the Hungarian violinist Eduard Reményi, Brahms met Franz Liszt, who praised the 20-year-old's Scherzo in E Flat Minor and his piano sonatas. Brahms, however, never became personally friendly with Liszt, and in 1860 he signed a manifesto attacking the so-called Music of the Future, which Liszt championed. More fruitful for Brahms was his meeting with Robert Schumann, who hailed the young composer as the coming genius of German music and arranged for the publication of his first songs and piano sonatas. Schumann died in 1856, and Brahms remained a devoted friend of his widow, Clara Schumann, until her death in 1896. Brahms never married, although he had a large circle of friends and patrons.

After Brahms was rejected for a post as conductor in Hamburg in 1862, he visited Vienna and later (1868) made his home there. The compositions written before his first visit to Vienna include several piano works—of which the "Edward" ballade is the most famous—the two serenades for orchestra, his first piano concerto, and the Piano Trio in B Major.

BRAHMS IN VIENNA

Brahms's work as a choral conductor in Vienna prepared him for the composition of *A German Requiem*, based on biblical texts rather than on the Roman Catholic requiem mass; it was first performed on Good Friday (April 10), 1868, in the cathedral of Bremen. Brahms's other major works from this period include the Piano Quintet in F Minor; the Magelone Romances based on poems by Ludwig Tieck; two piano quartets; and the trio for piano, violin, and French horn.

Brahms conducted the orchestra of the Society of the Friends of Music in Vienna from 1872 to 1875, after which he devoted himself entirely to composition. His conducting experience undoubtedly influenced his return to orchestral composition, marked by his first two symphonies (C minor and D major), his monumental violin concerto and second piano concerto, and two concert overtures—the *Tragic* and the jovial *Academic Festival*, based on student songs and written to celebrate an honorary doctorate awarded him by the University of Breslau in 1879. During this period Brahms did not neglect song or chamber music, although the number of his piano compositions diminished after he wrote Variations on a Theme by Handel (1862). During the 1880s, Brahms wrote his third (F major) and fourth (E minor) symphonies; the double concerto (A minor) for violin, cello, and orchestra; and choral works, chamber music, and songs.

Brahms made his will in 1891 and then embarked with renewed vigor on the composition of many of his best works. He returned to writing for the piano, creating in his short capriccios, ballades, and intermezzos a musical testament that sums up the musical achievements of German romanticism. During these years Brahms became friends with the clarinetist Richard Mühlfeld and wrote the finest works ever composed for the clarinet: two sonatas, the quintet for clarinet and string quartet, and the trio for clarinet, cello, and piano. Brahms's last two compositions were religious in nature: the *Four Serious Songs* on biblical texts, and the set of chorale preludes for organ. These works were published after Brahms died in Vienna on April 3, 1897.

SIGNIFICANCE

Brahms, more than any other composer of the second half of the 19th century, was responsible for reviving what is termed "absolute" music—compositions to be accepted on their own terms as interplays of sound rather than as works that depict a scene or tell a story (program music). Brahms was a master of the compositional craft. He often used established techniques, such as counterpoint, especially in his sets of variations, but in such novel and refreshing ways that the listener first perceives the beauty and strength of the music and only later becomes aware of the composer's technical mastery. Brahms's love of German folk song gave his music a sturdy Teutonic character. Although most of his music is serious, his intimate folk-song settings and his dazzling Hungarian-style finales, such as in the G Minor Piano Quartet or in the double concerto, reveal lighter sides of his musical personality. His choral music includes the finest Protestant church music since that of Bach, and in his *Lieder* (songs) he created the perfect partnership for voice and piano, although he selected many undeserving texts for them. His piano writing is more difficult than it sounds; hence, these works appeal to pianists who are more concerned with musicality than with virtuosity. Brahms's legacy of musical craftsmanship is evident in the works of Max REGER and Paul HINDEMITH.   R. M. LONGYEAR

Bibliography: Friedlander, Max, *Brahms's Lieder* (1928; repr. 1976); Gál, Hans, *Johannes Brahms* (1963); Geiringer, Karl, *Brahms: His Life and Work*, 3d ed. (1981); Holmes, Paul, *Brahms: His Life and Times* (1984); Jacobson, Bernard, *The Music of Johannes Brahms* (1977); McCorkle, Donald, ed., *The N. Simrock Thematic Catalogue of the Collected Works of Brahms* (1973); Musgrave, Michael, ed., *Brahms Two: Biographical, Documentary, and Analytical Studies* (1987).

braided stream

A braided stream is a natural watercourse marked by a complex pattern of numerous channels that divide and converge. Such streams tend to be relatively straight, wide, and shallow compared with meandering streams. The sediment of the bed and banks tends to be relatively coarse. Rapid shifts in channel position and sandbar pattern are characteristic, as is the process of channel splitting. Braided streams commonly occur on ALLUVIAL FANS along mountain fronts and in areas where streams of glacial MELTWATER issue from the margins of ice sheets and GLACIERS.

Bibliography: Leopold, L. B., Wolman, M. G., and Miller, J. P., *Fluvial Processes in Geomorphology* (1964).

Johannes Brahms was a major German composer of instrumental and vocal music during the 19th century. In his works, Brahms combined a profound grasp of technique with the warmth of romanticism.

A(1)	B(2)	C(3)	D(4)	E(5)	F(6)	G(7)	H(8)	I(9)	J(0)

| K | L | M | N | O | P | Q | R | S | T | U |

| V | W | X | Y | Z |

Braille Positions	Numeral Symbol	Capital Symbol
1 •• 4	• 4	
2 •• 5	• 5	
3 •• 6	3 •• 6	• 6

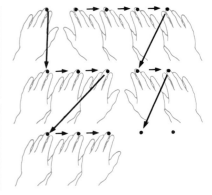

The braille system of printing and writing for the blind constitutes a different pattern of raised dots selected from among the 6 braille positions (63 possible combinations) for each letter of the alphabet. Numerals correspond to the patterns of letters A–J and are indicated when preceded by the numeral symbol. Capital letters are indicated when preceded by the dot in the number 6 position. In reading braille (right), the right hand picks up the messages, using one or more fingers, while the left hand reads and feels for the next line.

Braidwood, Robert

Robert John Braidwood, b. Detroit, July 29, 1907, is an American archaeologist who has pioneered research on the origins of village life in the Middle East. A faculty member at the University of Chicago (1940–76; emeritus 1976–   ), he excavated the Neolithic site of JARMO in Iraq in the 1940s. His many writings include *Prehistoric Men* (1948; rev. ed., 1975), *The Near East and the Foundations for Civilization* (1952), *Prehistoric Investigations in Southwestern Asia* (1972), and (with Halet Cambel) *Prehistoric Research in Southeastern Anatolia* (1980).

Brăila   [bra-ee'-lah]

Brăila, capital of the Brăila district, is a town located on the west bank of the Danube River in southeastern Romania. It has a population of 235,620 (1986 est.). Brăila is Romania's second largest port, and oceangoing ships carry grain from its enormous warehouses. The city is a rail center and has numerous buildings of historic significance, including churches and museums. Cement, textiles, wire products, and leather goods are manufactured. Average annual rainfall is only 440 mm (17 in).

First mentioned as part of Walachia in the 14th century, Brăila was under Turkish control from 1554 until 1829.

Braille, Louis   [bry]

The Frenchman Louis Braille, b. Jan. 4, 1809, d. Jan. 6, 1852, invented the braille system of printing and writing for the blind. He himself was blinded at the age of three in an accident. His early education, in a class with sighted pupils, depended on his memory of the teachers' lectures. Later he studied in Paris at the National Institute for Blind Youth, whose founder had developed cumbersome texts with large raised writing.

At the institute Braille witnessed a demonstration by Charles Barbier, an army officer, of a military code for night communications. The code used raised dots and dashes but was too complex and inconvenient for the blind to use. When Braille was only 15 years old, he improved this method, working on it and teaching throughout his life. Braille also adapted notations for music and for mathematics.

Bibliography: Keeler, Stephen, *Louis Braille* (1986); Kugelmass, J. Alvin, *Louis Braille: Windows for the Blind* (1951).

braille system   [brayl]

The braille system is a universally used tactile method of writing for the blind. Named for its inventor, Louis Braille, it employs groups of dots embossed on paper or some other flat surface to represent printed letters and numbers. The system's basic "braille cell" consists of six dots—like the points of a domino—arranged in vertical columns of three dots each. For convenience, the left column is numbered downward from one to three, the right from four to six. From the basic cell, 63 dot patterns can be formed. These patterns, easily identifiable to the touch, represent letters of the alphabet, numbers, punctuation signs, certain speech sounds (such as *ch* and *gh*), and a few common words (*and, for, of, the,* and *with*).

Braille designed the characters for the first 10 letters (A–J) from the 4 top dots, one, two, four, and five. A "backwards L" formation, consisting of dots three through six, preceding these 10 configurations indicates that they stand for the numbers 1 through 9, and 0. Braille used dots three and six along with the top four to represent the remaining letters of the alphabet and the other elements in the system. A single dot in the dot-six position and set just to the left of a formation indicates that the formation is a capital letter.

Braille first published his dot system in 1829; wide acceptance came slowly. A standard braille system for all English-speaking people was agreed upon in 1932. Grade 1 braille uses a separate cell for each letter, while grade 2 uses contractions for common word fragments such as "-ed" or "-ing"; grade 3 has even more contractions. Initially, people learn grade 1, but almost everyone moves on to grade 2, used for most books. Braille books are pressed from metal by a method that permits dots to be stamped on either side of the paper. Blind persons can write Braille with a stylus on a small metal or plastic slate or with a 6-key device called a braillewriter.

The number of blind persons who know braille is on the decline in the United States, with the development of machines that translate voice into print and greater access to computers and tape recorders. This is causing some controversy as blind persons who do not know braille are finding that they must learn it to be fully literate and get good jobs. A number of states have passed bills to make the teaching of braille mandatory for all blind persons able to learn it.

Bibliography: Croisdale, D. W., et al., eds., *Computerized Braille Production: Today and Tomorrow* (1982); Goldish, Louis, *Braille in the United States* (1967); Hampshire, Barry, *Working with Braille* (1981); Lowenfeld, Berthold, et al., *Blind Children Learn to Read* (1974).

brain

In the central NERVOUS SYSTEM of animals, the brain is a segregated group of nerve cells, or neurons, within the cranium, or skull, in vertebrates, and within the head segment in lower forms of animals. The brain varies in size and complexity from rudimentary ganglia (a group of nerve-cell bodies) in the central nervous systems of primitive worms to the large and complex human brain. As the central control organ of the body, the brain governs the functioning of the body's other organs. Sensory nerve cells feed external and internal information from all parts of the body to the brain. At least four medical subspecialties have a primary concern with the human brain: neurology, psychobiology, neurosurgery, and psychiatry.

The average human brain at birth weighs 390 g (14 oz); its average maximum weight, reached at age 15, is 1,315 g (46 oz). The total number of neurons in the human brain is approximately 10 billion. In contrast, the brain of a whale may weigh more than 5 kg (11 lb), four times as much as a human brain, and the brain of a grasshopper contains no more than a few thousand neurons. A theory has been proposed which states that behavioral capacity, a broad term indicating intelligence, is related not to the size of brain but to the index of cephalization—the amount of brain tissue in excess of that required for transmitting impulses to and from the brain. Studies have shown that a progressive evolutionary encephalization relative to body size occurs in vertebrates and culminates in humans. Of equal importance to encephalization has been the evolutionary development of the human forebrain, a greatly expanded and convoluted mantle containing neuronal centers necessary for understanding and producing language, for conceptualization and abstraction, for judgment, and for the capacity of humans to contemplate and influence their lives.

EVOLUTION

During the first few weeks of embryonic life the bodies and central nervous systems of different vertebrates are remarkably similar. It is difficult to differentiate between the human em-

bryo at the gestational age of one month and the embryo of an amphibian, fish, reptile, or rodent at a comparable stage. All have tails, primordial (primitive) gill clefts, and similar nervous systems, including primordial brains in the form of small bulges in the neural tube. The early embryos of these vertebrates most closely resemble, on a miniature scale, the adult fish, which is the oldest true vertebrate on the phylogenetic, or evolutionary, ladder. The developing human embryo, including the brain, passes through stages that, on a small scale, resemble the evolution of its ancestors. The embryological development of the human brain thus parallels the evolution of the brain. The small bulges in the primitive neural tube gradually enlarge and form the anatomical divisions of the future adult brain, or encephalon. These divisions are known as the hindbrain (rhombencephalon), the midbrain (mesencephalon), and the forebrain (prosencephalon). The prefixes describe either the shape (*rhomb,* derived from ''rhombus'') or the position (*meso,* meaning ''middle''; and *pros,* meaning ''before'' or ''in front of'') of the structure along the longitudinal axis of the brain.

In primitive animals, the forebrain lags in development, but certain parts of the brain that are essential to survival of the species develop much more than others. In fish and amphibians, the olfactory (smell) system, including the olfactory cortex, the cortex being the outer layer of the brain, is particularly well developed. The olfactory cortex and the adjacent

Lower vertebrate animals, such as frogs, have the most primitive brain, with only a brain stem, a cerebellum, and an undeveloped cerebrum. The brain stem controls such involuntary actions as breathing, digestion, and heart rate, and the cerebellum coordinates muscular activity. The most dramatic change in the course of brain evolution involves the development of the cerebrum. At the lower end of the evolutionary scale, the cerebrum is merely a center for the sense of smell and is small in size relative to the other areas, such as the cerebellum. As complexity increases to the level found in primates, the cerebrum controls more senses as well as fine muscle activity, limited memory, and learned behavior. Primate brains contain cerebrums that have four lobes: frontal, parietal, temporal, and occipital. Development of the cerebrum culminates in the highly convoluted cerebrum of humans, which makes sophisticated reasoning possible.

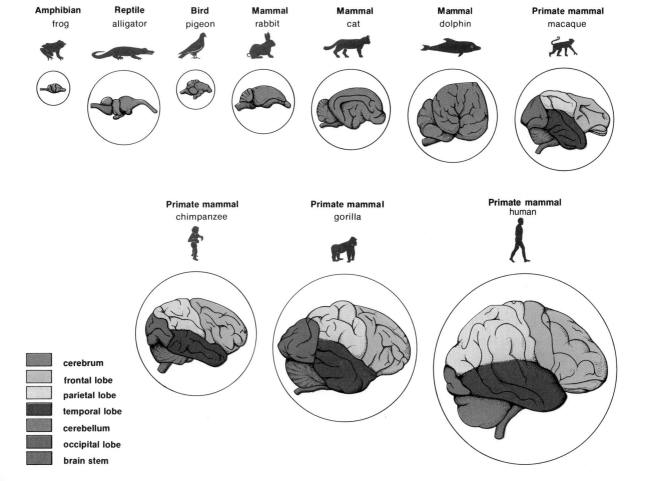

structures are old in terms of evolution, and the microscopic structure of this cortex consists of simple layers of neurons arranged fairly uniformly. This structure contrasts with the highly complex neocortex (most highly evolved cerebral tissue) in phylogenetically newer areas of the brain, such as the frontal lobes.

In reptiles and birds, both evolutionary descendants of the amphibians, the corpus striatum (a mass of gray matter close to the thalamus) is well developed and serves as a coordination center for reflexes involving the eye and ear. In addition, the cerebellum (part of the hindbrain) of birds is extremely large compared to the rest of the brain, because it controls the motor coordination and balance necessary for flight. The visual systems of reptiles and birds are also well developed. Reptiles and birds have a small cerebral cortex. Thus the brain of most submammalian vertebrates is characterized by a well-developed brain stem that may weigh more than the rest of the brain, as well as by the selective development of the cerebellum (in birds) and the areas of the forebrain that are vital for survival.

In the mammalian brain, the olfactory cortex is part of a larger neuronal system called the limbic system. The ancient olfactory system has been modified to serve not only smell but also the behavioral responses known as emotion and sexual behavior. Embryologically—and according to evolutionary development—the brain of the mammal gradually enlarges because of the expansion of the neocortex (composed of the frontal, parietal, occipital, and temporal lobes). The neocortex reaches its fullest development in the primates, specifically in humans.

In the forebrain, the primitive neural tube expands into a system of fluid-filled cavities, or ventricles. The thalamus and other parts of the diencephalon (literally, "between brain") develop as bulges on the neural tube above the developing brain stem. The two cerebral hemispheres at first grow out and then back over the two halves of the thalamus, eventually burying them completely. The hemispheres grow in a manner that is singular to individual species. Simultaneous

with the species-dependent development of the limbic lobe and neocortex is the development of the corpus striatum—three pairs of large nuclei, or ganglia—from the diencephalic part of the primitive forebrain. The main difference between the neocortex of humans and that of other primates is the more extensive development of the frontal, parietal, and temporal cortical areas in humans. An increase in weight and in the number and complexity of cortical gyri (elevated convolutions) occurs. The cortical areas essential for language function are located in the frontal and temporal lobes (see Cerebral Cortex below). The extensive infolding and overlapping of the human cerebral cortex makes possible the efficient connection by converging nerve fibers of a large area of gray matter in a small volume to much less voluminous areas of subcortical gray matter—the basal ganglia. Approximately 70 percent of the cerebral cortex of humans is not visible on the surface of the brain. If the human cerebral cortex were unfolded to its greatest extent, it would cover an area of several square feet.

MICROSCOPIC STRUCTURE AND APPEARANCE

The brain is composed of nerve cells (or neurons), glial cells, and nutrient blood vessels. Neurons transmit nerve impulses, and glial cells, which account for half of the brain's weight, form the supporting structure of the brain.

Each multipolar neuron has a soma, or cell body, from which extends a single large process, or axon, along which impulses are transmitted to other neurons when the soma is sufficiently excited by incoming impulses. Axons of functionally similar neurons are frequently grouped as more or less discrete fiber tracts. The somas from which they arise are grouped as nuclei, or ganglia (a group of nerve cell bodies). The soma also has shorter processes, called dendrites, whose principal function is to receive incoming nerve impulses. The area at the dendrites where the terminal branch of an axon comes into contact with another neuron is called a synapse. Nerve impulses are transmitted from one neuron to another across synapses. When the combined interplay of many incoming impulses reaches a certain threshold, the soma depo-

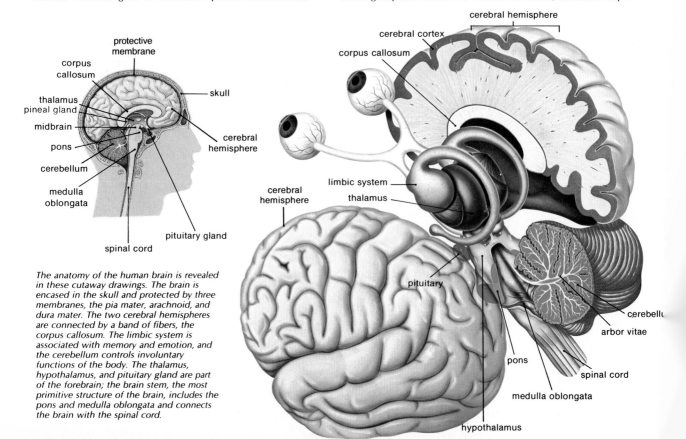

The anatomy of the human brain is revealed in these cutaway drawings. The brain is encased in the skull and protected by three membranes, the pia mater, arachnoid, and dura mater. The two cerebral hemispheres are connected by a band of fibers, the corpus callosum. The limbic system is associated with memory and emotion, and the cerebellum controls involuntary functions of the body. The thalamus, hypothalamus, and pituitary gland are part of the forebrain; the brain stem, the most primitive structure of the brain, includes the pons and medulla oblongata and connects the brain with the spinal cord.

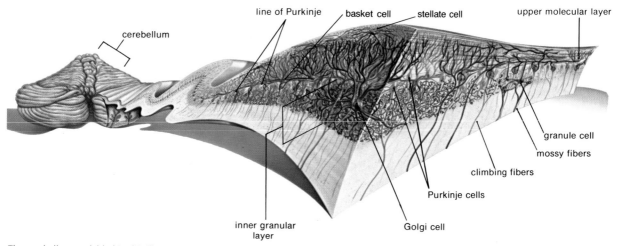

The cerebellum, unfolded in this illustration, comprises an upper molecular layer that contains stellate and basket cells, an inner granular layer, and an inner layer of nerve fibers (bottom) connecting the cerebellum to other parts of the brain and body. The molecular and granular layers are separated by the line of Purkinje, at which point lie the Purkinje cell bodies. Golgi cell bodies and granule cells, located within the granular layer, project nerve fibers throughout the molecular and granular layers. Mossy nerve fibers connect granule cells to other brain and body nerves, and climbing fibers wrap around the Purkinje cells, bringing information from outside the cerebellum to the molecular layer.

larizes and sends a nerve action potential down its axon to other nerve cells and their processes (see BIOPOTENTIAL; NEUROPHYSIOLOGY).

The terms *afferent* and *efferent* describe nerve tracts as going toward or away from the cerebral cortex or other higher brain structures. The corticospinal nerve tract from cortex to spinal cord is efferent, with somas of the cells of origin in the cortex, their axons traveling downward to the cord, away from the highest center. The terms *sensory* and *afferent* are used synonymously, as are *motor* and *efferent*.

The exposed living brain is a soft mass of glistening, grayish white tissue above which numerous small, bright red arteries and bluish veins are visible. The brain is protected by the skull and three membranes, called meninges. When the brain is "fixed" with chemicals, it becomes firm and can be sliced. A coronal section (that is, one that is vertical and cut from one side of the head to the other) shows an outer layer of gray matter 3 to 5 mm (0.12 to 0.20 in) thick, comprising the cerebral cortex, where the nerve-cell bodies lie. Beneath this is the white matter, nerve fibers sheathed in myelin. Below the white matter are globular areas of other gray matter; these are the thalamus and the subcortical nuclei, or basal ganglia, including the corpus striatum.

ANATOMY AND FUNCTION

Localization of function is defined by two investigative techniques: ablation and stimulation. Ablation, the removal of a small area of the brain, may result in a neurological deficit that is considered in terms of a lost function, one that is assigned to the area of the brain that was ablated. In humans, correlation of the indications of brain dysfunction during life with lesions of the brain found at autopsy has added greatly to the knowledge of localized functions. Movements and sensations can be produced in conscious humans by stimulating the brain electrically in appropriate areas. A portion of the skull may be removed (a craniotomy) under local anesthesia, giving access to the brain in a conscious patient. Gray and white matter may be cut, stimulated, or cauterized without the patient experiencing pain. Apparently no nerve endings sensitive to pain exist within the brain substance. Large blood vessels supplying the brain and certain sensory nerves attached to the brain stem are pain sensitive.

Brain Stem. The most notable structures of the adult human brain are the brain stem, the cerebellum, and the cerebrum (cerebral hemispheres). The lowest, or most caudal, portion of the brain stem, the medulla oblongata, is continuous with the spinal cord. Above it, the pons bulges prominently and is continuous with the midbrain, into which the cerebral peduncles (stemlike connections) extend. The cerebral pedun-

cles carry upper motor neuron fibers that originate in the cerebral cortex to the cell bodies of cranial nerves in the brain stem and to cells in the spinal cord, called lower motor neurons, which cause certain muscles to move.

The brain stem contains all afferent and efferent nerve fibers between the spinal cord and the higher brain centers. Some upper motor neuron fibers cross in the brain stem, whereas others do not. Most cranial nerves to each side of the head connect evenly with both cerebral hemispheres. In contrast, 80 percent of the fibers in the corticospinal tract from each side cross over in the medulla oblongata, so that the affected muscles are primarily controlled by one hemisphere. Thus a unilateral (single-sided) lesion in the cerebrum or brain stem above this crossover causes weakness or paralysis on the opposite side of the body.

Cranial Nerves. The human brain has 12 paired cranial nerves. The first 2, the olfactory and optic nerves, enter the brain above the brain stem and are actually extensions of the brain rather than peripheral nerves. Afferent impulses originating in peripheral sensory organs form ascending fiber tracts that cross either in the spinal cord or in the brain stem on their way to synapsing in nuclei above. The largest of these nuclei is the thalamus, whose many subdivisions act as relay stations to the cerebral cortex. Some thalamic nuclei project to specific receiving areas of the cerebral cortex, the primary cortical areas. Different afferent tracts and thalamic areas subserve sensations of pain; sensations of heat and cold; proprioception (the sensation of movement at joints); and special senses of sight, taste, and hearing. A knowledge of the level of crossing of the various afferent and efferent tracts, when correlated with symptoms and signs, enables physicians to localize with considerable accuracy the level and extent of lesions in the nervous system. The other 10 cranial nerves, in descending order of location, are the oculomotor, trochlear, trigeminal, abducens, facial, acoustic, glossopharyngeal, vagus, spinal accessory, and hypoglossal nerves.

Cerebellum. The cerebellum accounts for about 10 percent of the brain's weight and is a center for coordinating automatic (reflex) and voluntary movements of the body. It receives afferent impulses from the spinal cord as well as from various brain-stem nuclei. The cerebellum is connected by fibers, both going and coming, to parts of the basal ganglia and the extrapyramidal system (various nuclei and tracts governing motor function that are not part of the corticospinal, or pyramidal, tract). Fibers also go to the cerebral cortex by way of thalamic nuclear relays. The cerebral cortex (principally the frontal lobe) is connected to the cerebellum by numerous fibers. Lesions of the cerebellum and basal ganglia cause inco-

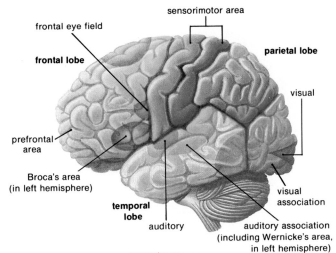

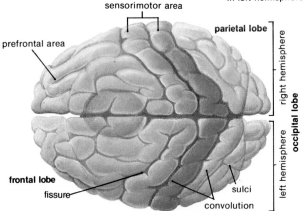

The cerebral cortex of a human brain—upon which all thought, memory, and perception depend—is arranged into hemispheres, lobes, convolutions (ridges), fissures (clefts), and sulci (furrows). The cortex is divided into a left hemisphere, associated largely with logical expression, and a right hemisphere, associated largely with creative expression. The prefrontal lobes of both hemispheres are considered the centers of reason, emotion, and judgment; the frontal lobes control voluntary muscle action. The parietal lobes regulate sensory information for taste and touch, and the temporal lobes do so for hearing, balance, and smell. The occipital lobes control visual perception, including color, image size, and movement.

ordination and other disorders of movement, such as tremor or choreiform movements (sudden involuntary movements or muscle contractions).

Reticular Formation. Deep within the brain stem is a large group of cells known as the reticular formation. Ascending fibers from this area project via thalamic nuclei to large association areas in the cortex. The reticular formation is a regulator of the state of alertness; its destruction at the midbrain level results in a state of coma. In contrast, large areas of the cerebrum may be destroyed without a loss of consciousness. The mechanism of cerebral concussion is thought to be a temporary derangement in the reticular formation.

Hypothalamus. The hypothalamus, located below the thalamus and including the pituitary gland, is an important part of the diencephalon. It contains centers for regulating body temperature, blood pressure, pulse rate, perspiration, and other functions controlled by the autonomic nervous system. The hypothalamus is the neural regulatory center for the production and release of hormones. Lesions of it that occur early in life may affect an individual's growth and sexual development. In adults, a sudden, destructive lesion such as an intraventricular hemorrhage may result in diabetes insipidus, hyperthermia (high body temperature), and frequently death. Emerging from the rear of the diencephalon is a small or-

gan, the PINEAL GLAND, which plays a role in controlling certain biorhythms such as the onset of puberty.

Cerebral Cortex. In terms of evolution, the cerebral cortex of humans has become increasingly complex. In present-day humans, it has a highly convoluted surface, greatly increasing the total area of the cortex. It comprises about 85 percent of the nerve cells in the brain. Because it is easily accessible, the cerebral cortex has been studied extensively, and some parts have been mapped in great detail. In primates, the deep horizontal Sylvian fissure (groove) separates in each hemisphere the temporal lobe, below, from the frontal, parietal, and occipital lobes, above. Running vertically, the less constant Rolandic fissure separates the frontal from the parietal lobe. Other landmarks separate the parietal from the occipital lobe on each side.

The motor cortex in the frontal lobe and the sensory cortex in the parietal lobe are involved in the integration of muscular action and sensations.

An important area of the frontal lobe is Broca's area, which lies in the left hemisphere of the brain of right-handed people, just forward of the lips–teeth–tongue areas of the sensorimotor strip. A lesion here causes a motor aphasia, the inability to produce meaningful spoken language (in the absence of any weakness of the muscles used in speech and with understanding preserved, including the ability to read and follow commands). In right-handed people, language dominance is located in the left hemisphere. About 50 percent of left-handed persons have right cerebral dominance. A lesion in Wernicke's area (the posterior, upper part of the temporal lobe on the dominant side) causes a receptive aphasia. The individual may verbalize extensively, talking in gibberish with occasional mispronounced words. The person is also unable to understand spoken or written language and may show a lack of concern over his or her plight.

Olfactory impulses enter the brain through the olfactory bulbs, and synapse occurs in the olfactory cortex of the limbic system. Visual impulses travel through the optic nerves to the optic chiasma, where half of the fibers from each eye cross to the opposite side. They then synapse in a part of the thalamus that projects to the primary visual cortex in the occipital lobe. A complete lesion in one optic tract behind the chiasma causes an inability to see objects on one side of the midline opposite the lesion. Auditory impulses travel up the brain

The sensorimotor areas of the cortex regulate muscular control and sensation of surface areas of the body. Sectors that control the fine movements and senses of the feet, lips, and fingers require more space in the sensorimotor area than do other body parts.

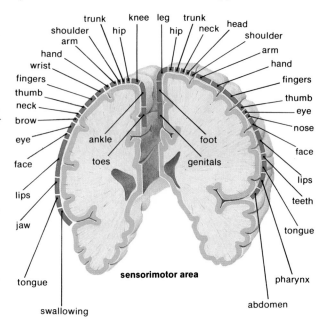

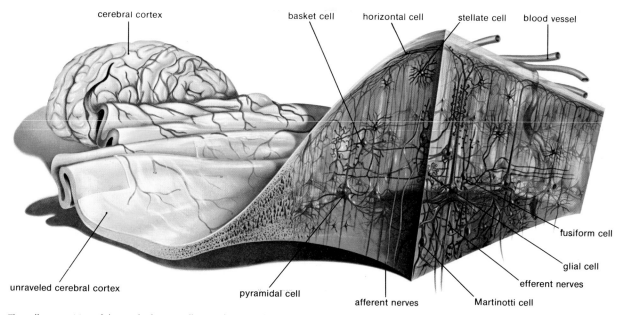

cerebral cortex   basket cell   horizontal cell   stellate cell   blood vessel

fusiform cell

glial cell

efferent nerves

unraveled cerebral cortex

pyramidal cell

afferent nerves   Martinotti cell

The cell composition of the cerebral cortex, illustrated as an unfolded layer, comprises a supportive glial cell and several types of neurons. Horizontal neuron cells run along the surface of the cerebral cortex and interconnect the vertical neuron layers that lie deeper in the cortex. Basket, fusiform, and stellate cells are vertical neurons that receive messages from areas of the body. Pyramidal and Martinotti cells are also vertical neurons, which relay messages to areas of the body. Glial cells support the cerebral cortex structure and transport nutrients and oxygen from blood vessels to neurons. Afferent nerves relay information from the body to the cerebral cortex; efferent nerves do so back to the body.

stem in a series of complex crossings and uncrossings with several synapses, ending in the auditory primary cortex deep in the temporal lobe.

The temporal lobe cortex and certain portions of the limbic system have important functions involving recall and memory. This was first observed by Wilder Graves Penfield (1891–1976) during surgical operations on people having an unusual type of temporal lobe seizure during which they had vivid auditory and visual hallucinations of previously experienced events. Their experiential hallucinations could be reproduced by stimulating the surface of the temporal lobe—an activation of a specific complex memory, or engram. Bilateral removal of the hippocampal gyri causes a loss of recent memory or an inability to retain new information or experiences longer than a few minutes. Memory of information acquired before the lesions occurred is preserved, however, as is abstract thinking and general intelligence.

BRAIN WAVES

In an electroencephalogram, or EEG, brain waves (oscillating electric currents) from the scalp are recorded. In 1874, brain waves were first recorded by the Englishman Richard Caton, who connected primitive equipment directly to the cerebral cortex of a rabbit. In 1929 the German psychiatrist Hans Berger published the first information about scalp-recorded brain waves of humans. The invention of the differential input amplifier by B. H. C. Matthews in 1934 revolutionized the high-gain amplification of biologic electrical signals, including brain waves. Frederic Gibbs, Hallowell Davis, and William Lennox, of the Harvard Medical School, published (1935) the first paper in English on the EEG in epilepsy in humans. The EEG is extensively used in diagnosing epilepsy and in the study of how the brain functions in animals and humans.

An EEG is painless and harmless. The data gained from it is interpreted and correlated with other medical data by physicians as an aid to diagnosis. The different types and causes of epileptic seizures are correlated with certain recognizable focal or diffuse brain wave abnormalities, such as spikes. Treatment with anticonvulsant drugs or, in rare instances, neurosurgical removal of brain scars often depends on the data furnished by an EEG. Minute brain wave currents in the scalp, measured in microvolts, are amplified as changes in potential, which are then written out in a series of wavy lines or channels, one above the other, each channel corre-

sponding to recording electrodes over different brain areas. Scalp-recorded activity originates primarily in the underlying cerebral cortex. During brain operations designed to ameliorate some forms of epilepsy, brain waves are recorded directly from the cerebral cortex and from depth electrodes in subcortical nuclei.

Brain waves are classified according to frequency bands in cycles per second (Hz), the most common of which are alpha activity (8 to 14 Hz), beta activity (above 14 Hz), delta activity (below 4 Hz), and theta activity (4 to less than 8 Hz), activity defined as a series of waves. Characteristic EEG patterns correspond to the level and type of behavioral activity. For example, alpha activity is usually produced during periods of relaxation. In most people alpha activity is abolished by attention. Beta activity occurs in bursts in the anterior part of the brain and is associated with mental activity.

SLEEP involves changes in EEG patterns as well as physiologic changes such as heart rate. In sleep slow rhythmic activity occurs. This activity tends to alternate with periods of low-voltage faster frequencies associated with rapid eye movements (REM).

CHEMICAL ACTIVITY

The transmission of nerve impulses across a synaptic gap involves the release of chemical transmitters called biogenic amines, formed from amino acids. NEUROTRANSMITTERS include ACETYLCHOLINE, dopamine, norepinephrine, SEROTONIN, and ATP. Acetylcholine is a transmitter in the reticular activating formation, involved in arousal and alertness. Dopamine is concentrated most heavily in the basal ganglia and is associated with muscular activity. Norepinephrine is found in high concentrations in the hypothalamus and in the limbic system. Serotonin is found in many parts of the central nervous system but particularly in the brain stem. ATP's function has not yet been fully defined.

Many temporary changes that occur in body chemistry would have a drastic effect on brain function if the brain were not protected by physiological barriers. One of these, the blood-brain barrier, depends on the unusually tight junctions between the endothelial cells in brain capillaries, which are triggered by the brain's astrocyte cells to keep otherwise harmful water-soluble substances from passing into the brain from the blood. Another barrier, called the blood-cerebrospinal fluid barrier, lies deep within the brain. These same systems, however, also make it difficult to introduce various therapeutic drugs into the brain. Such substances as antibiotics, hormones, and tranquilizers are admitted, along with various small or fat-soluble molecules. Other drugs are blocked, however, including a number of cancer drugs and other large, water-soluble compounds. One technique is to use glucose injections that apparently shrink capillary cells long enough for drugs to get in through openings in the walls of the brain's blood vessels. Different techniques are being studied and developed, such as the linking of fat-soluble with water-soluble molecules.

ADVANCED BRAIN RESEARCH TECHNIQUES

From a technical viewpoint the invention of the computerized axial tomograph (see CAT SCAN) in the early 1960s marked the opening of a new era in brain research. The machine uses a weak X-RAY beam rotated about a person's head to produce an image of a "slice" of the brain in terms of varying tissue densities. A computer then plots the results in an oscilloscope display or on photographic film. The CAT scan differentiates and localizes the extent and site of brain tumors, blood clots, and areas of cerebral damage.

Various other RADIOLOGY techniques have since been developed for imaging the brain. These include MAGNETIC RESONANCE IMAGING (MRI), which involves placing the subject in an intense magnetic field that magnetizes hydrogen nuclei (protons) within the brain's tissues. By means of radio-frequency pulses, the locations of the nuclei can then be transformed into diagnostic images that reveal different tissue characteristics. Another technique, called POSITRON EMISSION TOMOGRAPHY (PET), obtains images through the injection of a glucose-related compound that has been tagged by a radioactive isotope. As the isotope decays it emits positrons that collide with electrons in the brain to form photons, which are then recorded by a PET scanner. This technique yields information on the varying levels of glucose metabolism at different brain sites. Abnormal levels are observed, for example, at sites of tumors and stroke damage. A further imaging technique involves the use of ULTRASONIC waves.

All of these techniques have their relative advantages and disadvantages, depending on physiological differences between the brain sites under study and on the kind of brain activity or pathology being investigated. What all these noninvasive methods for studying the living brain have done has been to enable researchers to probe the interplay of chemical activities within different brain tissues in ways that had never before been possible.   HUNTINGTON MAVOR

Bibliography: Arbib, M. A., ed., *Vision, Brain and Cooperative Computation* (1990); Atlas, S. W., *Magnetic Resonance Imaging of the Brain and Spine* (1991); Caine, R. N. and G., *Making Connections* (1991); Coen, C. W., ed., *Functions of the Brain* (1985); Datta, A. K., ed., *Essentials of Human Anatomy, Volume II: Head, Neck and Brain* (1990); Klivington, K., *The Science of Mind* (1989); Llinas, R. R., ed., *The Biology of the Brain* (1989) and *The Workings of the Brain* (1989); McGeer, P. L., *Molecular Neurobiology of the Mammalian Brain,* 2d ed. (1987); Oakley, David, ed., *Brain and Mind* (1985); Thompson, R. F., *The Brain* (1993); Trehub, A., *The Cognitive Brain* (1991).

Brain, Dennis

Dennis Brain, b. May 17, 1921, d. Sept. 1, 1957, was an English virtuoso French horn player and a popular soloist. He studied with his father, Aubrey Brain, a virtuoso of the same instrument. Brain was principal horn player of the Royal Philharmonic and the Philharmonia Orchestra. Several composers wrote pieces for him, including the *Serenade* for tenor, horn, and strings (1943) by Benjamin Britten.

brain bilateralism

One of the most striking features of the BRAIN is its bilateralism, its organization into two largely symmetric anatomical structures—the left and right cerebral hemispheres. The brain is often compared to a computer, but the more appropriate analogy is two computers, for each hemisphere is capable of processing and storing information on its own, independent of the other half-brain.

EVIDENCE FOR BILATERALISM

In humans and other mammals the corpus callosum is the main pathway of interhemispheric communication. The callosum is the largest fiber tract in the human brain, containing more than 200 million nerve fibers (axons). The critical role of the corpus callosum was demonstrated by Ronald Myers and Roger Sperry in the 1950s. Using a special surgical procedure, they were able to show in cats that information reaching one half of the brain was unavailable to the other half in the absence of the corpus callosum.

In the 1960s, Sperry's laboratory had the opportunity to extend its earlier studies to human beings when Joseph Bogen and Peter Vogel cut the callosum in a group of epileptic patients in an effort to control their otherwise unmanageable seizures. The psychological follow-up of these patients by Michael Gazzaniga, Sperry, and Bogen confirmed the earlier animal studies. The patients were able to describe verbally information presented to the left hemisphere, usually the hemisphere that possesses linguistic functions. When information was presented exclusively to the right hemisphere, the patients were unable to describe it verbally but were able to demonstrate that they had perceived the information.

HEMISPHERE SPECIALIZATION

The presence of two separate and apparently different mental systems (one verbal and the other not) in split-brain human beings raised questions concerning the psychological uniqueness of the two hemispheres. The left hemisphere is normally dominant for language functions. The right hemisphere seems to be better equipped for handling spatial and other nonverbal relations. Observations like these led to theories suggesting hemispheric specialization through evolution.

According to some theories, the evolution of the human brain involved change from the bilateral symmetry that typifies the neural organization of lower animals to a bilateral specialization of function. Although this view has attracted popular attention, Joseph LeDoux and Gazzaniga, on the basis of recent studies, have suggested a more conservative theory to explain hemisphere differences. These investigators feel that hemisphere differences in human beings can be accounted for in terms of the evolutionary acquisition of language by one hemisphere. The other hemisphere continues to process information in essentially the same way that it did in prehumans. The superior performance of the right hemisphere on certain nonverbal tests, according to this view, is attributable to the sacrifice of nonverbal processing efficiency by the left hemisphere as a result of having acquired language, instead of to the improved capacities of the right hemisphere.

CONSCIOUSNESS

Perhaps the most intriguing aspect of studies of split-brain patients has been the possibility that, following brain bisection, each hemisphere is separately conscious. The question attracted the interest of philosophers and scientists alike. But while the conscious properties of the talking left hemisphere were apparent, the consciousness of the silent hemisphere was more doubtful. Further studies revealed the unequivocal presence of double consciousness in a split-brain patient. The possibility exists that a fully integrated consciousness does not develop until a child is several years old; research shows that the fibers of the corpus callosum do not begin to mature until one year after birth, and the process continues until the age of ten or older. The corpus callosum has also been found to be about 11% larger in left-handed and ambidextrous than in right-handed people.   JOSEPH LEDOUX

Bibliography: Bianki, V. L., *The Right and Left Hemispheres of the Animal Brain* (1987); Dunaif-Hattis, J., *Doubling the Brain: On the Evolution of Brain Lateralization and Its Implications for Language* (1984); Geschwind, N., and Galabunda, A. M., eds., *Cerebral Dominance* (1988).

Brain Trust

In American history, the *Brain Trust* was a term originally applied to Franklin D. ROOSEVELT's close advisors in his 1932 presidential campaign because most of them came from the academic world. They included Columbia University professors A. A. BERLE, Jr., Raymond Moley, and Rexford G. TUGWELL.

Later the name was applied to all professionally trained people in Roosevelt's administration.

Bibliography: Oulahan, Richard, *The Man Who . . .: The Story of the 1932 Democratic National Convention* (1971); Rosen, Elliot A., *Hoover, Roosevelt, and the Brain Trust: From Depression to New Deal* (1977).

Brainerd, David

David Brainerd, b. Haddam, Conn., Apr. 20, 1718, d. Oct. 9, 1747, was an American Presbyterian missionary to the Seneca and Delaware Indians in New York, New Jersey, and Pennsylvania. The part of his diary that was published during his lifetime was widely read. The remaining portions were edited by Jonathan EDWARDS in 1749; the work became a devotional classic. Brainerd died of tuberculosis just as he was beginning to enjoy his greatest success, but his work inspired colonial interest in the Indian missions.

Bibliography: Brainerd, D., ed., *The Life and Diary of David Brainerd,* 2d ed. (1989); Wynbeck, David, *David Brainerd* (1961).

brainwashing

Brainwashing is the process of deliberately subjecting individuals to physical and psychological hardship in order to alter their thoughts, attitudes, and actions. It differs from other forms of persuasion or instruction, not only in the key element of coercion but in the radical intent to clear the mind totally of one set of ideas and replace them by another, often completely opposed, set. The term *indoctrination* is applied to the implanting of new ideas, but indoctrination may take place without brainwashing.

The term *brainwashing* is a literal translation of the Chinese *hsi nao,* referring to thought reform. When the Chinese Communists came to power in 1949, they sought to reeducate the intellectuals and middle classes by brainwashing techniques; they applied the same methods to prisoners taken during the Korean War. Similar efforts to control the minds of individuals have been made by authorities in many other countries.

The two aspects of brainwashing are confession of past crimes or errors and reeducation to new beliefs. Prisoners are brought to confess by lack of sleep and food and other forms of intense physical discomfort, isolation from familiar surroundings, a prison routine requiring absolute obedience and humility, and social pressure from cell mates. The last includes mutual criticism and self-criticism sessions, which play particularly on the generalized guilt feeling that all people have to some extent. At the same time regular indoctrination sessions are conducted. The acceptance of the new ideas is again fostered by group pressure and the anticipated reward of freedom.

Improved understanding of psychology and neurophysiology has enabled modern totalitarian regimes to create extremely effective brainwashing programs. Some of their techniques, however, have been used for centuries: the INQUISITION, for example, elicited confessions from alleged heretics by similar methods. In the context of religion, some scholars have noted a parallel between brainwashing for political purposes and the techniques used by some religious groups to generate religious excitement and conversion. The parallel is observable in religions that use physical means (such as scourging, rhythmic dancing and drumming, and sometimes drugs) to induce a trancelike state in which the individual is open to conversion. It is also apparent in the mind-control practices of some of the RELIGIOUS CULTS of the 20th century, most notably the People's Temple group of JONESTOWN, Guyana, whose 900 members committed mass suicide in 1978.

Bibliography: Bromley, D. G., and Richardson, J. T., eds., *The Brainwashing-Deprogramming Controversy* (1984); Lifton, R. J., *Thought Reform and the Psychology of Totalism: A Study of "Brainwashing" in China* (1989); Schein, Edgar H., et al., *Coercive Persuasion* (1971).

brake

A brake is a device used to slow down or stop a moving object. It operates by converting the energy of motion, which is called kinetic energy, into some other form of energy, usually heat energy.

A stationary part—the brake shoe or pad—is pressed against a rotating part, commonly a shaft, disk, or drum, producing a large amount of friction. The brake shoe or pad has an expendable lining made of heat-resistant friction materials, usually organic or metallic compounds that wear away very slowly under conditions of high temperatures and pressures.

The brake shoe may be pressed against the rotating part mechanically, through a system of levers, linkages, or cables; pneumatically; electromagnetically; or hydraulically. A good brake system should provide adequate heat dissipation, smooth operation, and a simple means of adjustment.

Block, Disk, Drum, and Band Brakes. In the single block brake, the simplest brake type, the concave side of a block is pressed against the rotating part, which is usually a wheel or drum fastened to a shaft. This type of brake was used in horse-drawn vehicles. In the double block brake two blocks are symmetrically positioned on opposite sides of the shaft.

The disk brake has a block that presses against the flat surface of a disk rather than against the wheel rim. An example is the caliper disk brake, which was originally developed for aircraft and is now used in automobiles; the same type is used in bicycles. Two opposed blocks (brake shoes) squeeze the disk between them like a pair of calipers. Disk brakes dissipate heat rapidly because they are not enclosed, thus allowing air to flow over them and carry away heat.

A drum brake has two curved brake shoes that press against a rotating brake drum. Automobile drum brakes have internal brake shoes that are inside a tightly closed drum and are actuated by hydraulic pressure. Such a brake has the advantage that it can keep out water and dust effectively; its ability to dissipate heat is limited, however. When drum brakes heat up, they are subject to fading—a decrease in braking effectiveness during extended use of the brake. This happens because the increased temperature causes a decrease in the friction of the brake-lining material. Special materials have been developed that can be used for the linings to improve resistance to fading.

Newer, heavier cars are often equipped with disk brakes, especially on the front wheels. Rear-wheel braking is not as critical, because the weight of the vehicle is shifted to the front wheel during braking, thereby reducing the braking force needed at the rear wheels.

A band brake consists of a metal band lined with a friction material that can be tightened around the rotating part by using a lever. Band brakes are currently used mainly for hoists and excavating machinery.

Hydraulic Brakes. Until about 1930, automobiles were braked mechanically. Such a system, however, made it difficult to brake all the wheels equally. The increased weight and speed of vehicles also required that the driver exert a greater pedal pressure. Both these problems were solved with the development of modern HYDRAULIC SYSTEMS.

In a hydraulic system, depression of the brake pedal moves a piston in a master cylinder, forcing hydraulic fluid through piping to a cylinder at each wheel. Called wheel cylinders or slave cylinders, these are each fitted with pistons moved by the pressure of the fluid, which brings the brake lining into contact with the rotating brake drum or disk, producing a braking force.

Power Brakes. Even with the force-multiplying feature of hydraulic brakes, as vehicles became heavier and faster the pedal pressure required to brake the vehicle increased beyond a comfortable, safe level. Power brakes were developed to solve this problem. In automobiles they use the vacuum created by the engine during its intake stroke to increase the pressure applied to the piston in the master cylinder, reducing the required pedal pressure. If the power-assisting mechanism should fail, or if the engine stalls, the brakes will not fail completely, although greater pedal pressure will be needed.

Power-assisted brake systems are also needed in such heavy vehicles as buses, trucks, and railroad trains. One such system is the pneumatically operated Westinghouse air brake patented in 1869 by George WESTINGHOUSE, an American manu-

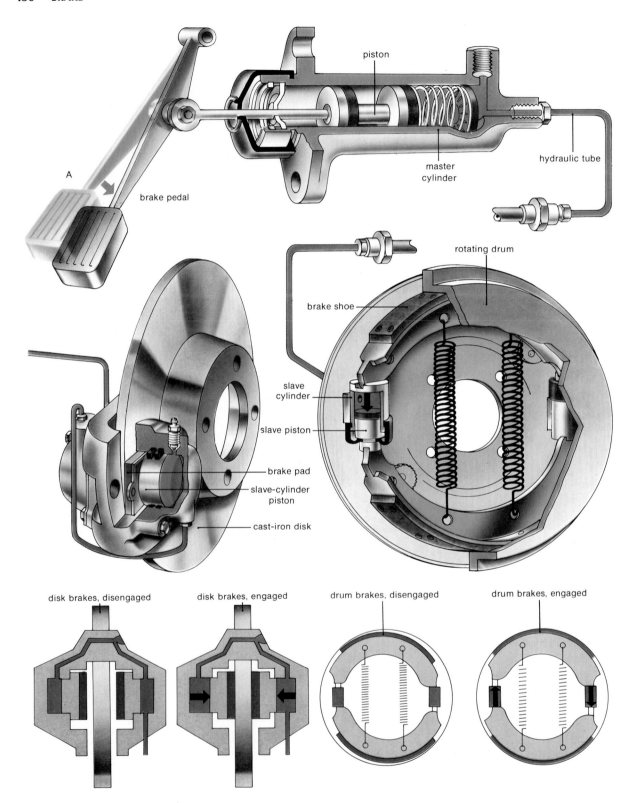

piston

hydraulic tube

master
cylinder

brake pedal

A

rotating drum

brake shoe

slave
cylinder

slave piston

brake pad

slave-cylinder
piston

cast-iron disk

disk brakes, disengaged

disk brakes, engaged

drum brakes, disengaged

drum brakes, engaged

Two major braking systems are used in automobiles—drum brakes (center right) and disk brakes (center left). In both, power is transmitted hydraulically from a master cylinder operated by the brake pedal. When the brake pedal is depressed (A), the piston in the master cylinder forces fluid through the hydraulic tube to slave cylinders located at each wheel. The fluid moves the slave pistons, pushing the brake shoes into contact with the rotating drum, and thus produces braking action. The disk brake is simply a cast-iron disk that rotates with the wheel. Fluid from the master cylinder moves the slave-cylinder pistons, thus bringing the brake pads in contact with the rotating disk and slowing it down. Shown are disk brakes (bottom) disengaged and engaged, and drum brakes disengaged and engaged.

facturer. This system, in a slightly improved form, is still used on trains. Each railroad car has its own reservoir, called an auxiliary reservoir, connected by means of a valve with a brake pipe extending the length of the train. To apply the brakes, the engineer lowers the pressure in the brake pipe by letting air escape. The valve arrangement closes the connection between the reservoir and the brake pipe while simultaneously opening a normally closed connection between the reservoir and the brake cylinder. This allows the compressed air in the reservoir to enter the brake cylinder, forcing the piston in the brake cylinder against the train wheel, braking the train. To release the brakes, the engineer builds up the pressure in the brake pipe. This shifts the valve back to its former position and allows the air in the brake cylinder to escape, releasing the brake. An important advantage of this system is that any sudden drop in brake-pipe air pressure, such as that caused by cars uncoupling, will automatically apply the brake. The brake will continue to act until the problem is corrected, a good example of a fail-safe mechanism.

Another brake system with a fail-safe feature is used in heavy trucks. The brake is applied by means of a spring, and the power system is used to release the brake—either by compressed air (an air brake) or by a vacuum (a vacuum brake). If the system should fail, the restraining force is removed, allowing the spring to apply the brake immediately.

A similar principle is used in some types of hoisting equipment. A heavy brake shoe is lifted off a brake drum by an electromagnet. When the brake is actuated by switching off the magnet, the shoe will drop onto the drum.

Other Types. A machine powered by an electric motor may be designed with electric braking. The circuitry of the motor can be switched so that the motor operates as a generator driven by the rotating axle. Not only does the conversion of the rotational energy into electricity slow down the machine, but the electricity produced can be returned to the power source or collected in storage batteries, thus saving much energy. This general principle is called dynamic braking; the special case in which the electricity is returned to the source is known as regenerative braking.

Braking can also be accomplished by reversing the thrust. In propeller-driven aircraft and ships, the pitch of the PROPELLER blades can be reversed so as to produce thrust in the opposite direction; in some ships the direction of propeller rotation can be reversed. Spacecraft are braked by first turning them around and then firing retrorockets—rockets that supply thrust in the direction opposite to the spacecraft's direction.

Air resistance, which is considerable at high speeds, can also be used for braking spacecraft and aircraft. Flaps on the wings of aircraft can be shifted to increase the air resistance to slow the aircraft.

Anti-Skid Braking Systems. Some jet aircraft and many newer passenger cars use an anti-skid braking system (ABS) for more controlled stops on wet, slippery, or irregular surfaces. In these systems an electronic rotation sensor at each wheel detects wheel lockup, a condition where severe brake action stops one or more wheels from turning although the vehicle is still moving. A central computer then modulates brake line hydraulic pressure to that wheel in bursts, allowing it to turn briefly under lower braking force.   Reviewed by GREGORY VON DARE

Bibliography: Birch, T. W., *Automotive Braking Systems* (1988); Hughes, J. G., *Brakes* (1987); Society of Automotive Engineers, *ABS Traction Control and Brake Components* (1990).

Brakhage, Stan   [brak'-ij]

Stan Brakhage, b. Kansas City, Mo., Jan. 14, 1933, is an experimental filmmaker whose lyric films have contributed radically to the nonnarrative form. His concern with the drama of subconscious seeing (described in the essay "Metaphors on Vision," 1963) has shaped his approach. His usually silent films use superimposition and rapid montage. They include *Anticipation of the Night* (1958), *Dog Star Man* (1964)—considered his major work—and such later films as *Salome* (1980), *Jane* (1985), and *Passage Through* (1990). *The Brakhage Scrapbook* (1982) contains his collected writings.   LESLIE CLARK

Bramah, Joseph

The English inventor of the hydraulic press, Joseph Bramah, b. Apr. 13, 1748, d. Dec. 9, 1814, was the son of a Yorkshire farmer. A locksmith and inventor, he designed and built a variety of new machine tools that were used in making his complicated, pickproof locks. His most celebrated invention, the Bramah press, provided a new source of power for England's iron and steel mills. A relatively simple two-pump hydraulic mechanism, it could exert forces of several thousand tons by means of liquid transmitting pressure from a smaller to a larger cylinder. The celebrated inventor Henry MAUDSLAY was for some years a foreman in Bramah's shop.

See also: HYDRAULIC SYSTEMS.

Bramante, Donato   [brah-mahn'-tay]

The High Renaissance architect Donato Bramante's Tempietto was built in 1502 in the courtyard of San Pietro in Montorio, Rome. It was erected to mark the site of the martyrdom of Saint Peter.

The architect Donato Bramante, b. 1444 at Monte Asdruvaldo, near Urbino, d. Mar. 11, 1514, was one of the most influential Italian architects of the Renaissance. His designs for St. Peter's Church and the TEMPIETTO in San Pietro in Montorio (both in Rome) influenced architects until the modern era. Bramante brought to Italian architecture renewed gravity and monumentality, which had been largely absent since the early 15th century.

Bramante received his architectural training in Urbino. In all likelihood he was employed in the workshops of the Ducal Palace, then being constructed (1462–70) under the direction of Luciano Laurana and Francesco di Giorgio. In 1477, Bramante was summoned to Milan by the new duke of Milan, Ludovico Sforza Il Moro. He soon began work on the enlargement of the church of Santa Maria presso San Satiro (1478).

The plan called for the reorientation of the church: the old nave was turned into a transept, and a new nave was constructed at right angles to it. The site was so limited that it was impossible to build a full chancel. Bramante therefore built a false choir that appears to continue the structural system of the nave. It is an early example of illusionistic architecture in the Renaissance.

Bramante's second great work in Milan was the enlargement of the church of Santa Maria della Grazie (c.1492–99) by adding a new choir intended as a memorial chapel for the Sforza family. The interior is a vast monumentalized version of Filippo BRUNELLESCHI's old sacristy in the church of San Lorenzo in Florence. Bramante was also active outside Milan. In 1488 he made a model for the cathedral of Pavia and about 1494 laid out the town square of Vigevano.

In 1499 Bramante left for Rome. His major work in Rome was the Tempietto in the courtyard of the church of San Pietro in Montorio (1502). Built on the supposed site of the martyrdom of St. Peter, it was the first Renaissance building to imitate precisely the form of the circular ancient temple, with its colonnade bearing an architrave. The Tempietto was originally to have been surrounded by a circular cloister of 16 columns, with niches at the corners to make a square ensemble.

In 1500 Bramante built the cloister of Santa Maria della Pace. He was also responsible for the choir of the church of Santa Maria del Popolo (1508) and the Palazzo Caprini (c.1510), which set the style for palace architecture for the next century.

In 1503 a new pope, JULIUS II, ascended the throne of St. Peter. He soon began a vast building program, of which Bramante became the director. Bramante's first work for Julius was the construction of the Belvedere Court of the Vatican (begun in 1505). The structure was intended to join the old villa of Innocent VIII with the Vatican Palace across a valley. The upper half of the huge court was to display the Vatican's collection of ancient sculpture, and the lower area was to be used for tournaments and pageants. At the far end was placed a giant *exedra*, an enormous semicircular niche capped with a half dome.

At the center of Julius's vast plans was the rebuilding of St. Peter's. The dilapidated old church was no longer large enough for the vast number of pilgrims who flocked there on feast days. In 1506 the job of dismantling the old church was begun. Based on a medal by Caradosso and a large drawing, now in the Uffizi, Florence, the plan apparently called for a Greek cross with a major dome over the crossing and minor domes and bell towers at the corners. Unfortunately the death of Julius II in 1513 and of Bramante the next year prevented the work from progressing much beyond the planning stage.

Bramante's work may be divided into two periods. Before his intense study of the Roman monuments, it seems to be a synthesis of major 15th-century sources (Leon Battista ALBERTI, Brunelleschi, and the decorative tradition of northern Italy). After he came to Rome, his style became more monumental, imposing, and evocative of the architecture of ancient Rome.

NICHOLAS ADAMS

Bibliography: Fraser, Douglas, et al., eds., *Essays in the History of Architecture* (1967); Godfrey, F. M., *Italian Architecture Up to 1750* (1971); Heydenreich, Ludwig H., *Architecture in Italy 1400–1600* (1974); Murray, Peter, *The Architecture of the Italian Renaissance* (1966).

bramble

Bramble is the common name for thorny berry bushes such as RASPBERRIES, BLACKBERRIES, and dewberries. They make up the genus *Rubus*, family Rosaceae; all species hybridize readily. *Rubus* plants have perennial underground parts and biennial aerial stems called canes. Flowers and fruits are produced on second-year canes; the five-petaled flowers are usually white. Brambles grow mainly in the Northern Hemisphere. Red raspberries usually thrive in cooler climates, whereas both black raspberries and blackberries thrive in warmer climates.

JANE PHILPOTT

bran

Bran is the outer layer of cereal grain, such as wheat and rye, that is removed in the process of manufacturing flour or meal. It is used primarily in livestock feed, although, when added to cereals or to bread flour, it is an important element in human nutrition, providing roughage in the form of cellulose.

Brancati, Vitaliano   [brahn-kah'-tee, vee-tahl-yah'-noh]

Vitaliano Brancati, b. July 24, 1907, d. Sept. 25, 1954, was an Italian writer of satirical novels. His first successful work, *Don Giovanni in Sicilia* (Don Juan in Sicily, 1941), is highly critical of the Sicilian obsession with eroticism and machismo, a theme that reappears in *Antonio, the Great Lover* (1949; Eng. trans., 1952). His *Diario romano* (1961) is autobiographical.

LOUIS KIBLER

Brancusi, Constantin   [brahn'-koosh]

Constantin Brancusi's Mademoiselle Pogany is one of a large series of similar busts executed between 1912 and 1933. All of Brancusi's work after 1908 is characterized by extreme simplicity, with the subject reduced to its elemental form.

Constantin Brancusi, b. Pestisani Gorj, Romania, Feb. 21, 1876, d. Mar. 16, 1957, was one of the most innovative and influential sculptors of the 20th century. He studied at the academies of Kraków, Bucharest, and Munich and, in 1904, went to Paris, where he studied sculpture for two years at the École des Beaux-Arts with Antonin Mercié. In 1906, Brancusi came into contact with Auguste Rodin but refused to work with him, seeking instead his own expressive form. The first important example of his personal style is the stone sculpture *The Kiss* (1908), which was erected over a friend's grave in the Cimetière Montparnasse in Paris. It demonstrates his use of primitivism in its simplicity of form and compactness.

Brancusi's primitivism is specifically modern; unlike the primitive art from which it takes its inspiration, it is symbolic rather than depictive, and it gives attention to form for its own sake. Brancusi subscribed to one of the most decisive ideas of modern sculpture, "truth to materials"; that is, he respected the medium and conserved its specific quality by doing the least possible to shape his works.

Brancusi, about 1910, began producing nonrepresentational sculptures in marble or metal, concentrating on two basic themes: variations of the egg shape and soaring bird motifs. Among these works are *The New-Born* (1915; marble, Philadelphia Museum of Art; and 1920; polished bronze, Museum of Modern Art, New York) and *Bird in Space* (1919–25, several versions in marble and bronze), both of which exemplify his sensuous, simply modeled, contemplative, and mystical style.

An important feature of Brancusi's work is the continuity it establishes between the space occupied by the object and the space outside it, a quality much emulated in subsequent sculpture from Henry Moore to Carl Andre. Brancusi's wood sculpture, which emphasizes the natural condition of both shape and surface, anticipates a similar quality in DADA and surrealist "found" sculpture and in the junk sculpture of the 1950s. In his independent search for elemental, organic forms that transmit the elemental ideas of life, Brancusi created an enigmatic and mystical art that is concerned with inner reality. He wrote: ". . . That which they call abstract is the most realist, because what is real is not the exterior form but the idea, the essence of things."   BARBARA CAVALIERE

Bibliography: Geist, Sidney, *Brancusi: A Study of the Sculpture* (1968; repr. 1983) and *Brancusi: The Sculpture and Drawings* (1975); Hulton, P., and Dumitresco, N., eds., *Brancusi*, trans. by M. Paris (1987); Spear, A. T., *Brancusi's Birds* (1969); Varia, Radu, *Brancusi* (1985).

Brand, Max

Max Brand was one of 20 pseudonyms used by Frederick Shiller Faust, b. Seattle, Wash., May 29, 1892, d. May 12, 1944, an American writer known as the King of the Pulps for his work in several popular genres, chiefly the western. Of more than 500 books, at least 7 were filmed from Faust's screenplays of them, including the Dr. Kildare movies (1930s) and *Destry Rides Again* (1930), filmed three times from 1932 to 1954. Faust was killed in action while serving as a war correspondent in Italy.

Bibliography: Nolan, William, *Max Brand* (1986).

Brand, Vance

The astronaut Vance Devoe Brand, b. Longmont, Colo., May 9, 1931, flew on the first international manned space mission. Brand was a Marine fighter pilot from 1953 to 1957 and worked as a test pilot for Lockheed Aircraft Corporation from 1960 until selection as an astronaut in 1966. On his first flight in space, he was command module pilot of the U.S. Apollo in the APOLLO-SOYUZ TEST PROJECT, a Soviet-American spaceflight made in 1975. He was chosen in 1978 as a mission commander for SPACE SHUTTLE flights; he served in that capacity for the first operational flight, in 1982, and for the 10th Shuttle flight, in 1984.   DAVID DOOLING

Brandeis, Louis D.   [bran'-dys]

Louis Brandeis, the first Jew to serve as a justice on the U.S. Supreme Court, was so gifted as a student that the Harvard Law School was forced to revise its rules so that he could graduate before his 21st birthday. As a jurist, Brandeis is best remembered as a liberal dissenter.

Louis Dembitz Brandeis, b. Louisville, Ky., Nov. 13, 1856, d. Oct. 5, 1941, was a justice of the Supreme Court of the United States, known for stressing the importance of social and economic information in his opinions. He graduated from Harvard Law School in 1877 and became a successful lawyer in Boston, often working without pay for causes in which he believed, such as consumer protection, labor unions, and small stockholders at odds with giant corporations.

Brandeis was the initiator of savings bank life insurance in Massachusetts. He also defended state minimum wage laws in Oregon, Illinois, Ohio, and California against the charge that they were unconstitutional. His method of arguing from masses of statistical data and other information became known as "the Brandeis brief." In his popular book, *Other People's Money, and How the Bankers Use It* (1914), Brandeis described the key role played by large banks in the corporate financial system. His antimonopoly views were adopted by Woodrow Wilson and became the basis for the antitrust legislation of Wilson's first administration.

As a Supreme Court justice from 1916 to 1939, Brandeis was frequently at odds with the Court's conservative majority. He tended to favor regulation of the economy, "to meet changing social and economic needs," at the same time opposing most government interference with freedom of speech or press. During the early 1930s, Brandeis was one of the minority favoring most of Franklin Roosevelt's New Deal legislation. After retirement, he devoted himself to the Zionist movement for a Jewish homeland.

Bibliography: Baker, Leonard, *Brandeis and Frankfurter: A Dual Biography* (1984); Dawson, Nelson, ed., *Brandeis and America* (1989); Gal, Allon, *Brandeis of Boston* (1980); Strum, Philippa, *Louis D. Brandeis: Justice for the People* (1984).

Brandeis University

Brandeis University (enrollment: 3,450; library: 798,900 volumes) was established in 1948 as the only Jewish-sponsored nonsectarian university in America. The coeducational institution, located in Waltham, Mass., offers a wide range of undergraduate and graduate programs.

Brandenburg   [bran'-den-burg]

Brandenburg (German: Brandenberg) is a historic region of Germany, centered around the city of BERLIN. Ruled from the 15th century by the HOHENZOLLERN family, it eventually formed the nucleus of the kingdom of PRUSSIA. Brandenburg was revived as a state in 1990.

Originally inhabited by Slavic peoples, Brandenburg was conquered in the 12th century by the German prince Albert the Bear (see ALBERT I, MARGRAVE OF BRANDENBURG), who colonized it with German settlers. Albert was made margrave of the Mark (border territory) of Brandenburg by Holy Roman Emperor Lothair II. As Albert's descendants—the Ascanians—expanded their domains, three divisions emerged: the Old Mark (Altmark), west of the Elbe River; the Middle Mark (Mittelmark), between the Elbe and the Oder; and the New Mark (Neumark), east of the Oder. The Old Mark and the Middle Mark occupied most of the central part of the former East Germany; the New Mark lay in present Poland.

Beginning in the 14th century the margraves of Brandenburg were designated electors (princes with a vote in imperial elections). In 1415, Brandenburg was acquired by the Hohenzollerns, who adopted Protestantism at the time of the Reformation and extended their rule west to the Rhine and east to Prussia on the Baltic Sea. Under FREDERICK WILLIAM, the Great Elector (r. 1640–88), Brandenburg became the most powerful state in northern Germany. His successor, FREDERICK I, assumed the title king of Prussia in 1701, and from then on Brandenburg's history merged with that of Prussia.

The city of Brandenburg An Der Havel is a river port 64 km (40 mi) west of Berlin at the eastern end of the Elbe-Havel Canal. Its population is 94,755 (1987 est.).

Bibliography: Mitchell, Otis, *A Concise History of Brandenburg-Prussia to 1786* (1980).

Brandenburg Gate   [bran'-den-burg]

Berlin's Brandenburg Gate (1789–93) was designed by the German neoclassical architect Carl Gotthard LANGHANS. Its enormous colonnade, flanked by twin temple pavilions, is crowned by Gottfried von SCHADOW's bronze *Quadriga of Victory*. Because of its proximity to the BERLIN WALL, the Brandenburg Gate often symbolized the division of the city in the period before 1989.

Brandes, Georg Morris Cohen [brahn'-des]

Georg Morris Cohen Brandes, b. Feb. 4, 1842, d. Feb. 19, 1927, the Danish literary critic and scholar, greatly influenced Scandinavian literature between 1870 and 1900. Through an extensive correspondence with such writers as Bjørnstjerne Bjørnson, Henrik Ibsen, Alexander Lange Kielland, Selma Lagerlöf, August Strindberg, and J. P. Jacobsen, he influenced an entire generation of writers in the direction of social criticism. Despite this, he was never accepted by the Danish establishment, who regarded him as a radical, atheistic, and at times poisoning influence on Denmark's cultural life.

Brandes was the first to introduce the ideas of such thinkers as John Stuart Mill and Friedrich Nietzsche to Scandinavia. In his early criticism he was influenced primarily by the French positivist philosopher Auguste Comte and the critic Hippolyte Taine, and in his most important work, *Main Currents in Nineteenth-Century European Literature* (6 vols., 1872–80; Eng. trans., 1901–05), he demonstrated a new consciousness of literature's social value.

Brandes's influence during these years is partly explained by his ability to formulate the ideas of the new socially engaged literature and partly by the fact that he was able to make direct personal contact with the young Scandinavian writers. His other important studies include *Søren Kierkegaard* (1877), *Danish Poets* (1877), and *The Men of the Modern Breakthrough* (1883). In later years, Brandes wrote about more comparative subjects, publishing studies about Goethe, Michelangelo, Voltaire, and Shakespeare.   KJETIL A. FLATIN

Bibliography: Nolin, Bertil, *Georg Brandes* (1976).

branding

Branding, widely used for the identification of cattle, usually involves the burning of a distinctive mark, or brand, into an animal's hide with a hot iron. A sign of ownership, a brand serves as an aid in recovering lost or stolen animals. Branding is especially important on open ranges, where grazing lands are not enclosed by fences. Pictures on the walls of Egyptian tombs indicate that humans branded oxen as early as 2000 BC. Spanish explorers introduced the practice of branding into the Americas in the 1500s. Besides cattle, animals such as horses, sheep, and pigs are also branded. The branding of people —slaves and criminals—was practiced in ancient and medieval times and continued as late as the 18th century in Britain and its colonies.

Animals are believed to suffer little from the branding process. Some ranchers use painless chemicals to mark their cattle. Other methods of identification, used alone or in conjunction with branding, include tattooing and tagging.

Brando, Marlon

The American actor Marlon Brando, b. Omaha, Nebr., Apr. 3,1924, achieved success on the stage and in films as the brutally sensuous Stanley Kowalski in Tennessee Williams's *A Streetcar Named Desire* (1947; film, 1951). Brando was trained in method acting in the Actors Studio. His mumbling, introspective, and often moving presence was used to great effect in such films as *The Men* (1950), *Viva Zapata!* (1952), *The Wild One* (1954), and *The Young Lions* (1958). After consecutive best-actor nominations for his roles as Kowalski, Zapata, and Mark Antony in *Julius Caesar* (1953), Brando won the Academy Award for his lead in Elia Kazan's *On the Waterfront* (1954). After less notable performances in *One-Eyed Jacks* (1961), which he also directed, *Mutiny on the Bounty* (1962), *The Chase* (1966), and *Reflections in a Golden Eye* (1967), he again achieved success in Francis Ford Coppola's first film about the Mafia, *The Godfather* (1972).

For his portrayal of aging New York Mafia chieftain Vito Corleone, Brando won a second Academy Award for best actor; he refused the honor, however, because of the film industry's treatment of native Americans. Although his support of unpopular causes has sometimes caused controversy, his stature as an actor is unquestioned. Bernardo Bertolucci's X-rated *Last Tango in Paris* (1973) provided another vehicle for Brando's act-

The American actor Marlon Brando was voted Broadway's most promising actor in 1946. The following year he became the rage of Broadway with his powerful performance as Stanley Kowalski, the brutal male lead of Tennessee Williams's play A Streetcar Named Desire. *Brando repeated that role in a 1951 motion picture version and went on to become one of the world's most celebrated screen personalities.*

ing prowess. The actor again gained public note in Coppola's Vietnam War epic, *Apocalypse Now* (1979), and later appeared in *The Freshman* (1990).   LESLIE HALLIWELL

Bibliography: Carey, Gary, *Marlon Brando* (1985); Downing, David, *Marlon Brando* (1984); Grobel, Lawrence, *Conversations with Brando* (1991); Higham, Charles, *Brando: The Unauthorized Biography* (1987); McCann, Graham, *Rebel Males: Clift, Brando, and Dean* (1993); Nickens, Christopher, *Brando: A Biography in Photographs* (1987); Schickel, Richard, *Brando* (1991); Thomas, Tony, *The Films of Marlon Brando* (1973).

Brandon

Brandon, a Canadian city of 38,567 (1991) on the Assiniboine River, is located in southwestern Manitoba. Established in the late 1870s, it was named after Brandon House, a Hudson's Bay Company trading post (1793). A major highway, two transcontinental railroads, and an airport make Brandon an important distribution center. A grain center, Brandon produces processed food, petrochemicals, woolens, metal products, and electrical and farm equipment. The city has medical and educational institutions, including Brandon University (1899).

Brandt, Bill

Bill Brandt, b. London, 1905, d. Dec. 20, 1983, was a photographer whose work is known for its variety, beauty, and daring. Much of his inspiration was originally derived from surrealism and the school of Paris—including a brief apprenticeship (1929) with Man Ray. Books that illustrate Brandt's technical skill and training include *The English at Home* (1936) and *London at Night* (1938). Disillusioned with realistic photography after World War II, he turned to experimental high-contrast studies of nudes. Brandt's ability to reveal his subject as both familiar and strange has become a hallmark of his style. His *Perspective of Nudes* was published in 1961.

Brandt, Willy

Willy Brandt, b. Karl Herbert Frahm on Dec. 18, 1913, d. Oct. 8, 1992, was chancellor of West Germany from 1969 to 1974. The illegitimate son of a Lübeck ship assistant, Brandt fled to Norway in 1933 when his activities as a socialist brought him to the attention of the Gestapo. He became a citizen of Norway but, following the German invasion of that country in 1940, took refuge in Sweden. In 1945 he returned to Germany as a Scandinavian press correspondent and became friendly with the leaders of the German Social Democratic party (SPD). With their influence he regained German citizenship and in 1949 was elected an SPD member of the Bundestag.

On Oct. 3, 1957, Brandt was elected mayor of West Berlin, a position that gave him international prominence. He was elected (1964) SPD leader, and in 1966 he joined the coalition

Willy Brandt, former West German chancellor, won the Nobel Peace Prize in 1971 for his willingness to open negotiations with the Communist governments of Eastern Europe. Brandt became a familiar figure in the United States, which he visited frequently to obtain support for his Eastern policy.

government of Kurt Kiesinger as foreign minister. When the SPD won the 1969 federal elections, Brandt became chancellor on October 21. Initiating a policy of conciliation toward Eastern Europe, he signed (1970) a treaty with Poland recognizing the Oder-Neisse line as Poland's western border and began negotiations to normalize relations with East Germany. In 1971 he was awarded the Nobel Peace Prize for these endeavors. On May 6, 1974, Brandt was forced to resign, after the discovery that an East German spy was serving on his personal staff. In the late 1970s he headed the Independent Commission on International Development Issues, which issued the report *North-South: A Programme for Survival* (1980). He continued as SPD chairman until 1987.

Bibliography: Homze, Alma and Edward, *Willy Brandt* (1974).

brandy

The term *brandy* (Dutch *brandewijn*, "burnt [that is, distilled] wine") refers to the unsweetened, distilled spirit derived from the juice of grapes. Brandy made from other fruits has the name of the fruit attached to it, as in the case of apple brandy or cherry brandy. As early as the 13th century, brandy was used as a medicine in Europe.

White wine, made from white grapes, is almost universally used for brandy. It is distilled and then aged in wood casks for a minimum of 2 years. Notable French brandies include cognac, a grape brandy distilled only in the Cognac region of France, and Armagnac, distilled in Gascony. The more alcoholic, harsh-tasting marc is made from the grape residue left after the wine has been pressed.

French grape brandies are the most celebrated, although California produces a light, smooth, highly fragrant product. Spanish brandies are generally full-flavored and sweeter than the French. Greek brandies tend to be dark and sweet, with a taste derived from resin.

The principal United States fruit brandy is apple brandy (applejack). Calvados is the apple brandy of the Normandy region of France. Slivovitz, a plum brandy made throughout central Europe, is called mirabelle in France; it has a fruity flavor with a slight taste of bitter almonds.

The white fruit brandies are not aged in wood and thus have virtually no color. They are costly to produce. Kirsch, or kirschwasser, is made from black cherries. Strawberry (*fraise*), raspberry (*framboise*), blackberry, and pear brandies are also produced. The finest of these come from Switzerland, from the Alsace, and from the Black Forest region of Germany.

RONALD A. KAPON

Bibliography: Blumberg, Robert S., and Hannum, Hurst, *Brandies and Liqueurs of the World* (1976); Mayer, Fred, *Cognac Country* (1984).

Brandy Station, Battle of

The Battle of Brandy Station, also called the Battle of Fleetwood Hill, was the largest cavalry clash of the U.S. CIVIL WAR. The engagement, involving 18,000 horses, was fought on June 9, 1863, in Culpeper County, Va. The Confederates under Jeb STUART held the field against the attacking Union general, Alfred Pleasonton. Pleasonton withdrew when he learned that Confederate forces were moving north toward Maryland and ultimately Pennsylvania, where the Battle of GETTYSBURG took place on July 1–3, 1863.

Brandywine, Battle of the

The Battle of the Brandywine, fought on Sept. 11, 1777, was a victory for the British during the AMERICAN REVOLUTION. Intending to capture Philadelphia, Gen. William HOWE landed on Chesapeake Bay with 15,000 men and moved north toward the city. George WASHINGTON met him at Brandywine Creek, near Chadds Ford, Pa., with an army of 11,000. Howe successfully used a flanking movement to drive the Americans from the field, but Washington managed to withdraw most of his troops safely.

Bibliography: Canby, H. S., *The Brandywine*, 2d ed. (1977); Smith, S. S., *The Battle of Brandywine* (1976).

Branner, Hans Christian   [brahn'-ur]

Hans Christian Branner, b. June 23, 1903, d. Apr. 24, 1966, was an outstanding Danish writer who excelled in his short fiction, collected in *Two Minutes of Silence* (1944; Eng. trans., 1966) and other volumes. His novels include *The Riding Master* (1949; Eng. trans., 1951) and *No Man Knows the Night* (1955; Eng. trans., 1958). Among his plays is *The Judge* (1952; Eng. trans., 1955). The recurrent theme of Branner's writings is the relationship of power to weakness and strength.

Bibliography: Markey, Thomas L., *H. C. Branner* (1973).

Brans-Dicke theory   see GRAVITATION.

Bransfield, Edward   [branz'-feeld]

Edward Bransfield, 1795–1852, was an English naval officer who probably made the first sighting of the Antarctic mainland. While stationed in Valparaiso, Chile, he was ordered to sail south to investigate reports of a southern mainland. Having claimed King George and Clarence islands for Britain, on Jan. 30, 1820, he sighted and charted what he called Trinity Land, near the South Shetland Islands. Ten months later the American Nathaniel PALMER made his sighting, and the United States subsequently claimed that Bransfield must have seen Trinity Island and not the mainland.

Brant, Joseph

Joseph Brant, b. 1742, d. Nov. 24, 1807, called Thayendanegea in his native tongue, was a MOHAWK Indian chief who is best known for his courageous military exploits in support of the British during the AMERICAN REVOLUTION. The son of a Mohawk chief, he became a Christian and served as an interpreter and translator for missionaries. The realization of his ambition for a political career was facilitated through his sister's liaison with Sir William JOHNSON, then superintendent of Indian affairs. In 1774, Brant was appointed secretary to Guy Johnson, Sir William's son-in-law and successor. Because of his efforts in enlisting the aid of the IROQUOIS for the British cause, he was granted a captain's commission in the British army and visited England.

In addition to participating in the Battle of Oriskany (1777), Brant directed the Cherry Valley Massacre of 1778 and numerous other campaigns during the Revolutionary War. At the war's end he opposed efforts to arrange a separate Iroquois peace with the new nation. Brant remained pro-British and did much toward acquiring compensation in money and land grants from the British for losses incurred by his people. One result of these efforts is the Six Nations Reserve located near what is today Brantford, Ontario.   JAMES HERRICK

Bibliography: Chalmers, Harvey, and Monture, Ethel B., *Joseph Brant: Mohawk* (1955); Wallace, Anthony F. C., *The Death and Rebirth of the Seneca* (1969).

Brant, Sebastian

Sebastian Brant, b. *c.*1457, d. May 10, 1521, was a German humanist, moralist, and satirist who edited and translated commonsense practical lore. He is best known for his satirical verse allegory *Ship of Fools* (1494; Eng. trans., 1509). The poem recounts the journey of a ship that never reaches its destination, Narragonia. Its 112 passengers are classified according to their shortcomings and foibles, rather than their social class. In form, the work resembles the DANCE OF DEATH and some of the earlier medieval Shrovetide plays (*Fastnachtsspiele*). It was widely distributed and translated, and its view of folly and the FOOL became a popular feature of humanistic and vernacular satire. Katherine Anne PORTER's novel *Ship of Fools* (1962) takes its title and theme from Brant's text.

PAUL SALMON

Brantford

Brantford (1991 pop., 81,997) is a Canadian city located in southern Ontario on the Grand River. The seat of Brant County, it is an agricultural and industrial center; its products include agricultural implements and truck bodies. It was named for Joseph BRANT, a Mohawk chief who was granted the site in 1784. Brantford is the site of the oldest Protestant church in Ontario—St. Paul's, Her Majesty's Chapel of the Mohawks (1785). Alexander Graham BELL worked to perfect the telephone while living (1874) nearby; the house is now a museum.

Branting, Hjalmar

Hjalmar Branting, b. Nov. 23, 1860, d. Feb. 24, 1925, was Sweden's first Social Democratic prime minister (1920, 1921–23, 1924–25). He was a founder (1889) of the Social Democratic party and party leader from 1907, a delegate at the conference on the future of the Åland Islands (disputed between Sweden and Finland), and a delegate to the League of Nations. Branting was corecipient of the 1921 Nobel Peace Prize.

Braque, Georges   [brahk]

Georges Braque, b. May 13, 1882, d. Aug. 31, 1963, in collaboration with Pablo PICASSO, was the founder of CUBISM. After receiving training at the local art school in Le Havre, Braque went to Paris in 1900. There he studied (1902–04) at the Académie Humbert and then at the École des Beaux-Arts in the studio of Léon Bonnat. Braque's early works (1903–05) were executed in the mood of early impressionism. Greatly influenced by André Derain, Henri Matisse, and Maurice de Vlaminck, Braque entered (1906 or 1907) his Fauve period, in which he used soft, undulating patterns and brilliant colors. Unlike the other Fauves (see FAUVISM), however, he showed an interest in architectonic solidity of composition and an emphasis on strongly defined volumes rather than color and brushwork.

A crucial change in Braque's art came in the fall of 1907, when he rediscovered Paul CÉZANNE at the memorial exhibitions at the Salon d'Automne and the Bernheim-Jeune Gallery. At this time, he also met Picasso. In the late work of Cézanne, both Braque and Picasso saw a new geometrization of form and new spatial relationships that were to become the basis of cubism. Spurred by his close association with Picasso, whose *Les Demoiselles d'Avignon* (1906–07) has been called "the first painting of the 20th century," Braque transformed his style radically. Within three years, Picasso and Braque invented analytic cubism, a new, completely nonillusionistic and nonimitative method of depicting the visual world. Their concerns were so mutual and their association so intense that in many instances only experts can distinguish Braque's paintings of 1910–12 from those of Picasso. *Violin and Pitcher* (1910; Kunstmuseum, Basel) is one of the best examples of Braque's analytic cubism. The paintings of this period are all executed in muted greens, grays, ochers, and browns. The objects are fragmented, as though seen from multiple viewpoints. This multiplicity introduced the element of time into vision. These fragments, or cubes, are organized along a grid, thereby creating a compact pictorial structure.

Violin and Pitcher (1910), one of Georges Braque's most characteristic still lifes, was executed in the style of analytic cubism that he cofounded with Pablo Picasso. (Kunstmuseum, Basel.)

Braque's works from the period 1917–20 are derived compositionally from synthetic cubism, the second phase of cubism, which began about 1914. Much flatter and more variegated in color, they include brightly dotted decorative passages. Around 1930–31, Braque moved to the coast of Normandy in France. As a result, he changed the subjects of his paintings; bathers, beach scenes, and seascapes were now his favorite themes. Stylistically, he became increasingly interested in ornamentation and patterned surfaces. During the late 1930s and early '40s, Braque was drawn to melancholy themes. From 1945, birds were a dominant subject. Braque's canvases done during the 1950s show a return to the brilliant colors of the Fauve period, as in the Louvre ceiling (1952–53) and the decoration for the villa at Saint Paul-de-Vence (1954). Active until the end of his life, Braque produced an oeuvre that includes sculpture, graphics, book illustration, and decorative art.

MAGDALENA DABROWSKI

Bibliography: Cogniat, Raymond, *Georges Braque* (1980); Cooper, Douglas, *Braque: The Great Years* (1973); Elderfield, John, The *"Wild Beasts"* : *Fauvism and Its Affinities* (1976); Leymarie, Jean, *Braque* (1961; repr. 1988); Mullins, Edwin, *The Art of Georges Braque* (1968); Rubin, William, *Picasso and Braque* (1990); Wilkin, Karen, *Georges Braque* (1991).

Bras d'Or Lake   [brah dor]

Bras d'Or Lake is a saltwater lake in central Cape Breton Island, Nova Scotia, Canada. About 71 km (44 mi) long and covering 932 km^2 (360 mi^2), it is connected to the Atlantic Ocean by two narrow channels and a canal. On Feb. 23, 1909, the ice-covered lake served as the site of Canada's first airplane flight.

Brasília [brah-zeel'-yah]

The Congress Building is one of the chief landmarks in Brasília, the capital of Brazil since 1960. The building was designed by Brazil's acclaimed architect Oscar Niemeyer, who was also commissioned to design the other monumental buildings in the planned city.

Brasília, the capital of Brazil, is located in a federal district of 5,814 km² (2,245 mi²) in Goias state, on Brazil's central plateau. The population of the city and the entire district is 1,576,657 (1985 est.).

An outstanding example of a planned city constructed in a rural setting, Brasília is situated at an elevation of 1,065 m (3,500 ft) on a drainage divide among three rivers—the Tocantins, Paraná, and São Francisco.

Brasília was laid out in the shape of an airplane. Government buildings, separated by broad avenues, form the fuselage, and various commercial and residential sectors form the wings. Because of Brasília's relatively remote location, its airport is an important link with the rest of Brazil. The planner Lúcio de Costa created the city's modernistic design after winning a national competition for the job. He worked in concert with architect Oscar Niemeyer, who designed the major structures. Critics claim that lack of low-cost housing has forced more than one million workers to seek homes in the unplanned satellite communities outside Brasília. The federal government is a major employer, and construction, publishing, and printing are important industries in the city. The National Theater, Museum of Brasília, and University of Brasília (1962) are located there.

The proposal to build a new capital in the interior of Brazil in order to stimulate development there was first made in 1763. A new federal district was first designated in 1889, although it was not precisely located until 1956. In 1957, during the presidency of Juscelino Kubitschek de Oliveira, construction was at last authorized. The seat of government was officially moved to Brasília from Rio de Janeiro in 1960.

JAMES N. SNADEN

Bibliography: Epstein, David G., *Brasília, Plan and Reality* (1973).

Braşov [brah-shawv']

Braşov is a city in central Romania on the northern slope of the Transylvanian Alps. It has a population of 335,000 (1984 est.). Surrounded on three sides by mountains, it is an important distribution center served by roads and railroads. Industrial growth since World War II has been substantial, and today its industries include truck and tractor plants, textile factories, and chemical plants. The cultural center of the Braşov district, the city contains numerous theaters, a museum, and a polytechnic school.

Braşov was founded by the Teutonic Knights in 1211, and through much of its history it was known by its German name, Kronstad. During the 13th century it was the regional trading center for such goods as cloth, wax, and metalwork. The heavily fortified town withstood Turkish attacks during the 15th century, and many historic buildings from this era, such as the Town Hall (1420), the Trumpeter's Tower (1528), and several churches, still stand.

brass

Brass is an ALLOY consisting of 50% or more of copper, to which zinc and smaller amounts of other elements—usually tin, lead, or aluminum—have been added. (BRONZE is a copper-base alloy where tin, rather than zinc, is used.) The color, strength, machinability, and corrosion resistance of brass are determined by the amount of zinc and other metals present. At about 15% zinc, copper's color changes from dark red to a reddish gold; as more zinc is added, the gold tint increases.

The percentage of zinc mixed with copper will affect ductility, the metal's ability to be permanently stretched or bent, as well as its hardness. The alloy known as cartridge brass, containing 30% zinc, provides the greatest measure of ductility and strength and is used for cold-forming operations, where brass is shaped by rolling, drawing (reducing the diameter of a rod by pulling it through a series of dies), deep drawing (using punches and dies to stamp out shapes), and other machining processes. Cold-forming produces high-strength brass objects such as bolts and screws. No heat is used in processing, although low-temperature annealing is sometimes used to remove the stresses caused by machining. The alloy known as Muntz metal contains 40% zinc and is used for hot-working, to make such low-strength items as handles and door fittings. Other alloy compositions are used to make brass foundry products.

Lead added to brass makes it softer and easier to machine. Iron, aluminum, nickel, or manganese improve the alloy's strength. The addition of tin increases corrosion resistance.

Brass has been a common metal since Roman times. Because it can be easily shaped, cast, and engraved, it was used in increasing quantities for decorative and utilitarian items—plaques, candlesticks, clocks—and for scientific instruments such as telescopes and compasses. Less-expensive metallic materials have replaced brass for decorative objects, however, and other, more technically appropriate metals or plastics are now used for instrumentation and for scientific and structural needs. Cities in New England—especially in Connecticut—that through the 19th century had flourishing economies based on brass production have had to find new enterprises to replace their failing brass industries.

MERLE C. NUTT

brass instruments: see WIND INSTRUMENTS.

Brassaï [brah-sah'-ee]

The Parisian photographer Brassaï, pseudonym of Gyula Halász, b. Brassó, Transylvania, Sept. 9, 1899, d. July 8, 1984, achieved success overnight with his revealing views of the street and night life of Paris during the 1930s, published in 1933 as *Paris de Nuit*. Along with other photographs of the period, these were reproduced and translated (1976) into English as *The Secret Paris of the 30's*. Using a camera borrowed from his photographer friend André Kertész, Brassaï from 1924 began recording the sights he saw on his nightly wanderings through the salons, streets, and bars of the French capital, concentrating on the brothels, criminal haunts, and other aspects of Parisian night life that fascinated him. The results were a new dimension in documentary photography and the nickname "the eye of Paris" bestowed on him by the American novelist Henry Miller. Brassaï's other books of photographs include *Camera in Paris* (1949), *Graffiti* (1961), and *The Artists of My Life* (1982).

ELIZABETH POLLOCK

Bibliography: Miller, Henry, *Brassaï* (1952).

Bratianu   (family)   [brah-tee-ah'-noo]

The Bratianus were a prominent Romanian family. **Ion Constantin Bratianu**, b. June 2, 1821, d. May 16, 1891, was instrumental in securing the union of Walachia and Moldavia as an independent Romania and was prime minister (1876–88) under King CAROL I. His son **Ionel Bratianu**, b. Aug. 20, 1864, d. Nov. 24, 1927, was also prime minister (1909–11, 1914–18, 1918–19, 1922–27). He led Romania into World War I (1916) on the Allied side, and after the Romanian defeat by Germany, resigned (May 1918) rather than sign the German-imposed peace treaty. Returning to office, he represented Romania at the PARIS PEACE CONFERENCE but resigned in protest against the Treaty of Trianon. In power from 1922 to 1927, he introduced a new constitution. His brother **Constantin** or **Dinu Bratianu**, b. Jan. 13, 1866, d. 1952?, opposed the dictatorships of CAROL II and Ion ANTONESCU and the postwar Communist regime. He died in prison under the Communists, as did various other family members.

Bratislava   [brah'-tee-slah-vah]

Bratislava is the capital of Slovakia. It has a population of 441,453 (1991). It is on the left bank of the Danube River, where the Little Carpathian Mountains cut across the valley from Austria, and lies near the point where the borders of Slovakia, Austria, and Hungary meet. Bratislava is served by highways, railroads, and an airport, and its docking facilities make it a busy trade center. The main industries include food processing, chemical manufacturing, oil refining, and textile and paper processing. Comenius University was established there in 1919. There are also the Slovak Academy of Sciences and several other schools and theaters, as well as many landmark buildings.

Occupied by the Slovaks in the 8th century, Bratislava became part of Hungary in the 11th century and was recognized as a city by the Hungarian king in 1291. It was the capital of Habsburg Hungary from 1541 to 1784. At that time the city was often known by its German name, Pressburg. The Habsburg rulers were crowned in the Cathedral of St. Martin, and the royal family lived in the castle that rises 91 m (300 ft) above the Danube River bank. Napoleon made peace with the Austrians there in 1805. From 1918 to 1992, Bratislava was the capital of the Slovak republic within Czechoslovakia.

Brattain, Walter   [brat'-uhn]

The American physicist Walter Houser Brattain, b. Amoy, China, Feb. 10, 1902, d. Oct. 13, 1987, shared the 1956 Nobel Prize for physics with John BARDEEN and William B. SHOCKLEY for his research on semiconductors and for the development of the TRANSISTOR. A graduate of Whitman College, Walla Walla, Wash. (1924), the University of Oregon (1926), and the University of Minnesota (1929), Brattain served as a research physicist at Bell Telephone Laboratories from 1929 to 1967, where he carried out his work on transistor physics.

Braudel, Fernand   [broh-del']

Fernand Braudel, b. Aug. 24, 1902, d. Nov. 28, 1985, was a French economic historian whose influential *The Mediterranean and the Mediterranean World in the Age of Philip II* (1949; Eng. trans., 2 vols., 1972–73) integrated geographic, economic, sociological, and historical factors in a new and elegant synthesis, an approach to historical scholarship Braudel had first practiced as editor of the journal *Annales*. Braudel also wrote an acclaimed 3-volume examination of the origins of capitalism, *Civilization and Capitalism, 15th–18th Centuries* (1979; Eng. trans., 1982–84).

Braun, Carol Moseley

Carol Moseley Braun, b. Chicago, Ill., Aug. 16, 1947, became the first black woman elected to the United States Senate when she carried half the white vote in Illinois to defeat her Republican opponent in 1992. A Chicago native and graduate of the University of Illinois and University of Chicago Law School, she was an assistant U.S. attorney in Chicago before serving in the state legislature (1979–89). She was the little known Cook County recorder of deeds (1989–92) when she defeated Senator Alan J. Dixon in the Democratic primary.

Braun, Eva

Eva Braun, b. Feb. 6, 1912, d. Apr. 30, 1945, was the mistress and later the wife of the German dictator Adolf HITLER. A photographer's assistant, she began living with Hitler about 1936. They were married on Apr. 29, 1945, in an air raid shelter in Berlin as Soviet troops advanced through the city, and committed suicide the next day.

Braun, Karl Ferdinand

The German physicist Karl Ferdinand Braun, b. June 6, 1850, d. Apr. 20, 1918, shared the 1909 Nobel Prize for physics with Guglielmo MARCONI for his work in developing the radio. Braun, who spent his career as a professor of physics at German universities, increased the range of Marconi's transmitter. He also invented the crystal RECTIFIER, a device that allows current to flow in only one direction and improves radio transmission. Braun later invented the OSCILLOSCOPE, a cathode-ray–tube laboratory device that was the forerunner of today's television and radar tubes.

Braunschweig   (city)   [brown'-shvyk]

Braunschweig (English: Brunswick) is a city in the state of Lower Saxony in northern Germany, on the Oker River. It is an industrial center with a population of 258,833 (1991 est.). Chief industries include the production of automobiles, optical instruments, office machinery, and food products (especially sugar). Founded in the 9th century, Brauschweig was chartered in the 12th century by HENRY THE LION, duke of Saxony, and in the 13th century it was an important member of the HANSEATIC LEAGUE. The city was the residence of the dukes of Braunschweig from 1753 until 1918, when the duchy was abolished. Saint Blasius, the 12th-century Romanesque cathedral where Henry the Lion and Holy Roman Emperor Otto IV are buried, survived World War II, during which the city was severely damaged. Known for scientific research, Braunschweig is the site of Germany's oldest technical university (est. 1745).

Braunschweig   (region):   see BRUNSWICK.

Brautigan, Richard   [brow'-ti-guhn]

Poet and novelist Richard Brautigan, b. Tacoma, Wash., Jan. 30, 1935, d. an apparent suicide, October 1984, is identified with the U.S. counterculture movement of the 1960s. From his first successful novel, *Trout Fishing in America* (1967), most of his work features eccentric plots related by gentle, self-deprecating narrators. Brautigan never shed his hippie persona, and his later writings attracted a younger audience than his contemporaries, who had once been his most ardent readers.

Bibliography: Boyer, Jay, *Richard Brautigan* (1987); Chenetier, Marc, *Richard Brautigan* (1983).

Brave New World

Brave New World (1932), a satirical, futuristic novel by Aldous HUXLEY, is a major work of utopian literature. Set in the year 632 AF (After Ford), it depicts a world in which art, religion, and individual achievement have been replaced by societal conformity, indifferent technology, and drugged stability. Human embryos, ranging from Alpha Plus Intellectuals to Epsilon Minus Morons, are produced by artificial, assembly-line fertilization. John, a naturally born "savage" individualist, is found in New Mexico, taken to London for experimentation, and driven to madness and destruction when his human emotions conflict with the brave new world of rigid predictability. Huxley's ironic title is taken from Shakespeare's *The Tempest*.

JEAN DWYER CORMICK

Bibliography: Firchow, P. E., *The End of Utopia* (1984).

Bray, Thomas

Thomas Bray, b. 1656, d. Feb. 15, 1730, was an English clergyman and philanthropist. After graduating from Oxford in 1678, he served as a country rector. In 1696 he was appointed commissary, or representative, of the bishop of London for Maryland. Although Bray made only one brief trip to Maryland, he was instrumental in securing the passage of legislation making the Church of England the established church there. He recruited other clergymen for the colonies and founded more than 30 colonial libraries. In England he engaged in many charitable works, especially the relief of prisoners. Bray was also active in founding the Society for Promoting Christian Knowledge (SPCK) and the Society for Propagating the Gospel (SPG); both societies are still active in Great Britain.

Bibliography: Thompson, H. P., *Thomas Bray* (1954).

Brazil

Brazil, the largest country in South America, stretches almost 4,350 km (2,700 mi), from the Andes Mountains eastward to the Atlantic Ocean, and borders on every country of the continent except Chile and Ecuador. Its official name is the Federative Republic of Brazil. Brazil occupies almost half of South America and is the world's fifth-largest country in area. Al-

FEDERATIVE REPUBLIC OF BRAZIL

LAND. Area: 8,511,965 km² (3,286,487 mi²). Capital: Brasília (1991 pop., 1,596,274). Largest city: São Paulo (1991 pop., 9,480,427).

PEOPLE. Population (1993 est.): 156,664,000; density: 18 persons per km² (48 per mi²). Distribution (1991): 75% urban, 25% rural. Annual growth (1993 est.): 1.4%. Official language: Portuguese. Major religions: Roman Catholicism, Protestantism.

EDUCATION AND HEALTH. Literacy (1991): 81% of adult population. Universities: (1992): 83. Hospital beds (1987): 501,660. Physicians (1987): 206,382. Life expectancy (1993 est.): women—67; men—58. Infant mortality (1993 est.): 62 per 1,000 live births.

ECONOMY. GNP (1992): $369 billion; $2,350 per capita. Labor distribution (1990): agriculture—22%; services—55%; industry—23%. Foreign trade (1992): imports—$20 billion; exports—$35 billion; principal trade partners—United States, European Community, Latin America. Currency: 1 real = 100 centavos.

GOVERNMENT. Type: federal republic. Legislature: National Congress. Political subdivisions: 27 states, 1 federal district.

COMMUNICATIONS. Railroads (1990): 28,828 km (17,913 mi) total. Roads (1990): 1,448,000 km (899,745 mi) total. Major ports: 11. Major airfields: 24.

Colonial tile-roofed buildings in Olinda help maintain Brazil's ties to its Portuguese past. Colonial settlement, impeded by coastal mountains and interior forests, was largely confined to the Atlantic coast.

though only slightly smaller in size than the United States, it has just 60% of the U.S. population. The capital, BRASÍLIA, was built in the central highlands beginning in 1957 in order to encourage development of the interior.

Brazil's name is derived from the Portuguese word for the reddish color of brazilwood, an important export during the 16th century. Today the country is normally the world's largest exporter of coffee and sugar. It is also a leading exporter of soybeans. Despite the availability of rich agricultural and mineral resources and recently modernized industry, Brazil has an economy that is hampered by a huge foreign debt.

Brazil gained independence from Portugal in 1822, and in the 19th century enjoyed a political stability unusual for Latin America. In the 20th century, however, social turmoil and political strife led to the overthrow of many administrations. The military controlled the government from 1964 until 1985, when a civilian president took office.

LAND AND RESOURCES

Brazil is mostly highland. Its major physiographic regions include the Guiana Highlands, which are north of the AMAZON RIVER; the Amazon Basin itself; the Brazilian Highlands, which are south of the Amazon; and the CHACO. Brazil's highest mountain, the Pico da Neblina (3,014 m/9,888 ft), is in the northwest of the country near the Venezuelan border.

Similar geologic processes formed all of Brazil's highland regions. The deepest and oldest rocks are crystalline granites and quartzites. Over several million years these large blocks of land were thrust upward, dissected by erosion, and then inundated by the sea; during this period, sedimentary layers of varying thicknesses were deposited. Finally, another episode of uplift and erosion took place. Resistant diabase is responsible for the buttes and mesas common to Brazil's highlands. Uplift along the eastern margin produced the coastal mountain ranges. The eastern margin of the Brazilian Highlands, known as the Great Escarpment, slopes abruptly toward the sea. A wealth of data indicates that Brazil was once joined to Africa.

The lowland areas of Brazil are composed mostly of undisturbed sedimentary rocks of alluvial origin. Brazil's coastal plain is narrow and discontinuous. This arrangement of landforms has acted as a deterrent to interior settlement.

Climate. The single most important influence on Brazil's climate is its location on the equator. Temperatures seldom exceed 35° C (95° F) in the tropics, owing to the moderating effects of high atmospheric humidity. At Rio de Janeiro, average temperatures vary from 22° C (71° F) in the coldest month, July, to 27° C (80° F) in the warmest month, January. The northern limit of frost passes through the state of Paraná. Most

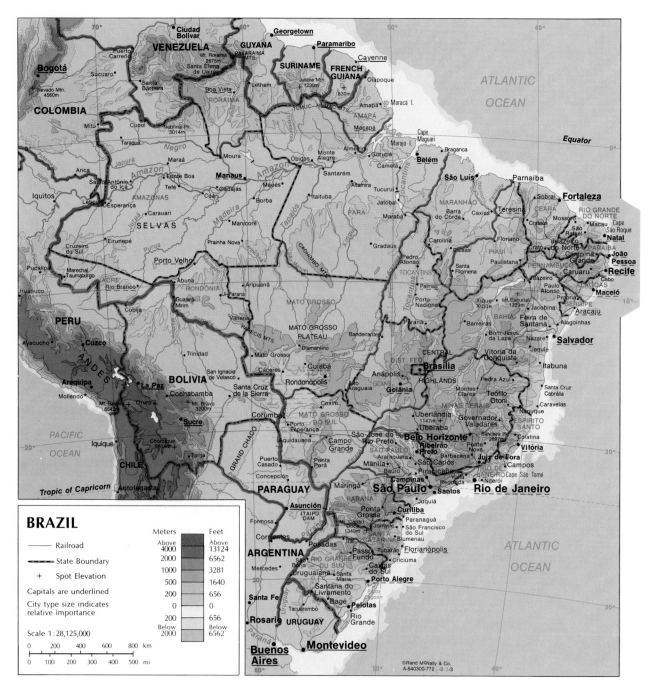

BRAZIL

— Railroad

■ ■ ■ ■ State Boundary

+   Spot Elevation

Capitals are underlined

City type size indicates
relative importance

Scale 1:28,125,000

Meters	Feet
Above 4000	Above 13124
2000	6562
1000	3281
500	1640
200	656
0	0
200	656
Below 2000	Below 6562

0   200   400   600   800 km

0   100   200   300   400   500 mi

©Rand McNally & Co.
A-540300-772 -2 -3-3

of Brazil receives a moderate rainfall of 1,000–1,500 mm (40–
60 in), but the Amazon lowlands and several other areas receive more than 2,030 mm (80 in) of rainfall annually.
Vegetation and Animal Life. Rainfall is the primary determi-
nant of vegetation patterns in Brazil. Tropical rain forest, or
selva, is found in the wettest part of the Amazon Basin. The
opening of this area to settlement through roadbuilding since
1970 has led to the large-scale burning of this forest—an
estimated 200,000 km² (77,220 mi²) was burned in 1987 alone—
arousing worldwide concern and prompting a government
conservation program. Much of Brazil is covered by savanna,
or tropical grassland. In the interior of the northeast, *caatinga,* a
low and bushy scrub and thorn forest, is characteristic. Wildlife is abundant in Brazil, although large mammals are rare. Ta-
pirs, capybaras, parrots, and monkeys are plentiful. The

small, flesh-eating piranha fish lives in the Amazon River.
Soils. Lateritic soils dominate the Brazilian countryside. Thick,
coarse, and reddish, they are deficient in plant nutrients. Rich
alluvial soils mark the river floodplains.
Drainage. Brazil is drained by three major river systems: the
Paraná-Paraguay-Plata in the south, the SÃO FRANCISCO in the
east, and the Amazon in the north. The highlands of southern Brazil are drained by the PARANÁ, PARAGUAY, and URUGUAY
rivers, water from which flows eventually into the Plata.
None of these rivers is navigable for any distance. The São
Francisco flows northward from the Brazilian Highlands for
about 1,600 km (1,000 mi). Waterfalls and currents prohibit
navigation in its lower course for about 322 km (200 mi). The
Amazon, the major river of South America, is the world's second longest (6,440 km/4,000 mi), and most of its basin lies

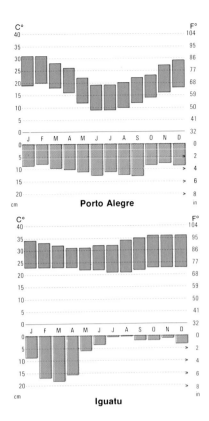

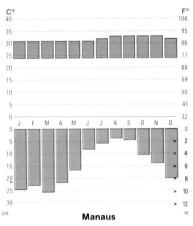

Annual climate charts for five cities in Brazil illustrate the distinct climate zones of the country. Bars indicate monthly ranges of temperatures (red) and precipitation (blue). Iguatu, in the northeastern state of Ceará, has a steppe climate; Rio de Janeiro, a coastal city on the Atlantic, a tropical wet climate modified by maritime influences; Pôrto Alegre, an important inland port on the Guaíba River in eastern Rio Grande do Sul, a subtropical humid climate; Brasília, the federal capital, a tropical wet-dry climate; and Manaus, a river port near the confluence of the Amazon and the Rio Negro, a tropical wet climate.

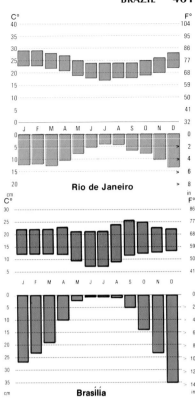

within Brazil. No other river approaches its discharge or volume of flow: more than 198,100 m³ (7,000,000 ft³) of water pass through its mouth into the Atlantic Ocean each second, more than ten times the volume of the Mississippi River. The river's channel reaches depths of 91 m (300 ft) in places, permitting oceangoing ships to navigate almost 1,600 km (1,000 mi) upstream. The Amazon's major tributaries are the TOCANTINS-ARAGUAIA, the MADEIRA, the NEGRO, the Xingu, and the Tapajós.

Resources. Brazil's mineral resources are superlative, but many are still unexploited. Sizable deposits of iron and manganese ores have been discovered, but Brazil lacks the high-grade coking coal needed to transform them into steel. Brazil is a leading world exporter of iron ore. New discoveries of oil

and increased domestic output permitted the country to reduce oil imports from over 58% of the nation's requirements in 1971 to 43% by 1991. Production of gold expanded markedly during the 1980s. Discoveries of other minerals—including phosphates, manganese, uranium, copper, coal, and gemstones—are regularly being made, particularly in the state of Minas Gerais and the Amazon area. Known reserves of bauxite and platinum are also extensive.

PEOPLE

Demography. Most Brazilians live in densely populated areas of eastern Brazil. Although urbanization has not produced actual declines in rural population, internal migration has caused cities to grow much faster than rural areas. The largest

Coffee growing in the temperate southeast (left) is Brazil's leading export industry, and the nation is the world's foremost coffee producer. Industry, fast catching up to the agricultural sector as a source of foreign exchange, is concentrated in the city of São Paulo (below), the most populous in South America.

cities are São Paulo, Rio de Janeiro, Belo Horizonte, Salvador, Recife, and Pôrto Alegre. Hundreds of thousands of homeless, a great many of them children, roam the streets. At the growth rate prevailing in the mid-1990s, the population of Brazil was expected to double in 40 years.

The Ethnic Mix. Because of the tremendous influx of immigrants into Brazil during the 19th century, the population is mostly Caucasian (60%) and mixed (30%). The Portuguese were followed by Italians, Germans, Syrians, and Lebanese. Asians, especially Japanese, arrived during the 1930s. About 1 million native Americans, mostly of Tupi-Guaraní, Carib, Arawak, and Ge linguistic stock, lived in Brazil when the first Portuguese explorers arrived early in the 16th century. Intermarriage between Portuguese and indigenous peoples produced a new race called *mamelucos* by the Brazilians. Beginning in 1538, African slaves were brought to Brazil. Almost 5 million slaves were admitted before the abolition of slavery in 1888. Mulattoes, those of mixed black and white ancestry, constitute perhaps 20% of the population. Today, the population of Brazil's three southernmost states is mostly white. Blacks and mulattoes are concentrated along the Atlantic Coast. Native Americans, who fish and practice slash-and-burn agriculture, live mostly in the Amazon Basin. Of the perhaps 200,000 native Americans living in the interior, many are threatened by the gradual encroachment of farmers and miners.

Language and Religion. Although Brazil has a racially mixed population, most of its citizens are united by language and religion. Portuguese is the official language. More than 90% of Brazilians are nominally Roman Catholic, although many practice folk religions that combine Catholic and African elements (see Afro-American cults). Church and state have been constitutionally separated since 1889. Brazil is the largest Portuguese-speaking and largest Catholic nation in the world.

Education and Health. The adult literacy rate in Brazil has risen only gradually. Despite the adult education program MOBRAL, which the government launched in 1971 to increase literacy, the illiteracy rate remained close to 20% in 1994. Official schools offer free preprimary education. Education is compulsory and free between the ages of 7 and 14 years. Secondary education is also free. The University of Rio de Janeiro (1920) is one of South America's leading universities.

The Arts. The vitality of the arts in Brazil owes much to the country's racial and ethnic mix. Rio's Carnaval, a spectacular folk festival held each year just before Lent, is a showcase for the samba, Brazil's most characteristic dance, which has a pronounced African beat. Heitor Villa-Lobos was one of the nation's most respected composers. Folk arts and crafts thrive in the rural areas, and many modern Brazilian painters take the everyday life of humble people as their subject. The influence of Mexican revolutionary muralists is apparent in the work of such famous modern artists as Cândido Portinari. Brazil's brilliant architects have created outstanding modern structures of a recognizably Brazilian stamp, most notably the nation's capital, Brasília, which was planned by Lúcio Costa. Its buildings, designed by Oscar Niemeyer, blend function and simple beauty. Prominent literary figures of the last two centuries include Jorge Amado, Joaquim Maria Machado de Assis, Euclydes da Cunha, and Gilberto Freyre. (See Brazilian literature.)

ECONOMIC ACTIVITY

Until recently Brazil's economy has been one of boom and bust; its development has been determined in succession by the world demand for sugarcane, rubber, and coffee. The country has now begun a drive to develop its vast resources and to industrialize. Nevertheless, Brazil is still primarily an agricultural country, with severe economic problems. The reforming "cruzado plan" (1986) in its first year spurred economic growth, but an inflation rate of more than 4,000% per year prevailed in the first six months of 1994. The world financial community has cooperated in rescheduling interest payments on Brazil's massive foreign debt.

Agriculture and Forestry. Despite its importance to the economy, Brazilian agriculture needs to modernize its farming methods. The most important commercial crop has traditionally been coffee, largely produced on *fazendas* ("plantations") in the states of Paraná and São Paulo and thus subject to frost damage. Even though the quality of coffee from other countries is considered better, Brazil is the world's leading producer and exporter. Other important commercial crops are bananas, soybeans, cacao (of which Brazil is the world's third-largest exporter), tobacco, maize, sugarcane, and oranges. Cattle raising is well developed, and Brazil produces more livestock than does Argentina. Brazil is Latin America's largest exporter of lumber and, despite environmental concerns, cut down more forest in the 1980s than any other country in the world

Mining and Manufacturing. Iron ore and aluminum ore are the mainstays of Brazilian mining. High-grade hematite has

The Carnival of Rio de Janeiro, Brazil's four-day national celebration of Mardi Gras, features gorgeously costumed street dancers and lively street parades. Rio, the former national capital, is a world-class tourist center, with wide beaches and lofty coastal mountains.

The opera house at Manaus, a once-thriving Amazon port, was built at the turn of the century when Manaus was the rubber capital of the world. Today the city exports bananas and other agricultural products grown in the country's tropical interior.

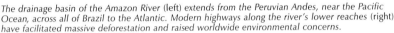

The drainage basin of the Amazon River (left) extends from the Peruvian Andes, near the Pacific Ocean, across all of Brazil to the Atlantic. Modern highways along the river's lower reaches (right) have facilitated massive deforestation and raised worldwide environmental concerns.

long been mined at Itabira in the state of Minas Gerais, and a new site in the Carajás Highlands in Para, estimated to be the largest deposit in the world, is now under development. The world's largest gold mine, opened in the 1980s, is at Serra Pelada in the Amazon Basin.

Brazil's leading industries manufacture processed foods, chemicals, textiles, metal products and machinery, transportation equipment (automobiles and ships), and petroleum products. Brazil is the seventh-largest steel-producing country in the world, and its automobile industry is the world's ninth largest. Most manufacturing is concentrated in the São Paulo area. The country drastically reduced its dependence on imported petroleum in the 1980s through the use of GASO-HOL and hydroelectric power. The ITAIPÚ hydroelectric station near Foz do Iguaçu on the Paraná River, opened in 1982, has the largest generating capacity in the world.

Transportation and Trade. Brazil has the longest road network in Latin America, as well as the most automobiles, trucks, and buses. Among the busiest seaports are Santos, Vitória, Rio de Janeiro, Paranaguá, and Recife. Rivers are major avenues of transportation, especially in the interior; topography has hindered the development of an inland rail network.

The value of Brazil's exports (including coffee, soybeans, iron ore, processed foods, machinery, vehicles, and vegetable products) is the highest in South America, although drought and fluctuating world prices can significantly alter the annual trade balance. Moreover, due to its crazy-quilt economy and lack of restraint in spending by government officials, Brazil has become one of the world's largest debtor nations.

GOVERNMENT

The constitution of 1969, suspended by a succession of military governments and amended in 1977 and 1978, vested executive power in the president, legislative power in a senate and a chamber of deputies, and judicial power in a supreme court. The country returned to full civilian rule in 1985, but the president was chosen by an electoral college. The new constitution, promulgated on Oct. 5, 1988, provides for a directly elected president and a bicameral legislature. Although the presidential system was retained, the constitution grants greater powers than previously to states and localities. It also created several new states from former territories and states.

HISTORY

Archaeological discoveries in northeastern Brazil in the 1980s indicate that humans may have settled in the area at least 32,000 years ago—far earlier than had been believed. The indigenous Indian population was widely scattered and probably numbered no more than 1 million when Vicente Pinzón, a Spaniard, touched the northern coast of Brazil in

1500. In the same year Pedro CABRAL claimed the land for Portugal, based on the Treaty of TORDESILLAS (1494). The first permanent Portuguese settlement (São Vicente in São Paulo state), however, was not founded until 1532. French Huguenots briefly settled at Rio de Janeiro, and the Dutch ruled at Recife from 1630 to 1654. Europe's demand for sugar led to the establishment of sugarcane plantations along the northeast coast in the 1530s, and the Portuguese crown granted 12 individuals feudal powers over large blocks of land called *capitanias*. This system ended in 1640. Starting in the 1600s colonists from São Paulo called *bandeirantes* settled the interior. Gold and diamonds were discovered in Minas Gerais about 1700. Rio de Janeiro was the only port from which gold could legally be exported, and it supplanted Bahía as the capital in 1763.

In 1807–08, during the Napoleonic Wars, King JOHN VI of Portugal took refuge in Rio de Janeiro. Brazil, now the seat of government for its mother country, witnessed great economic growth. When a threatened revolution in Portugal forced John VI to return to Lisbon, popular pressure compelled his son, Dom Pedro, to declare (1822) Brazil independent. Dom Pedro was crowned Emperor PEDRO I and ruled until he abdicated in 1831. His son, Dom PEDRO II, succeeded him.

During the reign of Dom Pedro II, Brazil enjoyed economic prosperity. After expanding the country's territory as the result of a successful war against Paraguay (1864–70), the emperor cultivated cordial relationships with the United States and with other Latin American countries. Nevertheless, prorepublican factions began to grow in power, and the army overthrew the emperor in 1889. Brazil was ruled directly or indirectly by the military until 1894, when the first civilian president, Prudente de Moraes, was elected. Coffee and rubber exports generated great profits around the turn of the century; the coffee and rubber boom, however, collapsed.

Political unrest led to a 1930 revolt led by Getúlio VARGAS. Vargas's tenure marked the start of industrialization for Brazil. Overthrown in 1945, he was reelected in 1950 but committed suicide when the army demanded his resignation in 1954.

A new capital was established at Brasília to encourage development of the interior, but the concern of the military and business leaders turned to the pressing problems of social unrest and excessive inflation. In 1964 the military overthrew President João GOULART, and Brazil came to be ruled by a succession of military governments. The military suspended constitutional guarantees and imposed strict press censorship. These policies were moderated under President Ernesto GEISEL, who was succeeded by Gen. João Baptista de Oliveira FIGUEIREDO in 1979. Civilian government was restored fully in

The Congress Building is a focal point of Brasília, the capital of Brazil since 1960 and a striking example of modern urban planning. The new city was sited more than 965 km (600 mi) inland in order to stimulate the development of Brazil's vast underpopulated interior.

1985 when an electoral college chose Tancredo de Almeida Neves as president. He died before taking office and was succeeded by José SARNEY. A new constitution took effect in October 1988. Sarney's successor, Fernando COLLOR DE MELLO, Brazil's first directly elected president, took office in March 1990. As a result of revelations of widespread corruption, Collor was impeached on Sept. 29, 1992. He was succeeded by Vice-President Itamar Franco, who became acting president and then president when Collor de Mello resigned on Dec. 29, 1992. Corruption charges continued to bedevil the government, however. In 1994 former finance minister Fernando Henrique Cardoso, a center-left economist with strong business support, was elected president.   JAMES N. SNADEN

Bibliography: Andrade, M. C., *The Land and People of Northeast Brazil* (1980); Baer, Werner, *The Brazilian Economy*, 3d ed. (1989); Becker, B. K., and Egler, C. A., *Brazil* (1992); Bethel, Leslie, ed., *Colonial Brazil* (1987); Bradford, B. E., *A History of Brazil*, 3d ed. (1993); Kinzo, M. D., ed., *Brazil: Economic, Social, and Political Challenges of the 1990s* (1993); Margolis, M. L., and Carter, W. E., eds., *Brazil: Anthropological Perspectives* (1979); Nyrop, R. F., ed., *Brazil*, 4th ed. (1983); Skidmore, T. E., *The Politics of Military Rule in Brazil, 1964–1985* (1988); Young, J. M., *Brazil: Emerging World Power*, rev. ed. (1991).

Brazil Current

The Brazil Current is a warm, very salty South Atlantic ocean current that flows southward along the east coast of South America from 5° south latitude. A branch of the Atlantic South equatorial current, it is deflected to the east by the Falkland Current at 35°–40° south latitude. Temperatures are 19°–27° C (66°–80° F), salinity is 35–37 parts per thousand, and depth is 100–200 m (330–660 ft).

Brazil nut

The tough-shelled, triangular Brazil nut is the seed of a tropical evergreen tree, *Bertholletia excelsa*, that grows in large forests in the Amazon River basin of South America. The trees, which can reach a height of 45 m (150 ft), are not cultivated; propagation is entirely by the chance sowing of the seeds, usually by animals. The fruits of the tree are melon-size—10–20 cm (4–8 in) in diameter—thick-walled pods, each of which contains some 18–30 nuts. The pods are gathered when they have fallen from the trees and must be chopped open to obtain the nuts. They can be shipped only during the rainy season, when stream and river waters are navigable. Belém, a port in the Brazilian state of Pará, is a center for Brazil nut

The Brazil nut tree, B. excelsa, a tall tropical evergreen, grows wild in the forests of the Amazon region. Up to 30 of its creamy-fleshed, triangular nuts grow inside a hard, coconutlike "fruit"; the nuts can be gathered only when the fruit falls to the ground. The woody coverings of the fruits are so tough that they must be opened with an ax.

export, and the nuts are often called Pará nuts. Brazil nut kernels are sweet tasting and an excellent source of protein. They are also rich in an oil that is used for lubricating and lighting.   DONALD K. OMECKY

Brazilian literature

A branch of Portuguese literature from the 16th to the early 19th century, Brazilian literature began to acquire its own identity only after 1822, when Brazil severed political ties with Portugal. Through World War II the model for Brazilian letters was French literature. Literary schools, therefore, followed French patterns: first romanticism, then realism, symbolism, and finally—after a transitional period between approximately 1900 and 1920—avant-garde modernism.

Critics and literary historians generally agree that the Brazilian Joaquim Maria MACHADO DE ASSIS was the outstanding Latin American novelist of the 19th century. Machado was the first major Brazilian writer to experiment with language and structure, beginning a tradition of openness to the avant-garde that continues to this day. Modernism shaped Brazilian letters in the period before World War II, and, like similar movements in Europe, it turned to folk sources for material and used the vernacular as its language. The leading exponent of modernism was Mário de ANDRADE, whose great novel *Macunaíma* (1928) is considered its outstanding example.

The anthropologist and historian Gilberto FREYRE, in such social histories as *The Masters and the Slaves* (1933; Eng. trans., 1946), had a significant influence, especially on writers of Brazil's northeast region. *The Devil to Pay in the Backlands* (1956; Eng. trans., 1963), by the great novelist João Guimarães ROSA, is a regional novel and one of the first contemporary Latin American literary works to achieve international acclaim. The novels of Jorge AMADO, one of Brazil's most popular writers (for example, *Dona Flor and Her Two Husbands,* 1966; Eng. trans., 1969), are also widely translated.

Bibliography: Bishop, Elizabeth, and Brasil, Emanuel, eds., *An Anthology of 20th Century Brazilian Poetry* (1972); Brookshaw, David, *Race and Color in Brazilian Literature* (1986); Johnson, Randal, ed., *Tropical Paths: Essays on Modern Brazilian Literature* (1992); Martins, Wilson, *The Modernist Idea* (1970; repr. 1979); Patai, Daphne, *Myth and Ideology in Contemporary Brazilian Fiction* (1983); Stern, Irwin, ed., *Dictionary of Brazilian Literature* (1988).

See also: LATIN AMERICAN LITERATURE.

brazilwood

Brazilwood, *Caesalpinia,* includes several tropical American trees in the pea family, Leguminosae. The heartwood of this tree is used to make violin bows and also yields a red dye that was used for dying and printing calico before coal-tar dyes became popular. Brazilwood was discovered in East India, but early European explorers found it in such abundance in the coastal forests of South America that they named the area Brazil.   JANE PHILPOTT

brazing

Brazing is a method of joining metal parts. It differs from WELDING in that no substantial amount of the metals to be joined is melted, and it differs from soldering in that the melting point of the filler metal is above 427° C (800° F). The metals to be joined, known as base metals, are fitted closely together and joined by a molten filler metal that wets the base metals and is distributed between the fitted surfaces of the base metals by capillary attraction. After the joined parts cool, the filler metal solidifies to form the newly brazed joint.

Brazing is one of the oldest joining processes; one of its earliest uses was to join ornamental gold and platinum. Silversmiths also used silver-base filler metals in their work. The process is used today in the manufacture of automobile radiators, aerospace structures, electronic equipment, structural building panels, and other items.

Brazing processes include the commonly used torch method, furnace brazing for mass production, induction heating, arc heating, block-and-flow brazing, dip brazing, and infrared brazing.   JOHN F. KANE AND PHILLIP W. MORTON

Brazos River   [braz'-uhs]

The Brazos River is formed by the junction of the Double Mountain and Salt rivers, which fork in north central Texas. Draining an area of about 108,000 mi² (44,500 mi²), it flows southeast to the Gulf of Mexico at Freeport. The Possum Kingdom and Whitney dams on the Brazos provide power and irrigation.

Brazza, Pierre Paul François Camille Savorgnan de   [brah-zah']

Pierre de Brazza, b. Jan. 26, 1852, d. Sept. 14, 1905, was a French colonial governor in Africa who founded (1880) the city of Brazzaville. An Italian nobleman, he took French citizenship in 1874. After 6 years of exploration in equatorial Africa, he arranged (1883) the treaties that eventually established the French Congo, which he governed from 1886 to 1897. Brazza later (1905) undertook an investigation that helped reduce the exploitation of native workers.

Bibliography: West, Richard, *Brazza of the Congo* (1972).

Brazzaville

Brazzaville (1984 pop., 595,102), the capital city of the People's Republic of the Congo, is located on the north bank of the Congo River below Stanley Pool.

Brazzaville is the center of transportation and communication for the Congo. Served by steamships, railroads, and a network of highways, it is a transit trade point for wood, rubber, agricultural products, and other commodities bound for central African countries. Its main industries produce building materials, textiles, beverages, leather products, and matches.

Founded in 1883 by the French explorer Pierre de Brazza, the city served as the capital of French Equatorial Africa from 1910 to 1958. Marien Ngoubai University (1972) is located there.

breach of the peace

Breach of the peace is a willful violation of public order or a disturbance of public tranquillity by disorderly conduct. (In law, "breach" is the violation of a duty or obligation; other principal types include breach of contract, breach of promise to marry, and breach of trust.) Examples of breach of the peace include rioting, unlawful discharge of firearms, public fighting, and the use of abusive or threatening language. Obstructing the flow of traffic and disturbing the enjoyment of others in public places are also acts constituting breach of the peace.

This offense was outlawed by common law, which considered peace essential to civil society, and is also punishable under modern statutes in many jurisdictions.

bread

Bread is a baked food made from a dough of ground or milled cereal grain, usually wheat flour, and leavened by chemical or microbiological action.

Because of the leavening process, the making of even the simplest kind of bread is a fairly complicated procedure. Only wheat flour contains gluten, a substance that supplies the structure needed for leavening. Many non-wheat-growing cultures have never known bread.

Bread making may have originated in Egypt. Archaeologists have found pieces of bread that show clear evidence of leavening action in deposits dating from about 3500 BC. The "sun bread" of Upper Egypt, made today by a method that must be very old, is prepared from a thick batter that is placed in the sun to leaven and partially dry before it is baked into a hard-crusted loaf with a sweet, soft interior. By the dynastic period, loaves of special shapes and sizes were made for religious purposes and for consumption by different social groups.

Bread was a common foodstuff in Rome, and a sophisticated baking industry developed, using mechanical kneading devices. During the early Middle Ages, baking technology regressed; although eventually the growth of bakers' guilds resulted in improvements in techniques and tools. During the Industrial Revolution, an acceleration occurred in the development of baking technology, and today the making of bread is a highly mechanized process in most Western countries.

LEAVENING

Dough was originally leavened by adding sourdough left over from a previous day's bread production. The relative acidity, alcohol content, and low oxygen tension in the interior of a sourdough mass tend to inhibit the growth of molds and undesirable bacteria while allowing preferred strains of YEAST to proliferate. The results are unpredictable, however, because varying amounts and types of yeast can develop in the sourdoughs. An improved method of ancient origin uses the relatively pure yeast that settles out from beer or wine.

Yeast. Today bread is leavened with yeast manufactured by inoculating pure cultures of the selected strain of microorganism into carefully formulated and sterilized liquid media. The yeast cells multiply under controlled conditions; they are harvested by centrifugation and filtering, washed free of media, and packaged for delivery. Bakers' yeast is composed of the living cells of *Saccharomyces cerevisiae*, a unicellular microorganism.

Yeast performs its leavening function by fermenting carbohydrates such as glucose, fructose, maltose, and sucrose. (It cannot metabolize lactose, the predominant carbohydrate in milk.) The principal products of fermentation are carbon dioxide, which produces the leavening effect, and ethanol. Yeast also produces many other chemical substances that flavor the baked product and change the dough's physical properties.

Although most breads and rolls are leavened by yeast, some breadlike products (Irish soda bread, corn bread, certain kinds of muffins) are leavened by chemical systems such as BAKING POWDER.

INGREDIENTS OF BREAD

Bread can be made using only flour, water, salt, and leavening. This simple recipe is used for the popular Italian and French breads, which are light in color and have a crisp crust and coarse, relatively tough crumb. The flavor and the texture of both crust and crumb deteriorate rather quickly, however. Other ingredients must be added to improve storage stability.

Bread flour is usually made from hard wheat, which produces a dough that is elastic enough to hold the gas produced during fermentation.

Nonfat dry milk is often added to improve the flavor and enhance the nutritional quality of commercial bread. Shortening improves the texture of the crumb and increases shelf life. It also makes the dough easier to handle. Some types of shortening, such as butter, contribute significantly to the flavor of the finished loaf. Eggs contribute their characteristic color and flavor to the bread, and their natural emulsifiers improve the handling properties of the dough and make the crumb softer. Sugar and corn syrup make the bread sweeter and supply fermentable carbohydrates for the yeast to metabolize. Molasses and honey add their typical flavors as well as sweetness. Most consumers prefer slightly sweet bread.

Other ingredients sometimes added to commercial bread and rolls include dough improvers (to adjust handling properties), yeast foods, mold inhibitors, vitamins, and minerals.
Whole Wheat Bread. Whole wheat bread is made from a meal that contains essentially all of the components of the cleaned wheat kernel in the same proportions as they are found in the grain. The loaves are dense, firm, dark in color, coarse in texture, and strong in flavor. Wheat and part-whole-wheat breads contain a mixture of whole grain meal and

enough white flour to assure good dough expansion and a lighter color and density.
Pumpernickel and Rye Bread. Pumpernickel, a dark, tough, and close-textured loaf, is made from crushed or ground whole rye kernels, without the admixture of wheat flour. Rye and wheat flours are added to produce rye bread, which has a better texture, lighter color, and milder flavor than pumpernickel. Caramel coloring and caraway seeds are often added to rye bread.

Rye bread can be made by the sourdough method, where leavening and flavor result from the addition of a small amount of old dough in which lactic-acid–producing bacteria have developed. These microorganisms ferment some of the carbohydrates in the fresh dough batch, producing characteristic sour tastes and odors.
Salt-Rising Bread. Salt-rising bread is made with a sourdough high in salt. The salt limits the growth of common bakers' yeast while creating a more favorable environment for growth of bacteria that influence the flavor.

A truck delivers flour to a modern bakery, where it is unloaded into a silo. The flour is sifted, weighed, and poured into a mixer, where it is combined with a premix of yeast, water, salt, and additives. The dough is allowed to stand for a few hours in order to rise and is then extruded onto a conveyor belt and sliced into loaves. The loaves are put into pans and go through a prover, where they rise a second time. A hot-air oven bakes the bread, and a depanner removes the bread from pans by pneumatic suction. Pans are cleaned and reused. The bread loaves are cooled, sliced and wrapped. Factory bakeries are situated close to their markets to facilitate daily deliveries.

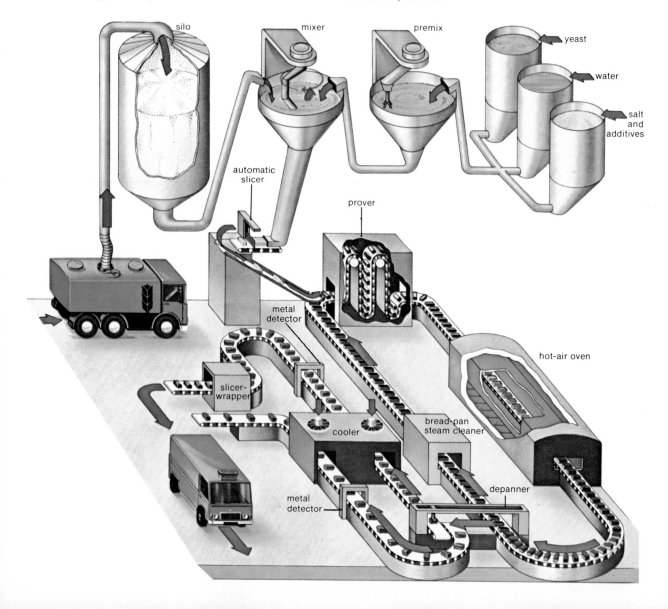

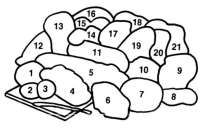

(1) *Jewish pumpernickel*, (2) *plain hard roll*, (3) *poppy-seed hard roll*, (4) *challah*, (5) *French bread*, (6) *white bread*, (7) *Italian ring*, (8) *corn bread*, (9) *pita*, (10) *pumpernickel*, (11) *seedless rye bread*, (12) *whole-wheat bread*, (13) *Russian black bread*, (14) *plain bagel*, (15) *pumpernickel bagel*, (16) *Italian round bread*, (17) *raisin bread*, (18) *Jewish rye*, (19) *honey bran bread*, (20) *bread sticks*, (21) *onion rolls*

PRODUCTION METHODS

All conventional bread production involves measuring the ingredients; mixing and kneading the ingredients to form an extensible dough; allowing the dough to ferment under controlled conditions; kneading the fermented dough; forming the dough piece; proofing, or allowing the dough piece to ferment; and baking. There are many variations of this simple scheme.

Mixing and kneading the ingredients to form a soft, elastic mass (called developing the dough) is a critical part of the baking process. Unless the proper physical properties are obtained at this stage, the dough will be very difficult to manipulate, either by hand or by machinery, and will not produce bread of optimal volume and texture. An adequately developed bread dough will exhibit a slight sheen on the surface but will be only slightly sticky to the touch. When the dough is stretched out to a thin film, it will not tear readily and will have a translucent, webbed appearance when viewed against the light.

The second kneading process collapses the expanded dough piece so that most of the leavening gas is pressed out of it. This is done to prevent the formation of large gas bubbles, which mar the appearance of the loaf and reduce the quality of the bread.

After the initial fermentation, the bulk dough mass is cut into pieces calculated to yield the desired size of roll or loaf. These pieces may be rounded to form a skin around the piece before it is fermented again, or they may be sheeted out and rolled into cylinders to be deposited in loaf pans. In one type of breadmaking the dough is deposited into pans immediately after it has been mixed. The panned or rounded dough pieces then undergo a second, and sometimes a third, fermentation, during which the leavening gas generated by the yeast causes them to expand considerably.

Bread and rolls can be baked in pans or on sheets; the latter method produces the so-called hearth breads. Most commercial ovens for large-scale production are of the tunnel type, in which multiple assemblies of loaf pans or sheets are carried through long baking chambers indirectly heated by gas, oil, or electricity.

NUTRITIONAL QUALITIES

Most white bread sold in the United States is enriched. Federal standards require that enriched bread contain not less than 1.1 mg of thiamin, 0.7 mg of riboflavin, 10 mg of niacin, and 8 mg of iron to a pound. (It must not contain more than 12.5 mg of iron in each pound.) It may contain enough added calcium to bring the total calcium content of the bread to 600 mg a pound. When so enriched, bread can supply significant percentages of the daily requirements of these and several other essential nutrients.

A serving of bread will vary in size depending on the desires of the individual consumer, but an average portion is generally considered to be 2 ounces, or about two slices. Consuming a 2-ounce serving of enriched white bread made with 4 percent nonfat dry milk at each of three daily meals will supply the following nutrients:

Calories	460
Protein	14.8 g
Fat	5.4 g
Carbohydrates	86 g
Fiber	38 g
Sodium	0.86 g
Potassium	0.18 g

The percentages of the U.S. recommended daily adult allowance supplied by the same daily servings are:

Protein	23
Calcium	22
Phosphorus	16
Iron	17
Vitamin A	trace
Thiamin	45
Riboflavin	24
Niacin	28
Ascorbic acid	trace

SPECIAL DIETARY BREADS

To meet the needs of people who experience adverse physiological reactions to some ingredients of bread, bakers have developed special products that do not contain the offending ingredients. A few bakers produce bread containing less than 10 mg of sodium to every 100 g. Although this bread is not as palatable as the regular product, it can be helpful in the diets of persons with edematous conditions, certain hypertensive states, and nephritis.

Gluten bread contains reduced amounts of starch and a higher percentage of protein than regular white bread. Persons who react adversely to the consumption of wheat starch can usually eat this food without developing symptoms. It is also recommended for high-protein, low-calorie diets.

Wheat gluten, as well as some other proteins, can cause celiac disease, a debilitating intestinal disorder affecting susceptible infants and small children. Foods resembling bread can be made for these patients from starch and a texturizing agent such as egg whites.   SAMUEL A. MATZ

Bibliography: Beard, J., *Beard on Bread* (1977); Clayton, B., Jr., *The New Complete Book of Breads* (1987); Jones, J. and E., *The Book of Bread* (1986); Matz, S., *Ingredients for Bakers* (1987); Miller, B., *Variety Breads in the U.S.* (1981); Pomeranz, Y., and Shellenberger, J. A., *Bread Science and Technology* (1971).

breadfruit

The breadfruit is the globular or oval fruit of the breadfruit tree, *Artocarpus altilis*, an evergreen member of the mulberry family, Moraceae. It is a staple crop in parts of the Pacific, particularly Polynesia, and a significant food elsewhere in the moister tropics.

The breadfruit tree grows to heights of 18 m (60 ft) or more. The yellow-green fruit is up to 30 cm (12 in) in diameter. Its pulp is starchy, bland, and very palatable when cooked. The fruit is seedless, and the tree is reproduced vegetatively, usually from root suckers. Breadfruit were once grown only in the Pacific. In 1789 plants were shipped from Tahiti on the ill-fated voyage of the BOUNTY; Captain William BLIGH's next voyage was more successful, and the breadfruit was established in 1793 in Jamaica and St. Vincent. Since then it has spread round the tropics and become a very valuable food crop. Malaysia's jackfruit, *A. heterophyllus*, is widely cultivated for its edible fruit and its durable wood.   N. W. SIMMONDS

Breadfruit, native to East Asia, is a source of wood, fiber, latex, and food for people in the tropics. The flower develops into a starchy, edible fruit, which is roasted, baked, boiled, or ground into flour.

breaker

A breaker is a WATER WAVE that breaks into foam against a shore or reef, or over a very shallow sea bottom. Breaking waves are commonly classified as spilling, plunging, or surging. Spilling breakers break gradually over long distances; they are usually associated with steep-wind waves and a relatively flat offshore sea-bottom. Plunging breakers break all at once; they result from long swells over bottom sloping up to the shore. Surging breakers tend to surge up the face of a steep beach. A wave breaks when the orbital velocity of the water in the crest exceeds the phase speed of the wave, usually when the ratio of wave height to wavelength exceeds 1:7, or when water depth is about 1.3 times wave height.
ROBERT E. WILSON

Bibliography: Tricker, R. A. R., *Bores, Breakers, Waves, and Wakes* (1964).

breakfast cereal

In 19th-century America, breakfast cereal was a cooked mixture of grain—usually oats—water, and salt. The processed, packaged, ready-to-eat cereal that has become a typical American breakfast food originated with a group of Seventh-Day ADVENTISTS seeking healthful additions to their vegetarian diet (see NUTRITION, HUMAN). During the 1860s, at their sanitarium in Battle Creek, Mich., they produced a new cereal food by grinding up and rebaking already baked sheets of thin dough. Both C. W. Post, a patient at the sanitarium, and W. K. Kellogg of Battle Creek improved and expanded the process and founded what was to become a giant industry.

Today, breakfast cereals are available in dozens of flavors, forms, and textures. They are mixtures of wheat, corn, oats, and rice, with added sugars, colorings and flavorings. These ingredients are cooked together under pressure; dried; ground, flaked, or shredded; then toasted and packaged. To produce puffed cereals, grains are heated in a pressure chamber; when the pressure is released, expanding water vapor puffs each grain to many times its original size.

Bibliography: Daniels, R., *Breakfast Cereal Technology* (1974).

breakwater: see COASTAL PROTECTION.

bream: see MINNOW; SUNFISH.

Bream, Julian

Julian Bream, b. London, July 15, 1933, has taken the place of his advisor and mentor, the late Andrés Segovia, as the world's premier guitarist. He is, as well, an accomplished lutenist. Tutored by his father on the guitar, Bream later studied piano and cello at the Royal College of Music. He made his debut in 1947. Like Segovia, Bream has extended the range of the guitar by commissioning works from such contemporary composers as Benjamin Britten, Hans Werner Henze, and Sir Michael Tippett. His work in earlier music includes many transcriptions and arrangements for guitar or lute. Bream is the founder (1960) of the Julian Bream Consort, among the first groups to play early ensemble music; in 1961 he established the Semley Festival in Wiltshire, England, for the performance of rare chamber music. Bream's 4-part videocassette series *Guitarra!* (1986) traces the evolution of the art of the Spanish guitar.

breast

Breasts, in human females, are two glandular organs that secrete milk for feeding newborn infants. Such GLANDS are present in all MAMMALS and are known in general as mammaries. Physiologically, they are highly modified sweat glands. No other animals possess such glands, and no related precedents exist in other classes of vertebrates.

Rudimentary breasts are present in both human sexes at birth. No further development takes place in males during normal GROWTH, but full development occurs in females in the early childbearing period. A projection called a nipple is found at the tip of each breast in both men and women. It is surrounded by a pigmented area, the areola, that is about 3.75 cm (1.5 in) in diameter and that enlarges and deepens in color in pregnancy (see PREGNANCY AND BIRTH).
Structure. The female human breast consists mainly of a round mass of glandular tissue comprising about 15–20 lobes, each having a duct leading to an opening on the nipple; the duct system and glandular tissue fully develop with pregnancy. The amount of fat sheathing the glandular tissue determines the size of the breast. In a well-developed, well-nourished woman who has not borne a child, the breasts extend from the second or third rib to the sixth or seventh rib, and from the outer border of the breastbone (sternum) to the folds of the armpit. Connective tissues, or stroma, form the foundation or framework of the breast. The layer of ligaments directly beneath the breast sends strands into the breast itself, providing the firm consistency of the organ. The deep layer of connective tissue sends strands in the opposite direction into the covering of the chest muscles; the connection is a loose one, enabling the breast to move freely over the chest wall.
Examination. Breast CANCER is an important medical problem, with women of age 35 or older at increasing risk of developing some form of the disease. Physicians urge that women conduct monthly self-examinations of their breasts to detect potentially cancerous lumps, because the disease is more curable when found at an early stage. Another screening method is the X-ray process called MAMMOGRAPHY. Medical groups agree on the desirability of yearly mammography tests for women of 50 and older. Some groups also advise an initial test for women between 35 and 40, and a test every one or two years for women between 40 and 50, but other groups argue that the medical gains for the population at large do not justify the costs of such procedures. The alternative screening process called thermography has been characterized as a waste of time by the American College of Radiology. Other techniques for screening are also being explored.

For many years, the most common approach taken in the treatment of breast cancer was MASTECTOMY—the removal of the breast and sometimes of surrounding tissues and muscles

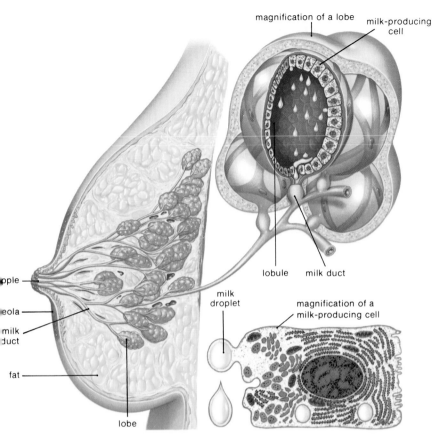

magnification of a lobe

milk-producing cell

lobule   milk duct

milk droplet

magnification of a milk-producing cell

pple

eola

milk duct

fat

lobe

An adult human female's breast comprises mostly fatty tissue, into which lobes are embedded. Each lobe connects to the nipple by means of a milk duct. A magnification of a lobe reveals a cluster of lobules, which are spheres of columnar, or milk-producing, cells. Milk produced by these cells contains fat, protein, carbohydrates, inorganic salts, vitamins, and antibodies that immunize the suckling infant from infections. Milk droplets accumulate in the lobule and travel through a duct to the nipple during lactation. The development of the breasts and the production of milk are controlled in a complex manner by four hormones. Estradiol and progesterone are hormones produced in the ovaries and uterus of a woman. Estradiol regulates duct development, and progesterone regulates lobule development. The hormones prolactin and oxytocin control milk production and secretion. Prolactin is released by the pituitary as pregnancy-induced levels of progesterone and estradiol in the blood drop. Prolactin stimulates the lobules to produce milk. Oxytocin is secreted by the pituitary in response to nerve impulses initiated when the infant sucks its mother's nipple. This hormone causes the contraction of muscle cells associated with the lobules and ducts, squeezing the milk toward the nipple. In addition, oxytocin causes uterine muscles to contract, restoring to the uterus of a nursing mother its original muscle tone.

as well—along with X-ray treatments. Many physicians instead urge less drastic lumpectomies, in combination with radiation therapy and chemotherapy, but the subject remains one of considerable controversy.

Bibliography: Day, N. E., and Miller, A. B., eds., *Screening for Breast Cancer* (1987); Haagensen, C. D., *The Breast* (1984) and *Diseases of the Breast,* 3d ed. (1986); Kopans, Daniel B., *Breast Imaging* (1988); Levy, Jerome, F., *Your Breasts* (1990); Love, Susan M., *Dr. Susan Love's Breast Book* (1990); Page, David L., and Anderson, Thomas J., *Diagnostic Histopathology of the Breast* (1988).

breast-feeding

Breast-feeding is giving a baby milk from the breast. After the birth of a child a mother's breast begins to produce milk, a natural process designed to provide complete nourishment for a baby for several months after its birth.

Before milk is produced the mother's breast produces colostrum, a deep-yellow liquid containing high levels of protein and antibodies. A newborn baby who feeds on colostrum in the first few days of life is better able to resist the bacteria and viruses that cause illness. The mother's milk, which begins to flow a few days after childbirth when the mother's hormones change, is a blue-white color with a very thin consistency. If the mother is well nourished, the milk provides the baby with the proper balance of nutrition.

The fat contained in human milk, compared with cow's milk, is more digestible for infants and allows greater absorption of fat-soluble vitamins into the bloodstream from the baby's intestine. Calcium and other important nutrients in human milk are also better utilized by infants. Antigens in cow's milk can cause allergic reactions in a newborn child, whereas such reactions to human milk are rare. Human milk also promotes growth, largely due to the presence of certain hormones and growth factors. Human milk banks have been established in several U.S. cities for the benefit of premature, ill, or allergic infants whose mothers are unable to breast-feed. Donor mothers are screened for certain diseases, and

their excess milk is frozen for later use.

The health of children in developing countries has suffered where dry formulas mixed with polluted water have replaced uncontaminated, nutritionally superior mother's milk. Controversy has erupted over commercial efforts to convert women in these countries to formula feeding. Conversely, studies have found toxic substances in human milk, often in areas affected by pesticide spraying programs.

While nursing, the mother may feel a tingling sensation as the milk glands, or lobules, produce milk and a slight tension when the milk is released from the glands to the nipple by the baby's sucking. The mother may feel some uterine contractions because the hormones that influence milk ejection also affect the uterus.

Many mothers attest to a special, intimate bond they have with their breast-fed infants. Although breast-feeding is a natural process, the actual techniques of breast-feeding are often not instinctive to new mothers. Some nursing mothers encounter difficulties with engorged breasts or chronically sore or leaking nipples. In some cases the nervous-hormonal reflex that ejects the milk can be blocked by anxiety and stress. Information on these problems and their solutions is available from physicians and organizations for nursing mothers, such as the La Leche League.   LISA L. PAINE

Bibliography: Conrad, Lynne H., *Maternal-Newborn Nursing* (1988); Dana, Nancy, *Successful Breastfeeding,* rev. ed. (1989); Goldfarb, Johanna, and Tibbetts, Edith, *Breastfeeding Handbook* (1989); Kitzinger, Sheila, *Breastfeeding Your Baby* (1989); Van Esterik, Penny, *Beyond the Breast-Bottle Controversy* (1989).

Breasted, James Henry

James Henry Breasted, b. Rockford, Ill., Aug. 27, 1865, d. Dec. 2, 1935, was an American Egyptologist, historian, and archaeologist. A graduate of Yale and Berlin universities, he joined the University of Chicago faculty in 1894. In 1899 he collaborated on the Berlin Egyptian Dictionary. He organized (1905) the University of Chicago Egyptian expedition, which carried out a major epigraphic survey of endangered inscriptions. His epigraphic researches formed the basis for his 5-volume *Ancient Records of Egypt: Historical Documents from the Earliest Times to the Persian Conquest* (1906–07). In 1919, Breasted was instrumental in founding the University of Chicago's Oriental Institute and became its first director. During his directorship many important archaeological projects were begun, including expeditions to Persepolis and Megiddo and further surveys in Egypt.

Breasted's publications include *A History of Egypt from the Earliest Times to the Persian Conquest* (1905), *The Development of Religion and Thought in Ancient Egypt* (1912), and the general textbook *Ancient Times: A History of the Early World* (1916), revised as *The Conquest of Civilization* (1926). He also originated the FERTILE CRESCENT concept to describe the development of civilization in the ancient Near East.

Bibliography: Breasted, Charles, *Pioneer to the Past* (1943; repr. 1977).

breath analyzer

The breath analyzer is an instrument that detects alcoholic impairment by measuring the concentration of alcohol in the breath; there is a definite relationship between the concentration of alcohol in breath and blood. The breath analyzer collects specimens of breath and, using any of a number of available chemical laboratory techniques, quickly determines the percentage of blood alcohol concentration (BAC). Under U.S. government standards, a BAC of 0.10 percent or more is evidence of alcoholic impairment. Breath analyzer results are accepted as evidence in all 50 states. In Great Britain and Europe, they must be corroborated by the results of blood analyses.   ROBERT F. BORKENSTEIN

Bibliography: Emerson, Vivian S., *The Measurement of Breath Alcohol* (1981); Stearn, Marshall B., *Drinking and Driving*, 2d ed. (1987).

breathing: see LUNGS; RESPIRATORY SYSTEM.

Brébeuf, Saint Jean de   [bray-buf']

Saint Jean de Brébeuf, b. Mar. 25, 1593, was a missionary to the Huron Indians and one of the JESUIT MARTYRS OF NORTH AMERICA. In 1625 he landed at Quebec with two other Jesuits and began missionary work among the Hurons, who eventually adopted him into their tribe. On Mar. 16, 1649, Brébeuf and his assistant Gabriel Lalemant were tortured to death by Iroquois Indians, who attacked the Huron settlement where they were working. They, and six other Jesuits and laymen killed by Indians during the same period, were canonized in 1930. Feast day: Sept. 26 (Mar. 16 for the Jesuits).

Bibliography: Donnelly, Joseph P., *Jean de Brébeuf, 1593–1649* (1976).

breccia   [brech'-ee-uh]

Breccia is a type of rock composed of large angular fragments that have become cemented together. Unlike the cobbles in conglomerates, which have been rounded by transport, the angular fragments of breccias have been formed in place rather than by erosion and sedimentation. Common in stratigraphic formations, they form in many ways: collapse of cave deposits, igneous activity, DIASTROPHISM, and meteorite crater impacts. Nearly all rocks are subject to some natural breakage, but they are considered breccias only when a considerable amount of fine-grained cementing material (matrix) is produced during fragmentation.   ROBERT S. DIETZ

Brecht, Bertolt   [brekht, bair'-tohld]

Bertolt Brecht, b. Feb. 10, 1898, d. Aug. 14, 1956, one of the great German poets and playwrights, had a key influence on modern drama. As an innovator he advanced such ideas as the "alienation effect," an attempt to divorce the audience from emotional identification with the play's characters, presumably preventing them from experiencing a catharsis of pity and fear—the Aristotelian requirements for dramatic effectiveness. "Gestic" acting, another Brechtian notion, trained ac-

Bertolt Brecht, an East German playwright, dramatized the Marxist themes of greed and corruption in capitalist society. He was a leader in the development of epic theater, a movement contending that the dramatic message of any play should be directed at viewers' senses of reason rather than evoking an emotional response.

tors to distance themselves from their stage characters, emphasizing stylized action, intonation, and facial expression rather than emotional empathy. These ideas were realized in many of Brecht's works, first in plays produced in Germany in the 1920s and early 1930s under the generic category of EPIC THEATER, and later in Brecht's own theater in East Berlin.

Brecht's reputation dates from 1922, when his second play, *Drums in the Night*, won the Kleist Prize, at that time Germany's chief literary award. With his love of unpretentious forms (the ballad, for example), his down-to-earth dialogue, and his use of American stereotypes such as the gangster, he foreshadowed the end of EXPRESSIONISM and the start of the style known as *neue Sachlichkeit* ("new objectivity"). Primarily, however, Brecht was the very concrete and intelligible poet of what he called the "Dark Times" in which he lived. It was his effort to understand these in Marxist terms that gave compelling unity to his varied work.

Early Life. The son of a paper manufacturer, Eugen Berthold Friedrich Brecht (he called himself Bertolt) grew up in his Bavarian birthplace, Augsburg, and entered Munich University as a medical student in the fall of 1917. He served briefly as a hospital orderly in his home town. He wrote his first play, *Baal*, in 1918, and during the revolutionary upheavals at the end of World War I he served on a soldiers' and workers' council. Brecht became a *dramaturg* (theatrical literary adviser) in Munich for two years following the success of *Drums*. Then he moved to Max REINHARDT's chief Berlin theater in 1924. Unsuccessful at first at the box office and unwanted as a director, he left after a year to work freelance. In 1927 he began his association with Erwin PISCATOR, another exponent of epic theater. In that year he met composer Kurt WEILL, with whom he wrote what is without doubt his most popular work, The THREEPENNY OPERA (first production, 1928; first film, 1931), freely adapted from John Gay's 1728 ballad-play, *The Beggar's Opera*. A full-scale opera, *The Rise and Fall of the City of Mahagonny*, followed in 1930. By then, however, Brecht had become interested in *Lehrstücke* (teaching plays), and after Weill scored two of these, their collaboration ceased. The music for the militantly Communist *The Measures Taken* (1930) and *The Mother* (1932) was composed by Hanns EISLER, a committed communist with whom Brecht wrote some of his best-known political songs.

Exile. When the Nazis took over in 1933, Brecht and his wife, the actress Helene WEIGEL, left Germany for Denmark, where they lived until the German invasion forced them once again to move. During the period of Scandinavian exile, however, Brecht composed the great poems of his maturity, collected in the *Svendborg Poems* (1939). Moreover, he returned to large-scale playwriting with *Mother Courage and Her Children* (1939), *The Life of Galileo* (1939), *The Good Person of Setzuan* (1940), and *The Resistable Rise of Arturo Ui* (1941).

In 1941, traveling by way of Helsinki, Moscow, and Vladivostok, the couple settled for six years in California, where Brecht collaborated on several films. In California he wrote the CAUCASIAN CHALK CIRCLE (1945), as well as a number of songs with Eisler, including "Hollywood Elegies" (1942), bitterly satirical verses on Hollywood. He worked with Charles Laughton on the adaptation and theatrical production of *Galileo* (1947). Despite his reputation as a Marxist, several of his other plays were produced on U.S. stages in the Cold War period of the late 1940s and early 1950s.

In 1947, Brecht was interrogated by the U.S. House of Representatives' Committee on UN-AMERICAN ACTIVITIES. Within days, he had returned to Europe. In Zurich (1947–48) he wrote his principal theoretical work, the *Short Organum for the Theater*. After settling in East Berlin in 1949, he devoted his last seven years to directing and training his own company, the BERLINER ENSEMBLE.

Appraisal. In the 1920s and '30s, Brecht was both celebrated and attacked as an author of the left vanguard. In the decade following World War II, his works came to assume the status of modern classics in both East and West Germany, and indeed throughout Europe. The high esteem with which he is regarded in the United States is of more recent vintage. The length of some of his plays and the sizes of their casts may account to some extent for their relatively rare appearance on commercial stages such as those of Broadway. However, his theatrical techniques have shaped the substance and structure of much modern drama.   Reviewed by PETER HELLER

Bibliography: Bentley, Eric, *Brecht Commentaries* (1981) and *Brecht Memoir* (1986); Brecht, Bertolt, *Brecht on Theatre*, trans. by John Willett (1964); Brooker, Peter, *Bertolt Brecht: Dialectics, Poetry, Politics* (1988); Esslin, Martin, *Brecht: A Choice of Evils*, 4th ed. (1984); Fuegi, John, et al, eds., *Brecht Performance: The Brecht Yearbook*, vol. 13, (1987); Hayman, Ronald, *Brecht: A Biography* (1984); Lyons, James K., *Bertolt Brecht in America* (1980); Willett, John, *The Theatre of Bertolt Brecht*, rev. ed. (1968) and *Brecht in Context* (1983).

Breckinridge, John Cabell

John Cabell Breckinridge, b. near Lexington, Ky., Jan. 15, 1821, d. May 17, 1875, was vice-president (1857–61) of the United States and the Southern Democrats' presidential nominee in 1860. A lawyer, he fought in the Mexican War and served in the Kentucky legislature (1849–50) and U.S. House of Representatives (1851–55) as a Democrat. As vice-president under James BUCHANAN, he presided over the Senate with impartiality despite his strong Southern sympathies. In the presidential election of 1860 he carried 11 states.

Breckinridge worked to prevent secession and civil war, but late in 1861 he fled to join the Confederacy. Made a general, he participated in several major battles, mostly in the West. He also administered a territorial command in western Virginia and on Feb. 6, 1865, was named Confederate secretary of war. After the war he went abroad. Returning to Kentucky in 1868, he practiced law and was vice-president of a railroad company.   RICHARD M. MCMURRY

Bibliography: Davis, W. C., *Breckinridge: Statesman, Soldier, Symbol* (1974); Klotter, J. C., *Breckinridges of Kentucky: 1760–1981* (1986).

Brecknock: see POWYS.

Breconshire: see POWYS.

Breda [bray-dah']

Breda is a city in North Brabant province of the southern Netherlands. Situated on the Mark River, it is about 43 km (27 mi) south of Rotterdam on the main road to Antwerp. Breda's population of 119,174 (1986 est.) is heavily Catholic. The main industries are canning and cloth and carpet manufacturing. Just north of Breda is the Beisbosch, a well-known park and bird sanctuary.

Settled in the 12th century, Breda was a strongpoint on the northern frontier of the duchy of Brabant and served as the capital of the barony of Breda from 1350. Taken alternately by the Spanish and Dutch during the 16th and 17th centuries, it was the site of the Compromise of Breda in 1566 (the beginning of the Dutch Revolt against Spain); the 1660 Declaration of Breda; and the 1667 Peace of Breda signed by England, France, Denmark, and the Netherlands. Notable buildings include the 15th-century Great Church of Our Lady, with a 45-bell belfry, and the Royal Military Academy (1536).

Bredero, Gerbrand   [bray'-de-roh, hair'-brahnt]

Gerbrand Adriaenszoon Bredero (Brederode or Breero), b. Mar. 16, 1585, d. Aug. 23, 1618, was a Dutch playwright and poet whose works were full-bodied portraits of 16th- and early 17th-century Dutch life. Although he was trained and worked as a painter, none of his paintings have survived. As a writer he was influenced by the style of the Dutch REDERIJKERS. Bredero is best known for such farces as *De Klucht van de Koe* (The Farce of the Cow, 1612), *De Klucht van de Molenaar* (The Farce of the Miller, 1613), and a boisterous comedy about Amsterdam life, *Spaanschen Brabander* (The Spanish Brabanter, 1617), loosely based on the Spanish picaresque novel *Lazarillo de Tormes* (1554). His lyrical and religious poetry, some of it in sonnet form, was collected in *Amoreus, Boertigh en Aendachtig Liedboeck* (Amorous, Humorous, and Religious Songbook, 1622).   R. P. MEIJER

breeder reactor

A nuclear fission reactor that produces as much fuel as (or more fuel than) it consumes is called a breeder reactor. Such a device is possible because when the URANIUM isotope U-238 absorbs a neutron during the operation of a reactor, it is converted into a fissionable isotope of PLUTONIUM, Pu-239, which can itself be used to fuel reactors. Breeding is also possible by the absorption of neutrons in thorium, Th-232, to produce the fissionable isotope U-233.

THEORY

A neutron in a nuclear reactor can meet one of several fates: it can be absorbed in the fuel, producing fission and more neutrons; it can be absorbed by nonfissionable materials in the reactor core and thus lost; it can be absorbed by a fertile material, such as U-238, thus producing more fissionable material; or it can escape from the system entirely. The maintenance of a chain reaction requires that at least one neutron be released, as the result of fission, for each neutron absorbed or lost for any reason. To replace the fuel that is burned and also sustain the chain reaction, at least two neutrons must be released. The accumulation of fuel, as in a breeder reactor, requires that the number of neutrons released per absorption in fuel, labeled η (eta), minus any losses, be greater than two. The parameter η depends on the type and degree of enrichment of fuel and on the energy of the neutrons in the reactor. In a reactor using natural uranium and containing a neutron-moderating material, such as graphite or heavy water, η is slightly more than 1.3; in one using slightly enriched uranium (about 3% U-235) and a water moderator, η is only about 1.8. Such reactors are merely converters. In a fast-neutron reactor that is fueled primarily with plutonium and has no moderator to slow neutrons, values of η of 2.3 are possible.

CONSTRUCTION AND IMPORTANCE

A typical breeder reactor has two regions: (a) an inner core, consisting of a large number of stainless-steel tubes filled with a mixture of uranium oxide (UO_2) and plutonium oxide (PuO_2), and (b) an outer blanket, consisting of tubes of natural uranium oxide, which captures neutrons that escape from the core to produce plutonium. Heat is removed from the core by a liquid coolant and used to produce steam; the steam powers a turbine that drives an electrical generator. Breeder reactors typically operate at high temperatures because fast (high-energy) neutrons are essential to their efficiency. Liquid sodium, which has excellent heat-transfer properties and, unlike water, does not readily absorb neutrons, is therefore commonly used as a coolant.

The potential importance of the breeder in the world's energy picture may be understood in terms of fuel utilization. In a typical present-day commercial light-water reactor, only

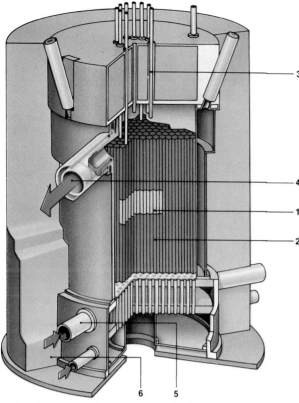

A breeder reactor produces more fissionable fuel than it consumes, supplying almost inexhaustible energy. The reaction in a breeder uses fast neutrons to generate plutonium-239 from uranium-238 (through uranium-239 and neptunium-239). The plutonium-239 in turn absorbs a neutron, giving off fission products and more neutrons. Reactions in the breeder reactor take place in the uranium-235 core (1), which produces fast neutrons, and the uranium-238 outer blanket (2), which absorbs them. Boron control rods (3) are interspersed throughout the core. Fission heat is carried away by liquid sodium coolant (4, 5) and used in a steam-driven electrical generator. The reactor is surrounded by a thick, concrete radiation shield (6).

about 2% of the uranium is burned, which implies that the resources of inexpensive natural uranium would be exhausted in a few decades if all reactors were converters. On the other hand, the breeder under ideal conditions uses almost 100% of the uranium, thus extending the uranium resources for many hundreds of years. Because the fuel used need not be enriched in the U-235 isotope, cost savings are effected.

In Europe the world's first commercial-size fast breeder—the Superphoenix, built in France by a consortium of European countries—began to produce electricity in 1986. In the United States, however, environmental concerns and fears of plutonium theft have halted the development of breeder reactors. The building of the controversial Clinch River reactor was slowed under the Carter administration, which also tried to discourage breeder technology development in other parts of the world, and was ended when Congress cut off its funding in 1983.

Worldwide, by the early 1990s, the need to amplify fuel sources with plutonium from fast breeder reactors had lessened considerably for several reasons. Uranium continued in strong supply, because fewer conventional reactors were being built; large amounts of stockpiled plutonium had been accumulated; the end of the Cold War ended the need for weapons-grade nuclear fuel; and reactor safety and nuclear theft problems remained unsolved. France's Superphoenix had been plagued with shutdowns; Britain's fast-breeder program was scheduled to end by the end of the decade. Only Japan continued its breeder development program; Monju, its sec-

ond breeder, with a 280-megawatt generating capacity, was due to go on-line in the mid-1990s.   RAYMOND L. MURRAY

Bibliography: Hirsch, P., ed., *The Fast-Neutron Breeder Fission Reactor* (1991); Waltar, A. E., and Reynolds, A. B., *Fast Breeder Reactors* (1981).

See also: NUCLEAR ENERGY; NUCLEAR REACTOR.

Breedlove, Craig

Norman Craig Breedlove, b. Los Angeles, Mar. 23, 1937, was the first person to set records of 400, 500, and 600 mph on land and the first to pursue the land speed record in a jet-powered vehicle. His first record (407.45 mph; 656 km/h) was established (1963) at the Bonneville Salt Flats, Utah, in a three-wheeled vehicle that was officially considered a motorcycle. He reached 526.28 mph (847 km/h) in 1964 in a four-wheeled vehicle. His two runs in 1965 averaged 600.601 mph (967 km/h), a record not broken until 1970. Breedlove held the land speed record five times between 1963 and 1965.

Bregenz   [bray'-gents]

Bregenz is the capital city of Vorarlberg province in western Austria. Located at the eastern end of Lake Constance, it is a winter and summer tourist center with a population of 27,236 (1991). During the Middle Ages it was ruled by the counts of Bregenz and the counts of Montfort. It was sold to the Habsburgs in the 16th century. A cable car runs up Mount Pfänder to a museum that displays Celtic and Roman artifacts.

Breitenfeld, Battle of: see THIRTY YEARS' WAR.

Bremen   [bray'-men]

Bremen is a port city in northern Germany, on the banks of the Weser River about 70 km (43 mi) from the North Sea. Bremen has a population of 537,600 (1989 est.). Bremen and its surrounding territory became a *Land*, or state, of the Federal Republic of Germany in 1947. The province has an area of 404 km² (156 mi²) and a population of 673,700 (1990 est.).

The Weser River is navigable by seagoing craft up to the city's docks. The Bremen docks are second in importance only to those of Hamburg; they line the Weser to the north of the Old Town. A considerable trade in cotton, grain, and tobacco is conducted in the city. Above the city the Weser River is used by barges and is linked with the canal system of Germany. On the estuary to the north is the outport of BREMERHAVEN, built on land purchased from Hanover. It was opened in 1830 to accommodate ships that were too large to sail up to Bremen itself. The chief industries of Bremen are shipbuilding, the production of iron and steel, and the manufacture of automobiles, electrical equipment, and machinery.

Bremen was founded about AD 787. By the 13th century it was a prosperous trading town, and in 1358 it became a member of the HANSEATIC LEAGUE. It was declared a free city in 1646 and maintained its independence until 1815, when it merged with the German Confederation. The city was heavily damaged during World War II but has since been completely rebuilt. The Altstadt, or Old Town, retains its Cathedral of Saint Peter (dating in part from the 11th century), its Gothic town hall, several other medieval churches, and the Guild Hall of the cloth merchants.   NORMAN J. G. POUNDS

Bremer, Fredrika   [bray'-mur, fred-ree'-kuh]

Fredrika Bremer, b. Aug. 17, 1801, d. Dec. 31, 1865, was a Swedish author and women's rights advocate. She published *Familjen H.* (The Family H.), Sweden's first realistic novel, in 1830. Among her many novels were *Hertha* (1856; Eng. trans., 1856) and *Father and Daughter* (1858; Eng. trans., 1859), both dealing with the domestic effects of the demand for women's rights. Much of her work was translated into English, and on her visit to the United States (1849–51) she was enthusiastically welcomed, especially by Ralph Waldo Emerson and his abolitionist friends, whose beliefs Bremer shared.

Bremerhaven   [bray'-mur-hah-fen]

Bremerhaven is a city in northern Germany in the state of Bremen. It lies on an inlet of the North Sea, where the Geest River and Weser Estuary enter the sea. The city has a population of 127,600 (1989 est.). Except during severe winters, its harbor is ice free. Major industries are shipbuilding, fish processing, and machinery construction. An oceanographic institute is located there.

The people of BREMEN, a city on the Weser 74 km (46 mi) to the south, founded (1827) Bremerhaven in order to have a port capable of handling large ships. It became important for passenger service and fishing. In 1939 the port and its neighboring towns were consolidated and named Wesermünde. The city was heavily bombed during World War II. In 1947 it was renamed Bremerhaven.

Brendan, Saint

Saint Brendan, 484–577, was an Irish abbot and missionary. Tradition holds that he founded the monastery at Clonfert, where he was the abbot. According to the medieval Irish epic *Voyage of Saint Brendan the Abbott*, he and 17 fellow monks sailed across the Atlantic to the land promised to the saints. This legend has led to speculation that Brendan may have reached America. In 1976 a group led by Timothy Severin crossed the Atlantic in the kind of leather boat Brendan would have used, proving that such a voyage was possible. Most scholars, however, accept only that Brendan visited Scotland and perhaps Wales on his missionary journeys. Feast day: May 16.

Bibliography: Severin, Timothy, *The Brendan Voyage* (1978; repr. 1987).

Brendel, Alfred

Alfred Brendel, b. Jan. 5, 1931, is one of the world's most acclaimed pianists. The Czech-born Austrian was a student of Edwin Fischer and commanded a large modern repertoire while still in his twenties. Preeminently an interpreter of the classical and romantic literature, he has recorded works of Schubert and Liszt, Beethoven's complete piano music, and the complete Mozart piano concertos with Sir Neville MARRINER conducting. Both a recitalist and concert artist, he combines refined pianism with interpretive passion. His *Musical Thoughts and Afterthoughts* (1977) and *Music Sounded Out* (1991) are collections of critical essays.

Brennan, William Joseph, Jr.

William Brennan, b. Newark, N.J., Apr. 25, 1906, a Democrat, was appointed to the U.S. Supreme Court by Republican President Dwight D. Eisenhower in 1956. Brennan graduated (1931) from Harvard Law School and specialized in labor law. In 1949 he was appointed to the New Jersey superior court and in 1952 to the state supreme court. On the U.S. Supreme Court Brennan cast consistently liberal votes on such major issues as abortion, equal rights, pornography, libel, religion, and criminal law. In the 1960s, Brennan was in the majority more often than any other justice; his landmark majority opinions include BAKER V. CARR and NEW YORK TIMES COMPANY V. SULLIVAN. He retired from the court in 1990.

Brenner Pass

The Brenner Pass is one of the lowest passes through the Alps, with an elevation of 1,370 m (4,495 ft). Since Roman times it has been the principal route between Germany and northern Italy. From Innsbruck, Austria, the route climbs steeply to its highest point, which marks the border between Austria and Italy. The first road was built through the pass in 1772, and between 1864 and 1867 a railroad was constructed, linking Innsbruck with Bolzano, Italy.

Brennus   [bren'-uhs]

Brennus was a Gallic king who captured Rome about 390 BC. According to legend, his attack on the Capitoline Hill failed when the Romans were alerted by the cries of the sacred geese. When the Gauls were found cheating in weighing the gold paid to secure their withdrawal, Brennus is said to have added his sword to the scales, justifying the action with the words *Vae victis* ("Woe to the vanquished").

Brent, Margaret

Margaret Brent, c.1600–c.1670, was a wealthy landowner in early Maryland and the first woman to hold land in her own right in the colony. As executor of Gov. Leonard Calvert's estate, she played a leading role in Maryland's affairs during the troubled period following his death (1647). She withdrew to Virginia after being denied a vote in the Maryland assembly because of her sex.

Brentano, Clemens   [bren-tah'-noh]

Clemens Maria Brentano, b. Sept. 9, 1778, d. July 28, 1842, brother of Bettina von Arnim, was a German romantic poet, playwright, and fiction writer. He was a leader of romanticism in Germany and of the patriotic revival of 1813. With his brother-in-law, Ludwig Joachim von Arnim, he published what has become the most famous collection of German folk poetry, *Des Knaben Wunderhorn* (The Youth's Magic Horn, 1805–08), which influenced such writers as Heinrich Heine and the Grimm brothers.

His original work is characterized by the simplicity found in genuine folk literature and avoids the vague atmosphere that often marked the work of the early romantics. He was particularly skilled in writing satire and fantastical literature. Because of his interest in folk literature, many of his works are based on folk themes.   CARL R. MUELLER

Bibliography: Brentano, Clemens, *Fairy Tales from Brentano* (1925); Dickens, David B., *Negative Spring* (1989); Fetzer, John, *Romantic Orpheus: Profiles of Clemens Brentano* (1974).

Brentano, Franz

Franz Brentano, b. Jan. 16, 1838, d. Mar. 17, 1917, was a German philosopher generally regarded as the initiator of act-psychology, the study of mental acts rather than the contents of consciousness. Because of his powerful influence on students, including the psychologist Christian von Ehrenfels and the philosophers Edmund Husserl and Alexius Meinong, Brentano is also acknowledged as a forerunner of Gestalt psychology and phenomenology. His best-known work is *Psychology from an Empirical Standpoint* (1874; Eng. trans., 1973). Recently, increasing attention has been given to his metaphysical, epistemological, and ethical writings.   BERNARD KAPLAN

Bibliography: Chisholm, Roderick M., *Brentano and Intrinsic Value* (1986); McAlister, Linda, ed., *The Philosophy of Brentano* (1976); Rancurello, Antos, *A Study of Franz Brentano* (1968).

Brescia   [bray'-shah]

Brescia is the capital city of Brescia province in the Lombardy region of northern Italy. Located in the southern foothills of the Alps east of Milan, it is a commercial, agricultural, and industrial center with a population of 196,935 (1990 est.). Firearms, machinery, vehicles, textiles, and iron and steel products are manufactured. Brescia's notable monuments include the Old Cathedral (11th-century Romanesque), the New Cathedral (17th-century baroque), the Lombard-Romanesque Church of San Francesco, the Pinacoteca (Picture Gallery) Tosio Martinengo, and the archaeological museum containing the bronze Winged Victory.

First a Gallic town, Brescia was successively a Roman town (from the 2d century BC), a Lombard duchy, and a free commune (from the 11th century). Thereafter it was dominated successively by Verona, Milan, Venice, France, and Austria. It was a revolutionary center during the 18th and 19th centuries and was united with Italy in 1859.   DANIEL R. LESNICK

Breslau: see WROCŁAW.

Breslin, Jimmy

Jimmy Breslin, b. Jamaica, N.Y., Oct. 17, 1930, is a writer whose work typifies the colorful, muckraking style of the "new journalism." Beginning as a sportswriter while still in his teens, he switched to political subjects in the 1960s, as a columnist for various New York newspapers and, from 1968 to 1971, for *New York* Magazine. His fiction includes *The Gang That Couldn't Shoot Straight* (1969; film, 1971), *Table Money* (1986), and *He Got Hungry and Forgot His Manners* (1988). Breslin won the Pulitzer Prize for commentary in 1986.

Bresson, Robert   [bre-sohn']

Robert Bresson, b. Sept. 25, 1907, is perhaps the most individualistic of all French film directors. His films are characterized by a single theme—the achievement or loss of spiritual grace—and by the subordination of plot, sound, and even acting (he uses nonprofessionals) to the photographic image. Beginning his career as a painter and photographer, Bresson worked with filmmaker René CLAIR in the 1930s and made his first major film, *Angels of Sin*, in 1943. Jean Cocteau wrote the dialogue for *The Ladies of the Bois de Boulogne* (1945). The prize-winning *Diary of a Country Priest* (1950) was based on a novel by Georges Bernanos. *A Man Escaped* (1956) uses Bresson's own experience as a wartime German prisoner. Later films include *Lancelot of the Lake* (1974) and *Money* (1983). Bresson's treatise on filmmaking, *Notes on Cinematography*, was published in 1975 (Eng. trans., 1977).

Bibliography: Hanlon, Lindley, *Fragments: Bresson's Film Style* (1986); Sloan, Jane, *Robert Bresson* (1983).

Brest   (Belarus)

Brest (1989 pop., 258,000) is a city in southwestern Belarus, near the Polish border. Situated on the Bug River and on the main route between Moscow and Warsaw, Brest is a major transportation center, with food-processing and textile industries. First mentioned in the 11th century, the city belonged to Lithuania (1319–1569) and then to Poland before being annexed by Russia in 1795; it was part of Poland again from 1919 to 1939 and of the USSR from 1939 to 1991. Brest was formerly known as Brest-Litovsk (Brest of Lithuania). The Treaty of Brest-Litovsk was signed there in 1918.

Brest   (France)

Brest is a city in Finistère department of Brittany, in northwestern France. Located on the Penfeld River, it is an important commercial port and naval base. The population is 153,100 (1990). Although the port is the main employer, some industry, including electronics, chemicals, metallurgy, and shipbuilding, is present. Brest is also the site of a national engineering school.

The recorded history of Brest goes back to Roman times. The growth of the city began in 1631 when Cardinal Richelieu improved the sheltered harbor and established a naval base. Fortified by Vauban in the 1680s, it withstood an attack by English and Dutch forces in 1694 and was the main base for France's Atlantic fleets during the 18th century. During World War I, Brest served as a supply base and debarkation point for U.S. troops. Occupied by the Germans during World War II, Brest was heavily damaged by Allied bombing.

Brest-Litovsk, Treaty of   [brest-lit-awfsk']

The Treaty of Brest-Litovsk, signed on Mar. 3, 1918, by Germany and Austria-Hungary on the one hand and the new Soviet government of Russia on the other, ended Russian participation in World War I. The Soviets had to agree to massive territorial losses. Germany and Austria had signed a separate treaty with Ukraine in February. Both treaties were annulled by the later armistice between Germany and the Western powers (November 1918).

Bibliography: Wheeler-Bennett, John, *Brest-Litovsk, the Forgotten Peace* (1938; repr. 1971).

Brethren

The term *Brethren* identifies several Christian groups of common origin, at an earlier date frequently called "Dunkers," of which the Church of the Brethren is today the largest. The movement began in Germany in 1708 as part of the spiritual awakening called PIETISM. In that year a small group led by Alexander Mack (1679–1735) baptized one another by immersion, facedown, three times in a flowing stream: this form of baptism became a distinctive practice. Mack and his followers migrated to Pennsylvania from Germany in 1719. Since then, small groups have broken away from the main body, either because it seemed too liberal or not liberal enough. Among all Brethren, trine immersion is practiced and a pacifist witness maintained. The Church of the Brethren lists 149,681 members in 1,102 congregations (1991). The Brethren Church and the Old German Baptist Brethren are much smaller.

CONRAD WRIGHT

Bibliography: Bowman, S. L., *Power and Polity among the Brethren* (1987); Stoffer, Dale, *Background and Development of Brethren Doctrine* (1989).

Brethren of the Common Life

The Brethren of the Common Life was a Christian religious group active in the Netherlands in the 14th and 15th centuries. Founded by Gerhard GROOTE, it included both clergy and lay people who lived together in communities but did not take monastic vows. Their spiritual teachings, known as the *Devotio Moderna,* are contained in *The Imitation of Christ,* a treatise attributed to THOMAS À KEMPIS.

Brétigny, Treaty of   [bray-teen-yee']

Signed on May 8, 1360, at Brétigny, near Chartres, the Treaty of Brétigny concluded the first phase of the HUNDRED YEARS' WAR between France and England. The English, under EDWARD III, had won a series of victories over the French, culminating in the Battle of Poitiers in 1356, in which JOHN II of France was taken prisoner. By the treaty, John was ransomed for the sum of 3 million crowns, and the French ceded to England Aquitaine, Calais, Ponthieu, and Guînes. In return, Edward renounced his claim to the French crown. The peace established at Brétigny lasted for only nine years.

Breton: see CELTIC LANGUAGES.

Breton, André   [bre-tohn']

André Breton, b. Feb. 18, 1896, d. Sept. 28, 1966, a French poet, essayist, critic, and editor, turned from Dadaism to outline the theoretical foundations of SURREALISM in *Manifeste du surréalisme* (Manifesto of Surrealism, 1924). Among the first writers in France to publicize Sigmund Freud's work, Breton explored the subject matter of dreams, the unconscious, and insanity.

Bibliography: Balakian, Anna, and Kuenzli, Rudolf, eds., *André Breton Today* (1989); Matthews, John F., *André Breton* (1987).

Breton, Jules Adolphe Aimé Louis

The French artist Jules Breton, b. May 1, 1827, d. July 5, 1906, won fame and official recognition with his often-sentimental paintings of peasants in landscape settings. After working under Félix de Vigne and Martin Drolling, he entered the École des Beaux-Arts, the official French art school, in 1847. Breton's first great success came in 1853 with his *Return of the Gleaners* (Musée d'Arras), painted in a very precise and detailed fashion and depicting the workers' graceful, harmonious body movements. Similar idyllic representations of peasant life won him honors and awards and led to his election to the Académie des Beaux-Arts in 1886. The French government purchased many of Breton's works, and his paintings were also frequently shown at official exhibitions abroad.

MARK ROSKILL

Breton literature   [bret'-uhn]

Breton literature, in the CELTIC LANGUAGE of the people who settled (5th–6th century) Brittany in France, began as a rich oral culture that strongly influenced medieval European literature, particularly through its Arthurian tales. (See also WELSH LITERATURE.)

Written literature of note began to appear only in the 19th century, after Jean François Le Gonidec (1775–1838) produced a Breton grammar (1807), a dictionary (1821), and the first Breton translation of the Bible (published in 1868). An anthology of Breton folksongs (1838) had a profound influence on the literature by inspiring a pride in the Celtic heritage and a national consciousness among Breton writers. In the 20th century the playwright Tangi Malmanche, the novelist Roparz Hémon, and other important Breton writers were all associated with the nationalist magazine *Gwalarn* (Northwest, 1925), which was suppressed by the French after World War II.

ELIZABETH A. GRAY AND AMY VARIN

Bretton Woods Conference

The Bretton Woods Conference, officially called the United Nations Monetary and Financial Conference, met (July 1–22, 1944) at Bretton Woods, N.H. It was attended by delegates from 44 states and nations. The conference laid the foundations of the postwar international monetary system, including plans for the WORLD BANK and the INTERNATIONAL MONETARY FUND.

Breuer, Marcel   [broy'-ur]

Marcel Lajos Breuer, b. Pécs, Hungary, May 21, 1902, d. July 1, 1981, was among the most influential figures in 20th-century architecture and design. Breuer became a student at the newly established BAUHAUS in Germany in 1920. The spirit of experimentation and functionalism there suited his own attitudes toward design so well that in 1924 he joined the teaching staff. From 1925 on, his revolutionary designs for furniture (particularly his S-shaped chairs) gained wide recognition.

Breuer left the Bauhaus in 1928 to establish an independent architectural practice in Berlin. When the Nazis assumed power in 1933 he left Germany, working first in Zurich and then in London. He had worked closely with Walter GROPIUS, the first director of the Bauhaus, and this collaboration resumed in 1937 when both Gropius and Breuer accepted professorships at Harvard University.

In 1946, Breuer left Harvard to establish an independent practice in New York City. Particularly characteristic of his architecture was the development of sculptural concrete forms and walls emphasizing solidity, pattern, and the play of sun and shadow. This work was influential in establishing a modern

The St. John's Abbey/University Church in Collegeville, Minn., is notable for its striking use of poured concrete. Marcel Breuer planned the church, one of the best known of his major commissions, in 1953.

aesthetic of reinforced concrete, especially in the use of prefabricated building elements.

Among Breuer's most notable buildings are the UNESCO headquarters in Paris (1953–57, with Pier Luigi NERVI and Bernard Zehrfuss); the headquarters of the Department of Housing and Urban Development, Washington (1963–68); the WHITNEY MUSEUM OF AMERICAN ART, New York City (1963–66); and the headquarters of the Department of Health, Education, and Welfare, Washington (1967–69).

RONALD WIEDENHOEFT

Bibliography: Breuer, Marcel, *Sun and Shadow* (1955); Caspar, Dale E., *Marcel Breuer* (1988); Masello, David, *Architecture without Rules: The Houses of Herbert Beckhard and Marcel Breuer* (1993).

Breughel: see BRUEGEL (family).

Breuil, Henri   [bruh'-ee, ahn-ree']

Henri Édouard Prosper Breuil, called Abbé Breuil, b. Feb. 28, 1877, d. Aug. 14, 1961, was a French archaeologist who became known as the father of prehistory within his lifetime. He was ordained a priest in 1900 and taught at the Institut de Paléontologie Humaine, Paris (1910–29), and the Collège de France (1929–47). Much of his career was spent at archaeological sites in Europe, Asia, and Africa, searching for prehistoric habitations and the works of prehistoric cave art.

Breuil is credited with reinterpreting in the early part of the 20th century the mass of poorly understood Old Stone Age tool industries of the Upper PALEOLITHIC and with establishing a chronology that remains fundamentally unchanged to the present. He is best known for his drawings of Paleolithic cave art, published as *Four Hundred Centuries of Cave Art* (Eng. trans., 1952), which helped establish the authenticity and antiquity of this art. Other works include *Les Subdivisions du paléolithique supérieur et leur signification* (Subdivisions of the Upper Paleolithic and Their Significance, 1937) and *Beyond the Bounds of History* (Eng. trans., 1949).

DAVID S. BROSE

Bibliography: Brodrick, Alan, *Father of Prehistory* (1963; repr. 1973).

breviary

In Roman Catholic worship, the breviary—from the Latin *breviarium* (summary, compendium)—is a book or books containing the DIVINE OFFICE, or Liturgy of the Hours, a collection of prayers, psalms, and biblical readings recited at different hours of the day. It dates from the Middle Ages, when it formed the basis of the BOOK OF HOURS. The breviary has been revised several times, most recently in 1971.

Brewer, David J.

David Josiah Brewer, b. Smyrna, Turkey, June 20, 1837, d. Mar. 28, 1910, was a justice of the U.S. Supreme Court who staunchly defended DUE PROCESS. The son of an American missionary in Turkey, Brewer graduated from Yale (1856) and the Albany (N.Y.) Law School (1858). He moved to Kansas, climbing up the judicial ladder to the federal circuit court before President Benjamin Harrison appointed him to the Supreme Court in 1889. During his 21 years on the court, Brewer usually joined conservatives to resist the growing power of the federal government. In a dissenting opinion in 1892 he wrote, "The paternal theory of government is to me odious."

brewing: see BEER.

Brewster, Sir David

The reputation of the Scottish physicist Sir David Brewster, b. Dec. 11, 1781, d. Feb. 10, 1868, rests mainly on his contributions to optics. An experimenter rather than a theorist, he discovered several constant relationships in the behavior of light polarized by reflection or refraction, including Brewster's law, which defines Brewster's angle of reflection (see POLARIZED LIGHT). Brewster also invented the kaleidoscope.

ROBERT SILLIMAN

Brewster, William

William Brewster, b. 1567, d. Apr. 10, 1644, was a leader of the PILGRIMS, who established PLYMOUTH COLONY. In England he studied briefly at Cambridge, the only Pilgrim Father to have some university training. A member of the local gentry in Scrooby, Yorkshire, he helped organize a separatist religious congregation in 1606 and financed its move to Holland in 1608. His influence was instrumental in winning the approval of the Virginia Company for the proposal to resettle the congregation in America, and he was one of the few original Scrooby separatists who sailed on the MAYFLOWER in 1620. As the church's ruling elder in Leyden and then in Plymouth, Brewster shared with William Bradford and Edward Winslow in the leadership of the Pilgrim enterprise.   OSCAR ZEICHNER

Bibliography: Sherwood, M. B., *Pilgrim* (1982).

Breyer, Stephen G.   [bry'-uhr]

Stephen Gerald Breyer, b. San Francisco, Aug. 15, 1938, was named an associate justice of the U.S. Supreme Court by President Bill Clinton in 1994. A graduate of Stanford and Harvard Law School, where he taught (1981–94), Breyer became a judge of the federal First Circuit Court of Appeals in Boston in 1980 and its chief judge in 1990. Earlier he had served as law clerk to Supreme Court Justice Arthur Goldberg (1965–67), as counsel on the Watergate Special Prosecution Force (1974–75), and as a special counsel to the Senate Judiciary Subcommittee on Administrative Practices (1979–80). Considered a moderate and a pragmatist, he achieved a rare degree of consensus while chief judge of the court of appeals.

Breytenbach, Breyten   [bry'-ten'-bahk]

Breyten Breytenbach, b. Sept. 16, 1939, was honored by his countrymen as South Africa's finest living poet writing in Afrikaans, even while he was scorned for his antiapartheid convictions. Born into a well-known Afrikaner family, Breytenbach has lived most of his adult life in France. On a visit to South Africa in 1975 he was convicted of antigovernment activities and imprisoned for seven years. Imprisonment resulted in three books: *A Season in Paradise* (1981) is the account of his return and of the activities for which he was imprisoned; *Mouroir* (1984), written while he was in solitary confinement, is a gathering of pieces on the themes of freedom and mortality; *The True Confessions of an Albino Terrorist* (1985) is the factual narrative of his prison experiences. In *Return to Paradise* (1993), he views, with some apprehension, a South Africa stumbling toward multiracial rule. Breytenbach's poetry is published in translation in *In Africa Even The Flies Are Happy: Selected Poems, 1964–77* (1986).

Brezhnev, Leonid Ilich   [brezh'-nef]

Leonid Brezhnev, b. Dec. 19, 1906, was the leader of the USSR from October 1964 until his death on Nov. 10, 1982. A native of Russified eastern Ukraine, he rose steadily in party ranks during the 1930s and in 1939 was appointed propaganda secretary of the Dnepropetrovsk regional committee. During World War II, he worked at the front as a political commissar attached to the armed forces, becoming a major general in 1944.

In the postwar years Brezhnev worked under Nikita KHRU-SHCHEV in Ukraine, later serving as Communist party chief in Moldavia (1950–53) and Kazakhstan (1954–56). He was elevated to the highest political body in the USSR (the Presidium, later called the Politburo) once Khrushchev's political opponents had been defeated (1957). For four years (1960–64) he served as the titular head of the USSR. After helping to oust Khrushchev in 1964, Brezhnev became first secretary (later general secretary) of the Communist party.

Brezhnev first ruled the country in tandem with Prime Minister Aleksei KOSYGIN and later as the first among the "collective leadership" of the party. But as he grew older, he resisted the economic reforms of Kosygin and kept conservative, often corrupt bureaucrats in positions of power. The economy faltered: industrial growth rates slowed down, and bad harvests

Leonid Brezhnev dominated the Soviet Union from 1964 to 1982. His repressive internal policies were resisted by a gradually developing dissident movement within the USSR, and his management of the economy led to industrial decline and increasing shortfalls in agricultural production.

—particularly in 1981—forced the Soviet Union to buy grain abroad. For this reason, the Brezhnev era was later dubbed the "period of stagnation." Brezhnev suppressed (1968) reform Communism in Czechoslovakia and formulated the Brezhnev Doctrine, which asserted the USSR's right to intervene against "anti-socialist degeneration" within the Soviet bloc. In his early years he continued the policy of DÉTENTE with the West, but he also expanded the Soviet arsenal, supported revolutionary movements in Africa and Asia, and in 1979 involved the USSR in a civil war in Afghanistan. When he died, he left the Soviet Union a military superpower but a country with deep economic problems and an increasingly discontented population.   RONALD SUNY

Bibliography: Anderson, Richard, *Public Politics in an Authoritarian State: Making Foreign Policy during the Brezhnev Years* (1993); Bialer, Seweryn, *The Soviet Paradox* (1986); Breslauer, George, *Khrushchev and Brezhnev as Leaders* (1982).

Brian Boru, King of Ireland   [buh-roo']

Brian Boru, b. c.941, king of Munster (978–1014), defeated other Irish rulers and the Norse to become high king of Ireland in 1002. His Norse and Irish enemies allied against him, but at Clontarf, on Apr. 23, 1014, Brian's army routed the coalition. Brian, too old to take part, was murdered by Norsemen fleeing the battle.

Briand, Aristide   [bree-awn', ahr-ees-teed']

Aristide Briand, b. Mar. 28, 1862, d. Mar. 7, 1932, served as premier of France many times and as foreign minister almost continually from 1925 to 1932. He is best known for his world peace efforts following World War I.

Briand first entered the Chamber of Deputies in 1902 and gained recognition in 1905 for his law separating church and state. He was a moderate who held no deep convictions, but his adaptability and oratorical skills brought him the premiership of 11 cabinets between 1909 and 1929.

After the war Briand demanded heavy reparations from Germany but later agreed with Britain's David LLOYD GEORGE to reduce reparations in exchange for British military aid if France were attacked. In 1925 he helped formulate the LOCARNO PACT to stabilize relations in postwar Europe. For this he was awarded the 1926 Nobel Peace Prize with Gustav Stresemann. Briand was also an architect of the KELLOGG-BRIAND PACT (1928), in which 63 nations agreed to outlaw war. In 1929–30 he advocated a vague plan for a United States of Europe. He retired in 1932 after an unsuccessful bid for the presidency.   P. M. EWY

Bibliography: Thompson, Valentine, *Briand, Man of Peace* (1930).

The briard is known in France as berger de Brie, or "the sheepdog of Brie." It has been used to defend sheep against predators.

briard   [bree-ahrd']

The briard is an alert, vigorous breed of herding dog with an almost catlike grace of movement. The male stands 58 to 68 cm (23 to 27 in) at the shoulder and weighs up to 36 kg (79 lb); the female is slightly smaller. The body is moderately long, and the heavily feathered tail, carried low, has a slight upward curl at the end. The ears may be cropped for show or work purposes but are otherwise short and straight. The outer coat is hard, coarse, flat, and moderately long; the undercoat is fine. Any solid color except white is permitted for show dogs; black, gray shades, and tan shades are the most common. A small patch of white on the chest is acceptable. The briard learns slowly but has a good memory and makes a faithful pet that tends to be reserved around strangers.

Bibliography: American Kennel Club, *The Complete Dog Book,* 18th ed. (1992).

bribery

Bribery is the crime of offering, giving, receiving, or soliciting anything of value with the intent of influencing someone in a responsible position to act contrary to his or her duty. Both the giver and the receiver of a bribe are guilty of the offense.

Under Anglo-Saxon law, bribery involved public officials. In modern statute law, it also includes certain acts by private citizens. The laws in some U.S. states punish bribery of voters, jurors, and witnesses. Some states also punish bribery in certain business transactions, including bribery of labor union officials by employers. In the 1970s the Securities and Exchange Commission took civil action against several U.S. corporations that had made improper payments, mostly to officials of foreign countries, without reporting the payments to their shareholders.

Brice, Fanny

Fanny Brice, b. New York City, Oct. 29, 1891, d. May 29, 1951, was an American comedienne and singer who became famous for her comic roles while a star with the ZIEGFELD FOLLIES, beginning in 1910. She starred in many other Broadway revues, in several films, and on radio—notably as the popular character Baby Snooks. A great farceur and satirist, she could also put over serious torch songs. Barbra STREISAND portrayed Brice on stage and screen in *Funny Girl* (1964; film, 1968), a musical based on her life, and in the sequel, *Funny Lady* (film, 1975).
ANDREW KELLY

brick and bricklaying

Building bricks are masonry units made of clay and hardened by heat or chemical action. Sun-dried, or ADOBE, bricks are a mixture of clay and vegetable fibers; kiln-burned bricks are made from clays and are formed in a mold and fired in a

kiln (oven) to hardness. Sand-lime bricks are a mixture of sand and lime that has been hardened under steam pressure. Concrete bricks are composed of portland cement and aggregate. The most commonly used type is kiln-burned brick.

HISTORY

In the Babylonian civilization (c. 3500 BC) that developed in the valley of the Tigris and Euphrates rivers, the thick clay and mud deposited by the rivers was well suited for making bricks. Immense pyramids (see ZIGGURAT) were constructed of sun-dried brick faced with kiln-burned glazed brick of many colors. The bricks were held together with bitumens (naturally occurring tars). The Romans made wide use of kiln-burned brick in conjunction with an efficient mortar of lime and volcanic ash (*pozzuolana*). As the Roman Empire declined, the art of brickmaking disappeared in most of Europe and was revived only in the late Middle Ages, influenced by the Italian and Byzantine artisans who had kept the technology alive.

In the earliest method of brickmaking, clay was pulverized, mixed with water to form a stiff paste, and pressed into molds by hand. The bricks were then turned out of the molds and dried in the sun. The kiln consisted of a series of arches made

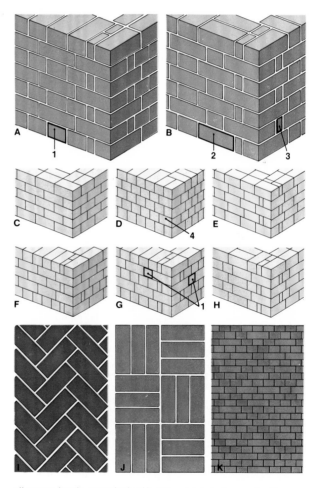

All pattern bonds, or methods of laying up bricks to form wall patterns, are based on the use of various combinations of headers (1) and stretchers (2). An English bond (A) and a Flemish bond (B) also use so-called blind headers, or half bricks (3) to obtain square corners. A stretching, or running, bond (C) uses stretchers only, except for a corner header in alternate courses. A heading bond (D) uses headers only, except for a 3/4-size corner brick (4) in alternate courses. Other variations in laying up bricks include a Flemish garden-wall bond (E), an English garden-wall, or common, bond (F), an English cross, or Dutch, bond (G), a monk bond (H), a herring (I), a basket-weave bond (J), and a diaper bond, in which colored headers are used to create different designs along the wall (K).

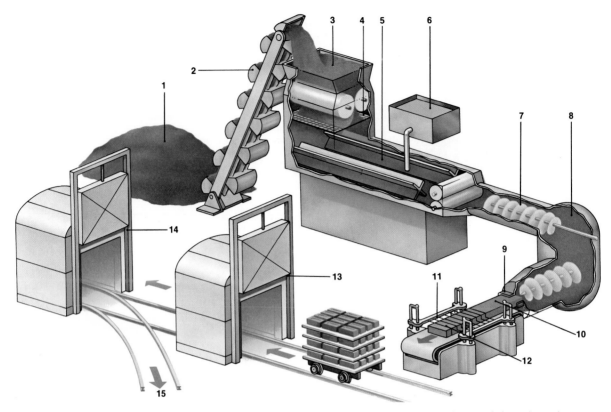

Bricklaying in modern plants begins with automatic feeding of clay (1) by a conveyor (2) into a grinder (3). The ground clay is dropped on a vibrating screen (4), which passes only fine-grained particles into a mill (5), in which the clay is mixed to a plastic consistency with water from a tank (6). The wet clay is mixed further in a screw-type mixer (7), degassed in a vacuum chamber to remove air bubbles (8), and extruded through a die (9) to form a continuous block (10), which is sliced by a wire-slicing machine (11) into bricks (12). These bricks are oven-dried slowly under carefully controlled conditions to prevent cracking (13), fired in a kiln at high temperatures and in various gaseous atmospheres (14), depending on the type of brick desired, cooled slowly, and stored or shipped (15).

from the naturally dried brick. More dried brick was piled atop the arches in a checkerboard pattern to form a beehive-shaped mound, and a fire was built under the arches. Because the heat of the fire was uneven, the bricks closest to the fire burned to a shining surface that was almost black. These occasionally warped bricks, called clinkers, were used for special architectural effects. Bricks on the outer shell of the mound fired to a lighter color and were called salmon brick.

MANUFACTURING

Most brick produced in the United States is made by the stiff-mud process, using mixtures of surface clays and shales. In the soft-mud process, a much wetter clay is pressed into molds or extruded, rather than sliced from a brick-sized column of clay. In the dry-press process high pressure is used to compress a fairly dry clay in a mold and is then used to manufacture refractory masonry, such as FIREBRICK.

Modern kilns are permanent enclosures with the heat usually generated by external ovens. The heated air is circulated through the bricks stacked in the kiln to produce a fairly uniform masonry unit. Kilns are classed as *intermittent* or *continuous*. In the intermittent kiln, the brick must be piled, fired, cooled, and the bricks removed before new dried brick is piled to be fired. The continuous, or tunnel, kiln consists of a tunnel with several zones in which the temperature is carefully controlled. The moist clay formed by machines is loaded onto special cars that are drawn through the kiln at a constant rate of speed. The bricks are successively shaped, dried, fired, and cooled to produce a uniform product.

The most widely used brick is called common brick. Its color will vary from a dark orange to a yellow or deep red, depending on the type of clay used. Face brick is manufactured to close tolerances in size, structural qualities, color, and finish. It is sometimes glazed and used as a facing on exposed wall surfaces. Firebrick is used for lining fireplaces and furnaces; it is beige to light brown in color and is weaker than common brick.

BRICKWORK

Brickwork is designed so that individual bricks are bonded into a structure that will act as a whole. The texture, strength, and watertightness of a brick wall depend greatly on the skill of the bricklayer. Mortar joints between individual bricks must be well formed and watertight. The mortar used to hold the bricks together consists usually of portland cement, lime, and sand, although mortar types vary throughout the world.

The "bond" of a brick wall is the arrangement of bricks in rows or courses. The type of bond used will determine the appearance of a wall. Bonds tie 2 or 3 tiers of brick together or they tie an outer brick facing to an inner backup wall.

Steel reinforcing bars increase the shearing and bending strength of a load-bearing brick wall. The steel bars may be placed in the mortar joints between bricks or in a double wall in the cavity between outer and inner walls. The cavity may be left as a dead-air space to provide for evaporation of moisture from the walls, or it is sometimes filled with grout, a mortar of pouring consistency.

New methods were developed in the 1970s for producing prefabricated reinforced brick masonry panels. Masonry panels as large as 2.4 x 6.1 m (8 x 20 ft) are fabricated in specially equipped shops and transported to the job site for erection. The steel-reinforced brick panels are hoisted into position by cranes and welded or bolted to the structural frame.

DON A. WATSON

Bibliography: Gurcke, Karl, *Bricks and Brickmaking* (1987); Hayward, Robert, *The Brick Book* (1977); Watson, D. A., *Construction Materials and Methods*, 2d ed. (1978).

Bridalveil Fall

Bridalveil Fall is a waterfall in Yosemite National Park, located in the Sierra Nevada range in east central California. The waters of Bridalveil Creek drop 189 m (620 ft) to the Merced River in Yosemite Valley.

bride-price

Bride-price, also known as bride-wealth, is the wealth transferred by the groom or his kin to the kin of the bride in order to validate MARRIAGE. The concept of bride-wealth is found throughout the world, primarily in preliterate societies; it is most highly developed in Africa, where it is almost universal in traditional areas.

Bride-price is most typical of patrilineal societies (see KINSHIP), in which its transfer to the bride's family entitles the groom to sexual access to the bride, the right to determine her residence, the right to her labor, and, most important, the right to claim any children she bears as belonging exclusively to his kin group, the patrilineage. Hence, some anthropologists refer to bride-price as progeny-price. In a matrilineal society, however, bride-price transfers only the right to sexual access to the bride; the other three rights remain with the woman's kin group.

Bride-price not only validates marriage; it also compensates the woman's kin for the loss of rights over her and symbolizes marriage linking two families as well as two individuals. Bride-price is returned (at least in part) in the case of divorce.

Bride-price may include goods, livestock, money, the groom's working for the bride's family, or even an exchange of women. It may be made in one payment or over a long period of time.   JAMES LOWELL GIBBS, JR.

Bibliography: Goody, Jack R., and Tambiah, S. J., *Bridewealth and Dowry* (1973); Radcliffe-Brown, Alfred R., and Forde, Daryll, eds., *African Systems of Kinship and Marriage* (1987).

See also: DOWRY.

bridge   (card game)

Bridge is a card game derived from WHIST. Although several variations exist, the most common form is contract bridge. Whatever form is played, bridge demands a high degree of skill, in both the bidding and the playing of each hand.
Bidding and Playing. Four players, in seating themselves at a table, form two partnerships, North and South against East and West. Only one score is kept for each side.

Each player, dealt 13 cards, determines the value of his or her hand. The cards in each suit are ranked downward from ace to deuce; the point count is four per ace, three per king, two per queen, and one per jack. Thus 40 points are in the deck, exclusive of points for distribution of cards.

A partnership usually must hold a total of at least 20 points to make a contract. A contract is the final bid of a hand made by a partnership that promises to win no fewer than the number of tricks bid, plus 6. (A trick is one round of cards played by the four players.) If, for example, the bid is four

WORLD BRIDGE TEAM CHAMPIONSHIP

Year	Winner	Year	Winner
1950–51*	United States	1980	France
1953–54	United States	1981	United States
1955	Great Britain	1982	France
1956	France	1983	United States
1957–59	Italy	1984	Poland
1960	France	1985–88	United States
1961–69	Italy	1989	Brazil
1970–71	United States	1990	Germany
1972–75	Italy	1991	Iceland
1976–77	United States	1992	France
1978	Poland	1993	Netherlands
1979	United States	1994	United States

*The world championship was not held in 1952.

hearts, the bidder must win at least ten tricks to make his contract. Penalties are assessed if the contract is not fulfilled, and bonuses are awarded for the number of tricks won over the contract.

Sometimes the defending partners will double the contract, saying, in effect, that they expect to defeat the bid. If they do defeat the contract, further penalties are exacted against the bidders; if they fail to defeat the contract, the bidders receive bonus points.

In addition to counting actual points for bidding purposes, a player adds the following points based on card distribution in the player's hand: three points for a void (that is, no cards in any one suit), two for each singleton (one card in a suit), and one for each doubleton (two cards in a suit).

The bidding proceeds clockwise around the table, beginning with the dealer. Any player who does not wish to bid says, "Pass." To overcall the preceding bid, a player must bid a greater number of tricks or the same number of tricks in a higher suit, with the rank being (in descending order) spades, hearts, diamonds, and clubs. Thus, one spade will overcall one heart, two or more clubs will overcall one spade, and so on. When a bid is followed by three consecutive passes, the bidding is closed, and every card of the suit named in the final bid becomes a trump. The exception to this occurs when the last bid is in no trump. In this case the bidders wish to play with no suit as trump; each trick will be won only by the highest card played in the suit that is led. The hand is played by the declarer, the player who made the first bid in the suit contracted for; the declarer's partner places his or her hand face up on the table; this hand is known as the dummy.

The object of play is to win tricks. When the bidding has been completed, the player on the declarer's left makes the opening lead (plays the first card). Thereafter, the declarer plays from the dummy's hand as well as from his or her own, in the proper order of play. A player must play a card from the suit that is led, if he or she holds one; otherwise, any card may be played. An uneven distribution of trump among the four players usually aids one team, although sometimes not the declarer's. The hand that wins a trick leads next, and play continues until all 13 tricks have been played.
Sample Hand. With East as dealer, the following hand might be played: West leads his diamond three, then North and South pursue a course toward making a four-heart contract.

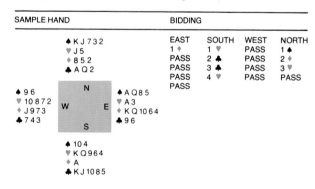

SAMPLE HAND				BIDDING			
	♠ K J 7 3 2			EAST	SOUTH	WEST	NORTH
	♥ J 5			1 ♦	1 ♥	PASS	1 ♠
	♦ 8 5 2			PASS	2 ♣	PASS	2 ♦
	♣ A Q 2			PASS	3 ♣	PASS	3 ♥
♠ 9 6	N	♠ A Q 8 5		PASS	4 ♥	PASS	PASS
♥ 10 8 7 2		♥ A 3		PASS			
♦ J 9 7 3	W E	♦ K Q 10 6 4					
♣ 7 4 3	S	♣ 9 6					
	♠ 10 4						
	♥ K Q 9 6 4						
	♦ A						
	♣ K J 10 8 5						

Bibliography: Goren, Charles H., *Fundamentals of Contract Bridge* (1989) and *Goren's New Complete Bridge* (1985).

bridge   (engineering)

A bridge is a structure designed to carry pedestrians or vehicles across such obstacles as ravines, rivers, or other roads or railroads. The earliest bridges may well have consisted of tree trunks or flat stones thrown across a stream—like the "clam" bridges of southeastern Cornwall or the "clapper" bridges of Dartmoor, which were the first beam bridges. Alternatively, the earliest types may have been primitive suspension spans formed of twisted bamboo or creepers hung across a stream, with their ends tied to tree trunks on either side; such bridges can still be seen in Africa and Asia. Both types were doubtless used long before the first masonry ARCH, even though both types were preceded by natural rock arches such as those at Ardèche in France or in Lexington, Va.

In all three types of bridge—beam, arch, and suspension—the foundations must carry the full weight of the bridge and the traffic on it. The vital differences, however, are that arched bridges, by virtue of their shape, are in compression and thrust outward on their end supports or bearings, whereas the cables of a suspension bridge are in tension and exert a continual pull on their end anchorages.

EARLY BRIDGES OF NOTE

The finest early bridges were the semicircular masonry arches of the Romans, built during the 500 years of their supremacy. Some of these—such as the Alcántara bridge over the Tagus in Spain, with its tall, majestic spans of 30 m (98 ft)—are still standing after nearly 2,000 years. The most significant contributions of the Romans were the use of a natural cement called *pozzuolana* that enabled them to make concrete below water in bridge foundations, and the use of timber cofferdams—made by driving piles around the site of a pier in midstream and then draining out the water inside—so that the ground could be excavated as necessary and the pier built on dry surface. The Ponte Sant' Angelo in Rome, which is still standing, was built on cofferdam foundations in the Tiber more than 1,800 years ago; most Roman bridges still standing, however, have piers built on solid rock.

By the Middle Ages the first ogival (pointed) arches were built in Europe; these arches resulted from Persian and Muslim influence. Bridges were often fortified to be used in defense of a city, such as the Pont Valentré at Cahors, France, which had arrow slits, machicolations, and protected stairways to the towers. To pay for the maintenance of many medieval bridges, tolls were levied not only on travelers crossing over but also on vessels passing under the bridge.

Toward the end of the 12th century, work began on two outstanding bridges, Old LONDON BRIDGE and the Pont St. Bénézet at Avignon on the Rhône in the south of France. Begun in 1177 and completed ten years later, the Pont St. Béné-

Three primary types of bridge are the beam bridge (A), the arch bridge (B), and the suspension bridge (C). The bascule bridge (D) is a beam bridge in which each section of the beam is supported only at one end. The types differ in the way they transmit loads (black arrows) to their supports, or piers. The beam bridge rests on its piers and exerts a downward force (red arrows). The arch bridge requires stronger piers because the arch exerts an outward as well as a downward force. The suspension bridge uses steel cables to support a load. The cables, always under tension, pass over high towers and transmit their tensional force to ground anchorages beyond them.

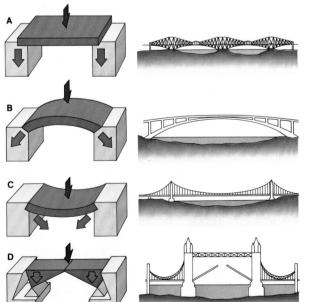

The Alcántara Bridge across the Tagus River in Spain is the highest arch bridge built by the Romans. Still in use after nearly 2,000 years, it was constructed with six semicircular granite arches 30 m (98 ft) long and rises 31 m (102 ft) above the river.

zet had 20 lofty elliptical arches, each spanning 30 m (98 ft). Unfortunately, little of the bridge remains today. The construction of the first stone bridge over the Thames in London, begun in 1176, presented even greater difficulties, for it was the first large bridge with masonry foundations to be built in a swiftly flowing river with a tidal range of 5 m (16 ft). The design consisted of 19 pointed arches on wide, protected piers and a drawbridge that served for defense and to let ships pass at high water. For more than 600 years the bridge supported a famous street of shops and houses flanking the narrow roadway. It even survived the Great Fire of London in 1666, which ravaged the northern end of the bridge. The street was not demolished until 1831, by which date a new bridge had been completed by Sir John RENNIE.

THE RENAISSANCE ERA

The next great bridge-building era occurred during the RENAISSANCE. An example of the unbounded confidence of the Renaissance was Leonardo da Vinci's offer to build a masonry arch bridge with a span of 240 m (787 ft) over the Golden Horn at Constantinople. In Florence, the Ponte Vecchio (c.1350), which still stands over the Arno, was eclipsed by the Santa Trinità bridge (1569) with its three "basket-handled" arches that had a rise-to-span ratio of only 1 to 7 instead of the usual 1 to 4. In 1588 Antonio da Ponte's design was accepted for the Rialto Bridge in Venice—a low circular arch that supports a 23-m-wide (75-ft) roadway lined with shops on a span of 27 m (89 ft) across the Grand Canal. To support the bridge in the soft alluvial soil of Venice, 6,000 wood piles were driven to a depth of 3.35 m (11 ft) beneath each abutment.

Other great examples of this age were the Pont Notre Dame (c.1500) and the Pont Neuf (1604), both masonry arch bridges over the Seine in Paris. These preceded the masterpieces of Jean Perronet (1708–94)—the Pont Neuilly over the Seine, the Pont de Sainte-Maxence over the Oise, and his last work, the Pont de la Concorde (1791).

BRIDGES OF THE 18TH AND 19TH CENTURIES

During the 18th and 19th centuries a wide variety of timber truss bridges were built in North America, including the Colossus bridge of 104-m (340-ft) span over the Schuylkill River. In the late 18th century another innovation began with the building of the world's first all-iron bridge, the semicircular arch of 30-m (100-ft) span at Coalbrookdale over the River Severn in England.

In the 19th century, as more and more railroads were built, cast iron was superseded by wrought iron, because the latter was malleable, ductile, much stronger, and could be riveted instead of bolted. In 1826, Thomas TELFORD completed the 177-m (580-ft) span Menai suspension bridge, which was sup-

Railway lines ran inside the iron tubes of the Britannia Railway Bridge (1850) over the Menai Straits. The tubes were floated out on pontoons, then lifted into position between the stone piers. The bridge's sole ornamentation was the lions mounted on the abutments.

The Brooklyn Bridge over the East River in New York City was dedicated on May 24, 1883. For 20 years it held the record as the largest suspension bridge in the world. It has a span of 486 m (1,595 ft) and uses four supporting cables spun from hundreds of steel wires.

ported by cables of wrought-iron links; it carried two lanes of roadway traffic over the straits. In addition, Robert STEPHEN-SON's Britannia Railway Bridge, also across the Menai Straits, was opened in 1850. It had four continuous spans, two of 70 m (230 ft) and two of 140 m (460 ft), consisting of wrought-iron tubes of rectangular cross section, through which the trains ran. This was the prototype of the modern steel box girders. The main difference today is that the traffic is carried on a roadway above the tubes or boxes instead of through them. Only a few years later, in 1859, I. K. BRUNEL completed his last and greatest project, the Royal Albert bridge at Salt-ash, England, with its two spans of 142 m (465 ft), each carry-ing one broad-gauge railway over the Tamar estuary.

Before the end of the 19th century the mass production of mild steel plates and sections, with an ultimate strength of about 4.1 kilonewtons (kN) per m² (30 tons per in²) in both tension and compression, led to their use in building bridges. The first large bridge in the world to be built of steel was the St. Louis bridge (1874) over the Mississippi River. Designed by James B. EADS, it had three arch spans of more than 152 m (500 ft) each. This was followed by the construction (1869–83) of the BROOKLYN BRIDGE, a suspension bridge of 486-m (1,595-ft) span traversing the East River and linking Brooklyn with Manhattan. Designed by John A. ROEBLING, the bridge is nearly half again as long as any bridge previously built; it has six lanes for vehicular traffic and a footpath. The four main cables each comprise parallel wires of galvanized cast steel 4.82 mm (0.19 in) thick, with an ultimate strength of 9.85 kN per m² (71.5 tons per in²). The cables were spun in place by a method that has subsequently been used in every large sus-pension bridge built in the United States. To prevent failure brought on by oscillations built up in the deck by wind or traffic, steel-stiffening trusses were incorporated in the deck over the entire length of the bridge.

The next major advance was the Forth Railway Bridge (1882–90), with two cantilever spans of 521 m (1,710 ft) each, which carries a double railway track over the Forth Estuary at South Queensferry, Scotland. Unlike the Britannia and Royal Albert bridges, where the spans were floated out and hoisted up, all the steelwork of the Forth bridge was cantilevered out at the site from the main piers and riveted in place.

NEW CONSTRUCTION TECHNIQUES
This period also saw the building of the first modern types of movable bridges, such as the bascule bridge, lift bridge, and swinging drawbridge. The largest bascule bridge to date—in which the opening spans swing upward as in the Tower Bridge in London—is the railway bridge built in 1941 at Sault Ste. Marie, Michigan. The bridge has an opening of 102 m (335 ft). In lift bridges, the opening span remains horizontal and is counterweighted at the ends and lifted vertically. The lifting span of the Arthur Kill bridge (1959) at Elizabeth, N.J., has a length of 170 m (558 ft). Swinging draw-bridges have swing spans that remain horizontal and are usually swung

round on a central pivot or pin; thus they cause more ob-struction to river traffic than do other movable bridges. The longest swing bridge yet built (1965) is that at al Firdan over the Suez Canal in Egypt; it has two arms that swing round on turntables at each end, giving an opening of 168 m (552 ft). Floating bridges have been built since the 1st millennium BC, but their life is short and they require much maintenance. The well-known BAILEY BRIDGES were standardized steel-lat-ticed trusses, designed to make quick replacements for bridges destroyed in wartime.

Various kinds of bridge foundations are also used. Coffer-dams are still used when the ground is suitable, and the use of steel-sheet piling has enabled much larger and deeper foundations to be laid. If the ground is too hard or too soft for piling, however, caissons or wells are used and are either sunk by open grabbing or, as in the Royal Albert bridge at Saltash, by means of compressed air. At Saltash, a wrought-iron cylinder 11 m (36 ft) in diameter was sunk to the rock at a depth of 26 m (85 ft) in midstream. The water was expelled from the working chamber at the bottom by pumping in compressed air; workmen entered through an air lock and ex-cavated the ground, so that the cylinder sank until hard rock was reached; then the caisson was plugged with concrete, and the piers were built up to the necessary height.

Compressed air cannot be used in foundations deeper than about 37 m (120 ft) because at that depth the pressure would be 3.6 N/m² (52 lb/in²), which is high enough to cause the BENDS (caisson disease) in workmen. For very large founda-tions, reinforced concrete monoliths can be sunk instead of steel caissons, as was done for the Howrah bridge in Calcutta,

The world's best-known cantilever bridge is the Forth Railway Bridge in Scotland, which has two 521-m (1,710-ft) cantilever spans. Opened on Mar. 4, 1890, it was the first long-span railway bridge to be made of steel and was designed to withstand the high winds at the site.

The Gladesville Bridge in Sydney, Australia, which opened officially in 1964, has the longest single arch span of reinforced concrete in the world. Columns located above its 305-m (1,000-ft) concrete arch span support a 22-m wide (72-ft) roadway and two footpaths.

A view of the New York Verrazano-Narrows Bridge during its construction reveals the spinning-in-place of one of the four main suspension cables. Each is 0.9 m (3 ft) in diameter; their total length of steel wire equals more than half the distance to the moon.

where the monoliths measured 55 by 25 m (180 by 82 ft) in plan and were sunk to a depth of 31 m (102 ft). The latest trend is away from pneumatic caissons, turning instead to the use of piles that may be 0.9 m (3 ft) or more in diameter and up to 60 m (200 ft) long, or to thin-walled cylinders of prestressed concrete up to 6 m (20 ft) in diameter that can be driven to depths of more than 30 m (98 ft).

THE 20TH CENTURY: CONCRETE AND STEEL

The 20th century ushered in the building of bridges using re-inforced concrete. Concrete resists compressive forces, and the steel reinforcement resists tensile stresses that concrete alone would be unable to withstand. The first spans to be built of re-inforced concrete were arches, a notable one being François Hennebique's Pont de Chatellerault (1898), with a span of 52 m (171 ft). In 1905, Robert Maillart built the first of his three-hinged arches, the Tavanasa bridge over the Rhine in Switzerland. He next built the Schwandbach bridge (1924), which was curved in plan and had a span of 34 m (112 ft) across a deep ravine. Eugène Freyssinet's masterpiece was the Pont Albert Louppe (1930) over the River Elorn in Brittany; it has three arched spans of 172 m (564 ft) each. Another major work was the Sandö bridge (1942) in Sweden, with a span of 264 m (866 ft) and a low arch with a rise of only 40 m (131 ft) at the center. The Gladesville Bridge (1964) in Sydney, New South Wales, has an even longer span—305 m (1,000 ft) of reinforced concrete that carries a 22-m (72-ft) wide roadway and two footpaths supported on columns above its low, graceful arch.

The process of prestressing concrete first developed by Freyssinet consists of putting the concrete into a state of compression by tensioning steel wires or bars that pass through it; this system was universally adopted after World War II. At the same time, marked improvements in concrete technology led to its allowable compression strength being doubled to 0.2 kN/m^2 (3,000 lbs/in^2). These improvements enabled design-

ers to save approximately one-third of the volume of concrete and three-quarters of the weight of steel reinforcement over what previously had to be used. Prestressed concrete bridges thus became strongly competitive and have been widely adopted for spans up to 180 m (600 ft) or even 305 m (1,000 ft) if the bridges are braced by cables.

For short spans, simple beams can be used, as is the case for the two Pontchartrain bridges in Louisiana (1958 and 1969), which have 2,170 and 2,174 spans, respectively, each 17 m (56 ft) long. As the spans become longer, they can be made continuous, as was done in the Moscow River bridge (1957) in Russia. This is a double-decked bridge carrying roadway traffic above and railway traffic below; it has two spans of 44 m (144 ft) each and one span of 148 m (485 ft). One of the longest prestressed concrete cantilever bridges is the Bendorf bridge (1964) in Koblenz, Germany, which has a clear span of 208 m (682 ft).

Various other types of prestressed concrete bridges exist: tied arch, lattice truss, box girder, multiple suspension, and cable braced. When constructed in 1970, the longest multiple suspension bridge was the Save River bridge in Mozambique, with two spans of 100 m (328 ft) each and three of 210 m (689 ft) each. The longest cable-braced bridge is the Wadi Kuf bridge in Libya, which has a single span of 300 m (983 ft).

After prestressed concrete, steel is the material most widely used for bridge construction. Research has been concentrated on production of high tensile steel, which can be used at a much higher working stress than mild steel and yet is still suitable for fabrication by flame-cutting and electric arc welding. Today, riveting has been superseded by welding in the shops during fabrication and by the use of friction grip bolts for making on-site connections.

Over the years bridges have failed, mostly during construction, and today much effort is being devoted to ensuring the

NOTABLE BRIDGES OF THE WORLD

Name of Bridge	Location	Length of Main Span		Year Opened
		meters	feet	
Suspension				
Humber River	Hull, England	1,410	4,626	1981
Verrazano-Narrows	Brooklyn-Staten Island, New York City	1,298	4,260	1964
Golden Gate	San Francisco, Calif.	1,280	4,200	1937
Mackinac	St. Ignace-Mackinaw City, Mich.	1,158	3,800	1957
Bosporus	Istanbul-Üsküdar, Turkey	1,073	3,520	1973
George Washington	New York City-Fort Lee, N.J.	1,067	3,500	1931
Brooklyn	Brooklyn-Manhattan, New York City	486	1,595	1883
Steel Cantilever				
Quebec Railway	Quebec, Canada	549	1,800	1917
Firth of Forth Railway	Queensferry, Scotland	521	1,710	1890
Commodore John Barry	Chester, Pa.-Bridgeport, N.J.	501	1,644	1974
Greater New Orleans	New Orleans, La.	480	1,575	1958
Howrah	Calcutta, India	457	1,500	1943
Transbay (East Bay)	San Francisco-Oakland, Calif.	427	1,400	1936
Simple Truss				
Metropolis Railway	Ohio River, Metropolis, Ill.	219	720	1917
Irvin Cobb (Paducah)	Ohio River, Paducah, Ky.	218	716	1930
Municipal	St. Louis, Mo.	204	668	1910
Continuous Truss				
Astoria	Astoria, Oreg.-Megler, Wash.	376	1,232	1966
Tenman	Kumamoto, Japan	300	984	1966
Steel Arch				
New River Gorge	Fayetteville, W.Va.	518	1,700	1977
Bayonne	Bayonne, N.J.-Staten Island, N.Y.	504	1,652	1931
Sydney Harbour	Sydney, Australia	503	1,650	1932
Fremont	Portland, Oreg.	383	1,255	1971
Ždákov (Orlik)	Ždákov, Czech Republic	380	1,244	1967
Concrete Arch				
Gladesville	Sydney, Australia	305	1,000	1964
Amizade	Foz do Iguassu, Brazil-Paraguay	290	951	1964
Arrábida	Porto, Portugal	270	885	1963
Sandö	Kramfors, Sweden	264	866	1943
Shibenik	Krka River, Croatia	246	808	1967
Steel Plate and Box Girders				
Rio-Niteröi	Rio de Janeiro, Brazil	300	984	1971
Sava I	Belgrade, Yugoslavia	261	856	1957
Zoobrücke	Cologne, Germany	259	850	1966
Sava II	Belgrade, Yugoslavia	250	820	1970
Auckland Harbour	Auckland, New Zealand	244	800	1969
Prestressed-Concrete other than Cantilever				
Wadi Kuf	Cyrenaica, Libya	300	983	1970
General Rafael Urdaneta	Maracaibo, Venezuela	236	775	1961
Save River	Mozambique	210	689	1970
Concrete Cantilever				
Bendorf	Koblenz, Germany	208	682	1964
Medway	Rochester, Kent, England	152	500	1963
Amakusa	Japan	146	479	1966
Alnö	Sweden	134	439	1964
New London	London, England	104	340	1971
Bascule				
South Capital Street	Washington, D.C.	118	386	1949
Saulte Sainte Marie Railway	Michigan-Ontario	102	336	1941
Black River	Lordin, Ohio	101	333	1940
Tennessee River	Chattanooga, Tenn.	94	310	1917
Swing				
al Firdan	Suez Canal, Egypt	168	552	1965
Mississippi River Railway	Fort Madison, Iowa	160	525	1927
Willamette River	Portland, Oreg.	159	521	1907
Missouri River	East Omaha, Nebr.	158	519	1893
Vertical lift				
Arthur Kill Railway	Elizabeth, N.J.-Staten Island, N.Y.	170	558	1959
Cape Cod Canal Railway	Cape Cod, Mass.	166	544	1935
Delair	Delair, N.J.	165	542	1960
Marine Parkway	New York, N.Y.	164	540	1937

safety of bridges during erection and, above all, to guaranteeing the safety of the personnel on site. A few of the most tragic failures during erection were the collapse of the cantilever of the Quebec bridge (1907) due to buckling of the main chords, in which 74 men died; and the collapse of the suspended span of the same bridge in 1916 as it was being lifted into place from the water, causing 13 more deaths. More recently, the failure of a large steel box girder during the erection (1970) of the West Gate bridge in Melbourne killed 35 men. The principal causes of other failures that have taken place after completion of the bridge have been high winds, which blew down 13 of the high level spans of the Tay bridge, Scotland, with a train on them, in 1879; aerodynamic oscillations, which brought down the Tacoma Narrows bridge in 1940; brittle fractures of steelwork; earthquakes; floods; and the impact of a ship on the bridge piers.

In the 20th century the United States has led the way in building great suspension bridges with spans from 610 m (2,000 ft) to more than 1,219 m (4,000 ft). The greatest of these, the VERRAZANO-NARROWS BRIDGE (1964) at the entrance to New York Harbor, carries a double-deck roadway for 12 lanes of traffic and has steel towers 207 m (680 ft) high. The four main cables, each 0.9 m (3 ft) in diameter, contain 229,300 km (142,200 mi) of wire. The Sydney Harbour bridge in New South Wales was opened in 1932; it has a 503-m (1,650-ft) span and carries four interurban railway tracks, a 17-m-wide (56-ft) roadway, and two footpaths. Three other major suspension bridges were completed in the United Kingdom. The Forth Road bridge (1964) and the Severn bridge (1966) both have spans exceeding 914 m (3,000 ft); the 1,410-m (4,626-ft) main span of the Humber bridge, near Hull, England, was the longest in the world when completed in 1981. The Bosporus bridge, of 1,073-m (3,520-ft) span, completed in 1973 in Istanbul, created the first permanent road link between Asian and European Turkey. Projects for the future include a bridge over the Messina Straits, where the 122-m (400-ft) depth of water poses a major problem.

The newest bridge design, the cable-stayed bridge, is suspended by cables that run directly down to the roadway from centrally positioned towers. Because they are less costly than conventional suspension bridges, cable-stayed bridges have been built, largely in Europe, for spans up to about 700 m (2,000 ft). The dynamics of these bridges, however, create special stresses on the cables, and improved technologies must be used to prevent cable corrosion.

SIR HUBERT SHIRLEY-SMITH

Bibliography: Hopkins, H. J., *The Span of Bridges* (1973); Jackson, D., *Great American Bridges and Dams* (1988); Lengyel, J., *The Bridge Builders* (1979); Leonhardt, F., *Bridges* (1984); Mock, E. B., *The Architecture of Bridges* (1949; repr. 1972); Plowden, D., *Bridges: The Span of North America* (1974; repr. 1987); Shirley-Smith, H., *The World's Great Bridges* (1964); Wittforth, H., *Building Bridges* (1984).

Bridge, Frank

Virtuoso English violist and conductor Frank Bridge, b. Feb. 26, 1879, d. Jan. 10, 1941, is best known for his many compositions. Bridge's early work was largely romantic in flavor and followed, while stretching, 19th-century conventions (as in his popular suite *The Sea*, 1910–11). After World War I he began experimenting with serial modes, although atonalities were often hidden by lush harmonies or brilliant counterpoint.

bridge circuit

A bridge circuit, in electricity, is a circuit comprising four impedances (combinations of resistors, inductors, and capacitors) arranged in a diamond-shaped network. Power is supplied at two opposite "corners" of the network, and an electrical load or meter is connected to the other two.

The earliest and most common bridge circuit is the WHEATSTONE BRIDGE (named for Charles Wheatstone, 1802–75), which is used to measure such electrical characteristics as resistance, capacitance, and frequency. In measuring resistance, for example, an unknown resistor and three known or variable resistors constitute the circuit along with a GALVANOM-

ETER for measuring current. One or more resistors are varied until the galvanometer indicates zero current; the value of the unknown resistor may then be calculated. The advantage of this method of measurement is its high accuracy.

Another common application of a bridge circuit is as a full-wave RECTIFIER; if the four impedances are DIODES (devices that transmit electricity in one direction only), alternating current (AC) applied to the bridge is rectified (transformed) into direct current (DC). Both halves of the AC cycle are sent through the load.

FORREST M. MIMS III

Bibliography: Simpson, Robert E., *Introductory Electronics for Scientists and Engineers,* 2d ed. (1985).

Bridge of San Luis Rey, The

The Bridge of San Luis Rey (1927; film, 1944), a Pulitzer Prize–winning novel by Thornton WILDER, traces the lives of five travelers killed when a bridge collapses in Peru. Brother Juniper, a Franciscan friar who had witnessed the collapse in 1714, wonders if the accident was merely random or a part of God's plan. His investigation into the lives of the victims constitutes the major part of the book. Although the friar considers his investigation a devout theological inquiry, both he and his book are burned by the church as heretical, leaving his question unanswered.

CHARLOTTE D. SOLOMON

Bridgeport

Bridgeport (1990 pop., 141,686) is a city in southwestern Connecticut situated on Long Island Sound, at the mouth of the Pequonnock River. In the 1970s, Bridgeport displaced Hartford as Connecticut's largest city in population. Long the state's leading industrial city, Bridgeport manufactures helicopters, trucks, electrical equipment, firearms and ammunition, gas turbine engines, metal products, sewing machines, pharmaceuticals, and radios. It is the site of the University of Bridgeport, Bridgeport Engineering Institute, and Housatonic Community College.

The city, settled in 1639 as an agrarian and fishing community, was first called Newfield. Known by various names until 1800, it was then renamed Bridgeport for the first drawbridge over the Pequonnock. Showman P. T. Barnum wintered his circus there and was for a time its mayor. Another noted mayor (1933–57) was the socialist Jasper McLevy.

Bridger, James

One of the American West's most famous MOUNTAIN MEN, James Bridger, b. Virginia, Mar. 17, 1804, d. July 17, 1881, also played an important role as an explorer and guide. He moved to an Illinois farm near St. Louis at the age of eight. In 1822 he took part in a trapping expedition led by William H. Ashley to the upper Missouri River, and in 1825 he was probably the first white to see the Great Salt Lake. In 1830 he and four others bought the Rocky Mountain Fur Company, and with this group and a later firm he helped direct trapping operations in the central and northern Rockies until 1838.

Between 1838 and 1843 he and Louis Vasquez planned and built Fort Bridger, on the Green River, which became an important trading post and later a military post and pony express station. After the fur trade waned, Bridger served as a government guide on several expeditions, including the 1857 campaign against the Mormons and the Yellowstone expedition of 1859–60. He later farmed in Missouri.

ELLIOTT WEST

Bibliography: Alter, J. Cecil, *Jim Bridger* (1962; repr. 1986); Vestal, Stanley, *Jim Bridger, Mountain Man* (1946; repr. 1970).

Bridges, Harry

Harry Bridges, b. Alfred Bryant Renton Bridges in Australia, July 28, 1901, d. Mar. 30, 1990, led the Longshoremen's Union on the U.S. West Coast for four decades. A sailor, he made the United States his base in 1920 and gained prominence as an organizer of San Francisco dockworkers in the 1930s. In 1937 he established the International Longshoremen's and Warehousemen's Union (ILWU), of which he was president from 1937 to 1977. Marxist in outlook and friendly to the USSR, he was accused of being a Communist; he denied party membership, and the federal government was unsuccessful in its attempts to deport him. In 1961, in a startling departure from traditional union attitudes, he negotiated a contract with the employers in which the union accepted automation of the docks. The contract resulted in reduction in jobs but yielded high wages and generous retirement benefits. When Bridges retired, maritime leaders praised him for his success in freeing the West Coast docks of corruption.

Bridges, Robert

Robert Seymour Bridges, b. Oct. 23, 1844, d. Apr. 21, 1930, was British poet laureate from 1913. He is now best remembered for his long philosophical poem, *The Testament of Beauty* (1929), for his metrical studies, and for his friendship with Gerard Manley HOPKINS, whose works he edited in 1918. Trained as a doctor, Bridges gave up medicine in 1882. His critical works include studies of John Keats and John Milton and a highly successful anthology, *The Spirit of Man* (1916).

ROBIN BUSS

Bibliography: Stanford, Donald E., *In the Classic Mode: The Achievement of Robert Bridges* (1978).

Bridges v. California

The case of *Bridges* v. *California* (1941) was decided with the companion case of *Times-Mirror Co.* v. *Superior Court of California*; both dealt with the conflict between contempt of court and freedom of speech and press. Harry BRIDGES, a union leader, had sent telegrams to the secretary of labor and to the newspapers, calling a judge's initial decision that had gone against his union "outrageous." In retaliation, he threatened that his union would strike the port of Los Angeles and possibly the entire West Coast. For these remarks he was cited for contempt. In the second case a judge had cited the *Times-Mirror* for contempt for a series of editorials warning the judge that he would be making a serious mistake if he granted probation to two labor union members awaiting sentence. In a 5–4 opinion delivered by Justice Hugo L. BLACK, the Supreme Court set aside both convictions, asserting that the First Amendment's guarantee of freedom of speech and press had been violated. Although the Bridges telegram could be construed as an announcement to call a strike, it had not intimidated the judge nor sidetracked the course of justice, Black commented, and the editorial, he said, had done no more than threaten future adverse criticism, which was to be expected anyway in the event of a lenient disposition of the case.

Bridget of Sweden, Saint

Bridget (Swedish, Birgitta), b. *c*.1303, d. July 23, 1373, is the patron saint of Sweden. She was lady-in-waiting at the royal court until her husband died in 1344. She founded the double order of monks and nuns, known as the Bridgettines, following one of her many visions and revelations. In 1349 she went to Rome, where she was prominent in religious and political life until her death. She was canonized in 1391. Feast day: July 23 (formerly Oct. 8).

Bridgetown

Bridgetown (1980 pop., 7,517) is the capital and chief port of the island-nation of Barbados in the West Indies. Settled in the 1620s, it has an economy based on tourism, shipping, sugar refining, and rum distilling.

Bridgewater Canal

The Bridgewater Canal extends from Worsley to Liverpool, England. The first section, built between Worsley and Manchester (16 km/10 mi) by James Brindley, was completed in 1761 and extended to Liverpool in 1776. The canal facilitated the shipment of coal within the region and greatly decreased its price in Manchester and Liverpool, stimulating their rapid industrial growth.

Bridgman, Percy Williams   [brij'-muhn]

The American physicist and philosopher of science Percy Williams Bridgman, b. Cambridge, Mass., Apr. 21, 1882, d. Aug. 20, 1961, made major contributions to the physics of high-pressure phenomena. He pursued his entire academic career at Harvard University, obtaining degrees in 1904, 1905, and 1908, and teaching from 1910 until 1954. A skillful experimentalist, Bridgman obtained unprecedented high pressures in his laboratory and published more than 260 articles on his work. He is best known, however, for his 13 books of commonsense logical philosophy, in which he argues that the meaning of any scientific term is expressed best by the operations it conveys. Stricken with an incurable disease, Bridgman committed suicide.

MICHAEL MEO

Bridie, James   [bry'-dee]

James Osborne Henry Mavor Bridie, b. Jan. 3, 1888, d. Jan. 29, 1951, was a Scottish dramatist and physician whose works are frequently compared to those of G. B. Shaw. His well-made plays on social and moral themes include his first, *The Anatomist* (1930), and *A Sleeping Clergyman* (1933). *Tobias and the Angel* (1930) is based on the Bible and folklore. Bridie wrote a play almost every year. His last, *The Queen's Comedy*, was completed in 1950.

ROBIN BUSS

brief

A lawyer's brief is a statement of his or her case, together with the arguments and authorities upon which it rests. United States appellate courts usually require a brief to be filed for the information of the judge and the opposing party. Generally, the party appealing presents the first brief, and the opponent files an answering brief. The first party may then file a reply brief. Occasionally a brief may incorporate considerable economic and sociological data, as in the brief presented by the plaintiff in BROWN v. BOARD OF EDUCATION OF TOPEKA, KANSAS, which argued that racially segregated schools provided unequal education.

A brief filed by someone not a party to the case but who wishes to present arguments is called a brief AMICUS CURIAE ("friend of the court").

In English practice a brief is a document prepared by the solicitor and given to the BARRISTER. It contains all the information necessary for the barrister's use in arguing the case in court.

brier

Brier, or briar, is a term used to designate prickly bushes, especially those belonging to the BRAMBLES (blackberries, raspberries, and dewberries). The name GREENBRIER, or catbrier, is applied to the plant genus *Smilax*. In Europe, certain kinds of wild ROSES are called briers; among these are the Austrian brier (*Rosa foetida*), the dog brier (*R. canina*), and the sweet brier, or EGLANTINE (*R. eglanteria*). The term *brier* is also used to refer to a white HEATH tree, *Erica arborea*, found in southern Europe, the flame-resistant root of which is used in making tobacco pipes. Briar pipes are sometimes made from roots of other plants as well, including some species of *Smilax*.

Brieux, Eugène   [bree-u']

Eugène Brieux, b. Jan. 19, 1858, d. Dec. 6, 1932, was a French dramatist whose more than 30 realistic problem plays were admired by George Bernard Shaw. Sometimes his forthright treatment of social themes scandalized his audiences. *Blanchette* (1892) examined social class, and *The Red Robe* (1900; Eng. trans., 1915) attacked judges. Later plays dealt frankly with sexual problems.

brig and brigantine: see SHIP.

brigade

A brigade is a military unit comprising a minimum of a head-quarters and two battalions. Since 1962 a U.S. Army division has comprised three brigades composed, in turn, of two or more battalions of varying size and type, depending on the division's mission.

Briggs, Henry

An English mathematician, Henry Briggs, b. February 1561, d. Jan. 26, 1630, was the man most responsible for scientists' acceptance of logarithms. He was educated at Cambridge University and was the first professor of geometry at Gresham College, London. In 1619 he was appointed professor of geometry at Oxford.

Briggs published works on navigation, astronomy, and mathematics. He proposed "common" logarithms, with ten as the base, and constructed a table of logarithms that was used until the 19th century.   STEVEN LUBAR

Brigham City

Brigham City, Utah (1990 pop., 15,644), was settled in 1851 by Mormons. Located at the foot of the Wasatch Range, it is the seat of Box Elder County. The city's leading industry is the processing of food staples grown on the surrounding irrigated farmland.

Brigham Young University

Established in 1875 and operated by the Church of Jesus Christ of Latter-Day Saints, Brigham Young University (enrollment: 27,748; library: 2,129,057 volumes) is a private coeducational institution in Provo, Utah. It has a graduate school and schools of law and management. A campus is located at Oahu, Hawaii.

Bright, John

John Bright, b. Nov. 16, 1811, d. Mar. 27, 1889, was a prominent British reform politician and orator during Queen Victoria's reign. The son of a Quaker cotton mill owner, he was a lifelong advocate of peace, free trade, and parliamentary reform. As an opponent of aristocratic rule (in his own Liberal party as well as among the Tories, or Conservatives), he was excluded from cabinet office until 1868 when William E. Gladstone became prime minister.

Bright first gained attention in the 1840s by opposing the Corn Laws. He represented Manchester in Parliament from 1847 to 1857, when his opposition to the British military intervention in China brought his defeat. He then, however, represented Birmingham from 1857 to 1889. His most famous parliamentary address was the "angel of death" speech, opposing the Crimean War. He then concentrated on the expansion of free trade and of voting rights. He served in Gladstone's cabinets three times but resigned finally (1882) in protest against the British bombardment of Alexandria. The newer radicalism of Joseph Chamberlain in the 1880s made him look old-fashioned, but Bright joined in opposing Gladstone's Irish Home Rule proposals (1886).   DONALD SOUTHGATE

Bibliography: Robbins, Keith, *John Bright* (1979); Trevelyan, G. M., *John Bright*, 2d ed. (1925).

Bright, Richard

Richard Bright, b. Sept. 28, 1789, d. Dec. 16, 1858, was an English physician famous for his description of kidney diseases that became known as BRIGHT'S DISEASE. In 1820 he became affiliated with Guy's Hospital in London. In his *Reports on Medical Cases* (1827), Bright described diseases in what was a new approach for that time. He correlated bedside observations, changes in body chemistry, and findings obtained at autopsies in an attempt to learn more about disease and facilitate future diagnosis and treatment.

Bibliography: Hale-White, W., *Great Doctors of the Nineteenth Century* (1935); Williamson, R. T., *English Physicians of the Past* (1923).

Brighton

Brighton is a borough and seaside resort in the county of East Sussex, England, 82 km (51 mi) south of London. The population is 144,700 (1988 est.). In 1783 the Prince of Wales (later George IV) became the important patron of the town. The ROYAL PAVILION, built in Oriental style, is now a museum and art gallery, and the town is noted for its Regency period squares and terraces. The main section of the town is the Front, which extends along the shore from the Palace to the West Pier, both of which are now amusement arcades. The old fishing port contains many antiques shops. The city is still a popular resort, and the University of Sussex was founded there in 1961.

Brighton Pavilion: see ROYAL PAVILION AT BRIGHTON.

Bright's disease

Bright's disease is an outmoded name for kidney disease in general. Between 1827 and 1836, the English physician Richard Bright performed pioneer work in describing the symptoms and physical signs of patients suffering from kidney disease. Since the 1960s, however, physicians have classified kidney diseases in more specific terms, according to cause, outcome, and the microscopic changes that occur in kidney tissue. The term *Bright's disease* is still used in many textbooks, however, to describe any of at least a dozen kidney diseases that involve inflammation and degeneration of kidney tissue and at least partial loss of kidney function.
                                        RICHARD B. FREEMAN, M.D.

Brillat-Savarin, Anthelme   [bree-ah'-sah-vah-ran', ahn-telm']

Jean Anthelme Brillat-Savarin, b. Apr. 1, 1755, d. Feb. 2, 1826, was the author of *La Physiologie du goût* (1825), a treatise on the fine art of gastronomy. Published in English as *The Physiology of Taste* (1825), it was the first work to treat dining as a form of art, and gastronomy as "the intelligent knowledge of whatever concerns man's nourishment." Born in France, Brillat-Savarin was trained as a jurist and fled the French Revolution in 1793. He lived for three years in the United States, supporting himself as a violinist and by teaching French. He returned to France and his legal career in 1796 and died in Paris one year after having published his great work.

brimstone: see SULFUR.

brine shrimp

The brine shrimp is a small, primitive crustacean found worldwide in the concentrated brine of salt lakes and ponds. Not a true shrimp, it has an elongated trunk of 20 or more segments and lacks a carapace. The nearly transparent body is rarely more than 1.3 cm (0.5 in) long. Flattened, unspecialized appendages on 11 to 19 of the segments are used for swimming and feeding, and the compound eyes are stalked. It usually swims upside down. The eggs can develop without fertilization and may hatch within the female's brood pouch. If laid, they can survive for years until hatching conditions are favorable. Both the adults and the eggs are used as fish food in aquariums. Brine shrimp are of the genus *Artemia*, order Anostraca, subclass Branchiopoda.

Brinkley, David

A television news personality noted for his acerbic wit, David Brinkley, b. July 10, 1920, started his journalism career as a writer for his hometown newspaper, the *Wilmington* (N.C.) *Star–News*. He studied at the University of North Carolina at Chapel Hill and Vanderbilt University and, after service in the army, joined NBC news in 1943. In 1956 he was teamed with Chet HUNTLEY for an evening news show, the "Huntley–Brinkley Report." He was also host of "David Brinkley's Journal" (1961) and of a number of specials. After Huntley's retirement in 1971, Brinkley continued on "NBC Nightly News" until 1981, when he moved to ABC. His *Washington Goes to War,* describing the city's growth during World War II, was published in 1988.   VINCENT TERRACE

Briosco, Andrea   [bree-aws'-koh]

Andrea Briosco, b. *c.*1470, d. June 1532, who was also known as Riccio, was an Italian Renaissance sculptor and goldsmith from Padua. He was renowned for his many small-scale bronzes that were inspired by classical art and represent mythological subjects. In addition to these refined and sophisticated statuettes, his major works include the magnificent bronze Paschal Candlestick in the Basilica del Santo (Sant' Antonio) in Padua (1506–15), with its abundance of antique-inspired ornament, and the tomb of the physicians Girolamo and Marcantonio della Torre (*c.*1516–21), with its eight classical reliefs (now in the Louvre, Paris) depicting the lives of the deceased in a frankly pagan spirit.   MARK J. ZUCKER

Brisbane   [briz'-buhn]

Brisbane is a port city in eastern Australia located at Moreton Bay, above the mouth of the Brisbane River. It is the capital of Queensland and the third largest city in Australia, with a population of 1,171,300 (1986 est.). It exports wool, sugar, meat, grain, and minerals from the surrounding, vast region.

Among its industries are shipyards, oil refineries, food processing plants, railroad shops, and factories that manufacture automobiles, rubber products, construction materials, and fertilizer. Two airports and a network of rail lines and highways serve the city. The University of Queensland at St. Lucia was established in 1909. Of interest are Parliament House (1869), Anglican and Roman Catholic cathedrals, and a new cultural center housing the Queensland Art Gallery, a performing arts center, the Queensland Museum, and the State Library.

In 1824 a convict settlement was moved to the site from Redcliffe. When this colony was designated a town in 1834, its name was changed from Edenglassie to Brisbane in honor of Sir Thomas Brisbane, former governor of New South Wales. A town of freemen began to grow up around the colony, and in 1842 the colony was disbanded. Brisbane became capital of Queensland in 1859. In 1988 the city was the site of World Expo 88, a world's fair held during the Australian Bicentennial.

Brisbane, Arthur

Arthur Brisbane, b. Buffalo, N.Y., Dec. 12, 1864, d. Dec. 25, 1936, was a newspaper editor whose sensational exploitation of news stories made him a central figure in American YELLOW JOURNALISM. As editor of William Randolph HEARST's *New York Journal,* he led the 1897–98 circulation battles against Joseph PULITZER's *New York World.* By sensationalizing and slanting the news from Cuba in an anti-Spanish direction, he was instrumental in stirring popular sentiment in favor of the Spanish-American War. His column, "Today," noted for its simple language and simplistic arguments, was syndicated to more than 1,000 weeklies. Beginning as a reporter on the *New York Sun* in 1883, Brisbane worked for the *World* from 1890 to 1897, when he became managing editor of the *Journal.* His policies, while criticized widely, boosted the paper's circulation—and his own fortune—enormously.

Bibliography: Carlson, Oliver, *Brisbane: A Candid Biography* (1937; repr. 1970).

Brissot de Warville, Jacques Pierre   [bree-soh' duh var-veel']

The French revolutionary Jacques Pierre Brissot de Warville, b. Jan. 15, 1754, was a leader of the Girondist moderates in the French Revolution. An antiroyalist, antislavery publicist be-

fore the Revolution and editor of *Le Patriote français* (May 1789–March 1793), he was elected to the Legislative Assembly in 1791. He urged war against European reactionary sovereigns but would have preserved the French monarchy, for which he was denounced. He spoke in the National Convention for the GIRONDISTS against the extremist Montagnards. He fled arrest but was caught and guillotined on Oct. 31, 1793.

bristlecone pine

A bristlecone, or hickory, pine, P. aristata, grows extremely slowly, and some bristlecones have lived to be more than 4,000 years old. The tree grows to a height of 3 to 14 m (10 to 45 ft). The cones are 6 to 10 cm (2.4 to 4 in) in length, topped with a sharp bristle.

The bristlecone pine, *Pinus aristata,* is an evergreen tree that belongs to the pine family, Pinaceae. It is named for the spiny scales on its cones; another distinguishing feature is the needlelike leaves, in groups of five, that are bluish green in color and covered with specks of resin. Some individuals of this species are probably the oldest things alive on Earth. Growing primarily in six states of the southwestern United States, bristlecone pines have been found at elevations of 3,050–3,350 m (10,000–11,000 ft) above sea level. Precipitation where they grow is light, averaging 30.5–33 cm (12–13 in) of rainfall a year. Most pines retain their needles for 2 or 3 years, but the bristlecone pine's short needles may be retained for 20 to 30 years before being replaced. The dense head of foliage resembles the tail of a fox; for this reason, the bristlecone pine and similar trees are popularly called foxtail pines. The bristlecone pine reaches a height of up to 14 m (45 ft); in Eastern states, however, it is a dwarf tree and may be only 1 m (3 ft) high. Bristlecone pines grow slowly and may take up to 3,000 years to reach full height.

Interest was drawn to the bristlecone pine in the 1950s when Edmund Schulman (1908–58) of the Laboratory for Tree-Ring Research in Tucson, Ariz., began trying to correlate climatic conditions with tree-ring diameter in the bristlecone pine. (Trees, in general, grow thicker rings during warm, wet years.) This type of work had been carried out before, notably with the ponderosa pine, but Schulman was the first to take up an analysis of bristlecone-pine tree rings. In the course of his research, Schulman established the great age of bristlecone pines; he found 17 that were more than 4,000 years old, one of which was about 4,600 years old. Analyzing core samples from living pines and preserved wood from long-dead trees, researchers have developed a bristlecone-pine tree-ring chronology dating back some 8,700 years.

Most of the research on the bristlecone pine has been done in the White Mountains of California. The U.S. Forest Service protects these trees, but they are available for public viewing.

The age of a living bristlecone pine is determined by using a hand-operated drill (increment borer) to remove a core of growth that can be microscopically examined to determine the width of the annual rings. Carbon-14 dating is also used on this material, although different results may be obtained. Nevertheless, DENDROCHRONOLOGY (tree-ring dating) is a valuable tool in determining the climatic history of the Earth in recent millennia. Valuable information has been gathered on the intensity of solar activity in ancient times.

Bibliography: Mirov, Nicholas T., and Hasbrouck, Jean, *The Story of Pines* (1976).

See also: RADIOMETRIC AGE-DATING.

bristlemouth

Bristlemouth is the common name for deep-sea fish of the family Gonostomatidae. These fishes resemble miniature herring and are characterized by a series of light organs, or photophores, along the sides of the body. Usually less than 5–7 cm (2–3 in) in length, they are the most numerous fish in the sea but are rarely noted except in the stomach contents of deep-sea carnivores or in deep-haul plankton nets.

EDWARD O. WILEY

bristletail

Bristletails are small, scaly, wingless insects with three taillike appendages at the end of the abdomen; hence, their name. Bristletails are members of the primitive order Thysanura. The species most commonly seen are the silverfish and the firebrat. These are active, fast-running insects that feed on such starchy materials as bookbindings, the paste in wallpaper, some fabrics, and many foods. The silverfish is silvery in appearance and is often seen in kitchens and bathrooms; the firebrat is brownish and is more commonly found around furnaces and boilers. The species most often seen outdoors are the jumping bristletails, which occur in leaf litter, under bark or stones, or in similar locations. DONALD J. BORROR

Bristol

Bristol is the largest city in southwestern England. It has a population of 396,600 (1984 est.). An international seaport, it is situated on the Avon River about 11 km (7 mi) from its mouth in the Bristol Channel. Supplemented by the docks of Avonmouth and Portishead, Bristol is a busy import point for food and petroleum and an export outlet for the city's many manufactures, notably heavy machinery and motor vehicles. Bristol is also noted for its aircraft production.

During the Middle Ages the city was a textile center. Its seaport was John Cabot's point of departure for the New World in 1497. William Penn and John Wesley both lived in Bristol. The city thrived on commerce with the colonies and was a crucial link in the slave trade. The end of that trade and the rising competition of Liverpool brought a decline in the early 1800s, but the expansion of the city's docks and the development of new industries allowed Bristol to regain its position as a major seaport by the early 20th century. Repeated bombing during World War II caused heavy damage, but many notable medieval edifices remain.

Bristol, University of

Founded in 1876 as University College, Bristol, and chartered in 1909 in its present form, the University of Bristol (enrollment: 7,500; library: 1,000,000 volumes) in Bristol, England, has faculties of arts, science, engineering, medicine, law, social sciences, and education, all of which grant undergraduate and graduate degrees. Among the associated institutions are the Baptist College, Wesley College, Bath College of Higher Education, College of St. Paul and St. Mary, and Bristol Polytechnic Faculty of Education.

Bristol Channel

The Bristol Channel is an inlet of the Atlantic Ocean between southwestern England and Wales. It is about 137 km (85 mi) long, and its width ranges from 69 km (43 mi) at its western

end to 8 km (5 mi) near Cardiff, Wales. The shores of Wales are marked by coalfields and industrial development. Somerset and Devon, on the south shore, are agricultural. The mouth of the Severn River lies to the east. Lundy Island, off the Devon coast, is near the channel's western entrance.

Much shipping traffic passes through the channel to Swansea, Cardiff, and Bristol. Bristol has solved shipping problems caused by the channel's unusually high tides by installing locks to create a tide-free port.

Bristow, Benjamin Helm

Benjamin Helm Bristow, b. June 20, 1832, d. June 22, 1896, served (1874–76) as U.S. secretary of the treasury under President Ulysses S. Grant and exposed the WHISKEY RING, a scandal that implicated many prominent Republicans, including Grant's private secretary, Orville Babcock. A Union officer in the Civil War, Bristow served as U.S. attorney for Kentucky (1866–70) and U.S. solicitor-general (1870–72) before his appointment to the cabinet. In 1876 he was an unsuccessful candidate for the Republican presidential nomination.

Britain: see GREAT BRITAIN; UNITED KINGDOM.

Britain, Battle of

The Battle of Britain was the air war (1940–41) fought over Great Britain between the German Luftwaffe and the Royal Air Force during World War II. Having decided (June 1940) to invade Britain, Adolf Hitler ordered a preliminary attack by the Luftwaffe to destroy the RAF and neutralize the Royal Navy. After a series of raids on British coastal defenses in July, the Luftwaffe's attack began in earnest on August 8. With a total force of 900 fighters (mostly Messerschmitt BF-109s) and 1,300 bombers, the Germans mounted massive daily raids on southern England. Although the RAF had much smaller forces, about 650 Hurricanes and Spitfires, the newly developed radar enabled it to concentrate in vital areas for effective resistance.

On August 24 the Luftwaffe began attacks further inland, seeking to destroy the RAF bases and fighter production centers. By September 5 the RAF Fighter Command had lost 450 planes and was close to defeat. At that point, however, Hitler and Luftwaffe chief Herman Goering changed their strategy. Infuriated by British bombing raids (August 24–29) on Berlin, they concentrated the German attacks on London. With its defense task simplified, the RAF inflicted heavy losses on the German bombing formations. Early in October the Luftwaffe switched entirely to night raids. By the end of that month Hitler had canceled his invasion plans.

German bombing attacks on British cities (the "Blitz") continued until May 1941, when most of the Luftwaffe planes were withdrawn to prepare for the German invasion of the USSR. The Battle of Britain, however, had been won by October 1940. Of the RAF fighter pilots, Winston Churchill said: "Never, in the field of human conflict, was so much owed by so many to so few." In saving Britain from invasion, they had inflicted the first major defeat on Germany in the war.

Bibliography: Deighton, Len, *Fighter: The True Story of the Battle of Britain* (1978); Gelb, N., *Scramble: A Narrative History of the Battle of Britain* (1985); Mosley, L., ed., *The Battle of Britain* (1977).

British Antarctic Territory

The British Antarctic Territory is a colony comprising a wedge of the Antarctic continent and offshore islands. It is an area bounded by 20° west longitude and 80° west longitude and by 60° south latitude. It includes the Antarctic Peninsula, the South Orkney Islands, and the South Shetland Islands. The territory is administered from the Falkland Islands in the South Atlantic. Before becoming a British colony in 1962, it was included in the Falkland Islands Dependencies. Parts of the territory are also claimed by Chile and Argentina.

The region is relatively mountainous and contains several large glaciers and the Filchner, Ronne, and Larsen ice shelves.

The highest peak, Mount Andrew Jackson on the Antarctic Peninsula, rises to 4,191 m (13,750 ft). The climate is polar, and although no permanent inhabitants reside there, about 100 scientists and support personnel work at various British Antarctic Survey stations that conduct meteorological and geological research.

British Broadcasting Corporation

The British Broadcasting Corporation—the BBC—is Great Britain's public radio and television broadcasting organization. It consists of a network of national and regional radio stations and a 2-channel television service. The corporation also broadcasts radio and television programs around the world through its World Service. BBC operations are largely financed by an annual license fee paid by television-set owners. No commercial advertising is carried.

Begun as a private effort in 1922, the BBC was chartered by Parliament in 1927 as the sole provider of British broadcasting. From its inception, it has been almost completely free of government oversight. The corporation is directed by a board of governors and administered by a director-general.

The first director-general, Sir John (later 1st Baron) Reith (1889–1971), served the corporation until 1938, and by fulfilling in the most literal fashion his commitment "to educate, to entertain, and to inform," he almost single-handedly created a broadcasting entity that has set still-unsurpassed standards for cultural richness and journalistic objectivity.

The BBC continued to maintain the quality of its programming even as it grew into the monolith it is today. It inaugurated the world's first regular TV service in 1936, opened BBC-2, its second TV channel, in 1964, and has produced innumerable TV and radio programs, documentaries, and series—many of them as memorable as fine theater pieces. Some of the TV series have been shown to great acclaim on U.S. television. In addition, the BBC publishes and sells books, magazines—notably, *The Listener,* on the arts of radio and television communication—and such other products as records and videocassettes.

The BBC's television monopoly ended in 1954, when Parliament established the Independent Television Authority (ITV), which grew into a consortium of 15 regional TV companies—now known collectively as Channel 3—each of which operates a single channel within its assigned area, produces many of its own programs, and is financed by the sale of commercial time. Channel 4, established in 1982, broadcasts programs bought from independent producers and moviemakers and is operated and financed by the ITV network.

The BBC was often accused of a kind of self-righteous stuffiness ("Auntie Beeb" was a popular name for the network), but competition from the commercial channels, cable, and from direct broadcast satellite networks forced the corporation to try new experiments of its own (see, for example, MONTY PYTHON'S FLYING CIRCUS) and to buy more programming from non-BBC sources. With its charter up for renewal in 1996, the organization has become more responsive to government pressures to increase its revenues.

In addition to World Service Television, its 24-hour all-news channel, the corporation announced plans in 1994 to open two satellite-delivered channels in Europe as well as a wide range of other initiatives around the world.

Bibliography: Briggs, Asa, *The BBC* (1985); Horner, R., *Inside BBC Television* (1984); Hughes, P., *British Broadcasting: Programmes and Power* (1981); Lucas, R., *The Voice of a Nation?* (1990); Scannell, P., and Cardiff, D., *A Social History of British Broadcasting*, vol. 1, 1922–39 (1991); Tusa, J., *Conversations with the World* (1992); Whitehead, Kate, *The Third Programme: A Literary History* (1989).

See also: RADIO AND TELEVISION BROADCASTING; TELEVISION, NONCOMMERCIAL.

British Columbia

British Columbia, the westernmost province of Canada, has an area of 947,800 km² (365,947 mi²), making it the third-largest province, after Quebec and Ontario. (The federally administered Northwest Territories is largest of all in area.)

BRITISH COLUMBIA

LAND. Area: 947,800 km² (365,947 mi²); rank: 3d. Capital: Victoria (1991 pop., 71,228). Largest city: Vancouver (1991 pop., 471,844). Municipalities: 218. Elevations: highest—4,663 m (15,300 ft) at Fairweather Mountain; lowest—sea level.

PEOPLE. Population (1993 est.): 3,535,000; rank: 3d; density: 3.8 persons per km² (9.8 per mi²). Distribution (1991): 80.5% urban, 19.5% rural. Average annual change (1986–91): +2.8%.

EDUCATION. Enrollment (1993–94 est.): elementary and secondary—646,780; higher—77,030. Institutions of higher education (1993–94): 25.

ECONOMY (monetary figures in Canadian dollars). Total personal income (1992): $78.2 billion; rank: 3d. Median family income (1992): $50,252. Labor force distribution (1993): agriculture—36,000 persons; other primary industries—50,000; manufacturing—190,000; construction—133,000; transportation, communication, and other utilities—135,000; trade—328,000; finance, insurance, and real estate—100,000; services—647,000; public administration—100,000. Agriculture: farm cash receipts (1990)—$1.2 billion. Fishing: landed value (1991)—$369 million. Forestry: lumber production (1990)—14.05 billion board feet. Mining: value (1991)—$3.6 billion. Manufacturing: value added (1991): $9.45 billion.

GOVERNMENT (1994). Lieutenant Governor: David C. Lam. Premier: Michael Harcourt, New Democratic Party. Parliament: Senate—6 members; House of Commons—24 Reform Party, 2 New Democrats, 6 Liberals. Provincial legislature: 75 members. Admitted to Confederation: July 20, 1871, the 6th province.

In population the province also ranks third, after Ontario and Quebec. About 70% of the population are concentrated in the southwestern section of the province, mainly in the largest city, VANCOUVER, and in VICTORIA, the capital, which is located on south VANCOUVER ISLAND.

"B.C.," as it is known to its people, became a crown colony of Britain (1858) and a Canadian province in 1871. Cut off from the rest of Canada in earlier years by a mountain barrier, British Columbia often had its closest links with trans-Pacific countries and with the West Coast of the United States.

LAND AND RESOURCES

The Cordilleran mountain system of western North America extends through British Columbia in a series of north-south mountain ranges, linear valleys, and high interior plateaus. On the east, the high wall of the ROCKY MOUNTAINS rises abruptly about 1,220 to 1,520 m (4,000 to 5,000 ft) above the Interior Plains of Alberta and has peaks that are 3,340 and 3,650 m (11,000 and 12,000 ft) above sea level. The western boundary of the Rockies is the longest valley in North America—the narrow Rocky Mountain Trench that extends the length of British Columbia from Montana to the Yukon Territory. To the west of the trench, groups of high, jagged mountain ranges and interconnected north-south valleys are collectively known as the Columbia Mountains in the south (named for the Columbia River) and the Cassiar-Omineca Mountains in the north. Much of south central British Columbia is an upland called the Interior Plateau, which is deeply incised by the FRASER RIVER. To the north the Stikine Plateau contains the headwaters of the Stikine River.

The western section of mountains comprises two lines along the coast. The northern edge of the Cascade Range of Washington State terminates at the Fraser River, and the high peaks of the Coast Mountains continue northward, capped by Mount Waddington (4,042 m/13,260 ft). The numerous fjords and narrow coastal valleys present spectacular scenery along the whole British Columbia coast and into the panhandle of Alaska. This sheltered water route along the coast is known as the Inside Passage. It is protected from the open ocean by another line of mountains extending through Vancouver Island and the QUEEN CHARLOTTE ISLANDS.

Soils. It is estimated that less than 5% of British Columbia has soil of agricultural value. As in most mountainous regions, soils on the rocky, barren upper slopes are not suitable for farming. Only in the narrow floodplains of the river valleys are there alluvial soils on which crops can grow.

Climate. British Columbia has two types of climate. The coastal section, facing the Pacific, has mild winters, cool summers, and heavy winter rainfall. The interior of the province, which may be affected in winter by cold air masses moving south from the Yukon Territory, has cold winters and has heavy snows on west-facing slopes. The northern valleys are cool in summer, but the southern interior valleys are hot and dry.

Vegetation and Animal Life. More than half the province is well forested with tall, straight coniferous trees that are the basis of the lumbering industry. These trees are the largest in the wet, mild coastal region. Grasslands occupy the dry, lower sections of the southern interior valleys and cover larger areas of the western part of the Interior Plateau, in the lee of the Coast Mountains.

Wildlife of the province includes the black and grizzly bear, deer, wolf, bighorn sheep, moose, and beaver. Numerous varieties of migratory waterfowl inhabit the coastal area and lakes. Sea lion and fur seal are found along the coast.

Natural Resources. Forestry is the major use of the natural environment of the province. The mountains contain abundant mineral deposits, and mining has been important for more than a century. Offshore and at river mouths salmon fishing is a major source of income. There is ample water power in the many rushing rivers of the mountainous region.

ECONOMIC ACTIVITIES

The economy of British Columbia is based to a considerable extent on the processing of natural resources. Most processing

The Canadian Pacific Railroad winds along a canyon carved by the Fraser River in central British Columbia. The discovery of gold along the river during the 1850s drew thousands of settlers into the province and promoted the exploration of British Columbia's interior.

of forest, fish, and agricultural products is concentrated in what is called the Georgia Strait region in southwest British Columbia. Manufacturing is carried on mainly in Vancouver and nearby cities at the mouth of the Fraser River and on the east side of Georgia Strait, but also in smaller cities on the east side of Vancouver Island. These industries and the urban residents are supplied with electrical power from nearby sites and from large power plants as far away as the Columbia and Peace rivers. Vancouver is the main transportation center on the south coast, being the western terminal of both transcontinental railroads and also the main port for ocean vessels. Prince Rupert is the only significant port along the north coast.

The economy of the interior of the province is based mainly on forestry, having both lumber and pulp and paper mills. Mining is carried on throughout the province, but the largest mines are in the southeast. The spectacular mountain scenery, the attraction of cool, sunny summers on the coast, and excellent interior highways have made British Columbia one of the main tourist attractions of North America.

PEOPLE

About half the population of British Columbia lives in metropolitan Vancouver, and 75% is in the small area of the southwest coast. The northern half of the province is almost empty, and the population of the southern interior is concentrated in

Vancouver, the largest city in British Columbia, offers both the modern and traditional with Canada Place (left), the shiplike trade and convention center built for the 1986 world's fair, and the totem poles of Stanley Park, representative of the city's native heritage.

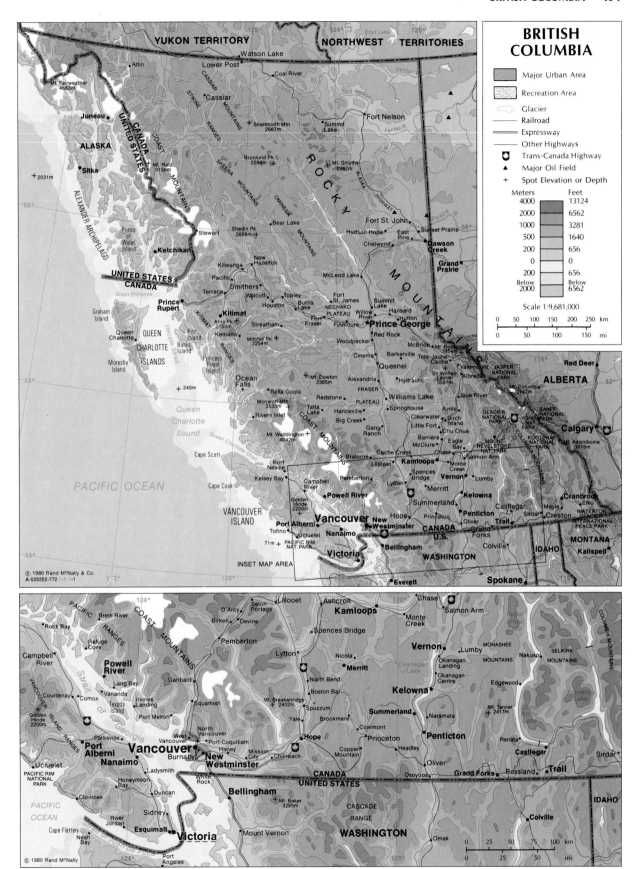

BRITISH COLUMBIA

Major Urban Area
Recreation Area
Glacier
Railroad
Expressway
Other Highways
Trans-Canada Highway
Major Oil Field
Spot Elevation or Depth

Meters	Feet
4000	13124
2000	6562
1000	3281
500	1640
200	656
0	0
200	656
Below 2000	Below 6562

Scale 1:9,681,000

0 50 100 150 200 250 km
0   50   100   150 mi

INSET MAP AREA

© 1980 Rand McNally & Co.
A-520202-772

© 1980 Rand McNally

(Above) *Fishing vessels lie at berth in Prince Rupert, near the Alaskan border. British Columbia leads all Canadian provinces in its fishing industry. Although salmon supply most of the province's catch, the waters off Prince Rupert are rich in halibut.*

(Left) *Victoria, the capital of British Columbia since its establishment as a province in 1871, occupies the southeastern tip of Vancouver Island. A significant center of the forest-products industry, the city also has spacious parks and gardens.*

the several narrow valleys. About 60% of the population are of British origin. As a result of post–World War II immigration from Europe and East Asia, this percentage has declined from about 80% a few decades ago. Chinese, Japanese, and East Indians are now noticeable elements in the urban population of British Columbia.

University education is provided by three institutions: the University of British Columbia on the western edge of Vancouver, Simon Fraser University in Burnaby, and the University of Victoria in the capital. The smaller cities in the rest of the province are served by a system of more than 15 community colleges, offering first- and second-year university courses and vocational and technical programs. Elementary and secondary schools, administered by local school boards, with financial help from the provincial government, are located wherever there are sufficient people. Major museums, archives, and art galleries are found in Vancouver and Victoria, and local museums are maintained in many smaller cities in the interior. The main theater productions are in Vancouver, but companies often go on tour to the smaller interior cities. All major cities have newspapers and radio and television stations. A widely scattered system of provincial parks and a few national parks supply recreational facilities.

GOVERNMENT

British Columbia is governed by a legislature consisting of members elected from defined electoral districts throughout the province. The premier is the leader of the party electing the greatest number of representatives. Elections must be held at least every five years. A cabinet is chosen by the premier, and government services are provided by the civil service, with headquarters in Victoria. As in other provinces, an appointed lieutenant governor represents the crown.

HISTORY

Indians have lived in both interior and coastal British Columbia since the waning of the last Ice Age, probably 7,000 to 10,000 years ago. Their numbers were probably sizable, and the Indians of the North Coast and Queen Charlotte Islands developed a well-organized and thriving culture. Among the most important tribes were the BELLA COOLA, HAIDA, KWAKIUTL, NOOTKA, SALISH, and TSIMSHIAN.

Exploration by Europeans took place in the late 18th century, both along the coast by ships from Spain, Britain, and Russia, and also overland from the interior by British fur-traders. The first settlements established by Europeans early in the 19th century were fur-trading posts located mainly in the interior but also near the southwest coast.

The first major influx of settlers did not occur until after 1858, when placer gold deposits were discovered in the Fraser River, and later in its upstream tributaries, particularly in those rivers east of present-day Quesnel. Because of the rush of prospectors, many of whom came from the California goldfields, two British colonies were established. Vancouver Island, with its capital at Victoria, controlled the sea entrances to the other colony, British Columbia, on the mainland with its capital at New Westminster. As goldfield activity in the interior declined, the two colonies were combined (1866), and the capital became (1868) Victoria.

In 1871 the people of British Columbia decided to join the Dominion of Canada, created in 1867. They had been promised a transcontinental railroad to link them with the eastern cities. The new province was to wait 15 years before the Canadian Pacific Railway reached the southwest coast. The western rail terminal and port of Vancouver was incorporated in 1887, and by 1901 it was the province's largest city.

In the 20th century, growth of British Columbia's population and economy has been based mainly on the exploitation of its vast natural resources. Lumber production expanded, particularly after World War I when the new Panama Canal gave access to the eastern United States and European markets. Fish canneries were built at the mouths of west-coast rivers to process the enormous runs of salmon.

The interior of British Columbia was less developed, and settlement was mainly near the few railroads. The Kootenay region of the southeast was a major mining area in Canada for a short time (1890-1910). Irrigation was introduced into the dry southern valleys, and the Okanagan Valley in particular became a significant fruit-growing area after World War I. Much of the population increase in the interior came after 1950, when the forestry industry expanded. The Social Credit party, under William A. C. Bennett (premier, 1952–72) and his son William R. (premier, 1975–86), has dominated post–World War II politics.   J. LEWIS ROBINSON

Bibliography: Cuddy, Mary L., comp., *British Columbia in Books: An Annotated Bibliography* (1975); Hilson, Stephen E., *Exploring Puget Sound and British Columbia*, rev. ed. (1981); McKeever, Harry P., *British Columbia* (1982); Ormsby, Margaret A., *British Columbia: A History* (1958; repr. 1971); Robinson, J. L., *British Columbia* (1972).

British Columbia, University of

Established in 1908, the University of British Columbia (enrollment: 26,175; library: 2,800,000 volumes) is a provincial institution in Vancouver, British Columbia, Canada. It has institutes of oceanography and of animal resource ecology and a full range of undergraduate and graduate programs.

British East India Company: see EAST INDIA COMPANY, BRITISH.

British education

British education has, for many centuries, influenced and been influenced by British society. It is an unusual system, characterized by national financing and local control.

Earliest education in the United Kingdom began in medieval churches and monasteries; for the most part, religious subjects were taught. Many people were educated by apprenticeship to an employer or in a guild.

The influence of humanism changed the focus of education: curricula were broadened to include history, literature, and languages, although religion continued to be taught. Church schools were secularized or closed after the Reformation. Charity schools for poor students and grammar schools for the more affluent were predominant in the 16th and 17th centuries and continued until the late 19th century. After the Restoration, in the middle of the 17th century, the number of endowed parish elementary and grammar schools increased. The 18th-century attitude toward education was influenced by French philosophers, who were great proponents of education for all. Political innovators in England advocated publicly provided education. Nineteenth-century schools—charity, privately endowed, village, or parish—flourished and helped to educate large numbers of children, and some adults.

Elementary education for children from the ages of 5 to 10 first became free and mandatory after the passage of the Elementary Education Act of 1870. An extensive network of voluntary schools, many of them provided by churches and charities, existed long before that date. Indeed, by contemporary European standards, a high proportion of the British population was already literate by 1870. Compulsory education was extended by law to 11-year-olds in 1893 and to 12-year-olds in 1899. At the end of World War I the minimum age at which children could leave school was raised to 14; at the end of World War II it was raised to 15. In 1973 it was raised again to 16, although a growing proportion of pupils stay in school until they are 17 or 18.

ADMINISTRATION AND FINANCE

After 1870 local school boards were established to assume control of the existing voluntary schools and to found new ones. In 1902 these independent boards were abolished, and their functions were taken over by all-purpose local authorities: county councils, which had been created in the 1880s, and city or borough councils, which had existed for many centuries. The local councils selected education committees from among their members; these Local Education Authorities were traditionally responsible for all education in Britain except in universities. The system as a whole—again, with the exception of universities—was presided over by a president of the board of education, who was a member of the cabinet. This title was later changed to minister of education and was changed again in 1964, when its holder became responsible for universities as well, to secretary of state for education and science.

Authority. The British education system is conventionally described as "a national system locally administered." It is a partnership between the central government (the Department of Education and Science) and the 104 Local Education Authorities, ranging from the gigantic Inner London Education Authority to those which administer schools in remote and mountainous counties of Wales such as Powys and Gwynedd. Scottish primary and secondary education are administered separately by a similar partnership between the Scottish Education Department (a division of the office of the secretary of state for Scotland) and the 12 regional authorities, ranging from Strathclyde, with about half the population of Scotland, to the Shetland Islands. Schools in Northern Ireland are also administered separately. The state schools are Protestant, and a Roman Catholic parochial school system also exists.

BRITISH UNIVERSITIES

University and Location	Date Founded*		Enrollment	Volumes in Library
England				
University of Aston in Birmingham	1895	(1966)	3,600	220,000
University of Bath	1856	(1966)	3,700	270,000
University of Birmingham	1880	(1900)	9,000	1,300,000
University of Bradford	1957	(1966)	4,200	400,000
University of Bristol	1876	(1909)	7,500	950,000
Brunel University, Uxbridge, Middlesex	1957	(1966)	3,400	160,000
University of Buckingham	1973	(1983)	600	20,000
Cambridge University	13th century		11,600	4,100,000
City University, London	1891	(1966)	4,100	110,000
University of Durham	1832		4,900	700,000
University of East Anglia, Norwich	1960	(1964)	4,700	550,000
University of Essex, Colchester	1961	(1965)	3,000	400,000
University of Exeter	1893	(1955)	4,900	750,000
University of Hull	1927	(1954)	4,700	750,000
University of Keele	1949	(1962)	2,700	496,000
University of Kent at Canterbury	1954	(1965)	4,100	505,000
University of Lancaster	1964	(1964)	4,400	710,000
University of Leeds	1884	(1904)	10,300	1,900,000
University of Leicester	1918	(1957)	4,700	850,000
University of Liverpool	1881	(1903)	8,100	1,000,000
University of London	1836	(1836)	65,800	1,000,000
Loughborough University of Technology	1952	(1966)	5,100	600,000
Victoria University of Manchester	1851	(1903)	17,900	3,350,000
University of Newcastle upon Tyne	1963		7,600	700,000
University of Nottingham	1881	(1948)	7,400	800,000
Open University, Milton Keynes	1969	(1969)	120,000	116,000
Oxford University	12th century		12,800	4,900,000
University of Reading	1892	(1926)	6,400	650,000
University of Salford	1896	(1967)	3,600	300,000
University of Sheffield	1897	(1905)	7,700	800,000
University of Southampton	1862	(1952)	6,400	750,000
University of Surrey, Guilford	1891	(1966)	4,000	325,000
University of Sussex, Brighton	1961	(1961)	4,500	500,000
University of Warwick, Coventry	1965	(1965)	5,600	600,000
University of York	1963	(1963)	3,600	350,000
Northern Ireland				
University of Ulster, Coleraine	1984		2,100	526,000
Queen's University of Belfast	1845	(1908)	6,900	755,000
Scotland				
University of Aberdeen	1495		6,000	1,000,000
University of Dundee	1881	(1967)	3,700	450,000
University of Edinburgh	1583	(1582)	11,500	2,000,000
University of Glasgow	1451	(1577)	13,000	1,400,000
Heriot-Watt University, Edinburgh	1821	(1966)	3,700	100,000
University of St. Andrews	1410		3,700	750,000
University of Stirling	1967	(1967)	2,800	450,000
University of Strathclyde, Glasgow	1796	(1964)	7,500	387,000
Wales				
University of Wales:				
University College of Wales, Aberystwyth	1872	(1889)	3,000	450,000
University College of North Wales, Bangor	1884	(1884)	2,800	400,000
University College, Cardiff	1883	(1884)	6,400	500,000
University College of Swansea	1920	(1920)	3,900	600,000
St. David's University College, Lampeter	1822	(1828)	750	130,000
University of Wales College of Medicine, Cardiff	1893	(1931)	650	60,000
University of Wales Institute of Science and Technology, Cardiff	1866	(1967)	3,100	200,000

*Date of university charter appears in parentheses.

(Above) *Tom Tower, a 16th-century bell tower, overlooks the courtyard of Oxford University's Christ Church. Oxford, England's oldest university, has been the site of an academic community since the 12th century. University College, founded in 1249, was the first of its self-governing colleges.*

(Left) *The 15th-century Gothic chapel of King's College, near the historic River Cam, is one of England's landmarks. King's College, one of 31 colleges that constitute Cambridge University, was founded in 1441 to further the education of Eton graduates.*

Although local authorities retain the primary responsibility for the administration of British schools, the Department of Education and Science planned to establish a national curriculum in the Great Education Reform Bill (1987). Individual schools would also be allowed to "opt out" of local control and be controlled nationally.

Funding. British schools, colleges, and universities, like those in most European countries, are financed almost entirely by public funds, either from the central government in London or from local education authorities. Only about 2,800 of Britain's more than 35,000 primary and secondary schools are private institutions. Unlike its European neighbors, however, the national government of Britain is not involved in the detailed administration of individual institutions or in determining the actual education they provide; the latter is the responsibility of teachers and professors alone.

Public expenditure on education in Britain in 1987–88 was projected at $24.6 billion. Local authorities receive only about one-third of their income from property taxes, known as rates. The rest is provided by the central government in the form of a rate-support grant, the amount of which is negotiated each autumn.

Local authorities, however, are free to spend this money as they wish, within limits established by law. They can, for instance, choose to spend more on education and less on housing than the government had assumed in its calculation of the grant. They can also supplement their income by increasing the rates they charge residents, although in the 1980s the central government assumed power to limit rates. The central government maintains tighter control over expenditures for capital improvements, such as new buildings and expensive equipment. Any large projects must be individually approved by the Department of Education and Science. The department is also directly involved in the negotiation of teachers' salaries, which are uniform throughout the country and constitute a large part of the education budget.

UNIVERSAL EDUCATION

There are more than 10 million students in Britain's 35,000 schools. About 50,000 attend the nation's 1,000 nursery schools, which accept children between the ages of 3 and 5—the start of compulsory schooling. About 4.8 million are educated in the 27,000 primary schools, which are usually divid-

ed into infants' departments, for children up to age 7, and junior schools for those aged 8 to 11. There are 4 million pupils enrolled in Britain's 5,400 secondary schools. In addition, about 150,000 students with learning difficulties and other handicaps attend 1,800 special schools.

Primary Schools. Since the 1950s the traditional approach to the education of younger children, having pupils sitting in rows and learning by rote, has been replaced by a more relaxed and informal approach. This change was highlighted by the report on primary schools (1967) by a committee under Lady Plowden. This report recommended, among other things, the abolition of corporal punishment and the hiring of more teachers. It also recommended that educational priority areas be established in the most deprived areas of cities.

The primary curriculum has also been greatly extended in recent years. New approaches to reading and mathematics have been developed, on the whole with considerable success. Modern languages, in particular French, have been introduced into primary schools, but with less success. The moves to liberalize the primary schools have been strongly supported by the teachers themselves, in particular by the National Union of Teachers, to which most British teachers belong.

Welsh is the main language of instruction in primary and some secondary schools in primarily Welsh-speaking areas of Wales; in English-speaking areas of the country, schools are bilingual, with classes taught in English or Welsh. Irish is taught as a second language in Roman Catholic schools in Northern Ireland.

Secondary Schools. Many of the beneficial changes in primary education have been made possible by the abolition of the notorious "11 plus" examination, named for the age at which children took it. This examination, based largely on verbal reasoning and mathematical ability, was used to decide which children would go on to strictly academic secondary schools (grammar schools) and which would go to the so-called secondary modern schools, which included vocational courses. Even in the few areas where this dual system of secondary schools still exists, children are now assessed on the basis of their total school performance, not by examinations.

In most parts of Britain the old grammar and secondary modern schools have been replaced by comprehensive secondary schools that all children in the district attend, whatever their academic ability. This change was initiated by the Labour government in 1966 and continued even after the Conservative party returned to power in 1970. After the return of Labour in 1974, the changeover to comprehensive schools was accelerated. The return of the Conservatives to power in 1979 has not affected this trend.

The creation of the comprehensive school has also led to radical changes in school examinations, which until recently were oriented almost exclusively to the academic pupil, and in particular to those wishing to enter higher education. Even today, the brighter children normally take the ordinary level (O level) of the Graduate Certificate of Education (GCE) in five to eight separate subjects at about the age of 16, and take the advanced level (A level) of the GCE in two or three subjects two years later. Their chances of being admitted to a university or other institution of higher education depend on their performance on A level examinations, which are graded A to E.

Almost one-fourth of those leaving school pass examinations in at least five subjects at O level, and about half of these receive two A level passes, the minimum required for entry to a university degree course. In the 1970s a less academic examination system, called the Certificate of Secondary Education (CSE), was introduced for the majority of students, those who do not aim for higher education. About a quarter of the British students, however, leave school without any formal qualification. In the late 1980s the O level examination was expected to be replaced by a broader General Certificate of Secondary Education (GCSE). Different systems of secondary examinations have been used in Northern Ireland and in Scotland. The Scottish examination system has not emphasized the dichotomy between academic and vocational subjects. In most Commonwealth countries, secondary students take qualifying examinations prepared in collaboration with Cambridge University. Pre–university-level education is the responsibility of each country.

Independent Schools. About 8% of British children attend independent schools—private, preparatory, and other independent schools—for which fees are charged. The education offered in these institutions is generally deemed superior to that offered in the state system. The educational privilege and social prestige have enabled many graduates of these schools to achieve high positions in all phases of British society. The "public schools"—so called because they were endowed, in contrast with private schools that operated at the financial risk of the master—include CHARTERHOUSE, ETON COLLEGE, HARROW SCHOOL, RUGBY SCHOOL, and WINCHESTER COLLEGE. Girls' public schools include Cheltenham Ladies' College and Roedean School.

HIGHER EDUCATION

The pinnacle of British education is the 45 universities, which enroll about 296,000 students, 65,000 of them postgraduates. Admission is highly competitive: only 9% in the 18-year-old age group are offered places. But the close attention undergraduates receive, which is still one of the most remarkable attributes of British higher education, makes it difficult for a student to fail. The dropout rate is just over 5%.

OXFORD (12th century) and CAMBRIDGE (13th century) are the two oldest and most famous universities, but four of the eight Scottish universities were established before 1600. The majority of universities began far more recently. The earliest, great civic universities (e.g., at Birmingham, Leeds, Liverpool, Manchester) of the Midlands and the North were founded in the Victorian era, as were the universities of London and Wales. More universities (e.g., at Exeter, Hull, Leicester, Southampton) were established by the mid-20th century. Twenty-one new universities (e.g., at Essex, Kent, Stirling, Sussex, Warwick, York) were founded in the 1960s and '70s.

British universities enjoy a high degree of autonomy: they admit whom they wish, teach them as they wish, and award their own degrees. Since the early days of the 20th century, however, they have received a growing proportion of their income from the government. Today taxation is almost their only significant source of support. Historically, the autonomy

of universities was safeguarded by the University Grants Committee (UGC), a buffer between them and the state consisting largely of academics, which advised the government on the financial needs of the universities. In the late 1980s, however, the UGC was slated to be replaced by a University Funding Council under direct political control.

Other Institutions. The British system of higher education also includes 32 new institutions called polytechnics, which have their roots in earlier technical education. In many respects they are similar to the universities, although their admission requirements are slightly less demanding, and they are more committed to vocational subjects, such as social work, teacher education, and business management. In the 1960s, the polytechnics absorbed the formerly independent colleges of art and business; in the late 1970s they assumed principal responsibility for teacher training, which had previously been done in independent colleges of education.

Altogether, more than 500,000 students are enrolled in full-time higher education, and almost 3 million students are enrolled part-time, most of them in the more than 600 colleges of further education and in adult education. Perhaps the most distinguished British contribution to educational development since World War II is the OPEN UNIVERSITY, which teaches about 120,000 degree-level students by radio, television, and correspondence.   PETER SCOTT

Bibliography: Burgess, Tyrrell, *A Guide to English Schools* (1972); Curtis, Stanley, *History of Education in Great Britain*, 7th ed. (1971); Dent, Harold C., *Education in England and Wales* (1977); Evans, Keith, *The English Educational System* (1975); Loukes, Harold, et al., *Education: An Introduction* (1984); Lowndes, George A. N., *The British Educational Systems* (1977); Morris, Max, and Griggs, Clive, *Education: The Wasted Years, 1973–1986* (1987); Smith, William O. L., *Education in Great Britain,* 5th ed. (1967).

British Empire

The British Empire was the product of many forces operating over a period of almost 400 years. The objectives behind Great Britain's acquisition of territories were varied: settlement, resources, markets, defense, trade, religion, and diplomacy. Government of these areas differed greatly. Some parts were ruled directly from Britain; some gained limited self-government, and others, virtual independence. At its peak, about 1914, the empire covered about one-fifth of the land surface of the globe and included one-quarter of the world's population. Its growth and decline encompass major themes in the history of Western civilization, from the problem of race relations to the reconciliation of authority with democratic institutions.

The empire began with the Elizabethan sea voyages of the 16th century, but its real foundations were laid in the next century. North America, from Hudson Bay to the Caribbean, was the principal focus of British expansion. Settlements were established in the central area, from New England to the Carolinas, and the fur trade and cultivation of sugar dominated the margins. Expansion extended also to the Indian Ocean and Southeast Asia, the attractions of the SPICE TRADE drawing Britain into competition with the Portuguese and with the Dutch. This thrust led the British to India, where the British

A key possession of the British Empire was India, where British rule was initially established through the East India Company. This Indian miniature painting (c. 1760) portrays an administrator enjoying his waterpipe, attended by servants.

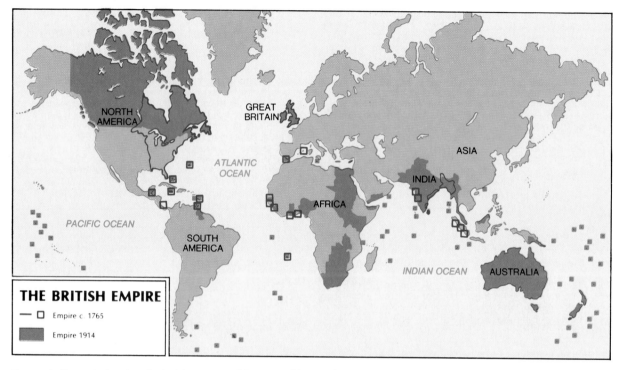

The map indicates the location of colonial outposts and the extent of the British Empire in 1765, shortly after Britain's victory over France in the Seven Years' War, which greatly expanded the empire's overseas possessions, and in 1914, at the outbreak of World War I.

EAST INDIA COMPANY soon supplemented commerce with the profitable occupations of tax collection and administration.

Although the North American colonies possessed virtual self-government in domestic affairs, the empire was tightly regulated in its trade and shipping by the NAVIGATION ACTS after 1651. The global struggle with France in the 18th century rocked the empire. At the end (1763) of the SEVEN YEARS' WAR, however, the French were forced to withdraw from North America and India. The removal of the French threat in North America contributed to the confidence of the American colonies in challenging Britain's authority. The AMERICAN REVOLUTION essentially ended the first British Empire.

The second British Empire grew from the ruins of the first. The LOYALIST refugees from the American states built new settlements in Canada, and territories such as the Cape of Good Hope (South Africa), Ceylon, and Trinidad were secured in the NAPOLEONIC WARS. Motives for acquisition were often strategic, although the settlements in Australia (begun in 1788) were intended originally to receive convicts. In central India British control was steadily extended, while farther east the creation (1819) of SINGAPORE supplied a base for a network of British trading contacts in South Asia and along the China coast. The long years of peace after 1815 allowed the steady growth of European settlement in the Canadian and Australian colonies, together with the development of an orderly overseas administration directed from the Colonial Office in London. The settlement colonies moved steadily toward greater self-government, a phase followed by the consolidation of these colonies into federal unions. Canada led the way in 1867, followed by Australia in 1901 and South Africa, which became a unitary state in 1910.

Meanwhile British traders, missionaries, and soldiers were penetrating the continent of Africa, carrying European values to primitive societies and staking out large areas for British suzerainty. By the end of the century, Africa had been partitioned among European powers through a rivalry that was as much related to national prestige as it was to economic factors.

World War I called forth a vast flow of men and materials from the empire to aid Britain and gave the senior colonies (now called dominions) participation in the direction of the empire's war effort. This association was continued at the PARIS PEACE CONFERENCE, where the dominions advanced their position internationally through charter membership in the League of Nations. The process of achieving equality of status with Britain was completed by the Statute of Westminster (1931), which, by granting full legislative authority to the dominions, provided a basis for their association in a novel world community, the COMMONWEALTH OF NATIONS. Through these developments the second British Empire ran its course. The final phase occurred after World War II, when virtually all the colonies that were still dependent won political freedom. Most then affiliated themselves with the Commonwealth.   D. M. L. FARR

Bibliography: Clayton, Anthony, *The British Empire as a Superpower: 1919–1939* (1986); Eldridge, Colin C., *British Imperialism in the Nineteenth Century* (1984); Lapping, Brian, *End of Empire* (1985); McIntyre, W. David, *The Commonwealth of Nations, Origins and Impact, 1869–1971* (1977); Mansergh, Nicholas, *The Commonwealth Experience*, 2 vols., rev. ed. (1982).

See also: AFRICA, HISTORY OF; AUSTRALIA, HISTORY OF; CANADA, HISTORY OF; COLONIALISM; GREAT BRITAIN, HISTORY OF; INDIA, HISTORY OF; NEW ZEALAND, HISTORY OF; UNITED STATES, HISTORY OF THE.

British Film Institute

The British Film Institute is a government-sponsored body active since 1933. A key, if controversial, element in British film culture, it comprises many units: the National Film Archive, the National Film Theatre, a production board, library, film distribution, and educational advisory services. It publishes the influential periodical *Sight and Sound*.   ROY ARMES

British Guiana: see GUYANA.

British Honduras: see BELIZE.

British Indian Ocean Territory

The British Indian Ocean Territory is a British colony in the western Indian Ocean comprising the Chagos Archipelago.

Formerly a dependency of Mauritius, it has a total area of 75 km² (29 mi²). Diego Garcia is the largest island. The failure of the island's main coconut plantation and the decision to lease (until the year 2025) the island to the United States for the construction of a military base prompted the removal of Diego Garcia's residents to Mauritius, which, in the early 1980s, renewed its claim of sovereignty over the island. Created in 1965, the territory originally included the islands of Aldabra, Farquhar, and Desroches, purchased from the Seychelles. These islands were returned to the Seychelles after its independence in 1976.

British Interplanetary Society

The British Interplanetary Society was founded in 1933 by P. E. Cleator to promote the advancement of knowledge relating to space research, technology, and applications. The society, whose headquarters are in London, had 2,500 fellows and 1,200 members in 1987. It publishes the monthly *Spaceflight* and the *Journal of the British Interplanetary Society*.

British Isles

The British Isles are a group of islands in the Atlantic Ocean northwest of the European continent. They comprise the two large islands of Great Britain and Ireland, the Orkney, Shetland, and Scilly islands, the Hebrides, the Isle of Man, and the Isle of Wight, and more than 5,000 smaller islands. The total area is about 315,000 km² (121,000 mi²).

British Library

The British Library, established in 1973 under an act of Parliament, has three main operating divisions: reference, lending, and bibliographic services. The reference division in London comprises the former library departments of the British Museum, including the science reference library. The British Museum, founded in 1753, incorporated the Royal Library in 1757 and also became the depository of a copy of every new book copyrighted in the United Kingdom. It benefited in the 19th century from the vigorous leadership of Antonio (later Sir Anthony) Panizzi (1787–1879). The holdings of the reference division total more than 11 million volumes, 85,000 Western manuscripts, 41,000 Oriental manuscripts, and 100,000 charters and rolls. The lending division, located at Boston Spa in West Yorkshire, is particularly strong in the literature of science and technology. It is the world's largest library devoted to supplying information by loan, photocopy, and microfilm.

COLIN STEELE

British Museum

The British Museum in London houses outstanding collections of antiquities and ethnographic art from around the world. The first public institution of its kind, the British Museum was founded in 1753 with the government's acquisition of a famous collection of books, manuscripts, and objects of natural history amassed by the physician and naturalist Sir Hans Sloane (1660–1753). The Sloane collection was joined with two earlier bequests, the important manuscript library of Edward and Robert Harley, earls of Oxford, and the so-called Cottonian manuscripts, coins, and antiquities donated by Sir Robert Bruce Cotton (1571–1631). George II presented the Royal Library of the Kings of England to the museum in 1757. Two years later the museum was opened to the public at Montagu House in Bloomsbury, its present site.

Interest in archaeology burgeoned during the 19th century. The British Museum acquired treasures of antiquity by gift or purchase, including, in 1816, the famous ELGIN MARBLES, classical Greek sculptures from the Acropolis at Athens. With the acquisition of George III's library in 1823, more space was needed to house the expanding collection. The present building, designed by Sir Robert Smirke, replaced Montagu House in 1847. Ten years later the immense domed library was completed according to plans drawn up by Sir Anthony Panizzi, the museum's chief librarian. In 1883 the museum's natural history collection was moved to South Kensington and renamed the Natural History Museum. The British Library was

The British Museum, London, designed by Sir Robert Smirke, is a fine example of 19th-century Greek Revival architecture. The museum is noted for its antiquities collection, including the Elgin Marbles, the Rosetta Stone, and other artifacts of the ancient and medieval periods.

formed in 1973 from the collections of manuscripts and printed books in the British Museum and other libraries.

The British Museum collections have four main areas: the antiquities department, the coins and medals department, the prints and drawings department, and the ethnographic department, now located in a separate building and known as the Museum of Mankind. The antiquities department comprises specialized collections of Egyptian, Western Asiatic, Greek and Roman, prehistoric British, medieval, and Oriental antiquities. Prized holdings include the ROSETTA STONE, which provided the key to deciphering Egyptian hieroglyphics, Assyrian reliefs from Ashurbanipal's palace at NINEVEH, sculptured friezes from the Mausoleum at HALICARNASSUS, the SUTTON HOO SHIP BURIAL, and fine African bronzes and carved ivories.

Bibliography: Miller, Edward, *That Noble Cabinet* (1974).

British North America Act

The British North America Act was the original name of the Canadian constitution, which was renamed the CONSTITUTION ACT in 1982. The original act, passed by the British Parliament in 1867, created the Canadian Confederation from the colonies of Nova Scotia, New Brunswick, and the United Province of Canada (Ontario and Quebec). It incorporated proposals worked out by Canadians themselves at a series of conferences in 1864 and 1866.

The act gave enumerated powers only to the provinces and reserved residual powers to the federal government. Subsequent decisions by the judicial committee of the imperial privy council, the final Canadian court of appeal until 1949, modified this considerably, however. As an imperial statute the British North America Act could be amended only by the British Parliament, which did so on several occasions. Transfer of this power to Canada was achieved in 1982 with the British Parliament's passage of the Canada Act, authorizing the patriation of Canada's renamed and amended constitution.

PETER J. KING

Bibliography: Abel, Albert S., *Towards a Constitutional Charter for Canada* (1980); Davenport, Paul, and Leach, Richard H., eds., *Reshaping Confederation* (1984); Kennedy, W. P. M., *The Constitution of Canada* (1938; repr. 1973).

British thermal unit

The British thermal unit (Btu) is a quantity of energy usually associated with the production or transfer of heat. Before 1929 it was defined as the amount of heat required to raise the temperature of 1 pound of water 1 degree Fahrenheit (from 59.5° F to 60.5° F). In 1929 it was redefined in terms of electrical units and is equivalent to 251.996 calories, 778.26 ft-lb, or approximately ⅓ watt-hours.

Brittany (dog)

The Brittany, formerly called the Brittany spaniel, is a French breed of sporting dog that hunts on land and occasionally is used to retrieve game from water.

The Brittany, formerly known as the Brittany spaniel, is a compact, medium-boned breed of sporting dog that stands 44–52 cm (17.5–20.5 in) at the shoulder and weighs 13.5–18 kg (30–40 lb). Long-legged, it is able to run great distances. The coat is dense and flat or wavy; the standard colors are dark orange and white, or liver and white. The color of the nose is fawn, tan, brown, or deep pink; a black nose is a disqualification from the show ring. The ears are high-set and lie flat and close to the head. The dog may be tailless or have a tail little more than 10 cm (4 in) long; it may be cropped for shows.

The Brittany is of ancient lineage, combining the earliest Spanish spaniel and pointing breeds with setters to produce today's breed. It is known for its ability to hunt under widely varying conditions and frequently points its quarry. Since its first importation to the United States in 1931, the Brittany has grown steadily in popularity as both a hunter and household companion.   JOHN MANDEVILLE

Bibliography: Pisano, B., and Monte, E., eds., *Brittany Spaniels* (1980).

Brittany (region)

Brittany (French: Bretagne; Breton: Breiz) is a region and former province of northwestern France corresponding with the departments of Finistère, Côtes-du-Nord, Morbihan, Ille-et-Vilaine, and Loire-Atlantique. A peninsula projecting into the Atlantic Ocean, the region is bordered on the north by the English Channel and on the south by the Bay of Biscay.

Brittany is distinct from other French regions because of its Celtic heritage. About one-quarter of its population of 2,750,000 (1985 est.) are able to speak Breton, a Celtic language similar to Cornish and Welsh. The language, customs, and costumes are preserved mainly in the more isolated west. RENNES (1982 pop., 192,000) is Brittany's route focus, traditional capital, and cultural center. Its university is a center of Celtic studies. (See also BRETON LITERATURE.)

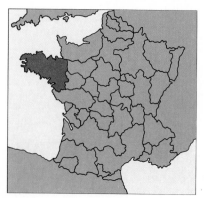

The locator map indicates the boundaries of Brittany, an historic French province occupying the Armorican peninsula separating the English Channel and the Bay of Biscay. The region is linguistically and culturally different from its neighboring provinces, a result of Brittany's settlement by Celtic peoples.

Brittany's rugged indented coast, called Armor (Breton for "country of the sea"), has only about a dozen frost days a year—no more than the Riviera. Early vegetables, soft fruit, and flowers are grown for the Parisian and British markets. Traditionally, Bretons have been sailors and fishermen. Their catch includes cod from the Grand Banks of Newfoundland, oysters, lobsters, sardines, and tuna.

The interior is a relatively barren, often misty, plateau called Argoat ("country of the woods"); only two woodland ridges rise above 245 m (800 ft). Hedgerows surround small fields, resulting in a picturesque landscape called *bocage*.

Between 3500 and 1800 BC early inhabitants built stone monuments at CARNAC and other sites. Celts later settled in the area, and in 56 BC they were conquered by Julius Caesar. The Anglo-Saxon invasions of Britain in the 5th and 6th centuries drove Celtic refugees to settle in Brittany. In the 9th century, under the leadership of Nomenoe, Brittany was united, winning independence from Carolingian rule. In the 10th century, Brittany became a duchy with its capital at Rennes. For the next 4 centuries it sought to retain its independence amid French and British rivalries. In the 15th century the duchy became closely linked to France with the marriage of ANNE OF BRITTANY to 2 successive kings of France. In 1532, it was formally incorporated into France.   TIMOTHY J. RICKARD

Britten, Benjamin

Benjamin Britten, one of the foremost English composers of the 20th century, was particularly skillful in writing vocal music and opera. A frequent theme in his operas is the conflict between innocence and corruption.

Benjamin Britten, b. Nov. 22, 1913, d. Dec. 4, 1976, was a highly acclaimed English composer. His operas—especially the first, *Peter Grimes* (1945)—helped revitalize English opera, languishing since the time of Henry Purcell.

Britten studied with the composer Frank BRIDGE and later attended the Royal College of Music. His early works comprise incidental music to documentary films, radio dramas, and expressionist plays by W. H. Auden and Christopher Isherwood. Recognition came early in Britten's career with a performance in 1934 of the Fantasy Quartet for Oboe and Strings, the choral piece *A Boy Was Born* (1933), and *Variations on a Theme of Frank Bridge* (1937). Three years (1939–42) of intense creativity in the United States produced a setting of Arthur Rimbaud's *Les Illuminations*, the Violin Concerto, and the *Seven Sonnets of Michelangelo*, the last written for his friend Peter Pears, the tenor, for whom Britten composed many of his operas and songs.

Britten worked in a traditional style and was not given to avant-garde experimentation. He possessed a remarkable ability to compose for voice and text, and his work is characterized by extremely personal instrumentation and melodies. *Peter Grimes*, based on George Crabbe's *The Borough*, is particularly impressive for its turbulent chorus scenes and atmospheric sea interludes. The conflict between a simple man and a corrupt society is one frequently addressed by Britten.

His nonoperatic works include *The Young Person's Guide to the Orchestra* (1946), suites for solo cello composed for the Russian cellist Mstislav Rostropovich, and the Serenade for Tenor, Horn, and Strings (1943). The *War Requiem* (1961), written for the consecration of the new Coventry Cathedral, is based on poems by Wilfred Owen.

The operas include the early, unpublished *Paul Bunyan* (text by Auden), *The Rape of Lucretia* (1946), the comic opera *Albert Herring* (1947), *Let's Make an Opera* (1949, written for children), *Billy Budd* (1951), *Gloriana* (1953, composed for Elizabeth II's coronation), *The Turn of the Screw* (1954), *A Midsummer Night's Dream* (1960), and *Death in Venice* (1973, based on the Thomas Mann novella). His music dramas for use in churches include *Curlew River* (1964) and *The Burning Fiery Furnace* (1966).

In addition to his frequent activities as a conductor and accompanist, Britten was also instrumental in founding (1947) the annual Aldeburgh Festival (Suffolk) and the English Opera Group. He was made a life peer in 1976.

Bibliography: Carpenter, H., *Benjamin Britten* (1993); Evans, John, et al., eds., *A Britten Sourcebook* (1987); Herbert, D., *The Operas of Benjamin Britten* (1989); Palmer, Christopher, *The Britten Companion* (1984); White, E. W., *Benjamin Britten: His Life and Operas*, rev. ed. (1983).

brittle star

The brittle star, an ECHINODERM, is found on all ocean floors to a depth of about 6,000 m (20,000 ft). It is so named because of its ability to break off arms or parts of arms when disturbed; it then regenerates new parts. The typical brittle star is about 7 cm (3 in) or less in total diameter and has five long, solid, cylindrical arms arising from a circular central disk. Tube feet arise in pairs from the underside of each arm joint; in basket stars the arms are branched. Brittle stars move by means of snakelike movements of the arms, aided by the tube feet. They are major ocean scavengers, feeding upon small organisms on the seafloor or catching small animals on their extended, sticky tube feet. They are also part of the diet of several commercially important fish. Brittle stars number about 2,000 species and comprise the class Ophiuroidea, phylum Echinodermata.

Britton, Nathaniel

Nathaniel Lord Britton, b. Staten Island, N.Y., Jan. 15, 1859, d. Jan. 25, 1934, was an American botanist who from 1896 to 1929 led the development of the New York Botanical Gardens into one of the foremost botanical gardens in the world. Britton was a professor of botany at Columbia University in New York City and wrote still-valuable descriptions of plants of the eastern United States and the West Indies. He coauthored with Addison Brown *An Illustrated Flora of the Northern United States, Canada, and the British Possessions.*

Brno [bur'-naw]

Brno (German: Brünn) is the second-largest city of the Czech Republic, with a population of 390,000 (1991). The historic capital of Moravia, and today the capital of the Czech region of Southern Moravia, it is located at the confluence of the Svratka and Svitava rivers, in the eastern foothills of the Bohemian-Moravian Highlands. Its name comes from the Celtic *brynn,* meaning "hill town." An industrial center, the city is known for its textile and steel mills, chemical plants, and arms factory, where the Bren gun was invented. Nearby are the famous Paleolithic site of DOLNÍ VĚSTONICE and the Napoleonic battlefield of AUSTERLITZ.

Founded in 1243 by German settlers as a trading center, Brno grew up around a fortress known as the Špílberk (Spielberg). In the 14th century it came under the control of the margraves of Moravia, and in the 16th century it passed to the Austrian Habsburgs. It was a well-fortified city that successfully withstood several sieges. In the 19th century the Špílberk became notorious as a place of confinement for opponents of Austrian rule in Italy. The botanist Gregor Mendel (1822–84) performed his genetic experiments at the Augustinian monastery in Brno; the composer Leoš Janáček was a native of the city, and its opera house bears his name. From 1918 to 1992, Brno was part of Czechoslovakia.

Broadbent, Donald Eric

Donald Eric Broadbent, b. May 6, 1926, is an English psychologist who pioneered in applying INFORMATION THEORY to psychology and in studying ATTENTION. He graduated from and taught at Cambridge until he moved to Oxford in 1974; he retired in 1991. Broadbent's *Perception and Communication* (1958) gave impetus to the development of COGNITIVE PSYCHOLOGY, presenting the techniques he had invented to study attention and the "filter theory" he had devised to explain attention. He utilized the concept of short-term MEMORY in applying his approach to problems of memory and learning.

broadbill

Broadbills are mainly forest birds that live in India, China, and Southeast Asia, as well as in Africa. The 14 species range from 13 to 28 cm (5 to 11 in) long; the head is broad, the body stout, and the tail ranges from short and square to long and slender. The birds are named for their wide, flat, slightly hooked bill. They are brightly colored, with blues and greens predominating; often they have a white dorsal patch. The sexes usually differ in color. Some broadbills eat mainly fruit, and others also feed on insects, frogs, and lizards. The pear-shaped nests, made of grass and other material, are decorated with streamers of moss and are usually built on limbs that hang over water. Ordinarily three to five eggs are produced. Some species are gregarious, and others are solitary. Their songs range from clear whistles to churring notes. The birds do not migrate.

Broadbills comprise the single family Eurylaimidae, in the suborder Eurylaimi, order Passeriformes. Recent studies, however, suggest that the Eurylaimi are less distinct from the suborder Tyranni—which includes such birds as COTINGAS and TYRANT FLYCATCHERS—than was formerly believed.

ROBERT J. RAIKOW

broadcasting: see RADIO AND TELEVISION BROADCASTING; TELEVISION TRANSMISSION; VIDEO TECHNOLOGY.

broadcloth

Broadcloth is a closely woven fabric usually made of cotton or wool. In medieval England, it was woven on a special wide loom, and the cloth measured 2 yds (1.8 m) in width, or double the width of ordinary cloth. Today, the width of the fabric is no longer its characterizing feature. Wool broadcloth is most often a TWILL weave, with a heavy sheared nap, or finish, that conceals the weave; cotton broadcloth is a glossy, sometimes slightly ribbed fabric.

DOROTHY SIEGERT LYLE

Broadway

Broadway is both a New York City street and a term that has become synonymous with New York theater. The street starts at Bowling Green, the southern tip of Manhattan Island, where it was the main thoroughfare in the Dutch settlement of New Amsterdam, and it runs northward 25 km (15 mi) through all of Manhattan and Bronx boroughs.

From New York's earliest days, theaters have been located on or near Broadway. The theater district has moved uptown along the street, starting at Bowling Green and going on to lower Broadway, then to Union Square, and finally to Times Square, where it is "The Great White Way." The commercial theater district now seems stabilized with boundaries at 42nd Street on the south, 53rd Street on the north, Avenue of the Americas (Sixth Avenue) on the east, and Eighth Avenue on the west.

The turn of the century saw the beginnings of Times Square as a major theater center. The Depression of the 1930s and the advent of talking pictures put an end to theater construction, and all the legitimate playhouses on 42nd Street eventually became cinemas. With the growth of television during the 1950s, many other theaters in the area became broadcasting studios. During the 1970s and 1980s pornography and drug sales and prostitution in the theater district led to public outcries and to plans for renovating the area. A few old theaters have disappeared, and new ones have been built.

Theatrical promoters long have used the phrase "Direct from Broadway" as a virtual guarantee of a professional polish on a touring production. Escalating production costs and other commercial pressures have beset theatrical Broadway, but in the late 1980s its shows collectively were earning more income than at any time in history. Broadway competes with OFF-BROADWAY, OFF-OFF BROADWAY, regional, and so-called alternative theaters, and survives. It has been described as a "fabulous invalid," always dying but never dead.

GLENN LONEY

Bibliography: Atkinson, Brooks, *Broadway* (1970); Churchill, Allen, *The Great White Way* (1962); Guernsey, Otis L., Jr., *Curtain Times: The New York Theatre, 1965–1987* (1987); Henderson, Mary, *The City and the Theater* (1973).

Broca, Paul   [broh-kah']

Paul Broca, b. June 28, 1824, d. July 9, 1880, a French surgeon and physical anthropologist, is noted for his comparative study of the brain and his contributions to the understanding of aphasia, impairment of the ability to use words. Professor of surgical pathology at the Faculté de Médecine, Paris, he founded the École des Hautes Études (1858), Paris, and the Société d'Anthropologie de Paris (1859). He identified (1861) the lobe of the brain controlling articulate speech, which became known as the convolution of Broca, or Broca's area.

brocade   [broh-kayd']

Brocade is a fabric characterized by a raised, decorative design that is not a structural part of the woven texture; it may be made with any fiber and weave. It is richly patterned, and gold or silver thread is often used to form the design. Although brocade can be woven on handlooms, it is usually factory-produced on Jacquard looms and is made in a variety of weights, from light dress fabrics to upholstery and drapery materials.

DOROTHY SIEGERT LYLE

broccoli   [brahk'-uh-lee]

Broccoli is a popular garden vegetable that is related to cauliflower. The edible head is about 15 cm (6 in) across.

Broccoli, grown for its edible blooms, which are harvested while in the bud stage, is classified along with CAULIFLOWER as *Brassica oleracea,* Botrytis group. Cabbage, cauliflower, Brussels sprouts, collards, and kohlrabi are grouped with broccoli as cole crops of the Cruciferae family. Wild cabbage is the common ancestor of this group.

Broccoli grows best at temperatures between 10° and 25° C (50° and 77° F), and commercial culture takes place primarily in coastal areas with moderate climates. An annual from spring plantings and a biennial from fall plantings, broccoli first produces a rosette of deeply divided, blue green leaves. The head develops from the terminal bud; it is harvested when 10 to 15 cm (4 to 6 in) in diameter and while the flower buds are tightly closed. Head-bearing side-shoots develop on some varieties after the terminal head is cut. If the head is not harvested, the branches will elongate rapidly, and the buds will develop into conspicuous yellow flowers.

Broccoli is usually grown from seed, but transplants are used for spring planting. Marketable heads, produced in 60 to 150 days, are harvested by hand. Numerous broccoli cultivars and HYBRIDS are grown, such as Italian, or asparagus, broccoli, *B. oleracea,* Italica group. California produces most of the U.S. commercial crop.

DONALD N. MAYNARD

broch   [brahk]

A broch is a fortified house of the pre-Roman Iron Age (50 BC–AD 100) of north and west Scotland. It is a thick-walled, circular, stone tower about 12–24 m (40–80 ft) in diameter, with storage chambers, and sometimes a stairway, built into the wall thickness. A timber gallery served as sleeping quarters. Of about 500 known examples, the broch at Mousa on Shetland is the best preserved.

R. J. C. ATKINSON

Broch, Hermann   [brohk]

Hermann Broch, b. Nov. 1, 1886, d. May 30, 1951, was an Austrian novelist best known for his long, philosophical novels *The Sleepwalkers* (1932; Eng. trans., 1932) and *The Death of Virgil* (1945; Eng. trans., 1945). The son of a Jewish textile manufacturer, he sold his family's factories at the age of 41 to return briefly to Vienna University and only then began his career as a writer. In 1938, following brief imprisonment by the Nazis, he emigrated to the United States. There he completed several novels about the Nazi catastrophe: *The Death of Virgil* (1945), *The Guiltless* (1950; Eng. trans., 1974), and *The Tempter* (1953). (*The Spell,* another novel about the coming of the Nazis, cast as an allegory in which a village is seduced into barbarism, was originally written in 1935 but remained unpublished until its English translation in 1987.)

Broch was a late-romantic prophet of apocalypse. Denouncing 19th-century Vienna as a "metropolis of kitsch," he wrote of the organic "decay" or moral values since the Middle Ages and termed modern man a "sleepwalker." These views culminated in *The Death of Virgil,* a massive monologue presenting the last hours of Vergil's life. In this novel the Roman poet, ready to burn his epic the *Aeneid* in despair over the impotence of art, suddenly experiences a mystical vision of hope for the world—a vision obviously inspired by Broch's own close encounter with death under the Nazis. The significance of Broch's works, despite their difficulty and length, lies in their ethical, almost mystical, belief in classical European humanism.

DAVID H. MILES

Bibliography: Cohn, Dorrit C., *The Sleepwalkers: Elucidations of Hermann Broch's Trilogy* (1966); Schlant, Ernestine, *Hermann Broch* (1986); Ziolkowski, Theodore, *Hermann Broch* (1964).

Brock, Sir Isaac

Sir Isaac Brock is known as the "Hero of Upper Canada" for his exploits in the WAR OF 1812. Born in Guernsey on Oct. 6, 1769, he entered the British army in 1785 and went to Canada as a regimental commander in 1802. In 1810 he assumed command of the troops in Upper Canada (Ontario) and in 1811 was promoted to major-general and administrator of the province. He was the main inspiration for the defense of Upper Canada when it was invaded by the Americans in 1812. Following his capture of Detroit (Aug. 15, 1812), Brock was knighted for his brilliant action. On Oct. 13, 1812, his troops defeated the enemy at Queenston Heights, Ontario, but Brock was killed. In 1854 a large monument, containing his grave, was erected at Queenston Heights.

GEORGE F. G. STANLEY

Bibliography: Goodspeed, D. J., *The Good Soldier: The Story of Isaac Brock* (1964); Lamb, W. K., *The Hero of Upper Canada* (1962).

Brock, Lou

Baseball Hall of Fame member Louis Clark Brock, b. El Dorado, Ark., June 18, 1939, is most famous for breaking Ty Cobb's record (892) for lifetime stolen bases in 1977 and for setting a new one-season mark (118; since surpassed) in 1974. Brock, an outfielder, played most of his 18-season career (1961–79) with the St. Louis Cardinals of the National League, accumulating 938 stolen bases (a record surpassed by Rickey Henderson in 1991), a .293 lifetime batting average, and 3,023 hits—the 14th player in baseball history to reach the 3,000-hit plateau. He also shares (with Eddie Collins) the record for most stolen bases in World Series play (14).

Brockton

Brockton (1990 pop., 92,788) is an industrial and residential city in Massachusetts, south of Boston. It was settled in 1700, and from about the time of the Civil War until recently it was a major shoe-manufacturing center. Brockton pioneered in the use of electric streetlights and electric streetcars.

Brod, Max   [broht]

The Austrian writer Max Brod, b. Prague, May 27, 1884, d. Tel Aviv, Dec. 20, 1968, is remembered chiefly as the editor, perceptive biographer, and loyal friend of Franz KAFKA. His *Franz Kafka: A Biography* (1937; Eng. trans., 1947) remains one of the most fascinating portraits of that tormented writer. Brod was a prolific author, notably of German prose fiction, but his only fictional work of enduring interest is his historical novel about the 16th-century astronomer Tycho Brahe, *The Redemption of Tycho Brahe* (1916; Eng. trans., 1928). His career as a Czech official and as the theater and music critic for Prague's leading German newspaper, *Prager Tagblatt*, ended in 1939, when he fled to Palestine. Brod's extensive essayistic work, such as *Paganism, Christianity, Judaism: A Confession* (1921; Eng. trans., 1970), reflects his dedication to Judaism.

PETER HELLER

Bibliography: Weltsch, Robert, *Max Brod and His Age* (1970).

Brodsky, Joseph

Poet, critic, essayist, and translator, Joseph Aleksandrovich Brodsky, b. Leningrad, May 27, 1940, is an expatriate writer who is held by many to be the leading contemporary Russian poet. He was awarded the Nobel Prize for literature in 1987.

Brodsky left school at age 15 and worked at a variety of jobs while he wrote the poetry that soon began to appear in the Russian underground press (see SAMIZDAT). His poems became known to a wide audience but also attracted the attention of the Soviet authorities. In 1964, Brodsky was tried and sentenced to five years in a labor camp. The protest that erupted, however, persuaded the authorities to release him after 18 months, but they continued to find his presence threatening, and in 1972 he was forced into exile.

Since leaving the USSR, Brodsky has lived and taught in the United States. He describes himself as a happy combination of Russian poet and English essayist (the Nobel citation mentions his "quite amazing mastery of the English idiom"). Work available in English includes several volumes of poetry—*Selected Poems* (1973), *A Part of Speech* (1980), and *To Urania* (1988)—as well as the essays in *Less than One* (1986). Brodsky was named the fifth U.S. poet laureate in 1991.

Broederlam, Melchior   [brur'-dur-lahm, mel'-kee-ohr]

Melchior Broederlam, fl. 1381–c.1409, was an important Franco-Flemish panel painter associated with the court of Philip the Bold, duke of Burgundy. Broederlam was one of the earliest artists of the Gothic International style, and his reputation is based on one authenticated work: the two wings he painted for a wooden altarpiece (c.1392–99; Musée des Beaux Arts, Dijon) carved by Jacques de Baerze. The piece is composed of the *Annunciation* and *Visitation* on one wing and the *Presentation in the Temple* and *Flight into Egypt* on the other and shows a new solution to the problem of spatial composition.

Bibliography: Panofsky, E., *Early Netherlandish Painting*, 2 vols. (1953; repr. 1971).

Broken Hill

Broken Hill is a mining city located at the southeastern base of the Main Barrier Range in New South Wales, Australia. It has a population of 27,200 (1984 est.). Settled in 1883 following the discovery of huge deposits of silver, lead, and zinc, the city was connected by rail to Adelaide in 1887 and Sydney in 1927. It remains Australia's largest producer of lead and zinc ores.

Broken Hill man

Broken Hill man, formerly called Rhodesian man, is the name given fossil remains discovered (1921) at the Broken Hill zinc mine in Zambia (former Northern Rhodesia). Recent investigations suggest the remains of the individual may be 130,000 years old or even older. Several features of the skull have been called NEANDERTHAL-like, including the brow ridges. Broken Hill man is generally grouped with *Homo sapiens,* but other features also link the fossil with the ancestral HOMO ERECTUS.

Broken Hill man is one of very few fossil specimens in which the probable cause of death can be determined. Extensive tooth decay appears to have caused serious infection in the region of the left ear, which is evident in the fossil remains and was the probable cause of death.

ALAN MANN AND NANCY MINUGH

Brome, Richard   [broom]

Richard Brome, d. c.1652, an English dramatist, wrote comedies that give a lively picture of life in his time. He was secretary to the dramatist Ben JONSON, and his work was influenced by his master's. His most popular play was *The Northern Lasse* (1632). His other comedies, of which 15 are known, include *A Joviall Crew*, the last play performed before the English theaters were closed in 1642.

ROBIN BUSS

bromeliad   [broh-mee'-lee-ad]

Bromeliads are herbaceous plants that are members of the pineapple family, Bromeliaceae. About 2,000 species and 46 verifiable genera of bromeliads have been identified. They are native to the tropical and subtropical regions of North, South, and Central America. The only exception is a single species of *Pitcairnia* found in West Africa. The bromeliad plant usually consists of a cluster of strap-shaped leaves, some of which have bizarre designs or striking colors. The flowers may be hidden in the center of the cluster or carried on showy center spikes. The plants vary in height from 2.5 cm to about 9 m (1 in to about 30 ft) or higher.

Bromeliads of Central and South America are companions to orchids and aroids, from the mountains (some over 4,200 m/13,800 ft) to the rocky seasides. They live either on the forest floor or as epiphytes (air plants) on trees and rocks. The roots of the epiphytic bromeliads function more as holdfasts than as absorbing organs. Some species, such as the Spanish moss, *Tillandsia usneoides,* and the *Tillandsia* species that live on the sand of central Peru, are almost rootless. They absorb food and water from a reservoir formed in the central cup of leaves. Terrestrial bromeliads such as the pineapple, *Ananas comosus,* have well-developed root systems, and their leaves play only a small part in absorption.

Bromeliads are adapted for a wide range of climatic conditions. Some need frequent rains, and others are able to subsist with fog as their sole source of moisture. All bromeliads have scales on their leaves that serve in the absorption of water and nutrients, and most tend to be xerophytic (able to withstand dry conditions). They are often grown as houseplants; any light growth-medium containing rich soil is suitable, but peat moss is best. Water should be maintained consistently in the central cup formed by the leaves, and the medium should be kept somewhat moist. Most bromeliads prefer filtered sunlight. One to 12 years may pass before they bloom. The mother plant dies 1 to 2 years after it flowers, but offshoots at the plant's base can be separated for propagation.

Bibliography: Benzing, David H., *Biology of the Bromeliads* (1980); Padilla, Victoria, *Bromeliads* (1986); Williams, B. E., and Hodgson, Ian, eds., *Growing Bromeliads* (1991).

See also: ANGIOSPERM; COTYLEDON.

Bromfield, Louis

Louis Bromfield, b. Mansfield, Ohio, Dec. 27, 1896, d. Mar. 18, 1956, was a regional novelist and journalist. He wrote such rurally accented novels as *The Green Bay Tree* (1924), the 1927 Pulitzer Prize–winning *Early Autumn* (1926), and *The Farm* (1933). He returned to Ohio after years as a foreign correspondent and began an agricultural research farm near Lucas, about which he wrote in *Malabar Farm* (1948).

bromine   [broh'-meen]

The chemical element bromine is a liquid with a powerful, unpleasant odor. Its symbol is Br, its atomic number 35, and its atomic weight 79.904. In its elemental state it is a deep red color, so dark as to appear almost black. It is a nonmetal appearing on the periodic chart of the elements as a member of family VIIa, the HALOGENS.

Discovery. In 1826 in the *Annales de Chimie et de Physique*, Antoine Jérôme BALARD published a paper in which he announced the discovery of a new element that he called *muride*. He was, at the time, 23 years of age and had not yet graduated from the École de Pharmacie. The Académie Française did not accept the proposed name, and instead *bromine*, meaning "stench," or "bad odor," is now used. Balard's investigations began in 1824 while he was studying salt marshes. Before publishing his conclusions he was able to characterize bromine and many of its compounds, noting that it was found in small quantities in seawater, in the mother liquor of the production of salts from several brines, in the ashes of several plants growing in the Mediterranean Sea, in kelp mollusks, and in certain mineral waters. His work progressed rapidly because of the similarity of bromine to chlorine and iodine.

Occurrence. In cosmic abundance bromine is 36th among the elements; in the Earth's crust it has been calculated as 48th. At 0.0065 percent by weight, it is the 7th most abundant element dissolved in seawater, gases excepted.

Because of its high reactivity it is never found free in nature, yet neither is it a major constituent in any mineral except a rare silver ore first identified in 1841 near Zacatecas, Mexico. It is more commonly found in underground brines such as those in Michigan and Arkansas and in saline basins such as Searles Lake in California and the Dead Sea. Much is also present in underground salt beds such as those near Stassfurt, Germany.

Both marine plants and animals are capable of concentrating bromine in their bodies and by doing so become sources of the element. Certain kelp and shellfish are examples, and the fabled Tyrian purple dye was prepared from the bromine-containing secretion of a Mediterranean mollusk, the murex.

Chemical Properties. Bromine is similar chemically to chlorine and combines directly with many elements and compounds, but it does so less energetically. It is completely miscible in several organic solvents such as carbon tetrachloride and benzene, which can be used to extract the element from water solutions.

Bromine reacts with most metals, explosively with potassium and vigorously with aluminum, but magnesium, nickel, and lead are unreactive with it. In some cases, as with iron and zinc, moisture must be present to initiate the reaction, and in other cases, as with sodium, an elevated temperature must be attained.

The reaction of bromine with organic compounds is called bromination. Bromine commonly adds across the bond of unsaturated hydrocarbons: $CH_2 = CH_2 + Br_2 \rightarrow CH_2Br - CH_2Br$,

and reacts with the ring structure of phenol by substitution for hydrogen atoms:

phenol   2, 4, 6-tribromophenol

Bromine is an oxidizing agent, as illustrated by these reactions: $2KI + Br_2 \rightarrow 2KBr + I_2$ and $H_2S + Br_2 \rightarrow 2HBr + S$. It hydrolyzes slightly in aqueous solution, producing hydrobromic acid (HBr) and hypobromous acid (HBrO). The hypobromous acid is unstable, resulting in the production of oxygen, which accounts for the bleaching capability of bromine water: $2HBrO \rightarrow 2HBr + O_2$. In a freezing mixture of saturated bromine in water, deposits of red crystals of bromine hydrate, $Br_2 \cdot H_2O$, will form.

Preparation. One laboratory preparation of small quantities of bromine requires the manganese dioxide oxidation of acidified bromides:
$2NaBr + 2H_2SO_4 + MnO_2 \rightarrow Na_2SO_4 + MnSO_4 + 2H_2O + Br_2$.
Here the bromine is distilled from the reaction mixture and cooled sufficiently to quickly condense to its normal liquid state. A second laboratory method involves the displacement of bromine from acidified bromide solutions by the addition of chlorine gas. Commercial sources of bromide solutions are the concentrated brines, or residual liquors (bitterns), that remain after the production of salt, or sodium chloride (NaCl), from seawater by evaporation. At large plants on the North Carolina and Texas coasts, bromine is commercially obtained using concentrated bromide solutions from seawater.

Uses. Bromine is chiefly used in the production of dibromoethane, which is added to automotive fuels containing tetraethyl lead. During combustion of the fuel within the automobile engine, the tetraethyl lead forms a volatile lead bromide that becomes part of the exhaust gases, thereby preventing lead buildup within the engine. It is also valuable in dyes, in photographic emulsions, as bleach modifiers, in fire retardants, in disinfectants, in methylene bromide fire extinguishers, and as a mild sedative, hence the term "an old bromide."

Hazards. Bromine is toxic and a severe irritant to the membranes of the respiratory tract and the eyes. It is a powerful oxidizer and may cause ignition of combustible materials upon contact; thus it is a moderate to high fire hazard.

CHARLES HOWARD

Bibliography: Downs, A., and Adams, C., *The Chemistry of Chlorine, Bromine, Iodine, and Astatine* (1975); Kirk, K., *Biochemistry of the Elemental Halogens and Inorganic Halides* (1991); Price, D., et al., eds., *Bromine Compounds* (1988); Sharpe, A., *Inorganic Chemistry*, 3d ed. (1992).

bronchial tube

Bronchial tubes are subdivisions of the bronchi within the LUNGS. At its lower end the TRACHEA, or windpipe, divides into two branches called bronchi, each bronchus leading into one lung. Successive branchings of the bronchi are called bronchial tubes, and these subdivide into still smaller tubes, or bronchioles. The bronchioles lead into thin-walled air sacs called alveoli, each terminal bronchiole supplying a small cluster of these sacs. The alveoli number in the hundreds of millions. Each alveolus is surrounded with a network of blood capillaries. Gas exchange—uptake of oxygen and loss of carbon dioxide by the blood—occurs across the alveolar surface, where blood in the capillaries and air in the lungs are separated by only a thin membrane.

The trachea and the bronchi are surrounded by rings of cartilage, which make the air passages resistant to collapse from external and internal pressures. The bronchial tubes have no cartilage, but their walls contain a layer of smooth muscle. Contraction or relaxation of this muscle layer can vary the internal diameter of each bronchial tube and regulate the amount of air reaching the alveoli. The muscle layer is controlled by the AUTONOMIC NERVOUS SYSTEM. Stimulation of the parasympathetic division of that system causes the muscle layer to contract. In an asthma attack, the bronchial tubes are in a contracted state because of parasympathetic overstimulation; this can be relieved by administration of BRONCHODILATORS. In an emergency situation, on the other hand, the sympathetic division of the autonomic nervous system is stimulated, relaxing the bronchial muscle. The resulting dilation of the bronchial tubes enables more oxygen to reach the alveoli.

PETER L. PETRAKIS

Bibliography: West, J. B., *Respiratory Physiology*, 3d ed. (1985).

bronchitis   [brahng-ky'-tis]

Bronchitis is an inflammation of the membrane that lines the air passages, or bronchial tubes, of the LUNGS and results in the narrowing of these air passages. This disorder may be of either an acute or chronic type. Irritation of mucus-producing glands within the membrane results in the production of excess bronchial secretions. The main symptoms of bronchitis are cough and increased expectoration of sputum, with or without associated wheezing and shortness of breath.

Acute bronchitis is usually caused by infection by one of the many viruses that cause the common COLD or INFLUENZA and is frequently associated with MEASLES. The patient may suffer from additional symptoms, such as chest discomfort, fever, and aching, that are characteristic of these diseases. WHOOPING COUGH is a form of severe bronchitis caused by the bacterium *Hemophilus pertussis*. Treatment of a pure viral infection is directed toward the relief of symptoms, but frequently secondary infections by bacteria complicate the condition. In such a case the patient's sputum may turn from white to yellow (purulent, or pus containing), and treatment with various antibiotics is recommended. Acute chemical bronchitis may be caused by the inhalation of irritating fumes, such as smoke, chlorine, ammonia, and ozone.

Chronic bronchitis results from prolonged irritation of the bronchial membrane, causing cough and the excessive secretion of mucus for extended periods. By far the most common cause of chronic bronchitis is cigarette SMOKING, but air pollution and industrial fume and dust inhalation are also important irritants. Patients with chronic bronchitis are subject to recurrent infections with *H. influenzae* and pneumococci. Pulmonary EMPHYSEMA often coexists, and over a long period of time the patient may suffer from increasing breathlessness, decreasing exercise tolerance, and, finally, total disability. In the most severe forms of the disease, the patient may have a blue, bloated appearance and a fatal heart disease, known as COR PULMONALE.

HOWARD BUECHNER, M.D.

Bibliography: Burrows, B., *Respiratory Disorders* (1983); Fletcher, C., et al., *The Natural History of Chronic Bronchitis and Emphysema* (1976); Pennington, J. E., ed., *Respiratory Infections* (1983).

See also: ASTHMA; ENVIRONMENTAL HEALTH; RESPIRATORY DISEASE.

bronchodilators   [brahng'-koh-dy'-lay-turz]

Drugs that tend to widen or open the bronchioles, the smaller air passages of the lungs, are known as bronchodilators. They are useful in the treatment of ASTHMA and bronchitis because some symptoms of these diseases are traceable to constricted bronchioles, which cause decreased volume and velocity of airflow into and from the lungs. For example, bronchioconstriction causes the wheezes typical of an asthma attack. The sites of bronchodilator action are those parts of the bronchial tree containing smooth muscle. The drugs either stimulate the autonomic nervous system to produce direct dilation, or inhibit enzymes that destroy dilator chemical messengers within the smooth muscle cell. Stimulating bronchodilators, which include ephedrine and isopoteranol, may be given orally or by injection or inhaled as fine droplets of liquid. Inhibiting bronchodilators include primarily theophylline and its derivatives, which are given orally.

Bibliography: McFadden, E. R., Jr., *Inhaled Aerosol Bronchodilators* (1985).

bronchoscope   [brahng'-koh-skohp]

The bronchoscope is a simple ENDOSCOPE that is used to examine visually the main air passages of the human body. It is composed basically of a tube with side holes at different distances from the lower end so that one lung can be ventilated while the other is being examined. Several instruments can be used with the bronchoscope to perform minor surgical operations.

DONALD LONGMORE

Bibliography: Stradling, Peter, *Diagnostic Bronchoscopy*, 5th ed. (1986).

Bronfenbrenner, Urie

Urie Bronfenbrenner, b. Apr. 29, 1917, a Russian-born American psychologist, has done influential studies of preschool and comparative education. A professor at Cornell University since 1948, he was president of the Task Force on Early Childhood (1966–67). After studying attempts to improve school performance by early compensatory education, he concluded that home-based programs involving the mothers are the most successful. He has studied the effects of child-raising practices in different cultures, particularly in the Soviet Union, and the influence of education on character.

Bibliography: Bronfenbrenner, Urie, *Influences on Human Development*, 2d ed. (1975), and *Two Worlds of Childhood* (1970).

Brongniart, Alexandre   [brohn-yar']

Alexandre Brongniart, b. Feb. 5, 1770, d. Oct. 7, 1847, was a French geologist who pioneered the use of fossils for identifying layers or strata of SEDIMENTARY ROCKS. After studying at the École des Mines, he became a mining engineer, a professor at the École Centrale des Quatre-Nations and the Muséum d'Histoire Naturelle, and, finally, a director of the Sèvres porcelain factory. With naturalist Georges CUVIER he determined the order of succession of strata in the Paris basin, laying the groundwork for recognition of the TERTIARY System.

Bronk, William

William Bronk, b. Fort Edward, N.Y., Feb. 17, 1918, is an American poet and essayist. Graduating from Dartmouth College in 1938, Bronk served in the army in World War II and had a career in business thereafter, mainly in Hudson Falls, N.Y. His poetry, influenced by Wallace Stevens, is simple in form but exhibits a complex interest in the philosophical aspects of the human situation. His first book of poetry was *Light and Dark* (1956); his collected poems, *Life Supports* (1981), won the 1982 National Book Award. His essays are collected in *Vectors and Smoothable Curves* (1983); other works include *Manifest and Furthermore* (1987).

Bronson, Charles

Charles Bronson, b. Ehrenfeld, Pa., Nov. 3, 1922, originally named Charles Bunchinsky, is an American film actor who became an international star after moving to France in 1968. He was first seen in *You're in the Navy Now* (1951) and later in *Machine Gun Kelly* (1958), *The Magnificent Seven* (1960), *The Great Escape* (1963), *The Dirty Dozen* (1967), *Once upon a Time in the West* (1969), *The Valachi Papers* (1972), *Death Wish* (1974) and its sequels, *Hard Times* (1975), and *Death Hunt* (1981). Bronson generally portrays unsentimental men of action who tend to take the law into their own hands.

Brønsted, Johannes Nicolaus   [brurn'-steth]

The Danish chemist Johannes Nicolaus Brønsted, b. Feb. 22, 1879, d. Dec. 17, 1947, is best known for his theory of ACIDS AND BASES (1923), according to which an acid is a proton donor and a base is a proton acceptor. While professor (1908–47) of physical and inorganic chemistry at the University of Copenhagen, he produced outstanding papers in thermodynamics (heat and its relationship to other forms of energy) and kinetics (the effect of forces upon the motion of material bodies).

HUGO ZAHND

Brønsted-Lowry theory: see ACIDS AND BASES.

Brontë (family) [brahn'-tee]

Anne, Emily, and Charlotte Brontë (left to right) appear in this painting by their brother, Branwell. After collaborating on an early volume of poetry, each of the sisters went on to write successful novels. (National Portrait Gallery, London.)

The English writers the Brontë sisters—Charlotte, Emily, and Anne—transmuted the sheltered thoughts of their lonely, circumscribed lives into the stuff of poetry and influenced the direction of the modern English novel.

Their father, the Rev. Patrick Brontë, was an Irishman who had been educated in England and ordained in the Anglican Church. Their mother, a Cornishwoman, bore six children: two daughters, Maria and Elizabeth; Charlotte, b. Apr. 21, 1816; Patrick Branwell, a son, b. June 26, 1817; Emily, b. July 30, 1818; and Anne, b. Jan. 17, 1820. Shortly after Anne's birth, Patrick Brontë became curate near the village of Haworth in Yorkshire. After Mrs. Brontë's death in 1821, an aunt assumed control of domestic duties and the children, and life at Haworth settled into a grim routine. Surrounded by the harsh beauty of the Yorkshire moors and living in a home where strong energies were kept in strict control, the Brontë children grew up in their own private worlds.

In 1824, Maria, Elizabeth, Charlotte, and Emily were enrolled at a school at Cowan Bridge, a school that would serve as the model for Lowood in Charlotte Brontë's JANE EYRE. Perhaps partly because of their harsh treatment at school, Maria and Elizabeth died. Charlotte and Emily returned to Haworth, received some education from their aunt, and resumed their quiet, introspective lives among the graves and moors of Haworth parsonage. It was at this time that Charlotte and Emily began to compose a series of adventure stories set in imaginary lands. Charlotte's world was "Angria," Emily's a chronicle of "Gondal," into which she would continue to incorporate the poems secretly composed in the years ahead.

During adolescence the Brontë sisters moved through a number of schools and minor teaching positions. Anne found a situation as governess in 1839, while Charlotte and Emily developed plans to establish a school at Haworth parsonage. To prepare themselves to teach foreign languages, the elder sisters traveled to Brussels in 1842 and studied for eight months at a school run by M. and Mme. Héger. Charlotte served in the school as a teacher in 1843, but, perhaps because of an attraction for her married employer, the time was

an unhappy one. The relationship is central to *Jane Eyre*. She returned to Haworth in 1844, but the plan for a school at their home was never realized, and domestic troubles became more severe. The Rev. Brontë's eyesight was failing, and Branwell, his unstable son, was sinking deeper into the opium habit, bad company, and drunkenness.

In these circumstances Charlotte, Emily, and Anne made the mutual discovery of each other's secret poetry. In 1846 they published the poems at their own expense as *Poems by Currer, Ellis, and Acton Bell*, the pseudonyms chosen to correspond with their real initials. The book attracted little attention, but each of the sisters was already at work on a novel. After *The Professor*, her first attempt, was rejected by a publisher, Charlotte submitted JANE EYRE (1847). The book was an immediate success, arousing intense public curiosity concerning its author. Emily's WUTHERING HEIGHTS and Anne's *Agnes Grey* were published later in the same year; Anne's second novel, *The Tenant of Wildfell Hall*, appeared in 1848. But a series of tragedies suddenly cut short the Brontës' happiness. Their brother, Branwell, died Sept. 24, 1848, Emily became ill and died on Dec. 19 the same year, and Anne died of consumption on May 28, 1849.

Charlotte, left alone to care for her father and writing in the intervals between domestic duties, completed a novel with strong autobiographical elements, *Shirley* (1849). She escaped the gloom of Haworth only by her trips to London, where William Makepeace THACKERAY and other writers sought her acquaintance, and by visits to friends in the north of England, where in 1850 she met Elizabeth GASKELL, the novelist who would become her first biographer.

In 1853, *Villette* was published, a novel in which Charlotte returned to the Brussels experience that she had used in her first and yet unpublished novel, *The Professor*. Having previously rejected several offers of marriage in the past, she married the Rev. Arthur Nicholls in 1854. Their happiness was brief; Charlotte Brontë died on Mar. 31, 1855. *The Professor* was published posthumously in 1857; *Emma*, a fragment of a novel, in 1860.

The Brontë sisters' poetry has recently received increased critical attention, but the major interest of most readers and critics remains centered on Charlotte's *Jane Eyre* and Emily's *Wuthering Heights*. Both novels developed elements from earlier literature (Gothic and romantic novels and melodrama), provided models for literature to come, and stand as unique works of art in their own right. In *Jane Eyre* there is an atmosphere of Gothic and Byronic romanticism, but it is incorporated into a broader tradition of novels that trace one troubled character's slow growth to maturity. In *Wuthering Heights* the Gothic and romantic elements are much more pronounced, but what had been mannered or mechanical in earlier writers was transformed in this novel by Emily's mystical religious sensibility. For most readers of the Brontës, *Wuthering Heights* will remain a symbol of the sisters' cumulative struggle for fulfillment.
                                                                                PHILIP FLYNN

Bibliography: Bentley, P., *The Brontës* (1973; repr. 1986); Bloom, H., ed., *The Brontës* (1987); Chitham, E., *A Life of Emily Brontë* (1987); Duthie, E., *The Brontës and Nature* (1986); Fraser, Rebecca, *The Brontës* (1988); Gaskell, E. C., *The Life of Charlotte Brontë* (1857; repr. 1975); Gerin, W., *Charlotte Brontë* (1967) and *Emily Brontë* (1971); Harrison, A., and Stanford, D., *Anne Brontë* (1959; repr. 1970); Myer, V. G., *Charlotte Brontë: Truculent Spirit* (1987); Smith, A., ed., *The Art of Emily Brontë* (1976); Winnifrith, T., *The Brontës* (1977).

Brontosaurus: see APATOSAURUS.

Brontotherium [brahn'-toh-thee'-ree-uhm]

Brontotherium was a huge mammal, now extinct, related to the horse. The animal lived about 35 million years ago, during the Oligocene epoch. It was one of the largest of the brontotheres, or titanotheres, family Brontotheriidae, which first appeared in North America 54 million years ago and spread to Asia and eastern Europe. The last members of the family died out 22 million years ago. *Brontotherium* stood 2.4 m (8 ft) high at the shoulder, was 4.5 m (15 ft) long, and weighed

The Brontotherium, *a member of the Titanothere family that flourished more than 30 million years ago, was a giant herbivore.*

about 5 tons. It had weak teeth and fed on soft vegetation. Like many of the late brontotheres, it bore a hornlike growth on its snout. This feature consisted of bone covered by thick skin. In *Brontotherium* it was Y-shaped, and it was larger in the male.

Bibliography: Savage, D. E., and Russell, D. E., *Mammalian Paleofauna of the World* (1983).

Bronx, the

The Bronx is the northernmost of the five boroughs of New York City and is the only borough entirely on the mainland. It has an area of 109 km² (42 mi²). It is coextensive with Bronx County and has a population of 1,203,789 (1990). First settled in 1639 and named for an early settler, Jonas Bronck, it was part of Westchester County until 1898, when it was incorporated into New York City.

Although primarily residential, the Bronx has a large waterfront area (over 129 km/80 mi) that is utilized for shipping and industry. The southern section experienced extreme urban deterioration in the 1970s. The noted Bronx Zoo and Yankee Stadium are located in the borough, as is the 101-ha (250-acre) New York Botanical Garden, which includes a National Landmark conservatory, museum, herbarium, and library.

Bronx Zoo

The Bronx Zoo, officially named the New York Zoological Park, is the largest zoo in the United States in acreage. The zoo has some of the rarest animals in the world; since it first opened in 1899 it has been the first to exhibit many exotic animals, such as the duck-billed platypus, the vampire bat, and the Komodo dragon. The zoo covers 102 ha (252 acres), 16 ha (40 acres) of which constitute the Wild Asia exhibit. Other exhibits include the World of Birds, the Rare Animals Range Exhibit, and the World of Darkness, in which the day-night cycle has been reversed so that visitors can see nocturnal animals in action. The New York Zoological Society, a private organization, operates the zoo.

bronze

Bronze is among the oldest artificially produced alloys. It was of such importance to technological development that the term Bronze Age was coined by archaeologists to characterize the period following the Neolithic when weapons and tools began to be constructed of bronze in a particular area.

In its narrowest definition, bronze is an alloy of copper and tin, with or without small proportions of other elements such as zinc and phosphorus. Certain copper-base alloys containing more manganese, iron, lead, or zinc than tin are also regarded as bronzes. Even some alloys that contain no tin are considered bronzes in modern usage, including aluminum bronze (copper-aluminum), silicon bronze (copper-silicon), and beryllium bronze (copper-beryllium). Some copper-base alloys that are actually brasses have been given bronze trade names, such as architectural bronze (57% copper, 40% zinc, 3% lead) and commercial bronze (90% copper, 10% zinc). Despite the broadened definition, tin is still the principal addition used in most bronzes.

Copper-tin alloys are important because of their strength, wear-resistance, and corrosion-resistance in a saltwater environment. The alloys in this system that are most useful from an engineering standpoint are those with less than 20% tin, although other elements are often added to give the best properties for certain applications. Copper-tin bronzes may be categorized readily according to their composition, which affects their machinability. Alloys with up to 8% tin are used mainly for cold-worked applications, such as sheets, wire, and coins; those with 8% to 12% tin are used mainly for gears, bearings, and marine hardware. Bearings are made largely from the 12%-to-20% tin-copper alloys, and bells are the principal product made from copper-tin alloys with from 20% to 25% tin. Alloys in this latter group are very hard and extremely brittle compared with other types. The substitution of zinc for tin results in an improvement in workability and the sacrifice of a measure of strength for hardness.

Beryllium bronzes are used for parts requiring good formability and high fatigue and yield strengths. They are also used for their resistance to creep, as in springs, and in hard parts required to wear well when used with hardened steel, such as dies and firing pins.   MERLE C. NUTT

Bronze Age

The Bronze Age is the stage of prehistoric cultural development when bronze, an alloy of copper and tin, first came into regular use in the manufacture of tools, weapons, and other objects. It marks the transition between the NEOLITHIC PERIOD (a phase of the Stone Age), when stone tools and weapons were predominant, and the succeeding IRON AGE, when the

This copper bull's head from Ur dates from the Early Dynastic period (3d millennium BC) of Sumerian history. Copper metallurgy marked the first phase of the Bronze Age. During the 3d millennium BC the use of bronze itself (blending copper with other metals) became widespread in Mesopotamia. (University Museum, University of Pennsylvania.)

large-scale use of various kinds of metals was introduced.

The term originated as part of the three-age system (Stone Age, Bronze Age, and Iron Age) introduced (1816) by Christian THOMSEN, a Danish museum curator. The three-age system, initially used purely for museum classification, was later validated in STRATIGRAPHY observed through archaeological excavations, first in Denmark and then in other parts of Europe.

The Bronze Age occurred at different times in different parts of the world. In most areas, the development of bronze technology was preceded by an intermediary period when copper was used. This stage, sometimes called the Copper Age, did not occur in some areas, including ancient China and prehistoric Britain, where the transition was made directly from stone to bronze technology. In certain ancient cultures in Africa and elsewhere, stone was replaced directly by iron technology, and the Bronze Age was bypassed completely. These and other variations raise the issue of how prehistoric cultures changed: whether objects of material culture were exchanged, were introduced through invasions or migrations, or were the result of the independent occurrences of technological advances. Archaeologists believe that in the development of bronze METALLURGY all these are possibilities.

Ancient Near East. Metallurgy was first practiced in the ore-rich highlands of eastern Anatolia, more than 10,000 years ago. Initially, during what is termed the CHALCOLITHIC ("copper-stone") Period, metals such as copper were treated like stone and beaten into shape with stones. The earliest known artifacts produced by the SMELTING of copper date from about 3800 BC at the site of Tepe Yahya, Iran. The bronze produced there presumably resulted from an accidental blending of copper with other metals, thus forming a new mixture with better properties than copper alone. Early forms of the new alloy were composed of copper combined with arsenic or antimony. From about 3000 BC, when bronze implements were in common use in the ancient Near East, copper was combined with tin ore, which produced a stronger bronze.

Bronze has many characteristics that make it more useful than copper. It is more durable and casts better than copper. When dented or bent, it can be reworked back into shape, and bronze cutting tools, such as axes or knives, can be easily resharpened. In the hands of artisans, bronze tools revolutionized the arts of woodworking and stoneworking. Bronze also served as a new medium of artistic expression, and from the beginning of the 3d millennium BC, members of the Mesopotamian elite were buried with luxurious bronze objects. The Royal Cemetery at UR, of about 2800 BC, contained some of the richest bronze finds known.

The development of bronze technology is associated with the rise of the earliest great urban CIVILIZATIONS. The scarcity of tin in the Near East prompted the budding civilizations of

The Trundholm sun chariot (c.1000 BC), an example of European Bronze Age art, was found in Trundholm, Denmark. The horse, chariot, and sun were cast in bronze, and the sun was plated with finely worked gold. (National Museum, Copenhagen.)

MESOPOTAMIA and SUMER to search for raw materials in new lands and thereby may have indirectly stimulated their expansion into new territories. In addition to specialized labor for the operation of mining, smelting, and casting, a complex trade network was established, which necessitated an administrative hierarchy, storage systems, computation and writing, and other characteristics of urbanism.

Other Areas. Elsewhere in Asia, the Bronze Age of the INDUS CIVILIZATION began about 2500 BC. In China, the use of bronze was introduced relatively late, probably during the early phases of the SHANG dynasty (c.1600–1027 BC). From about 2500 to 1200 BC, the AEGEAN CIVILIZATIONS of the Minoans and Mycenaeans established centers of metalworking and extensive trade routes into central Europe in order to obtain tin and copper.

The Bronze Age spread throughout Europe from about 1800 BC, chiefly through the influence of the Uneticians (named for the archaeological site of Unetice, in the Czech Republic), a farming and metalworking people living close to the ore sources. They supplanted the earlier European copper workers associated with the BEAKER CULTURE, widely distributed throughout Europe in about 2000 BC (see EUROPEAN PREHISTORY).

Succeeding the Bronze Age in the Old World was the Iron Age, which had its beginnings in the Near East near the end of the 2d millennium BC. In the pre-Columbian New World, although the AZTECS and the high cultures of the Andes worked with wrought copper and other metals, a full-fledged Bronze Age was not attained.   RALPH S. SOLECKI

Bibliography: Childe, V. Gordon, *The Bronze Age* (1930; repr. 1991); Dickinson, Oliver, *The Aegean Bronze Age* (1994); Drews, Robert, *The End of the Bronze Age* (1993); Fell, Barry, *Bronze-Age America* (1982); Fong, Wen, *The Great Bronze Age of China* (1980).

bronzes

The creation of bronzes, objects cast in bronze, is one of the most ancient and pervasive art forms. Magnificent bronze ritual vessels were made in China from the Shang dynasty of the 2d millennium BC through the Han dynasty of the 2d century AD. In southern Nigeria between the 14th and 18th centuries AD, the Bini culture produced the superb bronze ritual objects known as Benin bronzes (see BENIN, KINGDOM OF). For detailed treatment of these cultures see AFRICAN ARCHAEOLOGY; AFRICAN ART; CHINESE ARCHAEOLOGY; and CHINESE ART AND ARCHITECTURE.

Early Bronze Sculpture. In Western art, bronze has also played an important cultural role since the invention of this useful and beautiful alloy more than 4,000 years ago. It is made of a mixture of copper and tin, the tin content not exceeding 11 percent. In the ancient world the use of bronze was widely disseminated, and the alloy's origin cannot be precisely determined. It gave its name to the BRONZE AGE, the period during which bronze weapons and implements replaced those made of stone, preceding the invention of iron implements. Bronze was used by the Sumerians in the 3d millennium BC and by the Akkadians, who adopted their techniques.

The LOST-WAX PROCESS (or cire-perdue) was probably developed in Egypt during the 1st millennium BC, although the Chinese had used it, and probably invented it, during the 2d millennium BC. It was to be the most common method of casting bronze until the 19th century. The earliest bronzes discovered to date were cast solid and were of necessity small in scale, since bronze was scarce and costly. Bronze in sheet form was sometimes beaten into shape over wooden forms to produce such works as the life-size group of King Pepi I with his son (c.2300 BC; Egyptian Museum, Cairo); sometimes it was pressed into molds. Bronze casting was never of major importance to the Egyptians, although it came into common use during the 18th dynasty of the New Kingdom (1573 BC) for the manufacture of small-scale works. Sandcasting (using sand molds) is another ancient process still in use.

Bronze has been used not only for utilitarian objects (household utensils, bells, and weapons) but also for works of art ranging from votive statuettes to gigantic works, such as the *Co-*

lossus of Rhodes (destroyed 224 BC), one of the SEVEN WONDERS OF THE WORLD, which was 36 m (118 ft) high.

Greek and Roman Bronze Sculpture. With the Greeks, bronze assumed a role of great importance. The technique of solid casting continued in use for small works even after the discovery of hollow casting, traditionally ascribed to Rhoiko, Telekles, and Theodoros, craftsmen from Samos, in the 6th century BC. Most of the larger bronzes have disappeared, but the famous *Charioteer of Delphi* (c.470 BC; Delphi Museum) is an outstanding example of the high quality of Greek bronzes. The Etruscans made extensive use of bronze and were highly skilled in its working. In addition to the manufacture of household furnishings and military accoutrements, the Etruscans used bronze for freestanding works, as in the *Capitoline She-Wolf* (c.500 BC; Palazzo dei Conservatori, Rome). The Romans made considerable advances in the technical aspects of bronze casting, particularly in the use of prefabricated parts and in methods of joining metals to each other. Bronze was used for various kinds of military equipment, for the decoration of furniture, and for domestic utensils. It was also used for monumental works as noteworthy and subsequently influential in the history of art as the majestic equestrian statue of *Marcus Aurelius* (AD 161-80) in Rome.

Medieval Bronze Sculpture. During the centuries between the fall of the Roman Empire (476) and the first years of the ROMANESQUE period (c.1000), stone was used more frequently than bronze for SCULPTURE, although some outstanding works in bronze have survived. A late antique heroic statue, called the *Colossus of Barletta* and probably representing the Byzantine emperor Heraclius (610-41), is preserved in the town square of Barletta in Italy. The CAROLINGIAN renaissance of the 9th century brought bronze back into favor. Bronze doors decorated with lion-headed ring handles were cast (804) for the west portal of the Palatine Chapel at Aachen. In the OTTONIAN period, bronze was used extensively; the pair of bronze doors for Mainz Cathedral was cast in 988, and in 1015, Bishop Bernward of Hildesheim designed and had cast the celebrated pair of doors for Hildesheim Cathedral. An important center of bronze casting during the Romanesque and GOTHIC periods was in Dinant, a town in the Meuse Valley of Belgium, which became famous throughout Europe for its baptismal fonts, such as the massive font in the church of Saint Barthélemy in Liège (1107-18), Paschal candlesticks, lecterns, censers, altar services, and chandeliers.

Renaissance Bronze Sculpture. The RENAISSANCE in Italy brought about a major revival of bronze casting on a large scale. Bronze continued to be used for architectural features, as in the two splendid pairs of doors by Lorenzo GHIBERTI for the Florence Baptistery. More important for the future of bronze sculpture, however, was DONATELLO's decision to cast in bronze his *David* (1430-32; Bargello, Florence), the first freestanding nude statue created since classical times. Like the Romans, the Italians of the Renaissance devoted much of their talent to public monuments, two of the greatest being Donatello's equestrian statue of *Erasmo da Narni, General Gattemelata* (1446; Piazza del Santo, Padua) and Andrea del VERROCCHIO's equestrian statue of *Bartolommeo Colleoni* (c.1481-88) in Venice. Characteristic Renaissance interest in the classical world led to the fashion of collecting small bronzes, first in Padua and then in Venice and Florence. Among the most accomplished creators of small bronzes are Antonio POLLAIUOLO, Bertoldo di Giovanni (c.1420-91), and Andrea BRIOSCO, also called Riccio. Interest continued during the 16th century, when such sculptors as Benvenuto CELLINI, with his *Perseus* (1554; Loggia dei Lanzi, Florence), and Giovanni da BOLOGNA, with his *Mercury* (1564; Bargello), cast bronzes of great spatial daring and virtuosity. Giovanni Lorenzo BERNINI preferred marble for his sculpture, but his vast Baldachino (1624-33), a bronze canopy soaring 29 m (95 ft) over

(Right) This Greek bronze kouros (an idealized figure of a young man) was discovered (1959) in Piraeus by workmen digging a sewer. The statue, the oldest known bronze kouros figure, dates from c.520 BC, during the Archaic period of Greek art, and reveals a thorough understanding of human anatomy. (National Museum, Athens.)

(Left) The Roman bronze equestrian statue of Marcus Aurelius portrays the victorious emperor as a bringer of peace. The only well-preserved Roman equestrian monument, the statue survived during the medieval period because it was believed to represent Constantine I. The bronze, placed by Michelangelo in his Piazza del Campidoglio in Rome, served as a model for most subsequent equestrian statues.

(Right) King and Queen *(1952–53) by the British sculptor Henry Moore is in the powerful, abstract style he developed after World War II. The seated bronze group, reduced to the rudiments of the human figure and with masklike heads, recalls the austere, ageless regality of ancient tribal images and votive statues. (Openhecht Museum, Antwerp.)*

(Left) *The early Renaissance statue of* David *(1430–32) by the Florentine sculptor Donatello reveals the influence of classical sculpture in Donatello's conception of the beauty of the human figure and the relaxed contrapposto pose. Originally executed for the Medici family, the bronze was the first free-standing nude figure made since ancient times. (Bargello, Florence.)*

the high altar in Saint Peter's Basilica in the Vatican, is a measure of the enormous technical accomplishment of the 17th-century bronze foundries.

18th- and 19th-Century Bronze Sculpture. In the 18th century bronze sculpture was usually produced on a more modest scale. Works such as Étienne Maurice Falconet's huge *Equestrian Monument to Peter the Great* (1766; Leningrad) are the exception. More characteristic are examples in the decorative arts in the purest rococo style—the elegant furniture mounts, clock cases, candelabra, and andirons created by such French artists as Charles Cressent (1685–1768), Pierre Gouthière, and Pierre Thomire (1751–1843).

The use of bronze became widespread during the 19th century. The development of electrotyping made possible the inexpensive reproduction of bronzes through the mass production of copies. Replicas and reductions from all periods were made for bourgeois collectors. However, Antoine Louis Barye, the great animal sculptor, produced some of the finest bronzes of the century, such as *Theseus and the Minotaur* (1846; Hirshhorn Museum, Washington, D.C.). Auguste Rodin exploited all the effects of which bronze is capable, from the intense naturalism of *The Age of Bronze* (1876–77; Rodin Museum, Philadelphia) to small studies in which traces left by the casting processes are deliberately preserved.

Contemporary Bronze Sculpture. Since Rodin's death, the use of bronze has declined, due in part to the high cost of materials and labor. Although direct carving was preferred to

bronze casting at the beginning of the 20th century, many important sculptors—among them Constantin Brancusi, Jean Arp, Jacques Lipchitz, Alberto Giacometti, Henry Moore, and Aristide Maillol—have continued to work in the medium. With the increasing emphasis on welding, construction, and assemblage, bronze casting is now merely one of many techniques available to sculptors.   John Tancock

Bibliography: Berman, Harold, *Encyclopedia of Bronzes*, 4 vols. (1974–80); Broder, Patricia, *Bronzes of the American West* (1974); Cooper, Jeremy, *Nineteenth-Century Romantic Bronzes* (1975); Haynes, Sybile, *Etruscan Bronzes* (1986); Koop, Albert J., *Early Chinese Bronzes* (1924; repr. 1971); Shapiro, Michael E., *Bronze Casting and American Sculpture, 1850–1900* (1985); Underwood, Leon, *Bronzes of West Africa* (1949; repr. 1968).

Bronzino   [brohn-tsee'-noh]

The Florentine artist Angelo Bronzino (di Cosimo di Mariano), b. Nov. 17, 1503, d. Nov. 23, 1572, was the court painter to Cosimo I de' Medici, duke of Tuscany, and one of the most distinguished Mannerist portraitists (see Mannerism). He studied under Jacopo Pontormo, from whom he absorbed the traditionally Florentine artistic penchants for elegant linearism, emotional intensity, and brilliant color. From these and from his study of Michelangelo and Raphael, the artist developed his characteristic style, as seen in his *Allegory* (National Gallery, London) and in the decoration of the Chapel of Eleonora da Toledo (Palazzo Vecchio, Florence). In these works of the 1540s, the forms are painted with detailed accuracy and an extreme sensitivity to textures and surfaces, yet spatial relationships in the paintings are often highly unnatural. In his religious paintings, such as the *Deposition of Christ* (1545; Musée des Beaux-Arts, Besançon), Bronzino seems less concerned with subject than with formal allusions to the art of Pontormo and Michelangelo and even to classical art.

Cosimo I in Armor and *Eleonora da Toledo with Her Son*, both in the Uffizi Gallery, Florence, and dating from about 1545, are examples of Bronzino's court portraits, in which the sitters are portrayed as personifications of political power. *Andrea Doria* (Brera, Milan) and *Lodovico Capponi* (Frick Collection, New York), paintings probably of the 1550s, exemplify the cold naturalism and allegorical quality of Bronzino's portraits of private individuals.   William Hood

Bibliography: McComb, Arthur, *Agnolo Bronzino: His Life and Works* (1928); Smyth, C. H., *Bronzino as Draughtsman* (1972).

Bronzino's elegant portrait, Eleonora da Toledo with Her Son, *was painted about 1545. An important Mannerist artist who painted many prominent people of the time, Bronzino is noted for his precise, linear, sophisticated style. (Uffizi Gallery, Florence.)*

bronzite: see PYROXENE.

Brook, Alexander

Alexander Brook, b. Brooklyn, N.Y., July 14, 1898, d. Feb. 26, 1980, was an American realist painter. He studied at the Art Students League of New York, where he met his first wife, Peggy BACON. His subject matter is largely that of the studio—still lifes, nudes, portraits—treated in a style called romantic realism. His paintings of the American scene include *Georgia Jungle* (1939; Carnegie Inst., Pittsburgh). Brook was also a successful portraitist.   MARION BURLEIGH-MOTLEY

Bibliography: Baigell, M., *The American Scene* (1974).

Brook, Peter

Peter Brook, b. Mar. 21, 1925, is an English stage director whose controversial stagings of Shakespeare's plays, including a bleak, absurdist *King Lear* (1962; film, 1971) and an exuberant, circuslike *Midsummer Night's Dream* (1970), have been both critical and popular successes. Brook was educated at Oxford University and directed plays, operas, films, and television programs before becoming a codirector of the Royal Shakespeare Company in 1962. His avant-garde staging of Peter Weiss's *Marat/Sade* (1964; film, 1967), in the style of Antonin Artaud's Theater of Cruelty, was an enormous success. Brook's International Center for Theater Research, founded in Paris in 1970, studies primitive and ritualistic forms of theater. Brook's most ambitious project there was his 9½-hour-long production of the Indian epic *The Mahabharata* (Paris, 1985; New York, 1987). Among Brook's most memorable films are his 1952 production of *The Beggar's Opera* and *Lord of the Flies* (1963), from William Golding's novel.

Bibliography: Brook, P., *The Shifting Point, 1946–1987* (1987); Jones, E., *Following Directions* (1985); Trewin, J. C., *Peter Brook* (1971).

Brook Farm

Brook Farm, a short-lived American experimental community founded in 1841, attracted many of New England's best-known intellectual figures of the time. Located on 81 ha (200 acres) in West Roxbury, Mass., near Boston, it was founded by George RIPLEY, a former Unitarian minister, as a cooperative community uniting physical and mental labor within the framework of a simple but cultured way of life. All members, whether manual or intellectual workers, received the same wage. Profits were divided according to the number of days the members worked. The novelist Nathaniel HAWTHORNE and the editor Charles DANA were early members.

The farm had an excellent school, where Bronson ALCOTT, Ralph Waldo EMERSON, Margaret FULLER, and Theodore PARKER were visiting lecturers. In 1844 most of the members became converts to the socialism of Charles FOURIER, and the community was reorganized as the Brook Farm Phalanx. Because the new system required communal living, a phalanstery, or central building, was erected. Its destruction by fire in 1846 dealt Brook Farm a devastating financial blow, and the community was dissolved the next year.

Bibliography: Curtis, E. R., *A Season in Utopia* (1961; repr. 1971); Swift, L., *Brook Farm* (1900).

Brooke, Edward W.

Edward William Brooke, b. Washington, D.C., Oct. 26, 1919, was the first black U.S. senator (1967–79) since Reconstruction. A lawyer and a Republican, Brooke served as attorney general of Massachusetts from 1963 to 1966, gaining a reputation as a fighter against corruption and organized crime.

In 1966, Brooke became the first black popularly elected to the U.S. Senate, winning by almost 500,000 votes. He won reelection easily in 1972. His 1978 reelection campaign was clouded by a bitter divorce settlement, which led to an investigation of his fiscal records by the Senate Ethics Committee; he lost to Democratic candidate Paul Tsongas. Subsequently cleared of wrongdoing, Brooke took up private law practice in Washington, D.C. He wrote *The Challenge of Change* (1966).

Bibliography: Cutler, J. H., *Ed Brooke: Biography of a Senator* (1972).

Brooke, Sir James

Sir James Brooke, b. Apr. 29, 1803, d. June 11, 1868, was an English adventurer who became (1841) rajah of Sarawak on the island of Borneo and founded a dynasty that ruled there until 1941. After military service with the British East India Company, he undertook a private expedition to the East Indies in 1838. There he helped the rajah of Borneo put down a rebellion in Sarawak and was granted the title of rajah. He explored the interior of the region and created the government. The British also made (1847) him consul general for Borneo and governor of the nearby island of Laubuan. He was succeeded in Sarawak by a nephew.

Bibliography: Reece, R. W., *The Name of Brooke* (1982); Runciman, Sir Steven, *The White Rajahs* (1960).

Brooke, Rupert

Rupert Chawner Brooke, b. Aug. 3, 1887, d. Apr. 23, 1915, was an English poet whose sonnet series, *1914 and Other Poems* (1915), expressed the patriotism and romantic optimism of the early years of World War I. Handsome and talented, he became symbolic of youth wasted in war, when, on his way to serve in the Dardanelles, he died of blood poisoning. Although widely read during World War I, Brooke's poems were later accused of sentimentality.

Educated at King's College, Cambridge, Brooke adopted the Georgian style in his first volume, *Poems* (1911). He contributed to *Georgian Poetry*, a biennial anthology; wrote some charming and witty verse, such as "Grantchester" and "Wagner"; and composed vivid love lyrics. Brooke was an intelligent critic who took an interest in the imagism of Ezra Pound and the works of T. S. Eliot. His interest in 17th-century metaphysical poets and Elizabethan drama anticipated trends in modern criticism and poetry. His study *John Webster and the Elizabethan Drama* (1916) is a highly regarded critical work.

MARTIN SEYMOUR-SMITH

Bibliography: de la Mare, Walter, *Rupert Brooke and the Intellectual Imagination* (1919; repr. 1972); Delany, Paul, *The Neo-Pagans* (1987); Hassall, C., *Rupert Brooke* (1964; repr. 1972); Lehmann, John, *The Strange Case of Rupert Brooke* (1981).

Brookfield Zoo

The Brookfield Zoo, also known as the Chicago Zoological Park, was opened in 1934 and administered by the Chicago Zoological Society with financial support from the city. It was the first U.S. zoo with fenceless animal enclosures and the first inland U.S. zoo to have dolphins; in 1987, Brookfield opened the world's largest indoor dolphin exhibit. The animal collection comprises more than 2,500 specimens.

Brookhaven National Laboratory

The Brookhaven National Laboratory is a large, multidisciplinary center for fundamental and applied research in the nuclear sciences and high-energy physics. Established in 1947 on Long Island, N.Y., it is operated by Associated Universities, Inc., and funded by the U.S. Department of Energy. Major research equipment includes nuclear reactors (a high-flux beam reactor and a medical research reactor) and a variety of accelerators. The major accelerator is the 33-GeV Alternating Gradient Synchrotron. Brookhaven also houses the National Synchrotron Light Source, with 0.8-GeV and 2.5-GeV storage rings (see SYNCHROTRON RADIATION). BRIAN SOUTHWORTH

Brookings Institution

The Brookings Institution, located in Washington, D.C., is a nonprofit organization devoted to research in economics, government, and public affairs. It seeks to provide independent analysis and criticism of public policy. Its social scientists serve as a bridge between the world of scholarship, where new knowledge is formulated, and that of policy-making, where it is applied.

The institution, established in 1927, is maintained largely by endowment and private support. It conducts an extensive program of research and publication. It offers research associate positions to advanced graduate students and fellowships to teachers of economics or business. Critics of Brookings have charged that it is staffed predominantly by former advisors to Democratic administrations.

Bibliography: Critchlow, D. T., *The Brookings Institution* (1985); Saunders, C. B., Jr., *The Brookings Institution* (1966).

Brookline

Brookline, in eastern Massachusetts, is a prosperous residential suburb of Boston nearly surrounded by that city. It has a population of 54,718 (1990). Brookline, settled in 1638 as a part of Boston and separated from it in 1705, has resisted annexation by Boston. It was the birthplace of John F. Kennedy.

Brooklyn

Brooklyn, a borough of New York City with a population of 2,300,664 (1990), is located on southwestern Long Island. It has an area of 181 km² (70 mi²). Coterminous with Kings County, it is separated from the borough of Manhattan by the East River and borders the borough of Queens to the north and east. It is connected to Manhattan by three bridges and to Staten Island by the Verrazano Narrows Bridge. A huge shipping port, it clears 25 to 30% of the foreign commerce of the Port of New York through its terminals. The area, first settled by the Dutch in 1636, was named for one of the local towns, Breuckelen. The Battle of Long Island (1776) was fought there. Brooklyn, which became a borough of New York City in 1898, has diversified manufacturing, large residential areas, and many educational institutions, including the Polytechnic Institute of Brooklyn and Pratt Institute. Also of interest are the Brooklyn Museum and the Brooklyn Botanic Garden.

Bibliography: McCullough, D. W., *Brooklyn and How It Got That Way* (1983); Miller, Rita S., ed., *Brooklyn, U.S.A.* (1979).

Brooklyn Botanic Garden and Arboretum

Located in the Prospect Park section of Brooklyn, N.Y., the Brooklyn Botanic Garden and Arboretum is city-owned and privately operated. In addition to the 20-ha (50-acre) garden in Brooklyn, a 90-ha (223-acre) field station in Westchester County, N.Y., serves for plant cultivation and experimental research. The garden is noted for its magnificent display of blossoming cherry trees, its Japanese gardens, rose garden, orchids, and cacti; a garden of fragrances for the blind; a children's garden; and public education programs.

Bibliography: Stone, Doris M., *The Great Public Gardens of the Eastern United States: A Guide to Their Beauty and Botany* (1982).

Brooklyn Bridge

The Brooklyn Bridge (1869–83) was the first great suspension bridge in the United States that had cables formed from parallel steel wires that were spun in place. This fundamental method is still used today. Designed by John ROEBLING and completed by his son Washington Roebling, the Brooklyn Bridge links the boroughs of Brooklyn and Manhattan across the East River in New York City. The bridge carries six lanes of traffic on a span of 486 m (1,595 ft), 50 percent longer than the previous maximum span.

The foundations were built in timber caissons sunk to depths of 13.5 m (44 ft) on the Brooklyn piers and 24 m (78 ft) on the Manhattan piers. Compressed air pressurized the caissons. At that time little was known of the risks of working under such conditions, and more than a hundred workers suffered serious cases of the bends. But in spite of all hazards, the work was completed, and the bridge stands today as an enduring tribute to its daring engineers. New York City honored the bridge with a gala centennial celebration in 1983.

SIR HUBERT SHIRLEY-SMITH

Bibliography: Brooklyn Museum, *The Great East River Bridge, 1883–1983* (1983); McCullough, D. G., *The Great Bridge* (1972; repr. 1983); Shapiro, M. J., *A Picture History of the Brooklyn Bridge* (1984).

Brooklyn College: see NEW YORK, CITY UNIVERSITY OF.

Brooklyn Museum, The

The Brooklyn Museum, originally known as the Library Association, was founded in Brooklyn, N.Y., in 1823 as a wide-ranging educational institution. An art school was added in 1841, and it was renamed the Brooklyn Institute in 1844. Its importance as a center for the collection and study of American art began with the bequest of Augustus Graham in 1853, which required the annual purchase of a work by an American artist. Renamed the Brooklyn Museum in 1890, it moved to its present building on the edge of Prospect Park in 1897; the building was a major project of the architectural firm McKim, Mead, and White.

In the 20th century, major exhibits of Benjamin West (1922), Georgia O'Keefe (1927), Eastman Johnson (1940), and William Sidney Mount (1950) have consolidated the museum's scholarly position in its chief area of interest. Major collections of Egyptian and American Indian art have also been assembled. Recently, an energetic attempt has been made to return to the museum's original purpose: offering exhibits and educational services, both to the professional art world and to the surrounding community. CARTER RATCLIFF

Bibliography: Graham, J. S., "A Museum Grows in Brooklyn," *Horizon*, July–August 1985.

Brookner, Anita

Anita Brookner, b. July 16, 1928, is the English author of a series of novels whose central characters are women—usually intelligent, educated, literary—who have lost in the competition for love and see their lives, therefore, as blighted. A talented art historian, Brookner had written several scholarly works (among them, *Watteau,* 1968; *Jacques-Louis David,* 1974) before she published her first novel, *A Start in Life* (U.S. title, *The Debut*), in 1981. Subsequent novels include *Providence* (1982), *Look at Me* (1983), *Hotel du Lac* (1984; winner of Britain's Booker Prize), *A Misalliance* (1986), *Brief Lives* (1991), and *Fraud* (1993).

Brooks, Cleanth

Cleanth Brooks, b. Murray, Ky., Oct. 16, 1906, d. May 10, 1994, was a literary critic closely associated with NEW CRITICISM. Educated at Vanderbilt, Tulane, and Oxford universities, he taught English at Yale from 1947 until 1975. With Robert Penn WARREN, his coeditor on *The Southern Review,* Brooks wrote two influential textbooks, *Understanding Poetry* (1938) and *Understanding Fiction* (1943). These, together with his critical volume *The Well-Wrought Urn* (1947), helped establish the method of approaching literature through an analysis of the inner structure of a work. The method dominated U.S. literary criticism during the 1950s and '60s. Brooks wrote extensively on William Faulkner and published two books on the origins of Southern U.S. dialects.   RICHARD A. JOHNSON

Brooks, Gwendolyn

The poet Gwendolyn Brooks, b. Topeka, Kans., June 7, 1917, focuses much of her work on the conflict between the individual black American and the social pressures on the black community. She won a Pulitzer Prize for *Annie Allen* in 1950. Her later works include *Family Pictures* (1970), *Report from Part One: An Autobiography* (1972), and *To Disembark* (1981). *Blacks* (1987) is a collection of her writings.

Bibliography: Kent, G. E., *A Life of Gwendolyn Brooks* (1990); Melham, D. H., *Gwendolyn Brooks* (1987).

Brooks, Mel

Mel Brooks, an American comedy writer, actor, and film director, appears on the set of his 1977 film High Anxiety. *Distinguished by his fast-paced, parodic brand of humor, Brooks ranked among the most successful filmmakers of the 1970s.*

Mel Brooks is the professional name of Melvyn Kaminsky, b. Brooklyn, N.Y., June 28, 1926, a comic writer and film actor-director whose humor is based on outrageous insult and zany parody. He began his career as a television writer for Sid Caesar's "Your Show of Shows" (1950–54). His most successful films include *The Producers* (1968), *The 12 Chairs* (1970), *Blazing Saddles* (1973), *Young Frankenstein* (1974), *Silent Movie* (1976), *History of the World—Part I* (1981), and *To Be or Not To Be* (1983). Later work (including *Life Stinks,* 1991; *Robin Hood,* 1993) has been less well received.   FRANK MANCHEL

Brooks, Phillips

Phillips Brooks, b. Boston, Dec. 13, 1835, d. Jan. 23, 1893, was an American Episcopalian bishop noted for his pulpit oratory. He served as rector of churches in Philadelphia and Boston and as bishop of Massachusetts from 1891 to 1893. A "broad" churchman with great confidence in liberal theology and American culture, he stressed the undiscovered potential in human nature and the transforming power of Christianity. His lectures at Yale were published as *Lectures on Preaching* in 1877. Brooks also wrote poetry and hymns, including the Christmas carol "O Little Town of Bethlehem" (1868).

Bibliography: Albright, Raymond, *Focus on Infinity* (1961); Allen, Alexander V. G., ed., *Life and Letters of Phillips Brooks,* 2 vols. (1900).

Brooks, Van Wyck

Van Wyck Brooks, b. Plainfield, N.J., Feb. 16, 1886, d. May 2, 1963, was a literary critic and cultural historian who emphasized the vigor and clarity of American writing while he criticized the country's prevailing business ethic. Ralph Waldo Emerson (*The Life of Emerson,* 1932) was, for Brooks, the embodiment of the "dynamic idealism" he believed should be at the center of American culture, and his major works are an attempt to trace the Emersonian line through its literary and cultural history. The Pulitzer Prize–winning *The Flowering of New England, 1815–1865* (1936) and *New England: Indian Summer, 1865–1915* (1940) are evocative celebrations that seem now, however, to verge on chauvinism.

Bibliography: Hoopes, J., *Van Wyck Brooks* (1977); Kazin, A., *On Native Grounds* (1942); Sprague, C., ed., *Van Wyck Brooks: The Early Years, 1908–25,* rev. ed. (1993).

Brooks Range

The Brooks Range is a northern extension of the Rocky Mountains that runs east-west for 965 km (600 mi) across northern Alaska. The highest peak is Mount Michelson (2,816 m/9,239 ft) at the eastern end of the range. The mountains are sparsely populated by Nunamiut Eskimo.

broom

Broom is the common name for *Cytisus,* a genus with about 50 species of evergreen and deciduous small trees and shrubs in the pea family, Leguminosae. Brooms are native to the warmer and drier regions of Eurasia and North Africa; many, however, have become naturalized elsewhere. The common, or Scotch, broom is naturalized in eastern North America. Many species are cultivated for their yellow, purplish, or white flowers that grow singly or in clusters. Brooms have few leaves.

Broom, Jacob

Jacob Broom, b. Wilmington, Del., 1752, d. Apr. 25, 1810, was a delegate from Delaware to the Constitutional Convention in 1787. He began his career as a surveyor but soon took an active part in public life. In 1776 he was elected burgess of Wilmington and later he became Wilmington's first postmaster. In 1786 he attended the Annapolis Convention. Broom, a bank director, built a cotton mill in Brandywine in 1795. Seven years later he sold the site to E. I. du Pont (see DU PONT, family), who built a powder mill there.

broomrape

Broomrape, the common name for *Orobanche,* is a genus of about 140 species of flowering plants that are parasitic on the roots of other plants. They have reduced, scalelike leaves with little or no green pigment and thus do not make their food photosynthetically. The flowers are purple to yellowish or white. The plants are cosmopolitan in distribution, most species preferring the dry and sandy areas of temperate and subtropical regions of the Northern Hemisphere. Some species are natives of the Old World and are seldom found in North America. The plant may infest tobacco crops. Another name often used for these plants is cancer root.

Brophy, Brigid

Brigid Brophy, b. June 12, 1929, is an English novelist whose works frequently analyze sexual relationships. Her first novel, *Hackenfeller's Ape* (1953), was followed by *Black Ship to Hell* (1962), *The Snow Ball* (1964), *The Adventures of God in His Search for the Black Girl* (1974), and *Palace without Chairs* (1978). Brophy has also written plays, essays, and two studies of the artist Audrey Beardsley.   ROBIN BUSS

Brosse, Salomon de   [braws, sah-loh-mohn' duh]

Salomon de Brosse, b. 1571, d. Dec. 8, 1626, was the first French architect of the 17th century to conceive of a building in terms of mass rather than surface ornamentation. His robust classicism is derived in part from his 16th-century predecessor Philibert de l'Orme. Of de Brosse's three great houses—the châteaux of Blérancourt (1612) and Coulommiers (1613) and LUXEMBOURG PALACE (1615)—only the latter, built in Paris for Queen Marie de Médicis, is extant (with 19th-century alterations). For the Luxembourg, he followed the traditional French system of wings surrounding a courtyard; at Blérancourt, de Brosse broke away by designing a freestanding, symmetrical block. The simplicity of form and suave handling of the classical orders that characterize de Brosse's private commissions may also be found in his facade for the Church of Saint Gervais (1616) in Paris as well as his chief civic work, the Palais du Parlement at Rennes (1618). His overall goal was to imbue traditional French forms with elements of Italian Renaissance architecture; in this, he strongly influenced François MANSART.   ROBERT M. NEUMAN

Bibliography: Blunt, Anthony, *Art and Architecture in France, 1500–1700* (1970); Coope, Rosalys, *Salomon de Brosse* (1972).

Brothers Karamazov, The   [kar-rah-mah'-zawf]

The Brothers Karamazov (1879–80; Eng. trans., 1927) is Fyodor DOSTOYEVSKY's last work and greatest novel. In it, Dostoyevsky presents four Karamazov brothers—the passionate Dmitri, the intellectual Ivan, the mystical Alyosha, and the misanthropic Smerdyakov. He dramatizes their fate, their relationship to their father, and the guilt they suffer because of his murder. The novel concerns itself with everything that Dostoyevsky struggled with during his lifetime: faith and doubt, love of authority and hatred of it, sensuality and abstinence, hatred of the human race and love of it. All are taken up again on a scale that runs from precise realism to universal psychological and metaphysical generalizations. The central theme explores the possibility of the child raising his hand against his father and, by extension, the right of a human being to raise his hand against God.   EDWARD WASIOLEK

Bibliography: Jones, M., and Terry, G., eds., *New Essays on Dostoyevsky* (1983); Sandoz, Ellis, *Political Apocalypse, a Study of Dostoevsky's Grand Inquisitor* (1971); Wasiolek, Edward, *Dostoevsky* (1964); Wasserman, J., ed., *Fyodor Dostoevsky, the Grand Inquisitor* (1970).

Brougham and Vaux, Henry Peter Brougham, 1st Baron   [broo'-uhm, vawks]

An influential British reformer, lawyer, and politician, Henry Peter Brougham, b. Sept. 19, 1778, d. May 7, 1868, was born and educated in Scotland, where he began to practice law and was (1802) a founder of the *Edinburgh Review*. Moving to London in 1803, he distinguished himself as a supporter of the Whig party and an opponent of slavery. He was elected to Parliament in 1810, where he became known for both his eccentricity and the effectiveness of his oratory. As attorney general to Caroline of Brunswick, wife of King George IV, he successfully defended (1820) the queen in divorce proceedings brought against her by the king. In 1830, Brougham was raised to the peerage as Lord Brougham and Vaux. During a

term as lord chancellor (1830–34), he was responsible for major legal and educational reforms.

Lord Brougham popularized the French resort of Cannes, where he lived in later years, and the brougham, a light one-horse carriage designed to his specifications.

Bibliography: Stewart, Robert, *Henry Brougham* (1986).

Broun, Heywood   [broon]

Matthew Heywood Campbell Broun, b. Brooklyn, N.Y., Dec. 7, 1888, d. Dec. 18, 1939, was an aggressive, often humorous newspaper columnist who helped organize the newspaper writers' union, the American Newspaper Guild, in 1933 and served as its president until his death. He was a sportswriter, drama and literary critic, and war correspondent for the *New York Tribune* before becoming a columnist in 1921. His column, ''It Seems to Me,'' appeared first in the *New York World* and later in the *Telegram* and *World-Telegram*. A liberal, Broun often took an independent stance in his column, setting a new trend in American journalism. Broun also edited a literary and humorous weekly, the *Nutmeg*, for a time and wrote some longer works, including *The Boy Grew Older* (1922).   ERNEST C. HYNDS

Bibliography: O'Connor, Richard, *Heywood Broun* (1975).

Brouncker, William   [brung'-kur]

William Brouncker, 2d Viscount Brouncker of Castle Lyons, b. c.1620, d. Apr. 5, 1684, an English mathematician, was a founder and the first president (1662–1677) of the Royal Society. He graduated from Oxford University in 1647 and served as president (1664–67) of Gresham College, London. Brouncker's mathematical accomplishments include work on continued fractions and on the computation of logarithms by infinite series. He published only one book, a translation of Descartes's *Musicae compendium* (1653). Most of Brouncker's work was done with John WALLIS and appeared in the publications of Wallis.   STEVEN LUBAR

Brouwer, Adriaen   [brow'-ur, ah-dree-ahn']

Pain (n.d.), an oil painting by the Flemish genre painter Adriaen Brouwer, is an example of 17th-century Netherlandish naturalism in the tradition of Hals and the Elder Bruegel. (Alte Pinakothek, Munich.)

Adriaen Brouwer b. c.1606, d. January 1638, was a Flemish genre and landscape painter who spent most of his adult life in Holland, where his paintings were popular during his lifetime. Born in Oudenaarde, Brouwer studied drawing with his father, a tapestry designer. He traveled north to live in Amsterdam, probably from 1625 to 1627, then moved to Haarlem. There he became a friend and pupil of Frans HALS.

Brouwer's early Dutch paintings, such as *Pancake Man* (c.1625; Philadelphia Museum of Art), illustrate his appreciation for the Elder BRUEGEL's peasant types and Flemish warm colors, which through Brouwer influenced Dutch genre painters. Because of Brouwer's affiliation with Hals's studio and Dutch monochromatic paintings, he infused his rough drinking and tavern scenes (which frequently contained his self-portrait) with chiaroscuro atmosphere, as in *Fighting Card Players* (1630–35; Alte Pinakothek, Munich). In 1631, Brouwer left Holland for Antwerp, where he continued to paint and lead a dissolute life until his death, perhaps from the plague. In Antwerp, Brouwer's Dutch style influenced many Flemish painters, especially David TENIERS.   ALAN P. DARR

Bibliography: Knuttel, Gerard, *Adriaen Brouwer* (1962).

Brouwer, Dirk   [brow'-ur]

The Dutch-born American astronomer Dirk Brouwer, b. Sept. 1, 1902, d. Jan. 31, 1966, was a specialist in the field of CELESTIAL MECHANICS, the theory of the motion of celestial bodies. Brouwer first demonstrated a method for mathematically determining planetary perturbations, showed how to calculate long-term changes in the orbits of asteroids, and solved the problem of the effect of the Earth's oblateness on the motions of artificial satellites. A graduate (1927) of the University of Leiden, he taught (1928–66) at Yale University and directed (1941–66) the Yale Observatory.   STEVEN J. DICK

Brouwer, L. E. J.   [brow'-ur]

Luitzen Egbertus Jan Brouwer, b. Feb. 27, 1881, d. Dec. 2, 1966, a Dutch mathematician, founded the doctrine of mathematical intuitionism, which views mathematics as the formulation of mental constructions that are governed by self-evident laws. Brouwer's doctrine differed substantially from the formalism of David HILBERT and the logicism of Bertrand RUSSELL. He was a lecturer at the University of Amsterdam, where he taught set theory and other mathematical subjects. A major contributor to the theory of TOPOLOGY, he was considered by many to be its founder.   H. HOWARD FRISINGER

Browder, Earl

Earl Russell Browder, b. Wichita, Kans., May 20, 1891, d. June 27, 1973, led the U.S. COMMUNIST PARTY from 1930 to 1945. A Socialist as a youth, he joined the Communist party in 1921 and by 1930 was general secretary of the party. He twice ran for U.S. president (1936, 1940). Until 1945, Browder faithfully followed swings in party policy—from denunciation of the social democrats in the 1920s, to cooperation with them in a "popular front" against fascism in the 1930s, to justification of the NAZI-SOVIET PACT (1939), and to full Soviet-Western cooperation after 1941. After World War II, however, his continued espousal of cooperation with the bourgeois parties—at a time when Moscow was resuming its revolutionary ideology—led to his ouster from the party.

Bibliography: Browder, Earl, *Communism in the United States* (1935); Draper, Theodore, *The Roots of American Communism* (1957; repr. 1977); Isserman, Maurice, *Which Side Were You On?* (1982; repr. 1987).

Brown   (family)

Three members of the Edmund Brown family have held high state offices in California. **Edmund Gerald "Pat" Brown**, b. San Francisco, Apr. 21, 1905, was California's attorney general (1951–59) and governor (1959–67). A very popular Democrat, he defeated Richard Nixon in the gubernatorial election of 1962. His son, **Edmund Gerald "Jerry" Brown, Jr.**, b. San Francisco, Apr. 7, 1938, was California secretary of

Jerry Brown, governor of California from 1975 to 1983, poses with his father, Pat, who served as governor from 1959 to 1967. Pat Brown defeated Richard Nixon in a bitterly contested gubernatorial campaign in 1962. In 1966, however, he was defeated by Ronald Reagan.

state (1971–75) and governor (1975–83). An unconventional liberal who opposed high taxes and heavy government spending while favoring legislation that would benefit minorities, the poor, and consumers, as well as measures to protect the environment, he ran unsuccessfully for the Democratic presidential nomination in 1976, 1980, and 1992 and lost a U.S. Senate race to Republican Pete Wilson in 1982. His sister, **Kathleen Brown**, b. San Francisco, Sept. 25, 1945, was elected California's treasurer in 1990 and was the Democrats' unsuccessful candidate for governor (against Pete Wilson) in 1994.

Bibliography: Pack, R., *Jerry Brown: The Philosopher Prince* (1978).

Brown, Capability

Lancelot Brown, b. 1716, d. Feb. 5, 1783, better known as Capability Brown because of his customary optimistic comment to prospective clients, was the leading English landscape architect of the 18th century (see LANDSCAPE ARCHITECTURE). In 1740 he became a gardener at Stowe, Buckinghamshire, the greatest English landscape garden of the day, and worked with William KENT, the creator of the English "natural" garden; by the later 1740s he was in charge of Stowe. Brown established himself as an independent consulting landscape architect in 1749 and was eventually responsible for refashioning most of the major landscape gardens in England.

His picturesque style, characterized by broad lawns, asymmetrically placed groves of trees, and serpentine lakes, may still be seen at Bowood, Wiltshire (1763–71), BLENHEIM PALACE, Oxfordshire (c.1765), and Ashburnham Place, Sussex (1767). Brown also designed a number of buildings, including Croome Court, Worcestershire (1751–52; interiors by Robert ADAM), Claremont, Surrey (1770–72), the chapel at Compton Verney, Warwickshire (1772), and many garden structures. In 1772, Henry HOLLAND, who married Brown's daughter the next year, became his assistant; thereafter, most of the building assignments connected with Brown's commissions were turned over to Holland.

Bibliography: Clifford, J., *Capability Brown* (1989); Hyams, E., *Capability Brown and Humphry Repton* (1971); Turner, Roger, *Capability Brown and the 18th Century English Landscape* (1985).

Brown, Charles Brockden

Charles Brockden Brown, b. Jan. 17, 1771, d. Feb. 22, 1810, was America's first professional author. Over a two-year period he wrote the four novels for which he is best known: *Wieland* (1798), a first-person, Gothic narrative involving religious mania, ventriloquism, and spontaneous combustion; *Ormond* (1799); *Edgar Huntly; or, Memoirs of a Sleepwalker* (1799); and *Arthur Mervyn* (1799, 1800). Brown held the view that American literature should include material that is distinctly national in character and setting. He was fascinated with complex states of human consciousness, especially those of people under great stress. In this respect, Brown's work anticipates the psychological novels of Nathaniel Hawthorne, Edgar Allan Poe, and Henry James. Despite his imitativeness and slip-shod style, he wrote with great emotional intensity. Although after 1800 Brown continued to work as a novelist, critic, and editor, insufficient finances obliged him to join (1804) his family's mercantile business.   WAYNE R. KIME

Bibliography: Axelrod, Alan, *Charles Brockden Brown* (1983); Watts, Steven, *The Romance of Real Life* (1994).

Brown, Claude

Claude Brown, b. New York City, Feb. 23, 1937, is an African-American writer and lecturer whose autobiographical novel *Manchild in the Promised Land* (1965) candidly describes the physical and psychological brutalities of his Harlem childhood. In *The Children of Ham* (1976) he portrays even grimmer conditions in the black ghetto.

Brown, Dee

Dee Brown, b. Louisiana, Feb. 18, 1908, is a writer best known for his history of the Indian wars, *Bury My Heart at Wounded Knee* (1971), which details the Indians' loss of their lands and betrayal by the government, culminating in the massacre at Wounded Knee Creek, S.Dak. Brown, who has written prolifically about Western history, is also the author of *Hear That Lonesome Whistle Blow* (1977) about the building of the railroads, and the novel *Killdeer Mountain* (1983).

Brown, Ford Madox

Ford Madox Brown, b. Calais, Apr. 16, 1821, d. London, Oct. 6, 1893, was an English painter associated with the PRE-RAPHA-ELITES, although he was not a member of the group. He studied art on the Continent, coming under the influence of the NAZARENES (a group similar to the Pre-Raphaelites) and took the Pre-Raphaelite Dante Gabriel ROSSETTI as a pupil for a short time. Work executed by Brown during the 1840s included such romantic subjects as *Wycliff Reading His Translation of the Bible to John of Gaunt* (1847; Bradford City Art Gallery) and *Cordelia Washing the Feet of Lear* (1849; Tate Gallery). He soon began painting more characteristic works, such as *The Last of England* (1855; Birmingham City Art Gallery; another version is in the Fitzwilliam Museum, Cambridge), *Work* (1852–65; Manchester City Art Gallery), and *The Pretty Baa-Lambs* (Birmingham City Art Gallery; a smaller version is in the Ash-

The Last of England (1855) by Ford Madox Brown was inspired by the surge of emigration from England during the 1850s. Brown used his friend the Pre-Raphaelite sculptor Thomas Woolner and his wife as models for this forlorn couple. (Birmingham City Art Gallery.)

molean Museum, Oxford). The brilliant representation of natural lighting in the last caused the critic R. A. M. Stevenson to exclaim "By God! the whole history of modern art begins with that picture." Most of Brown's work is marked by great attention to detail.   RAYMOND LISTER

Bibliography: Hilton, T., *The Pre-Raphaelites* (1970; repr. 1977); Newman, T., and Watkinson, R., *Ford Madox Brown and the Pre-Raphaelite Circle* (1992); Rabin, L. F., *Ford Madox Brown and the Pre-Raphaelite History-Picture* (1979); Surtees, V., ed., *The Diaries of Madox Brown* (1981).

Brown, George

George Brown was a Canadian political leader and editor, associated with the Liberal party, who became one of the fathers of the federal union of the British North American colonies in 1867. Born in Alloa, Scotland, on Nov. 29, 1818, Brown immigrated first to New York (1837) and then to Toronto (1843). He founded the *Globe*, which became the voice of the Reform party in Canada West (Ontario) and the most influential paper in the region. His principal causes were "representation by population," to replace the equal standing that Canada West and Canada East (Quebec) held in the joint legislature, and the acquisition by Canada of the Hudson's Bay Company territories. Elected to the assembly in 1851, he served as joint premier in a short-lived Reform ministry in 1858. In 1864 he joined the coalition ministry that was to bring Confederation, but conflict with Conservative leader John A. Macdonald led him to resign in 1865. After Confederation, Brown remained active behind the scenes in the Liberal party. He was appointed to the Senate in 1873. On May 9, 1880, he was murdered by a former employee of the *Globe*.   D. M. L. FARR

Bibliography: Careless, J. M. S., *Brown of the Globe,* 2 vols. (1959–63).

Brown, Helen Gurley

Helen Gurley Brown, b. Green Forest, Ark., Feb. 18, 1922, has been the chief editor of *Cosmopolitan* magazine since its transformation in 1965 from a staid publication to a lively, working-woman's how-to guide to sex, careers, and adventure. She began her own career as a secretary. Her skill in writing, publicizing, and marketing her first book, *Sex and the Single Girl* (1962; rev. ed., 1970), a guide to self-improvement for the unmarried woman, led to her being named to *Cosmopolitan*'s top job.   SUZANNE EMERY

Brown, Jacob Jennings

Jacob Jennings Brown, b. Bucks County, Pa., May 9, 1775, d. Feb. 24, 1828, was a U.S. general in the War of 1812. As commander on the New York State border, he repelled an enemy attack at Sackets Harbor in 1813. In 1814 he invaded Canada and fought an indecisive battle with British forces at Lundy's Lane, near Niagara Falls. He was later (1821–28) commanding general of the U.S. Army.

Brown, James

James Brown, b. Macon, Ga., May 3, 1933, is one of the foremost African-American singer-performers. His career became established with his debut recording, "Please, Please, Please," in 1956. His intense, gospel-style rhythm-and-blues singing, combined with dramatic showmanship, has made his concerts box-office sellouts, and his records are among the most successful in pop-music history. His quasi-religious frenzy on such hits as "Cold Sweat" (1967) and "I Got the Feelin'" (1968) contributed to the revitalization of soul music.

Bibliography: Brown, James, and Tucker, Bruce, *James Brown* (1986).

Brown, Jerry: see BROWN (family).

Brown, Jim

James Nathaniel Brown, b. St. Simon Island, Ga., Feb. 17, 1936, was an exceptional all-around athlete who combined speed, size, and strength to become the foremost running back in football in the 1950s and '60s. Many experts have called him

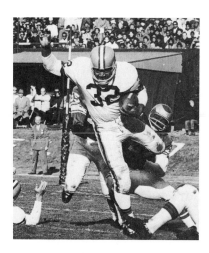

The football player Jim Brown carries the ball against the Philadelphia Eagles of the National Football League. A fullback both in college (Syracuse University) and professionally (Cleveland Browns, 1957–65), Brown possessed the ideal combination of power and grace in a running back.

the greatest running back of all time. During his youth, Brown was a standout in basketball, lacrosse, track, and baseball as well. Concentrating on football, he became an All-American fullback at Syracuse University in 1956, once scoring 43 points in a game. Drafted by the professional Cleveland Browns, he led the National Football League (NFL) in rushing in his rookie year (1957) and for seven of the next eight years he played. In his peak year, 1963, he rushed for 1,863 yd—then a record—and an astounding 6.4-yd average. He also set records for yards rushing in a career (12,312 yd, since broken by Walter Payton) and touchdowns (126). The durable 230-lb (104-kg) star never missed a game because of injury; he retired at his peak to pursue a Hollywood career. He has been selected to both the college and professional football halls of fame.   JIM BENAGH

Bibliography: Brown, Jim, with Myron Cope, *Off My Chest* (1964).

Brown, John

John Brown, who violently opposed slavery, is portrayed in his last moments before being hanged for insurrection, murder, and treason. He was captured after he and his small band raided the federal arsenal in Harpers Ferry, Va., on Oct. 16, 1859.

The American abolitionist John Brown is remembered especially for his raid on the federal arsenal at Harpers Ferry, Va., in 1859. Born on May 9, 1800, in Torrington, Conn., he grew up in Ohio. During most of his adult years Brown wandered from job to job. Ill fortune, business reverses, and charges of illegal practices followed him from the 1820s onward. By the 1850s, however, he had become deeply interested in the slavery question.

Brown envisioned emancipation by massive slave insurrection, but he did not pursue that goal until the 1859 raid on Harpers Ferry. Before then, he and five of his sons became embroiled in the struggle between proslavery and antislavery forces for control of the territorial government in Kansas. By the spring of 1855, civil war had broken out and Brown had assumed command of local Free-Soil militia. Within a year, proslavery forces had sacked the Free-Soil town of Lawrence, an event that triggered a bloody retaliation by Brown. During the night of May 24, 1856, Brown, four of his sons, and two other followers invaded the Pottawatomie River country and killed five helpless settlers, hacking them with sabers. Brown, who was never caught, took full responsibility for the act.

From then on, Brown became even more preoccupied with abolition by slave insurrection. Observers often remarked on his magnetic ability to dominate and involve others in his designs. By 1858 he had persuaded a number of the North's most prominent ABOLITIONISTS to finance his insurrectionary projects. After protracted conspiracy, delay, and diversion, Brown finally chose Harpers Ferry as his point of attack, hoping to establish a base in the mountains to which slaves and free blacks could flee. Brown assembled an armed force of 21 men about 8 km (5 mi) from Harpers Ferry, and on Oct. 16, 1859, they seized the town and occupied the federal arsenal. The town was soon surrounded by local militia, and federal troops under Robert E. LEE arrived the next day. Ten of Brown's army died in the ensuing battle, and Brown himself was wounded. Arrested and charged with treason, Brown conducted himself with great courage and displayed considerable skill in arousing Northern sympathy. Many hailed him as a noble martyr, even as Southern whites expressed deep outrage at his fanaticism. His hanging, on Dec. 2, 1859, symbolically foreshadowed the violence of the Civil War, which broke out two years later.   JAMES BREWER STEWART

Bibliography: Casdorph, Paul, *The Letters of John Brown* (1985); Oates, Stephen B., *To Purge This Land with Blood: A Biography of John Brown*, 2d ed. (1984); Rossbach, Jeffrey, *Ambivalent Conspirators* (1983); Scott, John A., *John Brown of Harper's Ferry* (1987).

Brown, Joseph Rogers

Joseph Rogers Brown, b. Warren, R.I., Jan. 26, 1810, d. July 23, 1876, is best remembered for his invention of the milling and grinding machines called universal because of their many uses in manufacturing. Brown also invented precision machinery and was a famous maker of watches, clocks, and surveying and mathematical instruments. His firm, the Brown and Sharpe Company, was an important tool manufacturer. A few of the tower clocks that he built are still in use.

Brown, Nicholas

Nicholas Brown, b. Providence, R.I., Apr. 4, 1769, d. Sept. 27, 1841, was a Rhode Island merchant and philanthropist. He expanded the family business and cofounded the shipping firm of Brown & Ives. He donated large sums of money to Rhode Island College, which in 1804 became Brown University. His son, John Carter Brown (1797–1874), built up a library of Americana, now housed at Brown University.

His uncle John (1736–1803) had been a leader in the American Revolution. Another uncle, Moses (1738–1836), worked with Samuel Slater to establish the first waterpowered cotton mill in the country.

Brown, Norman O.

Norman O. Brown, b. El Oro, Mexico, Sept. 25, 1913, is an Oxford-educated American scholar who is known for his radical reinterpretation of human culture and history. In *Life against Death* (1959), Brown concluded that the sublimation Sigmund Freud saw as essential to progress is destructive and death-oriented. Brown has also written *Hermes the Thief* (1947), *Love's Body* (1966), and *Closing Time* (1973), a treatise on James Joyce and Giambattista Vico.

Brown, Olympia

Olympia Brown, b. Prairie Ronde, Mich., Jan. 5, 1835, d. Oct. 23, 1926, was a Universalist minister and feminist leader. Ordained in 1863, she was the first American woman to join the clergy of a major ecclesiastical group. She served congregations in Massachusetts, Connecticut, and Wisconsin. After meeting with Susan B. ANTHONY in 1866, Brown spent more than 30 years lecturing and campaigning for women's rights and women's SUFFRAGE. Her autobiography was published as *Acquaintances, Old and New, Among Reformers* (1911).

Bibliography: Greene, Dana, ed., *Suffrage and Religious Principle: Speeches and Writings of Olympia Brown* (1983).

Brown, Paul

Paul Eugene Brown, b. Norwalk, Ohio, Sept. 7, 1908, d. Aug. 5, 1991, was a football executive who previously established one of the game's great coaching records, compiling 351 victories against 133 losses and 16 ties in 41 years. From 1932 to 1941 he coached Massillon, Ohio, high school teams to national prominence, and his 1942 Ohio State team was the national collegiate champion. Brown gained his greatest fame in the pros with the Cleveland Browns (1946–62). The Browns, named for him, won four titles in the All-America Conference (now defunct), then three National Football League titles and seven divisional titles. Brown also coached (1968–75) and is general manager of the Cincinnati Bengals. In pro football, he had 213 victories, 104 losses, and 9 ties. He wrote, with Jack Clary, *PB: The Paul Brown Story* (1979).

Bibliography: Collett, Ritter, *Super Stripes* (1982).

Brown, Robert

Scottish botanist Robert Brown, b. Dec. 21, 1773, d. June 10, 1858, is best known for his 1827 discovery of the motion of microscopic particles suspended in a liquid, now called BROWNIAN MOTION. At the invitation of Sir Joseph BANKS, Brown took part (1801–05) in a survey expedition to Australia, then spent several years classifying the nearly 4,000 plant specimens he had gathered. He was later made librarian of and granted a life interest in Banks's collection, which was eventually transferred to the British Museum with Brown as keeper. The first to observe (1831) the nucleus of a living cell, Brown contributed to plant classification techniques and pioneered in fossil-plant studies.

Bibliography: Mabberly, D. J., *Jupiter Botanicus* (1985).

Brown, Robert McAfee

The American Presbyterian minister and educator Robert McAfee Brown, b. Carthage, Ill., May 28, 1920, is a leading figure in the ecumenical movement. He served (1963–64) as a Protestant observer at the Second Vatican Council. Brown also taught at Union Theological Seminary in New York City and at Stanford University. His books include *The Ecumenical Revolution* (1967), *Is Faith Obsolete?* (1974), *Creative Dislocation* (1980), *Elie Wiesel* (1983), and *Unexpected News* (1984).

Brown, Roger

Roger Brown, b. Detroit, Apr. 14, 1925, is an American social psychologist and one of the first psycholinguists. He studied the effects of different languages on the memory of colors. In the 1970s he began studies of the systematic nature of children's acquisition of language. Among his books are *Words and Things* (1958) and *A First Language* (1973).

Brown-Séquard, Charles

The French physician and physiologist Charles Édouard Brown-Séquard, b. Apr. 8, 1817, d. Apr. 1, 1894, pioneered in endocrinology and made important contributions to an understanding of how the spinal cord functions. He demonstrated in 1856 that removal of the adrenal glands causes death in animals. His work on extracts from the testes influenced the later isolation of sex hormones. In his description of the syndrome now known as Brown-Séquard syndrome, he demonstrated that some nerve pathways cross in the spinal cord.

Bibliography: Olmsted, J., *Charles-Édouard Brown-Séquard* (1946).

Brown, Sterling

Sterling Allen Brown, b. Washington, D.C., May 1, 1901, d. Jan. 13, 1989, was an American poet, critic, and anthologist of black literature. *Southern Road* (1932), an early collection of his verse, is a minor classic of dialect poetry. Such widely anthologized poems as "Strong Men," "Slim in Hell," and "Southern Road" range in tone from broad humor to despair. Brown compiled *Negro Poetry and Drama* (1937), *The Negro in American Fiction* (1937; repr. 1969), and, with Arthur Davis and Ulysses Lee, *The Negro Caravan* (1941; repr. 1969). The verse of *The Last Ride of Wild Bill* (1975) and *The Collected Poems of Sterling A. Brown* (1980) was critically praised.

Brown, William Adams

William Adams Brown, b. New York City, Dec. 29, 1865, d. Dec. 15, 1943, was a liberal Presbyterian theologian active in the ecumenical movement and in Christian social work. After studying in Germany under Adolf von Harnack, he taught at Union Theological Seminary from 1892 to 1930. Following Harnack's lead in adapting theology to the modern world, Brown focused on the basic meaning of Christianity. His works include *The Essence of Christianity* (1902), *Modern Theology and the Preaching of the Gospel* (1914), and *Imperialistic Religion and the Religion of Democracy* (1923).

brown dwarf

In astronomy, a brown dwarf is a theorized celestial body with a starlike composition but a mass between that of a giant planet and the smallest possible stars. Too small to initiate the nuclear reactions by which stars shine, it would glow feebly in the infrared. The largest known planet, Jupiter, is itself starlike in composition and does radiate some energy, but it is about 50 times smaller than the smallest brown dwarfs that might be detected orbiting other stars. A few possible brown-dwarf candidates have been singled out thus far, but the readings remain in dispute. Various astronomers, using advanced infrared imaging techniques, are also searching star clusters such as the Hyades and Pleiades as likely sites for brown dwarfs and have found evidence for a number of them. If brown dwarfs do exist, they might help to account for the supposed "missing mass" of the universe that current theories in COSMOLOGY incorporate as an unexplained problem.

Bibliography: Bartusiak, Marcia, "The Hunt for Brown Dwarfs," *Discover*, April 1991; "Brown Dwarfs Lost (and Found?)" *Sky & Telescope*, August 1991; Tucker, Wallace and Karen, *The Dark Matter* (1988).

brown lung

Brown lung, or byssinosis, is an occupational disease that involves allergic reactions to dust or fungi on inhaled particles of natural fibers (see DISEASES, OCCUPATIONAL). Textile mill workers who are exposed to cotton, flax, or soft hemp dust are susceptible to this RESPIRATORY SYSTEM DISORDER.

Tissue reaction to small particles of dust in the lungs causes the accumulation of thick mucus, with a resulting constriction of air passages. The constriction may destroy air sacs, or alveoli, in the lungs, leading to breathing difficulty. Symptoms include wheezing, shortness of breath, dizziness, and headaches, and lung tissue takes on the discoloration that gives the disorder its name. If environmental conditions are corrected the symptoms may subside, but continued exposure to fiber dust can cause permanent damage to the lungs and bring on life-threatening chronic BRONCHITIS, EMPHYSEMA, or COR PULMONALE. Prevention of brown lung includes adequate ventilation of textile mills.

brown recluse spider

The brown recluse spider, *Loxosceles reclusa,* is one of the few poisonous spiders in the United States. Its range extends from Kansas and Missouri, south to Texas, and west to California. Found in sheltered sites indoors and outdoors, the brown recluse spider is about 10 mm (0.4 in) long and has an orange-yellow body with a dark violin-shaped design on the back. Although its bite is rarely fatal to humans, the venom kills the skin and the wound may take several months to heal. The brown recluse spider is active at night and feeds on small insects that it paralyzes with its poison.

Brown University

Established in 1764 by the Baptists, Brown University (enrollment: 7,490; library: 1,966,160 volumes) is a private nondenominational institution in Providence, R.I. It is the seventh-oldest U.S. college. Pembroke College, its coordinate women's school, merged with it in 1971. Brown has an outstanding collection of incunabula and of pre-1800 Americana.

Brown v. Board of Education of Topeka, Kansas

Brown v. *Board of Education of Topeka, Kansas,* decided on May 17, 1954, was one of the most important cases in the history of the U.S. Supreme Court. Linda Brown had been denied admission to an elementary school in Topeka because she was black. Brought together under the Brown designation were companion cases from South Carolina, Virginia, and Delaware, all of which involved the same basic question: Does the equal protection clause of the 14TH AMENDMENT prohibit racial segregation in the public schools?

In 1896 the Supreme Court had held in PLESSY V. FERGUSON that racial segregation was permissible as long as equal facilities were provided for both races. Although that decision involved only passenger accommodations on a railroad, the principle of "separate but equal" was applied thereafter to all aspects of public life in states with large black populations.

It was not until the late 1940s that the Court began to insist on equality of treatment, but it did not squarely face the constitutionality of the "separate but equal" doctrine until it decided the *Brown* case. In a brief, unanimous opinion delivered by Chief Justice Earl WARREN, the Court declared that "separate education facilities are inherently unequal" and that racial segregation violates the equal protection clause of the 14th Amendment. In a moving passage, the chief justice argued that separating children in the schools solely on racial grounds "generates a feeling of inferiority as to their status in the community that may affect their hearts and minds in a way unlikely ever to be undone." Although the decision did not bring about total integration of blacks in the schools, it resulted in efforts by many school systems to remove the imbalance by BUSING students. The Court's decision had far-reaching effects, influencing CIVIL RIGHTS legislation and the civil rights movement of the 1960s.   ROBERT J. STEAMER

Bibliography: Cushman, Robert F., ed., *Cases in Constitutional Law,* 6th ed. (1984); Mason, Alpheus T., *The Supreme Court from Taft to Burger* (1979); Swisher, Carl B., *Historic Decisions of the Supreme Court,* 2d ed. (1969; repr. 1979).

Brown v. Maryland

In *Brown* v. *Maryland* (1827), Chief Justice John Marshall enunciated what became known as the "original package doctrine." In 1821 the Maryland legislature had required all importers and sellers of foreign goods to pay a license fee. After Brown had imported and sold a package of foreign dry goods without the requisite license, he was prosecuted by the state and appealed his conviction to the U.S. Supreme Court.

Reversing the conviction, Chief Justice Marshall invalidated the Maryland law on two grounds. First, the law was, in effect, a tax on imports and was thus forbidden by Article 10 of the Constitution. The state may tax an imported article only after it has been mixed with the general property of the state, but not while it is in the original form in which it was imported. Second, observed Marshall, the law was repugnant to the commerce clause, since it was an attempt on the part of the state to regulate interstate commerce, a power that resided in Congress. This was one of several decisions handed down by Marshall that marked out the boundaries of federal and state power. Secondarily, the case was a strong defense of laissez-faire economics.   ROBERT J. STEAMER

Browne, Charles Farrar: see WARD, ARTEMUS.

Browne, Robert

Robert Browne, 1553–1633, was an English separatist and one of the founders of CONGREGATIONALISM. After adopting Presbyterian ideas of the church, he established independent congregations—an action for which he was imprisoned. Later, he migrated to Holland, where he wrote *A Treatise of Reformation without Tarrying for Any* (1582). Other separatists joined his followers, known as Brownists. A few years later, however, he lost favor with them and returned to the Church of England, in which he held several positions before his death.

Browne, Sir Thomas

Sir Thomas Browne, b. Oct. 19, 1605, d. Oct. 19, 1682, was an Anglican physician and a supreme prose stylist concerned with reconciling science and religion. *Religio Medici* (1643) is a delightful and sympathetic self-revelation. In *Pseudodoxia Epidemica* (1646), he applied reason, authority, and personal observation to expose erroneous beliefs: for example, that salamanders live in fire, that ostriches digest iron, and that Aristotle drowned himself in the Euripus because he could not explain its tides. *Hydriotaphia, or Urn Burial* (1658), a sometimes humorous discussion of burial customs, leads to an eloquent reflection on human vanity. "'Tis all one to lie in St. Innocent's churchyard," he wrote, "as in the sands of Egypt, ready to be anything in the ecstasy of being ever." *The Garden of Cyrus* (1658) begins as a discourse on the arrangement of ancient gardens in the pattern of a quincunx and ends as a mystical treatise on the number 5. A Royalist, Browne was knighted by Charles II in 1671.   DAVID M. ZESMER

Bibliography: Bush, Douglas, *English Literature in the Earlier Seventeenth Century,* 2d rev. ed. (1962); Dunn, W. P., *Sir Thomas Browne* (1950); Huntley, F. L., *Sir Thomas Browne* (1962); Keynes, Geoffrey, ed., *Works of Sir Thomas Browne,* 4 vols., rev. ed. (1964).

Browne, Thomas Alexander

Thomas Alexander Browne was the pen name of Rolf Boldrewood, b. Aug. 6, 1826, d. Mar. 11, 1915, a prolific Australian novelist who is best remembered for his adventure tales of pioneer life in Australia. One novel, *Robbery Under Arms* (1888), became a classic in his lifetime. *Old Melbourne Memories* (1884) and *Miner's Right* (1890) are among his most popular works.

Browne, William

William Browne, c.1591–c.1643, was an English poet who also wrote several dramatic masques. His *Britannia's Pastorals* (1613, 1616), a collection of pastoral poems written in the manner of Sir Philip Sidney and Edmund Spenser, influenced such later poets as John Keats and John Milton.   ROBIN BUSS

Brownian motion

Brownian motion is an erratic, zigzag motion of microscopic particles. It was first observed in 1827 by the English botanist Robert Brown, who was investigating a suspension of microscopic pollen particles in an aqueous solution. The effect was observed even in pollen samples that had been dead for more than 100 years. Brownian motion was investigated further by Brown and others during the 19th century. Experiments showed that the motion became more rapid and the particles moved farther in a given time interval when the temperature was raised, when the viscosity of the fluid was lowered, or when the average particle size was reduced.

The KINETIC THEORY OF MATTER, developed toward the end of the 19th century, gave a qualitative explanation for the motion of inanimate particles in solution. The atoms or molecules that make up a liquid or gas are in constant thermal motion, and their distribution of velocity is determined by the temperature of the system. Each suspended particle collides with surrounding molecules, and each collision changes the particle's velocity by a small amount. The net effect is an erratic, random motion of the particle through the fluid. A quantitative theory of Brownian motion was developed independently by Albert Einstein and Marian Smoluchowski in 1905–06; it accounts for the dependence of the effect on temperature, viscosity, and size. Collision with fluid molecules can also make a suspended particle rotate. This phenomenon, called rotational Brownian motion, has also been observed and explained.   DAVID W. OXTOBY

brownie

In English and Scottish folklore, a brownie is a tiny, helpful FAIRY. It is usually associated with houses, performing domestic chores while the occupants sleep. In many tales, brownies display a mischievous streak when criticized and leave if rewarded with anything other than cream, milk, or bread. German and Scandinavian folklore contains descriptions of similar household spirits.

In the SCOUTING movement the youngest age group of Girl Scouts and Girl Guides is the Brownies.

Browning, Elizabeth Barrett

Elizabeth Barrett Browning, 19th-century English poet, appears in this oil painting by Michele Gordigiani. Elizabeth Browning is remembered largely for a single publication, Sonnets from the Portuguese (1850), a collection of love poems dedicated to her husband, Robert Browning.

Elizabeth Barrett, b. Durham, Mar. 6, 1806, was an English poet who married Robert BROWNING. Raised at Hope End, her parents' country estate, amid natural beauty and familial love, Barrett was an avid reader and precocious writer. A riding accident at age 15 seriously injured her spine and left her an invalid. The subsequent death of her mother, Mary, and the financial reverses of her father, Edward, forced the family to move to London in 1836, where Barrett's continued ill health confined her to her bedroom for long periods of time. In 1838 the family moved to 50 Wimpole Street. At 20 she published her first volume of poetry, An Essay on Mind, with Other Poems (1826), which was followed by Prometheus Bound (1833), The Seraphim, and other Poems (1838), and Poems of E. Barrett (1844). The shock of her brother's drowning further undermined her health. One of the few new acquaintances allowed into her sitting room was the young poet Robert BROWNING.

When they first met Browning was still unknown, but Barrett's reputation was already established; her "Cry of the Children" was widely quoted. Their fervent courtship (the subject of the successful modern play The Barretts of Wimpole Street, 1930) led to their marriage in 1846 and the SONNETS FROM THE PORTUGUESE (1850), perhaps her finest work.

Shortly after their marriage, Elizabeth and Robert Browning left England for the Continent. They settled in Florence, where her health improved. Her fascination with Italian themes found expression in Casa Guidi Windows (1851), and her Aurora Leigh (1857), a blank-verse romance, became popular. In her own day Elizabeth Browning's verse was considered to be far better than her husband's, and today it is receiving renewed attention. She believed that her husband's fame was destined to eclipse her own. She died in Florence on June 30, 1861. Her Last Poems appeared posthumously in 1862.   PHILIP FLYNN

Bibliography: Clarke, Isabel C., Elizabeth Barrett Browning: A Portrait (1929; repr. 1985); Hewlett, Dorothy, Elizabeth Barrett Browning (1952; repr. 1972); Leighton, Angela, Elizabeth Barrett Browning (1986); Radley, Virginia, Elizabeth Barrett Browning (1972); Whiting, Lilian, A Study of Elizabeth Barrett Browning (1899; repr. 1973).

Browning, John Moses

John Moses Browning, b. Ogden, Utah, Jan. 21, 1855, d. Nov. 26, 1926, was unsurpassed as an inventor of small arms and automatic weapons. As a designer for the Winchester and Colt companies and for his own firm, he invented or improved firearms of almost every type. Browning received his first patent for a breech-loading single-shot rifle. His patents for repeating rifles, shotguns, and automatic pistols made him wealthy. The Browning automatic rifle (BAR), pistol, and machine gun became standard U.S. Army equipment.

Browning, Robert

Robert Browning, whose earliest poems met with severe criticism, finally achieved fame as a master of dramatic monologue. Browning used this poetic device to explore the complexities of his characters. A familiar Browning theme, humankind's noble, yet futile, quest for perfection, is reflected in a famous line from his "Andrea del Sarto," "Ah, but a man's reach should exceed his grasp,/Or what's a heaven for?"

Robert Browning ranks with TENNYSON as one of the greatest Victorian poets. Yet his optimistic sentiments and innovative style provoked mixed reactions among 19th-century readers and remain controversial even today. Born in London on May 7, 1812, Browning derived from his parents a deep, if unconventional, religious sense and a love of books, music, and painting. His first published poem, Pauline (1833), which was influenced by Shelley, was mainly a series of musings on poetic sensibility. The volume attracted little notice, but it did lead John Stuart Mill to censure Browning's self-absorption, an attack that may have prompted Browning's turn toward the dramatic monologue. Popular success long eluded him. Paracelsus (1835) was largely ignored; Strafford, a play, had a brief run at Covent Garden in 1837; Sordello (1840), a verse tale of medieval Italy, quickly became a byword for willful obscurity among the small circle of critics who read it. Yet

Browning was steadily improving his art, and a series of eight pamphlets, known collectively as *Bells and Pomegranates* (1841–46), included several of the poems on which his later reputation was to rest, including "My Last Duchess," "Soliloquy of the Spanish Cloister," and "The Bishop Orders His Tomb at Saint Praxed's Church."

After Browning married Elizabeth Barrett (see BROWNING, ELIZABETH BARRETT) in 1846, they settled at Casa Guidi in Florence, where he composed the poems that appeared in *Men and Women* (1855), including "Childe Roland to the Dark Tower Came." His sorrow at the death of his beloved wife in 1861 drove him back to England, where he gradually became a well-known figure in London literary circles. *Dramatis Personae* (1864), containing "Caliban upon Setebos" and "A Death in the Desert," showed his concern with 19th-century religious problems, but it was the publication of *The Ring and the Book* (1868–69) that finally established his reputation as a major poet. Considered by some modern critics to be the most important long poem in Victorian literature, *The Ring and the Book* synthesizes Browning's most abiding interests—the Italian scene, moral casuistry, and the complexity of human personality. Both pleased by and wary of his long-delayed public acclaim, Browning took pains to preserve his private life and creative energies. In *Balaustion's Adventure* (1871) and *Aristophanes' Apology* (1875) he explored the realm of classical literature, and in *Red Cotton Night-Cap Country* (1873) and *The Inn-Album* (1875) he developed his concern with crime and criminal psychology. The two *Dramatic Idyls* (1879, 1880) revealed again what was best and worst in Browning—a compressed, sometimes contorted style and an erudition that could alternately fascinate and bewilder readers. *Asolando*, his last volume of poetry, was published on the day of his death in Venice on Dec. 12, 1889. He was interred in Poets' Corner, Westminster Abbey.   PHILIP FLYNN

Bibliography: Browning, Robert, *Complete Works*, ed. by Roma A. King (1967–72); Eriksen, Lee, *Robert Browning* (1984); Gibson, Mary E., *History and the Prism of Art: Browning's Poetic Experiments* (1987); King, Roma, *The Bow and the Lyre: The Art of Robert Browning* (1957); Maynard, John, *Robert Browning's Youth* (1977); Pearsall, Robert, *Robert Browning* (1974); Pettigrew, John, ed., *Robert Browning: The Poems*, 2 vols. (1981).

Browning, Tod

The American film director Tod Browning, b. Louisville, Ky., July 12, 1882, d. Oct. 6, 1962, is considered the creator of the classic horror film. He began his professional career as a vaudeville comedian, joined Biograph film studios as an actor (1912), and was assistant director and writer on D. W. Griffith's *Intolerance* (1916). His best films include *The Unholy Three* (1925), which brought stardom to actor Lon Chaney; *Dracula* (1931), in which Bela Lugosi played the vampire count; and the critically acclaimed *Freaks* (1932). Browning's serious approach to the horror film made him one of the most respected directors of that genre.

Brownmiller, Susan

Susan Brownmiller, b. Brooklyn, N.Y., Feb. 15, 1935, is an American feminist and journalist whose 1975 study *Against Our Will: Men, Women, and Rape* was received as a comprehensive and illuminating treatment of the subject. Her thesis is that rape, or its threat, is a widespread social mechanism used by men to control women. *Femininity* (1984) analyzes male-imposed standards of beauty. *Waverly Place* (1989) examines a notorious case of child abuse in New York City.

Brownson, Orestes

Orestes Augustus Brownson, b. Stockbridge, Vt., Sept. 16, 1803, d. Apr. 17, 1876, was an American journalist and social and religious critic. As a reformer, Brownson championed transcendentalism, the Democratic party, and Catholicism; many of his writings were published in the journals he edited, *Boston Quarterly Review* (1838–42) and *Brownson's Quarterly Review* (1844–64; 1873–75). In his *New Views of Christianity, Society, and the Church* (1836) he criticized established religion, and in *The American Republic* (1865) he expressed his conservative political philosophy. Brownson's religious pilgrimage from universalism to skepticism to Unitarianism to Catholicism is chronicled in his novel *The Spirit-Rapper: An Autobiography* (1854) and in his autobiography *The Convert; or, Leaves from My Experience* (1857).

JOEL MYERSON

Bibliography: Ryan, T. R., *Orestes A. Brownson* (1976; repr. 1984).

Brownsville

Brownsville (1990 pop., 98,962) is the seat of Cameron County and the southernmost city in Texas, located on the Rio Grande opposite Matamoros, Mexico. A port with a deepwater channel to the Gulf of Mexico, Brownsville has a shrimp fleet and is the processing and shipping center of a rich citrus-growing area. It also has many industries based on oil and natural gas. Its warm climate and deep-sea fishing attract vacationers. The city grew around Fort Brown, the establishment of which (1846) helped provoke the Mexican War. The area was the scene of early Mexican War battles and of one of the last battles of the Civil War.

Brownsville Raid

The Brownsville Raid took place near Fort Brown, Brownsville, Tex., on Aug. 13, 1906, when a group of armed men fired into homes and stores located near the fort, killing one man. The episode was blamed on black soldiers garrisoned there, but no proof was ever established. Nevertheless, President Theodore Roosevelt ordered discharged "without honor" 167 black soldiers who had been stationed at Fort Brown. In 1972 the U.S. Army officially admitted Roosevelt's injustice by changing the discharges to honorable.

Bibliography: Weaver, John D., *The Brownsville Raid* (1970).

Brubeck   (family)

The Brubecks are American jazz musicians and composers who often play together as a group called Two Generations of Brubeck. The founder and most famous member is **David Warren Brubeck**, b. Concord, Calif., Dec. 6, 1920, a pianist who led a popular jazz quartet in the 1950s and '60s. A student of Darius Milhaud and Arnold Schoenberg, Brubeck has a harmonically complex style and uncommon time signatures that have influenced contemporary jazz pianists. He has also composed more than 250 songs, cantatas, oratorios, and symphonic pieces, some of them featuring a jazz quartet with orchestra. Brubeck's recordings include *Jazz Impressions of Japan* (1964), *Adventures in Time* (1971), *Quartet 25th Anniversary* (1976), and *Reflections* (1986). His sons, **David Darius**, b. June 6, 1947, **Chris**, b. Mar. 14, 1952, and **Daniel**, b. May 4, 1955, have performed and recorded with their father and with their own groups.   JONATHAN KAMIN

Bibliography: Berendt, Joachim, *The Jazz Book*, trans. by Dan Morgenstern et al. (1975); Collier, James L., *The Making of Jazz* (1978).

Bruce, Sir David

Sir David Bruce, b. May 29, 1855, d. Nov. 27, 1931, was a British microbiologist who discovered the cause of several diseases. While stationed in Malta in 1887, he isolated the organism responsible for Malta, or undulant, fever, later identified as one of the *Brucella* bacteria. It is responsible for a disease (now called BRUCELLOSIS) in humans, cattle, swine, and goats. While working in Africa some years later, Bruce found that the animal disease nagana is caused by the parasite *Trypanosoma brucei* and that African sleeping sickness is caused by the parasite *T. gambiense*, both parasites being transmitted by species of the tsetse fly.

Bibliography: deKruif, Paul, *Men against Death* (1932); Eberson, Frederick, *Man against Microbes* (1963).

Bruce, James

James Bruce, b. Dec. 14, 1730, d. Apr. 27, 1794, was a British traveler, who in 1770, after a treacherous journey, reached

Lake Tana, source of the Blue Nile. His 5-year journey, from 1768, took him through Egypt and Ethiopia to Lake Tana, which he mistakenly thought to be the main source of the Nile. His *Travels to Discover the Source of the Nile* (1790) is a classic of travel literature.

Bibliography: Moorhead, Alan, *The Blue Nile*, rev. ed. (1972; repr. 1983); Reid, J. R., *Traveller Extraordinary* (1968).

Bruce, Lenny

Lenny Bruce, one of the most controversial comics of the early 1960s, begins one of his aggressive, satirical routines. Bruce's often vulgar material resulted in a series of trials on obscenity charges. In 1966 he was found in a Hollywood mansion, dead from a drug overdose at the age of 39.

Lenny Bruce was the stage name of Leonard Alfred Schneider, b. Minneola, N.Y., Oct. 13, 1926, a nightclub performer and comedian who reached his peak of popularity in the early 1960s. His stinging, uninhibited comedy, now considered mild, was particularly aimed at contemporary mores. Delivered in a staccato fashion, his stand-up routines included vulgar jokes and sexually explicit observations, resulting in Bruce's 1964 criminal conviction for giving an obscene performance. The rest of his life was spent in battling this conviction. His autobiography, *How to Talk Dirty and Influence People*, was published in 1965. He died on Aug. 3, 1966, of a drug overdose. The play *Lenny* (1971; film, 1974), by Julian Barry, was based on Bruce's life.   FRANK MANCHEL

Bibliography: Goldman, Albert, with Schiller, Lawrence, *Ladies and Gentlemen, Lenny Bruce!!!* (1974).

Bruce, Robert: see ROBERT I, KING OF SCOTLAND.

Bruce, Stanley Melbourne, 1st Viscount of Melbourne

Stanley Bruce, b. Apr. 15, 1883, d. Aug. 25, 1967, was the first Australian to sit in the British House of Lords. Entering the Australian Parliament in 1918, he was federal treasurer from 1921 to 1923, when he succeeded William Morris HUGHES as leader of the Nationalist, or Liberal-Country party, coalition government. Prime minister until 1929, Bruce fostered scientific research and economic development, passed unemployment insurance and public health legislation, and extended the national railways. From 1933 to 1945, he was high commissioner in Britain, serving as Australia's representative in the British war cabinet during World War II. In 1947, Bruce chaired the World Food Council and was created a viscount.   E. J. TAPP

Bibliography: Edwards, Cecil, *Bruce of Melbourne* (1965).

Bruce, William Speirs

William Speirs Bruce, b. Aug. 1, 1867, d. Oct. 28, 1921, was a Scottish scientist and explorer. As head of the 1902-04 Scottish National Antarctic Expedition aboard the *Scotia*, he dis-

covered 241 km (150 mi) of the Antarctic coast along the Weddell Sea and named it Coats Land. He also set up a weather station in the South Orkney Islands and made soundings in the Scotia and Weddell seas. Bruce made other expeditions to both the Arctic and Antarctic.

brucellosis   [broo-suh-loh'-sis]

Brucellosis is primarily an infectious disease of animals, including domesticated species. Caused by any of several forms of *Brucella* bacteria, it is also known as Cyprus, Malta, Mediterranean, or Rio Grande fever or Bang's disease. Humans who handle or drink the milk of infected animals can catch the disease, which is then called undulant fever. In animals the disease is hard to control and can cause sterility and abortions. It is dealt with by slaughter but also, in cattle, by vaccination of calves. Brucellosis in humans is rarely fatal but often chronic, causing chills, fever, weight loss, joint and muscle pains, and an enlarged spleen. Serious complications such as encephalitis and meningitis may also arise. Treatment is with a combination of tetracycline and streptomycin.

J. MICHAEL S. DIXON, M.D.

Bruch, Max   [brook]

Max Christian Friedrich Bruch, b. Jan. 6, 1838, d. Oct. 2, 1920, was a prominent late romantic German composer. After training under Ferdinand Hiller and Carl Reinecke, among others, Bruch led an itinerant musical life as a teacher and conductor until 1892, when he became head of composition at the music conservatory in Berlin. His music adheres to the German romantic aesthetic of the late 19th century. Although his oratorios were once celebrated, he is now known mostly for the Violin Concerto in G Minor (op. 26), the *Scottish Fantasy* for violin and orchestra (op. 46), and the *Kol Nidrei* for cello and orchestra (op. 47).   F. E. KIRBY

Brücke, Die   [bruek-e, dee]

Ernst Ludwig Kirchner's A Group of Artists (1926–27) portrays some of the most important members of the expressionist group Die Brücke. The artists (left to right) are Otto Müller, Kirchner, Erich Heckel, and Karl Schmidt-Rottluff. (Wallraf-Richartz Museum, Cologne.)

Die Brücke ("The Bridge"), a German expressionist art movement, was founded in Dresden, Germany, in 1905 by Erich HECKEL, Ernst Ludwig KIRCHNER, Karl SCHMIDT-ROTTLUFF, and Fritz Bleyl. They were later joined by Max PECHSTEIN, Otto Müller, Axel Gallén-Kallela, and Cuno Amiet, and, briefly (1906–07), by Emil NOLDE. Their goal was the renewal of German art and a renaissance of German cultural life. In order to educate the public to new art forms, they mounted exhibitions and sent subscribers yearly portfolios of their prints.

Their first exhibition (1906) was accompanied by a manifesto calling on all future-minded artists to unite. They fashioned themselves after a medieval guild, at first living and working communally. By 1911 most of the members had moved to Berlin. They spent summers frolicking nude at nearby lakes or living in Baltic fishing villages in an effort to recapture a primal innocence and freshness of inspiration.

The expressionistic style of the Die Brücke artists is characterized by dynamic, animated brushwork, vibrant color, and emotionally distorted forms and spaces. With Paul GAUGUIN, Vincent VAN GOGH, and Edvard MUNCH as their heroes, they sought to evoke an emotional and psychological reality behind surface appearance. They excelled in woodcut printmaking, incorporating the angular forms of Oceanic and African art for heightened emotional impact. (See EXPRESSIONISM.)

Although their work bears formal affinities with that of the Fauves (see FAUVISM), the Brücke artists, unlike the Parisian group, were primarily concerned with psychological expression. Their art was permeated, to varying degrees, by angst over modern society.

Tensions in the group, present from about 1910, culminated in 1913 in its dissolution, the immediate result of protest over Kirchner's controversial history of the organization, *Chronicle of the Brücke*. An art collection and historical archive of the movement is housed in the Brücke Museum, West Berlin.

IDA K. RIGBY

Bibliography: Myers, Bernard S., *The German Expressionists* (1957); Selz, Peter, *German Expressionist Painting* (1957).

Bruckner, Anton   [bruk'-nur, ahn'-tohn]

The Austrian composer Anton Bruckner was first recognized for his masterful improvisations on the organ. Although his symphonies and masses earned Bruckner only a small following during the late 19th century, they are widely appreciated today. (Ferry Bératon, 1889; Art History Museum, Vienna.)

The Austrian composer Josef Anton Bruckner, b. Sept. 4, 1824, is famous for his nine monumental symphonies in the tradition of Beethoven—classic in form, richly romantic in harmony and orchestration. Often misinterpreted during his lifetime as a mere imitator of Richard Wagner, he is recognized today not only as a great composer but also as a link between the Viennese classical school (Beethoven, Haydn, Mozart, and Schubert) and the major Austrian composers of the late 19th and early 20th centuries, Gustav Mahler and Arnold Schoenberg.

The most important influence on Bruckner's early years was the magnificent baroque monastery of Saint Florian, where he was first a chorister and student and later a teacher and organist. It remained a spiritual refuge for him throughout his life. In 1861, after intensive studies with the theorist and organist Simon Sechter, he began to study orchestration and form with Otto Kitzler, a theater conductor in Linz. Kitzler introduced him to the music of Wagner, a revelation that caused Bruckner's breakthrough to full musical maturity—symbolized by his Mass in D Minor (1864). The Mass in E Minor and the First Symphony followed (1866). His third and last great Mass, the Mass in F Minor, was completed in 1868 in gratitude for his recovery from a nervous breakdown. He also wrote many shorter choral pieces, both religious and secular. His one important chamber work is a beautiful string quintet.

In 1868, Bruckner moved to Vienna, where he was appointed professor of thorough bass, counterpoint, and organ

at the Vienna Conservatory. He was to spend the rest of his life in Vienna, teaching, composing, and playing the organ at the Imperial Court Chapel. He made highly successful tours to France (1869) and England (1871) as an organ virtuoso.

His symphonies, however, were often viciously attacked by the Viennese critics. His self-confidence shaken, he revised his symphonies many times (some went through as many as three versions) and even allowed his pupils to make changes in them. He carefully kept his original manuscripts for posterity, however, and today performances of his symphonies are based on his authentic scores. The first versions of the symphonies were completed as follows: no. 1 in C Minor, 1865–66; no. 2 in C Minor, 1871–72; no. 3 in D Minor (dedicated to Wagner), 1873–74; no. 4 in E-flat Major, 1874; no. 5 in B-flat Major, 1875–76; no. 6 in A Major, 1879–81; no. 7 in E Major, 1881–83; no. 8 in C Minor, 1884–87; and no. 9 in D Minor (dedicated to God), begun in 1891. Bruckner died on the afternoon of Oct. 11, 1896, after a morning spent working on his Ninth Symphony. (Only the first three movements were completed; his mighty "Te Deum" for chorus and orchestra is sometimes performed as a finale.) At his own request, he was buried under the organ in Saint Florian.

DIKA NEWLIN

Bibliography: Doernberg, Erwin, *The Life and Symphonies of Anton Bruckner* (1960); Newlin, Dika, *Bruckner, Mahler, Schoenberg*, rev. ed. (1978); Redlich, Hans F., *Bruckner and Mahler* (1963); Schönzeler, Hans-Hubert, *Bruckner*, rev. ed. (1978); Simpson, Robert, *The Essence of Bruckner* (1968); Watson, Derek, *Bruckner* (1975); Wolff, Werner, *Anton Bruckner* (1942; repr. 1972).

See also: GERMAN AND AUSTRIAN MUSIC; SYMPHONY.

Bruegel   (family) [broy'-guhl]

The Bruegel family of Flemish painters was among the most notable families of professional artists. **Peter Bruegel the Elder**, c.1525–1569, is now considered the most important Northern painter of the mid-16th century. He established the independence of landscape and genre subjects (scenes of everyday life) from traditional figural painting (see GENRE PAINTING; LANDSCAPE PAINTING). Although he frequently depicted scenes of rustic life, "Peasant Bruegel," as he was known, was not a peasant but a townsman. His friends and patrons were humanists. Unlike his predecessors, Bruegel painted almost entirely for private patrons and produced no surviving works for churches or other public buildings. Consequently, he was known in his own time primarily as an inventor of moralistic figural scenes and landscapes, which were reproduced in engravings by other artists.

Many of Bruegel's paintings have been interpreted as disguised criticism of the harsh Spanish control of the Netherlands. Bruegel was patronized, however, by Cardinal Antoine Perrenot de Granville, advisor to PHILIP II, and about 1563 he moved from Antwerp to Brussels, the seat of the Spanish government in the Netherlands. Given the sparse and contradictory evidence, Bruegel's political convictions remain unknown. Modern scholars are also unable to determine his religious beliefs. Bruegel probably viewed organized religion as an obstacle between man and God; his *Parable of the Blind*, also known as *The Blind Leading the Blind* (1568; Museo Nazionale di Capodimonte, Naples) may be interpreted as illustrating this idea.

Upon completing his artistic training in 1551, Bruegel traveled to Italy. In spite of the influences of this journey, he continued throughout his life to paint in a manner that was strongly Northern in both subject and style. Only close study of his works reveals that he absorbed figural poses and compositional ideas from Italian art. The journey through the Alps had a more obvious impact on Bruegel's artistic imagination. In a number of his landscapes, among them *Hunters in the Snow* (1565; Kunsthistorisches Museum, Vienna), tall mountains are placed in the backgrounds of his panoramic views while the centers and foregrounds depict typical Netherlandish settings and subjects.

Bruegel's painting style changed considerably during the short span of his career. His early works (until c.1562) are characterized by a multiplicity of small elements, an overall

Hunters in the Snow *(1565), by the Flemish painter Peter Bruegel the Elder, is one of a series of paintings representing the months of the year. In a solemn January landscape, a band of hunters and their dogs trudge wearily toward their homes, where villagers skate on the frozen ponds. (Kunsthistorisches Museum, Vienna.)*

composition, and a bird's-eye perspective. A typical example is *Netherlandish Proverbs* (1559; Staatliche Museum, West Berlin). Here, as in so many of his paintings, Bruegel satirizes the folly and sinfulness of humankind.

Two religious paintings, the *Suicide of Saul* (1562) and the *Conversion of St. Paul* (1567; both Kunsthistorisches Museum, Vienna), exemplify the changes that took place in Bruegel's style during the mid-1560s. These two paintings also show Bruegel's practice of depicting religious subjects as contemporary events. After *c.*1562, Bruegel's compositions were increasingly concentrated and were often organized along diagonals; the main action was more frequently presented at eye level.

During the last years of his life Bruegel usually painted figures that appear more monumental in scale and closer to the viewer. As in *The Blind Leading the Blind*, he steadily reduced his cast of characters to a minimum in order to concentrate the composition on the essentials of the story.

Two of Peter Bruegel's children were painters. **Peter ("Hell") Bruegel the Younger,** 1564–1638, frequently imitated his father's works. **Jan I ("Velvet") Bruegel the Elder**, 1568–1625, the more talented of the two sons, was court painter to the regents of the Southern Netherlands after 1610. Jan I favored a miniaturistic style. His landscapes, such as *Outskirts of a Village* (1597; State Art Collections, Kassel), differ considerably from the panoramic "world views" of his father; their mood, like their spaces, is more intimate. In his life-size flower paintings, such as *Flowers in a Blue Vase* (Kunsthistorisches Museum, Vienna), Jan I created an encyclopedic arrangement of the many individual flowers he studied from life. In his allegorical and religious paintings, such as *Para-*

dise (*c.*1620; Mauritshuis, The Hague), he occasionally collaborated with Peter Paul RUBENS and other painters.

Three of the next generation were painters: **Peter III** (1589–*c.*1634), son of Peter the Younger; and **Ambrosius** (1617–75) and **Jan the Younger** (1601–78), both sons of Jan I. Each imitated the work of his father. Five sons of Jan the Younger were artists: **Jan Peter, Abraham, Filips, Ferdinand,** and **Jan Baptist.** Abraham (1631–90), a still-life painter, was the most talented. None of these members of the family attained the artistic stature of Peter the Elder.   ZIRKA FILIPCZAK

Bibliography: Delevoy, Robert L., *Bruegel: Historical and Critical Study,* trans. by Stuart Gilbert (1959); Foote, Timothy, *The World of Bruegel: c.1525–1569* (1968); Gibson, Walter S., *Bruegel* (1977; repr. 1985); Grossmann, Fritz, *Pieter Bruegel: Complete Edition of the Paintings,* 3d ed. (1973); Münz, Ludwig, *Bruegel: The Drawings* (1961); Winkelmann-Rhein, Gertraude, *The Painting and Drawings of Jan "Flower" Bruegel* (1969).

See also: FLEMISH ART AND ARCHITECTURE.

Bruges   [broozh]

Bruges (Flemish: Brugge) is the capital of West Flanders province in northwestern Belgium. It lies 16 km (10 mi) from the North Sea on the flat, alluvial northern plain. The name is derived from a Roman bridge that crossed one of the many streams of this region. The city has a population of 118,146 (1983 est.). The old section of Bruges has twisting streets and a large market square, which is dominated by a late medieval belfry and a market hall. The old city is enclosed by canals.

Bruges rose to prosperity during the 12th century as the chief port and one of the most important textile centers in

Flanders. It was also a hub of the English and Scandinavian trade. Its decline was initiated by the increasing difficulty of navigating the Zwin River, which linked it with the sea, and by civil strife. In the 16th century its place as a trade center was taken by Antwerp.

Bruges revived as a port in the 19th century when a canal was cut to the sea at Zeebrugge. Manufacturing subsequently increased. But Bruges depends primarily on tourists attracted by the city's famous Beguinage, a retreat for nuns, and its fine collections of Flemish art. Much of the medieval city has been preserved.   NORMAN J. G. POUNDS

Brugge: see BRUGES.

Brugmann, Karl   [brug'-mahn]

The German philologist Karl Brugmann, b. Mar. 16, 1849, d. June 29, 1919, is noted for his methodical research in comparative and historical linguistics. Brugmann's major contribution to the literature of the field is his 5-volume *Outline of the Comparative Grammar of Indo-Germanic Languages*, first published in 1886. The last revised volume appeared in 1916.
                                               F. P. DINNEEN, S. J.

Bruhn, Erik   [broon]

Erik Bruhn, b. Copenhagen, Oct. 3, 1928, d. Apr. 1, 1986, was one of the great *danseurs nobles* (classical male dancers) of his generation, noted for his pure technique and dramatic depth. His career began with the Royal Danish Ballet in 1947, and he soon began appearing internationally, notably with American Ballet Theatre (ABT). Bruhn's portrayals of James in August Bournonville's *La Sylphide*, of Don José in Roland Petit's *Carmen*, and of Jean in Birgit Cullberg's *Miss Julie* are justly celebrated. His own choreography included *Romeo and Juliet*, a pas de deux danced with his frequent partner Carla Fracci. Bruhn served (1967–71) as director of the Royal Swedish Ballet. After a period of retirement he returned to dancing in character roles. He also staged several works for the National Ballet of Canada and was that company's artistic director from 1983 to 1986.   MICHAEL ROBERTSON

Brûlé, Étienne   [brue'-lay]

The French explorer Étienne Brûlé, b. *c*.1592, was probably the first European to see the Great Lakes. He went to Canada in 1608 with Samuel de CHAMPLAIN, who sent him westward in 1610. Sometime in the following four years Brûlé apparently discovered Lake Huron. In 1615, Brûlé followed the Susquehanna River to Chesapeake Bay, and during the early 1620s he probably discovered Lakes Superior and Erie. He betrayed Champlain in 1629, guiding an English fleet up the St. Lawrence River to capture Quebec. From 1629, Brûlé lived with Huron Indians, who killed him in 1633.

Brummell, Beau   [bruhm'-uhl]

George Bryan Brummell, b. June 7, 1778, d. Mar. 30, 1840, was an English dandy popularly known as Beau Brummell. A friend of the prince regent (later GEORGE IV), he was the arbiter of English clothing fashions in the early 1800s, popularizing trousers and elaborate cravats. His sharp wit eventually alienated his patron, and Brummell fled to France in 1816 to avoid paying gambling debts. He died in an insane asylum.

Brundage, Avery   [bruhn'-dij]

Avery Brundage, b. Detroit, Sept. 28, 1887, d. May 8, 1975, was a leader in American and international amateur sports and served as vice-president (1945–52) and president (1952–72) of the International Olympic Committee. He was also a successful Chicago businessman and a collector of Oriental art. Brundage's interest in international sports began with his participation in the decathlon at the 1912 Olympic Games. He was also the U.S. all-around track champion three times. A defender of amateurism, the often controversial Brundage was

president of the Amateur Athletic Union for 7 terms and chairman of the U.S. Olympic Committee for 24 years.

Brundtland, Gro Harlem

Norway's first woman prime minister, Gro Harlem Brundtland, b. Apr. 20, 1939, served as environment minister from 1974 to 1979. After becoming Labor party leader, she was premier from February to October 1981, and from 1986 to 1989, returning to head a third government in November 1990.

Brunei   [broo'-ny]

Brunei, a small Islamic sultanate on the northwest coast of Borneo, is surrounded by the Malaysian state of SARAWAK. The center of a commercial empire before the 15th century, it was under British protection from 1888 to 1984.

LAND, PEOPLE, AND ECONOMY

The country is divided into two enclaves by the disputed Limbang River watershed, which Brunei has unsuccessfully attempted to recover from Malaysia. Most of the land is covered by tropical forests. Only 5% is cultivated, and Brunei must import food. The petroleum and natural-gas industry, concentrated along the northwest coast and offshore, accounts for 85% of the gross domestic product. At current rates of production, proven petroleum reserves should last until 2014, natural gas until 2022. The population is 68.8% Malay, 5% other indigenous groups, 18.3% Chinese, and 7.9% Indian and others. Malays are concentrated in public services, while Chinese dominate commerce. Malays and indigenous natives are citizens; most Chinese are stateless. New stringent naturalization laws permit very few permanent residents to become citizens, and 25–40% of the labor force consists of temporary immigrant workers. Petroleum has given Brunei a high per capita income; citizens pay no income tax and enjoy free education, health care, and other benefits.

NEGARA BRUNEI DARUSSALAM

LAND. Area: 5,765 km² (2,226 mi²). Capital and largest city: Bandar Seri Begawan (Brunei Town; 1988 est. pop., 52,300).
PEOPLE. Population (1990 est.): 372,108; density: 52 persons per km² (135 per mi²). Distribution (1989): 59% urban, 41% rural. Annual growth (1989): 2.7%. Official language: Malay. Major religions: Islam (official), Buddhism, animism, Christianity.
EDUCATION AND HEALTH. Literacy (1984): 80% of adult population. Universities (1989): 1. Hospital beds (1986): 876. Physicians (1986): 171. Life expectancy (1989): 71. Infant mortality (1989): 11 per 1,000 live births.
ECONOMY. GDP (1987): $3.1 billion; $13,663 per capita. Labor distribution (1988): agriculture and fishing—5%; manufacturing (1986)—8.6%; commerce and services—25%; construction—19%; government and public authorities (1986)—40%. Foreign trade (1987): imports—$650 million; exports—$2.3 billion; principal trade partners—Japan, Singapore, United States. Currency: 1 Brunei dollar = 100 sen.
GOVERNMENT. Type: constitutional sultanate. Political subdivisions: 4 districts.
COMMUNICATIONS. Railroads (1987): 19 km (12 mi) total. Roads (1986): 1,860 km (1,156 mi) total, 50% paved. Major ports: 1. Major airfields: 1.

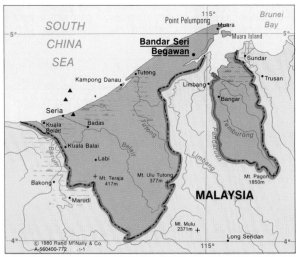

BRUNEI

Railroad

National capitals are underlined

Scale 1 : 2,000,000

▲   Major Oil Field

+   Spot Elevation

0   10   20   30   40   50 km

0   10   20   30 mi

HISTORY AND GOVERNMENT

Brunei may have existed as a commercial center as early as the 6th century. It emerged as a powerful independent sultanate after its ruler converted to Islam in the 15th century, collecting tribute from northern Borneo and the southern Philippines. After Malacca fell to the Portuguese in 1511, Brunei flourished as the most powerful Muslim state in Southeast Asia until the 17th century, when its power waned and it lost much of its territory. To avoid complete extinction as a state, it sought and received British protection in 1888. Japanese occupation during World War II was followed by renewed British protection. Brunei rejected an invitation to join the newly created Federation of Malaysia in 1964. Relations with Malaysia were strained but improved after Brunei became independent in January 1984. The current sultan heads a government composed mostly of family members and technocrats.

GORDON P. MEANS

Bibliography: Singh, D. S. R., *Brunei, 1839–1983* (1984); Tarling, N., *Britain, the Brookes, and Brunei* (1971); Tate, D. J. M., *The Making of Modern Southeast Asia*, 2 vols. (1977–79).

Brunel   (family)   [broo-nel']

Isambard Kingdom Brunel, an English engineer, is best known for building bridges and railroads, and for designing the first transatlantic steamer and the first large iron steamship. He is seen here in 1858 in front of the anchor chains of his Great Eastern, *at that time and for decades to come the largest steamship afloat.*

Two Brunels, father and son, were engineers, designers, and builders, both in Europe and America, during the 19th century. **Marc Isambard Brunel**, b. France, Apr. 25, 1769, d. London, Dec. 12, 1849, was a Royalist exile from the French Revolution who fled to America in 1793. After practicing as an architect and a canal designer, he became New York City's chief engineer. In 1799 he moved to England, where he made important contributions in shipbuilding and textile production. His most enduring work was the construction of the first Thames TUNNEL (1824–43), for which he invented an iron shield that reduced the risk of the water breakthroughs that had prevented previous tunneling under the Thames.

His son, **Isambard Kingdom Brunel**, b. Portsmouth, England, Apr. 9, 1806, d. Sept. 15, 1859, designed many bridges, tunnels, and viaducts and was one of the first to use compressed-air CAISSONS to sink bridge foundations into deep riverbeds. He was also a railroad builder and the designer of London's Paddington Station. His greatest work was the design and construction of three oceangoing steamships, each the first of its type. The paddle-steamer *Great Western* (1838) was the first transatlantic passenger steamship in regular service; it made the Bristol–New York crossing in a spectacular 15 days. The *Great Britain* (1845) was the first large screw-driven oceangoing steamship. The GREAT EASTERN (1858), the largest steam vessel of its time, was designed to make the round trip to Australia without recoaling.

Bibliography: Brunel, Isambard, *The Life of Isambard Kingdom Brunel* (1870; repr. 1972); Pugsley, A., ed., *The Works of Isambard Brunel* (1980).

Brunelleschi, Filippo   [broo-nel-les'-kee, fee-leep'-poh]

The Pazzi Chapel, designed by the early Florentine Renaissance architect Filippo Brunelleschi, was commissioned about 1429 by the Pazzi family to be a chapter house for the monastic church of Santa Croce in Florence. The chapel, begun about 1442, is noted for its subtle proportions and classical decoration.

Filippo Brunelleschi, b. 1377, d. Apr. 15, 1446, was one of the earliest and greatest architects of the Florentine Renaissance. The well-educated son of a lawyer, he engaged first in goldsmith work and sculpture but soon turned to architecture. In 1419 he received a major commission for the Ospedale degli Innocenti (Foundling Hospital); in 1421 he began work on the vast dome of Florence's cathedral, left unfinished in the 14th century because of seemingly insoluble structural problems; and in 1421 he began work on the church of San Lorenzo. These buildings, which took years to complete, mark the beginning of the Renaissance—the dome of the cathedral for its technical innovations, the other buildings for their style. The octagonal dome is 39 m (130 ft) in diameter and 91 m (300 ft) high, with a 16-m (52-ft) lantern crowning it. By devising new scaffolding and hoists, by making the dome a self-supporting double shell, and by using new and lighter masonry, Brunelleschi was able to solve the problems that had defeated his predecessors. To the astonishment of his contemporaries, the soaring structure was completed without centering (supporting scaffolding).

The church of San Lorenzo and the Ospedale were created in a new style, in which the details of classical architecture—columns, arches, and pilasters—are used with a fresh approach, each element being distinctly and visibly in proportion with all other elements. This system of harmonious proportions is the basis of most Renaissance architecture. Brunelleschi was able to begin much more; in 1434 he started work on the first centrally planned church of the Renaissance, Santa Maria degli Angeli; in 1436 the church of Santo Spirito was begun; and in the 1440s, the construction got under way on the elegant Pazzi Chapel in Santa Croce. Each building is a further refinement of his style, the details being purer and more delicate, the internal order and modular planning successively more consistent and more tightly organized.

Brunelleschi's biographer Antonio Manetti (1423–97) notes that sometime between 1417 and 1420, Brunelleschi painted two panels demonstrating new schemes of perspective, techniques he may have discovered in his painstaking architectural studies of actual buildings. These schemes established the form of all subsequent perspective painting in the Renaissance. The importance of Brunelleschi's buildings and methods cannot be overestimated. His work was the model for much that followed, and his influence on his successors, such as Michelangelo and Donato Bramante, was enormous. By his achievement he asserted a new position for the artist in Renaissance society.   DAVID CAST

Bibliography: Heydenreich, L. H., and Lotz, Wolfgang, *Architecture in Italy, 1400–1600* (1974); Manetti, Antonio, *The Life of Brunelleschi,* trans. by Catherine Engass (1970); Prager, Frank, and Scaglia, Gustina, *Brunelleschi* (1970); Saalman, Howard, *Filippo Brunelleschi,* ed. by John Harris and Alastair Laing (1986).

Bruner, Jerome Seymour

The American psychologist Jerome Seymour Bruner, b. New York City, Oct. 1, 1915, has made a significant contribution to the field of COGNITIVE PSYCHOLOGY, particularly through his research on perception and on how children learn. Bruner taught from 1945 to 1972 at Harvard, where he was a founder (1961) and codirector of the Center for Cognitive Studies. He later taught at Oxford University and, from 1981 to 1988, at the New School for Social Research in New York City.

Bruner, as a coauthor of *A Study of Thinking* (1965), developed a theory of CONCEPT FORMATION AND ATTAINMENT. Other books include *The Process of Education* (1960), *Toward a Theory of Instruction* (1966), *Child's Talk* (1983), the autobiographical *In Search of Mind* (1983), and *Actual Minds, Possible Worlds* (1986).

Brunetière, Ferdinand   [brue-nuh-tee-air']

Ferdinand Brunetière, b. July 19, 1849, d. Dec. 9, 1906, was a French literary historian and critic who became editor of the influential *Revue des Deux Mondes* in 1893. He is remembered chiefly for his opposition to naturalism and its leading exponent, Émile Zola.   ROBIN BUSS

Brunhild   [broon'-hilt]

In Norse mythology, Brunhild was the leader of the VALKYRIES. When she disobeyed Odin and spared Siegmund and Sieglinde, the incestuous siblings who parented Sigurd (SIEGFRIED), Odin made her mortal and surrounded her with a circle of fire, where she would sleep until roused by a hero's kiss. The "hero" Siegfried performed this chore, but a magic potion caused him to forget Brunhild (who believed he had forsaken her) and marry Gudrun. In disguise, Siegfried later caused Brunhild to marry Gudrun's brother, Gunther. When Brunhild learned of the deception, she had Siegfried murdered and then killed herself on his funeral pyre. In Wagner's opera cycle RING OF THE NIBELUNG, she is called Brünnehilde.

Brüning, Heinrich   [brue'-ning]

Heinrich Brüning, b. Nov. 26, 1885, d. Mar. 30, 1970, was chancellor of Germany (1930–32) in the period of crisis preceding the Nazi assumption of power. A financial expert and leader of the Roman Catholic Center party, Brüning proposed a program of tax increases and budget cuts to counter the economic depression. This conservative program was defeated in the Reichstag, but Brüning continued to govern under emergency powers granted him by President Hindenburg. Although these powers were constitutional, their use marked the breakdown of parliamentary government.

As the economic crisis worsened and political polarization increased, Brüning was replaced (May 30, 1932) by Franz von Papen. Brüning left Germany in 1933 and spent much of the rest of his life in the United States, where he taught (1939–52) at Harvard University.

Brunner, Emil

A Swiss Protestant, Heinrich Emil Brunner, b. Dec. 23, 1889, d. Apr. 6, 1966, was one of the best known of the neoorthodox theologians, who rejected 19th-century liberal theology. After serving as a pastor, he was appointed (1924) professor of theology at Zurich. Like other neoorthodox theologians, Brunner insisted on the primacy of revelation, but he also accorded reason a limited role in knowledge of God, and this partial acceptance of natural theology brought him into sharp conflict with Karl Barth. Influenced by Martin Buber, Brunner understood revelation as a personal encounter and believed that only secondarily does it assume propositional form. His theology as a whole is less rigid than Barth's but also less consistent and less profound. Among his many books translated into English are *The Theology of Crisis* (1929), *The Divine-Human Encounter* (1943), and *Christianity and Civilization* (1948–49).

JOHN MACQUARRIE

Bibliography: Humphrey, J. E., *Emil Brunner* (1976; repr. 1984); Kegley, C. W., ed., *The Theology of Emil Brunner* (1962).

Bruno, Giordano

Giordano Bruno, b. 1548, d. Feb. 17, 1600, is perhaps the best-known philosopher of the Italian Renaissance. Ordained a Dominican priest in 1575, he was accused of heresy and in 1576 left his order. After some travel and further study, he taught (1580–81) theology at Toulouse. Soon he found favor with Henry III, who in 1583 sent him to England, where he taught at Oxford. Following sojourns in Marburg, Wittenberg, Prague, and Frankfurt, he went back to Venice, where in 1592 he was imprisoned by the Inquisition. Refusing to recant, he was burned as a heretic. Bruno's philosophy owed much to such diverse sources as Thomas Aquinas, Averroës, Copernicus, John Scotus Erigena, Marsilio Ficino, Nicholas of Cusa, and the Hermetic literature. In his *De umbris idearum* (On Shadows of Ideas), Bruno pictured nature in all its multiplicity descending from divine unity to matter and darkness. At once, he distinguished God from the world and yet tended toward a completely contrary pantheism. His insistence on divine immanence, linked with a doctrine of panpsychism (belief that reality is constituted by the mind), anticipated both Gottfried Leibniz and Baruch Spinoza. He rejected the geocentric and anthropocentric universe, believing that the Earth and human individuals are ultimately accidents of a single living world-substance.   JOHN P. DOYLE

Bibliography: Michel, P. H., *The Cosmology of Giordano Bruno,* trans. by R. Maddison (1973); Yates, Frances, *Giordano Bruno and the Hermetic Tradition* (1969; repr. 1979).

Brunswick

A historic duchy and province in northwestern Germany, Brunswick (German: Braunschweig) is now part of the state of Lower Saxony (Niedersachsen). The region occupies a transition zone between the fertile North German Plain in the north and the Harz Mountains in the south. Its major cities include BRAUNSCHWEIG and Wolfsburg, the location of the main Volkswagen plant in Germany.

Brunswick was constituted as a duchy in the 13th century, but it was subsequently repeatedly divided among branches

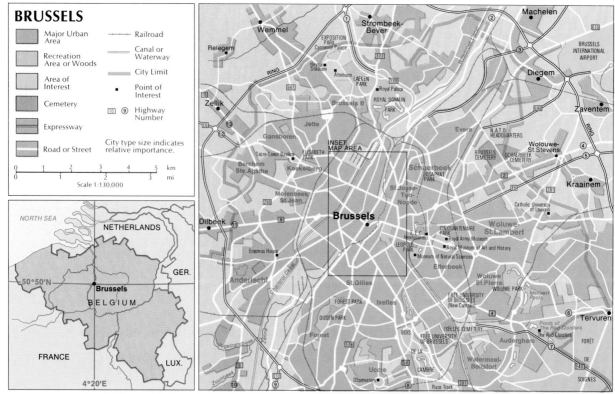

BRUSSELS

Major Urban Area	——— Railroad
Recreation Area or Woods	=== Canal or Waterway
Area of Interest	City Limit
Cemetery	▪ Point of Interest
Expressway	⑩ ⑨ Highway Number
Road or Street	City type size indicates relative importance.

Scale 1:130,000

of the ruling WELF family. One of its subdivisions became the electorate of HANOVER. In 1918, Brunswick became a state of the German (Weimar) Republic, and in 1946 it was incorporated into Lower Saxony.

Brunswik, Egon

Egon Brunswik, b. Mar. 18, 1903, d. July 7, 1955, was a Hungarian-born American psychologist noted for his research in stimulation and perception. He also raised the question of the ecological validity of experiments in psychology, that is, the extent to which laboratory findings could be applied to situations in real life.

Brusilov, Aleksei Alekseyevich   [broo-see'-lawf]

As commander (1915–16) of the Russian Southwestern Front during World War I, Aleksei Alekseyevich Brusilov, b. Aug. 19 (N.S.), 1853, d. Mar. 17, 1926, achieved a spectacular breakthrough against Austro-German forces. The Brusilov Offensive (June–September 1916) shattered the Austrian army, but the high Russian casualties also weakened the tsarist government. Supreme Russian commander in 1917, Brusilov sustained wounds in the Bolshevik Revolution of that year but served in the Soviet army until 1924. His memoirs, *A Soldier's Notebook, 1914–1918*, were published in English in 1930.

Brussels

Brussels (Flemish: Brussel; French: Bruxelles) is the capital of Belgium and of Brabant province. Greater Brussels is by far the country's largest metropolitan area, with a population of 970,500 (1989 est.). Brussels is located on the rolling plain in the center of the country, about 40 km (25 mi) south of Antwerp. It straddles the small Senne (Zenne) River, which joins the Rupel, a tributary of the Scheldt. The Willebroek Canal has been cut from the city to the Scheldt, permitting waterborne transportation to Antwerp. Southward, the Charleroi Canal connects Brussels to the Meuse River.

Brussels is mainly a French-speaking city, but it lies within the predominantly Flemish region of Belgium. Thus it is at the center of a long-standing struggle between the two linguistic

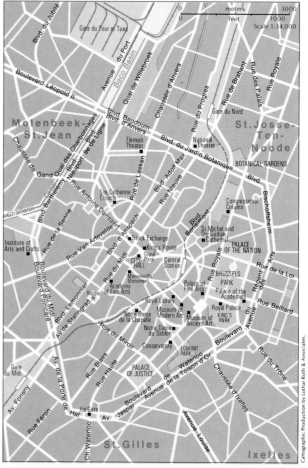

Cartographic Production by Lothar Roth & Associates.

communities of Belgium. In 1970 the Free University of Brussels (founded 1834) divided into two independent institutions, one French-speaking, the other Flemish.

Contemporary City. The old city in the Senne Valley is enclosed by a wide boulevard; this follows the course of the city walls, which were torn down in 1831. Within lies the Grande Place, or Great Square, noted for its 15th-century town hall and gabled 17th-century guild houses. The upper town lies on higher ground to the east and is, like the old city, within the line of the former city walls. It contains the Gothic Cathedral of Saint Michel and Sainte Gudule, the Royal Palace, the Palace of Justice, and the Palace of the Nation, where the Belgian legislature meets. The Senne River, which once formed the axis of the old city, now flows underground, beneath the central north-south boulevard.

During the 19th century, Brussels expanded far beyond the line of its medieval walls, but until 1970 it remained for purposes of local government an agglomeration of 19 separate communes. These were then merged, and in 1989 the city became one of Belgium's three federated regions, with its own elected administration. Brussels is the chief manufacturing center of Belgium. Industries include engineering, chemical and paper manufacture, and food processing. The major industrial quarters lie to the north along the Senne Valley. Brussels is the hub of Belgium's road and railroad network and has one of Europe's most important airports.

The government has long been a major employer in Brussels, and many additional jobs were created when the European Community (EC) established its headquarters there, beginning in 1958. By the 1990s the EC-related service sector represented a high proportion of the city's economy. Brussels is also the headquarters of NATO.

History. Brussels developed in the early Middle Ages around a castle beside the marshes of the Senne Valley, and its early name, Bruoc-sella, means "marshy settlement." By the 11th century it had become a small, walled town, which grew to be a center of the cloth industry and the seat of the dukes of Brabant. An illustrious period in Brussels's history began in 1430, when Brabant became a possession of the dukes of Burgundy. The city's wealth and importance declined in the 16th century, when it became the capital of the Spanish Netherlands. It was partially destroyed by war in 1695, after which the upper town was replanned.

The modern growth of Brussels dates from its establishment in 1830 as the capital of an independent Belgian state. The old walls were replaced by new boulevards, and new residential quarters were laid out.   NORMAN J. G. POUNDS

Brussels griffon

The Brussels griffon is a toy breed of dog. Its short muzzle, large, dark eyes, and long face hair give it a striking expression. It stands about 20 cm (8 in) at the shoulder and weighs 3.5–4.5 kg (8–10 lb); show dogs must not weigh more than 5.4 kg (12 lb). The large, domed head has high-set, semierect ears that may be cropped, and the erect tail is docked to about a third of its length for shows. The thickset body has either a hard, wiry coat or a smooth one. The color may be

The Brussels griffon, a toy dog, was developed from the affenpinscher and the griffon d'écurie of Belgium. This terrierlike dog was originally bred as a ratter and later became a driver's companion in the hansom cabs of 19th-century England.

reddish brown, black and reddish brown mixed, black with reddish brown markings, or solid black; the last is not permitted in smooth-coated dogs by official kennel clubs.

The breed originated in the 17th century from crosses between the affenpinscher and the Belgian street dog. Later the pug and the ruby spaniel were introduced, and the accepted standard for the breed was established in the late 19th century. Although generally obedient and easily managed, the Brussels griffon can be stubborn on the leash and may be difficult to train without persistent effort.   JOHN MANDEVILLE

brussels sprouts

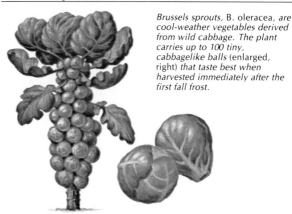

Brussels sprouts, B. oleracea, are cool-weather vegetables derived from wild cabbage. The plant carries up to 100 tiny, cabbagelike balls (enlarged, right) that taste best when harvested immediately after the first fall frost.

Brussels sprouts, *Brassica oleracea*, vegetables belonging to the mustard family, Cruciferae, are closely related to cabbage, cauliflower, collards, broccoli, and kohlrabi. Wild cabbage is the common ancestor for these plants, which are collectively termed *cole crops*. Brussels sprouts are grown for the numerous edible axillary buds on each plant. They are so named because they were first grown in quantity near Brussels, Belgium, during the 16th century.

Best growth occurs during an extended period of cool temperatures (10°–20° C/50°–68° F), and 90–120 days are required from transplanting to harvest. U.S. commercial production is limited to the midcoastal area of California and some areas of New York State. Production is extensive in Western Europe, where brussels sprouts are a popular vegetable.

The plant is biennial, producing an upright stout stem bearing many long petioled, round, waxy leaves and vegetative buds (the sprouts) in the leaf axils in the first year. Conspicuous yellow flowers are produced in the second year.

Seeds are usually planted in field nurseries, and the resulting seedlings are transplanted to the production field. Each plant requires about 60–90 cm (24–36 in) of field space.

Multiple hand-harvests have now been largely replaced by once-over harvests in which mechanical aids are used to remove the sprouts from the stems. Brussels sprouts are grown for sale both fresh and frozen.   DONALD N. MAYNARD

Brustein, Robert

The American theater critic and educator Robert Brustein, b. New York City, Apr. 21, 1927, was dean of the Yale Drama School and founder and artistic director of the Yale Repertory Theatre from 1966 to 1978, during which time Yale became one of the foremost theater training schools in the United States. Brustein's drama criticism has appeared for many years in *The New Republic* and other publications. Frequently aimed at what he considers the low state of theater in the United States, Brustein's work includes a study of modern drama, *The Theatre of Revolt* (1964), and such essay collections as *Seasons of Discontent* (1965), *Revolution as Theatre* (1971), and *Who Needs Theatre* (1987). Since 1979, Brustein has been director of the Loeb Drama Center at Harvard University, where he founded and directs the American Repertory Theatre Company.

Brustolon, Andrea   [broo-stoh-lohn']

Andrea Brustolon, b. July 20, 1662, d. Oct. 25, 1732, was an Italian woodcarver and furniture designer. By 1684 his earliest recorded work, a pair of angels, was completed for the Frari in Venice. His exotic baroque style culminated in a set of furniture (1690s; Palazzo Rezzonico, Venice), including 12 chairs, two *guéridons*, and a vase stand.   JUDITH APPLEGATE

Bibliography: Honour, Hugh, *Cabinet Makers and Furniture Designers*, (1969).

Brut

In the Arthurian legends, Brut was the founder of the Arthurian dynasty of ancient Britain. A great-grandson of the Trojan hero AENEAS, he led a group of Trojan exiles from Greece to Britain, where he ruled for 24 years.

brutalism

Brutalism, or new brutalism, was an avant-garde movement in modern architecture, in part growing out of the later work of LE CORBUSIER, that received its name in the early 1950s and gained wide acceptance in the 1960s. It is usually characterized by a preference for strong contrasts of simple shapes, a "puritanical" exposure of concrete as a building material, and expression of structural systems on the exteriors of buildings. It is particularly identified with the wife-husband team of Alison and Peter SMITHSON. Although the term was never intended to mean that buildings in this style are brutal to their occupants or their surroundings, the bold shapes of brutalist architecture have sometimes been criticized as insensitive impositions on the environment. Undercurrents of this connotation led to a decline of the style in the 1970s, although widely admired architects such as Louis KAHN successfully drew on stylistic aspects of both brutalism and the INTERNATIONAL STYLE.
                                                          RON WIEDENHOEFT

Bibliography: Banham, Reyner, *The New Brutalism* (1966); Pehnt, Wolfgang, ed., *Encyclopedia of Modern Architecture* (1964).

Brutus, Marcus Junius

Marcus Junius Brutus, b. *c.*85 BC, achieved fame as one of the chief assassins of Julius Caesar. His mother, Servilia, was a half-sister of CATO the Younger and reputed mistress of Caesar. Later adopted by Quintus Servilius Caepio, Brutus took the name Quintus Caepio Brutus. Brutus accompanied Cato to Cyprus in 58 and served the eminent Appius Claudius Pulcher as quaestor in Cilicia during 53 BC.

Although Brutus supported POMPEY THE GREAT, Caesar pardoned him after Pompey's defeat and treated him well. He became governor of Cisalpine Gaul in 46 and a praetor in 44. Nonetheless, Brutus joined the conspiracy against Caesar. Disappointed by the events after the assassination, he joined forces with Gaius CASSIUS LONGINUS to meet Mark ANTONY and Octavian (later Emperor AUGUSTUS) at Philippi. Defeated there, Brutus committed suicide in November 42 BC.

Brutus had a genuine appreciation of philosophy and was a sincere patriot within the narrow limits of the aristocratic republican tradition. He scrupulously opposed the assassination of anyone except Caesar and hoped for the restoration of the free republic without further violence. Unfortunately, he little understood the situation.   ALLEN M. WARD

Bibliography: Radin, Max, *Marcus Brutus* (1939); Syme, Ronald, *The Revolution* (1939).

Bry, Théodore de   [bree, tay-oh-dohr' duh]

Théodore de Bry, b. 1528, d. Mar. 27, 1598, was a Flemish publisher and engraver whose portraits of famous contemporaries and depictions of notable events, such as the 34 engravings of *The Funeral Procession of Sir Philip Sydney* (1587), are primary sources for the study of the 16th century. Assisted by renowned British cosmographer Richard HAKLUYT, de Bry produced a series of illustrated travel books, *Collectiones peregrinationum* (1590–1634). He also produced the engraved illustrations for the books of J. J. Boissard and Thomas HARRIOT.

Bryan, Kirk

Kirk Bryan, b. Albuquerque, N.Mex., July 22, 1888, d. Aug. 21, 1950, taught geology at Harvard from 1926 until his death. He first worked (1912–26) for the U.S. Geological Survey on the problems of water resources in arid regions and made the first geological study of desert landforms. He earned his Ph.D. at Yale in 1920. In 1924–25, he joined an archaeological excavation in Chaco Canyon, N.Mex., to study the history of climatic conditions on the site, the first of many collaborations with archaeologists. His work on climatic change in the recent geological past, using the evidence from ancient soils and pollen, stimulated much of the later general interest in such studies that led in turn to development of the scientific discipline known as paleoecology.

Bibliography: Johnson, Frederick, "Kirk Bryan: 1888–1950," *American Antiquity*, vol. 16 (1951).

Bryan, William Jennings

William Jennings Bryan, shown holding a baby during a political campaign, was three times the Democratic nominee for the U.S. presidency, but he never won. A charismatic speaker, he championed the Free Silver movement. Bryan is also remembered for his role as prosecution counsel in the 1925 "Monkey Trial" in which schoolteacher John T. Scopes was convicted for teaching evolutionary theory in the Tennessee public schools.

A U.S. congressman, three-time Democratic presidential nominee, and secretary of state, William Jennings Bryan was a major force in American politics for three decades. Bryan was born on Mar. 19, 1860, in Salem, Ill. He attended college, studied law, and entered legal practice in Illinois before moving to Lincoln, Nebr., in 1887. Elected to Congress in 1890 and reelected in 1892, he argued for inflationary policies, including FREE SILVER, and fought a losing battle against repeal (1893) of the Sherman Silver Purchase Act.

Failing in a bid for a U.S. Senate seat in 1894, Bryan became editor of the *Omaha World-Herald*. He was out of public office in 1895 and 1896, but he reached a wide audience as a speaker at political gatherings and Chautauqua meetings. By 1896 his party was bitterly divided between gold Democrats, led by Grover CLEVELAND, and free-silver advocates. The silverites controlled the party's 1896 convention, and Bryan, confirming his position as free silver's champion through his dramatic "Cross of Gold" speech, was nominated for president. He conducted an active campaign and received many more votes in losing than Cleveland had in winning in 1892.

When nominated for president again in 1900, Bryan insisted on a platform endorsing free silver but emphasized imperialism as a more important issue. He attacked the administration of incumbent William MCKINLEY for having fought the Spanish-American War (1898) and acquiring the Philippines. Bryan's antiimperialist credentials were not unblemished, however. He had volunteered for military service and had urged, albeit on tactical grounds, passage of the treaty annexing the Philippines. Defeated by a larger margin in 1900 than in 1896, Bryan nevertheless retained his hold on rank-and-file Democrats through frequent speaking engagements and distribution of the *Commoner*, a weekly newspaper he edited and published (1901–1913). In 1908 he won the Democratic nomination for a third time but again lost the election.

In 1912, Woodrow WILSON, whom Bryan had supported at the Democratic convention, won the presidential election and named Bryan secretary of state. Bryan supported Wilson's Mexican intervention (1914), but, preferring peaceful diplomacy, he persuaded 30 nations to sign treaties that committed them to arbitration of international disputes. When World War I broke out in Europe in 1914, Bryan advocated strict neutrality, including restrictions against American travel on belligerent vessels and the prohibition of loans to Britain and France. These views placed him at odds with the administration, and he resigned (June 1915) during the LUSITANIA crisis.

Bryan was a political evangelist. Often ahead of his time as a spokesman for liberal causes, he was also closely identified with traditionalism, particularly with fundamentalist Christianity. In 1924 he drafted legislation to prevent the teaching of Darwinist evolutionary theory in Florida's public schools, and in 1925 he served as a prosecution lawyer in the SCOPES TRIAL, a Tennessee case involving a similar law. Taking the stand in defense of the Bible's authority, Bryan was subjected to a devastating cross-examination by the defense attorney, Clarence DARROW. Bryan won the case, but he died less than a week later, on July 26, 1925.   GERALD W. McFARLAND

Bibliography: Bryan, William Jennings, *The First Battle*, 2 vols. (1896; repr. 1971), and *Memoirs*, ed. by Mary B. Bryan (1925; repr. 1970); Coletta, P. E., *William Jennings Bryan*, 3 vols. (1964–69); Curti, M., *Bryan and World Peace* (1971); Glad, P. W., *The Trumpet Soundeth: William Jennings Bryan and His Democracy, 1896–1912* (1960; repr. 1986); Levine, Lawrence W., *Defender of the Faith* (1987).

Bryant, Bear

Paul William "Bear" Bryant, b. Kingsland, Ark., Sept. 11, 1913, d. Jan. 26, 1983, was by popular and professional consensus the greatest American college football coach. After playing end for the University of Alabama and serving in the navy during World War II, Bryant was head coach at Maryland for one year (1945) before moving on to Kentucky (1946–53), Texas A&M (1954–57), and Alabama (1958–82). It was mostly at the last school that Bryant achieved his impressive record: 6 won or shared national championships, 3 Coach of the Year awards, 15 victories in a record 29 bowl-game appearances, and a won-lost record of 323-85, with 17 ties. His record of 323 lifetime victories was broken in 1985 by Eddie Robinson of Grambling State University (La.). Bryant coached 54 All-Americans, and 47 men who played for or coached under him became collegiate or professional head coaches. Bryant retired about a month before his death.

Bibliography: Bryant, Paul W., with John Underwood, *Bear* (1974); Peterson, J. A., and Cromartie, B., *Bear Bryant*, 2d ed. (1983).

Bryant, William Cullen

William Cullen Bryant was a 19th-century American journalist and romantic poet. When "Thanatopsis," his major work, was submitted for publication, it was initially rejected by the North American Review on the grounds that no American could have produced a work of such sophistication. During his career as a newspaper editor, Bryant took an active role in public affairs, speaking out against slavery and political corruption.

William Cullen Bryant, b. Cummington, Mass., Nov. 3, 1794, d. June 12, 1878, was a journalist, literary critic, and public speaker and the first significant poet in 19th-century American literature. Along with the landscapes of the Hudson River painters, a group that included many of his friends, his writings symbolize the intense love of nature prominent in the romantic period. Bryant's two best-known poems, composed in 1815, are "To a Waterfowl" and "Thanatopsis," a blank-verse lyric in which death is portrayed as the inevitable absorption into nature. Its metrical form, graveyard theme, melancholy tone, and panoramic imagery make "Thanatopsis" an important document of American romanticism. In 1815, Bryant was admitted to the Massachusetts bar, but in 1825 he switched his profession from law to literature and left his native New England for New York City. He edited the *New York Evening Post* for 50 years and made it one of the country's most noteworthy liberal newspapers. He supported Andrew Jackson and the Democrats, defended the right of workers to strike, spoke out against slavery, proposed a central park for the city, helped to organize the Republican party, and fought the Tweed ring. His literary criticism showed similar liberal concerns. Bryant wrote several of his best poems while in New York: "A Forest Hymn" (1825), "The Prairies" (1833), and "The Death of Lincoln" (1865).   JAMES T. CALLOW

Bibliography: Brown, Charles Henry, *William Cullen Bryant* (1971); Bryant, William C., 2d, and Voss, Thomas G., eds., *The Letters of William Cullen Bryant*, 6 vols. (1975–   ); McDowell, W. T., *William Cullen Bryant* (1935; repr. 1986); McLean, Albert, Jr., *William Cullen Bryant* (1964).

Bryant College

Established in 1863, Bryant College (enrollment: 6,152; library: 108,314 volumes) is a private coeducational 4-year school of business administration in Smithfield, R.I. Master's degrees are also awarded.

Bryce, James Bryce, 1st Viscount

The British statesman and scholar James Bryce, b. May 10, 1838, d. Jan. 22, 1922, served as ambassador to the United States from 1907 to 1913 and wrote one of the most perceptive studies of its institutions, *The American Commonwealth* (1888). Bryce studied at Oxford and Heidelberg before publishing his prizewinning history, *The Holy Roman Empire*, in 1864. Bryce also taught law at Oxford, sat in the House of Commons (1880–1907), and served in several Liberal cabinets; he remained until his death a tireless spokesman for better Anglo-American understanding.   JOEL COLTON

Bibliography: Fisher, H. A. L., *James Bryce*, 2 vols. (1927; repr. 1979); Ions, E. S., *James Bryce and American Democracy* (1968).

Bryce Canyon National Park

Bryce Canyon National Park, in southern Utah, is famous for its weirdly shaped, many-colored limestone cliffs. On Paunsaugunt Plateau, a series of amphitheaters have been formed by the cliffs, which stand as pinnacles and towers. The park, established in 1928, has an area of 145 km² (56 mi²).

Bryn Mawr College   [brin mahr]

Established in 1885 by the Quakers, Bryn Mawr College (enrollment: 1,794; library: 800,000 volumes) is a private 4-year liberal arts institution for women in Bryn Mawr, Pa. Men are admitted to the graduate schools. Bryn Mawr, Haverford, and Swarthmore participate in a plan that allows students to take courses for credit at any of the three colleges. Bryn Mawr and Haverford students may live on either campus. Bryn Mawr is known for its graduate program in classical archaeology.

Brynner, Yul   [brin'-ur]

Yul Brynner, b. July 11, 1915, d. Oct. 10, 1985, was a Russian-American actor noted for his stage and screen roles as the King of Siam in the musical comedy *The King and I* (1951; film, 1956). Brynner won both a 1952 Tony Award and a 1956 Academy Award for this part, and he returned to Broadway to play it again in 1977 and 1985. He appeared in many films, including *Anastasia* (1956), *The Brothers Karamazov* (1958), *The Magnificent Seven* (1960), and *Westworld* (1973).

LESLIE HALLIWELL

Bibliography: Robbins, Jhan, *Yul Brynner* (1987).

bryophyte [bry'-oh-fyt]

A bryophyte is any member of the plant phylum Bryophyta, which comprises the most primitive plants adapted to existence on dry land—the familiar MOSS, the common but unfamiliar LIVERWORT, and the relatively unknown HORNWORT. Like amphibians of the animal kingdom, the bryophytes cannot be wholly divorced from water, commonly growing in shady, perpetually moist regions, where the danger of drying out is minimized. Several species have secondarily adapted to an aquatic existence, living afloat or submerged in fresh water.

Bryophytes lack the true stem, leaf, and root of the vascular plants (see TRACHEOPHYTE) and grow in horizontal, prostrate forms or leafy mats on soil, tree trunks, stumps, rocks, or in the water. Bryophytes have rhizoids rather than roots. These simple projections penetrate the material the bryophytes live on and absorb water and minerals. The epidermal cells, interspersed with air pores, cover the photosynthetic cells. These pores allow for gaseous exchange of carbon dioxide, the carbon and oxygen source for photosynthesized organic compounds, and the photosynthetic by-product, molecular oxygen. Excessive water loss from the plant body is reduced by a waxy cuticle produced by the epidermal cells.

The ALTERNATION OF GENERATIONS common to many life forms is illustrated clearly by the bryophytes. Alternation of generations refers to the reproductive cycle of organisms in which the gametophyte and sporophyte stages succeed one another. Spores, produced by sporophytes, germinate and develop into gametophytes. Gametophytes develop sex organs called archegonia, which produce the female gametes (egg cells). Male gametes (sperm) are produced in structures called antheridia. Fertilization occurs when sperm are released under high-moisture conditions and actively swim to the archegonia, where they unite with the egg. The archegonium is a flask-shaped structure; disintegration of cells lining its neck results in a chemical secretion that attracts the sperm.

Following fertilization, the new sporophyte undergoes embryonic development within the archegonium, developing a base of foot cells, which grow into and absorb nutrition from the gametophyte parent. Most of the sporophyte body consists of a capsule in which spores are produced and released when the capsule opens. Spores are carried away by water, by wind, or on animal bodies to new locations where their germination will result in new gametophytes. The dominant phase of the life cycle of bryophytes is the gametophyte and is the form most recognizable to the professional and amateur botanist. In vascular plants, it is the sporophyte that is dominant and that is the recognizable form of each species.

Bibliography: Schofield, W. B., *Introduction to Bryology* (1985); Watson, Eric V., *Structure and Life of Bryophytes*, 3d ed. (1971).

See also: ANGIOSPERM; EVOLUTION; GYMNOSPERM.

bryozoan [bry-oh-zoh'-uhn]

A bryozoan is any member of the phylum Bryozoa, which contains approximately 4,000 living species of colonial invertebrate animals that live in fresh and marine waters. The bryozoans, also called ectoprocts or polyzoans, form colonies by the attachment and fusion of many individual bryozoans, called zooids. Although each zooid is usually less than 0.5 mm in length, the colonies are several centimeters or greater in diameter and height, with some reaching more than 1 m (about 3.3 ft). Most bryozoan colonies are sessile and are found attached to hard surfaces such as rocks, pilings, and shells; several are mobile or lie unattached. Many colonies are encrusting, but some are shrublike, fanlike, or low and nodular. Zooidal covers are shaped like small, rectangular boxes. Zooids have ciliated tentacles (lophophores) that are retracted when at rest and drive food particles down toward the mouth during feeding. Most bryozoans are bisexual (hermaphroditic). The eggs are released into a special brood chamber where they develop into larvae, which are then freed and settle to form new colonies. Individuals of some classes also bud. Most bryozoans form an external skeleton by secreting calcium carbonate, and the skeletons of dead animals afford an extensive fossil record dating from the Ordovician Period, almost 500 million years ago. Marine bryozoans have been abundant nearly all of that time. During the early Paleozoic Era, bryozoans formed massive domal and shrublike colonies in shallow, tropical-shelf seas. Later in the Paleozoic, fan-shaped colonies abounded in some of these habitats; in some areas, their skeletons acted as sediment traps and formed mounds. Such mounds have proved to be valuable sources of petroleum. Bryozoans enjoy wide geographic distribution. Small encrustations of them are most commonly seen on kelp or other seaweed.

WILLIAM B. N. BERRY

Bibliography: Ross, J. R., *Bryozoa* (1987).

Brythonic language: see CELTIC LANGUAGES.

Bryusov, Valery Yakovlevich [broo'-sawf, vul-yair'-ee yah'-kuhv-le-vich]

Valery Yakovlevich Bryusov, b. Dec. 13 (N.S.), 1873, d. Oct. 9, 1924, was a major poet of Russian SYMBOLISM as well as one of its organizers and leaders. He managed the Scorpion Press, the principal outlet for Russia's finest modernist poets, and edited (1904–09) *Vesy* (The Scales), one of the most esteemed literary journals in Europe. Despite his Mephistophelian poses and his association with the extreme themes of DECADENCE (sadism, masochism, voyeurism, necrophilia), Bryusov was scholarly and erudite, writing on numerous topics such as passion, the city, and antiquity. Among his best known works are *Russkie Simvolisty* (Russian Symbolism, 1894–95), *Chefs d'oeuvre* (Masterpieces, 1895), *Me eum esse* (This One—I, 1897), *Tertia Vigilia* (The Third Watch, 1900), and *Stephanos* (The Garlands, 1906), and the novel *The Fiery Angel* (1908; Eng. trans., 1930).

KENNETH N. BROSTROM

Bibliography: Grossman, Joan D., *Valery Bryusov and the Riddle of Russian Decadence* (1985).

Brzezinski, Zbigniew [bruh-zhin'-skee, zvig'-nee-ef]

Zbigniew Kazimierz Brzezinski, b. Warsaw, Poland, Mar. 28, 1928, is an American scholar of international relations who served (1977–81) as national security advisor under the Carter administration. From 1973 to 1977, Brzezinski was director of the Trilateral Commission, an organization devoted to common concerns of the United States, Western Europe, and Japan. In 1981, Brzezinski returned as a professor to Columbia University, where he had established (1962) the Research Institute on Communist Affairs (subsequently called the Research Institute on International Change) and also became senior advisor at Georgetown University's Center for Strategic and International Studies. He is author of *The Soviet Bloc: Unity and Conflict* (1960), *Power and Principle* (1983), and *Game Plan: How to Conduct the U.S.-Soviet Contest* (ed. by Harold Evans; 1986).

Btu: see BRITISH THERMAL UNIT.

Bubastis [boo-bas'-tis]

Bubastis (modern Tell Basta), located 83 km (52 mi) north of Cairo, is the site of an ancient Egyptian city. Its name is related to Bast, the feline-goddess of ancient Egypt. During the Old Kingdom, the site was dedicated to the leonine form of Bast, who continued to be venerated as a lioness through the New Kingdom. A blending of traditions occurred at some time after the end of the New Kingdom, and the syncretistic nature of Egyptian religion transformed the goddess into a graceful cat. Numerous bronze statuettes of cats, examples of which exist today, were made as votive offerings to Bast at Bubastis.

Bubastis was the center of the cult of the Egyptian goddess Bast. Represented here as a cat, she also took the form of a cat-headed woman. The temple of Bast and the annual festival held there are described in the History of Herodotus.

interaction of the fast particles with the atoms in the liquid. Various liquids, including propane, neon, xenon, deuterium, liquid hydrogen, and the refrigerant freon, have served this purpose. The paths of the particles are photographed in stereo by two cameras. By plotting coordinate points, the data can be fed into a computer via punched cards for analysis.

When liquid hydrogen is employed as the medium, a high magnetic field can cause the particles to move in a curved path, allowing measurement of their magnetic dipole moments or intrinsic spin characteristics. To save a large amount of power, the coils producing the magnetic field are held at a temperature approaching absolute zero, making them superconductive with proper wire material. Once introduced, a strong current will continue to circulate indefinitely.

FRANK J. OLIVER

Bibliography: Shutt, R. P., Bubble and Spark Chambers, 2 vols. (1967).

See also: DETECTOR, PARTICLE; NUCLEAR PHYSICS; PHOTOGRAPHY.

Founded in the 3d dynasty (2686–2613 BC), the site rose to prominence in the 19th dynasty (1320–1200 BC). It was at its peak of importance during the 22d dynasty (945–c.730 BC) when Osorkon II built the Hypostyle Hall. That pink granite structure, set within a landscaped palm grove at the confluence of two branches of the Nile, was still an impressive sight when visited by the Greek historian Herodotus. During the 30th dynasty (380–343 BC), Nectanebo II added an inner shrine with subsidiary chapels to the sanctuary of Osorkon II. Today the site lies in ruins.   ROBERT S. BIANCHI

bubble chamber

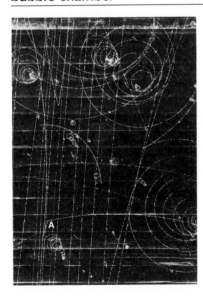

A bubble chamber displays tracks (bright lines) of high-energy particles. The photograph, showing the production of a negatively charged omega meson (A), was taken in 1964 in the 80-in (2-m) liquid hydrogen bubble chamber at Brookhaven National Laboratory.

A bubble chamber is a particle detector used in research on high-energy nuclear reactions. It is similar to a CLOUD CHAMBER but is a much more sophisticated instrument of greater size and complexity. The bubble chamber is attached to a subatomic particle accelerator of large size, such as a cyclotron. It was invented in 1953 by Donald A. Glaser, a physicist at the University of Michigan and later a Nobel laureate.

The bubble chamber consists of a large vessel with a volume of up to 20 m³ (706 ft³), in which as much as 500 l (132 gal) of a liquid is maintained at a temperature higher than its boiling point but prevented from boiling by high pressure. With the same pulse rate as the particle accelerator (typically 1–2 seconds), the pressure is suddenly released when the beam of subnuclear particles is diverted into the container. The liquid boils along the tracks of the particles by

Buber, Martin   [boo'-bur]

Martin Buber was a 20th-century Jewish existentialist who was influenced by Hasidic mysticism. After being expelled from Nazi Germany in 1938, he taught at Hebrew University in Jerusalem.

Martin Buber, b. Feb. 8, 1878, d. June 13, 1965, was an Austrian-born Jewish philosopher. Educated at the universities of Vienna, Leipzig, Zurich, and Berlin, he was an active Zionist (see ZIONISM). In 1901 he became the editor of Die Welt (The World), a Zionist journal; in 1916 he founded Der Jude (The Jew), an important journal for German-speaking Jewry. He became professor of Jewish theology at the University of Frankfurt in 1923. After Adolf Hitler came to power, Buber devoted most of his attention to strengthening German Jewry in the face of Nazi anti-Semitism. Finally forced to leave Germany in 1938, he settled in Palestine, where he became professor of social philosophy at Hebrew University, Jerusalem. He advocated creation of a binational state of Israel comprising both Jews and Arabs. During the 1950s he traveled and lectured widely, particularly in the United States.

Buber's philosophy, which was strongly influenced by HASIDISM, is sometimes referred to as Jewish EXISTENTIALISM. It is best set forth in Ich und Du (1923; I and Thou, 1937). Buber posited a basic difference between the way people relate to an inanimate object (the I-It relationship) and the way they relate to other people (the I-Thou relationship). In the former, no genuine relationship exists because the I and the It do not interrelate. The It is regarded as object, to be manipulated and used. Superficial human relationships tend to resemble the I-It type more than they do the I-Thou type. In the latter, a true dialogue exists because the I interrelates totally with the Thou, creating a union, a bonding, between the two. The I-Thou relationship involves risks, because total involvement cannot calculate injuries that may be inflicted on the I by the Thou. Human relationships can only approximate the perfect I-Thou dialogue. When people are in a genuine dialogue with God (the only perfect Thou), the true I-Thou relationship is present.

In his later years Buber tried to apply the I-Thou principle to biblical interpretation, psychotherapy, and political philosophy. Among his many writings are *The Origin and Meaning of Hasidism*, 2 vols. (Eng. trans., 1960), and *A Believing Humanism: My Testament, 1902–1965* (Eng. trans., 1967).

Bibliography: Aberbach, David, et al., *Jewish Thinkers* (1989); Friedman, Maurice, *Martin Buber*, 3d rev. ed. (1976), and *Martin Buber's Life and Works* (1987); Susser, Bernard, *Existence and Utopia* (1981).

Bubka, Sergei [buhb'-kah, sir-gay']

Soviet athlete Sergei Bubka, b. Dec. 4, 1963, has been the world's premier pole vaulter since his first world title in 1983. He has consistently broken his own records throughout his career, passing the 6-m barrier indoors in February 1991. He achieved the 20-ft (6.10-m) mark indoors in March 1991 and outdoors at the 1991 World Championships in August. Bubka won the gold medal in the 1988 Olympics.

bubonic plague [bue-bahn'-ik]

Bubonic plague is an acute infection in humans and various species of rodents, caused by *Yersinia pestis* (formerly called *Pasteurella pestis*), a bacterium transmitted by fleas that have fed on infected rodents. After a flea has fed on blood from the skin of an infected rodent, usually a rat, the ingested plague bacteria multiply in the flea's upper digestive tract and eventually obstruct it. Then, when the flea feeds again, on a human or another rodent, the obstruction causes the freshly ingested blood to be regurgitated back into the bite, along with plague bacteria. The circulatory system of the bitten individual then carries the bacteria throughout the body.

The first signs of illness in humans appear suddenly, within about a week. In a few hours the body temperature rises to about 40° C (104° F), and the victim becomes gravely ill, experiencing vomiting, muscular pain, mental disorganization, and delirium. The lymph nodes throughout the body, especially those in the groin and the thighs, become enlarged and extremely painful. The inflamed lymph nodes, called buboes (from which the disease gets its name), become filled with pus, and the disease spreads through the body by way of the infected bloodstream and the lymphatic system. In 60–90 percent of untreated cases, death occurs within a few days.

Plague pneumonia, or pneumonic plague, is caused by the same bacteria as bubonic plague but is acquired by inhaling infected droplets from the lungs of someone whose plague infection has spread to the respiratory system. This is the most contagious form of the disease and the form that progresses most rapidly, with death usually occurring in less than three days in virtually all untreated cases.

Historic Epidemics. Respiratory transmission was mainly responsible for the historic plague epidemics that swept across entire continents and wiped out tens of millions of people. One such epidemic killed an estimated 100 million people in the Middle East, Europe, and Asia during the 6th century. Another epidemic in the same regions during the 14th century—known as the Black Death—killed one-fourth to one-half the population of Europe, or about 75 million people.

Small epidemics of bubonic plague continue to occur in widespread regions of the world, including the United States. The epidemics fail to spread beyond local outbreaks, however, which may suggest that less virulent strains of the plague bacterium have developed over the years and conferred a relative immunity to many people. That plague does recur indicates its existence as a chronic disease among wild rodents.

Prevention. The most effective way to prevent plague is to reduce the rodent and flea populations by the use of proper sanitation and rodenticides and insecticides. The plague organism is vulnerable to the antibiotics streptomycin, chloramphenicol, and tetracycline, if treatment is started within about 15 hours of the first appearance of symptoms.

Bibliography: Gottfried, R. S., *The Black Death* (1983); McEvedy, C., "The Bubonic Plague," *Scientific American*, February 1988; McNeill, W. H., *Plagues and People* (1977); William, D., ed., *The Black Death* (1982).

buccaneer: see PIRACY.

Bucephalus [boo-sef'-uh-luhs]

Bucephalus was the horse of ALEXANDER THE GREAT. The animal, still untamed, was acquired by Alexander when he was a young man; it is said that he never rode any other horse. According to legend, the horse was capable of great speed. After Bucephalus died in 326 BC, Alexander built a city over its grave and named it Bucephala. The site of the city has been placed in modern Pakistan.

Bucer, Martin [boot'-sur]

Martin Bucer (or Butzer), b. Nov. 11, 1491, d. Feb. 28, 1551, was the leading German Protestant reformer in his adopted city, Strasbourg. With Matthew Zell and Wolfgang Capito, Bucer introduced the Reformation into that city. It was firmly established there through his preaching and his organizational ability, by which he promoted congregational discipline, evangelical confirmation, and education.

In his early career, Bucer was a Dominican friar (from 1506 to 1518) and had a humanist interest in classical studies. In 1518 he heard Martin LUTHER present his theology of the cross during a public disputation in Heidelberg and was moved to support the evangelical cause.

Theologically, Bucer was close to Luther, but he sought to mediate between Luther's views on the Eucharist and those of Ulrich ZWINGLI, the Swiss reformer. He was one of the authors of the *Confessio Tetrapolitana* (1530), a confession of faith based on the Augsburg Confession and subscribed to by four southwest German cities. After Emperor CHARLES V had defeated the Protestant princes in the Schmalkaldic War, Bucer was driven out of Strasbourg in 1549. He went to England and became a professor at Cambridge. LEWIS W. SPITZ

Bibliography: Abray, Lorna J., *The People's Reformation* (1985); Eells, Hastings, *Martin Bucer* (1931).

Buchan, John, 1st Baron Tweedsmuir [buhk'-uhn, tweedz'-muer]

John Buchan, b. Perth, Scotland, Aug. 26, 1875, d. Feb. 11, 1940, combined a successful political career with one as a writer of highly popular adventure stories, including *The Thirty-nine Steps* (1915; film, 1935) and *Greenmantle* (1916). He became governor-general of Canada in 1935 and held that post until his death. He also wrote history, biographies, and an autobiography, *Pilgrim's Way* (1940). ROBIN BUSS

Bibliography: Kruse, Juanita, *John Buchan and the Idea of Empire* (1989); Smith, Janet A., *John Buchan* (1985).

Buchanan, George

George Buchanan, b. February 1506, d. Sept. 29, 1582, was a Scottish humanist. Educated at the universities of Saint Andrews and Paris, he was considered one of the greatest Latin scholars and poets of the late Renaissance. Buchanan spent 30 years on the Continent, teaching and writing, before returning to Scotland as a Protestant in 1561 or 1562. He was initially engaged as tutor to the Roman Catholic MARY, QUEEN OF SCOTS, but he soon became one of her most implacable opponents. In his pamphlet *Detectio Mariae Reginae* (Exposure of Queen Mary, 1571), he accused the queen of complicity in the murder of her husband, Lord DARNLEY. After Mary's fall, Buchanan was tutor to her son, James VI (later JAMES I of England). The young king, however, did not absorb Buchanan's views on the limitations of royal power, set forth in *De jure regni apud Scotos* (On Royal Right Among the Scots, 1579).

Bibliography: Ford, P. J., *George Buchanan, Prince of Poets* (1982); McFarlane, I. D., *Buchanan* (1981).

Buchanan, James

James Buchanan, the 15th president of the United States (1857–1861), served during the beginning of the secession crisis that led to the Civil War. Of Scotch-Irish descent, he was born on Apr. 23, 1791, in Cove Gap, near Mercersburg, Pa., the son of James Buchanan, a prosperous storekeeper, and his wife, Elizabeth Speer.

Early Career. Young James received an academy education and attended Dickinson College, Carlisle, Pa., graduating in 1809. He then studied law in Lancaster, where he began practice in 1813. Although a Federalist in political sympathies, he supported the prosecution of the WAR OF 1812 and participated as a volunteer in the defense of Baltimore.

After serving in the Pennsylvania House of Representatives (1814–16), Buchanan devoted attention to his law practice, which soon prospered. In 1819 he became engaged to Ann Coleman, daughter of a wealthy Lancaster iron manufacturer, but as a result of a misunderstanding the engagement was ended. Her sudden death shortly thereafter left Buchanan desolate. He never married.

In 1820, Buchanan was elected to the U.S. House of Representatives. With the collapse of the Federalist party, he supported Andrew JACKSON for the presidency. In the late 1820s he emerged as the leader of the Amalgamation party, the dominant faction of Pennsylvania Jacksonians.

Buchanan retired from Congress in 1831 but later that year accepted Jackson's offer of the ministry to Russia. He remained at St. Petersburg from 1832 to 1834, where he concluded a commercial treaty. Shortly after his return he was elected to the U.S. Senate, where he served from 1834 to 1845.

Mentioned as a possible presidential candidate in 1844, Buchanan became (1845) secretary of state in the cabinet of President James K. POLK. Although Polk personally directed the formulation of foreign policy, Buchanan worked diligently in matters relating to the consummation of the annexation (1845) of Texas, the settlement of the OREGON QUESTION, and the MEXICAN WAR. He retired from office at the end of the Polk administration in 1849. Buchanan was a serious contender for the Democratic nomination in 1852 but lost to Franklin PIERCE, who named him minister to Great Britain. His mission in London (1853–56) accomplished little but benefited him politically, for he remained aloof from the controversy over the KANSAS-NEBRASKA ACT (1854).

Presidency. At the Democratic convention in 1856, Buchanan won the presidential nomination on the 17th ballot. In the fall he won an electoral victory, although he failed to get a popular majority over John C. FRÉMONT, the Republican, and Millard FILLMORE, the Know-Nothing candidate.

Two days after Buchanan's inauguration, the Supreme Court declared in the DRED SCOTT case that Congress had no power over slavery in the territories. He welcomed this ruling as the final word on that issue, but the Republicans and many Northern Democrats refused to accept the Court's opinion. Like Pierce, Buchanan met difficulties in organizing Kansas Territory. He urged Congress to accept the territory's proslavery LECOMPTON CONSTITUTION, even though it had been drawn up by an unrepresentative convention that had refused to submit it to the people. Stephen A. DOUGLAS, Democratic senator of Illinois, broke with Buchanan, arguing that the president's stand made a mockery of the doctrine of POPULAR SOVEREIGNTY. Ultimately the constitution was referred to the Kansas electorate, which overwhelmingly rejected it.

With his long experience in diplomacy, Buchanan expected his administration to conduct a vigorous foreign policy. He sought to extend American influence in the Caribbean, but congressional opposition forced him to give up efforts to purchase Cuba from Spain. Inevitably, domestic matters intruded upon his attention. The panic of 1857 added to the unpopularity of his administration and contributed to heavy Democratic losses in the congressional elections of 1858.

The sectional controversy grew steadily more serious during the last two years of Buchanan's presidency. The raid by John BROWN at Harpers Ferry and Brown's execution by Virginia authorities in 1859 intensified public feeling in both the South and the North. In the presidential campaign of 1860 the Democratic party split, and Buchanan endorsed Vice-President John C. BRECKINRIDGE of Kentucky, whom he considered the regular nominee, instead of Douglas, the candidate of the Northern Democrats.

The election of Abraham LINCOLN, the Republican candidate, prompted the secession of seven Southern states and the creation of the CONFEDERATE STATES OF AMERICA during Bu-

JAMES BUCHANAN
15th President of the United States (1857–61)

Nickname: "Old Buck"
Born: Apr. 23, 1791, Cove Gap (near Mercersburg), Pa.
Education: Dickinson College (graduated 1809)
Profession: Lawyer
Religious Affiliation: Presbyterian
Marriage: None
Political Affiliation: Democrat
Writings: *Mr. Buchanan's Administration on the Eve of the Rebellion* (1866); *Works of James Buchanan* (12 vols., 1908–11), ed. by John Bassett Moore
Died: June 1, 1868, near Lancaster, Pa.
Buried: Woodward Hill Cemetery, Lancaster, Pa.

Vice-President and Cabinet Members

Vice-President: John C. Breckinridge
Secretary of State: Lewis Cass (1857–60); Jeremiah S. Black (1860–61)
Secretary of the Treasury: Howell Cobb (1857–60); Philip F. Thomas (1860–61); John A. Dix (1861)
Secretary of War: John B. Floyd (1857–60); Joseph Holt (1861)
Attorney General: Jeremiah S. Black (1857–60); Edwin M. Stanton (1860–61)
Postmaster General: Aaron V. Brown (1857–59); Joseph Holt (1859–61); Horatio King (1861)
Secretary of the Navy: Isaac Toucey
Secretary of the Interior: Jacob Thompson

chanan's last months in office. The president was criticized by secessionists because he denied the legality of their action and by Northern advocates of a more vigorous policy because he believed that the executive lacked the power to coerce a state. He based his hopes for the survival of the Union on last-minute compromise efforts, which failed. As the more pro-Southern cabinet members resigned during the crisis, he took a stronger pro-Union stand, refusing to turn over Fort Pickens in Florida and FORT SUMTER in South Carolina to the authorities in those secessionist states.

During the Civil War Buchanan generally supported Lincoln's war policies while preparing a defense of his own administration, which he published in 1866. He died at his estate, Wheatland, near Lancaster, on June 1, 1868.

Buchanan's reputation is judged mainly by his conduct during the last months of his presidency, and he is therefore generally regarded as an ineffective executive. In his defense it can be said that he was a lame-duck president caught in a vicious cross fire between secessionists and Republicans. But at the same time his adherence to a conservative legalism led him to interpret narrowly his powers to deal with an unprecedented constitutional crisis.   EDWIN A. MILES

Bibliography: Klein, Philip S., *President James Buchanan: A Biography* (1962); Nevins, Allan, *The Emergence of Lincoln*, 2 vols. (1950); Potter, David M., *The Impending Crisis, 1848–1861* (1976); Reisman, David, ed., *The Political Economy of James Buchanan* (1990); Smith, Elbert, *The Presidency of James Buchanan* (1975).

Bucharest   [boo'-kuh-rest]

Bucharest, the capital and largest city of Romania, lies on the Walachian plain along the Dîmboviţa River. The city produces farm equipment, textiles, and automotive parts.

Bucharest (Romanian: Bucureşti) is the capital, largest city, and foremost industrial center of Romania. It lies on the Dîmboviţa River, which flows to the Danube River, 55 km (34 mi) away. It is surrounded by the rolling plain of Walachia; the Transylvanian Alps are 90 km (56 mi) to the north.

Bucharest covers an area of 525 km² (203 mi²) and has a population of 2,064,474 (1992). It lies 60–90 m (200–300 ft) above sea level. The Dîmboviţa is subject to floods and has been enclosed by levees.

Contemporary City. The city has grown rapidly, doubling its size since World War II. The earliest city lay on rising ground on the left bank of the Dîmboviţa. This rural town was replaced beginning in the 1860s by an elegant capital with French-inspired architecture that caused it to be known as the Paris of the Balkans.

The Communist regime extended the wide boulevards begun in the 19th century. The Communists also laid out squares and erected massive buildings, including the old Communist party headquarters and the giant Scînteia building, erected to house the government printing and publishing works. Among the new buildings are many huge, utilitarian apartment blocks of no particular aesthetic distinction. A number of historic churches and synagogues were razed to make way for these building projects under the regime of former Romanian president Nicolae Ceauşescu.

Economy. Under Communist rule the many small factories were nationalized and merged into large state-run enterprises. Since 1950 many new industries have been established, including clothing, mechanical engineering, and the manufacture of farm equipment. Bucharest also has many food processing factories.

Education and Culture. Bucharest has a university, founded in 1561, and is the site of the Academy of Sciences, the State Library, and the National Theater. Also located there are many professional colleges, galleries, and museums, among them, the Village Museum (1936), in which specimens of traditional village architecture have been gathered from all parts of the country. Several of the city's churches, Eastern Orthodox in style, date from the 18th century. Bucharest also boasts many parks and open spaces and a large sports stadium.

History. The founding of Bucharest is traditionally ascribed to a peasant named Bucur, but no record of the city exists prior to the late Middle Ages. Attacks by Tatars and Turks restricted its growth before the 17th century. It became the capital of Walachia in 1698 and grew during the more peaceful 18th century. By 1800 its population was about 50,000. In 1861, Bucharest became the capital of Romania. Its continued growth was helped by the proximity of the Romanian oil field, and it was one of the first cities to be lighted by natural gas.
                                                            NORMAN J. G. POUNDS

Buchenwald   [boo'-ken-vahlt]

Buchenwald, near Weimar in the German state of Thuringia, was one of the most notorious CONCENTRATION CAMPS of the German Nazi regime. It was used in particular for experiments by medical doctors interested in the effects of amputations, lethal germs, and poisons on the human body. Established in 1937, it was liberated by U.S. troops in April 1945, by which time more than 50,000 persons had died there.

Buchman, Frank   [buhk'-muhn]

Frank Nathan Daniel Buchman, b. Pennsburg, Pa., June 4, 1878, d. Aug. 7, 1961, was a Lutheran pastor, an evangelist, and the founder of MORAL RE-ARMAMENT (MRA). After experiencing a spiritual rebirth in 1908, he launched a program to bring a similar rebirth to others. His followers, known first as the Oxford Group and First-Century Christian Fellowship, became known as Moral Re-Armament in 1938. Buchman concentrated his effort on political and social leaders and other successful people because he believed they had the prestige and power to achieve change in society.   JOHN F. PIPER , JR.

Buchner, Eduard   [book'-nur, ay'-doo-art]

The German chemist Eduard Buchner, b. May 20, 1860, d. Aug. 13, 1917, is known for his work on fermentation. He did research in analytic and organic chemistry, establishing the norcaradiene system as bicyclic. In 1896, Buchner began a series of papers in which he presented the first satisfactory experimental proof that alcoholic fermentation of sugar is caused by a nonliving fermentable enzyme. For this achievement he was awarded the 1907 Nobel Prize for chemistry. Serving in the German army during World War I, Buchner was wounded and died at Focsani, Romania.   VIRGINIA F. McCONNELL

Büchner, Georg   [buesh'-nur, gay'-awrk]

Karl Georg Büchner, b. Oct. 17, 1813, d. Feb. 19, 1837, was a German playwright who produced, during his short life, one of the most influential, prophetic, and disturbing bodies of drama in the history of Western theater. Trained to be a medical research scientist, he was about to assume a position at the University of Zurich when he died of what may have been typhoid fever.

In his youth Büchner was a revolutionary. The reaction to his tract *The Hessian Courier* (1834; Eng. trans., 1963) forced him to flee Germany. He was greatly inspired by the French Revolution. His first play, *Danton's Death* (1835; Eng. trans., 1927, 1963), written in hiding, is about the hero of that revolution, but in the course of his research Büchner concluded that revolution was futile and that freedom was a naive, untenable concept.

Büchner's second play, the comic romance *Leonce and Lena* (1836; Eng. trans., 1927, 1963), is about a prince and princess whose marriage is arranged. While fleeing their fate, they meet each other, fall in love, and marry. His most innovative and influential play is *Woyzeck* (1837; Eng. trans., 1927, 1963), about a lowly barber whose existence is determined by the cruelty of his environment. It concerns the dehumanization of people, their use as guinea pigs, and their insignificance in the universe. The play was the subject of Alban Berg's 1925 opera *Wozzeck*. Büchner also wrote an uncompleted prose work, *Lenz* (1839; Eng. trans., 1963). His plays, unrecognized in his own time, presaged many modern theater movements, including absurdism, existentialism, expressionism, and naturalism.   CARL R. MUELLER

Bibliography: Benn, Maurice, *The Drama of Revolt: A Critical Study of Georg Büchner* (1976); Büchner, Georg, *Complete Plays and Prose*, trans. by Carl Mueller (1963); Grimm, Reinhold, *Love, Lust, and Rebellion* (1985); Lindenberger, Herbert, *Georg Büchner* (1964).

Buchwald, Art

Art Buchwald, b. Mount Vernon, N.Y., Oct. 20, 1925, is a humorist and syndicated newspaper columnist known for his satirical jibes at American politics and life-styles. Buchwald was Paris reporter for *Variety* (1948–49) and in 1949 joined the Paris staff of the *New York Herald Tribune*. A column he wrote in 1957 on briefings by the then presidential press secretary, James C. Hagerty, helped make his reputation. His numerous books include *Son of the Great Society* (1966), *I Never Danced at the White House* (1973), and *I Think I Don't Remember* (1987).   CALDER M. PICKETT

Buck, Pearl S.

Pearl Sydenstricker Buck, b. June 26, 1892, d. Mar. 6, 1973, was the third American to receive the Nobel Prize for literature (1938). The daughter of American missionaries in China and a missionary herself, she is best known for her novels set in China. She achieved success with her second novel, *The Good Earth* (1931), the first volume in her *House of Earth* trilogy. For this story about the fluctuating fortunes of the peasant family of Wang Lung, she won a 1932 Pulitzer Prize. In the subsequent volumes of the trilogy, *Sons* (1932) and *A House Divided* (1935), and even in the archetypal story "The Mother" (1934), however, the characters became superficial and stereotyped. In the view of many critics, her partisan didacticism and lack of subtlety showed that the missionary zeal that had inspired her parents had triumphed over artistic considerations in her own work.

In 1936, Buck wrote extremely successful twin biographies of her mother *(The Exile)* and her father *(Fighting Angel: Portrait of a Soul))*. These moving accounts of their lives in China are largely credited with winning her the Nobel Prize. After that she published voluminously, but beginning with *Dragon Seed* (1942), a harrowing story of China's struggle to maintain its independence against the Japanese invasions of the 1930s, her work was increasingly propagandistic.

Pearl S. Buck, a 20th-century American novelist, was raised and educated in China by missionary parents. Her best-known book, The Good Earth, *was published in 1931. Like several of her works, this Pulitzer Prize-winning novel sympathetically portrays Chinese peasant life.*

Buck was an indefatigable contributor to humanitarian causes, especially in behalf of orphaned Asian and retarded children. Her more than 85 works include many stories and journalistic pieces. In 1954 she published the autobiographical *My Several Worlds*.   WARREN FRENCH

Bibliography: Doyle, Paul, *Pearl S. Buck*, rev. ed. (1980); Harris, Theodore, *Pearl S. Buck: A Biography*, 2 vols. (1969); Stirling, N., *Pearl Buck* (1983).

buckeye

The yellow, or sweet, buckeye, A. octandra, is the largest U.S. species of its genus, reaching heights of 27 m (89 ft). It flourishes from Pennsylvania to Georgia and Illinois. The flowers grow in clusters (panicles), and two inedible nuts are in each case.

The buckeye is any of about 13 species of deciduous hardwood trees or shrubs that belong to the genus *Aesculus* in the horse-chestnut family, Hippocastanaceae. They are native to North America, southeastern Europe, and eastern Asia.

The Ohio buckeye, *A. glabra*, is the state tree of Ohio. Under poor conditions it appears bushlike, but it can grow to a height of 12.2 m (40 ft). Distribution is throughout the northern and northeastern United States and parts of the Southwest. The bark on young stems is scaly and light brown; on trunks it is ashy gray or whitish. The leaves are compound, formed of five leaflets arising from a common point, giving the leaf a starry shape. The fruit has a few spines and breaks into two or three valves that contain chestnut-colored seeds. This tree has mostly ornamental use.

The red buckeye, *A. pavia*, is sometimes used as a landscape tree because of its showy red flowers, which are borne in clusters 15–25 cm (6–10 in) long. The leaves are distinguishable from those of the Ohio buckeye by having seven rather than five leaflets.

Buckingham, George Villiers, 1st Duke of

George Villiers, 1st duke of Buckingham, b. Aug. 28, 1592, d. Aug. 23, 1628, was an English courtier and the favorite of both JAMES I and CHARLES I. His extravagant policies helped turn Parliament against the monarchy and thus contributed to the eventual outbreak of the ENGLISH CIVIL WAR.

Villiers went to court in 1614, and his good looks soon attracted James I. He rose rapidly, being made a gentleman of the bedchamber (1615), knight of the Garter (1616), earl of Buckingham (1617), lord high admiral (1619), and duke (1623). Lavishly endowed with pensions and monopolies, he became extremely rich. In 1623, Buckingham accompanied Prince Charles on a trip to Spain. After their negotiations to obtain Charles's marriage to the Spanish Infanta failed, the duke planned war against Spain. The following year he arranged Charles's marriage to the French princess HENRIETTA MARIA. Although he had promised to help the French crown suppress the HUGUENOTS (French Protestants), Buckingham reversed himself in the face of English opposition and in 1627 led a disastrous expedition to relieve the Huguenots at La Rochelle. In 1626, Parliament had threatened to impeach Buckingham, and Charles, now king, had dissolved it to save his friend. When Parliament met in 1628 it renewed its attack on the duke, "the grievance of grievances." Buckingham, however, was assassinated by John Felton, a disaffected naval officer, while preparing another expedition against La Rochelle. Buckingham's flirtation with the French queen ANNE OF AUSTRIA is a major theme of Alexandre Dumas's novel *The Three Musketeers*.

The first duke's son, George Villiers, 2d duke of Buckingham (1628–87), was a leading courtier under Charles II and a member of the notorious Cabal.   MAURICE ASHLEY

Bibliography: Erlanger, Philippe, *George Villiers, Duke of Buckingham*, trans. by Lionel Smith-Golden (1953); Lockyer, Roger, *Buckingham: The Life and Political Career of George Villiers, First Duke of Buckingham* (1981; repr. 1984).

Buckingham Palace

Buckingham Palace, the residence of British monarchs since 1837, was originally built during the reign of King James I but was reconstructed in 1703 for the Duke of Buckingham, for whom the building is named.

Buckingham Palace, the London residence of Britain's sovereigns, is situated at the west end of St. James's Park at the terminus of Pall Mall. Queen VICTORIA was the first British monarch to live there (1837).

The palace was originally built by Sir George Goring (later the earl of Norwich) during the reign (1603–25) of King JAMES I. It was rebuilt (1674, 1703) by John Sheffield, duke of Buckingham and of Normanby, and called Buckingham House. GEORGE III bought the building in 1761, and his eldest son and successor, GEORGE IV (r. 1820–30), commissioned the architect John NASH to remodel it in 1825, when it was renamed Buckingham Palace. George IV's successor, King WILLIAM IV (r. 1830–37), disliked the palace, however, and refused to live there. He was succeeded by Queen Victoria, who moved into the palace immediately after her accession. The east wing was added in 1847; the south wing and grand ballroom were added in 1853–55.

The garden front remains as designed by Nash. The front facing the Mall, however, which is the facade visible to the public, is set back from a large paved courtyard and was refaced by Sir Aston Webb in 1913, during the reign of King GEORGE V. Among the nearly 600 rooms are the Marble Hall and Sculpture Gallery, the throne room, the Blue and the White drawing rooms, and the library. The grounds cover 16 ha (40 acres). When the sovereign is in residence the Royal Standard is flown and the ceremonial changing of the guard takes place daily. The palace itself is not open to the public, but tourists may visit the Queen's Gallery, in which works from the Royal Collections are displayed, and the Royal Mews, which houses the state coaches and horses.

Buckinghamshire

Buckinghamshire (also called Buckingham) is a county in central England, northwest of London. Its area is 1,883 km^2 (727 mi^2), and the population is 594,600 (1984 est.). The county town is Aylesbury. Buckinghamshire is primarily fertile agricultural land, but the forested Chiltern Hills cross the central part of the county. The economy is based on grain cultivation and livestock raising; some light industry is located around Aylesbury and High Wycombe.

The Saxons invaded the area in 570, and it became part of the Anglo-Saxon kingdom of Mercia. During the English Civil War (1642–48), Buckinghamshire was an antiroyalist stronghold and, later, a refuge for Quakers.

Buckland, William

William Buckland, b. Mar. 12, 1784, d. Aug. 15, 1856, pioneered in the science of GEOLOGY in England. Seeking to reconcile his geologic observations with the biblical account of creation and the DELUGE, he espoused the catastrophist viewpoint then in vogue and taught that the Flood was responsible for the EROSION AND SEDIMENTATION that produced the modern landscape. The decline of this view of Earth history was hastened by Charles LYELL, who had been a student of Buckland's at Oxford.

See also: CATASTROPHISM; GEOLOGIC TIME; UNIFORMITARIANISM.

Buckle, Henry Thomas

Henry Thomas Buckle, b. Nov. 24, 1821, d. May 29, 1862, was an English historian who sought to make history a precise science. A positivist, Buckle believed that the development of various nations could be explained by scientific laws governing such natural factors as climate, soil, food, and environment. To demonstrate the workings of his laws of history, he outlined a general history of civilization, but his death prevented its completion. Buckle's reputation was earned through his earlier work, *History of Civilization in England*, the first volume of which appeared in 1857.   JOEL COLTON

Bibliography: St. Aubyn, Giles, *A Victorian Eminence: The Life and Works of Henry Thomas Buckle* (1958).

Buckley, William F., Jr.

The writer and editor William F. Buckley, Jr., b. New York City, Nov. 24, 1925, became the intellectual voice of American conservatism after publication of his book *God and Man at Yale* (1951). In 1955 he founded the magazine *National Review*, which he edits and publishes; in 1962 he began to write "On the Right," a syndicated newspaper column; and in 1966 he became host of the television interview program "Firing Line." In all of these capacities he demonstrated not only a strong intellectual grasp of public affairs but also a wit and charm that endeared him even to some on the left. Consis-

William F. Buckley, Jr., contemplates a question before the General Assembly during his service with the U.S. delegation to the United Nations in 1973. Among many other writings, Buckley is the author of a series of thrillers featuring clean-living CIA operative Blackford Oakes. His exploits are described in such works as Saving the Queen (1976) and High Jinx (1986).

tently, he emerged as an articulate defender of traditional values. His many books include several on politics (for example, *Up from Liberalism*, 1959); *United Nations Journal* (1974), about his experiences as a U.S. delegate to the UN, and *On the Firing Line* (1989), moments from his years with the program; sailing reminiscences (*Racing through Paradise*, 1987); and a mystery series.   CALDER M. PICKETT

Bucknell University

Established in 1846 by the Baptists, Bucknell University (enrollment: 3,595; library: 498,685 volumes) is a private independent liberal arts institution for men and women in Lewisburg, Pa. Master's degrees are offered in arts and in sciences.

Buckner, Simon Bolivar

Simon Bolivar Buckner, b. near Munfordville, Ky., Apr. 1, 1823, d. Jan. 8, 1914, was a Confederate general in the Civil War. He participated in Gen. Braxton BRAGG's invasion of Kentucky in 1862 and after 1864 was commander of Louisiana. Buckner was governor of Kentucky from 1887 to 1891.

Buckner's son, Simon Bolivar Buckner, Jr. (1886–1945), was an American general who commanded the Allied invasion (April–June 1945) of Okinawa during World War II.

Bibliography: Stickles, Arndt M., *Simon Bolivar Buckner* (1940).

buckthorn

The buckthorn R. purshiana is a small tree, about 12 m (40 ft) tall. The bark of the buckthorn contains a drug used in laxatives.

Buckthorn is the common name for some members of the buckthorn family, Rhamnaceae, which comprises about 55 genera with 900 species of mostly thorny or spiny shrubs, small trees, and climbing vines. They are widely distributed but most abundant in arid, temperate to subtropical regions. The JUJUBE is a member of the family.

More specifically, buckthorn refers to the genus *Rhamnus*, about 150 species of evergreen or deciduous shrubs and small trees found in temperate and subtropical regions on all continents except Australia; some species are also known as cascara. The black, fleshy fruit of buckthorn contains 2–4 hardened nutlets and in the U.S. west is an important food source for some birds and mammals. A related species known as COYOTILLO, however, can be poisonous to cattle. The leaves, bark, and berries of some buckthorns have purgative qualities.

Some species in the genus *Bumelia*, family Sapotaceae, are commonly referred to as false buckthorn.

buckwheat

Buckwheat, *Fagopyrum esculentum*, is an herb belonging to the family Polygonaceae and is not, as popularly believed, a

The buckwheat plant, Fagopyrum esculentum, *an herb that is grown as a cereal crop, has broad leaves and small, five-parted flowers. Its three-cornered seeds are ground for pancake flour and groats, and its blossoms are a source of strong, dark honey.*

cereal grain. Native to central Asia, buckwheat has been cultivated in China, Turkey, and Russia since the 10th century but was not introduced into Europe and North America until centuries later.

The buckwheat plant is shallow-rooted, grows rapidly to a height of 61–122 cm (2–4 ft), and produces extensive branches and small, white clusters of flowers from a single stem. The seeds are three-cornered. The plant is not usually damaged by diseases or insects and is often planted on nonproductive soil. On good soil and in a favorable environment, it does not yield as much as cereal grains. Buckwheat is planted and harvested in the manner of cereal grains.

Buckwheat production is largely confined to Europe and North America, but nowhere is it a major crop. The major countries producing buckwheat are Russia, France, Poland, and Canada. New York, Pennsylvania, Michigan, and Minnesota are the main producers in the United States. Approximately two-thirds of the production is used on the farm, almost all as feed, but some is plowed under for soil improvement. For human consumption, buckwheat is processed in much the same way as wheat flour. Buckwheat flour is used mainly for pancake mixes or for buckwheat noodles. The farina, the coarser flour particles plus the groat, can be used for breakfast foods, soups, porridge, and gravy. Buckwheat feed, a by-product of milling, is a mixture of middlings and hull. The hulls constitute about 18 to 25 percent of the kernel but have little feed value and are usually used as fuel, bedding for livestock, or packing material.

Bucovina   [boo-koh-vee'-nuh]

Bucovina (or Bukovina) is a region in the northeastern Carpathian Mountains of east central Europe that is now shared by Romania and Ukraine. The area is heavily wooded, and the Carpathians serve as the source of the Prut, Dnestr, and Siret rivers, which flow to the Black Sea. Bucovina covers an area of 8,796 km^2 (3,396 mi^2). The climate is moderate, with temperatures ranging from $-7°$ C (20° F) to 29° C (85° F) annually. Forest products, iron ore, and grains are the area's main output. The inhabitants are a mix of Ukrainians, Russians, and Romanians. The main Ukrainian city is Chernovtsy; Romanian cities include Suceava and Botosani.

Historically a part of the Moldavian principality, Bucovina was ruled by Austria from 1775 to 1918 and became a separate crown land in 1849. From 1918 to 1940 it was part of Romania; then the USSR annexed it and incorporated it with Bessarabia. It was reshaped in 1947, with the southern half becoming part of northern Romania and the northern half part of the Ukrainian SSR (since 1991 independent Ukraine).

Budapest

Budapest is the capital, largest city, and industrial center of Hungary, having about one-fifth of the country's population. Situated on both banks of the Danube River, 217 km (135 mi) southeast of Vienna, Austria, it embraces three older cities: Obuda, Buda, and Pest. An administrative county with an area of 526 km² (203 mi²) and a population of 2,018,035 (1991), the metropolis is flanked on the west by hills and on the east by the Hungarian Plain. The climate is one of severe winters and hot summers.

Budapest was a comparatively small city until the mid-19th century, when it began growing rapidly, reaching about 1,700,000 at the outbreak of World War II. The population declined during the war but increased again after 1950. The city developed as a major center of transportation and communication, and it remains the hub of the country's roads and railroads. Essential to its role as a transportation center are the bridges across the Danube, the first of which was built in the 1840s. Previously Buda and Pest, cut off periodically by flood or ice, formed two separate cities. They were merged in 1872.

The origins of Budapest's three separate urban districts are quite distinct. Obuda lay on the west bank of the Danube, close to the Roman frontier town of Aquincum. Buda lay to the west on a steep hill, Castle Hill, and in the Middle Ages it became a seat of the Hungarian kings. Pest spread out along the flat east bank of the Danube and became a commercial and industrial city.

Contemporary City. The people of Budapest are mainly Hungarian. The population includes Germans as well, however, and South Slavs remain from the period of the Ottoman invasion of southeastern Europe. In Buda are the remains of the former royal palace, the historic 13th-century Cathedral of Saint Matthias, 18th-century government buildings, and the former town houses of Hungarian noblemen. These are important tourist attractions. The architecture of Pest is mainly 19th century, although within the curving line of the boulevards, which follow early defenses, are recent industrial and residential quarters. Pest contains the 19th-century neo-

Gothic parliament building. Budapest is also the chief educational and cultural center of the country and is noteworthy for its museums and art collections. The city has a university and ten professional schools.

Economy. After the creation of the Dual Monarchy of AUSTRIA-HUNGARY in 1867, Budapest developed as the exclusive site of manufacturing in the Hungarian state. Almost every branch of Hungarian industry is located there. Flour milling and agriculture-related industries were among the first to develop, but engineering and metalworking have become the most important.

The chief industrial quarters are situated beside the Danube to the north and south and in the plain to the east. Commercial docks line the Pest side of the river, especially on Csepel Island to the south. Manufacturing employs more than half the population; government service, a quarter.

History. Roman Aquincum was destroyed during the barbarian invasions. A settlement (Buda) was later established on Castle Hill and resisted the Tatar invasion of 1241. It was the Hungarian capital thereafter until its capture by the Turks in 1541. In 1686 it was liberated from Ottoman rule by the Austrians and was the center of Austrian administration until Hungary became autonomous in 1867. Buda's union with the city of Pest in 1872 prepared the way for Budapest's growth into a large industrial city. The capital of the Hungarian republic from 1918, Budapest was severely damaged in World War II and again in the Hungarian Revolution of 1956, but it has been entirely repaired.

NORMAN J. G. POUNDS

Buddha

The word *Buddha* is a general term meaning one who is enlightened or awakened. It is primarily applied to the historical founder of Buddhism, a prince of a small kingdom spanning northern India and Nepal, who was known as Sakyamuni, which means "the silent sage of the Sakya tribe," and Gautama, his clan name. His personal name was Siddhartha, "he who will accomplish." Legend and controversy shroud Siddhartha's life. The core of accepted beliefs derive from traditions current during the reign of the Buddhist emperor ASOKA about three centuries after Buddha's life (c.560 to c.480 BC).

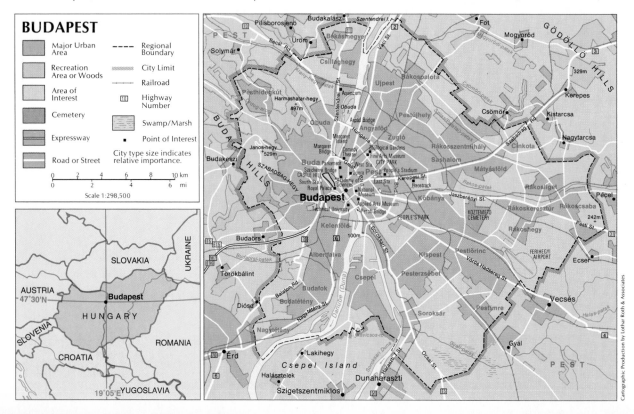

BUDAPEST

Major Urban Area	Regional Boundary
Recreation Area or Woods	City Limit
Area of Interest	Railroad
Cemetery	Highway Number
Expressway	Swamp/Marsh
Road or Street	Point of Interest

City type size indicates relative importance.

Scale 1:298,500

Cartographic Production by Lothar Roth & Associates

Some forms of Buddhism are based on the belief in an eternal, omnipresent Buddha, of which Gautama Buddha (the historical Buddha) was a physical incarnation. This statue is of Amitabha Buddha, meaning infinite light; in Japan he is called Amida. Amitabha is the fundamental buddha of Japanese Buddhism. The 15-m-high (49-ft) bronze statue was built in Kamakura, Japan, in 1252. It is an important shrine and place of pilgrimage.

The legend begins with divine conception. His mother, Maya, dreamed of a white elephant that entered her womb. She gave birth after ten months and died seven days later. A sage prophesied that the child would either become a great monarch or Buddha.

Siddhartha's father, seeking to prevent the child from becoming Buddha, allowed him to experience only pleasure. He married at age 16 and was on course to political leadership when he took a fateful chariot trip outside the palace. For the first time, Siddhartha witnessed irremediable suffering. Overwhelmed with sorrow, he began to contemplate renunciation. Despite the fact that Siddhartha had a newborn son, he left the palace, at the age of 29, to become a religious ascetic and recluse.

Siddhartha traveled from teacher to teacher failing to find enlightenment. After 6 years of ascetic self-mortification he remembered meditating as a young boy, abandoned his asceticism, and conceived of a "middle path" between luxuries and asceticism. He resolved to sit in meditation until attaining enlightenment. He sat one evening under a pipal tree, later called the bodhi ("enlightenment") tree (see BODH GAYA), and began to meditate. At dawn he was Supreme Buddha.

Buddha worried that his insights were too deep for ordinary human beings, but a high deity (Brahma) prevailed on him to delay his entry into NIRVANA and share his insight. He preached his first sermon at SARNATH, where he outlined his doctrine of the Four Noble Truths (see BUDDHISM). He accepted lay disciples (male and female) and converted his former ascetic companions as the first monks. Buddha's ministry continued for 45 years, after which, at the age of 80, he entered final nirvana. His body was cremated.

Although Theravada Buddhist doctrine takes the story of Siddhartha literally, it also places him in a series with several earlier Buddhas and one Buddha, Mettayya (or Maitreya), yet to come. From this view, Buddhahood endures only as long as life itself. In Mahayana Buddhist doctrine, this story is the tale of one historical manifestation of an eternal, ultimate Buddha. Manifestations of Buddha are called BODHISATTVA. The historical Buddha was a bodhisattva in the period

before his enlightenment. According to the Mahayana view, Buddhahood is a transcendental state of being of which the historical Buddha and other bodhisattvas partook. Siddhartha adopted the bodhisattva ethic—refusing to enter nirvana until all are saved. Chan (Ch'an), or ZEN BUDDHISM, pursues this logic to its ultimate conclusion. In Zen, all beings equally partake of this Buddha-nature and are as much Buddha as Siddhartha himself. Thus it denies the distinction between nirvana and samsara, or ordinary life.

Buddha is typically portrayed sitting on a lotus—a flower that arises pure from the muck. He sits in peaceful, compassionate meditation. The image grew more abstract over time as he came to be seen as a universal being.   CHAD HANSEN

Bibliography: De Bary, W. T., ed., *The Buddhist Tradition* (1969; repr. 1972); Marshall, G. N., *Buddha*, rev. ed. (1990); Oldenberg, H., *Buddha: His Life, His Doctrine, His Order*, trans. by W. Hoey (1971; repr. 1992); Snellgrove, D., ed., *The Image of Buddha* (1978).

Buddhism

Buddhism, one of the major religions of the world, was founded by Siddhartha Gautama, the Buddha, who lived in northern India from c.560 to c.480 BC. The time of the Buddha was one of social and religious change, marked by the further advance of Aryan civilization into the Ganges Plain, the development of trade and cities, the breakdown of old tribal structures, and the rise of a whole spectrum of new religious movements that responded to the demands of the times. These movements were derived from the Brahmanic tradition of HINDUISM but were also reactions against it. Of the new sects, Buddhism was the most successful and eventually spread throughout India and most of Asia.

Today it is common to divide Buddhism into two main branches. The Theravada, or "Way of the Elders," is the more conservative of the two; it is dominant in Sri Lanka, Burma (Myanmar), and Thailand. The Mahayana, or "Great Vehicle," is more diverse and liberal; it is found mainly in Taiwan, Korea, and Japan, and among Tibetan peoples, where it is distinguished by its emphasis on the Buddhist TANTRAS. In recent times both branches, as well as TIBETAN BUDDHISM, have gained followers in the West.

It is virtually impossible to tell the size of the Buddhist population today. Statistics are difficult to obtain because some individuals may have Buddhist beliefs and engage in Buddhist rites while maintaining folk or other (Shinto, Daoist, Hindu) religions; such persons may or may not call themselves or be counted as Buddhists. Nevertheless, the number of Buddhists worldwide is estimated at more than 300 million.

THE TEACHINGS OF THE BUDDHA

Just what the original teaching of the Buddha was is a matter of some debate. Yet, it may be said to have centered on certain basic doctrines. The first of the Four Noble Truths, the Buddha held, is suffering (*duhkha*). By this, he meant not only that human existence is occasionally painful but that all beings —humans, animals, ghosts, hell-beings, even the gods—are caught up in *samsara*, a cycle of rebirth, a maze of suffering in which their actions (KARMA) keep them wandering.

Samsara and *karma* are not doctrines specific to Buddhism. The Buddha, however, specified that *samsara* is characterized by three marks: suffering, impermanence, and no-self (*anatman*). Individuals not only suffer in a constantly changing world, but what appears to be the "self," the "soul," has no independent reality apart from its many separable elements.

The second Noble Truth is that suffering itself has a cause. At the simplest level, this may be said to be desire; but the theory was fully worked out in the complex doctrine of "dependent origination" (*pratityasamutpada*), which explains the interrelationship of all reality in terms of an unbroken chain of causation.

The third Noble Truth, however, is that this chain can be broken—that suffering can cease. The Buddhists called this end of suffering *nirvana* and conceived of it as a cessation of rebirth, an escape from *samsara*.

Finally, the fourth Noble Truth is that a way exists through which this cessation can be brought about: the practice of the noble Eightfold Path. This combines ethical and disciplinary practices (*sila*) and training in concentration and meditation (*samadhi*) with initial faith (*saddha*), which is ultimately transformed into enlightened wisdom (*panna*).

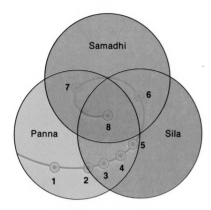

The Eightfold Path of (1) right views; (2) right intentions; (3) right speech; (4) right conduct; (5) right livelihood; (6) right effort; (7) right mindfulness; and (8) right concentration is possibly an expansion of an earlier three-part scheme of Buddhist life: saddha, or faith (ultimately, panna, or wisdom); sila, or ethics; and samadhi, or meditation.

THE DEVELOPMENT OF BUDDHISM

With the death of the Buddha, the community of his followers (the *sangha*) immediately faced a crisis: what were they to do in the absence of the master? The lay followers who had remained householders undertook to honor his bodily relics, which were enshrined in monuments called STUPAS. This was the beginning of a cult of devotion (BHAKTI) to the person of the Buddha that was to focus not only on *stupas* but on many holy sites (such as the bodhi tree), which became centers of pilgrimage, and eventually on Buddha images as well.

On the other hand, those Buddhists who had become monks and nuns undertook the gathering and preservation of their departed master's teachings (the DHARMA). According to tradition (the historicity of which many scholars have contested), a great council of 500 enlightened monks was held at Rajagriha, immediately after the Buddha's death, and all the Buddha's sermons (the *sutras*) and the rules of the discipline (*vinaya*) were remembered and recited.

In the years that followed, the monks gradually consolidated their communal life. Originally, like many other wandering mendicants of their time, they had tended to be constantly on the move, congregating only once a year for the three months of the monsoon. Gradually, these rain-retreats grew into more structured year-round monastic settlements. As new monastic communities developed, it was inevitable that some differences in their understanding of both the Buddha's teaching (*dharma*) and of the rules of the order (*vinaya*) should arise. Within 100 years of the Buddha's death, a second council took place at Vaisali, during which the advocates of certain relaxations in the *vinaya* rules were condemned. Then, c.250 BC, the great Buddhist emperor ASOKA is said to have held a third council at Pataliputra to settle certain doctrinal controversies.

It is clear from the accounts of these and other Buddhist councils that whatever the unity of early Buddhism may have been, it was rapidly split into various sectarian divisions. One of the earliest and most important of these divisions was that between the Sthavira (Elder) and the Mahasamghika (Great Council) schools. Within the former developed such important sects as the Sarvastivada (whose canon was in Sanskrit) and the Theravadins, whose canon is in Pali and who today are the only surviving representatives of the whole of the Hinayana, or "Lesser Vehicle," of Buddhism.

The Mahasamghika, also a Hinayanist sect, died out completely, but it is important because it represents one of the forerunners of the Mahayana doctrines. These doctrines were to include a different understanding of the nature of the Buddha, an emphasis on the figure of the BODHISATTVA, and on the practice of the perfections (*paramitas*).

In addition, within the Mahayana, a number of great thinkers were to add some new doctrinal dimensions to Buddhism. One of these was Nagarjuna, the 2d-century AD founder of the Madhyamika school. Using subtle and thoroughgoing analyses, Nagarjuna took the theory of dependent origination (*pratityasamutpada*) to its logical limits, showing that the absolute relativity of everything means finally the emptiness (*sunyata*) of all things.

Another important Mahayana school arose in the 4th century AD when the brothers Asanga and Vasubandhu sought to establish the doctrine of *Vijnanavada*—that the mind alone exists and that objects have no reality external to it. This idealist doctrine and Nagarjuna's emptiness were to play important roles in the further developments of Buddhist thought outside of India. Within India itself, they paved the way for yet another stage in the elaboration of the religion: the development of Buddhist tantra.

Tantric Buddhism, which is sometimes separated from the Mahayana as a distinct "Thunderbolt-Vehicle" (*Vajrayana*), became especially important in Tibet, where it was introduced starting in the 7th century. It was, however, the last phase of Buddhism in India, where the religion—partly by reabsorption into the Hindu tradition, partly by persecution by the Muslim invaders—ceased to exist by the 13th century.

THE EXPANSION OF BUDDHISM

Before its demise in India, Buddhism had already spread throughout Asia. This expansion started at least as early as the time of the emperor Asoka in the 3d century BC. According to tradition, this great monarch, who was himself a convert to Buddhism, actively supported the religion and sought to spread the *dharma*. He is said to have sent his own son, Mahinda, as a missionary to Sri Lanka. There Buddhism quickly took root and prospered, and the island was to become a stronghold of the Theravada sect. The Pali Canon was first written there in the 1st century BC; later the island was to be host to the great Theravadin systematizer and commentator Buddhaghosa (5th century AD). Asoka is also said to have sent missionaries to the East to what is now Burma and Thailand. Whatever the truth of this claim, it is clear that by the first several centuries AD, Buddhism, accompanying the spread of Indian culture, had established itself in large areas of Southeast Asia, even as far as Indonesia.

Also, tradition has it that another son of Asoka established a Buddhist kingdom in Central Asia. Whether or not this is true, it is clear that in subsequent centuries more missionaries (especially Mahayanists) followed the established trade routes west and north to this region, preaching the *dharma* as they went.

China. Central Asia was at that time a crossroads of creeds from all parts of Asia and the Near East, and by the 1st century AD Central Asian Buddhist monks were penetrating in turn into China. It is a matter of some debate what was transformed more in this process—China by Buddhism or Buddhism by China. On the one hand, at an early stage, Buddhists became very influential at the Chinese court, and soon their views penetrated the philosophical and literary circles of the gentry. On the other hand, early translators of Buddhist texts often adopted Daoist (Taoist) terminology in an attempt to make the Indian Buddhist concepts more understandable, and Buddhism adapted itself to Chinese worldviews, in particular to their stress on the importance of the family.

Buddhism in China also saw the rise of new sects, many of which were later transmitted to Japan. In the 6th century, the monk Zhiyi (Chih-i) consolidated the Tiantai (T'ien-t'ai) school, which sought to order all Buddhist teachings into a set hierarchy culminating in the text known as the *Lotus Sutra*. During the Tang (T'ang) dynasty (618–907), the so-called golden age of Chinese Buddhism, the Huayan (Hua-yen) school (based on the teachings of the Avatamsaka *sutra*), the Faxiang (Fa-hsiang) school (which taught Vijnanavada doctrines and was promoted by the great pilgrim and scholar XUANZANG, or Hsüan-tsang), and the Chan (Ch'an) school (better known in Japan as ZEN BUDDHISM) all prospered. At the same time, PURE LAND BUDDHISM became increasingly popular.

By 845, however, the *sangha* had grown so large and rich that its tax-exempt status now made it a severe drain on the empire's economy. For this and other reasons it became the object of a brief but effective imperial persecution. Many

(Above) *A group of Thai monks offer prayers during the ceremony of New Year, one of the most important events of the Buddhist calendar. On this holiday, Buddhists make pilgrimages to local shrines, where they are expected to present food and gifts to monks.*

(Left) *The gold Buddha of Bangkok's Wat Trimitr holds its hands in a* mudra, *one of the symbolic gestures that often appear in Buddhist statuary. This particular mudra, with the right hand touching the Earth, represents the Buddha's triumph over earthly temptations.*

temples were destroyed, thousands of monks and nuns were laicized, and the vast landholdings of monasteries were confiscated. Buddhism, especially the Chan school, did recover, but it never regained its former prestige in Chinese life.

Japan. Before 845, a number of Chinese schools had been transmitted to Japan. Buddhism was introduced to Japan from Korea about the 6th century and initially established itself as a superior means of magical power, especially for preserving and protecting the nation. Early in its history, it received the patronage of Prince SHOTOKU (7th century) and during the Nara period (710–84) became the state religion.

During the Heian period, in the early 9th century, two monks, Saicho and Kukai, traveled to China and on their return introduced to Japan the Tendai (or Chinese, Tiantai) sect and the Shingon sect, which was a form of Chinese Tantric Buddhism. Both of these esoteric sects were to take part in the mixing of Buddhism with various Japanese SHINTO folk, ascetic, and magical practices.

The Tendai sect, moreover, became a fountainhead of several later popular Japanese Buddhist movements. One of the Tendai's traits was the worship of the Buddha Amida and the belief in his Pure Land. With Honen (1133–1212) and Shinran (1173–1262), these Pure Land beliefs were systematized and made the exclusive focus of two new, popular sects, the Jodo and the Jodo Shin. Another Tendai trait was emphasis on the teachings of the *Lotus Sutra*. In the 13th century, the monk NICHIREN founded a dynamic and nationalistic sect that made the *Lotus* its sole basis of worship. Finally, it was also in this

(Left) *The Kinkaku-Ji, or Golden Pavilion, of Kyoto has been one of Japan's most important shrines of Zen Buddhism since its construction in 1934.*

(Below) *An exiled Tibetan monk in India works on his* mandala, *a diagram used as an aid in meditation. Tibetan Buddhism, or Lamaism, incorporates animist elements from pre-Buddhist history.*

same period that two schools of Zen Buddhism were introduced from China.

Under the feudal Tokugawa regime (1603–1867), all these sects became tools of the government; temples and priests were means of registering, educating, and controlling the populace. In the Meiji era (1868–1912), this Buddhist structure was disestablished in favor of Shinto. Finally, during the 20th century, new religious movements within Buddhism, such as the SOKA GAKKAI and the Risshokosei-kai, have arisen in response to the problems of the modern age.

INSTITUTIONS AND PRACTICES

Throughout Asia, wherever Buddhism was introduced, its leaders tended to seek the support of kings and other rulers of the state. The pattern of this relationship between a Buddhist king and the monastic community was given its definitive formulation by Emperor Asoka in the 3d century BC. This was a symbiotic relationship in which, in exchange for the allegiance and religious support of the *sangha*, the emperor became the patron and backer of the Buddhist *dharma*.

To some extent this pattern was extended to the laity as well. Everywhere, Buddhist monastic communities tended to depend on the laity for food and material support. Although in some places the *sangha* as a whole became well-to-do and the controller of vast monastic estates, traditionally monks were beggars and, in Southeast Asian countries, they still go on daily alms rounds.

Traditionally also, Buddhist monks have been celibate. Thus they depend on the faithful not only for food and financial support but for new recruits. Often children will enter a monastery and spend a number of years as novices, studying, learning, and doing chores. Then, following ordination, they become full members of the community, vowing to uphold its discipline. Henceforth their days will be taken up in ritual, devotions, meditation, study, teaching, and preaching. Twice a month, all the monks in a given monastery will gather for the recitation of the rules of the order (the *pratimoksha*) and the confession of any violation of those rules.

One of the pivotal concepts behind the rites and festivals of Buddhist laity and monks is that of offering (*dana*). This includes, for the laity, not just the giving of food and (in special ceremonies at the end of the rainy seasons) of new robes to the monks, but also the offering of flowers, incense, and

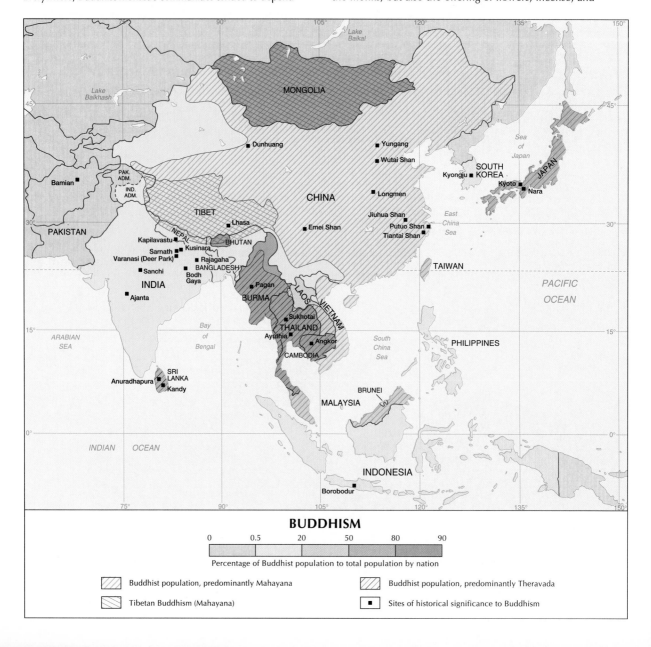

BUDDHISM

| 0 | 0.5 | 20 | 50 | 80 | 90 |

Percentage of Buddhist population to total population by nation

Buddhist population, predominantly Mahayana

Buddhist population, predominantly Theravada

Tibetan Buddhism (Mahayana)

■ Sites of historical significance to Buddhism

praise to the image of the Buddha, *stupas,* bodhi trees, or, especially in Mahayanist countries, to other members of the Buddhist pantheon such as bodhisattvas. For the monks, the notion of offering extends also to the giving of the *dharma* in the form of sermons, to the chanting of scriptures in rituals (which may also be thought of as magically protective and salutary), and to the recitation of *sutras* for the dead.

All of these acts of offering are intimately involved in the concept of merit-making. By performing them, individuals, through the working of *karma,* can seek to assure themselves rebirth in one of the heavens or a better station in life, from which they may be able to attain the goal of enlightenment.

BUDDHISM TODAY

During the 20th century, traditional Buddhist practices have been increasingly challenged by the advances of secularization and Westernization in Asia. In view of this, various modern Buddhist leaders have tended to deemphasize the popular Buddhist practices and expressions of faith and to stress the more rational and empirical aspects of Buddhist thought as well as the practice of meditation. At the same time, they have given to Buddhism a considerable role in the nationalist movements in their own countries and promoted contacts with other Buddhist nations through such ecumenical organizations as the World Fellowship of Buddhists, which now has chapters throughout the world.

In more recent years, however, some of the Buddhist leaders have lost their national influence. Vietnam, Laos, China (including Tibet), and North Korea are once-Buddhistic but now-Communist nations, although Buddhism has been restored in formerly Communist Cambodia and Mongolia. Even as Western ideology (whether in the form of communism or secular capitalism) has advanced into Asia, however, Buddhism has begun to spread in the West. Tibetan, Theravada, and Japanese sects especially have firm toeholds in America and Western Europe, and, in the face of further uncertainties in Asia, a few Buddhist leaders have even come to think that the future of their religion lies there.

JOSEPH M. KITAGAWA AND JOHN S. STRONG

Bibliography: Bechert, H., and Gombrich, R., eds., *The World of Buddhism* (1984); Becker, C. B., *Breaking the Circle: Death and the Afterlife in Buddhist Thought* (1994); Conze, E., *Buddhism* (1959; repr. 1982); Dumoulin, H., *Buddhism in the Modern World* (1976); Eliot, C., *Hinduism and Buddhism,* 3 vols. (1921); Humphreys, C., ed., *The Wisdom of Buddhism,* rev. ed. (1987); Ikeda, D., *The Flower of Japanese Buddhism* (1986); Ling, T., *A Dictionary of Buddhism* (1981); Robinson, R., and Johnson, W., *The Buddhist Religion,* 3d ed. (1982); Ross, N., *Buddhism* (1980); Snellgrove, D., *Indo-Tibetan Buddhism,* 2 vols. (1986); Wright, A. F., *Studies in Chinese Buddhism* (1990); Zurcher, E., *Buddhism* (1962).

Buddhist sacred literature

Buddhist sacred literature comprises a vast body of texts—hundreds of works—that were transmitted both orally and in written form and have been preserved principally in four languages: Pali, Sanskrit, Chinese, and Tibetan.

Of the several different Buddhist ways of classifying this material, perhaps the most important is the division into the three "baskets" (*tripitaka*): the *vinaya* (which deals with monastic discipline), the *sutra* (which contains discourses attributed to the BUDDHA himself), and the *abhidharma* (which comprises scholastic elaborations and classifications of the elements of reality). This three-basket division is most evident in the organization of the Theravada Pali Canon, which is said to have been written in the 1st century BC. Also extant in Pali are many important semicanonical and noncanonical texts, as well as a vast commentarial literature.

The Theravadins, moreover, were only one of several sects of Hinayana BUDDHISM, each of which compiled its own *tripitaka.* Only fragments of these other canons, which were in Sanskrit, are still extant in the original, but significant portions of them have been preserved in translation in the Chinese and Tibetan canons. In addition, these vast storehouses of texts (which are more eclectic than the Pali Canon) contain translations of great Mahayana *sutras* (such as the Lotus, Avatamsaka, Pure Land, and Mahaparinirvana *sutras* and the Perfec-

tion of Wisdom literature), original works in Chinese or Tibetan, TANTRAS, biographies, philosophical treatises, ritual manuals, and collections of legends.

JOSEPH M. KITAGAWA AND JOHN S. STRONG

Bibliography: Conze, Edward, ed., *Buddhist Texts through the Ages* (1954; repr. 1992); Goddard, D., ed., *A Buddhist Bible* (1994); Stryk, Lucien, ed., *World of the Buddha* (1969; repr. 1982).

Buddington, Arthur Francis

Arthur Francis Buddington, b. Wilmington, Del., Nov. 29, 1890, d. Dec. 29, 1981, was a professor of geology at Princeton University from 1920 to 1959. Buddington did extensive fieldwork (1943–61) for the U.S. and New York State Geological surveys. Focusing his research on iron-bearing ore deposits, he discovered a class of ores containing minerals formed at both high and low temperatures, and he analyzed the processes that transform sedimentary rock into metamorphic rock. In his survey of the Adirondack Mountains of northern New York, he located magnetic anomalies that were eventually traced to iron-titanium minerals having reverse magnetism. Working with iron-titanium compounds dissolved in magnetite, he developed techniques for determining the temperatures and pressures at which rocks form.

Budenny, Semyon Mikhailovich   [boo-dyawn'-ee, sem-yawn' mik-hy'-lo-vich]

Semyon Mikhailovich Budenny, b. Apr. 25 (N.S.), 1883, d. Oct. 17, 1973, was a Soviet general who organized the Red Army cavalry forces and commanded them with great success in the Russian Civil War (1918–20) and Polish-Soviet War (1920). He was made (1935) a marshal and in World War II assumed command (1941) of the southwestern front. He proved inept in modern mechanized war, however, and after a disastrous defeat by the Germans at Kiev (September 1941) he was relieved of command.

Budge, Don

John Donald Budge, b. Oakland, Calif., June 13, 1915, became the first tennis player in history to achieve the coveted "grand slam," winning the four most important singles championships—American, Australian, British, and French—in the same year (1938). He led the U.S. team in winning the Davis Cup in 1937 for the first time in ten years and helped to retain it in 1938. In addition, in 1937 and 1938 he won both the singles and doubles titles at Wimbledon, England, and captured the U.S. singles titles. The lanky Budge turned professional late in 1938 and was the best player on the tour in the year immediately before World War II.

budget

A budget is a document itemizing anticipated receipts and expenditures over a period of time, most commonly a year. Both a planning and a control instrument, it is a useful tool for individuals and families and an essential one for businesses and large organizations, such as governments, where subordinate units are responsible to a central authority. To assure control, the central authority dispenses funds only for those expenditures approved in the budget. For a government, the budget is also a political statement, reflecting the administration's primary goals and, in the amount of revenues anticipated, its forecasts of the volume of economic activity.

For the federal government of the United States, the major budget outlays are for income (including social security and welfare) and national defense payments, and the major revenue sources are individual income taxes and social insurance contributions and taxes. For state and local governments, the major expenditures are for education and public welfare, and the main revenue sources are sales taxes, property taxes, individual income taxes, and revenues from the federal government.

The U.S. federal budget is made for the fiscal year, which begins on October 1 and ends September 30 the following year. There are two stages in formulating the budget. In the first, the president and the executive branch of the government develop requests for funds and estimates of revenues for the fiscal year. Although government bureaus make rough expenditure plans running several years into the future, actual budget formulation begins about 18 months before the start of the fiscal year, when departments and agencies develop specific requests for funds. These requests are coordinated by the Office of Management and Budget (OMB; see MANAGEMENT AND BUDGET, U.S. OFFICE OF), which is a part of the Executive Office of the President. The OMB confers with the agencies in order to incorporate the president's priorities and then works with the president to prepare the administration's budget request, which is presented to Congress in January.

The second stage in formulating the budget is carried out by the Congress as it considers and acts upon the requests made by the president. Congressional consideration goes forward simultaneously on two levels; on one level, appropriations for specific agencies and departments are determined; the other level sets budgetary aggregates—that is, the total size of the budget. On the appropriations level, the president's requests are considered by subcommittees of the Appropriations Committee of the House of Representatives. Separate appropriations bills are recommended by the committees and acted upon by the House. These bills are considered by the Senate Appropriations Committee and are then acted on by the Senate. Final appropriations bills emerge after differences between the House and the Senate have been reconciled.

On the budget aggregates level, the grand total and the major functional breakdowns of the president's budget are considered by Budget Committees in both the Senate and the House. By about mid-May the Congress adopts a resolution setting target amounts for total expenditures and for broad functional areas of the budget. The CONGRESSIONAL BUDGET OFFICE maintains a running account of specific appropriations and how they match the totals established in the target resolution. In September the Congress compares the total of individual appropriations bills to the total established in the target resolution and takes action to reconcile any difference. (An important issue involves "off-budget" items, such as loan guarantees and financing arrangements. These are not included in the budget, which therefore does not state total anticipated expenditures with entire accuracy.) The appropriations bills then go to the president for signature or veto.

After budget action has been completed by the Congress, the control aspects of the budget process are carried out by the Office of Management and Budget, which releases funds to individual agencies as specified by the budget, and by the GENERAL ACCOUNTING OFFICE, which audits agency and department accounts to ensure that the directives of the budget have been followed.

The U.S. federal government budget process is incremental, for it focuses mainly on changes from previous budget appropriations. ZERO-BASED BUDGETING is an alternative method that gives regular periodic attention to all items in the budget. The zero-based process may be nonincremental—that is, it may ignore preceding budget levels and budget each program as if it were new. The process is often used to examine and justify budgeting levels of individual programs. Another variation is capital budgeting, which separates long-term investment expenditures from current operating expenditures. Program budgeting organizes budget considerations by functions and objectives rather than by administrative agencies.

In Great Britain and Canada the budget prepared by the government (in Great Britain, it is the responsibility of the British Treasury; in Canada, of the Treasury Board) must be accepted or rejected in its entirety by Parliament. Budget preparation in France and other European countries is usually carried out by the entire cabinet. The French Assembly, like the U.S. Congress, has the power to amend budgets submitted to it.   WAYLAND GARDNER

Bibliography: Cogan, John F., et al., *The Budget Puzzle: Understanding Federal Spending* (1993); Collender, Stanley E., *The Guide to the Federal Budget* (1994); Rubin, Irene, ed., *New Directions in Budget Theory* (1987); Wildavsky, Aaron, *The New Politics of the Budgetary Process,* 2d ed. (1991).

Buell, Don Carlos   [bue'-uhl]

Don Carlos Buell, b. near Marietta, Ohio, Mar. 23, 1818, d. Nov. 19, 1898, was a Union general during the American Civil War. An 1841 graduate of West Point, Buell served in the Mexican War. Promoted to brigadier general at the start of the Civil War, he was given command of the Army of the Ohio. Buell supported Ulysses S. GRANT's invasion of Tennessee by seizing (Feb. 25, 1862) Nashville, and he supplied vital reenforcement to Grant at the Battle of SHILOH (April 6–7). In September 1862 he marched north into Kentucky to oppose a Confederate offensive led by Braxton BRAGG. After a fierce but inconclusive battle at Perryville (October 8), Buell was criticized for allowing the Confederates to escape and relieved (October 24) of command.

Buell, John

John Edward Buell, b. Montreal, July 31, 1927, is an English-speaking Canadian novelist whose works have been translated into both French and German. His novels include *The Pyx* (1959), and *The Shrewsdale Exit* (1972), which are studies of the innocent victims of criminals, and *Playground* (1976), about a middle-aged man's naive attempts to return to nature. The novel *A Lot to Make Up For* was published in 1990.

Buen Retiro Palace   [bwayn ray-tee'-roh]

The Buen Retiro Palace was constructed in Madrid between 1631 and 1640 as a suburban pleasure palace for King PHILIP IV. Alonso Carbonell, the principal architect of the building, followed the so-called severe style of the ESCORIAL in his design. The palace and subsidiary buildings were set within an elaborate park still in use today. The interior decoration was planned by Diego VELÁZQUEZ, and other great baroque artists executed paintings. Although much of the palace has been destroyed, the ballroom and the throne room survive and now serve as museums.   EDWARD J. SULLIVAN

Bibliography: Brown, J., and Elliott, J. H., *A Palace for a King* (1980).

Buenaventura   [bway-nah-vayn-too'-rah]

Buenaventura (1985 pop., 157,528) is a port city on the Pacific Ocean in western Colombia, located on Cascajal Island in Buenaventura Bay. Its port facilities handle tobacco, sugar, and coffee from the Cauca Valley as well as platinum and gold from the Chocó region to the north. An oil pipeline has been constructed from Cali, 146 km (91 mi) to the northwest. Founded in 1540, the city developed slowly until construction of railroads and roadways in the early 1900s.

Bueno, Maria   [bway'-noh]

The grace, speed, and power of self-taught Brazilian tennis star Maria Ester Audion Bueno, b. Oct. 11, 1939, made her one of the sport's dominant players from 1958 to 1968. During this period she won 3 Wimbledon (1959–60, 1964) and 4 U.S. (1959, 1963–64, 1966) singles titles; she also captured 12 Grand Slam doubles crowns, despite a long bout with hepatitis (May 1961–September 1963). Bueno was voted Associated Press Female Athlete of the Year for 1959.

Buenos Aires   [bway'-nohs y'-rays]

Buenos Aires, the capital of Argentina and the industrial, political, and cultural center of the country, is located on the Río de la Plata estuary opposite Uruguay. The city proper has a population of 2,960,976 (1991) and an area of 200 km² (77 mi²). The metropolitan district has a population of 10,800,000 (1991) and covers 3,646 km² (1,408 mi²).

Contemporary City. The people of Buenos Aires call themselves *porteños*, or "people of the port." In the second half of the 19th century, a tremendous influx of immigrants from Europe greatly increased the size of the city. The majority of the people are of European origin, mostly Italian. The city also has sizable communities of English, French, and Germans, and smaller numbers of Poles, Russians, Portuguese, Syrians, Turks, and Paraguayans and other South Americans.

Manufacturing and service industries are the mainstays of the city's economy. Industrial products include textiles, automobiles, paper products, chemicals, metal products, and foodstuffs. The port itself, which handles nearly half of the entire nation's foreign trade, is another important employer. The major exports are foodstuffs, wool, and flax.

Buenos Aires constitutes the federal district of Argentina and is controlled by the country's president. The National Congress handles all of the city's legislative affairs, and the mayor is appointed by the president. The city is divided into 46 administrative districts.

Buenos Aires has excellent educational facilities, including more than 40 universities and a number of colleges and tech-

nical schools. Among the major universities are the University of Buenos Aires (1821), the National Technological University (1959), and several religious institutions. Cultural activities and recreational facilities are abundant. The city has 16 museums and approximately 40 theaters, including the world-famous opera house Teatro Colón, and is the home of the national ballet and symphony. Palermo Park, the city's oldest park, covers about 600 ha (1,500 acres). Several large industries have their headquarters here.

History. Buenos Aires was founded in 1536 by Pedro de MENDOZA but was not settled permanently until 1580. Throughout the 17th and 18th centuries, the city remained on the extreme southern periphery of the Spanish empire; Córdoba domi-

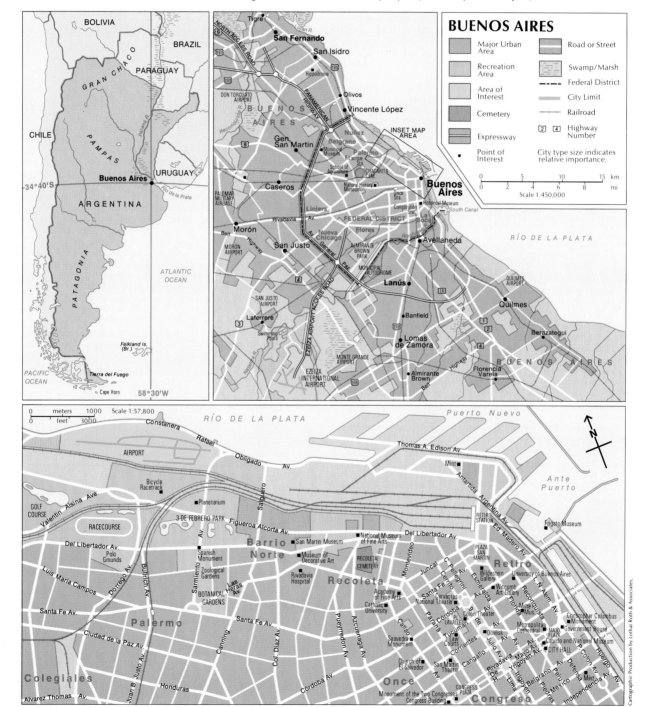

Cartographic Production by Lothar Roth & Associates.

nated the region, because all trade was through the north to Upper Peru and through Panama to Spain. Following the decline of silver production in the north in the late 18th century, Buenos Aires began to gain importance. In 1776 the city was made the center of the new viceroyalty of the Río de la Plata.

When Napoleon invaded Spain in 1810 and deposed the Spanish king, Buenos Aires established its own government. In 1816 it became the capital of the newly proclaimed United Provinces of the Río de la Plata. When the Argentine Republic was consolidated in 1880, Buenos Aires remained the capital. The arrival of the railroad, the development of mechanized farming, and the influx of European immigrants in the late 1800s contributed to the city's further growth.

The growth of Buenos Aires and its increased control over the commerce, industry, politics, and culture of the nation have become overriding problems in Argentina. As jobs, goods, and services became increasingly concentrated in one city, the growth of other metropolitan and middle-level centers slowed or stopped. Argentina recognized the implications of this trend; in 1987, Congress took action to limit further concentration in Buenos Aires. It approved a plan to move the national capital from Buenos Aires to the Patagonian twin cities of Viedma and Carmen de Patagones, with the move beginning in 1988. Buenos Aires will doubtless remain the dominant national center.   RICHARD W. WILKIE

Bibliography: Newton, Ronald, *German Buenos Aires, 1900–1933: Social Change and Cultural Crisis* (1977); Ross, S. R., and McGann, T. F., eds., *Buenos Aires: Four Hundred Years* (1982).

Buffalo

Located in western New York on Lake Erie and the Niagara River, Buffalo is the seat of Erie County. The city has a population of 328,123 (1990), and the metropolitan area, 1,189,288. Once a major Great Lakes port and East-West transshipment point, Buffalo was known as the door to the Midwest during the early 1900s. Today it is a transportation and wholesale-retail center with electronics, fabricated-metals, and food-products industries. Banking is also important.

An educational center, Buffalo is the site of the State University of New York at Buffalo (1846), the State University College at Buffalo (1867), and several other colleges. Its cultural and historic attractions include the noted Albright-Knox Art Gallery, Buffalo Museum of Science, Buffalo Zoological Gardens, and Theodore Roosevelt Inaugural National Historic Site, where Roosevelt was inaugurated president following William McKinley's assassination in Buffalo in 1901. Also a sports center, the city is the home of football's Buffalo Bills as well as a national hockey club and a minor-league baseball team.

Buffalo was founded in 1803, when Joseph Ellicott laid out a village for the Holland Land Company there. The British burned the settlement during the War of 1812, and recovery was slow until 1825, when the Erie Canal opened, bringing trade and prosperity to Buffalo, the canal's western terminus. Trade with the expanding West grew rapidly, and by the turn of the century the city was one of the world's largest grain and livestock markets and a major rail center. Its port bustled with activity as cargo was transferred from Great Lakes steamers to railroad cars, and with the opening (1959) of the St. Lawrence Seaway it began accommodating oceangoing vessels. More recently, since the signing (1988) of the U.S.-Canadian free-trade agreement and because of Buffalo's proximity to Toronto, the city's economy has benefited from Toronto-area shoppers and Canadian investment. Its mass transit system, opened in 1985, has experienced financial difficulties.

buffalo

The name buffalo generally refers to the Asian water buffalo, *Bubalus bubalis*, and the African buffalo, *Syncerus caffer*. Both species have triangular horn cores and other features distinguishing them from other bovids. The name is also, incorrectly, used to refer to the North American BISON.

The Asian water buffalo is found over most of southern

The domesticated water buffalo, B. bubalis, yields high-quality milk, from which yogurt and mozzarella cheese originally were made. Easily handled by people it knows, it is aggressive toward strangers.

Asia. Because it is docile, it has been widely domesticated and is quite common in most of Mediterranean Europe. In southern India these huge beasts with massive horns are often seen being led by children. They are widely used as draft animals, especially in rice paddies. The wide hooves, flexible joints, and short legs are adaptations for swimming or walking in mud. Because they have relatively few sweat glands, they spend much time cooling themselves in water.

The African buffalo was widely distributed in Africa south of the Sahara prior to 1890, but the cattle-virus disease called rinderpest spread through the herds and nearly exterminated them. Their original range is now fragmented, and they have been steadily disappearing from most areas of South Africa. Although they occupy diverse habitats, water is a necessity. Hunters' tales at one time indicated that this buffalo was one of the most dangerous of African mammals. Investigators now describe it as a peaceful grazer.

Males join the cow-calf herds during the breeding season. Calving reaches a peak in July after a gestation period of 330 to 346 days—the longest gestation period for any of the cow-like mammals.   HARVEY L. GUNDERSON

Bibliography: Unipub, *Buffaloes of China* (1976) and *The Water Buffalo* (1978).

buffalo berry

Buffalo berry, or soapberry, is the common name for two species of shrubs, genus *Shepherdia*, of the oleaster family. Native to wooded areas of North America, they bear small, bell-shaped flowers and usually have thorny branches. Their bitter-tasting berries foam in water. Buffalo berries are among the few plants besides legumes that can convert atmospheric nitrogen into compounds used as nutrients by the plants.

Buffalo Bill

William F. "Buffalo Bill" Cody participated in the westward expansion of the United States and helped shape the world's romantic image of the American frontier. Born on Feb. 26, 1846, in LeClair, Iowa, he moved with his family to Kansas and later rode for the pony express. He served briefly in the Civil War and was given the nickname Buffalo Bill when he supplied buffalo meat for workers on the Kansas Pacific Railroad in 1867–68. As chief of scouts for the Fifth U.S. Cavalry, he participated in several Indian fights between 1868 and 1872.

In 1869 his career took a new turn when he became the subject of a dime novel; he subsequently appeared in theatrical melodramas, touring successfully for 11 years. In 1883 he organized a Wild West show that staged Indian fights, roundups, stage robberies, and buffalo hunts and introduced such stars as Buck Taylor and Annie Oakley to the public. His Wild

Buffalo Bill, who posed for this photograph in 1903, inspired colorful myths of the cowboy hero. His Wild West Show captured the imagination of Europeans and Americans, drawing crowds at Queen Victoria's Jubilee (1887) and the Chicago World's Fair (1893).

West show toured Europe and the United States until 1913, after which Cody retired to the West until his death on Jan. 10, 1917.   ELLIOTT WEST

Bibliography: Russell, D., *The Lives and Legends of Buffalo Bill* (1969; repr. 1982).

buffalo fish

Buffalo fishes, genus *Ictiobus* of the sucker family, Catostomidae, are freshwater fishes of eastern America. They are native to large rivers and lakes from southern Canada to northeastern Mexico and have been introduced along the southeastern U.S. coastal plain; all three species broadly overlap in the central Mississippi Valley. Their color ranges from gray to bronze; they have a long dorsal fin; and they feed on insects, crustaceans, and algae. The largest, the bigmouth buffalo, *I. cyprinellus,* weighs up to 36 kg (80 lb); the black buffalo, *I. niger,* and smallmouth buffalo, *I. bubalus,* usually weigh 4.5–5.5 kg (10–12 lb) but may weigh more. The three species are fished commercially.

buffer

In chemistry, a buffer is a solution that resists changes in acidity or alkalinity (pH) when acid or alkali is added. This is accomplished through consumption of added hydrogen ions (H^+) or hydroxyl ions (OH^-) by chemical ASSOCIATION with other ions in the buffer. Usually a buffer comprises a water solution of a weak acid and its related, or conjugate, base (for example, citric acid and citrate ion, or in general, HA and A^-; see ACIDS AND BASES). The buffering action arises because the acid, its conjugate base, and the hydrogen ion participate in a rapid and reversible equilibrium reaction: $HA \rightleftharpoons H^+ + A^-$. Added hydrogen ion associates with A^- to form HA, and added hydroxyl ion associates with H^+ to form water, H_2O. As long as the amount of acid or base added (or formed from a chemical reaction) is small relative to the amount of buffer, it will be consumed with little change in the pH. An example of a buffer is a mixture of sodium acetate and acetic acid. The buffer could also be produced by mixing sodium acetate with a strong acid or mixing acetic acid with a strong base.

Of the many acidic and basic compounds in seawater, the bicarbonate ion (HCO_3^-) and its conjugate base carbonate ion (CO_3^{2-}) are present in the highest concentrations and establish the pH of seawater near 8. The same buffer controls the pH of blood, which is 7.4 (average). The rate or equilibrium position of many chemical reactions depends on the pH of the solutions in which they occur. Buffers often control such reactions in nature or are used for this purpose. Buffers are also widely used as reference solutions of known acidity in the measurement of pH.   C. F. BAES, JR.

Bibliography: Bates, R. G., *Determination of pH*, 2d ed. (1973).

See also: CHEMICAL EQUILIBRIUM; PH.

Buffet, Bernard   [bue-fay', bair-nahr']

Bernard Buffet, b. July 10, 1928, is one of the most successful French painters of *L'Homme témoin* ("the Witness") group. The melancholy and despair brought on by World War II found vivid expression in Buffet's somber canvases from 1945 to 1956. This pessimism is exemplified by his numerous depictions of the Crucifixion, typically with sticklike figures in black, brown, and olive-drab modern dress who reenact the familiar Christian tragedy. Buffet was awarded the Prix de la Critique, bestowed by vote of the major French critics, in 1948. Beginning with a series of paintings of Parisian monuments in 1957, Buffet's work has become increasingly trivial and sentimental in both subject matter and style, in the view of many critics. Buffet has nonetheless retained his great popularity with collectors worldwide.

Bibliography: Buffet, Bernard, *Bernard Buffet: Lithographs, 1952–1966,* pref. by Georges Simenon (1968); Dorival, Bernard, *French Painters: Twentieth Century Painters,* vol. 1, trans. by W. J. Strachan (1958).

Buffon, Georges, Comte de   [bue-fohn', zhawrzh, kohnt duh]

Georges Louis Leclerc, comte de Buffon, b. Sept. 7, 1707, d. Apr. 16, 1788, a French naturalist, wrote *Natural History,* one of the most widely read scientific works of the 18th century. In 1739 he became the intendant, or director, of the Jardin du Roi, the French botanical gardens. With the help of collaborators, Buffon spent almost 50 years until his death writing the eventually 44-volume *Natural History,* which concerns almost all nature, as well as presenting Buffon's views on the origin and age of the Earth—one of the first not based on biblical interpretations. Well known and respected, he was made a count in 1753 by King Louis XV.

Bibliography: Adams, Alexander B., *Eternal Quest* (1969); Fellows, Otis E., and Milliken, S. F., *Buffon* (1972); Lyon, John, and Sloan, Philip, *From Natural History to the History of Nature: Readings from Buffon and His Critics* (1981).

bug: see HEMIPTERA.

Bugaku   [boo-gah'-koo]

Bugaku is the classical dance of the Japanese court. It originated at the Chinese court and came to Japan by way of Korea in the 6th century. It is one of the oldest important dance forms known in the world. Adapted to Japanese tastes, Bugaku has been supported continuously at the emperor's palace to the present day. The dancers are men, dressed in elaborate ceremonial costumes and often masked. Dancers move in unison, forming geometric patterns with slow and dignified gestures, to the accompaniment of percussion, string, and wind music called *gagaku.*   JAMES R. BRANDON

Buganda: see GANDA; UGANDA.

Bugatti, Ettore Arco Isidoro

Ettore Bugatti, b. Sept. 15, 1881, d. Aug. 21, 1947, was an Italian designer of racing cars. His factory at Molsheim, Alsace, produced, between 1909 and the late 1940s, the best designed and fastest racers of the times (in the 1925–26 season his cars won over 1,000 races). Bugatti's Type 35, Type 41, and Type 57 models were especially highly praised.

bugbane

Bugbane, *Cimicifuga americana,* is an herb in the buttercup family, Ranunculaceae. The plants are tall, white, ill-smelling perennials found in damp woods in the Northern Hemisphere. Both the scientific and the common name refer to the insect-repelling properties of bugbane. The genus name, *Cimicifuga,* is a combination of the Latin words *cimex* ("bug") and *fugere* ("to repel").

Bugis [boo'-gis]

The Bugis (Buginese) are one of the two major ethnic groups (the other is the Macassarese) who occupy the southern peninsula of the island of Sulawesi (Celebes) in eastern Indonesia. They are closely related to the Toradja, who live in west central Sulawesi. Of all the peoples living in Sulawesi, the Bugis are the most culturally advanced, with a high literacy rate. The more than 3 million Bugis speak a language affiliated with the Malayo-Polynesian linguistic family.

The Bugis were early converts to Buddhism but in the 17th century adopted Islam. They developed a highly stratified society and adopted an Indian-derived script in which they produced a rich literature. The Bugis were famous as skilled traders and sailors; some of them were pirates who raided coastal principalities. In those regions they conquered, the local ruler was forced to accept a Bugis as advisor.

As rice farmers, the Bugis live in villages of several hundred residents. Some houses are so large that they are occupied by as many as 20 related families. They also raise cattle, horses, and water buffalo. Polygamy is allowed, but most married Bugis have only one wife. Although Muslim, the Bugis retain beliefs in ancestral spirits.   DONN V. HART

Bibliography: Le Bar, Frank M., ed., *Indonesia, Andaman Islands, and Madagascar* (1972), vol. 1 in *Ethnic Groups of Insular Southeast Asia*; Provencher, Ronald, *Mainland Southeast Asia* (1975).

bugle

The bugle is a wind instrument that comprises a coiled tube of metal, usually brass, without valves and ending in a bell. Its pitches, G or B flat, are limited to the lower tones of the harmonic series. The bugle was originally used for giving military signals, such as reveille, charge, retreat, or taps, but its use is now mostly ceremonial. In the mid-18th century the British army used the bugle, as did the Hessians during the American Revolution. The bugle has also been used for hunting calls. The American army used the bugle in World War I, but since then a mechanical apparatus has performed the bugle's former military function. The OPHICLEIDE, a bass bugle, was developed in 1817.   ELWYN A. WIENANDT

bugleweed

Bugleweed is the common name for two nonaromatic genera in the mint family, Labiatae. The genus *Ajuga* comprises about 40 species of annual or perennial herbs native to the Old World. The flowers are mainly blue, though sometimes white or pink, and are valued horticulturally as ground cover. Creeping species such as *A. reptans* have become naturalized throughout North America. The genus *Lycopus*, also known as water horehound, comprises perennial herbs found in the northern temperate regions. They grow in moist ground and have small, mostly white flowers.

Buhari, Mohammed [bu-hah'-ree]

Maj.-Gen. Mohammed Buhari, b. Dec. 17, 1942, became head of state of Nigeria in the Dec. 31, 1983, coup that ousted Shehu SHAGARI. Buhari, an officer involved in the 1975 coup against Gen. Yakubu GOWON, served as military governor of the North Eastern State (1975–76) and later as national oil minister. As a member of the Supreme Military Council (1976–77) he helped arrange the 1979 transition to civilian rule, but he later became disillusioned with the Shagari regime. After the 1983 coup Buhari became head of the ruling military council and commander in chief of the armed forces. The economy failed to improve, and he was overthrown in a coup led by Ibrahim BABANGIDA on Aug. 27, 1985.

Bühler, Karl [bue'-lur]

Karl Bühler, b. May 27, 1879, d. Oct. 24, 1963, was a German psychologist who was a leading spokesman for the Würzburg school and an advocate of imageless thought. He was one of the earliest proponents of an experimental psychology of cognition, and his work *The Mental Development of the Child* (1928; Eng. trans., 1930) was important in shaping the field of child psychology. He was also an important contributor to the psychological study of language, influencing Roman JAKOBSON and the PRAGUE SCHOOL. Bühler's studies led to a famous controversy with Wilhelm WUNDT concerning the nature and limits of introspection in the analysis of higher mental activities.

At the University of Vienna, from 1922, Bühler and his wife, Charlotte, developed a world-renowned psychological institute. Forced to flee Vienna in 1938, Bühler went eventually to the United States.   BERNARD KAPLAN

building construction

Building construction involves the techniques and procedures by which a building is erected. A building is generally classed by the material used to create its frame. The basic structural component of most large-scale modern buildings is steel; for buildings whose structure is primarily wood, see HOUSE. The principles used in steel construction have evolved from the era of CAST-IRON ARCHITECTURE, beginning in the late 18th century. Although steel has replaced iron as the primary structural element, the engineering principles associated with the development of the iron TRUSS and the ARCH, beam, and COLUMN are still in use today.

SKELETON STEEL FRAMING

Skeleton steel construction evolved in Chicago in the 1880s and '90s and has continued to be one of the most important techniques used in the construction of tall buildings. A skeleton steel frame comprises a braced steel framework of columns and beams connected by bolts, rivets, or electric welding (see RIVETING; WELDING AND SOLDERING). This steel framework, or skeleton, supports all floors and walls. The exterior, or curtain, walls are attached to the steel framework. Interior partitions, called nonbearing walls, do not add to the rigidity or strength of the building.

Built floor by floor, steel-frame structures can be erected to great heights. For many years the standard practice was to rivet the beams to the columns, thus forming a semirigid connection. Electric arc-welding had been perfected by the 1920s to a point where the entire frame could be welded into a rigid, homogeneous grid of interconnecting columns and beams. The most recent technique in joining steel structural members is the use of high-strength structural bolts. These bolts, made from special steels and finished to exact dimensions, are installed in predrilled holes and tightened by a pneumatic wrench to form an immobile joint.

Tall buildings rest on FOUNDATIONS usually of reinforced concrete piers drilled or dug to sufficient depth to support the building. PILES of wood, concrete, or steel are driven into the dense soils deep under the surface and then used to support reinforced concrete on which the steel skeleton rests.

The erection of structural steel is accomplished with cranes or DERRICKS. The steel is erected floor by floor. Each piece of structural steel is fabricated in a factory, where it is marked to show exactly where it will go in the finished frame. Beams and columns are hoisted into place, aligned, and temporarily bolted. When the steel members of a complete floor are in position, they are braced and checked for perfect alignment, and the joints are then permanently fixed by riveting, welding, or bolting. When the steel skeleton has been completed and beams and floors are in place, the curtain wall panels are attached to the structural frame. Mechanical equipment and interior finish material can then be installed.

CURTAIN WALLS

A curtain wall is an exterior wall that carries no floor loads; it usually is made principally of metal, stone, glass, or precast concrete. Prefabricated into panels, the curtain is attached to the structural frame by clips or anchors to form a continuous wall. Curtain walls may also be made of sandwich panels. In this case a metal exterior panel, a layer of insulation, and a layer of interior finish material are prefabricated into a single unit by joining the three layers; this unit then forms both the interior and exterior walls. The joints between the panels of curtain walls must be sealed to prevent water seepage.

FLOOR AND ROOF SYSTEMS

Floor and roof systems are closely related to the structural frame. The oldest type of floor used on steel skeleton framed buildings comprised reinforced concrete slabs about 10 cm (4 in) thick, laid between wrought-iron I beams. Today reinforced concrete slabs that span 3.7 to 5.5 m (12 to 18 ft) can be poured into place. Spaces of greater width may be spanned by ribbed reinforced concrete slabs, which are poured into place over hollow clay tile or metal pans to form reinforced concrete beams that span distances between the major steel beams.

One of the lightest floor- and roof-support members for long spans is the open-web steel joist, a variety of truss. It can be fabricated to span up to 44 m (144 ft). The top and bottom chords usually comprise two steel angles separated by diagonal round steel bars or steel angles. The top chord rests on the structural beam, where it is bolted or welded into place. The most commonly used material for spanning between open-web joists is steel decking, a light-gauge sheet steel prefabricated with corrugations to furnish stiffening. Cellular steel decking comprises two sheets of steel held apart to form hexagonally shaped open cells. These cells may be used as conduits for electrical and other wiring. The decking is usually welded to the structural beams, and a 50- to 100-cm (2- to 4-in) concrete fill completes the rough floor.

FIREPROOFING
Although steel is an incombustible material, it loses its strength and buckles or collapses when heated to 650°–950° C (1,200°–1,700° F). Early steel buildings were protected from the effects of fire by clay tile, masonry, or concrete surrounding each column and beam. Although these materials are still used to a limited extent, other methods have been developed that use lighter, thinner substances. Contact fireproofing uses GYPSUM or portland cement plaster mixed with PERLITE or ver-

miculite; this is sprayed directly onto columns, beams, and the underside of steel decking. H columns may be wrapped with metal lath, which is then plastered or sprayed with gypsum or portland cement to make a square column. Steel decks and floor beams may be protected by membrane fireproofing, a thin, lightweight ceiling attached to or hung underneath decks and beams on steel wires. The membrane is usually made of vermiculite or perlite and gypsum plaster. The space between the floor and the hung ceiling is used for ducts, piping, electrical wiring, and other mechanical equipment.

Traditionally, all exterior structural members were encased in insulation as fire protection. Three new forms of protection are now in use: hollow steel columns and beams are filled with liquid; flame shields are placed around window openings to direct the heat of a fire away from the structural steel; the structural steel is separated from building walls so that the air space between wall and steel prevents heat buildup.

LONG-SPAN STEEL FRAMING
Large buildings such as auditoriums, airports, and sports arenas require greater distances between supports than can be supplied by traditional column-and-beam framing. Large areas may be covered instead by long-span steel framing. The most common types of long-span framing include built-up girders—steel plates and shapes welded or riveted together to form a structural member of far greater strength than the single girder. Built-up girders offer great flexibility, because they may be arched or tapered to suit different design requirements and may be pierced in low-stress areas to allow pipes, ducts, and conduits to pass through. Trusses are also used to span large areas. Usually prefabricated in the shop, they are hoisted into place by cranes or derricks. As the trusses are set,

(Below) *Tower cranes were moved to successively higher levels to hoist structural materials into place during construction of the World Trade Center in New York City. The buildings used closely spaced columns to supply exterior load-bearing walls.*

(Above) *Different stages in skyscraper construction are illustrated in this urban renewal project in Portland, Ore. Reinforced concrete pillar foundation supports for the steel skeleton are being formed at the lower right. The uncoated skeletal steel framing is exposed in the upper stories of the building; in the lower levels, the steel already has been surfaced with cement to protect it against corrosion and fire. Floor joists and floors serve as platforms for the construction workers as the building proceeds upward.*

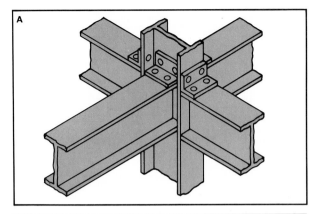

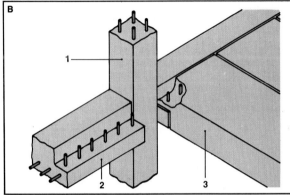

The rigid column-and-beam skeleton frames of skyscrapers are made either of steel sections connected by riveted, bolted, or welded iron brackets (A) or of reinforced concrete (B). In reinforced concrete construction, pillars (1), main beams (2), and floor slabs (3) are cast in place as integral units reinforced with steel rods to provide the tensile strength that concrete lacks.

they are held in alignment by horizontal beams called purlins, which span between trusses.

When very large clear spans are needed, open-web arches may be used. The arch may start from the ground and furnish support for the walls as well as for the roof. The bottom of the arch is connected to the foundation by heavy pin connections. These act as hinges and allow the bottom of the arch to move, thus relieving stresses that could build up in individual members of the arch. This type of arch is called a two-hinged arch. A three-hinged arch has a third pin connection at the center of the span. For long spans, tie rods, either in or under a concrete floor, tie the bottom of the two sides of the arch together. Arched trusses may radiate from a central point, forming a dome. The outward thrust is resisted by a tension ring on the outside of the circle thus formed. Covers over athletic facilities with spans as great as 200 m (660 ft) use this type of framing.

Space frames, known also as lattice structures, comprise three-dimensional, trusslike triangular frameworks used to span square or rectangular areas. The individual members are arranged to carry loads to four or more supports on all sides of the rectangle. Space frames are used for structures such as exhibition halls, where long spans and a column-free interior space are desired. Space frames with parallel top and bottom surfaces are usually constructed of standardized, prefabricated rods or tubes that can be quickly assembled and erected by simple methods. Joints, which may serve to connect as many as nine identical members, may be designed for bolted or welded connections. The framing members are fabricated and joined together in the shop in sections that can be conveniently transported to the job site and hoisted into place by a crane. The matching joints are finished on the site by welding

or bolting. Prefabricated metal or precast concrete roof deck, insulation, and roofing can then be applied to the top of the space frame to complete the assembly. The underside of the space frame may be left exposed, whereby it becomes an interior design feature.

CABLE-SUPPORTED STRUCTURES

In recent years a substantial upsurge has occurred in the design and construction of cable-supported structures. This type of system uses a wire-cable suspension bridge, which had reached a high state of development in the 1860s. Two types of cable-supported structures are in use today: the single-story hanging roof, and multistory systems using cables for vertical supports.

A cable is the most economical form of steel with which to span large areas. A steel cable has an extremely high tensile strength and flexibility. Roof decks supported entirely by steel cables take on a characteristic shape because the cables naturally sag downward. Cable-supported roofs introduce a new problem into design because they tend to be aerodynamically unstable (affected by wind). Several techniques have been used to overcome flutter in suspended roofs. One of the first major one-story, cable-supported roofs erected in the United States was the State Fair and Exhibition building in Raleigh, N.C., built in 1954. In this building the roofing rests on a tightly drawn two-layered grid of cables at right angles to one another. The cables are anchored to two parabolic reinforced concrete arches on a common axis. The arches slope outward and are joined at the low point of the roof to form a stable structure, putting all cables in tension. Another form of suspended roof construction is Eero SAARINEN's Dulles International Airport in Washington, D.C., completed in 1962. This building has a cable suspension system covered with heavy precast concrete decking. In the multistory suspension system a central reinforced concrete core or tower is erected first. The roof and floors are hung from a steel truss above the roof. Exterior curtain walls are then hung from the floors.

REINFORCED CONCRETE CONSTRUCTION

Concrete is a material with great compressive strength. It can be designed to resist a compressive load of 69 kilonewtons a square meter (10,000 lb/in²). Concrete, however, has little resistance to a pulling force or tension. Steel is produced with a tensile strength of 345 kN/m² (50,000 lb/in²). Concrete and steel are combined in reinforced concrete to take advantage of the strengths of each material. Modern reinforced concrete construction uses many smaller steel reinforcing bars exactly shaped and placed in each structural member.

The first high-rise concrete buildings were constructions of columns and beams similar to skeleton steel framing. The concrete was hoisted up temporary steel towers and poured into wooden forms to shape the columns and beams. When the concrete had set and gained sufficient strength, the forms were removed and reused. As the concrete skeleton progressed upward, new forms were set, and the floors were poured over the beams. The refinement of flat slab framing in the 1920s greatly reduced the weight of buildings by eliminating many of the heavy beams. In this system the reinforced floor slabs act as a continuous beam attached to, and spanning between, columns. A recent innovation in concrete construction is the design of exterior walls as load-bearing columns and beams. Flat slabs span from the exterior framework to solid interior walls that act as shear panels. This type of construction eliminates the use of a curtain wall.

The full potential of concrete in building construction resulted from the development of prestressing, which is the method of inducing a controlled stress in a beam before it is subjected to a load. In the first type of prestressing, called pretensioning, high-quality steel cables are imbedded in the lower portion of the beam or in areas where tension exists. The steel cables are placed in forms and stretched by heavy jacks; the concrete is poured into the form and allowed to set; and the jacks are then released, putting the concrete in compression. In the other type of prestressing, called posttensioning, the cables may be located in hollow tubes placed within the forms. The concrete is poured into the forms and allowed to set; and the cables are put in tension by screws or jacks and wedged into place against steel plates at opposite ends of the beam.

The labor of building forms and the equipment necessary to transport and place concrete in high structures are major cost items. Concrete formed and placed in factories or at ground level is simpler and less expensive. Intricate shapes and textures can be obtained in forms lined with metal, plastic, or plaster. Two major methods have been developed to erect precast walls or floors: tilt-up and lift-slab construction.

Tilt-up construction comprises casting wall panels in a horizontal position and, when they have gained sufficient strength, tilting them up into position by cranes. Individual panels are generally joined by poured-in-place concrete pilasters. Steel reinforcing rods projecting from the edges of adjacent panels are welded together, wood forms are erected, and the pilaster is poured to make a rigid wall.

Lift-slab construction is similar to tilt-up construction. Concrete or steel columns are erected, and the ground-floor slab is cast. The second, third, and subsequent floors are cast on top of the first floor; the final floor is the roof slab. The roof and floor slabs are lifted into position one at a time by hydraulic jacks at a rate of 2 to 3 m/h (7 to 10 ft/h). As each slab reaches its designated position, it is attached to the column. Buildings more than 12 stories high have been constructed by this method.

SHELL STRUCTURES
A shell structure is formed of single or double curved surfaces where the ratio of thickness to span is 1:500 or less. Column,

beam, and slab structures resist bending and shearing forces by their strength, and shell structures have stresses uniformly distributed over their entire surface and resist loading by their shape. The simplest of the shell structures comprise barrel vaults and domes. Builders in Europe and Latin America used thin shell structures in a variety of shapes derived from the geometry of double-warped surfaces, such as the conoid and hyperbolic paraboloid. Outstanding shell structures have been designed and constructed by Felix CANDELA of Mexico, Luigi NERVI of Italy, Oscar NIEMEYER of Brazil, and Eduardo Torroja of Spain. Relatively few outstanding structures have been constructed in North America and the United Kingdom. One of the most unusual shell structures, designed by the Danish architect Jorn Utzon, is the Opera House in Sydney, Australia.

Most shell structures can be constructed on forms made of straight pieces of lumber. The forms are erected on falsework, and the reinforcing, which comprises an intricate web of small reinforcing rods or wire, is spaced in such a way that it will be in the center of the finished slab. The concrete is pumped into place through flexible hoses. Sections of the shell may be precast in a shop or on the job site for future erection.

FACTORY-PRODUCED MODULES
In the future, building construction may be revolutionized by a new technology using preformed modular structures. Several systems have been developed that use factory-produced modules that can be assembled to form a complete high-rise building. In France more than 100,000 dwelling units are pro-

In the lift-slab method of building construction, the columns (1) of a building are erected first. All floors, including the roof, are then cast at ground level, one on top of the other. The complete stack of floors is hoisted up the columns one at a time by hydraulic jacks (2). As the stack rises, each of the lower floors (3) is secured in position by an anchor frame (4) at the appropriate level, and the outer walls (5) are constructed. The raising of the individual floors of a stack (6) is represented diagrammatically in the figure at right.

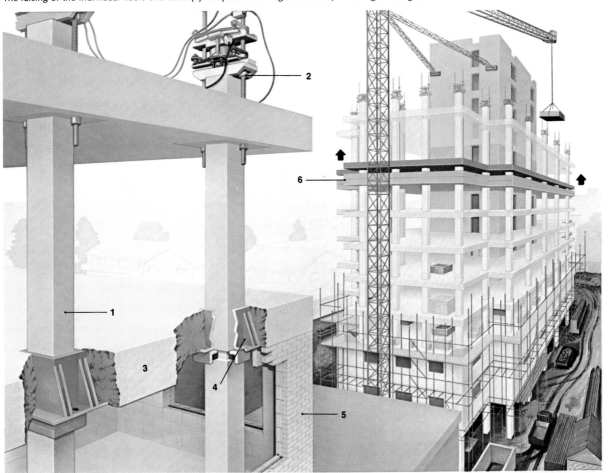

(Above) *Buckminster Fuller used a huge geodesic dome, a self-supporting sphere of interlocking steel triangles with a transparent interior skin of plastic, for the United States Pavilion at the 1967 Montreal world exposition.*

(Right) *The Opera House in Sydney, Australia, is a structure consisting of huge concrete shell vaults. The thick, arching concrete ribs that support the concrete walls were precast on the ground and later assembled and interlocked.*

(Below) *Prefabricated concrete modules— box-shaped units complete with utilities— were hoisted into place to form the apartment complex Habitat, displayed at the Montreal world exposition in 1967. This type of multistory modular construction is finding increasing use in Europe.*

duced annually that use precast concrete walls and slabs in room-sized units containing all utilities. The box-shaped units are assembled on the ground and hoisted into place in a structural steel frame by a crane. In London many multistory flats are now produced whose units are machine-molded from materials reinforced with glass fiber and are hoisted into place in modular steel-framed structures. Scandinavia has produced several industrialized building systems that are used throughout the world under licensing arrangements. One example is the Skarne system developed in Sweden. This system is used to construct multistory housing units up to 25 stories high. All components are delivered to the site prefabricated; vinyl coverings are on the floors, ceilings are painted, the partitions snap into premolded floor and ceiling tracks, and cabinet and closet walls are prefinished. These components are precision manufactured with tolerances of a few millimeters. Although Europe has moved toward modular buildings, U.S. progress has been slow, partially because of the multiplicity of building codes and regulations. Prefabricated modular systems will be successful only when such regulations are modified to the point where mass production is feasible.   DON A. WATSON

Bibliography: Cowan, H. J., and Smith, P. R., *Dictionary of Architectural and Building Technology* (1986); Olin, H. B., et al., *Construction Principles, Materials and Methods* (1983); Smith, R. C., and Andres, C. K., *Principles and Practices of Heavy Construction*, 3d ed. (1986); Smith, R. C., and Honkala, T. L., *Principles and Practices of Light Construction*, 4th ed. (1986); Watson, Don A., *Construction Materials and Methods* (1978).

See also: CEMENT AND CONCRETE; GEODESIC DOME; SKYSCRAPER.

Buisson, Ferdinand Édouard   [boo-ee-sohn', fair-dee-nahn' ay-dwar']

Ferdinand Édouard Buisson, b. Dec. 20, 1841, d. Feb. 16, 1932, a French educator and politician, advocated peace and civil rights. With Ludwig Quidde, he received the 1927 Nobel Peace Prize for his work as president of the League for the Rights of Man, which he helped found (1898), and for his efforts to promote Franco-German reconciliation. Buisson taught philosophy in Neuchâtel, Switzerland, from 1866 to 1870. He returned to France after the downfall of Napoleon III and the establishment of the Third Republic. In 1879 he became the director of elementary education. Buisson taught (1896–1902) pedagogy at the Sorbonne and edited (1882–93) the *Dictionnaire de pédagogie et d'instruction primaire*. He served in the Chamber of Deputies (1902–14, 1919–24).

Bujones, Fernando   [boo-hoh'-nays]

Fernando Bujones, b. Miami, Fla., Mar. 9, 1955, was a dancer with American Ballet Theatre (1972-85); since 1990 he has been a principal guest artist there. Since 1987 he also has been a permanent guest artist with the Boston Ballet. A 1974 gold medal winner at the Varna International Ballet Competition in Bulgaria, Bujones has a classical style and technique that has earned him leading roles in such showpieces as *Le Corsaire, La Bayadère,* and *Swan Lake.*   PETER ROSENWALD

Bujumbura   [boo-joom-boo'-rah]

Bujumbura is the capital and largest city (1990 pop., 236,334) of Burundi, in central Africa. Located at the northeastern end of Lake Tanganyika, it was formerly known as Usumbura and was renamed Bujumbura in 1962, when Burundi became independent. It has a university (1961).

Bukhari, al-   [bu-kah'-ree, ahl]

Muhammad Ibn Ismail al-Bukhari, b. July 21, 810, d. Aug. 31, 870, was a Muslim scholar who compiled a collection of *Hadith* (traditions about Muhammad) in a book, *Al-Jami al-sahih,* ranked second only to the Koran in influence among Muslims. Born in Bukhara, he made a pilgrimage to Mecca as a teenager and then spent 16 years traveling through Asia to listen to Muslim authorities, gathering traditions and sayings of the prophet. Al-Bukhari's tomb, near Samarkand, is an important shrine for pilgrims.

Bukharin, Nikolai Ivanovich   [boo-kar'-een, nik-oh-ly' ee-vah'-noh-vich]

Nikolai Ivanovich Bukharin, b. Oct. 9 (N.S.), 1888, d. Mar. 13, 1938, a leading Soviet theoretician of the 1920s, was executed during the Great Purge of the 1930s. He became a Bolshevik in 1906 and lived in exile from 1911 until 1917. In August 1917 he was elected to the Bolshevik Central Committee. After the Bolshevik Revolution in November (October, O.S.) 1917, he became editor of *Pravda.* Bukharin led the so-called Left Communist opposition to the Treaty of Brest-Litovsk (Mar. 3, 1918), but he later accepted Lenin's policies. Chosen a full member of the Politburo in 1924, he became president of the Communist International (Comintern) two years later.

When Joseph Stalin began the forced collectivization of agriculture in 1928, Bukharin opposed the new policy, becoming leader of the Right Opposition. He lost his posts in 1929. Although he soon recanted his criticisms, he never regained his former power. Arrested in 1937, Bukharin was tried publicly in March 1938 for conspiring to overthrow the Soviet state. He made a partial confession and was shot. Soviet authorities later acknowledged that the charge was false, and he was officially rehabilitated in 1988. Bukharin's most influential work was *Economic Theory of Leisure Class* (1927).

Bibliography: Cohen, Stephen F., *Bukharin and the Bolshevik Revolution* (1973; repr. 1980); Kemp-Welch, Anthony, ed., *The Ideas of Nikolai Bukharin* (1992); Larina, Anna, *This I Cannot Forget: The Memoirs of Nikolai Bukharin's Widow* (1993).

Bukowski, Charles

The American poet, short-story writer, and novelist Charles Bukowski, b. Andernach, Germany, Aug. 16, 1920, d. Mar. 9, 1994, was a literary cult hero who emerged in the early 1960s. Bukowski's voluminous works—unconventional, unrevised, uneven—reveal a powerfully negative worldview in their depiction of Los Angeles low life. The collection *War All the*

Time: Poems, 1981–1984 was published in 1984; *Pulp,* a detective novel parody, in 1994.

Bulawayo   [boo-lah-way'-yoh]

Bulawayo ("the Place of Slaughter"; 1992 pop., 620,936), in southeastern Africa, is the capital of Matabeleland and Zimbabwe's second largest city and chief industrial center. It was founded on its present site in 1894 by British settlers under the leadership of Cecil Rhodes. Bulawayo is a railroad junction and an educational and service center. Its industries include metal fabricating, food processing, auto assembly, and tobacco processing.   ALAN C. G. BEST

bulbul

The bulbuls comprise many species of birds, family Pycnonotidae, order Passeriformes, that inhabit tropical and subtropical Africa, southern Asia, the Malay archipelago, and the Philippines. The 120 species vary from sparrow- to thrush-size, and most have olive green, brown, and yellow plumage.   W. EARL GODFREY

Bulfinch, Charles

Charles Bulfinch, b. Boston, Aug. 8, 1763, d. Apr. 4, 1844, is considered the first native-born professional American architect. Although a graduate (1781) of Harvard College, he learned architecture through independent study. From 1785 to 1787, Bulfinch traveled throughout England, France, and Italy. He was particularly attracted to the English architecture of Robert Adam. Bulfinch's version of the Adam style is known in the United States as the FEDERAL STYLE.

With his designs for the Massachusetts State House, Boston (1795–98), and the Connecticut State House, now Hartford City Hall (1792–96), Bulfinch used a domed central block with heavy flanking wings, which reflects the influence of Andrea Palladio as much as that of Robert Adam. Another of Bulfinch's outstanding designs is the central part of the Massachusetts General Hospital (1817–20).

In 1818, Bulfinch became the Architect of the Capitol in Washington, D.C., succeeding Benjamin LATROBE. He continued Latrobe's restoration of those areas of the Capitol burned during the War of 1812, including the rotunda, and completed the west portico to his own designs.

Bibliography: Hunt, W. D., Jr., *Encyclopedia of American Architecture* (1980); Kirker, Harold, *The Architecture of Charles Bulfinch* (1969; repr. 1977); Place, Charles A., *Charles Bulfinch* (1925; repr. 1968).

Bulfinch, Thomas

Thomas Bulfinch, b. Newton, Mass., July 15, 1796, d. May 17, 1867, the son of the architect Charles Bulfinch, was the author of a popular account of classical and world mythology, *The Age of Fable* (1855). He also wrote an account of Arthurian and Carolingian legends, *The Age of Chivalry* (1858). The two are often published together as *Bulfinch's Mythology.*

Bulgakov, Mikhail Afanasievich   [bul-gah'-kawf, meek-hyl' ah-fuh-nah'-syuh-vich]

At the time of his death the Russian novelist and playwright Mikhail Bulgakov, b. May 15 (N.S.), 1891, d. Mar. 10, 1940, was known chiefly for his novel *The White Guard* (1925; Eng. trans., 1973) and its stage adaptation, *The Days of the Turbins* (1926; Eng. trans., 1938, 1963, 1972), which were probably the only Soviet works concerning the Russian Revolution in which the enemies of the Bolsheviks were described with a degree of sympathy. Paradoxically, the play was a favorite of Joseph Stalin, who protected Bulgakov from reprisals.

Bulgakov is regarded today as one of this century's finest Russian satirists and fantasy writers. His works include the uncompleted novel *Black Snow,* published in 1965 (Eng. trans., 1968); *The Master and Margarita,* published in a censored edition in 1966–67 (Eng. trans., 1968); *The Heart of a Dog* (1925; Eng. trans., 1968), a caustic satire on Soviet life; and numerous plays.   MAURICE FRIEDBERG

Bibliography: Curtis, J. A. E., *Bulgakov's Last Decade* (1987) and *Manuscripts Don't Burn: Mikhail Bulgakov, A Life in Letters and Diaries* (1992); Milne, Lesley, *Mikhail Bulgakov* (1990); Proffer, Ellendea, *Mikhail Bulgakov* (1984).

Bulgakov, Sergei Nikolayevich   [sir-gay' nik-oh-ly'-e-vich]

Sergei Nikolayevich Bulgakov, b. June 16 (N.S.), 1871, d. July 12, 1944, was a Russian theologian and philosopher. After studies at the seminary of Orel, he joined the Marxist movement during his years at the University of Moscow. While professor (1901–06) of political economy at the Kiev Polytechnic Institute, he published *From Marxism to Idealism* (1903), which signaled his conversion to Christianity. In 1918 he was ordained an Orthodox priest. Expelled from Russia, he died in Paris, where he was dean of the Orthodox Theological Institute. In his numerous books, Bulgakov developed a system known as sophiology; it affirms—not unlike the thought of Paul Tillich and Teilhard de Chardin—a metaphysical continuity between God and creation.   JOHN MEYENDORFF

Bulganin, Nikolai Aleksandrovich   [bool-gahn'-yin, nik'-oh-ly ah-lik-sahn'-droh-vich]

Nikolai Aleksandrovich Bulganin, b. June 11 (N.S.), 1895, d. Feb. 24, 1975, was the chairman of the Council of Ministers (premier) of the USSR (1955–58). A Communist party member from 1917, he was an industrial and economic administrator who was elected to the Central Committee of the party in 1934. He served as a political commissar in the army during World War II and became minister of the armed forces in 1947. After the death (1953) of Joseph Stalin, Bulganin supported Nikita KHRUSHCHEV in his power struggle with Georgy MALENKOV, whom he eventually replaced as premier. He later opposed Khrushchev, however, and was demoted.

Bulgaria

Bulgaria is located on the Balkan Peninsula in southeastern Europe. It is bordered by the Black Sea on the east, Turkey and Greece on the south, Serbia and Macedonia on the west, and Romania on the north.

Although a small country today, Bulgaria was once the dominant power in the Balkans. In the Middle Ages it competed with the Byzantine Empire and greatly influenced the cultural life of the region, until conquered by the Ottoman Turks in the late 14th century. The modern nation of Bulgaria was established in 1878. From 1947 until 1989 it was under dictatorial Communist rule.

LAND AND RESOURCES

Bulgaria is divided into four major geographic regions. The most northerly is the plateau of the Danube, which rises from the shore of the Danube River to the foothills of the east.

The ancient Rilski Monastrie, or Rila Monastery, lies in a valley of the Rila Mountains, in southwestern Bulgaria. The fortresslike monastery, a historic center of the Bulgarian Orthodox church, is a center of national culture and a major tourist attraction.

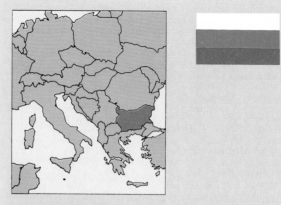

REPUBLIC OF BULGARIA

LAND. Area: 110,994 km² (42,855 mi²). Capital and largest city: Sofia (1991 est. pop., 1,140,795).
PEOPLE. Population (1993 est.): 8,831,168; density: 79.6 persons per km² (206 per mi²). Distribution (1993 est.): 67% urban, 33% rural. Annual growth (1993 est.): −0.39%. Official language: Bulgarian. Major religions: Eastern Orthodoxy, Islam.
EDUCATION AND HEALTH. Literacy (1990): 98% of adult population. Universities (1993): 3. Hospital beds (1992): 87,010. Physicians (1992): 27,117. Life expectancy (1993): women—76; men—69. Infant mortality (1992): 15.9 per 1,000 live births.
ECONOMY. GDP (1992): $34.1 billion; $3,861 per capita. Labor distribution (1990): agriculture—13.1%; manufacturing and mining—38.3%; construction—6.3%; transportation and communications—8.5%; trade—6.3%; public utilities and housing—1.9%; public administration and defense—25.4%; other—0.2%. Foreign trade (1992): imports—$3.2 billion; exports—$3.2 billion; principal trade partners (1992)—former USSR, Germany, Italy. Currency: 1 lev = 100 stotinki.
GOVERNMENT. Type: republic. Legislature: National Assembly. Political subdivisions: 9 provinces.
COMMUNICATIONS. Railroads (1992): 6,560 km (4,076 mi) total. Roads (1992): 36,922 km (22,942 mi) total. Major ports: 3. Major airfields: 1.

Its climate is continental, with hot summers and cold winters. The Balkan Mountains (or "Old Mountains" to the Bulgarians) are the second region. They are highest in the western part of the country and gradually diminish as they extend across the country to the Black Sea. These mountains serve to block the cold winds blowing from the plains of Russia, and the region to the south, the valley drained by the Maritsa River, enjoys a Mediterranean climate, with mild, rainy winters and warm, dry summers. Finally, south of the Maritsa River valley are the Rhodope Mountains, highest in the Balkan Peninsula, which form the border between Bulgaria and Greece.

The Danube Plateau and the Maritsa valley are important agricultural regions. The former produces wheat, corn, sugar beets, and sunflowers. The Maritsa valley grows tobacco

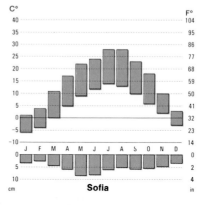

(Left) *Bars indicate monthly ranges of temperatures (red) and precipitation (blue) of Sofia. Bulgaria has a continental climate with Mediterranean influences.*

and contains the famous Valley of Roses, devoted to the production of attar of roses, a vital ingredient in the making of perfume. The mountains contain valuable forests, about three-quarters of which are broadleaf and the rest coniferous. Bears, wolves, foxes, squirrels, elk, and wildcats can still be found in Bulgaria's mountain forests.

The most important natural resources that Bulgaria possesses are the fertility of its land, which is the basis of the country's agricultural economy, and the beauty of its landscape, which has allowed an important tourist industry to develop, particularly along the Black Sea coast and in the mountains. Bulgaria is not well endowed with mineral wealth. It does contain significant deposits of coal, but it is of a low-grade kind called lignite (brown coal), which contributes to a serious problem of air pollution around industrial areas where it is burned. Iron, copper, zinc, and lead are also found, but not in the quantities sufficient to satisfy the country's needs.

PEOPLE

Ethnic Bulgarians, about 80% of the population, are Slavs, descendants of the people who settled in the region in the 6th century AD. The name *Bulgaria* comes from the Bulgars, a nomadic people from Central Asia who arrived a century later. They conquered the Slavs and created the First Bulgarian Kingdom but were gradually absorbed by the much larger Slavic population. The largest minority today are ethnic Turks, the descendants of Turks who settled in Bulgaria during the five hundred years it was a province of the Ottoman Empire. They make up approximately 9% of the population. Other minorities include Gypsies, Armenians, Greeks, Russians, and Jews. Ethnic Bulgarians who converted to Islam are recognized as a separate group called Pomaks. The Turks, persecuted under the Communist regime, have emerged as a potent political force in post-Communist Bulgaria.

Historically, Bulgarians belong to the Bulgarian Orthodox church, an autonomous branch of the Eastern Orthodox church. Most ethnic Turks and the Pomaks are Muslim. Small groups of Protestants, Jews, and Roman Catholics also exist.

During the Communist period, the practice of religion was discouraged by the government.

Education and Health Care. Basic education in Bulgaria is free, universal, and compulsory. Bulgarian children begin formal education at age seven, although most of them have experienced day-care classes from their earliest years. Compulsory education continues to age 16, after which most students continue on to receive specialized training. Students who qualify for advanced work are supported by the state. The University of Sofia trains most of the country's intellectual elite, although many Bulgarians also go abroad for study.

Like education, health services are provided by the state, although citizens may seek private care if they wish. Diseases such as cholera and tuberculosis, which were once serious threats to public health, have been eliminated.

Culture. Bulgaria's cultural life was quite rich during the Middle Ages but declined in the centuries of isolation under Ottoman rule. In the 19th century Bulgarians began to create a new cultural life that was influenced both by foreign models and by native traditions. Bulgaria developed particularly strong traditions in literature, music, and the arts. In music the opera singers Boris CHRISTOFF and Nikolai Ghaiouroff became world famous, and Milcho Leviev is an important contributor to American jazz. The artist CHRISTO Javacheff is famous for the vast scale of his productions.

ECONOMY

Under the pre-1989 Communist system, Bulgaria had a centrally planned economy in which the government set economic goals and directed the processes of production. Although this system worked effectively in the early stages of industrialization, it was not adequate for a more complex economy. With the fall of the Communist dictatorship in 1989, the country began moving toward a system based on free markets. Small, independent enterprises became legal right away, and similar measures were proposed for the larger industries.

Agriculture. About half of Bulgaria's land area is suitable for agriculture. The country's chief crops are wheat, corn, other grains, sugar beets, sunflower seeds, roses, fruits and vegetables, and tobacco. Bulgarian fruits and vegetables are exported to many countries in Europe, and much of what is called "Turkish" tobacco actually comes from southern Bulgaria. Bulgarian wines have become popular in many countries.

Under the Communists, collective farms managed Bulgarian agriculture. In 1990 the government began the process of restoring the land to its former owners or their descendants.

Industry. Bulgaria had little modern industry before World War II. Since that time, however, the government stressed the industrial sector, and it has become the main component of the economy, employing over 40% of the country's workers. Bulgaria's principal industrial products are processed foods, machinery, chemicals, and metal products. Tourism has also become an important industry, with many resorts built along the coast of the Black Sea, in the mountains, and near hot springs. Most of Bulgaria's energy needs must be satisfied by imports, although some progress has been made in developing nuclear power. With the breakup of the Communist system in the early 1990s, Bulgaria's economy, which had been heavily dependent on the USSR, experienced a precipitous decline. Inflation and unemployment rates soared as the country began its difficult transition to capitalism. Obstacles to economic progress included a large foreign debt inherited from the Communist era, and the YUGOSLAV WAR, which made foreign businesses reluctant to invest in the Balkans.

Bulgaria's largest cities are SOFIA, the capital and seat of government; PLOVDIV, the site of an annual world industrial fair; and the Black Sea cities of VARNA and BURGAS. RUSE, on the Danube, is also an important port.

GOVERNMENT

From 1947 to 1989 the Bulgarian government was run by the Communist party, whose Politburo (Political Bureau, or ruling council) was the real center of power. On Nov. 10, 1989, Todor ZHIVKOV, who had headed the Communist party and the government for 35 years, was forced to retire. The new Communist leadership condemned the party's past methods, changed its name from "Communist" to "Socialist," and promised to respect individual rights and to allow a political opposition.

At the same time, many other groups took advantage of these changes to form new political parties. The most important of them formed a coalition, the Union of Democratic Forces (UDF), led by Zheliu Zhelev. In August, Zhelev was elected to the presidency by the parliament. In July 1991 a new constitution was adopted that provided for basic civil rights, representative government, and the separation of executive, legislative, and judicial powers. In the first elections under the new constitution, a coalition of the UDF and the ethnic Turkish party (MRF) won a narrow majority over the former Communists in the 240-seat National Assembly and formed a government headed by Filip Dimitrov of the UDF. Zhelev won a popular vote for president in January 1992. Internal divisions in the UDF caused the fall of the Dimitrov government in October 1992, and Lyuben Berov, a former aide to the president, became premier in December. Between 1992 and 1994, numerous former Communist officials, including Zhivkov, were convicted of various offenses and sentenced to prison terms.

HISTORY

In the 6th and 7th centuries AD much of the Balkan Peninsula was settled by Slavic tribes. The Bulgars, a Turkic people, migrated to the Balkans from central Asia in the second half of the 7th century. They conquered the Slavic tribes and founded the First Bulgarian Kingdom in 681. The Bulgarians adopted Orthodox Christianity in the 9th century under BORIS I. Under Boris's son, Tsar SIMEON I (r. 893–927) the First Bulgarian Kingdom reached the height of its power. Its territory included most of the Balkan peninsula, and it enjoyed a vigorous cultural and intellectual life.

Bulgaria declined under Simeon's successors, and in 1014 the Byzantine emperor Basil II won a battle over the Bulgarian army after which he ordered 14,000 prisoners to be blinded. For this Basil II took the title *Bulgaroctonos,* or "Bulgar slayer," and Bulgaria was ruled by Byzantium until 1185. In that year the brothers Ivan and Peter Asen launched a successful revolt

that led to the establishment of the Second Bulgarian Kingdom, which reached its height under Tsar Ivan Asen II (r. 1218–41). After his death the kingdom weakened, retreating before the rising power of the Ottoman Turks.

Turnovo, the royal capital, was seized by the Turks in 1393, beginning for the Bulgarians a period of nearly 500 years of captivity in the Ottoman Empire. During this time Bulgaria's national customs and values were preserved in the monasteries and in mountain villages isolated from Turkish influence. In the 18th century Paissy, a Bulgarian monk of the Khilendar monastery on Mount Athos, used medieval texts to prepare a history of his people. Paissy called on Bulgarians to rediscover themselves, and in the following century a strong national revival developed. A Bulgarian school system was begun in 1835, and the national church was restored in 1870. Finally, the RUSSO-TURKISH WAR of 1877–78 resulted in the restoration of a self-governing Bulgarian state.

Because the European powers feared Russian influence in Bulgaria, they initially allowed only the northern part to become autonomous. In 1885, however, the southern portion, known as Eastern Rumelia, joined the new state. A German prince, Ferdinand of Saxe-Coburg-Gotha (see FERDINAND I, TSAR OF BULGARIA), became Bulgaria's monarch in 1887.

In 1908, Ferdinand took the old title of tsar, and his desire to regain all the old Bulgarian lands led to the formation of an alliance with Serbia, Montenegro, and Greece. In the First Balkan War (1912), the allies forced Turkey to relinquish its remaining Balkan territories. They could not agree among themselves, however, and fought the Second Balkan War (1913), which Bulgaria lost. (See BALKAN WARS.)

Bulgaria was also on the losing side in World War I and had to give up territory to Serbia and Greece. Ferdinand was forced to abdicate, and the throne passed to his son BORIS III

In the center of Sofia's National Assembly Square is a statue of Alexander II of Russia. Facing the monument is the National Assembly building; Alexander Nevsky Cathedral is in the background.

(r. 1918–43). Reparations, the influx of many refugees from the lost territories, and severe economic problems kept Bulgaria in turmoil after the war. In 1934, Boris and the army imposed a dictatorship on the country.

During World War II, Bulgaria was a reluctant ally of Germany. Boris's death in 1943 left the country without a strong leader, and in September 1944 the Soviet Union declared war on Bulgaria and quickly occupied its territory. Led by Georgi DIMITROV, the Bulgarian Communists seized power, and by the end of 1947 completely eliminated their opponents.

The Communist government industrialized Bulgaria and also expanded education, helping to prepare the way for a new reform-minded generation at the end of the 1980s.

JOHN D. BELL

Bibliography: Bell, John D., *The Bulgarian Communist Party* (1987); Crampton, Richard J., *A Short History of Modern Bulgaria* (1987); Curtis, Glenn, ed., *Bulgaria: A Country Study*, 2d ed. (1993); OECD Staff, *Bulgaria: An Economic Assessment* (1992); Runciman, S., *A History of the First Bulgarian Empire* (1930).

Bulgarian language: see SLAVIC LANGUAGES.

Bulgarian literature

A national literature in Bulgaria appeared only in the 19th century as an expression of patriotic agitation against Turkish rule. The most famous early writer was Khristo BOTEV, whose revolutionary and patriotic works are still popular. In 1878, when the process of national liberation was begun, the literature was dominated by poet and novelist Ivan Vazov, whose novel *Under the Yoke* (1893; Eng. trans., 1894), concerning the struggle against the Turks, had an international audience. Notable among the next generation were the avant-garde poets Peyo Yavorov and Dimcho Debelyanov. Elisaveta Bagryana, considered Bulgaria's finest poet, returned to the directness and simplicity of the Bulgarian folk tradition in the poetry she published between the wars.

After the Communist takeover in 1944, a few Bulgarian writers were able to escape the strictures of Soviet-imposed socialist realism by turning to the past. Dimitur Talev, for example, published a famous trilogy on the struggle for independence (*The Iron Candlestick, Ilinden, The Bells of Prespa,* 1952–54; Eng. trans., 1964–66). Political restrictions were somewhat relaxed after 1956 and writers such as Olga Krusteva and Blaga Dimitrova experimented with radical prose techniques. Playwright and novelist Yordan Radichkov is the most original and prolific contemporary Bulgarian writer.

Bibliography: Kirilov, N., and Kirk, F., eds., *Introduction to Modern Bulgarian Literature* (1969); Meredith, W., ed., *Poets of Bulgaria* (1985); Moser, C. A., *A History of Bulgarian Literature, 865–1944* (1972).

Bulge, Battle of the

The Battle of the Bulge, or Battle of the Ardennes, fought from Dec. 16, 1944, to Jan. 31, 1945, was Germany's last major attempt to turn back the Allied invasion of Europe in WORLD WAR II. German forces under generals Gerd von Rundstedt and Hasso von Manteuffel drove a wedge (the Bulge) into Allied lines through the Ardennes on the Franco-Belgian frontier. They were halted chiefly by the U.S. 1st and 3d armies, the latter under Gen. George PATTON, and forced to retreat. Snowstorms contributed to the heavy casualties on both sides.

Bibliography: Cortesi, L., *Valor in the Bulge* (1986); Goldstein, D., et al., *The Battle of the Bulge* (1994); Parker, D., *The Battle of the Bulge* (1991).

bulimia

Bulimia nervosa is an eating disorder characterized by cycles of intractable urges to overeat (with a sense of loss of control) and induced vomiting or abuse of laxatives to eliminate food eaten during a binge—and, as in ANOREXIA NERVOSA, by a morbid fear of becoming fat. It mostly occurs in adolescent and young adult females, with about 10% of cases in males. Bulimia can cause hormonal changes and associated menstrual irregu-

larities, as well as changes in metabolism and blood chemistry, which may affect the heart or gastrointestinal system. The brain chemical serotonin may become depleted as a result of the binge and purge cycles, contributing to carbohydrate craving. Bulimia results from an interplay of many factors, including social pressures on females to be thinner than natural. Many people who develop bulimia have been obese; they often suffer from low self-esteem and mental depression and have an impulsive personality; they may have a history of sexual or physical abuse; some also abuse alcohol or drugs. Treatment requires a combination of nutritional counseling, drugs, and psychotherapy. Fluoxetine (Prozac) is effective in treating bulimia.

PAUL E. GARFINKEL, M.D.

Bibliography: Helmi, K. A., ed., *Psychobiology and Treatment of Anorexia Nervosa and Bulimia Nervosa* (1992); Mitchell, J., *Bulimia Nervosa* (1989); Moorey, J., *Living with Anorexia and Bulimia* (1993).

Bull, John (composer)

John Bull, b. *c.*1562, d. Mar. 12 or 13, 1628, was a celebrated English organist, virginalist, and composer. Educated as a member of the choir of the Children of the Chapel Royal, he became a doctor of music at both Oxford and Cambridge universities and music professor at London's Gresham College. Bull served as organist to the Chapel Royal under both Elizabeth I and James I. In 1617 he was named organist to Antwerp Cathedral, and he remained there until his death. Bull's reputation rests principally on his works for organ and virginals, which show brilliance and great technical mastery.

Bibliography: Henry, Leigh, *Doctor John Bull* (1937; repr. 1968).

Bull, John (personification)

John Bull, in literature and cartoons, is the personification of England. He was created by the Scottish wit John Arbuthnot (1667–1735) in the *History of John Bull* (1712). The caricaturists of the humorous magazine *Punch* have represented him as an aroused countryman, a proud burgher, or a defiant sailor with a Union Jack waistcoat.

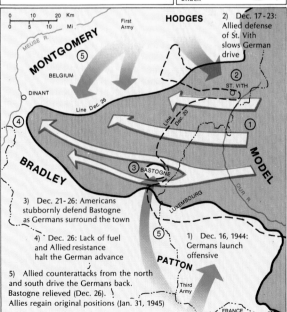

BATTLE OF THE BULGE
Dec. 16, 1944-Jan. 31, 1945

German attack
Allied counter-attack

2) Dec. 17-23: Allied defense of St. Vith slows German drive

3) Dec. 21-26: Americans stubbornly defend Bastogne as Germans surround the town

4) Dec. 26: Lack of fuel and Allied resistance halt the German advance

1) Dec. 16, 1944: Germans launch offensive

5) Allied counterattacks from the north and south drive the Germans back. Bastogne relieved (Dec. 26). Allies regain original positions (Jan. 31, 1945)

Bull, Olaf Jacob Martin Luther

Olaf Jacob Martin Luther Bull, b. Nov. 10, 1883, d. June 23, 1933, is one of the greatest modern Norwegian poets. He published his first volume, *Poems*, in 1909 and was soon recognized as a talent equal to Henrik WERGELAND, Norway's national poet.

Bull's most famous poem is "Metope," from the 1927 collection of the same name. It is a dialogue between lovers who are aware of the fragility of the moment and full of the pathos of their mortality.

Bull's poetry is marked by a concern for formal perfection, wide-ranging allusiveness, an often ironic tone, and careful attention to exact description. It is often pessimistic, depicting a fruitless search for purpose and meaning in nature.

WILLIAM MISHLER

Bull, Ole   [bool, oh'-le]

Ole Borneman Bull, b. Feb. 5, 1810, d. Aug. 17, 1880, was a celebrated Norwegian violinist. He first studied theology but gave this up for a career in music. In the 1830s he made his first concert appearances in the major capitals of Europe. Between 1843 and 1879 he made five highly successful concert tours of North America. With the fortune amassed from these tours he tried, unsuccessfully, to found a colony for Norwegian settlers in the United States. His recital programs included his own compositions, extemporizations, and renditions of Norwegian folk tunes.

ROBERT M. CAMMAROTA

Bibliography: Bull, Inez, *Ole Bull Returns to Pennsylvania* (1961); Bull, Sara Chapman, *Ole Bull: A Memoir* (1883; repr. 1981); Howard, John Tasker, *Our American Music*, 4th ed. (1965); Smith, Mortimer B., *The Life of Ole Bull* (1943; repr. 1973).

bull, papal

A bull, from the Latin *bulla* meaning "leaden seal," is a letter containing a mandate of the pope. In very early times, bulls were sealed with the pope's signet ring. Today, they are ordinarily sealed with a red stamp; only the most solemn bulls carry a leaden seal. Famous bulls include *Exsurge Domine* (1520) of Leo X against Martin Luther; *Pastor Aeternus* (1870) of Pius IX on papal infallibility; and *Humanae Salutis* (1961), issued by John XXIII to convoke the Second Vatican Council. Papal bulls are also issued to proclaim the canonization of a saint.

bull mastiff

The bull mastiff is a powerful and active breed of working dog. The male stands 64–69 cm (25–27 in) at the shoulder and weighs 50–59 kg (110–130 lb); the female stands 61–65 cm (24–26 in) and weighs 45–54 kg (100–120 lb). The head is massive, with a fair amount of wrinkling, and the V-shaped ears are medium in length. The short, dense coat may be red, fawn, or brindle; a dark muzzle is preferred.

The breed was developed in the second half of the 19th century by English gamekeepers to attack poachers on the

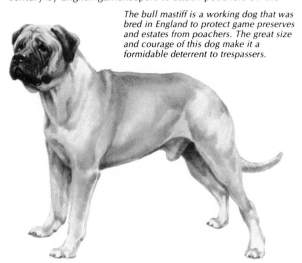

The bull mastiff is a working dog that was bred in England to protect game preserves and estates from poachers. The great size and courage of this dog make it a formidable deterrent to trespassers.

lands they managed. Crosses between the mastiff and the bulldog of that time produced the desired combination of courage, power, speed, and tenacity. By the 20th century the great game preserves were disappearing, but the need for guard dogs and watchdogs was still great, and the bull mastiff moved easily into this role. The breed was officially recognized by the English Kennel Club in 1924 and the American Kennel Club in 1933.

JOHN D. MANDEVILLE

Bibliography: American Kennel Club, *The Complete Dog Book*, 17th ed. (1985).

Bull Moose party

The Bull Moose party was the popular name for the U.S. PROGRESSIVE PARTY that Theodore Roosevelt organized for his 1912 presidential campaign. After being denied the Republican nomination that year, Roosevelt ran on his own third-party ticket.

The Bull Moose platform called for the direct election of senators; women's suffrage; monopoly-control laws; minimum-wage and child-labor legislation; tariff reform; and the initiative, recall, and referendum at the federal level. In the election, Roosevelt polled 4,118,571 popular and 88 electoral votes. He outpolled the Republican ticket but, by splitting the Republican vote, assured the election of Woodrow WILSON, the Democratic candidate. The Bull Moose party disappeared in 1916, when Roosevelt rejoined the Republicans.

Bibliography: Gable, John A., *The Bull Moose Years: Theodore Roosevelt and the Progressive Party* (1978); Mowry, George E., *Theodore Roosevelt and the Progressive Movement* (1960); Pinchot, Amos R., *History of the Progressive Party, 1912–1916* (1958; repr. 1978).

Bull Run, Battles of

Two battles in the U.S. CIVIL WAR were fought along Bull Run Creek near Manassas in northern Virginia. The first occurred on July 21, 1861, when Gen. Irwin McDOWELL led his 37,000

SECOND BATTLE OF BULL RUN
Aug. 29-30, 1862

I

LEE

JACKSON

SUDLEY MOUNTAIN

1) Aug. 29-30: Jackson repulses Union attacks

POPE

STONE BRIDGE

LEWIS FORD

BULL RUN

BALL'S FORD

HENRY HOUSE HILL

MANASSAS R.R. (INCOMPLETE)

WARRENTON TURNPIKE

MANASSAS JUNCTION

PORTER

BALD HILL

LONGSTREET

2) Aug. 30: Longstreet smashes the Union left flank and seizes Bald Hill. Pope falls back toward Henry House Hill

NEW MARKET

0   ½   1   1½ Km
0   ½   1 Mi

II

3) Aug. 30: Union troops re-form on Henry House Hill towards dusk

BULL RUN

SUDLEY MOUNTAIN

JACKSON

STONE BRIDGE

POPE

4) Aug. 30: Pope withdraws to Centerville during the night

LEE

MANASSAS R.R. (INCOMPLETE)

HENRY HOUSE HILL

WARRENTON TURNPIKE

LONGSTREET

Union advances
Union positions
Union retreat
Confederate advance
Confederate position
Battle

0   ½   1   1½ Km
0   ½   1 Mi

Union troops against 32,000 Confederates under Gen. P. G. T. BEAUREGARD in the first phase of an "on to Richmond" campaign. Beauregard, who had been reinforced on July 20 by about 10,000 men from the Shenandoah Valley under Gen. Joseph E. JOHNSTON, met McDowell near Manassas Junction. McDowell's swift start threatened to sweep the field. Resistance by Gen. T. J. Jackson's brigade at the Henry House Hill on the Confederate left, however, earned JACKSON the nickname "Stonewall" and won the day for Beauregard. First Bull Run (or Manassas) convinced the North of the war's seriousness and made the South overconfident.

A year later, after the Peninsular campaign and other major Virginia battles, Gen. Robert E. LEE met the Federals under Gen. John POPE near the First Bull Run fields. Second Bull Run (Aug. 29–30, 1862) marked the high point of Lee's campaign against both Gen. George B. McCLELLAN and Pope. Lee detached Jackson behind Pope, and Jackson held Pope off while Lee sent Gen. James LONGSTREET to defeat Pope's left flank. This great Southern victory cleared Virginia of Federal troops.

FRANK E. VANDIVER

Bibliography: Davis, William C., *Battle at Bull Run* (1977; repr. 1981); Foote, Shelby, *The Civil War*, 3 vols. (1958–74).

bull terrier

The bull terrier, a powerfully built dog, is one of the strongest dogs of its size. It was bred from the early bulldog and the white English terrier.

The bull terrier was probably developed about 1835 in England by mating a bulldog with a white English terrier, a breed now extinct. Created as a pit dog to fight other dogs, the bull terrier battled until it or its opponent was dead. It was well suited for such activity, having great agility, a low center of gravity, and a powerful set of jaws. Although dog fighting was outlawed in England in 1835, the breed continued to be used for this bloody sport through most of the 19th century. (See also PIT BULL.)

Bull terriers grow up to 56 cm (22 in) high at the shoulder, weigh up to 16.3 kg (36 lb), and are similar in size to bulldogs but longer-legged. They may be white, red, black, black and tan, or brindle, and the colored bull terriers usually have white markings.

Bibliography: Drewes, Marilyn, *Your Bull Terrier* (1978); Eberhard, Ernest, *The New Complete Bull Terrier*, 2d ed. (1971); Wells, Martin, *Bull Terriers* (1983).

Bullard, Sir Edward   [bul'-urd]

The English geophysicist Sir Edward Crisp Bullard, b. Sept. 21, 1907, d. Apr. 3, 1980, is known for his research and publications on the physics of the Earth's upper mantle. As an outgrowth of his research on the origin of the Earth's magnetic field, Bullard advanced the dynamo theory of Earth magnetism, according to which the outer core of the Earth is fluid and electrically conducting and, as such, acts as a self-exciting dynamo. In 1965, Bullard and his Cambridge associates published a reconstruction of how the continents on the two sides of the Atlantic Ocean fitted together during the Triassic Period (about 190 to 230 million years ago), thus lending support to the CONTINENTAL DRIFT hypothesis.

Bibliography: Hallam, Anthony, *A Revolution in the Earth Sciences* (1973).

bulldog

The bulldog is well known for its squat, muscular stance and pugnacious expression. Used from the Middle Ages to the 19th century to bait bulls, the bulldog attacked savagely and without regard to pain. The modern bulldog is more docile than its ancestor.

The bulldog is a British breed of dog created to bait bulls, a sport in which the dog grabbed the bull by the nose and hung on at all costs. The breed's massive head, dumpy body, and incredible tenacity were all qualities needed in bullbaiting. With the outlawing of bullbaiting in 1835, the bulldog's usefulness was thought to be finished. Breeders, however, were determined to preserve the breed, and in the process the deadly fighter was transformed into a good-natured, quiet companion.

The massive head of the bulldog, out of proportion to the rest of the animal, often necessitates a cesarean section for delivery. The pushed-in face makes the breed susceptible to breathing and respiratory troubles. The dogs suffer in hot weather and have many eye and ear problems.

Mature bulldogs weigh about 22.5 kg (50 lb) and stand 33–38 cm (13–15 in) high at the shoulder. They are popular in the United States.

Bibliography: Brearley, Joan, *The Book of the Bulldog* (1984); Hanes, Bailey C., *The New Complete Bulldog*, 3d ed. (1973).

bulldozer: see EARTH-MOVING MACHINERY.

bullfighting

Bullfighting is a spectacle in which a bullfighter, or matador, ceremoniously taunts and fights a bull in a public arena, usually with the goal of killing it with a sword, the *estoque*. Bullfighting is the national sport of Spain and is also popular in Mexico and other parts of Latin America, southern France,

El Cordobés, a great Spanish matador, avoids the charge of a toro bravo, *a bull bred specifically to attack in bullfights. The objective of this ritualized spectator sport is for the matador skillfully to assert his dominance over the animal prior to killing it.*

The illustration depicts the main participants of bullfighting, a sport of Hispanic heritage. Only after the mounted picador (left) has lanced the bull's neck and the banderillero (center) has placed darts in the animal's shoulders does the matador (right) confront his adversary. Armed with a sword and a muleta, a red cloth attached to a rod, the matador is expected to kill the bull with a single swordstroke.

and Portugal. As a sport, bullfighting can be traced back to the Minoans, when Cretan boys tested themselves by tossing their bodies over the sharp horns of pasturing bulls. After the Moors conquered Spain in AD 711, they restored the sport, which had been suppressed by Christians.

In its original form, bullfighting was practiced by men on horses. It was considered a noble sport, and it has been glamorized by historians in the *fiesta de toros* of 1090, when Roderigo Diaz de Bivar, known as "El Cid," performed. A common laborer, Francisco Romero, is credited with changing the style of bullfighting when, in 1725, he used a sword and killed a bull while fighting on foot. Soon after, in 1743, the first permanent bullring was erected in Madrid.

Bullfighting became a national pastime in Spain, and in this century such great matadors as Manolete, who was gored to death in 1947, Juan BELMONTE, Luis Dominguín, Antonio Ordóñez, Carlos Arruza, and Manuel Benítez (EL CORDOBÉS) have become wealthy and famous for their artistic killings of bulls.

In modern bullfighting, the star is a matador (although the Portuguese still attack by horseback and do not kill the bull). He has assistants, called *banderilleros* (on foot) and *picadores* (on horseback). The actual bullfight, which begins with a parade and ceremony, has several stages. First, the banderilleros enter the ring with the matador and proceed to taunt the bull by waving capes and forcing him to charge. This gives the matador an opportunity to evaluate the bull's temperament. Then the two picadores ride into the ring on padded, blindfolded horses. The picadores thrust long lances at the bull, enraging the bull in preparation for the next stage. The banderilleros return to the ring and further disturb the bull by waving brightly ribboned dart sticks at the animal and then placing these sticks in the bull's shoulders.

Finally comes the matador for the kill. Brightly dressed, he uses a sword draped with a red cloth, called a *muleta*. After a number of intricate passes with the *muleta*, during which the matador must work extremely close to the bull, the matador sights the bull along his sword, runs forward, and plunges it in, aiming for the half-dollar–size spot between the shoulders.

Although bullfighting has been described as inhumane and has been little practiced outside the Iberian peninsula and Latin America, its defenders say that it is too much ingrained in these cultures to ban.   GORDON STANG

Bibliography: Conrad, Barnaby, *Encyclopedia of Bullfighting* (1961); Fulton, John, *Bullfighting* (1971); Hemingway, Ernest, *Death in the Afternoon* (1932); Witwer, Kitty, *Divine Addiction* (1985).

bullfrog

The bullfrog, *Rana catesbeiana*, family Ranidae, is an aquatic amphibian that formerly was found in North America only east of the Rocky Mountains. It has now been introduced to other localities as a potential source of food; most frog legs sold commercially in the United States are from this species.

The bullfrog grows to 20 cm (8 in) in body length. The male's loud, bellowing voice establishes a territory, and defending males may engage in pushing or wrestling matches with intruding bullfrogs. The bullfrog matures slowly, usually taking about five years to become a full adult, and may live for up to 16 years.   JONATHAN CAMPBELL

Bibliography: Dickerson, Mary C., *The Frog Book: North American Toads and Frogs* (1969); Wright, Albert H. and Anna A., *Handbook of Toads and Frogs of the United States and Canada*, 3d ed. (1949).

The bullfrog, Rana catesbeiana, is a common, long-lived aquatic frog known for its loud, raucous croaking.

bullhead

Bullheads comprise two distinct families of fish: the bullhead SHARKS in the family Heterodontidae and the bullhead CATFISH in the family Ictaluridae, both of the genus *Ictalurus*. Bullheads are native to North America and have a truncated, or square, caudal fin. The four species are the flat bullhead, *I. platycephalus*, in coastal streams from North Carolina to Florida; the yellow bullhead, *I. natalis*; the black bullhead, *I. melas*; and the brown bullhead, *I. nebulosus*, found throughout eastern North America. All have been introduced into western North America. Bullheads prefer the quiet waters of ponds

The yellow bullhead, I. natalis, has eight characteristic whiskerlike barbels on its head that serve as sensitive organs for touch.

and streams. They are bottom-dwellers, most active at night. Like many other catfish, bullheads guard their nests and then herd the young around until they can fend for themselves.

The bullhead sharks are among the most primitive of the CHONDRICHTHYES. They are also called horned sharks or Port Jackson sharks. Six species of the genus *Heterodontus* are found in the tropical waters of the Indo-Pacific and the eastern Pacific from California to Peru and the Galápagos Islands. Bullhead sharks grow to about 1.2 m (4 ft). They are bottom-dwellers and usually eat shellfish.   EDWARD O. WILEY

Bibliography: Armstrong, Philip B., and Child, Julia S., *Stages in the Development of Ictalurus Nebulosus* (1962); Ellis, Richard, *The Book of Sharks* (1983); Moss, Sanford, *Sharks* (1984).

Bullinger, Heinrich   [bul'-ing-ur, hyn'-rik]

A Swiss theologian and reformer, Heinrich Bullinger, b. July 18, 1504, d. Sept. 17, 1575, was the successor of Ulrich ZWINGLI as the chief pastor at Zürich. Through the reading of Scripture, the Fathers of the Church, and the writings of the time, Bullinger was drawn to join the Reformation. He promoted various educational, social, and ecclesiastical reforms and joined John CALVIN in producing (1549) the *Consensus Tigurinus*, a statement setting forth their doctrine of the Eucharist. Later, Bullinger wrote (1566) the second Helvetic Confession. A prolific correspondent, he maintained a lively exchange of ideas and personal friendship with many English Reformers, supporting the church-state policies of Elizabeth I.

Bibliography: Keep, D., *Henry Bullinger and the Elizabethan Church* (1970).

Bullins, Ed   [bul'-inz]

The American writer Ed Bullins, b. Philadelphia, July 2, 1935, is best known for his plays; he has also written a novel, short stories, and poetry. Bullins, who did not begin to write plays until the mid-1960s, when many militant black writers emerged, bases his work in the black experience. His numerous plays include *In the Wine Time* (1968), *Goin' a Buffalo* (1969), *The Duplex* (1970), and *The Taking of Miss Janie* (1974; N.Y. Drama Critics Circle award). He is working on a projected cycle of 20 plays.   BONNIE MARRANCA

Bullock, Wynn

Wynn Bullock, b. Chicago, Apr. 18, 1902, d. Nov. 16, 1975, was an American photographer known for his large-format studies of nature and nudes. An accomplished singer, he turned to photography in 1938 when he began studies at the Art Center School in Los Angeles. His work is a blend of both straight and experimental photography. His early solarized images are previews of later experiments with long exposures and negative prints and of his mystical interest in space-time concepts and visual metaphors. His *Child in the Forest* (1954) was prominent in the Family of Man exhibition, which was held in New York in 1955 and published in book form.
                                            KEITH F. DAVIS

Bibliography: Bullock, Barbara, *Wynn Bullock* (1971); De Cock, Liliane, ed., *Wynn Bullock* (1973); Fuess, David, *Wynn Bullock* (1976).

Bülow, Bernhard Heinrich Martin, Fürst von   [bue'-loh]

Bernhard Heinrich Martin, Fürst von Bülow, b. May 3, 1849, d. Oct. 18, 1929, was the fourth chancellor of the German Empire. A career diplomat from 1874, he became German foreign secretary in 1897 and chancellor on Oct. 17, 1900. In foreign affairs Bülow supported Germany's colonial and naval expansion. His muddled diplomacy, however, forced France closer to Britain in the first Moroccan crisis, settled by the ALGECIRAS CONFERENCE (1906), and strengthened Russia's ties with Britain in the crisis over Bosnia in 1908. As a result Germany and Austria were isolated diplomatically.

A clever manipulator of parties and public opinion, and a flatterer of Emperor WILLIAM II, Bülow was essentially opportunistic in his domestic measures. He was dismissed on July 14, 1909, because of failure to defend William against public attacks and a split in the governmental coalition over a proposed inheritance tax. Later ambassador to Italy, he could only delay Italy's entrance into World War I on the Allied side (1915).   FREDERIC B. M. HOLLYDAY

Bülow, Hans von

Hans von Bülow, b. Jan. 8, 1830, d. Feb. 12, 1894, was a major German pianist, conductor, and music editor. He studied both law and music, but his association (1849–50) with Franz LISZT and Richard WAGNER in Weimar and Berlin caused him to turn wholly to music. After conducting, teaching, and touring (1850–64) throughout Europe, he went to Munich as conductor of the Bavarian State Opera; later (1867) he also became director of the Conservatory. After his wife, Cosima (Franz Liszt's daughter), left him (1869) for Richard Wagner, he resumed touring in the United States (1875–76) and also conducted in Hannover, Meiningen, Hamburg, and Berlin. Bülow's meticulous and elegant orchestral performances, prepared with detailed analysis of the scores, helped establish the present-day role of the conductor.   F. E. KIRBY

Bibliography: Bülow, Hans Guido von, *Letters*, trans. by Hannah Waller (1972).

bulrush

The bulrush, *Scirpus cernuus*, is a grasslike plant in the sedge family, Cyperaceae. Native to the East Indies, it has been naturalized in Europe and is valued for its graceful, drooping growth. Plants form numerous, round, threadlike, glossy-green stems about 30 cm (1 ft) tall, which become pendant. Small flowers form at the tips of the stems.

Other species include *S. lacustris*, which grows to a height of 3 m (9 ft) and is apparently leafless, producing a mass of spikes that terminate in dense clusters. *S. tabernaemontani* grows to 61 cm (2 ft) and produces spikelets in flat-topped clusters. The variety *zebrinus* has white-banded stems.

Bultmann, Rudolf

Rudolf Karl Bultmann, b. Germany, Aug. 20, 1884, d. July 30, 1976, was one of the greatest New Testament scholars of the 20th century. Educated at the universities of Marburg, Tübingen, and Berlin, he held professorships at Breslau and Giessen before returning in 1921 to Marburg as a professor of New Testament studies, a post he held until his retirement 30 years later.

Bultmann was one of the leaders in the development of the form criticism of the New Testament. According to this method, the Gospels comprise episodic fragments that can be classified according to their forms as apothegms (sayings set in the context of illustrative incidents), miracle stories, historical narratives, or similar categories. These fragments circulated as units of preaching and teaching in the primitive church and were later unified to form the Gospels.

Bultmann was skeptical about gaining reliable historical information about JESUS CHRIST. In his view, the Gospels concern instead the beliefs of the early church. Bultmann admitted that in a general way Jesus is correctly portrayed in the Gospels, and he made it clear that theologically he was not troubled by historical skepticism. Accepting the Lutheran principle "faith alone," he argued that faith cannot be established by historical research. This position was developed further in his program for demythologizing the New Testament. Bultmann felt that the history of Jesus had been transformed into myth and that the gospel thus comes clothed in mythological ideas. He felt that the gospel, therefore, must be translated out of mythical into existentialist language, such as that of Martin HEIDEGGER, and that Christianity would then be understood as a new possibility of existence. Bultmann's works include *Jesus and the Word* (1934); *Theology of the New Testament* (2 vols., 1952–55); *Jesus Christ and Mythology* (1958); *The History of the Synoptic Tradition* (1963); and *The Gospel of John: A Commentary* (1971).   JOHN MACQUARRIE

Bibliography: Barth, K., and Bultmann, R. K., *Barth-Bultmann Letters, 1922 to 1966* (1981); Kegley, C. W., ed., *The Theology of Rudolf Bultmann* (1966); Macquarrie, John, *The Scope of Demythologizing* (1960).

Bulwer-Lytton, Edward, 1st Baron Lytton

[bul'-wur-lit'-uhn]

Edward George Earle Lytton Bulwer-Lytton, b. May 25, 1803, d. Jan. 18, 1873, was an English member of Parliament (colonial secretary, 1858) and a writer now best remembered for his historical novel *The Last Days of Pompeii* (1834). Bulwer-Lytton's works include satires (*Pelham*, 1828), historical romances (*Reinzi*, 1835), realistic novels (*Kenelm Chillingly*, 1873), and plays (*Richelieu*, 1839).   ROBIN BUSS

Bibliography: Flower, Sibylla Jane, *Bulwer-Lytton* (1973); Shattuck, Charles, ed., *Bulwer and Macready* (1958).

Bulwer-Lytton, Edward Robert, 1st Earl of Lytton

Edward Robert Bulwer-Lytton, b. Nov. 8, 1831, d. Nov. 24, 1891, was a British career diplomat who achieved a reputation as a poet, publishing under the pseudonym of Owen Meredith. Viceroy of India (1876–80), he was created (1880) an earl in recognition of his services in the Afghan wars. He was later ambassador to France (1887–91). Bulwer-Lytton's poetry includes *Fables in Song* (1874).   ROBIN BUSS

Bumbry, Grace

Grace Melzia Bumbry, b. St. Louis, Mo., Jan. 4, 1937, is an American singer who achieved international fame following her debut (1961) as Venus in a controversial production of *Tannhäuser* in Bayreuth. She was the first black singer to appear there. Bumbry sings both soprano and mezzo-soprano roles, including Carmen, Tosca, and Salome. She is a frequent guest with major opera companies in the United States and Europe and is also active as a Lieder singer.

bumelia   [bue-mee'-lee-uh]

Bumelia is any one of a genus, *Bumelia*, of woody trees and shrubs in the sapodilla family, Sapotaceae. It is found in warm and tropical America. Because of their very hard woods, several species are also called ironwoods; other common names are chittamwood or shittimwood, false buckthorn, and gum elastic. The fruit of the bumelia is small and black and resembles a cherry; its branches, often thorny, bear small, white flower clusters; and its sap is milky or gummy.

Bumppo, Natty

Natty Bumppo is the central figure in James Fenimore Cooper's LEATHERSTOCKING TALES and a prototype of the natural man. A woodsman and solitary hunter, he is rudely noble, utterly competent, and owes final allegiance only to the American wilderness itself. In the novels, he is variously called Deerslayer, Hawkeye, Pathfinder, and Leatherstocking.

Bunau-Varilla, Philippe Jean   [bue-noh'-vah-ree-ah']

Philippe Jean Bunau-Varilla, b. July 21, 1860, d. May 18, 1940, was a French engineer who was instrumental in involving the United States in building the PANAMA CANAL. In 1884 he joined the French company run by Ferdinand de LESSEPS that had begun work on the canal. When that company collapsed in 1889 and France lost interest in the project, Bunau-Varilla organized (1894) another engineering firm, which bought the rights to the Panama site. In 1901–02 he helped persuade President Theodore ROOSEVELT, who had favored a canal through Nicaragua, to decide in favor of the Panama route and to buy out his company for $40 million.

The U.S. commitment, however, was contingent on the agreement of Colombia, of which Panama was then a part, to relinquish sovereignty over the proposed canal route. When Colombia held out for more than the $10 million offered, Bunau-Varilla helped Panamanian rebels launch (1903) a revolution that resulted in creation of an independent Panama. As the new republic's minister to the United States, he then negotiated the Hay-Bunau-Varilla Treaty (1903) by which the United States acquired full control over the Canal Zone.

Bibliography: Anguizola, G., *Philippe Bunau-Varilla* (1980); Bunau-Varilla, P. J., *Panama* (Eng. trans., 1914) and *From Panama to Verdun* (Eng. trans., 1940); Miner, D. C., *The Fight for the Panama Route* (1966).

See also: HAY-PAUNCEFOTE TREATY.

bunchberry: see DOGWOOD.

Bunche, Ralph

Ralph Bunche was a United Nations staff member who mediated the 1948–49 Arab-Israeli War and became the first black to receive (1950) the Nobel Peace Prize. He was a key UN diplomat until shortly before his death.

Ralph Bunche, b. Detroit, Aug. 7, 1904, d. Dec. 9, 1971, was a black American official of the United Nations who won the 1950 Nobel Peace Prize for his mediation of the 1948–49 Arab-Israeli War.

Educated at the University of California at Los Angeles and Harvard, Bunche taught (1928–50) at Howard University. From 1938 to 1940 he was chief assistant to the Swedish sociologist Gunnar MYRDAL in Myrdal's study of American blacks. During World War II, Bunche served in the Office of Strategic Services and in 1944 entered the State Department. He was the first black to head (1945) a division in that department.

Joining the UN staff in 1946, Bunche was appointed (1947) to the Palestine Commission and in 1948 became chief mediator in the Palestine conflict. Subsequently a UN under secretary, he directed the UN peacekeeping forces at Suez (1956), in the Congo (1960), and in Cyprus (1964). From 1967 until his resignation in 1971, Bunche was under secretary general of the UN.

Bibliography: Mann, Peggy, *Ralph Bunche: U.N. Peacemaker* (1975).

Buncho

Tani Buncho, 1764–1840, was a Japanese artist who introduced Nanga, a major school of later Japanese painting, to Edo (Tokyo). This school was inspired by literati painting traditions of Ming and Ch'ing China. A highly versatile artist, Buncho produced works ranging from academic, Kano-styled paintings to works influenced by European book illustration. These and other influences were incorporated into his mature Nanga style, as seen in the idiosyncratic landscape *True View of Mount Hiko* (1808; Tokyo National Museum). Buncho wrote a treatise on painting and illustrated a catalog of ancient artworks compiled by the chief advisor to the shogun in the middle Edo period.   BARBARA BRENNAN FORD

Bibliography: Cahill, James, *Scholar Painters of Japan: The Nanga School* (1972; repr. 1979); Yonezawa, Yoshiho, and Yoshizawa, Chu, *Japanese Painting in the Literati Style*, trans. by B. I. Monroe (1974).

Bundy, McGeorge

McGeorge Bundy, b. Boston, Mass., Mar. 30, 1919, was president of the Ford Foundation from 1966 to 1979. He taught (1949–54) government at Harvard University until named the dean of the Faculty of Arts and Sciences. President John F. Kennedy appointed Bundy his special assistant for National Security Affairs in 1961, a post that he also held under President Lyndon B. Johnson until 1966. At the Ford Foundation he encouraged a commitment to civil rights, environmental concerns, and the improvement of university management. He wrote *The Strength of Government* (1968). In 1979 he became a professor of history at New York University.

Bunin, Ivan Alekseyevich [boon'-yin, ee-vahn' ul-yik-syay'-yih-vich]

Ivan Alekseyevich Bunin, winner of the 1933 Nobel Prize for literature, was a major Russian prose writer and poet in the tradition of Aleksandr PUSHKIN and Ivan TURGENEV. He was born on Oct. 22 (Oct. 10, O.S.), 1870, to an impoverished aristocratic family and died on Nov. 8, 1953, in Paris, where he had gone in exile in 1919 after the Russian Revolution. At his death he was the last bard of the Russian aristocracy.

Bunin's career spanned about 60 years. He began writing poetry in the 1890s, but his lyric verse, although often exquisitely rendered, was dismissed as old-fashioned. A traditional realist, Bunin viewed with contempt such modern literary movements as symbolism, which to him were but passing fads. Bunin was also a gifted translator of verse; he is especially known for his Russian translation of Longfellow's "Song of Hiawatha," which was awarded the Pushkin Prize.

A world traveler, Bunin often wrote about distant lands. His most famous work is the novella *The Gentleman from San Francisco* (1916; Eng. trans., 1922), a story about an American millionaire who goes on a pleasure trip around the world but dies before being able to enjoy it. The work demonstrates Bunin's characteristic bitter irony, restraint, and understatement. The illusory pursuit of pleasure and the closeness of love to death are prominent themes in *The Elagin Affair* (1927; Eng. trans., 1935) and in Bunin's fictional autobiography, *Life of Arseniev* (1927; also translated as *The Well of Days*, 1933), which is set against the background of a disintegrating aristocratic family. Bunin's pessimism is also evident in his novel *The Village* (1910; Eng. trans., 1923) and in the short story "Sukhodol" (1911; also translated as "Dry Valley," 1934), in which he describes the peasants as drunken and cruel.

A meticulous and elegant craftsman who avoided sentimentality, Bunin is at his best in lyrical but terse descriptions of nature. His vocabulary remains one of the richest in Russian literature.   MAURICE FRIEDBERG

Bibliography: Kryzytski, Serge, *The Works of Ivan Bunin* (1971).

bunions: see FOOT DISORDERS.

Bunker, Ellsworth

Ellsworth Bunker, b. Yonkers, N.Y., May 11, 1894, d. Sept. 27, 1984, a businessman who became a diplomat, was best known for his role as U.S. ambassador to Vietnam in 1967–73. Serving during the years of peak U.S. involvement in the Vietnam War, he played a major part in making policy. Bunker began his diplomatic career as ambassador to Argentina (1951) and subsequently served in Italy (1952–53) and India (1956–61). He was mediator of the Dutch-Indonesian dispute over West New Guinea in 1962. In his eighties Bunker helped negotiate the Panama Canal treaty of 1977, by which the United States agreed to give Panama control of the canal by the year 2000.

Bunker Hill, Battle of

A misnamed engagement of the AMERICAN REVOLUTION, the Battle of Bunker Hill was fought between British regulars under Gen. William HOWE and New England militiamen under Col. William Prescott and Gen. Israel PUTNAM on June 17, 1775. When Americans learned that the British in Boston intended to secure certain heights outside the city, Gen. Artemas Ward ordered the fortification of Bunker Hill on the Charlestown peninsula. Inexplicably, his subordinates instead took position on nearby Breed's Hill. The British soon launched an attack. In several hours of bloody fighting the Americans were dislodged, but only after the British lost 228 dead and 826 wounded—42 percent of them.   DON HIGGINBOTHAM

Bibliography: Ketchum, Richard M., *Battle for Bunker Hill* (1962).

bunker: see FORTIFICATION.

Bunner, H. C.

Henry Cuyler Bunner, b. Oswego, N.Y., Aug. 3, 1855, d. May 11, 1896, was an American author and journalist who served for nearly 20 years as editor of *Puck*. Like its contemporaries *Judge* and the original *Life*, *Puck* was a national weekly magazine of humor, cartoons, and satire. Bunner began his journalistic career on the *Arcadian* magazine and joined *Puck* as an assistant editor at age 22. A prolific and gifted writer of great versatility, he produced more than 20 volumes of sketches, poems, short stories, and drama. His graceful style, dexterity, and economy of language showed the influence of de Maupassant and other French writers. A famous *Puck* cartoon suggested by Bunner, depicting James G. Blaine as a man "tattooed" with his own failure, was considered to have contributed to the Republican party's defeat in 1884.
                                                         CHARLES T. DUNCAN

Bunraku [boon'-rah-koo]

Bunraku is the popular name for Japan's classical puppet theater, also called *Jōruri*, for its musical style. Bunraku is a serious art intended for an adult audience. Each complex puppet is operated by three puppeteers while a chanter sings and speaks the text of the play to the accompaniment of *shamisen* music. Puppets are three-quarters life size and are exceptionally realistic, with movable fingers, eyes, and mouths.

Japanese doll theater, or *Ningyo shibai*, was given its distinctive form by Takemoto Gidayu (1651–1714) in Osaka about 1685. Among Japan's greatest plays are domestic puppet dramas, such as CHIKAMATSU MONZAEMON's *The Love Suicides of Sonezaki* (1703), and historical dramas, such as Takeda Izumo's *Chūshingura* or *The Treasury of Loyal Retainers* (1748). KABUKI and Bunraku competed for the same urban, commoner audience, troupes often performing side by side in Osaka, the capital of Japanese puppet theater, Kyoto, and Edo (Tokyo). Today many puppet plays are also perfomed by Kabuki actors. On the island of Awaji, in the Inland Sea, and in other areas, folk puppet theater is popular.
                                                         JAMES R. BRANDON

Bibliography: Ando, Tsuruo, *Bunraku: The Puppet Theatre* (1970); Keene, Donald, and Kaneko, Hiroshi, *Bunraku: The Art of the Japanese Puppet Theatre* (1965).

Bunsen, Robert Wilhelm

The German chemist Robert Wilhelm Bunsen, b. Mar. 31, 1811, d. Aug. 16, 1899, is best known for his improvement of methods for identifying, separating, and measuring quantities of inorganic substances. Emphasizing the experimental aspects of chemistry, Bunsen invented or improved numerous pieces of laboratory equipment, including an electrochemical BATTERY, the grease-spot PHOTOMETER, the SPECTROSCOPE, and the Bunsen burner.

In collaboration with Gustav KIRCHHOFF, Bunsen developed the foundations of SPECTROSCOPY in 1859 and demonstrated how spectral analysis of terrestrial matter could be used to determine its chemical composition. In 1860 and 1861 they further demonstrated the value of spectroscopic techniques by using them to discover cesium and rubidium. Because of his scientific fame, Bunsen attracted numerous students to his laboratory at the University of Heidelberg, where he established a major center for German chemical education.
                                                         RICHARD HIRSH

Bibliography: Ihde, Aaron J., *The Development of Modern Chemistry* (1964; repr. 1983).

Bunsen burner

A Bunsen burner produces a hot flame by mixing flammable gas under pressure with controlled quantities of air. It is named for Robert Wilhelm Bunsen, a German chemist who began using it in 1855. A Bunsen burner consists of a vertical metal tube with holes near the bottom to admit air and a mov-

Buntings are 11 to 14 cm (4 to 5.5 in) long and prefer to live in dry, open scrubland. Pictured are (left to right, male in foreground) the indigo bunting, Passerina cyanea, *whose black feathers diffract bright light and appear indigo; the lazuli bunting,* P. amoena; *and the painted bunting,* P. ciris, *also called "nonpareil" ("without equal") because it is one of the most colorful and unusually marked birds in North America.*

able collar that regulates the air flow. A stopcock controls the gas, and a short pipe at the bottom, connected to a rubber hose, carries the gas from its source to the burner. The Bunsen burner is widely used in laboratories.

Bunshaft, Gordon

Gordon Bunshaft, b. Buffalo, N.Y., May 9, 1909, d. Aug. 6, 1990, was an architect noted for his large-scale corporate and public buildings. He graduated from Massachusetts Institute of Technology (B.A., 1933; M.A., 1935) and in 1937 joined the firm of SKIDMORE, OWINGS, AND MERRILL, where he became a full partner (1949–79). The style of his earlier buildings, particularly the glass-and-aluminum Lever House (1952; New York), was influenced by the work of Ludwig Mies van der Rohe and helped establish the smooth-skinned rectilinear slab with adjacent plaza as the standard for corporate offices.

With the Beinecke Rare Book Library (1963) at Yale University, Bunshaft's mature style began to emerge. The deeply articulated external frames holding thin translucent marble panels evince a new feeling for texture and mass. In the Lyndon Baines Johnson Memorial Library (1971) at Austin, Tex., Bunshaft maintained his characteristic overall clarity of simple geometrical form but rejected the INTERNATIONAL STYLE with such frankly neoclassical components as a high podium, massive stone-clad walls, and a projecting attic story. A later major work, reminiscent of the visionary architectural projects of Étienne Louis Boullée, is the HIRSHHORN MUSEUM AND SCULPTURE GARDEN (1969–74) in Washington, D.C. Bunshaft was co-recipient of the Pritzker Architecture Prize in 1988.

Bibliography: Drexler, A., *Transformations in Modern Architecture* (1979); Drexler, A., and Menges, A., *Architecture of Skidmore, Owings and Merrill, 1963–1973* (1974); McCallum, I., *Architecture U.S.A.* (1959).

bunting

Bunting is the common name of various small to medium-sized birds, including members of the genus *Passerina*, of the Americas; the FINCHES and SPARROWS, in North America; the genus *Emberiza*, of Eurasia; the snow bunting (*Plectrophenax nivalis*), which is holarctic, or distributed in northern Europe, northern Asia, and North America; the Lapland bunting, or LONGSPUR (*Calcarius lapponicus*), and its North American relatives; and the lark bunting (*Calamospiza melanocorys*) of North America.

Among the buntings of *Passerina*, the males are bright blue, red, or green and the females are brown, gray, or green. Both

sexes of New World sparrows are plumaged alike in brown and gray, which is frequently streaked, but such finches as the rufous-sided towhee (*Pipilo erythrophthalmus*) are boldly marked. In *Emberiza*, the males are typically patterned in black, white, yellow, or rust, and the females are usually brown with streaks. Unlike other buntings, the snow bunting is mostly white. Many buntings have rich, varied songs. The open cup-shaped nests are usually on the ground or low in bushes or trees. Buntings eat seeds, berries, and insects.

DAVID EWERT

Buntline, Ned

Ned Buntline was the pen name for Edward Zane Carroll Judson, b. Stamford, N.Y., Mar. 20, 1823, d. July 16, 1886, who was the popular writer of some 400 so-called dime novels. His own colorful and violent life was often the subject of his adventure fiction. He is best known for transforming an obscure Indian scout, William F. Cody, into the romantic BUFFALO BILL. Cody figured in several of Buntline's novels and in his play *The Scouts of the Plains* (1872). Buntline was also a leader of the ASTOR PLACE RIOT (1849), and toward the end of his life was involved in the temperance movement.

Bibliography: Monaghan, James, *The Great Rascal* (1952).

Buñuel, Luis   [boon-yoo-el']

The iconoclastic wit of Luis Buñuel reached a zenith in the scene from his 1961 film Viridiana, *in which beggars and cripples reenact Da Vinci's* Last Supper. *A Spanish filmmaker, Buñuel was noted for his antipathy toward the Roman Catholic church.*

Luis Buñuel, b. Calanda, Spain, Feb. 22, 1900, d. July 29, 1983, was a film director whose works were characterized by mocking humor, a spirit of anarchy, and both irreverence and religious undertones. He was renowned for his ability to shock, instruct, and entertain.

Buñuel collaborated with Salvador DALÍ on his first film, *Un Chien andalou* (An Andalusian Dog, 1928), a demonstration of automatism and surrealistic techniques. His *L'Age d'or* (The Golden Age, 1930) created a scandal by depicting Christ and the Marquis de Sade together. He next directed a tough, socially conscious documentary, *Las Hurdes* (Land without Bread, 1932), a genre he continued to exploit during the Spanish Civil War. After a period in Hollywood, he settled in Mexico in 1947. There, in addition to making melodramas for the Mexican mass market, he directed *Los Olvidados* (The Young and the Damned, 1950), *Nazarin* (1958), *The Exterminating Angel* (1962), and *Simon of the Desert* (1965). Buñuel returned to Spain to make *Viridiana* (1961), only to see his completed film banned as anticlerical by the Franco regime. His *Milky Way* (1969) remains one of the cinema's most scathing attacks on Catholicism. From the mid-1960s, Buñuel worked largely in France on politically satirical films depicting the eccentricities of the affluent class. They include *Belle de jour* (1966); the Oscar-winning *Discreet Charm of the Bourgeoisie* (1972); *The Phantom of Liberty* (1974); and *That Obscure Object of Desire* (1977). Buñuel's autobiography is *My Last Sigh* (trans. by Abigail Israel; 1983).

GAUTAM DASGUPTA

Bibliography: Edwards, Gwynne, *The Discreet Art of Luis Buñuel* (1983); Mellen, Joan, ed., *The World of Luis Buñuel* (1978); Sandro, Paul, *Diversions of Pleasure* (1987).

Bunyan, John

John Bunyan, the self-educated tinker who became a Baptist preacher, was the author of the religious allegory Pilgrim's Progress, *in which the life of Christian is depicted as a pilgrimage from the City of Destruction to the Celestial City. Bunyan wrote almost all his 43 books and tracts while imprisoned for nonconformist beliefs.*

John Bunyan, b. Elstow, Bedfordshire, 1628, d. Aug. 31, 1688, was a fervent English Puritan and a supreme master of English prose, best known for his PILGRIM'S PROGRESS. Educated briefly in the local school, Bunyan early became a tinker like his father. During the English Civil War, he served (1646) in the parliamentary army. As a member of a Baptist congregation in Bedford after 1653, Bunyan clashed with his fellow nonconformists, the Quakers. This experience led to two religious pamphlets (published in 1656 and 1657) in defense of his faith and launched him on a new career as an itinerant preacher.

Arrested in 1660 for preaching without a license, Bunyan spent most of the next 12 years in jail. While there he produced 10 books, the most important of which was his powerful spiritual autobiography, *Grace Abounding to the Chief of Sinners* (1666). In this he chronicles his many battles with Satan and "the merciful working of God" on his sinful soul, leading to his salvation and the acceptance of his divine call to preach to other sinners. Following his release from prison in 1672 and his temporary reimprisonment for nonconform-

ism, Bunyan completed his most famous work, *Pilgrim's Progress,* an allegory of Christian salvation; it was published in two parts, in 1678 and 1684. Bunyan's other works—rich in biblical echoes and notable for their vigorous, colloquial, and highly personal style—include *The Life and Death of Mr. Badman* (1680), which presents, as a dialogue between Mr. Wiseman and Mr. Attentive, the biography of an unregenerate rogue, and *The Holy War* (1682), in which the City of Mansoul (symbolizing the human soul) is besieged by Diabolus and delivered by Emmanuel.

DAVID M. ZESMER

Bibliography: Batson, E. Beatrice, *John Bunyan: Allegory and Imagination* (1984); Bunyan, John, *Complete Works of John Bunyan,* ed. by Henry Stebbing (1859; repr. 1970); Forrest, James T., and Greaves, Richard L., *John Bunyan: A Reference Guide* (1982); Furlong, Monica, *Puritan's Progress* (1975); Sharrock, Roger, *John Bunyan,* new ed. (1968; repr. 1984); Tindall, William York, *John Bunyan, Mechanick Preacher* (1934; repr. 1964).

Bunyan, Paul

In American folklore, Paul Bunyan is a giant lumberjack of superhuman strength. The character is based on an oral tradition that apparently originated among French or Irish lumberjacks in 19th-century Canada, but most of the tales about him are literary creations of the 20th century. He first appeared in print in a Detroit newspaper article in 1910 and soon became a popular symbol of American bigness and energy. W. B. Laughead, who adopted Paul as the advertising symbol of a Minnesota lumber company, invented the name *Babe* for Paul's giant blue ox and the names of other characters in his legendary logging camp.

Bibliography: Hoffman, Daniel, *Paul Bunyan* (1966; repr. 1983); Stevens, James, *The Saginaw Paul Bunyan* (1987).

buoy

A buoy is a floating device fixed by an ANCHOR. The two basic types are mooring buoys and navigational buoys. Mooring buoys are moored in a dock or HARBOR so that ships or boats can be secured to them. Recently, large, elaborate, and costly mooring buoys have been used to secure large petroleum TANKERS in deep-water berths from which liquid cargoes can be pumped ashore along a pipeline laid on the seabed and connected to oil storage tanks on the land.

Most buoys, however, serve as floating marks to aid NAVIGATION. Navigational buoys are used to mark the sides and centers of navigation channels; wrecks and rocks; spoil grounds; underwater telegraph cables; boundaries of dangerous areas; and middle grounds in estuaries. The cable connecting a buoy to its anchor is usually made of chain and is sufficiently long to allow the buoy to rise and fall with changes in sea level. Navigational buoys are distinguished from one another by their shapes, colors, markings, and lights. (Some also carry bells, whistles, or radar reflectors.) By interpreting the buoy's characteristics, navigators can identify its purpose and avoid the hazard indicated. Multinational, but no universal codes, exist for these characteristics.

CHARLES H. COTTER

buoyancy: see ARCHIMEDES' PRINCIPLE.

bur reed

Bur reed, *Sparganium,* is the only genus in the bur reed family of perennial herbs, Sparganiaceae; about 15 species grow in the temperate and cool regions of the Northern Hemisphere, Australia, and New Zealand. The bur reeds are grasslike aquatic and marsh plants with creeping roots. The round female flowering heads become burlike because of the spreading tips of the mature pistil, giving rise to the common name. The scientific name is derived from the Greek word *sparganion* ("band"), referring to ribbonlike leaves.

Burbage, Richard   [bur'-bij]

Richard Burbage, b. *c.*1568, d. March 1619, was the son of the theater manager James Burbage and perhaps the greatest actor on the Elizabethan and Jacobean stage. One of the 26 "principal actors" in William SHAKESPEARE's company, the Lord CHAMBERLAIN's Men, he created such roles as Richard III, Henry V, Romeo, Lear, Hamlet, Othello, and Macbeth. He held a partial interest in the GLOBE THEATRE and owned the BLACKFRIARS theatre with his brother Cuthbert.   ANDREW KELLY

Burbank, Luther

Luther Burbank developed ingenious breeding methods prior to the rediscovery of Mendelian genetics. This 1923 photo was taken in his world-famous horticulture center at Santa Rosa, Calif.

Luther Burbank, b. Lancaster, Mass., Mar. 7, 1849, d. Apr. 11, 1926, was an American horticulturist who created hundreds of new varieties of fruits, vegetables, and flowers. At the age of 19, he read Charles Darwin's book *The Variation of Animals and Plants Under Domestication.* "It was without question the most inspiring book I had ever read," he later wrote; and the principle of natural selection postulated by Darwin influenced all Burbank's future work. Without the aid of any scientific theory, he taught himself the complicated techniques of plant crossing, selection, and hybridization. His Massachusetts garden began to produce the best and earliest vegetables in the area, among them his first creation, the famous Burbank potato, which is still grown today.

In 1875, Burbank moved to Santa Rosa, Calif., established a small nursery garden, greenhouse, and orchard, and began the systematic plant experimentation that was to continue for half a century. Primarily through hybridization—the crossbreeding of plants of different varieties—he culled from thousands of specimens those with special characteristics of size, color, aroma, or flavor. Some of his experiments were monumental undertakings: to produce his blackberry-raspberry hybrid, Phenomenal, he grew and discarded about 65,000 berry bushes. Burbank's principal work was with flowers (among many others, the Shasta daisy is his creation), fruits—especially plums and berries—and vegetables. Primarily pragmatic rather than scientific, he relied solely on his own perceptions, and the records of his experiments, which would have been invaluable to plant scientists, were invariably destroyed when he no longer needed them.

Bibliography: Beeson, E. B., *The Early Life and Letters of Luther Burbank* (1927); Dreyer, Peter, *A Gardener Touched with Genius: The Life of Luther Burbank,* rev. ed. (1987).

See also: PLANT BREEDING; PLANT PROPAGATION.

burbot   [bur'-buht]

Burbot, or ling, *Lota lota,* family Gadidae, is the only species of cod that inhabits fresh water, in Northern Eurasia and North America. Burbots once were abundant in the Great Lakes, but their number was reduced unintentionally by

The burbot, L. lota, is a freshwater codfish of northern waters. Although abundant in lakes, the burbot is not caught for commercial purposes because its flesh does not keep well.

whitefish anglers. Still common in many small, cold, deep lakes, they feed voraciously in shallow water at night on fish and on crayfish, returning to the depths with dawn. They spawn in the winter, the young remaining in near-shore areas until the age of two.   A. R. EMERY

Burchfield, Charles   [burch'-feeld]

American artist Charles Burchfield, b. Apr. 9, 1893, d. Jan. 10, 1967, painted landscapes and Midwestern towns. Burchfield often distorted forms and space to capture the inner spirit of these places. He grew up in Salem, Ohio, and claimed to be obsessed by childhood memories. In his *Church Bells Ringing, Rainy Winter Night* (1917; Cleveland Museum, Ohio), the windows of the old wooden church have been made to appear as faces, the steeple as a grotesque, hawk-shaped head; the falling rain evokes drops of blood or perhaps tears. Burchfield could visualize figments of invisible forces. In his *Night Wind* (1918; Museum of Modern Art, New York City), the wind is suggested by patterns of hunched figures, with protruding fingers and heads perched over the roof of the house.   ABRAHAM A. DAVIDSON

Bibliography: Baur, John I. H., *Charles Burchfield* (1956) and *The Inlander: Life and Work of Charles Burchfield, 1893–1967* (1982).

Charles Burchfield's *Ice Glare* (1933) is an indictment of the effects of industrialization on the small towns of midwestern America. The regenerative natural forces of water and snow are frequent motifs in his work. (Whitney Museum of American Art, New York City.)

Burckhardt, Jakob

Jakob Burckhardt, b. Basel, Switzerland, May 25, 1818, d. Aug. 8, 1897, one of the greatest modern historians, was one of the first scholars to emphasize the study of culture and the arts as crucial to understanding human history. Burckhardt studied history and art at the University of Berlin from 1839 to 1843. After a tour of Germany and Italy, he returned to his native city, where he lectured on history and art until his retirement in 1893.

Burckhardt is best known for his masterpiece, *The Civilization of the Renaissance in Italy* (1860), in which he formulated the present view of the RENAISSANCE as a distinct cultural period. Stressing individualism and secular values as hallmarks of modern culture, Burckhardt saw Italy as the school for Europe in the early modern period. Interested in all of Western history, he planned a history of culture from ancient to modern times; it remained unfinished at his death. From his papers was published his speculative *Reflections on History* (1905; Eng. trans., 1943), in which he argued that culture, conceived broadly to include technology as well as art and literature, has been the sole creative factor in history, and that the state and religion have been repressive forces.

BENJAMIN G. KOHL

Bibliography: Gay, Peter, *Style in History* (1974); Weintraub, K. J., *Visions of Culture* (1966).

burdock

Burdock, *Arctium*, in the sunflower family, Asteraceae, is native to the Old World but has established itself in North America as a weed that grows mainly in overgrown fields and along roadsides. The flower, surrounded by rough leaves, is usually purple; the modified leaves of the flowering head become hooked and woody when mature, thus forming the burrs that aid in seed dispersal.

bureaucracy

Bureaucracy is a system for administering large organizations involving a specific structure of authority and a clearly defined set of rules and regulations. Bureaucracy may be found in all large, formal organizations, such as government, corporations, churches, schools, prisons, and political parties. Bureaucracy is criticized for being plagued by red tape, indecisiveness, and excessive paperwork. Its defenders maintain that bureaucracy is necessary for the swift, smooth, and economical completion of large-scale tasks.
Theories about Bureaucracy. A key to the historical development of bureaucracy was supplied by the German sociologist Max WEBER, who saw it as characteristic of the movement toward rational social organization in modern societies. These societies differ from others in that government in them is based on a system of law; leaders obtain their offices by following certain legal procedures; and the power to rule is vested in their positions rather than in themselves as individuals. Bureaucracy is not a new system of administration, but it has become the pervasive pattern in modern industrial countries. "The decisive reason for the advancement of bureaucratic organization," Weber wrote, "has always been its purely technical superiority over any other form of organization."

Weber was concerned with governmental bureaucracy, but subsequent writers have approached bureaucracy as a form of organization for accomplishing large-scale tasks in general. The tasks may involve collecting taxes, administering workers' compensation, operating a bank, running a school system, managing a large corporation, or building highways.

The emergence of bureaucracy as a system of administration may also be seen as related to the growing complexity of society. Émile DURKHEIM, the French sociologist, saw societies in terms of the division of labor within them. In primitive societies, relatively little division of labor exists. As societies become more complex, their members no longer share the same experiences. A new basis of uniting individuals with the collectivity is required. A form of social organization develops to coordinate and moderate their diverse activities.

Bureaucracy in Modern Life. Forms of large-scale organization have become so predominant in modern life that a large literature has developed about bureaucracy and its characteristics. Many writers have seen it as a threat to freedom, a faceless system gradually acquiring control over most of industrial and political life. William H. Whyte, Jr., wrote, in *The Organization Man* (1956), of the executives whose lives and values are largely determined by the requirements of the organizations for which they work. C. Wright MILLS, in *The Sociological Imagination* (1959), described the employee who is coopted and controlled by his organization as "the cheerful robot." Robert MERTON, in *Social Theory and Social Structure* (1968), noted that in a bureaucracy the rules and procedures created to achieve certain ends may become ends in themselves; bureaucratic training may produce persons who are unable to act outside of the procedural rules to which they are accustomed.

Government has grown in both size and scope in recent decades. In the 19th century the government was thought to have only a limited sphere of usefulness, primarily in defense and the collection of taxes. In the 1930s, the scope of government in the United States was extended greatly, so that it covered such matters as the regulation of security markets and the supervision of labor-management relations. In the 1960s and '70s, governmental regulation was extended to such public concerns as pollution, health, and consumer safety. (See GOVERNMENT REGULATION.) In other countries the number of public officials has also expanded, not only in WELFARE STATES, such as the Scandinavian countries, but also in the new countries of Africa and Asia. In Communist countries, government bureaucracy is an omnipresent fact of life.

In Western countries, the expansion of government bureaucracy has been accompanied by restraints upon the powers exercised by officials. Most powers of public administrators are delegated to them by legislatures. The enormous expansion of record-keeping by government agencies has given rise to a fear that personal data may be used against citizens without their knowledge. In the United States, under the FREEDOM OF INFORMATION ACT, federal agencies are required to open their files to the public. (See also COMPUTERS AND PRIVACY.)

Large private corporations, such as General Electric or Ford Motor Company, have administrative staffs that resemble the administrative staffs of government agencies. An important difference, however, is that private corporations are owned by stockholders; their power of decision making is not delegated to them by a legislature, and they are not bound by standardized personnel procedures like those of the CIVIL SERVICE. Several schools of management philosophy have arisen.

One school is associated with the work of the industrial engineers Frederick W. TAYLOR, Frank and Lillian GILBRETH, and Henry Gantt (1861–1919) early in the 20th century. They were interested in the efficient organization of work and devoted much of their effort to the study of the industrial organization as a machine. They viewed the organization as a closed system with a single, unified structure; managers were responsible for maintaining that structure. A second school of management, known as the human-relations or behavioral school, developed in the 1950s and '60s. It applied concepts from the behavioral sciences to the study of activities in the workplace. In its view the organization was still a closed system, but one composed of multiple internal structures; managers were responsible for coordinating these structures to achieve the organization's goals.

The impact of bureaucracy on individual workers remains controversial. There is general agreement that bureaucracy will remain the predominant form of administrative organization for the foreseeable future, but more attention is now being given to the need to balance continued rationalization of production and control with concern for the individual.

PHYLLIS L. STEWART AND NANCY L. WITYAK

Bibliography: Aberbach, J. D., et al., *Bureaucrats and Politicians in Western Democracies* (1981); Blau, P. M., and Meyer, M. W., *Bureaucracy in Modern Society* (1987); Hummel, R. P., *The Bureaucratic Experience* (1987); Rourke, F. E., *Bureaucracy, Politics and Public Policy*, 3d ed. (1984).

Burgas   [boor-gahs']

Burgas (1991 est. pop., 226,121) is a major port town in southeastern Bulgaria that is located on the Gulf of Burgas, an inlet of the Black Sea, and handles much of Bulgaria's Black Sea trade. Established during the 18th century as a fishing village on the site of the 14th-century town of Pyrgos, Burgas continues to process most of the Bulgarian fish catch. Exports include tobacco, grain, wooden articles, and food products. Iron, steel, and petroleum are major imports.

Bürger, Gottfried August   [buer'-ger]

Gottfried August Bürger, b. Dec. 31, 1747, d. June 8, 1794, was a German writer of folk songs and ballads. He belonged to a group of poets called the Göttinger Hain (Gottingen Circle) and later to the STURM UND DRANG (Storm and Stress) movement. He is best known for his ballad "Lenore" (1773), which became famous throughout Europe and important for the development of the BALLAD.   LILIAN R. FURST

Burger, Warren Earl   [bur'-gur]

Warren Earl Burger, b. Saint Paul, Minn., Sept. 17, 1907, was the 15th chief justice of the United States, from 1969 until he retired in 1986. He worked his way through law school in Saint Paul and became active in Republican politics under Harold Stassen, supporting Stassen's presidential aspirations in 1948 and 1952. In 1955, President Dwight D. Eisenhower appointed Burger to the U.S. Court of Appeals for the District of Columbia, where he was known for his conservative approach to law. President Richard M. Nixon named Burger to succeed Earl Warren as chief justice in 1969; Burger's "strict constructionism" sharply contrasted with the broad activism of the Warren court.

Chief Justice Burger promoted administrative efficiency and reform in the courts. He usually took a conservative position on the bench, voting to uphold the death penalty, limit the rights of defendants in criminal cases, and restrict access to legal abortion. His views as chief justice, however, did not dominate those of his colleagues. The Burger court lacked a dominant philosophy. It was often divided and its opinions unpredictable. It was generally a moderate court, consolidating rather than undoing the Warren legacies. At times it was "activist," upholding school busing and ruling that women have a right to abortion.

Bibliography: Blasi, Vincent, *The Burger Court* (1986).

Burgess, Anthony   [bur'-jes]

Anthony Burgess, b. Feb. 25, 1917, d. Nov. 25, 1993, who also published as John Burgess Wilson and Joseph Kell, was a versatile essayist, linguist, translator, musician, and comic novelist whose inventive use of language and taste for parody reflected his interest in James Joyce, about whom he wrote in *Re Joyce* (1965). He is perhaps best known for his futuristic novel *A Clockwork Orange* (1962; film, 1971).

Raised a Roman Catholic in Manchester, England, he was trained as a composer and continued to use musical forms in his fiction, such as *Napoleon Symphony: A Novel in Four Movements* (1974). After serving in the British Army in World War II, he became a teacher and education officer, first in England (1950–54) and then in the Far East (1954–59), the setting of *Time for a Tiger* (1956), his first published novel. Sent back to England with a supposedly fatal brain tumor, he wrote five books in a year. His many other books include such novels as *The Right to an Answer* (1960), *Enderby Outside* (1968), and *MF* (1971); fictional (*Nothing Like the Sun*, 1964) and factual (*Shakespeare*, 1970) biographies of Shakespeare; variations on the Oedipus legend; and literary criticism, such as *Flame into Being* (1985) on D. H. Lawrence. *Little Wilson and Big God* (1986) and *You've Had Your Time!* (1990) are the two volumes of his autobiography.

ROBERT MURRAY DAVIS

Bibliography: Coale, Samuel, *Anthony Burgess* (1981); Stinson, John J., *Anthony Burgess Revisited* (1991).

Anthony Burgess, a versatile English author, reveals a grim and violent vision of the future in his novels A Clockwork Orange (1962) and The Wanting Seed (1962). In addition to his contributions to contemporary fiction, Burgess has written several important works in the field of linguistics.

Photo Jill Krementz © 1979

Burgh, Hubert de   [burg]

As justiciar (chief political and judicial leader) of England, Hubert de Burgh, d. 1243, was effectively ruler of England during the minority of King HENRY III. He was appointed justiciar at Runnymede in 1215, when King John granted the Magna Carta to his rebellious barons. After John's death (1216) and the succession of the 9-year-old Henry, Hubert repelled a French invasion and rapidly became the most powerful man in the realm, overshadowing the regent, the earl of Pembroke. He restored royal authority after the prolonged baronial revolt, but his self-aggrandizement alienated the barons and, eventually, the young king. Henry dismissed him in 1232.

Burghers of Calais: see RODIN, AUGUSTE.

Burghley, William Cecil, 1st Baron   [bur'-lee]

Sir William Cecil, b. Sept. 18, 1520, d. Aug. 4, 1598, later Lord Burghley, was the chief minister in the English government throughout most of the reign of ELIZABETH I. Educated at Cambridge and at Gray's Inn, one of the Inns of Court, he first entered the government as secretary to Edward Seymour, duke of Somerset, the Protector of Edward VI. Knighted in 1551, he continued to hold offices under Queen Mary.

One of Elizabeth's first acts upon succeeding to the throne in 1558 was to name Cecil her principal secretary. He shared many of the queen's views and worked closely with her. He was particularly active in foreign diplomacy; in Parliament, where he explained government policy and argued successfully for grants of taxation; and in the field of government finance, serving (1572–98) as lord treasurer. In religion he was a moderate Puritan, and he urged Elizabeth to execute the Roman Catholic claimant to the throne, Mary, Queen of Scots. He was ennobled as Baron Burghley in 1571. Cecil built several great country houses, of which Burghley House at Stamford still stands. His son Robert Cecil, 1st earl of Salisbury, was also a principal secretary.   STANFORD E. LEHMBERG

Bibliography: Read, Conyers, *Lord Burghley and Queen Elizabeth* (1960); Smith, Alan G., ed., *The Anonymous Life of William Cecil, Lord Burghley* (1990).

Burgkmair, Hans, the Elder   [boork'-my-ur]

Hans Burgkmair the Elder, 1473–1531, was a leading German Renaissance painter and graphic artist who was at the forefront of artistic life in 16th-century Augsburg. He studied with his father, Thoman, an important Augsburg painter, and possibly with Martin Schongauer in Colmar. He probably visited Venice and northern Italy several times. In his many religious paintings and portraits, he combined an Italianate sense of color and modeling with northern expressiveness and love of detail. One of his best-known paintings is the magnificent *St. John Altarpiece* (1517; Alte Pinakothek, Munich).

Burgkmair did many important woodcuts, often experimenting with chiaroscuro and color techniques. His patrons included the prominent Fuggers of Augsburg and Emperor Maximilian I, for whom he made woodcuts illustrating the emperor's genealogy and the major events of his reign. Many of the woodcuts in Maximilian's great *Triumphal Arch* (a multiartist project supervised by Albrecht DÜRER) and *Triumphal Procession* are by Burgkmair. For the *Triumphal Procession,* a great scroll 61 m (200 ft) long depicting a magnificent parade in honor of the emperor, he supplied 61 of the 137 woodcuts. His elegant decorative sense and superb understanding of woodcut techniques are demonstrated in these prints.

TANIA BAYARD

Bibliography: Appelbaum, Stanley, ed., *The Triumph of Maximilian I* (1964); Osten, Gert von der, and Vey, Horst, *Painting and Sculpture in Germany and the Netherlands: 1500–1600* (1969).

burglary

The crime of burglary, in common law, is the breaking and entering of the dwelling of another person with the intent to commit a felony. Breaking comprises opening a closed door or window by any means. Entry need only be slight—such as placing a hand or an instrument into the building. The dwelling also includes other structures located within the common enclosure (a garage, for example). The felony need not actually be committed if the intent to do so is established. Historically, in English common law (from which the U.S. states have derived their varying definitions of burglary), burglary was defined as occurring at night.

In the United States, many jurisdictions have altered the common-law conceptions of burglary in their statutes. Some states have eliminated the element of breaking into the building. Many states have abolished the requirement that the entry be made at night, although night entries are generally punished more severely. Most jurisdictions no longer require that the building be a dwelling. Some have extended it to include airplanes, automobiles, railroad cars, and ships. Certain states have broadened the element of intent to commit a felony so as to include the intent to commit any crime.

Burgos   [boor'-gohs]

Burgos (1984 est. pop., 155,849), a city in Old Castile, northern Spain, is situated on a high plateau overlooking the Arlanzón River. Burgos is the administrative, trade, and processing center (notably woolen and leather goods) for a fertile area. It is chiefly noted for its exceptional architecture and its historical role.

Founded in the 9th century, it became the capital of the Kingdom of Castile under Ferdinand I in 1035. It also prospered as the seat of the Burgos Guild, which from 1494 controlled all of Castile's foreign trade. After 1560, when the court moved to Madrid, the city declined in political importance, although it was the headquarters of Gen. Francisco FRANCO during the Spanish Civil War (1936–39). Its architecture is a present testimony to Burgos's former glory. Landmarks of special interest include the elaborate Gothic cathedral (1221–1567), which holds the remains of EL CID (Rodrigo Díaz de Vivar); the Arco de Santa María; the Gothic churches of Santa Agueda, San Estaban, and San Nicolás; the castle overlooking the city; and monasteries and convents nearby.

Burgoyne, John

John Burgoyne, b. 1722, d. Aug. 4, 1792, a British general in the American Revolution, was also a politician and playwright. Burgoyne conducted himself so well during military campaigns in Portugal in 1762 that he was called a man of promise. After serving (1763–75) in Parliament, he joined the army in America and in 1776 was given command of the northern army to carry out an invasion from Canada.

Burgoyne's campaign started successfully when he captured TICONDEROGA in July 1777, but he ran into difficulty when a detachment of his Hessians was defeated (August 16) near Bennington, Vt., while foraging for food. After two furious battles near Saratoga, N.Y. (September 19 and October 7), Burgoyne surrendered his entire army to Gen. Horatio GATES on Oct. 17, 1777 (see SARATOGA, BATTLES OF). Saratoga proved to be the turning point of the war, because it convinced France to become America's ally.

Burgoyne returned to England in disgrace and resigned his rank as lieutenant general after a parliamentary inquiry into his conduct of the war in America. Briefly reinstated, he was commander in chief of Ireland in 1782–83. He later retired from the army and occupied himself mainly with literary and dramatic writing. His best-known play is *The Heiress* (1786).

GEORGE ATHAN BILLIAS

Bibliography: De Flonblanque, Edward B., *Political and Military Episodes . . . derived from the Life and Correspondence of the Rt. Hon. John Burgoyne* (1876); Hargrove, R. J., *General John Burgoyne* (1982); Lewis, Paul, *The Man Who Lost America: A Biography of Gentleman Johnny Burgoyne* (1973).

Burgundy

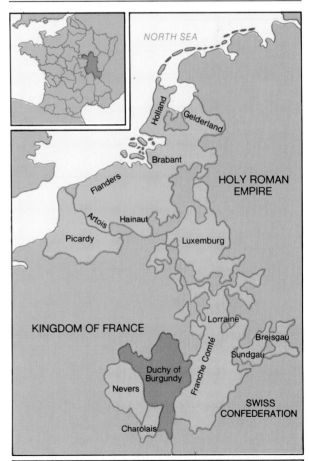

BURGUNDY IN THE MIDDLE AGES

 Duchy of Burgundy in 1363 (Inset shows later, province of Burgundy)

 Burgundian territories under Charles the Bold (1467-77)

The rule of the Valois dukes (1363–1477) expanded Burgundy to include not only Franche-Comté and Lorraine but land that later comprised the Netherlands, Belgium, and Luxembourg. At its height, Burgundy rivaled England and France in power and culture.

Burgundy (French: Bourgogne) is a historic region of east central France. The region's core is the fertile Rhône and Saône river valleys, where routes from Paris and the Rhineland to the Mediterranean converge. DIJON, a city famous as a gastronomic center, is the historic capital. Burgundy's wines, especially those of the celebrated Côte d'Or ("Golden Slope"), are among the world's most distinguished.

The region prospered under Roman rule, with Autun becoming a center of learning and the capital of northeastern GAUL. By the 5th century the Burgundii, a Germanic tribe, had settled in the area and established a kingdom. In 534, Burgundy became part of the Frankish kingdom under the MEROVINGIANS and, after 751, the CAROLINGIANS. During the various partitions of the Carolingian empire in the 9th century, two Burgundian states emerged: Lower (sometimes called Cisjurane) Burgundy, or PROVENCE, in the south; and Upper Burgundy, which was further divided into Transjurane and Cisjurane sections, in the north. These were united (933) as another Kingdom of Burgundy, later called Arles, which was part of the Holy Roman Empire from the 11th century until 1378, when it was ceded to France.

Two other, relatively independent, divisions had been formed in the 9th century: the duchy of Burgundy (corresponding to the modern region), which remained part of France, and the Free County of Burgundy, or FRANCHE-COMTÉ. The duchy was ruled by a cadet branch of the CAPETIANS from 1031 until 1361 when the line died out. The golden age of Burgundy commenced in 1363 when JOHN II, king of France, granted the duchy to his second son, PHILIP THE BOLD. With the death of his father-in-law in 1384, Philip added Flanders, Artois, Franche-Comté, and other lands to his holdings. Under his successors, JOHN THE FEARLESS, PHILIP THE GOOD, and CHARLES THE BOLD, Burgundy increased its territorial extent to include most of present-day Belgium and the Netherlands, as well as to Luxembourg, Alsace, and Lorraine (see LOW COUNTRIES, HISTORY OF).

In the early 15th century the dukes of Burgundy sought to dominate French affairs (see ARMAGNACS AND BURGUNDIANS). When thwarted, they allied (1419) with England in the HUNDRED YEARS' WAR. Antagonism between the kings of France and the dukes of Burgundy climaxed with the defeat and death (1477) of Charles the Bold in battle near Nancy. Burgundy's northern territories passed to Habsburg rule while the duchy itself was annexed by the French king, Louis XI. The Franche-Comté was acquired by France in 1678.

Bibliography: Armstrong, C. A., *England, France, and Burgundy in the 15th Century* (1983); Vaughan, Richard, *Philip the Bold: The Formation of the Burgundian State* (1962), *John the Fearless: The Growth of Burgundian Power* (1966), and *Philip the Good: The Apogee of Burgundy* (1970).

burial

Deliberate disposition of the human dead, generally referred to as burial, is practiced in virtually all cultures. Methods vary widely, but the most common form of burial is interment. Deliberate interment, also called inhumation, dates from at least 50,000 years ago, and evidence exists that some NEANDERTHALERS prepared graves for their dead. Another mode of burial is entombment in natural caves or rock-cut chambers, in specially prepared underground areas such as the CATACOMBS, or in buildings constructed to house the dead as in the MASTABAS and PYRAMIDS of the ancient Egyptians and the Mausoleum of HALICARNASSUS.

The rapid oxidation of the body to ash, called CREMATION, although technically not a form of burial, is often followed by containment of the ashes in a burial urn. In the platform burial of the Plains Indians the dead were exposed to the sun, air, and predators from the sky to hasten the decomposition of the flesh, after which the bones were collected and preserved in a safe place. Platform burial is also practiced by primitive societies in Indonesia, Melanesia, and Australia.

The consignment of a body to deep waters is an infrequently used form of burial. Other unusual burial procedures dependent upon specific climatic or physical conditions are burial in permafrost, which preserves the body by freezing, and burial in tannin-rich soil conditions, which also naturally preserves the body.

Graves are usually rectangular in shape and designed to accommodate only one person. Both individual and communal prehistoric burials have been found, but in historic times mass burial has rarely been practiced except in the case of natural disasters, pestilence, or mass killing during time of war.

Bodies are usually buried in a supine, extended position, encased in a casket, sometimes with an outer enclosure, or vault. At Paleolithic sites, crouched burials are common, with the skeleton bent at the knees and the hips.   ROBERT C. SLATER

Bibliography: Bendann, E., *Death Customs: An Analytical Study of Burial Rites* (1930; repr. 1971); Curl, J. S., *A Celebration of Death* (1980); Turner, Ann W., *Houses for the Dead* (1976).

See also: FUNERAL CUSTOMS; TOMB.

Buridan, Jean   [bue-ree-dahn']

Jean Buridan, 1300–58, was a French scholastic philosopher and logician. He produced critical commentaries on the works of Aristotle, advanced his own theory of causality, and wrote works on optics and mechanics. Buridan's story of an ass (or dog) that lacked the ability to choose and that starved to death when placed between two equidistant sources of food has caused him to be credited with originating PROBABILITY theory.   CATHERINE WILSON

burin: see PALEOLITHIC PERIOD.

Burke, Edmund

Edmund Burke, b. Dublin, Jan. 12, 1729, d. July 9, 1797, was perhaps the most brilliant and original thinker ever to sit in the British House of Commons. He graduated from Trinity College, Dublin, and led an impecunious life as a young man. He trained to become a lawyer in London but showed an inclination to literature and philosophy in his early essays *A Vindication of Natural Society* (1756) and *A Philosophical Enquiry into the Origin of Our Ideas of the Sublime and Beautiful* (1757). He committed himself to a political career by entering the service of the marquess of ROCKINGHAM in 1765 and took a seat in Parliament the same year.

In the following years Burke did much to mold and still more to express the principles of the Rockingham faction of the WHIG PARTY, notably in his *Thoughts on the Cause of the Present Discontents* (1770), in which he argued the value of political parties, and in his speeches defending the rights of the American colonists ("On American Taxation," 1774; "On Conciliation with the Colonies," 1775). He favored moderate reform to secure the independence of the House of Commons from crown influence, carrying a bill to that end as paymaster general of forces in the short-lived Rockingham ministry of 1782, but he opposed fundamental reform of Parliament and a reduction in the privileges of the Anglican church. He was concerned to defend the interests of the subjects of the British Empire in India as well as America and played a prominent, though controversial, part in the impeachment (1787–94) of Warren HASTINGS. In this, as in other periods of life, he was the object of much malicious criticism, some of it related to his relatively humble origins and Irish background.

Burke's last years were perhaps his most influential. He denounced the FRENCH REVOLUTION, advised the prime minister William PITT the Younger, and became a bitter enemy of his old friends in the Whig party. His most famous piece, *Reflections on the Revolution in France* (1790), was a forceful attack on the principles of the Revolution; although extravagantly expressed, it made him the international apostle of counter-revolution, and in some measure the founder of the modern conservative tradition.   PAUL LANGFORD

Bibliography: Burke, Edmund, *Correspondence*, ed. by Thomas Copeland, 10 vols. (1958–78); Freeman, Michael, *Edmund Burke and the Critique of Political Radicalism* (1980); Morley, John, *Edmund Burke* (1867; repr. 1979); Reid, Christopher, *Edmund Burke and the Practice of Political Writing* (1986).

Burke, Kenneth

Kenneth Duva Burke, b. Pittsburgh, Pa., May 5, 1897, d. Nov. 19, 1993, was a wide-ranging American literary critic notable for the extent of his influence. Educated at Ohio State and Columbia universities, he wrote music criticism, book reviews, and poetry for *The Dial* (1927–29) and *The Nation* (1934–35). With his innovative theory that literature is "symbolic action," he combined insights drawn from philosophy, sociology, psychology, and linguistics. Burke emphasized the social function of literature and the psychological basis of literary form, believing that a poet uses rhetoric to express himself in symbols. *The Philosophy of Literary Form* (1941), his central statement of this thesis, was followed by *A Grammar of Motives* (1945), *A Rhetoric of Motives* (1950), and *Language as Symbolic Action* (1966). His other major works include *Counterstatement* (1931; rev. ed., 1968) and *Attitudes toward History* (1937). His *Collected Poems, 1915–1967* (1967) was followed by a book of short stories, *The Complete White Oxen,* (1968) and *Dramatism and Development* (1972). A later work was *On Symbols and Society* (1989).　　　　CHARLES CANTALUPO

Bibliography: Bygrave, S., *Kenneth Burke* (1993); Frank, A. P., *Kenneth Burke* (1969); Henderson, G. E., *Kenneth Burke* (1989); Southwell, S. B., *Kenneth Burke and Martin Heidegger* (1983; repr. 1988).

Burke, Martha Jane:　　see CALAMITY JANE.

Burke, Robert O'Hara

Robert O'Hara Burke, b. 1820, d. June 28, 1861, was one of Australia's most famous early explorers. An Irishman, he migrated (1853) to Melbourne, where he joined the police force. In 1860, with William J. Wills, he led an expedition from Melbourne to cross the continent from south to north. Well provisioned and using camels, they reached the Gulf of Carpentaria, a distance of 2,400 km (1,500 mi), in 6 months. Affected by mishap, mismanagement, and failure to cooperate with the Aborigines on their return journey, both Burke and Wills died of starvation at Cooper Creek, in Central Australia. Only one expedition member, John King, survived.　　E. J. TAPP

Bibliography: Joy, William, *The Explorers* (1971); Moorehead, Alan, *Cooper's Creek* (1963; repr. 1987).

Burkina Faso

Burkina Faso, formerly Upper Volta, is a small, poor, landlocked country in West Africa. It is bounded by Niger to the east, Mali to the north and west, and Benin, Togo, Ghana, and Ivory Coast to the south. A French colony after 1896, it became independent in 1960. The renaming of the country in 1984 dramatized its break with the colonial past.

LAND AND PEOPLE

Distinctive aspects of the land have shaped the economy and way of life. Burkina Faso is located in the savanna zone on a granite and gneiss plateau some 200 to 300 m (650 to 1,000 ft) above sea level. The plateau is drained by the nonnavigable headwaters of the VOLTA RIVER, sources of river blindness, a scourge to the inhabitants. The poor, semiarid soil supports few crops, produces low yields, and loses its fertility rapidly. The tropical climate has rainy (June–October) and dry (November–May) seasons, with rainfall averaging 1,015–1,270 mm (40–50 in) annually in the south and only 510 mm (20 in) in the north. Extreme variations in rainfall led to severe droughts in 1969–74 and 1981–83, with large losses of life and livestock. Temperatures range from 10° C (50° F) in the early dry season to 40° C (104° F) just before the rains. Vegetation varies by ecological zone: there are fruit trees and some forests and woodlands in the center, and desert flora and scrub vegetation in the north.

There is great linguistic and ethnic diversity among the inhabitants (known as Burkinabe). The Voltaic linguistic grouping includes the MOSSI (48% of the population), Grunshi (5%), Bobo (7%), Lobi (7%), and SENUFO (5%). Mande-speakers (about 14%) include the Busani, Marka, and Samo and the Dyula, whose language is the commercial lingua franca. Other

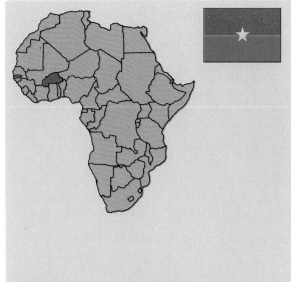

BURKINA FASO (REPUBLIC OF BURKINA)

LAND. Area: 274,200 km² (105,869 mi²). Capital and largest city: Ouagadougou (1985 pop., 441,514).
PEOPLE. Population (1993 est.): 10,000,000; density: 36.5 persons per km² (94.5 per mi²). Distribution (1993): 20% urban, 80% rural. Annual growth (1992): 3.1%. Official language: French. Major religions: traditional religions, Islam, Roman Catholicism.
EDUCATION AND HEALTH. Literacy (1991): 16% of adult population. Universities (1993): 1. Hospital beds (1984): 5,580. Physicians (1988): 280. Life expectancy (1993): women—53; men—52. Infant mortality (1993): 119 per 1,000 live births.
ECONOMY. GNP (1990): $2.96 billion; $330 per capita. Labor distribution (1985): agriculture—87%; industry and mining—4%; services—9%. Foreign trade (1990): imports—$540 million; exports—$151 million; principal trade partners—France, Ivory Coast, Taiwan, Italy. Currency: 1 C.F.A. franc = 100 centimes.
GOVERNMENT. Type: republic. Legislature: National Assembly. Political subdivisions: 30 provinces.
COMMUNICATIONS. Railroads (1991): 622 km (386 mi) total. Roads (1991): 13,134 km (8,161 mi) total (paved 12%). Major ports: none. Major airfields: 2.

groups include the FULANI and HAUSA. Most Burkinabe adhere to traditional religious beliefs. About 25% are Muslims, a faith that was historically resisted. Roman Catholics form a tiny but influential educated minority.

Most Burkinabe live in rural areas, where traditional leaders remain influential. The extended family and clan are the basic social units. Drought and population pressures in the south have increased the flight from the land, accelerating the traditional emigration of young (20–40) male Burkinabe to the plantations and cities of the more prosperous Ghana and Ivory Coast. An estimated 200,000 Burkinabe migrate annually to find jobs; many never return. This permanent migration reduces the labor force (and thus economic growth) and leaves women as the key producers in agriculture. OUAGADOUGOU, the capital, and Bobo Dioulasso, the home of the Bobo people, are the two largest cities. Both are growing rapidly as a result of an influx of job seekers, young people, and refugees from drought.

The wide dispersal of the rural population and the preference of the educated for city life make efforts to provide schools, health facilities, and other rural services very difficult. Poverty and lack of access to health care give the country one of the world's lowest life expectancies and one of its highest infant mortality rates. Endemic diseases such as meningitis, malaria, measles, and (to a lesser degree) leprosy and river blindness are pervasive in rural areas. The percentage of school-age children in primary school has increased since 1965 but to only 35% in 1989.

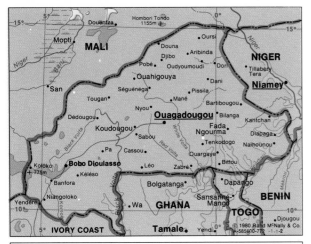

BURKINA FASO

——— Railroad

+   Spot Elevation

Scale 1:10,839,000

National capitals
are underlined

Meters	Feet
1000	3281
500	1640
200	656
0	0

0 50 100 150 200 250 km
0 50 100 150 mi

ECONOMIC ACTIVITY

Burkina Faso is one of Africa's poorest countries, and per capita caloric intake declined 5% between 1965 and 1984. The
economy is based upon agriculture and livestock (the second
largest export, shipped to neighbors to the south). Agriculture
contributes 45% of the gross national product (GNP) and employs most of the labor force. Peasants grow drought-resistant
crops such as millet, sorghum, and peanuts as well as cassava
and rice. Cash crops include cotton, the leading export, shea
nuts, and sesame. Known mineral deposits, including manganese and limestone, remain unexploited because of a lack of
transportation facilities and capital. Industry contributes 20–
22% of the GNP. Artisanship and small-scale agricultural processing predominate; there is little modern industry apart from

the Voltex textile factory. Services (including the urban ba-
zaar economy and the government work force, which consumes roughly 60% of the budget) constitute one-third of the
GNP.

Burkina Faso regularly imports far more than it exports—including much of its food. The trade deficit is financed by mi-
grant-worker remittances and by foreign aid, which also funds
roughly 90% of the development budget. With low economic
growth and negative national savings, Burkina Faso has had
recurring fiscal crises, but trade-union and public protests
have repeatedly slowed implementation of government austerity plans.

HISTORY AND GOVERNMENT

The Mossi arrived in this area in the 11th to 13th centuries
and established powerful kingdoms, including Ouagadougou,
Tenkodogo, and Yatenga. These linked kingdoms were centers of trade and contact between trans-Saharan traders and
the forest kingdoms to the south. The Mossi strongly resisted
the expansionist Islamic Mali (12th to 15th centuries) and
Songhai (14th to 16th centuries) empires. France asserted control over the area in the 1890s, dividing it among other French
colonies and reconstituting it within its present borders from
1919 to 1932 and again from 1947.

A Mossi-dominated political party headed by Maurice Yameogo led Upper Volta to independence in 1960. Political life
has since been dominated by the small educated elite, military officers, and labor unions. The nation's extreme poverty
has made it difficult to meet the demands of all these groups,
contributing to increasing political instability. Yameogo was
overthrown by the military in 1966 after trade-union protests.
Under the benign hand of Lt.-Col. (later Gen.) Sangoulé Lam-
izana (president, 1966–80), Upper Volta enjoyed more civil
liberties than most other African countries. It had a civilian
legislature from 1970 to early 1974 and again from 1978 to
1980, when renewed union pressures and military impatience
with squabbling civilian politicians led to a coup. A politicized officer corps mounted new coups in 1982 and 1983,
when Capt. Thomas Sankara and a young, radical officer
group seized power and sought to revolutionize society. Common people were encouraged to create Committees for the
Defense of the Revolution (CDRs) in cities and villages
through which to build schools and clinics, run local cooperatives, and exercise local power. The CDRs and Sankara
sought to divert funds from the costly urban civil service to ru-

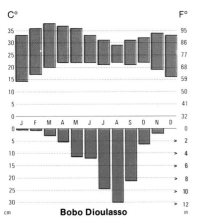

(Above) *Bars indicate monthly ranges of
temperatures* (red) *and precipitation* (blue)
*in Bobo Dioulasso, the second largest city
in Burkina. This southwestern regional
capital has a tropical wet-dry climate.*

(Right) *Washing laundry in a nearby stream
is one of the communal activities shared by
the women in a village in Burkina. This
landlocked West African nation was under
French control from the 1890s until 1960.*

ral development, and Sankara came to symbolize popular democracy. A border conflict with Mali that sparked military confrontations in 1974 and 1985 was settled amicably in 1986.

Disputes among the ruling group led to Sankara's assassination by his deputy, Capt. Blaise Compaore, in October 1987. This act and the new military government provoked popular revulsion and anger. Marxism-Leninism was abandoned as the official ideology. A new constitution approved by voters in June 1991 reduced the powers of the presidency and provided for direct multiparty elections. Campaore and his party won the presidential election of December 1991 and the nation's first legislative elections in 14 years, held May 1992.

JON KRAUS

Bibliography: Asante, S. K., *The Political Economy of Regionalism in West Africa* (1985); Harsch, E., "A Revolution Derailed," *Africa Report*, January–February 1988; Raymond, D., *Government and Economy in Upper Volta* (1967); Skinner, E., *African Urban Life* (1974) and *The Mossi of Upper Volta* (1964); Vengroff, R., *Upper Volta* (1983).

burlesque shows: see MUSIC HALL, VAUDEVILLE, AND BURLESQUE.

burlesque and travesty

Burlesque and travesty are forms of SATIRE in which the style and subject matter of an original work are ridiculed. Although the original may be almost any type of expression—there have been burlesques and travesties of musical works, pieces of art, political speeches, ballets, and so forth—the original use of the words was probably associated with literature. The differences between burlesque, travesty, and a third satiric form, PARODY, are subtle and often difficult to apply. Burlesque and travesty are both coarser, more grotesque forms of ridicule than parody, and come closer to the notion of caricature. Burlesque is often applied to extravagant imitations of form: John Gay's *The Beggar's Opera* (1728) burlesques the conventions of Italian opera. Parody, on the other hand, ridicules individual works, and the term might be derived from Paul Scarron's comic romance *Vergile travesti* (1648–58), a travesty of the *Aeneid* in which lofty characters are placed in prosaic situations, and low-life people speak in lofty tones.

Bibliography: Kitchin, G., *A Survey of Burlesque and Parody in English* (1931; repr. 1967); Rubsamen, W. H., *Satire, Burlesque, Protest, and Ridicule* (1975).

burletta [bur-let'-uh]

In the English theater of the late 18th and early 19th centuries, the burletta, performed at minor theaters that were legally forbidden to produce "legitimate," or prose, drama, was a short comic piece whose dialogue was sung or recited to music. Along with melodrama it was a popular dramatic form of the period.

A. H. SAXON

Burlington

Burlington (1990 pop., 39,127), the largest city in Vermont, is the seat of Chittenden County. At an altitude of 61 m (200 ft), it is a port city on the eastern shore of Lake Champlain, with the Green Mountains to the east. Industrial manufacturing and lumbering are important to the economy. The University of Vermont (1791), Trinity College (1925), and Saint Michael's College (1904) are in the area. The patriot leader Ethan Allen is buried in the city. The Shelburne Museum, a popular tourist attraction, is 11 km (7 mi) to the south. Settled in 1773, Burlington was named for the Burling family, colonial landholders. Early industries included lumbering and shipbuilding. During the War of 1812, Battery Park was the site of both land and water battles.

Burlington, Richard Boyle, 3d Earl of

Richard Boyle, 3d earl of Burlington and 4th earl of Cork, b. Apr. 25, 1694, d. Dec. 3, 1753, was the single most influential figure in English architecture between 1720 and 1750 and a dominant force in the establishment of the Palladian revival style. He made two grand tours of Italy, in 1714–15 and 1719,

during which he studied the architecture of Andrea Palladio and began a collection of Palladian drawings. On his second trip he met William Kent, who returned with Burlington and became a leading architect, landscape gardener, and interior designer of the Palladian movement. Burlington was greatly inspired by the publications of Colen CAMPBELL and Giacomo Leoni (*c.*1686–1746). As an architect, Burlington combined the inspiration of Palladio and of Inigo Jones. One of his best-known works is Chiswick House (begun 1725), London, which was directly inspired by Palladio's Villa Rotonda (1550–51) in Vicenza, Italy. Chiswick's rooms, decorated by Kent, are in a variety of forms that Burlington derived from his own study of Roman buildings. Through his personal patronage, his own architectural work, which includes the grandiose Assembly Rooms at York (1731–32), his ability to place his followers in important positions, and his encouragement of architectural publications, Burlington greatly influenced his age with his taste.

Bibliography: Summerson, John, *Architecture in Britain, 1530–1830,* 6th ed. (1977); Wilton-Ely, John, ed., *Apollo of the Arts* (1973); Wittkower, Rudolf, *Palladio and English Palladianism* (1974; repr. 1983).

Burma

Burma, officially called Myanmar since 1989, is the westernmost country of Southeast Asia's Indochina peninsula. It faces the Bay of Bengal on the south and is bounded on the northwest by Bangladesh and India, on the east by China and Laos, and on the southeast by Thailand. RANGOON (or Yangon), the capital, is the largest city and chief port. Although Burma today has one of the lowest per-capita incomes in Asia, people generally have enough to eat. The country was once the world's leading exporter of rice and remains one of the few developing countries that is a net exporter of food. Cut off from the outside world in ancient times by its mountains and its kings, Burma was again isolated after 1962 by the socialist policies of its government. Its various rulers have long struggled to impose their authority over minority groups in the rugged border regions.

LAND AND RESOURCES

Physical Regions. Laid out in a kitelike shape, the country has a central core of lowlands that are watered by the IRRAWADDY and Sittang rivers. The Irrawaddy itself is the most important feature of the region and is continuously navigable for almost 1,400 km (900 mi) upstream from the sea. Along it were sited Burma's great cities of ancient times. The Sittang River, by contrast, is of little navigational importance. The Arakan (western) and Tenasserim (southern) coastal lowlands are separated from the central core region by mountains or water bodies. The chief resource of the lowlands is soil, most of which is alluvial. Petroleum is the other major resource of the lowland core. The central Burma oil fields supplied the needs of the country until the early 1980s, and exploration continues.

The remainder of Burma comprises mountain and highland areas. In the north, near the border with China, is Mount Hkaka, the highest point in Burma (5,881 m/19,296 ft). To the west of the central core is the Patkai–Naga-Chin Hills and Arakan Yoma complex, which extends from Tibet to the sea. To the east the Shan Plateau rises sharply to more than 600 m (2,000 ft) high. The SALWEEN RIVER bisects this area. The Shan Highlands are rich in minerals, with substantial deposits of lead, zinc, and silver and more depleted reserves of rubies and other gemstones. Substantial tungsten deposits are found to the south of the Shan Plateau. Resource development has been limited by the general inaccessibility of the region and the inability of the government to provide effective administrative control. East of the Salween River, in the so-called Golden Triangle, poppies are cultivated for illicit opium traffic.

Climate. Burma has a tropical climate. The annual average temperature is 27° C (81° F) at Rangoon and 22° C (71° F) at Lashio on the Shan Highlands. Coastal and mountain regions receive up to 5,080 mm (200 in) of rain annually, and delta regions receive about 2,540 mm (100 in). Northern Burma is the driest part of the country, averaging 510 to 1,015 mm (20 to 40 in) a year.

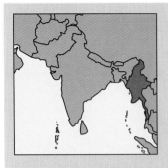

UNION OF MYANMAR

LAND. Area: 676,552 km² (261,218 mi²). Capital and largest city: Rangoon (Yangon; 1983 pop., 2,513,023).

PEOPLE. Population (1994 est.): 45,400,000; density: 67.1 persons per km² (173.8 per mi²). Distribution (1994): 25% urban, 75% rural. Annual growth (1994): 1.9%. Official language: Burmese. Major religions: Buddhism, animism, Islam, Hinduism, Christianity.

EDUCATION AND HEALTH. Literacy (1990): 81% of adult population. Universities (1989): 2. Hospital beds (1991): 26,294. Physicians (1991): 12,427. Life expectancy (1994): women—61; men—57. Infant mortality (1994): 98 per 1,000 live births.

ECONOMY. GDP (1992): $28 billion; $660 per capita. Labor distribution (1990): agriculture—68%; mining and manufacturing—8%; construction, public utilities, transport, and communications—4%; trade—9%; finance, public administration, services—6%. Foreign trade (1992): imports—$907 million; exports—$535 million; principal trade partners—Singapore, Japan, China. Currency: 1 kyat = 100 pyas.

GOVERNMENT. Type: military rule. Legislature: People's Assembly (suspended 1988). Political subdivisions: 7 divisions, 7 states.

COMMUNICATIONS. Railroads (1991): 3,137 km (1,949 mi) total. Roads (1988): 23,643 km (14,579 mi) total. Major ports: 3. Major airfields: 1.

PEOPLE

Ethnic Composition and Languages. Because of much ethnic intermarriage, Burma's population is best described as composed of ethnolinguistic groups rather than segregated racial or ethnic stocks. Its peoples speak more than 100 distinct languages. Most of this linguistic variety, however, is found among the hill peoples. The dominant (and official) tongue is Burmese, the language of the lowlanders. It is the medium of trade, communications, and education. Until modern times the only indigenous written languages were Burmese (a Sino-Tibetan language), Shan (of the Tai group), and Mon (Mon-Khmer). Large minorities include the KARENS and Kayahs (10%), SHANS (8%), Chins and Kachins (4%), Indians (2%), and Chinese (3%).

Religion. Most Burmese speakers are Buddhists; Theravada Buddhism is the practiced religion of about 85% of the population. Historically, Burmese Buddhists have perceived themselves as a bastion of Buddhist orthodoxy. In rural Burma, most males spend time in monasteries as *bhikkus* ("monks"). The folk religion of many Buddhists also includes adherence to astrology and *nat* spirit worship. About 5% of the population are Christian. Indians adhere to either Hinduism or Islam, and the Chinese to Buddhism or traditional Chinese religions. Most others practice various forms of animism.

Demography. Burma's crude birthrate is substantially higher than its crude death rate. Because approximately two-fifths of the populace are under 15 years of age, a substantial increase in population size may be expected regardless of any short-term decline in the birthrate.

In this land of villages, nearly one-half of all urban dwellers live in the Rangoon metropolitan area. Other large cities in-

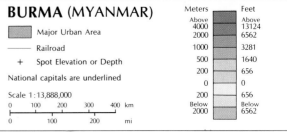

BURMA (MYANMAR)

	Major Urban Area
	Railroad
+	Spot Elevation or Depth

National capitals are underlined

Scale 1:13,888,000

0   100   200   300   400 km

0   100   200   mi

Meters		Feet
Above 4000		Above 13124
2000		6562
1000		3281
500		1640
200		656
0		0
200		656
Below 2000		Below 6562

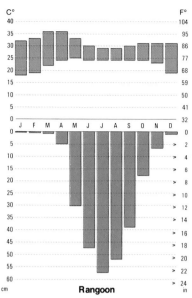

Bars on this climate chart indicate the monthly ranges of temperature (red) and precipitation (blue) at Rangoon, in the Irrawaddy Delta region. Rangoon and other places along the coast have a monsoon climate with heavy precipitation during the annual rainy season. Annual rainfall is much less in the interior, where mountains block the moisture-bearing monsoon winds.

Rangoon

clude MANDALAY in central Burma and MOULMEIN on the Tenasserim coast. Most small towns are villagelike in appearance and architecture. Houses are built mainly of wood and bamboo with thatch or tile roofs and typically are raised on piles off the ground.

Migration today is carefully controlled by the government, which has sought to restrict both immigration and emigration. After British colonial accession in the 19th century, a steady southward movement of people into the Irrawaddy Delta region occurred as the area came under commercial rice production. In previous centuries the Shans had immigrated from what is now southern China. Tibeto-Burmans preceded them from southeastern Tibet. The MONS immigrated even earlier from the east.

Social Conditions. Literacy in Burma has always been high. Monastery schools existed before modern educational curricula were introduced. Primary education today is free, but nominal fees are charged for secondary and higher education.

Student enrollment at all levels has greatly expanded in recent decades. Health-care programs are limited by lack of funds.

The Burmese folk arts remain largely un-Westernized; the state supports schools of dance, drama, music, and fine arts.

ECONOMIC ACTIVITY

Farming, forestry, and mining are the mainstays of the economy. Monoculture of rice characterizes the lower Burma delta. A diversified cropping system exists in the central dry zone, and shifting subsistence cultivation and forestry are carried on in the hills. The commercial rice industry began only about a century ago under British stimulus. Production came to be controlled during the 1930s by absentee landlords, many of them Indian or Chinese. Badly damaged by World War II, the economy failed to recover after independence.

The military officers who seized control in 1962 expanded earlier efforts to diminish the role of foreign enterprise and make Burma self-reliant by banning foreign investment, nationalizing all foreign and many domestic industries, and taking control of the import-export trade. By the 1970s, they began to accept limited foreign aid; state control over retail trade was lifted in 1987. Irrigation projects and the introduction of improved seed varieties and fertilizer led to a rise in agricultural productivity, but living standards continued to decline. Inflation, shortages, and official efforts to crush the flourishing black market contributed to massive antigovernment protests in 1988. In 1989 free-market policies were introduced in an effort to gain popular support.

The varied mineral output includes petroleum, natural gas, tin, tungsten, lead, zinc, precious stones, barite, gypsum, and limestone. Teak replaced rice as the leading export in 1985; manufactured goods constitute the chief imports.

GOVERNMENT

According to the constitution of 1974, which was suspended following a military coup on Sept. 18, 1988, supreme power of government resided in an elected unicameral legislature, which elected a council of state whose chairman was president of the republic. The Burma Socialist Program party (renamed the National Unity party in 1988) was the sole legal political party. After the coup, army leaders named a military council to rule the country. A March 1989 draft electoral law promised multiparty elections to transfer power to a civilian government within 14 months, and opposition parties were allowed to form. Military commanders administer the seven divisions of the Burmese heartland and the seven states in which national ethnic minorities form local majorities.

(Left) A monk prays before figures of Buddha at the Shwe Dagon temple in Rangoon. This temple and its massive pagoda, which is believed to be more than 2,500 years old, are Burma's most important Buddhist shrines. (Right) Pagan, the capital of an ancient Burmese empire, contains some of the most extensive ruins in southeastern Asia. Founded during the 9th century by the Burmese (Burmans), Pagan flourished until it was sacked in 1287 by Mongol invaders. The ruins were devastated by a 1975 earthquake, but much of the damage has since been repaired.

A fisherman guides his canoe past a rural dwelling on Lake Inle in central Burma. The use of stilts in housing construction is not unique to waterfront communities; throughout Burma's central lowlands homes must be raised off the ground to avoid damage from floods.

HISTORY

The early Mon inhabitants of the region established commercial and cultural ties with India and adopted Theravada Buddhism. After a period of domination by the Tibetan Pyu tribes, leadership passed to the Burmese, whose king ANAWRATHA united the region in 1044. Anawratha established his capital at PAGAN and accepted Theravada Buddhism. Pagan remained the capital until 1287, when it was conquered by the MONGOLS. Burma was again unified in the 16th century by the Toungoo dynasty. Early in the 18th century the Mons gained their independence and control of the Irrawaddy Delta, and in 1753 the whole of Burma came under Mon rule. In 1758, Alaungapaya led the Burmese in overthrowing the Mons, and a new capital was established in Rangoon. Alaungapaya's successors, members of the Konbaung dynasty, continued ruling, and their influence spread into India.

In 1824 war broke out between Britain and Burma over Burma's border with India, and as a result Burma had to cede the Arakan and Tenasserim coasts to Britain. In 1852, Britain gained control of the Irrawaddy Delta, and following the Anglo-Burmese War of 1885, Burma became a province of India in 1886. It remained as such until Britain gave Burma a constitution in 1937, thus separating it from India.

After the Japanese invasion during World War II, a nominal Burmese government was set up under Dr. Ba Maw. An anti-Japanese resistance movement was headed by the Anti-Fascist People's Freedom League, formed by U AUNG SAN.

Burma gained independence from British rule in 1948. Since that time, the country has followed a strictly neutralist foreign policy. Civil war broke out in the late 1950s, with selected minorities and Communist groups independently opposing the new government. In 1958, Premier U NU asked Gen. U NE WIN to take over the government and to quell civil disorder. Order was restored, and in the 1960 elections Nu and a civilian government were returned to power.

During 1962, in the face of mixed economic performance and threat of a second civil war, Ne Win staged a successful military coup. He and other government leaders resigned from the military in 1972 but kept their governmental positions. The 1974 constitution strengthened the hand of Ne Win and the ruling BSPP. Ne Win resigned as president in 1981 in favor of former army chief U San Yu, who was reelected in 1985, but he retained the powerful post of party chairman until 1988.

In that year the 26-year ascendancy of the BSPP appeared to unravel. Long beset by ethnic and Communist insurgencies in the northern and eastern regions, the government was now challenged, beginning in March 1988, by massive student and general urban unrest. Ne Win stepped down on July 23, announcing that a referendum on one-party rule would be held. His successor, the hard-line Gen. U Sein Lwin, resigned only 17 days later, but unrest continued under new leader U Maung Maung. Gen. U Saw Maung, who assumed control of

the government on Sept. 18, 1988, cracked down brutally on dissent. In June 1989 the name of the country was changed to Myanmar; the capital was renamed Yangon.

Since 1992, under new SLORC head Gen. Than Shwe, most martial law decrees have been lifted, the economy has improved, and peace agreements with several ethnic rebel groups have been reached. But human rights abuses continued. In 1994 a military-dominated constitution convention adopted guidelines intended to bar opposition leader AUNG SAN SUU KYI, who remained under house arrest, from politics.

DAVID G. DICKASON

Bibliography: American University, *Burma* (1984); Fredholm, M., *Burma: Ethnicity and Insurgency* (1993); Lintner, B., *Outrage* (1989); Luce, G. H., *Phases of Pre-Pagan Burma*, 2 vols. (1985); Maung, M., *The Burma Road to Poverty* (1991); Smith, M., *Burma* (1991); Steinberg, D. J., *Burma* (1982); Taylor, R. H., *The State in Burma* (1988); Tinker, H., *Burma* (1982); Trager, F. N., *From Kingdom to Republic* (1976).

Burma Road

The Burma Road connects Lashio in eastern Burma (Myanmar) with Kunming (K'un-ming) in Yunnan province in southern China and is more a Chinese than a Burmese roadway. Most of the 1,154 km (717 mi) of road is in China and traverses rough, mountainous country. Construction was begun in 1937 by the Chinese at the start of the Sino-Japanese War. From its completion in 1939, the Burma Road served as an overland supply route to China. In World War II, it was a major factor in supplying the Japanese-besieged CHIANG KAI-SHEK government in Kunming. The road has lost its importance and, especially in Burma, is not well maintained.   RICHARD BUTWELL

Burmese

Although the term *Burmese* is loosely used to describe all citizens of Burma (now Myanmar), the Burmese (Burmans) are the dominant ethnic group. Ethnic Burmese constitute about two-thirds of Burma's more than 45 million people (1994 est.); they are concentrated in the valleys and plains of the Irrawaddy, Sittang, and Salween rivers, and a smaller number live in the towns and cities. Their tonal language is affiliated with the Sino-Tibetan linguistic family. The first written knowledge of the Burmese dates from the end of the 1st century; their original homeland was in south China. Later they adopted Theravada Buddhism and other elements of Indian civilization from the Mon living in southern Burma

Typical Burmese are rice farmers who live in villages with the houses lining a dirt road or waterway or clustered among fruit trees and bamboo. The farmers also raise vegetables and fruits and fish the rivers. Their raised houses have wooden walls and thatched roofs; most houses have a shelf for a Buddha figure or a spirit (nat) shrine. Genealogical descent is traced through both parents, and the family is the most important social and economic unit.

Although Buddhists, the Burmese also believe in the ghosts of the dead and in a pantheon of environmental spirits incorporated into village religious practices. Buddhist priests direct numerous religious ceremonies and also sell protective magical charms. The Burmese are noted for their fine silverwork and goldwork, dances, and music.   DONN V. HART

Bibliography: Khaing, Mi Mi, *Burmese Family* (1946; repr. 1962); Nash, Manning, *The Golden Road to Modernity* (1965; repr. 1973); Pe, Hla, *Burma* (1986); Trager, Helen G., ed., *We the Burmese* (1969).

Burmese cat

The Burmese cat is a shorthaired breed of domestic cat closely related to the Siamese but with a rich, sable brown coat. (Burmese-Siamese hybrids are called Tonkinese or honey Siamese.) The body of the Burmese is compact and the head small and round. The eyes of the Burmese are golden or yellow; the large ears are narrow and long. The bones are as fine as those of the Siamese, and the hind legs slightly longer than the front legs. The tail is long and pointed and may be kinked near the tip. The Burmese is a playful and affectionate cat.   EVERETT SENTMAN

The Burmese cat is a breed of domestic cat developed in the United States during the 1930s from a Siamese and a brown cat native to Burma.

Burmese language: see SINO-TIBETAN LANGUAGES.

burn

Burns are contact injuries resulting from exposure to heat, electricity, radiation (mainly solar radiation), or caustic chemicals. They most often involve the SKIN, but swallowing caustic chemicals can burn the cells lining the inner surface of the esophagus.

The severity of a burn is indicated by its degree. First-degree burns damage only the epidermis, or outermost skin layer; the symptoms are redness, mild swelling, and stinging pain. Second-degree burns penetrate to the dermis, or second skin layer; they appear red or mottled, are more painful, and may be wet because of seepage of tissue fluids. Third-degree burns destroy all skin down to the fatty layer, and the skin appears white or charred. Such burns may actually feel less painful than second-degree burns because nerve endings are destroyed. In adults, second-degree burns affecting 15 percent of the body are considered a cause for hospitalization; in children, the figure is 10 percent.

FIRST AID for burns requires cooling by plain cold water; ice may induce shock. After this an ointment may help to soothe a minor burn, but ointments or greasy substances should never be applied to serious burns. For chemical burns, cool water should be run over the area until all of the chemical is removed. Recovery of persons with severe burns has improved greatly in recent years, following recognition of the special treatment needs of victims and the establishment of regional burn-treatment centers. Early replacement of tissue fluids has become routine at these centers, along with intravenous nutritional support. Infections account for a large percentage of the deaths among burn patients, because of injury to the immune system and because the skin is the first line of defense against pathogenic organisms. Burn patients are kept in sterile wards and treated with antibiotics; wounds are also closed by grafting as soon as possible.

Currently, burned areas eventually must be covered by grafts of the patient's own skin, sometimes first stretching the grafts. Temporary grafts from other humans or from pigs can be used as well, and epidermal skin has also been cloned into sheets (see SKIN DISEASES). An artificial skin being tested in the late 1980s consists of a synthetic epidermis called Silastic and a dermal layer of collagen and a cartilage derivative. The latter serves as a permanent scaffolding for dermal regrowth, while the Silastic is later replaced by grafts (see ARTIFICIAL ORGANS). In animal experiments, seeding of the artificial dermis with epidermal cells apparently causes a whole new skin to regenerate on the muscle substrate, so use of the artificial skin could become a one-time operation.   WILLIAM A. CHECK

Bibliography: Thygerson, Alton L., *The First Aid Book* (1982); Mannon, James M., *Caring for the Burned* (1985).

Burne-Jones, Sir Edward

Sir Edward Coley Burne-Jones, b. Aug. 28, 1833, d. June 17, 1898, was an important British PRE-RAPHAELITE painter of romantic legend and a decorative arts designer. Educated at Exeter College, Oxford, he became a friend of William MORRIS, a fellow divinity student. An inspiring acquaintance with Dante Gabriel ROSSETTI, which began in 1856, set both Burne-Jones and Morris on a career in art. In 1857 they joined Rossetti in the decoration of the Oxford Union with scenes from Thomas Malory's *Morte d'Arthur*. Burne-Jones's association with Morris as a designer was long and close. In 1861 he became a partner in the firm of Morris, Marshall, Faulkner & Co., for which he designed stained-glass windows, tapestries, and other forms of craft. He also designed book illustrations for Morris's KELMSCOTT PRESS, including the highly acclaimed Kelmscott *Chaucer* (1896).

As a painter, Burne-Jones owed much to Rossetti, but Sandro BOTTICELLI and Andrea MANTEGNA also influenced his style. Medieval subjects, including the Arthurian legends, and mythology were frequent themes in his work, for example, *The Beguiling of Merlin* (1872–77; Lady Lever Art Gallery, Port Sunlight, England). His paintings, "romantic dreams" in his own words, were a sensation at the Grosvenor Gallery exhibitions of 1877–87. His *King Cophetua and the Beggar Maid* (1884; Tate Gallery, London) made a great impression in France. He was made a baronet in 1894.

Burne-Jones's work was much neglected following his death, but a modern revival of interest in the late-19th-century aesthetic interchanges between England and France has directed fresh attention to and appreciation of his wistful idealism and its influence.   WILLIAM GAUNT

Bibliography: Cecil, David, *Visionary and Dreamer: Two Poetic Painters, Samuel Palmer and Edward Burne-Jones* (1969); Fitzgerald, Penelope, *Edward Burne-Jones: A Biography* (1975); Spalding, Frances, *Magnificent Dreams: Burne-Jones and the Late Victorians* (1978); Waters, Bill, and Harrison, Martin, *Burne-Jones* (1973).

The Baleful Head (1886-87) by Pre-Raphaelite painter Sir Edward Burne-Jones represents a mythological scene in which Perseus shows Andromeda the reflection of Medusa's severed head with its snaky locks. (Stadtsgalerie, Stuttgart.)

Burnet, Gilbert [bur'-nit]

A British churchman and historian, Gilbert Burnet, b. Sept. 18, 1643, d. Mar. 17, 1715, wrote the *History of My Own Times* (2 vols., 1724–34) and *History of the Reformation of the Church of England* (3 vols., 1679–1714). Both are valued sources. An advocate of religious tolerance, he had great influence under WILLIAM III, who made him bishop of Salisbury.

Burnet, Sir Macfarlane

Australian virologist Sir Frank Macfarlane Burnet, b. Sept. 3, 1899, d. Aug. 31, 1985, shared the 1960 Nobel Prize for physiology or medicine with Peter MEDAWAR for his 1949 theory, confirmed by Medawar, that an animal embryo can acquire immunological tolerance to an administered antigen. This discovery was important for later organ-transplant and cancer research. Burnet's early career was devoted to virus studies; in 1932 he developed the technique of culturing viruses in living chick embryos that remained standard practice for two decades, and he isolated the rickettsial organism that causes Q FEVER. His autobiography, *Changing Patterns*, was published in 1968.

Burnett, Carol

Carol Burnett, b. San Antonio, Tex., Apr. 26, 1934, is a popular American television and film comedienne. She began her career as a singer but switched to comedy in the mid-1950s. Burnett first gained national attention through television in 1956 on the "Garry Moore Show." In 1959 she starred in the off-Broadway musical *Once upon a Mattress*. Her highly popular "Carol Burnett Show" ran on CBS television for 11 years (1967–78). Among her film performances was a dramatic role in *The Four Seasons* (1981) and a comedic role in *Annie* (1982). Burnett was the first person to win (1981) a libel suit against the gossip tabloid *National Enquirer*. In 1986 she published *One More Time: A Memoir*.

Burnett, Frances Hodgson

The English-born American writer Frances Hodgson Burnett, b. Nov. 24, 1849, d. Oct. 29, 1924, is best known for her classic juvenile novel *Little Lord Fauntleroy* (1886; film, 1936). Her dramatization (1888) of the story was remarkably successful. Her other works include the play *Esmeralda* (1881) and a novel, *The Secret Garden* (1911).   F. M. PAULSEN

Bibliography: Bixler, Phyllis, *Frances Hodgson Burnett* (1984).

Burney, Charles

Charles Burney, b. Apr. 7, 1726, d. Apr. 12, 1814, was an important English historian of music. After studying with Thomas Arne, Burney worked as an organist, composer, and teacher. He then attended Oxford and received (1769) his doctor's degree. In 1770 and 1772 he traveled in Europe to gather materials for his books and met many important musicians. In his main writings—*The Present State of Music in France and Italy* (1771), *The Present State of Music in Germany, the Netherlands, and the United Provinces* (1773), and the 4-volume *A General History of Music* (1776–89)—he drew heavily on his personal experiences, and these works have become classics. Burney was an enthusiastic supporter of Franz Josef Haydn's music, and *A General History of Music* includes a long chapter on Italian opera in England. It also contains the first important critique in modern times of the great Renaissance composer Josquin des Prez.

Burney's large circle of friends included Samuel Johnson, Jean Jacques Rousseau, King George III, and William Pitt the Younger. His last appointment was as organist at Chelsea Hospital from 1783, and in 1806 he retired on a pension from the king. Burney's memoirs were compiled by his daughter, Fanny Burney, in 1832.   F. E. KIRBY

Bibliography: Grant, K. S., *Dr. Charles Burney as Critic and Historian of Music* (1983); Kilma, S., Gowers, G., and Grant, K. S., eds., *Memoirs of Dr. Charles Burney, 1726–1769* (1988).

Burney, Fanny

Fanny Burney, b. June 13, 1752, d. Jan. 6, 1840, was an English novelist whose diary and letters give a vivid picture of English society in the late 18th and early 19th century. Largely self-taught, she grew up in the brilliant circle of friends that surrounded her father, Dr. Charles Burney. Her first and probably best novel, *Evelina* (1778), was an immediate success, but after *Camilla* (1796) her powers declined, and *The Wanderer* (1814) had few readers. These works influenced the growth of the English novel, however. She spent an unhappy period (1786–91) at the court of Queen Charlotte and in 1793 married Alexandre d'Arblay, a French exile. The last volumes of her diary were published posthumously.   ROBIN BUSS

Bibliography: Masefield, M., *The Story of Fanny Burney* (1974); Simons, J., *Fanny Burney* (1987); Wallace, T. G., *A Busy Day* (1984).

Burnham, Daniel Hudson [bur'-nuhm]

Daniel Hudson Burnham, b. Sept. 4, 1846, d. June 1, 1912, was one of the earliest comprehensive modern city planners and, with his partner, John Wellborn ROOT, the architect of the first American SKYSCRAPER. In 1872, Burnham joined a Chicago architectural firm whose head draftsman was Root. The following year, sensing mutual interests, the two men established their own firm. The development of the skyscraper was necessitated by increasing land rents that forced architects to build vertically rather than horizontally. Simultaneously, such technological advances as the electric elevator (1889), the light bulb (1879), the telephone (1876), and the cast-iron skeleton made the skyscraper possible. These devices were first used together in Burnham & Root's Montauk Block (1881–82). Unlike today's glass and steel constructions, the earliest skyscrapers by Burnham & Root—the Calumet Building (1882–84), the Rookery (1885–88), the Monadnock Building (1889–92), and the Reliance Building (1890–94)—all had exterior walls of masonry and followed in the tradition of Henry Hobson RICHARDSON, whose influence in Chicago was particularly strong during this time. In 1891, Burnham & Root was assigned the architectural responsibility for the WORLD'S COLUMBIAN EXPOSITION OF 1893. In the same year, however, John Root died; Burnham asked leading Eastern architects to assist him, and the landscape architect F. L. OLMSTEAD collaborated in the planning. Burnham's subsequent projects included plans for the enlargement of Washington, D.C., and the improvement of such cities as Cleveland, San Francisco, and Manila. Between 1906 and 1909, at the request of the Commercial Club of Chicago, Burnham devoted himself to developing a plan for redesigning the city. It was the first comprehensive regional plan for an American city. (See URBAN PLANNING.)

Bibliography: Hines, Thomas S., *Burnham of Chicago* (1974; repr. 1979); Moore, Charles, *Daniel H. Burnham* (1921; repr. 1968).

Burnham, Forbes [burn'-uhm, forbz]

Linden Forbes Sampson Burnham, b. Feb. 20, 1923, d. Aug. 6, 1985, became prime minister of British Guiana in 1964 and two years later led the country to independence as Guyana, within the British Commonwealth. In the 1950s, Burnham worked with the Marxist Cheddi JAGAN in Jagan's pro-independence People's Progressive party but broke with Jagan in 1955 to found his own party, the People's National Congress. Burnham held power continuously from 1964 until his death. In 1980 he became Guyana's first president under a new constitution. Committed to a nonaligned socialist program, Burnham maintained control despite mounting opposition that stemmed from an economy in continuing crisis.

burning bush

Burning bush is a common name applied to a variety of shrubby plants. *Euonymus atropurpureus*, also called wahoo, is a large deciduous shrub or tree of North America that grows up to 7.6 m (25 ft) tall. Leaves turn yellow in the fall, and the fruit is scarlet. *Combretum microphyllum* is a large, rambling tropical shrub with small, notched leaves and scarlet flowers.

The dwarf burning bush, E. alatus compactus, *was named for the biblical burning bush, which burst into flames but was not consumed. The leaves of this plant turn fiery red in autumn.*

Dictamnus albus, also called fraxinella or gas plant, is a Eurasian shrub with strong-smelling foliage that emits flammable oil. The flowers are reddish purple. *Kochia scoparia* is a fast-growing shrub, native to Eurasia, with small but dense foliage that turns bronze red after frost.

Burns, Arthur F.

U.S. economist Arthur Frank Burns, b. Stanislau, Austria, Apr. 27, 1904, d. June 26, 1987, was chairman of the Federal Reserve System from 1970 to 1978. In that post he was often at odds with the federal government as he stressed the importance of a balanced budget and monetary stability. Earlier, he taught at Columbia and Rutgers universities. For years Burns was associated with the National Bureau of Economic Research where, with Wesley Clair MITCHELL, he did pathbreaking studies in the analysis of business cycles. He served President Eisenhower as chairman (1953–56) of the Council of Economic Advisers and President Nixon (1969–70) as economic counselor. From 1981 to 1985 he served as ambassador to West Germany. His books include *Economic Research and the Keynesian Thinking of Our Times* (1946) and *The United States and Germany* (1986).

Burns, George: see BURNS AND ALLEN.

Burns, Robert

Robert Burns is the best known of all Scottish poets. He is most admired for having voiced the attitudes of the common person and for his innate lyrical sense. His poems celebrate the simple, and often earthy, love between man and woman, the pleasures of convivial drinking, and the fierce pride of the independent individual. Writing in the last quarter of the 18th century, Burns combined the sentimental tradition of such poets as James Thomson and William Shenstone with the Scottish vernacular tradition of Allan Ramsay and Robert Fergusson to produce some of the best lyrics in English literature. His emphasis on natural simplicity and the rights of the individual exerted considerable influence on the English romantic poets.

Burns was born on Jan. 25, 1759, into the family of a peasant farmer in rural southwest Scotland. He took up farming at an early age but was not successful. At the same time, he began writing poems for local circulation and had them published in *Poems, Chiefly in the Scottish Dialect* (1786) in the small

town of Kilmarnock. This work, which contains most of his poems, was expanded in 1787 and again in 1793. Copies of the Kilmarnock edition reached the literati in Edinburgh, who were immediately impressed to find their theories about the sensitivity of the common man confirmed by what they called this "ploughman poet." Burns spent the winters of 1786–87 and 1787–88 in Edinburgh as a national celebrity, but he disliked the condescension with which he was treated and so returned to farming. In 1789 he obtained the post of exciseman, or inspector, but the hard labor of his early farming years, along with the heavy drinking, had ruined his health, and he died on July 21, 1796.

Most of Burns's poems are short, lyrical pieces. "Holy Willie's Prayer" is an exquisite satire revealing the hypocrisy of a sour, self-righteous man; it uses the dramatic monologue form to create a masterpiece of irony. "The Jolly Beggars," a collection of seven songs, depicts in vivid, dramatic detail a disreputable company of outcasts. "The Cotter's Saturday Night" was for a long time the most highly regarded of Burns's poems, but it is flawed by Burns's use of sentimental English diction to flood the reader with emotion in contemplating the homely details of peasant life. Burns's single narrative poem, "Tam o'Shanter," uses Gothic conventions for comic effect and is remarkable for its complex narrative voice, skillful meter and pacing, and successful fusion of English and Scots diction. His many songs, such as "Auld Lang Syne" and "A Red, Red Rose," are concise expressions of emotion ranging from the tender to the bawdy. In providing vivid details of pastoral life and in delicately fitting the words to music, Burns proved himself a master of this genre.

Burns has become a national hero in Scotland in the last two centuries. Many of his admirers have chosen to sentimentalize him, disregarding his true gifts and status as a poet. His overwhelming popularity led most 19th-century Scottish writers to create lifelessly sentimental imitations of Burns's pastoral verse. Not until the poems of Hugh MacDIARMID, written more than a century after Burns's death, did Scottish literature begin to free itself from Burns's influence. Although the sentimentalizing cult survives today, more astute scholars and critics now rank Burns as a major Scottish poet and one of the finest lyricists of the 18th century.   R. L. ABRAHAMSON

Bibliography: Burns, Robert, *Poems and Songs*, ed. by James Kinsley, 3 vols. (1968), and *Letters*, ed. by J. De Lancey Ferguson, 2 vols. (1931; repr. 1971); Crawford, Thomas, *Burns: A Study of the Poems and Songs*, 2d ed. (1965); Daiches, David, *Robert Burns*, rev. ed. (1966); Hecht, Hans, *Robert Burns: The Man and His Work* (1985); Jack, R. D., and Noble, Andrew, eds., *The Art of Robert Burns* (1982); Low, Donald, *Robert Burns* (1986).

Robert Burns, an 18th-century Scottish poet, appears in this oil portrait by Alexander Nasmyth. Burns's poetry, written in the Scottish vernacular, reflects his peasant origins. While editing a collection of folk music, Burns grew interested in that genre and composed lyrics from several earlier tunes. Today Burns is remembered for such traditional songs as "Coming Thro the Rye" and "Auld Lang Syne."

Burns and Allen

George Burns, originally named Nathan Birnbaum, b. New York City, Jan. 20, 1896, and Gracie Allen, b. San Francisco, July 20, 1906, d. Aug. 27, 1964, were one of the finest husband-and-wife comedy acts in American show business history. They became popular stars in vaudeville, radio, movies, and television. Burns first teamed with Allen on stage in the early 1920s and became her straight man. He played the unruffled but confused spouse whose simple questions elicited nitwit answers from his daffy but unflappable wife. They specialized in the humor of illogical logic. A master of the one liner, Burns worked as a stand-up comic and continued to appear in films and television in his nineties. He won an Academy Award for his role as an aging vaudevillian in the film version of Neil Simon's *The Sunshine Boys* (1975). Burns's autobiography is *Living It Up* (1976).   FRANK MANCHEL

Burnside, Ambrose E.

Although a man of lofty character and winning personality, Union general Ambrose Burnside failed to distinguish himself militarily during the Civil War. The public, however, admired his side-whiskers, calling them "burnsides" or "sideburns." Many men copied his style.

Ambrose Everett Burnside, b. Liberty, Ind., May 23, 1824, d. Sept. 13, 1881, was a Union army commander in the U.S. Civil War. He graduated (1847) from West Point and later headed an arms manufacturing company. After the Civil War began, Burnside inexpertly commanded a brigade at the First Battle of BULL RUN (August 1861). In 1862 he led a successful amphibious landing on the North Carolina coast, but did less well commanding George McClellan's left wing at ANTIETAM. As commander of the Army of the Potomac, he led that force to a terrible defeat at Fredericksburg, Va., in December 1862 (see FREDERICKSBURG, BATTLE OF). Burnside was able to hold Knoxville, Tenn., in 1863, but terminated his wartime service by undistinguished leadership of the IX Corps under Gen. Ulysses Grant in 1864.

After Appomattox, Burnside served as governor of Rhode Island (1866–69) and as U.S. senator from that state from 1875 until his death.   WARREN W. HASSLER, JR.

Burr, Aaron

Although Aaron Burr, b. Newark, N.J., Feb. 6, 1756, fought in the American Revolution and became an important political figure, serving a term (1801–05) as vice-president of the United States, he is best remembered today for having killed Alexander HAMILTON in a duel.

The son of a president of the College of New Jersey (now Princeton University) and the grandson of another (Jonathan EDWARDS), Burr could trace his ancestry back to the earliest Puritans. He entered Princeton at the age of 13, graduated at 16, and went on to become a Revolutionary War hero, rising to the rank of lieutenant colonel at the age of 21. In July 1782 he married Theodosia Bartow Prevost, the widow of a former British officer. They moved to New York City, where Burr built a reputation as an excellent attorney and made important political connections. He was "the most rising young man in the state," a contemporary noted.

Political Career. In 1789, Burr was appointed attorney general of New York by Gov. George CLINTON. Two years later the state assembly, which was controlled by partisans of Clinton and Robert LIVINGSTON, elected Burr to the U.S. Senate. His career in the Senate was not particularly memorable. Hamilton hated him, Clinton soon learned to distrust him, and George Washington refused his request to be appointed minister to France. But Burr managed to maneuver so skillfully, and with so much personal charm, that he won the support of many Federalists as well as Democratic Republicans.

In 1796 and 1800, Burr ran for vice-president with Thomas JEFFERSON on the Democratic-Republican ticket. Whatever doubts Virginia Republicans had about Burr—they had not voted for him in 1796—were put to rest when he carried New York City for his party in 1800. It was assumed that the outcome of the national election would follow that in New York, but under the confused electoral system then in use Jefferson and Burr received an equal number of electoral votes for the presidency (73 each), throwing the election into the House of Representatives. There the Federalists refused to heed the advice of Hamilton and unsuccessfully tried, against the obvious wishes of the public, to elect Burr. Jefferson won the contest and Burr became vice-president. Jefferson doubted his loyalty and soon began to withhold patronage from Burr and his followers. Although still a Republican, Burr began to cultivate Federalists; his strategy was to unite dissidents against the Virginia party of Jefferson and James Madison.

Dropped from the Republican ticket for 1804, Burr entered the 1804 gubernatorial race in New York. Some northern Federalists who were plotting secession called on Burr to support them, but his response was masterfully enigmatic. An old enemy, Alexander Hamilton, did everything he could to defeat Burr. Some of Hamilton's derogatory comments, personal in nature, appeared in print, and Burr, who lost the election, demanded a retraction, which Hamilton refused to make. The duel that followed at Weehawken, N.J., on July 11, 1804, resulted in Hamilton's death. Charged with murder, Burr fled to Philadelphia to escape arrest.

The Conspiracy. In his final eight months as vice-president, Burr's conduct was exemplary. He presided over the impeachment trial of Samuel CHASE with dignity, ability, and impartiality, and delivered a farewell address that favorably impressed the Senate. But his insatiable dream of personal glory led him to undertake a western scheme that ended in his arrest and trial for treason.

Precisely what Burr planned will probably never be known. Most likely he envisioned the creation of an empire stretching from the Ohio River to Mexico over which he would preside, and he intended to take whatever steps were necessary to achieve it. "The gods invite us to glory and fortune," Burr wrote to his coconspirator, Gen. James WILKINSON; "it remains to be seen whether we deserve the boon." While Burr and a handful of followers were on their way to New Orleans, however, Wilkinson informed Jefferson of the conspiracy. On Nov. 27, 1806, Jefferson issued a proclamation that led to the collapse of the plot and Burr's arrest.

Aaron Burr appears in this portrait by John Vanderlyn. Burr, vice-president during Thomas Jefferson's first term, was tried for treason in 1807. Although he was acquitted, evidence suggests his complicity in a plot to establish an independent nation in the west. (The Granger Collection.)

The subsequent trial, held in Richmond, Va., was presided over by Chief Justice John MARSHALL. He defined the law of treason so narrowly that the jury took a mere 25 minutes to acquit Burr. Marked as a traitor and threatened by angry mobs in Baltimore, Burr gathered some money from friends and left for Europe. He traveled to England, Sweden, Denmark, Germany, and France, and did not return to the United States until May 1812. Soon thereafter he suffered the deaths of his grandson and his daughter. At the age of 76 he married a wealthy New York widow, Eliza Jumel; but his wife sued for divorce, which was granted on Sept. 14, 1836, the day Burr died.   MORTON BORDEN

Bibliography: Abernethy, Thomas, *The Burr Conspiracy* (1954); Burr, Aaron, *Memoirs of Aaron Burr,* ed. by Matthew Davis (1836–37), and *Political Correspondence and Public Papers,* ed. by M. J. Kline and J. W. Ryan (1983); Daniels, Jonathan, *Ordeal of Ambition* (1970); Lomask, Milton, *Aaron Burr,* 2 vols. (1979–82); Schachner, Nathan, *Aaron Burr* (1937; repr. 1961); Wandell, S. H., and Minnigerode, Meade, *Aaron Burr,* 2 vols. (1925; repr. 1971).

burro: see DONKEY.

Burroughs, Edgar Rice

Edgar Rice Burroughs, b. Chicago, Sept. 1, 1875, d. Mar. 19, 1950, was an American adventure writer whose sales of more than 100 million copies of his novels in 56 languages make him one of the most widely read authors of the 20th century. Unsuccessful in a number of jobs and needing money to support his family, Burroughs began to write and sell pulp magazine fiction in 1911. The appearance in serial form of his second novel, TARZAN OF THE APES, in *All-Story Magazine* in 1912 and the publication of the novel in hardcover form in 1914 made Burroughs a best-selling novelist. Thereafter, he devoted himself exclusively to writing. By the end of his career in 1944, he had published about 70 novels, most of them in both pulp serial and hardcover forms. During the early 1960s additional millions of Burroughs's books were sold in paperback.

Although Burroughs wrote almost all types of popular fiction, including crime stories and westerns, he is most famous for his heroic adventure fantasies of lost cities and faraway civilizations. Of these, the 24 books in the Tarzan series, many of which were translated into films or comic strips, are the best known. Two other series often praised by Burroughs fans are the 7-novel "Pellucidar" series, featuring a world at the core of the Earth, and the 11-book "Barsoom" series, focusing on the adventures of an American, John Carter, on Mars.   JACK NACHBAR

Bibliography: Holtsmark, Erling B., *Edgar Rice Burroughs Dictionary* (1987); Lupoff, Richard A., *Edgar Rice Burroughs: Master of Adventure* (1965; repr. 1975); McWhorter, George T., *Burroughs Dictionary* (1987); Porges, Irwin, *Edgar Rice Burroughs: The Man Who Created Tarzan,* 2 vols. (1975).

Burroughs, John

John Burroughs, b. near Roxbury, N.Y., Apr. 3, 1837, d. Mar. 29, 1921, was an American naturalist and author and a friend to Walt Whitman and other important men of his day. He wrote the first biography of Walt Whitman, *Notes on Walt Whitman, As Poet and Person* (1867), and then a number of books that showed both poetic and spiritual appreciation and scientific knowledge of nature, particularly birds. Among these are *Wake Robin* (1871), *Locusts and Wild Honey* (1879), and *The Breath of Life* (1915).

Bibliography: Barrus, Clara, *Our Friend, John Burroughs* (1914; repr. 1983); Bergon, F., ed., *A Sharp Lookout: Selected Nature Essays of John Burroughs* (1987); Kelley, Elizabeth B., *John Burroughs, Naturalist* (1959); Westbrook, Perry D., *John Burroughs* (1974).

Burroughs, William S.

William Seward Burroughs, b. St. Louis, Mo., Feb. 5, 1914, is an American writer whose work has had a profound influence on modern American literature, particularly on the writers of the BEAT GENERATION.

William Burroughs, an American novelist, achieved distinction for writings based on his experiences as a former drug addict. His irreverent themes, related in a stream-of-consciousness style, established Burroughs as one of the most popular authors of the beat generation.

A grandson of William Seward Burroughs, founder of the Burroughs Adding Machine Company, the young Burroughs grew up in a wealthy milieu, studied at Harvard, and then, in the process of drifting through a series of odd jobs in New York City, became a drug addict. Both his first novel, *Junkie* (published as *Junk* in 1953 under the pseudonym William Lee; reissued in 1977), and his second, *The Naked Lunch* (Paris, 1959; N.Y., 1962), are based on his experiences as an addict. Because of its unique narrative technique—which creates a prismatic, multiviewed presentation of events—and its hallucinatory rendering of the addict's world, *The Naked Lunch* had a significant effect on American literary style. Burroughs's other works include *The Soft Machine* (1961) and *The Ticket That Exploded* (1962), both novels that experiment with narrative structure; *Letters to Allan Ginsberg, 1953–57* (1981); *The Adding Machine: Collected Essays* (1985); and several more recent novels including *Cities of the Red Night* (1981), *The Place of Dead Roads* (1983), and *Queer* (1986).

Bibliography: Ansen, Alan, *William Burroughs: An Essay* (1986); Bockris, Victor, *With William Burroughs: A Report from the Bunker* (1981); Burroughs, W. S., and Odier, Daniel, *The Job: Interviews with William S. Burroughs* (1974); Lyndenberg, Robin, *Word Cultures: Radical Theory and Practice in William S. Burroughs' Fiction* (1987); Tytell, John, *Naked Angels* (1976).

Burrows, Larry

Larry Burrows, b. May 29, 1926, d. Feb. 10, 1971, was an important British-born photojournalist and war photographer long associated with *Life* magazine. Although he did famous color essays on the great Asian monuments, the Taj Mahal and Angkor, he was best known for his photographs of the armed conflicts he covered in the Suez, Lebanon, the Belgian Congo, and Vietnam. His Vietnam photographs of war-crippled children and soldiers under fire depict the horrors of battle in powerful personal terms. Burrows died in a helicopter crash over Laos. Some of his work is collected in *Larry Burrows: Compassionate Photographer* (1972).   KEITH F. DAVIS

Bursa   [bur-sah']

Bursa (Brusa) is the capital of Bursa province in northwestern Turkey. Located about 21 km (13 mi) from the southeastern shore of the Sea of Marmara and about 88 km (55 mi) south of Istanbul, it is at the base of the Mysian Mount Olympus (Ulu Dag) in an area subject to frequent earthquakes. Its population is 614,133 (1985). The climate is subtropical, with dry, hot summers. The city is also known as Yesil (green) Bursa because many of its 15th-century buildings are painted this color. Bursa is the center of the Turkish silk industry. The ancient city called Prusa was founded in the 3d century BC and named for the Bithynian king Prusias I. Bursa's many mosques include the Ulu Cami (built 1396–1400) with its 20 domes.

bursitis   [bur-sy'-tis]

Bursitis is inflammation of bursae, which are closed sacs that contain fluid and are located at points of friction in joints. Bursitis can occur in several joints, but the shoulder joint is the most common site. The buildup of calcium deposits on tendons associated with a joint is a frequent precipitating cause. The calcium deposits trigger an inflammatory reaction that can spread to a nearby bursa and even rupture it. Bursitis may be acute or chronic. In the acute form of shoulder bursitis there is a sudden pain in the shoulder area that often radiates into the neck and upper arm. Shoulder movement is restricted by the pain. Treatment is usually with oral antiinflammatory drugs and painkillers. In most patients the condition clears up in a few days, but in severe cases it may be necessary to remove calcium material surgically or inject antiinflammatory agents directly into the inflamed area of the joint.

Burt, Sir Cyril

Cyril Lodowic Burt, b. Mar. 3, 1883, d. Oct. 10, 1971, was a leading British educational psychologist, especially in the areas of child development and statistical analysis. He also wrote extensively on mind-body problems and on mental telepathy. Burt studied at the University of Oxford and was appointed lecturer in psychology at Liverpool in 1908. In 1913 he became the first psychologist to be appointed to an education authority, namely the London County Council. In this post he adapted the Binet-Simon and Stanford-Binet intelligence tests for English use and produced a comprehensive series of educational attainment tests. His best-known works are *The Young Delinquent* (1925) and *The Backward Child* (1937). As professor of psychology at University College, London (1931–50), Burt made important contributions to FACTOR ANALYSIS and applied analysis of variance to the results of tests administered to twins and other relatives in order to demonstrate the importance of heredity in determining INTELLIGENCE. After prolonged controversy, it has been established that some of his results, published in his later years, were fraudulent. This does not affect the value of the work of his early years, nor does it demolish, although it reduces, the evidence for genetic factors in intelligence.   PHILIP E. VERNON

Bibliography: Boring, E. G., and Langfeld, H. S., eds., *A History of Psychology in Autobiography*, vol. 4 (1951); Hearnshaw, L. S., *Cyril Burt: Psychologist* (1979).

Burton, Richard

Richard Burton is the stage name of Richard Jenkins, b. Pontrhydfen, Wales, Nov. 10, 1925, d. Aug. 5, 1984, a British actor who first earned his reputation on the London stage with the Old Vic company in 1953–54. He later made New York stage appearances in *Camelot* (1960; revival 1980), *Hamlet* (1964), *Equus* (1976; film, 1977), and *Private Lives* (1983), but he worked primarily in films, including *Look Back in Anger* (1959), *Cleopatra* (1962), *Beckett* (1964), *Who's Afraid of Virginia Woolf?* (1966), *The Spy Who Came in from the Cold* (1966), and *The Taming of the Shrew* (1967).

Bibliography: Alpert, Hollis, *Burton* (1986); Ferris, Paul, *Richard Burton* (1981); Junor, Penny, *Burton* (1986).

Burton, Sir Richard

Sir Richard Francis Burton, an intrepid English explorer of inner Africa in the mid-19th century, discovered the great Central African lakes. Born on Mar. 19, 1821, he was brought up in France and Italy. He studied for a time at Oxford University and then purchased a commission in the Bombay Native Infantry. From 1843 to 1848 he soldiered in Sind in northwestern India (now Pakistan). Between 1853 and 1855, Burton visited the Muslim holy cities of Mecca and Medina in disguise and made a dangerous foray to the forbidden city of Harar in eastern Ethiopia.

Burton's greatest journey began in 1857 on the coast of what is now eastern Tanzania. Following African paths, he became (1858) the first white in modern times to view Lake Tanganyika. Ill with malaria, he did not travel north with John SPEKE to Lake Victoria and thus failed to discover the source of the Nile. Later, Burton crossed the United States to Salt Lake City and went on to Panama before returning to England in 1861. For the next three years he served as British consul at Fernando Po, off the coast of Nigeria, went up the Congo River, and journeyed to Dahomey (now Benin). He was later consul in Santos, Brazil (1865–69), Damascus, and Trieste (1872–90). Burton died on Oct. 20, 1890.

In addition to his travels, which he celebrated in 21 books, Burton produced books on swordsmanship and falconry and is widely remembered for his translation of the *Tales of the Arabian Nights*. A brilliant linguist, he also secretly translated a number of Eastern erotic manuals. Burton's frankness about sexuality in his publicly distributed works offended many Victorians, and after his death his widow destroyed his papers to avoid scandal.   ROBERT I. ROTBERG

Bibliography: Brodie, Fawn, *The Devil Drives: A Life of Sir Richard Burton* (1967; repr. 1984); Burne, G. F., *Richard F. Burton* (1985); Farwell, Byron, *Burton* (1963).

Burton, Robert

Robert Burton, b. Feb. 8, 1577, d. Jan. 25, 1640, was an English cleric and scholar best known for his ANATOMY OF MELANCHOLY (1621), which he wrote under the pseudonym Democritus Junior. This work, a vast, learned compendium of Elizabethan notions about psychology and medicine, history and politics, and miscellaneous knowledge, went through numerous editions and was widely read and often quoted by other authors. Burton entered Oxford as a student in 1593 and stayed the remainder of his life, serving as librarian of Christ Church College and vicar of St. Thomas's Church. He was an exceptional English prose stylist, but his verse and plays, written in Latin, were less successful.   W. L. GODSHALK

Bibliography: Babb, Lawrence, *Sanity in Bedlam* (1959); Donovan, D. G., and Herman, M. G., *Sir Thomas Browne and Robert Burton* (1981); O'Connell, Michael, *Robert Burton* (1986).

Burundi   [boo-roon'-dee]

Burundi is a small country located at the northern end of Lake Tanganyika in east central Africa. It is bordered by Tanzania, Zaire, and Rwanda. Formerly known as Urundi and joined with Rwanda in the Belgian-administered United Nations Trust Territory of Ruanda-Urundi, Burundi gained independence as the Kingdom of Burundi on July 1, 1962, and became a republic on Nov. 29, 1966. Burundi is one of the smallest countries in Africa but has one of the continent's highest population densities. The capital and largest city is BUJUMBURA, which has grown rapidly since independence.

LAND

Located near the remotest headwaters of the Nile and Congo rivers, Burundi is predominantly a country of high mountains and plateaus. The only lowland area (under 900 m/3,000 ft) is the narrow plain of the Ruzizi River, which, like Lake Tanganyika to the south, occupies the structural trough of the GREAT RIFT VALLEY that crosses this part of Africa from north to south. High mountains, rising to more than 2,400 m (8,000 ft), extend north-south across western and central Burundi, parallel to the eastern edge of this trough. Eastern Burundi is less mountainous and consists of a series of plateaus at elevations between 1,500 and 2,000 m (5,000 and 6,500 ft) that descend eastward to the Kagera and Malagarasi river valleys.

Burundi has a tropical climate, but one that is moderated by high elevation. The relatively constant temperatures throughout the year reflect the location near the equator. Bujumbura, in the lowlands, has an average temperature of 23° C (73° F), and average temperatures in the mountains and plateaus range between 17° and 20° C (63° and 68° F). Rainfall varies from more than 1,400 mm (55 in) in the mountains to less than 1,015 mm (40 in) along the shores of Lake Tanganyika. Rainfall is concentrated during the rainy season (February to May), which is followed by a pronounced dry season (June to early September).

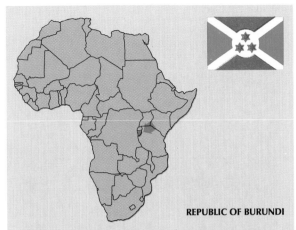

REPUBLIC OF BURUNDI

LAND. Area: 27,834 km² (10,747 mi²). Capital and largest city: Bujumbura (1990 pop., 236,334).

PEOPLE. Population (1994 est.): 6,000,000; density: 216 persons per km² (558 per mi²). Distribution (1994): 6% urban, 94% rural. Annual growth (1994): 2.9%. Official languages: French, Kirundi. Major religions: Roman Catholicism, traditional religions.

EDUCATION AND HEALTH. Literacy (1990): 50% of adult population. Universities (1994): 1. Hospital beds (1990): 10,370. Physicians (1990): 168. Life expectancy (1994): women—50; men—46. Infant mortality (1994): 105 per 1,000 live births.

ECONOMY. GNP (1992): $1.2 billion; $210 per capita. Labor distribution (1983): agriculture—93%; government—4%; other—3%. Foreign trade (1991): imports—$246 million; exports—$92 million; principal trade partners—Belgium-Luxembourg, Iran, France, Germany. Currency: 1 Burundi franc = 100 centimes.

GOVERNMENT. Type: republic. Legislature: National Assembly (suspended 1987). Political subdivisions: 15 provinces.

COMMUNICATIONS. Railroads (1994): none. Roads (1991): 6,265 km (3,893 mi) total. Major ports: 1. Major airfields: 1.

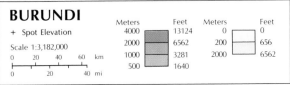

BURUNDI

+ Spot Elevation

Scale 1:3,182,000

Meters	Feet	Meters	Feet
4000	13124	0	0
2000	6562	200	656
1000	3281	2000	6562
500	1640		

The upper mountain slopes are cool, wet, and forested; the plateaus and lower-altitude regions are drier and have a savanna grassland type of vegetation cover. Much of the land is eroded as a result of a combination of conditions, including overgrazing, deforestation, heavy rains, and brushfires.

PEOPLE

Burundi has two major groups, the Nilotic Tutsi and the Bantu Hutu, who share a common language, Kirundi (Kinyarwanda), and cultural traditions. The Tutsi (14% of the population), Hutu (85%), and Twa (1%; see Pygmy) have intermarried and are considered by some to be castes within a single ethnic group. The Tutsi are predominantly pastoralists. They dominate the army and were the ruling elite of Burundi from their migration there between the 1300s and 1500s from the upper Nile area until 1993. The Hutu, who are believed to have migrated to the area about 800 years ago, are an agricultural people and are concentrated in the highlands. Traditionally, they cultivated the Tutsi fields and performed other services in exchange for Tutsi protection and the use of Tutsi cattle. Tensions between the two groups have periodically led to violence, most notably in 1972, 1988, and 1993. The Twa are mainly hunters and gatherers; they are believed to have been the region's first inhabitants. There are also large numbers of refugees from neighboring Rwanda.

Kirundi is the language of instruction in primary schools, and French in secondary schools. Much of the population, especially among the Hutu, is illiterate. Primary education is officially free and compulsory, and primary school enrollment tripled between 1980 and 1988. About 62% of the population are Roman Catholic and about 32% follow indigenous beliefs. Although Burundi is one of the most densely populated nations in Africa, it is predominantly rural; the only towns of note are Bujumbura and Gitega.

ECONOMIC ACTIVITIES

The economy of Burundi is based overwhelmingly on agricultural and pastoral activities. The principal subsistence crops are cassava (manioc) and sweet potatoes; corn, beans, peas, sorghum, and bananas are also grown. The main cash crop is arabica coffee, which accounts for more than 80% of all exports. Others are cotton, hides and skins, tea, and minerals. Most of the cash crops are exported to the United States, France, and Germany. Cattle raising is widespread.

The principal minerals produced are cassiterite (from which tin is obtained), bastnaesite (used in making television tubes), gold, tungsten, and tantalum. Large nickel deposits have recently been discovered. The country has almost no manufacturing, and many products are imported.

Burundi has no railroads and few paved roads, the most important of which link Bujumbura with Gitega and Kayanza. Bujumbura has an international airport and is the nation's main port on Lake Tanganyika.

HISTORY AND GOVERNMENT

Burundi history traditionally dates back to the arrival of the Tutsi, who ruled the area under successive *mwamis*, or kings, until recent times. In 1885 the region was designated a German sphere of interest by the Conference of Berlin. Burundi officially was incorporated into German East Africa in 1897, but effective German control over the kingdom was not established until 1903. In 1916, during World War I, Burundi was occupied by Belgian troops and was subsequently administered by Belgium as part of the Ruanda-Urundi mandate of the League of Nations (after World War I) and part of the United Nations Trust Territory of Ruanda-Urundi (after World War II).

Burundi became an independent constitutional monarchy on July 1, 1962, with Mwambutsa IV as king. Mwambutsa was overthrown in a military coup in July 1966 by his son Charles, who subsequently reigned for a few months as King Ntare V, with the military leader Michel Micombero as prime minister. King Ntare was deposed by Micombero on Nov. 29, 1966, and Burundi was declared a republic with Micombero as president. In 1972 an attempt to restore the monarchy was unsuccessful, and in the fighting that followed King Ntare was killed, and as many as 150,000 Hutu, who were blamed by the government for the uprising, were slaughtered by the Tutsi.

Micombero was ousted on Nov. 1, 1976, in a military coup led by Lt.-Col. Jean Baptiste Baganza, who remained president when civilian rule was formally restored in 1979. Baganza was overthrown in a 1987 coup led by Maj. Pierre Buyoya, who launched a program of national reconciliation after another eruption of tribal hostility led to the apparent massacre by the Tutsi of thousands of Hutu in 1988.

In 1992 voters overwhelmingly approved a multiparty constitution calling for a president and national assembly directly elected to 5-year terms. In June 1993, Melchior Ndadya defeated Buyoya to become Burundi's first elected civilian Hutu president. Ndadya was killed in an October coup by Tutsi soldiers. Although army leaders later supported the civilian government, thousands died in ethnic violence after the coup. The president of Rwanda and Burundi's new president, Cyprien Ntaryamira, were killed when their plane was shot down over Rwanda on Apr. 6, 1994. Violence engulfed Rwanda and threatened Burundi's tenuous stability. On Sept. 30, 1994, Sylvestre Ntibantunganya, a Hutu, was elected president in a new ethnically balanced government.   ALAN C. G. BEST

Bibliography: Lemarchand, R., *Burundi* (1994); McDonald, G. C., et al., *Area Handbook for Burundi* (1969); Melady, T., *Burundi* (1974); Ress, D., *The Burundi Ethnic Massacres, 1988* (1992); Weinstein, W., *Historical Dictionary of Burundi* (1976).

Bury St. Edmunds

Bury St. Edmunds ("bury" meaning burgh, or town) is a town in the county of Suffolk, England, in St. Edmundsbury district, on the River Lark. The district population is 93,100 (1991). The last king of the East Angles, St. Edmund, who was martyred by the Danes, was interred there in 903. In medieval times the town was a center of pilgrimage equal to Canterbury. It contains the ruins of a Benedictine abbey founded (*c.*1020) by Canute, king of England, Denmark, and Norway. In its church the English barons swore (1214) to force King John to accept the stipulations of the Magna Carta. The town is now an agricultural center with some brewing.

Buryat   [boor-yaht']

The Buryat are a Mongoloid people who live near Lake Baikal, in Russian Siberia. They speak a Mongol dialect of the Altaic language family. Their homeland is called Buryatia, or the Buryat autonomous republic, but many of them also live in the neighboring Russian provinces of Irkutsk and Chita and in northern Mongolia and northwestern China as well. The total population is estimated at about 400,000.

Most of the Buryat adhere to Tibetan Buddhism or else practice a shamanistic religion; Russian Orthodox traditions prevail among those west of Lake Baikal. Traditionally, the west-Baikal Buryat were seminomadic pastoralists who raised beef cattle and grew crops on a small scale. The east-Baikal Buryat were nomads whose livestock roamed the grasslands of Transbaikalia year-round. These Buryat lived in YURTS and drank koumiss, an alcoholic beverage derived from mare's milk. Kin groups were determined by male ancestry, and customs of mutual aid and of blood feud were maintained.

Historically, the Buryat people first appeared in their homeland in the 13th century. They represented a minority tribe of the MONGOL invaders of Eurasia. When the Russians arrived in the 17th century, Buryat tribal and kin groups were deteriorating. Today, less than 25 percent of the Buryat are urban. Nomadism, accompanied by material improvements under the Russian government, continues east of the lake. Most of the Buryat were collectivized during Soviet rule.   VICTOR L. MOTE

Bibliography: Symmons-Symonolewicz, K., ed., *The Non-Slavic Peoples of the Soviet Union* (1972); Wixman, R., *Peoples of the USSR* (1984).

bus

The bus of today is a large motor vehicle equipped with seats for passengers that is usually operated on a regular schedule along a fixed route. Because it is relatively inexpensive to purchase and operate and can be used on existing roads and highways, the motor bus is the most common form of public

transportation in the United States and throughout the world.

HISTORY

The motor bus is a descendant of the horse-drawn omnibus. The mathematician Blaise Pascal helped introduce (1662) the first known omnibus service in Paris. At first the service was free and very popular. As soon as a fare was charged, however, patronage declined, and the service was soon withdrawn.

In 1819 the omnibus was revived with the introduction in Paris and New York of vehicles that could carry up to 16 passengers. Soon most major cities had an omnibus service, and the Latin word *omnibus* ("for everyone") was shortened to the well-known term *bus*. (See COACH AND CARRIAGE.)

Common during the first two decades of the 20th century were large, long-frame automobiles that seated 12 to 20 people and had buslike bodies set on truck chassis, but this design was neither durable nor comfortable for passengers. In Oakland, Calif., Frank and William Fageol built (1920) a more suitably designed bus. The floor was lowered to allow easier boarding, the seats were made more comfortable, and the

The first London buses were horse-drawn carriages with passenger seats inside and on top (A). An early 1900 double-decker London bus had a gasoline engine and a rear stairway to the top (B). A typical mid-1920s bus used in New York City had a single deck, a front door entrance and exit, and an inside seat for the driver (C). Modern American intercity buses are supplied with air conditioning, washrooms, cushioned reclining seats, and baggage space (D).

brakes and engine were improved. Soon other manufacturers, usually from the trucking industry, followed this lead.

In the 1920s, large parlor coaches were built to take advantage of the network of intercity highways being constructed in the United States. Today, the typical intercity bus is a large vehicle powered by a diesel engine. The floor is placed fairly high to allow space below for baggage and package freight. Since the end of World War II, air-conditioning has become almost universal on U.S. buses, and air-suspension systems give a comfortable ride. Most new buses also have rest rooms, and automatic transmissions are becoming standard.

BUS INDUSTRY

The U.S. intercity bus industry is dominated by a few large companies, although more than a thousand smaller bus companies also offer service. Local transportation is dependent on the bus, and federal subsidy programs, especially in the 1970s, have given municipal bus systems a new lease on life.

In mass transit systems, new ways of using buses have increased their effectiveness. Express bus services pick up and deliver suburban riders to outlying automobile parking lots. In many cities, some streets are reserved exclusively for bus use, as in the busways in Pittsburgh, Pa., and Los Angeles. Small, van-type buses, carrying 10 to 15 passengers, cover inner-city routes, serving special groups, such as the handicapped or the elderly. Articulated buses 18 m (60 ft) long have two segments that pivot about a central joint to make turning possible, and can carry twice as many passengers as a conventional bus, as can the double-decker vehicles, which are common in Britain and have been used in some U.S. cities.

Although the bus is the dominant mode of mass transport within cities, the industry has problems. Bus companies are highly sensitive to the cost of labor, and since 1968 the local transit industry has operated at a loss, requiring heavy city and state subsidies to maintain service. In some cities, fares cover less than half of operating costs. Moreover, the cost of new buses has risen sharply.

Intercity bus service continues to be vital to transport in the United States. About 15,000 U.S. communities have no other form of public transportation, and more than 350 million intercity bus passengers are carried each year. Yet the intercity bus industry is only marginally profitable. Compounding the problem is the private automobile, a major competitor of the bus both for passengers and for road space.

Nevertheless, mass-transit planners see the bus as the most efficient and economical form of inner-city and intercity transport, and anticipate that bus systems will become even more important in future years. GEORGE M. SMERK

Bibliography: Dodgson, J. S., and Topham, N., *Bus Deregulation and Privatisation* (1987); Hibbs, J., ed., *The Omnibus* (1971); Savage, I., *The Deregulation of Bus Services* (1985); Smerk, G. M., *Urban Mass Transportation: A Dozen Years of Federal Policy* (1974); Stauss, Ed, *The Bus World Encyclopedia of Buses* (1988).

Busch, Adolf

The violinist and composer Adolf Busch, b. Germany, Aug. 8, 1891, d. June 9, 1952, made his debut at the age of 18. He toured the United States for the first time with Arturo Toscanini in 1931. After several years in Switzerland, he returned and became a U.S. citizen. He was one of the founders of the Marlboro Music School and Festival. He frequently appeared with his son-in-law Rudolf Serkin in recitals.

Busch, Wilhelm

Wilhelm Busch, b. Apr. 15, 1832, d. Jan. 9, 1908, was a German poet, painter, and caricaturist who combined his talents to satirize German culture of the late 19th century. Such works as *Max und Moritz* (1865) and *Pater Filucius* (1872), written in ironic humorous verse and illustrated with comic and intentionally naive drawings, brought him wide acclaim and are viewed as being precursors of the modern comic strip. His satire was fiercest in his treatment of the Catholic clergy, the military, and the newly rich. JOSEPH A. REITER

Bush, George

George Herbert Walker Bush was elected the 41st president of the United States on Nov. 8, 1988, and was inaugurated on Jan. 20, 1989. He had held an array of senior public positions and served (1981–89) as Ronald REAGAN's vice-president, becoming the first sitting vice-president to be elected in his own right since Martin Van Buren in 1836.

Early Life and Career. Born on June 12, 1924, in Milton, Mass., to Dorothy Walker Bush, daughter of a wealthy investor, and Prescott Sheldon Bush, a banker and later Republican U.S. senator from Connecticut, George Bush grew up in the New York City suburb of Greenwich, Conn., and attended Phillips Academy in Andover, Mass. During World War II he became the navy's youngest bomber pilot. Shot down over the Pacific island of Chichi Jima and rescued by a submarine, he was awarded the Distinguished Flying Cross and three Air Medals. In 1945 he married Barbara Pierce and then matriculated at Yale, where he majored in economics, was captain of the baseball team, and graduated with Phi Beta Kappa honors in 1948.

After Yale, "Poppy," as Bush was called, went to work for Dresser Industries in the west Texas oilfields. Two years later he and a partner established the Bush-Overby Development Company to trade oil leases and royalties, and in 1954 he became president of the Zapata Offshore Company, developing new oil-drilling equipment. Within a decade he had amassed about $2 million and began dabbling in local Republican politics in Houston. Defeated when he ran for the U.S. Senate in 1964, Bush became the first Republican to represent Houston in the U.S. House of Representatives in 1966. Known as one

GEORGE HERBERT WALKER BUSH
41st President of the United States (1989–93)

Born: June 12, 1924, Milton, Mass.
Education: Yale University (graduated 1948)
Profession: Businessman, Public Official
Religious Affiliation: Episcopalian
Marriage: Jan. 6, 1945, to Barbara Pierce (1925–   )
Children: George (1946–   ), Robin (1949–53), John
(1953–   ), Neil (1955–   ), Marvin (1956–   ),
Dorothy (1959–   )
Political Affiliation: Republican
Writings: *Looking Forward* (with Victor Gold; 1987)

Vice-President and Cabinet Members

Vice-President: Dan Quayle
Secretary of State: James A. Baker (1989–92);
   Lawrence S. Eagleburger (1992–93)
Secretary of the Treasury: Nicholas Brady
Secretary of Defense: Richard Cheney
Attorney General: Dick Thornburgh (1989–91);
   William P. Barr (1991–93)
Secretary of the Interior: Manuel Lujan
Secretary of Agriculture: Clayton Yeutter (1989–
   91); Edward R. Madigan (1991–93)
Secretary of Commerce: Robert Mosbacher (1989–
   92); Barbara H. Franklin (1992–93)
Secretary of Labor: Elizabeth Dole (1989–90);
   Lynn Morley Martin (1990–93)
Secretary of Health and Human Services: Louis
   Sullivan
Secretary of Housing and Urban Development:
   Jack Kemp
Secretary of Transportation: Samuel Skinner
   (1989–91); Andrew H. Card (1992–93)
Secretary of Energy: James Watkins
Secretary of Education: Lauro Cavazos (1989–91);
   Andrew Lamar Alexander (1991–93)
Secretary of Veterans Affairs: Edward Derwinski
   (1989–92)

of the new breed of centrist Republicans in the modern South, he voted for the 1968 Civil Rights Act despite its unpopularity with his constituents.

After a second unsuccessful bid for the Senate in 1970, Bush served as U.S. ambassador to the United Nations (1971–72) and in 1972 was named chairman of the Republican National Committee by Pres. Richard M. NIXON. He traveled the country for 20 months defending Nixon and the GOP against the widening WATERGATE scandal, which brought the president close to impeachment. Staunchly loyal almost to the end, Bush urged Nixon to step down on Aug. 7, 1974. Nixon announced his resignation the next day. His successor, Gerald

Ford, chose New York governor Nelson Rockefeller over Bush for the vice-presidency, and Bush departed for China to head the U.S. Liaison Office in Beijing. In December 1975, Ford suddenly recalled him to Washington to take over the Central Intelligence Agency.

Bush resigned from the CIA after Jimmy CARTER became president in 1976 and began his quest for the 1980 GOP presidential nomination. His victory in the Iowa caucuses of 1980 gave Bush an early lead, but his attacks on Ronald Reagan's ultraconservatism failed to attract a majority of Republican voters. After losing the Texas primary he withdrew from the race and asked his delegates to support Reagan. The GOP convention in July conferred on Bush the vice-presidential nomination after Ford declined to accept the position.

Vice-Presidency. In spite of their earlier political rivalry and policy differences, Reagan and Bush worked harmoniously for eight years in the White House. Bush traveled more than a million miles and visited some 75 nations as a special emissary for the president and headed the National Security Council's "crisis management team." He also chaired presidential task forces on deregulation, on combating terrorism, and on coordinating government efforts to stop drug smuggling in southern Florida.

The Presidential Election. After faltering in the Republican caucuses in Iowa in February 1988, Bush gained momentum with a victory in New Hampshire a week later and never relinquished the lead. He won the presidential nomination overwhelmingly on the first ballot at the Republican convention and picked Indiana senator Dan QUAYLE as his running mate. Immediately, doubts were raised about Quayle's qualifications. This cast a shadow over the Bush candidacy, and the late summer polls pointed to a landslide for his Democratic opponent, Michael DUKAKIS. Bush relentlessly attacked Dukakis as a soft-on-crime-and-defense liberal and as the candidate of unpatriotic marginal groups. Benefiting from the popularity and active assistance of President Reagan, and from public contentment with the peace and prosperity of the Reagan era, Bush surged ahead in the polls in the last several weeks of the campaign. He won the election with 54% of the popular vote and 426 of the 538 electoral votes.

Presidency. During the first two-and-a-half years of his administration Bush acted decisively abroad and cautiously in domestic affairs. The beneficiary of the crumbling of communism in Central and Eastern Europe in 1989–90 and the worsening chaos and economic crisis in the Soviet Union, Bush negotiated a treaty with the USSR to reduce nuclear and conventional arms and in 1989 he intervened militarily in Panama to depose its president, Manuel NORIEGA. In August 1990, following Iraq's invasion and annexation of Kuwait, Bush won widespread support throughout the world for an economic embargo of Iraq and stationed more than 400,000 American troops in the Persian Gulf region to defend Saudi Arabia. Having secured congressional approval for the use of force if Iraq defied his ultimatum to withdraw from Kuwait by mid-January 1991, Bush ordered a massive bombing attack on Iraq and its forces in Kuwait to begin on January 16, followed by a swift ground assault on February 24. Four days later Iraq capitulated. (See GULF WAR.)

Consistently gaining high ratings for his conduct of foreign affairs, including major reciprocal arms cuts with the USSR, and Russia, Bush shied from divisive domestic matters. Forced to deal with the pressing problem of a mounting federal deficit, he and moderates of both parties agreed to a compromise that increased taxes, reduced spending, and provided growth incentives for business. Nevertheless, persistent economic stagnation, which began when the nation's output fell to recession levels in July 1990, dogged the remainder of his term in office. Attacks on the cautious fiscal policies of his economic advisors and criticism of his optimistic assessments of future prospects fueled popular discontent. In the Republican presidential primaries of 1992 Bush faced a strong but unsuccessful challenge by conservative columnist Patrick Buchanan. The Democrats nominated Bill CLINTON, a centrist, in 1992. Bush appeared to move to the right in the campaign, focusing on so-called value issues, apologizing for breaking a no-new-taxes pledge, and allowing conservatives to dominate his party's convention. After weeks of lackluster campaigning, Bush resorted to strident attacks toward the end. In the election, Clinton won with a plurality of 43% to Bush's 38%. A month later, Bush ordered U.S. troops to strife-torn Somalia to ensure famine relief.   HARVARD SITKOFF

Bibliography: Graubard, Stephen R., *Mr. Bush's War: Adventures in the Politics of Illusion* (1992); Green, Fitzhugh, *George Bush* (1989); Sufrin, Mark, *George Bush* (1989).

Bush, Vannevar

Vannevar Bush, b. Everett, Mass., Mar. 11, 1890, d. June 28, 1974, was a pioneer in computer design who helped to direct the course of American science policy during the World War II era. Earning a doctorate in engineering from the Massachusetts Institute of Technology (MIT) and Harvard University in 1916, Bush served as a professor and dean of engineering at MIT from 1919 to 1938. During those years he was a major inventor in many fields. He is best known for inventing the DIFFERENTIAL ANALYZER, a predecessor of the analog computer. It incorporated concepts of great importance in the design of the first generation of electronic COMPUTERS.

Bush became president of the Carnegie Institute in Washington, D.C. (1939), and was chairman of the National Advisory Committee for Aeronautics (1939–41). In 1941, President Roosevelt appointed Bush the first director of the Office of Scientific Research and Development, an agency to coordinate federally funded defense research. Bush's proposal for a similar agency to coordinate peacetime research led to the creation of the NATIONAL SCIENCE FOUNDATION in 1950, and his writings, such as *Science: The Endless Frontier* (1945), *Endless Horizons* (1946), and *Modern Arms and Free Men* (1949), had a strong influence on national policy.

Bibliography: Cortada, J. W., *Historical Dictionary of Data Processing* (1987); Penick, J. L., et al., eds., *The Politics of American Science,* rev. ed. (1972); Weisner, J. B., ''Vannevar Bush,'' *National Academy of Sciences: Biographical Memoirs,* vol. 50 (1979).

bush baby: see GALAGO.

bushmaster

The bushmaster, *Lachesis muta,* is a venomous PIT VIPER related to the rattlesnake. It is found in Central America and tropical parts of South America. Its background color is usually reddish yellow, crossed by dark bands. A black streak runs from the eye to the corner of the mouth. Slender-bodied, the bushmaster is the longest member of the pit-viper group, reaching lengths up to 3.6 m (12 ft). The fangs may be more than 2.5 cm (1 in) long. The bushmaster is the only New World member of the snake family Crotalidae that lays eggs, usually about a dozen at a time.

Bibliography: Phelps, Tony, *Poisonous Snakes* (1989).

The bushmaster, Lachesis muta, *is second in size only to the king cobra among poisonous snakes. Lachesis is the goddess of fate in Greek mythology, who determines the duration of human life.*

Bushmen: see SAN.

Bushnell, David

David Bushnell, b. Saybrook, Conn., *c.*1742, d. 1824, was an American inventor credited with designing the first effective SUBMARINE. An early interest in gunpowder led him to the invention of an underwater mine triggered by a timer. To attach the mine to the hull of a ship, Bushnell designed the TURTLE, an egg-shaped, submersible wooden craft powered by a hand-cranked propeller. Although its attempt (1776) to sink the British ship *Eagle* in New York harbor during the American Revolution failed, the *Turtle* did maneuver effectively and had an important influence on submarine development. After the war Bushnell practiced medicine.

Bibliography: Burgess, Robert F., *Ships beneath the Sea* (1975).

Bushnell, Horace

Horace Bushnell, b. Bantam, Conn., Apr. 14, 1802, d. Feb. 17, 1876, was an American Congregational minister. He had planned for a career in law, but a religious conversion caused him to choose the ministry instead. Drawing most of his ideas from practical experience as a pastor (at the North Church, Hartford, Conn., 1833–59), Bushnell fashioned a new approach to theology. Noting that all language is metaphoric, he concluded that doctrinal arguments are relative. Personal experience of spiritual matters is much more important. Bushnell also considered the world as an organic whole. He saw no sharp distinctions between categories such as the natural and the supernatural, individual and society, humanity and divinity. Rather, he held that there is constant penetration and interaction between aspects where one affects the other, where God reunites the world to himself through reconciling love instead of punishment.

Bushnell's influential books earned him fame as the father of American religious liberalism. His works include *A Discourse on Christian Nurture* (1847; 2d ed., 1861), *God in Christ* (1849), and *Nature and the Supernatural* (1858).
                                          HENRY WARNER BOWDEN

Bibliography: Barnes, Howard A., *Horace Bushnell and the Virtuous Republic* (1991); Duke, James O., *Horace Bushnell* (1984); Smith, David L., *Symbolism and Growth* (1981).

bushrangers

Bushrangers were robbers in 19th-century Australia who usually operated in sparsely settled areas, using the bush, or forest, as their base. The early bushrangers were generally British convicts who had escaped from assigned service in the penal colonies of New South Wales (from 1788) and Van Diemen's Land (now Tasmania; from 1804).

After the discovery of gold in the 1850s, bushrangers increased their activities; many began ambushing gold shipments. The bushrangers of this period were often native Australians rather than convicts from the British Isles. A few claimed to be modern Robin Hoods, some adopting romanticized names such as ''Captain Moonlight'' or ''Captain Thunderbolt.'' One bushranger, Ned KELLY, was an especially famous folk hero.   E. J. TAPP

Bibliography: Boxell, G. E., *The Story of the Australian Bushrangers* (1924); Finn, Paul, *Law and Government in Colonial Australia* (1987); Prior, Tom, and Wannan, Bill, *Plundering Sons* (1966).

bushtit

The bushtit, genus *Psaltriparus,* family Paridae, order Passeriformes, is a small, long-tailed, brown-gray TITMOUSE of western North America. It inhabits scrubby woodlands and forages in roving flocks for insects. The bushtit nest is a remarkable pocketlike structure of soft plant and animal materials suspended from a tree branch.   WILLIAM EARL GODFREY

*The tiny bushtit is about 9 cm (3.5 in) long. The black-eared bushtit,
P. melanotis (left), is usually found only above 1,500 m (4,920 ft) and
is far less abundant than the common bushtit, P. minimus (right).*

business administration

Business administration comprises all the arts and techniques
of running a business. In capitalist countries, a business is
both an independent unit in the economy, run for profit, and
part of a complex political and legal system. Its managers
must not only satisfy customers, they must also comply with
the regulations of government agencies, meet the expectations
of employees, bargain with labor unions, keep watch on competitors, and make a good impression on the public. To operate under these often conflicting demands and pressures, businesses have departments and personnel that specialize in particular functions, such as ACCOUNTING and sales.

Forms of Business Ownership. The three major forms of business ownership are the sole proprietorship, the partnership,
and the CORPORATION. A sole proprietorship is a business
owned by one person, in which all the profits belong to the
owner. The major disadvantage of the sole proprietorship is
that the assets of the business are treated in law as part of the
owner's personal assets. In case of bankruptcy, all the personal assets of the owner, including home and car, can be sold to
settle the debts of the business. A partnership is an association
of two or more persons who own a business jointly. Like the
sole proprietorship, the partnership is easy to establish, and its
profits are not subject to federal corporation taxes. The major
disadvantage of the partnership is that each partner is liable
for the debts of the business. A corporation is a legal entity
chartered by the state in which it is incorporated. The corporation is owned by investors called stockholders. A corporation is a separate legal entity, which limits personal liability.

Major Components of a Business. Most businesses have three
major components: production, MARKETING, and finance. Production is the transformation of raw materials into goods and
services that are sold to other businesses or to the consumer.
In a wholesale or retail business, the purchase of articles for
resale takes the place of production. The need to organize
production as efficiently as possible has resulted in the specialties known as OPERATIONS RESEARCH and MANAGEMENT SCI-
ENCE, which use complex mathematical techniques to analyze
the way organizations function. On the production line itself,
a specialty called production management is concerned with
planning and routing materials so that time and energy will
not be wasted. The design of complex machines and systems
is called SYSTEMS ENGINEERING.

The function of marketing is the sale and distribution of the
firm's goods or services to the public. Marketing also includes
ADVERTISING. Financial management includes the search for adequate sources of capital and the management of the capital
already invested. It requires estimating the amount of cash the
company will need in its operations, deciding whether to use
short-term or long-term credit, choosing the right time to issue
STOCK or sell BONDS, budgeting, and planning expenditures.

The selection and training of employees is a continuous
process in every large organization. Most companies center
this in a personnel department. In large companies, personnel
management also involves recruiting and training administrators and negotiating with LABOR UNIONS.

The Task of Management. Management includes planning,
administering, and controlling. These are separate functions,
but they must all be handled competently if a company is to
achieve its goals. The planning function includes all manage-
rial activities that ultimately enable an organization to achieve
its goals. At the highest levels of business, planning involves
establishing company strategies, that is, determining how the
resources of the business will be used to reach its objective.
After plans, policies, and strategies have been established,
managers must organize the company to reach its objectives.
The internal structure of any company can be shown on an organization chart. The chart displays the relationship of the
various parts of the organization as well as indicating who reports to whom. Management must determine the functions to
be performed and the sequence for accomplishing each goal.
Once this is done, job classifications can be established.

An efficient business organization requires a system of controls for keeping the top management informed as to how well
the company is meeting its goals. No plan is ever carried out
exactly as conceived. Managers must always be ready to meet
new problems posed by competitors, labor unions, government regulatory agencies (see BUSINESS LAW; GOVERNMENT REG-
ULATION), changing business conditions, and public opinion.
Essentially, the control process requires establishing clear
standards of performance, measuring actual performance
against the standards, and making the necessary corrections.
Controls may include budgets, schedules, charts, statistics,
and personal observation.   THOMAS ZIMMERER

Bibliography: Ferrell, O. C., et al., *Business* (1989); Horowitz, David,
The Business of Business (1989); Koontz, Harold, and Fulmer, Robert,
A Practical Introduction to Business, 4th ed. (1984); Kreitner, Robert, et
al, *Business*, 2d ed. (1990).

business cycle

Fluctuations in the level of business activity are called business cycles. The term is inaccurate because it suggests that
business ups and downs occur at regular intervals. Fluctuations, however, do follow a typical cyclical pattern.

Economists generally distinguish four phases in a cycle, beginning from the bottom: (1) an expansion, or recovery,
marked by increasing employment and rising income in most
parts of the economy; (2) a peak, or prosperous period; (3) a
contraction, or recession, in which business investment tapers
off, stocks of unsold goods increase, and workers are laid off;
and (4) a new bottom, known as a trough.

In actuality the pattern of the cycle is not as clear as this description indicates, and observers often disagree as to whether
the economy is about to move up or down. The shift into a
new phase of a cycle may not be recognized until after it has
occurred. Pioneering analysts of these cycles include Wesley
Clair MITCHELL and Joseph A. SCHUMPETER.

Bibliography: Barro, R. J., ed., *Modern Business Cycle Theory* (1989);
Mullineux, A. W., *Business Cycles and Financial Crisis* (1990); Schum-
peter, Joseph A., *Business Cycles* (1939; repr. 1989); Valentine, Lloyd
M., *Business Cycles and Forecasting*, 8th ed. (1991).

business education

Formal business education in the United States was established in the late 18th century as a response to needs created
by the Industrial Revolution. It began with proprietary secre-
tarial schools and vocational secondary schools that sought to
train young men and women in specific skills such as bookkeeping, filing, stenography, and office procedures. Such institutions exist to the present day.

The growing complexity of industrial society encouraged
the development of business education at the collegiate level.
A few professors would typically apply the principles of economic theory to business problems, particularly in finance.

The first college specifically for business was the Wharton School of Finance and Commerce (1881) at the University of Pennsylvania. By 1900 several other universities had entered the field; the Harvard School of Business was established in 1908. By 1990, approximately 1,350 U.S. colleges and universities offered degrees in business.

Over the past century, the curriculum of the business college has undergone a substantial evolution. Until World War II, collegiate business education tended to prepare specialists in public accounting, corporation finance, investments, marketing, management, and aspects of business law. The curriculum consisted of a core of business courses supplemented by required studies in the liberal arts. The techniques of instruction were descriptive and not quantitative, stressing procedures rather than inquiry into those procedures. Moreover, business faculties were rarely research-oriented and relied on the conventional lecture method of instruction.

After World War II a broad curriculum reform was initiated in business education. The new approach discouraged specialization, stressed the disciplines underlying business decision making (mathematics, psychology, economic theory, organization theory, and others), fostered instruction by the case method, and sought to upgrade faculty qualifications for teaching and research. It took an executive management perspective, stressing analysis over the rote learning of techniques. This remains the method of business education, except that most schools blend the lecture and case methods.

Business education is most widespread in the United States, although the European economic resurgence following World War II spurred the growth of university-level business programs in Western Europe. These follow the U.S. model in many important respects.   JOHN J. CLARK

Bibliography: Barille, Judy A., *Introduction to Business* (1989); Business Week Editors, and Byrne, John A., *Business Week's Guide to the Best Business Schools* (1989); Collin, Eliza G., and Devanna, Mary Anne, *The MBA Kit* (1990); Osborne, David, *Laboratories of Democracy* (1990).

business law

Business law includes those branches of law that affect the formation, operation, and termination of a business firm, including CORPORATIONS. The legal system regulates or determines (1) the way a firm is organized, (2) the nature of its transactions with other firms, (3) employer-employee relationships, (4) its responsibility to consumers, and (5) the obligations it owes to society at large. Specific subjects in the field of business law include, among others, contracts, agency, sales law, bankruptcy, and negotiable instruments.

Contracts. A commercial CONTRACT may be viewed as a tool by which business people, often assisted by their lawyers, establish rules to govern a particular business or personal relationship. Contract law determines which contracts are enforceable in court and defines what must be done to comply with contractually established obligations.

Agency. The legal cornerstone of the entire area of business transactions is agency law. An AGENT is a person empowered to act so as to legally bind another, the principal. Agency enables principals to handle a multitude of transactions at once, to greatly extend their geographic reach, and to make use of professional expertise when incurring legal obligations.

Sales. The Uniform Commercial Code (UCC) sets forth the rules governing sales of goods, commercial paper, and sellers' security interests. Emphasizing honesty, the UCC holds merchants to high standards of conduct.

A written sales contract will generally specify the performance obligations of both buyer and seller. The seller's minimum obligation is to put conforming goods at the buyer's disposition and give the buyer notice thereof. If the contract obliges the seller to deliver the goods to the buyer or to a carrier, the seller must do so, obtaining the necessary documents and delivering them to the buyer.

Warranties. A warranty is a guarantee by a seller that the goods will be of a certain quality. If they are below that quality, the buyer may sue for the difference in value.

The UCC sets forth the implied warranties that exist in certain sales transactions unless they are specifically excluded. The effect of these warranties is to neutralize the old doctrine of *caveat emptor* ("let the buyer beware") by requiring either that the goods be of average quality or that the buyer be conspicuously warned that the goods may not be up to standard.

Secured Transactions. When a sales transaction involves an extension of credit, the seller naturally wants to ensure that the buyer will pay as promised by establishing a legal interest in property held by the buyer that may be enforced if the buyer defaults. The most logical property for the seller to hold a secured interest in or LIEN on is the merchandise sold. The UCC sets up a legal procedure for handling defaults, establishing priorities among various classes of creditors.

Bankruptcy. The law of BANKRUPTCY provides a method by which an honest but insolvent debtor may be discharged, or freed, from claims held by creditors.

Negotiable Instruments. Certain kinds of business documents, or paper, can be exchanged for money because they enable their holders to obtain legal interests on the basis of the documents themselves. NEGOTIABLE INSTRUMENTS are usually classified under the following three groupings: (1) commercial paper, which includes formal documents involving a promise (for example, a promissory note) or order (for example, a check) to pay a sum of money; (2) commodity paper, which represents an ownership interest in property held by another, such as a trucker or shipper (for example, a bill of lading); and (3) investment paper, which includes stocks and bonds.   THOMAS W. DUNFEE

Bibliography: Clark, L. S., and Kinder, P. D., *Law and Business* (1988); Dunfee, Thomas W., and Blackburn, John, *Modern Business Law*, 2d ed. (1989); Research and Education Association Staff, *Essentials of Business Law* (1990).

business machines

Business machines, devices originally designed to aid in the performance of routine clerical work in offices, have evolved radically from, for example, the first TYPEWRITER of the 1860s through today's WORD PROCESSOR. Among other devices often indispensable to business operations are the ADDING MACHINE, electronic CALCULATOR, COMPUTER, COPYING MACHINE (see also ELECTROSTATIC PRINTING), and FACSIMILE machine. Dictating machines and mail-handling machines are also used.

Business Week

Business Week, a McGraw-Hill publication, is a newsweekly that covers corporate administration, economics, finance, and other matters affecting commercial production and exchange. Launched in 1929, *Business Week* maintains many U.S. news bureaus and foreign correspondents. Its international circulation in 1990 exceeded 850,000.

busing, school

The transportation of children by bus has long been an integral part of U.S. public education, particularly in rural areas, where children may live a considerable distance from their schools. Busing became a controversial policy issue, however, when it was introduced in the early 1970s as a means of achieving racial balance in the schools. Supporters of the policy hold that busing is a necessary tool for ending school segregation (see INTEGRATION, RACIAL); opponents claim that mandatory busing infringes on the right of parents to enroll their children at neighborhood schools.

Busing for integration was an outgrowth of the U.S. Supreme Court decision in BROWN V. BOARD OF EDUCATION OF TOPEKA, KANSAS in 1954, declaring racial segregation in the public schools unconstitutional. *Brown* itself did not address the issue of busing, but eventually other court decisions did. In *Green* v. *New Kent County School Board* (1968) in Virginia, a court charged school authorities with the affirmative duty of taking whatever steps might be necessary to eliminate racial discrimination. In *Swann* v. *Charlotte-Mecklenburg Board of Education* (1971) in North Carolina, it was ruled that if school authorities failed to desegregate, then the courts had the power to provide remedies, including busing.

In a 1972 decision (*Bradley* v. *School Board of the City of Richmond*) the Virginia state court of appeals overturned a court-ordered consolidation of Richmond city schools with those of adjoining suburban counties, on the grounds that the city's segregated schools were not the result of de jure (legal) actions, such as those which had created the segregated systems of the South, but rather were caused by de facto conditions, such as residential patterns. Nevertheless, despite the difficulty of proving that segregation had resulted from de jure causes, throughout the 1970s compulsory busing was ordered by the courts in a number of cities, including Boston, Mass., Cleveland, Ohio, and Los Angeles, Calif. In Wilmington, Del., and Indianapolis, Ind., black students were bused from the cities to white suburban schools.

In the early 1980s, however, the courts and Congress began speaking of "deliberate" or "intentional" segregation as the necessary precondition to compulsory busing. A massive busing program instituted (1978) in Los Angeles was ended in 1981, after state courts approved the constitutionality of a statewide referendum banning compulsory busing, except in cases of deliberate school segregation. The U.S. Supreme Court, in affirming that ruling, implied a limitation on the power of the courts to impose busing on communities whose segregated schools are not the result of deliberate policy.

In 1986 the Supreme Court, by declining to review a busing case from Norfolk, Va., signaled that a city can end court-ordered busing systems once its schools are integrated. The case had been appealed by black parents and civil rights leaders fearing school "resegregation" with the end of busing. In 1991 the Court went further, ruling in an Oklahoma City case that court-ordered busing could end short of integration if everything "practicable" to eliminate the vestiges of past discrimination had been done.

In many cases busing to achieve integration has accelerated the flight of white families to the suburbs, thus contributing to resegregated urban schools. It has exacerbated already tense race relations in some cities. On the other hand, such studies as the COLEMAN REPORT (1966) have demonstrated that the academic performance of minority children improves when they are in classes where middle-class white pupils are the majority.   HOWARD OZMON AND SAM CRAVER

Bibliography: Dimond, Paul R., *Beyond Busing: Inside the Challenge to Urban Segregation* (1985); Lupo, Alan, *Liberty's Chosen Home: The Politics of Violence in Boston* (1988); Schwartz, Bernard, *Swann's Way: The School Busing Case and the Supreme Court* (1986).

Buson   [boo'-sahn]

Taniguchi Buson, b. 1716, d. Dec. 25, 1783, later called Yosa Buson, was a Japanese haiku poet and artist, generally ranked second only to Matsuo Basho among poets of the Tokugawa period (1600–1868). Buson's technical skill as an artist is reflected in the visual detail of his poetry. Besides haiku, he wrote longer verse influenced by both Chinese and Japanese classics.

Busoni, Ferruccio   [boo-zoh'-nee, fer-roo'-choh]

Ferruccio Busoni, b. Florence, Italy, Apr. 1, 1866, d. July 27, 1924, piano virtuoso, composer, and musical theorist, was one of the most influential musicians of his generation. His father was Italian and his mother of partly German parentage, and from an early age he experienced tension between his Italian and German backgrounds that he never fully resolved, although he spent most of his career in Germany. Both of Busoni's parents were musical, and he received his earliest training on the piano from his mother.

A child prodigy, Busoni gave his first public piano recital in Trieste at the age of seven and at nine he performed his own piano pieces in Vienna. He studied composition with Wilhelm Meyer-Remy in Graz. Busoni spent most of his twenties as a teacher in Helsinki, Moscow, and Boston before settling (1894) in Berlin. This was to be his home for most of the rest of his life, although he traveled extensively and gave concerts

and often visited the United States. In Berlin he taught, conducted concerts, and continued to give recitals. He championed the works of such modern composers as Béla Bartók and Arnold Schoenberg and espoused progressive and visionary ideals. Busoni also wrote brilliantly on the aesthetics of music, among other subjects.

Busoni composed in virtually every musical form. Two violin sonatas and two string quartets are among his early works, and he composed for the piano throughout his life. His numerous orchestral works include a violin concerto, a vast piano concerto (with a choral finale), and *Indian Fantasy* for piano and orchestra, one of several works based on American Indian themes. He turned his incidental music for Carlo Gozzi's play *Turandot* (1904) into an opera (1917). His other operas include *Die Brautwahl* (1912), *Arlecchino* (1916), and, perhaps his masterpiece, *Doktor Faust,* unfinished when he died and completed by Philipp Jarnach. In the tradition of Franz Liszt, Busoni also made piano transcriptions of other composers' works, especially those of Johann Sebastian Bach, whom he greatly admired.   J. W. BARKER

Bibliography: Busoni, Ferruccio, *Letters to His Wife,* trans. by Rosamond Ley (1938), and "Sketch of a New Aesthetic of Music," trans. by T. Baker, in *Three Classics in the Aesthetics of Music* (1962); Dent, E. J., *Ferruccio Busoni: A Biography* (1933; repr. 1982); Stuckenschmidt, N. H., *Ferruccio Busoni,* trans. by S. Morris (1970); Van Dieren, Bernard, *Down among the Dead Men and Other Essays* (1935).

Bustamante, Sir Alexander   [boos-tah-mahn'-tay]

William Alexander Bustamante, b. Feb. 24, 1884, d. Aug. 6, 1977, was the first prime minister of independent Jamaica. A labor organizer in the 1930s, he founded the Bustamante Industrial Trade Union, Jamaica's largest union. Subsequently he formed (1943) the moderate Jamaica Labour party to counteract the more radical People's National party of Norman Manley. He was chief minister (1953-55) and, becoming prime minister in 1962, presided over Jamaica's acquisition (August 1962) of independence. In office until 1967, he initiated extensive public works programs and land reform.

bustard

Great bustard, Otis tarda, one of the world's largest flying birds, may weigh up to 22 kg (48.5 lb). It lives on the plains and steppes of Eurasia; its population is concentrated in the western and central areas of Asia.

A bustard is any of 23 species of birds found in grasslands and brushlands of southern Eurasia, Africa, and Australia. The 16 genera of bustards constitute the family Otididae, or Otidae, order Gruiformes. With their long necks and legs, bustards look somewhat like turkeys, although they are more closely related to cranes and rails. They range in length from 37 to 132 cm (14.5 to 52 in) and have a broad wingspan.

Among them are the heaviest of all flying birds. Weights of up to 22 kg (48.5 lb) have been reported for the great bustard, *Otis tarda*, of Eurasia. The bill is flattened and fairly short. The feet, built for running, have three front toes and no hind toe. The plumage is gray or brown, often with bars or spots, and white, brown, or black beneath. Bustards can fly well but stay mainly on the ground, feeding on a wide variety of plants and insects. They tend to gather in flocks, and they put on striking courtship displays. Their nests are simple depressions in the ground, with one to five eggs. Because they are hunted for food, some species are endangered.

butane   [bue'-tayn]

Butane (C_4H_{10}) is a petroleum hydrocarbon with a molecular weight of 58.12. It exists in two isomers, n–butane (CH_3—CH_2—CH_2—CH_3) with a boiling point of $-0.5°$ C ($31°$ F), and isobutane (CH—$(CH_3)_3$) with a boiling point of $-11.7°$ C ($11°$ F)—both boiling points at atmospheric pressure. It can be compressed to form a liquid at this same pressure. Butane is an important fuel gas and a major constituent of liquefied petroleum gas (LPG), and is used as a fuel in homes and for cigarette lighters. In such applications, most properties are the same for both forms. Butane is also used in making synthetic rubbers and motor oils.   JOHN T. MCMULLAN

Bute   [buet]

Bute was a county in southwestern Scotland until 1975, when it became part of the Strathclyde administrative region. It comprised the islands of Bute, Arran, Cumbrae, Holy, Pladda, and Inchmarnock, all located in the Firth of Clyde. The county town was Rothesay. The sparsely populated, mountainous islands are covered with grasslands and are used primarily for sheep and cattle raising. Agriculture is practiced in the lowlands, with potatoes and grains the major crops. Coastal towns engage in fishing and boatbuilding. The islands are popular summer resorts. Prehistoric stone structures and castles built in the 11th century to defend against Norse invaders are found throughout the islands.

Butenandt, Adolf   [boo'-te-nahnt]

The German biochemist Adolf Friedrich Johann Butenandt, b. Mar. 24, 1903, isolated the female SEX HORMONES estrone (1929) and progesterone (1934). In 1939 he isolated and determined the structure of the male sex hormone androsterone and synthesized testosterone. That same year he shared the Nobel Prize for chemistry with Leopold RUŽIČKA. Butenandt later studied gene-mutation effects, isolated and determined the structure of the silk moth's sex pheromone, and did research on carcinogens and viruses.   ROBERT J. PARADOWSKI

Butkus, Dick

Richard "Dick" Butkus, b. Chicago, Dec. 9, 1942, is a former football player who is considered one of the best linebackers in football history. Butkus became famous at the University of Illinois, where he was twice named to the All-American team. Playing for the professional Chicago Bears, he was an all-pro seven of his first eight years (1965, 1967–72). The 111-kg (245-lb) Butkus ranged from sideline to sideline to get to ball-carriers and receivers from his middle-linebacker position. He had 25 fumble recoveries, a National Football League record at the time, and 19 interceptions, before injuries to his knees forced him to retire in 1973.

Butler, Alban

An English Roman Catholic priest, Alban Butler, b. Oct. 24, 1710, d. May 15, 1773, compiled *The Lives of the Fathers, Martyrs, and Other Principal Saints*, biographies of some 1,600 saints, published between 1756 and 1759. Revised several times, this monumental work was the basis for Herbert Thurston and Donald Attwater's *Butler's Lives of the Saints* (1956), now a standard reference.

Butler, Benjamin Franklin

Benjamin Franklin Butler, b. Deerfield, N.H., Nov. 5, 1818, d. Jan. 11, 1893, was a controversial American politician and general in the Civil War. Upon graduation from Waterville (now Colby) College, he practiced law in Lowell, Mass. In 1853 he began serving as a Democrat in the state legislature, where he espoused the causes of minority groups and labor.

Because of his political following in New England, Butler was named a general in the federal army when the Civil War began. His effrontery made it difficult to ignore or discipline him. Butler's most effective military action was his seizure of Baltimore and Annapolis, Md., early in the war, although he blundered into defeat at Big Bethel, near Fort Monroe, in June 1861. In command of Fort Monroe, Butler refused to return runaway slaves on the grounds that they were "contrabands." Later, his troops occupied (May 1, 1862) New Orleans after Admiral Farragut had captured it, but Butler's efficient administration there became notorious through dubious heavy-handed policies and ensuing corruption. His ineptness as a general was shown in his handling of Union soldiers at Fort Fisher, Wilmington, N.C., in December 1864, after which he was relieved of his command.

As a radical Republican in the U.S. House of Representatives (1867–75, 1877–79), Butler played a leading role in the impeachment of Andrew JOHNSON and supported tough Reconstruction policies in the South. A Democrat again, he was elected governor of Massachusetts in 1882 and in 1884 was the presidential candidate of the GREENBACK PARTY.   WARREN W. HASSLER, JR.

Bibliography: Driscoll, William D., *Benjamin F. Butler*, ed. by H. Hyman and S. Bruchey (1987).

Butler, John

John Butler, b. Memphis, Tenn., Sept. 29, 1920, d. Sept. 11, 1993, was one of the first choreographers to combine ballet and modern dance in his works. Trained as a dancer at the schools of both George Balanchine and Martha Graham, he danced with Graham (1945–55). Butler was a freelance choreographer for such ballet and modern-dance companies as the Alvin Ailey American Dance Theater and the Joffrey Ballet. Well known for his pas de deux *After Eden* (1966), he also choreographed works for opera companies, such as his *Carmina Burana* (1959) for New York City Opera.   ROBERT PIERCE

Butler, Joseph

Joseph Butler, b. May 18, 1692, d. June 16, 1752, was an English bishop, theologian, and philosopher. Educated as a Presbyterian, he joined the Church of England and became a priest (1714). Although he engaged in pastoral duties, he lived in seclusion while he prepared his major work, *The Analogy of Religion* (1736). A formidable rebuttal of Deism, it demonstrated the parallel between natural and religious knowledge. Butler was made bishop of Bristol in 1738 and later declined (1747) the see of Canterbury to become bishop in Durham (1750). David HUME was greatly influenced by Butler's critique of dogmatic RATIONALISM.   JAMES D. NELSON

Butler, Nicholas Murray

Nicholas Murray Butler, b. Elizabeth, N.J., Apr. 2, 1862, d. Dec. 7, 1947, was an American educator and Nobel Prize winner. During most of his life, he was associated with Columbia University, receiving his bachelor's degree from Columbia in 1882 and serving as its president from 1901 to 1945.

Butler was founder and president of the Industrial Education Association, which in 1889 established the New York College for the Training of Teachers. This became (1893) Teachers College, Columbia University, for a long period the most influential school of education in the country. In 1900, with Harvard's president Charles William Eliot, Butler created the College Entrance Examination Board. He was influential in appointing the National Education Association's Committee of Ten, whose 1894 report oriented the high school curriculum toward college preparation and away from vocational education.

Active in the Republican party, Butler was a delegate at many of its national conventions. He was particularly concerned with international understanding and was instrumental in establishing the Carnegie Endowment for International Peace (1910). He was president of the endowment from 1925 to 1945 and shared the 1931 Nobel Peace Prize with Jane Addams.

Bibliography: Marrin, Albert, *Nicholas Murray Butler* (1976).

Butler, Reg

Reginald Cottrell Butler, b. Apr. 28, 1913, d. Oct. 23, 1981, was one of the most popular contemporary sculptors in England. Trained as an architect, he began to sculpt after World War II. He learned blacksmithing and in 1948 began to create open wrought-iron sculpture in the tradition of Julio González. In 1953, Butler won first prize in the International Sculpture Exhibition for *The Unknown Political Prisoner* (1951–52). Influenced by primitive and African art, his work is noted for its images of taut human figures in movement. Butler's later works, less dynamic, fall into a kind of academicism.   HARRY RAND

Bibliography: Butler, Reginald Cottrell, *Reg Butler* (1962); Speed Memorial Museum, *Reg Butler: A Retrospective Exhibition* (1963).

Butler, Samuel   (1612–80)

Samuel Butler, baptized Feb. 8, 1612, d. Sept. 25, 1680, was an English satirist best known for *Hudibras* (1663–78). In this long mock-heroic poem modeled on Don Quixote, Butler ridiculed Puritan extremism, berating hypocrisy, bigotry, and selfishness. *Hudibras* is the source of many expressions that have become household phrases, such as "looking a gift-horse in the mouth."

Butler also derided contemporary science with *The Elephant in the Moon*, in which an elephant, viewed through a telescope, appears to be on the Moon, but is really only a mouse trapped inside the instrument.

Bibliography: Richards, Edward A., *Hudibras in the Burlesque Tradition* (1937; repr. 1972); Veldkamp, Jan, *Samuel Butler* (1923; repr. 1980); Wasserman, G. R., *Samuel "Hudibras" Butler* (1989).

Butler, Samuel   (1835–1902)

Samuel Butler, b. Dec. 4, 1835, d. June 18, 1902, was an English novelist and satirist who rebelled against the accepted ideas of his time. Born into an ecclesiastical family, Butler was expected to join the clergy, but after his graduation from Cambridge, instead of being ordained, he went to New Zealand, where he was a sheep farmer for 5 years. Upon his return (1864) to England, he tried painting but gradually settled on a literary career. His first novel, *Erewhon* (1872), a utopian romance (the name is an anagram of "Nowhere"), describes in a Swiftian manner a country in which most customs are contrary to those of the English: poverty, for example, is considered a crime.

Butler later became deeply involved in the evolutionary disputes of his day, suggesting intelligent modifications to Darwin's theories. In *The Authoress of the Odyssey* (1897), he postulated that a woman might have written *The Odyssey*, and he analyzed the archetypal feminine motif in the Homeric epics.

Just before his death, Butler published the sequel *Erewhon Revisited* (1901). His most durable work, The WAY OF ALL FLESH (1903), is a realistic but bitter study of English middle-class family life and a merciless indictment of the religious myopia, bigotry, and sanctimoniousness that Butler knew in his youth. The book set a trend for many later antiparental books and greatly influenced English society.

Bibliography: Cole, G. D., *Samuel Butler* (1973); Furbank, P. N., *Samuel Butler, 1835–1902*, 2d ed. (1971); Harris, J. F., *Samuel Butler, Author of Erewhon* (1973); Holt, L., *Samuel Butler*, rev. ed. (1989); Jeffers, Thomas L., *Samuel Butler Revalued* (1981).

Butler University

Established in 1855, Butler University (enrollment: 3,723; library: 130,000 volumes) is a private institution in Indianapolis, Ind. Bachelor's and master's degrees are offered in the colleges of arts and sciences, education, business administration, and pharmacy and in the Jordan College of Fine Arts.

Butlerov, Aleksandr   [boot'-luh-rawf, ul-yik-sahn'-dur]

The Russian chemist Aleksandr Mikhailovich Butlerov, b. Sept. 6 (N.S.), 1828, d. Aug. 17 (N.S.), 1886, was one of the first to use formulas to represent the relative position of atoms in organic compounds and introduced (1861) the term *chemical structure* for this concept. His textbook *Introduction to Organic Chemistry* (1864; German trans., 1868) had a far-reaching influence on the younger generation of chemists. Among other achievements, Butlerov prepared synthetic sugars from formaldehyde and recognized the existence of chemical isomers.   VIRGINIA F. MCCONNELL

Butor, Michel   [bue-tawr', mee-shel']

Michel Butor, b. Sept. 14, 1926, is a French essayist and a leading exponent of the *nouveau roman*, or NEW NOVEL. For Butor, neither linear plots nor characterization is important to the novel; rather, he seeks the almost "mathematical" order that lies behind reality. Typical of his novels, *Passage de Milan* (1954) reveals in minute detail the events in a Paris apartment house during a 12-hour period. *Passing Time* (1956; Eng. trans., 1960) recalls, via minutiae, two years of melancholy in England's gray city of Manchester. Later works available in English include *Letter from the Antipodes* (1978; Eng. trans., 1981) and *The Spirit of Mediterranean Places* (1960; Eng. trans., 1987).   BETTINA KNAPP

Bibliography: Hirsch, M., *Beyond the Single Vision: Henry James, Michel Butor, Uwe Johnson* (1981); McWilliams, D., *The Narratives of Michel Butor* (1978); Spencer, M., *Michel Butor* (1974).

Butte   [byoot]

Butte, the seat of Silver Bow County, is a city in southwestern Montana with a population of 33,941 (1990). Located on the western slope of the Continental Divide, it was long one of the principal copper-mining centers in the United States. Today, manufacturing has supplanted mining in importance.

By 1864 settlers were attracted to the area's rich mineral deposits, and in 1879 a city was incorporated and named for Big Butte, a nearby peak. The Montana College of Mineral Science and Technology (1893), with an excellent mineral and fossil museum, is located in Butte. In 1976, Butte and Silver Bow were consolidated for government purposes into Butte–Silver Bow, administered by a county board.

butte

A butte is an isolated, steep-sided hill of rock, often capped with a resistant rock layer. Commonly found in the plateau areas of the western and southwestern United States, it is usually a remnant of landscape left after erosion of material around it—analogous to a mesa but smaller. The term *butte* is also occasionally applied to an isolated cinder cone (see VOLCANO).   JOHN A. SHIMER

butter

Butter is a delicately flavored dairy food (see DAIRYING) made from milk fat, to which salt and coloring may be added. Cream, the concentrated fat from milk, is the basic constituent of butter. When chilled cream is violently agitated in a CHURN, the protective membranes of some individual fat globules break and the liquid fat that is released helps cement other globules together. Globules and free fat become granules, which lump together to form a semisolid mass in the liquid buttermilk, which is drained away. A modern barrel churn can produce up to 2,250 kg (5,000 lb) of butter an hour.

Nineteenth-century butter-making equipment included the conventional plunger churn (left) and a new invention, the barrel churn (right). In both churns, cream was agitated to separate the fat from the whey, and the fat then coagulated into butter. The plunger was moved up and down by hand; with the barrel churn, butter making was quicker and easier.

buttercup

Buttercup, *Ranunculus*, is a large genus of about 250 species of annual and perennial herbs in the crowfoot family, Ranunculaceae. They occur worldwide in various habitats, although they occur more commonly in temperate and cool zones of the Northern Hemisphere. The primitive flowers of the genus are mostly yellow—hence the name—but a few white species exist. The five or more carpels of the flower are separate. The common name for the family—crowfoot—refers to the shape of the deeply divided leaves. The Latin name (meaning "little frog") was applied by Pliny to the numerous aquatic forms that grew where frogs were abundant.

Buttercups are highly adaptive herbs found in nearly all parts of the world and in habitats ranging from aquatic to dry soil. The creeping buttercup, Ranunculus repens (left), is a prolific weed native to North American and Europe.

The butter granules are washed to remove the residual buttermilk, and the mass is then kneaded, or worked, until the remaining moisture droplets become minute and evenly distributed. Most butter has a moisture content ranging to a maximum of 16 to 18 percent. During the kneading process, coloring matter and salt may be added. The salt serves as a flavoring and often masks off-flavors present in the cream. Well-wrapped, refrigerated butter will keep several weeks, and frozen butter, several months.

May is the month of peak milk production in the United States. Of the yearly total of more than 500 million kg (more than 1 billion lb) of butter, about 10 percent is produced during this month. The skim milk left after the cream has been separated is processed, usually, into dried milk powder.

In the United States butter is graded by the U.S. Department of Agriculture. The highest grade of butter, and the one most frequently seen in grocery stores, is U.S. Grade AA. In a score-ranking established by the USDA for grading such qualities as flavor, body, and color, AA butter ranks at least 93 on a scale of 100. Sweet butter contains no salt. Sweet cream butter is made from unsoured cream. Whipped butter has been lightened, and its volume increased, by having air beaten into it.

Cultured or soured-cream butter, to which certain starter culture bacteria are added in order to impart flavor, is popular in Denmark and other European countries. Originally this flavor was imparted by growing the bacteria in cream before churning. Today, the flavors are usually distilled from a culture and added to the butter as it is worked.

Some societies consume milk fat in an even more concentrated form than butter. In Asia, Africa, and the Middle East, *ghee* is made by melting butter—often made from buffalo milk—pouring off the fat, and evaporating its moisture by heating to near boiling. Moisture content is about 1 percent. Butter oil and anhydrous milk fat, products similar to *ghee*, are often made in areas of surplus milk production.

Major butter producers include the republics of the former USSR—primarily, Russia, Ukraine, and Belarus; India, which converts most of its butterfat into ghee; and the United States, Germany, and France. Annual U.S. per-capita butter consumption has dropped significantly over the past decades, from 2.5 kg (5.4 lb) in 1970 to the present 1.9 kg (4.2 lb).

ROBERT T. MARSHALL

Bibliography: Robertson, R. K., ed., *Modern Dairy Technology*, 2d ed. (1993); Rosenthal, I., *Milk and Dairy Products* (1991).

Butterfield, John

John Butterfield, b. Berne, N.Y., Nov. 18, 1801, d. Nov. 14, 1869, was an American organizer of stagecoach companies and the founder of the first overland mail service to California. Butterfield organized the American Express Company in 1850 by merging several smaller firms. His Overland Mail Company carried mail during the 1850s and '60s from St. Louis to San Francisco and Portland, Oreg. He established the streetcar system in Utica, N.Y., and served as mayor of the city in 1865, living there until his death.

Butterfield, William

William Butterfield, b. Sept. 7, 1814, d. Feb. 23, 1900, was a prolific architect of the English GOTHIC REVIVAL whose work reflects his religious beliefs. Most often employed by wealthy clients who shared his High Church philosophy, Butterfield designed several dozen churches and parsonages throughout England. His most famous building is All Saints, Margaret Street (1849–55), London, where the architect capitalized on a cramped urban site by emphasizing the building's verticality with a prominent tower. Other significant examples of his work include Saint Matthias, Stoke Newington (1850–53), and Saint Augustine's, Queen's Gate (1868), London. Butterfield's largest commission was Keble College, Oxford (begun 1868), where he combined boxy shapes with his characteristic polychromy. Butterfield also produced many of the church furnishings.

LEON SATKOWSKI

Bibliography: Summerson, John, *Heavenly Mansions* (1949; repr. 1963); Thompson, Paul, *William Butterfield* (1971).

butterfish

Butterfishes inhabit the coastal waters of temperate and tropical oceans. Their name refers to their slippery coating of mucus. Also called harvest fish, they are harvested for food. The oval, laterally compressed body may reach a length of 30 cm (1 ft). The mouth is small, and pelvic fins are absent in the adult. The young frequently swim beneath some species of jellyfish to find shelter and, probably, food. The common butterfish, *Peprilus triacanthus*, is found along the Atlantic coast of North America, and the California pompano—unrelated to true pompanos—along the Pacific coast. Butterfish comprise 3 genera and about 13 species of the family Stromateidae, order Perciformes.

EDWARD O. WILEY

butterflies and moths

Butterflies and moths are insects comprising more than 100,000 species worldwide in the second largest insect order, Lepidoptera. The name, derived from the Greek *lepis*, meaning "scale," and *pteron*, meaning "wing," refers to the distinctive covering of minute scales, overlapping like shingles, on the wings. Variously colored with pigments or color-forming structures, the scales form distinctive color patterns, particularly in butterflies. Typically the adult mouthparts comprise two pairs of sensory palpi and a long, coiled, tubular proboscis through which liquids can be sucked. The metamorphosis is complete, or indirect, with four stages: EGG; larva, or CATERPILLAR; PUPA, or chrysalis; and adult. Adults range in size from about a 5-mm (0.2-in) wing expanse in the smallest moths to a 30-cm (11.8-in) expanse in the largest moths and butterflies. Nearly all larvae feed on plant matter, chiefly green foliage, but in some groups they are wood borers or scavengers of dead plant or, rarely, animal matter.

DISTINGUISHING FEATURES

The familiar butterflies and SKIPPERS comprise only about 12 families of a total of nearly 90, the remainder being moths. The moths range from very primitive groups to highly advanced ones. The butterflies and skippers are on different evolutionary lines, the butterflies highly advanced, the skippers a bit more primitive. In general, moths are duller in color than butterflies, have looser wing scales, fly at night, have a frenulum, or special mechanism for joining the fore and hind wings, and have threadlike and tapered, or plumy, antennae. The butterflies and skippers are more brightly colored, have firmer wing scales, fly during the day, lack wing-coupling structures, and have knobs at the end of the antennae. Many moths, however, are brilliantly colored, fly by day, and lack wing-coupling, and some have knobbed antennae.

CLASSIFICATION

The most important and most widely known families may be classified as follows.

Primitive Moths. In the two major families, Micropterygidae (mandibulate moths) and Hepialidae (ghost moths), the adult mouthparts of some are for chewing. Fore and hind wings are similar in size and venation and are linked by a special flap, the jugum.

Advanced Moths. The families of this group are often called microlepidoptera or micro moths because most of them are quite small, but some, such as the Cossidae (wood boring moths), are large. The very small larvae of some mine in single leaves. Many larvae live in rolled-up or tied-together leaves; others bore into fruits or stems. Many are serious agricultural or forest pests. The pyralids are perhaps the third largest family in the order, comprising thousands of species, and are very diverse. Some are leaf eaters; others bore into stems or sod; and in one subfamily the larvae are aquatic.

Most Advanced Moths. These are often called the macro moths, although some are quite small, and include the majority of the larger and more familiar species. The noctuids constitute the largest family in the order and geometrids the second largest family. In some families the mouthparts are greatly reduced, and the adults do not feed.

Skippers. The two families Megathymidae (giant skippers) and Hesperiidae (skippers) are exceedingly fast flyers and quick dodgers, flying by day, and eager flower visitors. The giant skippers are a small, New World group, whose larvae bore into the stems of yuccas and agaves. The true skippers are found worldwide, with thousands of species. Most skippers have a hook at the tip of the antenna beyond the knob. Their larvae have a distinct, narrow neck between the head and prothorax. The skippers share characteristics of both butterflies and moths and are placed in a separate group.

Butterflies. Several thousand species of butterflies are known worldwide. The nymphalids, brush-footed butterflies, are by far the largest family, but most of the other families include some familiar species seen everywhere. Many members of all families are brightly colored, but the morphos and some of the hairstreaks, especially in the tropics, are most brilliant with iridescent blues and greens caused by submicroscopic

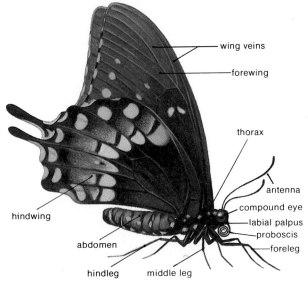

Spicebush Swallowtail Butterfly
Papilio troilus   North America

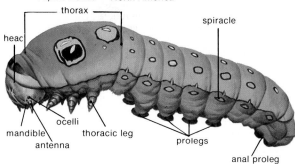

A butterfly and a moth share similar features of anatomy, such as mouthparts for sucking nectar and two pairs of wings that operate as one pair. The butterfly, however, is slender, has knobbed antennae, and folds its wings vertically when at rest. The moth is stout and hairy, has unknobbed, often feathered antennae, and spreads its wings when resting. The butterfly, active by day, has beautifully colored, often iridescent wings, and the moth, which is active by night, commonly has dull-colored wings. The spicebush swallowtail caterpillar, P. troilus, has a striking orange-and-black pattern, resembling eyes, on the back of its head that is believed to be used to startle its enemies.

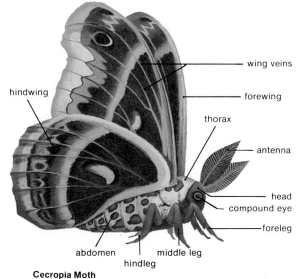

Cecropia Moth
Hyalophora cecropia   North America

structures on the scales. Many of the larvae and pupae (chrysalids) are brightly colored or grotesquely shaped and bear spines, horns, or peculiar filaments.

ANATOMY

Eggs are small, spherical to hemispherical, sometimes flat or spindle-shaped. At one end is an opening, the micropyle through which sperm can enter. Larvae are typically elongate and divided into head, thorax, and abdomen. The head bears a set of short mouthparts, and the mandibles are powerful. A tubular spinneret emits liquid silk. The antennae are very short, and the eyes are a group of very small stemmata on each side. The thorax has three segments, the prothorax, mesothorax, and metathorax, each with a pair of short, jointed legs. The abdomen has ten visible segments, with a pair of short, fleshy prolegs on each of segments 3–6 and 10; these bear many short hooks, or crotchets. The prothorax and abdominal segments 1–8 each bears a pair of respiratory openings, or spiracles. These admit air to a very complex system of air tubes, or tracheae. Internally the digestive system is very large and capacious, and a pair of silk glands is extremely long and complex. The very specialized larvae of leaf miners are flat and greatly reduced. Many larvae are smooth; many are hairy, sometimes very densely; others bear spines and horns, sometimes long and ornate.

The adult's head bears two usually long antennae, two large compound eyes, usually a pair of simple eyes (ocelli), one or two pairs of sensory palpi, and the tubular, coiled proboscis. The thorax bears a pair of long, jointed legs on each segment and a pair of wings on each of the mesothorax and metathorax. In many families a pair of tympanic hearing organs is located on the metathorax or the basal segment of the abdomen. The abdomen bears no appendages except for short genitalic structures at the end. A pair of spiracles is located on the prothorax and each of the first eight abdominal segments. The wings are membranous, supported by a series of branching, tubular veins; in all but the most primitive moths the fore wings are the larger. The number and arrangement of the veins are important in classification.

METAMORPHOSIS

Butterflies and moths develop through the four stages of a complete METAMORPHOSIS. The small, tough-shelled eggs are usually produced in large numbers and laid by the female in appropriate places or on suitable foodplants. The larva, or caterpillar, develops within the eggshell, then eats its way out. It then feeds and grows, periodically molting its old skin and head capsule several times. It may complete its growth in about one month, but some species remain larvae for as long as two years.

Eventually the last larva molt produces the pupa, typically a smooth, mummylike, almost immobile object with the adult structures showing in shallow relief. Many moth pupae are enclosed in a silk covering, or COCOON, spun by the larva; others are naked and uncovered, often underground or, as in most butterflies, suspended from a silk pad. Within the pupa the larval structures transform to those of the adult, in some species in as little as a few days, in others in as long as several months.

When fully formed the adult breaks out of the pupal shell. Its outer structures harden and its wings, at first small pads, expand greatly, flatten out, and harden. The adult does not molt but may live for as long as several months in some species, flying about, seeking a mate, and reproducing. In such a metamorphosis the larva is the nutritive stage; the pupa a transition stage between the larva and the adult; and the highly mobile adult, the reproductive and dispersive stage. Some butterflies migrate long distances, usually toward the equator in fall and away from it in spring. The North American monarch butterfly is noted for its mass migrations of thousands of kilometers.

IMPORTANCE

Abounding almost everywhere, and feeding, as a group, on an enormous variety of plants, the Lepidoptera have the greatest ecological and economic importance. Their larvae transform millions of tons of plant matter into animal matter and wastes and are eaten by other animals or eventually recy-

A single egg (1), laid on a milk parsley plant by a European swallow-tail butterfly, Papilio machaon, hatches out a caterpillar (2) that eats the leaves and develops to its full size (3). A three-week-old caterpillar (4) attaches itself to a stalk by a silk thread and then sheds its skin (5), revealing a bright green pupa, or chrysalis (6). An adult swallowtail (7) finally emerges from the chrysalis after weeks of metamorphosis. (Overleaf) A selection of butterflies of the world reveals the remarkable range of the insect's colors and varieties. Euptychia cymele is the little wood satyr of North America. Kallima parakleta of Malaya is known as a dead-leaf butterfly. When its wings are folded, revealing only the underside, it looks like a dead leaf. Heliconius charitonius is a zebra heliconian that ranges from South and Central America to South Carolina and the West Indies. Limenitis bredowi is a colorful butterfly of Arizona, southern California, and Mexico. It belongs to the same family as the monarch butterfly. Pieris rapae, the small cabbage butterfly, lives throughout the world and destroys cultivated crops of the cabbage family by eating the leaves. Limenitis astyanax, the red-spotted purple butterfly, lives in open, scrubby woods ranging from New England to Florida. Cyaniris pseudargiolus, a blue butterfly, ranges from Alaska to Panama. Epitula badura, also a blue butterfly, lives on the west coast of Africa. Libythea bachmanii, known as Bachman's snout butterfly, lives in woods and open country of the southern and midwestern United States. Caligo memnon, known as the owl butterfly, of Venezuela and central America, scares away its enemies with large markings that look like owl eyes. Melitaea diamina, a fritillary known as the checkerspots butterfly, ranges from northern Spain to central Asia. Colias cesonia, or dog-face butterfly, ranges from New York to Argentina. Erebia epipsodea, a common alpine butterfly, is found from Alaska to Colorado. Limenitis lorquini is a white admiral of the western United States. Speyeria idalia, or the Regal fritillary, of the eastern United States and Canada, prefers to live in open meadows and prairies. Graphium weiskei, a kite swallowtail, lives in New Guinea and Borneo. Batesia hypochlora lives in the upper Amazon region of South America. Chorinea faunus is a small swallowtail of Trinidad and South America. Papilio toboroi differs from other swallowtails by having no "tail." It lives in Bougainville in the Solomon Islands. Hades noctula is found in Mexico, Central America, and Venezuela. Danaus plexippus, the monarch butterfly, migrates in fall from Canada and the northern United States to the southern United States and Mexico. In spring it returns north by the same route. Amblyscirtes vialis is the roadside skipper of Canada and the western United States. Skippers are classed between butterflies and moths. Lycaena phlaeas americana, the American copper, lives in the northeastern United States and fearlessly chases after large butterflies, birds, and dogs. Parnassius apollo, an apollo butterfly of Europe and north Africa, makes beautiful soaring flights above its mountain habitat. Thecla teresina is a colorful hairstreak from South and Central America. Trogonoptera brookiana, Raja Brooke's birdwing, lives in Malaya. This large butterfly has wings that appear to have feathers like a bird. Thecla quercus, the purple hairstreak of South America, is so named because of its fine, hairlike tails and the streaks on its wings.

Wood Satyr
Euptychia cymele

Dead-leaf
Kallima parakleta

Zebra Heliconian
Heliconius charitonius

Limenitis bredowi

Cabbage
Pieris rapae

Red-spotted Purple
Limenitis astyanax

Cyaniris pseudargiolus

Epitola badura

Bachman's Snout
Libythea bachmanii

Owl
Caligo memnon

Checkerspots Fritillary
Melitaea diamina

Dogface
Colias cesonia

Common Alpine
Erebia epipsodea

White Admiral
Limenitis lorquini

Regal Fritillary
Speyeria idalia

Kite Swallowtail
Graphium weiskei

Batesia hypochlora

Chorinea faunus

Papilio toboroi

Hades noctula

Monarch
Danaus plexippus

Roadside Skipper
Amblyscirtes vialis

American Copper
Lycaena phlaeas americana

Apollo
Parnassius apollo

Thecla teresina

Raja Brooke's Birdwing
Trogonoptera brookiana

Purple Hairstreak
Thecla quercus

Alcidis aurora

Dark Crimson Underwing
Catocala sponsa

Peach-Tree Borer
Sanninoïdes exitosa

Isabella Tiger
Isia isabella

Luna Moth
Actia luna

Dysphania militaris

Erasmia sanguiflua

Death's Head
Acherontia atropos

Chrysiridia madagascariensis

Io Moth
Automeris io

(Opposite page) *A selection of moths hints at the range and variations in shape and color in these insects. Alcidis aurora, one species of Uranid moth, inhabits forests of New Guinea and other Indonesian islands. Unlike most moths, Uranids fly during the day and not at night. The peach-tree borer moth,* Sanninoides exitosa, *ranges throughout the United States and Canada. Larvae, or caterpillars, of this moth bore into trunks of peach trees, causing extensive damage in orchards. The Isabella tiger moth,* Isia isabella, *is also common to the United States. Its caterpillar, known as the "woolly bear," is kept as a children's pet and fed grass and plantain leaves.* Dysphania militaris *is a Geometrid moth found in India, Java, and Borneo.* Erasmia sanguiflua *is a moth native to mountainous regions of India and parts of Southeast Asia. It flies during the day, unlike most moths, and moves quickly and erratically. The Io moth,* Automeris io, *native to the United States, is sometimes known as the "bull's-eye moth" because of its spotted hindwings. The caterpillar also has poisonous spines as protection from its enemies. The dark crimson underwing moth,* Catocala sponsa, *is found only in the New Forest of England. Like other underwing moths, it has brightly decorative hind wings that are hidden by drab fore wings when the moth is resting. The luna moth,* Actia luna, *ranging throughout the United States and Canada, is easily recognized by its pale green color and the long tails on its hind wings. The male luna has feathery antennae that are sensitive enough to detect the scent of a female miles away. The death's-head moth,* Acherontia atropos, *ranging from southern Europe to Great Britain, is recognized by a skull-like mark on its thorax and its yellow and black striped abdomen. This moth belongs to the Sphingid family, so named because the resting larvae, with elevated head and thorax, supposedly resemble the profile of the Egyptian sphinx.* Chrysiridia madagascariensis *lives near trees and flowering shrubs of Madagascar. This moth, which belongs to the Uranid family, is commercially bred for its beautiful wings, which are made into jewelry.*

cled into plant matter. Inevitably many of them, feeding on plants valuable to humans, are severe economic pests. Among the most noted of these are: spruce budworm, *Choristoneura fumiferana;* GYPSY MOTH, *Porthetria dispar,* many forest and cultivated trees; armyworm, *Pseudaletia,* grain and forage crops; tent caterpillars, *Malacosoma;* and many CUTWORMS, Noctuidae. A few Lepidoptera are directly beneficial, notably the SILKWORM, *Bombyx mori.* Many help control weed plants.

Flower-visiting adults are second only to bees in the cross-pollination of many flowering plants. In the laboratory, many species are used in important research in evolution, genetics, and physiology.   ALEXANDER B. KLOTS

Bibliography: Ackery, P. R., and Vane-Wright, R. I., *Milkweed Butterflies* (1984); Brewer, Jo, and Winter, Dave, *Butterflies and Moths* (1986); Carter, David, and Phillips, Roger, eds., *Butterflies and Moths of Britain and Europe* (1982); Douglas, M. M., *The Lives of Butterflies* (1986); Gerardi, M. H., and Grimm, J. K., *The History, Biology, Damage, and Control of the Gypsy Moth* (1978); Sbordoni, V., and Foresterio, S., *Butterflies of the World* (1985); Scott, J. A., *The Butterflies of North America: A Natural History and Field Guide* (1986).

butterfly bush

Butterfly bushes are 100 or more species of deciduous or evergreen shrubs and small trees found in tropical and temperate regions of the Americas, Asia, and South Africa. They are so named because their fragrant, somewhat lilaclike flowers attract butterflies. They have tall, slender stems; toothed leaves that are whitish beneath; and small individual flowers produced in profusion on long spikes. The flowers may be white, yellowish, or lavender. Some species are used as ornamentals. Butterfly bushes constitute the genus *Buddleia* of the logania family, Loganiaceae.

butterfly fish

Butterfly fish are small fish with laterally compressed bodies. Most of the approximately 140 species occur in shallow, tropical reefs; a pair will often inhabit the same area of reef for up to 2 years. Butterfly fish are so called because they are brilliantly colored—usually yellow, black, white, or a combination of these. Most have patterns of black bars, or large eyelike spots, or both. It is still uncertain whether the spots truly frighten predators; perhaps they give them an incorrect target or are useful in displays directed at other butterfly fish. Small, bristlelike teeth that line the small mouths of butterfly fish are specialized for extracting small animals from the in-

Butterfly fish are so named because of their attractive coloration of yellow, black, white, or a combination of these colors and because of their rapid, butterflylike swimming motions. Shown (clockwise from top left) are the addis butterfly fish, Chaetodon semilarvatus; *black-back butterfly fish,* C. melanotus; *rainbow butterfly fish,* C. trifasciatus; *moon butterfly fish,* C. lunula; *and golden butterfly fish,* C. auriga.

terstices of coral and rock. Some species have long snouts for reaching into crevices. A small group of deep-water butterfly fish tolerate cooler water and penetrate the temperate region. Butterfly fish are classified in the family Chaetodontidae, order Perciformes. An unrelated freshwater species, *Pantodon bucholzi*, order Osteoglossiformes, of tropical western Africa, is also known as the butterfly fish.   CAMM SWIFT

butterfly lily: see GINGER LILY.

butterfly weed

Butterfly weed, *Asclepias tuberosa*, is a plant in the milkweed family, Asclepiadaceae, with a brilliant orange and yellow flower. It lives in dry open soils in North America and is one of the few milkweeds without a milky juice. The brilliant colors of the flowers attract butterflies. Another common name for butterfly weed is pleurisy root, since it was used to treat lung and throat ailments. The scientific name refers to the Greek god of medicine, Asclepius.

butternut

The butternut tree, J. cinerea, has wide, spreading branches and gray, deeply grooved bark. The inner shell of its nuts is rough and the outer, smooth and sticky.

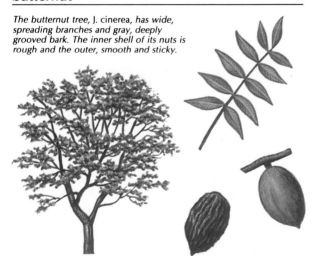

The butternut, *Juglans cinerea* (family Juglandaceae, order Juglandales), is a large tree that reaches a height of 30 m (100 ft); it has gray bark and 11–19 oblong and pointed leaflets. It is one of the hardiest northern NUT trees but is frequently short-lived because of its susceptibility to fungal and virus bunch diseases. The wood is hard, light colored, and is used in furnituremaking and for interior trim. Butternuts are propagated by SEED and, with difficulty, by GRAFTING. Black WALNUT, *J. nigra*, can be used as a rootstock. Juice from the nut husk and inner bark of the butternut and black walnut has a characteristic staining property. Butternuts are MONO-ECIOUS and grow better than the black walnut on poor soil. CATKINS elongate before shedding pollen. Female flowers are pubescent in short racemes of 2–5. Fruits are 5–10 cm (2–4 in) in length with four distinct, irregular ribs, and a sticky pubescent husk surrounding a thick shell containing a high-quality kernel.

Butterworth, George

George Sainton Kaye Butterworth, b. London, July 12, 1885, d. Aug. 5, 1916, was an English composer and folk song collector. He entered Trinity College, Oxford, in 1904 with the prospects of a legal career, but soon realized that his interests were in music. For a while he supported himself by writing music criticism for *The Times*, then by teaching (1909–10) music at Radley College. Because of his interest in folk music he worked with the folk song collector Cecil Sharp and Ralph Vaughan Williams. He enlisted in the British army in World War I and was killed in the Battle of the Somme. His published works include the orchestral piece *The Banks of Green*

Willows, based on folk themes, and songs based on texts of Percy Bysshe Shelley, A. E. Housman, Oscar Wilde, and William Ernest Henley.   ROBERT M. CAMMAROTA

Bibliography: Howes, Frank, *The English Musical Renaissance* (1966).

Button, Dick

Richard Button, b. Englewood, N.J., July 18, 1929, is a former figure skater who many believe contributed more to the sport—as competitor, innovator, and television commentator—than any other male. Button, whose serious skating career began when he was 12, became the youngest male (at the age of 16) to win the U.S. title, which he achieved six more times. In 1948 he became the first American to win an Olympic gold medal in skating, and he won the gold again in 1952. He also won three North American, one European, and five world titles during his career.   JIM BENAGH

buttonbush

Buttonbush, *Cephalanthus occidentalis*, is a shrub or small tree in the madder family, Rubiaceae. It is found along lake shores and streams in temperate and tropical North America, Asia and Africa. The common name refers to the fragrant white flowers that grow into round stalked heads.

buttress

A tower, or pier, buttress (1) is a solid mass of masonry built against a wall to absorb the lateral thrust of a vault. A flying buttress (2) and a double flying buttress (3), common in Gothic architecture, are masonry arches that transfer the thrust across open areas to piers at the side aisles. Gothic flying buttresses (4) support the roof vault, freeing the walls for vast stained-glass windows.

Used in architecture from ancient times, a buttress is a mass of masonry or brickwork that projects from or is built against a wall to give it additional strength. A pier, or tower, buttress is a vertical structural member that not only supports an adjacent wall but also receives and transmits the weight of a roof to the base or foundation of a building.

By 1175 architects had introduced the flying buttress in the construction of churches. This type is an arch or half-arch that displaces the thrust of a vaulted ceiling from the weakened upper portion of a wall onto the exterior supports, usually those along the side aisles. The introduction of the flying buttress made possible the rapid evolution of GOTHIC ARCHITECTURE, with its high, thin walls and large windows filled with elaborate stained glass. As the Gothic period advanced, the flying buttress itself became a decorative feature of great sculptural complexity.

butyl alcohol

Butyl alcohol, or butanol, C₄H₉OH, is an ALCOHOL that exists in four different structural forms, or isomers. Butyl alcohol is a colorless, toxic, combustible material that is soluble in most organic fluids. Its main uses are as chemical intermediates and industrial solvents.

Buxtehude, Dietrich   [buhks'-te-hoo-de]

The Danish-born organist and composer Dietrich (or Diderik) Buxtehude, b. 1637, d. May 9, 1707, was one of the most influential predecessors of J. S. Bach and other composers of the North German school. His first 30 years were spent in Scandinavia. In 1668 he obtained one of the finest musical positions in Europe, that of organist of the Marienkirche (Church of the Virgin Mary) in Lübeck. There he established an annual series of afternoon concerts during Advent that became famous throughout Europe. Buxtehude presented his own compositions for organ, chorus, and orchestra during these concerts. Bach traveled about 320 km (200 mi) on foot to hear them and remained for some time to study Buxtehude's music.

An unusual aspect of Buxtehude's life was the Lübeck tradition that the new organist should marry the daughter of his predecessor; Buxtehude thus married the daughter of Franz Tunder. This tradition later diminished both Bach's and Handel's interest in succeeding Buxtehude in Lübeck. Buxtehude composed chamber music for strings, harpsichord suites and variations, a large quantity of choral music, many solo cantatas, and various types of organ music.   FARLEY K. HUTCHINS

Bibliography: Hutchins, Farley K., *Dietrich Buxtehude: The Man, His Music, His Era* (1955).

Buys Ballot, Christoph Hendrik Diederik
[boys bah-laht', hine'-rik deed'-rik]

Christoph Hendrik Diederik Buys Ballot, a Dutch mathematician, physicist, and meteorologist, b. Oct. 10, 1817, d. Feb. 3, 1890, was one of the chief organizers of the science of METEOROLOGY and an early advocate of international cooperation in the field. A professor at the University of Utrecht and founder (1854) of the Royal Netherlands Meteorological Institute, he is best known for his empirical observation (1857), now known as Buys Ballot's law, that if one stands with one's back to the wind in the Northern Hemisphere, atmospheric pressure will be lower on the left than on the right (conversely in the Southern Hemisphere)—a rule that the American meteorologist William Ferrel had deduced theoretically a year earlier.
                                                    PETER J. WEBSTER

buzzard

The name *buzzard* is given to a miscellaneous assortment of scavenger birds—six New World VULTURES belonging to the Cathartidae family are often called buzzards—but in a more restricted sense the term applies to many Old World HAWKS, family Accipitridae, that may or may not be scavengers. An example is the common buzzard of Europe, *Buteo buteo*,

The common buzzard, B. buteo, is perhaps the most frequently sighted bird of prey in Europe. It nests in woodlands but hunts small rodents, reptiles, and amphibians in open country.

closely related to the American red-tailed hawk. Other hawks that are also often called vultures are widespread in Asia and Africa.   GEORGE J. WALLACE

Buzzards Bay

Buzzards Bay is an inlet (48 km/30 mi long) of the Atlantic Ocean, in southeastern Massachusetts at the base of CAPE COD. Fishing villages and resorts are located along it. The Cape Cod Canal connects it to Cape Cod Bay.

Buzzati, Dino   [boo-tsah'-tee]

Dino Buzzati, b. Oct. 16, 1906, d. Jan. 28, 1972, was a leading Italian writer of allegorical and surrealistic fiction and plays. His best novel, *The Tartar Steppe* (1940; Eng. trans., 1952), is typical of his works, in which the painful solitude of existence is tempered by Christianity. Buzzati also wrote for the stage and painted. His most performed play is *Un Caso Clinico* (A Clinical Case, 1953).   LOUIS KIBLER

Byblos   [bib'-luhs]

Byblos (biblical Gebal) was an ancient city of PHOENICIA, located on the Lebanese coast at present-day Jebeil. First occupied in Neolithic times (c.8000–4000 BC), the site was an active seaport and trade center from about 3000 BC. It was subject, in turn, to the Egyptian, Assyrian, Babylonian, and Persian empires, all of which extorted tribute in the form of timber from the Lebanon cedar forests. In the 1st millennium BC, Byblos was an important source of papyrus to the Greeks; *Bible* is derived from the city's name.

Excavations of Byblos, undertaken by the French since 1921, have yielded Early Bronze Age courtyard houses and a monumental temple of Baalat-Gebel, the Byblite form of the goddess ASTARTE, dating from the 3d millennium BC. Notable remains of the Middle Bronze Age (c.1900–1550 BC) include four royal tombs containing rich deposits of gold and silver jewelry, ivory plaques, and alabaster vessels. Also found at Byblos was the famous 10th-century BC sarcophagus of King Ahiram (now in the Beirut Archaeological Museum), bearing one of the earliest known alphabetic inscriptions.

Byblos was under Persian control from 539 to 333 BC, when the city fell to Alexander the Great and became completely Hellenized. During the Roman period it was the center of the cult of Adonis; remains of two temples and a theater, bath, and basilica have been unearthed. After its capture (1103) by the Crusaders the site fell into decline and was later abandoned.   JONATHAN N. TUBB

Bibliography: Jidejian, N., *Byblos through the Ages,* 2d ed. (1973); Moscati, S., ed., *The Phoenicians* (1989); Saghieh, M., *Byblos in the Third Millennium* (1984).

Bydgoszcz   [bid'-gawshch]

Bydgoszcz (German: Bromberg) is a city in north central Poland near the confluence of the Brda and Vistula rivers. The population is 372,600 (1988 est.). Grain and timber industries were central to the town's early economic growth, and the completion of the Bydgoszcz Canal in 1774, linking the Vistula and Oder river systems, caused the town to become an important inland port. The current economy is based on the food, pulp, metal, textile, and chemical industries. During the 13th century it was under control of the Teutonic Knights, and in 1346 it became an independent city. From 1772 to 1919 it was, except for a brief period, under Prussian rule. The city suffered damage during the German occupation of 1939–45.

Byelorussia: see BELARUS.

Byng, Julian Hedworth George, 1st Viscount Byng of Vimy   [bing, vee'-mee]

Viscount Byng, b. Sept. 11, 1862, d. June 6, 1935, was a British general who commanded the Canadian Corps in its capture (Apr. 9, 1917) of Vimy Ridge in northern France during World War I. He later commanded the British Third Army in the Cambrai offensive (November 1917), where he made the first large-scale use of tanks. Byng was governor general of Canada from 1921 to 1926. In the latter year he became involved in a political controversy—the so-called King–Byng Affair—because of his refusal to dissolve parliament when requested to do so by the Canadian prime minister, William Lyon McKenzie King. From 1928 to 1931, Byng served as chief commissioner of London's metropolitan police. He was made a viscount in 1925 and a field marshal in 1932.

Byrd, Harry F.

Harry Flood Byrd, b. Martinsburg, Va., June 10, 1887, d. Oct. 20, 1966, the brother of Richard E. Byrd, was a U.S. senator from Virginia from 1933 to 1965. Before that, he published a newspaper, served (1915–25) in the state senate, and was governor of Virginia from 1926 to 1930. Appointed to the Senate in 1933, he was subsequently elected to six terms. As chairman of the Senate Finance Committee for ten years, Byrd championed fiscal conservatism.

Byrd, Richard E.

Richard Evelyn Byrd, b. Winchester, Va., Oct. 25, 1888, d. Mar. 11, 1957, was an aviator, Antarctic explorer, and author. He attended the U.S. Naval Academy and later became an aviator. In 1925 he commanded a naval flying unit on the MacMillan expedition to the Arctic, and on May 9, 1926, he and Floyd BENNETT flew over the North Pole, for which Byrd was awarded the Congressional Medal of Honor. With backing from private donors, Byrd organized (1928) an expedition to Antarctica, establishing a base called Little America on the Ross Ice Shelf near Roosevelt Island. With three companions, he flew (1929) to the South Pole and back. On his return to the United States he was given a hero's welcome and promoted to the rank of rear admiral. Byrd led further Antarctic expeditions in 1933–35, 1939–41, 1946–47, and 1955–56. In 1934 he spent five months by himself near the South Pole, an experience described in his book, *Alone* (1938).

Bibliography: Gladych, Martin, *Admiral Byrd of Antarctica* (1960); Rodgers, Eugene, *Beyond the Barrier: The Story of Byrd's First Expedition to Antarctica* (1990).

Byrd, Robert C.

Robert Carlyle Byrd, originally named Cornelius Calvin Sale, Jr., b. North Wilkesboro, N.C., Nov. 20, 1917, was majority (Democratic) leader of the U.S. Senate from 1977 to 1981 and again from 1987 to 1989; in the interim he was minority leader (1981–87). Byrd was raised in West Virginia by relatives, who changed his name. He entered politics in 1946, sitting in the West Virginia House of Delegates (1947–51) and the Senate (1951–53). He served (1953–59) in the U.S. House of Representatives, was elected to the U.S. Senate in 1958, and became majority whip of the Senate in 1971.

Byrd, William   (composer)

William Byrd, b. 1543, d. July 4, 1623, the most famous and versatile English composer of his age, inherited a characteristically English musical style from his teacher Thomas TALLIS. When only 20 years of age he was appointed organist and master of the choristers at Lincoln Cathedral, but he left in 1572 for London, where he had been named a gentleman of the Chapel Royal. Although a steadfast Roman Catholic, Byrd remained a loyal member of the Anglican musical establishment until his death. The music he wrote for the Anglican church was surpassed only by his music for the Roman Catholic rite, most of which was privately performed in the houses of Catholic patrons. Despite the allusions to religious persecution in the text of Byrd's MOTETS, he was respected and admired by Queen Elizabeth I and King James I.

Byrd was a fine organist and a virtuoso performer on the virginals, for which he wrote numerous pieces, including fantasias, dances, variations, and program music. He was one of the pioneers of the consort song (for voice and viols) and also excelled in chamber music of many kinds: sacred and secular songs for domestic use, and a wide variety of forms and styles ranging from lullabies to theater music. He composed occasional music on the defeat of the Spanish Armada and on the death of Tallis. His secular music includes settings of poems by the earl of Oxford, Sir Philip Sidney, and Sir Edward Dyer and madrigals, most of which are adaptations of consort songs. Byrd's most important works include the motets of the *Cantiones sacrae* (1575, with Tallis; 1589; 1591), the *Gradualia* (1605, 1607), and the three masses (published without date but probably composed in 1592–95). In his finest work Byrd equaled the highest achievements of his European contemporaries.   DENIS STEVENS

Bibliography: Brown, Alan, and Turbet, Richard, eds., *Byrd Studies* (1991); Fellowes, Edmund H., *William Byrd,* 2d ed. (1948); Kerman, Joseph, *The Masses and Motets of William Byrd* (1981); Neighbour, Oliver, *The Consort and Keyboard Music of William Byrd* (1978).

Byrd, William   (writer)

Little published during his own lifetime, William Byrd of Westover, Va., b. Mar. 28, 1674, d. Aug. 26, 1744, is now recognized as the most important writer of pre–Revolutionary Virginia. Son and heir of William Byrd (1652–1704), he assumed his father's life, that of a wealthy planter and politician. Three fragments of the "Secret Diary," written in shorthand and covering the years 1709–12, 1717–19, and 1739–41, reveal a proud, well-educated, socially self-conscious man who strove to maintain the ideals of an English gentleman in rural Virginia. "Secret History of the Line" and "History of the Dividing Line betwixt Virginia and North Carolina, run in the year 1728" grew out of the diaries Byrd kept on an expedition to map the boundary between these two neighboring colonies. Written in mock epic style, the latter chronicles his complex feelings about the American frontier. Lesser works include "A Progress to the Mines" (c.1732), "A Journey to the Land of Eden" (1733), and letters.   ROBERT D. ARNER

Byrnes, James Francis

James Francis Byrnes, b. Charleston, S.C., May 2, 1879, d. Apr. 9, 1972, was politically active for nearly half a century as a legislator, jurist, wartime administrator, diplomat, and governor of his native South Carolina. After serving (1911–25) in the U.S. House of Representatives, he was elected to the Senate in 1930. There he acted as legislative whip for Franklin D. ROOSEVELT's domestic and foreign program, despite his objections to its unbalanced budgets.

Byrnes served briefly (1941–42) on the Supreme Court before being appointed director of economic stabilization (1942) and then head of the War Mobilization Board (1943). In this powerful position he managed the nation's economy, including wages, prices, production, transportation, and civilian manpower. He also accompanied President Roosevelt to the Yalta Conference in 1944, an act that influenced Harry S. TRUMAN's choice of Byrnes as secretary of state (1945–47). Byrnes moved from a position of conciliation to one of firm opposition to postwar Soviet expansion. He also participated in the decision to use the atom bomb.

Service as governor of South Carolina (1951–55) concluded Byrnes's career. Increasingly conservative, he pressed for economies and opposed desegregation of that state's public school system.   ELLIOT A. ROSEN

Bibliography: Byrnes, James F., *All in One Lifetime* (1958); Clements, K. A., ed., *James F. Byrnes and the Origins of the Cold War* (1982).

Byron, George Gordon, Lord

George Gordon Noel Byron, 6th baron Byron of Rochdale, b. Jan. 22, 1788, d. Apr. 19, 1824, was the most conspicuous and influential of the English romantic poets. His facetious and satirical poem *Don Juan* (1819–24) is often considered his masterpiece.

Early Years. After leaving Cambridge, Byron set out on a long expedition through the Middle East that furnished the subject matter of his first important poem, *Childe Harold's Pilgrimage*. The opening cantos appeared in 1812, and he became famous overnight.

During the next four years, Byron enjoyed a whirl of triumphs, wrote a number of equally successful verse-tales, each with a romantic Eastern background, and plunged into a series of exhausting and disturbing love affairs. His marriage early in 1815 was an ill-considered attempt to solve his many personal problems, among the worst of which was his illicit passion for his half sister, Augusta Leigh. Twelve months later his wife deserted him, taking their infant child with her. She obtained a separation, despite her husband's furious protests, and in the ensuing scandal Byron left England.

Exile. The poet's exile lasted until his death. In Switzerland he met PERCY and MARY SHELLEY, added a third canto to *Childe Harold* (1816), and began his symbolic drama *Manfred* (1817), in which he evoked the image of Augusta and sought to expiate his sense of guilt. He moved on to Venice, where his behavior was so dissolute that he became, again, a subject of much gossip. In Venice he started to compose *Don Juan*. Other satires, in a no less irreverent vein, are *Beppo* (1818) and

Lord Byron donned an Albanian costume for this portrait by Thomas Philips. Byron influenced romantic literature with his flamboyant life-style as well as with his poetry. He fled England to avoid a scandal and died in 1824 in the struggle for Greek independence.

The Vision of Judgment (1822). His historical dramas, *Marino Faliero, Sardanapalus,* and *The Two Foscari* (all published in 1821), are considered comparatively lesser works.

Meanwhile, Byron had met Teresa Guiccioli, a young Italian married woman with whom he established a joint household. He willingly gave up more promiscuous loves, and they shared a quasi-matrimonial life. He was still restive, however, and in 1823 he agreed to go to the aid of the Greek patriots, then struggling against their Turkish masters. In January 1824, Byron landed at Missolonghi, where he died of a fever.

Reputation. Byron achieved a wide reputation as a poet and had a profound effect on the literature of Europe. He typified the romantic revolt and the cult of personal freedom that opposed the "stupid old system" of monarchical government and the repressive dictates of conservative society. Young French writers, such as Victor Hugo, Alphonse de Lamartine, Alfred de Musset, and Alfred de Vigny, were deeply indebted to his influence, which extended through Germany and into Russia, where he was held in high esteem by Aleksandr Pushkin and Mikhail Lermontov. At times an undisciplined poet with a somewhat faulty ear, Byron was always an accomplished writer of prose. Officious friends destroyed his memoirs, but the private letters he casually dashed off give a fairly complete record of his adventures.   PETER QUENNELL

Bibliography: Calder, A., ed., *Byron* (1987); Knight, G. W., *Byron's Dramatic Prose* (1954; repr. 1976) and *Lord Byron* (1952; repr. 1976); McGann, J., *Byron* (1986); Marchand, L., *Byron: A Portrait* (1970), *Byron's Poetry* (1965), and, as ed., *Lord Byron: Selected Letters and Journals* (1984); Quennell, Peter, *Byron* (1974).

Byronic hero   [by-rahn'-ik]

The Byronic hero was the brooding and defiant romantic character who emerged from Lord Byron's finest works, *Childe Harold's Pilgrimage* (1812–17), *Manfred* (1817), *Don Juan* (1819–24), and *Cain* (1821). Alternately guilty and guiltless, the hero bore Byron's own stamp of personal revolt and had a profound effect on the literature of European ROMANTICISM and the German STURM UND DRANG. As seen in Byron's writings, the figure was both darkly satanic and thoroughly attractive. While cognizant of sin and evil, he sought to expiate guilt and conventional morality through acts of personal freedom. The Byronic hero is analogous to Goethe's Faust and the mythical Prometheus.   PETER QUENNELL

Bibliography: Thorslev, Peter, *The Byronic Hero* (1962).

byte   [byt]

In computer terminology, a byte is a unit of digital data consisting of eight so-called bits. Each BIT may take two values, usually referred to as zero and one or as low and high. In physical systems the values of the bits are often represented by voltages, with a zero-bit commonly represented by a low voltage and a one-bit by a high one.

Bytes may be used to represent characters, or they may represent binary or other data. In some systems one of the bits in a byte is used for parity—that is, to indicate whether the number of high bits in the byte is odd or even, thus serving as a check on the occurrence of errors in the byte. In such systems only seven bits in the byte serve as information bits. A byte is itself sometimes divided into two so-called nybbles (or nibbles) of four bits each.

Although 8-bit MICROPROCESSORS use data units that are equal to a byte, the data unit used by other processors and by larger computers is the *word*—the common term for all data units. For example, 16-bit microprocessors use words consisting of 2 bytes, and larger computers use still larger words. The size of a COMPUTER MEMORY is usually measured in kilobytes or megabytes (1,000 and 1,000,000 bytes, respectively). Because memory is usually provided in units that are powers of two, a kilobyte is sometimes used to represent 1,024 bytes instead of 1,000 bytes.   BRIAN ASTLE

Bytom   [bee'-tawm]

Bytom (German: Beuthen) is an industrial city in Katowice province in southwestern Poland, situated about 55 km

(34 mi) northeast of the Czech border. The population is 231,200 (1991 est.). Coal, zinc, lead, and silver are mined nearby, and the city has an institute of mining. Iron and steel, silver, heavy machinery, and furniture are produced there.

Bytom, chartered in 1254, was held by Bohemia and Austria until it passed to Prussia in 1742, forming part of Upper Silesia. In 1921 it voted to become part of Poland, but Germany retained control. It joined Poland after World War II.

bytownite: see FELDSPAR.

Byurakan Astrophysical Observatory

Byurakan Astrophysical Observatory, founded in 1946 by Soviet astrophysicist Vicktor A. AMBARTSUMIAN, is located 1,500 m (5,000 ft) above sea level on the south slope of Mount Aragatz, 27 km (17 mi) northwest of Yerevan, the capital of the Republic of Armenia. Its 2.6-m (102-in) reflecting telescope, installed in 1976, is used especially to study flare stars and peculiar galaxies. The 1-m (40-in) Schmidt telescope uses three of the world's largest objective prisms for spectroscopic work.

NORMAN SPERLING

See also: OBSERVATORY, ASTRONOMICAL.

Byzantine art and architecture   [biz'-uhn-teen]

Byzantine art is generally taken to include the arts of the Byzantine Empire from the foundation of the new capital of Constantinople (now ISTANBUL) in AD 330 in ancient BYZANTIUM to the capture of the city by the Ottoman Turks in 1453. The territory of the Byzantine Empire originally encompassed the entire eastern half of the Roman Empire around the Mediterranean Sea but shrank to little more than Greece, part of southern Italy, the southern Balkans, and Anatolia after the Islamic invasions of the 7th century. In the period after the 12th century, the empire comprised little more than Constantinople and a few other outposts. The influence of Byzantine art, however, extended far beyond these borders, because arts derived from Byzantium continued to be practiced in parts of Greece, the Balkans, and Russia into the 18th century and, in some isolated monasteries, to the present day.

Moreover, it was during the 12th century that the influence of Byzantium on western European art, already an important factor in the preceding period, reached its zenith and played a truly generative role in the development within RO-MANESQUE ART of a greater naturalism in style and humanism in content. Byzantine art could play this role because, throughout its long history, it maintained a connection with the artistic heritage of Greek and Roman art and architecture; it preserved and transmitted much of this heritage to the West until Western artists were able to approach antiquity directly.

BYZANTINE ARCHITECTURE

Although many local variants existed in different regions of the empire during most of the 4th and 5th centuries, Byzantine religious architecture used the two basic structures developed in EARLY CHRISTIAN ARCHITECTURE—longitudinal-plan BASILI-CAS, which served as meeting places for the eucharistic service, and centralized-plan buildings, which served as BAPTISTERIES and as martyria (memorials over tombs of martyrs).

Basilicas. Basilicas continued in use into the 6th century; splendidly preserved examples, with magnificent MOSAICS in the APSE above the ALTAR, may be seen at Sant'Apollinare in Classe (c.549), near RAVENNA in northern Italy and at Saint Catherine's monastery at Mount Sinai (c.560). At this time, however, during the reign of Emperor JUSTINIAN I (527–65), centralized plans began to be used for congregational churches as well as for martyrs' shrines, probably because of the growing importance of the cult of relics. Important examples of such centralized churches are Saints Sergius and Bacchus in Constantinople (527–36) and the stylistically related octagonal church of SAN VITALE in Ravenna (532–47).

Hagia Sophia. By far the most significant building is the great church of HAGIA SOPHIA (Church of the Holy Wisdom) in Constantinople (532–37), which retained a longitudinal axis but was dominated by its enormous central dome. Seventh-

century Syriac texts suggest that this design was meant to show the church as an image of the world with the dome of heaven suspended above, from which the Holy Spirit descended during the liturgical ceremony. The precise features of Hagia Sophia's complex design were not repeated in later buildings; from this time, however, most Byzantine churches were centrally planned structures organized around a large dome; they retained the cosmic symbolism and demonstrated with increasing clarity the close dependence of the design and decoration of the church on the liturgy performed in it.

Greek Cross Churches. Few major architectural projects were undertaken during the three troubled centuries following the death of Justinian in 565. During the late 9th- and 10th-century revival, however, the classic Byzantine church, generally small in scale but richly decorated with mosaics, was developed. The typical church comprised a high central dome with four vaults arranged about it to form an equal-armed cross known as the cross-in-square or the Greek-cross church. This period also saw the increasing emphasis on the practice of closing off the chancel from the rest of the church with an ICONOSTASIS, a screen hung with icons and with a large central door. This arrangement was intimately bound up with the Byzantine liturgy; the architectural setting intensified the mystery of the Mass, most of which was performed in secret behind closed doors but included splendid processions that were symbolic manifestations of the divinity. The classic Middle Byzantine Greek-cross church continued to be built without fundamental change down to the modern period and became the standard for Slavic churches of Russia and the Balkans.

MOSAICS AND MONUMENTAL PAINTING

Early Byzantine art must be considered in relation to the Early Christian condemnation of pagan idolatry and the consequent reluctance to depict sacred Christian figures and stories. Although many notable exceptions exist, figural scenes were usually avoided and were presented in an allusive symbolic mode or were embedded in complex programs that made the veneration of single images nearly impossible.

San Vitale Mosaics. The magnificent mosaic program (546–48) of San Vitale in Ravenna focuses on the ritual of making offerings to Christ. He is depicted in the apse mosaic, receiving a model of the church from Bishop Ecclesius and bestowing a martyr's crown on its patron, Saint Vitalis. The same theme of offering is picked up both in Old Testament scenes of the offerings of Abel, Abraham, and Melchizedek and the famous twin panels of Emperor Justinian and Empress Theodora.

The apse mosaic (c.549) in the Basilica of Sant'Apollinare in Classe, near Ravenna, depicts Saint Apollinaris in a symbolic scene of the Transfiguration. The 12 sheep represent the Apostles, and overhead is the symbol of Christ, with Moses and Elijah on either side.

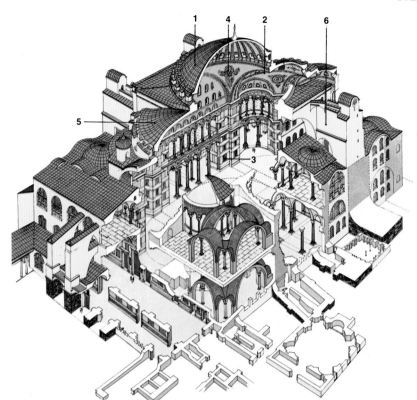

1 4 2 6

5

3

(Left) *Hagia Sophia (532–37) in Istanbul, designed by Anthemius of Tralles and Isidorus of Miletus, incorporates: a huge central dome (1) supported by four large arches (2) that transfer the thrust to the main piers (3); pendentives (4), spherical triangles in the four corners that rise to the base of the circular dome; semidomes (5) flanking the main piers; buttresses (6) that absorb the dome's north and south thrust.*

(Below) *An Ionic capital from Hagia Sophia combines the volute with an incised acanthus-leaf decoration. The monogram of Emperor Justinian I appears in the disk.*

Image Veneration. After about 550, such restraint weakened, and in 7th-century church decorations, such as those of the churches of Saint Demetrius at Salonika and Santa Maria Antiqua in Rome, small isolated panels depicting single figures begin to appear at or near eye level. The style of these works continues the tendency evident in the Theodora panel of San Vitale toward large-eyed, elongated figures arranged in formal hieratic frontal poses, almost compelling veneration. More important, these images are similar in style and subject matter to ICONS, whose great importance in Byzantine art dates from this period. Both panels and icons similarly invite overt veneration of the holy figures portrayed in this manner.

The Iconoclastic Crisis. In the next century the fear of idolatry that haunted the Byzantines broke out in ICONOCLASM (726–843), the imperially sponsored wholesale destruction or obliteration of all art that depicted sacred figures, and the violent persecution of its opponents. Subsequently, religious art was limited mainly to images of the cross and of symbolic birds and plants, as in the 8th-century mosaics of Hagia Eiene (Church of the Holy Peace) in Constantinople. Secular art, however, seems to have continued throughout the period and served as the foundation for the revival of Christian figural art in the succeeding period.

Macedonian Renaissance. Toward the end of the 9th century, Byzantine religious art entered its "second Golden Age," often called the Macedonian Renaissance for the ruling dynasty. The term may be too strong, but it does correctly indicate the extent to which the art of the period, in both subject matter and style, often draws directly and deliberately on the Hellenistic and Roman classical heritage. Monumental art again exhibited relatively naturalistic and strongly modeled three-dimensional figures, often characterized by a restrained dignity and noble grandeur, as in the mosaic of the Virgin and Child (867) still in place in the apse of Hagia Sophia. Within the newly developed and standardized Byzantine Greek-cross church, such figures were organized into consistent programs best preserved today in the churches of Hosios Lukas in central Greece (c.1000) and Daphni near Athens (c.1100). At Daphni, the Pantocrator—Christ as Lord of the Universe—appears at the summit of the central dome, and the Virgin is represented in the apse above the altar as the instrument of

Christ's incarnation. Below her the church on earth is represented by the saints, and around the upper parts of the vaults were arranged major scenes from the life of Christ. These scenes, which closely correspond to the major feast days of the Byzantine religious calendar, are often called a feast cycle and act as reminders of events in the life of Christ that are also reflected in the daily liturgy.

Spread of Byzantine Art. During the 11th and 12th centuries the mosaic system was carried by Byzantine mosaicists to Russia (Hagia Sophia at Kiev, 1043–46) and in Italy to Venice (Saint Mark's, after 1063) and to Norman Sicily (Palatine Chapel, Palermo, 1140s; Monreale Cathedral, 1180s). At the same time, Byzantine art began to develop a much stronger humanistic approach, now with a greater concern for naturalism and for conveying a strongly emotional quality. In icons such as *Our Lady of Vladimir* (Tretyakov Gallery, Moscow), produced in Constantinople about 1130, the Virgin no longer displays her divine child to the people but interacts with it in more human terms, as the child turns toward her and clings to her neck. The use of FRESCOES in churches spread throughout the Balkans; clearly derivative of lost works in Byzantium itself, they show an extreme emotional intensity.

Palaeologan Mosaics and Frescoes. After the capture and sack of Constantinople by the Fourth Crusade in 1204, the development of Byzantine art was severely disrupted, but not altogether ended. However, the period following the reestablishment of the empire (1261) in Constantinople under the Palaeologan dynasty saw a brilliant revival of intellectual life. Its greatest artistic monument is the splendid mosaic and fresco program of the small church of SAINT SAVIOR IN THE CHORA (Kariye Djami) in Constantinople, dating from the first decade of the 14th century, which combines a refined decorative quality with a delicate emotional sensibility, as in the striking Anastasis fresco in the pareccleseion, depicting Christ descending into Hell. Both the decorative and emotional qualities characterize the last phase of Byzantine painting. They occur, for example, in the frescoes of the churches of Mistra, the mountainside capital of the despotate of Morea in southern Greece. These frescoes date from the decades around the fall of Constantinople to the Turks in 1453 and mark the end of Byzantine art as such.

(Left) *The large apse mosaic from the Cathedral of Monreale in Sicily represents the Christ Pantocrator (Ruler of the Universe). Built by William II of Sicily, the cathedral is an example of late Byzantine art.*

(Right) *The elaborate 6th-century Throne of Maximian, the bishop of Ravenna, is decorated with ivory panels carved by several artists. The five front panels depict John the Baptist and the four Evangelists; the back of the chair contains scenes from the life of Christ. (Archiepiscopal Museum, Ravenna.)*

Gospels (Archiepiscopal Museum, Rossano, Italy) and the famous Vienna Genesis manuscript (Nationalbibliothek) are the outstanding examples; both contain many separate miniatures painted on purple parchment and may be dated to the 6th or 7th century. Secular books were also profusely illustrated, the Biblioteca Ambrosiana in Milan preserving a text of Homer's *Iliad* (c.500) and the Vienna Nationalbibliothek a pharmaceutical manual, *De materia medica* (512), by the Greek physician Dioscorides. A strongly classical element is particularly characteristic of illustrated manuscripts, perhaps reaching its high point during the Macedonian Renaissance of the 10th century. In the famous Paris Psalter (c.950; Bibliothèque Nationale) a portrait of David composing the Psalms is placed in a rich pastoral landscape closely paralleling the Hellenistic-Roman art of Pompeii.

Ivories and Enamels. Classical subjects and a classicizing style may also be found in a certain type of secular ivories produced during the 10th century, such as the Veroli Casket (Victoria and Albert Museum, London), with its scenes taken from classical literature (Euripides) and mythology. Ivories were more commonly intended to serve as book covers or altar objects. Christian subjects were presented in a sober version of the classicizing idiom, with hieratically arranged rows of holy figures, as in the beautiful 10th-century Harbaville triptych (Louvre, Paris). This noble classicizing style is even more characteristic of Byzantine enamel work executed in CLOISONNÉ, in which the glowing gemlike colored enamels enclosed in burnished gold heighten the splendor. Examples of such works, among the most prized possessions of the courts and treasuries of Europe, include the jeweled Pala d'Oro altarpiece (mostly 12th century) in SAINT MARK's BASILICA in Venice, and the reliquary at Limburgan der Lahn (964–65), decorated inside and out with enamel figures.   LAWRENCE NEES

Thereafter, Christian art languished in the former Byzantine lands, which were all subject to Turkish rule; only in the young Russian state, where the Orthodox church remained dominant, did the artistic tradition inspired by Byzantium continue to develop (see RUSSIAN ART AND ARCHITECTURE).

BYZANTINE APPLIED ART

In Byzantium the applied arts of manuscript illumination, IVORY CARVING, METALWORK, ENAMEL work, and textile manufacture held an importance and achieved a magnificence seldom matched in other cultures. They were produced largely for the imperial court, for the altars of churches, or as diplomatic presents for export, such as Saint Stephen's Crown of Hungary. Such objects were avidly sought by Western medieval rulers and churchmen. They frequently served as models for works later produced locally and survive in large numbers in the major European and American collections. From the 6th to the 12th century, Byzantium held a monopoly on the production of silk textiles, which were so treasured in the West that they were used to wrap relics of the saints.

Illuminated Manuscripts. For the development of Byzantine art the inherently conservative medium of ILLUMINATED MANUSCRIPTS had a particular importance in preserving ancient traditions. Only a handful of the magnificent books produced in the pre-Iconoclastic period survive, of which the Rossano

Bibliography: Beckwith, John, *The Art of Constantinople: An Introduction to Byzantine Art*, 2d ed. (1968); Demus, Otto, *Byzantine Art and the West* (1970) and *Byzantine Mosaic Decoration* (1976); Grabar, André, *The Art of the Byzantine Empire* (1966); Hutter, Irmgard, *Early Christian and Byzantine Art* (1988); Kitzinger, Ernst, *The Art of Byzantium and the Medieval West* (1976) and *Byzantine Art in the Making* (1977); Krautheimer, Richard, *Early Christian and Byzantine Architecture* (1965); Mango, Cyril, *The Art of the Byzantine Empire, 312–1453: Sources and Documents* (1972) and *Byzantine Architecture* (1976); Rice, D. Talbot, *Byzantine Painting* (1968); Runciman, Steven, *Byzantine Style and Civilization* (1975); Weitzmann, Kurt, *Greek Mythology in Byzantine Art* (1984).

Byzantine Empire

The Byzantine Empire is the name given to the continuation of the Roman Empire, which—converted to Christianity and using Greek as its principal language—flourished in the eastern Mediterranean area for more than 1,000 years until its fall in 1453. The name *Byzantine* is derived from BYZANTIUM, the city which CONSTANTINE I made his new capital and renamed Constantinople (now ISTANBUL, Turkey). The three major periods of Byzantine history—Early, Middle, and Late—are characterized by drastic changes in internal organization.

EARLY PERIOD

The Early Byzantine period (324–610) was highlighted by Constantine's conversion to Christianity and the foundation of Constantinople, Theodosius I's final division of the empire into eastern and western parts, and Justinian I's successful efforts to reconquer the West. The major foreign conflicts of the period were with the Persians under the SASSANIANS in the east and the Germans in the west. Constantine and his successors successfully withstood Persian attack, but the defeat and death (363) of JULIAN THE APOSTATE caused the loss of large parts of Armenia to the Persians. Conflict was renewed under JUSTINIAN I (527–65) and his successors; the Byzantines repeatedly had to buy peace, and the year 610 saw the Persians threatening to occupy the eastern provinces. German pressure (c.375) on the Rhine and Danube increased as the Huns drove the Germans westward. Early in the 5th century, the Germans occupied most of the western half of the empire; they took Italy in 476. Justinian regained North Africa and Italy, but his successors yielded northern and central Italy to the LOMBARDS.

Internally, the reforms of Constantine, who built on the major administrative changes of his predecessor DIOCLETIAN, brought an end to the previous anarchy. The person of the emperor was elevated to a semi-divine position and surrounded by Eastern-style ceremonial, to insulate him from military coups. At all levels, civil and military authorities were sharply divided, to hinder potential rebels. An elaborate and huge bureaucracy developed. Although exceptions occurred, subjects were bound to fixed social-economic positions; peasants could not leave the land, nor craftsmen their jobs. A sound currency and a money economy were restored.

Constantine's conversion to Christianity made it the most favored religion in the state; after 380 it was the sole official religion. The state, however, became deeply involved in religious disputes. Constantine was forced to confront the heresy of ARIANISM, and only THEODOSIUS I (r.379–95) was able to

Justinian I, 6th-century Byzantine emperor, appears in this mosaic (Church of St. Vitale, Ravenna) accompanied by ministers of state, men of the army, and clergy, including Archbishop Maximian. Under Justinian the Byzantine Empire reached its greatest extent.

subdue the Arians. During the 5th and 6th centuries, NESTORIANISM and MONOPHYSITISM disturbed religious peace. The Nestorians were expelled, but efforts to suppress or reconcile the Monophysites failed.

MIDDLE PERIOD

The Middle Byzantine period (610–1081) began with the triumph of HERACLIUS over the Persians and his subsequent defeat by the Arabs. After 634, Muslim ARABS seized Palestine, Syria, and Egypt (provinces largely inhabited by Monophysites) and raided deep into Anatolia. LEO III (r. 717–41) beat them back from the gates of Constantinople, and BASIL I

The map shows the contraction of the Byzantine Empire, from c.533, when the empire reached its greatest territorial extent under Justinian I, to 1355, by which time it was reduced to Thrace and Morea. The fall of Constantinople to the Ottomans in 1453 brought the end of the empire.

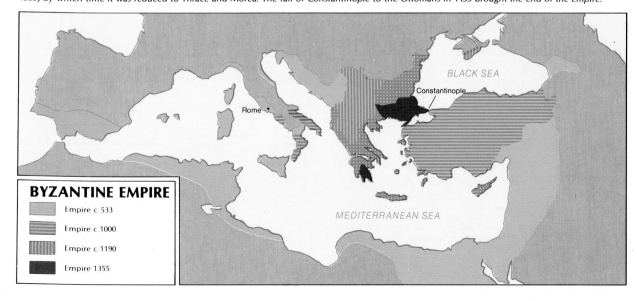

BYZANTINE EMPIRE

Empire c. 533
Empire c. 1000
Empire c. 1190
Empire 1355

(r. 867–86) started a campaign of reconquest that achieved considerable success in the 10th century. Slavs and Bulgarians meantime took possession of the Balkan peninsula. BASIL II (r. 976–1025) proved himself the greatest of Byzantine conquerors in defeating Arabs and Bulgarians.

The loss of the Monophysite provinces to the Arabs ended that religious problem, but Leo III commenced a dispute about ICONOCLASM when he attacked the veneration of images (726). Many monks were among those who suffered death or other penalties at the hands of Leo's son, Constantine V (r. 741–75), when iconoclasm reached its height. The images were briefly restored under Irene (787) and finally under Michael III in 843. The iconoclast rulers exacerbated relations with the papacy. Disputes over theological formulas, religious usages, and territorial jurisdiction led to a schism (867–870) under Patriarch PHOTIUS. Increasing disagreements with the papacy culminated in the Great SCHISM between the ORTHODOX CHURCH and Roman Catholicism in 1054.

Michael III's successor, Basil, inaugurated the Macedonian period (867–1056). Laws were codified by Basil I and LEO VI, new styles of church architecture developed, and a literary renaissance occurred.

The Arab and Bulgar invasions caused a perpetual state of military emergency. In response, civil and military authority was unified in the *theme* system. Each army unit, or *theme*, was settled on a specific region (also called a *theme*), which was governed by its commander. Soldiers received allotments of land, and their sons apparently became free peasants. Because these free peasants, as taxpayers and soldiers, were fundamental to the survival of the state, the 10th-century emperors strove to defend them from the great landlords.

In the 11th century, this effort to save the peasants failed, and the throne became the prize in a struggle between the bureaucrats and the generals (who were great landowners). Distracted by this struggle, the emperors were unable to resist the SELJUKS, who conquered Anatolia between 1048 and 1081.

LATE PERIOD

The triumph of the soldier-emperor ALEXIUS I COMNENUS in 1081 inaugurated the Late Byzantine period. Alexius and his immediate successors beat the Seljuk Turks back from the coasts of Anatolia, but were unable to cope with aggressive western Europeans. In 1204 the Fourth CRUSADE seized and brutally sacked the capital and established the Latin Empire of Constantinople, while refugee Byzantines created an empire at Nicaea, the despotate of Epirus and the Empire of Trebizond (Trabzon). In 1261 the ruler of Nicaea, MICHAEL VIII PALAEOLOGUS, regained Constantinople. The refounded Byzantine Empire had to face threats from Westerners and from Turks. Gradually reduced in area, it finally succumbed in 1453 to the Ottoman Turks, who made Constantinople the capital of the OTTOMAN EMPIRE.

In this final period the landed aristocracy dominated all provincial and central administrative positions of the Byzantine Empire. The peasantry was reduced to a servile status. The army consisted of mercenaries and a "feudal" levy based on government properties awarded to great landlords in return for military service. Venetian, Pisan, and Genoese merchants controlled Byzantine commerce. The emperors of the Palaeologan dynasty repeatedly tried to reunify the Orthodox and Catholic churches in return for Western aid against the Turks, but this effort proved futile.

The Byzantine Empire is notable for its ability to revive in times of disaster (as is shown in the cases of Heraclius, Leo III, Basil I, Alexius I, and Michael VIII), for its vigorous Greek culture, and for its outstanding Christian art and architecture.
C. M. BRAND

Bibliography: *Cambridge Medieval History*, vol. 4, new ed., parts 1–2 (1966–67); Hussey, Joan M., *The Byzantine World*, 3d rev. ed. (1967); Jones, A. H. M., *The Later Roman Empire, 284–602*, 2 vols. (1964); Mango, Cyril, *Byzantium: The Empire of New Rome* (1981); Ostrogorsky, George, *History of the Byzantine State*, 2d rev. ed., trans. by Joan M. Hussey (1969); Rice, Tamara, *Everyday Life in Byzantium* (1987).

See also: BYZANTINE ART AND ARCHITECTURE; CONSTANTINOPLE, LATIN EMPIRE OF; ROME, ANCIENT.

Byzantine music

Byzantine music is the body of music that is associated with the Byzantine Empire, from its foundation by Constantine I in AD 324 to the fall of Constantinople to the Turks in 1453. Most of what is known about Byzantine music is related to the liturgical chant of the Byzantine, or Eastern, church. Superficially, Byzantine music appears to have descended from GREEK MUSIC; but it is more similar to the music of Western Christianity than to that of ancient times. The language of the Byzantine church is Greek; there the similarity to the classical past ends. The modes used in the Eastern church are more closely related to the modes of the Western medieval church than to the Greek; the chant itself has features in common with its Gregorian counterpart, PLAINSONG, in that it consists of a single stepwise melodic line without accompaniment or strict meter. The greatest difference, however, lies in the texts: the Western chant is based primarily on psalms and other scriptural texts; most Eastern chants are nonscriptural HYMNS.

The Byzantine liturgy was firmly established with coronation of Justinian I in 527, barely two centuries after the Eastern Roman Empire was Christianized. Justinian, a hymn writer himself, recognized the need for trained singers to conduct the musical affairs of the church, especially because the varied Office hymns required more time in the service than did the masses of the Western church.

The principal forms of hymn, the major accomplishment in Byzantine music, were established early. The *troparion*, a monostrophic prayer, was known from the 4th century; the *kontakion*, a form having numerous stanzas, dates from the 6th century; and the *kanon*, which replaced the *kontakion* at the end of the 7th century, increased in length and had great mystical symbolism through its connection with the biblical canticles.

A musical staff was not developed in Byzantine notation; instead, signs were used to show the rise and fall of pitch levels. Because no intervals were shown, the signs must have been no more than a memory aid for music previously learned. The melodies of the hymns were built from formulas in common use; linking these formulas supplied what variety existed in the chant. Reiteration and VARIATION, important features of Oriental art, were evident in the rearrangement and modification of the chant formulas.

Outside the church the only surviving pieces are a few processional songs and some acclamations to the imperial pair and the patriarch; no other nonchurch music has survived. Instruments were commonly used, but not in church. The organ was important as a processional instrument, at the circus, and in theatrical performances. Christmas Eve was one of the rare occasions when instruments were permitted in church, and even then only wind and percussion instruments were allowed.
ELWYN A. WIENANDT

Bibliography: Conomos, Dimitri, *Byzantine Hymnography and Byzantine Chant* (1984); *Early Medieval Music up to 1300*, vol. 2 in *The New Oxford History of Music* (1954); Wellesz, Egon, *A History of Byzantine Music and Hymnography*, rev. ed. (1961).

See also: MASS (musical setting); MUSIC.

Byzantine Rite: see EASTERN RITE CHURCHES; ORTHODOX CHURCH.

Byzantium   [bi-zan'-tee-uhm]

Byzantium, the famed ancient city on the western side of the Bosporus, occupied the site of modern ISTANBUL. It is thought to have been founded (c.657 BC) by the Megarians and Argives. No trace of earlier inhabitants remains. Overrun by opposing forces during the PELOPONNESIAN WAR, it was a valuable port of the Roman Empire until it opposed Septimius SEVERUS and was destroyed (AD 196). Byzantium was splendidly rebuilt (AD 330) by Constantine I, who renamed it Constantinople; it became the capital of the BYZANTINE EMPIRE.

Bibliography: Downey, Glanville, *Constantinople in the Age of Justinian* (1981).